The Grants Register®

2010

Twenty-eighth Edition

palgrave
macmillan

The editor of *The Grants Register* cannot undertake any correspondence in relation to grants listed in this volume.

While every care has been taken in compiling the information contained in this publication, the publisher and editor do not accept any responsibility for any errors or omissions therein.

First published 2009 by
PALGRAVE MACMILLAN

Palgrave Macmillan in the UK is an imprint of Macmillan Publishers Limited, registered in England, company number 785998, of Houndmills, Basingstoke, Hampshire RG21 6XS.

Palgrave Macmillan in the US is a division of St Martin's Press LLC, 175 Fifth Avenue, New York, NY 10010

Palgrave Macmillan is the global academic imprint of the above companies and has companies and representatives throughout the world.

Palgrave® and Macmillan® are registered trademarks in the United States, the United Kingdom, Europe and other countries.

ISBN-13: 978-0-230-20600-7
ISBN-10: 0-230-20600-X
ISSN: 0072-5471

This book is printed on paper suitable for recycling and made from fully managed and sustained forest sources. Logging, pulping and manufacturing processes are expected to conform to the environmental regulations of the country of origin.

A catalogue record for this book is available from the British Library.

A catalog record for this book is available from the Library of Congress.

10 9 8 7 6 5 4 3 2 1
18 17 16 15 14 13 12 11 10 09

Printed in Hong Kong

LIST OF CONTENTS

PREFACE

The twenty-eighth edition of *The Grants Register* provides a detailed, accurate and comprehensive survey of awards intended for students at or above the postgraduate level, or those who require further professional or advanced vocational training.

Student numbers around the world continue to grow rapidly, and overseas study is now the first choice for many of these students. *The Grants Register* provides comprehensive, up-to-date information about the availability of, and eligibility for, non-refundable postgraduate and professional awards worldwide.

We remain grateful to the institutions which have supplied information for inclusion in this edition, and would also like to thank the International Association of Universities for continued permission to use their subject index within our Subject and Eligibility Guide to Awards.

The Grants Register database is updated continually in order to ensure that the information provided is the most current available. Therefore, if your details have changed or you would like to be included for the first time, please contact The Reference Administrator (The Grants Register), at the address below. If you wish to obtain further information relating to specific application procedures, please contact the relevant grant-awarding institution, rather than the publisher.

The Grants Register
Palgrave Macmillan
Houndmills
Basingstoke
RG21 6XS
United Kingdom
Tel: 144 (0)1256 329242
Fax: 144 (0)1256 357268

Website: www.palgrave.com
Email: grants.register@palgrave.com

HOW TO USE *THE GRANTS REGISTER*

For ease of use, *The Grants Register 2010* is divided into five sections:

- *The Grants Register*
- Subject and Eligibility Guide to Awards
- Index of Awards
- Index of Discontinued Awards
- Index of Awarding Organisations

The Grants Register

Information in this section is supplied directly by the awarding organisations. Entries are arranged alphabetically by name of organisation, and awards are listed alphabetically within the awarding organisation. This section includes details on subject area, eligibility, purpose, type, numbers offered, frequency, value, length of study, study establishment, country of study, and application procedure. Full contact details appear with each awarding organisation and also appended to individual awards where additional addresses are given.

Subject and Eligibility Guide to Awards

Awards can be located through the Subject and Eligibility Guide to Awards. This section allows the user to find an award within a specific subject area. *The Grants Register* uses a list of subjects endorsed by the International Association of Universities (IAU), the information centre on higher education, located at UNESCO, Paris (please see pp. 813–816 for the complete subject list). It is further subdivided into eligibility by nationality. Thereafter, awards are listed alphabetically within their designated category, along with a page reference where full details of the award can be found.

Index of Awards

All awards are indexed alphabetically with a page reference.

Index of Discontinued Awards

This Index lists awards previously included within *The Grants Register* which are no longer being offered, have been replaced by another programme, or are no longer relevant for inclusion in the publication.

Index of Awarding Organisations

A complete list of all awarding organisations, with country name and page reference.

ACADIA UNIVERSITY

Room 214B, Horton Hall, 18 University Avenue, Wolfville, NS, B4P 2R6, Canada
Tel: (1) 902 585 1914
Fax: (1) 902 585 1096
Email: theresa.starratt@acadiau.ca
Website: www.acadiau.ca
Contact: Ms Theresa Starratt, Graduate Studies Officer-Research and Graduate Studies

Acadia University is an institution that is commited to providing a liberal education based on the highest standards. The University houses a scholarly community that aims to ensure a broadening life experience for students, faculty and staff.

Acadia Graduate Awards

Subjects: English, political science, sociology, biology, chemistry, computer science, geology, psychology, education and recreation management, mathematics and statistics.
Purpose: To financially support students.
Eligibility: Open to registered full-time graduate students at Acadia University. In order to be eligible for an award students must have a GPA of not less than 3.00 in their major field in each of their last 2 years of undergraduate study.
Level of Study: Postgraduate
Type: Award.
Value: Up to Canadian $9,000
Length of Study: 1–2 years

ENGINEERING

GENERAL

Any Country

The Airey Neave Trust Scholarship, 12
Association for Women in Science Educational Foundation Predoctoral Awards, 118
AUC Assistantships, 96
AUC Laboratory Instruction Graduate Fellowships in Engineering and Computer Science, 97
AUC University Fellowships, 98
Australian Postgraduate Award Research Scholarship, 667
B K Krenzer Memorail Re-Entry Scholarship, 612
The Bernard Butler Trust Fund, 395

HOW TO USE THE GRANTS REGISTER

For ease of use, The Grants Register 2020 is divided into five sections:

- The Grants Register
- Subject and Eligibility Guide to Awards
- Index of Awards
- Index of Discontinued Awards
- Index of Awarding Organisations

The Grants Register

Information in this section is supplied directly by the awarding organisations. Entries are arranged alphabetically by name of organisation, and awards are listed alphabetically within the awarding organisation. This section includes details on subject area, eligibility, purpose, type, numbers offered, frequency, value, length of study, establishment, country of study, and application procedure. Full contact details appear with each awarding organisation and also appended to individual awards where additional addresses are given.

Subject and Eligibility Guide to Awards

Awards can be located through the Subject and Eligibility Guide to Awards. This section allows the user to find an award within a specific subject area. The Grants Register uses a list of subjects produced by the International Association of Universities (IAU), the information source on higher education, located in UNESCO, Paris (please see pp. 414–816 for the complete subject list). It is further subdivided into eligibility by nationality. Thereafter awards are listed alphabetically within their designated category, along with a page reference where full details of the award can be found.

Index of Awards

All awards are indexed alphabetically with a page reference.

Index of Discontinued Awards

This index lists awards previously included within The Grants Register which are no longer being offered, have been replaced by another programme, or are no longer relevant for inclusion in the publication.

Index of Awarding Organisations

A complete list of all awarding organisations, with contact name and page reference.

THE GRANTS REGISTER

A-T CHILDREN'S PROJECT

668 South Military Trail, Deerfield Beach, FL, 33442-3023, United States of America
Tel: (1) 954 481 6611
Fax: (1) 954 725 1153
Email: info@atcp.org
Website: www.atcp.org
Contact: Dr Cynthia Rothblum-Oviatt, Science Co-ordinator

The A-T Children's Project is a non-profit organization that raises funds to support and co-ordinate biomedical research projects, scientific conferences and a clinical centre aimed at finding a cure for ataxia-telangiectasia, a lethal genetic disease that attacks children, causing progressive loss of muscle control, as well as cancer and immune system problems.

Direct Research on Ataxia-Telangiectasia

Subjects: ATM biology.
Purpose: To accelerate first-rate, international scientific research in the area of ATM biology to help find a cure or life-improving treatments for children with ataxia-telangiectasia.
Eligibility: Open to applicants of all ages and nationalities.
Level of Study: Research
Type: Grant
Value: Up to US$75,000
Length of Study: 1–2 years
Frequency: Annual
Application Procedure: Application procedures can be found online at www.atcp.org
Closing Date: September 1st and March 1st
Funding: Private

AARON SISKIND FOUNDATION

C/o School of Visual Arts, MFA Photography, 209 East 23rd Street, New York, 10010, United States of America
Tel: (1) 609 348 5650
Fax: (1) (609) 348-8867
Email: info@aaronsiskind.org
Website: www.aaronsiskind.org

The Foundation works to preserve and protect Aaron Siskind's artistic legacy, and foster knowledge of and appreciation of his art.

Individual Photographer's Fellowship

Subjects: Photography-based art. Eligible work must be based on the idea of the lens-based still image, but grant recipients work in forms as diverse as digital imagery, video, installations, documentary projects and photo-generated print media.
Purpose: To stimulate excellence and the promise of future achievement in the photographic field.
Eligibility: Open to citizens or permanent residents of the United States of America. Applications sent from outside the United States of America will not be accepted.
Level of Study: Postgraduate
Type: Fellowship
Value: Up to $7,000
Country of Study: United States of America
No. of awards offered: 5
Application Procedure: Candidates must send an application form, 10 x 35 mm slides of their work, a slide list, stamped addressed return envelope together with their curriculum vitae and statement of plans for intended work to main address.
Closing Date: December 20th
Funding: Private
Additional Information: The application procedure is explicit and candidates are advised to check the website.

For further information contact:

United States of America

ABBEY AWARDS

43 Carson Road, London, SE21 8HT, England
Tel: (44) 20 8761 7980
Email: administrator@abbey.org.uk
Website: www.abbey.org.uk
Contact: Jane Reid, The Administrator

The Abbey Awards offer all-expenses-paid residencies for painters in excellent studio apartments at the British School in Rome. The 9-month Abbey Scholarship is awarded to an emergent artist while the 3-month Abbey Fellowships are for mid-career painters with an established record of achievement. Please see The Britsh School at Rome.

Abbey Awards

Subjects: Applicants must be fine artists specializing in painting.
Purpose: To enable painters to take up residencies at the British School at Rome.
Eligibility: Open to painters only, from UK or USA or from other countries provided they have lived for at least 5 years in UK or USA.
Level of Study: Unrestricted
Type: Scholarships and fellowships
Value: Scholarship – £16,000; Fellowships – £6,500
Length of Study: Scholarships - 9 months, Fellowships - 3 months
Frequency: Annual
Study Establishment: British School at Rome
Country of Study: Italy
No. of awards offered: 4
Application Procedure: Application forms are available from the administrator or from the website www.abbey.org.uk and must be accompanied by a CD showing a powerpoint presentation of not more than 8 images of recent work, alongwith a cheque for £20/US$50.
Closing Date: January 15th
Funding: Private
Contributor: The Incorporated Edwin Austin Abbey Memorial Scholarships Trust (in US)
No. of awards given last year: 4
No. of applicants last year: 123

Abbey Harris Mural Fund

Subjects: Mural painting.
Purpose: To provide grants to artists who have been commissioned to create murals in public places or in charitable institutions in the United Kingdom.
Eligibility: Awards are for mural painters and the work must be carried out in the United Kingdom. There are other restrictions.
Level of Study: Unrestricted
Type: Grant
Value: Approx. UK £3,000
Country of Study: United Kingdom
No. of awards offered: 1 or 2
Application Procedure: Applicants must send for an application form, enclosing a stamped addressed envelope. Requests for application forms can also be made by email or downloaded from www.abbey.org.uk
Closing Date: Applications are accepted at any time. Decisions may be made at twice-yearly meetings of the Trustees in May and November
Funding: Trusts
Contributor: E A Abbey Memorial Trust Fund for mural painting in Great Britain and E Vincent Harris Fund for mural decoration
No. of awards given last year: 1
No. of applicants last year: 3

ABDUS SALAM INTERNATIONAL CENTRE FOR THEORETICAL PHYSICS (ICTP)

Strada Costiera 11, Trieste, I-34014, Italy
Tel: (39) 040 224 0111
Fax: (39) 040 224 163
Email: sci_info@ictp.it
Website: www.ictp.it
Contact: Public Information Officer

3

The Abdus Salam International Centre for Theoretical Physics (ICTP) is an institution for research and high-level training in physics and mathematics, mainly for scientists from developing countries. It also maintains a network of associate members and federated institutes.

Abdus Salam ICTP Fellowships

Subjects: Physics and mathematics.
Purpose: To enable qualified applicants pursue research in the fields of condensed matter physics, mathematics and high-energy physics.
Eligibility: Open to qualified applicants of any nationality who have a PhD in physics or mathematics.
Level of Study: Postdoctorate
Type: Fellowship
Value: Monthly stipend and round-trip expenses where applicable, and allowances according to the length of the visit
Length of Study: Up to 1 year
Frequency: Dependent on funds available
Study Establishment: ICTP
Country of Study: Italy
No. of awards offered: Varies
Application Procedure: Applicants must request for appropriate application forms from the secretariat, or visit the ICTP website.
Closing Date: Applications are accepted at any time
Funding: Government
Contributor: The Italian government, IAEA and UNESCO

ABERYSTWYTH UNIVERSITY

Old College, King Street, Aberystwyth, Ceredigion, SY23 2AX, Wales
Tel: (44) 19 7062 2023
Fax: (44) 19 7062 2921
Email: pg-admissions@aber.ac.uk
Website: www.aber.ac.uk
Contact: Dr Rhys Williams, Postgraduate Admissions Officer

Located in beautiful surroundings, the Aberystwyth University provides an ideal learning environment. Its information services are among the best in the United Kingdom, and students also enjoy free access to one of the six copyright libraries in the United Kingdom, the National Library of Wales, which is adjacent to the University.

Aberystwyth Postgraduate Research Studentships

Subjects: Studies leading to the award of a PhD in any of the University's 17 academic departments. The university offers a wide range of research opportunities within the faculties of science, social sciences and arts.
Purpose: To enable United Kingdom and European Union students to undertake full-time doctoral study at Aberystwyth University.
Eligibility: Open to United Kingdom and European Union candidates who have obtained at least an Upper Second Class (Honours) Degree or equivalent in their degree examination and who wish to study full-time. To be eligible you must: (i) be a uk/eu fee payer. (ii) have or expect to obtain at least a second upper class Honours degree. (iii) apply and be offered a place for Doctoral study at Aberystwyth University.
Level of Study: Doctorate, Postgraduate, Research
Type: Studentship
Value: United Kingdom fees plus a subsistence allowance based on UK research council rates
Length of Study: 1 year, in the first instance, but usually renewable for up to 3 years subject to satisfactory academic progress
Frequency: Annual
Study Establishment: Aberystwyth University
Country of Study: United Kingdom
No. of awards offered: Usually 12 per year
Application Procedure: Applicants must complete an application form, available from the Postgraduate Admissions Office or from the website. Selection is based on the application for admission including a research proposal and references. There are no additional forms for this competition.
Closing Date: March 1st
Funding: Private
Contributor: Aberystwyth University
No. of awards given last year: 12

No. of applicants last year: 120
Additional Information: For all enquiries, please contact the Postgraduate Admissions Office: pg-admissions@aber.ac.uk

For further information contact:

United Kingdom

THE ACADEMY OF NATURAL SCIENCES

1900 Benjamin Franklin Parkway, Philadelphia, 19103, United States of America
Tel: (1) 215 299 1000
Fax: (1) 215 299 1028
Email: webmaster@ansp.org
Website: www.ansp.org
Contact: Dr Lois Kuter, Volunteer Coordinator

Founded in 1812, the Academy of Natural Sciences is the oldest continually operating museum of its kind in the Western Hemisphere. The Academy's mission is to create the basis for a healthy and sustainable planet through exploration, research, and education.

Böhlke Memorial Endowment Fund

Subjects: Ichthyology.
Purpose: To support graduate students and postdoctoral researchers to work with ichthyology collection and library at the academy.
Eligibility: Open to graduate students and recent postdoctoral researchers.
Level of Study: Postdoctorate
Type: Funding support
Value: less than $500
Study Establishment: The Academy of Natural Sciences
Country of Study: United States of America
Application Procedure: A letter of application outlining proposed research and tentative budget should be sent.
Additional Information: The Academy of Natural SciencesContact: Dr John Lundberg

For further information contact:

Contact: Dr John Lundberg

Jessup and McHenry Awards

Subjects: The Jessup award is for zoology and the McHenry award is for botany.
Purpose: To assist predoctoral and postdoctoral students working with biological collections at the Academy of Natural Sciences in Philadelphia.
Eligibility: Jessup funds are awarded competitively to students wishing to conduct studies at the postgraduate, doctoral and postdoctoral levels under the supervision or sponsorship of a member of the curatorial staff of the Academy. The awards are not available for undergraduate study. These awards are intended to assist predoctoral and postdoctoral students within several years of receiving their PhDs. Students commuting within the Philadelphia area are ineligible.
Level of Study: Doctorate, Postdoctorate, Postgraduate, Predoctorate
Type: Fellowship
Value: The stipend for subsistence is US$300 per week. Fellowships may include round trip travel costs of up to a total of US$500 for North American applicants, including Mexico and the Caribbean, and US$1,000 for applicants from other parts of the world. This is not guaranteed
Length of Study: 2–16 weeks
Frequency: Annual
Study Establishment: The Academy of Natural Sciences
Country of Study: United States of America
Application Procedure: Applicants must send queries, requests for information and supporting information to the given address.
Closing Date: March 1st or October 1st
Funding: Private
No. of awards given last year: 3

Additional Information: The provision of scientific supplies and equipment is the responsibility of the student and the sponsoring curator. Contact Dr Ted Daeschler, Jessup McHenry Fund Committee for further information.

For further information contact:

Jessup-McHenry Fund Commitee
Contact: Dr Edward Daeschler

John J. & Anna H. Gallagher Fellowship

Purpose: To offer an opportunity for the study of rarer microscopic, multicellular invertebrate animals.
Eligibility: Open to candidates involved in original postdoctoral or sabbatical research on the systematics of microscopic invertebrates with priority for the study of rotifers.
Level of Study: Postdoctorate
Type: Fellowship
Length of Study: 1 year
Study Establishment: The Academy of Natural Sciences
Country of Study: United States of America
Application Procedure: Application materials may be sent by email or post.
Closing Date: The position is currently filled. The next opening will probably be in 2010

For further information contact:

Chair, Gallagher Fellowship Committee, The Academy of Natural Sciences
Contact: Dr Ted Daeschler

ACADEMY OF TELEVISION ARTS & SCIENCES

5220 Lankershim Boulevard, North Hollywood, CA, 91601-3109, United States of America
Tel: (1) 818 754 2800
Fax: (1) 818 761 2827
Email: webmaster@emmys.org
Website: www.emmys.org

The Academy of Television Arts & Sciences promotes creativity, diversity, innovation and excellence through recognition, education and leadership in the advancement of the telecommunications arts and sciences. The Academy has become both a place for serious discussion and a place to celebrate the industries finest achievements with its annual Emmy Awards ceremonies.

Fred Rogers Memorial Scholarship

Subjects: Children's media.
Purpose: To support and encourage an aspiring upper division or graduate student to pursue a career in children's media that furthers the values and principles of Fred Rogers work.
Eligibility: Open to upper division graduate students of accredited colleges or universities. Candidates must have the ultimate goal of working in the field of children's media.
Level of Study: Doctorate, Postgraduate
Type: Scholarship
Value: US$10,000
Frequency: Annual
Country of Study: United States of America
Application Procedure: Candidates must complete an extensive form that includes background information about the themselves and plan for the use of the scholarship money. The application must also include recommendations from 2 people, either faculty members or professionals from the children's media industry who have worked with the applicant. Application forms are available online.
Closing Date: February 27th
Contributor: The Academy of Television Arts & Sciences in association with Ernst & Young LLP
Additional Information: In addition to the monetary award, successful applicants will work with a mentor from the Children's Programming Peer Group during the academic year.

ACADIA UNIVERSITY

Room 214B, Horton Hall, 18 University Avenue, Wolfville, NS, B4P 2R6, Canada
Tel: (1) 902 585 1914
Fax: (1) 902 585 1096
Email: theresa.starratt@acadiau.ca
Website: www.acadiau.ca
Contact: Ms Theresa Starratt, Graduate Studies Officer-Research and Graduate Studies

Acadia University is an institution that is committed to providing a liberal education based on the highest standards. The University houses a scholarly community that aims to ensure a broadening life experience for students, faculty and staff.

Acadia Graduate Awards

Subjects: English, political science, sociology, biology, chemistry, computer science, geology, psychology, education and recreation management, mathematics and statistics.
Purpose: To financially support students.
Eligibility: Open to registered full-time graduate students at Acadia University. In order to be eligible for an award students must have a GPA of not less than 3.00 in their major field in each of their last 2 years of undergraduate study.
Level of Study: Postgraduate
Type: Award
Value: Up to Canadian $9,000
Length of Study: 1–2 years
Frequency: Annual
Study Establishment: The Division of Research and Graduate Studies at Acadia University
Country of Study: Canada
No. of awards offered: Limited
Application Procedure: Applicants must write for details.
Closing Date: February 1st
Additional Information: Recipients of an Acadia Graduate Award should expect to undertake certain duties during the academic year (up to a minimum of 10 hours per week and a maximum of 120 hours per semester) as a condition of tenure of the award. The specific duties will be established by agreement at the beginning of each academic year.

THE ACOUSTICAL SOCIETY OF AMERICA (ASA)

Suite 1NO1, 2 Huntington Quadrangle, Melville, NY, 11747-4502, United States of America
Tel: (1) 516 576 2360
Fax: (1) 516 576 2377
Email: asa@aip.org
Website: http://asa.aip.org
Contact: Elaine Moran, ASA Office Manager

The Acoustical Society of America (ASA) is primarily a voluntary organization and attracts the interest, commitment and service of a large number of professionals. Since its inception in 1929, the Society has grown steadily in membership and stature.

ASA Frederick V. Hunt Postdoctoral Research Fellowship

Subjects: Acoustics.
Purpose: To carry out Professor Hunt's wish that his estate be used to further the science of, and education in, acoustics.
Eligibility: Open to candidates who have obtained a PhD and are members of the ASA.
Level of Study: Postdoctorate, Research
Type: Fellowship
Value: US$55,000
Length of Study: 1 year
Frequency: Annual
Country of Study: United States of America
No. of awards offered: 1
Application Procedure: Applicants can download the form from the website.
Closing Date: September 1st

ACTION CANADA

3306-515 West Hastings Street, c/o Morris J. Wosk Centre for
Dialogue, Simon Fraser University, Vancouver, BC, V6B 5K3, Canada
Tel: (1) 778 782 7961
Fax: (1) 778 782 7956
Email: actioncanada@actioncanada.ca
Website: www.actioncanada.ca

Action Canada is a national organization committed to building leadership for the future of Canada through an innovative fellowship program.

Action Canada Fellowships

Subjects: All subjects.
Purpose: To support applicants in the early years of their careers.
Eligibility: Open to applicants who are citizens of Canada.
Level of Study: Postgraduate
Type: Fellowship
Value: Canadian $20,000 each
Length of Study: 10 months
Frequency: Annual
Country of Study: Canada
No. of awards offered: Maximum 20
Application Procedure: A completed application form along with a curriculum vitae and proof of Canadian citizenship must be submitted. See the website for details.
Closing Date: See website for details
Contributor: Action Canada
No. of awards given last year: 16
No. of applicants last year: 199

ACTION CANCER

1 Marlborough Park, Belfast, BT9 6XS, Northern Ireland
Tel: (44) 28 9080 3344
Fax: (44) 28 9080 3356
Email: info@actioncancer.org
Website: www.actioncancer.org
Contact: Mr Robin McRoberts, Chief Executive

Action Cancer is a Northern Ireland cancer charity that relies entirely on voluntary donations. Founded in 1973, it offers awareness and health promotion, free early-detection clinics for men and women concerned about cancer and a support service for cancer patients and their families. Action Cancer also provides funding for research at local universities.

Action Cancer Pilot Grants

Subjects: Cancer-related projects.
Purpose: To help researchers in Northern Ireland carry out cancer-related projects by contributing to the cost of equipment or materials. Preference will be given to the support of individuals early in their career.
Eligibility: Researchers must be working in Northern Ireland.
Level of Study: Postdoctorate
Type: Grant
Value: UK £10,000
Length of Study: 1 year
Frequency: Annual
Country of Study: United Kingdom
No. of awards offered: 5
Application Procedure: Awards are advertised in the local press in March. Applicants must submit an application form, based on which a decision is made by the Scientific and Research Committee.
Closing Date: Early May
Funding: Private
Contributor: Voluntary donations
No. of awards given last year: 8
No. of applicants last year: 26

Action Cancer Project Grant

Subjects: Cancer-related projects.
Purpose: To help researchers in Northern Ireland carry out significant cancer-related projects by contributing to salaries, the purchase of materials and equipments and to other appropriate costs.

Eligibility: Researchers must be working in Northern Ireland.
Level of Study: Postdoctorate
Type: Project grant
Value: Up to UK £45,000 per year for up to 3 years
Length of Study: 3 years
Frequency: Every 2 years
Country of Study: United Kingdom
No. of awards offered: 1
Application Procedure: Awards are advertised in the local press in March. Applicants must submit a form, based on which a decision is taken by the Action Cancer Scientific and Research Committee, which also takes advice from external reviewers.
Closing Date: Early May
Funding: Private
Contributor: Voluntary donations
No. of awards given last year: None

Action Cancer Research Studentship

Subjects: Cancer-related projects.
Purpose: To provide an opportunity for an outstanding graduate in an appropriate chemical, biological or biomedical science, to work on a cancer-related research project and undergo research training with a view to being awarded a PhD from the Queen's University of Belfast or the University of Ulster.
Eligibility: Supervisors must be researchers in Northern Ireland.
Level of Study: Doctorate
Type: Studentship
Value: Approx. UK £17,800 per year
Length of Study: 3 years
Frequency: Annual
Country of Study: United Kingdom
No. of awards offered: 1
Application Procedure: Awards are advertised in the local press in December. Supervisors must submit an application form, and on receipt of the award must advertise for an appropriate student. Applications are reviewed externally and a decision is taken on the award by Action Cancer's Scientific and Research Committee.
Closing Date: April
Funding: Private
Contributor: Voluntary donations
No. of awards given last year: 1
No. of applicants last year: 10

For further information contact:

Tel: 028 9080 3348
Email: 028 9080 3348
Contact: Teresa Scott

ACTION MEDICAL RESEARCH

Vincent House, Horsham, West Sussex, RH12 2DP, England
Tel: (44) 14 0321 0406
Fax: (44) 14 0321 0541
Email: info@action.org.uk
Website: www.action.org.uk

Action Medical Research is dedicated to preventing and treating disease disability by funding vital medical research in UK-based hospitals and universities. The remit focuses on child health with an emphasis onclinical research or research at the clinical/basic interface. Research applications are judged by rigorous peer review.

Action Medical Research Project Grants

Subjects: A broad spectrum of research with the objective of preventing and treating disease and disability and alleviating physical disability. The remit focuses on child health to include problems affecting pregnancy, childbirth, babies, children and adolescents.
Purpose: To support one precisely formulated line of research.
Eligibility: Open to researchers based in the United Kingdom. Grants are not awarded to MRC units, other charities or for higher education.
Level of Study: Unrestricted
Type: Grant
Value: Varies
Length of Study: Up to 3 years, assessed annually
Frequency: Dependent on funds available, see the website

Study Establishment: Hospitals, universities and recognised research establishments in the UK
Country of Study: United Kingdom
No. of awards offered: Varies
Application Procedure: Applicants must submit a one-page outline of the project before an application form can be issued. Full details and outline proposals are available on the website.
Closing Date: See the website for details. Likely to be in April or November
Funding: Private, trusts
Contributor: Voluntary income
No. of awards given last year: 20
No. of applicants last year: 159

Action Medical Research Training Fellowship

Subjects: A broad spectrum of research with the objective of preventing and treating disease and disability and alleviating physical disability. The remit focuses on child health to include problems affecting pregnancy, childbirth, babies, children and adolescents.
Purpose: To enable the training of young medical and non-medical graduates in research techniques and methodology in areas of interest to Action Medical Research.
Eligibility: Open to medical and non-medical graduates. Although it is not limited to United Kingdom citizens, those who do not hold United Kingdom citizenship must be able to show that they have all the required statutory documentation, e.g. work permits, to cover the period of the fellowship. Preference will be given to candidates resident in the UK. No grants are made purely for higher education. Further guidelines are available on the organisation's website.
Level of Study: Postgraduate, Doctorate, Postdoctorate
Type: Fellowship
Value: Varies
Length of Study: Up to 3 years
Frequency: Dependent on funds available
Study Establishment: A hospital, university department or recognised research institute in the UK
Country of Study: United Kingdom
No. of awards offered: Varies
Application Procedure: Applicants must submit a one-page outline of the project before an application form can be issued. Full details and outline proposal forms are available on the website.
Closing Date: Please see the website; likely to be August 31st
Funding: Private, trusts
Contributor: Voluntary income
No. of awards given last year: 3
No. of applicants last year: 46
Additional Information: Fellowships are advertised separately each year in June/July.

ADELPHI UNIVERSITY

1 South Avenue, PO BOX 701, Garden City, NY, 11530-0701, United States of America
Tel: (1) 516 877 3080
Fax: (1) 516 877 3380
Email: financialservices@adelphi.edu
Website: www.senries.adelphi.edu

Adelphi University is the oldest institution of higher education for liberal arts and sciences on Long Island.

Adelphi University Athletic Grants

Subjects: Athletics.
Purpose: To support students who demonstrate exceptional ability in the area of athletics.
Eligibility: The student's athletic performance/record is the initial criterion for consideration of this award.
Level of Study: Postgraduate
Type: Scholarship
Value: Covers full tuition fees
Length of Study: 1 year
Frequency: Annual
Study Establishment: Adelphi University
Application Procedure: Students must file an admissions application.
Closing Date: February 15th

Adelphi University Dean's Award

Subjects: All subjects.
Purpose: To reward academic achievement and cocurricular activities.
Eligibility: The candidates should have combined critical reading and math SAT scores ranging from 1050 to 1190 and rank in the top 25% of their high school class. The performance on the writing section of the SAT will be carefully evaluated and will be considered in the determination of the final scholarship award.
Level of Study: Postgraduate
Type: Scholarship
Value: $8,000–$11,500
Length of Study: 1 year
Frequency: Annual
Study Establishment: Adelphi University
Application Procedure: Students must file an admissions application.
Closing Date: February 15th
Funding: Private

Adelphi University Presidential Scholarship

Subjects: All subjects.
Purpose: To reward exceptional academic achievement and co-curricular activities.
Eligibility: Open to Presidential scholars typically having combined critical reading and math SAT scores of at least 1300 and rank in the top 10% of their high school class. The performance on the writing section of the SAT will be carefully evaluated and will be considered in the determination of the final scholarship award.
Level of Study: Postgraduate
Type: Scholarship
Value: $15,000–$16,000
Length of Study: 1 year
Frequency: Annual
Study Establishment: Adelphi University
Application Procedure: Students must file an admissions application.
Closing Date: February 15th
Funding: Private

Adelphi University Provost Scholarship

Subjects: All subjects.
Purpose: To reward students with excellent academic performance and co curricular activities.
Eligibility: Open to Provost scholars having combined critical reading and math SAT scores exceeding 1200 and rank in the top 15% of their high school class or have a minimum transfer GPA of 3.5.
Level of Study: Postgraduate
Type: Scholarship
Value: $12,000–$14,500
Length of Study: 1 year
Frequency: Annual
Study Establishment: Adelphi University
Application Procedure: Students must file an admissions application.
Closing Date: February 15th
Funding: Private

Adelphi University Talent Awards

Subjects: Theater, dance, art and music.
Purpose: To support students who demonstrate exceptional talent in the areas of theater, dance, art, or music.
Eligibility: Open to candidates who demonstrate exceptional talent in the areas of theater, dance, art or music. Candidates must declare a major and will be required to initially submit a portfolio or audition in their area of concentration.
Level of Study: Postgraduate
Type: Award
Value: $4,000–$9,500
Length of Study: 1 year
Frequency: Annual
Study Establishment: Adelphi University
Application Procedure: Students must file an admissions application.
Closing Date: February 15th
Funding: Private

Adelphi University Trustee Scholarship

Subjects: All subjects.
Purpose: To support freshmen with the most outstanding academic achievement and cocurricular activities.
Eligibility: Open to trustee scholars having combined critical reading and math SAT scores exceeding 1350 and rank in the top 10% of their high school class.
Level of Study: Postgraduate
Type: Scholarship
Value: $16,500–$24,000
Length of Study: 1 year
Frequency: Annual
Application Procedure: Students must file an admissions application.
Closing Date: February 15th
Funding: Private
Contributor: Adelphi University

ADOLPH AND ESTHER GOTTLIEB FOUNDATION, INC.

380 West Broadway, New York, NY 10012, United States of America
Tel: (1) 212 226 0581
Fax: (1) 212 226 0584
Email: sross@gottliebfoundation.org
Website: www.gottliebfoundation.org
Contact: Sheila Ross, Grants Manager

The Adolph and Esther Gottlieb Foundation is a non-profit corporation registered with the state of New York. It was established to award financial aid to mature creative painters, sculptors and printmakers.

Gottlieb Foundation Emergency Assistance Grants

Subjects: Painting, sculpture and printmaking.
Purpose: To provide interim financial assistance to creative visual artists whose need is the result of unforeseen catastrophic incident.
Eligibility: Open to painters, sculptors and printmakers who can demonstrate a minimum of 10 years of involvement in a mature phase of their work and who do not have the resources to meet the costs incurred by a catastrophic event e.g. fire, flood or emergency medical expenses. The disciplines of film, photography or related forms are not eligible unless the work involves directly, or can be interpreted as, painting or sculpture.
Level of Study: Unrestricted
Type: Grant
Value: Up to US$10,000. US$4,000 is typical on a one time basis only
Frequency: Dependent on funds available
Country of Study: Any country
No. of awards offered: Varies
Application Procedure: Applicants must complete and submit an application form which is available from the Foundation throughout the year and may be requested by telephone. Second party requests are honoured only when the applicant is physically unable to communicate with the Foundation.
Closing Date: Please write for details
Funding: Private
Contributor: An endowment
Additional Information: Maturity is based on the level of technical, intellectual and creative development of the artist. The programme does not cover general indebtedness, dental work, unemployment, capital improvements, long-term disabilities or project funding. Review procedures for completed applications begin as soon as they are received. Full review generally takes about four weeks from the time an application is complete. Situations with imminent deadlines will receive priority. When a situation warrants it, reviews can be completed within 24 to 48 hours.

Gottlieb Foundation Individual Support Grants

Subjects: Painting, sculpture and printmaking.
Purpose: To recognize and support serious, fully committed painters, sculptors and printmakers who are in financial need.
Eligibility: Open to creative painters, sculptors and printmakers who have been in a mature phase of their work for at least 20 years and require financial assistance to continue this work. United States residency is not required. The Gottlieb Foundation does not provide funding for organizations, projects of any type, educational institutions, students, graphic artists or those working in crafts. The disciplines of photography, film, video or related forms are not eligible unless the work directly involves, or can be interpreted as, painting or sculpture.
Level of Study: Unrestricted
Type: Grant
Value: Varies
Length of Study: 1 year
Frequency: Annual
Country of Study: Any country
No. of awards offered: The number and amount of awards are annual decisions made by the Foundation's Board of Directors
Application Procedure: Applicants must include a current application form, available from the foundation, and a small group of slides of the artist's work that illustrates the progressive development of the art for at least a 20-year period. These slides must be properly labelled and dated. Applicants must also include a written statement in narrative form. This statement should include outside jobs which have helped support the artist's career, changes in artistic approach that have occurred, and other facts which can aid the review panel in forming an accurate picture. All aspects of artistic history, i.e. education, exhibitions, etc., should be described, and dates must be provided for all information. Financial disclosure, which entails completing a disclosure page and submitting a copy of a federal tax return for the past year, is necessary in the determination of financial need. A stamped addressed envelope for the return of supplementary materials must also be included.
Closing Date: December 15th
Funding: Private
Contributor: An endowment
Additional Information: Artists who have been awarded a grant must allow one year to elapse before reapplication. Only first person written requests for application forms will be honoured.

AFRICAN MATHEMATICS MILLENNIUM SCIENTIFIC INITIATIVE

School of Mathematics, University of Nairobi, PO Box 30197, Nairobi, GPO 00100, Kenya
Tel: (254) 254 20 445 0934
Email: ammsi@uonbi.ac.ke
Website: www.ammsi.org
Contact: Professor Wandera Ogana, AMMSI Programme Director

The African Mathematics Millennium Science Initiative (AMMSI) is a distributed network of mathematics research, training and promotion throughout sub-Saharan Africa. It has five regional offices located in Botswana, Cameroon, Kenya, Nigeria and Senegal. It is a project established by the Millenium Science Initiative (MSI), administered by the Science Initiative Group (SIG). The primary goal of the MSI is to create and nuture world-class science and scientific talent in the developing world by strengthening S&T capacity through integrated programmes of research and training, planned and driven by local scientists in the field of mathematics.

Research/Visiting Scientist Fellowships

Subjects: Mathematics.
Purpose: To encourage research and postgraduate teaching in mathematics.
Eligibility: Candidates should undertake research and postgraduate teaching in mathematics at any university in sub-Saharan Africa, should be a staff member at a university and hold at least a Master's degree, and should obtain an official invitation from the host institution.
Level of Study: Postgraduate
Type: Fellowships
Value: US$5,000
Length of Study: 1–12 months
Application Procedure: Application forms should be filled and submitted online. In exceptional circumstances, hard copy application forms may be obtained from the nearest AMMSI Regional Coordinator whose contact details can be found in the website.
Closing Date: September 15th
Additional Information: Successful applicants must take up the offer by December 31st.

For further information contact:

School of Mathematics, University of Nairobi, Nairobi, KENYA, 30197
Tel: (+254 20) 235 8569
Email: progoffice@ammsi.org
Contact: Wandera Ogana, AMMSI Programme Director

AFRICAN NETWORK OF SCIENTIFIC AND TECHNOLOGICAL INSTITUTIONS (ANSTI)

PO Box 30592, Nairobi, Kenya
Tel: (254) 2 7622 619
Fax: (254) 2 7622 538
Email: info@ansti.org
Website: www.ansti.org
Contact: Administrative Assistant

The African Network of Scientific and Technological Institutions (AN-STI) is an organ of co-operation that embraces institutions engaged in the fields of science and technology. To date it has 126 member institutions in 33 countries in Sub-Saharan Africa.

ANSTI/DAAD Postgraduate Fellowships

Subjects: Basic and engineering sciences.
Purpose: To enable students to pursue Master's and PhD courses in the basic and engineering sciences.
Eligibility: Open only to African nationals who are staff members of ANSTI member institutions. Applicants must possess a good Bachelor's degree and must be below 36 years of age.
Level of Study: Doctorate, Postgraduate
Type: Fellowship
Value: Varies, approx. US$12,000
Length of Study: Varies, approx. 1.5 years
Frequency: Annual
Study Establishment: ANSTI member institutions
Application Procedure: Applicants must complete an application form, available by contacting ANSTI by mail, fax or email, or by visiting our website.
Closing Date: May 31st
Funding: Government
Contributor: DAAD/UNESCO
No. of awards given last year: 5
No. of applicants last year: 52
Additional Information: The applicant is responsible for gaining admission into the university of his or her choice. Preference is given to graduates with a few years of experience.

AFRO-ASIAN INSTITUTE (AAI) IN VIENNA AND CATHOLIC WOMEN'S LEAGUE OF AUSTRIA

Student Division, Türkenstrasse 3, A-1090 Vienna, Austria
Tel: (43) 310 5145 311
Fax: (43) 310 5145 312
Email: s.angerler@aai-wien.at
Website: www.aai-wien.at
Contact: Mr Maga Susanne Angerler, Study Advisor

The Afro-Asian Institute (AAI) major function is to aid students from the developing countries of Africa, Asia and Latin America. Presently, the AAI provides services for more than 5,000 students from developing countries, which counts as an acknowledged contribution to Austrian development aid.

One World Scholarship Program

Subjects: All subjects.
Purpose: To promote cultural exchange, international development and international co-operation aid.
Eligibility: Open to nationals of developing countries in Africa, Asia and Latin America aged 18–35 years who have had adequate previous study or vocational practice in the specific field for which the scholarship is applied. Preference is given to candidates who are able to speak German. Only those in financial need will be considered, and the applicability of the special branch of study or training in the applicant's home country is essential. It is expected that scholars will return to their home country after studying. Good, and sometimes excellent, study results are also required. Preference is given to applicants from the least developed countries. It is a requirement that applicants have already started their studies in Austria.
Level of Study: Doctorate, Graduate, Unrestricted
Type: Scholarship
Value: UK £475–510 per month
Frequency: Annual
Study Establishment: Universities
Country of Study: Austria
No. of awards offered: Varies
Application Procedure: Applicants must complete an application form, which is available from the Institute. Only personal applications will be considered. Postal applications from abroad will not be answered.
Closing Date: April
Funding: Government, private
Contributor: The Catholic Church
Additional Information: It is one of AAI's essential aims to establish a 'partnership' contact between assisted students and the scholarship donor that continues beyond the termination of studies. Only about 10 per cent of applicants can be accepted.

THE AGA KHAN FOUNDATION

The Aga Khan Development Network, PO Box 2049, 1-3 Avenue de la Paix, Geneva 2, 1211, Switzerland
Tel: (41) 22 909 7200
Fax: (41) 22 909 7292
Email: info@akdn.org
Website: www.akdn.org

The Aga Khan Foundation is a non-denominational, international development agency established in 1967 by His Highness the Aga Khan. Its mission is to develop and promote creative solutions to problems that impede social development, primarily in Asia and East Africa. Created as a private, non-profit foundation under Swiss law, it has branches and independent affiliates in 15 countries. It is a modern vehicle for traditional philanthropy in the Ismaili Muslim community under the leadership of the Aga Khan.

Aga Khan Foundation International Scholarship Programme

Subjects: All subjects.
Purpose: To financially support outstanding students from developing countries who have no other means of financing their studies.
Eligibility: Open to candidates under the age of 30 with excellent academic records and genuine financial need. Candidates are expected to have some years of work experience in their field of interest.
Level of Study: Doctorate, Postgraduate
Type: Scholarship
Value: The Foundation assists students with tuition fees and living expenses only
Length of Study: 1–2 years
Frequency: Annual
Application Procedure: Application forms are available on January 1st each year from AKF offices or Aga Khan Education Services/ Boards in applicants countries of current residence. Completed applications should be returned to the agency or to the address indicated on the front of the form.
Closing Date: March 31st
Funding: Foundation, government, private
Contributor: Aga Khan Foundation
Additional Information: The foundation accepts applications from countries where it has branches, affiliates or other AKDN agencies which can help with processing applications and interviewing applicants. At present, these are Bangladesh, India, Pakistan, Afghanistan, Tajikistan, Syria, Kenya, Tanzania, Uganda, Mozambique, Madagascar, France, Portugal, UK, USA and Canada.

AGENCY FOR SCIENCE, TECHNOLOGY AND RESEARCH (A*STAR)

20 Biopolis Way, 07 01 Centros, 138668, Singapore
Tel: (65) 6826 6111
Fax: (65) 6777 1711
Email: tellusmore@a-star.edu.sg
Website: www.a-star.edu.sg/astar

A*STAR comprises of the Biomedical Research Council (BMRC), the Science and Engineering Research Council (SERC), Exploit Technologies Private Ltd (ETPL), the A*STAR Graduate Academy (AGA) and the Corporate Planning and Administration Division (CPAD). Both BMRC and SERC promote, support and oversee the public sector R&D research activities in Singapore.

A*STAR Graduate Scholarship
Subjects: Biomedical sciences, physical sciences and engineering.
Purpose: To provide financial assistance for a research intensive training programme at PhD level and to support Singapore's knowledge-based economy.
Eligibility: Open to citizens of Singaporeans, Singaporean permanent residents and ASEAN nationals. Successful candidates who are not Singaporeans are required to take up Singapore citizenship. Candidates must be graduates with First Class Honours Degree (or equivalent) or graduates with Second upper Class Honours and good 'A' levels results.
Level of Study: Doctorate, Research, PhD
Type: Scholarship
Value: Successful candidates will be given support for up to 4 years of academic pursuit leading to a PhD. Additional two years of post-doctoral training for selected partner universities will also be considered for those who qualify
Length of Study: 4 years
Frequency: Annual
Country of Study: Singapore
Application Procedure: Please check the website.
Closing Date: Please refer to the website
Additional Information: The AGS is tenable at the following partner universities: National University of Singapore, Nanyang Technological University, Imperial college of London, University of Illinois at Urbana-Champaign, Karolinska Institutet, University of Dundee, Carnegie Mellon University and University of Cambridge.

A*STAR Imperial Partnership (AIP) PhD Programme
Subjects: All subjects.
Eligibility: Open to Singaporeans, Singaporean permanent residents and ASEAN nationals. Successful candidates who are not Singaporeans are required to take up Singapore citizenship. Candidates must have a first degree in relevant disciplines, and have obtained 1st Class Honours. Those with 2nd Class (Upper) Honours and Good 'A' Levels results are also eligible to apply. Candidates must satisfy criteria for PhD admission to Imperial College London.
Type: Programme
Value: Full tuition fees, monthly sustenance allowance, annual book allowance, conference allowance, computer allowance, thesis allowance and travel and subsistence allowance for each permitted overseas visit
Closing Date: April 15th
Additional Information: This award is merged with the award A*Star Graduate Scholarship.

International Fellowship for Medical Doctors
Subjects: Medicine.
Purpose: The fellowship is offered with the main aim of developing clinician scientists.
Eligibility: Open to candidates who are medical doctors during their specialized training and possess excellent publication records, who are typically under 35 years of age and must be a Singapore Citizen.
Level of Study: Doctorate
Value: All rates and allowances vary according to country and university, and are subject to A*STAR adjustments from time to time
Length of Study: 2 years
Frequency: Annual
Country of Study: Singapore

No. of awards offered: Varies
Application Procedure: Please download application form from the website and submit by mail to A*STAR Graduate Academy.
Closing Date: A*STAR accepts and processes applications throughout the year

National Science PhD Scholarship
Subjects: Science, engineering and biomedical science disciplines.
Purpose: To offer support for PhD training in various Science, engineering and biomedical science disciplines. In return, scholars will return to make their mark on the R & D landscape in Singapore.
Eligibility: Open to Singaporeans, Singaporean permanent residents and ASEAN nationals. Successful candidates who are not Singaporeans are required to take up Singapore citizenship. Candidates must have a first degree honours in relevant disciplines, GPA of 3.8 and above from US universities or a CAP of 4.5 and above from local universities.
Level of Study: Research, PhD
Type: Scholarship
Value: All rates or allowances vary according to country and university
Length of Study: Varies
Frequency: Annual
No. of awards offered: Varies
Closing Date: A*STAR accepts and processes NSS (PhD) applications throughout the year. However, priority will be given to applications that reach us by 1st April for admissions to the overseas university in Fall the following year
Additional Information: For further information please visit the website www.a-star.edu.sg/astar/studentsandscholarships/action/scholarship_NSS_overseas_phd.do.

AGRICULTURAL HISTORY SOCIETY

1000 Holt Avenue - 2762, Rollins College, Winter Park, Florida, 32789, United States of America
Tel: (1) 407 646 2043
Fax: (1) 407 646 2363
Email: web@aghistorysociety.org
Website: www.aghistorysociety.org
Contact: Editor

The Agricultural History Society recognizes the roles of agriculture and agri-business in shaping the political, economic, social and historical profiles of different countries worldwide. Since 1927, the Society's publication, *Agricultural History*, has been the international journal for the field and publishes innovative research on agricultural and rural history.

Everett E Edwards Awards in Agricultural History
Subjects: Agricultural and rural history.
Purpose: To encourage and reward scholarly work in the field. The award was established in 1953 in memory and recognition of the outstanding services of Everett Eugene Edwards, a long-time agricultural historian and editor of *Agricultural History* from 1931 to 1951.
Eligibility: Open to any graduate or doctoral student submitting an article to *Agricultural History* during the calendar year.
Level of Study: Graduate
Type: Award
Value: US$200 plus publication in the Journal
Frequency: Annual
Country of Study: Any country
No. of awards offered: 1
Application Procedure: Applicants must submit three copies of their manuscript, prepared in accordance with the latest edition of the *Chicago Manual of Style*, to the editor.
Closing Date: December 31st
Additional Information: The award is presented annually to the author of the winning article at the Agricultural History Society's Presidential Luncheon. In addition, the winning submission is published in the fall issue of *Agricultural History*. Further information is available on request.

Gilbert C Fite Dissertation Award
Subjects: Agricultural and rural history.
Purpose: To reward the best dissertation.

Eligibility: Open to any doctoral student who has completed a PhD dissertation.
Level of Study: Doctorate
Type: Award
Value: US$300
Frequency: Annual
Country of Study: Any country
No. of awards offered: 1
Application Procedure: Applicants must complete forms and send three copies to the editor.
Closing Date: Please contact the organization
Additional Information: Further information is available on request.

Theodore Saloutos Award

Subjects: Agricultural and rural history in the United States of America.
Purpose: To reward the best book published annually in the United States of America on the subject of agricultural history.
Eligibility: Open to nationals of any country. Books must be based on substantial primary research and should represent a major new scholarly interpretation or reinterpretation of agricultural history scholarship.
Level of Study: Unrestricted
Type: Prize
Value: US$500
Frequency: Annual
Country of Study: Any country
Application Procedure: Applicants must send four copies of the book to the editor. Books may be nominated by their authors, the publisher, a member of the award committee, or a member of the Society.
Closing Date: Please contact the organization
Additional Information: Further information is available on request.

Vernon Carstensen Award in Agricultural History

Subjects: Agricultural and rural history.
Purpose: To promote research and publication. The award was established in 1980 to recognize Vernon Carstensen's services to agricultural history by his former students.
Eligibility: Open to any author who has been published in the quarterly journal of *Agricultural History* during the calendar year.
Level of Study: Doctorate, Postdoctorate
Type: Award
Value: US$200
Frequency: Annual
Country of Study: Any country
No. of awards offered: 1
Application Procedure: All published articles per issue and year are considered.
Closing Date: The Autumn issue of the Journal each year
Additional Information: Vernon Carstensen served as editor of Agricultural History from 1953 to 1957 and as president of the *Agricultural History* Society from 1957 to 1958. Further information is available on request.

AIDS ACTION

1730 M Street NW, Suite 611, Washington, DC, 20036, United States of America
Tel: (1) 202 530-8030
Fax: (1) 202 530-8031
Email: Zamora@aidsaction.org
Website: www.aidsaction.org
Contact: Coordinator, Pedro Zamora Fellowship Program

AIDS Action, founded in 1984, is the National AIDS Organization dedicated to the development, analysis, cultivation, and encouragement of sound policies and programs in response to the HIV epidemic.

The Pedro Zamora Public Policy Fellowship

Subjects: Research into a variety of public health and civil rights issues related to HIV prevention, treatment and care.
Purpose: To fund postgraduate students seeking experience in public policy and government affairs focussed on HIV/AIDS issues.

Eligibility: Open to graduate and undergraduate students and young professionals. Candidates need strong research, writing, and organizational skills and a willingness to work in a professional office. Ability to work independently in a fast-paced environment is critical. Familiarity with HIV-related issues and the legislative processes is preferred. Fellows must commit to working a minimum of 30 hours per week for 8 weeks. People of color, women, gay, lesbian, bisexual, and transgender individuals, and HIV positive individuals are encouraged to apply.
Level of Study: Postgraduate, Graduate
Type: Fellowship
Value: Stipend plus expenses
Length of Study: 26 weeks
Frequency: 3 times per year
Country of Study: United States of America
Application Procedure: Applicants must apply with covering letter, curriculum vitae, writing sample and essay. Check website for up-to-date details.
Closing Date: November 15th, April 15th, July 15th
Funding: Private

For further information contact:

1730 M Street NW, Suite 611 Washington, DC 20036
Tel: (202) 530-8030
Email: Zamora@aidsaction.org
Contact: Pedro Zamora, Coordinator

THE AIREY NEAVE TRUST

PO Box 36800, First Floor, 40 Bernard Street, London, WC1N 1WJ, England
Tel: (44) 20 7833 4440
Email: info@aveyneevetrust.org.uk
Website: www.aireyneavetrust.org.uk
Contact: Hannah Scott, The Trustees

Initiated in 1979, the Airey Neave Trust sponsors research into the protection of personal freedom under the law against the threat of terrorism, political violence and torture. It also provides financial support for any person who is a refugee, with particular emphasis on postgraduates and those retraining in their professions.

The Airey Neave Research Fellowships

Subjects: Research into the protection of personal freedom under the law against the threat of terrorism, political violence and torture.
Purpose: To support serious research connected with national and international law and human freedom.
Eligibility: Open to academics wishing to undertake research in the field of human freedom.
Level of Study: Postdoctorate, Research, Fellowships
Type: Fellowship
Value: £5,000 available for seminars and workshops, with certain guidelines
Length of Study: Up to 3 years
Study Establishment: An institution attached to a particular university in the United Kingdom
Country of Study: United Kingdom
No. of awards offered: 1–3 per year
Application Procedure: Contact the organisation for more details. No application form required but copy of an upto date curriculum vitae, certificate of mental fitness, 2 referees research plan up to 500 words.
Closing Date: None
Funding: Trusts
No. of awards given last year: 4
No. of applicants last year: 6
Additional Information: The trust also supports work in the following areas: (i) research into transnational networks and their implications for international security. The study will investigate the use of networks by criminal and terrorist organizations for activities such as money-laundering and arms sales (Centre of International Studies, Cambridge University); and (ii) research assistance to the Metropolitan Police in preventing, deterring, disrupting and detecting terrorist activity, particularly in its preparatory stages.

For further information contact:

Contact: Hannah Scott, Administrator

The Airey Neave Trust Scholarship

Purpose: To provide help for postgraduate refugees.
Eligibility: Open to postgraduate refugees
Level of Study: Doctorate, Postdoctorate, Postgraduate, Professional development, Medical Doctors
Value: Grants average UK £1,000–2,000 per year
Length of Study: 1 year
Frequency: Annual
Country of Study: United Kingdom
No. of awards offered: 20
Application Procedure: Applications are in March every year and must include completed application forms, two references and copies of home office documents confirming that the applicant is a refugee or has indefinite leave to stay in the United Kingdom.
Closing Date: May 31st
Funding: Trusts
No. of awards given last year: 11
No. of applicants last year: 30
Additional Information: Asylum seeker and refugees with British citizenship excluded.

AKADEMIE SCHLOSS SOLITUDE

Solitude 3, Stuttgart, 70197, Germany
Tel: (49) 711 99 6 19 0
Fax: (49) 711 99 6 19 50
Email: mail@akademie-solitude.de
Website: www.akademie-solitude.de

A public foundation located on the grounds of the baroque Castle Schloss Solitude near Stuttgart, the Akademie Schloss Solitude operates an international artist program awarding live/work fellowships to artists, emerging scholars, scientists, and professionals. Hundreds of fellows from more than 70 countries have used the Akademie to realize and advance their work and projects.

Akademie Schloss Solitude Fellowships

Subjects: Architecture, visual arts, performing arts, literature, music/sound, media, sciences, humanities, design, cinema and television.
Purpose: To promote young gifted artists, scholars, scientists and professionals.
Eligibility: Fellowships are awarded to artists, emerging scholars, scientists and professionals, who are not older than 35 or who have finished their basic studies not more than 5 years before applying to Akademie Schloss Solitude. Currently enrolled university or college students (at the time of application) will not be considered for selection. Several fellowships are also awarded regardless of the applicant's age.
Level of Study: Postdoctorate, Professional development, Unrestricted
Type: Fellowships
Value: €1,000 per month plus other benefits
Length of Study: 6 or 12 months
Frequency: Every 2 years
Country of Study: Germany
No. of awards offered: 50–60
Application Procedure: Applicants can download the application form from the website or request in writing during the application period i.e. July 1st to October 31st 2008 for a fellowship in 2009–2011
Closing Date: October 31st
Funding: Foundation
No. of awards given last year: 65
No. of applicants last year: 1,500
Additional Information: One specialist junior per artistic discipline is responsible for selecting the fellows. The Akademie, along with its fellows, presents a public program of events including exhibitions, concerts, readings, theatrical presentations, performance art, discussions, symposia or other forms of interdisciplinary artistic representations. Located on the grounds of the baroque castle Schloss Solitude in the outskirts of Stuttgart, a total of 45 furnished live/work studios are available to fellows and guests.

For further information contact:

Contact: Kristene Doyle

ALBERT ELLIS INSTITUTE

45 East 65th Street, New York, NY, 10021, United States of America
Tel: (1) 212 535 0822
Fax: (1) 212 249 3582
Email: info@albertellis.org
Website: www.albertellisinstitute.org
Contact: Fellowships Office

The Albert Ellis Institute is a non-profit training and therapy institute chartered by the regents of the University of the State of New York, specializing in cognitive behaviour therapy and rational emotive behaviour therapy.

Albert Ellis Institute Clinical Fellowship

Subjects: Psychology and counselling.
Purpose: To provide in-depth, hands-on training in cognitive behavioural therapy and rational emotive behaviour therapy.
Eligibility: Candidates must be in a doctoral programme, hold a PhD, MSW, MD or RN and be licence-eligible in their place of practice. There are no other restrictions.
Level of Study: Postdoctorate, Postgraduate, Predoctorate
Type: Fellowship
Value: US$9,000
Length of Study: 2 years
Frequency: Annual
Country of Study: United States of America
No. of awards offered: Varies
Application Procedure: Candidates must obtain applications and further information by writing to the Institute.
Closing Date: January 15th
Funding: Private
No. of awards given last year: 5
No. of applicants last year: 30
Additional Information: The programme begins in mid-July.

ALBERTA HERITAGE FOUNDATION FOR MEDICAL RESEARCH (AHFMR)

Suite 1500, Bell Tower, 10104-103 Avenue, Edmonton, AB, T5J 4A7, Canada
Tel: (1) 780 423 5727
Fax: (1) 780 429 3509
Email: pamela.valentine@ahfmr.ab.ca
Website: www.ahfmr.ab.ca
Contact: Dr Pamela Valentine, Acting Director, Grants and Awards

The Alberta Heritage Foundation for Medical Research (AHFMR) supports a community of researchers who generate knowledge that improves the health and quality of life of Albertans and people throughout the world. The Foundation's long-term commitment is to fund basic patient and health research based on international standards of excellence and carried out by new and established investigators and researchers in training.

Alberta Heritage Clinical Fellowships

Subjects: Medical research.
Purpose: To provide an opportunity for research training to candidates who have completed clinical sub-speciality training requirements.
Eligibility: Open to candidates who have completed all Canadian clinical requirements and licensable by the College of Physicians and Surgeons of Alberta or by the Alberta Dental Association, or they must be enrolled in, and nearing completion of, a subspecialty program recognized by the Royal College of Physicians and Surgeons of Canada, or must have completed the Fellowship program of the Canadian College of Family Practice.
Level of Study: Postgraduate
Type: Fellowship
Value: Canadian $3,000 research allowance plus stipend
Length of Study: 2 years, with a possibility of renewal for a further year
Frequency: Annual
Study Establishment: An appropriate institution, usually in Alberta
Country of Study: Canada
No. of awards offered: Approx. 10

Application Procedure: Applicants must complete an application form.
Closing Date: February 27th and October 1st
Funding: Government
No. of awards given last year: 11
No. of applicants last year: 29

For further information contact:

Tel: (780)423-5727
Email: grants@ahfmr.ab.ca.

Alberta Heritage Full-Time Fellowships

Subjects: Medical research.
Purpose: To enable doctoral graduates to prepare for careers as independent investigators.
Eligibility: Open to candidates with a PhD, MD, DDS, DVM or DPharm degree. Normally, support will not be provided beyond 6 years after receipt of the PhD degree, or beyond 8 years after receipt of the MD, DDS, DVM or DPharm degrees.
Level of Study: Postdoctorate
Type: Fellowship
Value: Canadian $3,000 research allowance plus stipend
Length of Study: Maximum 3 years
Frequency: Annual
Study Establishment: Usually at a university in Alberta
Country of Study: Canada
No. of awards offered: Varies
Application Procedure: Applicants must complete an application form.
Closing Date: February 27th and October 1st
Funding: Government
No. of awards given last year: 42
No. of applicants last year: 129

For further information contact:

Tel: (780)423-5727
Email: grants@ahfmr.ab.ca

Alberta Heritage Full-Time Studentship

Subjects: Medical research.
Purpose: To enable academically superior students to undertake full-time research training in a discipline relevant to the objectives of the Foundation.
Eligibility: Open to candidates sponsored by a faculty supervisor. The supervisor must have a record of productive health orientated research and sufficient competitively acquired research funding to ensure the satisfactory conduct of the student's research during the term of the award. Students must be engaged in, or accepted into, a full-time university graduate programme in a health related discipline leading to a Master's or doctoral degree. Candidates must also hold a record of superior academic performance in studies relevant to the proposed training.
Level of Study: Doctorate, Graduate
Type: Studentship
Length of Study: 2 years with the possibility to renewal for a maximum of 5 years' support
Frequency: Annual
Study Establishment: A university in Alberta
Country of Study: Canada
No. of awards offered: Approx. 40–60
Application Procedure: Candidates must submit, in full, the original application to the Foundation's offices by either of the deadlines.
Closing Date: February 27th and October 1st
Funding: Government
No. of awards given last year: 38
No. of applicants last year: 170

For further information contact:

Tel: (780)423-5727
Email: grants@ahfmr.ab.ca

Alberta Heritage Health Research Studentship

Subjects: Medical sciences.

Purpose: To enable academically superior students engaged in, or accepted in to, a full-time university programme to undertake full-time research training.
Eligibility: Candidates must have been accepted into, or be currently engaged in, a full-time, thesis-based, graduate program at an Alberta-based university in a health-related discipline leading to a Master's or doctoral degree.
Level of Study: Doctorate, Graduate
Type: Studentship
Value: Cost of purchasing scientific materials, supplies and expendables, to purchase of minor equipment (note: the policies of the host institution with respect to ownership of equipment will apply to equipment bought with these funds), computer software programs, costs for the use of libraries, or computers, costs associated with the publication of research results, travel expenses to attend scientific meetings, purchase of books, periodicals and journals
Length of Study: 2 years with a possibility to renewal for a maximum of 5 years' support
Frequency: Annual
Study Establishment: A university in Alberta
Country of Study: Canada
No. of awards offered: Varies
Application Procedure: Applicants must submit the original application to the Foundation's offices by either of the deadlines. They must be completed in full to be entered into the competition.
Closing Date: February 27th and October 1st
Funding: Government

Alberta Heritage Part-Time Fellowships

Subjects: Medical research.
Purpose: To enable continuing active participation in research during professional education.
Eligibility: Open to graduates holding a PhD in a science relevant to AHFMR objectives or who are registered in a health professional programme in Alberta.
Level of Study: Postdoctorate
Type: Fellowships
Value: Pro-rated on full-time fellowships stipend and dependent on the amount of time spent in research
Length of Study: 1 year, renewable
Frequency: Annual
Study Establishment: A university in Alberta
Country of Study: Canada
No. of awards offered: Approx. 5
Application Procedure: Candidates must complete an application form.
Closing Date: February 27th and October 1st
Funding: Government
No. of awards given last year: 2
No. of applicants last year: 2

Alberta Heritage Part-Time Studentship

Subjects: Medical research.
Purpose: To enable full-time degree students to continue research training on a part-time basis.
Eligibility: Candidates must normally have been accepted into, or be currently engaged in, a full-time graduate program at an Alberta-based university in a health-related discipline leading to a Master's or doctoral degree.
Level of Study: Doctorate, Graduate
Type: Studentship
Value: Pro-rated on full-time studentship stipend and dependent on the amount of time spent in research
Length of Study: 2 years, to a maximum of 5 years support
Frequency: Annual
Study Establishment: A university in Alberta
Country of Study: Canada
No. of awards offered: Approx. 5
Application Procedure: Applicants must complete an application form.
Closing Date: February 27th and October 1st
Funding: Government
No. of awards given last year: 1
No. of applicants last year: 1

Dr Lionel E Mcleod Health Research Scholarship

Subjects: Health.
Purpose: To enable academically superior students engaged in, or accepted on to, a full-time university programme to undertake full-time research training.
Eligibility: Open to Canadian citizens or permanent residents who attend the Universities of Alberta, Calgary or British Columbia.
Level of Study: Postgraduate
Type: Scholarship
Value: Canadian $21,500
Frequency: Annual
Country of Study: Canada
No. of awards offered: 1
Application Procedure: Applicants must write for details.
Funding: Government, private

Heritage Health Research Career Renewal Awards

Subjects: Epidemiology, biostatistics, psychosocial sciences or clinical experimental method and design.
Purpose: To enable carefully selected Alberta faculty members with a demonstrated interest in clinical or health research to obtain training.
Eligibility: Open to candidates proposed and sponsored by an Alberta institution, which is prepared to ensure an adequate environment for the candidate on their return to the province. This environment should encompass fostering the development of a group of scientists to be capable of independent research and to be able to assist others in the design of patient based and population based research.
Level of Study: Postdoctorate
Value: Please write for details
Frequency: Annual, but dependent upon tenure of current scholarship
Country of Study: Canada
No. of awards offered: Varies
Application Procedure: Applicants must write for details.
Closing Date: March 1st and October 1st
Funding: Government
No. of awards given last year: 1
No. of applicants last year: 2

ALCOHOL BEVERAGE MEDICAL RESEARCH FOUNDATION

1122 Kenilworth Drive, Suite 407, Baltimore, MD, 21204, United States of America
Tel: (1) 410 821 7066
Fax: (1) 410 821 7065
Email: info@abmrf.org
Website: www.abmrf.org
Contact: Dr Robin A Kroft, Vice President

The Alcohol Beverage Medical Research Foundation is a non-profit independent research organization that provides support for scientific studies on the use of alcoholic beverages. It awards grants to study changes in drinking patterns, effects of moderate use of alcohol on health and well being and the mechanisms underlying the behavioural and biomedical effects of alcohol.

Alcohol Beverage Medical Research Foundation Research Project Grant

Subjects: Medical and behavioural sciences.
Purpose: To support new knowledge in order to prevent alcohol related problems.
Level of Study: Doctorate
Type: Project grant
Value: Up to US$50,000 per year
Length of Study: Up to 2 years
Study Establishment: Non-profit universities and research institutions
Country of Study: United States of America or Canada
No. of awards offered: 30–40
Application Procedure: Applicants must complete an application form, available on request or from the website.

Closing Date: February 1st or September 1st
Funding: Private
No. of awards given last year: 40
No. of applicants last year: 150

ALEXANDER GRAHAM BELL ASSOCIATION FOR THE DEAF AND HARD OF HEARING

3417 Volta Place North West, Washington, DC, 20007, United States of America
Tel: (1) 202 337 5220
Fax: (1) 202 337 8314
Email: info@agbell.org
Website: www.agbell.org
Contact: Ms Lisa Ruffin Schauf

Alexander Graham Bell Association for the Deaf and Hard of Hearing (AG Bell) is a lifelong resource, support network and advocate for listening, learning, talking and living independently with hearing loss. Through publications, advocacy, training, scholarships and financial aid, AG Bell promotes the use of spoken language and hearing technology.

Alexander Graham Bell Scholarship Awards

Subjects: All subjects.
Purpose: To encourage severely or profoundly hearing-impaired students to attend mainstream colleges. A G Bell offers financial aid and scholarships through four major programmes, which are parent-infant (0–6 years), school age, arts and sciences and college scholarships.
Eligibility: Open to auditory oral students born with profound hearing loss, 80 dB loss in the better ear, average, or a severe hearing loss, who experienced such a loss before acquiring language. Candidates must use speech and residual hearing and/or speech reading as their preferred customary form of communication and demonstrate a potential for leadership. In addition, applicants must have applied to, or already be enrolled in, a regular full-time college or university programme for hearing students.
Level of Study: Unrestricted
Type: Scholarship
Value: US$250–2,000
Frequency: Annual
Country of Study: United States of America
No. of awards offered: Varies
Application Procedure: Applicants must request an application form in writing between September 1st and January 1st. Fax copies or telephone applications will not be accepted. Applicants may visit the website or send an email to financialaid@agbell.org for current information.
Closing Date: March 1st
Funding: Private
Contributor: Members and donors
No. of awards given last year: 31
No. of applicants last year: Approx. 150

ALEXANDER S ONASSIS PUBLIC BENEFIT FOUNDATION

7, Aeschinou Street, Athens, GR-105 58, Greece
Tel: (30) 210 371 3000
Fax: (30) 210 371 3013
Email: ffp@onassis.gr
Website: www.onassis.gr
Contact: Deputy Director, Human Resource Manager

The Alexander S Onassis Public Benefit Foundation establishes and supports public benefit projects, offers services and makes contributions to other public benefit institutions for medical care, education, literature, religion, science, research, journalism, art, cultural matters, history, archaeology and sport. It also awards prizes, grants and scholarships to both Greeks and foreigners.

Onassis Foreigners' Fellowship Programme Educational Scholarships Category B

Subjects: Greek language, Greek literature, Greek history and civilization.

Purpose: To render possible the acquaintance, collaboration and exchange of information between the scholarship recipients and their Greek colleagues in Greek schools, education or other relevant departments of Greek universities.

Eligibility: Open to active elementary or high school foreign teachers who teach the Greek language, modern or ancient, Greek literature, Greek history and Greek civilization. Only persons other than Greek nationals are eligible. However, persons of Greek descent, second generation and on, are also eligible providing they are permanently residing and working abroad or currently studying in foreign universities.

Type: Fellowship

Value: A monthly allowance of €1,200 plus hotel accommodation and a round trip air ticket

Length of Study: A maximum of 6 months

Frequency: Annual

Country of Study: Greece

No. of awards offered: 5

Application Procedure: Copies of the announcement and the relevant nomination and application forms are available daily at the Foundation's Secretariat or from the website.

Closing Date: January 31st

Additional Information: The programme presupposes that the scholarship recipients will continue offering their services to their country of origin after they have completed their training in Greece.

Onassis Foreigners' Fellowship Programme Educational Scholarships Category C

Subjects: All subjects.

Purpose: To render possible the acquaintance, collaboration and exchange of information between the scholarship recipients and their Greek colleagues in Greek schools, education or other relevant departments of Greek universities.

Eligibility: Open to foreign postgraduate students and PhD candidates up to 40 years of age who pursue studies in universities, scholarly or research centres or fine art schools either outside Greece or in Greece.

Level of Study: Doctorate, Postgraduate

Type: Fellowship

Value: A monthly allowance of €1,200 plus hotel accommodation and a round trip air ticket

Length of Study: 5–10 months

Frequency: Annual

Country of Study: Greece

No. of awards offered: 10

Application Procedure: Copies of the Announcement and the relevant nomination and application forms are available daily at the Foundation's Secretariat or from the website.

Closing Date: January 31st

Additional Information: The programme presupposes that the scholarship recipients will continue offering their services to their country of origin, after they have completed their training in Greece.

Onassis Foreigners' Fellowships Programme Research Grants Category AI

Subjects: Humanistic sciences, political sciences and the arts.

Purpose: To enable full members of national academies and full university professors whose scholarly or artistic work has been widely acclaimed and who wish to visit Greece in order to conduct scholarly research or to collaborate with educational institutions, research institutions or organizations.

Eligibility: Only people of non-Greek nationality are eligible. However, persons of Greek descent, second generation and on, are also eligible providing they are permanently residing and working abroad or currently studying in foreign universities. Candidates must have had a professional academic career of at least 10 years.

Level of Study: Postdoctorate

Type: Research grant

Value: A monthly allowance of €4,500 plus a round trip air ticket and hotel accommodation

Length of Study: 1 month

Frequency: Annual

Country of Study: Greece

No. of awards offered: 10

Application Procedure: Copies of the Announcement and the relevant nomination and application forms are available daily at the Foundation's Secretariat or from the website.

Closing Date: January 31st

Additional Information: Any candidate wishing to apply under this programme should specify the category in which they want to be considered in order to receive the relevant nomination and application form. Only one application form for one of the categories can be submitted.

Onassis Foreigners' Fellowships Programme Research Grants Category AII

Subjects: All subjects.

Purpose: To enable university or equivalent institutions' faculty, researchers, PhD holders, artists and musicians, and translators of Greek literature who wish to come to Greece either for scholarly research co-operation with a Greek university, research centre or institute or for their artistic creation or translation.

Eligibility: Only candidates who are not Greek nationals are eligible. However, candidates of Greek descent, second generation and on, are also eligible providing they are permanently residing and working abroad or currently studying in foreign universities. Candidates must have had a professional academic career of at least 10 years.

Level of Study: Postdoctorate

Type: Fellowship

Value: A monthly allowance of €2,500 plus hotel accommodation and a round trip air ticket

Length of Study: Up to 3–6 months

Frequency: Annual

Country of Study: Greece

No. of awards offered: 15

Application Procedure: Copies of the Announcement and the relevant nomination and application forms are available daily at the Foundation's Secretariat or from the website.

Closing Date: Please contact the organization

Additional Information: Any candidate wishing to apply under this programme should specify the category in which they want to be considered in order to receive the relevant nomination and application form. Only one application form for one of the categories can be submitted.

ALEXANDER VON HUMBOLDT FOUNDATION

Marketing and Mobility Centre, Jean-Paul-Str. 12, Bonn, D 53173, Germany
Tel: (49) 228 833 262
Fax: (49) 228 833 114
Email: andrea.berg@avh.de
Website: www.humboldt-foundation.de; www.euraxess.de
Contact: Mrs Berg Andrea

The Alexander von Humboldt Foundation is a non-profit foundation established by the Federal Republic of Germany for the promotion of international research co-operation. It enables highly qualified scientists and scholars not resident in Germany to spend extended periods of research in Germany and promotes the ensuing academic contacts. The Humboldt Foundation promotes an active world-wide network of researchers.

Alexander Von Humboldt Professorship

Subjects: All subjects.

Purpose: To recruit on a long-term basis top scientists and scholars from abroad for research in Germany and to give German universities–also in cooperation with non-university research institutions–the opportunity to establish or upgrade internationally visible research focus areas, thus raising their profile.

Eligibility: Academics of all disciplines from abroad, who are internationally recognized as leaders in their field.

Level of Study: Research

Type: Prize

Value: Academics in experimental disciplines: €5 million. Researchers in theoretical disciplines: €3.5 million for 5 years
Length of Study: 5 years
Frequency: Annual, 3 selection rounds each year
Study Establishment: German universities and research institutions
Country of Study: Germany
No. of awards offered: Up to 10
Application Procedure: Applications may be made by German universities. Non-university research institutions may also submit nominations jointly with a German university.
Closing Date: For the corresponding deadlines see the homepage
Funding: Government

Feodor Lynen Research Fellowships for Experienced Researchers

Subjects: All subjects.
Purpose: To enable researchers from Germany to carry out a long-term research project of their own choice in cooperation with an academic host at a research institution abroad. The host must be an academic working abroad who has already been sponsored by the Humboldt Foundation.
Eligibility: This programme targets outstanding academics from Germany who completed their doctorates less than twelve years ago and whose work demonstrates an independent academic profile. Typically applicants should be working at least at the level of an assistant professor or junior research group leader or as an independent researcher in a comparable position.
Level of Study: Postdoctorate
Type: Fellowship
Value: The provisions of the fellowship comprise a basic monthly sum and a monthly foreign allowance which may differ according to location and marital status. In addition marital and child allowances may be paid
Length of Study: 6–18 months; The fellowship is flexible and can be divided into as many as three stays within three years
Frequency: Annual, 3 selection rounds each year
Study Establishment: Research institutions or Universities
No. of awards offered: Up to 150 per year (For Postdoctoral and experienced researchers together)
Application Procedure: Information regarding the application procedure is available from the website.
Closing Date: Applications can be made at any time
Funding: Government
No. of awards given last year: 122 (For Postdoctoral and experienced researchers together)
No. of applicants last year: 221 (For Postdoctoral and experienced researchers together)

Feodor Lynen Research Fellowships for Postdoctoral Researchers

Subjects: All subjects.
Purpose: To enable researchers from Germany to carry out a long-term research project of theirown choice in cooperation with an academic host at a research institution abroad. The hostmust be an academic working abroad who has already been sponsored by the Humbldt Foundation
Eligibility: Open to researchers from Germany with above average qualifications, at the beginning of their academic career, who have only completed their doctorate or comparable academic degree (PhD, C.Sc or equivalent) in the last 4 years. Please check the website for further details.
Level of Study: Postdoctorate
Type: Fellowship
Value: A basic monthly sum and a monthly foreign allowance which may differ according to location and marital status. In addition marital and child allowances may be paid
Length of Study: 6–24 months
Frequency: Annual, 3 selection rounds each year
Study Establishment: Research institutions or universities
No. of awards offered: Up to 150 (For Postdoctoral and Experienced researchers together)
Application Procedure: Information regarding the application procedure is available from the website.
Closing Date: Applications can be made at any time
Funding: Government

No. of awards given last year: 122 (For Postdoctoral and Experienced researchers together)
No. of applicants last year: 221 (For Postdoctoral and Experienced researchers together)

Friedrich Wilhelm Bessel Research Award

Subjects: All subjects.
Purpose: To support scientists and scholars, internationally renowned in their field, who are expected to continue producing cutting-edge achievements which will have a seminal influence on their discipline beyond their immediate field of work.
Eligibility: The nominee must be recognised internationally as an outstanding researcher in his/her field and has a doctorate completed less than 12 years ago.
Level of Study: Research
Type: Prize
Value: €45,000
Length of Study: 6–12 months
Frequency: Annual, Two selection rounds each year
Study Establishment: Universities and research institutions
Country of Study: Germany
No. of awards offered: Up to 25
Application Procedure: Nominations may be submitted by established academics in Germany. Direct applications are not accepted.
Closing Date: Nominations are accepted throughout the year
Funding: Government
No. of awards given last year: 18
No. of applicants last year: 38
Additional Information: Selection committee meetings are held twice a year in Spring and Autumn.

Georg Forster Fellowships for Experienced Researchers

Subjects: The research proposal must address issues of significant relevance to the future development of the candidate's country of origin, and, in this context, promise to facilitate the transfer of knowledge and methods to developing and threshold countries.
Purpose: To enable researchers from developing and threshold countries to carry out long-term research project of their own choice with an academic host at a research institution in Germany.
Eligibility: This programme targets outstanding academics from developing and threshold countries (excluding the People's Republic of China, India and Turkey) who completed their doctorates less than 12 years ago and whose work demonstrates an independent academic profile. Typically, applicants should be working at least at the level of an assistant professor or junior research group leader, or as an independent researcher in a comparable position.
Level of Study: Postdoctorate
Type: Fellowship
Value: €2,450 per month (Includes a mobility lump sum and a contribution towards health and liability insurance as well as additional benefits)
Length of Study: 6–18 months; the fellowship is flexible and may be divided up into as many as three stay in Germany within three years
Frequency: 3 selection rounds each year
Study Establishment: Universities or research institution
Country of Study: Germany
No. of awards offered: Up to 60 per year (for Postdoctoral and Experienced Researchers together)
Application Procedure: Information regarding the application procedure is available from the website
Funding: Government
No. of awards given last year: 50 (for Postdoctoral and Experienced Researchers together)
No. of applicants last year: 134 (for Postdoctoral and Experienced Researchers together)
Additional Information: Applications should be sent directly to the Foundation. If this is not possible, applications may be submitted via the branch offices of the DAAD or the German embassy or consulate which will then forward them to the Humboldt Foundation.

Georg Forster Research Fellowships for Postdoctoral Researchers

Subjects: The research proposal must address issues of significant relevance to the future development of the candidate's country of origin, and in this context, promise to facilitate the transfer of knowledge and methods to developing and threshold countries.

Purpose: To enable researchers from developing and threshold countries to carry out long-term research projects of their own choice with an academic host at a research instituition in Germany.

Eligibility: Open to researchers from developing and threshold countries (excluding People's Republic of China, India and Turkey) with above average qualifications, at the beginning of their academic career who have only completed their doctorate or comparable academic degree (PhD, C.Sc or equivalent)in the last 4 years. Please check the website for further details.

Level of Study: Postdoctorate

Type: Fellowship

Value: €2,250 per month (including a mobility lump sum and a contribution towards health and liability insurance as well as additional benefits.)

Length of Study: 6–24 months

Frequency: Annual, 3 selection rounds each year

Study Establishment: Universities or research institutions

Country of Study: Germany

No. of awards offered: Up to 60 (For Postdoctoral and Experienced researchers together)

Application Procedure: Information regarding the application procedure is available from the website

Closing Date: Applications are accepted at any time

Funding: Government

No. of awards given last year: 50 (For Postdoctoral and Experienced researchers together)

No. of applicants last year: 134 (For Postdoctoral and Experienced researchers together)

Additional Information: Applications should be sent directly to the Foundation. If this is not possiblethey may be submitted via the branch offices of the DAAD or the consulate, which will then forward them to the Humboldt Foundation.

German Chancellor Fellowships for Prospective Leaders

Subjects: Candidates from all professions and disciplines, but especially from the humanities, law, social sciences and economics.

Purpose: To enable prospective leaders from the USA, the Russian Federation or the People's Republic of China to carry out an individual projects tailored to their professional development and goals in co-operation with a German host with whom they have established contact prior to the application.

Eligibility: Applicants must hold at least a Bachelor's degree completed less than 12 years prior to the start of the fellowship (September 1st of the year following the application) and be citizens of the United States, the Russian Federation, or the People's Republic of China. Candidates must have gained work experience and have already shown outstanding leadership potential in their careers

Level of Study: Postgraduate, Professional development, requires at least a Bachelor's degree

Type: Fellowship

Value: €2,150–2,750 monthly (in exceptional cases up to €3,650)

Length of Study: 1 year (beginning in September), preceded by a mandatory German language course for Fellows with little or no German language skills

Frequency: Annual, requires at least a Bachelor's degree

Study Establishment: Any institution/organization in Germany

Country of Study: Germany

No. of awards offered: 10 to US citizens, 10 to Russian citizens and 10 to Chinese citizens

Application Procedure: Information regarding the application procedure is available from the website of the Humboldt Foundation.

Closing Date: Varies, once per year. Please see our website for further information

Funding: Government

No. of awards given last year: 10 to US, 10 to Russian and 10 to Chinese citizens

Additional Information: The fellowship begins with a 4-week introductory seminar in Berlin and Bonn.

For further information contact:

Alexander van Humboldt Foundation, Jean-Paul-Strasse. 12, Bonn, D-53173, Germany

Hezekiah Wardwell Fellowships

Subjects: Music.

Purpose: To allow young, highly-gifted musicians from Spain to pursue further training or advanced studies at a college of music or conservatoire in Germany mentored by an established music teacher.

Eligibility: The Fellowship is aimed at candidates from Spain in transition to their professional careers. Therefore the Fellowship period applied for cannot start later than 3 years after the end of the graduation as a musician or musicologist. The Humboldt Foundation expects candidates to establish contact with supervisors prior to submitting their applications and to obtain binding clarification on whether the can be accepted as students and be given academic supervision.

Level of Study: Graduate, Postgraduate, Professional development

Type: Fellowships

Value: €800 per month and a sum of €250 on arrival for travel expenses

Length of Study: 10 months

Frequency: Annual

Study Establishment: College of Music, Conservatoire, University in Germany

Country of Study: Germany

No. of awards offered: Up to10

Application Procedure: Applicants must send a completed application form to the Foundation.

Closing Date: Please see the website for the deadline

Funding: Foundation

Humboldt Research Award

Subjects: All subjects.

Purpose: To support outstanding scientists and scholars from all disciplines from abroad whose fundamental discoveries, new theories, or insights have had a significant impact on their own discipline and who are expected to continue producing cutting-edge achievements in future.

Eligibility: Eminent foreign researchers at the peak of their academic careers and in leading positions, such as full professors or directors of institutes, may be nominated.

Level of Study: Research

Type: Prize

Value: Up to €60,000

Length of Study: 6–12 months

Frequency: Annual, 2 selection rounds each year

Study Establishment: Universities and research institutions

Country of Study: Germany

No. of awards offered: Up to 100

Application Procedure: Applicants are nominated by eminent German scientists and scholars. Direct applications are not accepted.

Closing Date: Nominations are accepted throughout the year

Funding: Government

No. of awards given last year: 714

No. of applicants last year: 171

Additional Information: Selection committee meetings are held twice a year in Spring and Autumn.

Humboldt Research Fellowships for Experienced Researchers

Subjects: All subjects.

Purpose: To enable researchers from abroad to carry out long-term research project of their own choice in cooperation with an academic host at a research institution in Germany.

Eligibility: This programme targets outstanding academics who completed their doctorates less than 12 years ago and whose work demonstrates an independent academic profile. Typically, applicants should be working at least at the level of an assistant professor or junior research group leader, or as an independent researcher in a comparable position.

Level of Study: Postdoctorate

Type: Fellowship

Value: €2,450 per month (includes a mobility lump sum and a contribution towards health and liability insurance as well as additional benefits)

Length of Study: 6–18 months; The fellowship is flexible and may be divided into as many as three stays in Germany within three years

Frequency: Annual, 3 selection rounds each year

Study Establishment: Universities or research institutions
Country of Study: Germany
No. of awards offered: Up to 600 per year (for Postdoctoral and Experienced Researchers together)
Application Procedure: Information regarding the application procedure is available from the website.
Closing Date: Applications are accepted at any time
Funding: Government
No. of awards given last year: 535 (for Postdoctoral and Experienced Researchers together)
No. of applicants last year: 1,276 (for Postdoctoral and Experienced Researchers together)
Additional Information: Applications should be sent directly to the Foundation or through diplomatic or consular offices of the federal Republic of germany in the candiadtes respective countries.

Humboldt Research Fellowships for Postdoctoral Researchers

Subjects: All subjects.
Purpose: To enable researchers from abroad to carry out a long-term research project of their own choice in cooperation with an academic host at a research instituition in Germany.
Eligibility: Open to researchers from abroad with above average qualifications, at the beginning of their academic career who have only completed their doctorate or comparable academic degree (PhD, C.Sc. or equivalent) in the last 4 years. Please check the website for further details.
Level of Study: Postdoctorate
Type: Fellowship
Value: €2,250 per month (including a mobility lump sum and a contribution towards health and liability insurance as well as additional benefits)
Length of Study: 6–24 months
Frequency: Annual, 3 selection rounds each year
Study Establishment: Universities or research institutions
Country of Study: Germany
No. of awards offered: Up to 600 per year (For Postdoctoral and Experienced researchers together)
Application Procedure: Information regarding the application procedure is available from the website.
Closing Date: Applications are accepted at any time
Funding: Government
No. of awards given last year: 552 (For Postdoctoral and Experienced researchers together)
No. of applicants last year: 1,299 (For Postdoctoral and Experienced researchers together)
Additional Information: Applications should be forwarded directly to the Foundation or through diplomatic or consular offices of the Federal Republic of Germany in the candidates' respective countries.

JSPS Research Fellowships for Postdoctoral Researchers

Subjects: All subjects.
Purpose: To enable highly qualified postdoctoral researchers from Germany to carry out research projects of their own choice in cooperation with an academic at a selected national research institution in Japan.
Eligibility: Open to highly qualified post-doctoral researchers from Germany, who have only completed their doctorate in the last 6 years.
Level of Study: Postdoctorate
Type: Fellowship
Value: ¥364,000 per month plus additional allowances
Length of Study: 15 days–24 months
Frequency: Annual, 3 selection rounds each year
Study Establishment: A university or other research institution
Country of Study: Japan
No. of awards offered: Up to 20
Application Procedure: Information regarding the application procedure is available from the website.
Closing Date: Applications can be made at any time
Funding: Government

Konrad Adenauer Research Award for Canadian Scholars in the Humanities and Social Sciences

Subjects: Humanities and social sciences.

Purpose: To promote academic collaboration between Canada and the Federal Republic of Germany.
Eligibility: Open to highly qualified Canadian scholars, whose research work in the humanities or the social sciences has earned international recognition and who are among the group of leading scholars in their respective area of specialization.
Level of Study: Research
Type: Prize
Value: Up to €60,000
Length of Study: Up to 1 year
Frequency: Annual
Study Establishment: Universities and research institutions
Country of Study: Germany
No. of awards offered: 1 per year
Application Procedure: Canadian universities and research institutions may nominate Canadian scholars of international renown in the humanities and social sciences for the award. Direct applications are not accepted. Nomination forms and further information can be obtained from the awards coordinator of the Royal Society of Canada.
Closing Date: Please see the website for the deadline
Funding: Government
Additional Information: Nominations will be made jointly by the Royal Society of Canada and the University of Toronto and submitted to the Humboldt Foundation.

For further information contact:

Awards Coordinator, The Royal Society of Canada, 170 Waller Street, Ottawa, ON, K1N 9B9, Canada

Max Planck Research Award

Subjects: On an annually alternating basis, the call for nominations addresses areas within the natural and engineering sciences, the life sciences, and the humanities.
Purpose: To enable excellent scientists and scholars of all nationalities who are expected to continue producing outstanding academic achievements in international collaboration to pursue research of their own choosing.
Eligibility: Open to scientists and scholars of all nationalities who are recognized internationally as outstandingly qualified academics.
Level of Study: Research
Type: Prize
Value: €750,000
Length of Study: 3–5 years
Frequency: Annual
Study Establishment: Universities and research institutions
Country of Study: Germany or abroad
No. of awards offered: 2 per year, 1 researcher working in Germany and 1 researcher working abroad.
Application Procedure: A detailed list of persons entitled to make a nomination can be found on our website.
Closing Date: Please see the website for the deadline
Funding: Government
Additional Information: Selection occurs once per year.

Sofja Kovalevskaja Award

Subjects: All subjects.
Purpose: To enable successful top ranking junior researchers from abroad to spend five years building up working groups and working on a high-profile, innovative research project of their own choice at a research institution of their own choice in Germany.
Eligibility: Open to highly qualified scientists and scholars who have a doctorate or comparable academic degree (PhD, C.Sc or equivalent), completed with distinction less than 6 years prior to the date of application.
Level of Study: Research
Type: Prize
Value: Up to €1.65 million
Length of Study: 5 years
Frequency: Every 2 years
Study Establishment: Universities and research institutions
Country of Study: Germany
No. of awards offered: 8–12
Application Procedure: Applicants may apply directly to the Humboldt Foundation. Applicants may send their inquiries to kovalevskaja.select@avh.de

Closing Date: October
Funding: Government
Additional Information: Selection committee meetings are held once every 2 years. Please check our website for further details.

ALFRED P SLOAN FOUNDATION

630, Fifth Avenue, Suite 2550, New York, NY, 10111, United States of America
Tel: (1) 212 649 1649
Fax: (1) 212 757 5117
Email: stella@sloan.org
Website: www.sloan.org
Contact: Erica Stella, Fellowship Administrator

The Alfred P Sloan Foundation is a philanthropic non-profit institution which was established in 1934 by Alfred Pritchard Sloan. The Foundation's programmes and interests fall into vast areas of science, technology and business programmes.

Sloan Industry Studies Fellowships
Subjects: Economics, management, engineering, political science, sociology and other related fields.
Purpose: To enhance the careers of the very best young faculty members in the interdisciplinary field of industry studies and to support the development of research in industry studies.
Eligibility: Open to candidates who hold a PhD or an equivalent degree and must be members of the regular faculty.
Level of Study: Postgraduate
Type: Fellowship
Value: US$45,000
Length of Study: 2 years
Frequency: Annual
Country of Study: United States of America
No. of awards offered: 5
Closing Date: October 15th
Funding: Foundation
No. of awards given last year: 5
No. of applicants last year: 33

Sloan Research Fellowships
Subjects: Chemistry, computational and evolutionary molecular biology, computer science, economics, mathematics, neuroscience, physics.
Purpose: To enhance the careers of the very best young faculty members in specified fields of science.
Level of Study: Postdoctorate
Type: Fellowship
Value: $50,000
Length of Study: 2 years
Frequency: Annual
No. of awards offered: 118
Application Procedure: Applicants must check the website for detailed procedure.
Closing Date: September 15th
No. of awards given last year: 118

ALFRED TOEPFER FOUNDATION

Georgsplatz 10, Hamburg, 20099, Germany
Tel: (49) 4033 4020
Fax: (49) 4033 5860
Email: mail@toepfer-fvs.de
Website: www.toepfer-fvs.de

Alfred Toepfer Scholarships
Subjects: Humanities, social sciences.
Purpose: To provide scholarships for doctoral candidates from the humanities and the social sciences who are in the final stages of research on European issues.
Eligibility: Candidates should be no older than 30 years and should be from Central and Eastern Europe: Albania, Armenia,

Azerbaijan, Belarus, Bosnia-Herzegovina, Bulgaria, Croatia, Czech Republic, Estonia, Georgia, Hungary, Kosovo, Latvia, Lithuania, Macedonia, Moldavia, Poland, Romania, Russia, Slovakia, Slovenia, Ukraine. Applicants should have a good knowledge of German.
Level of Study: Doctorate
Type: Scholarship
Value: €920 per month
Length of Study: 1 year
Frequency: Annual
Country of Study: Germany
No. of awards offered: 30–50
Application Procedure: Applications need not be submitted on a special form.
Closing Date: November 30th
Contributor: Alfred Toepfer Foundation
Additional Information: Available on www.toepfer-fvs.de

Max Brauer Award
Purpose: To honour personalities and institutions in the City of Hamburg for their services to the city's cultural, scientific, or intellectual life and for extraordinary impulses for the preservation of its architecture and architectural monuments, its city and landscape and renewal of the city, as well as its tradition and its customs.
Type: Award
Value: €5,000 each
Frequency: Annual
Contributor: Alfred Toepfer Foundation in association with European school
Additional Information: The selection of the Preisträgerin and/or the winner is decided by the Kuratorium Max Brauer award.

ALICIA PATTERSON FOUNDATION

1025 F St NW, Suite 700, Washington, DC, 20004, United States of America
Tel: (1) 202 393 5995
Fax: (1) 301 951 8512
Email: info@aliciapatterson.org
Website: www.aliciapatterson.org
Contact: Ms Margaret Engel, Executive Director

The Alicia Patterson Foundation gives grants to professional print reporters and photojournalists to investigate a subject of their choice. Their reports are published in a quarterly magazine, the *Alicia Patterson Foundation Reporter*, and on the Foundation's website.

Alicia Patterson Journalism Fellowships
Subjects: Journalism.
Purpose: To give working print journalists, a chance to spend a year researching and writing on a topic of their choosing.
Eligibility: Open to print journalists, e.g., reporters, editors, photographers with at least 5 years of full-time professional experience and who are citizens of the United States of the America.
Level of Study: Professional development
Type: Fellowships
Value: The fellowship stipend is $40,000 for twelve months and $20,000 for six months and must cover your travel and research costs
Length of Study: 1 year
Frequency: Annual
Country of Study: Any country
No. of awards offered: 5–9
Application Procedure: Candidates must use the Alicia Patterson Foundation application form and are also required to submit a three-page proposal, a two-page autobiographical essay, three clips, four letters of reference and a budget.
Closing Date: Postmarked October 1st
Funding: Private
No. of awards given last year: 6
No. of applicants last year: 231

ALL INDIA COUNCIL FOR TECHNICAL EDUCATION (AICTE)

4th Floor, NBCC Place, Bhishma Pitamaha Marg, Pragati Vihar, Lodhi Road, New Delhi, 110003, India
Tel: (91) 011 24369624
Fax: (91) 011 24369633
Email: prasad_krishna@aicte.ernet.in
Website: www.aicte.ernet.in
Contact: Professor Prasad Krishna, Advisor (Quality Assurance)

All India Council for Technical Education (AICTE) was set-up in November 1945 as a national-level Apex Advisory Body to conduct survey on the facilities on technical education and to promote development in the country in a coordinated and integrated manner. The statutory AICTE was established on May 12, 1988 with a view to proper planning and coordinated development of technical education system throughout the country, the promotion of qualitative improvement of such education in relation to planned quantitative growth and the regulation and proper maintenance of norms and standards in the technical education system. The purview of AICTE (the Council) covers programmes of technical education including training and research in engineering, technology, architecture, town planning, management, pharmacy, applied arts and crafts, hotel management, and catering technology etc. at different levels.

Career Awards for Young Teachers

Subjects: All subjects.
Purpose: To support young teachers.
Eligibility: Open to candidates below 35 years (relaxation of 5 years in age limit for women candidates), who are regular teachers in an AICTE-approved technical institutions/university departments and holds at least a postgraduate degree with consistent good academic career and an aptitude for research.
Level of Study: Postgraduate
Type: Award
Value: Total amount of grant–10.50 lakh for 3 years. (1st year–4.60 lakh, 2nd year–3.10 lakh, 3rd year–2.80 lakh) as per the norms of the scheme
Length of Study: 3 years
Frequency: Annual
Study Establishment: AICTE approved technical institutions/university departments
No. of awards offered: 100
Application Procedure: Candidates must apply to AICTE in prescribed format through the Head of the Institution to which the applicant is attached.
Closing Date: August 31st

ALL SAINTS EDUCATIONAL TRUST

St Katharine Cree Church, 86 Leadenhall Street, London, EC3A 3DH, England
Tel: (44) 20 7283 4485
Fax: (44) 20 7621 9758
Email: aset@aset.org.uk
Website: www.aset.org.uk
Contact: Mr Stephen Harrow FKC, Clerk to the Trustees

The Trust makes grants to help with the costs of the formal training or better qualification of individual teachers, and also funds educational advance by other means, e.g. research. There is particular emphasis on religious education, home economics or related subjects, and multi-cultural endeavour linked to those areas. (UK/EU and Commonwealth of Nations only.)

All Saints Educational Trust Corporate Awards

Subjects: Religious education, home economics and kindred subjects, as well as multicultural and interfaith education.
Purpose: To offer assistance to individuals and institutions within certain specified terms of reference.
Level of Study: Unrestricted
Type: Award
Value: Varies. UK £125,000 over 3 years is the maximum awarded
Length of Study: Up to 5 years
Country of Study: United Kingdom

No. of awards offered: Subject to the availability of funds
Application Procedure: Applicants must complete an application form, available on request from the Clerk to the Trust.
Closing Date: Applications are accepted at any time. March 1st is the deadline for the ensuing academic year
Funding: Private
No. of awards given last year: 6
No. of applicants last year: 16
Additional Information: The award must be used or applied for in the United Kingdom. Further information is available on request or from the website.

All Saints Educational Trust Personal Scholarships

Subjects: Religious education, home economics and multicultural education.
Purpose: To give support to persons who work in certain capacities associated with education.
Eligibility: Open to individuals over 18 years of age who are, or who intend to become, teachers. Grants for research are open to individuals. The award must be used with United Kingdom Awards to commonwealth citizens and will be for full-time postgraduate study at Marker's level only.
Level of Study: Foundation programme, Graduate, Postgraduate, Professional development
Type: Grant
Value: Varies, usually UK £500–10,000 but occasionally more (Commonwealth Scholars)
Length of Study: 1–3 years
Study Establishment: Recognized educational institutions in the United Kingdom
Country of Study: United Kingdom
No. of awards offered: Dependent on availability of funds
Application Procedure: Applicants must complete an application form, available on request from the Clerk to the Trust or from the website.
Closing Date: March 1st for UK/EU applications. April 1st for Commonwealth applications
Funding: Private
No. of awards given last year: 42 UK/EU, 33 Commonwealth
No. of applicants last year: 61 UK/EU, 69 Commonwealth
Additional Information: Enquiries should not be delayed until the offer of a place on a course of study has been confirmed.

For further information contact:

Further information is available on request or from the website

THE ALLEN FOUNDATION, INC.

PO Box 1606, Midland, MI, 48641-1606, United States of America
Tel: (1) 989 832 5678
Fax: (1) 989 832 8842
Email: dbaum@allenfoundation.org
Website: www.allenfoundation.org
Contact: Dale Baum, Secretary

Established in 1975 by agricultural chemist William Webster Allen, the Allen Foundation makes grants to projects that benefit human nutrition in the areas of education, training and research.

Allen Foundation Grants

Subjects: Human nutrition in the areas of health, education, training and research.
Purpose: To assist in the field of human nutrition, to fund relevant nutritional research and to encourage the dissemination of information regarding healthful nutritional practices and habits.
Eligibility: Open to non-profit organizations that are able to provide a copy of their federal Internal Revenue Service certification of 501(c)3 tax-exempt status. If applying from outside the United States of America, applicants must send their country's counterpart or equivalent of the tax-exempt form. Individuals, non-profit organizations without a current exempt status, conferences, seminars, symposia, sponsorship events, fund-raising events and religious organizations without a secular community designation are not eligible for the award.

If a grant proposal involves primarily academic research, the grant should be conducted under the leadership of a full-time, principal investigator who is a regular faculty member with tenure or on a tenure track.

Level of Study: Research
Type: Grant
Country of Study: United States of America
No. of awards offered: 1
Application Procedure: Applicants must submit an application form via email only. Application forms and further information can be obtained from the website.
Closing Date: December 31st
Additional Information: Any applications received after this deadline will be reviewed for the following year's applications. The Board of Trustees will announce their decision for successful applicants in June. Because of the number of proposals received and the limited resources of the Foundation, applicants should never view possible declinations to fund their proposals or delays in reviewing their proposals as judgements on the actual merits of their proposals. The Foundation does not directly administer the programmes it funds. For further information, visit the website or contact the Allen Foundation Inc.

ALPHA KAPPA ALPHA-EDUCATIONAL ADVANCEMENT ORGANIZATION (AKA-EAF)

5656 South Stony Island, Chicago, IL, 60637, United States of America
Tel: (1) 777 947 0026
Fax: (1) 773 947 0277
Email: akaeaf@akaeaf.net
Website: www.akaeaf.org

AKA-EAF Financial Need Scholarship

Subjects: All subjects.
Purpose: To provide funds to advance education in fulfillment of its mission: to promote life-long learning.
Eligibility: Applicants must be a full-time and currently enrolled student at an accredited campus based degree-granting institution, must plan to continue their academic pursuits in the fall of the grant year, demonstrated exceptional academic achievement/or financial need, leadership, volunteer, civic and academic services
Level of Study: Postgraduate, Graduate
Type: Scholarship
Value: US$750–2,500
Frequency: Annual
Application Procedure: The only means to obtain an application is through the website
Closing Date: April 15th
Funding: Foundation
No. of awards given last year: 26
No. of applicants last year: 94

AKA-EAF Merit Scholarships

Subjects: All subjects.
Purpose: To provide funds to advance education in fulfillment of it's mission: to promote life-long learning
Eligibility: Applicants must be a full-time and currently enrolled student at an accredited campus based degree-granting institution, must plan to continue their academic pursuits in the fall of the grant year, demonstrated exceptional academic achievement/or financial need, leadership, volunteer, civic and academic services
Type: Scholarship
Value: US$750–2,500
Frequency: Annual
Application Procedure: The only means to obtain an application is through the website
Closing Date: April 15th
Funding: Foundation
No. of awards given last year: 51
No. of applicants last year: 180

ALZHEIMER'S ASSOCIATION AUSTRALIA

Frewin Centre, Frewin Place, Scullin, ACT, 2615, Australia
Tel: (61) 02 6254 4233
Fax: (61) 02 6278 7225
Email: secretariat@alzheimers.org.au
Website: www.alzheimers.org.au

Alzheimer's Australia Research Ltd (AAR) was established as the research arm of Alzheimer's Association Australia to provide funds and disseminate into Alzheimer's disease and other forms of dementia. AAR provides annual research grants and a key priority is to support emerging researchers and to encourage the next generation of demantia researchers.

AAR Dementia Research Grants

Subjects: Behavioural and cognitive sciences, biological sciences, or medical and health sciences.
Purpose: To fund research into all aspects of dementia.
Eligibility: Open to new investigators who are citizens of Australia or permanent residents.
Level of Study: Postgraduate
Type: Scholarship
Value: Australian $20,000
Frequency: Annual
Country of Study: Australia
No. of awards offered: 4
Application Procedure: Check website for further details.
Closing Date: April 27th
Contributor: Alzheimer's Australia Research Limited (AAR)
No. of awards given last year: 4
No. of applicants last year: 19

For further information contact:

Alzheimer's Australia Research Ltd, PO Box 4019, Hawker, ACT 2614 Australia
Tel: (61) 02 6254 4233
Email: aar@alzheimers.org.au
Website: www.alzheimers.org.au
Contact: Dinusha Fernando

AAR Postdoctoral Fellowship in Dementia

Subjects: Fellowship can be for biological or psychosocial research, but the research proposal must be judged to relate to research in dementia.
Purpose: To support a PhD graduate undertaking research in an area related to dementia.
Eligibility: Open to citizens of Australia and permanent residents.
Level of Study: Postdoctorate
Type: Fellowship
Value: Australian $45,000 per year, on the condition that the applicants can raise matching funds from their institutions
Length of Study: 2 years
Frequency: Dependent on funds available
Country of Study: Australia
No. of awards offered: 3
Application Procedure: Please check the website for details.
Closing Date: April 27th
Contributor: Alzheimer's Australia Research Limited (AAR)

For further information contact:

Alzheimer's Australia Research Ltd., PO Box 4019, Hawker, ACT 2614, Australia
Tel: (61) 02 6254 4233
Email: aar@alzheimers.org.au
Website: www.alzheimers.org.au
Contact: Dinusha Fernando

AAR Rosemary Foundation Travel Grant

Subjects: Allow a researcher to travel overseas to learn new techniques in a variety of dementia-related fields and/or network with international research teams conducting dementia-related research.
Purpose: To enable an Australian researcher to travel overseas in order to learn new techniques and/or network with international dementia research teams.

Eligibility: Open to citizens of Australia or permanent residents.
Level of Study: Postgraduate, Research
Type: Scholarship
Value: Australian $15,000
Length of Study: 1 month
Frequency: Dependent on funds available
No. of awards offered: 1
Application Procedure: Please check the website for details.
Closing Date: April 27th
Contributor: The Rosemary Foundation for Memory Support Inc

For further information contact:

Alzheimer's Australia Research Ltd., PO Box 4019, Hawker, ACT 2614, Australia
Tel: (61) 02 6254 4233
Email: aar@alzheimers.org.au
Website: www.alzheimers.org.au
Contact: Dinusha Fernando

Hazel Hawke Research Grant in Dementia Care

Subjects: Suitable projects might include research in carer support, best quality care practices, activities and non-pharmaceutical therapies for people with dementia, or any other aspect of dementia care research.
Purpose: To fund research in dementia care.
Eligibility: Open to citizens of Australia or permanent residents.
Level of Study: Postdoctorate, Postgraduate, Research
Type: Scholarship
Value: Australian $20,000
Frequency: Annual
Country of Study: Australia
No. of awards offered: 2
Application Procedure: Please check the website for details.
Closing Date: April 27th
Funding: Foundation
Contributor: Hazel Hawke Alzheimer's Research and Care Fund
No. of awards given last year: 1
No. of applicants last year: 15

For further information contact:

Alzheimer's Australia Research Ltd., PO Box 4019, Hawker, ACT 2614, Australia
Tel: (61) 02 6254 4233
Email: aar@alzheimers.org.au
Website: www.alzheimers.org.au
Contact: Dinusha Fernando

ALZHEIMER'S DRUG DISCOVERY FOUNDATION (ADDF)

1414 Avenue of the Americas, Suite 1502, New York, NY, 10019, United States of America
Tel: (1) (212) 901-8005
Fax: (1) 212 935 2408
Email: mailto:jkeller@alzdiscovery.org
Website: www.alzdiscovery.org
Contact: Mr Grants Manager

The ADDF is an affiliated public charity of the Institute for the Study of Aging (ISOA), a private foundation founded by the Estèe Lauder family in 1998. The charity was established in 2004 to enable the public to work in advancing the common mission of supporting scientists and to rapidly accelerate the discovery and development of drugs to prevent, treat, and cure Alzheimer's disease, related dementias and cognitive aging.

ADDF Grants Program

Subjects: Early identification, prevention and treatment of Alzheimer's disease and cognitive decline.
Purpose: To promote the research and development of technology and therapies to identify, treat and prevent cognitive decline, Alzheimer's disease and related dementias.
Eligibility: There are no eligibility restrictions.
Level of Study: Unrestricted

Type: Grant
Value: Negotiable
Length of Study: 1–3 years
Frequency: There is no funding cycle
Study Establishment: A non-profit family foundation
Country of Study: Any country
Application Procedure: Candidates must submit a brief lay summary, a research proposal of up to five pages including background, aims, supporting data, experimental design and methods, a biosketch, a summary of resources and a budget with justification.
Closing Date: Applications are accepted at any time
Funding: Private
No. of awards given last year: 29
Additional Information: In addition to funding research activities, the Institute sponsors and/or co-sponsors conferences, scientific and medical workshops to advance knowledge on issues related to Alzheimer's disease and cognitive vitality.

For further information contact:

Email: lrefolo@aging-institute.org
Contact: Lorenzo Refolo, Scientific Director
Email: hfillit@aging-institute.org
Contact: Howard Fillit, Executive Director

ALZHEIMER'S RESEARCH TRUST

The Stables Station Road, Cambridge, Cambridgeshire, CB22 5LR, England
Tel: (44) 12 2384 3899
Fax: (44) 12 2384 3325
Email: enquiries@alzheimers-research.org.uk
Website: www.alzheimers-research.org.uk
Contact: Rebecca Wood, Chief Executive

Alzheimer's Research Trust is the leading United Kingdom research charity for dementia. The ART funds work in any area of research that promises to further the understanding of the basic disease process in Alzheimer's and related dementias, or that is directed to early detection, identifying risk factors, or progress towards effective treatments.

Alzheimer's Research Trust, Clinical Research Fellowship

Subjects: The basic disease process, symptoms and treatments in Alzheimer's disease and related dementias.
Purpose: To support clinical research by a medically qualified applicant in the field of dementia.
Eligibility: Applicants are required to have secured the sponsorship of a senior established investigator in the institution where the Fellowship is to be held. The Fellowship must be based in the UK with the lead supervisor.
Level of Study: Postdoctorate
Type: Fellowship
Value: Full salary plus contribution towards research and travel costs
Length of Study: Up to 3 years initially
Frequency: Annual
Country of Study: United Kingdom
No. of awards offered: 1
Application Procedure: Applicants must submit an application form that is available on the website.
Closing Date: February
Contributor: Charitable sources
No. of awards given last year: 1
No. of applicants last year: 3

Alzheimer's Research Trust, Emergency Support Grant

Subjects: The basic disease processes, symptoms and treatments in Alzheimer's disease and related dementias.
Purpose: To bridge funding shortfalls in research.
Eligibility: Members of the Alzheimer's Research Trust network only.
Level of Study: Research
Type: Grant
Value: Up to UK £30,000
Length of Study: A few weeks–2 years
Frequency: Annual, Anytime
Country of Study: United Kingdom
No. of awards offered: As necessary

Application Procedure: Applicants must submit an application form that is available on the website.
Closing Date: Can be submitted at any time
Contributor: Charitable sources
No. of awards given last year: 1
No. of applicants last year: 2

Alzheimer's Research Trust, Equipment Grant
Subjects: The basic disease process in Alzheimer's disease and related dementias.
Purpose: To speed up and increase the accuracy and efficiency of research.
Eligibility: Must be UK-based.
Level of Study: Research
Type: Grant
Value: UK £10,000–100,000
Frequency: Annual, Twice a year
Country of Study: United Kingdom
No. of awards offered: 1 or more
Application Procedure: Applicants must submit an application form that is available on the website.
Closing Date: December and April
Contributor: Charitable sources
No. of awards given last year: 3
No. of applicants last year: 5

Alzheimer's Research Trust, Major Project or Programme
Subjects: The basic disease process in Alzheimer's disease and related dementias.
Purpose: To support imaginative and high-quality research.
Eligibility: Collaborations with researchers outside the UK will be considered providing the lead applicant is UK-based.
Level of Study: Research
Type: Grant
Value: UK £150,000–1,000,000
Length of Study: 3–5 years
Frequency: Annual
Country of Study: United Kingdom
No. of awards offered: 1 or more
Application Procedure: Applicants must submit an application form that is available on the website.
Closing Date: February
Contributor: Charitable sources
No. of awards given last year: 6
No. of applicants last year: 30

Alzheimer's Research Trust, Network Co-operation Grant
Subjects: The basic disease process in Alzheimer's disease and related dementias.
Purpose: To promote collaborative research between members of the Trust's network.
Eligibility: Lead applicant must be a member of the Alzheimer's Research Trust network, but application can include non-network and non-United Kingdom researchers.
Level of Study: Research
Type: Grant
Value: Up to UK £50,000
Frequency: Annual, Twice a year if appropriate
Country of Study: United Kingdom
No. of awards offered: 1 or more
Application Procedure: Lead applicants must submit an application form that is available on the website.
Closing Date: Can be submitted at any time
Contributor: Charitable sources
No. of awards given last year: 2
No. of applicants last year: 3

Alzheimer's Research Trust, PhD Scholarship
Subjects: The basic disease processes in Alzheimer's disease and related dementias.
Purpose: To contribute towards research in the field, and to help ensure that bright young graduates are inducted into this area.
Eligibility: Must be UK-based supervisors to apply for grant.
Level of Study: Postgraduate
Type: Scholarship

Value: Full fees and stipend of UK £45,000 or £48,000 in London and research cost of UK £30,000
Length of Study: 3 years
Frequency: Annual
Country of Study: United Kingdom
No. of awards offered: Up to 5
Application Procedure: Applications must be submitted by individual or joint prospective supervisors, as laid down in the Guidelines for Applicants. Applicants must visit the organization's website for full details.
Closing Date: November prior to commencement in October of the following year
Contributor: Charitable sources
No. of awards given last year: 6
No. of applicants last year: 24

Alzheimer's Research Trust, Pilot Project Grant
Subjects: The basic disease process in Alzheimer's disease and related dementias.
Purpose: To fund innovative research projects and pilot studies.
Eligibility: Lead applicant must be based in the UK.
Level of Study: Research
Type: Grant
Value: Up to UK £30,000
Length of Study: Up to 2 years
Frequency: Annual, Twice a year
Country of Study: United Kingdom
No. of awards offered: 1 or more
Application Procedure: Applicants must submit an application form that is available on the website.
Closing Date: December and May
Contributor: Charitable sources
No. of awards given last year: 10
No. of applicants last year: 21

Alzheimer's Research Trust, Research Fellowships
Subjects: The basic disease process in Alzheimer's disease and related dementias.
Purpose: To allow junior postdoctoral researchers of demonstrated ability and high potential to carry out further research.
Eligibility: Sponsor must be UK-based.
Level of Study: Postdoctorate
Type: Fellowship
Value: Full salary plus contribution towards research and travel costs
Length of Study: 3 years
Frequency: Annual
Country of Study: United Kingdom
No. of awards offered: Up to 3
Application Procedure: Applicants must submit an application form that is available on the website.
Closing Date: February
Contributor: Charitable sources
No. of awards given last year: 3
No. of applicants last year: 16

ALZHEIMER'S SOCIETY

Gordon House, 10 Greencoat Place, London, SW1P 1PH, England
Tel: (44) 0171 306 0606
Fax: (44) 0171 306 0808
Email: research@alzheimers.org.uk
Website: www.alzheimers.org.uk
Contact: Dr Richard Harvey, Director of Research

The Alzheimer's Society is the leading care and research charity for people with all forms of dementia, their families and carers.

Alzheimer's Society Research Grants
Subjects: All forms of dementia, particularly Alzheimer's disease and vascular dementia.
Purpose: To support research into the cause, cure and care of dementia.
Eligibility: Awards may only be held by United Kingdom institutions. Non-United Kingdom-based researchers may be subcontractors.
Level of Study: Postdoctorate, Research

Value: UK £1,000,000 per year is committed to research. Fellowship Grants are approx. UK £250,000. Project Grants are approx. UK £650,000
Length of Study: Up to 5 years
Country of Study: United Kingdom
No. of awards offered: Varies
Application Procedure: Applicants must complete an application form available from the website.
Closing Date: The deadline for Fellowship Grants is in October. Deadlines for Project Grants applications are in July and January
Funding: Government, private, trusts, commercial
No. of awards given last year: 7
No. of applicants last year: 71

AMERICA–ISRAEL CULTURAL FOUNDATION (AICF)

32 Allenby Road, Tel Aviv, 63325, Israel
Tel: (972) 3 517 4177
Fax: (972) 3 517 8991
Email: info@aicf.co.il
Website: www.aicf.org
Contact: Mr Gideon Paz, Executive Director

The America–Israel Cultural Foundation (AICF) has been promoting and supporting the arts in Israel for over 60 years. Through its Sharett Scholarship Program, the AICF grants hundreds of study scholarships each year to Israeli students of the arts, music, dance, visual arts, film, television and theatre, mainly for studies in Israel. The AICF also provides short-term fellowships to artists and art teachers and financially supports various projects in art schools, workshops, master classes, etc.

AICF Sharett Scholarship Program
Subjects: Performing arts, visual arts, design, film or television.
Eligibility: Open to Israeli citizens only.
Level of Study: Unrestricted
Type: Scholarship
Value: US$750–2,000
Length of Study: Varies
Frequency: Annual
Country of Study: Any country
No. of awards offered: Approx. 1,100 scholarships, fellowships and grants, mostly for students in Israel
Application Procedure: Applicants must complete and submit an application form with recommendations and prerequired repertoire. Application forms are available from February 1st of each year.
Closing Date: End of February
Funding: Private
Contributor: America–Israel Cultural Foundation
No. of awards given last year: 1,110
No. of applicants last year: 2,300
Additional Information: The programme is revised on an annual basis. For more detailed information, please contact the Foundation after February 1st.

THE AMERICAN ACADEMY IN BERLIN

Hans Arnhold Center, Am Sandwerder 17-19, Berlin, D 14109, Germany
Tel: (49) 30 804 83 0
Fax: (49) 30 804 83 111
Email: applications@americanacademy.de
Website: www.americanacademy.de

The American Academy in Berlin provides a unique bridge between Germany and America – a bridge created through the scholarship and creativity of distinguished individuals involved in cultural, academic and public affairs.

American Academy in Berlin Prize Fellowships
Subjects: Public affairs, culture, humanities, journalism, law, fiction and non-fiction writing, poetry, history, sociology and literature.
Purpose: To provide residential fellowship opportunities to scholars and professionals.

Eligibility: Open to scholars, writers, and professionals who are citizens and permanent residents of the United States. US expatriates are not eligible. Candidates in academic fields must have completed their doctorates at the time of application. The Academy does not accept applications from visual artists.
Level of Study: Postgraduate
Type: Fellowship
Value: A stipend ranging from $3,500–5,000 per month of residency, round-trip airfare to Berlin, and a generous apartment with partial board
Frequency: Annual
Study Establishment: American Academy in Berlin
Country of Study: Germany
Application Procedure: For application guidelines, restrictions, and forms please visit our website: www.american academy.de/home/fellows/applications
Closing Date: October 15th
Funding: Private
Additional Information: The academy especially encourages people on sabbatical or study leave from their home institutions and organizations.

THE AMERICAN ACADEMY IN ROME

7 East 60 Street, New York, NY, 10022-1001, United States of America
Tel: (1) 212 751 7200
Fax: (1) 212 751 7220
Email: aainfo@aarome.org
Website: www.aarome.org
Contact: Grants Management Officer

The American Academy in Rome is the only American overseas centre for independent study and advanced research in the fine arts and the humanities. It provides a unique opportunity for interaction between artists and scholars working in up to 18 different disciplines. The Academy offers a number of fellowships, residencies and grants for visiting artists and scholars, as well as organizing a variety of events, including concerts, readings, symposia and exhibitions.

American Academy in Rome Fellowships in Design Art
Subjects: Interior design, industrial design, architecture, landscape architecture, set design, urban design, urban planning, conservation and historic preservation and graphic design.
Purpose: To financially support students of design art.
Eligibility: Open to citizens of the United States who have working experience in the related field for at least 7 years and are also currently working in the same field.
Level of Study: Professional development
Type: Fellowship
Value: US$12,500 for 6 months fellowship and US$25,000 for 11 months fellowship
Length of Study: 6 months or 11 months
Frequency: Annual
Country of Study: Italy
Application Procedure: Applicants can complete an online application posted on the Academy's website (www.aarome.org)
Closing Date: November 1 (extended deadline of November 15 for an additional fee)
No. of awards given last year: 30
No. of applicants last year: 692

AMERICAN ACADEMY OF CHILD AND ADOLESCENT PSYCHIATRY

3615 Wisconsin Avenue North West, Washington, DC, 20016-3007, United States of America
Tel: (1) 202 966 7300
Fax: (1) 202 966 2891
Email: shall@aacap.org
Website: www.aacap.org
Contact: Deputy Director of Research & Training

The American Academy of Child and Adolescent Psychiatry is a national, professional medical association established in 1953 as a non-profit organization to support and improve the quality of life for children, adolescents and families affected by mental illnesses.

AACAP Educational Outreach Program for Child and Adolescent Psychiatry Residents (former Travel Grant Program)

Subjects: Child and adolescent psychiatry.
Purpose: To help defray the cost of attending the AACAP's Annual Meeting in Boston, MA.
Eligibility: Candidates must be child and adolescent psychiatry residents at the time of the AACAP Annual Meeting and must be currently enrolled in a residency programme in the United States of America. All awardees must attend the Young Leaders Awards Luncheon and other stated events, and serve as a monitor for 1 day at the Annual Meeting.
Level of Study: Postdoctorate
Type: Travel grant
Value: US$750
Frequency: Annual
Country of Study: United States of America
No. of awards offered: 50
Application Procedure: For updated application guidelines, applicants must visit the AACAP website at www.aacap.org/awards/pfizertravel.htm
Closing Date: July 13th
Contributor: ACCAP
No. of awards given last year: 50

Jeanne Spurlock Minority Medical Student Clinical Fellowship in Child and Adolescent Psychiatry

Subjects: Psychiatry and mental health.
Purpose: To support work during the summer with a child and adolescent psychiatrist mentor.
Eligibility: Applications are accepted from African American, Asian American, Native American, Alaskan Native, Mexican American, Hispanic and Pacific Islander students in accredited United States of America medical schools.
Level of Study: Graduate
Type: Fellowship
Value: Up to US$3,500
Length of Study: 12 weeks
Frequency: Annual
Country of Study: United States of America
No. of awards offered: Up to 14
Application Procedure: For updated application information, applicants must visit the AACAP website at www.aacap.org/awards/index.htm
Closing Date: March 2nd
Funding: Government
Contributor: CMHS
No. of awards given last year: 12

Jeanne Spurlock Research Fellowship in Drug Abuse and Addiction for Minority Medical Students

Subjects: Psychiatry and mental health.
Purpose: To support work during the Summer with a child and adolescent psychiatrist research mentor.
Eligibility: Applications are accepted from African American, Asian American, Native American, Alaskan Native, Mexican American, Hispanic and Pacific Islander students in accredited United States of America medical schools. All applications must relate to substance abuse research.
Level of Study: Graduate
Type: Fellowship
Value: Up to US$3,500
Length of Study: 12 weeks
Frequency: Annual
Country of Study: United States of America
No. of awards offered: Up to 5
Application Procedure: For updated application information on the 2005 Spurlock Fellowships, applicants must visit the AACAP website at www.aacap.org/awards/index.htm
Closing Date: March 2nd

Funding: Government
Contributor: NIDA
No. of awards given last year: 1

THE AMERICAN ACADEMY OF FACIAL PLASTIC AND RECONSTRUCTIVE SURGERY (AAFPRS) FOUNDATION

310 S. Henry Street, Alexandria, VA, 22314, United States of America
Tel: (1) 703 299 9291
Fax: (1) 703 299 8898
Email: info@aafprs.org
Website: www.aafprs.org
Contact: Research Programme

The American Academy of Facial Plastic and Reconstructive Surgery (AAFPRS) Foundation represents 2,700 facial plastic and reconstructive surgeons throughout the world. Its main mission is to promote the highest quality facial plastic surgery through education, the dissemination of professional information and the establishment of professional standards. The AAFPRS was created to address the medical and scientific issues confronting facial plastic surgeons.

Leslie Bernstein Grant

Subjects: Facial plastic and reconstructive surgery.
Purpose: To encourage original research projects that will advance facial plastic and reconstructive surgery.
Eligibility: Open to all AAFPRS members.
Level of Study: Professional development
Value: US$25,000
Length of Study: 3 years
Study Establishment: The recipient's practice or institution
Country of Study: Any country
No. of awards offered: 1
Application Procedure: Applicants must submit an application form and other documentation including a curriculum vitae and research proposal. Application forms and guidelines are available on the web at www.entlink.net//research/grant/foundation.funding-opportunities.cfm
Closing Date: January 15th
Funding: Private
Contributor: Dr Leslie Bernstein
No. of awards given last year: 1
No. of applicants last year: 3
Additional Information: All applications must be submitted through the Centralized Otolaryngology Research Efforts (CORE) programme (see the website listed above for information and application).

Leslie Bernstein Investigator Development Grant

Subjects: Facial plastic surgery or clinical or laboratory research.
Purpose: To support the work of a young faculty member in facial plastic surgery conducting significant clinical or laboratory research, as well as the training of resident surgeons in research.
Eligibility: Open to AAFPRS members who are involved in the training of resident surgeons.
Level of Study: Postgraduate
Type: Research grant
Value: US$15,000
Length of Study: 2 years
Frequency: Annual
Study Establishment: The recipient's institution
Country of Study: United States of America
No. of awards offered: 1
Application Procedure: Applicants must submit an application form and other documentation including a curriculum vitae and research proposal. Application forms and guidelines are available on the web at www.entlink.net//research/grant/foundation-funding-opportunities.cfm
Closing Date: January 15th
Funding: Private
Contributor: Dr Leslie Bernstein
No. of awards given last year: 1
No. of applicants last year: 2
Additional Information: All applications must be submitted through the Centralized Otolaryngology Research Efforts (CORE) programme (see the website listed above for information and application).

Leslie Bernstein Resident Research Grants

Subjects: Facial plastic surgery.
Purpose: To stimulate resident research in projects that are well conceived and scientifically valid.
Eligibility: Open to AAFPRS members. Residents at any level may apply even if the research work will be done during their fellowship year. All applicants are required to have the sponsorship and oversight of the department chair or an AAFPRS member as mentor.
Level of Study: Postgraduate
Type: Research grant
Value: US$5,000
Length of Study: 2 years
Frequency: Annual
Study Establishment: The recipient's institution
Country of Study: United States of America
No. of awards offered: Up to 2
Application Procedure: Applicants must submit an application form and other documentation including a curriculum vitae and research proposal. Application forms and guidelines are available on the web www.entlink.net//research/grant/foundation-funding-opportunities.cfm
Closing Date: January 15th
Funding: Private
Contributor: Dr Leslie Bernstein
No. of awards given last year: 1
No. of applicants last year: 4
Additional Information: Residents are encouraged to enter early in their training so that their applications may be revised and resubmitted if not accepted the first time. All applications must be submitted through the Centralized Otolaryngology Research Efforts (CORE) programme (see the website listed above for information and appli-cation).

THE AMERICAN ALPINE CLUB (AAC)

710 Tenth Street, Suite 100, Golden, CO 80401, United States of America
Tel: (1) 303 384 0110
Fax: (1) 303 384 0111
Email: getinfo@americanalpineclub.org
Website: www.americanalpineclub.org
Contact: Corporate Support Co-ordinator

The American Alpine Club (AAC) is a national non-profit organization that has represented mountaineers and rock climbers for almost a century. Since its inception in 1902, the AAC has been the only national climbers' organization devoted to the exploration and scientific study of high mountain elevations and polar regions of the world, and the promotion and dissemination of knowledge about the mountains and mountaineering through its meetings, pub-lications and libraries. It is also dedicated to the conservation and preservation of mountain regions and other climbing areas and the representation of the interests and concerns of the American climbing community.

AAC Mountaineering Fellowship Fund Grants

Subjects: Rock climbing.
Purpose: To encourage young American climbers to visit remote ar-eas and seek out climbs more technically demanding than they would normally undertake.
Eligibility: Applicants must be 25 years of age or under, citizens of the United States of America and experienced climbers. Membership of the American Alpine Club is not a prerequisite. Members of a single expedition may apply individually, but organized groups or expeditions are ineligible. Grants are not available for the purpose of climbing instruction.
Level of Study: Unrestricted
Type: Grant
Value: US$300–800
Country of Study: United States of America
No. of awards offered: 5–16
Application Procedure: Applicants must write for application forms, which are also available from the website.
Closing Date: April 1st and November 1st
Funding: Private

Additional Information: Grants will be based on the excellence of the proposed project and evidence of mountaineering experience. A report must be written upon project completion.

AAC Research Grants

Subjects: Scientific research focusing on mountain and polar areas.
Purpose: To recognize a specific contribution to scientific endeavour germane to mountain regions and alpine research projects.
Eligibility: There are no restrictions on eligibility, but grants will not be awarded for academic tuition. Applications are considered in terms of their scientific or technical quality and the purposes for which the funds and the AAC are established.
Level of Study: Postgraduate
Type: Research grant
Value: US$200–1000
Frequency: Annual
Country of Study: Any country
No. of awards offered: Varies
Application Procedure: Applicants must write for application forms, which are also available from the website.
Closing Date: March 1st
Funding: Private
Contributor: The Arthur K. Gilkey Memorial Research Fund, the William Putnam Research Fund, and the Bedayn Research Fund
Additional Information: A report must be submitted upon completion of the project.

AMERICAN ANTIQUARIAN SOCIETY (AAS)

185 Salisbury Street, Worcester, MA, 01609-1634, United States of America
Tel: (1) 508 755 5221
Fax: (1) 508 754 9069
Email: perickson@mwa.org
Website: www.americanantiquarian.org
Contact: Paul Erickson, Director of Academic Programs

The American Antiquarian Society (AAS) is a learned society that was founded in 1812 in Worcester, MA. The Society maintains a research library of American history and culture up to 1876 in order to collect, preserve and make available for study the printed records of the United States of America.

AAS American Society for 18th Century Studies Fellowships

Subjects: American 18th century studies.
Eligibility: Open to a fellowship holder with an ABD graduate student or post-doctoral, holding the PhD or equivalent degree at the time of the application.
Level of Study: Doctorate, Postdoctorate
Type: Fellowships
Value: $1,700 per month or $1,200 per month including housing in the Society's Goddard-Daniels House
Length of Study: 1 year
Frequency: Annual
Study Establishment: The Society's Library in Worcester, Massa-chusetts
Country of Study: United States of America
No. of awards offered: 1
Application Procedure: All application material is available from our website: www.americanantiquarian.org
Closing Date: January 15th
Funding: Private
Contributor: The American Society for 18th Century Studies and the AAS
No. of awards given last year: 2

AAS Joyce Tracy Fellowship

Subjects: Early American history and culture.
Purpose: To support research on newspapers or magazines for projects using these resources as primary documentation.
Eligibility: Doctoral candidates may apply.
Level of Study: Doctorate, Postdoctorate

Type: Fellowship
Value: $1,700 per month or $1,200 per month including housing in the Society's Goddard-Daniels House
Length of Study: 1 year
Frequency: Annual
Study Establishment: The Society's Library in Worcester, Massachusetts
Country of Study: United States of America
No. of awards offered: 1
Application Procedure: All application material is available from our website: www.americanantiquarian.org
Closing Date: January 15th
Funding: Private
Contributor: An endowment established in memory of Joyce Tracy
No. of awards given last year: 1

AAS Kate B and Hall J Peterson Fellowships

Subjects: Early American history to 1876.
Purpose: To enable persons, who might not otherwise be able to do so, to travel to the Society in order to make use of its research facilities.
Eligibility: Doctoral candidates may apply
Level of Study: Doctorate, Postdoctorate
Type: Fellowship
Value: $1,700 per month or $1,200 per month including housing in the Society's Goddard-Daniels House
Length of Study: 1–3 months
Frequency: Annual
Study Establishment: The Society's Library in Worcester, Massachusetts
Country of Study: United States of America
No. of awards offered: 10
Application Procedure: All application material is available from our website: www.americanantiquarian.org
Closing Date: January 15th
Funding: Private
Contributor: The late Hall J Peterson and his wife Kate B Peterson

AAS Reese Fellowship

Subjects: American bibliography and the history of the book in America to 1876.
Purpose: To support research.
Eligibility: Doctoral candidates may apply
Level of Study: Postdoctorate, Doctorate
Type: Fellowship
Value: $1,700 per month or $1,200 per month including housing in the Society's Goddard-Daniels House
Length of Study: 1 month
Frequency: Annual
Study Establishment: The Society's Library in Worcester, Massachusetts
Country of Study: United States of America
Application Procedure: All application material is available from our website: www.americanantiquarian.org
Closing Date: January 15th
Contributor: The William Reese Company, New Haven, CT

AAS-National Endowment for the Humanities Visiting Fellowships

Subjects: Early American history and culture.
Purpose: To make the Society's research facilities more readily available to qualified scholars.
Eligibility: Fellowships may not be awarded to degree candidates or for study leading to advanced degrees, nor may they be granted to foreign nationals unless they have been resident in the United States of America for at least 3 years immediately prior to receiving the award.
Level of Study: Postdoctorate
Type: Fellowship
Value: The maximum stipend available is US$40,000
Length of Study: Either 4–5 months or 6 months–1 year
Frequency: Annual
Country of Study: United States of America
No. of awards offered: 3
Application Procedure: All application material is available from our website: www.americanantiquarian.org

Closing Date: January 15th
Funding: Government
Contributor: NEH
No. of awards given last year: 3
Additional Information: Fellows may not accept teaching assignments or undertake any other major activities during the tenure of the award. Other major fellowships may be held concurrently.

AAS-North East Modern Language Association Fellowship

Subjects: American literary studies.
Purpose: To support research.
Eligibility: Doctoral candidates may apply.
Level of Study: Postdoctorate
Type: Fellowship
Value: $1,700 per month or $1,200 per month including housing in the Society's Goddard-Daniels House
Length of Study: 1–3 months
Frequency: Annual
Study Establishment: The Society's Library in Worcester, Massachusetts
No. of awards offered: 1
Closing Date: January 15th
Funding: Private
Contributor: Jointly funded by NEMLA and AAS
No. of awards given last year: 1

ACLS Frederick Burkhardt Fellowship

Subjects: All subjects supported by the AAS library.
Purpose: To support research.
Eligibility: Candidates must be recently tenured humanists selected on the basis of their scholarly qualifications, the scholarly significance of the project and the appropriateness of the proposed study to the Society's collections.
Level of Study: Postdoctorate
Type: Fellowship
Value: A maximum stipend of US$65,000
Length of Study: 1 year
Frequency: Annual
Study Establishment: The Society's Library in Worcester, Massachusetts
Country of Study: United States of America
No. of awards offered: 11
Application Procedure: All application material is available from ACLS website: www.acls.org/burkguid.htm
Closing Date: October 3rd
Funding: Private
Contributor: The Andrew W Mellon Foundation and ACLS
No. of awards given last year: 8, 1 at AAS

American Historical Print Collectors Society Fellowship

Subjects: American prints of the 18th and 19th centuries.
Purpose: To support research or projects using prints as primary documentation.
Eligibility: Doctoral candidates may apply.
Level of Study: Doctorate, Postdoctorate
Type: Fellowship
Value: $1,700 per month or $1,200 per month including housing in the Society's Goddard-Daniels House
Length of Study: 1 month
Frequency: Annual
Study Establishment: The Society's Library in Worcester, Massachusetts
Country of Study: United States of America
Application Procedure: All application material is available from our website: www.americanantiquarian.org
Closing Date: January 15th
Funding: Private
Contributor: The American Historical Print Collectors Society and the AAS
No. of awards given last year: 1

Drawn to Art Fellowship

Subjects: American art, visual culture or other projects that will make substantial use of graphic materials as primary sources.

Purpose: To support research.
Eligibility: Doctoral candidates may apply.
Level of Study: Doctorate, Postdoctorate
Type: Fellowship
Value: $1,700 per month or $1,200 per month including housing in the Society's Goddard-Daniels House
Length of Study: 1 month
Frequency: Annual
Study Establishment: The Society's Library in Worcester, Massachusetts
Country of Study: United States of America
No. of awards offered: 1
Application Procedure: All application material is available from our website: www.americanantiquarian.org
Closing Date: January 15th
Funding: Private
Contributor: Diana Korzenik
No. of awards given last year: 1

Jay and Deborah Last Fellowship in American History Visual Culture

Subjects: American art, visual culture, or other projects that will make substancial use of graphic materials as primary sources.
Purpose: To support students who wish to carry out research in the related fields.
Eligibility: Doctoral candidates may apply.
Level of Study: Doctorate, Postdoctorate
Type: Fellowship
Value: $1,700 per month or $1,200 per month including housing in the Society's Goddard-Daniels House
Length of Study: 1–3 months
Frequency: Annual
Study Establishment: Study at the Society's library in Worcester, Massachusetts
No. of awards offered: 2
Application Procedure: You can find more information and down-loadable form at www.americanantiquarian.org
Closing Date: January 15th
Funding: Private
Contributor: Jay and Deborah Last

Stephen Botein Fellowship

Subjects: The history of the book in American culture to 1876.
Eligibility: Doctoral candidates may apply.
Level of Study: Doctorate, Postdoctorate
Type: Fellowship
Value: $1,700 per month or $1,200 per month including housing in the Society's Goddard-Daniels House
Length of Study: Up to 2 months
Frequency: Annual
Study Establishment: The Society's Library in Worcester, Massachusetts
Country of Study: United States of America
No. of awards offered: 1–2
Application Procedure: All application material is available from our website: www.americanantiquarian.org
Closing Date: January 15th
Funding: Private
Contributor: An endowment established by the family and friends of the late Mr Botein
No. of awards given last year: 2

AMERICAN ASSOCIATION FOR CANCER RESEARCH (AACR)

615 Chestnut Street, 17th Floor, Philadelphia, PA, 19106-4404, United States of America
Tel: (1) 215 440 9300
Fax: (1) (215) 440-9313
Email: awards@aacr.org
Website: www.aacr.org
Contact: Ms Sheri Ozard, Program Co-ordinator

The American Association for Cancer Research (AACR) is a scientific society of over 17,000 laboratory and clinical cancer researchers. It was founded in 1907 to facilitate communication and dissemination of knowledge among scientists and others dedicated to the cancer problem, and to foster research in cancer and related biomedical sciences. It is also dedicated to encouraging the presentation and discussion of new and important observations in the field, fostering public education, science education and training, and advancing the understanding of cancer etiology, prevention, diagnosis and treatment throughout the world.

AACR Career Development Awards in Cancer Research

Subjects: Cancer research.
Purpose: To support cancer research by junior faculty.
Eligibility: Open to junior faculty. Candidates must have completed productive postdoctoral research and demonstrated independent, investigator-initiated research. Employees of national government or private industry are not eligible.
Level of Study: Research, Postdoctorate
Type: Award
Value: US$50,000 per year
Length of Study: 2 years
Frequency: Annual
Study Establishment: Universities or research institutions
Country of Study: Any country
No. of awards offered: Varies
Application Procedure: Candidates must be nominated by a member of AACR and must be an AACR member or apply for membership by the time the application is submitted. Associate members may not be nominators. The online application is available at the AACR website.
Closing Date: December 18th
Funding: Private
Contributor: The Cancer Research and Prevention Foundation, the Susan G Komen Breast Cancer Foundation, Genentech Inc., the Pancreatic Cancer Action Network
No. of awards given last year: 6
No. of applicants last year: 75

For further information contact:

Tel: (267) 646-0655
Fax: (215) 440-9372
Email: grants@aacr.org
Contact: Julia Laurence

AACR Gertrude B. Elion Cancer Research Award

Subjects: Cancer research.
Purpose: To foster meritorious basic, clinical or translational cancer research.
Eligibility: Open to tenure-track scientists at the level of assistant professor at an institution worldwide, who have completed their postdoctoral studies or clinical research by July 1st of the award year, and ordinarily not more than 5 years earlier. Candidates must be members of the AACR or apply for membership by the time the applications are submitted.
Level of Study: Postdoctorate, Research
Type: Research award
Value: $50,000 for salary and benefits, laboratory supplies and limited travel for the grant recipient
Length of Study: 1 year
Frequency: Annual
Study Establishment: Universities or research institutions
Country of Study: Any country
No. of awards offered: 1
Application Procedure: Candidates must be nominated by a member of the AACR. The online application is available at the AACR website.
Closing Date: February 27th
Funding: Private
Contributor: GlaxoSmithKline
No. of awards given last year: 1
No. of applicants last year: 20

For further information contact:

Tel: (267) 646-0655
Fax: (215) 440-9372
Email: grants@aacr.org
Contact: Ms Julia Laurence

AACR Research Fellowships

Subjects: Cancer research.
Purpose: To foster meritorious cancer research.
Eligibility: Candidates must have completed a PhD or other doctoral degree and currently be a postdoctoral or Clinical Research Fellow. Academic faculty holding the rank of Instructor or higher, graduates and medical students, medical residents, permanent government employees and employees of private industry are not eligible.
Level of Study: Postdoctorate
Type: Fellowships
Value: US$30,000–40,000 per year
Length of Study: 1–3 years
Frequency: Annual
Study Establishment: Universities or research institutions
Country of Study: Any country
No. of awards offered: Varies
Application Procedure: Candidates must be nominated by a member of the AACR. Candidates must be an AACR member or apply for membership by the time the application is submitted. The online application is available from the AACR website.
Closing Date: December 10th
Funding: Private
Contributor: Amgen, Inc., AstraZeneca, Bristol-Myers Squibb Oncology, the Cancer Research and Prevention Foundation and Genentech BioOncology, Inc, MedImmune, National Brain Tumor Foundation
No. of awards given last year: 7
No. of applicants last year: 125

AACR Scholar-in-Training Awards

Subjects: Cancer research.
Purpose: To allow individuals to attend the AACR Annual Meeting and Special Conferences.
Eligibility: Open to first authors of an abstract submitted for presentation at the AACR Annual Meeting or Special Conference. Eligible candidates are graduate students, medical students and residents, clinical fellows or equivalent and postdoctoral Fellows.
Level of Study: Doctorate, Graduate, Postdoctorate, Postgraduate, Predoctorate
Type: Award
Value: US$400–2,000
Frequency: Annual
No. of awards offered: Varies
Application Procedure: No application is needed. Qualified persons who want to be considered should follow the instructions included in the abstract submission materials for the AACR Annual Meetings or Special Conference. If a candidate is eligible based on the above criteria, a certification form confirming his or her status will be requested at a later date.
Closing Date: Varies, please contact AACR for details
Funding: Corporation, individuals, private
Contributor: AFLAC Inc., AstraZeneca, Aventis, Bristol-Myers Squibb Oncology, Genentech, GlaxoSmithKline, ILEX, ITO EN Limited, Novartis Pharmaceuticals, the Avon Foundation, Susan G. Komen Breast Cancer Foundation and Pezcoller Foundation
No. of awards given last year: 300
No. of applicants last year: Approx. 2,000

AMERICAN ASSOCIATION FOR RESPIRATORY CARE

9425 N. MacArthur Boulevard, Suite 100, Irving, TX, 75063-4706,
United States of America
Tel: (1) 972 243 2272
Fax: (1) 972 484 2720
Email: info@aarc.org
Website: www.aarc.org
Contact: Administrative Assistant

The American Respiratory Care Foundation is dedicated to the art, science, quality and technology of respiratory care. It is a non-profit organization formed for the purpose of supporting research, education and charitable activities and to promote prevention, quality treatment and management of respiratory-related diseases.

NBRC/AMP Gareth B Gish, MS RRT Memorial Postgraduate Recognition Award

Subjects: Respiratory care and prevention.
Purpose: To assist qualified individuals in the pursuit of training leading to an advanced degree.
Eligibility: Open to professional respiratory therapists who have at least a Baccalaureate degree with a 3.0 cumulative grade point average or better on a 4.0 scale or equivalent. Candidates must be able to provide proof of acceptance into an advanced degree programme of a fully accredited school and proof that the applicant is a candidate for degree.
Level of Study: Postgraduate, Professional development
Type: Award
Value: Up to US$1,500 plus airfare, a certificate of recognition, one night's lodging and registration for the AARC International Respiratory Congress
Frequency: Annual
Country of Study: United States of America
No. of awards offered: 1
Application Procedure: Candidates must return a completed, signed and notarized application form, provide three letters of reference attesting to the applicant's character, academic ability and professional commitment and supply an essay of at least 1,200 words. This must describe how the award will assist the applicant in reaching the objective of an advanced degree and the candidate's ultimate goals of leadership in healthcare. Application forms can be downloaded and printed out from the website.
Closing Date: June 15th

Parker B Francis Respiratory Research Grant

Subjects: Respiratory care and related topics.
Purpose: To provide financial assistance for research programmes.
Eligibility: Open to qualified investigators in the field of respiratory care. The principal investigator may be a physician or respiratory therapist. However, a respiratory therapist must be the co-principal investigator if a physician is the principal applicant for the award.
Level of Study: Professional development
Type: Research grant
Value: The award is at the discretion of the Board of Trustees and is dependent on the quality of the proposal
Frequency: Annual
Country of Study: United States of America
Application Procedure: Candidates must apply directly to the Foundation Executive Office. Complete details can be found in the Application for Research Grant packet available from the Foundation.
Closing Date: Applications are accepted at any time
Funding: Private
Contributor: Parker B Francis Foundation
Additional Information: In 1993, the Parker B Francis Foundation provided an endowment to the American Respiratory Care Foundation to make funds available to provide financial assistance for research programmes.

William F Miller, MD Postgraduate Education Recognition Award

Subjects: Respiratory care and prevention.
Purpose: To assist a professional therapist pursuing postgraduate education which will lead to an advanced degree.
Eligibility: Open to professional respiratory therapists who have at least a baccalaureate degree with a 3.0 cumulative grade point average or better on a 4.0 scale or equivalent. Candidates must be able to provide proof of acceptance into an advanced degree programme of a fully accredited school and proof that the applicant is a candidate for degree.
Level of Study: Postgraduate, Professional development
Type: Award
Value: Up to US$1,500 plus airfare, certificate of recognition, one night's lodging and registration for the AARC International Respiratory Congress
Frequency: Annual
Country of Study: United States of America
No. of awards offered: 1
Application Procedure: Candidates must return a completed, signed and notarized application form, provide three letters of reference attesting to the candidate's character, academic ability and professional

commitment and supply an essay of at least 1,200 words. This must describe how the award will assist the candidate in reaching the objective of an advanced degree and the candidate's ultimate goals of leadership in healthcare.
Closing Date: June 15th
Funding: Private

AMERICAN ASSOCIATION FOR WOMEN RADIOLOGISTS (AAWR)

4550 Post Oak Place, Suite 342, Houston, Texas, TX 77027, United States of America
Tel: (1) 713 965 0566
Fax: (1) 713 960 0488
Email: kmacura@jhmi.edu
Website: www.aawr.org
Contact: Dr Katarzyna Macura , AAWR Account Manager

Alice Ettinger Distinguished Achievement Award
Subjects: Radiology.
Purpose: To recognize outstanding residents on the basis of contributions to clinical care, teaching, research or public service.
Eligibility: Open to candidates in the field of radiation oncology who are members of the AAWR as of January 1st of the year of the award.
Level of Study: Unrestricted
Type: Award
Value: Daily expenses and airfare to accept the award will be provided to the winner
Frequency: Annual
Country of Study: Any country
No. of awards offered: 1
Application Procedure: Candidates must submit an application including a nominating letter from the residency director, a letter of concurrence from the department chair, a curriculum vitae and a personal statement.
Closing Date: June 30th
Funding: Private
Contributor: Membership dues
Additional Information: Expenses to accept the award will be provided to the winner.

Eleanor Montague Distinguished Resident Award in Radiation Oncology
Subjects: Radiation oncology.
Purpose: To honour a resident radiation oncologist on the basis of outstanding contributions to clinical care, teaching, research and/or public service.
Eligibility: Open to candidates in the field who are members of the AAWR as of January 1st of the year of the award.
Level of Study: Unrestricted
Type: Award
Value: US$500 and reimbursement of expenses including travel and lodging per day
Frequency: Annual
Country of Study: Any country
No. of awards offered: 1
Application Procedure: Candidates must submit an application including a letter of nomination, a letter of concurrence and a curriculum vitae.
Closing Date: June 30th
Funding: Private

Lucy Frank Squire Distinguished Resident Award in Diagnostic Radiology
Subjects: Radiology.
Purpose: To honour a resident diagnostic radiologist on the basis of outstanding contributions to clinical care, teaching, research and/or public service.
Eligibility: Open to candidates in the field of diagnostic radiology who are members of the AAWR as of January 1st of the year of the award.
Level of Study: Unrestricted
Type: Award
Value: US$500 and reimbursement of expenses including travel and lodging per day

Frequency: Annual
Country of Study: Any country
No. of awards offered: 1
Application Procedure: Candidates must submit an application including a curriculum vitae, a letter of nomination and a letter of concurrence.
Closing Date: June 30th
Funding: Private
Contributor: Membership dues

Marie Sklodowska-Curie Award
Subjects: Radiology.
Purpose: To honour an individual who has made an outstanding contribution to the field of Radiology.
Eligibility: There are no nationality restrictions and nominees need not be members of the AAWR.
Level of Study: Unrestricted
Type: Award
Value: Expenses and airfare to accept the award will be provided to the winner (Less than £5,000. Estimated total funds £1,200)
Frequency: Annual
Country of Study: Any country
No. of awards offered: 1
Application Procedure: Candidates must submit an application including a letter of nomination, at least one letter of support and a curriculum vitae.
Closing Date: June 30th
Funding: Private
Contributor: Membership dues
Additional Information: Expenses to accept the award will be provided to the winner.

For further information contact:

Email: kmacura@jhmi.edu
Contact: Dr Katarzyna Macura

AMERICAN ASSOCIATION OF LAW LIBRARIES (AALL)

Scholarship Committee, 53 West Jackson Boulevard, Suite 940, Chicago, IL, 60604, United States of America
Tel: (1) 312 939 4764
Fax: (1) 312 431 1097
Email: scholarships@aall.org
Website: www.aallnet.org

The American Association of Law Libraries (AALL) was founded in 1906 to promote and enhance the value of law libraries to legal and public communities, to foster the profession of law librarianship and to provide leadership in the field of legal information. Today, the AALL represents law librarians and related professionals who are affiliated with a wide range of institutions including law firms, law schools, corporate legal departments and courts, and local, state and federal government agencies.

AALL and West-George A Strait Minority Scholarship Endowment
Subjects: Law librarianship.
Eligibility: Open to degree candidates in an accredited library or law school. Preference is given to individuals with previous service to, or interest in, law librarianship and who intend to pursue a career in law librarianship. Applicants must be members of a minority group as defined by the current United States of America government guidelines.
Level of Study: Graduate
Type: Scholarship
Value: Up to US$3,500 for tuition and school-related expenses
Frequency: Annual
Study Establishment: Accredited library schools or accredited law schools
Country of Study: Any country
No. of awards offered: Varies
Application Procedure: Applicants must write for details or download an application form from the website.
Closing Date: April 1st

AALL James F Connolly LexisNexis Academic and Library Solutions Scholarship

Subjects: Law librarianship.
Eligibility: Awarded to library school graduates with law library experience who are presently attending an accredited law school with the intention of pursuing a career as a law librarian. Preference will be given to individuals who have demonstrated an interest in government documents.
Level of Study: Graduate
Type: Scholarship
Value: Up to US$3,000 for tuition and school-related expenses
Frequency: Annual
Study Establishment: ABA-accredited Law Schools
Country of Study: Any country
No. of awards offered: Varies
Application Procedure: Applicants must write for details or download an application form from the website.
Closing Date: April 1st

AALL LexisNexis/John R Johnson Memorial Scholarship Endowment

Subjects: Law librarianship.
Eligibility: Candidates who apply for AALL educational scholarships, types I–IV, become automatically eligible to receive the LexisNexis/John R Johnson Memorial Scholarship.
Level of Study: Graduate
Type: Scholarship
Value: Up to US$2,000 for tuition and school-related expenses
Frequency: Annual
Study Establishment: ALA-accredited library schools or ABA-Accredited Law Schools
Country of Study: Any country
No. of awards offered: Varies
Application Procedure: Applicants must write for details or download an application form from the website.
Closing Date: April 1st

AMERICAN ASSOCIATION OF NEUROLOGICAL SURGEONS (AANS)

5550 Meadowbrook Drive, Rolling Meadows, IL, 60008, United States of America
Tel: (1) 847 378 0500
Fax: (1) 847 378 0600
Email: info@aans.org
Website: www.aans.org
Contact: Julie Qattrocchi, Development Coordinator

Founded in 1931 as the Harvey Cushing Society, the American Association of Neurological Surgeons (AANS) is a scientific and educational association with more than 6,500 members worldwide. The AANS is dedicated to advancing the speciality of neurological surgery in order to provide the highest quality of neurosurgical care to the public. All active members of the AANS are certified by the American Board of Neurological Surgery, The Royal College of Physicians and Surgeons (Neurosurgery) of Canada or the Mexican Council of Neurological Surgery, AC. Neurological surgery is the medical speciality concerned with the prevention, diagnosis, treatment and rehabilitation of disorders that affect the entire nervous system including the spinal column, spinal cord, brain and peripheral nerves.

NREF Research Fellowship

Subjects: Any field of neurosurgery.
Purpose: To provide training for neurosurgeons who are preparing for academic careers as clinician investigators.
Eligibility: Open to MDs who have been accepted into, or who are in, an approved residency training programme in neurological surgery in North America.
Level of Study: Postdoctorate
Type: Fellowship
Value: US$40,000 for a 1-year fellowship and US$70,000 for a 2-year fellowship
Length of Study: 1–2 years

Frequency: Annual
Country of Study: Other
Application Procedure: Applicants must send a completed application, sponsor statement, programme director comments and letters of recommendation. Responses to questions 1–9, a curriculum vitae and photographic images must also be submitted. Applications are available at the website www.aans.org
Closing Date: October 31st
Funding: Private
Contributor: Corporations and membership
No. of awards given last year: 5
No. of applicants last year: 25
Additional Information: Notification of awards will be made by February 28th. After notification of the award, the applicant must indicate acceptance, in writing, no later than April 1st. If unwilling to accept the award by that date, funds will be awarded to the first runner-up. A report of findings and accounting of funds will be expected at the halfway point and upon completion of the fellowship. Normally, no more than one award per year will be made to any one institution. Individuals who accept a grant from another source, NIH or private, for the same research project will become ineligible for the award. A budget must be prepared by the applicant and the sponsor indicating how the grant funds will be expended. It is the policy of the NREF to fund only direct costs involved with the research awards. This means no fringe benefits, publication costs or travel expenses. The signature representing the applicant's institution's financial officer on page four should be that of their chief financial officer or grants and contracts manager. The award will be made payable to the institution and disbursed by it according to its institutional policy.

For further information contact:

Email: nref@aans.org

NREF Young Clinician Investigator Award

Subjects: Any field of neurosurgery.
Purpose: To fund pilot studies that provide preliminary data used to strengthen applications for more permanent funding from other sources.
Eligibility: Candidates must be neurosurgeons who are full-time faculty in teaching institutions in North America and in the early years of their careers.
Level of Study: Postdoctorate
Type: Award
Value: US$40,000
Length of Study: 1 year
Frequency: Annual
No. of awards offered: 1
Application Procedure: Candidates must send a completed application, sponsor statement, programme director comments and letters of recommendation. Responses to questions 1–9, a curriculum vitae and photographic images must also be submitted. Applications are available at the website www.aans.org
Closing Date: October 31st
Funding: Private
Contributor: Corporations and membership
No. of awards given last year: 3
No. of applicants last year: 20
Additional Information: Notification of awards will be made by February 28th. After notification of the award, the applicant must indicate acceptance, in writing, no later than April 1st. If unwilling to accept the award by that date, funds will be awarded to the first runner-up. A summary report and an accounting of funds will be expected upon completion of the award. Normally, no more than one award per year will be made to any one institution. Individuals who accept a grant from another source, NIH or private, for the same research project will become ineligible for the award. The award is for those budget items necessary to pursue proper research. It may be used entirely, or in part, for stipend. A budget must be prepared by the applicant and sponsor indicating how the award funds will be expended. It is the policy of the NREF to fund only direct costs involved with the research awards. This means no fringe benefits, publication costs or travel expenses.

For further information contact:

Email: NREF@aans.org

William P. Van Wagenen Fellowship

Subjects: Any field of neurosurgery.
Purpose: To fund quality research in which the plan for a period abroad has been designed.
Eligibility: All senior neurological residents in approved neurosurgery residency programs.
Level of Study: Postdoctorate
Type: Travelling fellowship
Value: $60,000 stipend for living and travel expenses to a foreign country for a period of 12 months. A family travel and living allowance of $6,000 is available if spouse and/or children are accompanying the Fellow. In addition, $15,000 of research support is available to the University, hospital or laboratory, which has agreed to sponsor the Van Wagenen Fellow
Length of Study: 6 months–1 year
Frequency: Annual
Country of Study: Country of study must be different than the country of residence
No. of awards offered: 2
Application Procedure: Application should be submitted with letters of reference, including one from the applicant's Program Director. A letter from the proposed sponsor and documentation of intent to pursue an academic career, while not required, will strengthen the application.
Closing Date: October 1st
Funding: Private
Contributor: William P Van Wagenen
No. of awards given last year: 1
No. of applicants last year: 6
Additional Information: By December 31st, the Chairman of the Van Wagenen Selection Committee will notify the winning applicant, who will be expected to implement the fellowship within 6 months following notification. A formal announcement of the award will be made at the Annual Meeting of the AANS. Applications and additional information regarding the William P Van Wagenen Fellowship can be located at www.aans.org

For further information contact:

Email: info@aans.org

AMERICAN ASSOCIATION OF OCCUPATIONAL HEALTH NURSES FOUNDATION (AAOHN)

2920 Brandywine Road, Suite 100, Atlanta, GA 30341, United States of America
Tel: (1) 770 455 7757
Fax: (1) 770 455 7271
Email: ann@aaohn.org
Website: www.aaohn.org

Securing the future by improving the health and safety of the Nation's workers.

AAOHN Professional Development Scholarship

Subjects: Occupational and Environmental Health.
Eligibility: Candidates must be employed in the field of occupational and environmental health nursing.
Level of Study: Postgraduate, Professional development
Value: US$1,000–1,500
Length of Study: 1
Frequency: Annual
No. of awards offered: 13
Application Procedure: Submit an application form, a narrative of 500 words or less describing career goals and how the scholarship will enable continued education activity, and also supply a letter of support.
Closing Date: August 5th

THE AMERICAN ASSOCIATION OF PETROLEUM GEOLOGISTS (AAPG) FOUNDATION

PO Box 979, Tulsa, OK, 74101 0979, United States of America
Tel: (1) 918 584 2555
Fax: (1) 918 560 2642
Email: rgriffin@aapg.org
Website: http://foundation.aapg.org/
Contact: Ms Rebecca Griffin, Manager

Established by the American Association of Petroleum Geologists (AAPG) in 1967, the AAPG Foundation is a public foundation, qualified to receive gifts that are tax-deductible for United States of America taxpayers, in support of worthwhile educational and scientific programmes or projects related to the geosciences.

American Association of Petroleum Geologists Foundation Grants-in-Aid

Subjects: Earth and geological sciences.
Purpose: To support graduate (Master's or PhD) students whose research can be applied to the search for, and development of, petroleum and energy-minerals resources, and to related environmental geology issues.
Eligibility: Open to graduate and doctorate students of any nationality.
Level of Study: Doctorate, Graduate
Type: Grant
Value: A maximum of US$2,000
Country of Study: Any country
No. of awards offered: Varies
Application Procedure: Applicants must complete an application form and submit certified college academic transcripts and signed statements from professors commenting on the applicant's academic credentials and endorsements. Applicants must apply online the website being http://aapg.gia.confex.com/aapg_gia/2009/index.html
Closing Date: January 31st
Funding: Foundation
No. of awards given last year: 115
No. of applicants last year: 240
Additional Information: Grants are to be applied to expenses directly related to the student's thesis work, such as summer fieldwork, analytical analyses, etc. Funds are not to be used to purchase capital equipment, or to pay salaries, tuition or room and board during the school year.

AMERICAN ASSOCIATION OF UNIVERSITY WOMEN EDUCATIONAL FOUNDATION (AAUW)

1111 Sixteenth Street, NW, Washington, DC, 20036, United States of America
Tel: (1) 202 785 7700
Fax: (1) 202 872 1425
Email: foundation@aauw.org
Website: www.aauw.org
Contact: Tara McLoughlin, Director of Programs

The AAUW Educational Foundation is composed of three corporations. These are the Association, a 150,000 member organization with more than 1,500 branches nationwide that lobbies and advocates for education and equity; the AAUW Educational Foundation, which funds pioneering research on girls and education, community action projects, and fellowships and grants for outstanding women around the globe; and the AAUW Legal Advocacy Fund, which provides funds and a support system for women seeking judicial redress for sexual discrimination in higher education.

AAUW American Fellowships for Postdoctoral Research

Subjects: All subjects.
Purpose: To encourage and support women for conducting Doctoral/Postdoctoral research in related fields.

Eligibility: Open to women who are citizens or permanent residents of the United States and who have earned a Doctoral degree by November 15th.
Level of Study: Doctorate, Postdoctorate
Type: Fellowship
Value: US$30,000
Frequency: Annual
Study Establishment: American Association of University Women
Country of Study: Any country
Closing Date: November 15th
Additional Information: AAUW Educational Foundation, American Fellowships, PO Box 4030, Iowa City, 52243-4030, USA. Please note that materials sent to the Washington, D.C., office will be disqualified and will not be reviewed.

AAUW Career Development Grants

Purpose: To support women who hold a bachelor's degree and are preparing to advance their careers, change careers, or re-enter the work force.
Eligibility: Open to candidates with a bachelor's degree who are preparing to advance their careers, change careers, or re-enter the work force. Special consideration is given to women of color, and women pursuing their first advanced degree or credentials in non-traditional fields.
Level of Study: Graduate, Postgraduate
Type: Grant
Value: $2,000–12,000
Length of Study: 1 year
Frequency: Annual
No. of awards offered: Varies
Closing Date: December 15th
Additional Information: Materials sent to the Washington DC office will be disqualified and will not be reviewed.

For further information contact:

PO Box 4030, Iowa City, IA, 52243-4030
Contact: AAUW Educational Foundation Career Development Grants

AAUW Community Action Grants

Subjects: All subjects.
Purpose: To provide seed money to individual women, local community-based non-profit organizations, AAUW branches and AAUW state organizations for innovative programmes or non-degree research projects that engage girls in mathematics, science and technology.
Eligibility: Applicants must be women who are citizens or permanent residents of the United States of America. Special consideration will be given to AAUW members and AAUW branch and state applicants who seek partners for collaborative projects. Collaborators can include local schools or school districts, businesses and other community-based organizations. 2-year grants are restricted to projects focused on girls' achievement in mathematics, science or technology. Projects must involve community and school collaboration. The fund supports planning and coalition-building activities during the 1st year and implementation and evaluation the following year.
Type: Grant
Value: US$5,000–10,000
Length of Study: 1 or 2 years
Frequency: Annual
No. of awards offered: 5
Application Procedure: Applicants must write for an application form, which is also available from the website.
Closing Date: January 15th
Funding: Private
Additional Information: Please note that materials sent to the Washington, D.C., office will be disqualified and will not be reviewed. Two types of grant are available. 1-year grants are for short-term projects. Topic areas are unrestricted but should have a clearly defined educational activity. 2-year grants are for longer term programmes and are restricted to projects focused on K-12 girls achievement in mathematics, science and/or technology. Funds support planning activities and coalition-building during the 1st year and implementation and evaluation the following year.

AAUW Eleanor Roosevelt Fund Award

Subjects: Gender equity in Mathematics.
Purpose: To support professional development for teachers, educational opportunities for girls and the advancement of gender equity in the classroom, school or district.
Eligibility: Open to all public school, K-12 women teachers who are citizens of the United States of America or permanent residents.
Level of Study: Professional development
Type: Award
Value: $5,000 plus travel expenses to attend the AAUW National Convention
No. of awards offered: Approx. 25
Application Procedure: Candidates must write for an application form, which is also available from the website.
Closing Date: November 1st
Funding: Private
Additional Information: Please note that materials sent to the Washington, DC, office will be disqualified and will not be reviewed.

AAUW International Fellowships

Subjects: All subjects
Purpose: To support full-time study or research to women who are not US citizen or permanent residents.
Eligibility: Open to women who are not citizens of the United States of America or permanent residents, who hold a United States of America Bachelor's degree or equivalent. Applicants must be planning to return to their home country upon completion of degree and/or research. English proficiency is required
Level of Study: Postgraduate, Doctorate, Postdoctorate
Type: Fellowship
Value: $18,000 for Master's/professional, $20,000 for Doctorate, $30,000 for Postdoctoral fellowships
Length of Study: 1 year
Frequency: Annual
Study Establishment: Any accredited institution
Country of Study: United States of America
Application Procedure: Applicants must complete an application for each year applying. Applications must be obtained from the customer service centre or the AAUW website between August 1st and December 15th. Three letters of recommendation, transcripts and a minimum score of 550 on the Test of English as a Foreign Language (213 computer-based) are also required.
Closing Date: December 1st
Additional Information: Please note that materials sent to the Washington DC office will be disqualified and will not be reviewed.

For further information contact:

PO Box 4030, Iowa City, IA, 52243-4030
Contact: AAUW Educational Foundation International Fellowships

AAUW LAF Plaintiff Travel Grants

Subjects: All subjects.
Purpose: To help states and regions increase knowledge of LAF and equity issues in higher education.
Eligibility: See website for conditions.
Level of Study: Postgraduate, Research
Type: Grant
Value: Air travel and accommodation
Frequency: Annual
Application Procedure: Apply online.
Closing Date: October 15th
Additional Information: Please note that materials sent to the Washington, D.C., office will be disqualified and will not be reviewed.

AAUW Selected Professions Fellowships

Subjects: Architecture, computer/information sciences, engineering, mathematics/statistics, business administration, law and medicine.
Purpose: To support women who intend to pursue a full-time course of study at accredited institutions during the fellowship year in one of the designated degree programs where women's participation has been low.
Eligibility: Candidates must be US citizens or permanent residents. Fellowships are restricted to women of color, who have been underrepresented in these fields. Special consideration is given to

applicants who show professional promise in innovative or neglected areas of research or practice in areas of public interest.
Level of Study: Doctorate, Postdoctorate, Postgraduate
Type: Fellowships
Value: $5,000–12,000 for Master's and First Professional Awards and $20,000 for Engineering Dissertation Awards
Length of Study: 1 year
Frequency: Annual
Study Establishment: Any accredited institution
Application Procedure: Check website for details.
Closing Date: January 10th for Master's and First Professional Awards and December 15th for Engineering Dissertation Awards
Additional Information: Materials sent to the Washington DC office will be disqualified and will not be reviewed.

For further information contact:

PO Box 4030, Iowa City, IA, 52243-4030
Contact: AAUW Educational Foundation Selected Professions Fellowships

International Fellowship Scholarship Program for Women
Subjects: All subjects.
Purpose: To provide for full-time study or research to women who are not United States citizens.
Eligibility: Open to women who are citizens of countries other than the United States and have an academic degree equivalent to a bachelor's degree from a United States college or university.
Level of Study: Postgraduate
Type: Fellowship
Value: $18,000 (Master's), $20,000 (Doctorate), and $30,000 (Post-doctoral) Fellowship
Length of Study: 1 year
Frequency: Annual
Country of Study: Any country
No. of awards offered: 6
Application Procedure: Please check the website www.aauw.org for further details. Applications are available from August 1st.
Closing Date: December 1st
Funding: Foundation
No. of awards given last year: 74
Additional Information: AAUW members are not eligible to apply for international fellowships.

For further information contact:

Website: www.aauw.org

AMERICAN AUSTRALIAN ASSOCIATION (AAA)

599 Lexington Avenue, 17th Floor, New York, NY, 10022, United States of America
Tel: (1) 212 338 6860
Fax: (1) 212 338 6864
Email: information@aaanyc.org
Website: www.americanaustralian.org
Contact: Diane Sinclair, Director of Education

The American Australian Association (AAA), founded in 1948, is the largest non-profit organization in the United States devoted to relations between the United States, Australia and New Zealand, with operations throughout the tri-state and the New England regions. Its goal is to encourage stronger ties across the Pacific, particularly in the private sector.

AAA Education Fund Program
Subjects: Science, engineering, mining, medicine.
Purpose: To assist students doing research in the field of science, engineering, mining medicine and other related fields.
Eligibility: Open to applicants who are American citizens or permanent residents of the USA doing research or study at the graduate level. Applicants must also show proof of the arrangements made at an Australian university or institution where the research or study will be conducted for the next academic year.
Level of Study: Research

Value: The Fellowships will support part of the costs of 1 year of research or study in Australia
Frequency: Annual
No. of awards offered: Varies
Closing Date: October 31st

AMERICAN CENTER OF ORIENTAL RESEARCH (ACOR)

656 Beacon Street, 5th Floor, Boston, MA, 02215-2010, United States of America
Tel: (1) 617 353 6571
Fax: (1) 617 353 6575
Email: acor@bu.edu
Website: www.bu.edu/acor

The American Center of Oriental Research (ACOR) in Amman, Jordan, is a private, non-profit academic institution dedicated to promoting research and publication in the fields of archaeology, anthropology, history, languages, biblical studies, Arabic, Islamic studies and other aspects of near eastern studies.

ACOR-CAORC Fellowship
Subjects: Humanities, natural and social sciences.
Purpose: To provide fellowships for Master's and pre-doctoral students.
Eligibility: Open to masters and doctoral students candidates.
Level of Study: Postgraduate, Predoctorate
Type: Fellowship
Value: $22,600
Length of Study: 2–6 months
Frequency: Dependent on funds available
No. of awards offered: 3 or more
Closing Date: February 1st
Funding: Government
Additional Information: Topics should contribute to scholarship in Near Eastern studies.

ACOR-CAORC Postgraduate Fellowships
Subjects: Natural and social sciences and humanities.
Purpose: To financially support students undertaking research in Jordon.
Eligibility: Open to post-doctoral scholars and scholars with a terminal degree in their field, pursuing research or publication projects in the natural and social sciences, humanities and associated disciplines relating to the Near East. U.S. citizenship required.
Level of Study: Postdoctorate
Type: Fellowships
Value: Maximum award is $29,800. Awards may be subject to funding
Length of Study: 2–6 months
Frequency: Annual
Country of Study: Jordan
No. of awards offered: 2 or more
Application Procedure: Candidates need to submit letters of recommendation, health insurance and waiver forms along with the application packet.
Closing Date: February 1st
Funding: Government
Additional Information: A prior recipient of an ACOR-CAORC Fellowship is not eligible for this award for a period of 2 years.

Andrew W. Mellon Foundation East-Central European Research Fellows Program
Subjects: Humanities, social sciences.
Purpose: To provide fellowships for scholars who have a PhD, or equivalent experience, pursuing research in any field of humanities or social sciences that relates to the Near East.
Eligibility: Applicants must be a citizen of Bulgaria, the Czech Republic, Estonia, Hungary, Latvia, Lithuania, Poland, Romania or Slovakia.
Level of Study: Postgraduate
Type: Fellowship
Value: US$11,500
Length of Study: 3 months
Frequency: Annual

Country of Study: Jordan
No. of awards offered: 2
Closing Date: February 1st
Funding: Foundation

Bert and Sally de Vries Fellowship

Subjects: Archaeology.
Purpose: To support a student for participation on an archaeological project.
Eligibility: Open to enrolled undergraduate or graduate students of any nationality.
Level of Study: Graduate
Type: Fellowship
Value: $1,200
Frequency: Annual
Country of Study: Jordan
No. of awards offered: 1
Closing Date: February 1st
Funding: Private
Additional Information: Senior project staff whose expenses are being borne largely by the project are ineligible.

Frederick-Wenger Jordanian Educational Fellowship

Subjects: Related to Jordan's cultural heritage is preferred.
Purpose: To assist Jordanian student with the cost of their education.
Eligibility: Open to enrolled undergraduate or graduate students with Jordanian citizenship.
Level of Study: Graduate
Type: Fellowship
Value: $1,500
Frequency: Annual
Country of Study: Any country
No. of awards offered: 1
Closing Date: February 1st
Funding: Private
Additional Information: Eligibility is not limited to a specific field of study, but preference will be given to study related to Jordan's cultural heritage.

Harrell Family Fellowship

Subjects: Archaeology.
Purpose: To support a graduate student for participation on an archaeological project.
Eligibility: Open to enrolled graduate students of any nationality.
Level of Study: Graduate
Type: Fellowship
Value: $1,800
Frequency: Annual
Country of Study: Jordan
No. of awards offered: 1
Closing Date: February 1st
Funding: Private
Additional Information: Senior project staff whose expenses are being borne largely by the project are ineligible.

James A. Sauer Fellowship

Subjects: Archaeology.
Purpose: To assist Jordanian graduate student in Jordan or elsewhere.
Eligibility: Open to enrolled graduate students with US or Canadian citizenship participating on an archaeological project or research in Jordan.
Level of Study: Graduate
Type: Residential fellowships
Value: The fellowship includes room and board at ACOR and a stipend of $400
Length of Study: 1 month
Frequency: Annual
Country of Study: Jordan
No. of awards offered: 1
Closing Date: February 1st
Funding: Private

Jennifer C. Groot Fellowship

Subjects: Archaeology.

Purpose: To support beginners in archaeological fieldwork who have been accepted as staff members on archaeological projects with ASOR/CAP affiliation in Jordan.
Eligibility: Open to a graduate student with US or Canadian citizenship.
Level of Study: Graduate
Type: Fellowship
Value: $1,800 each
Frequency: Annual
Country of Study: Jordan
No. of awards offered: 2 or more
Closing Date: February 1st
Funding: Private

Kenneth W. Russell Fellowship

Subjects: Archaeology, anthropology, conservation or related areas.
Purpose: To assist non-Jordanian student, in Jordan.
Eligibility: Open to enrolled undergraduate or graduate students with Jordanian citizenship.
Level of Study: Graduate
Type: Fellowship
Value: The award for each student is 200 Jordanian Dinars ($280)
Frequency: Every 2 years
Country of Study: Jordan
No. of awards offered: 1
Closing Date: February 1st
Funding: Private

Kress Fellowship in the Art and Archaeology of Jordan

Subjects: Art history, archaeology, architectural history and classical studies.
Purpose: To support PhD candidates who are completing dissertation research in the field of history of art.
Eligibility: Open to applicants who are enrolled graduate students at the time of application. The applicants must be citizens of the United States or must have matriculated at United States institutions.
Level of Study: Doctorate, Predoctorate
Type: Fellowships
Value: Up to US$17,000. The award includes a living allowance, research funds, international transportation and accommodations at ACOR
Length of Study: 3–6 months
Frequency: Annual
Study Establishment: American Center of Oriental Research
Country of Study: Jordan
No. of awards offered: 1
Application Procedure: Applicants need to submit their application form along with letters of recommendations, transcripts, health insurance form and waiver form.
Closing Date: November 1st
Funding: Foundation

MacDonald/Sampson Fellowship

Subjects: Ancient Near Eastern languages and history, archaeology, Bible studies and comparative religion.
Purpose: To support Canadian students.
Eligibility: Open to enrolled undergraduate or graduate students with Canadian citizenship or landed immigrant status.
Level of Study: Graduate
Type: Fellowship
Value: The ACOR residency fellowship option includes room and board at ACOR and a stipend of US$600. The travel grant option provides a single payment of US$1,800 to help with any project-related expenses
Length of Study: 6 weeks
Frequency: Annual
Country of Study: Jordan
No. of awards offered: 1
Closing Date: February 1st
Funding: Private

National Endowment for the Humanities (NEH) Fellowship

Subjects: Modern and classical languages, linguistics, history, jurisprudence, philosophy, archaeology, comparative religion, ethics, and the history, criticism, and the theory of the arts.

Eligibility: Open to candidates who have a PhD or have completed their professional training. Social and political scientists are encouraged to apply. Candidates must be US citizens or foreign nationals living in the US three years immediately preceding the application deadline.
Level of Study: Doctorate
Type: Fellowship
Value: $27,800
Frequency: Every four months
No. of awards offered: 1
Closing Date: February 1st

Pierre and Patricia Bikai Fellowship

Subjects: Archaeology.
Eligibility: Open to enrolled graduate students of any nationality participating on an archaeological project or research in Jordan.
Level of Study: Graduate
Type: Fellowship
Value: The fellowship includes room and board at ACOR and a monthly stipend of $600.
Length of Study: 1–2 months residential
Frequency: Annual
Country of Study: Jordan
No. of awards offered: 1
Closing Date: February 1st
Funding: Private

THE AMERICAN CHEMICAL SOCIETY (ACS)

1155 16th Street, NW, Washington, DC, 20036, United States of America
Tel: (1) 202 872 4600
Fax: (1) 202 872 6067
Email: prfinfo@acs.org
Website: www.chemistry.org

The American Chemical Society is a self-governed individual membership organization that consists of more than 160,000 members at all degree levels and in all fields of chemistry. The organization provides a broad range of opportunities for peer interaction and career development, regardless of professional or scientific interests. The program and activities conducted by ACS today are the products of a tradition of excellence in meeting member needs that dates from the Society's founding in 1876.

ACS Ahmed Zewail Award in Ultrafast Science and Technology

Subjects: Physics, chemistry, biology, or related fields.
Purpose: To recognize outstanding and creative contributions to fundamental discoveries or inventions in ultrafast science and technology.
Eligibility: Open to candidates who have conducted original and insightful research that has had a significant impact on the field of ultrafast science and technology.
Level of Study: Postgraduate
Type: Award
Value: US$5,000
Frequency: Annual
Application Procedure: See website for details.
Closing Date: November 1st
Funding: Trusts
Contributor: Ahmed Zewail Endowment Fund

ACS Award for Achievement in Research for the Teaching and Learning of Chemistry

Subjects: Chemical sciences.
Purpose: To recognize outstanding contributions to experimental research that have increased our understanding of chemical pedagogy.
Eligibility: Open to candidates in the field of chemical pedagogy.
Level of Study: Postgraduate
Type: Award
Value: US$5,000
Length of Study: 1 year

Frequency: Annual
No. of awards offered: 1
Application Procedure: See website for details.
Closing Date: November 1st
Funding: Commercial
Contributor: Prentice-Hall Publishers
Additional Information: Experimental research should include one or more recognized techniques and designed such as: control-group designs with random assignments of subjects or the use of in-tact class sections; factorial designs, bi-variate or multivariate correlation studies, etc.

ACS Award for Creative Advances in Environmental Science and Technology

Subjects: Enviornmental science and technology.
Purpose: To encourage creativity in research and technology.
Eligibility: Open to all candidates without regard to age or nationality.
Level of Study: Postgraduate
Type: Award
Value: US$5,000 and a certificate
Frequency: Annual
Application Procedure: See the website for more details
Closing Date: November 1st
Contributor: Air Products and Chemicals, Inc. in memory of Joseph J. Breen

ACS Award for Creative Research and Applications of Iodine Chemistry

Subjects: Chemistry.
Purpose: To promote global research of iodine chemistry.
Eligibility: Open to applicants who have performed outstanding research related to iodine chemistry.
Level of Study: Postgraduate
Type: Award
Value: US$10,000, travel expenses of up to US$1,000 and a certificate
Frequency: Biennially in odd-numbered years
Application Procedure: A completed nomination form and curriculum vitae must be sent.
Closing Date: November 1st
Contributor: Sociedad Quimica y Minera de chile S.A. (SQM S.A.)

ACS Award for Creative Work in Synthetic Organic Chemistry

Subjects: Organic chemistry.
Purpose: To recognize and encourage creative work in synthetic organic chemistry.
Eligibility: Open to applicants who have accomplished outstanding creative work in synthetic organic chemistry, which has been published.
Level of Study: Postgraduate
Type: Award
Value: US$5,000 and a certificate. In addition up to US$1,000 is provided for travel expenses to the meeting
Frequency: Annual
Application Procedure: See the website for more details
Closing Date: November 1st
Contributor: Aldrich Chemical Company, Inc

ACS Award for Encouraging Disadvantaged Students into Careers in the Chemical Sciences

Subjects: Chemistry.
Purpose: To recognize significant accomplishments by individuals in stimulating students, underrepresented in the profession, to elect careers in the chemical sciences and engineering.
Eligibility: Open to all applicants of any nationality.
Level of Study: Postgraduate
Type: Award
Value: US$5,000 and a certificate along with a travel allowance of US$1,500
Frequency: Annual
Country of Study: United States of America
Application Procedure: Completed nomination and optional support forms must be submitted to the awards office.

Closing Date: November 1st
Contributor: The Camille and Henry Dreyfus Foundation, Inc
Additional Information: A grant of US$10,000 will be made to an academic institution chosen by the recipient.

For further information contact:

The Awards Office
Email: awards@acs.org

ACS Award for Encouraging Women into Careers in Chemical Sciences

Subjects: Chemistry.
Purpose: To recognize individuals who have significantly stimulated the interests of women in chemistry.
Eligibility: Open to candidates of all nationalities.
Level of Study: Professional development
Type: Award
Value: US$5,000 and a certificate plus US$1,500 towards travel expenses
Frequency: Annual
No. of awards offered: 1
Application Procedure: For more details visit the website.
Closing Date: November 1st
Contributor: The Camille and Henry Dreyfus Foundation, Inc
Additional Information: A grant of US$10,000 will be made to an academic institution chosen by the recipient.

ACS Award in Chromatography

Subjects: Chemistry.
Purpose: To recognize outstanding contributions to the fields of chromatography.
Eligibility: Open to all applicants.
Level of Study: Postgraduate
Type: Award
Value: The award consists of $5,000 and a certificate. Up to $2,500 for travel expenses to the meeting at which the award will be presented will be reimbursed
Frequency: Annual
Application Procedure: See the website for more details.
Closing Date: November 1st
Contributor: SUPELCO, Inc

For further information contact:

The Awards Office
Email: awards@acs.org

ACS Award in Colloid and Surface Chemistry

Subjects: Chemistry.
Purpose: To recognize outstanding scientific contributions to colloid and/or surface chemistry in North America.
Eligibility: Open to applicants who are residents of North America.
Level of Study: Postgraduate
Type: Award
Value: The award consists of $5,000 and a certificate. Up to $2,500 for travel expenses to the meeting at which the award will be presented will be reimbursed
Frequency: Annual
Application Procedure: Completed nomination and optional support forms must be submitted.
Closing Date: November 1st
Contributor: Procter & Gamble Company

For further information contact:

The Awards Office
Email: awards@acs.org

ACS National Awards

Subjects: Chemical sciences.
Purpose: To recognize premier chemical professionals in extraordinary ways.
Level of Study: Postgraduate
Type: Grant
Length of Study: 2 years
Frequency: Annual

No. of awards offered: 57
Application Procedure: See website for details.
Closing Date: November 1st

ACS Petroleum Research Fund

Subjects: Petroleum-related chemistry science.
Purpose: The ACS Petroleum Research Fund will support innovative fundamental research, advanced scientific education, and the careers of scientists, to aid in significantly increasing the world's energy options
Eligibility: Open to candidates in the field of petroleum-related chemistry science.
Type: Funding support
Value: US$90,000
Length of Study: 1–3 years
Frequency: Annual
Application Procedure: See website for details.
Closing Date: December 9th
Funding: Trusts
Contributor: Petroleum Research Fund

ACS PRF Summer Research Fellowships (SRF)

Subjects: Chemistry science.
Purpose: To support faculty guest researchers from non-doctoral institutions.
Eligibility: Only current grant holders are eligible to apply.
Level of Study: Postgraduate
Type: Fellowships
Value: US$8,000. Most or all of this amount shall constitute a stipend to the visiting faculty member (including the cost of benefits, if any). Up to $1,000 of the $8,000 may be used toward research expenses
Frequency: Annual
Application Procedure: See website for details.
Closing Date: December 2nd
Additional Information: Up to US$1,000 of the US$8,000 may be used towards research expenses.

ACS PRF Supplements for Underrepresented Minority Research (SUMR)

Subjects: Chemistry sciences.
Purpose: To support a student who is a member of a minority group underrepresented in science, i.e., African American, Hispanic/Latino or American Indian.
Eligibility: Only current grant holders are eligible to apply.
Level of Study: Postgraduate
Type: Supplement or Fellowship
Value: US$5,000. Most, or all, of this amount shall constitute a stipend to the SUMR Scholar (including the cost of benefits, if any). Up to $500 of the total may be used toward research expenses
Frequency: Annual
Application Procedure: See website for details.
Closing Date: December 5th

ACS PRF Type SE Grants

Subjects: Scientific education and fundamental research in the petroleum field.
Purpose: To provide partial funding for foreign speakers at major symposia.
Eligibility: Open to non-profit institutions throughout the United States of America and worldwide for speakers coming to conferences in the United States of America, Canada and Mexico and speaking within the PRF Trust.
Level of Study: Unrestricted
Type: Grant
Value: Up to $1,500 per foreign speaker with a maximum of $4,500 per symposium (three or more visiting speakers)
Frequency: Annual
Country of Study: United States of America
No. of awards offered: Varies
Closing Date: Applications are accepted at any time
Funding: Private
Contributor: A private trust

ACS Roger Adams Award in Organic Chemistry

Subjects: Organic chemistry.

Purpose: To recognize and encourage outstanding contributions to research in organic chemistry.
Eligibility: Open to applicants of any nationality.
Type: Award
Value: US$25,000, a medallion and a certificate
Frequency: Biennically in odd-numbered years
Application Procedure: A completed nomination form must be sent as an email attachment. See the website www.chemistry.org for further details.
Closing Date: November 1st
Contributor: Organic Reactions, Inc. and Organic Synthesis, Inc

ACS Stanley C. Israel Regional Award

Subjects: Chemical sciences.
Purpose: To recognize individuals who have advanced diversity in the chemical sciences and significantly stimulated or fostered activities that promote inclusiveness within the region.
Eligibility: Candidates nominated for the award may come from any professional setting: academia, industry, government, or other independent facility. Candidates may also be organizations, including ACS local sections and divisions. The awardees will have increased the participation and leadership of persons from diverse or underrepresented minority group(s), persons with disabilities, or women.
Level of Study: Postgraduate
Type: Award
Value: The award consists of a medal and a $1,000 grant to support and further the activities for which the award was made
Frequency: Annual
Application Procedure: See website for details.
Closing Date: May 1st and March 1st

For further information contact:

Committee on Minority Affairs, American Chemical Society, 1155, 16th Street NW, Washington, DC, 20036, United States of America
Tel: (1) 800 227 5558 ext. 6122
Email: p.christopher@acs.org
Contact: Paula Christoper

Alfred Burger Award in Medicinal Chemistry

Subjects: Medicinal chemistry.
Purpose: To acknowledge outstanding contributions to research in medicinal chemistry.
Eligibility: Open to all applicants without regard to age or nationality.
Level of Study: Postgraduate
Type: Award
Value: US$3,000 and a certificate. Up to $2,500 for travel expenses to the meeting at which the award will be presented will be reimbursed
Frequency: Biennically in even-numbered years
Application Procedure: A completed nomination form available on the website www.chemistry.org must be sent as an email attachment.
Closing Date: November 1st
Contributor: Glaxo SmithKline

Anselme Payen Award

Subjects: Chemistry.
Purpose: To encourage outstanding professional contributions to the science and chemical technologies of cellulose and its allied products.
Eligibility: Open to all scientists conducting research in the field of cellulose.
Level of Study: Postgraduate
Type: Award
Value: US$3,000 and a bronze medal
Frequency: Annual
Application Procedure: A completed nomination form available on the website www.membership.acs.org must be sent.
Closing Date: December 1st
Contributor: Cellulose, paper and textile division, ACS

For further information contact:

Awards committee chair, National Bioenergy Center, 1617 Cole Boulevard, Golden, CO 80401
Tel: 384 6123
Fax: 384 6363
Contact: Dr Stephen S. Kelley

Arthur C. Cope Scholar Awards

Subjects: Organic chemistry.
Purpose: To recognize outstanding achievement in the field of organic chemistry.
Eligibility: Open to all candidates irrespective of their nationality and age.
Level of Study: Postgraduate
Type: Award
Value: The award consists of $5,000, a certificate. Up to $2,500 for travel expenses to the fall national meeting will be reimbursed
Frequency: Annual
Application Procedure: See the website.
Closing Date: November 1st
Additional Information: A $40,000 unrestricted research grant to be assigned by the recipient to any university or non-profit institution.

Cognis Corporation Graduate Research Fellowship in Colloid and Surface Chemistry

Subjects: Chemistry.
Purpose: To support outstanding graduate students during their final 2 years of doctoral thesis research.
Eligibility: Open to candidates who are enrolled in a full-time graduate programme leading to a PhD degree at an accredited university within the United States.
Level of Study: Research
Type: Award
Value: US$20,000
Length of Study: 2 years
Frequency: Annual
Study Establishment: Any accredited university
Country of Study: United States of America
Application Procedure: See the website www.membership.acs.org
Closing Date: Novermber 1st
Funding: Corporation
Contributor: The Cognis Corporation

For further information contact:

Department of chemical and Materials Engineering, University of Kentucky, Lexington, KY 40506-0046
Contact: Professor Mark A. Keane

Earle B. Barnes Award for Leadership in Chemical Research Management

Subjects: Chemistry and chemical engineering.
Purpose: To recognize outstanding achievements in chemical research management.
Eligibility: Open to candidates who are citizens of the United States. The award is intended to recognize individuals who have demonstrated outstanding leadership and creativity in promoting the sciences of chemistry and chemical engineering in research management.
Level of Study: Postgraduate
Type: Award
Value: US$5,000 and a certificate. Up to $2,500 for travel expenses to the meeting at which the award will be presented will be reimbursed
Frequency: Annual
Application Procedure: A completed nomination form must be submitted to awards@acs.org as an email attachment.
Closing Date: November 1st
Contributor: The Dow Chemical Company

Ernest Guenther Award in the Chemistry of Natural Products

Subjects: Organic chemistry.
Purpose: To recognize and encourage outstanding achievements in analysis, structure elucidation and chemical synthesis of natural products.
Eligibility: Open to all applicants for their accomplished outstanding work.
Type: Award
Value: US$6,000
Frequency: Annual
Application Procedure: A completed nomination form and optional support forms must be mailed to awards@acs.org
Closing Date: November 1st

F. Albert Cotton Award in Synthetic Inorganic Chemistry
Subjects: Inorganic chemistry.
Purpose: To recognize distinguished work in synthetic inorganic chemistry.
Eligibility: Open to all candidates of all nationalities.
Level of Study: Postgraduate
Type: Award
Value: US$5,000
Frequency: Annual
Application Procedure: A completed application form to be submitted as an email attachment to awards@acs.org
Closing Date: November 1st
Funding: Private
Contributor: F. Albert Cotton Endowment Fund

Frederic Stanley Kipping Award in Silicon Chemistry
Subjects: Chemistry.
Purpose: To recognize distinguished contributions to the field of silicon chemistry.
Eligibility: Open to all candidates who have contributed to the field of silicon chemistry. There are no limits on age or on nationality. A nominee must have made distinguished contributions in the field of silicon chemistry during the 10 years preceding the current nomination
Level of Study: Postgraduate
Type: Award
Value: US$5,000 and a certificate
Frequency: Biennially in even-numbered years
Application Procedure: A completed nomination form to be mailed to awards@acs.org
Closing Date: November 1st
Funding: Corporation
Contributor: Dow Corning Corporation

Glenn T. Seaborg Award for Nuclear Chemistry
Subjects: Chemistry.
Purpose: To recognize and encourage research in nuclear and radiochemistry or their applications.
Eligibility: Open to all applicants without regard to nationality or age.
Level of Study: Postgraduate
Type: Award
Value: US$3,000 and a certificate
Frequency: Annual
Application Procedure: See the website.
Closing Date: November 1st
Contributor: ACS Division of Nuclear Chemistry and Technology

For further information contact:

The Awards Office
Email: awards@acs.org

Herbert C. Brown Award for Creative Research in Synthetic Methods
Subjects: Chemistry.
Purpose: To recognize and encourage outstanding and creative contributions to research in synthetic methods.
Eligibility: Open to all applicants without regard to age or nationality.
Level of Study: Postgraduate
Type: Award
Value: US$5,000 a medallion with a presentation box and a certificate
Frequency: Annual
Application Procedure: A completed application form available on the website must be sent as an email attachment to awards@acs.org
Closing Date: November 1st
Contributor: Purdue Borane Research Fund and Herbert C. Brown Award Endowment

Ipatieff Prize
Subjects: Chemistry.
Purpose: To recognize outstanding chemical experimental work in the field of catalysis.
Eligibility: Open to candidates who should not have passed his or her 40th birthday on April 30 of the year in which the award is presented, and must have done outstanding chemical experimental work in the field of catalysis or high pressure. Special weight will be given to independence

of thought and originality. The award may be made for investigations carried out in any country and without consideration of nationality.
Level of Study: Postgraduate
Type: Prize
Value: The award will consist of the income from a trust fund and a certificate. The financial value of the prize may vary, but it is expected that it will be approximately $5,000
Frequency: Every 3 years
Country of Study: Any country
Application Procedure: Contact the awards office.
Closing Date: November 1st
Contributor: Ipatieff Trust Fund
Additional Information: Preference will be given to American chemists.

For further information contact:

The Awards Office
Email: awards@acs.org

Irving Langmuir Award in Chemical Physics
Subjects: Chemistry and physics.
Purpose: To encourage research in chemistry and physics.
Eligibility: A candidate must have made an outstanding contribution to chemical physics or physical chemistry within the 10 years preceding the year in which the award is made. The award will be granted without restriction, except that the recipient must be a resident of the United States and the monetary prize must be used in the United States or its possessions.
Level of Study: Postgraduate
Type: Award
Value: US$10,000 and a certificate
Frequency: Biennially in even-numbered years
Country of Study: United States of America
Application Procedure: Contact the Awards office.
Closing Date: November 1st
Funding: Foundation
Contributor: GE Global Research

James Bryant Conant Award in High School Chemistry Teaching
Subjects: Teaching.
Purpose: To recognize outstanding teachers of high school chemistry in the United States.
Eligibility: Open to candidates who are actively engaged in the teaching of chemistry in high school.
Level of Study: Postgraduate
Type: Award
Value: US$5,000 and a certificate
Frequency: Annual
Country of Study: United States of America
Application Procedure: A completed nomination form must be submitted as an email attachment.
Closing Date: November 1st
Contributor: The Thermo Fisher Scientific, Inc
Additional Information: A certificate will also be provided to the recipient's institution for display.

For further information contact:

Email: awards@acs.org
Contact: The Awards Office

Peter Debye Award in Physical Chemistry
Subjects: Physical chemistry.
Purpose: To encourage and reward outstanding research in physical chemistry.
Eligibility: Open to all candidates without regard to age or nationality.
Level of Study: Postgraduate
Type: Award
Value: US$5,000 and a certificate
Frequency: Annual
Application Procedure: A completed nominations form to be sent as an email attachment to awards@acs.org
Closing Date: November 1st
Contributor: E.I. du Pont de Nemours and Company

39

Ronald Breslow Award for Achievement in Biomimetic Chemistry

Subjects: Chemistry.
Purpose: To recognize outstanding contributions to the field of biomimetic chemistry.
Eligibility: Open to all candidates without regard to age or nationality.
Level of Study: Postgraduate
Type: Award
Value: US$5,000 and a certificate
Frequency: Annual
Application Procedure: A completed application form along with a curriculum vitae must be submitted as an email attachment to awards@acs.org
Closing Date: November 1st
Funding: Trusts
Contributor: The Ronald Breslow Endowment

AMERICAN COLLEGE OF OBSTETRICIANS AND GYNECOLOGISTS (ACOG)

409, 12th Street South West, PO Box 96920, Washington, DC, 20090-6920, United States of America
Tel: (1) 202 863 2577
Fax: (1) 202 863 4992
Email: lcummings@acog.org
Website: www.acog.org
Contact: Mrs Lee Cummings, Director of Corporate Relations

The American College of Obstetricians and Gynecologists (ACOG) is a membership organization of obstetricians and gynecologists dedicated to the advancement of women's health through education, advocacy, practice and research.

ACOG Abbott Nutrition Research Award on Nutrition in Pregnancy

Subjects: Obstetrics and gynecology with a focus on nutrition in pregnancy with a special interest in the areas of obesity, diabetes and women age 20–39.
Purpose: To provide seed grant funds to a junior investigator for clinical research in the area nutrition in pregnancy.
Eligibility: Applicants must be ACOG Junior Fellows or Fellows at the time of application.
Level of Study: Postdoctorate
Type: Research grant
Value: US$25,000 plus $1,000 travel stipend to attend the ACOG Annual Clinical Meeting
Length of Study: 1 year
Frequency: Annual
Country of Study: United States of America or Canada
No. of awards offered: 1
Application Procedure: Applicants must sumit six copies of a proposal consisting of a hypothesis, objectives, specific aims, background and significance and experimental design, and references. One page budget is required, applicants's curriculum vitae and a letter of support from the program director, departmental chair or laboratory director.
Closing Date: October 1st
Funding: Commercial
Contributor: Abbott Nutrition
Additional Information: Further information can be found on the member side of the website www.acog.org

ACOG Bayer Health Care Pharmaceticals Research Award in Long Term Contraception

Subjects: Obstetrics and gynecology.
Purpose: To provide seed grant funds to junior investigators for clinical research in the area of non-daily contraception, such as proper use and administration, factors affecting patient acceptance and compliance, and non-contraceptive benefits.
Eligibility: Candidates must be an ACOG Junior Fellow or Fellow and in an approved obstetrics-gynecology residency program or within 3 years post-residency.
Level of Study: Postgraduate
Type: Research grant
Value: US$25,000 plus a US$1,000 travel stipend to attend the ACOG annual clinical meeting
Length of Study: 1 year
Frequency: Annual
Country of Study: United States of America or Canada
No. of awards offered: 1
Application Procedure: Candidates must submit six copies of a research proposal, written in eight pages or less, and should include the following: hypothesis, objectives, specific aims, background and significance, experimental design, and references. A one-page budget, curriculum vitae and letter of support from the program director, departmental chair or laboratory director must also be submitted.
Closing Date: October 1st
Funding: Commercial
Contributor: Bayer Healthcare Pharmaceuticals
No. of awards given last year: 1
No. of applicants last year: 4
Additional Information: Further information can be found on the member side of the website www.acog.org

ACOG/Bayer Health Care Pharmaceuticals Research Award in Contraceptive Counseling

Subjects: Obstetrics and gynecology.
Purpose: To provide seed grant funds to junior investigators for clinical research in the area of contraceptive counselling, such as education to parents to recognize the options available to them and the risks, benefits and total costs associated with each option, patient preference for contraception options and patient selection criteria for different forms of contraception.
Eligibility: Candidates must be ACOG Junior Fellows or Fellows who are in an approved obstetrics or gynecology residency programme or within 3 years of postresidency.
Level of Study: Postgraduate
Type: Research award
Value: US$25,000 plus a $1,000 travel stipend to attend the ACOG Annual Clinical Meeting
Length of Study: 1 year
Frequency: Annual
Country of Study: United States of America or Canada
No. of awards offered: 1
Application Procedure: Candidates must submit six copies of a proposal consisting of a hypothesis, objectives, specific aims, background and significance, experimental design and methods. These must not exceed six typewritten pages in total. A curriculum vitae, letter of support from the programme director, departmental chair or laboratory director, references and a one-page budget must also be submitted.
Closing Date: October 1st
Funding: Commercial
Contributor: Bayer Healthcare Pharmaceuticals
No. of awards given last year: 1
No. of applicants last year: 7
Additional Information: Further information can be found on the member side of the website www.acog.org

ACOG/Eli Lilly and Company Research Award for the Prevention and Treatment of Osteoporosis

Subjects: Obstetrics and gynecology with a focus on osteoporosis.
Purpose: To provide seed grant funds to a junior investigator for clinical research in the area of prevention and treatment for osteoporosis.
Eligibility: Candidates must be ACOG Junior Fellows or Fellows who are in an approved obstetrics/gynecology residency program, or within 3 years post-residency.
Level of Study: Postdoctorate
Type: Research award
Value: US$$15,000
Length of Study: 1 year
Frequency: Annual
Country of Study: United States of America or Canada
No. of awards offered: 1
Application Procedure: Candidates must submit six copies of a proposal consisting of a hypothesis, objectives, specific aims, background and significance, and experimental design and references.

A one page budget is required, applicant's curriculum vitae and a letter of support from the program director, departmental chair or laboratory director.

Closing Date: October 1st
Funding: Commercial
Contributor: Eli Lilly and Company
No. of awards given last year: 1
No. of applicants last year: 5
Additional Information: Further information can be found on the member side of the website www.acog.org

ACOG/Hologic Research Award for the Prevention of Cervical Cancer

Purpose: To provide seed grant funds to a junior investigator for clinical research in the area cervical cancer prevention and to provide opportunity to advance knowledge on issues related to cervical cancer.
Eligibility: Applicants must be ACOG Junior Fellows or Fellows who are in an approved obstetrics/gynecology residency program, or within three years post-residency.
Level of Study: Postdoctorate
Type: Research award
Value: US$15,000 plus a US$1,000 travel stipend to attend the ACOG Annual Clinical Meeting
Length of Study: 1 year
Frequency: Annual
Country of Study: United States of America & Canada
No. of awards offered: 1
Application Procedure: Applicants must submit six copies of a proposal consisting of a hypothesis; objectives, specific aims, background and significance, and experimental design, and references. A one-page budget is required, applicant's curriculum vitae and a letter of support from the program director, departmental chair, or laboratory director.
Closing Date: October 1st
Funding: Commercial
Contributor: Hologic
No. of awards given last year: 1
No. of applicants last year: 10
Additional Information: Please check the website for more details.

ACOG/Kenneth Gottesfeld-Charles Hohler Memorial Foundation Research Award in Ultrasound

Subjects: To provide grant funds to a junior investigator to support research or advanced training that is ultrasound specific and dedicated to a practical clinical use in a new or unique approach.
Purpose: To provide grant funds to support work in ultrasound and its application to obstetrics and gynecology.
Eligibility: Applicants must be ACOG Junior Fellows or Fellows who are in an approved obstetrics/gynecology residency programme, or within 5 years of completion of their residency or fellowship.
Level of Study: Postdoctorate
Value: One grant of US$10,000 or two grants of US$5,000 will be provided at the discretion of the review committee plus US$1,000 travel stipend to attend the ACOG Annual Clinical Meeting
Length of Study: 1 year
Frequency: Annual
Country of Study: United States of America or Canada
No. of awards offered: 1 or 2
Application Procedure: Applicants must submit six copies of a proposal or eight pages or less consisting of a hypothesis; objectives, specific aims, background and significance, and experimental design, and references. An advanced training proposal must be eight pages or less and include the site, the dates, the proposed curriculum and the individuals responsible for the training. A one-page budget is required and applicant's curriculum vitae.
Closing Date: October 1st
Funding: Foundation
Contributor: Kenneth Gottesfeld-Charles Hohler Memorial Foundation
No. of awards given last year: 1
No. of applicants last year: 8
Additional Information: Further information can be found on the member side of the website www.acog.org

ACOG/Merck and Company Research Award on Adolescent Health Preventive Services

Purpose: To provide seed grant funds to a junior investigator for research in the area of prevention in adolescent health and to provide opportunity to advance knowledge on issues related to adolescent health, specifically to develop and test strategies: to incorporate young adolescents into ob/gyn practice for the ACOG recommended initial adolescent reproductive health visit (ages 13–15) and on-going preventive care at all ages; to provide clinical preventive services such as immunization and screening; and, to provide health guidance and counseling to both adolescents and parents on issues such as sexual behavior, tobacco, alcohol and other drugs, safety, weight and exercise.
Eligibility: Applicants must be ACOG Junior Fellows or Fellows.
Level of Study: Postdoctorate
Type: Research grant
Value: US$15,000 plus a US$1,000 travel stipend to attend the ACOG Annual Clinical Meeting
Length of Study: 1 year
Frequency: Annual
Country of Study: United States of America & Canada
No. of awards offered: 1
Application Procedure: Applicants must submit 6 copies of a proposal consisting of a hypothesis; objectives, specific aims, background and significance, and experimental design, and references. A one-page budget is required, applicant's curriculum vitae and a letter of support from the program director, departmental chair, or laboratory director.
Closing Date: October 1st
Funding: Commercial
Contributor: Merck and Company
No. of awards given last year: 1
No. of applicants last year: 6
Additional Information: Please check the website for further details.

ACOG/Merck and Company Research Award on Immunization

Purpose: To provide seed grant funds to an ACOG Junior Fellow or Fellow for research in the area of immunization and to provide opportunity to advance knowledge on issues related to immunization in the ob/gyn practice. Topics of interest include, but are not limited to: immunization history of patients; frequency of immunization of patients by an ob/gyn; incidence of infectious diseases preventable by immunization; prohibitions to immunizations in ob/gyn patients; pregnancy and immunization; ob/gyn patients interest in immunization; and, any other related area.
Eligibility: Applicants must be ACOG Junior Fellows or Fellows.
Level of Study: Postdoctorate
Type: Research grant
Value: US$15,000 plus a US$1,000 travel stipend to attend the ACOG Annual Clinical Meeting
Length of Study: 1 year
Frequency: Annual
Country of Study: United States of America or Canada
No. of awards offered: 1
Application Procedure: Applicants must submit six copies of a proposal consisting of a hypothesis; objectives, specific aims, background and significance, and experimental design, and references. A one-page budget is required, applicant's curriculum vitae and a letter of support from the program director, departmental chair, or laboratory director.
Closing Date: October 1st
Funding: Commercial
Contributor: Merck and Company
No. of awards given last year: 1
No. of applicants last year: 7
Additional Information: Please check the website for further details.

ACOG/Ortho Women's Health and Urology Academic Training Fellowships in Obstetrics and Gynecology

Subjects: Obstetrics and gynecology.
Purpose: To provide opportunities for especially qualified residents or Fellows to spend an extra year involved in responsibilities that will train them for academic positions in the speciality.

Eligibility: Open to ACOG Junior Fellows or Fellows who have completed at least 1 year of training, and are considered by the director of their residency programme to be especially fitted for a career in medical education or academic obstetrics and gynecology.
Level of Study: Postgraduate
Type: Research grant
Value: US$30,000 stipend plus a $1,000 travel stipend to attend the ACOG Annual Clinical Meeting
Length of Study: 1 year
Frequency: Annual
Country of Study: United States of America or Canada
No. of awards offered: 2
Application Procedure: Applicants must submit six copies of a proposal consisting of a hypothesis, objectives, specific aims, background and significance, experimental design and references. These must not exceed eight typewritten pages in total. A curriculum vitae, letter of support from the programme director, departmental chair or laboratory director are also required.
Closing Date: October 1st
Funding: Commercial
Contributor: Ortho-Women's Health and Urology
No. of awards given last year: 2
No. of applicants last year: 14
Additional Information: Further information can be found on the member side of the website www.acog.org

Warren H Pearse/Wyeth Pharmaceuticals Women's Health Policy Research Award

Subjects: Obstetrics and gynecology.
Purpose: To provide funds to support research in the area of health care policy.
Eligibility: The principal or co-principal investigator must be an ACOG Junior Fellow or Fellow. Proposals will be considered with regard to innovation, potential utility of the research, ability to generalize results and demonstrated capability of the investigator.
Level of Study: Postgraduate
Type: Research award
Value: US$15,000 plus $1,000 travel stipend to attend the ACOG Annual Clinical Meeting
Length of Study: 1 year
Frequency: Annual
Country of Study: United States of America or Canada
No. of awards offered: 1
Application Procedure: Candidates must submit six copies of a proposal consisting of a hypothesis, objectives, specific aims, background and significance, experimental design and methods. These must not exceed eight typewritten pages in total. A curriculum vitae, letter of support from the programme director, departmental chair or laboratory director, references and a one-page budget must also be submitted.
Closing Date: October 1st
Funding: Commercial
Contributor: Wyeth Pharmaceuticals
No. of awards given last year: 1
No. of applicants last year: 7
Additional Information: Further information can be found on the member side of the website www.acog.org

AMERICAN COLLEGE OF RHEUMATOLOGY

1800 Century Place, Suite 250, Atlanta, GA, 30345-4300, United States of America
Tel: (1) 404 633 3777
Fax: (1) 404 633 1870
Email: ref@rheumatology.com
Website: www.rheumatology.org

The American College of Rheumatology (ACR) is the professional organization of rheumatologists and associated health professionals who share a dedication to healing, preventing disability and curing more than 100 types of arthritis and related disabling and sometimes fatal disorders of the joints, muscles and bones.

ACF/REF/Paula De Merieux Rheumatology Fellowship Award

Subjects: Rheumatic diseases.
Purpose: To help ensure that a diverse and highly trained workforce is available to provide competent clinical care to those affected by the rheumatic diseases.
Eligibility: Only training directors at ACGME-accredited institutions in good standing may apply. The trainee must be an underrepresented minority or a woman, i.e., either Black American, Native American (American Indian, Alaska Native, Native Hawaiian), Mexican American, Puerto Rican or any other minority category. Award applicant must be a citizen or non-citizen national of the United States of America, or be in lawful possession of a permanent resident card. Individuals on temporary (J1, H1) or student visas are not eligible.
Level of Study: Professional development
Type: Fellowship
Value: US$25,000
Length of Study: 1 year
Frequency: Annual
Country of Study: United States of America
Application Procedure: Applications forms are available on website.
Closing Date: August 1st
Funding: Private
Contributor: The Dr Paula de Merieux estate

ACR REF Lawren H. Daltroy Fellowship in Patient-Clinician Communication

Subjects: Rheumatology.
Purpose: To improve patient-clinician interactions through the development of more qualified and trained clinicians and investigators in the field of patient–clinician communication.
Eligibility: Eligible candidates must be ARHP members. A candidate must have either a doctoral degree or a clinical degree and apply in partnership with a mentor possessing a doctoral degree. The award is not intended for physician members of the ACR or ARHP.
Level of Study: Professional development
Type: Fellowship
Value: Up to US$7,000 per year
Length of Study: 1 year
Frequency: Annual
Country of Study: United States of America
Application Procedure: Application forms are available on website.
Closing Date: August 1st
Contributor: Rheuminations, Inc
No. of awards given last year: 1

ACR REF/Abbott Medical and Graduate Student Achievement Awards

Subjects: Rheumatology.
Purpose: To recognize outstanding medical and graduate students for significant work in the field of rheumatology and provide an opportunity to attend the ACR annual scientific meeting.
Eligibility: Medical student candidates must be enrolled in an LCME-accredited medical school; graduate student candidates must be enrolled in an accredited institution. In addition, students must submit an abstract to the annual scientific meeting. The student must have made a significant contribution to the work submitted in order to be considered for the award. Award applicant must be a citizen or non-citizen national of the United States of America, or be in lawful possession of a permanent resident card. Individuals on temporary (J1, H1) or student visas are not eligible.
Level of Study: Doctorate, Graduate, Postgraduate
Type: Award
Value: US$750 cash award, waiver of registration fees and hotel and travel expenses to attend the ACR annual scientific meeting
Length of Study: 1 year
Frequency: Annual
Application Procedure: Application forms are available on website.
Closing Date: August 1st
Contributor: Abbott Endowment for Rheumatology Development
No. of awards given last year: 17

ACR REF/Abbott Medical and Pediatric Resident Research Award

Subjects: Rheumatology.

Purpose: To motivate outstanding residents to pursue subspecialty training in rheumatology by providing an opportunity to attend the ACR annual scientific meeting.

Eligibility: A candidate must be a resident enrolled in an ACGME-accredited pediatric, medicine or combined medicine/pediatric residency programme who is interested in rheumatology. The candidate must be an author or co-author of an abstract submitted to the upcoming ACR annual meeting. He must be a citizen or non-citizen national of the United States of America, or be in lawful possession of a permanent resident card. Individuals on temporary (J1, H1) or student visas are not eligible.

Level of Study: Professional development

Type: Research award

Value: US$750 cash prize plus US$1,000 to cover travel expenses and hotel accommodations for the ACR annual scientific meeting. Registration fees will be waived

Frequency: Annual

Country of Study: United States of America

Application Procedure: Only online applications submitted through the REF Web site will be accepted.

Closing Date: August 1st

Funding: Foundation

Contributor: Abbott Endowment for Rheumatology

No. of awards given last year: 5

ACR REF/Amgen/Wyeth Rheumatology Fellowship Training Award

Subjects: Rheumatic diseases.

Purpose: To help ensure that a highly trained workforce is available to provide competent clinical care to those affected by rheumatic diseases.

Eligibility: Only training directors at ACGME-accredited institutions in good standing may apply. The rheumatology fellowship training programme director at the institution will be responsible for the selection and appointment of trainees. Award applicant must be a citizen or non-citizen national of the United States of America, or be in lawful possession of a permanent resident card. Individuals on temporary (J1, H1) or student visas are not eligible.

Level of Study: Professional development

Type: Training award

Value: Recipients will receive $25,000 to support the salary and fringe of one trainee. The award is paid directly to the sponsoring institution and payments are disbursed in two equal installments of $12,500

Length of Study: 1 year

Frequency: Annual

Country of Study: United States of America

Application Procedure: Application forms are available on website.

Closing Date: August 1st

Funding: Corporation

Contributor: Amgen Inc., and Wyeth

No. of awards given last year: 20

ACR REF/Ephraim P. Engleman Endowed Resident Research Preceptorship

Subjects: Rheumatology.

Purpose: To introduce residents to the speciality of rheumatology by supporting a full-time research experience.

Eligibility: Candidates currently enrolled in ACGME-accredited training programmes in internal medicine, paediatrics, or med/paeds are eligible. Candidates may apply during any year of their residency; however preference is given to 1st and 2nd year residents. Preceptors are responsible for approving the research plan and must be members of the ACR. Candidates must be citizen or non-citizen national of the United States of America or be in lawful possession of a permanent resident card. Individuals on temporary (J1, H1) or student visas are not eligible.

Level of Study: Research

Value: Up to US$15,000

Length of Study: 3 months

Frequency: Annual

Country of Study: United States of America

Application Procedure: Application forms are available on website.

Closing Date: February 1st

Funding: Private

Contributor: Funding for this award is made possible through an endowment from Dr Ephraim P. Engleman

ACR/REF Amgen Pediatric Rheumatology Research Award

Subjects: Rheumatology.

Purpose: To recognize and promote scholarship in the field of pediatric rheumatology.

Eligibility: Candidates must be trainees enrolled in a recognized ACGME-accredited pediatric rheumatology programme or a related research laboratory. Trainees must be preparing for a career in pediatric rheumatology. In addition, candidates must submit an abstract to the upcoming ACR Annual Scientific Meeting. There are no citizenship requirements for this award.

Level of Study: Research

Type: Award

Value: US$1,000

Length of Study: 1 year

Frequency: Annual

Country of Study: United States of America

Application Procedure: Application forms are available online at www.rheumatology.org

Closing Date: August 1st

Contributor: Amgen Inc

No. of awards given last year: 4

ACR/REF Association of Subspecialty Professors Junior Career Development Award in Geriatric Medicine Award

Subjects: Geriatrics, rheumatology.

Purpose: To provide support to academicians interested in careers focused on the geriatric and gerontology aspects of rheumatology.

Eligibility: To be eligible for the award, the candidate must: be a member of the ACR; have completed a rheumatology fellowship leading to certification by the ABIM and be within the first 3 years of his/her faculty appointment; and possess a faculty appointment at the time of the award. Award applicant must be a citizen or non-citizen national of the United States of America, or be in lawful possessions of a permanent resident card. Individuals on temporary (J1, H1) or student visas are not eligible.

Level of Study: Professional development

Type: Award

Value: US$75,000 per year plus US$3,000 in travel grants

Length of Study: 2 years

Frequency: Annual

Country of Study: United States of America

Application Procedure: Application forms are available on website.

Closing Date: August 1st

Funding: Private

Contributor: Association of Subspecialty Professors

No. of awards given last year: 1

ACR/REF Clinical Investigator Fellowship Award

Subjects: Rheumatology.

Purpose: To provide a training programme to rheumatology fellows or rheumatologists in the early stages of their career on aspects of clinical investigations through a structured, formal training programme.

Eligibility: Candidates must be an ACR member and a physician licenced to practice in the United States of America. Candidates may apply only within 6 years after starting their rheumatology training programme. MD/PhD candidates are not eligible. Candidates must be citizen or non-citizen national of the United States of America or a lawful permanent resident. Individuals on temporary (J1, H1) or student visas are not eligible.

Level of Study: Research, Professional development

Type: Fellowship

Value: Financial support of up to $90,000 will be provided for salary and tuition (fringe benefits areallowed). Salary will be provided based on the salary levels set by the institution, up to a maximum of $50,000 per year. The remainder may be applied towards educational needs (e.g. books, travel to conferences, computers and other research related supplies)

Length of Study: Up to 2 years

Frequency: Annual
Country of Study: United States of America
Application Procedure: Application forms are available online at www.rheumatology.org
Closing Date: August 1st
Funding: Corporation
Contributor: Merck and Co., Inc
No. of awards given last year: 3

ACR/REF Clinician Scholars Educator Award

Subjects: Rheumatology.
Purpose: To recognize and support rheumatologists dedicated to providing high-quality clinical educational experience to trainees.
Eligibility: Candidates must be ACR members with experience in the training of medical students, residents and fellows in rheumatology. Candidates must be affiliated with an LCCME-accredited school or an ACGME-accredited training programme in internal medicine, pediatrics or rheumatology. A faculty appointment is not essential. If the candidate is not a citizen or non-citizen national of the United States of America, the candidate must provide evidence that he or she is eligible to remain in the United States of America throughout the period of the award.
Level of Study: Professional development
Type: Award
Value: US$50,000 per year
Length of Study: 3 years
Frequency: Annual
Country of Study: United States of America
Application Procedure: Application forms are available on website.
Closing Date: August 1st
Funding: Corporation
Contributor: Pfizer Inc
No. of awards given last year: 3

ACR/REF Health Professional Graduate Student Research Preceptorship

Subjects: Rheumatic diseases.
Purpose: To introduce students to rheumatology-related healthcare by supporting full-time research by a graduate student in the broad area of rheumatic diseases.
Eligibility: Only students enrolled in graduate school are eligible. Preceptors are responsible for selecting student applicants and must be members of the ARHP.
Level of Study: Doctorate, Postgraduate
Value: US$3,500 student stipend, US$1,000 for laboratory expenses, US$1,500 stipend for the mentor and up to US$1,000 for travel funds for the student to attend the ACR/ARHP annual scientific meeting
Length of Study: 8 weeks
Frequency: Annual
Country of Study: United States of America
No. of awards offered: Up to 3
Application Procedure: Only complete applications submitted online by the deadline will be accepted.
Closing Date: February 1st
Contributor: Abbott Endowment for Rheumotology Development
No. of awards given last year: 4

ACR/REF Health Professional Investigator Award

Subjects: Rheumatic diseases.
Purpose: To provide support to health professionals in the research fields related to rheumatic diseases and to sustain individuals committed to a career in rheumatology-related research.
Eligibility: Applicants must have a doctoral degree and be members of the ARHP. Applicants should not apply for the health professional investigator award and the health professional new investigator award during the same cycle.
Level of Study: Research
Type: Award
Value: US$50,000 per year
Length of Study: 2 years
Frequency: Annual
Country of Study: United States of America
Application Procedure: Application forms are available on website.

Closing Date: August 1st
Funding: Private
Contributor: ACR
No. of awards given last year: 2

ACR/REF Health Professional New Investigator Award

Subjects: Rheumatology.
Purpose: To provide support to health professionals new to rheumatology and to individuals committed to a career in rheumatology-related research.
Eligibility: Candidates must be ARHP members and must be doctorally prepared (i.e., candidate must have PhD, DSc, or equivalent doctoral degree). Candidates may not apply for the Health Professional New Investigator Award and the Health Professional Investigator Award during the same cycle. Only two applications may be submitted per department in any institution.
Level of Study: Professional development
Type: Award
Value: US$50,000 per year
Length of Study: 2 years
Frequency: Annual
Country of Study: United States of America
Application Procedure: Application forms are available on website.
Closing Date: August 1st
Funding: Private
Contributor: ACR
No. of awards given last year: 2

ACR/REF Lupus Research Institute Lupus Investigator Fellowship Award

Subjects: Systemic lupus erythematosus.
Purpose: To encourage qualified physicians without significant prior research experience to develop a research career that will emphasize the better understanding of systemic lupus erythematosus.
Eligibility: Applicants must have received an MD, DO, or equivalent degree from an accredited institution; completed training in internal medicine or paediatrics; and will have completed at least 1 year of speciality training in rheumatology at the start of the award. MD/PhDs, DO/PhDs, and PhDs are not eligible for this award. Only physicians, with not more than 1 year of research training at the time of application, are eligible. Award applicant must be a citizen or non-citizen national of the United States of America, or be in lawful possession of a permanent resident card. Individuals on temporary (J1, H1) or student visas are not eligible.
Level of Study: Doctorate, Professional development, Research
Type: Fellowship
Value: US$50,000 per year
Length of Study: 3 years
Frequency: Annual
Country of Study: United States of America
Application Procedure: Application forms are available on website.
Closing Date: August 1st
Funding: Foundation
Contributor: Lupus Research Institute
No. of awards given last year: 1

ACR/REF Physician Scientist Development Award

Subjects: Arthritis and rheumatic diseases.
Purpose: To encourage qualified physicians without significant prior research experience to embark on careers in biomedical and/or clinical research in arthritis and rheumatic diseases.
Eligibility: Applicants must have received an MD, DO, or equivalent medical degree from an accredited institution; completed training in internal medicine or pediatrics; and will have completed at least 1 year of speciality training in rheumatology at the start of the award. MD/PhDs, and PhDs are not eligible for this award. Only physicians are eligible to apply. Award applicant must be a citizen or non-citizen national of the United States of America, or be in lawful possession of a permanent resident card. Individuals on temporary (J1, H1) or student visas are not eligible.
Level of Study: Postdoctorate
Type: Award
Value: US$50,000 per year
Length of Study: 3 years
Frequency: Annual

Country of Study: United States of America
Application Procedure: Application forms are available on website.
Closing Date: August 1st
Funding: Corporation
Contributor: Centocor Inc
No. of awards given last year: 6

AMERICAN COLLEGE OF SPORTS MEDICINE (ACSM)

PO Box 1440, Indianapolis, IN, 46206-1440, United States of America
Tel: (1) 317 637 9200
Fax: (1) 317 634 7817
Email: mwayne@acsm.org
Website: www.acsm.org
Contact: Megan Wayne, Coordinator

American College of Sports Medicine (ACSM) was founded in 1954. Since that time, they have applied their knowledge, training and dedication in sports medicine and exercise science to promote healthier lifestyles for people around the globe. Working in a wide range of medical specialities, allied health professions and scientific disciplines, their members are committed to the diagnosis, treatment and prevention of sports-related injuries and the advancement of the science of exercise.

ACSM Carl V. Gisolfi Memorial Fund

Subjects: Thermoregulation, exercise or hydration.
Purpose: To honor Carl V. Gisolfi's contributions to ACSM and the exercise science field and to encourage research in thermoregulation, exercise, and hydration.
Level of Study: Research
Type: Funding support
Value: $ 5,000
Frequency: Annual
Application Procedure: Check website for details.
Contributor: ACSM

ACSM Clinical Sports Medicine Fund

Subjects: Sports medicine.
Purpose: To stimulate clinical research in sports medicine and research in clinical sports medicine.
Eligibility: Open to MDs, DOs, PTs, ATCs, and other medical professionals (ACSM members only) involved in the conduct of patient-based clinical research.
Level of Study: Research
Type: Funding support
Value: $ 5,000
Frequency: Annual
No. of awards offered: 1
Application Procedure: Check website for details.
Funding: Foundation
Contributor: Clinical Sports Medicine Endowment

ACSM International Student Award

Purpose: To support students fees and personal expenses.
Eligibility: Applicants should be from countries outside North America.
Level of Study: Research
Type: Award
Value: $1,000 each to cover personal expenses related to presenting research abstracts at ACSM's Annual Meetings
Frequency: Annual
No. of awards offered: Up to 3
Application Procedure: Check website for details.
Closing Date: February 1st

ACSM Raymond Weiss Endowment Fund

Subjects: Physical, mental and emotional benefits of physical activity.
Purpose: To provide on-going financial support to sponsor research on the subject of the physical, mental and emotional benefits of physical activity.
Level of Study: Research
Type: Funding support

Frequency: Annual
Application Procedure: Check website for details.
Funding: Foundation

ACSM Research Endowment

Subjects: Basic and applied research in science.
Purpose: The Research Endowment is dedicated to the advancement of basic and applied research in exercise science.
Eligibility: Funding is primarily targeted for new or junior investigators, within 7 years of attaining a terminal degree (e.g., PhD, EdD). Only one application per person is allowed.
Level of Study: Research
Type: Research
Value: $10,000
Frequency: Annual
Funding: Foundation

Doctoral Student Research Grants

Subjects: All subjects.
Purpose: To assist doctoral students.
Eligibility: Doctoral students enrolled in full-time programs.
Level of Study: Doctorate, Postgraduate, Research
Type: Grant
Value: Up to US $5,000 for experimental subjects, supplies, and small equipment needs
Length of Study: 1 year
Frequency: Annual
Application Procedure: Check website for further details.

NASA Space Physiology Research Grants

Subjects: Exercise, weightlessness, and musculoskeletal physiology.
Eligibility: Open to US residents who are doctoral students enrolled in full-time programs.
Level of Study: Doctorate, MBA, Postgraduate, Research
Type: Research grant
Value: US $10,000
Length of Study: 1 year
Frequency: Annual
Application Procedure: Check website for further details.
Contributor: National Aeronautics and Space Administration (NASA)
Additional Information: Funds are available after October 1st.

Ralph S. Paffenbarger-Blair Fund for Epidemiological Research on Physical Activity.

Subjects: Sports medicine
Purpose: To encourage researchers early in their career to become involved with physical activity epidemiology.
Eligibility: Open to ACSM member at the time of application submission
Level of Study: Postdoctorate, Postgraduate
Type: Funding support
Value: Up to US$10,000
Length of Study: 1 year
Frequency: Annual
Country of Study: United States of America
Application Procedure: Applications can be downloaded from the ACSM website, applicants are expected to apply within 2 years of receiving a postgraduate degree or completion of clinical training
Closing Date: June 30th
Funding: Foundation

AMERICAN CONGRESS ON SURVEYING AND MAPPING (ACSM)

6, Montgomery Village Avenue, Suite 403 Gaithersburg, Maryland, 20879, United States of America
Tel: (1) (240) 632-9716
Fax: (1) (240) 632-1321
Email: Dawn.james@acsm.net
Website: www.acsm.net

The ACSM is a nonprofit association dedicated to serving the public interest and advancing the profession of surveying and mapping.

AAGS Graduate Fellowship Award
Subjects: Geodetic surveying.
Purpose: To support students in the field of geodetic surveying or geodesy.
Eligibility: Open to students enrolled in a programme in geodetic surveying. Preference will be given to applicants having at least two years of employment experience in the surveying profession.
Level of Study: Graduate
Type: Award
Value: $2,000
Length of Study: 2–4 years
Frequency: Annual
Application Procedure: See the website.
Closing Date: October 15th
Funding: Foundation
Contributor: American Association for Geodetic Surveying (AAGS)
No. of awards given last year: 1
No. of applicants last year: 5

AAGS Joseph F. Dracup Scholarship Award
Subjects: Surveying.
Purpose: To offer better opportunities to students in geodetic science programmes.
Eligibility: Open to students enrolled in 4-year programme in surveying. Preference will be given to applicants from programs with a significant focus on geodetic surveying.
Level of Study: Postgraduate
Value: US$2,000
Frequency: Annual
Application Procedure: A completed application form must be submitted.
Closing Date: October 15th
Funding: Foundation
No. of awards given last year: 1
No. of applicants last year: 5

ACSM Fellows Scholarship
Subjects: Any ACSM disciplines.
Purpose: To encourage, recognize and support exceptional surveying and mapping students.
Eligibility: Open to students with a junior or higher degree and enrolled in four-year degree programs in surveying or in closely related programs such as geomatics or surveying engineering.
Type: Scholarship
Value: US$2,000
Application Procedure: Applicants must submit a completed application form along with proof of membership in ACSM, a complete statement indicating educational objectives, future plans of study or research, professional activities and financial need, three letters of recommendation and a complete original official transcript.
Closing Date: October 15th
Additional Information: Prior scholarship winners are eligible to apply in succeeding years providing all appropriate criteria are satisfied.

Berntsen International Scholarship In Surveying
Subjects: Surveying.
Purpose: To encourage, recognize and support exceptional surveying and mapping students.
Eligibility: Open to students enrolled in four-year degree programs in surveying or in closely related programs such as geomatics or surveying engineering.
Type: Scholarship
Value: US$1,500
Application Procedure: Applicants must submit a completed application form along with proof of membership in ACSM, a complete statement indicating educational objectives, future plans of study or research, professional activities and financial need, three letters of recommendation and a complete original official transcript.
Closing Date: October 15th
Contributor: Berntsen International Inc., of Madison, Wisconsin
Additional Information: Prior scholarship winners are eligible to apply in succeeding years providing all appropriate criteria are satisfied.

Berntsen International Scholarship in Surveying Technology
Subjects: Surveying technology.
Purpose: To encourage exceptional students in surveying and mapping.
Eligibility: Open to students who are registered in a 2-year programme in surveying technology.
Level of Study: Postgraduate
Type: Scholarship
Value: US$500
Length of Study: 2 years
Frequency: Annual
No. of awards offered: 1
Application Procedure: A completed application form must be submitted.
Closing Date: October 15th
Funding: Foundation
Contributor: Bernsten International Inc., of Madison, Wisconsin
No. of awards given last year: 1
No. of applicants last year: 24

The Cady McDonnell Memorial Scholarship
Purpose: To recognize a women student enrolled in the field of surveying.
Eligibility: Open to female candidates who are residents of one of the following western states: Alaska, Arizona, California, Colorado, Hawaii, Idaho, Montana, Nevada, New Mexico, Oregon, Utah, Washington, Wyoming.
Level of Study: Postgraduate
Type: Scholarship
Value: US$1,000
Length of Study: 2–4 years
Frequency: Annual
No. of awards offered: 1
Application Procedure: A completed application along with proof of legal home residence and ACSM membership website form must be submitted. See the website for further information.
Closing Date: October 15th
Funding: Foundation
Contributor: National Society of Professional Surveyors
No. of awards given last year: 1
No. of applicants last year: 24

The Schonstedt Scholarships in Surveying
Subjects: Surveying.
Purpose: To provide opportunities for students in surveying.
Eligibility: Open to students enrolled in a four-year degree programme in surveying. Preference will be given to applicants with junior or senior standing.
Level of Study: Postgraduate
Type: Scholarship
Value: US$1,500
Frequency: Annual
No. of awards offered: 2
Application Procedure: See the website.
Closing Date: October 15th
Funding: Commercial
Contributor: Schonstedt Instrument Company of Kearneysville, West Virginia
No. of awards given last year: 2
No. of applicants last year: 7
Additional Information: Schonstedt donates a magnetic locator to the surveying program at each recipient's school.

Tri State Surveying and Photogrammetry Kris M. Kunze Memorial Scholarship
Subjects: Surveying.
Purpose: To provide financial assistance.
Eligibility: Open to candidates who are citizens of United States of America. First priority candidates are licensed Professional Land Surveyors or Certified Photogrammetrists pursuing college level courses in Business Administration or Business Management. Second priority candidates are certified Land Survey Interns pursuing college level courses in Business Administration or Business Management. Third priority candidates are full-time students enrolled in a two or four

year degree program in Surveying and Mapping pursuing a course study including Business Administration or Business Management.
Level of Study: Postgraduate
Type: Scholarship
Value: US$1,000
Frequency: Annual
Application Procedure: A completed application form along with proof of ACSM membership must be submitted. See the website for further information.
Closing Date: October 15th
Funding: Commercial
Contributor: Kris M. Kunze Memorial Scholarship Fund
No. of awards given last year: 1
No. of applicants last year: 12

AMERICAN COUNCIL OF LEARNED SOCIETIES (ACLS)

Office of Fellowships and Grants, 633 3rd Avenue, New York, NY, 10017-6795, United States of America
Tel: (1) 212 697 1505
Fax: (1) 212 949 8058
Email: sfisher@acls.org
Website: www.acls.org

The American Council of Learned Societies (ACLS) is a private non-profit federation of 68 national scholarly organizations. The mission of the ACLS, as set forth in its Constitution is the advancement of humanistic studies in all fields of learning in the humanities and the social sciences and the maintenance and strengthening of relations among the national societies devoted to such studies.

ACLS American Research in the Humanities in China
Subjects: Humanities.
Purpose: To enable scholars to carry out research in the People's Republic of China.
Eligibility: Open to United States citizens and permanent residents. Candidates must hold a PhD or equivalent.
Level of Study: Postdoctorate
Type: Research grant
Value: $40,000
Length of Study: 4–12 months
Frequency: Annual
Study Establishment: A university or research institute
Country of Study: China
No. of awards offered: Approx. 5
Application Procedure: Applicants must write for details.
Closing Date: November 12th
Contributor: The National Endowment for the Humanities

ACLS Charles A. Ryskamp Research Fellowship
Subjects: Humanities and related social sciences
Purpose: To support advanced assistant professors and untenured associate professors in the humanities and related social sciences whose scholarly contributions have advanced their fields and who have well designed and carefully developed plans for new research and to provide time and resources to enable research under optional conditions.
Eligibility: Open to candidates holding a PhD or equivalent and employed in tenure-track positions at degree-granting academic institutions in the United States, remaining so for the duration of the fellowship.
Level of Study: Postdoctorate
Type: Fellowship
Value: US$64,000 stipend, plus a US$2,500 travel allowance
Length of Study: one academic year, plus one summer if justified by a persuasive case
Frequency: Annual
Country of Study: United States of America
No. of awards offered: 12
Application Procedure: Apply online.
Closing Date: October 2nd
Funding: Foundation

Contributor: Andrew W. Mellon Foundation
Additional Information: An additional US$14,222 is available if justified by a persuasive case.

ACLS Chinese Fellowships for Scholarly Development
Subjects: Humanities.
Purpose: To support students with living allowance and health insurance.
Eligibility: Candidates must be nominated by the U.S. host; Chinese scholars may not apply directly. Nominees must currently reside in China.
Level of Study: Postdoctorate
Type: Fellowships
Value: Living allowance, health insurance and international airfare
Length of Study: 1–2 semesters
Frequency: Annual
Application Procedure: Apply online.
Funding: Foundation
Contributor: Li Foundation

ACLS Digital Innovation Fellowship
Subjects: Humanities and related social sciences, digital humanities
Purpose: To support an academic year dedicated to work on a major scholarly project that takes a digital form.
Eligibility: This program is open to scholars in all fields of the humanities and the humanistic social sciences. Candidates must have a PhD degree conferred prior to the application deadline. (An established scholar who can demonstrate the equivalent of the PhD in publications and professional experience may also qualify.) U.S. citizenship or permanent resident status is required as of the application deadline.
Level of Study: Postdoctorate
Type: Fellowship
Value: US$60,000 stipend (for academic year's leave from teaching), plus up to US$25,000 in project costs like access to tools, personnel for digital production, collaborative work and dissemination and preservation of digital projects created or enhanced under the Fellowship
Length of Study: one year
Frequency: Annual
Country of Study: United States of America
No. of awards offered: 6
Application Procedure: Completed applications must be submitted through the ACLS Online Fellowship Application system.
Closing Date: October 3rd
Funding: Foundation
Contributor: Andrew W. Mellon Foundation
Additional Information: Check website for further details.

ACLS Humanities Program in Belarus, Russia and Ukraine
Subjects: History, archeology, literature, linguistics, film studies, art history.
Purpose: To sustain individuals doing exemplary work, so as to assure continued future leadership in the humanities.
Eligibility: Applicants should be involved in studies related to performing arts, ethnographic and cultural studies, gender studies, philosophy or religious studies. ACLS organizes annual regional meetings for advisers and grant recipients.
Level of Study: Research
Type: Grant
Value: Varies
Frequency: Annual
No. of awards offered: Varies
Application Procedure: Application forms can be obtained by writing to hp@acls.org.
Closing Date: November 15th
Funding: Foundation

ACLS Postdoctoral Fellowships in East European Studies
Subjects: Humanities and social sciences.
Purpose: To offer support for postdoctoral research and a written account of the work in East European studies.
Eligibility: Open to candidates who are citizens or permanent residents of the United States. A candidate must hold a PhD degree

conferred prior to the application deadline; however, an established scholar who can demonstrate the equivalent of the PhD in publications and professional experience may also qualify. A candidate must be at an early career stage; tenured faculty are not eligible.

Level of Study: Postdoctorate, Research
Type: Fellowships
Value: US$25,000
Length of Study: 6–12 consecutive months
Frequency: Annual
Study Establishment: American Council of Learned Societies
Country of Study: United States of America or Germany
Application Procedure: Completed applications must be submitted through the ACLS Online Fellowship Application system
Closing Date: November 12th
Additional Information: These fellowships are to be used for work outside East Europe, although short visits to the area may be proposed as part of a coherent programme primarily based elsewhere. Project must clearly demonstrate the necessity to conduct research at German universities or research institutes on countries of East and Central Europe or on Germany's relations with those countries.

ACLS/Chiang Ching-kuo Foundation (CCK) New Perspectives on Chinese Culture and Society

Subjects: Humanities and related social science.
Purpose: To provide support for all conferences and publications on new perspectives on Chinese culture and society.
Eligibility: Open to candidates who are affiliated with a university or research institution and who hold a PhD degree. There are no restrictions as to citizenship of participants or location of the project.
Level of Study: Doctorate, Postgraduate
Type: Scholarship
Value: up to $25,000 for conferences; up to $15,000 for workshops and seminars; up to $6,000 for planning meetings
Frequency: Annual
Country of Study: Any country
Application Procedure: Applications should be submitted by mail or courier.
Closing Date: November 12th
Funding: Foundation
Contributor: Chiang Ching-kuo Foundation for International Scholarly Exchange

For further information contact:

New Perspectives on Chinese Culture and Society, Office of Fellowships and Grants, American Council of Learned Societies, 633 Third Avenue, New York, 10017-6795, United States of America

ACLS/New York Public Library Fellowship

Subjects: Humanities and humanistic social sciences
Purpose: The ACLS and the NYPL offer a collaborative programme to provide up to 5 residential fellowships at the Library's Dorothy and Lewis B. Cullman Center for Scholars and Writers. The center provides opportunities for up to 15 fellows to explore and use the collections of NYPL Humanities and Social sciences Library.
Eligibility: Application for an ACLS/NYPL residential fellowship has the same eligibility requirements, application form, and schedule as the ACLS fellowship programme
Level of Study: Postdoctorate
Type: Fellowship
Value: Stipend for the NYPL residential fellowships will be $65,000
Length of Study: 6–12 months
Frequency: Annual
Study Establishment: New York Public Library
Country of Study: United States of America
No. of awards offered: Up to 15
Application Procedure: Apply online.
Closing Date: Late September
Additional Information: Because this is a collaborative fellowship, applicants for the ACLS/NYPL residential fellowships must also apply to the Dorothy and Lewis B. Cullman Center for Scholars and Writers at the NYPL. An NYPL application form may be requested from csw@nypl.org

ACLS/SSRC/NEH International and Area Studies Fellowships

Subjects: The societies and cultures of Asia, Africa, the Near and Middle East, Latin America and the Caribbean, Eastern Europe and the former Soviet Union.
Purpose: To encourage humanistic research in area studies.
Eligibility: Applicants must be citizens or permanent residents of the United States as of the application deadline date, and hold a PhD degree. However, an established Scholar who can demonstrate the equivalent of a PhD in publications and professional experience may also qualify. Scholars pursuing research and writing on the societies and cultures of Asia, Africa, the Near and Middle East, Latin America and the Caribbean, East Europe and the Former Soviet Union are eligible. Scholars currently enrolled for any degree are not eligible.
Level of Study: Postdoctorate
Type: Fellowship
Value: Up to US$50,000 for full professor and equivalent, US$40,000 for associate professor and equivalent and US$30,000 for assistant professor and equivalent
Length of Study: 6–12 months
No. of awards offered: Approx. 10
Application Procedure: Applications must be made to the ACLS Fellowship Programme and all requirements and provisions of that programme must be met. The Fellow must submit a final report to both NEH and ACLS. Note that applications must also be made to the competition for residential fellowships administered separately by the NYPL Center for Scholars and Writers.
Closing Date: Please consult the organization
Contributor: American Council of Learned Societies (ACLS), Social Science Research Council (SSRC), National Endowment for the Humanities (NEH)

For further information contact:

Center for Scholars & Writers, The New York Public Library Humanities & Social Sciences Library, Fifth Avenue & 42nd Street, New York, NY, 10018-2788, United States of America
Email: csw@nypl.org

Andrew W. Mellon Foundation/ACLS Early Career Fellowships Program Dissertation Completion Fellowships

Subjects: Humanities and related social sciences.
Purpose: To assist graduates in the last year of their PhD dissertation writing.
Eligibility: Open to a PhD candidate in a humanities or social science department in an American University. Applicant should not be in the degree programme for more than 6 years and the successful candidates cannot hold this fellowship after the 7th year.
Level of Study: Doctorate
Type: Fellowships
Value: US$33,000
Length of Study: 1 year
Frequency: Annual
Country of Study: United States of America
No. of awards offered: 65
Application Procedure: Applicants can apply online.
Closing Date: November 14th

For further information contact:

Email: grants@acls.org

Andrew W. Mellon/ACLS Recent Doctoral Recipients Fellowships

Subjects: Humanities and social science.
Purpose: To provide support and assistance for young scholars to complete their dissertation and later to advance their research after being awarded the PhD.
Eligibility: Open to scholars who hold the Dissertation Completion Fellowships of any nation. Candidates must be in the final year of dissertation completion at the time of application. Those who have completed the dissertation are not eligible. Candidates for this program must be Ph.D. candidates in a humanities or social science department in the United States. Candidates from other departments

may be eligible if their project is in the humanities or related social sciences, and their principal dissertation advisor holds an appointment in a humanities or related social science field.
Level of Study: Doctorate, Postgraduate
Type: Fellowships
Value: US$30,000
Length of Study: 1 year
Frequency: Annual
Country of Study: United States of America
No. of awards offered: 25
Application Procedure: Applicants will have to fill an online application form.
Closing Date: December 10th
Funding: Foundation

Frederick Burkhardt Residential Fellowships

Subjects: Humanities.
Purpose: To encourage more adventurous, more wide-ranging and longer-term patterns of research; the specific goal of the fellowship year is a major piece of scholarly work.
Eligibility: Candidates must be employed in a tenured position at a degree-granting academic institution in the United States, remaining so for the duration of the fellowship.
Level of Study: Postdoctorate
Type: Fellowships
Value: US$75,000 stipend
Length of Study: 1 year
Frequency: Annual
Study Establishment: A participating national research centre
Country of Study: United States of America
No. of awards offered: 9
Application Procedure: Completed applications must be submitted through the ACLS Online Fellowship Application system.
Closing Date: October 2nd
Funding: Foundation
Contributor: Rockefeller Foundation

Henry Luce Foundation/ACLS Dissertation Fellowships in American Art

Subjects: Art history, focusing on a topic in the history of the visual arts of the United States.
Purpose: To assist students at any stage of PhD dissertation research or writing.
Eligibility: Applicants must be United States citizens and have completed all requirements for a PhD except the dissertation before beginning tenure. They must also be in a department of art history. A student whose degree will be granted by another department may be eligible if the principal dissertation advisor is in a department of the history of art. In all cases the dissertation topic should be object oriented. Students preparing theses for the Master's of Fine Arts degree are not eligible.
Level of Study: Graduate, Predoctoral
Type: Fellowship
Value: US$25,000
Length of Study: 1 year, non-renewable
Country of Study: United States of America
No. of awards offered: 10
Application Procedure: Apply online
Closing Date: November 12th
Contributor: The Henry Luce Foundation

AMERICAN COUNCIL ON RURAL SPECIAL EDUCATION (ACRES)

ACRES Headquarters, Montana Center on Disabilities/MSU-B, 1500 University Dr, Billings, MT 59101, United States of America
Tel: (1) 435 797 0697
Fax: (1) 435 797 3572
Email: davidf@cc.usu.edu
Website: www.acres-sped.org
Contact: David Forbush, Headquarters Co-ordinator

ACRES Scholarship

Subjects: Special education in the areas of the handicapped, those with specific learning disabilities and the socially disadvantaged.
Purpose: To give a rural teacher an opportunity to pursue education and training not otherwise affordable within his or her district.
Eligibility: Applicants must be citizens of the United States of America, currently employed by a rural school district as a certified teacher in regular or special education, working with students with disabilities or with regular education students and retraining to a special education career.
Level of Study: Graduate
Type: Scholarship
Value: Up to US$1,000
Length of Study: 1 year
Frequency: Annual
Country of Study: United States of America
No. of awards offered: 1
Application Procedure: Applicants must complete and submit an application form with an essay and two letters of recommendation. Applicants should access application materials online.
Closing Date: February 15th
Funding: Private
Additional Information: The award will be announced at the March ACRES conference.

AMERICAN COUNCILS FOR INTERNATIONAL EDUCATION ACTR/ACCELS

1776 Massachusetts Avenue, NW, Suite 700, Washington, DC, 20036, United States of America
Tel: (1) 202 833 7522
Fax: (1) 202 833 7523
Email: general@americancouncils.org
Website: www.americancouncils.org
Contact: American Councils Headquarters

American Councils for International Education ACTR/ACCELS was founded in 1974, as an association for area and language professionals, it is an international, non-profit organization working to advance education, research and mutual understanding across the United States of America, Canada and the nations of Southeastern Europe, Eurasia and South Asia.

National Endowment for the Humanities Grants for Collaborative Research in Eastern Europe and Eurasia

Subjects: Humanities and social sciences including such disciplines as anthropology, modern and classical languages, history, linguistics, literature, jurisprudence, philosophy, political science, archaeology, comparative religion, sociology and ethics.
Purpose: To provide fellowships for research in Eastern Europe and Eurasia.
Eligibility: Open to candidates with US citizenship, permanent resident status or residency in U.S. for 3 years before date of application.
Level of Study: Postdoctorate, Research
Type: Grant
Value: US$40,000
Length of Study: 4–9 months
Frequency: Annual
Country of Study: Eastern Europe and Eurasia
Application Procedure: Proposals must include plans to work with at least one collaborator in the field. Especially encouraged are applications with a strong regional focus and the potential to broaden and strengthen international academic linkages beyond the traditional centres such as Moscow, St Petersburg, Warsaw and Prague.
Closing Date: February 15th
Funding: Foundation
Contributor: National Endowment for the Humanities (NEH)
Additional Information: All applications will receive consideration without regard to any non-merit factor such as race, colour, religion, sex, sexual orientation, national origin, marital status, age, political affiliation or disability.

For further information contact:

NEH Collaborative Humanities Fellowship NCEEER, 2601 Fourth Ave, Suite 310,, Seattle, WA,
Tel: (206) 441-6433
Website: www.nceeer.org

Special Initiatives Research Fellowship

Subjects: Policy-relevant research in Armenia, Azerbaijan, Georgia, Kazakhstan, Kyrgyzstan, Tajikistan, Turkmenistan and Uzbekistan.
Purpose: To financially support innovative programmes in scholarly research.
Eligibility: Open to permanent residents or citizens of the United States who hold a PhD in a policy-relevant field.
Level of Study: Postdoctorate, Postgraduate, Predoctorate, Research
Type: Fellowships
Value: US$35,000
Length of Study: 4–9 months overseas
Frequency: Annual
Application Procedure: Applicants can download the application form from the website. The completed application form must be submitted along with a research proposal, research bibliography, a curriculum vitae, copy of the inside page of passport and 2 letters of recommendation.
Closing Date: January 15th (Fall and academic year programme) October 1st (Spring and Summer Programme)
Funding: Government
Contributor: Programme for the Study of Eastern Europe and the Independent States of the former Soviet Union (Title VIII), US Department of State
Additional Information: Applications sent through fax or email will not be considered.

Title VIII Combined Research and Language Training Program

Subjects: Humanities and social sciences.
Purpose: The American Councils Combined Research and Language Training (CRLT) Program serves graduate students, postdoctoral scholars and faculty who, in addition to support for research in Eurasia, require supplemental language instruction.
Eligibility: Applicants must be US citizens or permanent residents. All competitions for funding are open and merit based. Applicants must be scholars in humanities and social sciences who have attained at least an intermediate level of proficiency in Russian or their proposed host-country language, typically students at relatively early stages of their dissertation research. However, participants may be at more advanced stages in their careers and applications from established scholars seeking to develop their proficiency in new languages are welcome.
Level of Study: Postdoctorate, Postgraduate, Predoctorate, Research, Graduate
Type: Fellowship
Value: $5,000–25,000
Length of Study: 3–9 months
Frequency: Annual
Application Procedure: Applicants must submit a 2 to 3 page research proposal and bibliography, curriculum vitae, archive lists (if relevant), 1 page research synopsis in the host-country language, application form, copy of the inside page of their passport and 2 letters of recommendation from colleagues, professors or other qualified persons who are familiar with the applicant's work. At least one letter of recommendation must directly address the applicant's language skills and ability to conduct research in the host country.
Closing Date: January 15th (Fall and academic year programmes) and October 1st (Spring and summer programmes)
Funding: Government
Contributor: Programme for the Study of Eastern Europe and the Independent States of the former Soviet Union (Title VIII), US Department of State
Additional Information: Programmes are available in Belarus, Central Asia, Russia, South Caucasus, Ukraine and Moldova. A wide range of topics receive support each year, all funded research must contribute to a body of knowledge enabling the US to better understand the region and formulate effective policies within it. All applicants should clearly describe the policy-relevance of their work, be it in anthropology, literature, history, international relations, political science or some other field. Applications sent through fax or email will not be considered.

Title VIII Research Scholar Program

Subjects: Humanities and social sciences.
Purpose: To provide full support for graduate students, postdoctoral scholars and faculty seeking to conduct research for 3 to 9 months in Belarus, Central Asia, Russia, South Caucasus, Southeastern Europe, Ukraine and Moldova.
Eligibility: Applicants must be US citizens or permanent residents. All competitions for funding are open and merit based.
Level of Study: Postgraduate, Graduate, Postdoctorate, Predoctorate, Research
Type: Fellowship
Value: $5,000–25,000
Length of Study: 3–9 months
Frequency: Annual
Application Procedure: Applicants must submit a 2 to 3 page research proposal and bibliography, curriculum vitae, archive lists (if relevant), 1 page research synopsis in the host-country language, application form, copy of the inside page of their passport and 2 letters of recommendation from colleagues, professors or other qualified persons who are familiar with the applicant's work. At least 1 letter of recommendation must directly address the applicant's language skills and ability to conduct research in the host country.
Closing Date: January 15th (Fall and academic year programmes) and October 1st (Spring and summer programmes)
Funding: Government
Contributor: Programme for the Study of Eastern Europe and the Independent States of the former Soviet Union (Title VIII), US Department of State
Additional Information: Programmes are available in Belarus, Central Asia, Russia, South Caucasus, Southeastern Europe, Ukraine and Moldova. A wide range of topics receive support each year, all funded research must contribute to a body of knowledge enabling the US to better understand the region and formulate effective policies within it. All applicants should clearly describe the policy-relevance of their work, be it in anthropology, literature, history, international relations, political science, or some other field. Applications sent through fax or email will not be considered.

Title VIII Southeastern Europe Language Program

Purpose: The American Councils Southeastern Europe Language Program offers academic year, semester and summer programs for independent language study in Albania, Bosnia-Herzegovina, Bulgaria, Croatia, Macedonia, Montenegro, Romania and Serbia.
Eligibility: Open to students at the MA and PhD level, as well as postdoctoral scholars and faculty who have at least elementary language skills. Applicants must be US citizens or permanent residents.
Level of Study: Graduate, Postdoctorate, Postgraduate, Predoctorate, Research
Type: Fellowship
Value: Varies
Length of Study: 1–9 months
Frequency: Annual
Application Procedure: Applicants must plan to study for at least one month in the region. Study trips for periods of 4–9 months are particularly encouraged. Applicants should explain how their plans for language-study support their overall research goals. A wide range of interests and research goals have received support each year, all funded research must contribute to a body of knowledge enabling the US policy makers to better understand the region.
Closing Date: January 15th (Fall and academic year programmes) and October 1st (Spring and summer programmes)
Funding: Government
Contributor: Programme for the Study of Eastern Europe and the Independent States of the former Soviet Union (Title VIII), US Department of State
Additional Information: Fellowships provide: full tuition at major university or educational institution in Southeastern Europe, international round trip airfare from the fellow's home city to host city, a monthly living and housing stipend, health insurance of upto $50,000 per accident or illness, Visa support as necessary, graduate-level

academic credit through Bryn Mawr College for programmes providing 7 weeks or more of full-time instruction, ongoing logistical support from American Councils offices throughout the region. Applications sent through fax or email will not be considered.

THE AMERICAN DENTAL ASSOCIATION FOUNDATION (ADA)

211, East Chicago Avenue, Chicago, IL, 60611-2678, United States of America
Tel: (1) 312 440 2567
Fax: (1) 312 440 3526
Email: adaf@ada.org
Website: www.ada.org
Contact: The Director

The purpose of the ADA Foundation Charitable Assistance Programs is to provide a measure of financial assistance to individuals who have financial hardship, whether due to educational needs, chemical dependency, disability or disaster.

ADA Foundation Allied Dental Health Scholarship

Subjects: Dental hygiene, dental assisting and dental laboratory technology.
Purpose: To defray study expenses including tuition fees, books and living expenses.
Eligibility: Open to citizens of the United States of America only. Applicants must either be entering their 1st year (dental assisting) or final year (dental laboratory technology and dental hygiene). Applicants must have a minimum grade point average of 3.0 based on a 4.0 scale and show financial need of at least US$1,000.
Level of Study: Professional development
Type: Scholarship
Value: US$1,000
Frequency: Annual
Country of Study: United States of America
No. of awards offered: 15 dental hygiene, 10 dental assisting and 5 dental laboratory technology
Application Procedure: Application forms are available from the dental hygiene, dental laboratory technology and dental assisting programme directors, and are distributed by school officials. Application forms must be original, typed, completed and signed with the assistance of school officials. Applicants must submit a completed application form, including the Academic Achievement Record Form and Financial Needs Assessment Form signed by school officials, two typed reference forms sealed and noted on the back of the envelopes by the referees and a typed biographical sketch.
Closing Date: August 15th for dental hygiene and dental laboratory technology or September 15th for dental assisting
Funding: Private
Contributor: The ADA Foundation
No. of awards given last year: 15 for dental hygiene, 10 for dental assisting and 5 for dental laboratory technology
Additional Information: This scholarship is not renewable.

AMERICAN DIABETES ASSOCIATION (ADA)

1701 North Beauregard Street, Alexandria, VA, 22311, United States of America
Tel: (1) 703 549 1500
Fax: (1) 703 549 1715
Email: mgalindo@diabetes.org
Website: www.diabetes.org/research
Contact: Magda Galindo, Research Programs Manager

The American Diabetes Association (ADA) is the nation's leading non-profit health organization providing diabetes research information and advocacy. The mission of the organization is to prevent and cure diabetes, and to improve the lives of all people affected by diabetes. To fulfil this mission, the ADA funds research, publishes scientific findings and provides information and other services to people with diabetes, their families, healthcare professionals and the public.

ADA Career Development Awards

Subjects: Diabetes-related research.
Purpose: To allow exceptionally promising new investigators to conduct research.
Eligibility: Open to citizens of the United States of America and permanent residents or those who have applied for permanent resident status, who have MD or PhD degrees or, in the case of other health professions, an appropriate health or science-related degree. Applicants must hold an assistant professorship or provide documentation that he or she will receive this position upon receipt of this award. Career Development Award applicants no more than seven years out of their postdoctoral fellowship may apply. All applicants must have independent lab space and must be publishing independently in order to be eligible for this Award. Career Development Award applicants may hold an R01 at the time of applying provided that the R01 does not overlap with the ADA award. Applicants currently holding awards with similar intent from NIH or other agencies (i.e., career development award, new investigator award, etc.) are *not* eligible for applying or holding an ADA Career Development Award. However, applicants can have previously been recipients of an NIH KO1 or KO8 awards. If awarded the ADA Career Development Award and another career development award from another funding agency, the PI must relinquish one of the awards.
Level of Study: Professional development, Postdoctorate
Type: Research grant
Value: Up to US$150,000 per year and an additional 15 per cent for indirect costs. The funds are to be divided by the recipient between the salary of the principal investigator and other grant support. Each year of funding, after the first, is contingent upon approval by the ADA of the recipient's research progress report, and the availability of funds
Length of Study: 5 years, non-renewable
Frequency: Bi-annual
Country of Study: United States of America
No. of awards offered: Varies, depending on funds available
Application Procedure: Applicants must write for details. All applications must be submitted online via the website www.diabetes.org/research
Closing Date: January 15th for July 1st funding and July 15th for January 1st funding
Funding: Foundation, individuals, private

ADA Clinical Research Grants

Subjects: Diabetes-related research. For the purpose of this programme, clinical research is defined as research involving humans directly.
Purpose: To support patient-orientated research.
Eligibility: Open to citizens of the United States of America and permanent residents or those who have applied for permanent resident status, who have MD or PhD degrees or, in the case of other health professions, an appropriate health or science-related degree, and who hold full-time faculty positions or the equivalent at university-affiliated institutions within the United States of America and its possessions. Support will be provided for studies that focus on intact human subjects in which the effects of a change in the individual's external or internal environment is evaluated.
Level of Study: Research
Value: Up to US$200,000 per year for 3 years. Up to US$40,000 per year may be used for principal investigator salary support, and up to 15 per cent for indirect costs. Each year of funding after the first is contingent upon approval by the ADA of the recipient's research progress report and the availability of funds
Length of Study: 3 years
Frequency: Bi-annual
Country of Study: United States of America
No. of awards offered: Varies, depending on funds available
Application Procedure: Applicants must write for details. All applications must be submitted online via the website at www.diabetes.org/research
Closing Date: January 15th for July 1st funding and July 15th for January 1st funding
Funding: Foundation, individuals, private

ADA Junior Faculty Awards

Subjects: Diabetes.
Purpose: To support investigators who are establishing their independence as diabetes researchers.

Eligibility: Open to citizens of the United States of America and permanent residents or those who have applied for permanent resident status, who have an MD or a PhD degree or an appropriate health or science-related degree. Junior Faculty Award applicants may be senior postdoctoral or clinical fellows (with more than 3 years of experience since obtaining their doctoral degrees) and will receive their first faculty position by the starting date of the award; or junior faculty with less than 4 years from completion of their postdoctoral/clinical fellowships at the time of submission of their applications are eligible. Exceptions to these rules will be considered on an individual basis for applicants who experienced a major career change or interruption. Applicants in this situation must verify their eligibility with the ADA's Research Programmes Department prior to preparing their application. Applicants currently holding or having held awards with similar intent from NIH or other agencies (i.e., career development award, KO1 or KO8 award, new investigator award, etc.) are *not* eligible for applying or holding an ADA Junior Faculty Award. If awarded the ADA Junior Faculty Award and another career development award from another funding agency, the PI must relinquish one of the awards. Applicants who currently hold or have held an RO1 or VA Merit Review award are not eligible for the Junior Faculty Award. If an RO1 or VA Merit Review award is obtained during the 3 years after ADA funding has begun, the applicant will not be required to relinquish his/her ADA award.

Level of Study: Postdoctorate, Professional development
Type: Research grant
Value: Up to US$120,000 per year, and up to 15 per cent for indirect costs plus up to US$10,000 per year towards repayment of the principal on loans for a doctoral degree such as the MD or PhD
Length of Study: 3 years
Frequency: Bi-annual
Country of Study: United States of America
No. of awards offered: Varies, depending on funds available
Application Procedure: Applicants must write for details. All applications must be submitted online via the website at www.diabetes.org/research
Closing Date: January 15th for July 1st funding and July 15th for January 1st funding
Funding: Foundation, individuals, private

ADA Mentor-Based Postdoctoral Fellowship Program
Subjects: Diabetes.
Purpose: To support the training of scientists in an environment most conducive to beginning a career in research.
Eligibility: There are no citizenship requirements for the Fellow. However, the investigator must be a citizen of the United States of America or a permanent resident, and must also hold an appointment at a United States of America research institution and have sufficient research support to provide an appropriate training environment for the Fellow. The Fellow selected by the investigator must hold an MD or PhD degree and must not be serving an internship or residency during the fellowship period. The Fellow must not have more than 3 years of postdoctoral research experience in the field of diabetes or endocrinology at the commencement of this fellowship.
Level of Study: Postdoctorate
Type: Fellowship
Value: Up to US$45,000 per year
Length of Study: Up to 4 years
Frequency: Annual
Country of Study: United States of America
No. of awards offered: Varies, depending on funds available
Application Procedure: Applicants must complete an application form. All applications must be submitted online via the website www.diabetes.org/research
Closing Date: January 15th for July 1st funding
Funding: Foundation, individuals, private

ADA Research Awards
Subjects: Aetiology and pathophysiology of diabetes.
Purpose: To assist investigators, new or established, who have a particularly novel and exciting idea for which they need support.
Eligibility: Open to citizens of the United States of America and permanent residents or those who have applied for permanent resident status, who have MD or PhD degrees, or, in the case of other health professions, an appropriate health or science-related degree.

Applicants must hold full-time faculty positions or the equivalent at university-affiliated institutions within the United States of America and its possessions.
Level of Study: Research
Type: Research grant
Value: US$20,000–100,000 per year, for a maximum of 3 years, of which a maximum of US$20,000 can be used for principal investigator salary support, and up to 15 per cent for indirect costs. Each year of funding after the first is contingent upon approval by the ADA of the recipient's research progress report, and the availability of funds
Length of Study: Up to 3 years
Frequency: Bi-annual
Country of Study: United States of America
No. of awards offered: Varies, depending on funds available
Application Procedure: All applications must be submitted online via the website at www.diabetes.org/research
Closing Date: January 15th for July 1st funding and July 15th for January 1st funding
Funding: Foundation, individuals, private

Clinical Scholars Program
Subjects: Diabetes.
Purpose: To produce leaders in the fields of research, teaching and patient care, by giving physicians in training the opportunity to contribute to the process of discovery in basic and clinical research laboratories. The Medical Scholars Program will supply a unique opportunity to effectively integrate medical students into the process of discovery.
Eligibility: Open to institutions within the United States of America and its possessions. The application must be initiated by the student, and the student must have a qualified sponsor. The student must have completed at least 1 year of medical school and the sponsor must hold a faculty position within an accredited medical school in the United States of America and be a citizen of the United States of America or a permanent resident.
Level of Study: Doctorate, Postgraduate
Type: Scholarship
Value: Support for 1 year in a clinical or basic science research environment. The award will be up to US$30,000 per student, US$20,000 for the student's support and US$10,000 for materials, supplies and travel to the Association's scientific sessions
Length of Study: 1 year
Frequency: Annual
Country of Study: United States of America
No. of awards offered: Varies
Application Procedure: Applicants must write for details. All applications must be submitted online via the website at www.diabetes.org/research
Closing Date: January 15th for July 1st funding
Funding: Foundation, individuals, private

AMERICAN FEDERATION FOR AGING RESEARCH (AFAR)

55 West 39th Street, 16th Floor, New York, NY, 10018, United States of America
Tel: (1) 212 703 9977
Fax: (1) 212 997 0330
Email: grants@afar.org
Website: www.afar.org
Contact: Odette van der Willik, Director, Grant Programs

The American Federation for Aging Research (AFAR) is a leading non-profit organization supporting biomedical aging research. Since its founding in 1981, AFAR has provided more than US$113 million to close to 2,500 new investigators and students conducting cutting-edge biomedical research on the aging process and age-related diseases. The important work AFAR supports leads to a better understanding of the aging process and to improvements in the health of all Americans as they age.

AFAR Research Grants
Subjects: Biomedical and clinical topics. Basic mechanisms of aging.
Purpose: To help junior faculty to carry out research that will serve as the basis for longer term research efforts.

Eligibility: Open to junior faculty with an MD or PhD degree.
Level of Study: Postdoctorate, Research
Type: Research grant
Value: US$75,000 for junior faculty
Length of Study: 1–2 years
Frequency: Annual
Country of Study: United States of America
No. of awards offered: Approx. 15
Application Procedure: Applicants must complete and return the application by the annual deadline. These are available from the website.
Closing Date: December 16th
Funding: Foundation, private
Contributor: AFAR

The Cart Fund, Inc.

Subjects: Alzheimers disease.
Purpose: To encourage exploratory and developmental Alzheimers disease research projects.
Eligibility: Open to applicants whose projects have the potential to advance biomedical research.
Level of Study: Research
Value: US$250,000
Frequency: Annual
No. of awards offered: 1
Application Procedure: A letter-of-intent that includes sufficient details of the study must be submitted.
Closing Date: December 1st
Funding: Private

Ellison Medical Foundation/AFAR Postdoctoral Fellows in Aging Research Program

Subjects: The fundamental mechanisms of aging.
Purpose: The program addresses the current concerns about an adequate funding base for postdoctoral fellows (both MDs and Phds) who conduct research in the fundamental mechanisms of aging.
Eligibility: Postdoctoral fellows at all levels of training are eligible.
Level of Study: Postdoctorate
Type: Fellowship
Value: US$44,850–58,850
Length of Study: 1 year
Frequency: Annual
No. of awards offered: Up to 15 Fellowships
Application Procedure: Applications.

The Glenn/AFAR Breakthroughs in Gerontology Awards

Subjects: Projects that focus on genetic controls of aging and longevity, on delay of aging by pharmacological agents or dietary means, or which elucidate the mechanisms by which alterations in hormones, antioxidant defenses, or repair processes promote longevity are all well within the intended scope of this competition. Projects that focus instead on specific diseases or on assessment of health care strategies will receive much lower priority, unless the research plan makes clear and direct connections to fundamental issues in the biology of aging. Studies of invertebrates, mice, human clinical materials or cell lines are all potentially eligible for funding. Although preliminary data are always helpful for evaluating the feasibility of the experiments proposed, the emphasis in review will be on creativity and the likelihood that the findings will open new vistas and approaches to aging research that might merit intensive follow up studies.
Eligibility: To be eligible, applicants must at the time they submit their proposal be full time faculty members at the rank of Assistant Professor or higher. A strong record of independent publication beyond the postdoctoral level is a requirement. Applications from individuals not previously engaged in aging research are particularly encouraged, as long as the research proposals show high promise for leading to important new discoveries in biological gerontology. Applicants who are employees in the NIH Intramural programme are not eligible. The proposed research must be conducted at any type of non-profit setting in the United States.
Level of Study: Research
Value: US$200,000
Length of Study: 2 years
Frequency: Dependent on funds available
No. of awards offered: 1

Closing Date: December 16th
Funding: Private
Contributor: The Glenn Foundation for Medical Research

The Julie Martin Mid-Career Award in Aging Research

Subjects: Basic aging research.
Purpose: To encourage outstanding mid-career scientists.
Eligibility: Open to mid-career (Associate Professors) scientists whose research could lead to novel approaches to aging, and also whose research is high risk.
Level of Study: Research
Type: Award
Value: US$500,000, in addition up to US$50,000 may be requested for indirect costs
Length of Study: 4 years
Frequency: Annual
No. of awards offered: 2
Closing Date: December 16th
Funding: Foundation
Contributor: Ellison Medical Foundation

Medical Student Training in Aging Research (MSTAR) Program

Purpose: This programme provides medical students, early in their training, with an enriching experience in aging-related research and geriatrics.
Eligibility: Any allopathic or osteopathic medical student in good standing, who will have successfully completed 1 year of medical school at a US institution by June. Evidence of such likelihood must be provided at the time of application. Applicants must be citizens or non-citizen nationals of the United States, or must have been lawfully admitted for permanent residence (i.e., in procession of a currently valid Alien Registration Receipt Card I-551, or some other legal verification of such status.) Individuals on temporary or student visas and individuals holding PhD, MD, DVM, or equivalent doctoral degrees in the health sciences are not eligible. The NIA and other sponsoring organizations have a strong interest in continuing to diversify the research workforce committed to advancing the fields of aging and geriatric research. Therefore, students who are members of ethnic or racial groups underrepresented in these fields, students with disabilities, or students whose background and experience are likely to diversify the research or medical questions being addressed, are encouraged to apply.
Level of Study: Graduate, Medical student
Value: A stipend of US$1,731
Frequency: Annual
Application Procedure: Applications can be completed through www.afar.org
Closing Date: February 6th
Funding: Government, private

Paul Beeson Career Development Award in Aging Research

Subjects: Medical sciences.
Purpose: To bolster the current severe shortage of academic physicians who have the combination of medical, academic and scientific training relative to caring for other people.
Eligibility: Applicants must be citizens of the United States of America or permanent residents, be full-time faculty members with clear potential for long-term faculty appointments. To be eligible a candidate must (1) have clinical doctoral degree (e.g., MD, DO, DDS) or its equivalent and have completed clinical training; (2) commit at least 75 per cent of his/her full-time professional effort to the goals of this award; (3) be a US citizen or non-citizen national of the United States or a permanent resident alien; (4) be at a for-profit or non-profit organization, public or private institution (such as universities, colleges, hospitals and laboratories), units of state and local governments or eligible agencies of the federal government provided the demonstrated environment has a commitment to the geriatric population and capacity to support the scholar's career development.
Level of Study: Research, Professional development
Type: Grant
Value: US$600,000–800,000
Length of Study: 3–5 years
Frequency: Annual

Country of Study: United States of America
No. of awards offered: 10–12
Application Procedure: Applicants must complete and return the application by the annual deadline. Application forms can be found at: http://grants1.nih.gov/grants/guide/rfa-files/RFA-AG-09-012.html
Closing Date: November 3rd
Funding: Government, private
Contributor: The National Institute on Aging, John A Hartford Foundation, Commonwealth Fund, Atlantic Philanthropies and Starr Foundation

For further information contact:

Website: www.grants1.nih.gov/grants/guide/rfa-files/RFA-AG-08-006.html

The Paul Beeson Career Development Awards in Aging Research for the Island of Ireland

Subjects: Aging-related research.
Purpose: To encourage and assist the development of future leaders in the field of aging, deepen the commitment of research institutions to academic reserach in aging, and to expand medical research on aging.
Level of Study: Research
Type: Award
Value: €339,390/£228,000
Length of Study: 3 years
Country of Study: Ireland
Application Procedure: All candidates must submit applications endorsed by the Dean of School of Medicine (or equivalent). Scholars will be required to submit a brief annual narrative report on the progress of their research and career plans.
Closing Date: January 22nd
Funding: Private

For further information contact:

55 West 39th Street, 16th Floor, New York, NY 10018, United States of America
Email: beeson@afar.org
Website: www.afar.org

The Rosalinde and Arthur Gilbert Foundation/AFAR New Investigator Awards in Alzheimer's Disease

Subjects: Neurosciences, research related to Alzheimer's disease.
Purpose: To support important research and encourage junior investigators in the United States and Israel to pursue research and academic careers in the neurosciences, and Alzheimer's disease in particular.
Eligibility: Open to applicants in their first or second year of a junior faculty appointment and establishing independent research activities.
Level of Study: Research
Type: Grant
Value: $75,000
Length of Study: 1–2
Frequency: Annual
No. of awards offered: 5
Application Procedure: Check the website for instruction sheet and application.
Closing Date: December 16th

For further information contact:

Website: www.afar.org

AMERICAN FOUNDATION FOR AGING RESEARCH (AFAR)

Biochemistry Department, North Carolina State University, Campus Box 7622, Polk Hall, Raleigh, NC, 27695, United States of America
Tel: (1) 919 515 5679
Fax: (1) 919 515 2047
Email: afar_office@ncsu.edu
Website: www.ncsu.edu/project/afar/
Contact: Dr Paul F Agris, President

The American Foundation for Aging Research (AFAR) promotes and supports researchand education that will elucidate the basic processes involved in the biology of aging and age associated disease, by awarding scholarships and fellowships to young, motivated scientists.

Dr Vincent Cristofalo Memorial Fund, Cecille Gould Memorial Fund Award in Cancer Research, Richard Shepherd Fellowship

Subjects: Aging and cancer research.
Purpose: To encourage young people to pursue research in age-related health problems and the biology of aging.
Eligibility: Open to graduates enrolled in degree programmes such as MS, PhD, MD or DDS at institutions within the United States of America. Must be conducting cellular, molecular or genetic research on aging or age-related illnesses such as cancer, diabetes or Alzheimer's. Sociological and psychological research is not accepted in these programmes.
Level of Study: Doctorate, Graduate, Postgraduate
Type: Fellowship
Value: US$1,000 per semester or summer
Length of Study: Between 4 months and 1 year
Frequency: Annual
Study Establishment: Educational institutions
Country of Study: United States of America
No. of awards offered: 5–10
Application Procedure: Applicants must undertake the two levels of review: a pre-application form to determine eligibility, and a full application. Applicants should submit a request for a pre-application. There is no charge for the submission of the pre-application or the full application.
Closing Date: There is no deadline
Funding: Private
No. of awards given last year: 15
No. of applicants last year: 115
Additional Information: AFAR is a national, tax-exempt, non-profit, educational and scientific charity but not affiliated with North Carolina State University.

AMERICAN FOUNDATION FOR PHARMACEUTICAL EDUCATION (AFPE)

One Church Street, Suite 202, Rockville, MD, 20850-4, United States of America
Tel: (1) 301 738 2160
Fax: (1) 301 738 2161
Email: info@afpenet.org
Website: www.afpenet.org
Contact: Administrative Assistant

The mission of the AFPE is to advance and support pharmaceutical sciences education at US schools and colleges of pharmacy.

AAPS/AFPE Gateway to Research Scholarships

Subjects: Pharmaceutics.
Purpose: To encourage graduates from any discipline to pursue a PhD in a pharmacy graduate programme.
Eligibility: Open to students who are enrolled in the last 3 years of a Bachelor of science or PharmD programme at a United States school or college of pharmacy, or Baccalaureate degree programme in a related field of scientific study at any college. Candidates must have a demonstrated interest in, and potential for, a career in any of the pharmaceutical sciences and be enrolled for at least one full academic year following the award of the scholarship. United States citizenship or permanent resident status is not required.
Level of Study: Professional development, Postgraduate
Type: Scholarship
Value: No less than US$5,000 is provided as a student stipend for a full calendar year
Frequency: Annual
Country of Study: United States of America
No. of awards offered: 3
Application Procedure: Applicants must write for details.
Closing Date: January 25th 2008

AFPE Clinical Pharmacy Post-PharmD Fellowships in the Biomedical Research Sciences

Subjects: Pharmacology including topics such as cost benefit and cost effectiveness of pharmaceuticals, the impact of current or future legislation on drug innovation and healthcare in the nation, the economics of healthcare and the quality of life in changing patterns of healthcare delivery systems, the contribution of the pharmaceutical industry, the economic impact of research and new drugs, and healthcare cost containment issues.

Purpose: Outstanding Pharm.D. graduates who have completed one or more post-doctoral residencies or fellowships.To obtain advanced education and training in relevant areas of the biomedical and related basic sciences in order to become competent clinical scientists.

Eligibility: Open to all pharmacy faculty members who have a strong record of research.

Level of Study: Doctorate, Postdoctorate

Type: Fellowship

Value: US$27,500 per year

Length of Study: 1–2 years

Frequency: Annual

Study Establishment: An Institute of Higher Education

Country of Study: United States of America

No. of awards offered: 2

Application Procedure: Applicants must complete an application form and should write for details.

Closing Date: February 15th

AFPE Gateway to Research Scholarship Program

Subjects: Pharmacology.

Purpose: To encourage individuals in a pharmacy college to pursue a PhD within a pharmacy college.

Eligibility: Open to students who are enrolled in the last 3 years of a Bachelor of Science or PharmD programme at a United States school or college of pharmacy, or Baccalaureate degree programme in a related field of scientific study at any college. Candidates must have a demonstrated interest in, and potential for, a career in any of the pharmaceutical sciences and will be enrolled for at least one full academic year following the award of the scholarship. United States citizenship or permanent resident status is not required.

Level of Study: Postgraduate, Professional development

Type: Scholarship

Value: No less than US$5,000 is provided as a student stipend for a research project

Frequency: Annual

Study Establishment: An approved college of pharmacy

Country of Study: United States of America

No. of awards offered: 12

Application Procedure: Applicants must write for details.

Closing Date: January 25th 2008

AFPE Predoctoral Fellowships

Subjects: Any of the pharmaceutical sciences, including pharmaceutics, pharmacology, manufacturing pharmacy and medicinal chemistry.

Purpose: To offer fellowship support leading to a PhD degree.

Eligibility: Open to students who have completed at least three semesters of graduate study and who have no more than 3 years remaining to obtain a PhD degree in a graduate programme in the pharmaceutical sciences administered by, or affiliated with, a United States school or college of pharmacy. The award is also open to students enrolled in joint PharmD and PhDs, if a PhD degree will be awarded within three additional years. Applicants must be United States citizens or permanent residents.

Level of Study: Doctorate, Postdoctorate, Postgraduate

Type: Fellowships

Value: US$6,000 stipend

Length of Study: 1 year, renewable for 2 additional years

Frequency: Annual

Study Establishment: An appropriate university

Country of Study: United States of America

No. of awards offered: 70

Application Procedure: Applicants must write for details.

Closing Date: March 3rd

AMERICAN FOUNDATION FOR SUICIDE PREVENTION (AFSP)

120 Wall Street, 22nd Floor, New York, NY 10005, United States of America
Tel: (1) 212 363 3500
Fax: (1) 212 363 6237
Email: tauster@afsp.org
Website: www.afsp.org
Contact: Tracey Auster, Research Administrator

The American Foundation for Suicide Prevention (AFSP) is the only national non-profit organization exclusively dedicated to understanding and preventing suicide through research and education, and to reaching out to people with mood disorders and those affected by suicide.

AFSP Distinguished Investigator Awards

Subjects: The clinical, biological or psychosocial aspects of suicide.

Purpose: Awarded to investigators at the level of associate professor or higher with a proven history of research in the area of suicide.

Level of Study: Postdoctorate, Research

Type: Grant

Value: Up to US$100,000

Length of Study: 1–2 years

Frequency: Annual

Country of Study: Worldwide

No. of awards offered: Varies

Application Procedure: Applicants should consult the website or contact the organization for full details. Application form must be completed.

Closing Date: December 15th

Funding: Private

Additional Information: Decisions regarding awards are made in May and funding begins in July.

AFSP Pilot Grants

Subjects: The clinical, biological or psychosocial aspects of suicide.

Level of Study: Research, Postdoctorate

Type: Grant

Value: Up to US$30,000

Length of Study: 1–2 years

Frequency: Annual

Country of Study: Worldwide

No. of awards offered: Varies

Application Procedure: Applicants should consult the website or contact the organization for full details. Application form must be completed.

Closing Date: December 15th, June 15th

Funding: Private

Additional Information: Decisions regarding awards are made 2 times a year.

AFSP Postdoctoral Research Fellowships

Subjects: The clinical, biological or psychosocial aspects of suicide.

Purpose: Awarded to investigators who have received a PhD, an MD, or other doctoral degrees within the preceding 6 years.

Eligibility: Applicants must have received a PhD 3 years prior to application for the fellowship.

Level of Study: Research, Postdoctorate

Type: Fellowship

Value: US$100,000

Length of Study: 2 years

Frequency: Annual

Country of Study: Worldwide

No. of awards offered: Varies

Application Procedure: Applicants should consult the website or contact the organization. Application form must be completed.

Closing Date: December 15th

Funding: Private

Additional Information: Decisions regarding awards are made in May and funding begins in July.

AFSP Standard Research Grants

Subjects: The clinical, biological or psychosocial aspects of suicide.

Purpose: Awarded to individual investigators at any level.

Level of Study: Postdoctorate, Research

Type: Grant
Value: Up to US$75,000
Length of Study: 2 years
Frequency: Annual
Country of Study: Worldwide
No. of awards offered: Varies
Application Procedure: Applicants should consult the website or contact the organization. Application form must be completed.
Closing Date: December 15th
Funding: Private
Additional Information: Decisions regarding awards are made in May and funding begins in July.

AFSP Young Investigator Award

Subjects: The clinical, biological or psychosocial aspects of suicide.
Purpose: Awarded to those at the level of assistant professor or lower.
Level of Study: Research
Type: Award
Value: Up to US$85,000
Length of Study: 2 years
Frequency: Annual
Country of Study: Worldwide
No. of awards offered: Varies
Application Procedure: Applicants should consult the website or contact the organization. Application form must be completed.
Closing Date: December 15th
Funding: Private
Additional Information: Decisions regarding awards are made in May and funding begins in July. Investigators should be at the level of assistant professor or lower.

AMERICAN FOUNDATION FOR THE BLIND (AFB)

11 Penn Plaza, Suite 300, New York, NY 10001, United States of America
Tel: (1) 212 502 7600
Fax: (1) 212 502 7777
Email: afbinfo@afb.net
Website: www.afb.org

The American Foundation for the Blind (AFB) is a national non-profit organisation that expands possibilities for people with vision loss. AFB's priorities include broadening access to technology; elevating the quality of information and tools for the professionals who serve people with vision loss; and promoting independent and healthy living for people with vision loss by providing them and their families with relevant and timely resources.

Karen D. Carsel Memorial Scholarship

Purpose: To provide financial help to blind students who want to further a career.
Level of Study: Postgraduate
Type: Scholarship
Value: US$500
Frequency: Annual
No. of awards offered: 1
Application Procedure: The candidate will have to submit the evidence of legal blindness, official transcripts, proof of acceptance into a programme, evidence of economic need, 3 letters of recommendation, and typewritten statement describing educational and personal goals, work experience, extra-curricular activities and how scholarship monies will be used.
Closing Date: April 30th

AMERICAN GEOPHYSICAL UNION (AGU)

2000 Florida Avenue, N.W., Washington, DC, 20009-1277, United States of America
Tel: (1) 202 462 6900
Fax: (1) 202 328 0566
Email: service@agu.org
Website: www.agu.org
Contact: Director, Outreach and Research Support

The American Geophysical Union (AGU) is an international scientific society with more than 45,000 members, primarily research scientists, dedicated to advancing the understanding of Earth and space and making the results of the AGU's research available to the public.

F.L. Scarf Award

Subjects: Solar-planetary science.
Purpose: To award outstanding dissertation research that contributes directly to solar-planetary science.
Eligibility: Open to all candidates with a PhD (or equivalent) degree.
Level of Study: Doctorate
Value: US$1,000
Frequency: Annual
Application Procedure: Nominations to be sent to outreach administrator at AGU.
Closing Date: February 15th
Contributor: The Space Physics and Aeronomy section of AGU

For further information contact:

Tel: 1 202 777 7502
Email: leadership@agu.org

Horton (Hydrology) Research Grant

Subjects: Hydrology including its physical, chemical or biological aspects, life sciences, physical sciences, social sciences, school of public affairs, school of law.
Purpose: To support research in hydrology and water resources.
Eligibility: There are no eligibility restrictions.
Level of Study: Postdoctorate
Type: Grant
Value: US$10,000
Frequency: Annual
No. of awards offered: 2
Application Procedure: Applicants must submit four copies of the application form, an executive summary, a statement of purpose, a detailed budget and two letters of recommendation. Applicants should contact the AGU for further details.
Closing Date: April 13th
No. of awards given last year: 2
No. of applicants last year: 27

The Mineral and Rock Physics Outstanding Student Award

Subjects: Mineral and rock physics.
Purpose: To recognize outstanding contributions by young scientists.
Eligibility: Open to students who have completed their PhD.
Level of Study: Doctorate
Type: Award
Value: US$500, a certificate and public recognition at the annual Mineral and Rock Physics Reception at the AGU fall meeting
Frequency: Annual
No. of awards offered: Varies
Application Procedure: A letter of nomination along with a curriculum vitae, two supporting letters and 3 reprints or preprints of the nominee's work should be sent.
Closing Date: May 1st
Contributor: Mineral and Rock Physics community at AGU

For further information contact:

Department of Earth and Planetary Sciences, Northwestern University, 1850 Campus Drive, Evanston, IL, 60208-2150, United States of America
Tel: (1) 847 467 1825
Fax: (1) 847 491 8060
Email: steven@earth.northwestern.edu
Contact: Professor Steven D. Jacobsen

AMERICAN HEAD AND NECK SOCIETY (AHNS)

11300 W. Olympic Boulevard, Suite 600, Los Angeles, CA, 90064, United States of America
Tel: (1) 310 437 0559
Fax: (1) 310 437 0585
Email: admin@ahns.info
Website: www.headandneckcancer.org
Contact: Joyce Hasper, Research Grants Enquiries

The purpose of the American Head and Neck Society (AHNS) is to promote and advance the knowledge of prevention, diagnosis, treatment and rehabilitation of neoplasms and other diseases of the head and neck.

AHNS Pilot Research Grant
Subjects: Diseases of the head and neck.
Purpose: To support students who wish to try a pilot project in head and neck-related research.
Eligibility: Open to residents and fellows in the junior faculty.
Level of Study: Doctorate, Postgraduate
Type: Award
Value: US$10,000
Length of Study: 1 year
Frequency: Annual
Study Establishment: A university in the United States of America
Country of Study: United States of America
No. of awards offered: 1
Funding: Private

AHNS Surgeon Scientist Career Development Award (with AAOHNS)
Subjects: Cancer and other diseases of the head and neck.
Purpose: To support research in the pathogenesis, pathophysiology, diagnosis, prevention or treatment of head and neck neoplastic disease.
Eligibility: Open to surgeons beginning a clinician-scientist career.
Level of Study: Postdoctorate
Type: Award
Value: US$35,000 per year
Length of Study: 2 years
Frequency: Annual
Study Establishment: A university in the United States of America
Country of Study: United States of America
No. of awards offered: 1
Funding: Private

AHNS Young Investigator Award (with AAOHNS)
Subjects: Cancer and other diseases of the head and neck.
Purpose: To support research in neoplastic disease of the head and neck.
Eligibility: Candidate must be a member of AHNS.
Level of Study: Doctorate
Type: Award
Value: US$10,000 per year
Length of Study: Up to 2 years
Frequency: Annual
Study Establishment: A university in the United States of America
Country of Study: United States of America
No. of awards offered: 1
Funding: Private

AHNS-ACS Career Development Award
Subjects: Diseases of the head and neck.
Purpose: To facilitate research in connection with career development.
Eligibility: Applicants must be a member or candidate member of AHNS.
Level of Study: Postgraduate
Type: Award
Value: US$40,000 per year
Length of Study: 2 years
Frequency: Annual
Study Establishment: A university in the United States of America
Country of Study: United States of America
Funding: Private

AMERICAN HEALTH ASSISTANCE FOUNDATION (AHAF)

22512 Gateway Center Drive, Clarksburg, MD, 20871, United States of America
Tel: (1) 301 948 3244
Fax: (1) 301 258 9454
Email: psenda@ahaf.org
Website: www.ahaf.org
Contact: Dr Pam Senda, Grants Manager

The American Health Assistance Foundation (AHAF) is a non-profit charitable organization that funds research and public education on age related and degenerative diseases including: Alzheimer's disease, macular degeneration, glaucoma and heart and stroke diseases. The organization also provides emergency financial assistance to Alzheimer's disease patients and their care givers.

AHAF Alzheimer's Disease Research Grant
Subjects: Neurology, biomedicine, biochemistry, biophysics, molecular biology and pharmacology.
Purpose: To enable basic research on the causes of and treatments for Alzheimer's disease.
Eligibility: The principal investigator must hold the rank of assistant professor or equivalent, or higher.
Level of Study: Doctorate, Postdoctorate, Postgraduate
Type: Grant
Value: Standard grants are for US$150,000 per year for up to 2 years. Pilot project grants can receive US$50,000 per year up to 2 years
Length of Study: 1–2 years
Frequency: Annual
Study Establishment: Non-profit institutions and organizations
Country of Study: Any country
No. of awards offered: Varies
Application Procedure: Applicants must complete an application form. The current application form should be requested for each year or can be downloaded from the website.
Closing Date: October 11th
Funding: Private
No. of awards given last year: 14
No. of applicants last year: 89

AHAF Macular Degeneration Research
Subjects: Ophthalmology, biomedicine, biochemistry, biophysics, genetics, molecular biology and pharmacology.
Purpose: To enable basic research on the causes of, or the treatment for, macular degeneration.
Eligibility: The principal investigator must hold a tenure track or tenured position and the rank of assistant professor or higher.
Level of Study: Research
Type: Grant
Value: Up to US$50,000. Grants may be renewed on a competitive peer review basis
Length of Study: 1 year
Frequency: Annual
Study Establishment: Non-profit institutions and organizations
Country of Study: Any country
No. of awards offered: Varies
Application Procedure: Applicants must complete an application form. The current application form should be requested for each year or can be downloaded from the website.
Closing Date: Letters of intent due July 11th of each year. Application due in October
Funding: Private
No. of awards given last year: 7
No. of applicants last year: 31

AHAF National Glaucoma Research
Subjects: Ophthalmology, biomedicine and pharmacology.
Purpose: To enable basic research on the causes of or treatments for glaucoma.
Eligibility: The principal investigator must hold the rank of assistant professor or equivalent, or higher.
Level of Study: Research, Doctorate
Type: Grant
Value: Up to US$45,000 per year for up to 2 years
Length of Study: 1–2 years
Frequency: Annual
Study Establishment: Non-profit institutions and organizations
Country of Study: Any country
No. of awards offered: Varies
Application Procedure: Applicants must complete an application form. The current application form should be requested for each year and can also be downloaded from the website.
Closing Date: November 16th

Funding: Private
No. of awards given last year: 9
No. of applicants last year: 28

AHAF National Heart Foundation

Subjects: Cardiology, biomedicine, physiology and pharmacology.
Purpose: To provide start up grants for new investigators into the causes of, or treatments for, cardiovascular disease and stroke.
Eligibility: Open to young investigators who are beginning independent research careers at the assistant professor level and are head of an independent research laboratory group.
Level of Study: Research, Postgraduate, Predoctorate, Professional development
Type: Grant
Value: Up to US$25,000 may be requested for 1 year
Length of Study: 1 year, renewable for a further year
Frequency: Annual
Study Establishment: Non-profit institutions and organizations
Country of Study: Any country
No. of awards offered: Varies
Application Procedure: Applicants must complete an application form. The current application form should be requested for each year or can be downloaded from the website.
Closing Date: November 2nd
Funding: Private
No. of awards given last year: 5
No. of applicants last year: 18

AMERICAN HEART ASSOCIATION (AHA)

National Center, 7272 Greenville Avenue, Dallas, TX, 75231, United States of America
Tel: (1) 214 360 6104, 6106
Fax: (1) 214 706 1341
Email: juanita.morales@heart.org
Website: www.americanheart.org
Contact: Ms Juanita Morales, Manager

The American Heart Association (AHA) is a non-profit, voluntary health organization funded by private contributions. Its mission is to reduce disability and death from cardiovascular diseases and stroke. To support this goal, the Association has given more than US$2 billion to heart and blood vessel research since 1949.

AHA Fellowships

Subjects: Cardiovascular diseases, stroke, basic science, clinical, bioengineering/biotechnology and public health problems.
Purpose: To help students initiate careers in cardiovascular research by providing assistance and training in research activities broadly related to cardiovascular function and diseases.
Eligibility: Open to permanent residents or citizens of the United States. Also for exchange visitors under J-1, temporary worker under H-1, H-1B, O-1 visas. Canadian or Mexican citizens engaged in professional activities or student visa are also eligible.
Level of Study: Predoctorate, Research
Type: Fellowships
Value: Stipend of US$20,000 per year
Length of Study: 2 years
Frequency: Annual
Country of Study: United States of America
Closing Date: January 12th
Additional Information: Participation by women and minorities is encouraged.

AMERICAN HERPES FOUNDATION

433 Hackensack Avenue, 9th Floor, Hackensack, NJ, 07601, United States of America
Tel: (1) 201 883 5852
Fax: (1) 201 342 7555
Email: IHMF@hbase.com
Website: www.herpes-foundation.org
Contact: Loretla A. Ponesse

American Herpes Foundation is a non-profit organization dedicated to improving the management of herpes virus infections. Our initiatives focus primarily on clinician education and awareness.

American Herpes Foundation Stephen L Sacks Investigator Award

Subjects: Research areas include HSV1 and 2, VZV, EBV, CMV, and HHV6 and 8.
Purpose: To recognize and encourage newer researchers who have completed significant research in the herpes virus area.
Eligibility: Residents, fellows or junior faculty up to the 5th year of faculty appointment are eligible.
Level of Study: Physicians-in-training or researchers-in-training
Type: Cash prize
Value: US$5,000 cash prize
No. of awards offered: 2
Application Procedure: Candidates must submit a letter of nomination, completed application form, curriculum vitae, biographical sketch and documentation of research.
Closing Date: Call for details
Funding: Private

AMERICAN HISTORICAL ASSOCIATION

400 A Street, S.E., Washington, DC, 20003-3889, United States of America
Tel: (1) 202 544 2422
Fax: (1) 202 544 8307
Email: info@historians.org
Website: www.historians.org
Contact: Research Grant Administrator

The American Historial Association (AHA) is a non-profit membership organization founded in 1884 and was incorporated by Congress in 1889 for the promotion of historical studies, the preservation of historial documents and artefacts and the dissemination of historical research.

Albert J Beveridge Grant

Subjects: The history of the United States of America, Latin America or Canada.
Purpose: To promote and honor outstanding historical writing and to support research in the history of the Western hemisphere.
Eligibility: Open to American Historical Association members only.
Level of Study: Postgraduate, Doctorate, Postdoctorate
Type: Grant
Value: A maximum of US$1,000
Frequency: Annual
Country of Study: Any country
No. of awards offered: Varies
Application Procedure: Applicants must apply online at www.historians.org/prizes/beveridgegrantinfo.htm
Closing Date: February 15th
Funding: Private

Bernadotte E Schmitt Grants

Subjects: The history of Europe, Asia and Africa.
Purpose: To support research in the history of Europe, Africa and Asia, and to further research in progress.
Eligibility: Open to American Historical Association members only.
Level of Study: Postdoctorate, Postgraduate, Doctorate
Type: Grant
Value: Up to US$1,000
Frequency: Annual
Country of Study: Any country
No. of awards offered: Varies
Application Procedure: Applicants must apply online at www.historians.org/prizes/schmittgrantinfo.htm
Closing Date: February 15th
Funding: Private

J Franklin Jameson Fellowship

Subjects: The collections of the Library of Congress.
Purpose: To support significant scholarly research for 1 semester in the collections of the Library of Congress by scholars at an early stage in their careers in history.

Eligibility: Applicants must hold a PhD degree or equivalent, must have received this degree within the past 7 years, and must not have published or had accepted for publication a book-length historical work. The fellowship will not be awarded to complete a doctoral dissertation.
Level of Study: Postdoctorate
Type: Fellowship
Value: US$5,000
Length of Study: 1 semester
Frequency: Annual
Country of Study: United States of America
No. of awards offered: 1
Application Procedure: Applicants must refer to the website www.historians.org/prizes/jameson_fellowship.htm for instructions.
Closing Date: March 15th
Funding: Private, government

Littleton-Griswold Research Grant

Subjects: American legal history, law and society.
Purpose: To further research in progress.
Eligibility: Open to American Historical Association members only.
Level of Study: Doctorate, Postdoctorate, Postgraduate
Type: Research grant
Value: Up to US$1,000
Frequency: Annual
Country of Study: Any country
No. of awards offered: Varies
Application Procedure: Applicants must apply online at www.historians.org/prizes/littleton-griswaldgrantinfo.htm
Closing Date: February 15th
Funding: Private

AMERICAN INDIAN GRADUATE CENTER (AIGC)

4520 Montgomery Boulevard NE, Suite 1B, Albuquerque, NM, 87109, United States of America
Tel: (1) 505 881 4584
Fax: (1) 505 884 0427
Email: web@aigcs.org
Website: www.aigc.com

American Indian Graduate Center (AIGC) is the only national non-profit organization dedicated to aiding Indian graduate students in all fields of study. As a non-profit organization, AIGC prides itself on maintaining a very low administrative cost. In fact 90 per cent of all contributions goes directly to student services. AIGC will help plan and produce the social, economic and political changes needed to ensure the long-term positive development of the communities by providing extraordinary numbers of talented, highly skilled and exceptionally trained Indian professionals.

AIGC Accenture American Indian Scholarship Fund

Subjects: Fields of study: business, high technology, medicine, law and engineering fields
Purpose: To financially support American Indian and Alaskan Native students seeking higher education.
Eligibility: Open to candidates who are members of a U.S. federally recognized American Indian or Alaska Native Group and who are able to demonstrate involvement with Native American activities or affairs. Must be a full-time student. Undergraduates must have a 3.25 GPA Cumulative at their 7th semester of high school. Graduates must have a 3.00 Cumulative GPA in their undergraduate years.
Level of Study: Doctorate, Graduate, MBA
Type: Scholarships
Value: Varies
Frequency: Annual
Country of Study: United States of America
No. of awards offered: 10
Application Procedure: Application forms can be downloaded from the AIGC website.
Closing Date: Undergraduates: May 1st. Graduates: June 1st

AMERICAN INNS OF COURT

1229 King Street, 2nd Floor, Alexandria, VA 22314, United States of America
Tel: (1) (703) 684 3590
Fax: (1) (703) 684 3607
Email: info@innsofcourt.org
Website: www.innsofcourt.org

American Inns of Court is designed to improve the skills professionalism and ethics of the bench and bar. An American Inn of Court is an amalgam of judges, lawyers, and in some cases law professors and law students. In short it is our mission to foster excellence in professionalism, ethics, civility and legal skills.

Pegasus Scholarship Trust Program for Young Lawyers

Subjects: English legal system.
Purpose: To support talented young American lawyers travel to London, England.
Eligibility: Refer to website.
Level of Study: Graduate
Type: Scholarship
Value: All transportation costs to and from the United States, accommodation and a stipend sufficient for meals and public transport
Length of Study: 6 weeks
Frequency: Annual
Country of Study: United Kingdom
No. of awards offered: 2
Application Procedure: Complete available online application.
Closing Date: October 1st

Warren E. Burger Prize

Subjects: Any topic that addresses issues of legal excellence, civility, ethics, and professionalism.
Purpose: To encourage outstanding scholarship that promotes the ideals of excellence, civility, ethics, and professionalism within the legal profession.
Eligibility: Open to judges, lawyers, professors, students, scholars, and other authors.
Type: Prize
Value: US $5,000
Application Procedure: Check website for further details.
Closing Date: June 15th
Funding: Trusts
Additional Information: The winning essay will be published in the *South Carolina Law Review* and the Warren E. Burger Prize will be presented to the author at the American Inns of Court annual Celebration of Excellence at the United States Supreme Court on October 20th.

For further information contact:

Tel: 703 684 3590 ext 104
Contact: Cindy Dennis

AMERICAN INSTITUTE FOR ECONOMIC RESEARCH (AIER)

PO Box 1000, Great Barrington, MA, 01230, United States of America
Tel: (1) 413 528 1216
Fax: (1) 413 528 0103
Email: fellowship@aier.org
Website: www.aier.org
Contact: fellowships@aier.org

The American Institute for Economic Research (AIER), founded in 1933, is an independent scientific educational organization. The Institute conducts scientific enquiry into general economics with a focus on monetary issues. Attention is also given to business cycle analysis and forecasting as well as monetary economics.

AIER Summer Fellowship

Subjects: Scientific procedures of enquiry, monetary economics, business cycle analysis and forecasting.
Purpose: To further the development of economic scientists.

Eligibility: Open to graduating seniors who are entering doctoral programmes in economics, or those enrolled in doctoral programmes in economics for no longer than 2 years. The programme is not designed for those enrolling into business school.
Level of Study: Postgraduate
Type: Fellowship
Value: US$300 weekly stipend plus room and full board
Length of Study: Two 4-week sessions
Frequency: Annual
Study Establishment: AIER
Country of Study: United States of America
No. of awards offered: 10–12
Application Procedure: Applicants must submit a completed application form, curriculum vitae, personal statement, writing sample, an outline of the proposed course of study and official transcripts. Scholastic references should be sent directly to the director from the referees.
Closing Date: March 14th
Funding: Private
No. of awards given last year: 17
No. of applicants last year: 47

AMERICAN INSTITUTE FOR SRI LANKAN STUDIES (AISLS)

155 Pine Street, Belmont, MA 02478, United States of America
Email: rogersjohnd@aol.com
Website: www.aisls.org
Contact: John Rogers

The American Institute for Sri Lankan Studies (AISLS) was established in 1995, to foster excellence in American research and teaching on Sri Lanka, and to promote the exchange of scholars and scholarly information between the US and Sri Lanka. The Institute serves as the professional association for US-based scholars and other professionals who are interested in Sri Lanka.

AISLS Dissertation Planning Grant

Subjects: Social sciences and humanities with a focus on Sri Lanka.
Purpose: To fund students enrolled at an American university who intend to do dissertation research in Sri Lanka, to be able to make a predissertation visit to Sri Lanka and investigate the feasibility of their topic, sharpen their research design or make other practical arrangements for future research.
Eligibility: Open to candidates enrolled in a PhD programme (or equivalent) in a university in the US.
Level of Study: Doctorate
Type: Grant
Value: US$350 per week and reimbursement for roundtrip airfare and any visa fees paid to the Sri Lankan government
Length of Study: 8 weeks
Frequency: Annual
Application Procedure: Applicants can download the application cover sheet from the website. The completed application cover sheet along with curriculam vitae, a copy of graduate transcript, a project narrative, one-page project bibliography and confidential letter of recommendation is to be sent.
Closing Date: December 4th
Contributor: American Institute for Sri Lankan Studies
Additional Information: Submissions by fax or email will not be accepted.

AISLS Fellowship Program

Subjects: Social sciences and humanities with a focus on Sri Lanka.
Purpose: To encourage research and a better understanding of Sri Lanka.
Eligibility: Open to citizens of the United States who hold a PhD or equivalent academic degree.
Level of Study: Postdoctorate, Research
Type: Fellowship
Value: US$2,500 per month, reimbursement for roundtrip airfare and research expenses
Length of Study: 2–9 months
Frequency: Annual

Application Procedure: Applicants can download the application cover sheet from the website. The completed application cover sheet along with a curriculum vitae and a description of the proposed study should be sent.
Closing Date: December 1st
Contributor: American Institute for Sri Lankan Studies
Additional Information: Submissions by fax or email will not be accepted.

THE AMERICAN INSTITUTE OF BAKING (AIB)

1213 Bakers Way, PO Box 3999, Manhattan, Kansas, 66505-3999, United States of America
Tel: (1) 785 537 4750
Fax: (1) 785 537 1439
Email: kembers@aibonline.org
Website: www.aibonline.org
Contact: Mr Ken Embers, Registrar

The AIB is a non-project corporation, founded by the North American wholesale and retail baking industries in 1991. AIB's staff includes experts in the fields of baking production, research related to experimental baking, cereal science and nutrition; food safety and hygiene; occupational safety and maintenance engineering.

Baking Industry Scholarship

Subjects: Food processing.
Purpose: To support students who are planning to seek employment in the baking or food processing industry.
Eligibility: Open to applicants who are enrolled at the American Institute of Baking
Level of Study: Postgraduate
Type: Scholarship
Length of Study: US$500 to the cost of the full tuition
Frequency: Annual
Country of Study: United States of America
Application Procedure: See the website.
Closing Date: May 1 for fall scholarships and November 1 for spring scholarships

AMERICAN INSTITUTE OF BANGLADESH STUDIES (AIBS)

South Asia Center, 820 Williams Hall 36th Streets, University of Pennsylvania Philadelphia, PA, 19104-6305, United States of America
Tel: (1) 215 898 7475
Fax: (1) 215 573 2138
Email: gwelbon@ccat.sas.upenn.edu
Website: www.aibs.net
Contact: Guy Welbon, President

The American Institute of Bangladesh Studies (AIBS) is a consortium of US universities and colleges involved in research on Bangladesh. It strives to improve the scholarly understanding of Bangladesh culture and society in US and to promote educational exchange between the two countries.

AIBS Senior Fellowship

Subjects: Area and cultural studies.
Purpose: To improve the scholarly understanding of Bangladesh culture and society in the United States.
Eligibility: Open to citizens or permanent residents of the United States who have obtained a PhD.
Level of Study: Doctorate, Research
Type: Fellowships
Value: US$1,000 per month and other benefits
Length of Study: 4–12 months
Frequency: Annual
Country of Study: Bangladesh
Application Procedure: Applicants can download the application form from the website.
Closing Date: February 1st

AMERICAN INSTITUTE OF CERTIFIED PUBLIC ACCOUNTANTS (AICPA)

1211 Avenue of the Americas, New York, NY, 10036-8775, United States of America
Tel: (1) 212 596 6200
Fax: (1) 212 596 6213
Email: MIC_programs@aicpa.org
Website: www.aicpa.org

The American Institute of Certified Public Accountants (AICPA) is a national, professional organization for all Certified Public Accountants. Its mission is to provide members with the resources, information and leadership that enable them to provide valuable services in the highest professional manner to benefit the public as well as employers and clients. In fulfilling its mission, the AICPA works with state CPA organizations and gives priority to those areas where public reliance on CPA skills is most significant.

Fellowships for Minority Doctoral Students

Subjects: Accounting.
Purpose: To support minority students enrolled in a Doctoral programme with a concentration in accounting.
Eligibility: Open to applicants who have earned a Master's degree and/or completed a minimum of 3 years full-time experience in the practice of accounting. For purposes of this program, the AICPA defines minority students as those of Black, Native American, Pacific Island races, or of Hispanic ethnic origin. All applicants must be US citizens.
Level of Study: Doctorate
Type: Fellowship
Value: Up to US$12,000
Frequency: Annual
Country of Study: United States of America
Application Procedure: Applicants must submit their application form, transcript and reference letters.
Closing Date: April 1st
Funding: Foundation
Additional Information: Recipients of the fellowship will attend school on a full-time basis.

John L. Carey Scholarship

Purpose: To provide financial assistance to liberal arts degree holders pursuing graduate studies in accounting. These awards are intended to encourage liberal arts undergraduates to consider professional accounting careers.
Eligibility: Open to applicants who have obtained a liberal arts degree prior to enrolling in a graduate accounting programme. The applicants must be US citizens.
Level of Study: Postgraduate
Type: Scholarship
Value: US$5,000 for 1 year and is renewable for an additional year of study provided satisfactory scholastic progress is maintained
Frequency: Annual
No. of awards offered: 10
Closing Date: April 1st
Funding: Foundation
Contributor: AICPA Foundation fund

AMERICAN INSTITUTE OF INDIAN STUDIES (AIIS)

1130 East 59th Street, Chicago, Illinois, IL 60637, United States of America
Tel: (1) 773 702 8638
Email: aiis@uchicago.edu
Website: www.indiastudies.org
Contact: Mr Ralph W Nicholas, President

The American Institute of Indian Studies (AIIS) is a consortium of American colleges and universities that supports the understanding of India, its people and cultures. AIIS offers a range of fellowships for research in India. It also supports individuals studying the performing arts, operates language programmes in India and offers research facilities to scholars in India.

AIIS Junior Research Fellowships

Subjects: India, its people and culture.
Purpose: To support the advancement of knowledge and understanding.
Eligibility: Open to doctoral candidates at United States of America colleges and universities.
Level of Study: Doctorate
Length of Study: Up to 11 months
Frequency: Annual
Study Establishment: An Indian university
Country of Study: India
Application Procedure: Applicants must write for further information.
Closing Date: July 1st

AIIS Senior Performing and Creative Arts Fellowships

Subjects: Performing and creative arts.
Eligibility: Open to accomplished practitioners of the performing arts of India and creative artists who demonstrate that study in India would enhance their skills, develop their capabilities to teach or perform in the United States of America, enhance American involvement with India's artistic traditions and strengthen their links with peers in India.
Level of Study: Unrestricted
Type: Fellowship
Frequency: Annual
Country of Study: India
Application Procedure: Applicants must write for further information.
Closing Date: July 1st

AIIS Senior Research Fellowships

Subjects: South Asian studies.
Purpose: To enable scholars to pursue further research in India.
Eligibility: Open to scholars who hold a PhD or its equivalent and are either citizens of the United States of America or resident aliens teaching full-time at United States of America colleges and universities.
Level of Study: Postdoctorate
Type: Fellowship
Length of Study: Up to 9 months
Frequency: Annual
Country of Study: India
Application Procedure: Applicants must write for further information.
Closing Date: July 1st

AIIS Senior Scholarly/Professional Development Fellowships

Subjects: India, its people and culture.
Purpose: To support the advancement of knowledge and understanding.
Eligibility: Open to established scholars who have not previously specialized in Indian studies and to established professionals who have not previously worked or studied in India.
Level of Study: Professional development
Type: Fellowship
Length of Study: 6–9 months
Frequency: Annual
Country of Study: India
No. of awards offered: Varies
Application Procedure: Applicants must write for further information.
Closing Date: July 1st

AMERICAN LIBRARY ASSOCIATION (ALA)

50 East Huron Street, Chicago, IL, 60611, United States of America
Tel: (1) 800 545 2433 ext. 4274
Fax: (1) (312) 280 4392
Email: learvin@ala.org
Website: www.ala.org/work/
Contact: Ms Cheryl Malden, ALA Awards Co-ordinator

Each year the American Library Association (ALA) and its member units sponsor awards to honour distinguished service and foster professional growth.

ALA 3M/NMRT Professional Development Grant

Subjects: Library studies.
Purpose: To encourage professional development and participation by new ALA members in national ALA and NMRT activities.
Eligibility: Open to members of the ALA and the New Members Round Table (NMRT) who are working within the territorial United States.
Level of Study: Professional development
Type: Grant
Value: Airfare, hotel, conference registration and US$250
Frequency: Annual
Country of Study: Any country
No. of awards offered: 3
Application Procedure: Applicants must submit nominations to the NMRT Professional Development Grant at ALA.
Closing Date: December 15th
Funding: Commercial
Contributor: 3M

ALA AASL Frances Henne Award

Subjects: Library media.
Purpose: To enable an individual to attend an AASL national conference or ALA Annual Conference for the first time.
Eligibility: Open to school library media specialists with less than 5 years in the profession.
Level of Study: Unrestricted
Type: Grant
Value: US$1,250
Frequency: Annual
Country of Study: Any country
No. of awards offered: 1
Application Procedure: Applicants must write for details.
Funding: Commercial
Contributor: R R Bowker

ALA AASL Highsmith Research Grant

Subjects: Library science.
Purpose: To enable an individual to conduct innovative research aimed at measuring and evaluating the impact of school library media programmes on learning and education.
Eligibility: Open to qualified researchers of any nationality.
Level of Study: Professional development
Type: Research grant
Value: Up to US$5,000
Frequency: Annual
Country of Study: Any country
No. of awards offered: 1
Application Procedure: Applicants must write for details.
Funding: Commercial
Contributor: The Highsmith Company

ALA AASL Information Technology Pathfinder Award

Subjects: Library media.
Purpose: To recognize and honour a school library media specialist for demonstrating vision and leadership through the use of information technology to build lifelong learners.
Eligibility: Open to school library media specialists, supervisors or educators.
Level of Study: Professional development
Type: Scholarship
Value: US$1,000 to the specialist and US$500 to the library, a citation and travel expenses to the ALA Annual Conference
Frequency: Annual
Country of Study: Any country
No. of awards offered: 1
Application Procedure: Applicants must write for details.
Funding: Commercial
Contributor: Information Plus

ALA Beta Phi Mu Award

Subjects: Education for librarianship.
Purpose: To recognize distinguished service.
Eligibility: Open to library school faculty members or others in the library profession.
Level of Study: Professional development

Value: US$1000 and a citation
Frequency: Annual
No. of awards offered: 1
Application Procedure: Applicants must submit 6 copies of nominations to the ALA Awards Programme Office.
Closing Date: December 1st
Funding: Private
Contributor: The Beta Phi Mu International Library Science Honorary Society
No. of awards given last year: 1

ALA Bogle-Pratt International Library Travel Fund

Subjects: Library science.
Purpose: To enable ALA members to attend their first international conference.
Eligibility: Open to ALA members.
Level of Study: Professional development
Type: Travel grant
Value: US$1,000
Frequency: Annual
Country of Study: Any country
No. of awards offered: 1
Application Procedure: Applicants must write for details.
Closing Date: January 1st
Funding: Private
Contributor: The Bogle Memorial Fund
No. of awards given last year: 1

ALA Bound to Stay Bound Book Scholarships

Subjects: Library science.
Purpose: To support study in the field of library service to children in an ALA-accredited programme.
Eligibility: Open to qualified applicants of any nationality who have not started the programme.
Level of Study: Graduate, Postgraduate
Type: Scholarship
Value: US$6,500 each
Frequency: Annual
Country of Study: United States of America or Canada
No. of awards offered: 4
Application Procedure: Applicants must write or email for details.
Closing Date: March 1st
Funding: Commercial
Contributor: Bound to Stay Bound Books, Inc

ALA Carroll Preston Baber Research Grant

Subjects: Library service.
Purpose: To encourage innovative research that could lead to an improvement in library services to any specified group or groups of people.
Level of Study: Unrestricted
Type: Research grant
Value: Up to US$3,000
Frequency: Annual
Country of Study: Any country
No. of awards offered: 1
Application Procedure: Applicants must submit an application including a research proposal.
Funding: Private
Contributor: Eric R Baber
No. of awards given last year: 1
No. of applicants last year: 5
Additional Information: The project should aim to answer a question that is of vital importance to the library community and the researchers should plan to provide documentation of the results of their work. The jury would welcome proposals that involve innovative uses of technology and proposals that involve co-operation between libraries and other agencies, or between librarians and persons in other disciplines.

ALA Christopher J Hoy/ERT Scholarship

Subjects: Library and information studies.
Purpose: To allow individuals to attend an ALA-accredited programme of library and information studies.

Eligibility: Open to applicants who will be attending an ALA-accredited programme of library and information studies leading to a Master's degree.
Level of Study: Postgraduate
Type: Scholarship
Value: US$3,000
Frequency: Annual
Country of Study: Any country
No. of awards offered: 1
Application Procedure: Applicants must write for details.
Funding: Private
Contributor: The family of Christopher J Hoy

ALA David H Clift Scholarship

Subjects: Library science.
Purpose: To enable a worthy candidate to begin a Master's degree.
Eligibility: Open to qualified citizens of Canada or the United States of America pursuing a Master's degree in library science in an ALA-accredited programme.
Level of Study: Postgraduate
Type: Scholarship
Value: US$3,000
Frequency: Annual
Country of Study: Any country
No. of awards offered: 1
Application Procedure: Applicants must write for details.

ALA David Rozkuska Scholarship

Subjects: Library science.
Purpose: To provide financial assistance to an individual who is currently working with government documents in a library.
Eligibility: Open to applicants currently completing a Master's programme in library science.
Level of Study: Postgraduate
Type: Scholarship
Value: US$3,000
Frequency: Annual
Country of Study: Any country
No. of awards offered: 1
Application Procedure: Applicants must write for details.

ALA EBSCO Conference Sponsorship

Subjects: Library science.
Purpose: To allow librarians to attend the ALA Annual Conference.
Eligibility: Open to librarians.
Level of Study: Professional development
Type: Travel grant
Value: Up to US$1,000 for expenses
Frequency: Annual
Country of Study: Any country
No. of awards offered: 10
Application Procedure: Applicants must submit 6 copies of the application and essay.
Closing Date: December 1st
Funding: Commercial
Contributor: EBSCO Subscription Services

ALA Eli M Oboler Memorial Award

Subjects: Intellectual freedom and freedom to read.
Purpose: To award the best published work in the field.
Eligibility: There are no eligibility restrictions.
Level of Study: Unrestricted
Type: Award
Value: US$500 and a Certificate
Frequency: Every 2 years
Country of Study: Any country
No. of awards offered: 1
Application Procedure: Applicants must submit the nominated documents with nominating form.
Closing Date: December 1st
Funding: Private

ALA Elizabeth Futas Catalyst for Change Award

Subjects: Library science.
Purpose: To recognize and honour a librarian who invests time and talent to make positive changes in the profession of librarianship by

taking risks to further the cause, helping new librarians grow and achieve, working for change within the ALA or other library organizations and inspiring colleagues to excel or make the impossible possible.
Type: Award
Value: US$1,000 and a citation
Frequency: Annual
No. of awards offered: 1
Application Procedure: Applicants must submit 6 copies of the application.
Contributor: An endowment administered by the ALA
No. of awards given last year: 1

ALA Equality Award

Subjects: Pay equity, affirmative action, legislative work and non-sexist education.
Purpose: To recognize an outstanding contribution towards the promotion of equality in the library profession. The contribution may be either a sustained one or a single outstanding accomplishment.
Eligibility: Open to members of the library profession.
Level of Study: Professional development
Value: US$500 plus a citation
Frequency: Annual
No. of awards offered: 1
Application Procedure: Applicants must submit 6 copies of nominations to the ALA Awards Programme Office.
Funding: Commercial
Contributor: The Scarecrow Press
No. of awards given last year: 1

ALA Facts on File Grant

Subjects: Library science.
Purpose: To award a library for imaginative programming that would make current affairs more meaningful to an adult audience. Programmes, bibliographies, pamphlets, and innovative approaches of all types and in all media are eligible.
Eligibility: Open to adult librarians.
Level of Study: Professional development
Type: Grant
Value: US$2,000
Frequency: Annual
Country of Study: Any country
No. of awards offered: 1
Application Procedure: Applicants must submit a proposal accompanied by a statement of objective, identification of the current issues, the target audience and the extent of community involvement planned, an outline of planned activities for conducting and promoting the project, a budget summary and details of how the project will be evaluated.
Funding: Commercial
No. of awards given last year: 1

ALA Frances Henne/YALSA/VOYA Research Grant

Subjects: Library science.
Purpose: To provide seed money to an individual, institution or group for a project to encourage research on library service to young adults.
Eligibility: Open to applicants of any nationality.
Level of Study: Unrestricted
Type: Research grant
Value: US$500 minimum
Frequency: Annual
Country of Study: Any country
No. of awards offered: 1
Application Procedure: Applicants must write for details.

ALA Frederick G Melcher Scholarships

Subjects: Library service to children.
Purpose: To provide financial assistance for the professional education of men and women who intend to pursue children's librarianship in an ALA-accredited program.
Eligibility: Open to qualified young persons who have been accepted for admission to an appropriate school.
Level of Study: Postgraduate, Graduate
Type: Scholarship
Value: US$6,000

Frequency: Annual
Study Establishment: An ALA-accredited school
Country of Study: United States of America or Canada
No. of awards offered: 2
Application Procedure: Applicants must write or email for details.
Closing Date: March 1st
Funding: Private

ALA H W Wilson Library Staff Development Grant

Subjects: Library science.
Purpose: To award a library organization whose application demonstrates greatest merit for a programme of staff development designed to further goals and objectives of the library organization.
Type: Grant
Value: US$3,500 and a citation
Frequency: Annual
No. of awards offered: 1
Application Procedure: Applicants must submit 6 copies of the application and documentation to the ALA Awards Programme Office.
Contributor: The H W Wilson Company
No. of awards given last year: 1

ALA Jesse H Shera Award for Distinguished Published Research

Subjects: Library science.
Purpose: To honour an outstanding and original paper reporting the results of research related to libraries.
Eligibility: Authors of nominated articles need not be Library Research Round Table (LRRT) members but the nominations must be made by LRRT members. All entries must be research articles published in English during the calendar year previous to the competition. All nominated articles must relate in at least a general way to library and information studies.
Level of Study: Unrestricted
Type: Prize
Value: US$500
Frequency: Annual
Country of Study: Any country
No. of awards offered: 1
Application Procedure: Applicants wishing to nominate research articles for this award should send three copies of each article together with a covering letter stating that they are a current member of LRRT or that they are acting in their role as journal editor.
Closing Date: January 1st
Funding: Private
No. of awards given last year: 1
No. of applicants last year: 12

ALA John Philip Immroth Award for Intellectual Freedom

Subjects: Intellectual freedom.
Purpose: To recognize a notable contribution to intellectual freedom fuelled by personal courage.
Eligibility: Open to intellectual freedom fighters.
Level of Study: Unrestricted
Type: Award
Value: US$500 plus a citation
Frequency: Annual
Country of Study: Any country
No. of awards offered: 1
Application Procedure: Applicants must submit a detailed statement explaining why the nominator believes that the nominee should receive the award. Nominations should be submitted to IFRT Staff Liaison at the ALA.
Closing Date: December 1st
Funding: Private

ALA Joseph W Lippincott Award

Subjects: Library work with professional library associations.
Purpose: To recognize distinguished service in the profession of librarianship, including outstanding participation in professional library activities, notable published professional writing or other significant activities.
Eligibility: Open to librarians.
Level of Study: Professional development
Type: Award

Value: US$1,000 plus a citation
Frequency: Annual
No. of awards offered: 1
Application Procedure: Applicants must submit 6 copies of nominations to the ALA Awards Programme Office.
Closing Date: December 1st
Funding: Private
Contributor: The late Joseph W Lippincott
No. of awards given last year: 1

ALA Ken Haycock Award for Promoting Librarianship

Subjects: Library science.
Purpose: Honours an individual for contributing significantly to the public recognition and appreciation of librarianship through professional performance, teaching or writing.
Type: Award
Value: US$1,000 and a citation
Frequency: Annual
No. of awards offered: 1
Closing Date: Postmarked by February 2nd
Funding: Private
Contributor: Kenneth Haycock, PhD

ALA Lexis/Nexis/GODORT/ALA Documents to the People Award

Subjects: Library science.
Purpose: To provide funding for research in the field of documents librarianship or in a related area that would benefit the individual's performance as a documents librarian or make a contribution to the field.
Eligibility: Open to individuals and libraries, organizations and other appropriate non-commercial groups.
Level of Study: Unrestricted
Type: Award
Value: US$3,000
Frequency: Annual
Country of Study: Any country
No. of awards offered: 1
Application Procedure: Applicants must submit nominations to the GODORT Staff Liaison at the ALA.
Funding: Commercial
Contributor: Lexis/Nexis

ALA Loleta D Fyan Public Library Research Grant

Subjects: Library service.
Purpose: To facilitate the development and improvement of public libraries and the services they provide.
Eligibility: Applicants can include but are not limited to local, regional or state libraries, associations or organizations including units of the ALA, library schools or individuals.
Level of Study: Unrestricted
Type: Research grant
Value: Up to US$10,000
Frequency: Annual
Country of Study: Any country
No. of awards offered: 1 or more
Application Procedure: Applicants must submit an application form in addition to a proposal and budget.
Closing Date: Applications are accepted at any time
Funding: Private
No. of awards given last year: 1
No. of applicants last year: 10
Additional Information: The project must result in the development and improvement of public libraries and the services they provide, have the potential for broader impact and application beyond meeting a specific local need, should be designed to effect changes in public library services that are innovative and responsive to the future and should be capable of completion within 1 year.

ALA Marshall Cavendish Excellence in Library Programming

Subjects: Library science.
Purpose: To recognize a school or public library for programmes that have community impact and respond to community needs.
Type: Award

Value: US$2,000 and a citation
Frequency: Annual
No. of awards offered: 1
Application Procedure: Applicants must submit 6 copies of the application and supporting material.
Funding: Corporation
Contributor: Marshall Cavendish Corporation

ALA Mary V Gaver Scholarship

Subjects: Library science.
Purpose: To assist library support staff specializing in youth services.
Eligibility: Open to library support staff who are citizens of the United States of America or Canada who are pursuing a Master's degree in library science.
Level of Study: Unrestricted
Type: Scholarship
Value: US$3,000
Frequency: Annual
Country of Study: Any country
No. of awards offered: 1
Application Procedure: Applicants must write for details.
Closing Date: March 1st
No. of awards given last year: 1

ALA Melvil Dewey Medal

Subjects: Library science.
Purpose: To award an individual or group for recent creative professional achievement in library management, training, cataloguing, classification and the tools and techniques of librarianship.
Type: Award
Value: Medal and citation
Frequency: Annual
No. of awards offered: 1
Application Procedure: Applications can be downloaded from the ALA website. Applicants must submit 6 copies of nomination form.
Contributor: The OCLC Forest Press
No. of awards given last year: 1

ALA Miriam L Hornback Scholarship

Subjects: Library science.
Purpose: To assist an individual pursuing a Master's degree.
Eligibility: Open to ALA or library support staff who are pursuing a Master's degree in library science and who are citizens of the United States of America or Canada.
Level of Study: Postgraduate
Type: Scholarship
Value: US$3,000
Frequency: Annual
No. of awards offered: 1
Application Procedure: Applicants must write for details.
Closing Date: March 1st
No. of awards given last year: 2

ALA New Leaders Travel Grant

Subjects: Library science.
Purpose: To enhance professional development and improve the expertise of individuals new to the field by making possible their attendance at major professional development activities.
Eligibility: Open to qualified public librarians.
Level of Study: Professional development
Type: Travel grant
Value: Plaque and travel grant of up to US$1,500 per applicant
Frequency: Annual
Country of Study: Any country
No. of awards offered: 1
Application Procedure: Applicants must write for details.

ALA NMRT/EBSCO Scholarship

Subjects: Library science.
Purpose: To enable an individual to begin an MLS degree in an ALA-accredited programme.
Eligibility: Open to citizens of the United States of America and Canada.
Level of Study: Postgraduate
Type: Scholarship

Value: US$1,000
Frequency: Annual
Country of Study: Any country
No. of awards offered: 1
Application Procedure: Applicants must write for details.
Closing Date: April 1st

ALA Penguin Putnam Books for Young Readers Award

Subjects: Library science.
Purpose: To allow children's librarians to attend the Annual Conference of the ALA.
Eligibility: Open to members of the Association for Library Service to Children with between 1 and 10 years of experience who have never attended an ALA Annual Conference.
Level of Study: Professional development
Type: Award
Value: US$600
Frequency: Annual
Country of Study: Any country
No. of awards offered: 4
Application Procedure: Applicants must telephone or email for details.
Closing Date: December 3rd
Funding: Commercial
Contributor: Penguin Group, USA
No. of awards given last year: 4

ALA Samuel Lazerow Fellowship for Research in Acquisitions or Technical Services

Subjects: Acquisitions or technical services.
Purpose: To foster advances in acquisitions or technical services by providing a fellowship for travel or writing in those fields.
Eligibility: Open to qualified librarians.
Level of Study: Professional development
Type: Fellowship
Value: US$1,000 plus a citation
Frequency: Annual
Country of Study: Any country
No. of awards offered: 1
Application Procedure: Applicants must write for details and are advised to refer to the awards section of the ACRL website www.ala.org/acrl
Closing Date: First Friday in December
Funding: Corporation
Contributor: Thomson Scientific
No. of awards given last year: 1

For further information contact:

ACRL, 50 East Huron Street, Chicago, IL 60611, United States of America

ALA Schneider Family Book Award

Subjects: Library science.
Purpose: The Schneider Family Book Awards honour an author or illustrator for a book that embodies an artistic expression of the disability experience for child and adolescent audiences. The book must emphasize the artistic expression of the disability experience for children and or adolescent audiences. The book must portray some aspect of living with a disability or that of a friend or family member, whether the disability is physical, mental or emotional.
Type: Award
Value: US$5,000 and a citation for each winner
Frequency: Annual
No. of awards offered: 3
Application Procedure: Applicants must submit 8 copies of the application.
Closing Date: December 1st
Funding: Private
Contributor: Katherine Schneider

ALA Shirley Olofson Memorial Awards

Subjects: Library science.
Purpose: To allow individuals to attend ALA conferences.

Eligibility: Open to members of the ALA who are also current or potential members of the New Members Round Table. Applicants should not have attended any more than five conferences.
Level of Study: Unrestricted
Type: Award
Value: US$1,000
Frequency: Annual
Country of Study: Any country
No. of awards offered: Varies
Application Procedure: Applicants must write for details.
Closing Date: December 15th

ALA Spectrum Initiative Scholarship Program

Subjects: Library and information studies.
Purpose: To encourage admission to an ALA recognized Master's degree programme by the four largest underrepresented minority groups.
Eligibility: Open to citizens of the United States of America or Canada only, from one of the largest underrepresented groups. These are African American or African Canadian, Asian or Pacific Islander, Latino or Hispanic and native people of the United States of America or Canada.
Level of Study: Postgraduate
Type: Scholarship
Value: US$5,000
Frequency: Annual
Country of Study: United States of America or Canada
No. of awards offered: 25–50
Application Procedure: Applicants must request details via fax or visit the website.
Closing Date: March 1st

ALA Sullivan Award for Public Library Administrators Supporting Services to Children

Subjects: Library science.
Purpose: To an individual who has shown exceptional understanding and support of public library service to children while having general management/supervisory/administrative responsibility that has included public library service to children in its scope.
Type: Award
Value: Citation and commemorative gift
Frequency: Annual
No. of awards offered: 1
Application Procedure: Applicants must submit 6 copies of the application.
Closing Date: December 1st
Funding: Private
Contributor: Peggy Sullivan, PhD

ALA W Y Boyd Literary Award

Subjects: The writing and publishing of outstanding war-related fiction.
Purpose: To award an author who has written a military novel that honours the service of American veterans and military personnel during a time of war: 1861–1865, 1914–1918 or 1939–1945.
Type: Award
Value: US$5,000 and a citation
Frequency: Annual
No. of awards offered: 1
Application Procedure: Applicants must submit 6 copies of the application.
Closing Date: December 1st
Funding: Private
Contributor: William Young Boyd II

ALA YALSA/Baker and Taylor Conference Grants

Subjects: Library science.
Purpose: To allow young adult librarians who work directly with young adults in either a public library or a school library, to attend the Annual Conference of the ALA.
Eligibility: Open to members of the Young Adult Library Services Association with between 1 and 10 years of library experience who have never attended an ALA Annual Conference.
Level of Study: Professional development
Type: Grant
Value: US$1,000

Frequency: Annual
Country of Study: Any country
No. of awards offered: 2
Application Procedure: Applicants must submit applications to the Young Adult Library Services Association, ALA.
Closing Date: December 1st

ALA/Information Today Library of the Future Award

Subjects: Library science.
Purpose: To honour an individual library, library consortium, group of librarians or support organization for innovative planning for applications of, or development of, patron training programmes about information technology in a library setting.
Type: Award
Value: US$1,500 and a citation
Frequency: Annual
No. of awards offered: 1
Application Procedure: Applicants must submit 6 copies of the application.
Closing Date: December 1st
Funding: Private
Contributor: Information Today, Inc
Additional Information: The American Library Association offers a number of other awards in various fields related to library science, including the following medals and citations with no cash prizes: the Randolph Caldecott Medal, the James Bennett Childs Award, the Dartmouth Medal, the John Newberry Medal, the Laura Ingalls Wilder Medal, the ASCLA Exceptional Service Award, the Armed Forces Librarians Achievement Citation, the Francis Joseph Campbell Citation, the Margaret Mann Citation, the Isadore Gilbert Mudge Citation, the Esther J Piercy Award, the Distinguished Library Service Award for School Administrators and the Trustees Citations. A full list of awards is available from the ALA.

Scholastic Library Publishing Award

Subjects: Library work with children and young people to high school age.
Purpose: To recognize a librarian whose unusual contribution to the stimulation and guidance of reading by children and young people exemplifies outstanding achievement in the profession. The award is given either for outstanding continuing service, or in recognition of one particular contribution of lasting value.
Eligibility: Open to community and school librarians.
Level of Study: Professional development
Value: US$1,000 plus a citation
Frequency: Annual
No. of awards offered: 1
Application Procedure: Applicants must submit 6 copies of the application to the ALA Awards Programme Office.
Closing Date: December 1st
Funding: Commercial
Contributor: Gale, a part of Cengage learning
No. of awards given last year: 1

AMERICAN LUNG ASSOCIATION

61 Broadway 6th Floor, New York, NY, 10006, United States of America
Tel: (1) 212 889 3370
Fax: (1) 212 889 3375
Email: info@alany.org
Website: www.lungusa.org/research
Contact: Ms Evita Mendoza

The American Lung Association is the oldest voluntary health organization in the United States, with a National Office and constituent and affiliate associations around the country. Founded in 1904 to fight tuberculosis, the American Lung Association today fights lung disease in all its forms, with special emphasis on asthma, tobacco control and environmental health.

Lung Health (LH) Research Dissertation Grants

Subjects: Psychosocial, behavioral, health services, health policy, epidemiological, biostatistical and educational matters related to lung disease.

Purpose: To provide financial assistance for Doctoral research training for dissertation research on issues relevant to lung disease.
Eligibility: Open to citizens or permanent residents of the United States.
Level of Study: Doctorate
Type: Research grant
Value: US$21,000 per year
Frequency: Annual
Country of Study: United States of America
Closing Date: September 1st
Funding: Corporation, foundation, government

AMERICAN METEOROLOGICAL SOCIETY (AMS)

45 Beacon Street, Boston, MA, 02108-3693, United States of America
Tel: (1) 617 227 2426
Fax: (1) 617 742 8718
Email: dfernand@ametsoc.org
Website: www.ametsoc.org

The American Meteorological Society (AMS) promotes the development and dissemination of information and education on the atmospheric and related oceanic and hydrologic sciences and the advancement of their professional applications. Founded in 1919, AMS has a membership of more than 11,000 professionals, professors, students and weather enthusiasts.

AMS Graduate Fellowship in the History of Science
Subjects: History of the atmospheric or related oceanic or hydrologic sciences.
Purpose: To provide financial support to students who wish to complete a dissertation in the related fields.
Eligibility: Open to graduate students in good standing who propose to complete the dissertation in the subject mentioned above.
Level of Study: Graduate, Research
Type: Fellowship
Value: US$15,000 stipend
Length of Study: 1 year
Frequency: Annual
Country of Study: United States of America
Application Procedure: Applicants must submit a complete application form along with a cover letter with curriculum vitae, official transcripts from undergraduate and graduate institutions, a typewritten, detailed description of the dissertation topic and proposed research plan (maximum 10 pages) and 3 letters of recommendation.
Closing Date: February 9th
Funding: Foundation
Additional Information: Any questions regarding the fellowship opportunity may be directed to Donna Sampson, 617 227 2426 ext 246 or Stephanie Armstrong, (617) 227-2426 ext. 235.

AMS Industry/Government Graduate Fellowships
Subjects: Atmospheric or related oceanic or hydrologic sciences.
Purpose: To attract promising young scientists to prepare for careers in the atmospheric and related oceanic and hydrologic fields.
Eligibility: Applicants must be US citizens or hold permanent resident status entering their first year of graduate school and provide evidence of acceptance as a full-time student at an accredited US institution at the time of the award. Applicants must have a minimum grade point average of 3.25 on a 4.0-point scale.
Level of Study: Graduate
Type: Fellowship
Value: $23,000 to each recipient for a 9-month period
Length of Study: 9 months
Frequency: Annual
Application Procedure: Application form should be completed and written references, official transcripts, and GRE score reports, may be sent under separate cover.
Closing Date: February 22nd
Contributor: Industry leaders and government agencies
Additional Information: The evaluation of applicants will be based on applicant's performance as an undergraduate student, including academic records, recommendations and GRE scores.

AMERICAN MUSEUM OF NATURAL HISTORY (AMNH)

Central Park West, 79th Street, New York, NY, 10024-5192, United States of America
Tel: (1) 212 769 5040
Fax: (1) 212 769 5495
Email: yna@amnh.org
Website: www.amnh.org
Contact: Ms Maria Dixon, Office of Grants & Fellowships

For 125 years, the American Museum of Natural History (AMNH) has been one of the world's pre-eminent science and research institutions, renowned for its colletions and exhibitions that illuminate millions of years of the Earth's evolution.

AMNH Annette Kade Graduate Student Fellowship Program
Subjects: Vertebrate zoology, invertebrate zoology, paleontology, physical sciences and anthropology.
Purpose: To partner with French and German institutions and to permit an exchange of graduate students.
Eligibility: Open to students who are engaged in full-time research towards a Master's or PhD degree.
Level of Study: Postgraduate
Type: Fellowship
Value: US$2,500 monthly stipend for housing and food for a 3 month stay. Travel will be provided in the form of roundtrip airfare of up to US$1,500
Length of Study: 3 months
Frequency: Annual
Country of Study: United States of America and Europe
No. of awards offered: 4
Application Procedure: Applicants must submit their curriculum vitae, project description, reference letters and transcripts along with their application form.
Closing Date: March 8th/June 15th/October 8th
Funding: Foundation
Additional Information: Each student will pursue a predetermined research project with a science mentor. This mentor will also ensure that the student is exposed to the other disciplines in the Museum. Research interest must be in one of the subjects mentioned above and it must be in keeping with the Museum's research interests.

AMNH Research Fellowships
Subjects: Vertebrate zoology, invertebrate zoology, paleozoology, anthropology, astrophysics and Earth and planetary sciences.
Purpose: To provide financial support to recent postdoctoral investigators and established scientists to carry out a specific project within a limited time period.
Eligibility: Open to students with a Doctoral degree or an equivalent degree.
Level of Study: Postdoctorate, Research
Type: Research fellowship
Value: Varies
Length of Study: 2 years
Frequency: Annual
Study Establishment: American Museum of Natural History
Country of Study: United States of America
Application Procedure: Applicants can obtain the application form online or from the office of grants and fellowships. The application requires a project description with bibliography, budget, curriculum vitae including list of publications and letters of recommendation.
Closing Date: November 15th

AMERICAN MUSIC CENTER, INC.

30 West 26th Street, Suite 1001, New York, NY, 10010-2011, United States of America
Tel: (1) 212 366 5260
Fax: (1) 212 366 5265
Email: Anna@amc.net
Website: www.amc.net
Contact: Anna Smith, Manager of Grantmaking Programmes

The American Music Center is a non-profit membership and service organization. The Center's mission is to build a national community for new American music.

American Music Center Composer Assistance Program

Subjects: Music.
Purpose: To support individual composers to realize their music in performance.
Eligibility: American composers in good standing with the American Music Center.
Level of Study: Professional development
Type: Fellowship
Value: Up to US$5,000
Length of Study: Variable
Frequency: Annual
Country of Study: United States of America
Application Procedure: Applicants must download guidelines from website.
Closing Date: February 1st
Funding: Private
Contributor: The Helen F Whitaker Fund

For further information contact:

Grants Manager, American Music Center 30 West 26th Street, Suite 1001, New York, 10010-2011, United States of America
Contact: Jennifer Clarke

THE AMERICAN MUSIC SCHOLARSHIP ASSOCIATION, INC. (AMSA)

441 Vine Street, Suite 1030, Cincinnati, OH, 45202, United States of America
Tel: (1) 513 421 5342
Fax: (1) 513 421 2672
Email: wpc@cincinnatiwpc.org
Website: www.cincinnatiwpc.org
Contact: Founder/Artistic Director

The American Music Scholarship Association (AMSA) produces the annual world piano competition in Cincinnati. AMSA also provides outreach programmes to Cincinnati children (e.g. The Bach, Beethoven, and Brahms Club) and worldwide performances. The young artist division winners perform at Carnegie Hall and the gold medallist of the artist division performs at Lincoln Center's Alice Tully Hall.

AMSA World Piano Competition

Subjects: Musical performance on the piano.
Purpose: To encourage the careers of aspiring young pianists and expose them to the performances of great musicians.
Eligibility: Open to piano students of any nationality who are between the ages of 5 and 30.
Level of Study: Unrestricted
Type: Scholarship
Value: The Artist Division's first prize is US$10,000 plus a fully managed debut recital at the Lincoln Center in New York. The second prize is US$3,000, the third US$2,000, the fourth US$1,000, the fifth US$500 and the sixth US$300. The Young Artists Division grand prize at levels 9–12 is US$1,500
Country of Study: Any country
Application Procedure: Applicants must apply in compliance with the full competition rules and regulations, which are available on request and on the website.
Closing Date: January 1st
Funding: Private

AMERICAN MUSICOLOGICAL SOCIETY (AMS)

6010 College Station, Brunswick ME, 04011-8451, United States of America
Tel: (1) 207 798 4243
Fax: (1) 207 798 4254
Email: ams@ams-net.org
Website: www.ams-net.org
Contact: Executive Director

The American Musicological Society (AMS) was founded in 1934 as a non-profit organization, with the aim of advancing research in the various fields of music as a branch of learning and scholarship. In 1951, the Society became a constituent member of the American Council of Learned Societies.

Alfred Einstein Award

Subjects: Musicology.
Purpose: To honour a musicological article of exceptional merit by a scholar in the early stages of his or her career.
Eligibility: Open to citizens or permanent residents of Canada or the United States of America.
Level of Study: Professional development
Type: Prize
Value: Varies
Frequency: Annual
No. of awards offered: 1
Application Procedure: Applicants must be nominated. The committee will entertain articles from any individual, including eligible authors who are encouraged to nominate their own articles. Nominations should include the name of the author, the title of the article and the name and year of the periodical or other collection in which it was published. A curriculum vitae is also required.
Closing Date: May 1st
Funding: Private

Alvin H Johnson AMS 50 Dissertation One Year Fellowships

Subjects: Any field of musical research.
Purpose: To encourage research in the various fields of music as a branch of learning and scholarship.
Eligibility: Open to full-time students registered for a doctorate at a North American university, who have completed all formal degree requirements except the dissertation at the time of full application. Open to all students without regard to nationality, race, religion or gender.
Level of Study: Doctorate, Postgraduate
Type: Fellowship
Value: US$17,500
Length of Study: 1 year
Frequency: Annual
Country of Study: United States of America or Canada
No. of awards offered: 5–6
Application Procedure: Application forms will be sent via the Directors of Graduate Study at all doctorate-granting institutions in North America. They will also be available directly from the Society and the website. Applications must include a curriculum vitae, certification of enrolment and degree completed and two supporting letters from faculty members, one of whom must be the principal adviser of the dissertation. A detailed dissertation prospectus and a completed chapter or comparable written work on the dissertation should accompany the full application. All documents should be submitted in triplicate.
Closing Date: January 15th
Funding: Private
Additional Information: Any submission for a doctoral degree in which the emphasis is on musical scholarship is eligible. The award is not intended for support of early stages of research and it is expected that a recipient's dissertation will be completed within the fellowship year. An equivalent major award from another source may not normally be held concurrently unless the AMS award is accepted on an honorary basis.

AMS Subventions for Publications

Subjects: Musicology.

Purpose: To help individuals with expenses involved in the publication of works of musical scholarship, including books, articles and works in non-print media.

Eligibility: Open to younger scholars and scholars in the early stages of their careers. Proposals for projects that make use of newer technologies are welcomed.

Level of Study: Professional development

Type: Grant

Value: US$500–2,000 with a maximum of US$2,500 available

Application Procedure: Applicants must submit a short, written abstract of up to 1,000 words describing the project and its contribution to musical scholarship, a copy of the article or other equivalent sample, a copy of a contract or letter of agreement from the journal editor or publisher indicating final acceptance for publication, and a detailed budget and explanation of the expenses to which the subvention would be applied. Wherever possible expenses should be itemized. If the publication is a book a representative chapter should be submitted.

Closing Date: March 15th or September 15th

Funding: Private

Additional Information: No individual can receive a subvention more than once in a 3-year period.

Howard Mayer Brown Fellowship

Subjects: Musicology.

Purpose: To increase the presence of minority scholars and teachers in musicology.

Eligibility: Open to candidates who have completed at least 1 year of academic work at an institution with a graduate programme in musicology and who intend to complete a PhD in the field. Applicants must be members of a group historically underrepresented in the discipline, including African Americans, Native Americans, Hispanic Americans and Asian Americans. Candidates will normally be citizens or permanent residents of the United States of America or Canada. There are no restrictions on age or gender.

Level of Study: Postgraduate

Type: Fellowship

Value: US$17,000 for 12 months

Length of Study: 1 year

Frequency: Annual

Study Establishment: An institution which offers a graduate programme in musicology

Country of Study: United States of America or Canada

Application Procedure: Applicants must be nominated. Nominations may come from a faculty member of the institution at which the student is enrolled, from a member of the AMS at another institution, or directly from the student. Supporting documents must include a letter summarizing the candidate's academic background, letters of support from three faculty members and samples of the applicant's work such as term papers or any published material.

Closing Date: January 15th of the year in which the fellowship is awarded

Funding: Private

Additional Information: The AMS encourages the institution at which the recipient is pursuing his or her degree to offer continuing financial support. Further information is available on request.

Noah Greenberg Award

Subjects: Musicology.

Purpose: To provide a grant-in-aid to stimulate active co-operation between scholars and performers by recognizing and fostering outstanding contributions to historical performing practices.

Eligibility: Both scholars and performers may apply. Applicants need not be members of the Society.

Level of Study: Professional development

Type: Award

Value: Varies

Frequency: Annual

No. of awards offered: 1–2

Application Procedure: Applicants must submit three copies of a description of the project, a detailed budget and supporting materials such as articles or tapes of performances which are relevant to the project. Applications must be sent to the chair of the Noah Greenberg Award Committee.

Closing Date: August 15th

Funding: Private

Otto Kinkeldey Award

Subjects: Musicology.

Purpose: To award the work of musicological scholarship such as a major book, edition or other piece of scholarship that best exemplifies the highest quality of originality, interpretation, logic, clarity of thought and communication.

Eligibility: The work must have been published during the previous year in any language and in any country by a scholar who is a citizen or permanent resident of Canada or the United States of America.

Level of Study: Professional development

Type: Prize

Value: Varies

Frequency: Annual

Application Procedure: Applicants must write for details.

Closing Date: May 1st

Funding: Private

Additional Information: Further information is available on request.

Paul A Pisk Prize

Subjects: Musicology.

Purpose: To encourage scholarship.

Eligibility: Open to graduate students whose abstracts have been submitted to the Programme Committee of the Society and papers accepted for inclusion in the Annual Meeting. Open to all students without regard to nationality, race, religion or gender.

Level of Study: Graduate

Type: Prize

Value: US$1,000

Frequency: Annual

Country of Study: United States of America or Canada

No. of awards offered: 1

Application Procedure: Applicants must submit three copies of the complete text paper to the chair of the Pisk Prize Committee. The submission must be accompanied by a statement from the student's academic adviser affirming the graduate student status of the applicant.

Closing Date: October 1st

Funding: Private

Additional Information: Further information is available on request.

AMERICAN NUCLEAR SOCIETY (ANS)

555 North Kensington Avenue, La Grange Park, IL, 60526, United States of America

Tel: (1) 708 352 6611
Fax: (1) 708 352 0499
Email: outreach@ans.org
Website: www.ans.org
Contact: Scholarship Programme

The American Nuclear Society (ANS) is a non-profit, international, scientific and educational organization. It was established by a group of individuals who recognized the need to unify the professional activities within the diverse fields of nuclear science and technology.

Alan F Henry/Paul A Greebler Scholarship

Subjects: Reactor physics.

Purpose: To aid students pursuing studies in the field of nuclear science.

Eligibility: Open to full-time graduate students at a North American university engaged in Master's or PhD research in the area of nuclear reactor physics or radiation transport. Applicants may be of any nationality.

Level of Study: Postdoctorate, Graduate

Type: Scholarship

Value: US$3,500

Length of Study: Varies

Frequency: Annual

Study Establishment: An accredited institution

Country of Study: United States of America

No. of awards offered: 1

Application Procedure: Applicants must complete an application form available from the organization. An official grade transcript and three completed confidential reference forms are also required. Applications on line at www.ans.org/honors/scholarships

Closing Date: February 1st
No. of awards given last year: 1
Additional Information: Further information is available either on request or from the website.

ANS Undergraduate/Graduate Pittsbugh Local Section Scholarship

Subjects: Nuclear science and technology.
Value: US$2000-3,500; undergraduate/graduate US$ 3,000
Frequency: Annual
Study Establishment: An accredited institution
Country of Study: United States of America
Application Procedure: Applications on line at www.ans.org/honors/scholarships
Closing Date: February 1st

Delayed Education Scholarship for Women

Subjects: Must be a mature woman whose undergraduate studies in nuclear science, nuclear engineering or a nuclear-related field have been delayed.
Value: US$4,000
Frequency: Annual
Study Establishment: An accredited institution
Country of Study: United States of America
Application Procedure: Applications on line at www.ans.org/honors/scholarships
Closing Date: February 1st

Everitt P Blizard Scholarship

Subjects: Radiation protection and shielding.
Purpose: To aid students pursuing studies in the field of radiation protection and shielding.
Eligibility: Open to full-time graduate students in a programme leading to an advanced degree in nuclear science, nuclear engineering or a nuclear-related field. Applicants must be citizens of the United States of America or permanent residents and be enrolled in an accredited institution in the United States of America.
Level of Study: Graduate
Type: Scholarship
Value: US$3,000
Length of Study: Varies
Frequency: Annual
Study Establishment: An accredited institution
Country of Study: United States of America
No. of awards offered: 1
Application Procedure: Applicants must complete an application form available from the organization. An official grade transcript and three completed confidential reference forms are also required. Applications on line at www.ans.org/honors/scholarships
Closing Date: February 1st
No. of awards given last year: 1
Additional Information: Further information is available either on request or from the website.

James F Schumar Scholarship

Subjects: Materials science and technology for nuclear applications.
Eligibility: Open to citizens of the United States of America or holders of a permanent resident visa who are full-time graduate students enrolled in a programme leading to an advanced degree
Level of Study: Graduate
Type: Scholarship
Value: US$3,000
Frequency: Annual
Study Establishment: An accredited institution
Country of Study: United States of America
No. of awards offered: 1
Application Procedure: Applicants must submit a request for an application form that includes the name of the university the candidate will be attending, the year the candidate will be in during the autumn of the award, the major course of study and a stamped addressed envelope. Completed applications must include a grade transcript and three confidential reference forms. Candidates must be sponsored by an ANS section, division, student branch, committee, member or organization member. The applicant should indicate on the nomination

form that he or she is applying for the MSTD Scholarship. Applications on line at www.ans.org/honors/scholarships
Closing Date: February 1st
No. of awards given last year: 1
Additional Information: Further information is available either on request or from the website.

John and Muriel Landis Scholarship Awards

Subjects: Nuclear physics and engineering.
Purpose: To help students who have greater than average financial need.
Eligibility: Candidates should be planning to pursue a career in nuclear engineering or a nuclear-related field. Candidates must have greater than average financial need, and consideration will be given to conditions or experiences that render the student disadvantaged. Applicants need not be citizens of the United States of America.
Level of Study: Graduate
Type: Scholarship
Value: US$4,000
Frequency: Annual
Study Establishment: An accredited institution
Country of Study: United States of America
No. of awards offered: Up to 8
Application Procedure: Applicants must request an application form and include the name and a letter of commitment from the university the candidate will be attending, the year the candidate will be in the Autumn of the award, the major course of study and a stamped addressed envelope. Completed applications must include a grade transcript and three confidential reference forms. Candidates must be sponsored by an ANS section, division, student branch, committee, member or organization member. Applications on line at www.ans.org/honors/scholarships
Closing Date: February 1st

John R. Lamarsh Scholarship

Subjects: Nuclear science and technology.
Value: US$2,000
Frequency: Annual
Study Establishment: An accredited institution
Country of Study: United States of America
Application Procedure: Applications on line at www.ans.org/honors/scholarships
Closing Date: February 1st
No. of awards given last year: 1

Operations and Power Division Scholarship Award

Subjects: Nuclear science and technology.
Value: US$2,500
Frequency: Annual
Study Establishment: An accredited institution
Country of Study: United States of America
Application Procedure: Applications on line at www.ans.org/honors/scholarships
Closing Date: February 1st

Robert A Dannels Memorial Scholarship

Subjects: Nuclear science or nuclear engineering.
Eligibility: Open to citizens of the United States of America or holders of a permanent resident visa who are full-time graduate students enrolled in a programme leading to an advanced degree or in a graduate-level course of study leading towards a degree in mathematics and computation. Handicapped persons are encouraged to apply.
Level of Study: Graduate
Type: Scholarship
Value: US$3,500
Frequency: Annual
Study Establishment: An accredited institution
Country of Study: United States of America
No. of awards offered: 1
Application Procedure: Applicants must submit a request for an application form that includes the name of the university the candidate will be attending, the year the candidate will be in during the Autumn of the award, the major course of study and a stamped addressed envelope. Completed applications must include a grade transcript and three confidential reference forms. Candidates must be sponsored by

an ANS section, division, student branch, committee, member or organization member. Applications on line at www.ans.org/honors/scholarships

Closing Date: February 1st

Verne R Dapp Memorial Scholarship

Subjects: Nuclear science or nuclear engineering.
Eligibility: Open to citizens of the United States of America or holders of a permanent resident visa who are full-time graduate students enrolled in a programme leading to an advanced degree.
Level of Study: Graduate
Type: Scholarship
Value: US$3,000
Frequency: Every 2 years
Study Establishment: An accredited institution
Country of Study: United States of America
No. of awards offered: 1
Application Procedure: Applicants must submit a request for an application form that includes the name of the university the candidate will be attending, the year the candidate will be in during the Autumn of the award, the major course of study and a stamped addressed envelope. Completed applications must include a grade transcript and three confidential reference forms. Candidates must be sponsored by an ANS section, division, student branch, committee, member or organization member. Applications on line at www.ans.org/honors/scholarships
Closing Date: February 1st

Vogt Radiochemistry Scholarship Award

Subjects: Student must be enrolled in or proposing to undertake research in radioanalytical chemistry, analytical chemistry or analytical applications of nuclear science.
Level of Study: Graduate, or undergraduate
Value: US$2,000 if awarded to an undergraduate (Junior/Senior) US$3,000 if awarded to a graduate
Frequency: Annual
Country of Study: United States of America
No. of awards offered: 1 per year
Application Procedure: Applications on line at www.ans.org/honors/scholarships
Closing Date: February 1st
No. of awards given last year: 1

Walter Meyer Scholarship

Subjects: Nuclear physics and engineering.
Eligibility: Open to full-time graduate students in a programme leading to an advanced degree in nuclear science, nuclear engineering or a nuclear-related field. Applicants must be citizens of the United States of America or permanent residents and be enrolled in an accredited institution in the United States of America.
Type: Scholarship
Value: US$3,500
Length of Study: Varies
Frequency: Every 2 years
Study Establishment: An accredited institution
Country of Study: United States of America
No. of awards offered: 1
Application Procedure: Applicants must complete an application form available from the organization. An official grade transcript and three completed confidential reference forms are also required. Applications on line at www.ans.org/honors/scholarships.
Closing Date: February 1st
Additional Information: Further information is available either on request or from the website.

THE AMERICAN NUMISMATIC SOCIETY (ANS)

96 Fulton Street, New York, NY, 10038, United States of America
Tel: (1) 212 571 4470
Fax: (1) 212 571 4479
Email: wartenberg@numismatics.org
Website: www.numismatics.org
Contact: Dr Ute Wartenberg Kagan, Executive Director

The mission of the American Numismatic Society (ANS) is to be the preeminent national institution advancing the study and appreciation of coins, medals and related objects of all cultures as historical and artistic documents. It aims to do this by maintaining the foremost numismatic collection and library, supporting scholarly research and publications, and sponsoring educational and interpretative programmes for diverse audiences.

Donald Groves Fund

Subjects: Early American numismatics involving material dating no later than 1800.
Purpose: To promote publications in the field.
Level of Study: Postgraduate, Research
Value: Varies. Funding is available for travel and other expenses in association with research as well as for publication costs
Frequency: Annual
Country of Study: United States of America
No. of awards offered: Varies
Application Procedure: Applicants must address applications to the Secretary of the Society and must include an outline of the proposed research, the method of accomplishing the research, the funding requested and the specific use to which the funding will be put. Applications will be reviewed periodically by the Donald Groves Fund Committee.
Closing Date: Applications are accepted at any time
Funding: Private

For further information contact:

American Numismatic Society (ANS), 75 Varick Street, Floor 11, New York, NY, 10013, United States of America
Contact: Dr Ute Wartenberg Kagan, Executive Director

Frances M Schwartz Fellowship

Subjects: Numismatic methodology and museum practice.
Purpose: To assist the Fellow in the study of Greek and Roman fields relevant to the subject.
Eligibility: Open to students of numismatics who possess a Bachelor of Arts or equivalent degree.
Level of Study: Postgraduate, Professional development
Type: Fellowship
Value: Up to US$5,000
Frequency: Annual
Country of Study: United States of America
No. of awards offered: Varies
Application Procedure: Applicants must write for details.
Closing Date: March 1st
Funding: Private

Grants for ANS Summer Seminar in Numismatics

Subjects: Numismatics.
Purpose: To provide a selected number of graduate students with a deeper understanding of the contribution that this subject makes to other fields.
Eligibility: Open to applicants who have had at least 1 year's graduate study at a university in the United States of America or Canada and who are students of classical studies, history, near eastern studies or other humanistic fields.
Level of Study: Postgraduate
Type: Grant
Value: US$4,000
Length of Study: 9 weeks during the Summer
Frequency: Annual
Study Establishment: Museum of the American Numismatic Society
Country of Study: United States of America
No. of awards offered: Approx. 10
Application Procedure: Applicants must write well in advance for details of the application process.
Closing Date: February 15th
Funding: Private
No. of awards given last year: 12
No. of applicants last year: 21
Additional Information: One or two students from overseas are usually accepted to the seminar but will not receive a grant.

THE AMERICAN OCCUPATIONAL THERAPY FOUNDATION (AOTF)

4720 Montgomery Lane, PO Box 31220, Bethesda, MD, 20824-1220,
United States of America
Tel: (1) 301 652 6611
Fax: (1) 301 656 3620
Email: aotf@aotf.org
Website: www.aotf.org

The AOTF is a charitable, non-profit organization created in 1965 to advance the science of occupational therapy and increase public understanding of its value.

The A. Jean Ayres Award
Subjects: Occupational therapy.
Purpose: To recognize occupational therapy clinicians, educators and researchers who have made significant contributions to their profession.
Eligibility: Open to candidates who are members of the American Occupational Therapy Association.
Level of Study: Doctorate
Type: Award
Value: US$500, a plaque and acknowledgement at the Annual conference of the American Occupational Therapy Association
Frequency: Annual
No. of awards offered: 2
Application Procedure: Five copies of the nomination package must be sent to the chairman of the AOTF Awards of Recognition Committee.
Contributor: American Occupational Therapy Foundation

AOTF Certificate of Appreciation
Subjects: Occupational therapy.
Purpose: To recognize outstanding service toward the Foundation.
Eligibility: Open to any individual, agency, business or other institutions.
Level of Study: Doctorate, Postgraduate
Type: Award
Value: A certificate of appreciation and acknowledgement at the annual conference
Frequency: Annual
Application Procedure: Four copies of a letter of nomination and candidate's curriculum vitae must be sent.
Funding: Foundation
Contributor: American Occupational Therapy Foundation

AMERICAN ORCHID SOCIETY

16700 AOS Lane, Delray Beach, West Palm Beach, FL, 33446-4351,
United States of America
Tel: (1) 561 404 2000
Fax: (1) 561 404 2100
Email: theaos@aos.org
Website: www.aos.org
Contact: Ms Pamela Giust, Awards Registrar

Grants for Orchid Research
Subjects: Orchid research.
Purpose: To advance scientific study of orchids in every respect and to assist in the publication of scholarly and popular scientific literature on orchids.
Eligibility: There are no eligibility restrictions.
Level of Study: Postgraduate
Type: Grant
Value: US$500–12,000
Length of Study: Up to 3 years
Frequency: Annual
Country of Study: Any country
No. of awards offered: Varies
Application Procedure: Applicants must write for guidelines.
Closing Date: January 1st

For further information contact:

Tel: 561-404-2000
Email: theaos@aos.org

Website: www.aos.org
Contact: Executive Director

AMERICAN ORIENTAL SOCIETY

Hatcher Graduate Library, University of Michigan, Ann Arbor, MI,
48109-1205, United States of America
Tel: (1) 734 647 4760
Fax: (1) 734 763 6743
Email: jrodgers@umich.edu
Website: www.umich.edu/aos
Contact: Grants Management Officer

The American Oriental Society is primarily concerned with the encouragement of basic research in the languages and literatures of Asia.

Louise Wallace Hackney Fellowship
Subjects: Chinese art, with special relation to painting, and the translation into English of works on the subject.
Purpose: To remind scholars that Chinese art, like all art, is not a disembodied creation, but the outgrowth of the life and culture from which it has sprung. It is requested that scholars give special attention to this approach in their study.
Eligibility: Open to United States citizens who are doctoral or postdoctoral students and have successfully completed at least 3 years of Chinese language study at a recognized university, and have some knowledge or training in art. In no case shall a fellowship be awarded to Scholars of well-recognized standing, but shall be given to either men or women who show aptitude or promise in the said field of learning.
Level of Study: Postdoctorate
Type: Fellowship
Value: US$8,000
Length of Study: 1 year
Frequency: Annual
Study Establishment: Any institution where paintings and adequate language guidance is available
Country of Study: Any country
No. of awards offered: 1
Application Procedure: Applicants must submit the following materials in duplicate: a transcript of their undergraduate and graduate course work, a statement of personal finances, a four page summary of the proposed project to be undertaken including details of expense, and no less than three letters of recommendation.
Closing Date: March 1st
Funding: Private
Additional Information: It is possible to apply for a renewal of the fellowship, but this may not be done in consecutive years.

For further information contact:

Hackney Fellowship American Oriental Society Hatcher Graduate Library, Ann Arbor, MI, 48109-1205

THE AMERICAN OTOLOGICAL SOCIETY (AOS)

3096 Riverdale Road, The Villages, FL, 32162, United States of
America
Tel: (1) 352 751 0932
Fax: (1) 352 751 0696
Email: segossard@aol.com
Website: www.americanotologicalsociety.org
Contact: Ms Shirley Gossard, Administrator

The AOS is a society focused upon 'aural' medicine. The society's mission is to advance and promote medical and surgical otology, encouraging research in the related disciplines.

American Otological Society Research Grants
Subjects: All aspects of otosclerosis, Ménière's disease and related disorders.
Eligibility: Open to physicians and doctorate level investigators.
Level of Study: Postdoctorate, Postgraduate
Type: Research grant

Value: Up to US$55,000 per year. No funding is provided for the investigator's salary
Length of Study: 1 year, renewable
Frequency: Annual
Country of Study: United States of America or Canada
No. of awards offered: Varies
Closing Date: January 31st
Funding: Private
No. of awards given last year: 3
No. of applicants last year: 10

For further information contact:

Research Fund of the American Otological Society, Inc., Johns Hopkins University, School of Medicine, Department of Otolaryngology-Head & Neck Surgery, 601 N. Caroline Street, JHOC 6210, Baltimore, MD, 21287-0910
Tel: 410 955 1080
Fax: 410 955 6526
Email: lminor2@jhmi.edu
Contact: Lloyd B. Minor, MD, Executive Secretary

American Otological Society Research Training Fellowships

Subjects: All aspects of otosclerosis, Ménière's disease and related disorders.
Purpose: To support research.
Eligibility: Open to physicians, residents and medical students in the United States of America and Canada.
Level of Study: Postgraduate
Type: Fellowship
Value: Up to US$40,000 depending on position and institutional norms
Length of Study: 1–2 years
Frequency: Annual
Country of Study: United States of America or Canada
No. of awards offered: Varies
Closing Date: January 31st
No. of awards given last year: 1
No. of applicants last year: 1
Additional Information: The organization requires institutional documentation that facilities and faculty are appropriate for the requested research.

For further information contact:

Research Fund of the American Otological Society, Inc., Johns Hopkins University, School of Medicine, Department of Otolaryngology-Head & Neck Surgery, 601 N. Caroline Street, JHOC 6210, Baltimore, MD, 21287-0910, United States of America
Tel: (1) 410 955 1080
Fax: (1) 410 955 6526
Email: lminor2@jhmi.edu
Contact: Lloyd B. Minor, MD, Executive Secretary

AMERICAN PHILOSOPHICAL SOCIETY

104 South Fifth Street, Philadelphia, PA, 19106-3387, United States of America
Tel: (1) 215 440 3400
Fax: (1) 215 440 3423
Email: lmusumeci@amphilsoc.org
Website: www.amphilsoc.org
Contact: Linda Musumeci, Research Administrator

The American Philosophical Society is an eminent scholarly organization of international reputation, and promotes useful knowledge in the sciences and humanities through excellence in scholarly research, professional meetings, publications, library resources and community outreach.

Daland Fellowships in Clinical Investigation

Subjects: Internal medicine, neurology, pediatrics, psychiatry and surgery.
Purpose: To award a limited number of fellowships for research in clinical medicine including the fields of internal medicine, neurology, pediatrics, psychiatry and surgery. For the purposes of this award, the committee emphasizes patient-orientated research.
Eligibility: Candidates are expected to have held the MD degree for less than 8 years. The fellowship is intended to be the first postclinical fellowship, but each case will be decided on its merits. Preference is given to candidates who have less than 2 years of postdoctoral training. Applicants must expect to perform their research at an institution in the United States of America, under the supervision of a scientific adviser.
Level of Study: Research
Type: Fellowship
Value: US$50,000 each for the first and second year
Length of Study: 1 year, with renewal for a further year if satisfactory progress is demonstrated
Frequency: Annual
Application Procedure: Applicants must complete an application form. Information and forms are available from the website. If electronic access is denied, forms can be requested by mail and must indicate when the MD degree was awarded. Candidates must be nominated by their department chairman in a letter providing assurance that the nominee will work with the guidance of a scientific adviser of established reputation who has guaranteed adequate space, supplies, etc. for the Fellow. The adviser need not be a member of the department nominating the Fellow, nor need the activities of the Fellow be limited to the nominating department. As a general rule, no more than one fellowship will be awarded to a given institution in the same year of competition. Application forms must be sent to the Daland Fellowship Committee.
Closing Date: September 1st
Funding: Private
No. of awards given last year: 2
No. of applicants last year: 20

Franklin Research Grant Program

Subjects: Scholarly research: as the term is used here, covers most kinds of scholarly inquiry by individuals leading to publication. It does not include journalistic or other writing for general readership, the preparation of textbooks, case books, anthologies or other materials for use by students or the work of creative and performing artists.
Purpose: To contribute towards the cost of scholarly research in all areas of knowledge, except those in which support by government or corporate enterprise is more appropriate.
Eligibility: Applicants are normally expected to have a doctorate, but applications are considered from persons whose publications display equivalent scholarly achievement. Grants are rarely made to persons who have held the doctorate less than a year, and never for predoctoral study or research. It is the Society's long standing practice to encourage younger scholars. The Committee will seldom approve more than two grants to the same person within any 5 year period. Applicants may be residents of the United States of America, citizens of the United States of America on the staffs of foreign institutions or foreign nationals whose research can only be carried out in the United States of America. Institutions are not eligible to apply. Applicants expecting to conduct interviews in a foreign language must possess sufficient competence in that language, and must be able to read and translate all source materials.
Level of Study: Research
Type: Grant
Value: The maximum grant is US$6,000. The budget year corresponds to the calendar year, not the academic year. If an applicant receives an award for the same project from another granting institution, the Society will consider limiting its award to costs that are not covered by the other grant
Frequency: Annual
Country of Study: United States of America
Application Procedure: Applicants must complete an application form. Information and forms are available from the website. If electronic access is denied, forms can be requested by mail. These must indicate the eligibility of both applicant and project, state the nature of the research, e.g. laboratory, archival or fieldwork and proposed use of the grant, e.g. travel or purchase of microfilm. Foreign nationals must specify the objects of their research, only available in the United States of America, e.g. indigenous plants, archival materials or architectural sites. A stamped addressed envelope should also be included. If forms are downloaded from the website, applicants must ensure that the page format is maintained and must print enough copies of the form for the letters of support.

Closing Date: October 1st and December 1st
Funding: Private
Additional Information: If an award is made and accepted, the recipient is required to provide the Society with a 250-word report on the research accomplished during the tenure of the grant, and a one page financial statement.

Library Resident Research Fellowships

Subjects: Library collections research.
Purpose: To support research in the American Philosophical Society library's collections.
Eligibility: Scholars who reside beyond a 75-mile radius of Philadelphia will be given some preference. The fellowships are open to both citizens of the United States of America and foreign nationals who are holders of a PhD or equivalent, PhD candidates who have passed their preliminary exams and independent scholars. Applicants in any relevant field of scholarship may apply.
Level of Study: Research
Type: Fellowship
Value: US$2,000 per month
Length of Study: 1–3 months
Frequency: Annual
Application Procedure: Applicants must complete an application form. A complete application includes all information requested on the form, a project statement, the applicant's curriculum vitae and two letters of support; if the applicant is a graduate student, one of the letters must be from the dissertation supervisor. The project statement should briefly describe the project and how it relates to existing scholarship, state the specific relevance of the American Philosophical Society's collections to the project, and indicate expected results of the research, such as publications.
Closing Date: March 1st for a decision by May
Funding: Private
No. of awards given last year: 23
No. of applicants last year: 90
Additional Information: Published guides to the Society's collections are available in most research libraries. Applicants are strongly encouraged to consult the library staff by mail or phone regarding the collections. A list of these guides and further information can be found on the website or by contacting the American Philosophical Society Library.

Phillips Fund Grants for Native American Research

Subjects: Native American linguistics and ethnohistory, and the history of the study of Native Americans in the continental United States of America and Canada.
Purpose: To financially support research.
Eligibility: Open to graduate students who have passed their qualifying examinations for either the Master's or doctoral degrees. Postdoctoral applicants are eligible.
Level of Study: Research
Value: The average award is approx. US$2,500 and grants rarely exceed US$3,500. This is to cover travel, tapes and informants' fees and is not for general maintenance or the purchase of permanent equipment
Length of Study: 1 year
Frequency: Annual
Application Procedure: Applicants must complete an application form. A complete application includes all information requested on the form, the correct number of copies and three confidential letters supporting the application. It is the applicant's responsibility to ensure that all materials reach the society on time. Information and forms are available from the website. If electronic access is denied, forms can be requested by mail. These must indicate eligibility of both applicant and project, and state whether the field of research is linguistics or ethnohistory. Applications should be addressed to Phillips Fund for Native American Research at the main address.
Closing Date: March 1st
Funding: Private
Additional Information: If an award is made and accepted, the recipient is required to provide the Society's Library with a brief formal report and copies of any tape recordings, transcriptions, microfilms, etc., that may be acquired in the process of the grant-funded research, and a release for scholarly use.

Sabbatical Fellowship for the Humanities and Social Sciences

Subjects: Humanities and social sciences.
Purpose: To support the second half of an awarded sabbatical year.
Eligibility: Open to mid-career faculty of universities and 4-year colleges in the United States of America who have been granted a sabbatical or research year, but for whom financial support from the parent institution is available for only the first half of the year. Candidates must not have had a financially supported leave during the 3 years prior to date of application. At the discretion of the review panels, the fellowship may be used to supplement another external award of similar purpose. The total external support cannot exceed the half-year salary. The society encourages candidates to use the resources of the American Philosophical Society Library, but this is not a requirement of the fellowship. There is no restriction on where the Fellow resides during the fellowship year, but an indication of the appropriateness of the available library resources should be given. The PhD must have been awarded no fewer than 7 and no more than 2–3 years prior to the date of application.
Level of Study: Research
Type: Award
Value: US$30,000–40,000
Length of Study: Tenure of the fellowship is for the second half of the academic year
Frequency: Annual
Application Procedure: Applicants must submit an application form. Information and forms are available from the website. If electronic access is denied, applicants can request forms by mail, but must be sure to state the date that their PhD was awarded, the end date of the last financially supported leave and beginning date of sabbatical.
Closing Date: October 15th
Funding: Private
No. of awards given last year: 20
No. of applicants last year: More than 250

THE AMERICAN PHYSIOLOGICAL SOCIETY (APS)

9650 Rockville Pike, Bethesda, MD, 20814-3991, United States of America
Tel: (1) 301 634 7164
Fax: (1) 301 634 7241
Email: webmaster@the-aps.org
Website: www.the-aps.org
Contact: Ms Linda Jean Dresser, Executive Assistant

The American Physiological Society (APS) is a non-profit scientific society devoted to fostering education, scientific research and the dissemination of information in the physiological sciences. The Society strives to play a role in the progress of science and the advancement of knowledge.

APS Conference Student Award

Subjects: Biology and physiology.
Purpose: To encourage the participation of young scientists in training at the APS conferences.
Eligibility: Open to graduate students wishing to present a contributed paper at an APS conference.
Level of Study: Graduate
Type: Award
Value: Cash award and complimentary conference registration
Length of Study: The duration of the conference
Frequency: Dependent upon meetings scheduled
Study Establishment: Any APS conference
Country of Study: United States of America
No. of awards offered: Varies
Application Procedure: Applicants must submit an abstract to the APS. Candidates must indicate on the abstract page a desire to be considered for the award and should contact the APS for further details.
Closing Date: Please write for details

APS Mass Media Science and Engineering Fellowship

Subjects: Physiology or any related subject.
Purpose: To enable promising young scientists to work in the newsroom of a newspaper, magazine, radio or television station,

sharpening their ability to communicate complex scientific issues to non-scientists and helping to improve public understanding of science.
Eligibility: Open to graduate or postgraduate students of physiology, or a related subject, preferably with a background in scientific writing.
Level of Study: Graduate, Postgraduate
Type: Studentship
Value: US$4,500 stipend
Length of Study: 10 weeks
Frequency: Annual
Study Establishment: The newsroom of a newspaper, magazine or radio or television station
Country of Study: United States of America
No. of awards offered: 1
Application Procedure: Applicants must complete an application form, available from Alice Ra'anan, Public Affairs Office, American Physiological Society.
Closing Date: January 15th
No. of awards given last year: 1

APS Minority Travel Fellowship Awards
Subjects: Biology and physiology.
Purpose: To increase the participation of predoctoral and postdoctoral minority students in the physiological sciences.
Eligibility: Open to advanced predoctoral and postdoctoral students. Students in the APS Porter Physiology Development programme are also eligible. Minority faculty members at MBRS and MARC eligible institutions may also submit applications.
Level of Study: Predoctorate, Postdoctorate
Type: Travel grant
Value: Funds for travel to attend either the Experimental Biology meeting or one of the APS conferences
Length of Study: The duration of the conference or meeting
Country of Study: United States of America
No. of awards offered: Varies
Application Procedure: Applicants must contact the Education Office of the APS for further details.
Closing Date: January 15th
Contributor: NIDDK and NIGMS

For further information contact:

Email: education@the-aps.org
Contact: Dr Marsha Matyas

Caroline tum Suden/Frances Hellebrandt Professional Opportunity Awards
Subjects: Biology and physiology.
Purpose: To provide funds for junior physiologists to attend and fully participate in the Experimental Biology meeting.
Eligibility: Open to graduate students or postdoctoral Fellows who are APS members or sponsored by an APS member.
Level of Study: Graduate, Postdoctorate
Type: Award
Value: US$500 per award, complimentary registration for the meeting
Length of Study: The duration of the conference
Frequency: Annual
Study Establishment: An APS Experimental Biology meeting
Country of Study: United States of America
No. of awards offered: 36
Application Procedure: Applicants must submit an abstract to APS and should contact the Education Office for further details.
Closing Date: Please write for details
No. of awards given last year: 36
Additional Information: Recipients are obliged to attend the Experimental Biology meeting and present a paper.

Porter Physiology Fellowships for Minorities
Subjects: Biology and physiology.
Purpose: To support the training of talented students entering careers in physiology by providing predoctoral fellowships for underrepresented students (African Americans, Hispanics, Native Americans, Native Alaskans and Native Pacific Islanders).
Eligibility: Open to underrepresented ethnic minority applicants, i.e. African Americans, Hispanics, Native Americans, Native Alaskans or Native Pacific Islanders who are citizens or permanent residents of the United States of America or its territories.

Level of Study: Graduate, Postdoctorate, Predoctorate
Type: Fellowship
Value: US$20,772 stipend
Length of Study: Varies
Frequency: Annual
Study Establishment: Universities or research establishments
Country of Study: United States of America
No. of awards offered: Varies
Application Procedure: Applicants must contact the Education Office of the APS for further details.
Closing Date: January 15th

Procter and Gamble Professional Opportunity Awards
Subjects: Biology and physiology.
Purpose: To provide funds to predoctoral students allowing them to fully participate in the Experimental Biology meeting.
Eligibility: Open to predoctoral students who are within 1–1.5 years of completing a PhD degree and wish to present a paper at the meeting. Applicants must be student members of the APS or have an adviser or a supporting sponsor who is an APS member.
Level of Study: Predoctorate
Type: Award
Value: US$500 per award and complementary registration for the Experimental Biology meeting
Length of Study: The duration of the conference
Frequency: Annual
Study Establishment: The APS Experimental Biology meeting
Country of Study: United States of America
No. of awards offered: Varies
Application Procedure: Applicants must submit an abstract to APS and should contact the Education Office for further details.
Closing Date: Please write for details
No. of awards given last year: 9

AMERICAN PSYCHOLOGICAL ASSOCIATION MINORITY FELLOWSHIP PROGRAM (APA/MFP)

Minority Fellowships Program (MFP), 750 First Street, N.E., Washington, DC, 20002-4242, United States of America
Tel: (1) 202 336 6127
Fax: (1) 202 336 6012
Email: mfp@apa.org
Website: www.apa.org/mfp
Contact: Administrative Assistant

The American Psychological Association Minority Fellowships Program's (APA/MFP) objective is to increase the knowledge of issues related to ethnic minority mental health and to improve the quality of mental health and substance abuse treatment delivered to ethnic minority populations as consistent with Healthy People 2010, the Surgeon General's report on mental health, and other federal initiatives to reduce health disparities. This is done by providing financial support and professional guidance to individuals pursuing doctoral degrees in psychology and neuroscience.

Diversity Program in Neuroscience Doctoral Fellowship
Subjects: Behavioural neuroscience, cellular neurobiology, cognitive neuroscience, computational neuroscience, developmental neurobiology, membrane biophysics, molecular neurobiology, neuroanatomy, neurobiology, neurobiology of ageing, neurobiology of disease, neurochemistry, neurogenetics, neuroimmunology, neuropathology, neuropharmacology, neurophysiology, neurotoxicology or systems neuroscience.
Purpose: To increase the representation of underrepresented ethnic minorities in neuroscience as well as to increase the pool of researchers and teachers whose work focuses on ethnic minority persons and issues.
Eligibility: Applicants must be citizens of the United States of America or permanent residents who are enrolled full-time in a

doctoral programme. An important goal of the programme is to increase the representation of Black or African American, Alaskan Native, American Indian, Asian American, Hispanic or Latino and Pacific Islander students within neuroscience. However, the programme welcomes applications from all students, especially those interested in increasing the representation of underrepresented ethnic minorities in neuroscience as well as in increasing the pool of researchers and teachers in the field.

Level of Study: Doctorate
Type: Fellowship
Frequency: Annual
Country of Study: United States of America
Application Procedure: Applicants must submit a completed application, essay, references, transcripts, and Graduate Record Examination scores. Further information and application forms are available on request.
Closing Date: January 15th
Funding: Government
Contributor: National Institute of Mental Health

Diversity Program in Neuroscience Postdoctoral Fellowship

Subjects: Behavioural neuroscience, cellular neurobiology, cognitive neuroscience, computational neuroscience, developmental neurobiology, membrane biophysics, molecular neurobiology, neuroanatomy, neurobiology of ageing, neurobiology of disease, neurochemistry, neurogenetics, neuroimmunology, neuropathology, neuropharmacology, neurophysiology, neurotoxicology or systems neuroscience.
Purpose: To increase the number of ethnic minorities in neuroscience who conduct research in areas of importance to the National Institute of Mental Health.
Eligibility: Open to citizens or permanent residents of the United States of America with a PhD or MD degree and prior graduate training in neuroscience or in other basic sciences.
Level of Study: Postdoctorate, Predoctorate
Type: Fellowship
Frequency: Annual
Application Procedure: Applicants must visit the website.
Closing Date: January 15th
Additional Information: Benefits include travel funds to visit universities being considered for postdoctoral training, travel funds to attend the Society for Neuroscience's annual meeting and opportunities for mentoring and networking with neuroscientists.

MFP Mental Health and Substance Abuse Services Doctoral Fellowship

Subjects: Clinical, counselling and school psychology.
Purpose: To improve the quality of mental health treatment and research on issues of concern to ethnic minority populations by providing financial support and professional guidance to individuals pursuing doctoral degrees in psychology and by increasing the knowledge of issues related to ethnic minority health.
Eligibility: Applicants must be citizens or permanent residents of the United States of America enrolled full-time in an APA-accredited doctoral programme at the time the fellowship is awarded. An additional factor among the many considered is the applicant's ethnic minority group including, but not limited to, Blacks or African Americans, Alaskan Natives, American Indians, Asian Americans, Hispanics or Latinos and Pacific Islanders, and/or those who can demonstrate commitment to a career in psychology related to ethnic minority health.
Level of Study: Doctorate
Type: Fellowship
Frequency: Annual
Country of Study: Any country
Application Procedure: Applicants must submit a completed application, essay, references, transcripts and Graduate Record Examination scores. Further information and application forms are available on request.
Closing Date: January 15th
Funding: Government
Contributor: The Substance Abuse and Mental Health Administration

THE AMERICAN PSYCHOLOGICAL FOUNDATION (APF)

750 First Street NE, Washington, DC, 20002-4242, United States of America
Tel: (1) 202 336 5843
Fax: (1) 202 336 5812
Email: foundation@apa.org
Website: www.apa.org/apf

The American Psychological Foundation (APF) is affiliated with the American Psychological Association. It is a non-profit, philanthropic organization that advances the science and practice of psychology as a means of understanding behaviour and promoting health, education and human welfare. APF seeks to advance psychology and its impact on improving the human condition. The work of the Foundation is ongoing, sometimes urgent, always important and always growing.

Alexander Gralnick Research Investigator Prize

Subjects: Serious mental illness.
Purpose: To support exceptional research and mentoring accomplishments in the area of serious mental illness.
Eligibility: Applicants must have a doctoral degree (PhD, PsyD or MD) and must have a record of significant research productivity (for at least 8 years) and provide evidence of continuing creativity in the area of serious mental illness research. Applicants must have an affiliation with an accredited college, university or other research/treatment institution.
Level of Study: Doctorate
Type: Prize
Value: US$20,000
Frequency: Biennial
Application Procedure: Applicants should send 5 copies of letter of nomination addressing the award criteria and describing both the nominee's accomplishments and prospects for future contributions, applicant's current curriculum vitae and copies of two seminal publications.
Funding: Foundation

APF Division 29 Early Career Award

Subjects: Psychotherapy, psychology.
Purpose: To recognize promising contributions to psychotherapy and psychology.
Eligibility: Open to members of Division 29 who are within 10 years of receiving their Doctorate.
Level of Study: Doctorate
Type: Award
Value: US $1,000
Application Procedure: Check website for further details.
Closing Date: January 1st

APF Pre-college Psycology Grant Program

Purpose: To support proposals for programmes that support the science and application of psychological science among talented high school students.
Eligibility: Applicants must be educational institutions or a 501(c)(3) non-profit organizations or affiliated with such an organization. Check website for further details.
Level of Study: Research
Type: Grant
Value: Up to $30,000
Frequency: Annual
Application Procedure: Check website for details.
Closing Date: May 1st
Funding: Foundation

APF/COGDOP Graduate Research Scholarships

Eligibility: Applicants should be nominated by their department of psycology, which is a member in goodstanding of the Council of Graduate Departments of Psychology (COGDOP).
Level of Study: Graduate, Research
Type: Scholarships
Value: Up to $16,000, which includes $1,000 for each candidate, $3,000 for the top applicant and $2,000 for Clarence J. Rosecrans Scholarship

Frequency: Annual
No. of awards offered: Up to 11
Application Procedure: Applications will be sent to the departments and applicants can contact the department for nomination.
Closing Date: June 16th
Funding: Foundation

Benton Meier Neuropsychology Scholarships

Subjects: Neuropsychology and psychology.
Purpose: To provide financial asistance to students who wish to pursue a career in neuropsychology.
Eligibility: Open to candidates who present a record of achievement.
Level of Study: Postgraduate
Type: Scholarships
Value: US$2,500 per year
Frequency: Annual
Country of Study: United States of America
No. of awards offered: 2
Application Procedure: Applicants must send 7 copies of the nomination materials to the American Psychological Foundation.
Closing Date: June 1st
Funding: Foundation
Additional Information: Candidates must submit a letter that documents their scholarly or research accomplishments, explains their financial need and describes for what purpose the financial award will be used.

Charles L. Brewer Distinguished Teaching of Psychology Award

Subjects: Teaching of psychology.
Purpose: To recognize a significant career of contribution to the teaching of psychology.
Eligibility: Open to those who have a proven track record as an exceptional teacher of psychology.
Level of Study: Professional development, Research
Type: Award
Value: Australian $2,000, and paid round trip to the APA annual convention
Frequency: Annual
Application Procedure: Application can be filled online or downloaded.
Closing Date: December 1st

For further information contact:

Website: www.apa.org/apf/teaching.nom.guideline.pdf

Counseling Psychology Fund

Subjects: Counseling psychology.
Purpose: To support research on the implementation of innovative counseling programs and models.
Eligibility: Open to those who are members of APA Division 17 and educational institutions, or a 501(c)(3) nonprofit or affiliated organizations.
Level of Study: Research
Type: Grant
Value: Up to US $5,000
Frequency: Annual
Application Procedure: Check website for further details.

Cummings PSYCHE Prize

Subjects: Psychology.
Purpose: To recognize a licensed practicing psychologist whose career demonstrates a plan to effect significant and enduring contributions to expanding the role of the psychologist as primary care provider in the primary care setting of organized systems of healthcare delivery.
Eligibility: Applicants should be individuals whose career exemplifies the integration of behaviour and physical healthcare.
Level of Study: Research
Type: Prize
Value: $50,000
Frequency: Annual
No. of awards offered: 2
Closing Date: December 1st

Funding: Foundation
Additional Information: To create a centrifugal force that will encourage the ascendance of leadership by psychology in establishing innovative healthcare delivery systems and to spur training of future psychologists to become such leaders.

Elizabeth Munsterberg Koppitz Child Psychology Graduate Fellowships

Subjects: Child psychology.
Purpose: To help students in the advancement of knowledge and learning in the field of child psychology.
Eligibility: Open to applicants who have academically progressed through the qualifying exams for Doctoral study.
Level of Study: Graduate, Predoctorate
Type: Fellowships
Value: Up to US$28,000 for graduate work and professional development; US$4,000 travel stipends for runners-up
Frequency: Annual
Country of Study: United States of America
No. of awards offered: 5
Closing Date: November 15th
Funding: Foundation, trusts
Additional Information: Consideration will be given to psychological research that creates significant new understandings that facilitate the development and functioning of children and youth.

Esther Katz Rosen Grant for Research and Programs on Giftedness in Children

Eligibility: Check website for details.
Level of Study: Research
Type: Grant
Value: $25,000
No. of awards offered: Up to 3
Application Procedure: Applications can be completed online. Check website for details.
Closing Date: February 15th
Funding: Foundation

F J McGuigan Young Investigator Research Prize on Understanding the Human Mind

Purpose: To support a young psychologist engaged in research that seeks to explicate the concept of the human mind.
Eligibility: Applicants must have earned a doctoral degree in psychology or in a related field and be no more than 9 years postdoctoral degree at the nomination deadline. Applicants must have an affiliation with an accredited college, university or other research institution. The prize will be awarded to the recipient's institution for the benefit of his or her research. Applicants research must be from a primarily psychophysiological perspective, although physiological and behavioral research are also eligible. Dualistic approaches, such as those espoused by many contemporary cognitive psychologists are not eligible.
Level of Study: Research
Type: Research prize
Value: $25,000
Frequency: Biennial
Application Procedure: Check website for details.
Closing Date: March 1st
Funding: Foundation

Harry and Miriam Levinson Award for Exceptional Contributions to Consulting Organizational Psychology

Subjects: Organizational Psychology.
Purpose: To recognize an outstanding consulting organizational psychologist.
Eligibility: Open to an APA member who has demonstrated exceptional ability to integrate a wide variety of psychological theories and concepts.
Type: Award
Value: US $5,000
Frequency: Annual
No. of awards offered: 1
Application Procedure: Check website for further details.
Closing Date: March 15th
Contributor: The Harry Levinson Fund

Harry V McNeill Memorial Award for Innovative Community Mental Health

Subjects: Community mental health services.

Purpose: To support innovation in community mental health and encourage the participation of the local community.

Eligibility: Applicants can be individual practitioners, neighborhood organizations or community mental health centers. Applicants must demonstrate development of innovative practice in community mental health services, evidence of stimulating participation in local community activities and transfer of expertise to the community. Members or fellows of APA should nominate the applicants.

Type: Award

Frequency: Biennial

No. of awards offered: Varies

Application Procedure: Nomination forms should include four letters of support (two from local community citizens and/or organizations and two from members or fellows of APA), written documentation of the innovation (two page description plus supporting materials) and a copy of the curriculum vitae or resume of the individual or a brief description of the organizational unit.

Closing Date: February 15th

Funding: Foundation

For further information contact:

306H White Gravenor Bldg, 37th & P Streets NW, WA, 20057

Tel: 202 687 9258

Contact: Jennifer Wooland, Georgetown University Psychology Department

Henry P. David Grants for Research and International Travel in Human Reproductive Behavior and Population Studies

Subjects: Population studies or human reproductive behavior.

Purpose: To support young professionals with a demonstrated interest in behavioral aspects of human reproductive behavior or an area related to population concerns.

Eligibility: Open to those carrying out dissertation research or have a PhD, PsyD, or EdD, with not more than 5 years postgraduate experience.

Level of Study: Doctorate, Research

Type: Grant

Value: Up to US $1,500 for research, up to US $1,500 for International travel

Frequency: Annual

No. of awards offered: 2

Application Procedure: Check website for further details.

Closing Date: February 15th

Lizette Peterson Homer Memorial Injury Research Grant

Subjects: Psychology.

Purpose: To enable students to perform psychosocial research on injuries to children and young adults through accidents, violence, abuse or suicide.

Level of Study: Research

Type: Research grant

Value: US$1,500

Length of Study: 1 year

Frequency: Annual

Country of Study: United States of America

Application Procedure: Applicants must submit a research proposal describing objectives, rationale, hypotheses, design, method, procedures and a data analysis plan. Research relevance to pediatric psychology should be highlighted along with a detailed budget, a statement of qualifications and current curriculum vitae. Applicants must also produce a letter of recommendation from the nominee's faculty advisor, if the applicant is a student a statement regarding membership in professional organizations is required.

Closing Date: Feburary 16th

Funding: Foundation

For further information contact:

Email: sharon.berry@childrensmn.org

Paul E. Henkin Travel Grant

Purpose: To provide support to defer the costs of registration, lodging, and travel for student members of APA Division 16 to attend the APA annual convention.

Eligibility: Applicants must not be employed at the convention by the APA or receive compensation or reimbursement of expenses from the APA for convention travel or activities.

Type: Travel grant

Value: Up to $1,000 to defer the costs of registration, lodging and travel

Frequency: Annual

Application Procedure: Application form should include letter of recommendation, 500-word essay and curriculum vitae.

Closing Date: April 15th

Funding: Foundation

Additional Information: The grant money may not be used for food, drink, or any materials that are not included in the registration fee.

Randy Gerson Memorial Grant

Subjects: Understanding of couple, family dynamics or multi-generational processes.

Eligibility: Applicants for the professional-level grant must have a doctorate (e.g., PhD, PsyD, EdD or MD). Grants will be given in alternate years to students and professionals.

Level of Study: Doctorate, Graduate, Research

Type: Grant

Value: $6,000

Frequency: Annual

Application Procedure: Application can be completed online. Check website for details.

Closing Date: February 1st

Funding: Foundation

Raymond A and Rosalee G Weiss Innovative Research and Programs Grant

Subjects: Psychology.

Purpose: To support innovative psychological research and programmes and encourage creative, cutting-edge psychological endeavors.

Eligibility: Applicants must be affiliated with educational institutions or a 501(c)(3) non-profit organization or affiliated with such an organization.

Level of Study: Doctorate, Research

Type: Grant

Value: Up to $10,000

Frequency: Annual

Application Procedure: Applicants can submit a proposal and curriculum vitae of the project leader online at http://forms.apa.org/apf/grants/

Closing Date: July 1st

Funding: Foundation

Robert L Fantz Memorial Award for Young Psychologists

Subjects: Psychology.

Purpose: To encourage and support careers of promising young investigators in psychology or related disciplines through a grant, presented to the awardee's institution on their behalf.

Eligibility: Applicants must show evidence of basic scientific research or scholarly writing in perceptual-cognitive development and the development of selective attention and research and writing on the development of individuality, creativity and free-choice of behaviour.

Level of Study: Research

Type: Grant

Value: $2,000

Frequency: Annual

No. of awards offered: Varies

Application Procedure: The candidates are selected from the nominees for APA's Early Career Award.

Funding: Foundation

Roy Scrivner Memorial Research Grants

Subjects: All fields of the behavioral and social sciences.

Purpose: To support empirical research focused on lesbian, gay and bisexual family psychology and lesbian, gay and bisexual family therapy.

Eligibility: All applicants, including co-investigators, must have a doctoral-level degree.
Level of Study: Doctorate, Research
Type: Grant
Value: Up to $10,000 for postdoctoral research and up to $1,000 each for predoctoral research
Frequency: Annual
No. of awards offered: 1 postdoctoral and up to 2 predoctoral awards
Application Procedure: Check website for details.
Funding: Foundation

Theodore Millon Mid-Career Award in Personality Psychology
Subjects: Science of personality psychology including the areas of personology, personality theory, personality disorders and personality measurement.
Purpose: To support an outstanding mid-career psychologist engaged in advancing the science of personality psychology including the areas of personology, personality theory, personality disorders, and personality measurement.
Eligibility: Applicants should be no less than 10 years and no more than 20 years postdoctoral degree.
Level of Study: Research
Type: Award
Value: $1,000 and a plaque at the APA convention
Frequency: Annual
No. of awards offered: 1
Application Procedure: Applications should include a cover letter outlining the nominee's contributions to science of personality psychology and a copy of an abbreviated curriculum vitae. Self-nomination is permitted.
Closing Date: October 1st
Funding: Foundation

For further information contact:

PO Box 1082, Niwot, CO, 80544-1082
Contact: Diane J Willis, Division of Clinical Psychology

Timothy Jeffrey Memorial Award in Clinical Health Psychology
Subjects: Clinical health psychology.
Purpose: To recognize the outstanding commitment to clinical health psychology by a full-time provider of direct clinical services.
Eligibility: Applicants must be fully licensed clinical health psychologists and members of APA and APA Division 38 (Health Psychology).
Type: Award
Value: $3,000
Frequency: Annual
No. of awards offered: 1
Application Procedure: Nominations must be accompanied by a current curriculum vitae, at least one letter of support from a non-psychologist, professional colleague (letters will not be accepted from students or supervisees), and one letter from a psychologist colleague. Nomination letters should describe the nominee's practice, professional activities and commitment to the field.
Closing Date: May 1st
Funding: Foundation

For further information contact:

PO Box 1838, Ashland, VA, 23005
Website: www.healthpsych.org
Contact: APA Division 38 Awards Committee

Todd E. Husted Memorial Dissertation Award
Subjects: Psychology.
Purpose: To encourage contributions towards development of improved outreach and delivery of mental health services.
Eligibility: Open to applicants who are enrolled full-time in a graduate programme in psychology at a regionally accredited university or college located in the United States or Canada.
Level of Study: Postgraduate
Type: Fellowships
Value: US$2,000
Frequency: Annual

Country of Study: United States of America
Application Procedure: Applicants must submit a dissertation proposal or abstract that will indicate significant potential for the development or improvement of mental health services for those with severe and persistent mental illness.
Closing Date: September 15th
Funding: Foundation
Additional Information: The applicants must get their dissertation proposals approved by their dissertation committees prior to application and the applicants must not have previously received an APA Dissertation Research Award.

Violence Prevention and Intervention Grant
Purpose: To encourage the transfer of psychological science to the prevention of violence in our society and facilitate the implementation of innovative community programmes aimed at interventions to reduce violence.
Level of Study: Doctorate, Research
Type: Grant
Value: Up to $20,000
Frequency: Annual
Application Procedure: Application can be submitted online.
Closing Date: June 1st
Funding: Foundation

Visionary Funds Grants Program
Subjects: Psychology.
Purpose: To support projects and programmes that respond to pressing needs in society where psychology can help to find effective solutions.
Eligibility: Applicants can be educational institutions, 501(c)(3) non-profit organizations, or affiliated with such organizations.
Level of Study: Doctorate
Value: $5,000 for 1 year for one cycle grants and $5,000 per year for 5 years for multi cycle grants
Frequency: Annual
Application Procedure: Application forms can be downloaded from the website.
Closing Date: For one cycle grants: March 15th, July 1st, October 1st, December 1st. For multi cycle grants: September 1st
Funding: Foundation

Wayne F Placek Large Research Grants
Purpose: To encourage scientific research to increase the general public's understanding of homosexuality and to alleviate the stress that gay men and lesbians experience in this and future civilizations.
Eligibility: Applicants must have a doctoral degree at the time of application and must be affiliated with a college, university or research institute that meets US federal requirements for administering research awards.
Level of Study: Research, Doctorate
Value: Up to $65,000 in research support
Frequency: Annual
Application Procedure: Application forms can be downloaded from the website.
Closing Date: March 9th
Funding: Foundation

Wayne F Placek Small Research Grants
Purpose: To encourage scientific research to increase the general public's understanding of homosexuality and to alleviate the stress that gay men and lesbians experience in this and future civilizations.
Eligibility: Applicants must have a doctoral degree at the time of application and must be affiliated with a college, university or research institute that meets US federal requirements for administering research awards.
Level of Study: Doctorate, Research
Type: Grant
Value: $5,000 in research support and are intended to encourage small-scale scientific research
Frequency: Annual
Application Procedure: Application forms can be downloaded from the website.
Closing Date: January 31st
Funding: Foundation

AMERICAN PUBLIC POWER ASSOCIATION (APPA)

1875 Connecticut Avenue, NW, Suite 1200, Washington DC, 20009,
United States of America
Tel: (1) 202 467 2900
Fax: (1) 202 467 2992
Email: DEED@appanet.org
Website: www.appanet.org
Contact: Ms Michele Suddleson, DEED Administrator

APPA is a service organization for the nation's more than 2,000
community-owned electric utilities that serve more than 43 million
Americans. Its purpose is to advance the public policy interests of its
members and their consumers, and provide member services to ensure adequate, reliable electricity at a reasonable price with the proper
protection of the environment.

DEED (Demonstration of Energy-Efficient Developments) Student Research Grant/Internship

Subjects: Engineering, mathematics or computer science.
Purpose: To promote the involvement of students studying in energy-
related disciplines in the public power industry and to increase
awareness of career opportunities in public power.
Eligibility: Open to students studying in energy-related disciplines.
Applicants must be enrolled in an accredited university in the United
States or Canada and must be sponsored by a DEED member utility
(check APPA's website for instruction).
Level of Study: Graduate, Postdoctorate, Postgraduate, Doctorate
Type: Grant
Value: US$4,000
Frequency: Annual
Country of Study: United States of America
No. of awards offered: 10
Application Procedure: Applications must be completed, sponsored
and submitted by a DEED member utility, with the required signatures.
An official transcript must accompany the application or be sent sep-
arately to the attention of the DEED administrator by the deadline. A
second copy of the application must be sent to the local DEED Board
regional director. A listing of addresses for these are available on the
website.
Closing Date: February 15th and October 15th
Funding: Private
No. of awards given last year: 10
Additional Information: Currently only the United States of
America has DEED members. Applicants should visit the website
for a listing of members and for additional scholarship information
and tips.

THE AMERICAN RESEARCH CENTER IN EGYPT (ARCE)

Emory Briarcliff Campus, 1256 Briarcliff Road North East,
Building A, Suite 405-S, Atlanta, GA, 30306,
United States of America
Tel: (1) 404 712 9854
Fax: (1) 404 712 9849
Email: arce@emory.edu
Website: www.arce.org
Contact: Diane Springfield, Program Administrative Assistant

The American Research Center in Egypt (ARCE) is the
professional society in the United States of America for specialists
on all periods of Egypt's cultural history. It is also a consortium of
universities and museums that supports archaeological and academic
research in Egypt via fellowships, and whose membership is open to
the public.

ARCE Fellowships

Subjects: Arts and humanities, Near East studies and humanistic
social sciences.
Purpose: To support research in Egypt.
Eligibility: Open to citizens of the United States of America who are
predoctoral candidates. Postdoctoral candidates should be nationals

of the United States of America or foreign nationals who have been
teaching at an American university for 3 years or more.
Level of Study: Doctorate, Postdoctorate, Museum curators
Type: Fellowship
Value: Varies
Length of Study: 3 months–1 year
Frequency: Annual
Study Establishment: ARCE
Country of Study: Egypt
No. of awards offered: 10–17
Application Procedure: Applicants must write for materials or
download them from the website.
Closing Date: January 5th
Funding: Government
No. of awards given last year: 17
No. of applicants last year: 31

AMERICAN RESEARCH INSTITUTE IN TURKEY (ARIT)

University of Pennsylvania Museum, 3260 South Street, Philadelphia,
Pennsylvania, PA 19104-6324, United States of America
Tel: (1) 215 898 3474
Fax: (1) 215 898 0657
Email: leinwand@sas.upenn.edu
Website: www.ccat.sas.upenn.edu/ARIT
Contact: Administrative Assistant

The American Research Institute in Turkey's (ARIT) main aim is to
support scholarly research in all fields of the humanities and social
sciences in Turkey through administering fellowship programmes at
the doctoral and postdoctoral level and through maintaining research
centres in Ankara and Istanbul.

ARIT Fellowship Program

Subjects: Research on ancient, medieval, or modern times in Turkey,
in any field of the humanities and social sciences are eligible.
Purpose: To enable scholars and advanced graduate students
interested in research in the field of humanities and social
science.
Eligibility: Turkish law requires foreign scholars to obtain formal
permission to carry out research at institutions in Turkey.
Level of Study: Predoctorate, Doctorate, Postdoctorate, Postgradu-
ate, Research
Type: Fellowship
Value: US$4,000–16,000
Length of Study: 1 year
Frequency: Annual
Study Establishment: Turkey and its branch centres in Istanbul and
Ankara
Country of Study: Turkey
Application Procedure: In order to be considered, applicants
must provide complete information in their applications. Applications
and three letters of recommendation must be received by the due
date.
Closing Date: November 1st
Funding: Government, private
Contributor: United States Department of State, Bureau of Educa-
tional and Cultural Affairs
Additional Information: ARIT fellowships applicants are responsible
for obtaining their research permissions and visas. In general, researchers should seek permission to carry out research from the Directors of the Institutions in which they intend to work.

Fellowships for Intensive Advanced Turkish Language Study in Istanbul, Turkey

Subjects: Turkish.
Purpose: To provide full travel and fellowship to students and scholars for participation in the summer program in advanced Turkish
language at Bogazici University in Istanbul.
Eligibility: Applicant must be a citizen, national or permanent resident
of the United States; be enrolled in a graduate level academic programme or be a faculty members; have a minimum B average in your
studies, if still a student; and perform at the high-intermediate level on
a proficiency-based admissions examination.

Level of Study: Graduate
Type: Fellowship
Value: Fellowship includes round-trip airfare to Istanbul, application and tuition fees, and a maintenance stipend
Frequency: Annual
Study Establishment: Bogazici University
No. of awards offered: Approx. 15
Application Procedure: Application forms are available at the ARIT website http://ccat.sas.upenn.edu/ARIT
Closing Date: February 1st
Contributor: US Department of Education, Fulbright-Hays Group Projects Abroad Programme

For further information contact:

Near Eastern Studies, 110 Jones Hall, Princeton University, Princeton, NJ 08544-1008
Email: ehgilson@princeton.edu
Contact: Erika H Gilson, Director

Kenan T. Erim Fellowship for Research at Aphrodisias

Subjects: Excavation and/or research in the field of art history and archaeology to be carried out at the site of Aphrodisias in Turkey.
Purpose: To enable scholars to carry out research in the field of art history and archaeology to be carried out at the site of Aphrodisias in Turkey.
Eligibility: Scholars or advanced graduate students engaged in excavation at the site of Aphrodisias or research on material from that site are eligible to apply.
Level of Study: Doctorate, Research
Type: Fellowships
Value: US$2,375
Frequency: Annual
Application Procedure: In order to be considered, applicants must provide a complete application. The application, a letter of acceptance from Director or the ARIT President in addition to two letters of reference must be received by the due date.
Closing Date: November 1st
Contributor: American friends of Aphrodisias
Additional Information: Projects should be included within the Aphrodisias excavation permit.

KRESS/ARIT Pre-Doctoral Fellowship in the History of Art and Archaeology

Subjects: The history of art and architecture from antiquity to the present, and archaeology.
Eligibility: Open to advanced graduate students engaged in research in Turkey. Applicants must have fulfilled all preliminary requirements for the doctorate except the dissertation by June 2007, and before beginning any ARIT-sponsored research. Candidacy is open to US citizens and non-US applicants who matriculated at US or Canadian institutes. Pre-doctoral applicants may also qualify for ARIT Fellowship in the Humanities and Social Sciences.
Level of Study: Doctorate, Predoctorate, Research
Type: Fellowship
Value: Up to US$17,000
Length of Study: 1 academic year. Awards for shorter periods of time are also available
Frequency: Annual
Study Establishment: Either of ARIT's two research establishments in Ankara or Istanbul
Country of Study: Turkey
No. of awards offered: 2–4
Application Procedure: Applicants must submit an application form accompanied by three letters of recommendation.
Closing Date: November 1st
Funding: Private
Contributor: The Samuel H. Kress Foundation
No. of awards given last year: 2
No. of applicants last year: 14

Mellon Postdoctoral Fellowships In Turkey For East European Scholars

Subjects: Humanities and social sciences.
Purpose: To bring Eastern and Central European scholars to Turkey to carry out research.

Eligibility: Open to nationals of Bulgaria, Czech Republic, Slovakia, Poland, Hungary and Romania as well as Estonia, Latvia, Lithuania. Preference will be given to scholars in the early stages of their careers who have not had an opportunity for extensive travel.
Level of Study: Postdoctorate
Type: Fellowship
Value: Up to US$11,500
Length of Study: 2–3 months
Frequency: Annual
Study Establishment: Either of ARIT's two research establishments in Ankara or Istanbul
Country of Study: Turkey
No. of awards offered: 3–4
Application Procedure: Applicants must submit an application form, project statement and references.
Closing Date: March 5th
Funding: Private
Contributor: The Mellon Foundation
Additional Information: Further information is available on request or from the website www.mellon.org

NEH ARIT-National Endowment for the Humanities Fellowships for Research in Turkey

Subjects: All subjects of the humanities and interdisciplinary approaches to social sciences, prehistory, history, art, archaeology, language and literature.
Purpose: To support research on ancient, medieval or modern times.
Eligibility: Open to scholars who have completed their formal training and plan to carry out research in Turkey may apply. They may be US citizens or three year residents of the US. Please consult ARIT headquarters on questions of eligibility. Advanced scholars also may apply for ARIT Fellowships in the Humanities and Social Sciences.
Level of Study: Professional development, Postdoctorate, Research
Type: Fellowship
Value: Stipends generally range US$13,335–40,000
Length of Study: 4–12 months
Study Establishment: Either of ARIT's two research establishments in Ankara or Istanbul
Country of Study: Turkey
No. of awards offered: 2–4
Application Procedure: Applicants must submit an application form, project statement and references.
Closing Date: November 1st
Funding: Government
Contributor: The United States Information Agency (USIA)

W.D.E. Coulson and Toni M. Cross Aegean Exchange Program

Subjects: Any field of humanities and social sciences from prehistoric to modern times to conduct research in Greece.
Purpose: To provide an opportunity for Turkish scholars to meet with their Greek colleagues and to pursue research interests in the museum, archives and library collections and at the sites and monuments of Greece.
Eligibility: Applicants must be Turkish citizens and must have their primary academic affiliation with a university in Turkey. They must have completed all PhD work.
Level of Study: Doctorate, Postdoctorate, Predoctorate, Research
Type: Fellowship
Value: Up to $2,500
Length of Study: 1 month
Frequency: Annual
Study Establishment: American School of Classical Studies of Athens
Country of Study: Greece
No. of awards offered: Up to 3
Application Procedure: A 5-page statement of purpose, along with application and reference letter.
Closing Date: November 30th
Funding: Government

For further information contact:

Senit Ersan No 24/9, Gankaya, Ankara, 06680, Turkey
Contact: Arit-Ankara

THE AMERICAN SCHOOL OF CLASSICAL STUDIES AT ATHENS (ASCSA)

6-8 Charlton Street, Princeton, NJ, 08540-5232, United States of America
Tel: (1) 609 683 0800
Fax: (1) 609 924 0578
Email: ascsa@ascsa.org
Website: www.ascsa.edu.gr
Contact: Ms Mary E Darlington, Executive Assistant

Established in 1881, the American School of Classical Studies at Athens (ASCSA) offers both graduate students and scholars the opportunity to study Greek civilization, first hand, in Greece. The ASCSA supports and encourages the teaching of the archaeology, art, history, language and literature of Greece from early times to the present.

ASCSA Advanced Fellowships

Subjects: Classical art history, history of architecture, study of pottery.
Eligibility: Open to students from the United States of America or Canadian institutions who have completed 1 year as a regular or student associate member of the ASCSA.
Level of Study: Postgraduate, Predoctorate
Type: Fellowship
Value: Room and board, school fees and stipend of US$16,000
Length of Study: 1 academic year
Frequency: Annual
Study Establishment: ASCSA
Country of Study: Greece
No. of awards offered: 4–6
Application Procedure: Applicants must submit the following to the Director of the school: an up-to-date curriculum vitae; a project statement no longer than three, single-spaced pages; a list of other fellowships, if any applied for, with dates of notification of these awards; and one letter of reference from the applicant's dissertation advisor on the feasibility of the applicant's work. Applicants who were not at the School in the preceding year should also get a letter of reference from a scholar who can evaluate what they have done since they left the School.
Closing Date: February 21st
Funding: Private
No. of applicants last year: 24
Additional Information: The fellowships include: the Edward Capps, the Doreen C Spitzer and the Eugene Vanderpool Fellowships (subject unrestricted); the Samuel H Kress Fellowships in art history; the Gorham P Stevens Fellowship in the history of architecture; and the Homer A and Dorothy B Thompson Fellowship in the study of pottery. Ione Mylonas Shear in Mycenaean Archaeology or Athenian architecture.

For further information contact:

The American School of Classical Studies at Athens, 54 Soudias Street, Athens, GR-10676, Greece
Tel: (30) 210 723 6313
Fax: (30) 210 725 0584
Contact: School Director

ASCSA Fellowships

Subjects: Classical philology and archaeology, post-classical Greek studies or a related field.
Eligibility: Open to students who hold a Bachelor of Art degree but not a PhD, and who are preparing for an advanced degree in classical studies or a related field. Applicants must be affiliated with a college or university in the United States of America or Canada.
Level of Study: Graduate, Postgraduate, Predoctorate
Type: Fellowship
Value: US$11,500 stipend plus fees, room and partial board
Length of Study: 1 academic year
Frequency: Annual
Study Establishment: ASCSA
Country of Study: Greece
No. of awards offered: 13

Application Procedure: Applicants must complete an official application, either available on request or from the website. Applications are judged on the basis of credentials and competitive examinations in Greek language, history and archaeology.
Closing Date: January 15th
Funding: Private
No. of awards given last year: 13
No. of applicants last year: 29

ASCSA Research Fellowship in Environmental Studies

Subjects: Earth sciences, geological sciences and archaeological sciences.
Purpose: To support research on studies from archaeological contexts in Greece.
Eligibility: Doctoral candidates working on their dissertation and postdoctoral scholars with well-defined projects that can be completed during the academic year of the fellowship.
Level of Study: Postdoctorate, Doctorate, Postgraduate
Type: Fellowship
Value: US$15,500–25,000 stipend depending on seniority and experience
Length of Study: 1 academic year
Frequency: Annual
Study Establishment: The Malcolm H Wiener Research Laboratory for Archaeological Science, ASCSA
Country of Study: Greece
No. of awards offered: 1
Application Procedure: Applicants must contact the Chair of the Wiener Laboratory by fax or email. Alternatively, they should contact Dr Sherry C Fox by fax at (30) 210 725 0584, or by email at sfox@ascsa.edu.gr for application guidelines and further information.
Closing Date: January 15th
Funding: Private
No. of awards given last year: 1
No. of applicants last year: 11

ASCSA Research Fellowship in Faunal Studies

Subjects: Biological sciences, life sciences and archaeological sciences.
Purpose: To study faunal remains from archaeological contexts in Greece.
Eligibility: Doctoral candidates working on their dissertation and postdoctoral scholars with well-defined projects that can be completed during the academic year of the fellowship. There is no citizenship requirement.
Level of Study: Postdoctorate, Postgraduate, Doctorate
Type: Fellowship
Value: US$15,500–25,000 stipend depending on seniority and experience
Length of Study: 1 academic year
Frequency: Annual
Study Establishment: The Malcolm H Wiener Research Laboratory for Archaeological Science, ASCSA
Country of Study: Greece
No. of awards offered: 1
Application Procedure: Applicants must contact the Chair of the Wiener Laboratory by fax or email. Alternatively, they should contact Dr Sherry C Fox by fax at (30) 210 725 0584, or by email at sfox@ascsa.edu.gr for application guidelines and further information.
Closing Date: January 15th
Funding: Private
No. of awards given last year: 1
No. of applicants last year: 11

ASCSA Research Fellowship in Geoarchaeology

Subjects: Earth sciences, geological sciences and archaeological sciences.
Purpose: To support research on a geoarchaeological topic in Greece.
Eligibility: Doctoral candidates working on their dissertation and postdoctoral scholars with well-defined projects that can be completed during the academic year of the fellowship. There is no citizenship requirement.
Level of Study: Doctorate, Postdoctorate, Postgraduate
Type: Fellowship

Value: US$15,500–25,000 stipend depending on seniority and experience
Length of Study: 1 academic year
Frequency: Annual
Study Establishment: The Malcolm H Wiener Research Laboratory for Archaeological Science, ASCSA
Country of Study: Greece
No. of awards offered: 1
Application Procedure: Applicants must contact the Chair of the Wiener Laboratory by fax or email. Alternatively, they should contact Dr Sherry C Fox by fax at (30) 210 725 0584, or by email at sfox@ascsa.edu.gr for application guidelines and further information.
Closing Date: January 15th
Funding: Private
No. of awards given last year: 1
No. of applicants last year: 11

J Lawrence Angel Fellowship in Human Skeletal Studies

Subjects: Biological sciences, life sciences and archaeological sciences.
Purpose: To study human skeletal remains from archaeological contexts in Greece.
Eligibility: Doctoral candidates working on dissertations and scholars holding a PhD or equivalent degree.
Level of Study: Postgraduate, Doctorate, Postdoctorate
Type: Fellowship
Value: US$15,500–25,000 stipend, depending on seniority and experience
Length of Study: 1 academic year
Frequency: Annual
Study Establishment: The Malcolm H Wiener Research Laboratory for Archaeological Science, ASCSA
Country of Study: Greece
No. of awards offered: 1
Application Procedure: Applicants must contact Dr Sherry C Fox by fax at (30) 210 725 0584, or by email at sfox@ascsa.edu.gr for application guidelines and further information.
Closing Date: January 15th
Funding: Private
Contributor: The Malcolm H Wiener Research Laboratory for Archaeological Sciences at the American School at Athens
No. of awards given last year: 1
No. of applicants last year: 11

Jacob Hirsch Fellowship

Subjects: Pre-classical, classical or post-classical archaeology.
Purpose: To support individuals completing a project that requires a lengthy residence in Greece.
Eligibility: Open to graduate students of American or Israeli institutions who are writing a dissertation and to recent PhD graduates completing a project such as a dissertation for publication. Applications will be judged on the basis of appropriate credentials including referees.
Level of Study: Postdoctorate, Postgraduate, Predoctorate
Type: Fellowship
Value: US$11,000 stipend plus room, board and waiver of fees
Length of Study: 1 academic year, non-renewable
Frequency: Annual
Study Establishment: ASCSA
Country of Study: Greece
No. of awards offered: 1
Application Procedure: Applicants must submit three letters of recommendation, transcripts and a detailed description of projects to be pursued in Greece. Applicants must apply for membership at the School simultaneously with the application for the fellowship.
Closing Date: January 15th
Funding: Private
No. of awards given last year: 1
No. of applicants last year: 5

M Alison Frantz Fellowship in Post-Classical Studies at the Gennadius Library

Subjects: Post-classical studies in late antiquity, Byzantine studies, post-Byzantine studies and modern Greek studies.

Eligibility: Open to PhD candidates. Applicants from institutions in the United States of America or Canada must be recent PhD candidates and all candidates must show a need to use the Gennadius Library.
Level of Study: Postdoctorate, Doctorate, Predoctorate
Type: Fellowship
Value: US$10,000 stipend plus room, board and waiver of fees
Length of Study: 1 academic year
Frequency: Annual
Study Establishment: The Gennadius Library
Country of Study: Greece
No. of awards offered: 1
Application Procedure: Applicants must submit a curriculum vitae, project description and two letters of support to the Chair of Gennadius Library Committee.
Closing Date: January 15th
Funding: Private
No. of awards given last year: 1
No. of applicants last year: 8
Additional Information: This fellowship was formerly known as the Gennadeion Fellowship.

NEH Fellowships

Subjects: Ancient, classical and post-classical studies, including but not limited to the history, philosophy, language, art and archaeology of Greece and the Greek world, art history, literature, philology, architecture, archaeology, anthropology, metallurgy and environmental studies from prehistoric times to the present.
Eligibility: Open to doctoral and postdoctoral scholars who are citizens of the United States of America or foreign nationals with 3 years residency in the United States of America immediately preceding the application deadline.
Level of Study: Postdoctorate, Doctorate
Type: Fellowship
Value: A maximum stipend of US$20,000 for a 5-month project and US$40,000 for a 10-month project
Length of Study: 1 academic year
Frequency: Annual
Study Establishment: ASCSA
Country of Study: Greece
No. of awards offered: 2–5
Application Procedure: Applicants must write for details or visit the website.
Closing Date: December 1st
Funding: Government
No. of awards given last year: 3: 1 academic year, 2 partial year
No. of applicants last year: 21

AMERICAN SCHOOLS OF ORIENTAL RESEARCH (ASOR)

Boston University, 656 Beacon Street, 5th Floor, Boston, MA, 02215-2010, United States of America
Tel: (1) 617 353 6570
Fax: (1) 617 353 6575
Email: asor@bu.edu
Website: www.asor.org
Contact: Ms Alexandra Ratzlaff, Programme Co-ordinator

The American Schools of Oriental Research's (ASOR) mission is to initiate, encourage and support research and public understanding of the people and cultures of the Far East, by fostering original research, archaeological excavations and explorations and by encouraging scholarship in the basic languages, cultural histories and traditions of the Far Eastern world.

ASOR Mesopotamian Fellowship

Subjects: Social sciences, history, archaeology in Middle East studies.
Purpose: To financially support field research in ancient Mesopotamian civilization carried out in Middle East.
Eligibility: Open to applicants affiliated with an institution that is a corporate member of ASOR. See website for further details.
Level of Study: Research
Type: Fellowship
Value: US$7,000 plus

No. of awards offered: 1
Application Procedure: Applicants need to submit application form, transcript and reference letters.
Closing Date: April 1st
Additional Information: Research will be carried out in Middle East, ancient Mesopotamian civilization. Other research projects such as museum or archival research related to Mesopotamian studies may also be considered.

ASOR W.F. Albright Institute of Archaeological Research/ National Endowment of the Humanities Fellowships

Subjects: Archaeology, history, religion/theology, art history, literature/english/writing, social sciences, anthropology, geography, near and Middle East studies.
Purpose: To financially support scholars holding a PhD or equivalent degree with a research project.
Eligibility: Open to citizens of the United States or alien residents residing in the United States for the last 3 years.
Level of Study: Doctorate
Type: Fellowships
Value: Up to US$40,000. Stipend varies with the duration of the fellowship
Length of Study: 4–12 months
Frequency: Annual
Country of Study: United States of America
No. of awards offered: 2
Application Procedure: A completed application form must be sent.
Closing Date: October 1st
Additional Information: Residence at the Institute in Jerusalem is preferred.

AMERICAN SOCIETY FOR ENGINEERING EDUCATION (ASEE)

1818 North Street NW, Suite 600 Zip-2479, Washington, DC, 20036, United States of America
Tel: (1) 202 331 3500/3525
Fax: (1) 202 265 8504
Email: sttp@asee.org
Website: www.asee.org
Contact: Mr Michael More, Projects Department

The American Society for Engineering Education (ASEE) is committed to furthering education in engineering and engineering technology by promoting excellence in instruction, research, public service and practice, exercising worldwide leadership, fostering the technological education of society and providing quality products and services to members.

Air Force Summer Faculty Fellowship Program

Subjects: Engineering, science and mathematics.
Purpose: To stimulate professional relationships among SFFP participants, the scientist and engineers at Air Force Research facilities.
Eligibility: Applicants to the Air Force Summer Faculty Fellowship Program (SFFP) must be citizens or legal permanent residents of the United States. Applicants must hold a full-time appointment at a US college or university. Participants are expected to conduct research at an Air Force Research Laboratory Directorate, US Air Force Academy, or the Air Force Institute of Technology.
Level of Study: Doctorate, Postdoctorate, Postgraduate, Professional development, Research
Type: Fellowship
Value: Weekly stipend US$1,300–1,700
Length of Study: 8–12 weeks
Frequency: Annual
Country of Study: United States of America
Application Procedure: Apply online at www.asee.org/sffp
Closing Date: November
Funding: Government
Contributor: Air Force Office of Scientific Research, US Air Force Academy and the Air Force Institute of Technology
No. of awards given last year: 90
No. of applicants last year: 250

Naval Research Laboratory Post Doctoral Fellowship Program

Subjects: Computer science, artificial intelligence, plasma physics, acoustics, radar, fluid dynamics, chemistry, materials, science and many more specialist fields.
Purpose: To increase the involvement of creative and highly trained scientists to scientific and technical areas of interest and relevance to the US Navy.
Eligibility: US citizens and permanent residents.
Level of Study: Postdoctorate, Doctorate
Type: Fellowship
Value: US$69,000–71,000
Frequency: Annual
Study Establishment: Naval Research Laboratory
Country of Study: United States of America
No. of awards offered: 40
Application Procedure: Apply online at www.asee.org/nrl
Closing Date: No closing dates; rolling admission
Funding: Government
Contributor: US Navy
No. of awards given last year: 35

NDSEG Fellowship Program

Subjects: Aeronautical/astronautical engineering, biosciences, chemical engineering, chemistry, civil engineering, cognitive, neural and behavioral science, computer/computational sciences, electrical engineering, geosciences, materials science and engineering, mathematics, mechanical engineering, naval architecture and ocean engineering, oceanogrphy, physics.
Purpose: To increase the number of US citizens and nationals trained in science and engineering disciplines of military importance.
Eligibility: Must be a US citizen or national. Applicants must be at or near beginning of graduate studies in one of the above-named fields. Applicants must be either enrolled in their final year of undergraduate studies or have completed no more than the equivalent of 2 year's of full-time graduate study in the field in which they are applying. Exceptional circumstances may qualify other applicants as being at the early stages of their graduate studies.
Level of Study: Doctorate
Type: Fellowship
Value: Full tution fees, stipend of $30,500 for 1st year, $31,000 for 2nd year, $31,500 for 3rd year, $1,000/year medical insurance allowance
Length of Study: 3 years
Frequency: Annual
Country of Study: United States of America
No. of awards offered: 200
Application Procedure: Apply online at www.asee.org/ndseg
Closing Date: January 5th
Funding: Government
Contributor: US Department of Defense
No. of awards given last year: 200
No. of applicants last year: 2000

For further information contact:

Email: ndseg@asee.org
Contact: Rachel Kline

ONR Summer Faculty Research

Subjects: Science technology, engineering and mathematics.
Purpose: To allow university faculty members to collaborate with the Navy Scientist on issues of mutual interest.
Eligibility: US citizen or permanent resident, must hold teaching or research appointment at US college or university.
Level of Study: Postdoctorate
Type: Fellowship
Value: $14,000–19,000 (varies per award)
Length of Study: 1 Semester
Frequency: Annual
Country of Study: United States of America
No. of awards offered: Varies
Application Procedure: Apply online at www.asee.org/summer
Closing Date: December 4th
Funding: Government
No. of awards given last year: 73

No. of applicants last year: 544
Additional Information: Programme duration is for a continuous 10 weeks.

For further information contact:

Email: ONRSUMMER@asee.org
Contact: Artis Hicks

SMART Scholarship for Service Program

Subjects: Science, technology, mathematics and engineering.
Purpose: To support the education of future scientists and engineers.
Eligibility: Applicants must be a US citizen or national, pursuing a degree in science, technology, engineering or mathematics, at least 18 years old, have a minimum of 3.0 average on a 4.0 scale and must be enrolled in a US college or university if applying for undergraduate funding.
Level of Study: Doctorate, Graduate
Type: Scholarship
Value: Varies
Length of Study: Varies
Frequency: Annual
Country of Study: United States of America
No. of awards offered: Varies
Application Procedure: Apply online at www.asee.org/smart
Closing Date: December
Funding: Government
Contributor: US Department of Defense
No. of awards given last year: 200
No. of applicants last year: 1800

AMERICAN SOCIETY FOR MICROBIOLOGY (ASM)

1752 N Street North West, Washington, DC, 20036-2904, United States of America
Tel: (1) 202 942 9225
Fax: (1) 202 942 9353
Email: awards@asmusa.org
Website: www.asm.org
Contact: Ms Peggy McNult, Manager, Awards Programme

The American Society for Microbiology (ASM) is the oldest and largest single life science membership organization in the world. With 43,000 members throughout the world. The ASM represents all disciplines of microbiological specialization including microbiology education. The ASM's mission is to promote research and research training in the microbiological sciences and to assist communication between scientists, policymakers and the public to improve health, the environment and economic well-being.

Abbott Laboratories Award in Clinical and Diagnostic Immunology

Subjects: Clinical or diagnostic immunology.
Purpose: To honour a distinguished scientist in the field.
Eligibility: Nominees must demonstrate significant contributions to the understanding of the functioning of the host immune system in human disease, clinical approaches to diseases involving the immune system or development, or clinical application of immunodiagnostic procedures.
Level of Study: Unrestricted
Type: Award
Value: US$2,000 cash prize, a commemorative medal and domestic travel to the ASM General Meeting
Frequency: Annual
Country of Study: Any country
No. of awards offered: 1
Application Procedure: Self-nominations will not be accepted. Nominations must consist of a nomination cover page that includes a specific description of the nominee's contributions, a curriculum vitae including a list of the nominee's publications and two additional supporting letters.
Closing Date: October 1st
Funding: Commercial
Contributor: Abbott Laboratories, Diagnostic Division
No. of awards given last year: 1

No. of applicants last year: 5
Additional Information: ASM awards are granted at the discretion of award selection committees and may not be awarded every year.

Abbott-ASM Lifetime Achievement Award

Subjects: Microbiology.
Purpose: To honour a distinguished scientist for a lifetime of outstanding contributions in fundamental research in any of the microbiological sciences.
Eligibility: Open to mature scientists, both active and retired, from all relevant areas of microbiology.
Level of Study: Unrestricted
Type: Award
Value: US$20,000 cash prize, a commemorative medal and travel to the ASM General Meeting
Frequency: Annual
Country of Study: Any country
No. of awards offered: 1
Application Procedure: Self-nominations will not be accepted. Nominations must consist of a nomination cover page that includes a description of the nominee's outstanding research accomplishments, a curriculum vitae including a list of nominee's publications and two additional letters of support.
Closing Date: October 1st
Funding: Commercial
Contributor: Abbott Laboratories
No. of awards given last year: 1
No. of applicants last year: 15
Additional Information: ASM awards are granted at the discretion of the award selection committees and may not be awarded every year.

ASM Graduate Microbiology Teaching Award

Subjects: Microbiology.
Purpose: To recognize an individual for distinguished teaching of microbiology and mentoring of students at the graduate and postgraduate level and for encouraging them to subsequent achievement.
Eligibility: Nominees must be currently teaching microbiology in a recognized college or university, have devoted a substantial portion of their time during the past 5 years to teaching graduate students in microbiology and have a minimum of 10 years of total teaching experience. Nominees may have engaged in research or other concerns, provided that teaching graduate students remained a substantial activity.
Level of Study: Unrestricted
Type: Award
Value: US$2,000 cash prize, a commemorative medal and travel to the ASM General Meeting
Frequency: Annual
Country of Study: Any country
No. of awards offered: 1
Application Procedure: Self-nominations will not be accepted. Nominations must consist of a nomination cover page that specifically addresses how the nominee fulfils the award eligibility, including a record of teaching responsibilities, manifests of distinguished teaching, innovations, publications, special awards or other pertinent information, a curriculum vitae including a list of the nominee's publications and two additional supporting letters.
Closing Date: October 1st
Funding: Private
Contributor: American Society for Microbiology
No. of awards given last year: 1
No. of applicants last year: 8
Additional Information: ASM awards are granted at the discretion of award selection committees and may not be awarded every year.

BD Award for Research in Clinical Microbiology

Subjects: Clinical microbiology.
Purpose: To honour a distinguished microbiologist for outstanding research accomplishments leading to or forming the foundation for important applications in the field.
Eligibility: Open to clinical microbiologists.
Level of Study: Unrestricted
Type: Award
Value: US$2,000 cash prize, a commemorative medal and travel expenses to the ASM General Meeting

Frequency: Annual
Country of Study: Any country
No. of awards offered: 1
Application Procedure: Self-nominations will not be accepted. Nominations must consist of a nomination cover page that describes the nominee's activities and accomplishments pertinent to the award, a curriculum vitae including a list of publications and two additional supporting letters.
Closing Date: October 1st
Funding: Commercial
Contributor: BD Diagnostic Systems
No. of awards given last year: 1
No. of applicants last year: 4
Additional Information: ASM awards are granted at the discretion of award selection committees and may not be awarded every year.

bioMérieux Sonnenwirth Award for Leadership in Clinical Microbiology

Subjects: Microbiology.
Purpose: To honour a distinguished microbiologist who has exhibited exemplary leadership, recognizes the promotion of innovation in clinical laboratory science and demonstrates high dedication and commitment to ASM and to the advancement of clinical microbiology as a profession.
Eligibility: Open to distinguished microbiologists, who are identified with clinical microbiology.
Level of Study: Unrestricted
Value: US$2,000 cash prize, commemorative medal and travel to the ASM general meeting
Frequency: Annual
Country of Study: Any country
No. of awards offered: 1
Application Procedure: Self-nominations will not be accepted. Nominations must consist of a nomination cover page that describes the nominee's activities and accomplishments pertinent to the award, a curriculum vitae including a list of publications and two additional supporting letters.
Closing Date: October 1st
Funding: Commercial
Contributor: BioMérieux Inc
No. of awards given last year: 1
No. of applicants last year: 7
Additional Information: ASM awards are granted at the discretion of award selection committees and may not be awarded every year.

Carski Foundation Distinguished Undergraduate Teaching Award

Subjects: Science education.
Purpose: To recognize a mature individual for distinguished teaching of microbiology to pre-baccalaureate students and who has encouraged them to subsequent achievements.
Eligibility: Nominees must be currently teaching microbiology in a recognized college or university. A substantial portion of his or her time during the past 5 years must have been devoted to teaching undergraduate students in microbiology and a minimum of 10 years total teaching experience is required. Nominees may have engaged in research or other concerns, provided that teaching undergraduates remained a substantial activity.
Level of Study: Unrestricted
Type: Award
Value: US$2,000 cash prize, commemorative medal and travel to the ASM General Meeting
Frequency: Annual
Country of Study: Any country
No. of awards offered: 1
Application Procedure: Self-nominations will not be accepted. Nominations must consist of a nomination cover page, a nominating letter detailing teaching responsibilities, manifests of distinguished teaching, innovations, publications and special awards, a curriculum vitae and two additional supporting letters.
Closing Date: October 1st
Funding: Foundation, private
Contributor: The Carski Foundation
No. of awards given last year: 1
No. of applicants last year: 11

Additional Information: ASM awards are granted at the discretion of award selection committees and may not be awarded every year.

Eli Lilly and Company Research Award

Subjects: Microbiology and immunology.
Purpose: To reward fundamental research of unusual merit in microbiology or immunology by an individual on the threshold of his/her career.
Eligibility: Nominees must be working in the United States of America or Canada at the time of application and must be actively involved in the line of research for which the award is to be made. They must not have reached their 45th birthday by April 30th of the year the award is given.
Level of Study: Unrestricted
Type: Award
Value: US$5,000 cash prize, a commemorative medal and travel expenses to the ASM General Meeting
Frequency: Annual
Country of Study: Any country
No. of awards offered: 1
Application Procedure: Self-nominations will not be accepted. Nominations must consist of a nominating letter that includes a specific description of the research on which the nomination is based, verification of the date of birth, i.e. a photocopy of driver's licence, passport or birth certificate, a curriculum vitae including a list of publications and two additional supporting letters.
Closing Date: October 1st
Funding: Commercial
Contributor: Eli Lilly and Company
No. of awards given last year: 1
No. of applicants last year: 5
Additional Information: ASM awards are granted at the discretion of award selection committees and may not be awarded every year.

Gen-Probe Joseph Public Health Award

Subjects: Microbiology.
Purpose: To honour a distinguished microbiologist who has exhibited exemplary leadership and service in the field of public health.
Eligibility: Nominees must be a microbiologist identified with public health.
Level of Study: Unrestricted
Value: A cash prize of $2,000 a commemorative piece and a $2,000 travel stipend to attend the ASM general meeting
Frequency: Annual
Country of Study: Any country
No. of awards offered: 1
Application Procedure: Self nominations will not be accepted. Nominations must consist of a letter of nomination that describes the nominee's leadership and service in the field of public health, a curriculum vitae including a list of publications and two additional supporting letters.
Closing Date: October 1st
Funding: Commercial
Contributor: Gen-Probe
No. of awards given last year: 1
No. of applicants last year: 6
Additional Information: ASM awards are granted at the discretion of award selection committees and may not be awarded every year.

ICAAC Young Investigator Award

Subjects: Microbiology, including the discovery and application of chemotherapeutic agents and other sciences associated with infectious diseases.
Purpose: To recognize and reward young investigators for research excellence and potential in microbiology and infectious diseases.
Eligibility: Nominees must have completed postdoctoral research training in microbiology or infectious diseases no more than 3 years prior to presentation of the award.
Level of Study: Postdoctorate, Doctorate
Type: Award
Value: US$2,500 cash prize and commemorative medal
Country of Study: Any country
No. of awards offered: Up to 4
Application Procedure: Self-nominations will not be accepted. Nominations must consist of a nomination cover page including a

specific description of research, a curriculum vitae including a list of publications and two additional supporting letters.
Closing Date: April 1st
Funding: Commercial
Contributor: The Human Health Division of Merck USA and the American Society for Microbiology
No. of awards given last year: 4
No. of applicants last year: 12
Additional Information: ASM awards are granted at the discretion of award selection committees and may not be awarded every year.

Merck Irving S. Sigal Memorial Award
Subjects: Microbiology.
Purpose: To recognize excellence in basic research in medical microbiology and infectious diseases.
Eligibility: Nominees must be no more than 5 years beyond completion of postdoctoral research training in microbiology or infectious diseases at the time of the nomination deadline.
Level of Study: Unrestricted
Value: A commemorative piece and a cash prize of $2,500
Frequency: Annual
Country of Study: Any country
No. of awards offered: Up to 2
Application Procedure: Self nominations will not be accepted. Nominations must consist of a letter of nomination that describes the nominee's excellence in basic research in medical microbiology and infectious diseases, a curriculum vitae including a list of publications and two additional supporting letters.
Closing Date: October 1st
Funding: Commercial
Contributor: Merck Research Laboratories
No. of awards given last year: 2
No. of applicants last year: 7
Additional Information: ASM awards are granted at the discretion of award selection committees and may not be awarded every year.

Procter & Gamble Award in Applied and Environmental Microbiology
Subjects: Environmental microbiology, applied microbiology.
Purpose: To recognize distinguished achievement in research and development in applied (non-clinical) and environmental microbiology.
Eligibility: Nominees must show outstanding accomplishment in research or development in the appropriate field. They must be actively engaged in research or development at the time that the award is presented.
Level of Study: Unrestricted
Type: Award
Value: US$2,000 cash prize, a commemorative medal and travel to the ASM General Meeting
Frequency: Annual
Country of Study: Any country
No. of awards offered: 1
Application Procedure: Self-nominations will not be accepted. Nominations must consist of a nomination cover page that describes the work that has stimulated the nomination, a curriculum vitae including a list of publications and awards and two additional supporting letters.
Closing Date: October 1st
Funding: Commercial
Contributor: Procter & Gamble
No. of awards given last year: 1
No. of applicants last year: 10
Additional Information: ASM awards are granted at the discretion of award selection committees and may not be awarded every year.

Promega Biotechnology Research Award
Subjects: Biotechnology.
Purpose: To honour outstanding contributions to the application of biotechnology through fundamental research, developmental research or reduction to practice.
Eligibility: An outstanding contribution can be a single exceptionally significant achievement or the aggregate of a number of exemplary achievements.
Level of Study: Unrestricted
Type: Award

Value: US$5,000 cash prize, a commemorative medal and travel to the ASM General Meeting
Frequency: Annual
Country of Study: Any country
No. of awards offered: 1
Application Procedure: Self-nominations will not be accepted. Nominations must consist of a nominating letter that includes a description of the nominee's research, a curriculum vitae including a list of publications and two additional supporting letters.
Closing Date: October 1st
Funding: Commercial
Contributor: The Promega Corporation
No. of awards given last year: 1
No. of applicants last year: 15
Additional Information: ASM awards are granted at the discretion of the selection committee and may not be awarded every year.

Raymond W. Sarber Award
Subjects: Microbiology.
Purpose: To recognize students at the undergraduate or predoctoral levels for research excellence and potential.
Eligibility: Nominees must be at the undergraduate or predoctoral level, attending an accredited institution in United States, in an academic programme involving microbiology.
Level of Study: Predoctorate
Value: a cash prize of $1,500, a commemorative piece and travel to the ASM general meeting
Frequency: Annual
Country of Study: Any country
No. of awards offered: Up to 2
Application Procedure: Self nominations will not be accepted. Nominations must consist of a letter of nomination that describes the nominee's research excellence and potential, a personal statement from the student, a curriculum vitae, two additional supporting letters. One letter must be from a supervisor or mentor, while the other letter may be from an academic advisor or colleague.
Closing Date: October 1st
Funding: Private
Contributor: American Society for Microbiology
No. of awards given last year: 1
No. of applicants last year: 3
Additional Information: ASM awards are granted at the discretion of award selection committees and may not be awarded every year.

Roche Diagnostics Alice C. Evans Award
Subjects: Microbiology.
Purpose: To recognize contributions toward the full participation and advancement of women in microbiology.
Eligibility: Nominees can be any member of ASM who has made major contributions toward fostering the inclusion, development and advancement of women in careers in microbiology. Nominees must demonstrate commitment to women in science through mentorship and advocacy and by setting an example through scientific and professional achievement.
Level of Study: Unrestricted
Value: A commemorative plaque and travel to the ASM general meeting
Frequency: Annual
Country of Study: Any country
No. of awards offered: 1
Application Procedure: Self nominations will not be accepted. Nominations must consist of a letter of nomination that describes the nominees major contributions toward fostering the inclusion, development and advancement of women in careers in microbiology, a curriculum vitae including a list of publications and two additional supporting letters.
Closing Date: October 1st
Funding: Corporation
Contributor: Roche Diagnostics Corporation
No. of awards given last year: 1
No. of applicants last year: 6
Additional Information: ASM awards are granted at the discretion of award selection committees and may not be awarded every year.

sanofi-aventis US Award
Subjects: Microbiology.

Purpose: To stimulate research in antimicrobial chemotherapy and honour outstanding sustained achievement.
Eligibility: Nominees must be actively engaged in research involving development of new agents, investigation of antimicrobial action or resistance to antimicrobial agents and/or the pharmacology, toxicology or clinical use of those agents. They must not have served on an ICAAC Program Committee within the past 2 years.
Level of Study: Unrestricted
Type: Award
Value: US$20,000 cash prize, a commemorative medal and travel expenses
Frequency: Annual
Country of Study: Any country
No. of awards offered: 1
Application Procedure: Self-nominations will not be accepted. Nominations must consist of a nomination cover page that includes a specific description of the research on which the nomination is based, a curriculum vitae including a list of publications and two additional supporting letters.
Closing Date: April 1st
Funding: Commercial
Contributor: sanofi-aventis US
No. of awards given last year: 1
No. of applicants last year: 15
Additional Information: ASM awards are granted at the discretion of award selection committees and may not be awarded every year.

Scherago-Rubin Award

Subjects: Clinical microbiology.
Purpose: To recognize an outstanding, bench-level clinical microbiologist.
Eligibility: Nominees must be a non-doctoral level clinical microbiologists involved primarily in routine diagonostic work, rather than in research, who has distinguished himself or herself with excellent performance in clinical laboratory.
Level of Study: Graduate, Predoctorate
Value: A commemorative piece and $1,500 cash prize to defray costs of attending the ASM general meeting
Frequency: Annual
Country of Study: Any country
No. of awards offered: 1
Application Procedure: Self nominations will not be accepted. Nominations must consist of a letter of nomination from supervisor that describes the nominee's routine disgnostic work that has distinguished him or her in the clinical laboratory, a curriculum vitae including a list of publications and two additional supporting letters.
Closing Date: October 1st
Funding: Private
Contributor: American Society for Microbiology
No. of awards given last year: 1
No. of applicants last year: 4
Additional Information: ASM awards are granted at the discretion of award selection committees and may not be awarded every year.

Siemens Healthcare Diagnostics Young Investigator Award

Subjects: Microbiology.
Purpose: To recognize research excellence and potential and to further the educational or research objectives of an outstanding young clinical scientist.
Eligibility: The nominee must be no more than 5 years beyond completion of postdoctoral training
Level of Study: Postdoctorate
Type: Award
Value: US$2,000 cash prize, a commemorative medal and travel to the ASM General Meeting
Frequency: Annual
Country of Study: Any country
No. of awards offered: 1
Application Procedure: Self-nominations will not be accepted. Nominations must consist of a nomination cover page, a curriculum vitae including a list of publications, abstracts and manuscripts in preparation, 1 or 2 page statement from the nominee that describes

how educational or research objectives will be enhanced by the award, and 2 additional supporting letters documenting the nominee's research excellence and anticipated impact of the award on achievement of the nominee's career objectives.
Closing Date: October 1st
Funding: Commercial
Contributor: Siemens Healthcare Diagnostics
No. of awards given last year: 1
No. of applicants last year: 8
Additional Information: ASM awards are granted at the discretion of award selection committees and may not be awarded every year.

USFCC/J. Roger Porter Award

Subjects: Microbiology.
Purpose: To recognize outstanding efforts by a scientist who has demonstrated the importance of microbial biodiversity through sustained curatorial or stewardship activities for a major resource used by the scientific community.
Eligibility: Nominees will have greatly aided other scientists by demonstrating the fundamentals of culture collections and related resources and the rich biodiversity that such collections preserve.
Level of Study: Unrestricted
Value: A cash prize of $2,000, a commemorative piece and travel to the ASM general meeting
Frequency: Annual
Country of Study: Any country
No. of awards offered: 1
Application Procedure: Self nominations will not be accepted. Nominations must consist of a letter of nomination that describes the nominee's outstanding efforts demostrating the importance of microbial biodiversity through sustained curatorial or stewardship activities for a major resource used by the scientific community, a curriculum vitae including a list of publications and two additional supporting letters.
Closing Date: October 1st
Funding: Commercial, private
Contributor: The United States Ferderation for Cultural Collections and The American Society for Microbiology
No. of awards given last year: 1
No. of applicants last year: 5
Additional Information: ASM awards are granted at the discretion of award selection committees and may not be awarded every year.

William A Hinton Research Training Award

Subjects: Microbiology.
Purpose: To honour an individual who has made outstanding signif-icant contributions towards fostering the research training of under-represented minorities in microbiology.
Eligibility: Nominees must have contributed to the research training of undergraduate students, graduate students, postdoctoral Fellows or health professional students. Their efforts must have led to the in-creased participation of underrepresented minorities in microbiology.
Level of Study: Unrestricted
Type: Award
Value: US$2,000 cash prize, a commemorative medal and travel to the ASM General Meeting
Frequency: Annual
Country of Study: Any country
No. of awards offered: 1
Application Procedure: Self-nominations will not be accepted. Nominations must consist of a cover page, a nominating letter highlighting the nominee's activities and accomplishments pertinent to the award, a curriculum vitae and two additional supporting letters.
Closing Date: October 1st
Funding: Private
Contributor: ASM
No. of awards given last year: 1
No. of applicants last year: 3
Additional Information: ASM awards are granted at the discretion of award selection committees and may not be awarded every year.

AMERICAN SOCIETY FOR PHOTOGRAMMETRY AND REMOTE SENSING (ASPRS)

The Imaging and Geospatial Information Society, 5410 Grosvenor Lane Suite 210, Bethesda, MD, 20814-2160, United States of America
Tel: (1) 301 493 0290
Fax: (1) 301 493 0208
Email: asprs@asprs.org
Website: www.asprs.org

The American Society for Photogrammetry and Remote Sensing (ASPRS) was founded in 1934. It is a scientific association serving over 7,000 professional members around the world whose mission is to advance knowledge and improve understanding of mapping sciences to promote the responsible applications of photogrammetry, remote sensing, geographic information systems and supporting technologies.

ASPRS Robert N. Colwell Memorial Fellowship
Subjects: Remote sensing and geospatial information technologies.
Purpose: To encourage and commend college/university students or postdoctoral researchers who display exceptional interest, desire, ability and aptitude in the specified field and who have a special interest in developing practical uses of these technologies.
Eligibility: Open to students enrolled or intending to enrol in a college or university in the United States or Canada, or a recently graduated postdoctoral researcher who is pursuing a programme of study aimed at starting a professional career.
Level of Study: Doctorate, Postgraduate
Type: Fellowship
Value: US$5,000
Frequency: Annual
Country of Study: United States of America or Canada
Application Procedure: Applicants must include a listing of courses, transcripts, listing of internship, 3 letters of recommendation and statement of purpose along with a completed application form.
Closing Date: December 1st
Contributor: ASPRS Foundation

ASPRS Student Travel Grants
Purpose: To increase student exposure to the profession and to encourage continued student identification with and membership in ASPRS as their national professional organisation.
Level of Study: Graduate
Type: Travel grant
Value: US$500
Frequency: Annual
Country of Study: Any country
No. of awards offered: 2
Application Procedure: Applicants must submit a one-page written statement outlining the importance of attending this conference in relation to the applicant's course of study and career development plans, one letter of recommendation from a faculty advisor, agreement to serve as a student volunteer at the conference and attendence at the conference.
Closing Date: December 1st
Funding: Foundation

ASPRS Ta Liang Memorial Award
Subjects: Remote sensing.
Purpose: To facilitate research-related travel by outstanding graduate students.
Level of Study: Graduate
Type: Grant
Value: US$500
Frequency: Annual
Application Procedure: Applicants must submit an application form and recommendation letters. In addition to that they must also submit a 2 page statement detailing the plan for research-related travel, transcripts and Graduate Record Examination scores.
Closing Date: December 1st
Funding: Corporation, individuals
Contributor: ASPRS Foundation

Additional Information: The recipient is obligated to provide ASPRS and Ta Liang's family, a report of his/her accomplishments during the travel for which the award is granted.

ASPRS William A. Fischer Memorial Scholarship
Subjects: Remote sensing data/techniques.
Purpose: To facilitate graduate-level studies and career goals directed towards new and innovative uses of remote sensing data/techniques that relate to the natural, cultural or agricultural resources of the Earth.
Eligibility: Open to current or prospective graduate student.
Level of Study: Graduate
Type: Scholarship
Value: US$2,000 per scholarship
Frequency: Annual
Country of Study: United States of America
Application Procedure: Applicants must submit a 2-page statement detailing applicant's educational and career plans for continuing studies in remote sensing applications, letters of recommendation and transcripts.
Closing Date: December 1st
Funding: Corporation, individuals
Contributor: ASPRS Foundation

BAE Systems Award
Subjects: Photogrammetry, remote sensing.
Purpose: To reward top quality research and publication by young students at Master's or doctoral level and to encourage researchers to use the ASPRS annual conference as a vehicle to publish and present their findings.
Eligibility: Applicants must be a student enrolled in a Master's or doctoral programme at a recognised institution, must be the principal of the paper accepted for publication, must be a current student member of ASPRS.
Level of Study: Postgraduate, Doctorate
Type: Grant
Value: US$2,000 equally divided among the recipients, if more than one is selected
Frequency: Annual
Country of Study: Any country
Application Procedure: Applicants must submit an abstract and once it is accepted for presentation, the full paper should be submitted along with the application for the award.
Closing Date: December 1st
Funding: Private
Contributor: BAE Systems

GeoEye Award
Subjects: Remote sensing, image processing.
Purpose: To support remote sensing education and stimulate the development of applications high-resolution digital satellite imagery for applied research by graduate students.
Eligibility: Applicant should be full-time undergraduate or graduate student at an accredited college or university in the United States or Canada with image processing facilities appropriate for conducting the proposed work.
Level of Study: Graduate
Value: IKONOS satellite imagery (potential value upto US$2,000)
Frequency: Annual
Study Establishment: Accredited college or university in the United States or Canada
Country of Study: United States of America or Canada
Application Procedure: Applicants must submit the application form along with letters of recommendation and a brief 2-page proposal.
Closing Date: December 1st
Funding: Private
Contributor: GeoEye
Additional Information: The imagery award is one 100 sq. km scene from the GeoEye archive. Request for more square kilometers will be considered on a case-by-case basis.

Intergraph Scholarsip
Subjects: Signal processing, image processing, photogrammetry.
Purpose: To facilitate graduate-level studies and career goals adjudged to address new and innovative uses of signal processing,

image processing techniques and the application of photogrammetry to real-world techniques within the earthimaging industry.
Eligibility: Applicant should be a member of ASPRS. Should be a student currently pursuing graduate-level studies or who plans to enroll for graduate studies.
Level of Study: Graduate
Type: Scholarship
Value: US$2,000
Frequency: Annual
Study Establishment: Recognised college or university
Country of Study: Any country
Application Procedure: Applicants should submit the application forms along with 2-page statement detailing educational and career plans and two reference forms from faculty members who have knowledge of the applicant's capabilities.
Closing Date: December 1st
Funding: Private
Contributor: Intergraph

Leica Geosystems Internship
Subjects: Photogrammetry, remote sensing.
Purpose: The internship provides the award winner with an opportunity to carry out a small research project of his/her own choice or to work on an Leica Geosystems project as part of a team.
Eligibility: Applicants must be able to travel to the Leica Geosystems locations.
Level of Study: Graduate
Type: Internship
Value: US$2,500 plus an allowance for travel and living expences for the period of internship
Length of Study: 8 weeks
Frequency: Annual
Country of Study: Any country
Application Procedure: Applicants must submit application forms, letters of recommendation, official transcript and proposal for the type of research the intern would like to conduct.
Closing Date: December 1st
Funding: Private
Contributor: Leica Geosystems GIS & Mapping, LLC

Paul R. Wolf Memorial Scholarship
Subjects: Surveying, mapping, photogrammetry.
Purpose: To encourage and commend college students who display exceptional interest, desire, ability and aptitude to enter the profession of teaching surveying, mapping or photogrammetry.
Eligibility: Applicants must be a graduate student currently enrolled or intending to enroll in a college or university in the United States, who is pursuing a programme of study in preparation for entering the teaching profession in the general area of surveying, mapping or photogrammetry.
Level of Study: Graduate
Type: Scholarship
Value: US$1,500
Frequency: Annual
Country of Study: United States of America
Application Procedure: Applicants must submit the application forms along with list of courses taken, academic grades, a transcript of all college and university level courses completed, two letters of recommendation from faculty members, papers, reports, other items produced by the applicant, a statement of teaching experience and a 2 page statement detailing applicant's plans for continuing studies to become an educational professional in surveying, mapping or photogrammetry.
Closing Date: December 1st
Funding: Individuals
Contributor: Friends and colleagues of Paul R. Wolf

Robert E. Altenhofen Memorial Scholarship
Subjects: Theoretical photogrammetry.

Purpose: To encourage college students who display exceptional interest and ability in the theoretical aspects of photogrammetry.
Level of Study: Graduate
Type: Award
Value: US$2,000
Frequency: Annual
Country of Study: Any country
Application Procedure: Applicants should submit application form, letters of recommendation, 2-page statement regarding plans for continuing studies, papers, reports or other items and academic transcripts.
Closing Date: December 1st
Funding: Foundation

AMERICAN SOCIETY FOR QUALITY (ASQ)

600 North Plankinton Avenue, Milwaukee, WI, 53203, United States of America
Tel: (1) 414 272 8575
Fax: (1) 414 272 1734
Email: help@asq.org
Website: www.asq.org

The American Society for Quality (ASQ) is the world's leading authority on quality. With more than 100,000 individual and organizational members, this professional association advances learning, quality improvement and knowledge exchange to improve business results and to create better workplaces and communities worldwide.

ASQ Ellis R. Ott Scholarship for Applied Statistics and Quality Management
Subjects: Statistics.
Purpose: To encourage students to pursue a career in a field related to statistics and/or quality management.
Eligibility: Open to candidates who are planning to enroll or are enrolled in a Master's degree or higher level programme in the United States or Canada.
Level of Study: Doctorate, Postgraduate
Type: Scholarships
Value: US$5,000
Length of Study: 1 year
Frequency: Annual
Country of Study: United States of America
No. of awards offered: 6
Application Procedure: Applicants can download the application form from the website. The completed application form along with curriculum vitae, academic transcripts and 2 letters of recommendation are to be submitted.
Closing Date: April 1st

For further information contact:

Kraft Foods, Research - East 200 DeForest Avenue, East Hanover, NJ, 07936-1944, United States of America
Contact: Dr Lynne B Hare

The Richard A. Freund International Scholarship
Subjects: It covers the engineering, statistical, managerial and behavioral foundations of theory and application of quality control, quality assurance, quality improvement, and total quality management.
Purpose: This scholarship honours the memory of Richard A. Freund, a past president of ASQ. It is for graduate study of the theory and application of quality control, quality assurance, quality improvement and total quality management.
Level of Study: Postgraduate
Type: Scholarship
Value: US$5,000
Frequency: Annual
No. of awards offered: Varies
Closing Date: April 1st
Funding: Foundation

AMERICAN SOCIETY OF HEATING, REFRIGERATING AND AIR CONDITIONING ENGINEERS, INC. (ASHRAE)

1791 Tullie Circle North East, Atlanta, GA, 30329, United States of America
Tel: (1) 404 636 8400
Fax: (1) 678 539 2112
Email: mvaughn@ashrae.org
Website: www.ashrae.org
Contact: Mr Michael R Vaughn, Manager of Research and Technical Services

The American Society of Heating, Refrigerating and Air Conditioning Engineers, Inc. (ASHRAE) is an international organization of 50,000 people with chapters all over the world. The Society is organized for the sole purpose of advancing the arts and sciences of heating, ventilation, air conditioning and refrigerating for public's benefit through research, standards writing, continuing education and publications.

ASHRAE Grants-in-Aid for Graduate Students
Subjects: Heating, refrigeration, air conditioning and ventilation.
Purpose: To stimulate interest through the encouragement of original research.
Eligibility: Open to graduate engineering students capable of undertaking appropriate and scholarly research.
Level of Study: Doctorate, Postgraduate
Type: Grant
Value: Up to US$10,000 depending upon the needs and nature of request
Length of Study: Usually for 1 year or less, non-renewable
Frequency: Annual
Study Establishment: The grantee's institution
Country of Study: Any country
No. of awards offered: 12–18
Application Procedure: Applicants must complete an application form, available from the website. An application form must also be submitted by the faculty advisor.
Closing Date: December 15th
Funding: Private
No. of awards given last year: 18
No. of applicants last year: 48

AMERICAN SOCIETY OF HEMATOLOGY (ASH)

1900 M Street North West, Suite 200, Washington, DC, 20036, United States of America
Tel: (1) 202 776 0544
Fax: (1) 202 776 0545
Email: ash@hematology.org
Website: www.hematology.org
Contact: Administrative Assistant

The mission of the American Society of Hematology (ASH) is to further the understanding, diagnosis, treatment and prevention of disorders affecting the blood, bone marrow and the immunologic, hemostatic and vascular systems, by promoting research, clinical care, education, training and advocacy in hematology.

American Society of Hematology Minority Medical Student Award Program
Subjects: Haematology.
Purpose: To provide support for a summer research programme of 8–12 weeks and for travel to the Society's annual meeting.
Eligibility: Applicants must be minority medical students enrolled in either MD, MD/PhD or equivalent DO programmes and must be citizens or permanent residents of the United States of America or Canada.
Level of Study: Professional development, Research
Type: Grant
Value: US$7,000 plus US$1,000 travel allowance
Length of Study: 8–12 weeks
Frequency: Annual
Study Establishment: Depends on participant, US or Canadian university
Country of Study: United States of America or Canada
No. of awards offered: 10
Application Procedure: All applicants must complete the Minority Medical Student Award Program application available from the website.
Closing Date: March 14th
Funding: Commercial
No. of awards given last year: 9
No. of applicants last year: 11
Additional Information: For additional information, please contact Courtney Krier, Award Programme Coordinator, at ckrier@hematology.org or by phone at 202 776 0544, ext. 1168. Notification of awards will be by May 1st.

American Society of Hematology Scholar Award
Subjects: Haematology.
Purpose: To encourage haematologists to begin a career in research by providing partial salary or other support.
Eligibility: To be eligible for the Junior Faculty Scholar Award, applicants must be within the first 2 years of their initial faculty appointment as an assistant professor, and for the Fellow Scholar Award, applicants must have more than 2 years, but less than 6 years of postdoctoral research training. Applicants must work in a United States of America or Canadian institution.
Level of Study: Research
Type: Award
Value: US$100,000 for Fellow Scholars and US$150,000 for Junior Faculty Scholars
Length of Study: 2–3 years
Frequency: Annual
Application Procedure: A letter of intent must be submitted by early May and it should include a signed cover letter, abstract of the proposed project (350 words or less), applicant's curriculum vitae and should identify which award category the applicant is applying for.
Closing Date: August 28th
Funding: Commercial, foundation
No. of awards given last year: 17
No. of applicants last year: 83
Additional Information: For detailed information, applicants must visit the website or contact Courtney Krier at the American Society of Hematology.

American Society of Hematology Trainee Research Award Program
Subjects: Haematology.
Purpose: To provide support for a research project of 3 months and for travel to the Society's annual meeting.
Eligibility: Applicants must be medical students or residents and selected undergraduates only. The programme is open to ACGME-accredited institutions in the United States of America, Mexico and Canada that have a training programme director in haematology or a related area.
Level of Study: Professional development
Value: US$4,000 plus US$1,000 for travel
Length of Study: 3 months
Frequency: Annual
No. of awards offered: 1
Application Procedure: All applicants and institutions must complete the Trainee Award application form available from the website.
Closing Date: March 15th
Funding: Commercial
Additional Information: For any additional information regarding the programme, please contact Joe Basso, Training Manager, at 202 776 0544.

American Society of Hematology Travel and Merit Awards
Subjects: Haematology.
Purpose: To help individuals to defray annual meeting expenses.
Eligibility: Applicants must be medical students graduate students, resident physicians or postdoctoral Fellows who are both first author and present of an abstract.

Level of Study: Professional development
Type: Travel grant
Value: US$500
Frequency: Annual
Application Procedure: Applicants must submit an abstract for the annual meeting and identify themselves as 'travel/merit award' applicants. Applicants must also include a letter from their Training Programme Director requesting travel support and indentifying need.
Closing Date: Early August
Funding: Commercial, foundation
No. of awards given last year: 195

American Society of Hematology Visiting Trainee Program

Subjects: Haematology.
Purpose: To provide scientists and haematologists in developing countries an opportunity to gain valuable clinical experience, technology training or laboratory experience.
Eligibility: Applicants must be scientists and haematologists from developing countries as defined by the American Society of Hematology.
Level of Study: Professional development
Type: Grant
Length of Study: Up to 12 weeks
Frequency: Annual
Application Procedure: Applicants must complete the visiting trainee programme application and submit it with a letter of recommendation from the proposed host institution. They will need to identify a site and host for their proposed short-term clinical or laboratory experience and give a clear statement of the topic or goal of the training programme. Application forms are available from the website.
Closing Date: May 1st
Funding: Commercial
Additional Information: For any additional information regarding the programme, please contact Lafaundra Neville, Executive Assistant, by email at lneville@hematology.org or phone at 202 776 544 Ext. 1106.

ASH-AMFDP Award

Subjects: Heamatology.
Purpose: To increase the number of underrepresented minority scholars in the field of heamatology with academic and research appointments.
Eligibility: Applicants must be from historically disadvantaged backgrounds, US citizens or permanent residents at the time of application deadline, completing their formal clinical training.
Value: $75,000 and an annual grant of $30,000
Length of Study: 4 years
Frequency: Annual
Application Procedure: Applications are available online at www.amfdp.org.
Closing Date: March 23rd
Funding: Commercial, foundation

For further information contact:

8701 Georgia Ave. Suite 411, Silver Spring, MD, 20910-3713
Contact: Harold Amos, Medical Faculty Development Programme

EHA-ASH International Fellowship Award

Purpose: To provide heamatologists early in their careers or in training the opportunity to conduct research in another country.
Eligibility: Applicant should be a member of ASH or EHA, older than 38 years and from Europe or North America.
Level of Study: Postgraduate, Doctorate
Value: $75,000
Length of Study: 10 months–2 years
Frequency: Annual
No. of awards offered: 2
Application Procedure: Applicants must submit a letter of intent by early September. The letter of intent is available at the ASH website.
Closing Date: Early September
Funding: Foundation

AMERICAN SOCIETY OF INTERIOR DESIGNERS (ASID) EDUCATIONAL FOUNDATION, INC.

608 Massachusetts Avenue North East, Washington, DC, 20002-6006, United States of America
Tel: (1) 202 546 3480
Fax: (1) 202 546 3240
Email: education@asid.org
Website: www.asid.org
Contact: Education Department

The American Society of Interior Designers (ASID) Educational Foundation represents the interests of more than 30,500 members including interior design practitioners, students and industry and retail partners. ASID's mission is to be the definitive resource for professional education and knowledge sharing, advocacy of interior designers' right to practice and expansion of interior design markets.

ASID/Joel Polsky-Fixtures Furniture Academic Achievement Award

Subjects: Interior design.
Purpose: To recognise an outstanding student's interior design research or thesis project.
Eligibility: Open to applicants of any nationality. Research papers or doctoral and Master's theses should address such interior design topics as educational research, behavioural science, business practice, design process, theory or other technical subjects.
Level of Study: Postgraduate
Type: Prize
Value: US$1,000
Frequency: Annual
Country of Study: Any country
No. of awards offered: 1
Application Procedure: Applicants must write for details.
Closing Date: April 30th
Additional Information: Entries will be judged on actual content, breadth of material, comprehensive coverage of topic, innovative subject matter and bibliography or references.

ASID/Joel Polsky-Fixtures Furniture Prize

Subjects: Interior design.
Purpose: To recognise outstanding academic contributions to the discipline of interior design through literature or visual communication.
Eligibility: Entries should address the needs of the public, designers and students on topics such as educational research, behavioural science, business practice, design process, theory or other technical subjects.
Level of Study: Unrestricted
Type: Prize
Value: US$1,000
Frequency: Annual
Country of Study: Any country
No. of awards offered: 1
Application Procedure: Applicants must write for details.
Closing Date: April 30th
Additional Information: Material will be judged on innovative subject matter, comprehensive coverage of topic, organization, graphic presentation and bibliography or references.

ASID/Mabelle Wilhelmina Boldt Memorial Scholarship

Subjects: Interior design.
Eligibility: Applicants must have been practising designers for a period of at least five years prior to returning to graduate level. Preference will be given to those with a focus on design research. The scholarship will be awarded on the basis of academic or creative accomplishment, as demonstrated by school transcripts and a letter of recommendation.
Level of Study: Graduate
Type: Scholarship
Value: US$2,000
Frequency: Annual
Study Establishment: A degree granting institution
Country of Study: Any country

No. of awards offered: 1
Application Procedure: Applicants must write for details.
Closing Date: April 30th

AMERICAN SOCIETY OF MECHANICAL ENGINEERS (ASME INTERNATIONAL)

Three Park Avenue, New York, NY 10016-5990, United States of America
Tel: (1) 212 591 8131
Fax: (1) 212 591 7143
Email: oluwanifiset@asme.org
Website: www.asme.org/education/enged/aid
Contact: Theresa Oluwanifise, Coordinator Educational Operations

Founded in 1880 as the American Society of Mechanical Engineers (ASME International), today ASME International is a non-profit educational and technical organization serving a worldwide membership.

ASME Graduate Teaching Fellowship Program

Subjects: Mechanical engineering.
Purpose: To encourage outstanding students, especially women and minorities, to pursue a doctorate in mechanical engineering teaching and to encourage the engineering education as a profession.
Eligibility: Open to PhD students in mechanical engineering, with a demonstrated interest in a teaching career. A Master's degree or passage of qualifying exam is required as is a lecture responsibility/teaching assistantship commitment from the applicant's department. In addition, the applicant should be a citizen of the United States of America or permanent resident, with an undergraduate degree from an ABET-accredited programme, and a student member of ASME. The student must also study in the United States of America.
Level of Study: Doctorate, Postgraduate
Type: Fellowship
Value: US$5,000 per year
Length of Study: 2 years
Frequency: Annual
Country of Study: United States of America
No. of awards offered: 4
Application Procedure: Applicants must submit an undergraduate grade point average, Graduate Record Examination scores, two letters of recommendation from faculty or their MS committee, a graduate transcript, transcripts of all academic work, a statement about faculty career and a current curriculum vitae.
Closing Date: October 15th
No. of awards given last year: 4
No. of applicants last year: 10
Additional Information: In the terms of the fellowship, the awardee must teach at least one lecture course. The applicant's department head must certify, prior to the award or continuation notice, the commitment of a teaching assistantship and the lecture assignment anticipated.

Elisabeth M and Winchell M Parsons Scholarship

Subjects: Mechanical engineering.
Purpose: To assist ASME student members working towards a doctoral degree.
Eligibility: Selection is based on academic performance, character, need and ASME participation. Applicants must be citizens of the United States of America and be enrolled in a United States of America school in an ABET-accredited mechanical engineering department. No student may receive more than one auxiliary scholarship or loan in the same academic year.
Level of Study: Doctorate
Type: Grant
Value: US$2,000
Frequency: Annual
Country of Study: United States of America
No. of awards offered: Approx. 2
Application Procedure: Application forms are available from the website.
Closing Date: March 15th

For further information contact:

216 Churchill Crossing, Nicholasville, Kentucky, 40356, United States of America

Tel: (1) 859 887 3949
Email: mrsnyder@aol.com
Contact: Mary Snyder

Marjorie Roy Rothermel Scholarship

Subjects: Mechanical engineering.
Purpose: To assist students working towards a Master's degree.
Eligibility: Selection is based on academic performance, character, need and ASME participation. Applicants must be citizens of the United States of America and must be enrolled in a United States of America school in an ABET-accredited mechanical engineering department. No student may receive more than one auxiliary scholarship or loan in the same academic year.
Level of Study: Graduate
Type: Scholarship
Value: US$2,000
Frequency: Annual
Country of Study: United States of America
No. of awards offered: 6–8
Application Procedure: Application forms are available from the website.
Closing Date: March 15th

For further information contact:

332 Valencia Street, Gulf Breeze, FL, 32561, United States of America
Tel: (1) 850 932 3698
Email: eprocha340@aol.com
Contact: Mrs Otto Prochaska

Rice-Cullimore Scholarship

Subjects: Mechanical engineering.
Purpose: To aid a foreign student pursuing graduate work for a Master's or doctoral degree in the United States of America.
Eligibility: Open to candidates from any country except the United States of America. Selection is based on academic performance, character, need and ASME participation. No student may receive more than one auxiliary scholarship or loan in the same academic year.
Level of Study: Doctorate
Type: Scholarship
Value: US$2,000
Length of Study: 1 year
Frequency: Annual
Country of Study: United States of America
Application Procedure: Applicants must apply in their home country through the local institute of International Education Embassy (IEE) or Education Offices at the United States of America Embassy. Only applications received from the IEE will be considered.
Closing Date: Please contact the organization

AMERICAN SOCIETY OF NEPHROLOGY (ASN)

1725 I Street NW, Suite 510, Washington, DC, 20006, United States of America
Tel: (1) 202 659 0599
Fax: (1) 202 659 0709
Email: email@asn-online.org
Website: www.asn-online.org
Contact: Grants Co-ordinator

The American Society of Nephrology (ASN) was founded in 1967 as a non-profit corporation to enhance and assist the study and practice of nephrology, to provide a forum for the promulgation of research and to meet the professional and continuing education needs of its members.

ASN M James Scherbenske Grant

Subjects: Nephrology.
Purpose: To provide bridge funding for investigators from R01 to R01 whose application was scored, but not funded.
Eligibility: Applicants must be an active member of the ASN and hold an MD or PhD or equivalent degree. The applicants appointment to full-time faculty must be confirmed in writing by the department chair,

indicating the date of first full-time faculty appointment, and providing assurance that the department will provide needed resources for conducting independent research.

Type: Grant
Value: US$100,000
Length of Study: 1 year
Frequency: Annual
Country of Study: United States of America
Application Procedure: Applicants must submit four copies of the grant application form, available online, and the NIH grant proposal.
Closing Date: March 15th, June 15th, November 15th
Funding: Private
Contributor: ASN
Additional Information: Applicants will be considered ineligible should they submit more than one ASN grant application during any particular grants cycle. For detailed information contact Benjamin Schuster by email at bschuster@asn-online.org

ASN-ASP Junior Development Grant in Geriatric Nephrology

Subjects: Geriatric and gerontologic aspects of nephrology.
Purpose: To support developing academic subspecialists interested in careers in the field.
Eligibility: Open to individuals who are within the first 3 years of a faculty appointment. Candidates must have completed a subspecialty internal medicine fellowship leading to a certification in nephrology by the American Board of Internal Medicine. All candidates must have United States of America citizenship or permanent resident status classification in the United States of America, and must be active ASN members at the time of application.
Type: Grant
Value: US$75,000 per year. The award will also include a one-time travel grant of US$3,000, which must be used to attend the meetings of the American Geriatrics Society and the ASN during the second year of the award
Length of Study: 2 years
Frequency: Annual
No. of awards offered: 1
Application Procedure: Applicants must submit four copies of the grant application form, available online, which must include the department chairman's letter, division director's letter (if applicable) and three letters of reference.
Closing Date: February 1st
Contributor: ASP, ASN
No. of awards given last year: 2
No. of applicants last year: 7

ASN-AST John Merrill Grant in Transplantation

Subjects: Biomedical research related to transplantation.
Purpose: To foster the independent careers of young investigators in biomedical research related to transplantation.
Eligibility: Applicant must be an active member of the ASN and hold an MD or PhD or equivalent degree. At the time of submission the applicant's membership must be current and their dues paid. Appointment to full-time faculty must be confirmed in writing by the department chair.
Level of Study: Postdoctorate, Postgraduate
Value: US$100,000
Length of Study: 2 years
Frequency: Annual
Study Establishment: ASN and AST
Country of Study: United States of America
Application Procedure: Applicants must submit four copies of the grants application form, letters from the chairman and division director, a curriculum vitae and a research proposal (no longer than 10 pages).
Closing Date: February 1st
Additional Information: For more information contact Benjamin Schuster by email at bschuster@asn-online.org

Carl W Gottschalk Research Scholar Grant

Subjects: Nephrology.
Purpose: To provide funding for young faculty to foster evolution to an independent research career.
Eligibility: Applicants must an active member of the ASN and hold an MD or PhD or equivalent degree. At the time of submission the appli-

cant's membership must be current and their dues paid. Appointment to full-time faculty must be conformed in writing by the department chair.
Level of Study: Postgraduate, Postdoctorate
Type: Grant
Value: US$100,000 for 2 years. A maximum of 10 per cent of the whole amount can be used to cover indirect costs at the candidate's sponsoring institution
Length of Study: 2 years
Frequency: Annual
Country of Study: United States of America
Application Procedure: Applicants must submit four copies of the grant application form, the letters from the chairman and division director, a curriculum vitae and a research proposal (no longer than 10 pages).
Closing Date: February 1st
Contributor: Co-sponsored by the Kidney and Urology Foundation of America
Additional Information: For detailed information contact Benjamin Schuster by email at bschuster@asn-online.org

AMERICAN SOCIETY OF TRAVEL AGENTS (ASTA) FOUNDATION, INC.

Myriam Lechuga, 1101 King ST, Suite 200, Alexandria, VA 22314-2944, United States of America
Tel: (1) 703 739 2782
Fax: (1) 703 684 8319
Email: scholarship@astahq.com
Website: www.astanet.com

ASTA is the world's largest association of travel professionals. Its mission is to enhance the professionalism and profitability of member agents through effective representation in industry and government affairs, education and training, and by identifying and meeting the needs of the traveling public.

Alaska Airlines Scholarship

Subjects: Travel and tourism.
Purpose: To encourage students pursuing a career in the field of travel and tourism.
Eligibility: Open to applicants who are enrolled in a 4 year travel and tourism programme at a university.
Level of Study: Postgraduate
Type: Scholarship
Value: US$2,000
Frequency: Annual
No. of awards offered: 1
Application Procedure: Application form can be downloaded from the website.
Closing Date: August 30th
Funding: Foundation
Contributor: ASTA Foundation

Arizona Chapter Gold Scholarship

Subjects: Travel and tourism.
Purpose: To encourage serious academic study in the field of travel and tourism.
Eligibility: Open to students enrolled in an accredited university in the state of Arizona.
Level of Study: Postgraduate
Type: Scholarship
Value: US$3,000
Length of Study: 4 years
Frequency: Annual
Country of Study: United States of America
No. of awards offered: 1
Application Procedure: Application form available on the website.
Closing Date: August 30th
Funding: Foundation
Contributor: ASTA Foundation

Healy Scholarship

Subjects: Travel and tourism.
Eligibility: Open to candidates enrolled in a 4 year college/university course of study.

Level of Study: Postgraduate
Type: Scholarship
Value: US$2,000
Length of Study: 4 years
Application Procedure: See the website.
Closing Date: August 30th
Funding: Foundation
Contributor: ASTA Foundation

For further information contact:

Tel: 703-739-8721
Contact: Verlette Mitchell, Manager

Southern California Chapter/Pleasant Hawaiian
Subjects: Travel and tourism.
Purpose: To encourage people to take up travel and tourism business as their profession.
Eligibility: Open to US citizens enrolled in a 4-year college/university course of study.
Level of Study: Postgraduate
Type: Scholarship
Value: US$2,500
Length of Study: 4 years
Frequency: Annual
Application Procedure: A completed form and general application requirements must be submitted.
Closing Date: August 30th
Contributor: ASTA Foundation

AMERICAN SOCIOLOGICAL ASSOCIATION (ASA)

1307 New York Avenue NW, Suite 700, Washington, DC, 20005-4701, United States of America
Tel: (1) 202 383 9005 ext. 321
Fax: (1) 202 638 0882
Email: minority.affairs@asanet.org
Website: www.asanet.org
Contact: Minority Affairs Programme

The American Sociological Association (ASA), founded in 1905, is a non-profit membership association dedicated to advancing sociology as a scientific discipline and profession serving the public good. With over 13,200 members, the ASA encompasses sociologists who are faculty members at colleges and universities, researchers, practitioners and students. About 20 per cent of the members work in government, business or non-profit organizations.

ASA Minority Fellowship Program
Subjects: Sociological research on mental health and mental illness including attention to prevention and causes, consequences, adaptations and interventions.
Purpose: To support the development and training of minority sociologists, to attract talented minority students interested in mental health issues and to facilitate their placement, work and success in an appropriate graduate programme.
Eligibility: Open to citizens, non-citizen nationals or permanent residents of the United States of America. Applicants must have been accepted or be enrolled in a full-time sociology doctoral programme in the United States of America and must be members of one of the following minority racial and ethnic groups: Black/African American; Latino, e.g. Chicano, Cuban, Puerto Rican; American Indian or Alaskan Native; Asian, e.g. Chinese, Japanese, Korean, or South East Asian; or Pacific Islander, e.g. Hawaiian, Guamanian, Samoan or Filipino.
Level of Study: Graduate, Predoctorate
Type: Fellowship
Value: US$20,772
Length of Study: 1 year, renewable for up to 3 years
Frequency: Annual
Study Establishment: Varies
Country of Study: United States of America
No. of awards offered: Varies
Application Procedure: Applicants must submit their complete application package to the Minority Fellowship Program in one package.

The complete application package consists of a fellowship application, essays, three letters of recommendation, official transcripts and other optional supporting documents such as a curriculum vitae, published research papers and Graduate Record Examination scores.
Closing Date: January 31st
Funding: Government, private
Contributor: NIMH
No. of awards given last year: 8
No. of applicants last year: 60
Additional Information: Dissertation support is available through an NIMH Dissertation Research Grant to Fellows who have completed all coursework and who have advanced to degree candidacy.

AMERICAN STATISTICAL ASSOCIATION (ASA)

732 North Washington Street, Alexandria, VA, 22314-1943, United States of America
Tel: (1) 703 684 1221
Fax: (1) 703 684 2037
Email: asainfo@amstat.org
Website: www.amstat.org

The American Statistical Association (ASA) is a scientific and educational society, founded in 1839, to promote excellence in the application of statistical science across the wealth of human endeavour.

Gertrude M. Cox Scholarship
Subjects: Statistics.
Purpose: To provide financial assistance to students and encourage more women to enter statistically orientated professions.
Eligibility: Open to women who are citizens or permanent residents of the United States or Canada and who are in or entering the early stages of graduate training (MS or PhD).
Level of Study: Doctorate
Type: Scholarship
Value: US$1,000
Frequency: Annual
Application Procedure: Applicants can download the application form from the website.
Closing Date: April 1st

For further information contact:

Contact: Chair, Gertrude Cox Scholarship

AMERICAN SYMPHONY ORCHESTRA LEAGUE (ASOL)

New York Headquarters 33 West, 60th Street, 5th Floor, New York, NY, 10023-7905, United States of America
Tel: (1) 212 262 5161
Fax: (1) 212 262 5198
Email: league@symphony.org
Website: www.symphony.org

Founded in 1942, the American Symphony Orchestra League (ASOL) provides leadership and service to American orchestras while communicating to the public the value and importance of orchestras and the music they perform.

ASOL Orchestra Management Fellowship Program
Subjects: Orchestra management.
Purpose: To launch executive careers in orchestra management.
Eligibility: Open to citizens or permanent residents of the United States, or have been authorized by US Citizenship and Immigration Services (USCIS) to accept employment in the United States. Highly qualified candidates with experience in organizational management are also eligible.
Level of Study: Postgraduate, Professional development
Type: Fellowship
Value: US$32,500 plus health benefits and travel allowance
Length of Study: 1 year
Frequency: Annual
Study Establishment: American Symphony Orchestra League

Country of Study: United States of America
Application Procedure: Applicants must fill the application online. An interview is required.
Closing Date: February 1st
Funding: Foundation, individuals
No. of awards given last year: 5
No. of applicants last year: 120

AMERICAN TINNITUS ASSOCIATION (ATA)

National Headquarters, PO Box 5, Portland, OR 97207-0005, United States of America
Tel: (1) 503 248 9985 x218
Fax: (1) 503 248 0024
Email: amy@ata.org
Website: www.ata.org
Contact: Amy Harris, Director of Research

The American Tinnitus Association's (ATA) mission is to cure tinnitus through the development of resources that advance tinnitus research.

American Tinnitus Association Scientific Research Grants

Subjects: Tinnitus.
Purpose: To identify the mechanisms of tinnitus, to improve treatments and to identify a cure.
Eligibility: Student Award: Open only to students at US institutions. Primary Grant: Open to anyone at a non-profit institution worldwide
Level of Study: Doctorate, Graduate, Postdoctorate, Postgraduate, Predoctorate, Research
Value: Student Grant: US$10,000 for one year
Length of Study: 1–3 years
Frequency: Twice a year
Country of Study: Any country
No. of awards offered: Varies
Application Procedure: Applicants must write for grant application policies and a procedures brochure. These documents and also the applications can be downloaded from the ATA website.
Closing Date: June 30th and December 31st
Funding: Individuals, private
Contributor: Sufferers of tinnitus
No. of awards given last year: 7
No. of applicants last year: 30

THE AMERICAN UNIVERSITY IN CAIRO (AUC)

PO Box 2511, 113 Sharia Kasr El Aini, Cairo, 11511, Egypt
Tel: (20) 20-2-797-5194/5612
Fax: (20) 20-2-795-7565
Email: aucgrad@aucegypt.edu
Website: www.aucegypt.edu/graduate
Contact: Mrs Sawsan Mardini, Office of Graduate Studies & Research

The American University in Cairo (AUC) provides quality higher and continuing education for students from Egypt and the surrounding region. The University is an independent, non-profit, apolitical, non-sectarian and equal opportunity institution. English is the primary language of instruction. The University is accredited in the United States of America by the Commission of Higher Education of the Middle States Association of Colleges and Schools.

AUC African Graduate Fellowship

Subjects: Arts, humanities, business administration, engineering or information science.
Purpose: To enable outstanding young men and women from Africa to study for a Master's degree.
Eligibility: Open to African nationals, not including Egyptians, with Bachelor's degrees, an academic record of not less than 'Very Good' and an overall grade point average of 3.0 on a 4.0 scale or the equivalent. Candidates must also show proficiency in the English language by either submitting a Test of English as a Foreign Language with TWE score of 550 or above, or taking the AUC's ELPET exam.
Level of Study: Graduate
Type: Fellowship
Value: A waiver of tuition, incidental and graduation fees, health insurance on the AUC plan, a monthly stipend and, if needed, a housing allowance or accommodation at the University's residence
Length of Study: 2 academic years and the intervening Summer session
Frequency: Annual
Study Establishment: AUC only
Country of Study: Egypt
No. of awards offered: 5
Application Procedure: Applicants must complete an application form available from the Office of Graduate Studies and Research.
Closing Date: February 1st
Funding: Private
No. of awards given last year: 3
No. of applicants last year: 45

AUC Arabic Language Fellowships

Subjects: All subjects.
Purpose: To support fully admitted international graduate students who need to satisfy their degree requirement.
Eligibility: Open to candidates from any country except Egypt. Candidates must be full-time graduate students who need to take Arabic language classes in order to satisfy their requirements at AUC and would like to enrol in the Arabic Language Institute's (ALI) full-time Summer Arabic programme or take up to 6 credits of ALING classes in the Arabic Language not towards a degree.
Level of Study: Graduate, Postgraduate
Type: Fellowship
Value: 50 per cent waiver of tuition fees for the ALI full-time summer Arabic programme or 50 per cent of up to six credits of ALING classes (non-credit classes) during the academic year
Length of Study: 1 Summer session or 2 courses during the academic year
Frequency: Annual, every semester
Study Establishment: AUC
Country of Study: Egypt
No. of awards offered: 5
Application Procedure: Applicants must submit a completed application form, which can be found on the website www.aucegypt.edu/academic/gradstudies/Fellowship/arabic.html
Closing Date: February 1st for the Summer session, November 1st for Spring and June 1st for Fall
No. of awards given last year: 3
No. of applicants last year: 3
Additional Information: Fellows are assigned 5 hours per week of related academic or administrative work.

AUC Assistantships

Subjects: Arts, humanities, business administration, engineering and information science.
Purpose: To support graduate-level teaching or research assistants who do not receive tuition waivers.
Eligibility: Fully accepted graduate students enrolled in two or more courses or actively engaged in thesis work are given preference over those not enrolled in the graduate programme. Applicants who have completed their MA or MS, are preparing for a PhD, and have or are receiving academic degree training may also receive assistantships as postmaster's assistants.
Level of Study: Graduate
Type: Award
Value: Holders of a Master's degree receive monthly stipends of Egyptian £90 per hour of load per week. Bachelor's degree holders receive monthly stipends of Egyptian £75 per hour of load per week
Length of Study: 1 semester, renewable
Study Establishment: AUC
Country of Study: Egypt
Application Procedure: Applications must be made to the relevant department.
Closing Date: September 1st for the Fall, January 1st for the Spring, and June 1st for the Summer

AUC Graduate Merit Fellowships

Subjects: Business, communication, computer science, social and behavioural sciences.

Purpose: To recognize and reward outstanding new or continuing graduate students who wish to pursue full-time study in one of the graduate programmes.

Eligibility: Open to students who are fully admissible to one of the graduate programmes at AUC and who have a BA or BSc degree with a minimum overall grade point average of 3.4 on a 4.0 scale and a minimum of 3.5 in their major. Students who are already enrolled in one of AUC's graduate programmes and have a minimum grade point average of 3.7 in their graduate courses are also eligible to apply.

Level of Study: Graduate

Type: Fellowship

Value: A waiver of tuition Egyptian £36,900, student services and activities fees and a monthly stipend of Egyptian £780 for 10 months

Length of Study: 1 year, although the award may be renewed for a 2nd year with the approval of the school Dean

Frequency: Annual

Study Establishment: AUC

Country of Study: Egypt

No. of awards offered: 18

Application Procedure: Applicants must write to the Office of Graduate Studies and Research or the Dean's offices, or download forms from the web under Fellowships www.aucegypt.edu/academic/gradstudies/Fellowships/merit.html

Closing Date: May 15th

Contributor: AUC

No. of awards given last year: 18

No. of applicants last year: 100

Additional Information: Please note that the Merit Fellowship provides a partial tution waiver to international students.

AUC International Graduate Fellowships in Arabic Studies, Middle East Studies and Sociology/Anthropology

Subjects: Arabic studies, Middle East studies, sociology or anthropology.

Purpose: To recognize and award outstanding new international graduate students who wish to pursue full-time study.

Eligibility: Open to candidates from any country except Egypt. Candidates must have completed an appropriate undergraduate degree with a minimum overall grade point average of 3.4 on a 4.0 scale or equivalent.

Level of Study: Graduate, Postgraduate

Type: Fellowship

Value: A waiver of tuition fees, a monthly stipend of Egyptian £780 and housing allowance of Egyptian £950 or accommodation in the University's residence. The award also includes medical service and health insurance fees

Length of Study: 2 years

Frequency: Annual

Study Establishment: AUC

Country of Study: Egypt

No. of awards offered: 2

Application Procedure: Applicants must complete an application form, available from the website.

Closing Date: February 1st

No. of awards given last year: 2

No. of applicants last year: 30

Additional Information: Fellows are assigned 18 hours per week of related academic or administrative work.

AUC Laboratory Instruction Graduate Fellowships in Engineering and Computer Science

Subjects: Computer science and engineering.

Purpose: To recognize and support outstanding graduate students who wish to pursue full-time study in either engineering or computer science.

Eligibility: Students must have a BSc degree with a minimum overall grade point average of 3.2 on a 4.0 scale or its equivalent. Students already enrolled in a graduate programme with a minimum grade point average of 3.2 are also eligible.

Level of Study: Graduate

Type: Fellowship

Value: A waiver of tuition of Egyptian £36,900, student services and activities fees and a monthly stipend of Egyptian £780 for 10 months

Length of Study: Reviewed every semester and may be renewed for a maximum period of 2 years. The fellowship may cover a Summer session

Frequency: Annual

Study Establishment: AUC

Country of Study: Egypt

No. of awards offered: 13

Application Procedure: Application forms are available from the Departments of Engineering and Computer Science as well as the Office of Graduate Studies and Research, and are also downloadable from the web site under Fellowships www.aucegypt.edu/academic/gradstudies/Fellowships/lab.html

Closing Date: May 15th for the fall semester and December 15th for the spring semester

AUC Nadia Niazi Mostafa Fellowship in Islamic Art and Architecture

Subjects: Islamic art and architecture.

Purpose: To recognize and award outstanding Egyptian graduate students who wish to pursue full-time study in the programme. The award is for 2nd-year Egyptian students already enrolled in the programme.

Eligibility: Open to Egyptians. Candidates must be 2nd-year students enrolled in the graduate programme in Islamic art and architecture and have completed 12 credit hours with a minimum grade point average of 3.2.

Level of Study: Postgraduate

Type: Fellowship

Value: A waiver of tuition fees, student services and activities fee and a monthly stipend Egyptian £450 for 10 months

Length of Study: 1 academic year

Frequency: Annual

Study Establishment: AUC

Country of Study: Egypt

No. of awards offered: 1

Application Procedure: Application forms are available from the Office of Graduate Studies and Research or the Department of Arabic Studies.

Closing Date: May 15th

Funding: Private

No. of awards given last year: 1

Additional Information: Fellows are assigned 12 hours per week of related academic or administrative work.

AUC Ryoichi Sasakawa Young Leaders Graduate Scholarship

Subjects: Arts, humanities and social sciences.

Purpose: To educate outstanding young men and women who have demonstrated a high potential for future leadership in international affairs, public life and private endeavour.

Eligibility: Applicants must have a Bachelor's degree with a grade point average of 3.2 or above and have actively participated in extra-curricular activities. Preference is given to those students who require four semesters to complete their degree. The award is contingent upon full admission to one of AUC's graduate programmes in the humanities and social sciences.

Level of Study: Graduate

Type: Scholarship

Value: A waiver of tuition, student services and activities fee, medical service and health insurance fees

Length of Study: 2 years

Frequency: Annual

Study Establishment: AUC only

Country of Study: Egypt

No. of awards offered: 3

Application Procedure: Graduate application forms are available from the Office of Graduate Studies and Research or can be downloaded from the website.

Closing Date: February 1st

Funding: Private

Contributor: The Tokyo Foundation

No. of awards given last year: 3

No. of applicants last year: 25

AUC Teaching Arabic as a Foreign Language Fellowships

Subjects: Arabic, education and teacher training.
Purpose: To acquire language teaching skills.
Eligibility: Open to individuals who have Teaching Arabic as a Foreign Language experience or excellent qualifications in the Arabic language.
Level of Study: Graduate
Type: Fellowship
Value: A tuition waiver, a monthly stipend of Egyptian £780, medical service and health insurance fees
Length of Study: 2 academic years and the intervening Summer session
Frequency: Annual
Study Establishment: AUC
Country of Study: Egypt
No. of awards offered: 3
Application Procedure: Applicants must write to the Office of Graduate Admissions and the Arabic Language Institute.
Closing Date: February 1st
Contributor: AUC
No. of awards given last year: 3
No. of applicants last year: 10

AUC Teaching English as a Foreign Language Fellowships

Subjects: Education.
Purpose: To acquire language teaching experience.
Eligibility: Special consideration is given to applicants with previous Teaching English as a foreign language experience and/or excellent qualifications in the English language.
Level of Study: Graduate
Type: Fellowship
Value: A waiver of tuition fees and a monthly stipend of Egyptian £780 and medical insurance. Non-residents of Egypt are provided with accommodation in the University dormitory or with a monthly housing allowance of Egyptian £950 and one-way home travel
Length of Study: 2 academic years and the intervening summer session
Frequency: Annual
Study Establishment: AUC
Country of Study: Egypt
Application Procedure: Applicants must write to the English Language Institute in Cairo or the New York office at aucegypt@aucnyo.edu. The downloadable application for the TEFL fellowship is avaliable www.aucegypt.edu/academic/gradstudies/Fellowships/tefl.html apply.
Closing Date: February 1st
Contributor: AUC
No. of awards given last year: 10
No. of applicants last year: 50

AUC University Fellowships

Subjects: Art and humanities, business administration and management, engineering, mass communication and information, mathematics and computer science, social and behavioural sciences.
Purpose: To assist new and continuing graduate students who display superior performance in their academic endeavours and who wish to pursue full-time study.
Eligibility: Students must have a BSc or a BA degree with a minimum overall grade point average of 3.2 on a 4.0 scale or its equivalent. Students already enrolled in one of these graduate programmes with a minimum grade point average of 3.2 are also eligible. Preference is given to outstanding graduate students who are already enrolled.
Level of Study: Graduate
Type: Fellowship
Value: A waiver of tuition of Egyptian £36,900, student services and activities fees and a monthly stipend of Egyptian £515 for 10 months
Length of Study: Reviewed every semester and may be renewed for a maximum period of 2 years. The fellowship may cover a summer session
Frequency: Annual
Study Establishment: AUC
Country of Study: Egypt
Application Procedure: Applicants must complete applications, available from the chosen department in May.

Closing Date: May 15th for the fall semester and by December 15th for the spring semester
Contributor: AUC
No. of awards given last year: 18
No. of applicants last year: 123
Additional Information: Fellows are assigned 10–12 hours per week of work with faculty members in teaching and research activities.

AUC Writing Center Graduate Fellowships

Subjects: English, grammar, education and native language, literacy education, teaching and learning.
Purpose: To provide outstanding students with valuable teaching, academic experience and to involve them as tutors in AUC's Writing Center.
Eligibility: Open to students who are fully admissible to the graduate programme in English and Comparative Literature at AUC and who have a Bachelor of Arts degree with a minimum overall grade point average of 3.2 on a 4.0 scale or its equivalent. Students already enrolled in one of these graduate programmes with a minimum grade point average of 3.4 are also eligible.
Level of Study: Graduate
Type: Fellowship
Value: A waiver of tuition, student services and activities fee, a monthly stipend of Egyptian £515 for 10 months, medical service and health insurance fees
Length of Study: Reviewed every semester and may be renewed for a maximum period of 2 years. The fellowship may cover a Summer session
Frequency: Annual
Study Establishment: AUC
Country of Study: Egypt
No. of awards offered: 1
Application Procedure: Applicants must write for details to the Chair of the Department of English and Comparative Literature, and the Office of Graduate Studies and Research.
Closing Date: May 15th for the fall semester and December 15th for the spring semester
Contributor: AUC
No. of awards given last year: 1
No. of applicants last year: 5
Additional Information: As part of their fellowship and in support of their professional training, Fellows are assigned 10 hours of work per week in the Writing Center.

AMERICAN UROLOGICAL ASSOCIATION (AUA) FOUNDATION

1000 Corporate Boulevard, Linthicum, MD 21090, United States of America
Tel: (1) 410 689 3700
Fax: (1) 410 689 3800
Email: grants@auafoundation.org
Website: www.auafoundation.org

The association founded by Ramon Guiteras in 1902 takes care for the advancement of urologic patient care. Its wide range of services including publications, research, the annual meeting, continuing medical education (CME), and the formulation of health policy fosters the highest standards of urological care. Its main aim is to network and collaborate physicians to increase educational opportunities.

MD Post-Resident Fellowship in Urology

Subjects: Urology.
Purpose: To learn scientific techniques, to provide evidence of current and/or prior interest/accomplishments in research.
Eligibility: Open to applicants who are willing to spend at least 80% of their time on their research project, should prepare the scholar to become an independent investigator capable of obtaining independent research grant support, must have an interest in the delivery of health services, economics, and policy also are encouraged to submit applications for consideration.
Level of Study: Predoctorate
Type: Fellowship
Value: US$60,000 per year is paid (US$30,000 from the AUA Foundation and US$30,000 from the sponsoring institution)

Length of Study: 2 years
Frequency: Annual
Application Procedure: Check website for further details.
Closing Date: July 1st
Funding: Foundation
Contributor: An accredited medical education/research institution or department within such an institution must sponsor the Applicant.

MD/PhD One Year Fellowship in Urology
Subjects: Urology.
Purpose: To learn scientific techniques.
Eligibility: Open to candidates who are either a trained urologist or basic scientist within 5 years of completing residency or doctorate, must be willing to spend at least 80% of their time on their research project. PhD applicants must spend 100% of their time on their research project to prepare the scholar to subsequently become an independent investigator capable of obtaining independent research grant support.
Level of Study: Predoctorate, Doctorate
Type: Fellowship
Value: US$30,000
Length of Study: 1 year
Frequency: Annual
Application Procedure: Check website for further details.
Closing Date: July 1st
Funding: Foundation

PhD Post-Doctoral Fellowship in Urology
Subjects: Urology.
Purpose: To support researcher urologic diseases and conditions and/or related diseases and dysfunctions.
Eligibility: Open to candidates who must be a basic scientist within 5 years of earning a PhD with a research interest in urologic diseases.
Level of Study: Doctorate, Postdoctorate
Type: Fellowship
Value: AUA will provide a salary stipend of US$30,000. In addition, the sponsoring institution will provide up to US$30,000 in matching support for requisite supplies and equipment to complete the research
Length of Study: 2 years
Frequency: Every 2 years
Application Procedure: Check website for further details.
Funding: Foundation
Contributor: An accredited medical education/research institution or department within such an institution

Urology Research Scholarship program
Subjects: Urologic research.
Purpose: To support young scientists to begin a career in urologic research.
Eligibility: Open to young men and women who are interested in pursuing a career in urologic research.
Level of Study: Doctorate, Postgraduate
Type: Scholarship
Length of Study: 1–2 years
Application Procedure: Check website for further details.

AMERICAN VENOUS FORUM FOUNDATION

PMB 311, 203 Washington Street, Salem, MA 01970, United States of America
Tel: (1) 978 744 5005
Fax: (1) 978 744 5029
Email: venous-info@administrare.com
Website: www.venous-info.com

The American Venous Forum Foundation grants research awards and prizes that stimulate and recognize excellence in published (science) writing on laboratory and clinical research in the study of venous disease.

The BSN-Jobst Inc. Research Award
Subjects: Venous disease.

Purpose: To award a grant to a research fellow or a resident in an ACGME programme who has a specific interest in the diagnosis and treatment of venous disease.
Level of Study: Doctorate, Graduate, Postdoctorate
Type: Award
Value: US$25,000
Frequency: Annual
Country of Study: United States of America
No. of awards offered: 1
Application Procedure: Candidates must visit the website for details.
Closing Date: September 16th
Contributor: BSN-Jobst Inc. and the American Venous Forum Foundation
No. of awards given last year: 1
No. of applicants last year: 4

Sigvaris Travelling Fellowship
Subjects: Venous disease.
Purpose: To enable young physicians to travel throughout the United States of America and abroad to visit centres of excellence in the management of venous disease.
Level of Study: Doctorate, Graduate, Postdoctorate
Type: Travelling fellowship
Value: US$3,000
Frequency: Annual
Country of Study: United States of America and abroad
No. of awards offered: 4
Application Procedure: Applicants must visit the website for details.
Closing Date: September 7th
Contributor: Sigvaris Inc. and the American Venous Forum Foundation
No. of awards given last year: 1

THE AMERICAN-SCANDINAVIAN FOUNDATION (ASF)

58 Park Avenue, New York, NY 10016, United States of America
Tel: (1) 212 879 9779
Fax: (1) 212 249 3444
Email: grants@amscan.org
Website: www.amscan.org
Contact: Director of Fellowships and Grants

The ASF is a publicity supported, non-profit organization that promotes international understanding through educational and cultural exchange between the US and the Nordic countries

American-Scandinavian Foundation Award for Study in Scandinavia
Subjects: All subjects.
Eligibility: Applicants must be US citizens and must study in one of the Scandinavian countries for up to 1 year. They must be doing work at the graduate level or doing research in all fields. The applicants must have finished their undergraduate degrees before applying for this award, and the American-Scandinavian Foundation prefers to give the awards to people who speak a little Norwegian, Danish or Swedish.
Level of Study: Postgraduate, Research
Type: Award
Value: $23,000 or $5,000
Length of Study: 1 year
Frequency: Annual
No. of awards offered: 25–35
Application Procedure: Check website for further details.
Closing Date: November 1st
No. of awards given last year: 35
No. of applicants last year: 106

American-Scandinavian Foundation Scholarships for Advanced Study or Research in the U.S.A for Citizens of Nordic Countries
Subjects: All subjects.

99

Eligibility: Applicants must be Scandinavians (citizens of Denmark, Finland, Iceland, Norway or Sweden), study in the United States and be 21 years or older.
Level of Study: Postgraduate
Type: Scholarship
Value: $4,000–20,000
Length of Study: 1 year
Frequency: Annual
Country of Study: United States of America
Application Procedure: Check website for further details.
Closing Date: Varies by country
Funding: Private
Additional Information: There are several different awards, and there are also various requirements for each award. Therefore, it is important for the applicant to visit the websites for the American-Scandinavian Foundation.

The American-Scandinavian Foundation–Visiting Lectureship

Subjects: All subjects.
Eligibility: Applicants must be Norwegian or Swedish scholars or experts who shall go to the United States for up to six months. They must teach one course at an American institution on public policy, conflict resolution, environmental studies, healthcare or multicultural-ism. The scholars must participate at a NORTANA conference, SASS conference, and/or a Swedish Teachers' Conference.
Level of Study: Doctorate
Type: Grant
Value: $20,000 plus $5,000
Length of Study: 6 months
Application Procedure: Check website for further details.
Closing Date: November 1st and January 30th
Funding: Private
No. of awards given last year: 10
No. of applicants last year: 2

ASF Grants and Fellowships for Advanced Study or Research in Denmark, Finland, Iceland, Norway and Sweden

Subjects: All subjects.
Purpose: To encourage advanced study and research, and to increase understanding between the United States of America and Scandinavia.
Eligibility: Applicants must be citizens of the United States of America or permanent residents who have a well-defined research or study project that makes a stay in Scandinavia essential. Team projects are eligible, but each member must apply as an individual. Some ability in the language of the host country is desirable. Priority will be given to applicants who have not previously received an ASF award.
Level of Study: Postgraduate, Professional development, Research
Type: Fellowship
Value: Grants are usually US$5,000; fellowships are up to US$23,000
Length of Study: A maximum of 1 year
Frequency: Annual
Country of Study: Denmark, Finland, Iceland, Norway or Sweden
No. of awards offered: 25–35
Application Procedure: Applicants must complete an official appli-cation form and submit this with an application fee of US$20.
Closing Date: November 1st
Funding: Private
No. of awards given last year: 35
No. of applicants last year: 106
Additional Information: For further information please contact Valeria Hymas via email or visit the website.

Awards for Scandinavians

Subjects: All subjects.
Purpose: To fund Scandinavians to undertake study or research programs in the United States.
Eligibility: Applicants must be citizens of Denmark, Finland, Iceland, Norway or Sweden. Check website for further details.
Level of Study: Graduate, Postgraduate, Professional development, Research
Type: Award
Value: Varies
Length of Study: 1 year

Frequency: Annual
Country of Study: United States of America
No. of awards offered: Varies
Application Procedure: Check the website for further details.
Funding: Foundation

Visiting Lectureships

Subjects: Public policy, conflict resolution, environmental studies, multiculturalism and health care.
Purpose: To support American Universities and colleges to host Norwegian and Swedish lectures.
Eligibility: Open to Norwegian or Swedish citizens, and a scholar or expert in a field appropriate to the host department or program. Open to all American colleges and universities.
Type: Lectureship/Prize
Value: $20,000 as research/teaching stipend, travel stipend for lec-ture appearances outside home institution and J–1 visa sponsorship as a short-term scholar (up to 6 months) through the ASF Visitor Exchange Program
Application Procedure: Applicants are required to submit a pre-pro-posal, from which finalists will be selected. Finalists will then be re-quired to submit more detailed and specific information, including confirmation of the lecturer and institutional support, for a later deadline.
Closing Date: January 30th
Funding: Foundation
No. of awards given last year: 10
No. of applicants last year: 2

THE AMITY SCIENCE & TECHNOLOGY FOUNDATION (ASTF)

Amity University Campus, Sector 125 Noida, Adj, New Delhi, India
Tel: (91) 120 2432400
Fax: (91) 120 2432200
Email: ssaran@aib.amity.edu
Website: www.amity.edu
Contact: Professor Sunil

The Amity Science & Technology Foundation (ASTF) was established with the aim of helping India become a global leader in the field of science and technology.

ASTF PhD Fellowships

Subjects: Applied sciences, biotechnology, engineering, forestry and environment, herbal and microbial studies, high vacuum technology, Indian heritage crops and their products, nanotechnology, organic agriculture, telecommunication and other areas in science, engineer-ing and technology.
Purpose: To enable brilliant young researchers and scientists who possess the competence and motivation to carry out cutting edge research in thrust areas that will impact the development of the Indian Nation.
Level of Study: Doctorate
Type: Fellowships
Value: Indian Rs 2,70,700 per year. The fellowship includes aca-demic fees, subsidy towards cost of on-campus or off-campus ac-commodation, mediclaim for hospitalisation and a stipend of Indian Rs 1,000 per month
Length of Study: 3 years
Frequency: Annual
Study Establishment: Amity Science & Technology Foundation
Country of Study: India
No. of awards offered: 100
Additional Information: Please see the website for further informa-tion www.amity.edu/astf/fellowship.htm

ASTF Postdoctoral Research Associate Fellowships

Subjects: Applied sciences, biotechnology, engineering, forestry and environment, herbal and microbial studies, high vacuum technology, Indian heritage crops and their products, nanotechnology, organic agriculture, telecommunication and other areas in science, engineer-ing and technology.
Purpose: To enable brilliant young researchers and scientists who possess the competence and motivation for carrying out cutting-edge

research in thrust areas that will impact the development of the Indian nation.

Eligibility: Open to candidates with PhD in relevant area with evidence of sustained high quality research and throughout first class academic record.

Level of Study: Postdoctorate

Type: Fellowships

Value: Indian Rupees 1,87,900 per year. The fellowship includes a stipend of Indian Rupees 12,000 per month plus HRA, and mediclaim for hospitalization

Length of Study: 3 years

Frequency: Annual

Study Establishment: Amity Science & Technology Foundation

Country of Study: India

No. of awards offered: 100

Application Procedure: Please visit the website www.amity.edu/astf

Funding: Foundation

Additional Information: For further information, please see the website.

ANGLO-AUSTRIAN MUSIC SOCIETY

Richard Tauber Prize for Singers, 158 Rosendale Road, London,
SE21 8LG, England
Tel: (44) 20 8761 0444
Fax: (44) 20 8766 6151
Email: info@aams.org.uk
Website: www.aams.org.uk
Contact: Jane Avery, Secretary

The Anglo-Austrian Music Society promotes lectures and concerts and is closely associated with its parent organization, the Anglo-Austrian Society, which was founded in 1944 to promote friendship and understanding between the people of the United Kingdom and Austria through personal contacts, educational programmes and cultural exchanges. AAMS awards the Richard Tauber prize for singers every 2 years.

Richard Tauber Prize for Singers

Subjects: Vocal musical performance.

Eligibility: Open to singers of any country resident in the United Kingdom or Austria. Applicants must be aged over 21 years and not older than 30 years.

Level of Study: Postgraduate

Type: Prize

Value: First prize: UK £5,000 plus public recital in London; second prize: UK £2,500

Frequency: Every 2 years

Country of Study: Any country

No. of awards offered: 5

Application Procedure: Applicants must complete an application form.

Closing Date: February

Funding: Private

Additional Information: Preliminary auditions are held in London and Vienna in April. Applicants must attend these auditions at their own expense. A final public audition is held at Wigmore Hall London in June. Additional prizes are 1. Adele Leigh Memorial Prize – £2,000, 2. Ferdinand Rauter Memorial prize for Accompanists – £1,000, 3. Schubert Society Lied Prize – £500 plus recital for the Schubert Society of Britain.

For further information contact:

158 Rosendale Road, London, SE21 8LG, England
Tel: (44) 0208 761 0444
Email: info@aams.org.uk
Website: www.aams.org.uk

THE ANGLO-DANISH SOCIETY

c/o 6 Keats Avenue, Littleover, Derbyshire, Derby, DE23 4ED,
England
Tel: (44) 1332 517 160
Fax: (44) 1332 517 323
Email: margit.staehr@googlemail.com
Website: www.anglo-danish.society.org.uk
Contact: Mrs Margit Staehr, Administrator

The Anglo-Danish Society exists to promote closer understanding between the United Kingdom and Denmark by arranging lectures, outings, social gatherings and other events of interest for its members and their guests. The society administers scholarship funds which help Danish students visit the United Kingdom or British students visit Denmark, for the purpose of advanced or postgraduate studies.

The Anglo-Danish Society Scholarships

Subjects: Anglo-Danish cultural and scientific interests.

Purpose: To promote Anglo-Danish relations.

Eligibility: Open to graduates of Danish and British nationality. The country of study is Denmark (for the British) and the United Kingdom (for Danes).

Level of Study: Doctorate, Postdoctorate, Postgraduate, Professional development

Type: Scholarship

Value: Minimum UK £2,000 per month

Length of Study: A maximum of 6 months

Frequency: Dependent on funds available

Study Establishment: Universities

No. of awards offered: 4–6

Application Procedure: Application forms can be obtained by sending an e-mail to scholarships@anglo-danishsociety.org.uk from October 1st to March 1st. Applicants should submit their applications by e-mail or by post to the Administrator's address.

Closing Date: March 1st

Funding: Commercial, private

No. of awards given last year: 6

No. of applicants last year: 80

Anglo-Danish Society/CF Moller Architecture Scholarship

Subjects: Anglo-Danish architectural studies.

Purpose: To promote Anglo-Danish relations.

Eligibility: Open to graduates of British nationality.

Level of Study: Doctorate, Postdoctorate

Type: Scholarship

Value: UK £5,000

Length of Study: Maximum of 6 months

Frequency: Dependent on funds available

Study Establishment: The Royal Academy of Fine Arts School of Architecture, Copenhagen or The Danish School of Architecture in Aarhus

Country of Study: Denmark

No. of awards offered: 1

Application Procedure: Application forms can be obtained by sending an email to scholarships@anglo-danishsociety.org.uk

Closing Date: March 1st

Funding: Commercial

THE ANGLO-JEWISH ASSOCIATION

152 West End Lane, London, NW6 1SD, England
Tel: (44) 20 7443 5169
Email: info@anglojewish.org.uk
Website: www.anglojewish.org.uk
Contact: Julia Samuel, Chairman, Education Committee

The Anglo-Jewish Association gives grants to Jewish students in financial need at universities in the United Kingdom.

Anglo-Jewish Association Bursary

Subjects: All subjects.

Purpose: To assist Jewish students in full-time higher education who are in financial need.

Eligibility: Open to Jewish students of any nationality in financial need up to the age of 35.

Level of Study: Graduate

Type: Bursary

Value: Up to UK £2,000 per year

Frequency: Annual

Study Establishment: University

Country of Study: United Kingdom

No. of awards offered: 30

Application Procedure: Application form must be completed and returned with all enclosures. This form can be downloaded from the website.
Closing Date: April 27th
Funding: Trusts
No. of awards given last year: 130
No. of applicants last year: 950

APPRAISAL INSTITUTE EDUCATION TRUST

Headquarters Office, 550 West Van Buren Street, Suite 1000, Chicago, IL, 60607, United States of America
Tel: (1) 312 335 4100
Fax: (1) 312 335 4400
Email: ocarreon@appraisalinstitute.org
Website: www.appraisalinstitute.org
Contact: Fred Grubbe, Chief Executive Officer

The Appraisal Institute is an international membership association of professional real estate appraisers, with more than 21,000 members and 99 chapters throughout the United States of America, Canada and abroad. Its mission is to support and advance its members as the choice for real estate solutions and uphold professional credentials, standards of professional practice and ethics consistent with the public good.

Appraisal Institute Education Trust Scholarship
Subjects: Real estate appraisal, land economics, real estate and allied fields.
Purpose: The Education Trust scholarship is awarded on the basis of academic excellence and is intended to help finance the education endeavors of individuals concentrating in the fields listed.
Eligibility: Applicant must be a member of a racial, ethnic or gender group underrepresented in the appraisal profession and full- or part-time student enrolled-in real estate related courses at a degree-granting college/university or junior college/university. Individuals must have proof a cumulative grade point average of no less than 2.5 on 4.0 scale and have demonstrated financial need.
Level of Study: Graduate, Postgraduate
Type: Scholarship
Value: Undergraduates US$2,000, graduates US$3,000
Length of Study: 1 year
Frequency: Annual
Country of Study: United States of America
No. of awards offered: Varies
Application Procedure: A written statement from the Dean of your college recommending your application; A signed statement regarding your general activities and intellectual interests in college. (This statement should not exceed 1,000 words.); Official copies of all collegiate grade records; A proposed student programme, including a brief description of each course you plan to pursue in working toward the degree indicated, and a certificate of approval of this programme signed by the Dean of the college in which the work is to be completed; A graduate student must have served, or is about to serve, an internship with an appraiser or the appraisal department of a corporation (letter from employer required); Request two individuals to write a letter regarding your qualifications and character and to forward these letters to the Appraisal Institute, at the address below; Student must submit four copies of all information (one original and three copies).
Closing Date: March 15th
Funding: Private
Additional Information: visit the Appraisal Institute scholarships Web page at www.appraisalinstitute.org/education/scholarship.aspx, or contact Sylvia Davila at sdavila@appraisalinstitute.org.

For further information contact:

Email: Davila at sdavila@appraisalinstitute.org
Contact: Sylvia Davila

Minorities and Women Educational Scholarship Program
Subjects: Real estate appraisal or related fields.
Purpose: The Minority and Women Educational Scholarship is geared towards college students working towards a degree in real estate appraisal or a related field. The scholarship is to help offset the cost of tuition.
Eligibility: Applicant must be a member of a racial, ethnic or gender group underrepresented in the appraisal profession and full- or part-time student enrolled-in real estate related courses at a degree-granting college/university or junior college/university. Individuals must have proof a cumulative grade point average of no less than 2.5 on 4.0 scale and have demonstrated financial need. Scholarship award must be used in the same calendar year as awarded by the committee.
Level of Study: Graduate, Postgraduate
Type: Scholarship
Value: Minimum of US$1,000 per person
Frequency: Annual
Country of Study: United States of America
No. of awards offered: Varies
Application Procedure: An official student transcript for all college work completed to date. A 500-word written essay stating why applicant should be awarded the scholarship. Two letters of recommendation from previous employers and/or college professors. An attestation that the scholarship will be applied toward tuition/books expense as stated in the application. Optional: Applicants are asked to include a head and shoulders photograph as scholarship recipients may be profiled in Appraisal Institutenewsletter/news releases.
Closing Date: April 15th
Funding: Private
Additional Information: For further information or request for an application, contact Hillary Richmond.

For further information contact:

Appraisal Institute
Tel: 312 335 4278
Email: hrichmond@appraisalinstitute.org
Contact: Hillary Richmond

ARAB-BRITISH CHAMBER CHARITABLE FOUNDATION (ABCCF)

Longmead, Benhall Green, Saxmundham, Suffolk, IP17 1HU, England
Tel: (44) 17 2860 3359
Email: abccf@abcc.org.uk
Website: www.abcc.org.uk
Contact: Mr Hugh de Las Casas, Secretary to the Trustees

The Arab-British Chamber Charitable Foundation (ABCCF) provides funding for Arab postgraduate students studying at British universities.

ABCCF Student Grant
Subjects: Agriculture, forestry and fishery, architecture and town planning, business administration and management, education and teacher training, engineering, mathematics and computer science, mass communication and information science, social sciences or transport.
Purpose: To assist Arab nationals in financial need, while they are at United Kingdom universities, to undertake studies in subjects of potential value to the Arab world.
Eligibility: Open to nationals of an Arab League State. Applicants must have United Kingdom student visa status. Applicants must show a commitment to return to the Arab world on completion of the postgraduate programme.
Level of Study: Research, Doctorate, MBA, Postgraduate
Type: Grant
Value: Up to UK £2,000 per academic year
Length of Study: 3-4 years
Frequency: Annual
Study Establishment: A university in the United Kingdom
Country of Study: United Kingdom
No. of awards offered: Up to 30
Application Procedure: Applicants must complete an application form that is sent only to applicants who have confirmed that their circumstances meet with the ABCCF's criteria. Other supporting documentation is required, e.g. transcripts of degrees, academic references, proof of citizenship and visa status, university acceptance or

registration and a written undertaking to return to the Arab world after graduation.
Closing Date: None
Funding: Commercial
Contributor: The Arab-British Chamber of Commerce, London
No. of awards given last year: 30
No. of applicants last year: 200

THE ARC OF THE UNITED STATES

1010 Wayne Avenue, Suite 650, Silver Spring, MD, 20910, United States of America
Tel: (1) 301 565 3842
Fax: (1) 301 565 3843
Email: info@thearc.org
Website: www.thearc.org
Contact: Sue Swenson, Executive Director

The Arc of the United States advocates for the rights and full participation of all children and adults with intellectual and developmental disabilities. Together with our network of members and affiliation chapters, we improve systems of supports and services, connect families, inspire communities and influence public policy.

Distinguished Research Award
Subjects: The prevention or improvement of mental retardation.
Purpose: To reward an individual or individuals whose research has had a significant impact on the prevention or improvement of mental retardation.
Type: Award
Value: The recipient of the award will receive a plaque, US$1,000 and a trip to speak at the Research and Prevention Luncheon of The Arc's National Convention
Frequency: Annual
No. of awards offered: 1
Application Procedure: Applicants must send the original and five copies of a nomination to The Arc.
Closing Date: June 7
Funding: Private
No. of awards given last year: 1
No. of applicants last year: 5

ARCTIC INSTITUTE OF NORTH AMERICA (AINA)

The University of Calgary, 2500 University Drive North West, Calgary, AB, T2N 1N4, Canada
Tel: (1) 403 220 7515
Fax: (1) 403 282 4609
Email: www.arctic@ucalgary.ca
Website: www.ucalgary.ca/aina
Contact: Mr Benoit Beauchamp, Executive Director

Created in 1945, the Arctic Institute of North America (AINA) is a non-profit membership organization and a multidisciplinary research institute for the University of Calgary.

Jennifer Robinson Memorial Scholarship
Subjects: Northern biology.
Purpose: To award a graduate who best exemplifies the qualities of scholarship that the late Jennifer Robinson brought to her studies at the Kluane Lake Research Station. The scholarship committee looks for evidence of Northern relevance and a commitment to field orientated research.
Eligibility: Applicants should contact the organization for eligibility details and guidelines.
Level of Study: Graduate
Type: Scholarship
Value: Canadian $5,000
Length of Study: 1 year, with the possibility of renewal
Frequency: Annual
Country of Study: Canada
No. of awards offered: 1
Application Procedure: There is no application form. Applicants must submit a brief description, of 2–3 pages, of the proposed

research, including a clear hypothesis, relevance, title and statement of the purpose of the research, the area and type of study, and the methodology and plan for the evaluation of findings. Any collaborative relationship or work should be briefly identified. Three academic reference letters, a complete curriculum vitae with copies and a separate sheet of paper listing current sources and amounts of research funding including scholarships, grants and bursaries should also be submitted. Applicants are requested to include their email address, if they have one, upon submitting applications.
Closing Date: January 10th
Funding: Private
No. of awards given last year: 1
Additional Information: The winning applicant will be notified by the selection committee in February. Information is also available on our website www.arctic.ucalgary.ca

Jim Bourque Scholarship
Subjects: Education, environmental studies or traditional knowledge of telecommunications.
Purpose: To financially support those in post-secondary training.
Eligibility: Open to Canadian Aboriginal mature or matriculating students who are enrolled in postsecondary training in the relevant subject areas.
Type: Scholarship
Value: Canadian $1,000
Length of Study: 1 year
Frequency: Annual
Country of Study: Canada
No. of awards offered: 1
Application Procedure: There is no application form. Applicants must submit, in 500 words or less, a description of their intended programme of study and the reasons for their choice. In addition, applicants must include a copy of their most recent college or university transcript, a signed letter of recommendation from a community leader e.g. Town or Band Council, Chamber of Commerce, Metis Local, a statement of financial need indicating funding already received or expected and a proof of enrolment into, or application for, a post-secondary institution. Applications are evaluated based on need, relevance of study, achievements, return of investment and overall presentation of the application.
Closing Date: July 18th
Additional Information: The recepient of the award will be announced in August. Information is also available on our website www.arctic@ucalgary.ca

Lorraine Allison Scholarship
Subjects: Canadian issues.
Purpose: To promote the study of Northern issues.
Eligibility: Open to any student enrolled at a Canadian university in a programme of graduate study related to Northern issues, whose application best addresses academic excellence, a demonstrated commitment to Northern research and a desire for research results to be beneficial to Northerners, especially Native Northerners. Candidates in biological science fields will be preferred, but a social science topic will also be considered. Scholars from Yukon, the North West Territories and Nunavut are encouraged to apply.
Level of Study: Graduate
Type: Scholarship
Value: Canadian $2,000
Length of Study: 1 year with the possibility of renewal following receipt of a satisfactory progress report and reapplication
Frequency: Annual
Country of Study: Canada
No. of awards offered: 1
Application Procedure: Applicants must submit a two-page description of the Northern studies programme and relevant projects being undertaken, three letters of reference from the applicant's current or past professors, a complete curriculum vitae with academic transcripts and a separate sheet of paper listing current sources and amounts of research funding, including scholarships, grants and bursaries. There is no application form.
Closing Date: January 10th
Funding: International Office, trusts
Additional Information: The selection committee will notify the winning applicant in February.

ARD INTERNATIONAL MUSIC COMPETITION

Bayerischer Rundfunk, Munich, 80300, Germany
Tel: (49) 89 5 900 2471
Fax: (49) 89 5 900 3573
Email: ard.musikwettbewerb@brnet.de
Website: www.ard-musikwettbewerb.de

The ARD International Music Competition is an event organized by the Association of Public Broadcasting Station in Germany. The Competition, held annually in September in Munich, Germany, covers various categories and is open to all nationalities.

ARD International Music Competition Munich
Subjects: Music, categories vary annually.
Purpose: To support and reward a selection of young musicians who are at concert standard.
Eligibility: Open to musicians of any nationality. Age restrictions apply.
Level of Study: Graduate
Type: Competition
Frequency: Annual
Study Establishment: Conservatories, university schools of music and music academies, but also includes advanced private studies
Country of Study: Any country
No. of awards offered: The competition includes 4 categories. For each category 3 prizes are offered
Application Procedure: Applicants must complete and submit an application form, an application fee and an audio cassette. There is an entry fee of €100 per soloist, €120 for duos.
Closing Date: April 30th
Funding: Corporation
Contributor: Public radio stations in Germany
No. of awards given last year: 14
No. of applicants last year: 430

Prize Winner of the ARD International Music Competition Munich
Subjects: Music (categories are singer, solo instruments and chamber music ensembles. Categories vary annually).
Purpose: To support and reward a selection of young musicians who are at concert standard.
Eligibility: Open to musicians of any nationality. Age restrictions apply. Further information can be found in the brochure, which is available on request and on the website.
Level of Study: Graduate
Type: Prize
Value: €99,000 in cash awards per year. Please contact the organization for details
Frequency: Annual
Study Establishment: Conservatories, university schools of music and music academies, but also includes advanced private studies
Country of Study: Any country
No. of awards offered: The competition includes 4 categories and 3 prizes for each category
Application Procedure: Applicants must complete and submit an application form, an application fee and an audio cassette.
Closing Date: April 30th
Funding: Corporation
Contributor: Public radio stations in Germany
No. of awards given last year: 14
No. of applicants last year: 390

ARKANSAS SINGLE PARENT SCHOLARSHIP FUND (ASPSF)

614 East Emma Avenue, Suite 119, Springdale, AR 72764, United States of America
Tel: (1) 479 927 1402
Fax: (1) 479 927 0755
Email: rnesson@jtlshop.jonesnet.org
Website: www.aspsf.org

The ASPSF is a private, non-profit corporation, which was established in 1990 in recognition of the severe impoverishment of single-parent families in Arkansas.

Arkansas Single Parent Scholarships
Subjects: All subjects.
Purpose: To provide financial assistance to single parents who are pursuing a course of instruction that will improve their income-earning potential.
Eligibility: Open to applicants who are single parents living in Arkansas who are considered economically disadvantaged.
Level of Study: Professional development
Type: Scholarship
Value: US$500
Frequency: Annual
Country of Study: United States of America
Application Procedure: See the website.

Business and Professional Women's (BPN) Foundation Career Advancement Scholarship
Subjects: All subjects.
Purpose: To promote equity for all women in the workplace through advocacy, education and information.
Eligibility: Open to female candidates who are US citizens or US nationals and are above the age of 25.
Level of Study: Professional development
Type: Scholarship
Frequency: Annual
Country of Study: United States of America
Application Procedure: Application forms and details are available on the website.
Closing Date: April 15th
Funding: Foundation
Contributor: The BPW Foundation

Jeannette Rankin Foundation Grant
Subjects: All subjects.
Purpose: To financially support low-income women in their education.
Eligibility: Open to female candidates who are US citizens and 35 years of age or older.
Level of Study: Professional development
Type: Grant
Value: Up to US$2,000
Frequency: Annual
Country of Study: United States of America
No. of awards offered: 60
Application Procedure: Application form can be downloaded from the website.
Funding: Private

ARTHRITIS NATIONAL RESEARCH FOUNDATION (ANRF)

200 Oceangate, Suite 830, Long Beach, CA, 90802, United States of America
Tel: (1) 800 588 2873
Fax: (1) 562 983 1410
Email: anrf@ix.netcom.com
Website: www.curearthritis.org
Contact: Ms Helene Belisle, Executive Director

The Arthritis National Research Foundation (ANRF) provides funding for highly qualified postdoctoral researchers associated with major research institutes, universities and hospitals seeking to discover new knowledge for the prevention, treatment and cure of arthritis and related rheumatic diseases. The ANRF fills a much-needed niche in the field of rheumatic disease research by providing support for young postdoctoral investigators, often providing the first major funding in their research careers.

ANRF Research Grants
Subjects: Arthritis, rheumatic diseases and related immune disorders.
Purpose: To support research focusing on arthritic diseases, such as osteoarthritis, rheumatoid arthritis, lupus and related rheumatic and autoimmune diseases.

Eligibility: Applicants must hold an MD or PhD degree. Applicants need not be citizens of the United States of America, but must conduct their research at United States of America institutions. Applications will be accepted from postdoctorates and faculty members, with priority going to those scientists who do not already hold awards from the NIH or the Arthritis Foundation.
Level of Study: Postdoctorate, Research
Type: Research grant
Value: Grants may range from US$20,000 to 75,000
Length of Study: 1 year, with potential for renewal
Frequency: Annual
Study Establishment: Qualifying non-profit institutions in the United States of America
Country of Study: United States of America
No. of awards offered: 8 to 15 per year
Application Procedure: Applicants must visit the website for further information. A copy of the grants guidelines may be obtained via telephone or email.
Closing Date: January 16th
Funding: Foundation, individuals, private
Contributor: Individuals
No. of awards given last year: 13
No. of applicants last year: 52

ARTHRITIS RESEARCH CAMPAIGN

Copeman House, St Mary's Court, St Mary's Gate, Chesterfield, S41 7TD, England
Tel: (44) 12 4655 8033
Fax: (44) 12 4655 8007
Email: info@arc.org.uk
Website: www.arc.org.uk
Contact: Mr Michael Patnick, Head of Research & Education Funding

The Arthritis Research Campaign (arc) is the fourth largest medical research charity in the United Kingdom, and the only charity in the country dedicated to finding the cause of and cure for arthritis, relying entirely upon voluntary donations to sustain its wide-ranging research and educational programmes.

Allied Health Professionals Educational Training Bursaries

Subjects: Arthritis and related musculoskeletal diseases.
Purpose: To promote awareness and understanding of arthritis and related musculoskeletal diseases among allied health professionals through research, practical experience, presentation of research or formal education in rheumatology.
Eligibility: Open to allied health professionals who are, or are eligible to be, registered with the Health Professionals Council (HPC), Nursing and Midwifery Council (NMC) or other appropriate regulatory body. Applicants should have at least 3 years relevant post-registration work experience and at least 1 year's experience in rheumatology/arthritis.
Level of Study: Postgraduate, Professional development, Unrestricted
Type: Bursary
Value: Funding is offered towards the cost of tuition fees for full-time or part-time study
Length of Study: Full MSc course or short training/diploma course
Frequency: Annual
Study Establishment: A recognized training establishment in the UK
Country of Study: United Kingdom
No. of awards offered: Varies
Application Procedure: Applicants must complete an application form, available from the website.
Closing Date: January and July
Funding: Private
Contributor: Voluntary charitable donations
No. of awards given last year: 9
No. of applicants last year: 11

Allied Health Professionals Educational Travel Awards

Subjects: Arthritis and musculoskeletal diseases.
Purpose: To enable allied health professionals to attend a national or international meeting in order to present a paper or poster, chair a session or lead a discussion, provided the meeting has a clear relevance to the aims and interests of ARC or to visit wards/units in their speciality for the purpose of studying other methods of care of patients with arthritis and related musculoskeletal diseases.
Eligibility: Open to allied health professionals who are, or are eligible to be, registered with the Health Professions Council (HPC), Nursing and Midwifery Council (NMC) or other appropriate regulatory body. Applicants should have at least 3 years relevant post-registration work experience and at least 1 year's experience in rheumatology/arthritis.
Level of Study: Postgraduate, Professional development, Unrestricted
Type: Travel award
Value: Please see the website
Frequency: Annual
Study Establishment: A recognized training establishment, a national or an international congress
Country of Study: United Kingdom
No. of awards offered: Varies
Application Procedure: Applicants must complete an application form, available from the website.
Closing Date: April, July and September
Funding: Private
Contributor: Voluntary charitable donations
No. of awards given last year: 2
No. of applicants last year: 2

Allied Health Professionals Training Fellowships

Subjects: Arthritis and related musculoskeletal diseases.
Purpose: To enable allied health professionals to undertake training in clinical or basic science research at a UK institution leading to a PhD or other appropriate higher degree.
Eligibility: Open to allied health professionals who are, or are eligible to be, registered with the Health Professionals Council (HPC), Nursing and Midwifery Council (NMC) or other appropriate regulatory body. Applicants should have at least 3 years relevant post-registration work experience and be committed to the care of patients with arthritis and related musculoskeletal diseases.
Level of Study: Postgraduate, Professional development, Research
Type: Fellowship
Value: Salary plus reasonable running costs
Length of Study: Varies, full-time or part-time
Frequency: Annual
Study Establishment: A university, hospital or recognized research institute
Country of Study: United Kingdom
No. of awards offered: Varies
Application Procedure: Applicants must complete an application form, available from the website.
Closing Date: February 2nd
Funding: Private
Contributor: Voluntary charitable donations
No. of awards given last year: 1
No. of applicants last year: 9

Barbara Ansell Fellowships in Paediatric Rheumatology

Subjects: Paediatric rheumatology.
Purpose: To provide an opportunity for paediatricians or rheumatologists to develop research interests in paediatric rheumatology.
Eligibility: Open to medical graduates of the United Kingdom who are at specialist registrar level. Successful applicants will be expected to develop projects in paediatric rheumatology for further fellowship support.
Level of Study: Postgraduate, Professional development, Research
Type: Fellowship
Value: Salary plus reasonable running expenses
Length of Study: 1 year
Study Establishment: A university department, hospital or recognized research institution
Country of Study: United Kingdom
No. of awards offered: Varies
Application Procedure: Applicants must complete an application form, available from the website.
Closing Date: There is no deadline date
Funding: Private
Contributor: Voluntary charitable donations
Additional Information: These entry-level training fellowships are offered by ARC in memory of Dr Barbara Ansell.

Career Development Fellowships

Subjects: Arthritis and related musculoskeletal diseases.
Purpose: To attract and retain talented postdoctoral scientists and allied health professionals in research relevant to arthritis and related musculoskeletal diseases.
Eligibility: Open to candidates working in institutions in the United Kingdom who should normally have at least 3 years of postdoctoral research experience.
Level of Study: Postdoctorate, Professional development, Research
Type: Fellowship
Value: Salary plus an additional fixed salary supplement of £3,000 per year, plus reasonable running costs and small items of equipment
Length of Study: Up to 5 years
Frequency: Annual
Study Establishment: A university department or similar research institute preferably within a multidisciplinary research group
Country of Study: United Kingdom
No. of awards offered: Varies
Application Procedure: Applicants must complete an application form, available from the website.
Closing Date: March 2nd
Funding: Private
Contributor: Voluntary charitable contributions
No. of awards given last year: 3
No. of applicants last year: 8

Clinical PhD Studentships

Subjects: Arthritis and related musculoskeletal diseases.
Purpose: To provide training for medically qualified clinicians in a high-quality research environment leading to a PhD and allow institutions to recruit candidates of the highest calibre.
Eligibility: Open to university departments who can provide an appropriate scientific/clinical training environment and a scientifically robust project relevant to the aims of the Arthritis Research Campaign.
Level of Study: Postgraduate, Doctorate, Professional development, Research
Type: Studentship
Value: A clinical salary over 3 years at the appropriate level for the appointed candidate (usually at SpR level) with running expenses and essential equipment
Length of Study: 3 years
Frequency: Annual
Study Establishment: A university hospital or recognized research institute
Country of Study: United Kingdom
No. of awards offered: 2
Application Procedure: Applicants must complete an application form, available from the website.
Closing Date: July 13th
Funding: Private
Contributor: Voluntary charitable donations

Clinical Research Fellowships

Subjects: Arthritis and related musculoskeletal diseases.
Purpose: To encourage young clinicians to enter into an academic research career in rheumatology or any related field (including general practice) concerned with the treatment of arthritis and related musculoskeletal diseases.
Eligibility: Open to medical graduates who are registered for a higher degree usually a PhD.
Level of Study: Doctorate, Professional development, Research
Type: Fellowship
Value: Fellow's salary plus reasonable running costs
Length of Study: 2–3 years
Frequency: Annual
Study Establishment: A university, hospital or recognized research institute
Country of Study: United Kingdom
No. of awards offered: Varies
Application Procedure: Applicants must complete an application form available from the website.
Closing Date: January 5th
Funding: Private
Contributor: Voluntary charitable contributions
No. of awards given last year: 2
No. of applicants last year: 13

Educational Project Grants

Subjects: Arthritis and related musculoskeletal diseases.
Purpose: To fund a number of projects aimed at investigating innovative approaches to enhance the education of healthcare professionals and the public on musculoskeletal disorders.
Eligibility: Individuals working for universities, the NHS or other public institutions with an interest in educational research.
Level of Study: Professional development, Research
Type: Project grant
Value: Up to a maximum of £100,000 per project
Length of Study: Up to 2 years
Frequency: Annual
Study Establishment: A university, hospital or recognized research institute
Country of Study: United Kingdom
No. of awards offered: Varies
Application Procedure: Applicants must complete an application form available from the website.
Closing Date: March 30th
Funding: Private
Contributor: Voluntary charitable contributions
Additional Information: Intending applicants should see arc's education strategy on the website to gain insight into its global activities.

Educational Research Fellowships

Subjects: Arthritis and related musculoskeletal diseases.
Purpose: To provide an opportunity for an individual to gain training in educational research methodology and medical education.
Eligibility: Open to clinicians (usually at specialty training level in rheumatology or general practice) or non-clinicians (including allied health professionals and eucationists). Candidates will be expected to register for a higher degree (MD, MSc or PhD).
Level of Study: Postgraduate, Professional development, Research
Type: Fellowship
Value: Salary plus reasonable running costs
Length of Study: 2 or 3 years, full-time or part-time
Frequency: Annual
Study Establishment: A university, hospital or recognized research institute
Country of Study: United Kingdom
No. of awards offered: Varies
Application Procedure: Applicants must complete an application form, available from the website.
Closing Date: September 7th
Funding: Private
Contributor: Voluntary charitable contributions

Equipment Grants

Subjects: Arthritis and related musculoskeletal diseases.
Purpose: To fund major items of equipment costing in excess of UK £30,000 that will facilitate multiple projects and make a lasting impact on rheumatological research over many years.
Eligibility: Open to established units with a track record of research in arthritis and musculoskeletal disease.
Level of Study: Research
Type: Grant
Value: Varies
Length of Study: Up to 3 years
Study Establishment: A university, hospital or recognized research institute
Country of Study: United Kingdom
No. of awards offered: Varies
Application Procedure: Applicants must complete an application form, available from the website.
Closing Date: The last Monday of February, June and October
Funding: Private
Contributor: Voluntary charitable contributions
No. of awards given last year: 9
No. of applicants last year: 12

Foundation Fellowships

Subjects: Arthritis and related musculoskeletal diseases.
Purpose: To retain the best PhD students as postdoctoral researchers and provide an opportunity for Fellows to develop independent research ideas at an early stage in their career.

Eligibility: Open to PhD students in the final year of training, or within 1 year of completing their PhD at the time of application. Fellowships cannot be taken up until the PhD has been awarded.
Level of Study: Postdoctorate, Professional development, Research
Type: Fellowship
Value: Salary, plus an additional fixed salary supplement for non-clinical fellows, plus reasonable running costs and small items of equipment
Length of Study: 3 years
Frequency: Annual
Study Establishment: A university, hospital or recognized research institute
Country of Study: United Kingdom
No. of awards offered: Varies
Application Procedure: Applicants must complete an application form, available from the website.
Closing Date: April 6th
Funding: Private
Contributor: Voluntary charitable donations
No. of awards given last year: 3
No. of applicants last year: 6
Additional Information: Applications should be made by the applicant and their sponsor(s) (who should not be the applicant's previous PhD supervisor). Preference will be given to applicants who wish to move to another laboratory in the UK or, if remaining in the same institution, spend a period of time in another laboratory, preferably abroad.

Orthopaedic Clinical Research Fellowship
Subjects: Arthritis and related musculoskeletal diseases.
Purpose: To encourage trainee orthopaedic surgeons to undertake research relevant to arthritis and related musculoskeletal diseases.
Eligibility: Open to fellows or members of the Royal College of Surgeons of Edinburgh and/or the Royal College of Surgeons of England and in good standing.
Level of Study: Doctorate, Professional development, Research
Type: Fellowship
Value: Varies
Length of Study: Up to 3 years
Frequency: Annual
Study Establishment: A university, hospital or recognized research institute
Country of Study: United Kingdom
No. of awards offered: One
Application Procedure: Applicants must complete an application form, available from the website.
Closing Date: June 8th
Funding: Private
Contributor: Voluntary charitable contributions
No. of awards given last year: 1
No. of applicants last year: 3

PhD Studentships
Subjects: Arthritis and related musculoskeletal diseases.
Purpose: To encourage the best young science graduates to embark on a research career in any discipline relevant to arthritis and related musculoskeletal diseases.
Eligibility: Open to university departments allied to rheumatology.
Level of Study: Postgraduate, Doctorate, Professional development, Research
Type: Studentship
Value: Incremental stipend, United Kingdom tuition fees and limited running costs
Length of Study: 3 years
Frequency: Annual
Study Establishment: A university, hospital or recognized research institute
Country of Study: United Kingdom
No. of awards offered: Varies
Application Procedure: Applicants must complete an application form, available from the website.
Closing Date: August 10th
Funding: Private
Contributor: Voluntary charitable donations

No. of awards given last year: 5
No. of applicants last year: 30
Additional Information: Proposals may be submitted for collaborative studentships by universities with an industrial sponsor/supervisor.

Programme Grants
Subjects: Arthritis and related musculoskeletal diseases.
Purpose: To support work that cannot be carried out in the short-term, to attract and maintain high-quality staff in an effective research team and to enable established research workers of proven ability to concentrate their efforts in a specific area.
Eligibility: Established groups undertaking research relevant to the aims of ARC, and which have a substantial research track record based on either ARC support or peer-reviewed funding from other sources.
Level of Study: Research
Type: Grant
Value: Varies
Length of Study: Up to 5 years
Frequency: Annual
Study Establishment: A university, hospital or recognized research institute
Country of Study: United Kingdom
No. of awards offered: Varies
Application Procedure: Applicants must submit an outline proposal form in the first instance, available from the website.
Closing Date: June 8th
Funding: Private
Contributor: Voluntary charitable contributions
No. of awards given last year: 1
No. of applicants last year: 4
Additional Information: Applicants should note that up to 1 year should be allowed for the full process of the programme grant evaluation to take place.

Project Grants
Subjects: Arthritis and related musculoskeletal diseases.
Purpose: To provide support for projects designed to seek an answer to a single question or group of related questions, providing they offer promise of adancement in the understanding of arthritis and related musculoskeletal diseases.
Eligibility: Open to applicants working at institutions in the United Kingdom who must have previous investigation and research experience.
Level of Study: Professional development, Research
Type: Project grant
Value: Varies
Length of Study: Up to 3 years
Frequency: 3 times a year
Study Establishment: A university, hospital or recognized research institute
Country of Study: United Kingdom
No. of awards offered: Varies
Application Procedure: Applicants must complete an application form, available from the website.
Closing Date: The last Monday of February, June and October
Funding: Private
Contributor: Voluntary charitable contributions
No. of awards given last year: 29
No. of applicants last year: 134
Additional Information: Grants are made in support of specific research projects.

Travelling Fellowships
Subjects: Arthritis and related musculoskeletal diseases.
Purpose: To provide an opportunity for medical graduates to undertake research in any discipline relevant to arthritis and related musculoskeletal diseases in another institution, either abroad or in the UK, for up to 1 year.
Eligibility: Open to medical graduates usually during specialty training or equivalent level, or postdoctoral scientists. These fellowships are not renewable
Level of Study: Professional development, Research
Type: Fellowship
Value: Salary plus either reasonable running expenses (in the UK) or an allowance for airfares (overseas)

Length of Study: 1 year
Frequency: Annual
Study Establishment: A research centre of the Fellow's choice, subject to ARC's approval
Country of Study: Any country
No. of awards offered: Varies
Application Procedure: Applicants must complete an application form, available from the website.
Closing Date: June 8th
Funding: Private
Contributor: Voluntary charitable contributions
No. of awards given last year: 0
No. of applicants last year: 1
Additional Information: Applicants should have made their own arrangements with the unit to be visited and documentary evidence that the host institution would be prepared to accept the candidate should be submitted with the application.

THE ARTHRITIS SOCIETY

393 University Avenue, Suite 1700, Toronto, ON, M5G 1E6, Canada
Tel: (1) 416 979 7228 extn. 393
Fax: (1) 416 979 1149
Email: jwysocki@arthritis.ca
Website: www.arthritis.ca
Contact: Ms Julie Wysocki, Manager, Reserach and career Development Program

The Arthritis Society is Canada's only non-profit agency dedicated solely to funding and promoting arthritis research and care.

Arthritis Society Research Fellowships

Subjects: Arthritis.
Purpose: To provide financial support so that candidates can pursue full-time research.
Eligibility: Open to highly qualified candidates with preference given to candidates intending to embark on a research career in Canada. Candidates must hold a PhD, MD, DDS, DVM, PharmD or the equivalent.
Level of Study: Postdoctorate
Type: Fellowship
Value: Based on institution scales
Length of Study: 2 years, usually beginning on July 1st with a possibility of renewal
Frequency: Annual
Study Establishment: Ordinarily, universities. Out-of-country training may be arranged in order to obtain specific expertise
Country of Study: Canada
No. of awards offered: Varies
Application Procedure: Applicants must complete and submit an application form with further documentation as outlined in the regulations.
Closing Date: December 1st
Funding: Private
Contributor: Public donors
No. of awards given last year: 7
No. of applicants last year: 13
Additional Information: Fellowships are awarded by the Society on the advice of the Review Panel. The Society reserves the right to approve or decline any application without stating its reasons.

Geoff Carr Lupus Fellowship

Subjects: Lupus.
Purpose: To provide advanced training to a rheumatologist.
Eligibility: Open to nationals of any country specializing in lupus at an Ontario lupus clinic.
Level of Study: Postdoctorate
Type: Fellowship
Value: Canadian $55,000
Length of Study: 1 year
Frequency: Annual
Study Establishment: An approved Ontario lupus clinic
Country of Study: Canada
No. of awards offered: 1
Application Procedure: Applicants must submit an application with three letters of recommendation and a letter of acceptance from a

proposed supervisor. The letter of acceptance must include an outline proposed training programme and a certified transcript of their undergraduate record.
Closing Date: November 1st
Funding: Private
Contributor: The Ontario Lupus Association
No. of awards given last year: 1

Metro A Ogryzlo International Fellowship

Subjects: Clinical rheumatology.
Purpose: To provide advanced training to individuals from a developing country.
Eligibility: The successful candidate will have completed his or her training in general medicine and have a substantial prospect of returning to an academic position in his or her own country. Canadian citizens or landed immigrants are not eligible.
Level of Study: Postdoctorate
Type: Fellowship
Value: Up to a maximum of Canadian $31,000 per year
Length of Study: 1 year, non-renewable
Frequency: Annual
Study Establishment: A rheumatic disease unit or arthritis centre
Country of Study: Canada
No. of awards offered: 1
Application Procedure: Applicants must submit an application including letters of recommendation from three sponsors, letter of acceptance from the proposed supervisor, an outline of the proposed training programme and a certified transcript of their undergraduate record.
Closing Date: December 1st
Funding: Private
Contributor: Public donors
Additional Information: Fellows may not receive remuneration for any other work or hold a second major scholarship, except that, with the approval of their supervisors, they may engage in and accept remuneration for such departmental activities as are conducive to their development as clinicians, teachers or investigators. Ordinarily, a Fellow who is not a graduate of a medical school in the United States of America, the United Kingdom, Republic of Ireland, Australia, New Zealand or South Africa must take the Medical Council of Canada evaluating examination to obtain the Medical Council of Canada certificate before an education licence can be issued.

ARTHUR RUBINSTEIN INTERNATIONAL MUSIC SOCIETY

12 Huberman Street, Tel Aviv, 64075, Israel
Tel: (972) 3 685 6684
Fax: (972) 3 685 4924
Email: competition@arims.org.il
Website: www.arims.org.il
Contact: Ms Idith Zui, Director

The Arthur Rubinstein International Music Society was founded by Jan Jacob Bistritzky in 1980 in tribute to the artistry of Arthur Rubinstein (1887–1982) and to maintain his spiritual and artistic heritage in the art of the piano. The Society organizes and finances the Arthur Rubinstein International Piano Master Competition and the Hommage à Rubinstein worldwide concert series and festivals, awards scholarships, runs music courses and master classes, organizes lectures and memorial festivals and issues publications and recordings.

Arthur Rubinstein International Piano Master Competition

Subjects: Piano.
Purpose: To reward talented pianists with the capacity for multifaceted creative interpretation of composers, ranging from the pre-classic to the contemporary era.
Eligibility: Candidates must be 18–32 years of age.
Level of Study: Professional development
Type: Prize
Value: The first prize is a competition gold medal plus US$25,000, the second prize is a competition silver medal plus US$15,000 and the third prize is a competition bronze medal plus US$10,000. The fourth, fifth and sixth prizes are US$3,000 each
Frequency: Every 3 years

Country of Study: Any country
No. of awards offered: 10
Application Procedure: Applicants must complete an application form according to the rules stipulated in the prospectus of the Arthur Rubinstein International Piano Master Competition. Details are available from the organization.
Closing Date: October
Funding: Private, government
No. of applicants last year: 185
Additional Information: Next competition: March 28th–April 14th.

ARTIST TRUST

1835, 12th Ave, Seattle, WA, 98122, United States of America
Tel: (1) 206 467 8734
Fax: (1) 206 467 9633
Email: info@artisttrust.org
Website: www.artisttrust.org

Artist Trust is a non-profit organization whose sole mission is to support and encourage individual artists working in all disciplines in order to enhance community life throughout Washington state.

Artist Trust/WSAC Fellowships
Subjects: Art.
Purpose: To reward practicing professional artists of exceptional talent and demonstrated ability. The fellowship is a merit-based, not a project-based award.
Eligibility: Candidates must be 18 years or older, and should not be a matriculated student. Only Washington State residents may apply.
Level of Study: Unrestricted, Students may not apply
Type: Fellowship
Value: US$6,500
Frequency: Annual, Awarded in two-year cycles: music, media, literature and crafts disciplines are awarded in odd-numbered years. Dance, Design, Theater and Visual Arts disciplines are awarded in even-numbered years
No. of awards offered: 21
Application Procedure: Candidates must complete an application form (available online), submit work samples, proof of Washington State residency, a curriculum vitae and a work sample description.
Closing Date: June 12th
Funding: Commercial, corporation, foundation, government, individuals, private
Contributor: Washington State Arts Commission
No. of awards given last year: 21
No. of applicants last year: 333 applicants in visual arts, dance, design, theatre

Grants for Artist Projects (GAP) Program
Subjects: Art.
Purpose: To provide support for artist-generated projects, which can include (but are not limited to) the development, completion or presentation of new work.
Eligibility: All candidates must be 18 years or older, and Washington State residents. All disciplines and interdisciplinary projects are eligible.
Level of Study: Unrestricted, students may not apply
Type: Grant
Value: A maximum of US$1,500 for projects
Frequency: Annual
No. of awards offered: Varies
Application Procedure: Candidates must submit an application form (available online), work sample, proof of Washington State residency, a curriculum vitae and a work sample description.
Closing Date: February 20th
Funding: Commercial, government, private
No. of awards given last year: 40
No. of applicants last year: 675

Twining Humber Award for Lifetime Artistic Achievement
Subjects: Visual arts.
Purpose: To reward a female visual artist over the age of 60 from Washington State.

Eligibility: Artists must be nominated. Nominees must be female, over the age of 60, a Washington State resident and a visual artist who has been practicing for 25 years or more.
Level of Study: Unrestricted
Type: Award
Value: US$10,000
Frequency: Annual
No. of awards offered: 1
Application Procedure: Nomination forms are available by mail or online.
Closing Date: January
Funding: Commercial, corporation, foundation, government, individuals, private
Contributor: Mrs Twining Humber (deceased)
No. of awards given last year: 1
No. of applicants last year: 12

ARTS AND HUMANITIES RESEARCH COUNCIL (AHRC)

Postgraduate Awards Division, Whitefriars, Lewins Mead, Bristol, BS1 2AE, England
Tel: (44) 11 7987 6543
Fax: (44) 11 7987 6544
Email: pgenquiries@ahrc.ac.uk
Website: www.ahrc.ac.uk
Contact: Dr Emma Wakelin, Associate Director of Programmes

The Arts and Humanities Research Council (AHRC) funds postgraduate study and research within the United Kingdom's Institutions of Higher Education. The AHRC supports Master's courses and doctoral research within a huge subject domain ranging from history, modern languages and English literature, to music and the creative and performing arts. The AHRC makes awards on the basis of academic excellence.

AHRC Doctoral Awards Scheme
Subjects: Archaeology, classics and ancient history, cultural and media studies, English language and literature, history of art and architecture, law, linguistics, modern languages, music, drama, dance and performing arts, philosophy, religious studies, art and design, creative writing, musical performance, museum studies, librarianship and information studies and medieval and modern history.
Purpose: To support full-time and part-time study for students undertaking a doctoral degree in the arts and humanities.
Eligibility: Applicants must be resident in the United Kingdom or the European Union and be graduates of a recognized Institute of Higher Education or be expecting to graduate by July 31st preceding the start of the course. Applicants should refer to the AHRC guide for full details.
Level of Study: Doctorate
Type: Studentship
Value: UK £14,300 per year maintenance grant for London-based full-time students and UK £12,300 per year for full-time students based elsewhere. Tuition fees up to UK £3,168 per year, plus a study visit and conference costs. For part-time students, maintenance grant of UK £275 per year and tuition fees of UK £1,584 per year
Length of Study: Up to 3 years full-time and 5 years part-time
Frequency: Annual
Study Establishment: Any approved Institute of Higher Education
Country of Study: United Kingdom
No. of awards offered: Varies
Application Procedure: Applicants must download and complete an application form available on the website.
Closing Date: July 1st
Funding: Government
No. of awards given last year: 673
No. of applicants last year: 2,566

Professional Preparation Master's Scheme
Subjects: Art and design, interpreting and translation, librarianship, archives and information management, museum studies and heritage management, creative writing, archaeology, classics and literature, linguistics, modern languages, music, drama, dance and performing arts and medieval and modern history, conservation.

Purpose: To provide funding to allow students to undertake Master's or postgraduate diploma courses that focus on developing high-level skills and competencies for professional practice.

Eligibility: Applicants must be resident in the United Kingdom or the European Union and be graduates of a recognized Institute of Higher Education or be expecting to graduate by July 31st preceding the start of the course. Applicants should refer to the AHRC guide for full details.

Level of Study: Postgraduate

Type: Studentship

Value: For full-time, UK £10,000 in London, UK £8,000 elsewhere, plus tuition fees of up to UK £3,168. These amounts are subject to change. Please consult the organization. For part-time, maintenance grant of UK £250 per year and tuition fees of UK £1,584 per year

Length of Study: 9 months–1 year

Frequency: Annual

Study Establishment: An Institute of Higher Education

Country of Study: United Kingdom

No. of awards offered: Varies

Application Procedure: Applicants must download and complete an application form available on the website.

Closing Date: May 1st

Funding: Government

No. of awards given last year: 351

No. of applicants last year: 1,521

Research Preparation Master's Scheme

Subjects: Archaeology, classics and ancient history, cultural and media studies, English language and literature, history of art and architecture, law, linguistics, modern languages, music, drama, dance and performing arts, philosophy, religious studies, art and design, medieval and modern history, museum studies, librarianship, and information studies.

Purpose: To support students undertaking Master's courses that focus on advanced study and research training explicitly intended to provide a foundation for further research at doctoral level.

Eligibility: Applicants must be resident in the United Kingdom or the European Union, be graduates of a recognized Institute of Higher Education or be expecting to graduate by July 31st preceding the start of the course. Applicants should refer to the AHRC guide for full details.

Level of Study: Postgraduate

Type: Studentship

Value: For full-time, UK £10,600 per year maintenance grant for London-based students and UK £8,600 per year for students based elsewhere plus tuition fees up to UK £3,168 per year. For part-time, maintenance grant of UK £275 per year and tuition fees UK £1,584 per year

Length of Study: 1–2 years

Frequency: Annual

Study Establishment: An approved Institute of Higher Education

Country of Study: United Kingdom

No. of awards offered: Varies

Application Procedure: Applicants must download and complete an application form available on the website.

Closing Date: May 1st

Funding: Government

No. of awards given last year: 466

No. of applicants last year: 1,779

THE ARTS COUNCIL OF WALES

9 Museum Place, Cardiff, CF10 3NX, Wales
Tel: (44) 29 2037 6500
Fax: (44) 29 2022 1447
Email: info@artswales.org.uk
Website: www.artswales.org.uk
Contact: Angela Blackburn

The Arts Council of Wales is the national organization with specific responsibility for the funding and development of the arts in Wales. Most of its funds come from the National Assembly for Wales, but it also distributes National Lottery funds to the arts in Wales.

Arts Council of Wales Creative Wales Award

Subjects: Arts.

Purpose: To develop their creative practice.

Eligibility: Applicants must be aged 18 or above and not in full-time education. Must be able to demonstrate originality, excellence and purpose in their work. Applicants must live in Wales and demonstrate a commitment to Wales.

Type: Award

Value: £5,001–12,000

Frequency: Every 3 years

Country of Study: Wales

Contributor: Arts Council of Wales

Additional Information: The award might include the creation of new, experimental and innovative work that takes forward the art form and artistic practice.

Arts Council of Wales Major Creative Wales Award

Subjects: Arts.

Purpose: To develop their creative practice.

Eligibility: Applicants must be aged 18 or above and not in full-time education. Must be able to demonstrate originality, excellence and purpose in their work. applicants must live in Wales and demonstrate a commitment to Wales.

Type: Award

Value: £20,000–25,000

Frequency: Every 3 years

Country of Study: Wales

Contributor: Arts Council of Wales

Additional Information: Artists should demonstrate a consistent level of achievement and contribution within the area of professional practice in Wales.

Arts Council of Wales Production Grants

Subjects: Arts.

Purpose: To support artists in the creation of a new artistic product in collaboration with a new partner organisation who will present their work in Wales.

Eligibility: Applicants must be aged 18 or above and not in full-time education. Must be able to demonstrate originality, excellence and purpose in their work. Applicants must live in Wales and demonstrate a commitment to Wales. Work must be innovative and artistically challenging.

Type: Grant

Value: £5,001–20,000

Country of Study: Wales

Contributor: Arts Council of Wales

Arts Council of Wales Project Grants

Subjects: Arts.

Purpose: To allow individuals to explore project ideas or to build their creative, artistic and professional capability over time.

Eligibility: Applicants must be aged 18 or above and not in full-time education. Must be able to demonstrate originality, excellence and purpose in their work. Applicants must live in Wales and demonstrate a commitment to Wales. Applicants will need to demonatrate their ability to manage public funds effectively.

Type: Grant

Value: £250–5,000

Country of Study: Wales

Contributor: Arts Council of Wales

Additional Information: If applicant's project includes an element of production then they must have a partner organization who will present their work in Wales.

Arts Council of Wales Training

Subjects: Arts.

Purpose: To support individuals with the provision of all artistic, creative, technical, business and marketing training in the arts who wish to undertake training within Wales, the UK or abroad.

Eligibility: Applicants must be aged 18 or above and not in full-time education. Must be able to demonstrate originality, excellence and purpose in their work. applicants must live in Wales and demonstrate a commitment to Wales.

Type: Grant

Value: £250–2,000
Country of Study: Wales
Contributor: Arts Council of Wales

Steps to New Music

Subjects: Dance.
Purpose: To increase range of innovative and experimental work produced to inspire and accompany live dance.
Eligibility: Open to Wales individuals whose application is fully supported by a partner organisations. Open to organisations based in Wales or intend to present work in Wales.
Type: Grant
Value: £3,000–5,000
Country of Study: Wales
Application Procedure: Contact the music officer at regional ACW office for specifc guidelines.
Contributor: Arts Council of Wales and PRS Foundation for new music (PRSF)

For further information contact:

PRSF, 29-33 Berners street, London, W1T 3AB, United Kingdom
Website: www.prsfoundation.co.uk

Wales Arts International

Subjects: Arts.
Purpose: To support professional arts practitioners and arts organisations based in Wales to explore international partnerships and projects, outside the UK.
Eligibility: Applicants must be aged 18 or above and not in full-time education. Must be able to demonstrate originality, excellence and purpose in their work. applicants must live in Wales and demonstrate a commitment to Wales.
Type: Funding support

ARTS NSW

Level 9, St James Centre, 111 Elizabeth Street, Sydney, NSW, 2000, Australia
Tel: (61) 02 9228 5533
Fax: (61) 02 9228 4722
Email: mail@arts.nsw. gov.au
Website: www.arts.nsw.gov.au

Arts NSW is part of the NSW Department of the Arts, Sport and Recreation. Arts NSW advises the Minister for the Arts on all aspects of the arts and cultural activity. Arts NSW works closely with the state's 8 major cultural institutions, providing policy advice to Government on their operations. The institutions manage significant cultural heritage collections and provide services and programmes throughout the state and beyond.

Asialink Residency Program

Subjects: Arts management, literature, performing arts, and visual arts/crafts.
Purpose: To promote cultural understanding, information exchange and artistic endeavour between Australia and Asian countries.
Eligibility: Open to the Australian citizens or permanent residents who have at least 3 years professional experience in their field.
Level of Study: Unrestricted
Type: Grant
Value: Up to $12,000
Application Procedure: Check website for further details.
Closing Date: September 7th
Contributor: Arts NSW, in association with the Asialink Centre

For further information contact:

Arts Program, The Asialink Centre, The University of Melbourne, Sidney Myer Asia Centre, Vic 3010, Australia
Tel: (61) 03 8344 4800
Fax: (61) 03 9347 1768
Email: arts@asialink.unimelb.edu.au
Website: www.asialink.unimelb.edu.au/arts

David Paul Landa Memorial Scholarships for Pianists

Subjects: Music.
Eligibility: Open to the Australian citizens currently residing in New South Wales or holding residence visas who have been residents of New South Wales for two consecutive years.
Level of Study: Unrestricted
Type: Scholarship
Value: $25,000
Frequency: Every 2 years
Application Procedure: Applicants must forward the completed application form (and one copy of it), two copies of all written supporting material, single copies of other supporting material, the completed EFT authorization form and, if applicable, two copies of the completed RCTI to Program Support.
Additional Information: Previous recipients of Arts NSW's fellowships and scholarships are ineligible to apply for the same award twice.

For further information contact:

David Paul Landa Memorial Scholarship for Pianists, Musica Viva Australia, PO Box 1687, Strawberry Hills, NSW, 2012, Australia
Tel: (61) 02 8394 6666
Fax: (61) 02 9698 3878
Email: musicaviva@mva.org.au
Contact: The Administrator

Helen Lempriere Travelling Art Scholarship

Subjects: Arts.
Purpose: To enable visual artists who are at the beginning of their career to undertake a 1–2 year programme of study or training overseas.
Eligibility: Open to applicants who are within the first 5 years of their professional practice as artists.
Level of Study: Postgraduate
Type: Scholarship
Value: Australian $40,000
Length of Study: 1 year
Frequency: Annual
Country of Study: Australia
Application Procedure: Applicants must submit a completed application form, including a summary of their qualifications and professional record and an outline of the programme of study to be undertaken.
Closing Date: June
Funding: Government, trusts
Additional Information: The judging committee will make its decision on the basis of both artistic ability and potential, and the suitability of the proposed programme of study. The scholarship is not intended for established artists.

NSW History Fellowship

Subjects: History.
Purpose: To assist a person living in New South Wales to research and produce a work on a subject of historical interest relating to New South Wales.
Level of Study: Unrestricted
Type: Fellowship
Value: $20,000
Frequency: Annual
Application Procedure: Applicants must submit the form with details of the proposal, qualifications and experience along with the original and one copy of five pages of published material or five typewritten pages (if not published) demonstrating their research and writing skills.

NSW Indigenous Arts Fellowship

Subjects: Arts.
Purpose: To assist an Indigenous artist to further develop their career.
Eligibility: Applicants must be experienced as a practising professional.
Level of Study: Unrestricted
Type: Fellowship
Value: $15,000
Length of Study: 18 months

Frequency: Every 2 years
Country of Study: Australia
Application Procedure: Applicants must submit a completed application form (and a copy of it) which outlines: details of the proposal, their qualifications and experience, and samples of work as support material. Check website for details.

NSW Indigenous History Fellowship

Subjects: History.
Purpose: To assist a person living in New South Wales to research and produce a work on a subject of historical interest relating to New South Wales from an Indigenous point of view.
Eligibility: Open to the candidates who may be independent historians, or historians working in conjunction with indigenous communities.
Level of Study: Unrestricted
Type: Fellowship
Value: Australian $20,000
Length of Study: 2 years
Frequency: Every 2 years
Application Procedure: Applicants must submit form with details of the proposal and their qualifications and experience details. Check website for further details.
Additional Information: The fellowship will be administered by the History Council of New South Wales.

For further information contact:

History Council of New South Wales Inc., PO Box R1737, Royal Exchange, NSW 1225
Tel: 02 9252 8715
Fax: 02 9252 8716
Email: office@historycouncilnsw.org.au
Website: www.historycouncilnsw.org.au
Contact: The Executive Officer

NSW Premier's History Awards

Subjects: History.
Eligibility: Open only to the citizens of Australia.
Level of Study: Unrestricted
Type: Award
Value: Australian $15,000
Frequency: Annual
No. of awards offered: 6
Application Procedure: Check website for further details.
Closing Date: March 14th

For further information contact:

Literature and History Program Staff
Tel: 02 9228 5533

NSW Premier's Literary Awards

Subjects: Literature.
Eligibility: Open only to the residents of Australia.
Level of Study: Unrestricted
Type: Award
Value: $5,000–20,000
Frequency: Annual
No. of awards offered: 11
Application Procedure: Check website for further details.
Closing Date: November 9th

For further information contact:

Literature and History Program Staff
Tel: 02 9228 5533

NSW Premier's Translation Prize

Subjects: Poetry, stage and radio plays, and fiction and non–fiction works of literary merit.
Eligibility: Open to the Australian translators who translate literary works into English from other languages and whose body of literary translation has been published or performed in recent years.
Level of Study: Unrestricted
Type: Prize
Value: Australian $15,000

Frequency: Every 2 years
Application Procedure: Check website for further details.
Closing Date: December 5th
Contributor: Funded alternately by Arts NSW and the Community Relations Commission for a Multicultural NSW and presented as part of the NSW Premier's Literary Awards

For further information contact:

Literature and History Program Staff
Tel: 02 9228 5533

NSW Writer's Fellowship

Subjects: Novels, poems, plays, fiction or literary non-fiction.
Purpose: To assist the writing of a new literary work by a writer living in New South Wales.
Eligibility: Open to the candidates who demonstrate that their proposal will be of demonstrable benefit to their development as a writer and will contribute to the advancement of Australian literature.
Level of Study: Unrestricted
Type: Fellowship
Value: Australian $20,000
Frequency: Annual
Application Procedure: Applicants must submit a form with details of the proposal, their qualifications and experience details, evidence of their body of work as well as 10 pages of published material or, if they have not been previously published, 10 single-sided typewritten A4 pages demonstrating their writing ability. Check website for further details.
Funding: Government

Philip Parsons Young Playwright's Award

Subjects: Playwright.
Eligibility: Open to young playwrights under the age of 35 whose work demonstrates an original and compelling theatrical voice.
Level of Study: Unrestricted
Type: Scholarship
Value: Australian $5,000
Frequency: Annual
Application Procedure: Check website for further details.

For further information contact:

Company B Belvoir, 25 Belvoir Street, Surry Hills, NSW 2010
Tel: 02 8399 2190
Email: bsharp@belvoir.com.au
Website: www.belvoir.com.au
Contact: Downstairs Theatre Director

Rex Cramphorn Theatre Scholarship

Subjects: Theatre acting.
Purpose: To assist professional theatre artists to develop their career further.
Eligibility: Open to the candidates who have completed a body of work that suggests an inquiring mind and an original theatrical voice, and are able to demonstrate how the proposed program would assist them to develop a vision for future theatre practice.
Level of Study: Unrestricted
Type: Scholarship
Value: Australian $30,000
Length of Study: 1 year
Frequency: Every 2 years
Country of Study: Australia
Application Procedure: Applicants are required to submit the form with the details of the proposal, qualifications and experience, and samples of their work. Check website for further details.
Closing Date: April 6th
Funding: Government

Robert Helpmann Scholarship

Subjects: Arts.
Purpose: To financially assist professional dancers and choreographers to further develop their career by supporting a specific artistic programme put forward by them.

Eligibility: Open to Australian citizens currently residing in New South Wales or persons holding permanent residence visas.
Level of Study: Postgraduate
Type: Scholarship
Value: Australian $30,000
Length of Study: 1 year
Frequency: Every 2 years
Application Procedure: Applicants must submit a completed application form along with detailed proposal, qualifications and experience, support material such as videos or photographs of their work.
Closing Date: April
Funding: Government
Additional Information: The applicant's proposal can include further study or training, professional research or the undertaking of a particular dance project. The judging committee will favour applicants who demonstrate how their proposal will develop a vision for future dance practice and how it shares the spirit and general intention of the scholarship.

For further information contact:

Arts NSW, Sydney South, NSW 1235, PO Box A226, Australia
Contact: Programme Support

Western Sydney Artists' Fellowships
Subjects: Music and literature.
Purpose: To support the creative development of new work or professional development by Western Sydney artists.
Eligibility: Open to professional artists working in music or literature who are the residents of, or whose practice is located primarily in, Western Sydney.
Level of Study: Unrestricted
Type: Fellowship
Value: Australian $5,000–25,000
Application Procedure: Check website for further details.
Closing Date: June 8th

Women and Arts Fellowship
Subjects: Arts.
Purpose: To financially assist women in professional development as artists.
Eligibility: Open to Australian citizens or those with permanent residency status in Australia who have at least 3 years professional experience in their field.
Level of Study: Postgraduate
Type: Fellowship
Value: Australian $30,000
Frequency: Every 2 years
Country of Study: Australia
Application Procedure: Applicants must submit a completed application form along with details of the proposal, their qualifications and experience and samples of their work as support material.
Funding: Government, trusts
Additional Information: The fellowship increases recognition of the valuable contribution being made by Australian women artists and celebrates their creativity.

THE ASCAP FOUNDATION

One Lincoln Plaza, New York, NY, 10023, United States of America
Tel: (1) 212 621 6219
Fax: (1) 212 595 3342
Email: ascapfoundation@ascap.com
Website: www.ascapfoundation.org

The American Society of Composers, Authors and Publishers (ASCAP) is a membership association of over 260,000 composers, songwriters, lyricists and music publishers. It is dedicated to nurturing the music talent of tomorrow, preserving the legacy of the past and sustaining the creative incentive for today's creators through a variety of educational, professional and humanitarian programmes and activities which serve the entire music community. ASCAP's function is to protect the rights of its members by licensing and paying royalties for the public performances of their copyrighted works.

ASCAP Foundation Morton Gould Young Composer Awards
Subjects: Music composition.
Purpose: To encourage talented young composers by providing recognition, appreciation and monetary awards.
Eligibility: Open to United States citizens or permanent residents who have not reached their 30th birthday by March 1st in the year of competition. Original concert music of any style will be considered. However, works which have previously earned awards or prizes in any other national competition are ineligible. Arrangements are also ineligible.
Level of Study: Unrestricted
Type: Award
Value: Approx. US$40,000 in total (last year, Approx. US$40,000 in prizes)
Frequency: Annual
No. of awards offered: Varies from year to year
Application Procedure: Applicants must complete an application form and other materials.
Closing Date: March 1st
Funding: Foundation, private
No. of awards given last year: 39

The ASCAP Foundation Rudolf Nissim Prize
Subjects: Music composition.
Purpose: To encourage talented composers of concert music by providing recognition, appreciation and a monetary award to the composer of the winning score.
Eligibility: Open to all living concert composer members of ASCAP. Prior winners of this Prize are ineligible. The bound score (copy, not original manuscript), of one published or unpublished original concert work (no arrangements) requiring a conductor scored for full orchestra, chamber orchestra, or large wind/brass ensemble (with or without soloists and/or chorus) will be considered. The work must not have been previously premiered by paid professionals.
Level of Study: Unrestricted
Type: Award
Value: US$5,000
Frequency: Annual
No. of awards offered: 1
Application Procedure: Applicants must complete an application form and other materials.
Closing Date: November 15th
Additional Information: For guidelines and application: www.ascap.com/concert/nissimapp.pdf

The ASCAP Foundation Young Jazz Composer Awards
Subjects: Music composition.
Purpose: To encourage talented young jazz composers by providing recognition, appreciation and monetary awards.
Eligibility: Open to United States citizens or permanent residents who have not reached their 30th birthday by December 31st in the year of the competition. Only completely original music will be considered. Arrangements are not eligible. Compositions which have previously earned awards or prizes in any other national competition are ineligible.
Level of Study: Unrestricted
Type: Award
Value: US$25,000
Frequency: Annual
No. of awards offered: Varies from year to year
Application Procedure: Applicants must complete an application form and other materials.
Closing Date: December 1st
Additional Information: For guidelines and application: www.ascapfoundation.org/youngjazz/youngjazz.pdf

ASCAP/CBDNA Frederick Fennell Prize for the Best Original Score for Concert Band
Subjects: Music composition.
Purpose: ASCAP and the College Band Directors National Association (CBDNA) seek to recognize talented young composers who write for Concert Band.
Eligibility: Open to United States citizens or permanent residents who are under 30 years of age. Only original music for concert band

will be considered. Arrangements are not eligible. Compositions which have previously earned awards or prizes in any other national competition are ineligible.

Level of Study: Unrestricted
Type: Award
Value: US$5,000
Frequency: Every 2 years
Country of Study: Any country
No. of awards offered: 1
Application Procedure: Applicants must complete an application form and other materials.
Closing Date: September 15th
Additional Information: The winning score will be performed at the ensuing CBDNA national conference. For guidelines and application: www.ascap.com/about/sbdna.pdf

ASCAP/Lotte Lehmann Foundation Song Cycle Competition

Subjects: Music composition.
Purpose: ASCAP and the Lotte Lehmann Foundation seek to recognize talented young composers who write for voice.
Eligibility: Open to United States citizens or permanent residents who are below the age of 30 for next competition. Only one original work with English text will be considered. Arrangements are not eligible.
Level of Study: Unrestricted
Type: Commission
Value: US$3,500 (first prize); US$1,000 (second prize); US$500 (third prize)
Frequency: Every 2 years
No. of awards offered: 3
Application Procedure: Applicants must complete an application form and other materials.
Closing Date: September 15th
Additional Information: For guidelines and application: www.ascap.com/concert/lottelehmann/LLCompetition.pdf

ASCAP/LUS Awards Program

Subjects: Writing.
Purpose: To recognize active and established writers.
Eligibility: Open to writers who earn less than US$250,000 in annual domestic performance royalties.
Level of Study: Professional development, Postgraduate
Type: Award
Frequency: Annual
Closing Date: June 1st

ASHRIDGE MANAGEMENT COLLEGE

Berkhamsted, Hertfordshire, HP4 1NS, England
Tel: (44) 14 4284 1143
Fax: (44) 14 4284 1144
Email: mba@ashridge.org.uk
Website: www.ashridge.org.uk
Contact: Ms Jane Tobin, MBA Admissions Manager

Ashridge Business School's expertise, built up through many years of experience as a provider of executive development, has deliberately shaped their mission to help practicing and experienced managers become even more effective as leaders, and in so doing, fulfil their individual potential and that of the organization.

Ashridge Management College-Full-Time MBA and Executive MBA Scholarships

Subjects: MBA studies.
Purpose: To fund students pursuing a full-time MBA.
Eligibility: Applicant must be accepted in a full-time MBA programme. Preferably, the applicant should be an individual applying from a nonprofit organization, a female applicant or a need-based applicant. Applicants must have 3–5 years business or managerial experience.
Level of Study: MBA
Type: Scholarship
Value: UK £6,000
Length of Study: 1 year
Frequency: Annual

Study Establishment: Ashridge Business School
Country of Study: United Kingdom
No. of awards offered: 5
Application Procedure: Applicants must submit a form, with two references and either a Graduate Management Admission Test score or an Ashridge test score. English language skill is required. All candidates are asked to come for an interview.
Closing Date: December 1st
Funding: Commercial
Contributor: Natwest Bank, the Bank of Scotland and the Association of MBAs
No. of awards given last year: 5
No. of applicants last year: 7
Additional Information: Ashridge also awards two bursaries per year to suitable applicants who are employed in the charity sector, provided that the applicants carry out their project work for their employing charitable organization.

ASIA RESEARCH INSTITUTE(ARI) NATIONAL UNIVERSITY OF SINGAPORE

The Institute Manager, 469A Tower Block, 10-01 Bukit Timah Road, 259770, Singapore
Tel: (65) 65163810
Fax: (65) 67791428
Email: joinari@nus.edu.sg
Website: www.nus.edu.sg

The Asia Research Institute (ARI) was formed in July 2001 as one of the strategic initiatives of the National University of Singapore (NUS). The mission of the Institute is to provide a world class focus and resource for research on the Asian region, located at one of its communication hubs.

ARI (Senior) Visiting Fellowships

Subjects: Social sciences and humanities (areas of particular interest to the institute).
Purpose: Intended for outstanding active researchers from both the Asian region and the world, to complete an important programme of research in social sciences and humanities.
Eligibility: Open to active researchers from all over the world.
Level of Study: Postgraduate, Research
Type: Fellowship
Value: Up to Singaporean $12,000 per month
Length of Study: 1 year or less
Frequency: Annual
Country of Study: Asia
Application Procedure: Applicants must send their curriculum vitae, a synopsis of the research project and at least 1 sample of their published work.
Closing Date: January 15th
Additional Information: Applicants may send their applications through email, facsimile or mail.

ARI PhD Research Scholarship

Subjects: Social sciences and humanities, law, business or design and enviornment (areas of particular interest to the institute).
Purpose: To provide financial assistance to students to enable them to complete an important programme of research in the social sciences and humanities, law, business or design and environment.
Eligibility: Open to candidates who will be enrolled in a PhD proramme with the appropriate discipline-based department of the Faculty of Arts and Social Sciences, Faculty of Law, School of Business or School of Design and Environment at the National University of Singapore.
Level of Study: Postgraduate, Research
Type: Scholarship
Value: Stipend of Singaporean $1,500 per month and coverage of tuition/research fee
Length of Study: Up to 4 years
Frequency: Annual
Country of Study: Asia
Application Procedure: Applicants must send their research application form, academic referrals report forms, transcript request form, application fee payment form and acknowlegement form.

Closing Date: November 15th
No. of awards given last year: 3
No. of applicants last year: 14
Additional Information: The applicants may mail their applications simultaneously to the institute and the relevant discipline-based department in the faculty/school.

ARI Postdoctoral Fellowships

Subjects: Social sciences and humanities (areas of particular interest to the institute).
Purpose: Intended for outstanding active researchers from both the Asian region and the World, to complete an important programme of research in social sciences and humanities.
Eligibility: Open to candidates who have fulfilled all requirements of the PhD within the last 4 years.
Level of Study: Postdoctorate
Type: Fellowship
Value: Singaporean $4,500 per month (inclusive of housing allowance for expatriate staff who do not own properties in Singapore), with a one-time allowance of Singaporean $2,000, and support for fieldwork and conference attendance
Frequency: Annual
Country of Study: Asia
Application Procedure: Applicants must send their curriculum vitae, a synopsis of the research project and at least 1 sample of their published work.
Closing Date: December 31st
Additional Information: Applicants can email, facsimile or mail their applications.

Asian Graduate Students Fellowship

Subjects: Social sciences and humanities (areas of particular interest to the Institute).
Purpose: To enable students working in the social sciences and humanities on Asian topics to be based at the National University of Singapore for three months, and make use of the wide range of library resources.
Eligibility: Open to Asian citizens enrolled for a fulltime advanced degree at a university in an Asian country except Singapore.
Level of Study: Graduate
Type: Fellowship
Value: Monthly allowance of Singaporean $1,750 (inclusive of housing allowance) and a one- time travel subsidy of up to Singaporean $1,000
Length of Study: 3 months
Frequency: Annual
Country of Study: Asia
Application Procedure: Applicants must send their curriculum vitae, a synopsis of the research project and at least 2 letters of reference.
Closing Date: November 15th
Contributor: ARI
No. of awards given last year: 29
No. of applicants last year: 76
Additional Information: The applicants may email, facsimile or mail their applications.

THE ASIALINK CENTRE

Level 4, Sidney Myer Asia Centre, The University of Melbourne, Parkville, VIC, 3010, Australia
Tel: (61) 3 8344 4800
Fax: (61) 3 9347 1768
Email: j.shaw@asialink.unimelb.edu.au
Website: www.asialink.unimelb.edu.au
Contact: Jacyl Shaw, Chief Executive Officer

Asialink is Australia's leading centre for the promotion of public understanding of the countries of Asia and Australia's role in the region. Headquartered at the University of Melbourne, it engages the corporate, media, arts, education, health and community sectors in Australia and Asia through numerous, diverse programmes and initiatives.

Dunlop Asia Fellowships

Subjects: Social service, local community development, regional organisation building, peace-keeping, public health/welfare, appropriate technology, environment/resource management, arts/culture and sport.
Purpose: To provide opportunities for young Australians who are committed towards making a lasting contribution to Australia-Asia relations.
Eligibility: Open to candidates who are between 21–40 years of age, are Australian citizens and are able to demonstrate commitment to a career with a regional focus.
Level of Study: Professional development
Type: Fellowships
Value: AUS$15,000
Length of Study: 3 months–1 year
Frequency: Annual
Country of Study: Asia
No. of awards offered: 1–3 per year
Application Procedure: Applicants can download the form from the website.
Closing Date: September
Funding: Trusts
Contributor: Asialink is supported by the Myer Foundation and the University of Melbourne
No. of awards given last year: 2
No. of applicants last year: 20

ASIAN CULTURAL COUNCIL (ACC)

6 West 48th Street, 12th floor, New York, NY, 10036-1802, United States of America
Tel: (1) 212 843 0403
Fax: (1) 212 843 0343
Email: acc@accny.org
Website: www.asianculturalcouncil.org
Contact: Jennifer Goodall, Executive Director

The Asian Cultural Council (ACC) is a foundation that supports cultural exchange in the visual and performing arts between the United States and the countries of Asia. The emphasis of the ACC's programme is on providing individual fellowships to artists, scholars and specialists from Asia undertaking research, study and creative work in the United States. Grants are also made to United States citizens pursuing similar work in Asia.

ACC Fellowship Grants Program

Subjects: Visual and performing arts.
Purpose: To provide fellowship opportunities for research, training, travel and creative work.
Eligibility: The Asian Cultural Council grants are o[pen to citizens and permanent residents of the United States. In Asia, the council's grants are only open to citizens and permanent residents of the countries of Asia eastward through Japan and Indonesia
Level of Study: Doctorate, Postdoctorate, Postgraduate, Professional development
Value: Varies
Length of Study: 1–12 months
Frequency: Annual
No. of awards offered: Approx. 150
Application Procedure: Applicants must send a brief project description to the Council by October 15th. If the proposal falls within the Council's guidelines, application forms will be forwarded to individual candidates or more detailed information will be requested from institutional applicants.
Closing Date: November 15th
Funding: Corporation, foundation, individuals, private
No. of awards given last year: 158
No. of applicants last year: 281

ACC Humanities Fellowship Program

Subjects: Archaeology, conservation, museology and the theory, history and criticism of architecture, art, dance, film, music, photography and theater.
Purpose: To assist American scholars, graduate students and specialists in the humanities to undertake research, training and study in Asia.
Eligibility: Open to Asian individuals who are seeking grant assistance to conduct research, study, receive specialized training,

undertake observation tours or pursue creative activity in the United States in the visual and performing arts. Americans seeking aid to undertake activities in Asia are also eligible to apply.
Level of Study: Graduate, Postdoctorate, Postgraduate, Predoctorate, Professional development, Research, Unrestricted
Type: Fellowship or Grant
Value: Varies
Length of Study: 1–9 months
Frequency: Annual
Country of Study: United States of America or other countries if appropriate
Application Procedure: Applicants should send a brief description of the activity for which assistance is being sought to the Council.
Closing Date: November 15th
Funding: Foundation, government, individuals, private
Contributor: Endowment income
No. of awards given last year: 11 (Humanities Program only)
No. of applicants last year: 49 (Humanities Program only)
Additional Information: The programme also supports American and Asian scholars participating in international conferences, exhibitions, visiting professorships and similar projects.

ASIAN DEVELOPMENT BANK (ADB)

PO Box 789, Manila, 0980, Philippines
Tel: (63) 632 4444
Fax: (63) 636 2444
Email: information@adb.org
Website: www.adb.org

The Asian development bank is a multilateral development financial institution. Its work is aimed at improving the welfare of the people in Asia and the Pacific.

ADB Fully Funded Internships

Subjects: Finance.
Purpose: To help gain a deeper understanding of development finance and the impact of ADB.
Eligibility: Open to candidates enrolled in a Master's or PhD-level programme at a recognized academic institution.
Level of Study: Postgraduate
Type: Internship
Value: A daily stipend, round trip airfare and suitable accommodation and a certificate of completion to successful participants
Frequency: Annual
No. of awards offered: 6
Application Procedure: See the website.
Closing Date: January 31st

ADB Research Fellowships

Subjects: All subjects.
Purpose: To support research.
Eligibility: Open to nationals of one of ADB's member countries.
Type: Fellowship
Value: All costs covered by the fellow's academic institution, grant agency or research fellow
Frequency: Annual
No. of awards offered: Up to 5
Application Procedure: A completed application form along with curriculum vitae must be submitted.

ADB-Japan Scholarship Program

Subjects: Economics, management, science and technology.
Purpose: To provide an opportunity for further studies.
Eligibility: Open to applicants who are not more than 35 years of age.
Level of Study: Postgraduate
Type: Scholarship
Value: Full tuition fees, a monthly subsistence and housing allowance, travel expenses and an excellence for books
Length of Study: 1–2 years
Frequency: Annual
Application Procedure: See the website.

ASIAN MUSLIM ACTION NETWORK (AMAN)

House 1562/113 Soi 1/1 Mooban Pibul, Pracharaj Road, Bangkok, 10800, Thailand
Tel: (66) 662 913 0196
Fax: (66) 662 913 0197
Email: aman@arf-asia.org
Website: www.arf-asia.org/aman

Asian Muslim Action Network (AMAN) was established in 2002. t is a network of progressive Muslims in Asia that promotes human dignity and social justice for all by encouraging intercultural and inter religious dialogue and co-operation.

AMAN Research Fellowship Programme for Young Muslim Scholars

Subjects: Popular Islam, globalization and identity politics, Islam and changing gender realities and Islam values, economic activities and social responsibilities.
Purpose: To encourage innovative research on issues concerning economic, socio-political and cultural changes taking place in the diverse Muslim communities of Southeast Asia.
Eligibility: Open to nationals of Southeast Asian countries who are not more than 40 years of age.
Level of Study: Postgraduate, Research
Type: Grant
Value: US$5,000
Length of Study: 6 months
Frequency: Annual
Application Procedure: Applicants can download the application form from the website and submit the completed form along with a complete research proposal.
Closing Date: November 30th
Additional Information: Women are strongly encouraged to apply.

ASIAN SCHOLARSHIP FOUNDATION (ASF)

29 Vanissa Building, 4th Floor, Chidlom Ploenchit Road Pathumwan, Bangkok, 10330, Thailand
Tel: (66) 2655 1615/6/7
Fax: (66) 2655 7977
Email: info@asianscholarship.org
Website: www.asianscholarship.org

The Asian Scholarship Foundation (ASF) is an Asian led, non-profit organization funded by a grant from the Ford Foundation that is mandated to strengthen regional capacity to produce scholarly research on Asian societies, create a network of Asian specialists on Asian studies in Asia and develop a regional perspective among scholars working in the field of Asian studies.

ASF Asia Fellow Awards

Subjects: Arts, culture, humanities and social sciences.
Purpose: To increase the overall awareness of intellectual resources in the countries of Northeast, South and Southeast Asia and to contribute to the growth of long-range capabilities for cross-regional knowledge sharing.
Eligibility: Open to citizens and residents of Bangladesh, Bhutan, Brunei, Cambodia, the People's Republic of China, Hong Kong, India, Indonesia, Japan, Laos, Malaysia, the Republic of Maldives, Myanmar, Nepal, Pakistan, the Philippines, Singapore, South Korea, Sri Lanka, Taiwan, Thailand, and Vietnam. Applicants must not be more than 45 years of age. However, those up to 50 years old, proposing to do research in the field of humanities may be given special consideration.
Level of Study: Postgraduate, Research
Type: Fellowship
Value: Covers international travel allowance, monthly living allowance, limited accident and health insurance, field trip and language training allowance, research allowance, excess baggage/shipping allowance
Length of Study: 6–9 months
Frequency: Annual

Application Procedure: Applicants must download the application form from the website and send the completed application materials to the ASF office or affiliate offices in the country or region of their citizenship.

Funding: Foundation

Additional Information: Those who are currently enrolled in a degree programme, or have just completed a degree programme for less than 1–2 years will not be eligible to apply. Those who were recipients of a Ford Foundation fellowship grant within the last 2 years prior to the application are also ineligible.

ASSOCIATED BOARD OF THE ROYAL SCHOOLS OF MUSIC

24 Portland Place, London, W1B 1LU, England
Tel: (44) 20 7636 5400
Fax: (44) 20 7637 0234
Email: abrsm@abrsm.ac.uk
Website: www.abrsm.org
Contact: Director of Finance & Administration

The Associated Board of the Royal Schools of Music is the world's leading provider of graded music examinations with over 500,000 candidates each year in over 80 countries. It is also a major music publisher and a provider of professional development courses and seminars for music teachers.

Associated Board of the Royal Schools of Music Scholarships

Subjects: Instrumental and vocal performance.
Purpose: To enable exceptionally talented young musicians to study at one of the four Royal Schools of Music.
Eligibility: Candidates should normally be at least 21 years of age by January 31st in the year of entry. Entries can be received from any of the countries where the Associated Board organizes examinations. Candidates must have a good standard of general education and must normally have qualified by passing, with distinction, Grade 8 in a practical examination of the Board's, the Advanced Certificate or the LRSM diploma, plus one other practical examination of the Board's above Grade 5.
Level of Study: Professional development, Postgraduate
Type: Scholarship
Value: Tuition fees, grant of £4,500 per year towards living expenses and a flight ticket home upon satisfactory completion of the course
Length of Study: 1–4 years, according to designated course
Frequency: Annual
Study Establishment: The Royal Academy of Music, the Royal College of Music, the Royal Northern College of Music or the Royal Scottish Academy of Music and Drama
Country of Study: United Kingdom
No. of awards offered: 2
Application Procedure: Applicants must submit an application form, health certificate, examination marks, forms, testimonials, and an authenticated cassette tape of recent performance. Candidates should apply to the Board's representative in their own country or directly to the Board in London.
Closing Date: January 31st
Funding: Private

ASSOCIATED GENERAL CONTRACTORS OF AMERICA (AGC)

2300 Wilson Boulevard, Suite 400, Arlington, VA, 22201, United States of America
Tel: (1) 703 548 3118
Fax: (1) 703 548 3119
Email: info@agc.org
Website: www.agc.org

The Associated General Contractors of America (AGC), the voice of the construction industry, is an organization of qualified construction contractors and industry-related companies dedicated to skill, integrity and responsibility. Operating in partnership with its chapters, the association provides a full range of services satisfying the needs and concerns of its members, thereby improving the quality of construction and protecting the public interest.

AGC The Saul Horowitz, Jr. Memorial Graduate Award

Subjects: Construction or civil engineering.
Purpose: To provide financial assistance to students who wish to pursue higher studies.
Eligibility: Open to applicants enrolled or planning to enroll, in a Master's or Doctoral level construction or civil engineering programme as a full-time student.
Level of Study: Doctorate, Postgraduate
Type: Scholarship
Value: US$7,500. Paid in 2 installments of US$3,750
Frequency: Annual
Country of Study: United States of America
Application Procedure: Application form is available in the paper format as well as in the online format. To have the application mailed, applicants must send an email to foundation@agc.org.
Closing Date: November 1st

ASSOCIATION FOR INTERNATIONAL PRACTICAL TRAINING (AIPT)

10400 Little Patuxent Parkway Suite 250, Columbia, MD 21044-3519, United States of America
Tel: (1) 997 2200
Fax: (1) 992 3924
Email: aipt@aipt.org
Website: www.aipt.org

The AIPT is a non-profit organization that promotes international understanding through cross-cultural, on-the-job, practical training exchanges for students and professionals.

Jessica King Scholarship Fund

Subjects: Hotel management.
Purpose: To inspire young hospitality students and professionals.
Eligibility: Open to young Americans who wish to succeed in the international hospitality field.
Level of Study: Postgraduate
Type: Scholarship
Value: US$2,000
Frequency: Annual
Application Procedure: Contact AIPT.
Contributor: The King Family

For further information contact:

Email: aipt@aipt.org

ASSOCIATION FOR LIBRARY SERVICE TO CHILDREN

American Library Association, 50 East Huron, Chicago, IL, 60611-2795, United States of America
Tel: (1) 800/545 2433 ext. 2163
Fax: (1) 312 280 5271
Email: alsc@ala.org
Website: www.ala.org

The Association for Library Service to Children develops and supports the profession of children's librarianship by enabling and encouraging its practitioners to provide the best library service to our nation's children.

The Bound to stay Bound Books Scholarship.

Subjects: Library science.
Purpose: To support library services to children.
Eligibility: See the website.
Level of Study: Postgraduate
Type: Scholarship
Length of Study: US$6,500
Frequency: Annual
Country of Study: United States of America
No. of awards offered: 4

The Frederic G. Melcher Scholarship

Subjects: Library science.
Purpose: To provide financial assistance to professionals who plan to work in children's librarianship.
Eligibility: Open to candidates with academic excellence, leadership qualities, and desire to work with children.
Level of Study: Postgraduate
Type: Scholarship
Value: US$6,000
Frequency: Annual
Country of Study: United States of America
No. of awards offered: 2
Application Procedure: See the website.

ASSOCIATION FOR SPINA BIFIDA AND HYDROCEPHALUS (ASBAH)

ASBAH House, 42 Park Road, Peterborough, Cambridgeshire, PE1 2UQ, England
Tel: (44) 01733 555988
Fax: (44) 01733 555985
Email: info@asbah.org
Website: www.asbah.org
Contact: Mrs L Rylance, Secretary to the Directorate

The Association for Spina Bifida and Hydrocephalus (ASBAH) is a voluntary organization that works for people with spina bifida and hydrocephalus. The charity lobbies for improvements in legislation and provides advisory and support services to clients and their families or carers, in addition to supplying information to professionals and sponsoring medical, social and educational research.

ASBAH Bursary Fund

Subjects: Any subject that will improve the chances of employment for people with spina bifida, hydrocephalus or both.
Purpose: To help with expenses of further or higher education courses approved by, but not organized by, ASBAH.
Eligibility: Open to individuals with spina bifida and hydrocephalus. Applicants must be resident in the United Kingdom.
Level of Study: Unrestricted
Type: Bursary
Value: Course fees and other expenses
Length of Study: Varies
Frequency: Dependent on funds available
Study Establishment: Varies
Country of Study: England, Wales and Northern Ireland only
No. of awards offered: Varies
Application Procedure: Applicants must complete an application form, available from Mrs M Malcolm, the Director of Services.
Closing Date: Applications are accepted at any time
Funding: Private
Contributor: Charitable donations
No. of awards given last year: None
No. of applicants last year: None
Additional Information: Applicants are normally visited by an AS-BAH Area Adviser prior to an award being considered.

ASBAH Research Grant

Subjects: Medical sciences, natural sciences, education and teacher training, recreation, welfare and protective services.
Purpose: To support research in an area directly related to spina bifida and/or hydrocephalus, and to explore ways of improving the quality of life for people with these conditions through medical, scientific, educational and social research.
Eligibility: Applicants must be resident in the United Kingdom.
Level of Study: Postgraduate
Value: Varies
Length of Study: Varies
Frequency: Dependent on funds available
Study Establishment: Varies
Country of Study: United Kingdom
No. of awards offered: Varies
Application Procedure: Applicants must make an initial enquiry to the Chief Executive. If the proposed research is considered to be interesting, the applicant will be asked to complete an application

form. Applications must be submitted on time to the committees, which meet in February and September to October.
Closing Date: January 1st and August 1st
Funding: Private
Contributor: Charitable donations
No. of awards given last year: 3
No. of applicants last year: 3

ASSOCIATION FOR WOMEN IN SCIENCE EDUCATIONAL FOUNDATION

7008 Richard Drive, Bethesda, MD 20817-4838, United States of America
Email: awisedfd@awis.org
Website: www.awis.org/careers/edfoundation.html
Contact: Dr Barbara Filner, President

The Association for Women in Science Educational Foundation provides fellowships to assist women students studying the sciences.

Association for Women in Science Educational Foundation Predoctoral Awards

Subjects: Life, physical, behavioural or social science and engineering.
Purpose: To promote the participation of women in engineering and the sciences.
Eligibility: Open to female students enrolled in any life, physical, behavioural or social science or engineering programme leading to a PhD degree. Applicant must have passed the departmental qualifying exam and except to complete the PhD within two-and-one-half years, at the time of application.
Level of Study: Doctorate, Predoctorate
Value: Varies, usually US$300–1,000
Length of Study: 2 years
Frequency: Annual
Study Establishment: An Institute of Higher Education
Country of Study: Anywhere for United States of America citizens; in the United States of America for others
No. of awards offered: Varies
Application Procedure: Applicants must submit an application including a basic form, a five-page summary of the candidate's dissertation research, two recommendation report forms and official transcripts of all coursework conducted at postsecondary institutions. Forms are available on the website.
Closing Date: Mid-January
Funding: Foundation
No. of awards given last year: 10
No. of applicants last year: 100
Additional Information: Winners are notified by email in June and announced publicly in the Autumn issue of the AWIS Magazine.

ASSOCIATION OF AMERICAN GEOGRAPHERS (AAG)

1710 Sixteenth Street North West, Washington, DC, 20009-3198, United States of America
Tel: (1) 202 234 1450
Fax: (1) 202 234 2744
Email: ekhater@aag.org
Website: www.aag.org
Contact: Ms Ehsan Khater, Office Coordinator

The Association of American Geographers (AAG) is a non-profit organization founded in 1904 to advance professional studies in geography and to encourage the application of geographic research in business, education and government. The AAG was amalgamated with the American Society of Professional Geographers (ASPG) in 1948.

AAG Dissertation Research Grants

Subjects: Geography.
Purpose: To support dissertation research.
Eligibility: Open to candidates without a doctorate at the time of the award, who have been AAG members for at least 1 year at the time of

application and who have completed all PhD requirements except the dissertation by the end of the semester or term following the approval of the award. The candidates' dissertation supervisor must certify eligibility and proposals should demonstrate high standards of scholarship.

Level of Study: Postdoctorate
Type: Research grant
Value: A maximum of US$500
Frequency: Dependent on funds available
Country of Study: United States of America
No. of awards offered: 3
Application Procedure: Applicants must complete an application form, available on request from the executive assistant, Ehsan M Khater. Also, applicants must submit seven copies of a dissertation proposal of no more than 1,000 words and seven copies of the completed forms. The proposal should describe the problem that is to be solved, outline the methods and data to be used and summarize the results expected to be found. Budget items should also be included within the body of the proposal.
Closing Date: December 31st
Funding: Private
Contributor: Members
No. of awards given last year: 6
No. of applicants last year: 8
Additional Information: By accepting an AAG dissertation grant, awardees agree to submit a copy of the dissertation, and a report that documents expenses charged to the grant, to the AAG Executive Director. AAG support must also be acknowledged in presentations and publications. The awards include the Robert D Hodgson Memorial PhD Dissertation Fund the Paul Vouras Fund and the Otis Paul Starkey Fund. Please visit the website for any further information.

AAG General Research Fund

Subjects: Geography.
Purpose: To support research and field work expenses.
Eligibility: Open to candidates who have been AAG members for at least 2 years at the time of application. Proposals that, in the opinion of the committee, offer the prospect of obtaining substantial subsequent support from private foundations or federal agencies and that address questions of major import to the discipline will be given preference.
Level of Study: Professional development, Postdoctorate
Type: Research grant
Value: US$500–1,000
Country of Study: Any country
No. of awards offered: Varies
Application Procedure: Applicants must complete and send seven application forms, available on request from the executive assistant, Ehsan M Khater. Successful award applicants will be announced on or about March 31st.
Closing Date: December 31st
Funding: Private
Contributor: AAG members
No. of awards given last year: 5
No. of applicants last year: 8
Additional Information: No awards are made if proposals are not suitable or for Master's and doctoral dissertation research. Guidelines are printed in the AAG Newsletter.

Anne U White Fund

Subjects: Geochemistry.
Purpose: To enable people, regardless of any formal training in geography, to engage in useful field studies and to have the joy of working alongside their partners.
Eligibility: Open to candidates who have been AAG members for at least 2 years at the time of application. Proposals that, in the opinion of the committee, best meet the purposes for which Anne and Gilbert White set up the funds will be given preference.
Level of Study: Professional development
Type: Funding support
Value: US$1,500
Frequency: Annual
Application Procedure: Candidates must complete seven application forms, available from the website or by request from the executive assistant, Ehsan M Khater. Successful candidates will be announced on or about March 31st.

Closing Date: December 31st
Funding: Private
No. of awards given last year: 2
No. of applicants last year: 9
Additional Information: By accepting the Anne U White grant, awardees agree to submit a two-page report that summarizes results and documents expenses underwritten by the grant to the AAG Executive Director. In 1989, Gilbert and Anne White donated a sum of money to the Association of American Geographers to establish the Anne U White Fund. Gilbert White and other donors have subsequently added substantially to the original gift.

The George and Viola Hoffman Fund

Subjects: Historical, contemporary, systematic and regional geographic studies.
Purpose: To provide financial support towards a Master's thesis or doctoral dissertation on a geographical subject in Eastern Europe.
Level of Study: Doctorate, Postgraduate
Type: Grant
Value: US$350–500
Length of Study: 1 year
Frequency: Annual
No. of awards offered: 1
Application Procedure: Applicants must obtain application forms and precise guidelines from the main organization, or write to the Chair of the Hoffman Award, Michelle Behr, Western New Mexico University, behrm@cs.wnmu.edu
Closing Date: December 31st

For further information contact:

Email: behrm@cs.wnmu.edu

IGU Travel Grant

Subjects: Geography.
Purpose: To provide Travel Grants to the IGU conference.
Eligibility: Open to United States of America scholars and citizens.
Level of Study: Professional development
Type: Grant
Value: US$2,000 (Junior scholars); US$1,500 (Senior scholars)
Frequency: Annual
Country of Study: As applicable
No. of awards offered: 27 (Junior scholars); 18 (Senior scholars)
Application Procedure: Applicant must apply to the main organization address or download a form from the website.
Closing Date: February 23rd

J. Warren Nystrom Award

Subjects: Geography.
Purpose: To support a paper based upon recent dissertations in geography.
Eligibility: Open to AAG members who have received their doctorate within the last 2 years. The paper submitted should be based on the student's dissertation.
Level of Study: Doctorate, Postdoctorate
Value: Varies
Frequency: Annual
Country of Study: Any country
No. of awards offered: Varies
Application Procedure: Applicants must apply to the Association for information.
Closing Date: September 15th
Funding: Private
Contributor: AAG members
No. of awards given last year: 1
No. of applicants last year: 15
Additional Information: Awards are made for papers presented at the annual meeting of the Association.

Visiting Geographical Scientist Program

Subjects: Geography.
Purpose: To stimulate interest in geography.
Level of Study: Professional development
Type: Grant
Value: US$500
Frequency: Annual

Study Establishment: Institution with an active chapter of Gamma Theta Upsilon
Country of Study: United States of America
Application Procedure: Applicants must write to Oscar Laron, VGSP Coordinator, at the main organization address.

For further information contact:

Email: olarson@aag.org

ASSOCIATION OF CALIFORNIA WATER AGENCIES (ACWA)

910 K Street, Suit 100, Sacramento, CA 95814-3577, United States of America
Tel: (1) 916 441 4545
Fax: (1) 916 325 4849
Email: acwabox@acwa.com
Website: www.acwa.com

The Association of California Water Agencies has been a leader in California water issues since 1910. Its primary mission is to assist its members in promoting the development, management and reasonable beneficial use of water in an environmentally balanced manner.

ACWA Scholarship
Subjects: Water resources.
Purpose: To support students in water resources-related fields.
Eligibility: Open to applicants who are residents of California.
Level of Study: Postgraduate
Type: Scholarship
Value: US$3,000
Frequency: Annual
No. of awards offered: 2
Application Procedure: See the website.
Closing Date: April 1st

Clair A. Hill Scholarship
Purpose: To provide financial assistance to students in the water-related fields.
Eligibility: Open to applicants who are residents of California attending a California University.
Level of Study: Postgraduate
Type: Scholarship
Value: US$5,000
Frequency: Annual
Country of Study: United States of America
Application Procedure: See the website.
Closing Date: February 1st
Contributor: Association of California Water Agencies

ASSOCIATION OF CLINICAL PATHOLOGISTS

189 Dyke Road, Hove, East Sussex, BN3 1TJ, England
Tel: (44) 12 7377 5700
Fax: (44) 12 7377 3303
Email: info@pathologists.org.uk
Website: www.pathologists.org.uk
Contact: Administrative Assistant

The Association of Clinical Pathologists promotes the practice of clinical pathology by running postgraduate education courses and national scientific meetings and has a membership of 2,000 worldwide.

Student Research Fund
Subjects: Research projects within laboratory medicine (undergraduate) or to support students undertaking BSc/BMED Sci.
Purpose: To support medical students undertaking BSc degrees in any pathology discipline and contribute to the living expenses during their year of study or to fund small educational projects up to a maximum of UK £1,000.
Type: Scholarship
Value: Up to UK £5,000

Frequency: Annual
No. of awards offered: Up to 5
Application Procedure: Written application including a brief statement (400 words) outlining their interest in laboratory medicine; together with a full curriculum vitae. applications should include details of work to be undertaken as a part of the project or during the BSc and must be supported in writing by the project supervisor or head of the department in which the students will be placed.
Closing Date: Applications for BSc support must be received by June 30th. For project funding applications are considered throughout the year
Contributor: Association of Clinical Pathologists
No. of awards given last year: 3
No. of applicants last year: 5

ASSOCIATION OF MANAGEMENT DEVELOPMENT INSTITUTIONS IN SOUTH ASIA (AMDISA)

Secretariat, University of Hyderabad Campus, Central University Post Office, Hyderabad, 500-046, India
Tel: (91) 40 64545226; 40 64543774
Fax: (91) 40 23013346
Email: amdisa@amdisa.org
Website: www.amdisa.org
Contact: Executive Director

Association of Management Development Institutions in South Asia (AMDISA) was established in 1988, with the initiative of leading management development institutions in the SAARC region. It is the only association that networks management development centres across 8 nations and promotes partnership between business schools, business leaders and policy administrators for enhancing the quality and effectiveness of management education in South Asia.

Commonwealth AMDISA Regional Doctoral and Post Doctoral Fellowship
Subjects: Management and related social science and other disciplines.
Purpose: To provide financial and academic institutional assistance to PhD scholars and younger faculty in the South Asian countries, and to contribute to the developement of South Asian academic perspectives networks and communities in management and related areas.
Eligibility: Open to resident citizens of South Asian Commonwealth countries to undertake comparative studies in their home country or at least one of the countries listed. For doctoral fellowships, applicants must be registered PhD scholars in a recognized institution. For postdoctoral fellowships, applicants must be below 50 years of age, must have a doctorate degree and must be employed as a full-time teacher/researcher.
Level of Study: Doctorate, Postdoctorate
Type: Fellowship
Value: UK £1,500–4,500
Length of Study: 1 year
Frequency: Dependent on funds available
Study Establishment: Recognized institution where the fellow is a registered PhD scholar or full-time teacher-researcher in the home country
Country of Study: Home Country
No. of awards offered: 8
Application Procedure: Through the Fellowship Announcement a detailed outline of the research proposal and other supporting documents to be submitted in hard and soft copies is communicated to eligible applicants. The applications are evaluated and fellowships are awarded by a 5-member AMDISA Regional Fellowship Committee.
Closing Date: December 31st
Funding: International Office
Contributor: Commonwealth Fund for Technical Cooperation(CFTC)
No. of awards given last year: 8
No. of applicants last year: 15
Additional Information: Countries in which fellows can undertake comparative studies are Bangladesh, India, Malaysia, Maldives, Pakistan, Singapore, SriLanka.

ASSOCIATION OF MOVING IMAGE ARCHIVISTS (AMIA)

1313 North Vine Street, Hollywood, CA, 90028, United States of America
Tel: (1) 323 463 1500
Fax: (1) 323 463 1506
Email: amia@amianet.org
Website: www.amianet.org

The Association of Moving Image Archivists (AMIA) is a non-profit professional association established to advance the field of moving image archiving by fostering co-operation among individuals and organizations concerned with the acquisition, preservation, exhibition and use of moving image materials.

AMIA Kodak Fellowship in Film Preservation

Subjects: Filmmaking, video, historic preservation and conservation.
Purpose: To foster the education and training of the next generation of moving image archivists.
Eligibility: Open to applicants who are not below 21 years of age and are full time students with a grade point average of at least 3.0 in their recent academic programmes.
Level of Study: Postgraduate
Type: Fellowship
Value: Minimum award amount offered is US$4,000. In addition, up to US$2,000 will be provided to cover travel, hotel accommodations and other related costs
Frequency: Annual
Country of Study: United States of America
No. of awards offered: 1
Application Procedure: Applicants must submit an application form, official transcript, essay of no more than 1,000 words describing the applicant's interest and 2 reference letters.
Closing Date: May 1st
Funding: Foundation
Additional Information: A 6-week internship at Kodak and other film restoration facilities in Los Angeles will also be provided and the student will be paid an hourly wage to offset other living expenses.

AMIA Scholarship Program

Subjects: Filmmaking/video, historic preservation and conservation.
Purpose: To financially support students who wish to pursue careers in moving image archiving.
Eligibility: Open to students who have a minimum grade point average of 3.0. Applicants must be full-time students.
Level of Study: Postgraduate
Type: Scholarships
Value: Minimum of US$4,000
Frequency: Annual
Country of Study: United States of America
No. of awards offered: 4–5
Application Procedure: Applicants must submit an application form, transcript, essay and reference letters.
Closing Date: May 15th
Funding: Foundation
Contributor: Association of Moving Image Archivists

For further information contact:

Contact: Janice Simpson, AMIA Managing Director

The AMIA/Rockfeller Archive Center Visiting Archivist Fellowship

Purpose: To provide assistance and first hand experience, the AMIA/Rockfeller Archive Center Visiting Archivist Fellowship is awarded each year to a professional archivist from the developing world interested in improving their skills and knowledge through a study at the Centre.
Eligibility: The applicant must be employed as archivists or in a closely related field, the applicant must also have a BA or equivalent.
Type: Fellowship
Value: US$2,500–3,500

No. of awards offered: Varies
Contributor: Rockfeller Archive Center in cooperation with the Association of Moving Image Archivists

Image Permanence Institute Internship

Subjects: Imaging science and technology.
Purpose: To give a student of merit who is committed to the preservation of moving images the opportunity to acquire practical experience in preservation research.
Eligibility: The applicant must be enrolled in a moving image programme for the next academic year and must have a grade point average of atleast 3.0.
Level of Study: Postgraduate
Type: Internship
Value: US$5,000 stipend to be used for living expences during the 3 month internship
Closing Date: May 2nd

ASSOCIATION OF RHODES SCHOLARS IN AUSTRALIA

University of Melbourne, VIC, 3010, Australia
Tel: (61) 3 8344 2049
Fax: (61) 3 9347 6739
Email: d.cookson@unimelb.edu.au
Website: www.research.unimelb.edu.au/admin/rhodes/arsa.html
Contact: Dr David Cookson, Vice-Principal (Research)

Rhodes Scholarships were created under the will of Cecil John Rhodes, the British colonial pioneer and statesman, who died in 1902. Rhodes hoped to provide future leaders of the English-speaking world with an education, which would broaden their views and develop their abilities. Rhodes hoped that those who gained these benefits from Oxford and his scholarships would go on to improve the lot of humanity, and work towards maintaining peace between nations. The Rhodes Trust, which administers the scholarships, is based in Oxford. Its Secretary, also Warden of Rhodes House, assists, guides and advises Rhodes Scholars in residence, and the Warden's office administers financial and other aspects of the scholarships. The Secretary to the Trust is also responsible for the operation of all the Selection Committees in the various constituencies, and is assisted in this in most of the larger constituencies by national secretaries. The Australian Secretary of the Trust co-ordinates the work of the Selection Committees and generally represents the Trust in Australia.

Association of Rhodes Scholars in Australia Scholarship

Subjects: All subjects.
Purpose: To enable an overseas Commonwealth student to undertake research in Australia.
Eligibility: Open to graduates of a Commonwealth university approved by the committee administering the bursary. Graduates must currently be enrolled as higher degree research students at their home university, be Commonwealth citizens and may not be graduates of an Australian or New Zealand university.
Level of Study: Postgraduate, Research
Type: Scholarship
Value: Australian $20,000 including travel expenses and a monthly stipend
Length of Study: 6 months
Frequency: Dependent on funds available
Study Establishment: A university
Country of Study: Australia
No. of awards offered: 1
Application Procedure: Applicants must apply for information and application forms, available through the website.
Closing Date: October 12th
Funding: Private
Contributor: Charitable donations from former Australian Rhodes Scholars
Additional Information: For further information visit the website at www.research.unimelb.edu.au/admin/rhodes/arsa.html

ASSOCIATION OF SURGEONS OF GREAT BRITAIN AND IRELAND

The Royal College of Surgeons of England, 35-43 Lincoln's Inn Fields,
London, WC2A 3PN, England
Tel: (44) 20 7973 0300
Fax: (44) 20 7430 9235
Email: admin@asgbi.org.uk
Website: www.asgbi.org.uk
Contact: Mrs Nechema Lewis, Administrative Assistant

The founding objectives of the Association of Surgeons of Great Britain and Ireland, in 1920, were the advancement of the science and art of surgery and the promotion of friendship among surgeons. As other surgical specialities developed, the Association came to represent general surgery, encompassing breast, colorectal, endocrine, laparoscopic, transplant, upper gastrointestinal and vascular surgery.

Moynihan Travelling Fellowship

Subjects: General surgery.
Purpose: To enable specialist registrars or consultants to broaden their education, and to present and discuss their contribution to British or Irish surgery overseas.
Eligibility: Open to either specialist registrars approaching the end of their higher surgical training or consultants in general surgery within 5 years of appointment after the closing date for applications. Candidates must be nationals of and residents of the United Kingdom or the Republic of Ireland, but need not be Fellows or affiliate Fellows of the Association. They may be engaged in general surgery or a sub-speciality thereof.
Level of Study: Postdoctorate
Type: Fellowship
Value: Up to UK £5,000
Frequency: Annual
Country of Study: Any country
No. of awards offered: 1
Application Procedure: Applicants must submit 12 copies of an application, which must include a full curriculum vitae giving details of past and present appointments and publications, a detailed account of the proposed programme of travel, costs involved and the object to be achieved. Applications must be addressed to the Honorary Secretary at the Association of Surgeons.
Closing Date: October 2nd
Funding: Private
Contributor: Charitable association funds
No. of awards given last year: 1
No. of applicants last year: 6
Additional Information: Shortlisted candidates will be interviewed by the Scientific Committee of the Association, which will pay particular attention to the originality, scope and feasibility of the proposed itinerary. The successful candidate will be expected to act as an ambassador for British and Irish surgery and should therefore be fully acquainted with the aims and objectives of the Association of Surgeons and its role in surgery. After the completion of the fellowship, the successful candidate will be asked to address the Association at its annual general meeting and to provide a written report for inclusion in the Executive Newsletter. A critical appraisal of the centres visited should form the basis of the report.

ASSOCIATION OF UNIVERSITIES AND COLLEGES OF CANADA (AUCC)

Corporate Services and Scholarships Division, 350 Albert Street,
Suite 600, Ottawa, ON, K1R 1B1, Canada
Tel: (1) 613 563 1236
Fax: (1) 613 563 9745
Email: awards@aucc.ca
Website: www.aucc.ca
Contact: Mr Luc Poulin

The AUCC is a non-profit, non-governmental association that represents Canadian universities at home and abroad. The Association's mandate is to foster and promote the interests of higher education in the firm belief that strong universities are vital to the prosperity and wellbeing of Canada.

Department of National Defence Security and Defence Forum Internship Program

Subjects: Studies relating to current and future Canadian national security and defence issues including their political, international, historical, social, military, industrial and economic dimensions. Research in the pure and applied sciences is ineligible.
Purpose: To help recent MA graduates with a background in security and defence studies to obtain work experience.
Eligibility: Open to Canadian citizens or permanent residents who hold a Master's degree before taking up the award.
Level of Study: Intership
Type: Internship
Value: Up to Canadian $35,000
Length of Study: Up to 12 months, non-renewable
Frequency: Annual
Study Establishment: Private sector or non-governmental organizations. Contact the AUCC to obtain a list of potential organizations
Country of Study: Canada
No. of awards offered: Upto 4
Application Procedure: Applicants must contact the AUCC or visit the National Defense website (www.dnd.ca/admpol/eng/academic/sdf_e.htm) to obtain an application package.
Closing Date: Postmarked February 1st
Funding: Government
Additional Information: On completion of the award a reasonable detailed account of the internship and any research undertaken must be submitted to the AUCC who will forward it to the Department of National Defence. Further information is available on request or from the website.

Department of National Defence Security and Defence Forum MA Scholarship Program

Subjects: Current and future Canadian national security and defence issues including their political, international, historical, social, military, economic dimensions. Research in the pure or applied sciences is ineligible.
Eligibility: Open to Canadian citizens or permanent residents who, as a minimum requirement, hold a Bachelor's (Honours) Degree or its equivalent before taking up the award.
Level of Study: Graduate, MBA
Type: Scholarship
Value: Up to Canadian $10,000
Length of Study: At least 1 year, with possible renewal for a further year if evidence of satisfactory academic achievement is found
Frequency: Annual
Country of Study: Canada
No. of awards offered: Approx. 8
Application Procedure: Applicants must contact the AUCC or visit the National Defense wesite (www.dnd.ca/admpol/eng/academic/sdf_e.htm) to obtain an application package.
Closing Date: Postmarked February 1st
Funding: Government
Additional Information: Successful applicants may not hold more than one award from the federal government.

Department of National Defense Security and Defence Forum PhD Scholarship Program Including the Dr Ronald Baker Doctoral Scholarship

Subjects: Studies relating to current and future Canadian national security and defence issues including their political, international, historical, social, military and economic dimensions. Research in the pure or applied science is ineligible.
Eligibility: Applicants must be Canadian citizens or permanent residents at the time of application and, as a minimum requirement, hold a Master's degree or its equivalent before taking up the award. Candidates must have completed their coursework (first year of PhD study) to be eligible. Students applying to a PhD program not requiring coursework are eligible to apply as they begin their research program.
Level of Study: Doctorate, Graduate
Value: Up to Canadian $20,000. The Dr Ronald Baker Doctoral Scholarship is up to Canadian $22,500
Length of Study: 1 year, non renewable
Frequency: Annual
Country of Study: Canada

No. of awards offered: PhD Scholarship: 4; Ronald Baker PhD Scholarship: 1
Application Procedure: Applicants must contact the AUCC or visit the National Defense website (www.dnd.ca/admpol/eng/academic/ sdf_e.htm) to obtain an application package.
Closing Date: Postmarked February 1st
Funding: Government
Additional Information: On completion of the scholarship one copy of the dissertation or a reasonable detailed account of the research undertaken must be submitted to the AUCC who will forward it to the Department of National Defence.

Department of National Defense Security and Defense Forum Postdoctoral Fellowship including the R B Byers Postdoctoral Fellowship

Subjects: Studies relating to current and future Canadian national security and defence issues including their political, international, historical, social, military and economic dimensions. Research in the pure and applied sciences is ineligible.
Eligibility: Open to Canadian citizens or permanent residents who hold a PhD or its equivalent before taking up the award. Individuals who hold a tenure or tenure track appointment at any level are not eligible.
Level of Study: Postdoctorate, Postgraduate
Type: Fellowship
Value: Up to Canadian $35,000
Length of Study: 1 year, non renewable
Frequency: Annual
Country of Study: Canada
Application Procedure: Applicants must contact the AUCC or visit the National Defense website (www.dnd.ca/admpol/eng/academic/ sdf_e.htm) to obtain an application package.
Closing Date: Postmarked February 1st
Funding: Government
Additional Information: On completion of the award period a reasonably detailed account of the research undertaken, as well as copies of publications and unpublished conference presentations resulting from the award, are to be submitted to the AUCC who will forward them to the Department of National Defence. Successful applicants may not hold more than one award from the federal government.

Frank Knox Memorial Fellowships

Subjects: Arts and sciences including engineering, business administration, design, divinity studies, education, law, public administration at the John F Kennedy School of Government, medicine, dental medicine and public health.
Purpose: To offer an opportunity to students from Canada who wish to graduate from the Harvard University.
Eligibility: Open to Canadian citizens or permanent residents who have recently graduated or who are about to graduate from an institution in Canada which is a member or affiliated to a member of the AUCC. Applications from students presently studying in the United States of America will not be considered, although applications will be considered from recent graduates who are working in the United States of America and will be applying to the MBA programme.
Level of Study: MBA, Postgraduate
Type: Fellowship
Value: US$20,000 plus tuition fees and student health insurance
Length of Study: 1 academic year
Frequency: Annual
Study Establishment: Harvard University
Country of Study: United States of America
No. of awards offered: Up to 3
Application Procedure: Applicants must apply directly to the graduate school of their choice. Applicants are responsible for gaining admission to Harvard University by the deadline set by the various faculties. Further information and application forms are available on request or from the website.
Closing Date: November 30th
Additional Information: Holders of this award may not accept any other grant for the period of this fellowship unless approved by the Committee on General Scholarships and the Sheldon Fund of Harvard University.

L'ORÉAL Canada For Women in Science Fellowships, With Support of the Canadian Commission for UNESCO

Subjects: Engineering and pure and applied sciences and life sciences.
Purpose: To support research by Canadian female scientists.
Eligibility: Open to female Canadian citizens or permanent residents who are already engaged in pursuing research at the postdoctoral level.
Level of Study: Doctorate, Postdoctorate, Postgraduate
Type: Fellowship
Value: Canadian $20,000
Length of Study: 1 academic year
Frequency: Annual
Country of Study: Canada
No. of awards offered: 2
Application Procedure: Further information and application forms are available on request or from the website.
Closing Date: June 1st
Funding: Private
Contributor: L'ORÉAL Canada and Canadian Commission for UNESCO
No. of awards given last year: 2
Additional Information: Fellowships will alternate each year between the life sciences and engineering/pure and applied sciences.

Public Safety and Emergency Preparedness Canada Research Fellowship in Honour of Stuart Nesbitt White

Subjects: Research in Emergency Management. Preferred disciplines are regional planning, engineering, environmental studies, computer science, geography, sociology, economics and/or areas such as risk modeling and system science.
Purpose: Public Safety and Emergency Preparedness Canada is seeking to encourage PhD research in two areas of its mission, which is to enhance the safety and security of Canadians in their physical and cyber environments.
Eligibility: Open to Canadian citizens or permanent residents of Canada, who have completed their coursework (first year of PhD study) or applying to a PhD program not requiring coursework as they begin their research program. Candidates must intend to use the fellowship to assist them in completing a graduate degree (preferably a doctorate) that includes a thesis on a topic related to the fields of study, work must be carried out at an accredited university in Canada or abroad.
Level of Study: Doctorate
Type: Fellowship
Value: Canadian $19,250. Transportation and board will be paid in addition to the value of the award
Length of Study: One year; however, award holders may re-apply annually by submitting a new application form
Frequency: Annual
Study Establishment: Any accredited university in Canada or abroad
Country of Study: Canada
No. of awards offered: 8
Application Procedure: Application can be downloaded from the website.
Closing Date: March 31st
Funding: Government
Additional Information: Further information is available on request or from the website. Resources permitting, the award winners will attend a one day symposium in Ottawa in late spring/early summer to present information on the progress/results of their work. Attendees will include fellowship winners for the year, PSEPC representatives and other invited guests. Students cannot accept both this award and financial awards from other federal government programs (e.g. NSERC, SSHRC, or CIHR).

THE ASTHMA FOUNDATION OF NEW SOUTH WALES (AFNSW)

Level 7, Chandos Street 35, St Leonards, NSW, 2065, Australia
Tel: (61) 2 9906 3233
Fax: (61) 2 9906 4493
Email: ask@asthmansw.org.au
Website: www.asthmansw.org.au
Contact: Executive Director

The vision of the Asthma Foundation of New South Wales (AFNSW) is to eliminate asthma as a major cause of illness and disruption within the New South Wales community. Fundraising efforts assist with the promotion and funding of research activities that are aimed at helping the Foundation to achieve this vision. The Foundation has been supporting and helping people with asthma since 1961. It is a registered charity committed to helping people with asthma, their families and careers.

Asthma Research Postgraduate Scholarships

Subjects: Medical, scientific and clinical research into asthma, its causes, triggers and impact.
Purpose: To expand the body of knowledge towards the causes of asthma and its possible cure.
Level of Study: Postdoctorate, Postgraduate
Type: Scholarship
Value: Australian $20,000
Length of Study: 1 year
Frequency: Annual, (dependent on funds available)
Country of Study: Australia
No. of awards offered: Varies
Application Procedure: Applicants must complete application forms. Short-listed candidates will be interviewed.
Closing Date: November 19th
Funding: Private
Contributor: Private donors
No. of awards given last year: 2
No. of applicants last year: 3

Asthma Research Project Grants

Subjects: Medical, scientific and clinical research into asthma, its causes, triggers and impact.
Purpose: To expand the body of knowledge towards the causes of asthma and its possible cure.
Level of Study: Postgraduate, Postdoctorate
Type: Project grant
Value: Australian $50,000
Length of Study: 1 year
Frequency: Annual, (dependent on funds available)
Country of Study: Australia
No. of awards offered: Varies
Application Procedure: Applicants must complete application forms. Short-listed candidates will be interviewed.
Closing Date: November 19th
Funding: Private
Contributor: Private donors
No. of awards given last year: 4
No. of applicants last year: 11

ATAXIA UK

9 Winchester House, Kennington Park, London, SW9 6EJ, England
Tel: (44) 20 7820 3900
Fax: (44) 20 7582 9444
Email: research@ataxia.org.uk
Website: www.ataxia.org.uk
Contact: Mrs Julie Greenfield, Research Projects Manager

Ataxia UK is the leading charity in the United Kingdom working with and for people with ataxia. It will support research projects and related activities in order to enhance scientific understanding of ataxia, develop and evaluate therapeutic and supportive strategies and encourage wider involvement with ataxia research.

Ataxia UK PhD Studentship

Subjects: Any aspect of both inherited and sporadic progressive ataxias including Friedreich's ataxia and other cerebellar ataxias.
Purpose: To further research into causes and treatments for preventive for progressive ataxias.
Eligibility: Proposals are accepted from academic institutions, private sector research companies and suitably qualified individuals. There are no restrictions on age, nationality or residency.
Level of Study: Predoctorate
Type: Project grant
Value: Covers stipend, tuition fees and consumables for project

Length of Study: Varies
Country of Study: Any country
No. of awards offered: Varies
Application Procedure: Applicants must complete an application form available from ataxia's Research Projects Manager at research@ataxia.org.uk
Closing Date: Refer the website
Funding: Commercial, individuals, private, trusts
Additional Information: There are a number of priority areas of research and these can be obtained from the Research Projects Manager.

Ataxia UK Research Fellowship in Friedreich's ataxia

Subjects: Any aspect of Friedreich's ataxia which will have clear potential benefits for treatment development for the condition.
Purpose: To assist researchers wishing to establish a career in Friedreich's ataxia research.
Eligibility: Proposals are accepted from academic institutions, private sector research companies and suitably qualified individuals. There are no restrictions on age, nationality or residency.
Level of Study: Postdoctorate
Type: Fellowship
Value: UK £150,000
Length of Study: 5 years
Frequency: Dependent on funds available
Country of Study: United Kingdom
No. of awards offered: 1
Application Procedure: Applicants must complete an application form available from Ataxia's Research Projects Manager at research@ataxia.org.uk
Closing Date: Refer the website
Funding: Commercial, individuals

Ataxia UK Research Grant

Subjects: Any aspect of both inherited and sporadic progressive ataxias including Friedreich's ataxia and other cerebellar ataxias.
Purpose: To further research into causes of and treatments for progressive ataxias.
Eligibility: Proposals are accepted from academic institutions, private sector research companies and suitably qualified individuals. There are no restrictions on age, nationality or residency.
Level of Study: Unrestricted
Type: Project grant
Value: Varies
Frequency: Dependent on funds available
Country of Study: Any country
No. of awards offered: Varies
Application Procedure: Applicants must complete an application form available from Ataxia's Research Projects Manager at research@ataxia.org.uk
Closing Date: Refer the website
Funding: Commercial, individuals, private, trusts
No. of awards given last year: 11
Additional Information: There are a number of priority areas of research and these can be obtained from the Research Projects Manager.

Ataxia UK Travel Award

Subjects: Any aspect of both inherited and sporadic progressive ataxias including Friedreich's ataxia and other cerebellar ataxias.
Purpose: To enable researchers to present their ataxia research at national and international conferences.
Eligibility: Proposals are accepted from academic institutions, private sector research companies and suitably qualified individuals. There are no restrictions on age, nationality or residency, although preference will be given to events which could potentially benefit patients and researchers in the UK or Europe.
Level of Study: Unrestricted
Type: Travel grant
Value: Dependent on the conference
Frequency: Dependent on funds available
Country of Study: Any country
No. of awards offered: Varies

Application Procedure: Applicants must complete an application form available from Ataxia's Research Projects Manager at research@ataxia.org.uk
Closing Date: 3 times a year. Contact Research Projects Manager for precise dates
Funding: Commercial, individuals, private, trusts
No. of awards given last year: 1
No. of applicants last year: 3
Additional Information: There are a number of priority areas of research and these can be obtained from the Research Projects Manager.

ATHENAEUM INTERNATIONAL CULTURAL CENTRE

3 Adrianou Street, Athens, GR, 105 55, Greece
Tel: (30) 210 321 1987
Fax: (30) 210 321 1196
Email: contact@athenaeum.com.gr
Website: www.athenaeum.com.gr
Contact: Mrs Irene Mega, Executive Secretary

The Athenaeum International Cultural Centre is a non-profit association dedicated to preserving the memory of Maria Callas. The organization was founded in 1974 by a group of inspired artists who wanted to contribute to the development and evolution of musical education and culture in Greece.

Maria Callas International Music Competition
Subjects: Musical performance, although disciplines vary with each competition. Singing such as opera, oratorio-lied and the piano.
Purpose: To recognize outstanding artists.
Eligibility: Open to musicians of all nationalities.
Level of Study: Postgraduate, Unrestricted
Type: Competition
Value: Please contact the organization
Frequency: Annual
Country of Study: Any country
No. of awards offered: Varies according to the category
Application Procedure: Applicants must request for full details and application procedures or visit the website. There is a registration fee of €120.
Closing Date: November 15th
Funding: Government, private
Contributor: The Ministry of Culture and The Cultural Organization of the Municipality of Athens
No. of awards given last year: 9 in opera and 3 in piano
No. of applicants last year: 70 for singing and 63 for the piano competition
Additional Information: Concert appearances are arranged for the winners.

Paolo Montarsolo Special Prize
Subjects: Bass singing by males in the 2009 Maria Callas Grand Prix.
Purpose: To honour the best young bass singer of the 2009 Maria Callas Grand Prix.
Type: Prize
Value: €4,000
No. of awards offered: 1
Additional Information: For further details check the website: www.athenaeum.com.gr/english/grand.

ATLANTIC SALMON FEDERATION (ASF)

PO Box 5200, St Andrews, NB, E5B 3S8, Canada
Tel: (1) 506 529 4581
Fax: (1) 506 529 4438
Email: asfres@nb.aibn.com
Website: www.asf.ca/awards/awards.html
Contact: Ms Ellen Merrill, Executive Assistant

The Atlantic Salmon Federation (ASF) is an international, non-profit organization that promotes the conservation and management of the Atlantic salmon and its environment. ASF has a network of seven regional councils, a membership of over 150 river associations and 40,000 volunteers. Regional offices cover the salmon's freshwater range in Canada and the United States of America.

Olin Fellowship
Subjects: Salmon biology, management and conservation.
Purpose: To support individuals seeking to improve their knowledge or skills in advanced fields, while looking for solutions to current problems in Atlantic salmon biology, management and conservation.
Eligibility: Open to citizens and legal residents of the United States of America or Canada. Applicants need not be enrolled in a degree programme to be eligible.
Level of Study: Unrestricted
Type: Fellowship
Value: Canadian $1,000–3,000
Frequency: Annual
Study Establishment: Any accredited university, research laboratory or active management programme
Country of Study: United States of America or Canada
No. of awards offered: Varies
Application Procedure: Applicants must complete an application form, available on request or from the website. www.asf.ca/awards/awards
Closing Date: March 15th
Funding: Private
Contributor: Memberships and foundation grants
No. of awards given last year: 4
No. of applicants last year: 6

ATSUMI INTERNATIONAL SCHOLARSHIP FOUNDATION (AISF)

3-5-8 Sekiguchi, Bunkyo-ku, Tokyo, 112-0014, Japan
Tel: (81) 03 3943 7612
Fax: (81) 03 3943 1512
Email: office@aisf.or.jp
Website: www.aisf.or.jp/index.html

The Atsumi International Scholarship Foundation(AISF) was established to help promote a greater sense of Japan's role in the process of internationalization. Its goal is to provide financial assistance to foreign students with superior academic skills to further their studies at graduate schools in Japan.

AISF Scholarship
Subjects: All subjects with a focus on Japan.
Purpose: To help scholars to visit Japan and experience the diverse culture by not only developing a deeper academic knowledge of Japan but by cultivating a greater appreciation for its social richness as well.
Eligibility: Open to candidates of non-Japanese nationality who are PhD candidates enrolled in a graduate school in Kanto area.
Level of Study: Doctorate
Type: Scholarships
Value: ¥200,000 per month
Length of Study: 1 year
Frequency: Annual
Country of Study: Asia
No. of awards offered: 12
Application Procedure: Applicants can avail the application forms from the appropriate foreign students scholarship office school or from the AISF office.
Closing Date: September 30th

AUDI DESIGN FOUNDATION

Yeomans Drive, Blakelands, Milton Keynes, MK14 5AN, England
Tel: (44) 19 0860 1570
Fax: (44) 19 0860 1943
Email: audidesignfoundation@audidesignfoundation.org
Website: www.audidesignfoundation.org

The Audi Design Foundation is an independent charity established in 1997 by Audi UK. Our aim is to encourage designers to develop ideas that create a positive change in people's lives. Since its inception, the Foundation has given millions of pounds through a range of programmes that promote innovative design.

Designs for Life

Subjects: Sustainable and inclusive design.
Purpose: To encourage designers to develop ideas that create a positive change in people's lives.
Eligibility: Applicants may be individuals or small groups. The Foundation can only support applicants who are resident in the United Kingdom; however, applicants can be citizens of any European country.
Level of Study: Unrestricted
Type: Grant
Value: Dependent on the amount required to develop and produce a prototype as set out in the applicant's initial grant request document and approved by the Audi Design Foundation grant panel
Frequency: Annual, Ad hoc: Up to 10 times a year
Application Procedure: All applicants must complete a brief, online application form; please visit www.audidesignfoundation.org and follow the 'Designs For Life' link. Shortlisted applicants will be asked to submit a more detailed report and present their ideas to our trustees.
Closing Date: March 31st
Funding: Commercial
Contributor: Audi UK
No. of awards given last year: 3
No. of applicants last year: Approx. 60

THE AUSTRALIA COUNCIL (OZCO)

PO Box 788, Strawberry Hills, NSW, 2012, Australia
Tel: (61) 2 9215 9000
Fax: (61) 2 9215 9111
Email: mail@australiacouncil.gov.au
Website: www.ozco.gov.au

The Australia Council is the Australian Government's arts funding and advisory body. We support and promote the practice and enjoyment of the arts.

Aboriginal and Torres Strait Islander Arts Fellowship

Subjects: Craft art, literature, performing arts, new media.
Purpose: To support an Aboriginal and Torres Strait Islander artist undertaking a major creative project program in their artform.
Eligibility: Open to practicing Aboriginal and Torres Strait Islander artists who are able to demonstrate at least 10 years experience as a practicing professional artist.
Level of Study: Postgraduate
Type: Fellowship
Value: Australian $40,000 annual stipend
Length of Study: 2 years
Frequency: Annual
Country of Study: Australia
Application Procedure: Apply online.
Closing Date: November 15th
Funding: Government

For further information contact:

Email: atsia@ozco.gov.au

Aboriginal and Torres Strait Islander Arts Indigenous Arts Worker's Program Grant

Purpose: To provide funding for either the employment of an Indigenous art worker or a programme of activity.
Eligibility: Open to Aboriginal and Torres Strait Islander arts organisations only.
Length of Study: 3 years
Frequency: Annual
Application Procedure: Applications should include evidence of your eligibility and the required support material. Check website for further details.
Closing Date: July 15th

Aboriginal and Torres Strait Islander Arts Key Organisations Triennial

Purpose: To support a limited number of Aboriginal and Torres Strait Islander arts organisations to advance Aboriginal and Torres Strait Islander arts in Australia.
Eligibility: Open to Aboriginal and Torres Strait Islander arts organisations only and must be outstanding organisations with a substantial record of achievement in their field.
Frequency: Annual
Application Procedure: Application forms should include evidence of eligibility and the required support materials. Check website for further details.
Closing Date: July 15th

Aboriginal and Torres Strait Islander Arts Presentation and Promotion

Purpose: To support projects which promote Aboriginal and Torres Strait Islander artists and their work regionally and internationally through publications, recordings, performances, exhibitions and international export.
Eligibility: Open to Aboriginal and Torres Strait Islander artists and community organisations and Aboriginal and Torres Strait Islander and non-indigenous arts organisations (including publishers).
Frequency: 6 monthly
Application Procedure: Applications should include evidence of your eligibility and the required support materials. Check website for further details.
Closing Date: July 15th and November 15th
Additional Information: Overseas applicants for international projects must provide written evidence of co-funding from the host country or organisation.

Aboriginal and Torres Strait Islander Arts Program

Purpose: To provide support for 1 year towards the cost of an organisation wishing to employ an Aboriginal and Torres Strait Islander artworker or artist to organise, develop and initiate a programme or arts activities in their community or region.
Eligibility: Open to Aboriginal and Torres Strait Islander arts organisations only.
Frequency: Annual
Application Procedure: Applications should include evidence of eligibility and required support materials. Check website for further details.
Closing Date: July 15th

Aboriginal and Torres Strait Islander Arts Skills and Arts Development

Purpose: To assist Aboriginal and Torres Strait Islander artists and arts organisations to develop ideas and skills, not necessarily with a public outcome.
Eligibility: Applicants should be Aboriginal and Torres Strait Islander individuals, organisations or groups.
Frequency: 6 monthly
Application Procedure: Applications should include evidence of eligibility and the required support materials. Check website for further details.
Closing Date: July 15th

Aboriginal and Torres Strait Islander New Work Grant

Subjects: Theatre production, writing, music.
Purpose: To support Aboriginal and Torres Strait Islander artists, arts organizations or community organizations to create new work with an expected public outcome.
Eligibility: Open to Aboriginal and Torres Strait Islander artists who demonstrate artistic merit and innovation.
Level of Study: Professional development
Type: Grant
Value: Varies
Length of Study: Up to 12 months
Frequency: Annual
Country of Study: Australia
Application Procedure: Apply online.
Closing Date: July 15th and November 15th
Funding: Government

For further information contact:

Email: atsia@ozco.gov.au

Communities Cultural Development Grants Programme
Purpose: To provide support for an organisation to deliver a 1 year programme of specific community cultural development activities. This may involve the employment of an artist or artsworker in a particular region or community for a year.
Eligibility: Open only to organisations which meet the general eligibility requirements.
Frequency: Annual
Application Procedure: Applications should include required support materials. Check website for further details.
Closing Date: July 1st

Communities Cultural Development Grants Residency
Purpose: To offer an experienced community cultural development artist or artsworker the opportunity to undertake a period of professional development at Australia Council's studio.
Value: Travel and living expense
Length of Study: January–March
Frequency: Annual
Closing Date: April 15th

Communities Cultural Development Skills and Arts Development
Purpose: To support skills and arts development oppurtunities for communities and professional artists and artsworkers working in community cultural development. There are two subcategories: for individuals and for organisations and groups.
Eligibility: Open to individuals, groups and organisations who meet the general eligibility requirements.
Frequency: 6 monthly
Application Procedure: Applications should include required support materials. Check website for further details.
Closing Date: April 15th and August 1st

Community Cultural Development Category A
Purpose: To develop significant project ideas and/or extension of effective partnerships that enable future projects to take place.
Eligibility: Open to individuals, groups and organisations and who have discussed their proposal with Community Partnerships staff.
Type: Grant
Value: Up to $5,000 per grant
Frequency: Annual
Application Procedure: Applications should include required support materials. Check website for further details.
Closing Date: November 1st

Community Cultural Development Category B
Purpose: To support off community arts and culture projects which may have a public outcome and must involve a range of partners.
Eligibility: Open to individuals, groups and organisations.
Type: Grant
Value: Up to $20,000
Frequency: Annual
Application Procedure: Applications should include required support materials. Check website for further details.
Closing Date: July 1st

Community Cultural Development Category C
Purpose: To support one-off community arts and culture projects which have a public outcome and involve cross-sectoral partners.
Eligibility: Open to individuals, groups and organisations who meet the general eligibility requirements.
Value: $20,000–35,000
Frequency: Annual
Application Procedure: Applications should include required support materials. Check website for further details.
Closing Date: July 1st

Community Cultural Development Presentation and Promotion
Purpose: To support project that promote the value of community cultural development practice. This includes projects that create opportunities for practitioners to explore new ways of presenting the outcomes of existing best-practice models to new audiences.

Eligibility: Open to individuals and organisations who meet the general eligibility requirements.
Frequency: Annual
Application Procedure: Applications should include required support materials. Check website for further details.
Closing Date: August 1st

Community Partnerships New Work
Purpose: To support one-off project to create new artistic work through community-based arts and cultural activity.
Eligibility: Open to individuals, groups and organisations.
Frequency: Annual
Application Procedure: Applications should include the required support materials. Check website for further details.
Closing Date: April 15th

Community Partnerships Residency
Purpose: The programme affords an artist or artworker the opportunity to take time out of project based work and focus on professional development, reflection or individual arts practice.
Eligibility: Current recipients of a fellowship grant from the Community Cultural Development Board are not eligible to apply to this category.
Length of Study: 6–8 weeks
Frequency: Annual
Application Procedure: Applications should include curriculum vitae and outline the aims of the residency in terms of its benefit to the artist's professional development. Check website for further details.
Closing Date: August 1st

Dance Artform Development
Subjects: Dance.
Purpose: To support activities that contribute to the overall development of dance in Australia.
Eligibility: Open to young and emerging artists and will be assessed as a discrete group.
Frequency: 6 monthly
Closing Date: November 3rd

Dance Cite International des Arts Residency
Purpose: To offer an established dance practitioner the opportunity to undertake a period of professional development at Australia Council's studio at Cite Internationale des Arts in Paris.
Value: Allowance towards travel and living expenses for the period of the residency
Frequency: Annual
Closing Date: May 15th

Dance Initiative Project Workspace
Purpose: To assist individual dancers, choreographers and movement artists to gain acess to work space.
Eligibility: Open to individual choreographers, dancers/movement artists, as individuals only. Applicants should be Australian citizens or have permanent resident status in Australia.
Value: $1,000
Frequency: Annual
Application Procedure: Check website for details.
Closing Date: March 15th

Dance New Work Creative Development
Purpose: To support the creation of new dance works.
Eligibility: Open to individuals who meet the general eligibility requirements.
Frequency: 6 monthly
Application Procedure: Applications should include required support materials. Check website for further details.
Closing Date: May 15th and November 1st

Dance New Work Production
Purpose: To support public performance of a new work and any stages leading up to the production.
Eligibility: Open to individuals who meet the general eligibility requirements.
Frequency: 6 monthly

Application Procedure: Applications should include required support materials. Check website for further details.
Closing Date: May 15th and November 1st

Dance Presentation and Promotion

Purpose: To support international touring through the International Market Development Strategy of the Dance Board and Community Partnerships and Market Development.
Frequency: Annual
Additional Information: Contact Dance staff for further information.

Dance Program

Purpose: To provide 1 year funding to a limited number of significant organisations to enrich the diversity of dance practice.
Eligibility: Open to organisations which meet the general eligibility requirements.
Frequency: Annual
Application Procedure: Applications should include required support materials. Check website for further details.
Closing Date: June 15th

Dance Skill and Arts Development–Skills Development for Young Emerging Artists

Purpose: To provide professional development opportunities for young emerging artists.
Eligibility: Open to individuals and organisations who meet the general eligibility requirements. Applicants should be of 26 years of age or less and have had not more than 5 years of experience.
Value: Up to $10,000
Frequency: 6 monthly
No. of awards offered: Up to 4
Application Procedure: Applications should include required support materials. Check website for further details.
Closing Date: May 15th and November 1st

Inter-Arts Fellowship

Subjects: Interdisciplinary art, hybrid art or new artistic practice.
Purpose: Offered to artists working in interdisciplinary art, hybrid art or new artistic practice to further enhance their capacity to provide leadership to the field.
Eligibility: Open to individuals who meet the eligibility requirements and provide the necessary support materials.
Value: $45,000 per year for 2 years
Frequency: Annual
Application Procedure: Application form should include the required support materials. Check website for further details.
Closing Date: May 1st

Inter-Arts Hybrid Art Key Organisations Triennial

Purpose: To support leading organisations to develop creative programmes or services in the field of hybrid art and/or new media art.
Eligibility: Open to organisations which meet the eligibility requirements and provide the necessary support materials.
Frequency: Annual
Application Procedure: Application form should include the required support materials. Check website for further details.
Closing Date: June 1st

Inter-Arts Hybrid Art Program

Purpose: To support activities in relation to hybrid art: research and development, creative development, production.
Eligibility: Applicants should meet the eligibility requirements and provide the necessary support materials.
Frequency: Annual
Application Procedure: Application form should include the required support materials. Check website for further details.
Closing Date: May 1st

Inter-Arts Initiative–Artslab

Purpose: To promote the importance of research and development activity and provide artists with time to critically explore aspects of their practice.
Value: Up to $75,000
Frequency: Annual

Inter-Arts Initiative-Run_way 2006

Eligibility: Open to individuals who are 30 years of age or under.
Value: Up to $5,000
Frequency: Annual
Application Procedure: Applications can be downloaded from the website. Check website for further details.
Closing Date: October 15th

Inter-Arts International Residency

Subjects: Interdisciplinary art, hybrid art and new artistic practice.
Eligibility: Open to individuals who meet the eligibility requirements and provide the necessary support materials.
Value: $20,000 per residency
Frequency: Annual
Application Procedure: Application form should include the required support materials. Check website for further details.
Closing Date: October 15th

Inter-Arts National Residency

Subjects: All subjects.
Purpose: To provide six-month residency at SymbioticA sited in the School of Anatomy & Human Biology at the University of Western Australia in Perth. SymbioticA welcomes artists from all disciplines to work as individual researchers or as part of interdisciplinary research teams.
Frequency: Annual
Application Procedure: Application form should include the required support materials. Check website for further details.
Closing Date: November 1st

Inter-Arts Projects

Subjects: Interdisciplinary art, hybrid art and new artistic practice.
Purpose: To support the creation of new artistic practices providing funding for research and development, creative development and production.
Eligibility: Open to individuals and organisations which meet the eligibility requirements and provide the necessary support materials.
Frequency: Annual
Application Procedure: Application form should include the required support materials. Check website for further details.
Closing Date: May 1st

Inter-Arts Residency–International Residency

Purpose: To support an artist to participate in the Media and Visual Arts Thematic Residency Programme at the Banff Center for the Arts in Alberta, Canada.
Frequency: Annual
Closing Date: November 1st
Additional Information: Check website or contact staff for further details.

Literative Key Organisations Triennial

Purpose: To develop a viable strategic infrastructure to support the work and professional development of Australian writers and the general advancement of Australian literature.
Eligibility: Open to organisations, check website for eligibility criteria.
Frequency: Annual
Application Procedure: Application form should include the required support materials. Check website for further details.
Closing Date: June 15th

Literature New Work

Subjects: Fiction, literary non-fiction, children's and young adult literature, poetry and creative writing for performance or new media.
Purpose: To assist in the creation of new work by emerging, developing and established Australian writers and picture book illustrators.
Eligibility: Open to individuals who meet the eligibility requirements and provide the necessary support materials.
Frequency: Annual

Application Procedure: Application form should include the required support materials. Check website for further details.
Closing Date: May 15th

Literature Presentation and Promotion
Subjects: Fiction, literary non-fiction, children's literature, poetry and creative writing for performance or new media.
Purpose: To improve the vitality and viability of the Australian literature sector by supporting activities which foster greater awareness and appreciation of outstanding Australian creative writing.
Eligibility: Open to Australian and international organisations which meet the eligibility requirements.
Frequency: 6 monthly
Application Procedure: Application form should include the required support materials. Check website for further details.
Closing Date: March 15th and October 1st

Literature Program
Purpose: To provide 1 year funding to a limited number of significant organisations that contribute to a viable strategic infrastructure that supports the work and professional development of Australian writers and general advancement of Australian literature.
Eligibility: Open to organisations which meet the eligibility requirements and provide the necessary support materials.
Frequency: Annual
Application Procedure: Application form should include the required support materials. Check website for further details.
Closing Date: October 1st

Literature Skills and Arts Development
Purpose: To foster a supportive environment for professional development, research and creative risk-taking.
Eligibility: Open to individuals and organisations which meet the eligibility requirements and provide the necessary support materials.
Frequency: 6 monthly
Application Procedure: Application form should include the required support materials. Check website for further details.
Closing Date: March 15th and October 1st

Music Initiative
Purpose: To support young musicians, sound artists and music related arts workers through grants.
Eligibility: Check website for details.
Value: $2,500
Frequency: 6 monthly
Application Procedure: Application form should include the required support materials. Check website for further details.
Closing Date: March 1st and September 5th

Music Initiative Sounding Out
Subjects: Acoustic, electro-acoustic, electronic, virtual, interactive, automated, software, intermedia instruments and interfaces.
Purpose: To support and raise awareness of Australian-made music instruments and sound-interface practices through encouraging imaginative and innovative proposals from the field.
Eligibility: Open to individuals, collectives/groups and organisations involved in the making of Australian-made musical instruments and sound interfaces.
Value: Up to $100,000
Frequency: Annual
Application Procedure: Application form should include the required support materials. Check website for further details.
Closing Date: September 30th

Music International Market Development Program International Pathways
Purpose: To assist strategic international artistic and market development activities for Australian music and musicians.
Eligibility: Open to individuals, groups and organisations who meet the eligibility requirements and provide the necessary support materials. Applicants must be Australian citizens or have permanent resident status in Australia. Proof of citizenship or residency may be required.
Frequency: 3 monthly

Application Procedure: Applicants must complete the proposal cover sheet and submit this with the proposal. Check website for further details.
Closing Date: December 1st, March 15th, June 30th, September 1st

Music Key Organisations Triennial
Purpose: To develop a viable strategic infrastructure to advance the arts in Australia.
Eligibility: Open only to organisations currently in receipt of Key Organisations Triennial Grants from the Music Board.
Frequency: Annual
Application Procedure: Application form should include the required support materials. Check website for further details.
Closing Date: June 1st

Music National Residency
Purpose: It is a six-month residency for new media artists with ABC Radio National in Sydney.
Frequency: Annual
Application Procedure: Application form should include the required support materials. Check website for further details.
Closing Date: June 1st

Music New Work
Purpose: To support one-off project that involves the creation or development of new musical materials or music and media arts projects.
Eligibility: Open to individuals, performing groups/ensembles/bands and organisations which meet the eligibility requirements and provide the necessary support materials.
Frequency: 6 monthly
Application Procedure: Application form should include the required support materials. Check website for further details.
Closing Date: June 1st and November 15th

Music Presentation and Promotion
Purpose: To support one-off projects that present, publish, distribute and/or market quality music of any style.
Eligibility: Open to individuals, performing groups/ensembles/bands and organisations which meet the eligibility requirements and provide the necessary support materials.
Frequency: 6 monthly
Application Procedure: Application form should include the required support materials. Check website for further details.
Closing Date: June 1st and November 15th

Music Program
Purpose: To provide funding for 1 year to a limited number of organisations that play a significant role in enriching the quality and diversity of music practice in Australia through the delivery of specific activities.
Eligibility: Open to organisations which meet the eligibility requirements and provide the necessary support materials.
Frequency: Annual
Application Procedure: Application form should include the required support materials. Check website for further details.
Closing Date: June 1st

Music Skills and Development
Purpose: To support skills development for professional artists and artsworkers and programmes and services of organisations that contribute to the development of music practice in Australia. There are two subcategories: individuals and groups (established and emerging), and organisations (legally constituted).
Eligibility: Open to individuals and organisations which meet the eligibility requirements and provide the necessary support materials.
Frequency: 6 monthly
Application Procedure: Application form should include the required support materials. Check website for further details.
Closing Date: June 1st and November 15th

OZCO Community Cultural Development Fellowship
Subjects: Community-based arts.
Purpose: To enhance the capacity of artists and artsworkers to provide leadership in the field.

Eligibility: Applicants should have a solid record of achievement in community arts and culture, including community cultural development.
Level of Study: Postgraduate, Professional development
Type: Fellowship
Value: Australian $40,000
Length of Study: 2 years
Frequency: Annual
Country of Study: Australia
No. of awards offered: Varies
Application Procedure: Contact the department.
Closing Date: April 15th
Funding: Government

For further information contact:

Tel: 61 2 9215 9029
Email: ccd@ozco.gov.au

OZCO Dance Fellowship

Subjects: Dance.
Purpose: To strengthen an artist's current practice and ability to seek new challenges or test a new direction.
Level of Study: Postdoctorate, Professional development
Type: Fellowship
Value: Australian $40,000
Length of Study: 2 years
Frequency: Annual
Country of Study: Australia
No. of awards offered: Varies
Application Procedure: Contact the department.
Closing Date: November 15th
Funding: Government

For further information contact:

Email: dance@ozco.gov.au

OZCO Dance Grant Initiative: Take Your Partner

Subjects: Dance and movement arts.
Purpose: To support young and emerging dance artists and art workers to forge a new relationship or build on an existing one through a specific project.
Level of Study: Professional development
Type: Grant
Value: Australian $15,000
Frequency: Annual
Country of Study: Australia
Application Procedure: Contact the department.
Closing Date: May–June
Funding: Government

For further information contact:

Tel: 2 9215 9179
Email: s.woo@ozco.gov.au
Contact: Sandi Woo

OZCO Literature Fellowships

Subjects: Fiction, literary non-fiction (defined by the Literature Board as autobiography, biography, essays, histories criticism or other analytical prose); children's and young adult literature; poetry; and creative writing for performance or new media.
Purpose: To support excellence in Australian literature.
Eligibility: Applications will only be accepted from individuals who have had a minimum of major works published or performed and have achieved substantial critical recognition.
Level of Study: Postgraduate, Professional development
Type: Fellowship
Value: Australian $40,000
Length of Study: 2 years
Frequency: Annual
Country of Study: Australia
No. of awards offered: Varies
Application Procedure: Contact the department.
Closing Date: May 15th
Funding: Government

For further information contact:

Email: literature@ozco.gov.au

OZCO Literature Grants Initiative: Write in Your Face

Subjects: Writing in zines, e-zines, comics, multimedia, multi-art forms, websites, live performance and spoken word.
Purpose: To support young writers using language in innovative ways.
Eligibility: Applicant must be aged 30 years or under.
Level of Study: Professional development
Type: Grant
Value: A maximum of Australian $5,000
Frequency: Annual
Country of Study: Australia
No. of awards offered: Varies
Application Procedure: Contact the department.
Closing Date: December 9th

For further information contact:

Tel: 29215 9058
Email: j.jones@ozco.gov.au
Contact: J. Jones

OZCO Music Fellowship

Subjects: Music.
Purpose: To provide musicians with a record of outstanding achievement with financial support.
Level of Study: Postdoctorate, Professional development
Type: Fellowship
Value: Australian $40,000
Length of Study: 2 years
Frequency: Annual
Country of Study: Australia
No. of awards offered: Varies
Application Procedure: Contact the department.
Closing Date: June 1st
Funding: Government
Additional Information: Fellowship recipients may apply for funding from other categories during the term of the Fellowship, with the exception of the project Fellowships initiative.

For further information contact:

Email: music@ozco.gov.au

OZCO Music Project Fellowship

Subjects: Music.
Purpose: To fund artists for significant projects that will benefit their artistic development.
Eligibility: Music artists working in music theatre and indigenous music artists are particularly encouraged to apply.
Level of Study: Postgraduate, Professional development
Type: Fellowship
Value: Australian $20,000
Length of Study: 1 year
Frequency: Annual
Country of Study: Australia
No. of awards offered: Varies
Application Procedure: Contact the department.
Closing Date: June 1st
Funding: Government

For further information contact:

Email: music@ozco.gov.au

OZCO Theatre Fellowship

Subjects: Theatre studies.
Purpose: To financially support an individuals professional development.
Eligibility: It is for artists with a record of outstanding achievement.
Level of Study: Postgraduate, Professional development
Type: Fellowship
Value: Australian $40,000
Length of Study: 2 years

Frequency: Annual
Country of Study: Australia
Application Procedure: It is strongly recommended that you discuss your application with staff before applying.
Closing Date: November 15th
Funding: Government

For further information contact:

Email: theatre@ozco.gov.au

OZCO Visual Arts Fellowship
Subjects: Visual Arts.
Purpose: To provide financial support to visual artists, craftspeople and specialist visual arts and craft writers of outstanding achievement to enable them to create new work and further develop their practice.
Level of Study: Postgraduate
Type: Fellowship
Value: Australian $40,000
Length of Study: A maximum of 2 years
Frequency: Annual
Country of Study: Australia
Application Procedure: Apply online.
Closing Date: April 15th
Funding: Government
Additional Information: Fellowships are granted only once in an artist's lifetime.

For further information contact:

Email: vac@ozco.gov.au

Theatre Initiative Dramaturgy Fellowship
Purpose: To provide an opportunity for the consolidation of professional dramaturgical practice to an experienced dramaturg.
Eligibility: Applicants should be an experienced dramaturg and design a programme that includes their dramaturgy on one or a series of projects over the course of approximately 1 year or more, concluding the programme within 2 years.
Value: $25,000 each
Frequency: Annual
No. of awards offered: 2
Application Procedure: Applications can be downloaded from the website.
Closing Date: July 30th

Theatre Initiative-Playing the World
Purpose: To assist Australian theatre artists to develop international markets and reach new audiences overseas.
Frequency: Annual
Closing Date: February 14th
Additional Information: Check website for further details.

Theatre International Residency
Purpose: To provide a significant opportunity for an artist by offering a three-month studio residency at the Cite Internationale des Arts in Paris.
Value: $10,000 towards travel and living expenses
Length of Study: January–March
Frequency: Annual
Application Procedure: Contact staff of the Theatre Board for guidelines and selection criteria.
Closing Date: June 1st

Theatre Key Organisations Triennial
Purpose: To provide funding to a limited number of outstanding organisations to assist the development and advancement of theatre in Australia.
Eligibility: Open to organisations which meet the general eligibility requirements.
Value: Up to $20,000
Frequency: Annual
Application Procedure: Applications should include required support materials. Check website for further details.
Closing Date: June 1st

Theatre Presentation and Promotion
Purpose: The Theatre Board funds international activities through Playing the World, but does not offer a seperate grants programme for national and regional touring or for the development of marketing strategies.
Frequency: Annual
Application Procedure: Applicants should discuss with the Theatre staff before submitting the proposal.

Visual Arts Emeritus Award
Subjects: Relevant to visual arts.
Purpose: To acknowledge and honor the special achievements of Australian craftspeople, designers, new media artists, visual artists and arts writers who have made and are making an outstanding contribution to the development of Australian art.
Value: $40,000
Frequency: Annual
Closing Date: August 1st

Visual Arts Emeritus Medal
Subjects: Relevant to visual arts.
Purpose: To acknowledge and honor the special professional achievements of living curators, administrators and/or advocates of contemporary Australian art, who have made and are making an outstanding contribution to the development of the Australian cultural sector.
Value: $10,000
Frequency: Annual
Additional Information: August 1st.

Visual Arts Initiative Maker to Manufacturer to Market
Purpose: To encourage Australia's craft and design practitioners to be entrepreneurial with their art products and to succeed in the market place.
Eligibility: Open to individuals, groups and organisations that need financial assistance to create multiples of their art products and to get them to market.
Value: $30,000
Frequency: Annual
No. of awards offered: 3
Application Procedure: Check website for details.
Closing Date: June 1st

Visual Arts Initiative-Artista Run
Value: Up to $10,000
Frequency: Annual
Application Procedure: Applicants should complete the Visual Arts Board coversheet and submit with the proposal. Check the website for further details.
Closing Date: November 1st

Visual Arts Key Organisations Triennial
Purpose: Visual arts.
Frequency: Annual
Additional Information: Check website for further details.

Visual Arts New Work
Purpose: To support the creation of new work by emerging and established craftspeople, designers, new media artists, visual artists and arts writers.
Eligibility: Open to individuals and groups which meet the eligibility requirements and provide the necessary support materials.
Value: $10,000 for emerging and $20,000 for established craftpeople, designers, new media artists, visual artists and arts writers
Frequency: Annual
Application Procedure: Applications should include the required support materials. Check website for further details.
Closing Date: April 15th
Contributor: National Association for the Visual Arts (NAVA)

Visual Arts Presentation and Promotion
Purpose: To assist arts organisations to present and promote contemporary Australian craft, design, new media art and visual arts, to audiences in Australia and overseas.

Eligibility: Open to organisations which meet the eligibility require-
ments and porvide the necessary support materials.
Frequency: Annual
Application Procedure: Applications should include the required
support materials.
Closing Date: August 1st

Visual Arts Skills and Arts Development

Purpose: To promote excellence in the arts by providing professional
development oppurtunities for craftspeople, designers, new media
artists, visual artists, arts writers and curators. Three types of grants
are offered: Studio residencies, General professional development
and Young and emerging artists initiative grants.
Eligibility: Open to individuals and groups which meet the eligibility
requirements and provide the necessary support materials.
Frequency: Annual
Application Procedure: Applications should include the required
support materials. Check website for further details.
Closing Date: August 1st

AUSTRALIAN ACADEMY OF THE HUMANITIES (AAH)

GPO Box 93, Canberra, ACT, 2601, Australia
Tel: (61) 2 6125 9860
Fax: (61) 2 6248 6287
Email: enquiries@humanities.org.au
Website: www.humanities.org.au
Contact: Administration Officer

The Australian Academy of the Humanities (AAH) was established
under Royal Charter in 1969 for the advancement of the scholarship,
interest in and understanding of the humanities. Humanities disciplines include, but are not limited to, history, classics, English, European languages and cultures, Asian studies, philosophy, the arts,
linguistics, prehistory and archaeology and cultural and communications studies.

AAH Humanities Travelling Fellowships

Subjects: Humanities disciplines as per the Academy's charter.
Purpose: To enable short-term study abroad.
Eligibility: Open to scholars resident in Australia and who are working
in the field of humanities. Fellows of the Academy are ineligible for
awards. Preference shall be given to scholars in the earlier stages of
their careers, and who are not as well placed to receive funding from
other sources. They should have a project going forward that requires
a short visit overseas for its completion or advancement. The pro-
posed work should not form part of the requirement for a higher de-
gree. Funds are not given for conference attendance. Country of study
is any country except Australia.
Level of Study: Doctorate, Postdoctorate
Type: Fellowship
Value: Australian $4,000 each
Length of Study: At least 2 weeks
Frequency: Annual
Study Establishment: An appropriate research centre
Country of Study: Any country
No. of awards offered: 10
Application Procedure: Applicants can download application form
and guidelines from the academy website www.humanities.org.au
Closing Date: July 31st
Funding: Government
No. of awards given last year: 13
No. of applicants last year: 40
Additional Information: Please visit the Academy's website,
www.humanities.org.au for detailed information and application pro-
cedures.

AAH Visiting Scholar Programmes

Subjects: All subjects.
Purpose: To encourage scholarly contact with scholars from both
Russia/the former USSR and Indonesia/South–East Asia and to assist
scholars from those countries to obtain access to research materials
held in Australia.

Eligibility: Applicants must be identified as being appropriate repre-
sentatives at Australia-based conferences.
Level of Study: Doctorate
Type: Award
Value: $7,000 (for scholars from Russia and the Former USSR) and
$4,000 (for scholars from Indonesia and South–East Asia)
Frequency: Annual
No. of awards offered: 4
Application Procedure: Applicant (Australian host scholar) must
send to the Secretariat a brief explanation of the reason for the visit, a
copy of the visiting scholar's curriculum vitae and a list of their most
significant publications (in English), a provisional itinerary listing
speaking engagements, potential contact with Australian scholars and
research institutions to be visited and a provisional budget for the
expenditure of the funds.
Closing Date: July 31st
No. of awards given last year: 4
No. of applicants last year: 10

For further information contact:

Tel: 02 6125 8950
Email: grants@humanities.org.au
Contact: Jorge Salavert

The British Special Joint Project Funding Scheme

Subjects: All subjects.
Eligibility: The principal applicant on the Australian side should be
normally a resident of Australia. Other scholars associated with the
project will normally be expected to be of postdoctoral status.
Level of Study: Postdoctorate
Type: Award
Value: Up to £8,000 (if 1 award is given) or up to £4,000 per project (if
2 awards are given)
Length of Study: Up to 1 year
Frequency: Annual
No. of awards offered: 1 or 2
Application Procedure: Applicants from both sides must submit
applications to the appropriate Academy. Australian scholars should
apply through either the AAH or ASSA, depending on the nature of
their project. Australian partners should consult the AAH or ASSA for
application procedures. Equivalent information must be included on all
application forms. All applications for Academy grants are considered
in the light of referees comments.
Closing Date: September 30th
No. of awards given last year: 2
No. of applicants last year: 15

For further information contact:

Tel: 02 6125 8950
Email: grants@humanities.org.au
Contact: Jorge Salavert

AUSTRALIAN BIO SECURITY-CRC (AB-CRC)

Brisbane, OLD Building 76, Molecular Biosciences, The University of
Queens land, St Lucia, QLD 4072, Australia
Tel: (61) (0) 7 3346 8866
Fax: (61) (0) 7 3346 8862
Email: info@abcrc.org.au
Website: www1.abcrc.org.au

The mission of the ABCRC is to protect Australia's public health,
livestock, wildlife and economic resources through research and education that strengthens the national capability to detect, diagnose,
identify, monitor, assess, predict and to respond to emerging infectious disease threats.

AB-CRC Honours Scholarships

Subjects: Biosecurity and emerging infectious diseases.
Purpose: To encourage students of high academic ability to take the
first step in their career path as a researcher.
Eligibility: Scholarships will be awarded preferentially to Australian
residents and students from the Asia-Pacific region.

Level of Study: Postgraduate
Type: Scholarship
Value: Australian $5,000
Length of Study: 1 year
Frequency: Annual
Study Establishment: AB-CRC participating university
Country of Study: Australia
Application Procedure: Contact the scholarships Administrator officer.
Closing Date: October 31st

For further information contact:

Tel: 08 9266 1634
Email: debra.gendle@abcrc.org.au
Contact: Debra Gendle

AB-CRC PhD and Masters-by-Research Scholarships

Subjects: Bio security and emerging infectious diseases.
Purpose: To expand training opportunities.
Level of Study: Doctorate, Postdoctorate, Postgraduate
Type: Scholarship
Value: An annual stipend of up to Australian $25,000 and a development allowance of Australian $2,000
Length of Study: 1–3 years
Frequency: Annual
Study Establishment: AB-CRC participating university
Country of Study: Australia
Application Procedure: Request application form.
Closing Date: October 24th

AB-CRC Professional Development Scholarships

Subjects: Bio Security and emerging infectious diseases.
Purpose: To expand our capability to support the training of specialists.
Level of Study: Professional development
Type: Scholarship
Length of Study: Australian $2,000
Frequency: Annual
Study Establishment: AB-CRC participating university
Country of Study: Australia
No. of awards offered: 5
Application Procedure: Contact the Scholarships Administration officer.
Closing Date: November 16th
Additional Information: Candidates will be required to sign a confidentially agreement.

For further information contact:

Email: debra.gendle@abcrc.org.uk
Contact: Debra Gendle

AUSTRALIAN CATHOLIC UNIVERSITY (ACU)

PO Box 456, Virginia, Brisbane, QLD, 4014,
Australia
Tel: (61) 07 3623 7100
Email: futurestudents@acu.edu.au
Website: www.acu.edu.au

ACU National shares with universities worldwide a commitment to quality in teaching, research, and community engagement and to provide an excellent higher education experience for the entire student body, through upholding the principles of free enquiry, and academic integrity. The University strives to create an environment of support and challenge, where intellectual engagement and cognitive development occur as part of a deeper concern to help people learn intellectually, spiritually, culturally, and socially. It provides excellent higher education for its entire diversified and dispersed student body. Through fostering and advancing knowledge in education, health, commerce, the humanities, the sciences and technologies, and the creative arts, Australian Catholic University seeks to make a specific contribution to its local, national, and international communities.

Archdiocese of Brisbane Theology Scholarships

Subjects: Theology.
Purpose: To provide support and encouragement for postgraduate students undertaking higher degree studies in Theology at the University's Brisbane campus.
Level of Study: Postgraduate
Type: Scholarship
Value: Maximum of Australian $3,000
Frequency: Annual
Study Establishment: Australian Catholic University's Brisbane campus
Application Procedure: Candidates can obtain further information from the Course Co-ordinator.
Contributor: Archdiocese of Brisbane

Council of Catholic School Parents (NSW) Indigenous Postgraduate Scholarship (IES)

Subjects: Education.
Purpose: To encourage involvement of parents and the community in education.
Eligibility: Open to Indigenous students enrolled in a postgraduate course within the faculty of education at the Strathfield campus, and have a particular focus, interest, or understanding of the importance of parent and community involvement in education.
Type: Scholarship
Value: Australian $1,000
Frequency: Annual
Study Establishment: Strathfield campus
Country of Study: Australia
Application Procedure: Candidates can obtain further information from Yalbalinga Indigenous Unit, Strathfield campus.
Contributor: Council of Catholic School Parents (NSW)

Nano Nagle Scholarship (IES)

Subjects: All subjects.
Purpose: To commemorate and honour the work of their founder Nano Nagle who established the Congregation.
Eligibility: Open to Indigenous students undertaking postgraduate studies at ACU National's Brisbane Campus in areas of concern to the Presentation Sisters, with a preference given to study in education.
Level of Study: Graduate
Type: Scholarship
Value: Australian $1,250 per year
Frequency: Annual
Study Establishment: Australian Cahtolic University National's Brisbane Campus
Country of Study: Australia
Application Procedure: Candidates can obtain further information from Weemala Indigenous Unit, Brisbane campus.
Contributor: Presentation Sisters, Queensland Congregation

Pratt Foundation Bursary (IES)

Subjects: All subjects.
Purpose: To make available a bursary to a suitably qualified Aboriginal and Torres Strait Islander student undertaking postgraduate study at ACU National.
Eligibility: Open to suitably qualified Aboriginal and Torres Strait Islander student undertaking postgraduate study at ACU National.
Level of Study: Graduate
Type: Bursary
Value: Australian $2,500
Frequency: Annual
Study Establishment: Australian Catholic University (ACU) National
Country of Study: Australia
No. of awards offered: 1
Application Procedure: Candidates can obtain further information from Weemala Indigenous Unit, Brisbane campus.
Funding: Foundation
Contributor: The Pratt Foundation

Wexford Senate Bursary (IES)

Subjects: All subjects.
Purpose: To support a suitably qualified Indigenous student undertaking postgraduate study at ACU National with the specific goal of development of skills of emerging leaders of Aboriginal and Torres

Strait Islander communities through professional preparation at post-graduate level.
Eligibility: Open to suitably qualified Aboriginal and Torres Strait Islander student undertaking postgraduate study at ACU National.
Type: Bursary
Value: Australian $3,000
Study Establishment: Australian Catholic University (ACU) National
Country of Study: Australia
Application Procedure: Candidate can obtain further information from Weemala Indigenous Unit, Brisbane campus.
Contributor: The Wexford Senate

AUSTRALIAN CENTRE FOR BLOOD DISEASES (ACBD)

6th Floor, Burnet Tower, 89 Commercial Road, Melbourne, VIC, 3004, Australia
Tel: (61) 3 990 30122
Fax: (61) 3 990 30228
Email: acbd@med.monash.edu.au
Website: www.acbd.monash.org

The Australian Centre for Blood Diseases (ACBD) brings together the skills and facilities of separate yet complementary organizations to enhance understanding of blood and its diseases. Its aim is to provide excellence in the diagnosis and treatment of blood conditions as well as play a leading role in the advancement of knowledge in this increasingly important area of medicine.

Firkin PhD Scholarship
Subjects: Cardiovascular disciplines.
Purpose: To undertake a PhD programme at the ACBD or affiliated institutes comprising AMREP.
Eligibility: Open to students interested in pursuing doctorate studies in cardiovascular disciplines, and who have the appropriate graduate qualifications.
Level of Study: Graduate
Type: Scholarships
Value: Australian $22,500 per year
Length of Study: 3 years
Frequency: Annual
No. of awards offered: Up to 4
Application Procedure: For further information, please contact Dr Robert Medcalf.

For further information contact:

Australian Centre for Blood Diseases, Monash University, 6th Floor, Burnet Building, AMREP, Commercial Road, Melbourne, Victoria 3004, Australia
Email: Robert.Medcalf@med.monash.edu.au
Contact: Dr Robert Medcalf, Associate Professor

AUSTRALIAN FEDERATION OF UNIVERSITY WOMEN (AFUW) VICTORIA

LPO Box A344, Australian National University, Canberra, ACT 2601, Australia
Tel: (61) 03 9557 2556
Email: ireneaxup@hotmail.com
Website: www.afuw.org.au
Contact: Ms Irene Axup, Scholarship Secretary

Australian Federation of University Women (AFUW) Victoria was formed in 1922 as part of the international network of women Graduates for the benefit of women and society. AFUW Victoria is a member association of AFUW and serves a number of benefits both at personal and societal level in providing women with opportunities.

AFUW William and Elizabeth Fisher Scholarship
Subjects: All subjects.
Purpose: To promote the advancement of graduate women worldwide and their equality of opportunity through initiatives in education, friendship and peace.

Eligibility: Open to female students who are enrolled in postgraduate research degree at a Victorian University.
Level of Study: Postgraduate
Type: Scholarship
Value: Australian $1,500
Frequency: Annual
Study Establishment: Victorian University
Country of Study: Australia
No. of awards offered: 2
Application Procedure: A complete application form must be sent across by post.

For further information contact:

AFUW Fellowships Convenor, PO Box 4066, Bay Village, NSW, Australia

THE AUSTRALIAN FEDERATION OF UNIVERSITY WOMEN, SOUTH AUSTRALIA, INC. TRUST FUND (AFUW-SA, INC.)

GPO Box 634, Adelaide, SA, 5001, Australia
Website: www.afuwsa-bursaries.com.au
Contact: Ms Heather Latz, Fellowships Trustee

The Australian Federation of University Women's (AFUW) main activity is assisting women in tertiary education in Australia via bursaries. Funds for the bursaries are raised through volunteer work, academic dress hire, donations and bequests.

Diamond Jubilee Bursary
Subjects: All subjects.
Purpose: To assist in the completion of a coursework postgraduate degree.
Eligibility: Open to men or women of any nationality, enrolled in a postgraduate degree by coursework at South Australian Universities. Applicants must not be in full-time paid employment or on fully paid study leave during the tenure of the bursary.
Level of Study: Doctorate, Postgraduate
Type: Bursary
Value: Australian $4,000
Length of Study: The bursary must be used within 1 year of the date of the award
Frequency: Annual
Study Establishment: A South Australian university
Country of Study: Australia
No. of awards offered: 1
Application Procedure: Candidates should complete an application form and submit it with evidence of enrolment at the institution at which the qualification will be obtained, as well as copies of official transcripts and a curriculum vitae. Application forms can be downloaded from the website and sent by post.
Closing Date: March 1st
Funding: Private
No. of awards given last year: 3
No. of applicants last year: 9

Doreen McCarthy, Barbara Crase, Cathy Candler and Brenda Nettle Bursaries
Subjects: All subjects.
Purpose: To assist in the completion of a Master's or PhD research degree.
Eligibility: Open to men and women of any nationality. Applicants must have completed 1 year of postgraduate research, and must be enrolled at a university in South Australia. Applicants must not be in full-time paid employment or on fully paid study leave.
Level of Study: Postgraduate, Doctorate
Type: Bursary
Value: Australian $5,000
Length of Study: The bursary must be used within 1 year of the date of the award
Frequency: Annual
Study Establishment: A South Australian university

Country of Study: Australia
No. of awards offered: 4
Application Procedure: Candidates should complete an application form and submit it with evidence of enrolment at the institution at which the qualification will be obtained, as well as copies of official transcripts, a curriculum vitae and a list of publications. Application forms can be downloaded from the website and sent by post.
Closing Date: March 1st
Funding: Private
No. of awards given last year: 10
No. of applicants last year: 24

Heather Latz Bursary

Subjects: All subjects.
Purpose: To assist women complete their coursework postgraduate degrees.
Eligibility: Open to women of any nationality, enrolled for coursework postgraduate degrees at any Australian university. Applicants must not be in full-time paid employment or on fully paid study leave during the tenure of the bursary.
Level of Study: Postgraduate, Doctorate
Type: Bursary
Value: Australian $4,000
Length of Study: The bursary must be used within 1 year of the date of the award
Frequency: Annual
Study Establishment: A recognized Australian tertiary institution
Country of Study: Australia
No. of awards offered: 1
Application Procedure: Applicants must complete an application form and submit it with evidence of enrolment at the institution at which the qualification is to be obtained, as well as copies of official transcripts, a curriculum vitae and a list of publications. Application forms can be downloaded from the website and sent by post.
Closing Date: March 1st
Funding: Private
No. of awards given last year: 2
No. of applicants last year: 39

Jean Gilmore, Thenie Baddams and Daphne Elliott Bursary

Subjects: All subjects.
Purpose: To assist women to complete a Master's or PhD degree by research.
Eligibility: Open to female graduates of any nationality enrolled at Australian universities undertaking postgraduate degrees by research, who have completed 1 year of postgraduate research. Applicants must not be in full-time paid employment or on fully paid study leave during the tenure of the bursary.
Level of Study: Postgraduate, Doctorate
Type: Bursary
Value: Up to Australian $6,000 each; however, runners-up can be awarded a lesser amount
Length of Study: The bursary must be used within 1 year of the date of the award
Frequency: Annual
Study Establishment: A recognized Australian Institute of Higher Education
Country of Study: Australia
No. of awards offered: At least 1
Application Procedure: Applicants must complete an application form and submit this with evidence of enrolment at the institution at which the qualification is to be obtained, as well as copies of official transcripts, a curriculum vitae and a list of publications. There is an Australian $12 lodgement fee. Application forms can be downloaded from the website and sent by post.
Closing Date: March 1st
Funding: Private
No. of awards given last year: 13
No. of applicants last year: 138

Padnendadlu Graduate Bursary

Subjects: All subjects.
Purpose: To assist in the completion of a postgraduate degree.

Eligibility: Applicants must be Australian indigenous women undertaking postgraduate degrees at South Australian universities. Applicants must not be in full-time paid employment or on fully paid study leave.
Level of Study: Graduate
Type: Bursary
Value: Australian $2,000
Frequency: Annual
Study Establishment: A South Australian University
Country of Study: Australia
No. of awards offered: At least 1
Application Procedure: Candidates should complete an application form and submit it with evidence of enrolment at the institution at which the qualification will be obtained, as well as copies of official transcripts and a curriculum vitae. An application form can be downloaded from the website and sent by post.
Closing Date: March 1st
Funding: Private
Additional Information: Eligible applicants undertaking a postgraduate degree by coursework must apply for the Diamond Jubilee Bursary, and those undertaking a postgraduate degree by research must apply for the Doreen McCarthy, Barbara Crase, Cathy Candler and Brenda Nettle Bursaries. In each case, completion of a declaration of indigenous status will ensure that applicants are considered for the Padnendadlu Bursary.

Padnendadlu Postgraduate Bursary

Subjects: All subjects.
Purpose: To assist in the completion of a postgraduate degree.
Eligibility: Applicants must be Australian indigenous women undertaking postgraduate degrees at South Australian universities. Applicants must have completed 1 year postgraduate research and must not be in full-time paid employment or on fully paid study leave during the tenure of the bursary.
Level of Study: Doctorate, Postgraduate
Type: Bursary
Value: Australian $5,000 for those undertaking research degrees, or Australian $4,000 for those undertaking coursework degrees
Frequency: Annual
Study Establishment: A South Australian university
Country of Study: Australia
No. of awards offered: At least 1
Application Procedure: Candidates should complete an application form and submit it with evidence of enrolment at the institution at which the qualification will be obtained, as well as copies of official transcripts and a curriculum vitae. Application forms can be downloaded from the website and sent by post.
Closing Date: March 1st
Funding: Private
No. of awards given last year: 2
No. of applicants last year: 2
Additional Information: Eligible applicants undertaking a postgraduate degree by coursework must apply for the Diamond Jubilee Bursary, and those undertaking a postgraduate degree by research must apply for the Doreen McCarthy, Barbara Crase, Cathy Candler and Brenda Nettle Bursaries. In each case, completion of a declaration of indigenous status will ensure that applicants are considered for the Padnendadlu Bursary.

Winifred E Preedy Postgraduate Bursary

Subjects: Dentistry or a related field.
Purpose: To assist women in the completion of a higher degree.
Eligibility: Open to women of any nationality who are students of the University of Adelaide's Dental School in the past or present, and are enrolled as postgraduate students in dentistry or an allied field. The applicant must have completed 1 year of the postgraduate degree, and must not be in full-time paid employment or on fully paid study leave, and must not have previously won this bursary.
Level of Study: Doctorate, Postgraduate
Type: Bursary
Value: Australian $4,000
Length of Study: The bursary must be used within 1 year of the date of the award
Frequency: Annual

Study Establishment: Anywhere, if the applicant is a past student at the University of Adelaide's Dental Faculty in Australia. Otherwise, the applicant must be a student at the University of Adelaide's Dental Faculty

Country of Study: Australia

No. of awards offered: 1

Application Procedure: Applicants must complete an application form and submit it with evidence of enrolment at the institution at which the qualification will be obtained, as well as copies of official transcripts, a curriculum vitae and a list of publications. Application forms can be downloaded from the website and sent by post.

Closing Date: March 1st

Funding: Private

THE AUSTRALIAN INSTITUTE OF ABORIGINAL AND TORRES STRAIT ISLANDER STUDIES (AIATSIS)

Research Grants Administration, AIATSIS Research Program, GPO Box 553, Canberra, ACT 2601, Australia

Tel: (61) 61 2 6261 4221 or 61 2 6246 1111

Fax: (61) 61 2 6249 7714

Email: grants@aiatsis.gov.au

Website: www.aiatsis.gov.au/research_program/grants

The Australian Institute of Aboriginal and Torres Strait Islander Studies (AIATSIS) is the world's premier institution for information and research about the cultures and lifestyles of Aboriginal and Torres Strait Islander peoples. AIATSIS undertakes and encourages scholarly, ethical community-based research, holds a priceless collection of films, photographs, video and audio recordings and the world's largest collections of printed and other resource materials for indigenous studies. Its activities affirm and raise awareness among all Australians, and people of other nations, of the richness and diversity of Australian Indigenous cultures and histories.

AIATSIS Conference Support Grants

Subjects: Indigenous studies.

Purpose: To provide financial support for successful applicants to attend major international conferences held outside Australia.

Eligibility: Open for studies in countries except Australia. Applicants must be an Aboriginal or Torres Islander and citizens of Australia or New Zealand.

Level of Study: Postgraduate

Type: Grant

Value: Varies

Study Establishment: The Australian Institute of Aboriginal and Torres Strait Islander Studies

Country of Study: Australia

No. of awards offered: 2

Application Procedure: For application details, visit the website, www.aiatsis.gov.au/research_program/grants.

Closing Date: March 15th and August 31st

Funding: Government

AIATSIS Research Grants Program

Subjects: Indigenous studies.

Purpose: To support research into a wide range of research areas in aboriginal and Torres Strait Islander studies.

Eligibility: This scholarship is for study in Australia.

Level of Study: Postgraduate, Research

Type: Scholarship

Value: Varies

Frequency: Annual

Study Establishment: The Australian Institute of Aboriginal and Torres Strait Islander Studies

Country of Study: Australia

Application Procedure: Check website for further details, www.aiatsis.gov.au/rsrch/index.htm

Closing Date: December 15th

Funding: Government

THE AUSTRALIAN MUSIC FOUNDATION

4 Chelwood Vachery, Millbrook Hill, Nutley, East Sussex, TN22 3HB, United Kingdom

Email: info@amf-uk.com

Website: www.amf-uk.com

The Australian Music Foundation was established in 1980 and exists to offer financial support to outstanding young Australian musicians who wish to pursue post-graduate music courses in leading music education institutions in Europe. The Foundation aims to support and enhance that facet of modern Australian society, offering opportunities to outstanding young instrumentalists and singers to further their careers, studying with top teachers and coaches in the well-established music colleges and academies of Europe.

Australian Music Foundation Award

Subjects: Music.

Purpose: To offer financial support to outstanding young Australian musicians who wish to pursue post-graduate music courses in leading music education institutions in Europe.

Eligibility: Open to outstanding young Australian musicians who wish to pursue post-graduate music courses in leading music education institutions in Europe.

Level of Study: Graduate

Type: Award

Frequency: Annual

Study Establishment: Music colleges in Europe

Country of Study: European Union

No. of awards offered: Varies

Application Procedure: Check the website for further information.

Closing Date: April 30th

Funding: Foundation

AUSTRALIAN NATIONAL UNIVERSITY (ANU)

Building 11, Canberra, ACT, 0200, Australia

Tel: (61) 2 6249 5949

Fax: (61) 2 6125 5931

Email: student.information@anu.edu.au

Website: www.anu.edu.au

Contact: Research & Scholarships Office

The Australian National University (ANU) was founded by the Australian Government in 1946 as Australia's only completely re-search-orientated university. It comprises eight research schools, six teaching faculties, a graduate school and over a dozen other aca-demic schools or centres.

ANU Alumni Association PhD Scholarships

Subjects: All subjects.

Purpose: To assist international students with study in Australia.

Eligibility: Open to nationals of Hong Kong, Japan, Malaysia, Thai-land and Singapore.

Level of Study: Doctorate

Type: Scholarship

Value: Approx. Australian $19,231 per year (tax-free), payment of the programme fee for the duration of the stipend, an additional allowance for dependent children of married scholars, travel to Canberra and a grant for the reimbursement of some removal expenses. A thesis reimbursement allowance is also available

Length of Study: Normally tenable for 3 years, renewable for 6 months

Country of Study: Australia

No. of awards offered: 1 each for nationals of eligible countries

Application Procedure: Applicants must complete an application form, available on request or from the website.

Closing Date: Published through the Alumni Association of each country

Contributor: The Australian National University

ANU Doctoral Fellowships

Subjects: All subjects.

Purpose: To help Doctoral students pursue research and dissertation writing.

Eligibility: Open to candidates who have obtained their graduate degree from a university located in the United States.

Level of Study: Doctorate

Type: Fellowships

Value: Australian $1,600 per month, one round-trip economy class airfare and some funding for research

Length of Study: 3–9 months

Frequency: Annual

Study Establishment: Australian National University

Country of Study: Australia

Application Procedure: Applicants can download the application form from the website. The completed application form can be sent by post or electronically.

Closing Date: January 30th

Additional Information: Fellows accompanied by their family and staying for 6 months or more at the ANU will be entitled to family support of up to Australian $5,000, depending on the number of family members and other circumstances.

For further information contact:

ANU Southeast Asian Studies Fellowship Selection Committee, HR Academic Research School of Pacific and Asian Studies, The Australian National University, Canberra, ACT, 0200, Australia

Email: hr.rspas@anu.edu.au

ANU Graduate School Scholarships

Subjects: All subjects.

Purpose: To fund postgraduate study.

Eligibility: Open to individuals who are permanent residents of Australia. They need not necessarily have been resident in Australia for twelve months prior to the closing date. Applicants who have been in receipt of a PhD scholarship funded in the University for 1 year or more are ineligible.

Level of Study: Doctorate

Type: Scholarship

Value: A stipend of Australian $17,609 per year tax free, travel to Canberra from within Australia and a grant for the reimbursement of some removal expenses is available

Length of Study: 3 years in the first instance, with a possible extension of 6 months

Frequency: Annual

Country of Study: Australia

Application Procedure: Applicants must complete an application form, available on request or from the website.

Contributor: The Australian National University

ANU Indigenous Graduate Scholarship

Subjects: All subjects.

Purpose: To assist an Aboriginal or Torres Strait Islander to undertake a graduate diploma, Master's degree course or a course leading to a PhD.

Eligibility: Open to indigenous Australians who are Aborigines or Torres Strait Islanders.

Level of Study: Postgraduate

Type: Scholarship

Value: Australian $19,616 in fortnightly payments and travel to Canberra from within Australia; reimbursement of some removal expenses; thesis reimbursement allowance

Length of Study: Dependent upon the programme for which the scholarship is awarded

Frequency: Annual

Country of Study: Australia

No. of awards offered: 1

Application Procedure: Applicants must complete an application form, available on request or from the website.

Closing Date: October 31st

Contributor: The Australian National University

Additional Information: Open only to Australians citizens of indigenous.

ANU PhD Scholarships

Subjects: All subjects.

Purpose: To assist research.

Eligibility: Applicants should write for details.

Level of Study: Doctorate

Type: Scholarship

Value: A stipend of Australian $19,616 per year tax free, and if applicable, an additional allowance for dependent children of international scholars plus economy travel to Canberra and a grant for the reimbursement of some removal expenses thesis reimbursement allowance

Length of Study: 3 years, renewable for 6 months

Frequency: Annual

Country of Study: Australia

No. of awards offered: Varies

Application Procedure: Applicants must complete an application form, available on request or from the website.

Closing Date: October 31st for citizens or permanent residents of Australia and New Zealand, and August 31st for international applicants

Additional Information: Initial correspondence concerning graduate courses and scholarships should be sent to the main address or sent by email.

AUSTRALIAN PAIN SOCIETY (APS)

Secretariat Office, Dc Conferences Pty Ltd, PO Box 637, North Sydney, 2059, Australia
Tel: (61) 61 2 9954 4400
Fax: (61) 61 2 9954 0666

The Australian Pain Society (APS) is a non-profit organisation and is directed by an elected honorary council. The APS is anxious to enlist as members, other professionals interested in supporting the society in its goal of alleviating the suffering of our fellow citizens. Active membership in the APS is open to all health care professionals engaged in pain research or in the diagnosis and management of pain syndromes.

PhD Scholarships

Subjects: Health and life sciences.

Purpose: To improve the education, research and development, diagnosis and treatment of all forms of pain and to support education and research in pain.

Eligibility: Open to permanent residents and citizens of Australia and New Zealand citizens and applicants with permanent humanitarian visa.

Level of Study: Doctorate

Type: Scholarship

Value: Australian $23,000 per year. In addition to this, the Australian Pain Society (APS) and Australian Pain Relief Association (APRA) will provide financial support enabling the candidate to attend the Society's Annual Scientific Meeting

Length of Study: 3 years

Frequency: Annual

Country of Study: Australia

No. of awards offered: 2

Application Procedure: Further information about the PhD scholarship, including the conditions of award, can be obtained from the APS secretariat.

Closing Date: October 5th

Funding: Commercial

Contributor: Mundipharma Australia and Janssen-Cilag Australia and New Zealand

For further information contact:

PO Box 637, North Sydney, New South Wales, 2059, Australia
Tel: (61) 02 9954 4400
Fax: (61) 02 9954 0666
Email: aps@dcconferences.com.au
Website: www.apsoc.org.au
Contact: APS Secretariat: DC Conferences

AUSTRALIAN RESEARCH COUNCIL (ARC)

GPO Box 2702, Canberra, ACT, 2601, Australia
Tel: (61) 2 6287 6600
Fax: (61) 2 6287 6601
Email: ncgp@arc.gov.au
Website: www.arc.gov.au
Contact: Grants Management Officer

The Australian Research Council (ARC) plays a key role in the Australian Government's investment in the future prosperity and well-being of the Australian community. Its mission is to advance Australia's capacity to undertake quality research. ARC has various funding programmes under the umbrella of the National Competitive Grants Programme.

ARC Discovery Projects Postdoctoral Fellow (APD)
Subjects: All areas of science except clinical medicine or dentistry.
Purpose: To strengthen Australia's national research and development capability by providing opportunities for researchers to undertake research of national and international significance, and to broaden their research experience.
Eligibility: Applicants must have submitted their PhD thesis before the commencement of the fellowship. No more than 3 years should have elapsed since the awarding of their PhD and an excellent academic record is required.
Level of Study: Postdoctorate
Type: Fellowship
Value: Australian $67,494, including 26 per cent of costs
Length of Study: 3 years
Frequency: Annual
Country of Study: Australia
No. of awards offered: Approx. 110
Application Procedure: Applicants must submit applications through an Australian host institution. It is the responsibility of the applicant to approach potential host institutions.
Closing Date: March 8th
Funding: Government
No. of awards given last year: 112
No. of applicants last year: 568
Additional Information: Candidates must obtain Australian citizenship or temporary residency status at the time of commencing the fellowship.

ARC Discovery Projects: Australian Research Fellow/ Queen Elizabeth II Fellow (ARF/QEII)
Subjects: All areas of science except clinical medicine or dentistry.
Purpose: To strengthen Australia's national research and development capability by providing opportunities for established researchers to undertake research of national and international significance.
Eligibility: Open to candidates with a PhD and an excellent academic record. Applicants should have more than 3 years, but not more than 8 years of professional experience since the awarding of their PhD.
Level of Study: Postdoctorate
Type: Fellowship
Value: Australian Research Fellows are awarded Australian $84,252 and Queen Elizabeth II Fellows are awarded Australian $100,126. This includes 26 per cent of costs
Length of Study: 5 years
Frequency: Annual
Country of Study: Australia
No. of awards offered: Approx. 15 of each
Application Procedure: Applicants must submit applications through an Australian host institution. It is the responsibility of the applicant to approach potential host institutions.
Closing Date: March 8th
Funding: Government
No. of awards given last year: 30
No. of applicants last year: 265
Additional Information: Candidates must obtain Australian citizenship or temporary residency status at the time of commencing the fellowship.

ARC Projects: Professional Fellow (APF)
Subjects: All areas of science except clinical medicine or dentistry.
Purpose: To provide opportunities for outstanding researchers with proven international reputations to undertake research that is both of

major importance in its field and of significant benefit to Australia. Senior Research Fellowships are the premier fellowships offered by the Australian Research Council and, consequently, are highly sought after and extremely competitive.
Eligibility: Open to researchers who normally have more than 8 years of professional experience since the awarding of their PhD and extremely high-profile expatriate Australians and non-Australian researchers who wish to pursue their research in Australia.
Level of Study: Postdoctorate
Type: Fellowship
Value: Australian $115,656–135,822 including 26 per cent of costs
Length of Study: 5 years
Frequency: Annual
Country of Study: Australia
No. of awards offered: Approx. 15
Application Procedure: Applicants must submit applications through an Australian host institution. It is the responsibility of the applicant to approach potential host institutions.
Closing Date: March 8th
Funding: Government
No. of awards given last year: 23
No. of applicants last year: 176
Additional Information: Candidates must obtain Australian citizenship or temporary residency status at the time of commencing the fellowship.

AUSTRALIAN SPORTS COMMISSION (ASC)

PO Box 176, Belconnen, ACT 2616, Australia
Tel: (61) 61 02 6214 1111
Fax: (61) 61 02 6251 2680
Email: recruitment@ausport.gov.au
Website: www.ausport.gov.au

The Australian Sports Commission (ASC) is responsible for implementing the Australian Government's national sports policy, which is based on a sports philosophy of excellence and participation. It promotes an effective national sports system that offers improved participation in quality sports activities by all Australians and helps the talented and motivated to reach their potential excellence in sports performance. Its work is guided by the Australian Government's national sports policy, Building Australian Communities through Sport (BACTS).

Biomechanics Postgraduate Scholarship (General Sports)
Subjects: Sports.
Purpose: To provide an opportunity for graduates with degrees with a major emphasis in biomechanics to have experience in the application of biomechanics to enhance elite sports performance.
Eligibility: Applicants must have tertiary qualification in science, human movement, mathematics or a related area, should have an interest and/or understanding of research principles and some knowledge of biomechanical systems and equipment.
Level of Study: Graduate
Type: Scholarship
Value: Australian $21,434 per year
Length of Study: 48 weeks
No. of awards offered: 3
Application Procedure: Applicants must submit a covering letter, a statement of experience and curriculum vitae along with the application form.
Closing Date: September 29th

For further information contact:

Tel: 02 6214 1659
Email: recruitment@ausport.gov.au
Contact: Dale Barnes

Indigenous Sporting Excellence Scholarships
Subjects: Sports.
Purpose: To give indigenous sportspeople the opportunity to improve their sporting performance at an elite level.

Eligibility: Applicants must be over 12 years of age, representing their state in national competition or Australia internationally within sport or the school sport system, a coach with level 1 or level 2 accreditation, a sports trainer with level 1 accreditation, a sports official with accreditation, competing in a sport that is recognized by the Australian Sports Commission.
Type: Scholarship
Value: Australian $500
No. of awards offered: 100
Application Procedure: Check website for further details.
Additional Information: Athletes, coaches, sports trainers and officials who receive this scholarship are also eligible to apply for the Elite Indigenous Travel and Accommodation Assistance Program if they are selected for a state representative team attending national championships or an Australian team competing internationally.

National Coaching Scholarship Program

Subjects: Sports.
Purpose: To provide opportunities for potential and current elite coaches to develop skills and knowledge to coach effectively in high-performance programs.
Eligibility: Applicants should be a coach. They are expected to be integrally involved in the elite program in which they are placed.
Level of Study: Coach
Type: Scholarship
Length of Study: 1–2 years
Application Procedure: Check website for further details.
Funding: Government

Performance Analysis Scholarship

Subjects: Sports.
Purpose: To provide performance analysis services to AIS sport programmes through coaches as directed and as required work on projects relating to enhancement of knowledge and coach education.
Eligibility: Applicants must have a tertiary qualification in computer science, software engineering, information technology, human movement or a related area and an interest and/or understanding of research principles.
Type: Scholarship
Value: Australian $21,434 per year
Length of Study: 48 weeks
Application Procedure: Applicants must write a covering letter referencing the position title, prepare a thorough (but concise) statement that focuses on the relevant experience, curriculum vitae that summarize the qualifications including contact details for two referees and can be submitted by email.
Closing Date: September 29th

For further information contact:

Tel: 02 6214 1659
Email: recruitment@ausport.gov.au
Website: www.ausport.gov.au
Contact: Dale Barnes

Physiotherapy Postgraduate Scholarship

Subjects: Sports.
Purpose: To provide intensive technical and practical training combined with a research element aimed at providing a postgraduate with a good grounding in the field of sports physiotherapy.
Eligibility: Applicants must be Australian citizens and recent graduates of a physiotherapy degree having relevant sports-specific experience and a proven level of academic and professional excellence and should have an outstanding record and ambition to develop their professional skills in the sport physiotherapy area.
Level of Study: Graduate
Type: Scholarship
Value: Australian $26,266
Length of Study: 45 weeks
Application Procedure: Applications must provide personal particulars, academic qualifications, a history of experience, name of two referees who may be contacted to provide support for your application. Enquiries should be addressed to the Head of Department of Physical Therapies.
Closing Date: September 7th

For further information contact:

Australian Sports Commission, PO Box 176, Belconnen, ACT 2617
Contact: Craig Purdam, Head of Department of Physical Therapies

Postgraduate Scholarship Program–Physiology (Quality Control)

Subjects: Physiology.
Purpose: To provide opportunity for a graduate whose primary role will be to assist in the area of quality control under the direction of the laboratory manager.
Eligibility: Applicants must have a tertiary qualification in science or a related area, an interest and/or understanding of research principles and an experience in an administrative role and good computing skills.
Level of Study: Graduate
Type: Scholarship
Value: Australian $21,434 per year
Length of Study: 54 weeks
Application Procedure: Applicants must submit a covering letter, a statement of experience and curriculum vitae along with the application form.
Closing Date: September 29th

For further information contact:

Tel: 02 6214 1564
Email: recruitment@ausport.gov.au
Contact: Marilyn Dickson, Manager

Postgraduate Scholarship–Biomechanics (Swimming)

Subjects: Sports.
Purpose: To provide the opportunity for graduates of degrees with major emphasis in biomechanics and to have experience in the application of biomechanics to enhance elite sports performance.
Eligibility: Applicants must have a degree in biomechanics or human movement sciences, an interest and/or understanding of research principles, experience in biomechanics services and knowledge of and experience in a competitive swimming environment.
Level of Study: Graduate
Type: Scholarship
Value: Australian $21,434 per year
Length of Study: 48 weeks
Application Procedure: Applicants must submit a covering letter, a statement of experience and curriculum vitae along with the application form.
Closing Date: September 29th

For further information contact:

Tel: 02 6214 1732
Email: recruitment@ausport.gov.au
Contact: Clare Jones

Postgraduate Scholarship–Physiology (Biochemistry/Haematology)

Subjects: Physiology.
Purpose: To provide an opportunity for a graduate whose primary role will be to assist in the area of biochemistry and haematology under the direction of the biochemistry/haematology manager.
Eligibility: Applicants must have a degree in medical laboratory science or biological sciences and an interest and/or understanding of research principles, good computer skills.
Level of Study: Postgraduate
Type: Scholarship
Value: Australian $21,434 per year
Length of Study: 50 weeks
Application Procedure: Applicants must write a covering letter referencing the position title, prepare a thorough (but concise) statement that focuses on the relevant experience, curriculum vitae that summarize the qualifications including contact details for two referees and can be submitted by email.
Closing Date: September 29th

For further information contact:

Tel: (02) 6214 1700
Email: recruitment@ausport.gov.au

Website: www.ausport.gov.au
Contact: Graeme Allbon

Sport Leadership Grants for Women Program

Subjects: Sports.
Purpose: To provide women with an opportunity to undertake sport leadership training.
Eligibility: Applicants must be indigenous women, women in disability sport, women from culturally and linguistically diverse backgrounds and women in general sport leadership.
Type: Grant
Value: Up to Australian $5,000 for individuals and up to Australian $10,000 for incorporated organizations
Application Procedure: Check website for further details.
Funding: Government

For further information contact:

Tel: (02) 6214 7994
Email: leadershipgrants@ausport.gov.au

Sports Physiology Postgraduate Scholarship–Fatigue and Recovery

Subjects: Physiology.
Purpose: To offer an Honours graduate in science or a related field the opportunity to complete a scholarship in physiology (fatigue and recovery).
Eligibility: Applicants must have an Honours Degree in science or a related area, basic skills in conducting routine physiological testing procedures, good computing skills, outstanding organizational skills and a high level of initiative.
Level of Study: Graduate
Type: Scholarship
Value: Australian $19,890 per year
Length of Study: 12 months
Application Procedure: Applicants must submit a covering letter, a statement of experience and curriculum vitae along with the application form.
Closing Date: April 6th

For further information contact:

Tel: 02 6214 1589
Email: Recruitment@ausport.gov.au
Website: www.ausport.gov.au
Contact: Shona Halson

AUSTRALIAN–AMERICAN FULBRIGHT COMMISSION

PO Box 9541, Deakin, ACT 2600, Australia
Tel: (61) 2 6260 4460
Fax: (61) 2 6260 4461
Email: lwilson@fulbright.com.au
Website: www.fulbright.com.au
Contact: Ms Lyndell Wilson, Programme Manager

The Australian–American Fulbright Commision is a non-profit organization in Australia, established through a binational treaty between the Australian and United States governments in 1949 under the auspices of the United States Educational Foundation (USEFA) in Australia. The mission of the Commission is to further mutual understanding between the people of Australia and the United States through educational and cultural exchange.

Fulbright Postdoctoral Fellowships

Subjects: All subjects.
Purpose: To enable those who have recently completed their PhD to conduct postdoctoral research, to further their professional training or lecture at a university in the United States of America.
Eligibility: Open to Australian citizens by birth or naturalization. Those holding dual United States of America and Australian citizenship are not eligible. Applicants should have recently completed their PhD, normally less than 3 years prior to application, although those who have completed their PhD 4 or 5 years prior to application will be considered.

Level of Study: Postdoctorate
Type: Fellowship
Value: Up to Australian $30,000
Length of Study: 3–12 months
Frequency: Annual
Study Establishment: A university, college or research establishment or reputable private practice
Country of Study: United States of America
No. of awards offered: 1
Application Procedure: Applicants must complete and submit an application form along with three reference reports, already included in the application pack, documentation of citizenship and qualifications. Further information and application packs are available from the website.
Closing Date: August 31st
Funding: Government

Fulbright Postgraduate Awards

Subjects: All subjects.
Purpose: To enable students to undertake an approved course of study for an American higher degree or equivalent, or to engage in research relevant to an Australian higher degree.
Eligibility: Open to Australian citizens by birth or naturalization. Those holding dual United States of America and Australian citizenship are not eligible.
Level of Study: Doctorate, Postgraduate
Type: Studentship
Value: Up to Australian $40,000
Length of Study: 8–12 months funded, renewable for up to 5 years unfunded
Frequency: Annual
Study Establishment: An accredited institution
Country of Study: United States of America
No. of awards offered: Up to 12
Application Procedure: Applicants must complete an application form and submit this with three reference reports, already included in the application pack, and documentation of citizenship and qualifications. Naturalized citizens must provide a certificate of Australian citizenship with their application, and native-born Australians must provide a copy of their birth certificate. Further information and application packs are available from the website.
Closing Date: August 31st
Funding: Government
Additional Information: As the award does not include any provision for maintenance payments, applicants must be able to demonstrate that they have sufficient financial resources to support themselves and any dependants during their stay in the United States of America.

Fulbright Postgraduate Student Award for Science and Engineering

Subjects: Science and engineering.
Purpose: To enable candidates to undertake an approved course of study for an American higher degree, or to engage in research relevant to an Australian higher degree.
Eligibility: Open to Australian citizens. Those with dual United States of America and Australia citizenship are not eligible.
Level of Study: Postgraduate, Doctorate
Value: Up to Australian $40,000
Length of Study: 8–12 months funded or up to 4 years unfunded
Frequency: Annual
Study Establishment: An accredited institution
Country of Study: United States of America
No. of awards offered: 1
Application Procedure: Applicants must complete and submit an application form along with three reference reports, already included in the application pack, documentation of citizenship and qualifications. Further information and application packs are available from the website.
Closing Date: August 31st
Funding: Commercial, government
Contributor: Billiton Pvt. Ltd

Fulbright Postgraduate Student Award for the Visual and Performing Arts

Subjects: Fine and applied arts.
Purpose: To enable candidates to undertake a higher degree, or carry out research towards an Australian higher degree.

Eligibility: Open to Australian citizens. Those with dual United States of America and Australian citizenship are not eligible.
Level of Study: Doctorate, Postgraduate, Professional development
Value: Up to Australian $40,000
Length of Study: 8–12 months funded or up to 4 years unfunded
Frequency: Annual
Country of Study: United States of America
No. of awards offered: 1
Application Procedure: Applicants must complete and submit an application form along with three reference reports, already included in the application pack, documentation of citizenship and qualifications. Further information and application packs are available from the website.
Closing Date: August 31st
Funding: Commercial, government
Contributor: Anthony Joseph Pratt

Fulbright Professional Award

Subjects: All professional fields. Programmes should include an academic as well as a practical aspect.
Purpose: These awards are available to professionals from public and private sectors (junior to middle level staff poised for advancement to a senior level research or undertaking a programme of professional development in the United States of America.
Eligibility: Open to resident Australian citizens with a record of achievement poised for advancement to a senior management or policy role. Those holding dual United States of America and Australian citizenship are not eligible.
Level of Study: Professional development
Type: Award
Value: Up to Australian $25,000
Length of Study: 3–4 months. Programmes of longer duration may be proposed, but without additional funding
Frequency: Annual
Country of Study: United States of America
No. of awards offered: 4
Application Procedure: Applicants must complete and submit an application form along with three reference reports, already included in the application pack, documentation of citizenship and qualifications. Further information and application packs are available from the website.
Closing Date: August 31st
Funding: Government

Fulbright Professional Award for Vocational Education and Training

Subjects: Vocational education.
Purpose: To enable candidates to visit institutions or organizations and people in the United States of America from their own field.
Eligibility: Open to Australian citizens employed in the vocational education and training sector. Those holding dual United States of America and Australian citizenship are not eligible.
Level of Study: Professional development
Value: Up to Australian $20,000
Length of Study: 3–4 months funded
Frequency: Annual
Country of Study: United States of America
No. of awards offered: 1
Application Procedure: Applicants must complete and submit an application form along with three reference reports, already included in the application pack, documentation of citizenship and qualifications. Further information and application packs are available from the website.
Closing Date: August 31st
Funding: Government
Contributor: The Australian National Training Authority
No. of awards given last year: 1

Fulbright Senior Scholar Awards

Subjects: All subjects.
Purpose: To allow candidates to teach, undertake research, be an invited speaker or visit institutions within their field.
Eligibility: Open to Australian citizens by birth or naturalization. Those holding dual United States of America and Australian citizenship are not eligible. Applicants should be either scholars of estab-

lished reputation working in an academic institution, who intend to teach or research in the United States of America, leaders in the arts, e.g. music, drama, visual arts or senior members of the academically based professions who are currently engaged in the private practice of their profession.
Level of Study: Professional development
Value: Up to Australian $30,000
Length of Study: 4–6 months
Frequency: Annual
Study Establishment: A university, college, research establishment or reputable private organization
Country of Study: United States of America
No. of awards offered: 2
Application Procedure: Applicants must complete an application form and submit this with three reference reports, already included in the application pack, documentation of citizenship and qualifications. Further information and application packs are available from the website. Naturalized citizens must provide a certificate of Australian citizenship with their application, and native-born Australians must provide a copy of their birth certificate.
Closing Date: August 31st
Funding: Government

AUSTRIAN ACADEMY OF SCIENCES

Institute of Limnology, Mondseestrasse 9, A-5310 Mondsee, Austria
Tel: (43) 623 240 79
Fax: (43) 623 235 78
Email: ipgl.mondsee@oeaw.ac.at
Website: www.ipgl.at
Contact: Mr Gerold Winkler, IPGL Course Manager

With 1100 employee and 60 research institutions the Austrian Academy of Sciences is the leading organization promoting non-university academic research in Austria. The Institute of Limnology performs ecological research on inland waters to understand the structure, functions and dynamics of freshwater ecosystems. The IPGL office acts as a hub for postgraduate training, research and international networking.

Austrian Academy of Sciences, MSc Course in Limnology and Wetland Ecosystems

Subjects: Aquatic systems.
Purpose: To understand the structure and functioning of aquatic and wetland ecosystems for the conservation of biodiversity and sustainable management of natural resources. To acquire skills for interacting with stakeholders, managers and policy makers in the development of best practices.
Eligibility: Open to candidates from developing countries who are maximum 35 years of age, have a good working knowledge of English and have an academic degree in science, agriculture or veterinary medicine from a university or any other recognized Institute of Higher Education. Applicants should have 3 years practical experience in at least one special subject in their field of professional training. All applications are considered on their individual merits.
Level of Study: Postgraduate
Type: Scholarship
Value: US$1,350 paid monthly to cover food, lodging and personal needs plus free tuition, health insurance, study material and equipment for laboratory work, field work and travelling expenses
Length of Study: 18 months
Frequency: Annual
Study Establishment: Institute for Limnology, Mondsee; Institute UNESCO-IHE, Delft, The Netherlands; Makerere University, Kampala, Uganda; Egerton University, Kenya; Czech Academy of Sciences, Trebon, Czech Republic; Austrian Universities and Federal Institutes in Austria
No. of awards offered: 4
Application Procedure: Applicants must obtain application forms from the website. Filled application forms can be sent to
Closing Date: End of January
Funding: Government
Contributor: The Austrian Development Co-operation
No. of awards given last year: 4
No. of applicants last year: 70

Additional Information: No provisions are made for dependants. It is strongly advised that dependants do not accompany fellows due to frequent moves during the course. Fellows must also provide their own transportation to and from Austria.

For further information contact:

IPGL-Course, Institute for Limnology of the Austrian Academy of Sciences, Mondseestrasse 9, A-5310 Mondsee, Austria
Tel: (43) 6232/4079
Fax: (43) 6232/3578

AUSTRIAN SCIENCE FUND (FWF)

Haus der Forschung, Sensengasse 1, Vienna, 1090, Austria
Tel: (43) 43 1 505 67 40
Fax: (43) 43 1 505 67 39
Email: office@fwf.ac.at
Website: www.fwf.ac.at
Contact: Scientific Administrator

The Austrian Science Fund (FWF) is Austria's central body for the promotion of basic research. It is equally committed to all branches of science and in all its activities it is guided solely by the standards of the international scientific community. Its mission is the promotion of high-quality basic research, education and training through research and scientific culture and knowledge transfer.

Charlotte Bühler Habilitation Fellowships

Subjects: All subjects.
Purpose: To support and encourage young female scientists to become future university lecturers.
Eligibility: Open to female scientists up to the age of 40, who are residents of Austria.
Level of Study: Postdoctorate
Type: A variable number of fellowships
Value: Please contact the organization
Length of Study: 1–2 years
Frequency: 6 times per year
No. of awards offered: Varies
Application Procedure: Applicants must complete an application form, available from the Austrian Science Fund, from the website or by email.
Closing Date: Applications are accepted at any time
Funding: Government

Elise Richter Program

Subjects: All subjects.
Purpose: To support the career of highly qualified female scientists and scholars.
Eligibility: The candidate should possess appropriate postdoctoral experience.
Level of Study: Postdoctorate
Type: Research
Value: €15,000 (project specific costs), €59,670 (personal costs) and €1,950 (lump sum per child per year)
Length of Study: 12–48 months
Frequency: Twice a year
Closing Date: May 31st

For further information contact:

Tel: 43 1 505 67 40 ext. 8503
Email: susanne.menschik@fwf.ac.at
Contact: Susanne Menschik

Erwin Schrödinger Fellowships

Subjects: All subjects.
Purpose: To offer citizens the opportunity to work in leading foreign research institutions and research programmes.
Eligibility: Open to highly qualified Austrian citizens up to the age of 35.
Level of Study: Postdoctorate
Type: Fellowship
Value: €28,200–35,000
Length of Study: 10 months–2 years
Frequency: 6 times per year

Study Establishment: Universities or research institutions
No. of awards offered: Varies
Application Procedure: Applicants must complete an application form, available from the Austrian Science Fund, from the website or by email. All necessary details can be found on the website www.fwf. ac.at/en/projects/erwin-schroedinger.html
Closing Date: Applications are accepted at any time
Funding: Government
No. of awards given last year: 55
No. of applicants last year: 117

EURYI–Award

Subjects: All subjects.
Purpose: To enable young scientists all over the world to work in European research institution for 5 years.
Eligibility: Open to applicants who possess between 2 and a maximum of 8 years of postdoctoral experience.
Level of Study: Postdoctorate
Type: Award
Value: €150,000–250,000 per year
Length of Study: 5 years
No. of awards offered: 25
Application Procedure: Applicants should submit their application in English and the decision will be taken by EURYI–Jury on the basis of an international peer-review process.
Closing Date: November 30th
Contributor: EUROHORCS in co-operation with the European Science Foundation (ESF)

For further information contact:

Tel: 43 1 505 67 40 ext 8701
Email: reinhard.belocky@fwf.ac.at
Contact: Reinhard Belocky

Hertha Firnberg Research Positions for Women

Subjects: All subjects.
Purpose: To support and encourage young female scientists and expand scientific career opportunities for women.
Eligibility: Open to female scientists up to the age of 40 who are residents of Austria.
Level of Study: Postdoctorate
Type: Position (Employment)
Value: €52,790 personnel costs per year plus €8,000 for material, travel, assistance
Length of Study: 3 years
Frequency: Annual
Study Establishment: Any university
Country of Study: Austria
No. of awards offered: 10
Application Procedure: Applicants must complete an application form, available from the Austrian Science Fund, from the website or by email. All necessary details can be found on the website www.fwf. ac.at/en/projects/firnberg.html
Closing Date: December
Funding: Government
No. of awards given last year: 11
No. of applicants last year: 43

Lise Meitner Program

Subjects: All subjects.
Purpose: To offer foreign scientists an opportunity to carry out research in Austria and to enhance the Austrian scientific community through international contacts.
Eligibility: Open to highly qualified foreign scientists up to the age of 40.
Level of Study: Postdoctorate
Type: Position (Employment)
Value: €52,790 (Post Doctorate); €59,670 (Senior Post Doctorate) plus €8,000 for material, travel, assistance
Length of Study: 1–2 years
Frequency: Annual, 6 times per year
Study Establishment: Universities or research institutions
Country of Study: Austria
No. of awards offered: Varies

Application Procedure: Applicants must complete an application form, available from the Austrian Science Fund, from the website or by email. All necessary details can be found on the website: www.fwf. ac.at/en/projects/meitner.html
Closing Date: Applications are accepted at any time
Funding: Government
No. of awards given last year: 35
No. of applicants last year: 86

START Program
Subjects: All subjects.
Purpose: To support outstanding young researchers of any discipline.
Eligibility: Open to applicants who possess at least 2 and at most 10 years of postdoctoral experience at the time of application.
Level of Study: Postdoctorate
Value: Up to €200,000 per year
Length of Study: 6 years, with an interim review after 3 years
No. of awards offered: About 5
Funding: Government
Contributor: Federal Ministry for Science and Research (BMWF)

For further information contact:

Tel: 43 1 505 67 40 ext 8605
Email: mario.mandl@fwf.ac.at
Contact: Mario Mandl

Translational Research Program
Subjects: All subjects.
Purpose: To promote cooperation between scientists at universities with scientists at extra-university research institutions or other institutes of higher education.
Eligibility: Open to candidates who possess high scientific quality at international level.
Level of Study: Research
Value: €76,300 per year
Length of Study: Maximum 36 months
Closing Date: September 6th

For further information contact:

Tel: 43 1 505 67 40 ext. 8602
Email: milojka.gindl@fwf.ac.at
Contact: Milojka Gindl

Wittgenstein Award
Subjects: All subjects.
Purpose: To support outstanding researchers of any discipline.
Eligibility: The candidate should possess international recognition in the field and be employed in an Austrian research organization and should be aged 55 or under at the time of nomination.
Level of Study: Professional development, Research
Type: Research
Value: Up to €1.5 million per award
Length of Study: 5 years
Frequency: Annual
No. of awards offered: 1–2
Funding: Government
Contributor: Federal Minister for Science

For further information contact:

Tel: 43 1 505 67 40 ext 8605
Email: mario.mandl@fwf.ac.at
Contact: Mario Mandl

AUSTRO-AMERICAN ASSOCIATION OF BOSTON

82 Dover Road, Wellesley, MA, 02482, United States of America
Tel: (1) 781 283 2255
Email: thansen@wellesley.edu
Website: www.austria-boston.org
Contact: Professor Thomas S. Hansen, Chairman of Scholarship Committee

Membership of the Austro-American Association of Boston is open to any individual interested in any aspect of Austrian history, economy, culture, politics and tourism. The association conducts meetings and get togethers focussing on events and experiences related to Austria.

Austro-American Association of Boston Stipend
Subjects: Austrian cultural studies, history, folklore, literature, music, fine and applied arts, and film.
Purpose: To promote the understanding and dissemination of Austrian culture.
Eligibility: Junior faculty members and students enrolled in a college in New England.
Level of Study: Unrestricted
Type: Stipendiary
Value: US$1,000
Study Establishment: Any in New England
Country of Study: United States of America
No. of awards offered: 1
Application Procedure: Applicants must submit a detailed description of the project including the reasons for selecting it, a curriculum vitae and two letters of recommendation from faculty members who know the applicant well and can comment on the feasibility of the project.
Closing Date: March 15th
Funding: Private
Contributor: Association members
No. of applicants last year: 1
Additional Information: The award is limited to individuals living or studying in New England. Projects funded in the past have included the preparation of musical or dramatic performances, the facilitation of appropriate publications and research trips to Austria. Culture is defined to include the humanities and the arts. The recipient may be asked to present the results of the project at an event of the Austro-American Association. The award may not be used to pay tuition fees at a college or university in New England.

For further information contact:

Email: thansen@wellesley.edu
Contact: Professor T Hansen

AWSCPA

Administrative Offices, 136 South Keowee Street, Dayton, OH 45402, United States of America
Tel: (1) 937 222 1872
Fax: (1) 937 222 5794
Email: info@awscpa.org
Website: www.awscpa.org

The American Woman's Society of CPA provides annual scholarships to women working towards an accounting degree as well as to those working towards their Certified Public Accountant License.

AWSCPA National Scholarship
Subjects: Accounting.
Purpose: To fund women working towards an accounting degree.
Eligibility: Applicants must meet the minimum educational requirements to sit for the CPA exam within 1 year of the award of the scholarship.
Level of Study: Postgraduate
Type: Scholarship
Value: Approx. US$2,500
Frequency: Annual
No. of awards offered: 1 per year
Application Procedure: Apply through website.
Closing Date: March 15th
Funding: Foundation
Contributor: AWSCPA members and supporters
No. of awards given last year: 1
No. of applicants last year: 30

BACKCARE

16 Elmtree Road, Teddington, Middlesex, TW11 8ST, England
Tel: (44) 20 8977 5474
Fax: (44) 20 8943 5318
Email: info@backcare.org.uk
Website: www.backcare.org.uk
Contact: Dr Dries Hettinga, Chief Executive

BackCare is a national charity dedicated to educating people about how to avoid preventable back pain and support those living with back pain. BackCare provides education and information through its publications, telephone helpline, local branches and website. It also funds research and campaigns to raise the profile of issues surrounding back pain.

BackCare Research Grants

Subjects: Studies related to back pain.
Purpose: To reduce the incidences of disability from back pain and to improve its treatment by gaining, through research, a better understanding of its manifestation and causes.
Eligibility: Open to appropriately qualified and experienced persons.
Level of Study: Postgraduate
Type: Project grant
Value: Varies, dependent on funds available
Length of Study: Up to 2 years
Frequency: Dependent on funds available
Study Establishment: Suitable establishments
Country of Study: United Kingdom
No. of awards offered: Varies, depends on funds available
Application Procedure: Applicants must refer to the website for details of the application procedure.
Closing Date: Please check the website for details
Funding: Individuals, private, trusts
No. of awards given last year: 4
No. of applicants last year: 20

THE BANFF CENTRE

Arts Programming, Box 1020, Station 28, Banff, AB, T1L 1H5, Canada
Tel: (1) 403 762 6180/1 800 565 9989
Fax: (1) 403 762 6345
Email: arts_info@banffcentre.ca
Website: www.banffcentre.ca
Contact: Registrar

The Banff Centre is a catalyst for creativity, with a transformative impact on those who attend the programmes, conferences and events. Our alumni create, produce and perform works of art all over the world, lead our institutions, organizations and businesses, and play significant roles in our cultural, social, intellectual and economic well-being, and in the preservation of our environment.

Banff Centre Financial Assistance

Subjects: Studio art, photography, ceramics, performance art, video art, theatre production and design, stage management, opera, singing, dance, drama, music, writing, creative non-fiction and cultural journalism, publishing, media arts, television and video, audio recording, computer applications, research, audio engineering work study, theatre production, design stage management work study, Aboriginal arts programmes in dance training, programme publicity and theatre production work study and screenwriting.
Purpose: To provide financial assistance to deserving artists for a residency at The Banff Centre.
Eligibility: Open to advanced students who have been accepted for a residency at The Banff Centre.
Level of Study: Postgraduate, Professional development
Type: Grant
Value: A major contribution towards tuition
Length of Study: Varies
Frequency: Annual
Study Establishment: The Banff Centre, Arts Programming
Country of Study: Canada
No. of awards offered: Varies
Application Procedure: Applicants must submit a completed application form, accompanied by requested documentation. See website for details.

Closing Date: Varies according to programme
Funding: Government, private
Contributor: Individual donations and The Banff Centre revenues
No. of awards given last year: 1,000

Paul D. Fleck Fellowships in the Arts

Purpose: To allow artists in all disciplines to participate in independent artists residencies at the Banff centre to create new work or collaborate with other arts programmes at the centre.
Eligibility: Nomination.
Level of Study: Postgraduate, Professional development, Research
Type: Fellowship/Scholarship
Value: Tuition, accommodation, meals and in approved circumstances, a travel award
Frequency: Annual
Study Establishment: Arts programming, The Banff Centre
Country of Study: Canada
No. of awards offered: Varies
Application Procedure: See website for details.
Closing Date: Spring
Funding: Individuals, private, trusts
No. of awards given last year: Varies
No. of applicants last year: Varies

Susan and Graeme Mc Donald Music Scholarships

Purpose: To bring gifted musicians together from across Canada and around the world for transformational learning experiences in Banff centre music programs.
Level of Study: Graduate, Professional development
Type: Scholarship
Value: Varies
Length of Study: Varies
Frequency: Annual
Study Establishment: Music Programs, The Banff Centre
Country of Study: Canada
No. of awards offered: Varies
Application Procedure: See website for details.
Closing Date: Varies according to programme
Funding: Private, trusts
No. of awards given last year: Varies

BANGOR UNIVERSITY

Bangor, Gwynedd, LL57 2DG, Wales
Tel: (44) 12 4838 2025/18
Fax: (44) 12 4837 0451
Email: aos061@bangor.ac.uk
Website: www.bangor.ac.uk
Contact: Ms Sarah Wale, The Student Recruitment Unit

Bangor University is the principal seat of learning, scholarship and research in North Wales. Established in 1884, the University attaches considerable importance to research training in all disciplines and offers research studentships of a value similar to those of other United Kingdom public funding bodies.

Bursaries

Subjects: Electronic engineering and computer science.
Purpose: To provide financial support, based on academic performance, for full-time masters students of all courses.
Eligibility: Open to applicants who have already been offered a place in one of the postgraduate degree courses.
Level of Study: Postgraduate
Type: Bursary
Value: £1,000
Frequency: Dependent on funds available
Study Establishment: Bangor University
Country of Study: United Kingdom
No. of awards offered: Unspecified
Application Procedure: Refer to the website for further details.
Contributor: Bangor University

Doctoral Scholarships

Purpose: To provide financial support to those undertaking full-time and research degrees.

Eligibility: Refer to the website for further details.
Type: Studentship and scholarship
Value: £12,000 per annum
Frequency: Annual
Study Establishment: Bangor University
Country of Study: United Kingdom
No. of awards offered: Unspecified
Application Procedure: Refer to the website.
Contributor: Bangor University anfd UK Research Councils

Gold and Silver Scholarships
Subjects: Banking, Mangement, Business and Finance.
Purpose: To provide financial support to full-time students on all MSc, MBA and MA programmes.
Eligibility: Open to applicants who wish to apply for a postgraduate MSc, MBA or MA degree programme included in the scholarship scheme.
Level of Study: Postgraduate, MBA
Type: Scholarship
Value: UK £ 2,000–5,000 per year
Length of Study: 1 year
Frequency: Annual
Study Establishment: Bangor University
Country of Study: United Kingdom
Application Procedure: There is no application form for scholarships. Candidates who wish to be considered for the awards should include a letter listing their main academic and personal achievements together with a short essay on why they have chosen to study at Bangor.
Closing Date: July
Funding: Government

For further information contact:

Bangor Business School, Bangor University, Bangor, Gwynedd, LL57-2DG, Wales
Tel: (44) 1248 382644
Fax: (44) 01248 383228
Email: b.hamilton@bangor.ac.uk
Website: www.bbs.bangor.ac.uk
Contact: Bethan Hamilton-Hine Scholarships (Gold and Silver)

Llewellyn and Mary Williams Scholarship
Subjects: All biological sciences, including marine biology.
Purpose: To support doctoral studies and research training in the biological sciences.
Eligibility: Open to First Class (Honours) Degree holders who are classified as home or European Union students for fee purposes.
Level of Study: Doctorate, Postgraduate
Type: Scholarship
Value: Equal to that of a British Research Council Studentship
Length of Study: 3 years
Frequency: Dependent on funds available
Study Establishment: Bangor University
Country of Study: United Kingdom
No. of awards offered: 2
Application Procedure: This scholarship is allocated annually. Applicants must contact the Head of the School for details. Nominations are sought by the school of Biological Science and the School of Ocean Science.
Closing Date: May 15th
Funding: Private
No. of awards given last year: 3
No. of applicants last year: 10

MA/MPhil/PhD Scholarships
Subjects: English, history, Welsh history and archaeology, linguistics, modern linguistics, music, theology and religious studies and Welsh.
Eligibility: Open to students seeking places on MA, MPhil or PhD courses within the College of Arts and Humanities or in any of its research units or institutes.
Level of Study: Postgraduate, Doctorate, Postdoctorate
Type: Scholarship
Value: £2,000, subject to ratification
Frequency: Annual
Study Establishment: Bangor University

Country of Study: United Kingdom
No. of awards offered: Unspecified
Application Procedure: Refer to the website.
Closing Date: June 29th

For further information contact:

Email: s.lee@bangor.ac.uk

Mr and Mrs David Edward Memorial Award
Subjects: All subjects offered by the University.
Purpose: To support doctoral studies in any subject area.
Eligibility: Open to holders of a relevant First Class (Honours) Degree or, exceptionally, Upper Second Class (Honours) Degree, who are classified as United Kingdom or European Union students for fee purposes.
Level of Study: Doctorate, Postgraduate
Type: Award
Value: No less than that of a Research Council or British Academy Research Studentship, including fees
Length of Study: 1 year, renewable for a maximum of a further 2 years if satisfactory progress is maintained
Frequency: Dependent on funds available
Study Establishment: Bangor University
Country of Study: United Kingdom
No. of awards offered: 1
Application Procedure: Nominations are made by the University and nominees are invited to submit formal applications.
Funding: Private
No. of awards given last year: 1
No. of applicants last year: 20

MSc Bursaries
Subjects: Sports and exercise psychology, sports and exercise physiology, sports science and exercise rehabilitation.
Eligibility: Open to applicants with good second class honours degree in sports science or health and to students with a 2:2 degree or a degree from a different academic area will also be considered.
Level of Study: Postgraduate
Type: Bursary
Value: £2,500 (UK/EU students); £3,500 (non-EU international students)
Length of Study: 1 year (full-time); 2 years (part-time); 30 weeks full-time (Diploma)
Frequency: Dependent on funds available
Study Establishment: Bangor University
Country of Study: United Kingdom
No. of awards offered: Unspecified
Application Procedure: Refer to the website.
Contributor: Bangor University

For further information contact:

Tel: 01248 383493
Email: mscsport@bangor.ac.uk/
Website: www.shes.bangor.ac.uk/
Contact: Dr James Hardy

NERC Studentships
Subjects: Applied physical oceanography and marine environment protection.
Purpose: To support students who wish to pursue studies related to oceanography.
Eligibility: Open to applicants who already have, or expect to obtain, a first class or upper second class honours degree in an appropriate subject.
Level of Study: Doctorate, Postgraduate
Type: Studentship
Value: Stipend plus fees for UK nationals; fees only for EU nationals; UK residency qualification may allow funding for non-EU nationals. Refer NERC website for further details
Study Establishment: Bangor University
Country of Study: United Kingdom
No. of awards offered: 4 (for Applied physical oceanography), 5 (for Marine environment protection)

Application Procedure: Applicants must submit a completed application form, a curriculum vitae (with work and academic experience) and a covering letter with reasons for applying for the funding.
Closing Date: March 23rd
Contributor: NERC

For further information contact:

Postgraduate admissions office, Main Arts Building, College Road, Bangor, Gwynedd, LL57 2DG, United Kingdom

Open PhD Studentships

Subjects: English, history, Welsh history and archaeology, linguistics and English language, modern languages, music, theology and religious studies, Welsh creative industries.
Eligibility: Open to candidates who have applied unsuccessfully to a UK funding council (e.g. the AHRC or the ESRC) to study at Bangor.
Level of Study: Doctorate
Type: Studentship
Value: Fees plus maintenance grant
Frequency: Dependent on funds available
Application Procedure: Applicants must submit a scholarship application form along with a summary of your proposed research project in up to 500 words.
Closing Date: June 29th

For further information contact:

Email: s.lee@bangor.ac.uk

PhD Studentships

Subjects: Law.
Purpose: To fund research training at the PhD level.
Eligibility: Open to candidates classified as United Kingdom and European Union students for fee purposes who have attained a First Class (Honours) Degree or, exceptionally, an Upper Second Class (Honours) Degree or equivalent.
Level of Study: Postgraduate, Doctorate
Type: Studentship
Value: Equal to that of a British Research Council Studentship
Length of Study: 1 year, renewable for a maximum of 2 additional years
Frequency: Annual
Study Establishment: Bangor University
Country of Study: United Kingdom
No. of awards offered: Unspecified
Application Procedure: Applicants must contact the relevant department of proposed study. The department will nominate the most worthy and eligible stidents.
Closing Date: Refer to the website
Funding: Private
Contributor: Drapers Trust/Thomas Hovells Law PhD scholarship
No. of awards given last year: 11
No. of applicants last year: 90

Sir William Roberts Scholarship

Subjects: Agriculture and agricultural science (not forestry).
Purpose: To fund research training at the PhD level.
Eligibility: Open to candidates classified as home/EU based who have attained a First Class (Honours) Degree or Upper Second Class (Honours) Degree. These scholarships are allocated to the School of The Environment and Natural Resources and the School of Biological Sciences.
Level of Study: Postgraduate, Doctorate
Type: Scholarship
Value: Equal to that of a British Research Council Research Studentship
Length of Study: 1 year, renewable for a maximum of 2 additional years
Study Establishment: Bangor University
Country of Study: United Kingdom
No. of awards offered: 2
Application Procedure: Applicants must contact the Head of the relevant School.
Closing Date: June 1st
Funding: Private
No. of awards given last year: 2
No. of applicants last year: 20

BATTEN DISEASE SUPPORT AND RESEARCH ASSOCIATION

120 Humphries Drive, Reynoldsburg, OH, 43068, United States of America
Tel: (1) 740 927 4298
Fax: (1) 740 927 7683
Email: bdsra1@bdsra.org
Website: www.bdsra.org
Contact: Mr Lance W Johnston, Executive Director

The Batten Disease Support and Research Association provides information, education, medical referrals and support to families that have children with NCL or Batten Disease. The Association also provides funding for research into Batten Disease.

Batten Disease Support and Research Association Research Grant Awards

Subjects: NCL or Batten Disease in the areas of genetics, biochemistry, molecular biology and related areas with the eventual goal of developing a viable treatment.
Purpose: To support work that identifies genes, proteins, enzymes or additional NCLs and the development of novel therapeutic treatments.
Eligibility: There are no eligibility restrictions.
Level of Study: Doctorate, Postdoctorate, Research
Value: Varies
Length of Study: Research is for 1 year and doctorate and postdoctorate are up to 3 years
Frequency: Annual
Country of Study: Any country
Application Procedure: RFP (request for proposals) will be posted on website: www.bdsra.org, follow instructions contained in RFP.
Closing Date: June 15th
Funding: Private
No. of awards given last year: 8
No. of applicants last year: 25

BBC WRITERSROOM

Grafton House, 379–381 Euston Road, London, NW1 3AU, United Kingdom
Email: writersroom@bbc.co.uk
Website: www.bbc.co.uk/writersroom/opportunity

BBC Writersroom identifies and champions new writing talent and diversity across BBC Drama, Entertainment and Children's programmes. Writersroom is constantly on the lookout for writers of any age and experience who show real potential for the BBC. It invests in new writing projects nationwide and builds creative partnerships, including work with theatres, writer's organizations and film agencies across the country.

Alfred Bradley Bursary Award

Subjects: Drama.
Purpose: To encourage and develop new radio writing talent in the BBC North region.
Eligibility: Entrants must live or have been brought or born in the North of England.
Level of Study: Professional development
Type: Bursary
Value: Up to UK £6,000 and a BBC Radio Drama commission
Frequency: Every 2 years
Country of Study: United Kingdom
Application Procedure: Applicants must send completed afternoon play scripts for consideration. Details published on www.bbc.co.uk/writersroom
Closing Date: Varies-bi-annual
Funding: Corporation, private
Contributor: BBC
Additional Information: There is a change of focus for each award, e.g. previous years have targeted comedy, drama, verse drama, etc. In 2004, the brief was for a play suitable for the afternoon play slot.

Writers-in-Residence with NCH, the Children's Charity
Subjects: All subjects.
Purpose: To enable young writers to work in residence with selected NCH projects during their 'Growing Strong' campaign, which focuses on young people's emotional well-being, inner-strength and confidence.
Eligibility: Applicants must be talented writers with professional experience.
Type: Bursary
Value: £3,000
Length of Study: 3 months
Country of Study: United Kingdom
No. of awards offered: 5
Application Procedure: Applicants must write a covering letter explaining why he/she would like to take part in the residency and a brief outline of a proposed project idea, a curriculum vitae detailing their relevant professional experience and a writing sample (full script) and send hard copies marked 'NCH Writer in Residence' to BBC Writersroom.
Closing Date: October 19th
Additional Information: Residencies will be based in London, Glasgow, Belfast, Cardiff and Liverpool.

BEINECKE SCHOLARSHIP PROGRAM

c/o Office of International Education and Fellowship Programs, Box 208351, Yale Station, New Haven, CT 06520-8351, United States of America
Tel: (1) 203 432 8685
Email: BeineckeScholarship@earthlink.net
Website: www.beineckescholarship.org

The Beinecke Scholarship Program, established in 1970, seeks to encourage and enable highly motivated students to take the fullest advantage of graduate opportunities available to them and be courageous in the selection of graduate study programmes.

Beinecke Scholarship
Subjects: Liberal arts mathematics and natural sciences.
Purpose: To encourage and enable highly motivated students to pursue opportunities available to them.
Eligibility: Open to US citizens or US national from American Samoa or the commonwealth of Northern Mariana Islands with superior standards of intellectual ability, scholastic achievement and personal.
Level of Study: Postgraduate
Type: Scholarship
Value: US$34,000
Length of Study: 1–5 years
Study Establishment: Any accredited university
No. of awards offered: 20
Application Procedure: Request and submit a completed application form a curriculum vitae, a personal statement of 1,000 words and three letters of recommendation from faculty members.
Closing Date: March 1st
Funding: Corporation
Contributor: The Sperry Fund

For further information contact:

Scholarship Connection 301 Compbell Hall
Email: scholarships@learning.berkeley.edu
Website: www.//scholarships.berkeley.edu

BEIT MEMORIAL FELLOWSHIPS FOR MEDICAL RESEARCH

c/o Institute of Molecular Medicine, John Radcliffe Hospital, Headington, Oxford, Oxfordshire, OX3 9DS, England
Email: beit.fellowships@hammer.imm.ox.ac.uk
Contact: Mrs Melanie J Goble, Administrative Secretary

Beit Memorial Fellowships for Medical Research
Subjects: Medical research.
Purpose: To promote research into medicine and allied sciences.
Eligibility: Open to postdoctoral level or medically qualified applicants who are graduates of any faculty at an approved university in the United Kingdom, or in any country that is or has been, since 1910, a British Dominion, Protectorate or Mandated Territory.
Level of Study: Postdoctorate, Research
Type: Fellowship
Value: United Kingdom salary plus research expenses
Length of Study: 3 years
Frequency: Annual
Study Establishment: An approved university, research institute or medical school in the UK or Ireland
No. of awards offered: Approx. 4
Application Procedure: Applicants must write for details.
Closing Date: March 1st

BEIT TRUST (ZIMBABWE, ZAMBIA AND MALAWI)

PO Box CH 76, Chisipite, Harare, Zimbabwe
Tel: (263) 4 496132
Fax: (263) 4 494046
Email: beitrust@africaonline.co.zw
Contact: T M Johnson, Representative

Beit Trust Postgraduate Scholarships
Subjects: All subjects.
Purpose: To support postgraduate study or research.
Eligibility: Open to persons under 30 years of age or 35 years for medical doctors, who are university graduates domiciled in Zambia, Zimbabwe or Malawi. Applicants must be nationals of those countries.
Level of Study: Postgraduate
Type: Scholarship
Value: A variable personal allowance and fees plus books, clothing, thesis and departure allowances
Length of Study: 1–3 years depending on course sought
Frequency: Annual
Study Establishment: Approved universities and other institutions in South Africa, Britain and Ireland
No. of awards offered: 10
Application Procedure: Applicants must complete an application form.
Closing Date: August 31st
Funding: Private
No. of awards given last year: 8
No. of applicants last year: 400
Additional Information: Zambian applicants should contact the BEIT Trust UK office. Zimbabwe and Malawi applicants should contact the Zimbabwe office.

For further information contact:

The BEIT Trust, BEIT House, Grove Road, Woking, Surrey, GU21 5JB, England
Tel: (44) 01483 772 575
Fax: (44) 01483 725 833
Email: enquiries@beittrust.org.uk

BELGIAN AMERICAN EDUCATIONAL FOUNDATION (BAEF)

Marie-Claude Hayoit, Egmontstraat 11 Rue d'Egmont, 1000 Brussels, Belgium
Tel: (32) 2 513 59 55
Fax: (32) 2 672 53 81
Email: mail@baef.be
Website: www.baef.be

The BAEF is a nonprofit organization, funded by the general public under United States Law, and engaged in fostering the higher education of deserving Belgians and Americans.

BAEF Alumni Award
Subjects: Mathematics, physics, chemistry, physical chemistry, geology, physical geography, and astronomy.

Purpose: To encourage young researchers in mathematics, physics, chemistry, physical chemistry, geology, physical geography, and astronomy.

Eligibility: Open to Belgian researchers who are below the age of 36 years.

Level of Study: Postgraduate

Type: Award

Length of Study: €5,000

Frequency: Annual

Application Procedure: A completed application form along with 10 copies of curriculum vitae and summary of complete scientific work must be sent.

Closing Date: March 1st

Fellowships for Biomedical Engineering Research

Subjects: Biomedical Engineering.

Purpose: To provide a stipend covering living and travel expenses and including health insurances.

Eligibility: Open to candidates who hold a university degree of a regular second cycle from a Belgian institution; should be nominated by a Rector or a Dean of Faculty from a recognized Belgian university; should have an outstanding academic record; should have good command of the English language, and engage in doctoral or post-doctoral biomedical engineering research in the USA.

Level of Study: Doctorate, Postdoctorate

Type: Fellowship

Value: $40,000

Length of Study: 1 year

Frequency: Annual

Country of Study: United States of America

Application Procedure: Check website for details.

Closing Date: October 31st

Funding: Foundation

Fellowships for Research in the U.S.A

Subjects: All subjects.

Purpose: To support advanced study or research.

Eligibility: Open to Belgian citizen holding a university degree of a regular second cycle or doctorate from a Belgian institution with an outstanding academic record and with a good command of the English language.

Type: Fellowship

Value: US$19,000 (for pre-doctoral fellows) and US$30,000 (for post-doctoral fellows) to cover living and travel expenses plus health insurance

Length of Study: 1 year

Frequency: Annual

Country of Study: Belgium

No. of awards offered: 8

Application Procedure: A completed application form along with three letters of recommendation must be sent.

Closing Date: October 31st

Fellowships for Study or Research in Belgium

Subjects: All subjects.

Purpose: To encourage advanced study or research.

Eligibility: Open to applicants who are citizens of the United States, either with a Masters degree or equivalent degree, or working towards a PhD or equivalent degree. Preference is given to applicants under the age of 30 with a reading and speaking knowledge of Dutch, French, or German, and must reside in Belgium during the tenure of their fellowship.

Level of Study: Doctorate, Postgraduate

Value: $21,000

Length of Study: Minimum of 6 months, up to 12 months

Frequency: Annual

Country of Study: Belgium

No. of awards offered: Up to eight

Application Procedure: For additional information contact the Foundation.

Closing Date: October 31st

Funding: Foundation

Additional Information: Applicants should make their own arrangements to register or affiliate with a Belgian university or research institution.

Postdoctoral Fellowships for Biomedical or Biotechnology Research

Subjects: Biomedical or Biotechnology Research.

Purpose: To cover living and travel expenses and includes health insurance.

Eligibility: Open to candidates who are Belgian citizens, holding a university degree of a regular second cycle from a Belgian institution; have an outstanding academic record; have a good command of the English language, and engage in doctoral or postdoctoral biomedical research or biotechnology research in the USA.

Level of Study: Doctorate, Postdoctorate

Value: $35,000

Length of Study: 1 year

Frequency: Annual

Country of Study: United States of America

Application Procedure: Check website for details.

Closing Date: October 31st

Funding: Foundation

Contributor: D. Collen Research Foundation vzw and BAEF

Additional Information: Fellows who have their own means to finance their research in the USA may apply for an Honorary Fellowship of the Foundation.

BERTHOLD LEIBINGER STIFTUNG

Johann-Maus-Strasse 2, D-71254 Ditzingen, Germany

Tel: (49) 7156 303 35202

Fax: (49) 7156 303 35205

Email: innovationspreis@leibinger-stiftung.de

Website: www.leibinger-stiftung.de

Contact: Mr Sven Ederer, Project Manager

Berthold Leibinger Innovation Prize

Subjects: Applied laser technology (application or generation of laser light).

Purpose: To promote the advancement of science.

Eligibility: Open to individuals and project groups who have completed an innovative scientific or technical development work on applying or generating laser light.

Level of Study: Unrestricted

Type: Prize

Value: €20,000, €10,000 and €5,000

Frequency: Every 2 years

No. of awards offered: 3

Application Procedure: Applicants must submit a completed application form, short documentation of up to ten pages in accordance with stipulated structure, biography and explanation describing the context of work. Upto eight nominees are invited to present their work in the jury session. Candidates can also be suggested by a third party. Suggestions must include the reasons for the project's merit.

Closing Date: Varying, refer to the website

Funding: Private

Contributor: Berthold Leibinger

No. of awards given last year: 3

No. of applicants last year: Approx. 30

Additional Information: The foundation bears travelling expenses for nominees to jury session and for prize winners to the prize ceremony.

For further information contact:

Berthold Leibinger Stiftung, Innovation Prize, 71252 Ditzingen, Germany

BETA PHI MU

College of Information Studies, Florida State University, Tallahassee, FL, 32306-2100, United States of America

Tel: (1) 850 644 3907

Fax: (1) 850 644 6253

Email: beta_phi_mu@lis.fsu.edu

Website: www.beta-phi-mu.org

Contact: Mr Wayne Wiegand Executive, Secretary

Beta Phi Mu is a library and information studies society, founded in 1948, with over 25,000 graduates of the ALA-initiated accredited professional programmes. Beta Phi Mu was founded at the University of Illinois by a group of leading librarians and library educators. Aware of the notable achievements of honour societies in other professions, they believed that such a society would have much to offer librarianship and library education.

Blance E Woolls Scholarship for School Library Media Service

Subjects: Library science.
Purpose: To assist a new student who plans to become a school media specialist.
Eligibility: Open to new students who have not completed more than 12 hours by Autumn. Applicants must be accepted into an ALA-accredited programme.
Level of Study: Graduate
Type: Scholarship
Value: US$1,500
Frequency: Annual
Study Establishment: An ALA-accredited school
Country of Study: United States of America
Application Procedure: Applicants must send three references and a completed application form, available by sending a stamped addressed envelope to Beta Phi Mu headquarters.
Closing Date: March 15th
No. of awards given last year: 1

Doctoral Dissertation Scholarship

Subjects: Library science and information studies.
Purpose: To support library and information science doctoral students who are working on their dissertations.
Eligibility: Applicants must be doctoral students who have completed their coursework. Scholarships will be awarded based on the usefulness of the research topic to the profession.
Level of Study: Doctorate
Type: Scholarship
Value: US$2,000
Length of Study: 1 year
Frequency: Annual
Country of Study: Any country
No. of awards offered: 1
Application Procedure: Applicants must provide a 300-word abstract of dissertation, a curriculum vitae, a letter from their Dean or Director approving a topic and a work plan for the study.
Closing Date: March 15th
Funding: Private
No. of awards given last year: 1

Eugene Garfield Doctoral Dissertation Fellowship

Subjects: Library and information science.
Purpose: To fund library and information science doctoral students who are working on their dissertations.
Eligibility: All requirements for the degree except the writing and defense of dissertation must have been completed.
Level of Study: Doctorate
Type: Fellowship
Value: US$3,000
Frequency: Annual
Study Establishment: Florida State University
Country of Study: United States of America
No. of awards offered: 2
Application Procedure: Applicants should provide a personal statement not exceeding 500 words relating to post-dissertation plans, three letters of reference, a completed application form, abstract of dissertation (300-word limit) and a letter of approval of topic from the Dean or Director.
Closing Date: March 15th
Funding: Government

Frank B Sessa Award

Subjects: Library science or information studies.
Purpose: To enable the continuing professional education of a Beta Phi Mu member.
Eligibility: Open to Beta Phi Mu members only.
Level of Study: Professional development
Type: Scholarship
Value: US$1,250

Frequency: Annual
Country of Study: Any country
Application Procedure: Applicants must request an application form from Beta Phi Mu. Further details are also available from the website.
Closing Date: March 15th
Funding: Private
No. of awards given last year: 1

Harold Lancour Scholarship For Foreign Study

Subjects: Library science.
Purpose: To assist a librarian or library school student to undertake short-term research in a foreign country.
Eligibility: Open to nationals of any country.
Level of Study: Unrestricted
Type: Scholarship
Value: US$1,000
Frequency: Annual
Country of Study: Any country
No. of awards offered: 1
Application Procedure: Applicants must write to Beta Phi Mu for further details, enclosing a stamped addressed envelope. Further details are also available from the website.
Closing Date: March 15th
Funding: Private
No. of awards given last year: 1
No. of applicants last year: 10

Sarah Rebecca Reed Award

Subjects: Library and information science.
Purpose: To assist a new student in library and information science at an ALA-accredited school.
Eligibility: Open to beginning students who have not completed more than 12 hours by Autumn. Applicants must also be accepted into an ALA-accredited programme and provide five references. Nationals of any country can apply.
Level of Study: Graduate
Type: Scholarship
Value: US$2,700
Frequency: Annual
Study Establishment: An ALA-accredited school
Country of Study: United States of America
No. of awards offered: 1
Application Procedure: Applicants must request an application from the address shown, enclosing a stamped addressed envelope. Further details are also available from the website.
Closing Date: March 15th
Funding: Private
No. of awards given last year: 1
No. of applicants last year: 30

BIAL FOUNDATION

Avenida da Siderurgia Nacional A, S. Mamede do Coronado, 4745-457, Portugal
Tel: (351) 22 986 6100
Fax: (351) 22 986 6190
Email: fundacao@bial.com
Website: www.bial.com
Contact: Chairman

The BIAL Foundation, a non-profit institution, was set up in 1994 with the aim of encouraging and supporting research focused on humans. It manages the BIAL award, one of the most distinguished awards for Health in Europe, and the BIAL Fellowship Programme, which focuses largely on psychophysiology and parapsychology.

BIAL Award

Subjects: Medical sciences and clinical medicine.
Purpose: To award intellectual written work in the subject area of health. To award work of a high quality and scientific relevance in clinical practice.
Eligibility: At least one of the authors must be a physician.
Level of Study: Doctorate, Graduate, MBA, Postdoctorate, Postgraduate, Predoctorate, Professional development, Research
Type: Prize

Value: €220
Frequency: Every 2 years
No. of awards offered: 6
Application Procedure: Applicants must submit eight copies of an original written specimen in either English or Portuguese to the Foundation. Further requirements are listed on its regulation, which will be forwarded to prospective applicants on request or can be downloaded from www.bial.com
Closing Date: October 31st
Funding: Private
Contributor: The BIAL Foundation
No. of awards given last year: 6
No. of applicants last year: 49

THE BIBLIOGRAPHICAL SOCIETY

Fellowship and Bursaries Subcommitte, The Bibliographical Society, Centre for Urban History, University of Leicester, Leicester, LE1 7RH, England
Tel: (44) 0116 252 5925
Fax: (44) 0116 252 5769
Email: jh241@le.ac.uk
Website: www.bibsoc.org.uk
Contact: Dr John Hinks, Secretary

Founded in 1892, the Bibliographical Society is the senior learned society dealing with the study of the book and its history.

Antiquarian Booksellers Award

Subjects: Book trade and history of publishing.
Purpose: To support research into the history of the book trade and publishing industry.
Eligibility: Applicants may be of any age or nationality and need not be members of the Society.
Level of Study: Research
Type: Grant
Value: Up to US$1,500
Frequency: Annual
No. of awards offered: 1
Application Procedure: Application form (obtainable from the society's administrator), supported by letters from two referees familiar with the applicant's work.
Closing Date: December 1st in preceding year
Funding: Private
Contributor: Antiquarian Booksellers Association
No. of awards given last year: 1
Additional Information: Successful applicants will be asked to report briefly on the progress of their project by December of the same year.

Barry Bloomfield Bursary

Subjects: Research.
Purpose: To honour Barry Bloomfield by supporting research in bibliography, particularly pertaining to book history in areas of the former British Empire.
Eligibility: Applicants may be of any age or nationality and need not be members of the society.
Level of Study: Research
Type: Bursary
Value: Up to UK £2,000
Frequency: Annual
No. of awards offered: 1
Application Procedure: Application form (obtainable from the Society's administrator) supported by letters from two referees familiar with the applicant's work.
Closing Date: December 1st for preceding year
Funding: Private
Additional Information: Successful applicants will be asked to report briefly on the progress of their project by December of the same year.

Bibliographical Society Small Grants

Subjects: Bibliographic research.
Purpose: To support bibliographic research projects by providing small grants for specific purposes.
Eligibility: Applicants may be of any age or nationality and need not be members of the society.

Level of Study: Research
Type: Grant
Value: UK £50–200
Frequency: Any time
Application Procedure: Application by letter to the above address. If the applicant is registered for a research degree the application should be accompanied by a letter of support from their academic supervisor.
Closing Date: Applications are accepted any time
Funding: Private

Falconer Madan Award

Subjects: Any subject connected with Oxford or available to research specifically in an Oxford library.
Purpose: To support a scholar's research in an Oxford library.
Eligibility: Applicants may be of any age or nationality.
Level of Study: Research
Value: Up to UK £500 plus eligibility for accommodation at Wolfson College, Oxford
Frequency: At the discretion of the Society
Study Establishment: An Oxford library
Country of Study: United Kingdom
No. of awards offered: 1
Application Procedure: Application form (obtainable from the Society's administrator) supported by letters from two referees familiar with the applicant's work.
Closing Date: December 1st in preceding year
Funding: Private
Contributor: Oxford Bibliographical Society
Additional Information: Successful applicants will be asked to report briefly on the progress of their project by December of the same year.

The Fredson Bowers Award

Subjects: Bibliographic research.
Purpose: To support a bibliographic research project in the name of Fredson Bowers.
Eligibility: Applicants may be of any age or nationality and need not be members of the society.
Level of Study: Research
Type: Award
Value: US$1,500
Frequency: Annual
No. of awards offered: 1
Application Procedure: Application form (obtainable from the society's administrator) supported by letters from two referees familiar with the applicant's work.
Closing Date: December 1st in preceding year
Funding: Private
Contributor: The Bibliographical Society of America
Additional Information: Successful applicants will be asked to report briefly on the progress of their project by December of the same year.

BIBLIOGRAPHICAL SOCIETY OF AMERICA (BSA)

PO Box 1537, Lenox Hill Station, New York, NY, 10021, United States of America
Tel: (1) 212 452 2710
Fax: (1) 212 452 2710
Email: bsa@bibsocamer.org
Website: www.bibsocamer.org
Contact: Ms Michele Randall, Executive Secretary

The Bibliographical Society of America (BSA) invites applications for its annual short-term fellowships, which supports bibliographical inquiry as well as research in the history of the book trades and in publishing history.

BSA Fellowship Program

Subjects: Books or manuscripts as historical evidence. Topics may include establishing a text or studying the history of book production, publication, distribution, collecting or reading.
Purpose: To support bibliographical inquiry and research in the history of the book trades and publishing.
Eligibility: This programme is open to applicants of any nationality.
Level of Study: Doctorate, Postdoctorate, Postgraduate

Type: Fellowship
Value: US$2,000
Length of Study: 1 month
Frequency: Annual
Country of Study: Any country
No. of awards offered: 10
Application Procedure: Applicants must complete an application form. The original plus six photocopies must be posted to the Executive Secretary of the Fellowship Committee at the Bibliographical Society of America.
Closing Date: December 1st
Funding: Private
No. of awards given last year: 10
Additional Information: For applications now only available on website visit the BSA's website.

THE BIOCHEMICAL SOCIETY

Third Floor, Eagle House, 16 Procter Street, London, W1CV 6NX, England
Tel: (44) 207 280 4131
Fax: (44) 207 280 4170
Email: alison.mcwhinnie@biochemistry.org
Website: www.biochemistry.org
Contact: Miss Alison McWhinnie, Head of Human Resources and Corporate Affairs

Serving biochemistry and biochemists since 1911, the aim of The Biochemical Society is to promote the advancement of the science of biochemistry. It does so in the context of cellular and molecular life sciences. Through its regular scientific meetings with special interest groups, its publishing company Portland Press Limited and its policy, professional and education contacts, the Society provides a forum for current research to be shared.

The Biochemical Society General Travel Fund
Subjects: The Society helps scientists become established and maintain their status to promote Biochemistry in the UK and international communities.
Purpose: To assist scientists of the British Biochemical Society who wish to attend scientific meetings, or make short visits to other laboratories.
Eligibility: New members may apply for their first travel grants after they have been a member of the British Biochemical Society for 1 year. Applicants will not be eligible if they have been awarded a Student Travel Grant within the last year and a Travel Grant from the Society during the previous 2 years. No age or career stage limitations. Post-graduate research students (3rd or 4th year of PhD programme) should provide a reference from their Head of Department.
Level of Study: Predoctorate, Postdoctorate, Postgraduate
Type: Travel grant
Value: Not exceeding £500. The committee may consider awarding more for exceptionally well-argued and well-supported cases describing high quality research from outstanding scientists or those with recognized potential
Country of Study: Any country
No. of awards offered: Varies
Application Procedure: Please apply online through the website www.biochemistry.org. Applications should be for meetings that will be taking place at least 1 month after the closing date. The Travel Grants Committee meets six times a year.
Closing Date: January 1st, March 1st, May 1st, June 1st, September 1st and November 1st
Funding: Private, foundation
Contributor: Biochemical society
Additional Information: Log on to www.biochemistry.org for more details on 'guidelines to application'.

The Krebs Memorial Scholarship
Subjects: Biochemistry or allied biomedical science.
Purpose: To help candidates who wish to study for a PhD degree in biochemistry or in an allied biomedical science, but whose otherwise very promising research careers have been interrupted for quite extraordinary non-academic reasons totally beyond their control and who do not qualify for an award from public funds.

Eligibility: Open primarily to PhD students, but a post-doctoral fellowship might be considered for a candidate whose circumstances merit such consideration.
Level of Study: Doctorate, Postdoctorate, Postgraduate, Predoctorate
Type: Scholarship
Value: A maintenance grant and all necessary fees
Length of Study: 1 year, maximum of 3 years
Frequency: Every 2 years
Study Establishment: Any British university
Country of Study: United Kingdom
No. of awards offered: 1
Application Procedure: Application form is available in the autumn and can be downloaded from www.biochemistry.org or by contacting the Head of Human Resources and Corporate Affairs. Applications should be completed and forwarded through the Head of Department concerned, who should be able to place the applicant in the top 5 per cent of PhD candidates. Two references are required.
Closing Date: March 1st, September 1st
Funding: Private
No. of awards given last year: 1
Additional Information: Logon on to www.biochemistry.org for more details.

Visiting Biochemist Bursaries
Subjects: Biochemistry
Eligibility: Open to an overseas researcher on a laboratory visit to the sponsor's research facility or to go out to visit a research facility in a developing region or to enable a member give seminars and undergraduate or postgraduate training.
Level of Study: Research
Type: Bursary
Value: UK £2,000
Frequency: Twice a year
No. of awards offered: Varies
Application Procedure: Please apply online www.biochemistry.org
Closing Date: March 1st, September 1st
Funding: Foundation, private
Contributor: The Biochemical Society

BIOTECHNOLOGY AND BIOLOGICAL SCIENCES RESEARCH COUNCIL (BBSRC)

Polaris House, North Star Avenue, Swindon, SN2 1UH, United Kingdom
Tel: (44) 44 (0)1793 413200
Fax: (44) 44 (0)1793 413201
Email: postdoc.felloships@bbsrc.ac.uk
Website: www.bbsrc.ac.uk/Welcome.html

BBSRC is the UK's principal funder of basic and strategic biological research. It is a non-departmental public body, one of the seven Research Councils supported through the Science and Innovation Group of the Department for Innovation, Universities and Skills (DIUS). It supports research and research training in universities and research centres throughout the UK, including BBSRC–sponsored institutes, and promotes knowledge transfer from research to applications in business, industry and policy, and public engagement in the biosciences. It funds research in some exciting areas including genomics, stem cell biology, and bionanotechnology.

David Phillips Fellowships
Subjects: All subjects.
Purpose: To support outstanding early-career scientists who wish to establish themselves as independent researchers.
Eligibility: Open to candidates who have a minimum of 2 years and no more than 6 years of active postdoctoral research experience.
Level of Study: Postdoctorate
Type: Fellowship
Value: Personal salary and a significant research support grant to support the costs of the research
Length of Study: 5 years
No. of awards offered: 10
Application Procedure: All applications must be submitted online.
Closing Date: November 14th

Additional Information: Further queries, please contact Postgraduate Training and Research Career Development Branch.

For further information contact:

Email: postdoc.fellowships@bbsrc.ac.uk
Website: www.bbsrc.ac.uk/funding/fellowships

Institute Career Path Fellowships

Subjects: Animal biology.
Purpose: To support early-career researchers wishing to be based at the Institute for Animal Health (IAH) or Roslin Neuropathogenesis Unit (Roslin – NPU). Integrative biology and/or systems approaches are particularly encouraged.
Eligibility: Open to candidates who have a minimum of 2 years and no more than 6 years of active postdoctoral research experience.
Level of Study: Doctorate, Postdoctorate
Type: Fellowships
No. of awards offered: Up to 4
Application Procedure: Check website for further details.
Closing Date: November 14th
Additional Information: Further queries, please contact Postgraduate Training and Research Career Development Branch.

For further information contact:

Email: fiona.tomley@bbsrc.ac.uk or bruce.whitelaw@bbsrc.ac.uk
Website: www.bbsrc.ac.uk/funding/fellowships

Institute Development Fellowships

Subjects: Mathematics.
Purpose: To enable BBSRC scientists to spend a period of collaborative work at another research organization and to provide a mechanism for the influx of new ideas and new skills in strategically important areas to enhance the quality of science in BBSRC sponsored institutes.
Eligibility: Open to all BBSRC scientists at Band 5 and above on an open-ended contract, who have worked for a minimum of 5 years in their current or similar post.
Level of Study: Research
Type: Fellowships
Value: To cover the costs associated with the proposed research development activities
Length of Study: 6–12 months
No. of awards offered: Up to 4
Application Procedure: All applications must be submitted online.
Closing Date: November 14th
Additional Information: Further queries, please contact Postgraduate Training and Research Career Development Branch.

For further information contact:

Email: postdoc.fellowships@bbsrc.ac.uk
Website: www.bbsrc.ac.uk/funding/fellowships

Professorial Fellowships

Subjects: All subjects.
Purpose: To support world-class scientists with a proven track record of developing new and innovative directions of research and who have the potential to use a fellowship to open up dramatic and novel lines of work.
Eligibility: Open to scientists who are already recognized at an international level as outstanding researchers with exceptional research and interpretative achievements.
Type: Fellowships
Value: Grant to cover the costs of the research programme
Length of Study: 5 years
No. of awards offered: Up to 2
Application Procedure: Check website for further details.
Closing Date: November 14th
Additional Information: Further queries, please contact Postgraduate Training and Research Career Development Branch.

For further information contact:

Email: postdoc.fellowships@bbsrc.ac.uk
Website: www.bbsrc.ac.uk/funding/fellowships

Research Development Fellowships

Subjects: All subjects.
Purpose: To support scientists wishing to undertake new directions in their research. Applicants seeking to develop interdisciplinary dimensions by integrating new techniques or methodologies into their research are particularly encouraged.
Eligibility: Open to scientists who are full-time members of academic staff of a UK university who have worked for a minimum of 5 years in their current or similar post.
Type: Fellowship
Value: To cover the costs associated with the proposed research development activities
Length of Study: 1–3 years
No. of awards offered: Up to 5
Application Procedure: Applications must be submitted online.
Closing Date: November 14th
Additional Information: Further queries, please contact Postgraduate Training and Research Career Development Branch.

For further information contact:

Email: postdoc.fellowships@bbsrc.ac.uk
Website: www.bbsrc.ac.uk/funding/fellowships

THE BIRLA INSTITUTE OF TECHNOLOGY & SCIENCE (BITS)

Vidhya Vihar Campus, Pilani, Rajasthan, 333031, India
Tel: (91) 1 596 245073
Fax: (91) 1 01596 244183
Email: lkm@bits-pilani.ac.in
Website: http://discovery.bits-pilani.ac.in

The Birla Institute of Technology & Science (BITS) is an all India institute for higher education. An important aspect of education at BITS is its institutionalized linkages with the industry. The Institute attaches great importance to university industry alliances. The primary motive of BITS is to train young men and women able and eager to create and put into action such ideas, methods, techniques and information.

BITS HP Labs India PhD Fellowship

Subjects: Information and communication technologies.
Purpose: To aid aspiring and deserving students for research in the area of information and communication technologies (ICT) relevant to fast-growing markets such as India.
Eligibility: Open to candidates with a higher degree in computer science, interested in doing Doctoral work in web based print distribution, data on paper, intelligent storage management, distributed operating systems and related areas.
Level of Study: Doctorate
Type: Fellowship
Value: A monthly stipend of Indian Rupees 20,000. HP Labs India will pay the fees involved to BITS. An additional monthly allowance of Indian Rupees 20,000 will be available to cover living expenses for the duration the candidate spends at HP Labs India, Bangalore
Length of Study: 3 years or more
Frequency: Annual
Study Establishment: BITS Pilani
Country of Study: India
Application Procedure: Downloadable application forms are available at www.bits-pilani.ac.in
Closing Date: June and November 15th every year
Funding: Corporation
Contributor: HP Labs India
No. of awards given last year: 2
No. of applicants last year: 180
Additional Information: Additional information can be got from www.hpl.hp.com/india or www.bits-pilani.ac.in

BIRMINGHAM COLLEGE OF FOOD, TOURISM AND CREATIVE STUDIES

Summer Row, Birmingham, B3 1JB, England
Tel: (44) 12 1604 1000
Fax: (44) 12 1608 7100
Email: Registry@bcftcs.ac.uk
Website: www.bcftcs.ac.uk
Contact: Student Scholarships

Gill Boydol Scholarship

Subjects: Hospitality subjects.
Purpose: Reduction in tuition fee for new international students.
Type: Scholarship
Value: Up to UK £1,500
Length of Study: 1 year
Frequency: Annual
Study Establishment: Birmingham College of Food, Tourism and Creative Studies
Country of Study: United Kingdom
No. of awards offered: 2
Closing Date: 1 month before the start of the programme

James Liu Scholarship

Subjects: Hospitality and tourism.
Purpose: Reduction in tuition fee for international students from the continent of Asia.
Level of Study: Unrestricted
Type: Scholarship
Value: Up to UK £1,500
Length of Study: 1 year
Frequency: Annual
Study Establishment: Birmingham College of Food, Tourism and Creative Studies
Country of Study: United Kingdom
No. of awards offered: 5
Closing Date: 1 month before the start of the programme

Tim Brighouse Scholarship

Subjects: Childcare, care subjects.
Purpose: Reduction in tuition fees for new international students.
Level of Study: Unrestricted
Type: Scholarship
Value: Up to UK £1,500
Length of Study: 1 year
Frequency: Annual
Study Establishment: Birmingham College of Food, Tourism and Creative Studies
Country of Study: United Kingdom
No. of awards offered: 2
Closing Date: 1 month before the start of the programme

BIRTH DEFECTS FOUNDATION

BDF Centre, Hemlock Way, Cannock, Staffordshire, WS11 7GF, England
Tel: (44) 15 4346 8888
Fax: (44) 15 4346 8999
Email: info@bdfnewlife.co.uk
Website: www.bdfcharity.co.uk
Contact: Mrs Sheila Brown, Chief Executive Officer

The Birth Defects Foundation, more recently known as BDF Newlife, is a United Kingdom registered charity whose mission is to improve child health, aid families and raise awareness. BDF Newlife is committed to funding basic, clinical and ethically approved research into the causes, prevention and treatment of birth defects.

BDF Newlife-Full and Small Grants Schemes

Subjects: Aetiology, prevention and treatment of birth defects.
Level of Study: Research, Graduate, Postgraduate
Type: Fellowship
Value: Varies. Small grants up to UK £10,000, full grants up to UK £80,000
Length of Study: Varies

Frequency: Annual, Small Grants available throughout the year
No. of awards offered: Varies
Application Procedure: Applicants must fill in an application form for the full grant. Application for the small grant is by a brief proposal and then by application form if the proposal is of interest to the Foundation.
Closing Date: For full grants, applicants should consult advertisements and the website in June and July for the closing date. There is no closing date for small grants
Contributor: Charitable trading activity
No. of awards given last year: 14
No. of applicants last year: Over 30

BLACKLOCK NATURE SANCTUARY (BNS)

Catherine Jordan, Artists Fellowship Programs, 3853 County Line Road, PO 426, Moose Lake, MN 55767-0426, United States of America
Tel: (1) 612 823 6257
Email: jorda021@tc.umn.edu
Website: www.blacklock.org

The Blacklock Nature Sanctuary, founded in 1994, is dedicated to preserving undeveloped land in Minnesota and providing artists and naturalists with working space.

BNS Arts Administrator Renewal Fellowship

Subjects: Arts.
Purpose: To recognize the contributions made by artists.
Eligibility: Open to administrators who manage Minnesota arts organization or programmes.
Level of Study: Postgraduate
Type: Scholarship
Value: Up to US$300 per week
Frequency: Annual
Country of Study: United States of America
Application Procedure: See website.
Funding: Foundation
Contributor: Jerome Foundation

BNS Emerging Artists Fellowship

Subjects: Arts.
Purpose: To recognize the valuable cultural contributions of artists to society.
Eligibility: Open to candidates who are not less than 21 years of age and who are residents of Minnesota for at least one year.
Level of Study: Postgraduate
Type: Scholarship
Value: Up to US$2,000
Frequency: Annual
Country of Study: United States of America
Application Procedure: A completed application form must be submitted.
Contributor: Jerome Foundation

The Nadine Blacklock Nature Photography for Women

Subjects: Photography.
Purpose: To give recognition to women working in the nature photography genre.
Eligibility: Open to all women nature photographers who are at least 21 years of age.
Level of Study: Postgraduate
Type: Scholarship
Value: Free use of Sanctuary land and studios plus accommodation
Length of Study: One month
Frequency: Annual
Country of Study: United States of America
Application Procedure: See the website www.blacklockgallery.com
Contributor: Blacklock Nature Photography

THE BLAKEMORE FOUNDATION

1201 3rd Avenue, Suite 4800, Seattle, WA, 98101-3266, United States of America
Tel: (1) 206 359 8778
Fax: (1) 206 359 9778
Email: blakemore@perkinscoie.com
Website: www.blakemorefoundation.org
Contact: Mr Griffith Way, Trustee

The Blakemore Foundation was established in 1990 by Thomas and Frances Blakemore. The Blakemore Foundation makes grants for the advanced study of East and Southeast Asian languages and to improve the understanding of Asian fine art in the United States.

Blakemore Freeman Fellowships for Advanced Asian Language Study

Subjects: Asian language (Chinese, Vietnamese, Tibetan, Japanese, Indonesian, Thai, Korean, Khmer, Burmese, Malaysian).
Purpose: To provide financial aid and encourage the advanced study of Asian languages and to improve the understanding of Asian fine arts in the United States.
Eligibility: Applicants must be citizens or permanent residents of the United States. The candidates must be pursuing an academic, professional or business career that involves the regular use of a modern East or Southeast Asian language.
Level of Study: Advanced study
Type: Fellowships
Value: Tuition or tutoring fees and stipend for travel, living and study expenses
Length of Study: 1 year
Frequency: Annual
Country of Study: Asia
Application Procedure: Applicants must download the application form from the website.
Closing Date: December 30th
Funding: Foundation
No. of awards given last year: varies
No. of applicants last year: more than 200

Blakemore Refresher Grants: Short-Term Grants for Advanced Asian Language Study

Subjects: Asian language (Chinese, Vietnamese, Tibetan, Japanese, Indonesian, Thai, Korean, Khmer, Burmese, Malaysian).
Purpose: To encourage the advanced study of Asian languages and to improve the understanding of Asian fine arts in the United States.
Eligibility: Open to former Blakemore Fellows, professors teaching in an Asian field at a university or college in the United States or postdoctoral professionals whose degree and work is in an Asian field and graduates of the advanced-level academic-year programme at the given study establishment.
Level of Study: Advanced Study
Type: Grant
Value: Tuition and a maintenance stipend for travel, living and study expenses
Length of Study: Less than an academic year
Frequency: Annual
Study Establishment: Inter-University Center (IUC) for Japanese Language Studies in Yokohama, Japan or Inter-University Program (IUP) for Chinese Language Studies at Tsinghua University or International Chinese Language Program (ICLP) at National Taiwan University
Country of Study: Asia
Application Procedure: Applicants must give a written request stating prior Blakemore grant, the proposed language programme and dates of study. The request should include a statement of why additional language study is desired and how the applicant has used the language since last receiving a Blakemore grant. For other eligible applicants, applications can be downloaded from the website.
Closing Date: December 30th
Funding: Foundation

THE BLUE MOUNTAINS HOTEL SCHOOL (BMHS)

45 Hume Street, PO Box 905, Crows Nest, NSW, 2065, Australia
Tel: (61) 9437 0300
Fax: (61) 9437 0299
Email: communications@sha.cornell.edu
Website: www.hotelschool.com.au

The Blue Mountain Hotel School is a university level institution, recognized and accredited in Australia by the vocational education and training accreditation board.

BMHS Hospitality and Tourism Management Scholarship

Subjects: Hospitality and tourism management.
Purpose: To encourage students in the field of hospitality and tourism.
Eligibility: Open to Australian or New Zealand citizen who is eligible for entry into the firstyear in February or July under normal entry criteria.
Type: Scholarship
Value: Australian $15,000
Length of Study: 2–5
Frequency: Annual
No. of awards offered: 2
Application Procedure: Applications should arrive no later than September 30th for the February enrollment and no later than April 30th for the July enrollment.
Closing Date: September 30th and April 30th

For further information contact:

The Principal, Blue Mountains Hotel School, PO Box 905, Crows Nest, NSW, 2065

BOEHRINGER INGELHEIM FONDS

Schlossmühle, Grabenstrasse 46, 55262 Heidesheim, Germany
Tel: (49) 6132 89 85 0
Fax: (49) 6132 89 85 11
Email: secretariat@bifonds.de
Website: www.bifonds.de
Contact: Foundation for Basic Research in Medicine

The Boehringer Ingelheim Fonds is a foundation – an independent, not-for-profit institution – for the promotion of basic research in biomedicine. It pays particular attention to up-and-coming junior scientists and makes every attempts to assist them and create an atmosphere conductive to creative research.

PhD Scholarships (B.I.F.)

Subjects: Basic research in Biomedicine.
Purpose: Promote basic research in biomedicine by funding and fostering the best young scientists who are given a comprehensive support in addition to a competitive monthly stipend.
Eligibility: Candidates must not be older than 27 years for doctoral research. All nationalities are eligible to apply. European citizens are supported while in Europe and overseas; non-European citizens receive support while conducting research in Europe. The PhD project must be ambitious and pursued in internationally leading laboratories.
Level of Study: Doctorate, 3
Type: Scholarship
Value: €1,400 per month plus an additional flat rate sum of €100 per month to cover minor project-related costs, spouse allowance and/or child care allowance). A supplement for the respective countries may be added
Length of Study: Up to 2 years for doctoral research (extension possible up to 1 additional year)
Frequency: 3 times per year
No. of awards offered: 45 per year
Application Procedure: Applications must be submitted online and a paper version in English. Applications must be written by the applicants personally; however, consultation with scientific supervisors is recommended.
Closing Date: February 1st, June 1st, October 1st
Funding: Individuals, foundation

Contributor: C.H. Boehringer Sohn (Boehringer Ingelheim)
No. of awards given last year: 44
No. of applicants last year: 494
Additional Information: The foundation sponsors participation in research-oriented courses and summer or winter schools, where the selected participants learn special techniques in practical exercises as well as in lectures and discussions.

BOLOGNA CENTER OF THE JOHNS HOPKINS UNIVERSITY

Via Belmeloro 11, 40126 Bologna, Italy
Tel: (39) 051 291 7811
Fax: (39) 051 228 505
Email: admission@jhubc.it
Website: www.jhubc.it
Contact: Ms Bernadette O'Toole, Assistant Registrar

The Bologna Center is an integral part of the Paul H. Nitze School of Advanced International Studies (SAIS), one of the leading United States of America graduate schools devoted to the study of international relations. The programme seeks to merge the wisdom of universities, business and labour with the knowledge and expertise of those presently engaged in government, foreign affairs and international economic practice.

Paul H. Nitze School of Advanced International Studies (SAIS) Financial Aid and Fellowships

Subjects: International economics, European studies, international relations and international development. In addition to fundamental courses, international economics covers European economic integration, environmental and resource economics, commercial policies, corporate finance, economic development and public sector economics. European studies examines history, economics, contemporary politics and culture, as well as demographic and enlargement issues. International relations explores international law, international non-governmental organizations, human rights, conflict management, ethnic conflict and security issues.
Purpose: To facilitate graduate study in International relations.
Eligibility: Open to students who have completed their first university degree. Students who are in the process of completing their first degree may apply provided they obtain the degree prior to entry to the Bologna Center in the Autumn. All candidates must have an excellent command of written and spoken English and ideally have some background knowledge in economics, history, political or other social sciences. All fellowships and financial aid awards are based on need as well as academic merit.
Level of Study: Postgraduate
Type: Fellowships and financial aid
Value: Varies. Grants may cover partial or full tuition. Maintenance stipends are rarely provided
Frequency: Annual
Study Establishment: The Bologna Center of the Johns Hopkins University and the Paul H. Nitze School of Advanced International Studies
Country of Study: Italy
No. of awards offered: Varies, depending on funds available
Application Procedure: Applicants must submit an application form and financial aid application. Certain donor organizations require a separate application. Admission and financial aid for citizens of United States of America and permanent residents are administered by SAIS in Washington and all enquiries from United States of America students should be addressed to the Admissions Office in Washington. Financial aid and admission for non-United States of America students is administered in Bologna and all enquiries from non-United States of America students should be addressed to the Registrar's Office in Bologna.
Closing Date: The deadline for United States of America applicants is January 7th and February 1st for non-United States of America students
Funding: Government, individuals, private, trusts, commercial, corporation, foundation
No. of applicants last year: 600
Additional Information: Courses are also offered in the United States of America foreign policy, as well as Latin American, African

and Middle East issues. Language instruction is offered in Arabic, English, French, German, Portuguese, Spanish and Russian. Special fellowships administered by the Bologna Center on behalf of other donor organizations have certain restrictions, which vary depending upon the donor. Many of the fellowships available to non-United States of America students are provided by government ministries and other European organizations and are reserved for citizens of the country providing the fellowship.

For further information contact:

United States of America Citizens: Admissions Office, 1740 Massachusetts Avenue North West, Washington, DC 20036, United States of America
Email: admission.sais@jhu.eduNon-United States of America Citizens: Registrar's Office, Bologna Center, Via Belmeloro 11, 40126 Bologna, Italy
Email: admission@jhubc.it

THE BOSTON SOCIETY OF ARCHITECTS (BSA)

52 Broad Street, 4th Floor, Boston, MA 02109-4301, United States of America
Tel: (1) 617 951 1433
Fax: (1) 617 951 0845
Email: bsa@architects.org
Website: www.architects.org
Contact: Kate Miller, Awards Committee

The Boston Society of Architects (BSA) is the regional and professional association of over 3,000 architects and 1,000 affiliate members. The BSA's affiliate members include engineers, contractors, clients or owners, public officials, other allied professionals, students and lay people. The BSA administers many programmes that enhance the public understanding of design as well as the practice of architecture.

Rotch Travelling Scholarship

Subjects: Architecture.
Purpose: To provide young architects with the opportunity to travel and study in foreign countries.
Eligibility: Open to United States of America architects who will be under 35 years of age on January 1 of the competition year and a degree from an accredited U.S. school of architecture and one year of full-time professional experience in a Massachusetts architecture firm as of January 1 of the competition year.
Level of Study: Professional development
Type: Scholarship
Value: A stipend of US$35,000
Length of Study: 9 months
Frequency: Annual
Country of Study: Other
No. of awards offered: 1–2
Application Procedure: Applicants must complete an application form, available on written request.
Closing Date: August
Funding: Private
Additional Information: The scholar is selected through a two-stage design competition. The first year of professional experience required should be completed prior to the beginning of the preliminary competition. Scholars are required to return to the United States of America after the duration of the scholarship and submit a report of their travels.

BRADFORD CHAMBER OF COMMERCE AND INDUSTRY

Devere House, Vicar Lane, Little Germany, Bradford, Yorkshire, BD1 5AH, England
Tel: (44) 12 7477 2777
Fax: (44) 12 7422 4549
Email: john.speak@bradfordchamber.co.uk
Website: www.bradfordchamber.co.uk
Contact: Julie Snook

The Bradford Chamber of Commerce and Industry represents member companies in the Bradford and district area. It works with local partners to develop the economic health of the district and has a major voice within the British Chamber of Commerce movement in order to promote the needs of local business on a national basis.

John Speak Trust Scholarships

Subjects: Modern languages.
Purpose: To promote British trade abroad by assisting people in perfecting their basic knowledge of a foreign language.
Eligibility: Open to British nationals intending to follow a career connected with the export trade in the United Kingdom. Applicants must be over 18 years of age with a sound, basic knowledge of at least one language.
Level of Study: Professional development
Type: Scholarship
Value: Contribution towards living expenses and an amount towards the cost of travel
Length of Study: Between 3 months and 1 full academic year abroad depending on the circumstances and each candidate's level of knowledge of the language. It is non-renewable
Frequency: Annual
Study Establishment: A recognized college or university
No. of awards offered: 10
Application Procedure: Applicants must complete an application form and undertake an interview.
Closing Date: February 28th, May 31st or October 31st
Funding: Private
No. of awards given last year: 10
No. of applicants last year: 14

BRAIN RESEARCH INSTITUTE

Neurosciences Building, Austin Health, Waterdale Road, Heidelberg West, VIC 3081, Australia
Tel: (61) 3 9496 4137
Fax: (61) 3 9496 4071
Email: BRI@brain.org.au
Website: www.brain.org.au

The Brain Research Institute (BRI) was established at Austin Health, Melbourne, Australia in 1996. It supports collaboration between specialities in order to develop a better understanding of how a healthy or diseased brain functions. It is an affiliated institution of The University of Melbourne, an administering institution of the National Health & Medical Research Council and a member of Research Australia.

BRI PhD Scholarships

Subjects: Engineering and technology information, computing and communication sciences, medical and health sciences or physical sciences.
Purpose: To encourage competitive research in understanding the structure and function of the human brain.
Eligibility: Open to candidates who have obtained Honours 1 or equivalent, or Honours 2a or equivalent.
Level of Study: Doctorate
Type: Scholarship
Value: Varies
Length of Study: 3 years
Frequency: Annual
Country of Study: Australia
Application Procedure: Applicants must send a curriculum vitae, academic transcripts, expression of interest for area of research and details of 2 academic referees.

For further information contact:

Email: scholarships@brain.org.au
Contact: Karen van Nugteren, Scholarships Officer

BRAIN TUMOR SOCIETY

124 Watertown Street, Suite 3H, PO BOX 5225, Carefree, AZ, 85377, United States of America
Tel: (1) 800 770 8287
Fax: (1) 617 924 9998
Email: grants@tbts.org
Website: www.tbts.org
Contact: Carrie Treadwell, Director of Research Programs

The Brain Tumor Society exists to find a cure for brain tumours. It strives to improve the quality of life of brain tumour patients and their families. It disseminates educational information and provides access to psycho-social support. It raises funds to advance carefully selected scientific research projects, improve clinical care and find a cure.

BTS Research Grant

Subjects: Brain tumours.
Purpose: To fund scientific research aimed at finding a cure for brain tumours, and to support students working on a doctoral thesis in the subject.
Level of Study: Postgraduate, Doctorate
Type: Scholarship
Value: US$100,000 per year
Length of Study: 2 years
Country of Study: United States of America
Application Procedure: Applicants must check the website.
Closing Date: April 16th
Funding: Private

BRANDEIS UNIVERSITY

415 South Street, Waltham, MA 02454-9110, United States of America
Tel: (1) 781 736 2000
Email: goldfiel@brandeis.edu
Website: www.brandeis.edu

Brandeis University is a community of scholars and students united by their commitment to the pursuit of knowledge and its transmission from generation to generation. As a research university, Brandeis is dedicated to the advancement of the humanities, arts, and social, natural and physical sciences. As a liberal arts college, Brandeis affirms the importance of a broad and critical education in enriching the lives of students and preparing them for full participation in a changing society, capable of promoting their own welfare, yet remaining deeply concerned about the welfare of others.

International Visiting Scholarship

Subjects: Arts.
Purpose: For one academic year in any liberal arts subject.
Eligibility: Open to candidates from any country aged 18–23, with strong academic records in their home country. English proficiency and 600 TOEFL are required.
Type: Scholarship
Value: Full tuition fee waiver
Frequency: Annual
Study Establishment: Brandeis University
Country of Study: United States of America
No. of awards offered: 3
Application Procedure: Check website for further details.
Closing Date: January 1st
Funding: Government

For further information contact:

Waltham, Massachusetts, United States of America
Tel: (1) 02254 911
Email: www.brandeis.edu
Contact: Kutz Hall

BREAST CANCER CAMPAIGN

Clifton Centre, 110 Clifton Street, London, EC2A 4HT,
England
Tel: (44) 20 7749 3700
Fax: (44) 20 7749 3701
Email: research@breastcancercampaign.org
Website: www.breastcancercampaign.org
Contact: Research Grants Administrator

Breast Cancer Campaign aims to beat breast cancer by funding innovative world-class research into breast cancer throughout the UK and Republic of Ireland. The charity currently funds 105 projects worth over £13 million.

Breast Cancer Campaign PhD Studentships
Subjects: Breast cancer research including prevention, causes, diagnosis, treatment and management.
Purpose: To induct new and highly qualified science graduates into a career of breast cancer research.
Eligibility: See website for details.
Level of Study: Graduate, Postdoctorate
Type: Studentship
Value: Stipend and consumables
Length of Study: 3 years
Frequency: Annual
Country of Study: United Kingdom, Republic of Ireland
Application Procedure: Application forms can be downloaded from the website www.breastcancercampaign.org
Closing Date: July – Refer to website for the exact date
Funding: Individuals, trusts

Breast Cancer Campaign Project Grants
Subjects: Breast cancer research including prevention, causes, diagnosis, treatment and management.
Purpose: To support innovative research into breast cancer.
Eligibility: Open to candidates working in universities, medical schools/teaching hospitals and research institutes within the UK and Republic of Ireland
Level of Study: Postdoctorate, Research
Type: Grant
Value: UK £65,000 per year for up to 3 years
Length of Study: 3 years
Frequency: Annual
Country of Study: United Kingdom, Republic of Ireland
No. of awards offered: Variable
Application Procedure: Application forms can be downloaded from the website: www.breastcancercampaign.org
Closing Date: January and July (refer to website for exact dates)
Funding: Individuals, trusts

Breast Cancer Campaign Scientific Fellowships
Subjects: Breast cancer research including prevention, causes, diagnosis, treatment and management.
Purpose: To provide an opportunity for postdoctoral scientists to become independent researchers specializing in the breast cancer field and to undertake research of the highest quality.
Eligibility: Open to candidates who are working in universities, medical schools/teaching hospitals and research institutions within the UK and the Republic of Ireland
Level of Study: Research, Postdoctorate, Professional development
Type: Fellowship
Value: Not more than UK £450,000
Length of Study: 5 years
Frequency: Annual
Country of Study: United Kingdom, Republic of Ireland
Application Procedure: Application forms can be downloaded from the website www.breastcancercampaign.org
Closing Date: December (refer to website for exact date)

Breast Cancer Campaign Small Pilot Grants
Subjects: Breast cancer research including prevention, causes, diagnosis, treatment and management.
Purpose: To support established scientists to investigate and develop new ideas in the field of breast cancer research.

Eligibility: Open to candidates working in universities, medical schools/teaching hospitals and research institutes within the UK and Republic of Ireland.
Level of Study: Postdoctorate, Research
Type: Grant
Value: Not more than UK £20,000
Length of Study: Up to 1 year
Frequency: Annual
Country of Study: United Kingdom, Republic of Ireland
No. of awards offered: Variable
Application Procedure: Application forms can be downloaded from the website: www.breastcancercampaign.org
Closing Date: March and September (refer to website for exact dates)
Funding: Individuals, private, trusts

BRIAN MAY TRUST

ffrench.commercial lawyers, PO box 2656, Southport, QLD, 4215,
Australia
Tel: (61) 07 5591 7555
Fax: (61) 07 55917 450
Email: bms@ffcomlaw.com.au
Website: www.brianmayscholarship.org

The Trust is a charitable testamentary trust established under the will of the late Brian May, Australias leading film composer to finance promising Australian film composers.

The Brian May Scholarship
Subjects: Creative arts.
Purpose: To provide financial assistance to promising Australian film composers to study film scoring.
Eligibility: Candidates must be ordinarily resident in Australia. Candidates must hold a Bachelor's Degree from a University, preferably in music composition.
Level of Study: Postgraduate
Type: Scholarship
Value: Australian $80,000
Frequency: Every 2 years
Study Establishment: Thornton School of Music
Country of Study: United States of America
No. of awards offered: 1
Application Procedure: Contact the trust or apply online.
Funding: Trusts
Contributor: The Brian May Trust
No. of awards given last year: 1

THE BRITISH ACADEMY

10 Carlton House Terrace, London, SW1Y 5AH, England
Tel: (44) 20 7969 5200
Fax: (44) 20 7969 5300
Email: secretary@britac.ac.uk
Website: www.britac.ac.uk
Contact: Ms Jane Lyddon, Assistant Secretary (International Relations)

The British Academy is the premier national learned society in the United Kingdom devoted to the promotion of advanced research and scholarship in the humanities and social sciences.

British Academy 44th International Congress of Americanists Fund
Subjects: Latin American studies.
Purpose: To enable British scholars to visit Latin America or Latin American scholars to visit Britain.
Eligibility: Open to support British or Latin American scholars. Applicants must be resident in the UK.
Level of Study: Postdoctorate
Type: Travel grant
Value: Awards do not generally exceed UK £1,000
Frequency: Annual
No. of awards offered: Varies
Closing Date: October 15th, January 15th, April 15th
Funding: Private

British Academy Ancient Persia Fund

Subjects: Iranian, Central Asian studies in the pre-Islamic period.
Purpose: To encourage and support the study of Iranian or Central Asian studies in the pre-Islamic period. Grants are offered towards travel costs.
Eligibility: Preference will be given to scholars undertaking archaeological research or engaged in an archaeological project. Postdoctoral scholars of any nationality are eligible to apply.
Level of Study: Postdoctorate
Type: Travel grant
Value: Awards do not generally exceed UK £500
Length of Study: Tenable for 1 year
Frequency: Annual
Country of Study: Any country
No. of awards offered: 1–2
Closing Date: March 15th
Funding: Private
Contributor: in memory of the distinguished Russian scholar Vladimir G Lukonin
Additional Information: For United Kingdom residents, an application to this fund for travel costs may be combined with an application for a small research grant for other costs, up to a total of UK £5,000.

British Academy Elie Kedourie Memorial Fund

Subjects: Middle Eastern, modern European history and political thought.
Purpose: To promote the study of Middle Eastern, modern European history or history of political thought.
Eligibility: Awards are offered to support any aspect of research, including travel and publication.
Level of Study: Postdoctorate
Value: £1,000
Frequency: Annual
Country of Study: Any country
No. of awards offered: 1–2
Closing Date: March 15th
Funding: Private
Additional Information: Funds are not available to support travel to or attendance at conferences, workshops or seminars, either in the United Kingdom or elsewhere.

British Academy Overseas Conference Grants

Subjects: Humanities and social sciences.
Purpose: To help meet the costs of travel by British scholars to overseas conferences.
Eligibility: Open to scholars presenting an academic paper. Applicants must be resident in the United Kingdom and of postdoctoral or equivalent status. Postgraduate students are not eligible to apply.
Level of Study: Postdoctorate
Type: Grant
Value: Usually restricted to a maximum of UK £900
Country of Study: Any country
No. of awards offered: Approx. 800
Closing Date: October 15th, January 15th, April 15th
Funding: Government

British Academy Postdoctoral Fellowships

Subjects: Academic career development in humanities and social science.
Purpose: To enable outstanding young scholars to obtain experience of research and teaching in the university environment, which will strengthen their curriculum vitae and improve their prospects of obtaining permanent posts by the end of the fellowship.
Eligibility: Applicants must have obtained their doctorate no earlier than July 1st and must not have held an established teaching post in an Institute of Higher Education. Applicants must be United Kingdom nationals, or nationals of any country who have a doctorate from United Kingdom university or European Union nationals resident in the United Kingdom.
Level of Study: Postdoctorate
Type: Fellowship
Value: Salary equivalent to relevant early career plus limited research expences, payment towards mentors time and indirect costs
Length of Study: Tenable for 3 years and not renewable
Frequency: Annual

Country of Study: United Kingdom
No. of awards offered: Up to 45
Application Procedure: Applications must be made on the post-doctoral fellowship application form.
Closing Date: February 29th
Funding: Government
No. of awards given last year: See the website
No. of applicants last year: 593

British Academy Research Development Awards (BARDAs)

Subjects: Humanities and social sciences.
Purpose: To support research projects at the postdoctoral level in the humanities and social sciences.
Eligibility: Applicants must be resident in the United Kingdom.
Level of Study: Postdoctorate
Type: Grant
Value: €15,000 to €150,000 full economic costs-academy contribution at 80 per cent FEC
Length of Study: 3 years
Frequency: Annual
Country of Study: Any country
No. of awards offered: Approx. 50
Closing Date: October 15th
Funding: Government

British Academy Sino-British Fellowship Trust

Subjects: Humanities and social sciences.
Purpose: To support individual or co-operative research projects.
Eligibility: Research may be conducted either in the United Kingdom or China, or in both countries and must involve person to person contact.
Level of Study: Postdoctorate
Type: Fellowship
Value: Up to £7,500
Length of Study: 3 years
Frequency: As per availability of funds
No. of awards offered: 3–4
Closing Date: March 15th
Funding: Private
Contributor: Sino-British Fellowship Trust (SBFT)
Additional Information: Successful applications will be forwarded to the SBFT for approval in the Autumn of each year. It should be noted that the Academy will be unable to offer support should the SBFT decline to confirm funding. Priority funding will be provided to projects which help to achieve sustainable development in the problems arising from environmental issues and pollution.

British Academy Small Research Grants

Subjects: Humanities and social sciences.
Purpose: For original research at postdoctoral level.
Eligibility: Applicants must be resident in the United Kingdom and be of postdoctoral or equivalent status. Postgraduate students are not eligible to apply.
Level of Study: Postdoctorate
Type: Grant
Value: Maximum UK £7,500
Length of Study: 2 years
Frequency: As per availability of funds
Country of Study: Any country
No. of awards offered: Approx. 500
Application Procedure: All applications should demonstrate that Academy funds are sought for a clearly defined, discrete piece of research, which will have an identifiable outcome on completion of the Academy-funded component of the research.
Closing Date: March 15th
Funding: Government

British Academy Stein-Arnold Exploration Fund

Subjects: History, geography and the arts.
Purpose: To encourage research into the antiquities or historical geography or early history or arts of those parts of Asia that come within the sphere of the ancient civilizations of India, China and Iran, including Central Asia.

Eligibility: Research should be as far as possible by means of exploratory work. Candidates must be British or Hungarian subjects.
Level of Study: Postdoctorate
Type: Funding support
Value: Not to exceed UK £2,500
Frequency: Annual
No. of awards offered: 3–4
Closing Date: March 15th
Funding: Private

British Academy Worldwide Congress Grant

Subjects: Humanities and social sciences.
Purpose: To help meet the costs of organizing major international congresses in the United Kingdom, but only where the congress is one of an established series and where it is clearly the United Kingdom's turn to host the conference.
Eligibility: Open to organizers of worldwide congresses in the United Kingdom.
Level of Study: Postdoctorate
Type: Grant
Value: Maximum UK £20,000
Frequency: Dependent on funds available
Country of Study: Any country
No. of awards offered: 2–3 per year
Application Procedure: Applicants must apply on the prescribed forms, and there is a two-stage consideration procedure.
Closing Date: October 15th
Funding: Government

British Conference Grants

Subjects: Humanities and social sciences.
Purpose: To bring key speakers to conferences held in the United Kingdom.
Eligibility: Applicants must be resident in the United Kingdom and be of postdoctoral or equivalent status.
Level of Study: Postdoctorate
Type: Grant
Value: UK £1,000–20,000
Frequency: As per availability of funds
Country of Study: United Kingdom
No. of awards offered: Approx. 200
Closing Date: April 30th
Funding: Government

Elisabeth Barker Fund

Subjects: Recent European history, particularly of Eastern and Central Europe.
Purpose: To support studies in recent European history, particularly the history of Central and Eastern Europe.
Eligibility: Open to scholars of postdoctoral or equivalent status ordinarily resident in the United Kingdom. Candidates need not be British nationals. Applications must be made by a British resident and not a foreign scholar.
Level of Study: Postdoctorate
Value: Up to UK £1,000
Frequency: Annual
No. of awards offered: Up to 6
Closing Date: March 15th
Funding: Private

Neil Ker Memorial Fund

Subjects: Western medieval manuscripts, particularly those of British interest.
Purpose: To promote the study of Western medieval manuscripts.
Eligibility: Candidates should be of postdoctoral status, or have comparable experience. Normally grants will only be given for monographs, secondary works, editions or studies of documents, texts or illustrations, that include analysis of the distinctive features of original manuscripts.
Level of Study: Postdoctorate
Type: Funding support
Value: Approx. UK £2,000
Frequency: Annual
Country of Study: Any country

No. of awards offered: 3–4
Closing Date: March15th
Funding: Private

Thank-Offering to Britain Fellowships

Subjects: Topics of an economic, industrial, social, political, literary or historical character relating to the British Isles. Preference will be given to projects in the modern period.
Purpose: To fund a research fellowship.
Eligibility: Open to persons ordinarily resident in the United Kingdom and of postdoctoral status. Candidates should be in mid-career and must be employed at a United Kingdom university in an established teaching post.
Level of Study: Postdoctorate
Type: Fellowship
Value: Equivlent to a junior lecturers' salary. The award pays for a replacement to undertake the teaching and administrative duties of the award holders for 1 year
Length of Study: Normally for 1 year
Frequency: Dependent on funds available
Country of Study: United Kingdom
No. of awards offered: 1
Closing Date: November 14th
Funding: Private
Contributor: Association of Jewish Refugees
No. of awards given last year: 1
No. of applicants last year: 74

BRITISH ASSOCIATION FOR AMERICAN STUDIES (BAAS)

Department of English, Oxford Brookes University, Oxford, OX3 OBP, United Kingdom
Tel: (44) 17 7289 3040
Fax: (44) 17 7289 2970
Email: hrsmacpherson@uclan.ac.uk
Website: www.baas.ac.uk
Contact: Dr Catherine Morley, Secretary

The British Association for American Studies (BAAS), established in 1955, promotes research and teaching in all aspects of American studies. The Association organizes annual conferences and specialist regional meetings for students, teachers and researchers. The publications produced are The Journal of American Studies with Cambridge University Press, BAAS Paperbacks with Edinburgh University Press and British Records Relating to America in Microform with Microform Publishing.

BAAS Short Term Awards

Subjects: Culture and society of the United States of America.
Purpose: To fund travel to the United States of America for short-term research projects.
Eligibility: Open to residents in the United Kingdom. Preference is given to young postgraduates and to members of BAAS.
Level of Study: Doctorate, Postdoctorate, Postgraduate, Professional development
Type: Award
Value: UK £750
Frequency: Annual
Country of Study: United States of America
No. of awards offered: 5–10
Application Procedure: Applicants must complete an application form.
Closing Date: December 12th
Funding: Foundation
Contributor: American Embassy
No. of awards given last year: 6
No. of applicants last year: 35
Additional Information: Successful candidates must write a report and acknowledge BAAS assistance in any related publication.

BRITISH ASSOCIATION FOR CANADIAN STUDIES (BACS)

31 Tavistock Square, London, WC1H 9HA, England
Tel: (44) 20 7862 8687
Fax: (44) 20 7117 1875
Email: jodie.robson@canadian-studies.net
Website: www.canadian-studies.net
Contact: Ms Jodie Robson

In response to the growing academic interest in Canada, the British Association for Canadian Studies (BACS) was established in 1975. Its aim is to foster teaching and research on Canada and Canadian issues by locating study resources in Britain, facilitating travel and exchange schemes for professorial staff and ensuring that the expertise of Canadian scholars who visit the United Kingdom is put to effective use. Principal activities include the publication of The British Journal of Canadian Studies and the BACS Newsletter, and the organization of the Association's annual multidisciplinary conference, which attracts scholars from Canada and Europe as well as from the United Kingdom.

BACS Travel Awards

Subjects: Canadian studies, humanities and social sciences.
Purpose: To encourage and fund visits to Canada directly related to the applicant's actual or proposed teaching or research. The awards are intended to increase contact between academics and other scholars in Canada and the United Kingdom, and to assist in the preparation of teaching about Canada.
Eligibility: Open to academics from universities, colleges of higher education and polytechnics of the United Kingdom. Applicants must be citizens or long-term residents of the United Kingdom. Priority will be given to BACS members.
Level of Study: Doctorate, Postdoctorate
Type: Travel grant
Value: Up to UK £500
Frequency: Annual
Study Establishment: Universities or research institutions
Country of Study: Canada
No. of awards offered: 3–5
Application Procedure: Applicants must complete an application form and submit it with a covering letter, his or her curriculum vitae and the names of two referees.
Closing Date: October 1st, February 1st or May 1st
No. of awards given last year: 6
No. of applicants last year: 20
Additional Information: The BACS administers these awards on behalf of the Foundation for Canadian Studies in the United Kingdom.

Prix du Québec Award

Subjects: Humanities and social sciences.
Purpose: To assist British academics carrying out research related to Québec.
Eligibility: Open to citizens or long-term residents of the United Kingdom.
Level of Study: Doctorate, Postdoctorate, Professional development
Type: Award
Value: UK £1,000
Frequency: Dependent on funds available
Study Establishment: Universities, research institutions and schools
Country of Study: Canada
No. of awards offered: 1 award to doctoral and postdoctoral students and 1 award to full-time teaching staff
Application Procedure: Applicants must contact Jodie Robson, Administrator of BACS, for application guidelines.
Closing Date: March 1st
Funding: Government
Contributor: The Office of the Government of Québec in the United Kingdom
No. of awards given last year: 2
Additional Information: The award also seeks to encourage projects that incorporate Québec in a comparative approach. The Québec component must be more than 50 per cent.

BRITISH ASSOCIATION OF PLASTIC RECONSTRUCTIVE AND AESTHETIC SURGEONS (BAPRAS)

The Royal College of Surgeons, 35-43 Lincoln's Inn Fields, London, WC2A 3PE, England
Tel: (44) 20 7831 5161
Fax: (44) 20 7831 4041
Email: secretariat@bapras.org.uk
Website: www.bapras.org.uk
Contact: Ms Angela Rausch, Administrator

Founded in 1946 as British Association of Plastic Surgeons. The objective of the association is to relieve sickness and to protect and preserve public health by the promotion and development of Plastic Surgery. A name change to British Association of Plastic Reconstructive and Aesthetic Surgeons (BAPRAS) took effect in July 2006.

BAPRAS Barron Videotape Prize

Subjects: CD-ROMs or DVDs made on any subject that should run for a maximum of 20 minutes, and will be judged on its technical quality, production and editing, clinical content, educational value and the amount of information, visual and auditory, which is presented in the given time.
Purpose: To award the best videotape submitted by any member or associate of the association or plastic surgery trainee.
Type: Prize
Value: £500
Frequency: Annual
Closing Date: August 31st
Additional Information: The selection will be made by the Education & Research Sub-Committee of the BAPRAS at their meeting in September 2007. The name of the winner will be included in the BAPRAS handbook and a certificate will be presented.

BAPRAS European Travelling Scholarships

Purpose: To enable Specialist Registrars from UK to visit any plastic surgical centre in Europe.
Eligibility: Specialist Registrars (4–6) enrolled on a recognised training programme with the Specialist Advisory Committtee in plastic surgery are eligible to apply. Preference will be given to trainees travelling abroad without other financial awards and those applying for funding prior travel. Candidates seeking funds to travel abroad in paid jobs are less preferred.
Type: Scholarship
Value: £1,000
Frequency: Annual
No. of awards offered: 6
Application Procedure: Applicants should complete an application form, submit a proposed itinerary that should be detailed and give costs and the reasons for particular visits and a curriculum vitae (maximum length of two pages) to the Chairman of the Education and Research Sub-Committee, BAPRAS.
Closing Date: December 31st

BAPRAS Student Bursaries

Subjects: Plastic surgery.
Purpose: To help medical students to cover expenses of travel and research related to plastic surgery.
Eligibility: Medical students in the United Kingdom.
Level of Study: Predoctorate
Type: Bursary
Value: UK £500
Length of Study: Varies
Frequency: Annual
Study Establishment: Hospital plastic surgery units or research laboratories
Country of Study: Any country
No. of awards offered: 20
Application Procedure: Application forms are available on request from the BAPRAS or from the BAPRAS website: www.bapras.org.uk
Closing Date: December 31st
Funding: Private

Contributor: BAPRAS
No. of awards given last year: 20
No. of applicants last year: 33

BAPRAS Travelling Bursary
Subjects: Plastic surgery.
Purpose: To enable a plastic surgeon in the United Kingdom to study new techniques abroad.
Eligibility: Open to members of the Association who are either specialist registrars in years 4–6, enrolled in a recognized training programme or who have not had more than 3 years as consultant plastic surgeons.
Level of Study: Professional development
Type: Bursary
Value: Up to UK £5,000
Length of Study: Varies
Frequency: Annual
Study Establishment: Any approved hospital plastic surgery units
Country of Study: Any country
No. of awards offered: 5
Application Procedure: Applicants must complete an application form and submit it with a proposed itinerary giving details of costs and reasons for wanting to attend a particular unit. A curriculum vitae of not more than two pages must also be submitted.
Closing Date: December 31st
Funding: Private
Contributor: BAPRAS
No. of awards given last year: 5
No. of applicants last year: 11

Paton/Masser Memorial Fund
Subjects: Plastic surgery.
Purpose: To provide funds towards research projects.
Eligibility: Open to consultants and specialist registrars in plastic surgery working in the British Isles.
Level of Study: Research
Value: UK £10,000
Length of Study: Varies
Frequency: Annual
Study Establishment: A hospital or research laboratory
Country of Study: United Kingdom
No. of awards offered: Varies
Application Procedure: Application forms are available on the BAPRAS website: www.bapras.org.uk, or can be obtained by e-mailing a request to the secretariat@bapras.org.uk
Closing Date: December 31st
Funding: Private
Contributor: BAPRAS
No. of awards given last year: 1
No. of applicants last year: 5

Travelling Bursaries for Presentation at Overseas Meetings
Purpose: To cover the expenses for overseas travel by a consultant or trainee to present papers at international meetings.
Eligibility: Applicants must submit an application form to the Chairman of the Education and Research Sub-Committee, BAPRAS.
Type: Travel award
Value: £600
Frequency: Annual
No. of awards offered: 4
Closing Date: December 31st

THE BRITISH COUNCIL INDIA

Mittal Towers C Wing, Nariman Point, Mumbai, 400021, India
Tel: (91) 22790147
Email: mumbai.scholarship@in.britishcouncil.org
Website: www.britishcouncil.org/india

The British Council is the United Kingdom's public diplomacy and cultural organization working in more than 100 countries, in arts, education, governance and science. The British Council promotes the diversity and creativity of British society and culture. The Foreign and Commonwealth Office provides The British Council with the core grant-in-aid.

The De Souza Trust Goa Scholarships
Subjects: Media management, architecture, computing and design, TV documentary, music therapy, architectural conservation and human rights, communication systems and signal processing and innovation technology and the law.
Purpose: To provide opportunities for dynamic young men and women of Goan origin who have demonstrated academic excellence and extra-curricular achievements to study or train in the United Kingdom.
Eligibility: Open to Indian nationals, domiciled and resident in or born of Goan parents, who are not more than 35 years of age and have an excellent academic track record. Candidates must have confirmed admission for any technical/vocational/academic course of study in the United Kingdom for up to 1 year.
Level of Study: Postgraduate
Type: Scholarship
Value: The scholarship covers full or part fees and a gratis student visa for the duration of the course in the United Kingdom
Length of Study: 1 year
Frequency: Annual
Country of Study: United Kingdom
Application Procedure: A completed application form must be sent by post.
Closing Date: May 15th

BRITISH ECOLOGICAL SOCIETY (BES)

26 Blades Court, Putney, London, SW15 2NU, England
Tel: (44) 20 8871 9797
Fax: (44) 20 8871 9779
Email: info@britishecologicalsociety.org; grants@britishecologicalsociety.org
Website: www.britishecologicalsociety.org
Contact: Mr Dominic Burton, Grants Officer

As a learned society and registered charity, the British Ecological Society (BES) is an independent organization receiving no outside funds. The aims of the Society are to promote the science of ecology through research, publications and conferences and to use the findings of such research to educate the public and to influence policy decisions that involve ecological matters. The BES is an active and thriving organization with something to offer anyone with an interest in ecology. Academic journals, teaching resources, meetings for scientists and policy makers, career advice and grants for ecologists are first a few of the societies areas of activity.

BES Early Career Project Grants
Subjects: Ecology.
Purpose: To assist promising young ecologists by supporting innovative or important research of a pure or applied nature, and to provide an opportunity for ecologists recently appointed to academic posts to establish themselves.
Eligibility: Candidates must be in the early stages of their career and will normally be expected to have a PhD before applying. Must be a current BES member.
Type: Project grant
Value: Up to UK £20,000
Length of Study: 1 year
Frequency: Annual
Country of Study: Any country
Application Procedure: Candidates must complete an online application form, available from the BES office. Application form available from BES and from website.
Closing Date: January 31st
No. of awards given last year: 4
No. of applicants last year: 39

Additional Information: Successful candidates will be expected to submit a brief report within 15 months of receipt of the award. Further information is available on request or from the website.

BES Overseas Bursary

Subjects: Ecology.
Purpose: To support ecologists from developing countries in undertaking innovative ecological research.
Eligibility: Open to ecologist based in African or its associated Islands.
Level of Study: Professional development
Type: Grant
Value: Up to UK £7,000
Length of Study: 18 months
Frequency: Annual
Country of Study: Africa
Application Procedure: Applicants must complete an online application form, available from the BES website. Further information is available on request and from the website. By application available from the BES website.
Closing Date: September 1st
Contributor: British Ecological Society

BES Small Ecological Project (SEPG) Grants

Subjects: Ecological research and ecological survey.
Purpose: To promote all aspects of ecological research and ecological survey.
Eligibility: Open to ecological researchers. Support will not normally be given to projects forming part of an expedition proposal. All recipients will be required to submit a report on the work undertaken. (1) Must be a current BES member. (2) Must not be as part of a degree. (3) Applications require two referees. (4) UEPG's are given to an individual student who is responsible for completion of a report can be as part of an expedition but applicant has to take responsibility of completing own part of expedition.
Level of Study: Professional development
Type: Project grant
Value: Up to UK £1,000 for travel and up to UK £1,500 for other costs
Frequency: Annual
Country of Study: Any country
Application Procedure: Applicants must complete an online application form, available from the BES website.
Closing Date: April 1st and November 1st
Contributor: British Ecological Society
No. of awards given last year: 37
No. of applicants last year: 450
Additional Information: Published papers and reports to other organizations should include an acknowledgement of the support from the BES. Other conditions may apply. The Coalbourn Trust is an independent trust that looks to the BES to nominate suitable projects for funding. Recommendations for funding will be made from among the applicants for Small Ecological Project Grants. All applicants for Small Ecological Project Grants will automatically be eligible for funding from the Coalbourn Trust. Further information is available on request or from the website.

BES Specialist Course Grants

Subjects: Ecology.
Purpose: To help meet the costs of specialist field courses.
Eligibility: Open to postgraduates and recent graduates who are not in full-time employment. The Society will not fund applicants where a specialist course is a formal part of a credit-bearing programme e.g., a degree, diploma, or certificate. There are a limited number of grants, which are allocated on a first-come first-served basis.
Level of Study: Graduate, Postgraduate
Type: Grant
Value: The course fee, which may also include accommodation. There is limit of £300 per person
Frequency: Annual
Country of Study: United Kingdom
Application Procedure: Applicants must complete an application form, available from the BES office. See the BES and the BES website.
Closing Date: As advertised in the Bulletin and on BES website

Additional Information: The Education, Training and Careers Committee decides upon the courses that will receive available grants. Successful applicants are bound by the booking conditions of the institution running the course, and non-attendance on a booked course will result in the applicants being personally liable for the cancellation fee. Grantees are required to produce a short report on the course. Further information is available from the website.

Student Support for Attendance at BES and Specialist Group

Subjects: Ecology.
Purpose: To support students attending the Society's Winter and Annual General Meeting, Annual Symposium and Special Symposium.
Eligibility: Open to BES members. Applications must be endorsed by the student's Head of Department or research supervisor. Bulk applications on behalf of a group of students are not accepted. Undergraduates who at the time of the meeting will have graduated but not yet be enrolled on a postgraduate course and postgraduates.
Level of Study: Graduate, Postgraduate
Type: Grant
Value: 50 per cent of the cost of the registration fee plus meals and accommodation while at the meeting can only be claimed on a first-come first served basis on the online registration form
Frequency: Annual
No. of awards offered: Varies
Application Procedure: Applicants must complete an application form, available from the BES office. When all funds have been committed the price reduction for students will not be available on the online registration form.
Closing Date: By registration deadline of the Annual meeting. Other meetings are advertised in the Bulletin and on BES website
Contributor: British Ecological Society
Additional Information: Registration procedure and form available online at the BES website.

Travel Grants for Ecologists from Developing Countries to Attend BES Meetings

Subjects: Ecology.
Purpose: To make travel grants available to ecologists who wish to attend Society Annual meetings and Symposia within the UK.
Eligibility: Open to scientists and citizens of a country that is classified as low-income or low-middle-income economies according to the World Bank categorization.
Type: Grant
Value: UK £2,000
Country of Study: United Kingdom
Application Procedure: A completed application form along with supporting statements from the UK host institution and the applicants institution should be submitted.
Closing Date: February 1st
Additional Information: Applicants for a BES Travel Grant for Ecologists from Developing Countries should be a scientist and a citizen of a country that is classified as 'low-income economy' or 'lower-middle-income economy' according to the World Bank categorization. Applicants from countries classified as 'low-income economies' will have priority. Normally have at least a B.Sc. or equivalent degree. Usually be working or studying at a University or Research Institution (including field centres, NGOs, museums, etc.) that provides basic research facilities. Be working in scientific areas within the remit of the BES (the science of ecology) and of relevance to the Meeting they are applying to attend.

BRITISH FEDERATION OF WOMEN GRADUATES (BFWG)

4 Mandeville Courtyard, 142 Battersea Park Road, London, SW11 4NB, England
Tel: (44) 20 7498 8037
Fax: (44) 20 7498 5213
Email: awards@bfwg.org.uk
Website: www.bfwg.org.uk
Contact: Secretary

The British Federation of Women Graduates (BFWG) provides opportunities to women in education and public life. BFWG works as part of an international organization to improve the lives of women and girls, fosters local, national and international friendship and offers scholarships for final year postgraduate research.

AAUW Rose Sidgwick Memorial Fellowship

Subjects: All subjects.

Purpose: To assist with study or research that demonstrates a continued interest in the advancement of women.

Eligibility: Open to female members of the British Federation of Women Graduates (BFWG) or another national federation or association (NFA) of the International Federation of University Women (IFUW), who are not US citizens, are below 30 years of age, with acceptance by an institution in America at which the applicant proposes to undertake her work.

Level of Study: Graduate, Postdoctorate, Postgraduate, Predoctorate, Research

Type: Fellowship

Value: From US$18,000–30,000. The fellowship does not cover travel costs

Length of Study: 1 year

Frequency: Annual

Study Establishment: An Institute of Higher Education

Country of Study: United States of America

No. of awards offered: 1

Application Procedure: Applicants studying in Great Britain must apply through BFWG. Application material and membership details can be downloaded from their website or for paper copies via BFWG; or write to BFWG enclosing a C5 self-addressed stamped envelope.

Closing Date: Late March in the year preceding the competition for applicants studying in Great Britain. October 31st for applicants applying direct to America

Funding: Private

Contributor: AAUW members

Additional Information: If studying outside Great Britain, candidates should check the list of NFAs on IFUW's website (www.ifuw.org) or contact the AAUW Educational Foundation via their website. BFWG will interview those short-listed in June then write a letter of recommendation to AFUW.

For further information contact:

AAUW Educational Foundation, International Fellowships, PO Box 4030, Iowa City, IA, 52243-4030, United States of America
Website: www.act.org/fga/fellowships_grants/international.cfm

AAUW/IFUW International Fellowships

Subjects: All subjects.

Purpose: To assist study or research that demonstrates a continued interest in the advancement of women.

Eligibility: Open to female members of the British Federation of Women Graduates (BFWG) or another national federation or association (NFA) of the International Federation of University Women (IFUW), who are not US citizens, with acceptance by an institution in America at which the applicant proposes to undertake her work.

Level of Study: Graduate, Postdoctorate, Postgraduate, Predoctorate, Research

Type: Fellowships

Value: From US$18,000–30,000. These fellowships do not cover travel costs

Length of Study: 1 year

Frequency: Annual

Study Establishment: An Institute of Higher Education

Country of Study: United States of America

No. of awards offered: 6

Application Procedure: Application material can be downloaded from AAUW's website.

Closing Date: December 1st of the year preceding the competition

Funding: Private

Contributor: AAUW members

Additional Information: A list of NFA's can be found on IFUW's website (www.ifuw.org). Applicants studying in Great Britain (England, Scotland or Wales) must be members of BFWG. See BFWG website or for paper membership application forms write to the BFWG contact

address enclosing a C5 self addressed stamped envelope. A money order of US$20 must accompany all applications.

For further information contact:

AAUW Educational Foundation, International Fellowships, PO Box 4030, Iowa City, IA, 52243-4030, United States of America
Email: aauw@act.org
Website: www.act.org/fga/fellowships_grants/international.cfm

AFFDU Grants

Subjects: All subjects.

Purpose: To assist those at doctoral or postdoctoral levels whose studies or research take place in France.

Eligibility: Open to female members of the British Federation of Women Graduates (BFWG) or another national federation or association (NFA) of the International Federation of University Women (IFUW), who know the language of the country in which they plan to study.

Level of Study: Postgraduate, Doctorate, Postdoctorate, Research

Type: Grant

Value: From €300–1,500. The award does not cover travel costs

Length of Study: Up to 12 months

Frequency: Annual

Study Establishment: An Institute of Higher Education

Country of Study: France

No. of awards offered: 2 or 3

Application Procedure: Applicants should be undergraduate or postgradaute students, should have applied for admission to the University for a full-time scheme and have satisfied the entry requirements.

Closing Date: April 1st of the year preceding the competition

Funding: Private

Contributor: AFFDU members

Additional Information: A list of NFA's can be found on IFUW's website (www.ifuw.org). Applicants studying in Great Britain (England, Scotland or Wales) must be members of BFWG. See BFWG's website or for paper membership details write to BFWG, enclosing a C5 self-addressed stamped envelope.

For further information contact:

AFFDU, Reid Hall, 4 rue de Chevreuse, Paris, F-75006, France
Email: affdu@club-internet.fr
Website: www.int-evry.fr/affdu

AFFDU Monique Fouet Grant

Subjects: Political Sciences

Purpose: To support a women postgraduate studying Political Science.

Eligibility: Open to female members of the British Federation of Women Graduates (BFWG) or another National Federation of Association (NFA) of the International Federation of University Women (IFUW), who wish to undertake research on the AFFDU project site in Nabasdju Civol. Candidates must speak French.

Level of Study: Postgraduate, Research

Type: Grant

Value: From €1,000–1,500. The award does not cover travel costs

Length of Study: Up to 1 year

Frequency: Annual

Study Establishment: A university or institution of university status

Country of Study: Any country

No. of awards offered: 1

Application Procedure: Application materials can be downloaded from AFFDU's website or obtained via e-mail.

Closing Date: Mid-March of the year preceding the competition

Funding: Private

Contributor: AFFDU members

Additional Information: A list of NFA's can be found on IFUW's website (www.ifuw.org). Applicants studying in Great Britain (England, Scotland or Wales) must be members of BFWG. See BFWG's website or for paper membership details write to BFWG, enclosing a C5 self-addressed stamped envelope.

For further information contact:

AFFDU, Reid Hall, 4 rue de Chevreuse, Paris, F-75006, France

Email: affdu@club-internet.fr
Website: www.int.evry.fr/affdu

AFUW Australian Capital Territory Bursary

Subjects: All subjects.
Purpose: To offer free board and lodging in Canberra.
Eligibility: Open to female members of the British Federation of Women Graduates (BFWG) or another National Federation of Association (NFA) of the International Federation of University Women (IFUW), who graduated from a university or a tertiary institution in Australia, New Zealand, Papua-New Guinea or South Pacific countries for board and lodging at a residential college in Canberra.
Level of Study: Graduate, Postgraduate, Research
Type: Bursary
Value: Australian $1,000 onwards. The Bursary does not cover travel costs
Length of Study: Up to 4 weeks
Frequency: Annual
Study Establishment: A university or tertiary instituition
Country of Study: Australia
Application Procedure: Application material can be downloaded from the AFUW's website (www.afuw.org.au).
Closing Date: July 31st of the year preceding the competition
Funding: Private
Contributor: AFUW members
Additional Information: A list of NFA's can be found on the IFUW's website (www.ifuw.org). Applicants studying in Great Britain (England, Scotland or Wales) must be members of BFWG. See BFWG's website or for paper membership details write to BFWG, enclosing a C5 self- addressed stamped envelope.

For further information contact:

AFUW-ACT Inc, 138 LaPerouse Street, Red Hill, ACT 2603, Australia
Website: www.afuw-act.com
Contact: Fellowship Convenor

AFUW Georgina Sweet Fellowship

Subjects: Study or research in any discipline.
Purpose: To support a female postgraduate student in undertaking an advanced post-first degree.
Eligibility: Open to female members of the British Federation of Women Graduates (BFWG) or another National Federation of Association (NFA) of the International Federation of University Women (IFUW), who are not Australian citizens, with acceptance by the institution in Australia at which the applicant proposes to undertake her work.
Level of Study: Doctorate, Postgraduate, Research
Type: Fellowship
Value: Australian $6,000. The fellowship does not cover travel costs
Length of Study: 4–12 months
Frequency: Every 2 years
Study Establishment: A university or institution of university status
Country of Study: Australia
No. of awards offered: 1
Application Procedure: Applicants studying in Great Britain must apply through BFWG. Application material and membership details can be downloaded from their website or for paper copies via BFWG, write to BFWG enclosing a C5 self-addressed stamped envelope.
Closing Date: Late March in the year preceding the competition for applicants studying in Great Britain. July 31st for applicants applying direct to Australia
Funding: Private
Contributor: AFUW members
Additional Information: BFWG will interview those short-listed in June then write a letter of recommendation to AFUW.

For further information contact:

53 Verulam Road, Lampton, NSW 2299, Australia
Website: www.afuw.org.au
Contact: AFUW Fellowships Convenor

AFUW Western Australian Bursaries

Subjects: Study or research in mathematics, science, humanities or social sciences.

Purpose: To assist in the completion of a higher degree by research; academic support for further writing and research; research in mathematics or science or research or coursework in the humanities or social sciences.
Eligibility: Open to female members of British Federation of Women Graduates (BFWG) or another national federation or association (NFA) of the International Federation of University Women (IFUW), with acceptance by an institution in WA at which the applicant proposes to undertake her work.
Level of Study: Postgraduate
Type: Bursary
Value: Australian $3,500–5,000. The bursaries do not cover travel costs
Length of Study: 4–12 months
Frequency: Annual
Study Establishment: A university or institution of university status
Country of Study: Australia
No. of awards offered: Varies
Application Procedure: Applications can be downloaded from the AFUW website www.afuw.org.au
Closing Date: July 31st of the year preceding the competition
Funding: Private
Contributor: AFUW members
Additional Information: A list of NFA's can be found on the IFUW's website www.ifuw.org. Applicants studying in Great Britain (England, Scotland or Wales) must be members of BFWF. See the website for more information or write to BFWG for paper memberships.

For further information contact:

AFUW-WA Inc., PO Box 48, Nedlands, WA 6909, Australia
Contact: Bursary Liaision Officer

ASFDU/SVA International Fellowship

Subjects: All subjects.
Purpose: To support postgraduate study and research in Switzerland.
Eligibility: Open to female members of the British Federation of Women Graduates (BFWG) or another national federation or association (NFA) of the International Federation of University Women (IFUW) with acceptance by a Swiss institution at which the applicant proposes to undertake her work. Preference will be given to younger women starting their academic careers; competence in French or German is desirable.
Level of Study: Postgraduate, Research
Type: Scholarship
Value: Swiss francs 14,000. The scholarship does not cover travel costs
Length of Study: Up to 1 year
Study Establishment: A university of instituition of university status
Country of Study: Switzerland
No. of awards offered: 1
Application Procedure: Application materials can be downloaded from ASFDU/SVA's website.
Closing Date: January 31st in the year preceding the competition
Funding: Private
Contributor: ASFDU/SVA members
Additional Information: A list of NFA's can be found on IFUW's website (www.ifuw.org). Applicants studying in Great Britain (England, scotland or Wales) must be members of BFWG. See BFWG's website or for paper membership details write to BFWG, enclosing a C5 self-addressed stamped envelope.

For further information contact:

AFFDU/SVA, Schlossbergerstrasse 26, Zollikon, CH-8700, Switzerland
Website: www.unifemmes.ch
Contact: Fellowship Secretariat

BFWG Eila Campbell Scholarship

Subjects: Geography.
Purpose: To assist in final-year PhD research.
Eligibility: Academic excellence as evidenced by a proven ability to carry out independent research is the chief criterion. Open to female students, regardless of nationality, whose studies take place in Great Britain. Research students should be entering into their final year of formal study towards a PhD degree. Taught Master's degrees do not

count as research, although MPhil research students would need to be upgraded to a PhD around the close of the competition or thereabouts.
Level of Study: Research, Predoctorate
Type: Scholarship
Value: UK £2,500–6,000
Length of Study: 1 year
Frequency: Annual
Study Establishment: A university or institution of university status
Country of Study: Great Britain
No. of awards offered: Normally 1
Application Procedure: Application materials can be downloaded from our website or for paper copies write to BFWG enclosing a C5 self-addressed stamped envelope.
Closing Date: Late March for the academic year commencing in the Autumn
Funding: Private
Contributor: BFWG members
No. of awards given last year: 7
No. of applicants last year: 235
Additional Information: Recipients must submit a written report within 6 months of being awarded their PhD.

For further information contact:

BFWG, 4 Mandeville Courtyard, 142 Battersea Park Road, London, SW11 4NB, United Kingdom

BFWG Johnstone and Florence Stoney Studentship

Subjects: Biological, geological, meteorological or radiological science.
Purpose: To assist in final-year PhD research.
Eligibility: Academic excellence as evidenced by a proven ability to carry out independent research is the chief criterion. Open to female students, regardless of nationality, whose studies take place in Great Britain. Research students should be entering into their final year of formal study towards a PhD degree. Taught Master's degrees do not count as research, although MPhil research students would need to be upgraded to a PhD during the close of the competition or thereabouts.
Level of Study: Predoctorate, Research
Type: Studentship
Value: UK £2,500–6,000; the studentship does not cover travel costs
Length of Study: 1 year
Frequency: Annual
Study Establishment: A university or institution of university status
Country of Study: Australia, New Zealand or South Africa
No. of awards offered: 1
Application Procedure: Application materials can be downloaded from BFWG's website or for paper copies write to BFWG enclosing a stamped self-addressed envelope.
Closing Date: Late March in the year of the competition
Funding: Private
Contributor: BFWG members
No. of awards given last year: 7
No. of applicants last year: 235
Additional Information: Recipients must submit a written report within 6 months of being awarded their PhD.

For further information contact:

BFWG, 4 Mandeville Courtyard, 142 Battersea Park Road, London, SW11 4NB, United Kingdom

BFWG Kathleen Hall Fellowship

Subjects: All subjects.
Purpose: To assist final-year PhD research students.
Eligibility: Academic excellence as evidenced by a proven ability to carry out independent research is the chief criterion. Open to female students preferably from countries of low per capita income, whose studies take place in Great Britain. Research students should be entering into their final year of formal study towards a PhD degree. Taught Master's degrees do not count as research, although MPhil research students would need to be upgraded to a PhD during the close of the competition or thereabouts.
Level of Study: Predoctorate, Research
Type: Fellowship
Value: UK £2,500–6,000

Length of Study: 1 year
Frequency: Annual
Study Establishment: A university or institution of university status
Country of Study: Great Britain
No. of awards offered: 1
Application Procedure: Application materials can be downloaded from BFWG's website or for paper copies write to BFWG enclosing a stamped self-addressed envelope.
Closing Date: Late March in the year of the competition
Funding: Private
Contributor: BFWG members
No. of awards given last year: 7
No. of applicants last year: 235
Additional Information: Recipients must submit a written report within 6 months of being awarded their PhD.

For further information contact:

BFWG, 4 Mandeville Courtyard, 142 Battersea Park Road, London, SW11 4NB, United Kingdom

BFWG M H Joseph Prize

Subjects: Architecture or engineering.
Purpose: To assist final-year PhD research students.
Eligibility: Academic excellence as evidenced by a proven ability to carry out independent research is the chief criterion. Open to female students, regardless of nationality, whose studies take place in Great Britain. Research students should be entering into their final year of formal study towards a PhD degree. Taught Master's degrees do not count as research, although MPhil research students would need to be upgraded to a PhD during the close of the competition or thereabouts.
Level of Study: Predoctorate, Research
Type: Prize
Value: UK £2,500–6,000
Length of Study: 1 year
Frequency: Annual
Study Establishment: A university or institution of university status
Country of Study: Great Britain
No. of awards offered: 1
Application Procedure: Application materials can be downloaded from BFWG's website or for paper copies write to BFWG enclosing a stamped self-addressed envelope.
Closing Date: Late March in the year of the competition
Funding: Private
Contributor: BFWG members
No. of awards given last year: 7
No. of applicants last year: 235
Additional Information: Recipients must submit a written report within 6 months of being awarded their PhD.

For further information contact:

BFWG, 4 Mandeville Courtyard, 142 Battersea Park Road, London, SW11 4NB, United Kingdom

BFWG Ruth Bowden Scholarship

Subjects: Medical sciences.
Purpose: To assist final-year PhD research students.
Eligibility: Academic excellence as evidenced by a proven ability to carry out independent research is the chief criterion. Open to female students, regardless of nationality, whose studies take place in Great Britain. Research students should be entering into their final year of formal study towards a PhD degree. Taught Master's degrees do not count as research, although MPhil research students would need to be upgraded to a PhD during the close of the competition or thereabouts.
Level of Study: Research, Predoctorate
Type: Scholarship
Value: UK £2,500–6,000
Length of Study: 1 year
Frequency: Annual
Study Establishment: A university or institution of university status
Country of Study: Great Britain
No. of awards offered: 1
Application Procedure: Application materials can be downloaded from BFWG's website or for paper copies write to BFWG enclosing a C5 stamped self-addressed envelope.

Closing Date: Late March in the year of the competition
Funding: Private
Contributor: BFWG members
No. of awards given last year: 7
No. of applicants last year: 235
Additional Information: Recipients must submit a written report within 6 months of being awarded their PhD.

For further information contact:

BFWG, 4 Mandeville Courtyard, 142 Battersea Park Road, London, SW11 4NB, United Kingdom

BFWG Scholarships

Subjects: Research in any discipline.
Purpose: To assist final-year PhD research students.
Eligibility: Academic excellence as evidenced by a proven ability to carry out independent research is the chief criterion. Open to female students, regardless of nationality, whose studies take place in Great Britain. Research students should be entering into their final year of formal study towards a PhD degree. Taught Master's degrees do not count as research, although MPhil research students would need to be upgraded to a PhD during the close of the competition or thereabouts.
Level of Study: Predoctorate, Research
Type: Scholarship
Value: UK £2,500–6,000
Frequency: Annual
Study Establishment: A university or institution of university status
Country of Study: Great Britain
No. of awards offered: Varies but not normally more than 8
Application Procedure: Application materials can be downloaded from BFWG's website or for paper copies write to BFWG enclosing a stamped self-addressed envelope.
Closing Date: Late March in the year of the competition
Funding: Private
Contributor: BFWG members
No. of awards given last year: 7
No. of applicants last year: 235
Additional Information: Recipients must submit a written report within 6 months of being awarded their PhD.

For further information contact:

BFWG, 4 Mandeville Courtyard, 142 Battersea Park Road, London, SW11 4NB, United Kingdom

IAUW International Scholarship

Subjects: Arts and humanities, Jewish area and cultural studies, international law.
Purpose: To foster friendly relations between university women in Israel and abroad.
Eligibility: Open to female members of the British Federation of Women Graduates (BFWG) or another national federation or association (NFA) of the International Federation of University Women (IFUW) with acceptance by an institution in Israel at which the applicant proposes to undertake her work.
Level of Study: Postgraduate, Research
Type: Scholarship
Value: US$3,000 onwards. The scholarship does not cover travel costs
Length of Study: Up to 1 year
Frequency: Every 3 years
Study Establishment: A university or institution of university status
Country of Study: Israel
No. of awards offered: 1
Application Procedure: Application materials can be downloaded from IAUW's website www.ifuw.org/israel
Funding: Private
Contributor: IAUW members
Additional Information: A list of NFA's can be found on IFUW's website (www.ifuw.org). Applicants studying in Great Britain (England, scotland or Wales) must be members of BFWG. See BFWG's website or for paper membership details write to BFWG, enclosing a C5 self-addressed stamped envelope.

For further information contact:

IAUW, PO Box 7505, Jerusalem, 91074, Israel
Website: www.ifuw.org/israel
Contact: Chairwoman Fellowship Committee

IFUW International Fellowships

Subjects: Research or study in any discipline. However, priority will be given to proposals related to IFUW's priorities.
Purpose: To assist research, study or training to improve the status of women and girls and the promotion of women in scientific and technological careers.
Eligibility: Open to female members of the British Federation of Women Graduates (BFWG) or another national federation or association (NFA) of the International Federation of University Women (IFUW) with acceptance by the institution at which the applicant proposes to undertake her work.
Level of Study: Doctorate, Postdoctorate, Professional development, Research
Type: Fellowships
Value: Between 8,000 and 10,000 Swiss Francs. The awards do not cover travel costs, travel to conferences or direct family support
Length of Study: Up to 12 months
Frequency: Every 3 years
Study Establishment: A university or institution of university status
Country of Study: Any country
No. of awards offered: Varies
Application Procedure: Applicants studying in Great Britain must apply through BFWG. Application material and membership details can be downloaded from their website or for paper copies via BFWG, write to BFWG enclosing a C5 stamped self addressed envelope.
Closing Date: Late March in the year preceding the competition for applicants studying in Great Britain. November 1st for applicants applying direct to Switzerland
Funding: Private
Contributor: IFUW/NFA members
Additional Information: If studying outside Great Britain, candidates should check the list of NFAs on IFUW's website (www.ifuw.org) or contact IFUW. BFWG will interview those short-listed in June then write a letter of recommendation to IFUW. Grants between 3,000 and 6,000 Swiss Francs and Awards of about 1,000 Swiss Francs are also awarded.

For further information contact:

IFUW International Fellowships and Grants, 10 rue du Lac, Geneva, CH-1207, Switzerland

IFUWA Amy Rustomjee International Scholarship

Subjects: All subjects.
Purpose: To offer free accommodation and partially free board to a woman undertaking advanced research in Mumbai.
Eligibility: Open to female members of the British Federation of Women Graduates (BFWG) or another national federation or association (NFA) of the International Federation of University Women (IFUW) with acceptance by an institution in Mumbai at which the applicant proposes to undertake her work.
Level of Study: Postgraduate, Research
Type: Scholarship
Value: A stipend. The scholarship does not cover travel costs
Length of Study: Up to 1 year
Frequency: Annual
Study Establishment: A university or institution of university status
Country of Study: India
No. of awards offered: 1
Application Procedure: Application materials can be downloaded from IFUWA's website www.ifuw.org or obtained via an e-mail to wgu1915@bom2.vsnl.net.in.
Funding: Private
Contributor: IFUWA members
Additional Information: A list of NFA's can be found on IFUW's website (www.ifuw.org). Applicants studying in Great Britain (England, scotland or Wales) must be members of BFWG. See BFWG's website or for paper membership details write to BFWG, enclosing a C5 self- addressed stamped envelope.

For further information contact:

Scholarship Committee, Women Graduates Union, Union Road, Colaba, Mumbai, 400005, India
Contact: Chairman

IFUWA Sarojini Naidu Memorial Scholarship
Subjects: Indian culture.
Purpose: To encourage the exchange of scholars between India and other countries, to foster global understanding and to promote studies on Indian culture and women's development.
Eligibility: Open to female members of the British Federation of Women Graduates (BFWG) or another national federation or association (NFA) of the International Federation of University Women (IFUW) with acceptance by an institution in Delhi at which the applicant proposes to undertake her work.
Level of Study: Postgraduate, Research
Type: Scholarship
Value: Indian Rupees 30,000. The scholarship does not cover travel costs
Length of Study: 12 months
Frequency: Annual
Study Establishment: An Institute of Higher Education
Country of Study: India
No. of awards offered: 1
Application Procedure: Application materials can be downloaded from IFUWA's website www.ifuw.org oror obtained via an e-mail to ladcollege@yahoo.co.uk
Closing Date: December 31st of the year preceding the competition
Funding: Private
Contributor: IFUWA members
Additional Information: A list of NFA's can be found on IFUW's website (www.ifuw.org). Applicants studying in Great Britain (England, Scotland or Wales) must be members of BFWG. See BFWG's website or for paper membership details write to BFWG, enclosing a C5 self-addressed stamped envelope.

For further information contact:

University Women's Association of Delhi, Room 12, Kamla Devi Hostel, 6 Bhagwan Das Road, New Delhi, 110 001, India
Contact: The Convenor (Scholarships)

JAUW International Fellowship
Subjects: All subjects.
Purpose: To assist independent research or advanced study in Japan.
Eligibility: Open to female members of the British Federation of Women Graduates (BFWG) or another national federation or association (NFA) of the International Federation of University Women (IFUW) with acceptance by a Japanese institution at which the applicant proposes to undertake her work.
Level of Study: Research, Postgraduate
Type: Fellowship
Value: ¥500,000–1,000,000. The fellowships do not cover travel costs
Length of Study: 3 months minimum
Frequency: Annual
Study Establishment: A university or instituition of university status
Country of Study: Japan
No. of awards offered: 2
Application Procedure: Applicants studying in Great Britain must apply through BFWG. Application material and membership details can be downloaded from their website or for paper copies write to BFWG, 4 Mandeville Courtyard, 142 Battersea Park Road, London SW11 4NB enclosing a C5 self-addressed stamped envelope.
Closing Date: Late March in the year preceding the competition for applicants studying in Great Britain
Funding: Private
Contributor: JAUW members
Additional Information: If studying outside Great Britain, candidates should check the list of NFAs on IFUW's website (www.ifuw.org) or contact JAUW or via their website. BFWG will interview those short-listed in June then write a letter of recommendation to JAUW.

For further information contact:

JAUW, 11-6-101 Samoncho, Shinjuku-ku, Tokyo, 160-0017, Japan
Website: www.jauw.org

NKA Ellen Gleditsch Scholarship
Subjects: All subjects.
Purpose: To assist independent research or advanced studies by women at the post-graduate or doctoral level.
Eligibility: Open to female members of the British Federation of Women Graduates (BFWG) or another national federation or association (NFA) of the International Federation of University Women (IFUW) with acceptance by a Norwegian institution at which the applicant proposes to undertake her work and proof of adequate health insurance.
Level of Study: Doctorate, Postgraduate, Research
Type: Scholarship
Value: Norwegian krone 40,000. The scholarship does not cover tavel costs
Length of Study: 3–4 months
Frequency: Every 3 years
Study Establishment: A university or institution of university status
Country of Study: Norway
No. of awards offered: 1
Application Procedure: Applicants studying in Great Britain must apply through BFWG. Application material and membership details can be downloaded from their website or for paper copies write to BFWG, 4 Mandeville Courtyard, 142 Battersea Park Road, London SW11 4NB enclosing a C5 self-addressed stamped envelope.
Closing Date: Late March in the year preceding the competition for applicants studying in Great Britain. September 1st for applicants applying direct to Norway
Funding: Private
Contributor: NKA members
Additional Information: If studying outside Great Britain, candidates should check the list of NFAs on IFUW's website (www.ifuw.org) or contact EGS or via their website. BFWG will interview those short-listed in June then write a letter of recommendation to NKA.

For further information contact:

EGS, PO Box 251, Bergen, N-5000, Norway
Email: elisabeth.haavet@hi.uib.no
Website: www.fou.uib.no/nka/

SAAWG International Fellowship
Subjects: All subjects.
Purpose: To enable a non-South African postgraduate female student to undertake research in South Africa.
Eligibility: Open to female members of the British Federation of Women Graduates (BFWG) or another national federation of association (NFA) of the International Federation of University Women (IFUW) with acceptance by an institution in South Africa at which the applicant proposes to undertake her work.
Level of Study: Postgraduate, Research
Type: Fellowship
Value: South African Rand 2,500. The scholarship does not cover travel costs
Length of Study: 1 year
Frequency: Every 3 years
Study Establishment: A university or instituition of university status
Country of Study: South Africa
No. of awards offered: 1
Application Procedure: Application material can be downloaded from SAAWG's website www.ifuw.org/southafrica/awards.htm
Closing Date: February in the year preceding the competition
Funding: Private
Contributor: SAAWG members
Additional Information: A list of NFA's can be found on IFUW's website (www.ifuw.org). Applicants studying in Great Britain (England, Scotland or Wales) must be members of BFWG. See BFWG's website or for paper membership details write to BFWG, enclosing a C5 self- addressed stamped envelope.

For further information contact:

Postnet Suite 495, Private Bag, Benmore, Gauteng, 2010, South Africa
Contact: Fellowship Secretariat

THE BRITISH INSTITUTE AT ANKARA (BIAA)

10 Carlton House Terrace, London, SW1Y 5AH, United Kingdom
Tel: (44) 020 7969 5204
Fax: (44) 020 7969 5401
Email: biaa@britac.ac.uk
Website: www.biaa.ac.uk/index.html

BIAA aims to support, promote, facilitate, and publish British research focused on Turkey and the Black Sea littoral in all academic disciplines within the arts, humanities, and social sciences and to maintain a centre of excellence in Ankara focused on the archaeology and related subjects of Turkey.

BIAA Post-Doctoral Research Fellowship

Subjects: Turkey and Black Sea littoral and may fall within any of the academic disciplines of the arts, humanities, and social sciences.
Purpose: To focus on Turkey and/or the Black Sea littoral within any of the academic disciplines of the arts, humanities, and social sciences leading to a substantial publication either in monograph or in article form.
Eligibility: Open to candidates who hold a doctorate and who have a demonstrable connection to UK academia.
Level of Study: Doctorate
Type: Fellowship or Grant
Value: £14,000 per year and the cost of one return flight between the UK and Turkey to be paid by BIAA
Length of Study: 1 year from September
Frequency: Annual
Study Establishment: British Institute at Ankara
Country of Study: Turkey
No. of awards offered: 1
Application Procedure: Applicants should submit an application form to the London address. Applications can be filed from March 15th.
Closing Date: April 15th
No. of awards given last year: 1
Additional Information: Shortlisted candidates will be interviewed in London in May.

BIAA Research Scholarship

Subjects: Turkey and Black Sea littoral in any disciplines of the arts, humanities, and social sciences.
Purpose: To conduct their own research at doctoral level.
Eligibility: Open to candidates who hold a Master's degree and have a demonstrable connection to UK academia.
Level of Study: Postgraduate, Research
Type: Research scholarship
Value: £800 per month and the cost of one return flight between the United Kingdom and Turkey
Length of Study: 9 months
Frequency: Annual
Country of Study: Turkey
No. of awards offered: 1
Application Procedure: Applications can be filed from July 11th. Check website for further details.
Additional Information: The study starts from October 1st.

For further information contact:

British Institute at Ankara, Ankara, Turkey
Tel: (90) 020 7969 5204
Fax: (90) 020 7969 5401
Email: biaa@britac.ac.uk
Website: www.biaa.ac.uk
Contact: Siobhan McKeown

BIAA Study Grants

Subjects: Research in the fields of the arts, humanities, and the social sciences related to Turkey and the Black Sea littoral.
Purpose: To support doctoral or postdoctoral research in the fields of the arts, humanities, and the social sciences related to Turkey and the Black Sea littoral.
Eligibility: Open to postgraduate students or postdoctoral scholars based in a British university.

Level of Study: Graduate, Postdoctorate, Postgraduate
Type: Grant
Value: £500 per month for basic subsistence and accommodation and an airfare of £300
Length of Study: Upto 3 months
Frequency: Twice a year
Study Establishment: BIAA
Country of Study: Turkey
Application Procedure: Applicants must complete a copy of the form downloaded from the Institute's website, supported by a reference from the supervisor of postgraduate research or, for postdoctoral applicants, another suitable academic (who are not members of the BIAA Research Committee or staff of the Institute) and send the completed form to the London address.
Closing Date: November 1st and April 1st
Additional Information: Do not enclose any attachments unless they have been specifically asked for by BIAA.

BIAA Travel Grants

Subjects: Turkey and the Black Sea littoral and may fall within any of the academic disciplines of the arts, humanities, and social sciences.
Purpose: To enable students in the fields of the arts, humanities, and social sciences to travel to and in Turkey and the Black Sea region.
Eligibility: Open to postgraduate candidates based at a British university. The study should be undertaken in Turkey and the Black Sea region.
Level of Study: Postgraduate
Type: Travel grant
Value: UK £500
Frequency: Annual
Study Establishment: BIAA
Country of Study: Turkey
Application Procedure: Applicants must submit an application form to the London address.
Closing Date: February 1st

BIAA/SPBS Fieldwork Award

Subjects: Turkey and Black Sea littoral relating to Byzantine studies.
Purpose: To support fieldwork in Turkey and/or the Black Sea littoral relating to Byzantine studies.
Eligibility: Open to postgraduate students based at a British university. The study should be undertaken in Turkey and the Black Sea region and should relate to Byzantine studies.
Level of Study: Doctorate, Postgraduate
Type: Award
Value: Up to £400
Frequency: Annual
Study Establishment: British Institute of Ankara/Society for the Promotion of Byzantine Studies
Country of Study: Turkey
No. of awards offered: 1–2
Application Procedure: Applications must be submitted to the London address.
Closing Date: February 1st

BIAA/SPHS Fieldwork Award

Subjects: Turkey and Black Sea relating to Hellenic studies.
Purpose: To support fieldwork by a postgraduate on Turkey or the Black Sea region relating to Hellenic studies.
Eligibility: Open to postgraduate students based at a British university. The study should be undertaken in Turkey and the Black Sea region and should relate to Hellenic studies.
Level of Study: Postgraduate
Type: Grant
Value: Up to UK £400
Frequency: Annual
Study Establishment: British Institute of Ankara/Society for the Promotion of Hellenic Studies
Country of Study: Turkey
No. of awards offered: 1–2
Application Procedure: Applicants should submit an application form to the London address.
Closing Date: February 1st
Additional Information: Shortlisted candidates will be interviewed in London in May.

Martin Harrison Memorial Fellowship

Subjects: Archaeology.

Purpose: To assist junior Turkish archaeologists, who are not able to take advantage of travelling, working in any area of the archaeology of Anatolia from Prehistory to the Ottoman period, to visit the United Kingdom, especially Oxford, in connection with their research work.

Eligibility: Open to Turkish citizens residing in Turkey who have completed at least 2 years of postgraduate research and at most held a doctorate for 5 years, working in any area of the archaeology of Anatolia (from the Prehistoric to the Ottoman period).

Level of Study: Doctorate, Postgraduate, Research

Type: Short-term fellowship

Value: £1,500 and travel expenses from and to Turkey

Length of Study: 6–13 weeks

Frequency: Annual

Study Establishment: University of Oxford

Country of Study: United Kingdom

No. of awards offered: 1

Application Procedure: Completed applications, including a curriculum vitae, should be sent to the Turkey address.

Closing Date: March 31st

Funding: Foundation

Contributor: Martin Harrison Fund for living expenses and British Institute at Ankara (BIAA) for travel

Additional Information: The selection will be made on the basis of the applicant's academic record, coherent research proposal, ability to benefit from libraries and scholars in Oxford, and a working knowledge of spoken and written English.

For further information contact:

The British Institute at Ankara, 24 Tahran Caddesi, Kavaklidere, Ankara, TR 06700, Turkey
Tel: (90) 90 312 427 54 87
Fax: (90) 90 312 428 01 59
Email: ggirdivan@biaatr.org

BRITISH INSTITUTE FOR THE STUDY OF IRAQ (GERTRUDE BELL MEMORIAL)

10 Carlton House Terrace, London, SW1Y 5AH, United Kingdom
Tel: (44) 207 969 5274
Fax: (44) 207 969 5401
Email: bsai@britac.ac.uk or bisi@britac.ac.uk
Website: www.britac.ac.uk/institutes/iraq/
Contact: Mrs Joan Porter MacIver, Administrator

The institute was established in 1932 to promote, support and undertake research in Iraq and neighbouring countries. The schools academic coverage includes the subjects of archeology, history, anthropology, geology, language and other related domaind from the earliest times until the present. In 2007 it changed its name from the British School of Archaeology in Iraq to reflect its expanded remit.

British School of Archaeology in Iraq Grants

Subjects: Archaeology, history and the languages of Iraq and neighbouring countries from the earliest times to the present.

Purpose: To encourage and support research into the archaeology (and cognate subjects), history and languages of Iraq and its neighbouring countries.

Eligibility: Open to United Kingdom or Commonwealth citizens who are graduates or postgraduates with a knowledge of Western-Asiatic archaeology.

Level of Study: Doctorate, Graduate, Postdoctorate, Postgraduate

Type: Grant

Value: Usually between UK £4,000, depending on the nature of the research

Length of Study: 1 academic year

Frequency: Annual, Twice a year

No. of awards offered: Varies

Application Procedure: The School considers applications for individual research grants twice a year in January and October and Autumn. Information and application forms are available from either the Administrator or the website. Two academic references are required.

Closing Date: January 31st or October 31st

Funding: Government, trusts

Contributor: British Academy

No. of awards given last year: 12

Additional Information: Details of the British School of Archaeology in Iraq are available on the website under 'Institutes Overseas and Sponsored Societies.' Grantees will be required to provide a written report of their work and abstracts from these reports will be published in future issues of the School's newsletter. Individual research and travel grants are offered.

BRITISH INSTITUTE IN EASTERN AFRICA

PO Box 30710, Nairobi, GPO 00100, Kenya
Tel: (254) 020 43 43330/43190
Fax: (254) 020 43 43365
Email: justin.willis@biea.ac.uk
Website: www.biea.ac.uk
Contact: Dr Justin Willis, Director

The British Institute in Eastern Africa (BIEA) exists to promote research in the humanities and social sciences. BIEA is based in Nairobi, but supports work across Eastern Africa, and is one of the schools and institutes supported by the British Academy.

British Institute in Eastern Africa Graduate Attachments

Subjects: Humanities and social sciences.

Purpose: To provide opportunities for research experience to recent university graduates.

Eligibility: Open to recent graduates from UK and East African universities.

Level of Study: Postgraduate

Type: Studentship

Value: Covers travel and subsistence

Length of Study: 3–6 months

Frequency: Annual

Study Establishment: The British Institute in Eastern Africa

No. of awards offered: Up to 12

Application Procedure: Candidates must submit a letter of application to the Director, BIEA with the names of two academic referees and a curriculum vitae.

Closing Date: March 31st

Funding: Government

Contributor: British Academy

No. of awards given last year: 13

No. of applicants last year: 72

Additional Information: Small grants and assistance may be offered on a discretionary basis to scholars of other nationalities. Archaeology students may be required to assist in excavation carried out by the Institute's staff. Details of activities are published in the *Archaeology Abroad* bulletin and in the Institute's annual report, copies of which are available on request.

British Institute in Eastern Africa Minor Grants

Subjects: Humanities and social sciences.

Purpose: To assist with the costs of research projects in Eastern Africa.

Eligibility: Open to applicants from United Kingdom and Eastern Africa.

Level of Study: Postgraduate

Type: Grant

Value: Up to UK £1,000

Frequency: Twice each year

Study Establishment: The British Institute in Eastern Africa

No. of awards offered: Up to 10

Application Procedure: Application forms can be downloaded from the BIEA website.

Closing Date: April 30th and October 31st

Funding: Government

Contributor: British Academy

No. of awards given last year: 22

No. of applicants last year: 45

Additional Information: Applicants must contact the Director for further information on relevant topics likely to receive support. Those awarded grants will be required to keep the Institute regularly informed of the progress of their research, to provide a preliminary statement of accounts within 18 months of the award dates and to provide the Institute with copies of all relevant publications. They are encouraged to discuss with the Director the possibility of publishing their results in the Institute's journal, *Azania*. Results for the Minor Grants Award may be expected within 2 months of either May 30th or November 30th. Those awarded grants are required to become members of the BIEA.

For further information contact:

Email: pjlane@insightkenya.com

BRITISH LIBRARY

96 Euston Road, London, NW1 2DB, England
Tel: (44) 20 7412 7702
Fax: (44) 20 7412 7780
Email: maps@bl.uk
Website: www.maphistory.info/wallis.html
Contact: Mr Peter Barber, Map Librarian

Helen Wallis Fellowship

Subjects: The history of cartography, preferably with an international dimension, history.
Purpose: To promote the extended and complementary use of the British Library's book and cartographic collections in historical investigation.
Eligibility: Applicants should write for details.
Level of Study: Doctorate, Postdoctorate, Postgraduate
Type: Fellowship
Value: Up to UK £300
Length of Study: 6 months–1 year
Frequency: Annual
Study Establishment: British Library, London
Country of Study: United Kingdom
No. of awards offered: 1
Application Procedure: Applicants must submit a letter indicating the proposed period and outlining the research project together with a full curriculum vitae and give three references.
Closing Date: May 1st
Funding: Private
No. of awards given last year: 1
Additional Information: The award honours the memory of Dr Helen Wallis, OBE (1924–1995), Map Librarian at the British Museum and then the British Library between the years 1967–1986. Further information can be found on the website.

BRITISH LUNG FOUNDATION

73-75 Goswell Road, London, EC1V 7ER, England
Tel: (44) 20 7688 5555
Fax: (44) 20 7688 5556
Email: blf@britishlungfoundation.com
Website: www.lunguk.org
Contact: Julia Heidsta, Research Manager

The British Lung Foundation provides information to the public on lung conditions and all aspects of lung health. The Foundation provides support to those who live with a lung condition every day of their lives through the Breathe Easy Club, a nationwide network of local voluntary support groups, and finds solutions to lung disease by funding world-class medical research.

British Lung Foundation Project Grants

Subjects: Respiratory diseases.
Purpose: To promote medical research into the prevention, diagnosis and treatment of all types of lung diseases.
Eligibility: Open to graduates working within the United Kingdom who have relevant research experience. The principal applicant must be based in a research centre in the United Kingdom.
Level of Study: Professional development, Postgraduate, Postdoctorate, Doctorate, Predoctorate, Research
Type: Project grant
Value: Up to UK £120,000
Length of Study: Up to 3 years
Frequency: Annual
Study Establishment: An approved research centre

Country of Study: United Kingdom
No. of awards offered: Approx. 10
Application Procedure: Applicants must complete an application form, available from the British Lung Foundation.
Closing Date: Spring, for preliminary applications for awards in October
Funding: Private, commercial
Contributor: Voluntary donations
No. of awards given last year: Approx. 10
No. of applicants last year: 132

BRITISH MEDICAL ASSOCIATION (BMA)

BMA House, Tavistock Square, London, WC1H 9JP, England
Tel: (44) 20 7383 6755
Fax: (44) 20 7383 6383
Email: info.sciencegrants@bma.org.uk
Website: www.bma.org.uk
Contact: Luke Garland, Research Grants Executive

The BMA is a voluntary professional association with over two-thirds of practising UK doctors in membership and an independent trade union dedicated to protecting individual members and the collective interests of doctors.

Doris Hillier Research Grant

Subjects: Research into rheumatism and arthritis (and every 3rd year into Parkinson's disease).
Purpose: To assist and support research.
Eligibility: Open to registered medical practitioners in the United Kingdom.
Level of Study: Research
Type: Research grant
Value: Approx. UK £50,000
Length of Study: 3 years
Frequency: Annual
Country of Study: United Kingdom
No. of awards offered: 1
Application Procedure: Applicants must complete an application form.
Closing Date: Mid-March
Funding: Private
No. of awards given last year: 1
Additional Information: Grants are advertised in January, on the BMA website and in the *British Medical Journal*.

H C Roscoe Research Grant

Subjects: Research into the common cold and/or other viral diseases of the human respiratory system.
Purpose: To assist and support research.
Eligibility: Open to members of the BMA and non-medical scientists working in association with a BMA member.
Level of Study: Research
Type: Research grant
Value: Approx. UK £50,000
Length of Study: 3 years
Frequency: Annual
No. of awards offered: 1
Application Procedure: Applicants must complete an application form.
Closing Date: Mid-March
Funding: Private
No. of awards given last year: 1
Additional Information: Grants are advertised in January, on the BMA website and in the *British Medical Journal*.

Helen Lawson Research Grant

Subjects: Varies each year.
Purpose: To assist and support research.
Eligibility: Open to registered medical practitioners in the United Kingdom who are BMA members.
Level of Study: Research
Type: Research grant
Value: Approx. UK £50,000

Length of Study: 3 years
Frequency: Annual
Country of Study: United Kingdom
No. of awards offered: 1
Application Procedure: Applicants must complete an application form.
Closing Date: Mid-March
Funding: Private
No. of awards given last year: 1
Additional Information: Grants are advertised in January, on the BMA website and in the *British Medical Journal*.

The James Trust Research Grant

Subjects: Research into asthma.
Purpose: To assist and support research.
Eligibility: Open to registered medical practitioners in the United Kingdom who are BMA members.
Level of Study: Research
Type: Research grant
Value: Approx. UK £55,000
Length of Study: 3 years
Frequency: Annual
Country of Study: United Kingdom
No. of awards offered: 1
Application Procedure: Applicants must complete an application form.
Closing Date: Mid-March
Funding: Private
No. of awards given last year: 1
Additional Information: Grants are advertised in January, on the BMA website and in the *British Medical Journal*.

Joan Dawkins Research Grant

Subjects: Varies each year.
Purpose: To assist and support research.
Eligibility: Open to registered medical practitioners. Non-medical scientists may also apply. Projects must relate to the United Kingdom.
Level of Study: Research
Type: Research grant
Value: Approx. UK £50,000
Length of Study: 3 years
Frequency: Annual
Country of Study: United Kingdom
No. of awards offered: 1
Application Procedure: Applicants must complete an application form.
Closing Date: Mid-March
Funding: Private
No. of awards given last year: 1
Additional Information: Grants are advertised in January, on the BMA website and in the *British Medical Journal*.

Josephine Lansdell Research Grant

Subjects: Research in the field of heart disease.
Purpose: To assist and support research.
Eligibility: Open to registered medical practitioners in the United Kingdom who are BMA members.
Level of Study: Research
Type: Research grant
Value: Approx. UK £50,000
Length of Study: 3 years
Frequency: Annual
Country of Study: United Kingdom
No. of awards offered: 1
Application Procedure: Applicants must complete an application form.
Closing Date: Mid-March
Funding: Private
No. of awards given last year: 1
Additional Information: Grants are advertised in January, on the BMA website and in the *British Medical Journal*.

Kathleen Harper

Subjects: Varies each year.
Purpose: To assist and support research.

Eligibility: Registered medical practitioners in the United Kingdom who are also BMA members.
Value: Approx. UK £50,000
Length of Study: 3 years
Frequency: Annual
Application Procedure: Applicants should complete an application form.
Closing Date: Mid-March
Funding: Private
No. of awards given last year: 1
Additional Information: Grants are advertised in January on the BMA website and in the British Medical Journal.

Margaret Temple Research Grant

Subjects: Research into schizophrenia.
Purpose: To assist and support research.
Eligibility: Open to medical practitioners. Non-medical scientists may also apply. Projects must relate to the United Kingdom.
Level of Study: Research
Type: Research grant
Value: Approx. UK £50,000
Length of Study: 3 years
Frequency: Annual
Country of Study: United Kingdom
No. of awards offered: 1
Application Procedure: Applicants must complete an application form.
Closing Date: Mid-March
Funding: Private
No. of awards given last year: 2
Additional Information: Grants are advertised in January, on the BMA website and in the *British Medical Journal*.

Samuel Strutt Research Grant

Subjects: Subject varies every year.
Purpose: To assist and support research.
Eligibility: Registered medical practitioners in the UK.
Level of Study: Research
Type: Research grant
Value: Approx. UK £1,500
Length of Study: 3 years
Frequency: Annual
Country of Study: United Kingdom
No. of awards offered: 1
Application Procedure: Applicants must complete an application form.
Closing Date: Mid-March
Funding: Private
No. of awards given last year: 1
Additional Information: Grants are advertised in January, on the BMA website and in the *British Medical Journal*.

T P Gunton Research Grant

Subjects: Research into public health relating to cancer.
Purpose: To assist and support research.
Eligibility: Open to both medical practitioners and non-medical scientists in the United Kingdom.
Level of Study: Research
Type: Research grant
Value: Approx. UK £40,000
Length of Study: 3 years
Frequency: Annual
Country of Study: United Kingdom
No. of awards offered: 1
Application Procedure: Applicants must complete an application form.
Closing Date: Mid-March
Funding: Private
No. of awards given last year: 1
Additional Information: Grants are advertised in January, on the BMA website and in the *British Medical Journal*.

Vera Down Research Grant

Subjects: Research into neurological disorders.
Purpose: To assist and support research.

Eligibility: Open to registered medical practitioners in the United Kingdom.
Level of Study: Research
Type: Research grant
Value: Approx. UK £50,000
Length of Study: 3 years
Frequency: Annual
Country of Study: United Kingdom
No. of awards offered: 1
Application Procedure: Applicants must complete an application form.
Closing Date: Mid-March
Funding: Private
No. of awards given last year: 1
Additional Information: Grants are advertised in January, on the BMA website and in the *British Medical Journal*.

BRITISH MOUNTAINEERING COUNCIL (BMC)

177-179 Burton Road, Manchester, M20 2BB, United Kingdom
Tel: (44) (00 44) 0161 445 6111
Fax: (44) (00 44) 0161 445 4500
Email: office@thebmc.co.uk
Website: www.thebmc.co.uk

The BMC is the representative body that exists to protect the freedoms and promote the interests of climbers, hill walkers and mountaineers.

Alpine Ski Club Kenneth Smith Scholarship

Subjects: Ski research.
Purpose: To assist skiers and mountaineers in improving their touring and ski mountaineering skills and qualifications.
Level of Study: Professional development
Type: Scholarship
Value: UK £600
Length of Study: 1 year
Frequency: Annual
No. of awards offered: 2
Application Procedure: Contact organization.
Closing Date: October 31st
Funding: Trusts
Contributor: Kenneth Smith Trust

For further information contact:

The ASC Awards Sub-Committee, 22 Hatton Court, Hatton of Fintray, Aberdeenshire, AB21 OYA
Contact: Mrs Jay Turner

BMC Grant

Purpose: To fund innovative-style ascents in the greater mountain ranges by professional mountaineers.
Level of Study: Professional development
Type: Grant
Value: UK £1,000
Length of Study: 1 year
Frequency: Annual
No. of awards offered: Varies
Application Procedure: Contact the British Mountaineering Council.
Closing Date: No closing date

BRITISH RETINITIS PIGMENTOSA SOCIETY (BRPS)

PO Box 350, Buckingham, Buckinghamshire, MK18 1GZ, England
Tel: (44) 12 8082 1334
Fax: (44) 12 8081 5900
Email: info@brps.org.uk
Website: www.brps.org.uk
Contact: Mrs Lynda Cantor MBE, Trustee/Hon President

The British Retinitis Pigmentosa Society (BRPS) is a membership organization run by volunteers with branches throughout the United Kingdom. The BRPS aims to raise funds for scientific research to provide treatments leading to a cure for retinitis pigmentosa. The Society provides a welfare support and guidance service to its members and their families.

BRPS Research Grants

Subjects: Retinitis pigmentosa.
Purpose: To financially support research into treatments leading to a cure for retinitis pigmentosa.
Eligibility: Please contact the Society.
Level of Study: Postgraduate
Type: Research grant
Value: Varies
Length of Study: Varies
Frequency: Twice a year
Country of Study: Any country
No. of awards offered: Varies
Application Procedure: Applicants must submit their application to the BRPS office.
Closing Date: March 10th, September 10th
Funding: Individuals, private, trusts

BRITISH SCHOOL AT ATHENS

52 Souedias Street, Athens, 106 76, Greece
Tel: (30) 210 721 0974
Fax: (30) 210 723 6560
Email: admin@bsa.ac.uk
Website: www.bsa.gla.ac.uk
Contact: Assistant Director

The British School at Athens promotes research into the archaeology, architecture, art, history, language, literature, religion and topography of Greece in ancient, medieval and modern times. It consists of the Library, Fitch Laboratory for Archaeological Science, Archive, Museum, hostel and a second base at Knossos for research and fieldwork.

The Elizabeth Catling Memorial Fund for Archaeological Draughtmanship

Purpose: To encourage excellence in archaeological drawing, including the preparation of finished drawings for publication. It is hoped that awards will help individuals to improve their standards of draughtsmanship and also enable the preparation of a larger number of drawings, of higher quality, than might otherwise have been possible.
Eligibility: Individual applicants must show that drawings are an essential part of their research. Furthermore, although not a precondition, it is hoped that they may be draughtsmen themselves. Applications from project directors, who may also apply during the course of a field campaign, are limited to unexpected expenses that are not provided for in the project's budget, such as extra maintenance costs to enable a draughtsman to draw unforeseen material and finds.
Level of Study: Predoctorate
Value: £200
Frequency: Annual
No. of awards offered: 3
Application Procedure: Candidates should submit letters of application to the School's London office by post in four copies or by e-mail. Letters should not be longer than two pages and should include a statement of the purposes of the application and a budget and timetable for the proposed work, together with the name and address of a referee whom the awarding panel(s) may consult. Applications may be made for but are not limited to, grants towards the maintenance costs of longer stays at museums and other study centres so as to achieve work that would not otherwise have been attempted. Recipients of awards must have been admitted as Students of the School for the appropriate Session before receiving their grants, and must submit a short report on the use of the grant to the London office.
Closing Date: May 1st
Additional Information: The Fund does not support printing expenses, or site drawings such as plans and sections, or computer graphics.

For further information contact:

British School at Athens, Senate House, Malet Street, London, WC1E 7HU

Email: bsa@sas.ac.uk

Hector and Elizabeth Catling Bursary

Subjects: Greek studies including the archaeology, art, history, language, literature, religion, ethnography, anthropology or geography of any period and all branches of archaeological science.
Purpose: To assist travel, maintenace costs and for the purchase of scientific equipments.
Eligibility: Open to researchers of British, Irish or Commonwealth nationality.
Level of Study: Doctorate, Postdoctorate, Postgraduate, Research
Type: Bursary
Value: A maximum of UK £500 per bursary to assist with travel and maintenance costs incurred in fieldwork, to pay for the use of scientific or other specialized equipment in or outside the laboratory in Greece or elsewhere and to buy necessary supplies
Frequency: Annual
Study Establishment: The British School at Athens
No. of awards offered: 1–2
Application Procedure: Applicants must submit a curriculum vitae and state concisely the nature of the intended work, a breakdown of budget, the amount requested from the Fund and how this will be spent. Applications should include two sealed letters of reference. Bursary holders must submit a short report to the Committee upon completion of the project.
Closing Date: January 1st
Funding: Private
Additional Information: The bursary is not intended for publication costs, and cannot be awarded to an excavation or field survey team.

The John Morrison Memorial Fund for Hellenic Maritime Studies

Purpose: To further research into all branches of Hellenic maritime studies of any period.
Value: £500
No. of awards offered: 1–2
Application Procedure: Candidates should submit letters of application to the School's London office by post in four copies or by e-mail. Letters should not be longer than two pages and should include a statement of the purposes of the application and a budget and timetable for the proposed work, together with the name and address of a referee whom the awarding panel(s) may consult. Applications may be made for but are not limited to, grants towards the maintenance costs of longer stays at museums and other study centres so as to achieve work that would not otherwise have been attempted. Recipients of awards must have been admitted as Students of the School for the appropriate Session before receiving their grants, and must submit a short report on the use of the grant to the London office.
Closing Date: May 1st
Additional Information: Grants may also be available from the Fund for buying maritime books and journals for the School's Library.

For further information contact:

British School at Athens, Senate House, Malet Street, London, WC1E 7HU

Email: bsa@sas.ac.uk

The Richard Bradford McConnell Fund for Landscape Studies

Subjects: All disciplines of the arts, humanities and sciences (or any combination of them).
Purpose: To assist research in the interaction of place and people in Greece and Cyprus at any period(s).
Value: £400
Frequency: Annual
Application Procedure: Candidates should submit letters of application to the School's London office by post in four copies or by e-mail. Letters should not be longer than two pages and should include a statement of the purposes of the application and a budget and timetable for the proposed work, together with the name and address of a referee whom the awarding panel(s) may consult. Applications may be made for but are not limited to, grants towards the maintenance costs of longer stays at museums and other study centres so as to achieve work that would not otherwise have been attempted. Recipients of awards must have been admitted as Students of the School for the appropriate Session before receiving their grants, and must submit a short report on the use of the grant to the London office.
Closing Date: April 1st
Contributor: Richard Bradford Trust

For further information contact:

British School at Athens, Senate House, Malet Street, London, WC1E 7HU

Email: bsa@sas.ac.uk

The Vronwy Hankey Memorial Fund for Aegean Studies

Purpose: To support research in the prehistory of the Aegean and its connections with the East Mediterranean.
Eligibility: Preference may be given to younger Students.
Value: £500 are available for the expenses (including, but not limited to, attending conferences to present papers, photography, and travel to museums and sites)
Application Procedure: Candidates should submit letters of application to the School's London office by post in four copies or by e-mail. Letters should not be longer than two pages and should include a statement of the purposes of the application and a budget and timetable for the proposed work, together with the name and address of a referee whom the awarding panel(s) may consult. Applications may be made for but are not limited to, grants towards the maintenance costs of longer stays at museums and other study centres so as to achieve work that would not otherwise have been attempted. Recipients of awards must have been admitted as Students of the School for the appropriate Session before receiving their grants, and must submit a short report on the use of the grant to the London office.
Closing Date: May 1st

For further information contact:

British School at Athens, Senate House, Malet Street, London, WC1E 7HU

Email: bsa@sas.ac.uk

BRITISH SCHOOL AT ROME (BSR)

The British Academy, 10 Carlton House Terrace, London, SW1Y 5AH, England
Tel: (44) 20 7969 5202
Fax: (44) 20 7969 5401
Email: bsr@britac.ac.uk
Website: www.bsr.ac.uk
Contact: Dr Gill Clark, Registrar

The British School at Rome (BSR) is an interdisciplinary research centre for the humanities, visual arts and architecture. Each year, the School offers a range of awards in its principal fields of interest. These interests are further promoted by lectures, conferences, publications, exhibitions, archaeological research and an excellent reference library.

Abbey Fellowships in Painting

Subjects: Painting.
Purpose: To give mid-career artists the opportunity of working in Rome.
Eligibility: Open to mid-career painters with an established record of achievement. Applicants must be citizens of the United Kingdom or United States of America or have been resident in either country for at least 5 years.
Level of Study: Doctorate, Postdoctorate, Research, Postgraduate, Professional development
Type: Fellowship
Value: UK £700 per month plus full board and lodging
Length of Study: 3 months
Frequency: Annual
Study Establishment: The British School at Rome
Country of Study: Italy
No. of awards offered: 3

Application Procedure: Applicants must complete an application form and pay an application fee.
Closing Date: Mid-January
Funding: Private
Contributor: The Abbey Council
No. of awards given last year: 3

For further information contact:

Abbey Awards, 43 Carson Road, London, SE21 8HT, England
Contact: The Administrator

Abbey Scholarship in Painting

Subjects: Painting.
Purpose: To give exceptionally promising emergent painters the opportunity to work in Rome.
Eligibility: Open to citizens of the United Kingdom and United States of America and to those of any other nationality provided that they have been resident in either country for at least 5 years.
Level of Study: Doctorate, Graduate, Postdoctorate, Postgraduate
Type: Scholarship
Value: UK £500 per month plus board and lodging
Length of Study: 9 months
Frequency: Annual
Study Establishment: The British School at Rome
Country of Study: Italy
No. of awards offered: 1
Application Procedure: Applicants must complete an application form and pay an application fee.
Closing Date: Mid-January
Funding: Private
Contributor: The Abbey Council
No. of awards given last year: 1

For further information contact:

Abbey Awards, 43 Carson Road, London, SE21 8HT, England
Contact: The Administrator

Arts Council England Helen Chadwick Fellowship

Subjects: Visual arts.
Purpose: To allow artists to pursue a project that could be made possible or enhanced by spending time in Rome and in Oxford.
Eligibility: Open to visual artists who have established their practices in the years following graduation. Applicants must be United Kingdom nationals or have been continuously resident in the United Kingdom for the last 3 years.
Level of Study: Graduate, Postdoctorate, Postgraduate, Professional development, Research
Type: Fellowship
Value: UK £2,000 per month plus travel and materials allowances, and board and lodging at the British School at Rome and in Oxford
Length of Study: 6 months
Frequency: Annual
Study Establishment: The British School at Rome, the Ruskin School of Drawing and Fine Art at the University of Oxford and St Peter's College, Oxford
Country of Study: United Kingdom and Italy
No. of awards offered: 1
Application Procedure: Applicants must write for details of the application procedure.
Closing Date: January-February
Contributor: Arts Council England
No. of awards given last year: 1

Arts Council of Northern Ireland Fellowship

Subjects: Visual arts.
Eligibility: Visual artists resident in Northern Ireland.
Level of Study: Professional development, Doctorate, Graduate, Postgraduate
Value: UK £650 per month plus board and lodging
Length of Study: 9 months
Frequency: Every 2 years
Study Establishment: The British School at Rome
Country of Study: Italy
No. of awards offered: 1

Application Procedure: Application form must be completed.
Funding: Government
Contributor: Arts Council of Northern Ireland
No. of awards given last year: 1

For further information contact:

The Arts Council of Northern Ireland, MacNeice House, 77 Malone Road, Belfast, BT9 6AQ

Balsdon Fellowship

Subjects: Archaeology, art history, history, society and culture of Italy from prehistory to the modern period.
Purpose: To enable senior scholars engaged in research to spend time in Rome to further their studies.
Eligibility: Open to established scholars normally in a post in a university of the United Kingdom. Applicants must be British or Commonwealth citizens, or must be studying or have studied at postgraduate level in a higher education institution in the UK, having completed not less than 4 years of residence in the UK, or must hold a post in a higher education institution in the UK.
Level of Study: Postdoctorate, Professional development, Research
Type: Fellowship
Value: UK £650 plus board and lodging
Length of Study: 3 months
Frequency: Annual
Study Establishment: The British School at Rome
Country of Study: Italy
No. of awards offered: 1
Application Procedure: Applicants must complete an application form.
Closing Date: Early January
Funding: Private
Contributor: A bequest to the British School at Rome
No. of awards given last year: 1

Derek Hill Foundation Scholarship

Subjects: Painting, drawing.
Purpose: To encourage artists for whom the use of paint and/or drawing is important to the development of their work.
Eligibility: Open to those who are of British or Irish nationality who will be aged 24 years or over on September 1st of the academic year in which the award would be taken up.
Level of Study: Postgraduate, Professional development
Type: Scholarship
Value: Approx. UK £950 per month plus full board and lodging at the British School in Rome
Length of Study: 3 months
Frequency: Annual
Study Establishment: The British School at Rome
Country of Study: Italy
No. of awards offered: 1
Application Procedure: Applicants must complete an application form and pay an entry fee.
Closing Date: Early December
Funding: Foundation
Contributor: Derek Hill Foundation
No. of awards given last year: 1

Giles Worsley Travel Fellowship

Subjects: Architecture, architectural history.
Purpose: To enable an architect or architectural historian to spend 3 months in Rome studying an architectural topic of his choice.
Eligibility: Open to those who are of British nationality or who have been living and studying in Britain for at least the last 3 years.
Level of Study: Postdoctorate, Postgraduate, Professional development
Type: Fellowship
Value: Approx. £700 per month plus full board and lodging at the British School at Rome
Length of Study: 3 months
Frequency: Annual
Study Establishment: The British School at Rome
Country of Study: Italy
No. of awards offered: 1

Application Procedure: Applicants must submit a curriculum vitae, a statement indicating the subject of their proposal and arrange for two references to be sent.
Closing Date: January
No. of awards given last year: 1

Hugh Last Fellowship
Subjects: Classical antiquity.
Purpose: To enable established scholars to collect research material concerning classical antiquity.
Eligibility: Open to established scholars normally in a post at a United Kingdom university. Applicants must be British or Commonwealth citizens, or must be studying or have studied at postgaduate level in a higher education institution in the UK, having completed not less than four years of residence in the UK; or must hold a post in a higher education institution in the UK.
Level of Study: Postdoctorate, Professional development, Research
Type: Fellowship
Value: Board and lodging at the British School at Rome plus a research grant of UK £650
Length of Study: 3 months
Frequency: Annual
Study Establishment: The British School at Rome
Country of Study: Italy
No. of awards offered: 1
Application Procedure: Applicants must complete an application form.
Closing Date: Early January
Funding: Private
Contributor: A bequest to the British School at Rome
No. of awards given last year: 1

Paul Mellon Centre Rome Fellowship
Subjects: The Grand Tour and Anglo-Italian cultural and artistic relations.
Purpose: To assist research on grand tour subjects or on Anglo-Italian cultural and artistic relations.
Eligibility: Open to established scholars in the United Kingdom, United States of America or elsewhere. Applicants should be fluent in Italian.
Level of Study: Graduate, Postdoctorate, Postgraduate, Professional development, Research, Doctorate
Type: Fellowship
Value: Full board at the British School at Rome. For independent scholars, the fellowship offers a stipend of UK £6,000 plus travel to and from Rome. For scholars in full-time university employment, the fellowship offers an honorarium of UK £2,000, travel to and from Rome and a sum of UK £6,000 towards replacement teaching costs for a term at the Fellow's home institution
Length of Study: 4 months
Frequency: Annual
Study Establishment: The British School at Rome
Country of Study: Italy
No. of awards offered: 1
Application Procedure: Applicants must contact the Paul Mellon Centre for Studies in British Art for details.
Closing Date: January
Funding: Private
Contributor: The Paul Mellon Centre for Studies in British Art
No. of awards given last year: 1

For further information contact:

The Paul Mellon Centre for Studies in British Art, 16 Bedford Square, London, WC1B 3JA, England
Email: info@paul-mellon-centre.ac.uk
Website: www.paul-mellon-centre.ac.uk/support/PDFs/4rome.pdf
Contact: The Grants Administrator

Rome Awards
Subjects: Archaeology, art history, history, society and culture of Italy from prehistory to the modern period.
Purpose: To enable persons engaged in research, either for a higher degree or at early postdoctoral level, to spend time in Rome to further their studies.

Eligibility: Applicants must be British or Commonwealth citizens, or must be studying or have studied at postgraduate level in a higher education institution in the UK, having completed not less than 4 years of residence in the UK. Applicants will normally have begun a programme of research in the general field for which the award is sought, whether or not registered for a higher degree. Preference may be given to applicants attached to or registered at a university in the UK or Commonwealth.
Level of Study: Doctorate, Graduate, Postdoctorate, Postgraduate, Research
Type: Grant
Value: UK £150 per month plus UK £180 travel with board and lodging
Length of Study: 3 months
Frequency: Annual
Study Establishment: The British School at Rome
Country of Study: Italy
No. of awards offered: 4
Application Procedure: Applicants must complete an application form.
Closing Date: Early January
Funding: Private
No. of awards given last year: 4

Rome Fellowship
Subjects: Archaeology, art history, history, society and culture of Italy from prehistory to the modern period.
Purpose: To enable those who are at an early post-doctoral stage of their career to launch a major piece of postdoctoral research.
Eligibility: Applicants must be British or Commonwealth citizens, or must be studying or have studied at postgraduate level in a higher education institution in the UK, having completed not less than 4 years of residence in the UK. Successful applicants will need to have been awarded their doctorate prior to taking up the award. Preference may be given to applicants attached to, registered at or working at a university in the UK or Commonwealth.
Level of Study: Postdoctorate
Type: Fellowship
Value: UK £475 per month plus full board and lodging at the British School at Rome
Length of Study: 9 months
Frequency: Annual
Study Establishment: The British School at Rome
Country of Study: Italy
No. of awards offered: Varies
Application Procedure: Applicants must complete an application form.
Closing Date: Early January
Funding: Private
No. of awards given last year: 2

Rome Scholarship in Architecture
Subjects: Architecture and urbanism relevant to Rome and Italy.
Purpose: To encourage the pursuit of projects in architecture and urbanism relevant to Rome and Italy.
Eligibility: Open to architects, students of architecture and associated disciplines of at least postdiploma level who are United Kingdom or Commonwealth nationals, and to those who have been working professionally or studying at postgraduate level for more than 3 years in the United Kingdom or Commonwealth.
Level of Study: Doctorate, Graduate, Postdoctorate, Postgraduate, Professional development, Research
Type: Scholarship
Value: UK £500 per month plus board and lodging
Length of Study: 3–9 months
Frequency: Annual
Study Establishment: The British School at Rome
Country of Study: Italy
No. of awards offered: 1–2
Application Procedure: Applicants must complete an application form and pay an application fee. Application forms are available from the British School at Rome Registrar.
Closing Date: Mid-January
Funding: Private
No. of awards given last year: 1

Rome Scholarship in Landscape Architecture

Subjects: Landscape architecture.

Purpose: To encourage a recent graduate or an individual in mid-career to propose a contemporary response to the Roman landscape and to pursue a topic with direct bearing on modern design in the landscape.

Eligibility: Open to United Kingdom or Commonwealth citizens and to those who have been working professionally or studying at post-graduate level for more than 3 years in the United Kingdom or Commonwealth.

Level of Study: Doctorate, Graduate, Postdoctorate, Postgraduate, Professional development, Research

Type: Fellowship

Value: UK £500 per month plus full board and lodging at the British School at Rome

Length of Study: 3 months

Frequency: Annual

Study Establishment: The British School at Rome

Country of Study: Italy

No. of awards offered: 1

Application Procedure: Applicants must complete an application form and pay an entry fee.

Closing Date: Early January

No. of awards given last year: 1

Rome Scholarships in Ancient, Medieval and Later Italian Studies

Subjects: Archaeology, art history, history, society and culture of Italy from prehistory to the modern period.

Purpose: To enable persons engaged in research, at a predoctoral level, to spend time in Rome to further their studies.

Eligibility: Applicants must be British or Commonwealth citizens, or must be studying or have studied at postgraduate level in a higher education institution in the UK, having completed not less than 4 years of residence in the UK, or must hold a post in a higher education institution in the UK. Applicants must have begun a programme of research in the general field for which the scholarship is being sought, whether or not registered for a higher degree. Preference may be given to applicants attached to, registered at or working at a university in the UK or Commonwealth.

Level of Study: Doctorate, Graduate, Postgraduate, Predoctorate, Research

Type: Scholarship

Value: UK £444 plus board and lodging at the British School at Rome

Length of Study: 9 months

Frequency: Annual

Study Establishment: The British School at Rome

Country of Study: Italy

No. of awards offered: Varies

Application Procedure: Applicants must complete an application form.

Closing Date: Early January

Funding: Private

No. of awards given last year: 3

Rome Scholarships in the Fine Arts

Subjects: Visual arts in any media.

Purpose: To give emerging, early and mid-career artists the opportunity to work in Rome.

Eligibility: Open to United Kingdom or Commonwealth citizens who have been working professionally or studying at postgraduate level for more than 3 years in the United Kingdom or Commonwealth.

Level of Study: Professional development, Doctorate, Graduate, Postdoctorate, Postgraduate, Research

Type: Scholarship

Value: UK £500 per month plus board and lodging

Length of Study: 3–6 months

Frequency: Every 2 years

Study Establishment: The British School at Rome

Country of Study: Italy

No. of awards offered: Varies

Application Procedure: Applicants must complete an application form and pay an application fee.

Closing Date: Early December

Funding: Private

Sainsbury Scholarship in Painting and Sculpture

Subjects: Painting and sculpture, with drawing.

Purpose: To give emerging artists the opportunity to work in Rome.

Eligibility: Open to United Kingdom citizens and to those who have been working professionally or studying at postgraduate level for at least last 5 years in the United Kingdom. Applicants must be under 30 on October 1st in the year in which they would begin to hold the scholarship.

Level of Study: Doctorate, Graduate, Postdoctorate, Postgraduate, Research

Type: Scholarship

Value: UK £900 per month plus board, lodging and a travel grant of UK £1,000

Length of Study: 1 year, with an opportunity for a further 9 months in the following academic year, at the discretion of the selection committee

Frequency: Annual

Study Establishment: The British School at Rome

Country of Study: Italy

No. of awards offered: 1

Application Procedure: Applicants must complete an application form and pay an application fee.

Closing Date: Early December

Funding: Trusts

Contributor: The Linbury Trust

No. of awards given last year: 2

Sargant Fellowship

Subjects: Visual art and architecture.

Purpose: To enable a distinguished artist or architect to research and do new work within the historical context of Rome, away from the pressures associated with exhibiting and deadlines.

Eligibility: Open to United Kingdom or Commonwealth citizens and to those who have been working professionally or studying at postgraduate level for more than 3 years in the United Kingdom or Commonwealth.

Level of Study: Research, Graduate, Postdoctorate, Postgraduate, Professional development

Type: Fellowship

Value: UK £2,000 per month plus board and lodging at the British School at Rome

Length of Study: 3 or 6 months

Frequency: Every 2 years

Study Establishment: The British School at Rome

Country of Study: Italy

No. of awards offered: 1

Application Procedure: Applicants must complete an application form and pay an entry fee.

Closing Date: Mid-December

Funding: Private

Contributor: A bequest to the British School at Rome

No. of awards given last year: 1

Sargant Fellowship in Critical and Curatorial Studies

Subjects: Modern and contemporary art.

Purpose: To allow an established critic, writer, art historian or curator looking at modern and contemporary art, who can present a well-argued case for spending time in Rome to undertake research to inform future publications and/or exhibitions.

Eligibility: Open to citizens of the UK and the Commonwealth nations and to those who have been working professionally or studying at postgraduate level for at least the last 3 years in the UK or Commonwealth.

Level of Study: Professional development, Research

Type: Fellowships

Value: UK £2,000 per month, plus boarding and lodging, plus one-off travel allowance of UK £500

Length of Study: 3 months

Frequency: Dependent on funds available

Study Establishment: The British School at Rome

Country of Study: Italy

No. of awards offered: 1

Application Procedure: Applicants must complete an application form. For further information please visit the website.

Closing Date: Mid-January
Funding: Private
Contributor: A bequest to the British School at Rome

Tim Potter Memorial Award

Subjects: Archaeology.
Purpose: To promote the study of Italian archaeological material by those of high academic potential who have previously had limited opportunity to visit Italy.
Eligibility: Applicants must be British or Commonwealth citizens, or must be studying or have studied at postgraduate level in a higher education institution in the UK, having completed not less than 4 years of residence in the UK or must hold a post in a higher education institution in the UK. Applicants must have graduated prior to taking up the Award, but need not necessarily be registered for postgraduate study. Applications are also invited from those working in museums who could benefit from studying comparable Italian material.
Level of Study: Doctorate, Graduate, Postgraduate, Professional development, Research
Type: Grant
Value: UK £150 per month plus UK £500 travel allowance and full board and lodging at the British School at Rome
Length of Study: 3 months
Frequency: Annual
Study Establishment: The British School at Rome
Country of Study: Italy
No. of awards offered: 1
Application Procedure: Applicants must complete an application form.
Closing Date: Early January
Funding: Private
No. of awards given last year: 1

BRITISH SKIN FOUNDATION

19 Fitzroy Square, London, W1T 6EH,
England
Tel: (44) 20 7383 0266
Fax: (44) 20 7388 5263
Email: bsf@bad.org.uk
Website: britishskinfoundation.org.uk
Contact: Mr James Stalley

The British Skin Foundation exists to support research and education into skin diseases. Working closely with patient support groups as well as many of the country's leading dermatology departments, the foundation aims to help the 7 million people in the United Kingdom who suffer with a serious skin condition.

British Skin Foundation Large Grants

Subjects: Skin diseases in the UK.
Purpose: To support anybody wishing to carry out United Kingdom or Republic of Ireland-based research into skin disease.
Eligibility: Open to medical gradutes.
Value: UK £60,000–75,000
Length of Study: 1–3 years
Country of Study: United Kingdom
Application Procedure: Application forms are available from the website www.britishskinfoundation.org.
Closing Date: September 25th
No. of awards given last year: 8
No. of applicants last year: 44

British Skin Foundation Small Grants

Subjects: Skin diseases in the UK.
Purpose: To support anybody wishing to carry out United Kingdom or Republic of Ireland-based research into skin disease.
Level of Study: Unrestricted
Value: Up to UK £10,000
Length of Study: 1 year
Frequency: Annual
Country of Study: United Kingdom

Application Procedure: Application forms are available from the website www.britishskinfoundation.org
Closing Date: April 24th
Funding: Commercial, private
No. of awards given last year: 5
No. of applicants last year: 11

THE BRITISH SOCIETY FOR HAEMATOLOGY

100 White Lion Street, London, N1 9PF, United Kingdom
Tel: (44) 020 7713 0990
Fax: (44) 020 7837 1931
Email: info@b-s-h.org.uk
Website: www.b-s-h.org.uk

The British Society of Haematology advances the practice and study of haematology and to facilitate contact between persons interested in haematology. It offers scientific scholarships, is an active participant of the International Society of Haematology (ISH) and the International Council for Standardization in Haematology (ICSH) and publishes regular bulletins. The society also provides financial support to regional and national scientific meetings.

Annual Scientific Meeting Scholarships for Haematology Professionals

Subjects: Haematology.
Purpose: To support attendance at the British Society for haematology annual scientific meeting.
Eligibility: Open to clinical scientists, biomedical scientists, academic scientists, PhD students and nurse practitioners working in the United Kingdom.
Level of Study: Doctorate
Type: Scholarship
Value: Up to UK £500 to support registration, travel and accommodation
Frequency: Annual
Country of Study: United Kingdom
No. of awards offered: 40
Application Procedure: Check website for further details.
Closing Date: March 1st
Funding: Private

BRITISH SOCIOLOGICAL ASSOCIATION (BSA)

Bailey Suite, Palatine House, Belmont Business Park, Belmont, Durham, DH1 1TW, England
Tel: (44) 19 1383 0839
Fax: (44) 19 1383 0782
Email: enquiries@britsoc.org.uk
Website: www.britsoc.co.uk

The British Sociological Association (BSA) is the learned society and professional association for sociology in Britain. The Association was founded in 1951 and membership is drawn from a wide range of backgrounds, including research, teaching, students and practitioners in many fields. The BSA provides services to all concerned with the promotion and use of sociology and sociological research.

BSA Support Fund

Subjects: Sociology.
Purpose: To enable members of the association pursue their research interests by way of fieldwork/interview costs, conference attendance in the United Kingdom and overseas (including non-BSA events), thesis production costs.
Eligibility: Open to only fully paid-up members of the association, who are registered under the United Kingdom Concessionary or United Kingdom Lower Payment category, and new members. There is no holding period.
Level of Study: Postgraduate, Unrestricted, Research
Type: Grant

Value: Up to UK £200 per year, to cover costs associated with research, but not tuition fees, equipment or textbook purchase
Country of Study: United Kingdom
No. of awards offered: Approx. 60
Application Procedure: The application form can be downloaded from the BSA website: www.britsoc.co.uk/ students/SupportFund.htm. Applications are processed upon receipt and applicants can expect a response within 14 days.
Closing Date: There is no closing date. Applications are considered as and when received by the Support Fund Committee
Funding: Private
No. of awards given last year: 70
No. of applicants last year: 69

THE BRITISH UNIVERSITIES NORTH AMERICA CLUB (BUNAC)

16 Bowling Green Lane, London, EC1R 0QH,
England
Tel: (44) 20 7251 3472
Fax: (44) 20 7251 0215
Email: scholarships@bunac.org.uk
Website: www.bunac.org
Contact: Scholarships Department

The British Universities North America Club (BUNAC) is a leader in the field of international work and travel exchange programmes. A non-profit, non-political organization offering an ever-increasing range of programmes worldwide, BUNAC is dedicated to serving students and other young people everywhere by providing opportunities to live and work abroad legally.

BUNAC Educational Scholarship Trust (BEST)
Subjects: All subjects. Some awards are specifically for sports and geography-related courses.
Purpose: To help further transatlantic understanding.
Eligibility: Open to citizens of the United Kingdom who have graduated from a United Kingdom university within the last 5 years.
Level of Study: Postgraduate
Type: Scholarship
Value: Approx. US$5,000 per award
Length of Study: 3 months–3 years
Frequency: Annual
Country of Study: United States of America or Canada
No. of awards offered: Up to 10
Application Procedure: Applicants must complete an application form, available from the BUNAC website from January of each year.
Closing Date: Mid-March
Funding: Foundation
No. of awards given last year: 8
No. of applicants last year: 50

BRITISH VETERINARY ASSOCIATION

7 Mansfield Street, London, W1G 9NQ, England
Tel: (44) 20 7636 6541
Fax: (44) 20 7436 2970
Email: bvahq@bva.co.uk
Website: www.bva.co.uk
Contact: Mrs Helena Cotton

The British Veterinary Association's chief interests are the standards of animal health and veterinary surgeons' working practices. The organization's main functions are the development of policy in areas affecting the profession, protecting and promoting the profession in matters propounded by government and other external bodies and the provision of services to members.

Harry Steele-Bodger Memorial Travelling Scholarship
Subjects: Veterinary science and agriculture.
Purpose: To further the aims and aspirations of the late Harry Steele-Bodger.

Eligibility: Open to graduates of veterinary schools in the United Kingdom or the Republic of Ireland who have been qualified for not more than 3 years, and to penultimate or final-year students at those schools.
Level of Study: Unrestricted
Type: Scholarship
Value: Approx. UK £1,100
Frequency: Annual
Study Establishment: A veterinary or agricultural research institute or some other course of study approved by the governing committee
Country of Study: Any country
No. of awards offered: 1 or 2
Application Procedure: Applicants must complete an application form, available on request.
Closing Date: April 24th
Funding: Private
No. of awards given last year: 1
No. of applicants last year: 5
Additional Information: Recipients must be prepared to submit a record of their study abroad.

BROAD MEDICAL RESEARCH PROGRAM (BMRP)

The Eli and Edythe Broad Foundation, 10900 Wilshire Boulevard, 12th Floor, Los Angeles, CA 90024-6532, United States of America
Tel: (1) 310 954 5091
Fax: (1) 310 954 5092
Email: info@broadmedical.org
Website: www.broadmedical.org
Contact: Dr Daniel Hollander, Director

The Eli and Edythe Broad Foundation established the Broad Medical Research Program (BMRP) for Inflammatory Bowel Disease (IBD) Grants in 2001. The BMRP funds innovative and early exploratory clinical and basic research projects that will improve diagnosis, therapy, or prevention of IBD and will lead to long-term funding by more traditional granting agencies.

Broad Medical Research Program for Inflammatory Bowel Disease Grants
Subjects: Understanding, treating and preventing IBD, particularly Crohn's disease and ulcerative colitis.
Purpose: The BMRP is interested in providing funding for clinical or basic research in IBD that will improve the lives of patients with IBD by stimulating innovative early stage research that opens avenues for the diagnosis therapy and prevention of these diseases.
Eligibility: Open to non-profit organizations, such as universities, hospitals and research institutes. There are no other eligibility restrictions. In addition to experienced IBD researchers, the BMRP encourages applications from well-trained scientists who are not presently working in IBD to apply their knowledge, expertise and techniques to IBD research. Interdisciplinary collaboration is strongly encouraged.
Level of Study: Research
Type: Research grant
Value: Budgets should be commensurate with the scope of the work. Those who will need significantly more than US$150,000 per year should contact the BMRP before preparing their letters of interest
Length of Study: 1–2 years, with possible renewal
Frequency: Continuous; letters of interest accepted year round (no deadlines)
Country of Study: Any country
No. of awards offered: Varies
Application Procedure: Applicants must submit a brief letter of interest of up to three pages and also visit the website for further information. Investigators whose letters of interest appear to fit the BMRP's aims will be invited to submit full proposals.
Closing Date: There are no deadlines for receipt of letters of interest
Funding: Foundation
Contributor: Eli and Edythe L Broad
No. of awards given last year: 29
No. of applicants last year: 126

BROADCAST EDUCATION ASSOCIATION (BEA)

Scholarship Committee, 344 Moore Hall, Central Michigan University,
Mount Pleasant, MI 48859, United States of America
Tel: (1) 989 774 3851
Fax: (1) 989 774 2426
Email: orlik1pb@cmich.edu
Website: www.beaweb.org
Contact: Dr Peter B Orlik, Scholarship Chair

The Broadcast Education Association (BEA) is the professional association for professors, industry professionals and graduate students interested in teaching and research related to television, radio and the electronic media industry.

BEA Abe Voron Scholarship

Subjects: Radio.
Purpose: To assist study towards a career in radio.
Eligibility: Open to individuals who can show substantial evidence of superior academic performance and potential to be an outstanding radio professionals.
Level of Study: Unrestricted
Type: Scholarship
Value: US$5,000
Frequency: Annual
Study Establishment: BEA member institutions
No. of awards offered: 2
Application Procedure: Applicants must obtain an official application form from the BEA or from campus faculty. Applicants should refer to the website for more details.
Closing Date: October 10th
Funding: Private
Contributor: The Abe Voron Committee
No. of awards given last year: 2
No. of applicants last year: 45

BEA Alexander M Tanger Scholarship

Subjects: Broadcasting.
Purpose: To assist study for a career in any area of broadcasting.
Eligibility: The applicant must be able to show substantial evidence of superior academic performance and potential to be an outstanding electronic media professional.
Level of Study: Unrestricted
Type: Scholarship
Value: US$5,000
Frequency: Annual
Study Establishment: BEA member institutions
No. of awards offered: 1
Application Procedure: Applicants must obtain an official application form from the BEA or from campus faculty. Applicants should refer to the website for more details.
Closing Date: October 10th
Funding: Private
Contributor: Alexander M Tanger
No. of awards given last year: 1
No. of applicants last year: 94

BEA Harold E Fellows Scholarship

Subjects: Broadcasting.
Purpose: To assist those who are studying towards a career in broadcasting.
Eligibility: The applicant must be able to show substantial evidence of superior academic performance and potential to be an outstanding electronic media professional and must have worked, or their parent must have worked, at an NAB-member station.
Level of Study: Unrestricted
Value: US$2,250
Frequency: Annual
Study Establishment: BEA member institutions
No. of awards offered: 4
Application Procedure: Applicants must obtain an official application form from the BEA or campus faculty. Applicants should refer to the website for more details.
Closing Date: October 10th

Funding: Private
Contributor: National Association of Broadcasters (NAB)
No. of awards given last year: 4
No. of applicants last year: 55

BEA Harold E Fellows Scholarships

Subjects: Broadcasting.
Purpose: To assist study in any area of broadcasting.
Eligibility: The applicant must be able to show substantial evidence of superior academic performance and potential to be an outstanding electronic media professional. The applicant must have worked for pay or college credit at an NAB-member station.
Level of Study: Unrestricted
Type: Scholarship
Value: US$1,250 each
Frequency: Annual
Study Establishment: BEA member institutions
No. of awards offered: 4
Application Procedure: Applicants must obtain an official application form from the BEA or campus faculty. Applicants should refer to the website for more details.
Closing Date: October 10th
Funding: Private
Contributor: NAB
No. of awards given last year: 4
No. of applicants last year: 80

BEA Helen J Sioussat/Fay Wells Scholarships

Subjects: Any area of broadcasting.
Purpose: To assist study in any area of broadcasting.
Eligibility: The applicant must be able to show substantial evidence of superior academic performance and potential to be an outstanding electronic media professional.
Level of Study: Unrestricted
Type: Scholarship
Value: US$1,250 each
Frequency: Annual
Study Establishment: BEA member institutions
No. of awards offered: 2
Application Procedure: Applicants must obtain an official application form from the BEA or campus faculty. Applicants should refer to the website for more details.
Closing Date: October 10th
Funding: Private
Contributor: Broadcasters' Foundation
No. of awards given last year: 2
No. of applicants last year: 96

BEA Vincent T Wasilewski Scholarship

Subjects: Broadcasting.
Purpose: To assist graduate study in any area of broadcasting.
Eligibility: The applicant must be able to show substantial evidence of superior academic performance and potential to be an outstanding electronic media professional. Available to graduate students only
Level of Study: Graduate
Type: Scholarship
Value: US$5,000
Frequency: Annual
Study Establishment: BEA member institutions
No. of awards offered: 1
Application Procedure: Applicants must obtain an official application form from the BEA or campus faculty. Applicants should refer to the website for more details.
Closing Date: October 10th
Funding: Private
Contributor: Patrick Communications Corporation
No. of awards given last year: 1
No. of applicants last year: 35

BEA Walter S Patterson Scholarships

Subjects: Radio.
Purpose: To assist study towards a career in radio.
Eligibility: The applicant must be able to show substantial evidence of superior academic performance and potential to be an outstanding radio professional.

Level of Study: Unrestricted
Type: Scholarship
Value: US$2,250 each
Frequency: Annual
Study Establishment: BEA member institutions
No. of awards offered: 2
Application Procedure: Applicants must obtain an official application form from the BEA or campus faculty. Applicants should refer to the website for more details.
Closing Date: October 10th
Funding: Private
Contributor: NAB
No. of awards given last year: 2
No. of applicants last year: 45

Broadcast Education Two Year College Scholarship

Subjects: Electronic media.
Purpose: To assist study towards an electronic media career.
Eligibility: The applicant must be able to show substantial evidence of superior academic performance and potential to be an outstanding electronic media professional. There should be compelling evidence that the applicant possesses high integrity and a well articulated sense of personal and professional responsibility. The applicant must be studying at, or have studied at, a BEA two-year campus.
Type: Scholarship
Value: US$1,500
Frequency: Annual
Study Establishment: BEA member institutions
No. of awards offered: 2
Application Procedure: Applicants must obtain an official application form from the BEA or campus faculty. Applicants should refer to the website for more details.
Closing Date: October 10th
Funding: Private
Contributor: Sponsored by the Broadcast Education Association
No. of awards given last year: 2
No. of applicants last year: 22

BROOKHAVEN NATIONAL LABORATORY

Brookhaven Women in Science, PO Box 5000, Upton, NY, 11973-5000, United States of America
Tel: (1) 631 344 8000
Email: greenb@bnl.gov
Website: www.bnl.gov
Contact: Ms Loralie Smart

Brookhaven National Laboratory is a multi-programme national laboratory operated by Brookhaven Science Associates for the United States Department of Energy. The Laboratory's broad mission is to produce excellent science in a safe, environmentally benign manner with the co-operation, support and appropriate involvement of many communities.

Renate W Chasman Scholarship

Subjects: Natural sciences, engineering and mathematics.
Purpose: To encourage women whose education was interrupted to pursue formal studies or a career in the natural sciences, engineering or mathematics.
Eligibility: Open to re-entry women residing in Nassau County, Suffolk County, Brooklyn or Queens, who must be citizens of the United States of America or permanent residents. They must be currently enrolled in or have applied for a degree-orientated programme at an accredited institution.
Level of Study: Postgraduate
Type: Scholarship
Value: US$2,000
Frequency: Annual
Country of Study: Any country
No. of awards offered: 1
Application Procedure: Applicants must submit a completed application, academic record, letters of reference and a short essay on career goals.
Closing Date: April 1st
Funding: Private

No. of awards given last year: 1
Additional Information: Please write to the given address for further information. Application forms are also available in PDF on the website.

BUDAPEST INTERNATIONAL MUSIC COMPETITION

Philharmonia Budapest, Kazinczy u.24-26, Budapest, H-1075, Hungary
Tel: (36) 1 266 1459, 302 4961
Fax: (36) 1 302 4962
Email: liszkay.maria@hu.inter.net
Website: www.filharmoniabp.hu
Contact: Ms Maria Liszkay, Secretary

The Budapest Music Competition has been held since 1933. Competitions in different categories alternate annually.

Budapest International Music Competition

Subjects: Musical performance.
Eligibility: Open to young artists of all nationalities who are under 32 years of age.
Level of Study: Professional development
Type: Competition
Value: Up to €24,000
Frequency: Annual
Country of Study: Any country
No. of awards offered: 3
Application Procedure: Applicants must complete an application form to be submitted with other required documentation and should contact the office for further information.
Closing Date: May 1st
Funding: Government
No. of awards given last year: 3

THE BUPA FOUNDATION

Bupa House, 15-19 Bloomsbury Way, London, WC1A 2BA, United Kingdom
Tel: (44) 20 7656 2591
Fax: (44) 20 7656 2708
Email: saunderl@bupa.com
Website: www.bupafoundation.co.uk
Contact: Lee Saunders, Registrar

The Bupa Foundation is an independent medical research charity that funds medical research to prevent, relieve and cure sickness and ill health.

Bupa Foundation Annual Specialist Grant

Subjects: The subject of study may change each year.
Purpose: To provide project funding for studies in a specified area of the Foundation's interests. Please see www.bupafoundation.co.uk for details.
Eligibility: The competition is open to those based in the UK, Australia, Denmark, Hong Kong, New Zealand, Saudi Arabia, Spain and Thailand. Entries must be compliant with the local health and safety legislation if applicable. The Foundation will seek peer reviews from the home country of each shortlisted entry. Researchers and health professionals working for public or private organisations may apply for Bupa Foundation specialist grants for UK-based projects. Study for higher or further degrees, medical electives, educational courses, seminars, conferences, although valuable activities, are not eligible for themed grants. The Foundation will consider specialist grant applications for the creation of research reviews in the field specified in the current year's theme.
Level of Study: Project
Value: Up to UK £750,000 for a project over 1–3 years
Frequency: Annual
Application Procedure: Apply online at bupafoundation.co.uk and one original signed copy to be posted to the Bupa Foundation.
Closing Date: February 28th
Contributor: Bupa Foundation
No. of awards given last year: 4
No. of applicants last year: 31

Additional Information: See medical press and website.

For further information contact:

The Bupa Foundation
Contact: Mrs Lee Saunders, Registrar

Bupa Foundation Medical Research Grant for Health at Work

Subjects: To encourage promotion of good health by not only making people aware of healthy behaviour but also by motivating them to practice it.
Purpose: To support research into the feasibility and potential value of workplace conditions for health promotion and active management of employee health.
Eligibility: Open to health professionals and health researchers.
Level of Study: Doctorate, Postdoctorate, Postgraduate, Research, Project funding
Type: Project grant
Value: Restricted by project need only
Length of Study: A maximum of 3 years
Frequency: Twice yearly
Country of Study: United Kingdom
No. of awards offered: Varies
Application Procedure: For all queries contact Lee Saunders, the Foundation's Registrar. Apply online to www.bupafoundation.co.uk
Closing Date: End July for November intake and end October for February intake
Funding: Foundation
Contributor: Bupa Foundation
No. of awards given last year: 1
No. of applicants last year: 5

Bupa Foundation Medical Research Grant for Information and Communication

Subjects: Health information and communication.
Purpose: To support research designed to enhance partnership between health professionals and public/patients.
Eligibility: Open to health professional and health researchers.
Level of Study: Doctorate, Postdoctorate, Postgraduate, Research
Type: Project grant
Value: Restricted by project needs only
Length of Study: Maximum of 3 years
Frequency: Twice per year
Country of Study: United Kingdom
No. of awards offered: Varies
Application Procedure: For all queries contact Lee Saunders, the Foundation's Registrar. Apply online to www.bupafoundation.co.uk
Closing Date: End July for November intake and end October for February intake
Funding: Foundation
Contributor: Bupa Foundation
No. of awards given last year: 6
No. of applicants last year: 13

Bupa Foundation Medical Research Grant for Preventive Health

Subjects: Preventive health.
Purpose: To support research for preventive health projects in all health environments from epidemiology to health maintenance.
Eligibility: Open to health professionals and health researchers.
Level of Study: Doctorate, Postdoctorate, Postgraduate, Research
Type: Project grant
Value: Restricted by project needs only
Length of Study: A maximum of 3 years
Country of Study: United Kingdom
No. of awards offered: Varies
Application Procedure: For all queries contact Lee Saunders, the Foundation's Registrar. Apply online towww.bupafoundation.co.uk
Closing Date: End July for November intake and end October for February intake
Funding: Foundation
Contributor: Bupa Foundation
No. of awards given last year: 7
No. of applicants last year: 12

Bupa Foundation Medical Research Grant for Surgery

Subjects: Surgery.
Purpose: To support research into surgical practices, outcomes and new surgical techniques.
Eligibility: Open to health professionals and health researchers.
Level of Study: Doctorate, Postdoctorate, Postgraduate, Research
Type: Project grant
Value: Restricted by project needs only
Length of Study: A maximum of 3 years
Frequency: Twice per year
Country of Study: United Kingdom
No. of awards offered: Varies
Application Procedure: For all queries contact Lee Saunders, the Foundation's Registrar. Apply online towww.bupafoundation.co.uk
Closing Date: End July for November intake and end October for February intake
Funding: Foundation
Contributor: Bupa Foundation
No. of awards given last year: 6
No. of applicants last year: 19

Bupa Foundation Medical Research Grant for Work on Older People

Subjects: Prevention, treatment and palliative care of mental ill health in older people.
Purpose: To support research aimed at preventing, treating and caring for mental ill-health in older people.
Eligibility: Open to health professionals and health researchers.
Level of Study: Doctorate, Postgraduate, Research, Postdoctorate
Type: Project grant
Length of Study: A maximum of 3 years
Frequency: 6 months
Country of Study: United Kingdom
No. of awards offered: Varies
Application Procedure: For all queries contact Lee Saunders, the Foundation's Registrar. Apply online.
Closing Date: End July for November intake and end October for February intake
Funding: Foundation
Contributor: Bupa Foundation
No. of awards given last year: 4
No. of applicants last year: 8

THE CALEDONIAN RESEARCH FOUNDATION

Carnegie Trust for the Universities of Scotland, Cameron House, Abbey Park Place, Dunfermline, Fife, KY12 7PZ, Scotland
Tel: (44) 1383 72 4990
Fax: (44) 1383 729799
Email: jgray@carnegie-trust.org
Website: www.carnegie-trust.org
Contact: Ms Jackie Gray, Assistant Secretary

The Caledonian Research Foundation is a Scottish charity that has supported independent research in Scotland since 1990. See also the entries for the Carnegie Trust for the Universities of Scotland.

Caledonian Scholarship

Subjects: All subjects.
Purpose: To support postgraduate research in any subject.
Eligibility: Open to persons possessing a First Class (Honours) Degree from a Scottish university. Scholarship to be held at an instituition in Scotland.
Level of Study: Postgraduate
Type: Scholarship
Value: UK £14,000 plus tuition fees and allowances
Length of Study: Up to 3 years subject to annual renewal
Frequency: Annual
Study Establishment: Any university
Country of Study: Scotland
No. of awards offered: 2 (At least 1 in a non-scientific discipline)
Application Procedure: Application forms available on website or from trust office.
Closing Date: March 15th

Funding: Private
No. of awards given last year: 2
No. of applicants last year: 142
Additional Information: This award is considered along with Carnegie Scholarships.

CRF (Caledonian Research Foundation)/RSE Personal Research Fellowships

Subjects: Biological, biochemical, physical and clinical sciences.
Purpose: To aid independent research.
Eligibility: Open to students of all nationalities who have a PhD and who have 2–6 years of postdoctoral experience.
Level of Study: Postdoctorate
Type: Fellowship
Value: A salary according to age, qualifications and experience. Salaries are within the scales RGIA-2 for research staff in Institutes of Higher Education. Financial support towards expenses involved in carrying out the research is available, including a start up grant of UK £1,000 in the first year only. Fellows receive UK £1,000 for travel and subsistence each year
Length of Study: Up to 3 years
Frequency: Annual
Study Establishment: Any Institute of Higher Education
Country of Study: Scotland
No. of awards offered: Varies
Application Procedure: Applicants must complete an application form, available from the CRF. Candidates must negotiate with the relevant Head of Department of the proposed host institution.
Closing Date: Mid-March
Funding: Private
Contributor: The CRF
No. of awards given last year: 2
No. of applicants last year: 20
Additional Information: The fellowships are administered by the Caledonian Research Foundation (CRF). Fellows will be expected to devote their full time to research and will not be allowed to hold other paid appointments without the express permission of the Council of the RSE.

For further information contact:

The CRF (Caledonian Research Foundation), 39 Castle Street, Edinburgh, EH2 3BH, Scotland
Contact: Grants Management Officer

Henry Dryerre Scholarship

Subjects: Medical and veterinary physiology.
Purpose: To support postgraduate research.
Eligibility: Open to European citizens holding a First Class (Honours) Degree from a Scottish university.
Level of Study: Postgraduate, Predoctorate
Type: Scholarship
Value: Tuition fees, research costs and travel expenses up to UK £1050 per year and a maintenance grant of UK £14,000
Length of Study: 3 years full-time research
Frequency: Every 3 years
Study Establishment: A Scottish institution
Country of Study: Scotland
No. of awards offered: 1
Application Procedure: Applicants must be nominated by a professor, reader or lecturer in a Scottish university.
Closing Date: March
Funding: Private
Additional Information: The scholarships are administered by the Carnegie Trust for the Universities of Scotland.

For further information contact:

Carnegie Trust for the Universities of Scotland, Carnegie House, Pittencrieff Street, Dunfermline, Fife, KY12 8AW, Scotland
Tel: (44) 1383 724990
Fax: (44) 1383 749799
Email: jgray@carnegie-trust.org
Contact: Miss J Gray

THE CAMARGO FOUNDATION

1, avenue Jermini, 13260 Cassis, France
Tel: (33) 4 42 01 11 57
Fax: (33) 4 42 01 36 57
Email: apply@camargofoundation.org
Website: www.camargofoundation.org
Contact: Mr J P. Dautricourt, Executive Director

The Camargo Foundation maintains a study centre to assist scholars who wish to pursue projects in the humanities and social sciences related to French and Francophone cultures, and to support projects by visual artists, photographers, filmmakers, video artists, media artists, composers and writers.

Camargo Fellowships

Subjects: Humanities and social sciences, visual arts, music composition and creative writing.
Purpose: To assist scholars who wish to pursue projects in the humanities and social sciences related to French and Francophone cultures, and to support projects by visual artists, photographers, filmmakers, video artists, media artists, composers and writers. This interdisciplinary residency program is intended to give fellows the time and space they need to realise their projects.
Eligibility: Open to members of university and college faculties who wish to pursue special studies while on leave from their institutions, independent scholars working on specific projects and graduate students whose academic residence and general examination requirements have been met and for whom a stay in France would be beneficial in completing the dissertation required for their degree. The award is also open to writers, visual artists, photographers, filmmakers, video artists, multimedia artists and composers with specific projects to complete.
Level of Study: Professional development, Doctorate, Postgraduate
Type: Residency
Value: The use of furnished apartments, the reference library, darkroom, artist's studio and music composition studio, and a stipend of US$2,500
Length of Study: Varies
Frequency: Annual
Study Establishment: The Camargo Foundation, study centre in Cassis
Country of Study: France
No. of awards offered: Varies, approx. 20–26
Application Procedure: Applicants must apply online, submitting a completed application form, a curriculum vitae, a detailed description of their project of up to 1,000 words in length and three letters of recommendation by individuals familiar with the applicant's professional work. At least two of the letters should come from persons outside the applicant's own institution; graduate students are exempt from this requirement. Artists should submit 10 JPEGs showing samples of their work, composers should submit a score, MP3 or compact disc and writers should send 10–20 pages of text. For further information applicants should log on to the Foundation's website at: www.camargofoundation-apply.org
Closing Date: January 12th of the following academic year
Funding: Private
Contributor: The Jerome Hill endowment
No. of awards given last year: 26
No. of applicants last year: 500
Additional Information: A written report will be required at the end of the stay.

CAMBRIDGE COMMONWEALTH TRUST, CAMBRIDGE OVERSEAS TRUST, GATES CAMBRIDGE TRUST, CAMBRIDGE EUROPEAN TRUST AND ASSOCIATED TRUSTS

Cambridge Trusts, Trinity College, Trinity Street, Cambridge, CB2 1TQ, United Kingdom
Tel: (44) 1223 351 449
Fax: (44) 1223 323 322
Email: info@overseastrusts.cam.ac.uk
Website: www.admin.cam.ac.uk

The Cambridge Commonwealth Trust and the Cambridge Overseas Trust (formerly the Chancellor's Fund) were established in 1982 by the University of Cambridge under the Chairmanship of his Royal Highness the Prime of Wales to provide financial assistance for students from overseas who, without help, would be unable to take up their places at Cambridge. Since 1982, the Cambridge Commonwealth Trust has brought 6,600 students from 51 countries to Cambridge, the Cambridge Overseas trust 4,252 students from 76 countries.

Arab-British Chamber Chevening Cambridge Scholarships

Subjects: All subjects relevants to their country's needs.
Purpose: To financially support those undertaking postgraduate study.
Eligibility: Applicants must be citizens of Algeria, the Comoro Islands, Djibouti, Egypt, Jordan, Lebanon, Mauritania, Morocco, Palestine, Somalia, Sudan, Syria, Tunisia or the Yemen. They must apply to the University of Cambridge and be offered a place at Cambridge in the normal way. All applicants must have a First Class or High Second Class (Honours) Degree or equivalent and normally be under 26. After completion of their studies, scholars must undertake to return to their country or to another member state of the Arab League.
Level of Study: Postgraduate
Type: Scholarship
Value: The University Composition Fee at the overseas rate, approved college fees, a maintenance allowance sufficient for a single student and a contribution towards return economy airfare
Length of Study: 1 year
Frequency: Annual
Study Establishment: The University of Cambridge
Country of Study: United Kingdom
No. of awards offered: 5
Application Procedure: Applicants must complete a preliminary application form, which can be obtained from local universities, offices of the British Council or the Trust. Completed forms must be returned to the main address. Shortlisted candidates will be sent forms for admission to the University of Cambridge.
Closing Date: January 30th
Contributor: Offered in collaboration with the Arab-British Chamber Charitable Foundation and the Foreign & Commonwealth Office

BAT Cambridge Scholarships for PhD Study (China)

Subjects: All subjects.
Purpose: To financially support study towards a PhD.
Eligibility: Open to students from China. Applicants must apply to the University of Cambridge and be offered a place at Cambridge in the normal way. All applicants must have a First Class or High Second Class (Honours) Degree or equivalent and normally be under 26.
Level of Study: Postdoctorate, Doctorate
Type: Scholarship
Value: The University Composition Fee at the appropriate rate, approved college fees, a maintenance allowance sufficient for a single student and a contribution towards return economy airfare
Length of Study: 3 years
Frequency: Annual
Study Establishment: The University of Cambridge
Country of Study: United Kingdom
No. of awards offered: Varies
Application Procedure: The British American Tobacco Cambridge scholars will be selected by British American Tobacco, in consultation with the Cambridge Overseas Trust, from among those candidates who have been conditionally offered a place at Cambridge and nominated to British American Tobacco by the Cambridge Overseas Trust.
Contributor: Offered in collaboration with the British-American Tobacco (BAT) Company

BAT Cambridge Scholarships for PhD Study (Russia)

Subjects: All subjects.
Purpose: To financially support study towards a PhD.
Eligibility: The British American Tobacco Cambridge scholars will be selected by British American Tobacco, in consultation with the Cambridge Overseas Trust, from among those candidates who have been conditionally offered a place at Cambridge and nominated to British American Tobacco by the Cambridge Overseas Trust.
Level of Study: Doctorate, Predoctorate

Type: Scholarship
Value: The University Composition Fee at the appropriate rate, approved college fees, a maintenance allowance sufficient for a single student and a contribution towards return economy airfare
Length of Study: Up to 3 years
Frequency: Annual
Study Establishment: The University of Cambridge
Country of Study: United Kingdom
No. of awards offered: Varies
Application Procedure: Applicants must complete a preliminary application form, which can be obtained from local universities, offices of the British Council or the Trust. Completed forms must be returned to the main address. Shortlisted candidates will be sent forms for admission to the University of Cambridge. The preliminary application form can also be downloaded from www.admin.cam.ac.uk/offices/gradstud/admissions/forms/
Contributor: Offered in collaboration with the British-American Tobacco (BAT) Company

BAT Cambridge Scholarships for Postgraduate Study (China)

Subjects: All subjects.
Purpose: To financially support those undertaking postgraduate study.
Eligibility: The British American Tobacco Cambridge scholars will be selected by British American Tobacco, in consultation with the Cambridge Overseas Trust, from among those candidates who have been conditionally offered a place at Cambridge and nominated to British American Tobacco by the Cambridge Overseas Trust.
Level of Study: Postgraduate
Type: Scholarship
Value: The University Composition Fee at the appropriate rate, approved college fees, a maintenance allowance sufficient for a single student and a contribution towards return economy airfare
Length of Study: 1 year
Frequency: Annual
Study Establishment: The University of Cambridge
Country of Study: United Kingdom
No. of awards offered: Varies
Application Procedure: Applicants must complete a preliminary application form, which can be obtained from local universities, offices of the British Council or the Trust. Completed forms must be returned to the main address. Shortlisted candidates will be sent forms for admission to the University of Cambridge. The preliminary application form can also be downloaded from www.admin.cam.ac.uk/offices/gradstud/admissions/forms/
Closing Date: February 28th
Contributor: Offered in collaboration with the British-American Tobacco (BAT) Company

BAT Cambridge Scholarships for Postgraduate Study (Russia)

Subjects: All subjects.
Purpose: To financially support those undertaking postgraduate study.
Eligibility: Open to citizens of Russia. Applicants must apply to the University of Cambridge and be offered a place at Cambridge in the normal way. All applicants must have a First Class or High Second Class (Honours) Degree or equivalent and normally be under 26.
Level of Study: Postgraduate
Type: Scholarship
Value: The University Composition Fee at the appropriate rate, approved college fees, a maintenance allowance sufficient for a single student and a contribution towards return economy airfare
Length of Study: 1 year
Frequency: Annual
Study Establishment: The University of Cambridge
Country of Study: United Kingdom
No. of awards offered: Varies
Application Procedure: The British American Tobacco Cambridge scholars will be selected by British American Tobacco, in consultation with the Cambridge Overseas Trust, from among those candidates who have been conditionally offered a place at Cambridge and nominated to British American Tobacco by the Cambridge Overseas Trust.
Closing Date: February 28th

Contributor: Offered in collaboration with the British–American Tobacco (BAT) Company

BG Cambridge Scholarships

Eligibility: Applicants should already hold (or expect to hold by the time of taking up the award) a degree equivalent to a first-class from a UK university.
Level of Study: Postgraduate
Type: Scholarships
Value: Covers up to the University Composition Fee at the overseas rate approved College fees a maintenance allowance sufficient for a single student a return economy airfare by the cheapest available route
Length of Study: 1 year
Study Establishment: University of Cambridge
Application Procedure: Suitably qualified candidates must apply for admission to the University of Cambridge by submitting a Graduate Application Form to the Board of Graduate Studies. The Graduate Admission and Scholarship Application Form can be downloaded from: www.admin.cam.ac.uk/offices/gradstud/admissions/forms/ or, alternatively, the form may be requested, in writing, from the Board of Graduate Studies, 4 Mill Lane, Cambridge, CB2 1RZ, England.
Contributor: In collaboration with BG International Limited, the Cambridge Trusts
Additional Information: Scholarships are offered as two for Nigeria, one for Egypt, one for Oman and two for other priority countries including India, Trinidad & Tobago, Bolivia, Brazil, China, Kazakhstan, Tunisia, Mauritaniaand Madagascar. Successful applicants must undertake to return to their own country and take up permanent residence there after completing the course at Cambridge.

BG Cambridge Scholarships

Subjects: All subjects.
Purpose: To support one-year postgraduate courses of study.
Eligibility: Applicants should already hold (or expect to hold by the time of taking up the award) a degree equivalent to a first-class from a UK university. Applicants should be the citizens of India, Trinidad & Tobago, Bolivia, Brazil, China, Kazakhstan, Tunisia, Mauritania, Madagascar, Nigeria, Egypt and Oman.
Type: Scholarships
Value: Covers the University Composition Fee at the overseas rate, approved college fees, a maintenance allowance sufficient for a single student, a return economy airfare by the cheapest available route
Length of Study: 1 year
No. of awards offered: 6
Application Procedure: Suitably qualified candidates must apply for admission to the University of Cambridge by submitting a Graduate Application Form to the Board of Graduate Studies.
Contributor: The Cambridge Trusts

For further information contact:

Board of Graduate Studies, 4 Mill Lane, Cambridge, England, CB2 1RZ

BP Cambridge Scholarships for PhD Study (Egypt)

Subjects: Preference will be given to candidates who intend to pursue courses in petroleum-related or business-related subjects, but candidates proposing to study other subjects particularly relevant to Egypt's needs will also be eligible to apply.
Purpose: To financially support study towards a PhD.
Eligibility: Candidate must be a citizen of Egypt. Applicants should normally have a first-class degree or its equivalent from a recognised university. Any person employed by BP Egypt at the time of application is not eligible to apply for the BP Cambridge Scholarships for Egypt. However, dependants of those employed by BP Egypt are welcome to apply through the normal competitive process. Conditions: BP Egypt will request successful applicants to sign an 'Enrolment Agreement' that they return and reside in Egypt after the completion of their course of study, for double the amount of time they spent at Cambridge supported by a BP Cambridge Scholarship for Egypt. This agreement shall be concluded between BP Egypt and the successful candidate prior to his/her departure for Cambridge. Candidates will, upon returning to Egypt, also undertake, according to the 'Enrolment Agreement', to work for BP or an affiliated company, nominated by BP. If a candidate breaches his obligation to return to Egypt or to work

for BP, he/she shall refund and reimburse an amount equal to the cost of the scholarship paid by BP.
Level of Study: Doctorate, Predoctorate
Type: Scholarship
Value: The University Composition Fee at the overseas rate, approved college fees, a maintenance allowance sufficient for a single student and a contribution towards return economy airfare
Length of Study: Up to 3 years
Frequency: Annual
Study Establishment: The University of Cambridge
Country of Study: United Kingdom
No. of awards offered: Up to 10
Application Procedure: Applicants must complete a preliminary application form, which can be obtained from local universities, offices of the British Council or the Trust. Completed forms must be returned to the main address. Shortlisted candidates will be sent forms for admission to the University of Cambridge. The preliminary application form can also be downloaded from www.admin.cam.ac.uk/offices/gradstud/admissions/forms/
Contributor: Offered in collaboration with BP

BP Cambridge Scholarships for Postgraduate Study (Egypt)

Subjects: Preference will be given to candidates who intend to pursue courses in petroleum-related or business-related subjects, but candidates proposing to study other subjects particularly relevant to Egypt's needs will also be eligible to apply.
Purpose: To financially support those undertaking postgraduate study.
Eligibility: Candidate must be a citizen of Egypt. Applicants should normally have a first-class degree or its equivalent from a recognised university. Any person employed by BP Egypt at the time of application is not eligible to apply for the BP Cambridge Scholarships for Egypt. However, dependants of those employed by BP Egypt are welcome to apply through the normal competitive process. Conditions: BP Egypt will request successful applicants to sign an 'Enrolment Agreement' that they return and reside in Egypt after the completion of their course of study, for double the amount of time they spent at Cambridge supported by a BP Cambridge Scholarship for Egypt. This agreement shall be concluded between BP Egypt and the successful candidate prior to his/her departure for Cambridge. Candidates will, upon returning to Egypt, also undertake, according to the 'Enrolment Agreement', to work for BP or an affiliated company, nominated by BP. If a candidate breaches his obligation to return to Egypt or to work for BP, he/she shall refund and reimburse an amount equal to the cost of the scholarship paid by BP.
Level of Study: Postgraduate
Type: Scholarship
Value: The University Composition Fee at the appropriate rate, approved college fees, a maintenance allowance sufficient for a single student and a contribution towards return economy airfare
Length of Study: 1 year
Frequency: Annual
Study Establishment: The University of Cambridge
Country of Study: United Kingdom
No. of awards offered: Up to 10
Application Procedure: Applicants must complete a preliminary application form, which can be obtained from local universities, offices of the British Council or the Trust. Completed forms must be returned to the main address. Shortlisted candidates will be sent forms for admission to the University of Cambridge. The preliminary application form can also be downloaded from www.admin.cam.ac.uk/offices/gradstud/admissions/forms/
Closing Date: February 28th
Contributor: Offered in collaboration with BP

BP Chevening Cambridge Scholarships for Egypt

Subjects: Petroleum-related or business related subjects, and subjects relevant to Egypt's need.
Eligibility: Candidate should be from Egypt. Preference will be given to candidates who intend to pursue one-year postgraduate courses of study in petroleum-related or business related subjects, but candidates proposing to study other subjects particularly relevant to Egypt's needs will also be eligible to apply.
Type: Scholarships

Value: University Composition Fee at the overseas rate, approved college fees, a maintenance allowance sufficient for a single student, a contribution towards a return economy airfare by the cheapest available route
Length of Study: 1 year
No. of awards offered: Varies
Contributor: In collaboration with BP and the Foreign & Commonwealth Office

Britain-Australia Bicentennial Scholarships for Postgraduate Study

Subjects: All subjects.
Purpose: To financially support those undertaking postgraduate study.
Eligibility: Candidates must be citizens of Australia, must apply to the University of Cambridge and be offered a place at Cambridge in the normal way. All applicants must have a First Class or High Second Class (Honours) Degree or equivalent and normally be under 26.
Level of Study: Postgraduate
Type: Scholarship
Value: Contribution to the overall costs
Length of Study: 1 year
Frequency: Annual
Study Establishment: Jesus College, the University of Cambridge
Country of Study: United Kingdom
No. of awards offered: 2
Application Procedure: Applicants must contact the Board of Graduate Studies.
Closing Date: January 30th
Contributor: Offered in collaboration with the Foreign and Commonwealth Office (FCO) and Jesus College, Cambridge

For further information contact:

The Board of Graduate Studies, 4 Mill Lane, Cambridge, Cambridgeshire, CB2 1RZ, England
Contact: The Secretary

British Chevening Cambridge Foundation Chile Scholarships.

Subjects: All subjects.
Purpose: To financially support study towards a PhD.
Eligibility: Applicants must be from Chile, must apply to the University of Cambridge and be offered a place at Cambridge in the normal way. All applicants must have a First Class or High Second Class (Honours) Degree or equivalent and normally be under 26. They must be successfully nominated for an Overseas Research Student (ORS) award.
Level of Study: Postgraduate
Type: Scholarship
Value: The University Composition Fee at the overseas rate, approved college fees and a maintenance allowance sufficient for a single student and contribution towards return airfare
Length of Study: 1 year
Frequency: Annual
Study Establishment: The University of Cambridge
Country of Study: United Kingdom
No. of awards offered: 2
Application Procedure: candidates for the above awards must apply directly to the British Council in their home country. Candidates are reminded that they will also need to apply to the Cambridge Trusts on the Scholarship Application Form (SAF) in the usual way.
Contributor: Offered in collaboration with the Foreign and Commonwealth Office (FCO)

For further information contact:

The British Council, Eliodoro Yanez 832, Santiago de Chile, Chile

British Chevening Cambridge Scholarships for Postgraduate Study (Australia)

Subjects: All subjects.
Purpose: To financially support those undertaking postgraduate study.

Eligibility: Open for students from Australia. They should have a first-class or high second-class honours degree from a recognised university.
Level of Study: Postgraduate
Type: Scholarship
Value: The University Composition Fee at the overseas rate, approved college fees, a maintenance allowance sufficient for a single student and a contribution towards return economy airfare
Length of Study: 1 year
Frequency: Annual
Study Establishment: The University of Cambridge
Country of Study: United Kingdom
No. of awards offered: 2
Application Procedure: Applicants must write for information.
Closing Date: January 30th
Contributor: Offered in collaboration with the Foreign and Commonwealth Office (FCO)

For further information contact:

The Board of Graduate Studies, 4 Mill Lane, Cambridge, Cambridgeshire, CN2 1RZ, England
Contact: The Secretary

British Chevening Cambridge Scholarships for Postgraduate Study (Hong Kong)

Subjects: All subjects.
Purpose: To financially support those undertaking postgraduate study.
Eligibility: Applicants must be from Hong Kong, must apply to the University of Cambridge and be offered a place at Cambridge in the normal way. All applicants must have a First Class or High Second Class (Honours) Degree or equivalent and normally be under 26.
Level of Study: Postgraduate
Type: Scholarship
Value: The University Composition Fee at the overseas rate, approved college fees, a maintenance allowance sufficient for a single student and a contribution towards return economy airfare
Length of Study: 1 year
Frequency: Annual
Study Establishment: The University of Cambridge
Country of Study: United Kingdom
No. of awards offered: Up to 8
Application Procedure: Applicants must complete a preliminary application form, which can be obtained from local universities, offices of the British Council or the main address. Completed forms must be returned to the main address. Shortlisted candidates will be sent forms for admission to the University of Cambridge and a scholarship application form. These forms must be returned to the Board of Graduate Studies at the address below.
Closing Date: February 28th
Contributor: Offered in collaboration with the Foreign and Commonwealth Office (FCO)

For further information contact:

The Board of Graduate Studies, 4 Mill Lane, Cambridge, Cambridgeshire, CB2 1RZ, England
Contact: The Secretary

British Chevening Cambridge Scholarships for Postgraduate Study (Mexico)

Subjects: All subjects.
Purpose: To financially support those undertaking postgraduate study.
Eligibility: Applicants must be from Mexico, must apply to the University of Cambridge and be offered a place at Cambridge in the normal way. All applicants must have a First Class or High Second Class (Honours) Degree or equivalent and normally be under 26.
Level of Study: Postgraduate
Type: Scholarship
Value: The University Composition Fee at the overseas rate, approved college fees and a maintenance allowance sufficient for a single student
Length of Study: 1 year
Frequency: Annual

Study Establishment: The University of Cambridge
Country of Study: United Kingdom
No. of awards offered: 2
Application Procedure: Applicants for this scholarship must complete a preliminary application form, which can only be obtained from the British Council, Mexico City.
Closing Date: February 28th
Contributor: Offered in collaboration with the Foreign and Commonwealth Office (FCO)

For further information contact:

The British Council, Maestro Antonio Caso 127, Col San Rafael, Delegacion Cuauhtemoc, Apartado Postal 30-588, Mexico City, DF, 06470, Mexico

British Chevening Cambridge Scholarships for Postgraduate Study (Vietnam)
Subjects: All subjects.
Purpose: To financially support those undertaking postgraduate study.
Eligibility: Applicants must be from Vietnam, must apply to the University of Cambridge and be offered a place at Cambridge in the normal way. All applicants must have a First Class or High Second Class (Honours) Degree or equivalent and normally be under 26. They must be successfully nominated for an Overseas Research Student (ORS) award.
Level of Study: Postgraduate
Type: Scholarship
Value: The University Composition Fee at the overseas rate, approved college fees, a maintenance allowance sufficient for a single student and a contribution towards return economy airfare
Length of Study: 1 year
Frequency: Annual
Study Establishment: The University of Cambridge
Country of Study: United Kingdom
No. of awards offered: Up to 2
Application Procedure: Applicants for these scholarships should apply directly to the British Embassy in Vietnam.
Closing Date: February 28th
Contributor: Offered in collaboration with the Foreign and Commonwealth Office (FCO)

For further information contact:

The British Embassy, 16 Ly Thuong Kiet, Hanoi, Vietnam

British Prize Cambridge Scholarships (Barbados and The Eastern Caribbean)
Subjects: All subjects relevant to their country's development.
Purpose: To financially support those undertaking postgraduate study.
Eligibility: Applicants must be from Barbados, Antigua & Barbuda, Dominica, Grenada Grenadines, St Kitts-Nevis, St Vincent, and have a First Class or High Second Class (Honours) Degree or equivalent. Normally they should be under 26.
Level of Study: Postgraduate
Type: Scholarship
Value: The University Composition Fee at the overseas rate, approved college fees, maintenance allowance for a single student and a contribution towards return economy airfare
Length of Study: 1 year
Frequency: Dependent on funds available
Study Establishment: The University of Cambridge
Country of Study: United Kingdom
No. of awards offered: Up to 2
Application Procedure: Applicants for a place to do a PhD should apply for an ORS award and should normally be successfully nominated for an ORS award or an ORS equivalent award, which meets the difference between the higher overseas rate and the lower domestic rate of the University composition fee.
Funding: Trusts
Contributor: Offered in collaboration with the Foreign and Commonwealth Office (FCO)

Calbee Cambridge Scholarship
Subjects: All subjects.
Purpose: To financially support postgraduate study.
Eligibility: Offer for students from Japan. Preference being given to candidates who have been offered a place at Pembroke College.
Level of Study: Postgraduate
Type: Scholarship
Value: Contribution towards fees
Length of Study: 1 year
Frequency: Annual
Study Establishment: The University of Cambridge
Country of Study: United Kingdom
No. of awards offered: 1
Application Procedure: Applicants must apply to the university of Cambridge and be offered a place at Cambridge in the normal way. Applicants should complete only one scholarship form, which will enable them to be considered for all awards for which they are eligible. Application forms can be downloaded from the website.
Closing Date: February 28th
Funding: Trusts
Contributor: Cambridge Trusts

Cambridge Assessment Cambridge Scholarships (for PHD)
Purpose: To support research leading to the degree or PhD.
Eligibility: Open to candidates already having, or expecting to obtain, a first class honours degree or its equivalent from a recognised university.
Type: Scholarships
Value: University Composition Fee at the appropriate rate, approved college fees, a maintenance allowance sufficient for a single student, a contribution towards a return economy airfare by the cheapest available route
No. of awards offered: 2
Contributor: In collaboration with Cambridge Assessment

Cambridge Assessment Cambridge Scholarships (for postgraduate – Zimbabwe)
Eligibility: Open to students from Zimbabwe. The candidate should already have, or expect to obtain, a first class honours degree or its equivalent from a recognised university.
Type: Scholarships
Value: University Composition Fee at the appropriate rate, approved college fees, a maintenance allowance sufficient for a single student, a contribution towards a return economy airfare by the cheapest available route
No. of awards offered: 2
Contributor: in collaboration with Cambridge Assessment

Cambridge Australia Trust Scholarships
Subjects: Science.
Purpose: To financially support those undertaking postgraduate study through a number of award schemes.
Eligibility: Open to citizens of Australia. Applicants must apply to the University of Cambridge and be offered a place at Cambridge in the normal way. All applicants must have a First Class or High Second Class (Honours) Degree or equivalent and normally be under 26.
Level of Study: Doctorate
Type: Scholarship
Value: The University Composition Fee at the overseas rate, approved college fees, a maintenance allowance sufficient for a single student and a contribution towards return economy airfare
Frequency: Varies
Study Establishment: The University of Cambridge
Country of Study: United Kingdom
No. of awards offered: Varies
Application Procedure: Applicants must contact the Board of Graduate Studies.
Closing Date: January 30th
Contributor: Offered in collaboration with the Foreign and Commonwealth Office (FCO) and the Cambridge Australia Trust
Additional Information: Further information is available on request. For details of scholarships offered in collaboration with the Cambridge Australia Trust please see the website www.anu.edu.au/graduate/scholarships

For further information contact:

The Board of Graduate Studies, 4 Mill Lane, Cambridge, Cambridgeshire, CB2 1RZ, England
Contact: The Secretary

Cambridge Canada Scholarships for PhD Study

Subjects: All subjects.
Purpose: To financially support study towards a PhD.
Eligibility: Open to students from Canada. Applicants must apply to the University of Cambridge and be offered a place at Cambridge in the normal way. All applicants must have a First Class or High Second Class (Honours) Degree or equivalent and normally be under 26. They must be successfully nominated for an Overseas Research Student (ORS) award.
Level of Study: Doctorate, Predoctorate
Type: Scholarship
Value: The University Composition Fee at the home rate and approved college fees
Length of Study: Up to 3 years
Frequency: Annual
Study Establishment: The University of Cambridge
Country of Study: United Kingdom
No. of awards offered: Up to 5
Application Procedure: Application forms for the scholarship will be sent out to eligible candidates once the completed form for admission to the University of Cambridge has reached the Board of Graduate Studies.

For further information contact:

The Board of Graduate Studies, 4 Mill Lane, Cambridge, Cambridgeshire, CB2 1RZ, England
Contact: The Secretary

Cambridge Mandela Scholarships for PhD Study

Subjects: All subjects relevant to South Africa's needs.
Purpose: To financially support study towards a PhD.
Eligibility: Applicants must be from South Africa. Applicants must apply to the University of Cambridge and be offered a place at Cambridge in the normal way. All applicants must have a First Class or High Second Class (Honours) Degree or equivalent and normally be under 26. They must be successfully nominated for an Overseas Research Student (ORS) award.
Level of Study: Doctorate, Predoctorate
Type: Scholarship
Value: The University Composition Fee at the appropriate rate, approved college fees, a maintenance allowance sufficient for a single student and a contribution to return economy airfare
Length of Study: Up to 3 years
Frequency: Annual
Study Establishment: The University of Cambridge
Country of Study: United Kingdom
No. of awards offered: Up to 10
Application Procedure: Applicants must complete a preliminary application form, which can be obtained from local universities, offices of the British Council or the Trust. The preliminary application form can also be downloaded from www.admin.cam.ac.uk/offices/gradstud/admissions/forms/ completed forms must be returned to the main address. Shortlisted candidates will be sent forms for admission to the University of Cambridge.
Contributor: Offered by the Malaysian Commonwealth Studies Centre, Trinity College, Cambridge, and the Cambridge University Press, Cambridge Assessment (formerly LES)
Additional Information: These scholarships are offered in honour of former South African President Nelson Mandela.

Cambridge Mandela Scholarships for Postgraduate Study

Subjects: All subjects relevant to South Africa's needs.
Purpose: To financially support those undertaking postgraduate study.
Eligibility: Applicants must be from South Africa, must apply to the University of Cambridge and be offered a place at Cambridge in the normal way. All applicants must have a First Class or High Second Class (Honours) Degree or equivalent and normally be under 26. They

must be successfully nominated for an Overseas Research Student (ORS) award.
Level of Study: Postgraduate
Type: Scholarship
Value: The University Composition Fee at the overseas rate, approved college fees, a maintenance allowance sufficient for a single student and a contribution towards return economy airfare
Length of Study: 1 year
Frequency: Annual
Study Establishment: The University of Cambridge
Country of Study: United Kingdom
No. of awards offered: Up to 20
Application Procedure: Applicants must complete a preliminary application form, which can be obtained from local universities, offices of the British Council or the Trust. The preliminary application form can also be downloaded from www.admin.cam.ac.uk/offices/gradstud/admissions/forms/ completed forms must be returned to the main address. Shortlisted candidates will be sent forms for admission to the University of Cambridge.
Closing Date: February 28th
Contributor: Offered by the Malaysian Commonwealth Studies Centre, Trinity College, Cambridge, and the Cambridge University Press, Cambridge Assessment (formerly LES)
Additional Information: These scholarships are offered in honour of former South African President Nelson Mandela.

Cambridge Shared Scholarships

Subjects: All subjects, preference to study related to the economic and social development of their country.
Purpose: To partly support those undertaking postgraduate study.
Eligibility: Open to citizens from developing countries of the Commonwealth – Anguilla, Antigua & Barbuda, Bangladesh, Barbados, Belize, Bermuda, Botswana, British Virgin Islands, Cameroon, Cayman Islands, Dominica, Falkland Islands, Fiji, Gambia, Ghana, Gibraltar, Grenada, Guyana, India, Jamaica, Kenya, Kiribati, Lesotho, Malawi, Malaysia, Maldives, Mauritius, Montserrat, Mozambique, Namibia, Nauru, Nigeria, Pakistan, Papua New Guinea, Pitcairn, St Helena, St Kitts Nevis, St Lucia, St Vincent, Seychelles, Sierra Leone, Soloman Islands, South Africa, Sri Lanka, Swaziland, Tanzania, Tonga, Trinidad & Tobaga, Tristan da Cunha, Turks & Caicos Islands, Tuvalu, Uganda, Vanuatu, Western Samoa, or Zambia. Applicants must apply to the University of Cambridge and be offered a place at Cambridge in the normal way. All applicants must have a First Class or High Second Class (Honours) Degree or equivalent and be under the age of 35 on October 1st of the year they are applying for, with priority given to those candidates under the age of 30. Applicants should not be presently living or studying in a developing country.
Level of Study: Postgraduate
Type: Scholarship
Value: The University Composition Fee at the overseas rate, approved college fees, a maintenance allowance sufficient for a single student and a contribution towards return economy airfare
Length of Study: 1 year
Frequency: Annual
Study Establishment: The University of Cambridge
Country of Study: United Kingdom
No. of awards offered: 40
Application Procedure: Applicants must complete a preliminary application form, which can be obtained from local universities, offices of the British Council or the Trust. Completed forms must be returned to the main address. Shortlisted candidates will be sent forms for admission to the University of Cambridge. The preliminary application form can also be downloaded from www.admin.cam.ac.uk/offices/gradstud/admissions/forms/
Closing Date: February 28th
Contributor: Offered in collaboration with the Department for International Development (DFID)

Charles Wallace India Trust

Subjects: All subjects.
Purpose: To financially assist postgraduate study for applicants who are not successful in winning a scholarship.
Eligibility: Applicants for a place to do a PhD should apply for an ORS award and should be successfully nominated for an ORS award or an ORS equivalent award, which meets the difference between the

higher overseas rate and the lower domestic rate of the University Composition Fee.
Level of Study: Any level
Type: Bursary
Value: Part Cost
Frequency: Annual
Study Establishment: The University of Cambridge
Contributor: Charles Wallace India Trust

China Scholarship Council Cambridge International Scholarships
Subjects: Priority subjects set each year by the China Scholarship Council.
Purpose: To support research leading to the degree of PhD.
Eligibility: Candidate should be from China. Candidates should normally have a first-class honours degree and, preferably, a Masters degree or its equivalent from a recognised university in China.
Type: Scholarship
Value: University Composition Fee at the overseas rate, approved college fees, a maintenance allowance sufficient for a single student, a contribution towards a return airfare by the cheapest available route
No. of awards offered: 30
Application Procedure: Candidates must submit a copy of their GRADSAF form and supporting documents to the China Scholarship Council at the same time as they send their application for admission at the University of Cambridge to the Board of Graduate Studies, Cambridge.
Closing Date: February 20th
Contributor: In collaboration with the China Scholarship Council

CIALS Cambridge Scholarships
Subjects: Law.
Purpose: To support study towards the Master of Law (LLM) degree.
Eligibility: Open to graduates of Canadian law schools who have completed a Bachelor of Law degree on or before June 1st. Applicants must be Canadian citizens. Applicants must apply to the University of Cambridge and be offered a place at Cambridge in the normal way. All applicants must have a First Class or High Second Class (Honours) Degree or equivalent and normally be under 26.
Level of Study: Postgraduate
Type: Scholarship
Value: The scholarships will normally cover the University Composition Fee at the overseas rate, approved College fees. A maintenance allowance sufficient for a single student and a contribution towards a return economy airfare by the cheapest available route.
Also payable by the Commonwealth Scholarship Commission as applicable, thesis expenses of up to £225, study travel grant up to £100 and possible grant, upon application, towards excess baggage allowance for accompanied books up to 10k on return home
Length of Study: 1 year
Frequency: Annual
Study Establishment: The University of Cambridge
Country of Study: United Kingdom
No. of awards offered: 2
Application Procedure: Applicants must apply in writing to the Executive Director of the Canadian Institute for Advanced Legal Studies (CIALS).
Closing Date: December 31st
Contributor: Offered in collaboration with the CIALS

For further information contact:

The Canadian Institute of Advanced Legal Studies, 4 Beechwood Avenue, Ottawa, ON, K1L 8L9, Canada
Contact: Mr Frank E McArdle, Executive Director

Clutton-Brock Scholarship for PhD Study
Subjects: All subjects.
Purpose: To financially support study towards a PhD.
Eligibility: For a student from Zimbabwe who has been offered a place at Magdalene College, Cambridge in the normal way. All applicants must have a First Class or High Second Class (Honours) Degree or equivalent and normally be under 26. They must be successfully nominated for an Overseas Research Student (ORS) award.
Level of Study: Doctorate, Predoctorate
Type: Scholarship

Value: The University Composition Fee at the home rate, approved college fees, a maintenance allowance sufficient for a single student and a contribution towards return economy airfare
Length of Study: Up to 3 years
Frequency: Annual
Study Establishment: Magdalene College, the University of Cambridge
Country of Study: United Kingdom
No. of awards offered: 1
Application Procedure: Applicants for a place to do a PhD should apply for an ORS award and should normally be successfully nominated for an ORS award or an ORS equivalent award, which meets the difference between the higher overseas rate and the lower domestic rate of the university composition fee.
Contributor: Offered by the Government of Zimbabwe in collaboration with Magdalene College, Cambridge in honour of Guy Clutton-Brock, hero of Zimbabwe

Clutton-Brock Scholarship for Postgraduate Study
Subjects: All subjects.
Purpose: To financially support those undertaking postgraduate study.
Eligibility: Open to students from Zimbabwe who have been offered a place at Magdalene College, Cambridge in the normal way. All applicants must have a First Class or High Second Class (Honours) Degree or equivalent and normally be under 26. They must be successfully nominated for an Overseas Research Student (ORS) award.
Level of Study: Postgraduate
Type: Scholarship
Value: The University Composition Fee at the overseas rate, approved college fees, a maintenance allowance sufficient for a single student and a contribution towards return economy airfare
Length of Study: 1 year
Frequency: Dependent on funds available
Study Establishment: Magdalene College, the University of Cambridge
Country of Study: United Kingdom
No. of awards offered: 1
Application Procedure: Applicants must complete a preliminary application form, which can be obtained from local universities, offices of the British Council or the Trust. Completed forms must be returned to the main address. Shortlisted candidates will be sent forms for admission to the University of Cambridge. The preliminary application form can also be downloaded from www.admin.cam.ac.uk/offices/gradstud/admissions/forms/
Closing Date: February 28th
Contributor: Offered by the Government of Zimbabwe in collaboration with Magdalene College, Cambridge, in honour of Guy Clutton-Brock, hero of Zimbabwe

Corpus Christi Research Scholarship
Subjects: All subjects.
Purpose: To financially assist study towards a PhD.
Eligibility: Applicants must be from India, and already hold a degree equivalent to a first-class or a high upper second from a UK university.
Level of Study: Doctorate
Type: Scholarship
Value: The University Composition Fee at the appropriate rate, approved College fees, a maintenance allowance sufficient for a single student
Study Establishment: Corpus Christi College, The University of Cambridge
Country of Study: United Kingdom
Application Procedure: Applicants for a place to do a PhD should apply for an ORS award and should normally be successfully nominated for an ORS award or an ORS equivalent award, which meets the difference between the higher overseas rate and the lower domestic rate of the University Composition Fee.
Contributor: In collaboration with the Corpus Christi College

Developing World Education Fund Scholarships for PhD Study
Subjects: All subjects.
Purpose: To financially support study towards a PhD.

Eligibility: For citizens from Bangladesh, China, India, Pakistan, Sri Lanka or Zambia. Applicants must apply to the University of Cambridge and be offered a place at Cambridge in the normal way. All applicants must have a degree equivalent to a First Class from a UK university, and normally be under 26.
Level of Study: Doctorate
Type: Scholarship
Value: The University Composition Fee at the appropriate rate, approve College fees, a maintenance allowance sufficient for a single student, contribution towards an economy return airfare
Frequency: Varies
Study Establishment: The University of Cambridge
Country of Study: United Kingdom
No. of awards offered: Varies
Application Procedure: Applicants for a place to do a PhD should apply for an ORS award and should normally be successfully nominated for an ORS award or an ORS equivalent award, which meets the difference between the higher overseas rate and the lower domestic rate of the University Composition Fee.

Developing World Education Fund Scholarships for Postgraduate Study

Subjects: All subjects.
Purpose: To financially support those undertaking postgraduate study.
Eligibility: For citizens from Bangladesh, China, India, Pakistan, Sri Lanka, or Zambia. Applicants must apply to the University of Cambridge and be offered a place at Cambridge in the normal way. All applicants must have a degree equivalent to a First Class from a UK university and normally be under 26.
Level of Study: Postgraduate
Type: Scholarship
Value: The University Composition Fee at the overseas rate, approved college fees, a maintenance allowance sufficient for a single student and a contribution towards return economy airfare
Length of Study: 1 year
Frequency: Varies
Study Establishment: The University of Cambridge
Country of Study: United Kingdom
No. of awards offered: Varies
Application Procedure: Applicants must complete a preliminary application form, which can be obtained from local universities, offices of the British Council or the Trust. Completed forms must be returned to the main address. Shortlisted candidates will be sent forms for admission to the University of Cambridge. The preliminary application form can also be downloaded from www.admin.cam.ac.uk/offices/gradstud/admissions/forms/
Closing Date: February 28th
Contributor: Offered in collaboration with the Developing World Education Fund

Dharam Hinduja Cambridge Bursaries

Subjects: All subjects.
Purpose: To financially support students from India.
Eligibility: Applicants from India should already hold a degree equivalent to a first class or a high upper second from a UK university.
Level of Study: Any level
Type: Bursary
Value: Part cost Bursaries
Frequency: Varies
Study Establishment: The University of Cambridge
Country of Study: United Kingdom
No. of awards offered: 8
Application Procedure: Applicants for a place to do a PhD should apply for an ORS award and should be successfully nominated for an ORS award or an ORS equivalent award, which meets the difference between the higher overseas rate and the lower domestic rate of the University Composition Fee.
Contributor: In collaboration with Hinduja Cambridge Trust

Dharam Hinduja Cambridge Scholarships

Subjects: All subjects.
Purpose: To financially support study towards a PhD.
Eligibility: Applicants must be from India, and must be successful in winning an Overseas Research Student (ORS) award. Those who

have, in addition, to a First Class (Honours) Degree, a First Class Master's Degree or its equivalent may be given preference.
Level of Study: Doctorate
Type: Scholarship
Value: The University Composition Fee at the home rate, approved college fees, a maintenance allowance sufficient for a single student and a contribution towards return economy airfare
Length of Study: Up to 3 years
Frequency: Annual
Study Establishment: The University of Cambridge
Country of Study: United Kingdom
No. of awards offered: 2
Application Procedure: Applicants must obtain further details and a preliminary application form by writing before August 16th of the year before entry to the address given below with details of academic qualifications.
Contributor: Offered in collaboration with the Hinduja Cambridge Trust

For further information contact:

The Nehru Trust for Cambridge University, Teen Murti House, Teen Murti Marg, New Delhi, 110011, India
Contact: The Joint Secretary

Dharam Hinduja Commonwealth Shared Scholarships

Subjects: All subjects relevant to the needs of India.
Purpose: To offer financial support.
Eligibility: Applicants must be from India, and must be under the age of 35 on October 1st, with priority given to those candidates under the age of 30. Applicants must not be employed by a national or local government department or by a parastatal organization, or at present be living or studying in a developed country. Priority will be given to candidates wishing to pursue a course of study related to the economic and social development of their country. Applicants should have a first class degree.
Level of Study: Postgraduate
Type: Scholarship
Value: The University Composition Fee at the appropriate rate, approved college fees, a maintenance allowance sufficient for a single student and a contribution towards return economy airfare
Length of Study: 1 year
Frequency: Annual
Study Establishment: The University of Cambridge
Country of Study: United Kingdom
No. of awards offered: 4
Application Procedure: Applicants may obtain further details and a preliminary application form by writing before August 16th of the year before entry to the address given below with details of academic qualifications.
Closing Date: February 28th
Contributor: Offered in collaboration with the Hinduja Cambridge Trust and the Department for International Development

For further information contact:

The Nehru Trust for Cambridge University, Teen Murti House, Teen Murti Marg, New Delhi, 110011, India
Contact: The Joint Secretary

Entente Cordiale Scholarships for Postgraduate Study

Subjects: All subjects.
Purpose: To financially support those undertaking postgraduate study.
Eligibility: Applicants must be citizens of France.
Level of Study: Postgraduate
Type: Scholarship
Value: Applicants must contact the British Council for details
Length of Study: 1 year
Frequency: Annual
Study Establishment: The University of Cambridge, St Edmund's College
Country of Study: United Kingdom
No. of awards offered: Up to 6
Application Procedure: Applicants must obtain details of the application procedure from the British Council.
Closing Date: February 28th

Contributor: Offered in collaboration with the United Kingdom's Foreign and Commonwealth Office (FCO)

For further information contact:

British Council, 9-11 rue de Constantine, 75007 Paris, France
Tel: (33) 1 49 55 73 43180
Fax: (33) 1 47 05 77 02

FCO-China Chevening Fellowships for Postgraduate Study (China)

Subjects: All subjects.
Purpose: To financially support those undertaking postgraduate study.
Eligibility: Open to citizens of China. Applicants must apply to the University of Cambridge and be offered a place at Cambridge in the normal way. All applicants must have a First Class or High Second Class (Honours) Degree or equivalent and normally be under 26.
Level of Study: Postgraduate
Type: Scholarship
Value: The University Composition Fee at the overseas rate, approved college fees, a maintenance allowance sufficient for a single student and a contribution towards return economy airfare
Length of Study: 1 year
Frequency: Annual
Study Establishment: The University of Cambridge
Country of Study: United Kingdom
No. of awards offered: 3
Application Procedure: Applicants must complete a preliminary application form, which can be obtained from local universities, offices of the British Council or the Trust. Completed forms must be returned to the main address. Shortlisted candidates will be sent forms for admission to the University of Cambridge. The preliminary application form can also be downloaded from www.admin.cam.ac.uk/offices/gradstud/admissions/forms/
Closing Date: February 28th
Contributor: Offered in collaboration with the Foreign and Commonwealth Office (FCO)

First Canadian Donner Foundation Research Cambridge Scholarship

Subjects: All subjects.
Purpose: To financially support study towards a PhD.
Eligibility: Open to citizens of Canada or the USA, who excel in sport. Candidates must gain admission to Magdalene College, Cambridge in the normal way. All applicants must be successfully nominated for an Overseas Research Student (ORS) award.
Level of Study: Doctorate, Postgraduate, Predoctorate
Type: Scholarship
Value: Worth up to £15,000 per annum
Length of Study: 3 years or 1 year postgraduate
Frequency: Annual
Study Establishment: Magdalene College, the University of Cambridge
Country of Study: United Kingdom
No. of awards offered: 1
Application Procedure: Applicants for a place to do a PhD should apply for an ORS award and should normally be successfully nominated for an ORS award or an ORS equivalent award, which meets the difference between the higher overseas rate and the lower domestic rate of the university composition fee.
Contributor: Offered in collaboration with the Canadian Donner Foundation and Magdalene College and the Centre for International Studies

George and Mary Vergottis Cambridge Bursaries

Subjects: All subjects.
Purpose: To financially support those undertaking postgraduate study.
Eligibility: Open to citizens of Greece.
Level of Study: Doctorate, Postgraduate
Type: Bursary
Value: Varies
Length of Study: Varies
Frequency: Annual

Study Establishment: The University of Cambridge
Country of Study: United Kingdom
No. of awards offered: Varies
Contributor: In collaboration with The George and Mary Vergottis Cambridge Fund

Grosvenor Cambridge Scholarship

Subjects: MPhil in Real Estate Finance.
Purpose: To financially support those undertaking postgraduate study.
Eligibility: Applicants should normally have a first class degree or its equivalent from a recognised university.
Level of Study: Postgraduate
Type: Scholarship
Value: The University Composition Fee at the appropriate rate, approved College fees, a maintenance allowance sufficient for a single student, contribution towards an economy return airfare
Length of Study: 1 year
Frequency: Annual
Study Establishment: The University of Cambridge
Country of Study: United Kingdom
No. of awards offered: 3
Additional Information: Preference will normally be given to scholars with places at Pembroke College or Gonville & Caius College.

Guan Ruijun Memorial Bursary

Subjects: All subjects.
Purpose: To support postgraduate study in memory of Miss Guan Ruijun.
Eligibility: Preference will be given to students from Peking University. Applicants must have a First Class or High Second Class (Honours) Degree or equivalent and normally be under 26, from China.
Level of Study: Postgraduate
Type: Bursary
Value: Part-cost contribution towards the fees of the bursary
Length of Study: 1 year
Frequency: Dependent on funds available
Study Establishment: Wolfson College, Cambridge
Country of Study: United Kingdom
No. of awards offered: 1
Application Procedure: Applicants must apply to the university of Cambridge and be offered a place at Cambridge in the normal way. Applicants should complete only one scholarship form, which will enable them to be considered for all awards for which they are eligible. Application forms can be downloaded from the website.
Closing Date: February 28th
Contributor: Wolfson College and Cambridge Trusts

Hutchison Whampoa Chevening Cambridge Scholarships

Subjects: All subjects.
Purpose: To financially support those undertaking postgraduate study.
Eligibility: Open to students from China and Hong Kong. Applicants must apply to the University of Cambridge and be offered a place at Cambridge in the normal way. All applicants must have a First Class or High Second Class (Honours) Degree or equivalent.
Level of Study: Postgraduate
Type: Scholarship
Value: The University Composition Fee at the overseas rate, approved college fees, a maintenance allowance sufficient for a single student and a contribution towards return economy airfare
Length of Study: 1 year
Study Establishment: The University of Cambridge
Country of Study: United Kingdom
No. of awards offered: Up to 21
Application Procedure: Applicants must complete a preliminary application form, which can be obtained from local universities, offices of the British Council or the Trust. Completed forms must be returned to the main address. Shortlisted candidates will be sent forms for admission to the University of Cambridge. The preliminary application form can also be downloaded from www.admin.cam.ac.uk/offices/gradstud/admissions/forms/
Closing Date: February 28th

Contributor: In collaboration with Hutchison Whampoa and the Foreign and Commonwealth Office (FCO)

ICBC Cambridge Scholarship

Subjects: Education.
Purpose: To financially support those undertaking postgraduate study.
Eligibility: Open to students from Chile.
Level of Study: Postgraduate
Type: Scholarship
Value: The University composition fee at the overseas rate, approved college fees, a maintenance allowance sufficient for a single student, contribution towards an economy return airfare
Length of Study: 1 year
Frequency: Annual
Study Establishment: The University of Cambridge
Country of Study: United Kingdom
No. of awards offered: 1
Application Procedure: Apply directly to the British Council in Chile. Applicants are reminded that they will also need to apply to the Cambridge Trusts on the Scholarship Application Form (SAF) in the usual way.
Contributor: Offered in collaboration with the Instituto Chileno Britanico de Cultura, the British Council, Chile and Cambridge Assessment (formerly the Local Examinations Syndicate), University of Cambridge

Isaac Newton Trust European Research Studentships

Subjects: All subjects.
Purpose: To support research leading to a PhD.
Eligibility: Open to candidates from the European Union.
Level of Study: Doctorate
Type: Studentship
Value: UK £2,000 per year
Length of Study: 3 years
Frequency: Annual
Study Establishment: The University of Cambridge
Country of Study: United Kingdom
No. of awards offered: 33
Application Procedure: Applicants must contact the Trust.
Contributor: Offered in collaboration with the Isaac Newton Trust and the Cambridge European Trust

Jawaharlal Nehru Memorial Trust Cambridge Scholarships

Subjects: All subjects.
Purpose: To financially support study towards a PhD.
Eligibility: Open to candidates from India. All applicants must be successful in winning an Overseas Research Student (ORS) award. Those who have, in addition to a First Class (Honours) Degree, a First Class Master's Degree or equivalent, may be given preference.
Level of Study: Doctorate
Type: Scholarship
Value: The University Composition Fee at the overseas rate, approved college fees, a contribution towards a maintenance allowance and a contribution to return economy airfare
Length of Study: 2 years
Frequency: Annual
Study Establishment: Trinity College, the University of Cambridge
Country of Study: United Kingdom
No. of awards offered: 1
Application Procedure: Applicants may obtain further details and a preliminary application form by writing before August 16th of the year before entry to the Joint Secretary of the Nehru Trust for Cambridge University, giving details of academic qualifications.
Contributor: Offered in collaboration with the Jawaharlal Nehru Memorial Trust and Trinity College, Cambridge

For further information contact:

The Nehru Trust for Cambridge University, Teen Murti House, Teen Murti Marg, New Delhi, 110011, India
Contact: The Joint Secretary

Jawaharlal Nehru Memorial Trust Commonwealth Shared Scholarships

Subjects: All subjects.
Purpose: To offer financial support.
Eligibility: Open to citizens from India. All applicants must be under the age of 35 on October 1st with priority given to those candidates under the age of 30. They must not be employed by a national or local government department or by a parastatal organization, nor at present be living or studying in a developed country and not have undertaken studies lasting a year or more in a developed country. Priority will be given to candidates wishing to pursue a study related to the economic and social development of their country.
Level of Study: Postgraduate
Type: Scholarship
Value: The University Composition Fee at the overseas rate, approved college fees, a maintenance allowance sufficient for a single student and a contribution towards return economy airfare
Length of Study: 1 year
Frequency: Annual
Study Establishment: The University of Cambridge, Trinity College
Country of Study: United Kingdom
No. of awards offered: 2
Application Procedure: Applicants may obtain further details and a preliminary application form by writing before August 16th of the year before entry to the Joint Secretary of the Nehru Trust for Cambridge University, giving details of their academic qualifications.
Closing Date: February 28th
Contributor: Offered in collaboration with the Jawaharlal Nehru Memorial Trust and the Commonwealth Scholarship Commission

For further information contact:

The Nehru Trust for Cambridge University, Teen Murti House, Teen Murti Marg, New Delhi, 110011, India
Contact: The Joint Secretary

Kapitza Cambridge Scholarships

Subjects: All subjects.
Purpose: To financially support study towards a PhD.
Eligibility: Open to students from countries of the former Soviet Union. Applicants must apply to the University of Cambridge and be offered a place at Cambridge in the normal way. All applicants must have a First Class degree or a master's degree or its equivalent and normally be under 26.
Level of Study: Postdoctorate
Type: Scholarship
Value: The University Composition Fees at the overseas rate, approved college fees, a maintenance allowance sufficient for a single student and a contribution towards return economy airfare
Length of Study: 1 year
Frequency: Annual
Study Establishment: The University of Cambridge
No. of awards offered: Varies
Application Procedure: Applicants must complete a preliminary application form, which can be obtained from local universities, offices of the British Council or the Trust. Completed forms must be returned to the main address. Shortlisted candidates will be sent forms for admission to the University of Cambridge. The preliminary application form can also be downloaded from www.admin.cam.ac.uk/offices/gradstud/admissions/forms/
Closing Date: February 28th
Contributor: Offered in collaboration with Trinity College, Cambridge and Mr Stephen Anderman

Karim Rida Said Cambridge Scholarship for Postgraduate Study

Subjects: All subjects.
Purpose: To financially support those undertaking postgraduate study.
Eligibility: Applicants must be from Iraq, Jordan, Lebanon, Israel, Palestine or Syria. Applicants must apply to the University of Cambridge and be offered a place at Cambridge in the normal way. All applicants must have a First Class or High Second Class (Honours) Degree or equivalent and may be up to the age of 40. They must be successfully nominated for an Overseas Research Student (ORS) award. Priority given to those with at least 2 years of work experience.

Level of Study: Postgraduate
Type: Scholarship
Value: The University Composition Fee at the overseas rate, approved college fees, a maintenance allowance sufficient for a single student and a contribution towards a return economy airfare
Length of Study: 1 year
Frequency: Annual
Study Establishment: The University of Cambridge
Country of Study: United Kingdom
No. of awards offered: 7
Application Procedure: Applicants must complete a preliminary application form, which can be obtained from local universities, offices of the British Council or the Trust. Completed forms must be returned to the main address. Shortlisted candidates will be sent forms for admission to the University of Cambridge. The preliminary application form can also be downloaded from www.admin.cam.ac.uk/offices/gradstud/admissions/forms/
Closing Date: February 28th
Contributor: Offered in collaboration with the Karim Rida Said Foundation
Additional Information: This scholarship is offered in memory of Karim Rida Said.

Kenneth Sutherland Memorial Cambridge Scholarship

Subjects: Engineering.
Purpose: To support study towards a PhD.
Eligibility: Applicants must be from Canada and must be successfully nominated for an ORS award. All applicants must have a First Class or High Second Class (Honours) Degree or equivalent and normally be under 30.
Level of Study: Doctorate
Type: Scholarship
Value: The university composition fee and approved college fees
Length of Study: 3 years
Frequency: Dependent on funds available
Study Establishment: Jesus College, University of Cambridge
Country of Study: United Kingdom
No. of awards offered: 1
Application Procedure: Applicants must apply to the university of Cambridge and be offered a place at Cambridge in the normal way. Applicants should complete only one scholarship form, which will enable them to be considered for all awards for which they are eligible. Application forms can be downloaded from the website. Candidates must also apply for an ORS award.
Closing Date: February 28th
Funding: Trusts
Contributor: Cambridge Trust and Jesus college

Lady Noon Cambridge Shared Scholarships

Subjects: All subjects.
Purpose: To financially support those undertaking postgraduate study.
Eligibility: Open to students from Pakistan. All applicants must be under the age of 35 on October 1st with priority given to those candidates under the age of 30. They must not be employed by a national or local government department or by a parastatal organization, nor at present be living or studying in a developed country. Priority will be given to candidates wishing to pursue a course of study related to the economic and social development of their own country.
Level of Study: Postgraduate
Type: Scholarship
Value: The University Composition Fee at overseas rate, approved college fees, a maintenance allowance sufficient for a single student and a contribution towards return economy airfare
Length of Study: 1 year
Frequency: Annual
Study Establishment: The University of Cambridge
Country of Study: United Kingdom
No. of awards offered: Varies
Application Procedure: Applicants must complete a preliminary application form, which can be obtained from local universities, offices of the British Council or the Trust. Completed forms must be returned to the main address. Shortlisted candidates will be sent forms for admission to the University of Cambridge. The preliminary application

form can also be downloaded from www.admin.cam.ac.uk/offices/gradstud/admissions/forms/
Closing Date: February 28th
Contributor: Offered in collaboration with the Noon Educational Foundation and the Commonwealth Scholarship Commission

Link Foundation/Cambridge Bursaries

Subjects: All subjects relevant to their country's needs.
Purpose: To financially support those undertaking postgraduate study.
Eligibility: Open to citizens of New Zealand. Applicants must apply to the University of Cambridge and be offered a place at Cambridge in the normal way. All applicants must have a First Class or High Second Class (Honours) Degree or equivalent and normally be under 26.
Level of Study: Postgraduate
Type: Bursary
Value: Part-cost bursaries
Length of Study: 1 year
Frequency: Annual
Study Establishment: The University of Cambridge
Country of Study: United Kingdom
No. of awards offered: 3
Application Procedure: Applicants must contact the Board of Graduate Studies.
Closing Date: February 28th
Contributor: Offered in collaboration with the Link Foundation for UK-New Zealand Relations (formerly known as the Waitangi Foundation) and the Foreign and Commonwealth Office (FCO)

For further information contact:

The Board of Graduate Studies, 4 Mill Hill, Cambridge, Cambridgeshire, CB2 1RZ, England
Contact: The Secretary

The LMB Cambridge Scholarships for PhD Study

Subjects: Molecular biology.
Purpose: To financially support study towards a PhD.
Eligibility: Applicants must apply to the University of Cambridge and be offered a place at Cambridge in the normal way. All applicants must have a First Class or High Second Class (Honours) Degree or equivalent and normally be under 26.
Level of Study: Doctorate, Predoctorate
Type: Scholarship
Value: Full maintenance allowance at the single student rate, after taking account of other awards from public sources towards maintenance for which the students are eligible and have received funding
Length of Study: Up to 3 years
Frequency: Annual
Study Establishment: The Laboratory of Molecular Biology (LMB), the University of Cambridge
Country of Study: United Kingdom
No. of awards offered: Up to 5
Application Procedure: Candidates for LMB Cambridge Scholarships should apply directly to the LMB by: nominating up to four possible PhD supervisors and projects from the list of available projects as published by the LMB; providing a personal statement of not more than one page (for each proposed supervisor) explaining why they wish to work in that chosen area of research and their reasons for nominating that supervisor; providing a copy of an up-to-date curriculum vitae; and providing a copy of their transcripts.
Closing Date: December 13th
Contributor: Offered in collaboration with the Laboratory of Molecular Biology, Cambridge

For further information contact:

The MRC Laboratory of Molecular Biology, Hills Road, Cambridge, Cambridgeshire, CB2 2QH, England
Website: www.mrc-lmb.cam.ac.uk
Contact: Director of Studies

Malaysian Commonwealth Scholarship for PhD Study

Subjects: Any subject.
Purpose: To financially support study towards a PhD.
Eligibility: Open to outstanding calibre students from Malaysia and the countries of the Commonwealth.

Level of Study: Doctorate
Type: Scholarship/Bursary
Value: A means tested contribution towards fees only or towards the overall costs of studying at Cambridge
Frequency: Annual
Study Establishment: The Cambridge Commonwealth Trust
Country of Study: United Kingdom
No. of awards offered: Varies
Application Procedure: Applicants for a place to do a PhD should apply for an ORS award and should normally be successfully nominated for an ORS award or an ORS equivalent award, which meets the difference between the higher overseas rate and the lower domestic rate of the University Composition Fee.
Contributor: In collaboration with the Trustees of the Malaysian Commonwealth Studies Centre and of the Cambridge Commonwealth Trust

Malaysian Commonwealth Scholarship for Postgraduate Study

Subjects: Any subject.
Purpose: To financially support study to the students undertaking postgraduate study.
Eligibility: Open to outstanding calibre students from Malaysia and the countries of the Commonwealth.
Level of Study: Postgraduate
Type: Scholarship/Bursary
Value: A means tested contribution towards fees only or towards the total overall costs of studying at Cambridge
Length of Study: 1 Year
Frequency: Annual
Study Establishment: The University of Cambridge
Country of Study: United Kingdom
No. of awards offered: Varies
Contributor: In collaboration with the Trustees of the Malaysian Commonwealth Studies Centre and of the Cambridge Commmonwealth Trust

Mandela Magdalene College Scholarships for Postgraduate Scholarships

Subjects: All subjects relevant to South Africa's needs.
Purpose: To financially support those undertaking postgraduate study and research.
Eligibility: Students must have been offered a place at Magdalene College, Cambridge and be citizens of South Africa. All applicants must have a First Class or High Second Class (Honours) Degree or equivalent and normally be under 26.
Level of Study: Postgraduate
Type: Scholarship
Value: The University Composition Fee at the overseas rate, approved college fees, a maintenance allowance sufficient for a single student and a contribution to return economy airfare
Length of Study: 1 year
Frequency: Annual
Study Establishment: Magdalene College, the University of Cambridge
Country of Study: United Kingdom
No. of awards offered: Up to 3
Application Procedure: Applicants must complete a preliminary application form, which can be obtained from local universities, offices of the British Council or the Trust. Completed forms must be returned to the main address. Shortlisted candidates will be sent forms for admission to the University of Cambridge. The preliminary application form can also be downloaded from www.admin.cam.ac.uk/offices/gradstud/admissions/forms/
Closing Date: February 28th
Contributor: Offered in collaboration with Magdalene College, Cambridge and Mr Chris von Christierson

National Research Foundation Cambridge Scholarships

Subjects: Any subject relevant to South Africa's identified research priority needs.
Purpose: To financially support research study courses leading towards PhD, in order to contribute towards the building of a highly skilled doctoral community in South Africa.

Eligibility: Open to students form South Africa. After completion of their degree, candidates must return to South Agrica for a period equivalent to the duration of support.
Level of Study: Doctorate
Type: Scholarship
Value: A means tested scholarship, usually a contribution of UK £14,000 per annum towards the overall annual costs of doing a PhD at Cambridge
Frequency: Annual
Study Establishment: The University of Cambridge
Country of Study: United Kingdom
No. of awards offered: Up to 5
Application Procedure: Applicants for a place to do a PhD should apply for an ORS award and should normally be successfully nominated for an ORS award or an ORS equivalent award, which meets the difference between the higher overseas rate and the lower domestic rate of the University Composition Fee.
Contributor: In collaboration with the National Research Foundation, South Africa

Nedcor Cambridge Awards

Subjects: Economics or Finance.
Purpose: To financially support study towards MPhil in Economics or Finance.
Eligibility: Open to students of South Africa doing a MPhil in Economics or Finance.
Level of Study: Postgraduate
Type: Award
Value: The award is a substantial cash prize from Nedcor which is awarded to the winner of the annual Nedbank Old Mutual Budget Speech competition. If the winner of the prize has been offered a place at Cambridge to read Economics or Finance, the cash prize will be tenable in conjunction with a substantial grant from the Cambridge Commonwealth Trust
Frequency: Dependent on funds available
Study Establishment: The University of Cambridge
Country of Study: United Kingdom
No. of awards offered: 1
Application Procedure: Participants in the Nedbank Old Mutual Budget Speech competition who wish to apply to Cambridge by the deadlines set by the Departments of Economics and the Judge Business School.
Contributor: In collaboration with Nedcor Bank, South Africa

Nehru Cambridge Scholarship

Subjects: Any subject.
Purpose: To financially support study towards a PhD.
Type: Scholarship
Value: The University Composition Fee at the appropriate rate, approved college fees, a maintenance allowance sufficient for a single student and a contribution towards a return economy airfare
Frequency: Annual
Study Establishment: Robinson College, The University of Cambridge
Country of Study: United Kingdom
No. of awards offered: Up to 8
Application Procedure: Applicants for a place to do a PhD should apply for an ORS award and should normally be successfully nominated for an ORS award or an ORS equivalent award, which meets the difference between the higher overseas rate and the lower domestic rate of the University Composition Fee.
Contributor: In collaboration with Nehru Trust for Cambridge University

Nestle Cambridge Scholarships

Subjects: Any subject.
Purpose: To financially support study towards a PhD.
Eligibility: Open to students from a disadvantaged background from the Commonwealth countries of Africa.
Type: Scholarship
Value: The University Composition Fee at the appropriate rate, approved College fees, a maintenance allowance sufficient for a single student and a contribution towards a return economy airfair
Length of Study: Doctorate
Frequency: Dependent on funds available

Study Establishment: Robinson College, The University of Cambridge
Country of Study: United Kingdom
No. of awards offered: 1
Application Procedure: Applicants for a place to do a PhD should apply for an ORS award and should normally be successfully nominated for an ORS award or an ORS equivalent award, which meets the difference between the higher overseas rate and the lower domestic rate of the University Composition Fee.
Contributor: In cooaboration with Nestle Charitable Trust and Robinson College

OSI Chevening Cambridge Scholarships for Postgraduate Study

Subjects: Subjects relevant to the needs of the scholar's country.
Purpose: To financially support those undertaking postgraduate study.
Eligibility: Open to nationals of, and normally residents in Albania, Azerbaijan, Bangladesh, Bosnia, Croatia, Kazakhstan, Kosovo, Macedonia, Montenegro, Pakistan, Tajikistan, Turkmenistan, Turkey, Ukraine, Yugoslavia. Applicants must apply to the University of Cambridge and be offered a place at Cambridge in the normal way. All applicants must have a First Class or High Second Class (Honours) Degree or equivalent and normally be under 26. Preference will be given to candidates who have not previously studied outside of their home country.
Level of Study: Postgraduate
Type: Scholarship
Value: The University Composition Fee at the overseas rate, approved college fees, a maintenance allowance sufficient for a single student and a contribution towards return economy airfare
Length of Study: 1 year
Frequency: Annual
Study Establishment: The University of Cambridge
Country of Study: United Kingdom
No. of awards offered: Up to 34
Application Procedure: Applicants must complete a preliminary application form, which can be obtained from local universities, offices of the British Council or the Trust. Completed forms must be returned to the main address. Shortlisted candidates will be sent forms for admission to the University of Cambridge.
Closing Date: February 28th
Contributor: Offered in collaboration with the Open Society Institute (OSI) and the Foreign and Commonwealth Office (FCO)

OSI Noon Chevening Cambridge Scholarships

Subjects: All subjects relevant to the needs of Pakistan or criminology, developmental studies, economics, economics & development, education, historical studies, history & philosophy of science, international relations, law, philosophy, political thought & intellectual history or socisl anthropology.
Purpose: To financially support postgraduate study.
Eligibility: Candidates should be nationals of and normally resident in, Pakistan during the academic year in which they apply for an award. They must preferably have not already spent a full academic year or more studying in an Institution of Higher Education in the West, and must return to their home country at the end of their scholarship period to continue their studies/work there.
Level of Study: Postgraduate
Type: Scholarship
Length of Study: 1 year
Study Establishment: University of Cambridge
Country of Study: United Kingdom
No. of awards offered: Up to 5
Application Procedure: Applicants must complete a preliminary application form, which can be obtained from local universities, offices of the British Council or the Trust. Completed forms must be returned to the main address. Shortlisted candidates will be sent forms for admission to the University of Cambridge. The preliminary application form can also be downloaded from www.admin.cam.ac.uk/offices/gradstud/admissions/forms/
Closing Date: February 28th
Funding: Foundation, trusts
Contributor: Cambridge Trusts, Noon Educational Foundation, Foreign and Commonwealth Office and the Open Society Institute (OSI)

Pegasus Cambridge Scholarships for Postgraduate Study

Subjects: Law.
Purpose: To financially assist students who have gained an offer of a place to read for the Master of Law degree (LLM).
Eligibility: Applicants must be from one of the following countries: Australia, Antigua & Barbuda, Barbados, Bermuda, Canada, Dominica, Grenada, Hong Kong, India, Jamaica, Kenya, New Zealand, Nigeria, St Kitts & Nevis, St Lucia, St Vincent & the Grenadines, Singapore, Trinidad & Tobago, or Zambia.
Level of Study: Postgraduate
Type: Scholarship
Value: The scholarships are held in conjunction with other awards from the Cambridge Commonwealth Trust and other sources and enable the successful applicants to spend three months in London on work placements at Clifford Chance and the Inner Temple after completing the LLM at Cambridge
Frequency: Annual
Study Establishment: The University of Cambridge
Country of Study: United Kingdom
No. of awards offered: Up to 6
Application Procedure: Applicants must complete a preliminary application form, which can be obtained from local universities, offices of the British Council or the Trust. Completed forms must be returned to the main address. Shortlisted candidates will be sent forms for admission to the University of Cambridge.
Closing Date: February 28th
Contributor: Offered in collaboration with the Pegasus Scholarships Trust

Prince of Wales Scholarships for PhD Study

Subjects: All subjects.
Purpose: To financially support study towards a PhD.
Eligibility: Candidates must be citizens of New Zealand, must apply to the University of Cambridge and be offered a place at Cambridge in the normal way. All applicants must have a First Class or High Second Class (Honours) Degree or equivalent and normally be under 26. They must be successfully nominated for an Overseas Research Student (ORS) award.
Level of Study: Doctorate, Predoctorate
Type: Scholarship
Value: Means-tested contribution
Length of Study: Up to 3 years
Frequency: Annual
Study Establishment: The University of Cambridge
Country of Study: United Kingdom
No. of awards offered: Up to 5
Application Procedure: Applicants must apply directly to the Scholarships Officer at their own university. Otherwise, they should apply directly to the New Zealand Vice Chancellor's Committee.
Closing Date: February 28th
Contributor: Offered in collaboration with the New Zealand Vice Chancellor's Committee

For further information contact:

The New Zealand Vice Chancellor's Committee, Level 11, 94 Dixon Street, Wellington 6034, PO Box 11-915, New Zealand
Contact: Scholarships Officer

Prince Philip Graduate Exhibitions

Purpose: For courses of research leading to the degree or PhD.
Eligibility: For students from Hong Kong. Applicants for a place to do a PhD should apply for an ORS award and should normally be successfully nominated for an ORS award or an ORS equivalent award, which meets the difference between the higher overseas rate and the lower domestic rate of the University Composition Fee.
Frequency: Annual
No. of awards offered: 2
Contributor: In collaboration with the Friends of Cambridge University in Hong Kong
Additional Information: One scholarship being awarded to a student who has graduated from the Chinese University of Hong Kong. One scholarship to a student who has graduated from the University of Hong Kong.

Prince Philip Graduate Exhibitions For PhD Study

Subjects: All subjects.
Purpose: To financially support study towards a PhD.
Eligibility: Students who have graduated from the Chinese University of Hong Kong and the University of Hong Kong. Applicants must apply to the University of Cambridge and be offered a place at Cambridge in the normal way. All applicants must have a First Class or High Second Class (Honours) Degree or equivalent and normally be under 26. They must be successfully nominated for an Overseas Research Student (ORS) award.
Level of Study: Doctorate
Type: Scholarship
Value: Means-tested substantial part-cost awards towards the overall costs
Length of Study: Up to 3 years
Frequency: Annual
Study Establishment: The University of Cambridge
Country of Study: United Kingdom
No. of awards offered: 2
Application Procedure: Applicants must complete a preliminary application form, which can be obtained from local universities, offices of the British Council or the Trust. Completed forms must be returned to the main address. Shortlisted candidates will be sent forms for admission to the University of Cambridge. The preliminary application form can also be downloaded from www.admin.cam.ac.uk/offices/gradstud/admissions/forms/
Contributor: Offered in collaboration with the Friends of Cambridge University in Hong Kong

PTDF Cambridge Scholarships

Subjects: Science-related subjects contributing to an improvement in technical manpower for the oil and gas industry.
Purpose: To financially support postgraduate study.
Eligibility: Candidates must be from Nigeria, must apply to the University of Cambridge and be offered a place at Cambridge in the normal way. All applicants must have a First Class or High Second Class (Honours) Degree or equivalent and normally be under 26. They must be successfully nominated for an Overseas Research Student (ORS) award. The students may apply to MPhil in Environment and Development, Environmental Engineering and Sustainable Development, Environmental Policy, Fluid Flow in Industry and the Environment, or Geographical Information Systems and Remote Sensing.
Level of Study: Postgraduate
Type: Scholarship
Value: The university composition fee at the appropriate rate, approved college fees, a maintenance allowance sufficient for a single student and a contribution towards a return economy airfare
Length of Study: 1 year
Frequency: Annual
Study Establishment: University of Cambridge
Country of Study: United Kingdom
No. of awards offered: Varies
Application Procedure: Applicants must complete a preliminary application form, which can be obtained from local universities, offices of the British Council or the Trust. Completed forms must be returned to the main address. Shortlisted candidates will be sent forms for admission to the University of Cambridge.
Closing Date: February 28th
Funding: Trusts
Contributor: Offered in collaboration with Univation at the Robert Gordon University, Aberdeen

Rajiv Gandhi (UK) Foundation Cambridge Scholarship

Subjects: All subjects.
Purpose: To financially support study towards a PhD.
Eligibility: Applicants must be from India, must apply to the University of Cambridge and be offered a place at Cambridge in the normal way. All applicants must have a First Class (Honours) Degree. Those with a First Class Master's Degree may be given preference.
Level of Study: Doctorate, Postgraduate
Type: Scholarship
Value: University composition fee, approved college fees, maintenance allowance
Length of Study: 2 years
Frequency: Annual

Study Establishment: The University of Cambridge
Country of Study: United Kingdom
No. of awards offered: 1
Application Procedure: Applicants must contact the organization.
Closing Date: February 28th
Contributor: Offered in collaboration with the Rajiv Gandhi Foundation

For further information contact:

The Nehru Trust for Cambridge University, Teen Murti House, Teen Murti Marg, New Delhi, 110011, India
Contact: The Joint Secretary

Raymond and Helen Kwok Research Scholarship

Subjects: Any subject relevant to China's needs.
Purpose: To financially support study leading to a PhD.
Eligibility: Applicants must be from China, and must have been awarded a First Class (Honours) Degree or equivalent.
Level of Study: Doctorate
Type: Scholarship
Value: University composition fee approved college fees maintenance allowance
Length of Study: 3 years
Frequency: Annual
Study Establishment: Jesus College, The University of Cambridge
Country of Study: United Kingdom
No. of awards offered: 2
Application Procedure: Applicants must complete a preliminary application form, which can be obtained from local universities, offices of the British Council or the Trust. Completed forms must be returned to the main address. Shortlisted candidates will be sent forms for admission to the University of Cambridge. Applicants must also apply for an ORS award. The preliminary application form can also be downloaded from www.admin.cam.ac.uk/offices/gradstud/admissions/forms/
Closing Date: March 31st
Funding: Individuals, trusts
Contributor: Mr Raymond Kowk and Jesus College

Royal Government of Thailand Cambridge Scholarship for PhD Study

Subjects: All subjects.
Purpose: To financially support study towards a PhD.
Eligibility: Applicants must be from Thailand, must apply to the University of Cambridge and be offered a place at Cambridge in the normal way. All applicants must have a First Class or High Second Class (Honours) Degree or equivalent and normally be under 26. For PhD study they be successfully nominated for an Overseas Research Student (ORS) award.
Level of Study: Doctorate
Type: Scholarship
Value: The University Composition Fee at the appropriate rate, approved college fees, a maintenance allowance sufficient for a single student and a contribution towards return economy airfare
Length of Study: Up to 3 years
Frequency: Annual
Study Establishment: The University of Cambridge
Country of Study: United Kingdom
No. of awards offered: 1
Application Procedure: Applicants must complete a preliminary application form, which can be obtained from local universities, offices of the British Council or the main address. Completed forms must be returned to the main address. Shortlisted candidates will be sent forms for admission to the University of Cambridge. These forms must be returned to the Board of Graduate Studies.
Contributor: Offered in collaboration with the Cambridge Thai Foundation and Civil Service Commission, Royal Government of Thailand

Royal Government of Thailand Cambridge Scholarship for Postgraduate Study

Subjects: All subjects.
Purpose: To financially support those undertaking postgraduate study.

Eligibility: Applicants must be from Thailand, must apply to the University of Cambridge and be offered a place at Cambridge in the normal way. All applicants must have a First Class or High Second Class (Honours) Degree or equivalent and normally be under 26 years of age. They must be successfully nominated for an Overseas Research Student (ORS) award.

Level of Study: Postgraduate

Type: Scholarship

Value: The University Composition Fee at the overseas rate, approved college fees, a maintenance allowance sufficient for a single student and a contribution towards return economy airfare

Length of Study: 1 year

Frequency: Annual

Study Establishment: The University of Cambridge

Country of Study: United Kingdom

No. of awards offered: Up to 4

Application Procedure: Applicants must complete a preliminary application form, which can be obtained from local universities, offices of the British Council or the Trust. Completed forms must be returned to the main address. Shortlisted candidates will be sent forms for admission to the University of Cambridge. The preliminary application form can also be downloaded from www.admin.cam.ac.uk/offices/gradstud/admissions/forms/

Closing Date: February 28th

Contributor: The Cambridge Thai Foundation and the Civil Service Commission, Royal Government of Thailand

Shell Centenary Cambridge Scholarships (Countries Outside of the Commonwealth)

Subjects: Subjects relevant to the needs of the scholar's country.

Purpose: To financially support those undertaking postgraduate study.

Eligibility: Open to citizens from all countries except: Australia, Austria, Belgium, Canada, Denmark, Finland, France, Germany, Greece, Iceland, Ireland, Italy, Japan, Luxembourg, The Netherlands, New Zealand, Norway, Portugal, Spain, Sweden, Switzerland, UK or USA. Applicants must apply to the University of Cambridge and be offered a place at Cambridge in the normal way. All applicants must have a First Class or High Second Class (Honours) Degree or equivalent and normally be under 26.

Level of Study: Postgraduate

Type: Scholarship

Value: The University Composition Fee at the overseas rate, approved college fees, a maintenance allowance sufficient for a single student and a contribution towards return economy airfare

Length of Study: 1 year

Frequency: Annual

Study Establishment: The University of Cambridge

Country of Study: United Kingdom

No. of awards offered: Up to 20

Application Procedure: Applicants must complete a preliminary application form, which can be obtained from local universities, offices of the British Council or the Trust. Completed forms must be returned to the main address. Shortlisted candidates will be sent forms for admission to the University of Cambridge. The preliminary application form can also be downloaded from www.admin.cam.ac.uk/offices/gradstud/admissions/forms/

Closing Date: February 28th

Contributor: Offered in collaboration with Shell Centenary Scholarship Fund

Shell Centenary Chevening Scholarships for Postgraduate Study

Subjects: Subjects relevant to the needs of the scholar's country.

Purpose: To financially support those undertaking postgraduate study.

Eligibility: Open to citizens from all countries except: Australia, Austria, Belgium, Canada, Denmark, Finland, France, Germany, Greece, Iceland, Ireland, Italy, Japan, Luxembourg, The Netherlands, New Zealand, Norway, Portugal, Spain, Sweden, Switzerland, UK or USA. Applicants must apply to the University of Cambridge and be offered a place at Cambridge in the normal way. All applicants must have a First Class or High Second Class (Honours) Degree or equivalent and normally be under 26.

Level of Study: Postgraduate

Type: Scholarship

Value: The University Composition Fee at the overseas rate, approved college fees, a maintenance allowance sufficient for a single student and a contribution to return economy airfare

Length of Study: 1 year

Frequency: Annual

Study Establishment: The University of Cambridge

Country of Study: United Kingdom

No. of awards offered: 10

Application Procedure: Applicants must complete a preliminary application form, which can be obtained from local universities, offices of the British Council or the Trust. Completed forms must be returned to the main address. Shortlisted candidates will be sent forms for admission to the University of Cambridge. The preliminary application form can also be downloaded from www.admin.cam.ac.uk/offices/gradstud/admissions/forms/

Closing Date: February 28th

Contributor: Offered in collaboration with Shell Centenary Scholarship Fund and the Foreign and Commonwealth Office (FCO)

South African College Bursaries

Subjects: All subjects.

Purpose: To enable citizens of South and Southern Africa to study at the University of Cambridge.

Eligibility: Applicants must be from South or Southern Africa, must apply to the University of Cambridge and be offered a place at Cambridge in the normal way. All applicants must have a First Class or High Second Class (Honours) Degree or equivalent and normally be under 26. They must be successfully nominated for an Overseas Research Student (ORS) award.

Level of Study: Postgraduate

Type: Bursary

Value: Part-cost bursaries

Length of Study: 1 year

Frequency: Annual

Study Establishment: The University of Cambridge

Country of Study: United Kingdom

No. of awards offered: Varies

Application Procedure: Applicants must complete a preliminary application form, which can be obtained from local universities, offices of the British Council or the Trust. Completed forms must be returned to the main address. Shortlisted candidates will be sent forms for admission to the University of Cambridge. The preliminary application form can also be downloaded from www.admin.cam.ac.uk/offices/gradstud/admissions/forms/

Closing Date: February 28th

Contributor: Offered in collaboration with Churchill College, Newnham College, Selwyn College, St Catherine's College and Sidney Sussex College, Cambridge

Additional Information: The bursaries are normally held in conjunction with other awards from the Cambridge Commonwealth Trust and other sources.

Sun Hung Kai Cambridge Scholarship and Bursaries for Postgraduate Study

Subjects: Any subject.

Purpose: To financially support postgraduate study.

Eligibility: For students from China.

Level of Study: Postgraduate

Type: Scholarship/Bursary

Value: The University Composition Fee at the appropriate rate, approved College fees, a maintenance allowance sufficient for a single student and a contribution towards a return economy airfare

Length of Study: 1 year

Frequency: Annual

Study Establishment: The University of Cambridge

Country of Study: United Kingdom

No. of awards offered: Up to 15 scholarships, and a number of bursaries

Application Procedure: Applicants must complete a preliminary application form, which can be obtained from local universities, offices of the British Council or the Trust. Completed forms must be returned to the main address. Shortlisted candidates will be sent forms for admission to the University of Cambridge.

Closing Date: February 28th
Contributor: In collaboration wih the Sun Hung Kai Properties Limited

Sun Hung Kai Cambridge Scholarships for PhD Study

Subjects: All subjects.
Purpose: To financially support study towards a PhD.
Eligibility: Open to students from China. All applicants must have a First Class or High Second Class (Honours) Degree or equivalent and normally be under 26. They must be successfully nominated for an Overseas Research Student (ORS) award.
Level of Study: Doctorate
Type: Scholarships
Value: University Composition Fee, approved college fees, maintenance allowance for a single student, contribution to return economy airfare
Length of Study: Up to 3 years
Frequency: Annual
No. of awards offered: 2
Application Procedure: Applicants must complete a preliminary application form, which can be obtained from local universities, offices of the British Council or the Trust. Completed forms must be returned to the main address. Shortlisted candidates will be sent forms for admission to the University of Cambridge. The preliminary application form can also be downloaded from www.admin.cam.ac.uk/offices/gradstud/admissions/forms/
Contributor: Cambridge Trusts and Sun Hung Kai properties limited

Tidmarsh Cambridge Scholarship for PhD Study

Subjects: All subjects.
Purpose: To financially support study towards a PhD.
Eligibility: Open to citizens of Canada. Applicants must apply to the University of Cambridge and be offered a place at Cambridge in the normal way. All applicants must have a First Class or High Second Class (Honours) Degree or equivalent and normally be under 26. They must have been successfully nominated for an Overseas Research Student (ORS) award.
Level of Study: Doctorate
Type: Scholarship
Value: The University Composition Fee at the home rate, approved college fees and a maintenance allowance sufficient for a single student
Frequency: Dependent on funds available
Study Establishment: Trinity Hall, the University of Cambridge
Country of Study: United Kingdom
No. of awards offered: 1
Application Procedure: Application forms for the scholarship will be sent out to eligible candidates once the completed form for admission to the University of Cambridge has reached the Board of Graduate Studies.
Closing Date: February 28th
Contributor: A benefaction from Dr Evan Schulman

For further information contact:

The Board of Graduate Studies, 4 Mill Lane, Cambridge, Cambridgeshire, CB2 1RZ, England
Contact: The Secretary

TNK/BP Kapitza Cambridge Scholarships.

Subjects: All subjects relevant to the needs of their country.
Purpose: To financially support study towards a PhD.
Eligibility: Open to citizens of Russia and Ukraine. Preference may be given to candidates intending to pursue research in the broad fields of engineering, economics, management studies, law, mathematics and natural sciences. Applicants should normally have a first class honours degree and, preferably, a Masters degree or its equivalent from a recognised university. Applicants should apply for an Overseas Research Student (ORS) award.
Level of Study: Doctorate
Type: Scholarship
Value: The University composition fee at the appropriate rate, approved college fees, a maintenance allowance sufficient for a single student, a contribution towards a return economy airfare, and an annual dicretionary allowance for study-related expenses
Frequency: Annual
Study Establishment: Trinity College, the University of Cambridge

Country of Study: United Kingdom
No. of awards offered: Up to 8
Application Procedure: Application forms for the scholarship will be sent out to eligible candidates once the completed form for admission to the University of Cambridge has reached the Board of Graduate Studies.
Closing Date: February 28th
Contributor: Offered in collaboration with the TNK/BP and Trinity College

UK Commonwealth (Cambridge) Scholarships for PhD Study

Subjects: All subjects.
Purpose: To offer the opportunity for individuals with proven academic merit to study towards a PhD at Cambridge.
Eligibility: Open to candidates from Australia, New Zealand and Canada. Scholars should be nominated for an Overseas Research Student (ORS) award.
Level of Study: Doctorate, Predoctorate
Type: Scholarship
Value: The University Composition Fee at the home rate, approved college fees, a maintenance allowance sufficient for a single student and a contribution towards return economy airfare
Length of Study: Up to 3 years
Frequency: Annual
Study Establishment: The University of Cambridge
Country of Study: United Kingdom
No. of awards offered: Up to 15
Application Procedure: Candidates must apply to the local Commonwealth scholarship agency in their home country.
Contributor: Offered in collaboration with the Commonwealth Scholarship Commission in the United Kingdom

UK Commonwealth (Cambridge) Scholarships for Postgraduate Study

Subjects: All subjects.
Purpose: To financially support those undertaking postgraduate study.
Eligibility: Open to candidates from Australia, New Zealand and Canada.
Level of Study: Postgraduate
Type: Scholarship
Value: The University Composition Fee at the overseas rate, approved college fees, a maintenance allowance sufficient for a single student and a contribution towards return economy airfare
Length of Study: 1 year
Frequency: Annual
Study Establishment: The University of Cambridge
Country of Study: United Kingdom
No. of awards offered: Up to 10
Application Procedure: Candidates must apply to the local Commonwealth scholarship agency in their home country.
Closing Date: February 28th
Contributor: Offered in collaboration with the Commonwealth Scholarship Association in the United Kingdom

UK-Germany Millenium Studentships

Subjects: All subjects.
Purpose: To financially support postgraduate study.
Eligibility: Applicants must be German nationals. All applicants must have a First Class or High Second Class (Honours) Degree or equivalent and normally be under 26.
Level of Study: Postgraduate
Type: Studentship
Value: UK £2,000 per year
Length of Study: 1 year
Frequency: Annual
Study Establishment: St Edmund's College, Cambridge
No. of awards offered: 2
Application Procedure: Applicants must apply to the University of Cambridge and be offered a place at Cambridge in the normal way. Applicants should complete only one scholarship form, which will enable them to be considered for all awards for which they are eligible. Application form can be downloaded from the website.
Contributor: Cambridge Trusts and St Edmund's College

William and Margaret Brown Cambridge Scholarship for PhD Study

Subjects: Engineering, natural sciences, physical sciences or political sciences.

Purpose: To financially support study towards a PhD.

Eligibility: Open to students from Canada. Applicants must apply to the University of Cambridge and be offered a place at Cambridge in the normal way. All applicants must have a First Class or High Second Class (Honours) Degree or equivalent and normally be under 26. They must be successfully nominated for an Overseas Research Student (ORS) award.

Level of Study: Predoctorate, Doctorate

Type: Scholarship

Value: The University Composition Fee at the home rate and approved college fees

Length of Study: Up to 3 years

Frequency: Dependent on funds available

Study Establishment: The University of Cambridge

Country of Study: United Kingdom

No. of awards offered: 1

Application Procedure: Application forms for the scholarship will be sent out to eligible candidates once the completed form for admission to the University of Cambridge has reached the Board of Graduate Studies.

Contributor: A benefaction from Dr Donald Pinchin

For further information contact:

The Board of Graduate Studies, 4 Mill Hill, Cambridge, Cambridge-shire, CB2 1RZ, England

Contact: The Secretary

Wing Yip Cambridge Scholarships

Subjects: All subjects.

Purpose: For postgraduate courses of study.

Eligibility: Open to students from Canada. Preference will be given to applicants intending to apply for a PhD in Engineering, Natural Sciences, Physical Sciences or Political Sciences.

Level of Study: Postgraduate

Value: University Composition Fee, approved college fees, maintenance allowance, return economy airfare

Length of Study: 1 year

Frequency: Annual

Study Establishment: Churchill College, The University of Cambridge

No. of awards offered: 2

Application Procedure: Applicants must apply to the University of Cambridge and be offered a place at Cambridge in the normal way. Applicants should complete only one scholarship form, which will enable them to be considered for all awards for which they are eligible. Application forms can be downloaded from the website.

Closing Date: February 28th

Contributor: Cambridge Trusts, Mr Wing Yip and the Education Section of the Chinese Embassy, London

Woolf Fisher Scholarship

Subjects: Any subject.

Purpose: To financially support study towards a PhD.

Eligibility: Open to students from New Zealand, and have attended a secondary school in New Zealand. Students should have a first calss honours degree from a university in New Zealand. Applicants for a place to do a PhD should apply for an ORS award and should normally be successfully nominated for an ORS award or an ORS equivalent award.

Level of Study: Doctorate

Type: Scholarship

Value: The University Composition Fee at the appropriate rate, approved college fees, a maintenance allowance of UK £10,000 a year

Frequency: Annual

Study Establishment: Trinity College, The University of Cambridge

Country of Study: United Kingdom

No. of awards offered: Up to 3

Application Procedure: Candidates must apply on the prescribed forms to the Scholarships Manager, New Zealand Vice Chancellors Committee, PO Box 11-915, Wellington by September 1st in the year prior to that in which the scholarship will be taken up.

Closing Date: February 28th

Contributor: in collaboration with the Woolf Fisher Trust

World Bank Cambridge Scholarships for Postgraduate Study

Subjects: Subjects related to development.

Purpose: To financially support those undertaking postgraduate study.

Eligibility: Candidates must be nationals of a World Bank member country, be under the age of 45, with priority given to those candidates under 35, have or be about to obtain a First Class or High Second Class Degree from a recognized university in a development-related field. Other prerequisites include 2, but preferably 4–5 years of recent full-time professional experience in their home country or other developing country, usually in public service. Candidates must not hold resident status in the United States of America or another industrialized country. They should not hold a Master's degree or diploma or at present be studying towards a Master's degree or diploma from an industrialized country.

Level of Study: Postgraduate

Type: Scholarship

Value: The University Composition Fee at the overseas rate, approved college fees, a maintenance allowance sufficient for a single student and a contribution towards return economy airfare

Length of Study: 1 year

Frequency: Annual

Study Establishment: The University of Cambridge

Country of Study: United Kingdom

No. of awards offered: Up to 20

Application Procedure: Applicants must contact the organization.

Closing Date: February 28th

Contributor: Offered in collaboration with the World Bank

THE CANADA COUNCIL FOR THE ARTS

350 Albert Street, PO Box 1047, Ottawa, ON, K1P 5V8, Canada
Tel: (1) 613 566 4414 ext 5060/800 263 5588
Fax: (1) 613 566 4390
Email: lise.rochon@canadacouncil.ca
Website: www.canadacouncil.ca
Contact: Ms Lise Rochon

The Canada Council for the Arts is a national agency that provides grants and services to professional Canadian artists and art organizations in dance, media arts, music, theatre, writing and publishing, inter-arts and the visual arts.

Canada Council Grants for Professional Artists

Subjects: Art: dance, music, theatre, media arts, visual arts, creative writing and inter-arts.

Purpose: To help professional Canadian artists pursue professional development and/or independent artistic creation or production.

Eligibility: Open to Canadian citizens or permanent residents of Canada who have finished their basic training in the arts and/or are recognized as professionals within their own disciplines.

Level of Study: Postgraduate, Professional development

Value: Canadian $3,000–60,000

Frequency: Varies

Country of Study: Any country

No. of awards offered: Varies

Closing Date: Varies

Funding: Government

Additional Information: Interested Canadian individuals should see the website for detailed information on the grants offered in each discipline.

Canada Council Travel Grants

Subjects: Arts: dance, music, theatre, media art, visual art, creative writing and inter-arts.

Purpose: To enable Canadian artists to travel on occasions important to their professional careers.

Eligibility: Open to Canadian citizens or permanent residents of Canada who have finished their basic training in the arts and are recognized as professionals within their own disciplines.

Type: Travel grant

Value: A maximum of Canadian $2,500 to cover travel costs
Frequency: Varies
Country of Study: Any country
No. of awards offered: Varies
Funding: Government
Additional Information: Interested Canadian individuals should see the website for detailed information on the grants offered within each discipline.

J B C Watkins Award

Subjects: Architecture, music, theatre.
Purpose: To allow Canadian artists to pursue graduate study outside Canada in theatre, architecture and music.
Eligibility: Open to Canadian artists who are graduates of a Canadian university or postsecondary art institution or training school in the above subjects.
Level of Study: Postgraduate
Value: Canadian $5,000
Frequency: Annual
Country of Study: Canada
No. of awards offered: Varies
Application Procedure: Applicants must see the Canada Council's website for details. www.canadacouncil.ca/prizes/jbc_watkins
Closing Date: Varies
Funding: Private
Additional Information: All eligible candidates in the grants to individual program within the discipline of music, theatre or architecture will automatically be considered.

Killam Prizes

Subjects: Health sciences, natural sciences, engineering, social sciences and humanities.
Purpose: Intended to honour eminent Canadian scholars actively engaged in research in Canada in universities, hospitals, research and scientific institutes or other equivalent or similar institutions.
Eligibility: Only Canadian citizens are eligible for this honour, and the prizes are awarded only to living candidates. To be nominated for the prizes, candidates must have made a substantial and distinguished contribution, over a significant period, to scholarly research in Canada. Their outstanding achievements must have been clearly demonstrated already, and they are expected to make further contributions to the scholarly and scientific heritage of Canada.
Level of Study: Postgraduate
Type: Prize
Value: Canadian $100,000
Length of Study: Varies
Frequency: Annual
Study Establishment: Universities, hospitals, research institutes or scientific institutes
Country of Study: Canada
No. of awards offered: 5
Application Procedure: Candidates may not apply on their own behalf; they must be nominated by an expert in their field. Information is available on the Canada Council website www.canadacouncil.ca/prizes/killam
Closing Date: June 15th
Funding: Private
Contributor: Killam Trust
No. of awards given last year: 5
Additional Information: Detailed guidelines for the application process are available in the website.

Killam Research Fellowships

Subjects: Humanities, social sciences, natural sciences, health sciences, engineering and studies linking any of the disciplines within these broad fields.
Purpose: To support Canadian scholars of exceptional ability engaged in advanced research projects.
Eligibility: Open to Canadian citizens or permanent residents of Canada. Killam Research Fellowships are aimed at established scholars who have demonstrated outstanding ability through substantial publications in their fields over a period of several years.

Level of Study: Postgraduate
Type: Fellowship
Value: Canadian $70,000, paid to the university or research institution which employs the fellow
Length of Study: 2 years
Frequency: Annual
No. of awards offered: Varies
Application Procedure: There are no hard copy application forms: applicants must submit their requests through the Canada Council's online application system at killam.canadacouncil.ca
Closing Date: May 15th
Funding: Private
Contributor: Killam Trust
No. of awards given last year: 10

Robert Fleming Prize

Subjects: Composition in classical music.
Purpose: To encourage young Canadian composers.
Eligibility: It is intended to encourage the career development of young composers and is awarded to the most talented Canadian music composer in the competition for Canada Council Grants to Professional musicians in classical music.
Level of Study: Postgraduate
Value: Canadian $2,000
Length of Study: Up to 1 year
Frequency: Annual
Country of Study: Any country
No. of awards offered: 1
Closing Date: March 1st
Funding: Government
Additional Information: Artists may not apply for this prize. All successful candidates in the Canada Council Grants to professional musicians in classical music are considered automatically.

THE CANADIAN ASSOCIATION FOR GRADUATE STUDIES (CAGS)

205-260 Dalhousie Street, Ottawa, ON, K1N-7E4, Canada
Tel: (1) 613 562 0949
Fax: (1) 613 562 9009
Email: cags@uottawa.ca
Website: www.cags.ca

Canadian Association for Graduate Studies (CAGS) brings together 52 Canadian universities with graduate and post graduate programmes and 3 national graduate student associations. Its mandate is to promote graduate and post graduate education and research in Canada.

CAGS UMI Dissertation Awards

Subjects: Engineering, medical sciences and the natural sciences, fine arts, humanities and social sciences.
Purpose: To recognize Canadian Doctoral dissertations that make unusually significant and original contributions to the related academic field.
Eligibility: Open to students whose dissertation is completed and accepted by the graduate school.
Level of Study: Doctorate
Type: Award
Value: Canadian $1,000 and travel expenses of up to Canadian $1,500 to attend the CAGS Annual Conference
Frequency: Annual
Country of Study: Canada
No. of awards offered: 2
Application Procedure: Applications must be submitted by a Canadian university.
Closing Date: February 15th
Funding: Private
Contributor: University Microfilms International
No. of awards given last year: 2
No. of applicants last year: 50

CANADIAN ASSOCIATION FOR THE PRACTICAL STUDY OF LAW IN EDUCATION (CAPSLE)

c/o Secretariat (Lori Pollock), 37 Moultrey Crescent, Georgetown, ON,
L7G 4N4, Canada
Tel: (1) 905 702 1710
Fax: (1) 905 873 0662
Email: info@capsle.ca
Website: www.capsle.ca

CAPSLE is a national organization whose aim is to provide an open forum for the practical study of legal issues related to and affecting the education system and its stakeholders.

CAPSLE Fellowship

Subjects: Law.
Purpose: To provide an open forum for the practical study of legal issues affecting education.
Eligibility: Open to Canadian citizens or landed immigrants enrolled in a faculty of law or a Graduate School of Education at Canadian university.
Level of Study: Postgraduate
Type: Fellowship
Value: Canadian $3,000
Frequency: Annual
Study Establishment: Any accredited university or institution
Country of Study: Canada
Application Procedure: See the website.
Closing Date: April 15th
No. of awards given last year: 1
No. of applicants last year: 6
Additional Information: The successful candidate is invited to speak at the annual CAPSLE conference and to publish in our newsletter of CAPSLE or conference proceedings.

For further information contact:

CAPSLE, 37 Moultrey Crescent, Georgetown, Ontario, CANADA, L7G 4N4

CANADIAN ASSOCIATION OF BROADCASTERS (CAB)

PO Box 627, Station B, Ottawa, ON, K1P 5S2, Canada
Tel: (1) 613 233 4035
Fax: (1) 613 233 6961
Email: cab@cab-acr.ca
Website: www.cab-acr.ca
Contact: Vanessa Dawson, Special Events and Projects Co-ordinator

The Canadian Association of Broadcasters (CAB) is the collective voice of Canada's private radio and television stations and speciality services. The CAB develops industry-wide strategic plans, works to improve the financial health of the industry, and promotes private broadcasting's role as Canada's leading programmer and local service provider.

BBM Scholarship

Subjects: Statistical and quantitative research methodology.
Purpose: To ensure that there is an investment in the development of individuals, skilled and knowledgeable in research, who may be of future benefit to the Canadian broadcasting industry.
Eligibility: Open to students enrolled in a graduate studies programme, or in the final year of an Honours degree with the intention of entering a graduate programme, anywhere in Canada. Candidates must have demonstrated achievement in, and knowledge of, statistical and/or quantitative research methodology in a course of study at a Canadian university or postsecondary institution.
Level of Study: Graduate
Type: Scholarship
Value: Canadian $4,000 plus a commemorative certificate
Frequency: Annual
Country of Study: Canada
No. of awards offered: 1

Application Procedure: Applicants must complete an application form and submit a 250-word essay outlining their interest in audience research. Application forms are available from the website. Three references should be attached to the completed application form, including one from the course director.
Closing Date: June 30th
Funding: Private
Contributor: The BBM Bureau of Measurement and the Canadian Association of Broadcasters

CANADIAN BAR ASSOCIATION (CBA)

Canadian Bar Association (CBA) Suite 500, 865 Carling Avenue,
Ottawa, ON, K1S 5S8, Canada
Tel: (1) 613 237 2925
Fax: (1) 613 237 0185
Email: info@cba.org
Website: www.cba.org
Contact: Senior Director of Communications

The Canadian Bar Association (CBA) represents more than 36,000 lawyers across Canada. Offers national perspective on legal issues, federal legislation and trends in law. Provides explanations, analysis and commentary on all areas of law from practising lawyers, academics and in-house counsel. CBA is dedicated to improvement in the law, the administration of justice, lawyer education and advocacy in the public interest.

Viscount Bennett Fellowship

Subjects: Law.
Purpose: To encourage a high standard of legal education, training and ethics.
Eligibility: Open to Canadian citizens only.
Level of Study: Postgraduate
Type: Fellowship
Value: Canadian $40,000
Length of Study: 1 year
Frequency: Annual
Study Establishment: An approved institution
Country of Study: Any country
No. of awards offered: 1
Application Procedure: Please refer to www.cba.org/cba/awards/viscount_bennett for full details and an application form.
Closing Date: November 15th
Funding: Trusts
No. of awards given last year: 1
No. of applicants last year: Average: 48

CANADIAN BLOOD SERVICES (CBS)

1800 Alta Vista Drive, Ottawa, ON, K1G 4J5, Canada
Tel: (1) 613 739 2300
Fax: (1) 613 731 1411
Email: elaine.konecny@bloodservices.ca
Website: www.bloodservices.ca
Contact: Ms Elaine Konecny, Program Assistant, Research & Development

Canadian Blood Services (CBS) is a non-profit, charitable organization whose sole mission is to manage the blood system for Canadians. CBS collects approx. 900,000 units of blood annually and processes it into components and products that are administered to thousands of patients each year.

CBS Graduate Fellowship Program

Subjects: Blood transfusion science focusing on aspects of the collection and preparation of blood from volunteer donors as well as on the biological materials derived from blood or their substitutes obtained through biotechnology. Research may encompass a broad variety of disciplines including, but not restricted to, epidemiology, surveillance, social sciences, blood banking, immunohaematology, haematology, infectious diseases, immunology, genetics, protein chemistry, molecular and cell biology, clinical medicine, laboratory sciences, virology, bioengineering, process engineering or biotechnology.

Purpose: To attract and support young investigators to initiate or continue training in the field of blood or blood products research.

Eligibility: Open to graduate students who are undertaking full-time research training leading to a PhD degree. Students registering solely for a Master's degree will not be considered and only those demonstrating acceptance into a PhD programme will receive continued support. Candidates must have completed sufficient academic work to be admitted in good standing to a graduate school by the time the award is to take effect, or be already engaged in a PhD programme. Applicants possessing a medical degree but not licensed to practice medicine in Canada are eligible to apply for this award providing they meet the above criteria.

Level of Study: Graduate

Type: Fellowship

Value: Canadian $21,000 per year plus a yearly research and travel allowance of Canadian $1,000 per year

Length of Study: Up to 4 years. The initial term is for 2 years, with the option for a 2 year renewal. Renewals must be requested in the form of a complete new application

Frequency: 2 times per year

Country of Study: Canada

Application Procedure: Candidates are required to submit a completed application form (GFP-01) that is available either from the website, from or the main address.

Closing Date: May 15th and November 15th

Funding: Government

No. of awards given last year: 8

No. of applicants last year: 13

For further information contact:

Program Assistant, R&D, Canadian Blood Services, 1800 Alta Vista Drive, Ottawa, ON, K1G 4J5

Tel: 613-739-2230

Fax: 613-739-2201

Email: elaine.konecny@blood.ca

Contact: Elaine Konecny

CBS Postdoctoral Fellowship (PDF)

Subjects: Transfusion science. The CBS has active research programmes within transfusion science emphasizing platelets, stem cells, plasma proteins, infectious disease, epidemiology and chemical transfusion practice.

Purpose: To support Fellows working with CBS-affiliated research and development groups across Canada and to foster careers related to transfusion science in Canada.

Eligibility: Candidates must hold a recent PhD or equivalent research degree or an MD, DDS, DVM, plus a recent research degree in an appropriate health field (minimum of a MSc) or equivalent research experience, neither must be registered for a higher degree at the time of acceptance of the award and nor undertake formal studies for such a degree during the period of appointment.

Level of Study: Postdoctorate, Professional development

Type: Fellowship

Value: The value of each fellowship is related to the major degree(s) and experience that the applicant holds. The fellowship offers a stipend based on current Medical Research Council rates for each of the 3 years as well as a 1st year research allowance of Canadian $10,000

Length of Study: 1–3 years

Frequency: Annual

Country of Study: Canada

No. of awards offered: 6

Application Procedure: Applicants must complete CBS Form RD40. Applications must be made through and with the support of a CBS-affiliated scientist. Application forms and guidelines are available from any of the CBS centres or from the main address.

Closing Date: July 1st

Funding: Government

No. of awards given last year: 2

No. of applicants last year: 4

CANADIAN BUREAU FOR INTERNATIONAL EDUCATION (CBIE)

220 Laivier Avenue West Suite 1550, Ottawa, ON, K1P 5Z9, Canada
Tel: (1) 613 237 4820
Fax: (1) 613 237 1073
Email: scholarships-bourses@cbie.ca
Website: www.cbie.ca

The Canadian Bureau for International Education (CBIE) is a national non-profit association comprising educational institutions, organizations and individuals dedicated to internal education and intercultural training. CBIE's mission is to promote the free movement of learners and trainees across national borders.

Canadian Commonwealth Scholarship and Fellowship Plan

Subjects: Science, Law, environment studies, economics, sociology, geography, electronics and education.

Purpose: To offer scholarships to citizens of other common wealth countries to study in Canada.

Eligibility: Open to candidates who are not more than 40 years of age with completion of tertiary education from an English medium.

Level of Study: Postgraduate

Type: Scholarship

Value: Expenses of travel, living and study

Length of Study: 12–36 months

Frequency: Annual

Country of Study: Canada

Application Procedure: Further information available on the website www.scholarships.gc.ca

Closing Date: Please see the website

Contributor: Commonwealth Scholarship Commission

Canadian Studies Postdoctoral Fellowship

Subjects: Area and cultural studies.

Purpose: To enable young academics who have completed a doctoral thesis to visit a Canadian or foreign university with a Canadian studies programme for a teaching or research fellowship.

Eligibility: Open to students with a doctoral degree.

Level of Study: Postdoctorate

Type: Fellowship

Value: Canadian $2,500 per month plus the cost of a return airline ticket

Length of Study: 1 year

Frequency: Annual

Study Establishment: Any accredited Canadian university

Country of Study: Canada

Application Procedure: Application form and a recommendation from the national Canadian studies Association must be submitted. For country specific information and addresses please see the website www.scholarships.gc.ca/pdrfcountries-en.html

Closing Date: Varies

Contributor: Foreign Affairs and International Trade Canada

For further information contact:

Website: www.scholarships.gc.ca/pdrfcountries-en.html

Organization of American States (OAS) Fellowships Programs

Subjects: Human development.

Purpose: To fund education of Canadian residents and nationals in other American nations.

Eligibility: Open to Canadian residents and nationals.

Type: Fellowship

Value: Travel and tuition fees

Length of Study: 1–2 years

Frequency: Annual

Country of Study: United States of America

Application Procedure: A completed application form must be submitted. Please see the website www.scholarships.gc.ca

Funding: Government

CANADIAN CENTENNIAL SCHOLARSHIP FUND

Canadian Women's Club, MacDonald House, 1 Grosvenor Square,
London, W1K 4AB, England
Tel: (44) 20 7258 6344
Fax: (44) 20 7258 6637
Email: applications@canadianscholarshipfund.co.uk
Website: www.canadianscholarshipfund.co.uk
Contact: The Bursar

The Canadian Centennial Scholarship fund gives annual awards to Canadian men and women who are already studying in the United Kingdom. Scholarships are awarded on the basis of high academic standards, financial need and relevance of the proposed course of study to Canada.

Canadian Centennial Scholarship Fund

Subjects: All subjects.
Purpose: To assist Canadians studying in the United Kingdom and are exclusively for students who have already commenced their studies in the UK.
Eligibility: Canadian citizens currently enrolled in a United Kingdom programme of studies are eligible to apply.
Level of Study: Doctorate, Graduate, MBA, Postgraduate, Professional development
Type: Scholarship
Value: UK £500–2,500
Length of Study: 1 year. Recipients may re-apply
No. of awards offered: 12–15
Application Procedure: Candidates submit a written application and those short listed are interviewed. Applications can be downloaded from our website.
Closing Date: March 2nd
Funding: Trusts
Contributor: Maple Leaf Trust
No. of awards given last year: 20
No. of applicants last year: 103

CANADIAN CYSTIC FIBROSIS FOUNDATION (CCFF)

2221 Yonge Street, Suite 601, Toronto, ON, M4S 2B4, Canada
Tel: (1) 416 485 9149
Fax: (1) 416 485 0960
Email: amackesy@cysticfibrosis.ca
Website: www.cysticfibrosis.ca
Contact: Manager, Research Programs

Since 1960, the Canadian Cystic Fibrosis Foundation (CCFF) has worked to provide a brighter future for every child born with cystic fibrosis. Through its research and clinical programmes, the Foundation helps to provide outstanding care for affected individuals, while pursuing the quest for a cure or control.

CCFF Clinic Incentive Grants

Subjects: Cystic fibrosis.
Purpose: To enhance the standard of clinical care available to Canadians with cystic fibrosis, by providing funds to initiate a comprehensive programme for patient care, research and teaching or to strengthen an existing programme.
Eligibility: Canadian hospitals and medical schools are eligible to apply. Applicants must demonstrate the regional need for specialized clinical care for cystic fibrosis, the need of the institution for assistance and its plans to attract complementary funding from other sources to develop a complete cystic fibrosis programme, the potential for the development of a comprehensive programme for care, clinical research and teaching and the desire to collaborate with the CCFF and other Canadian cystic fibrosis clinics.
Level of Study: Research
Type: Grant
Value: Honorarium and travel allowance
Length of Study: 1 year, renewable on an annual basis
Frequency: Annual
Country of Study: Canada

Application Procedure: Applicants must complete an application form. Late applications will be subject to a penalty equal to 10 per cent of the value of the award. This penalty will be deducted from the clinic director's honorarium.
Closing Date: October 1st

CCFF Fellowships

Subjects: Cystic fibrosis.
Purpose: To support basic or clinical research training in areas of the biomedical or behavioural sciences pertinent to cystic fibrosis.
Eligibility: Applicants must hold a PhD or MD. Medical graduates should have already completed basic residency training and must be eligible for Canadian licensure. Equitable consideration will be given to Fellowship applicants from outside of Canada, who intend to return to their own country on completion of a fellowship.
Level of Study: Postgraduate
Type: Fellowship
Value: Dependent upon academic qualifications and research experience, Canadian $40,000–50,000 stipend and Canadian $1,500 travel allowance
Length of Study: 2 years, renewable for up to 1 more year
Frequency: Annual
Study Establishment: An approved university department, hospital or research institute in Canada
Country of Study: Canada
Application Procedure: Applicants must arrange to send three letters of recommendation, one of which should be from the applicant's current or most recent supervisor.
Closing Date: October 1st

CCFF Research Grants

Subjects: Cystic fibrosis.
Purpose: To facilitate scientific investigation of all aspects of cystic fibrosis.
Eligibility: A principal investigator should hold a recognized, full-time faculty appointment in a relevant discipline at a Canadian university or hospital. Under exceptional circumstances and at the discretion of the Research Subcommittee, applications from other individuals may be evaluated on a case-by-case basis.
Level of Study: Doctorate
Type: Research grant
Value: Determined by the Medical or Scientific Advisory Committee following a detailed review of the applicant's proposed budget
Length of Study: Usually 1 or 2 years or, in a limited number of instances, 3 years
Frequency: Annual
Study Establishment: A Canadian institution
Country of Study: Canada
Application Procedure: Applicants must write for details. Incomplete or late applications will be returned to the applicant.
Closing Date: October 1st
Additional Information: Investigators are eligible to hold more than one Research Grant. No more than one initial application may be submitted to a single competition, and it is a requirement that the focus of a second grant be clearly delineated from the first one. The specific aims of a second grant should represent new approaches to the cystic fibrosis problem and not an extension of an existing research programme.

CCFF Scholarships

Subjects: Cystic fibrosis.
Purpose: To provide salary support for a limited number of exceptional investigators, offering them an opportunity to develop outstanding cystic fibrosis research programmes, unhampered by heavy teaching or clinical loads. Intended to attract gifted investigators to cystic fibrosis research.
Eligibility: Open to holders of an MD or PhD degree who are sponsored by the Chairman of the appropriate department and by the Dean of Faculty. They may have recently completed training or be established investigators wishing to devote major research effort to cystic fibrosis. The beginning investigator should have demonstrated promise of ability to initiate and carry out independent research and the established investigator should have a published record of excellent scientific research.
Level of Study: Postgraduate, Doctorate

Type: Scholarship
Value: Salary support, which is dependent on the qualifications and experience of the successful candidate, will be determined by prevailing Canadian scholarship rates and the nominating university. The salary of the scholar may be supplemented by the institution or by clinical income and up to 50 per cent of the salary will be paid by the Foundation
Length of Study: 3 years, renewable for an additional 2 years on receipt of a satisfactory progress report. In no case will an award be for more than 5 years
Frequency: Every 2 years
Study Establishment: Any approved university, hospital or research institute
Country of Study: Canada
No. of awards offered: Varies, subject to availability of funds
Application Procedure: Applicants must write for details.
Closing Date: October 1st
Additional Information: Applications will be accepted only in odd-numbered years.

CCFF Senior Scientist Research Training Award

Subjects: Cystic fibrosis.
Purpose: To provide support to a limited number of cystic fibrosis investigators by offering them an opportunity to obtain additional training that will enhance their capacity to conduct research directly relevant to cystic fibrosis.
Eligibility: Applicants must have held a recognized, full-time faculty appointment in a relevant discipline at a Canadian university or hospital for at least 6 years.
Level of Study: Postgraduate
Type: Training award
Value: Canadian $30,000
Length of Study: 3 months–1 year
Frequency: Annual
Study Establishment: An approved university department or hospital in Canada
Country of Study: Canada
Application Procedure: Applications must be received by the Foundation no later than October 1st. Incomplete or late applications will be returned to the applicant.
Closing Date: October 1st
Additional Information: This award can be used for sabbatical support for qualified individuals.

CCFF Small Conference Grants

Subjects: Cystic fibrosis.
Purpose: To support small conferences that are focused on subjects of direct relevance to cystic fibrosis and to facilitate the exchange of special expertise between larger, university-based cystic fibrosis clinics and smaller, more remote clinics.
Eligibility: Open to clinic directors and CCFF-funded investigators.
Level of Study: Professional development
Type: Grant
Value: Grants to conferences will be up to a maximum of Canadian $2,500 and grants for the exchange of expertise will not normally exceed Canadian $1,000
No. of awards offered: Dependent on availability of funds
Application Procedure: Applicants must make applications in the form of a letter. For medical and/or scientific conferences, the application should indicate who is organizing and attending the conference, and the specific topics and purpose of the conference. For inter-clinic exchanges, the application should specify the proposed arrangements for, and the specific purpose of the exchange.
Closing Date: Applications may be submitted at any time, but the Foundation should be consulted in advance with respect to the availability of funds
Additional Information: Grants are available on a first-come, first-served basis. Frequency of application from any particular individual or group should be reasonable.

CCFF Special Travel Allowances

Subjects: Cystic fibrosis.
Purpose: To enable fellows and students to attend and participate in scientific meetings related to cystic fibrosis.
Eligibility: Fellows and other CCFF-supported scientists.

Level of Study: Postgraduate, Doctorate
Type: Award
Value: Travel and meal allowance
Length of Study: As determined by seminar length
Frequency: Annual
Study Establishment: Appropriate seminar
Country of Study: Any country
Application Procedure: Applications should be made in the form of a letter and must be submitted prior to travel.
Closing Date: Any time, but the Foundation must be consulted in advance

CCFF Studentships

Subjects: Cystic fibrosis.
Purpose: To support highly qualified graduate students who are registered for a higher degree, and who are undertaking full-time research training in areas of the biomedical or behavioural sciences relevant to cystic fibrosis.
Eligibility: Applicants must be highly qualified graduate students who are registered for a higher degree and who are undertaking full-time research training in areas relevant to cystic fibrosis, or highly qualified students who are registered in a joint MD/MSc or MD/PhD programme. Equitable consideration will be given to studentship applicants from outside of Canada who intend to return to their own country on completion of a studentship.
Level of Study: Doctorate, Postgraduate
Type: Studentship
Value: Salary and cost-of-living award at the discretion of the Medical/Scientific Advisory Committee
Length of Study: Master's level: 2–3 years, doctorate level: 2–5 years
Frequency: 3 times per year
Study Establishment: Studentships are tenable only at Canadian universities
Country of Study: Canada
Application Procedure: The Foundation sponsors a studentship competition in October and April. Candidates for initial awards are eligible to apply to either competition. Similar to all CCFF grants, studentships are subject to the availability of funds, and the availability of funds is generally more certain with respect to the October competition.
Closing Date: October 1st
Additional Information: Studentships are awarded for studies at the Master's or doctoral level. If a student receiving support for studies leading to a Master's degree elects to continue to a doctorate degree, he or she must reapply for an initial CCFF studentship at the doctoral level.

CCFF Transplant Centre Incentive Grants

Subjects: Cystic fibrosis.
Purpose: To enhance the quality of care available to cystic fibrosis transplant candidates by providing eligible centres with supplementary funding.
Eligibility: Open to any Canadian lung transplant centre that currently has one or more individuals with cystic fibrosis listed for transplant. Please note that under no circumstances will funding be provided to more than one transplant centre in the same city. Applicants must demonstrate how funds awarded would serve to enhance the quality of care available to patients in their centre.
Level of Study: Research
Type: Grant
Value: Determined in accordance with a formula that takes account of the number of patients assessed, accepted and followed preoperatively, transplanted and followed postoperatively in a given centre during the calendar year ending December 31st of the year preceding the application
Length of Study: 1 year
Frequency: Annual
Country of Study: Canada
Application Procedure: Applicants must contact the Foundation. Applicants must provide a rationale for the funding request and a detailed report on patient care and research within the lung transplant programme. All applications will be adjudicated by the Clinic Subcommittee of the Canadian Cystic Fibrosis Foundation.
Closing Date: October 1st

Additional Information: Late applications will be subject to a penalty equal to 10 per cent of the value of the award.

CCFF Visiting Scientist Awards

Subjects: Cystic fibrosis.
Purpose: To enable senior investigators from abroad who are invited to engage in cystic fibrosis research at a Canadian institution to travel to Canada or to assist junior or senior investigators who wish to work in another laboratory in Canada or abroad. This experience should, in some way, benefit the Canadian cystic fibrosis research effort.
Eligibility: A senior investigator can be considered such if he or she has attained at least the position of an associate professor, or has 6 years of equivalent experience.
Level of Study: Professional development, Doctorate
Type: Award
Value: Varies
Length of Study: Varies
Frequency: Dependent on funds available
Country of Study: Any country
Application Procedure: Applicants must send an application letter, accompanied by supporting letters from the head of the appropriate department of the host university. Supporting letters should also be provided by the Head of the Department and the Dean of the Faculty of the applicant's own university.

CCFF/Canadian Institutes of Health Research (CIHR) Fellowships

Subjects: Cystic fibrosis.
Eligibility: The general CIHR fellowship eligibility and award guidelines apply. Please consult the Foundation for details.
Type: Fellowship
Value: The value of the award will be in accordance with regular CIHR stipends. A yearly research and travel allowance is provided
Length of Study: 1–3 years, based on peer review recommendations
No. of awards offered: Up to 5
Application Procedure: Applications are to be submitted to the Canadian Institutes of Health Research using the CIHR Fellowship application package.
Closing Date: November 1st

Clinical Fellowships

Subjects: Cystic fibrosis care.
Purpose: Intended for those individuals who have already obtained their clinical training and wish to pursue training in CF care, and also acquire the competencethat would allow them to participate in clinical trails.
Eligibility: Canadian citizens or permanent reidents who have an MD degree, have recently completed their clinical training and have obtained medical licensure in Canada are eligible to apply.
Level of Study: Research, MD degree
Type: Fellowship
Value: Depends on academic qualifications and/or research experience
Length of Study: 2 years; Fellows can apply for 1 year renewal for further research training
Country of Study: Canada and abroad
No. of awards offered: 1
Application Procedure: Applicants must submit three letters of recommendation, one of which should be from the applicants' current or most recent supervisor. The application form should also include a description of the proposed research and clinical training program and official transcripts of the applicants' complete academic record. Applications that do not include these documents will be rejected.
Closing Date: October 1st

Clinical Projects Grants

Purpose: Intended to bolster the CCFF's commitment to clinical research and to promote the further development of the Clinical Studies Network. It provides a mechanism whereby the most important ideas for clinical studies can be forged into viable protocols and strategies of urgent clinical relevance can be pursued (seed money for small, start-up pilot projects).
Eligibility: Awarded at the discretion of the leaders of the Medical/Scientific Advisory Committee in consultation with the Clinical Studies Network.

Level of Study: Research
Frequency: Dependent on funds available
No. of awards offered: Varies
Application Procedure: Applications should be made in the form of a letter in which a clear hypothesis is detailed, relevance to CF is demonstrated, and a brief budget is outlined.
Additional Information: Applications may be submitted at any time but the Foundation should be consulted in advance with respect to the availability of funds.

Travel Supplement Grants for the European CF Society Conference

Purpose: To assist a limited number of individuals who plan to play an active role in ECFS conferences.
Eligibility: Applicants must be CCFF-funded investigators, Canadian CF clinic directors or clinicians, or Canadian CF clinic coordinators and allied health professionals. Applicants must show evidence of active participation at the conference.
Value: Maximum $2,000 per person
Frequency: Annual
No. of awards offered: Up to 5
Application Procedure: Applications should include a brief budget and frequency of application from any particular individual should be reasonable (once every 4 years).
Closing Date: April 1st
Additional Information: Incomplete or late applications will be returned to the applicant.

For further information contact:

Email: amackesy@cysticfibrosis.ca

Visiting Allied Health Professional Awards

Subjects: Cystic Fibrosis.
Purpose: To support allied health professionals from abroad who are invited to engage in CF clinical observation or activity at a Canadian institution or Canadian allied health professionals who wish to visit another clinic in Canada or abroad.
Eligibility: Applicants must be associated with a recognized CF clinic, and be an active member in CF clinical care. It is intended that this experience will in some way benefit Canadian CF clinical care.
Frequency: Dependent on funds available
Country of Study: Canada or abroad
No. of awards offered: Varies
Application Procedure: Applications should be made in the form of a letter, accompanied by a supporting letter from the head of the appropriate department of the applicants' institution. A supporting letter signed by the department head of the host institution should also be provided.
Additional Information: Applications may be submitted at any time, but the Foundation should be consulted in advance with respect to the availability of funds.

Visiting Clinician Awards

Subjects: Cystic Fibrosis.
Purpose: To support clinicians from abroad who are invited to engage in CF clinical observation or activity at a Canadian institution or Canadian clinicians who wish to visit another clinic in Canada or abroad.
Eligibility: Applicants must be associated with a recognized CF clinic, and be an active member in CF clinical care. It is intended that this experience will in some way benefit Canadian CF clinical care.
Frequency: Dependent on funds available
No. of awards offered: Varies
Application Procedure: Applications should be made in the form of a letter, accompanied by a supporting letter from the head of the appropriate department of the applicants' institution. A supporting letter signed by the department head of the host institution should also be provided.
Additional Information: Applications may be submitted at any time, but the Foundation should be consulted in advance with respect to the availability of funds.

CANADIAN EMBASSY (USA)

Foreign Affairs and International Trade Canada, 501 Pennsylvania
Ave NW, Washington, DC, 20001, United States of America
Tel: (1) 202 682 1740
Fax: (1) 202 682 7619
Email: enqserv@dfait-maeci.gc.ca
Website: www.canadianembassy.org
Contact: Daniel Abele, Academic Relations Officer

Canadian Embassy (USA) Research Grant Program

Subjects: Business and economic issues, Canadian values and culture, communications, environment, national and international security or natural resources e.g. energy, fisheries, forestry and trade.
Purpose: To assist individual scholars or a group of scholars in writing an article length manuscript of publishable quality and reporting their findings in scholarly publications.
Eligibility: Open to full-time faculty members at accredited 4 year United States colleges and universities, as well as scholars at American research and policy planning institutes who undertake significant research projects concerning Canada, Canada and the United States, or Canada and North America. Recent PhD recipients who are citizens or permanent residents of the United States are also eligible to apply.
Level of Study: Postgraduate
Value: Maximum award amount: upto $10000
Frequency: Annual
Study Establishment: An accredited 4 year college or university
Country of Study: United States of America
Application Procedure: Applicants must provide 6 copies of the following in this order: the completed application form, a concise proposal of 4–8 pages which will identify all members of the research team, if a team project, and specify each member's affiliation and role in the study, identify the key issues or the main theoretical problem, describe and justify the appropriate methodology, present a general schedule of research activities, indicate clearly both the nature and scope of the projects contribution to the advancement of Canadian Studies, include a detailed budget including all other funding sources and a description of anticipated expenditures. A curriculum vitae, and the names and addresses of two scholars from whom the applicants will solicit recommendations should also be included. Application forms are available on request.
Closing Date: September 30th
Funding: Government
Additional Information: The Research Grant Program promotes research in the social sciences and humanities with a view to contributing to a better knowledge and understanding of Canada and its relationship with the United States or other countries of the world.

For further information contact:

Tel: 202-682-7717
Email: daniel.abele@dfait-maeci.gc.ca
Contact: Dan Abele Academic Relations Officer

Canadian Embassy Faculty Enrichment Program

Subjects: Priority topics include bilateral trade and economics, Canada United States border issues, cultural policy and values, environment, natural resources, energy issues and security co-operation, projects that examine Canadian politics, economics, culture and society as well as Canada's role in international affairs.
Purpose: To provide faculty members with the opportunity to develop or redevelop courses with substantial Canadian content that will be offered as part of their regular teaching load, or as a special offering to select audiences in continuing or distance education.
Eligibility: Open to full-time, tenured or tenure track faculty members at accredited four year United States colleges and universities. Candidates should be able to demonstrate that they are already teaching, or will be authorized to teach, courses with substantial Canadian content (33 per cent or more). Team teaching applications are welcome. Applicants are ineligible to receive the same grant in two consecutive years or to receive two individual category Canadian Studies grants in the same grant period.
Value: Up to US$5,000
Frequency: Annual
Country of Study: United States of America
No. of awards offered: Varies

Application Procedure: Applicants must contact the organization for an application form.
Closing Date: October 31st
Additional Information: The Embassy especially encourages the use of new Internet technology to enhance existing courses, including the creation of instructional websites, interactive technologies and distance learning links to Canadian Universities.

For further information contact:

Tel: 202-682-7717
Email: daniel.abele@dfait-maeci.gc.ca
Contact: Dan Abele Academic Relations Officer

Canadian Embassy Graduate Student Fellowship Program

Subjects: Business and economic issues, Canadian values and culture, communications, environment, national and international security or natural resources e.g. energy, fisheries, forestry and trade.
Purpose: To offer graduate students the opportunity to conduct part of their doctoral research in Canada.
Eligibility: Open to full-time doctoral students at accredited 4 year colleges and universities in the United States or Canada whose dissertations are related in substantial part to the study of Canada, Canada and the United States or Canada and North America. Candidates must be citizens or permanent residents of the United States and should have completed all doctoral requirements except the dissertation when they apply for a grant.
Level of Study: Graduate
Type: Fellowship
Value: Up to US$8,000
Frequency: Annual
Study Establishment: An accredited four year college or university
Country of Study: Other
Application Procedure: Applicants must provide six copies of the following in the order listed: the completed application form, a concise letter of three to four pages which will explain clearly the present status of the candidate's doctoral studies, describe the candidate's study plans in Canada, list Canadian contacts such as Scholars, research institutes, academic institutions or libraries, state clearly the exact number of months for which financial support is needed, provide a complete and detailed budget, indicate what other funding sources are available, give the names and addresses of two referees, one of which must be the dissertation advisor, contain the dissertation prospectus which must identify the key issues or the main theoretical problem, justify the methodology and indicate clearly the nature of the dissertation's contribution to the advancement of Canadian Studies. An unofficial transcript of grades, a curriculum vitae and proof of United States citizenship or permanent residency must also be included. Application forms are available on request.
Closing Date: October 31st
Funding: Government
Additional Information: The Graduate Student Fellowship Program promotes research in the social sciences and humanities with a view to contributing to a better knowledge and understanding of Canada and its relationship with the United States or other countries of the world.

For further information contact:

Tel: 202-682-7717
Email: daniel.abele@dfait-maeci.gc.ca
Contact: Dan Abele Academic Relations Officer

Conference Grant Program

Subjects: Social science and humanities.
Purpose: To assist an institution in holding a conference and publishing the resulting papers and proceedings in a scholarly fashion.
Eligibility: Open to US institutions and universities who wish to undertake a conference on Canada–US issues.
Level of Study: Postgraduate
Type: Grant
Value: US$15,000
Frequency: Annual
Country of Study: United States of America
Application Procedure: Applicants must complete the online application form.

Closing Date: June 30th
Funding: Government
Contributor: Foreign Affairs Canada

Program Enhancement Grant

Subjects: International relations.
Purpose: To encourage innovative projects that promote awareness among students and the public about Canada–US relations.
Eligibility: Open to US colleges, research institutions and universities who wish to undertake professional academic activities.
Level of Study: Postgraduate
Type: Grant
Value: Up to US$18,000 per year
Length of Study: 1 year
Frequency: Annual
Country of Study: United States of America
Application Procedure: A completed online application form must be submitted.
Closing Date: June 16th

CANADIAN FEDERATION OF UNIVERSITY WOMEN (CFUW)

251 Bank Street, Suite 305, Ottawa, ON, K2P 1X3, Canada
Tel: (1) 613 234 8252 Extn 104
Fax: (1) 613 234 8221
Email: cfuwfls@rogers.com
Website: www.cfuw.org
Contact: Betty A Dunlop, CFUW Fellowships Program Manager

Found in 1919, the Canadian Federation of University Women (CFUW) is a voluntary, non-partisan, non-profit, self-funded bilingual organization of 10,000 women university graduates. CFUW members are active in public affairs, working to raise the social, economic, and legal status of women as well as to improve education, the environment, peace, justice and human rights.

Canadian Home Economics Association (CHEA) Fellowship

Subjects: Home economics.
Purpose: To provide funding for studying one or more aspects in the field of home economics, at the masters or doctoral level in Canada.
Eligibility: Open to female Canadian citizens or women who have landed immigrant status or permanent residence prior to the submission of an application. Candidates should hold a Bachelor's degree or its equivalent from a recognized university, not necessarily in Canada.
Level of Study: Doctorate, Postgraduate, Masters
Type: Fellowship
Value: Canadian $6,000
Frequency: Annual
Study Establishment: A recognized university
Country of Study: Canada
No. of awards offered: 1
Application Procedure: Applicants must complete an application form, available from the Federation website.
Closing Date: November 1st
Funding: Private
No. of awards given last year: 1
No. of applicants last year: 15
Additional Information: The fellowship is not renewable.

CFUW 1989 ÉCole Poytechnique Commemorative Award

Subjects: All subjects. (The applicant must justify the relevance of her work to women).
Purpose: To provide funding for graduate studies in any field.
Eligibility: Open to female Canadian citizens or women who have landed immigrant status or permanent residence prior to the submission of an application. Candidates should hold a Bachelor's degree or its equivalent from a recognized university, not necessarily in Canada.
Level of Study: Postgraduate
Type: Fellowship
Value: Canadian $7,000
Frequency: Annual

Study Establishment: A recognized university
Country of Study: Any country
No. of awards offered: 1
Application Procedure: Applicants must complete an application form, available from the Federation website.
Closing Date: November 1st
Funding: Private
No. of awards given last year: 1
No. of applicants last year: 80
Additional Information: The fellowship is not renewable.

CFUW Beverley Jackson Fellowship

Subjects: All subjects.
Purpose: To provide funding for graduate studies at an Ontario university.
Eligibility: Open to female Canadian citizens or women who have landed immigrant status or permanent residence prior to the submission of an application. Candidates should hold a Bachelor's degree or its equivalent from a recognized university, not necessarily in Canada. The applicant must be over the age of 35.
Level of Study: Postgraduate
Type: Fellowship
Value: Canadian $2,000
Frequency: Annual
Study Establishment: A recognized university
Country of Study: Canada
No. of awards offered: 1
Application Procedure: Applicants must complete an application form, available from the Federation website.
Closing Date: November 1st
Funding: Private
No. of awards given last year: 1
No. of applicants last year: 20
Additional Information: The fellowship is not renewable.

CFUW Bourse Georgette Lemoyne

Subjects: All subjects. The applicant must be studying in French.
Purpose: To provide funding for graduate study in any field at a Canadian university.
Eligibility: Open to female Canadian citizens or women who have landed immigrant status or permanent residence prior to the submission of an application. Candidates should hold a Bachelor's degree or its equivalent from a recognized university, not necessarily in Canada.
Level of Study: Postgraduate
Type: Fellowship
Value: Canadian $7,000
Frequency: Annual
Study Establishment: A recognized university
Country of Study: Canada
No. of awards offered: 1
Application Procedure: Applicants must complete an application form, available from the Federation website.
Closing Date: November 1st
Funding: Private
No. of awards given last year: 1
No. of applicants last year: 40
Additional Information: The fellowship is not renewable.

CFUW Dr Alice E. Wilson Awards

Subjects: All subjects.
Purpose: Awarded to mature students returning to graduate studies in any field, with special consideration given to those returning to study after at least three years.
Eligibility: Open to female Canadian citizens or women who have landed immigrant status or permanent residence prior to the submission of an application. Candidates should hold a Bachelor's degree or its equivalent from a recognized university, not necessarily in Canada.
Level of Study: Postgraduate
Type: Fellowship
Value: Canadian $6,000
Frequency: Annual
Study Establishment: A recognized university
Country of Study: Any country
No. of awards offered: 5

Application Procedure: Applicants must complete an application form, available from the Federation website.
Closing Date: November 1st
Funding: Private
No. of awards given last year: 6
No. of applicants last year: 160
Additional Information: The fellowship is not renewable.

CFUW Dr Marion Elder Grant Fellowship
Subjects: All subjects.
Purpose: To provide funding for full-time courses of studies at any level of a doctoral program.
Eligibility: Open to female Canadian citizens or women who have landed immigrant status or permanent residence prior to the submission of an application. Candidates should hold a Bachelor's degree or its equivalent from a recognized university, not necessarily in Canada, and be a full-time student at an advanced stage, i.e. doctoral programme or second masters.
Level of Study: Doctorate
Type: Fellowship
Value: Canadian $11,000
Frequency: Annual
Study Establishment: A recognized university
Country of Study: Any country
No. of awards offered: 1
Application Procedure: Applicants must complete an application form, available from the Federation website.
Closing Date: November 1st
Funding: Private
No. of awards given last year: 1
No. of applicants last year: 40
Additional Information: The fellowship is not renewable.

CFUW Elizabeth Massey Award
Subjects: Music, painting or sculpture.
Purpose: To provide funding for postgraduate studies in music, painting or sculpture in Canada or abroad.
Eligibility: Open to female Canadian citizens or women who have landed immigrant status or permanent residence prior to the submission of an application. Candidates should hold a Bachelor's degree or its equivalent from a recognized university, not necessarily in Canada.
Level of Study: Doctorate, Postgraduate
Type: Award
Value: Canadian $2,000
Frequency: Annual
Study Establishment: A recognized university
Country of Study: Any country
No. of awards offered: 1
Application Procedure: Candidates must complete an application form, available from the Federation website.
Closing Date: November 1st
Funding: Private
No. of awards given last year: 1
No. of applicants last year: 10
Additional Information: The fellowship is not renewable.

CFUW Margaret Dale Philp Award
Subjects: Humanities or social sciences and Canadian history.
Purpose: To provide funding for graduate studies in the humanities or social sciences. Special consideration given to study in Canadian history only as a deciding factor, all these being equal.
Eligibility: Open to female Canadian citizens or women who have landed immigrant status or permanent residence prior to the submission of an application. Candidates should hold a Bachelor's degree or its equivalent from a recognized university, not necessarily in Canada.
Level of Study: Postgraduate
Type: Award
Value: Canadian $3,000
Frequency: Annual
Study Establishment: A recognized university
Country of Study: Canada
No. of awards offered: 1
Application Procedure: Candidates must complete an application form, available from the Federation website.
Closing Date: November 1st

Funding: Private
Contributor: CFUW Kitchener-Waterloo funds
No. of awards given last year: 1
No. of applicants last year: 30
Additional Information: The fellowship is not renewable.

CFUW Margaret McWilliams Predoctoral Fellowship
Subjects: All subjects.
Purpose: To provide funding for full-time doctoral study.
Eligibility: Open to female Canadian citizens or women who have landed immigrant status or permanent residence prior to the submission of an application. Candidates should hold a Bachelor's degree or its equivalent from a recognized university, not necessarily in Canada, and be a full-time student at an advanced stage, i.e. at least 1 year into her doctoral programme.
Level of Study: Doctorate
Type: Fellowship
Value: Canadian $13,000
Frequency: Annual
Study Establishment: A recognized university
Country of Study: Any country
No. of awards offered: 1
Application Procedure: Applicants must complete an application form, available from the Federation website.
Closing Date: November 1st
Funding: Private
No. of awards given last year: 1
No. of applicants last year: 119
Additional Information: The fellowship is not renewable.

CFUW Memorial Fellowship
Subjects: Science, mathematics, or engineering.
Purpose: To provide funding for postgraduate degree studies in science, mathematics, or engineering.
Eligibility: Open to female Canadian citizens or women who have landed immigrant status or permanent residence prior to the submission of an application. Candidates should hold a Bachelor's degree or its equivalent from a recognized university, not necessarily in Canada.
Level of Study: Postgraduate, Masters
Type: Fellowship
Value: Canadian $10,000
Frequency: Annual
Study Establishment: A recognized university
Country of Study: Any country
No. of awards offered: 1
Application Procedure: Applicants must complete an application form, available from the Federation website.
Closing Date: November 1st
Funding: Private
No. of awards given last year: 1
No. of applicants last year: 60
Additional Information: The fellowship is not renewable.

Ruth Binnie Fellowship
Subjects: Home economics.
Purpose: To provide funding for Master's studies with a focus on one or more aspects of home economics.
Eligibility: Open to female Canadian citizens or women who have landed immigrant status or permanent residence prior to the submission of an application. Candidates should hold a Bachelor's degree or its equivalent from a recognized university, not necessarily in Canada.
Level of Study: Masters
Type: Fellowship
Value: Canadian $6,000
Frequency: Annual
Study Establishment: A recognized university
Country of Study: Any country
No. of awards offered: 1
Application Procedure: Applicants must complete an application form, available from the Federation website.
Closing Date: November 1st
Funding: Private
No. of awards given last year: 1
No. of applicants last year: 17
Additional Information: The fellowship is not renewable.

CANADIAN HOSPITALITY FOUNDATION

300 Adelaide Street East, Suite 213, Toronto, ON, M5A-1N1, Canada
Tel: (1) 363 3401
Fax: (1) 363 3403
Email: chf@theohi.ca
Website: www.chfscholarships.com

The Canadian Hospitality Foundation is Canada's largest industry driven source of scholarships for students pursuing careers in the foodservice/hospitality industry.

Canadian Hospitality Foundation Scholarship

Subjects: Hotel, food, tourism.
Level of Study: Postgraduate
Type: Scholarship
Value: Canadian $1,000–3,500
Frequency: Annual
Study Establishment: University of Calgary, University of Guelph, Ryerson Polytechnical Institute or Mount Saint Vincent University
Country of Study: Canada
No. of awards offered: 8
Application Procedure: More information and application forms available online.
Closing Date: March 20th

CANADIAN INSTITUTE FOR ADVANCED LEGAL STUDIES

PO Box 321, Station R, Toronto, ON, M4G 4C3, Canada
Tel: (1) 416 429 3292
Fax: (1) 416 429 9805
Email: info@canadian-institute.com
Website: www.canadian-institute.com
Contact: Mrs Lynn Morrison, Executive Secretary

The Canadian Institute for Advanced Legal Studies conducts legal seminars for judges and lawyers in Cambridge, England and Strasbourg, France.

The Right Honorable Paul Martin Sr. Scholarship

Subjects: Law.
Purpose: To study for an LLM at the University of Cambridge.
Eligibility: Open to graduates of Canadian faculties of law at the time of application, law students in their articling year at the time of application, or to students registered in their Bar Admission course at the time of application.
Level of Study: Postgraduate
Type: Scholarship
Value: Canadian $23,000
Length of Study: 1 year
Frequency: Annual
Study Establishment: The University of Cambridge
Country of Study: England
No. of awards offered: 2
Application Procedure: Applicants must submit a letter of application, undergraduate and faculty of law transcripts and no more than three letters of recommendation. There is no application form.
Closing Date: December 31st
Funding: Private
No. of awards given last year: 2
No. of applicants last year: 36
Additional Information: The scholarship may be held with another small award as approved by the Institute.

THE CANADIAN INSTITUTE FOR NORDIC STUDIES (CINS)

Department of Modern Languages and Cultural, University of Alberta, 200 Arts Building, Edmonton, AB, T6G 2E6, Canada
Email: chale@ualberta.ca
Website: www.ualberta.ca
Contact: Chair of the Board

The Canadian Institute for Nordic Studies (CINS) was established in 1987 to promote multidisciplinary academic and cultural interest in the Nordic countries of Denmark, Finland, Iceland, Norway and Sweden, including the Faroe Islands and Greenland. The mandate of the Institute is national and it co-operates with the national organization, the Association for the Advancement of Scandinavian Studies in Canada (AASSC).

CINS Graduate Scholarship

Subjects: Fine arts, humanities, natural, physical, applied and social sciences and more.
Purpose: To provide financial assistance to students who wish to pursue higher studies.
Eligibility: Open to Canadian citizens or landed immigrants, who have completed a Bachelor's degree from a Canadian university or college with high scholastic achievement. Applicants must be in residency at the Nordic destination for a minimum of 6 months and provide a written report to CINS no later than 6 months after completing the proposed programme of study.
Level of Study: Postgraduate
Type: Scholarship
Value: Canadian $5,000
Frequency: Annual
No. of awards offered: Usually 1 award per year
Application Procedure: Applicants should include the following in their application: contact details, citizenship status, social insurance number and date of birth, current academic status with formal transcripts, written acceptance from the host Nordic institution and reference letters.
Closing Date: February 15th
Additional Information: Applicants can study at any recognized institution granting earned degrees at the postbaccalaureate level in the applicant's field of study and located in one of the Nordic countries: Denmark, Finland, Iceland, Norway, Sweden, the Faroe Islands and Greenland.

For further information contact:

Chair of the Board, Canadian Institute for Nordic Studies, c/o Canadian Circumpolar Institute, 1-37 Pembina Hall, University of Alberta, Edmonton, Alberta, T6G 2H8

CANADIAN INSTITUTE OF GEOMATICS (CIG)

1390 Prince of Wales Drive, Suite 400, Ottawa, ON, K2C 3N6, Canada
Tel: (1) 613 224 9851
Fax: (1) 613 224 9577
Email: exdircig@magma.ca
Website: www.cig-acsg.ca
Contact: Jean Thie, Executive Director

The Canadian Institute of Geomatics (CIG) was founded in 1882. CIG has evolved to be a non-profit, scientific and technical association and represents the largest and most influential geospatial knowledge network in Canada. Over 50 per cent of its members are senior managers and researchers in government and private sectors, academic and NGO organizations.

Geomatics Canada Scholarship Program

Subjects: Geomatics.
Purpose: To enable Canadian students to pursue their postgraduate studies in the field of geomatics in Canada.
Eligibility: Open to students who are registered full-time in a recognized university, technical institution or community college in Canada. Students must be Canadian citizens or landed immigrants. Students must also be continuing a course of study in the field of geomatics within a full-time, co-op programme or postgraduate studies.
Level of Study: Postgraduate
Type: Scholarships
Value: Canadian $2,500
Frequency: Annual
Study Establishment: Canadian Institute of Geomatics
Country of Study: Canada
No. of awards offered: 4
Closing Date: March 14th

Contributor: Natural Resources Canada
Additional Information: The Canadian Institute of Geomatics will also present each of the scholarship winners with a complimentary 1 year student membership, which includes a subscription to Geomatica.

The Hans Klinkenberg Memorial Fund
Subjects: Geomatics sciences.
Purpose: The Hans Klinkenberg Memorial Scholarship Fund provides scholarships to students in the Geomatics sciences at technical institutes and community colleges in Canada.
Eligibility: The candidate must be a Canadian citizen or a landed immigrant.
Type: Funding support
Value: Awards range from Canadian $500–2000
Frequency: Annual
Country of Study: Canada
No. of awards offered: 2
Closing Date: February 15th
Funding: Trusts
Contributor: Hans Klinkenberg Memorial Fund

CANADIAN INSTITUTE OF UKRAINIAN STUDIES (CIUS)

University of Alberta, 450 Athabasca Hall, Edmonton, AB, T6G 2E8, Canada
Tel: (1) 780 492 2972
Fax: (1) 780 492 4967
Email: cius@ualberta.ca
Website: www.cius.ca
Contact: Ms Khrystyna Jendyk, Administrator

The Canadian Institute of Ukrainian Studies (CIUS) is part of the University of Alberta under the jurisdiction of the University's Vice President of Research. It was founded in 1976 in order to provide an institutional home to develop Ukrainian scholarship and Ukrainian language education in Canada. It also supports such studies internationally, through organizing research and scholarship in Ukrainian and Ukrainian and Canadian studies, by publishing books and a scholarly journal, developing materials for Ukrainian language education largely for the bilingual school programme, and organizing conferences, lectures and a seminar series. Policy is developed by the director in consultation with CIUS units, programme directors and an advisory council.

CIUS Research Grants
Subjects: Ukrainian or Ukrainian and Canadian studies in history, literature, language, education, social sciences and library sciences.
Purpose: To fund research by scholars on Ukrainian or Ukrainian-Canadian topic in the humanities and social sciences.
Eligibility: Please write for details.
Level of Study: Postdoctorate, Research
Type: Grant
Value: Up to Canadian $8,000
Length of Study: 1 year
Frequency: Annual
Country of Study: Any country
No. of awards offered: 1
Application Procedure: Candidates may request an application form and guide either from the main address or by email, or download from them the website.
Closing Date: March 1st
Funding: Private
No. of awards given last year: 38

For further information contact:

Canadian Institute of Ukrainian Studies, 430 Pembina Hall, University of Alberta, Edmonton, Alberta, Canada, T6G 2H8
Tel: 780-492-2973
Fax: 780-492-4967

Helen Darcovich Memorial Doctoral Fellowship
Subjects: Ukrainian or Ukrainian and Canadian topics in education, history, law, humanities, social sciences, women's studies and library sciences.

Purpose: To aid students to complete a thesis on a Ukrainian or Ukrainian and Canadian topic in education, history, law, humanities, social sciences, women's studies or library sciences.
Eligibility: Open to qualified applicants of any nationality. For non-Canadian applicants, preference will be given to students enrolled at the University of Alberta.
Level of Study: Doctorate
Type: Fellowship
Value: Up to Canadian $12,000
Length of Study: 1 academic year
Frequency: Annual
Study Establishment: Any approved Institute of Higher Education
Country of Study: Any country
No. of awards offered: 1
Application Procedure: Applicants may write to the main address for application form and guide. Application forms can also be downloaded from the website or received by email.
Closing Date: March 1st
Funding: Private
Contributor: The Helen Darcovich Memorial Endowment Fund
No. of awards given last year: 3
Additional Information: Only in exceptional circumstances may an award be held concurrently with other awards.

For further information contact:

Canadian Institute of Ukrainian Studies, 430 Pembina Hall, University of Alberta, Edmonton AB, Canada, T6G 2H8
Tel: 780-492-2973
Fax: 780-492-4967

John Kolasky Memorial Fellowship
Subjects: Research in social sciences or humanities specializing in Ukrainian studies.
Purpose: To allow scholars from Ukraine to undertake research in Candada.
Eligibility: Limited to scholar from Ukraine.
Level of Study: Postdoctorate
Type: Fellowship
Value: Canadian $7,500–30,000
Length of Study: 3–12 months
Frequency: Annual
No. of awards offered: 1 or more
Funding: Private
No. of awards given last year: 3

Marusia and Michael Dorosh Master's Fellowship
Subjects: Ukrainian or Ukrainian and Canadian topic in education, history, law, humanities, social sciences, women's studies and library sciences.
Purpose: To aid a student to complete a thesis on a Ukrainian or Ukrainian and Canadian topic in education, history, law, humanities, social sciences, women's studies or library sciences.
Eligibility: Open to qualified applicants of any nationality. For non-Canadian applicants, preference will be given to students enrolled at the University of Alberta.
Level of Study: Graduate
Type: Fellowship
Value: Up to Canadian $10,000
Length of Study: 1 academic year
Frequency: Annual
Study Establishment: Any approved Institute of Higher Education
Country of Study: Any country
No. of awards offered: 1
Application Procedure: Applicants may write to the main address for application form. Information and application forms can also be obtained by email or downloaded from the website.
Closing Date: March 1st
Funding: Private
Contributor: The Marusia and Michael Dorosh Endowment Fund
No. of awards given last year: 2
Additional Information: Only in exceptional circumstances may an award be held concurrently with other major awards.

For further information contact:

Canadian Institute of Ukrainian Studies, 430 Pembina Hall, University of Alberta, Edmonton AB, Canada, T6G 2H8

Neporany Doctoral Fellowship

Subjects: Awarded to one or more doctoral students specializing on Ukraine in political science, economics and related fields (social sciences and political, economic, and social history).
Purpose: To fund research of doctoral students writing dissertation in Ukrainian studies.
Eligibility: Applicants must be a PhD student writing a PhD thesis on Ukrainian studies.
Level of Study: Doctorate, Postdoctorate
Type: Fellowship
Value: Ranges from Canadian $5,000–15,000
Length of Study: 1 academic year
Frequency: Annual
Country of Study: Any country
No. of awards offered: 1 or more
Application Procedure: Applicants must write for further details to the main address. Information can be obtained by email or downloaded from the website.
Closing Date: March 1st
Funding: Private
Contributor: The Osyp and Josaphat Neporany Educational Fund
No. of awards given last year: 1

For further information contact:

Canadian Institute of Ukrainian Studies, 430 Pembina Hall, University of Alberta, Edmonton AB, Canada, T6G 2H8

CANADIAN INSTITUTES OF HEALTH RESEARCH (CIHR)

160 Elgin Street, 9th Floor, Address Locator 4809A, Ottawa, ON, K1A 0W9, Canada
Tel: (1) 613 946 7232
Fax: (1) 613 954 1800
Email: JLacroix@cihr-irsc.gc.ca
Website: www.cihr.ca
Contact: Jose Lacroix, Program Officer

CIHR Canadian Graduate Scholarships Doctoral Awards

Purpose: To provide special recognition and support to students who are pursuing a doctoral degree in a health-related field in Canada.
Eligibility: These candidates are expected to have an exceptionally high potential for future research achievement and productivity.
Level of Study: Doctorate
Value: Canadian $30,000 annual stipend and Canadian $5,000 annual research allowance
Length of Study: Maximum of 3 years
Frequency: Annual
Study Establishment: A Canadian Institution
Country of Study: Canada
Application Procedure: Applicants must complete an application form in accordance with programme guidelines, available on the website.
Closing Date: October 15th
Funding: Government
No. of awards given last year: 199
Additional Information: This funding program will be administered through the CIHR Doctoral Award competition, with the top candidates meeting eligibility criteria below receiving a CGS award.

CIHR Doctoral Research Awards

Subjects: General medical sciences and health sciences.
Purpose: To provide recognition and funding to students early in their academic research career, providing them with an opportunity to gain research experience. To provide a reliable supply of highly skilled and qualified researchers.
Eligibility: Open to Canadian citizens and permanent residents of Canada at the time of application, who are engaged in full-time research training in a graduate school. Please check the website for further details.
Level of Study: Graduate
Type: Award

Value: An annual stipend of Canadian $21,000 for awards held inside Canada and Canadian $27,000 for awards held outside Canada, Awards are valued in Canadian dollars and are taxable
Length of Study: A maximum of 3 years
Frequency: Annual
Study Establishment: Universities or research institutions
Country of Study: Canada and abroad
No. of awards offered: Varies
Application Procedure: Applicants must complete an application form in accordance with programme guidelines, available on the CIHR website.
Closing Date: October 15th
Funding: Government
Contributor: CIHR
No. of awards given last year: 113
No. of applicants last year: 814
Additional Information: Please consult the CIHR website for the complete programme description.

CIHR Fellowships Program

Subjects: Applicants must hold, or be completing, a PhD, health professional degree or equivalent. The health professional degree must be in a regulated health profession such as medicine, dentistry, pharmacy, optometry, veterinary medicine, chiropractic, nursing or rehabilitative science which requires at least a Bachelor's degree to be eligible for licensure in Canada.
Purpose: To provide support for highly qualified candidates at the post PhD or post health professional degree stages to add to their experience by engaging in health research either in Canada or abroad.
Eligibility: Candidates must hold or be completing a PhD or health professional degree. Candidates with more than 3 years of post-PhD training by the competition deadline are not eligible to apply. Candidates may not hold more than 3 years of federal to undertake post PhD studies. Please consult CIHR's website for full eligibility requirements. www.cihr-irsc.ge.cale/22340.html
Level of Study: Doctorate, Graduate, Postdoctorate, Postgraduate, Professional development, Research
Type: Fellowship
Value: The annual stipend level for those with a PhD degree (or equivalent) is $40,000 per annum. The following stipend levels apply to health professionals who hold licensure (full or educational) in Canada at the time of taking up the award. The stipend level is dependent upon the number of years of research or clinical training completed since obtaining the health professional degree. Upon completion of two years of postgraduate research training, the awardees may be eligible to receive a stipend increase to the higher level. (Updated: 2008-09-03) Less than 2 years of research or clinical training experience: $40,000 Two or more years of research or clinical training experience: $50,000 The stipend for health professionals who do not hold licensure in Canada is $21,000 per annum (i.e., equivalent to a Doctoral Research Award). Upon completion of two years of postgraduate research training the stipend may increase to $40,000 per annum. For awards held outside Canada $5,000 is added to the annual stipend. Stipends are valued in Canadian dollars and are taxable
Length of Study: 5 years maximum for health professionals intending to proceed to a PhD degree, 4 years maximum for health professionals who do not intend to proceed to a PhD degree, 3 years maximum for those with a PhD degree or a PhD and health professional degree
Frequency: Twice a year
Study Establishment: Universities or research institutions
Country of Study: Any country
No. of awards offered: Varies
Application Procedure: Applicants must submit a training module, a curriculum vitae module for both the candidate and the supervisor(s), official transcripts of the candidate's graduate and/or professional training including proof of any degrees completed, proof of Canadian licensure, three assessments from persons under whom the candidate has studied and a letter of support from the proposed supervisor of foreign candidates and proof of residency/citizenship for Canadians wishing to hold their award outside of Canada.
Closing Date: February 1st and October 1st
Funding: Government

No. of awards given last year: 132
No. of applicants last year: 988
Additional Information: Consult the CIHR website, www.cihr-irsc.gc.ca for the full programme description.

CIHR MD/PhD Studentships

Subjects: General medical sciences.
Purpose: To promote promising students embarking on a combined MD or PhD programme at approved Canadian Universities.
Eligibility: Candidates for this Studentship Award must be enrolled in a combined MD/PhD programme at one of the approved Canadian institutions. Research supervisors should normally be holders of operating grants or salary funding obtained through a CIHR peer review process.
Level of Study: Doctorate, Graduate, Research
Type: Grant
Value: A stipend of Canadian $21,000 per year plus a yearly research allowance of Canadian $1,000 is provided
Length of Study: 6 years maximum
Study Establishment: The universities of British Columbia, Calgary, Manitoba, McGill, Memorial, Montreal, Toronto, Western Ontario, Alberta
Country of Study: Canada
Application Procedure: Applicants must be nominated by the director of the MD/PhD programme at each institution.
Closing Date: April 1st
Funding: Government
Contributor: CIHR
Additional Information: For further information please contact the CIHR or refer to the website.

CANADIAN LIBRARY ASSOCIATION (CLA)

Scholarships and Awards Committee, 328 Frank Street, Ottawa, ON, K2P 0X8, Canada
Tel: (1) 613 232 9625
Fax: (1) 613 563 9895
Email: info@cla.ca
Website: www.cla.ca
Contact: V Delrue, Member Services

The Canadian Library Association works to maintain a tradition of commitment to excellence in library education and to advance continuing research in the field of library and information science.

CLA Dafoe Scholarship

Subjects: Library and information studies.
Eligibility: Open to Canadian citizens and landed immigrants, commencing studies for their first professional library degree at an ALA-accredited institution.
Level of Study: Postgraduate
Type: Scholarship
Value: Canadian $5,000
Length of Study: 1 year
Frequency: Annual
Study Establishment: An accredited library school
Country of Study: United States of America or Canada
No. of awards offered: 1
Application Procedure: Applicants must complete an application form. Applicants must submit transcripts, references and proof of admission to a library school.
Closing Date: May 1st
Funding: Commercial
No. of awards given last year: 1

CLA H.W. Wilson Scholarship

Subjects: Library and information studies.
Purpose: To support students who wish to pursue higher studies in library and information studies.
Eligibility: Open to candidates who are commencing studies for their first professional library degree at an ALA-accredited institution. Should have Canadian citizenship or hold a landed immigrant status.
Level of Study: Postgraduate
Type: Scholarship

Value: Canadian $2,000
Length of Study: 1 year
Frequency: Annual
Country of Study: Canada
Application Procedure: Applicants are required to complete CLA Scholarship application forms and supply transcripts, reference and proof of admission to a library school. Scholarship applications are reviewed by a committee of members of the CLA.
Closing Date: May 1st
Funding: Foundation
No. of awards given last year: 1

CLA Library Research and Development Grants

Subjects: Library and information sciences.
Purpose: To support members of the Canadian Library Association for theoretical and applied research in the related fields. To encourage and support research undertaken by practitionares in the field of library and information services. To promote research in the field of library and information services by and/or about Canadians.
Eligibility: Open to personal members of the Canadian Library Association.
Level of Study: Postgraduate
Type: Grant
Value: Canadian $1,000
Frequency: Annual
Country of Study: Canada
No. of awards offered: 1
Application Procedure: Applicants must submit grant applications via emails and MS word document in either French or English containing contact details, description of the research project, duration of the project, detailed assessment of costs and statement of other grants/awards received.
Closing Date: February 28th

For further information contact:

University of Ontario Institute of Technology Library
Email: pamela.drayson@dc-uoit.ca
Contact: Pamela Drayson

World Book Graduate Scholarship in Library Science

Subjects: Library science.
Eligibility: Open to Canadian citizens or landed immigrants pursuing a MLS or MLIS degree. In exceptional circumstances, consideration will be given to an outstanding candidate who is pursuing a MLS or MLIS degree at an ALA accredited institution in either Canada or the United States.
Level of Study: Postgraduate
Type: Scholarship
Value: Canadian $2,500
Length of Study: 1 year
Frequency: Annual
Study Establishment: An accredited library school
Country of Study: United States of America or Canada
No. of awards offered: 1
Application Procedure: Applicants must complete an application form and must submit transcripts, references.
Closing Date: May 1st
Funding: Private
Contributor: World Book Incorporated
No. of awards given last year: 1
Additional Information: The scholarship is given for study leading to a further library degree or related to library work in which the candidate is currently engaged, or to library work that will be undertaken upon completion of the studies.

CANADIAN LIVER FOUNDATION

2235 Sheppard Avenue East, Suite 1500, Toronto, ON, M2J 5B5, Canada
Tel: (1) 416 491 3353
Fax: (1) 416 491 4952
Email: clf@liver.ca
Website: www.liver.ca
Contact: National Director of Health Promotion and Patient Services

The Canadian Liver Foundation provides support for research and education into the causes, diagnosis, prevention and treatment of diseases of the liver.

Canadian Liver Foundation Graduate Studentships

Subjects: Hepatology, chemistry and biochemistry.
Purpose: To enable academically superior students to undertake full-time studies in a Canadian university in a discipline relevant to the objectives of the Foundation.
Eligibility: Candidates must be accepted into a full-time university graduate science programme in a medically related discipline related to a Master's or doctoral degree, and hold a record of superior academic performance in studies relevant to the proposed training.
Level of Study: Doctorate, Postgraduate
Type: Studentship
Value: Canadian $20,000 per year
Length of Study: 2 years, renewable once. Transfer from an MSc to a PhD programme will permit the student to apply for renewal of the award for a total of 4 years support
Country of Study: Canada
No. of awards offered: Dependent on availability of funds
Application Procedure: Applicants must submit application forms along with supporting documents. Application forms can be obtained from the applicant's institution or from the Canadian Liver Foundation website.
Closing Date: March 30th
Funding: Private
No. of awards given last year: 3
No. of applicants last year: 19
Additional Information: A student supported by the Foundation must not hold a current stipend award from another granting agency.

Canadian Liver Foundation Operating Grant

Subjects: Hepatology.
Purpose: To support research projects directed towards a defined objective.
Eligibility: Open to hepatobiliary research investigators who hold an academic appointment in a Canadian university or affiliated institution.
Level of Study: Research
Type: Grant
Value: Up to Canadian $60,000 per year
Length of Study: 2 years, after which time renewal may be sought
Country of Study: Canada
No. of awards offered: Dependent on availability of funds
Application Procedure: Applicants must submit application forms along with supporting documentation. Application forms can be obtained from the applicant's institution or from the Canadian Liver Foundation website.
Closing Date: March 15th
Funding: Private
No. of awards given last year: 5
No. of applicants last year: 30

THE CANADIAN NATIONAL INSTITUTE FOR THE BLIND (CNIB)

1929 Bayview Avenue, Toronto, ON, M4G 3E8, Canada
Tel: (1) 416 486 2500
Fax: (1) 416 480 7677
Email: barbara.marjeram@cnib.ca
Website: www.cnib.ca
Contact: Ms Barbara J. Marjeram, Corporate Secretary

CNIB is a nationwide, community-based, registered charity committed to public education, research and the vision health of all Canadians. CNIB provides the services and support necessary to enjoy a good quality of life while living with vision loss. Founded in 1918, CNIB reaches out to communities across the country, offering access to rehabilitation training, innovative consumer products and peer support programs as well as one of the world's largest libraries for people with a print disability. CNIB supports research to advance knowledge in the field of vision health. Our research program funds projects that focus on ways to cure, treat and prevent eye disease, and improve the quality of life for people with vision loss.

CNIB Baker Applied Research Fund

Subjects: Research focused on the social, educational, and cultural needs of Canadians who are blind or visually impaired.
Purpose: To promote non-medical applied research that will enhance the life of the blind or visually impaired.
Eligibility: Open to residents of Canada enrolled in graduate study in Canada, and includes a co-applicant who is either a supervisor or mentor with an academic appointment in Canada, or a supervisory position at a healthcare facility. Refer to the website for complete details.
Level of Study: Research
Type: Grant
Value: Up to Canadian $40,000 plus travel and publications costs up to $2,000
Length of Study: One year
Frequency: Annual
Country of Study: Canada
No. of awards offered: Varies
Application Procedure: Application forms are available at www.cnib.ca
Closing Date: December 1st
Funding: Private

CNIB Baker Fellowship Fund

Subjects: Ophthalmology and optometry.
Purpose: To further the prevention of blindness in Canada.
Eligibility: Open to Canadians for research or study in Canada, or abroad if returning to practice in Canada, with priority given to university teaching.
Level of Study: Professional development, Postgraduate, Research
Type: Fellowship or Grant
Value: Canadian $40,000
Length of Study: 1–2 years
Frequency: Annual
Country of Study: Any country
No. of awards offered: Varies
Application Procedure: Applicants must visit the website for information and an application form. For application forms see www.cnib.ca
Closing Date: December 1st
Funding: Private
No. of awards given last year: 13

CNIB Baker New Researcher Fund

Purpose: To further the prevention of blindness in Canada.
Level of Study: Postdoctorate, Professional development, Research
Type: Grant
Value: Up to Canadian $40,000
Length of Study: 1 year
Frequency: Annual
Country of Study: Canada
No. of awards offered: Varies
Application Procedure: For application forms see www.cnib.ca
Closing Date: December 1st
Funding: Private

CNIB Winston Gordon Award

Subjects: Product Development assistive technology for the blind.
Purpose: The award is given for significant advances in the field of technology benefiting people with vision loss.
Eligibility: The significant advances in, or application of, technology must have occurred within 10 years of nomination. The device or application must have a documented benefit to people who are blind or visually impaired. The award may be presented to an individual, group, or organization, including corporations and academic institutions.
Value: The award consists of a 24-carat gold medal and Canadian $15,000
Country of Study: Any country
No. of awards offered: 1
Application Procedure: Application form-www.cnib.ca
Closing Date: April 3rd
Funding: Private

The E. (Ben) & Mary Hochhausen Access Technology Research Award
Subjects: Research awards may be applied to: research projects, study at centers of excellence in Archnology, fellowships, development of prototypes and development costs of bringing important new products to market.
Purpose: To encourage research in the field of access technology for people living with vision loss.
Eligibility: The award will be available to individuals, including CNIB staff, volunteers and clients, with a post-secondary degree.
Level of Study: Research
Type: Research award
Value: Canadian $10,000
Country of Study: International
No. of awards offered: 1
Application Procedure: See website for details www.cnib.ca
Closing Date: December 31st
Funding: Private
No. of awards given last year: 1

Gretzky Scholarship Foundation for the Blind Youth of Canada
Subjects: The Gretzky family continue a tradition of assisting the blind youth of Canada to pursue their academic and lifelong dreams.
Purpose: To provide scholarships to eligible blind and visually impaired students planning to study at the post-secondary level.
Eligibility: All applicants must be blind or visually impaired, a graduate from secondary school entering their first year of post-secondary education, and a Canadian citizen.
Level of Study: Post secondary for blind or visually impaired students.
Type: Scholarship
Value: Canadian $3,000
Frequency: Annual
Country of Study: Canada
No. of awards offered: 20
Application Procedure: For application forms see www.cnib.ca
Closing Date: May 31st
Funding: Private
No. of awards given last year: 23

Ross Purse Doctoral Fellowship
Subjects: The fellowship will be awarded for research in social sciences, engineering and other fields of study that are immediately relevant to the field of vision loss.
Purpose: To encourage and support theoretical and practical research and studies at the postgraduate or doctoral level in the field of vision loss in Canada.
Eligibility: Applications will be considered from persons studying at a Canadian University or college, or at a foreign University, where a commitment to work in the field of vision loss in Canada for at least 2 years can be demonstrated.
Level of Study: Doctorate, Postgraduate
Type: Fellowship
Value: Up to Canadian $12,500
Length of Study: 2 years
Frequency: Annual
Country of Study: Any country
No. of awards offered: 1
Application Procedure: Application form-www.cnib.ca
Closing Date: April 2nd
Funding: Private

Tuck MacPhee Award
Subjects: Ophthalmology and optometry.
Purpose: To provide a 1-year grant in support of research in macular degeneration.
Eligibility: Open to all researchers, however applicants must be residents of Canada and research must be conducted primarily in Canada.
Level of Study: Research
Type: Grant
Value: Up to Canadian $50,000
Length of Study: One year
Frequency: Annual

Country of Study: Canada
No. of awards offered: Varies
Application Procedure: See application website www.cnib.ca
Closing Date: December 1st
Funding: Private

CANADIAN NURSES FOUNDATION (CNF)

50 Driveway, Ottawa, ON, K2P 1E2, Canada
Tel: (1) 613 237 2133
Fax: (1) 613 237 3520
Email: info@cnursesfdn.ca
Website: www.canadiannursesfoundation.com
Contact: CNF Scholarship Co-ordinator

The Canadian Nurses Foundation (CNF) is a registered charity founded in 1962. It is committed to promoting the health of Canadians through the advancement of the nurses' profession by financially supporting Canadian nurses in pursuing further education, research, or certification in their speciality. CNF is funded through donations from corporations, nursing associations and individuals.

CNF Scholarships and Fellowships
Subjects: All nursing specialities. Several awards are identified for neurosurgery, oncology, community health nursing, epidemiology, gerontology, child or family healthcare, nursing administration, occupational health, dialysis nursing, home care nursing and aplastic anaemia.
Purpose: To assist Canadian nurses pursuing further education and research.
Eligibility: Open to Canadian nurses who are members of the Foundation.
Level of Study: Doctorate, Predoctorate, Professional development, Graduate, Research, Postgraduate, Baccalaureate
Type: Scholarships, fellowships, bursaries
Value: US$3,000–3,500
Length of Study: 1 year
Frequency: Annual
Country of Study: Canada
No. of awards offered: Varies
Application Procedure: Applicants must visit the website for the application forms, criteria and requirements at www.canadiannurses-foundation.com
Closing Date: April 15th
Funding: Private
Contributor: Corporations, other foundations, individuals
No. of awards given last year: 35
Additional Information: Recipients must submit a summary of any thesis, study or major paper undertaken as part of the course to the CNF.

CANADIAN SOCIETY FOR CHEMICAL TECHNOLOGY

The Chemical Institute of Canada (CIC), 130 Slater Street, Suite 550, Ottawa, ON, K1P 6E2, Canada
Tel: (1) 613 232 6252 ext 223
Fax: (1) 613 232 5862
Email: awards@cheminst.ca
Website: www.chem-tech.ca
Contact: Gale Thirlwall, Awards Manager

The Canadian Society for Chemical Technology is the national technical association of chemical and biochemical technicians and technologists with members across Canada who work in industry, government or academia. The purpose of the Society is the advancement of chemical technology, the maintenance and improvement of practitioners and educators and the continual evaluation of chemical technology in Canada. The Society hopes to maintain a dialogue with educators, government and industry, to assist in the technology content of the education process of technologists, to attract qualified people into the professions and the Society, to develop and maintain high standards and enhance the usefulness of chemical technology to both the industry and the public.

CIC Fellowships

Subjects: Chemistry, chemical engineering, chemical technology.
Purpose: A senior class of membership that recognizes the merits of CIC members who have made outstanding contributions.
Frequency: Annual
No. of awards offered: Multiple
Application Procedure: Nomination form, Letters of support must be from a member of CIC for a minimum of 10 years.
Closing Date: October 1st

CIC Honorary Fellowship

Subjects: Chemistry, chemical engineering, chemical technology
Purpose: To an individual for exceptional contributions in the chemical profession (no more than 25 living honorary fellows).
Application Procedure: Nomination form.
No. of applicants last year: 1

CNC/IUPAC Travel Awards

Subjects: Chemistry, chemical engineering.
Purpose: Helps young Canadian scientists and engineers who are within 10 years of gaining their PhD present a paper at an IUPAC-sponsored conference.
Eligibility: Evidence of an independent research programme. High quality publication record. Ability to attract research funding.
Level of Study: Postdoctorate
Value: Up to US$2,000
No. of awards offered: Multiple
Application Procedure: Curriculum vitae, 2 letters of reference, name and location of conference amount ($) needed.
Closing Date: October 16th
Funding: Private
Contributor: Gendron Fund and CNC/IUPAC company associates
No. of awards given last year: 4

For further information contact:

Steacie Institute for Molecular Sciences, NRC, 100 Sussex Dr, Ottawa, OW KIA OR6
Contact: Dr C.I. Ratcliffe

CANADIAN SOCIETY FOR CHEMISTRY (CSC)

130 Slater Street, Suite 550, Ottawa, ON K1P 6E2, Canada
Tel: (1) 613 232 6252 ext 223
Fax: (1) 613 232 5862
Email: awards@cheminst.ca
Website: www.chemistry.ca
Contact: Gale Thirlwall, Awards Manager

The Canadian Society for Chemistry (CSC), one of three constituent societies of The Chemical Institute of Canada, is the national scientific and educational society of chemists. The purpose of the CSC is to promote the practice and application of chemistry in Canada.

Boehringer Ingelheim Award for Organic or Bioorganic Chemistry

Subjects: Organic chemistry.
Purpose: For a Canadian citizen or landed immigrant whose PhD thesis in the field of organic or bioorganic chemistry who was formally accepted by a Canadian university in the 12 month period preceding the nomination deadline and whose doctoral research is judged to be of outstanding quality.
Level of Study: Postdoctorate, Postgraduate
Value: A framed scroll, Canadian $2,000 cash, reasonable travel expenses
Frequency: Annual
No. of awards offered: 1
Application Procedure: Curriculum vitae, nomination form, brief synopsis of PhD thesis and 2 letters of support.
Closing Date: July 2nd
Funding: Corporation
Contributor: Boehringer Ingelheim (Canada) Ltd

Ichikizaki Fund for Young Chemists

Subjects: Synthetic organic chemistry.
Purpose: To provide financial assistance to young chemists who are showing unique achievements in basic research by facilitating their participation in international conferences or symposia.
Eligibility: Open to members of the Canadian Society for Chemistry or the Chemical Society of Japanwho have not passed their 34th birthday as of December 31st of the year in which the application is submitted, who have a research speciality in synthetic organic chemistry and are scheduled to attend an international conference or symposium directly related to synthetic organic chemistry within 1 yearof submission.
Level of Study: Postdoctorate, Professional development, Postgraduate, Doctorate
Value: The maximum value of any one award is Canadian $10,000. Successful applicants may re-apply in subsequent years, provided the cumulative total of all awards does not exceed Canadian $15,000
Frequency: Annual
Study Establishment: Ichikizaki Fund
Country of Study: Any country
Application Procedure: Applicants must submit an application, including a curriculum vitae, copies of recent research papers, the title and brief description of the conference that the applicant wishes to attend, the title and abstract, if available, of the research paper that the applicant intends to present and a proposed budget. Applications from graduate students must be accompanied by a letter of reference from the research supervisor. Resume, research papers, description of conference attending, title and abstract and budget and letter of reference.
Closing Date: December 31st for conferences scheduled between March 1st and February 28th of the following year
Funding: Foundation
Additional Information: The number of applicants to be recommended by the Society is limited to 10 per year. Although the awards are intended primarily for established researchers, applications from postgraduate students and postdoctoral Fellows will be considered. However, only one application per year from a graduate student can be recommended to the Fund.

CANADIAN SPACE AGENCY

6767 Route de l'Aéroport, Saint-Hubert, QC J3Y 8Y9, Canada
Tel: (1) 450 926 4770
Fax: (1) 450 926 4766
Email: dave.kendall@space.gc.ca
Website: www.space.gc.ca/asc/eng/default.asp
Contact: David Kendall, Director General, Space Science

The Canadian Space Agency (CSA) was established in 1989 by the Canadian Space Agency Act. The agency operates like a government department.

Canadian Space Agency Supplements Postgraduate Scholarships

Subjects: Space science.
Purpose: To foster advanced studies in space science by offering a supplement to the regular National Science and Engineering Research Council (NSERC) postgraduate scholarships.
Eligibility: Open to graduate and permanent resident and citizen of Canada engaged in Masters or Doctoral studies in the natural sciences or engineering, or intend to pursue such studies in the following year, is successful in obtaining a NSERC postgraduate scholarship (PGS) or a Canada graduate scholarships (CGS-Master's).
Level of Study: Postgraduate
Type: Scholarship
Value: $5,767 a year, $5,833 a year and $7,000 a year, respectively
Length of Study: 2 years
Frequency: Annual
Country of Study: Canada
No. of awards offered: 6
Application Procedure: Candidates should apply to the NSERC postgraduate scholarship or Canada graduate scholarship programs by completing Form 200. After reviewing the forms, notification of award will be sent to the selected applicants.
Closing Date: May 1st
Funding: Government

Contributor: National Science and Engineering Research Council
Additional Information: A candidate who is in receipt of a scholarship from federal sources other than NSERC will not be eligible for this supplement.

CANADIAN THORACIC SOCIETY (CTS)

The Lung Association, National Office, 1750 Courtwood Cres, Suite 300, Ottawa, ON, K2C 2B5, Canada
Tel: (1) 613 569 6411
Fax: (1) 613 569 8860
Email: sdesmarais@lung.ca
Website: www.lung.ca/cts
Contact: Grants Management Officer

The Canadian Thoracic Society (CTS) is the medical section of the Canadian Lung Association. It advises the Association on scientific matters and programmes including policies regarding support for research and professional education. The CTS provides a forum whereby medical practitioners and investigators may join in the study of thoracic diseases and other medical fields that may come within the scope of the Lung Association. The CTS's objectives are to maintain the highest professional and scientific standards in all aspects of respiratory diseases, to collect, interpret and distribute scientific information, to encourage epidemiological, clinical and other scientific studies in the prevention, diagnosis and treatment of respiratory diseases and to stimulate and support undergraduate, postgraduate and continuing medical education in respiratory diseases.

CTS Research Fellowship Program

Subjects: Pulmonary disease.
Purpose: To support research training in pulmonary disease.
Eligibility: Applicants must be Canadian citizens or permanent residents of Canada. Candidates for the award must have obtained an MD or PhD degree or the equivalent and must not hold a university-level academic position. Those expected to receive a PhD degree within the following year are eligible to apply but may not begin the fellowship until the PhD requirements have been completed. CLA Fellows may not work on projects that have not been approved by the appropriate institutional ethics committees.
Level of Study: Postdoctorate, Postgraduate
Type: Fellowship
Length of Study: 2 years, with a possibility of renewal for a further year
Frequency: Annual
Country of Study: Canada
Application Procedure: Applicants must submit applications on CIHR forms.
Closing Date: November 1st
Funding: Commercial, government
Contributor: The Canadian Lung Association, the Canadian Institutes of Health Research, Industry Partners, e.g. Glaxo Smithkline Inc. Merck Frosst Can, Bayer Inc, Boehringer Ingelheim and Astrazeneca
Additional Information: Recipients are selected based on priority ratings provided by the CIHR and are subject to the approval of the Canadian Thoracic Society and the Canadian Lung Association (CLA) Board of Directors. Applicants are screened to ensure proposed research areas are appropriate to the goals of the CLA. Fellowships are awarded in each case for research training in a specific institution, and may not be transferred without the explicit approval of both institutions involved.

For further information contact:

Canadian Institutes of Health Research, 410 Laurier Avenue West, 9th Floor, Address Locator 4209A, Ottawa, ON, KIA 0W9, Canada
Website: www.cihr.ca

CANADIAN TOBACCO CONTROL RESEARCH INITIATIVE (CTCRI)

CCS/NCIC National Office, 10 Acom Ave. Suite 200, Toronto, ON, M4V 3B1, Canada
Tel: (1) 416 934 5666
Fax: (1) 416 961 4189
Email: info@ctcri.ca
Website: www.ctcri.ca
Contact: Dr Agnes O'Donohue, Research Grants Manager

The Canadian Tobacco Control Research Initiative (CTCRI) is a national partnership of research organizations working to increase capacity and innovation in research relevant to tobacco control policies and programmes. The goal of the CTCRI is to provide strategic leadership to catalyse, co-ordinate and sustain research that has a direct impact on programmes and policies aimed at reducing toacco abuse and nicotine addiction.

Idea Grants

Subjects: Tobacco-related research.
Purpose: To support innovative research and young researchers in the health and social sciences in the area of tobacco control and encourage unique to original research that has the potential to advance knowledge in this area.
Eligibility: Open to Canadian citizens or those residing legally in Canada. Candidates will have to sign a waiver affirming lack of support from tobacco companies International candidates are welcome in all grant programmes.
Level of Study: Graduate, Research
Type: Grant
Value: Up to Canadian $50,000
Country of Study: Canada
Application Procedure: Candidates must visit the website for details.
Closing Date: April 1st and October 1st
Funding: Government
Contributor: NCIC

For further information contact:

CTCRI, Research Grant Programs, Canadian Tobacco Control Research Initiative, 10 Alcorn Ave., Suite 200, Toronto, ON, M4V 3B1
Tel: (416) 934-5666
Fax: (416) 961-4189

Knowledge Synthesis Grant

Subjects: Tobacco-related cancer research.
Purpose: To aid interdisciplinary research teams of researchers, practitioners and decision makers to conduct collaborative reviews of evidence for particular tobacco control interventions.
Eligibility: Open to candidate teams that include both researchers and those responsible for tobacco policy or programmes. International co-applicants are welcome.
Type: Grant
Value: The total amount available for this initiative is Canadian $360,000. The maximum amount awarded for a single grant is Canadian $120,000
Length of Study: 1 year
Country of Study: Canada
No. of awards offered: Up to 4
Application Procedure: Candidates must visit the website for application details.
Closing Date: April 1st
Contributor: Canadian Career Society/National Cancer Institute of Canada and Canadian Institutes of Health Research
No. of awards given last year: 3
No. of applicants last year: 7

Policy Research Grants

Subjects: Tobacco-related research.
Purpose: To stimulate research that will influence and guide policy decisions in tobacco control.
Eligibility: The Principal Applicant (PA) is a Canadian citizen or legal resident (Co-applicants may be citizens or residents of other countries). Research proposal is relevant to public policy issues surrounding tobacco control in Canada. Proposal includes a description of expected outcomes and/or a preliminary dissemination plan (not applicable for travel grants).
Level of Study: Postgraduate
Type: Grant
Value: Canadian $80,000
Length of Study: 2 years
Frequency: Annual
Country of Study: Canada
No. of awards offered: 6
Application Procedure: Applicants must visit the website for details.
Closing Date: October 1st

Funding: Government
Contributor: Canadian Institutes of Health Research (CIHR), Institutes of: Neurosciences, Mental Health and Addiction, Cancer Research, Aboriginal Peoples' Health, Circulatory and Respiratory Health, Gender and Health, Human Development Child and Youth Health

For further information contact:

CTCRI Research Grant Programs, Canadian Tobacco Control Research Initiative, 10 Alcorn Ave., Suite 200, Toronto, ON, M4V 3B1
Tel: (416) 934-5666
Fax: (416) 961-4189

Research Planning Grants

Subjects: Tobacco-related research, literature review or other background information gathering.
Purpose: To aid the development of new interdisciplinary research teams for the purpose of developing a well-formed and competitive research proposal for submission to traditional funding sources in tobacco control.
Eligibility: Open to Canadian citizens or permanent residents living legally in Canada. Applicants will be required to sign a waiver affirming lack of support from tobacco companies.
Level of Study: Professional development, Research
Value: Up to Canadian $15,000
Country of Study: Canada
No. of awards offered: 8
Application Procedure: Applicants must visit the website for details.
Closing Date: February 28th, May 30th, August 30th and November 30th
Funding: Government
Contributor: National Cancer Institute of Canada/Canadian Cancer Society
No. of awards given last year: 4
No. of applicants last year: 10

Researcher Travel Grant

Subjects: Tobacco-related cancer, social, behavioural research.
Purpose: To support travel for a student or member of a non-profit community group to attend a conference or similar event and present results of their research or high-quality evaluation.
Eligibility: The Principal Applicant must be conducting graduate or post-doctoral work and must be affiliated with an accredited academic program. OR The Principal Applicant must be affiliated with a non-governmental organization or community group conducting tobacco control research or evaluation. The proposal demonstrates that any current funding will not adequately support the stated objectives of the proposal. The Principal Applicant has not been awarded another CTCRI travel grant to present at a conference or event in the same calendar year as the current application. This does not include attendance at the special tobacco control conferences such as the World Conference on Tobacco or Health (WCOTH) or the Society for Research on Nicotine and Tobacco (SRNT) conference.
Level of Study: Graduate, Postgraduate, Professional development, Research
Value: Up to Canadian $3,000
Country of Study: Canada
No. of awards offered: 10
Application Procedure: Applicants must visit the website for details.
Closing Date: September 30th, January 10th, April 1st and June 30th
Funding: Government, private
Contributor: Canadian Institutes of Health Research (CIHR), Institutes of Neurosciences, Mental Health and Addiction, Cancer Research, Aboriginal Peoples' Health, Circulatory and Respiratory Health, Gender and Health, Human Development Child and Youth Health
No. of awards given last year: 18
No. of applicants last year: 20

Student Research Grant

Subjects: Tobacco-control research.
Purpose: To create new opportunities for graduate and post-doctoral students in Canada to undertake independent research projects related to tobacco control and nicotine addiction interventions.

Eligibility: Open to students enrolled at an accredited university in Canada. Candidates must be Canadian citizens living legally in Canada and will be expected to sign a waiver affirming lack of support from a tobacco company.
Type: Grant
Value: Up to Canadian $10,000
Country of Study: Canada
No. of awards offered: 16
Application Procedure: Candidates must visit the website for details.
Closing Date: March 31st, June 30th, September 30th and December 30th
Funding: Government, private
Contributor: Canadian Institutes of Health Research (CIHR), Institutes of: Neurosciences, Mental Health and Addiction, Cancer Research, Aboriginal Peoples' Health, Circulatory and Respiratory Health, Gender and Health, Human Development Child and Youth Health

Workshop and Learning Opportunity Grants

Subjects: Tobacco-related research.
Purpose: To support events that aim to build research capacity and promote collaboration between researchers and end-users.
Eligibility: Research could involve identifying research priorities, discussing and/or developing research frameworks and/or disseminating research results. Approach is innovative and deals with engaging new topics and methods or involves new populations (e.g., researchers or practitioners new to tobacco control, historically underrepresented regions or populations).
Level of Study: Postgraduate
Type: Grant
Value: Canadian $15,000
Length of Study: 4 months
Frequency: Annual
Country of Study: Canada
No. of awards offered: 6
Application Procedure: Applicants must visit the website for details.
Closing Date: Rolling deadline
Funding: Government
Contributor: Canadian Institutes of Health Research (CIHR), Institutes of: Neurosciences, Mental Health and Addiction, Cancer Research, Aboriginal Peoples' Health, Circulatory and Respiratory Health, Gender and Health, Human Development Child and Youth Health

CANADIAN WATER RESOURCES ASSOCIATION (CWRA)

280 Albert Street, Suite 900, Ottawa, ON, K1P-5G8, Canada
Tel: (1) 613 237 9363
Fax: (1) 613 594 5190
Email: services@aic.ca
Website: www.cwra.org

The Canadian Water Resources Association (CWRA) is a national organization of individuals and organizations interested in the management of Canada's water resources. The membership is composed of private and public sector water resource professionals including managers, administrators, scientists, academics, students and users. CWRA has branch organizations in 9 provinces and members throughout Canada and beyond.

CWRA Dillon Consulting Scholarship/Ken Thomson Scholarship

Subjects: Applied, natural or social science aspects of water resources.
Purpose: These scholarship are available to graduate students whose programs of study focus upon applied, natural, or social science aspects of water resources.
Eligibility: Open to Canadian citizens or landed immigrants attending a Canadian university or college who are enrolled in full-time graduate studies in any discipline.
Level of Study: Postgraduate
Type: Scholarship
Value: 4 awards available – Canadian $2,000(1) $5,000(1)
Frequency: Annual
Country of Study: Canada
No. of awards offered: 1

Application Procedure: Candidates must submit a 500 word statement that outlines the applicant's research project and its relevance to sustainable water resources, transcripts, reference letters, a statement from the programme chairman or director endorsing the application form that programme along with the completed application form. Applications are available from the award office of any university.
Closing Date: February 15th
Funding: Commercial, foundation
Contributor: Dillon Consulting Ltd
No. of awards given last year: 4
Additional Information: All candidates will receive a 1 year membership in the CWRA.

THE CANCER COUNCIL N.S.W.

Research Strategy Unit, New South Wales Cancer Council, PO Box 572, Kings Cross, NSW 1340, Australia
Tel: (61) 2 9334 1766
Fax: (61) 2 9326 9328
Email: rong@nswcc.org.au
Website: www.cancercouncil.com.au
Contact: Mr Ron Gale, Administrative Assistant

The Cancer Council NSW is one of the leading cancer charity organizations in New South Wales. Its mission is to defeat cancer and is working to build a cancer-smart community. In building a cancer-smart community, the Council undertakes high-quality research and is an advocate on cancer issues, providing information and services to the public and raising funds for cancer programmes.

The Cancer Council NSW Research Project Grants
Subjects: All aspects of cancer that elucidate its origin, cause and control at a fundamental and applied level. Grants are open to all research disciplines relevant to cancer including behavioural, biomedical, clinical, epidemiological, psychosocial and health services.
Purpose: To provide flexible support for cancer researchers.
Eligibility: Open to Australian residents from New South Wales. Recipients of tobacco sponsorship are ineligible. Applicants must complete an application form available through the NHMARC website. Applications are submitted through the researcher's institution to the NHMRC.
Level of Study: Unrestricted
Type: Project grant
Value: Generally a maximum of Australian $100,000 per year for 3 years
Length of Study: 1–3 years
Frequency: Annual
Study Establishment: An approved institution in New South Wales
Country of Study: Australia
No. of awards offered: Varies
Application Procedure: Applicants must complete an application form, available on request or from the website. Applications are submitted through the researcher's institution to NHMRC. Applicants must also complete a supplementary question form and a consumer review form.
Closing Date: March
Funding: Private
Contributor: Community fund-raising
No. of awards given last year: 19 grants awarded in 2007
No. of applicants last year: 106

For further information contact:

NHMRC, GPO Box 9848, Canberra, ACT, 2601, Australia

THE CANCER COUNCIL SOUTH AUSTRALIA

202 Grenhill Road, Eastwood, SA 5063, Australia
Tel: (61) 8 8291 4111
Fax: (61) 8 8291 4122
Email: msmith@cancersa.org.au
Website: www.cancersa.org.au
Contact: Ms Nicole Polglase, Executive Assistant Research & Development

The Cancer Council South Australia is a community-based charity independent of government control that has developed since 1928 with the support of South Australians. The Foundation's mission is to pursue the eradication of cancer through research and education on the prevention and early detection of cancer, thus enhancing the quality of life for people living with cancer.

PhD Scholarships
Subjects: Cancer research.
Purpose: To support cancer researchers in South Australia through the provision of research and senior research fellowships.
Eligibility: Applicant must be a student judged to be the best applicant from University of Adelaide, Flinders University or University of South Australia, who is commencing PhD studies. The applicant must not be currently enrolled in a PhD, must be eligible for the Research Training Scheme and must not have been previously enrolled for a Research Degree. Students are eligible to apply for the scholarship if they are enrolled in the Faculty or Division of Health Sciences at their institution and if their PhD topic is in an area of cancer research.
Level of Study: Postgraduate
Type: Scholarship
Value: Equivalent to the value of the stipend for an APA award
Length of Study: 3 years
Frequency: Annual
Country of Study: Australia
No. of awards offered: 1
Application Procedure: Applicants must contact the relevant Scholarships Offices of The University of Adelaide, University of South Australia and Flinders University for further information and closing dates.

For further information contact:

Tel: 08 8291 4297
Email: npolglase@cancersa.org.au
Contact: Nicole Polglase, Executive Assistant Research and Development

Research Project Grants
Subjects: Any scientific or medical field directly concerned with the cause, diagnosis, prevention and treatment of cancer.
Purpose: To assist postgraduate research workers undertaking research into cancer.
Eligibility: Open to postgraduate research workers who show promise of establishing themselves or to those who have already established themselves in the field of cancer research.
Level of Study: Postdoctorate
Type: Research grant
Value: Up to Australian $25,000
Length of Study: 1–2 years
Frequency: Annual
Study Establishment: An appropriate research organization
Country of Study: Australia
No. of awards offered: Approx. 20
Application Procedure: Visit our website for details www.cancersa.org.au
Closing Date: March 14th
Funding: Private
Contributor: South Australian community
No. of awards given last year: 19
No. of applicants last year: 48

THE CANCER RESEARCH SOCIETY, INC.

625 Avenue du President-Kennedy, Suite 402, Montréal, QC H3A 3S5, Canada
Tel: (1) (26) 514 861 9227
Fax: (1) 514 861 9220
Email: ldoolan@src-crs.ca
Website: www.cancerresearchsociety.ca
Contact: Ms Louise Langlois, Executive Director

The Cancer Research Society, founded in 1945, is a national organization that devotes its funds exclusively to research on cancer. The Society is committed to funding basic cancer research or seed money for original ideas. The funds are allocated in the form of grants and fellowships to universities and hospitals across Canada.

Cancer Research Society, Inc. (Canada) Operating Grants

Subjects: Fundamental research on cancer.
Purpose: To provide support for new or continuing research activities by independent scientists or groups of investigators in the field of cancer.
Eligibility: Candidates must hold an academic position on the staff of a Canadian university.
Level of Study: Professional development, Doctorate, Research
Type: Grant
Value: Canadian $30,000–60,000 to cover the cost of research. No equipment or travel is permitted
Frequency: Annual
Study Establishment: Universities and their affiliated institutions
Country of Study: Canada
No. of awards offered: Varies
Application Procedure: Applicants must visit the website for details of application procedures.
Closing Date: February 15th
Funding: Commercial, private
No. of awards given last year: 60
No. of applicants last year: 110

Cancer Research Society, Inc. (Canada) Postdoctoral Fellowships

Subjects: Basic medical sciences.
Purpose: To provide financial support to recent PhD and MD's.
Eligibility: Open to holders of a PhD or MD degree of any nationality.
Level of Study: Postdoctorate
Type: Fellowship
Value: Canadian $35,000
Length of Study: 1 year, renewable
Frequency: Annual
Study Establishment: Universities and their affiliated institutions
Country of Study: Canada
No. of awards offered: Varies
Application Procedure: Applicants must visit the website for details.
Closing Date: February 17th
Funding: Private, commercial
No. of awards given last year: 3
No. of applicants last year: 50

Strategic Research Program on Genomics and Proteomics of Metastasic Cancer

Subjects: Medicine.
Purpose: To support basic research in cancer.
Eligibility: The research has to be done in Canada and that all applicants, must be registered in a recognized Canadian Institution.
Level of Study: Doctorate, Research
Type: Programme
Value: Canadian $150,000
Length of Study: 3 years
Frequency: Dependent on funds available
No. of awards offered: Up to 2
Application Procedure: Application forms are available on the website.
Closing Date: February 26th
Funding: Private
Contributor: Cancer Research Society, Inc

THE CANON FOUNDATION IN EUROPE

Bovenkerkerweg 59-61, 1185 XB Amstelveen, Netherlands
Tel: (31) 20 5458934
Fax: (31) 20 7128934
Email: foundation@canon-europe.com
Website: www.canonfoundation.org
Contact: Secretary

The Canon Foundation is a non-profit, grant-making philanthropic organization founded to promote, develop and spread science, knowledge and understanding, in particular, between Europe and Japan.

Canon Foundation Research Fellowships

Subjects: All subjects.
Purpose: To contribute to scientific knowledge and international understanding, in particular between Europe and Japan.
Eligibility: Open to Japanese and European nationals only.
Level of Study: Doctorate, Postdoctorate, Postgraduate, Research
Type: Fellowship
Value: A maximum of award of €27,500
Length of Study: 1 year maximum
Frequency: Annual
No. of awards offered: 10–15
Application Procedure: Applicants must complete an application form, which is to be submitted with two reference letters, a curriculum vitae, a list of papers, two photographs and copies of certificates of higher education.
Closing Date: September 15th
Funding: Corporation, private
Contributor: Canon Europa NV
No. of awards given last year: 12
No. of applicants last year: 136

CANTERBURY HISTORICAL ASSOCIATION

c/o History Department, University of Canterbury, Private Bag 4800, Christchurch, New Zealand
Fax: (64) 3 364 2003
Email: geoff.rice@canterbury.ac.nz
Website: www.hist.canterbury.ac.nz
Contact: Dr G W Rice, Secretary

The Canterbury Historical Association (founded 1922, but in recess between 1940 and 1953) aims to foster public interest in all fields of history by holding meetings for the discussion of historical issues, and to promote historical research and writing through its administration of the J M Sherrard Award in New Zealand local and regional history.

J M Sherrard Award

Subjects: New Zealand regional and local history writing.
Purpose: To foster high standards of scholarship in New Zealand regional and local history.
Eligibility: Open to qualified applicants from New Zealand only. Major awards are normally restricted to substantial monograph length publications that meet scholarly standards. Small-scale works, biographies and family histories are not eligible.
Level of Study: Unrestricted
Type: Prize
Value: New Zealand $1,000
Country of Study: New Zealand
No. of awards offered: Varies
Application Procedure: No application is required, as judges assess all potential titles appearing in the New Zealand National Bibliography.
Funding: Private
No. of awards given last year: 3 major awards
No. of applicants last year: 45 works considered, 10 were shortlisted
Additional Information: The prize money is often divided among two or three finalists. A commendation list is also published.

CARNEGIE MELLON UNIVERSITY

The Heinz College, Australia, Torrens Building, 220 Victoria Square, Adelaide, SA 5000, Australia
Tel: (61) 08 8110 9900
Email: Monicar@cmu.edu.au and fdoyle@cmu.edu.au
Website: www.heinz.cmu.edu.au

Carnegie Mellon is home to the world's leading experts in a range of fields. From computing to the arts to the environment to biotechnology, the students, faculty and staff of the University are shaping the future with a strong focus on finding practical answers to complex problems. These scholarships are available to full-time students.

Carnegie Mellon University–Aus AID Scholarships

Subjects: Public policy, management and information technology.

Purpose: To support a limited number of students from countries where Australia has a bilateral aid program, to undertake a Masters Degree at the H. John Heinz III College at Carnegie Mellon University's campus in Adelaide, Australia.

Eligibility: For detailed listing of eligible countries, criteria (general eligibility and country specific), and scholarship benefits, please visit the website www.heinz.cmu.edu.au/.

Type: Scholarship

Value: Full tuition fee, return economy airfares, a contribution to living expenses, and basic medical insurance

Length of Study: 1 year

Frequency: Annual

Study Establishment: Carnegie Mellon University

Country of Study: Australia

Application Procedure: Check website for further details.

Funding: Government

Contributor: Government of Australia

THE CARNEGIE TRUST FOR THE UNIVERSITIES OF SCOTLAND

Andrew Carnegie House, Pittencrieff Street, Dunfermline, Fife, KY12 8AW, Scotland
Tel: (44) 1383 724990
Fax: (44) 1383 749799
Email: jgray@carnegie-trust.org
Website: www.carnegie-trust.org
Contact: Ms Jackie Gray, Assistant Secretary

The Carnegie Trust for the Universities of Scotland, founded in 1901, is one of the many philanthropic agencies established by Andrew Carnegie. The trust aims to offer assistance to students, to aid the expansion of the Scottish universities and to stimulate research. See also the entry for the Caledonian Research Foundation.

Carnegie Grants

Subjects: All subjects in the universities' curriculum.

Purpose: To support personal research projects or aid in the publication of books likely to benefit the universities of Scotland.

Eligibility: Open to graduates of Scottish universities and to full-time members of staff of Scottish universities.

Level of Study: Postdoctorate, Postgraduate, Professional development, Research

Type: Grant

Value: Varies according to requests but the maximum is usually UK £2,500

Length of Study: Up to 3 months

Frequency: 3 meetings per year

Country of Study: Any country

No. of awards offered: Varies

Application Procedure: Applicants must complete an application form, available from the Trust office or on the Trust's website.

Closing Date: January 15th, May 15th or October 15th prior to Executive Committee meetings in February, June and November

Funding: Private

No. of awards given last year: 273

No. of applicants last year: 334

Carnegie Scholarships

Subjects: All subjects in the universities curriculum.

Purpose: To support postgraduate research.

Eligibility: Open to candidates possessing a First Class (Honours) Degree from a Scottish university.

Level of Study: Postgraduate

Type: Scholarship

Value: UK £14,000 per year plus tuition fees and allowances

Length of Study: Up to 3 years, subject to annual review

Frequency: Annual

Study Establishment: Any university

Country of Study: United Kingdom

No. of awards offered: 15

Application Procedure: Applicants must be nominated by a senior member of staff at a Scottish university and an application form completed, available from the Trust office.

Closing Date: March 15th

Funding: Private

No. of awards given last year: 15

No. of applicants last year: 122

Additional Information: Scholarship is to support postgraduate research leading to a PhD. Applications for 1 year postgraduate courses are not eligible.

Carnegie-Cameron Taught Post-Graduate Bursaries

Purpose: To qualified and deserving, industrious and ambitious candidate, who would derive particular benefit from a one-year, taught, postgraduate degree which he or she would be unlikely to enjoy without the award.

Eligibility: Applicants must be Scottish by birth, descent (at least one parent born in Scotland) or have been continuously resident in Scotland for a period of at least 3 years for the purpose of secondary or tertiary education in Scotland. Vacations, periods of absence through illness and periods spent outside Scotland as part of a Scottish educational course shall not be taken into account in determining whether the residence has been 'continuous'.

Level of Study: Postgraduate

Type: Bursary

Length of Study: 1-year full-time or 2-year part-time, taught, postgraduate degree course at the awarding university

Country of Study: Scotland

Application Procedure: A completed application form, together with a copy of your degree transcript, two academic references and proof of either Scottish birth, descent or residency should be provided.

Additional Information: The bursaries are awarded directly by the universities and candidates wishing to be considered for these bursaries should make application to the university where they wish to study and not to the Trust.

CATHOLIC ACADEMIC EXCHANGE SERVICE (KAAD)

Hausdorffstrasse 151, 53129, Bonn, Germany
Tel: (49) 228 91758 0
Fax: (49) 228 91758 58
Email: zentrale@kaad.de
Website: www.kaad.de

Catholic Academic Exchange Service (KAAD) provides financial and civic educational support as well as pastoral assistance for high-potential post-graduate scholars from Africa, Asia, Latin America, the Middle East and Eastern Europe. The KAAD has been registered as a charity of the German Catholic Church since 1958-today it is the largest Catholic Organization offering scholarships in the area of International educational collaboration in the world.

Research Scholarships: Programme I

Subjects: All subjects.

Purpose: To support candidates from developing nations, who are still in their home countries, for doctoral and postdoctoral research.

Eligibility: Applicants must be young academics from Asia, Africa, Latin America, Near and Middle East or Eastern Europe, with a commitment to return to their home country upon completion of their research stay.

Level of Study: Postgraduate, Research, Doctorate, MBA, Postdoctorate

Type: Scholarship

Value: In accordance with KAAD scholarship guidelines

Length of Study: 1 year (extendable up to 3 years)

Study Establishment: A German university

Country of Study: Germany

No. of awards offered: 250

Application Procedure: Application forms are available on request. Applications can be submitted to the KAAD partner organizations in the home country, which in turn will propose the applicants to the KAAD.

Closing Date: January 15th and June 15th

Contributor: Catholic Academic Exchange Service (KAAD)

Research Scholarships: Programme II

Subjects: All subjects.
Purpose: To support candidates from developing nations, who are already in Germany and are in an advanced stage of their research and whose research is not yet promoted by KAAD.
Eligibility: Applicants must be young academics from Asia, Africa, Latin America, Near and Middle East or Eastern Europe, with a commitment to return to their home country upon completion of their research stay.
Level of Study: MBA, Postdoctorate, Postgraduate, Doctorate
Type: Scholarship
Value: In accordance with KAAD scholarship guidelines
Length of Study: 1 year (extendable up to 3 years)
Study Establishment: A German university
Country of Study: Germany
Application Procedure: Application forms are available on request. Applications can be submitted to the KAAD partner organizations in Germany, which in turn will propose the applicants to the KAAD.
Closing Date: January 15th and June 15th
Contributor: Catholic Academic Exchange Service (KAAD)

CATHOLIC LIBRARY ASSOCIATION (CLA)

100 North Street, Suite 224, Pittsfield, MA 01201-5109, United States of America
Tel: (1) 413 443 2252
Fax: (1) 413 442 2252
Email: cla@cathla.org
Website: www.cathla.org
Contact: Jean R Bostley, SSJ, Executive Director

The Catholic Library Association (CLA) represents all segments of the library community. Members strive to initiate, foster and encourage any activity or library programme that will promote literature and libraries, not only of a Catholic nature, but also of an ecumenical spirit.

Rev Andrew L Bouwhuis Memorial Scholarship

Subjects: Library science.
Purpose: To encourage promising and talented individuals to enter librarianship and to foster advanced study in the library profession.
Eligibility: Open to individuals who have been accepted into a graduate school programme, show promise of success based on collegiate record and who demonstrate the need for financial aid.
Level of Study: Graduate, Postgraduate
Type: Scholarship
Value: US$1,500
Frequency: Annual
Country of Study: United States of America
No. of awards offered: 1
Application Procedure: Applicants must complete an application form, available on request. Please send a stamped addressed envelope.
Closing Date: February 1st
Funding: Private
No. of awards given last year: 1

Sister Sally Daly – Junior Library Guild Grant

Purpose: To enable a new CLA/CLSS member to attend the Association's annual convention.
Eligibility: Only new members of the Catholic Library Association (CLA)/Children's Library Services Section (CLSS) are eligible.
Value: US$1,500
Application Procedure: Applications may be obtained by writing to the Association or downloaded from the Association's website www.cathla.org.
Closing Date: December 1st

World Book, Inc. Grant

Subjects: Continuing education in school or children's librarianship.
Purpose: Establish scholarships for continuing education in school or children's librarianship.
Eligibility: Open to national members of the CLA.
Level of Study: Postgraduate, Professional development
Type: Grant

Value: US$1,500 to be divided among no more than three recipients
Frequency: Annual
Study Establishment: Special workshops, institutes, or seminars and summer sessions at Institutes of Higher Education
Country of Study: Any country
No. of awards offered: 1–3
Application Procedure: Applicants must send a stamped addressed envelope for details.
Closing Date: March 15th
Funding: Commercial
No. of awards given last year: 1
Additional Information: This award may not be used for study leading to a degree in library science.

CAUZ GROUP

PO Box 229, BC, Pymble, NSW 2073, Australia
Tel: (61) 2 9144 2415
Email: trustawards@cauzgroup.com.au
Website: www.trust.com.au/philanthropy/awards
Contact: Mr Petrea Salter, Director

Cauz Group is the organizer and PR agency for a number of high profile awards and scholarships. These include the Miles Franklin Literary Award, Kathleen Mitchell Award (literary), Portia Geach Memorial Award (for female artists), the Sir Robert William Askin Operatic Travelling Scholarship (for male singers), the Lady Mollie Isabelle Askin Ballet Travelling Scholarship, and the Marten Bequest Travelling Scholarship.

Lady Mollie Isabelle Askin Ballet Travelling Scholarship

Subjects: Dancing or classical ballet.
Purpose: To support the advancement of culture and education in Australia and elsewhere. To reward Australian citizens of outstanding ability and promise in ballet.
Eligibility: Open to Australian citizens who are over the age of 17 and under the age of 30 at the closing date for entries for the award.
Level of Study: Unrestricted
Type: Scholarship
Value: Australian $15,000
Length of Study: More than 2 years
Frequency: Every 2 years
Country of Study: Any country
No. of awards offered: 1
Application Procedure: Applicants must complete an application form to be submitted with specified documents and enclosures.
Closing Date: The last Friday in November in the year preceding the award
Funding: Private
Contributor: The Estate of Lady Mollie Isabelle Askin
No. of awards given last year: 1

Marten Bequest Travelling Scholarships

Subjects: Two scholarships are available in each of the following categories, which rotate in two groups on an annual basis as follows: first category–architecture, ballet, instrumental music, painting, sculpture and singing. Second category–acting, instrumental music, painting, poetry, prose and singing.
Purpose: To augment a scholar's own resources towards affording him or her a cultural education by means of a travelling scholarship.
Eligibility: Applicants must have been born in Australia, and be aged 21–35 years (other than ballet) or 17–35 years for ballet.
Level of Study: Unrestricted
Type: Scholarship
Value: Australian $25,000 over 2 years
Length of Study: 2 years
Frequency: Annual
Country of Study: Any country
No. of awards offered: 12 per year
Application Procedure: Applicants must complete an application form and submit this with a study outline and supporting material as required.
Closing Date: The last Friday in October of the year preceding the award
Funding: Private

Contributor: The estate of the late John Chisholm Marten
No. of awards given last year: 12

Miles Franklin Literary Award

Subjects: Writing.
Purpose: To reward the novel of the year that is of the highest literary merit and presents Australian life in any of its phases.
Eligibility: Refer to the application form. The novel must have been first published in any country in the year preceding the award. Biographies, collections of short stories, children's books and poetry are not eligible. All works must be in English.
Level of Study: Unrestricted
Type: Award
Value: Australian $42,000
Frequency: Annual
Country of Study: Any country
No. of awards offered: 1
Application Procedure: Applicants must complete an application form and send six copies of their novel.
Closing Date: 2nd Friday in December in the year preceding the award
Funding: Private
Contributor: The estate of the late Miss S M S Miles Franklin
No. of awards given last year: 1
Additional Information: If there is no novel worthy of the prize, the award may be given to the author of a play.

Portia Geach Memorial Award

Subjects: Fine and applied arts.
Purpose: To award the best portraits painted from life of a man or woman distinguished in art, letters or the sciences, by a female artist.
Eligibility: Entrants must be female Australian residents who are either Australian or British-born or naturalized. Works must be executed entirely in the previous year.
Level of Study: Unrestricted
Type: Award
Value: Australian $18,000
Frequency: Annual
Country of Study: Any country
No. of awards offered: 1
Application Procedure: Applicants must complete an application form and submit this with an entry fee and the work.
Closing Date: The last Friday in August in the year of the award
Funding: Private
Contributor: The estate of the late Miss Florence Kate Geach
No. of awards given last year: 1
Additional Information: The winning portrait and selected works are exhibited for 1 month at the S H Ervin Gallery in Sydney, Australia.

Sir Robert William Askin Operatic Travelling Scholarship

Subjects: Operatic singing.
Purpose: To support the advancement of culture and education in Australia and elsewhere. To reward male Australian citizens of outstanding ability and promise as an operatic singer.
Eligibility: Applicants must be male Australian citizens between the ages of 18 and 30 at the time of application.
Level of Study: Unrestricted
Type: Scholarship
Value: Australian $15,000
Length of Study: 2 years
Frequency: Every 2 years
Country of Study: Any country
No. of awards offered: 1
Application Procedure: Applicants must complete an application form to be submitted along with specified documents and enclosures.
Closing Date: The last Friday in November in the year preceding the award
Funding: Private
Contributor: The estate of Sir Robert William Askin
No. of awards given last year: 1

CDS INTERNATIONAL, INC.

871 United Nations Plaza, New York, NY 10017-1814,
United States of America
Tel: (1) 212 497 3513
Fax: (1) 212 497 3535
Email: rdelfino@cdsintl.org
Website: www.cdsintl.org
Contact: Ms Anna F Oberle, Programme Officer

CDS International, Inc. is a non-profit organization that administers work exchange programmes. CDS International's goal is to further the international exchange of knowledge and technological skills, and to contribute to the development of a pool of highly trained and interculturally experienced business, academic and government leaders.

Congress Bundestag Youth Exchange for Young Professionals

Subjects: Business, technical, computer science, social and service fields.
Purpose: To foster the exchange of knowledge and culture between German and American youth, while providing career-enhancing theoretical and practical work experience.
Eligibility: Open to citizens of the United States of America and permanent residents aged 18–24 years who have well-defined career goals and related part or full-time work experience. Applicants must be able to communicate and work well with others, have maturity enabling them to adapt to new situations, an intellectual curiosity and a sense of diplomacy.
Level of Study: Professional development
Type: Scholarship
Value: International airfare and partial domestic transportation, language training and study at a German professional school, seminars, including transportation and insurance, host family stay
Length of Study: 1 year: 2-month language; 4-month study; 5-month internship
Frequency: Annual
Study Establishment: A field-specific postsecondary professional school
Country of Study: Germany
No. of awards offered: 75
Application Procedure: Apply online at www.cdsintl.org/cbyx
Closing Date: December 1st
Funding: Government
Contributor: US Congress and German Bundestag
No. of awards given last year: 75
No. of applicants last year: 250–350
Additional Information: Participants must have US$300–350 pocket money per month. During the year of the award, American exchange students will have the opportunity to improve their skills through formal study and work experience. The programme also includes intensive language instruction and housing with a host family or in a dormitory.

CEC ARTSLINK

435 Hudson Street, 8th Floor, New York, NY, 10014,
United States of America
Tel: (1) 212 643 1985
Fax: (1) 212 643 1996
Email: al@cecartslink.org
Website: www.cecartslink.org
Contact: Program Coordinator, ArtsLink Awards

CEC Artslink is an international arts service organization. Our programmes encourage and support exchange of artists and cultural managers between the United States and Central Europe, Russia and Eurasia. We believe that the arts are a society's most deliberate and complex means of communication.

ArtsLink Independent Projects

Subjects: Performing, design, media, literary and visual arts.
Purpose: To provide funding to artists and arts managers who propose to undertake projects in the United States in collaboration with a US non-profit arts organization.

Eligibility: Candidates must be citizens of, and reside in, an eligible countries Albania, Armenia, Azerbaijan, Belarus, Bosnia and Herzegovina, Bulgaria, Croatia, Czech Republic, Estonia, Georgia, Hungary, Kazakhstan, Kosovo, Kyrgyzstan, Latvia, Lithuania, Macedonia, Moldova, Mongolia, Montenegro, Poland, Romania, Russia, Serbia, Slovak Republic, Slovenia, Tajikistan, Turkmenistan, Ukraine and Uzbekistan. There are no age limitations. Arts managers must be affiliated with an organization in the non-commercial sector.
Type: Fellowship
Value: US$5,000
Length of Study: 1 year
Frequency: Annual
Country of Study: United States of America
Application Procedure: Complete online application form.
Closing Date: November 5th
Funding: Private, trusts
No. of awards given last year: 5

For further information contact:

CEC ArtsLink, 435 Hudson Street, 8th Floor, New York, NY 10014

ArtsLink Projects

Subjects: Performing Arts, visual and media arts.
Purpose: To support US artists, curators, presenters and non-profit arts organizations undertaking projects in Eastern and Central Europe, Russia, Central Asia and the Caucasus.
Eligibility: Candidates must be citizens of, and reside in, an eligible countries Albania, Armenia, Azerbaijan, Belarus, Bosnia and Herzegovina, Bulgaria, Croatia, Czech Republic, Estonia, Georgia, Hungary, Kazakhstan, Kosovo, Kyrgyzstan, Latvia, Lithuania, Macedonia, Moldova, Mongolia, Montenegro, Poland, Romania, Russia, Serbia, Slovak Republic, Slovenia, Tajikistan, Turkmenistan, Ukraine, and Uzbekistan.
Level of Study: Postgraduate
Type: Fellowship
Value: US$2,500–10,000
Length of Study: 1 year
Frequency: Annual
Application Procedure: Complete online application form.
Closing Date: January 15th
Funding: Private, trusts
No. of awards given last year: 10

ArtsLink Residencies

Subjects: Literature, Performing arts, Visual and Media Arts.
Eligibility: Applicants must be citizens of, and reside in, an eligible countries Albania, Armenia, Azerbaijan, Belarus, Bosnia and Herzegovina, Bulgaria, Croatia, Czech Republic, Estonia, Georgia, Hungary, Kazakhstan, Kosovo, Kyrgyzstan, Latvia, Lithuania, Macedonia, Moldova, Mongolia, Montenegro, Poland, Romania, Russia, Serbia, Slovak Republic, Slovenia, Tajikistan, Turkmenistan, Ukraine and Uzbekistan.
Level of Study: Postgraduate
Type: Fellowship
Length of Study: 5 weeks
Frequency: Annual
Country of Study: United States of America
No. of awards offered: 14–16
Application Procedure: Complete online application form.
Closing Date: November 5th
Funding: Private, trusts
Contributor: ArtsLink Residencies are funded through public and private sources including CEC ArtsLink, the National Endowment for the Arts, the Trust for Mutual Understanding, the Ohio Arts Council, the Kettering Fund and the Milton and Sally Avery Arts Foundation with additional support from the Polish Cultural Institute and the Romanian Cultural Institute
No. of awards given last year: 16

CENTER FOR CALIFORNIA STUDIES, CSU-SACRAMENTO, CALIFORNIA LEGISLATURE (CSUS)

CSUS 6000 J Street, Sacramento, CA, 95819-6081, United States of America
Tel: (1) 916 278 6906
Fax: (1) 916 278 5199
Email: calstudies@csus.edu
Website: www.csus.edu
Contact: Timothy Hodson, Executive Director

Center for California Studies, CSU-Sacramento, California Legislature (CSUS) was founded in 1984. It is located on the capital campus of the California State University. Center for California Studies is a public service, educational support and applied research institute of CSUS. It is dedicated to promoting a better understanding of California's government, politics, people, cultures and history.

California Senate Fellows

Subjects: Public policy and politics.
Purpose: To expose people with diverse life experiences and backgrounds to the legislative process and provide research and other professional staff assistance to the Senate.
Eligibility: Open to candidates who have obtained a degree from a 4 year college or university.
Level of Study: Professional development
Type: Fellowships
Value: US$1,972 per month and full health, vision and dental benefits
Length of Study: 11 months
Frequency: Annual
Country of Study: United States of America
No. of awards offered: 18
Application Procedure: Applicants can download the application form from the website.
Closing Date: February 27th
Funding: Government
Additional Information: For further information please contact David Pacheco, the program director, at 916 278 5408 (Sacramento State), 916 651 4160 (Senate) or email to david.pacheco@sen.ca.gov

Jesse M. Unruh Assembly Fellowship Program

Subjects: Public policy formation.
Purpose: To provide an opportunity for individuals of all ages, ethnic backgrounds and experiences to directly participate in the legislative process.
Eligibility: Applicants must have completed a Bachelor's degree by the end of Summer of the fellowship year. There are no preferred majors.
Level of Study: Professional development
Type: Fellowship
Value: US$1,972 per month and medical, dental and vision benefits
Length of Study: 11 months
Frequency: Annual
Study Establishment: Center for California Studies
Country of Study: United States of America
Application Procedure: Applicants must download the complete application form from the website. Applicants must furnish academic, employment and activities data, unofficial transcripts from colleges attended, a personal statement, a policy statement on a specific topic contained in the application and 3 references.
Closing Date: February 27th
Additional Information: Individuals with advanced degrees or those in mid-career are encouraged to apply.

CENTER FOR CREATIVE PHOTOGRAPHY (CCP)

The University of Arizona, 1030 North Olive Road PO Box 210103 Tucson, AZ, 85721-0103, United States of America
Tel: (1) 520 621 7968
Fax: (1) 520 621 9444
Email: oncenter@ccp.library.arizona.edu
Website: www.ccp.arizona.edu

The Center for Creative Photography (CCP) is an archive and research centre located on the University of Arizona campus.

CCP Ansel Adams Research Fellowship

Subjects: Photography.
Purpose: To promote and support research on the Center's photograph, archive and library collections.
Eligibility: Open to researchers from any discipline who are engaged in studies that require an extended period of research in the collections of the Center.
Level of Study: Research
Type: Fellowship
Value: US$5,000
Length of Study: 2–4 weeks
Frequency: Annual
Country of Study: United States of America
Application Procedure: Applicants must send a cover letter along with 5 copies each of a curriculum vitae and a statement detailing the applicant's research interests.
Closing Date: October 31st

For further information contact:

Center for Creative Photography, 1030 N. Olive Road, Tucson, AZ 85721-0103
Email: rulea@ccp.library.arizona.edu
Contact: Amy Rule, Head of Research

THE CENTER FOR CROSS-CULTURAL STUDY (CC-CS)

446 Main Street, Massachusetts, Amherst, 01002-2314,
United States of America
Tel: (1) 256 0011
Fax: (1) 256 1968
Email: admin@cccs.com
Website: www.cccs.com

The CC-CS provides unique learning experiences for students in a true cross-cultural exchange by inviting them to expand their worldview through intense immersion in Seville, Havana and Cordoba. The CC-CS has developed it's reputation from an emphasis on the personal growth of students.

CC-CS Scholarship Program

Subjects: Cultural studies, Spanish studies.
Purpose: To fund continuing excellence in Spanish studies.
Eligibility: Open to all students enrolled on the cross-cultural scholarship programme in Spain, Argentina and Cuba.
Level of Study: Doctorate, Postdoctorate, Postgraduate
Type: Scholarship
Value: Up to US$2,500
Length of Study: 1 year
Frequency: Annual
Study Establishment: The center for cross-cultural study
Country of Study: Argentina
No. of awards offered: Varies
Application Procedure: Submit application accompanied by an original essay in Spanish, Portuguese and English, and a faculty recommendation.
Closing Date: 60 days prior to taking up a past
No. of awards given last year: 11

CENTER FOR DEFENSE INFORMATION (CDI)

1779 Massachusetts Avenue North West, Washington,
DC 20036-2109, United States of America
Tel: (1) 202 332 0600
Fax: (1) 202 462 4559
Email: info@cdi.org
Website: www.cdi.org
Contact: Development Director

The Center for Defense Information (CDI) provides responsible, non-partisan research and analysis on the social, economic, environmental, political and military components of national and global security, and aims to educate the public and inform policy makers about these issues. The organization is staffed by retired senior government officials and knowledgeable researchers and is directed by Dr Bruce G Blair.

CDI Internship

Subjects: Weapons proliferation, military spending, military policy, diplomacy and foreign affairs.
Purpose: To support the work of CDI's senior staff while gaining exposure to research, issues and communications related to national security and foreign policy.
Eligibility: There are no eligibility restrictions. Paid internships are available for nationals of the United States of America and legal immigrants.
Level of Study: Unrestricted
Type: Internship
Value: US$1,000 per month
Length of Study: 3–5 months
Study Establishment: CDI
Country of Study: Any country
No. of awards offered: 5 per trimester, 15 per year
Application Procedure: Applicants must submit a curriculum vitae, covering letter, brief writing sample, transcript and two letters of recommendation.
Closing Date: July 1st for the Autumn deadline, October 1st for the Spring deadline and March 1st for the Summer deadline
Funding: Private
No. of awards given last year: 12
No. of applicants last year: 200

World Security Institute Internship

Subjects: Policy issues, including; weapons proliferation, military spending and reform, diplomacy and foreign affairs, small aims trade, terrorism, missile defense and space weaponization.
Purpose: To support work of one of the World Security Institute's four divisions: the Center of Defense Information, Azimuth Media, International Media, or International Programs.
Eligibility: Internships are open to recent graduates, graduate students, and highly qualified undergraduates with a strong interest in military policy, national security, foreign affairs, and related public policy issues who are willing to undertake some small administrative tasks. Although course work in these areas is not required, strong writing capabilities, prior experience in CDI's issue areas, and solid computer skills are appreciated. U.S. citizenship is not required.
Level of Study: Postgraduate
Type: Internship
Value: All fees and agreed allowance
Length of Study: 1 year
Frequency: Annual
Study Establishment: World Security Institute
No. of awards offered: 18
No. of awards given last year: 16

CENTER FOR HELLENIC STUDIES

3100 Whitehaven Street North West, Washington, DC 20008, United
States of America
Tel: (1) 202 745 4400
Fax: (1) 202 332 8688
Email: chs@fas.harvard.edu
Website: www.chs.harvard.edu
Contact: Programs Officer

The Center for Hellenic Studies (Trustees for Harvard University) offers residential research fellowships for professional scholars in ancient Greek studies.

Center for Hellenic Studies Junior Fellowships

Subjects: Ancient Greek studies, primarily literature, language, philosophy, history, religion, archaeology and art history, with restrictions.

Purpose: To provide selected classics scholars fairly early in their careers with an academic year free of other responsibilities to work on a publishable project.
Eligibility: Open to scholars and teachers of Ancient Greek studies with a PhD degree or equivalent qualification and some published work.
Level of Study: Postdoctorate
Type: Fellowship
Value: Up to US$26,000, plus private living quarters and a study at the Center building. Limited funds up to US$1,000 for research expenses and research related travel expenses are available
Length of Study: 9 months from September–June, non-renewable
Frequency: Annual
Study Establishment: The Center for Hellenic Studies, Washington, DC
Country of Study: United States of America
No. of awards offered: 12
Application Procedure: Applicants must submit an application form, a curriculum vitae, description of research project, samples of publications and three letters of recommendation. Enquiries about eligibility and early applications are encouraged. Applicants who are unable to stay for the full academic year may apply for a one-semester fellowship and should include a note explaining the circumstances that make this necessary with their application.
Closing Date: October 15th
Funding: Private
Additional Information: Residence at the Center is required.

CENTER FOR INTERNATIONAL STUDIES, UNIVERSITY OF MISSOURI-ST LOUIS

366 Social Sciences and Business Building, University of Missouri-St Louis, One University Boulevard, St Louis, MO, 63121-4400, United States of America
Tel: (1) 314 516 5753
Fax: (1) 314 516 6757
Email: jglassman@umsl.edu
Website: www.umsl.edu
Contact: Mr Robert Baumann, Assistant Director

The Center for International Studies supports a wide range of academic programmes designed to promote research and interest in international studies and to improve the teaching of international affairs.

Theodore Lentz Postdoctoral or Sabbatical Fellowship in Peace and Conflict Resolution Research

Subjects: International relations.
Purpose: To provide an opportunity for the recipient to conduct research projects in peace and conflict resolution, and to teach an introductory peace studies course in the Autumn semester and one course in the Spring semester at the University of Missouri-St Louis.
Eligibility: A completed PhD is required and preference is given to graduates of university programmes in peace studies and conflict resolution. Graduates of political science, international relations and other social science programmes who specialize in peace and conflict resolution are also invited to apply.
Level of Study: Postdoctorate
Type: Fellowship
Value: Approx. US$23,400 and university benefits and US$1,000 travel and expense allowance
Length of Study: 9 months
Frequency: Annual
Study Establishment: The University of Missouri-St Louis
Country of Study: United States of America
No. of awards offered: 1
Application Procedure: Applicants must submit a curriculum vitae, a letter of application, evidence of completion of PhD, three letters of recommendation and a research proposal of approx. 750 words.
Closing Date: April 15th
Funding: Private
Contributor: The Lentz Peace Research Association
No. of awards given last year: 1
No. of applicants last year: 10

Additional Information: Supported in part by the Lentz Peace Research Association.

CENTER FOR PHILOSOPHY OF RELIGION

418 Malloy Hall, University of Notre Dame, Notre Dame, IN, 46556, United States of America
Tel: (1) 574 631 7339
Email: cprelig@nd.edu
Website: www.nd.edu/~cprelig
Contact: Michael C Rea, Director

The Center for Philosophy of Religion at the University of Notre Dame was established in 1976 in order to promote, support and disseminate scholarly work in the philosophy of religion and Christian philosophy. The center aims to promote work concerned with the traditional topics and questions that fall under the rubric of the philosophy of religion: the theistic proofs, the rationality of belief in God, the problem of evil, the nature of religious language and the like. At least as important, however, is the Center's effort to support and encourage the development and exploration of specifically Christian and theistic philosophy, the sort of philosophy which takes Christianity (or, more broadly, theism) for granted and then proceeds to work on philosophical questions and problems from that perspective. As one of the world's leading Catholic institution, the University of Notre Dame provides an ideal home for such work.

The Alvin Plantinga Fellowship

Subjects: Philosophy.
Purpose: To provide time for reflection and writing to a distinguished senior scholar whose work is in the forefront of current research in the philosophy of religion and Christian philosophy.
Level of Study: Research
Type: Stipendiary
Value: $60,000
Frequency: Annual
No. of awards offered: 1
Application Procedure: Applications should include a complete curriculum vitae, three letters of recommendation, a statement of no more than three pages decribing the project and one published or unpublished paper.
Closing Date: Mid-January
Contributor: Center's endowment and College of Arts and Letters at Notre Dame
No. of awards given last year: 1
No. of applicants last year: 15

Center for Philosophy of Religion's Postdoctoral Fellowships

Subjects: Philosophy.
Purpose: Offered to those whose tenure at the Center would allow them to grow and make progress in the Center's areas of interest and subsequently disseminate and expand such work through their own teaching and writing.
Level of Study: Postdoctorate
Type: Fellowship
Value: $30,000 each
Frequency: Annual
No. of awards offered: 2
Application Procedure: Applications should include a complete curriculum vitae, three letters of recommendation, a statement of no more than three pages decribing the project and one published or unpublished paper.
Closing Date: March 2nd
Contributor: Center's endowment and College of Arts and Letters at Notre Dame
No. of awards given last year: 2
No. of applicants last year: 50

Center for Philosophy of Religion's Visiting Graduate Fellowship

Subjects: Philosophy.

Purpose: Awarded to philosophy graduate students from other institutions who are working on dissertations in philosophy of religion or Christian philosophy.
Level of Study: Graduate
Type: Fellowship
Value: $16,000
Frequency: Annual
No. of awards offered: 1
Application Procedure: Applications should include a complete curriculum vitae, three letters of recommendation, a statement of no more than three pages decribing the project and one published or unpublished paper.
Closing Date: March 2nd
Contributor: Center's endowment and College of Arts and Letters at Notre Dame
No. of awards given last year: 1
No. of applicants last year: 10

The Frederick J. Crosson Fellowship

Subjects: Philosophy.
Purpose: To support a foreign scholar (especially one outside the Anglo-American philosophical community) or to a scholar outside the field of philosophy (e.g. a theologian) who would benefit from a year at the center.
Level of Study: Research
Type: Fellowship
Value: $40,000–50,000, depending on rank
Frequency: Annual
No. of awards offered: 1
Application Procedure: Applications should include a complete curriculum vitae, three letters of recommendation, a statement of no more than three pages decribing the project and one published or unpublished paper.
Closing Date: Mid-January
Contributor: Center's endowment and College of Arts and Letters at Notre Dame
No. of awards given last year: 1
No. of applicants last year: 12

CENTRAL ASIA RESEARCH AND TRAINING INITIATIVE (CARTI)

Open Society Institute/International Higher Education, Október 6 u.12,
Budapest, 1051, Hungary
Tel: (36) 1 327 3854
Fax: (36) 1 411 4401
Email: carti@osi.hu
Website: www.soros.org
Contact: Edit Köblös, Programme Coordinator

Central Asia Research and Training Initiative (CARTI) is a regional higher education support programme of the Open Society Institute, a private operating and grantmaking foundation. CARTI promotes the development of indigenous capacities for original scholarly and academic work and internationalization of scholarship in the region of Central Asia including, but not limited to, the post Soviet states of Central Asia and Mongolia.

CARTI Junior Fellowships

Subjects: Humanities and social sciences.
Purpose: To support young individuals in early stages of their formal Doctoral studies (such as aspirantura) and focus on development of ideas and skills for high-quality research work.
Eligibility: Open to candidates holding a Master's degree or equivalent and formally registered at a Doctoral studies programme (PhD or equivalent programme) from Afghanistan, Kazakhstan, Mangolia, Tajikistan, Turkmenistan or Uzbekistan.
Level of Study: Doctorate
Type: Fellowships
Value: Varies
Length of Study: 2 years
Frequency: Annual
Application Procedure: Applicants can download the application form from the website.
Closing Date: October 20th

Additional Information: The programme is open to citizens who are also residents of Afghanistan, Kazakhstan, Kyrgyzstan, Mongolia, Tajikistan, Turkmenistan or Uzbekistan.

CENTRAL INTELLIGENCE AGENCY (CIA)

Office of Public Affairs, Washington, DC 20505,
United States of America
Tel: (1) 402 0623
Fax: (1) 482 1739
Website: www.cia.gov

The Central Intelligence Agency (CIA) is an agency exclusively devoted to the business of intelligence. The CIA engages in research, development and deployment of technology for intelligence purposes.

CIA Graduate Studies Program Scholarship

Subjects: International affairs, languages, economics, geography, cartography, physical sciences and engineering.
Purpose: To offer programmes that relate to the respective college major.
Eligibility: Open to candidates who are US citizens.
Level of Study: Postgraduate
Type: Scholarship
Value: Varies
Frequency: Annual
Country of Study: United States of America
Application Procedure: See the website.
Closing Date: November 1st
Funding: Government

CENTRAL QUEENSLAND UNIVERSITY

Office of Research, Building 351, Central Queensland University,
Rockhampton, QLD 4700, Australia
Tel: (61) 07 4923 2607
Fax: (61) 07 4923 2600
Email: research-enquiries@cqu.edu.au
Website: www.research.cqu.edu.au

The Central Queensland University (CQU) is committed to excellence in research and innovation with a particular emphasis on issues that affect the region. CQU achieves relevance in its research goals through linkages with industry, business, government and the community and through collaboration with national and international researchers and research networks. CQU provides a range of exciting and relevant research opportunities for Masters and PhD candidates and is committed to excellence and quality in the research training experience of its candidates.

Central Queensland University Postgraduate Research Award

Subjects: Any subject.
Purpose: For the higher research degree programs of Masters and PhD.
Eligibility: Open to citizens or permanent residents of Australia and New Zealand.
Level of Study: Graduate, Postgraduate
Type: Research award
Value: Australian $19,616 per year
Frequency: Annual
Study Establishment: Central Queensland University
Country of Study: Australia
No. of awards offered: 7
Application Procedure: Check website for further details.
Closing Date: October 31st
Funding: Government
Additional Information: This scholarship is paid fortnightly for the period of 2 years (Masters) or 3 years (PhD). Open for applications from July 1st.

For further information contact:

Office of Research, Building 351, Central Queensland University,
Rockhampton, QLD 4700, Australia
Tel: (61) 07 4923 2607

Fax: (61) 07 4923 2600
Website: www.research.cqu.edu.au/FCWViewer/view.do?page = 297
Contact: Kerry Hand, Executive Office

CQU/Industry Collaborative Grants Scheme
Subjects: Any subject.
Purpose: To encourage active research collaboration between the university and eligible industry partners.
Eligibility: Open for candidates who are full-time members of staff (either individuals or teams) and are able to demonstrate through their track record that they have the capability to successfully complete the proposed project.
Type: Grant
Value: Up to Australian $10,000 is tenable for 1 year, commencing 1 January and ending 31 December
Length of Study: 12 months
Study Establishment: Central Queensland University
Country of Study: Australia
Application Procedure: Applications must be submitted on the current application form, in the required format with the required number of copies. One original application, and one identical copy must be submitted in hard copy, and one copy must be submitted electronically, either as a word or pdf document.
Closing Date: August 11

For further information contact:

Bldg 351, Rockhampton (City) Campus, Rockhampton, Australia
Tel: (61) 4923 2601
Fax: (61) 4923 2600
Email: l.walker@cqu.edu.au
Contact: Leslie Walker, Grants and Industry Liaison Officer

Merit Grants Scheme
Subjects: Any subject.
Purpose: To provide opportunities for individuals or groups with well established or developing track records in research to initiate high quality research projects.
Eligibility: Members of the full-time staff of the University with a proven research record 'relative to opportunity' are eligible to compete for Merit Research Grants. Candidates must not be absent for a period exceeding eight weeks during the proposed period of grant. A researcher may be in receipt of only one Merit Grant at any one time.
Type: Grant
Value: Australian $10,000–30,000
Length of Study: 1 year
Study Establishment: Central Queensland University
Country of Study: Australia
Application Procedure: Applications must be submitted on the current application form, in the required format, and with the required number of copies.
Funding: Government
Additional Information: A researcher may be in receipt of only one Merit Grant at any one time.

For further information contact:

Office of Research, Bldg 351, Rockhampton (City) Campus, Rockhampton, Australia
Tel: (61) 4923 2601
Fax: (61) 4923 2600
Email: l.walker@cqu.edu.au
Contact: Leslie Walker, Grants and Industry Liaison Officer

RAAS Postdoctoral Award
Subjects: Any subject.
Purpose: To provide for the university's intellectual environment by facilitating mentoring, team building, and career development in areas of current or future research strength.
Eligibility: The applicant must remain based on a Central Queensland University campus (excluding international campuses) for the duration of the award.
Level of Study: Postdoctorate
Type: Award
Value: On-costs of 28 per cent will be paid in addition to salary
Frequency: Annual
Study Establishment: Central Queensland University

Country of Study: Australia
Application Procedure: Applications must be submitted on the current application form, in the required format, and with the required number of copies.
Funding: Government
Additional Information: Applicants may seek funding for 1, 2, or 3 years.

For further information contact:

Bldg 351, Rockhampton (City) Campus, Rockhampton, Australia
Tel: (61) 4923 2601
Fax: (61) 4923 2600
Email: l.walker@cqu.edu.au
Contact: Leslie Walker, Grants and Industry Liaison Officer

Seed Grants Scheme
Subjects: Any subject.
Purpose: To provide seed funding to encourage new research-trained staff to undertake a funded research project.
Eligibility: Open to newly trained researchers, who are currently within the first 5 years of academic or other research-related performance allowing uninterrupted, stable research development following completion of their postgraduate research training.
Level of Study: Research
Type: Grant
Value: Up to Australian $10,000
Length of Study: 1 year
Study Establishment: Central Queensland University
Country of Study: Australia
Application Procedure: Applications must be submitted on the current application form, in the required format, and with the required number of copies.
Closing Date: August 11
Funding: Government

For further information contact:

Office of Research, Bldg 351, Rockhampton (City) Campus, Rockhampton, Australia
Tel: (61) 4923 2601
Fax: (61) 4923 2600
Email: l.walker@cqu.edu.au
Contact: Leslie Walker, Grants and Industry Liaison Officer

CENTRE FOR ASIA-PACIFIC INITIATIVES (CAPI)

University of Victoria, 131 Murray and Anne Fraser Building,
PO Box 1700, Victoria, BC, V8W 2Y2, Canada
Tel: (1) 250 721 7020
Fax: (1) 250 721 3107
Email: capi@uvic.ca
Website: www.capi.uvic.ca

The Centre for Asia-Pacific Initiatives (CAPI) was established in 1987 as an important element of the University of Victoria's (Canada) plan to expand and strengthen its links with universities and other institutions in the Asia Pacific region, especially with China, Japan, Southeast Asia, Korea and the developing island states of the Southwest Pacific.

CAPI Student Fellowship for Thesis Research
Subjects: Languages and research on the Asia-Pacific region.
Purpose: To encourage excellence in research and in the study of languages and research of the Asia-Pacific region.
Eligibility: Open to Canadian citizens or landed immigrants who are working towards a Master's degree or PhD.
Level of Study: Graduate, Research
Type: Fellowships
Value: Canadian $2,000
Length of Study: 1 year
Frequency: Annual
Study Establishment: Centre for Asia-Pacific Initiatives

Application Procedure: Applicants must submit their curriculum vitae, a 2-page description of the proposed research project and activities, plus a letter of support from the faculty supervisor.
Closing Date: February 29th

CENTRE FOR THE HISTORY OF SCIENCE, TECHNOLOGY AND MEDICINE (CHSTM)

Simon Building, Oxford Road. The University of Manchester, Manchester, M13 9PL, England
Tel: (44) 16 306 6000
Email: chstm@manchester.ac.uk
Website: www.manchester.ac.uk/chstm

The Centre for the History of Science, Technology and Medicine (CHSTM) maintains teaching and research programmes of the highest standards. It acts as a focus for the history of science, technology and medicine in the northwest of England. CHSTM houses a Welcome Unit for the History of Medicine and the National Archive for the History of Computing.

AHRC Studentships
Subjects: The history of science, technology and medicine.
Purpose: To support students working for their MSc and/or PhD in the history of science, technology and medicine.
Level of Study: Doctorate, Postgraduate
Type: Studentship
Length of Study: 1 and/or 3 years
Frequency: Annual
Study Establishment: CHSTM
Country of Study: United Kingdom
Application Procedure: The AHRB deadline is May 1st. In order to ensure completion of paperwork and prompt submission of applications, the CHSTM deadline for AHRB forms is April 12th. We expect to work closely with applicants as they complete the forms, so early contact with CHSTM staff is advisable.
Closing Date: March 14th
Funding: Government
Contributor: Arts and Humanities Research Council

Wellcome Trust Studentships
Subjects: The history of medicine.
Purpose: To support applicants whose main interests are in the history of medicine.
Level of Study: Doctorate, Graduate, Postgraduate, Research
Type: Studentship
Value: Currently ranging from £16,853–18,580
Frequency: Annual
Study Establishment: CHSTM
Country of Study: United Kingdom
No. of awards offered: 5 per year
Application Procedure: Applicants must complete the university application form (with two references), the Wellcome Trust Studentship application form and submit a curriculum vitae and samples of written work.
Closing Date: May 1st each year
Funding: Foundation
Contributor: Wellcome Trust
Additional Information: Applicants are encouraged to discuss their application informally with Professor Michael Worboys and to submit their applications as soon as possible.

CERIES (CENTRE DE RECHERCHES ET D'INVESTIGATIONS EPIDERMIQUES ET SENSORIELLES)

20 rue Victor Noir, 92200, Neuilly-sur-Seine, France
Tel: (33) 146 434 900
Fax: (33) 146 434 600
Email: contact@ceries.com
Website: www.ceries.com

CERIES (Centre de Recherches et d'Investigations Epidermiques et Sensorielles or Centre for Epidermal and Sensory Research and Investigation) is the healthy skin research centre of Chanel.

CERIES Research Award
Subjects: The biology and physiology of healthy skin and/or its reactions to environmental factors.
Purpose: To honour a scientific researcher for a fundamental or clinical research project in the field of healthy skin.
Eligibility: There are no eligibility restrictions.
Level of Study: Research
Value: €40,000
Length of Study: 2 years
Frequency: Annual
Country of Study: Any country
Application Procedure: Applicants must consult the website.
Closing Date: June 1st
Funding: Private
Contributor: Chanel
No. of awards given last year: 1
No. of applicants last year: 26

For further information contact:

CE.R.I.E.S. Research Award, 20 rue Victor Noir, 92521 NEUILLY sur Seine Cedex, FRANCE
Contact: Claire BERNIN-JUNG / Marie-Hélène LAIR

CERN EUROPEAN LABORATORY FOR PARTICLE PHYSICS

Human Resources Division, CH-1211 Geneva 23, Switzerland
Tel: (41) 22 767 2735
Fax: (41) 22 767 2750
Email: recruitment.service@cern.ch
Website: www.cern.ch
Contact: Administrative Assistant

CERN European Laboratory for Particle Physics is the world's leading laboratory in its field, that being the study of the smallest constituents of matter and of the forces that hold them together. The laboratory's tools are its particle accelerators and detectors, which are among the largest and most complex scientific instruments ever built.

CERN Summer Student Programme
Subjects: Physics, computing and engineering.
Purpose: To awaken the interest of undergraduates in CERN's activities by offering them hands-on experience during their long summer vacation.
Eligibility: Open to all interested students who have completed at least 3 years of full-time studies at university level.
Value: Travel allowance and a daily stipend
Length of Study: 8–13 weeks
Study Establishment: CERN
Country of Study: Switzerland
Application Procedure: A completed application and curriculum vitae along with 2 references must be submitted to CERN.
Closing Date: January 31st

For further information contact:

CERN Recruitment Services via the e-recruitment system
Email: jkrich@umich.edu

CERN Technical Student Programme
Subjects: Accelerator physics, computing, mathematics, engineering, geotechnics, instrumentation for accelerators and particle physics experiments, low temperature physics and superconductivity, materials science, radiation protection, environmental and safety engineering, solid state, surface physics and ultra-high vacuum.
Purpose: To provide placements for students who are specializing in different technical fields.

Eligibility: Open to applicants attending an educational establishment in a CERN member state and following a full-time course in one of the subjects listed, at university or advanced technical level. Students must be less than 30 years of age at the time of the Selection Committee meeting. Candidates must be nationals of the member states of CERN. Students specializing in theoretical or experimental particle physics are not eligible for the programme.

Value: A subsistence allowance of Swiss franc 3,164 per month to cover the expenses of a single person in the Geneva area and medical costs arising from illnesses and accidents of a professional and non-professional nature. Travel expenses equivalent to a second class return rail fare to Geneva for one person may be paid

Length of Study: Appointments can last for 6 consecutive months, but mostly 1 year. Appointments can start throughout the year

Study Establishment: The European Laboratory for Particle Physics

Country of Study: Switzerland

No. of awards offered: Approx. 80–90

Application Procedure: Applications must be made electronically via the website.

Closing Date: March 14th

Funding: Government

No. of awards given last year: Approx. 80–90

No. of applicants last year: Approx. 240

Additional Information: The official languages of CERN are English and French. A good knowledge of at least one of these languages is essential. CERN member states include Austria, Belgium, Bulgaria, the Czech Republic, Denmark, Finland, France, Germany, Greece, Hungary, Italy, the Netherlands, Norway, Poland, Portugal, Slovakia Republic, Spain, Sweden, Switzerland and the United Kingdom.

CERN-Japan Fellowship Programme

Purpose: To support young researchers who are interested in LHC data analysis and physics studies.

Eligibility: The schlorship open either to scientists who are nationals of Asian countries or who wish to spend a fraction of the year at CERN, or to researchers at CERN who are nationals of a CERN Member State and who wish to spend part of the year at a Japanese laboratory.

Level of Study: Doctorate

Type: Fellowship

Value: Covers travel expense and insurance coverage

Length of Study: Up to 3 years

Frequency: Annual

Application Procedure: A completed electronic application form along with a curriculum vitae should be submitted.

Closing Date: December 1st

Contributor: CERN

For further information contact:

Recruitment Service, Human Resource Department, CERN, Geneva 23, CH-1211, Switzerland

Email: recruitment.science@cern.ch

Marie Curie Fellowships for Early Stage Training at CERN

Subjects: Scientific training.

Purpose: To offer structured scientific and/or technological training and to encourage participants to take up long-term research careers.

Eligibility: Open to researchers in the first 4 years of their research activity. Persons who have obtained a doctorate are ineligible.

Study Establishment: CERN

Application Procedure: Candidates should register and apply for the Marie Curie Fellowship programme using the CERN e-recruitment system.

Contributor: European Comission

For further information contact:

Please contact the Recruitment Service

Email: recruitment.service@cern.ch

THE CHARLES AND ANNE MORROW LINDBERGH FOUNDATION

2150 Third Avenue North, Suite 310, Anoka, MN 55303-2200, United States of America
Tel: (1) 763 576 1596
Fax: (1) 763 576 1664
Email: info@lindberghfoundation.org
Website: www.lindberghfoundation.org
Contact: Ms Shelley Nehl, Grants Administrator

Charles and Anne Morrow Lindbergh believed that balancing technology and the environment was vital to sustaining a healthy quality of life. The Lindbergh Foundation is committed to putting balance into action by giving research grants and awards to individuals whose scientific and educational innovations address important environmental issues around the world.

Lindbergh Grants

Subjects: Agriculture, aviation, aerospace, conservation of natural resources including animal plant and water resources,general conservation including land, air, energy etc., education including humanities/education, the arts and intercultural communication, exploration, health including biomedical research, health and population sciences, adaptive technologies and waste minimizaton and management.

Purpose: To support innovative projects that foster the environment and keep the planet in balance.

Eligibility: Lindbergh Grants are awarded to individuals for research or public education projects, not affiliated to organizations for institutional programs. The Foundation does not provide support for overhead costs of organizations, tuition or scholarships. The Foundation welcomes candidates who may or may not be afiiliated with an academic, non-profit or for-profit organization. Candidates for grants are not required to hold any graduate or postgraduate academic degrees. The Lindbergh Grants Program is international in scope. All letters, applications, endorsers reports, and required progress and final reports must be submitted in English.

Level of Study: Unrestricted

Type: Grant

Value: Up to $10,580

Length of Study: 1 year, but in exceptional cases up to 2 years

Frequency: Annual

Country of Study: Any country

No. of awards offered: Approx.8–10

Application Procedure: Applications must be submitted according to the relevant guidelines. Seven copies of the application by mail and one pdf by email must be sent to the Foundation's office.

Closing Date: The second Thursday in June

Funding: Foundation, individuals

No. of awards given last year: 10

No. of applicants last year: 166

Additional Information: Please check the Foundation's website www.lindberghfoundation.org for further information.

CHARLES BABBAGE INSTITUTE (CBI)

University of Minnesota 222 21st Avenue, Minneapolis, MN, 55455, United States of America
Tel: (1) 612 624 5050
Fax: (1) 612 625 8054
Email: yostx003@umn.edu
Website: www.cbi.umn.edu
Contact: Jeffrey Yost, CBI Assoc. Director

The Charles Babbage Institute (CBI) is a research centre dedicated to promoting the study of the history of computing, its impact on society and preserving relevant documentation. CBI fosters research and writing in the history of computing by providing fellowship support, archival resources and information to scholars, computer scientists and the general public.

Adelle and Erwin Tomash Fellowship in the History of Information Processing

Subjects: The history of computing and information processing.

Purpose: To advance the professional development of historians in the field.

Eligibility: Open to graduate students whose dissertations deal with a historical aspect of information processing. Priority will be given to students who have completed all requirements for the doctoral degree except the research and writing of the dissertation.
Level of Study: Doctorate
Type: Fellowship
Value: US$14,000 stipend, plus up to an additional $2,000 for tuition, fees, travel to the Babbage Institute, and other approved research expenses
Length of Study: 1 year
Frequency: Annual
Country of Study: Any country
No. of awards offered: 1
Application Procedure: Applicants must send their curriculum vitae, a five page statement and justification of the research problem, and a discussion of methods, research materials and evidence of faculty support for the project. Applicants should also arrange for three letters of reference and certified transcripts of graduate school credits to be sent directly to the Institute.
Closing Date: January 15th
Funding: Private

For further information contact:

Charles Babbage Institute University of Minnesota 103 Walter Library 117 Pleasant Street, SE, Minneapolis, MN 55455
Tel: 624-5050
Fax: 625-8054
Email: cbi@tx.umn.edu
Contact: Associative Director

CHARLES DARWIN UNIVERSITY (CDU)

Darwin, NT, 0909, Australia
Tel: (61) 8 8946 6868
Fax: (61) 8 8946 7199
Email: bob.wasson@cdu.edu.au
Website: www.cdu.edu.au
Contact: Professor Robert Wasson, Deputy Vice Chancellor (Research)

The Charles Darwin University (CDU) offers programmes from certificate level to PhD, incorporating the full range of vocational education courses. CDU has a distinctive research profile, reflecting the priorities appropriate to its location. It is a participating member of several CRCs.

ARC Australian Postgraduate Award – Industry
Subjects: Indigenous and developing country problems and opportunities.
Purpose: To identify and quantify the current patterns of natural resource use in livelihood strategies, to analyze the constraints to, and opportunities for, natural resource management and natural product enterprise development, and to identify strategies based on natural resources that will lead to livelihood improvement.
Eligibility: Open to the Australian or New Zealand citizens who have an Honours IIA Degree or equivalent in a relevant discipline.
Level of Study: Postgraduate
Type: Scholarship
Value: $26,140 as well as relocation and thesis production allowance
Length of Study: 3 years
Application Procedure: Check website for further details.
Closing Date: October 31st
Additional Information: For general university information and scholarship application forms, contact Research Degrees and Scholarships Officer. Email: research@cdu.edu.au

For further information contact:

Tel: 08 8946 6548 (Int. +61 8 8946 6548)
Email: bruce.campbell@cdu.edu.au
Contact: Professor Bruce Campbell

CHARLES STURT UNIVERSITY (CSU)

Locked Bag 588, Wagga Wagga,
NSW 2678, Australia
Tel: (61) 02 6933 2000
Fax: (61) 02 6933 2639
Email: inquiry@csu.edu.au
Website: www.csu.edu.au

CSU is one of the leading Australian universities for graduate employment and largest provider in distance education. Utilizing our expertise in distance education, CSU provides educational opportunities to students around the world. Around 36,000 students undertake their choice of study with CSU on one of our campuses, from home, their workplace or anywhere around the globe.

Charles Sturt University Postgraduate Research Studentships (CSUPRS)
Eligibility: Open to the candidates who hold or expect to hold, at least a Bachelor degree with upper second class honours or a qualification deemed equivalent.
Level of Study: Graduate, Research
Type: Studentship
Frequency: Annual
No. of awards offered: Up to 8
Application Procedure: Scholarship application form can be downloaded from the website. Send in the filled application to the center with original referee report and five copies of their report.
Closing Date: October 30th
Additional Information: Offers of scholarships cannot be made to candidates until their enrolment as Research Higher Degree students has been approved by the Board of Graduate Studies.

For further information contact:

Postgraduate Scholarships, Center for Research & Graduate Training, Charles Sturt University, Locked Bag 588, Wagga Wagga, NSW 2678, Australia
Tel: (61) 02 6933 4162
Email: pgscholars@csu.edu.au

THE CHARLIE TROTTER CULINARY EDUCATION FOUNDATION

816 West Armitage, Chicago, IL 60614,
United States of America
Tel: (1) 773 248 6228
Fax: (1) 773 248 6088
Email: info@charlietrotters.com
Website: www.charlietrotters.com/about/foundation.asp

Charlie Trotter's is regarded as one of the finest restaurants in the world, dedicated to excellence in the culinary arts. It has been instrumental in establishing new standards for fine dining. Its main goal is to educate and expose the youth to the great culinary arts in as many ways as possible. The Charlie Trotter Culinary Education Foundation, a non-profit organization, has been established to promote culinary arts among youth. The foundation is involved in awarding scholarships to students who are seeking careers in the culinary arts and working with Chicago-area youth to promote the enthusiastic quest for education as well as an interest in the cooking and food.

Charlie Trotter's Culinary Education Foundation Culinary Study Scholarship
Subjects: Cooking.
Eligibility: Open to an Illinois resident at the time of application.
Type: Scholarship
Value: US $5,000 cash scholarship for a pre-enrolled student
Length of Study: 1 year
Frequency: Annual
Country of Study: United States of America
Application Procedure: Check website for further details.
Closing Date: June 30th
Funding: Foundation, private
Contributor: Charlie Trotter's

CHEMICAL HERITAGE FOUNDATION (CHF)

315 Chestnut Street, Philadelphia, PA 19106-2702, United States of America
Tel: (1) 215 873 8269
Fax: (1) 215 629 5269
Email: fellowships@chemheritage.org
Website: www.chemheritage.org
Contact: Fellowship Co-ordinator

The Beckman Center for the History of Chemistry is the historical unit of the Chemical Heritage Foundation (CHF), which is located in Philadelphia. The Center is devoted to preserving, making known and applying the history of the chemical and molecular science technologies and associated industries.

Charles C Price Fellowship

Subjects: History of chemical sciences and technologies.
Purpose: To fund scholars who are pursuing research.
Eligibility: Open to scholars pursuing research on the history of the chemical sciences; preference given to projects in the history of polymers.
Level of Study: Doctorate, Postdoctorate
Type: Fellowship
Value: US$20,000
Length of Study: 9 months
Frequency: Annual
Study Establishment: Chemical Heritage Foundation
Country of Study: United States of America
No. of awards offered: 1
Application Procedure: Applications along with two letters of reference have to be sent directly to CHF and postmarked by the deadline. Printed materials should be sent to the fellowships coordinator and/or faxed to 215-629-5269.
Closing Date: February 15th
Funding: Private
No. of awards given last year: 1

Glenn E and Barbara Hodsdon Ullyot Scholarship

Subjects: The history of science.
Purpose: To advance understanding of the importance of the chemical sciences to the public's welfare.
Eligibility: To fund students to pursue postgraduate research.
Level of Study: Doctorate, Postdoctorate, Postgraduate
Type: Scholarship
Value: US$4,500
Length of Study: A minimum of 2 months
Frequency: Annual
Study Establishment: Chemical Heritage Foundation
Country of Study: United States of America
No. of awards offered: 1
Application Procedure: Applications along with two letters of reference have to be sent directly to CHF and postmarked by the deadline. Printed materials should be sent to the fellowships coordinator and/or faxed to 215-629-5269.
Closing Date: February 15th
Funding: Private
No. of awards given last year: 1
Additional Information: Applications are invited from scholars, science writers and journalists.

Gordon Cain Fellowship

Subjects: The history of the development of the chemical industry. The outcome of the research should further the understanding of the relationship between technology, policy, management and entrepreneurship and should shed light on the complex development of modern society and commerce.
Purpose: To support historical research on the development of the chemical industries.
Eligibility: Open to a scholar with a PhD who will carry out historical research on the development of chemical industries.
Level of Study: Postgraduate
Type: Fellowship
Value: US$43,000

Length of Study: 9 months
Frequency: Annual
Study Establishment: Chemical Heritage Foundation
Country of Study: United States of America
Application Procedure: Applications along with two letters of reference have to be sent directly to CHF and postmarked by the deadline. Printed materials should be sent to the fellowships coordinator and/or faxed to 215-629-5269.
Closing Date: February 15th
Funding: Private
No. of awards given last year: 1
Additional Information: The Fellow will be required to organize a one day conference at CHF.

John C. Hass Fellowship

Subjects: Chemical industries in relation to societal, environmental, health and safety issues.
Purpose: To enhance public understanding of the role of the chemical industries in relation to environmental, societal, health, and safety issues.
Eligibility: Open to PhD scholars whose research will enhance public understanding of the chemical industries.
Level of Study: Doctorate, Postdoctorate
Type: Fellowship
Value: US$43,000
Length of Study: 9 months
Frequency: Annual
Study Establishment: Chemical Heritage Foundation
Country of Study: United States of America
No. of awards offered: 2
Application Procedure: Applications along with two letters of reference have to be sent directly to CHF and postmarked by the deadline. Printed materials should be sent to the fellowships coordinator and/or faxed to 215-629-5269.
Closing Date: February 15th
Funding: Foundation
No. of awards given last year: 2

Robert W. Allington Fellowship

Subjects: History of the chemical sciences and technologies.
Purpose: To fund scholars who are pursuing research on history of the chemical and molecular sciences, technologies, and industries.
Eligibility: Open to scholars pursuing research on the history of the chemical sciences.
Level of Study: Postdoctorate
Type: Fellowship
Value: US$43,000
Length of Study: 9 months
Frequency: Annual
Study Establishment: Chemical Heritage Foundation
No. of awards offered: 1
Application Procedure: Applicants must visit the website for details on application procedure.
Closing Date: February 15th
Funding: Private

Robert W. Gore Fellowship

Subjects: Contemporary issues in the chemical and molecular sciences and technologies, their industrial linkages, and related policy topics through historical perspective.
Purpose: To conduct historical case studies of materials innovation of the past 30 years and to communicate findings to academic, policy, and industrial audiences.
Eligibility: Open to advanced PhD candidates with the research expertise, writing skills and technical background to conduct case studies.
Level of Study: Doctorate, Postdoctorate
Type: Fellowship
Value: US$35,000
Length of Study: 1 year
Frequency: Annual
Study Establishment: Chemical Heritage Foundation
Country of Study: United States of America
No. of awards offered: 1

Application Procedure: Applications along with two letters of reference have to be sent directly to CHF and postmarked by the deadline. Printed materials should be sent to the fellowships coordinator and/or faxed to 215-629-5269.
Closing Date: February 15th
Funding: Foundation
No. of awards given last year: 1
Additional Information: The Gore fellow will undertake one case study to be published by CHF. The case study will be about material innovations since 1980.

Roy G. Neville Fellowship
Subjects: The history of science.
Purpose: To study the history of science.
Eligibility: Open to historians of science, technology and allied fields, as well as to historians of book and print culture, bibliographers and librarians, who will make use of the Roy G. Neville Historical Chemical Library.
Level of Study: Doctorate, Postdoctorate, Postgraduate
Type: Fellowship
Value: US$3,000
Length of Study: A minimum of 3 months
Frequency: Annual
Study Establishment: Chemical Heritage Foundation
Country of Study: United States of America
No. of awards offered: 1
Application Procedure: Applications along with two letters of reference have to be sent directly to CHF and postmarked by the deadline. Printed materials should be sent to the fellowships coordinator and/or faxed to 215-629-5269.
Closing Date: February 15th
Funding: Private
No. of awards given last year: 2

Société de Chimie Industrielle (American Section) Fellowship
Subjects: The history of science.
Purpose: To stimulate public understanding of the chemical industries, using both terms in their widest sense.
Eligibility: Applications are encouraged from writers, journalists, educators and historians of science, technology and business.
Level of Study: Postdoctorate, Doctorate, Postgraduate
Type: Fellowship
Value: US$15,000
Length of Study: A minimum of 3 months
Frequency: Annual
Study Establishment: Chemical Heritage Foundation
Country of Study: United States of America
No. of awards offered: 1
Application Procedure: Applications along with two letters of reference have to be sent directly to CHF and postmarked by the deadline. Printed materials should be sent to the fellowships coordinator and/or faxed to 215-629-5269.
Closing Date: February 15th
Funding: Private
No. of awards given last year: 1
Additional Information: Multimedia, popular book projects and Web-based projects are encouraged.

Sydney M. Edelstein Fellowship
Subjects: History of chemical sciences and technologies.
Purpose: To fund scholars who are pursuing research on the history of the chemical and molecular sciences, technologies, and industries.
Eligibility: Open to scholars pursuing research on the history of the chemical sciences.
Level of Study: Doctorate, Postdoctorate
Type: Fellowship
Value: US$43,000
Length of Study: 9 months
Frequency: Annual
Study Establishment: Chemical Heritage Fund
No. of awards offered: 1
Application Procedure: Applicants must visit the website for details on application procedure.

Closing Date: February 15th
Funding: Private

THE CHEMICAL INSTITUTE OF CANADA

Suite 550, 130 Slater Street, Ottawa,
ON, K1P 6E2, Canada
Tel: (1) 613 232 6252 ext 223
Fax: (1) 613 232 5862
Email: awards@cheminst.ca
Website: www.cheminst.ca
Contact: Gale Thirlwall, Awards Manager

The Chemical Institute of Canada (CIC) is the umbrella organization for three Constituent Societies - the Canadian Society for Chemistry (CSC), the Canadian Society for Chemical Engineering (CSChE) and the Canadian Society for Chemical Technology (CSCT). The CIC establishes strategic direction and identifies synergies in matters of common interest to the Constituent Societies, to enhance the image of the chemical sciences and engineering with all sectors of the public and to deliver common services to individual members.

CIC Award for Chemical Education
Subjects: Chemistry and chemical engineering.
Purpose: To recognize a person who has made outstanding contributions in Canada to education at the post-secondary level in the field of chemistry or chemical engineering.
Level of Study: Professional development
Type: Award
Value: A framed scroll, a cash prize of Canadian $1,000 and up to Canadian $400 for travel expenses
Frequency: Annual
Country of Study: Canada
No. of awards offered: 1
Application Procedure: Applicants must be nominated. The applicant should submit a curriculum vitae with letters of support and the CIC nomination.
Closing Date: July 2nd
Funding: Private
Contributor: CIC Chemical Education Fund
No. of awards given last year: 1

CIC Catalysis Award
Subjects: Chemistry/chemical engineering.
Purpose: To recognize an individual who has made a distinguished contribution to the field of catalysis while resident in Canada.
Level of Study: Research
Type: Award
Value: A rhodium-plated silver medal and travel expenses to present the Award Lecture
Frequency: Every 2 years
Country of Study: Canada
No. of awards offered: 1
Application Procedure: Applicants must be nominated. They should submit (1) nomination form, (2) curriculum vitae, (3) bio and citation, (4) letters of support.
Closing Date: October 1st (odd years only)
Funding: Foundation
Contributor: Catalysis Foundation

CIC Macromolecular Science and Engineering Lecture Award
Subjects: Macromolecular science and engineering
Purpose: To recognize an individual who has made a distinguished contribution to macromolecular science or engineering.
Level of Study: Research
Type: Award
Value: A framed scroll, a cash prize, and travel expenses
Frequency: Annual
Country of Study: Canada
No. of awards offered: 1
Application Procedure: Applicants must be nominated. The applicant must submit a nomination form, curriculum vitae, bio and citation and letters of support.

Closing Date: July 2nd
Funding: Private
Contributor: NOVA Chemicals Limited
No. of awards given last year: 1

CIC Medal

Subjects: Chemistry, chemical engineering and chemical technology.
Purpose: To recognize a person who has made an outstanding contribution to the science of chemistry or chemical engineering in Canada.
Level of Study: Research
Type: Award
Value: A medal and travel expenses
Frequency: Annual
Country of Study: Canada
No. of awards offered: 1
Application Procedure: Applicants must be nominated. The applicant must submit (1) nomination form, (2) curriculum vitae, (3) bio and citation, (4) letters of support.
Closing Date: July 2nd
Funding: Private
No. of awards given last year: 1

CIC Montreal Medal

Subjects: Chemistry, chemical engineering and chemical technology.
Purpose: To honour a person who has shown significant leadership in or outstanding contribution to the profession of chemistry or chemical engineering in Canada.
Eligibility: Open to administrative contributions within the Chemical Institute of Canada and other professional organizations that contribute to the advancement of the professions of chemistry and chemical engineering. Contributions to the sciences of chemistry and chemical engineering are not considered. Administrative contributions to the CIC, contributions by chemical educators and by staff members of chemical industries and single individual exploits which contribute to the advancement of the chemical profession.
Type: Award
Value: A medal and travel expenses if required
Frequency: Annual
Country of Study: Canada
No. of awards offered: 1
Application Procedure: Applicants must be nominated. The applicant must submit an application form, curriculum vitae, bio and citation and letters of support.
Closing Date: July 2nd
Funding: Private
Contributor: Montréal CIC Local Section
No. of awards given last year: 1

CSCT Norman and Marion Bright Memorial Award

Subjects: Chemical technology.
Purpose: To reward an individual who has made an outstanding contribution in Canada to the furtherance of chemical technology.
Eligibility: Open to chemical sciences technologists or persons from outside the field who have made significant or noteworthy contributions to its advancement. May be either a chemical sciences technologist or a person from outside the field who has made a significant and noteworthy contribution to its advancement.
Type: Award
Value: An engraved medallion, together with an honorarium of $500
Frequency: Annual
Country of Study: Canada
No. of awards offered: 1
Application Procedure: Applicants must complete a nomination form and submit alongside it (1) a curriculum vitae, (2) a bio and citation and (3) letters of support.
Closing Date: December 1st
Funding: Trusts
Contributor: Norman and Marion Bright Trust Fund
Additional Information: Award winners are welcome to submit papers at either the CSC or CSChE conferences.

CHIANG CHING KUO FOUNDATION FOR INTERNATIONAL SCHOLARLY EXCHANGE

13F, 65 Tun Hwa South Road Sector 2, Taipei, 106-ROC, Taiwan
Tel: (886) 2 2704 5333
Fax: (886) 2 2701 6762
Email: cckf@ms1.hinet.net
Website: www.cckf.org

The Chiang Ching Kuo Foundation for International Scholarly Exchange is a non-profit organization headquartered in Taipei, the capital of the Republic of China. The Foundation was established in 1989 in honour of the late President Chiang Ching kuo. The main objective of the Foundation is to promote the study of Chinese culture and society, broadly defined.

Chiang Ching Kuo Foundation Doctoral Fellowships

Subjects: Chinese studies in the field of humanities and social sciences.
Purpose: To financially support Doctoral candidates while writing their dissertations.
Eligibility: Open to applicants who have completed all other requirements for their PhD degree except the dissertation. Candidates must not be employed or receive grants from other sources.
Level of Study: Doctorate
Type: Fellowships
Value: Up to US$15,000
Frequency: Annual
Application Procedure: Applicants need to submit a 1 page summary of the proposed project, budget, curriculum vitae and detailed description of the proposed project along with the application form. Application forms are available online.
Closing Date: October 15th
Funding: Commercial, private

Chiang Ching Kuo Foundation for International Scholarly Exchange Publication Subsidies

Subjects: Academic works, periodicals, and journals.
Purpose: To assist in the final stages of publishing academic works.
Eligibility: Open to scholars in the final stages of publishing academic works. Applications from scholars affiliated with institutions in Taiwan must involve cooperation with one or more scholars from other countries. Applicants for publication subsidies must be affiliated with a university or other academic institution.
Type: Grant
Value: New Taiwan $1,000,000, for periodicals and journals, the Foundation will support the publication of 2 issues, however, the Foundation will not fund an inaugural issue
Application Procedure: Applicants must use the application forms provided directly from the Foundation Secretariat. Three copies of the application and supporting documents must be submitted by registered mail to the Secretariat. In addition, electronic version of all application materials must be enclosed on diskette or sent as e-mail attachment to: cckf@ms1.hinet.net with heading "Application Materials from (Name)" in the header of the message.
Closing Date: September 15th (for conferences and publications from January–June) and February 15th (for conferences and publications from July–December)
Funding: Trusts

Chiang Ching–Kuo Foundation for Scholarly Exchange Eminent Scholar Lectureship

Subjects: Any subject.
Purpose: To sponsor eminent foreign scholars to come to Taiwan to take up lectureships or positions as visiting scholars.
Eligibility: Open to eminent scholars invited by universities or academic institutions of Taiwan.
Level of Study: Lectureship
Type: Lectureship/Prize
Value: New Taiwan $2,000,000
Length of Study: 1 year
Frequency: Annual
Study Establishment: Universities or academic institutions in Taiwan
Country of Study: Taiwan

Application Procedure: Applicants must use the application forms provided by the Foundation. The application must be sent by registered mail to the Secretariat. Electronic version of all application materials must be enclosed on diskette or sent as e-mail attachment to: cckf@ms1.hinet.net with heading "Application Materials from (Name)" in the header of the message. Applications are accepted from June 1st.
Closing Date: October 15th
Funding: Foundation
Additional Information: Project directors who are currently receiving Foundation aid are ineligible to apply. Project directors may not submit more than one application.

THE CHICAGO TRIBUNE

Tribune Books, 435 North Michigan Avenue, Chicago, IL, 60611, United States of America
Tel: (1) 312 222 4429
Fax: (1) 312 222 3751
Email: jwoelffer@tribune.com
Website: www.chicagotribune.com

The Chicago Tribune is the Midwest's leading newspaper. The Chicago Tribune Literary Awards are part of a continued dedication to readers, writers and ideas.

Nelson Algren Awards
Subjects: Short fiction.
Purpose: To award writers of short fiction.
Eligibility: Submissions must be unpublished, written by an American writer, and within 2,500–10,000 words in length.
Level of Study: Unrestricted
Type: Award
Value: One $5,000 prize and three runner-up prizes of $1,500
Frequency: Annual
Country of Study: Any country
No. of awards offered: 4
Application Procedure: Applicants must send a stamped addressed envelope with a request for written guidelines. The competition will begin accepting entries from November 1st.
Closing Date: March 12th
Funding: Corporation

For further information contact:

Chicago Tribune, Nelson Algren Awards, 435 N. Michigan Avenue, TT200, Chicago, IL 60611

CHILDREN'S LITERATURE ASSOCIATION

PO Box 138, Battle Creek, MI 49016-0138, United States of America
Tel: (1) 269 965 8180
Fax: (1) 269 965 3568
Email: kkiessling@childlitassn.org
Website: www.childlitassn.org
Contact: Ms Kathy Kiessling, Administrator

The Children's Literature Association is an international organization of persons interested in the promotion of scholarship about children's literature. The goals of the association are to enhance the professional stature of the graduate and undergraduate teaching of childrens literature and to encourage serious scholarship and research.

ChLA Beiter Graduate Student Research Grant
Subjects: Children's literature.
Purpose: To fund proposals of original scholarship with the expectation that the undertaking will lead to a publication or a conference presentation and contribute to the field.
Eligibility: Winners must be, or become, members of the Children's Literature Association. Students of the ChLA Executive Board members or Grant Committee members are not eligible to apply. Previous recipients are not eligible to reapply until the third year from the date of the first award.
Level of Study: Graduate

Type: Grant
Value: From US$500–1,500, which may be used to purchase supplies and materials e.g. books and videos, and as research support e.g. photocopying, or to underwrite travel to special collections or libraries
Frequency: Annual
Country of Study: Any country
No. of awards offered: 1–4
Application Procedure: Applicants must send six copies of their contact details including email address, academic institution and status, the expected date of their degree, a detailed description of the research proposal, a curriculum vitae and two letters of reference, one of which must be from the applicant's dissertation or thesis advisor.
Closing Date: February 1st
Funding: Private
No. of awards given last year: 2
No. of applicants last year: 6
Additional Information: Applicants should visit the website for further details. If applicants wish to receive guidelines by mail, a stamped addressed envelope must be provided.

ChLA Faculty Research Grant
Subjects: Children's literature.
Purpose: To award proposals dealing with criticism or original scholarship with the expectation that the undertaking will lead to publication and make a significant contribution to the field of children's literature in the area of scholarship or criticism.
Eligibility: Applicants must be, or become, members of the Children's Literature Association.
Level of Study: Doctorate, Postdoctorate, Postgraduate, Predoctorate, Research
Type: Grant
Value: Up to US$1,500. Individual awards may range US$500–1,500 and may be used only for research-related expenses such as travel to special collections or materials and supplies. Funds are not intended for work leading to the completion of a professional degree
Frequency: Annual
Country of Study: Any country
No. of awards offered: 1–4
Application Procedure: Applicants must send six copies of the application in English and a curriculum vitae. Applications must include the applicant's name, address, telephone number and email address, details of the academic institution the applicant is affiliated with and a detailed description of the research proposal, not exceeding three single spaced pages, and indicating the nature and significance of the project, where it will be carried out and the expected date of completion.
Closing Date: February 1st
Funding: Private
No. of awards given last year: 1
No. of applicants last year: 8
Additional Information: In honour of the achievement and dedication of Dr Margaret P Esmonde, proposals that deal with critical or original work in the areas of science fantasy or science fiction for children or adolescents will be awarded the Margaret P Esmonde Memorial Grant. Applicants should visit the website for further details. If applicants wish to receive guidelines by mail, a stamped addressed envelope must be provided.

THE CHINA SCHOLARSHIP COUNCIL

160 Fuxingmennei Street, Beijing, 100031, China
Tel: (86) 86 10 664 3249
Fax: (86) 86 10 664 3198
Email: webmaster@csc.edu.cn
Website: www.csc.edu.cn

The China Scholarship council (CSC) is a non-profit institution, which is affiliated with the ministry of education. The main objective of the CSC is to develop the educational, scientific and technological, and cultural exchanges and economic and trade cooperation between China and other countries.

The Barbara and Fred Kort Chinese Fellowship Program
Subjects: All subjects.
Eligibility: Open to Chinese scholars who wish to do post-doctoral research at Bar-Ilan university. The candidates should obtain formal approval from the academic supervisors of Bar-Ilan University.
Level of Study: Postdoctorate
Type: Fellowship
Value: US$15,000 per year
Length of Study: 1 year
Frequency: Annual
Study Establishment: Bar-Ilan University
Country of Study: Israel
No. of awards offered: 100 award within 4 years
Application Procedure: The candidates should obtain formal approval from the academic supervisors of Bar-Ilan universtiy.
Funding: Government
Contributor: China Scholarship Council and Bar-Ilan University, Israel

Hang Seng Bank Overseas Scholarships Program
Subjects: All subjects.
Eligibility: The candidates should have been formally offered places by Harvard University or Princeton University.
Type: Scholarships
Value: Tuition fees, textbooks, livings expenses
Length of Study: 2 Years
Frequency: Annual
Study Establishment: Harvard University and Princeton University
Country of Study: United States of America
No. of awards offered: 2
Application Procedure: See the website.
Funding: Government

K C Wong Postgraduate Scholarship Programme
Subjects: All subjects.
Purpose: To support students who intend to study further at King's College London.
Eligibility: Open to applicants who are citizens and permanent residents of People's Republic of china.
Type: Scholarship
Value: UK £8,400
Length of Study: 3 years
Frequency: Annual
Study Establishment: King's College London
Country of Study: United Kingdom
No. of awards offered: Up to 5
Application Procedure: A completed application form, which is available online, must be sent.
Closing Date: March 1st
Funding: Government
Contributor: K C Wong Education Foundation

For further information contact:

Quality Assurance Section King's College London 7.38 James Derk Maxwell Building 57 Waterloo Road, London, SE1 8WA, United Kingdom

Sino-French Training Programme in the Law in Europe
Subjects: French language, law.
Purpose: To provide training in French language and 1 year training in law in Europe.
Eligibility: Open to young teachers and postgraduate students in law.
Type: Scholarship
Value: Living expenses and international airfares
Frequency: Every 2 years
Country of Study: Europe, Germany
No. of awards offered: 10
Application Procedure: A completed application form must be submitted.
Funding: Government
Contributor: French Government and European union

CHINESE AMERICAN MEDICAL SOCIETY (CAMS)

281 Edgewood Avenue, Teaneck, NJ 07666, United States of America
Tel: (1) 201 833 1506
Fax: (1) 201 833 8252
Email: hw5@columbia.edu
Website: www.camsociety.org
Contact: Dr H H Wang, Executive Director

The Chinese American Medical Society (CAMS) is a non-profit, charitable, educational and scientific society that aims to promote the scientific association of medical professionals of Chinese descent. It also aims to advance medical knowledge and scientific research with emphasis on aspects unique to the Chinese and to promote the health status of Chinese Americans. The Society makes scholarships available to medical dental students and provides summer fellowships for students conducting research in health problems related to the Chinese.

CAMS Scholarship
Subjects: Medical or dental studies.
Purpose: To help defray the cost of study.
Eligibility: Open to Chinese Americans, or Chinese students who are residing in the United States of America. Applicants must be full-time medical or dental students at approved schools within the United States of America and must be able to show academic proficiency and financial hardship.
Level of Study: Doctorate
Type: Scholarship
Value: US$1,500–2,500
Frequency: Annual
Country of Study: United States of America
No. of awards offered: 3–5
Application Procedure: Applicants must complete an application form and send it together with a letter for the Dean of Students verifying good standing, two to three letters of recommendation, a personal statement, a curriculum vitae and a financial statement. Application forms can also be downloaded from the website.
Closing Date: April 30th
Funding: Private
Contributor: Membership and fund-raising
No. of awards given last year: 7
No. of applicants last year: 13

For further information contact:

CAMS Scholarship Committee, 41 Elizabeth Street, Suite 403, New York, New York 10013, NY 10013
Tel: (212) 334-4760
Contact: Jerry Huo, M.D. Chairman

CHINOOK REGIONAL CAREER TRANSITIONS FOR YOUTH

3305 18th Avenue North, Lethbridge, AB, T1H 5S1, Canada
Tel: (1) 403 328 3996
Fax: (1) 403 320 2365
Email: mvennard@pallisersd.ab.ca
Website: www.careertransitionsnews.ca

The Chinook regional career transitions for youth aims to improve the school-to-work transitions for students, promoting lifelong learning and coordinating and implementing career development activities and programming for youth.

Alberta Blue Cross 50th Anniversary Scholarships
Subjects: All subjects.
Purpose: To provide financial support.
Eligibility: Open to applicants who are registered Indian, Inuit, or Melis and are residents of Alberta.
Level of Study: Postgraduate
Type: Scholarship
Value: Canadian $375–1,250
Frequency: Annual

Country of Study: Canada
No. of awards offered: 63 awards
Application Procedure: A completed application form must be sent. For further information, see the website www.ab.bluecross.ca
Closing Date: June 1st

For further information contact:

Alberta Scholarship Programs, 9th Floor, 9940-106 Street, Box 28000 Station Main, Edmonton, AB 75J 4R4

Canadian Millenium Excellence Awards
Subjects: Social welfare.
Purpose: To recognize talented Canadians who make positive and significant contributions to the betterment of communities across the country.
Eligibility: Open to applicants who are Canadian citizens.
Level of Study: Professional development
Type: Award
Value: Canadian $4,000–20,000
Frequency: Annual
Country of Study: Canada
No. of awards offered: 931
Application Procedure: More information and application forms are available online.
Closing Date: December 15th

For further information contact:

Canadian Milleniuni Scholarship Foundation, PO Box 1386, Station M, Calgary, AB T2P 2L6

CanWest Global System Broadcasters of the Future Awards
Subjects: Broadcasting.
Purpose: To encourage careers in Canadian broadcast industry.
Eligibility: Open to citizens of Canadian with strong English language communications skills.
Level of Study: Professional development
Type: Scholarship
Value: Up to Canadian $10,000
Length of Study: 4 months
Frequency: Annual
No. of awards offered: 1
Application Procedure: A completed application form and copy of transcript of marks must be sent.
Closing Date: August 24th

For further information contact:

CanWest Global System Broadcasters of the Future Awards, 81 Barber Greene Road, Don Mills, Ontario, M3C 2A2

Robin Rousseau Memorial Mountain Achievement Scholarship
Subjects: Mountain leadership and safety.
Purpose: To bring about awareness of ways to improve safety in the mountains.
Eligibility: Open to all applicants who demonstrate volunteer commitment.
Level of Study: Professional development
Type: Scholarship
Length of Study: Course fee
Frequency: Annual
No. of awards offered: 1
Application Procedure: A completed application form must be sent.
Closing Date: January 30th

For further information contact:

Alberta Scholarship Programs, Box 28000 Stn. Mam, Edmonton, AB T5J 4R4

Terry Fox Humanitarian Award
Subjects: Social services.
Purpose: To encourage voluntary humanitarian work.

Eligibility: Open to Canadian citizens who are not more than 25 years of age.
Level of Study: Professional development
Type: Scholarship
Value: Canadian $3,500–7,000
Frequency: Annual
No. of awards offered: 20
Application Procedure: A completed application form must be submitted.
Closing Date: February 1st

For further information contact:

AQ5003, Simon Fraser University, Burnaby, BC V5A 153

Toyota Earth Day Scholarship Program
Subjects: Environmental community service.
Purpose: To encourage community service.
Eligibility: Open to students who have achieved academic excellence and distinguished themselves in environmental community service and extracurricular and volunteer activities.
Level of Study: Professional development
Type: Scholarship
Value: Canadian $5,000
Frequency: Annual
No. of awards offered: 15
Application Procedure: Application form available online.
Closing Date: January 31st

For further information contact:

Toyota Earth Day Scholarship Program, III Peter Street, Suite 503, Toronto, ON M5V 2H1

CHOIRS ONTARIO

330 Walmer Road, Toronto, ON, M5R 2Y4, Canada
Tel: (1) 416 923 1144
Fax: (1) 416 929 0415
Email: info@choirsontario.org
Website: www.choirsontario.org
Contact: Melva Graham

Choirs Ontario is an arts service organization dedicated to the promotion of choral activities and standards of excellence. Established in 1971 as the Ontario Choral Federation, Choirs Ontario provides services to choirs, conductors, choristers, composers, administrators and educators as well as anyone who enjoys listening to the sound of choral music. Choirs Ontario operates with the financial assistance of the Ministry of Culture, the Ontario Arts Council, the Trillium Foundation, the Toronto Arts Council and numerous foundations, corporations and individual donors.

Ruth Watson Henderson Choral Competition
Subjects: Singing: treble voice choirs.
Purpose: To reward new choral works.
Eligibility: This year's competition is for an SSA work for treble voice choir. Suggested time limit is 4–8 minutes. Compositions may be a capella or accompanied by up to three instruments. Texts may be sacred or secular and need not be limited to English. Submissions must not have been previously commissioned or published and must have been composed within the last 2 years. Composers must be Canadian citizens or landed immigrants. There is no age limit.
Level of Study: Unrestricted
Type: Award
Value: Canadian $1,000
Frequency: Every 2 years
Country of Study: Canada
Application Procedure: Applicants must submit four legible photocopies of the score (not original manuscripts). More than one entry may be submitted, but each entry must be accompanied by a separate entry form and a fee of Canadian $20. The composer's name must not appear on any score. Scores will be returned if a stamped addressed envelope is included. Application forms can be downloaded from the website www.choirsontario.org/ruthwatsonhenderson.html
Closing Date: September 1st
Funding: Private

Contributor: Choirs Ontario
Additional Information: Ruth Watson Henderson, one of Canada's foremost musicians, is internationally known both as a composer and pianist. Her compositions have been commissioned, performed and recorded worldwide.

CHRISTOPHER AND DANA REEVE FOUNDATION (CDRF)

636 Morris Turnpike, Suite 3A, Short Hills, NJ, NJ 07078,
United States of America
Tel: (1) 973 379 2690
Fax: (1) 973 912 9433
Email: dlandsman@christopherreeve.org
Website: www.ChristopherReeve.org
Contact: Dr Douglas S Landsman, Director of Individual Grants

The Christopher and Dana Reeve Foundation (CDRF) is committed to funding research that develops treatments and cures for paralysis caused by spinal cord injury and other central nervous system disorders. The Foundation also vigorously works to improve the quality of life for people living with disabilities through its grants programme, paralysis resource centre and advocacy efforts.

CRF Research Grant
Subjects: Spinal cord injury-related research.
Purpose: To fund research that will lead to effective treatments and ultimately a cure for spinal cord injury.
Eligibility: Open to American and international investigators located at institutions that have clearly established lines of accountability and fiscal responsibility. Institutional assurances regarding animal research and human subjects are required.
Level of Study: Postdoctorate, Research
Value: US$75,000 per year for a maximum total of US$150,000
Length of Study: A maximum of 2 years
Frequency: Annual
Country of Study: Any country
No. of awards offered: Usually 40 per year. Varies depending on the level of science and the amount of funds available
Application Procedure: Applicants must complete an application form and forward five copies of it to the Foundation. Forms are available from the website.
Closing Date: December 15th and June 15th
Funding: Foundation, private
Contributor: Private sector donations
No. of awards given last year: 40
No. of applicants last year: 200
Additional Information: The intent of these awards is to promote innovative and ground-breaking work, not to provide ongoing long-term support. CDRF funds activities that hold promise of identifying therapies for paralysis. For further information visit the website.

CHRONIC DISEASE RESEARCH FOUNDATION (CDRF)

St Thomas' Hospital, 1st Floor, South Wing, Lambeth Palace Road,
London, SE1 7EH, England
Tel: (44) 20 7188 6723
Fax: (44) 20 7188 6718
Email: ChristelMB77@aol.com
Website: www.cdrf.org.uk
Contact: Ms Christel Barnetson, Chief Administrator

The Chronic Disease Research Foundation (CDRF) was established to look at new ways of exploring the genetics of diseases associated with ageing. Its mission is to target those common diseases such as osteoporosis, arthritis, back pain, migraine, asthma and diabetes, inherited from our parents, and prevent and alleviate them now and for future generations. Its principal focus is on comparative studies of identical and non-identical twins, undertaken at the Twin Research Unit of St Thomas' Hospital.

CDRF Project Grants
Subjects: The genetic basis of diseases associated with ageing.

Purpose: To carry out comparative studies of identical and non-identical twins to pinpoint the genetic cause of common diseases associated with ageing.
Level of Study: Postgraduate, Research
Type: Project grant
Value: UK £30,000–150,000
Length of Study: 2–3 years
Frequency: Dependent on funds available
Country of Study: United Kingdom
No. of awards offered: Dependent on availability of funds
Application Procedure: Applicants must submit a preliminary proposal of no more than one side of A4-size paper including an outline of the proposal, a list of principal aims and objectives and scale of funding. If the CDRF's panel of experts consider the project to be of relevance, applicants must then submit a full grant proposal.
Funding: Private
No. of awards given last year: None

CDRF Research Fellowship
Subjects: The genetic basis of disease associated with ageing.
Purpose: To promote postgraduate education and enable the charity to carry out further research projects.
Level of Study: Postgraduate, Research
Type: Fellowship
Value: UK £30,000–175,000
Length of Study: 2–5 years
Frequency: Dependent on funds available
Country of Study: United Kingdom
No. of awards offered: Dependent on availability of funds
Application Procedure: Applicants must submit a preliminary proposal of no more than one side of an A4-size paper including an outline of the proposal, a list of principal aims and objectives and the scale of funding. If the CDRF's panel of experts consider the project to be of relevance, applicants must then submit a proposal for a full grant.
Funding: Private
No. of awards given last year: 2

CHRONIC GRANULOMATOUS DISORDER (CGD) RESEARCH TRUST

CGD Research Trust, 110 Bloomfield Rd, Bath, BA2 2AR, United
Kingdom
Tel: (44) 1725 517977
Fax: (44) 1725 517977
Email: cgd@cgdrt.co.uk
Website: www.cgd.org.uk
Contact: Dr Susan Walsh

The CGD Research Trust is a member of the Association of medical research charities and the International Patient Organization for Primary Immunodeficiencies (IPOPI). The Trust, founded in 1991, exists to promote research into the cases, inheritance, management, symptoms and cure of CGD.

CGD Research Trust Grants
Subjects: Topics pertaining to potential cures and treatment of inflammation and infection in chronic granulomatous disorder, basic understanding of the molecular defect and the impact of chronic granulomatous disorder on quality of life.
Purpose: To support thorough research that aims to increase understanding of the cause, inheritance, management and symptoms of chronic granulomatous disorder, and to disseminate the useful results of such research.
Level of Study: Doctorate, Postdoctorate, Postgraduate, Predoctorate, Research
Type: Grant
Value: UK £40,000–250,000
Length of Study: Usually 1–3 years depending on the programme
Frequency: Dependent on funds available
No. of awards offered: 2–3 each year
Application Procedure: Grants are advertised annually every June in Nature. Applicants must initially submit a four-page outline. These are reviewed by lay reviewers and members of the scientific and medical panel. A number of these are then invited to complete full

applications. These are then subjected to a peer review. The medical panel then makes recommendations and trustees announce grant offers the following February.

Closing Date: The end of September
Funding: Private
Contributor: Voluntary donations
No. of awards given last year: 3
No. of applicants last year: 12
Additional Information: Preliminary applications must be made on a form available from the CGD office in Bath.

THE CIRCULATION FOUNDATION

35-43 Lincoln's Inn Fields, London, WC2A 3PE, England
Tel: (44) 7304 4779
Fax: (44) 7430 9235
Email: terrie@vascularsociety.org.uk
Website: www.circulationfoundation.org.uk
Contact: T McCann, Fundraising Manager

The Circulation Foundation aims to provide research funding to find cures, better treatments and improve diagnosis of vascular disease. The Foundation also hopes to raise awareness of the disease's prevalence and impact and to provide information and support to sufferers, their families and friends.

Owen Shaw Award
Subjects: The rehabilitation of amputees.
Purpose: To devise better methods of helping patients to attain early mobilization.
Eligibility: Open to all those with an interest in amputee rehabilitation.
Level of Study: Unrestricted
Type: Award
Value: UK £3,000
Length of Study: 1 year
Frequency: Annual
Study Establishment: Any restricted research establishment
Country of Study: United Kingdom
No. of awards offered: 1
Application Procedure: Candidates must complete an outline proposal form, available from the Foundation.
Closing Date: June 5th
Funding: Private, trusts
Contributor: Owen Shaw
No. of awards given last year: 1
No. of applicants last year: 8

CITY UNIVERSITY, LONDON

Northampton Square, London, EC1V 0HB, United Kingdom
Tel: (44) 0 20 7040 5060
Fax: (44) 0 20 7040 5070
Email: enquiries@city.ac.uk
Website: www.city.ac.uk

The City University, London has developed into an innovative, forward-looking centre of excellence, with a well-deserved reputation in professional and business education and research. Today, it is ready and equipped to face the educational and professional challenges of the knowledge economy. It has close contacts with the leading professional institutions and with business and industry, both at home and abroad. Their professional links are reflected in their teaching and research staff.

Davis and Lyons Bursaries in Music
Subjects: Music.
Eligibility: Open to all students (UK/EU and overseas, full-time and part-time) beginning any postgraduate programme in music at city.
Type: Bursary
Value: UK £1,000
Length of Study: 1 year
Frequency: Annual
Country of Study: United Kingdom
No. of awards offered: 2
Application Procedure: Check website, www.city.ac.uk/music/

Closing Date: March
Additional Information: An announcement of the Davis and Lyons Bursaries in music outcome will be made in late July.

CLARA HASKIL COMPETITION

Case Postale 234, 31 rue du Conseil, 1800 Vevey 1, Switzerland
Tel: (41) 21 922 6704
Fax: (41) 21 922 6734
Email: clara.haskil@bluewin.ch
Website: www.regart.ch/clara-haskil
Contact: Mr Patrick Peikert, Director

The Clara Haskil Competition exists to recognize and help a young pianist whose approach to piano interpretation is of the same spirit that constantly inspired Clara Haskil, and that she illustrated so perfectly.

Clara Haskil Competition
Subjects: Piano performance.
Purpose: To recognize and financially help a young pianist.
Eligibility: Open to pianists of any nationality and either sex who are no more than 27 years of age.
Level of Study: Postgraduate
Type: Prize
Value: Swiss Francs 20,000
Frequency: Every 2 years
Country of Study: Any country
No. of awards offered: 1
Application Procedure: Applicants must pay an entry fee of Swiss Franc 260.
Closing Date: April 30th
Funding: Corporation, international office, trusts
Additional Information: The competition is usually held during the last weeks of August or the beginning of September.

THE CLAUDE LEON FOUNDATION

PO Box 13187, Mowbray 7705, Cape Town, South Africa
Tel: (27) 21 531 6910
Email: tanya@conferencewise.co.za
Website: www.leonfoundation.co.za
Contact: Mrs Tanya Stone, Postdoctoral Fellowships Administrator

The Claude Leon Foundation is a charitable trust, resulting from a bequest by Claude Leon (1887–1972). A founder and managing director of the Elephant Trading Company, a wholesale business based in Johannesburg, Claude Leon also helped develop several well-known South African companies, including Edgars, OK Bazaars and the mining house Anglo Transvaal (later Anglovaal). He served for many years on the Council of the University of the Witwatersrand, which in 1971 awarded him an honorary Doctorate of Law. The university postdoctoral fellowship award programme is now in its eighth year, and has as its goal the building of research capacity at South African universities and technikons.

Postdoctoral Fellowships (Claude Leon)
Subjects: Science, engineering, medical sciences.
Purpose: To fund postdoctoral research.
Eligibility: South African and foreign nationals may apply. Preference will be given to candidates who have received their doctoral degrees in the last 5 years and are currently underrepresented in South African science, engineering and medical science.
Level of Study: Postdoctorate
Type: Fellowship
Value: Rand 150,000 per annum
Length of Study: 2 years
Frequency: Annual
Study Establishment: South African universities and technikons
Country of Study: South Africa
Application Procedure: Application forms are available from the website or the Postdoctoral Fellowships Administrator.
Closing Date: May 31st
Funding: Foundation
Contributor: The Claude Leon Foundation

For further information contact:

Foundation's Postdoctoral Fellowships administrator, PO Box 13187, Cape Town, South Africa, Mowbray 7705
Contact: Tanya Stone

CLEMSON UNIVERSITY

G01 Sikes Hall, Box 345123, Clemson, SC, 29634-5123, United States of America
Tel: (1) 864 656 2280
Fax: (1) 864 656 1831
Email: finaid@clemson.edu
Website: www.clemson.edu
Contact: Associate Director

Uemson University is a selective, public, land-grant university, which is committed to world-class teaching, research and public service in the context of general education, student development and continuing education.

Clemson Graduate Assistantships
Subjects: MBA.
Eligibility: Decisions regarding the awarding of these assistantships and the duties and work period assigned are separately determined by each university department or office that employs graduate assistants.
Level of Study: MBA
Type: Graduate assistantship
Value: The assistantships pay stipends starting at US$6.18 per hour. The pay depends upon job duties and candidate qualifications. In addition, graduate assistants are granted partial remission of academic fees and enjoy some benefits provided to the University faculty and staff. Graduate assistantship presently pay US$1,044 per semester in tuition and fees
Length of Study: 2 years
Frequency: Dependent on funds available, on an annual or 9-month basis
Study Establishment: Clemson University
Country of Study: United States of America
No. of awards offered: Varies
Application Procedure: Applicants must contact the various university departments or offices for information or submit a general application with a curriculum vitae to the MBA office.

CLEVELAND INSTITUTE OF MUSIC

11201 East Boulevard, Cleveland, OH 44106, United States of America
Tel: (1) 216 791 5000 Ext. 262
Fax: (1) 216 795 3141
Email: kxg26@cwru.edu
Website: www.cim.edu
Contact: Kristie Gripp, Director of Financial Aid

The Cleveland Institute of Music's mission is to provide talented students with a professional, world-class education in the art of music. The Institute ranks among the top tier music schools across the nation, granting degrees up to the doctoral level. More than 80 per cent of the Institute's alumni perform in major national and international orchestras and opera companies, while others hold prominent teaching positions.

Cleveland Institute of Music Scholarships and Accompanying Fellowships
Subjects: Music.
Eligibility: Candidates for the accompanying fellowships should have a Bachelor of Music Degree or equivalent and must be proficient in English.
Level of Study: Graduate, Postgraduate
Type: Scholarships and fellowships
Value: US$1,000–28,000 for scholarships and US$1,000–3,000 for accompanying fellowships. No travel grants are provided
Length of Study: 1 academic year for scholarships or from August to the following May for accompanying fellowships. Scholarships are renewable

Frequency: Annual
Study Establishment: The Cleveland Institute of Music
Country of Study: United States of America
No. of awards offered: Approx. 400 scholarships and 15 accompanying fellowships
Application Procedure: Applicants must apply online.
Closing Date: December 1st
Funding: Private

THE COLLEGE OF OPTOMETRISTS

41-42 Craven Street, London, WC2N 5N6, United Kingdom
Tel: (44) 0 20 7839 6000
Fax: (44) 0 20 7839 6800
Email: optometry@college-optometrists.org
Website: www.college-optometrists.org

The College of Optometrists, founded in 1980, is a registered charity incorporated by Royal Charter in 1995. It is the single successor body to the British Optical Association, founded in 1895, and The Scottish Association of Opticians, formed in 1921.

College of Optometrists Postgraduate Scholarships
Subjects: Optometry.
Purpose: To support research work in optometry or a closely related subject.
Eligibility: Open to candidates who have obtained a First Class or upper Second Class Bachelor's degree.
Level of Study: Postgraduate
Type: Scholarships
Value: Check website for further details
Length of Study: 3 years
Frequency: Annual
Country of Study: United Kingdom
No. of awards offered: 10
Closing Date: March 31st
Additional Information: For a copy of the regulations, the conditions of awards and application forms, contact murtagh@college-optometrists.org or through Tel: 020 7766 4364.

COLLEGEVILLE INSTITUTE FOR ECUMENICAL AND CULTURAL RESEARCH

14027 Fruit Farm Road, Box 2000, Collegeville, MN, 56321, United States of America
Tel: (1) 320 363 3366
Fax: (1) 320 363 3313
Email: staff@collegevilleinstitute.org
Website: www.collegevilleinstitute.org
Contact: Patrick Henry, Executive Director

The Institute for Ecumenical and Cultural Research seeks to discern the meaning of Christian identity and unity in a religiously and culturally diverse nation and world and to communicate that meaning for the mission of the church and the renewal of human community. The Institute is committed to research, study, prayer, reflection and dialogue, in a place shaped by the Benedictine tradition of worship and work.

Bishop Thomas Hoyt Jr Fellowship
Subjects: Ecumenical and cultural research.
Purpose: To provide the Institute's residency fee to a North American person of colour writing a doctoral dissertation, in order to help the churches to increase the number of persons of colour working in ecumenical and cultural research.
Eligibility: Open to a North American, Canadian or Mexican person of colour writing a doctoral dissertation within the general area of the Institute's concern.
Level of Study: Postgraduate
Type: Fellowship
Value: US$3,600, this figure is slated to rise gradually in future years; check the website for projections
Length of Study: 1 academic year

Frequency: Annual
Study Establishment: The Institute
Country of Study: United States of America
No. of awards offered: 1 each year (or 2 if for semesters)
Application Procedure: Applicants must apply in the usual way to the Resident Scholars Programme (see separate listing). If invited by the admissions committee to be a Resident Scholar, the person will then be eligible for consideration for the Hoyt Fellowship.
Closing Date: November 1st
Funding: Private
No. of awards given last year: None
No. of applicants last year: None

COLLEGIO CARLO ALBERTO FOUNDATION (CCAF)

Via Real Collegio 30, Moncalieri, Turin, 10024, Italy
Tel: (39) 11 670 5000
Fax: (39) 11 647 68 47
Email: segreteria@collegiocarloalberto.it
Website: www.collegiocarloalberto.it

The Collegio Carlo Alberto Foundation (CCAF) was legally constituted on April 27, 2004, at the joint initiative of the Compagnia di San Paolo Foundation and the University of Turin. The Foundation aims to promote, manage and develop, in conjunction with the University of Turin, research and postgraduate education in the fields of economics, finance and law, as well as in related disciplines.

CCAF Junior Research Fellowship
Subjects: Economics and finance.
Purpose: To help in the creation of a stimulating interactive environment with Doctoral students and junior researchers.
Eligibility: Open to candidates who have obtained a PhD.
Level of Study: Postdoctorate
Type: Fellowships
Value: €50,000 per year
Length of Study: 2 years
Frequency: Annual
Country of Study: Italy
No. of awards offered: 2
Application Procedure: Applicants must send a curriculum vitae, a completed research paper, a 1–2 page research proposal and 2 letters of reference.
Closing Date: December 10th

COLT FOUNDATION

New Lane, Havant, Hampshire, PO9 2LY, England
Tel: (44) 23 9249 1400
Fax: (44) 23 9249 1363
Email: jackie.douglas@uk.coltgroup.com
Website: www.coltfoundation.org.uk
Contact: Ms Jackie Douglas, Director

The primary interest of the Colt Foundation is the promotion of research into medical and environmental problems created by commerce and industry and is aimed particularly at discovering the cause of illnesses arising from conditions at the place of work. The Foundation also makes grants to students taking higher degrees in related subjects.

Colt Foundation PhD Fellowship
Subjects: Medical and natural sciences including public health and hygiene, sports medicine, biological and life sciences, physiology or toxicology.
Purpose: To encourage the young scientists of the future.
Eligibility: Open to any student proposing to take a PhD in the correct subject area in a United Kingdom university or college.
Level of Study: Doctorate
Type: Fellowship
Value: UK £39,700 maintenance and travel plus fees/bench fees as incurred
Length of Study: 3 years
Frequency: Annual

Application Procedure: Applicants must visit the website where details are posted in August each year.
Closing Date: October 20th
Funding: Foundation
No. of awards given last year: 3

COLUMBIA UNIVERSITY

The Earth Institute at Columbia University, 405 Low Library 535 West 116th Street, NY, 10027, United States of America
Tel: (1) 845 365 8565
Fax: (1) 845 365 8164
Email: support@ei.columbia.edu
Website: www.earth.columbia.edu

The Earth Institute at Columbia University brings together talent from throughout the University to address complex issues facing the planet and its inhabitants, with particular focus on sustainable development and the needs of the world's poor.

Marie Tharp Visiting Fellowships
Subjects: Geosciences, social sciences, engineering and environmental health sciences.
Purpose: To provide an opportunity for women scientists to conduct research at one of the related departments within the Earth Institute.
Eligibility: Open to women candidates who have obtained their PhD and are citizens of the United States.
Level of Study: Research, Doctorate
Type: Fellowships
Value: US$30,000
Length of Study: 3 months
Frequency: Annual
Country of Study: United States of America
Application Procedure: Applicants must submit a 3 page proposal, a curriculum vitae, a proposed budget and complete contact information of 3 references.
Closing Date: January 11th
Additional Information: All application materials may be submitted by mail or by email.

For further information contact:

Lamont-Doherty Earth Observatory of Columbia University, PO Box 1000, 61 Route 9W, Palisades, NY, 10964, United States of America
Tel: (1) 845 365 8546/8729
Fax: (1) 845 365 8162
Email: director@ldeo.columbia.edu
Website: www.ldeo.columbia.edu
Contact: The Office of the Director

THE COMMONWEALTH FUND OF NEW YORK

Harkness House, 1 East 75th Street, New York, NY, 10021, United States of America
Tel: (1) 212 606 3809
Fax: (1) 212 606 3875
Email: ro@cmwf.org
Website: www.cmwf.org
Contact: Ms Robin Osborn, International Programs in Health Policy Director

The Commonwealth Fund of New York is a philanthropic foundation established in 1918. The Fund supports independent research on health and social issues and makes grants to improve healthcare practice and policy.

The Commonwealth Fund/Harvard University Fellowship in Minority Health Policy
Subjects: Health policy, public health and management, with special programme activities on minority health issues.
Purpose: To create physician-leaders who will pursue careers in minority health policy.
Eligibility: Open to physicians who are citizens of the United States of America and who have completed their residency. Additional

239

experience beyond residency is preferred. Applicants must demonstrate an awareness of, or interest and experience in dealing, with the health needs of minority populations, strong evidence of past leadership experience, as related to community efforts and health policy and the intention to pursue a career in public health practice, policy, or academia.

Level of Study: Graduate, Research, Postgraduate, Professional development
Type: Fellowship
Value: US$50,000 stipend, full tuition, health insurance, books, travel and related expenses
Length of Study: 1 year
Frequency: Annual
Study Establishment: Harvard Medical School
Country of Study: United States of America
Application Procedure: Applications available online at the website: www.cmwf.org/fellowships
Closing Date: January 2nd
Funding: Foundation

For further information contact:

c/o Minority Faculty Development Program, 164 Longwood Avenue, 2nd Floor, Boston, MA, 02115-5818, United States of America
Tel: (1) 617 432 2922
Contact: CFHUF Programme Co-ordinator

Harkness Fellowships in Healthcare Policy

Subjects: Healthcare policy and health services research.
Purpose: To encourage the professional development of promising healthcare policy researchers and practitioners who will contribute to innovation in healthcare policy and practice in the United States of America and their home countries.
Eligibility: Open to individuals who have completed a Master's degree or PhD in health services or health policy research. Applicants must also have shown significant promise as a policy-orientated researcher or practitioner, e.g. physicians or health service managers, journalists and government officials, with a strong interest in policy issues. Candidates should also be at the research Fellow to senior lecturer level, if academically based; be in their late 20s to early 40s, and have been nominated by their department chair or the director of their institution.
Level of Study: Postgraduate, Professional development, Research
Type: Fellowship
Value: Basic expenses of travel, residence and research, up to a maximum of US$107,000
Length of Study: Up to 1 year. A minimum of 6 months must be spent in the United States of America
Frequency: Annual
Study Establishment: An academic or other research policy institution
Country of Study: United States of America
No. of awards offered: 3 for Australia and New Zealand 3 for Germany, 2 from the Netherlands, 1 from Switzerland, and 5 from the United Kingdom
Application Procedure: Applicants must complete a formal application available online at the website www.cmwf.org/fellowships Applicants must be submitted via email.
Closing Date: September 7th
Funding: Private
Contributor: The Commonwealth Fund
Additional Information: Successful candidates will have a policy orientated research project, on a topic relevant to the Fund's programme areas. Projects will be supervised by senior researchers and each Fellow will be expected to produce a publishable report contributing to a better understanding of health policy issues.

For further information contact:

Associate Professor & Director (Australia), Center for Health Economics Research & Evaluation, University of Sydney, Mallett Street Campus, 88 Mallett Street, Level 6, Building F, Camperdown, NSW, 2050, Australia
Tel: (61) 2 9351 0900
Fax: (61) 2 9351 0930
Email: sylviab@pub.health.usyd.edu.au

Contact: Dr Jane HallPolicy Representative, Executive Director (New Zealand), New Zealand-United States Educational Foundation, PO Box 3465, Wellington, New Zealand
Tel: (64) 4 722 065
Fax: (64) 4 995 364
Email: jennifer@fulbright.org.nz
Contact: Ms Jennifer M Gill

Packer Fellowships

Subjects: Health policy issues in Australia and the United States of America, and shared lessons of both policies.
Purpose: To allow outstanding, mid-career health policy researchers from the United States of America to spend up to 10 months in Australia conducting original research and working with leading Australian health policy experts on issues relevant to both countries.
Eligibility: Accomplished, mid-career health policy researchers and practitioners including academics, physicians, decision makers in managed care and other private organizations, federal and state health officials and journalists.
Level of Study: Research
Type: Fellowship
Value: Australian $55,000 plus family allowance
Length of Study: Up to 10 months
Frequency: Annual
Study Establishment: Suitable establishment in Australia
Country of Study: Australia
Application Procedure: Applicants must submit a formal application, including a project proposal that falls within an area of mutual policy interest, such as: healthcare quality and safety, the private/public mix of insurance and providers, the fiscal sustainability of health systems, the healthcare workforce and investment in preventive care strategies. Applications are available online (www.cmwf.org/fellowships) and must be submitted via email.
Closing Date: August 15th
Funding: Government

COMMONWEALTH SCHOLARSHIP COMMISSION IN THE UNITED KINGDOM

c/o Association of Commonwealth Universities, Woburn House, 20–24 Tavistock Square, London, WC1H 9HF, England
Tel: (44) 20 7380 6700
Fax: (44) 20 7387 2655
Email: info@acu.ac.uk
Website: www.acu.ac.uk
Contact: Awards Administrator

The Commonwealth Scholarship Commission in the United Kingdom was set up as the body responsible for the United Kingdom's participation in the Commonwealth Scholarship and Fellowship Plan in 1959. It is responsible for the selection and placement of recipients coming to the United Kingdom and for the selection of candidates from the United Kingdom to be put forward for awards in other Commonwealth countries.

ACU Titular Fellowships

Subjects: All subjects, but preference is given to those fields that are needed in developing countries.
Purpose: To enable the universities of the commonwealth to develop the human resources of their institutions and countries through the interchanging of people, knowledge, skills and technologies. Not intended for degree courses, or for immediately postdoctoral programmes.
Eligibility: Applicants must be on the staff of member universities under the ACU, the Commonwealth interuniversity organization or working in industry, commerce or public service in a Commonwealth country. Applicant must be within 28–50 years of age.
Level of Study: Professional development
Type: Scholarship
Value: UK £5,000 for travel, board, insurance and fees where the approved programme includes a training programme
Length of Study: 6 months
Frequency: Annual

Study Establishment: ACU member university or in industry, commerce or public sector
Country of Study: Commonwealth countries
No. of awards offered: Up to 12
Application Procedure: Candidates must be nominated by executive heads of ACU member universities or by the chief executive officer of a Commonwealth interuniversity organization. Full application details on ACU website.
Closing Date: August 31st
Contributor: ACU
No. of awards given last year: 8
No. of applicants last year: 50

ACU/FCO Chevening Scholarships

Subjects: Human resource management.
Purpose: To support full-time study in the United Kingdom on Master's degree in human resource management offered by the University of Westminister. The principal aim of the programme is to improve human resource management in higher education in developing countries.
Eligibility: Open to persons currently working in human resource or personnel departments in ACU member universities in developing countries. Award holders must undertake to return to their employing university at the end of the scholarship.
Level of Study: Postgraduate
Type: Scholarship
Value: Full cost of study, including return airfare fees and maintenance allowance
Length of Study: 1 year
Frequency: Annual
Study Establishment: University of Westminister
Country of Study: United Kingdom
No. of awards offered: Up to 2 annually
Application Procedure: Application should be sent directly to ACU. Must be nominated for this award by the vice-chancellor or executive head of their employee ACU member university. Full application details on ACU website.
Closing Date: April
Contributor: Funded jointly by ACU, FCO, the University of Westminister and International Students House, London
No. of awards given last year: 2
No. of applicants last year: 55
Additional Information: Preference is given to candidates who have a combination of strong record of achievement in their careers to date and clear plans on how the benefits of the scholarships would be used in future. For details on the university and course check website www.wmin.ac.uk

ACU/FCO Chevening Scholarships: Public Relations, Media and Communications Programme

Subjects: Public communication and public relations.
Purpose: To support full-time study in the United Kingdom for a Master's degree in Public Communication and Public Relations offered by the University of Westminister. (The principal aim is to allow members to share best practice in this fast-growing field.) Intended for administrative or related staff currently employed by ACU render universities in developing commonwealth countries who wish to develop their success in media, public relations or marketing.
Eligibility: Open to administrative or related staff currently employed by ACU member universities in developing countries to develop their skills in public relations, media and external communications. Candidates should hold a good Honours degree or equivalent, although other professional qualifications or substantial work experience may also be acceptable. Award holders must undertake to return to their own university at the end of the scholarship.
Level of Study: Postgraduate
Type: Scholarship
Value: Full cost of study, including return airfare, fees and maintenance allowance
Frequency: Annual
Study Establishment: University of Westminister
Country of Study: United Kingdom
No. of awards offered: Up to 2
Application Procedure: Application should be sent directly to the ACU. Even candidates must be nominated for this award of the

vice-chancellor or executive members of their employing ACU member university. Full application details on ACU website.
Closing Date: April 30th
Funding: Foundation
Contributor: ACU, FCO, the University of Westminister and International Students House, London
No. of awards given last year: 1
No. of applicants last year: 29
Additional Information: For details on the University and course check the website www.wmiw.ac.uk or contact the Director, Human Capacity Development, ACU.

British Academy/Association of Commonwealth Universities: Grants for International Collaboration

Subjects: Humanities and social sciences.
Purpose: To support international joint activities involving British scholars in collaboration with Commonwealth partners.
Eligibility: Open to staff of ACU member institutions.
Level of Study: Postdoctorate, Research
Type: Grant
Value: Up to UK £5,000. Intended to cover travel, maintenance costs plus approved necessary expenditure (not intended to cover institutional overheads or permanent staff costs)
Length of Study: 1 year
Frequency: Annual
Study Establishment: An advanced research institution
Country of Study: Commonwealth countries
No. of awards offered: Up to 12
Application Procedure: Application should be submitted by the British partner. Full application details on ACU website.
Closing Date: September 30th
Contributor: British academy and ACU
No. of awards given last year: 10
No. of applicants last year: 50
Additional Information: Priority is given to new programmes with an expectation of continued collaboration or a defined overcome such as a joint publication.

Canada Memorial Foundation Scholarship

Subjects: All subjects.
Purpose: To fund postdoctorate study in Canada.
Eligibility: The candidate must be a United Kingdom citizen and must hold a First Class (Honours) Degree or equivalent (with at least Upper Second Class Honours), and should not be more than 30 years of age. To cover 1 year of taught postgraduate study. Not intended for doctoral level study.
Level of Study: Postgraduate
Type: Scholarship
Value: Maintenance allowance, return airfare, approved fees, book, thesis, travel and health insurance allowances
Length of Study: 1 year
Frequency: Annual
Study Establishment: Any institution or university in Canada approved by the Canada Memorial Foundation
Country of Study: Canada
No. of awards offered: Up to 2
Application Procedure: Full application details can be got on ACU website, or by mailing cmf@acu.ac.uk
Closing Date: November 10th
Funding: Foundation
Contributor: Canada Memorial Foundation
No. of awards given last year: 1
No. of applicants last year: 17

Commonwealth Academic Fellowships

Subjects: All subjects, but preference given to applications which fit with the development plans of the candidate's own institution.
Purpose: To support the cost of up to six months in the United Kingdom for staff of universities in certain developing Commonwealth countries.
Eligibility: Open to commonwealth citizens or British protected persons who have completed their doctorate in no less than 5 years by the time of taxing up an award. Candidates should be a permanent resident of and a teaching staff of a university in a developing

commonwealth country candidates should not be more than 50 years of age with at least 2 years of teaching experience.
Level of Study: Postdoctorate
Type: Fellowship
Value: Maintenance and travel allowances
Length of Study: 6 months
Frequency: Annual
Study Establishment: A university level institution
Country of Study: United Kingdom
No. of awards offered: Approx. 80
Application Procedure: Application by nomination only. Full application details, including special for awards involving clinical training in available on CSFP website.
Closing Date: December 31st for receipt of nominations in London
Funding: Government
Contributor: Commonwealth Scholarship Commission
Additional Information: Fellows are required to sign an undertaking to return to and resume their academic post in their country on completion of the fellowships. Candidates must be nominated by the vice chancellor of the university on whose permanent staff the applicant serves. Heads of Indian universities should send their nominations to the University Grants Commission in New Delhi, heads of Pakistani universities to the Ministry of Education in Islamabad, heads of Sri-Lankan universities to the Ministry of tertiary education and training in Colombo and heads of Bangladeshi universities to the University Grants Commission in Dhaka. The fellowship may not be held concurrently with other awards or with paid employment.

Commonwealth Academic Staff Scholarships

Subjects: All subjects.
Purpose: To enable promising staff members from universities and similar institutions in the developing commonwealth to obtain experience in a higher education institution in the UK.
Eligibility: Open to Commonwealth citizens or British protected persons who are permanently resident in Commonwealth countries other than the United Kingdom, not older than 42 years of age and holding or returning to a teaching appointment in a university in a developing Commonwealth country.
Level of Study: Research, Postgraduate
Type: Scholarship
Value: University fees, scholar's return travel, allowance for books, apparatus, approved travel within the country of tenure, and personal maintenance (plus family allowances for awards over 1 year in duration)
Length of Study: 1–2 years initially, maximum 3 years
Frequency: Annual
Study Establishment: An approved Institution of Higher Education
Country of Study: United Kingdom
No. of awards offered: 45–50
Application Procedure: Applicant should be nominated by the executive head of the university to which the candidate belongs. Full application details available on CSFP website.
Closing Date: December 31st
Additional Information: For detailed information check the website www.cspf-online.org, To be incorporated into given scholarship scheme with effect from 2006.

Commonwealth Professional Fellowships

Subjects: Education, engineering, environment, governance, public health and technology.
Purpose: To enable mid-career professionals to visit the United Kingdom for professional updating purposes.
Eligibility: Open to citizens and residents of Commonwealth countries with at least 5 years of appropriate experience in a profession. Fellows can be drawn from any sector.
Level of Study: Professional development
Type: Fellowship
Value: Maintenance and travel allowances, with fixed contributions to the costs of the host organization. Appropriate conference/short course fees are also available
Length of Study: 3
Frequency: Annual
Study Establishment: Appropriate host organizations in the United Kingdom
Country of Study: United Kingdom

No. of awards offered: 60–70 per year
Application Procedure: Application by nomination from a range of professional, charitable, public and private sector organizations based in the United Kingdom. Nominating and host organizations are expected to be the same wherever possible, though not essential. Full application details available on CSFP website.
Closing Date: April 30th
Funding: Foundation, government
Additional Information: The scholarship is not intended for those undertaking full-time study, those seeking assistance for commencing or completing formal academic or professional qualifications or to develop academic research for its own sake. Fellowships are not open to full-time academic staff.

Commonwealth Scholarships

Subjects: All subjects.
Purpose: Awards to commonwealth citizens for postgraduate study in commonwealth countries other than their own.
Eligibility: Open to Commonwealth citizens or British protected persons who have completed a First Class (Honours) Degree or Master's degree, and who are permanently resident in Commonwealth countries other than the United Kingdom. Candidates should hold a good Honours degree or equivalent.
Level of Study: Postgraduate, Research
Type: Scholarship
Value: University fees, scholar's return travel, allowance for books, apparatus, approved travel within the country of tenure, personal maintenance (plus family allowances for over 1 year in duration)
Length of Study: 1–2 years initially, maximum 3 years
Frequency: Annual
Study Establishment: An approved Institution of Higher Education
Country of Study: Designated Commonwealth countries other than candidates own
No. of awards offered: Up to 200
Application Procedure: Application by nomination through the Commonwealth Scholarship Agency in the country in which the scholar resides. Application forms and detailed application information available from CSFP agencies in relevant country. Full application details available on CSFP website.
Closing Date: Varies according to the country in which the candidate applies, usually some 12–18 months before the intended period of study
Additional Information: For detailed information check the website www.csfp-online.org

Commonwealth Shared Scholarship

Subjects: Subjects related to economic, social on technological development of the candidates; home country.
Purpose: To provide financial assistance to students from developing Commonwealth countries wishing to pursue a talent Master's degree in the United Kingdom.
Eligibility: Open to students from developing Commonwealth countries who are not living or studying in a developing country. Priority is given to candidates from poorer developing countries and to those under 30 years of age. Age limit is 35 years. Fluency in English is required. Candidates should not have previously studied for one term or none in a developed country.
Level of Study: Postgraduate
Type: Scholarship
Value: Full cost of study, including return airfare, maintenance and thesis allowances
Length of Study: 1 year
Frequency: Annual
Study Establishment: Participants institution in the UK (information on these available on the CSFP website)
Country of Study: United Kingdom
No. of awards offered: Between 150 and 200 annaully
Application Procedure: Application must be made to participating institutions, not directly to the ACU. Full application details available on CSFP website.
Closing Date: May 31st
Contributor: Department for International Development (DFID)

Commonwealth Split-Site Doctoral Scholarships

Subjects: All subjects.

Purpose: To support attendance for 1 year at a UK university, for those students for a PhD in a developing commonwealth country.
Eligibility: Open to Commonwealth citizens and British protected persons who are permanently resident in Commonwealth countries other than the United Kingdom. Candidates should hold a good Honours degree or equivalent and should be studying for a doctoral degree at their home institution.
Level of Study: Doctorate
Type: Scholarship
Value: University fees, scholar's return travel, allowances for books, apparatus, approved travel, personal maintenance (and family allowances for awards over 1 year in duration). Awards does not support the period of study at the home country university
Length of Study: 1 year of full-time study or two 6-month periods of full-time study
Frequency: Annual
Study Establishment: An approved Institution of Higher Education in the UK
Country of Study: United Kingdom
No. of awards offered: 30–35
Application Procedure: Applications are accepted directly from certain developing country universities. Otherwise, by nomination through the Commonwealth Scholarship Agency in the country in which candidate permanently resides. Full application details on the CSFP website.
Closing Date: December 31st
Funding: Government
Additional Information: For detailed information check the website: www.csfp-online.org

Scholarships by Distance Learning

Subjects: All subjects.
Purpose: To support study by distance learning for courses at UK universities chosen on the grounds of their impact on international development and oriented in partnership with institutions in developing commonwealth countries.
Eligibility: Open only to Commonwealth citizens.
Level of Study: Postgraduate
Type: Scholarship
Value: Fees
Frequency: Annual
Study Establishment: UK universities in partnership with institutions in developing commonwealth countries
Country of Study: United Kingdom
No. of awards offered: Depends on the availability of funds
Application Procedure: Application can be sent directly to United Kingdom providers. Full application details on CSFP website.
Closing Date: June and November
Additional Information: For details check the website www.csfp-online.org

CONCORDIA UNIVERSITY

École des Études Supérieures, 1455 boulevard de Maisonneuve, Montréal, QC, H3G 1M8, Canada
Tel: (1) 514 848 3809
Fax: (1) 514 848 2812
Email: verret@vax2.concordia.ca
Website: www.concordia.ca
Contact: Ms Patricia Verret, Graduate Awards Manager

Concordia University is the result of the 1974 merger between Sir George Williams University and Loyola College. The University incorporates superior teaching methods with an interdisciplinary approach to learning and is dedicated to offering the best possible scholarship to the student body and to promoting research beneficial to society.

Bank of Montréal Pauline Varnier Fellowship

Subjects: Business and administration management.
Eligibility: Open to women with 2 years of cumulative business experience who are Canadian citizens or landed immigrants intending to pursue a full-time course of study for the MBA. This is an entrance fellowship.
Level of Study: MBA

Type: Fellowship
Value: Canadian $10,000 per year
Length of Study: 2 years
Frequency: Annual
Study Establishment: Concordia University
Country of Study: Canada
No. of awards offered: 1
Application Procedure: Applicants must submit a completed application form, three letters of recommendation and official transcripts of all university studies by the closing date.
Closing Date: April 30th
Funding: Private
No. of awards given last year: 1
Additional Information: Academic merit is the prime consideration in the granting of the awards.

Concordia University Graduate Fellowships

Subjects: All subjects.
Eligibility: Open to graduates of any nationality. Candidates must be planning to pursue a full-time Master's or doctoral study at the University.
Level of Study: Postgraduate
Type: Fellowship
Value: Canadian $2,900 per term for Master's level and Canadian $3,600 per term for doctoral level
Length of Study: A maximum of 4 terms at the Master's level and 9 terms at the doctoral level, calculated from the date of entry into the programme
Frequency: Annual
Study Establishment: Concordia University
Country of Study: Canada
No. of awards offered: Varies
Application Procedure: Applicants must submit a completed application form, three letters of recommendation and official transcripts of all university studies by the closing date.
Closing Date: December 15th
Funding: Government, private
No. of awards given last year: 25
No. of applicants last year: 1050
Additional Information: Academic merit is the prime consideration in the granting of the award.

David J Azrieli Graduate Fellowship

Subjects: All subjects.
Eligibility: Open to Master's or doctoral students of any nationality. Candidates must be planning to pursue a full-time Master's or doctoral study at the University.
Level of Study: Postgraduate
Type: Fellowship
Value: Canadian $17,500 per year
Length of Study: 1 year, non-renewable
Frequency: Annual
Study Establishment: Concordia University
Country of Study: Canada
No. of awards offered: 1
Application Procedure: Applicants must submit a completed application form, three letters of recommendation and official transcripts of all university studies by the closing date.
Closing Date: December 15th
Funding: Private
No. of awards given last year: 1
No. of applicants last year: 1050
Additional Information: Academic merit is the prime consideration in the granting of the award.

J W McConnell Memorial Fellowships

Subjects: All subjects.
Eligibility: Open to Canadian citizens and permanent residents of Canada who are planning to pursue full-time Master's or doctoral study at the University. Fellowships are awarded on academic merit.
Level of Study: Postgraduate
Type: Fellowship
Value: Canadian $2,900 per term at the Master's level and Canadian $3,600 per term at the doctoral level

Length of Study: A maximum of 4 terms at the Master's level and 9 terms at the doctoral level, calculated from the date of entry into the programme
Frequency: Annual
Study Establishment: Concordia University
Country of Study: Canada
No. of awards offered: Varies
Application Procedure: Applicants must submit a completed application form, three letters of recommendation and official transcripts of all university studies by the closing date.
Closing Date: December 15th
Funding: Private
No. of awards given last year: 15
No. of applicants last year: 800
Additional Information: Academic merit is the prime consideration in granting the awards.

John W O'Brien Graduate Fellowship

Subjects: All subjects.
Eligibility: Open to full-time graduate students of any nationality. Candidates must be planning to pursue a full-time Master's or doctoral study at the University.
Type: Fellowship
Value: Canadian $3,300 per term at the Master's level and Canadian $4,000 per term at the doctoral level
Length of Study: A maximum of 3 terms
Frequency: Annual
Study Establishment: Concordia University
Country of Study: Canada
No. of awards offered: 1
Application Procedure: Applicants must submit a completed application form, three letters of recommendation and official transcripts of all university studies by the closing date.
Closing Date: December 15th
Funding: Private
No. of awards given last year: 1
No. of applicants last year: 1050
Additional Information: Academic merit is the prime consideration in the granting of awards.

Stanley G French Graduate Fellowship

Subjects: All subjects.
Eligibility: Open to graduates of any nationality. Candidates must be planning to pursue full-time Master's or doctoral study at the University.
Level of Study: Postgraduate
Type: Fellowship
Value: Canadian $3,300 per term for Master's level and Canadian $4,000 per term for doctoral level
Length of Study: A maximum of 3 terms
Frequency: Annual
Study Establishment: Concordia University
Country of Study: Canada
No. of awards offered: 1
Application Procedure: Applicants must submit a completed application form, three letters of recommendation and official transcripts of all university studies by the closing date.
Closing Date: December 15th
Funding: Private
No. of awards given last year: 1
No. of applicants last year: 1050
Additional Information: Academic merit is the prime consideration in the granting of awards.

CONSERVATION LEADERSHIP PROGRAMME

Conservation Leadership Programme, Birdlife International, Wellbrook Court, Girton Road, Cambridge, Cambridgeshire, CB3 0NA, England
Tel: (44) 12 2327 7318
Fax: (44) 12 2327 7200
Email: clp@birdlife.org
Website: www.conservationleadershipprogramme.org
Contact: The Programme Manager

Since 1985, the Conservation Leadership Programme has supported and encouraged international conservation projects that address global conservation priorities at a local level. This is achieved through a comprehensive system of advice, training and awards. The programme is managed through a partnership between BP, FFI, CI, WCS and Birdlife International.

Future Conservationist Awards

Subjects: Awards are presented annually to innovative international student conservation projects. All projects must address a conservation priority of global importance, have local support and collaboration, and have a majority of team members in either university education, or who are early career conservationists.
Purpose: To research species, sites and habitats with the highest priority for biodiversity conservation worldwide and develop the skills and networks of future generations of young professionals.
Eligibility: The project must address a globally recognized conservation priority, involve people, have host government approval, be run by teams of at least three people, be student-led, have over 50 per cent students registered, last for less than 1 year and take place in Africa, Asia Pacific, Middle East, Eastern Europe, Latin America or the Caribbean.
Level of Study: Doctorate, Graduate, Postgraduate, Undergraduate
Type: Award
Value: Up to $12,500
Length of Study: Projects should be less than 1 year in length
Frequency: Annual
Country of Study: This is a global programme
No. of awards offered: Up to 30
Application Procedure: Application forms are available from the website. Applications should be made electronically.
Closing Date: November 6th
Funding: Private
Contributor: BP, BirdLife International, Conservation International, WildLife Conservation Society, and Fauna and Flora International
No. of awards given last year: 29
No. of applicants last year: 360

CONSERVATION TRUST

National Geographic Society 1/45 17th Street NW, Washington, DC 20090-8244, United States of America
Email: conservationtrust@ngs.org
Website: www.nationalgeographic.com/conservation

The objective of the Conservation Trust is to support conservation activities around the world as they fit within the mission of the National Geographic Society. The trust will fund projects that contribute significantly to the preservation and sustainable use of the Earth's biological, cultural, and historical resources.

National Geographic Conservation Trust Grant

Subjects: Conservation.
Purpose: To support cutting programmes that contribute to the preservation and sustainable use of the Earth's resources.
Eligibility: Applicants must provide a record of prior research or conservation action. Researchers planning work in foreign countries should include at least one local collaboration as part of their research teams. Grants recipients are excepted to provide the National Geographic Society with rights of first refusal for popular publication of their findings.
Level of Study: Research
Type: Research grant
Value: US$15,000–20,000
Frequency: Annual
No. of awards offered: Varies
Application Procedure: Apply online.
Closing Date: 8 months prior to anticipated field dates
Funding: Trusts
Contributor: National Geographic Society

For further information contact:

Conservation Trust, National Geographic Society, 1145 17th Street NW, Washington, DC, 20090-8249

CONSULATE GENERAL OF SWEDEN

1 Dag Hammarskjold Plaza 45th Floor, New York, NY, 10017-2201,
United States of America
Tel: (1) 212 583 2550
Fax: (1) 212 752 4787
Email: generalkonsulat.new-york@foreign.ministry.se
Website: www.swedennewyork.com

The Consulate General of Sweden in New York represents Sweden in the United States, specifically in the New York area. Its broad mission is to provide assistance to Swedes and to promote Swedish interests in the United States.

Bicentennial Swedish-American Exchange Fund Travel Grants

Subjects: Area/ethnic studies, foreign language, social sciences, humanities, business/consumer services and education.
Purpose: To provide financial support for faculty, researchers and professionals to study in Sweden.
Eligibility: Open to citizens or permanent residents of the United States.
Level of Study: Professional development, Research, Postgraduate
Type: Grant
Value: Up to 25,000 SEK
Length of Study: 2–4 weeks
Frequency: Annual
Country of Study: Sweden
No. of awards offered: 2–4
Application Procedure: Applicants must submit 2 letters of recommendation and a detailed project plan. Application forms are available online.
Contributor: Consulate General of Sweden

COOLEY'S ANEMIA FOUNDATION

330 Seventh Avenue suite 900, New York, NY, 10001, United States
of America
Tel: (1) 212 279 8090
Fax: (1) 212 279 5999
Email: info@cooleysanemia.org
Website: www.cooleysanemia.org
Contact: Ms Sophie Buczynski, Accounting Department

The Cooley's Anemia Foundation is dedicated to serving people afflicted with various forms of thalassemia, most notably the major form of this genetic blood disease, Cooley's anemia/thalassemia major.

Cooley's Anemia Foundation Research Fellowship

Subjects: Clinical or basic research related to thalassemia. Applications on topics such as cardiac and endocrine complications of iron overload, hepatitis C, osteoporosis, bone marrow transplantation, iron chelation and gene therapy are encouraged.
Purpose: The research fellowship programme of the Cooley's Anemia Foundation exists to promote an increased understanding of Cooley's anemia, develop improved treatment and achieve a final cure for this life-threatening genetic blood disorder.
Eligibility: Fellows must have adequate preceptorship and guidance by an experienced investigator. The application is expected to be the original work of the candidate, but should reflect the close advice of the interested and involved sponsor. Applicants who are Fellows must have an MD, PhD or equivalent degree, and must not hold a faculty position. Applicants who are junior faculty must have an MD, PhD or equivalent degree, and must have completed less than 5 years at the assistant professor level at the time the applications are due.
Level of Study: Postgraduate
Type: Fellowship
Value: US$40,000
Length of Study: 1 year
Frequency: Annual
Study Establishment: Any suitable establishment
Country of Study: Any country
No. of awards offered: 10–15
Application Procedure: Qualified applicants should download an application form from the website.
Closing Date: March 5th

Funding: Private
Contributor: Study is supported by a grant from the Cooley's Anemia Foundation
No. of awards given last year: 11
Additional Information: The foundation seeks to make an extraordinary commitment towards recruiting doctors to pursue a career investigating thalassemia, especially due to the relatively small patient base in the United States of America.

COOPERATIVE RESEARCH CENTRE FOR WATER QUALITY AND TREATMENT (CRCWQT)

Australia Water Quality Centre, Private Mail Bag 3, Salisbury, SA,
5108, Australia
Tel: (61) 08 8259 0326
Fax: (61) 08 8259 0228
Email: dennis.steffensen@sawater.com.au
Website: www.waterquality.crc.org.au
Contact: Professor Dennis Mulcahy, Training Leader

The Cooperative Research Centre for Water Quality and Treatment (CRCWQT) provides a national strategic research capacity for the Australian water industry and focuses on issues relating to water quality management and health risk reduction.

CRCWQT Young Water Scientist of the Year Scholarship

Subjects: Agriculture and natural resources, environmental studies and sciences.
Purpose: To provide support to PhD students for research done within the Water Forum CRC.
Eligibility: Open to candidates who are in the final year of their PhD.
Level of Study: Doctorate
Type: Scholarship
Value: Australian $2,500
Length of Study: 1 year
Frequency: Annual
Country of Study: Australia

CORE

3 St Andrew's Place, London, NW1 4LB, England
Tel: (44) 20 7486 0341
Fax: (44) 20 7224 2012
Email: info@corecharity.org.uk
Website: www.corecharity.org.uk
Contact: Research Grants Administrator

CORE (the new name for the Digestive Disorders Foundation) supports research into the cause, prevention and treatment of digestive disorders, including digestive cancers, ulcers, irritable bowel syndrome, inflammatory bowel disease, diverticulitis, liver disease and pancreatitis. CORE also provides information for the public that explains the symptoms and treatment of these and other common digestive conditions.

CORE Fellowships and Grants

Subjects: Gastroenterology, such as basic or applied clinical research into normal and abnormal aspects of the gastrointestinal tract, liver and pancreas, and the prevention of and treatment for digestive disorders.
Purpose: To provide funding for gastroenterological research.
Eligibility: Open to applicants resident within the United Kingdom. Fellowship projects must contain an element of basic science training.
Level of Study: Doctorate, Postdoctorate, Postgraduate, Research
Type: Fellowship or Grant
Value: Up to UK £50,000 plus consumables for Research Grants. For fellowships, payment of a full-time, if medically qualified, is available
Length of Study: 1–3 years
Frequency: Dependent on funds available
Study Establishment: Recognized and established research centres
Country of Study: United Kingdom
No. of awards offered: Approx. 10 annually

Application Procedure: Applicants must complete an application form for consideration in a research competition. Details are available from the website.

Closing Date: June 1

Funding: Commercial, individuals, private, trusts

Contributor: Charitable donations

No. of applicants last year: Varies

Additional Information: Conditions are advertised in the medical press. Research grants are awarded for specific projects in the same field of interest.

CORNELL UNIVERSITY

Center for the Humanities, Andrew D White House, 27 East Avenue, Ithaca, NY 14853-1101, United States of America

Tel: (1) 607 255 9274

Email: humctr-mailbox@cornell.edu

Website: www.arts.cornell.edu/sochum

Contact: Program Administrator

Cornell University is a learning community that seeks to serve society by educating the leaders of the future and extending the frontiers of knowledge. The university aims to pursue understanding beyond the limitations of existing knowledge, ideology and disciplinary structure, and to affirm the value of the cultivation and enrichment of the human mind to individuals and society.

Mellon Postdoctoral Fellowships

Subjects: Arts and humanities.

Eligibility: Open to citizens of the United States of America and Canada and permanent residents who have completed requirements for a PhD before the application deadline and within the last 5 years.

Level of Study: Postdoctorate

Type: Fellowship

Value: US$45,000

Length of Study: 9 months

Frequency: Annual

Study Establishment: Cornell University

Country of Study: United States of America

No. of awards offered: 3–4

Application Procedure: Applicants must write for details.

Closing Date: Postmarked on or before October 1st

No. of awards given last year: 3

No. of applicants last year: 150

Additional Information: While in residence at Cornell, postdoctoral Fellows have department affiliation, limited teaching duties and the opportunity for scholarly work. Areas of specialization change each year.

Society for the Humanities Postdoctoral Fellowships

Subjects: Humanities.

Eligibility: Open to holders of a PhD degree who have at least 1 or 2 years of teaching experience at the college level. Applicants should be scholars with interests that are not confined to a narrow humanistic speciality and whose research coincides with the focal theme for the year. Fellows of the Society devote most of their time to research writing, but they are encouraged to offer a weekly seminar related to their special projects.

Level of Study: Postdoctorate

Type: Fellowship

Value: US$45,000

Length of Study: 1 academic year

Frequency: Annual

Study Establishment: Cornell University

Country of Study: United States of America

No. of awards offered: 6–7

Application Procedure: Applicants must contact the office to receive information on the theme and application materials.

Closing Date: Postmarked on or before October 1st

No. of awards given last year: 7

No. of applicants last year: 180

Additional Information: Information about this year's theme is available upon request.

THE COSTUME SOCIETY

Moore Stephens, St Paul's House, 8 Warwick Lane, London, EC4P 4BN, United Kingdom

Email: costumesociety@tiscali.co.uk

Website: www.costumesociety.org.uk

The Costume Society was formed in 1965 to promote the study and preservation of significant examples of historic and contemporary costumes.

The Costume Society Museum Placement Award

Purpose: To support students seeking museum work experience with a clothing/fashion/dress/costume collection and to help UK museums accomplish projects essential to the care, knowledge and interpretation of these types of collections. The award has been introduced to fund a student volunteer working on a clothing/fashion/dress/costume-related project in a public museum collection in the United Kingdom. The museum project/work experience should involve at least one of the following activities: documentation, numbering objects, preparing mannequins, mounting garments for display or photography, improving storage. Other appropriate object-related museum activities will be considered. The placement must be for a minimum of two months, either full or part-time.

Eligibility: The volunteer should be a student (minimum 2nd year) or graduate of an appropriate UK university course, such as dress/fashion history, museum studies, fashion design, theatre costume design, history, social history, art history.

Level of Study: Postgraduate, Graduate

Value: Up to £1,000

Length of Study: 2 months

Frequency: Annual

Country of Study: United Kingdom

No. of awards offered: 1

Application Procedure: The curator/administrator shall submit the application form with the name of the proposed volunteer and his/her CV and a proposal of not more than 500 words detailing the work the volunteer will be engaged in, its benefits to the museum and to the volunteer.

Closing Date: April 1st

Contributor: The Costume Society

No. of awards given last year: 1

No. of applicants last year: 7

Additional Information: Full details of the award are published on the Society's website www.costumesociety.org.uk and in *Costume*, the annual journal of the society.

For further information contact:

Costume Society Museum Placement Award Co-ordinator, Textiles & Fashion, V&A Museum, Cromwell Road, London, SW7 2RL

Contact: Susan North

The Costume Society Patterns of Fashion Award

Subjects: Historic and contemporary dress.

Purpose: To support a student on a theatre–wardrobe course at the graduate or post-graduate level who produces a reconstruction of a garment from a pattern in Janet Arnold's books *The Patterns of Fashion* to a standard which reflects that presented in the books.

Eligibility: The award is open to United Kingdom students studying costume-related higher education courses which involve the design and realization of costume.

Level of Study: Graduate, Postgraduate

Type: Grant

Value: UK £500 plus assisted travel for presentation for submitted work

Length of Study: As applicable to the course

Frequency: Annual

Study Establishment: Open to all courses applicable

Country of Study: United Kingdom

No. of awards offered: 1

Application Procedure: Applicants must submit photographs of a finished garment reconstructed from a pattern selected from one of the *Patterns of Fashion* books by Janet Arnold. The application must be supported by the Head of Department and Academic Supervisor of the course for which the applicant is enrolled.

Closing Date: April 30th

Funding: Trusts
Contributor: The Costume Society
No. of awards given last year: 1
Additional Information: Full details of the Award are published on the Society's website www.costumesociety.org.uk and in *Costume*, the annual journal of the society.

For further information contact:

The Awards Co-ordinator, The Patterns of Fashion Award, The Costume Society, Moore Stephens, St Paul's House, 8 Warwick Lane, London, EC4P 4BN, England

The Costume Society Student Bursary
Subjects: Historic and contemporary dress.
Purpose: To offer a postgraduate student full attendance at the Costume Society's annual conference/symposium exclusive of transport.
Eligibility: Open to UK students at the graduate and postgraduate level engaged in research directed towards a dissertation or thesis on the history and theory of dress. The research should reflect the theme of the Costume Society's current symposium or be an object-based project on the history of dress.
Level of Study: Graduate, Postgraduate
Type: Bursary
Value: Full-time attendance at the 3-day symposium inclusive of accommodation, meals and lecturer visits upto a maximum of £400
Length of Study: The award offers an intensive three days of study
Frequency: Annual
Study Establishment: Not specified
Country of Study: United Kingdom
No. of awards offered: 1
Application Procedure: The applicant should submit a curriculum vitae and a proposal of no more than 200 words identifying the subject area of the proposed research. The applicant should specify the institution and course attended and the names of the Head of Department and the academic supervisor who will be required as referees for awarding the bursary.
Closing Date: April 30th
Funding: Trusts
Contributor: The Costume Society
No. of awards given last year: 1
Additional Information: Full details of the Award are published on the Society's website www.costumesociety.org.uk and with *Costume*, the annual journal of the society.

For further information contact:

The Student Bursary, The Costume Society, c/o Moore Stephens, St Paul's House, 8 Warwick Lane, London, EC4P 4BN
Contact: The Awards Co-ordinator

The Costume Society Yarwood Award
Subjects: The history of historic and contempory dress.
Purpose: The award is made to a student on a specified MA course in the history of dress or theatre wardrobe design.
Eligibility: MA courses in the history of dress and theatre wardrobe design.
Level of Study: Postgraduate
Type: Award
Value: Up to UK £500
Frequency: Annual
Study Establishment: An academic institution is selected for a 3-year period
Country of Study: United Kingdom
No. of awards offered: 1
Application Procedure: Applications should be made by course leaders in writing to the Yarwood Award Sub-Committee giving details of the course accompanied by a course prospectus. Members of the Sub-Committee will wish to visit the course and meet the staff.
Funding: Trusts
Contributor: The Costume Society
No. of awards given last year: 1
Additional Information: The Award is offered at a specified academic institution for a period of 3 years and will subsequently be offered to another academic institution for a similar period so that all MA courses involving the history of dress or theatre wardrobe design

may benefit. The Yarwood Award is made in consultation with the course leader following the presentation of final year students' research leading to a final major project. The Award may be used for travel, research materials and publishing costs.

For further information contact:

The Costume Society, St Paul's House, 8 Warwick Lane, London, EC4P 4BN
Contact: The Yarwood Award Co-ordinator

THE COSTUME SOCIETY OF AMERICA (CSA)

PO Box 73, Earleville, MD 21919, United States of America
Tel: (1) 410 275 1619
Fax: (1) 410 275 8936
Email: national.office@costumesocietyamerica.com
Website: www.costumesocietyamerica.com
Contact: Administrative Assistant

The Costume Society of America (CSA) advances the global understanding of all aspects of dress and appearance. The Society seeks as members those who are involved in the study, education, collection, preservation, presentation and interpretation of dress and appearance in past, present and future societies.

CSA Adele Filene Travel Award
Subjects: Cultural heritage, museum studies and related areas.
Purpose: To assist student members in their travel to the CSA National Symposium to present an accepted paper or poster.
Eligibility: Open to current students with CSA membership who have been accepted to present a juried paper or poster at the CSA National Symposium.
Level of Study: Unrestricted
Type: Travel grant
Value: Up to US$500
Frequency: Annual
Country of Study: United States of America
No. of awards offered: 1–3
Application Procedure: Applicants must send three letters of support with a copy of the juried abstract and a one-page letter of application.
Closing Date: March 1st
No. of awards given last year: 4
No. of applicants last year: 3

CSA Stella Blum Research Grant
Subjects: North American costume.
Purpose: Support for research projects on North American costume by CSA student members.
Eligibility: Open to student members of the Society, who are enrolled on a degree programme at an accredited institution.
Level of Study: Postgraduate, Doctorate, Graduate, Postdoctorate, Predoctorate
Type: Grant
Value: Up to US$2,000 plus a travel component of up to $500 to attend National Symposium to present the completed research
Frequency: Annual
Study Establishment: An accredited institution
Country of Study: United States of America
No. of awards offered: 1
Application Procedure: Candidates must complete an application form, available upon request.
Closing Date: September 1st
No. of awards given last year: 1
No. of applicants last year: 4
Additional Information: The award will be given based on merit rather than need. Judging criteria will include creativity and innovation, specific awareness of and attention to costume matters, impact on the broad field of costume, awareness of the interdisciplinary nature of the field, ability to successfully implement the proposed project in a timely manner and faculty adviser recommendation.

For further information contact:

National Office, Costume Society of America, 203 Towne Centre Drive, Hillsborough NJ 08844, 800-CSA-9447

CSA Travel Research Grant

Subjects: Textile and fashion design, museum studies and related areas.
Purpose: To allow an individual to travel to collections for research purposes.
Eligibility: Applicants must be current, non-student CSA members and must have held membership for 2 years or more. Applicants must give proof of work in progress and indicate why the particular collection is important to the project.
Level of Study: Professional development
Value: Up to US$1,500
Frequency: Annual
Country of Study: Any country
No. of awards offered: 1
Application Procedure: Applicants must send a letter of application of no more than two pages and include the name of the collection and projected date of visit, a description of the project underway, evidence of work accomplished to date, reasons for visiting the designated collection, projected completion date of project, what audience the project will be directed to, as well as a current curriculum vitae.
Closing Date: September 1st
No. of awards given last year: 1
No. of applicants last year: 3

THE COUNCIL FOR BRITISH RESEARCH IN THE LEVANT (CBRL)

The British Academy, 10 Carlton House Terrace, London,
SW1Y 5AH, England
Tel: (44) 20 7969 5296
Fax: (44) 20 7969 5401
Email: cbrl@britac.ac.uk
Website: www.cbrl.org.uk

In 1998, the British Institute at Amman for Archaeology and History and the British School of Archaeology in Jerusalem amalgamated to create the Council for British Research in the Levant (CBRL). The CBRL promotes the study of the humanities and social sciences as relevant to the countries of the Levant (Cyprus, Israel, Jordan, Lebanon, Palestinian Territories and Syria).

CBRL Research Award

Subjects: Humanities and social sciences subjects, e.g. archaeology, economics, geography, historical studies, legal studies, languages and literature, linguistics, music, philosophy, politics, social anthropology, sociology and theology or religious studies.
Purpose: To support research projects from initial exploratory work through to publication.
Eligibility: Applicants must be of British nationality or ordinarily resident in the United Kingdom, Isle of Man or the Channel Islands.
Level of Study: Postdoctorate, Research
Type: Research award
Value: The value of individual awards does not normally exceed UK £10,000 and in most cases will be below that level
Frequency: Annual
Study Establishment: Council for British Research in the Levant
No. of awards offered: Varies
Application Procedure: Applicants must complete an application form, available from the United Kingdom Secretary at the main address or from the website.
Closing Date: December 1st
Funding: Government
Contributor: The British Academy
No. of awards given last year: 11
No. of applicants last year: 21

CBRL Travel Grant

Subjects: Humanities and social sciences subjects, e.g. archaeology, economics, geography, historical studies, legal studies, languages and literature, linguistics, music, philosophy, politics, social anthropology, sociology and theology or religious studies.
Purpose: To cover the travel and subsistence costs of students, academics and researchers undertaking reconnaissance tours or smaller research projects in the countries of the Levant.

Eligibility: Applicants must be of British nationality, a citizen of the European Union or ordinarily resident in the United Kingdom, Isle of Man or the Channel Islands, or registered for a full-time undergraduate or postgraduate degree in a United Kingdom university.
Level of Study: Unrestricted
Type: Travel grant
Value: A maximum of UK £800
Frequency: Annual
Study Establishment: Council for British Research in the Levant
No. of awards offered: Varies
Application Procedure: Applicants must complete an application form, available from the United Kingdom Secretary at the main address or from the CBRL website.
Closing Date: January 15th
Funding: Government
Contributor: The British Academy
No. of awards given last year: 18
No. of applicants last year: 31

CBRL Visiting Research Fellowships

Subjects: Humanities and social sciences subjects, e.g. archaeology, economics, geography, historical studies, legal studies, languages and literature, linguistics, music, philosophy, politics, social anthropology, sociology and theology or religious studies.
Purpose: To enable individuals to spend a period of between 3 and 9 months in the Levant, which is to include a minimum of 1 month residency at the British Institute in Amman or the Kenyon Institute in Jerusalem.
Eligibility: Applicants must be of British nationality or ordinarily resident in the UK, Isle of Man or the Channel Islands, or registered on a full-time doctoral degree in a UK university.
Level of Study: Postdoctorate, Research, Doctorate
Type: Research award
Value: Fellowship will provide: a return airfare between the UK and Levant, a subsistence allowance of £10 per day, free hostel accomodation whilst resident at the British Institute in Amman or the Kenyon Institute in Jerusalem
Study Establishment: Council for British Research in the Levant
No. of awards offered: Varies
Application Procedure: Applicants must complete an application form, available from the UK Secretary at the main address or from the website.
Closing Date: January 15th
Funding: Government
Contributor: The British Academy
No. of awards given last year: 5
No. of applicants last year: 8

COUNCIL FOR INTERNATIONAL EXCHANGE OF SCHOLARS (CIES)

3007 Tilden Street North West, Suite 5L, Washington, DC 20008-3009, United States of America
Tel: (1) 202 686 4000
Fax: (1) 202 362 3442
Email: apprequest@cies.iie.org
Website: www.cies.org
Contact: Ms Nancy Gainer, Director of External Relations

The Council for International Exchange of Scholars (CIES) is a private, non-profit organization that facilitates international exchanges in higher education. Under a co-operative agreement with the United States of America Department of State Bureau of Educational and Cultural Affairs, it assists in the administration of the Fulbright Scholar Program for faculty and professionals. CIES is affiliated with the Institute of International Education.

Fulbright Distinguished Chairs Program

Subjects: American studies (history, politics and literature), humanities, law, social sciences, computer science and e-commerce, business and management, fine arts, mass communications and journalism.
Purpose: To increase mutual understanding between the people of the United States of America and other countries and to promote international educational co-operation.

Eligibility: Open to citizens of the United States of America who hold a PhD or equivalent qualification. Candidates should have a prominent record of scholarly achievement.
Level of Study: Postdoctorate
Value: Varies by country
Length of Study: 3 months–1 academic year
Frequency: Annual
No. of awards offered: Approx. 30
Application Procedure: Applicants must submit a letter of intent and an eight-page curriculum vitae, and should telephone CIES or visit the website for more information.
Closing Date: August 1st
Funding: Government, private
No. of awards given last year: 30
No. of applicants last year: 300
Additional Information: Applicants must contact Dario Teutonico at dteutonico@cies.iie.org for more information.

Fulbright Senior Specialists Program

Subjects: Anthropology, archaeology, business administration, communications and journalism, economics, education, environmental science, information technology, law, library science, political science, public administration, sociology, social work, United States of America studies and urban planning.
Purpose: To offer short-term grants and encourage new types of activities in the Fulbright context. The programme also aims to advance mutual understanding, establish long-term co-operation and create opportunities for institutional linkages.
Eligibility: Open to citizens of the United States of America with a PhD or comparable professional qualification.
Level of Study: Postdoctorate, Professional development
Type: Grant
Value: An honorarium and international travel expenses
Length of Study: 2–6 weeks
Frequency: Annual
Country of Study: Other
No. of awards offered: Varies
Application Procedure: Applicants must complete the application form, available on the CIES website.
Closing Date: Applications and grants are processed on a rolling basis
Funding: Government
Additional Information: Successful candidates are expected to lecture, lead seminars, work with foreign counterparts on curriculum and program and institutional development. Applicants must contact fulspec@cies.iie.org for more information.

COUNCIL FOR THE ADVANCEMENT OF SCIENCE WRITING, INC. (CASW)

PO Box 910, Hedgesville, WV 25427, United States of America
Tel: (1) 304 754 5077
Fax: (1) 304 754 5076
Email: diane@nasw.org
Website: www.casw.org
Contact: Ms Diane McGurgan, Administration Secretary

The CASW is a group of distinguished journalists and scientists committed to improving the quality of science news reaching the general public.

Taylor/Blakeslee Fellowships for Graduate Study in Science Writing

Subjects: Journalism.
Purpose: To support graduate study in science writing.
Eligibility: Applicants must have a degree in science or journalism and must convince the CASW selection committee of their ability to pursue a career in science writing for the general public.
Level of Study: Postgraduate
Type: Fellowship
Value: A maximum of US$2,000
Length of Study: 1 year
Frequency: Annual
Country of Study: United States of America
No. of awards offered: 2–4

Application Procedure: Applicants must submit four collated sets of a completed application form, a curriculum vitae, a transcript of undergraduate studies if a student, three faculty recommendations or employer recommendations, three samples of writing on 8.5 by 11 inch sheets only and a short statement of career goals.
Closing Date: July 1st
Funding: Private
No. of awards given last year: 4
No. of applicants last year: 16
Additional Information: Science writing is defined as writing about science, medicine, health, technology and the environment for the general public via the mass media.

COUNCIL OF AMERICAN OVERSEAS RESEARCH CENTERS (CAORC)

PO Box 37012 NHB Room CE-123 MRC 178, Washington, DC, 20013-7012, United States of America
Tel: (1) 202 633 1599
Fax: (1) 202 786 2430
Email: fellowships@caorc.org
Website: www.caorc.org

Council of American Overseas Research Centers (CAORC) serve as a base for virtually every American scholar undertaking research in the host countries. The members have centres in many locations across the world.

CAORC Andrew W. Mellon East-Central European Research Fellows

Subjects: Humanities and allied social sciences.
Purpose: To help scholars in the humanities and allied social sciences to carry out research at institutes of advanced study in other countries.
Eligibility: Open to candidates who have obtained a PhD and are nationals of Bulgaria, Czech, Estonia, Hungary, Latvia, Lithuania, Poland, Romania or Slovakia.
Level of Study: Research
Type: Fellowships
Value: Varies
Length of Study: Short-term residencies
Frequency: Annual
No. of awards offered: 3

CAORC Multi-Country Research Fellowship Program For Advanced Multi-Country Research

Subjects: Humanities, social sciences or allied natural sciences.
Purpose: To advance higher learning and scholarly research and to conduct research of regional or trans-regional significance.
Eligibility: Applicants must have obtained a PhD or be established postdoctoral scholars. The candidates should be a citizens of the United States.
Level of Study: Research
Type: Fellowships
Value: US$9,000
Frequency: Annual
No. of awards offered: Approx. 10
Application Procedure: The application can be downloaded from the website. To obtain hard copy of the application, please contact CAORC.
Closing Date: January 16th
Additional Information: Scholars must carry out research in at least one of the countries that host overseas research centres.

COUNCIL OF SCIENTIFIC & INDUSTRIAL RESEARCH (CSIR)

CSIR Complex, Library Avenue, Pusa, New Delhi, 110-012, India
Tel: (91) 011 2574 8632, 011 2572 1585
Fax: (91) 011 2572 0997
Email: csircx@nda.vsnl.net.in
Website: www.csir.res.in

Council of Scientific & Industrial Research (CSIR) is a premier national research and development organization in India. It is among the world's largest publicly funded research and development organization. Human Resource Development Group, a division of CSIR, realises this objective through various grants, fellowship, schemes, etc.

CSIR Senior Research Associateship (SRA) Scheme

Subjects: Agriculture sciences, chemical sciences, earth, atmosphere, ocean and planetary sciences, life sciences, material sciences, mathematical statistics, operation research and computer sciences, physical sciences, engineering sciences, medical sciences and social sciences and humanities.
Purpose: To financially support highly qualified, but unemployed Indian nationals including those returning from abroad, to carry out independent research.
Eligibility: Open to Indian citizens who are not more than 35 years of age and have obtained M.Tech/ME/MD/MS/MVSc/MPharma/PhD in any branch of science/PhD in social sciences and humanities. The candidate should have followed it by 2 years of research/teaching experience or PhD in engineering/technology.
Level of Study: Doctorate, Postdoctorate, Predoctorate, Research
Type: Fellowship
Value: Indian Rupees 9,000–9,500 or Indian Rupees per month
Length of Study: 2 years, possible extension
Frequency: Annual
Country of Study: India
Application Procedure: Applicants must download the complete application form from the website.

COUNCIL OF SUPPLY CHAIN MANAGEMENT PROFESSIONALS (CSCMP)

333 East Butterfield Road, Suite 140, Lombard, IL 60148, United States of America
Tel: (1) 630 574 0985
Fax: (1) 630 574 0989
Email: cscmpadmin@cscmp.org
Website: www.cscmp.org
Contact: Kathleen Hedland, Director Education and Roundtable Services

The Council of Supply Chain Management Professionals (CSCMP) is a non-profit organization of business personnel who are interested in improving their logistics management skills. CSCMP works in cooperation with private industry and various organizations to further the understanding and development of the logistics concept. This is accomplished through a continuing programme of organized activities, research and meetings designed to develop the theory and understanding of the logistics process, promote the art and science of managing logistics systems, and foster professional dialogue and development within the profession.

CSCMP Distinguished Service Award

Subjects: Logistics.
Purpose: To recognize all those involved in logistics.
Eligibility: All individuals who have made contributions to the field of supply chain management are eligible for the DSA. This includes practitioners with responsibilities in a functional area of supply chain management, consultants, and educators anyone who has made a significant contribution to the advancement of supply chain management.
Type: Award
Frequency: Annual
Closing Date: April 30th

CSCMP Doctoral Dissertation Award

Subjects: Logistics.
Purpose: To encourage research leading to advancement of the theory and practice to logistics management.
Eligibility: Open to all candidates whose doctoral dissertation demonstrates signified originality and contributes to the logistics knowledge base.
Level of Study: Postdoctorate

Value: $5,000
Length of Study:
Frequency: Annual
Closing Date: March 21st

CSCMP George A Gecowets Graduate Scholarship Program

Subjects: Logistics management.
Purpose: To acknowledge the importance of logistics in a tangible way, while emphasising the Council's commitment to promote the art and science of managing logistics systems.
Eligibility: Applicants must be planning to pursue a career in logistics management, be a senior at an accredited 4 year college or university, and already be enrolled in the first year of a logistics or logistics related Master's degree programme.
Level of Study: Graduate
Type: Scholarship
Value: $2,000
Frequency: Annual
No. of awards offered: 15
Application Procedure: Applicants must submit a completed application, official college transcripts, Graduate Record Examination scores or Graduate Management Admission Test scores, and notification of any changes in address, school enrolment, or other pertinent information. The Citizens' Scholarship Foundation of America (CSFA) will then send a complete application package upon request.
Closing Date: Postmarked April 1st
Funding: Private
Contributor: The Council of Logistics Management
Additional Information: The Council wishes to make high potential students aware of the tremendous opportunities and challenges that await them in a career in logistics management, as the last 10 years have seen an exponential increase in the importance of the logistics manager.

For further information contact:

Council of Supply Chain Management Professionals, George A Gecowets Graduate Scholarship Program, Scholarship Management Services CSFA, 1505 Riverview Road, PO Box 297, St Peter, MN, 56082, United States of America

COUNCIL ON FOREIGN RELATIONS (CFR)

The Harold Pratt House, 58 East 68th Street, New York, NY 10021, United States of America
Tel: (1) 212 434 9489
Fax: (1) 212 434 9801
Email: fellowships@cfr.org
Website: www.cfr.org
Contact: Ms Elise Lewis, Vice President, Membership and Fellowship Affairs

The Council on Foreign Relations (CFR) is dedicated to increasing America's understanding of the world and contributing ideas to United States of America foreign policy. The Council accomplishes this mainly by promoting constructive debates and discussions, clarifying world issues and publishing *Foreign Affairs*, the leading journal on global issues.

CFR International Affairs Fellowship Program in Japan

Subjects: International relations.
Purpose: To cultivate the United States of America's understanding of Japan and to strengthen communication between emerging leaders of the two nations.
Eligibility: Open to citizens of the United States of America aged 27–45 who have not had prior substantial experience in Japan. Fellows will be drawn from academia, government institutions, the business community and the media. The programme does not fund pre- or postdoctoral scholarly research, work towards a degree or the completion of projects on which substantial progress has been made prior to the fellowship period. Knowledge of the Japanese language is not a requirement.
Level of Study: Professional development

Type: Fellowship
Value: Living expenses in Japan plus international transportation, health and travel insurance and necessary research expenses
Length of Study: 3 months to 1 year
Frequency: Annual
Country of Study: Japan
No. of awards offered: 2–5
Application Procedure: Application is primarily by invitation, on the recommendation of individuals in academic, government and other institutions who have occasion to know candidates particularly well suited for the experience offered by this fellowship. Others who inquire directly and who meet preliminary requirements may also be invited to apply without formal nomination. Those invited to apply will be forwarded application materials.
Closing Date: September 15th is the deadline for nominations and October 31st is the application deadline. Nominations and applications will also be accepted out of cycle
Funding: Private
Contributor: Hitachi Limited
No. of awards given last year: 3
No. of applicants last year: 6
Additional Information: While the Fellow is not required to produce a book, article or report, it is hoped that some written output will result.

CFR International Affairs Fellowships

Subjects: Important problems in international affairs and their implications for the interests and policies of the United States of America, foreign states or international organizations.
Purpose: To bridge the gap between analysis and action in foreign policy by supporting a variety of policy studies and active experiences in policy making.
Eligibility: Open to United States citizens aged 27–35. While a PhD is not a requirement, successful candidates should generally hold advanced degrees and possess a solid record of work experience. The programme does not fund pre- or postdoctoral research, work towards a degree, or the completion of projects for which substantial progress has been made prior to the fellowship period.
Level of Study: Professional development, Research
Type: Fellowship
Value: Determined according to individual budget statements in consultation with the programme administration. The programme will attempt to meet the major portion of a Fellow's current income, up to a maximum of US$60,000. The programme does not provide support for research assistance. Fellows may receive a travel grant of up to US$3,000
Length of Study: 1 year
Frequency: Annual
Country of Study: Any country
No. of awards offered: 8–12
Application Procedure: Application is primarily by invitation, on the recommendation of individuals in academic, government and other institutions who have occasion to know candidates particularly well suited for the experience offered by this fellowship. Others who enquire directly and who meet preliminary requirements may also be invited to apply without formal nomination. Those invited to apply will be forwarded application materials.
Closing Date: September 15th is the deadline for nominations and October 31st is the application deadline
Funding: Private
No. of awards given last year: 11
No. of applicants last year: 30
Additional Information: While the Fellow is not required to produce a book, article or report, it is hoped that some written output will result.

Edward R Murrow Fellowship for Foreign Correspondents

Subjects: Issues in international affairs and their implications for the interests and policies of the United States of America, foreign states or international organizations.
Purpose: To help the Fellow increase his or her competency in reporting and interpreting events abroad and to give him or her a period of nearly a year of sustained analysis and writing, free from the daily pressures that characterize journalistic life.
Eligibility: Open to any correspondent, editor or producer for radio, television, a newspaper or a magazine widely available in the United States of America who has covered international news. Eligibility is limited to those individuals who are authorized to work in the United States and who will continue to be authorized for the duration of the fellowship.
Level of Study: Professional development
Type: Fellowship
Value: A stipend equivalent to the salary relinquished, not to exceed US$65,000 for 9 months
Length of Study: Normally a period of 9 months
Frequency: Annual
Study Establishment: The Council headquarters in New York City
No. of awards offered: 1
Application Procedure: Application is primarily by nomination. A nomination letter must be submitted to the main address. The nomination letter may be submitted by a Council member, a former or current Murrow Fellow, the candidate's employer, or the candidates themselves. The nomination letter should confirm the candidate's eligibility as well as provide a brief description of their background and why the nominator believes the candidate to be an appropriate prospect for the Fellowship. For those candidates who choose to nominate themselves, their letter should address the same aforementioned issues in addition to providing a copy of their most recent curriculum vitae. Nominees who meet the criteria of the programme will then be forwarded an application form.
Closing Date: February 29th
Funding: Private
No. of awards given last year: 1
No. of applicants last year: 10

COUNCIL ON LIBRARY AND INFORMATION RESOURCES (CLIR)

1752 N Street NW Suite 800, Washington DC, 20036, United States of America
Tel: (1) 202 939 4750/4751
Fax: (1) 202 939 4765
Email: abishop@clir.org
Website: www.clir.org
Contact: Alice Bishop, Special Projects Associate

Council on Library and Information Resources (CLIR) is an independent, non-profit organization. Through publications, projects and programmes, CLIR works to maintain and improve access to information. In partnership with other institutions, CLIR helps create services that expand the concept of the term library and supports the providers and preservers of information.

Postdoctoral Fellowship in Academic Libraries for Humanists

Subjects: Humanities.
Purpose: To provide a unique opportunity to develop expertise in the new forms of scholarly research and the information resources.
Eligibility: Open to candidates who have received a PhD in the field of humanities.
Level of Study: Postdoctorate
Type: Fellowships
Value: Varies
Length of Study: 1–2 years
Frequency: Annual
Country of Study: United States of America
Application Procedure: Applicants can download the application form and the reference form from the website and 2 copies of completed application forms along with 2 copies of curriculum vitae, 3 letters of reference and graduate school transcripts are to be mailed.
Closing Date: December 30th
Funding: Private

COUNCIL ON SOCIAL WORK EDUCATION (CSWE)

1725 Duke Street, Suite 500, Alexandria, VA 22314-3457, United States of America
Tel: (1) 703 683 8080
Fax: (1) 703 683 8099
Email: jjones@cswe.org
Website: www.cswe.org
Contact: Dr Jenny Jones, Director, Minority Fellowship Programmes

The Council on Social Work Education (CSWE) provides national leadership and a forum for collective action designed to ensure the preparation of competent and committed social work professionals. Founded in 1952, CSWE is a non-profit, tax exempt, national organization representing 2,700 individual members as well as 650 graduate and undergraduate programmes of professional social work education. CSWE's goals include improving the quality of social work education, preparing competent human service professionals and developing new programmes to meet the demands of the changing services delivery systems.

CSWE Doctoral Fellowships in Social Work for Ethnic Minority Students Preparing for Leadership Roles in Mental Health and/or Substance Abuse

Subjects: Mental health or substance abuse.
Purpose: To equip ethnic minority individuals for the provision of leadership, teaching, consultation, training, policy development and administration in mental health or substance abuse programmes and to enhance the development and dissemination of knowledge that is required for the provision of relevant clinical and social services to ethnic minority individuals and communities.
Eligibility: Applicants must be citizens or permanent residents of the United States of America, including, but not limited to, persons who are American Indian or Alaskan Native, Asian or Pacific Islander, Chinese, East Indian and other South Asians, Filipino, Hawaiian, Japanese, Korean or Samoan, black or Hispanic, e.g. Mexican or Chicano, Puerto Rican, Cuban, Central or South American. This programme is open to students who have a Master's degree in social work and who will begin full-time study leading to a doctoral degree in social work or who are currently enrolled as full-time students in a doctoral social work programme.
Level of Study: Graduate
Type: Fellowship
Value: Monthly stipends to help defray living expenses. Some tuition support may be provided depending upon the availability of funds
Length of Study: 1 year, award is renewable for up to 3 years upon reapplication if the fellow maintains satisfactory progress
Study Establishment: Schools of Social Work
Country of Study: United States of America
No. of awards offered: Varies
Application Procedure: Applicants must write to the CSWE for an application pack and further information or visit the website.
Closing Date: February 28th
Funding: Government
Contributor: The Substance Abuse and Mental Health Services Administration
Additional Information: Applicants should demonstrate potential for assuming leadership roles, as well as potential for success in doctoral studies and commitment to a career in providing mental health and/or substance abuse services to ethnic minority clients and communities.

CSWE Doctoral Fellowships in Social Work for Ethnic Minority Students Specializing in Mental Health

Subjects: Mental health research.
Purpose: To educate leaders of the nation's next generation of mental health researchers.
Eligibility: Applicants must be citizens of the United States of America or permanent residents, including, but not limited to, persons who are American Indian or Alaskan Native, Asian or Pacific Islander, Chinese, East Indian and other South Asians, Filipino, Hawaiian, Japanese, Korean or Samoan, black or Hispanic, e.g. Mexican or Chicano, Puerto Rican, Cuban, Central or South American. This programme is open to students who have a Master's degree in social work and who will begin full-time study leading to a doctoral degree in social work or are currently enrolled as full-time students in a doctoral social work programme.
Level of Study: Graduate
Type: Fellowship
Value: Monthly stipends to help defray living expenses. Tuition support provided according to the National Insititute of Health tuition formula
Length of Study: 1 year, although the award is renewable upon reapplication if the Fellow maintains satisfactory progress towards degree objectives and funding is available
Study Establishment: Schools of Social Work

Country of Study: United States of America
No. of awards offered: Varies
Application Procedure: Applicants must write to the CSWE for an application pack and further information or visit the website.
Closing Date: February 28th
Funding: Government
Contributor: The Division of Epidemiology and Services Research, NIMH
Additional Information: Applicants should demonstrate potential for, and interest in, mental health research, as well as potential for success in doctoral studies and commitment to a career in mental health research.

For further information contact:

CSWE Minority Research Fellowship Program, 1600 Duke Street, Suite 300, Alexandria, VA 22314-3421

THE COUNTESS OF MUNSTER MUSICAL TRUST

Wormley Hill, Godalming, Surrey,
GU8 5SG, England
Tel: (44) 14 2868 5427
Fax: (44) 14 2868 5064
Email: admin@munstertrust.org.uk
Website: www.munstertrust.org.uk
Contact: Mrs Gillian Ure, Secretary

The Countess of Munster Musical Trust provides financial assistance towards the cost of studies and maintenance of outstanding postgraduate students who merit further training at home or abroad. Each year, the Trust is able to offer a small number of interest-free loans for instrument purchase to former beneficiaries.

Countess of Munster Musical Trust Awards

Subjects: Musical studies.
Purpose: To enable students, selected after interview and audition, to pursue a course of specialist or advanced performance studies.
Eligibility: Open to United Kingdom or British Commonwealth citizens who are aged 18–24 years (for instrumentalists, conductors and composers) or under 28 (for singers) who show outstanding musical ability and potential.
Level of Study: Postgraduate, Professional development, Private Lessons
Type: Grant
Value: By individual assessment to meet tuition fees and maintenance according to need, usually between UK £500–6,000
Length of Study: 1 year, with the possibility of renewal
Frequency: Annual
Country of Study: Any country
No. of awards offered: Up to 80 per year
Application Procedure: Applicants must complete an application form and will have to attend an audition and interview.
Closing Date: Application forms must be received between January and February 14th for awards to go through in September
Funding: Private
No. of awards given last year: 64
No. of applicants last year: 268

CRANFIELD UNIVERSITY

School of Applied Sciences, Bedfordshire, Cranfield,
MK43 OAL, England
Tel: (44) 1234 754086
Fax: (44) 1234 754109
Email: appliedsciences@cranfield.ac.uk
Website: www.cranfield.ac.uk/sas
Contact: Emma Longstaff

The school of applied sciences is recognized globally for its multidisciplinary approach to teaching and research in the key areas of manufacturing, materials, natural resources and sustainable systems. Our focus is on fundamental research and its application, together with teaching, to meet the needs of industry and society.

Department of Agriculture and Rural Development (DARD) for Northern Ireland

Subjects: Agricultural and environmental engineering, innovation and design for sustainability, environmental diagnostics and management, environmental management for business, geographical information management, waste and resource management, land management, water management.

Purpose: To assist candidates to obtain the necessary qualifications and experience to fit them for advisory, teaching, research and other technical work in agricultural and food industries and development of the economy and social infrastructure of rural areas.

Eligibility: Open to full time students only.

Level of Study: Postgraduate

Type: Studentship

Length of Study: 1 year

Frequency: Annual

Study Establishment: Cranfield University, School of Applied Sciences

Country of Study: United Kingdom, Republic of Ireland

Application Procedure: Application form can be downloaded from www.dardni.gov.uk

Funding: Government

Contributor: DARD

Douglas Bomford Trust

Subjects: Agricultural and environmental engineering, environmental diagnostics and management, environmental management for business, geographical information management, innovation and design for sustainability, land management, water management, waste and resource management, water and wastewater engineering, water and wastewater technology.

Purpose: To advance knowledge, understanding, practice, competence and capability in the application of engineering and physical science to agriculture, horticulture, forestry, amenity, and allied land basal and biological activities for sustainable benefit of the environment and mankind.

Eligibility: Individuals must demonstrate a long-term commitment to the areas of concern to the trust and have some connection with the United Kingdom through nationality, residency, or place of learning/registration.

Level of Study: Postgraduate

Value: Two options: either more or less than £1,500

Length of Study: 1 year

Frequency: Annual

Study Establishment: Cranfield University, School of Applied Sciences

Country of Study: United Kingdom

Application Procedure: Please check the website www.dbt.org.uk for details.

Funding: Trusts

Contributor: Douglas Bomford Trust

Environmental Issues Award

Subjects: Land management, geographical information management, water management, water science, innovation and design for sustainability, environmental management for business, environmental diagnostics and management.

Purpose: To support educational programmes dealing with environmental issues or support environmental project work.

Eligibility: Applicants must be members of the Institution of Mechanical Engineers and hold a degree accredited by the institution.

Level of Study: Postgraduate

Value: Up to £1,000

Frequency: Annual

Study Establishment: Cranfield University, School of Applied Sciences

Country of Study: United Kingdom

Application Procedure: Applicants must complete a form titled "Edcational Awards Committee for Financial Support" available from www.imeche.org/industries/prizeaward/postgraduate development awards/environmental issues award.htm

Contributor: IMechE

Grand Prix Mechanics Charitable Trust Fund

Subjects: Motorsport engineering and management.

Purpose: To subsidise study and living expenses for individuals wishing to pusue a career in F1.

Eligibility: Full time UK students are eligible to apply.

Level of Study: Postgraduate

Length of Study: 1 year

Frequency: Annual

Study Establishment: Cranfield University, School of Applied Sciences

Country of Study: United Kingdom

No. of awards offered: 2

Closing Date: End of June

Funding: Trusts

Contributor: Grand Prix Mechanics

The Lorch MSc Student Bursary

Subjects: Availabe to students wishing to study full-time MSc Water and Wastewater Engineering or MSc Water and Wastewater Technology.

Purpose: To assist postgraduate study.

Eligibility: Applicants should be UK citizens and possess a minimum 2:1 UK Honours degree in Engineering or Physical Sciences or related discipline, and have been offered a place on the 1-year full-time MSc in Water and Wastewater Engineering or Water and Wastewater Technology.

Level of Study: Postgraduate

Type: Bursary

Value: UK £5,000 plus tuition fees

Length of Study: 1 year

Frequency: Annual

Study Establishment: Cranfield University, School of Applied Sciences

Country of Study: United Kingdom

No. of awards offered: 1

Application Procedure: Applicants must apply directly to the university.

Closing Date: July

Funding: Foundation

Contributor: The Lorch Foundation

No. of awards given last year: 1

Additional Information: The bursary is provided by the Lorch Foundation, a charitable institution founded to support and promote education and research in the field of water purification and related sciences for the benefit of mankind. The successful applicant will undertake thesis research on processes of water purification and industrial effluent recycling as part of the MSc programme.

Natural Environment Research Council (NERC) Masters Studentships

Subjects: Available for students wishing to study MSc Water Management (Environmental Water Management option).

Purpose: To cover course fees and contribute towards research and fieldwork costs.

Eligibility: Open to UK candidates only who have a good UK honours degree or equivalent and have been offered a place on the MSc in Water Management. Students from other countries may be eligible for the fees only award

Level of Study: Postgraduate

Value: Award covers course fees and include a stipend

Length of Study: 1 year

Frequency: Annual

Study Establishment: Cranfield University, School of Applied Sciences

Country of Study: United Kingdom

No. of awards offered: Approx. 5–10

Application Procedure: Applicants must apply directly to the university.

Closing Date: July

Funding: Government

Contributor: NERC

No. of applicants last year: 75+

Panasonic Trust Fellowships

Subjects: Water and wastewater engineering, water and wastewater technology, and waste and resource management, engineering and management of manufacturing systems, manufacturing consultancy,

253

management and information systems, decision engineering, IT for product engineering, knowledge management for innovation and enterprise system implementation.

Purpose: To provide financial support to selected graduate engineers wishing to undertake full time Masters courses in subjects related to the environment and sustainability.

Level of Study: Postgraduate
Type: Fellowship
Value: £8,000
Frequency: Annual
Study Establishment: Cranfield University, School of Applied Sciences
Country of Study: United Kingdom
Application Procedure: Application form can be downloaded from www.raeng.org.uk or contact the Panasonic Trust.
Closing Date: August
Funding: Trusts
Contributor: The Royal Academy of Engineering

For further information contact:

Tel: 44(0)20 7222 2688

School of Applied Sciences Overseas Scholarships
Subjects: A wide range of disciplines, including advanced materials, motorsport engineering, nanotechnology, offshore engineering, welding, manufacturing, water and waste management sustainability, sports surface technology and management.
Purpose: To complement an individual overseas student's fees (50 per cent of total).
Level of Study: Postgraduate
Type: Scholarship
Value: Approx. UK £8,000
Length of Study: 1 year
Frequency: Annual
Study Establishment: Cranfield University, School of Applied Sciences
Country of Study: United Kingdom
No. of awards offered: 5
Application Procedure: Complete and submit an application form along with two references.
Closing Date: April of each year although early application is advised
Funding: Trusts
Contributor: School of Applied Sciences
No. of awards given last year: 5
No. of applicants last year: 48
Additional Information: Candidates must demonstrate their ability to fund the remaining 50 per cent of the overseas fees and to be able to support themselves while at Cranfield University.

Society for Underwater Technology (SUT)
Subjects: Offshore and ocean technology.
Purpose: To sponsor gifted students in Marine, Science and Engineering to meet industry's critical shortage of suitably qualified entrants.
Eligibility: First degree in an engineering or science subject.
Level of Study: Postgraduate
Value: Up to £4,000
Length of Study: 1 year
Frequency: Annual
Study Establishment: Cranfield University, School of Applied Sciences
Country of Study: United Kingdom
Application Procedure: Please check the website www.sut.org.uk
Closing Date: July 31st
Funding: Corporation
Contributor: SUT

For further information contact:

SUT, 80 Coleman Street, London,

Ultra Precision Technologies Industrial Studentships
Subjects: Ultra precision technologies.
Eligibility: Applications can be downloaded from the website www.cranfield.ac.uk/sas. Funding details are provided once an applicant has been accepted for the course.

Frequency: Annual
Study Establishment: Cranfield University, School of Applied Sciences
Country of Study: United Kingdom
Funding: Commercial
Contributor: Various

Utilities and Service Industries Training (USIT)
Subjects: Economics for natural resources and environmental management, innovation and design for sustainability, environmental diagnostics and management, environmental management for business, water and wastewater engineering, water and wastewater technology, and water management.
Purpose: To support students attending an established academic course in the UK, which is relevant to one water utility industry.
Level of Study: Postgraduate
Value: Up to £7,500
Length of Study: 1 year
Frequency: Annual
Study Establishment: Cranfield University, School of Applied Sciences
Country of Study: United Kingdom
Application Procedure: Application form can be downloaded from the website www.usit.org.uk. Applicants must submit a short paper to support the application.
Closing Date: March 31st
Funding: Foundation
Contributor: USIT
No. of awards given last year: 2

Williams F1 Bursaries
Subjects: Motorsport engineering and management.
Purpose: To support students whose interest is in mechanical/design engineering in relation to motorsport.
Level of Study: Postgraduate
Value: £4,800
Length of Study: 1 year
Frequency: Annual
Study Establishment: Cranfield University, School of Applied Sciences
Country of Study: United Kingdom
No. of awards offered: 2
Application Procedure: Please check the website www.motorsport.cranfield.ac.uk for more details.
Funding: Commercial
Contributor: Williams F1

CRIMINOLOGY RESEARCH COUNCIL (CRC)

GPO Box 2944, Canberra, ACT 2601, Australia
Tel: (61) 2 6260 9295
Fax: (61) 2 6260 9201
Email: crc@aic.gov.au
Website: www.aic.gov.au/crc
Contact: Administrator

The Criminology Research Council (CRC) funds methodologically sound research in the areas of sociology, psychology, law, statistics, police, judiciary, corrections, mental health, social welfare, education and related fields. The research to be conducted is policy-orientated, and research outcomes should have the potential for application nationally or in other jurisdictions.

CRC Grants
Subjects: Criminological research in the areas of sociology, psychology, law, statistics, police, judiciary and corrections, etc. From time to time the Council will call for research in specific areas.
Eligibility: Open to Australian residents or visitors (actual or intending) who are pursuing or intend to pursue studies of consequence to the furtherance of criminological research in Australia. Grants are not likely to be given for assistance with research leading to the award of postgraduate degrees.
Level of Study: Doctorate, Postdoctorate
Type: Grant

Value: Variable
Length of Study: Usually 1 year, with a possibility of renewal for up to 3 years
Frequency: Annual
Country of Study: Australia
No. of awards offered: Approx. 6
Application Procedure: Applicants must complete an application form, available from the CRC.
Closing Date: 12 weeks prior to meetings
Funding: Government
No. of awards given last year: 3
No. of applicants last year: 45
Additional Information: The Council does not ordinarily consider applications involving travelling expenses outside Australia. Meetings are held in March, July and November. The November meeting is for general grants funding in any area the council deems relevant.

THE CROHN'S AND COLITIS FOUNDATION OF AMERICA

386 Park Avenue South, 17th Floor, New York, NY, 10016-8804, United States of America
Tel: (1) 800 932 2423
Fax: (1) 212 779 4098
Email: info@ccfa.org
Website: www.ccfa.org
Contact: Ms Carol M Cox, Research Co-ordinator

The Crohn's and Colitis Foundation of America is a non-profit, voluntary health organization dedicated to improving the quality of life for persons with Crohn's disease or ulcerative colitis. It supports basic and clinical scientific research to find the causes and cure for these diseases, provides educational programmes for patients, medical and healthcare professionals and the general public, alongside offering supportive services to patients, their families and friends.

Crohn's and Colitis Foundation Career Development Award
Subjects: Crohn's disease and ulcerative colitis.
Purpose: To stimulate and encourage innovative research that is likely to increase our understanding of the aetiology, pathogenesis, therapy and prevention of Crohn's disease and ulcerative colitis (IBD).
Eligibility: Candidates should hold an MD and must have 5 years of experience (with 2 years of research relevant to IBD).
Level of Study: Research, Postdoctorate
Type: Award
Value: Not to exceed US$90,000 per year
Length of Study: 1–3 years
Study Establishment: An approved research institute
Country of Study: United States of America
Application Procedure: The full application must be submitted electronically via the IGAM and paper (master) of the full application must be sent to the CCFA National office.
Closing Date: January 14th or July 1st
Funding: Corporation, foundation

For further information contact:

Crohn's & Colitis Foundation of America, Research and Scientific Programs Department, 386 Park Avenue South 17th Floor, New York, NY 10016-8804

Crohn's and Colitis Foundation Research Fellowship Awards
Subjects: Crohn's disease and ulcerative colitis (IBD).
Purpose: To stimulate and encourage innovative research that is likely to increase our understanding of the aetiology, pathogenesis, therapy and prevention of Crohn's disease and ulcerative colitis (IBD).
Eligibility: Applicants must hold an MD, PhD or equivalent with at least 2 years of research experience.
Level of Study: Postdoctorate, Research
Value: Not to exceed US$58,250 per year
Length of Study: 1–3 years
Frequency: Every 2 years
Study Establishment: An approved research institute

Country of Study: United States of America
Application Procedure: The full application must be submitted electronically via the IGAM and paper (master) of the full application must be sent to the CCFA National office.
Funding: Foundation, individuals, corporation

Crohn's and Colitis Foundation Senior Research Award
Subjects: Crohn's disease and ulcerative colitis (IBD).
Purpose: To stimulate and encourage innovative research that is likely to increase our understanding of the aetiology, pathogenesis, therapy and prevention of Crohn's disease and ulcerative colitis (IBD).
Eligibility: Applicants should be researchers who hold an MD, PhD or equivalent.
Level of Study: Postdoctorate, Research
Type: Research award
Value: Up to US$130,000 direct cost per year plus indirect cost of 10 per cent of direct cost
Length of Study: Up to 2 years
Frequency: Annual
Study Establishment: An approved research institute
Country of Study: United States of America
Application Procedure: The full application must be submitted electronically via the IGAM and paper (master) of the full application must be sent to the CCFA National office.
Closing Date: January 14th and July 1st
Funding: Corporation, foundation, individuals

Crohn's and Colitis Foundation Student Research Fellowship Awards
Subjects: Crohn's disease and ulcerative colitis (IBD).
Purpose: To stimulate and encourage innovative research that is likely to increase our understanding of the aetiology, pathogenesis, therapy and prevention of Crohn's disease and ulcerative colitis (IBD).
Eligibility: Applicants should be a medical student or graduate student studying at an accredited North American institution.
Level of Study: Postgraduate
Length of Study: US$2,500 per year
Frequency: Annual
Study Establishment: An approved research institute
Country of Study: United States of America
No. of awards offered: 16
Application Procedure: The full application must be submitted electronically via the IGAM and paper (master) of the full application must be sent to the CCFA National office.
Closing Date: March 15th or June 15th
Funding: Corporation, foundation, individuals

THE CROSS TRUST

PO Box 17, 25 South Methven Street, Perth, Perthshire, PH1 5ES, Scotland
Tel: (44) 17 3862 0451
Fax: (44) 17 3863 1155
Email: Crosstrust@mccash.co.uk
Website: www.thecrosstrust.org.uk
Contact: Ms Kathleen Carnegie, Assistant Secretary

The aim of the Cross Trust is to provide opportunities to young people of Scottish birth or parentage to extend the boundaries of their knowledge of human life. Proposals are to be of demonstrable merit from applicants with a record of academic distinction.

Cross Trust Grants
Subjects: Any approved subject.
Purpose: To enable young Scottish people to extend the boundaries of their knowledge and experience or encourage performance and participation in drama or opera.
Eligibility: Open to graduates of Scottish universities, Scottish secondary school pupils or graduates of central institutions in Scotland. Applicants must be of Scottish birth or parentage.
Level of Study: Unrestricted
Type: Grant
Value: Varies
Length of Study: Varies
Frequency: Annual

Study Establishment: Any approved institute
Country of Study: Any country
No. of awards offered: Varies
Application Procedure: Applicants must complete an application form.
Closing Date: Deadlines for each of 4 trustees meetings given in advance
Funding: Private
No. of awards given last year: 210
No. of applicants last year: 363
Additional Information: Awards will only be considered from postgraduate students who have part funding in place from another organization. The Trust may support the pursuit of studies or research.

For further information contact:

McCash & Hunter, 25 South Methven Street, Perth, Perthshire, PH1 5ES, Scotland
Contact: The Secretaries

THE CROUCHER FOUNDATION

Suite 501, Nine Queen's Road Central, Hong Kong
Tel: (852) 2 736 6337
Fax: (852) 2 730 0742
Email: cfadmin@croucher.org.hk
Website: www.croucher.org.hk
Contact: Ms Elaine Sit, Administrative Officer

Founded to promote education, learning and research in the areas of natural science, technology and medicine, the Croucher Foundation operates a scholarship and fellowship scheme for individual applicants who are permanent residents of Hong Kong wishing to pursue doctoral or postdoctoral research overseas. The Foundation otherwise makes grants to institutions only.

Croucher Foundation Fellowships and Scholarships

Subjects: Natural science, medicine and technology.
Purpose: To enable selected students of outstanding promise to devote themselves to full-time postgraduate study or research in approved academic institutions outside Hong Kong.
Eligibility: Open to permanent residents of Hong Kong. Fellowships are intended for recent PhD graduates and not for the funding of career vacancies in universities. Scholarships are intended for those undertaking PhD studies.
Level of Study: Doctorate, Postdoctorate
Type: Scholarships, fellowships
Value: UK £20,640 per year for fellowships, and UK £11,520 per year and tution fees for scholarships, plus airfare assistance and other allowances
Length of Study: 1–2 years for fellowships, 1–3 years for scholarships
Frequency: Annual
Country of Study: Outside Hong Kong
No. of awards offered: Approx. 20–25
Application Procedure: Applicants can download an application form from the website (www.croucher.org.hk).
Closing Date: November 14th. Applicants should visit the website for the exact date every year
Funding: Private
No. of awards given last year: 20
No. of applicants last year: 110

THE CULINARY INSTITUTE OF AMERICA (CIA)

Admissions Department, 1946 Campus Drive, Hyde Park, NY 12538-1499, United States of America
Tel: (1) 845 452 9430
Email: admissions@culinary.edu
Website: www.ciachef.edu

The Culinary Institute of America (CIA) is a private, non-profit college dedicated to providing the world's best professional culinary education. CIA has been setting the standard for excellence in professional culinary education. The faculty, facilities, and academic programmes are offered at our campuses in Hyde Park, New York and St Helena, California.

The Culinary Institute of America Scholarship – Greystone

Subjects: Cooking.
Type: Scholarship
Value: US$5,000
Length of Study: 30 weeks
Frequency: Annual
Study Establishment: The Culinary Institute of America
Country of Study: United States of America
No. of awards offered: 1
Funding: Private

For further information contact:

Website: www.ciaprochef.edu

THE CULINARY TRUST

304 West Liberty Street Suite 201, Louisville, KY, 40202, United States of America
Tel: (1) 502 581 9786
Fax: (1) 502 589 3602
Email: tgribbins@hqtrs.com
Website: www.theculinarytrust.com

The Culinary Trust has been the philanthropic partner to over 4,000 members of the International Association of Culinary Professionals (IACP) for over 20 years. The Trust solicits, manages and distributes funds for educational and charitable programmes related to the culinary industry in many areas.

Centro Culinario Ambrosia Mexican Cuisine Scholarship

Subjects: Mexican cuisine.
Purpose: To provide continuing education in Mexican cuisine.
Eligibility: Open to an experienced cook.
Level of Study: Unrestricted
Type: Scholarship
Value: Includes tuition, supplies, uniforms, and cutlery
Length of Study: 15 weeks
Frequency: Annual
No. of awards offered: 1
Application Procedure: Check website for further details.
Additional Information: Scholarship is valid from July 1st. Transportation and accommodations are not provided.

For further information contact:

Website: www.ambrosia.com.mx

Cuisinart Culinary Arts Scholarship

Subjects: Cuisine art.
Purpose: To encourage students in the culinary schools.
Eligibility: Check website for further details.
Level of Study: Unrestricted
Type: Scholarship
Value: Open to student enrolled in a Culinary Certificate or Degree programme at any nationally accredited culinary school
Length of Study: $1,500
Frequency: Annual
No. of awards offered: 1
Application Procedure: Scholarship valid from July 1st.

For further information contact:

Website: www.cuisinart.com

Culinary Arts Scholarship

Subjects: Culinary arts.
Eligibility: Open to a candidate who has pre-enrolled toward the 6–10 month Culinary Arts or Pastry & Baking Arts Diploma Program.
Type: Scholarship
Value: $5,000
Length of Study: 6–10 months
Frequency: Annual

Study Establishment: The Institute of Culinary Education New York
No. of awards offered: 1
Application Procedure: Check the website for further information.
Additional Information: Scholarship may only be awarded to a student prior to their enrollment at The Institute of Culinary Education.

For further information contact:

Admissions Department, Institute of Culinary Education (ICE)
Tel: 212 847 0757
Website: www.iceculinary.com

Harry A. Bell Travel Grant

Subjects: Culinary research.
Purpose: For travel and research to food writers during the pre-contract phase of their book proposal.
Eligibility: Open to writers who are in the pre-contract phase of their book.
Level of Study: Unrestricted
Type: Grant
Value: $3,000–4,000
Frequency: Annual
No. of awards offered: Varies
Application Procedure: Check the website for further details.

For further information contact:

Website: www.theculinarytrust.com

The Julia Child Endowment Fund Scholarship

Subjects: Culinary arts.
Purpose: To support a career professional to conduct independent study and research in France, as it relates to French food, wine, history, culture and traditions. This programme also encourages, enables and assists aspiring students and career professionals to advance their knowledge of the culinary arts.
Eligibility: Open to applicants who have 2 years of food service experience.
Level of Study: Professional development
Type: Scholarship
Value: US$5,000
Frequency: Annual
Country of Study: France
Application Procedure: Applicants are required to submit a 2 page essay illustrating their culinary goals along with 2 letters of professional reference.
Closing Date: December 15th
Funding: Trusts

The Julia Child Fund at the Boston Foundation Independent Study Scholarship

Subjects: Culinary art.
Purpose: For independent study in France on French food, wine, and culinary disciplines.
Eligibility: Open to a career professional doing research in writing and teaching related to French food, wine and culinary disciplines.
Level of Study: Professional development
Type: Scholarship
Value: $5,000
Frequency: Annual
Country of Study: France
No. of awards offered: 1
Application Procedure: Check the website for further details.

For further information contact:

Website: www.tbf.org

L'Academie de Cuisine Culinary Arts Scholarship

Subjects: Culinary arts.
Eligibility: Open to a student pre-enrolled for the 12 months Culinary Arts or Pastry Arts Certificate Program.
Type: Scholarship
Value: $5,000
Length of Study: 1 year
No. of awards offered: 1
Application Procedure: Check the website for further details.

Additional Information: Scholarship is valid for enrollment during July or October only.

For further information contact:

Website: www.lacademie.com

Zwilling, J.A. Henckels Culinary Arts Scholarship

Subjects: Culinary arts.
Eligibility: Open to any pre-enrolled student, currently enrolled student or career professional toward any culinary arts degree or certificate program at any nationally accredited culinary school.
Level of Study: Postgraduate
Type: Scholarship
Value: $5,000
No. of awards offered: 1
Application Procedure: Check the website for further details.
Contributor: Zwilling, J.A. Henckels Trust

For further information contact:

Website: www.jahenckels.com

CURTIN UNIVERSITY OF TECHNOLOGY

GPO Box U1987, Scholarships Department, Perth, Western Australia, 6845, Australia
Tel: (61) 8 9266 9266
Fax: (61) 8 9266 2255
Email: scholarships@curtin.edu.au
Website: www.curtin.edu.au

Curtin University of Technology is a world class, internationally focused, culturally diverse institution. They foster tolerance and encourage the development of the individual. Their programmes centre around the provision of knowledge and skills to meet industry and workplace standards. A combination of first rate resources, staff and technology makes Curtin a forerunner in tertiary education both within Australia and internationally.

APA(I) – Innovation, Competition and Economic Performance

Subjects: Economics and industrial organization.
Purpose: To encourage students to undertake a Higher Degree by Research within the the the Centre for Research in Applied Economics (CRAE).
Eligibility: Candidates must be Australian citizens or permanent residents or New Zealand citizens, should hold or are expected to hold a First Class Honours Degree or its equivalent and must meet Curtin University of Technology's requirements for admission to a PhD.
Level of Study: Graduate
Type: Competition
Value: Australian $25,118 per year
Length of Study: 3 years
Application Procedure: Candidates must forward the completed application for admission to a higher degree by research to the Centre for Research into Applied Economics (CRAE).
Closing Date: March 31st

For further information contact:

The Centre for Research into Applied Economics (CRAE), Curtin Business School, Curtin University of Technology, GPO Box U1987, Perth, WA 6845
Tel: 61 8 9266 2035
Email: H.Bloch@exchange.curtin.edu.au
Contact: Professor Harry Bloch

Australian Biological Resources Study Postgraduate Scholarship

Subjects: Agricultural science.
Purpose: To foster research training compatible with ABRS and national research priorities.
Eligibility: Applicants must be Australian citizens or permanent residents, must hold a First or Upper Second Class Honours or equivalent degree in an appropriate discipline and be enrolled as a full-time student in a PhD degree at an Australian institution.

257

Level of Study: Graduate
Type: Scholarship
Value: $25,627 plus annual research support grant of $2,500
Country of Study: Australia
No. of awards offered: 1
Application Procedure: Applicants must submit the application to ABRS through the host institution. The application form will then be submitted to the ABRS Advisory Committee for consideration and assessment using the selection criteria. The individual selected as most worthy of funding will be awarded the scholarship.
Closing Date: November 3rd

For further information contact:

Australian Biological Resources Study, GPO Box 787
Tel: 02 6250 9554
Fax: 02 6250 9555
Email: abrs@deh.gov.au
Website: www.environment.gov.au/biodiversity/abrs/admin/training/index.html
Contact: Business Manager

Curtin Business School Doctoral Scholarship

Subjects: Business law and corporate administration, economics, management, marketing.
Purpose: To enable doctoral (PhD, DBA) students to study at the Curtin Business School.
Eligibility: Applicants must have completed at least four years of tertiary education studies at a high level of achievement and have First/Upper Second Class Honours or equivalent results. Check website for further details.
Level of Study: Postgraduate
Type: Scholarship
Value: $25,000
Length of Study: 3 years
Frequency: Annual
No. of awards offered: 3
Application Procedure: Applicants can download the application form and obtain further information from the website.
Closing Date: October 31st

For further information contact:

CBS HDR Unit, Curtin University of Technology, GPO Box U 1987, PERTH, WA 6845, Australia
Tel: (61) 61 08 9266 4301
Email: j.boycott@curtin.edu.au
Contact: Ms Jo Boycott, Research Student Coordinator

Curtin University Postgraduate Scholarship (CUPS)

Subjects: All subjects.
Purpose: To assist with general living costs.
Eligibility: Applicants must be Australian or New Zealand citizens or Australian permanent residents and must have completed four years of higher education studies at a high level of achievement and must hold, or are expected to obtain, First Class Honours or equivalent results.
Level of Study: Graduate
Type: Scholarship
Value: $25,427 per year
No. of awards offered: 35
Application Procedure: Check website for further details.
Closing Date: October 31st

For further information contact:

Office of Research & Development, Curtin University of Technology, GPO Box U1987, PERTH, WA 6845
Tel: 08 9266 4905
Fax: 08 9266 3793
Email: scholarships@curtin.edu.au
Website: http://scholarships.curtin.edu.au/
Contact: Manager, Scholarships

Establishing the Source of Gas in Australia's Offshore Petroleum Basins–Scholarship

Subjects: Chemistry, geochemistry, geology.

Purpose: To develop an isotopic method to analyze gases in fluid inclusions and to establish the source of gas in Australia's offshore petroleum basins.
Eligibility: Applicants must have First Class Honours or equivalent science degree, preferably in chemistry/geology/geochemistry. Interests in analytical organic chemistry, laboratory skills in trace analysis, wet chemical methods, GC/GCMS or GC–IRMS instrumentation and awareness of stable isotopic concepts is desirable.
Level of Study: Postgraduate
Type: Scholarship
Value: $20,000 per year
No. of awards offered: 1
Application Procedure: Check website for further details.
Contributor: The Stable Isotope and Molecular Biogeochemistry Research Group, Geoscience Australia, GFZ

For further information contact:

Stable Isotope and Molecular Biogeochemistry Group, Centre for Applied Organic Geochemistry, Department of Applied Chemistry, Curtin Universitiy of Technology, GPO Box U1987, Perth, WA 6845
Tel: 61 08 9266 2474
Fax: 61 08 9266 2300
Email: K.grice@curtin.edu.au
Website: www.caog.chemistry.curtin.edu.au
Contact: Professor Kliti Grice

French–Australian Cotutelle

Subjects: Agri-science, biomedical sciences, engineering, health and life sciences, physical sciences.
Purpose: To support the development of the double doctoral degree 'Cotutelle' between Australia and France.
Eligibility: Applicants must be PhD students (of any nationality) enrolled in a Cotutelle project between a French and an Australian university; should not have benefited from the French Embassy Cotutelle grant in previous years and should be registered with FEAST-France.
Level of Study: Postgraduate
Type: Grant
Value: $2,500
No. of awards offered: 10
Application Procedure: Applicants must provide the French Embassy with the completed application form and a copy of the Cotutelle convention.
Closing Date: December 8th

For further information contact:

Higher Education Attache, Embassy of France in Australia
Email: Stephane.GRIVELET@diplomatie.gouv.fr
Website: www.ambafrance-au.org
Contact: Mr Stephane GRIVELET

The General Sir John Monash Awards

Subjects: All subjects.
Purpose: To enable them to undertake postgraduate study abroad at the world's best Universities, appropriate to their field of study.
Eligibility: Applicants must be Australian citizens who have graduated from an Australian University with outstanding levels of academic achievement.
Level of Study: Graduate
Type: Award
Value: $150,000
Length of Study: 3 years
Frequency: Annual
No. of awards offered: 8
Application Procedure: Check website for further details.
Closing Date: August 31st

For further information contact:

Website: www.monashawards.org

Gowrie Research Scholarship

Subjects: All subjects.
Purpose: To assist members of the defence forces and direct descendants of members of the defence force to aid with their research study.

Eligibility: Candidates must be enrolled full-time in a Higher Degree by Research at the University of Southern Queensland, be a member of the Australian Armed Forces or be a direct lineal descendant of a member of the Australian Armed Forces.commence the degree by the date specified by the University of Southern Queensland.
Level of Study: Graduate
Type: Scholarship
Value: $4,000 per year
Length of Study: 2 years
No. of awards offered: 1 or 2
Application Procedure: Candidates must submit applications in duplicate on the prescribed form. If space is insufficient, a separate statement should be added.
Closing Date: October 31st
Contributor: Gowrie Scholarship Trust Fund

For further information contact:

The Gowrie Scholarship Fund Trust, 3/32 Beaconsfield Road, Mosman, NSW 2088, Australia
Contact: The Secretary

Hunter Postgraduate Scholarship
Subjects: Alzheimer's disease.
Purpose: To support a PhD student undertaking research in an area relevant to understanding the causes of Alzheimer's disease.
Eligibility: Candidates must be PhD students undertaking research in an area relevant to understanding the causes of Alzheimer's disease.
Level of Study: Postgraduate
Type: Scholarship
Value: $23,000 per year
Length of Study: 3 years
Application Procedure: Check website for further details.
Closing Date: October 31st

For further information contact:

Tel: 02 6254 7233
Email: aar@alzheimers.org.au
Website: www.alzheimers.org.au/content.cfm?infopageid=3102
Contact: Anna Conn

Scots Australia Council Scholarship
Subjects: All subjects.
Purpose: To develop lasting links between young Scots and Australians by offering outstanding graduates and young professionals the opportunity to study at a Scottish university.
Eligibility: Applicants must be Australian citizens or Australian permanent residents or New Zealand citizens or on permanent Humanitarian Visa. They must be indigenous or Torres Strait Islander students or students with a disability or students from rural or regional areas or mature students or sole parents or current students or prospective students.
Level of Study: Graduate
Type: Scholarship
Value: £12,000
Application Procedure: Check website for further details.
Closing Date: January 17th
Contributor: Scottish universities, Scottish business and industry, British Foreign and Commonwealth Office

For further information contact:

The Scots Australian Council, 19 Dean Terrace, Edinburgh, EH4 1NL, Scotland
Email: scholarships@scotsoz.org
Contact: The Secretary

Sediment and Asphaltite Transport by Canyon Upwelling – Top Up Scholarship
Subjects: Chemistry, geochemistry, geology.
Purpose: To investigate the role of upwelling currents in transporting material across the continental slope of the Morum Sub-Basin, southern Australia using an integrated geological, oceanographic and organic geochemical approach.
Eligibility: Applicants must be First Class Honours or equivalent science degree holders, preferably in chemistry/geology/

geochemistry. Interests in analytical organic chemistry, laboratory skills in trace analysis, wet chemical methods, GC/GCMS or GC-IRMS instrumentation; awareness of stable isotopic concepts is desirable.
Level of Study: Graduate
Type: Scholarship
No. of awards offered: 1
Application Procedure: Applicants must forward their interests, curriculum vitae and names of two referees to Stable Isotope and Molecular Biogeochemistry Group, Centre for Applied Organic Geochemistry, Department of Applied Chemistry.
Contributor: The Stable Isotope and Molecular Biogeochemistry Research Group, Adelaide University, a petroleum industry partner

For further information contact:

Stable Isotope and Molecular Biogeochemistry Group, Centre for Applied Organic Geochemistry, Department of Applied Chemistry, Curtin Universitiy of Technology, GPO Box U1987, Perth, WA 6845
Tel: 61 08 9266 2474
Fax: 61 08 9266 2474
Email: K.grice@curtin.edu.au
Website: www.caog.chemistry.curtin.edu.au
Contact: Professor Kliti Grice

Water Corporation Scholarship in Biosolids Research
Subjects: Agri-science, environmental science.
Purpose: To investigate the potential impacts to soil and plants following the agricultural land application of alum-dosed wastewater sludge.
Eligibility: Applicants must be Australian Citizens, Australian permanent residents or must hold an Australian permanent Humanitarian Visa. They must hold a relevant degree from a recognized University in the preferred fields of Agriculture, Environmental Science or the equivalent and demonstrate a high level in their Honours project or equivalent.
Level of Study: Graduate, Postgraduate
Type: Scholarship
Value: $23,400 per year
Length of Study: 3 years for a doctoral program and 2 years for a masters program
Application Procedure: Check website for further details.
Closing Date: October 31st

For further information contact:

Muresk Institute, Curtin University of Technology, GPO Box U1987, PERTH, WA 6845
Email: D.Pritchard@curtin.edu.au
Contact: Dr Deborah Pritchard

DAAD

German Academic Exchange Service, 34 Belgrave Square, London, SW1X 8QB, England
Tel: (44) 020 7235 1736
Fax: (44) 020 7235 9602
Email: reese@daad.org.uk
Website: http://london.daad.de
Contact: Ms Cecile Rees

Long-Term Research Grants for Doctoral Studies
Subjects: All subjects.
Purpose: To support long-term research for Doctoral studies.
Eligibility: Open to the candidates with Masters Degree (S2 Degree) with minimum GPA of 3.00 (from 1–4 scale) and excellently qualified teaching staff from universities, researchers from research institutions in any field of study/research applicants from private sectors with at least 2 years of working experience. Any teaching staff predominantly or exclusively involved in non-degree programs is not eligible.
Level of Study: Doctorate, Postgraduate
Type: Grant
Value: €975 per month plus travel and luggage cost and a health insurance allowance along with study and research allowance
Length of Study: Up to 3 years (full doctoral programs), maximum of 2 years (sandwich scholarships)

Country of Study: Germany

Application Procedure: Applicants should attach written confirmation of the supervision by a professor in Germany commenting on your research program. Doctoral candidates wishing to take a doctorate/PhD in their home country (Sandwich Program) must register for the doctorate at their home university.

Additional Information: When award holders take doctoral programs run under the "DAAD Sandwich Model" and obtain the degree at the home university, the award may include the travel expenses of both academic supervisors.

Study Scholarships for Graduates of All Disciplines for Master's Degree

Subjects: All subjects.

Eligibility: Open to excellently qualified junior teaching staff from state universities and from private universities and researchers from state-run research institutions in any field of study/research who hold a first degree (Bachelor's degree) with some teaching/research experience. Check website for further details.

Level of Study: Postgraduate

Type: Scholarship

Value: €715 plus travel and luggage cost and health insurance allowance along with a study and research allowance. Tuition fees cannot be paid by the DAAD

Length of Study: 10–24 months (initially, scholarships are awarded for one academic year and can be extended for students with good study achievements to cover the full length of the chosen degree course)

Additional Information: Any teaching staff predominantly or exclusively involved in non-degree programs is not eligible. Even if an applicant has qualified for a scholarship after the interview, the DAAD scholarship will only be granted after admission to the study program chosen.

For further information contact:

Website: www.daad.de/deutschland/studium/idp/04709.en.html

DALHOUSIE UNIVERSITY

15th Floor, Sir Charles Tupper Building, 5850 College Street, Halifax, NS, B3H 4H7, Canada
Tel: (1) 902 494 3502
Fax: (1) 902 494 1372
Email: dmrf@dal.ca
Website: www.dmrf.ca

Dalhousie University is one of Canada's leading universities, Dalhousie is widely recognized for outstanding academic quality and teaching, and a broad range of educational and research opportunities.

Dalhousie Medical Research Foundation Fellowships

Subjects: Basic or clinical science, medical research, health law, bioethics, medical informatics, population health, medical education and medical humanities.

Purpose: To acknowledge the exemplary work in basic medical research and clinical medical research by the junior researchers.

Eligibility: Open to outstanding junior researchers.

Level of Study: Postgraduate, Medical research

Type: Award

Value: Canadian $7,000

Length of Study: 1–3 years

Frequency: Annual

Study Establishment: Dalhousie University

Country of Study: Canada

Funding: Foundation

Contributor: Donations

DAMON RUNYON CANCER RESEARCH FOUNDATION

675 Third Avenue, 25th Floor, New York, NY 10017,
United States of America
Tel: (1) 212 455 0520
Email: info@drcrf.org
Website: www.drcrf.org

The Damon Runyon Cancer Research Foundation identifies and supports extraordinary young scientists across the nation who are committed to discovering the causes and cures for cancer.

Damon Runyon Clinical Investigator Award

Subjects: Understanding the causes and mechanisms of cancer and developing more effective cancer therapies and preventions.

Purpose: To support young scientists conducting patient-orientated cancer research.

Eligibility: Open to a U.S. citizen or permanent legal resident and must have received an MD or MD/PhD degree(s) from an accredited institution and be board-eligible.

Level of Study: Research, Professional development

Type: Award

Value: Funding will amount to $450,000 over three years. Each year the researcher will receive a $100,000 stipend and $50,000 for research support

Length of Study: Up to 5 years

Frequency: Annual

Study Establishment: Suitable facilities within the United States of America

Country of Study: United States of America

No. of awards offered: 5

Application Procedure: Application form can be downloaded from the website.

Closing Date: Januray 15th

Funding: Private

Contributor: Eli-Lilly

No. of awards given last year: 5

No. of applicants last year: 41

Additional Information: In addition, the Foundation will retire up to $100,000 of any medical school debt owed by the awardee.

Damon Runyon Fellowship Award

Subjects: Understanding the causes and mechanisms of cancer and developing more effective cancer therapies and preventions.

Purpose: To encourage all theoretical and experimental research relevant to the study of cancer and the search for cancer causes, mechanisms, therapies and prevention.

Eligibility: Legal residents or citizens of the United States of America working abroad. Candidates must be at the beginning of their 1st full-time postdoctoral fellowship. Candidate cannot be in the sponsor's laboratory for more than 1 year.

Level of Study: Postdoctorate

Type: Fellowship

Value: US$43,000–57,000 per year

Length of Study: 3 years

Study Establishment: Suitable accredited establishment within the United States of America

Country of Study: United States of America

No. of awards offered: 50–60 per year

Application Procedure: Applicants should download an application from the website. Fellowship awards are to be approved by the Board of Directors of the Damon Runyon Cancer Research Foundation acting upon the recommendation of the Scientific Advisory Committee.

Funding: Private

No. of awards given last year: 53

No. of applicants last year: 477

Damon Runyon Scholar Award

Subjects: Understanding the causes and mechanisms of cancer and developing more effective cancer therapies and preventions.

Purpose: To support the development of outstanding scientists as independent investigators in the cancer field by helping foster their research productivity during the first few years of their first faculty position.

Eligibility: Researchers must show exceptional promise within the first 3 years of their appointment as assistant professor.

Level of Study: Professional development, Postdoctorate

Type: Grant

Value: US$100,000 per year

Length of Study: 3 years

Frequency: Annual

Country of Study: United States of America

No. of awards offered: 5

Application Procedure: The application must be made within 3 years of the initial faculty appointment. The institution and department must guarantee, in written form, a commitment to the individual and the development of their laboratory and career.
Closing Date: July 1st
Funding: Private
No. of awards given last year: 5
No. of applicants last year: 87
Additional Information: The award will be allocated to the awardee's institution, with the understanding that it is to be used for the awardee's salary, technical support and/or equipment. The award may not be used for institutional overhead or indirect costs.

THE DAVIES CHARITABLE FOUNDATION

245 Alwington Place, Kingston, ON, K7L 4P9, Canada
Tel: (1) 613 546 4000
Fax: (1) 613 546 9130
Email: daviesfoundation@cogeco.ca
Website: www.daviesfoundation.ca

The Davies Charitable Foundation is a registered, non-profit, charitable organization founded in 1990 by Michael R.L. Davies, former owner and publisher of the Kingston Whig Standard. The purpose of the Foundation is to support individuals and organizations within the local district in the areas of the arts, education, health and sports. Since its inception the Davies Charitable Foundation has donated over $7.5 million to over 400 individuals and institutions.

The Davies Charitable Foundation Fellowship
Subjects: All subjects.
Purpose: To support a native of the Kingston, Ontario, area at the peak of academic excellence.
Eligibility: Open to candidates born in the Kingston area or have resided in the area for at least 5 years prior to their 20th birthday and must have been accepted into a postdoctoral or fellowship position at the university of their choice.
Level of Study: Postdoctorate
Type: Fellowship
Value: Canadian $10,000
Length of Study: 1 year
Frequency: Annual
Country of Study: Canada
No. of awards offered: 1
Application Procedure: Application form can be downloaded from the website.
Closing Date: April 15th
Funding: Foundation
Contributor: Davies Charitable Foundation

THE DAYTON AREA GRADUATE STUDIES INSTITUTE (DAGSI)

3155 Research Boulevard Suite 205, Kettering, OH, 45420, United States of America
Tel: (1) 937 781 4000
Fax: (1) 937 781 4005
Email: kelam@dagsi.org
Website: www.dagsi.org
Contact: Dr Elizabeth Downie, Director

The Dayton Area Graduate Studies Institute (DAGSI) is a consortium of graduate engineering schools at the University of Dayton, a private institution, Wright State University, a state assisted institution and the Air Force Institute of Technology, a federal institution. It integrates and leverages the combined resources of the partnership, including faculty, facilities, equipment and other assets of the institutions.

DAGSI Research Fellowships
Subjects: Engineering and computer science.
Purpose: To financially support full-time students pursuing a research-based Doctoral study.

Eligibility: Open to candidates with a minimum of Bachelor's degree in engineering, computer science or a related field.
Level of Study: Doctorate
Type: Fellowships
Value: US$27,500 plus full tution
Length of Study: 3 years
Frequency: Annual
No. of awards offered: 15
Application Procedure: Applicants can download the application form from the website.
Closing Date: December 15th
Additional Information: DAGSI encourages women, minorities and persons with disabilities to participate in the fellowship.

DEAKIN UNIVERSITY

221 Burwood Highway, Burwood, Victoria, 3125, Australia
Tel: (61) 3 9244 6100
Fax: (61) 3 9244 5094
Email: dconnect@deakin.edu.au
Website: www.deakin.edu

Established in the 1970s, Deakin University is one of Australia's largest universities providing all the resources of a major university to more than 32,000 award students. The University's reputation for excellent teaching and innovative course delivery has been recognized through many awards over the past few years.

Coltman Scholarship
Subjects: Biomedical science.
Purpose: To recognize outstanding achievement and ability within the student's particular area of research.
Eligibility: Open to students undertaking research in biomedical sciences.
Level of Study: Postgraduate
Type: Scholarship
Value: Australian $3,000 and a framed certificate
Frequency: Annual
Application Procedure: Check website for further details
Contributor: Dr Kay and Mrs Barbara

Edward Wilson Scholarship for Graduate Diploma of Journalism
Subjects: Journalism.
Purpose: To assist students pursuing journalism.
Eligibility: Open to Australian citizens undertaking postgraduate studies in journalism.
Level of Study: Postgraduate
Type: Scholarship
Value: Tuition fees
Length of Study: 2 years
Frequency: Annual
No. of awards offered: 1
Application Procedure: A completed application form must be submitted.
Closing Date: October 7th

Helen Macpherson Smith Trust Scholarship
Subjects: Arts and entertainment management.
Purpose: To financially support outstanding students.
Eligibility: Open to students who may benefit from financial assistance.
Level of Study: Postgraduate
Type: Scholarship
Value: Australian $500
Length of Study: 1 year
Frequency: Annual
No. of awards offered: 2
Application Procedure: Check website for further details
Closing Date: October 31st

The Isi Leibler Prize
Subjects: Area and cultural studies.
Purpose: To advance knowledge of multiculturism and community relations in Australia.

261

Eligibility: Open to students who have submitted a postgraduate or doctoral thesis at the university.
Level of Study: Doctorate, Postgraduate
Type: Award
Value: Australian $250
Frequency: Annual
Study Establishment: Deakin University
Country of Study: Australia
Application Procedure: Completed application form plus additional information must be submitted.
Closing Date: January 18th

For further information contact:

Vice-Chancellor's Prizes Committee, Academic Administrative Services Division, Geelong Waterfront Campus, Deakin University, Geelong, Vic 3217

Rex Williamson Prize

Subjects: Chemistry.
Purpose: To award students showing the best research potential and academic merit.
Eligibility: Open to students enrolled within the school of biological and chemical sciences.
Level of Study: Postgraduate
Type: Award
Value: Australian $5,000 and a framed certificate
Frequency: Annual
Application Procedure: Check website for further details

Tennis Australia Prize

Subjects: Sport management.
Purpose: To recognize outstanding achievement.
Eligibility: Open to outstanding students of Master's/graduate certificate of business.
Level of Study: Postgraduate
Type: Award
Value: Australian $750
Frequency: Annual
Application Procedure: A completed application form must be submitted.
Closing Date: October 31st

DEBRA UK

DebRA House, 13 Wellington Business Park, Dukes Ride, Crowthorne, Berkshire, RG45 6LS, England
Tel: (44) 13 4477 1961
Fax: (44) 13 4476 2661
Email: debra@debra.org.uk
Website: www.debra.org.uk

DebRA UK is the national charity working on behalf of people with the genetic skin blistering condition, Epidermolysis bullosa (EB).

DebRA UK Research Grant Scheme

Subjects: Epidermolysis bullosa.
Purpose: To fund research into epidermolysis bullosa (EB).
Eligibility: Applicants must be productive postdoctorates, usually with a track record as a principal investigator.
Level of Study: Postdoctorate, Research
Type: Project grant
Value: Average UK £40,000–50,000 per year
Length of Study: Grants for projects are usually for 1–3 years
Frequency: Twice per year
Country of Study: Any country
No. of awards offered: Varies
Application Procedure: Application form can be downloaded from the website www.debra-international.org or from the DebRA UK Office.
Closing Date: March 15th and September 15th
Funding: Private
Contributor: Charitable funding
No. of awards given last year: 5
No. of applicants last year: 8

DEMOCRATIC NURSING ORGANIZATION OF SOUTH AFRICA (DENOSA)

PO Box 1280, Pretoria, 0001, South Africa
Tel: (27) 12 343 2315
Fax: (27) 12 344 0750
Email: info@denosa.org.za
Website: www.denosa.org.za
Contact: Executive Director

The Democratic Nursing Organization of South Africa (DENOSA) is a professional organization and labour union for nurses in South Africa.

DENOSA Bursaries, Scholarships and Grants

Subjects: Nursing.
Purpose: To encourage postbasic studies at a South African teaching institution.
Eligibility: Open to members of the organization in good standing who hold the required registered nursing qualifications.
Level of Study: Doctorate, Graduate, Postgraduate, Professional development
Type: Bursary
Value: Varies
Frequency: Annual
Study Establishment: A South African teaching institution
Country of Study: South Africa
No. of awards offered: Varies
Application Procedure: Applicants must complete an application form.
Closing Date: January 31st
Funding: Private
Contributor: Donor funding
No. of awards given last year: 153
No. of applicants last year: 173

THE DENMARK-AMERICA FOUNDATION

Fiolstraede 24, 3rd Floor, DK-1171, Copenhagen, Denmark
Tel: (45) 3312 8323
Fax: (45) 3332 5323
Email: daf-fulb@daf-fulb.dk
Website: www.daf-fulb.dk
Contact: Ms Marie Monsted, Executive Director

The Denmark-America Foundation was founded in 1914 as a private foundation, and today its work remains based on donations from Danish firms, foundations and individuals. The Foundation offers scholarships for studies in the United States of America at the graduate and postgraduate university level and also has a trainee programme.

Denmark-America Foundation Grants

Subjects: All subjects.
Purpose: To further understanding between Denmark and the United States of America.
Eligibility: Open to Danes and Danish-American citizens.
Level of Study: Professional development, MBA, Postdoctorate, Graduate, Postgraduate, Research
Type: Bursary
Value: Varies
Length of Study: 3 months–1 year
Frequency: Annual
Country of Study: United States of America
No. of awards offered: Varies
Application Procedure: Applicants must complete a special application form, available by contacting the secretariat.
Funding: Private
No. of awards given last year: 34–35
No. of applicants last year: 250

DENTISTRY CANADA FUND (DCF)

Scican Suite, 1815 Alta Vista Drive, Ottawa, ON, KIG 3Y6, Canada
Tel: (1) 613 236 4763
Fax: (1) 613 236 3935
Email: information@dcf-fdc.ca
Website: www.dcf-fdc.ca
Contact: Office Manager

The Dentistry Canada Fund (DCF) is the national charitable foundation dedicated to assisting in the encouragement of optimal oral health in Canada through education, research and public outreach.

DCF Biennial Research Award
Subjects: Dentistry.
Purpose: To encourage research.
Eligibility: Open to graduate or postgraduate students who have conducted their research in association with a Canadian dental faculty. Applicants must either be in their graduating year or the ensuing year.
Level of Study: Graduate, Postgraduate
Type: Research grant
Value: Canadian $2,000
Frequency: Every 2 years
Country of Study: Canada
No. of awards offered: 1
Application Procedure: Applicants must submit one typewritten double-spaced copy, not exceeding 25 pages, and four copies of an original research project in the form of a paper. The manuscript should not be a previously published paper of the candidate's graduate work currently in press or already published in a scientific journal. Each applicant must also send a current curriculum vitae.
Closing Date: September 30th, every two years
Funding: Private
Additional Information: Each entry will be reviewed by three referees appointed by the CDA Committee on Dental Materials and Devices. The decision of the Committee is final.

DCF Fellowships for Teacher/Researcher Training
Subjects: Dentistry.
Purpose: To provide financial assistance to students who wish to pursue a career in dentistry research or teaching at the graduate level.
Eligibility: Applicants must be Canadian citizens or permanent residents who have completed a course in dentistry, a dental hygiene programme or a programme in science and also be eligible for admission to a graduate or other advanced education programme.
Level of Study: Postgraduate
Type: Fellowship
Value: The value of the award is dependent on the funds available and the number of applications received
Country of Study: Canada
Application Procedure: Applicants must submit an application including official transcripts of previous postsecondary education and a letter of recommendation from a faculty member of the applicant's postsecondary institution and from the administrative head of the institution and department where he or she expects to be employed. All applications must include a curriculum vitae.
Closing Date: January 31st/September 30th
Funding: Corporation
Contributor: Johnson & Johnson
No. of awards given last year: 2
No. of applicants last year: 3

DEPARTMENT OF BIOTECHNOLOGY, MINISTRY OF SCIENCE AND TECHNOLOGY

Indian Institute of Science, Bangalore, 560 012, India
Email: kmbc@biochem.iisc.ernet.in
Website: www.dbtindia.nic.in
Contact: Professor K Muniyappa, Coordinator DBT-PDF Program

The Government of India, Ministry of Science and Technology established the Department of Biotechnology in 1986 to give a new impetus to the development of the field of modern biology and biotechnology in India. The Department has made significant achievements in the growth and application of biotechnology in the broad areas of agriculture, health care, animal sciences, environment and industry.

Postdoctoral Fellowship Programme
Subjects: Biotechnology.
Purpose: To train scientists in the frontier areas of research in biotechnology at institutions in India which are engaged in major biotechnological research activities.
Eligibility: Open to Indian citizens who have obtained a PhD in science, engineering or MD or MS in any area of medicine with research interests in biotechnology and life sciences. Those who have already submitted the PhD/MD/MS theses are also eligible to apply. The applicants should preferably be below the age of 40 years and 45 years in case of female candidates.
Level of Study: Research
Type: Fellowships
Value: Indian Rupees 11,000–12,000 per month and a research contingency grant of Indian Rupees 50,000 per year, payable to the host institution. Candidates who are yet to be awarded their PhD/MD/MS degree, if selected, will be paid Indian Rupees 10,000 per month until being awarded the degree. The Fellows will also be entitled to HRA and other benefits
Length of Study: 2 years
Frequency: Annual, Biannual
Country of Study: India
No. of awards offered: 75
Application Procedure: Candidates must submit their application along with their curriculum vitae, list of publications (attach reprints of 2 important papers), copies of certificates, 1 page synopsis of PhD/MD thesis, 2 letters of recommendation (academic). The applicants are advised to propose their place of work, name of the supervisor, enclose 1 page synopsis of proposed research, which must be compatible with the ongoing research of the proposed supervisor, and his/her consent, for availing the fellowship. They should also enclose a declaration stating that if selected for the fellowship, they will complete the tenure of the fellowship.
Closing Date: August 31st
Funding: Government

DEPARTMENT OF EDUCATION SERVICES

22 Hasler Road, Osborne Park, Perth, WA, 6017, Australia
Tel: (61) 8 9441 1900
Fax: (61) 8 9441 1901
Email: des@des.wa.gov.au
Website: www.des.wa.gov.au

The Department of Education Services provides policy advice to the Minister for Education and Training and supporting universities, non-government schools and international education providers and in some cases individual students and teachers through scholarship programmes in Western Australia

Western Australian Government Japanese Studies Scholarship
Subjects: Japanese studies.
Purpose: To provide students with the opportunity to spend 1 year studying at a tertiary institution in Japan.
Eligibility: Candidates must have Australian citizenship, or evidence that Australian citizenship status will be approved prior to departure for Japan; be a student of a higher education institution in Western Australia, or an institution of equivalent standing, and have completed at least two years of full-time study (or equivalent of part-time study) in an appropriate Japanese language course; or be a graduate from a university, having a reasonable command of the Japanese language and developed an interest in Japan through employment or further studies.
Level of Study: Postgraduate
Type: Scholarship
Value: The scholarship includes a return airfare, an initial payment of Australian $3,000 for fees and other expenses and a monthly maintenance allowance of ¥226,600
Length of Study: 1 year

Frequency: Annual
Country of Study: Australia
Closing Date: July

DEPARTMENT OF INFRASTRUCTURE (DOI)

Level 14, 80 Collins Street Melbourne, VIC, 3000, Australia
Tel: (61) 3 96556666/341
Fax: (61) 3 96556752/2074
Email: salwa.andrews@doi.vic.gov.au
Website: www.doi.vic.gov.au

The Department of Infrastructure (DOI) is the lead provider of essential infrastructure in Victoria, with responsibility for transport, ports and marine, freight, information and communication technology, major development, energy and security.

DOI Women in Freight, Logistics and Marine Management Scholarship

Subjects: Freight, Logistics or Marine-related fields.
Purpose: To prepare women across Victoria for management positions within the freight, marine and logistics industries and help address the gender imbalance in an industry that has traditionally been male domonated.
Eligibility: Open to female candidates who are commencing or completing a PhD, Master's or postgraduate degree in the freight, logistics and marine fields. Candidates must be an Australian citizen and reside in Victoria, Australia to be eligible for the scholarship.
Level of Study: Postgraduate, Doctorate
Type: Scholarship
Value: Australian $10,000
Length of Study: 1 year (full-time), 2 years (part-time)
Frequency: Annual
Study Establishment: University of Victoria
Country of Study: Australia
No. of awards offered: 1
Application Procedure: Applicants must send a completed application form along with curriculum vitae, academic record and a statement about suitability for the scholarship. Refer the website for full details of the application process.
Closing Date: October 31st
Funding: Government
No. of awards given last year: 1

For further information contact:

Department of Infrastructure, GPO Box 2797, Melbourne, Vic 3001

DOI Women in Science, Engineering, Technology and Construction Scholarship

Subjects: Science, engineering, technology and construction.
Purpose: To provide encouragement and support to women with excellent technical and business skills and support women who wish to enter a non-traditional field of study.
Eligibility: Open to women who are undertaking postgraduate studies in science, engineering, technology and construction.
Level of Study: Postgraduate
Type: Scholarship
Value: Australian $10,000
Length of Study: 1 year
Frequency: Annual
Country of Study: Australia
Closing Date: December

DEPARTMENT OF INNOVATION, INDUSTRY AND REGIONAL DEVELOPMENT

GPO Box 4509RR, Melbourne, VIC, Australia
Tel: (61) 9651 9038/9266
Fax: (61) 9651 9236
Email: innovation@iird.vic.gov.au
Website: www.innovation.vic.gov.au

The Office of Science and Technology at the Department of Innovation, Industry and Regional Development, supports the ongoing development and advancement of a scientifically and technologically advanced Victoria.

Victoria Fellowships

Subjects: Engineering, science, innovation or technology.
Purpose: To offer support and encouragement to aspiring students to broaden their experience and develop networks. The fellowship also provides an opportunity for recipients to develop commercial ideas.
Eligibility: Open to candidates who are either currently employed or enrolled in post-graduate studies in Victoria in a field relating to science, engineering or technology and Australian citizens or hold permanent residence in Australia and a current resident of Victoria.
Level of Study: Postgraduate, Professional development
Type: Fellowships
Value: Australian $18,000
Length of Study: 1 year
Frequency: Annual
No. of awards offered: Upto 6
Application Procedure: A completed application form should be submitted.
Closing Date: April (Check website for closing date)
Funding: Government
Contributor: Government of Victoria
No. of awards given last year: 6

DEPARTMENT OF SCIENCE AND TECHNOLOGY (DST)

Technology Bhavan, New Mehrauli Road, New Delhi, 110-016, India
Tel: (91) 11 2656 7373 Ext. 223
Fax: (91) 11 2651 7186, 2685 4416
Email: neerajs@nic.in
Website: www.dst.gov.in
Contact: Mr Neeraj Sharma, Scientist

Department of Science and Technology (DST) Government of India was established in May 1971 with the objective to promote new areas of science and technology and to play the role of a nodal department for organizing, co-ordinating and promoting science and technology activities in the country.

DST Swarnajayanti Fellowships

Subjects: Life sciences, physical sciences, chemical sciences, earth and atmospheric sciences, mathematical sciences and engineering sciences.
Purpose: To provide special assistance and support to a select number of young scientists, with a proven track record and enable them to pursue basic research in frontier areas of science and technology.
Eligibility: Open to Indian nationals who have obtained PhD in science, engineering, Masters in engineering or technology or MD in medicine. The fellowship is open to scientists between 30 and 40 years of age.
Level of Study: Research, Doctorate
Type: Fellowship
Value: Indian Rupees 25,000 per month for those scientists who do not draw any salary from any other source and Indian Rupees 10,000 per month for those who draw salary from another source
Length of Study: 5 years
Frequency: Annual
Study Establishment: Any science and technology institute
Country of Study: India
Application Procedure: The complete application form is available on the website.
Funding: Government
Additional Information: The fellowships are not institution specific, are very selective and have close academic monitoring. In addition to fellowship, grants for equipment, computational and communication facilities, consumables, contingencies, administrative support, national and international travel and other special requirements will be covered.

DESCENDANTS OF THE SIGNERS OF THE DECLARATION OF INDEPENDENCE (DSDI)

DSDI Scholarship Committee, 3137 Periwinkle Court, Adamstown, MD, 21710, United States of America
Email: registrar@dsdi1776.com
Website: www.dsdi1776.com
Contact: Mr Frederick Wallace Pyne

Descendants of the Signers of the Declaration of Independence Scholarships

Subjects: All subjects.
Purpose: To financially assist descendants of the signers of the Declaration of Independence (those who prove eligibility and become members of this Society) to pursue their goals in higher education.
Eligibility: Open to proven direct lineal descendants of a signer of the Declaration of Independence. Proof of lineage must be established before an application is sent. Applicants must give the name of their ancestor signer in their first communication or they will not receive a reply. Applicants must be attending an accredited 4-year college or university course full-time, in graduate or undergraduate study.
Level of Study: Unrestricted
Type: Scholarship
Value: US$3,000, paid directly to the institution. Funds may be applied towards any costs chargeable to the students college account, ie. room, board, books, fees, tuition
Frequency: Annual
Country of Study: United States of America
No. of awards offered: 3
Closing Date: March 15th
Funding: Private
No. of awards given last year: 3
No. of applicants last year: 25
Additional Information: Only those with proven descent (a Society member number) will receive an application. Competition among eligible applicants is based on merit, need and length of time to graduation.

DEUTSCHE FORSCHUNGSGEMEINSCHAFT (DFG)

Kennedyallee 40, Bonn, 53175, Germany
Tel: (49) 0228 885 1
Fax: (49) 0228 885 2777
Email: postmaster@dfg.de
Website: www.dfg.de

The DFG is a central, self-governing research organization, which promotes research at universities and other publicity financial research institutions in Germany. The DFG serves all branches of science and the humanities by funding research projects and facilitating cooperation among researchers.

Albert Maucher Prize

Subjects: Geosciences.
Purpose: To promote outstanding young scientists and scholars in the field of geosciences.
Eligibility: Open to promising young scientists and scholars up to the age of 35 years who are German nationals or permanent residents of Germany.
Level of Study: Postdoctorate
Type: Award
Value: €10,000 each
Length of Study: Varies
Frequency: Every 2 years
Study Establishment: Approved universities or research institutions
Country of Study: Germany
No. of awards offered: 2
Application Procedure: Applicants must write for details or visit the website. Application is by nomination.
Contributor: Professor Albert Maucher

Bernd Rendel Prize in Geoscience

Subjects: Geoscience – geologists, mineralogists, geophysicists, oceanographers, geodesists.

Purpose: For the young geoscientists who have graduated, but do not yet hold a doctorate, and who have demonstrated great potential in their scientific career. The award must be used for scientific purposes, e.g. enabling prizewinners to attend international conferences and congresses.
Eligibility: Open to researchers from natural-science oriented fields in geoscience, researchers from humanities-oriented branches of geography are not eligible.
Level of Study: Predoctorate
Type: Prize
Value: €2,000
Frequency: Annual
No. of awards offered: 4
Application Procedure: Nominations may be submitted either by the researchers themselves, or by any researcher or academic working in a closely related field. Detailed information on the nominee's research to date (e.g. thesis, manuscripts, special publications) and future research plans, tabular curriculum vitae, list of publications, copies of certificates, statement on the proposed use of the prize money should be provided.
Contributor: The Bernd Rendel Foundation, which is administered by the Donors' Association for the Promotion of Sciences and Humanities in Germany

For further information contact:

Tel: (228) 885-2012
Email: Annett.Uhmann@dfg.de
Contact: Dr Annett Uhmann, Programme Officer

Copernicus Award

Subjects: All subjects.
Purpose: To promote young researchers to further advance research and contribute to the German–Polish research cooperation.
Eligibility: Open to outstanding researchers in Germany and Poland who work at universities or research institutions.
Type: Award
Value: €50,000
Length of Study: 5 years
Frequency: Every 2 years
No. of awards offered: 2 (1 in Germany and 1 in Poland)
Application Procedure: A completed application form along with the required documents should be submitted.
Contributor: The Foundation for Polish Science and the DFG

For further information contact:

Tel: (0) 228 885 2372
Email: torsten.fischer@dfg.de
Contact: Dr Torsten Fischer

DFG Collaborative Research Grants

Subjects: All subjects.
Purpose: To promote long-term co-operative research in universities and academic research.
Eligibility: Open to promising groups of German nationals and permanent residents of Germany.
Level of Study: Postdoctorate, Research
Type: Research grant
Value: Dependent on the requirements of the project
Length of Study: Up to 12 years
Study Establishment: Universities and academic institutions
Country of Study: Germany
No. of awards offered: Varies
Application Procedure: Applicants must write or visit the website for further information. Applications must be formally filed by the universities.
Closing Date: No submission deadline
Additional Information: A list of collaborative research centres is available in Germany only from the DFG.

DFG Individual Research Grants

Subjects: All subjects.
Purpose: To foster the proposed research projects of promising academic scientists or scholars.
Eligibility: Open to promising researchers and scholars who are German nationals or permanent residents of Germany.

Level of Study: Doctorate
Type: Grant
Value: Dependent on the requirements of the project
Length of Study: Based on individual project needs
Study Establishment: Universities
Country of Study: Any country
No. of awards offered: Varies
Application Procedure: Applicants must submit a proposal for a research project. Applicants must write for more details or visit the website.
Closing Date: Applications are accepted at any time

DFG Mercator Programme Guest Professorships

Subjects: All subjects.
Purpose: To support stays of foreign scientists at German universities.
Eligibility: Open to foreign scientists whose individual research is of special interest to research and teaching in Germany.
Level of Study: Postdoctorate
Type: Fellowship
Value: Dependent on the duration of the stay
Length of Study: 3 months–1 year
Frequency: Annual
Study Establishment: German universities
Country of Study: Germany
No. of awards offered: Varies
Application Procedure: A proposal must be submitted by the university intending to host the guest professor.

For further information contact:

Tel: 49 (228) 885 2232
Email: Cora.Laforet@dfg.de
Contact: Cora Laforet

DFG Priority Programme Funds

Subjects: All subjects.
Purpose: To promote proposals made by interested groups of scientists in selected fields.
Eligibility: Open to interested groups of scientists from Germany or any country participating in the scheme.
Level of Study: Postdoctorate, Research
Type: Grant
Value: The Senate decides on the financial ceiling for each programme
Length of Study: Up to 6 years
Frequency: Annual
Study Establishment: Universities or academic establishments
Country of Study: Germany
No. of awards offered: 30
Application Procedure: Applicants must write or visit the website for further information. Priority programmes are operated through calls for proposals, with all applications subject to open panel review, usually after discussion with the applicants.
Closing Date: November 15th

DFG Research Training Grant

Subjects: All subjects.
Purpose: To promote high-quality graduate studies at the doctoral level through the participation of graduate students recruited through countrywide calls in research programmes.
Eligibility: Open to highly qualified graduate and doctoral students of any nationality.
Level of Study: Postgraduate, Predoctorate
Type: Grant
Length of Study: Upto 9 years
Frequency: Annual
Study Establishment: Any approved university
Country of Study: Germany
No. of awards offered: Varies
Application Procedure: Applications should be submitted in response to calls. For further information applicants must visit the website.
Closing Date: April 1st and October 1st, preliminary version to be submitted 3 months prior to these dates

Additional Information: A list of graduate colleges presently funded is available (in Germany only) from the DFG.

DFG Research Unit Grants

Subjects: All subjects.
Purpose: To promote intensive co-operation between highly qualified researchers in one or several institutions in fields of high scientific promise.
Eligibility: Open to interested groups of German nationals and permanent residents of Germany.
Level of Study: Postdoctorate, Research
Type: Research grant
Value: Dependent on the requirements of the project
Length of Study: Up to 6 years
Frequency: Annual
Study Establishment: An approved university
Country of Study: Germany
No. of awards offered: Varies
Application Procedure: Applicants must submit proposals to the Senate of the DFG. They may write or visit the website for further information.
Closing Date: No submission deadline
Additional Information: A list of currently operating research groups is available in Germany only from the DFG.

Emmy Noether Programme

Subjects: All subjects.
Purpose: To give outstanding young scholars the opportunity to obtain the scientific qualifications needed to be appointed as a lecturer.
Eligibility: Open to promising young postdoctoral scientists within 5 years of receiving their PhD, who are up to 30 years of age and who are German nationals or permanent residents of Germany.
Level of Study: Postdoctorate
Type: Project grant
Value: For the 2 years of research spent abroad the candidate will receive a project grant in keeping with the requirements of the project including an allowance for subsistence and travel. For the 3 years of research spent at a German university or research institution the candidate will receive a project grant
Length of Study: 5 years
Frequency: Annual
Study Establishment: Universities or research institutions
Country of Study: Any country
No. of awards offered: 100
Application Procedure: Applicants must complete an application form. For further information applicants must write or visit the website.
Closing Date: Applications may be submitted at any time

For further information contact:

Tel: (0) 228 885 2124
Email: vera.herkommer@dfg.de
Contact: Dr Vera Herkommer

Eugen and Ilse Seibold Award

Subjects: Humanities, social science, law, economics, natural sciences, engineering and medicine.
Purpose: To promote outstanding young scientists and scholars who have made significant contributions to the scientific interchange between Japan and Germany.
Eligibility: Open to outstanding young German or Japanese scholars.
Level of Study: Postdoctorate
Type: Award
Value: €10,000
Length of Study: Varies
Frequency: Every 2 years
Study Establishment: Universities or research institutions
No. of awards offered: 2
Application Procedure: Applicants must write for details or visit the website. Application is by nomination.
Closing Date: August 31st

For further information contact:

Tel: (0) 228 885 2724
Email: ina.sauer@dfg.de
Contact: Dr Ina Sauer

European Young Investigator Award

Purpose: To enable and encourage outstanding young researchers from all over the world, to work in an European environment for the benefit of the development of European science and the building up of the next generation of leading European researchers.

Eligibility: The program is open to scientists of all disciplines and is open to candidates throughout the world.

Type: Prize

Length of Study: 5 years

Application Procedure: Applicants should provide a completed application form, letters of recommendation and the letter of support from the host institution to the DFG.

Closing Date: November 30th

Contributor: The European Union Research Organisations Heads of Research Councils (EuroHORCS)

Additional Information: For further information log on to: www.dfg.de/en/news/scientific_prizes/euryi_award/index.html

For further information contact:

Tel: (228) 885-2845
Email: Anjana.Buckow@dfg.de
Contact: Dr Anjana Buckow

Excellence Initiative

Purpose: To promote top-level research and improve the quality of German universities and research institutions in general, thus making Germany a more attractive research location, and more internationally competitive and focussing attention on the outstanding achievements of German universities and the German scientific community.

Eligibility: The precise conditions for receiving funding were defined in accordance with the criteria specified by the federal and state governments.

Type: Funding support

Length of Study: 5 years

Contributor: German federal and state governments

Additional Information: The three funding lines of the initiative: graduate schools to promote young scientists, clusters of excellence to promote top-level research, institutional strategies to promote top-level university research. For more details log on to www.dfg.de/en/research_funding/coordinated_programmes/excellence_initiative/

Gottfried Wilhelm Leibniz Prize

Subjects: All subjects.

Purpose: To promote outstanding scientists and scholars in German universities and research institutions.

Eligibility: Open to outstanding scholars in German universities.

Level of Study: Predoctorate, Research

Type: Research grant

Value: €2.5 million per award

Length of Study: 5 years

Frequency: Annual

Study Establishment: Any approved university or research institution

Country of Study: Germany

No. of awards offered: Up to 10

Application Procedure: Applicants must write for details or visit the website. Application is by nomination. Nominations are restricted to selected institutions such as DFG member organizations or individuals e.g. former prize winners or chairpersons of DFG review committees.

Additional Information: A list of prize winners is available in Germany only from the DFG.

For further information contact:

Tel: 49 (228) 885 2726
Email: Ursula.Rogmans-Beucher@dfg.de
Contact: Ursula Rogmans-Beucher

Heinz Maier–Leibnitz Prize

Subjects: All subjects.

Purpose: To promote outstanding young scientists at the doctorate level.

Eligibility: Open to promising young scholars up to 33 years of age, who are German nationals or permanent residents of Germany.

Level of Study: Doctorate, Postdoctorate

Type: Award

Value: €16,000

Length of Study: Varies

Frequency: Annual

Study Establishment: Any approved university or research institution

Country of Study: Germany

No. of awards offered: 6

Application Procedure: Applicants must write for details or visit the website. Application is by nomination.

Closing Date: August 31st

Funding: Government

Contributor: The Federal Ministry of Education and Research

For further information contact:

Tel: (0) 228 885 2724
Email: ina.sauer@dfg.de
Contact: Dr Ina Sauer

Heisenberg Programme

Subjects: All subjects.

Purpose: To promote outstanding young scientists.

Eligibility: Open to high-calibre young scientists up to the age of 35 years who are German nationals or permanent residents of Germany.

Level of Study: Postdoctorate

Type: Scholarship

Value: Varies

Length of Study: 5 years

Frequency: Annual

Study Establishment: Any approved university or research institution

Country of Study: Germany

No. of awards offered: Varies

Application Procedure: Applicants must submit a research proposal, a detailed curriculum vitae, copies of degree certificates, a copy of the thesis, a letter explaining the choice of host institution, a list of all previously published material and a letter outlining financial requirements in duplicate. For further information applicants must contact the DFG.

Closing Date: Applications are accepted at any time

For further information contact:

Tel: (0) 228 885 2398
Email: paul.heuermann@dfg.de
Contact: Paul Heuermann

Reinhart Koselleck Projects

Subjects: Research projects that are highly innovative and risky in a positive sense, which are not supported by other programmes of DFG.

Purpose: To enable outstanding researchers with a proven scientific track record to pursue exceptionally innovative or higher-risk projects.

Eligibility: Researchers who hold or are eligible to hold professorships, especially at universities, and who have an outstanding curriculum vitae and great scientific potential.

Type: Funding support

Value: €500,000–1.25 million

Length of Study: 5 years

Closing Date: June 1st

Contributor: Deutsche Forschungsgemeinschaft

Additional Information: For more details log on to www.dfg.de/en/research_funding/individual_grants_programme/reinhart_koselleck_projects/index.html

Ursula M. Händel Animal Welfare Prize

Subjects: Animal welfare.

Purpose: To award scientists who make, through research, a significant contribution to the welfare of animals.

Eligibility: Open to scientists who aim at improving the welfare of animals through research.

Level of Study: Postdoctorate

Type: Award

Value: €25,000

Frequency: Annual

No. of awards offered: Varies

Application Procedure: A completed application form and required documents must be submitted.

Funding: Trusts

Contributor: Mrs. Ursula M. Händel

For further information contact:

Tel: +49 (0) 228-885-2658
Email: Sonja.lhle@dfg.de
Contact: Dr Sonja Ihle

Von Kaven Award

Subjects: Instrumental mathematics.
Purpose: The award is granted as a fellowship or as a support for research in the field of instrumental mathematics.
Eligibility: Persons who meet the general eligibility criteria stipulated by the DFG within the individual grants programme.
Type: Research award
Value: €5,000
Application Procedure: Nominations for the von Kaven (Prize and) award may be made by the members of the mathematics review board, its previous chairs and other DFG committee members in the field of mathematics (such as senators and members of the senate committee working in the field of mathematics). It is not possible to apply directly for the von Kaven (Prize and) award.
Closing Date: January 31st

For further information contact:

Tel: 49 (228) 885-2567
Email: frank.kiefer@dfg.de
Contact: Dr Frank Kiefer

DIABETES RESEARCH & WELLNESS FOUNDATION

Office 101–102, Northney Marina, Hayling Island, Hampshire, PO11
0NH, England
Tel: (44) 23 9263 7808
Fax: (44) 23 9263 6137
Email: drwf@drwf.org.uk
Website: www.drwf.org.uk
Contact: Mrs S. Dixon, Grants Administrator

The Diabetes Research & Wellness Foundation was established in 1998 to fund research into finding a cure for diabetes. Each year this goal becomes more important as the number of people diagnosed continues to rise. The organization hopes to make diabetes a thing of the past, and, until then, alleviate its awful complications.

DRWF Open Funding

Subjects: Endocrinology or diabetes.
Purpose: To encourage research into the complications and cure of diabetes.
Level of Study: Postgraduate, Doctorate, Research
Type: Grant
Value: Up to UK £30,000
Length of Study: 1 year
Frequency: Annual
Study Establishment: A recognized institution or research group in the United Kingdom
Country of Study: United Kingdom
No. of awards offered: Up to 6, depending on grant amount
Application Procedure: Applications should be no more than 4 sides of A4 paper, typed using single-line spacing and an 11 or 12 point clearly readable font. They should include (as appropriate): applicant's name, qualifications, present post and contact details; name and address of the institution(s) where the work will be carried out; head of department/institution and major participants in the project; signed verification of funding application by HOD, outline of the proposed research comprising title, research question, relevance to diabetes, expected outcome; lay summary of the research question; any additional information to support the application; amount of funding requested, with a general breakdown of costs; and a (brief) curriculum vitae of the main applicant on separate single sheet of A4.
Closing Date: June 6th
Funding: Commercial, individuals, private
No. of awards given last year: 4
No. of applicants last year: 33
Additional Information: Notification of awards in November.

DRWF Research Fellowship

Subjects: Endocrinology or diabetes.
Purpose: To encourage research into the complications or cure of diabetes.
Eligibility: Open to suitable candidates who are working at an institution within the United Kingdom in an established position.
Level of Study: Doctorate, Postdoctorate, Research
Type: Fellowship
Value: Up to UK £55,000 each for both non-clinical and clinical fellowship
Length of Study: Up to 3 years
Frequency: Annual
Study Establishment: A recognized institution or research group in the United Kingdom
Country of Study: United Kingdom
No. of awards offered: 1
Application Procedure: Applicants must undergo a three-stage selection procedure starting with a pre-application. This is a single side of A4 paper, with single-line spacing and a clearly readable font in 11 or 12 points. The pre-application must include the applicant's name, qualifications, contact details and present post. The pre-application must also include the name of the head of the group, see open funding addition where the grant will be held, the post held or expected post to be held within the group and the relevant contact details of the group. There should also be a 300-word abstract of the proposed research work including the title, a research question of approximately 300 words, relevance to diabetes, expected outcome and any additional information to support the application, but no references. Lastly, a brief curriculum vitae of the applicant on a separate single sheet of A4 paper must be provided. Successful applicants at the pre-selection stage are required to submit a full application by August.
Closing Date: January 14th (for Non-Clinical Fellowship); April 27th (for Clinical Fellowship)
Funding: Commercial, individuals, private
No. of awards given last year: 1
No. of applicants last year: 10
Additional Information: Fellowships are alternated between clinical and non-clinical, year by year. Final interviews of selected candidates are held in October. The recipient of the fellowship is expected to take it up early in the following year.

For further information contact:

Email: sarah.brown@drwf.org.uk
Contact: Sarah Brown Grants Administrator

DIABETES UK

10 Parkway, London, NW1 7AA, England
Tel: (44) 20 7424 1833
Fax: (44) 20 7424 1082
Email: research@diabetes.org.uk
Website: www.diabetes.org.uk
Contact: Dr Eleanor Kennedy, Research Manager

Diabetes UK's overall aim is to help and care for both people with diabetes and those closest to them, to represent and campaign for their interests and to fund research into diabetes. Diabetes UK continues to encourage research into all areas of diabetes.

Diabetes UK Equipment Grant

Subjects: Endocrinology, diabetes and subjects relevant to diabetes.
Purpose: To enable the purchase of a specific large item of multi user equipment necessary for diabetes related research projects.
Eligibility: Open to suitably qualified members of the medical or scientific professions who are resident in the United Kingdom.
Level of Study: Postdoctorate
Type: Grant
Value: Up to £100,000
Length of Study: 1 year–3 years
Frequency: 3 times a year
Country of Study: United Kingdom
No. of awards offered: Varies
Application Procedure: Candidates must complete an application form that will be assessed by a peer review. Please write or telephone for details. Details can be found on the website.

Closing Date: June 1st, August 1st and December 1st
Funding: Private
Contributor: Voluntary contributions
No. of awards given last year: 3

Diabetes UK Project Grants

Subjects: Endocrinology, diabetes and subjects relevant to diabetes.
Purpose: To provide funding for a well-defined research proposal of timeliness and promise that, in terms of the application, may be expected to lead to a significant advance in our knowledge of diabetes.
Eligibility: Open to suitably qualified members of the medical or scientific professions who are resident in the United Kingdom.
Level of Study: Postdoctorate
Type: Project grant
Value: There is no limit to research expenses that may be requested, however, all requests must be fully justified
Length of Study: 1–3 years
Frequency: Every 3 years
Country of Study: United Kingdom
No. of awards offered: Varies
Application Procedure: Candidates must complete an application form, which will be assessed by a peer review and should write or telephone for details. Details can be found on the website.
Closing Date: June 1st and December 1st
Funding: Private
Contributor: Voluntary contributions
No. of awards given last year: 9
No. of applicants last year: 10
Additional Information: Candidates applying for £500,000 or more must contact the office in the first instance and should normally hold substantial funding from Diabetes UK. Candidates applying for £15,000 or less should follow the Guidelines for Small Grant Applications.

Diabetes UK Small Grant Scheme

Subjects: Endocrinology, diabetes and subjects relevant to diabetes.
Purpose: To enable research workers to develop new ideas in the field of diabetes research.
Eligibility: Open to suitably qualified members of the medical or scientific professions who are resident in the United Kingdom.
Level of Study: Postdoctorate
Type: Grant
Value: A maximum of UK £15,000
Length of Study: 1–3 years
Country of Study: United Kingdom
No. of awards offered: Varies
Application Procedure: Applicants must complete an application form which will be assessed by a peer review within 6–8 weeks. Please write or telephone for details. Details can also be found on the website.
Closing Date: Applications are accepted at any time
Funding: Private
Contributor: Voluntary contributions
No. of awards given last year: 14
No. of applicants last year: 30

DIRKSEN CONGRESSIONAL CENTER

2815 Broadway, Pekin, IL, 61554, United States of America
Tel: (1) 309 347 7113
Fax: (1) 309 347 6432
Email: fmackaman@dirksencenter.org
Website: www.dirksencenter.org
Contact: Executive Director

The Dirksen Congressional Center sponsors educational and research programmes to help people understand better the United States of America Congress, its members and leaders and the public policies it produces.

Dirksen Congressional Research Grants Program

Subjects: Political science and government.
Purpose: To fund the study of the United States of America Congress.

Eligibility: Open to citizens or residents of the United States of America. Awards are to individuals only. No institutional overhead charges are permitted. Political scientists, historians, biographers, scholars of public administration or American studies, and journalists are among those eligible.
Level of Study: Doctorate, Postdoctorate, Research
Type: Research grant
Value: Up to US$3,500
Length of Study: Varies
Frequency: Annual
Study Establishment: Unrestricted
Country of Study: United States of America
No. of awards offered: 10–15 per year
Application Procedure: Candidates should visit the Center's website for application information. Candidates are responsible for showing the relationship between their work and the awards program guidelines.
Closing Date: February 1st
Funding: Private

DONATELLA FLICK CONDUCTING COMPETITION

PO Box 34227, London, NW5 1XP, England
Tel: (44) 20 7482 1353
Fax: (44) 20 7267 0068
Email: administrator@conducting.org
Website: www.conducting.org
Contact: The Administrator

The Donatella Flick Associazione organizes the Donatella Flick Conducting Competition, which, in association with the London Symphony Orchestra, aims to help advance career opportunities for young conductors. The award subsidizes study and concert engagements for the winner who will work as Assistant Conductor with the London Symphony Orchestra for 1 year.

Donatella Flick Conducting Competition

Subjects: Conducting.
Purpose: To assist a young conductor in establishing an international conducting career.
Eligibility: Open to conductors who are under 35 years of age and are citizens of member countries of the European Union.
Level of Study: Professional development
Type: Prize
Frequency: Every 2 years
Study Establishment: London Symphony Orchestra
Country of Study: Any country
Application Procedure: Applicants must complete an application form and submit this with references specific to the competition, as well as videos and other supporting documentation such as other prizes, reviews, a curriculum vitae, etc.
Closing Date: Mid-April
Funding: Private
Contributor: Mrs Donatella Flick
Additional Information: Entry is by recommendation, documentation and supporting video. Finalists are then selected for audition, and three finalists conduct a public concert. The course of study of entrants must be approved by the organizing committee.

DOSHISHA UNIVERSITY

Keimeikan building, Karasuma-Higashi-iru Imadegawa-dori, Kyoto Kamigyo-ku, 602-8580, Japan
Tel: (81) 81 75 251 3260
Fax: (81) 81 75 251 3057
Email: ji-kksai@mail.doshisha.ac.jp
Website: www.doshisha.ac.jp

Located in the heart of Kyoto, Doshisha University occupies 3 separate campuses and is home to over 24,000 students engaged in both undergraduate and graduate studies. As one of Japan's most highly esteemed educational institutions, Doshisha offers students a wide ranging liberal arts education as well as studies in business and science. Doshisha has respected faculties of theology, letters, social studies, law, economics, commerce, policy studies, culture and information science and engineering.

Doshisha University Harris Science School Foundation Grant

Subjects: Engineering.
Purpose: To support students who wish to pursue higher studies in the field of engineering.
Eligibility: Open to full-time international students enrolled in the Graduate School of Engineering. Those who have received this grant in the previous academic year and those who received the Kato Yamazaki Memorial Foundation Grant are not eligible.
Level of Study: Postgraduate, Doctorate
Type: Grant
Value: ¥100,000 for the Master's degree course, ¥120,000 for the Doctoral degree course
Length of Study: 1 year
Frequency: Annual
Study Establishment: Doshisha University
Country of Study: Japan
No. of awards offered: Undetermined

DR HADWEN TRUST FOR HUMANE RESEARCH

84A Tilehouse Street, Hitchin, Hertfordshire, SG5 2DY, England
Tel: (44) 14 6243 6819
Fax: (44) 14 6243 6844
Email: info@drhadwentrust.org.uk
Website: www.drhadwentrust.org.uk
Contact: Dr Carol Newman, Scientific Officer

The Dr Hadwen Trust for Humane Research is a registered charity, established in 1970, to promote research into techniques and procedures to replace the use of living animals in biomedical research, teaching and testing.

Dr Hadwen Trust Research Assistant or Technician

Subjects: The development, validation or implementation of a technique or procedure that would replace one currently using living animals.
Purpose: To provide additional scientific or technical support for a research project to replace animal experiments
Eligibility: Open to applicants resident in the United Kingdom.
Type: Research
Value: Salary for research assistant or technician plus an allowance for consumables
Length of Study: 3 years
Frequency: Annual
Study Establishment: Varies
Country of Study: United Kingdom
No. of awards offered: Varies
Application Procedure: Applicants must make initial enquiries by contacting Carol Newman, Scientific Officer. Applications must be made by the senior researcher who will oversee the work. Preliminary applications are usually invited in October. Details are posted on the website.
Closing Date: See website for details
Funding: Private
No. of awards given last year: 5
No. of applicants last year: 40
Additional Information: For further details and policy information see website www.scienceroom.org

Dr Hadwen Trust Research Fellowship

Subjects: The development, validation or implementation of a technique or procedure that would replace one currently using living animals.
Purpose: To attract and retain talented young scientists in non-animal research fields. The funds provide personal support and a contribution to direct research costs for research to replace animal experiments.
Eligibility: Open to applicants resident in the United Kingdom.
Level of Study: Postdoctorate
Type: Fellowship

Value: Usually a maximum of £135,000 total for 3 years, to cover salary, consumables or small items of equipment
Length of Study: 3 years maximum
Study Establishment: Varies
Country of Study: United Kingdom
No. of awards offered: Varies
Application Procedure: Applicants must make initial enquiries by contacting Carol Newman, Scientific Officer. Application forms must be submitted by a senior researcher who will oversee the work. Preliminary applications are usually invited in October. Details and guidelines are posted on the website.
Funding: Private
Contributor: Public donations
No. of awards given last year: 5
No. of applicants last year: 40
Additional Information: Further policy information and application details are available on the website. www.scienceroom.org

DUBLIN INSTITUTE FOR ADVANCED STUDIES

10 Burlington Road, Dublin 4, Ireland
Tel: (353) 1 614 0100
Fax: (353) 1 668 0561
Email: registrarsoffice@admin.dias.ie
Website: www.dias.ie
Contact: Ms Ruth Graham, Administrative Assistant

The Dublin Institute for Advanced Studies is a statutory corporation established in 1940, under the Institute for Advanced Studies Act of that year. It is a publicly funded independent centre for research in basic disciplines. Research is currently carried out in the fields of Celtic studies, theoretical physics and cosmic physics including astronomy, astrophysics and geophysics.

Dublin Institute for Advanced Studies Scholarship in Astronomy, Astrophysics and Geophysics

Subjects: Astronomy, astrophysics and geophysics.
Purpose: To enable training in advanced research methods in the fields of astronomy, astrophysics and geophysics.
Eligibility: Open to candidates from any country.
Level of Study: Doctorate, Graduate, Postdoctorate, Postgraduate, Predoctorate
Type: Scholarship
Value: Please contact the Institute for details
Length of Study: 1 year
Frequency: Annual
Study Establishment: The Dublin Institute for Advanced Studies
Country of Study: Ireland
No. of awards offered: 3
Application Procedure: Applicants must complete an application form, available upon request.
Closing Date: Please write to the Institute for details
Funding: Government
Contributor: State
No. of awards given last year: 2
No. of applicants last year: 12

Dublin Institute for Advanced Studies Scholarship in Celtic Studies

Subjects: Celtic studies.
Purpose: To enable training in advanced research methods in the field of Celtic studies.
Eligibility: Open to nationals of any country.
Level of Study: Doctorate, Postdoctorate, Postgraduate, Predoctorate
Type: Scholarship
Value: Please contact the Institute for details
Length of Study: 1 year
Frequency: Annual
Study Establishment: The Dublin Institute for Advanced Studies
Country of Study: Ireland
No. of awards offered: 3

Application Procedure: Applicants must complete an application form, available upon request.
Closing Date: Applications are accepted at any time
Funding: Government
No. of awards given last year: 3
No. of applicants last year: 10

Dublin Institute for Advanced Studies Scholarship in Theoretical Physics

Subjects: Physics.
Purpose: To enable training in advanced research methods in the field of theoretical physics.
Eligibility: Open to candidates of any country.
Level of Study: Postdoctorate
Type: Scholarship
Value: Please contact the Institute for details
Length of Study: 1 year
Frequency: Annual
Study Establishment: The Dublin Institute for Advanced Studies
Country of Study: Ireland
No. of awards offered: 5
Application Procedure: Applicants must complete an application form, available upon request.
Closing Date: Please write to the Institute for details
Funding: Government
Contributor: State
No. of awards given last year: 3
No. of applicants last year: 30

DUKE UNIVERSITY

116 Allen Building, PO Box 90061, Durham, NC, 27708, United States of America
Tel: (1) 919 684 5708
Fax: (1) 919 668 0434
Email: grm@duke.edu
Website: www.gradschool.duke.edu
Contact: Co-ordinator

The Duke University ideally has a small number of superior students working closely with esteemed scholars. It has approximately 2,200 graduate students enrolled there, working with more than 1,000 graduate faculty members.

James B. Duke Fellowships

Subjects: All subjects.
Purpose: To pursue a programme leading to the PhD in the Graduate School at Duke University.
Level of Study: Doctorate
Type: Fellowship
Value: US$5,000 stipend
Length of Study: 4 years
Frequency: Annual
Country of Study: United States of America
Closing Date: February 28th
Additional Information: Its objective is to aid in attracting and developing outstanding scholars at Duke

For further information contact:

Contact: Director of Graduate Studies

DUMBARTON OAKS: TRUSTEES FOR HARVARD UNIVERSITY

1703, 32nd Street North West, Washington, DC, 20007, United States of America
Tel: (1) 202 339 6410
Email: DumbartonOaks@doaks.org
Website: www.doaks.org
Contact: Fellowship Programme Manager

Dumbarton Oaks houses important research and study collections in the areas of Byzantine and Medieval studies, landscape architecture studies and pre-Columbian studies. While the gallery holds exhibitions and the gardens are open to the public, the research facilities exist primarily to serve scholars who hold appointments at Dumbarton Oaks.

Dumbarton Oaks Fellowships and Junior Fellowships

Subjects: Byzantine civilization in all its aspects, including the late Roman and Early Christian period and the Middle Ages generally, studies of Byzantine cultural exchanges with the Latin West, Slavic and Near Eastern countries, pre-Columbian studies and garden and landscape studies.
Purpose: To promote study and research or to support writing of doctoral dissertations.
Eligibility: Junior fellowships are open to persons of any nationality who have passed all preliminary examinations for a higher degree and are writing a dissertation. Candidates must have a working knowledge of any languages required for the research. Fellowships are open to scholars of any nationality holding a PhD or relevant advanced degree and wishing to pursue research on a project of their own at Dumbarton Oaks.
Level of Study: Doctorate, Postdoctorate
Type: Fellowship
Value: US$22,110 per year for junior fellowships, US$43,400 per year for fellowships. Both junior and regular Fellows receive furnished accommodation or a housing allowance and US$2,000, if needed, to assist with the cost of bringing and maintaining dependants in Washington plus an expense account of US$1000 for approved research expenditure during the academic year. Fellows are also provided with travel assistance
Length of Study: Up to 1 academic year of full-time study, non-renewable
Frequency: Annual
Study Establishment: Dumbarton Oaks
Country of Study: United States of America
No. of awards offered: 10–11 fellowships in Byzantine studies and 3–4 in each of the other fields
Application Procedure: Applicants must contact Dumbarton Oaks for the current application brochure.
Closing Date: November 1st of the academic year preceding that for which the fellowship is required
No. of awards given last year: 35
No. of applicants last year: 200
Additional Information: Dumbarton Oaks also awards a limited number of Summer fellowships.

DUTCH MINISTRY OF FOREIGN AFFAIRS

PO Box 20061, 2500 EB The Hague, Netherlands
Tel: (31) 31 70 3486486
Fax: (31) 31 70 3484848
Email: dsi-my@minbuza.nl
Website: www.minbuza.nl

Dutch foreign policy is driven by the conviction that international co-operation brings peace and promotes security, prosperity, and justice. It is bound by the obligation to promote Dutch interests abroad as effectively and efficiently as possible. To do so, the Netherlands needs a worldwide network of embassies, consulates, and permanent representations to international organisations. The activities, composition, and size of each mission depend on its host country and region. Embassies and consulates-bilateral missions-concern themselves with relations between the Netherlands and other countries.

Netherlands Fellowship Programme

Subjects: All subjects.
Purpose: To support mid-career professionals nominated by their employers.
Eligibility: Open to candidates who are employed by an organization other than a large industrial, commercial and/or multinational firm, must be nationals of one of the 57 selected countries (see 'Eligible countries'), must declare that they will return to their home country immediately after they complete the master programme, must have gained admission to a TU/e master course, which is on the NFP course list and have sufficient mastery of the English language.

Priority is given to female candidates and to candidates coming from sub-Saharan Africa.
Level of Study: Postgraduate
Type: Fellowships
Value: Full-cost scholarship (including international travel, monthly subsistence allowance, tuition fee, books, and health insurance)
Length of Study: 2 years
Frequency: Annual
Country of Study: Netherlands
Application Procedure: Applicants must apply for an NFP fellowship through the Netherlands embassy or consulate in their own country by completing an NFP Application Form and submitting it together with all the required documents and information to the embassy or consulate. Then the Embassy checks and sends the forms to the Nufficchecks. Nuffic decides how many fellowships will be available for each program and sends TU/e the list of NFP candidates.
Closing Date: March 1st
Funding: Government
Contributor: Dutch Ministry of Foreign Affairs
Additional Information: Eligible countries: Afghanistan, Albania, Armenia, Autonomous Palestinian Territories, Bangladesh, Benin, Bhutan, Bolivia, Bosnia–Hercegovina, Brazil, Burkina Faso, Cambodia, Cape Verde, China*, Colombia, Costa Rica, Cuba, Ecuador, Egypt, El Salvador, Eritrea, Ethiopia, Georgia, Ghana, Guatemala, Guinea–Bissau, Honduras, India, Indonesia, Iran, Ivory Coast, Jordan, Kenya, Macedonia, Mali, Moldova, Mongolia, Mozambique, Namibia, Nepal, Nicaragua, Nigeria, Pakistan, Peru, Philippines, Rwanda, Senegal, South Africa, Sri Lanka, Suriname, Tanzania, Thailand, Uganda, Vietnam, Yemen, Zambia, Zimbabwe. For a more detailed list of criteria, please check website.

For further information contact:

International Relations Office, Education and Student Service Center
Tel: 31 (0)40 247 4690
Fax: 31 (0)40 244 1692
Email: io@remove-this.tue.nl
Website: www.nuffic.nl/nfp/

EARLY AMERICAN INDUSTRIES ASSOCIATION

1324 Shallcross Avenue, Wilmington, DE, 19806, United States of America
Tel: (1) 302 652 7297
Email: eaiainfo@worldnet.att.net
Website: www.eaiainfo.org
Contact: Ms Justine J Mataleno, Co-ordinator

The Early American Industries Association seeks to encourage the study and better understanding of early American industries in the home, in the shop, on the farm and on the sea. It also wishes to discover, identify, classify and exhibit obsolete tools, implements and mechanical devices that were used in early America.

Early American Industries Association Research Grants Program
Subjects: Early American industrial development, including craft practices, industrial technology and identification and use of obsolete tools, implements and mechanical devices used prior to 1900.
Purpose: To encourage research leading to a publication, exhibition or audio-visual material for educational purposes.
Eligibility: Open to citizens or permanent residents of the United States of America. Individuals may be either sponsored by an institution or engaged in self-directed projects.
Level of Study: Predoctorate, Research, Doctorate, Graduate, Postdoctorate, Postgraduate
Type: Grant
Value: Up to US$2,000
Length of Study: 1 year, non-renewable
Frequency: Annual
Country of Study: United States of America
No. of awards offered: 3–5
Application Procedure: Applicants must submit a completed application form plus three letters of recommendation.
Closing Date: March 15th

Funding: Private
Contributor: Membership dues and donations
No. of awards given last year: 3
No. of applicants last year: 10
Additional Information: Awards may be used to supplement existing financial awards. Successful applicants are required to file a project report on forms supplied by the Association. These are not scholarship funds.

EARTHWATCH INSTITUTE

Research Program, 3 Clock Tower Place, Suite 100, Maynard, MA, 01754, United States of America
Tel: (1) 978 461 0081
Fax: (1) 978 461 2332
Email: research@earthwatch.org
Website: www.earthwatch.org/research

Earthwatch Institute supports diverse research projects of high scientific merit worldwide that address critical environmental and social issues at local, national and international levels. Researchers are given both funding and field assistance from layperson volunteers. Volunteers are recruited by Earthwatch, who pay for the opportunity to assist them in the field.

Earthwatch Fellowships
Subjects: Global conservation priority areas including climate change, ocean ecosystem, sustainable resource management and sustainable cultures.
Purpose: To give teachers and students the opportunity to experience field research first hand and share this experience with their students and local communities. It sends volunteers around the world to assist scientists in gathering data on some of the most critical environmental issues facing the planet today.
Eligibility: Fellowships are awarded through a competitive process. Fellows are assigned to projects according to their interests, skills, availability, project need and grant restrictions. Fellowships are awarded to those with leadership potential in initiating and supporting environmental stewardship within the communities in which they work and live.
Level of Study: Professional development, Research
Type: Fellowship/Scholarship
Length of Study: 2–3 weeks
Frequency: Annual
Country of Study: Any country
No. of awards offered: 500
Application Procedure: Applicants must complete an application form and submit it with the other requested documents. Incomplete applications will not be considered.
Closing Date: Applications are accepted on an ongoing basis
Funding: Private, corporation, foundation, government, individuals
Contributor: Over 100 donors including foundations and corporations
No. of awards given last year: 450
Additional Information: Recipients are limited to two education awards and cannot receive an award in two consecutive years.

Earthwatch Field Research Grants
Subjects: Disciplines include, but are not limited to, anthropology, archaeology, biology, botany, cartography, conservation, ethnology, folklore, geography, geology, hydrology, marine sciences, meteorology, musicology, nutrition, ornithology, restoration, sociology and sustainable development.
Purpose: To provide grants for field research projects that can constructively utilize teams of non-specialist field assistants in accomplishing their research goals.
Eligibility: There are no residency requirements or nomination processes. Preference is given to applicants who hold a PhD and have both field and teaching experience, however, support is also offered for outstanding projects by younger postdoctoral scholars and, in special cases, graduate students. Women and minority applicants are encouraged. Research teams must include qualified volunteers from the Earthwatch Institute.
Level of Study: Postgraduate, Doctorate, Postdoctorate, Research
Type: Grant

Value: Varies. The normal range of support is US$17,000–51,000. Grants are awarded on a per capita basis, depending upon the number of volunteer participants who are recruited by Earthwatch
Length of Study: Teams last for 2–3 weeks and projects can go on all year
Frequency: Annual
Study Establishment: Research sites
Country of Study: Any country
No. of awards offered: Approx. 130
Application Procedure: Applicants must complete an application form, which can be obtained from the Earthwatch headquarters or by visiting the website. Concept notes must be submitted 18 months prior to field dates.
Closing Date: There is no deadline
Funding: Private
Contributor: Volunteers' contributions
No. of awards given last year: 130
No. of applicants last year: 400

EAST ASIA INSTITUTE (EAI)

909 Sampoong Building, 310-68 Euljiro 4-ga, Jung-gu, Seoul, 100-786, Korea
Tel: (82) 02 2277 1683 ext 107
Fax: (82) 02 2277 1684
Email: fellowship@eai.or.kr
Website: www.eai.or.kr

East Asia Institute (EAI), based in Seoul, Korea, was founded in May 2002, as an independent and non-partisan organization devoted to research, publication and education on public policy, institutions and East Asian affairs. The EAI strives to become a prominent think tank in Korea.

EAI Fellows Program on Peace, Governance and Development in East Asia

Subjects: Political science, international relations and sociology.
Purpose: To encourage interdisciplinary research with a comparative perspective in the study of East Asia.
Eligibility: Open to tenured, tenure-track as well as non-tenured East Asian professors, based in the United States.
Level of Study: Research
Type: Fellowships
Value: US$10,000
Length of Study: 3 weeks
Frequency: Annual
No. of awards offered: 5
Application Procedure: Applicants can download the application form from the website. A completed application cover sheet, applicant data form along with letters of recommendation and a curriculum vitae are to be submitted.
Closing Date: May 31st
Funding: Foundation
No. of awards given last year: 6
No. of applicants last year: 18

For further information contact:

Tel: 02 2277 1683 ext 107
Fax: 02 2277 1684
Email: fellowships@eai.or.kr

EAST LOTHIAN EDUCATIONAL TRUST

Finance Department, John Muir House, Haddington, East Lothian, EH41 3HA, Scotland
Tel: (44) 16 2082 7436
Fax: (44) 16 2082 7446
Email: eleducationaltrust@eastlothian.gov.uk
Website: www.eastlothian.gov.uk
Contact: Kim Brand, Clerk

The East Lothian Educational Trust provides grants to individuals who are undertaking studies, courses or projects of an educational nature, including scholarships abroad and educational travel. Applicants must be residents of East Lothian.

East Lothian Educational Trust General Grant

Subjects: All subjects, but must be of an educational nature.
Purpose: To provide supplementary support to individuals who undertake studies.
Eligibility: Open to residents of East Lothian, excluding Musselburgh, Wallyford and Whitecraig.
Level of Study: Unrestricted
Type: Grant
Value: Variable
Length of Study: Unrestricted
Frequency: Annual
No. of awards offered: Varies
Application Procedure: Applicants must complete an application form.
Closing Date: August 10th and November 10th
Funding: Private
No. of awards given last year: 103
No. of applicants last year: Approx. 130

THE ECONOMIC AND SOCIAL RESEARCH CONSORTIUM (CIES)

Calle Antero Aspillaga, 584 San Isidro, Lima, 27, Peru
Tel: (511) 421 8082
Email: postmaster@cies.org.pe
Website: www.consorcio.org/novedades

The Economicc and Social Research Consortium (CIES) is a private umbrella organization of 34 institutions, private and public universities, research centres and the National Statistics Institute. It seeks to strengthen the economic and social research community by supporting it's research as well as promoting it's use as a tool for decision making in government, civil society and academic community. Its final goal is to contribute to the development of Peru by improving the level of the national debate concerning key policy options for economic and social development.

CIES Fellowship Program

Subjects: Economics and social sciences.
Purpose: To facilitate the development of long-term partnerships between Canadian institutions and CIES members.
Eligibility: Open to citizens or permanent residents of Canada who are proficient in Spanish up to an academic level and must be a regular, full-time faculty member or researcher at a recognized Canadian university or research institute or full-time graduate student at a Canadian university or at a recognized Canadian research institute.
Level of Study: Postdoctorate, Postgraduate
Type: Fellowships
Value: Up to Canadian $8,000 for justifiable field research expenses and airfare to Peru
Length of Study: Minimum 30 days
Frequency: Annual
Study Establishment: Canadian university or research institute
Country of Study: Canada or abroad
No. of awards offered: 3
Application Procedure: Applicants must submit their application form, research proposal, curriculum vitae, letter of support, reference letter, authorized transcripts, proof of citizenship, proof of Spanish language competence and budget. Applications are available online.
Closing Date: June 30th

For further information contact:

Tel: 511 421 8082
Website: www.consorcio.org
Contact: Miguel Lerzundi, Analyst

ECONOMIC AND SOCIAL RESEARCH COUNCIL (ESRC)

Polaris House, North Star Avenue, Swindon, Wiltshire, SN2 1UJ, England
Tel: (44) 17 9341 3000
Fax: (44) 17 9341 3001
Email: ptd@esrc.ac.uk
Website: www.esrc.ac.uk
Contact: Ms Zoë Grimwood, Research Training & Development

The Economic and Social Research Council (ESRC) is an independent, government-funded body set up by royal charter. The mission of the ESRC is to promote and support, by any means, high-quality basic, strategic and applied research and related postgraduate training in the social sciences. It also aims to advance knowledge and provide trained social scientists who meet the needs of users and beneficiaries, thereby contributing to the economic competitiveness of the United Kingdom, the effectiveness of public services and policy and quality of life. ESRC also provides advice, disseminates knowledge and promotes public understanding of the social sciences.

ESRC 1+3 Awards and +3 Awards

Subjects: Social sciences.
Purpose: To promote social science research and postgraduate training. The ESRC aims to provide continuous support for high quality postgraduate training and research on issues of importance to business, the public sector and the government.
Eligibility: Open to United Kingdom or European Community nationals with a First or Upper Second Class (Honours) Degree in any subject, or a United Kingdom professional qualification acceptable to the ESRC as of degree standard plus 3 years of subsequent full-time, relevant professional work experience. Candidates must have ordinarily been resident in the United Kingdom throughout the 3-year period preceding the date of application.
Level of Study: Postgraduate
Type: Studentship
Value: ESRC 1+3 awards cover fees and/or maintenance, depending on the student's situation, circumstances and the type of award
Length of Study: Up to 3 years
Frequency: Annual
Study Establishment: ESRC-recognized institutional outlets and courses
Country of Study: United Kingdom
No. of awards offered: Varies
Application Procedure: Applicants must complete an application form. Information sheets and application forms are available from February each year and must be collected from the social science department of any university or Institute of Higher Education or career guidance outlet. Forms are available from the website. Studentships are allocated under the quota system.
Closing Date: May 1st
Funding: Government
No. of awards given last year: 85
No. of applicants last year: 465
Additional Information: The 1 refers to the 1-year Master's and the 3 refers to the 3-year PhD.

EDITH COWAN UNIVERSITY (ECU)

100 Joondalup Drive, Joondalup, WA 6027, Australia
Tel: (61) 61 8 6304 0000
Email: enquiries@ecu.edu.au
Website: www.ecu.edu.au

ECU is a contemporary university providing quality tertiary education for the students of today. It provides a different learning approach, developed to maximize the student outcome and experience, as well as providing state-of-the-art facilities and infrastructure. ECU awards are recognized nationally and internationally. Research areas of strength include health and wellness, education, environment and sustainability, electronic engineering, ICT, social and community, business and society, communications and creative arts, and security, law and justice.

Barbara MacLeod Scholarship

Subjects: Classical music.
Purpose: To enable students in the classical music programme to develop specialist skills in their chosen field by undertaking a short intensive programme of study in another world-class institution.
Eligibility: Open to female students who are Australian citizens and have completed 1 year full-time in the programme receiving high distinctions for their principal study.

Level of Study: Postgraduate
Type: Scholarship
Value: Up to Australian $12,000
Application Procedure: Check website for further details.
Additional Information: Applications are not invited from Percussionists.

Luke Pen Fund-Honours Scholarships

Subjects: Waterways research.
Purpose: To encourage young people to be involved in the gaining of scientific knowledge of river characteristics.
Level of Study: Graduate
Type: Scholarship
Value: Australian $50,000
Length of Study: 1 year
Frequency: Annual
Application Procedure: Check website address for further details.
Closing Date: March 31st
Funding: Trusts
Contributor: Luke Pen Scholarship Trust

For further information contact:

Department of Water, Drainage and Waterways Branch, PO Box K822, Perth WA 6842,
Email: mail: james.mackintosh@water.wa.gov.au
Contact: Verity Klemm

EDMUND NILES HUYCK PRESERVE, INC.

PO Box 189, Rensselaerville, NY, 12147,
United States of America
Tel: (1) 518 797 3440
Fax: (1) 518 797 3440
Email: info@huyckpreserve.org
Website: www.huyckpreserve.org/ggl.htm
Contact: Mr Chad Jemison, Executive Director

The Edmund Niles Huyck Preserve is a 2,000-acre nature preserve and biological research station with a newly expanded laboratory and housing for 20. The habitat is the north-eastern hardwood Hemlock forest with lakes, streams, bogs and plantations.

Edmund Niles Huyck Preserve, Inc. Graduate and Postgraduate Grants

Subjects: Ecology, behaviour evolution and natural resources of the area and conservation biology.
Purpose: To promote scientific research on the flora and fauna of the Huyck Preserve and its vicinity.
Eligibility: Open to all nationalities. Awards are made without regard to sex, colour, religion, ethnic origin or academic affiliation of the applicant, and support is based solely on the quality of the proposed research and its appropriateness to the natural resources and facilities of the Preserve.
Level of Study: Doctorate, Graduate, Postdoctorate, Postgraduate
Type: Grant
Value: A maximum of US$2,500 plus laboratory space and lodging (renewable)
Length of Study: Varies
Frequency: Annual
Study Establishment: The Preserve
Country of Study: United States of America
No. of awards offered: 10
Application Procedure: Applicants must complete an application form, available on written request or online. Proposals must contain an abstract of not more than 200 words describing the background and significance of the proposal. A literature cited section should be included and an up-to-date curriculum vitae provided. The researcher should submit three references that deal specifically with their proposed work. Please see the website www.huyckpreserve.org for further details.
Closing Date: February 1st
Funding: Private
No. of awards given last year: 6
No. of applicants last year: 12

EDUCATION AND RESEARCH FOUNDATION FOR THE SOCIETY OF NUCLEAR MEDICINE (SNM)

6500 Appalaloosa Avenue, Forest Lake, MN, 55025,
United States of America
Tel: (1) 703 708 9000
Fax: (1) 703 708 9015
Email: sueweiss@sueweiss.cnc.net
Website: erf.snm.org
Contact: Dr Samuel Morse

The Society of Nuclear Medicine (SNM) is an international, scientific and professional organization founded in 1954 to promote the science, technology and practical application of nuclear medicine. Its 16,000 members are physicians, technologists and scientists specializing in the research and practice of nuclear medicine.

Cassen Post-Doctoral Fellowships

Subjects: Nuclear medicine.
Purpose: To provide financial support and attract scientists from other fields to study nuclear medicine.
Eligibility: Open to citizens of the United States.
Level of Study: Postgraduate
Type: Fellowships
Value: US$25,000
Frequency: Annual
Study Establishment: Society of Nuclear Medicine
Country of Study: United States of America
No. of awards offered: 2
Application Procedure: Applicants must send in reference letters and research proposal.
Closing Date: November 15th

For further information contact:

Leadership Services, United States of America
Tel: (1) 703 708 9000
Contact: Sue Weiss

SNM Pilot Research Grants in Nuclear Medicine/ Molecular Imaging

Subjects: Health and medical sciences and nuclear science.
Purpose: To support Master's or PhD students to start research in nuclear medicine.
Eligibility: Open to basic and clinical scientists in early stages of their career.
Level of Study: Doctorate, Postgraduate
Type: Grant
Value: US$25,000
Frequency: Annual
Study Establishment: Society of Nuclear Medicine
Country of Study: United States of America
No. of awards offered: 2
Application Procedure: Applicants must submit a completed application form along with abstract of project proposal and budget proposal.
Closing Date: February 20th

For further information contact:

Leadership Services, United States of America
Tel: (1) 703 708 9000
Contact: Travis Stiltner, Manager

EDUCATION NEW ZEALAND

Scholarships Manager Education New Zealand Trust, PO Box 10-500, Wellington, 6143, New Zealand
Tel: (64) 4 917 0872
Email: Scholarships@educationnz.org.nz
Website: www.newzealandeducated.com/scholarships

Education New Zealand (ENZ) is a not-for-profit charitable trust that is governed by the New Zealand export education industry, and is committed to an "NZ Inc" approach to the export of New Zealand's education services offshore. ENZ is recognised by the New Zealand Government as the umbrella industry body for education exporters in New Zealand. The New Zealand Scholarships Programme is funded by the New Zealand Government and administered by Education New Zealand.

New Zealand International Doctoral Research Scholarships (NZIDRS)

Subjects: All subjects.
Purpose: To provide financial support to top achieving international students seeking doctoral degrees by research in New Zealand universities
Eligibility: The candidate must hold an 'A' average or equivalent (GPA 8.00/9.00) in their prior tertiary level studies and meet the requirements for entry into a research-based doctoral programme at a New Zealand University.
Level of Study: Doctorate
Type: Research scholarship
Value: Full tuition fees student services levies, an annual living allowance of New Zealand$20,500, travel allowance up to New Zealand$2000, annual health insurance allowance up to New Zealand$600, an establishment allowance of New Zealand$600 and a book and thesis allowance of New Zealand$800
Length of Study: 3 years
Frequency: Annual
Study Establishment: All New Zealand Universities
Country of Study: New Zealand
No. of awards offered: 38
Application Procedure: The candidate must complete the application form in English and attach supporting documents as stipulated within the NZIDRS application form etc.
Closing Date: July 15th
Funding: Government
Contributor: New Zealand Ministry of Education
No. of awards given last year: 38
No. of applicants last year: 385

For further information contact:

(For courier services) Scholarships Manager Education New Zealand Trust, 6th Floor, 138 The Terrace, Wellington, 6011, New ZealandEducation New Zealand Trust, PO Box 10-500, Wellington, 6143, New Zealand
Contact: (For Post Services) Scholarships Manager

New Zealand Postgraduate Study Abroad Award (NZPSAA)

Subjects: All subjects.
Purpose: To maximize the research capability and output of New Zealand tertiary providers, to help students to gain short-term access to the best educational institutions and opportunities abroad, to raise the international profile and reputation of New Zealand's tertiary educational institutions and increase international education linkages and partnerships.
Eligibility: Applicants must be enrolled full-time at a New Zealand institution and hold good standing in a doctoral or postgraduate degree programme, both at the time of application and throughout the tenure of the award. This award relates to travel outside New Zealand only and does not relate to incoming students who are not yet enrolled.
Level of Study: Doctorate, MBA, Postgraduate, Research
Type: Travel award
Value: Up to a maximum of $10,000
Length of Study: Up to 6 months
Frequency: Twice annually
Study Establishment: All New Zealand Universities
No. of awards offered: Varies
Application Procedure: Check website for further details.
Closing Date: May 1st, November 1st of each year
Funding: Government
Contributor: New Zealand Government via the New Zealand Ministry of Education
No. of awards given last year: 156
No. of applicants last year: 325
Additional Information: No funding is available for accompanying dependants. International students are eligible to apply, but priority

may be given to New Zealand citizens and permanent residents. New Zealand Masters and doctoral students may apply for funding to cover short-term study or research abroad in the following categories: (1) Seminars, workshops or courses, (2) Conferences, if the candidate is presenting, (3) Cooperative research with researchers abroad and (4) Independent research at facilities not available in New Zealand.

EDUCATIONAL TESTING SERVICE (ETS)

Rosedale Road, Princeton, NJ, 08541-0001, United States of America
Tel: (1) 609 734 1806
Fax: (1) 609 734 1755
Email: ldelauro@ets.org
Website: www.ets.org
Contact: Ms Linda J DeLauro

The Educational Testing Service (ETS) is a non-profit organization whose goal is to help advance quality and equity in education by providing fair and valid assessments, research, and related services.

ETS Harold Gulliksen Psychometric Fellowship Program
Subjects: Educational measurement, psychometrics, and statistics.
Purpose: To increase the number of well-trained scientists in educational measurement, psychometrics, and statistics.
Eligibility: Open to candidates who are enrolled in a doctoral program at the time of application and have completed all the coursework toward the PhD, and be at the dissertation stage of their program.
Level of Study: Predoctorate
Type: Fellowship
Value: US$15,000 (stipend), US$7,500 (tuition fees, and work-study program commitments), and a small grant for the purchase of equipment or software
Length of Study: 1 year
Frequency: Annual
Country of Study: United States of America or other countries if appropriate
No. of awards offered: Varies
Application Procedure: Refer website for further information about the application procedures.
Closing Date: February 1st
Funding: Private
Contributor: ETS
No. of awards given last year: 1
No. of applicants last year: 10
Additional Information: During the academic year selected fellows at their universities participate in a research project under the supervision of an academic mentor and in consultation with an ETS research scientist. During the summer, fellows are invited to participate in the Summer Internship program for graduate students working under the guidance of an ETS researcher.

For further information contact:

Email: internfellowships@ets.org
Website: www.ets.org/research/fellowships.html

ETS Postdoctoral Fellowships
Subjects: Measurement theory, validity, natural language, processing and computational linguistics, cognitive psychology, learning theory, linguistics, speech recognition and processing, teaching and classroom research, and statistics.
Purpose: To provide research opportunities to individuals who hold a doctorate in education and related fields, and to increase the number of women and minority professionals conducting research in educational measurement and related fields.
Eligibility: Open to applicants who have received their doctoral degree within the past three years. Selections will be based on the candidate's scholarship, the technical strength of the proposed topic of research, and the explicit objective of the research and its relationship to ETS research goals and priorities.
Level of Study: Postdoctorate
Type: Fellowship
Value: US$50,000. In addition, limited relocation expenses, consistent with ETS guidelines, will be reimbursed upon presentation of receipts

Length of Study: Up to 2 years, renewable after the first year by mutual agreement
Frequency: Annual, renewable
Country of Study: United States of America
No. of awards offered: Up to 3
Application Procedure: Refer the ETS website for further details. All application materials should be sent electronically as attachments.
Closing Date: February 1st
Funding: Private
Contributor: ETS
No. of awards given last year: 1
No. of applicants last year: 15

For further information contact:

Email: internfellowships@ets.org

ETS Summer Internship Program for Graduate Students
Subjects: Measurement theory, validity, natural language, processing and computational linguistics, cognitive psychology, learning theory, linguistics, speech recognition and processing, teaching and classroom research, and statistics, and international large scale assessents.
Purpose: To provide research opportunities to individuals enrolled in a doctoral program and to increase the number of women and underrepresented minority professionals conducting research in educational and related fields.
Eligibility: Open to graduate students who are pursuing a doctorate in a relevant discipline and have completed 2 years of coursework towards a PhD or EdD by June 1st of the internship year. The main criteria for selection will be scholarship and the match of applicant interests with participating ETS staff. Affirmative action goals will also be considered.
Level of Study: Predoctorate
Type: Internship
Value: US$5,000 stipend, limited round-trip travel from the intern's university to Princeton (consistent with ETS travel policy), and a US$1,500 housing allowance for interns residing outside a 50 mile radius of ETS facilities
Length of Study: June–July (8 weeks)
Frequency: Annual
Country of Study: United States of America
Application Procedure: Refer the ETS website for further details. All application materials should be sent electronically as attachments.
Closing Date: February 1st
Funding: Private
Contributor: ETS
No. of awards given last year: 18
No. of applicants last year: 180

For further information contact:

Email: internfellowships@ets.org

ETS Sylvia Taylor Johnson Minority Fellowship in Educational Measurement
Subjects: Measurement theory, validity, natural language, processing and computational linguistics, cognitive psychology, learning theory, linguistics, speech recognition and processing, teaching and classroom research, statistics and minority issues in education.
Purpose: To promote excellence, to encourage original and significant research for early career scholars and to provide talented minority scholars an opportunity to carry out independent research under the mentorship of ETS senior researchers. Studies focused on issues concerning the education of minority students are especially encouraged.
Eligibility: Open to applicants who have received their doctoral degree within the past 10 years and who are citizens or permanent residents of the United States of America. Selections will be based on the applicant's record of accomplishment, and proposed topic of research. Applicants should have a commitment to education and an independent body of scholarship that signals the promise of continuing outstanding contributions to educational measurement.
Level of Study: Postdoctorate
Type: Fellowship

Value: The stipend is set in relation to the compensation applicants receive in home institution. In addition, limited relocation expenses, consistent with ETS guidelines, will be reimbursed

Length of Study: Up to 2 years, renewable after the first year by mutual agreement

Frequency: Annual

Country of Study: United States of America

No. of awards offered: 1

Application Procedure: Refer the ETS website for further details. All application materials should be sent electronically as attachments.

Closing Date: February 1st

Funding: Private

Contributor: ETS

No. of awards given last year: 1

No. of applicants last year: 15

Additional Information: Through her research, extensive writings and service to the educational community as an educator, editor, counsellor, committee member and collaborator during her lifetime, Sylvia Taylor Johnson had a significant influence in educational measurement and assessment nationally. In honour of Dr Johnson's important contributions to the field of education, the ETS has established the Sylvia Taylor Johnson Minority Fellowship in educational measurement.

For further information contact:

Email: internfellowships@ets.org

THE EDWARD F ALBEE FOUNDATION, INC.

14 Harrison Street, New York, NY, 10013, United States of America
Tel: (1) 212 226 2020
Fax: (1) 212 226 5551
Email: info@albeefoundation.org
Website: www.albeefoundation.org
Contact: Mr Jakob Holder, Foundation Secretary

The Edward F Albee Foundation provides residence and working space to writers and visual artists at its facilities in Montauk, New York. The residency is offered at no charge to the participants and imposes no obligations, except diligent application to their work and respect for the privacy of others.

William Flanagan Memorial Creative Persons Center

Subjects: Writing, painting, sculpting and musical composition.

Purpose: To provide accommodation.

Eligibility: Open to artists and writers in need who have displayed evidence of their talent.

Level of Study: Unrestricted

Value: Accommodation only

Length of Study: 6 months (May 1st–November 1st); individual residencies are 4 weeks and 6 weeks

Frequency: Annual

Study Establishment: The William Flanagan Memorial Creative Persons Center in Montauk, Long Island

Country of Study: United States of America

No. of awards offered: 20

Application Procedure: Applicants must complete an application form. Forms are available upon request and should be accompanied by a stamped addressed envelope. Other materials are also required, and applicants should write for further details.

Closing Date: January 1st–April 1st

Funding: Private

No. of awards given last year: 20

No. of applicants last year: 300

Additional Information: The environment is communal and residents are expected to do their share in maintaining the conditions of the Center.

EDWIN O. REISCHAUER INSTITUTE OF JAPANESE STUDIES

1730 Cambridge Street, Room 8233, Cambridge, MA, 02138, United States of America
Tel: (1) 617 495 3220
Fax: (1) 617 496 8083
Email: rijs@fas.harvard.edu
Website: www.fas.harvard.edu

The Edwin O. Reischauer Institute of Japanese Studies at Harvard University supports research on Japan and provides a forum for related academic activities and the exchange of ideas. It seeks to stimulate scholarly and public interest in Japan and Japanese studies at Harvard and around the world.

Harvard Postdoctoral Fellowships in Japanese Studies

Subjects: Japanese studies.

Purpose: To aid Japanese studies to recent PhDs of exceptional promise, to give them the opportunity to turn their dissertation into publishable manuscripts.

Eligibility: Open to candidates who have received their PhD degree in Japanese studies in any area of the humanities or social sciences.

Level of Study: Postdoctorate

Type: Fellowships

Value: US$44,000 and health insurance coverage

Length of Study: 10 months

Frequency: Annual

No. of awards offered: 4

Closing Date: January 15th

Additional Information: Residence in the Cambridge/Boston area and participation in Institute activities are required during the appointment.

For further information contact:

Reischauer Institute Harvard University, 1730 Cambridge Street, Room S233, Cambridge, MA, 02138, United States of America
Contact: Dr Theodore J Gilman, Associate Director Postdoctoral Fellowships

THE EGULLET SOCIETY FOR CULINARY ARTS & LETTERS

20 East 93rd Street #1B, NY 10128, United States of America
Tel: (1) 1 212 828 0133
Email: sponsors@eGullet.org
Website: www.egsociety.org

The mission of the eGullet Society for Culinary Arts & Letters is to increase awareness and knowledge of the arts of cooking, eating and drinking, as well as the literature of food and drink. The Society sponsors the opportunity to present offerings to a rarefied audience by supporting the program services of the eGullet Society. The membership of the Society represents an audience of dedicated food enthusiasts who are knowledgeable, enthusiastic and care deeply about food.

The eGullet Society for Culinary Arts & Letters Culinary Journalist Independent Study Scholarship

Subjects: Culinary arts.

Purpose: To conduct independent study and research worldwide; designed to further writing on an original and innovative culinary topic.

Eligibility: Open to career journalist who demonstrates commitment to advancing his or her skills as a writer and whose work is primarily based on food, wine or some other aspects of gastronomy and the culinary arts.

Value: US $5,000

Length of Study: 1 year

No. of awards offered: 1

Application Procedure: Applicants are required to include a project proposal that demonstrates true literary merit in both promise and achievement at writing; an itemized budget detailing the use of this award; a tentative travel schedule with dates and locations; and a current curriculum vitae.

Closing Date: June 30th

Funding: Private

Additional Information: For further information check the website.

The eGullet Society for Culinary Arts & Letters Humanitarian Scholarship

Subjects: Culinary arts.

Purpose: To cover the expenses of a displaced victim of Hurricane Katrina, towards any culinary degree or certificate program at any accredited domestic or foreign culinary school.

Eligibility: Applicants must be pre-enrolled students, currently enrolled students, or career professionals.
Type: Scholarship
Value: US $5,000
Length of Study: 1 year
Application Procedure: Check website for further details.
Closing Date: June 30th
Funding: Private

The eGullet Society for Culinary Arts & Letters Matthew X. Hassett Memorial Culinary Arts Scholarship

Subjects: Culinary arts.
Purpose: To currently enrolled student or career professional, toward any culinary degree or certificate program at any accredited domestic or foreign culinary school.
Eligibility: Candidates must be pre-enrolled student, currently enrolled student or career professional, toward any culinary degree or certificate program at any accredited domestic orforeign culinary school.
Type: Scholarship
Value: US $5,000
Length of Study: 1 year
No. of awards offered: 1
Application Procedure: Check website for further details.
Closing Date: June 30th
Funding: Private
Contributor: James and Dora Hassett in memory of their son, eGullet Society staff member Matthew X. Hassett

The eGullet Society for Culinary Arts & Letters Professional Chef Independent Study Scholarship

Subjects: Culinary arts.
Purpose: To conduct independent study on culinary arts worldwide.
Eligibility: Open to a professional chef with a demonstrated commitment to advancing his or her skills as a chef or pastry chef.
Type: Scholarship
Value: US $5,000
Length of Study: 1 year
No. of awards offered: 1
Application Procedure: Check website for further details.
Closing Date: June 30th
Funding: Private

ELECTORAL COMMISSION NEW ZEALAND

Level 6, Greenock House 39, The Terrace, PO Box 3050, Wellington, 6140, New Zealand
Tel: (64) 4 474 0670
Fax: (64) 4 474 0674
Email: helena@elections.govt.nz
Website: www.elections.org.nz

The Electoral Commission New Zealand is an independent Crown entity, which registers political parties and party logos. It also receives registered parties annual returns of donations and returns of election expenses and allocates election broadcasting time and funds to eligible political parties. The Commission also encourages and conducts public education on electoral matters.

Wallace Scholarships

Subjects: Specific subjects are set each year, all are in the general areas of electoral participation.
Purpose: To encourage research work that will be useful in designing electoral education and information programmes and help raise public awareness of electoral issues.
Eligibility: Scholarships are for research as part of a New Zealand university degree.
Level of Study: Research
Type: Scholarships
Value: New Zealand $500–2,000
Length of Study: usually 1 year
Frequency: Annual
Country of Study: New Zealand

Application Procedure: Applicants must send a 1 page research proposal, letter of endorsement from a academic supervisor and contact details and enrollment qualifications.
Closing Date: February 2nd
Funding: Government
No. of awards given last year: 3
No. of applicants last year: 6
Additional Information: All queries should be directed to Dr Helena Catt at catt@elections.govt.nz or phone 04 474 0676.

For further information contact:

Electoral Commission
Email: Wellingtonorcatt@elections.govt.nz

ELIMINATION OF LEUKAEMIA FUND (ELF)

The Director, ELF, Regent House, 291 Kirkdale, Sydenham, London, SE26 4QD, United Kingdom
Tel: (44) 0 20 8778 5353
Fax: (44) 0 20 8778 7117
Email: elffund@ukonline.co.uk
Website: www.leukaemia-elf.org.uk

The Elimination of Leukaemia Fund's mission is to advance the cure and treatment of leukaemia and related blood disorders. This mission is implemented in four ways explained below. ELF is a major funder of leukaemia research at King's College Hospital, London, and is also funding work at a number of other major centres including the Institute of Child Health, Great Ormond Street Hospital and Belfast City Hospital. ELF favours 'patient-centred' work so that there is an immediate or near future benefit to sufferers of leukaemia and the related blood disorders.

Elimination of Leukaemia Fund Travelling and Training Fellowships

Subjects: Oncology and haematology.
Purpose: To advance the treatment and cure of leukaemia and related blood cancers.
Eligibility: Suitably qualified persons working in the field of haematological malignancies who wish to visit other departments or attend meetings in the UK or overseas.
Level of Study: Research
Type: Fellowship
Value: Travelling fellowships to attend meetings will not normally exceed UK £1500 and training fellowships to visit departments include a contribution to subsistence that will not normally exceed UK £4000
Frequency: Twice a year
Application Procedure: Successful applicants will be notified within 1 month. Application forms are available on written application.
Closing Date: working day in August, November, February and May

ELIZABETH GLASER PEDIATRIC AIDS FOUNDATION

1140 Connecticut Avenue NW, Suite 200, Washington, DC 20036, United States of America
Tel: (1) 202-296-9165
Fax: (1) 202-296-9185
Email: research@pedaids.org
Website: www.pedaids.org
Contact: Research Grants Enquiries

Elizabeth Glaser Pediatric Scientist Award

Subjects: Research in paediatric HIV/AIDS.
Purpose: To build a network of scientists focusing on issues of paediatric HIV/AIDS and create a generation of children born free of this infection.
Eligibility: Applicants must have an MD, PhD, DDS or DVM degree.
Level of Study: Research
Type: Grant
Value: Up to US$682,500
Length of Study: 5 years
Frequency: Annual

No. of awards offered: 1
Application Procedure: Applicants must visit the website to download instructions for the letter of intent and application form.
Closing Date: September 10th
Funding: Foundation
Contributor: The Elizabeth Glaser Pediatric AIDS Foundation

International Leadership Award

Subjects: Research in paediatric HIV/AIDS.
Purpose: To invest in medically trained individuals in developing countries who have the potential to develop local programmes that will have a direct impact on the paediatric HIV epidemic, but who lack resources.
Eligibility: Applicants should be developing country leaders in HIV/AIDS programme implementation and research.
Level of Study: Professional development
Type: Grant
Value: Up to US$450,000
Length of Study: 3 years
No. of awards offered: 1
Application Procedure: Application forms and instructions for letter of intent can be downloaded from the website.
Closing Date: September 10th
Funding: Foundation
Contributor: The Elizabeth Glaser Pediatric AIDS Foundation

Two-Year International Scholar Awards

Subjects: Research in paediatric HIV/AIDS.
Purpose: To assist clinicians and scientists in paediatric HIV/AIDS.
Eligibility: Applicants must be clinicians and scientists from developing countries and must work in developing countries.
Level of Study: Research, Postdoctorate
Type: Postdoctoral fellowship
Value: US$10,000–30,000 plus US$10,000
Length of Study: 2 years
Frequency: Annual
Application Procedure: Applicants must select an experienced sponsor who is a faculty member with an advanced degree and who will oversee the research, provide guidance to the applicant and can provide evidence of the institution's commitment to the career development of the applicant. Application form is available from the website.
Closing Date: September 10th
Funding: Foundation
Contributor: The Elizabeth Glaser Pediatric AIDS Foundation

Two-Year Scholar Awards

Subjects: Research in paediatric HIV/AIDS.
Purpose: To assist clinicians and scientists in paediatric HIV/AIDS.
Eligibility: Applicants should be clinicians and scientists in developed countries.
Level of Study: Postdoctorate, Research
Type: Postdoctoral fellowship
Value: US$30,000–46,000 plus US$10,000
Length of Study: 2 years
Frequency: Annual
Application Procedure: Applicants must select an experienced sponsor who is a faculty member with an advanced degree and who will oversee the research, provide guidance to the applicant and can provide evidence of the institution's commitment to the career development of the applicant. Application form is available from the website.
Closing Date: September 10th
Funding: Foundation
Contributor: The Elizabeth Glaser Pediatric AIDS Foundation

EMBASSY OF FRANCE IN AUSTRALIA

6 Perth Avenue, Yarralumla, Canberra, ACT, 2600, Australia
Tel: (61) 262 160 137
Fax: (61) 262 160 156
Email: education@ambafrance-au.org
Website: www.ambafrance-au.org
Contact: Higher Education Attaché

The Embassy of France in Australia supports the partnership between French and Australian Universities and offers grants and scholarships to help the students' mobility.

French Government Postgraduate Scholarships

Subjects: Engineering (general) 6.1 political sciences and government 17.2.
Purpose: To offers scholarships for one year university studies of master degree in France.
Eligibility: Open to Australian citizens who hold a Bachelor's degree and who have completed 3 years at a university.
Level of Study: Postgraduate
Type: Scholarships
Value: €730 monthly maintenance allowance plus medical cover
Length of Study: 2 years
Frequency: Annual
Study Establishment: Institut D'etudes Politiques De Paris or the "N + i" network of engineering schools
Country of Study: France
No. of awards offered: 2
Application Procedure: Candidates must submit an application after their admission to the postgraduate programme of a French university. Application forms are available from the French Embassy website www.ambafrance-au.org
Closing Date: April for Engineering and March for Political Sciences
Funding: Government
No. of awards given last year: 2

For further information contact:

Ambassade De France, 6 Perth Avenue, Yerralumla, Service De Cooperation, et d'Action Culturelle, ACT 2600, Australia

EMBASSY OF JAPAN IN PAKISTAN

PO Box 1119, 53–70, Ramna 5/4 Diplomatic Enclave 1, Islamabad, 44000, Pakistan
Tel: (92) (51) 2279320, 2279330
Fax: (92) (51) 2279340
Email: japanembculture@dslplus.net.pk
Website: www.pk.emb-japan.go.jp

The Japan Exchange and Teaching (JET) Programme

Subjects: International relations.
Purpose: To enhance the mutual understanding and relations that currently exist between Japan and Pakistan.
Eligibility: Open to applicants who are interested in Japan and who are below the age of 40 years.
Type: Scholarship
Length of Study: ¥3,600,000 per annum
Frequency: Annual
Country of Study: Japan
Application Procedure: A completed application form must be submitted.

ENGINEERS CANADA

180 Elgin Street Suite 1100, Ottawa, ON, K2P-2K3, Canada
Tel: (1) 613 232 2474
Fax: (1) 613 230 5759
Email: awards@engineerscanada.ca
Website: www.engineerscanada.ca

Engineers Canada is the national organization of the provincial and territorial associations and ordre that regulate the practice of engineering in Canada.

Engineers Canada's National Scholarship Program

Subjects: Engineering.
Purpose: To reward excellence in the Canadian engineering profession and support advanced studies and research.
Eligibility: Open to citizens or permanent residents of Canada who are registered as professional engineers in good standing with a provincial/territorial engineering association/order.
Level of Study: Doctorate, Graduate, MBA, Postgraduate

Type: Scholarships
Value: Canadian $62,500 in total
Frequency: Annual
Country of Study: Canada
No. of awards offered: 7
Application Procedure: Applicants must contact Marc Bourgeois for further details.
Closing Date: March 1st
Contributor: TD Insurance Meloche-Monnex Manulife Financial Insurance
No. of awards given last year: 7
No. of applicants last year: Approx. 50
Additional Information: Postdoctoral Fellows are not eligible to apply.

For further information contact:

Tel: 613 232 2474 ext 238
Email: marc.bourgeois@engineerscanada.ca
Contact: Marc Bourgeois, Director, Communications

ENGLISH-SPEAKING UNION (ESU)

Dartmouth House, 37 Charles Street, London, W1J 5ED, England
Tel: (44) 20 7529 1550
Fax: (44) 20 7495 6108
Email: esu@esu.org
Website: www.esu.org
Contact: Cultural Affairs Officer

The English-Speaking Union (ESU) is an independent, non-political educational charity with members throughout the world, promoting international and human achievement through the worldwide use of the English language.

ESU Chautauqua Institution Scholarships
Subjects: Art (painting, ceramics and sculpture), music education, literature and international relations and drama.
Purpose: To enable teachers from the United Kingdom to study at the Chautauqua Institution's Summer School.
Eligibility: Open to teachers from the United Kingdom with a particular interest in the arts.
Level of Study: Professional development
Type: Scholarship
Value: UK £850 plus board, room, tuition and lecture sessions at the Summer School
Length of Study: 6 weeks
Frequency: Annual
Study Establishment: Chautauqua Institution's Summer School
Country of Study: United States of America
No. of awards offered: 1
Application Procedure: Applicants must write for details or email education@esu.org
Closing Date: November
Funding: Private
No. of awards given last year: 2
No. of applicants last year: 5

ESU Music Scholarships
Subjects: Music.
Purpose: To enable musicians of outstanding ability to study at summer schools in the United States of America, Canada, France, United Kingdom, Czech Republic or Hungary.
Eligibility: Candidates must be students or graduates from a recognized United Kingdom conservatory or university music department.
Level of Study: Professional development
Type: Scholarship
Value: Tuition, board and lodging and relevant flight costs
Length of Study: 2–9 weeks, depending on the particular scholarship
Frequency: Annual
Study Establishment: Summer school
No. of awards offered: 10
Application Procedure: Applications must be supported by a teacher's reference.
Closing Date: Late October
Funding: Commercial, private

Contributor: Private trust funds
No. of awards given last year: 6
No. of applicants last year: 50

ESU Travelling Librarian Award
Subjects: Library science.
Purpose: To encourage United States of America and United Kingdom contacts in the library world and establish links between pairs of libraries.
Eligibility: Open to professionally qualified United Kingdom and United States of America librarians.
Level of Study: Professional development
Type: Award
Value: Upto £3,000. Board and lodging and relevant flight costs
Length of Study: A minimum of 3 weeks
Frequency: Annual
No. of awards offered: 1
Application Procedure: Candidates must submit a curriculum vitae and a covering letter explaining why they are the ideal candidates for the award.
Closing Date: Please write for details
Funding: Private, commercial
Additional Information: Candidates should contact the Librarian by telephone or email: library@esu.org

Lindemann Trust Fellowships
Subjects: Astronomy, chemistry, engineering, geology, geophysics, mathematics, physics and biophysics.
Purpose: To allow postdoctoral research to be carried out at a university in the United States of America.
Eligibility: Open to United Kingdom and Commonwealth citizens who are graduates of a United Kingdom university and to United Kingdom and Commonwealth citizens who are pursuing postgraduate research at a United Kingdom university, although are not graduates of that institution. Preference is given to those who have demonstrated their capacity for original research.
Level of Study: Postdoctorate, Postgraduate
Type: Fellowship
Value: US$30,000 stipend per year
Length of Study: 1 year
Frequency: Annual
Study Establishment: A university
Country of Study: United States of America
No. of awards offered: 2
Application Procedure: Applicants must write for details or email education@esu.org
Closing Date: February 25th
Funding: Private
No. of awards given last year: 3
No. of applicants last year: 20
Additional Information: Fellows are not required to work for an American degree, but are expected to be attached to a university, college or seat of advanced learning and technical repute in the United States of America. The place of study and research programme must be approved by the Committee. A limited amount of teaching as an adjunct to research activities is not excluded.

ENTENTE CORDIALE SCHOLARSHIPS

French Cultural Department, 23 Cromwell Road, London, SW7 2EL, England
Tel: (44) 20 7073 1312
Fax: (44) 20 7073 1326
Email: entente.cordiale@ambafrance.org.uk
Website: www.ambascience.co.uk/entente-cordiale
Contact: Administrative Officer

Launched by an agreement between the United Kingdom and French governments in 1995, the Entente Cordiale Scholarships enable outstanding British postgraduates to study or carry out research on the other side of the Channel, with a view to dispel preconceived ideas and promote good relations between the two countries.

Bourses Scholarships
Subjects: All subjects.

Purpose: To allow individuals to study or carry out research in France.
Eligibility: Open to British citizens.
Level of Study: Postgraduate
Type: Scholarship
Value: UK £8,000 for students living in Paris and UK £7,500 for those studying outside Paris
Length of Study: 1 academic year
Frequency: Annual
Study Establishment: Approved universities or grande écoles
Country of Study: France
No. of awards offered: 10
Application Procedure: Applicants must complete an application form, available from the website.
Closing Date: March 4th
Funding: Private
Contributor: Blue Circle (Lafarge), BP, Kingfisher PLC, EDF Energy, UBS, Xerox, Paul Minet, Sir Patrick Sheehy Schlumberger, French Embassy
No. of awards given last year: 7
No. of applicants last year: 60
Additional Information: Scholarships are also awarded to French postgraduates to study in the United Kingdom. Interested parties should contact the British Council in Paris.

ENTOMOLOGICAL SOCIETY OF CANADA (ESC)

Department of Zoology, University of British Columbia, 6270 University Blv, Vancouver, BC, V6T 1Z4, Canada
Tel: (1) 613 725 2619
Fax: (1) 613 725 9349
Email: myers@zoology.ubc.ca
Website: www.esc-sec.org

The Entomological Society of Canada (ESC) is one of the largest and oldest professional societies in Canada. Founded in Toronto on April 16, 1863, the Society was open to all students and lovers of entomology. ESC is a dynamic force in promoting research, disseminating knowledge of insects and encouraging the continued participation of all lovers of entomology in the most fascinating of all natural sciences. It is especially well known for its widely distributed and used publications.

Graduate Research Travel Scholarship

Subjects: Scientific studies on insects or other related terrestrial arthropods.
Purpose: To help students increase the scope of the graduate training.
Eligibility: Open to applicants who are full-time graduate student, studying at a Canadian university and are pursuing scientific studies on insects or other related terrestrial arthropods.
Level of Study: Graduate
Type: Scholarship
Value: Canadian $2,000
Frequency: Annual
Country of Study: Canada
No. of awards offered: 2
Closing Date: February 16th
No. of awards given last year: 2
Additional Information: The scientific merit of each application will be evaluated by a committee that has the option of sending specific projects out for external review by experts in the field.

For further information contact:

Department of Zoology, University of British Columbia, 6270 University Boulevard, Vancouver, BC V6T 1Z4, Canada
Contact: Dr Judith Myers, Chair, ESC Student Awards Committee

John H. Borden Scholarship

Subjects: Entomology and integrated pest management.
Purpose: To financially support students who are studying integrated pest management with an entomological emphasis.
Eligibility: Open to postgraduate students of Integrated Pest Management.

Level of Study: Postgraduate
Type: Scholarship
Value: Canadian $1,000
Frequency: Annual
Country of Study: Canada
Application Procedure: Applicants must submit their application form, curriculum vitae, transcripts and reference letters. Application forms are available online.
Closing Date: February 13th

For further information contact:

Email: Floate@agr.gc.ac
Contact: Dr Judith Myers, Chair ESC Students Award Committe

ENVIRONMENTAL LEADERSHIP PROGRAM

1609, Connecticut Avenue NW 400, Washington, DC, 20009, United States of America
Tel: (1) 202 332 3320
Fax: (1) 202 332 3327
Email: info@elpnet.org
Website: www.elpnet.org

The Environmental Leadership Program (ELP) inspires visionary, action-oriented and diverse leadership to work for a just and sustainable future. ELP nurtures a new generation of environmental leaders characterized by diversity, innovation, collaboration and effective communications. ELP addresses the needs of relatively new environmental activists and professionals.

Environmental Leadership Fellowships

Subjects: Enviromental leadership.
Purpose: To build the leadership capacity of the environmental field's most promising and emerging practitioners.
Eligibility: Open to citizens of the United States only.
Level of Study: Postgraduate
Type: Fellowship
Value: US$2,000 participation stipend, travel and accommodations for training retreats, as well as US$1,000–10,000 to support leadership-building activities and projects
Length of Study: 2 years
Frequency: Annual
Country of Study: United States of America
No. of awards offered: 20–25
Closing Date: October 1st

ENVIRONMENTAL RESEARCH AND EDUCATION FOUNDATION (EREF)

901 North Pitt Street, Suite 270, Alexandria, VA, 22314, United States of America
Tel: (1) 703 299 5139
Fax: (1) 703 299 5145
Email: mjcagney@erefdn.org
Website: www.erefdn.org
Contact: Mr Michael J Cagney, President

The Environmental Research and Education Foundation (EREF) deals with solid waste and recycling research and technologies as well as special events that support and highlight EREF's commitment to creating a clean and safe environment not only today, but for future generations.

EREF Scholarships in Waste Management Research and Education

Subjects: Waste management, environmental science, industrial ecology and waste services.
Purpose: To recognize excellence in masters, doctoral or postdoctoral students studying some aspect of solid waste management.
Eligibility: Open to full-time masters, doctoral or postdoctoral students and researchers irrespective of race, religion, national or ethnic origin, citizenship or disability. Applicant must have a clearly demonstrated interest in waste management research.

Level of Study: Graduate, Postdoctorate, Postgraduate, Doctorate
Type: Scholarship
Value: Up to US$12,000
Length of Study: Up to 3 years
Frequency: Annual
Country of Study: The United States of America or the United Kingdom
Application Procedure: Application forms can be downloaded from the website www.erefdn.org
Closing Date: April 30th
Funding: Foundation
No. of awards given last year: 4
No. of applicants last year: 40

EPILEPSY ACTION

New Anstey House, Gate Way Drive, Yeadon, Leeds, LS19 7XY, England
Tel: (44) 11 3210 8800
Fax: (44) 11 3391 0300
Email: research@epilepsy.org.uk
Website: www.epilepsy.org.uk
Contact: Margaret Rawnsley, Research Administration Officer

Epilepsy Action is the largest member-led epilepsy organization in the United Kingdom. As well as campaigning to improve epilepsy services and raise awareness of the condition, we offer assistance to people in a number of ways including a national network of branches, volunteers, free telephone and an email helpline.

Postgraduate Research Bursaries (Epilepsy Action)

Subjects: Social, healthcare and psychological aspects of epilepsy.
Purpose: To support postgraduate research in the social and medical aspects of epilepsy and all non-laboratory research into epilepsy.
Eligibility: Students should be registered for a postgraduate degree or study at a United Kingdom University.
Level of Study: Research, Doctorate, Postdoctorate, Postgraduate, Predoctorate
Type: Bursary
Value: UK £1,500
Length of Study: Varies
Frequency: Annual
Study Establishment: A university in UK
Country of Study: United Kingdom
No. of awards offered: 3
Application Procedure: Applicants must contact the Research Administration Office.
Closing Date: October
Funding: Foundation
Contributor: Organization's own funds
No. of awards given last year: 3
No. of applicants last year: 7

Postgraduate Research PhD Studentship (Epilepsy Action)

Subjects: Social, healthcare and psychological aspects of epilepsy.
Purpose: To support postgraduate research in the social and medical aspect of epilepsy and all non-laboratory research into epilepsy.
Eligibility: Proposals must be submitted by a supervisor.
Level of Study: Doctorate
Type: Studentship
Value: Up to £75,000
Length of Study: 3 years
Frequency: Annual
Study Establishment: UK university
Country of Study: United Kingdom
No. of awards offered: 1
Application Procedure: Applicants must contact the Research Administration Office.
Closing Date: October
Funding: Foundation
No. of awards given last year: 1
No. of applicants last year: 6

EPILEPSY FOUNDATION (EF)

4351 Garden City Drive, Landover, MD, 20785, United States of America
Tel: (1) 301 459 3700
Fax: (1) 301 577 4941
Email: ResearchWebSupport@EFA.org
Website: www.epilepsyfoundation.org
Contact: Ms Cassandra Richard, Research Co-ordinator

The Epilepsy Foundation (EF) is a national, charitable organization, founded in 1968 as the Epilepsy Foundation of America. It is the only organization wholly dedicated to the welfare of people with epilepsy and to working on their behalf through research, education, advocacy and service.

Behavioral Sciences Postdoctoral Fellowships

Subjects: Epilepsy research relevant to the behavioural sciences. Appropriate fields of study include sociology, social work, psychology, anthropology, nursing, political science and others fields relevant to epilepsy research and practice.
Purpose: To offer qualified individuals the opportunity to develop expertise in epilepsy research through a training experience or involvement in an epilepsy research project.
Eligibility: Open to individuals who have received their doctoral degree in a field of the behavioural sciences by the time the fellowship commences and desire additional postdoctoral research experience in epilepsy. Applications from women and minorities are encouraged.
Level of Study: Postdoctorate
Type: Fellowship
Value: Up to US$3,000 stipend, depending on the experience and qualifications of the applicant and the scope and duration of the proposed project
Length of Study: 3 months
Frequency: Annual
Study Establishment: An approved facility
Country of Study: United States of America
No. of awards offered: 1
Application Procedure: Candidates must complete an application form, available from the Foundation. Candidates may also visit the website research page for details.
Closing Date: March 2nd
Funding: Private
No. of awards given last year: 1
Additional Information: The closing date for applications may vary from year to year. Candidates should email: cmorris@efa.org for details.

Postdoctoral Research Fellowships

Subjects: Basic or clinical epilepsy.
Purpose: To offer qualified individuals the opportunity to develop expertise in epilepsy research through involvement in an epilepsy research project.
Eligibility: Open to physicians and neuroscientist PhDs who desire postdoctoral research experience. Preference is given to applicants whose proposals have a paediatric or developmental emphasis. Research must address a question of fundamental importance. A clinical training component is not required. Applications from women and minorities are encouraged.
Level of Study: Postdoctorate
Type: Fellowships
Value: US$45,000 stipend
Length of Study: 1 year
Frequency: Annual
Study Establishment: A facility where there is an ongoing epilepsy research programme
Country of Study: United States of America or Canada
No. of awards offered: Varies
Application Procedure: Candidates must complete an application form, available from the Foundation. Candidates may also look at the website research page for details.
Closing Date: August 29th
Funding: Private

Research Grants (EF)

Subjects: Basic biomedical, behavioural and social science.

Purpose: To support basic and clinical research that will advance the understanding, treatment and prevention of epilepsy.
Eligibility: Open to United States of America researchers. Priority is given to investigators just entering the field of epilepsy, to new or innovative projects or to investigators whose research is relevant to developmental or paediatric aspects of epilepsy. Applications from women and minorities are encouraged, while applications from established investigators with other sources of support are discouraged. Research grants are not intended to provide support for postdoctoral Fellows.
Level of Study: Postdoctorate, Postgraduate
Type: Grant
Value: Up to US$50,000 oer year (maximum $100,000 for two years)
Length of Study: 1 year
Frequency: Annual
Country of Study: United States of America
No. of awards offered: Varies
Application Procedure: Candidates must complete an application form, available from the Foundation. Candidates may also visit the website research page for details.
Closing Date: August 29th
Funding: Private
Additional Information: The closing date for applications may vary from year to year. Candidates should email: cmorris@efa.org for details.

EPILEPSY RESEARCH UK

PO Box 3004, London, W4 4XT, England
Tel: (44) 20 8995 4781
Fax: (44) 20 8995 4781
Email: info@eruk.org.uk
Website: www.epilepsyresearch.org.uk
Contact: Ms Isabella Von Holstein

Epilepsy Research UK promotes and supports basic and clinical and qualitative scientific research into the causes, treatment and prevention of epilepsy. Application are encouraged on all aspects of Epilepsy including basic and social science, clinical management and holistic management of patients.

Epilepsy Research UK Fellowship
Subjects: All aspects of Epilepsy including basic and social science, clinical management and holistic management of patients.
Purpose: To support a researcher in the field of epilepsy.
Eligibility: Open to researchers resident in the United Kingdom and affiliated to an academic institution in the United Kingdom. Applicants must be graduates in medicine or in one of the sciences allied to medicine.
Level of Study: Research, Unrestricted
Type: Fellowship
Value: UK £150,000–200,000
Length of Study: 1–3 years
Country of Study: United Kingdom
No. of awards offered: 2
Application Procedure: Application is a two-stage process: A preliminary application form must be completed and submitted. If shortlisted, a full application form must be completed. Further details from our website www.epilepsyresearch.org.uk. An interview may be required.
Closing Date: 3rd Friday in October
Funding: Individuals, private, trusts
No. of awards given last year: 2
No. of applicants last year: 11
Additional Information: Financial correspondent must be in UK for any application.

Epilepsy Research UK Research Grant
Subjects: All aspects of Epilepsy including basic and social science, clinical management and holistic managemenat of patients.
Purpose: To support a researcher in the field of epilepsy.
Eligibility: Open to researchers resident in the United Kingdom. And affiliated to an academic institution in the United Kingdom. Applicants must be graduates in medicine or in one of the sciences allied to medicine.

Level of Study: Unrestricted, Research
Type: Project
Value: A maximum of UK £100,000
Length of Study: Upto 3 years
Frequency: Annual
Country of Study: United Kingdom
No. of awards offered: 2
Application Procedure: Application is a two-stage process: A preliminary application form must be completed and submitted. If shortlisted, a full application form must be completed. Further details from the website www.epilepsyresearch.org.uk
Closing Date: 3rd Friday in October
Funding: Individuals, private, trusts
No. of awards given last year: 7
No. of applicants last year: 45
Additional Information: Financial correspondent must be UK-based for any application.

THE ERIC THOMPSON TRUST

The Royal Philharmonic Society, 10 Stratford Place, London, W1C 1BA, England
Tel: (44) 20 7491 8110
Fax: (44) 20 7493 7463
Email: ett@royalphilharmonicsociety.org.uk
Website: www.etorgantrust.co.uk
Contact: Mr David Lowe, Clerk to The Trustees

The Eric Thompson Trust aims to provide modest grants to help aspiring professional organists. Preference will be given to students seeking assistance towards specific projects, rather than continuing academic tuition, e.g. summer schools or special lessons in addition to normal studies and opportunities to play on historical instruments in the context of further study.

Eric Thompson Charitable Trust for Organists
Subjects: The organ.
Purpose: To provide aspiring professional organists with financial assistance for special studies such as summer schools, travel and subsistence for auditions or performance or other incidental costs incurred in their work.
Eligibility: Some professional training as an organist is required.
Level of Study: Professional development
Value: Determined by the Trustees, but normally limited to a contribution towards costs
Frequency: Twice a year
Country of Study: Any country
No. of awards offered: Varies
Application Procedure: An application form can be downloaded from the website. Applicants must send full details of their needs together with information on their training and career, two written references from organists of good standing in the profession and other relevant material to the Clerk to the Trustees.
Closing Date: December 31st or June 30th for consideration in January and July, respectively
Funding: Private
Contributor: Personal and corporate donors
No. of awards given last year: 4
No. of applicants last year: 7
Additional Information: An annual scholarship is also offered for a two-week period of study in the Netherlands with organ-builders Flentrop. The successful candidate will also have the opportunity of lessons with two eminent Dutch organists.

ESADE

MBA Office, Avenue d'Espluges 92–96, E-08034 Barcelona, Spain
Tel: (34) 34.93.280.61.62
Fax: (34) 34 93.204.81.05
Email: mba@esade.edu
Website: www.esade.edu
Contact: Ms Nuria Guilera, MBA Admissions Director

Established in 1958, ESADE is a private, non-profit Institute of Higher Education with a distinctly international outlook. It consists of three schools: the Business School, the Law School and the Language School. Located in one of Barcelona's most attractive residential areas, ESADE's three buildings provide a total of 26,850 square metres of space for teaching and study.

ESADE MBA Scholarships

Subjects: MBA (18-month and 1 Year).
Purpose: To assist full-time MBA students with tuition fees.
Eligibility: All candidates admitted to the programme. Scholarships are awarded on the basis of applicants academic records, professional experience, personal merits and how well they fit the required profile of the programme.
Level of Study: MBA
Type: Scholarship
Value: (1) ESADE Business School awards two grants for 20 per cent of the tuition fees to female candidates of any nationality. These two grants are awarded based on the candidate's professional career, their personal qualifications and their suitability for an MBA programme. (2) ESADE Business School awards two grants for 20 per cent of the tuition fees to candidates (men or women) from developing countries, especially from Eastern Europe and Asia. Selection will be based mainly on the candidate's international experience and professional career. (3) ESADE Business School awards a grant for 20 per cent of the tuition fees to candidates (men or women) in recognition of their exceptional academic and professional career. (4) ESADE Business School, together with Foundatión Carolina, awards two grants covering 25 per cent of the tuition fees, a return awardees will have access to favourable bank loan conditions to finance the rest of the programme. These grants are available as per suitability of each candidate to the programme
Length of Study: 12–18 months
Frequency: Annual
Study Establishment: ESADE
Country of Study: Spain
No. of awards offered: 7
Application Procedure: Applicants must apply for a scholarship along with their course application. Scholarship applications are reviewed once candidates have been admitted to the MBA programme by the admissions committee.
Closing Date: May

For further information contact:

Website: www.mbafinaid@esade.edu

EUROPEAN CALCIFIED TISSUE SOCIETY

PO Box 337, Patchway, Bristol, BS32 4ZR, United Kingdom
Tel: (44) 1454 610255
Fax: (44) 1454 610255
Email: admin@ectsoc.org
Website: www.ectsoc.org

The European Calcified Tissue Society is the major organization in Europe for researchers and clinicians working on calcified tissues and related fields.

ECTS Career Establishment Award

Subjects: Calcified tissue and related fields.
Purpose: To assist newly appointed faculty members in launching a successful research career.
Eligibility: Applicants must be members of the ECTS.
Level of Study: Set-up grant not dependent on study
Value: €50,000 (over 2–3 years)
Frequency: Dependent on funds available
No. of awards offered: Dependent on funds available
Application Procedure: Applicants must complete an application form, available from the website.
Funding: Foundation
Contributor: ECTS
No. of awards given last year: 2
No. of applicants last year: 7
Additional Information: Country of study can be anywhere in the Europe.

ECTS Exchange Scholarship Grants

Subjects: Calcified tissue and related fields.
Purpose: To enable researchers to spend time in another laboratory to learn new techniques.
Eligibility: Applicants must be members of the ECTS.
Level of Study: Professional development
Type: Scholarship
Value: Depends on anticipated expenses
Frequency: Dependent on funds available
No. of awards offered: Dependent on funds
Application Procedure: Applicants must complete an application form, available from the website.
Closing Date: There is no deadline
Funding: Foundation
Contributor: ECTS
No. of awards given last year: 3
No. of applicants last year: 5

ECTS PhD Studentship

Subjects: Calcified tissue and related fields.
Purpose: To assist European PhD students with expenses incurred for their PhD project.
Eligibility: Applicants must be members of the ECTS.
Level of Study: Predoctorate, Professional development
Type: Scholarship
Value: €75,000
Length of Study: 3 years
Frequency: Dependent on funds available
No. of awards offered: Up to 4
Application Procedure: Applicants must complete an application form, available from the website.
Funding: Foundation
No. of awards given last year: 4
No. of applicants last year: 25

ECTS Postdoctoral Fellowship

Subjects: Calcified tissue and related fields.
Purpose: To assist European postdoctoral fellows with expenses relating to their own research project.
Eligibility: Applicants must be a member of the ECTS.
Level of Study: Professional development
Type: Fellowship
Value: €60,000
Length of Study: 2 years
Frequency: Dependent on funds available
No. of awards offered: Up to 3
Application Procedure: Applicants must complete an application form, available from the website.
Funding: Foundation
No. of awards given last year: 3
No. of applicants last year: 15

ECTS/AMGEN Bone Biology Fellowship

Subjects: Relevant areas of bone biology.
Purpose: To enable scientists who are at the beginning of their research career and who wish to conduct research into basic or clinical aspects of bone disease.
Eligibility: Any scientist or clinician working in the field of bone biology in Europe.
Level of Study: Research
Type: Fellowship
Value: €125,000, of which 50 per cent shall be deployed to cover salary costs
Length of Study: 3 years
Frequency: Dependent on funds available
Study Establishment: European Calcified Tissue Society
Country of Study: United Kingdom
Application Procedure: Applicants must complete an application form available from the website.
No. of awards given last year: 1
No. of applicants last year: 16
Additional Information: All applications must be supported by the Head of the host laboratory.

ECTS/Servier Fellowship 2009

Subjects: Pathophysiology of osteoporosis.

Purpose: To encourage the research involving pathophysiology of osteoporosis, particularly the coupling and uncoupling processes between bone formation and bone resorption and all related matters.

Eligibility: Open for ECTS members who qualified PhD/MD within the last 10 years and are resident/working in Europe. Applications to include details of a preclinical or clinical research project on the pathophysiology of osteoporosis, particularly the coupling and uncoupling processes between bone formation and bone resorption and all related matters.

Level of Study: Research

Value: €40,000

Length of Study: 2 years

Application Procedure: Applicants should fill an application form. For further details log on to www.ectsoc.org

Closing Date: November 14th

Contributor: Servier

EUROPEAN LEAGUE AGAINST RHEUMATISM

Seestrasse 240, CH 8802 Kilchberg (Zürich), Switzerland
Tel: (41) 44 716 30 30
Fax: (41) 44 716 30 39
Email: eular@eular.org
Website: www.eular.org
Contact: Elly Wyss, EULAR Training Bursaries

EULAR Research Grants

Subjects: Research into diagnostic and therapeutic aspects of rheumatic diseases.

Purpose: To support work programmes that improve the quality of care in the field of rheumatology.

Level of Study: Research

Type: Project grant

Value: €30,000 per year

Length of Study: Up to 3 years

Frequency: Annual

Application Procedure: Applications for grants should include: an abstract, a rationale of the need and relevance of the project, an account of strategic objectives, resources, budget and organization, a description of the implementation and relevance of the project for EULAR, and a list of references of participating university/hospital centres relating to the topic of the proposal.

Closing Date: December 31st

Contributor: European League Against Rheumatism

Additional Information: For further information contact the EULAR Secretariat.

EUROPEAN MOLECULAR BIOLOGY ORGANIZATION (EMBO)

PO Box 1022.40, D-69012 Heidelberg, Germany
Tel: (49) 622 188 910
Fax: (49) 622 188 91200
Email: embo@embo.org
Website: www.embo.org
Contact: Mr Lindsay Johnson, Communications Officer

The European Molecular Biology Organization (EMBO) was established in 1964 to promote biosciences in Europe. Today EMBO supports transnational mobility, training and exchange through initiatives such as fellowships, courses, workshops and its young investigator activities.

EMBO Installation Grants

Subjects: Molecular biology and disciplines relying on molecular biology.

Purpose: To strengthen science in participating EMBC member states (Croatia, the Czech Republic, Estonia, Hungary, Portugal Poland and Turkey).

Eligibility: Eligible scientists should have an excellent publication record and should have spent at least two consecutive years prior to the application deadline, outside the country in which they are applying to establish their lab. The applicant should be negotiating a

full-time position at an institute/university in participating member states by the date of the application. Candidates who are planning to establish independent labs in the country that they are applying for can be in that country for 2 years at the time of the deadline.

Level of Study: Postdoctorate

Value: €50,000

Length of Study: 3–5 years

Frequency: Annual

No. of awards offered: Varies

Application Procedure: Applicants must visit the organization's website www.embo.org for details of the application forms, letters of reference and online application.

Closing Date: April 15th

Funding: Government

Contributor: The 27 EMBC member states

No. of awards given last year: 7

EMBO Long-Term Fellowships in Molecular Biology

Subjects: Molecular biology and disciplines relying on molecular biology.

Purpose: To promote the development of research in Europe and Israel.

Eligibility: Open to holders of a doctoral degree. EMBO fellowships are not awarded for exchanges between laboratories within one country. Applicants must be nationals from a European Molecular Biology Conference (EMBC) member state or be wishing to travel to a EMBC member state.

Level of Study: Postdoctorate

Type: Fellowship

Value: A return travel allowance for the Fellow and any dependants plus a stipend and dependants' allowance

Length of Study: 1 year, renewable for a further year

Frequency: Every 2 years, Twice a year

Study Establishment: A suitable laboratory

Country of Study: Any country

No. of awards offered: Approx. 150–200 per year

Application Procedure: Please see the EMBO website (www.embo.org/fellowships)

Closing Date: February 15th and August 15th

Funding: Government

Contributor: The 27 EMBC member states

No. of awards given last year: 215

No. of applicants last year: 1218

Additional Information: The following countries form the EMBC: Austria, Belgium, Croatia, the Czech Republic, Denmark, Estonia, Finland, France, Germany, Greece, Hungary, Iceland, Ireland, Israel, Italy, the Netherlands, Norway, Poland, Portugal, the Slovak Republic, Slovenia, Spain, Sweden, Switzerland, Turkey and the United Kingdom. Special provision is also made for applications involving Cyprus. For further information, email: fellows@embo.org

EMBO Short-Term Fellowships in Molecular Biology

Subjects: Molecular biology and disciplines relying on molecular biology.

Purpose: To advance molecular biology research by helping scientists to visit another laboratory with a view to applying a technique not available in the home laboratory and to foster collaboration.

Eligibility: Please see the EMBO website (www.embo.org/fellowships)

Level of Study: Predoctorate, Research, Doctorate, Postdoctorate, Postgraduate

Type: Fellowship

Value: Return travel for the Fellow and a daily subsistance for the duration of the fellowship

Length of Study: 2 weeks–3 months

Frequency: Ongoing process

Study Establishment: A suitable laboratory

Country of Study: Any country

No. of awards offered: Varies

Application Procedure: Application form and guidelines are available on the EMBO website.

Closing Date: There is no deadline, but applications should be made at least 3 months before proposed start date

Funding: Government

Contributor: The 27 EMBC member states

No. of awards given last year: 225
No. of applicants last year: 406

EMBO Young Investigator

Subjects: Molecular biology and disciplines relying on molecular biology.
Purpose: To promote the development of research in Europe and Israel.
Eligibility: Applicants should: be leading their first independent laboratory for at least 1 and not more then 4 years in an EMBC member state; have at least 2 years of post-PhD scientific experience, have an excellent track record; be working in the very broadly defined area of Molecular Biology; be supported by sufficient funds to run their laboratories; have published at least one last author paper after establishing an independent laboratory. Only in exceptional cases will applications from scientists over 40 years in age be considered.
Level of Study: Postdoctorate, Professional development
Value: €15,000
Length of Study: 3 years
Frequency: Annual
Study Establishment: The applicant's own independent laboratory
No. of awards offered: Varies
Application Procedure: Applicants must visit the website for details on Application forms, letters of reference and on-line application.
Closing Date: April 1st
Funding: Government
Contributor: The 27 EMBC member states
No. of awards given last year: 12
No. of applicants last year: 116

EUROPEAN RESEARCH CONSORTIUM FOR INFORMATICS AND MATHEMATICS (ERCIM)

2004, Route des Lucioles BP 93, F 06902, Sophia Antipolis, Cedex, France
Tel: (33) 4 92 38 50 10
Fax: (33) 4 92 38 50 11
Email: contact@ercim.org
Website: www.ercim.org

The European Research Consortium for Informatics and Mathematics (ERCIM) aims to foster collaborative work within the European research community and to increase co-operation with European industry.

Alain Bensoussan Fellowship Programme

Subjects: Applications of numerical mathematics in science, biomedical informatics, constraints technology and applications.
Purpose: To enable bright young scientists from all over the world to work on challenging problems as Fellows of leading European research centres.
Eligibility: Open to candidates who have obtained a PhD, and are fluent in English.
Level of Study: Research
Type: Fellowship
Value: Varies by country
Length of Study: 18 months
Frequency: Annual
Application Procedure: Applicants must submit the application form online.
Closing Date: April 30th
Additional Information: Not only are researchers from academic institutions encouraged to apply, but also scientists working in the industry. All queries should be directed to Emma Lière at emma.liereercim.org.

EUROPEAN SOCIETY OF SURGICAL ONCOLOGY (ESSO)

Avenue E. Mounier 83, B-1200, Brussels, Belgium
Tel: (32) 2 537 31 06
Fax: (32) 2 539 03 74
Email: fellowship@esso-surgeonline.be
Website: www.esso-surgeonline.be
Contact: Secretariat

ESSO was founded to advance the art, science and practice of surgery for the treatment of cancer. ESSO endeavours to ensure that the highest possible standard of surgical treatment is available to cancer patients throughout Europe by organizing congresses, granting fellowships and publishing the *EJSO*.

ESSO Training Fellowships

Subjects: Surgical oncology.
Purpose: To provide young surgeons a chance to spend time in another specialist centre to either expand their experience or learn new techniques.
Eligibility: Open to applicants who are specialists/specializing in surgery (or in any other medical discipline where cancer surgery is performed). Applicants must be less than 40 years of age. European applicants may choose to visit European or non-European units, while non-European applicants must choose to visit a European center.
Level of Study: Postdoctorate
Type: Fellowship
Value: €2,500 for standard fellowships and €10,000 for the major international training fellowship
Length of Study: 1 month for standard fellowships and upto 1 year for the major training fellowship
Frequency: Annual
Country of Study: Any country
No. of awards offered: 10 standard and 1 major training fellowships
Application Procedure: Applicants must submit a full curriculum vitae with their application, together with a note of their career intentions. Applicants should also outline what they hope to gain from the training fellowship, including what specific experience is sought and how this will fit in with the applicant's career development. Applicants should provide details as to which institution they wish to visit, together with details of the clinical or research training opportunities that the department can offer. A letter of support from the applicant's head of department must be included and this can be in the form of a reference. A letter of support from the head of the department they wish to visit must also be supplied, indicating that the department to be visited will be in a position to provide the experience required by the applicant.
Closing Date: August 31st
No. of awards given last year: 11
No. of applicants last year: 18
Additional Information: Applicants must be or become ESSO members.

For further information contact:

Email: carine@esso-surgeonline.org
Website: www.esso-surgeonline.org
Contact: Ms Carine Lecoq, ESSO Administrator

EUROPEAN SOUTHERN OBSERVATORY (ESO)

Karl-Schwarzschild-Strasse 2, D-85748 Garching bei Muenchen, Germany
Tel: (49) 893 200 60
Fax: (49) 893 202 362
Email: vacancy@eso.org
Website: www.eso.org
Contact: Mr Roland Block, Head of Personnel Department

The European Southern Observatory (ESO) is an intergovernmental organization for research in astronomy. At present ESO is operating the Very Large Telescope (VLT) at Cerro Paranal in Chile, the world's most powerful facility for optical astronomy, and La Silla Observatory.

ESO Fellowship

Subjects: Astronomy and astrophysics.
Purpose: To provide a unique opportunity to learn and participate in the process of observational astronomy while pursuing a research programme.
Level of Study: Postdoctorate
Type: Fellowship
Value: A basic monthly salary of not less than €2,918, to which is added an expatriation allowance as well as some family allowances, if

applicable. The Fellow will also have an annual travel budget for scientific meetings, collaborations and observing trips
Length of Study: 1 year, with a possible extension to 3 years in Garching. Fellowships in Chile are for 1 year with a possible extension to 4 years
Frequency: Annual
Study Establishment: The European Southern Observatory
No. of awards offered: 6–9
Application Procedure: Applicants must visit the ESO website for an application form and further information.
Closing Date: October 15th
Funding: Government
Additional Information: Fellowships begin between April and October of the year in which they are awarded. Selected Fellows can join ESO only after having completed their doctorate.

EUROPEAN SYNCHROTRON RADIATION FACILITY (ESRF)

6 rue Jules Horowitz, BP 220, Grenoble Cedex, 38043, France
Tel: (33) 4 76 88 20 00
Fax: (33) 4 76 88 20 20
Email: stuck@esrf.fr
Website: www.esrf.fr
Contact: Ms Elizabeth Moulin

The European Synchrotron Radiation Facility (ESRF) supports scientists in the implementation of fundamental and applied research on the structure of condensed matter in fields such as physics, chemistry, crystallography, Earth science, biology, medicine, surface science and materials science.

ESRF Postdoctoral Fellowships
Subjects: Physics, biology, chemistry, mineralogy and crystallography, computer engineering and accelerators science.
Purpose: To enable postdoctoral fellows develop their own research programme and motivate them to collaborate with external users.
Eligibility: Preference is given to member-country nationals, but other nationals may be accepted for the postdoctoral positions.
Level of Study: Postdoctorate
Value: €3,348 each month, plus a possible expatriation allowance of up to €418 each month. These amounts correspond to a gross remuneration and are subject to social charges and income tax in France
Length of Study: 2–3 years
Frequency: Dependent on funds available
No. of awards offered: Up to 20
Application Procedure: Applicants must complete an application form, available on request from the personnel department of the ESRF.
Closing Date: Individual deadlines exist for each position. Please contact the organization
Funding: Private
Contributor: Public funds from 18 countries, mostly European
No. of awards given last year: 27
No. of applicants last year: 400
Additional Information: Member countries are Belgium, Denmark, Finland, France, Germany, Italy, the Netherlands, Norway, Spain, Sweden, Switzerland and the United Kingdom. New associated members are the Czech Republic, Israel, Portugal and the Republic of Hungary, Poland and Austria.

ESRF Thesis Studentships
Subjects: Physics, biology, chemistry, mineralogy and crystallography, computer engineering and accelerators science. The ESRF proposes subjects related to the use of synchrotron radiation or synchrotron or storage ring technology.
Purpose: To enable grant holders pursue a PhD at the ESRF and to enable young scientists acquire knowledge of the use of synchrotron radiation or its generation.
Eligibility: Preference is given to member-country nationals, but other nationals may be accepted for the postdoctoral positions.
Level of Study: Doctorate

Value: €2,245 per month. These amounts correspond to a gross remuneration and are subject to social charges and income tax in France
Length of Study: 2–3 years
Frequency: Dependent on funds available
Study Establishment: Universities
No. of awards offered: Up to 10
Application Procedure: Applicants must complete an application form, available on request from the personnel department of the ESRF.
Closing Date: There is an individual deadline for each position
Funding: Private
Contributor: Public funds from 18 countries, mainly European
No. of awards given last year: 20
No. of applicants last year: 300
Additional Information: Member countries are Belgium, Denmark, Finland, France, Germany, Italy, the Netherlands, Norway, Spain, Sweden, Switzerland and the United Kingdom. Newly associated members are the Czech Republic, Israel, Portugal and the Republic of Hungary, Poland and Austria.

EUROPEAN UNIVERSITY INSTITUTE (EUI)

Via dei Roccettini 9, I-50014 San Domenico di Fiesole, Italy
Tel: (39) 55 4685 322
Fax: (39) 55 468 5444
Email: ken.hulley@eui.eu
Website: www.eui.eu
Contact: Mr Kenneth Hulley, Assistant Administrator (Academic Service)

The European University Institute's (EUI) main aim is to make a contribution to the intellectual life of Europe. Created by the European Union member states, it is a postgraduate research institution, pursuing interdisciplinary research programmes on the main issues confronting European society and the construction of Europe.

EUI Postgraduate Scholarships
Subjects: History and civilization, economics, law or political and social sciences.
Purpose: To provide the opportunity for study leading to the doctorate or Master's degree from the Institute.
Eligibility: Open to nationals of European Union member states. Candidates must possess a good Honours degree or its equivalent, and have full written and spoken command of at least two of the Institute's official languages. Nationals of countries other than the European Union may be admitted to the Institute subject to scholarship agreements being in place.
Level of Study: Doctorate, Postgraduate
Type: Scholarship
Value: Varies, from €1,150 to 1,500
Length of Study: 1 year, renewable for up to an additional 3 years
Frequency: Annual
Study Establishment: EUI
Country of Study: Italy
No. of awards offered: Approx. 150
Application Procedure: Applications must be submitted online at www.eui.eu
Closing Date: January 31st
Funding: Government
Contributor: Member states of the European Union
No. of awards given last year: 150
No. of applicants last year: 1,200

Fernand Braudel Senior Fellowships
Subjects: Economics, history and civilization, law, political and social sciences.
Purpose: Research.
Eligibility: Established academics with international reputation
Level of Study: Postdoctorate
Type: Fellowship
Value: €3,000 per month
Length of Study: 3–10 months
Frequency: Annual

Study Establishment: The EUI
Country of Study: Italy
No. of awards offered: 15
Application Procedure: Applicants must complete an online application form available via the internet at www.eui.eu
Closing Date: March 30th/September 30th
Contributor: The EU Commission/Members states of the European Union
No. of applicants last year: 100

Jean Monnet Fellowships

Subjects: Economics, history and civilization, law, political and social sciences
Purpose: To encourage postdoctoral research.
Eligibility: Open to candidates with a doctoral degree at an early stage of their academic career.
Level of Study: Postdoctorate
Type: Fellowship
Value: €1,250–2,000 per month depending on whether the applicant is on a paid sabbatical or not
Length of Study: 12 months
Frequency: Annual
Study Establishment: The EUI
Country of Study: Italy
No. of awards offered: 20
Application Procedure: Applicants must complete an online application form available via the Internet at www.eui.eu
Closing Date: October 25th
Funding: Government
Contributor: The EU commission Member states of the European Union
No. of awards given last year: 20
No. of applicants last year: 270

Max Weber Fellowships

Subjects: Economics, history and civilization, law, political and social sciences.
Purpose: To encourage postdoctoral research.
Eligibility: Open to candidates with a doctoral degree at an early stage of their academic career.
Level of Study: Postdoctorate
Type: Fellowship
Value: €1,250–2,000 per month depending on whether the applicant is on a paid sabbatical or not
Length of Study: 12 or 24 months
Frequency: Annual
Study Establishment: The EUI
Country of Study: Italy
No. of awards offered: 40
Application Procedure: Applicants must complete an online application form available via the internet at www.eui.eu
Closing Date: October 25th
Contributor: The EU Commission/Members State of European Union
No. of awards given last year: 40
No. of applicants last year: 920

EVANGELICAL LUTHERAN CHURCH IN AMERICA (ELCA)

Division for Ministry, 8765 West Higgins Road, Chicago, IL, 60631-4195, United States of America
Tel: (1) 773 380 2873
Fax: (1) 773 380 2829
Email: pwilder@elca.org
Website: www.elca.org
Contact: Mr Pat Wilder, Executive Secretary

ELCA Educational Grant Program

Subjects: Theological studies.
Eligibility: Open to members of the Evangelical Lutheran Church in America who are enrolled in an accredited graduate institution for study in a PhD, EdD or ThD programme in a theological area appropriate to seminary teaching. Priority is given to women and minority students.

Level of Study: Doctorate
Type: Grant
Value: US$250–5,000. Funds are distributed according to need and the contribution the applicant will make towards the future of the Church
Length of Study: Grants are awarded for a maximum of 4 years with a 5th-year award for the dissertation
Frequency: Annual
Country of Study: United States of America
No. of awards offered: 40–65
Application Procedure: Applications are available online at www.elca.org/dm/te/grants.html in January. Two recommendations are required for each applicant.
Closing Date: March 15th
Funding: Private
No. of awards given last year: 65
No. of applicants last year: 72

EXETER COLLEGE

Oxford, Oxfordshire, OX1 3DP, England
Tel: (44) 18 6527 9660
Fax: (44) 18 6527 9630
Email: joan.himpson@exeter.ox.ac.uk
Website: www.exeter.ox.ac.uk
Contact: Mrs Joan Himpson, Academic Administrator

Exeter College is one of the University of Oxford's oldest colleges. Founded in 1314, the college currently has 606 students, of which 374 are undergraduates and 232 are postgraduate students.

Exeter College Monsanto Senior Research Fellowship

Subjects: Molecular biology, cellular biology and biochemistry.
Purpose: To support research.
Eligibility: Open to qualified applicants of any nationality.
Level of Study: Postdoctorate
Type: Fellowship
Value: UK £23,692–30,913
Length of Study: 3–5 years
Frequency: Every 5 years
Study Establishment: Exeter College, the University of Oxford
Country of Study: United Kingdom
No. of awards offered: 1
Application Procedure: Applicants must address enquiries to the Academic Administrator.
Funding: Private

For further information contact:

Exeter college, Oxford, OX1 3DP
Email: academic.administrator@exeter.ox.ac.uk
Website: www.exeter.ox.ac.uk
Contact: Academic Administrator

Exeter College Queen Sofia Research Fellowship

Subjects: Peninsular Spanish literature.
Purpose: To support research.
Eligibility: Applicants should be close to completing doctoral or postdoctoral work and must be under 31 years of age at the time of taking up the fellowship. They must also be fluent in Spanish.
Level of Study: Doctorate, Postdoctorate
Type: Fellowship
Value: Up to UK £12,000 stipend per year. Fellows are entitled to free lunch and dinner, free rooms in the college if unmarried and a housing allowance if not resident in the college
Length of Study: 2–3 years
Frequency: Every 3 years
Study Establishment: Exeter College, the University of Oxford
Country of Study: United Kingdom
No. of awards offered: 1
Application Procedure: Applicants must address enquiries to the Academic Administrator or see the website www.exeter.ox.ac.uk for details
Funding: Private
Contributor: Endowment

Exeter College Senior Scholarship in Theology
Subjects: Theology or philosophy and theology.
Purpose: To support a graduate who wishes to read for the Final Honour School of Theology or Philosophy and Theology.
Eligibility: Applicants must hold at least a Second Class (Honours) Degree by the time of admission in a subject other than theology.
Level of Study: Postgraduate, 2ND BA
Type: Scholarship
Value: Fees at home/EU rate and maintenance equivalent to current research council rates
Length of Study: 1 year with possible renewal for 2nd year
Frequency: Every 3 years
Study Establishment: Exeter College, the University of Oxford
Country of Study: United Kingdom
No. of awards offered: 1
Application Procedure: Applicants must apply in writing to the Academic Administrator or see the website www.exeter.ox.ac.uk for details.
Funding: Private
Contributor: Endowment

Exeter College Staines Medical Research Fellowship
Subjects: Medical science.
Purpose: To support research in medical science.
Eligibility: Applicants should be close to completing doctoral or postdoctoral work and must be under 31 years of age at the time of taking up the fellowship.
Level of Study: Postdoctorate, Doctorate
Type: Fellowship
Value: UK £300–10,240 stipend per year. Fellows are entitled to free lunch and dinner, free rooms in the college if unmarried and a housing allowance if not resident in the college
Length of Study: 2–3 years
Frequency: Every 3 years
Study Establishment: Exeter College, the University of Oxford
Country of Study: United Kingdom
No. of awards offered: 1
Application Procedure: Applicants must address enquiries to the Academic Administrator, Exeter College or see www.exeter.ox.ac.uk for details.
Funding: Private
Contributor: Endowment
No. of awards given last year: 1
No. of applicants last year: 35
Additional Information: Next award not likely to be until 2009.

THE EXPLORERS CLUB

Exploration Fund, 46 East 70th Street, New York, NY 10021, United States of America
Tel: (1) 212 628 8383
Fax: (1) 212 288 4449
Email: asstmgr@explorers.org
Website: www.explorers.org

The Explores Club funds projects with scientific purpose to broaden our knowledge of the universe through remote travel and exploration.

Explorers Club Exploration Fund
Purpose: To support scientific expeditions.
Level of Study: Postgraduate, Professional development
Type: Grant
Value: US$500–1,500
Frequency: Annual
No. of awards offered: Varies
Application Procedure: Request application form.
Closing Date: January 15th

Scott Pearlman Field Award for Science and Exploration
Purpose: To support scientific expeditions.
Eligibility: Open to any professional artist, writer, photographer, filmmaker or journalist who has excelled in their field.
Level of Study: Postgraduate, Professional development
Type: Grant
Value: US$1,500

No. of awards offered: Varies
Application Procedure: Samples of the candidates work must be submitted along with an application form and two references.
Closing Date: March 31st
Funding: Trusts
Contributor: Scott Pearlman Fund

For further information contact:

Scott Pearlman Field Awards, The Explorers Club, 46 East 70th Street, New York, NY 10021, United States of America
Contact: Executive Assistant

F BUSONI FOUNDATION

Conservatorio Statale di Musica 'C Monteverdi'-Piazza Domenicani, 25-PO Box 368, I-39100 Bolzano, Italy
Tel: (39) 047 197 6568
Fax: (39) 047 132 6127
Email: info@concorsobusoni.it
Website: www.concorsobusoni.it
Contact: Ms Silvia Torresin, Secretary

The Busoni International Piano Competition was first held in 1949 to commemorate the 25th anniversary of the death of composer Ferruccio Busoni. The aim of the competition is to create a forum for Busoni's music as well as for promising young pianists.

Foundation Busoni International Piano Competition
Subjects: Piano performance.
Purpose: To award excellence in piano performance.
Eligibility: Open to pianists of any nationality between 16 and 30 years of age.
Level of Study: Unrestricted
Type: Prize
Value: The 1st prize is €22,000 plus 60 important concert contracts, the 2nd prize is €10,000, the 3rd prize is €5,000, the 4th prize is €4,000, the 5th prize is €3,000 and the 6th prize is €2,500. There are also other special prizes
Frequency: Every 2 years
Country of Study: Italy
No. of awards offered: 10
Application Procedure: Applicants must complete and submit an application form with a birth certificate, reports or certificates of study, a brief curriculum vitae and documentation of any artistic activity. Three recent photographs, the entrance fee and written evidence of any prizes and international competitions should also be included.
Closing Date: May 31st
Funding: Commercial, government, private
Contributor: The Municipality of Bolzano
No. of awards given last year: 10
No. of applicants last year: 150
Additional Information: The competition lasts for 2 years, with the pre-selection phase taking place in the 1st year.

FAIRBANK CENTER

Harvard University, CGIS South Building, 1730 Cambridge Street Cambridge, MA, 02138, United States of America
Tel: (1) 617 495 4046/8120
Fax: (1) 617 496 2420
Email: wtien@fas.harvard.edu
Website: www.fas.harvard.edu
Contact: Wen-Hao Tien, Program Officer

The Fairbank Center was founded in 1955 by Professor John King Fairbank. The Center was originally called the Center for East Asian Research. It supports research by offering hospitality to visiting scholars from all over the world, by awarding a limited but increasing number of Postdoctoral fellowships and by maintaining its own specialized library.

An Wang Postdoctoral Fellowship
Subjects: Chinese studies.
Purpose: To financially support research in Chinese studies.
Eligibility: Open to candidates who have obtained their PhD.

Level of Study: Postdoctorate
Type: Fellowships
Value: US$40,000
Length of Study: 1 year
Frequency: Annual
No. of awards offered: 6
Application Procedure: Applicants can download the application form from the website. The completed application form along with a curriculum vitae, a 5 page plan of research, 2 letters of reference and a chapter of the dissertation or another writing sample must be mailed.
Closing Date: February 1st
Additional Information: Those who have received their PhD from the Harvard University are normally not considered for this fellowship.

FANCONI ANEMIA RESEARCH FUND, INC.

1801 Willamette Street, Suite 200, Eugene, OR, 97401, United States of America
Tel: (1) 541 687 4658
Fax: (1) 541 687 0548
Email: info@fanconi.org
Website: www.fanconi.org
Contact: Ms Mary Ellen Eiler, Executive Director

To support research into effective treatments and a cure for Fanconi anaemia.

Fanconi Anemia Research Award

Subjects: Fanconi anaemia.
Purpose: To support research into effective treatments and a cure for Fanconi anaemia.
Eligibility: There are no restrictions on eligibility in terms of nationality, residency, age, gender, sexual orientation, race, religion or politics.
Level of Study: Doctorate, Postdoctorate
Type: Award
Value: Varies
Length of Study: 1–2 years
Country of Study: Any country
No. of awards offered: Unlimited
Application Procedure: Applicants must email to obtain information about the application process and complete an application form.
Closing Date: Ongoing
Funding: Foundation
No. of awards given last year: 11
No. of applicants last year: 19
Additional Information: The Internal Revenue Service has confirmed that the Fund is not a private foundation for the purposes of tax-exempt donations but a public charitable organization under 501(c) 3 of the Internal Revenue Code.

For further information contact:

Email: info@fanconi.org

FEDERATION OF EUROPEAN MICROBIOLOGICAL SOCIETIES (FEMS)

Keverling Buismanweg 4, 2628 CL Delft, Netherlands
Tel: (31) 15 269 3920
Fax: (31) 15 269 3921
Email: fems@fems-microbiology.org
Website: www.fems-microbiology.org
Contact: Dr D Van Rossum, Executive Officer

The Federation of European Microbiological Societies (FEMS) is devoted to the promotion of microbiology in Europe. FEMS advances research and education in the science of microbiology within Europe, by encouraging joint activities and facilitating communication among microbiologists, supporting meetings and laboratory courses and publishing books and journals.

FEMS Fellowship

Subjects: Microbiology.

Purpose: To foster transnational research in microbiology and to enable young scientists to pursue a short-term research project in another European country.
Eligibility: The award is restricted to members of FEMS member societies.
Level of Study: Doctorate, Postgraduate, Research, Graduate, Pre-doctorate, Professional development, Postdoctorate
Type: Fellowship
Value: A maximum of €3,500
Length of Study: A maximum of 3 months
No. of awards offered: Approx. 50
Application Procedure: Applicants must complete and submit an application form to a society that is a member of FEMS. The delegate of the member society will handle the application and submit it to the Federation for funding. FEMS will then make a decision on the application. Addresses of the Federation's delegates are published on the website.
Closing Date: December 1st and June 15th
Funding: Foundation
No. of awards given last year: 35
No. of applicants last year: 37

FFWG

BFWG Charitable Foundation, 20 Fern Road, Storrington, Pulborough, RH20 4LW, United Kingdom
Tel: (44) 44 01732 3211 39
Fax: (44) 44 01732 3211 39
Email: jean.c@blueyonder.co.uk
Website: http://ffwg.org.uk/
Contact: Mrs J V Considine

FfWG was registered in 2006 as a Trading name for the BFWG Charitable Foundation. The Charitable Foundation was incorporated in 1925 as the Crosby Hall Association. It took charitable status in 1971 and changed its name to BFWG Charitable Foundation in 1993.

BFWG Funds for Women Graduates–Charitable Foundation Grants and Emergency Grants

Subjects: All subjects.
Purpose: To financially assist female graduates registered for study or research at an approved Institute of Higher Education within Great Britain.
Eligibility: Main Foundation Grants: Open to female graduates who are in their final year or writing-up year. Foundation Grants are awarded to female students in their final year of a PhD. There is no restriction on nationality or age. Emergency Grants: Open to female graduates engaged in study or research at Institutes of Higher Education, who face an unexpected financial crisis.
Level of Study: Postgraduate, Doctorate, Postdoctorate
Type: Grant
Value: Foundation Grants are up to UK £4,000 and Emergency Grants are up to UK £1,500. (these values are being reviewed)
Length of Study: Courses that exceed 1 full year in length
Frequency: Annual, Annually for main Foundation Grants and twice a year for Emergency Grants
Study Establishment: Approved Institutes of Higher Education
Country of Study: Great Britain
No. of awards offered: Approx. 30–40 Foundation Grants and approx. 30 Emergency Grants
Application Procedure: For Foundation grants, applicants must complete an application form and submit it with two references, a copy of their graduation certificate, evidence of acceptance for the year, a postal order for UK £12 and a brief summary of the thesis, if applicable. Requests for application forms must be made by e-mail. For Emergency grants requests for application forms must be made by e-mail.
Closing Date: The deadline for Foundation Grants is March 31st and for Emergency Grants are Feb 19th and Oct 14
Funding: Private
Contributor: Investment income
No. of awards given last year: 46 Foundation Grants and 44 Emergency Grants
No. of applicants last year: Several hundreds

For further information contact:

Email: jean.c@blueyonder.co.uk

Theodora Bosanquet Bursary

Subjects: English Literature/History.
Purpose: This bursary is offered to women postgraduate students whose research in History or English Literature requires a short residence in London in the summer.
Eligibility: Open to female postgraduate students of any age from the United Kingdom and overseas.
Level of Study: Graduate
Type: Bursary
Value: Will be decided by the BFWG charitable foundation trading as FFWG
Length of Study: Up to 4 weeks
Frequency: Annual
Study Establishment: Any approved Institute of Higher Education in Great Britain
Country of Study: Great Britain
Application Procedure: Applicants must request an application form by e-mail or download it from the website. Forms should then be returned either by email or post enclosing a large stamped self-addressed envelope or international reply coupons. The envelope should be marked TBB.
Closing Date: October 31st
Funding: Private
Contributor: Investment income
No. of awards given last year: 2
No. of applicants last year: 8

For further information contact:

BFUG Charitable Foundation, Larkfield, Aylesford, Kent, 13 Brookfield Avenue, ME20-6RU
Tel: 017 3232 1139
Contact: The Grants Administrator

THE FIELD PSYCH TRUST

301 Dixie Street, Carrollton, GA, 30117, United States of America
Tel: (1) 770 834 8143
Email: arichard@westga.edu
Website: www.fieldpsychtrust.org
Contact: Dr Anne C Richards, Trustee

The Field Psych Trust is a charitable trust honouring the professional life and contributions of psychologist/educator Dr Arthur W Combs. It provides grant funding to encourage graduate student research grounded in perceptual (field) psychology perspectives. It also supports the publication of manuscripts related to Dr Combs' professional life and work.

Field Psych Trust Grant

Subjects: As a psychological theory, perceptual (field) psychology is applicable to any subject area in which links between human experience, meaning and/or perception and human behavior can be explored.
Purpose: To encourage graduate student research exploring the history, contributions and further development of perceptual (field) psychology as related to the research and writings of Arthur W Combs
Eligibility: Open to graduate students in good standing through a competitive review process.
Level of Study: Doctorate, Graduate, Postdoctorate, Predoctorate
Type: Research grant
Value: Varies according to the itemized budget request of successful applicants and their projects. Awards range from US$500–1,500
Length of Study: Varies, although 1 year is preferable
Frequency: Bi-annual
Study Establishment: An accredited Institution of Higher Education
Country of Study: Any country
No. of awards offered: 2
Application Procedure: Applicants must complete an application form and submit references. Application forms can be found on the website. Applications are judged with respect to the relevance of the proposed project to the mission of the Field Psych Trust, substance, conceptual quality and clarity of the proposal, significance of the project in addressing matters of consequence to the human condition, and the degree of confidence that the prospective grant recipient has in his or her ability to produce the proposed project.

Closing Date: January 31st and October 5th of each year
Funding: Private
Contributor: The estate of Arthur W Combs
No. of applicants last year: 2
Additional Information: Awards are subject to conditions, which are described, and include an obligation to submit a final report on conclusion of the project, which can take the form of a completed Master's thesis, research project report, doctoral dissertation or published manuscript. More information is available from the website, or by contacting Anne Richards at the main address.

FIGHT FOR SIGHT

1st Floor, 36-38 Botolph Lane, London, EC3R 8DE, United Kingdom
Tel: (44) 0207 929 7755
Fax: (44) 0207 929 4341
Email: info@fightforsight.org.uk
Website: http://fightforsight.org.uk
Contact: Chief executive

Fight for sight is dedicated to funding world-class research into the prevention and treatment of blindness and eye-disease at leading universities and hospitals. Current research projects include age-related macular degeneration, glaucoma, cataract, diabetic retinopathy and childhood blindness.

Fight for Sight Awards

Subjects: Ophthalmology.
Purpose: For the prevention and treatment of blindness and eye disease.
Eligibility: Open to suitably qualified individuals. Most grants are allocated to research teams throughout UK. But the charity may fund UK-based teams undertaking research overseas.
Level of Study: Postgraduate, Postdoctorate, Research
Type: Grant
Value: Determined each year
Length of Study: 2, 3 or 5 years
Frequency: Annual
Country of Study: United Kingdom
No. of awards offered: Varies
Application Procedure: See website www.fightforsight.org.uk for details.
Closing Date: Various
Funding: Trusts, commercial, individuals, private
No. of awards given last year: 16
No. of applicants last year: 88
Additional Information: The British Eye Research Foundation merged with Fight for Sight in 2005.

FINE ARTS WORK CENTER IN PROVINCETOWN, INC.

24 Pearl Street, Provincetown, MA 02657, United States of America
Tel: (1) 508 487 9960
Fax: (1) 508 487 8873
Email: general@fawc.org
Website: www.fawc.org
Contact: Ms Margaret Murphy, Executive Director

Established in 1968, the Fine Arts Work Center offers 7-month fellowships to emerging visual artists and creative writers. Housing, studios and monthly stipends are provided to create a community of peers as a catalyst for artistic growth.

Fine Arts Work Center in Provincetown Fellowships

Subjects: Visual arts and creative writing in fiction and poetry.
Purpose: To give emerging artists and writers the opportunity to work in a congenial and stimulating environment and to devote all of their time to art and writing.
Eligibility: Open to emerging artists and writers of outstanding promise. Applicants are accepted on the basis of work submitted.
Level of Study: Unrestricted
Type: Fellowship
Value: US$650 per month, plus housing and studio space
Length of Study: 7 months

Frequency: Annual
Study Establishment: Provincetown, MA
Country of Study: United States of America
No. of awards offered: 10 for visual arts and 10 for writing
Application Procedure: Applicants must send a stamped addressed envelope for applications, the fee for which is US$45. Alternatively, application forms can be downloaded from the website.
Closing Date: February 1st for visual artists and December 1st for writers
Funding: Corporation, foundation, government, individuals, private
No. of awards given last year: 20
No. of applicants last year: 1,000
Additional Information: The Center is a working community, not a school.

FLINDERS UNIVERSITY

GPO Box 2100, Adelaide, SA, 5001, Australia
Tel: (61) 08 8201 3911
Fax: (61) 8 8201 3177
Email: wwwperson@flinders.edu.au
Website: www.flinders.edu.au

Flinders University is an integral part of Australia's respected higher education system and makes an important economic and social contribution to South Australia and to the nation. Flinders has a high research profile and consistently ranks among Australia's top universities on a per capita basis for research. It emphasizes innovation and excellence in its educational programs and researches across a wide range of disciplines.

Advanced Community Care Scholarship
Subjects: Community care.
Purpose: To undertake a research project within the Faculty of Health Sciences related to the practical clinical, organizational and financial implications of home-based alternatives to hospital care.
Eligibility: Applicants must be Australian citizens or permanent residents of Australia and have completed at least 4 years of tertiary education studies at a high level of achievement and have an appropriate Honours 1 or high 2A (or equivalent) undergraduate degree. They must enroll as full-time students (part-time awards are available in certain circumstances).
Level of Study: Postgraduate
Type: Scholarship
Value: $19,616 per year
Length of Study: 3 years
No. of awards offered: 1
Application Procedure: Applicants must obtain the application kits from the Higher Degree Administration and Scholarships Office or can download it from the scholarships website.
Closing Date: October 31st
Contributor: Advanced Community Care Association

For further information contact:

Tel: (08) 8201 3115
Email: scholarships@flinders.edu.au

Australian Health Inequities Program Research Scholarship
Subjects: Public health, labour market economics, housing and geography.
Purpose: To address health inequities, understand the social determinants of health and analyze policy and program strategies that aim to reduce inequities.
Eligibility: Applicants should be Australian citizens, permanent residents of Australia or New Zealand citizens and have completed at least four years of tertiary education studies at a high level of achievement and have an appropriate Honours 1 or high 2A (or equivalent) undergraduate degree. They should enroll as full-time students (a part-time award may be available in certain circumstances) and should commence a Doctorate by research.
Level of Study: Postgraduate
Type: Scholarship
Value: $19,616 per year
Length of Study: 3 years

Application Procedure: Applicants can obtain the application kits from the Higher Degree Administration and Scholarships Office or download it from Flinders University scholarships website.
Closing Date: October 31st

For further information contact:

Department of Public Health
Tel: 08 8204 5983
Email: fran.baum@flinders.edu.au
Contact: Professor Fran Baum, AHIP Lead Investigator

Faculty of Science and Engineering Research Awards (FSERA)
Subjects: Biological sciences, chemical sciences, earth sciences, engineering and technology, information, computing and communication sciences, mathematical sciences, physical sciences or science in general.
Purpose: To enable students to pursue a Masters Degree by research or Doctorate by research in the Faculty of Science and Engineering.
Eligibility: Applicants should have achieved Honours 1 or equivalent, or Honours 2a or equivalent. Only citizens of Australia or New Zealand or permanent residents can apply.
Level of Study: Graduate, Postgraduate
Type: Research award
Value: Australian $19,616 per year
Length of Study: 2 years if masters or 3 years if PhD
Country of Study: Australia
No. of awards offered: 9
Application Procedure: Applicants must apply directly to the university.
Closing Date: October 31st

For further information contact:

Scholarships Office (Flinders University), GPO Box 2100, Adelaide, SA, 5001, Australia
Tel: (61) 08 8201 3115
Fax: (61) 08 8201 5175
Email: scholarships@flinders.edu.au
Website: www.flinders.edu.au/scholarships

Flinders University Australian Postgraduate Awards
Subjects: All subjects.
Purpose: To enable suitably qualified applicants to proceed to a full-time Masters by research or Doctorate by research.
Eligibility: Applicants must have achieved Honours 1 or equivalent. Only citizens of Australia or New Zealand or permanent residents can apply.
Level of Study: Postgraduate
Type: Award
Value: Australian $19,231 per year
Length of Study: 2 years for Masters or 3 years for PhD
Frequency: Annual
Country of Study: Australia
No. of awards offered: 27
Application Procedure: Applicants must apply directly to the scholarship provider.
Closing Date: October 31st

Flinders University Research Scholarships (FURS)
Subjects: All subjects.
Purpose: To enable suitably qualified applicants to proceed to a full-time Masters by research or Doctorate by research.
Eligibility: Applicants must have achieved Honours 1 or equivalent, or Honours 2a or equivalent. Only citizens of Australia or New Zealand or permanent residents can apply.
Level of Study: Postgraduate
Type: Scholarship
Value: Australian $19,616
Length of Study: 2 years for masters or 3 years for PhD
Frequency: Annual
Country of Study: Australia
No. of awards offered: 30

Application Procedure: Applicants must apply directly to the university.
Closing Date: October 31st

For further information contact:

Scholarships Office (Flinders University), GPO Box 2100, Adelaide, SA, 5001, Australia
Tel: (61) 08 8201 3115
Fax: (61) 08 8201 5175
Email: scholarships@flinders.edu.au
Website: www.flinders.edu.au/scholarships

FMC Foundation Pink Ribbon Ball Committee Breast Cancer Research Scholarship

Subjects: Biomedical.
Purpose: To undertake a breast cancer biomedical research project within the Faculty of Health Sciences.
Eligibility: Applicants must be Australian citizens or permanent residents of Australia and have completed at least 4 years of tertiary education studies at a high level of achievement and have an appropriate Honours 1 or high 2A (or equivalent) undergraduate degree. They must enroll as full-time students (part-time awards are available in certain circumstances) and must commence a Doctorate by research.
Level of Study: Postgraduate
Type: Scholarship
Value: Australian $25,000 plus up to $2,000 per year for conference travel and consumables
Length of Study: 3 years
Frequency: Annual
No. of awards offered: 1
Application Procedure: Applicants can obtain the application kits from the Higher Degree Administration and Scholarships Office and can download it from the scholarship website.
Closing Date: October 31st
Contributor: Flinders Medical Centre Foundation

For further information contact:

Department of Human Physiology, Flinders University, Australia
Tel: (61) (08) 8204 4100
Email: johnno.oliver@flinders.edu.au
Contact: Professor John Oliver, Associate Professor

FMC Foundation Research Scholarship

Subjects: Health sciences.
Purpose: To undertake a health-related project within the Faculty of Health Sciences.
Eligibility: Applicants should be Australian citizens or permanent residents of Australia and have completed at least 4 years of tertiary education studies at a high level of achievement and have an appropriate Honours 1 or high 2A (or equivalent) undergraduate degree. They should enroll as full-time students (part-time awards are available in certain circumstances) and should commence a Doctorate by research.
Level of Study: Postgraduate
Type: Scholarship
Value: $25,000 plus up to $2,000 per year for conference travel and consumables
Length of Study: 3 years
Frequency: Annual
No. of awards offered: 1
Application Procedure: Applicants can obtain application kits from the Higher Degree Administration and Scholarships Office or download from the scholarships website.
Closing Date: October 31st
Funding: Foundation
Contributor: FMC Foundation

For further information contact:

Department of Human Physiology, Flinders University
Tel: 08 8204 4100
Email: johnno.oliver@flinders.edu.au
Contact: Professor John Oliver, Associate Professor

Honours/Masters Scholarship for AI, User Interface or Robotics

Subjects: AI, user interface or robotics.
Purpose: To enable students to undertake an Honours or Masters project in the Artificial Intelligence Laboratory in the School of Informatics and Engineering at Flinders University.
Eligibility: Applicants must have Australian citizenship or permanent residence, plus distinction-level completion of the requirements of 3 years of undergraduate degree in cognitive science, computer science, mathematics, or engineering program.
Level of Study: Graduate
Type: Scholarship
Value: Australian $5,000
Application Procedure: Check website for further details.
Closing Date: November 15th

For further information contact:

Email: David.Powers@flinders.edu.au
Contact: David Powers

Investigation of the Human Intestinal Nervous System

Subjects: Physiology.
Purpose: To support investigation of the human intestinal nervous system.
Eligibility: Applicants must be Australian citizens or permanent residents of Australia and have completed at least 4 years of tertiary education studies at a high level of achievement and have an appropriate undergraduate medical degree. They should enroll as full-time students and commence a Doctorate by research.
Level of Study: Graduate
Type: Scholarship
Value: $29,172
Length of Study: 3 years
Frequency: Annual
No. of awards offered: 1
Application Procedure: Applicants can obtain application kits from the Higher Degree Administration and Scholarships Office or can download from the scholarships website.
Closing Date: October 31st

For further information contact:

Department of Surgery, Flinders University
Tel: 08 8204 4253
Email: david.wattchow@flinders.edu.au
Contact: David Wattchow, Associate Professor

The Jack Loader Top-Up Scholarship

Subjects: Dementia.
Purpose: To encourage research into dementia, in particular Alzheimer's Disease, and related disorders and/or the consequences of these diseases.
Eligibility: Applicants must be Australian citizens or permanent residents of Australia and be enrolled full time in a research degree at one of the South Australian universities. Applicants should have received an Australian Postgraduate Award or equivalent University Scholarship.
Level of Study: Graduate
Type: Scholarship
Value: Australian $8,000
Length of Study: 12 months
Frequency: Annual
Application Procedure: Check website for further details.
Closing Date: October 31st
Funding: Foundation
Contributor: The Rosemary Foundation for Memory Support Inc and Alzheimer's Australia South Australia

For further information contact:

Email: jmck1279@bigpond.net.au
Website: www.rosemaryfoundation.org.au/available_scholarships.html

May Mills Scholarship for Women

Subjects: All subjects.

Purpose: To encourage women, who have experienced significant interruptions to their studies due to family responsibilities, to proceed to a research higher degree at Flinders University.
Eligibility: Applicants must be female citizens or permanent residents of Australia.
Level of Study: Graduate, Postgraduate
Type: Scholarship
Value: Maximum Australian $9,000 per year
Length of Study: 1 year
Frequency: Annual
Country of Study: Australia
No. of awards offered: 2
Application Procedure: Applicants may consult the scholarship website.
Closing Date: January 31st

For further information contact:

Scholarships Office (Flinders University), GPO Box 2100, Adelaide, SA, 5001, Australia
Tel: (61) 08 8201 3115
Fax: (61) 08 8201 5175
Email: scholarships@flinders.edu.au
Website: www.flinders.edu.au/scholarships

Multi Scale Biomechanical Investigations of the Intervertebral Disc

Subjects: Orthopaedics.
Purpose: To undertake a challenging program of research that combines both analytical (finite element analysis) and experimental.
Eligibility: Applicants must be Australian or international students who have completed at least 4 years of tertiary education studies at a high level of achievement and have an appropriate Honours 1 or high 2A (or equivalent) undergraduate degree in mechanical/biomedical/civil/chemical engineering or related fields.
Level of Study: Postgraduate
Type: Scholarship
Value: $25,313
Length of Study: 3 years
Frequency: Annual
No. of awards offered: 1
Application Procedure: Applicants can obtain the application kits from the Higher Degree Administration and Scholarships Office at Flinders University.
Closing Date: June 1st

For further information contact:

Department of Orthopaedics, School of Medicine
Tel: 61 8 8275 1751
Email: john.costi@rgh.sa.gov.au
Contact: Dr John Costi

NHMRC Centre of Clinical Eye Research: PhD Scholarships

Subjects: Ophthalmology.
Purpose: To conduct clinical research in the major blinding diseases – cataract, glaucoma, diabetic retinopathy and corneal disease.
Eligibility: Applicants must be Australian citizens, permanent residents of Australia or New Zealand citizens and have completed at least 4 years of tertiary education studies at a high level of achievement and have an appropriate Honours 1 or high 2A (or equivalent) undergraduate degree.
Level of Study: Postgraduate
Type: Scholarship
Value: A stipend of Australian $20,007–29,172 plus $2,000 for conference travel and consumables
Length of Study: 3 years
Frequency: Annual
No. of awards offered: 3
Application Procedure: Applicants can obtain the application kits from the Higher Degree Administration and Scholarships Office or can download it from the scholarships website.
Closing Date: October 31st

For further information contact:

Department of Ophthalmology, Flinders University
Tel: 08 8204 4899
Email: Konrad.Pesudovs@flinders.edu.au
Contact: Konrad Pesudovs

NHMRC Medical and Dental Postgraduate Research Scholarships

Subjects: Medical and dental.
Purpose: To provide full-time research experience to medical or dental graduates registered to practice in Australia.
Eligibility: Applicants must be medical or dental graduates registered to practice in Australia. Graduates from overseas who hold permanent resident status and are currently resident in Australia are eligible to apply.
Level of Study: Graduate
Type: Scholarship
Value: Australian $29,172 per year plus $2,250 per year towards the cost of consumables and travel to approved conferences
Length of Study: 3 years
Country of Study: Australia
Application Procedure: Applicants can obtain application forms, instruction booklets, referee report pro formae and various attachments to the instructions from the NHMRC website.
Closing Date: July 25th

For further information contact:

Email: research@nhmrc.gov.au
Website: www.nhmrc.gov.au/fellows/types/granttype/scholars/index.htm

NHMRC Public Health Postgraduate Scholarships

Subjects: Public health.
Purpose: To encourage graduates to obtain formal training in public health research.
Eligibility: Applicants must be Australian citizens who have already completed a degree in an area applicable in public health research at the time of submission of the application or graduates in areas applicable to public health who are from overseas, have permanent resident status and are currently residing in Australia. All candidates must enroll for a higher degree requiring full-time research.
Level of Study: Graduate
Type: Scholarship
Value: $19,616 (Australian postgraduate award), $25,313 (nursing and allied health professionals) and $29,172 (medical/dental)
Frequency: Annual
Country of Study: Australia
Application Procedure: Applicants must submit the application forms to the Higher Degree Administration and Scholarships Office and should include one additional copy for University records. Application forms, instruction booklets, referee report pro formae and various attachments to the instructions are available from the NHMRC website.
Closing Date: July 25th

For further information contact:

Email: research@nhmrc.gov.au
Website: www.nhmrc.gov.au/fellows/types/granttype/scholars/index.htm

NHMRC: Primary Health Care Postgraduate Research Scholarships

Subjects: Health care.
Purpose: To encourage graduates to obtain formal training in primary health care related research, with an emphasis on rural communities.
Eligibility: Applicants must be Australian citizens or have permanent resident status, who are medical, dental or health-related graduates currently registered to practice within Australia or who have already completed a degree (or equivalent) at the time of submission of the application.
Level of Study: Graduate
Type: Scholarship
Value: $19,616 (Australian postgraduate award), $25,313 (nursing and allied health professionals) and $29,172 (medical/dental) per year
Country of Study: Australia

Application Procedure: Applications must be submitted to the Higher Degree Administration and Scholarships Office and should include one additional copy for University records. Application forms, instruction booklets, referee report pro formae and various attachments to the instructions are available from the NHMRC website.
Closing Date: July 25th

For further information contact:

Email: research@nhmrc.gov.au
Website: www.nhmrc.gov.au/fellows/types/granttype/scholars/index.htm

The Nita Curtis Scholarship
Subjects: Disability studies.
Purpose: To encourage postgraduate training in disability studies and provide financial support to students in the Department of Disability Studies at Flinders University.
Eligibility: Applicants must be Australian citizens or permanent residents of Australia and be undertaking one of the following programs offered by the Department of Disability Studies at the University: Honours or Graduate Certificate in Disability Studies or Master of Disability Studies or Masters degree by research or Doctorate by research and be undertaking a research project relevant to the Community Accommodation and Respite Agency (CARA) and its client population.
Level of Study: Graduate
Type: Scholarship
Value: Australian $5,000
Frequency: Annual
No. of awards offered: 1 or more (subject to the availability of funds)
Application Procedure: Applicants must contact the Higher Degree Administration and Scholarships Office or its website for application forms and further information.
Closing Date: February 28th

Overseas Field Trip Grant
Subjects: All subjects.
Purpose: To provide funding towards overseas field trips for competent postgraduate research students whose theses would be greatly improved by the opportunity to undertake research and collection of data which is inaccessible in Australia.
Eligibility: Applicants must be enrolled in the University for a PhD degree, normally in their second or early third year of candidature (or an equivalent period part-time) or be enrolled in the University for a Masters degree by research, normally in their first year of candidature (or an equivalent period part-time) and have clearly demonstrated during this period a capacity for research and have gained unqualified support from his/her supervisor for the proposed overseas visit.
Level of Study: Graduate
Type: Grant
Value: Australian $2,500
Application Procedure: Applicants can obtain further information and application forms from the Higher Degree Administration and Scholarships Office or the scholarships website.
Closing Date: May 31st

PhD Scholarship for Vascular and Metabolic Research
Subjects: Medicine.
Purpose: To focus on the relationship between obesity, adipose tissue distribution, endothelial function and cardiovascular risk in humans using established techniques such as liver MRI and spectroscopy, pulse-wave analysis, and forearm occlusion plethysmography.
Eligibility: Applicants should be Australian citizens or permanent residents of Australia and have completed at least 4 years of tertiary education studies at a high level of achievement and have an appropriate undergraduate medical degree.
Level of Study: Postgraduate
Type: Scholarship
Value: $20,007 per year
Length of Study: Up to 3 years
Frequency: Annual
Study Establishment: Faculty of Health Sciences, Flinders University
Country of Study: Australia

No. of awards offered: 1
Application Procedure: Applicants can obtain the application kits from the Higher Degree Administration and Scholarships Office or can download it from the scholarships website.
Closing Date: October 31st

For further information contact:

Department of Clinical Pharmacology, Flinders Medical Centre
Tel: 08 8204 5202
Email: arduino.mangoni@flinders.edu.au
Contact: Dr Arduino Mangoni

Professor Lowitja O'Donoghue Indigenous Student Postgraduate Research Scholarship
Subjects: All subjects.
Purpose: To enable suitably qualified applicants to proceed to a full-time Masters by research or Doctorate by research.
Eligibility: Applicants must be Australian citizen, must have achieved Honours 1 or equivalent or Honours 2a or equivalent and must be an Aboriginal or Torres Strait Islander.
Level of Study: Graduate
Type: Scholarship
Value: Australian $$25,627
Length of Study: 2 years if Masters and 3 years if PhD
Frequency: Annual
Study Establishment: Flinders University
Country of Study: Australia
No. of awards offered: 1
Application Procedure: Applicants must apply directly to the university.
Closing Date: October 31st

For further information contact:

Scholarships Office (Flinders University), GPO Box 2100, Adelaide, SA, 5001, Australia
Tel: (61) 08 8201 3115
Fax: (61) 08 8201 5175
Email: scholarships@flinders.edu.au
Website: www.flinders.edu.au/scholarships

RA Simpson International Scholarship
Subjects: All subjects.
Purpose: To assist students to undertake part of their course of study overseas to enhance their Flinders University studies by providing an international perspective.
Eligibility: Applicants must be students enrolled in an undergraduate or coursework postgraduate course of Flinders University and be Australian citizens or permanent residents of Australia and have not previously received a RA Simpson International Scholarship. Check website for specific details.
Level of Study: Graduate
Type: Scholarship
Value: Australian $1,500 each semester
Frequency: Dependent on funds available
No. of awards offered: 1 or more (subject to the availability of funding)
Application Procedure: Applicants must obtain the application forms from the Higher Degree Administration and Scholarships Office or the scholarships website.
Closing Date: November 15th
Additional Information: The RA Simpson International Scholarships will be awarded on the basis of academic merit and the extent to which an applicant's proposed program of study will enhance their Flinders University studies by providing an international perspective.

Reconciliation SA Aboriginal Education Leaders Fund Postgraduate Research Scholarship
Subjects: All subjects.
Purpose: To foster leadership potential and skill development and to promote the vision of the Council for Aboriginal Reconciliation in South Australia.
Eligibility: Applicants must have applied for admission to, or be enrolled in, a research higher degree on a full or part-time basis at Flinders University, University of Adelaide or University of South

Australia and normally reside in South Australia and be of Australian Aboriginal or Torres Strait Islander descent and be identified and be accepted as an Australian Aboriginal or Torres Strait Islander by the community in which he or she lives or has lived.
Level of Study: Graduate
Type: Scholarship
Value: Australian $5,000
Frequency: Annual
No. of awards offered: 1 or more (subject to availability of funds)
Application Procedure: Applicants must contact the Yunggorendi First Nations Centre for Higher Education for further information and application forms.
Closing Date: January 31st

For further information contact:

Email: shane.carr@flinders.edu.au

Repatriation General Hospital Department of Rehabilitation and Aged Care: Health Professionals Research Scholarship
Subjects: Rehabilitation.
Purpose: To undertake research in an area of rehabilitation (cerebral palsy, driving rehabilitation, hydrotherapy, multiple sclerosis rehabilitation, hip fracture recovery).
Eligibility: Applicants must normally be Australian citizens, permanent residents of Australia or New Zealand citizens, who hold a First Class or upper Second Class Honours Degree in an appropriate health-related discipline, or an equivalent qualification.
Level of Study: Graduate
Type: Scholarship
Value: Australian $25,000–29,172
Length of Study: 3 years
Frequency: Annual
No. of awards offered: 1
Application Procedure: Applicants can obtain the application kits and further information from the scholarships web site or from the Higher Degree Administration and Scholarships Office.
Closing Date: October 31st

For further information contact:

Department of Rehabilitation and Aged Care, Flinders University
Tel: 08 8275 1103
Email: maria.crotty@rgh.sa.gov.au
Contact: Professor Maria Crotty

Repatriation General Hospital Department of Rehabilitation and Aged Care: Medical Research Scholarship
Subjects: Health care.
Purpose: To join a world class research team and improve health care.
Eligibility: Applicants must be medical graduates and normally Australian citizens, permanent residents of Australia or New Zealand citizens, who hold a First Class or upper Second Class Honours Degree in an appropriate health-related discipline, or an equivalent qualification.
Level of Study: Graduate
Type: Scholarship
Value: $29,172
Length of Study: 3 years
No. of awards offered: 1
Application Procedure: Applicants can obtain the application kits and further information from the scholarships web site or from the Higher Degree Administration and Scholarships Office.
Closing Date: October 31st

For further information contact:

Department of Rehabilitation and Aged Care, Flinders University
Tel: 08 8275 1103
Email: maria.crotty@rgh.sa.gov.au
Contact: Professor Maria Crotty

Repatriation General Hospital Department of Rehabilitation and Aged Care: Nursing Research Scholarship
Subjects: Health care.
Eligibility: Applicants must be nursing graduates and normally Australian citizens, permanent residents of Australia or New Zealand citizens, who hold a First Class or upper Second Class Honours Degree in an appropriate health-related discipline, or an equivalent qualification.
Level of Study: Graduate
Type: Scholarship
Value: $25,000–29,172 per year
Length of Study: 3 years
No. of awards offered: 1
Application Procedure: Applicants can obtain the application kits and further information from the scholarships web site or from the Higher Degree Administration and Scholarships Office.
Closing Date: October 31st

For further information contact:

Department of Rehabilitation and Aged Care, Flinders University
Tel: 08 8275 1103
Email: maria.crotty@rgh.sa.gov.au
Contact: Professor Maria Crotty

South Australian Department of Health Research Award
Subjects: Medical and health sciences or public health and health services.
Purpose: To undertake a research project relevant to the health of South Australians, the South Australian health system, or the health-related targets in South Australia's Strategic Plan.
Eligibility: Applicants must have achieved Honours 1 or equivalent, or Honours 2a or equivalent. Only citizens of Australia or permanent residents can apply.
Level of Study: Postgraduate
Type: Scholarship
Value: Australian $19,231 per year
Length of Study: 3 years
Frequency: Annual
Country of Study: Australia
No. of awards offered: 2
Application Procedure: Applicants must apply directly to the university.
Closing Date: October 31st

For further information contact:

Scholarships Office (Flinders University), GPO Box 2100, Adelaide, SA, 5001, Australia
Tel: (61) 08 8201 3115
Fax: (61) 08 8201 5175
Email: scholarships@flinders.edu.au
Website: www.flinders.edu.au/scholarships

University Hall Dean's Scholarship
Subjects: All subjects.
Eligibility: Applicants must be resident in University Hall and enrolled in a degree course at the Flinders University at the time of application. Only citizens of Australia or New Zealand living in Australia over 1 year can apply.
Level of Study: Graduate
Type: Scholarship
Value: Australian $2,000 per year
Length of Study: 1 year
Frequency: Annual
Country of Study: Australia
No. of awards offered: 1
Application Procedure: Applicants must apply directly to the scholarship provider.
Closing Date: October 20th

For further information contact:

Scholarships Office (Flinders University), GPO Box 2100, Adelaide, SA, Australia
Tel: (61) 08 8201 3115

Fax: (61) 08 8201 5175
Email: scholarships@flinders.edu.au
Website: www.flinders.edu.au/scholarships

University Hall Eurest Overseas Study Scholarship
Subjects: All subjects.
Purpose: To enable full-time students residing in University Hall, who have demonstrated outstanding aptitude for research, to undertake a period of further study or research in approved universities or other institutions outside Australia.
Eligibility: Applicants must have lived in University Hall for a period of not less than one academic year, have gained unqualified support for his/her supervisor for the proposed overseas visit, have gained approval from the overseas institution that he/she is acceptable for the proposed period of study and have demonstrated a suitable academic record in the previous academic year.
Level of Study: Postgraduate
Type: Scholarship
Value: Australian $2,500
Length of Study: 1 year
Frequency: Annual
No. of awards offered: 1
Application Procedure: Applicants must contact the Higher Degree Administration and Scholarships Office and University Hall for application forms and further information.
Closing Date: October 20th

For further information contact:

Email: flinders.housing@flinders.edu.au

FLORIDA FEDERATION OF GARDEN CLUBS (FFGC)

1400 South Denning Drive, Winter Park, FL 32789-5662, United States of America
Tel: (1) 647 7016
Fax: (1) 647 5479
Email: office_manager@ffgc.org
Website: www.ffgc.org

The FFGC is the first state garden club on the Internet, which features FFGC activities, scholarships, youth programmes, floral design courses, arrangements, educational opportunities, tours, shows and special events of the various affiliated garden clubs in the state of Florida.

FFGC Scholarship in Ecology
Subjects: Ecology.
Purpose: To provide financial assistance to students in field of ecology.
Eligibility: Open to applicants who are residents of Florida and who demonstrate financial needs.
Level of Study: Postgraduate
Type: Scholarship
Value: US$1,500
Frequency: Annual
Country of Study: United States of America
No. of awards offered: 13
Application Procedure: Check website for details
Closing Date: May 1st
Contributor: Florida Federation of Garden Clubs
No. of awards given last year: 9

FFGC Scholarship in Environmental Issues
Subjects: Environmental studies.
Purpose: To support students in the field of environmental studies.
Eligibility: Open to students who are residents of Florida.
Level of Study: Postgraduate
Type: Scholarship
Value: Up to US$3,500
Frequency: Annual
Country of Study: United States of America
No. of awards offered: 13

Application Procedure: A completed application form must be submitted.
Closing Date: May 1st
Contributor: Florida Federation of Garden Clubs

FONDATION DES ETATS-UNIS

15 boulevard Jourdan, Paris, 75014, France
Tel: (33) 1 53 80 68 80
Fax: (33) 1 53 80 68 99
Email: administration@feusa.org
Website: www.feusa.org
Contact: Mr Terence Murphy, Director

For the past 75 years the Fondation des Etats-Unis has been welcoming American and International Students during their studies in Paris.

Harriet Hale Woolley Scholarships
Subjects: Visual fine arts, music.
Purpose: To support the study of visual fine arts and music in Paris.
Eligibility: Open to citizens of the United States of America, who are 21–35 years of age and have graduated with high academic standing from a US college, university or professional school of recognized standing. Preference is given to mature students who have already completed graduate study. Applicants should provide evidence of artistic or musical accomplishment. Applicants should have a good working knowledge of French, sufficient to enable the student to benefit from his or her study in France. Grants are for those doing painting, printmaking or sculpture and for instrumentalists, not for research in art history, musicology or composition, nor for students of dance or theatre. Successful candidates propose a unique and detailed project related to their study, which requires a 1-year residency in Paris.
Level of Study: Doctorate, Graduate, Postgraduate, Predoctorate
Type: Scholarship
Value: A stipend of €8,500
Length of Study: 1 academic year
Frequency: Annual
Country of Study: France
No. of awards offered: 3–5
Application Procedure: For a complete description of the scholarship including a list of general requirements, an application checklist and an application form, please visit: www.feusa.org, chapter 'Nos activités culturelles', sub-chapter 'The Harriet Hale Woolley Scholarship'.
Closing Date: January 31st
Funding: Private
No. of awards given last year: 4
No. of applicants last year: 25

For further information contact:

Tel: 1 53 80 68 87
Email: culture@feusa.org
Contact: Miss Elizabeth Askren-Brie, Attachée culturelle

FONDATION FYSSEN

194 Rue de Rivoli, F-75001 Paris, France
Tel: (33) 1 42 97 53 16
Fax: (33) 1 42 60 17 95
Email: secretariat@fondation-fyssen.org
Website: www.fondation-fyssen.org
Contact: Mrs Nadia Ferchal, Director

The aim of the Fyssen Foundation is to encourage all forms of scientific enquiry into cognitive mechanisms, including thought and reasoning, that underlie animal and human behaviour, their biological and cultural bases and phylogenetic and ontogenetic development.

Fondation Fyssen Postdoctoral Study Grants
Subjects: Disciplines relevant to the aims of the Foundation such as ethology, palaeontology, archaeology, anthropology, psychology, ethnology, neurobiology.

Purpose: To assist French or foreign postdoctoral researchers, under 35 years of age, to work on topics in keeping with the Foundation's goals.

Eligibility: Open to a first post-doctorate with a PhD of less than a year on September 1st of the year of application. Open to French or foreign research scientists holder of a French doctorate (PhD) and attached to a laboratory in France who wish to work in laboratories abroad (except country of origin or joint supervision) and foreign or French research scientists holder of a foreign doctorate (PhD) and attached to a foreign laboratory who wish to work in French laboratories. Applicants should be under 35 years of age.

Level of Study: Postdoctorate
Type: Study grant
Value: €25,000
Length of Study: 1&macndash2 years
Frequency: Annual
Application Procedure: Applicants must complete an application form, available from the Secretariat of the Foundation or from the website and send the same within the due date along with 15 copies.
Closing Date: March 31st
Funding: Private

International Prize

Subjects: Neuropsychology
Purpose: To encourage a scientist who has conducted distinguished research in the areas supported by the Foundation.
Eligibility: Open to a first post-doctorate with a PhD of less than a year on September 1st of the year of application. Open to French or foreign research scientists holder of a French doctorate (PhD) and attached to a laboratory in France who wish to work in laboratories abroad (except country of origin or joint supervision) and foreign or French research scientists holder of a foreign doctorate (PhD) and attached to a foreign laboratory who wish to work in French laboratories. Applicants should be under 35 years of age.
Value: €50,000
Frequency: Annual
Application Procedure: Candidates cannot apply directly but should be proposed by recognized scientists. Proposals for candidates should consist of (i) curriculum vitae, (ii) a list of publications, (iii) a summary (4 pages maximum) of the research. The proposal should be submitted in 15 copies to Secrétariat de la Fondation Fyssen.
Closing Date: October 30th
Funding: Private

FOOD AND DRUG LAW INSTITUTE (FDLI)

1155, 15th Street, NW, Suite 800, Washington, DC, 20005, United States of America
Tel: (1) 202 371 1420
Fax: (1) 202 371 0649
Email: comments@fdli.org
Website: www.fdli.org
Contact: Ms Rita M. Fullem, Vice President-Programs Publications

The Food and Drug Law Institute (FDLI) is a non-profit educational association dedicated to advancing public health by providing a neutral forum for a critical examination of the laws, regulations and policies related to drugs, medical devices, other healthcare technologies and food.

H Thomas Austern Memorial Writing Competition–Food and Drug Law Institute(FDLI)

Subjects: Current issues relevant to the food and drug field including relevant case law, legislative history and other authorities, particularly where the United States Food and Drug Administration is involved. Additional topic possibilities are available from the website.
Purpose: To encourage law students interested in the areas of law affecting foods, drugs, devices, cosmetics and biologics.
Eligibility: Entrants must currently be enrolled in a JD programme at any of the United States of America law schools. Anyone currently enrolled in a Juris Doctorate program in any US college or university.
Level of Study: Postgraduate
Value: Two first prizes of US$1,500; two second prizes of US$1,000
Frequency: Annual

Country of Study: United States of America
No. of awards offered: 4
Application Procedure: Applicants must submit a typewritten, double-spaced paper on 8.5 by 11 inch paper or submit a Word document electronically. The cover sheet must list the applicant's full name, address and telephone number, law school and year, and the date of submission of the paper. Papers must not exceed 40 pages in length, including footnotes for shorter paper competition. There is a 100 page limit for papers longer than 41 pages for long paper competition.
Closing Date: June 15th
Funding: Private
Contributor: Association funds and Association member dues
No. of awards given last year: 4
No. of applicants last year: Approx. 50
Additional Information: Winning papers will be considered for publication in the *Food and Drug Law Journal.*

FOOD SCIENCE AUSTRALIA

11 Julius Avenue, Riverside Corporate Park, North Ryde, NSW, 2113, Australia
Tel: (61) 2 9490 8333
Fax: (61) 2 9490 8499
Email: fsacontact@csiro.au
Website: www.foodscience.csiro.au

Food Science Australia is Australia's largest and most diversified food research organisation and a joint venture of CSIRO and the Victorian Government. They are committed to turning scientific research into innovative solutions for the food industry in Australia and overseas.

Food Science Australia CSIRO Postgraduate Scholarship Program

Subjects: Science and engineering.
Purpose: To provide opportunities in science and engineering for outstanding graduates who enroll each year at Australian tertiary institutions as full-time postgraduate students for research leading to the award of a PhD.
Eligibility: Open to doctoral students who have Australian Permanent Residency or citizenship and also who gain or expect to gain an Australian Postgraduate Award (APA) or equivalent university award.
Level of Study: Doctorate, Postgraduate
Type: Scholarship
Country of Study: Australia
Application Procedure: Check website for further details.
Funding: Government

FOULKES FOUNDATION

37 Ringwood Avenue, London, N2 9NT, England
Tel: (44) 20 8444 2526
Fax: (44) 20 8444 2526
Website: www.foulkes-foundation.org
Contact: M Foulkes, The Registrar

The aim of the Foulkes Foundation Fellowship is to promote medical research by providing financial support for postdoctoral science graduates who need a medical degree before they can undertake medical research, and similarly for medical graduates who need a science PhD degree.

Foulkes Foundation Fellowship

Subjects: All aspects of medical research, especially the areas of molecular biology and biological sciences.
Purpose: To promote research by providing financial support for postdoctoral study.
Eligibility: Open to recently qualified scientists who have a PhD or equivalent and intend to contribute to medical research.
Level of Study: Postdoctorate
Type: Fellowship
Value: Varies depending on individual need, but the scale for the basic SRC Studentship is used as a guideline. Fellowships do not cover fees
Length of Study: Up to 3 years
Frequency: Annual

Country of Study: United Kingdom
No. of awards offered: Varies
Application Procedure: Applicants must send an application form and a stamped addressed envelope to the Registrar for additional information.
Closing Date: March 15th
Funding: Private
No. of awards given last year: 5
No. of applicants last year: 75
Additional Information: Applicants must be undertaking medical training in the United Kingdom.

FOUNDATION FOR ANESTHESIA EDUCATION AND RESEARCH (FAER)

200 First Street South West, WF6-674,
Rochester, MN, 55905,
United States of America
Tel: (1) 507 266 6866
Fax: (1) 507 284 0291
Email: schrandt.mary@mayo.edu
Website: www.faer.org
Contact: Ms Mary Schrandt, Associate Director

The Foundation for Anesthesia Education and Research (FAER) strives to foster progress in anaesthesiology, critical care, pain and all areas of perioperative medicine. The organization aims to generate new knowledge that advances health and patient care by facilitating the career development of anaesthesiologists dedicated to research and education.

FAER Mentored Research Training Grant (MRTG)
Subjects: Anaesthesiology.
Purpose: To allow the applicant to become an independent investigator.
Eligibility: Applicants must be instructors or assistant professors who are within 10 years of their initial appointment.
Level of Study: Postdoctorate
Type: Grant
Value: US$75,000 in the 1st year and US$100,000 in the 2nd.
Length of Study: 2 years
Frequency: Annual
Application Procedure: Applicants must visit the website www.faer.org.
Closing Date: February 15th

FAER Research Education Grant
Subjects: Anaesthesiology.
Purpose: To improve the quality and productivity of education and research.
Eligibility: Open to anaesthesiology residents or faculty.
Level of Study: Postgraduate
Type: Grant
Value: US$50,000 in the 1st year and US$50,000 in the 2nd year
Length of Study: 2 years
Frequency: Annual
Application Procedure: Applicants must visit the website.
Closing Date: February 15th

FAER Research Fellowship Grant
Subjects: Anaesthesiology.
Purpose: To provide significant training in research techniques and scientific methods.
Eligibility: Open to anaesthesiology residents after CA-1 training.
Level of Study: Postdoctorate
Type: Fellowship
Value: US$75,000
Length of Study: 1 year
Frequency: Annual
Application Procedure: Applicants must visit the website.
Closing Date: February 15th

FOUNDATION FOR DIGESTIVE HEALTH AND NUTRITION

4930 Del Ray Avenue, Bethesda, MD, 20814, United States of America
Tel: (1) 301 222 4012
Fax: (1) 301 652 3890
Email: awards@fdhn.org
Website: www.fdhn.org
Contact: Ms Wykenna S.C.Vailor, Research Awards Manager

The Foundation for Digestive Health and Nutrition is the foundation of the American Gastroenterological Association (AGA), the leading professional society representing gastroenterological and heptatologists worldwide. It is separately incorporated and governed by a distinguished board of AGA physicians and members of the lay public. The Foundation raises funds for research and public education in the prevention, diagnosis, treatment and cure of digestive diseases. Along with the AGA, it conducts public education initiatives related to digestive diseases. The Foundation also administers the disbursement of grants on the behalf of the AGA and other funders.

AGA Fellowship to Faculty Transition Awards
Subjects: Medical science, specifically gastroenterology and hepatology.
Purpose: To prepare and support physicians for independent research careers in digestive diseases.
Eligibility: Applicants must be MDs currently in a gastroenterology-related fellowship at an accredited United States of America or Canadian institution and be committed to academic careers. They should have completed 2 years of research training at the start of this award. The additional training could be considered the equivalent of practical training ordinarily involved in a PhD programme. Therefore, individuals who hold a PhD are ineligible. Please note that non-United States of America or Canadian citizens based at United States of America or Canadian institutions are eligible to apply. Women and minority investigators are strongly encouraged to apply. Applicants must be AGA members or sponsored by an AGA member.
Level of Study: Postgraduate
Type: Award
Value: US$40,000 per year
Length of Study: 2 years
Frequency: Annual
Country of Study: The United States of America, Canada or Mexico
No. of awards offered: 4
Application Procedure: Electronic applications only.
Closing Date: September 5th
Funding: Private
Contributor: The AGA
Additional Information: At the end of the award, the recipient will be required to indicate how the funds were used, the accomplishments made during the training project and how this training has contributed to his or her research career development. A complete financial statement and scientific progress report are required annually and upon completion of the programme. All publications arising from work funded by this programme must acknowledge support of the award.

AGA June and Donald O Castell, MD, Esophageal Clinical Research Award
Subjects: Oesophageal diseases.
Purpose: To support investigators who have demonstrated a high potential to develop an independent, productive research career.
Eligibility: Applicants must have an MD or PhD equivalent to hold a full-time faculty position at a United States of America or Canadian university or professional institute and be members of the AGA. The recipient must be at or below the level of assistant professor, and his/her initial appointment to the faculty position must have been within 7 years of the time of application. This award is not intended for Fellows, but for juniors who have demonstrated unusual promise, have some record of accomplishment in research and have established independent research programmes at the time of the award. Candidates must devote at least 50 per cent of their efforts to research related to oesophageal function or diseases. Applicants may not simultaneously apply for an AGA Research Scholar Award, AGA Fiterman Foundation Basic Research Award or AGA/Elsevier Research Initiative Award.

Level of Study: Graduate
Value: US$35,000
Length of Study: 1 year
Frequency: Annual
Country of Study: United States of America
No. of awards offered: 1
Application Procedure: Electronic applications only.
Closing Date: January 14th
Funding: Private

AGA R Robert and Sally D Funderburg Research Scholar Award in Gastric Biology Related to Cancer

Subjects: Gastric mucosal cell biology, regeneration and regulation of cell growth, inflammation, genetics of gastric carcinoma, epidemiology of gastric cancer, etiology of gastric epithelial malignancies, or clinical research in the diagnosis of gastric carcinoma.
Purpose: To support an active established investigator in the field of gastric biology and who enhances the fundamental understanding of gastric cancer pathobiology in order to ultimately develop a cure for the disease.
Eligibility: Applicants must hold faculty positions at accredited United States of America or Canadian institutions and must have established themselves as independent investigators in the field of gastric biology. Women and minority investigators are strongly encouraged to apply. Applicants must be individual members of the AGA.
Level of Study: Postgraduate
Type: Award
Value: US$50,000
Length of Study: 2 years
Frequency: Annual
Country of Study: The United States of America, Canada or Mexico
No. of awards offered: 1
Application Procedure: Electronic applications only.
Closing Date: September 5th
Contributor: The AGA, the late R Robert and the late Sally D Funderburg

AGA Research Scholar Awards

Subjects: Gastroenterology and hepatology.
Purpose: To enable young investigators to develop independent and productive research careers in digestive diseases by ensuring that a major proportion of their time is protected for research.
Eligibility: Applicants must hold full-time faculty positions at United States of America or Canadian universities or professional institutes at the time of application and be members of the AGA. The award is not intended for Fellows, but for young faculty who have demonstrated unusual promise and have some record of accomplishment in research. Candidates should be in the beginning years of their careers. Those who have been at the assistant professor level or equivalent for more than 5 years at the time the award would begin are not eligible. Candidates must hold an MD, PhD or equivalent degree. Candidates must devote at least 70 per cent of their efforts to research related to the gastrointestinal tract or liver. Women and minority investigators are strongly encouraged to apply.
Level of Study: Graduate
Type: Research grant
Value: US$75,000 per year
Length of Study: 3 years
Frequency: Annual
Country of Study: United States of America
No. of awards offered: 6
Application Procedure: Electronic applications only.
Closing Date: September 5th
Funding: Private
Additional Information: A complete financial statement and scientific progress report are required upon completion of the programme. All publications arising from work funded by this programme must acknowledge the support of the award. Awardees must submit their work for presentation at Digestive Disease Week during the last year of the award.

AGA Student Research Fellowship Awards

Subjects: Research related to the gastrointestinal tract, liver or pancreas.

Purpose: To provide salary support for graduate students performing doctoral research related to the gastrointestinal tract, liver or pancreas.
Eligibility: Applicants should be US citizens, permanent residents or overseas students who have a current visa to pursue education within North America. Check website for further details.
Level of Study: Postgraduate, Professional development, Graduate
Type: Award
Value: US$20,000 (Includes $18,000 for stipend and $2,000 for fringe benefits)
Length of Study: 2 years
Frequency: Annual
Country of Study: The United States of America, Canada or Mexico
No. of awards offered: 2
Application Procedure: Applicants must visit the website.
Closing Date: March 3rd
Funding: Private
Contributor: The AGA

Pilot Research Awards

Subjects: Medical science, specifically gastroenterology and hepatology.
Purpose: To provide non-salary funds for new investigators to help them establish their research careers and to support pilot projects that represent new research directions for established investigators. The intent is to stimulate research in gastroenterology or hepatology-related areas by permitting investigators to obtain new data that can ultimately provide the basis for subsequent grant applications of more substantial funding and duration.
Eligibility: Investigators must possess an MD, PhD or equivalent and must hold a faculty position at accredited United States of America or Canadian institutions. They may not hold awards on a similar topic from other agencies. Applicants must be members of the AGA. Women and minorities are strongly encouraged to apply. Applicants for this award may not simultaneously apply for the AGA/Miles and Shirley Fiterman Foundation Basic Research Award.
Level of Study: Postdoctorate, Postgraduate, Predoctorate
Type: Award
Value: US$25,000
Length of Study: 1 year
Frequency: Annual
Country of Study: The United States of America, Canada or Mexico
No. of awards offered: 1
Application Procedure: Electronic applications only.
Closing Date: January 14th
Funding: Private
Contributor: The AGA

FOUNDATION FOR HIGH BLOOD PRESSURE RESEARCH

4/184 Main Street, Lilydale, VIC, 3140, Australia
Tel: (61) 3 9905 2555
Fax: (61) 3 9905 2566
Email: hbprca@meetingsfirst.com.au
Website: www.hbprca.com.au
Contact: Administrative Officer

The Foundation for High Blood Pressure Research was established to support research into any aspect of blood pressure, hypertension and associated cardiovascular diseases.

Foundation for High Blood Pressure Research Postdoctoral Fellowship

Subjects: The understanding of the causes, prevention, treatment or effects of hypertension.
Purpose: To fund a scientist to perform research.
Eligibility: Open to applicants who are Australian citizens or have permanent residency in Australia, who have a degree in medicine or science, or an appropriate PhD.
Level of Study: Postdoctorate
Type: Fellowship
Value: Salary plus project maintenance costs
Length of Study: 2 years
Frequency: Annual

Study Establishment: An approved institute, university or hospital
Country of Study: Australia
No. of awards offered: 1
Application Procedure: Applicants must complete and submit an application with a curriculum vitae and relevant publications.
Closing Date: Please consult the Foundation
Funding: Private
Contributor: The Foundation
No. of awards given last year: 1
No. of applicants last year: 10
Additional Information: The award is advertised in Australia and overseas. Interested applicants should contact the Honorary Secretary for further information.

ISH Postdoctoral Award

Subjects: The understanding of the causes, prevention, treatment or effects of hypertension.
Purpose: To fund an international scientist to perform research at an Australian research institution.
Eligibility: Open to applicants who have a degree in medicine or science, or appropriate PhD.
Level of Study: Postdoctorate
Type: Fellowship
Value: Some assistance is provided to the employing institution comprising part salary only
Length of Study: 2 years
Frequency: Every 2 years
Study Establishment: An approved institute, university or hospital
Country of Study: Australia
No. of awards offered: 1
Application Procedure: Applicants must complete and submit an application with a curriculum vitae and relevant publications.
Closing Date: Please consult the Foundation
Funding: Private
Contributor: The Foundation
No. of awards given last year: 1
No. of applicants last year: 4
Additional Information: Details are advertised in Australia and overseas. Interested applicants should contact the Honorary Secretary for further information.

FOUNDATION FOR JEWISH CULTURE

PO Box 489, New York, NY, 10011, United States of America
Tel: (1) 212 629 0500
Fax: (1) 212 629 0508
Email: grants@jewishculture.org
Website: www.jewishculture.org

The Foundation for Jewish Culture (formerly the National Foundation for Jewish Culture) is the leading advocate for Jewish cultural creativity and preservation in America. Since 1960, it has nurtured new generations of writers, filmmakers, artists, composers, choreographers and scholars. The Foundation invests in creative individuals in order to nurture a vibrant and enduring Jewish identity, culture and community. Its goals are achieved through the provision of grants, recognition awards, networking opportunities and professional development services. They collaborate with cultural institutions, Jewish organizations, consortia and funders to support the work of these artists and scholars. The Foundation also educates and builds audiences to provide meaningful Jewish cultural experiences to the American public, and advocates for the importance of Jewish culture as a core component of Jewish life.

Maurice and Marilyn Cohen Fund for Doctoral Dissertation Fellowships in Jewish Studies

Subjects: Jewish studies.
Purpose: To encourage study and research in the various disciplines related to Judaica and Jewish life.
Eligibility: Open to citizens or permanent residents of the United States who have completed all requirements for the PhD degree except the dissertation and are proficient in a Jewish language.
Level of Study: Doctorate
Type: Fellowships
Value: US$16,000–20,000

Length of Study: 1 year
Frequency: Annual
Application Procedure: Please see the website for current application and guidelines.
Closing Date: November 30th
No. of awards given last year: 8
No. of applicants last year: 50–75

FOUNDATION FOR PHYSICAL THERAPY

1111 North Fairax Street, Alexandria, VA, 22314, United States of America
Tel: (1) 800 999 2782 ext 8505
Fax: (1) 703 706 8536
Email: foundation@apta.org
Website: www.foundationforphysicaltherapy.org
Contact: Victoria Matthews, Scientific Program Administrator

The Foundation for Physical Therapy is a national, independent, non-profit corporation founded to support the physical therapy profession's research needs in the areas of scientific research, clinical research and health services research.

Florence P Kendall Doctoral Scholarships

Subjects: Physical therapy, rehabilitation medicine, neuroscience, sports medicine, paediatrics, medical sciences and social or preventative medicine.
Purpose: To assist physical therapists with outstanding potential for doctoral studies in the 1st year of study towards a doctorate.
Eligibility: Open to candidates who possess a licence to practice physical therapy, or as a physical therapist assistant in the United States of America and fulfil specific requirements with regard to research experience.
Level of Study: Doctorate
Type: Scholarship
Value: US$5,000
Length of Study: 1 year
Frequency: Annual
Country of Study: United States of America
No. of awards offered: Varies
Application Procedure: Applicants must apply online. Guidelines, instructions and access to the online system are available in the website.
Closing Date: August 12th
Funding: Private
No. of awards given last year: 4
No. of applicants last year: 9

New Investigator Fellowships Training Initiative (NIFTI)

Subjects: Physical therapy, rehabilitation medicine, neuroscience, sports medicine, paediatrics, medical sciences and social or preventative medicine.
Purpose: To fund doctorally prepared physical therapists as developing researchers and improve their competitiveness in securing external funding for future research.
Eligibility: Open to candidates who possess a licence to practice physical therapy, or as a physical therapist assistant in the United States of America, have received the required postprofessional doctoral degree no earlier than 5 years prior to the year of application or, for those already holding a postprofessional doctorates, a professional education degree in physical therapy no earlier than 5 years prior to the year of application. Candidates must also have completed a research experience as part of their postprofessional doctoral education.
Level of Study: Postdoctorate
Type: Fellowship
Value: US$78,000
Length of Study: 2 years
Frequency: Annual
Country of Study: United States of America
No. of awards offered: Varies
Application Procedure: Applicants must apply online. Guidlines, instructions and access to online system are available in the website.
Closing Date: January 14th
Funding: Private
No. of awards given last year: 1
No. of applicants last year: 7

Promotion of Doctoral Studies (PODS)

Subjects: Physical therapy, rehabilitation medicine, neuroscience, sports medicine, paediatrics, medical sciences and social or preventative medicine.

Purpose: To fund doctoral students who, having completed 1 full year of coursework, wish to continue their coursework or enter the dissertation phase.

Eligibility: Open to candidates who possess a licence to practice physical therapy, or as a physical therapist assistant in the United States of America and who are enrolled as students in a regionally accredited postprofessional, doctoral programme. The content of this programme should have a demonstrated relationship to physical therapy. Applicants must also be able to demonstrate continuous progress towards the completion of their postprofessional doctoral programme in a timely fashion and with a commitment to further the physical therapy profession through research and teaching within the United States of America and its territories.

Level of Study: Doctorate

Type: Scholarship

Value: Two levels, at US$7,500 or US$15,000

Length of Study: 1 year

Frequency: Annual

Country of Study: United States of America

No. of awards offered: Varies

Application Procedure: Applicants must apply online. Guidelines, instructions and access to the online system are available in the website.

Closing Date: January 14th

Funding: Private

No. of awards given last year: 20

No. of applicants last year: 46

Research Grants (FPT)

Subjects: Physical therapy, rehabilitation medicine, neuroscience, sports medicine, paediatrics, medical sciences and social or preventative medicine.

Purpose: The purpose of the Foundation's Research Grant programme is to fund research studies in specific areas initiated by emerging investigators.

Eligibility: Open to citizens or permanent residents of the United States of America or its territories who possess a licence to practice physical therapy or as a physical therapist assistant. Projects to be completed in fulfilment of requirements for an academic degree are not eligible to be funded by a Foundation Research Grant. A doctoral student in the latter stage of the dissertation phase of his/her programme may submit an application, but must provide evidence of completion of the degree by October 15th. In addition, the proposed study must differ substantially from any thesis research being conducted by graduate assistant(s) to be supported by this Research Grant.

Level of Study: Research

Type: Grant

Value: US$40,000

Frequency: Annual

Country of Study: United States of America

No. of awards offered: Varies

Application Procedure: Applicants must apply online. Guidelines, instructions and access to the online system are available in the website.

Closing Date: August 12th

Funding: Private

No. of awards given last year: 3

No. of applicants last year: 21

Additional Information: Guidelines and application forms are available online in the spring at www.apta.org/foundation/applications online. A paper version of the RFP is available from the Foundation.

FOUNDATION FOR SCIENCE AND DISABILITY, INC.

503 North West, 89th Street, Gainesville, FL, 32607,
United States of America
Tel: (1) 352 374 5774
Fax: (1) 352 374 5781
Email: rmankin@nersp.nerdc.ufl.edu
Website: http://stemd.org
Contact: Dr Richard Mankin, Grants Committee Chair

The Foundation for Science and Disability aims to promote the integration of scientists with disabilities into all activities of the scientific community and of society as a whole, and to promote the removal of barriers in order to enable students with disabilities to choose careers in science.

Foundation for Science and Disability Student Grant Fund

Subjects: Engineering, mathematics, medicine, natural sciences and computer science.

Purpose: To increase opportunities in science for physically disabled students at the graduate or professional level.

Eligibility: Open to candidates from the United States of America.

Level of Study: Doctorate, Postgraduate

Type: Grant

Value: US$1,000

Length of Study: 1 year

Frequency: Annual

Country of Study: United States of America

No. of awards offered: 1–3

Application Procedure: Applicants must submit a completed application form, copies of official college transcripts, a letter from the research or academic supervisor in support of the request and a second letter from another faculty member.

Closing Date: December 1st

Funding: Private

No. of awards given last year: 1

No. of applicants last year: 7

Additional Information: The award may be used for an assistive device or instrument, or as financial support to work with a professor on an individual research project or for some other special need.

FRANK KNOX MEMORIAL FELLOWSHIPS

3 Birdcage Walk, Westminster, London, SW1H 9JJ, England
Tel: (44) 20 7222 1151
Fax: (44) 20 7222 7189
Email: scholarships@ed.ac.uk
Website: www.frankknox.harvard.edu
Contact: Ms Annie Thomas, Secretary

The Frank Knox Memorial Fellowships were established at Harvard University in 1945 by a gift from Mrs Annie Reid Knox, widow of the late Colonel Frank Knox, to allow students from the United Kingdom to participate in an educational exchange programme.

Frank Knox Fellowships at Harvard University

Subjects: Arts, sciences including engineering and medical sciences, business administration and management, design, divinity, education, law, public administration and public health.

Eligibility: Open to citizens of the United Kingdom who, at the time of application, have spent at least 2 of the last 4 years at a university or university college in the United Kingdom and will have graduated by the start of tenure. Fellowships are not awarded for postdoctoral study and no application will be considered from persons already in the United States of America. A period of full-time work since graduation is necessary before embarking on the MBA programme.

Level of Study: Postgraduate

Type: Fellowship

Value: US$23,000 plus tuition fees. Unmarried fellows may be accommodated in one of the university dormitories or halls

Length of Study: 1 academic year. Depending on the availability of sufficient funds fellowships may be renewed for those fellows registered for a degree programme of more than 1 year

Frequency: Annual

Study Establishment: Harvard University

Country of Study: United States of America

No. of awards offered: 5

Application Procedure: Applicants must file an admissions application directly with the graduate school of their choice by the relevant closing date.

Closing Date: October 27th

Funding: Private

Contributor: The estate of the late Frank Knox

No. of awards given last year: 7
No. of applicants last year: 119
Additional Information: Travel Grants are not awarded, although in cases of extreme hardship applications can be made to Harvard University for travel cost assistance.

FRANKLIN AND ELEANOR ROOSEVELT INSTITUTE

Franklin D Roosevelt Library, 4079 Albany Post Road, Hyde Park, NY 12538, United States of America
Tel: (1) 845 486 1150
Fax: (1) 845 486 1150
Email: info@feri.org
Website: www.feri.org
Contact: The Chairman, Grants Committee

The Franklin and Eleanor Roosevelt Institute is a private non-profit corporation dedicated to preserving the legacy and promoting the ideals of Franklin and Eleanor Roosevelt.

Roosevelt Institute Research Grant
Subjects: Research on the Roosevelt years and clearly related subjects.
Purpose: To encourage younger scholars to expand their knowledge and understanding of the Roosevelt period and to give continued support to more experienced researchers who have already made a mark in the field.
Eligibility: Open to qualified researchers of any nationality with a viable plan of work. Proposals are recommended for funding by an independent panel of Scholars which reports to the Institute Board.
Level of Study: Doctorate, Graduate, Postdoctorate
Type: Research grant
Value: Up to US$2,500
Frequency: Annual
Study Establishment: The Franklin D Roosevelt Library, Hyde Park in New York
Country of Study: United States of America
No. of awards offered: 15–20
Application Procedure: Applicants must submit two copies of each of the following: an application front sheet, research proposal, relevance of holdings, travel plans, time estimate, curriculum vitae, three letters of reference and budget. Application forms and guidelines are available from the website or by emailing, faxing or writing to the Roosevelt Institute.
Closing Date: January 30th
Funding: Private

For further information contact:

The Franklin and Eleanor Roosevelt Institute, 511 Albany Post Road, Hyde Park, NY 12538
Contact: Chairman, Grants Committee

FRAXA RESEARCH FOUNDATION

45 Pleasant Street, Newburyport, MA, 01950, United States of America
Tel: (1) 978 462 1866
Fax: (1) 978 463 9985
Email: info@fraxa.org
Website: www.fraxa.org
Contact: Ms Katherine Clapp, President

The FRAXA Research Foundation funds postdoctoral fellowships and investigator-initiated grants to support medical research aimed at the treatment of Fragile X Syndrome. FRAXA is particularly interested in preclinical studies of potential pharmacological and genetic treatments and studies aimed at understanding the function of the FMRI gene.

FRAXA Grants and Fellowships
Subjects: The treatment of Fragile X Syndrome and potential pharmacological and genetic treatments and studies aimed at understanding the function of the FMRI gene.
Purpose: To promote research aimed at finding a specific treatment for Fragile X Syndrome.

Eligibility: There are no eligibility restrictions.
Level of Study: Postdoctorate, Research
Type: Fellowships
Value: $45,000 per year for postdoctoral fellowship for 2 years (for salary, fringe benefits and consumable costs)
Length of Study: 1 year, renewable
Country of Study: Any country
No. of awards offered: 25–35 each year
Application Procedure: Candidates must complete an application form, available from the FRAXA Research Foundation or from the website. Potential candidates are welcome to submit a one-page initial inquiry letter describing the proposed research before submitting a full application.
Closing Date: February 1st
Funding: Private
No. of awards given last year: 38
No. of applicants last year: 60

THE FREDERIC CHOPIN SOCIETY

Ostrogski Castle, Ul Okolnik 1, Warsaw, PL, 00-368, Poland
Tel: (48) 22 826 81 90
Fax: (48) 22 827 95 99
Email: konkurs@chopin.pl
Website: www.konkurs.chopin.pl
Contact: Administrative Assistant

The Frederic Chopin Society organizes the International Chopin Piano Competition, the Scholarly Piano Competition for Polish Pianists, the Grand Prix du Disque Frederic Chopin, courses in Chopin's music interpretation and Chopin music recitals as well as running a museum and collection.

International Frederic Chopin Piano Competition
Subjects: Piano performance of Chopin's music.
Purpose: To recognize the best artistic interpretation of Chopin's music and to encourage professional development.
Eligibility: Open to pianists of any nationality, born between 1977 and 1988.
Level of Study: Unrestricted
Type: Prize
Value: First Prize €30,000 and gold medal; Second Prize €25,000 and silver medal; Third Prize €20,000 and bronze medal; Fourth Prize €15,000; Fifth Prize €10,000; Sixth Prize €7,000 plus special prizes. Check website for complete details
Frequency: Every 5 years
Country of Study: Any country
No. of awards offered: 6
Application Procedure: Applicants must complete and submit an application form attached with the rules.
Closing Date: December 1st
Funding: Government, private
No. of awards given last year: 14

FREDERICK DOUGLASS INSTITUTE FOR AFRICAN AND AFRICAN-AMERICAN STUDIES

University of Rochester, 302 Morey Hall, Rochester, NY, 14627-0440, United States of America
Tel: (1) 585 275 7235
Fax: (1) 585 256 2594
Email: fdi@mail.rochester.edu
Website: www.rochester.edu/college/aas
Contact: G R Radegonde-Eison, Administrative Assistant

The Frederick Douglass Institute for African and African-American Studies was established in 1986 to promote the development of African and African-American studies and graduate education through advanced research at the University of Rochester. It has served as an interdisciplinary centre, its focus being on the social sciences, though not excluding the humanities and the natural sciences.

Frederick Douglass Institute Postdoctoral Fellowship

Subjects: Historical and contemporary topics on the economy, society, politics and culture of Africa and its diaspora. Broadly conceived projects on human and technological aspects of energy development and agriculture in Africa are welcomed.

Purpose: To support the completion of a project.

Eligibility: Open to scholars who hold a PhD degree in a field related to the African and African-American experience.

Level of Study: Postdoctorate

Type: Fellowship

Value: A stipend of US$35,000 as well as full access to the university's facilities and office space in the Institute. It also supports the completion of a research project for 1 academic year

Frequency: Annual

Country of Study: Any country

No. of awards offered: 1

Application Procedure: Applicants must submit a completed application, a curriculum vitae, a three- to five-page description of the project plus a short bibliography and a sample of published or unpublished writing on a topic related to the proposal. Three letters of recommendation that comment upon the value and feasibility of the work proposed are to be sent by referees.

Closing Date: January 31st

No. of awards given last year: 1

Additional Information: All Fellows receive office space in the Institute and opportunities to interact and collaborate with scholars of their respective disciplines within the University. Fellows must be in full-time residence during the tenure of their awards and are expected to be engaged in scholarly activity on a full-time basis. They must be available for consultation with students and professional colleagues, make at least two formal presentations based on their research and contribute generally to the intellectual discourse on African and African-American Studies.

Frederick Douglass Institute Predoctoral Dissertation Fellowship

Subjects: Historical and contemporary topics on the economy, society, politics and culture of Africa and its diaspora. Broadly conceived projects on human and technological aspects of energy development and agriculture in Africa are welcomed.

Purpose: To support the completion of a dissertation.

Eligibility: Open to graduate students of any university who study aspects of the African and African- American experience. Applicants must have completed and passed all required courses, any qualifying oral and/or written exams and have written at least one chapter of the dissertation, which then becomes part of the application package, to qualify for this award.

Level of Study: Predoctorate

Type: Fellowship

Value: A stipend of US$23,000 as well as full access to the university's facilities and office space in the institute

Frequency: Annual

Country of Study: Any country

Application Procedure: Applicants must complete and send the FDI fellowship application form, a curriculum vitae, an official transcript showing completion of all preliminary coursework and qualifying examinations, the dissertation prospectus, a sample chapter from the dissertation and three letters of recommendation to be sent out by the referees, including one from the dissertation supervisor assessing the candidate's prospects for completing the project within a year.

Closing Date: January 31st

No. of awards given last year: 1

Additional Information: All Fellows receive office space in the Institute and opportunities to interact and collaborate with scholars of their respective disciplines within the University. Fellows must be in full-time residence during the tenure of their awards and are expected to be engaged in scholarly activity on a full-time basis. They must be available for consultation with students and professional colleagues, make at least two formal presentations based upon their research and contribute generally to the intellectual discourse on African and African-American Studies.

FREIE UNIVERSITÄT BERLIN

Lansstrasse 7–9, Berlin, 14195, Germany
Tel: (49) 030 838 52703
Fax: (49) 030 838 52882
Email: jfki@zedat.fu-berlin.de
Website: www.jfki.fu-berlin.de/en
Contact: JFK Institut für Nordamerikastudien

Freie Universität Berlin John-F.-Kennedy-Institut für Nordamerikastudien Research Grants

Subjects: Culture, economy, geography, history, language, literature, politics and society.

Purpose: To financially assist scholars who are interested in conducting research on topics concerning the United States or Canada.

Eligibility: Open to scholars with permanent residence in a European country working on research projects on topics concerning the United States and/or Canada.

Level of Study: Research

Type: Research grant

Value: The full scholarship awards €921 monthly to doctoral candidates and €1,330 monthly to postdoctoral candidates. The guest scholarship complements the salary of guest scholars by €665. The theses scholarship offers €562 to candidates working on their final theses

Frequency: Annual

Study Establishment: Freie Universität Berlin, John-F.-Kennedy-Institut für Nordamerikastudien

Country of Study: Germany

Application Procedure: Applicants must submit the applications including completed application form, a letter of reference, curriculum vitae, a project proposal and a bibliography of works and references needed at the Institute.

Closing Date: October 31st, May 31st

Funding: Government

Contributor: The research grants are supported by the Freie University of Berlin, in conjunction with the United States Information Agency and the Canadian Embassy in Berlin

THE FRENCH CULINARY INSTITUTE

Office of Financial Aid, 462 Broadway, 4th Floor, New York, NY 10013, United States of America
Tel: (1) 888 324 2433
Email: finaid@frenchculinary.com
Website: www.frenchculinary.com

The French Culinary Institute accredited by the Accrediting Commission of Career Schools and Colleges of Technology (ACCSCT) launches the bright careers of the next generation of culinary leaders. Chefs, pastry chefs, bread bakers, sommeliers, restaurant owners, managers, and food writers can hone their craft and shape their dreams with the incomparable training, experience, and career connections of the institute.

The French Culinary Institute Italian Culinary Experience Scholarship

Subjects: Italian culinary.

Purpose: For experience in Italian culinary.

Eligibility: Open to a student pre-enrolled for the Italian Culinary Experience Diploma Program.

Type: Scholarship

Value: $5,000

Study Establishment: ALMA La Scuola Internazionale di Cucina Italiana, Parma and The French Culinary Institute, New York

No. of awards offered: 1

Application Procedure: Check website for further details.

FRIENDS OF ISRAEL EDUCATIONAL FOUNDATION

Academic Study Group, POB 42763, London, N2 0YJ, England
Tel: (44) 020 8444 0777
Fax: (44) 020 8444 0681
Email: info@foi-asg.org
Website: www.foi-asg.org
Contact: Mr John D A Levy

The Friends of Israel Educational Foundation and its sister operation, the Academic Study Group, aim to encourage a critical understanding of the achievements, hopes and problems of modern Israel, and to forge new collaborative working links between the United Kingdom and Israel.

Friends of Israel Educational Foundation Academic Study Bursary

Subjects: All subjects.
Purpose: To provide funding for British academics planning to pay a first research or study visit to Israel.
Eligibility: Open to research or teaching postgraduates. The Academic Study Group will only consider proposals from British academics who have already linked up with professional counterparts in Israel and agreed terms of reference for an initial visit.
Level of Study: Postdoctorate
Type: Bursary
Value: UK £300 per person
Frequency: Annual
Country of Study: Israel
No. of awards offered: 30
Application Procedure: Applicants must contact the organization. There is no application form.
Closing Date: November 15th or March 15th
Funding: Private
Contributor: Trusts and individual donations
No. of awards given last year: 10
No. of applicants last year: Approx. 50

Friends of Israel Educational Foundation Young Artist Award

Subjects: Fine arts.
Purpose: To enable a promising British artist to pay a working visit to Israel and prepare work for an exhibition on Israeli themes in the United Kingdom.
Eligibility: Open to promising young British painters, print makers and illustrators.
Level of Study: Postgraduate, Professional development
Type: Award
Value: Airfares, accommodation and basic living costs
Length of Study: A minimum of 2 months
Frequency: Annual
Study Establishment: A kibbutz
Country of Study: Israel
No. of awards offered: 1–2
Application Procedure: Applicants must submit a personal curriculum vitae, an academic letter of reference, a statement of reasons for wishing to visit Israel and a representative selection of work.
Closing Date: May
Funding: Private
Contributor: Individual donations
Additional Information: Shortlisted candidates will be interviewed and artwork examined by a distinguished panel of judges.

Jerusalem Botanical Gardens Scholarship

Subjects: Botany and horticulture.
Purpose: To provide opportunities for botanists and horticulturists to work at the Jerusalem Botanical Gardens.
Eligibility: Preference is given to permanent residents of the United Kingdom who hold a degree in a relevant subject. Landscape architects with practical plant skills are also eligible.
Level of Study: Professional development, Postgraduate
Type: Scholarship
Value: Return airfare to Israel, subsidized accommodation in the vicinity of the Hebrew University campus and a subsistence allowance that covers the full placement. Participants receive no formal salary
Length of Study: 6 months–1 year
Frequency: Annual
Study Establishment: The Jerusalem Botanical Gardens
Country of Study: Israel
No. of awards offered: Varies
Application Procedure: Applicants must submit a curriculum vitae, an academic letter of reference, a statement of reasons for wishing to work in Jerusalem, two passport-sized photographs and a handwritten covering letter.

Closing Date: March 31st
Funding: Private
Contributor: Trusts and individual donations
No. of awards given last year: 4

FRIENDS OF JOSÉ CARRERAS INTERNATIONAL LEUKEMIA FOUNDATION

1100 Fairview Avenue North, D5-100 PO Box 19024, Seattle, WA, 98109-1024, United States of America
Tel: (1) 206 667 7108
Fax: (1) 206 667 6124
Email: friendsjc@carrerasfoundation.org
Website: www.carrerasfoundation.org
Contact: Administrator

The Friends of José Carreras International Leukemia Foundation funds Medical Research Fellowships.

Friends of José Carreras International Leukemia Foundation E D Thomas Postdoctoral Fellowship

Subjects: Medical sciences or leukaemia.
Purpose: To support research in the field of leukaemia or related haematological disorders.
Eligibility: Candidates must hold an MD or PhD degree and have completed at least 3 years of postdoctoral training but must be less than 10 years past their first doctoral degree when the award begins.
Level of Study: Postdoctorate
Type: Fellowship
Value: US$50,000 per year
Length of Study: 1 year, renewable for an additional 2 years
Frequency: Annual
Study Establishment: A suitable institution with the academic environment to provide adequate support for the proposal project
Country of Study: Any country
No. of awards offered: 1
Application Procedure: Applicants must complete an application form, available from the website. All applications must be typed, single spaced, in English and must follow the format specified in the application packet. Award announcements will be made by letter in January. Please do not contact the Foundation for results. Reapplication by unsuccessful candidates will be necessary for the following year.
Closing Date: Early November
Funding: Foundation
Contributor: Individual donors
No. of awards given last year: 1
No. of applicants last year: 15

FROMM MUSIC FOUNDATION

c/o Department of Music, Harvard University, Cambridge, MA, 02138, United States of America
Tel: (1) 617 495 2791
Fax: (1) 617 496 8081
Email: moncrieff@fas.harvard.edu
Website: www.fas.harvard.edu
Contact: Ms Jean Moncrieff

The Fromm Music Foundation at Harvard University, founded by the late Paul Fromm in the fifties, has been located at Harvard since 1972. Over, the course of its existence, the foundation has commissioned over 300 new compositions and their performances, and has sponsored hundreds of new music concerts and concert series.

Fromm Foundation Commission

Subjects: Music composition.
Purpose: To support compositions by young and lesser known as well as established composers who are citizens or residents of the United States of America. The award includes a stipend for premiere performance of commissioned work.
Eligibility: There are no eligibility restrictions. Applicants must be citizens or residents of the United States of America.
Level of Study: Unrestricted

Value: US$10,000
Frequency: Annual
Country of Study: United States of America
No. of awards offered: Up to 12
Application Procedure: Applicants must obtain guidelines from the Fromm Music Foundation.
Closing Date: June 1st
Funding: Foundation, private
No. of awards given last year: 12
No. of applicants last year: 200

FULBRIGHT COMMISSION (ARGENTINA)

Viamonte 1653, 2 Piso, Buenos Aires, C1055 ABE, Argentina
Tel: (54) 11 4814 3561
Fax: (54) 11 4814 1377
Email: info@fulbright.com.ar
Website: www.fulbright.edu.ar
Contact: Melina Ginszparg, Educational Advisor

The Fulbright Programme is an educational exchange programme that sponsors awards for individuals approved by the J William Fulbright Board. The programme's major aim is to promote international co-operation and contribute to the development of friendly, sympathetic and peaceful relations between the United States and other countries in the world.

Fulbright Commission (Argentina) Awards for US Lecturers and Researchers

Subjects: All subjects except medical science.
Purpose: To enable United States lecturers to teach at an Argentine university for one semester, and to enable United States researchers to conduct research at an Argentine institution for three months.
Eligibility: Open to United States researchers and lecturers. Applicants must be proficient in spoken Spanish.
Level of Study: Professional development
Value: Varies according to professional experience
Length of Study: 3 months
Frequency: Annual
Country of Study: Argentina
Closing Date: July 31st
Funding: Government
Contributor: The United States of America and the Argentine governments

For further information contact:

The Council for International Exchange of Scholars, 3001 Tilden Street, Washington, DC, 20008-3009
Tel: (202) 686-4000
Email: info@ciesnet.cies.org

Fulbright Commission (Argentina) Master's Program

Subjects: All subjects except medical science.
Purpose: To support Argentines pursuing a Master's degree in the United States of America.
Eligibility: Open to Argentines only.
Level of Study: Postgraduate
Frequency: Annual
Country of Study: United States of America
Application Procedure: Applicants must contact the Fulbright Commission in Argentina between February 1st and April 30th.
Funding: Private, government
Contributor: The Binational Commission and private sources

Fulbright Institutional Linkages Program

Subjects: Social sciences, public administration, business, economics, law, journalism and communications and educational administration.
Purpose: To support educational partnerships between US universities and foreign post-secondary institutions.
Level of Study: Postgraduate
Frequency: Annual

Contributor: The US department of state's institutional linkage programmes

For further information contact:

Humphrey Fellowships and Institutional linkage Branch, Office of Global Educational Programs, Bureau of Educational and Cultural Affairs, SA-44, 301 4th street, Washington, DC, 20547

Fulbright Scholar-in Residence

Subjects: Education administration.
Purpose: To enable visiting scholars to teach in the US about their home country or world region.
Eligibility: Open to candidates with strong international interest and some experience in study abroad and exchange programmes.
Level of Study: Professional development
Type: Grant
Value: Fulbright funding plus salary supplement and in-kind support from the host institution
Length of Study: 1 year
Frequency: Annual
Application Procedure: Candidates must submit a Fulbright visiting scholar application form and a brief project statement.

For further information contact:

Tel: (011) 4814-3561/62
Email: info@fulbright.edu.ar

Fulbright Student Awards

Purpose: To enable students working for their PhD dissertation or towards a Master's degree to carry out independent research.
Eligibility: Applications are restricted to US citizens who are proficient in spoken and written Spanish.
Level of Study: Doctorate, Postgraduate
Value: Round-trip international travel, monthly stipend and health insurance
Length of Study: 8 months
Frequency: Annual
Closing Date: October 31st

For further information contact:

US Student Programs Institute of International Education, 809 United Nations Plaza, New York, 10017-3580
Tel: (212) 984-5330
Fax: (212) 984-5325

Fulbright Teacher and Administrator Exchange Awards – Elementary & High School Administrator

Subjects: Educational Administration.
Purpose: To support US Administrators who wish to shadow an Argentine counterpart and then host a reciprocal visit of the Argentine counterpart in the US.
Eligibility: Open to both Argentine and US candidates with considerable expenses as school principals, vice principal or other high level administrative position within the education sector.
Level of Study: Professional development
Type: Grant
Length of Study: 3 weeks
Frequency: Annual
Closing Date: May 14th

For further information contact:

Fulbright Teacher Exchange Program, 600 Maryland Avenue, SW, Room 235, Washington, DC, 20024-2520, United States of America

Fulbright Teacher and Administrator Exchange Awards – Teacher Exchange Awards

Subjects: Educational administration.
Purpose: To enable US teachers to exchange jobs for one semester with Argentine colleagues.
Eligibility: Applicants must have at least 3 years of teaching experience after graduation.
Level of Study: Professional development
Type: Grant

Value: Round-trip international travel, salary supplement and health services
Length of Study: One semester
Frequency: Annual
Closing Date: October 15th

For further information contact:

Fullbright Teacher Exchange Program, 600 Maryland Avenue, SW, Room 235, Washington, DC, 20024-2520

Fulbright Teaching Assistant Awards

Purpose: To provide young English teachers of Argentina with an opportunity to work as Language Assistants at US college or universities.
Eligibility: Open to candidates with Argentine citizenship who show interest in interacting closely with the host community.
Level of Study: Professional development
Value: Roundtrip ticket, monthly stipend and health insurance
Length of Study: 9–10 months
Frequency: Annual
No. of awards offered: 15
Application Procedure: Download application form from the website.
Closing Date: November 12th

Fulbright Teaching Assistant Awards (FTA)

Purpose: To provide young Spanish teachers of the United states with an opportunity to work as language assistants at Teacher Training Colleges.
Eligibility: Open to all Humphrey fellows.
Level of Study: Postdoctorate
Type: Grant
Frequency: Annual
Country of Study: Argentina
No. of awards offered: 15–20
Application Procedure: Download application form from the website.
Closing Date: September 1st
Funding: Government
Contributor: IIE and US Department of State

Hubert H. Humphrey Fellowship Program

Purpose: To help mid-career professionals for one year of non-degree study and professional internships in the United States.
Eligibility: Open to all alumni who have been home for at least 3 years.
Level of Study: Postdoctorate, Professional development
Type: Grant
Frequency: Annual
Country of Study: United States of America
Application Procedure: Download the application form from the website.
Funding: Government

For further information contact:

Institute of International Education, 1400 K street, N.W., Suite 650, Washington, DC, 20005, United States of America
Tel: (1) (202) 326-7701
Fax: (1) (202) 326-7702

Research Grant

Purpose: To enable Argentine junior and senior scholars to conduct research in the United States.
Eligibility: Open to United States of America citizens who hold a Bachelor's degree, are writing a Master's thesis or PhD dissertation and are proficient in Spanish.
Level of Study: Doctorate, Graduate, Postdoctorate, Postgraduate, Research
Type: Research grant
Length of Study: 3 months
Frequency: Annual
Country of Study: United States of America
No. of awards offered: 15–20
Application Procedure: Applicants must complete an application form.
Funding: Government

Contributor: The United States of America and Argentine government

FULBRIGHT TEACHER EXCHANGE

600 Maryland Avenue SW, Room 320, Washington, DC, 20024, United States of America
Tel: (1) 202 314 3537
Fax: (1) 202 479 6806
Email: fulbright@grad.usda.gov
Website: www.fulbrightexchanges.org
Contact: Administrative Officer

Sponsored by the United States Department of State, the Fulbright Teacher Exchange arranges direct one-to-one classroom exchanges to over 25 countries for teachers at the elementary, secondary, 2-year and 4-year college levels. Administrators may participate in six-week seminars in eleven countries.

Fulbright Teacher Exchange

Subjects: Education and cultural exchange.
Purpose: To promote cultural understanding between peoples of other countries and the people of the United States of America through educational exchange.
Eligibility: Open to administrators and teachers of all subjects and levels from elementary through to community college. Applicants must be citizens of the United States of America, be fluent in English, have a current full-time academic position, be in at least their 3rd year of teaching and hold a Bachelor's degree.
Level of Study: Professional development
Type: Grant
Value: Varies by country
Length of Study: 6 weeks–1 year
Frequency: Annual
Study Establishment: K-12 schools and, 2-year and 4-year colleges
Country of Study: Any country
No. of awards offered: Varies
Application Procedure: Applicants must submit a basic application that includes a two-page essay, three letters of recommendation, administrative approval and a peer interview.
Closing Date: October 15th
Funding: Government
No. of awards given last year: 250
No. of applicants last year: 800

FUND FOR THEOLOGICAL EDUCATION, INC.

825 Houston Mill Road, Suite 250, Atlanta, GA, 30329, United States of America
Tel: (1) 404 727 1450
Fax: (1) 404 727 1490
Email: fte@thefund.org
Website: www.thefund.org
Contact: Ms Sharon Watson Fluker, Director

The Fund for Theological Education advocates excellence and diversity in pastoral ministry and theological scholarship. Through our initiatives, we enable gifted young people throughout the Christian community to explore and respond to God's calling in their lives. We seek to be a creative, informed catalyst for educational and faith communities in developing their own capacities to nurture men and women for vocations in ministry and teaching. We also aim to awaken the larger community to the contributions of pastoral leaders and educators who act with faith, imagination and courage to serve the common good.

Congregational Fellowship

Subjects: Religion, theology, divinity.
Purpose: To provide financial aid and mentoring support in a Master of Divinity degree programme.
Eligibility: Open to applicants aged 35 or younger and entering a Master of Divinity degree programme in the fall semester. The award is to be used for education and living expenses.
Level of Study: Postgraduate

Type: Fellowship
Value: US$2,000–5,000 (one-to-one match with contribution from student's congregation)
Frequency: Annual
Study Establishment: A school accredited by the ATS of North America
Country of Study: United States of America or Canada
No. of awards offered: 40
Application Procedure: Applicants must be nominated by their congregations, who have made a $2,000–5,000 financial commitment to educational costs and must complete and submit an application form together with supporting documentation. Forms are available from the website or by request.
Closing Date: April 1st
Funding: Private
No. of awards given last year: 40

Dissertation Fellowship for African Americans

Subjects: Religion and theology.
Purpose: To support African American students in PhD and ThD programmes in the final writing stages of their dissertation.
Eligibility: Open to African-American students in the final writing stages of their dissertation. The dissertation proposal must have been approved prior to application.
Level of Study: Doctorate
Type: Fellowship
Value: Up to US$18,000
Length of Study: 1 year, non-renewable
Frequency: Annual
Study Establishment: Graduate or theological schools
Country of Study: United States of America
No. of awards offered: Up to 10 per year
Application Procedure: Applicants must complete an application form, available from the programme office or the website.
Closing Date: February 1st
Funding: Private
Contributor: Lilly Endowment, Inc
No. of awards given last year: 7
No. of applicants last year: Varies

Doctoral Fellowship for African-Americans

Subjects: Religion and theology.
Eligibility: Open to African-American students entering the 1st year of a PhD or ThD programme and studying at an ATS (Association of Theological Schools) accredited school or in another accredited graduate programme in religion/theology.
Level of Study: Doctorate
Type: Fellowship
Value: Up to US$18,000
Length of Study: 1 year, with a possibility of renewal for a 2nd year
Frequency: Annual
Study Establishment: Graduate or theological schools
Country of Study: United States of America
No. of awards offered: Up to 10
Application Procedure: Applicants must complete an application form, available from the programme office or website.
Closing Date: March 1st
Funding: Private
Contributor: Lilly Endowment, Inc
No. of awards given last year: 11
No. of applicants last year: Varies

Ministry Fellowship

Subjects: Religion, theology and divinity.
Purpose: To provide financial aid and to enrich theological education in a Master of Divinity degree programme.
Eligibility: Open to applicants aged 35 or younger in the second year of a Master of Divinity degree programme. The award is to be used for education and living expenses, and for the design and implementation of creative projects during the Summer.
Level of Study: Postgraduate
Type: Fellowship
Value: US$10,000 plus conference attendance
Frequency: Annual

Study Establishment: A school accredited by the ATS of North America
Country of Study: United States of America or Canada
No. of awards offered: 20
Application Procedure: Applicants must be nominated by their seminary dean or president, and must complete and submit an application form together with supporting documentation. Forms are available from the website or by request.
Closing Date: March 1st
Funding: Private
No. of awards given last year: 40
No. of applicants last year: 165

North American Doctoral Fellowship

Subjects: Religion and theology.
Purpose: To support students from African American, Asian American, Hispanic American and Native American populations already in doctoral programmes leading towards completion of a PhD or ThD.
Eligibility: Open to students from targeted racial or ethnic groups at any point in their graduate programme, although preference is given to students further along in their programmes. Students must be currently enrolled in PhD or ThD programmes of religion or theology.
Level of Study: Doctorate
Type: Fellowship
Value: US$5,000–10,000
Length of Study: 1 year
Frequency: Annual
Country of Study: United States of America or Canada
No. of awards offered: 10–12 per year
Application Procedure: Applicants must complete an application form, available from the programme office or website.
Closing Date: March 1st
Funding: Private
Contributor: National Council of Churches and others
No. of awards given last year: 12
No. of applicants last year: Varies

FUNGAL RESEARCH TRUST

PO Box 482, Macclesfield, Cheshire, SK10 9AR, England
Tel: (44) 16 2550 0228
Email: secretary@fungalresearchtrust.org
Website: www.fungalresearchtrust.org
Contact: Secretary

The Fungal Research Trust is a small charity that funds small research and travel grants and the aspergillus website (www.aspergillus.man.ac.uk). The website is the most comprehensive source of data on the aspergillus fungus and the diseases it causes.

Fungal Research Trust Travel Grants

Subjects: Fungal diseases and fungi.
Purpose: To enable researchers to attend national and international fungal meetings.
Eligibility: No restrictions.
Level of Study: Doctorate, Professional development, Postdoctorate, Postgraduate, Research
Type: Travel grant
Value: UK £1,000
Length of Study: Up to 1 week
Frequency: Dependent on funds available
No. of awards offered: Up to 4
Application Procedure: Applicants must submit a letter of application.
Closing Date: Applications are considered at any time, but 3 months notice before travel is required
Funding: Commercial, private
Contributor: Numerous
No. of awards given last year: 4
No. of applicants last year: 4
Additional Information: Advertisements for other awards are placed in the *Lancet*.

THE GARDEN CLUB OF AMERICA

14 East 60th Street 3rd Floor, New York, NY, 10022, United States of America
Tel: (1) 212 753 8287
Fax: (1) 212 753 0134
Email: scholarships@gcamerica.org
Website: www.gcamerica.org

The Garden Club of America stimulates the knowledge and love of gardening, shares the advantages of association by means of educational meetings, conferences, correspondence and publications, and restores, improves and protects the quality of the environment through educational programmes and action in the fields of conservation and civic improvement.

The Anne S. Chatham Fellowship
Subjects: Medicinal botany.
Purpose: To protect and preserve knowledge about the medicinal use of plants and thus prevent the disappearance of plants with therapeutic potential.
Eligibility: Open to candidates who are currently enrolled in PhD programmes or have obtained a PhD or a graduate degree.
Level of Study: Doctorate, Postdoctorate
Type: Fellowship
Value: US$4,000
Frequency: Annual
No. of awards offered: 1
Application Procedure: Applicants must submit an application letter, an abstract, a research proposal and a curriculum vitae.
Closing Date: January 15th

For further information contact:

Missouri Botanical Garden, PO Box 299, St Louis, MO, 63166-0299, United States of America
Tel: (1) 314 577 9503
Email: james.miller@mobot.org
Contact: Dr James S Miller

GENERAL BOARD OF HIGHER EDUCATION AND MINISTRY

PO Box 340007, Nashville, TN, 37203-0007, United States of America
Tel: (1) 615 340 7388
Fax: (1) 615 340 7377
Email: bkohler@gbhem.org
Website: www@gbhem.org
Contact: Dr Robert F Kohler

The General Board of Higher Education and Ministry of the United Methodist Church prepares and assists those whose ministry in Christ is exercised through ordination, the diaconate, licencing or certification. It also provides general oversight and care for United Methodist Institutions of Higher Education and campus ministries as well as financial resources for students to attend Institutions of Higher Education through church offerings and investments.

Dempster Fellowship
Subjects: Theology.
Purpose: To increase the effectiveness of teaching in United Methodist schools of theology by assisting worthy PhD candidates who are committed to serving the church through theological education.
Eligibility: The fellowships are open only to members of the United Methodist Church who plan to teach in seminaries, or to teach one of the technological disciplines (Bible, church history, theology, ethics, and the arts of ministry) in universities or colleges. The applicant must have received the MDiv degree or its equivalent from one of the United Methodist seminaries, or be in a PhD programme or its equivalent at a university affiliated with a United Methodist seminary at the time the award is granted.
Level of Study: Doctorate
Type: Fellowship
Value: Up to US$30,000 over a 5 year period
Length of Study: 1 year, with a possibility of renewal at the discretion of the Committee on Awards

Frequency: Annual
Country of Study: Any country
No. of awards offered: 5
Application Procedure: Applicants must submit a completed application form, transcripts of all previous academic work, letters of reference, a term or other paper of essay length, Graduate Record Examination scores, summary statement of academic plans and a curriculum vitae. Further information is available on request.
Closing Date: October 15th
Funding: Private
Contributor: The United Methodist Church
No. of awards given last year: 5
No. of applicants last year: 20

GEOLOGICAL SOCIETY OF AMERICA (GSA)

3300 Penrose Place, PO Box 9140, Boulder, CO 80301-9140, United States of America
Tel: (1) 303 447 2020
Fax: (1) 303 357 1070
Email: awards@geosociety.org
Website: www.geosociety.org
Contact: Ms Diane C Lorenz, Program Officer, Grants, Awards, and Recognition

Established in 1888, the GSA is a non-profit organization dedicated to the advancement of the science of geology. GSA membership is for the generalist and the specialist in the field of geology and offers something for everyone.

Alexander & Geraldine Wanek Fund
Subjects: Earth and geological sciences.
Purpose: To support research projects.
Eligibility: Open to GSA members.
Level of Study: Research
Type: Funding support
Value: $3,300
Frequency: Annual
Closing Date: February 1st
No. of awards given last year: 2

Alexander Sisson Award
Subjects: Geology.
Purpose: To support research.
Eligibility: Open to candidates who wish to pursue studies in Alaska and the Caribbean.
Type: Award
Value: $2400
Frequency: Annual
Application Procedure: Applications are available online.
Closing Date: February 1st
Contributor: Geological Society of America
No. of awards given last year: 1

Bruce L. "Biff" Reed Award
Subjects: Geology.
Purpose: To support students pursuing geologic research.
Eligibility: Open to candidates who are enrolled in a US, Canadian, Mexican or Central American university or college.
Type: Award
Value: Minimum award amount: $500. Maximum award amount: $2000
Frequency: Annual
Application Procedure: For further details contact the Program Officer-Grants, Awards and Recognition.
Closing Date: February 1st
Funding: Private
No. of awards given last year: 1

Charles A. & June R.P. Ross Research Fund
Subjects: Biostratigraphy.
Purpose: To support research projects.
Eligibility: Open to GSA members.

Level of Study: Postgraduate
Type: Funding support
Value: $1,300
Frequency: Annual
Application Procedure: Applications available online.
Closing Date: February 1st

Claude C. Albritton, Jr. Scholarships

Subjects: Earth science and archaeology.
Purpose: To encourage students who want to pursue higher studies in the field of Earth science and archaeology.
Level of Study: Postgraduate
Type: Scholarship
Length of Study: Minimum award amount - $500. Maximum award amount - $1000
Frequency: Annual
Closing Date: March 1st
Funding: Foundation
Contributor: GSA foundation

For further information contact:

Institute for Applied Sciences, PO Box 13078, University of North Texas, Denton, TX 76203
Contact: Reid Feming

Gladys W Cole Memorial Research Award

Subjects: Investigation of the geomorphology of semi-arid and arid terrain in the United States of America and Mexico.
Purpose: To provide financial support for research.
Eligibility: Open to GSA members or Fellows aged 30–65 who have published one or more significant papers on geomorphology. Funds cannot be used to pay for work already accomplished, but previous recipients may reapply if additional support is needed to complete their work. All qualified applicants are urged to apply.
Level of Study: Postdoctorate
Type: Research grant
Value: US$9,900
Frequency: Annual
Country of Study: Other
No. of awards offered: 1
Application Procedure: Applicants must complete an application form available from the website.
Closing Date: February 1st
Funding: Private
Contributor: Dr W Storrs Cole
No. of awards given last year: 1

Gretchen L. Blechschmidt Award

Subjects: Geological sciences.
Purpose: To support research by women interested in achieving a PhD.
Eligibility: Open to all women candidates who are GSA members and wish to achieve a PhD.
Level of Study: Postdoctorate, Postgraduate, Research
Type: Award
Value: $1,300
Frequency: Annual
Application Procedure: For additional information contact: Program Officer Grants, Awards and Recognition.
Closing Date: February 1st

GSA Research Grants

Subjects: Earth science.
Purpose: To provide partial support for Master's and doctoral thesis research.
Eligibility: Open to students attending colleges and universities within the United States of America, Canada, Mexico and Central America. Applicants must be members of the GSA in order to apply.
Level of Study: Postgraduate, Research
Type: Research grant
Value: There are no set limits
Length of Study: 1 year, renewable
Frequency: Annual
Country of Study: Other
No. of awards offered: Varies

Application Procedure: Applicants must complete current application forms.
Closing Date: February 1st
Funding: Government, private
Contributor: GSA's Penrose and Pardee endowments, the National Science Foundation, industry, individual GSA members through the GEOSTAR and Research Grants funds, and numerous dedicated research funds that have been endowed at the GSA Foundation by members
No. of awards given last year: 251
No. of applicants last year: 571
Additional Information: Grants are awarded on the basis of the scientific merits of the problem, the capability of the investigator and the feasibility of the budget, and as an aid to a research project, not to sustain the entire cost. Students may receive the award once at the Master's level and once at the PhD level.

Harold T. Stearns Fellowship Award

Subjects: Geology of Pacific Island and the circum-pacific region.
Purpose: To support research projects.
Eligibility: Open to GSA members.
Level of Study: Research
Type: Award
Value: Minimum no. of awards: 1. Maximum no. of awards: 4. Minimum award amount: $500. Maximum award amount: $3000
Frequency: Annual
Application Procedure: For more information contact the Program Officer-Grants, Awards and Recognition.
Closing Date: February 1st
No. of awards given last year: 3 scholarship(s), totalling $3,000.

History of Geology Student Award

Subjects: Geology.
Purpose: To award best proposals for a history of Geology paper.
Eligibility: Open to applicants who are enrolled in a US, Canadian, Mexican or Central American university or college.
Level of Study: Research
Type: Grant
Value: $500
Frequency: Annual
Application Procedure: Applications available online.
Closing Date: February 1st

J. Hoover Mackin and Arthur D. Howard Research Grants

Subjects: Quaternary geology/geomorphology.
Purpose: To support outstanding student research.
Eligibility: Applicants must be GSA members.
Level of Study: Research
Type: Grant
Value: upto $2,500
Frequency: Annual
No. of awards offered: 1–2
Application Procedure: Application forms are available online.
Closing Date: February 1st

John Montagne Fund

Subjects: Geomorphology.
Purpose: To support research.
Eligibility: Open to GSA members.
Type: Award
Frequency: Annual
Application Procedure: Applications are available online.
Closing Date: February 1st
Funding: Private

John T. Dillon Alaska Research Award

Subjects: Earth science.
Purpose: To support research on earth science problems.
Eligibility: Open to applicants who are GSA members.
Level of Study: Research
Type: Award
Frequency: Annual
Closing Date: February 1st

Lipman Research Award

Subjects: Volcanology and Petrology.
Purpose: To promote and support graduate research.
Eligibility: Open to applicants who are GSA members.
Level of Study: Research
Type: Award
Frequency: Annual
Application Procedure: Contact the Program officer for further information.
Closing Date: February 1st
Funding: Private

Parke D. Snavely, Jr. Cascadia Research Award Fund

Subjects: Geology.
Purpose: To support field-oriented graduate student research.
Eligibility: Open to applicants enrolled in a US, Canadian, Mexican or Central American university or college.
Level of Study: Research
Type: Award
Frequency: Annual
Application Procedure: For more information contact: Program Officer-Grants, Awards and Recognition.
Closing Date: February 1st

Robert K. Fahnestock Memorial Award

Subjects: Earth and geological science.
Purpose: To award applicants with the best application in the field of sediment transport.
Eligibility: Applicants must be enrolled in a US, Canadian, Mexican or Central American university or college and must be GSA members.
Level of Study: Research
Type: Award
Value: Minimum award amount: $500. Maximum award amount: $2000
Frequency: Annual
Application Procedure: For more details contact the Program Officer-Grants, Awards and Recognition.
Closing Date: February 1st
No. of awards given last year: 1 grant(s), totalling $1,500.

Roy J. Shlemon Scholarship Awards

Subjects: Engineering geology.
Purpose: To award best research proposals.
Eligibility: Open to student members of the Engineering Geology Division.
Level of Study: Doctorate, Research
Type: Scholarship
Value: US$1,000 stipend and US$500 allowance
Frequency: Annual
No. of awards offered: 4
Application Procedure: Application forms are available online.
Closing Date: March 15th
Additional Information: The scholarship award committee strongly encouraged women, minorities and persons with disabilities to participate in this programme.

For further information contact:

13376 Azores Avenue, Sylmar, CA 91342
Contact: Robert A. Larson

S.E. Dwornik Student Paper Awards

Subjects: Planetary geology.
Purpose: To encourage students to become involved with NASA and planetary science.
Eligibility: Open to all American students interested in planetary science.
Level of Study: Postgraduate
Type: Award
Value: US$500
Frequency: Annual
Application Procedure: Students must submit abstract of the paper along with the application form.
No. of awards given last year: 2 prize(s), totalling $1,000.

W Storrs Cole Memorial Research Award

Subjects: Invertebrate micropalaeontology.
Purpose: To support research into invertebrate micropalaeontology.
Eligibility: Open to GSA members or Fellows aged 30–65 who have published one or more significant papers on micropalaeontology. Funds cannot be used for work already accomplished but recipients of previous awards may reapply if additional support is needed to complete their work. All qualified applicants are urged to apply.
Level of Study: Postdoctorate
Type: Research grant
Value: US$9,100
Frequency: Annual
Application Procedure: Applicants must write for further details and an application form or visit the website.
Closing Date: February 1st
Funding: Private
Contributor: Dr W Storrs Cole
No. of awards given last year: 1

GEORGE WALFORD INTERNATIONAL ESSAY PRIZE (GWIEP)

Flat 143, 6 Slington House, Rankine Road, Basingstoke, London, RG24 8PH, United Kingdom
Email: richenda@gwiep.net
Website: www.gwiep.net
Contact: Ms Richenda Walford, Trustee

The George Walford International Essay Prize (GWIEP) is a registered charity that awards a cash prize each year to the winner of an essay on the subject of systematic ideology.

George Walford International Essay Prize (GWIEP)

Subjects: Any subject.
Purpose: To award a prize to the best essay on systematic ideology.
Eligibility: Everyone is eligible, with the exception of the trustees and judges themselves. There are no bars regarding age, race, nationality or gender.
Level of Study: Unrestricted
Type: Prize
Value: UK £3,500
Length of Study: Varies
Frequency: Annual
Country of Study: Any country
No. of awards offered: 1
Application Procedure: Applicants must contact GWIEP for details. Information can be requested by mail though communication via email and the website is greatly preferred.
Closing Date: May 31st
Funding: Private
Contributor: The family of the late George Walford
No. of awards given last year: 1
Additional Information: For more information about the prize and systematic ideology, please visit the website.

GEORGIA LIBRARY ASSOCIATION (GLA)

PO Box 793, Rex, Georgia, GA 30273, United States of America
Tel: (1) 678 466 4325
Fax: (1) 404 413 7761
Email: bpetersohn@gsu.edu
Website: gla.georgialibraries.org
Contact: Scholarship Committee Chair

The Georgia Library Association's (GLA) mission is to provide an understanding of the place that libraries should take in advancing the educational, cultural and economic life of the state, to promote the expansion and improvement of library service and to stimulate activities toward these ends.

Beard Scholarship

Subjects: Library science.
Purpose: To recruit excellent librarians for Georgia and provide financial assistance toward completing a degree in library science, for

candidates who show strong potential to inspire and motivate their peers in the profession and in professional associations.

Eligibility: Open to United States citizens accepted for admission to a Master's programme at an American Library Association (ALA) accredited library school, who intend to complete the course of study within 2 years.

Level of Study: Postgraduate

Type: Scholarship

Value: US$1,000, paid in equal instalments at the beginning of each term, semester or quarter

Length of Study: 2 years

Frequency: Annual

Study Establishment: An ALA accredited school

Country of Study: United States of America

No. of awards offered: 1

Application Procedure: Applicants must submit an official form of application, proof of acceptance in an accredited library school and official transcripts of all academic work sent directly from each institution of higher education. Three letters of reference must also be sent directly from the referee.

Closing Date: May 21st

Additional Information: The Scholar is required to work in a library or library-related capacity in Georgia for 1 year following completion of the programme, or agree to pay back a pro-rated amount of the scholarship plus interest within a 2 year period.

Hubbard Scholarship

Subjects: Library science.

Purpose: To recruit excellent librarians for Georgia and provide financial assistance toward completing a degree in library science.

Eligibility: Open to United States citizens accepted for admission to a Master's programme at an American Library Association (ALA) accredited library school, who intend to complete the course of study within 2 years.

Level of Study: Postgraduate

Type: Scholarship

Value: US$3,000, paid in equal instalments at the beginning of each term, semester or quarter

Length of Study: 2 years

Frequency: Annual

Study Establishment: An ALA accredited school

Country of Study: United States of America

No. of awards offered: 1

Application Procedure: Applicants must submit an official form of application, proof of acceptance in an accredited library school and official transcripts of all academic work sent directly from each institution of higher education. Three letters of reference must also be sent directly from the referee.

Closing Date: May 21st

Additional Information: The Scholar is required to work in a library or library related capacity in Georgia for 1 year following completion of the programme, or agree to pay back a pro-rated amount of the scholarship plus interest within a 2 year period.

THE GERALDINE R. DODGE FOUNDATION

163 Madison Avenue, Post Office Box 1239, Morris town, NJ 07962-12 39, United States of America

Tel: (1) 973 540 8442

Fax: (1) 973 540 1211

Email: info@grdodge.org

Website: www.grdodge.org

The Geraldine R. Dodge Foundation was established in 1974 with funds from the will of Geraldine Rockefeller Dodge. The mission of the foundation is to support and encourage those educational, cultural, social and environmental values that contribute to making our society more humane and our world more livable.

Dodge Foundation Frontiers for Veterinary Medicine Fellowships

Subjects: Veterinary medicine.

Purpose: To provide opportunities to veterinary students to explore and bring new problem-solving perspectives to animal-related issues.

Eligibility: Open to candidates who are enrolled as full-time veterinary students at a US or Canadian college of Veterinary medicine.

Level of Study: Postgraduate

Type: Fellowship

Length of Study: US$7,000

Frequency: Annual

Study Establishment: Any American Veterinary Medical Association accredited college of veterinary medicine

Country of Study: United States of America or Canada

Application Procedure: Check website for details

Closing Date: December 16th

For further information contact:

Contact: Michelle Knapik, Director for Environmental and Welfare of Animals

Dodge Foundation Teacher Fellowships

Subjects: Teacher training.

Purpose: To enable teachers to grow as educational leaders to better impact their scholars and communities.

Eligibility: Open to K-12 full-time teachers who are employed in New Jersey public and public charter schools in Camden Country, New Jersey.

Level of Study: Postgraduate

Type: Fellowship

Value: US$2,000–7,500 for individuals, and between US$5,000 and 10,000 for teams

Frequency: Annual

Country of Study: United States of America

Application Procedure: Application form and details available on the website.

Closing Date: January 12th

Funding: Foundation

Dodge Foundation Visual Arts Initiative

Subjects: Visual art.

Purpose: To provide a unique professional infrastructure and sprinted network for the artist/educator.

Eligibility: Open to candidates who have taught the visual arts for at least 3 years and will be continuing as visual arts teachers.

Level of Study: Professional development

Type: Grant

Value: US$5,000 plus US$2,000 for visual arts project

Frequency: Annual

Country of Study: United States of America

No. of awards offered: 20

Application Procedure: Check website for details

Closing Date: January 31st

Funding: Foundation

For further information contact:

Tel: 973 540 8443, ext. 118

Email: erastocky@grdodge.org

Contact: Elaine Rastocky

GERMAN ACADEMIC EXCHANGE SERVICE (DAAD)

New York Office, 871 United Nations Plaza, New York, NY, 10017, United States of America

Tel: (1) 212 758 3223

Fax: (1) 212 755 5780

Email: daadny@daad.org/ kim@daad.org

Website: www.daad.org

The German Academic Exchange Service (DAAD) is the German national agency for the support of international academic cooperation. It offers programmes and funding for students, faculty, researchers and others in higher education, providing financial support to over 55,000 individuals per year.

DAAD Research Grant

Subjects: All subjects.

Purpose: To provide opportunities to students to study and research in Germany.
Eligibility: Open to citizens of Canada and the United States who have obtained a graduate, Master's, Doctoral or postdoctoral degree.
Level of Study: Research
Type: Grant
Value: Approx €1,000 per month
Length of Study: 1 to 10 months
Frequency: Annual
Country of Study: Germany
Application Procedure: Applicants must download the application form from the website. The completed application form along with a curriculum vitae, research proposal and 2 letters of recommendation must be submitted.
Closing Date: November 15th
Funding: Government

GERMAN HISTORICAL INSTITUTE

1607 New Hampshire Avenue North West, Washington, DC, 20009, United States of America
Tel: (1) 202 387 3355
Fax: (1) 202 483 3430
Email: fellowships@ghi-dc.org
Website: www.ghi-dc.org
Contact: Philipp Gassert, Deputy Director

The German Historical Institute is an independent research institute dedicated to the promotion of historical research in the Federal Republic of Germany and the United States of America. The Institute supports and advises German and American historians and political scientists and encourages co-operation between them. It is part of the foundation Deutsche Geisteswissenschaftliche Institute im Ausland (DGIA).

Fritz Stern Dissertation Prize

Subjects: German history, history of Germans in North America, German-American relations.
Purpose: To award the two best doctoral dissertations submitted on German history, German-American relations or the history of Germans in North America. The winners are invited to the GHI to present their research at the annual symposium of the Friends, each November. Candidates are nominated by their dissertation advisers at a North American university during the previous academic year.
Eligibility: Open to PhDs from the United States of America.
Level of Study: Doctorate
Type: Prize
Value: US$2,000 and reimbursement for the travel to Washington DC
Frequency: Annual
Country of Study: United States of America
No. of awards offered: 2
Application Procedure: Applicants must refer to the website for further information.
Closing Date: May 1st
Funding: Private
Contributor: Friends of the German Historical Institute
No. of awards given last year: 2

German Historical Institute Doctoral and Postdoctoral Fellowships

Subjects: Humanities and social sciences, comparative studies in social, cultural and political history, studies of German-American relations and transatlantic studies.
Purpose: To give support to German and United States of America doctoral and postdoctoral students working on topics related to the Institute's general scope of interest.
Eligibility: Open to German and United States of America doctoral students. Applications from women and minorities are especially encouraged.
Level of Study: Postdoctorate, Doctorate
Type: Fellowship
Value: €1,600 for doctoral students; €2,800 for postdoctoral students
Length of Study: Up to 6 months
Frequency: Twice per year
Country of Study: United States of America

No. of awards offered: Open
Application Procedure: Applicants must refer to the website for details.
Closing Date: May 20th and October 15th
Funding: Government
No. of awards given last year: 20
No. of applicants last year: 75
Additional Information: All candidates are expected to evaluate source material in the United States of America that is important for their research. At the end of the scholarship they are required to report on their findings or give a presentation at the GHI.

German Historical Institute Summer Seminar in Germany

Subjects: German handwriting, German archives, German history and transatlantic studies.
Purpose: To introduce students to German handwriting of previous centuries by exposing them to a variety of German archives, familiarizing them with major research topics in German culture and history and encouraging the exchange of ideas among the next generation of United States of America scholars.
Eligibility: Open to United States of America doctoral students. Applications from women and minorities are especially encouraged.
Level of Study: Doctorate
Type: Scholarship
Value: US$2,500
Length of Study: 2 weeks
Frequency: Annual
Country of Study: Germany
Application Procedure: Applicants must refer to the website for details.
Closing Date: December 31st
Funding: Government
No. of awards given last year: 13

German Historical Institute Transatlantic Doctoral Seminar in German History

Subjects: German history and transatlantic studies.
Purpose: To bring together young scholars from Germany and the United States of America who are nearing completion of their doctoral degrees. It provides an opportunity to debate doctoral projects in a transatlantic setting.
Eligibility: Open to German and United States of America doctoral students. Applications from women and minorities are especially encouraged.
Level of Study: Doctorate
Type: Scholarship
Value: US$2,000
Length of Study: 4 days
Frequency: Annual
Country of Study: Other
Application Procedure: Applicants must refer to the website for details.
Closing Date: December 1st
Funding: Government
No. of awards given last year: 16

Kade-Heideking Fellowship

Subjects: American history, German history in the 20th century, comparative international history, German-American relations.
Purpose: To support a German doctoral student working in one of the three areas to which the late Professor Jürgen Heideking made significant contributions: American history and German-American relations from the early modern period to the present; international history of the 19th and 20th centuries, including the history of international relations and the comparative history of colonial systems and societies; and 20th-century German history, with an emphasis on the United States of America's influence on German society between 1918 and 1949.
Eligibility: Open to German doctoral students only.
Level of Study: Doctorate
Type: Fellowship
Value: US$30,000
Length of Study: 1 year
Frequency: Annual
Country of Study: United States of America

No. of awards offered: 1
Application Procedure: Applicants must refer to the website for details.
Closing Date: November 15th
Funding: Private
Contributor: Annette Kade Charitable Trust Fund
No. of awards given last year: 1

Medieval History Seminar

Subjects: Medieval history.
Purpose: The Medieval History Seminar is devoted to the latest research in the field of European medieval studies. Similar to the Transatlantic Doctoral Seminar, this programme invites 16 doctoral students from Europe and North America to discuss their dissertation projects with peers and senior scholars from both sides of the Atlantic.
Eligibility: Open to citizens of North America and Europe.
Level of Study: Doctorate
Type: Grant
Value: US$2,000
Length of Study: 4 days
Frequency: Every 2 years
Country of Study: Germany
No. of awards offered: 16
Application Procedure: Applicants must refer to the website for details.
Closing Date: May 1st
Funding: Government
No. of awards given last year: 16

Thyssen-Heideking Fellowship

Subjects: American history, German history in the 20th century, comparative international history, German-American relations.
Purpose: To support American scholars working in one of the three areas to which the late Professor Jürgen Heideking made important contributions: American history and German-American relations from the early modern period to the present; international history of the 19th and 20th centuries, including the history of international relations and the comparative history of colonial systems and societies; and 20th-century German history, with emphasis on America's influence on German society between 1918 and 1949.
Eligibility: Open to American scholars only.
Level of Study: Postdoctorate
Type: Fellowship
Value: €25,000
Length of Study: 6 months–1 year
Frequency: Annual
Country of Study: Germany
No. of awards offered: 1
Application Procedure: Applicants must refer to the website for details.
Closing Date: November 15th
Funding: Private
Contributor: Fritz Thyssen Foundation
No. of awards given last year: 1

Young Scholars Forum

Subjects: Humanities and social sciences, comparative studies in social cultural and political history, studies of German-American relations, German history, European history.
Purpose: To gather together PhD candidates and recent PhD recipients from the United States of America and Europe who work in the fields of German, German-American or European history and to give them the opportunity to present their work to peers and distinguished academics from both sides of the Atlantic.
Eligibility: Open to applicants from the United States of America and Europe, and Germans in particular.
Level of Study: Doctorate, Postdoctorate
Type: Grant
Value: US$2,000
Length of Study: 3 days
Frequency: Annual
Country of Study: United States of America
Application Procedure: Applicants must refer to the website for details.
Closing Date: January 10th

Funding: Government
No. of awards given last year: 15

GERMAN ISRAELI FOUNDATION FOR SCIENTIFIC RESEARCH AND DEVELOPMENT

GSF Forschungszentrum, Neuherberg, PO Box 1129, D-85758, Oberschleissheim, Germany
Tel: (49) 89 3187 3106
Fax: (49) 89 3187 3365
Email: gif.stepper@gsf.de
Website: www.gifres.org.il
Contact: GIF Verbindungsbuero

German Israeli Foundation Young Scientist's Programme

Subjects: Natural sciences, social sciences and humanities.
Purpose: This new initiative aims to encourage young German and Israeli scientists to establish initial contacts with potential counterparts in Israel or Germany. An integral part of the programme will be a visit of at least 2–3 weeks to Germany or Israel, to give a presentation of their research activities and results and to meet possible partners for future co-operation.
Eligibility: Scientists below 40 years, within the first 7 years after receiving their PhD, MD or equivalent degree, and recognized staff members of a GIF-eligible institution with legal status are eligible to apply.
Level of Study: Research
Type: Grant
Value: Up to €40,000 for the 1-year programme, for project-related equipment, disposable materials, computer services, auxiliary personnel, foreign travel, reports and publications
Length of Study: 1 year
Study Establishment: Any GIF-eligible institution
Country of Study: Germany and Israel
Application Procedure: Application forms are available on request.
Closing Date: Application deadlines vary. For details see www.gifres.org.il

Research Grant (GIF)

Subjects: Natural sciences, social sciences and humanities.
Purpose: To promote doctoral studies as well as basic and applied research projects within the framework of co-operative research programmes.
Eligibility: GIF projects must involve active collaboration between Israeli and German scientists. Special consideration will be given to young scientists, partners applying for the first time, scientists from the former East Germany and new immigrants to Israel from the former Soviet Union. Scientists applying for grants must be recognized staff members of a GIF-eligible institution with legal status. The principal investigators must hold a doctoral degree or equivalent at the time of application.
Level of Study: Doctorate, Research
Type: Grant
Value: €225,000–600,000 per project
Length of Study: 3 years
Study Establishment: Any GIF-eligible institution
Country of Study: Germany and Israel
Application Procedure: Doctoral candidates can apply to the GIF project co-ordinators, either in Germany or Israel, to pursue their doctoral research within the framework of the co-operative research project.
Closing Date: Application deadlines vary. For details see website
Contributor: German Israeli Foundation for Scientific Research and Development
Additional Information: The joint research programme must be presented as a single, co-ordinated proposal in which the roles and tasks of both groups are clearly defined. If institutional academic regulations permit the granting of fellowships, the GIF may support a fellowship for tasks within the research plan.

GERMAN MARSHALL FUND OF THE UNITED STATES (GMF)

1744 R Street NW, Washington, DC 20009, United States of America
Tel: (1) 202 745 3950
Fax: (1) 202 265 1662
Email: info@gmfus.org
Website: www.gmfus.org
Contact: Lea Rosenbohm, Administrative Assistant

The German Marshall Fund of the United States (GMF) is an American institution that stimulates the exchange of ideas and promotes cooperation between the United States and Europe in the spirit of the post war Marshall Plan. GMF was created in 1972 by a gift from Germany as a permanent memorial to Marshall Plan Aid.

GMF Journalism Fellowships

Subjects: Journalism.
Purpose: To contribute to better reporting on transatlantic issues by both American and European journalist.
Eligibility: Open to American and European journalists who have an outstanding record in reporting on foreign affairs.
Level of Study: Postdoctorate, Professional development
Type: Fellowship
Value: US$2,000–25,000 and funds for travel
Frequency: Annual
Application Procedure: Applicants including a description of the proposed project, current resume and samples of previous work must be sent.
Funding: Foundation
Contributor: The German Marshall Fund

For further information contact:

Email: usoyez@gmfus.org
Contact: Ursula Soyez

Manfred Wörner Seminar

Purpose: To provide an opportunity to broaden professional networks.
Level of Study: Professional development
Value: Travel, accommodation and meals
Length of Study: 10 days
Frequency: Annual
Country of Study: Germany
No. of awards offered: 30
Closing Date: January 23rd
Funding: Government
Contributor: The German Government

For further information contact:

Email: nhagen@gmfus.org
Website: www.gmfus.org/fellowships/manfred.cfm
Contact: Nicola Hagen, Program assistant

Marshall Memorial Fellowship

Subjects: Politics, government business, media and non-profit sector committed to strengthening the transatlantic relationship.
Purpose: To provide opportunities for emerging leaders from the United States and Europe to explore societies, institutions and people from the other side of the Atlantic.
Eligibility: Open to candidates who are citizens or permanent residents of one of the 15MMF countries.
Level of Study: Postdoctorate
Length of Study: 3–4 weeks
Frequency: Annual
Application Procedure: Candidates are required to submit a written application and undergo an interview in person.
Closing Date: Varies
Contributor: German Marshall Fund

For further information contact:

Website: www.gmfus.org/fellowships/mmf.cfm

Peter R. Weitz Journalism Prize

Subjects: Journalism.

Purpose: To acknowledge outstanding coverage of transatlantic and European issues by American media.
Eligibility: The senior prize is open to all journalists covering European issues and the young journalist prize is open to American journalists under 35 years of age.
Type: Award
Value: Senior prize worth US$10,000 and junior prize US$5,000
Frequency: Annual
Application Procedure: A completed application form must be submitted.
Closing Date: February 29th
Funding: Foundation
Contributor: The German Marshall Fund

Transatlantic Community Foundation Fellowship

Subjects: International relations.
Purpose: To create strengthen networks of people and share international expenses.
Eligibility: Open to staff of American and European community foundation.
Level of Study: Postdoctorate, Professional development
Value: Roundtrip airfare, a daily stipend and reimbursement for car rental expenses as needed
Frequency: Annual
No. of awards offered: 10
Funding: Foundation
Contributor: Charles Stewart Mott Foundation

For further information contact:

Website: www.gmfus.org/fellowships/tcff.cfm

Transatlantic Fellows Program

Subjects: Foreign policy, international security, trade and economic development, immigration and other topics important to transatlantic cooperation.
Purpose: To build important networks of policymakers analysts in the Euro-Atlantic community.
Eligibility: Open to senior policy-practitioners, journalists businesspeople and academics.
Level of Study: Postdoctorate
Frequency: Annual

For further information contact:

Website: www.gmfus.org/fellowships/taf.cfm

GERMAN STUDIES ASSOCIATION

Kalamazoo College 1200 Academy Street, Kalamazoo, MI, 49006-3295, United States of America
Tel: (1) 269-337-7364
Fax: (1) 269-337-7251
Email: director@thegsa.org
Website: www.g-s-a.org
Contact: Gerald R. Kleinfeld, Exectuive Director

The German Studies Association (GSA) is a non-profit educational organization that promotes the research and study of Germany, Austria and Switzerland. The GSA Endowment Fund provides financial support to Association projects, the annual conference, and general operations.

Berlin Program Fellowship

Subjects: Modern and contemporary German and European affairs.
Purpose: To support doctoral dissertation research as well as postdoctoral research leading to the completion of a monograph.
Eligibility: Applicants for a dissertation fellowship must be full-time graduate students who have completed all coursework required for the PhD and must have achieved ABD status by the time the proposed research stay in Berlin begins. Also eligible are United States of America and Canadian PhDs who have received their doctorates within the past 2 calendar years.
Level of Study: Doctorate, Postdoctorate
Type: Fellowship
Value: €1,100 per month for dissertation fellows, €1,400 per month for postdoctoral fellows

Length of Study: 10–12 months
Frequency: Annual
Study Establishment: Freie Universität Berlin
Country of Study: Germany
No. of awards offered: 12
Application Procedure: Applicants must submit a single application packet consisting of completed application forms, a proposal, three letters of reference, language evaluation(s) and graduate school transcripts. Proposals should be no longer than 2,500 words or 10 pages, followed by a one- or two-page bibliography or bibliographic essay.
Closing Date: December 1st
Contributor: Halle Foundation and the National Endowment for the Humanities

For further information contact:

Berlin Program for Advanced German and European Studies, Freie Universität Berlin, Garystrasse 45, D-14195, Berlin, Germany
Tel: (49) 30 838 56671
Fax: (49) 30 838 56672
Email: bprogram@zedat.fu-berlin.de
Website: www.userpage.fu-berlin.de/~bprogram

THE GETTY FOUNDATION

1200 Getty Center Drive, Suite 800, Los Angeles, CA, 90049-1685, United States of America
Tel: (1) 310 440 7320
Fax: (1) 310 440 7703
Email: researchgrants@getty.edu
Website: www.getty.edu/grants
Contact: Grants Administration

The J Paul Getty Trust is a privately operating foundation dedicated to the visual arts and the humanities. The Getty supports a wide range of projects that promote research in fields related to the history of art, the advancement of the understanding of art and the conservation of cultural heritage.

The Conservation Guest Scholar Program
Subjects: All subjects.
Purpose: To supports new ideas and perspectives in the field of conservation, with an emphasis on the visual arts and to provide an opportunity for professionals to pursue scholarly research in an interdisciplinary manner.
Eligibility: Open to established conservators, scientists, and professionals who have attained distinction in conservation and allied fields.
Level of Study: Research
Type: Grant
Value: US $3,500–31,500
Application Procedure: Applications are available for viewing and printing in Portable Document Format (PDF) or by contacting the Getty Grant Program office.
Closing Date: November 1st

The Getty Foundation Collaborative Research Grants
Subjects: History of art and related fields.
Purpose: To provide opportunities for teams of scholars to collaborate on interpretative research projects that offer new explanations of art and its history.
Eligibility: Collaborative Research Grant teams must consist of two or more art historians, or of an art historian and one or more scholars from other disciplines. Funding is also available for the research and planning of scholarly exhibitions. Teams for these projects must include scholars from both museums and universities.
Level of Study: Postgraduate, Professional development, Postdoctorate
Type: Research grant
Value: Varies according to the needs of the project
Length of Study: 1–2 years
Frequency: Annual
Country of Study: Any country
No. of awards offered: Varies
Application Procedure: Applicants must complete an application form. Additional information, detailed guidelines and application forms

are available from the website or by contacting the Getty Grant Program Office.
Closing Date: November 1st
Funding: Private
Additional Information: Further information is available on request.

The Getty Foundation Curatorial Research Fellowships
Subjects: History of art and related fields.
Purpose: To support the professional scholarly development of curators by providing them with time off from regular museum duties to undertake short-term research or study projects.
Eligibility: Open to full-time curators who have a minimum of 3 years of professional experience and are employed at museums with art collections.
Level of Study: Professional development
Type: Fellowship
Value: Up to US$3,500 per month toward salary replacement and travel expenses of up to $5,000 for a three-month period
Length of Study: 1–3 months
Frequency: Annual
Country of Study: Any country
No. of awards offered: Varies
Application Procedure: Applicants must complete an application form. Additional information, detailed guidelines and application forms are available from the website or by contacting the Getty Grant Program Office.
Closing Date: November 1st
Funding: Private
Additional Information: Further information is available on request.

The Getty Foundation Postdoctoral Fellowships
Subjects: History of art or related fields.
Purpose: To provide support for outstanding scholars in the early stages of their careers to pursue interpretative research projects that make a substantial and original contribution to the understanding of art and its history.
Eligibility: Open to scholars of all nationalities who have earned a doctoral degree within the past 6 years.
Level of Study: Postdoctorate
Type: Fellowship
Value: US$22,000
Length of Study: 1 year
Frequency: Annual
Country of Study: Any country
Application Procedure: Applicants must complete an application form. Additional information, detailed guidelines and application forms are available from the website or by contacting the Getty Grant Program Office.
Closing Date: November 1st
Funding: Private
Additional Information: Further information is available on request.

Graduate Internships
Subjects: Curatorial, education, conservation, research, information management, public programs, and grant making.
Purpose: To support full-time positions for students who intend to pursue careers in fields related to the visual arts.
Eligibility: Open to applicants of all nationalities who have currently enrolled in a graduate program leading to an advanced degree in a field relevant to the internship(s).
Type: Scholarship
Value: US$17,400 for 8 months; US$26,000 for 12 months
Length of Study: 8 months and 12 months
Application Procedure: Applications are available for viewing and printing in Portable Document Format (PDF) or by contacting the Getty Grant Program office.
Closing Date: December 15th
Additional Information: Students whose degrees were conferred prior to January 1, 2005 are not eligible.

Library Research Grants
Subjects: All subjects.
Purpose: To provide partial, short-term support for costs relating to travel and living expenses to scholars.

Eligibility: Open to scholars of all nationalities and at any level who demonstrate a compelling need to use materials housed in the research library, and whose place of residence is more than 80 miles from the Getty Center.
Type: Research grant
Value: US$500 up to US$2,500
Study Establishment: Getty Research Institute
Application Procedure: Applications are available for viewing and printing in Portable Document Format (PDF) or by contacting the Getty Grant Program office.
Closing Date: November 1st
Additional Information: Projects must relate to specific items in the library collection.

Postdoctoral Fellowships in Conservation Science
Subjects: Chemistry or physical sciences.
Purpose: To provide recent PhDs in chemistry or the physical sciences with experience in the GCI's Museum Research Laboratory.
Eligibility: Open to scientists of all nationalities who are interested in pursuing a career in conservation science and have received a PhD in chemistry/physical science and have excellent written and oral communication skills.
Level of Study: Research
Type: Fellowship
Value: US $29,300 per year
Length of Study: 2 years
Application Procedure: Applications are available for viewing and printing in Portable Document Format (PDF) or by contacting the Getty Grant Program office.
Closing Date: November 1st
Additional Information: The successful candidate will have a record of scientific accomplishment combined with a strong interest in the visual arts.

Research Grants for Getty Scholars and Visiting Scholars
Subjects: Arts, humanities, or social sciences.
Purpose: To provide a unique research experience.
Eligibility: Open to established scholars, artists, or writers of all nationalities who have attained distinction in their fields and also for those who are working in the arts, humanities, or social sciences.
Level of Study: Research
Type: Scholarship
Value: US$75,000 (For Scholars); US$3,500 (For Visiting Scholars)
Application Procedure: Applications are available for viewing and printing in Portable Document Format (PDF) or by contacting the Getty Grant Program office.
Closing Date: November 1st
Contributor: Getty Research Institute
Additional Information: Applicants will be notified of the Research Institute's decision by the Spring.

Residential Grants at the Getty Center and Getty Villa
Subjects: Arts and humanities.
Purpose: To provide support for established scholars to undertake research related to a specific theme while in residence at the Getty Center and Getty Villa in Los Angeles.
Eligibility: Open to established scholars who are working on projects that address the given scholarly theme.
Level of Study: Professional development, Postdoctorate, Postgraduate, Research
Type: Grant
Value: Please contact the organization
Frequency: Annual
Country of Study: Any country
No. of awards offered: Varies
Application Procedure: Applicants must complete an application form. Additional information, detailed guidelines and application forms are available from the website or by contacting the Getty Grant Program office.
Closing Date: November 1st
Funding: Private

USA – Getty Foundation Research Grants for Predoctoral and Postdoctoral Fellowships
Subjects: Arts, humanities, or social sciences.

Purpose: To support emerging scholars to complete work on projects related to the Getty Research Institute's annual theme.
Eligibility: Open to scholars of all nationalities who are working in the arts, humanities, or social sciences. Predoctoral fellowship applicants must have advanced to candidacy by the time of the fellowship start date and expect to complete their dissertations during the fellowship period.
Level of Study: Postdoctorate, Predoctorate
Type: Fellowship
Value: US $18,000 predoctoral fellows (9–month residency) and US $22,000 for the postdoctoral fellows (9–month residency)
Length of Study: 1 year
Application Procedure: Applications are available for viewing and printing in Portable Document Format (PDF) or by contacting the Getty Grant Program office.
Closing Date: November 1st

Villa Predoctoral and Postdoctoral Fellowships
Subjects: Arts, humanities, or social sciences.
Purpose: To provide support for emerging scholars to complete work on projects related to the Getty Villa's annual theme.
Eligibility: Open to scholars of all nationalities who are working in the arts, humanities, or social sciences. Predoctoral fellowship applicants must have advanced to candidacy by the time of the fellowship start date and expect to complete their dissertations during the fellowship period.
Level of Study: Postdoctorate, Predoctorate
Type: Fellowship
Value: US $18,000 for the predoctoral fellows (9–month residency) and US $22,000 for the postdoctoral fellows (9–month residency)
Length of Study: 1 year
Application Procedure: Applications are available for viewing and printing in Portable Document Format (PDF) or by contacting the Getty Grant Program office.
Closing Date: November 1st

GÉZA ANDA FOUNDATION

Bleicherweg 18, CH-8002, Zurich, Switzerland
Tel: (41) 44 205 1423
Fax: (41) 44 205 1429
Email: info@gezaanda.org
Website: www.gezaanda.org
Contact: Ms Ruth Bossart

The Géza Anda Foundation was established in 1978 in memory of the pianist, Géza Anda. It holds the Géza Anda Concours, an international piano competition, every 3 years, and awards prize to winners and special prizes, and providing an opportunity for the laureates to appear as soloists in concerts and recitals.

International Géza Anda Piano Competition
Subjects: Piano playing.
Purpose: To sponsor young pianists in the musical spirit of Géza Anda.
Eligibility: Open to pianists born after June 5th, 1977.
Level of Study: Unrestricted
Type: Prize
Value: Cash prizes of Swiss francs 60,000 and other benefits such as free concert management services for 3 years
Frequency: Every 3 years
Country of Study: Switzerland
No. of awards offered: 3
Application Procedure: Applicants must complete four rounds in the competition: an audition, a recital, Mozart and a final concert with orchestra. Date of the competition: June 5–16
Closing Date: January 31st
Funding: Private
No. of awards given last year: 3 official awards and 5 special awards

GILBERT MURRAY TRUST

Department of International Relations, LSE, Houghton Street, London, WC2A 2AE, England
Tel: (44) 18 6555 6633
Contact: Dr Peter Wilson, International Studies Committee

The International Studies Committee of the Gilbert Murray Trust is a small foundation dedicated to the promotion of international education, especially with regard to the theory and practice of the United Nations.

Gilbert Murray Trust Junior Awards

Subjects: International affairs or international law.
Purpose: To study the purposes and work of the United Nations.
Eligibility: Open to persons of any nationality who are, or who have been, students at a university or similar institution in the United Kingdom. Candidates should currently be taking or should have taken part in a course of international affairs or international law and must not be over 25 years of age, although consideration will be given to those over that age in special cases.
Level of Study: Postgraduate, Undergraduate
Type: Award
Value: UK £500
Frequency: Annual
Country of Study: Any country
No. of awards offered: 6
Application Procedure: Applicants must submit five copies, typed and on one side only, of a letter of application, a curriculum vitae, an outline of their intention with regard to a future career, full particulars of the purpose for which the award would be used and a supporting testimonial from a person capable of judging the candidate's ability to use the award profitably.
Closing Date: April 1st
Funding: Private
Contributor: Small individual contributions
No. of awards given last year: 9
No. of applicants last year: 18
Additional Information: Awards are only given to support a specific project, such as a research visit to the headquarters of an international organization, or to a particular country, or a short research course at an institution abroad that will assist the applicant in his or her study of international affairs in relation to the purpose and work of the United Nations. The Junior Awards are not intended as general financial support for the study of international affairs.

GILCHRIST EDUCATIONAL TRUST (GET)

20 Fern Road, Storrington, Pulborough, West Sussex, RH20 4LW, England
Tel: (44) 01903 746723
Email: gilchrist.et@blueyonder.co.uk
Website: www.gilchristgrants.org.uk
Contact: Mrs J.V Considine, Secretary

Gilchrist Educational Trust awards grants to: individuals who face unexpected financial difficulties, which may prevent completion of a degree or higher education course; organizations if it seems likely that a project for which funds are sought will fill an educational gap or make more widely available for a particular aspect of education or learning; British expeditions proposing to carry out research of a scientific nature abroad.

GET Grants

Subjects: All subjects.
Purpose: To promote the advancement of education and learning.
Eligibility: Open to: students in the United Kingdom who have made proper provision to fund a degree or higher education course but find themselves facing unexpected financial difficulties which may prevent completion of it; students who are required to spend a short period abroad as part of their course; and British expeditions proposing to carry out scientific research in another country.
Level of Study: Doctorate, Graduate, Postgraduate, Research
Type: Grant
Value: £500–1,000 (Individual Awards), £500–4,000 (Organization Grants), £500–1,500 (Expeditions Grants)
Study Establishment: Any university
Country of Study: United Kingdom
No. of awards offered: Varies
Application Procedure: Application forms must be completed in all cases. For grants to individuals, please contact The Grants Officer on gilchrist.et@blueyonder.co.uk, or write to: 13 Brookfield Avenue, Larkfield, Aylesford ME20 6RU. For other grants contact the Secretary

of the Trust on valconsidine@toucansurf.com or write to her at 20 Fern Road, Storrington, Pulborough, West Sussex, RH20 4LW
Closing Date: Last day of February for organizations and expeditions. No deadline for applications from individuals
Funding: Private
No. of awards given last year: Organization Grants - 14; Expedition Grants - 13; Adult Study Grants - 28; Travel Grants - 35
No. of applicants last year: Approx. 110 (Organization Grants), approx. 40 (Expedition Grants), many for Adult study and Travel Grants
Additional Information: These are awarded in four different categories as 1. Individual awards (a) Travel study grants (b) Adult study grants, 2. Organization grants and 3. Expedition grants.

Gilchrist Fieldwork Award

Subjects: All scientific subjects.
Purpose: To fund a period of fieldwork by established scientists or academics.
Eligibility: Open to teams wishing to undertake a field season of over 6 weeks in relation to one or more scientific objectives. Teams should consist of not more than 10 members, most of whom should be British and holding established positions in research departments at universities or similar establishments. The proposed research must be original and challenging, achievable within the timetable and preferably of benefit to the host country or region.
Level of Study: Research
Type: Grant
Value: UK £15,000
Frequency: Every 2 years
Country of Study: Any country
No. of awards offered: 1
Application Procedure: Applicants must write for details. There is no application form. Applicants must send a proposal to the Grants Officer at RGS by email (grants@rgs.org) in word format
Closing Date: February 26th in even-numbered years
Funding: Private
No. of awards given last year: None
Additional Information: The award is competitive.

For further information contact:

1 Kensington Gore, London, SW7 2AR, England
Email: grants@rgs.org
Contact: RGS-IBG

THE GILO CENTER FOR CITENZENSHIP, DEMOCRACY AND CIVIC EDUCATION

Faculty of Social Sciences, The Hebrew University of Jerusalem, Mount Scopus, Jerusalem, 91905, Israel
Tel: (972) 02 5882267
Fax: (972) 02 5881532
Email: gilocentre@savion.huji.ac.il
Website: http://gilocenter.mscc.huji.ac.il

The Gilo Center for Citizenship, Democracy and Civic Education at the Hebrew University of Jerusalem was established in 2001, with the generous support of the Gilo Family Foundation in order to promote research on citizenship and democracy in Israel and actively encourage its study and praxis within the education system. The establishment of the Center was made possible by the joint effort of the Hebrew University and Department of Political Science with the Ministry of Education.

The Yitzhak Rabin Fellowship Fund for the Advancement of Peace and Tolerance

Subjects: Advancement of peace and tolerance.
Purpose: To promote research on issues pertaining to citizenship, democracy and civic education by awarding excellent young researchers in their advanced studies.
Eligibility: Open to applicants enrolled in an accredited doctoral or postdoctoral programme focusing on areas relating to the pursuit of peace and/or to the enhancement of peaceful forms of social life. Open to one Canadian applicant, one Jewish and one Arab Israeli.
Level of Study: Doctorate, Postdoctorate, Postgraduate

Type: Fellowship
Value: US$10,000
Length of Study: 1 year
Frequency: Annual
Country of Study: Israel
No. of awards offered: 3
Application Procedure: Applicants must provide a research essay or a completed project.
Additional Information: The selected Fellow commits to a period of normally 1 month during which he or she spends time with the Rabin Scholars in seminars and/or field trips, as well as lectures, and undertakes pertinent research within the network of the Hebrew University.

For further information contact:

Email: inquiry@cfhu.org

GLADYS KRIEBLE DELMAS FOUNDATION

521 Fifth Avenue, Suite 1612, New York, NY, 10175-1699, United States of America
Tel: (1) 212 687 0011
Fax: (1) 212 687 8877
Email: info@delmas.org
Website: www.delmas.org
Contact: Ms Shirley Lockwood

The Gladys Krieble Delmas Foundation promotes the advancement and perpetuation of humanistic enquiry and artistic creativity by encouraging excellence in scholarship and in the performing arts, and by supporting research libraries and other institutions that preserve the resources that transmit this cultural heritage.

Gladys Krieble Delmas Foundation Grants

Subjects: The history of Venice, the former Venetian empire and contemporary Venetian society and culture. Disciplines of the humanities and social sciences are eligible areas of study, including but not limited to art, architecture, archaeology, theatre, music, literature, political science, economics and law.
Purpose: To promote research into Venice and the Veneto.
Eligibility: Open to citizens and permanent residents of the United States of America who have some experience in advanced research. Graduate students must have fulfilled all doctoral requirements except for completion of the dissertation. The dissertation proposal must, however, have been approved by the time of application for the grant. There is also a programme for scholars from Commonwealth countries.
Level of Study: Postdoctorate, Predoctorate
Type: Grant
Value: US$500–19,900 depending on the length of study. At the discretion of the trustees and advisory board of the Foundation, funds may be made available for aid on the publication of results
Length of Study: Up to 1 academic year
Frequency: Annual
Country of Study: Italy
No. of awards offered: Usually 15–25
Application Procedure: Applicants must complete an application form. Instruction sheets and forms are available from the website.
Closing Date: December 15th
Funding: Private
No. of awards given last year: 17
No. of applicants last year: 43

GLASGOW EDUCATIONAL AND MARSHALL TRUST

21 Beaton Road, Glasgow, G41 4NW, Scotland
Tel: (44) 0141 423 2169
Fax: (44) 0141 424 1731
Email: enquiries@gemt.org.uk
Website: www.gemt.org.uk

The Glasgow Educational and Marshall Trust is a charitable trust that meets quarterly and awards bursaries to, among others, mature students and postgraduate students. It also awards grants to aid travel.

Glasgow Educational and Marshall Trust Bursary

Subjects: All subjects.
Purpose: To offer financial support to those who have lived, or are currently living within the Glasgow Municipal Boundary.
Eligibility: Applicants must have a minimum of 5 years of residence within the Glasgow Municipal Boundary, as it was prior to 1975. Years spent within the Boundary purely for the purpose of study do not count.
Level of Study: Unrestricted
Type: Bursary
Value: UK £100–1,200
Frequency: Dependent on funds available
Country of Study: United Kingdom
Application Procedure: Applicants must complete and submit an application form together with two written references prior to the start of the course. No retrospective awards are available.
Closing Date: July 31st
Funding: Private
No. of awards given last year: 58
No. of applicants last year: 59

THE GLASGOW SCHOOL OF ART (GSA)

167 Renfrew Street, Glasgow, Scotland, G3 6RQ, United Kingdom
Tel: (44) 44 0 141 353 4509
Fax: (44) 44 0 141 353 4746
Email: welfare@gsa.ac.uk
Website: www.gsa.ac.uk

The Glasgow School of Art, internationally recognized as one of Britain's foremost higher education institutions for the study and advancement of fine art, design and architecture. GSA is a small, specialist and highly focused international community of artists, designers and architects and, as a prospective student, visitor, research partner or supporter of the School, and one can find the GSA an immensely stimulating and creative place.

Austin Merrills Scholarship

Subjects: Digital design studio programmes.
Eligibility: Open to individuals who meet the academic entry requirements for study at the GSA and hold an offer letter (either conditional or unconditional) to study.
Level of Study: Postgraduate
Type: Scholarship
Value: £700 to cover maintenance
Frequency: Annual
Study Establishment: The Glasgow School of Art
Country of Study: United Kingdom
No. of awards offered: 1
Application Procedure: Applicants should complete the standard application form and financial need form which can be downloaded from the GSA website.
Additional Information: A candidate may apply only for two awards.

For further information contact:

The Glasgow School of Art, 167 Renfrew Street, Glasgow, G3 6RQ, United Kingdom
Tel: (44) 141 353 4509
Fax: (44) 141 353 4746
Website: www.gsa.ac.uk/scholarships

Bellahouston Bequest Scholarship

Subjects: Related to digital design studio.
Eligibility: Open to citizens of Glasgow and west of Scotland, who meet the academic entry requirements for study at the GSA and hold an offer letter (either conditional or unconditional) to study here.
Level of Study: Postgraduate
Type: Scholarship
Value: £1,000 per year to cover fees
Length of Study: 1 or 2 years
Frequency: Annual

Study Establishment: The Glasgow School of Art
Country of Study: United Kingdom
No. of awards offered: 1
Application Procedure: Applicants should complete the standard application form and financial need form which can be downloaded from the GSA website.
Additional Information: A candidate may apply only for two awards.

For further information contact:

The Glasgow School of Art, 167 Renfrew Street, Glasgow, G3 6RQ, United Kingdom
Tel: (44) 141 353 4509
Fax: (44) 141 353 4746
Website: www.gsa.ac.uk/scholarships

Cargill Thomson Scholarships

Subjects: Silversmithing and jewellery.
Eligibility: Open to individuals who meet the academic entry requirements for study at the GSA and hold an offer letter (either conditional or unconditional) to study.
Level of Study: Postgraduate
Type: Scholarship
Value: £3,085 to cover fees
Length of Study: 3 years
Frequency: Annual
Study Establishment: The Glasgow School of Art
Country of Study: United Kingdom
No. of awards offered: 1
Application Procedure: Applicants should complete the standard application form and financial need form which can be downloaded from the GSA website.
Additional Information: A candidate may apply only for two awards.

For further information contact:

The Glasgow School of Art, 167 Renfrew Street, Glasgow, G3 6RQ, United Kingdom
Tel: (44) 141 353 4509
Fax: (44) 141 353 4746
Website: www.gsa.ac.uk/scholarships

DOG Digital Scholarship

Subjects: Related to digital design studio.
Purpose: Fees or maintenance.
Eligibility: Open to individuals who meet the academic entry requirements for study at the GSA and hold an offer letter (either conditional or unconditional) to study.
Level of Study: Postgraduate
Type: Scholarship
Value: £2,750 to cover fees or maintenance
Length of Study: 2 years
Frequency: Annual
Study Establishment: The Glasgow School of Art
Country of Study: United Kingdom
No. of awards offered: 1
Application Procedure: Applicants should complete the standard application form and financial need form which can be downloaded from the GSA website.
Additional Information: A candidate may apply only for two awards.

For further information contact:

Website: www.gsa.ac.uk/scholarships

Glasgow and West of Scotland Postgraduate Scholarships

Subjects: All subjects.
Eligibility: Open to citizens of Glasgow and west of Scotland. Applicants should be exceptional students undertaking taught or research master's programmes.
Level of Study: Postgraduate
Type: Scholarship
Value: £5,000 per year to cover fees and maintenance
Length of Study: 1 or 2 years, depending on length of course
Frequency: Annual
Study Establishment: The Glasgow School of Art

Country of Study: United Kingdom
No. of awards offered: 5
Application Procedure: Applicants should complete the standard application form and financial need form which can be downloaded from the GSA website.
Additional Information: A candidate may apply only for two awards. For the scholarship to continue to year 2, students must have satisfactorily completed year 1.

For further information contact:

Website: www.gsa.ac.uk/scholarships

Governors International Postgraduate Scholarships

Subjects: All subjects.
Eligibility: Open to applicants who are non EU (students paying full international fees). Applicants should be exceptional students undertaking one-year masters programmes. A report is required at the end of each academic year.
Level of Study: Postgraduate
Type: Scholarship
Value: £2,000 to cover fees
Length of Study: 1 year
Frequency: Annual
Country of Study: United Kingdom
No. of awards offered: 8
Application Procedure: Applicants should complete the standard application form and financial need form which can be downloaded from the GSA website.
Contributor: The Glasgow School of Art
Additional Information: A candidate may apply only for two awards.

For further information contact:

Website: www.gsa.ac.uk/scholarships

Grace and Clark Fyfe Architecture Masters Scholarships

Subjects: Architecture.
Eligibility: Open to individuals who meet the academic entry requirements for study at the GSA and hold an offer letter (either conditional or unconditional) to study MArch (Taught).
Level of Study: Postgraduate
Type: Scholarship
Value: £3,085 to cover fees or maintenance
Length of Study: 1 year
Frequency: Annual
Study Establishment: The Glasgow School of Art
Country of Study: United Kingdom
No. of awards offered: 1
Application Procedure: Applicants should complete the standard application form and financial need form which can be downloaded from the GSA website.
Additional Information: A candidate may apply only for two awards.

For further information contact:

Website: www.gsa.ac.uk/scholarships

Grace and Clark Fyfe Architecture PhD Scholarship

Subjects: Architecture.
Eligibility: Open to individuals who meet the academic entry requirements for study at the GSA and hold an offer letter (either conditional or unconditional) to study PhD in Architecture.
Level of Study: Postgraduate
Type: Scholarship
Value: £3,085 per year to cover fees or maintenance
Length of Study: 3 years
Frequency: Annual
Study Establishment: The Glasgow School of Art
Country of Study: United Kingdom
No. of awards offered: 1
Application Procedure: Applicants should complete the standard application form and financial need form which can be downloaded from the GSA website.
Additional Information: A candidate may apply only for two awards.

For further information contact:

Website: www.gsa.ac.uk/scholarships

John Keppie Scholarship

Subjects: Architecture, sculpture.
Eligibility: Open to individuals who meet the academic entry requirements for study at the GSA and hold an offer letter (either conditional or unconditional) to study architecture (Diploma and above) or sculpture (including MFA where the applicant specializes in sculpture).
Level of Study: Postgraduate
Type: Scholarship
Value: £500 to cover maintenance
Length of Study: 1 year
Frequency: Annual
Study Establishment: The Glasgow School of Art
Country of Study: United Kingdom
No. of awards offered: 2
Application Procedure: Applicants should complete the standard application form and financial need form which can be downloaded from the GSA website.
Additional Information: A candidate may apply only for two awards.

For further information contact:

Website: www.gsa.ac.uk/scholarships

Leverhulme Scholarships for Architecture

Subjects: Architecture.
Eligibility: Open to UK citizens who meet the academic entry requirements for study at the GSA and hold an offer letter (either conditional or unconditional) to study architecture specializing in urban building and design, creative urban practices, advanced computing and visualization or energy and environmental studies.
Level of Study: Postgraduate
Type: Scholarship
Value: £9,000 per year to cover fees and maintenance (students have home fees paid with balance given as a stipend)
Length of Study: 2 years
Frequency: Annual
Study Establishment: The Glasgow School of Art
Country of Study: United Kingdom
No. of awards offered: 2
Application Procedure: Applicants should complete the standard application form and financial need form which can be downloaded from the GSA website.
Additional Information: A candidate may apply only for two awards. Candidates are expected to develop a PhD proposal during their course of study.

For further information contact:

Website: www.gsa.ac.uk/scholarships

Leverhulme Scholarships for Masters of Fine Art

Subjects: Fine arts.
Eligibility: Open to UK citizens who meet the academic entry requirements for study at the GSA and hold an offer letter (either conditional or unconditional) to study Master of fine arts.
Level of Study: Postgraduate
Type: Scholarship
Value: £9,000 per year to cover fees and maintenance (students have home fees paid with balance given as a stipend)
Length of Study: 2 years
Frequency: Annual
Study Establishment: The Glasgow School of Art
Country of Study: United Kingdom
No. of awards offered: 2
Application Procedure: Applicants should complete the standard application form and financial need form which can be downloaded from the GSA website.
Additional Information: A candidate may apply only for two awards. For the scholarship to continue to year 2, students must have satisfactory completed year 1.

For further information contact:

Website: www.gsa.ac.uk/scholarships

Mackendrick Scholarship

Subjects: Painting.

Eligibility: Open to individuals who meet the academic entry requirements for study at the GSA and hold an offer letter (either conditional or unconditional) to study postgraduate painting. Applicants must submit one painting based on the theme 'The City of Glasgow'.
Level of Study: Postgraduate
Type: Scholarship
Value: £2,500 per year to cover fees or maintenance
Length of Study: 1 or 2 years, depending on length of course
Frequency: Annual
Country of Study: United Kingdom and Australia
No. of awards offered: 1
Application Procedure: Applicants should complete the standard application form and financial need form which can be downloaded from the GSA website.
Contributor: The Glasgow School of Art
Additional Information: A candidate may apply only for two awards. For the scholarship to continue to year 2, students must have satisfactorily completed year 1.

For further information contact:

Website: www.gsa.ac.uk/scholarships

Sir Harry Barnes Scholarship

Subjects: All subjects.
Eligibility: Open to individuals who meet the academic entry requirements for study at the GSA and hold an offer letter (either conditional or unconditional) to study.
Level of Study: Postgraduate
Type: Scholarship
Value: £1,500 to cover maintenance
Length of Study: 1 year
Frequency: Annual
Study Establishment: The Glasgow School of Art
Country of Study: United Kingdom
No. of awards offered: 1
Application Procedure: Applicants should complete the standard application form and financial need form which can be downloaded from the GSA website.
Additional Information: A candidate may apply only for two awards.

For further information contact:

Website: www.gsa.ac.uk/scholarships

Tetsuya Mukai Scholarship

Subjects: All subjects.
Eligibility: Open to Japanese (i.e., those paying full international fees) and UK students to undertake taught or research postgraduate study at the GSA.
Level of Study: Postgraduate
Type: Scholarship
Value: £3,000 to cover fees
Length of Study: 1 year
Frequency: Annual
Study Establishment: The Glasgow School of Art
Country of Study: United Kingdom
No. of awards offered: 1
Application Procedure: Applicants should complete the standard application form and financial need form which can be downloaded from the GSA website.
Additional Information: A candidate may apply only for two awards.

For further information contact:

Website: www.gsa.ac.uk/scholarships

Weavers Postgraduate Textiles Scholarships

Subjects: Textiles.
Eligibility: Open to individuals who meet the academic entry requirements for study at the GSA and hold an offer letter (either conditional or unconditional) to study MDes textiles as fashion.
Level of Study: Postgraduate
Type: Scholarship
Value: £1,500 to cover fees or maintenance
Length of Study: 1 year
Frequency: Annual

Study Establishment: The Glasgow School of Art
Country of Study: United Kingdom
No. of awards offered: 1
Application Procedure: Applicants should complete the standard application form and financial need form which can be downloaded from the GSA website.
Additional Information: A candidate may apply only for two awards.

For further information contact:

Website: www.gsa.ac.uk/scholarships

William and Mary Armour Fellowships

Subjects: Painting.
Eligibility: Open to individuals who meet the academic entry requirements for study at the GSA and hold an offer letter (either conditional or unconditional) to study postgraduate painting (including MFA where the applicant specializes in painting).
Level of Study: Postgraduate
Type: Fellowship
Value: £1,500 to cover maintenance
Length of Study: 1 year
Frequency: Annual
Study Establishment: The Glasgow School of Art
Country of Study: United Kingdom
No. of awards offered: 1
Application Procedure: Applicants should complete the standard application form and financial need form which can be downloaded from the GSA website.
Additional Information: A candidate may apply only for two awards.

For further information contact:

Website: www.gsa.ac.uk/scholarships

THE GOLDSMITHS' COMPANY

Goldsmiths' Hall, Foster Lane, London, EC2V 6BN, England
Tel: (44) 20 7606 7010
Fax: (44) 20 7606 1511
Email: education@thegoldsmiths.co.uk
Website: www.thegoldsmiths.co.uk
Contact: The Assistant Clerk

The Goldsmiths' Company is one of the Great Twelve Companies of the City of London. It has been responsible for hallmarking since 1300 and today operates the Assay Office London and supports the craft and industry of silversmithing and precious metal jewellery.

Goldsmiths' Company Science for Society Courses

Subjects: Genetics, particle physics, complementary medicine, astrophysics, sustainable development, materials science, and mathematics.
Purpose: To provide teachers of A levels with first-hand, practical experience of the theory that they teach.
Eligibility: Open to United Kingdom science teachers of secondary age children, but teachers from other disciplines are also accepted.
Level of Study: Professional development
Value: Free tuition, accommodation and travel after joining
Length of Study: 1 week in July
Frequency: Annual
Study Establishment: Various locations around the United Kingdom
Country of Study: United Kingdom
No. of awards offered: Approx. 120 vacancies each year
Application Procedure: Please write for details.
Closing Date: Vacancies are on a first come, first served basis
Funding: Private

GOOGLE SYDNEY

Google headquarters, Google Inc., 1600 Amphitheatre Parkway,
Mountain View, CA, 94043, United States of America
Tel: (1) +1.650.253.0000
Fax: (1) +1.650.253.0001
Website: www.google.com

Google is a public and profitable company focused on search services. Google operates web sites at many international domains. Google is widely recognized as the "world's best search engine" because it is fast, accurate and easy to use. The company also serves corporate clients, including advertisers, content publishers and site managers with cost–effective advertising and a wide range of revenue generating search services. Google's breakthrough technology and continued innovation serve the company's mission of "organizing the world's information and making it universally accessible and useful".

Google Australia Anita Borg Memorial Scholarship

Subjects: Computer science, computer engineering, informatics, or related technical field.
Purpose: To encourage women to excel in computing and technology and become active role models and leaders.
Eligibility: Candidates must be a female student who has studied one or more years of a B.Sc/B.Eng, or is enrolled in an M.Sc/M.Eng or PhD program (or equivalent) at a university in Australia and can be an Australian citizen, Australian permanent resident or international student maintaining an excellent academic record.
Level of Study: Doctorate, Graduate, Postgraduate, Research
Value: Australian $5,000 (or equivalent)
Frequency: Annual
Study Establishment: Google's Sydney Engineering centre
Country of Study: Australia

GOTTLIEB DAIMLER AND KARL BENZ FOUNDATION

Carl Benz Platz 2, Ladenburg, 68526, Germany
Tel: (49) 06203 109216
Fax: (49) 06203 10925
Email: info@daimler-benz-stiftung.de
Website: www.daimler-benz-stiftung.de
Contact: Ms Petra Jung, Dr

The Gottlieb Daimler and Karl Benz Foundation established in 1986, sponsors interdisciplinary research and scientific discussion on the interrelationships between humanity, environment and technology. In addition, the foundation awards fellowships to young doctoral students doing research, whether as foreign students in Germany, or as German students abroad.

Grants for Young Scholars with Research Projects Abroad

Subjects: This programme is open to all disciplines.
Purpose: To provide support for foreign academics working towards a dissertation and planning a research stay at a German host institution and for Germans working for a PhD in foreign countries.
Eligibility: Open to applicants who are not older than 30 years of age and who have been awarded their last academic degrees within the last year. Postdoctoral research, diploma theses, study visits and practical training will not be supported. Applicants must have a clearly defined research project of their own and an invitation for their research stay at a host institution.
Level of Study: Doctorate, Research
Type: Fellowships
Value: €970 for foreign students in Germany
Length of Study: 2 years
Frequency: Twice a year
Country of Study: Germany
Application Procedure: Application forms may be obtained by contacting the Daimler-Benz Foundation.
Closing Date: March 1st/October 1st
Funding: Foundation
Contributor: Gottlieb Daimler and Karl Benz Foundation
Additional Information: After an initial review of all applications, selected applicants will be invited to present their projects in a seminar at the Karl-Benz-Haus in Ladenburg. Representatives of the Foundation and outside referees will choose the final candidates who will receive fellowships among the participants of this seminar.

GOVERNMENT FINANCE OFFICERS ASSOCIATION (GFOA)

203 North LaSalle Street, Suite 2700, Chicago, IL, 60601-1210,
United States of America
Tel: (1) 312 977 9700
Fax: (1) 312 977 4806
Website: www.gfoa.org
Contact: Scholarship Committee

Government Finance Officers Association (GFOA) is the professional association of state/provincial and local finance officers in the United States and Canada and has served the public finance profession since 1906. More than 16,500 GFOA members are dedicated to the sound management of government financial resources.

Daniel B. Goldberg Scholarship
Subjects: State and local government finance.
Purpose: To fund a students enrolled in full-time Master's study preparing for a career in state and local government finance.
Eligibility: Open to candiates who are currently a full-time students in a graduate programme, have a Baccalaureate degree or its equivalent. Applicants must be a citizens or permanent residents of the United States or Canada.
Level of Study: Postgraduate
Type: Scholarship
Value: US$10,000
Frequency: Annual
Country of Study: United States of America
Application Procedure: Applicants must submit their application form, curriculum vitae, transcripts, statement of proposed career plan in state and local government finance and letters of recommendation.
Closing Date: March 6th
Funding: Foundation
Contributor: Girard Miller Foundation

Minorities in Government Finance Scholarship
Subjects: State and local government finance.
Purpose: To support a graduate student enrolled in a course of study preparing for a career in state and local government finance and recognize outstanding performance by minority students preparing for careers in state and local government finance.
Eligibility: Open to applicants who are currently a full or part-time student in public administration, (governmental) accounting, finance, political science, economics or business administration. The applicant must be a Black or African American, American Indian or Alaskan Native, Asian, Native Hawaiian or Other Pacific Islander, Hispanic or Latino and should be a citizen or permanent resident of the United States or Canada.
Level of Study: Graduate
Type: Scholarship
Value: US$5,000
Frequency: Annual
Country of Study: United States of America
Application Procedure: Applicants must submit the aplication form, transcripts, curriculum vitae, letters of recommendation and statement of proposed state and local government finance career plan and, if applicable, plan of graduate study.
Closing Date: March 6th
Contributor: Microsoft

GRADUATE INSTITUTE OF INTERNATIONAL STUDIES, GENEVA

132, rue de Lausanne, Case postale 36, Genève 21, CH-1211,
Switzerland
Tel: (41) 22 908 5700
Fax: (41) 22 908 5710
Email: info@hei.unige.ch
Website: www.hei.unige.ch

The Graduate Institute of International Studies, best known as HEI, was founded in 1927 as one of the first instituions in the world dedicated to the study of international relations. A small and selective institute with about 1100 undergraduate and graduate students from over 90 countries, HEI owes its reputation to the quality of its cosmopolitan faculty, the strength of its core disciplines (economics, history, law and political science), its policy-relevent approach to international affairs, and its bilingual English-French education programmes.

Graduate Institute of International Studies (HEI-Geneva) Scholarships
Subjects: History and international politics, international economics, international law and political science.
Eligibility: Open to any applicant who can prove sound knowledge of the French language and sufficient prior study in political science, economics, law or modern history through the presentation of a college or university degree.
Level of Study: Postgraduate, Doctorate
Type: Scholarship
Value: Swiss francs 1,500 per month on 10 months
Length of Study: 1 year, possibly renewable
Frequency: Annual
Study Establishment: Graduate Institute of International Studies, Geneva
Country of Study: Switzerland
No. of awards offered: 50
Application Procedure: Applicants must contact the Institute for details.
Closing Date: January 1st
Funding: Government
Contributor: The Canton of Geneva and the Swiss Confederation
No. of awards given last year: 24
No. of applicants last year: 49
Additional Information: Scholars are exempt from Institute fees, but not from the obligatory fees of the University of Geneva, which confers the degree.

GRAINS RESEARCH AND DEVELOPMENT CORPORATION (GRDC)

PO Box 5367, Kingston, ACT 2604, Australia
Tel: (61) 2 6272 5525
Fax: (61) 2 6271 6430
Email: grdc@grdc.com.au
Website: www.grdc.com.au
Contact: Ms Sonia Yanni, Program Support Coordinator

The Grains Research and Development Corporation's (GRDC) mission is to invest in innovation for the greatest benefit stakeholders. This will be achieved by being a global leader in linking science, technology and its adoption with industry and community needs. The Corporation's vision is for a profitable, internationally competitive and ecologically sustainable grains industry.

GRDC Grains Industry Research Scholarships
Subjects: Fields of high priority to the grains industry.
Purpose: To give support to students of excellence proceeding to postgraduate study in a field relevant to the future of the Australian grains industry.
Eligibility: Open to permanent residents of Australia who hold academic qualifications equivalent to a First Class (Honours) Degree or have otherwise demonstrated a high level of postgraduate achievement in research, teaching or extension activities.
Level of Study: Doctorate, Postgraduate
Type: Scholarship
Value: A tax-free stipend of Australian $25,000 with no allowances for dependants. An additional grant of up to Australian $5,000 per year may be provided to the host organization to support the work
Length of Study: 3 years
Frequency: Annual
Study Establishment: Any university with a record of achievement for full-time research in the subject area leading to a DPhil
Country of Study: Australia
No. of awards offered: Several
Application Procedure: Applicants must complete an application form, available on request. Applications (six copies) should include the curriculum vitae of the applicant and the report of at least two referees.

323

Evidence that the university and collaborating organizations will provide facilities and supervision of the project must also be supplied.
Closing Date: October 26th
Funding: Government
Contributor: The government and Australian grain growers
No. of awards given last year: 13
No. of applicants last year: Approx. 30
Additional Information: The Corporation's 5-year research and development plan outlines the objectives and programmes to be covered. Copies of this may be obtained from the Secretariat.

GRDC In-Service Training
Subjects: Grains research and development.
Purpose: To support training on an industry-wide basis by funding younger scientists, technical staff or other persons engaged in work relevant to the Corporation's objectives who may not be eligible for other forms of support. Funds may be provided for travel, secondment or interchange between institutions.
Eligibility: Open to permanent residents of Australia only.
Level of Study: Unrestricted
Type: Grant
Value: Up to a maximum of Australian $25,000
Length of Study: Up to 6 months
Frequency: Annual
Country of Study: Any country
Application Procedure: Applicants must submit six copies of a curriculum vitae, details of the proposed in-service training, the names, positions and locations of the proposed collaborators and training venue and approximate dates for the programme, which must fall within the appropriate funding year. Details of any travel directly related to the proposed programme, a proposed budget, including the cost of travel and expected accommodation and living expenses, an indication of other forms of support available to the applicant, evidence that the proposed collaborators are agreeable to the training programme, supporting comments from two referees and a covering letter should also be included.
Closing Date: October 26th
Contributor: The government and Australian grain growers
Additional Information: On completion of their award, trainees must provide the Board with a report.

GRDC Industry Development Awards
Subjects: Grains research and development.
Purpose: To fund study tours or for other purposes approved by the Corporation.
Eligibility: Open to permanent residents of Australia who are experienced growers, processors or other contributors to the work of the Corporation who are not engaged in research and development activity.
Level of Study: Unrestricted
Type: Award
Value: Up to a total of Australian $15,000 towards personal travel costs, including economy class airfares and contribution to living expenses
Frequency: Annual
Country of Study: Any country
No. of awards offered: Several
Application Procedure: Applicants must submit five copies of the nominee's curriculum vitae, details of the proposed programme, the names, positions and locations of the proposed collaborators, approximate dates for the programme and details of any internal travel directly related to the proposed programme. A proposed budget, including the cost of international and internal travel, and expected accommodation and living expenses, an indication of other forms of support available to the nominee, evidence that the proposed collaborators are agreeable to the programme, supporting comments from two referees and a covering letter should also be included.
Closing Date: February 29th and August 29th
Contributor: The government and Australian grain growers
Additional Information: On completion of the award, a report must be given to the Board. Preference may be given to applicants who have access to matching funds.

GRDC Senior Fellowships
Subjects: Grains research and development.

Purpose: To allow experienced research and development personnel to enhance their experience and their potential to contribute to the work of the Corporation by working at an institution in Australia or overseas.
Eligibility: Open to permanent residents of Australia only.
Level of Study: Unrestricted
Type: Fellowship
Value: Up to a total of Australian $50,000 towards personal travel costs, including economy class airfares and a contribution to living expenses
Length of Study: Up to 1 year
Frequency: Annual
Country of Study: Any country
No. of awards offered: Up to 2 per year
Application Procedure: Applicants must submit six copies of the following documentation: the nominee's curriculum vitae, including a list of publications, details of the nominee's research project and its relationship to the host institution's programme of research (this should include evidence that the host institution already has an interest and competence in the area of research proposed by the applicant and that it is relevant to the Corporation's objectives) and the names, positions and major publications of the proposed collaborators, together with a letter of invitation from the Head of the host institution. They should also include approximate dates for the programme, which must fall within the appropriate funding year, details of any internal travel directly related to the proposed programme, a proposed budget, including the cost of international and internal travel, and expected accommodation and living expenses, an indication of other forms of support available to the applicant, evidence that the host institution has available the necessary facilities and is willing to accept the Fellow, supporting comments from two referees, and a covering letter. On completion of their award Fellows must furnish the Board with a report. Preference may be given to applicants who have access to matching funds.
Closing Date: October 26th
Funding: Government
Contributor: The government and Australian grain growers

GRDC Visiting Fellowships
Subjects: Grains research and development.
Purpose: To give support and stimulus to research programmes supported by the Corporation by funding visits by overseas personnel who could enhance those programmes.
Eligibility: Open to candidates of any nationality.
Level of Study: Postgraduate
Type: Fellowship
Value: The Corporation will consider paying the nominee's personal travel costs, contributing to living expenses and providing some support to the host institution or company. The maximum total level of support will normally be Australian $17,500
Length of Study: Up to 1 year
Frequency: Annual
Country of Study: Australia
No. of awards offered: Several
Application Procedure: Applicants must submit six copies of the following documentation: the nominee's curriculum vitae, details of the nominee's research project or itinerary for study and its relationship to the host institution's or company's programme of research, development or other industry contribution, the name, position and industry contributions of the person proposing the nominee, together with a letter of support from the Head of the host institution or company, where appropriate, the names, positions and institutions of collaborators of the proposed project or study tour. They should also include approximate dates for the programme, which must fall within the appropriate funding year, details of any travel directly related to the proposed programme, a proposed budget, including the cost of international and internal travel, and expected accommodation and living expenses, an indication of other forms of support available to the nominee, including those from the home institution or company, evidence that the host institution or company has accepted the nomination, supporting comments from two referees and a covering letter.
Closing Date: October 26th
Contributor: The government and Australian grain growers
No. of awards given last year: 4
No. of applicants last year: 6

Additional Information: On completion of the award, a report must be given to the Board. Preference may be given to nominees who have access to matching funds.

THE GREAT BRITAIN-CHINA EDUCATIONAL TRUST

The Great Britain-China Centre, 15 Belgrave Square, London, SW1X 8PS, England
Tel: (44) 020 7235 6696
Fax: (44) 020 7245 6885
Email: contact@gbcc.org.uk
Website: www.gbcc.org.uk
Contact: Administrative Assistant

The Great Britain-China Centre nourishes understanding between Britain and China particularly in the areas of legal and judicial reform, and labour reform. It exchanges projects with Chinese partners and many UK organizations. It responds and facilitates the need for dialogue in a particular and acts as a trust facilitator for both Chinese and UK sides. The current policy of the trust is to support Chinese students in Britain via the Chinese Student Awards and the study of Chinese language through the annual Chinese Language Awards.

Chinese Student Awards
Subjects: All subjects.
Eligibility: Open to Chinese candidates (from the PRC inc., Hong Kong) studying for a PhD in any subject and British postgraduate students (UK citizens only) giving conference papers in China, or traveling to China to pursue essential doctoral research.
Level of Study: Doctorate, Graduate, Postgraduate
Type: Award
Value: UK £500–5000
Frequency: Twice a year
Application Procedure: Check website for further details.
Closing Date: October 17th
Funding: Trusts
Contributor: Sino-British Fellowship Trust, the Universities' China Committee in London, and the Han Suyin Trust
Additional Information: Eligibility criteria vary very slightly for those people studying in the relevant subject area. For further details, check website address.

For further information contact:

15 Belgrave Square, London, SW1X 8PS, United Kingdom
Tel: (44) 020 7821 3221 or 020 7963 9446
Email: trust@gbcc.org.uk
Website: www.gbcc.org.uk
Contact: Trust Administrator

GREEK MINISTRY OF NATIONAL EDUCATION AND RELIGIOUS AFFAIRS

37, A. Papandreou Street, Marousi, 15180, Greece
Tel: (30) 00302103442469, 00302103443129
Fax: (30) 00302103442469
Email: des-a@ypepth.gr
Website: www.ypeplh.gr
Contact: Directorate of International Relations in Education

The Ministry handles affairs that relate to student's welfare (studies, diplomas, athletic organizations, cost estimation of university course-books, etc.). Also responsible for the cultural an educational exchanges (long-term scholarships) with other countries.

Scholarships for Greek Language Studies in Greece
Subjects: Greek language.
Purpose: To allow nationals from the Balkans, Eastern Europe, Asia and Africa to study Greek Language.
Eligibility: Applicants must be nationals of Albania, Armenia, Azerbaijan, Bosnia and Herzegovina, China, Egypt, Ethiopia, FYROM, Georgia, India, Indonesia, Iran, Iraq, Jordan, Kazakhstan, Korea, Lebanon, Moldova, Montenegro, Pakistan, Palestine, Russia, Serbia, Sudan, Syria, Thailand, Tunisia, Turkey, Ukraine or Uzbekistan.

Applicants should be students of Greek language abroad and have an excellent knowledge of modern Greek. Applicant must be foreign citizens, not of Greek orgin under 35 years of age.
Level of Study: Postgraduate
Type: Scholarship
Value: €600 for initial expenses, stay permit dues, tuition fees, free medical care and €500 for living expenses
Length of Study: Up to 1 year
Frequency: Annual
Country of Study: Greece
No. of awards offered: Up to 10
Application Procedure: Applicants should complete an application form, as well as provide letters of recommendation and relevant documentation.
Closing Date: April 30th
Funding: Government
No. of awards given last year: 11

Scholarships for Postdoctoral Studies in Greece
Subjects: Any subject.
Purpose: To allow nationals from the Balkans, Eastern Europe, Asia and Africa to undergo postdoctoral research in Greece.
Eligibility: Applicants must be nationals of Albania, Armenia, Azerbaijan, Bosnia and Herzegovina, China, Egypt, Ethiopia, FYROM, Georgia, India, Indonesia, Iran, Iraq, Jordan, Kazakhstan, Korea, Lebanon, Moldova, Montenegro, Pakistan, Palestine, Russia, Serbia, Sudan, Syria, Thailand, Tunisia, Turkey, Ukraine or Uzbekistan. Applicants should have an excellent knowledge of Greek or French or English language. Applicant must be of foreign nationality and hold a doctorate degree and their first degree must be from a foreign university.
Level of Study: Postdoctorate
Type: Scholarship
Value: €800 for initial expenses, stay permit dues, tuition fees, free medical care and €700 for living expenses
Length of Study: 3 months
Frequency: Annual
Country of Study: Greece
No. of awards offered: Up to 5
Application Procedure: Applicants should complete an application form as well as provide letters of recommendation and relevant documentation. Applications should be submitted to the Greek embassies.
Closing Date: April 30th
Funding: Government
No. of awards given last year: 4

Scholarships for Postgraduate Studies in Greece
Subjects: Any subject.
Purpose: To allow nationals from the Balkans, Eastern Europe, Asia and Africa to study in Greece.
Eligibility: Applicants must be nationals of Albania, Armenia, Azerbaijan, Bosnia and Herzegovina, China, Egypt, Ethiopia, FYROM, Georgia, India, Indonesia, Iran, Iraq, Jordan, Kazakhstan, Korea, Lebanon, Moldova, Montenegro, Pakistan, Palestine, Russia, Serbia, Sudan, Syria, Thailand, Tunisia, Turkey, Ukraine or Uzbekistan. Applicants should be students of Greek language abroad and have an excellent knowledge of modern Greek. Applicant must be of foreign citizens, not of Greek origin under 35 years of age.
Level of Study: Graduate, Postgraduate
Type: Scholarship
Value: €650 for initial expenses, stay permit dues, tuition fees, free medical care, and €550 for living expenses
Length of Study: 2 year MA plus 1 year Greek Language study
Frequency: Annual
Country of Study: Greece
No. of awards offered: Up to 10
Application Procedure: Applicants should complete an application form, as well as provide letters of recommendation and relevant documentation. Applications should be submitted to Greek embassies.
Closing Date: April 30th
Funding: Government
No. of awards given last year: 11

Scholarships Granted by the GR Government to Foreign Citizens

Subjects: All subjects.
Purpose: To support candidates who wish to study or conduct research project in Greek Universities.
Eligibility: Applicants must be nationals of Albania, Armenia, Azerbaijan, China, Egypt, Ethiopia, FYROM, Georgia, India, Iran, Iraq, Jordan, Korea, Lebanon, Montenegro, Pakistan, Russia, Serbia, Syria, Tunisia, Turkey or Ukraine. Applicants should have an excellent knowledge of Greek or French or English language. Applicant must be of foreign nationality and hold a doctorate degree and their first degree must be from a foreign university.
Level of Study: Doctorate, Graduate, MBA, Postdoctorate, Postgraduate, Predoctorate, Research
Type: Scholarship
Value: €550 per month, €500 lump sum for establishment expenses, €150 for transport expenses, exemption from tuition fees
Length of Study: Varies
Frequency: Annual
Study Establishment: Greek public universities
Country of Study: Greece
No. of awards offered: Up to 350
Application Procedure: Check with Ministry of Education or Ministry of Foreign Affairs in Individual country. Applicants must apply through their home countries.
Closing Date: March 31st
Funding: Government
Contributor: Greek Ministry of National Education and Religious Affairs
No. of awards given last year: 250

For further information contact:

Contact: Applicants must apply through their home countries

GRIFFITH UNIVERSITY

Student Administration, Room 0.07, Bray Centre (N54), Griffith University, 170 Kessels Road, Nathan, QLD, 4111, Australia
Tel: (61) (07) 3735 3870
Fax: (61) (07) 3735 7957
Email: scholarships@griffith.edu.au
Website: www.gu.edu.au

In the pursuit of excellence in teaching, research and community service, Griffith University is committed to innovation, bringing disciplines together, internationalization, equity and social justice and life-long learning, for the enrichment of Queensland, Australia and the international community.

APAI Water Resources Management Scholarship

Subjects: Engineering, environmental planning, science.
Purpose: To utilize smart meters and loggers to gauge the degree of water savings attributable to the execution of various water conservation strategies.
Eligibility: Open only to the citizens of Australia or New Zealand or permanent residents who have achieved Honours 1 or equivalent, Honours 2a or equivalent, or Masters or equivalent.
Level of Study: Graduate, Postgraduate
Type: Scholarship
Value: Australian $25,118 per year
Frequency: Annual
Study Establishment: Griffith University
Country of Study: Australia
No. of awards offered: 1
Application Procedure: Applicants must apply directly to the scholarship provider. Check the website for further details.
Closing Date: December 31st

For further information contact:

Griffith University
Tel: 07 3735 6596
Email: M.Mitchell@griffith.edu.au

Website: www.griffith.edu.au
Contact: Marianne Mitchell, Postgraduate Scholarships Coordinator

Griffith University Postgraduate Research Scholarships

Subjects: All subjects.
Purpose: To provide financial support for candidates undertaking full-time research leading to the award of the degree of MPhil or PhD.
Eligibility: Open to any person, irrespective of nationality, holding or expecting to hold a First Class (Honours) Degree or equivalent from a recognized institution. Applicants must demonstrate proficiency in the English language by scoring an overall score of 6.5 in the International English Language Testing System test, or have a score of at least 580 on the Teaching of English as a Foreign Language test or hold a test score of 237 (new Teaching of English as a Foreign Language) with an essay rating of 5.0.
Level of Study: Postgraduate
Type: Scholarship
Value: Australian $18,484 per year, tax exempt
Length of Study: Up to 2 years for a research Master's and up to 3 years for PhD candidates, with a possible extension of up to 6 months for the PhD, subject to satisfactory progress
Frequency: Annual
Study Establishment: Griffith University
Country of Study: Australia
No. of awards offered: Varies
Application Procedure: Applicants must complete an application form.
Closing Date: October 31st
Additional Information: The scholarship does not cover the cost of tuition fees, which ranges from Australian $15,000 to 19,000 per year.

Jackson Memorial Fellowship

Subjects: The application of the social, political, economic, environmental or technological sciences to the analysis and resolution of substantial policy issues at the national or regional levels.
Purpose: To consolidate links with a variety of institutions in South East Asia and to provide funding to facilitate visits to Griffith University by faculty staff of the Association of South East Asian Institutions of Higher Learning (ASAIHL) member institutions.
Eligibility: Open to senior members of faculty staff of the ASAIHL member institutions.
Level of Study: Professional development
Type: Fellowship
Frequency: Annual
Study Establishment: Griffith University
Country of Study: Australia
Application Procedure: Applicants must apply through the heads of their employing institutions.
Closing Date: September 10th
Funding: Private
No. of awards given last year: 1
No. of applicants last year: Varies

Sir Allan Sewell Visiting Fellowship

Subjects: All subjects offered by Griffith University.
Purpose: To commemorate the distinguished service of Sir Allan Sewell to Griffith University by offering awards to enable visits by distinguished scholars engaged in academic work who can contribute to research and teaching in one or more areas of interest at a faculty or college of the university.
Eligibility: Open to researchers of any nationality.
Level of Study: Professional development
Type: Fellowship
Frequency: Annual
Study Establishment: Griffith University
Country of Study: Australia
Application Procedure: Applicants must be invited to apply by faculties or colleges of the University.
Closing Date: September 10th
Funding: Private
No. of awards given last year: Varies
No. of applicants last year: Varies

GROUPE DE RECHERCHE SUR LE SYSTÈME NERVEUX CENTRAL

Faculty of Medicine, Universite de Montréal, PO Box 6128, Station Centre-Ville, Montréal, QC, H3C 3J7, Canada
Tel: (1) 514 343 6366
Fax: (1) 514 343 6113
Email: louis-eric.trudeau@umontreal.ca,
sonia.gosselin@umontreal.ca
Website: www.grsnc.umontreal.ca
Contact: Dr Trevor Drew, Director

Founded in 1991, the Groupe de Recherche sur le Système Nerveux Central (GRSNC) is a multidisciplinary research group that includes researchers from several departments within the Faculties of Medicine and Dentistry at the Universite de Montréal. It receives funding from both the University and from the provincial government to support its research infrastructure. It organizes an annual international symposium and has weekly research seminars by invited speakers.

Herbert H Jasper Fellowship

Subjects: Neurology and neurosciences.
Purpose: To enable the use of the exceptional research facilities of the Groupe de Recherche sur le Système Nerveux Central of the University of Montréal.
Eligibility: Open to Canadian citizens or permanent residents.
Level of Study: Postdoctorate
Type: Fellowship
Value: Canadian $40,000 per year
Length of Study: 2 years
Frequency: Annual
Study Establishment: Group de Recherche sur le Système Nerveux Central, University of Montréal
Country of Study: Canada
No. of awards offered: 1
Application Procedure: Applicants must complete an application form, which can be obtained from the website or by writing to the Fellowship Committee.
Closing Date: January 31st
Funding: Government
No. of awards given last year: 1
No. of applicants last year: 20
Additional Information: The fellowship provides the opportunity for the recipient to work closely with the investigator of his or her choice within a large active group of neuroscientists who are members of the group.

THE GRUNDY EDUCATIONAL TRUST

Jefford Cottage, 3 Parkside Lane, Ropley, Hants, S024 0BB, England
Tel: (44) 1962 773118
Email: alicia.hardy@hotmail.co.uk
Website: www.grundyeducationaltrust.org.uk
Contact: Mrs A Hardy, Secretary to the Trustees

The Grundy Educational Trust was established in 1991 to advance education by providing or assisting in the provision of graduate and postgraduate awards to students for research and higher learning at selected institutions in the United Kingdom, namely, Surrey University, Loughborough University, Nottingham University, Imperial College, London, and University of Manchester (UMIST).

Grundy Educational Trust

Subjects: Technologically or scientifically based disciplines in industry and commerce.
Purpose: To assist in covering maintenance costs while obtaining postgraduate or second degrees.
Eligibility: Open to United Kingdom citizens under 30 years of age.
Level of Study: Postgraduate
Type: Award
Value: Up to UK £4,500
Length of Study: 1–5 years
Frequency: Annual
Study Establishment: Surrey University, Loughborough University, Imperial College, London, Nottingham University and University of Manchester (UMIST)

Country of Study: United Kingdom
No. of awards offered: Up to 16
Application Procedure: Applicants must apply through the five selected universities only and not directly.
Closing Date: Approximately at the end of May. Refer to the universities
Funding: Private
No. of awards given last year: 12
No. of applicants last year: 25

GUIDE DOGS FOR THE BLIND ASSOCIATION

Hillfields Burghfield Common, Reading, Berkshire, RG7 3YG, England
Tel: (44) 11 8983 5555
Email: guidedogs@guidedogs.org.uk
Website: www.guidedogs.org.uk
Contact: H Perryman, Research co ordinator

Founded in 1931, the Guide Dogs for the Blind Association's mission is to provide guide dogs, mobility and other rehabilitation services that meet the needs of blind and partially sighted people. The Association also supports other activities that enhance the quality of life of visually impaired people, including funding research into eye conditions.

Guide Dogs Ophthalmic Research Grant

Subjects: Guide dogs funds ophthalmic research to encourage developments in ophthalmology (including optometry) that may lead to improved mobility for blind and visually impaired people, or better diagnosis or treatment to aid the preservation of sight and prevent further visual loss in those who are visually impaired.
Purpose: To promote high-quality research relating to the preservation and improvement of sight in those already visually impaired.
Eligibility: Applicants and any research workers must be resident in the United Kingdom. The principal applicant must be in a tenured post for the duration of the requested grant.
Level of Study: Research
Value: Up to UK £60,000 per year
Length of Study: Maximum of 3 years
Frequency: Annual
Study Establishment: Specialist ophthalmic departments or organizations
Country of Study: United Kingdom
No. of awards offered: 4–6, depending on funds
Application Procedure: Applicants must submit an application in accordance with Guide Dogs Ophthalmic Research Grant application guidelines.
Closing Date: Refer to Guide Dogs Ophthalmic Research Grant applicaton guidelines
Funding: Private
Contributor: Donations to the Guide Dogs for the Blind Association
No. of awards given last year: 4
Additional Information: The Guide Dogs for the Blind Association is committed to avoiding the use of experimental animals or tissues from laboratory animals in funded research and will not accept any application that involves these procedures.

GUILLAIN-BARRÉ SYNDROME SUPPORT GROUP

Lincolnshire County Council Offices, Eastgate, Sleaford, Lincolnshire, NG34 8NR, England
Tel: (44) 15 2930 0328
Fax: (44) 15 2930 0328
Email: admin@gbs.org
Website: www.gbs.org.uk
Contact: Administration Officer

The Guillain-Barré Syndrome Support Group provides emotional support, personal visits and comprehensive literature to patients and their relatives and friends. The Group also educates the public and the medical community about the Support Group and maintains their awareness of the illness. The Group fosters research into the causes, treatment and other aspects of the illness and encourages fund raising and support for its activities.

Guillain-Barré Syndrome Support Group Research Fellowship

Subjects: Any aspect of Guillain-Barré syndrome (GBS) or related diseases including chronic inflammatory demyelinating poly-radiculoneuropathy (CIDP).
Purpose: To advance research into the prevention and cure of GBS and CIDP.
Level of Study: Doctorate, Postgraduate, Professional development, Research
Type: Fellowship
Value: Up to UK £65,000
Length of Study: Up to 3 years
Frequency: Dependent on funds available
Study Establishment: Any suitable hospital, university laboratory or department
No. of awards offered: 1
Application Procedure: Applicants must write for an application form.
Closing Date: Please contact the organization
Contributor: Members' donations, fund raising and trust funds
No. of awards given last year: 1
Additional Information: Further information is available on request.

THE GYPSY LORE SOCIETY

5607 Greenleaf Road, Cheverly, MD, 20785, United States of America
Tel: (1) 301 341 1261
Fax: (1) 301 341 1261
Email: headquarters@gypsyloresociety.org
Website: www.gypsyloresociety.org
Contact: Ms Sheila Salo, Treasurer

The Gypsy Lore Society, an international association of persons interested in Gypsy Studies, was formed in the United Kingdom in 1888. The Gypsy Lore Society, North American Chapter, was founded in 1977 in the United States of America and since 1989, has continued as the Gypsy Lore Society. The Society's goals include the promotion of the study of the Gypsy peoples and analogous itinerant or nomadic groups, dissemination of information aimed at increasing understanding of Gypsy culture in its diverse forms and establishment of closer contacts among Gypsy scholars.

Gypsy Lore Society Young Scholar's Prize in Romani Studies

Subjects: Any topic in Romani (Gypsy) studies.
Purpose: To recognize outstanding work by young scholars in Romani (Gypsy) studies.
Eligibility: Graduate students beyond the 1st year of study and PhD holders no more than 3 years beyond the degree. An unpublished paper not under consideration for publication is eligible for this award as well as self-contained scholarly articles of publishable quality that treat a relevant topic in an interesting and insightful way.
Level of Study: Doctorate, Graduate, Postdoctorate
Type: Cash prize
Value: US$500
Frequency: Varies
Study Establishment: Any
Country of Study: Any country
No. of awards offered: 1
Application Procedure: Submission file format is rich text file (RTF, PDF, MS word compatible). Files bigger than 5 MB should be presented on CD to the postal address below. A cover sheet should be included with the title of the paper, the author's name, affiliation, mailing, email address, telephone and fax number, date of entrance into an appropriate program or of awarding of the PhD, and US social security number, if the author has one. The applicant's name should appear on the cover sheet only.
Closing Date: October 30th
Funding: Corporation
Contributor: Gypsy Lore Society
No. of awards given last year: 1
No. of applicants last year: 3

For further information contact:

Gypsy Lore Society Prize Competition, Institute of Musicology, Hungarian Academy of Sciences, H-1250 Budapest, Pf 28, Hungary

Email: kovalcsik@zti.hu
Contact: Katalin Kovalcsik

H·E·A·R·T UK - THE CHOLESTEROL CHARITY

7 North Road, Maidenhead, Berkshire, SL6 1PE, United Kingdom
Tel: (44) 44 (0) 1628 777 046
Fax: (44) 44 (0) 1628 628 698
Email: cr@heartuk.org.uk
Website: www.heartuk.org.uk
Contact: Cathy Ratcliffe , Deputy Director

HEART UK sponsors research in the field of hyperlipidaemia, atherosclerosis (including coronary heart disease, stroke, peripheral arterial disease) with a special emphasis on genetic hyperlipidaemias including familial hypercholesterolaemia, familial combined hyperlipidaema and genetic hypertriglyceridaemia syndromes. Awards are open to basic scientists, professions allied to medicine and medical graduates to assist in travel for the purposes of either direct costs involved in research or to visit other laboratories to learn new techniques.

Conference Awards

Subjects: The charity's Annual Conference.
Eligibility: Open to students, junior clinical, scientific and paramedical staff. Applicants who have been successful in obtaining a conference grant in the last 2 years are not eligible to apply.
Value: Cover travel and registration to the charity's Annual Conference
Application Procedure: Submit your request by email to the Secretariat office (wheldonevents@btconnect.com) detailing why you should be given a grant to attend in no more than 200 words. Attach a supporting letter from your head of department explaining why the travel grant is needed and cannot be locally funded. All applicants will be notified no later than mid April and advised if their application has been successful.
Closing Date: March 24th

Sue McCarthy Travelling Scholarship

Subjects: Medical sciences.
Purpose: The award is designed to support career development for healthcare professionals or for doctors or scientists in training.
Eligibility: Open to senior medical and scientific professionals.
Level of Study: Unrestricted
Type: Scholarship
Value: UK £1,500
Frequency: Annual
Study Establishment: A university, hospital or research institution
Country of Study: United Kingdom
No. of awards offered: 1
Application Procedure: Contact Cathy Ratcliffe, Deputy Director, at HEART UK (cr@heartuk.org.uk) for application information.
Funding: Private
No. of awards given last year: 1
No. of applicants last year: 11
Additional Information: The subject shall include the diagnosis and treatment of lipid disorders including familial genetic disorders; familial hypercholestrolaemia (FH); familial combined hypercholestrolaemia (FCH), etc.

HAEMATOLOGY SOCIETY OF AUSTRALIA AND NEW ZEALAND (HSANZ)

145 Macquarie Street, Sydney, NSW 2000, Australia
Tel: (61) 2 9256 5456
Fax: (61) 2 9252 0294
Email: stephen.ackland@newcastle.edu.au
Website: www.hsanz.org.au
Contact: Lexy Harris

Haematology Society of Australia promote, foster, develop and assist the study and application of haematology. Its main aim is to promote improved standards, interest and research in all aspects of haematology and opportunities for meeting others in related fields of interest and discussing matters of common interest. It nourishes interest haematology amongst other interested persons including regional and international bodies.

Baikie Award

Subjects: Haematology.
Purpose: To recognize the best presentation (either oral or poster) at the annual scientific meeting by a new investigator who is a financial member of the society.
Eligibility: Open to new investigators who were awarded their postgraduate qualification (MSc, FRACP, FRCPA or PhD) within the past 5 years.
Level of Study: Doctorate, Postgraduate, Research
Type: Award
Value: Australian $3,000 plus Baikie Medal
Application Procedure: Applications will be called for in the registration brochure of the annual meeting with the closing date the same as the abstract submission. The award is announced on the last day of the annual meeting.

Celgene/Hsanz Educational Grants

Subjects: All subjects.
Purpose: To support trainee members of the society to attend and present at an international meeting.
Eligibility: Applicants need to be trainee Members of the Society.
Level of Study: Postgraduate
Type: Grant
Value: Australian $3,000 each
No. of awards offered: 4
Application Procedure: Check website for further details.
Closing Date: October 2nd
Additional Information: All applications will be considered by HSANZ Council and the successful applicants will be announced at the annual meeting.

Hott Fellowship Awards

Subjects: All subjects.
Purpose: To support clinical or translational research, or other project initiatives of benefit to the clinical oncology or haematology community within Australia.
Eligibility: Open to individuals undertaking advanced training in medical oncology or haematology, or to more senior oncologists or haematologists with limited research experience.
Type: Grant
Value: Australian $50,000 each
No. of awards offered: 2
Application Procedure: Check the website for further details.
Closing Date: July 2nd

For further information contact:

Website: www.cosa.org.au

Hsanz Travel Grant

Subjects: Science and medicine.
Purpose: To assist members (scientists and medical) with attendance at annual scientific meetings.
Eligibility: Applicants must submit an abstract and register for the meeting.
Level of Study: Research
Type: Grant
Value: Up to Australian $1,000
Application Procedure: Tenable at the HSANZ Annual Scientific Meeting. Please check the website address.

New Investigator Scholarships

Subjects: Haematology.
Purpose: To enhance the scientific stature of Australian and New Zealand haematology by providing the opportunity for medical or science graduates who are undertaking advanced training in haematology to gain experience in acknowledged centres of excellence.
Eligibility: Open for medical or science graduates who are undertaking advanced training in haematology.

Level of Study: Graduate
Value: Australian $30,000 (tax free status if enrolled for a full-time higher degree)
Length of Study: 1 year
Application Procedure: Check website for further details.
Contributor: AMGEN, Bayer Schering Pharma, Novartis. HSANZ matches sponsors' funds dollar for dollar

HAGLEY MUSEUM AND LIBRARY

PO Box 3630, Wilmington, Delaware, DE 19807-0630, United States of America
Tel: (1) 302 658 2400 ext. 243
Fax: (1) 302 655 3188
Email: clockman@hagley.org
Website: www.hagley.org
Contact: Ms Carol Ressler Lockman, Center Co-ordinator

Located along the Brandywine River on the site of the first du Pont black powder works, the Hagley Museum and Library provide a unique glimpse into American life at home and at work in the 19th century. Set among more than 230 acres of trees and flowering shrubs, Hagley offers a diversity of restorations, exhibits and live demonstrations for visitors of all ages.

Hagley Museum and Library Grants-in-Aid of Research

Subjects: American economic and technological history and 18th century French history.
Purpose: To support travel to the Hagley Library for scholarly research in the collections.
Eligibility: Open to degree candidates and advanced scholars of any nationality. Research must be relevant to Hagley's collections.
Level of Study: Doctorate, Graduate, Postdoctorate, Predoctorate
Value: Up to US$1,400 per month
Length of Study: 2–8 weeks
Frequency: Quarterly
Study Establishment: The Library
Country of Study: United States of America
No. of awards offered: 25
Application Procedure: Applicants must submit a completed application form with a five-page proposal.
Closing Date: March 30th, June 29th or October 30th
Funding: Private
Contributor: Foundation funds
No. of awards given last year: 19
No. of applicants last year: 40
Additional Information: Candidates may apply for research in the imprint, manuscript, pictorial and artefact collections of the Hagley Museum and Library. In addition the resources of the 125 libraries in the greater Philadelphia area will be at the disposal of the visiting scholar. The Research Fellowship is to be used only in the Hagley Library.

Henry Belin du Pont Dissertation Fellowship in Business, Technology and Society

Subjects: Business and technology.
Purpose: To aid students whose research on important historical questions would benefit from the use of Hagley's research collections.
Eligibility: Open to graduate students or PhD candidates.
Level of Study: Graduate, Predoctorate
Type: Fellowship
Value: US$6,000, free housing, use of computer, email and internet access and an office
Length of Study: 4 months
Frequency: Annual
Study Establishment: The Center for the History of Business, Technology and Society at Hagley
Country of Study: United States of America
Application Procedure: Applicants must submit an application dossier including a dissertation prospectus, a statement concerning the relevance of Hagley's research collections to the project and at least two letters of recommendation. Writing samples are also welcome. Potential applicants are strongly encouraged to consult with Hagley staff prior to submitting their dossier.
Closing Date: November 15th

Funding: Private
No. of awards given last year: 2
No. of applicants last year: 12
Additional Information: Recipients are expected to have no other obligations during the term of the fellowship, to maintain continuous residence at Hagley for its duration and to participate in events organized by Hagley's Center for the History of Business, Technology and Society. Towards the end of the residency the recipient will make a presentation at Hagley based on research conducted during the Fellowship. Hagley should also receive a copy of the dissertation, as well as any publications aided by the Fellowship.

Henry Belin du Pont Fellowship

Subjects: Areas of study relevant to the library's archival and artefact collections.
Purpose: To support access to and use of Hagley's research collections and to enable individual out-of-state scholars to pursue their own research and to participate in the interchange of ideas among the Center's scholars.
Eligibility: Open to applicants who have already completed their formal professional training. Consequently, degree candidates and persons seeking support for degree work are not eligible to apply. Applicants must not be residents of Delaware and preference will be given to those whose travel costs to Hagley will be higher. Research must be relevant to Hagley's collections.
Level of Study: Doctorate, Postdoctorate, Predoctorate
Type: Fellowship
Value: US$1,500 stipend per month
Length of Study: 2–6 months
Frequency: Quarterly
Study Establishment: The Library
Country of Study: United States of America
No. of awards offered: Varies
Application Procedure: Applicants must submit a completed application form with a five-page proposal.
Closing Date: March 31st, June 30th or October 30th
Funding: Private
Contributor: Foundation funds
No. of awards given last year: 3
No. of applicants last year: 10
Additional Information: Fellows must devote all their time to study and may not accept teaching assignments or undertake any other major activities during the tenure of their fellowships. At the end of their tenure, Fellows must submit a final report on their activities and accomplishments. As a centre for advanced study in the humanities, Hagley is a focal point of a community of scholars. Fellows are expected to participate in seminars, which are conducted periodically, as well as attend colloquia, lectures, concerts, exhibits and other public programmes offered during their tenure. Research fellowships are to be used in the Hagley Library only, not as scholarships for college.

THE HAGUE ACADEMY OF INTERNATIONAL LAW

Peace Palace, Carnegieplein 2, The Hague, NL-2517 KJ, Netherlands
Tel: (31) 70 302 4154
Fax: (31) 70 302 4153
Email: registration@hagueacademy.nl
Website: www.hagueacademy.nl
Contact: The Secretariat

The Hague Academy organizes summer courses in public and private international law, with the aim of furthering scientific and advanced studies of the legal aspects of international relations. The summer courses take place over a period of six weeks in July and August. Please visit our website at www.hagueacademy.nl for all pertinent information.

Centre for Studies and Research

Subjects: Private or public international law.
Purpose: To bring together young international lawyers of a high standard from all over the world to undertake original research and work under the direction of professors on a common general theme determined each year by the Academy.

Eligibility: Open only to academics or lawyers who are less than 40 years of age as on the opening date of the Centre.
Level of Study: Postdoctorate
Type: Scholarship
Value: €35 (daily allowance) and reimbursement of half of the travel expenses upto a maximum of €910
Length of Study: 3 weeks
Frequency: Annual
Study Establishment: Hague Academy of International Law
Country of Study: Netherlands
No. of awards offered: 24 (12 English speaking, 12 French speaking)
Funding: Private
Contributor: Governments
Additional Information: Preference is given to bilingual applicants.

Hague Academy of International Law/Doctoral Scholarships

Subjects: Private or Public International law.
Purpose: To aid individuals with the completion of their theses through research assistance at the Peace Palace Library.
Eligibility: Open to doctoral candidates, up to the age of 35 years, from developing countries who reside in their home country and do not have access to scientific sources.
Level of Study: Doctorate
Type: Scholarships
Value: Travel cost
Length of Study: 2 months
Frequency: Annual
Country of Study: The Netherlands
No. of awards offered: 22 for English and 22 for French speaking participants
Application Procedure: Applicants must submit their applications with a letter of recommendation from the professor under whose direction the thesis is being written. The thesis may be concerned with either private or public international law and the title should be mentioned.
Closing Date: March 15th
Funding: Government
Contributor: The Hague Academy of International Law
No. of awards given last year: 4
No. of applicants last year: 30

Hague Academy of International Law/Scholarships for Sessions of Courses

Subjects: International private or public law.
Purpose: To assist students with living expenses, including the registration fee, during summer courses.
Eligibility: Open to candidates up to the age of 30 years, who have not yet received an Academy scholarship. Applicants must have sufficient knowledge of English or French.
Level of Study: Doctorate
Type: Scholarship
Value: Applicants should contact the Academy for details. Scholars are exempt from registration fees and examination fees. Travelling expenses will not be refunded
Length of Study: 3 weeks
Frequency: Annual
Study Establishment: The Hague Academy of International Law
Country of Study: The Netherlands
No. of awards offered: Varies, 100
Application Procedure: Applicants must apply personally by submitting a curriculum vitae, one photograph and a statement of evidence that the candidate considers to be of value in support of their application. Every application must be typed and accompanied by a recommendation from a professor of international law in a closed envelop. As documents forwarded by applicants are not returned, university certificates or other documents must be submitted in the form of copies, duly verified by a competent authority. The teaching period for which the candidate wants to be registered should be stated clearly.
Closing Date: March 1st
Funding: Private
Contributor: Foundations, institutions and personalities
No. of awards given last year: 110
No. of applicants last year: 600

THE HAMBIDGE

PO Box 339, Rabun Gap, GA, 30568,
United States of America
Tel: (1) 706 746 5718
Fax: (1) 706 746 9933
Email: center@hambidge.org
Website: www.hambidge.org
Contact: The Residency Director

The Hambidge Center's primary function is an artist residency programme with the following aims: to provide artists with time and space to pursue their work, to enhance their communities' art environment, provide public accessibility and to protect and sustain the natural environment, land and endangered species. The Center is set in 600 acres of mountain and valley terrain with waterfalls and nature trails.

Hambidge Residency Program Scholarships

Subjects: Any field or discipline of creative work.
Purpose: To provide applicants with an environment for creative work in the arts and sciences.
Eligibility: Open to qualified applicants in all disciplines who can demonstrate seriousness, dedication and professionalism. International residents are welcome. The Fulton County Arts Council Fellowship is open to residents of Fulton County, Georgia only.
Level of Study: Unrestricted
Type: Fellowship
Length of Study: 2 weeks–2 months
Frequency: Dependent on funds available
Study Establishment: Hambidge
Country of Study: United States of America
Application Procedure: Applicants must submit an application form and work samples to the centre marked for the attention of the Residency Program. The application form can be downloaded from the website.
Closing Date: January 15th, April 15th or September 15th
Funding: Foundation, government, private
No. of awards given last year: 102
Additional Information: The scholarships that are offered by the Center are the Nellie Mae Rowe Fellowship, the Fulton County Arts Council Fellowship and teaching fellowships at public or independent schools.

Nellie Mae Rowe Fellowship

Subjects: Any field or discipline of creative work.
Purpose: The scholarship was established to serve the memory of Nellie Mae Rowe, to recognize the creativity of those artists who come to Hambidge in her name and to encourage the artistic growth of African-American visual artists.
Eligibility: African-American
Level of Study: Unrestricted
Type: Fellowship
Value: All fees
Length of Study: 2 weeks
Frequency: Annual
Study Establishment: Hambidge
Country of Study: United States of America
No. of awards offered: 1
Application Procedure: Applicants must submit an application and work samples to the Center. The application form cabn be downloaded from the website.
Contributor: Judith Alexander
No. of awards given last year: 1

Rabun Gap-Nacoochee School Teaching Fellowship

Subjects: Any field or discipline of creative work.
Purpose: To develop the calibre of creative thinkers.
Level of Study: Unrestricted
Type: Fellowship
Value: All fees
Frequency: Dependent on funds available
Study Establishment: Hambidge
Country of Study: United States of America
No. of awards offered: 1

HAND WEAVERS, SPINNERS & DYERS OF ALBERTA (HWSDA)

228 Park Ridge Close, Camrose, AB T4V 4P1, Canada
Tel: (1) 780 672 2551
Fax: (1) 780 672 5887
Email: studioword@studioword.com
Website: www.hwsda.org

The HWSDA is an exciting network of fibre artisans whose objectives are to foster and promote the development of fibre arts in the province of Alberta for both amateur and professional crafts people.

HWSDA Scholarship Program

Subjects: Textile design.
Purpose: To gain more knowledge in the field of weaving, spinning, dying, felting, basketry.
Eligibility: Open to HWSDA members who are involved in the art of textile design and who need financial help.
Level of Study: Professional development
Type: Scholarship
Value: Up to US$600 in total
Length of Study: 2 years
Frequency: Annual
Country of Study: Canada
Application Procedure: A complete application form and proposals should be submitted to the Vice President.
Closing Date: April 30th
Funding: Foundation
Contributor: The memorial scholarship fund
No. of awards given last year: 3
No. of applicants last year: 3

HARNESS TRACKS OF AMERICA

4640 East Sunrise Drive, Suite 200, Tucson, AZ 85718,
United States of America
Tel: (1) 520 529 2525
Fax: (1) 520 529 3235
Email: info@harnesstracks.com
Website: www.harnesstracks.com

Harness Tracks of America, Inc. is an association of the finest harness racing establishments in the world, dedicated to the advancement and progress of the sport.

Harness Track of America Scholarship

Subjects: Sports.
Purpose: To provide financial assistance to young people actively engaged in the harness racing industry.
Eligibility: Open to applicants with active harness racing involvement.
Level of Study: Professional development
Type: Scholarship
Value: US$5,000
Length of Study: 1 year
Frequency: Annual
No. of awards offered: 4% of the applications
Application Procedure: A completed application form and official academic transcripts must be submitted.
Closing Date: June 15th
No. of awards given last year: 6
No. of applicants last year: 54

THE HARRY FRANK GUGGENHEIM FOUNDATION (HFG)

25 West 53rd Street, 16th Floor, New York, NY, 10019-5401, United
States of America
Tel: (1) 646 428 0971
Fax: (1) 646 428 0981
Email: info@hfg.org
Website: www.hfg.org
Contact: Administrative Assistant

The Harry Frank Guggenheim Foundation (HFG) sponsors scholarly research on problems of violence, aggression and dominance. HFG provides both research grants to established scholars and dissertation fellowships to graduate students during the dissertation writing year. The *HFG Review of Research* is published and a report ID published occasionally every 3 years.

HFG Foundation Dissertation Fellowships

Subjects: Natural and social sciences, humanities.
Purpose: To financially support the research students and increase understanding of the causes, manifestations and control of violence, aggression and dominance. Highest priority is given to research that can increase understanding and amelioration of urgent problems of violence, aggression and dominance in the modern world.
Eligibility: Open to PhD candidates of any nationality who are in the writing stage of their dissertation.
Level of Study: Research, Doctorate, Postdoctorate
Type: Fellowships
Value: US$15,000 each
Frequency: Annual
Country of Study: United States of America
No. of awards offered: 10 or more
Application Procedure: Applicants must submit their application form, abstract, advisor's letter, curriculum vitae, a list of any relevant publications, transcripts and research plan. Application forms are available on the website or on request from the foundation.
Closing Date: February 1st
Funding: Foundation

HFG Research Program

Subjects: The social, behavioural and biological sciences. Research that is related to the Foundation's programme will be considered regardless of the disciplines involved.
Purpose: To promote understanding of the human social condition through the study of the causes and consequences of dominance, aggression and violence.
Eligibility: Open to individuals or institutions in any country.
Level of Study: Postdoctorate, Predoctorate
Value: Up to US$35,000 per year for research grants and $15,000 for dissertation fellowship. Applicants should contact the organization for more details
Length of Study: 1 year, but 2- or 3-year projects may also be considered
Frequency: Annual
Country of Study: Any country
No. of awards offered: 15–35 per year
Application Procedure: Applicants must submit an application form and research proposal along with a curriculum vitae and budget request. Application materials are available by contacting the Foundation.
Closing Date: August 1st for research grant and February 1st for dissertation fellowship
Funding: Foundation
No. of awards given last year: 15
No. of applicants last year: 200
Additional Information: The Foundation operates a programme of specific and innovative study and research. Proposals should be for a specific project and should describe well-defined aims and methods, not general institutional support.

THE HARRY S TRUMAN LIBRARY INSTITUTE

500 West US Highway 24, Independence, MO 64050-1798, United States of America
Tel: (1) 816 268 8248
Fax: (1) 816 268 8299
Email: lisa.sullivan@nara.gov
Website: www.trumanlibrary.org
Contact: Lisa Sullivan, Grants Administrator

The Harry S Truman Library Institute is a non-profit partner of the Harry S Truman Library. The institute's purpose is to foster the Truman Library as a centre for research and as a provider of educational and public programmes.

Harry S Truman Library Institute Dissertation Year Fellowships

Subjects: The public career of Harry S Truman and the history of the Truman administration.
Purpose: To encourage historical scholarship in the Truman era.
Eligibility: Open to graduates who have completed their dissertation research and are ready to begin writing. Dissertations must be on some aspect of the life and career of Harry S Truman or of the public and policy issues that were prominent during the Truman years.
Level of Study: Graduate, Postgraduate
Type: Fellowship
Value: US$16,000, payable in two instalments
Length of Study: 1 year
Frequency: Annual
Country of Study: United States of America
No. of awards offered: 1–2
Application Procedure: Application forms are available from the website.
Closing Date: February 1st for notification in April
Funding: Private
Additional Information: Recipients will not be required to come to the Truman Library but will be expected to furnish the Library with a copy of their dissertation.

THE HASTINGS CENTER

21 Malcolm Gordon Road, Garrison, NY, 10524, United States of America
Tel: (1) 845 424 4040
Fax: (1) 845 424 4545
Email: mail@thehastingscenter.org
Website: www.thehastingscenter.org
Contact: Ms Lori P Knowles, Executive Vice President

The Hastings Center is an independent, non-profit research and educational institute that studies ethical, social and legal issues in medicine, the life sciences, health policy and environment policy.

Hastings Center International Visiting Scholars Program

Subjects: Ethical, legal and policy issues in medicine, the life sciences and the professions.
Purpose: To enable international visiting scholars to spend time at the Center for advanced study and research.
Eligibility: Open to international scholars.
Level of Study: Doctorate, Graduate, Predoctorate, Professional development, Unrestricted, Postdoctorate, Research, Postgraduate
Type: Grant
Value: Assistance with accommodation costs is available based on need
Length of Study: Usually 4–6 weeks
Frequency: Annual
Study Establishment: The Hastings Center
Country of Study: United States of America
No. of awards offered: Varies
Application Procedure: Applicants must visit the website for applications. A detailed description of a research topic and work plan is also required as well as a copy of a recent writing sample, a curriculum vitae and the names and addresses of two referees.
Closing Date: Applications are accepted at any time, but should be submitted at least 3 months prior to the proposed stay
Funding: Private
No. of awards given last year: 13
No. of applicants last year: 15
Additional Information: Participation in the ongoing activities of the Center such as conferences, seminars and workshops is encouraged.

HATTORI FOUNDATION

7 Exton Street, London, SE1 8UE, England
Tel: (44) 20 7620 3055
Fax: (44) 20 7620 3054
Email: admin@hattorifoundation.org.uk
Website: www.hattorifoundation.org.uk
Contact: Mrs Sarah C Dickinson, Administrator

The chief aim of the Hattori Foundation is to encourage and assist exceptionally talented young instrumental soloists or chamber ensembles who are British nationals or resident in the United Kingdom, and whose talent and achievement give promise of an international career.

Hattori Foundation Awards
Subjects: Instrumental, solo performance and ensembles.
Purpose: To assist young instrumentalists of exceptional talent in establishing a solo or chamber music career at international level.
Eligibility: Open to British or foreign nationals aged 21–27 years studying full-time in the United Kingdom. Candidates should be of postgraduate performance level.
Level of Study: Postgraduate, Professional development
Type: Award
Value: No pre-determined amounts. The grant is based on the requirements of the approved project
Length of Study: Varies
Frequency: Annual
Country of Study: British Nationals can study in any country. Foreign nationals must be resident in the United Kingdom only
No. of awards offered: Up to 20
Application Procedure: Applicants must submit a completed application form with reference forms and a 30 minute performance (recital) on cassette tape or compact disc.
Closing Date: April 30th
Funding: Private
Contributor: Hattori family
No. of awards given last year: 13
No. of applicants last year: 59
Additional Information: Grants may be made for study, concert experience and international competitions, but course fees and the purchase of instruments are not funded. Projects must be submitted for approval and discussion with the Director of Music and the trustees. Auditions take place in June and are in two stages.

HAYSTACK MOUNTAIN SCHOOL OF CRAFTS

PO Box 518, Deer Isle, ME, 04627, United States of America
Tel: (1) 207 348 2306
Fax: (1) 207 348 2307
Email: haystack@haystack-mtn.org
Website: www.haystack-mtn.org
Contact: Ginger Aldrich, Development Director

The Haystack Mountain School of Crafts studio programme in the arts offers 1 and 2 week workshops in a variety of craft and visual media including blacksmithing, clay, wood, glass, metals, fibres and graphics.

Haystack Scholarship
Subjects: Fine crafts.
Purpose: To allow craftspeople of all skill levels to study at Haystack sessions for 1 or 2 week periods. Technical assistant and work study positions as well as minority scholarships and fellowships are awarded.
Eligibility: Open to nationals of any country, who are 18 years or older. Technical Assistant Scholarship: 1 year of graduate specialization or the equivalent in the craft area for which is requested. Work study Scholarship: Intended for those who show high promise in their craft field. Criteria include stated financial need, commitment to and growing knowledge of the craft area for which application is made, and the ability to work in a supportive, close-knit community. Minority Scholarship: Haystack awards up to six full scholarships to students of colour. Same criteria as work study scholarships.
Level of Study: Postgraduate, Research, Unrestricted
Type: Scholarships and fellowships
Value: US$600–1,800
Length of Study: 1 and 2 week sessions
Frequency: Annual
Country of Study: Any country
No. of awards offered: 100

Application Procedure: Applications available on the website or by contacting the school. Applicants must include references and supporting materials in their application.
Closing Date: March 1st
Funding: Foundation, individuals, private
No. of awards given last year: 100
No. of applicants last year: 300
Additional Information: Technical assistance are responsible for assisting the instructor and for shop maintenance and organization. Expected to be familiar with general technical requirements of the particular studio/medium. Responsibilities take precedence, but there is ample time for personal work and study. Work study and minority scholarship students will be assigned periodic tasks in the kitchen, or around the school campus. Assigned tasks will not exceed three hours daily, and students have ample time for personal work and study in the studio.

HEALTH RESEARCH BOARD (HRB)

Research & Development for Health, 73 Lower Baggot Street,
Dublin 2, Ireland
Tel: (353) 1 676 1176
Fax: (353) 1 661 1856
Email: hrb@hrb.ie
Website: www.hrb.ie
Contact: The Research Grants Manager

The Health Research Board (HRB) comprises 16 members appointed by the Minister of Health, with eight of the members being nominated on the co-joint nomination of the universities and colleges. The main functions of the HRB are to promote or commission health research, to promote and conduct epidemiological research as may be appropriate at national level, to promote or commission health services research, to liase and co-operate with other research bodies in Ireland and overseas in the promotion of relevant research and to undertake such other cognate functions as the Minister may from time to time determine.

Clinical Research Training Fellowship in Nursing and Midwifery
Subjects: Nursing and midwifery.
Purpose: To provide experienced nurses and midwives with an opportunity to carry out research in clinical nursing or midwifery, leading to a postgraduate degree at the Master's or doctoral level. These fellowships will provide nurses with the research experience necessary to develop their expertise as specialists in their chosen field of nursing or midwifery.
Eligibility: To be eligible for a fellowship a candidate must: be registered as a nurse or midwife; have practised professional nursing or midwifery for at least 5 years; hold a post in nursing or midwifery practice or a post related to nursing or midwifery; have been employed in the Irish health services or an Irish academic Department of Nursing and/or Midwifery, within 2 years prior to the closing date for application to the Fellowship; confirm support approval from Head of Department in which the research study is being carried out; and provide evidence of academic supervision from a suitably qualified nurse or a midwife.
Level of Study: Predoctorate, Graduate
Type: Fellowship
Value: Salary on postdoctoral scale and consumables of €7,500 p.a
Length of Study: Up to 3 years
Frequency: Annual
Study Establishment: Fellowships are tenable by nurses or midwives employed in a recognized health service or an Irish academic Department of Nursing and/or Midwifery and registered with an academic Department of Nursing and/or Midwifery or other relevant academic department
Country of Study: Ireland
Application Procedure: Applicants can obtain an application form from our website.
Closing Date: December 14th
Funding: Government
No. of awards given last year: 4
No. of applicants last year: 20

Clinician Scientist Award for Clinical Health Professionals

Subjects: Word class research clinical and translational research with a strong relevance to human health.

Purpose: To release outstanding medically or professionally qualified researchers in the health professions from some or all of their service commitment to conduct.

Eligibility: Medical consultants in the Irish health system or senior clinicians in health related disciplines who are qualified to hold a post in the Irish health service.

Level of Study: Research

Value: €1.5 million

Length of Study: 5 years

Frequency: Annual

Study Establishment: Any Irish teaching hospital or academic institution

Country of Study: Ireland

No. of awards offered: 2–3

Application Procedure: Online application form available from website. Full applications from invited applicants only.

Closing Date: October 13th

Funding: Government

No. of awards given last year: 1

No. of applicants last year: 5

Health Services Research Training Fellowships and Palliative Care Fellowships

Subjects: Clinical, epidemiological, public health, statistics, health economics, social science, operational and management disciplines.

Purpose: To enable graduates with some appropriate relevant experience to pursue a career in health devices and research in Ireland.

Eligibility: Candidates must normally hold a primary degree in a discipline relevant to health services research, have acquired appropriate postgraduate experience in the field of health services and research, have support from an approved academic department or centre, have obtained the prior approval of a head of department for the research study being proposed and be Irish citizens or graduates from overseas with a permanent Irish resident status.

Level of Study: Postgraduate

Type: Fellowship

Value: Please consult the organization salary on a postdoctorate scale up to €7,500 p.a for consumables

Length of Study: The maximum period of the award will be 3 years,

Frequency: Annual

Study Establishment: Institutions approved by the Board, such as teaching hospitals, universities, research institutes and health boards in Ireland

Country of Study: Ireland

No. of awards offered: Varies

Application Procedure: Applicants must complete an online application form, available from the website.

Closing Date: October 12th

Funding: Government

No. of awards given last year: 4

No. of applicants last year: 20

HRB Clinical Research Training Fellowships

Subjects: Biomedicine.

Purpose: To support medical and dental graduates with appropriate experience who are interested in gaining specialized clinical research training in a biomedical field in Ireland, leading to a PhD.

Eligibility: Candidates should be graduates in medicine or dentistry up to and including senior registrar or equivalent academic level. Applicants must be registered or have completed their higher specialized training.

Level of Study: Doctorate

Value: Please consult the organization salary on registrar's scale consumables of €15,000 p.a

Length of Study: Up to 3 years

Frequency: Annual

Study Establishment: At an appropriate academic department in the Republic of Ireland or Northern Ireland

Country of Study: Ireland

No. of awards offered: Varies

Application Procedure: Applicants must apply with the support of the head of an appropriate sponsoring laboratory in the Republic of Ireland. Candidates may apply to remain in their current laboratory, to return to one where they have worked before or to move to a new laboratory. Applicants have to fill in on online form available on the website.

Closing Date: October 19th

Funding: Government

No. of awards given last year: 8

No. of applicants last year: 42

Additional Information: Proposals may be submitted for specialized research training or for training in a basic subject relevant to a particular clinical interest.

HRB Postdoctoral Research Fellowships

Subjects: Researchers who hold a PhD and want to develop their career, as an advanced level in a health-related discipline.

Purpose: Career development in health related disciplines.

Eligibility: Applicants must be postdoctorates with less than 5 years of postdoctoral experience.

Level of Study: Postdoctorate

Type: Fellowship

Value: Salary on senior postdoctorate scale plus consumables of €15,000 p.a

Length of Study: Up to 3 years

Frequency: Annual

Study Establishment: A university, research hospital or institute

Country of Study: Ireland

No. of awards offered: Varies

Application Procedure: Applicants must complete an online application form, available from the website.

Closing Date: October 5th

Funding: Government

No. of awards given last year: 8

No. of applicants last year: 50

HRB Project Grants-General

Subjects: Biomedical sciences, public health and epidemiology, health services research or health research.

Purpose: To facilitate research in biomedical sciences, public health, epidemiology and health service research.

Eligibility: Postdoctoral researches can apply for their own salary support his or her speciality should be within the range of disciplines stated in the subject index. Applicants must reside in the Republic of Ireland and grants are tenable in this country.

Level of Study: Doctorate, Postdoctorate

Type: Project funding

Value: Please consult the organization. €100,000 p.a. if employing salaried researcher, €75,000 p.a if training PhD student

Length of Study: Up to 3 years

Frequency: Annual

Study Establishment: An Irish academic institution of research

Country of Study: Ireland

No. of awards offered: Varies

Application Procedure: Applicants must complete an online application form, available from the website.

Closing Date: November 2nd

Funding: Government

No. of awards given last year: 74

No. of applicants last year: 339

HRB Summer Student Grants

Subjects: Medical, biomedical, dental science, health service and science.

Purpose: To develop interest in research and give the student the opportunity to become familiar with research techniques.

Eligibility: Open to students from medical, dental science, biomedical or health service-related disciplines.

Level of Study: Undergraduate

Type: Grant

Value: €250 per week for up to 8 weeks

Length of Study: 8 weeks

Frequency: Annual

Study Establishment: A university, research hospital or institution

Country of Study: Ireland

No. of awards offered: Varies
Application Procedure: Applicants must complete an online application form, available from the website.
Closing Date: April 11th
Funding: Government
No. of awards given last year: 50
No. of applicants last year: 100

HRB Translational Research Programmes
Purpose: To enable researchers to establish and support teams working full-time or extensive or long-term research programmes that have a clear link to patient care; to support the development of clinical research in Ireland; to improve patient outcomes and to contribute to the creation of IPR.
Eligibility: Open to candidates who hold a post in an established academic research centre, have an outstanding track record and have at least 5 years of research experience.
Value: €1.5 million
Length of Study: 5 years
Frequency: Annual
Study Establishment: Any Irish academic or research institution
Country of Study: Ireland
Application Procedure: Online application form available from the HRB website.
Closing Date: October 6th
Funding: Government
No. of awards given last year: 4
No. of applicants last year: 12

THE HEART AND STROKE FOUNDATION

1402-222 Queen Street, Ottawa, Ontario, K1P 5V9, Canada
Tel: (1) 613 569 4361 ext 275
Fax: (1) 613 569 3278
Email: research@hsf.ca
Website: www.heartandstroke.ca

The Heart and Stroke Foundation is involved in eliminating heart disease and stroke and reducing their impact through the advancement of research and its application, and advocacy for the promotion of healthy living. It is a federation of 10 provincial foundations, led and supported by a force of more than 140,000 volunteers.

Canada Doctoral Research Award
Subjects: Cardiology.
Purpose: To award highly qualified graduate students enrolled in a PhD program, undertaking full-time research training in the cardiovascular or cerebrovascular fields.
Eligibility: Open to students enrolled in a PhD program and must be a full-time medical student.
Level of Study: Doctorate, Research
Type: Research
Value: $21,000
Country of Study: Canada
No. of awards offered: 20–30
Application Procedure: Applicants must send the application form along with the transcript, essay references and a self-addressed stamped envelope.
Closing Date: November 1st

For further information contact:

Research Department
Tel: 613 569 4361 ext. 327
Fax: 613 569 3278
Email: lhodgson@hsf.ca
Contact: Lise Hodgson, Administrative Assistant

Career Investigator Award
Subjects: Cardiology.
Purpose: To make their research a full-time career.
Eligibility: Applicants must possess a MD, PhD, or equivalent degree and working in the field of cardiovascular and/or cerebrovascular disease. Applicants must provide proof of national recognition.
Level of Study: Postgraduate
Type: Scholarship

Value: Minimum $48,282
Application Procedure: Applicants must send the application form along with the transcript, essay references and a self-addressed stamped envelope and must provide proof of national recognition.
Closing Date: September 1st
Contributor: Heart and Stroke Foundations of Ontario and British Columbia and the Yukon

For further information contact:

Research Department
Tel: 613 569 4361 ext. 327
Fax: 613 569 3278
Email: lhodgson@hsf.ca
Contact: Lise Hodgson, Administrative Assistant

Dr Andres Petrasovits Fellowship in Cardiovascular Health Policy Research
Subjects: Cardiology.
Eligibility: Please visit the website www.hsf.ca/research/application/index.html
Level of Study: Postgraduate
Type: Fellowship
Value: Maximum $44,568
No. of awards offered: 1
Application Procedure: Check website www.hsf.ca/research/application/index.html
Closing Date: November 14th

For further information contact:

Research Department
Tel: 613 569 4361 ext. 327
Fax: 613 569 3278
Email: lhodgson@hsf.ca
Website: www.hsf.ca/research/application/index.html
Contact: Lise Hodgson, Administrative Assistant

Grants-in-Aid of Research and Development
Subjects: Cardiology.
Purpose: To support researchers in projects of experimental nature in cardiovascular or cerebrovascular development.
Eligibility: Open for full-time medical student.
Level of Study: Postgraduate
Type: Grant
Value: $20,798,400
Frequency: Every 3 years
Application Procedure: Applicants must send the application form along with the transcript, essay references and a self-addressed stamped envelope.
Closing Date: September 1st

For further information contact:

Research Department
Tel: 613 569 4361 ext. 327
Fax: 613 569 3278
Email: lhodgson@hsf.ca
Contact: Lise Hodgson, Administrative Assistant

Heart and Stroke Foundation of Canada New Investigator Research Scholarships
Subjects: Cardiology.
Eligibility: Open to candidates who possess a MD, PhD, or equivalent degree and working in the field of cardiovascular and/or cerebrovascular disease.
Level of Study: Postgraduate
Type: Scholarship
Value: Maximum $37,140
No. of awards offered: 8–10
Application Procedure: Applicants must send the application form along with the transcript, essay references and a self-addressed stamped envelope.
Closing Date: September 1st

For further information contact:

Research Department

Tel: 613 569 4361 ext. 327
Fax: 613 569 3278
Email: lhodgson@hsf.ca
Contact: Lise Hodgson, Administrative Assistant

Heart and Stroke Foundation of Canada Nursing Research Fellowships

Subjects: Cardiology.
Eligibility: Applicants must possess a Nursing degree. For master's degree candidates, the programmes must include a thesis or project requirement.
Level of Study: Postgraduate
Type: Fellowship
Value: $18,570
Country of Study: Canada
No. of awards offered: 1–3
Application Procedure: Applicants must send the application form along with the transcript, essay references and a self-addressed stamped envelope.
Closing Date: March 14th

For further information contact:

Research Department
Tel: 613 569 4361 ext. 327
Fax: 613 569 3278
Email: lhodgson@hsf.ca
Contact: Lise Hodgson, Administrative Assistant

Heart and Stroke Foundation of Canada Research Fellowships

Subjects: Cardiology.
Eligibility: Applicants must possess a full-time degree for study towards an MSc or PhD.
Level of Study: Postgraduate
Type: Fellowship
Value: Up to $1,500 per annum is available for travel for scientific purposes
Country of Study: Canada
No. of awards offered: 10–20
Application Procedure: Applicants must send the application form along with the transcript, essay references and a self-addressed stamped envelope.
Closing Date: November 1st

For further information contact:

Research Department
Tel: 613 569 4361 ext. 327
Fax: 613 569 3278
Email: lhodgson@hsf.ca
Contact: Lise Hodgson, Administrative Assistant

Heart and Stroke Foundation of Canada Visiting Scientist Program

Subjects: Cardiology.
Eligibility: Applicants must be Canadians studying abroad or in Canada or for foreign visitors to Canada. The fellowship is open to citizens of United States of America.
Level of Study: Postgraduate
Type: Fellowship
Value: $2,228–8,914
Country of Study: Canada
Application Procedure: Applicants must send the application form along with the transcript, essay references and a self-addressed stamped envelope.
Closing Date: December 15th

For further information contact:

Research Department
Tel: 613 569 4361 ext. 327
Fax: 613 569 3278
Email: lhodgson@hsf.ca
Contact: Lise Hodgson, Administrative Assistant

HEART RESEARCH UK

Suite 12D, Joseph's Well, Leeds, LS3 1AB, England
Tel: (44) 11 3234 7474
Fax: (44) 11 3297 6208
Email: mail@heartresearch.org.uk
Website: www.heartresearch.org.uk

Heart Research UK funds pioneering medical research into the prevention, treatment and cure of heart disease. Heart Research UK is a visionary charity leading the way in funding ground-breaking, innovative medical research projects at the cutting edge of science into the prevention, treatment and cure of heart disease. There is a strong emphasis on clinical and surgical projects and young researchers. Heart Research UK encourages and supports original health lifestyle initiatives exploring novel ways of preventing heart disease in all sectors of the community.

Heart Research UK Clinical Research Training Fellowships

Subjects: Training for clinicians who wish to develop an academic research career in cardiovascular medicine.
Purpose: To support ground-breaking, innovative medical research into prevention, treatment and cure of heart disease and related conditions.
Eligibility: Medical graduates wishing to develop an academic research career with a view to acquiring a higher degree. Clinicians who are postdoctorates with less than 5 years experience can also apply.
Level of Study: Doctorate, Postdoctorate, Postgraduate, Predoctorate, Research
Type: Fellowship
Value: A maximum of £150,000
Length of Study: A maximum of 3 years
Frequency: Annual
Study Establishment: Centres of health and educational establishments
Country of Study: United Kingdom
No. of awards offered: 2
Application Procedure: Application forms can also be downloaded from the Heart Research UK website www.heartresearch.org.uk.
Closing Date: See website www.heartresearch.org.uk
Funding: Corporation, foundation, individuals, private, trusts
Contributor: Voluntary funding from supporters and grant-making trusts
Additional Information: Grants are specifically to give high calibre and talented clinicians the opportunity to undertake research training in the area of cardiovascular disease.

Heart Research UK Novel and Emerging Technologies Grant

Subjects: Research on new and emerging technologies and applications of bio-engineering and molecular strategies for cardiovascular diseases
Purpose: To support ground-breaking, innovative medical research into the prevention, treatment and cure of heart disease and related conditions.
Eligibility: Graduates or those holding a suitable professional qualification. Research must be carried out in the United Kingdom at a university, hospital or other recognized research institution.
Level of Study: Research, Unrestricted
Type: Project grant
Value: Maximum UK £200,000
Length of Study: Maximum 3 years
Frequency: Annual
Study Establishment: Centres of health and educational establishments
Country of Study: United Kingdom
No. of awards offered: 1
Application Procedure: Applicants must send 7 copies of application, outlining aims and objectives, to the Heart Research Medical Review Panel on the appropriate form.
Closing Date: Please see our website, www.heartresearch.org.uk for details
Funding: Trusts
Contributor: Voluntary funds from supporters and grant-making trusts

Additional Information: Appropriate approaches would include tissue and bio-engineering, development and evaluation of new therapeutic devices, bioimaging nanotechnology, biomaterials, genomic and proteomic approaches, computational biology and bioinformatics.

Heart Research UK Translational Research Project Grants

Subjects: Translational research projects that convert fundamental research into clinical benefits.
Purpose: To support ground-breaking, innovative medical research into prevention, treatment and cure of heart disease and related conditions.
Eligibility: Graduates or those holding a suitable professional qualification. Research must be carried out in the UK at a university, hospital or other recognized research institution.
Type: Project grant
Value: A maximum of £150,000
Length of Study: A maximum of 3 years
Frequency: Annual
Study Establishment: Centres of health and educational establishments
Country of Study: United Kingdom
No. of awards offered: Varies
Application Procedure: Application forms can also be downloaded from the Heart Research UK website www.heartresearch.org.uk
Closing Date: See website www.heartresearch.org.uk
Funding: Corporation, foundation, private, trusts
Contributor: Voluntary funding from supporters and grant-making trusts
Additional Information: Grants are for research which efficiently transfers innovative discoveries into practical tools to prevent, diagnose and treat cardiovascular disease.

HEBREW IMMIGRANT AID SOCIETY (HIAS)

333 Seventh Avenue, 16th Floor, New York, NY, 10001, United States of America
Tel: (1) 212 613 1358
Fax: (1) 212 967 4356
Email: scholarship@hias.org
Website: www.hias.org
Contact: Scholarship Department

The Hebrew Immigrant Aid Society (HIAS) is the oldest international and refugee resettlement agency in the United States of America, dedicated to assisting persecuted and opressed people worldwide and delivering them to safe havens. HIAS has helped more than 4.5 million people in its 126 years of existence.

HIAS Scholarship Awards Competition

Subjects: All subjects.
Purpose: To help HIAS-assisted refugees and asylees in pursuing higher education.
Eligibility: Open to HIAS-assisted refugees and asylees in the United States of America. United States of America applicants must have completed 1 year, i.e. two semesters, at a United States of America high school, college, or graduate school. The student must have immigrated after January 1, 1992.
Level of Study: Postgraduate, Doctorate, Graduate, MBA, Postdoctorate, Predoctorate, Professional development, Research, Unrestricted, and trade programs
Type: Scholarship
Value: Average US$2,000
Length of Study: 1 year must be completed in a US School prior to beginning the award and applicant must be poised to start another academic year
Frequency: Annual
Country of Study: United States of America
No. of awards offered: Varies, approx. 150
Application Procedure: Applicants must complete an official application form, which must be filled online. Application forms are available from mid-November to mid-February of each year.
Closing Date: February 24th
Funding: Individuals, private

No. of awards given last year: 131
No. of applicants last year: 420
Additional Information: Applications are judged on financial need, academic scholarship and community service. The HIAS Scholarship Awards Competition in Israel has a different deadline, award amount, specifications, etc. For further information visit the website www.hias.org/scholarships/apply.html

HEINRICH-BÖLL FOUNDATION

Studienwerk, Rosenthaler Street. 40/41, Berlin, 10178, Germany
Tel: (49) 030 285 340
Fax: (49) 030 285 34109
Email: info@boell.de
Website: www.boell.de

Heinrich-Boll Foundation, affiliated with the Green Party, is a legally independent political foundation working in the spirit of intellectual openness. Its primary objective is to support political education both within Germany and abroad, thus promoting democratic involvement, socio-political activism and cross-cultural understanding.

Heinrich Böll Foundation Doctoral Scholarships

Subjects: All subjects.
Purpose: To provide support to students pursuing their Doctoral studies.
Eligibility: Open to those who have either fulfilled the Doctorate entry requirements of a state or state-recognized university or college in Germany or have a foreign university or college degree.
Level of Study: Doctorate, Postgraduate
Type: Scholarship
Value: Varies
Length of Study: 1–3 years
Frequency: Annual
Country of Study: Germany
Application Procedure: Please check the website for details.
Closing Date: September 1st
Funding: Foundation
Contributor: German Ministry of Foreign Affairs

Heinrich Böll Foundation Scholarships for Postgraduate Studies

Subjects: All subjects.
Purpose: To provide support to students pursuing their postgraduate studies (MA/MSc).
Eligibility: Open to applicants who have completed their undergraduate studies (bachelor's degree, diploma, magister, state examination).
Level of Study: Postgraduate
Type: Scholarship
Value: Varies
Length of Study: 2 years
Frequency: Twice a year
Country of Study: Germany
Application Procedure: Refer the foundation website for further details.
Closing Date: March 1st and September 1st
Funding: Foundation
Contributor: German Ministry of Foreign Affairs

THE HENRY MOORE INSTITUTE

74 The Headrow, Leeds, LS1 3AH, United Kingdom
Tel: (44) 11 3246 7467
Fax: (44) 11 3246 1481
Email: hmi@henry-moore.ac.uk
Website: www.henry-moore-fdn.co.uk/hmi
Contact: Ellen Tait

The Henry Moore Institute aims to enlarge the understanding of how sculpture makes meaning at different times and in different places through a programme of exhibitions, talks, conferences, publications and through its collection activities and research fellowship programme.

Henry Moore Institute Research Fellowship

Subjects: Sculpture, both historical and contemporary.
Purpose: To enable scholars to use the Institute's facilities, which include the sculpture collection, library, archive and slide library, to assist them in researching their particular field.
Eligibility: There are no restrictions.
Level of Study: Doctorate, Postdoctorate, Postgraduate, Research
Type: Fellowship
Value: Accommodation, travel and daily living expenses
Length of Study: 1 month
Frequency: Annual
Study Establishment: The Henry Moore Institute
Country of Study: United Kingdom
No. of awards offered: 4
Application Procedure: Applicants must send a letter of application (marked RF), a proposal (maximum 1,000 words) and a curriculum vitae.
Closing Date: January 12th
Funding: Private
Contributor: The Henry Moore Foundation
No. of awards given last year: 4
No. of applicants last year: 70

Henry Moore Institute Senior Research Fellowships

Subjects: Any aspect of sculpture. Fellows are asked to make a small contribution to the research programme in Leeds in the form of a talk or a seminar.
Purpose: Senior fellowships are intended to give established scholars (working on any aspect of sculpture) time and space to develop a research project free from their usual work commitments.
Level of Study: Postdoctorate, Doctorate
Type: Fellowship
Value: Fellowships provide accommodation, travel expenses and a per diem
Length of Study: 3–6 weeks
Frequency: Annual
Study Establishment: Henry Moore Institute
Country of Study: United Kingdom
No. of awards offered: Up to 2 senior fellowships
Application Procedure: Full details are available from the website www.henry-moore.ac.uk. Applicants can also contact the institute at its address for details. An applicant must send a curriculum vitae and a proposal along with his or her letter of application.
Closing Date: January
Funding: Foundation
Contributor: Henry Moore Foundation
No. of awards given last year: 1
Additional Information: Research fellowships are also available. The institute offers the possibilty of presenting finished research in published form as a seminar or as a small exhibition.

For further information contact:

Tel: 0113 246 7467
Email: kirstie@henry-moore.ac.uk
Contact: Kirstie Gregory, Research Programme Assistant

THE HERB SOCIETY OF AMERICA, INC.

9019 Kirtland Chardon Road, Kirtland, OH, 44094,
United States of America
Tel: (1) 440 256 0514
Fax: (1) 440 256 0541
Email: herbs@herbsociety.org
Website: www.herbsociety.org
Contact: Ms Michelle Milks, Office Administrator

The aim of the Herb Society of America Inc. is to promote the knowledge, use and delight of herbs through educational programmes, research and sharing the experience of its members with the community.

Herb Society of America Research Grant

Subjects: Herbal projects.

Purpose: To further the knowledge and use of herbs and to contribute the results of study and research to the records of horticulture, science, literature, history, art or economics.
Eligibility: Open to persons with a proposed programme of scientific, academic or artistic investigation of herbal plants.
Level of Study: Unrestricted
Value: Up to US$5,000
Length of Study: Up to 1 year
Frequency: Annual
Country of Study: Any country
Application Procedure: Applicants must submit an application clearly defining all their research in 500 words or less and a proposed budget with specific budget items listed. Requests for funds will not be considered unless accompanied by five copies of the application form and proposal.
Closing Date: January 31st
Contributor: Members
Additional Information: Finalists will be interviewed.

HSA Grant for Educators

Subjects: Herbal projects.
Purpose: To deliver herbal education in schools, communities, or any public forum.
Level of Study: Unrestricted
Value: Up to US$5,000
Length of Study: Up to 1 year
Frequency: Annual
Country of Study: Any country
Application Procedure: Please submit application cover sheet, statement of qualifications, a comprehensive descriptions of the programme, and detailed budget (8 copies).
Closing Date: December 31st
Contributor: Members
No. of awards given last year: 1
Additional Information: Finalists will be interviewed.

HERBERT HOOVER PRESIDENTIAL LIBRARY ASSOCIATION

302 Parkside Drive, PO Box 696, West Branch, IA, 52358, United
States of America
Tel: (1) 319 643 5327
Fax: (1) 319 643 2391
Email: info@hooverassociation.org
Website: www.hooverassociation.org
Contact: Ms Patricia A Hand, Manager of Promotions & Academic Programs

The Herbert Hoover Presidential Library Association is a private, non-profit support group for the Herbert Hoover Presidential Library Museum and National Historic Site in West Branch, Iowa.

Herbert Hoover Presidential Library Association Travel Grants

Subjects: American history, journalism, political science and economic history.
Purpose: To encourage the scholarly use of the holdings, and to promote the study of subjects of interest and concern to Herbert Hoover, Lou Henry Hoover and other public figures.
Eligibility: Open to current graduate students, postdoctoral students and qualified independent scholars. Priority is given to well-developed proposals that utilize the resources of the Library, have the greatest likelihood of publication and subsequently, greatest likelihood of use by educators, students and policy makers.
Level of Study: Doctorate, Graduate, Postdoctorate, Postgraduate, Predoctorate, Professional development, Research
Type: Travel grant
Value: US$500–1,500 to cover the cost of a trip to the Library. There is no money available for any purpose other than to defray the expense of travel to West Branch, IA
Length of Study: Varies by individual
Frequency: Annual
Study Establishment: The Herbert Hoover Presidential Library-Museum in West Branch, IA
Country of Study: United States of America

No. of awards offered: Varies
Application Procedure: Applicants must submit a completed application form, a project proposal of up to 1,200 words and three letters of reference, mailed separately. The application form can be obtained from the website.
Closing Date: March 1st
Funding: Private
No. of awards given last year: 8
No. of applicants last year: 12
Additional Information: For archival holdings information please contact the Hoover Library on (1) 319 643 5301, email: hoover.library@nara.gov or visit the website: www.hoover.archives.gov

HERBERT SCOVILLE JR PEACE FELLOWSHIP

322 4th Street, NE, Washington, DC, 20002, United States of America
Tel: (1) 202 543 4100
Fax: (1) 202 543 6297
Email: scoville@clw.org
Website: www.scoville.org
Contact: Paul Revsine, Program Director

The Herbert Scoville Jr Peace Fellowship was established in 1987 to provide college graduates with the opportunity to gain a Washington perspective on key issues of peace and security.

Herbert Scoville Jr Peace Fellowship

Subjects: Arms control and disarmament.
Purpose: To provide a unique educational experience to outstanding graduates, that will allow them to develop leadership skills that can serve them throughout a career in arms control or a related area of public service, to contribute to the work of the participating arms control and disarmament organizations and to continue the work of Herbert Scoville Jr.
Eligibility: Open to United States of America college graduates with experience or interest in arms control, disarmament, international security and/or peace issues. A fellowship is awarded periodically to a foreign national from a country of arms proliferation concern to the United States of America.
Level of Study: Postgraduate
Type: Fellowship
Value: Please contact the organization
Length of Study: 4–6 months
Country of Study: United States of America
Application Procedure: Applicants must telephone, write or consult the website for information on application requirements.

THE HEREDITARY DISEASE FOUNDATION (HDF)

3960 Broadway 6th Floor, New York, NY, 10032, United States of America
Tel: (1) 202 326 6666
Email: carljohnson@hdfoundation.org
Website: www.hdfoundation.org
Contact: Carl D Johnson

The Hereditary Disease Foundation (HDF) was formed in 1968. HDF spearheaded the Venezuela Collaborative Huntington's Disease Project, which led to the identification in 1983 of a genetic marker for Huntington's disease. The HDF offers support for research projects that will contribute to identifying and understanding the basic defect of Huntington's disease.

John J. Wasmuth Postdoctoral Fellowships

Subjects: Trinucleotide expansions, animal models, gene therapy, neurobiology and development of the basal ganglia, cell survival and death and intercellular signalling in striatal neurons.
Purpose: To support research on Huntington's disease.
Level of Study: Postdoctorate, Research
Type: Fellowship
Value: Up to US$56,000
Length of Study: 1 year

Frequency: Annual
Country of Study: United States of America
Application Procedure: A completed application form must be submitted online.
Closing Date: February 15th, June 15th, October 15th
Funding: Foundation

HERIOT-WATT UNIVERSITY

Postgraduate Admissions Office, Edinburgh, EH14 4AS, England
Tel: (44) 131 451 3866
Email: research@rgu.ac.uk.
Website: www.rgu.ac.uk
Contact: The Bursar

Chevening Scholarship

Subjects: Any subject.
Purpose: To enable talented graduates and young professionals to become familiar with the UK and gain skills which will benefit their countries.
Eligibility: Details available at the website www.chevening.com
Level of Study: Doctorate, Postgraduate
Type: Scholarship
Value: Variable
Length of Study: Variable
Frequency: Annual
Country of Study: United Kingdom
No. of awards offered: 1000 plus
Application Procedure: Apply direct at www.chevening.com
Closing Date: Variable
Funding: Government
Contributor: Foreign and Commonwealth Office
Additional Information: Further details are available at www.chevening.com

For further information contact:

Website: www.chevening.com

DFID Shared Scholarship Scheme

Subjects: All subjects.
Purpose: To assist students from developing Commonwealth countries to come to the UK for a 1-year taught Master's degree when they would otherwise be financially unable to do so.
Eligibility: The award has an upper age limit of 35 years with preference given to applicants under 30 years of age. Government employees are ineligible. Awards made must be relevant to the economic, scientific and social development of the applicant's home country which must be a part of the Commonwealth.
Level of Study: Postdoctorate
Value: Tuition fees plus a maintenance grant
Length of Study: 1 year
Frequency: Annual
Study Establishment: Heriot-Watt University
Country of Study: United Kingdom
No. of awards offered: 2
Application Procedure: Applicants should apply through their school of study.

James Watt Scholarships

Subjects: All research areas.
Purpose: To support suitably qualified students undertake research activities at Heriot-Watt University.
Eligibility: All students.
Type: Scholarship
Value: Full university fees plus a contribution to maintenance costs
Length of Study: Up to 3 years
Frequency: Annual
Study Establishment: Heriot-Watt University
Country of Study: United Kingdom
No. of awards offered: Variable
Application Procedure: Please contact your school for further details.
Closing Date: April 30th

Music Scholarships

Subjects: All subjects.
Purpose: To support musicians in obtaining a postgraduate qualification whilst developing their musical skills.
Eligibility: All instrumentalists and vocalists who have been accepted for a course.
Level of Study: Postgraduate
Value: Free music tuition
Length of Study: 1 year
Frequency: Annual
Study Establishment: Heriot-Watt University
Country of Study: United Kingdom
No. of awards offered: 40
Application Procedure: Please contact your school for further details.

Overseas Scholarships Scheme

Subjects: All taught courses.
Purpose: To support high-calibre students pursue postgraduate study at Heriot-Watt University.
Eligibility: Open to all suitably qualified overseas students on a competitive basis.
Level of Study: Postgraduate
Type: Scholarship
Value: Value varies by school but offers a partial fee remission
Length of Study: 1 year
Frequency: Annual
Study Establishment: Heriot-Watt University
Country of Study: United Kingdom
No. of awards offered: Variable
Application Procedure: Please contact your school directly for advice on making an application.
Closing Date: Varies

Partial Fee Remission Scholarships

Subjects: Subjects covered are in the school of management and languages and include economics, management, accounting and finance and translating and interpreting.
Purpose: To support high-calibre students pursue postgraduate study at Heriot-Watt University.
Eligibility: Open to UK/EU students on a competive basis.
Level of Study: Postgraduate
Type: Scholarship
Value: Up to £1,500
Length of Study: 1 year
Frequency: Annual
Study Establishment: Heriot-Watt University
Country of Study: United Kingdom
No. of awards offered: Varies
Application Procedure: Please contact the school of management and languages directly for advice on applying.

Scotland–USA Graduate Scholarships

Subjects: All subjects.
Purpose: To allow US nationals to undertake postgraduate study at Heriot-Watt University.
Eligibility: Applicants must be US nationals normally resident in the USA. Awards will be made on the basis of academic merit.
Level of Study: Postgraduate
Type: Scholarship
Value: Up to £2,000
Length of Study: 1 year
Frequency: Annual
Study Establishment: Heriot-Watt University
Country of Study: United Kingdom
No. of awards offered: Up to 3
Application Procedure: Applications can be made online at www.scotland-usa-scholarship.com

Sports Scholarships

Subjects: All subjects.
Purpose: To support atheletes in obtaining a postgraduate qualification whilst continuing to develop their sporting prowess.
Eligibility: All students competing at a national level in any sport.
Level of Study: Postgraduate

Type: Scholarship
Value: Between £500 and £1,500
Length of Study: 1 year
Frequency: Annual
Study Establishment: Heriot-Watt University
Country of Study: United Kingdom
No. of awards offered: 30
Application Procedure: Applications should be made to the Sports Scholarship Co-ordinator if an offer of a place to study at Heriot-Watt University is held.
Closing Date: March 15th

THE HERTZ FOUNDATION

2456 Research Drive Zip-3850, Livermore, CA, 94550, United States of America
Tel: (1) 925 373 1642
Fax: (1) 925 373 6329
Email: askhertz@hertzfoundation.org
Website: www.hertzfoundation.org
Contact: Ms Linda Kubiak, Fellowship Administrator

The Fannie and John Hertz Foundation runs a national competition for graduate fellowships in the applied physical sciences.

The Graduate Fellowship Award

Subjects: Applied physical and biophysical sciences.
Purpose: To support students of outstanding potential in the applied physical sciences.
Eligibility: Open to citizens or permanent residents of the United States of America who have received a Bachelor's degree by the start of tenure and who propose to complete a programme of graduate study leading to a PhD. Students who have commenced graduate study are also eligible. The Foundation does not support candidates pursuing joint PhD and professional degree programmes.
Level of Study: Doctorate
Type: Fellowship
Value: US$31,000 per 9 month academic year, plus cost-of education allowance
Length of Study: 1 academic year and may be renewed annually for up to 5 years
Frequency: Annual
Study Establishment: Specific universities listed on the website
Country of Study: United States of America
No. of awards offered: 20
Application Procedure: Applicants must complete a Hertz application form, four reference reports on the supplied specific forms and official transcripts of all college work must be submitted. The application form is available from the Foundation's website.
Closing Date: October 28th
Funding: Private
No. of awards given last year: 15
No. of applicants last year: Approx. 550

HERZOG AUGUST LIBRARY

PO Box 1364, D-38299, Wolfenbuettel, Germany
Tel: (49) 5331 808 208
Fax: (49) 5331 808 266
Email: bepler@hab.de
Website: www.hab.de
Contact: Dr Gillian Bepler

The Herzog August Library is an independent research library devoted to the study of the cultural history of Europe from the middle ages to the early modern period. Its rich book manuscript holdings were founded in the 17th century and have survived intact until today.

Findel Scholarships and Schneider Scholarships

Subjects: History and related disciplines.
Purpose: The Herzog August Library administers the doctoral fellowships funded by the Dr Guenther Findel Foundation and Rolf and Ursula Schneider Foundation towards the advancement of history and other related disciplines.

Eligibility: Outstanding doctoral candidates from all over the world, whose research requires an intensive use of the rich collections at Herzog August Library, may apply.
Level of Study: Doctorate, Predoctorate
Type: Scholarship
Value: €700 per month. Additionally, the Herzog August Library provides accommodation for Fellows in its guest house
Length of Study: 3–6 months
Frequency: Twice a year
Study Establishment: Herzog August Library
Country of Study: Germany
Application Procedure: An application form is available on request.
Closing Date: April 1st and November 1st
Funding: Foundation
Contributor: Findel and Schneider Foundations
No. of awards given last year: 15
Additional Information: If researchers are already supported by another grant/fellowship, the foundation will only provide free accommodation, but no subsistence allowance.

Herzog August Library Fellowship

Subjects: History and all related disciplines.
Purpose: Awards to post-doctoral researchers whose projects are based on the historical book and manuscript holdings of the Wolfenbuettel Library.
Eligibility: Qualified researchers whose projects are partly or fully based on the library's holdings.
Type: Fellowship
Value: €1,600 per month
Length of Study: 2–12 months
Study Establishment: Herzog August Library
Country of Study: Germany
Application Procedure: Application forms available on request.
Closing Date: January 31st
Contributor: State of Lower Saxony
No. of awards given last year: 20
No. of applicants last year: 80
Additional Information: Fellowship holders have a residence requirement in Wolfenbuttel during their tenure. The library has its own guest accomodation.

Mellon Research Fellowships

Subjects: Humanities.
Eligibility: Postdoctoral researchers from Bulgaria, Hungary, Poland, Rumania, Czech Republic, Slovakia and Baltic countries, whose research requires an intensive use of the rich collections at Herzog August Library, are eligible to apply.
Level of Study: Postdoctorate
Type: Fellowship
Value: US$11,500
Length of Study: 3 months
Study Establishment: Herzog August Library
Country of Study: Germany
Application Procedure: Application forms are available on request.
Closing Date: January 31st and March 31st
Contributor: Andrew W. Mellon Foundation
No. of awards given last year: 3

HIGHER EDUCATION COMMISSION

Islamabad, H-9, Pakistan
Tel: (92) 92 51 9257651 60
Fax: (92) 92 51 9290128
Email: info@hec.gov.pk
Website: www.hec.gov.pk

The Higher Education Commission has been set up to facilitate the development of the universities of Pakistan to be world-class centers of education, research and development.

International Research Support Initiative Program

Subjects: All subjects.
Purpose: To provide a training programme.
Eligibility: Open to candidates who have completed their PhD. studies and who are under the age of 45 years.

Level of Study: Doctorate
Type: Scholarship
Value: Travel costs (up to Rs 80,000), monthly stipend (up to Rs 70,000) and bench fee (up to Rs 200,000)
Length of Study: 6 months
Frequency: Annual
Application Procedure: A completed application form, which is available on the website, must be sent.
Closing Date: November 21st
Funding: Government
Additional Information: The candidates will have to enter into a bond with HEC to serve the country at least for 3 years.

Overseas Scholarship for MS (Engineering) in South Korean Universities

Subjects: Engineering.
Purpose: To create a critical mass of highly qualified engineering manpower in high-tech field.
Eligibility: Open to Pakistan and AJK nationals who are the below the age of 35 years.
Level of Study: Doctorate
Type: Scholarship
Value: US$9,600 and round-trip expenses from South Korea
Length of Study: 24 months
Frequency: Annual
Country of Study: South Africa
No. of awards offered: 250
Application Procedure: A completed application form along with all other requirements must be sent.
Funding: Government

For further information contact:

HRD Divison Higher Education Commission
Contact: Reznana Siddiqui, Project Director (SK/FFSP)

Partial Support for PhD Studies Abroad

Subjects: All subjects.
Purpose: To financially support Pakistan students who are in the final stage of completion of their PhD studies abroad.
Eligibility: Open to candidate who are Pakistan nationals who are studying abroad.
Level of Study: Doctorate
Type: Scholarship
Value: Up to US$15,000
Frequency: Annual
Application Procedure: A completed application form along with photocopies of all academic documents must be sent.
Funding: Government
Additional Information: An awardee is required to execute a bond with HEC to serve Pakistan for 2 years.

HILDA MARTINDALE EDUCATIONAL TRUST

Royal Holloway University of London, Egham, Surrey, TW20 0EX, England
Tel: (44) 17 8443 4455
Fax: (44) 17 8443 7520
Email: francesca.chiarelli@rhul.ac.uk
Contact: Miss J L Hurn, Secretary to the Trustees

The Hilda Martindale Educational Trust was set up by Miss Hilda Martindale in order to help women of the British Isles with the costs of vocational training for any profession or career likely to be of use or value to the community. Applications are considered annually by six women trustees.

Hilda Martindale Exhibitions

Subjects: Any vocational training for a profession or career likely to be of value to the community.
Purpose: To assist with the costs of vocational training.
Eligibility: Open to women of the British Isles. Assistance is not given for short courses, courses abroad, elective studies, intercalated BSc years, access courses or academic research. Awards are not given to

those who are eligible for grants from research councils, the British Academy or other public sources.
Level of Study: Graduate, Postgraduate, Professional development
Type: Grant
Value: Varies, normally UK £200–1,000
Length of Study: 1 year
Frequency: Annual
Study Establishment: Any establishment approved by the trustees
Country of Study: United Kingdom
No. of awards offered: 15–20
Application Procedure: Applicants must complete two copies of an application form, which must be obtained from and returned to the Secretary to the Trustees.
Closing Date: March 1st for the following academic year. Late or retrospective applications will not be considered
Funding: Private
Contributor: Private trust
No. of awards given last year: 16
No. of applicants last year: 69

THE HINRICHSEN FOUNDATION

2-6 Baches Street, London, N1 6DN, England
Email: hinrichsen.foundation@editionpeters.com
Contact: L Adamson, Administrator

Hinrichsen Foundation Awards

Subjects: Contemporary music composition, performance and research.
Purpose: To promote the written areas of music.
Eligibility: Preference will be given to United Kingdom applicants and projects taking place in the United Kingdom. Grants are not given for recordings, for the funding of commissions, for degree or other study courses or for the purchase of instruments or equipment.
Level of Study: Unrestricted
Value: Varies
Frequency: Dependent on funds available
No. of awards offered: Varies
Application Procedure: Applicants must submit a completed application form along with two references.
Closing Date: Applications are accepted at any time
No. of awards given last year: 37 grants, 1 composition bursary
No. of applicants last year: 105

For further information contact:

The Hinrichsen Foundation, PO Box 309, KT22 2AT

HISPANIC ENGINEER NATIONAL ACHIEVEMENT AWARDS CONFERENCE (HEENAL)

3900 Whiteside, Los Angeles, CA 90063-1615, United States of America
Tel: (1) 323 292 0997
Website: www.henaac.org
Contact: Kathy Borunda, The Administrator

HENAAL Scholars program

Purpose: To award scholarships to graduate and undergraduate science, technology, engineering and mathematics (STEM) students.
Eligibility: Full-time students majoring in STEM, with a minimum grade of 3.0 in their GPA, and active in student and community organizations and attending school in the US.
Level of Study: Predoctorate, Doctorate
Type: Scholarship
Value: US$500–5,000 but varies
Frequency: Annual
Country of Study: United States of America
No. of awards offered: Approx. 75
Application Procedure: Application forms can be downloaded from the HENAAL website www.henaal.org
Closing Date: April 30th
Funding: Corporation, foundation, individuals

No. of awards given last year: 75
No. of applicants last year: 410

HISTORY OF SCIENCE SOCIETY (HSS)

Executive Office, PO Box 117360, University of Florida, Gainesville, FL 32611-7360, United States of America
Tel: (1) 352 392 1677
Fax: (1) 352 392 2795
Email: info@hssonline.org
Website: www.hssonline.org
Contact: Mr Robert J Malone, Executive Director

The History of Science Society (HSS) is the world's largest society dedicated to understanding science, technology, medicine and their interactions with society within their historical context.

The George Sarton Medal

Subjects: History of science.
Purpose: To honour an outstanding historian of science for lifetime scholarly achievement.
Eligibility: Open to candidates who have devoted their entire career to the field of the history of science.
Level of Study: Postgraduate
Type: Award
Value: The George Sarton Medal
Frequency: Annual
Application Procedure: A completed nomination form that is available online must be sent.
Closing Date: February1st
Funding: Foundation
Contributor: Dibner Fund
No. of awards given last year: 1

Joseph H. Hazen Education Prize

Subjects: Science education.
Purpose: To promote exemplary teaching and educational service in the history of science.
Eligibility: Open to applicants who have made outstanding contributions to the teaching of history sciences.
Level of Study: Postgraduate
Type: Award
Value: US$1,000
Frequency: Annual
Application Procedure: A completed application form along with the nominee's curriculum vitae must be sent.
Closing Date: April 1st
Funding: Foundation
No. of awards given last year: 1
No. of applicants last year: 10

Margaret W. Rossiter History of Women in Science Prize

Subjects: Medicine, technology, social and national sciences.
Purpose: To recognize an outstanding book (in odd–numbered years) or article (in even–numbered years) on the history of women in science.
Eligibility: Open to authors of books/articles that have been published no more than 4 years before the year of award.
Level of Study: Postgraduate
Type: Prize
Value: US$1,000
Frequency: Annual
No. of awards offered: 1
Application Procedure: A completed nomination form, available on the website, must be sent.
Closing Date: April 1st
Funding: Foundation
No. of awards given last year: 1
No. of applicants last year: 25

The Nathan Reingold Prize

Subjects: History of science.
Purpose: To recognize an outstanding student essay in the history of science and its cultural influences.

Eligibility: Open to all original student essays that have not been published.
Level of Study: Doctorate
Type: Prize
Value: US$500 and up to US$500 towards travel reimbursement
Frequency: Annual
No. of awards offered: 1
Application Procedure: A complete application form along with an electronic copy of the essay and proof of student status must be submitted.
Closing Date: April 1st
Funding: Foundation
Contributor: Friends and family of Nathan Reingold
No. of awards given last year: 1
No. of applicants last year: 12

Pfizer Award

Subjects: History of science.
Purpose: To honour outstanding books related to the history of science.
Eligibility: Open to authors books of that are published in the last 3 years.
Level of Study: Postgraduate
Type: Award
Value: US$2,500
Frequency: Annual
Application Procedure: A completed nomination form that is available on the website must be sent.
Closing Date: April 1st
Funding: Corporation
No. of awards given last year: 1
No. of applicants last year: 65

Suzanne J. Levinson Prize

Subjects: History of the life sciences or natural history.
Purpose: To be awarded for an outstanding book on the history of the life sciences and natural history.
Eligibility: Books on the history of natural history or evolutionary theory published 4 years prior to the award year are eligible.
Type: Prize
Value: $1,000
Frequency: Every 2 years, Biennial
No. of awards offered: 1
Application Procedure: Nominations can be downloaded from the website.
Funding: Foundation
No. of awards given last year: 1
No. of applicants last year: 40

Watson Davis and Helen Miles Davis Prize

Subjects: Writing.
Purpose: To promote a book that helps in public understanding of the history of science.
Eligibility: Open to authors of books published in the last 3 years.
Level of Study: Postgraduate
Type: Prize
Value: US$1,000
Frequency: Annual
Application Procedure: A completed nomination form that is available on the website must be submitted.
Closing Date: April 1st
Funding: Private
No. of awards given last year: 1
No. of applicants last year: 70

THE HITACHI FOUNDATION

21F Akihabara UDX Building, 14-1, Soto-Kanda 4-chome,
Chiyoda-ku, Tokyo, 101-8010, Japan
Website: www.hitachi.com

The Hitachi Foundation is an independent, nonprofit, philanthropic organization established by Hitachi Ltd. in 1985. Our purpose is to enhance the well being of economically isolated people in the United States of America, especially by exploring the value and limits of good corporate citizenship. The Foundation operates three programmes, each with its own mission and guidelines. Though autonomous, the Foundation plays an important role in assisting Hitachi in its effort to be a good corporate citizen in North America and its own corporate social responsibility (CSR) initiatives.

Hitachi Foundation Scholarship

Subjects: Science and technology.
Purpose: To encourage Southeast Asian students to study at Japanese graduate schools as full-time students for Master's or Doctoral course in the field of science and technology.
Eligibility: Open to candidates employed in a firm postion in the university, who are below 30 years of age and has obtained a Bachelor's degree (for master's course) and who are below 35 years of age and has obtained a Master's degree (for doctoral course).
Level of Study: Doctorate, Postgraduate
Type: Scholarship
Value: Travel expenses, arrival and return allowance (¥50,000), stipend (¥180,000), housing allowance, tuition and other school expenses, field study expenses (¥50,000), expenses to make presentation at international conferences and expenses to attend the Foundation activities
Length of Study: For Master's course, two and half years and for doctoral course, three and half years (including half a year for the study of Japanese language prior to commencement of the course)
Country of Study: Japan
Application Procedure: Applications should be endorsed by the President's office of the university to which the Foundation has offered the scholarship award and submitted to the Foundation address through registered mail.
Closing Date: November 30th

HONDA FOUNDATION

2nd Floor, Honda Yaesu Bldg, 6–20 Yaesu 2-chome, Chuo-ku, Tokyo,
104, Japan
Tel: (81) 3 3274 5125
Fax: (81) 3 3274 5103
Email: xv6m-nkmr@asahi-net.or.jp
Website: www.soc.nii.ac.jp/hf
Contact: Yutaka Ishihara, Secretary General

The Honda Foundation was established in December 1977 to contribute to the creation of true human civilization on the basis of the philosophy of the late Mr Soichiro Honda, the founder of Honda Motor Company Limited.

Honda Prize

Subjects: Ecotechnology.
Purpose: To recognize a distinguished achievement in the field of ecotechnology.
Eligibility: Open to individuals or an organization, irrespective of nationality.
Type: Prize
Value: The prize includes a donation of ¥10,000,000 and a medal
Frequency: Annual
Application Procedure: Approved recommenders of the Honda Foundation are able to recommend.
Closing Date: March 31st
Funding: Private
Contributor: The late Mr Soichiro Honda, the founder of Honda Motor Company Limited
No. of awards given last year: 1
No. of applicants last year: 1
Additional Information: Ecotechnology is a new concept that harmonizes the progress of technology and civilization, rather than pursuing technology designed solely for efficiency and profit.

HONG KONG JOCKEY CLUB MUSIC AND DANCE FUND

Secretariat Home Affairs Bureau, 41/F Revenue Tower, 5 Gloucester
Road, Wanchai, Hong Kong
Tel: (852) 2594 5628/ 5621
Email: customer.care@hkjc.com
Website: www.info.hkjc.com

Hong Kong Jockey Club Music and Dance Fund as a contributer of the Hong Kong Arts Festival, the Club provides grants to the Festival each year with the aim of bringing new arts and cultural experiences to local audiences as well as building a growing international reputation for Hong Kong.

Hong Kong Jockey Club Music and Dance Fund Scholarship

Subjects: Music and dance.
Purpose: To enable exceptionally talented candidates to pursue an integrated programme of postgraduate studies or professional training in music or dance outside Hong Kong at a world-renowned institution.
Eligibility: Applicants for the scholarship must be permanent Hong Kong residents who have resided in Hong Kong for 7 continuous years immediately preceding the application period. Applicants must not be above 32 years of age and must hold a relevant degree or post-form 7 tertiary qualification in either music or dance specifically.
Level of Study: Professional development, Postgraduate
Type: Scholarship
Value: Varies
Frequency: Annual
Application Procedure: Application forms can be downloaded from the website.
Closing Date: January
Additional Information: For further information, please call the Secretariat during office hours at 2594 5628 (Ms WONG) or 2594 5621 (Mr LEUNG).

THE HOROWITZ FOUNDATION FOR SOCIAL POLICY

PO Box 7, Rocky Hill, NJ, 08553 0007, United States of America
Tel: (1) 609 921 1479
Fax: (1) 732 445 3138
Email: ihorowitz@transactionpub.com
Website: www.horowitz-foundation.org
Contact: Mr Irving Louis Horowitz, The Chairman

An independent foundation for the support and advancement of social science research in related to issues of social and economic policies in press related to issue of social and economic policies.

Eli Ginzberg Award

Subjects: Social sciences, including anthropology, area studies, economics, political science, psychology, sociology and urban studies as well as newer areas such as evaluation research.
Purpose: To support a project involving solutions to major urban health problems in urban settings.
Eligibility: Open to nationals of any country. Candidates may propose new projects, or also solicit support for research in progress, travel, or preparing a work for publication.
Level of Study: Unrestricted
Type: Grant
Value: US$3,000–5,000 with an additional stipend
Length of Study: 1 year
Frequency: Annual
Country of Study: Any country
No. of awards offered: 1
Application Procedure: Application forms may be requested from the Horowitz Foundation or downloaded from the website. The application should be accompanied by a cover sheet listing the name of the applicant, the title of the project, a 50-word abstract stating what is to be done and why including the methodology to be used and a 50-word summary of the policy implications of the research. The application must be signed.
Closing Date: January 31st
Funding: Private

Harold D. Lasswell Award

Subjects: Social sciences, including anthropology, area studies, economics, political science, psychology, sociology and urban studies as well as newer areas such as evaluation research.
Purpose: To support policy-related projects in international relations and foreign affairs.

Eligibility: Open to nationals of any country. Candidates may propose new projects, or also solicit support for research in progress, including final work on a dissertation, supplementing research in progress, travel funds, or preparing a work for publication.
Level of Study: Unrestricted
Type: Grant
Value: US$3,000–5,000 with additional stipend
Length of Study: 1 year
Frequency: Annual
Country of Study: Any country
No. of awards offered: 1
Application Procedure: Applications forms may be requested from The Horowitz Foundation or downloaded from the website. The application should be accompanied by a cover sheet listing the name of the applicant, the title of the project, a 50-word abstract stating what is to be done and why, including the methodology to be used and a 50-word summary policy implication of the research. The application must be signed.
Closing Date: January 31st
Funding: Private
Additional Information: The cover sheet in the application is most important, as it is the basis for the initial screening of prospects.

John L Stanley Award

Subjects: Social sciences, including anthropology, area studies, economics, political science, psychology, sociology and urban studies as well as newer areas such as evaluation research.
Purpose: To support a work that seeks to expand our understanding of the political and ethical foundations of policy research.
Eligibility: Open to nationals of any country. Candidates may propose new projects or also solicit support for research in progress, including final work on a dissertation, supplementing research in progress, travel funds, or preparing a work for publication.
Level of Study: Graduate, Unrestricted
Type: Grant
Value: US$3,000–5,000 with additional stipend
Length of Study: 1 year
Frequency: Annual
Country of Study: Any country
No. of awards offered: 1
Application Procedure: Application forms may be requested from the Horowitz Foundation or downloaded from the website. The application should be accompanied by a cover sheet listing the name of the applicant, the title of the project, a 50-word abstract stating what is to be done and why including the methodology to be used and a 50-word summary of the policy implications of the research. The application must be signed.
Closing Date: January 31st
Funding: Private
Additional Information: The cover sheet in the application is most important, as it is the basis for the initial screening of prospects.

Joshua Feigenbaum Award

Subjects: Social sciences, including anthropology, area studies, economics, political science, psychology, sociology and urban studies as well as newer areas such as evaluation research.
Purpose: To support empirical research on policy aspects of the arts and popular culture, with special reference to mass communication.
Eligibility: Open to nationals of any country. Candidates may propose new projects, or also solicit support for research in progress, including final work on a dissertation, supplementing research in progress, travel funds, or preparing a work for publication.
Level of Study: Unrestricted
Type: Grant
Value: US$3,000–5,000 with additional stipend
Length of Study: 1 year
Frequency: Annual
Country of Study: Any country
No. of awards offered: 1
Application Procedure: Applications forms may be requested from The Horowitz Foundation or downloaded from the website. The application should be accompanied by a cover sheet listing the name of the applicant, the title of the project, a 50-word abstract stating what is to be done and why, including the methodology to be used and a 50-word summary policy implication of the research. The application must be signed.

Closing Date: January 31st
Funding: Private
Additional Information: The cover sheet in the application is most important, as it is the basis for the initial screening of prospects.

Martinus Nijhoff Award

Subjects: Social sciences, including anthropology, area studies, economics, political science, psychology, sociology and urban studies as well as newer areas such as evaluation research.
Purpose: To support policy implications of scientific, technological and medical research.
Eligibility: Open to nationals of any country. Candidates may propose new projects, or also solicit support for research in progress, including final work on a dissertation, supplementing research in progress, travel funds, or preparing a work for publication.
Level of Study: Unrestricted
Type: Grant
Value: US$3,000–5,000 with additional stipend
Length of Study: 1 year
Frequency: Annual
Country of Study: Any country
No. of awards offered: 1
Application Procedure: Applications forms may be requested from The Horowitz Foundation or downloaded from the website. The application should be accompanied by a cover sheet listing the name of the applicant, the title of the project, a 50-word abstract stating what is to be done and why, including the methodology to be used and a 50-word summary policy implication of the research. The application must be signed.
Closing Date: January 31st
Funding: Private
Additional Information: The cover sheet in the application is most important, as it is the basis for the initial screening of prospects.

Robert K Merton Award

Subjects: Social sciences including anthropology, area studies, economics, political science, psychology, sociology and urban studies as well as newer areas such as evaluation research.
Purpose: To support studies in the relation between social theory and public policy.
Eligibility: Open to nationals of any country. Candidates may propose new projects, or also solicit support for research in progress, travel funds, or preparing a work for publication.
Level of Study: Unrestricted
Type: Grant
Value: US$3,000–5,000 with additional stipend
Length of Study: 1 year
Frequency: Annual
Country of Study: Any country
No. of awards offered: 1
Application Procedure: Application forms may be requested from the Horowitz Foundation or downloaded from the website. The application should be accompanied by a cover sheet listing the name of the applicant, the title of the project, a 50-word abstract stating what is to be done and why including the methodology to be used and a 50-word summary of the policy implications of the research. The application must be signed.
Closing Date: January 31st
Funding: Private
Additional Information: The cover sheet in the application is most important, as it is the basis for the initial screening of prospects.

HORSERACE BETTING LEVY BOARD (HBLB)

52 Grosvenor Gardens, London, SW1W 0AU, England
Tel: (44) 20 7333 0043
Fax: (44) 20 7333 0041
Email: equine.grants@hblb.org.uk
Website: www.hblb.org.uk
Contact: Equine Grants Team

The Horserace Betting Levy Board (HBLB) operates in accordance with the Betting, Gaming and Lotteries Act 1963. It assesses and collects contributions from bookmakers and the Horserace Totalisator Board and uses these for the advancement of equine veterinary science and education and other improvements within the horseracing industry.

Horserace Betting Levy Board Senior Equine Clinical Scholarships

Subjects: Equine veterinary studies with emphasis on the Thoroughbred horse.
Purpose: To support postgraduate equine veterinary clinical training.
Eligibility: Open to holders of veterinary degrees recognised by the RCVS, who have at least 2 years experience in veterinary practice.
Level of Study: Postgraduate
Type: Scholarship
Value: €19,100 stipend in year 1 with increments for years 2, 3 and 4. The institution receives €9,200 to cover expenses directly relevant to the scholarship
Length of Study: Up to 4 years, subject to satisfactory progress
Frequency: Annual
Study Establishment: At any of the University veterinary schools, or in a joint venture with any appropriate university department, research institute or veterinary practice in the United Kingdom
Country of Study: United Kingdom
No. of awards offered: Usually 1, sometimes 2 per year
Application Procedure: The study establishment must submit applications in appropriate forms.
Closing Date: Early September. Please check with the HBLB for further details
Funding: Government
No. of awards given last year: 1
No. of applicants last year: Not limited
Additional Information: Awards normally commence on October 1st. The study establishment is responsible for the appointment of clinical scholars.

Horserace Betting Levy Board Veterinary Research Training Scholarship

Subjects: Equine veterinary medicine or science, with emphasis on the Thoroughbred.
Purpose: To support postgraduate equine veterinary research training.
Eligibility: Open to holders of a veterinary degree who wish to undertake full-time training in research in the equine veterinary field leading to a PhD.
Level of Study: Postgraduate
Type: Scholarship
Value: UK £19,100 stipend in year 1, with increments for years 2 and 3. UK £4,000 (accountable) per year for fees and expenses, and UK £5,200 (unaccountable) per year to the department in which the holder works. Scales are reviewed annually
Length of Study: Up to 3 years, subject to satisfactory progress
Frequency: Annual
Study Establishment: Any of the University veterinary schools, any appropriate university department or research institute in the United Kingdom
Country of Study: United Kingdom
No. of awards offered: Up to 2 per year
Application Procedure: Applicants must submit applications in appropriate forms.
Closing Date: Usually early September. Please check with the HBLB for further details
Funding: Government
No. of awards given last year: 2
No. of applicants last year: Maximum 3 per institution
Additional Information: The study establishment is responsible for the appointment of research scholars. Awards normally commence on October 1st.

HORTICULTURAL RESEARCH INSTITUTE

1000 Vermont Street North West, Suite 300, Washington, DC, 20005, United States of America
Tel: (1) 202 789 2900 ext. 3014
Fax: (1) 202 789 1893
Email: tjodon@anla.org
Website: www.anla.org/research
Contact: Ms Teresa A Jodon, Endowment Program Administrator

The aim of the Horticultural Research Institute is to direct, fund, promote and communicate research that increases the quality and value of plants, improves the productivity and profitability of the nursery and landscape industry and protects and enhances the environment.

Horticultural Research Institute Grants

Subjects: Nursery and landscape industry, especially woody and perennial landscape plants, their production, marketing, landscape, water management or the environment.
Purpose: To support necessary research for the advancement of the nursery, greenhouse and landscape industry.
Eligibility: Open to nationals and permanent residents of the United States of America and Canada. Candidates must submit an appropriate project that the Institute feels is deserving of support.
Level of Study: Unrestricted
Type: Grant
Value: US$5,000–30,000
Length of Study: 1 year, occasionally renewable by reapplication
Frequency: Annual
Study Establishment: State or federal research laboratories, land grant universities, forest research stations, botanical gardens and arboreta
Country of Study: United States of America
No. of awards offered: 15–30
Application Procedure: Applicants must submit the application electronically.
Closing Date: May 15th
Funding: Private
Contributor: Nursery and landscape firms, as well as state and regional nursery and landscape associations
No. of awards given last year: 18
No. of applicants last year: 105
Additional Information: Applicants should visit the website to download an application form.

HOSPITAL FOR SICK CHILDREN RESEARCH TRAINING CENTRE (RESTRACOMP)

555 University Avenue, Toronto,
ON, M5G 1X8, Canada
Tel: (1) 416 813 6825
Fax: (1) 416 813 7311
Email: jennifer.ng@sickkids.ca
Website: www.sickkids.on.ca
Contact: N. Ramsundar

RESTRACOMP Research Fellowship

Subjects: Paediatric research, biomedical research.
Purpose: To provide funds to postgraduate students or Fellows seeking research training.
Eligibility: Open to those nominated by the active senior staff of the Research Institute of the Hospital for Sick children. Postdoctoral trainees at the hospital for Sick Children, working under sick kids scientific staff.
Level of Study: Postdoctorate, Postgraduate, Graduate
Type: Fellowship
Value: Up to Canadian $36,750 per year
Length of Study: 2 years
Frequency: Biannual
Study Establishment: The Hospital for Sick Children, Toronto
Country of Study: Canada
No. of awards offered: 20–30 per annum
Application Procedure: Applicants must submit a completed application form.
Closing Date: Applications are accepted in mid-April and mid-October
Funding: Foundation
No. of applicants last year: 30% success rate

HOUBLON-NORMAN FUND

Bank of England, Threadneedle Street, London, EC2R 8AH, England
Tel: (44) 20 7601 3778
Fax: (44) 20 7601 4423
Email: MA-HNGfund@bankofengland.co.uk
Website: www.bankofengland.co.uk/about/fellowships/index.htm
Contact: Miss Emma-Jayne Coker, Business Support Unit

Houblon-Norman Fellowships/George Fellowships

Subjects: Economics and finance.
Purpose: To promote research into and disseminate knowledge and understanding of the working, interaction and function of financial and business institutions in the United Kingdom and elsewhere and the economic conditions affecting them.
Eligibility: Open to distinguished research workers as well as younger postdoctoral or equivalent applicants of any nationality. Preference will be given to the United Kingdom and European Union nationals.
Level of Study: Postdoctorate
Type: Fellowship
Value: The value of a fellowship is dependent on the candidate's circumstances and will be of such amount as seems necessary for undertaking the work. It might take the form of payment to the individual's employer
Length of Study: 1 month–1 year
Frequency: Annual
Study Establishment: The Bank of England
Country of Study: United Kingdom
No. of awards offered: Varies
Application Procedure: Applicants must complete an application form advertised through one Economist, one Royal economic society and our website, where an application form can be found www.bankofengland.co.uk/education/fellowships/index.htm
Closing Date: As advertised in the press
No. of awards given last year: 3
No. of applicants last year: 16

HUDSON RIVER FOUNDATION (HRF)

17 Battery Place, Suite 915, New York, NY 10004, United States of America
Tel: (1) 212 924 7667
Fax: (1) 212 924 8325
Email: info@hudsonriver.org
Website: www.hudsonriver.org
Contact: Grants Management Officer

The Hudson River Foundation (HRF) supports scientific research, education and projects to enhance public access to the Hudson River. The purpose of the Foundation is to make science integral to the decision-making process with regard to the Hudson River and its watershed and to support competent stewardship of this extraordinary resource.

Hudson River Graduate Fellowships

Subjects: Research on the resources, key species, toxic substances, abundances of key organisms, dynamics of Hudson River trophic webs, hydrodynamics, sediment transport, public policy and social science of the Hudson Bay River.
Purpose: To fund research fellowships to advanced graduate students conducting research on the Hudson River system.
Eligibility: Applicants must be in an accredited doctoral programme, and must have a thesis advisor and a research plan approved by the applicant's institution.
Level of Study: Doctorate, Postgraduate
Type: Full-time research fellowship
Value: US$11,000 stipend plus US$1,000 expenses for Master's and US$15,000 stipend plus US$1,000 expenses for doctorate
Length of Study: 1 year
Frequency: Annual
Study Establishment: Any
Country of Study: Any country
No. of awards offered: Up to 6
Application Procedure: Applicants must supply a description, timetable, statement of significance and relevance, estimate of the cost,

curriculum vitae and two letters of recommendation. The original and ten copies of the proposal must be forwarded to the Science Director at the main organization address.
Closing Date: April 14th

Tibor T Polgar Fellowship

Subjects: All aspects of the environment of the Hudson River, from Troy, New York, to the New York Harbor and Bight. Previous projects have studied hydrodynamics, larval fish, zooplankton, terrapins, landscape ecology, nutrients and public policy.
Purpose: To fund Summer research on the Hudson River.
Eligibility: There are no eligibility restrictions.
Level of Study: Graduate
Type: Fellowship
Value: US$3,800 and limited research funds
Length of Study: From May–June to August–September
Frequency: Annual
Country of Study: United States of America
No. of awards offered: 8 every Summer
Application Procedure: Applicants must submit the original and five copies of their application, which must include letters of interest from the student and of support from the sponsor, a short description of the research project including its significance of between four and six pages, a detailed timetable for the completion of the project, a detailed budget with estimated cost of supplies, travel and other expenses, and the student's curriculum vitae. Because of the training and educational aspects of this programme, each potential fellow must be sponsored by a primary advisor. The advisor must be willing to commit sufficient time for supervision of the research and to attend at least one meeting to review the progress of the research. Advisors will receive a stipend of US$500.
Closing Date: March 3rd
Funding: Private
Additional Information: The objectives of the programme are to gather important information on all aspects of the river and to train students in conducting estuarine studies and public policy research. Polgar Fellowships may be awarded for studies anywhere within the tidal Hudson estuary from the Federal Dam at Troy, to the New York Harbor.

HUMANE RESEARCH TRUST

Brook House, 29 Bramhall Lane South, Bramhall, Stockport, Cheshire, SK7 2DN, England
Tel: (44) 161 439 8041
Fax: (44) 161 439 3713
Email: info@humaneresearch.org.uk
Website: www.humaneresearch.org.uk
Contact: Jane McAllister, Trust Administrator

The Humane Research Trust is a registered charity encouraging and supporting new medical research which does not include the use of animals, with the objectives of advancing the diagnosis and treatment of disease in humans. The Trust encourages scientists to develop innovative alternatives to the use of animals and eliminate the suffering of animals, which occurs in medical research and testing.

Humane Research Trust Grant

Subjects: Humane research.
Purpose: To encourage scientific programmes where the use of animals is replaced by other methods.
Eligibility: Open to established scientific workers engaged in productive research. Nationals of any country are considered but for the sake of overseeing, projects should be undertaken in a United Kingdom establishment.
Level of Study: Unrestricted
Type: Grant
Value: Varies
Length of Study: Varies
Frequency: Dependent on funds available
Study Establishment: Various
Country of Study: United Kingdom
No. of awards offered: Varies
Application Procedure: Applicants must complete an application form, available on the website www.humaneresearch.org.uk

Closing Date: Varies
Funding: Private
Contributor: Supporters and legacies
No. of awards given last year: 2
No. of applicants last year: 12
Additional Information: The Trust is a registered charity and donations are encouraged.

HUMANITIES RESEARCH CENTRE (HRC)

Australian National University (ANU), Canberra, ACT, 0200, Australia
Tel: (61) 2 6125 2700
Fax: (61) 2 6248 0054
Email: administration.hrc@anu.edu.au
Website: www.anu.edu.au/hrc
Contact: Ms Judy Buchanan, Administrator

The Humanities Research Centre (HRC) was established in 1972, specifically to stimulate humanities research and debate at the Australian National University (ANU), within Australia and beyond.

HRC Visiting Fellowships

Subjects: Applications are particularly welcomed from scholars with interests in one or more of the HRC's Research Platforms: Humanities, biography and society, creativity and human rights, historical re-enactment and public memory.
Purpose: To provide scholars with time to pursue their own work in congenial and stimulating surroundings.
Eligibility: Open to candidates of any nationality who are at the postdoctoral level.
Level of Study: Postdoctorate
Type: Fellowship
Value: Return economy airfare up to Australian $3,000, plus accommodation
Length of Study: 12 weeks
Frequency: Annual
Study Establishment: The Humanities Research Centre at the Australian National University
Country of Study: Australia
No. of awards offered: Up to 20
Application Procedure: Applicants must complete a formal application, available from the website.
Closing Date: January 5th
Funding: Government
No. of awards given last year: 20
Additional Information: Fellows are required to spend all of their time in residence at the Centre, but are encouraged to visit other institutions. Please refer to the website for further information.

THE HUNTINGTON

1151 Oxford Road, San Marino, CA, 91108, United States of America
Tel: (1) 626 405 2194
Fax: (1) 626 449 5703
Email: cpowell@huntington.org
Website: www.huntington.org
Contact: Committee on Awards

The Huntington is an independent research center with holdings in British and American history, literature, art history, and the history of science.

Barbara Thom Postdoctoral Fellowship

Subjects: British and American history, literature, art history, and history of science.
Purpose: To support non-tenured faculty members who are revising a manuscript for publication.
Eligibility: Applicants must have received their PhD between 2004 and 2006.
Level of Study: Postdoctorate
Type: Fellowship
Value: US$45,000
Length of Study: 1 year
Frequency: Annual
Study Establishment: The Huntington

Country of Study: United States of America
No. of awards offered: 2
Application Procedure: Applicants must contact the Committee on Fellowships.
Closing Date: Applications are accepted between October 1st and December 15th
Funding: Private
No. of awards given last year: 2
No. of applicants last year: 10

Huntington Short-Term Fellowships

Subjects: British and American history, literature, art history, and history of science.
Purpose: To enable outstanding scholars to carry out significant research in the collections of the Library and Art Gallery, by assisting in balancing the budgets of such persons, on leave at reduced pay and living away from home.
Eligibility: Open to nationals of any country who have demonstrated, to a degree commensurate with their age and experience, unusual abilities as scholars through publications of a high order of merit. Attention is paid to the value of the candidate's project and the degree to which the special strengths of the Library and Art Gallery will be used.
Level of Study: Doctorate, Postdoctorate
Type: Fellowship
Value: US$2,500 per month
Length of Study: 1–5 months
Frequency: Annual
Study Establishment: The Huntington
Country of Study: United States of America
No. of awards offered: Approx. 100, depending on funds available
Application Procedure: Applicants must contact the Committee on Fellowships.
Closing Date: Applications are accepted between October 1st and December 15th
Funding: Private
No. of awards given last year: 105
No. of applicants last year: 202
Additional Information: Fellowships are available for work towards doctoral dissertations.

Mellon Fellowships

Subjects: British and American history, literature, art history, and history of science.
Purpose: To support scholarship in a field appropriate to the Huntington's collections.
Eligibility: Preference will be given to scholars who have not held a major award in the 3 years preceding the year of this award. Applicants must have received the PhD by June of 2008.
Level of Study: Postdoctorate
Type: Fellowship
Value: US$50,000
Length of Study: 1 year
Frequency: Annual
Study Establishment: The Huntington
Country of Study: United States of America
No. of awards offered: 2
Application Procedure: Applicants must contact the Committee on Fellowships.
Closing Date: Applications are accepted between October 1st and December 15th
Funding: Foundation
No. of awards given last year: 3
No. of applicants last year: 30

National Endowment for the Humanities Fellowships

Subjects: British and American history, literature, art history, and history of science.
Purpose: To support scholarship in a field appropriate to the Huntington's collections.
Eligibility: Preference will be given to scholars who have not held a major award in the 3 years preceding the year of this award. Applicants must have received the PhD by June of 2007.
Level of Study: Postdoctorate
Type: Fellowship
Value: Up to US$40,000

Length of Study: 4 months–1 year
Frequency: Annual
Study Establishment: The Huntington
Country of Study: United States of America
No. of awards offered: 3
Application Procedure: Applicants must contact the Committee on Fellowships.
Closing Date: Applications are accepted between October 1st and December 15th
Funding: Government
No. of awards given last year: 3
No. of applicants last year: 46

HUNTINGTON'S DISEASE ASSOCIATION

Neurosupport Centre, Norton Street, Liverpool, L3 8LR, England
Tel: (44) 0151 298 3298
Fax: (44) 0151 298 9440
Email: info@hda.org.uk
Website: www.hda.org.uk
Contact: Karen Jones

The Association provides a team of regional care advisers, who offer care, advice, support and education to families and professionals who care for people with Huntington's Disease.

HDA Research Project Grants

Subjects: Furthering the understanding of Huntington's Disease, improving its treatment or otherwise improving the quality of life for patients and their careers.
Purpose: To support research projects on Huntington's Disease in a direct way. Preference is given to small 'pump priming grants' likely to lead to support from a major funding body.
Eligibility: Open to suitably qualified researchers of any nationality.
Level of Study: Postgraduate, Research
Value: Up to UK £140,000
Length of Study: 1–3 years
Frequency: Annual
Study Establishment: A suitable institution in England or Wales
Country of Study: England, Wales and Northern Ireland only
Application Procedure: Applicants should apply to the main organization. Please check the website for more information.
Closing Date: March 1st
Funding: Private
No. of awards given last year: 1
No. of applicants last year: 9

HDA Studentship

Subjects: Furthering understanding into Huntington's Disease, improving its treatment or otherwise improving the quality of life for patients and their carers.
Purpose: To support a postgraduate student undertaking research into Huntington's Disease.
Level of Study: Postgraduate
Type: Studentship
Value: Up to UK£90,000–100,000
Length of Study: Up to 3 years
Frequency: Annual
Study Establishment: An institution in England or Wales
Country of Study: England, Wales and Northern Ireland only
Application Procedure: Applicants should apply to the main organization.
Closing Date: March 1st
Funding: Private
No. of awards given last year: 1
No. of applicants last year: 9

THE HURSTON-WRIGHT FOUNDATION

6525 Belcrest Road, Suite 531, Hyattsville, MD, 20782, United States of America
Tel: (1) 301 683-2134
Email: info@hurston-wright.org
Website: www.hurston-wright.org

The Foundation was established in September 1990 by novelist Marita Golden. Our mission is to develop, nurture and sustain the world community of writers of African descent.

The Hurston-Wright Award for College Writers

Subjects: Fiction or nonfiction writing in any genre.
Purpose: To support students of African descent enrolled full time as undergraduate or graduate students in any college or university in the United States of America.
Eligibility: Students of African descent from any area of the diaspora.
Level of Study: Graduate, Postgraduate
Type: Scholarship
Value: US$1,000 or US$500
Length of Study: Varies
Frequency: Annual
Study Establishment: Any suitable college or university
Country of Study: United States of America
No. of awards offered: 3
Application Procedure: Applicants must submit an application form to the main organization. Please check the website for details.
Closing Date: January 15th
Funding: Private
No. of awards given last year: 3

Hurston-Wright Legacy Award

Subjects: Works by published writers of African descent from any area of the diaspora.
Purpose: To support published writers of African descent in furthering their art.
Eligibility: Writers of African descent from any area of the diaspora.
Level of Study: Unrestricted, Professional development
Type: Scholarship
Value: US$10,000 or US$5,000
Length of Study: Varies
Frequency: Annual
No. of awards offered: 9
Application Procedure: Book must be submitted by the publisher with permission of the writer.
Closing Date: November 15th
Funding: Private
No. of awards given last year: 9

The Hurston-Wright Writer's Week Scholarships

Subjects: Fiction or nonfiction writing in any genre.
Purpose: To support promising writers attending Writer's Week.
Eligibility: Students of African descent from any area of the diaspora.
Level of Study: Professional development
Type: Scholarship
Value: Up to US$1,100
Length of Study: Duration of workshop
Frequency: Annual
Study Establishment: Howard University, Washington, DC
Country of Study: United States of America
No. of awards offered: Variable
Application Procedure: Applicants must write a brief letter of no more than two paragraphs stating their financial situation and the amount of assistance they are requesting.
Closing Date: April 20th
Funding: Private

THE HYPERTENSION TRUST

113–119 High Street, Hampton Hill, Middlesex, TW12 INJ, England
Tel: (44) 20 8979 8300
Fax: (44) 20 8979 6700
Email: gmccarthy@hamptonmedical.com
Website: www.hypertensiontrust.org
Contact: Mrs G McCarthy, Administrator

The Hypertension Trust is a registered charity established to support research in hypertension and related cardiovascular conditions. Funds are available to support annual awards for Research Fellowships and Research Studentships.

Hypertension Trust Fellowship

Subjects: Hypertension and related cardiovascular conditions.

Purpose: To support research into hypertension and related cardiovascular conditions.
Eligibility: Applicants must hold a medical degree or higher degree in science, e.g. doctorate, and provide evidence of research aptitude or clinical experience in hypertension. The fellowship is open to United Kingdom citizens or European Union nationals working in the United Kingdom.
Level of Study: Graduate, Postgraduate
Type: Fellowship
Value: A salary of approx. UK £25,000–35,000 per year. Up to UK £5,000 per year in expenses is available
Length of Study: 2 years
Frequency: Annual
Country of Study: United Kingdom
No. of awards offered: 1
Application Procedure: Applicants must complete an application form.
Closing Date: March 2nd
Contributor: Surplus funds following the 16th Scientific Meeting of the International Society of Hypertension in June 1996
No. of applicants last year: 13
Additional Information: Applicants should visit the website for additional information.

Hypertension Trust Studentship

Subjects: Hypertension and related cardiovascular conditions.
Purpose: To support research into hypertension and related cardiovascular conditions.
Eligibility: Open to graduates of a European Union university or those currently working in a United Kingdom or Republic of Ireland hospital or institution.
Level of Study: Postgraduate, Graduate
Type: Studentship
Value: A salary based on MRC rates and PhD fees and up to UK £5,000 in expenses
Length of Study: 3 years
Frequency: Annual
No. of awards offered: 1
Application Procedure: Applicants must complete an application form.
Closing Date: March 2nd
Contributor: Surplus funds following the 16th Scientific Meeting of the International Society of Hypertension in June 1996
No. of awards given last year: 2
No. of applicants last year: 3
Additional Information: Applicants should visit the website for additional information.

IBM CORPORATION

1 New Orchard Road, Armonk, New York, NY, 10504 1722, United States of America
Tel: (1) 877 426 6006
Fax: (1) 866 722 9226
Email: ews@us.ibm.com
Website: www.ibm.com

IBM stands today at the forefront of a worldwide industry that is revolutionizing the way in which enterprises, organizations and people operate and thrive. IBM strives to lead in the invention, development and manufacture of the industry's most advanced information technologies, including computer systems, software, storage systems and microelectronics.

IBM Herman Goldstine Postdoctoral Fellowship

Subjects: Mathematics and computer science.
Purpose: To provide an opportunity to scientists of outstanding ability.
Eligibility: Open to candidates who have obtained a PhD.
Level of Study: Research
Type: Fellowship
Value: US$95,000–115,000
Length of Study: 1 year
Frequency: Annual
Country of Study: United States of America
No. of awards offered: 1

Application Procedure: Applicants can download the application form from the website. The completed application form, curriculum vitae and abstract of PhD dissertation must be sent.
Closing Date: January 5th
Additional Information: Applications shall be accepted through email at goldpost@watson.ibm.com

IBM PhD Fellowship Program

Subjects: All subjects.
Purpose: To honour exceptional PhD students in an array of focus areas of interest to IBM and fundamental to innovation.
Eligibility: Open to students nominated by a faculty member. They must be enrolled full-time in a college or university PhD programme and they should have completed at least 1 year of study in their Doctoral programme at the time of their nomination.
Level of Study: Doctorate
Type: Fellowships
Value: US$17,500
Length of Study: 3 years
Frequency: Annual
Application Procedure: All nominations for the IBM PhD Fellowship must be submitted by faculty electronically over the web on a standardized form. The nomination form will be available on the IBM PhD Fellowship nomination website from September 19th to October 31st.
Closing Date: October 31st
Additional Information: Non-US citizens who wish to participate in an internship in the United Stated must obtain work authorization under the specifics of their particular visa.

ICMA CENTRE

The University of Reading, Whiteknights Park, PO Box 242, Reading, Berkshire, RG6 6BA, England
Tel: (44) 11 8378 8239
Fax: (44) 11 8931 4741
Email: admin@icmacentre.rdg.ac.uk
Website: www.icmacentre.ac.uk
Contact: Mrs Lucy Hogg, Marketing Manager

The ICMA Centre at the University of Reading is a leader in the research and education of applied securities and investment banking education. Its graduate study opportunities include Master's degrees and doctoral research programmes. The Centre is part of the School of Business at the University, but is housed in its own facilities with two financial dealing rooms.

ICMA Centre Doctoral Scholarship

Subjects: Asset pricing, corporate finance, corporate governance, credit risk, equity and futures markets, football finance, hedge funds, hedging strategies, high frequency econometrics, market microstructure, pension schemes, portfolio management and performance assessment, quantitative finance, real estate finance, real estate options, mortgage-backed securities, historical finance, regulation and compliance in the capital markets, volatility models.
Purpose: To support research in the field.
Eligibility: Open to candidates with an excellent academic background who have completed, or who are in the process of completing, a Master's degree with grade averages at distinction level, in a course containing a significant proportion of finance.
Level of Study: Doctorate
Type: Scholarship
Value: Minimum UK £10,000 paid quarterly plus PhD fee waiver
Length of Study: 3 years
Frequency: Annual
Study Establishment: ICMA Centre, University of Reading
Country of Study: United Kingdom
No. of awards offered: 8
Application Procedure: Applicants must complete an application form, available from the Centre.
Funding: Commercial, government, private
Contributor: ICMA Centre and the University of Reading
No. of awards given last year: 4
No. of applicants last year: 63

IDP EDUCATION AUSTRALIA LIMITED

Level 2, 410 Lonsdale Street, Melbourne, VIC 3000, Australia
Tel: (61) 3 9642 2920
Fax: (61) 3 9670 8172
Email: carlie.blake@idp.com
Website: www.idp.com
Contact: Carlie Blake, Manager, Community Relations and the Peace Scholarship Program

IDP Education is a global organization that informs and advises international students on Australian education, assists in enrolment in Australian institutions across all sectors, provides a portfolio of assessment, evaluation and credentialing tools, including English language testing, for education and immigration purposes, assists governments and communities around the world to achieve their goals through delivering expertise in education, health, financial management, environmental management, governance, and public sector management.

Peace Scholarship Program-Mexico-Postgraduate Scholarships

Subjects: All subjects.
Purpose: To provide opportunities for students in selected countries worldwide to study abroad in Australia at undergraduate or postgraduate level and at a later stage to provide opportunities for Australian students to study abroad.
Eligibility: Open to citizens of Mexico who do not hold citizenship or permanent residency in Australia or New Zealand, have completed an approved undergraduate degree equivalent to an Australian Bachelor's Degree of a 3 year minimum length, and have achieved at least an 8.5/10 grade point average.
Level of Study: Postgraduate
Value: Australian $1,000 per month plus tuition fees
Closing Date: September 31st
Contributor: Secretariat of Public Education (SEP), Mexico and Queensland Education and Training International

For further information contact:

Peace Scholarship Program – Postgraduate, Donceles 100, planta baja oficina 1016, Centro Historico, Delegacion Cuauhtemoc, 06010, Mexico
Contact: Direccion General de Relaciones Internacionales SEP

Peace Scholarship Program-Peace Scholarships for Afghanistan

Subjects: Law.
Purpose: To offer female law students from Afghanistan the opportunity for postgraduate study in Australia.
Eligibility: Open to female citizens of Afghanistan (do not hold citizenship or permanent residency in Australia) and who have completed an undergraduate law degree at the University of Kabul, and have achieved at least an 80 per cent average in the degree level.
Level of Study: Postgraduate
Type: Scholarship
Value: Tuition fees, travel and living allowances
Length of Study: 2 semesters
Study Establishment: Macquarie University or the University of Technology Sydney
Country of Study: Australia
No. of awards offered: 2
Closing Date: August 31st
Contributor: UNIFEM Australia

IEEE (INSTITUTE OF ELECTRICAL AND ELECTRONICS ENGINEERS, INC.) HISTORY CENTER

39 Union Street, New Brunswick, NJ, 08901, United States of America
Tel: (1) 732 932 1066
Fax: (1) 732 932 1193
Email: ieee_history@ieee.org
Website: www.ieee.org
Contact: Mr Robert Colburn, Research Co-ordinator

The mission of the IEEE History Center is to preserve, research and promote the history of information and electrical technologies.

IEEE Fellowship in Electrical History

Subjects: The history of electrical engineering and computer technology.
Purpose: To support graduate work in the history of electrical engineering.
Eligibility: Open to suitably qualified graduate students.
Level of Study: Doctorate, Postgraduate, Postdoctorate
Type: Fellowship
Value: US$17,000 plus US$3,000 research budget
Length of Study: 1 year
Frequency: Annual
Study Establishment: A college or university of recognized standing
Country of Study: Any country
No. of awards offered: 1
Application Procedure: Applicants must submit a completed application, transcripts, three letters of recommendation and a research proposal. Application materials can be downloaded from the website.
Closing Date: February 15th
Funding: Corporation
No. of awards given last year: 1
No. of applicants last year: 12
Additional Information: The fellowship is made possible by a grant from the IEEE Life Member Fund and is awarded by the IEEE History Committee. Application materials become available in October.

IESE BUSINESS SCHOOL

Avenida Pearson, 21, Barcelona, 08034, Spain
Tel: (34) 93 253 4200
Fax: (34) 93 253 4343
Email: info@iese.edu
Website: www.iese.edu

IESE Business School seeks to impact the management profession by offering high-quality learning to students and senior executives from around the world. Our programs are designed and delivered by faculty who are recognized for their dedication to teaching and research, with close ties with international business community.

The Cámara de Comercio Scholarship

Subjects: Business management.
Eligibility: Preference is given to students from developing countries.
Level of Study: MBA
Type: Scholarship
Value: All tuition fees
Length of Study: 1 year
Frequency: Annual
Study Establishment: IESE Business School
Country of Study: Spain
No. of awards offered: 2
Application Procedure: See website.
Closing Date: April 26th
Funding: Corporation
Contributor: Cámara de Comercio, Industria, Navegació de Barcelona

Ficosa International Scholarship

Subjects: Business management.
Eligibility: Preference is given to students from Central or Eastern Europe.
Level of Study: MBA
Type: Scholarship
Value: All agreed costs
Length of Study: 1 year
Frequency: Annual
Study Establishment: IESE Business School
Country of Study: Spain
No. of awards offered: 1
Application Procedure: See website.
Closing Date: April 26th
Funding: Corporation
Contributor: Ficosa International

Fundación Ramón Areces Scholarship

Subjects: Business management.
Eligibility: Open to applicants of Spanish nationality only.
Level of Study: MBA
Type: Scholarship
Value: All tuition fees
Length of Study: 1 year
Frequency: Annual
Study Establishment: IESE Business School
Country of Study: Spain
Application Procedure: See website.
Closing Date: April 26th
Funding: Foundation
Contributor: Fudación Ramón Arces

IESE AECI/Becas MAE

Subjects: Business management.
Eligibility: Preference is given to candidates from nations designated as priority countries by the Director de la Cooperacion Espanola.
Level of Study: Professional development
Type: Scholarship
Value: All living expenses
Length of Study: 1 year
Frequency: Annual
Study Establishment: IESE Business School
Country of Study: Spain
No. of awards offered: Varies
Application Procedure: Check website for details.
Funding: Government
Contributor: The Spanish Ministry of Foreign Affairs

For further information contact:

Website: www.becasmal.es

IESE Alumini Association Scholarships

Subjects: Business management and MBA.
Purpose: To reward candidates who have demonstrated excellent work experience and personal merit.
Eligibility: See website for conditions.
Level of Study: MBA
Type: Scholarship
Value: 50% of tuition fees
Length of Study: 1 year
Frequency: Annual
Study Establishment: IESE Business School
Country of Study: Spain
No. of awards offered: 4
Application Procedure: Contact Admission's office.
Closing Date: June 28th

For further information contact:

MBA Admissions Department, Avda. Pearson 21, Barcelona, 08034, Spain

IESE Donovan Data Systems Anniversary

Subjects: Business management.
Purpose: To commemorate 30 years of DDS partnership with the advertising industry.
Eligibility: Preference is given to students interested in pursuing a career in advertising, marketing or communications.
Level of Study: Professional development
Type: Scholarship
Value: All agreed costs
Length of Study: 1 year
Frequency: Annual
Study Establishment: IESE Business School
No. of awards offered: 1
Application Procedure: See website.
Funding: Corporation
Contributor: Donovan Data Systems
Additional Information: The scholarship alternates each year between a European studying in North American and a North American Studying in Europe.

For further information contact:

Website: www.donovandata.com

IESE Private Foundation Scholarships

Subjects: Business management and MBA.
Eligibility: Priority is given to students from developing countries.
Level of Study: MBA
Type: Scholarship
Value: All agreed costs
Length of Study: 1 year
Frequency: Annual
Study Establishment: IESE Business School
Country of Study: Spain
No. of awards offered: 4
Application Procedure: See website.
Closing Date: April 26th
Funding: Private

IESE Trust Scholarships

Subjects: Business management.
Eligibility: See website for conditions.
Level of Study: Professional development
Type: Scholarship
Value: All tuition fees
Length of Study: 1 year
Frequency: Annual
Study Establishment: IESE Business School
Country of Study: Spain
No. of awards offered: Varies
Application Procedure: Contact Admissions Office.
Closing Date: June 28th
Funding: Trusts

For further information contact:

MBA Admissions Department, Avda. Pearson, 21, Barcelona, 08034, Spain

ILLINOIS TEACHERS ESOL & BILINGUAL EDUCATION (ITBE)

PMB 232 8926 N. Greenwood, Niles, IL 60714-5163,
United States of America
Tel: (1) 312 409 4770
Email: awards@itbe.org
Website: www.itbe.org

The ITBE is a non-profit organization of individuals involved in professional development legislation, government issues and specialist interest groups for the teaching of English to speakers of other languages and bilingual education.

ITBE Graduate Scholarship

Subjects: Bilingual education and teaching English to speakers of other languages.
Level of Study: Postgraduate
Type: Scholarship
Value: US$1,000
Length of Study: 1 year
Frequency: Annual
Application Procedure: Submit application form and follow further instructions on the website.
Closing Date: January 14th

For further information contact:

c/o Albany Park Community Center, 5101 N Kimball Ave, 2nd Floor, Chicago, IL, 60625
Contact: Britt Johnson, Illinois TESOL-BE Awards Chair

INDIA HABITAT CENTRE

Visual Arts Galley, Lodhi Road, New Delhi, 110-003, India
Tel: (91) 11 24682001/09
Fax: (91) 11 24682010
Email: info@indiahabitat.org
Website: www.indiahabitat.org

The India Habitat Centre was conceived to provide a physical environment that would serve as a catalyst for a synergetic relationship between individuals and institutions working in diverse habitat related areas and, therefore, maximize their total effectiveness.

India Habitat Centre Fellowship for Photography

Subjects: Photography.
Purpose: To promote photography as an art form.
Eligibility: Open to Indian nationals who are between 21 and 40 years of age and who do not hold any other fellowship.
Level of Study: Professional development
Type: Fellowship
Value: Indian Rupees 1,20,000
Frequency: Annual
Country of Study: India
Application Procedure: Applicants must send a project summary, curriculum vitae and reference letters.
Closing Date: August 31st

For further information contact:

Visual Arts Gallery
Email: alkapande@indiahabitat.org
Contact: Dr Alka Pande

INDIAN COUNCIL OF SOCIAL SCIENCE RESEARCH (ICSSR)

35 Firozshah Road, New Delhi, 110-001, India
Tel: (91) 11 2617 9838
Fax: (91) 11 2724 7370
Email: info@icssr.org
Website: www.icssr.org
Contact: Deputy Director

The Indian Council of Social Science Research (ICSSR) is an autonomous organization, funded by the Indian Government to promote research in the social sciences. It provides grants in aid for research projects, fellowships and study grants for young people and gives publication grants. It established the National Social Science Documentation Centre and Archives for providing information to social scientists.

Doctoral Fellowships

Subjects: Social science.
Purpose: To provide opportunities for social scientists to engage themselves in full-time research on important themes of their choice or to write books about their research.
Eligibility: Open to applicants who are not above 35 years of age, who hold a Master's degree in social sciences from a recognized university with a minimum overall aggregate of 55 per cent. Applicants must be registered for PhD in social sciences and cleared the MPhil, National Eligibility Test.
Level of Study: Doctorate
Type: Fellowships
Value: Indian Rupees 6,000 per month (unemployed scholars) and salary protection (employed scholars). Contingency grant of Indian Rupees 12,000
Frequency: Annual
Country of Study: India
No. of awards offered: 55
Application Procedure: Application forms can be downloaded from www.icssr.org

General Fellowships

Subjects: Humanities and social science.
Purpose: To encourage promising and potential scholars in further research.
Eligibility: Open to candidates who are below the age of 45 years, who have shown significant promise and potential for research.
Level of Study: Research, Postgraduate
Type: Fellowship
Value: Indian Rupees 6,000 per month (unemployed scholars) and salary protection (employed scholars). Contingency grant of Indian Rupees 12,000 per year

Length of Study: 2 years
Frequency: Annual
Country of Study: India

National Fellowships
Subjects: Social science.
Purpose: To enable eminent social scientists, who have made outstanding contributions to research in their respective fields, to further continue their academic work.
Eligibility: Open to social scientists of eminence, preferably below the age of 70 years.
Level of Study: Research
Type: Fellowships
Value: Indian Rupees 25,000 per month plus a contingency grant of Indian Rupees 50,000 per year
Length of Study: 2 years
Frequency: Annual
Country of Study: India
No. of awards offered: 6

Senior Fellowships
Subjects: Social science and humanities.
Purpose: To encourage professional social scientists who have their PhD and quality publications in the form of books and papers in professional journals to their credit.
Eligibility: Open to scientists who are not above 65 years of age and who hold a PhD. Social workers, journalists and civil servants known for their academic interests with record of publications may be considered.
Level of Study: Postgraduate, Research
Type: Fellowship
Value: Indian Rupees 8,000 per month (unemployed scholars) and salary protection (employed scholars). Contingency grant of Indian Rupees 36,000 per year
Length of Study: 2 years
Frequency: Annual
Country of Study: India

INDIAN EDUCATION DEPARTMENT

Government of India, Ministry of Human Resource Department,
Shastri Bhavan, New Delhi, 110001, India
Tel: (91) 11 23382947
Fax: (91) 11 23381355
Email: webmaster.edu@nic.in
Website: www.education.nic.in

The origin of the Indian Education Department, Government of India, dates back to pre-independence days when for the first time a separate Department was created in 1910 to look after education. However, soon after India achieved its independence, a full fledged ministry of Education was established.

Agatha Harrison Memorial Fellowship (St Antony's College, Oxford)
Subjects: Modern Indian studies in history, economics,and political science.
Eligibility: Open to the residents of India with 60 per cent marks at Master's Degree level, PhD Degree in the subject field or published works of equivalent merit and minimum 3 years teaching experience at graduate/postgraduate level.
Level of Study: Postgraduate
Type: Fellowship
Value: UK £18,580
Length of Study: 1 year
Application Procedure: Applicants must send typed application with attested copies of testimonials, programme of study, photograph and other documents on plain paper.
Funding: Government
Contributor: The Government of India

For further information contact:

Es. 4 Section (Scholarships), Ministry of Human Resource Development, Department of Education, (ES 4) External Scholarships

Division, A1/w3 Curzon Road Barracks, K G Marg, New Delhi, 110 001, India
Contact: Section Officer

Belgium Scholarships
Subjects: Agronomy, environmental science, and technical metallurgy.
Eligibility: Open to the candidates up to the age of 35 who are graduates in agronomy/micro-electronics/chemical eng/technology/metallurgy/vet. science/environmental studies with 60 per cent or above marks with two years experience in the field for postgraduate studies.
Level of Study: Graduate
Type: Scholarship
Value: €675
Length of Study: 10 months
No. of awards offered: 3
Application Procedure: Applicants must send typed application with attested copies of testimonials, programme of study and other documents on plain paper by notified date.

For further information contact:

ES. 5, Ministry of Human Resource Development, Department of Education, A1/w3 Curzon Road Barracks, KG Marg, New Delhi, 110 001, India
Contact: Section officer

Canada Fellowships
Subjects: Political science/International relations with particular emphasis on Canada-India relations, geography, social administration, economic planning, management studies or computer science.
Eligibility: Open to Indian nationals residing in India, who have obtained first Graduation or the Master's degree within the last 5 years as on September of the in-take year with 2 years teaching, research or practical experience after obtaining postgraduate degree relating to the opted field of study.
Level of Study: Postgraduate
Type: Fellowship
Value: Fellowships cover return travel from India, University fee, living allowance in addition to supplement for books, preparation of thesis, warm clothing
Length of Study: 4 years (PhD) and 2 years (Masters)
Frequency: Annual
Application Procedure: Applicants must send typed application with attested copies of testimonials, photograph, plans for employment, and other documents on plain paper in prescribed format by notified date (Employed persons are expected to send their applications through their employer).
Additional Information: The candidates must have completed tertiary education in English medium.

China Scholarships
Subjects: Chinese language and literature, fine arts, (painting and sculpture) economics, history, bio-technology, botany, zoology, environmental science, plant breeding and genetics, fisheries, political science, sericulture agronomy.
Eligibility: Open to the Indian nationals below 40 years who have 2–3 year Cert/Dip in basic Chinese Language from a recognized Institution or University, have degree in fine arts with 60 per cent and 60 per cent for other subjects at postgraduate level with work research experience of 2 years.
Level of Study: Graduate
Type: Scholarship
Value: Expenditure on board and lodging. Tuition fees, pocket expenses paid by the Chinese Government
Length of Study: 1–2 years
No. of awards offered: 25
Application Procedure: Applicants must send the application duly sponsored by the employers (if employed) furnishing particulars (as per notified format) by the prescribed date.
Contributor: Government of China in association with the government of India

For further information contact:

ES. 3 Section, Ministry of Human Resource Development, Department of Education, External Scholarship Division, A1/w3 Curzon Road Barracks, KG Marg, New Delhi, 110 001, India
Contact: Section Officer

Commonwealth Scholarship/Fellowships in UK

Subjects: All subject.
Eligibility: Open to the Indian national residing in India completing tertiary education in English medium and graduated first Master's Degree as per requirement within the last 10 years as on October of the in-take year. For more details, check website.
Level of Study: Doctorate, Postgraduate
Type: Fellowship/Scholarship
Value: Tourist-class air passage (both ways), fee with adequate maintenance and other allowance
Length of Study: 1 year for postgraduation, 1 year for clinical training and 3 years for PhD
Application Procedure: Check the website for further details.
Additional Information: Candidate should give one page academic justification for pursuing Master Degree course in United Kingdom.

For further information contact:

ES. 1 Section(Scholarships), Ministry of Human Resource Development, Department of Education, (ES 1) External Scholarships Division, A1/W3 Curzon Road Barracks, K G Marg, New Delhi, 110 001, India
Contact: Section Officer

CZECH Scholarships

Subjects: Environment protection, mining and geology, and electronics/electrical engineering.
Eligibility: Open to the candidates up to the age of 35 years or less who have postgraduate degree with 60 per cent or more in science/engineering/technology in the related subjects or equivalent qualification in the subject selected or in the allied field.
Level of Study: Postgraduate
Type: Scholarship
Value: 5,500 Czech Crowns per month
Length of Study: As per rules of Czech Universities
No. of awards offered: 2
Application Procedure: Applicants must send their typed application on plain paper in the prescribed format along with photocopies of certificates through a employer, if employed.
Additional Information: Selected candidates who do not have the knowledge of Czech language are required to undergo language and preparatory course for 6–12 months depending on their command on Czech language.

For further information contact:

ES-I Section, Department of Education, Ministry of Human Resource Development, A1/W3 Curzon Road Barracks, K.G. Marg, New Delhi, 110 001, India
Contact: Section officer

Erasmus Mundus Scholarship Programme

Subjects: All subjects.
Purpose: For the benefit of Indian students.
Eligibility: Open to Indian nationals who are graduates from recognized institutions or universities.
Level of Study: Graduate
Type: Scholarships
Value: Covers airfare and living expenses
Length of Study: 1–2 years duration depending on the subject areas of study
Application Procedure: Applicants must apply directly to the universities/consortium of universities constituted under the Erasmus Mundus Programme.
Closing Date: December 30th
Contributor: European Union (EU)

For further information contact:

Email: eac-info@cec.eu.int

Website: www.europa.eu.int/comm/education/programmes/socrates/erasmus/students_en.html

Germany Scholarships

Subjects: Mechanical engineering, electronics and communication engineering, bio-pharmacology, metallurgy, environmental science, bio-technology, agriculture and forestry, veterinary sciences and animal husbandry, electrical engineering.
Eligibility: Open to the candidates with 60 per cent marks at Master's Degree in the subject/related field, sociology and economics candidates possessing adequate knowledge of German language with 2 years experience in teaching, research or practical training after obtaining the prescribed qualification.
Level of Study: Postgraduate
Type: Fellowship
Value: DM 1,800 per month and other allowances
Length of Study: 1 year
No. of awards offered: 7
Application Procedure: Applicants must send typed application, duly sponsored by employer, with research programme, attested copies of testimonials and other documents submitted on plain paper (as per notified format) by the prescribed date.
Additional Information: Period of fellowship is preceded by a compulsory 4 months German language course to be conducted at one of the branches of the Geothe Institute in Germany. Preference is given to candidates having contacts with German Professors or placement at the German Institute.

For further information contact:

ES.1 Section, Ministry of Human Resource Development, Department of Education (ES-I), External Scholarship Division, Curzon Road Barracks, K.G. Marg, New Delhi, 110 001, India
Contact: Section Officer

Greece Scholarships

Subjects: Mathematics, political philosophy/political thought.
Eligibility: Open to the candidates below 40 years who have Masters Degree with 60 per cent or more marks with 2 years teaching/research/practical experience. Candidates should be pursuing studies in universities or research centres.
Level of Study: Postgraduate
Type: Scholarship
Value: 150,000 drachmas. Check website for more details
Length of Study: 10 months
No. of awards offered: 1
Application Procedure: Applicants must send typed format along with photocopies of certificates through employer, if employed.
Additional Information: Travelling expenses from India to Greece and back to be borne by the candidate or his/her sponsor/employee.

For further information contact:

ES. 5 Section, Ministry of Human Resource Development, Department of Education (ES-5), A1/W3 Curzon Road Barracks, K.G. Marg, New Delhi, 110 001, India

Ireland Scholarships

Subjects: Environmental resources management, community health, remedial and special education and developmental studies.
Eligibility: Open to the candidates up to the age 30 having First Class Bachelor's Degree in related subjects along with good knowledge about Ireland, and have stayed in India after return from abroad for study/training.
Level of Study: Graduate
Type: Fellowship
Value: Fellowships cover return travel from India, university fee, living allowance in addition to supplement for books, preparation of thesis, warm clothing, etc
Length of Study: 1 year
No. of awards offered: 6
Application Procedure: Applicants must send the typed application with attested copies of testimonials, photograph, plans for employment, and other documents on plain paper in prescribed format by notified date.

For further information contact:

ES. 1 Section, Ministry of Human Resource Development, Department of Education, A.1/W.3 Curzon Road Barracks, K.G. Marg, New Delhi, 110 001, India
Contact: Section Officer

Israel Scholarships

Subjects: International relations, Judaism, Hebrew language, history of the Jewish people, agriculture, political science.
Eligibility: Open to the candidates of age 35 years who have 55 per cent or more for humanities, 60 per cent or more for agriculture, and have 2 years research/work/teaching experience.
Level of Study: Graduate
Type: Scholarship
Value: Paid by Israeli Government to cover stay, tuition fees, health insurance, etc
Length of Study: 8 month for research, 1 year for P.D
No. of awards offered: 6 (4 for 8 months research and 2 for P.D.)
Application Procedure: Applicants must send typed application on plain paper as per format notified, along with attested photocopies of the certificates, through employer, if employed.
Funding: Government
Contributor: Israeli Government for P.D. candidates
Additional Information: Passage cost from India to Israel and back is payable by the candidate/sponsor/employer who will apply for 8 months research. Candidates who are staying abroad will not be considered. Candidate who are already abroad for more than 6 months for study/research/training are eligible to apply only if they stayed in India for 2 consecutive years after their return from abroad.

For further information contact:

ES. 3 Section, Ministry of Human Resource Development, Department of Education, A.1/W.3 Curzon Road Barracks, K.G.Marg, New Delhi, 110 001, India
Contact: Section Officer

Italy Scholarships

Subjects: Italian language.
Eligibility: Open to the candidates of age not more than 45 years who have Graduate or equivalent degree from a recognized university along with good knowledge of Italian.
Level of Study: Graduate
Type: Scholarship
Value: 1,200,000 Lire per month
No. of awards offered: Check website for details
Application Procedure: Applicants must send typed application on plain paper as per format notified, along with two letters of introduction from Indian academic authorities attested photocopies of the certificates, through employer, if employed.

For further information contact:

ES. 5 Section, Ministry of Human Resource Development, Department of Education, A.1/W.3 Curzon Road Barracks, K.G. Marg, New Delhi, 110 001, India
Contact: Section Officer

Japan Scholarships

Subjects: All subject.
Eligibility: Open to the Indian nationals residing in India of age below 35 years. Candidates who have enrolled in the postgraduate degree in Japanese language or completed undergraduate degree in Japanese language or completed Level 2 of JLPT conducted in Japan foundation and have completed at least 3 years of Japanese language study in a university. For more details, check website address.
Level of Study: Graduate
Type: Scholarship
Value: Covers study allowance, fee, part payment of medical expenses, accommodation, etc
No. of awards offered: 30
Application Procedure: Applicants must send typed application on plain paper as per format notified, along with attested photocopies of the certificates, through employer, if employed.
Funding: Government

Contributor: Government of Japan

For further information contact:

ES. 3 Section, Ministry of Human Resource Development, Department of Education, A.1/W.3 Curzon Road Barracks, K.G. Marg, New Delhi, 110 001, India
Contact: Section Officer

Mexican Government Scholarship

Subjects: Electronics and communication, architecture, psychology, economics, management studies, biotechnology, environment science, history and geography.
Eligibility: Open to the candidates of age below 26 years for PG (Masters) and below 30 years for PhD who have Bachelor's Degree or equivalent with minimum 65 per cent marks in relevant subject for postgraduate studies and postgraduate degree with minimum 65 per cent marks in relevant subject for PhD.
Level of Study: Graduate, Postgraduate
Type: Scholarship
Value: Approx 5,840.40 pesos for Bachelor's and Master's research and approx 7,300.50 pesos for Doctorate or Doctoral research and other expenses
No. of awards offered: 4
Application Procedure: Applications can be submitted online at the Department website www.education.nic.in or application on plain paper (in prescribed format) along with photocopies of educational certificates (including proof of age) and other documents, with a copy of recent passport size photograph pasted on the application.
Closing Date: September 17th
Funding: Government
Contributor: Government of Mexico

For further information contact:

ES. 5 Section, Department of Higher Education, A.2/W.4, Curzon Road Barracks, Kasturba Gandhi Marg, New Delhi, 110 001, India
Contact: The Section Officer

Mongolia Scholarships

Subjects: Mongolian language and Mongolian study.
Eligibility: Open to the Indian nationals residing within the country of age below 45 years who have Bachelor's Degree along with good knowledge of English, and have stayed in India for 2 years consecutively after return from abroad for study/training.
Level of Study: Graduate
Type: Scholarship
Value: Course fees, living allowance, and free accommodation in hostel for the duration of stay
Length of Study: 1 semester
No. of awards offered: 2
Application Procedure: Applicants must send a typed application duly sponsored by employer, with attested copies of testimonials, photograph, programme of study/research and other documents on plain paper.
Additional Information: Advance applications may be considered provisionally pending sponsorship by employer within 2 weeks.

For further information contact:

ES. 1 Section(Scholarships), Ministry of Human Resource Development, Department of Education, (ES 1) External Scholarships Division, A1/W3 Curzon Road Barracks, K G Marg, New Delhi, 110 001, India
Contact: Section Officer

N.C.P.E.D.P. Rajiv Gandhi Postgraduate Scholarship Scheme

Subjects: Any other course that may be notified by the awarding authority. Check website for further details.
Purpose: To enable disabled students with limited means to receive education or professional training at postgraduate and doctoral levels.
Eligibility: Open to Indian nationals between 18 and 35 years of age. The scholarship may be awarded to students with the disabilities as recognized by N.C.P.E.D.P. The candidate should be either pursuing or should have gained admission to a full-time course in an Indian university established by law or in a recognized equivalent institution.

Level of Study: Doctorate, Graduate, Postgraduate
Type: Scholarship
Value: Rs 1,200 per month
Frequency: Annual
Application Procedure: Applicants must apply to the National Centre for Promotion of Employment for Disabled People.
Funding: Government
Additional Information: A scholarship will be provided for the entire duration of the approved course. Scholarship money will be released every 3 months. N.C.P.E.D.P. reserves the right to change the scheme and/or amend the rules without any notice. The income of the candidate or his parents/guardians should not exceed Rs 5,000 per month.

For further information contact:

National Centre for Promotion of Employment for Disabled People, A-77, South Extension, Part II, New Delhi, 110 049
Tel: +91 11 26265647, 26265648
Email: secretariat@ncpedp.org
Website: www.ncpedp.org

Narotam Sekhsaria Foundation Scholarship (Tribal)

Subjects: Engineering, technology, and sciences.
Purpose: For upliftment of SC candidates.
Eligibility: Open to candidates with a Bachelor degree (minimum 50 per cent and 2 years of relevant work experience) and Masters degree (2 years teaching/professional experience), or MPhil. For PhD, minimum 5 years of teaching/professional experience is required. Age limit applicable is 35 years.
Level of Study: Doctorate, Graduate, Postgraduate
Type: Scholarship
Value: A fellowship of Rs 26,000 per month is offered and a contingency grant of Rs 100,000 per year is also offered
Length of Study: 2 years Masters degree 3 years PhD, and 1–6 months postdoctoral research
Country of Study: India
No. of awards offered: 10
Application Procedure: Check the website for further details.
Funding: Government
Additional Information: Income limits is Rs 18,000 per month for all categories.

For further information contact:

Information Facilitation Centre, Ministry of Environment and Forests, Paryavaran Bhawan, CGO Complex, Lodi Road, New Delhi, 110003, India
Website: www.envfor.nic.in

Narotam Sekhsaria Foundation Scholarships

Subjects: Pure sciences, applied sciences, engineering, information technology, management, and business administration.
Purpose: To offer various scholarships for pursuing higher education in different streams.
Eligibility: Open to candidates who have an excellent background of academic and extra curricular activities for pursuing postgraduate studies in India or abroad. The upper age limit is 30 years.
Level of Study: Graduate
Type: Postgraduate scholarships
Value: Up to Rs 10 lakh
Country of Study: India
Application Procedure: Application forms can be downloaded from the website.
Funding: Foundation

For further information contact:

Narottam Sekhsaria Foundation, 46, Maker Chambers III, Nariman Point, Mumbai, Maharashtra, 400021, India
Website: www.nsscholarship.com

National Doctoral Fellowships

Subjects: All subjects.
Eligibility: Open to candidates who are below 35 years as on August 31st of the year of application. A relaxation of 5 years for SC/ST, physically handicapped, and women.

Level of Study: Doctorate, Postdoctorate
Type: Fellowship
Value: Rs 12,000 per month, a contingency grant of Rs 25,000 per year, and overhead charges of Rs 20,000 per year to be paid to the host institution
Length of Study: 3 years plus an extension up to 1 year
Frequency: Annual
No. of awards offered: 50
Application Procedure: Short-listed candidates will be called for interview in September/October. Final selection will be made from merit list prepared on the basis of candidate's performance in interview.
Closing Date: July
Funding: Government
Contributor: All India Council For Technical Education (AICTE)
Additional Information: Short-listed candidates will be called for interview sometime in September/October. The candidate should be in the first year of full-time doctoral programme in one of the host institutions listed in the Annexure.

For further information contact:

All India Council For Technical Education, Indira Gandhi Sports Complex, I.P. Estate, New Delhi, 110 002, India
Tel: (91) 011-23392506/63/64/65/68/71/73/74/78
Fax: (91) 0112339255

New Zealand Scholarship

Subjects: Soil science and dairy technology.
Eligibility: Open to the Indian nationals residing in India who have completed their Master's Degree with 60 per cent marks in respect of soil science and dairy technology and have 2 years experience in teaching, research or practical experience after obtaining Master's Degree.
Level of Study: Postgraduate
Type: Scholarship
Value: Travel expenses
Application Procedure: Applicants must send the application typed in English on plain paper as per format notified, with attested photocopies of the certificates, through their employer, if employed, within the date as notified along with the name of the scholarship scheme and the country, namely, United Kingdom, Canada, or New Zealand to the below address.
Additional Information: Applicants must have knowledge of India and of the donor country. Candidates qualifying from universities which do not award class/division, requirements in lieu of First Class 60 per cent marks. For candidates who are doing PhD/MPhil after completion of Master's Degree, actual period of research is taken into consideration as experience.

For further information contact:

ES. 1 Section (Scholarships), Ministry of Human Resource Development, Department of Education, (ES 1) External Scholarships Division, A1/W3 Curzon Road Barracks, K G Marg, New Delhi, 110 001, India
Contact: Section Officer

Norway Scholarships

Subjects: All subjects.
Eligibility: Open to the residents of India.
Type: Scholarship
Value: Centre for International University Co-operation (SIU) will pay a return air ticket from the fellow's home country, monthly allowance sufficient to cover food, rent and other ordinary living expenses and an installation allowance equivalent to half a monthly fellowship allowance
Length of Study: 2 years
Application Procedure: Applicants must send a typed application on plain paper as per format notified, along with attested photocopies of the certificates, duly sponsored, if employed.
Additional Information: Advanced applications are not considered.

For further information contact:

ES. 5 Section (Scholarships), Ministry of Human Resource Development, Department of Education, (ES 1) External Scholarships

Division, A1/W3 Curzon Road Barracks, K G Marg, New Delhi, 110 001, India
Contact: Section Officer

Portugal Scholarships

Subjects: All subject.
Eligibility: Open to the university teachers of age below 45 who possess a Masters Degree in the concerned subject, know Portuguese language and be willing to undertake research in the Portuguese language and culture and have secured admissions or acceptance in a Portuguese Institute or university.
Type: Scholarship
Value: €500 (equivalent to INR 21,000) per month. €450 (equivalent INR 19,000. First month grant will be €825 equivalent to INR 34,500)
No. of awards offered: 1 scholarship per month for postgraduate studies, 2 for research scholarships and 6 scholarships of 8 months duration each for pursuing annual course of Portuguese language and culture
Application Procedure: Applicants must send typed application on plain paper as per format notified, along with attested photocopies of the certificates, medical fitness report, duly sponsored, if employed.
Funding: Government
Contributor: Government of Portugal
Additional Information: Advanced application may be considered if the 'NOC' from employer can be produced at the time of interview.

For further information contact:

ES.1 Section(Scholarships), Ministry of Human Resource Development, Department of Education, (ES 5) External Scholarships Division, A1/W3 Curzon Road Barracks, K G Marg, New Delhi, 110 001, India
Contact: Section Officer

Postgraduate Indira Gandhi Scholarship Scheme for Single Girl Child

Subjects: All subject.
Purpose: To support higher education of girls who happen to be the only child in their families and also to provide incentive for the parents to observe small family norm.
Eligibility: Open to any single girl child of her parents who has taken admission in Master's degree programmes in any recognized university or a postgraduate college.
Level of Study: Postgraduate, Graduate
Type: Scholarship
Value: Rs 2,000 per month. No tuition fees will be charged
Length of Study: 2 years
Frequency: Annual
No. of awards offered: 1,200
Application Procedure: Check the website address for further details.
Closing Date: Check the website address for further details
Funding: Government
Contributor: The University Grants Commission
Additional Information: A student leaving the studies mid-way will have to take prior approval from the University Grants Commission by submitting an application along with justification through the concerned university and will have to refund the whole amount and the concerned institution will be responsible for this.

For further information contact:

University Grants Commission (UGC), Selections and Awards Bureau, Delhi University South Campus, Benito Juarez Marg, New Delhi, 110021, India

INDIAN INSTITUTE OF SCIENCE BANGALORE (IISC)

Bangalore, 560012, India
Tel: (91) 1 80 233 44411, 1 80 236 00757
Fax: (91) 1 80 2334 1683, 1 80 236 00683
Email: regr@admin.iisc.ernet.in
Website: www.iisc.ernet.in
Contact: The Registrar

The Indian Institute of Science (IISc) was started in 1909 through the pioneering vision of J N Tata. Since then, it has grown into a premier institution of research and advanced instruction, with more than 2,000 active researchers working in almost all frontier areas of science and technology.

IISc Kishore Vaigyanik Protsahan Yojana Fellowships

Subjects: Science, engineering and medicine.
Purpose: To assist students in realising their potential and to ensure that the best scientific talent is developed for research and growth in the country.
Eligibility: Open to Indian citizens.
Level of Study: Postgraduate, Graduate, Postdoctorate, Predoctorate, Research
Type: Fellowship
Value: Indian Rupees 2,000–5,000 per month and contingency grants
Frequency: Annual
Study Establishment: Indian Institute of Science, Bangalore
Country of Study: India
Application Procedure: Applicants can download the application form from the website.
Closing Date: September

For further information contact:

Indian Institute of Science, Bangalore, Kishore Vaigyanik Protsahan Yojana, 560 012, India
Tel: (91) 80 2360 1008, 80 2293 2976
Email: kvpy@admin.iisc.ernet.in
Website: www.iisc.ernet.in/kvpy
Contact: The Convener

INDIAN INSTITUTE OF TECHNOLOGY (IIT)

Department of Computer Science and Engineering, Kanpur, UP, 208016, India
Tel: (91) 512 259 7338/7638
Fax: (91) 512 259 7586
Email: pgadm@cse.iitk.ac.in
Website: www.cse.iitk.ac.in

Indian Institute of Technology (IIT) imparts training to students to make them competent, motivated engineers and scientists. The Institute not only celebrates freedom of thought, cultivates vision and encourages growth, but also inculcates human values and concern for the environment and the society.

Infosys Fellowship for PhD Students

Subjects: Computer science and engineering.
Purpose: To support those interested in pursuing the PhD programme in the Department of computer science and engineering at IIT Kanpur.
Eligibility: Open to deserving students who have a MTech/ME in any branch of engineering and who have secured admission into the PhD programme.
Level of Study: Postgraduate
Type: Fellowship
Value: Indian Rupees 15,000 per month Plus Contingency Indian Rupees 45,000–75,000 per year
Length of Study: 1 year
Frequency: Annual
Study Establishment: IIT Kanpur
Country of Study: India
Application Procedure: The applicant must submit a separate application form to the Deptartment of computer science and engineering.

For further information contact:

Kanpur, Uttar Pradesh, 208016, India
Contact: Admissions In-Charge (PhD) Computer science and engineering department, Indian Institute of Technology

THE INDIANAPOLIS STAR

307 N Pennsylvania Street, PO Box 145, Indianapolis, IN, 46206,
United States of America
Tel: (1) 317 444 4000
Email: rpulliam@indystar.com
Website: www.indystar.com

The Indianapolis Star celebrated its 100th anniversary on June 6, 2003. The brainchild of Muncie industrialist George F. McCulloch, The Star challenged the two existing morning newspapers, the Journal and the Sentinel.

Pulliam Journalism Fellowship
Subjects: Reporting, news design and graphics and photojournalism.
Purpose: To support newspaper journalism.
Eligibility: Open to candidates who have obtained graduate degrees.
Level of Study: Professional development
Type: Fellowships
Value: US$6,500
Length of Study: 10 weeks
Frequency: Annual
Country of Study: United States of America
No. of awards offered: 20
Application Procedure: Applicants can download the application form from the website. The completed application form along with samples of the best published writings, transcript of college credits, 3 letters of recommendation and a recent photograph must be sent.
Closing Date: November 15th
Additional Information: Please call Russ Pulliam in Indianapolis at 317 444 6001 or Bill Hill in Phoenix at 602 444 4368 for any further information.

For further information contact:

Website: www2.indystar.com/pjf
Contact: Russell B Pulliam, Pulliam Fellowship Director

INDICORPS

3418 Highway 6 South, Suite B309, Houston, TX, 77082, United
States of America
Tel: (1) 202 360 4150
Email: info@indicorps.org
Website: www.indicorps.org

Indicorps is a non-partisan, non-religious, non-profit organization that encourages Indians around the world to actively participate in India's progress.

Indicorps Fellowship
Subjects: Social work with grassroots service organizations in India.
Purpose: To implement projects that are in the organizations' and India's best interest.
Eligibility: Open to Indian citizens only.
Level of Study: Professional development
Type: Fellowship
Value: Varies
Length of Study: 1–2 years
Frequency: Annual
Country of Study: India
No. of awards offered: 10–15
Application Procedure: Applicants must apply online.
Closing Date: April 1st
Additional Information: For further information about the application procedure mail to apply@indicorps.org

INSEAD

Boulevard de Constance, F-77305 Fontainebleau Cedex, France
Tel: (33) 1 60 72 40 05
Fax: (33) 1 60 74 55 30
Email: mba.europe@insead.edu
Website: www.insead.edu/mba
Contact: Ms Helen Henderson, Director, Financial Aid

INSEAD is widely recognized as one of the most influential business schools in the world. With its second campus in Asia to complement its established presence in Europe, INSEAD is setting the pace in globalizing the MBA. The 1-year intensive MBA programme is focused on international general management.

INSEAD Alumni Fund (IAF) Diversity Scholarship(s)
Subjects: MBA.
Purpose: To assist candidates admitted to the MBA programme.
Eligibility: Open to applicants from emerging or developing countries.
Level of Study: MBA
Type: Scholarship
Value: €3,000–10,000
Frequency: Annual
Study Establishment: INSEAD
No. of awards offered: Varies
Application Procedure: Applicants must complete a specific assignment, details of which are available from the website.
Closing Date: April 18th and September 19th
Contributor: Alumni

INSEAD Asia Enterprise Fund Scholarship
Subjects: MBA.
Eligibility: Open to candidates admitted to and starting their course at INSEAD's Asian campus.
Level of Study: MBA
Type: Scholarship
Value: Up to €20,000
Frequency: Annual
Study Establishment: INSEAD
Country of Study: Singapore
No. of awards offered: 3
Application Procedure: Applicants must complete a specific assignment, details of which are available from the organization or from the website.
Closing Date: May 5th for the September intake of the same year and September 30th for the January intake of the following year
Contributor: Alumni and a gift from a private individual

INSEAD Belgian Alumni and Council Scholarship Fund
Subjects: MBA.
Purpose: To assist MBA participants.
Eligibility: Open to candidates of merit of Belgian nationality and those who have lived in Belgium for at least 5 years. Priority will be given to admitted applicants who intend to return to Belgium after their MBA.
Level of Study: MBA
Type: Scholarship
Value: €6,000
Frequency: Annual
Study Establishment: INSEAD
No. of awards offered: 2
Application Procedure: Applicants must complete a specific assignment, details of which are available from the organization or from the website.
Closing Date: May 5th for the September class of the same year and September 30th for the January class of the following year
Contributor: Alumni and the Belgian Council

INSEAD Børsen/Danish Council Scholarship
Subjects: MBA.
Purpose: To assist MBA participants.
Eligibility: Open to candidates of Danish nationality, admitted to the INSEAD MBA programme.
Level of Study: MBA
Type: Scholarship
Value: €15,000
Frequency: Annual
Study Establishment: INSEAD
Country of Study: Other
No. of awards offered: 2
Application Procedure: Applicants must complete an application form, available from the website.
Closing Date: May 15th for the September class of the same year and September 15th for the January class of the following year
Contributor: The Danish Council/Børsen

INSEAD Canadian Foundation Scholarship

Subjects: MBA.
Purpose: To provide financial assistance and scholarships to deserving Canadians admitted to the INSEAD MBA programme.
Eligibility: Open to candidates of Canadian nationality, preferably resident in Canada, who have been admitted to the INSEAD MBA programme and who intend to return to Canada.
Level of Study: MBA
Type: Scholarship
Value: Up to Canadian $10,000
Frequency: Annual
Study Establishment: INSEAD
No. of awards offered: Varies
Application Procedure: Applicants must submit the following in support of their application: a covering letter requesting a scholarship specifying which campus the applicant is applying to, a budget detailing the need for financial assistance including current and expected sources of funding, a copy of a completed INSEAD admission form with essay and supporting documents, a copy of reference letters submitted in support of application to INSEAD, a copy of Graduate Management Admissions Test results, a copy of university transcripts and a copy of confirmation of admission to INSEAD.
Closing Date: June 30th for candidates admitted to the September intake of the same year and October 31st for candidates admitted to the January class of the following year
Contributor: Alumni
Additional Information: The Canadian INSEAD Foundation is a non-profit corporation whose purpose is to encourage Canadian students to develop an international business understanding and perspective.

For further information contact:

The Board of Trustees, Canadian INSEAD Foundation, c/o Richard Tarte, Société générale de financement du Québec, 600 de La Gauchetière Street, West Suite 1700, Montréal, QC, H3B 4L8, Canada
Tel: (1) 514 876 9290 ext 2171

INSEAD Eli Lilly and Company Innovation Scholarship

Subjects: MBA.
Eligibility: Open to students of merit who demonstrate the capacity for innovative thinking and actions. Nationals from Africa, Asia, Central and Eastern Europe, Middle East, Central and South America, Turkey and Canada may apply.
Level of Study: MBA
Type: Scholarship
Value: Partial tuition
Frequency: Annual
Study Establishment: INSEAD
No. of awards offered: 2 per class
Application Procedure: Applicants must complete a specific assignment, details of which are available from the organization or from the website.
Closing Date: May 5th for the September intake of the same year and September 30th for the January intake of the following year
Contributor: Eli Lilly Foundation
Additional Information: Eli Lilly creates and delivers innovative pharmaceutical-based healthcare solutions that enable people worldwide to live longer, healthier and more active lives.

INSEAD Elmar Schulte Diversity Scholarship

Subjects: MBA.
Purpose: To encourage diversity in the INSEAD MBA programme.
Eligibility: Open to candidates from non-traditional MBA backgrounds who have been admitted to the programme.
Level of Study: MBA
Type: Scholarship
Value: Varies
Frequency: Annual
Study Establishment: INSEAD
No. of awards offered: Varies
Application Procedure: Applicants must complete an application form, available from the website.

Closing Date: May 5th for the September intake of the same year and September 30th for the January intake of the following year
Contributor: Alumni

INSEAD Elof Hansson Scholarship Fund

Subjects: MBA.
Purpose: To assist MBA participants.
Eligibility: Open to candidates of Swedish nationality who have been admitted to the INSEAD MBA programme.
Level of Study: MBA
Type: Scholarship
Value: €6,000
Frequency: Annual
Study Establishment: INSEAD
No. of awards offered: 2
Application Procedure: Applicants must complete an application form, available from the website.
Closing Date: May 15th for the September class of the same year and September 15th for the January class of the following year
Contributor: The Elof Hansson Foundation

INSEAD Giovanni Agnelli Scholarship

Subjects: MBA.
Purpose: To support MBA participants.
Eligibility: Open to Italian candidates of high merit, admitted to the INSEAD MBA programme.
Level of Study: MBA
Type: Scholarship
Value: €1,500
Frequency: Annual
Study Establishment: INSEAD
No. of awards offered: 1–2
Application Procedure: Applicants must complete an application form, available from the website.
Closing Date: May 5th for the September class of the same year and September 30th for the January class of the following year
Contributor: Fiat
Additional Information: This endowed scholarship is offered by the Fiat Group.

INSEAD Henry Grunfeld Foundation Scholarship

Subjects: MBA.
Purpose: To aid MBA students who can demonstrate a commitment to a career in investment banking.
Eligibility: Open to participants from a United Kingdom background with an interest in pursuing a career in investment banking.
Level of Study: MBA
Type: Scholarship
Value: Up to €12,500
Frequency: Annual
Study Establishment: INSEAD
Country of Study: Other
No. of awards offered: 1
Application Procedure: Applicants must complete a specific assignment, details of which are available from the organization or from the website.
Closing Date: May 5th for the September class of the same year and September 30th for the January class of the following year
Contributor: The Henry Grunfeld Foundation
Additional Information: Henry Grunfeld was a co-founder of S G Warburg, the United Kingdom investment bank that became one of the largest securities firms in the world, combining merchant banking, securities broking and market-making.

INSEAD Judith Connelly Delouvrier Scholarship

Subjects: MBA.
Purpose: To support women undertaking the MBA.
Eligibility: Open to deserving American women admitted to the September MBA programme.
Level of Study: MBA
Type: Scholarship
Value: US$15,000
Frequency: Annual
Study Establishment: INSEAD
No. of awards offered: 1

Application Procedure: Applicants must complete a specific assignment, details of which are available from the website.
Closing Date: May 5th for the September class of the same year
Contributor: Alumni
Additional Information: This scholarship is offered in memory of Judith Connelly Delouvrier, wife of Phillippe Delouvrier, an INSEAD MBA of 1977, who was a victim of the TWA Flight 800 tragedy in 1996.

INSEAD L'Oréal Scholarship

Subjects: MBA.
Purpose: To foster creativity, diversity and entrepreneurial spirit within the MBA population.
Eligibility: Open to candidates of any nationality who demonstrate a capacity for creativity, innovation and entrepreneurial activity and who can demonstrate financial need.
Level of Study: MBA
Type: Scholarship
Value: Partial tuition fees
Length of Study: 1 year
Frequency: Annual
Study Establishment: INSEAD
No. of awards offered: 2 per year, 1 per intake
Closing Date: May 5th for the September class of the same year and September 30th for the January class of the following year
Contributor: L'Oréal

INSEAD Lord Kitchener National Memorial Scholarship

Subjects: MBA.
Purpose: To assist MBA participants from the United Kingdom.
Eligibility: Open to candidates who are British subjects and have served, or are the son or daughter of a parent who has at any time served or is serving on a full-time engagement in HM Armed Forces. This includes members and former members of the Territorial Army and other Reserve Forces of the Crown, and their sons and daughters, providing that the former have served an element of full-time or permanent service for a minimum consecutive period of 3 months.
Level of Study: MBA
Type: Scholarship
Value: UK £2,000 each
Frequency: Annual
Study Establishment: INSEAD
No. of awards offered: 2 per year, 1 per intake
Application Procedure: Applicants must complete an application form, available from the website and send it to INSEAD with documentary evidence of either the candidate's or the candidate's parent's service in the British Armed Forces.
Closing Date: May 5th for the September class of the same year and September 30th for the January class of the following year
Additional Information: The Lord Kitchener National Memorial Fund was created in memory of the first Earl Kitchener of Khartoum who died in action in June 1916 when he went down with his ship.

INSEAD Louis Franck Scholarship

Subjects: MBA.
Eligibility: Open to candidates of United Kingdom nationality admitted to INSEAD. Financial need is neither a necessary nor a sufficient condition for being granted an award. Nevertheless, the candidate's financial position will be taken into account, and awards will not necessarily be granted to the best candidates if there is a sound candidate who is in financial need. Selected scholars are required to write a thesis or report, the subject of which is to be agreed upon with the trustees, and is to be presented to the trustees within 3 months of graduation.
Type: Scholarship
Value: €15,000
Frequency: Annual
Study Establishment: INSEAD
No. of awards offered: Up to 8
Application Procedure: Applicants must complete a specific assignment, details of which are available from the website.
Closing Date: May 5th for the September class of the same year and September 30th for the January class of the following year
Funding: Private
Contributor: The Louis Franck Trust

Additional Information: This scholarship was established in 1983 by Louis Franck, who served for many years on the Board of INSEAD.

INSEAD Sasakawa (SYLLF) Scholarships

Subjects: MBA.
Purpose: To encourage candidates to broaden their knowledge and enhance their career leadership through the INSEAD MBA programme.
Eligibility: Open to candidates of any nationality. The awards will be made on a competitive basis.
Level of Study: MBA
Type: Scholarship
Value: €3,000–11,000 depending on the number and quality of applications
Frequency: Annual
Study Establishment: INSEAD
No. of awards offered: 1 or more per intake
Application Procedure: Applicants must complete a specific assignment, details of which are available from the website.
Closing Date: May 5th for the September class of the same year and September 30th for the January class of the following year
Funding: Private
Contributor: The Sasakawa Young Leaders Fellowship Fund (SYLFF)

INSEAD Sisley-Marc d'Ornano Scholarship

Subjects: MBA.
Purpose: To support young graduates seeking further education in order to contribute to the economic development of Poland.
Eligibility: Open to Polish nationals admitted to the INSEAD MBA programme who demonstrate a commitment to work in Poland for 3 years after the INSEAD MBA programme. The winner of the scholarship will agree to take up a professional activity in Poland for at least 3 years, and if not, the candidate is obliged to reimburse the scholarship.
Level of Study: MBA
Type: Scholarship
Value: Up to €40,000. Tuition fees and a living allowance. Partial scholarships, i.e. tuition fees only, may be awarded for residence outside Poland
Frequency: Annual
Study Establishment: INSEAD
No. of awards offered: 1
Application Procedure: Applicants must submit an essay addressing the following question: Give the main reason for your applying for the scholarship and describe your aspirations for your future career development. Scholarship applications may be submitted with the admissions application form. Application forms are available from the website.
Closing Date: May 5th for the September intake of the same year and September 30th for the January intake of the following year
Contributor: Sisley
Additional Information: This scholarship is offered in memory of the late Marc d'Ornano, who lost his life in a car accident while at the start of an excellent career.

INSTITUT DE RECHERCHE ROBERT-SAUVÉN SANTÉT EN SÉCURITÉ DU TRAVAIL (IRSST)

505 boulevard de Maisonneuve Ouest, Montréal, QC, H3A 3C2, Canada
Tel: (1) 514 288 1551
Email: grants@irsst.qc.ca
Website: www.irsst.qc.ca

Institut de recherche Robert-Sauvén santét en sécurité du travail (IRSST), established in Quebec since 1980, is a scientific research organization known for the quality of its work and the expertise of its personnel. The Institute is a private, non-profit agency.

IRSST Graduate Studies Scholarships

Subjects: Occupational health and safety.

Purpose: To support Masters and doctoral students who wish to acquire research training in the occupational health and safety field.
Eligibility: Open to students who are registered full-time in a Masters or doctoral programme and have obtained a cumulative average of B+ for all of their undergraduate studies.
Level of Study: Doctorate, Postgraduate
Type: Scholarship
Value: $14,100 per year. In addition, a scholarship recipient whose training and research program is outside Canada is reimbursed for the amount exceeding the first $750 in annual tuition fees; the cost of travelling to the training and research location, representing the cost of one round-trip economy airplane ticket or one round trip by car, for each year of the effective period of the scholarship (maximum of two years)
Length of Study: 2–3 years
Frequency: Annual
Closing Date: First Tuesday of November
Contributor: The CSST provides most of the Institute's funding from the contributions it collects from the employers

INSTITUT FRANÇAIS DE WASHINGTON

238 Dey Hall, CB 3170, UNC-CH, Chapel Hill, NC, 27599-3170, United States of America
Tel: (1) 919 962 2032
Fax: (1) 919 962 5457
Email: cmaley@email.unc.edu
Website: www.unc.edu/depts/institut
Contact: Dr Catherine A Maley, President

The mission of the Institut Français de Washington is to promote the American study of French culture, language, history and society, and to encourage the work of teachers, scholars and students in these fields. The Institute also sponsors events to foster public understanding of French-American relations. The IFW provides funds for fellowships, prizes, and conferences that serve this mission.

Edouard Morot-Sir Fellowship in Literature

Subjects: French studies in the areas of art, economics, history, history of science, linguistics, literature or social sciences.
Eligibility: Open to those in the final stages of a PhD dissertation or who have held a PhD for no longer than 3 years before the application deadline.
Level of Study: Doctorate, Postdoctorate
Type: Fellowship
Value: US$1,500
Length of Study: At least 2 months
Frequency: Annual
Country of Study: France
Application Procedure: Applicants must write a maximum of two pages describing the research project and planned trip and enclose a curriculum vitae. A letter of recommendation from the dissertation director is required and a letter from a specialist in the field for assistant professors.
Closing Date: January 15th
Funding: Foundation, private
No. of awards given last year: 1
No. of applicants last year: 35
Additional Information: Awards are for maintenance during research in France and should not be used for travel.

Gilbert Chinard Fellowships

Subjects: French studies in the areas of art, economics, history, history of science, linguistics, literature or social sciences.
Eligibility: Open to those in the final stages of a PhD dissertation or who have held a PhD for no longer than 3 years before the application deadline.
Level of Study: Doctorate, Postdoctorate
Type: Fellowship
Value: US$1,500
Length of Study: At least 2 months
Frequency: Annual
Country of Study: France

No. of awards offered: 2
Application Procedure: Applicants must write a maximum of two pages describing the research project and planned trip and enclose a curriculum vitae. A letter of recommendation from the dissertation director is also required for PhD candidates and a letter from a specialist in the field for assistant professors.
Closing Date: January 15th
Funding: Private
No. of awards given last year: 2
No. of applicants last year: 35
Additional Information: Awards are for maintenance during research in France and should not be used for travel.

Harmon Chadbourn Rorison Fellowship

Subjects: French studies in the areas of art, economics, history, history of science, linguistics, literature or social sciences.
Eligibility: Open to those in the final stages of a PhD dissertation or who have held a PhD for no longer than 3 years before the application deadline.
Level of Study: Doctorate, Postdoctorate
Type: Fellowship
Value: US$1,500
Length of Study: At least 1 month
Frequency: Every 2 years
Country of Study: France
No. of awards offered: 1
Application Procedure: Applicants must write a maximum of two pages describing the research project and planned trip and enclose a curriculum vitae. A letter of recommendation from the dissertation director is required for PhD candidates and a letter from a specialist in the field for assistant professors.
Closing Date: January 15th
Funding: Foundation, private
No. of awards given last year: 1
No. of applicants last year: 35
Additional Information: Awards are for maintenance during research in France and should not be used for travel.

THE INSTITUT MITTAG-LEFFLER

Auravägen 17, SE-18260 Djursholm, Sweden
Tel: (46) 8 6220560
Fax: (46) 8 6220589
Email: koskull@mittag-leffler.se
Website: www.mittag-leffler.se
Contact: Marie-Louise Koskull, Administrator of the Visiting Programme

Institut Mittag-Leffler is a Nordic research institute for mathematics, under the auspices of the Royal Swedish Academy of Sciences, created by Gösta and Signe Mittag-Leffler, who donated their house, library and fortune to the Academy in 1916.

Institut Mittag-Leffler Grants

Subjects: Mathematics. Programs can run for the whole academic year, or be of semester length (September 1–December 15 and January 15–June 15, respectively).
Eligibility: Open to recent PhDs and advanced graduate students. Preference will be given to applications for long stays.
Level of Study: Graduate, Postdoctorate
Type: Grant
Value: 10,000–13,000 Swedish Krona per month; travel expenses to and from Stockholm, accommodation free of charge and office space
Length of Study: 1 academic year, from September through to June 15th. Sometimes there are two differnt topics during one academic year
Frequency: Annual, semi-annual
Country of Study: Sweden
No. of awards offered: Varies
Application Procedure: In addition to the completed application form, applicants should send a short description of the candidate's

361

research interests and plans, copies of the applicant's papers and preprints and two or (preferably) three letters of recommendation. See the website for further details: www.mittag-leffler.se/programs/0910/grants.php

Closing Date: January 20th
Additional Information: For further information, please turn to Marie-Louise Koskull at Institut Mittage-Leffler or email to koskull@mittag-leffler.se

INSTITUTE FOR ADVANCED STUDIES IN THE HUMANITIES

University of Edinburgh, Hope Park Square, Edinburgh, EH8 9NW, Scotland
Tel: (44) 13 1650 4671
Fax: (44) 13 1668 2252
Email: iash@ed.ac.uk
Website: www.iash.ed.ac.uk
Contact: Ms Anthea Taylor, Institute Administrator

The Institute for Advanced Studies in the Humanities aims to promote scholarship in the humanities, and, wherever possible, to foster interdisciplinary enquiries. This is achieved by means of fellowships awarded for the pursuit of relevant research and by the public dissemination of findings in seminars, lectures, conferences, exhibitions, cultural events and publications.

Andrew W Mellon Foundation East-Central European Fellowships in the Humanities

Subjects: Humanities.
Purpose: To promote advanced research within the field of humanities and to sponsor interdisciplinary research.
Eligibility: Open to Bulgarian, Czech, Estonian, Hungarian, Latvian, Lithuanian, Polish, Romanian and Slovak scholars only. Fellows must be able to speak English and be under 45 years of age.
Level of Study: Postdoctorate
Type: Fellowships
Length of Study: 3 months
Frequency: Annual
Study Establishment: The Institute for Advanced Studies in the Humanities at the University of Edinburgh
Country of Study: Scotland
No. of awards offered: 4
Application Procedure: Applicants must complete an application form, available from the Institute.
Closing Date: February 20th
Funding: Private
Contributor: Andrew W Mellon Foundation
No. of awards given last year: 4
No. of applicants last year: 35

Institute for Advanced Studies in the Humanities Visiting Research Fellowships

Subjects: Any discipline within the humanities and social sciences, but priority will be given to those whose work falls within the scope of one of the institute's research themes.
Purpose: To promote advanced research within the field and also to sponsor interdisciplinary research.
Eligibility: Open to scholars of any nationality holding a doctorate or offering equivalent evidence of aptitude for advanced studies. Degree candidates are not eligible.
Level of Study: Postdoctorate
Type: Fellowship
Length of Study: 2–6 months
Frequency: Annual
Study Establishment: The Institute for Advanced Studies in the Humanities at the University of Edinburgh
Country of Study: United Kingdom
No. of awards offered: 15
Application Procedure: Applicants must complete an application form, available from the Institute. Candidates should advise their referees to write on their behalf directly to the Institute.
Closing Date: February 27th
Funding: Private

No. of awards given last year: 13
No. of applicants last year: 23
Additional Information: Fellows have the use of study rooms at the Institute, near the library and within easy reach of the National Library of Scotland, the Central City Library, the National Galleries and Museums, the Library of the Society of Antiquaries in Scotland and the National Archives of Scotland.

Postdoctoral Bursaries

Subjects: Humanities and social sciences.
Purpose: To support candidates in any area of the Humanities and Social Sciences, whose work falls within the scope of one of the Institute for Advanced Studies current research themes or across disciplinary boundaries in the Humanities.
Eligibility: Applicants must have been awarded a doctorate, normally within the last three years, and should not have held a permanent position at a university, or a previous fellowship at the Institute for Advanced Studies. Those who have held temporary and/or short term appointments are eligible to apply.
Level of Study: Postdoctorate
Type: Bursary
Value: Up to UK£10,000
Length of Study: 3–9 months
No. of awards offered: 6
Application Procedure: Application form can be downloaded from the Institute's website.
Closing Date: July 11th
Additional Information: Check website for further details.

INSTITUTE FOR ADVANCED STUDIES ON SCIENCE, TECHNOLOGY AND SOCIETY (IAS-STS)

Kopernikusgasse 9, Graz, 8010, Austria
Tel: (43) 316 813909
Email: info@sts.tugraz.at
Website: www.ifz.tugraz.at

In 1999 the Inter University Research Centre for Technology, Work and Culture launched the IAS-STS in Graz, Austria. It promotes the interdisciplinary investigation of the links and interaction between science, technology and society as well as research on the development and implementation of socially and environmentally sound, sustainable technologies.

IAS-STS Fellowship Programme

Subjects: Gender (technology and environment), biotechnology, technology studies, information and communication technologies.
Purpose: To give the students the opportunity to explore issues.
Level of Study: Research
Type: Fellowships
Value: €1,000 per month
Length of Study: 9 months
No. of awards offered: 5
Application Procedure: Application forms can be download from the website.
Closing Date: December 31st

INSTITUTE FOR ADVANCED STUDY

Einstein Drive, Princeton, NJ, 08540, United States of America
Tel: (1) 609 734 8239
Fax: (1) 609 951 4451
Email: cferrara@ias.edu
Website: www.ias.edu
Contact: Ms Christine Ferrara, Senior Public Affairs Officer

The Institute for Advanced Study is an independent, private institution whose mission is to support advanced scholarship and fundamental research in historical studies, mathematics, natural sciences and social science. It is a community of scholars where theoretical research and intellectual enquiry are carried out under the most favourable conditions.

Institute for Advanced Study Postdoctoral Residential Fellowships

Subjects: Social science, history, astronomy, astrophysics, theoretical physics, mathematics theoretical computer science or theoretical biology.
Purpose: To support advanced study and scholarly exploration.
Eligibility: There are no restrictions on eligibility.
Level of Study: Postdoctorate
Type: Fellowship
Value: US$40,000–65,000
Length of Study: Generally 1 year
Frequency: Annual
Country of Study: United States of America
No. of awards offered: Approx. 190
Application Procedure: Applicants must complete an application. Materials are available from the school administrative officers.
Closing Date: Varies, but is between November 1st and December 15th
Funding: Corporation, foundation, government, individuals
No. of awards given last year: Approx. 190
No. of applicants last year: Approx. 2,400

INSTITUTE FOR HUMANE STUDIES (IHS)

3301 North Fairfax Drive, Suite 440, Arlington, VA, 22201-4432, United States of America
Tel: (1) 703 993 4880
Fax: (1) 703 993 4890
Email: abrand@gmu.edu
Website: www.theihs.org
Contact: Ms Amanda Bland, Director of Academic Programs

The Institute for Humane Studies (IHS) is a unique organization that assists graduate students worldwide with a special interest in individual liberty. IHS awards over US$400,000 a year in scholarships to students from universities around the world. They also sponsor the attendance of hundreds of students at free summer seminars and provide various forms of career assistance. Through these and other programmes, IHS and a network of faculty associates promote the study of liberty across a broad range of disciplines, encouraging understanding, open enquiry, rigorous scholarship and creative problem-solving.

Hayek Fund for Scholars

Subjects: Social sciences, law, the humanities, journalism.
Purpose: To help offset expenses for participating in professional conferences and job interviews.
Eligibility: Open to graduate students and untenured faculty members.
Level of Study: Postgraduate
Value: US$1,000
Frequency: Annual
Country of Study: Any country
Application Procedure: For application requirements visit the website.

For further information contact:

George Mason University, 4400 University Drive, Fairfax, VA, 22030, United States of America
Tel: (1) 703 323 1055
Fax: (1) 703 425 1536
Contact: Keri Anderson, Programme Director

IHS Film & Fiction Scholarships

Subjects: Filmmaking, fiction writing and playwriting.
Eligibility: Open to graduate students pursuing a Master of Fine Arts degree. Applicants should have a demonstrated interest in classical liberal ideas and their application in contemporary society. They should also demonstrate the desire, motivation and creative ability to succeed in their chosen profession.
Level of Study: Graduate
Type: Scholarship
Value: Up to US$10,000
Frequency: Annual

Application Procedure: Applicants must apply online at www. theihs.org/film & fiction
Closing Date: January 15th
Funding: Private

IHS Humane Studies Fellowships

Subjects: Arts and humanities, fine and applied art, law, mass communication and information, religion and theology and social and behavioural science.
Purpose: To support outstanding students with a demonstrated interest in the classical liberal tradition intent on pursuing an intellectual and scholarly career.
Eligibility: Open to graduate students who have enrolled for the next academic year at accredited colleges and universities.
Level of Study: Graduate, Postgraduate
Type: Fellowship
Value: Up to US$12,000
Frequency: Annual
Country of Study: Any country
Application Procedure: Applicants must complete and submit an application form with three completed evaluations, three essays, official test scores, official transcripts and a term paper or writing sample. Applications can be downloaded at www.theihs.org/hsf
Closing Date: December 31
Funding: Private
No. of awards given last year: 100
No. of applicants last year: 650

IHS Summer Graduate Research Fellowship

Subjects: The humane sciences, e.g. history, political and moral philosophy, political economy, economic history, legal and social theory.
Purpose: To give students who share an interest in scholarly research in the classical liberal tradition the opportunity to work on a thesis chapter or a paper of publishable quality and to participate in interdisciplinary seminars under the guidance of a faculty supervisor.
Eligibility: Open to graduate students in the humanities, social sciences and law who intend to pursue academic careers and who are currently pursuing research in the classical liberal tradition.
Level of Study: Doctorate, Graduate, Postgraduate
Type: Fellowship
Value: $3,000 stipend and travel expenses for two IHS seminars
Frequency: Annual
Country of Study: United States of America
No. of awards offered: 8–10
Application Procedure: Applicants must submit a proposal, curriculum vitae, a copy of Graduate Record Examination scores or Law School Admission Test scores and transcripts, a writing sample and reference details. Visit the website for further information.
Closing Date: February 15th
Funding: Private

THE INSTITUTE FOR SUPPLY MANAGEMENT (ISM)

PO Box 22160 Tempe, Tempe, AZ, 85285-2160, United States of America
Tel: (1) 480 752 6276
Fax: (1) 480 752 7890
Email: kspencer@ism.ws
Website: www.ism.ws
Contact: Karin Spencer

The Institute for Supply Management (ISM) is a non-profit association that provides national and international leadership in purchasing and supply management research and education. ISM provides more than 40,000 members with opportunities to expand their professional skills and knowledge.

ISM Doctoral Dissertation Grant In Supply Management

Subjects: Purchasing materials and supply management.
Purpose: To financially assist individuals in preparation for a career in the field, for university teaching and to encourage research.
Eligibility: Open to doctoral candidates who are pursuing a PhD or DBA in purchasing, business, logistics, management, economics,

industrial engineering or a related field and who are at the dissertation stage. Applicants must be enrolled in an accredited United States of America university are eligible for the award.

Level of Study: Doctorate
Type: Grant
Value: Up to US$12,000
Frequency: Annual
Country of Study: United States of America
No. of awards offered: 3
Application Procedure: Applicants must submit an application form and documents including letters of recommendation, transcripts and a research proposal.
Closing Date: January 31st
Funding: Private
Contributor: ISM
No. of awards given last year: 4
No. of applicants last year: 20
Additional Information: Upon successful completion of the research, the ISM will be interested in the publication of material from the study. Nominations are invited from departments of economics, management, marketing and business administration at United States of America universities offering a doctoral degree in appropriate fields.

ISM Senior Research Fellowship Program

Subjects: Topics include but are not limited to the integration of purchasing with other functions, the impact of globalization on purchasing, the role of purchasing in supply chain management, measuring purchasing effectiveness, historical analysis of trends in purchasing, objective measures of supplier performance, the application of electronic commerce in purchasing and supply, the use of purchasing as a strategic tool, the identification of educational or training tools and skills for purchasing and supply management, forecasting methods, ERP and purchasing, alliances and supplier development.
Purpose: To help support emerging, high-potential scholars who teach and conduct research in purchasing and supply management.
Eligibility: Open to assistant professors, associate professors or equivalent who have demonstrated exceptional academic productivity in research and teaching. Candidates are chosen from those who can help produce useful research that can be applied to the advancement of purchasing and supply management. Candidates must be full-time faculty members within or outside the United States of America and be present or past members of ISM committees, groups, forums or affiliated organizations. An assistant professor should have 3 or more years of post-degree experience. Previous awardees are ineligible.
Level of Study: Postdoctorate
Type: Fellowship
Value: US$5,000
Frequency: Annual
Country of Study: United States of America
No. of awards offered: 1
Application Procedure: Applicants must submit four copies of each of the following items in one complete package: a letter of application explaining qualifications for the fellowship, a research proposal of not more than five pages including a problem statement or hypothesis, research methodology with data sources, collection and analysis, value to the field of purchasing and supply and a curriculum vitae including works in progress.
Closing Date: January 31st
Funding: Private
Contributor: ISM
No. of applicants last year: 5–10
Additional Information: It is expected that the ISM Fellows will present the results of their research at an ISM forum, e.g. research symposium, ISM Annual International Purchasing Conference and/or an ISM publication such as *The Journal of Supply Chain Management*.

INSTITUTE FOR WORK AND HEALTH

481 University Avenue Suite 800, Toronto, ON, M5G-2E9, Canada
Tel: (1) 416 927 2027
Fax: (1) 416 927 4167
Email: info@iwh.on.ca
Website: www.iwh.on.ca

Institute for Work and Health is an independent, non-profit research organization whose mission is to conduct and share research with

workers, labourers, employers, clinicians and policy makers to promote, protect and improve the health of working people.

S. Leonard Syme Training Fellowships in Work & Health

Subjects: Work and health.
Purpose: To financially support young researchers at the Master's or Doctoral level who intend studying in the field of work and health.
Eligibility: Open to candidates who are enrolled at an Ontario university that has a formal affiliation with the Institute for Work & Health. Candidates who are part-way through their programme of study will also be considered.
Level of Study: Doctorate, Postgraduate
Type: Fellowship
Value: Canadian $15,000–20,000
Length of Study: 1 year
Frequency: Annual
Study Establishment: Several universities
Country of Study: Canada
Application Procedure: Applicants must provide a completed application form, a 300-word statement of their research interests and a 200-word statement of their career objectives, a reference letter and curriculum vitae. Application form is available online.
Closing Date: June 2nd
Additional Information: Preference will be given to candidates whose research interests include understanding the social determinants of health and illness in work environments, and/or evaluating workplace interventions to improve health and/or the associated measurement issues.

For further information contact:

Website: www.iwh.on.ca
Contact: Ms Lyudmila Marsurova

INSTITUTE OF ADVANCED LEGAL STUDIES (IALS)

School of Advanced Study, Charles Clore House, 17 Russell Square, London, WC1B 5DR, England
Tel: (44) 20 7862 5883
Fax: (44) 20 7862 5850
Email: peter.niven@sas.ac.uk
Website: www.ials.sas.ac.uk
Contact: Mr Peter Niven, Administrator

The Institute of Advanced Legal Studies (IALS) plays a national and international role in the promotion and facilitation of legal research. It possesses one of the leading research libraries in Europe and organizes a regular programme of conferences, seminars and lectures. It also offers postgraduate taught and research programmes and specialized training courses.

IALS Visiting Fellowship in Law Librarianship

Subjects: Law and library science.
Purpose: To enable experienced law librarians, who are undertaking research in, appropriate fields, to relate their work to activities in which the Institutes own library is involved.
Eligibility: Open to experienced law librarians from any country.
Level of Study: Unrestricted
Type: Fellowship
Value: Fellowships can consist of or include a period working with Institute library staff or be a period of research based in a research carrel
Length of Study: A minimum of 3 months and a maximum of 1 year
Frequency: Annual
Study Establishment: The IALS
Country of Study: United Kingdom
No. of awards offered: 1
Application Procedure: Applicants must submit a full curriculum vitae, the names, addresses and telephone numbers of two referees and a brief statement of the research programme to be undertaken to the Administrative Secretary.
Closing Date: Applications may be considered at any time of the year
No. of awards given last year: 1
No. of applicants last year: 1

IALS Visiting Fellowship in Legislative Studies
Subjects: Law.
Purpose: To enable individuals in the field to undertake research.
Eligibility: Open to established academics and practitioners from any country. This award is not available for postgraduate research.
Level of Study: Unrestricted
Type: Fellowship
Value: Non-stipendary
Length of Study: A minimum of 3 months and a maximum of 1 year
Frequency: Annual
Study Establishment: The IALS
Country of Study: United Kingdom
No. of awards offered: 1
Application Procedure: Applicants must submit a full curriculum vitae, the names, addresses and telephone numbers of two referees and a brief statement of the research programme to be undertaken.
Closing Date: January 31st for the following academic year
No. of awards given last year: None
No. of applicants last year: 1

IALS Visiting Fellowships
Subjects: Law: legal skills, legal profession, legal education, legal implementation studies, company and commercial law, financial services law, access to legal information.
Purpose: Visiting fellowships are designed for persons already established in their own field of activity who are undertaking work within fields covered by or adjacent to the Institute's own research programmes or interests.
Eligibility: Open to nationals of any country who are established legal scholars and are undertaking research in appropriate fields.
Level of Study: Unrestricted
Type: Fellowship
Value: Non-stipendary
Length of Study: A minimum of 3 months and a maximum of 1 year
Frequency: Annual
Study Establishment: The IALS
Country of Study: United Kingdom
No. of awards offered: Up to 6
Application Procedure: Applicants must submit a full curriculum vitae, the names, addresses and telephone numbers of two referees and a brief statement of the research programme to be undertaken.
Closing Date: January 31st for the following academic year
No. of awards given last year: 7
No. of applicants last year: 16
Additional Information: This award is not available for postgraduate research.

THE INSTITUTE OF CANCER RESEARCH (ICR)

Genetic Epidemiology Building, 15 Cotswold Road, Sutton, Surrey, SM2 5NG, England
Tel: (44) 20 8643 8901 ext 4253
Fax: (44) 20 8643 6940
Email: jane.boland@icr.ac.uk
Website: www.icr.ac.uk
Contact: Simon Hobson, Registrar

Over the past 90 years, the Institute of Cancer Research (ICR) has become one of the largest, most successful and innovative cancer research centres in the world. The Institute and the Royal Marsden NHS Trust exist side by side in Chelsea and on a joint site at Sutton, and this close association allows for maximum interaction between fundamental laboratory work and clinical environment.

ICR Studentships
Subjects: Cancer research.
Purpose: Research degree studentships.
Eligibility: First class or upper second class undergraduate degree required in a relevent subject.
Level of Study: Doctorate
Type: Studentship
Value: £19,096 (inner London - Chester Beatty Laboratories, Fulham Road) or £17,770 (outer London - Sutton Campus), is increased annually in-line with the increase in cost-of-living

Length of Study: Up to 4 years
Frequency: Annual
Study Establishment: The Institute of Cancer Research, University of London
Country of Study: United Kingdom
No. of awards offered: 20–30
Application Procedure: See website www.icr.ac.uk/phds
Funding: Government, trusts
Contributor: Cancer Research UK
No. of awards given last year: 28
No. of applicants last year: 300
Additional Information: A limited number of Institute postdoctoral fellowships are offered from time to time as vacancies occur.

INSTITUTE OF CURRENT WORLD AFFAIRS

4545 42nd St NW, Suite 311, Washington, DC 20016, United States of America
Tel: (1) 202 364 4068
Fax: (1) 202 364 0498
Email: icwa@icwa.org
Website: www.icwa.org

Institute of Current World Affairs Fellowships
Subjects: International affairs.
Purpose: To enable young adults of outstanding promise and character to study and write about areas or issues of the world outside the United States of America.
Eligibility: Open to individuals under 36 who have finished their formal education. Applicants must have a good command of spoken and written English.
Level of Study: Postgraduate, Professional development
Type: Fellowship
Value: The Institute provides fellows with sufficient funding to allow them and their families to live in good health and reasonable comfort
Length of Study: A minimum of 2 years
Country of Study: Any country
No. of awards offered: 4
Application Procedure: Applicants must write to the Executive Director and briefly explain their personal background and the professional experience that would qualify them in the Institute's current areas of concern, details of which are available upon request. They should also describe the activities they would like to carry out during the 2 years overseas. This initial letter is followed by a more detailed written application process and must be completed prior to the deadline.
Closing Date: September 1st
Funding: Private
Additional Information: Fellowships are not awarded to support work toward academic degrees nor to underwrite specific studies or research projects. The Institute is also known as the Crane-Rogers Foundation.

INSTITUTE OF EDUCATION

20 Bedford Way, London, WC1H 0AL, England
Tel: (44) 20 7612 6000
Fax: (44) 20 7612 6126
Email: info@ioe.ac.uk
Website: www.ioe.ac.uk
Contact: Josie Charlton, Head of Marketing and Development

Founded in 1902, the Institute of Education is a world-class centre of excellence for research, teacher training, higher degrees and consultancy in education and education-related areas of social science. Our pre-eminent scholars and talented students from all walks of life make up an intellectually rich and diverse learning community.

Nicholas Hans Comparative Education Scholarship
Subjects: Comparative education.
Purpose: To assist a well-qualified student to study for a PhD in comparative education at the Institute.

Eligibility: Candidates must be registered Institute students not normally resident in the United Kingdom.
Level of Study: Doctorate
Type: Scholarship
Value: Full time tuition fees
Length of Study: 3–7 years
Frequency: Annual
Study Establishment: Institute of Education
Country of Study: United Kingdom
No. of awards offered: 1
Application Procedure: Candidates are required to submit an extended essay of 25,000–30,000 words, based upon their research or proposed research, that exemplifies, extends or develops by critique the concerns of Nicholas Hans in comparative education.
Closing Date: June 1st
Funding: Trusts
Contributor: Trust fund based upon money left in the will of Nicholas Hans' widow

For further information contact:

Email: mailto:p.kelly@ioe.ac.uk
Contact: Patricia Kelly

INSTITUTE OF EUROPEAN HISTORY

Alte Universitätsstrasse 19, D-55116 Mainz, Germany
Tel: (49) 613 1393 9365
Fax: (49) 613 1393 5326
Email: ieg3@ieg-mainz.de
Website: www.ieg-mainz.de
Contact: Dr Joachim Berger, Staff unit/management

The Institute of European History in Mainz, founded in 1950, is dedicated to the promotion of interdisciplinary historical research that focuses on European communication and transfer processes since 1450. Its research groups and international fellows focus on the interplay of religious, political and social phenomena relating to these processes.

Institute of European History Fellowships

Subjects: Transnational and comparative history of Europe since c. 1500, especially religious and political.
Purpose: To support young scientists in the completion of their doctoral work or in the execution of shorter postdoctoral projects. Participation in the Institute's research groups is particularly welcome.
Eligibility: Open to holders of a Master's degree and to Fellows in the advanced stages of graduate work, at least 2 years after admission to doctoral candidacy. Applicants must have successfully completed their comprehensive oral examinations.
Level of Study: Doctorate, Postdoctorate
Type: Fellowship
Value: A monthly stipend, a family allowance, health insurance and a travel allowance, all of which are in line with the guidelines of the German Academic Exchange Service (DAAD)
Length of Study: 6–18 months
Frequency: Annual
Study Establishment: The Institute of European History
Country of Study: Germany
Application Procedure: Applicants must contact the directors of the institute. For details and deadlines see the website.
Closing Date: February and August
Funding: Government
No. of awards given last year: 20
No. of applicants last year: 100

INSTITUTE OF FOOD TECHNOLOGISTS (IFT)

525 W. Van Buren, Suite 1000, Chicago, IL 60607, United States of America
Tel: (1) 312 782 8424
Fax: (1) 312 416 7919
Email: info@ift.org
Website: www.ift.org
Contact: Dr Robert A. Vitas

The Institute of Food Technologists (IFT), founded in 1939, is a non-profit scientific society with 29,000 members working in food science, technology and related professions in industry, academia and government. IFT's mission is to advance the science and technology of food through the exchange of knowledge. As a society for food science and technology, IFT brings a scientific perspective to the public discussion of food issues.

IFT Graduate Fellowships

Subjects: Food technology and food science.
Purpose: To encourage and support outstanding research.
Eligibility: Open to current graduates pursuing a course of study leading to an MS or PhD degree. Candidates must possess an above-average interest in research together with demonstrated scientific aptitude.
Level of Study: Graduate, Postgraduate, Doctorate
Type: Fellowship
Value: Varies
Frequency: Annual
Study Establishment: Any educational institution that is conducting fundamental investigations in the advancement of food science and technology
Country of Study: United States of America or other countries if appropriate
Application Procedure: Applicants must contact IFT for details.
Closing Date: February 1st
Funding: Commercial, individuals, private
Contributor: Contributors include General Mills, Inc., PepsiCo, Gerber and Proctor & Gamble Company
No. of awards given last year: 21

Marcel Loncin Research Prize

Subjects: Chemistry/Physics/Engineering research applied to food processing and the improvement of food quality.
Purpose: To provide funds for research in food processing and the improvement of food quality.
Eligibility: Open to all individuals who are capable of conducting research.
Level of Study: Research
Type: Prize
Value: US$50,000 and a plaque
Frequency: Every 2 years
Application Procedure: A completed application form accompanied by a grant proposal and a biographical sketch must be submitted.
Closing Date: December 1st
Funding: Foundation
Contributor: Institute of Food Technologists

INSTITUTE OF HISTORICAL RESEARCH (IHR)

Senate House, Malet Street, London, WC1E 7HU, England
Tel: (44) 20 7862 8740
Fax: (44) 20 7862 8811
Email: ihr.reception@sas.ac.uk
Website: www.ihr.sas.ac.uk
Contact: Director

The Institute of Historical Research (IHR) is a centre for advanced study in history. It is the meeting place for scholars from around the world, housing the largest open access collection of primary sources for historians in the United Kingdom, administering research and providing courses, seminars and conferences.

IHR Past and Present Postdoctoral Fellowships in History

Subjects: History.
Purpose: To fund 1 year of postdoctoral research.
Eligibility: Applicants may be of any nationality and their PhD may have been awarded in any country. Those who have previously held another postdoctoral fellowship will normally not be eligible.

The fellowship may not be held in conjunction with any other award. Fellowships will begin on October 1st each year and it is a strict condition of these awards that a PhD thesis should have been submitted by that date.
Level of Study: Postdoctorate
Type: Fellowship
Value: Approx. UK £15,000
Length of Study: 1 year
Frequency: Dependent on funds available
Study Establishment: IHR
Country of Study: United Kingdom
No. of awards offered: 2 (may vary according to funds)
Application Procedure: Applicants must complete an application form, available from the Fellowship Officer in early January.
Closing Date: April 15th
Funding: Private
Contributor: The Past and Present Society and IHR
No. of awards given last year: 2

Isobel Thornley Research Fellowship

Subjects: Medieval history, modern history or contemporary history.
Purpose: To help candidates at an advanced stage of a PhD to complete their doctorates.
Eligibility: Open to nationals of any country, but only to those who are registered for a PhD at the University of London.
Level of Study: Doctorate
Type: Fellowship
Value: UK £10,000
Length of Study: 1 year
Frequency: Dependent on funds available
Study Establishment: IHR
Country of Study: United Kingdom
No. of awards offered: 1
Application Procedure: Applicants must complete an application form, available from the Fellowship Assistant in early January.
Closing Date: March 2nd
Funding: Private
Contributor: Isobel Thornley Bequest
No. of awards given last year: 1

Royal History Society Fellowship

Subjects: Medieval history, modern history and contemporary history.
Purpose: To help candidates at an advanced stage of a PhD to complete their doctorates.
Eligibility: Open to nationals of any country.
Level of Study: Doctorate
Type: Fellowship
Value: Approx. UK £10,000
Length of Study: 1 year
Frequency: Dependent on funds available
Study Establishment: IHR
Country of Study: United Kingdom
No. of awards offered: 1
Application Procedure: Applicants must complete an application form, available from the Fellowship Officer in early January.
Closing Date: Early March
Funding: Private
Contributor: The Royal Historical Society
No. of awards given last year: 1

Scouloudi Fellowships

Subjects: Medieval history, modern history and contemporary history.
Purpose: To help candidates at an advanced stage of a PhD to complete their doctorates.
Eligibility: Only open to United Kingdom citizens or to candidates with a first degree from a United Kingdom university.
Level of Study: Doctorate
Type: Fellowship
Value: UK £10,000
Length of Study: 1 year
Frequency: Dependent on funds available
Study Establishment: IHR
Country of Study: United Kingdom

No. of awards offered: 5
Application Procedure: Applicants must complete an application form, available from the Fellowship Officer in early January.
Closing Date: March 2nd
Funding: Private
Contributor: The Scouloudi Foundation
No. of awards given last year: 4

INSTITUTE OF HORTICULTURE (IOH)

The Garden Club of America, 14 East 60th Street, New York, 10022, United States of America
Tel: (1) (212) 753-8287
Fax: (1) (212) 753-0134
Email: ioh@horticulture.org.uk
Website: www.horticulture.org.uk
Contact: A Clarke, General Secretary

The Institute of Horticulture (IOH) is the professional institute for horticulturists of all disciplines in the industry.

Martin McLaren Horticultural Scholarship

Subjects: Horticulture, botany and landscape architecture.
Purpose: To fund 1 year of an MSc course at an American university.
Eligibility: Applicants must have gained a botany, horticulture or landscape architecture degree, and be in the early stages of their career. The age limit is 27 years of age.
Level of Study: Postgraduate
Type: Scholarship
Value: US$29,000
Length of Study: 1 year
Frequency: Annual
Study Establishment: A university
Country of Study: United States of America
No. of awards offered: 1
Application Procedure: Applicants must complete an application form, available from the IOH.
Closing Date: November 10th
Funding: Private
Contributor: The Martin McLaren Trust
No. of awards given last year: 1

INSTITUTE OF IRISH STUDIES

Queen's University of Belfast, Belfast, BT7 INN, Northern Ireland
Tel: (44) 28 9097 3386
Fax: (44) 28 9097 3388
Email: irish.studies@qub.ac.uk
Website: www.qub.ac.uk/iis
Contact: Director

The Institute of Irish Studies at Queen's University was established in 1965 and was one of the first of its kind. It is one of the leading centres for research-based teaching in Irish studies and is an internationally renowned centre of interdisciplinary Irish scholarship attracting academics from all over the world.

Institute of Irish Studies Research Fellowships

Subjects: Any field of Irish studies.
Purpose: To promote research.
Eligibility: Candidates must hold at least a Second Class (Honours) Degree, have research experience and a viable research proposal.
Level of Study: Postdoctorate
Type: Fellowship
Value: UK £28,000
Length of Study: 1 year
Frequency: Annual
Study Establishment: The Institute of Irish Studies, Queen's University Belfast
Country of Study: Northern Ireland
No. of awards offered: Up to 3
Application Procedure: Applicants must see the website for details. Awards are usually advertised in February to March.
Closing Date: Varies
Funding: Government
No. of awards given last year: 3
No. of applicants last year: 50

Mary McNeill Scholarship in Irish Studies

Subjects: Irish studies.
Eligibility: Open to well-qualified students enrolled in the 1-year MA course in Irish studies at Queen's University. Applicants must be citizens of the United States of America or Canada and be enrolled as overseas students in this course.
Level of Study: Postgraduate
Type: Scholarship
Value: UK £3,000
Length of Study: 1 year
Frequency: Dependent on funds available
Study Establishment: Queen's University Belfast
Country of Study: Northern Ireland
No. of awards offered: 1
Application Procedure: Application form can be downloaded from the website.
Closing Date: May 31st
No. of awards given last year: 1

THE INSTITUTE OF MATERIALS, MINERALS AND MINING

Danum House, South Parade, Doncaster, DN1 2DY, United Kingdom
Tel: (44) 1302 320486
Fax: (44) 1302 380900
Email: graham.woodrow@iom3.org
Website: www.iom3.org/index.htm
Contact: Dr G J M Woodrow, Deputy Chief Executive

The Institute of Materials, Minerals and Mining (IOM3) was officially recognised by the UK's Privy Council on 26 June 2002, created from the merger of The Institute of Materials (IOM) and The Institution of Mining and Metallurgy (IMM). The Institute intends to be the leading international professional body for the advancement of materials, minerals and mining to governments, industry, academia, the public and the professionals.

Bosworth Smith Trust Fund

Subjects: Metal mining and non-ferrous extraction metallurgy or mineral dressing.
Purpose: To assist research.
Eligibility: Open to applicants who possess a degree in a relevant subject.
Level of Study: Postgraduate
Value: Approx. UK £5,500 to cover working expenses, visits to mines and plants in connection with research and the purchase of apparatus
Length of Study: 1 year
Frequency: Annual
Study Establishment: An approved university
Country of Study: United Kingdom
No. of awards offered: Varies
Application Procedure: Applicants must complete an application form, available on request.
Closing Date: March 28th

Edgar Pam Fellowship

Subjects: All subjects within field of interest ranging from explorative geology to extractive metallurgy.
Eligibility: Open to young graduates resident in Australia, Canada, New Zealand, South Africa or the United Kingdom who wish to undertake advanced study or research in the United Kingdom.
Level of Study: Postgraduate
Type: Fellowship
Value: UK £2,000
Length of Study: 1 year
Frequency: Annual
Study Establishment: Approved universities
Country of Study: United Kingdom
No. of awards offered: 1
Application Procedure: Applicants must complete an application form, available on request.
Closing Date: March 28th

G Vernon Hobson Bequest

Subjects: Mining geology.

Purpose: To advance the teaching and practice of geology as applied to mining.
Eligibility: Open to university staff throughout the United Kingdom.
Level of Study: Professional development
Value: Approx. UK £1,300 to cover travel, research or other objects in accordance with the terms of the bequest
Frequency: Annual
Country of Study: United Kingdom
No. of awards offered: More than 1
Application Procedure: Applicants must complete an application form, available on request.
Closing Date: March 28th

Mining Club Award

Subjects: Mineral industry operations.
Purpose: To enable candidates to study in the United Kingdom or overseas, to present a paper at an international minerals industry conference or to assist the candidate in attending a full-time course of study related to the minerals industry outside the United Kingdom.
Eligibility: Open to British citizens aged 21–35 years who are actively engaged in full or part-time postgraduate study or employment in the minerals industry.
Level of Study: Postgraduate, Professional development
Type: Award
Value: Approx. UK £1,500
Frequency: Annual
Country of Study: Any country
No. of awards offered: Varies
Application Procedure: Applicants must complete an application form, available on request.
Closing Date: March 28th

Stanley Elmore Fellowship Fund

Subjects: Extractive metallurgy and mineral processing.
Purpose: To provide funds for research that is related to metallurgy and mineral processing.
Level of Study: Postdoctorate, Doctorate
Type: Fellowship
Value: UK £14,000
Length of Study: 1 year
Frequency: Annual
No. of awards offered: 2
Closing Date: March 28th

The Tom Seaman Travelling Scholarship

Subjects: Mining and/or related technologies.
Purpose: To assist the study for an aspect of engineering in the minerals industry.
Eligibility: Open to candidates who are training or have been trained for a career in mining.
Level of Study: Postgraduate, Professional development
Type: Scholarship
Value: Up to UK £5,500
Frequency: Annual
Application Procedure: A completed application form must be submitted.
Closing Date: March 28th
Additional Information: Check the website for further details (www.iom3.org/content/scholarships-bursaries).

For further information contact:

The Institute of Materials, Minerals and Mining
Tel: (0) 1302 320486
Fax: (0) 1302 380900
Contact: Dr GJM Woodrow, Deputy Chief Executive

THE INSTITUTE OF SPORTS AND EXERCISE MEDICINE

30 Devonshire Street, London, W1G 6PU, England
Email: d.patterson@ucl.ac.uk
Website: www.fsem.co.uk
Contact: Miss Diana Meynell, Secretary

The Institute of Sports and Exercise Medicine is a postgraduate medical institute, which was established to develop research, teaching and treatment in sports medicine. It offers annual awards to medical practitioners and runs courses on different aspects of this specialist subject. It has recently become the research arm of the Faculty of Sport and Exercise Medicine (UK), with a remit to promote sport and exercise medicine research throughout the UK.

Duke of Edinburgh Prize for Sports Medicine

Subjects: Sports medicine in the community.
Purpose: To promote postgraduate work and signify standards of excellence.
Eligibility: Open to medical practitioners in the United Kingdom.
Level of Study: Postgraduate
Type: Prize
Value: Varies, but usually a substantial cash prize
Frequency: Annual
Country of Study: United Kingdom
No. of awards offered: 1
Application Procedure: Applicants must write for an entry or nomination form in the first instance.
Closing Date: Varies annually. The exact date is specified in the conditions of entry
Funding: Private

Sir Robert Atkins Award

Subjects: Sports medicine.
Purpose: To increase medical support and active involvement in the field and to recognize a doctor who has provided the most consistently valuable medical, clinical or preventive service to a national sporting organization or sport in general.
Eligibility: Open to medical practitioners in the United Kingdom.
Level of Study: Postgraduate
Type: Award
Value: Varies, but usually a substantial cash prize
Frequency: Annual
Country of Study: United Kingdom
No. of awards offered: 1
Application Procedure: Applicants must write for an entry or nomination form in the first instance.
Closing Date: Varies
Funding: Private
No. of awards given last year: 0
No. of applicants last year: 0

INSTITUTE OF TURKISH STUDIES (ITS)

Intercultural Center-Box 571033, Georgetown University, Washington DC, 20057-1033, United States of America
Tel: (1) 202 687 0295
Fax: (1) 202 687 3780
Email: dcc@turkishstudies.org
Website: www.turkishstudies.org
Contact: David C Cuthell, Director

The Institute of Turkish Studies (ITS) was founded and incorporated in the District of Columbia in 1982. It is the only non-profit, private educational foundation in the United States that is exclusively dedicated to the support and development of Turkish Studies in United States higher education.

Dissertation Writing Grants for Graduate Students

Subjects: Social sciences and humanities.
Purpose: To fund advanced students who have finished the research stage of their dissertation.
Eligibility: Applicants must be graduate students currently enrolled in a PhD degree programme in the United States of America, expected to complete all PhD requirements except their dissertation by March. Open to citizens of the United States of America or permanent residents.
Level of Study: Doctorate
Type: Grant
Value: US$5,000–10,000
Length of Study: 1 academic year
Frequency: Annual

Application Procedure: A complete application must include the two-page grant application cover sheet completed in full, a project proposal (maximum six double-spaced pages), a budget statement, three letters of recommendation sent directly to ITS, an updated curriculum vitae and academic transcripts of all graduate work.
Closing Date: March 11th
Funding: Private
Additional Information: Decisions on applications will be announced in May. For further details check the website.

Post-Doctoral Summer Travel-Research Grants

Subjects: Ottoman and modern Turkish Studies.
Purpose: To provide partial support for travel and research to Turkey.
Eligibility: Open to citizens or permanent residents of the United States who currently live/work in the United States. The candidates must have obtained a PhD in humanities or social sciences.
Level of Study: Research
Type: Grant
Value: Varies
Length of Study: 4 weeks
Frequency: Annual
Country of Study: Turkey
Application Procedure: Applicants can download the application cover sheet from the website. The completed cover sheet along with a project proposal, budget, letters of recommendation and curriculum vitae must be submitted.
Closing Date: March 9th
Additional Information: Application forms and supporting materials submitted by fax will not be accepted.

Research Grants in Comparative Studies of Modern Turkey

Subjects: Ottoman and modern Turkish studies.
Purpose: To support and encourage the development of research, scholarship and learning in the field of Turkish Studies in the United States.
Eligibility: Open to postdoctoral scholars in the United States who study aspects of the Republic of Turkey (post-1922). The applicants must be citizens or permanent residents of the United States and affiliated with a university in the United States.
Level of Study: Doctorate, Graduate, Postdoctorate
Type: Grant
Value: US$10,000
Length of Study: 1 year
Frequency: Annual
Application Procedure: Applicants can download the application cover sheet from the website. The completed cover sheet must be sent along with a project proposal, budget, letters of recommendation, curriculum vitae and academic transcripts.
Closing Date: March 9th
Additional Information: Application forms and supporting materials submitted by fax will not be accepted.

Summer Language Study Grants in Turkey for Graduate Studies

Subjects: Turkish language.
Purpose: To fund summer travel to Turkey for language study in preparation for graduate research.
Eligibility: Applicants must be graduate students in any field of the social sciences or humanities, currently enrolled in a university in the United States of America. Open to citizens of the United States of America or permanent residents.
Level of Study: Graduate
Type: Grant
Value: US$1,000–2,000
Length of Study: Varies, minimum of 2 months
Frequency: Annual
Study Establishment: An established Ottoman or Turkish language training facility
Application Procedure: A complete application must include the two-page grant application cover sheet completed in full, a project proposal (maximum three double-spaced pages), a budget statement, three letters of recommendation sent directly to ITS, an updated curriculum vitae and academic transcripts of all graduate work.
Closing Date: March 11th

Funding: Private
Additional Information: Decisions on applications will be announced in May. For further details check the website.

Summer Research Grants in Turkey for Graduate Students

Subjects: Social sciences and humanities.
Purpose: To fund summer travel to carry out projects.
Eligibility: Applicants must be graduate students in any field of the social sciences or humanities in the United States of America, currently not engaged in dissertation writing. Applicants must be citizens of the United States of America or permanent residents.
Level of Study: Graduate, Postgraduate
Type: Grant
Value: US$1,000–2,000
Length of Study: Varies, minimum of 2 months
Frequency: Annual
Application Procedure: A complete application must include the grant application cover sheet completed in full, a project proposal (maximum five double-spaced pages), a detailed budget stating the amount requested from ITS, three letters of recommendation sent directly to ITS, an updated curriculum vitae and academic transcripts of all graduates work.
Closing Date: March 11th
Funding: Private
Additional Information: Decisions on applications will be announced in May. For further details check the website.

THE INSTITUTION OF CIVIL ENGINEERS

1 Great George Street, Westminster, London, SW1P 3AA, England
Tel: (44) 20 7222 7722
Fax: (44) 20 7233 0515
Email: quest.awards@ice.org.uk
Website: www.ice.org.uk
Contact: Ms Ellen Ryan, Education Officer

QUEST Institution of Civil Engineers Continuing Education Award

Subjects: Civil engineering.
Purpose: To enable approved persons to undertake MSc courses after some years of industrial experience.
Eligibility: Open to graduates of any nationality who hold an accredited First Class Degree in civil engineering and have been members of the Institution at any grade for not less than 2 years.
Level of Study: Postgraduate
Type: Award
Value: Up to UK £1,500
Frequency: Annual
Country of Study: United Kingdom
No. of awards offered: 10–15
Application Procedure: Applicants must complete an application form, available from Ms Coverdale.
Closing Date: Feburary 13th, April 30th, June 25th, September 25th
No. of awards given last year: 13
No. of applicants last year: 20

QUEST Institution of Civil Engineers Overseas Travel Awards

Subjects: Civil engineering, environmental engineering, transportation and agricultural engineering.
Purpose: To support overseas travel by institution members to overseas universities, specific overseas projects and mid-career support and development.
Eligibility: Open to institution members, preference being given to postgraduate applicants proposing individual overseas projects or requiring mid-career support.
Level of Study: Postgraduate
Value: Up to UK £1,500
Length of Study: 3 months–1 year
Frequency: Annual
Country of Study: Any country
No. of awards offered: Approx. 15
Application Procedure: Applicants must complete an application form, available from Mrs Coverdale.

Closing Date: Feburary 13th, April 30th, June 25th, September 25th
Additional Information: Applications are not necessarily restricted to technical developments, but may be concerned with organizational, managerial or financial aspects of civil engineering. Awards will be judged on merit.

THE INSTITUTION OF ENGINEERING AND TECHNOLOGY (IET)

Michael Faraday House, Six Hills Way, Stevenage, Hertfordshire, SG1 2AY, England
Tel: (44) 01438 767272
Fax: (44) 01438 767305
Email: awards@theiet.org
Website: www.theiet.org/awards
Contact: The Scholarships Officer

With more than 150,000 members spanning 127 countries, and offices in Asia, Europe and America, the IET is Europe's leading organization of engineering and tecnical professionals. Join us for the exchange of ideas, the sharing of knowledege nad the positive promotiion of science, engineering and technologyaround the world.

D H Thomas Travel Bursary

Subjects: Electrical, electronic, information engineering, manufacturing engineering and related disciplines.
Purpose: To support IET members undertaking research in Europe.
Eligibility: Open to IET members undertaking personal and professional research in Europe. Preference is given to research taking place in Germany.
Level of Study: Postdoctorate, Professional development, Postgraduate, Doctorate, Research
Type: Travel grant
Value: UK £500
Length of Study: Up to 3 years
Frequency: Every 2 years
Country of Study: Europe, Germany
No. of awards offered: 1
Application Procedure: Applicants should download an application form from the Travel Awards section at www.theiet.org/ambition. Given that there are a limited number of awards, applicants are advised to apply as early as possible.
Closing Date: Applications are accepted throughout the year
Funding: Trusts

Hudswell Bequest Travelling Fellowships

Subjects: Electrical, electronic, manufacturing, engineering and related disciplines.
Purpose: Enables IET members who are UK research students to travel overseas in order to further their research.
Eligibility: Open to IET members undertaking postgraduate research in the United Kingdom.
Level of Study: Postgraduate
Type: Fellowship
Value: Up to UK £1,000
Frequency: Annual
Country of Study: United Kingdom
No. of awards offered: 4
Application Procedure: Applicants should download an application form from the Travel Awards section at www.theiet.org/ambition
Closing Date: April 30th, July 31st and November 30th
Funding: Trusts
No. of awards given last year: 4
Additional Information: Given that there are a limited number of awards, applicants are advised to apply as early as possible.

Hudswell International Research Scholarships

Subjects: Electrical, electronic, information technology, manufacturing engineering and related disciplines.
Purpose: To assist members of the IET with advanced research work, leading to the award of a doctorate, to be undertaken outside the applicant's home country.
Eligibility: Applicants should be members of the IET and must have commenced their studies prior to applying for this scholarship
Level of Study: Doctorate, Postgraduate

Type: Scholarship
Value: UK £5,000
Length of Study: 1 year
Frequency: Annual
Study Establishment: Internationally recognized universities or research establishments with a high reputation for research
Country of Study: Any country
No. of awards offered: 3
Application Procedure: Applicants should download an application form from www.theiet.org/postgradawards. Given that there are a limited number of awards, applicants are advised to apply as early as possible.
Closing Date: April 30th
Funding: Trusts
No. of awards given last year: 3

IET Master's Degree Scholarship
Subjects: Electrical, electronic, manufacturing and information engineering.
Purpose: To assist IET members undertaking postgraduate research studies for MSc degrees.
Eligibility: Applicants should be members of the IET and must have commenced their studies prior to applying for this scholarship
Level of Study: Postgraduate
Type: Scholarship
Value: UK £1,500
Frequency: Annual
Country of Study: United Kingdom
No. of awards offered: 6
Application Procedure: Applicants should download an application form from www.theiet.org/postgradawards
Closing Date: April 30th
Funding: Trusts
Additional Information: Given that there are a limited number of awards available, applicants are advised to apply as early as possible.

IET Postgraduate Scholarships
Subjects: Electrical, electronic, communications, manufacturing and power engineering.
Purpose: To assist IET members with research studies.
Eligibility: Applicants should be members of the IET and must have commenced their studies prior to applying for this scholarship
Level of Study: Doctorate, Postgraduate, Research
Type: Scholarship
Value: UK £1,250
Length of Study: 1 year
Frequency: Annual
Study Establishment: University in the UK
Country of Study: United Kingdom
No. of awards offered: 3
Application Procedure: Applicants should download an application form from www.theiet.org/postgradawards
Closing Date: April 30th
Funding: Trusts
No. of awards given last year: 3

IET Younger Members Conference Bursary
Subjects: Electrical engineering and related disciplines.
Purpose: To assist IET members with presenting papers at IET conferences.
Eligibility: Bursaries are open to members carrying out career development activities who have had papers accepted for formal presentation at an IET conference or other conference sponsored by the IET
Level of Study: Postgraduate, Professional development
Type: Travel grant
Value: Up to UK £350
Frequency: Annual
No. of awards offered: 2 per conference
Application Procedure: Applicants should download an application form from the Travel Awards section at www.theiet.org/ambition
Closing Date: At least 2 months prior to the date of the conference
Funding: Trusts
Additional Information: This award is subject to complete revision and substantial changes in terms and conditions.

J R Beard Travelling Fund
Subjects: Electrical, electronic, manufacturing and related engineering.
Purpose: To enable members of the IET to travel overseas and thus broaden their professional experience.
Eligibility: Enables IET members carrying out career development activities to travel overseas in order to broaden their professional experience. Preference is given to younger members who are at the early stages of their professional careers and who are unable to readily find assistance from conventional sources.
Level of Study: Unrestricted
Type: Travel grant
Value: Up to UK £500
Frequency: Annual
Country of Study: Any country
No. of awards offered: 10
Application Procedure: Applicants should download an application form from the Travel Awards section at www.theiet.org/ambition
Closing Date: Applications are accepted throughout the year
Funding: Trusts
Additional Information: Given that there are a limited number of awards applicants are advised to apply as early as possible.

Leonard Research Grant
Subjects: Electrical, electronic, manufacturing and related engineering.
Purpose: To assist engineering graduates who might not otherwise be able to undertake or complete work leading to a higher degree.
Eligibility: Applicants should be members of the IET and must have commenced their studies prior to applying for this scholarship
Level of Study: Postgraduate, Doctorate
Type: Research grant
Value: UK £1,000 per annum
Frequency: Every 3 years
Country of Study: United Kingdom
No. of awards offered: 1
Application Procedure: Applicants should download an application form from www.theiet.org/postgradawards
Closing Date: April 30th
Funding: Trusts

Leslie H Paddle Scholarship
Subjects: Electronic and radio engineering.
Purpose: To assist IET members with research studies.
Eligibility: Applicants should be members of the IET and must have commenced their studies prior to applying for this scholarship
Level of Study: Doctorate, Postgraduate
Type: Scholarship
Value: UK £10,000
Length of Study: 2 years
Frequency: Annual
Country of Study: United Kingdom
No. of awards offered: 1
Application Procedure: Applicants should download an application form from www.theiet.org/postgradawards
Closing Date: April 30th
Funding: Trusts
No. of awards given last year: 1
Additional Information: It is hoped that the fellowship will encourage co-operation between industry and the higher education sector and that an industrial organization will be associated with the fellowship. Leslie H Paddle Scholarship holders who satisfactorily complete their research studies may use the appendage IET Scholar.

Lord Lloyd of Kilgerran Memorial Prize
Subjects: Mobile radio and RF engineering.
Purpose: To aid a candidate who intends to undertake an MSc, MPhil or PhD in mobile radio and RF engineering.
Eligibility: Applicants should currently be resident in the United Kingdom and should have been professional, practising engineers for a minimum of 3 years.
Level of Study: Postgraduate
Type: Prize
Value: UK £1,000
Length of Study: 1 year for full-time study, 2 years for part-time study

Frequency: Annual
Study Establishment: A suitable university
Country of Study: United Kingdom
No. of awards offered: 1
Application Procedure: Applicants must complete an application form.
Closing Date: December 31st
Funding: Trusts
No. of awards given last year: 2

Princess Royal Scholarship

Subjects: Engineering work commensurate with the activities of the IET.
Purpose: To enable an IET member to use his or her professional knowledge and experience in a way that is beneficial to an under-privileged community in a developing country.
Eligibility: Open to applicants undertaking a specific programme of work with a charitable organization. The nature of the work must be commensurate with the activities of the IET. The programme must be undertaken for a period of not less than 3 months and conducted in co-operation with an organization in the receiving country.
Level of Study: Postgraduate
Type: Scholarship
Value: UK £1,000
Frequency: Annual
Country of Study: Any developing country
No. of awards offered: 1
Application Procedure: Applicants should download an application form from the Travel Awards section at www.theiet.org/ambition
Closing Date: Applications are accepted throughout the year
Funding: Trusts
No. of awards given last year: 1

Robinson Research Scholarship

Subjects: Electrical, electronic, communications, information or manufacturing engineering and related disciplines.
Purpose: To assist IET members with research leading to the award of a PhD or postdoctoral qualification.
Eligibility: Open to first-year research students currently resident in the United Kingdom. Applicants must be members of the IET
Level of Study: Postgraduate, Doctorate
Type: Scholarship
Value: UK £1,250 per year
Length of Study: 2 years
Frequency: Annual
Country of Study: United Kingdom
No. of awards offered: 2
Application Procedure: Applicants should download an application form from www.theiet.org/postgradawards
Closing Date: April 30th
Funding: Trusts
Additional Information: Given that there are a limited number of awards available, applicants are advised to apply as early as possible.

INSTITUTION OF MECHANICAL ENGINEERS (IMECHE)

1 Birdcage Walk, Westminster, London, SW1H 9JJ, England
Tel: (44) (0) 20 7222 7899
Fax: (44) (0) 20 7222 4557
Email: prizesandawards@imeche.org.uk
Website: www.imeche.org.uk
Contact: The Prizes and Awards Officer

The Institution of Mechanical Engineers (IMechE) was founded in 1847 by engineers. They formed an institution to promote the exchange of ideas and encourage individuals or groups in creating inventions that would be crucial to the development of the world as a whole. Now, over 150 years later, IMechE is one of the largest engineering institutions in the world, with over 88,000 members in 120 countries.

Donald Julius Groen Prizes

Subjects: Engineering.
Purpose: To award the author of outstanding papers or for outstanding achievements in the group's sphere of activity.

Eligibility: Open to authors of papers or those who have achievements of a sufficiently high standard to warrant the award of an IMechE prize. As a general rule, but with certain exceptions, grants are normally awarded only to members of the Institution.
Type: Prize
Value: UK £250
Frequency: Annual
No. of awards offered: 1
Application Procedure: Applicants must contact the Institution of Mechanical Engineers for details.
Funding: Private

James Clayton Awards

Subjects: Mechanical engineering.
Purpose: To enable the recipient to pursue advanced postgraduate studies or programmes of research.
Eligibility: Open to IMechE members who hold an accredited engineering degree or who have satisfied the academic requirements for IMechE membership by other means. Applicants must not have had less than 2 years of acceptable professional training in mechanical engineering.
Level of Study: Postgraduate
Type: Grant
Value: Up to UK £1,000 per year
Length of Study: Up to 3 years
Frequency: Annual
Study Establishment: An approved centre
Country of Study: United Kingdom
No. of awards offered: Approx. 10
Application Procedure: Applicants must complete and submit an application form with three references.
Closing Date: 3 months before a decision is required
Funding: Private
Additional Information: A report is required within 3 months of the completion of the project.

James Clayton Overseas Conference Travel for Senior Engineers

Subjects: Mechanical engineering.
Purpose: To assist members of the Institution who have been invited to contribute in some way to a conference or who could be expected to make a significant contribution to the aims of a conference by their attendance.
Eligibility: Open to IMechE members over the age of 40 years.
Level of Study: Professional development
Type: Travel grant
Value: Up to UK £1,000
Country of Study: Any country
No. of awards offered: Varies
Application Procedure: Applicants must submit a completed application form with 3 references.
Funding: Private
Additional Information: A report is required three months after the conference.

James Clayton Postgraduate Hardship Award

Subjects: Mechanical engineering.
Purpose: To assist outstanding postgraduates who experience hardship while undertaking courses of advanced study, training or research work on a course approved by the Institution.
Eligibility: Open to candidates who have completed a degree course in mechanical engineering accredited by IMechE and who have gained graduate membership of IMechE.
Level of Study: Postgraduate
Type: Grant
Value: Up to UK £1,000
Length of Study: 1 year
Frequency: Annual
Country of Study: United Kingdom
No. of awards offered: Up to 3
Application Procedure: Applicants must complete and submit an application form with three references.
Closing Date: 3 months before a decision is required
Funding: Private

Additional Information: A report is required 3 months after the activity has been completed.

James Watt International Medal

Subjects: Mechanical engineering.

Purpose: To award an eminent engineer who has attained worldwide recognition in mechanical engineering.

Eligibility: Open to United Kingdom engineers and those nominated from overseas.

Type: Prize

Frequency: Every 2 years (odd-numbered years)

No. of awards offered: 1

Application Procedure: Applicants must write for details.

Funding: Private

Additional Information: This award is the premier international award of the Institution.

INTEL CORPORATION

Corporate Affairs, Rita Holiday, 2200 Mission College Blvd, M/S RN3-75, Santa Clara, CA, 95052-8119, United States of America

Tel: (1) (408) 765-2016

Fax: (1) (408) 765-3804

Website: www.intel.com/community

Intel Corporation is committed to maintaining and enhancing the quality of life in the communities where the company has a major presence.

Intel Public Affairs China Grant

Subjects: Science, mathematics, environmental studies and technology education.

Purpose: To support further study programmes with educational and technological components in India.

Eligibility: Each request will be evaluated on the basis of the services offered and the programme's impact on the community and the potential for Intel employee involvement.

Level of Study: Professional development

Type: Grant

Value: Varies

Length of Study: 1 year

Frequency: Annual

Country of Study: China

No. of awards offered: Varies

Application Procedure: Apply online or contact the office.

Funding: Corporation

Contributor: Intel Corporation

For further information contact:

Intel Technology (China) Ltd, Shanghai city

Tel: +86 21 504818818 ext. 32707

Contact: Joanna Chen, Community Affairs Manger

Intel Public Affairs Costa Rica Grant

Subjects: Science, mathematics, environmental studies and technology education.

Purpose: To support further study programmes with educational and technological components Costa Rica.

Eligibility: Each request will be evaluated on the basis of the services offered and the programme's impact on the community and the potential for Intel employee involvement.

Level of Study: Professional development

Type: Grant

Value: Varies

Length of Study: 1 year

Frequency: Annual

Country of Study: Costa Rica

No. of awards offered: Varies

Application Procedure: Apply online or contact the office.

Funding: Corporation

Contributor: Intel Corporation

For further information contact:

Intel Education Program Components Intel de Costa Rica Calle 129 La Ribera de Belen, Heredia, Costa Rica

Tel: (506) 256-6032

Contact: Public Affairs

Intel Public Affairs India Grant

Subjects: Science, mathematics, environmental studies and technology education.

Purpose: To support further study programmes with educational and technological components India.

Eligibility: Each request will be evaluated on the basis of the services offered and the programme's impact on the community and the potential for Intel employee involvement.

Level of Study: Professional development

Type: Grant

Value: Varies

Length of Study: 1 year

Frequency: Annual

Country of Study: India

No. of awards offered: Varies

Application Procedure: Apply online or contact the office.

Funding: Corporation

Contributor: Intel Corporation

For further information contact:

Intel Technology India Ltd Upper Ground Floor International Trade Tower Nehru place, New Delhi, 110019, India

Tel: (91) 11 51226055

Fax: (91) 11 51226000

Intel Public Affairs Malaysia Grant

Subjects: Science, mathematics, environmental studies and technology education.

Purpose: To support further study programmes with educational and technological components in Malaysia.

Eligibility: Each request will be evaluated on the basis of the services offered and the programme's impact on the community and the potential for Intel employee involvement.

Level of Study: Professional development

Type: Grant

Value: Varies

Length of Study: 1 year

Frequency: Annual

Country of Study: Malaysia

No. of awards offered: Varies

Application Procedure: Apply online or contact the office.

Funding: Corporation

Contributor: Intel Corporation

For further information contact:

Intel Technology Sdn Bhd Selina Saiu, Public Affairs Dept. Bayan Lepas Free International Zone Phase 3, Halaman Kampung Jawa, Penang, 11900, Malaysia

Tel: (60) 604-6422222

Fax: (60) 604-8596403

Intel Public Affairs Russia Grant

Subjects: Science, mathematics, environmental students and technology education.

Purpose: To support further study programmes with educational and technological components in Russia.

Eligibility: Each request will be evaluated on the basis of the services offered and the programme's impact on the community and the potential for Intel employee involvement.

Type: Grant

Frequency: Annual

Country of Study: Russia

No. of awards offered: Varies

Application Procedure: Apply online or contact the office.

Funding: Corporation

Contributor: Intel Corporation

For further information contact:

Intel Russia 30 Turgenev Street, Novgorod, Nizhny, 603950, Russia

Tel: (7) (8312) 16 2496

Email: paris@intel.com

Contact: Mr Evgeny Zakablukovsky, Public Affairs Manager

INTENSIVE CARE SOCIETY (ICS)

29B Montague Street, London, WC1B 5BH, England
Tel: (44) 20 7291 0690
Fax: (44) 20 7580 0689
Email: shaba@ics.ac.uk
Website: www.ics.ac.uk
Contact: Shaba Haque, Research Grant and Visiting Scholarship
Enquiries & Educational Events Team Leader

The Intensive Care Society (ICS) is a charitable organization promoting advances in the care of the critically ill. This is largely accomplished through educational means and promoting research activity.

ICS Visiting Fellowship

Subjects: Medicine.
Purpose: To provide the cost of travel to ICS members who wish to travel to an institution other than their own, either within the UK, or overseas.
Eligibility: Open to all members of ICS.
Level of Study: Doctorate, Postdoctorate
Type: Fellowship
Value: Up to UK £5,000
Application Procedure: A written proposal of not more than 1000 words should be submitted, outlining the proposed use of the grant, appropriate costs and the benefits accruing from the visit.
Closing Date: June 27th

ICS Young Investigator Award (Research Grants)

Subjects: Any aspect of intensive care medicine and care of the critically ill.
Purpose: To promote research.
Eligibility: Applicants must be ICS members.
Level of Study: Unrestricted
Type: Research grant
Value: £10,000
Frequency: Dependent on funds available
Country of Study: Any country
No. of awards offered: Varies
Application Procedure: Applicants must complete an application form, available from the website.
Closing Date: June 27th
Funding: Private
Additional Information: Further information is available on the Society's website.

INTER AMERICAN PRESS ASSOCIATION (IAPA)

Inter American Press Association, Jules Dubois Building, 1801 SW, 3rd Avenue, 8th Floor, Miami, FL 33129, United States of America
Tel: (1) 305 634-2465
Fax: (1) 305 635-2272
Email: gbryan@sipiapa.org
Website: www.sipiapa.org
Contact: Gloria Bryan, Assistant to the Executive Director

The Inter American Press Association (IAPA) was established in 1942 to defend and promote the right of the peoples of the America to be fully and freely informed through an independent press.

IAPA Scholarship Fund, Inc.

Subjects: Journalism in the print media.
Purpose: To help develop more rounded journalists through cultural exposure and study in a foreign country.
Eligibility: Open to all journalists or journalism school seniors between 21 and 35 years of age.
Level of Study: Professional development, Postgraduate
Type: Scholarship
Value: US$20,000 and a one-time round-trip airfare for the year
Length of Study: 1 year
Frequency: Annual
Study Establishment: An American or Canadian university school of journalism approved by the Fund for Latin American and West Indian

candidates, or an approved university or field work in a Latin American country for United States and Canadian candidates
Country of Study: Other
No. of awards offered: 4–6
Application Procedure: Applicants must complete an application form, available from the Scholarships Director.
Closing Date: January 31st
Additional Information: Candidates should have good command of the language of the country they intend to visit. United States and Canadian Scholars must take a minimum of three university courses, participate in the Fund's Reporting Program, and undertake a major research project. The Association also gives IAPA awards of US$500–1,000 and a scroll or plaque to Latin American and American journalists.

INTERNATIONAL AGENCY FOR RESEARCH ON CANCER (IARC)

150 Cours Albert Thomas, F-69372 Lyon Cedex 08, France
Tel: (33) 4 72 73 84 48
Fax: (33) 4 72 73 80 80
Email: fel@iarc.fr
Website: www.iarc.fr
Contact: Ms Eve Elakroud, Administrative Assistant IARC Fellowship Programme

The International Agency for Research on Cancer (IARC) is part of the World Health Organization. IARC's mission is to co-ordinate and conduct research into the causes of human cancer and the disease's mechanisms and to develop scientific strategies for cancer control. The Agency is involved in both epidemiological and laboratory research and disseminates scientific information through publications, meetings, courses and fellowships.

IARC Postdoctoral Fellowships for Training in Cancer Research

Subjects: Epidemiology and biostatistics of cancer, environmental chemical carcinogenesis, cancer etiology and prevention, infection and cancer molecular cell biology, molecular genetics, molecular pathology and mechanisms of carcinogenesis with emphasis on interdisciplinary projects
Purpose: To provide training in cancer research to junior scientists from low- or medium-resource countries.
Eligibility: Applicants from any country other than those classified as high-income economies by the World Bank are eligible. Candidates should have spent less than 5 years abroad (including doctoral studies), and have finished their doctoral degree within 5 years of the closing date for application. The working languages at IARC are English and French. Candidates must be proficient in English at a level sufficient for scientific communication. Candidates should contact the host group of their choice at IARC before application in order to establish a proposed programme of mutual interest. Candidates already working as a postdoctoral fellow at the Agency at the time of application or who have had any contractual relationship with IARC during the 6 months preceding the deadline for applications cannot be considered.
Level of Study: Postdoctorate
Type: Fellowship
Value: Travel for the Fellow and for dependents if accompanying the Fellow for at least 8 months; an annual stipend of approx. €32,000, net of tax; an annual family allowance of €400 for spouses and €450 for each child; and health insurance covered
Length of Study: 2 years, the 2nd year being subject to satisfactory appraisal
Frequency: Annual
Study Establishment: IARC in Lyon, France
Country of Study: France
No. of awards offered: Approx. 6
Application Procedure: Applicants must complete and submit an application form. Applications must be supported by the Director of the applicant's own institution.
Closing Date: November 30th
No. of awards given last year: 6
No. of applicants last year: 25

Additional Information: Applicants should provide evidence of their ability to return to their home country at the end of the fellowship and to continue their work in cancer research.

THE INTERNATIONAL AIR CARGO ASSOCIATION (TIACA)

PO Box 661510, Miami, FL, 33266-1510, United States of America
Tel: (1) 786 265 7011
Fax: (1) 786 265 7012
Email: secgen@tiaca.org
Website: www.tiaca.org

The International Air Cargo Association (TIACA) is the only worldwide organization that brings together all the links of the Air Logistics Chain. This organization supports and assists progressive liberalization of the global market and easier, enhanced trade between developing and developed economies.

TIACA Masters Scholarship Program

Subjects: This award is for a working thesis for expenses related to research i.e., books, tuition fees or living expenses.
Purpose: To provided support to students who are intending to enroll or have already enrolled in a Masters degree programme.
Eligibility: Open to all university students worldwide.
Level of Study: MBA, Doctorate, Postdoctorate, Postgraduate, Predoctorate, Research
Type: Scholarship
Value: US$5,000
Frequency: Annual
Country of Study: United States of America
Application Procedure: A completed application form must be submitted online.
Closing Date: November 15th
Funding: International Office
Contributor: The International Air Cargo Association (TIACA)
No. of awards given last year: 1
No. of applicants last year: 4

TIACA Walter H. Johnson, Jr. Scholarship Award

Subjects: Business and logistics management, engineering science and technology, and law.
Purpose: To financially assist students who wish to build a career in air commerce.
Eligibility: Open to PhD candidates in logistics, aviation management, transportation, international business, law or related fields with a focus on air commerce.
Level of Study: Doctorate, Postgraduate
Type: Scholarship
Value: US$25,000
Length of Study: 1 year
Frequency: Annual
Country of Study: Worldwide
Application Procedure: The student's proposed theses will be the primary source of information used to select the recipient.
Closing Date: March 30th
Funding: Corporation, international office
Contributor: The International Air Cargo Association (TIACA)
No. of awards given last year: 1
No. of applicants last year: 4

INTERNATIONAL ANESTHESIA RESEARCH SOCIETY

2 Summit Park Drive, Suite 140, Cleveland, Ohio 44131, United States of America
Tel: (1) 216 642 1124
Fax: (1) 216 642 1127
Email: iarshq@iars.org
Website: www.iars.org

An International society committed to improving clinical care, education and research in anaesthesia, pain management and perioperative medicine.

Clinical Scholar Research Award

Subjects: Anesthesiology.
Purpose: To further the understanding of clinical practice in anesthesiology and related sciences through clinical investigations.
Eligibility: For eligibilty requirements please see the website www.iars.org
Type: Research grant
Value: US$80,000 maximum per award
Length of Study: 2 years
Frequency: Annual
Study Establishment: International Anesthesia Research Society
No. of awards offered: 4
Application Procedure: Applicants must submit an application, which can be downloaded from the website www.iars.org, to the IARS by the deadline. Applicants must be a member of the IARS.
Closing Date: October 15th
No. of awards given last year: 4

Frontiers in Anesthesia Research Award

Subjects: Anesthesiology.
Purpose: To foster innovation and creativity by an individual researcher in the field of anesthesiology.
Eligibility: Eligibility requirements are available at www.iars.org
Level of Study: Unrestricted
Type: Research grant
Value: US$500,000
Length of Study: 3 years
Frequency: Every 2 years
No. of awards offered: 1
Application Procedure: Applicants must submit a formal application to the IARS by the published deadline. Applicants must be a member of the IARS. Please see the website www.iars.org for complete application procedures.
Closing Date: September
Funding: Corporation
Contributor: International Anesthesia Research Society
No. of applicants last year: 13–15

Teaching Recognition Award

Subjects: Anaesthesiology.
Purpose: The IARS Teaching Recognition Award for Achievement in Education is designed to recognize outstanding career contrbutions by seior faculty. The IARS Teaching Recognition Award for Innovation in Education is designed to recognize extraordinary educational programs devised by junior or middle-level faculty.
Eligibility: Please see the website www.iars.org for the eligibility requirements
Level of Study: Unrestricted
Type: Grant
Value: US$5,000 to the recipient, US$10,000 to the recipient's institution to be used for education in anesthesia
Frequency: Annual
Study Establishment: International Anesthesia Research Society
No. of awards offered: 2
Application Procedure: Application must be submitted to the IARS by the published deadline. Applicant must be a member of the IARS. For more details please see the website www.iars.org
Closing Date: April
No. of awards given last year: 3

INTERNATIONAL ASSOCIATION FOR THE STUDY OF INSURANCE ECONOMICS

53 Route de Malagnou, CH-1208 Geneva, Switzerland
Tel: (41) 22 707 6600
Fax: (41) 22 736 7536
Email: secretariat@genevaassociation.org
Website: www.genevaassociation.org
Contact: Professor Patrick Liedtke, Secretary General

The International Association for the Study of Insurance Economics was established in 1973 for the purpose of promoting economic research in the sector of risk and insurance.

Ernst Meyer Prize

Subjects: Risk and insurance economics.
Purpose: To recognize research work that makes a significant and original contribution.
Eligibility: Open to professors, researchers or students of economics.
Level of Study: Unrestricted
Type: Prize
Value: Swiss Francs 5,000
Frequency: Annual
Country of Study: Any country
No. of awards offered: 1
Application Procedure: Applicants must write for details.
Closing Date: January 14th
Funding: Private
No. of applicants last year: 7

Geneva Association

Subjects: Topics of interest in risk management or insurance.
Purpose: To defray printing costs of university theses.
Eligibility: Open to authors of university theses already submitted.
Level of Study: Doctorate, Postdoctorate
Type: Grant
Value: $10,000 to help defray printing costs
Frequency: Annual
Application Procedure: Applicants must write for further information.
Closing Date: September 30th
Funding: Private

International Association for the Study of Insurance Economics Research Grants

Subjects: Risk management and insurance economics.
Purpose: To promote economic research.
Eligibility: Open to graduates involved in research for a thesis leading to a doctoral degree in economics.
Level of Study: Postgraduate
Type: Research grant
Value: Swiss Francs 10,000
Length of Study: 10 months
Frequency: Annual
Country of Study: Any country
No. of awards offered: 2
Application Procedure: Applicants must submit an application accompanied by a personal history, a description of the research undertaken and a letter of recommendation from two professors of economics.
Closing Date: September 30th
Funding: Private
Additional Information: The Association reserves the right to support research on other subjects for which applications are submitted. The Association also grants authors of university theses already submitted, dealing in depth with a subject in the field of risk and insurance economics, a subsidy of up to Swiss francs 3,000 towards printing costs.

INTERNATIONAL ASSOCIATION FOR THE STUDY OF OBESITY

231 North Gower Street, London, NW1 2NS, England
Tel: (44) 20 7691 1900
Fax: (44) 20 7387 6033
Email: kate.baillie@iaso.org
Website: www.iaso.org
Contact: Kate Baillie, Director

The International Association for the Study of Obesity (IASO) aims to improve global health by promoting the understanding of obesity and weight-related diseases through scientific research and dialogue whilst encouraging the development of effective policies for their prevention and management. IASO is the leading global professional organization concerned with obesity, operating in over 50 countries around the world.

The IASO New Investigator Award

Subjects: Obesity research.
Purpose: To promote interest in obesity research among investigators who are still in training. IASO aims to increase the number of individuals choosing a career in the field and encourage attendance of students, fellows and mentors at the International Congress of Obesity.
Eligibility: Applicant must be a member of an IASO National Association.
Level of Study: Doctorate, Postgraduate, Research
Type: Award
Value: Cash prize of US$500 and a commemorative plaque
Length of Study: Variable
Frequency: Every 4 years
Study Establishment: Any
Country of Study: Any country
No. of awards offered: 1
Application Procedure: Applicants must check the website for details.

Per Björntorp Travelling Fellowship

Subjects: Obesity research.
Purpose: In memory of Professor Per Björntorp, to provide travel grants to enable young researchers to attend the International Congress of Obesity.
Eligibility: Applicant must be a member of an IASO National Association.
Level of Study: Doctorate, Postdoctorate, Postgraduate, Predoctorate, Research
Type: Travelling bursary
Value: Up to $2,000 of return economy flights, congress Registration and hotel accommodation at the International Congress of Obesity
Frequency: 4 years
Study Establishment: Any
Country of Study: Any country
Application Procedure: Applicant must check the website for details.

INTERNATIONAL ASSOCIATION OF FIRE CHIEFS (IAFC) FOUNDATION

4025, Fair Ridge Drive, Fairfax, VA, 22033, United States of America
Tel: (1) 703 273 0911
Fax: (1) 703 273 9363
Email: foundation@iafc.org
Website: www.iafc.org
Contact: Ms Patricia Hessenauer

Each year, the International Association of Fire Chiefs (IAFC) Foundation co-ordinates a scholarship programme made possible through the generosity of corporations throughout the United States of America as well as donations from individuals and persons sponsoring a scholarship as a memorial to a friend or colleague.

IAFC Foundation Scholarship

Subjects: All subjects.
Purpose: To assist fire service personnel towards college degrees.
Eligibility: Open to any person who is an active member of a state, county, provincial, municipal, community, industrial or federal fire department who has demonstrated proficiency as a member. Dependants of members are not eligible.
Level of Study: Professional development, Doctorate, Graduate, MBA, Postdoctorate, Postgraduate, Predoctorate
Type: Scholarship
Value: US$250–4,000
Frequency: Annual
Country of Study: Any country
No. of awards offered: 20
Application Procedure: Applicants must complete an application form. This includes a 250-word statement outlining reasons for applying for assistance and an explanation as to why the candidate thinks that the course will be useful in their chosen field of course description.
Closing Date: June 1st
Funding: Commercial, individuals, private
No. of awards given last year: 13
No. of applicants last year: 65

Additional Information: In evaluating the applications, preference will be given to those demonstrating need, desire and initiative.

INTERNATIONAL ASTRONOMICAL UNION (IAU)

98-bis, boulevard Arago, F-75014 Paris, France
Tel: (33) 1 43 25 83 58
Fax: (33) 1 43 25 26 16
Email: iau@iap.fr
Website: www.iau.org
Contact: Administrative Assistant

The mission of the International Astronomical Union (IAU), founded in 1919, is to promote and safeguard the science of astronomy in all its aspects through international co-operation. The IAU, through its 12 scientific divisions and 40 commissions covering the full spectrum of astronomy, continues to play a key role in promoting and co-ordinating worldwide co-operation in astronomy.

IAU Travel Grant

Subjects: Astronomy and astrophysics.
Purpose: To provide funds to qualified individuals to enable them to visit institutions abroad. It is intended that the visitors have ample time and opportunity to interact with the intellectual life of the host institution. It is a specific objective of the programme that astronomy in the home country is enriched after the applicant returns.
Eligibility: Open to faculty members, staff members, postdoctoral Fellows or graduate students at any recognized educational or research institution.
Level of Study: Postdoctorate, Research, Postgraduate, Graduate
Value: One return economy fare between home and host institutions
Length of Study: At least 3 months at a single host institution
Country of Study: Any country
No. of awards offered: 12–15 per year
Application Procedure: Applicants must submit an application including a curriculum vitae, a plan of scientific activity, letters of support from the home and host institutions, information on responsibility for subsistence at the host institution, and information on the lowest available fare. Applications should be submitted in time for the Officers of the Commission to consult by post.
Closing Date: There is no deadline
Contributor: Academy of Sciences
No. of awards given last year: 15
No. of applicants last year: 30

For further information contact:

University of Virginia-University of Station, Box 3818, Charlottesville, VA, 22 903 0818, United States of America
Tel: (1) 4349247494
Fax: (1) 434 924 3104
Email: crt@viginia.edu
Contact: Dr Charles R Tolbert, PresidentUniversity of Toronto, Erindale College, Mississauga, ON, L5l 1C6, Canada
Tel: (1) 905 828 5351
Fax: (1) 905 828 5328
Email: jpercy@credit.erin.utoronto.ca
Contact: John R Percy, Vice-President

INTERNATIONAL ATOMIC ENERGY AGENCY (IAEA)

Vienna International Centre, Wagramerstrasse 5, PO Box 100, A-1400 Vienna, Austria
Tel: (43) 1 26 00 0
Fax: (43) 1 26 00 7
Email: crp.research@iaea.org
Website: http://cra.iaea.org
Contact: Research Contract Administrator

The IAEA is the world's center of cooperation in the nuclear field. It was set up as the world's "Atoms of Peace" in 1957 within the United Nations family. The agency works with its Member States and multiple partners worldwide to promote safe, secure and peaceful nuclear technologies.

Research Contracts (IAEA)

Subjects: Any scientific or technical field related to the peaceful uses of atomic energy and the use of radio-isotopes in agriculture, industries, medicine, research, etc.
Purpose: To encourage and assist research on the development and practical application of atomic energy for peaceful purposes throughout the world.
Eligibility: Institutions with research projects developed in line with the overall goals of the agency. Priority is normally given to proposals received from institutions in developing countries.
Level of Study: Research
Type: Research
Value: Approx. €5,000 per year per contract
Length of Study: 1 year (extension possible up to 3 years)
Application Procedure: Application forms are available on request or can be downloaded from http://cra.iaea.org. Research proposals could be submitted either based on a proposal made by the agency or a proposal developed by the research institute itself.

INTERNATIONAL BEETHOVEN PIANO COMPETITION VIENNA

Universität für Musik und darstellende Kunst Wien, Lothringerstr. 18, A-1030 Vienna, Austria
Tel: (43) 171 155 6050
Fax: (43) 171 155 6059
Email: info@beethoven-comp.at
Website: www.beethoven-comp.at
Contact: Ms Elga Ponzer, Secretary General

The artistic reputation of musicians is highly dependent upon the quality of their Beethoven interpretations. The International Beethoven Piano Competition in Vienna gives young pianists the possibility to demonstrate their musicianship and artistic maturity.

International Beethoven Piano Competition Vienna

Subjects: Piano.
Purpose: To encourage the artistic development of young pianists.
Eligibility: Open to pianists of all nationalities born between January 1st 1977 and December 31st 1992.
Level of Study: Unrestricted
Type: Competition
Value: The first prize is €7,000, a Boesendorfer Model 200 piano and engagements, the second prize is €5,500, the third prize is €4,000, and there are three further prizes of €1,500
Frequency: Every 4 years
Country of Study: Austria
No. of awards offered: 6
Application Procedure: Apply online through the website www.beethoven-comp.at
Closing Date: September 30th
Funding: Government, private
No. of awards given last year: 6 plus special prizes
No. of applicants last year: 276
Additional Information: For more details please visit the website: www.beethoven-comp.at

INTERNATIONAL CENTER FOR JOURNALISTS (ICFJ)

1616 H Street NW, Third floor, Washington, DC 20006, United States of America
Tel: (1) 1 202 737 3700
Fax: (1) 1 202 737 0530
Email: editor@icfj.org
Website: www.icfj.com

Since 1984 the ICFJ has sought to share professional knowledge and information with journalists and their news organizations around the world, promoting excellence in news coverage of critical community and global issues.

Knight International Press Fellowship

Subjects: Journalism, media.
Level of Study: Postdoctorate
Type: Fellowship
Value: Transportation costs, living expenses and a daily US$100 honorarium
Length of Study: 2–9 months
Frequency: Annual
Study Establishment: International Center for Journalists
No. of awards offered: 25
Application Procedure: Apply online.
Closing Date: February 15th and August 15th
Funding: Foundation
Contributor: Knight Foundation

The McGee Journalism Fellowship in Southern Africa

Subjects: Journalism and technical, management and business aspects of the media.
Purpose: To help journalists improve the skills and standards they need to carry out their work.
Eligibility: Open candidates of outstanding personal and professional achievement in journalism, with experience of teaching overseas, a readiness to work under difficult conditions and an interest in Southern Africa.
Level of Study: Postdoctorate
Type: Fellowship
Value: The fellowship covers all travel, housing, health insurance, living expenses and an honorarium of US$100 per day
Frequency: Annual
Study Establishment: An approved South African University
Country of Study: South Africa
No. of awards offered: 1
Application Procedure: Submit a completed application form, an essay of 500 words or less and three letters of personal or professional recommendation.
Closing Date: April 16th
Funding: Foundation
Contributor: McGee Foundation

INTERNATIONAL CENTRE FOR GENETIC ENGINEERING AND BIOTECHNOLOGY (ICGEB)

Padriciano 99, I-34012 Trieste, Italy
Tel: (39) 040 375 71
Fax: (39) 040 226 555
Email: fellowships@icgeb.org
Website: www.icgeb.org
Contact: Human Resources Unit

The International Centre for Genetic Engineering and Biotechnology (ICGEB) is an organization devoted to advanced research and training in molecular biology and biotechnology, with special regard to the needs of the developing world. The component host countries are Italy, India and South Africa. The full member states of ICGEB are Afghanistan, Algeria, Argentina, Bangladesh, Bhutan, Bosnia and Herzegovina, Brazil, Bulgaria, Cameroon, Chile, China, Colombia, Costa Rica, Côte d'Ivoire, Croatia, Cuba, Ecuador, Egypt, FYR Macedonia, Hungary, Iran, Iraq, Jordan, Kuwait, Kyrgyzstan, Liberia, Libyan Arab Jamahiriya, Malaysia, Mauritius, Mexico, Morocco, Nigeria, Pakistan, Panama, Peru, Poland, Qatar, Romania, Russia, Saudi Arabia, Senegal, Serbia, Slovakia, Slovenia, Sri Lanka, Sudan, Syria, Tanzania, Trinidad and Tobago, Tunisia, Turkey, United Arab Emirates, Uruguay, Venezuela and Vietnam.

ICGEB Flexible Fellowships

Subjects: Molecular biology, proteomics, molecular medicine, tumour virology, yeast molecular genetics, bacteriology, protein structure and bioinformatics, molecular pathology, molecular immunology, biosafety, biotechnology development, human molecular genetics, virology, molecular virology, mouse molecular genetics, immunology, neurobiology, protein networks, mammalian biology, malaria, recombinant gene products, immunology, structural and computational biology, virology, plant biology, plant molecular biology, plant transformation,

insect resistance, molecular haematology, plant virology/bacteriology, cancer molecular and cell biology, cytokines and disease
Purpose: To provide short-term training in genetic engineering and biotechnology for scientists from the member states of ICGEB, and to promote academic and industrial research in an international context.
Eligibility: Open to promising pre- and postdoctoral students, who are nationals of one of the member states of ICGEB.
Level of Study: Postdoctorate, Predoctorate
Type: Fellowship
Value: An allowance to cover travel costs as well as boarding and lodging
Length of Study: 3–12 months
Frequency: Annual
Study Establishment: ICGEB laboratories in Trieste, Italy; New Delhi, India; Cape Town, South Africa; and at ICGEB outstations at Monterotondo (Rome) and Ca' Tron (Treviso), Italy
Country of Study: India or Italy
No. of awards offered: Varies
Application Procedure: Applicants must submit a completed application form through the ICGEB Liaison Officer of the applicant's country of origin. Application forms can be found on the website.
Closing Date: Applications are accepted at any time
Additional Information: For further information please refer to the website.

ICGEB Postdoctoral Fellowships

Subjects: Mammalian biology: virology, immunology, malaria, recombinant gene products, strucutral and computational biology. Plant biology: plant molecular biology, plant transformation, insect resistance; Bacteriology, Biosafety, Biotechnology Development, Human Molecular Genetics, Molecular Biology, Molecular Immunology, Molecular Medicine, Molecular Pathology, Molecular Virology, Mouse Molecular Genetics, Neurobiology, Protein Networks, Protein Structure and Bioinformatics, Proteomics, Tumour Virology, Yeast Molecular Genetics; Cancer Molecular and Cell Biology, Cytokines and Diseases, Biotechnology Development and Transfer; Plant Bacteriology, Plant Virology; Molecular Hematology.
Purpose: To provide long-term training in genetic engineering and biotechnology for scientists from the member states and to promote state-of-the art academic and industrial research training in an international context and for the scientific development of the Fellow's home country.
Eligibility: Open to promising postdoctoral or established research students under the age of 35, who are nationals of one of the ICGEB member states and carry out their study in India, Italy or South Africa.
Level of Study: Postdoctorate
Type: Fellowship
Value: US$19,000–31,000 per Fellow per year, depending on the place of study, as well as travel costs and medical insurance
Length of Study: 1–2 years
Frequency: Annual
Study Establishment: ICGEB laboratories in Trieste, Italy; New Delhi, India; Cape Town, South Africa; and Outstations at Monterotondo (Rome) and Ca' Tron (Treviso), Italy
Country of Study: India or Italy
No. of awards offered: Varies
Application Procedure: Applicants must submit a completed application form through the respective National Liaison Officer in their country of origin.
Closing Date: Refer to website
Additional Information: For further information please refer to the website.

Predoctoral Fellowships – ICGEB Cape Town International PhD Programme

Subjects: Cancer molecular and cell biology, cytokines and disease.
Purpose: To offer postgraduate training with the aim of obtaining a PhD degree in the field of life sciences at the University of Cape Town, South Africa, in collaboration with the ICGEB.
Eligibility: Open to promising young students in possession of an MSc from a recognized university, who are nationals of one of the ICGEB member-states.
Level of Study: Predoctorate
Type: Fellowship
Value: €10,200

Length of Study: 3–4 years
Frequency: Annual
Study Establishment: ICGEB laboratories in Cape Town
Country of Study: South Africa
No. of awards offered: Various
Application Procedure: Applicants must refer to the website.
Additional Information: For more information on this programme please refer to the website.

Predoctoral Fellowships – ICGEB JNU PhD Programme in Life Sciences

Subjects: Mammalian biology: virology, immunology, malaria, recombinant gene products, structural and computational biology. Plant biology: plant molecular biology, plant transformation, insect resistance.
Purpose: To offer postgraduate training with the aim of obtaining a PhD degree in the field of life sciences at the Jawaharlal Nehru University in New Delhi, in collaboration with the ICGEB.
Eligibility: Open to promising young students in possession of an MSc from a recognized university, who are nationals of one of the ICGEB member states.
Level of Study: Postgraduate, Predoctorate
Type: Fellowship
Value: US$12,240
Length of Study: 3–4 years
Frequency: Annual
Study Establishment: ICGEB laboratories in New Delhi
Country of Study: India
No. of awards offered: Various
Application Procedure: Applicants must refer to the website.
Closing Date: Please refer to the website
Additional Information: For more information on this programme please refer to the website.

Predoctoral Fellowships – ICGEB Trieste International PhD Programme

Subjects: Molecular biology, molecular medicine, tumour virology, bacteriology, protein structure and bioinformatics, molecular pathology, molecular immunology, proteomics, human molecular genetics, molecular virology, mouse molecular genetics, neurobiology, protein networks, yeast molecular genetics.
Purpose: To enable promising young students to attend and complete the PhD programme at ICGEB Trieste in Italy. The programme is in collaboration with the Scuola Normale Superiore (SNS) Pisa, Italy and is validated by the Open University, UK, and the University of Nova Gorica, Slovenia.
Eligibility: Open to promising predoctoral students under the age of 32 from any member state of the ICGEB.
Level of Study: Predoctorate
Type: Fellowship
Value: €15,600
Length of Study: 3 years
Frequency: Annual
Study Establishment: ICGEB component laboratories in Trieste
Country of Study: Italy
No. of awards offered: Various
Application Procedure: Applicants must refer to the website.
Closing Date: Please refer to website
Additional Information: For more information on this programme please refer to the website.

INTERNATIONAL CENTRE FOR PHYSICAL LAND RESOURCES

University of Ghent, Krijgslaan 281/S8, B-9000 Ghent, Belgium
Tel: (32) 9 264 4626
Fax: (32) 9 264 4991
Email: plrprog.adm@ugent.be
Website: www.plr.ugent.be
Contact: Professor E Van Ranst

The International Centre for Physical Land Resources has a long-standing tradition in academic formation and training in physical land resources, including soil science, soil survey, land evaluation, agricultural applications and eremology, e.g. dryland and desertification. Since 1997, the scope of the courses has been widened with courses on the non-agricultural use and application of physical land resources. Students can major in either soil science or land resources engineering. Teaching is provided by lecturers of the University of Ghent and of the Free University of Brussels (VUB).

Master Studies in Physical Land Resources Scholarship

Subjects: Fundamental soil science, soil genesis, prospection and classification, non-agricultural use and applications of land and soils, geotechnical engineering, soil mechanics and hydrogeology, management of physical and land resources, agricultural applications, soil fertility, soil erosion and conservation or land evaluation.
Purpose: To provide MSc training opportunities to nationals from developing countries.
Eligibility: Open to nationals of the developing world or non-European Union members.
Level of Study: Postgraduate
Type: Scholarship
Value: €950 per month
Length of Study: 1 year, with a possible maximum extension to 2 years
Frequency: Annual
Study Establishment: Ghent University
Country of Study: Belgium
No. of awards offered: Approx. 2
Application Procedure: Applicants must complete an application form and submit this with certified diplomas and transcripts to the Programme Secretariat to obtain academic admission.
Closing Date: March 31st
Funding: Government
No. of awards given last year: 1
No. of applicants last year: 45

INTERNATIONAL COLLEGE OF SURGEONS

1516 North Lake Shore Drive, Chicago, IL, 60610-1694, United States of America
Tel: (1) 312 642 3555
Fax: (1) 312 787 1624
Email: max@icsglobal.org
Website: www.icsglobal.org
Contact: International Executive Director

Postgraduate Scholarships

Purpose: To bring surgeons and surgical specialists of all nations, races, and creeds together, to promote surgical excellence for the benefit of all of mankind and to foster fellowship worldwide.
Eligibility: Open to practicing surgeons worldwide.
Level of Study: Postgraduate
Study Establishment: Established treatment, research facilities or educational institutions
Application Procedure: Completed applications should be sent to the Executive Director.

THE INTERNATIONAL DAIRY-DELI-BAKERY ASSOCIATION

IDDBA, PO Box 5528, Madison, W1 53705 0528, United States of America
Tel: (1) 608 238 5000
Fax: (1) 608 238 6330
Email: iddba@iddba.org
Website: www.iddba.org

Our mission is to expand our leadership role in promoting the growth and development of daily, deli and bakery sales in the food industry. Our vision is to be the essential resource for relevant information and services that add value across all food channels for the dairy, deli and bakery categories.

IDDBA Graduate Scholarships

Subjects: Culinary arts, baking/party arts, food service, business and marketing.

Purpose: To support employees of IDDBA-member companies.
Eligibility: Applicants must be a current full- or part-time employee of an IDDBA-member company with an academic background in a food-related field.
Level of Study: Postgraduate
Type: Scholarship
Value: US$250–1,000
Length of Study: 1 year
Frequency: Annual
Country of Study: United States of America
No. of awards offered: Varies
Application Procedure: Contact the Education Information Specialist.
Closing Date: January 1st, April 1st, July 1st, October 1st
Funding: Foundation
Contributor: IDDBA

For further information contact:

Email: kpeckham@iddba.org

INTERNATIONAL DEVELOPMENT RESEARCH CENTRE (IDRC)

Centre Training & Awards Program, 250 Albert Street, PO Box 8500, 150 Kent Street, Ottawa, ON K1G 3H9, Canada
Tel: (1) 613 236 6163
Fax: (1) 613 567 7748
Email: cta@idrc.ca
Website: www.idrc.ca/awards
Contact: Ms Carole Labrie, Program Assistant

The International Development Research Centre (IDRC) is a Canadian crown corporation created by the Canadian government to help communities in the developing world find solutions to social, economic and environmental problems through research.

The Bentley Cropping Systems Fellowship
Subjects: Use of fertility-enhancing plants such as leguminous forages, cover crops and grain legumes in small farms.
Purpose: To provide assistance to Canadian and a developing country's graduate students with a university degree in agriculture, forestry or biology, who wish to undertake post-graduate, applied on-farm research with co-operating farmers in a developing country.
Eligibility: Applicants must be Canadian citizens, permanent residents of Canada or citizens of a developing country who are enrolled full-time in a graduate program (Master's, doctoral, postdoctoral) at a recognized university in Canada or in a developing country for the duration of the award period.
Level of Study: Doctorate, Graduate, Postdoctorate, Postgraduate, Unrestricted
Type: Fellowship
Value: Up to Canadian $30,000
Length of Study: 1.5–2 years
Frequency: Every 2 years
Study Establishment: Universities
No. of awards offered: 1–2
Application Procedure: Applicants must complete and submit an application form with various supporting documents. For further information see the IDRC website.
Closing Date: October
Funding: Private
No. of applicants last year: Varies

Canadian Window on International Development
Purpose: The programme includes two types of awards: the first type is granted for doctoral students who will conduct comparative research in Canada and in developing countries on a common problem for both; the second type is granted to Master's or doctoral students for research projects that address a problem that is common to First Nations or Inuit communities in Canada and a developing region of the world.
Eligibility: Successful candidates will propose comparative research requiring data from both Canada and a developing region of the world to better understand the common, interrelated problem or issue identified for in-depth study. Selection will favour those proposals that

demonstrate the relevance of the research topic for Canada and for the less-developed country or countries being studied, and the close linkage between the international and national character of the topic. Competition is open to Canadian citizens, permanent residents of Canada and a developing country's nationals. Applicants must be registered at a Canadian university.
Level of Study: Graduate, Postgraduate, Doctorate, Master's
Value: Up to Canadian $20,000
Length of Study: 3 months–1 year
Frequency: Annual
Study Establishment: Universities
Country of Study: Canada
No. of awards offered: 2 or 3 per year
Application Procedure: Applicants must complete an application form. Please refer to the website www.idrc.ca/awards for details.
Closing Date: April 1st
Funding: Government
No. of awards given last year: 1
No. of applicants last year: Varies

Community Forestry: Trees and People-John G Bene Fellowship
Subjects: Forestry management.
Purpose: To assist Canadian graduate students in undertaking research on the relationship between forest resources and the social, economic, cultural and environmental welfare of people in developing countries.
Eligibility: Open to Canadian citizens and permanent residents who are registered at a Canadian university at the Master's or doctoral level. Applicants must have an academic background that combines forestry or agroforestry with social sciences.
Level of Study: Doctorate, Graduate, Postgraduate
Type: Fellowship
Value: Canadian $15,000
Length of Study: 3 months–1 year
Frequency: Annual
Study Establishment: Universities
Country of Study: Canada
No. of awards offered: 1
Application Procedure: Applicants must submit a research proposal and various supporting documents as part of their application. For further information, please see the website www.idrc.ca/awards/
Closing Date: March 1st
Funding: Private
Contributor: Endowment
No. of awards given last year: 1
No. of applicants last year: Varies

ECOPOLIS Graduate Research and Design Awards
Subjects: Environmental issues borne by the poor.
Purpose: To promote research and design projects that help lighten the environmental problems borne by the urban poor.
Eligibility: Open to Canadian citizens or permanent residents of Canada as well as citizens of developing countries.
Level of Study: Graduate, Doctorate, Master's
Type: Award
Value: Research awards – maximum of Canadian $20,000 covers justifiable field work expenses. Design awards – maximum of Canadian $40,000
Frequency: Annual
No. of awards offered: Up to 10 in total. Up to 5 – Research awards, Up to 5 – Design awards
Application Procedure: Visit the IDRC website for further information.
Closing Date: October
Funding: Government
No. of awards given last year: 9
No. of applicants last year: Varies

IDRC Doctoral Research Awards
Subjects: IDRC's research activities focus on four programme areas: social and economic policy;environment and natural resource management; information and communication technologies (ICTs) for development; innovation, policy and science.

Purpose: To promote the growth of Canadian capacity in research on sustainable and equitable development from an international perspective.
Eligibility: Open to Canadian citizens and permanent residents and a developing country's nationals. Applicants must be enrolled in a Canadian university, have a research proposal that has been approved by the thesis supervisor and be affiliated with an institution or organization in the region where the research will take place.
Level of Study: Doctorate
Type: Award
Value: Up to Canadian $20,000
Length of Study: 3 months–1 year
Frequency: Twice a year
Study Establishment: Universities. Normally, such research is conducted in Latin America, Africa, the Middle East or Asia
Country of Study: Canada
No. of awards offered: Varies (Varies; 18 to 20 per year)
Application Procedure: Applicants must complete and submit an application form with a research proposal and various supporting documents. Information on required documents is available on the IDRC website.
Closing Date: April 1st and November 1st
Funding: Government
Contributor: The Canadian government
No. of awards given last year: 18 to 20
No. of applicants last year: Varies

IDRC Evaluation Research Awards

Subjects: Theory and practice of evaluation
Purpose: To promote the growth of Canadian and developing country capacity in evaluation and to better the theory and practice of evaluation. Normally, such research is conducted in Latin America, Africa, the Middle East or Asia.
Eligibility: Applicants must be Canadian citizens, permanent residents of Canada or citizens of a developing country and be enrolled at the Master's or Doctoral level in a Canadian university or a recognized university in a developing country.
Level of Study: Doctorate, Graduate, Master's
Type: Award
Value: Canadian $20,000
Frequency: Annual
No. of awards offered: 2
Application Procedure: Applicants must submit a research proposal and various supporting documents as part of their application. Information on required documents and the application form are available on the IDRC website.
Closing Date: January 15th
Funding: Government
No. of applicants last year: Varies
Additional Information: The evaluation research awards will not be granted for Evaluation reserach that only judges the effectiveness of particular development interventions (projects, programs, activities, etc)

IDRC Internship Awards

Subjects: Research for international development through a program of training in research management and grant administration under the guidance of th IDRC program staff.
Purpose: To provide hands-on learning experiences in research program management – in the creation, dissemination and utilization of knowledge from an international perspective.
Eligibility: Applicants must be Canadian citizens, permanent residents of Canada or citizens of a developing country and be enrolled in the postgraduate studies or have obtained a postgraduate degree.
Level of Study: Doctorate, Graduate, Master's
Type: Award
Frequency: Annual
No. of awards offered: Varies
Application Procedure: Applicants must submit a research proposal and various supporting documents as part of their application. Information on required documents and application forms are available on the IDRC website. As outlined by IDRC, applicants are required to specify an area of interest in which the internship will take place. A list of possible areas of interest is available on the website.
Closing Date: September 12th

Funding: Government
No. of awards given last year: 14
No. of applicants last year: 120

INTERNATIONAL FEDERATION OF LIBRARY ASSOCIATIONS AND INSTITUTIONS (IFLA)

PO Box 95312, The Hague, NL-2509 CH, Netherlands
Tel: (31) 70 314 0884
Fax: (31) 70 383 4827
Email: ifla@ifla.org
Website: www.ifla.org
Contact: Anne Korhonen

Established in 1927, the primary function of the International Federation of Library Associations and Institutions (IFLA) is to encourage, sponsor and promote research and development in all aspects of library activity and to share its findings with the library community as a whole for the greater good of librarianship.

The Guust van Wesemael Literacy Prize

Subjects: Library science.
Purpose: To recognize an achievement in the field of literacy promotion in a developing country.
Eligibility: Open to candidates from developing countries.
Level of Study: Unrestricted
Value: €2,725
Frequency: Every 2 years
Country of Study: Any country
No. of awards offered: 1
Application Procedure: Applicants must complete an application form, available from IFLA headquarters.
Closing Date: March 1st every odd-numbered year
Funding: Private
No. of awards given last year: 1
No. of applicants last year: 10
Additional Information: The prize should be used for follow-up activities such as purchasing targeted collections of appropriate books.

THE INTERNATIONAL FEDERATION OF UNIVERSITY WOMEN (IFUW)

IFUW Headquarters, 10 rue de Lac, Geneva, CH-1207, Switzerland
Tel: (41) 22 731 23 80
Fax: (41) 22 738 04 40
Email: info@ifuw.org
Website: www.ifuw.org

The International Federation of University Women (IFUW) is a non-profit, non-governmental organization comprising graduate women working locally, nationally and internationally to advocate the improvement of the status of women and girls at the international level, by promoting lifelong education and enabling graduate women to use their expertise to effect change.

British Federation Crosby Hall Fellowship

Subjects: All subjects.
Purpose: To encourage advanced scholarship and original research.
Eligibility: Open to female applicants who are either members of one of IFUW's national federations or associations or, in the case of female graduates living in countries where there is not yet a national affiliate, independent members of IFUW. Applicants should be well started on a research programme and should have completed at least 1 year of graduate work.
Level of Study: Doctorate, Postdoctorate, Research
Type: Fellowship
Value: UK £2,500
Frequency: Dependent on funds available
Study Establishment: An approved Institute of Higher Education
Country of Study: United Kingdom
No. of awards offered: 1
Application Procedure: Applicants must apply through their respective federation or association. A list of IFUW national federations

can be sent upon request or obtained from the website. IFUW independent members and international individual members must apply directly to the IFUW headquarters in Geneva.
Closing Date: Early September in the year preceding the competition
Funding: Private
No. of awards given last year: 1

The CFUW/A Vibert Douglas International Fellowship
Subjects: Conservation biology, ecology and evolution.
Purpose: To financially assist women in pursuing advanced research, study and training.
Eligibility: Open to graduate women who are either members of one of IFUW's 74 national federations and associations or, if living in a country where there is not yet a national affiliate, an independent member of IFUW, or an international individual member of IFUW.
Level of Study: Doctorate, Postgraduate
Type: Fellowship or Grant
Value: Canadian $12,000
Frequency: Every 2 years
Country of Study: Any country

Dorothy Leet Grants
Subjects: All subjects.
Purpose: To enable recipients to carry out research, obtain specialized training essential to research or training in new techniques.
Eligibility: Open to female applicants who are either a member of one of IFUW's national federations or associations or, in the case of female graduates living in countries where there is not yet a national affiliate, an independent member of IFUW. Applicants should be well started on a research programme and should have completed at least 1 year of graduate work.
Level of Study: Doctorate, Graduate, Postdoctorate, Postgraduate
Type: Grant
Value: Swiss Franc 4,500
Length of Study: A minimum of 2 months
Frequency: Dependent on funds available
Country of Study: Any country
No. of awards offered: Varies
Application Procedure: Applicants must write for details enclosing a stamped addressed envelope. Applicants should apply through their respective federation or association. A list of IFUW national federations can be sent upon request or obtained from the Internet.
Closing Date: Early September in the year preceding the competition
Funding: Individuals, private
No. of awards given last year: 15–20
Additional Information: Further information is available from the website.

Ida Smedley MacLean Fellowship
Subjects: All subjects.
Purpose: To encourage advanced scholarship and original research.
Eligibility: Open to female applicants who are either members of one of IFUW's national federations or associations or, in the case of female graduates living in countries where there is not yet a national affiliate, independent members of IFUW. Applicants should be well started on a research programme and should have completed at least 1 year of graduate work.
Level of Study: Postgraduate, Doctorate, Postdoctorate
Type: Fellowship
Value: Swiss Francs 8,000
Length of Study: More than 8 months
Frequency: Dependent on funds available
Study Establishment: An approved Institute of Higher Education other than that in which the applicant received her education
Country of Study: Any country
No. of awards offered: 1 of each fellowship
Application Procedure: Applicants must write for details enclosing a stamped addressed envelope. Applicants should apply through their respective federation or association. A list of IFUW national federations can be sent upon request or obtained from the website.
Closing Date: Early September in the year preceding the competition
Funding: Individuals, private
No. of awards given last year: 1 of each

INTERNATIONAL FOUNDATION FOR ETHICAL RESEARCH (IFER)

53 West Jackson Boulevard, Suite 1552, Chicago, IL, 60604, United States of America
Tel: (1) 312 427 6025
Fax: (1) 312 427 6524
Email: ifer@navs.org
Website: www.ifer.org
Contact: Mr Peter O'Donovan, Deputy Director

The International Foundation for Ethical Research (IFER) supports the development and implementation of viable, scientifically valid alternatives to the use of animals in research, product testing and classroom education. IFER is dedicated to the belief that through new technologies and diligent research, solutions can be found that will create a better world for all, without using animals.

IFER Graduate Fellowship Program
Subjects: Tissue cultures, cell cultures, organ cultures, gas chromatography, mathematical and computer models and clinical and epidemiological surveys.
Purpose: To develop, validate and disseminate alternatives to the use of live animals in research, education and product testing. Alternatives are defined as methods that replace, refine or reduce the number of animals traditionally used.
Eligibility: Open to students enrolled in Master's and PhD programmes.
Level of Study: Graduate, Postgraduate
Type: Fellowship
Value: Up to US$12,500 in stipendiary support and up to $2,500 for supplies
Length of Study: 1 year, renewable for up to 3 years based on eligibility and funding
Frequency: Annual
Country of Study: Any country
No. of awards offered: Varies
Application Procedure: Applicants must write for details or refer to the website www.ifer@navs.org
Closing Date: March 15th
Funding: Private

INTERNATIONAL FOUNDATION FOR SCIENCE (IFS)

Karlavägen 108, 5th Floor, SE-115 26 Stockholm, Sweden
Tel: (46) 85 458 1800
Fax: (46) 85 458 1801
Email: info@ifs.se
Website: www.ifs.se
Contact: Head of Finance & Administration

Founded in 1972, the International Foundation for Science (IFS), a non-government organisation, has its largest presence in developing countries where it contributes to the strengthening of capacity to conduct relevant and high-quality research on the management, use and conservation of biological resources and the environment in which these resources occur and upon which they depend.

IFS Research Grants
Subjects: Aquatic resources, animal production, crop science, forestry/agroforestry, food science, water resources, social science and natural products.
Purpose: To provide opportunities for young researchers to contribute to the generation of scientific knowledge.
Eligibility: Applicants must be from, and do research in, a developing country. Countries in Eastern Europe, Turkey, Cyprus and the former Soviet Union are not eligible for support.
Level of Study: Postdoctorate, Research
Type: Grant
Value: Up to US$12,000
Length of Study: 1–3 year
Frequency: Bi-Annual
Application Procedure: Applications can be downloaded from the IFS website.
Closing Date: December 31st

Funding: Foundation
Contributor: International Foundation for Science
No. of awards given last year: 263
No. of applicants last year: 1500

For further information contact:

International Foundation for Science, Karlavägen 108, Stockholm, SE-11526, Sweden
Tel: (46) 545 818 00
Fax: (46) 545 818 01
Email: info@ifs.se
Website: www.ifs.se

INTERNATIONAL HARP CONTEST IN ISRAEL

4 Aharonowitz Street, IL-63566 Tel Aviv, Israel
Tel: (972) 3 5280 233
Fax: (972) 3 6299 9524
Email: harzimco@netvision.net.il
Website: www.harpcontest-israel.org.il
Contact: Ms Ilana Barnea, Director

The International Harp Contest takes place in Israel every 3 years and is judged by a jury of internationally known musicians. It was founded in 1959, and since then, harpists from all over the world gather in Jerusalem to participate in the contest, the only one of its kind.

International Harp Contest in Israel
Subjects: Harp playing.
Purpose: To encourage excellence in harp playing.
Eligibility: Open to harpists of any nationality who are aged 35 years or younger.
Level of Study: Professional development
Type: Prize
Value: The first prize is a grand concert harp from the House of Lyon and Healy, Chicago, the second prize is US$6,000 and the third prize is US$4,000. The Propes Prize is US$1,500 for the best performance of the required Israeli composition in stage one and the Herlitz Prize is US$1,000 for the best performance of a contemporary piece in stage three. The Chamber Music Prize is US$1,000 for the best performance of Ravel's Introduction and Allegro in stage three. Board and lodging is provided by the Contest Committee. The Gulbenkian Prize is awarded for a contemporary work
Frequency: Every 3 years
Country of Study: Any country
No. of awards offered: 7
Application Procedure: Applicants must complete an application form and submit this with recommendations, a record of concert experience, curriculum vitae and birth certificate. There is a registration fee of US$150.
Closing Date: April 1st
Funding: Trusts, private, government
Contributor: Culture Authority, the Government of Israel, the Ministry of Culture, foundations and donors
No. of awards given last year: 6
No. of applicants last year: 36

THE INTERNATIONAL HUMAN FRONTIER SCIENCE PROGRAM ORGANIZATION (HFSPO)

12 quai Saint-Jean, BP 10034, F-67080 Strasbourg Cedex, France
Fax: (33) (33) 388215289
Email: jhusser@hfsp.org
Website: www.hfsp.org

The Human Frontier Science Program (HFSP) promotes basic research in the life sciences that is original, interdisciplinary and requires international collaboration. The support and training of young investigators is given special emphasis.

HFSPO Cross-Disciplinary Fellowships
Subjects: Life sciences, biology. The aim is to support basic research focused on elucidating the complex mechanisms of living organisms.

The fields supported range from biological functions at the molecular level to higher brain functions.
Purpose: Cross-Disciplinary Fellowships are intended for postdoctoral fellows with a PhD in the physical sciences, chemistry, mathematics, engineering or computer science who wish to receive training in biology. The fellowships provide young scientists with up to 3 years of postdoctoral research training in an outstanding laboratory in another country. The conditions are the same as for Long-Term Fellowships.
Eligibility: For details, see HFSP website.
Level of Study: Postdoctorate
Type: Fellowship
Value: Approx. US$46,000 per year, including allowances for travel and research expenses
Frequency: Annual
Country of Study: Nationals of one of the supporting countries can apply to receive training in any country. Nationals of any other country must apply to train in a supporting country.
No. of awards offered: Varies
Application Procedure: Applications must be submitted online.
Closing Date: September
Funding: Government
Contributor: Member countries: Australia, Canada, France, Germany, India, Italy, Japan, New Zealand, Norway, Republic of Korea, Switzerland, United Kingdom, United States of America, European Union
No. of awards given last year: 12
No. of applicants last year: 56
Additional Information: Fellowships for up to 3 years. The 3rd year can be used to support 1 year of postdoctoral training in the home country and can be deferred for up to 2 years. Former awardees are eligible to apply for a Career Development Award upon repatriation to their home country to help establish themselves as individual investigators.

HFSPO Long-Term Fellowships
Subjects: Life sciences, biology. The aim is to support basic research focused on elucidating the complex mechanisms of living organisms. The fields supported range from biological functions at the molecular level to higher brain functions.
Purpose: Long-Term Fellowships provide young scientists with up to 3 years of postdoctoral research training in an outstanding laboratory in another country.
Eligibility: Applicants must see the website for details.
Level of Study: Postdoctorate
Type: Fellowship
Value: Approx. US$46,000 per year, including allowances for travel and research expenses
Frequency: Annual
Country of Study: Worldwide
No. of awards offered: Varies
Application Procedure: Applications must be submitted online through the website.
Closing Date: September
Funding: Government
Contributor: Member countries: Australia, Canada, France, Germany, India, Italy, Japan, New Zealand, Republic of Korea, Switzerland, United Kingdom, United States of America, European Union
No. of awards given last year: 100
No. of applicants last year: 700
Additional Information: Fellowships for up to 3 years. The 3rd year can be used to support 1 year of postdoctoral training in the home country and can be deferred up to 2 years. Former awardees are eligible to apply for a Career Development Award upon repatriation to their home country to help establish themselves as independent investigators.

HFSPO Program Grant
Subjects: Life sciences, biology. The aim is to support basic research focused on elucidating the complex mechanisms of living organisms. The fields supported range from biological functions at the molecular level to higher brain functions.
Purpose: To enable teams of independent researchers at any stage of their careers to develop new lines of research.
Eligibility: Independent investigators early on in their careers are encouraged to apply.

Level of Study: Research
Type: Collaborative research grant
Value: Up to US$450,000 per grant per year
Length of Study: Max. 3 years
Frequency: Annual
Country of Study: The Principal applicant must have his/her laboratory in a member country. Atleast one other team member must be located in another country.
No. of awards offered: Varies
Application Procedure: Application online, by letter of intent; submission of full application by invitation.
Closing Date: Spring. See website for details
Funding: Government
Contributor: Member countries: Australia, Canada, France, Germany, India, Italy, Japan, New Zealand, Norway, Republic of Korea, Switzerland, United Kingdom, United States of America, European Union
No. of awards given last year: 18
No. of applicants last year: 611 letters of intent 62 full applications received

HFSPO Short-Term Fellowships

Subjects: Life sciences, biology. The aim is to support basic research focused on elucidating the complex mechanisms of living organisms. The fields supported range from biological functions at the molecular level to higher brain functions.
Purpose: Short-Term Fellowships enable researchers, who are early on in their careers, to spend 2 weeks–3 months working in a laboratory in another country to learn new techniques or establish new collaborations.
Eligibility: Applicants must see the website for details.
Level of Study: Postdoctorate
Type: Fellowship
Value: Travel and per diem support
Length of Study: 2 weeks–3 months
Country of Study: Nationals of one of the supporting countries can apply to receive training in any country. Nationals of any other country must apply to train in a supporting country.
No. of awards offered: Varies
Application Procedure: Applications must be submitted online.
Closing Date: Applications are accepted throughout the year
Funding: Government
Contributor: Member countries: Australia, Canada, France, Germany, India, Italy, Japan, New Zealand, Norway, Republic of Korea, Switzerland, United Kingdom, United States of America, European Union
No. of awards given last year: 28
No. of applicants last year: 58
Additional Information: Former holders of HFSP Long-term or Cross-disciplinary Fellowships who have returned to their home country are also eligible to use HFSP Short-Term Fellowships to return to their former host laboratory to complete or extend their research.

HFSPO Young Investigator Grant

Subjects: Life sciences, biology. The aim is to support basic research focused on elucidating the complex mechanisms of living organisms. The fields supported range from biological at the molecular level to higher brain functions.
Purpose: Young investigator grants are awarded to teams of researchers, all of whom are within the first 5 years of obtaining an independent position (e.g. Assistant Professor, Lecturer or equivalent). They must also be within 10 years of receiving their PhD before the deadline for submission of the letter of intent.
Level of Study: Research
Type: Collaborative research grant
Value: Up to US$450,000 per grant, per year
Length of Study: Maximum 3 years
Frequency: Annual
Country of Study: The Principal applicant must have his/her laboratory in a member country. Atleast one other team member must be located in another country.
No. of awards offered: Varies
Application Procedure: Application online by letter of intent; submission of full application by invitation.

Closing Date: Spring. See website for details
Funding: Government
Contributor: Member countries: Australia, Canada, France, Germany, India, Italy, Japan, New Zealand, Norway, Republic of Korea, Switzerland, United Kingdom, United States of America, European Union
No. of awards given last year: 14
No. of applicants last year: 163 letters of intent and 25 full applications

INTERNATIONAL INSTITUTE FOR APPLIED SYSTEMS ANALYSIS (IIASA)

Schlossplatz 1 A-2361, Laxenburg, Austria
Tel: (43) 2236 807 402
Fax: (43) 2236 71 313
Email: ysspinfo@iiasa.ac.at
Website: www.iiasa.ac.at

The International Institute for Applied Systems Analysis (IIASA) is a non-governmental research organization. It conducts inter-disciplinary scientific studies on environmental, economic, technological and social issues in the context of human dimensions of global change. It is located in Austria near Vienna.

IIASA Postdoctoral Program

Subjects: Environment, economics, technology and social issues.
Purpose: To enrich IIASA's intellectual environment and help achieve research programme goals.
Eligibility: Open to candidates who have an advanced university degree equivalent to a PhD.
Level of Study: Postdoctorate
Type: Funding support
Value: Allowance for relocation expenses to and from Laxenburg, limited support for business travel and salary
Length of Study: 1–2 years
Frequency: Annual
No. of awards offered: 2
Application Procedure: Candidates must fill a personal information form online. In addition to this a research plan, a discussion of the relevance, a letter of support and names of 3 referees should be mailed.

For further information contact:

Website: www.iiasa.ac.at
Contact: Barbara Hauser, Postdoctoral Co-ordinator

INTERNATIONAL INSTITUTE FOR MANAGEMENT DEVELOPMENT (IMD)

Chemin de Bellerive 23, PO Box 915, CH-1001 Lausanne, Switzerland
Tel: (41) 21 618 0298
Fax: (41) 21 618 0615
Email: mbainfo@imd.ch
Website: www.imd.ch/mba
Contact: Ms Janet Shaner, Director, MBA Marketing

The International Institute for Management Development (IMD), created by industry to serve industry, develops cutting-edge research and programmes that meet real world needs. Their clients include dozens of leading international companies and their experienced faculty incorporate new management practices into the small and exclusive MBA programme. With no nationality dominating, IMD is truly global, practical and relevant.

The IMD MBA Future Leaders Scholarships

Subjects: MBA.
Purpose: To financially support candidates with exceptionally strong leadership potential undertaking an MBA at IMD.
Eligibility: Candidates must have gained acceptance into the IMD MBA programme and demonstrate exceptionally strong leadership potential.
Level of Study: MBA

Type: Scholarship
Value: Swiss Franc 30,000 towards tuition fees and book expenses
Length of Study: 1 year
Frequency: Annual
Study Establishment: IMD
Country of Study: Switzerland
No. of awards offered: 3
Application Procedure: Applicants must submit an essay of maximum of 750 words on the topic 'Leadership in an era of globalization' and should contact the organization for details.
Closing Date: September 30th
Funding: Private
No. of awards given last year: 3
No. of applicants last year: 43

Jim Ellert Scholarship

Subjects: MBA.
Purpose: To financially support candidates from China, Hong Kong, Estonia, Czech Republic, Bulgaria, Rumania, Hungary, Slovenia or Switzerland undertaking an MBA at IMD.
Eligibility: Candidates must have already gained acceptance into the IMD MBA programme and must demonstrate financial need.
Level of Study: MBA
Type: Scholarship
Value: Swiss Francs 20,000
Length of Study: 1 year
Frequency: Annual
Study Establishment: IMD
Country of Study: Switzerland
No. of awards offered: 1
Application Procedure: Applicants must complete and submit the IMD MBA application form for financial assistance and the MBA application form. In addition, candidates must submit a 500-word essay on the topic: Why I would like to do an MBA at IMD.
Closing Date: September 30th
Funding: Private
No. of awards given last year: 1
No. of applicants last year: 6

Nestlé Scholarship for Women

Subjects: MBA.
Purpose: To financially support women applicants with financial need undertaking an MBA at IMD.
Eligibility: Candidates must be female, have gained acceptance into the IMD MBA programme and must demonstrate financial need.
Level of Study: Graduate, MBA
Type: Scholarship
Value: Swiss Francs 25,000 towards tuition and living expenses
Length of Study: 1 year
Frequency: Annual
Study Establishment: IMD
Country of Study: Switzerland
No. of awards offered: 1
Application Procedure: Applicants must complete and submit the IMD MBA application form for financial assistance and the MBA application form. In addition, applicants must submit a 750 word on the topic: Does Diversity in Management impact the bottom line? If so, how?
Closing Date: September 30th
Funding: Corporation
No. of awards given last year: 1
No. of applicants last year: 10

Shell and IMD MBA Alumni Scholarships

Subjects: MBA.
Purpose: To financially support applicants from Africa, Middle East, Asia, Latin America, Eastern Europe, Western Europe, North America and Oceania undertaking an MBA at IMD.
Eligibility: Candidates must have gained acceptance into the IMD MBA programme, and must be citizens of the appropriate geographical area and must demonstrate financial need.
Level of Study: Graduate, MBA
Type: Scholarship

Value: Swiss Francs 30,000 towards tuition fees and book expenses
Frequency: Annual
Study Establishment: The International Institute for Management Development (IMD)
Country of Study: Switzerland
No. of awards offered: 5
Application Procedure: Applicants must complete and submit the IMD MBA application form for financial assistance and the MBA application form. In addition, applicants must submit an essay of 750 words on the topic: As a business leader, which issue would you set as your first priority to address in your region? Why would you choose this issue? How would you, personally address it? and should contact the organization for details.
Closing Date: September 30th
Funding: Corporation, private
Contributor: IMD Alumni Loan Fund and Shell
No. of awards given last year: 4
No. of applicants last year: 31

Staton Scholarship

Subjects: MBA.
Purpose: To financially support applicants from South America (excluding Brazil) undertaking an MBA at IMD.
Eligibility: Candidates must be from South America, must have already gained acceptance into the IMD MBA programme, and must return to South America (except Brazil) for at least 3 years after graduation.
Level of Study: Graduate, MBA
Type: Scholarship
Value: US$50,000 towards tuition fees and book expenses
Length of Study: 1 year
Frequency: Annual
Study Establishment: IMD
Country of Study: Switzerland
No. of awards offered: 1
Application Procedure: Applicants must complete and submit the IMD MBA application form. In addition, applicants must submit a 750-word essay on the topic: The role of entrepreneurship in moving my country forward and my contribution to that goal.
Closing Date: September 30th
Funding: Private
Contributor: Woods Staton
No. of awards given last year: 1
No. of applicants last year: 3
Additional Information: It is a condition of the scholarship that candidates return to South America for at least 3 years after graduation.

Von Muralt-Lo Scholarship

Subjects: MBA.
Purpose: To financially support two candidates from China or Hong Kong undertaking an MBA at IMD.
Eligibility: Candidates must be living and working in China or Hong Kong, must have already gained acceptance into the IMD MBA programme and must demonstrate financial need.
Level of Study: Graduate, MBA
Type: Scholarship
Value: Swiss Francs 25,000
Length of Study: 1 year
Frequency: Annual
Study Establishment: IMD
Country of Study: Switzerland
No. of awards offered: 2
Application Procedure: Applicants must complete and submit the IMD MBA application form for financial assistance and the MBA application form. In addition, candidates must submit a 500-word essay on the topic: How will you post the IMD MBA make a difference in your home country?
Closing Date: September 30th
Funding: Private
Contributor: Mr and Mrs Peter von Muralt-Lo
No. of awards given last year: 2
No. of applicants last year: 3

INTERNATIONAL NAVIGATION ASSOCIATION (PIANC)

Graaf de Ferraris Building, 11th Floor, boulevard du Roi Albert II,
20-Box 3, B-1000 Brussels, Belgium
Tel: (32) 32 2 553 71 61
Fax: (32) 32 2 553 71 55
Email: info@pianc-aipcn.org
Website: www.pianc-aipcn.org
Contact: Secretary General

The International Navigation Association (PIANC) is a worldwide non-political and non-profit technical and scientific organization of private individuals, corporations and national governments. PIANC's objective is to promote the maintenance and operation of both inland and maritime navigation by fostering progress in the planning, design, construction, improvement, maintenance and operations of inland and maritime waterways, ports and coastal areas for general use in industrialized and industrializing countries. Facilities for fisheries, sport and recreational navigation are included in PIANC's activities.

De Paepe-Willems Award

Subjects: The design, construction, improvement, maintenance or operation of inland and maritime waterways such as rivers, estuaries, canals, port, inland and maritime ports and coastal areas and related fields.
Purpose: To encourage young professionals to submit for presentation outstanding technical articles in the fields of interest to PIANC.
Eligibility: Open to members of PIANC or candidates sponsored by a member, who are under the age of 35.
Level of Study: Unrestricted
Type: Award
Value: A monetary award of €5,000 and free membership of PIANC for a 5-year period. Free hotel accommodation will be provided, together with a coverage of travel expenses to the venue of the General Assembly
Frequency: Annual
Country of Study: Any country
No. of awards offered: 1
Application Procedure: Applicants must complete an application form, available on request from the PIANC General Secretariat or on the PIANC website, and submit this together with the article. Articles must be written by a single author, not have been previously published elsewhere, not exceed 12,000 words, be in type script, and in English or French with a summary in the same language. Articles may be accompanied by illustrations or diagrams.
Closing Date: August 31st
Funding: Private, government
Additional Information: The prize will be awarded to the individual candidate who submits the most outstanding article in the calendar year preceding the Annual General Assembly at which the prize is awarded, provided the article is judged to be of sufficiently high standard. The prize winner will be invited to present a commentary on his or her article during the General Assembly of the PIANC or during the Congress. In judging the articles the jury shall take into account their technical level, originality and practical value and the quality of presentation. Candidates are advised that the Bulletin is designed for readers with a wide range of engineering interests and highly specialized articles should be written with this in mind.

INTERNATIONAL PEACE SCHOLARSHIP FUND

PEO, 3700 Grand Avenue, Des Moines, IA, 50312, United States of America
Tel: (1) 515 255 3153
Fax: (1) 515 255 3820
Email: www.peointernational.org.
Website: www.peointernational.org
Contact: Ms Carolyn J Larson, Project Supervisor

PEO International Peace Scholarship

Subjects: All subjects.
Purpose: To support international women studying for graduate degrees.

Eligibility: Applicants of any nationality may apply, with the exception of residents of the United States of America or Canada. Eligibility is based on financial need, nationality, degree, full-time status and residence.
Level of Study: Doctorate, Graduate
Type: Scholarship (grant-in-aid)
Value: US$10,000 maximum per year
Length of Study: A maximum of 2 years
Frequency: Annual
Country of Study: United States of America or Canada
No. of awards offered: Approx. 200
Application Procedure: Eligibility must be established before application material is sent. Candidates should write to the main address and request an eligibility form or download one from our website: www.peointernational.org. Completed forms should be returned to the IPS office. If the applicant is deemed eligible, the application material will be sent.
Closing Date: December 15th for receipt of the eligibility forms and January 31st for receipt of the application forms
Funding: Private
Contributor: PEO members
No. of awards given last year: 200
No. of applicants last year: 340
Additional Information: Scholarships cannot be used for travel, research dissertations, internships or practical training. An applicant must have a contact person who is a citizen of the United States of America or Canada and who will act as a non-academic adviser. Applicants must also have round-trip return travel expense guaranteed at the time of the application and promise to return to their own country within 60 days of completion of their studies.

INTERNATIONAL READING ASSOCIATION

800 Barksdale Road, PO Box 8139, Newark, DE, 19714-8139, United States of America
Tel: (1) 302 731 1600 ext 423
Fax: (1) 302 731 1057
Email: research@reading.org
Website: www.reading.org
Contact: Marcella Moore, Research & Policy Division

The International Reading Association seeks to promote high levels of literacy for all by improving the quality of reading instruction through studying the reading processes and teaching techniques, serving as a clearing house for the dissemination of reading research through conferences, journals and other publications and actively encouraging the lifetime reading habit.

Albert J Harris Award

Subjects: Reading and literacy.
Purpose: To recognize outstanding published works on the topics of reading disabilities and the prevention, assessment or instruction of learners experiencing difficulty learning to read.
Eligibility: Open to all literacy professionals.
Level of Study: Postgraduate
Type: Award
Value: US$1,000
Frequency: Annual
Country of Study: Any country
No. of awards offered: 1
Application Procedure: Applicants must obtain guidelines with specific information from the main address or by visiting the website.
Closing Date: September 1st
Funding: Private

Dina Feitelson Research Award

Subjects: Literacy.
Purpose: To recognize an outstanding empirical study that was published in English in a refereed journal that specifically reports on an investigation of aspects of literary acquisition such as phonemic awareness, the alphabetic principle, bilingualism, home influences on literacy development or cross-cultural studies of beginning reading.
Eligibility: Articles must have been published in a refereed journal within the past 18 months and may be submitted by the author or

anyone else. Empirical studies involve the collection of original data from direct experimentation or observation, and articles that develop theory without data, secondary reviews of the literature or descriptions of the theory are not eligible for this competition. Nominees for this award do not need to be members of the International Reading Association.

Level of Study: Unrestricted
Type: Award
Value: US$500 award
Frequency: Dependent on funds available
Country of Study: Any country
No. of awards offered: 1
Application Procedure: Applicants must obtain guidelines with specific information from the main address or by visiting the website.
Closing Date: September 1st
Funding: Private
Additional Information: The Dina Feitelson Research Award was established to honour the memory of Dina Feitelson. This award began in 1997.

Elva Knight Research Grant

Subjects: Literacy education.
Purpose: To assist a researcher in a reading and literacy project that addresses significant questions about literacy instruction and practice.
Eligibility: Applicants must be members of the International Reading Association and projects should be completed within 2 years.
Level of Study: Postgraduate, Research
Value: Upto a maximum of US$10,000
Length of Study: 2 years
Frequency: Annual
Country of Study: Any country
No. of awards offered: Up to 4 awards. It is expected that at least 1 award will go to a researcher outside the United States of America and/or Canada and at least 1 to a teacher-initiated research project
Application Procedure: Applicants must obtain guidelines with specific information from the main address or by visiting the website.
Closing Date: January 15th
Funding: Private
Additional Information: This award began in 1982.

Helen M Robinson Award

Subjects: Literacy education.
Purpose: To support doctoral students at the early stages of their dissertation research in the area reading and literacy.
Eligibility: Open to all doctoral students at the early stages of their dissertation research worldwide who are members of the International Reading Association.
Level of Study: Doctorate
Value: US$1,500
Frequency: Annual
Country of Study: Any country
No. of awards offered: 1
Application Procedure: Applicants must obtain guidelines with specific information from the main address or by visiting the website.
Closing Date: January 15th
Funding: Private
Additional Information: This award began in 1991.

International Reading Association Outstanding Dissertation of the Year Award

Subjects: Reading and literacy.
Purpose: To recognize dissertations in the field of reading and literacy.
Eligibility: Open to all doctoral students worldwide who are members of the International Reading Association.
Level of Study: Doctorate
Type: Prize
Value: US$1,000
Frequency: Annual
Country of Study: Any country
No. of awards offered: 1
Application Procedure: Applicants must obtain guidelines with specific information from the main address or by visiting the website.
Closing Date: October 1st

Funding: Private
Additional Information: This award began in 1964.

International Reading Association Teacher as Researcher Grant

Subjects: Literacy.
Purpose: To support teachers in their enquiries about literacy learning and instruction.
Eligibility: All applicants must be members of the International Reading Association and practicing pre-K-12 teachers with full-time teaching responsibilities, including librarians, classroom teachers and resource teachers. Applicants are limited to one proposal per year. There must be a span of 3 years before past grant recipients can apply for another Teacher as Researcher Grant.
Level of Study: Research
Value: Up to US$5,000 maximum, but priority is given to smaller grants of between US$1,000 and 2,000
Frequency: Annual
Country of Study: Any country
No. of awards offered: Several
Application Procedure: Applicants must obtain guidelines with specific information from the main address or by visiting the website.
Closing Date: January 15th
Funding: Private
Additional Information: This award began in 1997.

Jeanne S Chall Research Fellowship

Subjects: Reading and literacy.
Purpose: To encourage and support doctoral research investigating issues in beginning research, readability, reading difficulty and stages of reading development.
Eligibility: Open to doctoral students who are members of the International Reading Association and are planning or beginning dissertations.
Level of Study: Doctorate, Research
Type: Fellowship
Value: US$6,000 maximum
Frequency: Annual
Country of Study: Any country
No. of awards offered: 1
Application Procedure: Applicants must obtain guidelines with specific information from the main address or by visiting the website.
Closing Date: January 15th
Funding: Private
Additional Information: This award began in 1997.

Nila Banton Smith Research Dissemination Support Grant

Subjects: Reading and literacy.
Purpose: To facilitate the dissemination of literacy research to the educational community.
Eligibility: Open to any International Reading Association member, including student members, working on a research dissemination activity, (e.g., a literature review, meta-analysis, monograph, or other work) designed to disseminate research to the educational community.
Level of Study: Research, Professional development
Type: Grant
Value: US$5,000
Length of Study: 2–10 months
Frequency: Annual
Country of Study: Any country
No. of awards offered: 1
Application Procedure: Applicants must obtain guidelines with specific information from the main address or by visiting the website.
Closing Date: January 15th
Contributor: Nila Banton Smith Endowment
Additional Information: This award began in 1991.

Reading/Literacy Research Fellowship

Subjects: Literacy education.
Purpose: To provide support to a researcher who has shown exceptional promise in reading or literacy research.

Eligibility: Open to a researcher outside the United States or Canada who has evidenced exceptional promise in reading research and deserves encouragement to continue working in the field of reading.
Level of Study: Postdoctorate
Type: Fellowship
Value: US$5,000
Frequency: Annual
No. of awards offered: 1
Application Procedure: Applicants must obtain guidelines with specific information from the main address or by visiting the website.
Closing Date: January 15th
Funding: Private
Additional Information: This award began in 1974.

Steven A Stahl Research Grant

Subjects: Literacy education
Purpose: To encourage and support promising graduate students in their research.
Eligibility: Applicants must have at least 3 years of teaching experience and conduct classroom research (including action research) focused on improving reading instruction and children's reading achievement.
Level of Study: Research, Graduate
Type: Grant
Value: US$1,000
Frequency: Annual
Country of Study: Any country
Application Procedure: Applicants can write to Research and policy division, e-mail: research@reading.org
Closing Date: Feburary 16th
Funding: Private

INTERNATIONAL RESEARCH AND EXCHANGE BOARD (IREX)

2121 K Street North West, Suite 700, Washington, DC, 20037, United States of America
Tel: (1) 202 628 8188
Fax: (1) 202 628 8189
Email: irex@irex.org
Website: www.irex.org
Contact: Ms Michelle Duplissis, Senior Program Officer

The International Research and Exchange Board (IREX) is an international non-profit organization specializing in education, independent media, internet development and civil society programmes. Through training, partnerships, education, research and grant programmes, IREX develops the capacity of individuals to contribute to their societies. Since its founding in 1968, IREX has supported over 15,000 students, scholars, policymakers, business leaders, journalists and other professionals.

ECA/IREX/FSA Contemporary Issues Fellowship Program

Subjects: Business administration, civic education, educational policy, economics, energy policy, environmental policy, human rights, international relations, the internet, journalism and media, law enforcement, military/security issues, non-governmental organization development and management, political science, public administration (government), public health policy, rule of law and social welfare.
Purpose: To provide opportunities for experienced professionals and specialists to conduct policy-orientated research in the United States of America.
Eligibility: Open to citizens and residents of Armenia, Azerbaijan, Belarus, Georgia, Kazakhstan, Kyrgyzstan, Moldova, the Russian Federation, Tajikistan, Turkmenistan, Ukraine or Uzbekistan. Candidates must be aged 25–55, have an academic degree at least equivalent to a United States of America Master's degree, have at least 3 years experience in the listed topic of research and possess a high level of proficiency in written and spoken English. Applicants must not have participated in a United States of America government-sponsored grant of more than 6 weeks in the past 2 years.
Level of Study: Professional development
Type: Fellowship

Value: Travel, housing, a stipend, medical insurance, a research allowance and return trip transportation from the home city to the placement city
Length of Study: 4 months
Frequency: Annual
Study Establishment: A university, research centre, government institution or non-governmental organization
Country of Study: United States of America
No. of awards offered: Approx. 60
Application Procedure: Applicants must submit a completed application form, research proposal, two letters of recommendation, curriculum vitae and a short personal biography. All applications must contain developed and focused research projects that are policy-driven with practical application in Eurasia. Please contact the organization for further details.
Closing Date: November
Funding: Government
Contributor: The Bureau of Cultural and Educational Affairs, at the United States of America Department of State
No. of awards given last year: 100
No. of applicants last year: 1000
Additional Information: Prospective applicants are encouraged to contact IREX's Eurasia field offices and educational advising centres before submitting an application. Further information and field office contacts are available on the website.

IREX Individual Advanced Research Opportunities

Subjects: Policy-relevant research in the social sciences and humanities.
Purpose: To provide opportunities for scholars from the United States of America wishing to pursue research in the humanities and social sciences in Europe and Eurasia.
Eligibility: Open to citizens and 3-year permanent residents of the United States of America. Applicants must hold a PhD or other terminal graduate degree or be pursuing a PhD or a Master's degree. Doctoral candidates must have completed all requirements for the PhD except for the dissertation. Master's candidates are eligible for grants of 1–3 months to conduct policy relevant research for a thesis or comparable project. Normally, command of the host country's language sufficient for advanced research is required of all applicants. Further details can be found on the website.
Level of Study: Postdoctorate, Doctorate, Graduate, Predoctorate, Professional development, Research, MBA, Postgraduate
Type: Grant
Value: Up to a maximum of US$40,000. Covers travel and visa fees, dollar stipend and a housing allowance
Length of Study: 2–9 months
Frequency: Annual
Study Establishment: Appropriate institutions
No. of awards offered: Varies
Application Procedure: Applicants must visit the website for application forms and further information.
Closing Date: November 17th
Funding: Government, private
Contributor: The United States of America Department of State (Title VIII) and the IREX Scholar Support Fund
No. of awards given last year: 25
Additional Information: Applicants must study in one of the following countries: Albania, Armenia, Azerbaijan, Belarus, Bosnia and Herzegovina, Bulgaria, Croatia, Czech Republic, Estonia, Georgia, Hungary, Iran, Kazakhstan, Kyrgyzstan, Latvia, Lithuania, Macedonia, Moldova, Mongolia, Romania, Russia, Serbia and Montenegro, Slovakia, Slovenia, Tajikistan, Turkey, Turkmenistan, Ukraine and Uzbekistan. Further information is available on request; however, please contact IREX for programme information well in advance of the deadline.

IREX Policy-Connect Collaborative Research Grants Program

Subjects: Social sciences concerned with Europe, Eurasia, the Near East and Asia. Applicants should refer to the website as there will be a theme each year limiting the geographical focus and the eligible fields of research.
Purpose: To provide grants for collaborative cutting-edge research.

Eligibility: Open to citizens and 3-year permanent residents of the United States of America. Applicants must hold a PhD or other terminal graduate degree at the time of application. Collaborative research programmes involving international colleagues are strongly encouraged.

Level of Study: Postdoctorate, Postgraduate

Type: Grant

Value: Up to US$30,000

Length of Study: Up to 1 year

Frequency: Annual

No. of awards offered: 4

Application Procedure: Applicants must contact IREX or visit the website for application forms.

Funding: Government, private

Contributor: United States of America Department of State (Title VIII), John J and Nancy Lee Roberts

No. of awards given last year: 1

Additional Information: Further information is available on request. The programme is limited to specific geographic areas and topics each year.

IREX Short-Term Travel Grants

Subjects: Policy-relevant research.

Purpose: To provide opportunities for scholars from the United States of America to pursue research in the social sciences in Europe and Eurasia.

Eligibility: Open to citizens and permanent residents of the United States of America who have a PhD or other terminal graduate degree and need project support.

Level of Study: Postdoctorate, Postgraduate

Type: Travel grant

Value: International coach class roundtrip transportation from the US to the host country(ies) for the period of grant awarded; a monthly allowance for housing and living expenses, based on IREX's pre-established country-specific rates; travel visas; emergency evacuation insurance

Length of Study: Up to 60 days

Frequency: Annual

Country of Study: Eastern Europe and Eurasia

No. of awards offered: Varies

Application Procedure: Candidates must contact Amy Schulz, Program Officer, at stg@irex.org for details or application guidelines. Application forms can be downloaded from the website.

Closing Date: February 2nd

Funding: Government

Contributor: The United States of America Department of State's Title VIII Program

No. of awards given last year: Approx. 40

No. of applicants last year: Varies

Additional Information: Candidates will be notified of award decisions approx. 8 weeks after the application deadline. Candidates must study in one of the following countries: Albania, Armenia, Azerbaijan, Belarus, Bosnia and Herzegovina, Bulgaria, Croatia, Czech Republic, Estonia, Georgia, Hungary, Kazakhstan, Kyrgyzstan, Latvia, Lithuania, Macedonia, Moldova, Poland, Romania, Russia, Serbia and Montenegro, Slovakia, Tajikistan, Turkmenistan, Ukraine or Uzbekistan.

INTERNATIONAL TROPICAL TIMBER ORGANIZATION (ITTO)

International Organizations Center, 5th floor Pacifico-Yokohama 1-1-1, Minato-Mirai, Nishi-ku, Yokohama, 220-0012, Japan

Tel: (81) 45 223 1110

Fax: (81) 45 223 1111

Email: itto@itto.or.jp

Website: www.itto.or.jp

ITTO is an intergovernmental organization promoting the conservation and sustainable management, use and the trade of tropical forest resources.

International Tropical Timber Organization (ITTO) Fellowship Programme

Subjects: Forestry management including forest industry development and trade in forest products and services

Purpose: To promote human resource development and to strengthen professional expertise in tropical forestry.

Eligibility: Only nationals of ITTO member countries are eligible to apply and fellowships are awarded mainly to nationals of developing member countries.

Level of Study: Doctorate, Postgraduate, Professional development, Research

Type: Fellowship

Value: Up to US$10,000

Frequency: Twice a year

Study Establishment: Varies

No. of awards offered: 50 to 60 per year

Application Procedure: Application form must be completed and sent with required documebts to the ITTO Secretariat by post. Application procedure is found in the ITTO website www.itto.or.jp

Closing Date: March and September. Dates varies every year

Funding: Government

Contributor: International Tropical Timber Organization

No. of awards given last year: 45

No. of applicants last year: 245

Additional Information: Eligibal activities include participation in international/regional conferences, short term training courses, training internships at industries, research and educational institutions, study tours and lecture/demonstratin tours; Small grants for post graduate studies.

INTERNATIONAL UNION AGAINST CANCER (UICC)

62 route de Frontenex, 1207 Geneva, Switzerland

Tel: (41) 22 809 1843

Fax: (41) 22 809 1810

Email: vought@uicc.org

Website: www.uicc.org

Contact: Ms Beate Vought, Fellowships Manager

The International Union Against Cancer (UICC) Fellowships Programme provides long-, medium- and short-term fellowships to qualified investigators, clinicians and nurses, who are actively involved in cancer research, clinical oncology or oncology nursing.

American Cancer Society UICC International Fellowships for Beginning Investigators (ACSBI)

Subjects: Oncology.

Purpose: To facilitate cancer investigators and clinicians, who are in the early stages of their careers, to conduct cancer research projects into the pre-clinical, clinical, epidemiological, psychological, behavioural, health services, health policy, outcomes and cancer-control aspects of the disease.

Eligibility: 1. Beginning investigators and clinicians in the early stages of their academic careers, generally with a minimum of 10 years post-doctoral experience. 2. PhD candidates with appropriate earlier degrees, if returning to an academic track position. 3. Candidates must hold an academic university or hospital position with an explicit commitment to return to home institute. 4. Please note that fellowships are awarded only to individuals who will be conducting their research at not-for-profit institutions. Unsolicited applications will not be accepted from, nor will fellowship be awarded for, the support of research conducted at for-profit institutions.

Level of Study: Research

Type: Fellowship

Value: US$45,000 for travel and stipend

Length of Study: 1 year

Frequency: Annual

Study Establishment: A suitable host institute abroad

Country of Study: Any country

No. of awards offered: 6–8 per year

Application Procedure: Application forms can be obtained from the fellowships department or downloaded from the UICC website.

Closing Date: December 1st

Funding: Commercial

Contributor: American Cancer Society

No. of awards given last year: 4

No. of applicants last year: 16

Additional Information: Awards are conditional on the return of the fellow to the home institute at the end of fellowship and on the availability of appropriate facilities and resources to apply the newly acquired skills.

UICC Asia-Pacific Cancer Society Training Grants

Subjects: Oncology.
Purpose: To increase the capacity of volunteers and staff of voluntary cancer societies located in the Asia Pacific region by participating in, and learning from activities conducted by established collaborating cancer societies in the region.
Eligibility: Staff or accredited volunteers of voluntary cancer societies located in the Asia-Pacific region
Level of Study: Professional development, Unrestricted
Type: Grant
Value: US$1,800
Length of Study: 1 week
Frequency: Annual
Country of Study: India, Australia, Singapore
No. of awards offered: 5–10 per year
Application Procedure: Candidates must choose one of the projects offered and submit their curriculum vitae together with a letter of justification to the host society with a request for a formal invitation to participate in the specific project. The letter of justification must describe why a specific project was chosen, how candidates and their organizations would benefit from this experience and how they would disseminate the new skills upon return. All application material can be obtained from the UICC Fellowships Department or downloaded from the website.
Closing Date: September 1st
Funding: Trusts
Contributor: 1. William Rudder Memorial Fund (Australia) 2. The Cancer Council New South Wales, Sydney, Australia 3. The Cancer Council Queensland, Brisbane, Australia 4. Cancer Patients Aid Association, Mumbai, India 5. Singapore Cancer Society, Singapore
No. of awards given last year: 6
No. of applicants last year: 8
Additional Information: Selection results will be notified in mid-December. Awards are subject to the UICC general conditions for fellowships.

UICC International Cancer Research Technology Transfer Fellowships (ICRETT)

Subjects: Cancer control and prevention, epidemiology and cancer registration, public education and behavioural sciences.
Purpose: To facilitate the rapid international transfer of cancer research and clinical technology; to exchange knowledge and enhance skills in basic, clinical, behavourial and epidemiological areas of cancer research, and in cancer control and prevention; and to acquire up-to-date clinical management, diagnostic and therapeutic expertise.
Eligibility: Investigators and clinicians should be working in places where such teaching is not yet available and where the necessary facilities exist to apply and disseminate the new skills upon return. Qualified cancer investigators should be at the early stages in their careers, while clinicians should be well established in their oncology practice.
Level of Study: Professional development
Type: Fellowship
Value: US$3,400
Length of Study: 1–3 months with stipend support for 1 month
Study Establishment: A suitable host institute abroad
Country of Study: Any country
No. of awards offered: 120–150 per year
Application Procedure: Application forms can be obtained from the fellowships department or downloaded from the UICC website.
Closing Date: Any time
Funding: Commercial, government, private
Contributor: The fellowships are funded by a group of cancer institutes societies, leagues, associations and governmental agencies in North America, Europe and Australia
No. of awards given last year: 122
No. of applicants last year: 164
Additional Information: Candidates who are already physically present at the proposed host institute while their applications are under consideration are not eligible for a UICC fellowship.

UICC International Cancer Technology Transfer Training Workshops

Subjects: Basic, clinical, behavourial and epidemiological aspects of cancer research, cancer control and prevention, clinical management, and diagnostic and therapeutic skills.
Purpose: To facilitate teaching and training courses on cancer research.
Eligibility: Applicants should be internationally recognized leaders in their respective fields.
Level of Study: Teaching
Type: Fellowship
Value: A maximum of US$15,000 for travel and stipend for 3 international faculty members
Length of Study: 3–5 days
Frequency: Annual
Study Establishment: A suitable host institute in a resource-constrained abroad country
Country of Study: Any developing country
No. of awards offered: 10–20 per year
Application Procedure: Application forms can be obtained from the UICC fellowships department or downloaded from the website.
Closing Date: Accepted at any time
Funding: Private
Contributor: The fellowships are funded by a group of cancer institutes, societies, leagues, associations and governmental agencies in North America, Europe and Australia
No. of awards given last year: 8
No. of applicants last year: 11
Additional Information: Awards are subject to the UICC general conditions for fellowships.

UICC Trish Greene International Cancer Nursing Training Fellowships

Subjects: Training for nursing cancer patients.
Purpose: To support nurses who are actively engaged in the care of cancer patients and who come from developing and Eastern European countries.
Eligibility: Open to English or French speaking nurses who are actively engaged in the care of cancer patients in their home institutes and who come from developing or East European countries where specialist cancer nurse training is not yet widely available.
Level of Study: Professional development
Type: Fellowship
Value: A maximum of US$15,000 for travel and stipend for 3 international faculty members
Length of Study: 3–5 days
Frequency: Annual
Study Establishment: A suitable host institute in a resource-constrained country
Country of Study: Any developing country
No. of awards offered: 5–15
Application Procedure: Applicants must submit applications complete with supporting documentation to the UICC Geneva Office by the application closing date. Application forms can be obtained from the Fellowships department or the website.
Closing Date: November 1st for notification in mid-February
Funding: Private
Contributor: The Oncology Nursing Society (USA) and the Norwegian Cancer Society
No. of awards given last year: 15
No. of applicants last year: 24

UICC Yamagiwa-Yoshida Memorial International Cancer Study Grants

Subjects: Basic, translational or applied research
Purpose: To enable cancer investigators from any country to carry out bilateral research projects that exploit complementary materials or skills, including advanced training in experimental methods or special techniques.
Eligibility: Open to appropriately qualified investigators from any country who are actively engaged in cancer research. Candidates who are already physically present at the proposed host institute are not eligible.
Level of Study: Professional development, Research
Type: Grant

Value: The average stipend is US$10,000. If a Fellow's return home is delayed beyond the extra approved period, 50 per cent of the travel award, the return portion has to be reimbursed to the UICC. Calculation of travel and stipend awards are based on the candidate's estimates which are adjusted, if need be, to published fares and UICC scales. Travel awards contribute to the least expensive international return air fares or other appropriate form of transport. Travel estimates should not include costs for internal travel within the home or host countries. These and extra costs for visa, passports, airport taxes and insurance are the responsibility of the Fellow. No financial support is provided for dependants

Length of Study: 3 months. May be extended by their original duration, subject to written approval of the home and host supervisors. Funding for these additional periods may be secured from other funding agencies

Frequency: Annual

Study Establishment: A suitable host institute abroad

Country of Study: Any country

No. of awards offered: 15

Application Procedure: Applicants must complete an application form, available from the Fellowships Department or from the website.

Closing Date: January 15th for notification by mid April, July 1st for notification by mid October

Funding: Commercial, private

Contributor: Kyowa Hakko Kyoga Company Limited, Toray Industries, Inc. and the Japan National Committee for UICC

No. of awards given last year: 12

No. of applicants last year: 31

Additional Information: Awards are subject to the UICC general conditions for fellowships

INTERNATIONAL UNION FOR VACUUM SCIENCE AND TECHNOLOGY (IUVSTA)

84 Oldfield Drive, Vicars Cross, Chester, CH3 5LW, United Kingdom
Tel: (44) 12 44 34 2675
Fax: (44) 77 1340 3525
Email: iuvsta.secretary.general@ronreid.me.uk
Website: www.iuvsta.org
Contact: Dr R J Reid, Secretary General

The International Union for Vacuum Science and Technology (IUVSTA) is a non-government organization whose member societies represent all vacuum scientists, engineers and technologists in their country.

Welch Foundation Scholarship

Subjects: Vacuum science.

Purpose: To encourage promising scholars who wish to study vacuum science, techniques or their application in any field.

Eligibility: Open to applicants of any nationality who hold the minimum of a Bachelor's degree, although preference is given to those holding a doctoral degree.

Level of Study: Doctorate, Postdoctorate, Postgraduate

Type: Scholarship

Value: US$15,500

Length of Study: 1 year

Frequency: Annual

Study Establishment: An appropriate laboratory

Country of Study: Any country

No. of awards offered: 1

Application Procedure: Applicants must complete and submit an application form with a research proposal, a curriculum vitae and two letters of reference. More information and application forms can be obtained from the website.

Closing Date: April 15th

Funding: Private

Contributor: IUVSTA

No. of awards given last year: 1

No. of applicants last year: 6

For further information contact:

Canadian Photorics Fabrication Centre, Institute for Microstructural Sciences, National Research Council, Building M-50, Montréal Road, Ottawa, ON, K1A 0R6, Canada

Email: Frank.Shepherd@nrc-cnrc.gc.ca
Contact: Dr FR Shepherd, Administrator Technical Manager

INTERNATIONAL UNION OF BIOCHEMISTRY AND MOLECULAR BIOLOGY (IUBMB)

Institut de Botanique, 28 rue Goethe, Strasbourg Cedex, 67083, France
Tel: (33) 33 390 24 1832
Fax: (33) 33 390 24 1921
Email: jacques-henry.weil@ibmp-ulp.u-strasbg.fr
Website: www.iubmb.org
Contact: Professor Jacques Henry Weil

The International Union of Biochemistry and Molecular Biology (IUBMB) promotes the norms, values, standards and ethics of science and the free and unhampered movement of scientists of all nations interested in participation in activities related to biochemistry and molecular biology. Its mission is to foster and support the growth and advancement of biochemistry and molecular biology as the foundation from which the biomolecular sciences derive their basic ideas and techniques in the service of mankind.

Wood-Whelan Research Fellowships

Subjects: Biochemistry and molecular biology.

Purpose: To provide financial assistance to young biochemists and molecular biologists to carry out experiments.

Eligibility: Open to applicants who are residents of countries that are members of IUBMB and students or young researchers less than 35 years old. Retroactive applications will not be considered.

Level of Study: Postgraduate, Research

Type: Fellowship

Value: US$3,000. It covers travel and incidental costs, as well as living expenses

Length of Study: 1–4 months

Frequency: Annual

No. of awards offered: 14

Application Procedure: Applicants must submit a completed application form along with details of the research proposal, budget, curriculum vitae with a list of publications and a letter of recommendation. The original application should be sent by the applicant by email as PDF files.

Closing Date: Continuous

Contributor: The main sources of income for IUBMB are dues from adhering bodies (member societies) and revenue from publications

No. of awards given last year: 14

No. of applicants last year: 32

Additional Information: Travel should commence within 4 months of the award being made.

INTERNATIONAL UNIVERSITY OF JAPAN

Kokusai-cho, Minami Uonuma-shi, Nilgata, 949-7277, Japan
Tel: (81) 25 779 1111
Fax: (81) 25 779 4441
Email: ofcgsir@iuj.ac.jp
Website: www.iuj.ac.jp

From our vantage point in the heart of Asia, we offer a unique perspective of the world in a lively global setting. Our culturally diverse campus, coupled with our location and our insight, will enrich your educational experience.

Japanese Grant Aid for Human Resource Development Scholarship

Purpose: To provide students in Cambodia with opportunities for academic research at a Japanese University and thereby enhance bilateral relations between Cambodia and Japan.

Eligibility: Open to all University Graduates with advanced English language skills, and who are between the ages of 22 and 34 and nations of: Bangladesh, Cambodia, china, Indonesia, Laos, Mongolia, Myanmar, Phillipines, Uzbekistan, or Vietnam.

Level of Study: Postgraduate
Value: The scholarship includes tuition, a living allowance and travel expenses
Frequency: Annual
Country of Study: Japan
No. of awards offered: 20
Application Procedure: Submit application form available online.
Closing Date: September 9th
Contributor: The Ministry of Education, youth and sport

For further information contact:

JICE JDS Project Office PO Box 1592, Phnom Penh, Cambodia,

INTERNATIONAL VIOLIN COMPETITION–PREMIO PAGANINI

Secretariat of the International Violin Competition Premio Paganini,
Comune di Genova, Via Sottoripa, 5,
Genova, I-16124, Italy
Tel: (39) 010 557 4215
Fax: (39) 010 557 4326
Email: violinopaganini@comune.genova.it
Website: www.paganini.comune.genova.it
Contact: Ms Anna Rita Certo, Secretary General

The international violin competition "Premio Paganini" is a competition for young violinists between 16 and 30 years of age. It offers prizes for a total amount of €40,000 plus special prizes and an opportunity for the winner to play Paganini's violin on October 12th, on the occasion of the closing ceremony of the Christopher Columbus Celebrations.

International Violin Competition–Premio Paganini
Subjects: Violin.
Purpose: To discover new talented young violinists and encourage them to spread the values which Paganini himself and his music stands for.
Eligibility: Violinists between 16 and 30 years of age
Level of Study: Unrestricted
Type: Prize
Value: 1st prize €25,000 Premio Paganini (indivisible); 2nd prize €10,000; 3rd prize €5,000; special prizes will also be awarded
Frequency: Every 2 years
Country of Study: Italy
No. of awards offered: 3 awards and special prizes
Application Procedure: Applicants must send the application form by mail together with a CD and the documents required to the address indicated below. The application form and the rules of the competition may be obtained from obtained by writing to the Competition Secretariat or they can be downloaded at: www.paganini.comune.genova.it. A pre-selection will be made to enter the competition.
Closing Date: April 30th
Funding: Government
Contributor: Comune di Genova
No. of awards given last year: 3 plus prizes
No. of applicants last year: 107
Additional Information: Registration fee of €100 to be paid only after having passed the pre-selection. The next competition may be held in 2010.

For further information contact:

Segreteria del Cancorso Internazionale di Violino Premio Paganini, Comune di Genova-Archivio Generale, Via XX Settember, 15-2 Piano, Genova, I-16121, Italy

INTERNATIONAL WATER MANAGEMENT INSTITUTE (IWMI)

127 Sunil Mawatha, Pelawatte, Battaramulla, Sri Lanka
Tel: (94) 11 2787404/4080
Fax: (94) 11 2786854
Email: iwmi@cgiar.org
Website: www.iwmi.cgiar.org

The International Water Management Institute (IWMI) is a non-profit, scientific research organization specializing in water use in agriculture and integrated management of water and land resources. IWMI works to develop tools and methods to help poverty and ensure food security through more effective management of water and land resources.

IWMI PhD Scholarship
Subjects: Water resource management.
Purpose: To strengthen its own field-research capacity and make a strong contribution to professional development of water resources researchers, especially those from developing countries.
Eligibility: Open to postdoctoral scientists.
Level of Study: Postdoctorate
Type: Scholarships
Value: Complete coursework, living and travel expenses and research cost
Length of Study: 2 years
Frequency: Annual
Application Procedure: Applicants must submit a brief research proposal, curriculum vitae, copy of academic certificates and letter of support.
Additional Information: All queries should be directed to d.vaneyck@cgiar.org

INTERNATIONALER ROBERT-SCHUMANN-WETTBEWERB ZWICKAU

Stadtverwaltung Zwickau, PF 200933, 08009 Zwickau, Kulturamt, Germany
Tel: (49) (0) 375 83 4130
Fax: (49) (0) 375 83 4141
Email: kulturbuero@zwickau.de
Website: www.zwickau-schumann.de

International Robert Schumann Competition
Subjects: Piano performance and individual singing.
Purpose: To support the interpretation of the work of Robert Schumann.
Eligibility: Open to pianists up to the age of 30 and to individual singers up to the age of 32.
Level of Study: Professional development
Type: Competition
Value: 1. Piano: 3 prizes with a total amount of €15,0002. Singers (female): 3 prizes with a total amount of €15,0003. Singers (male): 3 prizes with a total amount of €15,0004. Special prize of €2,500 will be awarded to the best lied pianist
Frequency: Every 4 years
Country of Study: Any country
No. of awards offered: 10
Application Procedure: Applicants must write for further details.
Closing Date: February 15th
Funding: Commercial, government
No. of awards given last year: 10
No. of applicants last year: 108

IOTA SIGMA PI

Microelectronics Technology, Lord Corporation, 110 Lord Drive, Cary, NC, 27511, United States of America
Tel: (1) 919 469 2500, 2490
Fax: (1) 919 469 9688
Email: sara.paisner@lord.com
Website: www.iotasigmapi.info
Contact: Sara Paisner, Senior Scientist

Iota Sigma Pi, founded in 1902, is a National Honor Society that serves to promote the advancement of women in chemistry by granting recognition to women who have demonstrated superior scholastic achievement and high professional competence by election into Iota Sigma Pi.

Agnes Fay Morgan Research Award
Subjects: Chemistry and biochemistry.

Purpose: To acknowledge research achievements in chemistry or biochemistry.
Eligibility: Open to female applicants who are not more than 40 years of age.
Level of Study: Postgraduate
Type: Award
Value: The Award will consist of $500, a certificate, and membership in Iota Sigma Pi with a waiver of dues for one year
Frequency: Annual
Study Establishment: Any accredited institution
Country of Study: Any country
Application Procedure: See the website.
Closing Date: February 15th
Contributor: Iota Sigma Pi

For further information contact:

PO Box 6949 Radford university, Radford, VA 24142
Email: chermann@radford.edu
Contact: Dr Christine Hermann, Chemistry of Physics Department

Anna Louise Hoffman Award

Subjects: Chemistry.
Purpose: To recognize outstanding achievement in research.
Eligibility: The candidate must be a full-time (as defined by the nominee's institution) woman graduate student who is a candidate for a graduate degree in an accredited institution. The research presented by the candidate must be original research which can be described by one of the main chemical divisions (e.g., analytical, biochemical, inorganic, organic, physical, and/or ancillary divisions of chemistry). The nominee may be, but need not be, a member of Iota Sigma Pi.
Level of Study: Postgraduate
Type: Award
Value: The award will be $500, a certificate, and a waiver of dues for one year
Frequency: Annual
Study Establishment: Any accredited institution
Country of Study: Any country
Application Procedure: A completed application form along with two recommendations must be sent.
Closing Date: February 15th
Contributor: Iota Sigma Pi

Gladys Anderson Emerson Scholarship

Subjects: Chemistry and biochemistry.
Purpose: To award excellence in chemistry or biochemistry.
Eligibility: Open to applicants who are members of Iota Sigma Pi.
Level of Study: Postgraduate
Type: Scholarship
Value: US$2,000 and a certificate
Frequency: Annual
Study Establishment: Any accredited institution
Country of Study: Any country
Application Procedure: A completed application form, available on the website, must be sent.
Closing Date: February 15th
Contributor: Iota Sigma Pi

For further information contact:

University of North Dakota Chemistry Department, Box 9024, Grand Forks, ND 58202-9024
Email: kthomasson@mail.chem.und.nodak.edu
Contact: Kathryn A. Thomasson

Iota Sigma Pi Centennial Award

Subjects: Chemistry, biochemistry.
Purpose: To award excellence in teaching chemistry, biochemistry or chemistry-related subjects.
Eligibility: Open to female applicants who are chemists or biochemists.
Level of Study: Postgraduate
Type: Award
Value: US$500, a certificate and membership in Iota Sigma Pi with a waiver of dues for 1 year
Frequency: Annual
Application Procedure: See the website.

Closing Date: Feburary 15th
Contributor: Iota Sigma Pi

For further information contact:

Email: paisners@research.ge.com
Contact: Dr Sara Paisner

Iota Sigma Pi National Honorary Member Award

Subjects: Chemistry.
Purpose: To honour outstanding women chemists.
Eligibility: Open to female candidate with exceptional achievements in chemistry. Applicants may or may not be members of Iota Sigma Pi.
Type: Award
Value: US$1,000 a certificate and membership in Iota Sigma Pi with a lifetime waiver of dues
Frequency: Every 3 years
Application Procedure: See the website.
Closing Date: February 15th

For further information contact:

GE Global Research One Research Circle K1-4D17, Niskayuna, NY 12309
Email: paisners@research.ge.com
Contact: Dr Sara Paisner, Director for Professional Awards

Members-at-Large (MAL) Reentry Award

Subjects: Chemistry.
Purpose: To recognize potential excellence in chemistry and related fields.
Eligibility: Open to a candidate with a degree at any level in chemistry or a related field at an accredited four-year college or university.
Level of Study: Postgraduate
Type: Award
Value: US$1,500, a certificate and a year's complimentary membership in Iota Sigma Pi
Study Establishment: Any accredited institution
Country of Study: Any country
Application Procedure: A completed application form must be sent.
Closing Date: March 20th
Contributor: Iota Sigma Pi

For further information contact:

Joanne Bedlek-Anslow, PhD Camden High School 1022 Ehrenclou Drive, Camden, SC 29020
Contact: MAL National Coordinator

Violet Diller Professional Excellence Award

Subjects: Chemistry.
Purpose: To recognize significant accomplishments in academic, governmental or industrial chemistry.
Eligibility: Open to female applicants who have contributed to the scientific community or society on a national level.
Level of Study: Postgraduate
Type: Award
Value: US$1,000 a certificate and membership in Iota sigma Pi with a lifetime of dues
Frequency: Every 3 years
Application Procedure: See the website.
Closing Date: February 15th
Contributor: Iota Sigma Pi

For further information contact:

One Research Circle K1-4D17, Niskayuna, NY 12309
Email: paisners@research.ge.com
Contact: Dr Sara Paisner

IRELAND ALLIANCE

2800 Clarendon Boulevard # 502 West, Arlington, VA 22201, United States of America
Tel: (1) 703/841-5843
Email: vargo@us-irelandalliance.org
Website: www.us-irelandalliance.org
Contact: Trina Vargo, President

The US-Ireland Alliance is a proactive, non-partisan, non-profit organization dedicated to consolidating existing relations between the United States and Ireland and building that relationship for the future.

George J. Mitchell Scholarships

Subjects: All subjects.
Purpose: To familiarize and connect the next generation of American leadership with the island of Ireland.
Eligibility: Open to American citizens between the ages of 18 and 30.
Type: Scholarship
Value: Tuition, housing, a living expenses stipend, and an international travel stipend
Length of Study: 1 year
Frequency: Annual
Study Establishment: Any accredited institution of higher learning
Country of Study: United Kingdom
No. of awards offered: 12
Application Procedure: Applications forms are available online.
Funding: Foundation
Contributor: US-Ireland Alliance
No. of applicants last year: 20

IRISH RESEARCH COUNCIL FOR THE HUMANITIES AND SOCIAL SCIENCES (IRCHSS)

First Floor Brooklawn House, Crompton Avenue (off Shelbourne Road), Ballsbridge, Dublin 4, Ireland
Tel: (353) 1 660 3652
Fax: (353) 1 660 3728
Email: info@irchss.ie
Website: www.irchss.ie

Irish Research Council for the Humanities and Social Sciences (IRCHSS) was established in 2000, by the Minister for Education and Science in response to the need to develop Ireland's research capacity and skills base in a rapidly changing global environment where knowledge is the key to economic and social growth.

IRCHSS Postdoctoral Fellowship

Subjects: Humanities and social sciences.
Purpose: To encourage excellence and the highest standards in the humanities and social sciences.
Eligibility: Open to candidates of any nationality who have been awarded their Doctoral degrees within the past 5 years.
Level of Study: Postdoctorate
Type: Fellowship
Value: €31,745 per year
Frequency: Annual
Closing Date: Janurary 23rd

IRCHSS Postgraduate Scholarship

Subjects: Humanities and social sciences.
Purpose: To facilitate the integration of Irish researchers in the humanities and social sciences within the European Research Area.
Eligibility: Open to citizens of Ireland or citizens of a Member State of the European Union who have been residing within Ireland for less than 3 years. The candidates should be registered as full-time postgraduate research students.
Level of Study: Postgraduate
Type: Scholarship
Value: €16,000 per year
Length of Study: 1 year
Frequency: Annual
Application Procedure: Applicants can download the application form from the website.
Closing Date: January 30th

Thematic Research Project Grants

Subjects: Humanities and social sciences.
Purpose: To support projects that require medium to long-term support.
Eligibility: Open to academic staff employed at third-level institutions in Ireland.

Level of Study: Research
Type: Grant
Value: €6,500–3,00,000
Length of Study: 3 years
Frequency: Annual
Application Procedure: Applicants can download the application form from the website and send the completed form along with a description of the project.
Closing Date: September 14th

IRISH-AMERICAN CULTURAL INSTITUTE (IACI)

1 Lackawanna Place, Morristown, NJ, 07960, United States of America
Tel: (1) 973 605 1991
Fax: (1) 973 605 8875
Email: info@iaci-usa.org
Website: www.iaci-usa.org

The Irish-American Cultural Institute (IACI), a non-profit educational institute, is dedicated to preserving and promoting the highest standards of artistic development, education, research and entertainment in fostering the cultural understanding of Irish heritage in America. With international headquarters in Morristown, NJ, the Institute has a long history of supporting the arts and humanities through grants and awards as well as through programming. The Institute is strictly non-political and non-sectarian. Founded in 1962, the IACI is the sole United States of America organization with the distinction of having the President of Ireland as patron.

IACI Visiting Fellowship in Irish Studies at the National University of Ireland, Galway

Subjects: Irish studies.
Purpose: To allow scholars whose work relates to any aspect of Irish studies to spend a semester at the University of Ireland, Galway.
Eligibility: Open to scholars who normally reside in the United States of America, and whose work relates to any aspect of Irish studies.
Level of Study: Research, Postdoctorate
Type: Fellowship
Value: A stipend of over US$15,000 plus transatlantic transportation
Length of Study: A period of not less than 4 months
Frequency: Annual
Country of Study: Ireland
No. of awards offered: 1
Application Procedure: Applicants must complete an application form and submit this with a current curriculum vitae and list of publications. Application forms are available on request. Applications can be downloaded from the IACI website.
Closing Date: December 31st for the forthcoming academic year
Funding: Foundation
Contributor: Jointly funded with the National University International-Galway
Additional Information: The holder of the fellowship will be provided with services appropriate to a visiting faculty member during his or her time at NUI-Galway. There are certain relatively minor departmental responsibilities expected of the holder during his or her time at UCG, and certain other expectations regarding publication, upon completion of the fellowship.

Irish Research Funds

Subjects: All subjects; historical research has predominated, but other areas of research will be given equal consideration.
Purpose: To promote scholarly enquiry and publication regarding the Irish–American experience.
Eligibility: Open to individuals of any nationality. Media production costs and journal subventions will not be considered for funding.
Level of Study: Postgraduate
Type: Grant
Value: US$1,000–5,000
Country of Study: Any country
No. of awards offered: Varies
Application Procedure: Applicants must complete an application form.
Funding: Foundation

THE ISLAMIC DEVELOPMENT BANK (IDB)

PO Box 5925, Jeddah 21432, Kingdom of Saudi Arabia, Saudi Arabia
Tel: (966) 9662 6361400
Fax: (966) 9662 6366871
Email: idbarchives@isdb.org
Website: www.isdb.org

The Islamic Development Bank is an international financial institution, which aims to foster the economic development and social progress of member countries and Muslim countries.

IDB Merit Scholarship for High Technology

Subjects: Science and high technology.
Purpose: To encourage advanced studies/research in science and high technology areas.
Eligibility: Open to scholars may pursuing full-time 3-year PhD study or 6–12 months of post-doctoral research in any of the approved fields in science and high technology at renowned institutions of higher learning in the world.
Level of Study: Postgraduate
Type: Scholarship
Value: Tuition/bench fee, monthly living allowance, monthly family allowance (for PhD study only), clothing/books allowance (for PhD study only), installation allowance (for PhD study only), computer allowance (for PhD study only), conference/thesis preparation allowance and medical coverage# Return air tickets "
Frequency: Annual
Application Procedure: See the website.
Closing Date: December 31st

IDB Scholarship Programme in Science and Technology

Subjects: Science, technology, engineering and medicine.
Purpose: To assist IDB least developed member countries in the development of science and technology.
Eligibility: Open to candidates from least developed member countries, who are below the age of 30 years.
Level of Study: Postgraduate
Type: Scholarship
Value: The scholarship covers the tuition fees, living allowance, clothing and books allowances, computer allowance, conference allowance, medical coverage and a return air ticket
Length of Study: 2 years
Frequency: Annual
Application Procedure: A completed application form must be sent.

IWHM BERNARD BUTLER TRUST FUND

37 Oasthouse Drive, Fleet, Hampshire, GU51 2UL, United Kingdom
Tel: (44) 12 5262 7748
Fax: (44) 12 5262 7748
Email: info@bernardbutlertrust.org
Website: www.bernardbutlertrust.org
Contact: The Secretary

The Trust was established in 1998 from the assets of the Institution of Works and Highways Management after the merger of its professional activities with the Institution of Civil Engineers in 1994.

The Bernard Butler Trust Fund

Subjects: Civil and Municipal Engineering.
Purpose: To encourage men and women engaged in the engineering field to improve their education, training and professional standing together with aiding and promoting individuals/organizations to advance engineering training, safety and methods of working.
Eligibility: Those who can show practical and personal qualities needed to promote engineering.
Level of Study: Graduate, Postgraduate, Professional development, Research
Type: Training, education and research grants
Value: UK £1,000 upwards depending on submission
Study Establishment: Variable
Country of Study: Worldwide

Application Procedure: Applicants must download an application form from the website or on request from the Trust secretary. In addition to this an online application can also be made.
Closing Date: None
Funding: Private
Contributor: Institution of Works and Highways Management
No. of awards given last year: 36
No. of applicants last year: 96

J N TATA ENDOWMENT

Bombay House, 2nd Floor 24 Homi Mody Street Fort, Mumbai, 400001, India
Tel: (91) 022 6665 7643
Fax: (91) 022 2204 5432
Email: nbmody@sdtatatrust.com
Website: www.dorabjitatatrust.org/allied_trust/endowment.asp#sco
Contact: J. N. Tata Endowment, Director

The J N Tata Endowment awards loan scholarships to scholars of conspicuous distinction for postgraduate, PhD or postdoctoral studies abroad in all fields. Mid-career professionals with an outstanding academic background and experience in the field, who are going abroad for further specialization, are also considered for the scholarship.

J N Tata Endowment Loan Scholarship

Subjects: All subjects.
Purpose: To provide an opportunity to the gifted to pursue higher studies abroad in all disciplines.
Eligibility: Open only to Indian nationals. Applicants must be graduates of a recognized Indian university with a sound academic and extracurricular record. Deserving mid-career professionals are also eligible.
Level of Study: Doctorate, MBA, Postdoctorate, Postgraduate, Professional development, Research
Type: Loan scholarship
Value: Please contact the organization
Length of Study: Minimum 1 year; minimum 6 months for mid-career professionals
Frequency: Annual
Country of Study: Any country except India
No. of awards offered: 100+
Application Procedure: Applicants must complete an application form. Forms are issued against an application fee of Indian Rupees 100 only.
Closing Date: February 15th for the Autumn and Spring semesters
Funding: Private, trusts
Contributor: Tata Trusts
No. of awards given last year: 112
No. of applicants last year: 607
Additional Information: The award is primarily for the Autumn semester. The selection of scholars is made on the basis of a personal interview that assesses the student's competence in the field of graduation, general knowledge and maturity and suitability for the proposed field of study. Interviews are conducted between March and June for the Autumn and Spring semesters.

For further information contact:

Administrative Office Mulla House, 4th Floor, 51, M. G. Road, Fort, Mumbai, 400001, India
Contact: J. N. Tata, Endowment Regd. Off: Bombay House, 2nd floor 24, Homi Mody Street, Fort, Mumbai, 400 001, India
Contact: J. N. Tata

THE J.H. STEWART REID MEMORIAL FELLOWSHIP TRUST

Canadian Association of University Teachers, 2675 Queensview Drive, Ottawa, ON, K2B 8K2, Canada
Email: stewartreid@caut.ca
Website: http://stewartreid.caut.ca
Contact: Johanne Smith, Awards Officer

The J.H. Stewart Reid Memorial Fellowship Trust was founded to honour the memory of the 1st Executive Secretary of the Canadian Association of University Teachers.

J.H. Stewart Reid Memorial Fellowship Trust

Subjects: All subjects.
Purpose: To financially support students who wish to study further.
Eligibility: Open to Canadian citizens or landed immigrants, or those who have convention refugee status from April 30th of the year prior to application. Must be registered in doctoral programme and have first class academic record in the graduate programme
Level of Study: Doctorate
Type: Fellowship
Value: Canadian $5,000
Length of Study: 1 year
Frequency: Annual
Study Establishment: Any Canadian university
Country of Study: Canada
No. of awards offered: 1
Funding: Trusts
No. of awards given last year: 1
Additional Information: Applicants must be registered in a doctoral programme at a Canadian university and have completed their comprehensive examinations or equivalent and have had their doctoral theses proposal accepted by April 30th.

JACK KENT COOKE FOUNDATION

44325 Woodridge Parkway, Suite 200, Virginia, Lansdowne, 20176-5199, United States of America
Tel: (1) 703 723 8000
Fax: (1) 703 723 8030
Email: jkc@jackkentcookefoundation.org
Website: www.jackkentcookefoundation.org

The Jack Kent Cooke Foundation is a private, independent foundation, established in 2000 to help young people of exceptional reach their full potential through education.

Jack Kent Cooke Scholarship

Subjects: Any subjects.
Purpose: To goal of this scholarship is to enable the next generation of leaders to follow their dreams through graduate study.
Eligibility: Open to outstanding students from an accredited US college or university with financial need.
Level of Study: Postgraduate
Type: Scholarship
Value: US$50,000
Length of Study: Varies
Frequency: Annual
Study Establishment: A US University
Country of Study: United States of America
No. of awards offered: 45–50
Application Procedure: Application to be submitted which will undergo a rigorous review process by expert selection committee members. Visit Foundation website for information.
Closing Date: Feburary 2nd
Funding: Foundation
Contributor: Jack Kent Cooke Foundation

JACKI TUCKFIELD MEMORIAL GRADUATE BUSINESS SCHOLARSHIP FUND (JTMGBSF)

1160 NW 87th Street, Miami, FL, 33150-2544, United States of America
Tel: (1) 305 371 2711
Fax: (1) 305 371 5342
Email: saadya.rivera@dadecommunityfoundation.org
Website: www.jackituckfield.org
Contact: Scholarship Committee

On October 21, 1997, Drs Jack and Gloria Tuckfield established Jacki Tuckfield Memorial Graduate Business Scholarship Fund (JTMGBSF) at the non-profit, tax-exempt Dade Community Foundation to commemorate the vibrant life of their extraordinary daughter. Jacki Tuckfield Memorial Graduate Business Scholarship Fund (JTMGBSF) provides financial support to African-American residents of South Florida who are enrolled in Master's and Doctoral degree business programmes in Florida universities.The fund's mission is to improve the diversity of career professionals in the executive, administrative and managerial levels of south Florida's workforce by funding tuition scholarships.

Jacki Tuckfield Memorial Graduate Business Scholarship Fund

Subjects: Business, consumer services.
Purpose: To improve the diversity of career professionals employed in the executive, administrative and managerial levels of the South Florida workforce.
Eligibility: Open to full-time students. They must be African-American United States citizens of South Florida, enrolled in a graduate business programme at a Florida University.
Level of Study: Doctorate, Graduate, MBA, Postgraduate
Type: Scholarships
Value: US$1,000–2,000 in tuition scholarships; US$30,000 in US$1,000 scholarships offered for the 2009-2010 academic year
Frequency: Annual
Country of Study: United States of America
No. of awards offered: 20–30
Application Procedure: Applicants must submit their application form, transcript, interview, essay, reference letters, photograph and curriculum vitae. Application forms can be downloaded from the website www.jackituckfield.org or www.dadecommunityfoundation.org
Closing Date: May 11th
Funding: Foundation
Contributor: JTMGBSF
No. of awards given last year: 30
Additional Information: JTMGBSF awards 256 graduate business tuition scholarships, totalling $261,000 to South Florida residents.

JACOB'S PILLOW DANCE

358 George Canter Road, Becket, MA 01223,
United States of America
Tel: (1) 413 243 9919
Fax: (1) 413 243 4744
Email: info@jacobspillow.org
Website: www.jacobspillow.org

Jacob's Pillow is America's premier dance festival. Founded in 1930s, the Pillow today is renowned not only for producing a premier festival, but also for its professional school, intern programme, archives of rare holdings, artist residencies and year-round community programmes.

Jacob's Pillow Intern Program

Subjects: The following fields related to Dance studies: business, development, education, general management, graphic design, marketing, photojournalism, technical theatre production, ticket services, video documentation, archives/preservation, operations.
Purpose: To offer on-the-job training and experience working alongside professional staff.
Eligibility: Open to all candidates without regard to age, gender or national or ethnic origin.
Level of Study: Professional development
Type: Internship
Value: US$500 stipend, free room and board, access to festival activities, and expense allowance
Length of Study: 3 months
Frequency: Annual
Country of Study: United States of America
No. of awards offered: 31
Application Procedure: See the website www.jacobspillow.org/home/summer-internships.asp
Closing Date: February 28th
Funding: Corporation, foundation, government, individuals
No. of awards given last year: 32
No. of applicants last year: 142

Jacob's Pillow Summer Festival Internship Program

Subjects: Archives/preservation, business, development/individuals, development/institutional, editorial/press, education, graphic design, operations, photojournalism, presenting, production, ticket services, house management and video documentation.
Purpose: To those aspiring to professional careers in arts administration and technical theatre production. Offers on-the-job trainingand experience working alongside professional staff.
Eligibility: Open to all candidates without regard to age, gender, or national or ethnic origin.
Level of Study: Professional development
Type: Internship
Value: A monetary stipend, free room and board and access to festival activities
Length of Study: May 26 - September 3
Frequency: Annual
Country of Study: United States of America
No. of awards offered: 31
Application Procedure: Visit the website www.jacobspillow.org/home/summer-internships.asp for application procedures and more information.
Closing Date: February 6th for priority consideration; March 2nd for consideration
Funding: Corporation, foundation, government, individuals
No. of awards given last year: 31
No. of applicants last year: 180
Additional Information: Interns are selected through a competitive process of written and phone interviews.

JAMES AND GRACE ANDERSON TRUST

32 Wardie Road, Edinburgh, EH5 3LG, Scotland
Tel: (44) 13 1552 4062
Fax: (44) 13 1467 1333
Email: tim.straton@virgin.net
Contact: Mr Tim Straton, Trustee

The James and Grace Anderson Trust funds research into the cure or alleviation of cerebral palsy.

James and Grace Anderson Trust Research Grant

Subjects: Research into cure or alleviation of cerebral palsy.
Purpose: To advance by investigation, research or any other way, knowledge with regard to the causes of cerebral palsy and related conditions and, if possible, curing or alleviating the same.
Level of Study: Research
Type: Grant
Value: Maximum UK £25,000
Length of Study: 1–3 years
Frequency: Dependent on funds available
Country of Study: Scotland
Application Procedure: Application must be made in writing, giving full details of the research being carried out and the anticipated value. A copy of the ethical approval, if granted, should also be included.
Closing Date: April 15th and October 15th
Funding: Private
No. of awards given last year: 7
No. of applicants last year: 35
Additional Information: Grants will not be given to organizations that have no involvement with cerebral palsy

THE JAMES BEARD FOUNDATION

The Beard House, 167 West 12th Street, New York, NY, 10011, United States of America
Tel: (1) 212 627 2308
Email: info@jamesbeard.org
Website: www.jamesbeard.org

It is our mission to celebrate, preserve, nurture American's culinary heritage and diversity in order to elevate the appreciation of our culinary excellence.

James Beard Scholarship

Subjects: Fine cuisine.

Purpose: To fund aspiring culinary professionals.
Level of Study: Professional development
Type: Scholarship
Value: US$20,000 (awarded in US$5,000 increments)
Length of Study: 1–4 years
Frequency: Annual
No. of awards offered: 50
Application Procedure: Supply two letters of reference, mailed with a completed application.
Closing Date: May
Funding: Foundation
Contributor: James Beard Foundation
No. of awards given last year: 50

James Beard Scholarship II

Subjects: Fine cuisine.
Purpose: To offer unstinting help and encouragement to people embracing on a culinary career.
Level of Study: Professional development
Type: Scholarship
Value: US$500–5,000
Length of Study: 1 year
Frequency: Annual
No. of awards offered: 50
Application Procedure: Supply two letters of reference, mailed with a completed application.
Closing Date: May
Funding: Foundation
Contributor: The James Beard Foundation
No. of awards given last year: 50

JAMES COOK UNIVERSITY

Graduate Research School, Townsville, QLD, 4811, Australia
Tel: (61) 7 4781 4575
Fax: (61) 7 4781 6204
Email: researchstudenthelp@jcu.edu.au
Website: www.jcu.edu.au
Contact: Ms Susan Meehan, Manager

James Cook University prides itself on its international reputation for research and discovery and teaching that is enhanced and enlivened by that research activity.

James Cook University Postgraduate Research Scholarship

Subjects: All disciplines.
Purpose: To encourage full-time postgraduate research leading to a Master's or PhD degree.
Eligibility: Open to any student who has attained at least an Upper Second Class (Honours) Bachelor's Degree.
Level of Study: Postgraduate
Type: Scholarship
Value: Australian $20,007 per year
Length of Study: 3 years with a possible additional 6 months in exceptional circumstances for the PhD, or 2 years for the Master's programme
Frequency: Annual
Study Establishment: James Cook University
Country of Study: Australia
No. of awards offered: Up to 12
Closing Date: October 31st

Noel and Kate Monkman Postgraduate Award

Subjects: Marine biology.
Purpose: To encourage full-time study towards an MSc or PhD degree in marine biology.
Eligibility: Open to Australian citizens or those with permanent resident status in Australia who hold, or are expecting to hold, an Upper Second Class (Honours) Degree, or its equivalent, in marine biology or a related science.
Level of Study: Postgraduate
Type: Scholarship
Value: To be determined

397

Length of Study: 3 years for the PhD or 2 years for the Master's programme
Frequency: Dependent on funds available
Study Establishment: James Cook University
Country of Study: Australia
No. of awards offered: 1

Sustainable Tourism CRC – Climate Change PhD Scholarship

Subjects: Impacts of climate change on Great Barrier Reef tourism operators.
Eligibility: Open to the candidates who have achieved Honours 1 or equivalent.
Level of Study: Postgraduate, Research
Type: Scholarship
Value: Australian $19,930 per year
Length of Study: 3 years
Frequency: Annual
No. of awards offered: 1
Application Procedure: Applicants must apply directly to the scholarship provider. Check the website for further details.
Closing Date: October 31st
Contributor: James Cook University

For further information contact:

STCRC Education Program, Sustainable Tourism CRC
Tel: 61 7 5552 9063
Email: Jane@crctourism.com.au
Website: www.crctourism.com.au
Contact: Jane Malady

JAMES MADISON MEMORIAL FELLOWSHIP FOUNDATION

2000 K Street North West, Suite 303, Washington, DC, 20006, United States of America
Tel: (1) 202 653 8700
Fax: (1) 202 653 6045
Email: madison@act.org
Website: www.jamesmadison.gov
Contact: Mr Lewis F Larsen, Director of Programs

The mission of the James Madison Memorial Fellowship Foundation is to strengthen the teaching of the principles, framing and development of the United States of America Constitution in secondary schools.

James Madison Fellowship Program

Subjects: History, political science and education.
Eligibility: Applicants must be citizens of the United States of America.
Level of Study: Graduate
Type: Fellowship
Value: Up to US$24,000
Length of Study: Up to 5 years
Frequency: Annual
Country of Study: United States of America
No. of awards offered: 60 +
Application Procedure: Applications may be downloaded from the Foundation's website.
Closing Date: March 1st
Funding: Foundation, government, private
No. of awards given last year: 65

JAMES PANTYFEDWEN FOUNDATION

9 Market Street, Aberystwyth, Ceredigion, SY23 1DL, Wales
Tel: (44) 19 7061 2806
Fax: (44) 19 7061 2806
Email: pantyfedwen@btinternet.com
Website: www.jamespantyfedwenfoundation.org.uk
Contact: Mr Richard H Morgan, Executive Secretary

James Pantyfedwen Foundation Grants

Subjects: All subjects.

Purpose: To promote mainly postgraduate research.
Eligibility: Open to Welsh nationals, especially those who wish to train as ministers of religion of any denomination. The qualifying criteria for this are defined by the benefactor.
Level of Study: Postgraduate
Type: Grant
Value: Varies, usually linked to the cost of postgraduate tution fees (up to a maximum of UK £7,000)
Length of Study: Up to 3 years
Frequency: Annual
Country of Study: United Kingdom
No. of awards offered: Varies
Application Procedure: Applicants must submit applications on the appropriate forms, accepted on an ongoing basis. Closing date for students in each year is June 30th.
Closing Date: Please contact the organization by June 30th in each year
Funding: Private
Contributor: Exclusive to private investment portfolio
No. of awards given last year: 45
No. of applicants last year: 165

JANSON JOHAN HELMICH OG MARCIA JANSONS LEGAT

Blommeseter, Norderhov, N-3512, Hönefoss, Norway
Tel: (47) 3 213 5465
Fax: (47) 3 213 5626
Email: janlegat@online.no
Website: www.jansonslegat.no
Contact: Mr Reidun Haugen, Manager

Janson Johan Helmich Scholarships and Travel Grants

Subjects: All subjects.
Purpose: To support practical or academic training.
Eligibility: Open to qualified Norwegian postgraduate students with practical experience for advanced study abroad.
Level of Study: Doctorate, MBA, Postgraduate, Professional development, Research
Type: Scholarship
Value: A maximum of Norwegian Krone 100,000
Length of Study: 1 year
Frequency: Annual
Country of Study: Any country
No. of awards offered: 30
Application Procedure: Applicants must complete an application form.
Closing Date: March 15th
No. of awards given last year: 43
No. of applicants last year: 188

JAPAN SOCIETY FOR THE PROMOTION OF SCIENCE (JSPS)

Overseas Fellowship Division, 6 Ichiban-cho, Chiyoda-ku, Tokyo, 102-8471, Japan
Tel: (81) 3263 9094
Fax: (81) 3263 1854
Email: gaitoku@jsps.go.jp
Website: www.jsps.go.jp

The Japan Society for the Promotion of Science (JSPS) is an independent administrative institution, established for the purpose of contributing to the advancement of science in all fields of the natural and social sciences and the humanities. The JSPS plays a pivotal role in the administration of a wide specrum of Japan's scientific and academic programmes.

JSPS Award for Eminent Scientists

Subjects: Humanities, social sciences and natural sciences.
Purpose: To enable Nobel Laureates and other leading scientists to come to Japan for the purpose of associating directly with younger Japanese researchers so as to mentor, stimulate and inspire them to greater achievements.

Eligibility: Foreign researchers such as Nobel laureates, who possess a record of excellent research achievements and who are mentors and leaders in their respective fields are eligible to apply.

Level of Study: Professional development

Type: Award

Value: Business class round-trip air tickets, ¥42,000 as per day stipend and a family allowance of ¥10,000

Length of Study: 1–3 years

Frequency: Annual

Study Establishment: Any eligible host institution (see the website for details)

Country of Study: Japan

No. of awards offered: Approx. 4

Application Procedure: JSPS invites universities and institutions in Japan that wish to invite a Nobel laureate or other leading scientists to their campus to submit an invitation plan. JSPS reviews the plan and decides whether or not to fund the award. JSPS does not accept applications directly. It is the host institution that submits the application and supports the invitee's stay in Japan.

Additional Information: www.jsps.go.jp/english/e-awards/

JSPS Invitation Fellowship Programme for Research in Japan

Subjects: Humanities, social sciences, natural sciences.

Purpose: To enable Japanese scientists to invite their foreign colleagues to Japan to participate in co-operative work and other academic activities. This programme also aims to promote international co-operation in mutual understanding through scientific research.

Eligibility: The candidate must be a researcher with an excellent record of research achievements who, in principle, is employed full time at an overseas research institution and is a citizen of a country that has diplomatic relations with Japan. Senior scientists, university professors and other persons with substantial professional experience are welcome to apply. Japanese applicants must have lived abroad and been engaged in research for over 10 years.

Level of Study: Research

Type: Fellowship

Value: Long-term fellowships: Round-trip air ticket, Monthly stipend ¥369,000, Domestic travel allowance, ¥100,000, Research expense ¥40,000; short-term fellowships: Round-trip air ticket, Per diem ¥18,000, Domestic travel allowance ¥150,000

Length of Study: 14–60 days for short-term and 2–10 months for long-term fellowships

Study Establishment: Any eligible host institution (see the website for details)

Country of Study: Japan

No. of awards offered: 220 short-term and 70 long-term fellowships

Application Procedure: Applications for these programmes must be submitted to JSPS by a host scientist in Japan through the head of his/her university or institution. Foreign scientists wishing to participate in this programme are advised to establish contact with a Japanese or foreign-resident researcher in their field and to ask him/her to submit an application. An application form and all supporting documents must be submitted by the deadline.

Closing Date: September and May for short-term fellowships and September for long-term fellowships

Additional Information: www.jsps.go.jp/english/e-inv/main.htm

JSPS Postdoctoral Fellowships for Foreign Researchers

Subjects: Humanities, social sciences, natural sciences, engineering and medicine.

Purpose: To assist promising and highly qualified young foreign researchers wishing to conduct research in Japan.

Eligibility: Open to citizens of countries that have diplomatic relations with Japan. Applicants must hold a doctoral degree when the fellowship goes into effect which must have been received within the past 6 years

Level of Study: Postdoctorate

Type: Fellowship

Value: Round-trip air ticket, monthly maintenance allowance of ¥364,000, setting-in allowance of ¥200,000 and overseas travel accident and sickness insurance coverage

Length of Study: 2 years but a minimum of 1 year

Frequency: Annual

Study Establishment: Universities and research institutions

Country of Study: Japan

No. of awards offered: Varies

Application Procedure: Applicants must write for details. Application must be submitted to JSPS by the host researcher in Japan.

Closing Date: May and September

Funding: Government

Additional Information: www.jsps.go.jp/english/e-fellow/postdoctoral.htm/#long

JSPS Summer Programme

Subjects: Humanities, social sciences and natural sciences.

Purpose: To provide opportunities for young pre- and postdoctoral researchers from the US, UK, France, Germany and Canada to receive an orientation on Japanese culture and research systems and to pursue research under the guidance of host researchers at Japanese universities and research institutes.

Eligibility: Candidates must hold a doctorate, which must have been received within 6 years prior to April 1st of the year of the summer programme or must be enrolled in a university graduate programme. The candidate should also possess the nationality, citizenship, permanent residence or equivalent status in one of the countries represented by the five designated nominating agencies (i.e. the United States of America, United Kingdom, France, Germany or Canada).

Level of Study: Doctorate

Type: Fellowship

Value: International travel, maintenance allowances (534,000 yen), Domestic Research Trip Allowance (58,500 yen), insurance, research-related expenses at the host Institution (up to 100,000 yen). Hotel room charges at Narita and Tokyo, and meals and accommodation charges at SOKENDAI will be covered separately

Length of Study: 2 months (June–August)

Frequency: Annual

Study Establishment: Eligible host institutes (see the website for details)

Country of Study: Japan

Application Procedure: Candidates must contact the nominating authority in their respective countries for detailed application procedures and consult the website for further details.

Funding: Government

No. of awards given last year: 114

Additional Information: www.jsps.go.jp/english/e-summer/

For further information contact:

Contact: Check website for further details

JAPANESE AMERICAN CITIZENS LEAGUE (JACL)

1765 Sutter Street, San Francisco, CA, 94115, United States of America
Tel: (1) 41 5921 5225
Fax: (1) 41 5931 4671
Email: jacl@jacl.org
Website: www.jacl.org
Contact: Scholarships Officer

The Japanese American Citizens League (JACL) was founded in 1929 to fight discrimination against people of Japanese ancestry. It is the largest and one of the oldest Asian American organizations in the United States of America. The JACL has over 24,500 members in 112 chapters located in 25 states, Washington, DC, and Japan. The organization operates within a structure of eight district councils, with headquarters in San Francisco, CA.

Abe & Esther Hagiwara Student Aid Award

Subjects: All subjects.

Purpose: To provide financial assistance to students who are JACL members.

Eligibility: Open to members of JACL who demonstrate financial needs.

Level of Study: Postgraduate

Type: Scholarship

Value: US$5,000

Frequency: Annual

Application Procedure: See the website.

Closing Date: April 1st
Contributor: Japanese American Citizens League

Mike M. Masaoka Congressional Fellowship

Subjects: Public service.
Purpose: To financially support and develop leaders for public service.
Eligibility: Open to citizens of the United States who are seniors or students of a graduate college.
Level of Study: Postgraduate, Professional development
Type: Fellowship
Value: US$10,000
Length of Study: 3 months
Frequency: Annual
Country of Study: United States of America
Application Procedure: Applicants must send a completed application form and a letter of reference to the JACL national headquarters.
Closing Date: April 15th
Funding: Foundation
Additional Information: Preference will be given to those who have demonstrated a commitment to Asian American issues, particularly those affecting the Japanese American community.

For further information contact:

Japanese American Citizens League Headquarters, Mike M. Masaoka Fellowship,1765 Sutter Street, San Francisco, CA, 94115, United States of America

Norman Y. Mineta Fellowship

Subjects: All subjects.
Purpose: To focus on public policy advocacy as well as programs of safety awareness in the Asian Pacific American (APA) community.
Eligibility: Open to the members of the JACL with 4 year degree from an accredited college or university having excellent writing, analytical, and computer skills.
Level of Study: Postgraduate
Type: Fellowship
Value: US $1,500–2,500 per month
Length of Study: 6–10 months
Application Procedure: Applicants must submit a resume, a sample of writing, and names and contact information for two references to the Washington, DC office of the JACL via email or Fax.
Closing Date: Available until filled
Contributor: State Farm Insurance
Additional Information: Candidates must have ability to take directions and follow through with assignments, must work well with others, and have good interpersonal skills.

For further information contact:

JACL, 1828 L Street, NW Suite 802, Washington, DC, 20036, United States of America
Tel: (1) 202 223 1240
Fax: (1) 202 296 8082
Email: dc@jacl.org
Contact: Floyd Mori, National Director

JAPANESE GOVERNMENT

Embassy of Japan, 112 Empire Circuit, Yarralumla, ACT, 2600, Australia
Tel: (61) 2 6273 3244
Fax: (61) 2 6273 1848
Email: cultural@japan.org.au
Website: www.au.emb-japan.go.jp/
Contact: Ms Eriko Prior, Monbukagakusho Scholarship Co-ordinator

Japanese Government (Monbukagakusho) Scholarships In-Service Training for Teachers Category

Subjects: Teacher training.
Eligibility: Open to Australians under 35 years of age who are university or teacher training graduates currently in active service in primary or secondary schools, or who are on the staff at teacher training institutions or educational administrative institutions. Applicants must

have at least 5 years of experience in their terms of service. University academic staff members should not be selected as grantees.
Level of Study: Postgraduate
Type: Scholarship
Value: Return airfare plus ¥170,000 per month
Length of Study: 18 months
Frequency: Annual
Study Establishment: A Japanese university
Country of Study: Japan
No. of awards offered: 1–2
Application Procedure: Applicants must complete an application form available from the Embassy of Japan in their own country. Applications are not available from the main organization.
Closing Date: March 16th
Funding: Government
No. of awards given last year: 2
No. of applicants last year: 6
Additional Information: Applicants must be willing to study the Japanese language.

Japanese Government (Monbukagakusho) Scholarships Research Category

Subjects: Humanities, social sciences, literature, history, aesthetics, law, politics, economics, commerce, pedagogy, psychology, sociology, music and fine arts, natural sciences, pure science, engineering, agriculture, fisheries, pharmacology, medicine, dentistry and home economics.
Eligibility: Open to Australian graduates under 35 years of age.
Level of Study: Doctorate, Postgraduate
Type: Scholarship
Value: Return airfare plus ¥170,000 per month
Length of Study: 18–24 months
Frequency: Annual
Study Establishment: A Japanese university
Country of Study: Japan
No. of awards offered: Approx. 17
Application Procedure: Applicants must complete an application form available from the Embassy of Japan in their own country. Applications are not available from the main organization.
Closing Date: June 19th
Funding: Government
No. of awards given last year: 15
No. of applicants last year: 50
Additional Information: Applicants must be willing to study the Japanese language.

JEWISH COMMUNITY CENTERS ASSOCIATION (JCCA)

520 8th Avenue, 4th Floor, New York, NY, 10018, United States of America
Tel: (1) 212 532 4949 ext 246
Fax: (1) 212 481 4174
Email: info@jcca.org
Website: www.jccworks.com
Contact: Ms Naomi Marks, Scholarships Co-ordinator

The Jewish Community Centers Association (JCCA) of North America is the leadership network of, and central agency for, over 275 Jewish Community Centers, YM-YWHAs and camps in the United States of America and Canada, which annually serve more than one million members. The Association offers a wide range of services and resources to enable its affiliates to provide educational, cultural and recreational programmes to enhance the lives of North American Jewry. The JCCA is also the United States of America government-accredited agency for serving the religious and social needs of Jewish military personnel, their families and patients in Virginia hospitals through the JWB Chaplains Council.

JCCA Graduate Education Scholarship

Subjects: Social work, Jewish education, health, physical education, recreation, education and non-profit business administration.
Purpose: To provide scholarships for graduate study at the Master's level in areas leading to full-time professional employment at a Jewish Community Center.

Eligibility: Open to applicants who have obtained a BA (Honours) Degree with a grade point average of at least 3.0 and a strong commitment to the Jewish Community Center Movement. It is preferred that applicants have knowledge of Jewish community practices, customs, rituals and organization.
Level of Study: Graduate, MBA
Type: Scholarship
Value: Up to US$10,000 for tuition costs
Length of Study: 1 year, renewable for 1 extra year based on satisfactory academic performance
Frequency: Annual
Country of Study: United States of America or Canada
No. of awards offered: 6–8
Application Procedure: Applicants must submit an application, reference letters, personal statement and transcripts. Application forms and information are available on the website. Applications are available online on: www.jccworks.com
Closing Date: February 1st
Funding: Private
No. of awards given last year: 7
No. of applicants last year: 50
Additional Information: Candidates must make the commitment of working at a Jewish Community Center for a minimum of 2 years following the completion of graduate work.

JEWISH FOUNDATION FOR EDUCATION OF WOMEN

135 East 64th Street, New York, NY, 10065,
United States of America
Tel: (1) 212 288 3931
Fax: (1) 212 288 5798
Email: info@jfew.org
Website: www.jfew.org
Contact: Ms Elizabeth Leiman Kraiem, Executive Director

The Jewish Foundation for Education of Women is a private, nonsectarian organization. It provides scholarship assistance for higher education to women with financial need within a 50-mile radius of New York City through several specific programmes.

Scholarships for Émigrés from the FSU in the Health Professions

Subjects: Medicine, dentistry, dental hygiene, nursing, pharmacy, occupational and physical therapy and physician assistant programmes.
Eligibility: Applicants must be female émigrés from the former Soviet Union who live within a 50-mile radius of New York City and demonstrate financial need.
Level of Study: Graduate
Type: Scholarship
Value: US$5,000 per year
Frequency: Annual
Study Establishment: Schools within a 50-mile radius of New York City
Country of Study: United States of America
No. of awards offered: Approx. 80
Application Procedure: Applicants must request an application in writing from the financial aid office. Application forms are available in mid-March.
Closing Date: May 15th
Funding: Private

JILA (FORMERLY JOINT INSTITUTE FOR LABORATORY ASTROPHYSICS)

440, University of Colorado, Boulder, CO, 80309-0440,
United States of America
Tel: (1) 303 492 7789
Fax: (1) 303 492 5235
Email: jilavf@jila.colorado.edu
Website: www.colorado.edu
Contact: Programme Assistant

JILA's interests are at present research and applications in the fields of laser technology, opto-electronics, precision measurement, surface science and semiconductors, information and image processing, and materials and process science, as well as basic research in atomic, molecular and optical physics, precision measurement, gravitational physics, chemical physics, astrophysics and geophysical measurements. To provide an opportunity for persons actively contributing to these fields, JILA operates the Visiting Fellowship Programme as well as the Postdoctoral Research Associate Programme.

JILA Postdoctoral Research Associateship and Visiting Fellowships

Subjects: Natural sciences.
Purpose: To support additional training beyond the PhD and sabbatical research.
Eligibility: There are no restrictions other than those that might be required by the grant that supports the research.
Level of Study: Postdoctorate, Professional development
Type: Fellowship
Value: Varies
Length of Study: Visiting fellowships are for 4–12 months and Postdoctoral Research Associateships are for 1 year or more
Frequency: Annual
Country of Study: United States of America
No. of awards offered: Varies
Funding: Government
Contributor: Varies

JOHN CARTER BROWN LIBRARY AT BROWN UNIVERSITY

Box 1894, Providence, RI, 02912, United States of America
Tel: (1) 401 863 2725
Fax: (1) 401 863 3477
Email: jcbl_fellowships@brown.edu
Website: www.jcbl.org
Contact: Ms Nan Sumner-Mack, Programme Administration

The John Carter Brown Library, an independently funded and administered institution for advanced research in history and the humanities, is located on the campus of Brown University. The Library supports research focused on the colonial history of the Americas, including all aspects of the European, African and Native American involvement.

Alexander O Vietor Memorial Fellowship

Subjects: European and American maritime history 1450–1800.
Purpose: To assist students conducting research into early maritime history.
Eligibility: Open to scholars engaged in predoctoral, postdoctoral or independent research. Graduate students must have passed their preliminary or general examinations at the time of application.
Level of Study: Doctorate, Postdoctorate, Predoctorate
Type: Fellowship
Value: US$2,000 per month
Length of Study: 2–4 months
Frequency: Annual
Country of Study: United States of America
No. of awards offered: 1
Application Procedure: Applicants must complete an application form. Candidates should write to or email the Director.
Closing Date: January 15th
Funding: Private
No. of awards given last year: 1

Andrew W Mellon Postdoctoral Research Fellowship at Brown University

Purpose: To assist scholars in any area of research related to the Library's holdings.
Level of Study: Postdoctorate, Research
Value: US$4,000 per month
Length of Study: 5–10 months
Frequency: Annual
Study Establishment: The John Carter Brown Library

Country of Study: United States of America
No. of awards offered: Approx. 4
Application Procedure: Applicants must complete an application form. Candidates should write to or email the Director.
Closing Date: January 15th
Funding: Private, government
Contributor: The Andrew W Mellon Foundation and the National Endowment for the Humanities

Center for New World Comparative Studies Fellowship
Subjects: The early history of the Americas from the late 15th century to 1830 and all aspects of the discovery, exploration, settlements and development of the New World.
Purpose: To enable research with a definite comparative dimension relating to the history of the colonial Americas.
Eligibility: Open to scholars engaged in predoctoral, postdoctoral or independent research. Graduate students must have passed their preliminary or general examinations at the time of application.
Level of Study: Doctorate, Postdoctorate, Predoctorate
Type: Fellowship
Value: US$2,000 per month
Length of Study: 2–4 months
Frequency: Annual
Country of Study: United States of America
No. of awards offered: 2
Application Procedure: Applicants must complete an application form. Candidates should write to or email the Director.
Closing Date: January 15th
Funding: Private
No. of awards given last year: 1

Donald L. Saunders Fellowship
Type: Fellowship
Value: $4,000 per month
Length of Study: 5–10 months
Country of Study: United States of America
Closing Date: January 10th

For further information contact:

John Carter Brown Library, Box 1894, Providence, RI, 02912
Tel: (401) 863-2725
Email: JCBL_Fellowships@Brown.edu
Contact: Director

Helen Watson Buckner Memorial Fellowship
Subjects: All aspects of the discovery, exploration, settlement and development of the New World and the related history of Europe and Africa prior to 1825.
Purpose: To assist scholars in any area of research related to the Library's holdings.
Eligibility: Open to scholars engaged in predoctoral, postdoctoral or independent research. Graduate students must have passed their preliminary or general examinations at the time of application.
Level of Study: Postdoctorate, Predoctorate, Research
Type: Fellowship
Value: US$2,000 per month
Length of Study: 2–4 months
Country of Study: United States of America
No. of awards offered: Varies
Application Procedure: Applicants must complete an application form. Candidates should write to or email the Director.
Closing Date: January 15th
Funding: Private
No. of awards given last year: 1

The InterAmericas Fund
Subjects: History of the West Indies and the Carribean basin.
Purpose: To study the history of exploration and discovery.
Type: Funding support
Value: $4,000 per month
Length of Study: 5–10 months
Country of Study: United States of America
Closing Date: January 10th

For further information contact:

John Carter Brown Library, Box 1894, Providence, RI, 02912
Tel: (401) 863-2725
Email: JCBL_Fellowships@Brown.edu
Contact: Director

J.M. Stuart Fellowship
Level of Study: Graduate
Type: Fellowship
Value: $2,000 per month
Length of Study: 2–4 months
Country of Study: United States of America
Closing Date: January 10th

For further information contact:

John Carter Brown Library, Box 1894, Providence, RI, 02912
Tel: (401) 863-2725
Email: JCBL_Fellowships@Brown.edu
Contact: Director

Jeannette D Black Memorial Fellowship
Subjects: The early history of the Americas from the late 15th century to 1830 and all aspects of the discovery, exploration, settlements and development of the New World.
Purpose: To enable research into the history of cartography or a closely related area.
Eligibility: Open to scholars engaged in predoctoral, postdoctoral or independent research. Graduate students must have passed their preliminary or general examinations at the time of application.
Level of Study: Doctorate, Graduate, Postdoctorate, Predoctorate
Type: Fellowship
Value: US$2,000 per month
Length of Study: 2–4 months
Frequency: Annual
Country of Study: United States of America
No. of awards offered: 1
Application Procedure: Applicants must write to, or email the Director.
Closing Date: January 15th
Funding: Private
No. of awards given last year: 1

Library Associates Fellowship
Subjects: All aspects of the discovery, exploration, settlement and development of the New World and the related history of Europe and Africa prior to 1825.
Purpose: To assist scholars in any area of research related to the Library's holdings.
Eligibility: Open to scholars engaged in predoctoral, postdoctoral or independent research. Graduate students must have passed their preliminary or general examinations at the time of application.
Level of Study: Postdoctorate, Predoctorate, Research
Type: Fellowship
Value: US$2,000 per month
Length of Study: 2–4 months
Frequency: Annual
Country of Study: United States of America
No. of awards offered: 1
Application Procedure: Applicants must complete an application form. Candidates should write to, or email the Director.
Closing Date: January 15th
Funding: Private
Contributor: Associates of the John Carter Brown Library

Maury A. Bromsen Fellowship
Subjects: Colonial Spanish American history.
Level of Study: Doctorate, Postdoctorate, Predoctorate
Type: Fellowship
Value: $2,000 per month
Length of Study: 2–4 months
Country of Study: United States of America
Closing Date: January 10th

For further information contact:

John Carter Brown Library, Box 1894, Providence, RI, 02912, United States of America

Tel: (1) (401) 863-2725
Email: JCBL_Fellowships@Brown.edu
Contact: Director

Norman Fiering Fund
Subjects: Library's holdings.
Type: Funding support
Value: $2,000 per month
Length of Study: 2–4 months
Country of Study: United States of America
Closing Date: January 10th

For further information contact:

John Carter Brown Library, Box 1894, Providence, RI, 02912, United States of America
Tel: (1) (401) 863-2725
Email: JCBL_Fellowships@Brown.edu
Contact: Director

Paul W McQuillen Memorial Fellowship
Subjects: All aspects of the discovery, exploration, settlement and development of the New World and the related history of Europe and Africa prior to 1825.
Purpose: To assist scholars in any area of research related to the Library's holdings.
Eligibility: Open to scholars engaged in predoctoral, postdoctoral or independent research. Graduate students must have passed their preliminary or general examinations at the time of application.
Level of Study: Postdoctorate, Research, Predoctorate
Type: Fellowship
Value: US$2,000 per month
Length of Study: 2–4 months
Frequency: Annual
Country of Study: United States of America
No. of awards offered: Varies
Application Procedure: Applicants must complete an application form. Candidates should write to, or email the Director.
Closing Date: January 15th
Funding: Private
No. of awards given last year: 1

R. David Parsons Long-Term Fellowship
Purpose: To study the history of exploration and discovery.
Type: Fellowship
Value: $4,000 per month
Length of Study: 5–10 months
Country of Study: United States of America
Closing Date: January 10th

For further information contact:

John Carter Brown Library, Box 1894, Providence, RI, United States of America
Tel: (1) (401) 863-2725
Email: JCBL_Fellowships@Brown.edu
Contact: Director

Ruth and Lincoln Ekstrom Fellowship
Subjects: The history of women and the family in the Americas prior to 1825, including the question of cultural influences on gender formation.
Purpose: To sponsor historical research.
Eligibility: Open to scholars engaged in predoctoral, postdoctoral or independent research. Graduate students must have passed their preliminary or general examinations at the time of application.
Level of Study: Postdoctorate, Predoctorate, Research
Type: Fellowship
Value: US$2,000 per month
Length of Study: 2–4 months
Frequency: Annual
Country of Study: United States of America
No. of awards offered: 1–2
Application Procedure: Applicants must complete an application form. Candidates should write to, or email the Director.
Closing Date: January 15th

Funding: Private
No. of awards given last year: 1

Touro National Heritage Trust Fellowship
Subjects: Some aspect of the Jewish experience in the Western hemisphere prior to 1830.
Purpose: To sponsor historical research.
Eligibility: Open to graduates of any nationality engaged in predoctoral, postdoctoral or independent research. Applicants must have passed their preliminary or general examinations at the time of application.
Level of Study: Doctorate, Postdoctorate, Predoctorate
Type: Fellowship
Value: US$2,000 per month
Length of Study: 2–4 months
Frequency: Annual
Country of Study: United States of America
No. of awards offered: 1
Application Procedure: Applicants must complete and submit an application form. Candidates should write to or email the Director.
Closing Date: January 15th
Funding: Private
No. of awards given last year: 1
Additional Information: The Touro Fellow will be selected by an academic committee consisting of representatives from Brown University, the American Jewish Historical Society, Brandeis University, the Newport Historical Society and the John Carter Brown Library, as well as a representative of the Executive Committee of the Touro National Heritage Trust. The Touro Fellow must be prepared to participate in symposia or other academic activities organized by these institutions and may be called upon to deliver one or two public lectures.

William R. Hartland Fellowship
Subjects: Early martitime history.
Type: Fellowship
Value: $2,000 per month
Length of Study: 2–4 months
Country of Study: United States of America
Closing Date: January 10th

For further information contact:

John Carter Brown Library, Box 1894, Providence, RI, 02912, United States of America
Email: JCBL_Fellowships@Brown.edu
Contact: Director

JOHN E FOGARTY INTERNATIONAL CENTER (FIC) FOR ADVANCED STUDY IN THE HEALTH SCIENCES

Division of International Training & Research Building 31, Room B2C39, Fogarty International Center, 31 Center Drive, MSC 2220, Bethesda, MD, 20892, United States of America
Tel: (1) 301 496 2075
Fax: (1) 301 594 1211
Email: FICinfo@mail.nih.gov
Website: www.fic.nih.gov
Contact: Program Officer

The John E Fogarty International Center (FIC) for Advanced Study in the Health Sciences, a component of the National Institutes of Health (NIH), promotes international co-operation in the biomedical and behavioural sciences. This is accomplished primarily through long- and short-term fellowships, small grants and training grants. This compendium of international opportunities is prepared by the FIC with the hope that it will stimulate scientists to seek research enhancing experiences abroad.

AIDS International Training and Research Programme (AITRP)
Subjects: Biomedical and behavioural research related to AIDS.
Purpose: To enable scientists from developing countries to increase their proficiency to undertake biomedical and behavioural research

related to AIDS and HIV, related TB infections and to develop these acquired skills in clinical trials, prevention and related research.
Eligibility: Decisions about whom to accept for training are made by the programme directors. All current programme directors have developed collaborative activities with specific countries. The relevant United States programme director should be contacted for country specific information, necessary qualifications, eligibility and application procedures. Scientists from the participating countries are eligible to apply for these training programmes.
Level of Study: Research
Type: Research grant
Frequency: Annual
No. of awards offered: Varies
Application Procedure: Applications are accepted from United States institutions in response to a specific request for applications. Individuals who wish to become trainees must apply to the project director of an awarded grant. Application forms are available from the website.
Closing Date: August 14th
Funding: Government

Fogarty International Research Collaboration Award (FIRCA)

Subjects: Biomedical and behavioural sciences.
Purpose: To foster international research partnerships between NIH supported United States scientists and their collaborators in regions of the developing world.
Eligibility: Open to principal investigators of a United States based NIH sponsored research project grant that will be active for at least 1 year beyond the submission date of the FIRCA application. It is also open to scientists affiliated with public and private research institutions in Africa, Asia, (except Japan, Singapore, South Korea and Taiwan), Central and Eastern Europe, Russia and the Newly Independent States of the Former Soviet Union, Latin America and the non-United States Caribbean, the Middle East and the Pacific Islands except Australia and New Zealand. The United States scientist will apply as principal investigator with a colleague from a single laboratory or research site in an eligible country.
Level of Study: Unrestricted
Value: This program provides funds ($150,000 over three years) to foster international research partnerships between NIH-supported scientists and their collaborators in countries of the developing world
Length of Study: 1–3 years
Frequency: Annual
Study Establishment: The foreign collaborator's research site
Country of Study: Other
No. of awards offered: Approx. 35 depending on funds available
Application Procedure: Applicants must submit applications on the grant application form PHS 398. Special instructions and conditions apply. Please refer to the website for further information.
Closing Date: January 21st, May 21st, and September 21st
Funding: Government

Global Health Research Initiative Program for New Foreign Investigators (GRIP)

Subjects: Medicine.
Purpose: To assist well-trained young investigators to contribute to health care advances in their home countries.
Eligibility: Open to all well-trained young investigators.
Level of Study: Postgraduate
Type: Grant
Value: US$50,000 per year
Length of Study: 5 years
Frequency: Annual
Application Procedure: Application form on request.
Funding: Foundation
Contributor: Fugarty International Center

For further information contact:

Email: butrumb@mail.nih.gov
Contact: Bruce Butrum, Grants Management Officer

John E Fogarty International Research Scientist Development Award

Subjects: Medical research.

Purpose: To forge working relationships between future heads of health research programmes in the United States of America and established researchers in developing countries that will lead to on-going collaborations in the study of health problems of mutual interest.
Eligibility: Applicants must be American citizens or permanent residents, have a doctoral or medical degree, or the equivalent, in a health science field earned within the last 7 years. Applicants must have a demonstrated commitment and competence in health research, and have an invitation from a sponsor affiliated with an internationally recognized research facility in Africa, Asia (except Japan, Singapore, South Korea and Taiwan), Central and Eastern Europe, Russia and the Newly Independent States of the Former Soviet Union, Latin America and the non United States Caribbean, the Middle East and the Pacific Islands except Australia and New Zealand. Applications to work in institutions in Sub-Saharan Africa are especially encouraged. Applicants must have a United States sponsor or mentor at a research institution with ongoing collaborative research funding in one of the eligible countries listed above.
Value: Up to US$50,000 based on the level of experience, an allowance of up to US$20,000 for materials and an administrative supplement of up to US$20,000 during the 3rd year if the candidate is promoted to junior faculty status upon return. An economy class round trip airfare is also provided
Application Procedure: Applicants must refer to the website for further information and application forms.
Closing Date: January 16th

JOHN F AND ANNA LEE STACEY SCHOLARSHIP FUND

National Cowboy Hall of Fame, 1700 North East 63rd Street, Oklahoma City, OK, 73111, United States of America
Tel: (1) 405 478 2250
Email: emuno@nationalcowboymuseum.org
Contact: Mr Ed Muno

In accordance with the will of the late Anna Lee Stacey, a trust fund has been created for the education of young men and women who aim to make art their profession.

John F and Anna Lee Stacey Scholarships

Subjects: Painting and drawing in the classical tradition of western culture.
Purpose: To foster a high standard in the study of form, colour, drawing, painting, design and technique, as these are expressed in modes showing patent affinity with the classical tradition of western culture.
Eligibility: Open to citizens of the United States of America of 18–35 years of age who are skilled in printing and drawing and devoted to the classical or conservative tradition of western culture.
Level of Study: Graduate, Postgraduate, High-School Graduate
Type: Scholarship
Value: A total of approx. US$5,000
Length of Study: 1 year
Frequency: Annual
Country of Study: Any country
No. of awards offered: 1–5
Application Procedure: Applicants must complete and submit an application form with up to 10–35 mm slides of their work. Digital images or slides and completed application forms should be sent by United States of America mail, not rail or air express. Digital images are prefered. Applicants should also enclose a recent photograph, a letter outlining plans and objectives and at least four letters of reference.
Closing Date: February 1st
Funding: Private
Contributor: A bequest from the John F and Anna Lee Stacey Foundation
No. of awards given last year: 5
No. of applicants last year: 100
Additional Information: The Committee does not maintain storage facilities, so applicants must not send slides or any materials before November 1st. Each successful competitor will be required to submit a brief quarterly report together with 35 mm slides or we would prefer

digital images of their work and a more complete report at the termination of the scholarship.

JOHN F. KENNEDY LIBRARY FOUNDATION

Columbia Point, Boston, MA, 02125, United States of America
Tel: (1) 617 514 1624
Fax: (1) 617 514 1625
Email: Kennedy.library@nara.gov
Website: www.jfklibrary. org
Contact: Fellowships Administrator

The John F. Kennedy Library Foundation is a non-profit organization that provides financial support, staffing and creative resources for the John F. Kennedy Presidential Library and Museum whose purpose is to advance the study and understanding of President Kennedy's life and career, and the times in which he lived and to promote a greater appreciation of America's political and cultural heritage, the process of governing and the importance of public service.

Arthur M. Schlesinger, Jr. Fellowship
Subjects: Political science and history.
Purpose: To financially support scholars in the production of substantial work on the foreign policy of the Kennedy years.
Eligibility: Open to citizens of the United States only.
Level of Study: Postgraduate
Type: Fellowships
Value: Up to US$5,000
Frequency: Annual
Country of Study: United States of America
No. of awards offered: Up to 2
Application Procedure: Applicants must submit application form, financial need analysis, essay, reference letters and curriculum vitae.
Closing Date: August 15th
Funding: Foundation
Contributor: Schlesinger Fund
Additional Information: Proposals are invited from all sources, but preference will be given to applicants specializing in the work on the foreign policy of the Kennedy years especially with regard to the western hemisphere, or on Kennedy domestic policy, especially with regard to racial justice and to the conservation of natural resources. Preference is also given to projects not supported by large grants from other institutions.

Ernest Hemingway Research Grants
Subjects: Literature/English/writing, social sciences and humanities.
Purpose: To provide funds for the related costs incurred during research in the Hemingway Collection.
Eligibility: Open to citizens of the United States only.
Level of Study: Postgraduate
Type: Grant
Value: US$200–1,000
Frequency: Annual
Country of Study: United States of America
No. of awards offered: 6
Application Procedure: Applicants must submit application form, financial need analysis, essay, reference letters and curriculum vitae.
Closing Date: November 1st
Funding: Foundation
Contributor: John F. Kennedy Library Foundation
Additional Information: Preference is given to dissertation research by PhD candidates working in newly opened or relatively unused portions of the Collection, but all proposals are welcome and will receive careful consideration.

Kennedy Research Grants
Subjects: Social sciences, criminal justice/criminology, economics, history, political science, library and information sciences, humanities, education, literature/english/writing and architecture.
Purpose: To award a number of research grants in various fields.
Eligibility: Open to citizens of the United States only.
Level of Study: Postgraduate
Type: Grant
Value: US$500–2,500

Frequency: Annual
Country of Study: United States of America
No. of awards offered: 15–20
Application Procedure: Applicants must submit application form, financial need analysis, essay, reference letters and curriculum vitae.
Closing Date: March 15th and August 15th
Funding: Foundation
Contributor: John F. Kennedy Library Foundation

Marjorie Kovler Fellowship
Subjects: Political science.
Purpose: To financially support scholars in the production of a substantial work in the area of foreign intelligence and the presidency or a related topic.
Eligibility: Open to citizens of the United States only.
Level of Study: Postgraduate
Type: Fellowship
Value: US$2,500
Frequency: Annual
Country of Study: United States of America
No. of awards offered: 1
Application Procedure: Applicants must submit application form, financial need analysis, essay, reference letters and curriculum vitae.
Closing Date: March 15th
Funding: Foundation
Contributor: John F. Kennedy Library Foundation

JOHN SIMON GUGGENHEIM MEMORIAL FOUNDATION

90 Park Avenue, New York, NY, 10016, United States of America
Tel: (1) 212 687 4470
Fax: (1) 212 697 3248
Email: fellowships@gf.org
Website: www.gf.org

The John Simon Guggenheim Memorial Foundation is concerned with encouraging and supporting scholars and artists to engage in research in any field of knowledge and creation within the arts. The Foundation was established by United States Senator Simon Guggenheim and his wife as a memorial to their son who died on April 26, 1922.

Guggenheim Fellowships to Assist Research and Artistic Creation (Latin America and the Caribbean)
Subjects: Sciences, humanities, social sciences and creative arts.
Purpose: To further the development of scholars and artists by assisting them to engage in research in any field of knowledge and creation in any of the arts, under the freest possible conditions irrespective of race, colour or creed.
Eligibility: Open to citizens and permanent residents of countries of Latin America and the Caribbean who have demonstrated an exceptional capacity for productive scholarship or exceptional creative ability in the arts.
Level of Study: Professional development, Postdoctorate
Type: Fellowship
Value: Grants will be adjusted to the needs of Fellows, taking into consideration their other resources and the purpose and scope of their plans. The average grant is US$33,000
Length of Study: Ordinarily for 1 year, but in no instance for a period shorter than 6 consecutive months
Frequency: Annual
Country of Study: Any country
No. of awards offered: 36
Application Procedure: Applicants must complete an application form. Further information is available on the Foundation's website.
Closing Date: December 1st
Funding: Private
Contributor: The Foundation
No. of awards given last year: 35
Additional Information: Members of the teaching profession receiving sabbatical leave on full or part salary are eligible for appointment, as are holders of other fellowships and of appointments at research centres. Fellowships are awarded by the Trustees upon nominations made by a committee of selection.

Guggenheim Fellowships to Assist Research and Artistic Creation (USA and Canada)

Subjects: Sciences, humanities, social sciences and creative arts.
Purpose: To further the development of scholars and artists by assisting them to engage in research in any field of knowledge and creation in any of the arts, under the freest possible conditions irrespective of race, colour or creed.
Eligibility: Open to citizens and permanent residents of the United States of America and Canada who have demonstrated an exceptional capacity for productive scholarship or exceptional creative ability in the arts.
Level of Study: Postdoctorate, Professional development
Type: Fellowship
Value: Grants will be adjusted to the needs of Fellows, taking into consideration their other resources and the purpose and scope of their plans. The average grant is US$37,360
Length of Study: Ordinarily for 1 year, but in no instance for a period shorter than 6 consecutive months
Frequency: Annual
Country of Study: Any country
Application Procedure: Applicants must complete an application form. Further information is available on the Foundation's website.
Closing Date: October 1st
Funding: Private
Contributor: The Foundation
No. of awards given last year: 186
Additional Information: Members of the teaching profession receiving sabbatical leave on full or part salary are eligible for appointment, as are holders of other fellowships and of appointments at research centres. Fellowships are awarded by the Trustees upon nominations made by a committee of selection.

JOHNS HOPKINS UNIVERSITY

Bloomberg School of Public Health, Center for Alternatives to Animal Testing, 111 Market Place, Suite 840, Baltimore, MD, 21202, United States of America
Tel: (1) 410 223 1692
Fax: (1) 410 223 1603
Email: admiss@jhsph.edu
Website: www.caat.jhsph.edu
Contact: Grants Co-ordinator

The vision of the Johns Hopkins Center for Alternatives to Animal Testing is to be a leading force in the development and use of reduction, refinement and replacement alternatives in research, testing and education to protect and enhance the health of the public.

CAAT Research Grants

Subjects: Alternatives to current testing methods to replace, reduce and refine the use of animals.
Purpose: To serve as starter grants.
Eligibility: No eligibility restrictions.
Level of Study: Unrestricted
Value: A maximum of US$20,000
Length of Study: 1 year
Frequency: Annual
Country of Study: United States of America
No. of awards offered: Approx. 12
Application Procedure: Applicants must complete a preproposal. After review, selected applicants are invited to submit a full application.
Closing Date: The preproposal deadline is March 15th
Funding: Private
No. of awards given last year: 12
No. of applicants last year: 30

Greenwall Fellowship

Subjects: Biomedical science, ethics, public health, health policy and clinical care.
Purpose: To provide an unparalleled opportunity for fellowship and faculty development training in bioethics and health policy.
Eligibility: Open to applicants who have Doctoral degrees in medicine, nursing, philosophy, law, public health, biomedical sciences, social sciences or a related field.

Level of Study: Postdoctorate
Type: Fellowship
Value: US$82,521
Length of Study: 2 years
Frequency: Annual
Study Establishment: Johns Hopkins University
Country of Study: United States of America
Application Procedure: Applicants must send a cover letter, a personal statement describing why they want to be a Greenwall Fellow, a copy of their curriculum vitae, 3 reference letters, official copies of undergraduate and graduate/professional school transcripts and copies of their written and/or published work.
Closing Date: December 1st

For further information contact:

The John Hopkins Bermer Bioethics Institute, 100 North Charles Street, Suite 740, Baltimore, MS, 21201, United States of America
Email: fellows@ihsph.edu
Contact: Kathy Chen

JOSEPHINE DE KÁRMÁN FELLOWSHIP TRUST

PO Box 3389, San Dimas, CA, 91773, United States of America
Tel: (1) 909 592 0607
Email: info@dekarman.org
Website: www.dekarman.org
Contact: Ms Judy McLain, Secretary

The Josephine De Kármán Fellowship Trust was established in 1954 by the late Dr Theodore von Kármán, world renowned aeronautics expert and teacher, in memory of his sister, Josephine, who passed away in 1951. The purpose of this Fellowship programme is to recognize and assist students whose scholastic achievements reflect Professor von Kármán's high standards.

Josephine De Kármán Fellowships

Subjects: All subjects.
Purpose: To provide financial support to students pursuing their PhD.
Eligibility: Open to candidates with a PhD who will defend his/her dissertation by June. Postdoctoral students are not eligible.
Level of Study: Graduate, Doctorate
Type: Fellowships
Value: US$22,000
Length of Study: 1 year
Frequency: Annual, Fall and Spring semesters
Country of Study: United States of America
No. of awards offered: 10
Application Procedure: Applicants must submit completed application form including transcripts and 2 letters of recommendation before the deadline date.
Closing Date: January 31st
Funding: Foundation
Contributor: Josephine De Kármán Fellowship Trust
Additional Information: Special consideration will be given to applicants in the humanities field.

JUVENILE DIABETES FOUNDATION INTERNATIONAL/THE DIABETES RESEARCH FOUNDATION

120 Wall Street, 19th Floor, New York, NY, 10005-4001, United States of America
Tel: (1) 1-800-533-CURE (2873)
Fax: (1) 212 785 9595
Email: info@jdrf.org
Website: www.jdrf.org
Contact: Grant Adminstrator

JDRF Career Development Award

Subjects: Diabetes: the prevention of diabetes and its recurrence, restoration of normal metabolism and the avoidance of and reversal of complications.

Purpose: To provide salary and research support for exceptional scientists in research related to diabetes who are beginning their careers as junior staff members.
Eligibility: Open to highly qualified researchers of all nationalities, holding a PhD, MD, DMD, DVM or equivalent at a college, university, medical school or other research facility who have directed their expertise to target JDRF research priority areas. Both new and established researchers are supported. Proposals must be for a scientific research project involving the cause, treatment, prevention and/or cure of diabetes and its complications.
Level of Study: Professional development
Type: Award
Value: Maximum of US $150,000 total costs per year for up to 5 years. Indirect costs cannot exceed 10 per cent of total costs
Length of Study: 5 years
Closing Date: Varies. For details see the JDRF website

JDRF Conference Grant

Subjects: Diabetes: the prevention of diabetes and its recurrence, restoration of normal metabolism and the avoidance of and reversal of complications.
Purpose: To support scientific meetings, conferences and workshops relevant to the JDRF's mission.
Eligibility: Open to highly qualified researchers of all nationalities, holding a PhD, MD, DMD, DVM or equivalent at a college, university, medical school or other research facility, who have directed their expertise to target JDRF research priority areas. Both new and established researchers are supported. Proposals must be for a scientific research project involving the cause, treatment, prevention and/or cure of diabetes and its complications.
Level of Study: Professional development
Type: Grant
Value: Up to US$10,000 or above
Closing Date: Varies. For details see the JDRF website

JDRF Innovative Grant

Subjects: Diabetes: the prevention of diabetes and its recurrence, restoration of normal metabolism and the avoidance of and reversal of complications.
Purpose: To support highly innovative basic and clinical research that is at the developmental stage.
Eligibility: Open to highly qualified researchers of all nationalities, holding a PhD, MD, DMD, DVM or equivalent at a college, university, medical school or other research facility, who have directed their expertise to target JDRF research priority areas. Both new and established researchers are supported. Proposals must be for a scientific research project involving the cause, treatment, prevention and/or cure of diabetes and its complications.
Level of Study: Research
Type: Grant
Value: Maximum of US$100,000 in direct cost costs and indirect cost of 10 per cent for a total of US$110,000
Length of Study: 1 year
Closing Date: Varies. For details see the JDRF website

JDRF Postdoctoral Fellowships

Subjects: Diabetes: the prevention of diabetes and its recurrence, restoration of normal metabolism and the avoidance of and reversal of complications.
Purpose: To attract qualified, promising scientists entering their professional careers in diabetes.
Eligibility: Open to highly qualified researchers of all nationalities, holding a PhD, MD, DMD, DVM or equivalent at a college, university, medical school or other research facility, who have directed their expertise to target JDRF research priority areas. Both new and established researchers are supported. Proposals must be for a scientific research project involving the cause, treatment, prevention and/or cure of diabetes and its complications.
Level of Study: Postdoctorate
Type: Fellowship
Value: Includes allowance for travel to scientific meetings (up to $2000 per year), journal subscriptions, books, training courses, etc. The purchase of a personal computer is allowed up to $US 2000 only during Year 1 of the award. Health insurance costs are permissible

Length of Study: 2 years
Closing Date: Varies. For details see the JDRF website

JDRF Regular Research Grant

Subjects: Diabetes: the prevention of diabetes and its recurrence, restoration of normal metabolism and the avoidance of and reversal of complications.
Purpose: To support and fund research to find a cure for diabetes.
Eligibility: Open to highly qualified researchers of all nationalities, holding a PhD, MD, DMD, DVM or equivalent at a college, university, medical school or other research facility, who have directed their expertise to target JDRF research priority areas. Both new and established researchers are supported. Proposals must be for a scientific research project involving the cause, treatment, prevention and/or cure of diabetes and its complications.
Level of Study: Research
Type: Grant
Value: Maximum of US$ 165,000 total costs per year for a period up to 3 years. Indirect costs cannot exceed 10 per cent of direct costs
Length of Study: 3 years
Closing Date: Varies. For details see the JDRF website

KAISER FAMILY FOUNDATION (KFF)

Kaiser Media Fellowship Program, 2400 Sand Hill Road, Menlo Park, CA, 94025, United States of America
Tel: (1) 650 854 9400/234 9220
Fax: (1) 650 854 4800/7465
Email: pduckham@kff.org
Website: www.kff.org
Contact: Penny Duckham, Executive Director

Kaiser Family Foundation (KFF) is a non-profit, private operating foundation that focuses on the major health care issues facing the nation. KFF is an independent voice and source of facts and analysis for policymakers, the media, the health care community and the general public.

The Kaiser Media Fellowships in Health

Subjects: Journalism.
Purpose: To help journalists and commentators do the best possible job of keeping the public informed about health issues at this critical time in the evolution of our health care system.
Eligibility: Open to any journalist, editor or producer specializing in health reporting. The applicants must be citizens of the United States or must work for an accredited US media organization.
Level of Study: Professional development
Type: Fellowship
Value: Up to 10 stipends will be awarded based on the length of the fellowship - up to US$50,000 for a 9-month fellowship. The programme also covers travel costs and computer equipment based on the needs of the project
Length of Study: 9 months
Country of Study: United States of America
Application Procedure: There is no application form. For details of the procedure see the website.
Closing Date: March 3rd
Funding: Foundation
Additional Information: There is no age restriction, but typically fellows must be in the early to mid-career range, with at least 5 years experience as a journalist.

KATHOLIEKE UNIVERSITEIT LEUVEN

Office for International Students and Scholars, Naamsestraat 22, Leuven, 3000, Belgium
Tel: (32) 16 32 42 71
Fax: (32) 16 32 37 73
Email: csb@dir.kuleuven.be
Website: www.kuleuven.be

Situated at the heart of Western Europe, Katholieke Universiteit Leuven has been a centre of learning for almost 6 centuries. Founded in 1425, by Pope Martin V, Katholieke Universiteit Leuven bears the double honour of being the oldest extant Catholic university in the world and the oldest university in the Low Countries.

Doctoral Students Grants for Advanced Doctoral Students
Subjects: All subjects.
Purpose: To encourage fundamental and applied research in all academic disciplines.
Eligibility: Open to doctoral students from non-EEA countries who wish to complete their project at Katholieke
Level of Study: Doctorate
Type: Scholarships
Value: €1,085 per month
Length of Study: 15 months
Frequency: Annual
No. of awards offered: 3
Closing Date: January 31st or September 4th
Contributor: Katholieke Universiteit Leuven

KAY KENDALL LEUKAEMIA FUND

Allington House, 1st Floor, 150 Victoria Street, London, SW1E 5AE, England
Tel: (44) 20 7410 7045
Fax: (44) 20 7410 0332
Email: info@skklf.org.uk
Website: www.kklf.org.uk/
Contact: Ms Helen McLeod, Fund Executive

The Kay Kendall Leukaemia Fund awards grants for research on aspects of leukaemia and for relevant studies on related haematological malignancies. Applications are welcomed for first class research on innovative proposals via the fellowship or project grant routes. Please see website for full details.

Kay Kendall Leukaemia Fund Research Fellowship
Subjects: Aspects of leukaemia or relevant studies on related haematological malignancies.
Purpose: To encourage researchers in the field of leukaemia research to submit applications.
Eligibility: Open to applicants of any nationality intending to work mainly in the United Kingdom. Applicants must hold a recognized higher degree, but need not be medically qualified.
Level of Study: Postdoctorate
Type: Fellowship
Value: Salary and laboratory expenses
Length of Study: Junior (3 years), Intermediate (4 years), Senior (5 years)
Frequency: Annual
Country of Study: United Kingdom
No. of awards offered: 2–3
Application Procedure: Applicants must submit a research proposal form and details of support from the intended United Kingdom institution.
Closing Date: Junior Fellowship (October), Intermediate and Senior Fellowship (April)
Funding: Private
No. of awards given last year: Junior (2), Intermediate (1)

KENNAN INSTITUTE

Woodrow Wilson International Center for Scholars, One Woodrow Wilson Plaza, 1300 Pennsylvania Avenue North West, Washington, DC, 20004-3027, United States of America
Tel: (1) 202 691 4100
Fax: (1) 202 691 4247
Email: kennan@wilsoncenter.org
Website: www.wilsoncenter.org
Contact: Ms Edita Krunkaityte, Program Assistant

The Kennan Institute for Advanced Russian Studies sponsors advanced research on the successor states to the USSR and encourages Eurasian studies with its public lecture and publication programmes, maintaining contact with scholars and research centres abroad. The Institute seeks to function as a forum where the scholarly community can interact with public policymakers.

Kennan Institute Research Scholarship
Subjects: Social sciences and humanities. Research proposals examining topics in Eurasian studies are eligible, with those topics relating to regional Russia, the NIS and contemporary issues especially welcome.
Purpose: To offer support to junior scholars studying the former Soviet Union, allowing them time and resources in the Washington DC area to work on their first published work or to continue their research.
Eligibility: Open to academic participants in the early stages of their career before tenure, or scholars whose careers have been interrupted or delayed. For non-academics, an equivalent degree of professional achievement is expected. The scholarship is open to US citizens or permanent residents only.
Level of Study: Postdoctorate
Type: Scholarship
Value: US$3,300 per month plus research facilities, computer support and some research assistance
Length of Study: 3–9 months
Frequency: Dependent on funds available
Study Establishment: The Kennan Institute
Country of Study: United States of America
No. of awards offered: 5
Application Procedure: Applicants must complete an application form. The application must include a project proposal, publications list, bibliography, biographical data and three letters of recommendation specifically in support of the research to be conducted at the Institute. Applications received by fax or email will not be accepted.
Closing Date: December 1st
Funding: Government
No. of awards given last year: 5
No. of applicants last year: 14

Kennan Institute Short-Term Grants
Subjects: Eurasian studies in the social sciences and humanities. Social sciences and humanities focusing on the former Soviet Union, excluding the Baltic States.
Purpose: To support scholars in need of the academic and archival resources of the Washington, DC area in order to complete their research.
Eligibility: Open to academic participants with a doctoral degree or those who have nearly completed their dissertations. For non-academic participants, an equivalent level of professional development is required. Applicants can be citizens of any country, but must note their citizenship while applying.
Level of Study: Doctorate, Postdoctorate, Postgraduate, Predoctorate, Professional development, Research
Type: Scholarship
Value: US$100 per day
Length of Study: Up to 31 days
Frequency: Dependent on funds available
Study Establishment: The Kennan Institute
Country of Study: United States of America
No. of awards offered: 4 are available to non-United States of America citizens and 4 to citizens of the United States of America
Application Procedure: Applicants must submit a concise description of their research project of 700–800 words, a curriculum vitae, a statement on preferred dates of residence in Washington DC and two letters of recommendation specifically in support of the research to be conducted at the institute. No application form is required for short-term grants.
Closing Date: March 1st, June 1st, September 1st and December 1st
Funding: Government, private
No. of awards given last year: 40
No. of applicants last year: 97

KENNEDY MEMORIAL TRUST

3 Birdcage Walk, Westminster, London, SW1H 9JJ, England
Tel: (44) 20 7222 1151
Fax: (44) 20 7222 7189
Website: www.kennedytrust.org.uk
Contact: Ms Annie Thomas, Secretary

As part of the British national memorial to President Kennedy, the Kennedy Memorial Trust awards scholarships to British postgraduate students for study at Harvard University or the Massachusetts Institute of Technology. The awards are offered annually following a national competition and cover tuition costs and a stipend to meet living expenses.

Kennedy Scholarships

Subjects: All fields of arts, science, social science and political studies.

Purpose: To enable students to undertake a course of study in the United States of America.

Eligibility: Open to resident citizens of the United Kingdom who have been wholly or mainly educated in the United Kingdom. At the time of application, candidates must have spent at least 2 of the last 5 years at a university in the United Kingdom and must either have graduated by the start of tenure in the following year or have graduated not more than 3 years before the commencement of studies. Applications will not be considered from persons already in the United States of America.

Level of Study: Postgraduate

Type: Scholarship

Value: US$22,000 to cover support costs, special equipment and some travel in the United States of America, plus tuition fees and travelling expenses to and from the United States of America

Length of Study: 1 year. In certain circumstances, students who are applying for PhD or 2-year Master's programmes may be considered for extra funding to support a second year of study

Frequency: Annual

Study Establishment: Harvard University and the Massachusetts Institute of Technology (MIT), Cambridge, MA

Country of Study: United States of America

No. of awards offered: 10

Application Procedure: Applicants must submit a form, statement of purpose, references and a letter of endorsement from the applicant's university. Completed applications should be sent via the applicant's university.

Closing Date: November 3rd

Funding: Private

Contributor: Public donation

No. of awards given last year: 10

No. of applicants last year: 163

Additional Information: Scholars are not required to study for a degree in the United States of America, but are encouraged to do so if they are eligible and able to complete the requirements for it.

KIDNEY HEALTH AUSTRALIA

GPO Box 9993, Adelaide, SA, 5001, Australia
Tel: (61) 8 8334 7509
Fax: (61) 8 8334 7540
Email: teresa.taylor@kidney.org.au
Website: www.kidney.org.au
Contact: National Communications Manager

Founded in 1968, the Australian Kidney Foundation's mission is to be recognized as the leading non-profit national organization providing funding for, and taking the initiative in, the prevention of kidney and urinary tract diseases.

Australian Kidney Foundation Biomedical Scholarships

Subjects: Medical and scientific kidney and urology-related research.

Purpose: To provide scholarships for individuals wishing to study full-time for the research degrees.

Eligibility: Open to applicants who are graduates, or proposing to graduate in the current academic year.

Level of Study: Doctorate, Postgraduate

Value: Australian $25,000 for science and Australian $31,000 for medical

Length of Study: Up to 2 years for a Master's by research or up to 3 years for a PhD degree

Frequency: Annual

Closing Date: August 30th

Contributor: Kidney Health Australia

Australian Kidney Foundation Medical Research Grants and Scholarships

Subjects: The functions and disease of the kidney, urinary tract and related organs.

Purpose: To support medical research.

Eligibility: Open to Australian citizens who are graduates of Australian medical schools or overseas graduates who are eligible for Australian citizenship and for registration as medical practitioners in Australia.

Level of Study: Doctorate, Postgraduate

Type: Scholarship

Value: Please contact the organization

Length of Study: Up to 3 years

Frequency: Annual

Study Establishment: Any approved medical centre, university or research institute

Country of Study: Australia

No. of awards offered: Up to 6

Application Procedure: Guidelines at www.kidney.org.au

Closing Date: Grants applications closes on June 30th and Scholarships application on September 30th

Australian Kidney Foundation Seeding and Equipment Grants

Subjects: The functions or diseases of the kidney, urinary tract and related organs, or relevant problems, dialysis, transplantation, organ donation and research.

Purpose: To provide financial support for research projects related to the kidney and urinary tract.

Eligibility: Open to Australian citizens connected with Australian universities or medical centres with requisite research facilities.

Level of Study: Unrestricted

Type: Grant

Value: Up to Australian $15,000 per year

Length of Study: Up to 2 years

Frequency: Annual

Study Establishment: Any medical centre, university or research institute

Country of Study: Australia

No. of awards offered: 30–35

Application Procedure: Applicants must contact the Foundation for details.

Closing Date: June 30th

Investigator Driven Research Grants and Scholars

Purpose: To award investigators who have applied to the NHMRC for funding but have just missed the cut-off mark.

Eligibility: Open to projects that are ranked as worthy of funding.

Type: Scholarship

Frequency: Annual

No. of awards offered: 1

Contributor: Kidney Health Australia

KIDNEY RESEARCH UK

King's Chambers, Priestgate, Peterborough, Cambridgeshire, PE1 1FG, England
Tel: (44) 1733 704658
Fax: (44) 1733 704685
Email: grants@kidneyresearchuk.org
Website: www.nkrf.org.uk
Contact: Mrs Elaine Davies, Grants Manager

The Kidney Research UK aims to advance and promote research into kidney and renal disease. These may include epidemiological, clinical or biological approaches to relevant problems. All research must be carried out in the United Kingdom.

Kidney Research UK Non-clinical Senior Fellowships

Subjects: Renal medicine and related scientific studies.

Eligibility: Open to postdoctoral researchers in the biomedical field with evidence of independent research. Applicants may be of any nationality but project work must be carried out in the United Kingdom.

Level of Study: Research, Postdoctorate, Professional development

Type: Fellowship

Value: Up to UK £375,000 over a maximum of 5 years. Salary will be at the established academic level at the appropriate university scale. Includes a UK £12,000 per year bench allowance for consumables

Length of Study: 3–5 years, subject to review in the 3rd year

Frequency: Annual
Study Establishment: Any institution
Country of Study: United Kingdom
No. of awards offered: Varies
Application Procedure: Applicants must complete an application form available from the Grants Department or website.
Closing Date: November 21st
Funding: Private
Contributor: Public donations
No. of awards given last year: 1
No. of applicants last year: 2
Additional Information: www.kidneyresearchuk.org/content/view/63/90/

Kidney Research UK Research Project and Innovation Grants

Subjects: Renal medicine.
Purpose: To support both basic scientific and clinical research towards improving the understanding of renal disease, its causes, treatment and management.
Eligibility: Open to suitably qualified researchers of any nationality. Work must be carried out in the United Kingdom.
Level of Study: Unrestricted
Type: Project grant
Value: Up to UK £150,000 over 1–3 years for a full research project grant, and up to UK £40,000 over 1–2 years for an innovation grant
Length of Study: 1–3 years
Frequency: Annual
Study Establishment: Any institution
Country of Study: United Kingdom
No. of awards offered: Varies
Application Procedure: Applicants must complete an application form available from the Grants Department or website.
Closing Date: Provisional dates: February 20th, March
Funding: Private
Contributor: Public donations
No. of awards given last year: 14
No. of applicants last year: 59
Additional Information: www.kidneyresearchuk.org/content/view/63/90/

Kidney Research UK Training Fellowships/Career Development Fellowships

Subjects: Renal medicine and related scientific studies.
Purpose: To enable medical or scientific graduates undertake specialized training in renal research.
Eligibility: Open to medical candidates of immediate postregistration to registrar level and to science candidates with a PhD or DPhil and at least 2 years of postdoctoral experience. Project work must be carried out in the United Kingdom.
Level of Study: Postdoctorate, Professional development, Research
Type: Fellowship
Value: Up to £250,000 over a maximum of 3 years. Salary will be at the SHO/Specialist Registrar or the established academic level of the appropriate university scale. The fellowship includes a UK £5,000 per year bench allowance for consumables
Length of Study: 1–3 years, subject to annual review
Frequency: Annual
Study Establishment: Any institution
Country of Study: United Kingdom
No. of awards offered: Varies
Application Procedure: Applicants must complete an application form available from the Grants Department, the website or via email.
Closing Date: November 21st
Funding: Private
Contributor: Public donations
No. of awards given last year: 3
No. of applicants last year: 15
Additional Information: Please check the website www.kidney-researchuk.org/content/view/63/90/

PhD Studentships

Subjects: Renal medicine.
Purpose: To enable postgraduates to start a career in renal medicine by completing a course of training including submitting a PhD thesis.

Eligibility: Open to applicants of any nationality. Work must take place in the United Kingdom.
Level of Study: Postgraduate
Type: Studentship
Value: Up to UK £50,000. University fees are met by the Kidney Research UK and a bench fee is available to the host institution
Length of Study: 3 years, subject to a satisfactory annual report
Frequency: Annual
Study Establishment: Any institution
Country of Study: United Kingdom
No. of awards offered: Varies (only offered to current grant holders)
Application Procedure: Applicants must complete an application form available from the Grants Department or website.
Closing Date: November 28th, provisional date November 26th
Funding: Private
Contributor: Public donations
No. of awards given last year: 1
No. of applicants last year: 8
Additional Information: Those eligible to apply will be contacted directly.

KING'S COLLEGE LONDON

Strand, London, WC2R 2LS, United Kingdom
Tel: (44) 020 7836 5454
Fax: (44) 020 7848 3460
Email: ceu@kcl.ac.uk
Website: www.kcl.ac.uk

King's College is one of the oldest and largest colleges of the University of London with 13,800 undergraduate students and some 5,300 postgraduates in 9 schools of study. It was founded in 1829 as a university college in the tradition of the Church of England.

Australian Bicentennial (Australia) Scholarships and Fellowships

Purpose: To promote scholarship, intellectual links, and mutual awareness and understanding between the United Kingdom and Australia.
Eligibility: An applicant for a scholarship must be registered as a postgraduate student at an Australian tertiary institution, and must have at least an upper second class Honours degree.
Level of Study: Postgraduate
Type: Fellowship/Scholarship
Value: UK £4,000 per year
Frequency: Annual
Application Procedure: The application should include a curriculum vitae, the names of two referees, a statement of the research project (approximately 2 sides of A4) and where it is to be carried out.
Closing Date: March 30th

KOSCIUSZKO FOUNDATION

15 East 65th Street, New York, NY, 10021-6595, United States of America
Tel: (1) 212 734 2130
Fax: (1) 212 628 4552
Email: thekf@aol.com
Website: www.kosciuszkofoundation.org
Contact: Mr Thomas J Pniewski, Director, Cultural Affairs

The Kosciuszko Foundation, founded in 1925, is dedicated to promoting educational and cultural relations between the United States of America and Poland and increasing American awareness of Polish culture and history. In addition to its grants and scholarships, which total more than US$1 million annually, the Foundation presents cultural programmes including lectures, concerts and exhibitions, promotes Polish culture in the United States of America and nurtures the spirit of multicultural co-operation.

Chopin Piano Competition

Subjects: Piano performance of Chopin or other composers.
Purpose: To encourage highly talented students of piano to study and play works of Chopin and other Polish composers.

Eligibility: Open to students between the age of 16 and 22 who are citizens of the United States of America or full-time international students in the United States of America with a valid visa who wish to pursue a career in piano performance.

Level of Study: Unrestricted

Type: Prize

Value: First prize of US$5,000, a second prize of US$2,500 and a third prize of US$1,500. Scholarships may be awarded in the form of shared prizes

Frequency: Annual

Country of Study: United States of America

No. of awards offered: 3

Application Procedure: Applicants must complete an application form, available in December via the Kosciuszko Foundation's Cultural Department. Applications should be marked Chopin Piano Competition.

Closing Date: March 7th

Additional Information: The required repertoire is as follows: Chopin: one Mazurka of the contestant's choice and two major works; Szymanowski: one Mazurka of the contestant's choice; a major work by Bach, excluding The Well-Tempered Clavier; a complete sonata by Beethoven, Hadyn, Mozart or Schubert; a major 19th-century work (including Debussy, Ravel, Prokofiev and Rachmaninoff but excluding those already mentioned); and a substantial work by an American, Polish or Polish-American composer written after 1950. The competition is held on 3 consecutive days in mid-April.

Dr Marie E Zakrzewski Medical Scholarship

Subjects: Medical studies.

Purpose: To fund a young woman of Polish ancestry for the 1st, 2nd or 3rd year of medical studies at an accredited school of medicine in the United States of America.

Eligibility: The applicant must be a woman of Polish descent who is a citizen of the United States of America or a Polish citizen with permanent residency status in the United States of America, entering the 1st, 2nd or 3rd year of studies towards an MD degree with a minimum grade point average of 3.0.

Level of Study: Postgraduate

Type: Scholarship

Value: US$3,500

Frequency: Annual

Study Establishment: An accredited school of medicine in the United States of America

Country of Study: United States of America

No. of awards offered: 1

Application Procedure: Applicants must submit a tuition scholarship application form, a US$25 non-refundable application fee and supporting materials to the Kosciuszko Foundation. Emailed and faxed materials will not be considered.

Closing Date: January 15th

Funding: Private

Additional Information: First preference is given to residents of the state of Massachusetts or former presentees of the federation ball. Qualified residents of New England are considered if no first-preference candidates apply.

Graduate Study and Research in Poland Scholarship

Subjects: All subjects.

Purpose: To enable American students to pursue a course of graduate or postgraduate study and research in Poland for an academic year or semester.

Eligibility: Open to United States of America graduates and postgraduate students who wish to pursue a course of study and research at Institutes of Higher Education in Poland. University faculty members who wish to spend a sabbatical pursuing research in Poland are also eligible. All entrants must have the requisite Polish language ability commensurate with the proposed research project and must be under the supervision of a Polish university academic advisor.

Level of Study: Graduate, Postgraduate

Type: Grant

Value: Stipend for dormitory housing and living expenses

Length of Study: 1 academic year or semester

Frequency: Annual

Country of Study: Poland

No. of awards offered: 13

Application Procedure: Applicants must complete an application form, available in the Autumn, by mail or from the website.

Closing Date: January 15th

Contributor: The Foundation and the Polish Ministry of National Education

Kosciuszko Foundation Tuition Scholarships

Subjects: Polish-American related issues and activities.

Purpose: To provide financial aid to students in the United States of America and Poland.

Eligibility: Open to citizens of the United States of America of Polish descent who are pursuing or Polish citizens who are legal and permanent residents who are pursuing graduate studies in any field at a United States of America Institute of Higher Education, or citizens of the United States of America who are pursuing a major in Polish studies at the graduate level. All entrants must have a grade point average of 3.0.

Level of Study: Graduate

Type: Scholarship

Value: US$1,000–7,000

Length of Study: 1 academic year, renewable for a further academic year

Frequency: Annual

Country of Study: United States of America

No. of awards offered: Varies

Application Procedure: Applicants must write for details.

Closing Date: January 15th

Additional Information: Information and guidelines are available all year round. A student can receive funding through the Tuition Scholarship programme no more than twice. Only one member per immediate family may receive a Tuition Scholarship during a given academic year.

The Kosciuszko Foundation Year Abroad Program

Subjects: Polish language, history, literature and culture.

Eligibility: Open to citizens of the United States of America who are students in an MA or PhD programme, but not at the dissertation level.

Level of Study: Doctorate, Graduate, Postgraduate

Type: Grant

Value: Includes a tuition waiver and a stipend for housing and living expenses

Length of Study: 1 year

Frequency: Annual

Country of Study: Poland

No. of awards offered: Varies

Application Procedure: Applicants must complete an application form, available in the Autumn by mail or from the website.

Closing Date: January 15th

Contributor: Polish Ministry of Education and Sports

No. of awards given last year: 12

Additional Information: Applicants should mention the Year Abroad Program in their request letter and complete a physician's certificate as part of the application procedure.

Marcella Sembrich Memorial Voice Scholarship Competition

Subjects: Polish music.

Purpose: To encourage young singers to study the repertoire of Polish composers and to honour the great Polish soprano, Marcella Sembrich.

Eligibility: Open to all singers preparing for professional careers who are citizens of the United States of America or international full-time students with valid student visas, at least 18 years of age and born after May 13, 1969.

Level of Study: Unrestricted

Type: Scholarship

Value: 1st prize: US$2,000; 2nd prize: US$1,250; 3rd prize: US$750, (1st prize also includes round-trip airfare from New York City to the International Moniuszko competition in Warsaw, recital at the Moniuszko festival and an invitation to perform at the Sembrich Memorial Association (Lake George, NY))

Frequency: Every 3 years

Country of Study: Any country

No. of awards offered: 3

Application Procedure: Applicants must submit a competition application form and a non-refundable fee of US$35 with supporting documents, suggested programme and two copies of an audio cassette recording of approx. 10 min.
Closing Date: January 18th
Funding: Private

The Metchie J E Budka Award of the Kosciuszko Foundation

Subjects: Polish literature from the 14th century to 1939, and Polish history, the state, the nation and the people.
Purpose: To reward outstanding scholarly work in Polish literature, Polish history and Polish-American relations.
Eligibility: Applicants must be graduate students in colleges and universities of United States of America and Doctoral degree recipients from these institutions who apply during, or at the close of, the first 3 years of their postdoctoral scholarly careers.
Level of Study: Doctorate, Graduate
Type: Award
Value: US $3,000
Study Establishment: Colleges and universities of United States of America
Country of Study: United States of America
Application Procedure: Applicants must send four copies of each complete submission together with a cover letter.
Closing Date: July 16th
Funding: Private
Additional Information: Materials to be submitted: two original articles, or comparable material written in English in a form appropriate for publication or published in a refereed scholarly journal, or annotated translations into English from the original Polish of one or more significant works, which fall within the designated guidelines.

The Polish-American Club of North Jersey Scholarships

Subjects: All subjects.
Purpose: To financially aid full-time graduate students in the United States of America.
Eligibility: Applicants must be citizens of the United States of America or permanent residents of Polish descent, active members of the Polish-American Club of North Jersey, have a minimum grade point average of 3.0 and be children or grandchildren of Polish-American Club of North Jersey members.
Level of Study: Postgraduate, Predoctorate
Type: Scholarship
Value: US$5,00 to US$2,000
Length of Study: 1 year
Frequency: Annual
Country of Study: United States of America
Application Procedure: Applicants must complete an application form, available on the website from October to the end of December.
Closing Date: January 15th
Additional Information: Only one member per immediate family may receive a Polish-American Club of North Jersey Scholarship during any given academic year.

THE KRELL INSTITUTE

1609 Golden Aspen Drive, Suite 101, Ames, IA, 50010, United States of America
Tel: (1) 515 956 3696
Fax: (1) 515 956 3699
Email: csgf@krellinst.org
Website: www.krellinst.org
Contact: Rachel Huisman

Krell Institute was founded in 1997. The goal of the Krell Institute has been to provide superior technical resources, knowledge and experience in managing technology-based education and information programmes. They have done just that, developing outstanding fellowship programmes, educational outreach programmes and information management and exchange programmes.

Krell Institute Computational Science Graduate Fellowship Program

Subjects: Computational science.

Purpose: To support highly capable students pursuing graduate study at universities in the United States.
Eligibility: Open to citizens and permanent residents of the United States, undergraduate seniors, 1st and 2nd year graduate student in a PhD programme.
Level of Study: Graduate, Research
Type: Fellowship
Value: Minimum award amount: $45000. Maximum award amount: $50000
Frequency: Annual
Country of Study: United States of America
No. of awards:
Application Procedure: Apply online through the website www.krellinst.org/csgf/application
Closing Date: January 16th
Funding: Government
Contributor: Department of Energy (Office of Science and National Nuclear Security Administration)
No. of awards given last year: 16
No. of applicants last year: 396

THE KURT WEILL FOUNDATION FOR MUSIC

7 East 20th Street, 3rd Floor, New York, NY, 10003, United States of America
Tel: (1) 212 505 5240
Fax: (1) 212 353 9663
Email: kwfinfo@kwf.org
Website: www.kwf.org
Contact: Mr Brady Sansone, Office Manager

The Kurt Weill Foundation for Music is a non-profit, private foundation chartered to preserve and perpetuate the legacies of the composer Kurt Weill (1900–1950) and his wife, singer and actress Lotte Lenya (1898–1981). The Foundation awards grants and prizes, sponsors print and online publications, maintains the Weill-Lenya Research Center and administers Weill's copyrights.

Kurt Weill Foundation for Music Grants Program

Subjects: Any subject related to the perpetuation of Kurt Weill's artistic legacy. This includes performances or recordings of his compositions in their original form, scholarly projects focusing on Kurt Weill and other related activities as outlined in the printed guidelines.
Purpose: To fund projects that aim to perpetuate Kurt Weill's artistic legacy.
Eligibility: There are no eligibility restrictions.
Level of Study: Doctorate, Postdoctorate, Postgraduate, Professional development
Value: For college and university production performances, a maximum of US$5,000; otherwise no restrictions on requested amounts
Frequency: Annual
Country of Study: Any country
No. of awards offered: Varies
Application Procedure: Applicants must complete an application form for all but performances over US$5,000. Guidelines and forms are available from the website or from the Foundation directly.
Closing Date: November 1st. There is no deadline for professional proposals over US$5,000
Funding: Private

Kurt Weill Prize

Subjects: Music theatre of the 20th century.
Purpose: To encourage scholarship focusing on musical theatre in the 20th century.
Eligibility: Open to nationals of any country.
Level of Study: Unrestricted
Type: Prize
Value: US$2,500 for books, US$500 for articles
Frequency: Every 2 years
Country of Study: Any country
No. of awards offered: 2
Application Procedure: Applicants must submit five copies of their published work. Works must have been published within the 2 years preceding the award year.
Closing Date: April 30th
Funding: Private

KUWAIT FOUNDATION FOR THE ADVANCEMENT OF SCIENCE (KFAS)

PO Box 25263, Safat, Kuwait City, 13113, Kuwait
Tel: (965) 242 5912
Fax: (965) 240 3912
Email: prize@kfas.org.kw
Website: www.kfas.org
Contact: Dr Ali A Al-Shamlan, Director General

The Kuwait Foundation for the Advancement of Science (KFAS) aims to support efforts for modernization and scientific development within Kuwait by sponsoring basic and applied research, awarding grants to support and encourage research and awarding grants, prizes and recognition to enhance intellectual development. The KFAS also grants scholarships and fellowships for academic or training purposes, holds symposia and scientific conferences and encourages, supports and develops research projects and scientific programmes.

Islamic Organization for Medical Sciences Prize

Subjects: Medical practice addressing professional and well-documented clinical and laboratory experiments as well as the appropriate documentation of Islamic medical heritage, including Islamic jurisprudence.
Purpose: To support and promote scientific research in the field of Islamic medical sciences.
Level of Study: Unrestricted
Type: Prize
Frequency: Every 2 years
No. of awards offered: 2
Application Procedure: Nominations must be proposed by universities, scientific institutes, international organizations, individuals, past recipients of the prize and academic bodies.
Closing Date: December 31st
Funding: Private
Contributor: KFAS

KFAS Kuwait Prize

Subjects: Basic sciences, applied sciences economics and social sciences, arts and letters and Arabic and Islamic scientific heritage.
Purpose: To recognize the scientific achievements of outstanding Arab and Kuwaiti researchers and scientists worldwide.
Level of Study: Unrestricted
Type: Prize
Value: Kuwaiti Dinar 30,000, which is approx. US$100,000, for each prize. The combined value of the prizes is more than US$1 million
Frequency: Annual
No. of awards offered: 10
Application Procedure: Applicants must apply themselves or through non-political organizations and may also be recommended by search committees.
Closing Date: October 31st
Funding: Private
Contributor: KFAS
No. of awards given last year: 5
No. of applicants last year: 91

LA TROBE UNIVERSITY

Research and Graduate Studies Office, Bundoora Campus, Melbourne, VIC, 3083, Australia
Tel: (61) 3 9479 2971
Fax: (61) 3 9479 1464
Email: c.cocks@latrobe.edu.au
Website: www.latrobe.edu.au/rgso
Contact: Manager, Scholarships & Candidature Research

La Trobe University is one of the leading research universities in Australia. The University has internationally regarded strengths across a diverse range of disciplines. It offers a detailed and broad research training programme and provides unique access to technology transfer and collaboration with end users of its research and training via its Research and Development Park.

Australian Postgraduate Awards

Subjects: Health sciences, humanities, social sciences, science, technology, engineering, law, management and education.

Purpose: To support research leading to Master's or Doctoral degrees.
Eligibility: Open to applicants who have completed at least 4 years of tertiary education studies with a high level of achievement, e.g. a First Class (Honours) Degree or its equivalent at an Australian university. Applicants must be Australian citizens or have permanent resident status. Applicants who have previously held an Australian Government Award (APA, APRA or CPRA) for more than 3 months are not eligible for an APA and applicants who have previously held an Australian Postgraduate Course Award (APCA) may apply only for an APA to support PhD research. The awards may be held concurrently with other non-Australian government awards.
Level of Study: Doctorate, Postgraduate, Research
Type: Award
Value: Australian $20,427 per year full-time, which is tax exempt plus allowances and Australian $10,957 per year part-time, which is taxable plus allowances
Length of Study: 2 years for the Master's and 3 years for the PhD. Periods of study already undertaken towards the degree will be deducted from the tenure of the award
Frequency: Annual
Study Establishment: Bundoora Campus, La Trobe University
Country of Study: Australia
No. of awards offered: 32
Application Procedure: Applicants must write for application kits, available from the school in which the candidate wishes to study. Applications must be submitted in duplicate to the Research and Graduate Studies Office.
Closing Date: October 31st
Funding: Government
No. of awards given last year: 32
Additional Information: Paid work may be permitted for up to a maximum of 8 hours per week for the full-time award or up to 4 hours per week for the part-time award.

David Myers Research Scholarship

Subjects: All subjects.
Eligibility: Open to outstanding individuals of any nationality.
Level of Study: Postgraduate, Research
Type: Scholarship
Value: $22,000 per year, a research support grant of up to $3,000, and a $900 thesis allowance per year
Length of Study: 3 years full-time study for a PhD or 2 years full-time study for a Master's degree
Frequency: Annual
No. of awards offered: 1
Application Procedure: Check website for further details.
Closing Date: October 31st
No. of awards given last year: 1

International Postgraduate Research Scholarships (IPRS)

Subjects: Health sciences, humanities, social sciences, science, technology, engineering, law, management and education.
Purpose: To attract top quality overseas postgraduate students to areas of research in institutes of higher education and to support Australia's research efforts.
Eligibility: Open to suitably qualified overseas graduates (excluding New Zealand) eligible to commence a doctoral or Master's degree by research. The IPRS may be held concurrently with a university research scholarship and applicants for an IPRS are advised to apply for a La Trobe University Postgraduate Research Scholarship (LTUPRS). Applicants who have already commenced a Master's or PhD candidature or applicants for Master's candidature by coursework and a minor thesis are not eligible to apply for an IPRS. IPRSs are awarded on the basis of academic merit and research capacity alone.
Level of Study: Doctorate, Postgraduate, Research
Type: Scholarship
Value: Tuition fees
Length of Study: 2 years for the Master's and 3 years for the PhD
Frequency: Annual
Study Establishment: Bundoora Campus, La Trobe University
Country of Study: Australia
No. of awards offered: 7
Application Procedure: Applicants must submit the application form for international candidates available from the International

Programmes Office. Email: international@latrobe.edu.au for further information.
Funding: Government
Contributor: The Australian government
No. of awards given last year: 6
Additional Information: Applicants in most instances will become members of a research team working under the direction of senior researchers.

La Trobe University Fee Remission Research Scholarship

Purpose: For international students commencing a research doctorate or research Master's degree.
Eligibility: Students who are offered an LTUPS or some other competitive scholarship for living expenses.
Level of Study: Research
Value: Tuition fees waiver
Length of Study: 4 years for doctoral and 2 years for Masters
No. of awards offered: 40
Application Procedure: Please check the website for details.
Closing Date: September 30th
No. of awards given last year: 30
Additional Information: Candidate is liable for overseas student health cover.

La Trobe University Postgraduate Scholarship

Subjects: Education, engineering, health sciences, humanities and social sciences, law, management, science and technology.
Purpose: To provide financial assistance.
Eligibility: Open to applicants of any nationality having qualifications deemed to be equivalent to an Australian First Class (Honours) Degree.
Level of Study: Doctorate, Postgraduate, Research
Type: Scholarship
Value: Approx. Australian $20,427 per year. There is no spouse allowance, but Australian $919 per year is available per dependent child, along with a thesis allowance, partial removal and travel allowance. All amounts are dependent on funds available
Length of Study: Up to 2 years for the Master's and up to 3 years for the PhD
Frequency: Annual
Country of Study: Australia
No. of awards offered: Approx. 59
Application Procedure: Applicants must complete an application form, available directly from the department offering the relevant course of study.
Closing Date: September 30th for overseas applicants and October 31st for Australian citizens and permanent residents
No. of awards given last year: 59

LADY TATA MEMORIAL TRUST

Academic Department of Haematology and Cytogenetics, The Royal Marsden Hospital, Fulham Road, London, SW3 6JJ, United Kingdom
Tel: (44) (0) 20-7235-8281
Fax: (44) (0) 20-7351-6420
Email: daphne@tata.co.uk
Website: www.icr.ac.uk/research/research_sections/ haemato_oncology/4480.shtml

Established in 1932, the Trust has an international advisory committee, based in London, which supports research on Leukaemia worldwide, and spends four-fifths of its income on this initiative.

Lady Tata Memorial Trust Scholarships

Subjects: Leukaemia.
Purpose: To encourage study and research in diseases of the blood, with special reference to leukaemias and furthering knowledge in connection with such diseases.
Eligibility: Open to qualified applicants of any nationality. No restrictions regarding age or country.
Level of Study: Doctorate, Postdoctorate
Type: Scholarship
Value: Ranging between UK £20,000–25,000 per year
Length of Study: Studentship for 2–3 years
Frequency: Annual

Country of Study: Any country
No. of awards offered: Normally 15
Application Procedure: Applicants must submit eight copies of the application, including the application form, summary of proposed research, and two letters of reference.
Closing Date: March 1st
Funding: Private
Contributor: Tata Memorial Trust (India)
No. of awards given last year: 12
No. of applicants last year: 28

For further information contact:

Tata Limited c/o Tata Awards or c/o Mrs Daphne Harris, 18 Grosvenor Place, SWIX 7H5

LAHORE UNIVERSITY OF MANAGEMENT SCIENCES (LUMS)

Opposite Sector U, DHA, Lahore, 54792, Pakistan
Tel: (92) 92 42 5722670 9
Fax: (92) 92 42 5722591
Email: zahoor@lums.edu.pk
Website: www.lums.edu.pk

The Lahore university of Management Sciences is a national university, which aims to provide rigorous academic and intellectual training and a viable alternative to education comparable to leading universities around the world.

Khushhali Bank - USAID Scholarship

Subjects: Management.
Purpose: To support talented students who have a high financial need.
Eligibility: Open to candidates studying at Lahore university of Management Science.
Value: Tuition fees, books and materials, lodging and transportation
Study Establishment: LUMS
Country of Study: Pakistan
No. of awards offered: 21
Application Procedure: A completed application form must be sent.
Closing Date: January 25th
Contributor: Higher Education Commission

Unilever-LUMS MBA Fund for Women

Subjects: Management.
Purpose: To provide financial support for female candidates who aspire for a career in management.
Eligibility: Open to all female candidates from Pakistan.
Level of Study: Postgraduate
Type: Fellowship
Value: 7-year interest-free loan
Length of Study: 2 years
Frequency: Annual
Country of Study: Pakistan
No. of awards offered: 5
Application Procedure: A completed application form must be sent.
Contributor: Unilever Pakistan

LANCASTER UNIVERSITY

Student Services, Lancaster University, Bailrigg, Lancaster LA1 4YW, England
Tel: (44) 1524 594848
Email: studentfunding@lancaster.ac.uk
Website: www.lancs.ac.uk/funding
Contact: Craig Lowe

Lancaster University is a campus university dedicated to excellence in teaching and research, offering a wide range of nationally and internationally recognized postgraduate courses. For updated information on all the University's funding opportunities, please see our website www.lancs.ac.uk/funding

Cartmel College Scholarship Fund

Purpose: To assist prospective students who are unable to obtain adequate grants from other bodies.

Eligibility: Priority given to applicants who are past or present members of Cartmel College.
Level of Study: Postgraduate
Type: Bursary
Value: UK £500–1,000
Length of Study: 1 Year
Frequency: Annual
Application Procedure: Application form available from the Student Services website.
Closing Date: June 1st
Funding: Government

Peel Studentship Trust Award

Subjects: All subjects.
Purpose: To enable students who are unable to secure finance from other sources to study at Lancaster University.
Eligibility: Open to candidates of any nationality who have a place at Lancaster University and who will be over 21 years of age at the commencement of the course.
Level of Study: Postgraduate
Value: UK £1,500
Frequency: Annual
Study Establishment: Lancaster University
Country of Study: United Kingdom
No. of awards offered: 25–30
Application Procedure: Applicants must complete an application form, available on request from the Student Support Office.
Closing Date: June 1st
Funding: Trusts
Contributor: Dowager Countess Eleanor Peel Trust
No. of awards given last year: 25

LANCASTER UNIVERSITY MANAGEMENT SCHOOL

MBA Office, Lancaster, Lancashire, LA1 4YX, England
Tel: (44) 15 2459 4068
Fax: (44) 15 2459 2417
Email: mba@lancaster.ac.uk
Website: www.lums.lancs.ac.uk
Contact: Angela Graves

Lancaster University Management School (LUMS) is one of the only two United Kingdom to business schools have the coveted 6-star (6*) rating for research quality, and has been rated 'excellent' for teaching quality by the Higher Education Funding Council for England and Wales. LUMS is EQUIS-accredited and its MBA programmes are AMBA-accredited and winners of the Association of MBAs Student of the Year Award twice. In the Financial Times MBA rankings 2006, LUMS was placed joint 30th in the world. The Lancaster MBA is ranked 1st in Europe (and 2nd in the world) for the value for money it delivers to its students and alumini.

Lancaster MBA Director's Leadership Scholarships

Subjects: Full-time MBA.
Purpose: To assist exceptional highly motivated candidates to pursue the full-time MBA.
Eligibility: Open to candidates who hold an offer of a place on the Lancaster MBA.
Level of Study: Postgraduate, Full-Time MBA
Type: Scholarship
Value: Up to £5,000
Length of Study: 1 year
Frequency: Annual
Study Establishment: Lancaster University Management School
Country of Study: United Kingdom
No. of awards offered: Up to 5
Application Procedure: Applicants must contact the MBA Office for an application form. Candidates must write a 1,000 words statement.
Closing Date: March 13th
Funding: Private

Lancaster MBA Open Scholarships

Subjects: Full-time MBA.
Purpose: To assist candidates to pursue the full-time MBA.

Eligibility: Open to candidates who already hold an offer of a place or a Lancaster MBA.
Level of Study: Postgraduate, full-time MBA.
Value: Up to £3,000
Length of Study: 1 year
Frequency: Annual
Study Establishment: Lancaster University Management School
Country of Study: United Kingdom
No. of awards offered: Dependent on demand and funds available
Application Procedure: Applicants should contact the MBA Office for an application form. Candidates must write a 1,000 word statement.
Closing Date: March 14th and May 16th (two rounds of selections)
Funding: Private
No. of awards given last year: None
No. of applicants last year: None

LE CORDON BLEU AUSTRALIA

Days Road, Regency Park, SA 5010, Australia
Tel: (61) 618 8346 3700
Fax: (61) 618 8346 3755
Email: australia@cordonbleu.edu
Website: www.lecordonbleu.com

Le Cordon bleu, a global leader hospitality education, provides professional development for existing executives.

The James Beard Foundation Award

Subjects: International Hotel & Restaurant Management.
Purpose: To provide financial assistance.
Level of Study: Postgraduate
Type: Scholarship
Value: Australian $5,000
Frequency: Annual
Country of Study: Australia
Application Procedure: A copy of educational history statement of culinary goals, financial statement and two letters of reference must be submitted.

For further information contact:

The Beard House 167 West 12th Street, New York, NY 10011
Website: www.jamesbeard.org

Le Cordon Bleu Australia Masters in Gastronomy Scholarship

Subjects: Gastronomy.
Purpose: Designed for an individual seeking postgraduate qualifications with a passion for the study of gastronomy or a professional seeking a related career in media and tourism.
Eligibility: Open to the candidates who meet pre-requisites for the Masters programme at Le Cordon bleu Adelaide and speak fluent English.
Level of Study: Postgraduate
Type: Scholarship
Value: $5,000
Length of Study: 18 months of full-time study and 5 years of part-time study
Study Establishment: The University of Adelaide
No. of awards offered: 1
Application Procedure: Check website for further details.

For further information contact:

Website: www.lecordonbleu.com.au

Le Cordon Bleu Master of Arts in Gastronomy Scholarship

Subjects: Gastronomy.
Purpose: To encourage candidates seeking a gastronomy-related career.
Eligibility: Open to those with a passion for anything culinary.
Level of Study: Postgraduate

Type: Scholarship
Value: Varies
Frequency: Annual
Country of Study: Australia
Application Procedure: A completed application form must be submitted.

Le Cordon Bleu Master of Business Administration Scholarship.

Subjects: Hotel and Restaurant management.
Purpose: To help in advancement to senior or corporate management positions.
Eligibility: Open to Hoteliers restaurateurs, industry consultants and aspiring management executives.
Level of Study: Postgraduate
Type: Scholarship
Length of Study: Varies
Frequency: Annual
Country of Study: Australia
Application Procedure: See the website.

New Zealand Guild of Food Writers Scholarship

Purpose: Gastronomy.
Eligibility: Open to applicants who are permanent residents of New Zealand.
Level of Study: Postgraduate
Type: Scholarship
Value: Australian $12,750
Length of Study: 15–18 months
Frequency: Annual
Country of Study: New Zealand
Application Procedure: See the website.
Closing Date: October 27th

LE CORDON BLEU OTTAWA

453 Laurier Avenue East, Ottawa, Ontario, K1N 6R4, Canada
Tel: (1) 613 236 2433
Fax: (1) 888 289 6302
Email: ottawa@cordonbleu.edu
Website: www.lcbottawa.com

Le Cordon Bleu Ottawa Culinary Arts Institute has evolved from a Parisian culinary school, which has international culinary network with more than 30 schools in 15 countries. It has a team of over 80 distinguished Master chefs whose learning is crafted into the course of study. In addition to teaching, Le Cordon Bleu has expanded its activities to include culinary publications, video cassettes, TV series, and cooking equipment.It has incorporated its culinary expertise into the restaurant Le Cordon Bleu Signatures Restaurant and has also developed accessories and table settings with its sister company Pierre Deux–French Country.

Le Cordon Bleu Ottawa Culinary Arts Institute Basic Cuisine Certificate Scholarship

Subjects: Culinary arts.
Eligibility: Open to the career professionals.
Level of Study: Graduate
Type: Scholarship
Value: Full-tuition fees
No. of awards offered: 1

Le Cordon Bleu Paris Certificat De Perfectionnement Professionel En Cuisine Scholarship

Subjects: Cuisine.
Eligibility: Open to the graduates from Le Cordon Bleu Diplôme de Cuisine who have a moderate command of the French language.
Level of Study: Graduate
Value: $2,500, tuition fees only
No. of awards offered: 1
Application Procedure: Check website for further details.

LEAGUE OF UNITED LATIN AMERICAN CITIZENS (LULAC)

2000 L Street NW, Suite 610, Washington DC, 20036, United States of America
Tel: (1) 202 833 6130
Fax: (1) 202 833 6135
Email: scholarships@lnesc.org
Website: www.lulac.org
Contact: Rosa Rosales, National President

League of United Latin American Citizens (LULAC) consists of approximately 115,000 members throughout the United States of America and Puerto Rico. It is the largest and oldest Hispanic organization in the United States of America. LULAC advances the economic condition, educational attainment, political influence, health and civil rights of Hispanic Americans through community-based programmes operating at more than 700 LULAC councils nationwide. The organization involves and serves all Hispanic nationality groups.

LULAC National Scholarship Fund

Subjects: All subjects.
Purpose: To fund Hispanic students attending colleges and universities.
Eligibility: Open to citizens or legal residents of the United States who have applied to or enrolled in a college, university or graduate school.
Level of Study: Postgraduate
Type: Scholarships
Value: US$250–1,000
Frequency: Annual
Country of Study: United States of America
Application Procedure: Applications should be mailed to local council www.lnesc.org
Closing Date: March 31st

LEEDS INTERNATIONAL PIANOFORTE COMPETITION

Piano Competition Office, The University of Leeds, Leeds, LS2 9JT, United Kingdom
Tel: (44) (0) 113 244 6586
Fax: (44) (0) 113 234 6106
Email: pianocompetition@leeds.ac.uk
Website: www.leedspiano.com
Contact: Office Manager

The leeds International Pianoforte competition is a member of the World Federation of International Music competitions. It was founded in 1961 and since then has developed to become the world's greatest piano competition producing prizewinners who have gone onto successful international careers.

Henry Rudolf Meisels Bursary Awards

Subjects: Music.
Purpose: To award competitors accepted in the first stage of the competition.
Eligibility: Open to candidates who are accepted to perform in the first stage of the competition.
Level of Study: Professional development
Type: Scholarship
Value: UK £100
Frequency: Every 3 years
Study Establishment: The University of Leeds
Country of Study: United Kingdom
Application Procedure: Entry by competitive audition. Application forms should be submitted by the closing date.
Closing Date: February 1st
Contributor: Henry Rudolf Meisels Bequest
Additional Information: A non-refundable entrance fee of UK £50 must be paid no later than February 1st.

Leeds International Pianoforte Competition Award

Subjects: Music.
Purpose: To promote the careers of the winners.
Eligibility: Open to young, talented, professional pianists, who were born on or after September 1st, 1979.

Level of Study: Professional development
Type: Scholarship
Value: UK £65,750
Frequency: Every 3 years, Once every 3 years
Study Establishment: University of Leeds
Country of Study: United Kingdom
No. of awards offered: 33
Application Procedure: Application forms, completed in English, and repertoire to be submitted before the closing date.
Closing Date: February 1st
Funding: Individuals, trusts, private, foundation
Contributor: Leeds International Pianoforte Competition
No. of awards given last year: 33
No. of applicants last year: 235
Additional Information: A non-refundable entrance fee of UK £50 must be paid no later than 1st February.

LENTZ PEACE RESEARCH ASSOCIATION (LPRA)

c/o University of Missouri-St Louis, One University Boulevard, St Louis, MO, 63121-4400, United States of America
Tel: (1) 314 516 5798
Fax: (1) 314 516 6757
Email: bob.baumann@umsl.edu
Contact: Mr Robert Baumann, Board Member

The Lentz Peace Research Association, which Theodore F. Lentz founded originally in 1930 as the Character Research Institute, is the oldest continuously operating peace research center in the world.

Theodore Lentz Fellowship in Peace and Conflict Resolution Research

Subjects: International relations.
Purpose: To support research projects in peace and conflict resolution and to enable the recipient to teach an introductory peace studies course in the Fall semester and one course in the Spring semester at the University of Missouri-St Louis.
Eligibility: A completed PhD is required and preference is given to graduates of university programmes in peace studies and conflict resolution. Graduates of political science, international relations and other social science programmes that specialize in peace and conflict resolution are also invited to apply.
Level of Study: Postdoctorate
Type: Fellowship
Value: Approx. US$23,400 plus university benefits plus US$1,000 travel and expense allowance
Length of Study: 9 months
Frequency: Annual
Study Establishment: The University of Missouri-St Louis
Country of Study: United States of America
No. of awards offered: 1
Application Procedure: Applicants must send a curriculum vitae, a letter of application, evidence of completion of the PhD, three letters of recommendation and a research proposal of approximately 750 words to the Center for International Studies.
Closing Date: April 15th
Funding: Private
Contributor: The Lentz Peace Research Association
No. of awards given last year: 1
No. of applicants last year: 10
Additional Information: The fellowship is supported in part by the University of Missouri-St Louis. The Fellow must serve in residence at University of Missouri-St Louis.

LEO BAECK INSTITUTE (LBI)

15 West 16th Street, New York, NY, 10011 6301,
United States of America
Tel: (1) 212 744 6400
Fax: (1) 212 988 1305
Email: lbaeck@lbi.cjh.org
Website: www.lbi.org
Contact: Secretary

The Leo Baeck Institute (LBI) is a research, study and lecture centre, a library and repository for archival and art materials. It is devoted to the preservation of original materials pertaining to the history and culture of German-speaking Jewry.

David Baumgardt Memorial Fellowship

Subjects: Modern intellectual history of German-speaking Jewry.
Purpose: To provide financial support to scholars whose research projects are connected with the writings of Professor David Baumgardt or his scholarly interests.
Level of Study: Postdoctorate, Postgraduate, Doctorate
Type: Fellowship
Value: US$3,000
Length of Study: 1 year
Frequency: Annual
Study Establishment: The Leo Baeck Institute
Country of Study: United States of America
No. of awards offered: 1
Application Procedure: Applicants must submit an application form, a curriculum vitae and a full description of the research project. Doctoral students must submit official transcripts of graduate and undergraduate work, written evidence that they are enrolled in a PhD programme and two letters of recommendation, one by their doctoral adviser and one by another scholar familiar with the work. Postdoctoral candidates must submit evidence of their degree, of which transcripts are not required, and two letters of recommendation from two colleagues familiar with their research.
Closing Date: November 1st
Funding: Private
Contributor: The Leo Baeck Institute
No. of awards given last year: 1
No. of applicants last year: 2

Fritz Halbers Fellowship

Subjects: Culture and history of German-speaking Jewry.
Purpose: To provide financial assistance to scholars whose projects are connected with the culture and history of German-speaking Jewry.
Level of Study: Graduate, Postgraduate, Predoctorate, Doctorate, Postdoctorate
Type: Fellowship
Value: US$3,000
Length of Study: 1 year
Frequency: Annual
Country of Study: United States of America
No. of awards offered: More than 1
Application Procedure: Applicants must submit an application form, curriculum vitae and a full description of the research project. Doctoral students must submit official transcripts of graduate and undergraduate work, written evidence that they are enrolled in a PhD programme and two letters of recommendation, one by their doctoral adviser and one by another scholar familiar with the work. Postdoctoral candidates must submit evidence of their degree, of which transcripts are not required, and two letters of recommendation from two colleagues familiar with their research.
Closing Date: November 1st
Funding: Private
Contributor: The Leo Baeck Institute
No. of awards given last year: 1
No. of applicants last year: 7

LBI/DAAD Fellowship for Research at the Leo Baeck Institute, New York

Subjects: Social, communal and intellectual history of German-speaking Jewry.
Purpose: To provide assistance to students for dissertation research and to academics for writing a scholarly essay or book.
Level of Study: Doctorate, Graduate, Postdoctorate
Type: Fellowship
Value: US$2,000
Length of Study: 1 year
Frequency: Annual
Study Establishment: The Leo Baeck Institute
Country of Study: United States of America
No. of awards offered: 2

Application Procedure: Applicants must submit an application form, a curriculum vitae and a full description of the research project. Doctoral students must submit official transcripts of graduate and undergraduate work, written evidence that they are enrolled in a PhD programme and two letters of recommendation, one by their doctoral adviser and one by another scholar familiar with the work. Postdoctoral candidates must submit evidence of their degree, of which transcripts are not required, and two letters of recommendation from two colleagues familiar with their research.
Closing Date: November 1st
Funding: Private
Contributor: The Leo Baeck Institute
No. of awards given last year: 2
Additional Information: The fellowship holders must agree to submit a brief report on their research activities after the period for which the fellowship was granted.

LBI/DAAD Fellowships for Research in the Federal Republic of Germany

Subjects: Social, communal and intellectual history of German-speaking Jewry.
Purpose: To provide financial assistance to doctoral students conducting research for their dissertation and to academics in the preparation of a scholarly essay or book.
Eligibility: Applicants must be citizens of the United States of America and PhD candidates or recent PhDs who have received their degrees within the preceding 2 years.
Level of Study: Doctorate, Postdoctorate
Type: Fellowship
Value: Up to €975 and travel allowance of €520
Length of Study: 1 year
Frequency: Annual
Country of Study: Germany
No. of awards offered: 1–2
Application Procedure: Applicants must submit an application form, a curriculum vitae and a full description of the research project. Doctoral students must submit official transcripts of graduate and undergraduate work, written evidence that they are enrolled in a PhD programme and two letters of recommendation, one by their doctoral adviser and one by another scholar familiar with the work. Postdoctoral candidates must submit evidence of their degree, of which transcripts are not required, and two letters of recommendation from two colleagues familiar with their research.
Closing Date: November 1st
Funding: Private
Contributor: The Leo Baeck Institute
Additional Information: The fellowship holders must agree to submit a brief report on their research activities upon conclusion of their fellowship. These awards are in conjunction with awards offered by the German Academic Exchange Service (DAAD) in New York, United States of America.

LEPRA

28 Middleborough, Colchester, England, Essex, CO1 1TG, United Kingdom
Tel: (44) 12 0216 700
Fax: (44) 12 0676 2151
Email: lepra@lepra.org.uk
Website: www.lepra.org.uk
Contact: Programmes Department

LEPRA is a health development international organisation working to restore health, home and dignity to people affected by leprosy and other diseases of poverty such as malaria, tuberculosis and HIV/AIDS, among others. LEPRA is currently working in Angola, Brazil, Bangladesh, Guatemala, India, Mozambique, Nepal and Malawi.

Medical Elective Funding and Annual Essay Competition

Subjects: Leprosy.
Purpose: To encourage UK-based medical students wishing to undertake a leprosy assignment overseas.
Eligibility: Students in the UK of any nationality. LEPRA would also like to encourage medical students to apply for the annual essay competition.

Level of Study: Graduate, Postgraduate
Type: Grant
Value: Dependent on funds available and up to UK£1,000 fund for essay competition
Length of Study: Up to 3 years
Study Establishment: As appropriate to the nature of the research or training
Country of Study: Any country
No. of awards offered: Varies
Application Procedure: Applicants must complete a research application pack, available on request. Applications must be submitted using the appropriate forms and should observe the time scales involved in the approval process.
Closing Date: Applications are accepted at any time
Additional Information: Occasionally also funded to physiotherapy students or students taking a BSc in nursing. Please check the website for more details.

For further information contact:

Email: Yasmin_entwistle@lepra.org.uk
Contact: Yasmin Entwistle, Programmes Assistant

LEUKAEMIA FOUNDATION

PO Box 2126, 230 Lutwyche Road, Windsor QLD, 4030, Australia
Tel: (61) 7 3866 4038
Fax: (61) 7 3866 4011
Email: sobrien@leukaemia.org.au
Website: www.leukaemia.org.au
Contact: Susan O'Brien, Mission and Vision Project Officer

The Leukaemia Foundation has offices across Australia and it is the only national non-profit organization dedicated to the care and cure of patients and families living with leukaemia, lymphoma, myeloma and related blood disorders.

Leukaemia Foundation PhD Scholarships

Subjects: Leukaemia.
Purpose: To enhance the knowledge or treatment of haematological malignancies to improve the care of the patients and their families.
Eligibility: Open to candidates who are citizens or permanent residents of Australia.
Level of Study: Doctorate
Type: Scholarships
Value: US$40,000
Frequency: Annual
Country of Study: Australia
No. of awards offered: 4
Application Procedure: Applicants can download the application forms from the website.
Closing Date: September 28th
Funding: Foundation
Contributor: Leukaemia Foundation
Additional Information: All queries should be directed to Dr Anna Williamson, General Manager, Research, Advocacy and Patient Care, Leukaemia Foundation, National Research Program, PO Box 2126, Windsor, Queensland 4030, Australia. Email: awilliamson@leukaemia.org.au

Leukaemia Foundation Postdoctoral Fellowship

Subjects: Leukaemia.
Purpose: To encourage and support young researchers and to foster cutting-edge research to improve the understanding of leukaemia and related malignancies and to benefit patients and families in the short-term or long-term.
Eligibility: Open to candidates who have obtained a PhD no more than 3 years before the closing date for applications. Their PhD must be obtained by December of the year of application.
Level of Study: Postdoctorate
Type: Fellowship
Value: US$100,000
Frequency: Annual
Country of Study: Australia
No. of awards offered: 1

Application Procedure: Applicants can download the application form from the website.
Closing Date: July 28th
Funding: Foundation
Contributor: Leukaemia Foundation
Additional Information: All queries should be directed to Dr Susan O'Brien, Project Officer, Mission and Vision, Leukaemia Foundation, National Research Program, PO Box 2126, Windsor, Queensland 4030, Australia. Email: sobrien@leukaemia.org.au

LEUKAEMIA RESEARCH FUND

43 Great Ormond Street, London, WC1N 3JJ, England
Tel: (44) 20 7405 0101
Fax: (44) 020 7405 3139
Email: info@lrf.org.uk
Website: www.lrf.org.uk

Leukaemia research is devoted exclusively to leukaemia, Hodgkin's disease and other lymphomas, myeloma, myelodysplastic syndromes, aplastic anaemia and the myeloproliferative disorders. We are committed to finding causes, improving and developing new treatments and diagnostic methods as well as supplying free information booklets and answering written and telephone enquiries.

Gordon Piller Studentships
Subjects: All life science disciplines. The research topic must be applicable to blood cancers.
Purpose: To train graduates in life sciences in research and allow them to obtain a PhD degree.
Eligibility: Open to graduates of any nationality who work and reside in the United Kingdom.
Level of Study: Postgraduate
Type: Studentship
Value: Varies
Length of Study: 3 years
Frequency: Annual
Study Establishment: Universities, medical schools and research institutes
Country of Study: United Kingdom
No. of awards offered: 4
Application Procedure: Applicants must be invited to apply and must complete the appropriate form.
Closing Date: Advertised in *Nature* every January
No. of awards given last year: 4

Leukaemia Research Clinical Research Training Fellowships
Subjects: All life science disciplines. The research topic must be applicable to blood cancers.
Purpose: To train registrar grade clinicians in research and allow them to obtain a higher degree.
Eligibility: Open to researchers of any nationality who work and reside in the United Kingdom.
Level of Study: Research
Type: Fellowship
Value: Varies
Length of Study: 3 years
Frequency: 3 times per year
Study Establishment: Universities, medical schools, research institutes and teaching hospitals
Country of Study: United Kingdom
No. of awards offered: Varies
Application Procedure: Applicants must complete an application form.
Closing Date: Varies, available on request

Leukaemia Research Grant Programme
Subjects: All life science disciplines.
Purpose: To give long-term support to research groups studying the causes and treatment of haematological malignancies.
Eligibility: Open to researchers who work and reside in the United Kingdom.
Level of Study: Unrestricted
Type: Research grant

Value: Varies
Length of Study: Varies
Study Establishment: Universities, medical schools, research institutes and teaching hospitals
Country of Study: United Kingdom
No. of awards offered: Varies
Application Procedure: Applicants must complete an application form only after discussion with the Scientific Director.
Closing Date: Available on request

THE LEUKEMIA & LYMPHOMA SOCIETY OF CANADA (LLSC)

936 The East Mall, Toronto, ON, M9B 6J9, Canada
Tel: (1) 416 661 9541
Fax: (1) 416 661 7799
Email: laila.ali@lls.org
Website: www.lls.org/canada
Contact: CEO

The Leukaemia & Lymphoma Society of Canada's mission is to cure leukaemia, lymphoma, Hodgkin's disease and myeloma and to improve the quality of life of patients and their families. Since its founding, the Society has invested millions of dollars in research specifically targeting leukaemia, lymphoma and myeloma.

LLSC Awards
Subjects: Leukaemia, lymphoma (Hodgkin's and non-Hodgkin's) and myeloma.
Purpose: To support peer-reviewed research in leukaemia, lymphoma (Hodgkin's and non-Hodgkin's) and myeloma.
Eligibility: Open to applicants with a faculty appointment at a Canadian university.
Level of Study: Postdoctorate, Research
Type: Research grant
Value: Varies
Length of Study: 1 year. (fellowships are renewable for a further year)
Frequency: Annual
Country of Study: Canada
No. of awards offered: Varies
Application Procedure: Applicants must complete an official application. Applications are available from Deans of Medicine, the LLSC Office, the website, by contacting (1) 877 668 8326 or via email laila.ali@lls.org
Closing Date: February 1st
Funding: Private
No. of awards given last year: 11
Additional Information: A special grant is available for the study of CLL.

LEUKEMIA AND LYMPHOMA SOCIETY

1311 Mamoroneck Avenue, White Plains, NY, 10605, United States of America
Tel: (1) 914 821 8843
Fax: (1) 914 821 8946
Email: researchprograms@lls.org
Website: www.lls.org
Contact: Director of Research Administration

The Leukemia and Lymphoma Society is a national voluntary health agency dedicated to the conquest of leukaemia, lymphoma and myeloma through research. Through its research programme, the Society hopes to encourage and promote research activity of the highest quality. In addition, the Society also supports patient aid, public and professional education and community service programmes.

Career Development Program
Subjects: Leukaemia, lymphoma, Hodgkin's disease and myeloma research.
Purpose: To provide support for individuals pursuing careers in basic, clinical or translational research.
Eligibility: Applications may be submitted by individuals working in domestic or non-profit organizations such as universities, hospitals or

units of state and local governments. International applicants are welcome to apply.
Level of Study: Postdoctorate
Type: Fellowship
Value: US$45,000–110,000 per year
Length of Study: 3–5 years, based on experience and training
Frequency: Annual
Study Establishment: International and domestic non-profit organizations, including hospitals, universities and research institutes
Country of Study: Any country
No. of awards offered: Varies
Application Procedure: Applicants can visit the website for details of the Career Development Award application packet at www.lls.org/cdp
Closing Date: October 1st
Funding: Private

Translational Research Program

Subjects: Leukaemia, lymphoma, Hodgkin's disease and myeloma research.
Purpose: To encourage and provide early stage support for clinical research.
Eligibility: Open to individuals working in domestic or foreign non-profit organizations such as universities, hospitals or units of state and local governments. International applicants are welcome to apply.
Level of Study: Postdoctorate, Research
Value: Up to US$200,000 per year
Length of Study: 3 years, with the possibility of 2 additional years
Frequency: Annual
Study Establishment: International and domestic non-profit organizations, including hospitals, universities and research institutes
No. of awards offered: Varies
Application Procedure: Applicants must contact the Society or visit the website for details.
Closing Date: March 1st
Funding: Private

LEUKEMIA RESEARCH FOUNDATION (LRF)

Research Grants Administrator, Leukemia Research Foundation, 3520 Lake Avenue, Suite 202,, Wilmette, IL, 60091, United States of America
Tel: (1) 847 424 0600, 888 558 5385
Fax: (1) 847 424 0606
Email: Linda@lrfmail.org
Website: www.leukemia-research.org/
Contact: Linda Kabot, Director of Programs

The Leukaemia Research Foundation (LRF) was established in 1946. It aims to conquer leukemia, lymphoma and myelodysplastic syndromes by funding research into their causes and cures and to enrich the quality of life of those touched by these diseases.

LRF New Investigator Research Grant

Subjects: Health and medical sciences, oncology.
Purpose: To enable an investigator to initiate and develop a project sufficiently to obtain continued funding from national agencies.
Eligibility: Open to principal investigators who are members of the staff of a university, hospital or non-profit research institute and deemed eligible by that institution to apply for research grants.
Level of Study: Postgraduate
Type: Grant
Value: Up to US$100,000
Length of Study: 1 year
Frequency: Annual
Country of Study: United States of America
No. of awards offered: 5–10
Application Procedure: Applicants must submit application form, references, self-addressed stamped envelope and 1 paragraph abstract in lay terms.
Closing Date: February 15th
Contributor: Leukaemia Research Foundation

THE LEVERHULME TRUST

Research Awards Advisory Committee, 1 Pemberton Row London, EC4A 3BG, England
Tel: (44) 20 7822 6964
Fax: (44) 20 7822 5084
Email: jcater@leverhulme.org.uk
Website: www.leverhulme.org.uk
Contact: Mrs Bridget Kerr, Grants Officer

The Trust, established at the wish of William Hesketh Lever, makes awards for the support of research and education. The Trust emphasises individuals and encompasses all subject areas.

Leverhulme Trust Emeritus Fellowships

Subjects: All subjects.
Purpose: To assist experienced researchers in the completion of research already begun.
Eligibility: Open to individuals who have retired or who are about to retire. Applicants must hold, or have recently held, teaching and/or research posts in universities or institutions of similar status in the United Kingdom. Applicants must also have an established record of research.
Level of Study: Postdoctorate
Type: Fellowship
Value: Up to UK £20,000 by individual assessment. The awards are to meet incidental costs and do not provide a personal allowance or pension supplementation
Length of Study: 3 months–2 years
Frequency: Annual
No. of awards offered: Approx. 30
Application Procedure: Applicants must complete an application form that is downloadable from the website www.leverhulme.ac.uk
Closing Date: February 5th
Funding: Private
No. of awards given last year: 33
No. of applicants last year: 105

Leverhulme Trust Research Fellowships

Subjects: All subjects.
Purpose: To assist experienced researchers pursuing investigations who are prevented, by routine duties or other causes, from undertaking or completing a research programme.
Eligibility: Open to persons educated in the United Kingdom or the Commonwealth or who are permanent members of the United Kingdom scholarly community and who are normally resident in the United Kingdom. Awards are not normally made to those aged under 30 and are not made to those registered for first or higher degrees, professional or vocational qualifications.
Type: Fellowship
Value: Up to UK £45,000 by individual assessment
Length of Study: 3 months–2 years
Frequency: Annual
Country of Study: Any country
No. of awards offered: Approx. 90
Application Procedure: Applicants must complete an application form that is accessible from the website www.leverhulme.ac.uk
Closing Date: November 10th
Funding: Private
No. of awards given last year: 92
No. of applicants last year: 603

Leverhulme Trust Study Abroad Studentships

Subjects: All subjects.
Purpose: To fund advanced study or research at a centre of learning.
Eligibility: Open to candidates who have obtained a first degree from a United Kingdom university at the time of application or who are able to show evidence of equivalent education in the United Kingdom. Applicants must also have been educated at a school or schools in the United Kingdom or other parts of the Commonwealth. They must be normally resident in the United Kingdom and under 30 years of age on June 1st. If older than this, candidates must make a strong and appropriate case for special consideration. Students wishing only to improve knowledge of modern languages are not eligible.
Level of Study: MBA, Research, Postdoctorate, Postgraduate, Predoctorate, Professional development, Doctorate, Graduate

Type: Studentship
Value: UK £17,000 per year plus return airfare and other allowances at the discretion of the Committee
Length of Study: 1 or 2 years
Frequency: Annual
Study Establishment: Any centre of learning
No. of awards offered: Approx. 20
Application Procedure: Applicants must complete an application form that is downloadable from the website www.leverhulme.ac.uk
Closing Date: January 8th
Funding: Private
No. of awards given last year: 17
No. of applicants last year: 113

LEWIS & CLARK COLLEGE

0615 SW Palatine Hill Road, Portland, OR, 97219 7899, United States of America
Tel: (1) 503 768 7090
Email: sfs@lclark.edu
Website: www.lclark.edu
Contact: The Bursar

The College was founded by Presbyterian pioneers as Albany Collegiate Institute in 1867. The school moved to the former Lloyd Frank estate in Portland's southwest hills in 1942 and took the name Lewis & Clark College.

Mary Stuart Rogers Scholarship

Subjects: Teacher education.
Purpose: To support postgraduate students by funding study at Master's degree or PhD level.
Level of Study: Postgraduate
Value: US$3,000 for a single academic year
Frequency: Annual
Study Establishment: Lewis & Clark College
Country of Study: United States of America
No. of awards offered: Variable
Application Procedure: Applicants must contact the Department of Teacher Education.

LEWIS WALPOLE LIBRARY

PO Box 1408, Farmington, CT, 06034, United States of America
Tel: (1) 860 677 2140
Fax: (1) 860 677 6369
Email: walpole@yale.edu
Website: www.library.yale.edu/Walpole
Contact: Dr Margaret K Powell, The Librarian

The Lewis Walpole Library is a research centre for the study of all aspects of English 18th-century studies and is a prime centre for the study of Horace Walpole and Strawberry Hill.

Lewis Walpole Library Fellowship

Subjects: 18th-century British studies including history, literature, theatre, drama, art, architecture, politics, philosophy or social history.
Purpose: To fund study into any aspect of the Library's collection of 18th-century British prints, paintings, books and manuscripts.
Eligibility: Applicants should normally be pursuing an advanced degree or must be engaged in postdoctoral or equivalent research.
Level of Study: Doctorate, Postdoctorate, Postgraduate, Research
Type: Fellowship
Value: US$1,800 plus travel expenses and on-site accommodation
Length of Study: 1 month
Frequency: Annual
Study Establishment: Lewis Walpole Library, Yale University
Country of Study: United States of America
No. of awards offered: More than 2
Application Procedure: Applicants must submit a curriculum vitae, a brief research proposal of up to three pages and two confidential letters of recommendation.
Closing Date: January 15th
Funding: Private
No. of awards given last year: 13
No. of applicants last year: 35

LIBRARY AND INFORMATION TECHNOLOGY ASSOCIATION (LITA)

50 East Huron Street, Chicago, IL, 60611 2795, United States of America
Tel: (1) 312 280 4270
Fax: (1) 312 280 3257
Email: lita@ala.org
Website: www.lita.org
Contact: Grants Management Officer

The Library and Information Technology Association (LITA) provides a forum for discussion, an environment for learning and a programme for action on the design, development and implementation of automated and technological systems in the library and information science field.

LITA/Christian Larew Memorial Scholarship in Library and Information Technology

Subjects: Library and information science, with an emphasis on information technology.
Purpose: To encourage the entry of qualified people into the library and information technology field.
Eligibility: Open to students at the Master's degree level in an ALA-accredited programme.
Level of Study: Postgraduate
Type: Scholarship
Value: US$3,000
Frequency: Annual
Study Establishment: An ALA-accredited programme
Country of Study: United States of America
No. of awards offered: 1
Application Procedure: Candidates must send a statement indicating their previous experience in the field and what he or she can bring to the profession. Application forms and instructions are available from the website.
Contributor: The Electronic Business and Information Services (EBIS), a unit of Baker & Taylor, Inc
Additional Information: Factors considered in awarding the scholarship are academic excellence, leadership, evidence of commitment to a career in library automation and information technology and prior activity and experience in those fields.

LITA/LSSI Minority Scholarship in Library and Information Technology

Subjects: Library science and information technology.
Purpose: To encourage the entry of qualified persons into the library automation field.
Eligibility: Open to citizens of the United States of America or Canada who are qualified members of a principal minority group: American Indian or Alaskan Native, Asian or Pacific Islander, African American or Hispanic.
Level of Study: Postgraduate
Type: Scholarship
Value: US$2,500
Frequency: Annual
Study Establishment: An ALA-accredited programme
Country of Study: United States of America
No. of awards offered: 1
Application Procedure: Applicants must write, phone or visit the website for application forms.
Funding: Commercial
Contributor: Library Systems and Service, Inc

LITA/OCLC Minority Scholarship in Library and Information Technology

Subjects: Library information science, with an emphasis on library automation.
Purpose: To encourage the entry of qualified minority persons into the library automation field who plan to follow a career in that field and who evidence potential leadership in, and a strong commitment to, the use of automated systems in libraries.
Eligibility: Open to citizens of the United States of America or Canada who are qualified members of a principal minority

group: American Indian or Alaskan Native, Asian or Pacific Islander, African American or Hispanic.

Level of Study: Postgraduate
Type: Scholarship
Value: US$3,000
Frequency: Annual
Study Establishment: An ALA-accredited programme
Country of Study: United States of America
No. of awards offered: 1
Application Procedure: Applicants must write, phone or visit the website for application forms.
Funding: Commercial
Contributor: Online Computer Library Center
Additional Information: Factors considered in awarding the scholarship are academic excellence, leadership, evidence of commitment to a career in library automation and information technology and prior activity and experience in those fields.

LIBRARY COMPANY OF PHILADELPHIA

1314 Locust Street, Philadelphia, PA, 19107, United States of America
Tel: (1) 215 546 3181
Fax: (1) 215 546 5167
Email: jgreen@librarycompany.org
Website: www.librarycompany.org
Contact: Fellowship Office

Founded in 1731, the Library Company of Philadelphia was the largest public library in America until the 1850s and contains printed materials on aspects of American culture and society in that period. It is a research library with a collection of 500,000 books, pamphlets, newspapers and periodicals, 75,000 prints, maps and photographs and 150,000 manuscripts.

Library Company of Philadelphia and Historical Society of Pennsylvania Research Fellowships in American History and Culture

Subjects: 18th- and 19th-century American social and cultural history, African American history, literary history or the history of the book in America.
Purpose: To offer short-term fellowships for research in residence in their collections.
Eligibility: The fellowship supports both postdoctoral and dissertation research. The project proposal should demonstrate that the Library Company and/or the Historical Society of Pennsylvania has a primary source central to the research topic. Candidates are encouraged to enquire about the appropriateness of a proposed topic before applying.
Level of Study: Doctorate, Postdoctorate
Type: Fellowship
Value: US$2,000
Length of Study: 1 month
Frequency: Annual
Study Establishment: An independent research library
Country of Study: United States of America
No. of awards offered: Usually 30–35
Application Procedure: Applicants must send five copies each of a curriculum vitae, a description of the proposed project of 2–4 pages in length and a letter of reference.
Closing Date: March 1st. Fellows may take up residence at any time from the following June to May of the next year
Funding: Private
Contributor: The Andrew W Mellon Foundation, the Barra Foundation, the Albert M Greenfield Foundation and the McLean Contributionship
No. of awards given last year: 34
No. of applicants last year: 150
Additional Information: Fellows will be assisted in finding reasonably priced accommodation. International applications are especially encouraged since two fellowships, jointly sponsored with the Historical Society of Pennsylvania, are reserved for scholars whose residence is outside the United States of America. A partial catalogue of the Library's holdings is available through the website. This programme includes fellowships offered by the Library Company's programme in Early American Economy and Society and by the Balch Institute for Ethnic studies.

Library Company of Philadelphia Dissertation Fellowships

Subjects: 18th- and 19th-century American social, cultural and literary history, pre-1860 American economic and business history.
Purpose: To promote scholarship by offering long-term dissertation fellowships.
Eligibility: The fellowship supports dissertation research in the collections of the Library Company and other Philadelphia repositories.
Level of Study: Doctorate
Type: Fellowship
Value: US$10,000
Length of Study: 4.5 months (one semester)
Frequency: Annual
Study Establishment: An independent research library
Country of Study: United States of America
No. of awards offered: 4
Application Procedure: Applicants must send five copies each of a curriculum vitae, a description of the proposed project of 2–4 pages in length, two letters of recommendation and a relevant writing sample of up to 24 pages in length. Candidates are encouraged to enquire about the appropriateness of a proposed topic before applying.
Closing Date: March 1st. Fellows may take up residence for either the following Fall or the Spring semester
Funding: Private
Contributor: Albert M Greenfield Foundation
No. of awards given last year: 4
No. of applicants last year: 21
Additional Information: Further information can be found on the website, which also includes fellowships offered by the Library Company's programme in early American economy and society.

Library Company of Philadelphia Postdoctoral Research Fellowship

Subjects: 18th- and 19th-century American social, cultural and literary history.
Purpose: To promote scholarship by offering long-term postdoctoral and advanced research fellowships.
Eligibility: The fellowship supports both postdoctoral and advanced research in the collections of the Library Company and often Philadelphia repositories. Applicants must hold a doctoral degree.
Level of Study: Postdoctorate, Research
Type: Fellowship
Value: US$20,000
Length of Study: 4.5 months (1 semester)
Frequency: Annual
Study Establishment: An independent research library
Country of Study: United States of America
No. of awards offered: 4
Application Procedure: Applicants must send seven copies of a curriculum vitae, a description of the proposed project of 2–4 pages in length, two letters of recommendation and a relevant writing sample of up to 24 pages in length. Candidates are encouraged to enquire about the appropriateness of a proposed topic before applying.
Closing Date: November 1st. Fellows may take up residence for either the following Fall or the Spring semester
Funding: Government, private
Contributor: National Endowment for the Humanities
No. of awards given last year: 4
No. of applicants last year: 25
Additional Information: Two of the fellowships are offered by the Library Company's programme in early American economy and society. Two are supported by the National Endowment for the Humanities.

LIFE SCIENCES RESEARCH FOUNDATION (LSRF)

Lewis Thomas Laboratories, Princeton University, Washington Road, Princeton, NJ, 08544, United States of America
Tel: (1) 609 258 3551
Email: sdirenzo@princeton.edu
Website: www.lsrf.org
Contact: Assistant Director

The Life Sciences Research Foundation (LSRF) solicits monies from industry, foundations and individuals to support postdoctoral fellowships in the life sciences. The LSRF recognizes that discoveries and the application of innovations in biology for the public's good will depend upon the training and support of the highest quality young scientists in the very best research environments. The LSRF awards fellowships across the spectrum of life sciences: biochemistry, cell, developmental, molecular, plant, structural, organismic population and evolutionary biology, endocrinology, immunology, microbiology, neurobiology, physiology and virology.

LSRF 3-Year Postdoctoral Fellowships

Subjects: Biological and life sciences.
Purpose: To offer research support for aspiring scientists.
Eligibility: Open to researchers of any nationality, who are graduates of medical or graduate schools in the biological sciences and who hold an MD or PhD degree. Awards will be based solely on the quality of the individual applicant's previous accomplishments and on the merit of the proposal for postdoctoral research.
Level of Study: Postdoctorate
Type: Fellowship
Value: US$50,000 per year. The salary scale begins at US$33,000 for a 1st-year postdoctoral Fellow and a 5 per cent raise thereafter. The Fellow will control expenditure of the remainder. It can be used for fringe benefits, travel to the host institution, travel to visit the sponsor and to the LSRF annual meeting. However, its main purpose is to support the Fellow's research expenses
Length of Study: 3 years
Frequency: Annual
Study Establishment: Appropriate research institutions
No. of awards offered: 16–18
Application Procedure: Electronic submission only. See website.
Closing Date: October 1st
Funding: Private
No. of awards given last year: 16
No. of applicants last year: 820
Additional Information: LSRF Fellows must carry out their research at non-profit institutions. The fellowship cannot be used to support research that has any patent commitment or other kind of agreement with a commercial profit-making company.

LIGHT WORK

316 Waverly Avenue, Syracuse, NY 13244, United States of America
Tel: (1) 315 443 1300
Fax: (1) 315 443 9516
Email: jjhoone@syr.edu
Website: www.lightwork.org
Contact: Jessica Heckman

Light Work is an artist-run space that focuses on providing direct support for artists working in photography through its Artist-in-Residence Program, exhibitions, publications, and online permanent collection.

Light Work Artist-in-Residence Program

Subjects: Photography and digital imaging.
Purpose: To support and encourage the production of new work by emerging and mid-career artists.
Eligibility: Open to artists of any nationality working in photography with experience and demonstrable, serious intent in the field. Students are not eligible.
Level of Study: Professional development
Type: Residency
Value: US$4,000 stipend plus a darkroom and apartment
Length of Study: 1 month, non-renewable
Frequency: Annual
Country of Study: United States of America
No. of awards offered: 12–15
Application Procedure: Applicants must send a letter of intent describing in general terms the project or type work they would like to accomplish while in residence. In addition, 20 slides of work or proof prints, a curriculum vitae, and a short statement about the work must be included with a stamped addressed envelope for the return of materials. There are no application forms.
Closing Date: Applications are accepted at any time

Funding: Government, private
No. of awards given last year: 12
No. of applicants last year: 300
Additional Information: Participants in the residency program are expected to use their month to pursue their own projects: photographing in the area, printing for a specific project or book, etc. Artists are not obligated to teach at our facility, though we hope that the artists are friendly and accessible to local artists. Work produced by the Artist-in-Residence will also be published in Light Work's publication *Contact Sheet*.

LINK FOUNDATION

C/O Binghamton University Foundation, PO Box 6005, Binghamton, NY, 13902 6005, United States of America
Email: thompson@ist.ucf.edu
Website: www.binghamton.edu
Contact: Cheryl Dimick

The Link Foundation was established in 1953 to perpetuate and enhance the recognized Link legacy of technical leadership and excellence established by the founders in their fields of interest.

Advanced Simulation and Training Fellowships

Purpose: To support research in the field of flight training and to other qualifying doctoral students studying in the simulation and training field at US universities
Level of Study: Doctorate, Postdoctorate, Research
Type: Fellowships
Value: US$25,000
Length of Study: 1 year
Frequency: Annual
Study Establishment: University of Central Florida
Country of Study: United States of America
No. of awards offered: 5
Application Procedure: Application forms can be downloaded from the website.
Closing Date: January 17th
Funding: Foundation
Contributor: Administered by the Institute for simulation and training at the University of Central Florida

Energy Fellowships

Subjects: Energy.
Purpose: To foster education and innovation in the area of societal production and utilization of energy.
Eligibility: Open to candidates working towards a PhD in an academic institution.
Level of Study: Doctorate
Type: Fellowships
Value: US$50,000
Length of Study: 2 years
Frequency: Annual
Study Establishment: Any accredited academic institution
Country of Study: United States of America or Canada
Application Procedure: Applicants can download the application cover sheet from the website. The completed cover sheet along with project description, endorsement letter, letters of recommendation, budget and a curriculum vitae is to be submitted.
Closing Date: December 1st
Additional Information: Fellowships are only tenable at United States and Canadian Universities.

For further information contact:

Thayer School of Engineering Dartmouth College, Hanover NH, 03755, United States of America
Contact: Dr Lee R Lynd, Manager, Link Foundation Energy Programs

THE LIONEL MURPHY FOUNDATION

GPO Box 4545, Sydney, NSW 1044, Australia
Tel: (61) 9223 5151
Fax: (61) 9223 5267
Email: lmf@wran.com.au
Website: http://lionelmurphy.anu.edu.au/

The Lionel Murphy Foundation was established in 1986 to provide postgraduates scholarship opportunities for the study of law and/or science, or other disciplines where there are opportunities for some common good in Australia or overseas.

The Lionel Murphy Australian Postgraduate Scholarships

Subjects: All subjects. Please check website for details.
Purpose: To support candidates who wish to study further and wish to use their knowledge and ability to further common goal.
Eligibility: Open to Australian Citizens only.
Level of Study: Postgraduate
Type: Scholarship
Value: Australian $15,000 (may vary)
Length of Study: 1 year
Frequency: Annual
Study Establishment: Australian tertiary institution
Country of Study: Australia
No. of awards offered: 1
Application Procedure: See the website.
Closing Date: September 1st
Contributor: Private donations
No. of awards given last year: 1
No. of applicants last year: Approx. 20

The Lionel Murphy Overseas Postgraduate Scholarships

Subjects: All subjects. Check website for details.
Purpose: To support candidates in postgraduate work who wish to use their knowledge and ability to further the common goal.
Eligibility: Open to Australian citizens only.
Level of Study: Postgraduate
Type: Scholarship
Value: Australian $30,000 (may vary)
Length of Study: 1 year
Frequency: Annual
Study Establishment: Overseas tertiary institution
Country of Study: Any country
Application Procedure: A completed application form must be submitted.
Closing Date: September 1st
Contributor: Private donations
No. of awards given last year: 1
No. of applicants last year: Above 60

THE LISTER INSTITUTE OF PREVENTIVE MEDICINE

PO Box 1083, Bushey, HERTS, WD23 9AG, England
Tel: (44) 01923 801886
Fax: (44) 01923 801886
Email: secretary@lister-institute.org.uk
Website: www.lister-institute.org.uk
Contact: The Administrator

The Lister Institute of Preventive Medicine, originally founded in 1891, operates as a medical research charity whose sole function is to award research prizes to young clinical and non-clinical scientists working in the biological and biomedical sciences. The prizes are awarded on the basis of the quality of the proposed research and its potential implications.

Lister Institute Research Prizes

Subjects: Biomedical and biological science.
Purpose: To promote biomedical excellence in the United Kingdom through the support of postdoctoral scientific research into the causes and prevention of disease in man, thereby enhancing the state of public health.
Eligibility: Open to residents of the United Kingdom who have obtained a PhD, DPhil, MD or MBBCh, with membership of the Royal College of Physicians. Candidates must have a minimum of 3 and a maximum of 10 years postgraduate research experience. Applicants must have guaranteed support for the period of the award. The bulk of the work should be United Kingdom-based.
Level of Study: Postdoctorate, Research
Type: Research prize

Value: UK £200,000 to be spent in support of the recipient's research for a period of 3 years. The only restriction is 'no personal salaries'
Length of Study: 5 years
Frequency: Annual
Study Establishment: An employing United Kingdom university, research institute unit, hospital or charity laboratory
Country of Study: United Kingdom
No. of awards offered: 3–4
Application Procedure: Applicants must complete and submit an application form, curriculum vitae and two letters of reference.
Closing Date: December 5th
Funding: Private
Contributor: Investment income
No. of awards given last year: 4
No. of applicants last year: 48
Additional Information: Research topics are of the applicant's own choosing, but are primarily laboratory-based and targeted at generating understanding and underpinning knowledge through fundamental research. Epidemiological, bioinformatics and small clinical projects may also be considered but not social research. Projects are assessed on scientific merit and potential. The awards are personal and are transferable within the United Kingdom.

THE LONDON GOODENOUGH ASSOCIATION OF CANADA

PO Box 5896, Station A, Toronto, ON, M5W 1P3, Canada
Email: lgac@lgac.ca
Website: www.lgac.ca
Contact: Brian Cardie

The London Goodenough Association of Canada (LGAC) is an association of Canadians who lived as graduate students at Goodenough College in Mecklenburgh Square, London. The LGAC offers member events and provides a Scholarship Programme for Canadian graduate students studying in London and staying in London House or William Goodenough, the Goodenough College residence halls.

London Goodenough Association of Canada Scholarship Program

Subjects: All subjects.
Purpose: To support Canadian nationals who wish to pursue their higher studies in London.
Eligibility: Open to candidates who are full-time students enrolled in an accredited graduate programme in London or undertaking theses research in London while enrolled elsewhere.
Level of Study: Postgraduate, Research
Type: Scholarships
Value: Canadian $8,400 each
Frequency: Annual
Study Establishment: The London Goodenough Association of Canada
Country of Study: United Kingdom
No. of awards offered: 6 or more
Application Procedure: Application form can be downloaded from the website. Candidates must also arrange to have all post-secondary institution transcripts and 3 letters of reference sent to the address below.
Closing Date: January 11th
Funding: Foundation, individuals
Additional Information: For further information contact Dr Kathleen McCrone at the above address.

THE LONDON MATHEMATICAL SOCIETY

De Morgan House, 57-58 Russell Square, London, WC1B 4HS, England
Tel: (44) 020 7637 3686
Fax: (44) 020 7323 3655
Email: lms@lms.ac.uk
Website: www.lms.ac.uk
Contact: Mr P Cooper, Executive Secretary

The UK national learned society for the promotion and extension of mathematical knowledge, by means of publishing, grants, meetings and contribution to national debate on mathematics, research and education.

Cecil King Travel Scholarship

Subjects: All areas of mathematical research. Proposals must describe the intended programme of work and the benefits to be gained from the visit.
Purpose: To enable a young mathematician of outstanding promise to spend a period of 3 months undertaking study or reserach overseas.
Eligibility: Nationals of the UK or Republic of Ireland, having recently completed a doctoral degree at a UK university.
Level of Study: Postdoctorate, Postgraduate
Type: Scholarship
Value: Up to £5000
Length of Study: 3 months
Frequency: Annual
Study Establishment: University or research institute
Country of Study: Outside the United Kingdom
No. of awards offered: 1
Application Procedure: Application forms are available on request from the society or can be downloaded from the website.
Closing Date: February
Funding: Trusts
Contributor: Cecil King Memorial Fund
No. of awards given last year: 1
No. of applicants last year: 5
Additional Information: For complete details about the Scholarship check the website: www.lms.ac.uk

LONDON METROPOLITAN UNIVERSITY

Admissions Office, 166-220 Holloway Road, London, N7 8DB,
United Kingdom
Tel: (44) 20 7133 4200
Fax: (44) 20 7133 4202
Email: scholarships@londonmet.ac.uk
Website: www.londonmet.ac.uk

London Metropolitan University is one of Britain's largest universities, which offers a wide variety of courses in a huge range of subject areas. The University aims to provide education and training that will help students to achieve their potential and London to succeed us a world city.

Cannon Collins Scholarship

Subjects: Public administration.
Purpose: To provide financial support and accommodation to international students in the centre of London.
Eligibility: Open to nationals of Botswana, Lesotho, Malawi, Mozambique, Namibia, South Africa, Zambia and Zimbabwe who have been offered admission to the University.
Level of Study: Postgraduate
Type: Scholarship
Value: Full-fee or half-fee waiver and support in the form of stipend, fares and books
Frequency: Annual
Study Establishment: London Metropolitan University
Country of Study: United Kingdom
Application Procedure: Application should be sent to the Canon Collins Trust and the Trust will forward it to the university. Please see the website www.londonmet.ac.uk/how to apply. Applications that have been emailed or faxed or those that have been received after the deadline will not be considered.
Closing Date: May 31st or October 31st
Funding: Trusts
Contributor: Cannon Collins Educational Trust and Department of Applied Social Sciences

For further information contact:

Canon Collins Educational Trust for Southern Africa, PO Box 34692, Groote Schuur, 7937 Cape Town, South Africa
Website: www.londonmet.ac.uk/scholarships

ISH/London Metropolitan Scholarship Scheme

Subjects: All subjects.
Purpose: To support international students in the centre of London.

Eligibility: Open to students from Afghanistan, Algeria, Armenia, Botswana, Cameroon, Cuba, Democratic people's Republic of Korea, East Timor, Gambia, Iran, Libya, Nepal, Tanzania, Tibet, Uganda, Uzbekistan, Vietnam and Zimbabwe who have been offered admission to the University.
Level of Study: Postgraduate
Type: Scholarship
Value: Free tuition and accommodation
Length of Study: 1–2 years
Frequency: Annual
Study Establishment: London Metropolitan University
Country of Study: United Kingdom
Application Procedure: Please see the website www.londonmet.ac.uk/courses. Applications that have been emailed or faxed or those that have been received after the deadline will not be considered.
Closing Date: May 31st and October 31st
Contributor: International Students House (ISH) and London Metropolitan University

For further information contact:

Scholarship Section, c/o Student Recruitment Services, London Metropolitan, City Campus, 133 whitechapel High Street, London, E1 7QA, United Kingdom

The Katrina Mihaere Scholarship

Subjects: Sports Management.
Purpose: To honour the memory of Katrina Mihaere, a former London Metropolitan Women's Tennis team member.
Eligibility: Open to all women tennis players who have been offered admission to the University, with an excellent track record in Women's sports.
Level of Study: Postgraduate
Type: Scholarship
Value: Full tuition and accommodation
Frequency: Annual
Study Establishment: London Metropolitan University
Country of Study: United Kingdom
Application Procedure: Please see the website www.londonmet.ac.uk/how to apply. Applications that have been emailed or faxed or those that have been received after the deadline will not be considered.
Closing Date: May 31st and October 31st

For further information contact:

Email: i.jennings@londonmet.ac.uk
Website: www.londonmet.ac.uk/scholarships
Contact: Ian Jennings, Sports Manager

Savoy Educational Trust Scholarships

Subjects: Hospitality and Tourism.
Purpose: To financially assist students wishing to pursue students in the field of Hospitality and Tourism.
Eligibility: Open to applicants from any country in the world who have been offered admission to the University.
Level of Study: Postgraduate
Type: Bursary
Value: Up to UK £9,000
Frequency: Annual
Study Establishment: London Metropolitan University
Country of Study: United Kingdom
No. of awards offered: 1
Application Procedure: Please see the website www.londonmet.ac.uk/how to apply. Applications that have been emailed or faxed or those that have been received after the deadline will not be considered.
Closing Date: 31st May and October 31st
Funding: Trusts
Contributor: Savoy Educational Trust

For further information contact:

Scholarship Department, c/o Student Recruitment Services, Room 210, London Metropolitan University, London, E1 7NT, United Kingdom
Website: www.londonmet.ac.uk/scholarships

LONDON SCHOOL OF ECONOMICS (LSE)

Asia Research Centre, Houghton Street, London, WC2A 2AE,
United Kingdom
Tel: (44) 020 7955 7388
Fax: (44) 020 7107 5285
Email: c.s.lee2@lse.ac.uk
Website: www.lse.ac.uk
Contact: Chris Soo-Jeong Lee, Centre Manager

London School of Economics (LSE) was founded in 1895 by Beatrice and Sidney Webb. LSE has an outstanding reputation for academic excellence. LSE is a world class centre for its concentration of teaching and research across the full range of the social, political and economic sciences.

CR Parekh Fellowship

Subjects: Poverty, inequality, human development and social exclusion, quality of public life, regional disparities, identities – gender, ethnicity, language, economy and environment, political structures and processes, constitutional debates.
Purpose: To encourage research that is of social, economic, political and constitutional concern to India.
Eligibility: Open to established Indian scholars who are below 40 years of age and hold a PhD or comparable qualifications and experience.
Level of Study: Doctorate, Research
Type: Fellowship
Value: UK £1,200 per month
Length of Study: 3 months
Frequency: Annual
Country of Study: United Kingdom
Application Procedure: Applications should include a curriculum vitae and an outline of proposed research and the names and addresses of 2 referees who are familiar with their work, to be contacted by the chairman.
Closing Date: January 13th
Additional Information: Applications will not be accepted via email or fax.

Sir Ratan Tata Fellowship

Subjects: Poverty, inequality, human development and social exclusion, quality of public life, regional disparities, identities – gender, ethnicity, language, economy and environment.
Purpose: To encourage research on contemporary social and economic concerns of South Asia.
Eligibility: Open to candidates from SAARC region and who hold a PhD or comparable qualifications and experience.
Level of Study: Research
Type: Fellowship
Value: UK £1,500 per month
Length of Study: 6–8 months
Frequency: Annual
Country of Study: United Kingdom
Application Procedure: Applications should include a curriculum vitae and an outline of proposed research and the names and addresses of 2 referees who are familiar with their work, to be contacted by the Chairman.
Closing Date: January 19th
Additional Information: The fellowship is not intended for students registered for a degree or diploma, nor is it intended for senior academics. Applications will not be accepted via email or fax.

LONDON STRING QUARTET FOUNDATION

8 Woodlands Road, Romford, London, RM1 4HD, England
Tel: (44) 1708 761423
Fax: (44) 1708 761423
Email: info@playquartet.com
Website: www.playquartet.com
Contact: General Manager

The London String Quartet Foundation is a registered charity whose purpose is to promote the discovery and development of talent and audiences for the string quartet. The main activity of the Foundation is organizing the triennial London International String Quartet Competition.

London International String Quartet Competition

Subjects: Musical performance.
Purpose: To encourage young string quartets to develop further on the world stage and take part in this prestigious competition.
Eligibility: There are no restrictions except that each musician in the quartet must be under 35 years of age at the date of the final.
Level of Study: Unrestricted
Type: Award
Value: Prizes total UK £27,500, and are split into five different awards of differing amounts and a menu of development prizes for three prize winners. Concerts are also organized for the first three prize winners
Frequency: Every 3 years
Country of Study: Any country
No. of awards offered: 7
Application Procedure: Applicants must complete an application form, available on the website.
Closing Date: September 1st in the year preceding the award
Funding: Individuals, commercial, foundation, private, trusts

LOREN L ZACHARY SOCIETY FOR THE PERFORMING ARTS

2250 Gloaming Way, Beverly Hills, CA, 90210, United States of
America
Tel: (1) 310 276 2731
Fax: (1) 310 275 8245
Email: info@zacharysociety.org
Website: www.zacharysociety.org
Contact: Mrs Nedra Zachary, Director, National Vocal Competition

The Loren L Zachary Society for the Performing Arts was founded in 1972 by the late Dr Loren L Zachary and Nedra Zachary. The purpose of the organization is to help further the careers of young opera singers by providing financial assistance. The National Vocal Competition, now in its 37th year, has helped over 100 singers to embark on international careers.

Loren L Zachary National Vocal Competition for Young Opera Singers

Subjects: Operatic singing.
Purpose: To assist in the development of the careers of young opera singers through competitive auditions and monetary awards.
Eligibility: Open to female singers between 21–33 years of age and male singers between 21–35 years of age who have completed operatic training and are fully prepared to pursue professional operatic stage careers. Applicants must reside in the United States of America, Mexico or Canada. Applicants who have, or have had, a 2 year contract in a European opera house are not eligible.
Level of Study: Professional development
Type: Competition
Value: US$12,000 for the top winner. Approx. US$58,000 is distributed among the finalists and the minimum award is US$1,000–$2,000
Frequency: Annual
Study Establishment: must be thoroughly trained and be ready to pursue an operatic career
Country of Study: Any country
No. of awards offered: 10
Application Procedure: Applicants must complete an application form accompanied by a proof of age and an application fee of US$35. For application forms and exact dates, singers should send a stamped addressed business-sized envelope to the Society in November. Faxed requests will not be accepted. Applications and rules may be obtained by visiting www.zacharysociety.org
Closing Date: The deadline for the New York preliminary auditions is in January and the Los Angeles deadline is in March
Funding: Individuals, private
No. of awards given last year: 10
No. of applicants last year: 250
Additional Information: Applicants must be present at all phases of the auditions. Recordings are not acceptable. Preliminary and semifinal auditions take place in New York in February, and in Los Angeles

in March. The grand finals and awards distribution occurs on May 31st, 2008 in Los Angeles.

LOS ALAMOS NATIONAL LABORATORY (LANL)

PO Box 1663, MS P219, Los Alamos, NM, 87545, United States of America
Tel: (1) 505 667 4866
Fax: (1) 505 665 6932
Email: bmontoya@lanl.gov
Website: www.lanl.gov

Los Alamos National Laboratory (LANL) is the largest institution in Northern New Mexico with more than 9,000 employees plus approximately 650 contractor personnel. From its origins as a secret Manhattan Project Laboratory, Los Alamos has attracted world-class scientists and applied their energy and creativity to solving the nation's most challenging problems.

Los Alamos Graduate Research Assistant Program
Subjects: Technical and scientific disciplines.
Purpose: To provide students with relevant research experience while they are pursuing a graduate degree.
Level of Study: Doctorate, Research
Type: Research
Value: US$33,300–44,600, including benefits, travel and moving expenses
Length of Study: 3–12 months
Frequency: Annual
Closing Date: Continuous
Additional Information: For further inquiries contact Brenda Montoya, 505/667 4866, bmontoya@lanl.gov

LOUGHBOROUGH UNIVERSITY

Leicestershire, LE11 3TU, United Kingdom
Tel: (44) 1509 263171
Email: international-office@lboro.ac.uk
Website: www.lboro.ac.uk
Contact: The International Office

With 3,000 staff and 12,000 students Loughbrough, with its impressive 410 acre campus, is one of the largest university's in the UK. Our mission is to increase knowledge through research, provide the highest quality of educational experience and the widest opportunities for students, advance industry and the profession, and benefit society.

Business School Scholarships
Subjects: Finance, international and marketing management.
Level of Study: Postgraduate
Type: Scholarship
Value: UK £1,000
Length of Study: 1 year
Frequency: Annual
Study Establishment: Loughborough University
Country of Study: United Kingdom
No. of awards offered: 28
Application Procedure: See website.

For further information contact:

Email: msc.management@lboro.ac.uk

Design and Technology Scholarships
Subjects: Design and technology.
Level of Study: Postgraduate
Type: Scholarship
Value: All tuition fees and agreed maintenance costs
Frequency: Annual
Study Establishment: Loughborough University
Country of Study: United Kingdom
Application Procedure: See website.

For further information contact:

Email: r.i.campbell@lboro.ac.uk

Eli Lilly Scholarship
Subjects: Chemistry.
Level of Study: Postgraduate
Type: Scholarship
Value: UK £1,000
Length of Study: 1 year
Frequency: Annual
Study Establishment: Loughborough University
Country of Study: United Kingdom
No. of awards offered: 1
Application Procedure: See website.

For further information contact:

Email: l.e.child@lboro.ac.uk

ESPRC Studentships
Subjects: Chemistry.
Level of Study: Postgraduate
Type: Studentship
Value: All tuition fees and maintenance grant up to UK £6,000 p.a
Length of Study: 1 year
Frequency: Annual
Study Establishment: Loughborough University
Country of Study: United Kingdom
No. of awards offered: 8
Application Procedure: See website.
Funding: Government
Contributor: EPSRC

For further information contact:

Email: l.e.child@lboro.ac.uk

Industrial Design Studentship
Subjects: Industrial design.
Eligibility: Open to British nationals, resident in UK, intending to make a career in British Industry normally aged 21–24, but older candidates may apply.
Level of Study: Doctorate
Type: Studentship
Value: All tuition fees, stipend of UK £9,000 p.a., allowance of UK £850 p.a. for materials and agreed travel costs
Length of Study: 1–3 years
Frequency: Annual
Study Establishment: Loughborough University
Country of Study: United Kingdom
Application Procedure: See website.
Funding: Foundation
Contributor: Royal Commission for the Exhibition of 1851

For further information contact:

Email: royalcom1851@imperial.ac.uk

IPTME (Materials) Scholarships
Subjects: Polymer technology.
Level of Study: Postgraduate
Type: Scholarship
Value: All tuition fees
Length of Study: 1 year
Frequency: Annual
Study Establishment: Loughborough University
Country of Study: United Kingdom
No. of awards offered: 6
Application Procedure: See website.
Funding: Foundation
Contributor: Institute of Polymer Technology and Materials Engineering

For further information contact:

Email: iptme@lboro.ac.uk

Jean Scott Scholarships
Level of Study: Postgraduate
Type: Scholarship
Value: A maximum of US$5,000

Frequency: Annual
Study Establishment: Loughborough University
Country of Study: United Kingdom
No. of awards offered: 2
Application Procedure: See website.

For further information contact:

Email: msc.economics@lboro.ac.uk

Loughborough Sports Scholarships

Subjects: Athletics, cricket, football, golf, hockey, rugby, swimming, tennis and triathlon.
Purpose: To support elite athletes.
Type: Scholarship
Value: An annual UK £1,000 stipend, first class coaching, sports massage, expert nutritional advice and all
Frequency: Annual
Study Establishment: Loughborough University
Country of Study: United Kingdom
Application Procedure: See website.

For further information contact:

Email: sports-scholars@lboro.ac.uk

Mathematical Sciences Scholarship

Subjects: Industrial mathematical modelling.
Level of Study: Postgraduate
Type: Scholarship
Value: All tuition fees
Length of Study: 1–3 years
Frequency: Annual
Study Establishment: Loughborough University
Country of Study: United Kingdom
No. of awards offered: 3
Application Procedure: See website.

For further information contact:

Email: maths-admissions@lboro.ac.uk

MBA Scholarships

Subjects: Business management.
Level of Study: MBA
Type: Scholarship
Value: UK £500 annual stipend
Length of Study: 1–2 years
Frequency: Annual
Study Establishment: Loughborough University
Country of Study: United Kingdom
No. of awards offered: 10
Application Procedure: See website.

For further information contact:

Email: exec.mba@lboro.ac.uk

Politics Scholarships

Subjects: Politics, international relations and european studies.
Level of Study: Postgraduate
Type: Scholarship
Value: UK £1,000
Frequency: Annual
Study Establishment: Loughborough University
Country of Study: United Kingdom
Application Procedure: See website.

School of Art and Design Scholarships

Subjects: Art and design.
Level of Study: Postgraduate
Type: Scholarship
Value: All UK/EU tuition fees
Length of Study: 1–3 years
Frequency: Annual
Study Establishment: Loughborough University
Country of Study: United Kingdom
No. of awards offered: 6
Application Procedure: See website.

For further information contact:

Email: p.sawdon@lboro.ac.uk

THE LOUISVILLE INSTITUTE

1044 Alta Vista Road, Louisville, KY, 40205-1798, United States of America
Tel: (1) 502 992 5432
Fax: (1) 502 894 2286
Email: jlewis@louisville-institute.org
Website: www.louisville-institute.org
Contact: Dr James W Lewis, Executive Director

The Louisville Institute seeks to nurture inquiry and conversation regarding the character, problems, contributions and prospects of the historic institutions and commitments of American Christianity. In all of its work, the Louisville Institute is guided by its fundamental mission to enrich the religious life of American Christians and to encourage the revitalization of their institutions, by bringing together those who lead religious institutions with those who study them, so that the work of each might inform and strengthen the other.

Louisville Institute Dissertation Fellowship Program

Subjects: Religion/theology.
Purpose: To support the final year of writing on promising PhD and ThD dissertation projects dealing with aspects of American religious life that are related to the concerns of the Louisville Institute.
Eligibility: Applicants must be candidates for the PhD or ThD degree who have fulfilled all predissertation requirements, including approval of the dissertation proposal before the deadline and expect to complete the dissertation by the end of the following academic year.
Level of Study: Doctorate
Type: Fellowships
Value: US$18,000
Length of Study: 1 year
Frequency: Annual
Country of Study: United States of America
No. of awards offered: 10
Application Procedure: Applications should include applicant information and project summary form, dissertation fellowship programme, additional information form, dissertation adviser's letter of recommendation form and faculty letter of recommendation form.
Closing Date: January 15th
No. of awards given last year: 7
No. of applicants last year: 55
Additional Information: All tuition, medical insurance and required fees are the responsibility of the student. Travel and lodging expenses for the seminar will be covered by the Louisville Institute.

LOWE SYNDROME ASSOCIATION (LSA)

18919 Voss Road, Dallas, TX, 75287, United States of America
Tel: (1) 972 733 1339
Email: info@lowesyndrome.org
Website: www.lowesyndrome.org
Contact: Ms Christine Knight, Director of Public & Scientific Affairs

The Lowe Syndrome Association (LSA) is an international non-profit organization made up of families, friends and professionals dedicated to helping children with Lowe Syndrome and their families. Its main purposes are to foster communication among families, provide information and support research.

LSA Medical Research Grant

Subjects: Understanding and treatment of Lowe Syndrome.
Purpose: To support research projects that will lead to a better understanding of the metabolic basis of Lowe Syndrome, better treatments of the major complications of the disease and the prevention of and/or a cure for it.
Eligibility: Open to researchers who are affiliated with a non-profit institution.
Level of Study: Unrestricted
Type: Grant
Value: Varies, approx. US$30,000
Length of Study: 1 year

Frequency: Dependent on funds available
No. of awards offered: Varies
Application Procedure: Applicants must submit their application in writing. Specific instructions are available in the grant proposal guidelines document.
Closing Date: Varies
Funding: Private
Contributor: Members of the LSA and fund-raising events
No. of awards given last year: 2
No. of applicants last year: 2

THE LUISS UNIVERSITY OF ROME (LUR)

Research Center on Human Rights, Via Tommasini 1, Rome, 00-162, Italy
Tel: (39) 06 8650 6568
Fax: (39) 06 8650 6503
Email: infophd@luiss.it
Website: www.luiss.it

In 1974 a group of businessmen led by Umberto Agnelli decided to invest people and money in an innovative project for the education and training of a managerial class. Luiss adopted a new educational model along the lines of those to be found in the leading international universities.

LUR PhD Studentships in Political Theory

Subjects: Political theory.
Purpose: To support students enrolled in the Doctoral programme in political theory.
Eligibility: Open to applicants who have majored in an area of social sciences, human sciences or philosophy; however, applicants who have degrees in other disciplines will also be considered on the basis of their curriculum vitae and research proposals.
Level of Study: Doctorate
Type: Scholarships
Value: €900 per month
Length of Study: 3 years
Frequency: Annual
Study Establishment: The Luiss University of Rome (LUR)
Country of Study: Italy
No. of awards offered: 4
Application Procedure: Students interested in the PhD programme must apply by completing the application form. Applications must abide by the format attached to the call for application. Applications must be addressed to the Dean of Luiss Guido Carli and sent to the address below.
Closing Date: September 1st
Funding: Foundation
Additional Information: Applicants must submit a writing sample representative of the best work in an area consistent with the core-issues of the programme.

For further information contact:

Direzione Didattica e Ricerca Luiss Guido Carli-Viale Pola 12, Rome, 00198, Italy

THE MACDOWELL COLONY

100 High Street, Peterborough, NH, 03458, United States of America
Tel: (1) 603 924 3886
Fax: (1) 603 924 9142
Email: info@macdowellcolony.org,
admissions@macdowellcolony.org
Website: www.macdowellcolony.org
Contact: Ms Courtney Bethel, Admissions Director

The MacDowell Colony was founded in 1907 to provide creative artists with uninterrupted time and seclusion to work and enjoy the experience of living in a community with gifted artists. Residencies are up to eight weeks for writers, and playwrights, composers, film and video makers, visual artists, architects and interdisciplinary artists. Artists in residence receive room, board and the exclusive use of a studio. There are no residency fees. A travel grant and limited artist grants are available to artists in residence, based on need.

MacDowell Colony Residencies

Subjects: Creative writing, visual arts, musical composition, film and video making, architecture and interdisciplinary arts, playwriting.
Purpose: To provide a place where creative artists can take advantage of uninterrupted work time and seclusion in which to work and enjoy the experience of living in a community of gifted artists.
Eligibility: Open to established and emerging artists in the fields specified.
Level of Study: Unrestricted
Type: Residency
Value: Up to US$1,000 for artists in need of financial assistance (stipends), plus limited travel grants for any artist based on need
Length of Study: Usually 4 weeks, maximum of 8 weeks
Frequency: 3 deadlines annually: January 15, April 15 and September 15
Study Establishment: The Colony
Country of Study: United States of America
No. of awards offered: A total of 32 studios are available during each application period for individual residencies
Application Procedure: Applicants must write, telephone or refer to the website for information and an application form.
Closing Date: Summer (June 1st–September 30th), Autumn (October–January 31st), Winter-Spring (February 1st–May 31st)
Funding: Private
No. of awards given last year: 250 residencies
No. of applicants last year: 1800
Additional Information: The studios are offered for the independent pursuit of the applicant's art. No workshops or courses are given.

MACKENZIE KING SCHOLARSHIP SELECTION COMMITTEE

Faculty of Law, University of British Columbia, 1822 East Mall, Vancouver, BC, V6T 1Z1, Canada
Tel: (1) 604 822 4564
Fax: (1) 604 822 8108
Email: blom@law.ubc.ca
Website: www.mkingscholarships.ca
Contact: Professor Joost Blom

The Mackenzie King Scholarship Trust consists of two funds established under the will of the Right Honourable William Lyon Mackenzie King (1874–1950). Both scholarships are to support postgraduate study for graduates of Canadian universities.

Mackenzie King Open Scholarship

Subjects: All subjects.
Eligibility: Open to graduates of any Canadian university. Applicants should be persons of unusual worth or promise as awards are determined on the basis of academic achievement, personal qualities and demonstrated aptitudes. Consideration is also given to the applicant's proposed programme of postgraduate study.
Level of Study: Postgraduate
Type: Scholarship
Value: Canadian $9,000
Length of Study: 1 year, non-renewable
Frequency: Annual
Country of Study: Any country
No. of awards offered: 1
Application Procedure: Applicants must complete an application form available from the Faculty of Graduate Studies at each Canadian university and from the website. Applications must be submitted to the Dean of Graduate Studies at the Canadian university from which the candidate most recently graduated.
Closing Date: February 1st
Funding: Private
No. of awards given last year: 1

Mackenzie King Travelling Scholarship

Subjects: International or industrial relations, including international aspects of law, history, politics and economics.
Purpose: To give Canadian students the opportunity to broaden their outlook and sympathies and to contribute in some measure to the understanding of the problems and policies of other countries.

Eligibility: Open to graduates of any Canadian university who propose to engage in postgraduate studies in the given fields in the United States of America or the United Kingdom.
Level of Study: Postgraduate
Type: Scholarship
Value: Canadian $10,000
Length of Study: 1 year, non-renewable
Frequency: Annual
Study Establishment: Suitable institutions
Country of Study: United Kingdom or United States of America
No. of awards offered: 4
Application Procedure: Applicants must complete an application form available from the Faculty of Graduate Studies at each Canadian university or from the website. Applications must be submitted to the Dean of Graduate Studies at the Canadian university from which the candidate most recently graduated.
Closing Date: February 1st
Funding: Private
No. of awards given last year: 4

MACQUARIE UNIVERSITY

Balaclava Road, North Ryde, NSW 2109, Australia
Tel: (61) 2 9850 7111
Email: tgreen@ling.mq.edu.au
Website: www.mq.edu.au

Established in 1964, Macquarie attracts students from all walks of life, including large numbers from overseas. As the new millennium dawned, Macquarie had conferred some 58,000 degrees, diplomas and postgraduate certificates.

Centre for Lasers and Applications Scholarships
Subjects: Experimental and theoretical laser studies.
Purpose: To enable holders to pursue a research programme leading to the degree of MsC or PhD in experimental and theoretical laser studies.
Eligibility: Open to the Australian citizens, permanent residents, or citizens of overseas countries.
Level of Study: Postgraduate, Research
Type: Scholarship
Value: Australian $19,231 per year
Length of Study: 2 years (Masters) or 3 years (PhD)
Frequency: Annual
Study Establishment: Macquarie University
Country of Study: Australia
No. of awards offered: Varies
Application Procedure: Check website for further details.
Closing Date: Not specified

For further information contact:

Centre for Lasers and Applications
Tel: 02 9850 8911
Email: jpiper@ics.mq.edu.au
Website: www.mq.edu.au
Contact: Professor Jim Piper, Director

Macquarie University PhD Scholarship in Knowledge Acquisition and Cognitive Modelling
Subjects: Virtual training environment for risk assessment and spans the fields of cognitive modelling, knowledge acquisition, agent based systems for human learning, virtual reality and game technology.
Purpose: To enable students to undertake research in related fields.
Eligibility: Open to applicants who have completed, an Australian 4 year undergraduate degree with at least Second Class (Honours) division 1 in computing or a related field, or equivalent qualifications.
Level of Study: Postdoctorate, Postgraduate
Type: Scholarships
Value: Australian $19,231 plus Australian $5,000 top-up per year subject to satisfactory progress
Length of Study: 3 years
Frequency: Annual
Study Establishment: Macquarie University
Country of Study: Australia
No. of awards offered: 2

Application Procedure: Applicants must download the form from the website.
Closing Date: May
Additional Information: Additional Information can be obtained from the Higher Degree Research Unit by phoning 61 02 9850 7277, by emailing pgschol@mq.edu.au or by downloading the form from the website www.ro.mq.edu.au/hdru/scholar.htm

For further information contact:

Higher Degree Research Unit, Cottage C4C, Macquarie University, North Ryde, NSW, 2109, Australia
Email: richards@mq.edu.au
Contact: Professor Debbie Richards

MAKING MUSIC, THE NATIONAL FEDERATION OF MUSIC SOCIETIES (NFMS)

2-4 Great Eastern Street, London, EC2A 3NW, England
Tel: (44) 20 7422 8280
Fax: (44) 20 7422 8299
Email: ayca@makingmusic.org.uk
Website: www.makingmusic.org.uk/awards
Contact: Awards Administrator

Making Music, The National Federation of Music Societies (NFMS), is the leading umbrella group for the voluntary and semi-professional music sector. Making Music represents and supports over 2,650 music groups throughout the United Kingdom. Making Music groups also promote over 10,000 performances, spending over UK £10 million on professional artists per year and perform to audiences of around 1.6 million.

Philip and Dorothy Green Award for Young Concert Artists in Association with Making Music
Subjects: Music.
Purpose: To support young musicians at the start of their professional careers.
Eligibility: Open to singers under 32 years of age and instrumentalists under 28 years of age. All applicants must be European Union or Commonwealth citizens normally resident within the United Kingdom.
Level of Study: Professional development
Type: Award
Value: Up to 50 performance engagements with affiliated societies throughout the United Kingdom and Northern Ireland
Frequency: Annual
No. of awards offered: 4–6
Application Procedure: Applicants must submit a completed application form with their curriculum vitae.
Closing Date: As advertised in the national press and on the website
Funding: Trusts
No. of awards given last year: 6
No. of applicants last year: 60+
Additional Information: There is also a bursary available each year of around £400, for which candidates may be considered.

MANITOBA LIBRARY ASSOCIATION (MLA)

606-100 Arthur Street, Winnipeg MB, R3B 1H3, Canada
Tel: (1) 204 943 4567
Fax: (1) 204 942 1555
Email: manitobalibrary@gmail.com
Website: www.mla.mb.ca

The Manitoba Association (MLA) is a provincial, voluntary, non-incorporated association that provides leadership in the promotion, development and support of library and information services in Manitoba.

Jean Thorunn Law Scholarship
Subjects: Library science.
Purpose: To encourage careers in library and information science.

Eligibility: Open to applicants who have completed 12 months of library employment in Manitoba. The applicants must be a resident of Manitoba or returning to Manitoba after graduation.
Level of Study: Postgraduate
Type: Scholarship
Value: Up to Canadian $3,000
Frequency: Annual
Country of Study: Canada
Application Procedure: A completed application form, which is available online, must be sent. see website www.mla.mb.ca
Closing Date: June 1
Funding: Foundation, trusts
No. of awards given last year: 3

John Edwin Bissett Scholarship

Subjects: Library science.
Purpose: To encourage careers in library and information science.
Eligibility: Open to candidates attending an accredited library school. An applicant must be resident of Manitoba or returning to Manitoba on completion of the degree course.
Level of Study: Postgraduate
Type: Scholarship
Value: Up to Canadian $6,500
Frequency: Annual
Country of Study: Canada
Application Procedure: Please see the website www.mla.mb.ca
Closing Date: June 1st
Funding: Foundation, trusts
No. of awards given last year: 3

MARCH OF DIMES BIRTH DEFECTS FOUNDATION

1275 Mamaroneck Avenue, White Plains, NY, 10605, United States of America
Tel: (1) 914 997 4555
Fax: (1) 914 997 4560
Email: researchgrants@marchofdimes.com
Website: www.marchofdimes.com/professionals
Contact: Research and Grants Administration

Four major problems threaten the health of America's babies, birth defects, infant mortality, low birth weight and lack of prenatal care. The goal of the March of Dimes Birth Defects Foundation is to eliminate these problems so that all babies can be born healthy.

March of Dimes Graduate Nursing Scholarship

Subjects: Nursing.
Purpose: To recognize and promote excellence in nursing care of mothers and babies.
Eligibility: Open to applicants who are registered nurses currently enrolled in a graduate or postgraduate programme in maternal-child nursing at the Master's or Doctorate level. Applicant must be a member of at least 1 of the following professional organizations: the Association of Women's Health, Obstetric and Neonatal Nurses, the American College of Nurse-Midwives or the National Association of Neonatal Nurses.
Level of Study: Postgraduate
Type: Scholarships
Value: US$5,000
Frequency: Annual
Country of Study: United States of America
No. of awards offered: 4
Application Procedure: Applicants need to submit their application form, essay, reference letters and curriculum vitae.
Closing Date: January 15th
Funding: Foundation
Contributor: Scholarship supported in part by an educational grant from Pampers
Additional Information: Scholarship recipients are announced in May each year.

March of Dimes Research Grants

Subjects: Health and medical sciences.

Purpose: To support research scientists with faculty appointments or equivalent at universities, hospitals or research institutions.
Eligibility: Open to citizens of the United States and to employees or relatives of employees in the teaching industry.
Level of Study: Postgraduate
Type: Grant
Value: US$12,500–101,380
Frequency: Annual
Country of Study: United States of America
Application Procedure: Applicants must submit their application form, letter of intent and list of current financial support.
Closing Date: April 30th
Funding: Foundation
Contributor: March of Dimes Birth Defects Foundation

THE MARCUS CENTER OF THE AMERICAN JEWISH ARCHIVES

3101 Clifton Avenue, Cincinnati, OH, 45220-2488, United States of America
Tel: (1) 513 221 7444
Fax: (1) 513 221 7812
Email: kproffitt@huc.edu
Website: www.americanjewisharchives.org
Contact: Mr Kevin Proffitt, Director, Fellowship Programmes

The Marcus Center of the American Jewish Archives was founded by Dr Jacob Rader Marcus in 1947 in the aftermath of World War II and the Holocaust. It is committed to preserving a documentary heritage of the religious, organizational, economic, cultural, personal, social and family life of American Jewry. It contains nearly 5,000 linear feet of archives, manuscripts, newsprint materials, photographs, audio and video tapes, microfilm and genealogical materials.

Bernard and Audre Rapoport Fellowships

Subjects: American Jewish studies, preserving a documentary heritage of the religious, organizational, economic, cultural, personal, social and family life of American Jewry and imparting it to the next generation.
Eligibility: Open to postdoctoral candidates of any nationality.
Level of Study: Predoctorate, Doctorate, Postdoctorate, Postgraduate
Type: Fellowship
Value: Award is determined at the discretion of the selection committee
Length of Study: 1 month
Study Establishment: The Archives
Country of Study: Any country
Application Procedure: Applicants can refer to the website for related information.
Closing Date: March 1st

Ethel Marcus Memorial Fellowship

Subjects: American Jewish studies, preserving a documentary heritage of the religious, organizational, economic, cultural, personal, social and family life of American Jewry and imparting it to the next generation.
Eligibility: Open to ABDs.
Level of Study: Doctorate, Postdoctorate, Postgraduate, Predoctorate
Type: Fellowship
Value: Award is determined at the discretion of the selection committee
Length of Study: 1 month
Study Establishment: The Archives
Country of Study: Any country
Application Procedure: Applicants can refer to the website for related information.
Closing Date: March 1st

Jacob Rader Marcus Center of the American Jewish Archives Fellowship Program

Subjects: American Jewish studies, including – but not limited to – the religious, organizational, economic, cultural, personal, social and family life of American Jewry.

431

Purpose: To provide fellowships for research and writing in some area of the American Jewish experience using the vast collection of the American Jewish Archives.

Eligibility: Applicants must submit a fellowship application together with a five-page (maximum) research proposal that outlines the scope of their project and lists those collections at the American Jewish Archives that are crucial to their research. Applicants should also submit two letters of support, preferably from academic colleagues. For graduate and doctoral students, one of these two letters must be from their dissertation advisor.

Level of Study: Doctorate, Postdoctorate

Type: Fellowship

Value: Covers transportation and living expenses while in residence in Cincinnati

Frequency: Annual

No. of awards offered: Varies

Application Procedure: Fellowship application can be downloaded from the website or a request can be made to have one sent via postal mail.

Closing Date: March 18th

For further information contact:

Tel: 513 221 7444, ext. 304

Contact: Kevin Proffitt, The Director of the Fellowship Program

The Joseph and Eva R Dave Fellowship

Subjects: American Jewish studies, preserving a documentary heritage of the religious, organizational, economic, cultural, personal, social and family life of American Jewry and imparting it to the next generation.

Purpose: To facilitate research and writing using the vast collection at the American Jewish Archives, and to preserve a documentary heritage of the religious, organizational, economic, cultural, personal, social and family life of American Jewry and impart it to the next generation.

Eligibility: Open to ABDs.

Level of Study: Postdoctorate, Doctorate, Postgraduate, Predoctorate, Senior or independent scholars

Type: Fellowship

Value: Award is determined at the discretion of the selection committee

Length of Study: 1 month

Frequency: Annual

Study Establishment: The Archives

Country of Study: Any country

No. of awards offered: 1

Application Procedure: Applicants can refer to the website for related information.

Closing Date: March 18th in the year of proposed study

Funding: Private

Loewenstein-Wiener Fellowship Awards

Subjects: American Jewish studies, preserving a documentary heritage of the religious, organizational, economic, cultural, personal, social and family life of American Jewry and imparting it to the next generation.

Eligibility: Open to ABDs who have completed all but the dissertation requirement, and to postdoctoral candidates.

Level of Study: Doctorate, Postgraduate, Postdoctorate, Predoctorate

Type: Fellowship

Value: Award is determined at the discretion of the selection committee

Length of Study: 1 month

Study Establishment: The Archives

Country of Study: Any country

Application Procedure: Applicants can refer to the website for related information.

Closing Date: March 1st

Marguerite R Jacobs Memorial Award

Subjects: American Jewish studies, preserving a documentary heritage of the religious, organizational, economic, cultural, personal, social and family life of American Jewry and imparting it to the next generation.

Eligibility: Open to postdoctoral candidates of any nationality.

Level of Study: Doctorate, Postdoctorate, Postgraduate, Predoctorate, Senior or independent scholars

Value: Award is determined at the discretion of the selection committee

Length of Study: 1 month

Frequency: Annual

Study Establishment: The Archives

Country of Study: Any country

No. of awards offered: 1

Application Procedure: Applicants can refer to the website for related information.

Closing Date: March 1st

Funding: Private

The Natalie Feld Memorial Fellowship

Subjects: American Jewish studies, preserving a documentary heritage of the religious, organizational, economic, cultural, personal, social and family life of American Jewry and imparting it to the next generation.

Purpose: To facilitate research and writing using the vast collection at the American Jewish Archives, and to preserve a documentary heritage of the religious, organizational, economic, cultural, personal, social and family life of American Jewry for the next generation.

Eligibility: Open to ABDs.

Level of Study: Doctorate, Postdoctorate, Postgraduate, Predoctorate, Senior or independent scholars

Type: Fellowship

Value: Award is determined at the discretion of the selection committee

Frequency: Annual

Study Establishment: The Archives

Country of Study: Any country

No. of awards offered: 1

Application Procedure: Applicants can refer to the website for related information.

Closing Date: March 18th

Funding: Private

The Rabbi Harold D Hahn Memorial Fellowship

Subjects: American Jewish studies, preserving a documentary heritage of the religious, organizational, economic, cultural, personal, social and family life of American Jewry and imparting it to the next generation.

Purpose: A perpetual scholarship created to enable scholars to conduct independent research in subject areas relating to the history of North American Jewry.

Eligibility: Open to ABDs.

Level of Study: Doctorate, Postdoctorate, Postgraduate, Predoctorate, Senior or independent scholars

Type: Fellowship

Value: Award is determined at the discretion of the Selection Committee

Length of Study: 1 month

Frequency: Annual

Study Establishment: The Archives

Country of Study: Any country

No. of awards offered: 1

Application Procedure: Applicants can refer to the website for related information.

Closing Date: March 18th in year of proposed study

Funding: Private

The Rabbi Joachin Prinz Memorial Fellowship

Subjects: American Jewish studies, preserving a documentary heritage of the religious, organizational, economic, cultural, personal, social and family life of American Jewry and imparting it to the next generation.

Purpose: To enable the recipient to conduct an extensive study of the Rabbi Joachin Prinz collection in preparation for a doctoral dissertation or other scholarly publication.

Eligibility: Open to ABDs.

Level of Study: Doctorate, Postdoctorate, Postgraduate, Predoctorate, Senior or independent scholars

Type: Fellowship

Value: Award is determined at the discretion of the selection committee

Length of Study: 1 month
Frequency: Annual
Study Establishment: The Archives
Country of Study: Any country
No. of awards offered: 1
Application Procedure: Applicants can refer to the website for related information.
Closing Date: March 18th in the year of the proposed study
Funding: Private
Contributor: Deutsche Bank American Foundation

Rabbi Levi A Olan Memorial Fellowship

Subjects: American Jewish studies, preserving a documentary heritage of the religious, organizational, economic, cultural, personal, social and family life of American Jewry and imparting it to the next generation.
Eligibility: Open to ABDs.
Level of Study: Doctorate, Postdoctorate, Postgraduate, Predoctorate
Type: Fellowship
Value: Award is determined at the discretion of the selection committee
Length of Study: 1 month
Study Establishment: The Archives
Country of Study: Any country
Application Procedure: Applicants can refer to the website for related information.
Closing Date: March 1st

Rabbi Theodore S Levy Tribute Fellowship

Subjects: American Jewish studies, preserving a documentary heritage of the religious, organizational, economic, cultural, personal, social and family life of American Jewry and imparting it to the next generation.
Eligibility: Open to ABDs.
Level of Study: Doctorate, Postdoctorate, Postgraduate, Predoctorate, Senior or independent scholars
Type: Fellowship
Value: Award is determined at the discretion of the selection committee
Length of Study: 1 month
Frequency: Annual
Study Establishment: The Archives
Country of Study: Any country
No. of awards offered: 1
Application Procedure: Applicants can refer to the website for related information.
Closing Date: March 1st
Funding: Private

Starkoff Fellowship

Subjects: American Jewish studies, preserving a documentary heritage of the religious, organizational, economic, cultural, personal, social and family life of American Jewry and imparting it to the next generation.
Eligibility: Open to ABDs.
Level of Study: Doctorate, Postdoctorate, Postgraduate, Predoctorate
Type: Fellowship
Value: Award is determined at the discretion of the committee
Length of Study: 1 month
Study Establishment: The Archives
Country of Study: United States of America
Application Procedure: Applicants can refer to the website for related information.
Closing Date: March 1st

MARINE CORPS HISTORICAL CENTER

3079 Moreell Avenue, Quantico, Virginia, 22134, United States of America
Tel: (1) (703) 432-4877
Fax: (1) 202 433 7265
Website: www.usmc.mil
Contact: Attn: Coordinator Grants and Fellowships

The Marine Corps Historical Center houses the History and Museums Divisions. The History Division provides reference services to the public and government agencies, maintains the Marine Corps' archives and oral history collection and produces official histories of Marine activities, units and bases. The Museums Division maintains the artefact and personal papers collection, and operates the Marine Corps Museum and the Air-Ground Museum.

General Lemuel C. Shepherd, Jr. Memorial Dissertation Fellowship

Subjects: US military and naval history, as well as history and history-based studies in the social and behavioural sciences, with a direct relationship to the history of the United States Marine Corps.
Purpose: To fund a doctoral dissertation pertinent to Marine Corps history.
Eligibility: Awards are based on merit, without regard to race, creed, colour, or gender subject to a screening by the Director of Marine Corps History.
Level of Study: Predoctorate
Type: Fellowship
Value: US$10,000
Frequency: Annual
Country of Study: United States of America
No. of awards offered: 1
Application Procedure: Please check the website, www.history.usmc.mil for further details.
Closing Date: May 1st
Funding: Foundation
Contributor: The Marine Corps Heritage Foundation
No. of awards given last year: 1
No. of applicants last year: 3

Lieutenant Colonel Lily H Gridley Memorial Master's Thesis Fellowships

Subjects: Topics in United States of America military and naval history, as well as history and history-based studies in the social and behavioural sciences, with a direct relationship to the United States Marine Corps. This programme gives preference to projects covering the pre-1975 period where records are declassified or can be most readily declassified and made available to scholars.
Purpose: To award a number of fellowships to qualified graduate students working on topics pertinent to Marine Corps history.
Eligibility: Applicants must be actively enrolled in an accredited Master's degree programme that requires a Master's thesis. A fellowship will not be awarded to anyone who has held or accepted an equivalent fellowship from any other Department of Defence agency.
Level of Study: Postgraduate
Type: Fellowship
Value: US$3,500
Length of Study: 1–3 years
Frequency: Annual
Country of Study: United States of America
No. of awards offered: 2
Application Procedure: Applicants must complete an application form, available at www.history.usmc.mil. The applicant is responsible for ensuring that all required documentation is mailed before the closing date.
Closing Date: May 1st
Funding: Foundation, private
Contributor: The Marine Corps Heritage Foundation
No. of awards given last year: 1
No. of applicants last year: 2
Additional Information: The Director of Marine Corps History will notify all applicants individually of the application committee's decision not later than mid-July.

Marine Corps History College Internships

Subjects: History.
Purpose: To offer opportunities for college students to participate on a professional level in the Marine Corps Historical Center's many activities. The programme aims to give promising and talented student interns a chance to earn college credits while gaining meaningful experience in fields in which they might choose to seek employment after school or pursue a vocational interest.

Eligibility: Applicants must be registered students at a college or university. While there are no restrictions on individuals applying for intern positions, it has been found that mature and academically superior students are most successful.
Level of Study: Postgraduate
Type: Internship
Value: A small grant of daily expense money is provided. Any other costs of the internship must be borne by the student
Frequency: Annual
Study Establishment: Internships are served either at the Marine Corps Historical Center in Quantico, Virginia
Country of Study: United States of America
No. of awards offered: Varies
Application Procedure: Please check the website, www.history.usmc.mil for further details.
Funding: Foundation, private
Contributor: The Marine Corps Heritage Foundation

Marine Corps History Research Grants
Subjects: Topics in United States of America military and naval history, as well as history and history-based studies in the social and behavioural sciences, with a direct relationship to the United States Marine Corps. This programme gives preference to projects covering the pre-1975 period where records are declassified or can be most readily declassified and made available to scholars.
Purpose: To encourage research.
Eligibility: While the programme concentrates on graduate students, grants are available to other qualified persons. Applicants for grants should have the ability to conduct advanced study in those aspects of American military history and museum activities related to the United States Marine Corps.
Level of Study: Research
Type: Grant
Value: US$400–3,000
Frequency: Annual
Country of Study: United States of America
No. of awards offered: 5
Application Procedure: Applicants must submit a preliminary application to the Director of Marine Corps History outlining their qualifications, and either proposing a specific topic or requesting a suggested topic based on their interests and qualifications. If the evaluation of the preliminary application is favourable, the applicant will be asked to make a formal application on a form provided in www.history.usmc.mil
Funding: Foundation, private
Contributor: The Marine Corps Heritage Foundation
No. of awards given last year: 5
No. of applicants last year: 6

MARINES' MEMORIAL ASSOCIATION

609 Sutter Street, San Francisco, California, 94102-1027, United States of America
Tel: (1) 415 673 6672
Fax: (1) 415 441 3649
Email: michaelallen@marineclub.com
Website: www.marineclub.com

The Marines' Memorial Association is a non-profit veterans organization chartered to honor the memory of and commemorate the valor of Marines who have sacrificed in the nation's wars.

The Marine Corps Scholarship
Subjects: All subjects.
Purpose: To provide financial assistance to children of active and former members of the US Marines Corps.
Eligibility: Open to children of the MMA members scholastic aptitude, community involvement and civic spirit.
Level of Study: Postgraduate
Type: Scholarship
Value: Varies
Length of Study: Renewable
Frequency: Annual
Country of Study: Any country
No. of awards offered: 4

Application Procedure: See the website.
Closing Date: April 15th
Funding: Foundation
Contributor: The Marine Corps Foundation

MARQUETTE UNIVERSITY

PO Box 1881, Milwaukee, WI, 53201-1881, United States of America
Tel: (1) 414 288 7137
Fax: (1) 414 288 1902
Email: mugs@marquette.edu
Website: www.grad.marquette.edu
Contact: Thomas Marek, Student Services Co-ordinator

Marquette University is a private, Jesuit university situated about 100 miles north of Chicago. It is a graduate research institution with 18 doctoral and over 40 Master's and certificate programmes.

Alpha Sigma Nu Graduate Scholarship
Subjects: All subjects.
Purpose: To offer tuition scholarships for members of Alpha Sigma Nu.
Eligibility: Open to 1st-year graduate students who are members of Alpha Sigma Nu.
Level of Study: Graduate
Type: Scholarship
Value: Up to 18 credits of tuition scholarship
Length of Study: 2 years
Frequency: Annual
Country of Study: United States of America
No. of awards offered: 2
Application Procedure: Applicants must send a letter of application to the Graduate School.
Closing Date: February 15th
Funding: Private
No. of awards given last year: 2

Johnson's Wax Research Fellowship
Subjects: Engineering, chemistry and biology.
Purpose: To provide financial assistance for doctoral students.
Eligibility: Applicants must be admitted to a doctoral programme in engineering, biology or chemistry.
Level of Study: Doctorate
Type: Fellowship
Value: Approx. US$5,500 stipend and a tuition scholarship
Length of Study: 1 year
Frequency: Annual
No. of awards offered: 1
Application Procedure: Qualified applicants will be contacted by their department.
Closing Date: February 15th
Funding: Private
No. of awards given last year: 1
Additional Information: The award is offered to a different programme each year.

Marquette University Graduate Assistantship
Subjects: All subjects.
Purpose: To financially support teaching and research.
Eligibility: Open to full-time Master's and doctoral students.
Level of Study: Graduate
Type: Assistantship
Value: US$11,970 plus an 18-credit tuition scholarship, the value of which is approx. US$22,000
Length of Study: 1 year
Frequency: Annual
No. of awards offered: 289
Application Procedure: Applicants must submit an application to the Graduate School by the deadline. The graduate bulletin or the website should be consulted for further details.
Closing Date: February 15th for Autumn and November 15th for Spring
Funding: Private
Contributor: Marquette University
No. of awards given last year: 289

Marquette University Women's Club Fellowship
Subjects: All subjects.
Purpose: To support students who received their baccalaureate degrees from Marquette University.
Eligibility: Applicants must be admitted to a degree programme and have received a Bachelor's degree from Marquette University.
Level of Study: Graduate
Type: Fellowship
Value: US$2,000 stipend
Length of Study: 1 year
Frequency: Annual
No. of awards offered: 1
Application Procedure: Qualified students will be contacted by their department.
Closing Date: February 15th
Funding: Private
No. of awards given last year: 1
Additional Information: The award is offered to a different graduate programme each year.

Milwaukee Foundation's Frank Rogers Bacon Research Assistantship
Subjects: Electrical and computer engineering.
Purpose: To provide research support for students.
Eligibility: Open to full-time Master's and doctoral students.
Level of Study: Graduate
Type: Fellowship
Value: Up to US$12,450 stipend and possible scholarship
Length of Study: Varies
Frequency: Annual
Country of Study: United States of America
No. of awards offered: Varies depending on funds
Application Procedure: Applicants must contact the Department of Electrical and Computer Engineering at the University.
Closing Date: February 15th
Funding: Private
No. of awards given last year: 7

R A Bournique Memorial Fellowship
Subjects: Chemistry.
Eligibility: Open to graduate students in chemistry.
Level of Study: Graduate
Type: Fellowship
Value: Varies
Length of Study: The Summer
Frequency: Annual
No. of awards offered: 2
Application Procedure: Applicants must contact the Department of Chemistry.
Funding: Private
No. of awards given last year: 2

MARSHALL AID COMMEMORATION COMMISSION

Woburn House, 20-24 Tavistock Square, London, WC1H 9HF, United Kingdom
Tel: (44) 20 7380 6700
Fax: (44) 20 7387 2655
Email: info@marshallscholarship.org
Website: www.marshallscholarship.org

The Marshall Aid Commemoration Commission is responsible for the selection and placement of recipients of Marshall scholarships from the United States of America to the United Kingdom. The first awards were presented in 1954.

Marshall Scholarships
Subjects: All subjects.
Purpose: To provide intellectually distinguished young Americans with the opportunity to study in the United Kingdom, and thus to understand and appreciate the British way of life.
Eligibility: Open to citizens of the United States of America who have graduated with a minimum grade point average of 3.7 or A from an accredited US college not more than 2 years previously. Recipients are required to take a degree at their United Kingdom university. Preference is given to candidates who combine high academic ability with the capacity to play an active part in the United Kingdom university.
Level of Study: Postgraduate
Type: Scholarship
Value: Approx. UK £23,000 per year, which comprises tuition fees, residence, travel and related costs
Length of Study: 2 academic years, with a possible extension for a third year
Frequency: Annual
Study Establishment: Any suitable institution
Country of Study: United Kingdom
No. of awards offered: 40
Application Procedure: Applicants must submit an application form, university or college endorsement and four references. Information and application forms can be obtained from the British consulate in selected cities. Full details on application procedures can be obtained from the website. Application online: http://www.marshallscholarship.org/applications
Closing Date: October
Funding: Government
No. of awards given last year: 37
No. of applicants last year: 900

For further information contact:

Georgia Pacific Center, Suite 3400, 133 Peachtree Street NE, Atlanta, GA, 30303, United States of America
Tel: (1) (404) 954-7708
Contact: British Consulate-GeneralBritish Consulate-General, 33 North Dearborn Street, Chicago, IL, 60602, United States of AmericaBritish Consulate-General, 1 Sansome Street, San Francisco, CA, 94104, United States of AmericaBritish Consulate-General, 11766 Wiltshire Boulevard, Suite 400, Los Angeles, CA, 90025, United States of AmericaBritish Consulate-General, Wells Fayo Plaza, 1000 Louisiana, No 1900, Houston, TX, 77002, United States of America

MARYLAND INSTITUTE COLLEGE OF ART (MICA)

1300 West Mount Royal Avenue, Baltimore, MD, 21217, United States of America
Tel: (1) 410 225 2256
Fax: (1) 410 225 5275
Email: graduate@mica.edu
Website: www.mica.edu
Contact: Mr Scott G Kelly, Associate Dean for Graduate Studies

The Maryland Institute College of Art (MICA) offers a Master of Fine Arts (MFA) degree in painting, sculpture, photographic and electronic media, graphic design and digital imaging. It also offers excellent art education degrees such as an MAT and an MA in Art Education as well as Community Arts. The college has private studios, a strong visiting artists program, housing and excellent exhibition opportunities.

MICA Fellowship
Subjects: Fine and applied arts: art, design, art education, photo and general.
Purpose: To serve as a tuition scholarship.
Eligibility: Each applicant is considered.
Level of Study: Graduate
Type: Fellowship
Value: US$15,000 per year
Length of Study: 1–2 years
Frequency: Annual
Study Establishment: MICA
Country of Study: United States of America
No. of awards offered: 12
Application Procedure: All accepted applicants are automatically considered.
Closing Date: February 15th
Funding: Private
Contributor: MICA
No. of awards given last year: 1
No. of applicants last year: 823

MICA International Fellowship Award

Subjects: Fine and applied arts.
Purpose: To serve as a tuition scholarship.
Eligibility: Open to all international students accepted to the Institute.
Level of Study: Graduate
Type: Fellowship
Value: US$15,000 per year
Length of Study: 1–2 years
Frequency: Annual
Study Establishment: MICA
Country of Study: United States of America
No. of awards offered: 1
Application Procedure: All accepted applicants are automatically considered.
Closing Date: February 15th
Funding: Private
Contributor: MICA
No. of awards given last year: 1
No. of applicants last year: 67

MASSEY UNIVERSITY

Albany Expressway, Private Bag 102-904, Albany, North Shore Mail Centre, Auckland, New Zealand
Tel: (64) 09 414 0800
Fax: (64) 09 443 9704
Email: contact@massey.ac.nz
Website: www.massey.ac.nz

Massey University is a state funded university with a proud 80-year tradition of academic excellence. Its distance-learning programme delivers university qualifications to all parts of the country. It has a strong national and international reputation for the quality of research, research-led teaching, and the contributions of staff and graduates. It is a leader in advancing the economic, social, and cultural well being of the people of New Zealand.

C. Alma Baker Postgraduate Scholarship

Subjects: Agriculture, agriculture-related technologies, or the study of rural society.
Purpose: To encourage students enrolling in Master's or doctoral thesis programmes.
Eligibility: Open to candidates who are graduates and citizens of New Zealand. Awards are available for those intending to undertake postgraduate research either in New Zealand or overseas. Scholarships will be based on academic achievement.
Level of Study: Graduate, Postgraduate
Type: Scholarship
Value: Maximum $13,000 a year for a Master's student and $20,000 a year for a doctoral student
Length of Study: I year for Master's and up to 3 years for a Doctoral programme
Frequency: Dependent on funds available
Country of Study: New Zealand
No. of awards offered: Up to 6
Application Procedure: Applicants must apply on the prescribed form to the Secretary, C. Alma Baker Trust. A certified copy of Academic Record, birth certificate, passport, or other proof of citizenship, and an outline of proposed research (not more than one page) must be enclosed with the application.
Closing Date: February 1st
Funding: Trusts
Additional Information: Do not send original documents as application and attachments will not be returned. Information provided will be used by the trust or its representatives only for awarding scholarships and may be subject to verification procedures as appropriate.

For further information contact:

C. Alma Baker Trust, Room 550, Social Sciences Extension, Massey University, Mail Code 352, Private Bag 11-222, Palmerston North, New Zealand
Email: Contact@massey.ac.nz
Contact: Professor Barrie Macdonald, Secretary

Hurley Fraser Postgraduate Scholarship

Subjects: Applied sciences.

Purpose: To support postgraduate research in agriculture and horticulture.
Eligibility: Applicants must have enrolled for a full-time postgraduate degree or a diploma in one of the Applied Sciences. The award is based on the candidate's academic attainment.
Level of Study: Graduate
Type: Scholarship
Value: Up to $2,000 per year
Study Establishment: Massey University
Country of Study: New Zealand
Application Procedure: Applicants must apply to the Scholarships Office, Graduate Research School on forms (ASSC.3) available from Massey Contact or can be downloaded from the website.
Closing Date: March 10th
Contributor: John Alexander Hurley Scholarship and the Edith Fraser Agricultural and Horticultural Research Fund
Additional Information: The award shall be paid in May. Applications will not be accepted more than 3 months in advance of the closing date.

For further information contact:

Tel: 0800 627 739

Sir Alan Stewart Postgraduate Scholarships

Subjects: All subjects.
Purpose: To encourage new postgraduate enrolments from other tertiary institutions and to assist Massey students to progress from undergraduate to postgraduate study.
Eligibility: Open to New Zealand citizens or permanent residents who have completed an undergraduate degree at a New Zealand university.
Level of Study: Graduate
Type: Scholarship
Value: $4,000 per year for full-time students and pro-rated for part-time students
Frequency: Annual
Study Establishment: Any Massey University campus
Country of Study: New Zealand
No. of awards offered: Up to 10
Application Procedure: Check website for further details.
Closing Date: January 31st
Additional Information: Consideration will normally only be given to students with a B+ average or better. Full-time students may hold the scholarship only once. Part-time students may re-apply to the maximum of $4,000 in a period of 4 years from first enrolment in the postgraduate programme. Applications will NOT be accepted more than 3 months in advance of the closing date.

For further information contact:

Massey University, Private Bag 11-222, Palmerston North, New Zealand
Email: Contact@massey.ac.nz

THE MATSUMAE INTERNATIONAL FOUNDATION

4-14-46 Kamiogi, Suginami-ku, Tokyo, 167-0043, Japan
Tel: (81) 3 3301 7600
Fax: (81) 3 3301 7601
Email: contact2mif@mist.dti.ne.jp
Website: www.matsumae-if.org
Contact: Mr S Nakajima

Matsumae International Foundation Research Fellowship

Subjects: Engineering, mathematics, medicine, natural sciences and agriculture.
Purpose: To provide an opportunity for foreign scientists to conduct research at Japanese institutions.
Eligibility: Open to applicants under 40 years of age, of non-Japanese nationality who hold a Doctorate, and who have not previously been to Japan.
Level of Study: Professional development, Postdoctorate
Type: Fellowship

Value: ¥240,000 is provided monthly for the purpose of payment of tution, expenses for research material etc. ¥100,000 is provided to assist with local travel expenses on arrival, the initial cost of lodging etc
Length of Study: 3–6 months
Frequency: Annual
Study Establishment: Unrestricted
Country of Study: Japan
No. of awards offered: 20
Application Procedure: Applicants must obtain the current issue of the fellowship announcement from the Foundation.
Closing Date: July 31st
Funding: Private
Contributor: Charitable donations from individuals
No. of awards given last year: 20
No. of applicants last year: 124
Additional Information: Priority will be given to the fields of natural science, engineering and medicine.

MCDONNELL CENTER FOR THE SPACE SCIENCES

Washington University, Campus Box 1105, One Brookings Drive, St Louis, MO, 63130-4899, United States of America
Tel: (1) 314 935 4439
Fax: (1) 314 935 4134
Email: cowsik@physics.wustl.edu
Website: www.mcss.wustl.edu
Contact: Professor Ramanath Cowsik, Director

The McDonnell Center for the Space Sciences supports and stimulates scientists to work on fundamental problems in Space Sciences and Astroparticle Physics transcending borders between scientific disciplines.

McDonnell Center Astronaut Fellowships in the Space Sciences

Subjects: Space sciences, physics, earth sciences, astronomy, chemistry and planetary studies.
Purpose: To encourage scholarship and research in graduate students interest in the space sciences.
Eligibility: Open to citizens of the United States of America who have applied for and been accepted into a graduate programme in the departments of physics or earth and planetary sciences or chemistry at Washington University, St Louis. Candidates must have an excellent academic background and a particular interest in the space sciences.
Level of Study: Doctorate
Type: Fellowship
Value: Full tuition plus a stipend
Length of Study: 3 years
Frequency: Annual
Study Establishment: Washington University
Country of Study: United States of America
No. of awards offered: 3
Application Procedure: Applicants who have been accepted into a Washington University graduate programme in physics, earth and planetary sciences, chemistry, biology or electrical engineering and who have exhibited an interest in the space sciences are eligible to be considered for a McDonnell Center Astronaut Fellowship
Closing Date: January 15th
Funding: Private
No. of awards given last year: 1

McDonnell Graduate Fellowship in the Space Sciences

Subjects: Space sciences, physics, earth sciences, astronomy, chemistry and planetary studies.
Purpose: To encourage scholarship and research in graduate students in the space sciences.
Eligibility: Open to candidates who have applied for and been accepted into a graduate programme in the department of physics or earth and planetary sciences at Washington University, St Louis. Candidates must have an excellent academic background and a particular interest in the space sciences.
Level of Study: Doctorate
Type: Fellowship

Value: Full tuition plus a stipend
Length of Study: 3 years
Frequency: Annual
Study Establishment: Washington University
Country of Study: United States of America
No. of awards offered: 4–6
Application Procedure: Applicants who have been accepted into a Washington University graduate programme in physics, earth and planetary sciences, chemistry, biology or electrical engineering and who have exhibited an interest in the space sciences are automatically considered for a McDonnell Center Fellowship.
Closing Date: January 15th
Funding: Private
No. of awards given last year: 3

MCGILL UNIVERSITY

845 Sherbrooke Street West, Montréal, QC, H3A 2T5, Canada
Tel: (1) 514 398 4066/4455
Fax: (1) 514 398 2499
Email: graduate.admissions@mcgill.ca
Website: www.mcgill.ca

McGill University is Canada's best known university, renowned internationally for the highest standards in teaching and research and the outstanding record of achievement of professors and students. In fields like neurosciences, pain, cancer research and public policy to name but a few McGill is at the forefront of achievement nationally and internationally.

Maxwell Boulton QC Fellowship

Subjects: Law, especially with significance to the Canadian legal system and legal community.
Purpose: To provide young scholars with an opportunity to pursue a major research project or to complete the research requirements for a higher degree.
Eligibility: Open to candidates who have completed the residency requirements for a doctoral degree in law.
Level of Study: Postdoctorate, Doctorate
Type: Fellowship
Value: Canadian $30,000–35,000 per year
Length of Study: 1 year
Frequency: Annual
Country of Study: Canada
No. of awards offered: 2
Application Procedure: Applicants must write for details.
Closing Date: February 1st
No. of awards given last year: 2
No. of applicants last year: 20

MEDICAL LIBRARY ASSOCIATION (MLA)

65 East Wacker Place, Suite 1900, Chicago, IL, 60601 7246, United States of America
Tel: (1) 312 419 9094
Fax: (1) 312 419 8950
Email: mlapd2@mlahq.org
Website: www.mlanet.org
Contact: Lisa C. Fried, Coordinator, Credentialing, Professional Recognition and Careers

The Medical Library Association (MLA) is organized exclusively for scientific and educational purposes, and is dedicated to the support of health sciences research, education and patient care. MLA fosters excellence in the professional achievement and leadership of health sciences libraries and information professionals to enhance the quality of healthcare, education and research.

Cunningham Memorial International Fellowship

Subjects: Medical librarianship.
Purpose: To provide foreign medical librarians the opportunity to participate in and attend the Annual Meeting of the Library Association.

Eligibility: Open to those with a baccalaureate degree and a library degree who are working in a medical library. The applicant must submit a signed statement from a home country official stating that he or she is guaranteed a position in a medical library upon returning home. A satisfactory score must be achieved on the Test of English as a Foreign Language competency examination. Nationals of the United States of America or Canada are not eligible.

Level of Study: Professional development
Type: Fellowship
Value: US$3,500 to cover travel and expenses to the MLA's Annual Meeting
Length of Study: 2–3 weeks
Frequency: Annual
Study Establishment: Medical libraries
Country of Study: United States of America or Canada
No. of awards offered: 1–2
Application Procedure: Applicants must submit a completed application form with three letters of reference in English, a project overview, a certificate of health, Test of English as a Foreign Language examination result and an audio or video tape.
Closing Date: December 1st
Funding: Private
No. of awards given last year: 1

MLA Continuing Education Grants

Subjects: The theoretical, administrative and technical aspects of library and information science.
Purpose: To provide professional health science librarians with the opportunity to continue their education.
Eligibility: Open to citizens of the United States of America or Canada or permanent residents who are medical librarians with a graduate degree in library science and at least 2 years of work experience at the professional level.
Level of Study: Professional development
Type: Fellowship
Value: US$100–500
Length of Study: 1 year
Frequency: Annual
Country of Study: United States of America
No. of awards offered: 1
Application Procedure: Applicants must complete and submit an application form along with three references. Candidates should also identify a continuing education programme.
Closing Date: December 1st
Funding: Private
No. of awards given last year: 1
Additional Information: The award does not support work towards a degree or certificate.

MLA Doctoral Fellowship

Subjects: Medical librarianship and information science.
Purpose: To encourage superior students to conduct doctoral work in the field of health sciences librarianship or information sciences.
Eligibility: Open to citizens or permanent residents of the United States of America or Canada who are graduates of an ALA-accredited library school and are enrolled in a PhD programme with an emphasis on biomedical and health-related information science.
Level of Study: Doctorate
Type: Fellowship
Value: US$2,000
Length of Study: 1 year, non-renewable
Frequency: Every 2 years
Country of Study: United States of America or Canada
No. of awards offered: 1
Application Procedure: Applicants must submit a completed application form with two letters of reference, transcripts of graduate work completed, a summary of the project and a detailed budget plus a signed statement of terms and conditions.
Closing Date: December 1st
Funding: Commercial
Contributor: Thomson ISI
No. of awards given last year: 1

Additional Information: The award supports research or travel applicable to the candidate's study and may not be used for tuition.

MLA Research, Development and Demonstration Project Award

Subjects: Health science librarianship and the information sciences.
Purpose: To provide support for research, development and demonstration projects that will help to promote excellence in the field of health sciences librarianship.
Eligibility: Open to members of the Association who have a graduate degree in library science, are practicing medical librarians with at least 2 years of experience at the professional level and are citizens or permanent residents of the United States of America or Canada. Grants will not be given to support an activity that is only operational in nature or that has only local usefulness.
Level of Study: Postgraduate
Type: Award
Value: US$100–1,000
Length of Study: 1 year
Frequency: Annual
Country of Study: United States of America or Canada
No. of awards offered: 1
Application Procedure: Applicants must submit a completed application form with three references, a detailed description of the project design and budget.
Closing Date: December 1st
Funding: Private
No. of awards given last year: 1

MLA Scholarship

Subjects: Library science.
Purpose: To provide an opportunity to study at an ALA-accredited library school.
Eligibility: Open to citizens and permanent residents of the United States of America or Canada who are entering an ALA-accredited library school or who have at least one half of the academic requirements of the programme to finish in the year following the granting of the scholarship.
Level of Study: Graduate
Type: Scholarship
Value: US$5,000
Length of Study: 1 academic year
Frequency: Annual
Country of Study: United States of America or Canada
No. of awards offered: 1
Application Procedure: Applicants must submit a completed application form with two letters of reference, official transcripts and a statement of career objectives.
Closing Date: December 1st
Funding: Private
No. of awards given last year: 1

MLA Scholarship for Minority Students

Subjects: Medical librarianship.
Purpose: To provide a minority student with the opportunity to begin or continue graduate study in the field of library and information science.
Eligibility: Open to African, American, Hispanic, Asian, Pacific Island or Native American students who are entering an ALA-accredited library school and have at least one half of the academic requirements of the programme to finish in the year following the granting of the scholarship.
Level of Study: Graduate
Type: Scholarship
Value: US$5,000
Length of Study: 1 academic year
Frequency: Annual
Study Establishment: An ALA-accredited school
Country of Study: United States of America or Canada
No. of awards offered: 1
Application Procedure: Applicants must submit a completed application form with two letters of reference, official transcripts and a statement of career objectives.
Closing Date: December 1st
No. of awards given last year: 1

MEDICAL RESEARCH COUNCIL (MRC)

20 Park Crescent, London, W1B 1AL, England
Tel: (44) 20 7636 5422
Fax: (44) 20 7670 5002
Email: joaune.mccallum@headoffice.mrc.ac.uk
Website: www.mrc.ac.uk
Contact: Ms Joaune McCallum

The Medical Research Council (MRC) offers support for talented individuals who want to pursue a career in the biomedical sciences, public health and health services research. It provides its support through a variety of personal award schemes that are aimed at each stage in a clinical or non-clinical research career.

Collaborative Career Development Fellowship in Stem Cell Research

Subjects: Biomedical sciences.
Purpose: To provide specialized training in stem cell research to support fundamental stem cell biology or work towards new stem cell-derived treatments for major diseases and disabilities.
Eligibility: Applicants are normally expected to have a PhD/DPhil in a relevant discipline or hold a relevant research-orientated Master's degree, and to have undertaken not less than 3 years of appropriate research training.
Level of Study: Postdoctorate
Type: Fellowship
Value: An appropriate clinical or academic salary along with a fixed sum for research expenses and a travel allowance for attendance at scientific conferences
Length of Study: Up to 3 years
Frequency: Annual
Study Establishment: A suitable university or similar institution
Country of Study: United Kingdom
No. of awards offered: Varies
Application Procedure: Applicants must submit a personal application. Forms and further details are available from the MRC.
Closing Date: Usually around February, but applicants are advised to check the website for details
Funding: Government
No. of awards given last year: 6
No. of applicants last year: 19
Additional Information: Awards may be jointly funded with the MRC, or funded by bodies other than the MRC. Please contact the Fellowships Section at the MRC for further details.

MRC Career Development Award

Subjects: Biomedical sciences.
Purpose: To award outstanding researchers who wish to consolidate and develop their research skills and make the transition from post-doctoral research and training to becoming independent investigators, but who do not hold established positions.
Eligibility: It is expected that all applicants will hold a PhD or MPhil in a basic science and will have at least 3 years of postdoctoral research experience.
Level of Study: Postdoctorate, Research
Type: Fellowship
Value: Competitive personal salary support plus research support staff at the technical level, research expenses, capital equipment and a travel allowance for attendance at scientific conferences
Length of Study: Up to 4 years
Frequency: Annual
Study Establishment: A suitable university department or similar institution
Country of Study: United Kingdom
No. of awards offered: Up to 8
Application Procedure: Applicants must submit a personal application. Forms and further details are available from the MRC.
Closing Date: Usually around November, but applicants are advised to check the website for details
Funding: Government
No. of awards given last year: 13
No. of applicants last year: 86
Additional Information: Awards may occasionally be jointly funded with other bodies. Please contact the Fellowships Section at the MRC for further details.

MRC Clinical Research Training Fellowships

Subjects: Biomedical sciences.
Purpose: To provide an opportunity for specialized or further research training leading to the submission of a PhD, DPhil or MD.
Eligibility: Open to hospital doctors, dentists, general practitioners, nurses, midwives and allied health professionals. Residence requirements apply.
Level of Study: Postgraduate, Research
Type: Fellowship
Value: An appropriate clinical academic salary will be provided along with a fixed sum for research expenses and a travel allowance for attendance at scientific conferences
Length of Study: Up to 3 years
Study Establishment: A suitable university department or similar institution
Country of Study: United Kingdom
No. of awards offered: Up to 32
Application Procedure: Applicants must submit a personal application. Forms and further details are available from the MRC.
Closing Date: Round one is in August/September, and round two is in January/February, but applicants are advised to check the website for details
Funding: Government
No. of awards given last year: 39
No. of applicants last year: 169
Additional Information: In addition to this scheme, the MRC also offers Joint Training Fellowships with the Royal Colleges of Surgeons of England and Edinburgh and the Royal College of Obstetricians and Gynaecologists. These awards are aimed at individuals whose long-term career aspirations involve undertaking academic clinical research. Fellowships may also be jointly funded with the MS Society or the Prior Group. Please contact the Fellowships Section at the MRC for further details.

MRC Clinician Scientist Fellowship

Subjects: Biomedical sciences.
Purpose: To provide an opportunity for outstanding clinical researchers who wish to consolidate their research skills and make the transition from postdoctoral research and training to becoming independent investigators.
Eligibility: The scheme is open to hospital doctors, dentists, general practitioners, nurses, midwives and allied health professionals. All applicants must have obtained their PhD or MD in a basic science or clinical project, or expect to have received their doctorate by the time they intend to take up an award, and must not hold tenured positions.
Level of Study: Postdoctorate, Research
Type: Fellowship
Value: Competitive personal salary support plus research support staff at the technical level, research expenses, capital equipment and a travel allowance for attendance at scientific conferences
Length of Study: Up to 5 years
Frequency: Annual
Study Establishment: A suitable university department or similar institution
Country of Study: United Kingdom
No. of awards offered: Up to 7
Application Procedure: Applicants must submit a personal application. Forms and further details are available from the MRC.
Closing Date: August to December, but applicants are advised to check the website for details
Funding: Government
No. of awards given last year: 10
No. of applicants last year: 40

MRC Industrial Collaborative Studentships

Subjects: Any biomedical science.
Purpose: To enhance links between academia and industry in the provision of high-quality research training.
Eligibility: Candidates should have graduated with a good Honours Degree from a United Kingdom academic institution in a subject relevant to the MRC's scientific remit. This should be an Upper Second Class (Honours) Degree or higher. The MRC will, however, consider qualifications or a combination of qualifications and experience that demonstrates equivalent ability and attainment, e.g. a Lower Second Class (Honours) Degree can be enhanced by a Master's degree. A

439

copy of the regulations governing residence eligibility may be obtained from the Council.

Level of Study: Postgraduate

Value: A tax-free maintenance stipend depending on United Kingdom location, university tuition fees up to the current DFEE recommended limit plus college fees, where applicable. Awards also include a fixed sum for conference travel expenses and a support grant to the university department to help cover incidental costs of students' training. As a measure of interest and involvement the industrial company is expected to make a financial contribution to the cost of the studentship

Length of Study: Up to 4 years

Frequency: Annual

Study Establishment: Universities, medical schools, industry and other academic institutions

Country of Study: United Kingdom

No. of awards offered: Approx. 10

Application Procedure: The MRC does not make awards directly to students. Awards are made to industrial partners who apply for studentships by application. The individual or academic partner will then advertise for students to apply for their awards. Students who wish to apply for a studentship are advised to contact the department where they wish to study to see if it has an allocation of awards.

Closing Date: This competition is advertised in the Autumn

Funding: Commercial

No. of awards given last year: 10

No. of applicants last year: 23

Additional Information: The industrial company is expected to make a contribution.

MRC Master's Studentships

Subjects: Any biomedical science.

Purpose: To enable students to undertake early research training relevant to strategic research or strategic employment in a research-related capacity in academia or industry.

Eligibility: Candidates should have graduated with a good Honours Degree. A copy of the regulations governing residence eligibility may be obtained from the Council.

Level of Study: Postgraduate

Type: Studentship

Value: Tax-free maintenance stipend, depending on United Kingdom location, and university tuition fees up to the current DFEE recommended limit. Awards also include a fixed sum for conference travel expenses

Length of Study: 1 year

Frequency: Annual

Study Establishment: Universities, medical schools and other academic organizations

Country of Study: United Kingdom

Application Procedure: The MRC does not make awards directly to students. Awards are made to Institutes of Higher Education (IHE) based on the level of MCR grant and fellowship awards to that IHE. The IHE is responsible for recruiting students. Students who wish to apply for a studentship are advised to contact the department where they wish to study to see if it has an allocation of awards.

Closing Date: IHE's are notified of funding available for awards in March each year

Funding: Government

No. of awards given last year: 50

No. of applicants last year: 85

Additional Information: The MRC also has awards in strategic capacity building areas from time to time. Studentship awards have been replaced by Doctoral Training Accounts (DTA) from October 2004. Further details can be obtained from the MRC website.

MRC Research Studentships

Subjects: Any biomedical science.

Purpose: To enable individuals to undertake a training programme under the guidance of named supervisors that includes a research project plus training in research methods and personal key skills.

Eligibility: Candidates should have graduated with a good Honours Degree from a United Kingdom academic institution in a subject relevant to the MRC's scientific remit. This should be an Upper second class (Honours) degree or higher. The MRC will, however, consider

qualifications or a combination of qualifications and experience that demonstrates equivalent ability and attainment e.g. a Lower second class (Honours) degree can be enhanced by a Master's degree. A copy of the regulations governing residence eligibility may be obtained from the Council.

Level of Study: Predoctorate

Type: Studentship

Value: A tax-free maintenance stipend depending on United Kingdom location, university tuition fees up to the current DFEE recommended limit plus college fees, where applicable. Awards also include a fixed sum for conference travel expenses and a support grant to the university department to help cover incidental costs of students' training

Length of Study: Most studentships are 3 years, but they can be linked to a Master's course, making it a 4 year programme

Frequency: Annual

Study Establishment: Universities, medical schools, MRC research establishments and other academic organizations

Country of Study: United Kingdom

No. of awards offered: Approx. 400

Application Procedure: The MRC does not make awards directly to students. Awards are made to Institutes of Higher Education (IHE) based at the level of MRC grant and fellowship awards to that IHE. The IHE is responsible for recruiting students. Students who wish to apply for a studentship are advised to contact the department where they wish to study to see if it has an allocation of awards.

Closing Date: IHEs are notified of awards in March each year. The capacity building studentship competition is advertised in the Autumn

Funding: Government

No. of awards given last year: 50

No. of applicants last year: 203

MRC Royal College of Obstetricians and Gynaecologists (RCOG) Training Fellowship

Subjects: Biomedical sciences.

Purpose: To provide members of the RCOG with an opportunity for specialized or further research training in a basic science relevant to obstetrics and gynaecology leading to the submission of a PhD, DPhil or MD.

Eligibility: Open to members of the RCOG wishing to pursue research at PhD or MD level. Applicants must have a minimum of 1 year of experience in clinical obstetrics and gynaecology and hold part one membership of the college. Residence requirements apply.

Level of Study: Postgraduate, Research

Type: Fellowship

Value: An appropriate clinical academic salary will be provided along with a fixed sum for research expenses and a travel allowance for attendance at scientific conferences

Length of Study: Up to 3 years

Frequency: Annual

Study Establishment: A suitable university or similar institution

Country of Study: United Kingdom

No. of awards offered: 1

Application Procedure: Applicants must contact the Fellowships Section, Research Career Awards of the MRC for details.

Closing Date: Applicants are advised to check the MRC website for details

Funding: Government

No. of awards given last year: 2

No. of applicants last year: 2

MRC Royal College of Surgeons of Edinburgh Clinical Research Training Fellowship

Subjects: Biomedical sciences.

Purpose: To provide an opportunity for specialized or further research training within the United Kingdom leading to the submission of a PhD, DPhil or MD.

Eligibility: Open to members of the Royal College of Surgeons of Edinburgh wishing to pursue research at the PhD or MD level. Residence requirements apply.

Level of Study: Postgraduate, Research

Type: Fellowship

Value: An appropriate clinical academic salary will be provided along with a fixed sum for research expenses and a travel allowance for attendance at scientific conferences

Length of Study: Up to 3 years
Frequency: Annual
Study Establishment: A suitable university department or similar institution
Country of Study: United Kingdom
No. of awards offered: 1–2
Application Procedure: Applicants must submit a personal application. Forms and further details are available from the MRC.
Closing Date: Applicants are advised to check the MRC website for details
Funding: Government
No. of awards given last year: 2
No. of applicants last year: 17

MRC Royal College of Surgeons of England Training Fellowship

Subjects: Biomedical sciences.
Purpose: To provide an opportunity for specialized or further research training within the United Kingdom leading to the submission of a PhD, DPhil or MD.
Eligibility: Open to members of the Royal College of Surgeons of England wishing to pursue research at the PhD or MD level. Residence requirements apply.
Level of Study: Postgraduate, Research
Type: Fellowship
Value: An appropriate clinical academic salary will be provided along with a fixed sum for research expenses and a travel allowance for attendance at scientific conferences
Length of Study: Up to 3 years
Frequency: Annual
Study Establishment: A suitable university department or similar institution
Country of Study: United Kingdom
No. of awards offered: Up to 2
Application Procedure: Applicants must submit a personal application. Forms and further details are available from the MRC.
Closing Date: Round one is in August/September, and round two is in January/February, but applicants are advised to check the website for details
Funding: Government
No. of awards given last year: 2
No. of applicants last year: 20

MRC Senior Clinical Fellowship

Subjects: Biomedical sciences.
Purpose: To provide an opportunity for clinical researchers of exceptional ability to concentrate on a period of research.
Eligibility: Open to nationals of any country. Applicants are expected to have proven themselves to be independent researchers, be well qualified for an academic research career and demonstrate the promise of becoming future research leaders. The scheme is open to hospital doctors, dentists, general practitioners, nurses, midwives and allied health professionals. Applicants must hold a PhD or MD in a basic science or clinical project and have at least 3 years of postdoctoral research experience.
Level of Study: Postdoctorate, Research
Type: Fellowship
Value: Competitive personal salary support is provided plus research support staff at the technical and postdoctoral level, research expenses, capital equipment and a travel allowance for attendance at scientific conferences
Length of Study: Up to 5 years, with a possibility of renewal through open competition for a further 5 years
Frequency: Annual
Study Establishment: A suitable university department or similar institution
Country of Study: United Kingdom
No. of awards offered: Up to 4
Application Procedure: Applicants must submit a personal application. Forms and further details are available from the MRC.
Closing Date: Usually around August, but applicants are advised to check the website for details
Funding: Government
No. of awards given last year: 1
No. of applicants last year: 8

MRC Senior Non-Clinical Fellowship

Subjects: Biomedical sciences.
Purpose: To provide support for non-clinical scientists of exceptional ability to concentrate on a period of research.
Eligibility: Open to nationals of any country. Applicants are expected to have proven themselves to be independent researchers, be well qualified for an academic research career and demonstrate the promise of becoming future research leaders. It is expected that all applicants will hold a PhD or DPhil in a basic science project, have at least 6 years of relevant postdoctoral research experience and not hold a tenured position.
Level of Study: Postdoctorate, Research
Type: Fellowship
Value: Competitive personal salary support is provided plus research support staff at the technical and postdoctoral level, research expenses, capital equipment and a travel allowance for attendance at scientific conferences
Length of Study: Up to 5 years, with a possibility of renewal through open competition for a further 5 years
Frequency: Annual
Study Establishment: A suitable university department or similar institution
Country of Study: United Kingdom
No. of awards offered: Up to 6
Application Procedure: Applicants must submit a personal application. Forms and further details are available from the MRC.
Closing Date: Usually around September, but applicants are advised to check the website for details
Funding: Government
No. of awards given last year: 3
No. of applicants last year: 24

MRC Special Training Fellowships in Bioinformatics, Neuroinformatics and Computational Biology

Subjects: Biomedical sciences.
Purpose: To provide specialist, multidisciplinary research training at the doctoral or postdoctoral level.
Eligibility: The scheme is aimed at individuals from a variety of backgrounds such as non-biological as well as biological, non-clinical as well as clinical, and individuals with PhDs or MDs or with informatics research experience at the predoctoral level.
Level of Study: Postgraduate, Research
Type: Fellowship
Value: An appropriate academic salary will be provided along with a fixed sum for research expenses and a travel allowance for attendance at scientific conferences
Length of Study: Up to 4 years
Frequency: Annual
Study Establishment: A suitable university department or similar institution
Country of Study: United Kingdom
No. of awards offered: Up to 4
Application Procedure: Applicants must submit a personal application. Forms and further details are available from the MRC.
Closing Date: Applicants are advised to check the website for details
Funding: Government
No. of awards given last year: 5
No. of applicants last year: 23
Additional Information: Award holders are encouraged to apply for a PhD or MD if they do not already have one.

MRC Special Training Fellowships in Health Services and Health of the Public Research

Subjects: Biomedical sciences in health services research and health of the public, as defined by the MRC.
Purpose: To provide support for researchers wishing to gain further training in multidisciplinary research to address problems of direct relevance to the health services within the United Kingdom.
Eligibility: Open to non-medical graduates, hospital doctors, dentists, general practitioners, nurses, midwives and allied health professionals who are seeking a research career in health services and research.
Level of Study: Postdoctorate, Research
Type: Fellowship

Value: An appropriate academic salary will be provided along with a fixed sum for research expenses and a travel allowance for attendance at scientific conferences
Length of Study: Up to 4 years
Frequency: Annual
Study Establishment: A suitable university department or similar institution
Country of Study: United Kingdom
No. of awards offered: Up to 15
Application Procedure: Applicants must submit a personal application. Forms and further details are available from the MRC.
Closing Date: Usually around September/October, but applicants are advised to check the website for details
Funding: Government
No. of awards given last year: 10
No. of applicants last year: 52
Additional Information: Some awards are jointly funded with the Department of Health.

MRC/Academy of Medical Sciences Tenure Track Clinician Scientist Fellowship

Subjects: Biomedical sciences.
Purpose: To allow outstanding clinical researchers to consolidate their research skills and make the transition from postdoctoral research and training to becoming independent investigators, and to support career development and promote recruitment into clinical academic medicine.
Eligibility: Open to hospital doctors, dentists and general practitioners.
Level of Study: Postdoctorate, Research
Type: Fellowship
Value: Competitive personal salary support plus research support staff at the technical level, research expenses, capital equipment and a travel allowance for attendance at scientific conferences
Length of Study: Up to 5 years
Frequency: Annual
Study Establishment: A suitable university department or similar institution
Country of Study: United Kingdom
No. of awards offered: Varies
Application Procedure: Applicants must submit a personal application. Forms and further details are available from the MRC.
Closing Date: August/December, but applicants are advised to check the website for details
Funding: Government
No. of applicants last year: 40

MEDICAL RESEARCH SCOTLAND

Turcan Connell, Princes Exchange, 1 Earl Grey Street, Edinburgh, EH3 9EE, Scotland
Tel: (44) 131 659 8800
Fax: (44) 131 228 8118
Email: enquiries@medicalresearchscotland.org.uk
Website: www.medicalresearchscotland.org.uk
Contact: The Trust Administrator

Medical Research Scotland is comprehensive in its support of medical research and is not focused on research into any one disease or disorder. It supports the broad spectrum of clinical and laboratory-based medical research, all of which is aimed at improving the understanding of the basic mechanisms of disease processes, or improving the diagnosis, treatment or prevention of disease or the advancement of medical technology.

Research Project Grant

Purpose: To support people in the early stages of their careers in medical research, working in the medical, biological and physical sciences and whose research proposals are judged by international peer review to be of the highest quality.
Eligibility: Open to those who are under 35 years and hold a clinical or other professional qualification and are registered with the appropriate professional body, or hold a PhD (or equivalent) and have some years of research experience. Applicants from the physical sciences should have a co-applicant with expertise in the biomedical sciences. Research should be carried out in universities, recognized research

instituitions or NHS teaching hospitals in Scotland. Applicants may be based anywhere in the world at the time of application, but their research will be supported only if carried out in Scotland and hosted by a recognized research organization in Scotland.
Level of Study: Postdoctorate
Type: Project grant
Value: Currently up to £150,000
Length of Study: Up to 3 years
Frequency: Twice a year
Study Establishment: Universities, hospital research units or research institutions recognised as such
Country of Study: Scotland
No. of awards offered: Variable
Application Procedure: Applications must be submitted electronically, on forms available from the secure website. Full information about the application process is available on the website: www.medicalresearchscotland.org.uk
Closing Date: Mid-May and mid-October. Check the website for exact dates
Contributor: Income from the original endowment fund, established when the charity came into being in 1953, invested and augmented by voluntary donations and bequests
No. of awards given last year: 6
No. of applicants last year: 67
Additional Information: Applications are subject to a two-stage online process. Full applications are invited following rigorous peer review of outline applications. For complete details log on to www.medicalresearchscotland.org.uk

MEET THE COMPOSER, INC.

90 John Street, Suite 312, New York, NY, 10038, United States of America
Tel: (1) 212 645 6949
Fax: (1) 212 645 9669
Email: mtc@meetthecomposer.org
Website: www.meetthecomposer.org

Meet The Composer's mission is to increase artistic and financial opportunities for American composers by fostering the creation, performance, dissemination and appreciation of their music.

Commissioning Music/USA

Subjects: Music commissioning.
Purpose: To support the commissioning of new works.
Eligibility: Open to citizens of the United States of America only. Organizations that have been producing or presenting for at least 3 years are eligible and may be dance, chorus, orchestra, opera, theatre and music-theatre companies, festivals, arts presenters, public radio and television stations, internet providers, soloists and small performing ensembles of all kinds, e.g. jazz, chamber, new music, etc.
Level of Study: Professional development
Type: Grant
Value: Up to US$10,000–20,000
Frequency: Annual
Country of Study: United States of America
Application Procedure: Individuals cannot apply on their own. Host organizations must submit completed application forms and accompanying materials.
Closing Date: March 13th
Contributor: Offered in partnership with the National Endowment for the Arts
No. of awards given last year: 20–30
No. of applicants last year: 150–200

J P Morgan Chase Regrant Program for Small Ensembles

Subjects: Musical performance.
Purpose: To support small New York City-based ensembles and music organizations committed to performing the work of living composers and contemporary music.
Eligibility: Open to organizations focused primarily or exclusively on new music and living composers, improvisers, sound artists or singer/songwriters.
Level of Study: Professional development
Type: Grant

Value: US$1,000–5,000
Frequency: Annual
Country of Study: United States of America
Application Procedure: Applicants must contact the organization.
Closing Date: Contact organization
Funding: Commercial
Contributor: In partnership with J P Morgan Chase
No. of awards given last year: 15–20
No. of applicants last year: 75–100

MetLife Creative Connections

Subjects: Musical performance.
Purpose: To support US composers for the participation in public activities related to specific performances of their original music. Creative Connections aims to increase awareness and enhance the creative artist's role in society by strengthening the connections between living composers, performing musicians, presenters, communities and audiences.
Eligibility: Open to citizens of the United States of America only. Organizations may be choruses, dance, opera, theatre and music-theatre companies, symphonies, arts presenters, musical organizations, festivals, television production companies, radio stations and performing ensembles of all kinds, for example, jazz, chamber, new music etc. Awards are based solely on the overall quality of the application, which includes the merit of the composer, participation, and level of audience or community involvement.
Level of Study: Professional development
Type: Award
Value: Up to US$250–5,000
Country of Study: United States of America
Application Procedure: Individuals cannot apply themselves, as performing organizations apply on behalf of the composer. Interested parties should contact the organization for further details.
Closing Date: Application deadlines are quarterly: January 7th, April 1st, June 1st and October 1st
Contributor: MetLife
No. of awards given last year: 85
No. of applicants last year: 800–1,000

Music Alive

Subjects: Music.
Purpose: To offer financial and administrative support for composer-in-residence positions with orchestral ensembles. Residencies may be structured around one or multiple composers. The residency duration may range from one to three years with a minimum onsite composer presence of three weeks per season as well as a minimum performance of one work (created within the last ten years) per season by each resident composer.
Eligibility: Open to all League American Orchestra and youth member orchestras.
Level of Study: Professional development
Type: Residency
Value: US $10,000–100,000
Length of Study: 3 weeks per year, up to 3 years total
Frequency: Annual
Country of Study: United States of America
Application Procedure: Individuals cannot apply themselves, as performing organizations apply on behalf of the composer.
Closing Date: Contact organization
Contributor: Offered in partnership with the League American Orchestras
No. of awards given last year: 6
No. of applicants last year: 37

MELVILLE TRUST FOR CARE AND CURE OF CANCER

Tods Murray LLP, Edinburgh Quay, 133 Fountain Bridge, Edinburgh, EH3 9AG, Scotland
Tel: (44) 131 656 2000
Fax: (44) 131 656 2020
Email: maildesk@todsmurray.com

Melville Trust for Care and Cure of Cancer Research Fellowships

Subjects: The care and cure of cancer.
Purpose: To fund innovative research work.
Eligibility: Applicants need not necessarily hold a medical qualification or have experience of research.
Level of Study: Research
Type: Fellowship
Length of Study: Up to 2 years
Frequency: Annual
Study Establishment: One of the clinical or scientific departments in Lothian, Borders, Fife or Dundee
Application Procedure: Applicants must complete an application form and then be interviewed.
Closing Date: February 28th
Funding: Private
No. of awards given last year: 2
No. of applicants last year: 4

Melville Trust for Care and Cure of Cancer Research Grants

Subjects: The care and cure of cancer.
Purpose: To fund innovative research work.
Eligibility: Applicants need not necessarily hold a medical qualification or have experience of research.
Level of Study: Research
Type: Grant
Value: Up to UK £25,000
Length of Study: Up to 2 years
Frequency: Annual
Study Establishment: One of the clinical or scientific departments in Lothian, Borders, Fife or Dundee
Application Procedure: Applicants must complete an application form.
Closing Date: February 28th
Funding: Private
No. of awards given last year: 5
No. of applicants last year: 7

MEMORIAL FOUNDATION FOR JEWISH CULTURE

50 Broadway, 34th Floor, New York, NY, 10004, United States of America
Tel: (1) 212 425 6606
Fax: (1) 212 425 6602
Email: office@mfjc.org
Website: www.mfjc.org
Contact: Dr Jerry Hochbaum, Executive Vice President

The Memorial Foundation for Jewish Culture was established in 1965 to help assure a creative future for Jewish life throughout the world. The Foundation encourages Jewish scholarship, Jewish cultural creativity, and makes possible the training of professionals to serve in communities deprived of a large Jewish presence.

Memorial Foundation for Jewish Culture International Doctoral Scholarships

Subjects: Jewish studies.
Purpose: To assist in the training of future Jewish scholars for careers in Jewish scholarship and research, and to enable religious, educational and other Jewish communal workers to obtain advanced training for leadership positions.
Eligibility: Open to graduate students of any nationality who are specializing in a field of Jewish studies. Applicants must be officially enrolled or registered in a doctoral programme at a recognized university.
Level of Study: Doctorate
Type: Scholarship
Value: Up to US$10,000 a year
Length of Study: 1 academic year, renewable for a maximum of 4 years
Frequency: Annual
Study Establishment: A recognized university

Country of Study: Any country
No. of awards offered: Varies
Application Procedure: Applicants must write requesting an application form.
Closing Date: October 31st

Memorial Foundation for Jewish Culture International Fellowships in Jewish Studies

Subjects: A specialized field of Jewish studies that will make a significant contribution to the understanding, preservation, enhancement or transmission of Jewish culture.
Purpose: To allow well-qualified individuals to carry out independent scholarly, literary or artistic projects.
Eligibility: Open to recognized or qualified scholars, researchers or artists of any nationality who possess the knowledge and experience to formulate and implement a project in a specialized field of Jewish studies.
Level of Study: Unrestricted
Type: Fellowship
Value: Up to US$10,000 a year
Length of Study: 1 academic year, in exceptional cases renewable for a further year
Frequency: Annual
Country of Study: Any country
No. of awards offered: Varies
Application Procedure: Applicants must write requesting an application form.
Closing Date: October 31st

Memorial Foundation for Jewish Culture International Scholarship Programme for Community Service

Subjects: The rabbinate, Jewish education, communal service or religious functionaries, e.g. shohatim, mohalim.
Purpose: To assist well-qualified individuals for career training.
Eligibility: Open to any individual who is planning or who is currently undertaking training in his or her chosen field in a recognized Yeshiva, teacher training seminary, school of social work, university or other educational institution.
Level of Study: Unrestricted
Type: Scholarship
Value: US$1,000–3,000, but varies depending on the country in which the recipient is trained and other considerations
Length of Study: 1 year, renewable
Frequency: Annual
Study Establishment: Diaspora Jewish communities in need of such personnel
No. of awards offered: Varies
Application Procedure: Applicants must write for details.
Closing Date: November 30th
Additional Information: Recipients must commit themselves to serve a community of need. They should also be knowledgeable in the language and culture of that country or be prepared to learn it.

Memorial Foundation for Jewish Culture Scholarships for Post-Rabbinical Students

Subjects: Jewish studies.
Purpose: To assist in the training of future Jewish religious scholars and leaders and to assist newly ordained rabbis to obtain advanced training for careers as head of Yeshivot, as Dayanim and other leadership positions.
Eligibility: Open to recently ordained rabbis engaged in full-time studies at a Yeshiva, Kollel or a rabbinical seminary.
Level of Study: Unrestricted
Type: Scholarship
Value: Minimum award US$1,000 and maximum US$3,000
Length of Study: 1 year
Frequency: Annual
Country of Study: Any country
No. of awards offered: Varies
Application Procedure: Applicants must write for details.
Closing Date: October 31st
Additional Information: The Foundation also provides grants to bolster Jewish educational programmes in areas of need. Grants are awarded on the understanding that the recipient institution will assume responsibility for the programme following the initial limited period of Foundation support. Grants are made only for team or collaborative projects.

MEMORIAL UNIVERSITY OF NEWFOUNDLAND (MUN)

PO Box 4200 Station C, St Johns, NF, A1C 5S7, Canada
Tel: (1) 709 737 2445
Fax: (1) 709 737 4702
Email: info@mun.ca
Website: www.mun.ca

Located in Canada's most easterly province, Newfoundland and Labrador, Memorial University of Newfoundland (MUN) offers a diverse selection of Graduate programmes leading to diplomas, Master's and Doctoral degrees in the arts, sciences, professional and interdisciplinary areas of study. Their goal is to promote excellence in all aspects of Graduate education in order to assist students to fulfil their personal goals and to prepare for a productive career.

AG Hatcher Memorial Scholarship

Purpose: To provide financial assistance to students who have demonstrated high academic merit.
Eligibility: Open to applicants who have a high academic merit.
Level of Study: Graduate
Type: Scholarship
Value: Canadian $15,000
Frequency: Annual
No. of awards offered: 3
Closing Date: June 1st

The Dr Ethel M. Janes Memorial Scholarship in Education

Subjects: Reading or language arts.
Purpose: To aid students who want to specialize in reading and language arts and to those who want to make a career in research and teaching in primary and elementary education.
Level of Study: Graduate
Type: Scholarship
Value: Canadian $2,000
Frequency: Annual
No. of awards offered: 1

The ECHOS DU MONDE CLASSIQUE/Classical Views Internship Fund

Subjects: Editorial.
Purpose: To support a full time graduate student in Classics to train as an editorial intern with EMC/CV.
Eligibility: The applicant must be a full time graduate student in Classics to train as an editorial intern with EMC/CV.
Level of Study: Graduate
Type: Internship
Value: Canadian $10,000
Frequency: Annual
Contributor: Jointly sponsored by the journal ECHOS DU MONDE CLASSIQUE/ Classical Views and the school of Graduate studies

F.A. Aldrich Graduate Award

Subjects: All subjects.
Purpose: To enable students to undertake full time graduate programme based on academic merit and need only if all other things are equal.
Eligibility: Applicant must be enrolled in a full time graduate programme.
Type: Award
Value: US $2,000
Frequency: Annual
No. of awards offered: 3

The Imperial Tobacco Canada Limited Graduate Scholarship in Business Studies

Subjects: Business studies.
Purpose: To assist students whose area of specialization is business studies.

Level of Study: Graduate
Type: Scholarship
Value: Canadian $3,000
Frequency: Annual
No. of awards offered: 2
Contributor: Imperial Tobacco Canada Limited

The Maritime Awards Society of Canada (MASC) Maritime Studies Scholarship

Subjects: Maritime based Programme.
Purpose: To aid outstanding students who wish to study further.
Level of Study: Doctorate, Postdoctorate, Predoctorate
Type: Scholarship
Value: Canadian $5,000
Frequency: Annual
Study Establishment: Memorial University of Newfoundland
No. of awards offered: 3

Maritime History Internship

Subjects: Editorial.
Purpose: To support graduate students in history to train as an editorial intern with the journal The Northerner Mariner/Le Marin du nord.
Level of Study: Graduate, Postdoctorate, Predoctorate
Type: Internship
Value: Canadian $12,000
Frequency: Annual
No. of awards offered: Varies
Funding: Foundation
Contributor: Sponsored by Canadian Nautical Research Society and the School of Graduate Studies

The National Scholarship in Ocean Studies at Memorial University of Newfoundland

Subjects: Chemistry, biochemistry, biology, physics, earth science, geography, economics or engineering.
Purpose: To financially assist outstanding PhD candidates in an aspect of ocean studies.
Eligibility: Open to applicants who are outstanding PhD candidates in an aspect of ocean studies.
Level of Study: PhD
Value: CAN $18,000 and a one time grant of up to CAN $2,000 may be made in support of travel to appropriate conference where the student is presenting research findings
Frequency: Annual
Application Procedure: Application forms are available at the School of Graduate studies.
Closing Date: July 1st
Funding: Foundation

The P.J. Gardiner Award for Small Business and Entrepreneurship

Subjects: Business Programme.
Purpose: To recognize student creativity, innovation and entrepreneurship as evidenced by the establishment or plan to establish a new venture.
Eligibility: The applicant must submit a Venture Plan in the case of a proposed venture or a detailed description of a venture that they have already established.
Level of Study: Graduate
Value: CAN $5,000
Frequency: Annual
No. of awards offered: Varies
Funding: Foundation

The Peter Gardiner Award for International Study

Subjects: Business Studies.
Purpose: To support Business students to study at Memorial University of Newfoundland Harlow Campus or at another university outside Canada.
Level of Study: Graduate
Type: Award
Value: CAN $2,500
Frequency: Annual

Study Establishment: Memorial University of Newfoundland Harlow Campus or at another university outside Canada
No. of awards offered: 2
Funding: Foundation

The Sally Davis Scholarship

Subjects: Peace and international understanding, literacy, labour movement, gun control and environment.
Purpose: To provide financial support and celebrate the memory and life work of Sally Davis.
Eligibility: Open to candidates who are full-time students in the Master of Women's Studies programme.
Level of Study: Graduate
Type: Scholarship
Value: Canadian $1,000 will be awarded every year in the Spring semester
Frequency: Annual
Study Establishment: Memorial University of Newfoundland
Country of Study: Canada
Contributor: Family and friends of Sally

School of Graduate Studies F.A. Aldrich Fellowship

Purpose: To financially assist students with exceptional academic achievement to study further.
Eligibility: Open to full-time Canadian students on the basis of exceptional academic achievement.
Level of Study: Postdoctorate, Predoctorate
Type: Fellowship
Value: CAN $20,000 on the doctoral level and CAN $15,000 on the Master's level
Frequency: Annual
Study Establishment: Memorial University of Newfoundland
No. of awards offered: 6 to 8

MENINGITIS RESEARCH FOUNDATION

Midland Way, Thornbury, Bristol, BS35 2BS, England
Tel: (44) 14 5428 1811
Fax: (44) 14 5428 1094
Email: lindaglennie@meningitis.org
Website: www.meningitis.org
Contact: Mrs Joy Pepper, Research Administrator

Meningitis Research Foundation is a registered charity that supports an international programme of independently peer-reviewed research into the prevention, detection and treatment of meningitis and septicaemia. The Foundation also provides information for public and health professionals, runs medical and scientific meetings and provides support to people affected by the disease.

Meningitis Research Foundation Project Grant

Subjects: Meningitis and associated infections.
Purpose: To fight death and disability from meningitis and septicaemia by supporting research with the potential to produce results in immediate problem areas. Priority is given to work that is likely to bring clinical or public health benefits.
Eligibility: Meningitis Research Foundation research grants may be held in any country; nationality is not a restriction. Employees of commercial companies are not eligible to apply.
Level of Study: Research
Type: Project grant
Value: Up to UK £150,000 per year
Length of Study: Up to 5 years
Frequency: Annual
Study Establishment: Universities, research medical institutions and hospitals
Country of Study: Any country
No. of awards offered: 1
Application Procedure: Applicants must submit a two- or three-page outline proposal by email summarizing the work planned, the approximate cost and the duration of the project. This must include approximately ten lines explaining: (a) how the work described falls within the Foundation's research strategy, (b) the potential for clinical/public health benefit arising from this study and (c) why the applicant has chosen to apply to the Foundation for funding for this particular

project. Applicants who are invited to apply in full; submit a detailed research plan with other supporting documents. These are accessed by external referees and the Foundations scientific advisory panel.

Closing Date: Preliminary proposals will be accepted between September 13th and November 26th

Funding: Private

Contributor: Voluntary donations from the public

No. of awards given last year: 1

MESA STATE COLLEGE

PO Box 2647, 1100 North Avenue, Grand Junction, CO 81501, United States of America
Tel: (1) 970 248 1020
Fax: (1) 970 248 1973
Email: webmaster@mesastate.edu
Website: www.mesastate.edu
Contact: MBA Admissions Officer

Mesa State College, founded in 1925, is a comprehensive, liberal arts college that offers programmes at the Master's, baccalaureate, associate degree and certificate levels.

Brach, Louis and Betty Scholarship

Subjects: Natural science and mathematics.
Purpose: To provide financial assistance.
Eligibility: Open to full-time students who are in need of financial help.
Level of Study: Postgraduate
Type: Scholarship
Value: US$500
Length of Study: 1 year
Frequency: Annual
Study Establishment: Mesa State College
Country of Study: United States of America
Application Procedure: See the website.
Closing Date: March 1st

Bray Leadership Scholarship

Subjects: Business administration.
Eligibility: Open to full-time students pursuing a Bachelor of Business Administration degree.
Level of Study: Postgraduate
Type: Scholarship
Value: US$ 500 (value may vary)
Frequency: Annual
Study Establishment: Mesa State College
Country of Study: United States of America
Application Procedure: A completed application form must be submitted.
Closing Date: March 1st

Burkey Family Memorial Scholarship

Subjects: All subjects.
Eligibility: Open to candidates who are full-time seniors at the College.
Level of Study: Postgraduate
Type: Scholarship
Value: US$500
Length of Study: 1 year
Frequency: Annual
Study Establishment: Mesa State College
Country of Study: United States of America
Application Procedure: See the website.
Closing Date: March 1st

Hawkins, Edwin and Harriet History of Mathematics Scholarship

Subjects: Mathematics.
Eligibility: Open to full-time students enrolled in the spring mathematics course.
Level of Study: Postgraduate
Type: Scholarship
Value: US$1,000
Frequency: Annual

Study Establishment: Mesa State College
Country of Study: United States of America
Application Procedure: See the website.
Closing Date: March 3rd

Mesa State College Academic (Colorado) Scholarship

Subjects: Natural sciences and mathematics.
Eligibility: Open to students of Meta State College who are citizens of United States of America.
Level of Study: Postgraduate
Type: Scholarship
Value: Up to US$1,000
Length of Study: 1 year
Frequency: Annual
Study Establishment: Mesa State College
Country of Study: United States of America
Application Procedure: A completed application form, available on the website, must be submitted.
Closing Date: April 1st

MÉTIS CENTRE AT NAHO

220 Laurier Avenue, Suite 1200, Ottawa, ON, K1P-5Z9, Canada
Tel: (1) 613 237 9462
Fax: (1) 613 237 8707
Email: metiscentre@naho.ca
Website: www.naho.ca
Tel: 877 602 4445

The Métis Centre is a national, non-profit, Métis-controlled centre of the National Aboriginal Health Organization. The Métis Centre is dedicated to improving the mental, physical, spiritual, emotional and social health of all Métis in Canada through public education and health promotion.

Métis Centre Fellowship Program

Subjects: Health research.
Purpose: To financially support graduate students of Métis ancestry currently engaging in, or with an interest in, developing research on Métis population health.
Eligibility: Open to all students of Métis ancestry registered in a full-time graduate level programme at any Canadian university.
Level of Study: Postgraduate
Type: Fellowships
Value: Canadian $5,000
Frequency: Annual
Country of Study: Canada
No. of awards offered: 3
Application Procedure: There is no application form, the application package must consist of a cover letter, concise summary of the proposed research paper, official transcripts and letter of support from a faculty member familiar with the applicant's research, as well as from a Métis community member.
Closing Date: August 11th
Additional Information: Fellowship recipients will be required to submit a detailed methodology, literature review and research paper to the Métis Centre at NAHO within a specified timeframe.

THE METROPOLITAN MUSEUM OF ART

1000 Fifth Avenue, New York, NY, 10028-0198, United States of America
Tel: (1) 212 650 2763
Fax: (1) 212 570 3782
Email: communications@metmuseum.org
Website: www.metmuseum.org
Contact: Internship Programmes & Education

The Metropolitan Museum of Art is one of the world's largest and finest art museums. Its collections include more than two million works of art spanning 5,000 years of world culture, from prehistory to the present, and from every part of the world. As one of the greatest research institutions in the world, the Metropolitan Museum welcomes the responsibility to train future scholars and museum professionals. The Museum offers opportunities for students at several stages in their academic careers, from high school to the postgraduate level. Internships and apprenticeships can be either paid or unpaid, full- or part-time and can last from 9 weeks to an academic year.

Editorial, Design, and Video Internships in Educational Media

Subjects: Design, education and art history.
Purpose: To support students who wish to participate in the production of print, online and video publications created for families, teachers, students and the general museum public.
Eligibility: Open to candidates interested in careers in art museums.
Level of Study: Postgraduate
Type: Internship
Value: US$25,000
Length of Study: 1 year
Frequency: Annual
Study Establishment: The Metropolitan Museum of Art
Country of Study: United States of America
Application Procedure: For detailed information see the website.
Closing Date: January 4th

Lifchez/Stronach Curatorial Internship

Subjects: Art history.
Purpose: To support students interested in a curatorial career.
Eligibility: Open to students who are in need of financial assistance to pursue a career in art history.
Level of Study: Postgraduate
Type: Internship
Value: US$16,500
Frequency: Annual
Study Establishment: The Metropolitan Museum of Art
Country of Study: United States of America
Application Procedure: A typed application along with supporting materials must be sent.
Closing Date: January 4th
Contributor: Judith Lee Stronach and Raymond Lifchez

Metropolitan Museum of Art Roswell L Gilpatric Internship

Subjects: Museum studies.
Purpose: To support students showing an interest in museum careers.
Eligibility: Open to graduate students showing special interest in museum careers.
Level of Study: Graduate
Type: Internship
Value: Please contact organization for details
Length of Study: 9 weeks, from mid-June to mid-August
Frequency: Annual
Study Establishment: The Metropolitan Museum of Art
Country of Study: United States of America
No. of awards offered: Varies
Application Procedure: Applicants must submit a typed application including their name and address, a full curriculum vitae, two academic recommendations, official transcripts, a list of art history or other relevant courses taken and an essay or letter of not more than 500 words describing their career goals, interest in museum work and their reasons for applying. There are no application forms.
Closing Date: Please contact the Museum
Funding: Private
Contributor: The Thorne Foundation

Metropolitan Museum of Art Summer Internships for College Students

Subjects: Art history and related fields.
Purpose: To support students showing an interest in museum careers.
Eligibility: Open to recent graduates who have not yet entered graduate school. Candidates should have a strong background in art history and intend to pursue careers in art museums. It is not always possible to obtain a visa for foreign nationals.
Level of Study: Graduate
Type: Internship
Value: US$3,250

Length of Study: 10 weeks, full-time from June to August including 2 weeks of orientation
Frequency: Annual
Study Establishment: The Metropolitan Museum of Art
Country of Study: United States of America
No. of awards offered: Varies
Application Procedure: Applicants must submit a typed application including their name and address, a full curriculum vitae, two academic recommendations, official transcripts, a list of art history or other relevant courses taken and an essay or letter of not more than 500 words describing their career goals, interest in museum work and their reasons for applying. There are no application forms.
Closing Date: January 4th
Funding: Private
Contributor: The Lebensfeld Foundation, The Billy Rose Foundation, The Solow Art and Architecture Foundation and the Ittleson Foundation, Inc

Metropolitan Museum of Art Summer Internships for Graduate Students

Subjects: Art history and related fields.
Purpose: To support students showing an interest in museum careers.
Eligibility: Open to individuals who have completed at least 1 year of graduate work in art history or an allied field and who intend to pursue careers in art museums. It is not always possible to obtain a visa for foreign nationals.
Level of Study: Graduate
Type: Internship
Value: US$3,500 for graduate students
Length of Study: 10 weeks, full-time
Frequency: Annual
Study Establishment: The Metropolitan Museum of Art
Country of Study: United States of America
No. of awards offered: Varies
Application Procedure: Applicants must submit a typed application including their name and address, a full curriculum vitae, two academic recommendations, official transcripts, a list of art history or other relevant courses taken and an essay or letter of not more than 500 words describing their career goals, interest in museum work and their reasons for applying. There are no application forms.
Closing Date: January 19th
Funding: Private
Contributor: The Lebensfeld Foundation, The Billy Rose Foundation, Francine LeFrak Friedburg, the Solow Art and Architecture Foundation and the Ittleson Foundation, Inc
Additional Information: Graduate interns work on projects related to the Museum's collection or to a special exhibition as well as administrative areas.

The Tiffany & Co. Foundation Curatorial Internship in American Decorative Arts

Subjects: Museum management.
Eligibility: Open to postgraduates who are interested in careers in art museums.
Level of Study: Postgraduate, Research
Type: Internship
Value: US$25,000; stipend of US$3,000 available for research and educational travel
Length of Study: 1 year
Frequency: Annual
Application Procedure: See the website.
Closing Date: January 4th

MICHIGAN SOCIETY OF FELLOWS

University of Michigan, 0540 Rackham Building, 915 E Washington Street, Ann Arbor, MI, 48109-1070, United States of America
Tel: (1) 734 763 1259
Email: society.of.fellows@umich.edu
Website: www.rackham.umich.edu/Faculty/society.html
Contact: Administrative Assistant

The Michigan Society of Fellows with support from the Andrew W.Mellon Foundation promotes academic and creative excellence in the humanities and the arts, the social, physical and life sciences and the professions. The objective of the Society is to provide financial and intellectual support for individuals selected for outstanding achievement, professional promise and interdisciplinary interests.

Michigan Society of Fellows Postdoctoral Fellowships

Subjects: All subjects.
Purpose: To provide financial and intellectual support for individuals selected for outstanding achievement, professional promise and interdisciplinary interests.
Eligibility: Applicants must be near the beginning of their professional careers and have completed a PhD or comparable professional or artistic degree 3 years prior to application.
Level of Study: Postdoctorate
Type: Fellowship
Value: A stipend of US$51,500 per year
Length of Study: 3 years
Frequency: Annual
Study Establishment: The University of Michigan
Country of Study: United States of America
No. of awards offered: 8
Application Procedure: Applicants must complete an application form available from the website.
Closing Date: October 1st
Funding: Private
Contributor: The University of Michigan, Andrew W.Mellon Foundation
No. of awards given last year: 8
No. of applicants last year: 498

MICROSOFT RESEARCH

Microsoft Corporation, 1 Microsoft Way, Redmond, Washington, DC 98052-6399, United States of America
Tel: (1) 800 642 7676
Fax: (1) 425 93 936 7329
Email: erpinq@microsoft.com
Website: www.research.microsoft.com

In 1991, Microsoft Corporation became the first software company to create its own computer science research organization. It has developed into a unique entity among corporate research laboratories, balancing an open academic model with an effective process for transferring its research to product development teams.

Microsoft Fellowship

Subjects: Computer science.
Purpose: To empower and encourage PhD students in the Asia-Pacific region to realize their potential in computer science-related research and to recognize and award outstanding PhD students.
Eligibility: Open to candidates who specialize in computer science, electronic engineering, information technology or applied mathematics and are in their first or second year of PhD programme.
Level of Study: Research
Type: Fellowships
Value: US$6,000
Length of Study: 2 years
Frequency: Annual
Application Procedure: Applicants must send the completed application form (downloaded from the website), 2 recommendation letters, curriculum vitae and a video or Power Point presentation with audio introduction (on compact disk), including statement of purpose, previous, on-going and future projects, research interests and accomplishments.
Closing Date: May 31st
Additional Information: Previous Microsoft Fellows are excluded.

For further information contact:

MS Fellow 2006 Committee Microsoft Research Asia 3F Beijing Sigma Center No 49 Zhichun Road, Beijing PR, Haidian District, 100080, China
Email: fellowRA@microsoft.com

Microsoft Research European PhD Scholarship Programme

Subjects: Intersection of computing and the sciences including biology, chemistry and physics.

Purpose: To recognize and support exceptional students who show the potential to make an outstanding contribution to science.
Eligibility: Open to Europeans citizens.
Level of Study: Doctorate
Type: Scholarships
Value: €30,000 per year and a Tablet PC with a range of software applications
Length of Study: 3 years
Frequency: Annual
Closing Date: April
Additional Information: All queries shoud be sent to msrphd@microsoft.com.

Microsoft Research India PhD Fellowships

Subjects: Computer science.
Purpose: To encourage students to take up research as a career, a key qualification for which is to get a Doctoral degree.
Level of Study: Doctorate
Type: Grant
Value: US$5,000 per year and US$5,000 for attending seminars and conferences during the term of the fellowship
Length of Study: 4 years
Frequency: Annual
No. of awards offered: 5
Application Procedure: For application procedure information see the website.
Additional Information: The Fellows will also have the option of a 3–6 months internship at Microsoft Research India.

MINDA DE GUNZBURG CENTER FOR EUROPEAN STUDIES (CES) AT HARVARD UNIVERSITY

27 Kirkland Street, Cobotway, Cambridge, MA, 02138, United States of America
Tel: (1) 617 495 4303
Fax: (1) 617 495 8509
Email: ces@fas.harvard.edu
Website: www.ces.fas.harvard.edu/grants

The Minda de Gunzburg Center for European Studies at Harvard is dedicated to fostering the study of European history, politics and society. Through graduates, who go on to teach others about Europe and to many other roles in society, the Center sustains America's knowledge base about Europe, an important contribution to international understanding in difficult times.

Ariadne Graduate Summer Travel Grants to Greece

Subjects: Political, historical, economic, social, cultural,and intellectual trends in modern contemporary Greece.
Eligibility: Harvard doctoral students in the Faculty of Arts and Sciences may apply. Recepients must have completed two years of graduate school and have passed their general examinations. Grants must be used for research abroad during the summer break, and may not be used for language study, for expenses in the US, for special equipment such as tape recorders, or for fees for transcription or translation.
Level of Study: Research
Type: Travel grant
Value: A maximum of $6,000
Frequency: Annual
Study Establishment: Harvard University
Country of Study: United States of America
Application Procedure: Application forms can be downloaded from the CES website.
Closing Date: February 27th
Contributor: Gift from the Greek Ministry of Foreign Affairs to the Center for European Studies

Graduate Dissertation Research Fellowship

Subjects: Cultural, economic, historical, intellectual, political or social trends or on public policy in contemporary Europe (1750–present).
Purpose: To fund students from Harvard and the Massachusetts Institute of Technology who wish to conduct dissertation research.

Eligibility: Open to applicants from Harvard University in the faculty of arts and sciences and from Massachusetts Institute of Technology students of history, cultural studies and the social sciences. Recipients must have completed 2 years of graduate school and passed their general examinations but can be at any stage of research.
Level of Study: Doctorate, Research
Type: Fellowship
Value: US$24,000
Length of Study: 1 year
Frequency: Annual
Study Establishment: Harvard University
Country of Study: United States of America
Application Procedure: The application in pdf format is available on the CES website.
Closing Date: February 27th
Funding: Foundation
Contributor: Krupp Foundation and Minda de Gunzburg Center for European Studies
No. of awards given last year: 10
No. of applicants last year: 18
Additional Information: The fellowships cannot be deferred and must be used within the 12 month period for which they are awarded.

Graduate Summer Travel Grants

Subjects: Political, historical, economic, social, cultural and intellectual trends in contemporary Europe (1750–present).
Purpose: To fund summer research in Europe for doctoral students writing dissertations.
Eligibility: Open to Harvard doctoral students in the faculty of arts and sciences and Massachusetts Institute of Technology doctoral students in the social sciences or cultural studies.
Level of Study: Research
Type: Travel grant
Value: Maximum of US$6,000
Frequency: Annual
Study Establishment: Harvard University
Country of Study: United States of America
Application Procedure: The application form is available on the CES website.
Closing Date: February 27th
Contributor: Krupp Foundation and Minda de Gunzburg Center for European Studies
No. of awards given last year: 9
No. of applicants last year: 22
Additional Information: The Center funds research in Western and Central Europe. These grants are intended for students who have formulated a dissertation topic but do not require a long period of research abroad. Recipients must have completed 2 years of graduate school and have passed their general examinations.

Minda de Gunzberg Graduate Dissertation Writing Fellowship

Subjects: History, social sciences and cultural studies in modern or contemporary Europe(1750–present).
Purpose: To support students conducting dissertation work on contemporary Europe.
Eligibility: Open to advanced Harvard and Massachusetts Institute of Technology doctoral students. Students must have completed two draft dissertation chapters and submitted them to their advisor at the time of application.
Level of Study: Doctorate
Type: Fellowship
Value: US$22,000
Length of Study: 1 year
Frequency: Annual
Study Establishment: Harvard University
Country of Study: United States of America
Application Procedure: Application form is available on the CES website.
Closing Date: February 27th
Funding: Foundation
Contributor: Krupp Foundation and Minda de Gunzburg Center for European Studies
No. of awards given last year: 2
No. of applicants last year: 14

Additional Information: The fellowships cannot be deferred and must be used within the 12 month period for which they are awarded. No other employment is allowed under the grant except serving as an adviser for an undergraduate senior thesis. Students who have previously received writing/completion grants from other sources are not eligible.

MINERVA FOUNDATION

Society for Research Ltd., Hofgartenstrasse 8, D-80539, Munich, Germany
Tel: (49) 89 2108 1242
Fax: (49) 89 2108 1451
Email: info@theminervafoundation.com
Website: www.minerva.mpg.de

Minerva Fellowships

Subjects: All subjects.
Purpose: To fund scientific visits of Israeli scholars and scientists and to promote Israeli-German scientific co-operation.
Eligibility: Open to young scientists and researchers working in Israeli research institutes and universities. Candidates may be young doctoral and postdoctoral scientists, senior scientists or university teaching staff.
Level of Study: Research, Doctorate, Postdoctorate
Type: Fellowship
Value: €1,128 per month for scientists working on their PhD thesis, €2,100 per month for scientists (PhD) with 2 years working experience and €2,300 per month for scientists (PhD) with 5 years working experience
Length of Study: 6 months–3 years for doctoral candidates, 6 months–2 years for postdoctoral candidates
Study Establishment: A German university or research institute
Country of Study: Germany
Closing Date: January 15th and July 15th

Minerva Short-Term Research Grants

Subjects: All subjects.
Purpose: To fund scientific visits of Israeli scholars and scientists and to promote Israeli–German scientific co-operation.
Eligibility: Open to young scientists and researchers working in Israeli research institutes and universities. Candidates may be young doctoral and postdoctoral scientists, senior scientists or university teaching staff.
Level of Study: Research
Type: Grant
Value: €300 per week for doctoral candidates and €425 per week for postdoctoral candidates. (Additional payments like travel grants and family allowances are possible, depending on the type of the fellowship/grant)
Length of Study: 1–8 weeks
Study Establishment: A German university or research institute
Country of Study: Germany

MINISTRY OF EDUCATION, SCIENCE AND CULTURE (ICELAND)

Sölvhólsgata 4, IS-150, Reykjavik, Iceland
Tel: (354) 545 9500
Fax: (354) 562 3068
Email: postur@mrn.stjr.is
Website: www.eng.menntamalaraduneyti.is
Contact: Mrs Thórunn Bragadóttir, Division for Higher Education, Science & Research

The University of Iceland is a state university, founded in 1911. During its first year of operation 45 students were enrolled. Today, the university serves a nation of approximately 300,000 people and provides instruction for some 13,000 students studying in 5 schools and 26 faculties.

Ministry of Education, Science and Culture (Iceland) Scholarships in Icelandic Studies

Subjects: Icelandic studies for foreign students provides students with a good practical and theoretical basis for the Icelandic language and Icelandic culture. It facilitates further study in linguistics, literature, history and translation.

Eligibility: Citizens of the following countries may apply: Austria, Belgium, Bulgaria, Canada (if of Icelandic origin), China, Croatia, the Czech Republic, Denmark, Estonia, Faroe Islands, Finland, France, Germany, Greenland, Holland, Hungary, Ireland, Italy, Japan, Latvia, Lithuania, Norway, Poland, Russia, Slovakia, Spain, Sweden, Switzerland, Taiwan, the United Kingdom and United States of America. The scholarships are intended for students of language and literature. Preference will, as a rule, be given to a candidate under 35 years of age.

Level of Study: Unrestricted
Type: Scholarship
Value: Icelandic Krona 720,000 plus tuition
Length of Study: 8 months
Frequency: Annual
Study Establishment: The University of Iceland, Reykjavik
Country of Study: Iceland
No. of awards offered: 27–28
Application Procedure: The scholarship authorities of each cooperating country are invited to present applications for up to 3 candidates. Applicants must therefore apply to the relevant government department in their own country. Candidates from the United States of America should apply to the Institute of International Education. Candidates from the United Kingdomshould apply to the Icelandic Embassy. Candidates of Icelandic origin from Canada or the United States of America should apply to the Icelandic National League of North America, 103-94 1st Avenue, Gimli, MB ROC 1B1, Canada.
Closing Date: April 1st
Funding: Government
No. of awards given last year: 26
No. of applicants last year: 60
Additional Information: All applications must have been evaluated and forwarded to the Icelandic Ministry of Education, Science and Culture through the home country's scholarship authorities. A special committee in Iceland will decide on the outcome of the applications and its evaluation will be announced to the candidates in June/July. No one will be granted a scholarship more than 3 times.

For further information contact:

Icelandic Embassy, 2A Hans Street, London, SW1X 0JE, England
Email: icemb.london@utn.stjr.is
Website: www.iceland.org/uk

MINISTRY OF ENVIRONMENT & FORESTS (MOEF) GOVERNMENT OF INDIA

Wild Life Preservation, Paryavaran Bhavan CGO Complex, Lodhi Road, New Delhi, 110-003, India
Tel: (91) 11 2436 1147
Email: envisect@nic.in
Website: www.envfor.nic.in
Contact: The Director

The Ministry of Environment & Forests (MoEF) is an agency in the administrative structure of the Central Government, for the planning, promotion, co-ordination and overseeing the implementation of environmental and forestry programmes. The principal activities undertaken by MoEF are conservation and survey of flora, fauna, forests and wildlife, prevention and control of pollution, afforestation and regeneration of degraded areas and protection of environment in the frame-work of legislations.

Rajiv Gandhi Wildlife Conservation Award
Subjects: Wildlife conservation.
Purpose: To encourage individuals who will make a significant contribution in the field of wildlife and also a major impact on the protection and conservation of wildlife in the country.
Eligibility: Open to Indian citizens who are engaged in scientific work for the cause of protection and conservation of wildlife. There is no age limit.
Level of Study: Postgraduate
Type: Award

Value: Indian Rupees 1,00,000
Frequency: Annual
Country of Study: India
No. of awards offered: 2
Funding: Government

MINTEK

Human Resources Division, Private Bag X3015, Randburg, 2125, South Africa
Tel: (27) 11 709 4648
Fax: (27) 11 709 4465
Email: info@mintek.co.za
Website: www.mintek.co.za
Contact: Head of Academic Support

Mintek is the partially state-funded South African metallurgical research organization. Its mission is to serve the national interest through high-calibre research and development and technology transfer that promotes mineral technology, and to foster the establishment of small, medium and large industries in the field of minerals and products derived from them.

Mintek Bursaries
Subjects: Chemical, metallurgical and electrical engineering, light current and electronics, chemistry, with an emphasis on inorganic, physical or analytical chemistry, metallurgy, extraction and mineralogy, geology and physics.
Purpose: To promote the training of research workers for the minerals industry in general and to meet its own needs for technically trained people.
Eligibility: Open to graduates of any nationality who possess an appropriate 4-year degree or higher qualification. A knowledge of English is essential. Preference is given to South African citizens. Merit and excellence are the criteria for selection. The project should be a promising development that will contribute to Mintek's activities and is in line with its strategic purpose. The student must have a strong academic background and show the potential to develop expertise that would benefit Mintek, and the institution where the project is carried out should be a centre of excellence in the subject.
Level of Study: Postgraduate
Type: Bursary
Value: Rand 32,400 per year for a MSc degree and Rand 40,200 per year for a PhD degree
Length of Study: Up to 2 years. Extension of this period can be granted by the President of Mintek
Frequency: Annual
Study Establishment: Any university or technikons in fields that complement its own activities
Country of Study: South Africa
No. of awards offered: 35
Application Procedure: Applicants must write for details.
Closing Date: There is no deadline
Funding: Government
Additional Information: Candidates are requested to sign a contract before starting their project. Usually, Mintek insists on a service commitment from the bursar on the completion of his or her studies on a year-to-year basis. Bursars are paid a monthly bursary-salary and Mintek pays the institution an amount to cover the project's running costs.

MINTRAC NATIONAL MEAT INDUSTRY TRAINING ADVISORY COUNCIL LIMITED

Suite 2, 150 Victoria Road, Drummoyne, NSW 2047, Australia
Tel: (61) (02) 9819 6699
Fax: (61) (02) 9819 6099
Email: mintrac@mintrac.com.au
Website: www.mintrac.com.au/index.php

Aims to provide highly valued services to the Meat Industry in the areas of education and training development and advocacy along with providing products and services in accordance with world's best practice, satisfying and rewarding career paths for industry participants at every level, and securing and maintaining the ongoing commitment of the industry and its financial supporters.

MINTRAC Postgraduate Scholarship

Subjects: Research related to meat industry.
Purpose: To offer scholarships to students undertaking Honours, Masters or Doctorate programs with research in the meat industry.
Eligibility: Open to the candidates who want to undertake postgraduate research degrees (for Masters and Doctorate students) in disciplines relevant to the meat industry.
Level of Study: Doctorate, Postgraduate
Type: Scholarship
Value: $25,000 (full-time) and $12,500 (part-time) per year to students proceeding to Masters or Doctorate. $19,000 (full-time) and $9,500 (part-time) per year to students proceeding towards an Honours degree
Frequency: Ongoing
Study Establishment: Australian Universities
Country of Study: Australia
Application Procedure: Applicants must send the applications along with academic transcript(s), Overview of R&D project, Supervisor's letter confirming acceptance of proposed study, Meat industry conformation letter (unless forwarded separately), and Referee's reports (unless forwarded separately).
Funding: Private
Contributor: Red meat industry
Additional Information: A thesis allowance of $800 will be paid to the student on receipt of their thesis and précis and on the condition that progress reports have been received in a timely manner.

MISSOURI BOTANICAL GARDEN

PO Box 299, St Louis, MO, 63166-0299, United States of America
Tel: (1) 314 577 0253
Fax: (1) 314 577 0800
Email: ruthann.bizoff@mobot.org
Website: www.wlbcenter.org
Contact: Rainer W Bussman, Head & Curator of Economic Botany

Missouri Botanical Garden was founded in 1859 and is one of the oldest botanical institutions in the country. The Garden is a centre for botanical research and science education.

Anne S. Chatham Fellowship in Medicinal Botany

Subjects: Biology.
Purpose: To support candidates who wish to pursue their studies in medicinal botany.
Eligibility: Open to all nationalities.
Level of Study: Doctorate
Type: Fellowships
Value: Up to US$4,000
Frequency: Annual
Country of Study: United States of America
No. of awards offered: 1–2 awards
Application Procedure: Applicants need to submit their application forms along with statement of purpose, financial need analysis, essay and reference letters.
Closing Date: January 15th
Funding: Foundation
No. of awards given last year: 2
Additional Information: The fellowship was established to protect and preserve knowledge about the medicinal use of plants, and thus prevent the disappearance of plants with therapeutic potential.

MISSOURI STATE UNIVERSITY

College of Business Administration, 400 David D Glass Hall, Springfield, MO 65897, United States of America
Tel: (1) 417 836 5646
Fax: (1) 417 836 4407
Email: mbaprogram@missouristate.edu
Website: www.coba.missouristate.edu
Contact: MBA Admissions Officer

Missouri State University is a college of business administration offering courses in various departments. The programme will provide the background knowledge necessary for professional practice in the field of business. In the eyes of MBA students at Missouri State University, educational value is defined by a high-quality programme, low tuition rates and low living costs in an attractive locale.

Missouri State University Carr Foundation Scholarship

Subjects: MBA.
Purpose: To assist students with expenses and to enhance learning.
Eligibility: Students must be enrolled in the MBA programme and display financial need.
Level of Study: Graduate
Type: Scholarship
Value: US$600
Length of Study: Varies
Study Establishment: Missouri State University
Country of Study: United States of America
No. of awards offered: 1
Application Procedure: Applicants must contact the organization for application details.
Closing Date: Please contact the organization
Additional Information: The scholarship is automatically renewed as long as the student maintains satisfactory academic progress; however, the recipient must reapply to renew.

Missouri State University Graduate Assistantships

Subjects: All subjects.
Purpose: To assist students with expenses and to enhance learning while studying for advanced degrees at Missouri State University.
Eligibility: Applicants must be admitted to a graduate programme at MSU to be eligible. A minimum grade point average of 3.00 on the last 60 hours of undergraduate coursework or a minimum grade point average of 3.00 on 9 hours or more of graduate coursework is required. Graduate students who did not receive both their primary and secondary education where English was the primary language must meet the following requirements to qualify for graduate assistantships: successful completion of one semester of graduate studies at MSU, during which they complete cultural orientation to prepare them for a teaching appointment and pass an MSU-juried examination, in which the candidate must demonstrate his or her ability to interpret written English passages and to communicate orally in English in a classroom setting.
Level of Study: Graduate, MBA
Value: A minimum stipend of US$7,340 for the academic year (9 months). In a few situations, a stipend of US$9,730 may be awarded
Length of Study: A maximum of 2 years (including Fall, Spring, and Summer)
Frequency: Annual
Study Establishment: Missouri State University
Country of Study: United States of America
No. of awards offered: Varies
Application Procedure: Applicants must submit an application directly to the department in which the assistantship is sought. It is wise to check with the department before applying. Information from an applicant must include employment history, academic history and the addresses of referees. Applications are available from the Graduate Research College and on the website.
Additional Information: For further information visit the website or contact the Graduate Research College.

Missouri State University Robert and Charlotte Bitter Graduate Scholarship

Subjects: MBA.
Purpose: To assist students with expenses and to enhance learning.
Eligibility: Applicants must have been admitted to the MBA or MACC programme, be enrolled in 12 hours or more each semester or enrolled in 6 hours or more each semester if the student is a graduate assistant, have a combined formula score (200 x grade point average Graduate Management Admission Test score) of 1,100 or higher and minimum 3.33 graduate grade point average, have completed a minimum of 24 hours or 15 hours if the student is a graduate assistant,

and have completed all prerequisite courses or be currently enrolled in final prerequisite courses.
Level of Study: Graduate, MBA
Type: Scholarship
Value: US$1,000
Length of Study: Varies
Frequency: Annual
Study Establishment: Missouri State University
Country of Study: United States of America
No. of awards offered: 1
Application Procedure: Applicants must contact the organization for application details.
Closing Date: Please contact the organization

MIZUTANI FOUNDATION FOR GLYCOSCIENCE

Marunouchi Center Bldg. 10f, 1-6-1 Marunouchi, Chiyoda-ku, Tokyo, 100-0005, Japan
Tel: (81) 3 5220 8977
Fax: (81) 3 5220 8978
Email: info@mizutanifdn.or.jp
Website: www.mizutanifdn.or.jp
Contact: Takashi Kato, Executive Secretary

The Mizutani Foundation for Glycoscience undertakes major programmes such as the worldwide distribution of research grants to qualified glycoscientists for their outstanding basic research, assistance of international exchanges between Japanese and foreign glycosciences, contributions to glycoscience-related meetings in Japan and practice of other activities that are necessary to achieve the aims of the Foundation.

Mizutani Foundation for Glycoscience Research Grants
Subjects: Glycoscience.
Purpose: To contribute to human welfare, through the enhancement of glycoscience, by awarding grants for creative research in glycoscience conducted by domestic and overseas researchers, by awarding grants for international exchanges and for convening conferences in the field of glycoscience.
Eligibility: Open to those with a doctorate corresponding to a PhD or MD in the United States of America in a field relevant to the proposed project, who have documented capability in performing independent studies and are members of a scientific institution where they can carry out the proposed study. An applicant who has been awarded the grant previously may reapply after 5 years.
Level of Study: Doctorate, Postdoctorate
Value: ¥3,000,000–7,000,000
Length of Study: 1 year
Frequency: Annual
Country of Study: Any country
No. of awards offered: 10–15
Application Procedure: Applicants must download an application form from the website.
Closing Date: The term for applications is from July 1st to September 1st
Funding: Foundation
Contributor: Seikagaku Corporation
No. of awards given last year: 15
No. of applicants last year: 99

MODERN LANGUAGE ASSOCIATION OF AMERICA (MLA)

26 Broadway, 3rd Floor, New York, NY, 10004-1789, United States of America
Tel: (1) 646 576 5141
Fax: (1) 646 458 0030
Email: awards@mla.org
Website: www.mla.org
Contact: Ms Annie Reiser, Co-ordinator, MLA Book Prizes

The Modern Language Association of America (MLA) is a non-profit membership organization that promotes the study and teaching of language and literature in English and foreign languages.

Aldo and Jeanne Scaglione Prize for a Translation of a Literary Work
Subjects: Translation.
Purpose: To award an outstanding translation of a book-length literary work into English.
Eligibility: Open to translations published in the year preceding the year in which the award is given.
Type: Prize
Value: US$2,000
Frequency: Every 2 years
No. of awards offered: 1
Application Procedure: Applicants must send six copies of the work. For detailed information about specific prizes, applicants should contact the MLA.
Closing Date: April 1st
Funding: Private

Aldo and Jeanne Scaglione Prize for Comparative Literary Studies
Subjects: Comparative literary and cultural studies involving at least two literatures.
Purpose: To recognize outstanding scholarly work in comparative literary studies.
Eligibility: Open to books published in the year preceding the year in which the award is given. Authors must be members of the MLA.
Level of Study: Postdoctorate
Type: Prize
Value: US$2,000
Frequency: Annual
No. of awards offered: 1
Application Procedure: Applicants must send four copies of the work. For detailed information about specific prizes, applicants should contact the MLA.
Closing Date: May 1st
Funding: Private

Aldo and Jeanne Scaglione Prize for French and Francophone Literary Studies
Subjects: French and Francophone linguistic or literary studies.
Purpose: To recognize outstanding scholarly work.
Eligibility: Open to books published in the year preceding the year in which the prize is given. Authors must be members of the MLA.
Level of Study: Postdoctorate
Type: Prize
Value: US$2,000
Frequency: Annual
No. of awards offered: 1
Application Procedure: Applicants must send four copies of the work. For detailed information about specific prizes, applicants should contact the MLA.
Closing Date: May 1st
Funding: Private

Aldo and Jeanne Scaglione Prize for Italian Studies
Subjects: Italian literature, culture or comparative literature involving Italy.
Purpose: To award an outstanding scholarly work.
Eligibility: Open to books published in the year preceding the year in which the award is given. Authors must be members of the MLA.
Level of Study: Postdoctorate
Type: Prize
Value: US$2,000
Frequency: Every 2 years
No. of awards offered: 1
Application Procedure: Applicants must send four copies of the work. For detailed information about specific prizes, applicants should contact the MLA.
Closing Date: May 1st
Funding: Private

Aldo and Jeanne Scaglione Prize for Studies in Germanic Languages and Literatures

Subjects: The linguistics or literatures of any of the Germanic languages including Danish, Dutch, German, Norwegian, Swedish or Yiddish.

Purpose: To recognize an outstanding scholarly work.

Eligibility: Authors must be members of the MLA. Books must have been published in the 2 years preceding the year of the award.

Level of Study: Postdoctorate

Type: Prize

Value: US$2,000

Frequency: Every 2 years

No. of awards offered: 1

Application Procedure: Applicants must send four copies of the work. For detailed information about specific prizes, applicants should contact the MLA.

Closing Date: May 1st

Funding: Private

Aldo and Jeanne Scaglione Prize for Studies in Slavic Languages and Literatures

Subjects: Linguistic or literary study of a work in a Slavic language.

Purpose: To recognize an outstanding scholarly work.

Eligibility: Open to books published no more than two years preceding the year in which the prize is given. Authors need not be members of the MLA.

Level of Study: Postdoctorate

Type: Prize

Value: US$2,000

Frequency: Every 2 years

No. of awards offered: 1

Application Procedure: Applicants must send four copies of the work. For detailed information about specific prizes, applicants should contact the MLA.

Closing Date: May 1st

Funding: Private

Aldo and Jeanne Scaglione Prize for Translation of a Scholarly Study of Literature

Subjects: Translation.

Purpose: To recognize an outstanding translation of a book-length work of literary history, literary criticism, philology and literary theory into English.

Eligibility: Open to books published no more than 2 years preceding the year in which the prize is given. Authors need not be members of the MLA.

Level of Study: Postdoctorate

Type: Prize

Value: US$2,000

Frequency: Every 2 years

No. of awards offered: 1

Application Procedure: Applicants must send four copies of the work. For detailed information about specific prizes, applicants should contact the MLA.

Closing Date: May 1st

Funding: Private

Fenia and Yaakov Leviant Memorial Prize in Yiddish Studies

Subjects: English translation of a Yiddish literary work and/or Yiddish literature and culture.

Purpose: To recognize an outstanding translation into English or an outstanding scholarly work in the field of Yiddish.

Eligibility: The prize is awarded alternately to a translation or scholarly work in the field of Yiddish.

Level of Study: Postdoctorate

Type: Prize

Value: US$1,000

Frequency: Every 2 years

No. of awards offered: 1

Application Procedure: Applicants must send four copies of the work. For detailed information about specific prizes, applicants should contact the MLA.

Closing Date: May 1st

Funding: Private

Howard R Marraro Prize

Subjects: Italian literature or comparative literature involving Italian.

Purpose: To award an outstanding scholarly work.

Eligibility: Authors must be members of the MLA.

Level of Study: Postdoctorate

Type: Prize

Value: US$1,000

Frequency: Every 2 years

No. of awards offered: 1

Application Procedure: Applicants must send four copies of the work. For detailed information about specific prizes, applicants should contact the MLA.

Closing Date: May 1st

Funding: Private

James Russell Lowell Prize

Subjects: Literary theory, media, cultural history and interdisciplinary topics.

Purpose: To recognize an outstanding literary or linguistic study, a critical edition of an important work or a critical biography.

Eligibility: Open to books published the year preceding the year in which the award is due to be given. Authors must be current members of the MLA.

Level of Study: Postdoctorate

Type: Prize

Value: US$1,000

Frequency: Annual

No. of awards offered: 1

Application Procedure: Applicants must send six copies of the work. For detailed information about specific prizes, applicants should contact the MLA.

Closing Date: March 1st

Funding: Private

Katherine Singer Kovacs Prize

Subjects: Latin American or Spanish literatures and cultures.

Purpose: To recognize an outstanding book published in English in the field.

Eligibility: Open to books published the year preceding the year in which the prize is given. Competing books should be broadly interpretative works that enhance the understanding of the interrelations among literature, the arts and society.

Level of Study: Postdoctorate

Type: Prize

Value: US$1,000

Frequency: Annual

No. of awards offered: 1

Application Procedure: Applicants must send six copies of the work. For detailed information about specific prizes, applicants should contact the MLA.

Closing Date: May 1st

Funding: Private

Kenneth W Mildenberger Prize

Subjects: The teaching of languages and literatures, other than English.

Purpose: To support work in the field of the teaching of languages and literatures, other than English.

Eligibility: Authors need not be members of the MLA. Open to books published in the year preceding the year in which the prize is given.

Level of Study: Postdoctorate

Type: Prize

Value: US$1,000

Frequency: Annual

No. of awards offered: 1

Application Procedure: Applicants must send four copies of the work. For detailed information about specific prizes, applicants should contact the MLA.

Closing Date: May 1st

Funding: Private

Additional Information: The prize is given for a research article in odd-numbered years and a book in even-numbered years.

Lois Roth Award for a Translation of Literary Work

Subjects: Translation.

Purpose: To recognize an outstanding translation of a book-length literary work into English.

Eligibility: Open to translations published in the year preceding the year in which the prize is given. Translators need not be members of the MLA.

Level of Study: Postdoctorate

Type: Prize

Value: US$1,000

Frequency: Every 2 years

No. of awards offered: 1

Application Procedure: Applicants must send six copies of the work. For detailed information about specific prizes, applicants should contact the MLA.

Closing Date: April 1st

Funding: Private

Mina P Shaughnessy Prize

Subjects: Teaching English language, literature, rhetoric and composition.

Purpose: To recognize a research publication in the field of teaching English language, literature, rhetoric and composition.

Eligibility: Open to books published in the year preceding the year in which the prize is given. Authors need not be members of the MLA.

Level of Study: Postdoctorate

Type: Prize

Value: US$1,000

Frequency: Annual

No. of awards offered: 1

Application Procedure: Applicants must send four copies of the work. For detailed information about specific prizes, applicants should contact the MLA.

Closing Date: May 1st

MLA Prize for a Distinguished Bibliography

Subjects: Bibliography.

Purpose: To award an outstanding enumerative or descriptive bibliography.

Eligibility: Editors need not be members of the MLA. Open to books published during the 2 years preceding the year in which the prize is given.

Level of Study: Postdoctorate

Type: Prize

Value: US$1,000

Frequency: Every 2 years

No. of awards offered: 1

Application Procedure: Applicants must send four copies of the work. For detailed information applicants should contact the MLA.

Closing Date: May 1st

Funding: Private

MLA Prize for a Distinguished Scholarly Edition

Subjects: Works in any of the modern languages.

Purpose: To recognize an outstanding scholarly edition.

Eligibility: At least 1 volume must have been published during the 2 years preceding the year in which the award is given. Editors need not be members of the MLA. Editions may be single or multiple volumes.

Level of Study: Postdoctorate

Type: Prize

Value: US$1,000

Frequency: Every 2 years

No. of awards offered: 1

Application Procedure: Applicants must send four copies of the work. For detailed information about specific prizes, applicants should contact the MLA.

Closing Date: May 1st

Funding: Private

MLA Prize for a First Book

Subjects: Literary theory, media, cultural history or interdisciplinary topics.

Purpose: To recognize an outstanding literary or linguistic study, or a critical biography.

Eligibility: Open to books published in the year preceding the year in which the prize is given as the first book-length publication of a current MLA member.

Level of Study: Postdoctorate

Type: Prize

Value: US$1,000

Frequency: Annual

No. of awards offered: 1

Application Procedure: Applicants must send six copies of the work. For detailed information about specific prizes, applicants should contact the MLA.

Closing Date: April 1st

Funding: Private

MLA Prize for Independent Scholars

Subjects: English or other modern languages and literatures.

Purpose: To award a scholarly book in the field of modern languages.

Eligibility: Open to books published in the year preceding the year in which the prize is given. At the time of publication of the book, the author must not be enrolled in a programme leading to an academic degree or hold a tenured, tenure-accruing or tenure-track position in postsecondary education. Authors need not be members of the MLA.

Level of Study: Postdoctorate

Type: Prize

Value: US$1,000

Frequency: Annual

No. of awards offered: 1

Application Procedure: Applicants must send six copies of the work. For detailed information about specific prizes, applicants should contact the MLA.

Closing Date: May 1st

Funding: Private

MLA Prize in Latina and Latino or Chicana and Chicano Literary and Cultural Studies

Subjects: Chicana and Chicano, Latina and Latino literary or cultural studies.

Purpose: To award an outstanding scholarly study.

Eligibility: Open to authors who are members of the MLA.

Level of Study: Postdoctorate

Type: Prize

Value: US$1,000

Frequency: Annual

No. of awards offered: 1

Application Procedure: Applicants must send four copies of their work. For detailed information about specific prizes, applicants should contact the MLA.

Closing Date: May 1st

Funding: Private

Morton N Cohen Award for A Distinguished Edition of Letters

Subjects: Edition of letters in any of the modern languages.

Eligibility: At least one volume must have been published during the 2 years preceding the year in which the award is given. Editors need not be members of the MLA. Editions may be single or multiple volumes.

Level of Study: Postdoctorate

Type: Award

Value: US$1,000

Frequency: Every 2 years

No. of awards offered: 1

Application Procedure: Applicants must send four copies of the work. For detailed information about specific prizes, applicants should contact the MLA.

Closing Date: May 1st

Funding: Private

William Sanders Scarborough Prize

Subjects: Black American literature and culture.

Purpose: To recognize an outstanding scholarly book in the field of Black American literature or culture.

Eligibility: Books that are primarily translations will not be considered.

Level of Study: Postdoctorate

Type: Prize

Value: US$1,000
Frequency: Annual
No. of awards offered: 1
Application Procedure: Applicants must send four copies of the work. For detailed information about specific prizes, applicants should contact the MLA.
Closing Date: May 1st

MONASH UNIVERSITY

Wellington Road, Clayton, VIC 3800, Australia
Tel: (61) 3 9905 3009
Fax: (61) 3 9905 5042
Email: mrgs@adm.monash.edu.au
Website: www.mrgs.monash.edu.au
Contact: Monash Research Graduate School

Monash University is one of Australia's largest universities, with ten faculties covering every major area of intellectual activity, six campuses in Australia and an increasing global presence. Research at Monash covers the full spectrum from fundamental to applied research and ranges across the arts and humanities, social, natural, health and medical sciences and the technological sciences. The University is determined to preserve its strength in fundamental research, which underpins its successes in applied research, and to continue to make a distinguished contribution to intellectual and cultural life.

Monash Graduate Scholarship

Subjects: All subjects.
Purpose: To provide support for supervised full-time research at the masters and doctoral levels.
Eligibility: Open to graduates of any Australian or overseas university who holds a First Class (Honours) Bachelors degree or equivalent.
Level of Study: Doctorate, Postgraduate, Research
Type: Scholarship
Value: Australian $20,427
Length of Study: Upto 2 years for the Master's degree and upto 3 years witha possible extension for 6 months for the doctoral degree
Frequency: Annual
Study Establishment: Monash University
Country of Study: Australia
No. of awards offered: 150
Application Procedure: Applicants must apply directly to the university. Check website www.mrgs.monash.edu.au/scholarships for further details.
Closing Date: October 31st

For further information contact:

Monash Research Graduate School, Building 3d (Ground Floor), Wellington Road, Clayton, Vic, Australia
Tel: (61) 03 9905 2070
Fax: (61) 03 9905 5042
Email: arun.kumar@adm.monash.edu.au
Website: www.mrgs.monash.edu.au
Contact: Arun Kumar

Monash International Postgraduate Research Scholarship (MIPRS)

Subjects: All subjects.
Purpose: To provide support for supervised full-time research at the Master's and doctoral level.
Eligibility: Open to graduates of any Australian or overseas university who hold a First Class (Honours) Bachelor's Degree or equivalent.
Level of Study: Doctorate, Master's by Research
Type: Scholarship
Value: The award meets the full cost of international tuition fees and overseas student health cover (OSHC)
Length of Study: Up to 2 years for the Master's degree and up to 3 years with the possibility of an additional 6-month extension for the doctoral degree
Frequency: Annual
Study Establishment: Monash University
Country of Study: Australia
No. of awards offered: 70

Application Procedure: Please see the website www.mrgs.monash.edu.au/scholarships for further details.
Closing Date: October 31st
Additional Information: International students must meet English language proficiency requirements.

Monash University Silver Jubilee Postgraduate Scholarship

Subjects: Different subjects areawarded by rotation to faculties.
Purpose: To provide supervised full-time research at the Master's and doctoral level.
Eligibility: Open to graduates of any Australian or overseas university who hold a First Class (Honours) Bachelor's Degree or equivalent.
Level of Study: Doctorate, Master's by Research candidates
Type: Scholarship
Value: Australian $26,140 per year plus relocation, research and thesis allowance
Length of Study: Up to 2 years for the Master's degree and up to 3 years with the possibility of an additional 6-month extension for the doctoral degree
Frequency: Annual
Study Establishment: Monash University
Country of Study: Australia
No. of awards offered: 1
Application Procedure: Please visit our website ww.mrgs.monash.edu.au/scholarships for further details.
Closing Date: October 31st
Additional Information: International students must meet English language proficiency requirements.

Sir James McNeill Foundation Postgraduate Scholarship

Subjects: Engineering, medicine, music and science.
Purpose: To enable a PhD scholar to pursue a full-time programme of research that is both environmentally responsible and socially beneficial to the community.
Eligibility: Open to graduates of any Australian or overseas university who hold a First Class (Honours) Bachelor's Degree or equivalent.
Level of Study: Doctorate
Type: Scholarship
Value: Australian $26,640
Length of Study: Up to 3 years, with the possibility of an additional 6-month extension
Frequency: Annual
Study Establishment: Monash University
Country of Study: Australia
No. of awards offered: 1
Application Procedure: Please see the website www.mrgs.monash.edu.au/scholarships for further details
Closing Date: October 31st
No. of awards given last year: 1
No. of applicants last year: N/A
Additional Information: International students must meet English language proficiency requirements.

Vera Moore International Postgraduate Research Scholarships

Subjects: All subjects.
Purpose: To provide support for supervised full-time research at the Master's and doctoral level.
Eligibility: Open to graduates of any Australian or overseas university who hold a First Class (Honours) Bachelor's Degree or equivalent.
Level of Study: Doctorate
Type: Scholarship
Value: The full cost of tuition fees plus a research allowance of up to Australian $550 per year, and overseas student health cover
Length of Study: Up to 2 years for the Master's degree and up to 3 years with the possibility of an additional 6 months extension for the doctoral degree
Frequency: Annual
Study Establishment: Monash University
Country of Study: Australia
No. of awards offered: 1
Closing Date: October 31st
Additional Information: International students must meet English language proficiency requirements.

MONTANA STATE UNIVERSITY-BILLINGS

1500 University Drive, Billings, MT 59101-0298, United States of America
Tel: (1) 657 2244
Fax: (1) 657 1600
Email: finaid@msubillings.edu
Website: www.msubillings.edu

The Montana State University-Billings is dedicated to the development of workforce capacity by providing top quality learning opportunities and services to meet a variety of career choices and customer needs by being responsive, flexible and market driven.

Abrahamson Family Endowed Scholarship

Subjects: All subjects.
Purpose: To provide financial assistance.
Eligibility: Open to full-time enrolled students who are residents of Montana or Wyoming.
Level of Study: Postgraduate
Type: Scholarship
Value: US$1,300
Frequency: Annual
Study Establishment: Montana State University-Billings
Country of Study: United States of America
Application Procedure: See website.
Closing Date: February 1st

The Berg Family Endowed Scholarship

Subjects: Humanities area including English, philosophy and history.
Purpose: To provide financial assistance.
Eligibility: Open to residents of Montana Community who are between the age of 18 and 22.
Level of Study: Postgraduate
Type: Scholarship
Length of Study: US$1,150
Frequency: Annual
Study Establishment: Montana State University-Billings
Country of Study: United States of America
No. of awards offered: 2
Application Procedure: Complete details available on the website.
Closing Date: February 1st
Contributor: The Billings Foundation

Billings Broadcasters MSU-Billings Media Scholarship

Subjects: Communication, public relations, marketing, business management, graphic design, information technology, promotions and other areas related to the broadcast industry.
Purpose: To support students by offering financial assistance.
Eligibility: Open to full-time students at MSU-Billings.
Level of Study: Postgraduate
Type: Scholarship
Value: US$2,000
Frequency: Annual
Study Establishment: Montana State University-Billings
Country of Study: United States of America
No. of awards offered: Varies
Application Procedure: A completed application form along with scholarship application must be submitted.
Closing Date: February 1st

For further information contact:

MSU-Billings University, Relations, McMuller Hall, Room 201

Briggs Distributing Co., Inc./John & Claudia Decker Endowed Scholarship

Subjects: All subjects.
Purpose: To provide financial assistance.
Eligibility: Open to full-time students with financial needs.
Level of Study: Postgraduate
Type: Scholarship
Value: US$3,000
Frequency: Annual
Study Establishment: Montana State University-Billings

Country of Study: United States of America
Application Procedure: See the website.
Closing Date: February 1st
Additional Information: Preference will be given to Children of employers of Briggs Distributing Co., Inc.

The Bruce H. Carpenter Non-Traditional Endowed Scholarship

Subjects: All subjects.
Purpose: To provide financial assistance.
Eligibility: Open to non-traditional students who reside in Montana.
Level of Study: Postgraduate
Type: Scholarship
Value: US$3,100
Frequency: Annual
Study Establishment: Montana State University-Billings
Country of Study: United States of America
Application Procedure: A completed application form along with 3 letters of recommendation and a copy of college transcript must be submitted.
Closing Date: February 1st

Ellen Shields Endowed Scholarship

Subjects: All subjects.
Purpose: To assist a student with economic need.
Eligibility: Open to candidates who are not entitled to scholarships provided by the larger companies based on achievement.
Level of Study: Postgraduate
Type: Scholarship
Value: US$5,500
Frequency: Annual
Study Establishment: Montana State University-Billings
Country of Study: United States of America
No. of awards offered: 1
Application Procedure: See the website for details.
Closing Date: February 1st

Energy Laboratories Chemistry Endowed Scholarship

Subjects: Chemistry.
Purpose: To encourage students who wish to major in chemistry.
Eligibility: Open to full-time students residing in Montana.
Level of Study: Postgraduate
Type: Scholarship
Value: US$2,200
Frequency: Annual
Study Establishment: Montana State University-Billings
Country of Study: United States of America
Application Procedure: See the website.
Closing Date: February 1st

Eric Robert Anderson Memorial Scholarship

Subjects: Arts.
Purpose: To support art students.
Eligibility: Open to paid members of Art students league who are enrolled as full-time students.
Type: Scholarship
Value: US$1,000
Frequency: Annual
No. of awards offered: 2
Application Procedure: A completed application form along with curriculum vitae and artist's statement must be submitted. See the website for complete details.
Closing Date: February 1st

For further information contact:

MSU-Billings Art Office Secretary, First floor, liberal Arts Building

Frances S. Barker Endowed Scholarship

Subjects: All subjects.
Purpose: To support students with financial needs.
Eligibility: Open to full-time students who demonstrate a definite financial need.
Level of Study: Postgraduate
Type: Scholarship

Value: US$1,000
Frequency: Annual
Study Establishment: Montana State University-Billings
Country of Study: United States of America
No. of awards offered: 3
Application Procedure: See the website.
Closing Date: February 1st
Contributor: The MSU-Billings Foundation Athletics Scholarship Committee
Additional Information: Preference will be given to student athletes.

The Haynes Foundation Scholarships
Subjects: All subjects.
Purpose: To provide financial assistance.
Eligibility: Open to candidates who are residents of Montana.
Level of Study: Postgraduate
Type: Scholarship
Value: US$2,000
Frequency: Annual
Study Establishment: Montana State University-Billings
Country of Study: United States of America
No. of awards offered: 52
Application Procedure: See the website.
Closing Date: February 1st

Jarussi Sisters Scholarships Endowment
Subjects: All subjects.
Eligibility: Open to applicants who have enrolled as full-time students.
Level of Study: Postgraduate
Type: Scholarship
Value: Up to US$5,000 each
Frequency: Annual
Study Establishment: Montana State University-Billing
Country of Study: United States of America
No. of awards offered: 2
Application Procedure: See the website.
Closing Date: February 1st

John F. and Winifred M. Griffith Endowed Scholarship
Subjects: All subjects.
Purpose: To encourage students who demonstrate academic and leadership potential.
Eligibility: Open to candidates who are full-time students at Montana State University-Billings.
Level of Study: Postgraduate
Type: Scholarship
Value: Up to US$4,500 each
Frequency: Annual
Study Establishment: Montana State University-Billing
Country of Study: United States of America
No. of awards offered: 3
Application Procedure: See website.
Closing Date: February 1st

Kenneth W. Heikes Family Endowed Scholarship
Subjects: Accounting and information system. It varies every year.
Purpose: To assist students who wish to study further.
Eligibility: Open to full-time students who demonstrate academic or disciplinary potential.
Level of Study: Postgraduate
Type: Scholarship
Value: US$2,000
Frequency: Annual
Study Establishment: Montana State University-Billings
Country of Study: United States of America
Application Procedure: See the website.
Closing Date: February 1st

MSU-Billings Chancellor's Excellence Awards
Subjects: All subjects.
Purpose: To recognize academic achievement and leadership qualities.

Eligibility: Open to applicants with evidence of leadership and a record of community service.
Level of Study: Postgraduate
Type: Scholarship
Value: US$2,500 per year
Length of Study: 4 years
Frequency: Annual
Study Establishment: Montana State University-Billings
Country of Study: United States of America
Application Procedure: A completed Chancellor's Excellence Awards application must be submitted.
Closing Date: January 15th
Additional Information: Chancellor Scholars who meet or exceed all awards criteria may have their awards renewed for 4 years for a maximum award of US$10,000.

For further information contact:
Chancellor's Excellence Awards Committee, Montana State University-Billings Foundation

MONTREAL NEUROLOGICAL INSTITUTE

McGill University, 3801 University Street, Montréal, QC, H3A 2B4, Canada
Tel: (1) 514 398 8998
Fax: (1) 514 398 8248
Email: fil.lumia@mcgill.ca
Website: www.mcgill.ca/mni
Contact: Ms Filomena Lumia, Personnel Liaison Officer

The Montreal Neurological Institute is dedicated to the study of the nervous system and neurological disorders. Its 70 principal researchers hold teaching positions at McGill University. The Institute is characterized by close interaction between basic science researchers and the clinicians at its affiliated hospital.

Jeanne Timmins Costello Fellowships
Subjects: Neurology, neurosurgery and neuroscience research and study.
Purpose: To support research.
Eligibility: Open to candidates of any nationality who have an MD or PhD degree. Those with MD degrees will ordinarily have completed clinical studies in neurology or neurosurgery.
Level of Study: Doctorate, Postgraduate
Type: Fellowship
Value: Canadian $25,000 per year
Length of Study: 1 year, with the possibility of renewal for a further year
Frequency: Annual
Study Establishment: The Montreal Neurological Institute
Country of Study: Canada
No. of awards offered: 4
Application Procedure: Applicants must write for details.
Closing Date: October 15th
Funding: Private
Contributor: Jean Timmins Costello
No. of awards given last year: 4

Preston Robb Fellowship
Subjects: Neurology, neurosurgery and neuroscience.
Purpose: To support research.
Eligibility: Open to researchers of any nationality.
Level of Study: Doctorate, Postdoctorate, Postgraduate
Type: Fellowship
Value: Canadian $25,000
Length of Study: 1 year
Frequency: Annual
Country of Study: Canada
No. of awards offered: 1
Application Procedure: Applicants must write for details.
Closing Date: October 15th
Funding: Private
Contributor: Preston Robb
No. of awards given last year: 1

MORRIS K UDALL FOUNDATION

130 South Scott Avenue, Tucson, Arizona, AZ 85701-1922, United
States of America
Tel: (1) 520 901 8500
Fax: (1) 520 901 8570
Email: curlin@udall.gov
Website: www.udall.gov
Contact: Ellen Wheeler, Executive Director

The Morris K Udall Foundation is dedicated to educating a new generation of Americans to preserve and protect their national heritage
through studies in the environment and Native American health and
tribal public policy. The Foundation is also committed to the principles
and practices of environmental conflict resolution.

Environmental Public Policy and Conflict Resolution PhD Fellowship

Subjects: US environmental public policy and environmental conflict
resolution.
Purpose: To provide funds for doctoral candidates whose research
concerns US environmental public policy and environmental conflict
resolution and who are entering their final year of writing the dissertation.
Eligibility: Open to scholars in all fields of study whose dissertation
topic has significant relevance to US environmental public policy and
environmental conflict resolution. The applicant must be a US natonal
or citizen or have permanent residence in the US, be entering their
final year of writing the dissertation, have necessary approval for the
dissertation research proposal and completed all PhD coursework and
passed all preliminary examinations. Furthermore the applicant must
be enrolled at a US institute of higher education; US citizens attending
universities outside the US are not eligible to apply. It is the Foun-
dation's intent that work conducted during the Fellowship be done in
the US.
Level of Study: Doctorate
Type: Fellowship
Value: US$24,000
Length of Study: 1 year
Frequency: Annual
Study Establishment: Any US university
Country of Study: United States of America
No. of awards offered: 2
Application Procedure: Application forms are available from the
Foundation's website www.udall.gov
Closing Date: February 20th
Funding: Government
No. of awards given last year: 2
No. of applicants last year: 40

MOSCOW UNIVERSITY TOURO

20/12 Podsosenski Pereulok, Moscow, 103062, Russia
Tel: (7) (095) 917 4169
Fax: (7) (495) 917-5348
Email: admin@touro.ru
Website: www.touro.ru
Contact: Admissions Office

Moscow University Touro is an independent, non-profit institution of
higher education, established in 1991, which promotes international-
style business education in Russia.

Moscow University Touro Corporate Scholarships

Subjects: Any subject.
Purpose: To fund exceptionally talented students or employees with
the intellectual potential to become future business leaders in Russia.
Eligibility: Candidates of award are determined by the company or
association sponsor in consultation with Moscow University Touro.
Level of Study: Postgraduate
Type: Scholarship
Length of Study: 1 year
Frequency: Annual
Study Establishment: Moscow University Touro
Country of Study: Russia
Application Procedure: Apply online or contact the admissions
office.

Closing Date: August 1st
Funding: Corporation
Contributor: Russian and International Corporations

Moscow University Touro Universal Scholarships

Subjects: Any subject.
Purpose: To provide financial assistance to ready student with strong
scholarship potential.
Eligibility: Only available to student studying full time at the Moscow
campus.
Level of Study: Postgraduate
Type: Scholarship
Value: Payment of an approved tuition sum
Length of Study: 1 year
Frequency: Annual
Study Establishment: Moscow University Touro
Country of Study: Russia
Application Procedure: Apply online or contact the admissions office.
Closing Date: August 1st

For further information contact:

Tel: +7 (0) 95 917 4052
Contact: Eugenij Pouchinkin

MOTOR NEURONE DISEASE ASSOCIATION

PO Box 246, Northampton, Northamptonshire, NN1 2PR, England
Tel: (44) 16 0425 0505
Fax: (44) 16 0463 8289
Email: research@mndassociation.org
Website: www.mndassociation.org
Contact: Mrs M D Reicale, Research Administrator

The Motor Neurone Disease Association supports research on fundamental aspects of motor neurone disease (MND) and on its management and alleviation. It provides information and advice to patients
and carers, and runs a nationwide care service. MND paralyzes se-
lectively or generally and is fatal, irreversible and at present, incurable.

MND PhD Studentship Award

Subjects: Research on all aspects of MND in all relevant disciplines.
Purpose: To stimulate interest in MND research by encouraging
young scientists into the field.
Eligibility: Restricted to researchers from United Kingdom laborato-
ries.
Level of Study: Postdoctorate
Type: Studentship
Value: The Association will provide a student stipend of £12,500 per
annum (£13,500 in London), £7,500 per annum for laboratory ex-
penses and a total budget of £1,000, over 3 years, for conference
attendance
Length of Study: 3 years
Frequency: Annual
Country of Study: United Kingdom
No. of awards offered: 1–2
Application Procedure: Applicants must submit a summary of their
proposal, which is first considered by 3 members of the research
advisory panel (RAP). Full applications are invited thereafter and ap-
plication forms are provided. Full applications are submitted to 2 or
more independent referees and then to the RAP for consideration.
Closing Date: May 9th
No. of awards given last year: 3
No. of applicants last year: 9
Additional Information: The studentships are awarded on the basis
of scientific merit and the value of research training offered.

MND Research Project Grants

Subjects: Research into all aspects of MND in all disciplines.
Purpose: To understand and research the cause and effective
treatments of MND.
Eligibility: Overseas applicants must have a project that is unique in
concept or design and that involves some aspect of collaboration with
a United Kingdom institute.

Level of Study: Postdoctorate, Professional development, Research
Type: Grant
Value: UK £85,000 per year, maximum
Length of Study: 1–3 years
Frequency: Six monthly
Study Establishment: A research institution
No. of awards offered: Varies
Application Procedure: Applicants must submit a summary of their proposal, which is first considered by three members of the research advisory panel (RAP). Full applications are invited thereafter and application forms are provided. Full applications are submitted to two or more independent referees and then to the RAP for consideration.
Closing Date: May 9th
No. of awards given last year: 8
No. of applicants last year: 24

MOUNT DESERT ISLAND BIOLOGICAL LABORATORY

PO Box 35, Department NIA, Old Bar Harbor Road, Salisbury Cove, ME, 04672, United States of America
Tel: (1) 207 288 3605
Fax: (1) 207 288 2130
Email: phand@mdibl.org
Website: www.mdibl.org
Contact: Ms Patricia Hand, Administrative Director

The Mount Desert Island Biological Laboratory is a marine and biomedical research laboratory that uses unique models such as shark, skate and flounder to solve questions related to human and environmental health.

Mount Desert Island New Investigator Award

Subjects: Biological and life sciences.
Purpose: To support independent investigators spending 2–3 months in the Summer doing physiological research on marine animals at the Mount Desert Island Biological Laboratory.
Eligibility: Open to scientists at all stages of their career who wish to use marine systems for research studies at the Laboratory.
Level of Study: Professional development, Postdoctorate
Type: Fellowship
Value: US$4,000–12,000. Special awards from the Salisbury Cove Research Fund (Thomas H Maren Foundation) are available for up to US$20,000 depending on need and potential long-term commitment to the laboratory
Length of Study: 2–3 months
Study Establishment: Mount Desert Island Biological Laboratory
Country of Study: United States of America
No. of awards offered: 15–20
Application Procedure: Applicants must obtain an application form from the organization. Please visit the website for application information.
Closing Date: February 1st
Funding: Foundation, government, private
No. of awards given last year: 19
No. of applicants last year: 20
Additional Information: The Mount Desert Island Biological Laboratory, located in Salisbury Cove, Maine is a 105-year-old research institution and an international centre for comparative physiology, toxicology, tissue culture biology and marine functional genomics studies. Awards can be used to defray the cost of laboratory space, housing, equipment fees and other costs depending on individual needs. Additional information can be found on the website.

THE MOUNTAINEERING COUNCIL OF SCOTLAND (MCOFS)

The Old Granary, West Mill Street, Perth, PH1 5QP, Scotland
Tel: (44) 44 1738 493946
Email: info@mcofs.org.uk
Website: www.mcofs.org.uk
Contact: The Development Officer

MCofS administers the SportScotland grants for Scotland's mountaineers and is also the national governing body for sport climbing.

Mountaineering Council of Scotland Climbing and Mountaineering Bursary

Subjects: Climbing expeditions.
Purpose: To support Scots who undertake mountaineering or rock or ice climbing expeditions worthy ofinternational recognition.
Eligibility: Applicants must be Scottish or resident in Scotland and aged 14 years or above.
Level of Study: Professional development, Research
Type: Grant
Value: UK £1,000–3,500
Length of Study: Event specific
Frequency: Annual
Country of Study: Any country
No. of awards offered: Approx. 5
Application Procedure: Request a bursary information pack from the Development Officer.
Closing Date: March
Funding: Government
Contributor: sportscotland
No. of awards given last year: 6
No. of applicants last year: 6

MULTIPLE SCLEROSIS RESEARCH AUSTRALIA (MSRA)

Department of Neurology, Sir Charles Gairdner Hospital, Nedlands, WA 6009, Australia
Tel: (61) 08 9346 2471
Fax: (61) 08 9346 2455
Email: sumsr@iinet.net.au
Website: www.msaustralia.org.au
Contact: Sue Barham, Research Coordinator

In August 2004, Multiple Sclerosis (MS) Australia, the national organization of MS Societies, launched a new MS-specific research organization called Multiple Sclerosis Research Australia (MSRA). Its aim is to substantially lift the Australian MS research effort and accelerate the progress towards knowledge of a cause and cure for MS.

The Betty Cuthbert Postgraduate Scholarship

Subjects: Multiple sclerosis.
Purpose: To accelerate progress in research on cure for multiple sclerosis.
Eligibility: Open to candidates who have obtained a graduate degree.
Level of Study: Postgraduate
Type: Scholarships
Value: Varies
Length of Study: 3 years
Frequency: Annual
Application Procedure: Applicants must send an application form, which is available on the website.
Closing Date: September 1st
Additional Information: For more information please see the website www.msaustralia.org/au/msra/funding. This scholarship is awarded jointly with NHMRC.

MULTIPLE SCLEROSIS SOCIETY OF CANADA (MSSC)

175 Bloor Street East, Suite 700, North Tower, Toronto, Ontario, M4W 3R8, Canada
Tel: (1) 416 922 6065
Fax: (1) 416 922 7538
Email: jackie.munroe@mssociety.ca
Website: www.mssociety.ca
Contact: Ms Jackie Munroe, Research Grants Programme Manager

The mission of the MSSC is to be a leader in finding a cure for multiple sclerosis and enabling people affected by the disease to enhance their quality of life.

MSSC Career Development Award

Subjects: Multiple sclerosis.
Purpose: To encourage full-time research.

Eligibility: Open to individuals holding a doctoral degree who have recently completed their training in research and are capable of carrying out independent research relevant to multiple sclerosis on a full-time basis. Must hold an operating grant.
Level of Study: Postdoctorate
Value: $50,000 per annum for 3 years with the opportunity to apply for a renewal twice (total 9 years)
Length of Study: 1–3 years
Frequency: Annual
Study Establishment: A Canadian school of medicine/recognized institution
Country of Study: Canada
No. of awards offered: Limited
Application Procedure: Further information from Dean of graduate studies office.
Closing Date: October 1st
Funding: Private
No. of awards given last year: 2
No. of applicants last year: 3

MSSC Postdoctoral Fellowship

Subjects: Multiple sclerosis and allied diseases.
Purpose: To encourage research.
Eligibility: Open to qualified persons holding an MD or PhD degree and intending to pursue research work relevant to multiple sclerosis and allied diseases. The applicant must be associated to an appropriate authority in the field he or she wishes to study.
Level of Study: Postdoctorate
Type: Fellowship
Value: Salary scales will be similar to those suggested by the Canadian Institutes for Health Research
Length of Study: 1–3 years
Frequency: Annual
Study Establishment: A recognized institution which deals that problems relevant to multiple sclerosis
Country of Study: Other
No. of awards offered: Varies
Application Procedure: Contact Dean of Graduate studies office for further information.
Closing Date: October 1st
Funding: Private
No. of awards given last year: 18
No. of applicants last year: 26

MSSC Research Grant

Subjects: Multiple sclerosis.
Purpose: To fund research projects.
Eligibility: Open to researchers working in Canada or intending to return to Canada.
Level of Study: Postgraduate
Type: Research grant
Value: Varies
Length of Study: 1–3 years
Frequency: Annual
Study Establishment: A Canadian school of medicine or recognized institution
Country of Study: Any country
No. of awards offered: Varies
Application Procedure: Contact Dean of Graduate studies office for further information.
Closing Date: October 1st
Funding: Private
No. of awards given last year: 16
No. of applicants last year: 30

MSSC Research Studentships

Subjects: Multiple sclerosis and allied diseases.
Purpose: To support qualified persons to pursue specialized training in multiple sclerosis and allied diseases.
Eligibility: Eligible to qualified persons holding other than a MD or PhD degree wishing further training in a specialized area related to research in multiple sclerosis and allied diseases.
Level of Study: Doctorate, Research
Type: Studentship

Length of Study: The maximum period of a studentship will be four years but under exceptional circumstances may be extended by one additional year
Frequency: Annual
No. of awards offered: Limited
Application Procedure: Applicants must submit the completed application form, academic transcripts and letters of reference to the chairman. For further details please refer the website.
Closing Date: October 1st
Additional Information: Applications directed towards understanding the pathogenesis and potential treatment of multiple sclerosis will receive priority.

MUSCULAR DYSTROPHY ASSOCIATION (MDA)

Research Department, 3300 East Sunrise Drive, Tucson, AZ, 85718, United States of America
Tel: (1) 520 529 2000
Fax: (1) 520 529 5300
Email: grants@mdausa.org
Website: www.mdausa.org
Contact: Grants Manager

The Muscular Dystrophy Association (MDA) supports research into over 40 diseases of the neuromuscular system to identify the causes of, and effective treatments for, the muscular dystrophies and related diseases including spinal muscular atrophies and motor neuron diseases, peripheral neuropathies, inflammatory myopathies, metabolic myopathies and diseases of the neuromuscular junction.

MDA Grant Programs

Subjects: The muscular dystrophies and related diseases.
Purpose: To support research into over 40 diseases of the neuromuscular system, and to identify the causes of, and effective treatments for, the muscular dystrophies and related diseases.
Eligibility: Open to persons who are professional or faculty members at appropriate educational, medical or research institutions, qualified to conduct and supervise a programme of original research, who have access to institutional resources necessary to conduct the proposed research project and who hold an MD or PhD.
Level of Study: Postdoctorate
Type: Grant
Value: Please contact the Association
Length of Study: Maximum of 3 years
Frequency: Annual
Country of Study: Any country
No. of awards offered: Varies
Application Procedure: Applicants must complete the Request for Research Grant Application.
Closing Date: Pre-applications are due no later than December 15th or June 15th
Funding: Private
Contributor: Voluntary contributions
No. of awards given last year: 140
Additional Information: Proposals from applicants outside the United States of America will only be considered for projects of highest priority to the MDA. Other conditions apply. Research is sponsored under the following grant programmes: Neuromuscular Disease Research and Neuromuscular Disease Research Development. Further information is available from the website.

MUSCULAR DYSTROPHY CAMPAIGN OF GREAT BRITAIN AND NORTHERN IRELAND

61 Southwark Street, London, SE1 0HL, England
Tel: (44) 20 7720 8055
Fax: (44) 020 7401 3495
Email: research@muscular-dystrophy.org
Website: www.muscular-dystrophy.org
Contact: Mrs Jenny Versnel, Head of Research

The Muscular Dystrophy Campaign is a United Kingdom-based charity funding medical research and support services for people with muscular dystrophy and related conditions.

Muscular Dystrophy Research Grants

Subjects: Muscular dystrophy and allied neuromuscular conditions.
Purpose: To provide continuity of funding for high-quality research of central importance to the Muscular Dystrophy Campaign's research objectives.
Eligibility: The MDC will only fund United Kingdom-based research. Principal Investigators must hold a contract that extends beyond the duration of the grant at an institution approved by the MDC.
Level of Study: Research, Postdoctorate
Value: Salary of research staff, equipment and consumables. Salary of grant holder is not funded
Length of Study: 1–3 years
Frequency: Annual
Study Establishment: Universities, hospitals or research institutions
Country of Study: United Kingdom
No. of awards offered: Varies
Application Procedure: Applicants must contact the Head of Research with a summary of proposed research on A4-size paper. More details are available on the website.
Closing Date: October
Funding: Private
No. of awards given last year: 10
No. of applicants last year: 30

MUSEUM OF COMPARATIVE ZOOLOGY

26 Oxford Street, Cambridge, MA, 02138, United States of America
Tel: (1) 617 495 2460
Fax: (1) 617 496 8308
Email: ernstmayrgrant@oeb.harvard.edu
Website: www.mcz.harvard.edu
Contact: Ms Andrea Prill, Assistant to the Director

The Museum of Comparative Zoology was founded in 1859 through the efforts of Louis Agassiz (1807–1873). Agassiz, a zoologist from Neuchatel, Switzerland, served as the Director of the Museum from 1859 until his death in 1873. A brilliant lecturer and scholar, he established the Museum and its collections as a centre for research and education.

Ernst Mayr Travel Grant

Subjects: Animal systematics.
Purpose: To stimulate taxonomic work on neglected taxa.
Eligibility: There are no restrictions on eligibility. Preference is given to studies that use the Museum of Comparative Zoology's collections, although applications to work at other museums will be considered.
Level of Study: Research, Unrestricted
Type: Travel grant
Value: Up to US$1,500
Length of Study: 1 year
Frequency: Twice a year
Study Establishment: An accredited museum
Country of Study: Any country
No. of awards offered: Varies
Application Procedure: Applicants must submit a short project description, itinerary, budget, a curriculum vitae and three letters of support. No proposal forms are required or provided. Proposals may be submitted through standard mail or electronically. Submissions through standard mail must include five copies of all materials and be received by the closing date. Proposals submitted electronically must be created in Microsoft Word or plain ASCII text format. For additional information visit the website, www.oeb.harvard.edu/mayr-grant.htm or emailing grants@oeb.harvard.edu
Closing Date: October 15th and April 15th
Funding: Trusts
Contributor: Ernst Mayr
No. of awards given last year: 13
No. of applicants last year: 25
Additional Information: Announcements of awards will be made within 2 months of the closing date.

THE MUSICIANS BENEVOLENT FUND (MBF)

16 Ogle Street, London, W1W 6JA, England
Tel: (44) 20 7299 8356
Fax: (44) 20 7637 4307
Email: education@mbf.org.uk
Website: www.mbf.org.uk
Contact: Ms Susan Dolton, Education Administrator

The Musicians Benevolent Fund is the music business's own charity, the largest of its kind in the United Kingdom. Last year, it helped about 1,500 people of any age and in any area of the music business who were in need as a result of illness, accident or other misfortune, and spent over UK £2 million on its benevolent work. The MBF also plays a significant role in education, fulfilling its remit to encourage the next generation of young musicians.

Guilhermina Suggia Gift

Subjects: Musical performance of the cello.
Purpose: To assist with the studies of an outstanding cellist.
Eligibility: Open to cellists of any nationality, under 21 years of age. Students who are not British or Irish must be studying full time in the UK.
Level of Study: Professional development
Value: £3,000
Frequency: Annual
Country of Study: Any country
No. of awards offered: 1. There may be further discretionary awards
Application Procedure: Applicants must complete an application form and provide two references.
Closing Date: Autumn
Funding: Private
No. of awards given last year: 1
No. of applicants last year: 17

Manoug Parikian Award

Subjects: Musical performance on the violin.
Purpose: To assist with the studies of an outstanding young violinist.
Eligibility: Open to violinists of any nationality, under 21 years of age.
Level of Study: Graduate
Value: UK £3,000
Frequency: Annual
Country of Study: Any country
No. of awards offered: 1. There may be further discretionary awards
Application Procedure: Applicants must complete an application form and provide two references.
Closing Date: Autumn
Funding: Private
No. of awards given last year: 1
No. of applicants last year: 19
Additional Information: The Manoug Parikian Award is run in conjunction with the RPS Emily Anderson Prize. The Award must be used for study costs or instrument purchase.

MBF Music Education Awards

Subjects: Musical performance.
Purpose: To support outstandingly talented instrumentalists and singers and help with full-time postgraduate study costs.
Eligibility: Open to singers and instrumentalists possessing the potential to become first-class performers, who are British or Irish or have been resident in the United Kingdom for 3 years. Applicants must be studying fulltime at postgraduate level in the UK for the academic year.
Level of Study: Postgraduate, Professional development
Value: Varies, to cover tuition, maintenance and the purchase of instruments. Awards range from UK £1,000 to £5,000
Frequency: Annual
Country of Study: United Kingdom
Application Procedure: Applicants must complete an application form and provide two references.
Closing Date: February 6th
Funding: Private
No. of awards given last year: 81
No. of applicants last year: 514
Additional Information: The following major awards are also available through these auditions: Ian Fleming Charitable Trust Music

461

Education Awards, Professor Charles Leggett Awards, Emily English Scholarship, Maidment Scholarships, Myra Hess Scholarships, Sybil Tutton Awards, Sir Henry Richardson Scholarships, Eleanor Warren Award and MBF Awards for Accompanists and Repetiteurs.

Miriam Licette Scholarships

Subjects: Musical performance and song.
Purpose: To assist a female student of French song.
Eligibility: Open to female singers in full-time postgraduate vocal study or in the first year of entering a professional career. Applicants must be able to demonstrate considerable success at this level. Applicants should be British or Irish or be living or studying full-time in the UK.
Level of Study: Postgraduate, Professional development
Type: Scholarship
Value: UK £1,500
Frequency: Annual
Country of Study: Any country
No. of awards offered: Up to 4 awards. There may be further discretionary awards
Application Procedure: Selected students will be asked to audition. An application form must be completed and two references must be provided.
Closing Date: November 28th
Funding: Private
No. of awards given last year: 4
No. of applicants last year: 45
Additional Information: The award is run in conjunction with the Maggie Teyte Prize.

Peter Whittingham Award

Subjects: Jazz.
Purpose: To promote both composition and performance through an innovative jazz project.
Eligibility: Open to individuals ordinarily resident in the United Kingdom to work independently or with a project group. The project should be in creation or performance in the field of cutting-edge jazz. Money is not given for course fees.
Level of Study: Graduate, Postgraduate, Professional development
Value: UK £4,000
Frequency: Annual
No. of awards offered:
Application Procedure: A written description of the project must be provided together with a budget, a reference and a recording demonstrating composition and/or performance.
Closing Date: October
Funding: Private
No. of awards given last year: 1 + 1 MBF Development Award
No. of applicants last year: 10
Additional Information: Selected applicants will be asked to attend an interview.

THE MYASTHENIA GRAVIS FOUNDATION OF AMERICA

1821 University Ave W, Suite 8256, St Paul, MN 55104, United States
of America
Tel: (1) 800 541 5454
Fax: (1) 651 917 1835
Email: mgfa@myasthenia.org
Website: www.myasthenia.org
Contact: Ms Janet Golden, Chief Executive

The Myasthenia Gravis Foundation of America's mission is to facilitate the timely diagnosis and optimal care of individuals affected by myasthenia gravis and to improve their lives through programmes of patient services, public information, medical research, professional education, advocacy and patient care.

Myasthenia Gravis Nursing Research Fellowship

Subjects: Myasthenia gravis.
Purpose: To fund research specific to myasthenia gravis.
Eligibility: There are no eligibility restrictions.
Level of Study: Graduate, Postgraduate, Research
Type: Fellowship
Value: Up to US$5,000

Length of Study: Short-term
Frequency: Dependent on funds available
Country of Study: Any country
No. of awards offered: 2–3
Application Procedure: Applicants must contact the Foundation for further details.
Closing Date: March 15th
Funding: Private
No. of awards given last year: None
No. of applicants last year: None

Post-Doctoral Research Fellowship

Subjects: Research pertinent to myasthenia gravis that is concerned with neuromuscular transmission, immunology, molecular cell biology of the neuromuscular synapse and the aetiology and pathogenesis, diagnosis or treatment of the disease.
Purpose: To investigate the fundamental nature of myasthenia gravis.
Eligibility: There are no eligibility restrictions. The research preceptor must be an established investigator at an institution in the United States of America, Canada or abroad deemed appropriate by the MGFA Medical/Scientific Advisory Board. The applicant must either be (a) a permanent resident of the United States of America or Canada who has been accepted to work in the laboratory of an established investigator at an institution in the United States of America, Canada or abroad or (b) a foreign national who has been accepted to work in the laboratory of an established investigator at an institution in the United States of America or Canada deemed appropriate by the Medical/Scientific Advisory Board of MGFA.
Level of Study: Postdoctorate
Type: Fellowship
Value: US$50,000
Length of Study: 1 year
Frequency: Annual
Country of Study: Any country
No. of awards offered: 2–4
Application Procedure: Applicants must submit a ten-page proposal, a lay summary, budget, applicant's and preceptor's curriculum vitae and letters of recommendation.
Closing Date: October 1st
Funding: Foundation, private
No. of awards given last year: 3
No. of applicants last year: 11

Student Research Fellowship

Subjects: The scientific basis of myasthenia gravis or related neuromuscular conditions.
Purpose: To promote research into the cause and cure of myasthenia gravis.
Eligibility: There are no eligibility restrictions.
Level of Study: Doctorate, Graduate, Research
Type: Fellowship
Value: Maximum of US$5,000
Length of Study: Short-term
Frequency: Annual
Country of Study: Any country
No. of awards offered: Up to 3
Application Procedure: Applicants must briefly describe, in abstract form, the question proposed for study, its association to myasthenia gravis or related neuromuscular conditions and research methodology. Further information may then be requested by the Foundation.
Closing Date: March 15th
Funding: Private

NANTUCKET HISTORICAL ASSOCIATION (NHA)

15 Broad Street, PO Box 1016, Nantucket, MA, 02554, United States
of America
Tel: (1) 508 228 1894
Fax: (1) 508 228 5618
Email: bsimons@nha.org
Website: www.nha.org
Contact: Ben Simons, Curator and Editor of Historic Nantucket

The Nantucket Historical Association (NHA) is the principal repository of Nantucket history, with extensive archives, collections of historic properties and art and artefacts that broadly illustrate Nantucket's past. The Research Library at the NHA contains a rich collection of primary and secondary sources that document all facets of Nantucket's cultural, social, economic and spiritual history for more than three centuries. More than 400 manuscript collections relate to Nantucket individuals and families, ships, businesses and trades, churches, schools and organizations. Searchable inventories of the library's manuscript, map and book holdings can be accessed via the NHA website. The NHA art and artefacts collections include paintings, drawings, prints, baskets, silver, whaling tools, scrimshaw, furniture and textiles. The particular strengths of the collection lie in artefacts that document Nantucket's whaling industry.

E Geoffrey and Elizabeth Thayer Verney Research Fellowship

Subjects: History.
Purpose: To enhance the public's knowledge and understanding of the heritage of Nantucket, Massachusetts.
Eligibility: Open to graduate students and independent Scholars in any field to conduct research in the collections of the NHA.
Level of Study: Graduate
Type: Residency
Value: A stipend of US$300 per week and travel expenses will be reimbursed for expenses up to US$600
Length of Study: 3 weeks
Frequency: Annual
Study Establishment: The NHA
Country of Study: United States of America
No. of awards offered: 1
Application Procedure: Applicants must send a full description of the proposed project, a preliminary bibliography and a complete curriculum vitae. An account of travel expenses must also be included with the anticipated time and duration of stay. Applications must be addressed to the Library Director.
Closing Date: December 31st
No. of awards given last year: 1
Additional Information: Applicants will be notified by December 21st.

NANYANG TECHNOLOGICAL UNIVERSITY (NTU)

MBA Office, Nanyang Business School, Nanyang Avenue, Singapore, 639798, Singapore
Tel: (65) 65 6790 6183
Fax: (65) 65 6791 3561
Email: fellows@ntu.edu.sg
Website: www.ntu.edu.sg
Contact: Administrative Officer

Nanyang Technological University (NTU) is an established, research intensive tertiary institution with a vision to be a global university of excellence in science and technology. Asian Communication Resource Centre (ACRC) is a regional centre of NTU, dedicated to develop information resources on different aspects of communication, information and media.

The Lien Foundation Scholarship for Social Service Leaders

Subjects: Full-time or part-time local post-graduate studies in management and selected specialist fields at the National University of Singapore (NUS) and the Nanyang Technological University (NTU).
Purpose: To provide scholarships to support education and professional development.
Eligibility: The scholarship is open to candidates with academic excellence, notable performance record and the potential to take up leadership positions in voluntary welfare organizations.
Value: The award includes tuition fees, maintenance allowance (for full-time studies), book allowance and any other compulsory fees
Application Procedure: For more information on the scholarship do visit the websites www.ncss.org.sg/lien, http://lienfoundation.org/ScholarshipSSL.htm. For more information on the scholarship contact

Ms Ng Hwee Choon: ng_hwee_choon@ncss.gov.sg and Ms Pamela Biswas: Pamela_biswas@ncss.gov.sg.
Closing Date: May 31st

Nanyang Fellows Scholarship

Subjects: An elite MBA in collaboration with MIT.
Purpose: To allow outstanding candidates from the world, except Singapore, to pursue the Nanyang fellows programme at NTU on a full-time basis.
Eligibility: Open to all nationals but study should be undertaken in Singapore or USA.
Level of Study: MBA
Type: Scholarship
Value: Tuition fees for NTU and MIT
Length of Study: 12 months
Frequency: Annual
Study Establishment: NTU and MIT
No. of awards offered: 10
Application Procedure: Application details are available at the university website.
Closing Date: December 30th
Funding: Government
No. of awards given last year: 10
No. of applicants last year: 500
Additional Information: Applications open in September/October and close in December each year.

NTU Alumni Scholarship

Subjects: MBA.
Purpose: To provide financial support to alumni of Nanyang Technological University admitted to the MBA programme on a full-time or part-time basis.
Eligibility: Open to alumni of Nanyang Technological University admitted to the MBA programme on a full-time or part-time basis. Recipients of other scholarships or bursaries are not eligible to apply.
Level of Study: MBA
Type: Scholarship
Value: Singaporean $3,000 per year
Length of Study: Each scholarship shall be tenable only for the academic year in which it is awarded
Frequency: Annual
Study Establishment: NTU
Country of Study: Singapore
No. of awards offered: 1 for MBA
Application Procedure: Applicants must submit a completed application form (available at http://admissions.ntu.edu.sg/graduate/documents/alumnischolarship.pdf).
Closing Date: End of July
Funding: Private
Contributor: NTU Alumni Fund
No. of awards given last year: None

For further information contact:

Nanyang Technological University, Student Services Centre, Level 3, 42 Nanyang Avenue, Singapore, 639815, Singapore
Contact: Ms Jessica Wee, Assistant Director, Graduate Studies Office,

NTU APEC Scholarship

Subjects: MBA.
Purpose: To allow outstanding candidates from the APEC member economies except Singapore to pursue the MBA programme at NTU on a full-time basis.
Eligibility: Open to nationals from the following APEC member economies: Australia, Brunei Darussalem, Canada, Chile, Chinese Taipei, Hong Kong, China, Indonesia, Japan, Malaysia, Mexico, New Zealand, Papua New Guinea, People's Republic of China, Peru, Philippines, Republic of Korea, Russia, Thailand, United States of America and Vietnam. Singaporeans, Singapore permanent residents and recipients of other scholarships or bursaries are not eligible to apply.
Level of Study: MBA
Type: Scholarship
Value: Monthly stipend of Singaporean $1,400, book allowance of Singaporean $500, tuition fees, health insurance, examination fees

and other approved fees, allowances and expenses, cost of one overseas Business Study Mission, cost of travel from home country to Singapore on award of the scholarship, and cost of travel from Singapore to home country on successful completion of the Master's programme. Each scholarship is tenable for a period of 4 trimesters only

Length of Study: Full-time for 16 months
Frequency: Annual
Study Establishment: NTU
Country of Study: Singapore
No. of awards offered: 1–2
Application Procedure: Application details are available at the University website.
Closing Date: December
Funding: Government
Contributor: NTU
No. of awards given last year: 2
No. of applicants last year: 50
Additional Information: Applications open in November and close in December each year. Invitations for applications will be placed in the newspapers in the capital cities of the APEC countries and on the University's website. International students have to apply for a student's pass from Singapore immigration in order to pursue a full-time course of study in Singapore. The University will assist successful international applicants in their applications for the student's pass.

NTU ASEAN Graduate Scholarship

Subjects: MBA.
Purpose: To allow outstanding candidates from the ASEAN (Association of South East Asian Nations) member economies, except Singapore, to pursue the MBA programme at NTU on a full-time basis.
Eligibility: Open to nationals of the member countries of ASEAN (Brunei Darussalem, Cambodia, Indonesia, Laos, Malaysia, Myanmar, Philippines, Thailand and Vietnam). Singaporeans, Singapore permanent residents and recipients of other scholarships or bursaries are not eligible to apply.
Level of Study: MBA
Type: Scholarship
Value: Monthly stipend of Singaporean $1,350; book allowance of Singaporean $500; tuition fees, health insurance, examination fees and other approved fees, allowances and expenses; cost of one overseas Business Study Mission; cost of travel from home country to Singapore on award of the scholarship; and cost of travel from Singapore to home country on successful completion of the Master's programme. Each scholarship is tenable for a period of 4 trimesters only
Length of Study: Full-time for 16 months
Frequency: Annual
Study Establishment: NTU
Country of Study: Singapore
No. of awards offered: 1–2
Application Procedure: Application details available at the University website.
Closing Date: December
Funding: Government
No. of awards given last year: 1
No. of applicants last year: 50
Additional Information: Applications open in November and close in December each year. Invitations for applications will be placed in the newspapers in the capital cities of the ASEAN countries and on the University's website. International students have to apply for a student's pass from Singapore immigration in order to pursue a full-time course of study in Singapore. The University will assist successful international applicants in their applications for the student's pass.

NTU Asian Communication Resource Centre (ACRC) Fellowship Award

Subjects: Communication and information research from Asian perspective.
Purpose: To encourage in-depth research, promote cooperation and support scholars who wish to pursue research in communication, information and ICT-related disciplines in Asia.
Eligibility: Open to candidates pursuing their Master's degree and working on a research project in communication, media, information or related areas that would be able to exploit the materials in the ACRC.

Level of Study: Postgraduate, Research
Type: Fellowships
Value: Singaporean $600 for faculty or Singaporean $450 for postgraduate Fellows per month and an economy class return air ticket with on-campus accommodation
Length of Study: 1–3 months
Frequency: Annual
No. of awards offered: 2
Application Procedure: Applicants can download the application form from the website and send in their completed application form along with a copy of their latest curriculum vitae.
Closing Date: October 15th

For further information contact:

School of Communication and Information Nanyang Technological University 31 Nanyang Link, 637718, Singapore
Tel: (65) 6790 4577
Fax: (65) 6791 5214

NTU MBA Scholarship

Subjects: MBA.
Purpose: To enable outstanding overseas candidates to pursue the MBA programme on a full-time basis.
Eligibility: Open to international applicants. Singaporeans, Singapore permanent residents and recipients of other scholarships or bursaries are not eligible to apply.
Level of Study: MBA
Type: Scholarship
Value: Full or partial tuition fees of a full-time programme
Length of Study: Full-time for 16 months
Frequency: Annual
Study Establishment: NTU
Country of Study: Singapore
No. of awards offered: 4
Application Procedure: Applicants must submit only one application form for application to the NTU MBA and scholarship. Online application is available at www.nanyangmba.ntu.edu.sg/applynow.asp
Closing Date: End of February
Funding: Private
No. of awards given last year: 4
No. of applicants last year: 81
Additional Information: Applications open in October each year and close at the end of February each year. International students have to apply for a student's pass from Singapore immigration in order to pursue a full-time course of study in Singapore. The University will assist successful international applicants in their applications for the student's pass.

Sampoerna Foundation MBA Scholarship Program

Subjects: MBA.
Purpose: To help Indonesian citizens below 35 years pursue their MBA studies.
Eligibility: Open to Indonesian citizens under 35 years.
Value: Approx.US$70,000–150,000. This will cover GMAT and TOEFL/IELTS reimbursement, university application fee, student visa application fee, return airfares from Jakarta to the place of study, tuition fees for the duration of study, living allowance to support living costs during period of study and literature allowance to purchase textbooks required for study
Closing Date: April 30
Additional Information: For further information see www. nanyangmba.edu.sg/Admissions/FinancialAid.asp.

SPRING Management Development Scholarship (MDS)

Subjects: MBA.
Purpose: to nurture the next generation of leaders for the trailblazer companies of tomorrow.
Eligibility: Those who are currently working in an SME or are interested to join one, are citizens or permanent residents of Singapore, have less than 5 years of working experience and successfully apply for one of the approved MBA programmes.
Value: Full-time MBA: SPRING Singapore will provide grant value of up to 70% of expenses which includes tuition fees, basic stipend and other related costs, including monthly allowance for full-time MBA scholars. Part-time MBA: SPRING Singapore will provide grant value

of up to 90% of tuition fees and other related expenses. The smal-medium enterprise (SME) co-funding the scholarship will bear the full salaries throughout the course of study.
Study Establishment: Nanyang Business School
Country of Study: Singapore
Application Procedure: Applicants will have to go through a joint selection process by SPRING and the participating SME, serve a 3 month internship in the SME prior to embarking on the approved MBA course (performance must be deemed satisfactory by the SME), and serve a bond of up to 2 years in the SME upon completion of studies. For more information on government assistance programmes, please contact the EnterpriseOne hotline at Tel: (65) 6898 1800 or email enterpriseone@spring.gov.sg or visit their website at www.spring.gov.sg/mds.
Contributor: SPRING Singapore and small medium enterprises(SME)
Additional Information: For more information on government assistance programmes, please contact the EnterpriseOne hotline at Tel: (65) 6898 1800 or email enterpriseone@spring.gov.sg or visit their website at www.spring.gov.sg/mds.

NARSAD

60 Cutter Mill Road, Suite 404, Great Neck, NY, 11021, United States of America
Tel: (1) 516 829 5576
Fax: (1) 516 487 6930
Email: grants@narsad.org
Website: www.narsad.org
Contact: Ms Audra Moran, Director of Scientific Affairs

NARSAD the world's leading charity dedicated to mental health research raises and distributes funds for scientific research into the causes, cures, treatments and prevention of psychiatric brain and behaviour disorders. NARSAD is the largest donor-supported organization devoted exclusively to supporting scientific research on psychiatric disorders in the world.

NARSAD Distinguished Investigator Awards
Subjects: Schizophrenia, major mood disorders, other serious mental illnesses such as anxiety disorders, borderline personality disorder, suicide and children's psychiatric disorders.
Purpose: To encourage experienced scientists to pursue innovative projects in diverse areas of neurobiological research.
Eligibility: Open to senior researchers at the rank of professor or equivalent who maintain their own laboratory.
Level of Study: Postdoctorate, Research
Type: Grant
Value: Up to US$100,000
Length of Study: 1 year
Frequency: Annual
Country of Study: Any country
No. of awards offered: Varies
Application Procedure: Electronic applications are available at www.narsad.org.
Closing Date: May 15th
Funding: Private
Contributor: Donors
No. of awards given last year: 15
No. of applicants last year: 155
Additional Information: Further information is available from the website.

NARSAD Independent Investigator Awards
Subjects: Schizophrenia, major mood disorders, other serious mental illnesses such as anxiety disorders, borderline personality disorder, suicide and children's psychiatric disorders.
Purpose: To facilitate innovative research opportunities in diverse areas of neurobiological research.
Eligibility: Open to scientists at the academic level of associate professor or equivalent. Candidates must have won national competitive support as a principal investigator.
Level of Study: Postdoctorate, Research
Type: Grant
Value: Up to US$50,000 maximum per year

Length of Study: 2 years
Frequency: Annual
Country of Study: Any country
No. of awards offered: Varies
Application Procedure: Electronic applications are accepted through the NARSAD website.
Closing Date: March 3rd
Funding: Private
Contributor: Donors
No. of awards given last year: 42
No. of applicants last year: 242
Additional Information: Further information is available from the website.

NARSAD Young Investigator Awards
Subjects: Schizophrenia, major mood disorders, other serious mental illnesses such as anxiety disorders, borderline personality disorder, suicide and children's psychiatric disorders.
Purpose: To enable promising investigators to either extend their research fellowship training or to begin careers as independent research faculty.
Eligibility: Open to investigators who have attained a Doctorate or equivalent degree, are affiliated with a specific research institution and who have a mentor or senior collaborator who is performing significant research in an area relevant to schizophrenia, depression or other serious mental illnesses. Candidates should be at the postdoctoral to assistant professor level.
Level of Study: Postdoctorate, Research
Type: Grant
Value: Up to US$30,000 maximum per year
Length of Study: 1 or 2 years
Frequency: Annual
Country of Study: Any country
No. of awards offered: Varies
Application Procedure: Electronic applications are accepted through the NARSAD website.
Closing Date: July 25th
Funding: Private
Contributor: Donors
No. of awards given last year: 220
No. of applicants last year: 847
Additional Information: This award is intended to support only advanced Fellows through assistant professors or their equivalent. Further information is available from the website.

THE NATIONAL ACADEMIES

500 5th Street NW, Washington, DC, 20001, United States of America
Tel: (1) 202 334 2455
Fax: (1) 202 334 1667
Email: infofell@nas.edu
Website: www.nationalacademies.org

The National Academies perform an unparalleled public service by bringing together committees of experts in all areas of scientific and technological endeavor. These experts serve pro bono to address critical national issues and give advice to the federal government and the public.

The Ford Foundation Diversity Fellowships – Dissertation Awards
Subjects: Check website for details.
Purpose: To achieve excellence in college and university teaching.
Eligibility: Open to all citizens or nationals of the United States regardless of race, national origin, religion, gender, age, disability, or sexual orientation, individuals with evidence of superior academic achievement and committed to a career in teaching and research at the college or university level, PhD or ScD degree candidates studying in an eligible research-based discipline at a US educational institution. Also individuals who have not earned a doctoral degree at any time, in any field.
Level of Study: Doctorate
Type: Award

Value: Stipend: US $21,000. Expenses paid to attend one Conference of Ford Fellows. Access to Ford Fellow Liaisons, a network of former Ford Fellows who have volunteered to provide mentoring and support to current fellows
Length of Study: 9–12 months
Frequency: Annual
Country of Study: United States of America
No. of awards offered: 35
Application Procedure: Applicants must register and establish a personal user ID and password. Check website for further details.
Closing Date: On-line application must be submitted by November 29th. Supplementary Materials must be received in the Fellowships Office by January 18
Contributor: The National Research Council

For further information contact:

Fellowships Office, Keck 576, National Research Council, 500 Fifth Street, NW, WA, 20001
Tel: 202 334 2872
Email: infofell@nas.edu
Website: www.national-academies.org/fellowships

The Ford Foundation Diversity Fellowships – Postdoctoral Awards

Subjects: Check website for further details.
Purpose: For achieving excellence in college and university teaching and to increase the diversity of the nation's college and university faculties by increasing their ethnic and racial diversity, to maximize the educational benefits of diversity, and to increase the number of professors who can and will use diversity as a resource for enriching the education of all students.
Eligibility: Open to all citizens or nationals of the United States regardless of race, national origin, religion, gender, age, disability, or sexual orientation, individuals with evidence of superior academic achievement and committed to a career in teaching and research at the college or university level. Individuals should hold a PhD or ScD degree in an eligible research-based field from a US educational institution.
Level of Study: Postdoctorate
Type: Fellowships
Value: Stipend: US $40,000 and Employing Institution Allowance: US $1,500
Length of Study: 9–12 months
No. of awards offered: 20
Application Procedure: Applicants must register and establish a personal user ID and password. Check website for further details.
Closing Date: On-line application deadline: November 29th. Supplementary materials must be received in the fellowships office by January 18th
Funding: Foundation, government
Contributor: National Research Council (NRC) on behalf of the Ford Foundation
Additional Information: Candidates demonstrating superior academic achievement according to the judgement panels will be awarded.

For further information contact:

Fellowships Office, Keck 576, National Research Council, 500 Fifth Street, NW, Washington, DC, 20001, United States of America
Tel: (1) 202 334 2872
Email: infofell@nas.edu
Website: www.national-academies.org/fellowships

The Ford Foundation Diversity Fellowships – Predoctoral Awards

Subjects: Check website for further details.
Purpose: For achieving excellence in college and university teaching and increasing the diversity of the nation's college and university faculties to maximize the educational benefits of diversity, and to increase the number of professors who can use diversity as a resource for enriching the education of all students.
Eligibility: Open to all citizens or nationals of the United States regardless of race, national origin, religion, gender, age, disability, or sexual orientation, individuals with evidence of superior academic

achievement and committed to a career in teaching and research at the college or university level, should enroll in or planning to enroll in an eligible research-based program leading to a PhD or ScD degree at a US educational institution and who have not earned a doctoral degree at any time, in any field.
Level of Study: Predoctorate
Type: Award
Value: Annual stipend: $20,000. Award to the institution in lieu of tuition and fees: $2,000. Expenses paid to attend at least one Conference of Ford Fellows
Length of Study: 3 years
No. of awards offered: 60
Application Procedure: Applicants must register and establish a personal user ID and password. Check website for further details.
Closing Date: November 1st for on-line applications and postmark deadline for paper applications is November 15th. Supplementary materials must be received in the fellowships office by January 18th
Funding: Foundation, government
Contributor: National Research Council on behalf of the Ford Foundation
Additional Information: Predoctoral fellows are required to enroll full-time in a program leading to a PhD or ScD degree in an eligible field of study.

For further information contact:

Fellowships Office, Keck 576, National Research Council, 500 Fifth Street, NW, Washington, DC, 20001
Tel: 202 334 2872
Email: infofell@nas.edu
Website: www.national-academies.org/fellowships

Jefferson Science Fellows at the U.S. Department of State

Subjects: Science, technology, and engineering (STE).
Purpose: To offset the costs of temporary living quarters in the Washington, DC area.
Eligibility: Applicants must be US citizens and holding a tenured faculty position at a US degree granting academic institution of higher learning. For terms and conditions as well as further details log on to the website.
Level of Study: Postgraduate
Value: A stipend of US $50,000
Length of Study: 1 year
Frequency: Annual
No. of awards offered: 2
Application Procedure: A complete nomination/application package consists of nomination/application form in PDF format and in word format; curriculum vitae (limit 10 pages); statements of qualifications (limit 2 pages each); and at least three (3), and no more than five (5), letters of recommendation from peers of the nominee/applicant.
Closing Date: January 15th
Contributor: National Academies supported through a partnership between American philanthropic foundations, the US STE academic community, professional scientific societies, and the US Department of State
Additional Information: Applicants should notify their institution while applying and encourage them to initiate a JSF/MOU as described on the website. Incomplete nomination/application packages, or those received after the deadline, will not be reviewed.

For further information contact:

The National Academies, Fellowships office, 500 fifth street, NW, Keck 568, WA, 20001, United States of America
Tel: (1) 202 334 2643
Fax: (1) 202 334 2759
Email: jsf@nas.edu
Website: www.nationalacademies.org

National Academics Christine Mirzayan Science and Technology Policy Graduate Fellowship Program

Subjects: Science, engineering, medicine, veterinary medicine, business and law.
Purpose: To engage students in science and technology policy.
Eligibility: Graduate students and postdoctoral scholars and those who have completed graduate studies or postdoctoral research within the last 5 years are eligible to apply.

Level of Study: Postgraduate
Type: Fellowship
Length of Study: 10 weeks
Frequency: Annual
Application Procedure: A completed application form must be submitted. Application forms are available on the website.
Closing Date: November 1st

National Energy Technology (NETL) Methane Hydrates Fellowship Programs (MHFP)

Subjects: Chemistry (Methane Hydrate).
Purpose: To provide postgraduate and postdoctoral candidates opportunities for career development, largely of their own choice in the Methane Hydrates field that are compatible with the interests of the sponsoring laboratories and universities, and to contribute thereby to the overall efforts of NETL in their support in the development of Methane Hydrate Science.
Eligibility: Open to candidates holding appropriate prior degree for the level of fellowship they intend to pursue. An applicant's training, professional experience, and research experience may be in any appropriate discipline or combination of disciplines required for the proposed project. Each Methane Hydrate Program fellow will be closely affiliated with a Research Adviser at the host venue.
Level of Study: Doctorate, Postdoctorate, Postgraduate
Type: Fellowship
Value: $30,000 for Masters, $35,000 for PhD level, and for a postdoctoral researcher, it starts at $60,000 with increments for additional experience
Length of Study: 3 years
Application Procedure: Application must be submitted only in hard copy and sent by Express Delivery to the Associateship Programs office. After completing the WebRAP application, you must also mail your supporting documents (transcripts and references) to the same address.
Closing Date: February 1st and August 1st
Additional Information: Please check the website for further details. Please direct all Application inquiries directly to the Research Associateship Programs at rap@nas.edu or by phone at 202 334 2760.

For further information contact:

Associateship Programs, Keck 555, National Research Council, 500 Fifth Street, NW, Washington, DC, 20001, United States of America
Tel: (1) 202 334 2707
Email: ebasquest@nas.edu@nas.edu
Website: www.national-academies.org/rap
Contact: Dr Eric O Basques, Research Adviser

NATIONAL ALLIANCE FOR MEDIA ARTS AND CULTURE (NAMAC)

145 Ninth Street, Suite 250, San Francisco, CA 94103, United States of America
Tel: (1) 415 431 1391
Fax: (1) 415 431 1392
Email: helen@namac.org
Website: www.namac.org

NAMAC, founded in 1980, is a non-profit association whose membership comprises a diverse mix of organizations and individuals dedicated to a common goal: the support and advocacy of independent film, video, audio and online/multimedia arts.

McKnight Artist Fellowship for Filmmakers

Subjects: Cinema and television.
Purpose: To honour the professional and artistic accomplishments of Minnesota artists working in the medium of film/video.
Eligibility: Open to candidates who are residents of Minnesota.
Level of Study: Postgraduate
Type: Fellowship
Value: Varies
Frequency: Annual
Country of Study: United States of America
Application Procedure: See the website.
Closing Date: August 13th

McKnight Artists Fellowship for Screenwriters

Subjects: Screenwriting.
Purpose: To recognize screenwriters who have excelled in the artistic discipline of writing for cinema.
Eligibility: Open to resident screenwriters of Minnesota.
Level of Study: Postgraduate
Type: Fellowship
Value: Varies
Frequency: Annual
Country of Study: United States of America
Application Procedure: See the website.
Closing Date: August 13th

NATIONAL ASSOCIATION BLACK JOURNALISTS (NABJ)

University of Maryland, 8701-A Adelphi Road, Adelphi, MD, 20783-1716, United States of America
Tel: (1) 445 7100
Fax: (1) 445 7101
Email: nabj@nabj.org
Website: www.nabj.org

NABJ is an organization of journalists, students and media-related professionals that provides quality programmes and services to black journalists worldwide.

Ethel Payne Fellowships

Subjects: Journalism.
Purpose: To fund journalists wanting international reporting experience through self-conceived assignments in Africa.
Eligibility: Applicants should be an NABJ member with 5 years journalism experience, full-time freelance.
Level of Study: Postdoctorate
Type: Fellowship
Value: US$5,000
Study Establishment: University of Maryland
Country of Study: United States of America
Application Procedure: A completed application should be submitted accompanied by an 800-word project proposal, a 300 word essay on the applicant's journalism experience, 3 samples of work published or aired and 2 letters of recommendation.
Closing Date: December 15th
Contributor: The National Association of black Journalists (NABJ)
No. of awards given last year: 2

NATIONAL ASSOCIATION OF COMPOSERS

PO Box 49256, Barrington Station, Los Angeles, CA, 90049, United States of America
Tel: (1) 310 838 4465
Fax: (1) 310 838 4465
Email: info@music-usa.org/nacusa
Website: www.music-usa.org/nacusa
Contact: President

The National Association of Composers presents concerts of music by American composers throughout the United States of America, and sponsors a Young composers competition.

National Association of Composers Young Composers Competition

Subjects: Music composition.
Purpose: To foster the creation of new American concert hall music.
Eligibility: Open to nationals of any country between the ages of 18 and 30.
Level of Study: Unrestricted, Postdoctorate, Postgraduate
Type: Competition
Value: Please contact the organization
Frequency: Annual
Country of Study: Any country
No. of awards offered: 2

Application Procedure: Applicants must send in their music as there are no application forms.
Closing Date: October 30th
Funding: Private
No. of awards given last year: 2

NATIONAL ASSOCIATION OF DENTAL ASSISTANTS

900 St Washington Street, Suite G-13, Falls Church, VA, 22046, United States of America
Tel: (1) 703 237 8616
Fax: (1) 703 533 1153
Email: carloss@umich.edu
Website: www.ndaonline.org
Contact: Scholarship Department

National Association of Dental Assistants Annual Scholarship Award

Subjects: Dental assistant certification, recertification, dental training, continuing dental education seminars or any course that is related to, or required in, the dental degree programme.
Purpose: To enable dental assistants to further their education.
Eligibility: Open to dental assistants who have a minimum of 2 years of membership in good standing. Applicants may also be a member's dependent, spouse or grandchild. All courses must be approved by the board.
Level of Study: Unrestricted
Type: Scholarship
Value: US$250, varies
Frequency: Annual
Study Establishment: Appropriate institutions
Country of Study: Any country
No. of awards offered: 1–2
Application Procedure: Applicants must submit one recommendation from their current or previous employer, one recommendation from someone other than a member, if a member's dependent, such as a school counsellor or another dental assistant, a completed application form and an updated student transcript.
Closing Date: May 31st
Funding: Commercial
No. of awards given last year: 2
No. of applicants last year: Approx. 10

THE NATIONAL ASSOCIATION OF TEACHERS OF SINGING (NATS)

9957 Moorings Drive, Suite 401, Jacksonville, FL, 32257, United States of America
Tel: (1) 904 992 9101; Toll Free: 888 262 2065
Fax: (1) 904 262 2587
Email: violetdlg@aol.com
Website: www.nats.org

The National Association of Teachers of Singing (NATS) is now the largest association of teachers of singing in the world. NATS offers a variety of lifelong learning experiences to its members, such as workshops, intern programmes, master classes, and conferences, all beginning at the chapter level and progressing to national events.

NATS Art Song Composition Award

Subjects: Singing.
Purpose: To stimulate the creation of quality vocal literature through the cooperation of singer and composer.
Eligibility: Open to any composer whose submitted work meets the prescribed requirements, and who pays the competition entry fee.
Type: Cash prize
Value: $1,000 plus the composer's expenses to the NATS National Convention where the premiere performance of the winning composition will be given
Study Establishment: Valdosta State University
Country of Study: United States of America
No. of awards offered: 1

Application Procedure: Check the website for further details.
Closing Date: December 1st

For further information contact:

Department of Music, Valdosta State University, 1500 N. Patterson Street, Valdosta, GA, 31698, United States of America
Website: www.nats.org/competitions.php
Contact: Dr Carol Mikkelsen

THE NATIONAL ATAXIA FOUNDATION

2600 Fernbrook Lane Suite 119, Minneapolis, MN, 55447-4752, United States of America
Tel: (1) (763) 553 0020
Fax: (1) (763) 553 0167
Email: naf@ataxia.org
Website: www.ataxia.org

The National Ataxia Foundation is dedicated to improving the lives of persons affected by ataxia through support, education, and research. In 1978, the Foundation first began direct funding of ataxia research through the NAF Research "Seed-Money" Program. Since that time, the Foundation has established two additional research programs including the NAF Young Investigator Award and the NAF Fellowship Award.

Ataxia Research Grant

Subjects: Behavioural and cognitive sciences or medical and health sciences.
Purpose: To assist investigators in the early or pilot phase of their studies relevant to the cause, pathogenesis or treatment of the hereditary or sporadic ataxias.
Eligibility: Open to all nationals.
Level of Study: Postgraduate, Research
Type: Grant
Value: $5,000–15,000 range. Funding may be considered for up to $35,000 for projects deserving special consideration
Frequency: Annual
No. of awards offered: 1
Application Procedure: Application forms can be downloaded from the website.
Closing Date: July 15th

Research Fellowship Award

Subjects: Hereditary and sporadic ataxias.
Purpose: To promote and support research to find the cause, treatment, and cure for the hereditary and sporadic ataxias.
Eligibility: Applicants should have completed at least one year of post-doctoral training, but not more than two at the time of application, and should have shown a commitment to research in the field of ataxia. A letter from the mentor should outline a program of studies for the applicant, and delineate the candidate's plans.
Level of Study: Postdoctorate
Type: Fellowship
Value: $35,000–45,000
Length of Study: 1 year
Frequency: Annual
Application Procedure: The signed original plus four (4) copies of the completed application should be mailed to the Foundation.
Closing Date: August 15th

Young Investigator Award

Subjects: Friedreich's ataxia and spinocerebellar ataxia type 3 (SCA 3).
Purpose: To encourage young clinical and scientific investigators to pursue a career in the field of ataxia research.
Eligibility: Open to candidates who have attained a MD or PhD degree, and have an appointment as a junior faculty member. Individuals as the Associate Professor level are not eligible. Clinicians must have finished their residency no more than 5 years prior to applying.
Level of Study: Doctorate, Postgraduate
Value: $50,000
Length of Study: 2 years
Application Procedure: Applicants should submit a completed research application form with a list of past, present and pending funding

including project title, funding source, and amount of funding. Applications must also contain a letter of nomination from a faculty sponsor to make appropriate resources available to support the project.
Closing Date: September 1st

NATIONAL BREAST CANCER FOUNDATION (NBCF)

Level 3, 18-20 York Street, GPO Box 4126, Sydney, NSW, 2000, Australia
Tel: (61) 2 9299 4090
Fax: (61) 2 9299 4092
Email: info@nbcf.org.au
Website: www.nbcf.org.au

The ultimate goal of the National Breast Cancer Foundation (NBCF) is to raise enough money to fund a cure for breast cancer. The NBCF supports and promotes research into breast cancer, facilitates consumer participation in all aspects of their work, acts as an advocate for breast cancer research, and provides opportunities for all Australians to contribute to breast cancer research.

NBCF Doctoral Scholarship
Subjects: All aspects of breast cancer research will be considered.
Purpose: To provide outstanding graduates with a strong interest in breast cancer research with an opportunity to pursue full-time PhD studies at an Australian University.
Eligibility: Open to applicants who are permanent residents of Australia.
Level of Study: Doctorate, Research
Type: Scholarship
Value: Australian $31,000 plus Australian $2,250 allowance per year
Length of Study: 3 years
Frequency: Annual
Country of Study: Australia
Application Procedure: The applications are judged under peer review by experts in the field for their scientific merit and contribution to either new knowledge or building on existing knowledge of breast cancer.
Closing Date: June 6th
Funding: Foundation
Contributor: Australian community and corporate funding
No. of awards given last year: 5
No. of applicants last year: 11

For further information contact:

Email: lhan.gannon@nbcf.org.au
Contact: Lhan Gannon

NBCF Postdoctoral Fellowship
Subjects: All aspects of breast cancer research will be considered.
Purpose: To provide outstanding researchers who have recently completed a PhD with support to pursue their breast cancer research interest and increase their research capability.
Eligibility: Open to applicants who are permanent residents of Australia.
Level of Study: Postdoctorate, Research
Type: Fellowship
Value: Australian $63,500 plus Australian $5,000 allowances per year
Length of Study: 4 years
Frequency: Annual
Country of Study: Australia
Application Procedure: The applications are judged under peer review by experts in the field for their scientific merit and the contribution to either new knowledge or building on existing knowledge of breast cancer.
Closing Date: June 6th
Funding: Foundation
Contributor: Australian community and corporate
No. of awards given last year: 3
No. of applicants last year: 7

Novel Concept Awards
Subjects: Oncology (Breast cancer research).

Purpose: To provide investigators with the opportunity to pursue serendipitous observations and explore new, innovative, and untested ideas.
Eligibility: Open to those undertaking research in the entire continuum of breast cancer research.
Level of Study: Unrestricted
Type: Award
Value: Australian $200,000
Length of Study: 2 years
No. of awards offered: Up to 5
Application Procedure: Please contact the Research Administrator or check the website for further details.
Funding: Trusts

Pilot Study Grants
Subjects: Oncology (breast cancer research).
Purpose: To obtain preliminary data regarding methodology, effect sizes and possible findings relating to new research ideas relevant to breast cancer.
Eligibility: Open to Australian citizens, or graduates from overseas with permanent Australian resident.
Level of Study: Research, Unrestricted
Type: Grant
Value: Australian $100,000
Length of Study: 2 years
No. of awards offered: Up to 5
Application Procedure: Check website for further details.
Contributor: NBCF
Additional Information: Researchers are not eligible to apply if they receive tobacco sponsorship or are from institutions that allow sponsorship from the tobacco industry. Please contact the Research Administrator.

NATIONAL CANCER INSTITUTE OF CANADA (NCIC)

Suite 200, 10 Alcorn Avenue, Toronto, Ontario, M4V 3B1, Canada
Tel: (1) 416 961 7223
Fax: (1) 416 961 4189
Email: research@cancer.ca
Website: www.ncic.cancer.ca
Contact: Carol Bishop, Assistant Director, Operations Research Program

The National Cancer Institute of Canada (NCIC) is the largest non-government funder of cancer research in Canada. In concert with its partner, the Canadian Cancer Society, and with the Terry Fox Foundation, the NCIC provides support for research and related programmes undertaken at Canadian universities, hospitals and other research institutions.

CCS Feasibility Grants
Subjects: Cancer research.
Purpose: To provide a modest level of funding as the NCIC recognizes that it is difficult to submit a full application for a research grant without having first conducted preliminary studies.
Eligibility: This programme is open to all applicants but priority will be given where it is apparent that no other resources are available. These grants will not be awarded to support travel to conduct planning meetings. These funds will also not be awarded for conference travel or for the purchase of permanent equipment.
Level of Study: Postgraduate
Type: Grant
Value: Up to Canadian $35,000
Length of Study: 1 year, but funds may be spent over a 2 year period
Frequency: Annual
Country of Study: Canada
No. of awards offered: Varies
Application Procedure: Applicants must refer to the website.
Closing Date: Please contact the organization
Funding: Private
Contributor: The Canadian Cancer Society
No. of awards given last year: 7
No. of applicants last year: 25

Additional Information: Further information is available from the website.

NCIC Clinical Research Fellowship

Subjects: Clinical cancer research.

Purpose: To assist outstanding individuals who hold a doctoral degree in medicine and who seek specialized training.

Eligibility: Open to Canadian citizens or residents who possess a doctoral degree in medicine from a recognized institution and be licensed to practice in Canada. Preference will be given to those who can demonstrate research commitment by having completed, or being enrolled in, a relevant graduate course.

Level of Study: Postdoctorate, Professional development

Type: Fellowship

Value: Minimum Canadian $40,000 rising for each year of postdoctoral experience to a maximum of Canadian $47,500 per year

Length of Study: Up to 3 years

Frequency: Annual

Study Establishment: An approved institution

Country of Study: Canada, or abroad as approved

No. of awards offered: Varies

Application Procedure: Applicants must write for details or refer to the website.

Closing Date: September 15th

Funding: Private

Contributor: The Terry Fox Foundation and the Canadian Cancer Society

No. of awards given last year: 6

No. of applicants last year: 5

Additional Information: Further information is available from the website. Stipends are subject to annual review. Recipients of these fellowships are eligible for a research and travel allowance of Canadian $1,200 per award year.

NCIC Equipment Grants for New Investigators

Subjects: Cancer research.

Purpose: To make it possible for new investigators to set up cancer research facilities in Canada. The award is designed to assist young investigators beginning their career.

Eligibility: Applicants should be new investigators who have no more than 2 years of experience as an independent investigator and have not received an operational research grant from the National Cancer Institute or another comparable agency.

Level of Study: Postgraduate

Type: Grant

Value: Up to Canadian $75,000

Frequency: Dependent on funds available

Country of Study: Canada

No. of awards offered: Varies

Application Procedure: Applicants must write for details or refer to the website.

Closing Date: October 15th

Funding: Private

Contributor: The Terry Fox Foundation and the Canadian Cancer Society

No. of awards given last year: 6

No. of applicants last year: 21

Additional Information: The award is not intended to facilitate the relocation of individuals from one laboratory to another. Further information is available from the website.

NCIC Post-PhD Research Fellowships

Subjects: Cancer research.

Purpose: To provide training in cancer research for outstanding candidates who plan a career in Canada in this field of investigation.

Eligibility: Candidates must be graduates of a university recognized by the NCIC and must be accepted for postdoctoral training in the field of cancer research in an academic environment also recognized. If the fellowship is to be taken outside Canada the applicant must be either a Canadian citizen or Canadian landed immigrant. Post MD candidates must be licensed to practice in Canada. For applicants with both PhD and MD degrees, the degree obtained most recently will determine the fellowship category for which they should apply.

Level of Study: Postdoctorate

Type: Fellowship

Value: Minimum Canadian $35,000 rising for each year of postdoctoral experience to a maximum of Canadian $47,500 per year

Length of Study: Up to a maximum of 3 years

Frequency: Annual

Study Establishment: A Canadian institute or abroad if the applicant is Canadian or a Canadian landed immigrant

Country of Study: Canada and abroad

No. of awards offered: Varies

Application Procedure: Applicants must refer to the website.

Closing Date: February 1st

Funding: Private

Contributor: The Terry Fox Foundation and the Canadian Cancer Society

No. of awards given last year: 22

No. of applicants last year: 111

Additional Information: Further information is available from the website.

NCIC Research Grants for New Investigators

Subjects: Cancer research.

Purpose: To facilitate the greatest possibility for new investigators to obtain grant support for cancer research. The award is designed to assist new investigators who are beginning a career in cancer research.

Eligibility: Applicants should be new investigators who have no more than 2 years of experience as an independent investigator and have not previously received a research grant from the National Cancer Institute of Canada or another comparable agency.

Level of Study: Postgraduate

Type: Research grant

Value: Varies

Frequency: Annual

Study Establishment: An approved institution

Country of Study: Canada

No. of awards offered: Varies

Application Procedure: Applicants must write for details or refer to the website.

Closing Date: October 17th

Funding: Private

Contributor: The Terry Fox Foundation and the Canadian Cancer Society

No. of awards given last year: 6

No. of applicants last year: 34

NCIC Research Grants to Individuals

Subjects: Cancer research.

Purpose: To stimulate Canadian investigators in a very broad spectrum of research.

Eligibility: Open to a researcher who is designated as the principal investigator and must be based in, or formally affiliated with, but not necessarily receive salary support from, an eligible Canadian host institution such as a university, research institute or healthcare agency. Graduate students, postdoctoral Fellows, research associates, technical support staff, or investigators based outside Canada are not eligible to be a principal investigator.

Level of Study: Postgraduate

Type: Research grant

Value: Awards will be granted for the purchase and maintenance of animals, for expendable supplies, minor items of equipment, for payment of graduate students, postdoctoral Fellows and technical and professional assistants, and for research travel and permanent equipment. An allocation for conference travel may be added automatically by the NCIC. These grants do not provide for personal salary support of the principal investigator and/or co-applicants or for institutional overhead costs

Length of Study: 1–5 years

Frequency: Annual

Study Establishment: Universities or other institutions

Country of Study: Canada

No. of awards offered: Varies

Application Procedure: Applicants must complete an application form. Further details are available on request or from the website.

Closing Date: October 15th

Funding: Private

Contributor: The Terry Fox Foundation and the Canadian Cancer Society
No. of awards given last year: 81
No. of applicants last year: 413
Additional Information: Further information is available from the website. Grants will be awarded to projects deemed worthy of support, provided that the basic equipment and research facilities are available in the institution concerned and that it will provide the necessary administrative services. Grants are made only with the consent and knowledge of the administrative head of the institution at which they are to be held and applications must be countersigned accordingly.

NCIC Research Studentships
Subjects: Cancer research.
Purpose: To award outstanding PhD students who plan a career in cancer research in Canada.
Eligibility: Applicants must be Canadian residents enrolled in a PhD programme at a Canadian institute. Applicants must have completed at least 2 years of research training at graduate level or have equivalent research experience.
Level of Study: Postgraduate
Value: Canadian $22,500 per year
Length of Study: A maximum of 4 years
Frequency: Annual
Study Establishment: An approved institution
Country of Study: Canada
No. of awards offered: Varies
Application Procedure: Applicants must refer to the website for details and application forms.
Closing Date: Please contact the organization
Funding: Private
Contributor: The Terry Fox Foundation and the Canadian Cancer Society
No. of awards given last year: 15
No. of applicants last year: 77
Additional Information: Further information is available from the website. The NCIC invites all members of the research community to identify and approach qualified individuals, and encourages them to apply.

NCIC Travel Awards for Senior Level PhD Students
Subjects: Cancer research.
Purpose: To provide financial assistance by helping to defray the travel costs associated with making a scientific presentation at a conference, symposium or other appropriate professional gathering.
Eligibility: Applicants must be students enrolled in a PhD or MD programme at a Canadian institution and be in the final phase of their studies. Candidates must be attending a conference for the purpose of presenting data from a cancer-related project on a first author basis.
Level of Study: Postgraduate
Type: Travel grant
Value: Up to Canadian $1,500
Country of Study: Canada
No. of awards offered: Up to 20 per calendar year
Application Procedure: Applicants must refer to the website.
Closing Date: April 1st, September 1st or December 1st
Funding: Private
Contributor: The Canadian Cancer Society
No. of awards given last year: 13
No. of applicants last year: 31
Additional Information: Further information is available from the website.

NATIONAL CENTER FOR ATMOSPHERIC RESEARCH (NCAR)

PO Box 3000, Advanced Study Program, Boulder, CO, 80307-3000, United States of America
Tel: (1) 303 497 1328
Fax: (1) 303 497 1646
Email: paulad@ucar.edu
Website: www.asp.ucar.edu
Contact: Ms Paula Fisher, Co-ordinator

The National Center for Atmospheric Research (NCAR) is a national research center focused on atmospheric science.

NCAR Faculty Fellowship Programme
Subjects: Atmospheric sciences.
Purpose: To facilitate residency study at NCAR.
Eligibility: Open to all faculty employed full-time at a college or university. Diversity concerns will also be addressed in the selection process.
Level of Study: Doctorate, Postdoctorate
Type: Fellowships
Value: Applicants may be eligible for the following: travel, temporary living per diem, shipping allowance
Frequency: Annual
Study Establishment: The NCAR Centre
Country of Study: United States of America
No. of awards offered: 5–10
Application Procedure: Apply online.
Closing Date: Fall – Dates vary
Funding: Government
Additional Information: If you have any questions please contact Paula Fisher; and email: paulad@ucar.edu or please see the website.

NCAR Graduate Visitor Programme
Subjects: Atmospheric sciences.
Level of Study: Graduate
Type: Scholarship
Value: US$500 per month for living expenses plus travel expenses
Length of Study: 3–12 months
Frequency: Annual
Study Establishment: The NCAR Center
Country of Study: United States of America
No. of awards offered: Varies
Application Procedure: Applicants must apply through an advisor and NCAR scientist.
Closing Date: Fall
Funding: Government
Additional Information: If you have any questions about this new programme, please contact Paula Fisher; email: paulad@ucar.edu or please visit the website.

NCAR Postdoctoral Appointments in the Advanced Study Program
Subjects: Atmospheric sciences.
Purpose: To assist and support research.
Eligibility: Open to those who have recently received their PhD and scientists with no more than 4 years of applicable experience since receiving their PhD. Foreign nationals may also apply.
Level of Study: Postdoctorate
Type: Fellowship
Value: US$53,000 per year for recent PhDs and US$55,000 for appointees in the second year at NCAR-ASP. All appointees are eligible for life and health insurance, and travel expenses to the center are reimbursed for the appointee and family. Fellows living abroad will have round-trip travel expenses for themselves and their families paid up to a maximum of US$2,500. A small allowance for moving and storing personal belongings is provided. Scientific travel and registration fees that cost up to US$1,500 per year are normally available
Length of Study: Up to 1 year, with a possibility of renewal for a further year
Frequency: Annual
Study Establishment: The Center
Country of Study: United States of America
No. of awards offered: 7–10
Application Procedure: Applicants must apply online at www.asp.ucar.edu
Closing Date: January 5th
Funding: Government
No. of awards given last year: 8
No. of applicants last year: 120
Additional Information: NCAR is an equal opportunity employer with an affirmative-action programme.

For further information contact:

1850 Table Mesa Drive, Boulder, CO, 80305, United States of America

THE NATIONAL COLLEGIATE ATHLETIC ASSOCIATION

NCAA Postgraduate Scholarship Program, 700 W. Washington Street, PO Box 6222, Indianapolis, IN, 46206-6222, United States of America
Tel: (1) 317 917 6222
Fax: (1) 317 917 6888
Email: pmr@ncaa.org
Website: www.ncaa.org

The National Collegiate Athletic Association is the organization through which the nation's colleges and universities speak and act on athletics matters at the national level. It is a voluntary association of more than 1,265 institutions, conferences, organizations and individuals devoted to the sound administration of intercollegiate athletics.

Freedom Forum/NCAA Foundation Sports Journalism Scholarships
Subjects: Arts and media.
Purpose: To foster freedoms of the press and speech while promoting quality sports journalism education at the college level.
Eligibility: Open to applicants in their junior year in an NCAA member institution, have career goals in sports journalism, and major in journalism or experience in sports journalism on campus.
Level of Study: Postgraduate
Type: Scholarship
Value: US $3,000
Frequency: Annual
Study Establishment: NCAA member institution
No. of awards offered: 8
Application Procedure: Check website for further details.
Closing Date: December 8th

For further information contact:

Website: www.ncaa.org/leadership_advisory_board/programs.html
Contact: The NCAA Leadership Advisory Board

NCAA Postgraduate Scholarship
Subjects: All subjects.
Purpose: To honour outstanding student-athletes who are also outstanding scholars.
Eligibility: Open to student-athletes enrolled at an NCAA member institution, in the last year of intercollegiate competition and with a minimum grade point average of 3.2 on a 4.0 scale or its equivalent.
Level of Study: Postgraduate
Type: Scholarship
Value: One-time grant of US$7,500. This is not earmarked for a specific area of postgraduate study but the awardee must use it as a part-time or full-time graduate student in a graduate or professional school of an academically accredited institution within 3 years of winning the award
Frequency: Each Academic year
Country of Study: Any country
No. of awards offered: 174
Application Procedure: Applicants must be nominated by their faculty athletics representative or designee. Student may be any nationality but must be attending an NCAA member institution and be in final year of eligibility in the sport they are nominated.
Closing Date: There are three deadlines (may vary slightly each year): December 9th for Fall sports; February 24th for Winter sports; and May 5th for Spring sports
Funding: Foundation
No. of awards given last year: 174
No. of applicants last year: 374

Walter Byers Postgraduate Scholarship Program
Subjects: All subjects.

Purpose: Encouraging excellence in academic performance by student-athletes and in recognition of outstanding academic achievement and potential for success in postgraduate study.
Eligibility: Open to undergraduates with cumulative grade-point average of 3.500, or graduating senior who have competed in intercollegiate athletics as a member of a varsity team at an NCAA member institution; have demonstrated that participation in athletics has been a positive influence on their personal and intellectual development.
Level of Study: Postgraduate
Type: Scholarship
Value: US $24,000 per academic year; may be renewed for a second year
Frequency: Annual
No. of awards offered: 2
Application Procedure: Check website for further details.
Closing Date: Late January
Additional Information: Generally, applications are available on-line in October of each year and the completed applications are due back to the national office in late January. Please refer to the current application packet for the current year's due date.

For further information contact:

The National Collegiate Athletic Association, PO Box 6222, Indianapolis, Indiana, 46206 6222
Contact: The Walter Byers Scholarship Committee Staff Liaison

NATIONAL DAIRY SHRINE

1224 Atton Darby Creek Road, Columbus, OH 43228 9792, United States of America
Tel: (1) 614 870 5333
Fax: (1) 614 870 2622
Email: shrine@cobaselect.com
Website: www.dairyshrine.org
Contact: Maurice E. Core, Executive Director

Founded in 1949 by a small group of visionary dairy leaders, National Dairy Shrine brings together dairy producers, scientists, students, educators, marketers and others who share a desire to preserve the dairy heritage and keep the dairy industry strong.

Dairy Student Recognition Program Award
Subjects: Related to dairy: production agriculture, manufacturing, marketing, agriculture law, business, veterinary medicine and environmental sciences.
Purpose: To recognize graduating seniors planning a career related to dairy who have demonstrated leadership skills, academic ability and interest in dairy cattle.
Eligibility: Only two applicants per college or university are accepted for this contest in any given year.
Level of Study: Graduate
Type: Award
Value: 1st $1,500; 2nd $1,000; 3rd -9th $500
Frequency: Annual
Country of Study: United States of America
No. of awards offered: 2 per college
Application Procedure: Applicants must submit a letter of recommendation from the department head or a faculty member who is familiar with the applicant's activities and academic achievements and an official transcript showing all courses along with the application form.
Closing Date: March 15th
Additional Information: The total number of awards will be determined by the number and quality of applicants. Winners will be recognized at the National Dairy Shrine awards banquet.

Iager Dairy Scholarship
Subjects: Food science and production.
Purpose: To encourage students with an explicit interest in a career in the dairy industry.
Eligibility: Open to applicants studying in the agricultural schools.
Level of Study: Postgraduate
Type: Scholarship
Value: US$1,000
Frequency: Annual

Country of Study: United States of America
No. of awards offered: Varies
Application Procedure: A completed, typed, application form must be submitted to the National Dairy Shrine.
Closing Date: March 15th
Funding: Private
Contributor: Charles and Judy lager
No. of awards given last year: 1

Kildee Scholarship (Advanced Study)

Subjects: Related to dairy industry: production agriculture, manufacturing, marketing, agricultural law, business, veterinary medicine and environmental sciences.
Purpose: The scholarship is offered in honour of late H.H. Kildee, Dean Emeritus at Iowa State University, whose counsel, encouragement and teaching inspired many of today's dairy leaders, for graduate study to a student who excelled in dairy judging.
Eligibility: The awards are based on rank in the national contests, academic standing, leadership ability, student activities, interest and experience with dairy cattle and future plans.
Level of Study: Graduate
Type: Scholarship
Value: US$3,000
Length of Study: 4 semesters
Frequency: Annual
Country of Study: United States of America
No. of awards offered: 2
Application Procedure: Applicants must submit the application form along with 2 letters of recommendation, one from department head and other from a faculty member who is familiar with the applicant's activities and academic achievements. An official transcript showing all courses should also be submittted.
Closing Date: March 15th
Additional Information: The winners will be recognized at the National Dairy Shrine award banquet.

THE NATIONAL EDUCATION ASSOCIATION (NEA) FOUNDATION FOR THE IMPROVEMENT OF EDUCATION

1201 16th Street North West, Suite 417, Washington, DC, 20036 3207, United States of America
Tel: (1) 202 822 7840
Fax: (1) 202 822 7779
Email: info@neafoundation.org
Website: www.neafoundation.org

The NEA Foundation offers programs and grants that support public school educators' efforts to close the achievement gaps, increase student achievement, salute excellence in education and provide professional development.

NEA Foundation Learning and Leadership Grants

Subjects: All subjects.
Purpose: To support individuals participating in high-quality professional development experiences.
Eligibility: Open to practising public school classroom teachers, public school education support personnel and faculty and staff of public higher education institutions. Two or more collaborating educators may also apply for a group grant.
Level of Study: Professional development
Type: Grant
Value: US$2000 for individuals and US$5,000 for groups
Length of Study: 1 year
Frequency: Annual
Country of Study: United States of America
No. of awards offered: Up to 75
Application Procedure: Applicants should consult the website for details.
Closing Date: October 15th, February 15th, June 1st

NEA Foundation Student Achievement Grants

Subjects: Education.

Purpose: To support collaborative efforts by two or more colleagues to develop and implement creative project-based learning that results in high student achievement.
Eligibility: Open to teams of two or more practising United States public school teachers in grades K–12, public school education support personnel, public higher education faculty and staff.
Level of Study: Postgraduate
Type: Grant
Value: US$5,000
Length of Study: 12 months
Frequency: Annual
Country of Study: United States of America
Application Procedure: Applicants must consult the website for details.
Closing Date: October 15th, February 15th, June 1st

Student Grants

Subjects: Education.
Purpose: To promote collaborative, innovative ideas that lead to student achievement of high standards.
Eligibility: Open to teams of two or more practising United States public school teachers in grades K–12, public school education support personnel, public higher education faculty and staff. Preference will be given to National Education Association members, and to educators who serve economically disadvantaged and/or underserved students.
Level of Study: Postgraduate
Type: Grant
Value: US$5,000
Length of Study: 12 months
Frequency: Annual
Country of Study: United States of America
Application Procedure: Applicants must consult the organization for details.
Closing Date: June 1st

NATIONAL FEDERATION OF THE BLIND (NFB)

1800 Johnson Street, Baltimore, MD, 21230, United States of America
Tel: (1) 410 659 9314
Fax: (1) 410 685 5653
Email: pmaurer@nfb.org
Website: www.nfb.org

Founded in 1940, the National Federation of the Blind (NFB) is the nation's largest and most influential membership organization of blind people. With 50,000 members, the NFB has affiliates in all 50 states as well as Washington, DC and Puerto Rico, and over 700 local chapters. As a consumer and advocacy organization, the NFB is considered the leading force in the blindness field today.

Charles and Melva T Owen Memorial Scholarship

Subjects: Any subject excluding religion and general or cultural education.
Purpose: To assist blind people and to recognize achievements by blind scholars.
Eligibility: All applicants for the scholarship must be legally blind and pursuing or planning to pursue a full-time postsecondary course.
Level of Study: Unrestricted
Type: Scholarship
Value: US$3,000
Frequency: Annual
Study Establishment: A United States of America institution
Country of Study: United States of America
No. of awards offered: 1
Application Procedure: All applications must include a personal letter from the applicant, two letters of recommendation, all transcripts related to institutions attended, a letter from a federation state president or designee and score reports (for high school seniors).
Closing Date: March 31st
Funding: Private
Additional Information: First established by Charles Owen in loving memory of his blind wife and now endowed by his last will and testament to honour the memory of both.

EU Parker Scholarship

Subjects: All subjects.
Purpose: To assist blind people and to recognize achievements by blind scholars.
Eligibility: All applicants for the scholarship must be legally blind and pursuing or planning to pursue a full-time postsecondary course.
Level of Study: Unrestricted
Type: Scholarship
Value: US$3,000
Frequency: Annual
Study Establishment: A United States of America Institution
Country of Study: United States of America
No. of awards offered: 1
Application Procedure: All applications must include a personal letter from the applicant, two letters of recommendation, all transcripts related to institutions attended, a letter from a federation state president or designee and score reports (for high school seniors).
Closing Date: March 31st
Funding: Private
Additional Information: Given in honour of a long-time leader of the NFB, E U Parker.

Hank Lebonne Scholarship

Subjects: All subjects.
Purpose: To assist blind people and to recognize achievements by blind scholars.
Eligibility: All applicants for the scholarship must be legally blind and pursuing or planning to pursue a full-time postsecondary course.
Level of Study: Unrestricted
Type: Scholarship
Length of Study: US$5,000
Frequency: Annual
Study Establishment: A United States of America Institution
Country of Study: United States of America
No. of awards offered: 1
Application Procedure: All applications must include a personal letter from the applicant, two letters of recommendation, all transcripts related to institutions attended, a letter from a federation state president or designee and score reports (for high school seniors).
Closing Date: March 31st
Funding: Private
Additional Information: The scholarship is given in the memory of Hank Lebonne.

Hermione Grant Calhoun Scholarship

Subjects: All subjects.
Purpose: To assist blind people and to recognize achievements by blind scholars.
Eligibility: All applicants for the scholarship must be legally blind and pursuing or planning to pursue a full-time postsecondary course. The applicant must be a woman.
Level of Study: Unrestricted
Type: Scholarship
Value: US$3,000
Frequency: Annual
Study Establishment: A United States of America Institution
Country of Study: United States of America
No. of awards offered: 1
Application Procedure: All applications must include a personal letter from the applicant, two letters of recommendation, all transcripts related to institutions attended, a letter from a federation state president or designee and score reports (for high school seniors).
Closing Date: March 31st
Funding: Private

Howard Brown Rickard Scholarship

Subjects: Law, medicine, engineering, architecture and natural sciences.
Purpose: To assist blind people and to recognize achievements by blind people.
Eligibility: All applicants for the scholarship must be legally blind and pursuing or planning to pursue a full-time postsecondary course.
Level of Study: Unrestricted

Type: Scholarship
Value: US$3,000
Frequency: Annual
Study Establishment: A United States of America Institution
Country of Study: United States of America
No. of awards offered: 1
Application Procedure: All applications must include a personal letter from the applicant, two letters of recommendation, all transcripts related to institutions attended, a letter from a federation state president or designee and score reports (for high school seniors).
Closing Date: March 31st

Jennica Ferguson Memorial Scholarship

Subjects: All subjects.
Purpose: To assist blind people and to recognize achievements by blind scholars.
Eligibility: All applicants for the scholarship must be legally blind and pursuing or planning to pursue a full-time postsecondary course.
Level of Study: Unrestricted
Type: Scholarship
Value: US$5,000
Frequency: Annual
Study Establishment: A United States of America Institution
Country of Study: United States of America
No. of awards offered: 1
Application Procedure: All applications must include a personal letter from the applicant, two letters of recommendation, all transcripts related to institutions attended, a letter from a federation state president or designee and score reports (for high school seniors).
Closing Date: March 31st
Additional Information: The scholarship is given in the memory of Jennica Ferguson.

Kenneth Jernigan Scholarship

Subjects: All subjects.
Purpose: To assist blind people and to recognize achievements by blind scholars.
Eligibility: All applicants for the scholarship must be legally blind and pursuing or planning to pursue a full-time postsecondary course.
Level of Study: Unrestricted
Type: Scholarship
Value: US$12,000
Frequency: Annual
Study Establishment: A United States of America Institution
Country of Study: United States of America
No. of awards offered: 1
Application Procedure: All applications must include a personal letter from the applicant, two letters of recommendation, all transcripts related to institutions attended, a letter from a federation state president or designee and score reports (for high school seniors).
Closing Date: March 31st
Funding: Private
Contributor: The American Action Fund for Blind Children and Adults
Additional Information: The scholarship is given in memory of Kenneth Jernigan.

Kuchler-Killian Memorial Scholarship

Subjects: All subjects.
Purpose: To assist blind people and to recognize achievements by blind scholars.
Eligibility: All applicants for the scholarship must be legally blind and pursuing or planning to pursue a full-time postsecondary course.
Level of Study: Unrestricted
Type: Scholarship
Value: US$3,000
Frequency: Annual
Study Establishment: A United States of America Institution
Country of Study: United States of America
No. of awards offered: 1
Application Procedure: All applications must include a personal letter from the applicant, two letters of recommendation, all transcripts related to institutions attended, a letter from a federation state president or designee and score reports (for high school seniors).
Closing Date: March 31st
Funding: Private

Michael and Marie Marucci Scholarship

Subjects: Foreign languages, comparative literature, history, geography, political science with a concentration in international studies or any other discipline requiring study abroad.

Purpose: To assist blind people and to recognize achievements by blind scholars.

Eligibility: All applicants for the scholarship must be legally blind and pursuing or planning to pursue a full-time postsecondary course. The applicants must show evidence of competence in a foreign language.

Level of Study: Unrestricted

Type: Scholarship

Value: US$5,000

Frequency: Annual

Study Establishment: A United States of America Institution

Country of Study: United States of America

No. of awards offered: 1

Application Procedure: All applications must include a personal letter from the applicant, two letters of recommendation, all transcripts related to institutions attended, a letter from a federation state president or designee and score reports (for high school seniors).

Closing Date: March 31st

Funding: Private

Additional Information: Given by two dedicated and valued members of the NFB, Maryland.

National Federation of the Blind Computer Science Scholarship

Subjects: Computer science.

Purpose: To assist blind people and to recognize achievements by blind scholars.

Eligibility: All applicants must be legally blind and studying in the computer science field.

Level of Study: Unrestricted

Type: Scholarship

Value: US$3,000

Frequency: Annual

Study Establishment: A United States of America Institution

Country of Study: United States of America

No. of awards offered: 1

Application Procedure: All applications must include a personal letter from the applicant, two letters of recommendation, all transcripts related to institutions attended, a letter from a federation state president or designee and score reports (for high school seniors).

Closing Date: March 31st

Funding: Private

National Federation of the Blind Educator of Tommorow Award

Subjects: Education.

Purpose: To assist blind people and to recognize achievements by blind scholars.

Eligibility: All applicants for the award must be legally blind and planning a career in elementary, secondary or postsecondary teaching.

Level of Study: Unrestricted

Type: Award

Value: US$3,000

Frequency: Annual

Study Establishment: At a United States of America Institution

Country of Study: United States of America

No. of awards offered: 1

Application Procedure: All applications must include a personal letter from the applicant, two letters of recommendation, all transcripts related to institutions attended, a letter from a federation state president or designee and score reports (for high school seniors).

Closing Date: March 31st

National Federation of the Blind Scholarships

Subjects: All subjects.

Purpose: To assist blind people and to recognize achievements by blind scholars.

Eligibility: All applicants for the scholarships must be legally blind.

Level of Study: Unrestricted

Type: Scholarship

Value: US$3,000 each

Frequency: Annual

Study Establishment: A United States of America Institution

Country of Study: United States of America

No. of awards offered: 15

Application Procedure: All applications must include a personal letter from the applicant, two letters of recommendation, all transcripts related to institutions attended, a letter from a federation state president or designee and score reports (for high school seniors).

Closing Date: March 31st

Funding: Private

Additional Information: Given for academic excellence, community service and financial need.

NFB Computer Science Scholarship

Subjects: Computer science.

Eligibility: Open to legally blind persons pursuing, or planning to pursue, a full-time post secondary course of training. The scholarship is awarded on the basis of academic excellence, service to the community and financial need. Candidates need not be members of the Federation.

Level of Study: Unrestricted

Type: Scholarship

Value: US$3,000

Frequency: Annual

Country of Study: United States of America

No. of awards offered: 1

Application Procedure: Applicants must complete an application form, available on request.

Closing Date: March 31st

Funding: Private

Sally S Jacobsen Scholarship

Subjects: Education.

Purpose: To assist blind people and to recognize achievements by blind scholars.

Eligibility: All applicants for the scholarship must be legally blind and pursuing or planning to pursue a full-time postsecondary course.

Level of Study: Unrestricted

Type: Scholarship

Value: US$5,000

Frequency: Annual

Study Establishment: A United States of America Institution

Country of Study: United States of America

No. of awards offered: 1

Application Procedure: All applications must include a personal letter from the applicant, two letters of recommendation, all transcripts related to institutions attended, a letter from a federation state president or designee and score reports (for high school seniors).

Closing Date: March 31st

Funding: Private

Additional Information: The scholarship is given in memory of a long-time New York state leader Sally S Jacobsen.

NATIONAL FISH AND WILDLIFE FOUNDATION

1120 Connecticut Avenue, NW Suite 900, Washington, DC, 20036, United States of America
Tel: (1) 202 857 0166
Fax: (1) 202 857 0162
Email: brian.gratwicke@nfwf.org
Website: www.nfwf.org
Contact: Ms Alison Bolz, Budweiser Scholarship Programme

The National Fish and Wildlife Foundation is a private, non-profit organization dedicated to the conservation of fish, wildlife and plants, and the habitats on which they depend. Our goals are to promote healthy populations of fish, wildlife and plants by generating new commerce for conservation.

Budweiser Conservation Scholarship

Subjects: The Budweiser Conservation Scholarship programme is designed to respond to many of the most significant challenges in fish, wildlife and plant conservation in the United States of America.

Purpose: To support and promote innovative research or study that seeks to respond to today's most pressing conservation issues.
Eligibility: To be eligible for consideration, a student must be a citizen of the United States of America, at least 21 years of age and enrolled in an accredited Institute of Higher Education in the United States of America. The applicant must be pursuing a graduate or undergraduate degree (sophomores and juniors in the current academic year only) in environmental science, natural resource management, biology, public policy, geography, political science or related disciplines.
Level of Study: Doctorate, Graduate
Type: Scholarship
Value: US$10,000
Length of Study: 1 year
Frequency: Annual
Country of Study: United States of America
No. of awards offered: 10–15
Application Procedure: Our website at www.nfwf.org/budscholarship/ has application guidelines and an application form. Applicants must submit an application form, essay of 1,500 words, title for proposed research and short abstract, transcripts and three letters of recommendation.
Closing Date: January 26th (check website for future dates)
Funding: Corporation, government
Contributor: Anheuser-Busch Companies, Inc., United States of America; Fish and Wildlife Service
No. of awards given last year: 15
No. of applicants last year: 300+

NATIONAL FOUNDATION FOR INFECTIOUS DISEASES (NFID)

4733 Bethesda Avenue, Suite 750, Bethesda, MD, 20814, United States of America
Tel: (1) 301 656 0003
Fax: (1) 301 907 0878
Email: info@nfid.org
Website: www.nfid.org
Contact: Mr Charlotte Lazrus, Grants Manager

The National Foundation for Infectious Diseases (NFID) is a non-profit, non-governmental organization whose mission is public and professional education and promotion of research on the causes, treatment and prevention of infectious diseases.

NFID Advanced Vaccinology Course Travel Grant

Subjects: Immunology, vaccinology.
Purpose: To defray expenses related to attending the course, registration, airfare, ground transportation, lodging, meals and incidentals.
Eligibility: Applicants must be recent postdoctoral graduates (doctoral degree within past 3 years)/physicians who have completed speciality or subspeciality training within the past 2 years, with a demonstrated interest in a career in vaccinology. The applicant must be conducting research or working in a recognized and accredited United States of America Institution of Higher Learning or in a government agency.
Level of Study: Professional development
Type: Travel grant
Value: US$4,000
Length of Study: 10 days
Frequency: Annual
Study Establishment: Les Pensières, Veyrier-du-Lac
Country of Study: France
No. of awards offered: 2
Application Procedure: Applicant must submit an application and two copies, containing a letter from the applicant, letter of support from the department chairman, curriculum vitae and a copy of the application to the advanced vaccinology course, to be sent to the institution's main address.
Closing Date: November 15th
Funding: Foundation
Contributor: NFID Aventis Pasteur

NFID Travelling Professorship in Rural Areas

Subjects: Infectious diseases education, antimicrobial resistance and antimicrobial stewardship, new and future antimicrobials, tuberculosis, adult and adolescent immunizations, etc.

Purpose: To provide support for the applicant to provide face-to-face infectious diseases education to practicing physicians in rural areas in the applicant's state of residence or primary practice.
Eligibility: Applicant must be board certified in infectious diseases and must be a citizen of the United States of America.
Level of Study: Professional development
Type: Professorship
Value: US$10,000 cash payment that may be used for travel expenses, handout production, and supplies. Personal honorarium will not exceed US$5,000 of the grant
Length of Study: 5 working days
Frequency: Annual
Country of Study: United States of America
No. of awards offered: 1
Application Procedure: Applicant must submit an original application and four copies including cover letter, curriculum vitae and proposal (three pages), to be sent to the institution's main address.
Closing Date: February 1st
Funding: Foundation
Contributor: NFID Steven R. Mostow Endowment for Outreach Programs

THE NATIONAL GALLERY

Information Department, The National Gallery, Trafalgar Square, London, WC2N 5DN, United Kingdom
Tel: (44) (0) 20 7747 2885
Fax: (44) (0) 20 7747 2423
Email: information@ng-london.org.uk
Website: www.nationalgallery.org.uk

The National Gallery, London houses one of the largest collections of European painting in the world.

The Pilgrim Trust Grants

Subjects: Art history.
Purpose: To fund research into regional collections, which will make a contribution to the National Inventory Research Project.
Level of Study: Research
Type: Grant
Value: A maximum of UK £5,000
Frequency: Twice yearly
Country of Study: United Kingdom
No. of awards offered: Varies
Application Procedure: There is no application form. Please submit a project plan including a list of paintings to be researched and a detailed budget, together with a letter of support from a senior curator or other responsible person and a curriculum vitae for the person who carry out the research.
Closing Date: April 30th and October 30th
Funding: Trusts
Contributor: The Pilgrim Trust
Additional Information: Researchers are most welcome to spend all or some part of the research period in the National Gallery Library, but this is not obligatory.

NATIONAL HEADACHE FOUNDATION

820 N Orleans, Suite 217, Chicago, IL, 60610, United States of America
Tel: (1) 1 888 NHF 5552
Fax: (1) 312 640 9049
Email: info@headaches.org
Website: www.headaches.org
Contact: Executive Director

The National Headache Foundation disseminates information, funds research, sponsors public and professional education programmes and has a nationwide network of support groups, with 20,000 subscribers. The Foundation is the recognized authority in headache and head pain, and offers the award winning newsletter NHF Head Lines, patient education brochures, and audio and video tapes.

National Headache Foundation Research Grant

Subjects: Treatment and causes of headache.

Purpose: To encourage better understanding and treatment of headache and head pain.

Eligibility: Open to researchers in neurology and pharmacology departments in medical schools throughout the United States of America. Submissions from other departments and individual investigators are also welcome.

Level of Study: Postgraduate, Doctorate, Postdoctorate

Type: Research grant

Value: Dependent on funds available. Grants only cover direct costs of carrying out research and do not cover overheads or salaries

Length of Study: 1 year

Frequency: Annual

Country of Study: United States of America

No. of awards offered: Varies, depending on funds available and the number of worthy projects submitted

Application Procedure: Applicants must complete an application form.

Closing Date: December 1st for notification by the following March

Funding: Private

Contributor: Dues and donations

No. of awards given last year: 8

No. of applicants last year: 25

NATIONAL HEALTH AND MEDICAL RESEARCH COUNCIL (NHMRC)

Centre for Research Management and Policy, MDP 33, NHMRC,
GPO Box 9848, Canberra, ACT, 2601, Australia
Tel: (61) 2 6213 4153
Fax: (61) 2 6289 9132
Email: research@nhmrc.gov.au
Website: www.nhmrc.gov.au
Contact: Executive Director

The National Health and Medical Research Council (NHMRC) (Australia) consolidates within a single national organization the often independent functions of research funding and development of advice. One of its strengths is that it brings together and draws upon the resources of all components of the health system, including governments, medical practitioners, nurses and allied health professionals, researchers, teaching and research institutions, public and private programme managers, service administrators, community health organizations, social health researchers and consumers.

Australian Clinical Research Postdoctoral Fellowship

Subjects: Scientific research, including the social and behavioural sciences, that can be applied to any area of clinical or community medicine.

Purpose: To provide training in scientific research methods.

Eligibility: Open to Australian citizens or graduates from overseas with permanent Australian resident status, who are not under bond to any foreign government. Candidates should hold a Doctorate in a health-related field of research or have submitted a thesis for such by December of the year of application, be actively engaged in such research in Australia or overseas and have no more than 2 years postdoctoral experience at the time of application.

Level of Study: Postdoctorate

Type: Fellowship

Value: Australian $59,000 and Australian $5,000 per year

Length of Study: 4 years

Frequency: Annual

Study Establishment: Institutions approved by the NHMRC, such as teaching hospitals, universities and research institutes

Country of Study: Australia

No. of awards offered: Varies

Application Procedure: Application forms are available from the website.

Closing Date: First Friday in July each year

Funding: Government

No. of awards given last year: 7

No. of applicants last year: 26

Biomedical (Dora Lush) and Public Health Postgraduate Scholarships

Subjects: Biomedical sciences and public health.

Purpose: To encourage science Honours or equivalent graduates of outstanding ability to gain full-time health and medical research experience.

Eligibility: Open to Australian citizens who have already completed a science Honours degree (or equivalent) at the time of submission of the application, science Honours graduates and unregistered medical or dental graduates from overseas, who have permanent resident status and are currently residing in Australia. The scholarship shall be held within Australia.

Level of Study: Postgraduate

Type: Scholarship

Value: Varies

Length of Study: 1 year, renewable for up to 2 further years

Frequency: Annual

Study Establishment: Institutions approved by the NHMRC, such as teaching hospitals, universities and research institutes

Country of Study: Australia

No. of awards offered: Varies

Application Procedure: Applicants should visit the website at www.nhmrc.gov.au/funding/schlorships.htm for details.

Closing Date: First Friday of August each year

Funding: Government

No. of awards given last year: 95

No. of applicants last year: 220

C J Martin Fellowships (Overseas Biomedical)

Subjects: Biomedical sciences.

Purpose: To enable fellows to develop their research skills and work overseas on specific research projects within the biomedical sciences under nominated advisers.

Eligibility: Open to Australian citizens or graduates from overseas with permanent Australian resident status who are not under bond to any foreign government. Candidates should hold a Doctorate in a medical, dental or related field of research, be actively engaged in such research in Australia and have no more than 2 years postdoctoral experience at the time of application.

Level of Study: Postdoctorate

Type: Fellowship

Value: Australian $60,000 and allowances per year

Length of Study: 4 years, the first 2 of which are to be spent overseas and the final 2 in Australia

Frequency: Annual

Study Establishment: Institutions approved by the NHMRC, such as teaching hospitals, universities and research institutes

Country of Study: Any country

No. of awards offered: Varies

Application Procedure: Application forms available from the website.

Closing Date: First Friday in July each year

Funding: Government

No. of awards given last year: 30

No. of applicants last year: 89

Career Development Awards

Subjects: Any human health-related research area.

Purpose: To help researchers to conduct research that is internationally competitive and to develop a capacity for independent research.

Eligibility: Open to Australian citizens or permanent residents, normally between 3 and 9 years postdoctoral experience.

Type: Fellowship

Value: Australian $87,000 per year

Length of Study: 5 years

Frequency: Annual

Study Establishment: Institutions approved by NHMRC, such as teaching hospitals, universities and research institutes

Country of Study: Australia

No. of awards offered: Varies

Application Procedure: Application forms available from the website www.nhmrc.gov.au

Closing Date: Second Friday in April each year

Funding: Government

No. of awards given last year: 42

No. of applicants last year: 170

Howard Florey Centenary Fellowship

Subjects: Any human health-related research area.
Purpose: To provide a vehicle for Australian researchers working overseas to return to Australia to pursue biomedical/health related research.
Eligibility: Open to Australian citizens currently researching overseas, normally with between 2 and 5 years postdoctoral experience.
Type: Fellowship
Value: Australian $70,750 and Australian $10,000 per year
Length of Study: 2 years
Frequency: Annual
Study Establishment: Institutions approved by the NHMRC, such as teaching hospitals, universities and research institutes
Country of Study: Australia
No. of awards offered: Varies
Application Procedure: Application forms available from the website.
Closing Date: First Friday in July each year
Funding: Government
No. of awards given last year: 8
No. of applicants last year: 25

Industry Fellowships

Subjects: Human health-related field.
Purpose: To enable Australian researchers to gain experience in industrial research and increase knowledge of commercial aspects of R & D within research institutions.
Eligibility: Open to Australian citizens or permanent residents, normally with between 3 and 9 years postdoctoral experience in medical research.
Type: Fellowship
Value: Australian $87,000 per year
Length of Study: 4 years
Frequency: Annual
Study Establishment: Institutions approved by the NHMRC, such as teaching hospitals, universities and research institutes
Country of Study: Any country
No. of awards offered: Varies
Application Procedure: Application forms available from the website.
Closing Date: Last Friday in June each year
Funding: Government
No. of awards given last year: 4
No. of applicants last year: 10

Neil Hamilton Fairley Fellowships (Overseas Clinical)

Subjects: Scientific research, including the social and behavioural sciences, that can be applied to any area of clinical or community medicine.
Purpose: To provide training in scientific research methods.
Eligibility: Open to Australian citizens or graduates from overseas with permanent Australian resident status who are not under bond to any foreign government. Candidates should hold a Doctorate in a health-related field of research or have submitted a thesis for such by December of the year of application, be actively engaged in such research in Australia and have no more than 2 years postdoctoral experience at the time of application.
Level of Study: Postdoctorate
Type: Fellowship
Value: Australian $65,000 and allowances per year
Length of Study: 4 years, the first 2 of which are to be spent overseas and the final 2 in Australia
Frequency: Annual
Study Establishment: Institutions approved by the NHMRC, such as teaching hospitals, universities and research institutes
Country of Study: Any country
No. of awards offered: Varies
Application Procedure: Application form available from the website.
Closing Date: First Friday in July each year
Funding: Government
No. of awards given last year: 3
No. of applicants last year: 11

NHMRC Medical and Dental and Public Health Postgraduate Research Scholarships

Subjects: Medical or dental research.

Purpose: To encourage medical and dental graduates to gain full-time research experience.
Eligibility: Open to Australian citizens who are medical or dental graduates registered to practice in Australia, with the proviso that medical graduates can also apply during their intern year and that dental postgraduate research scholarships may be awarded prior to graduation provided that the evidence of high quality work is shown. Also open to medical and dental graduates from overseas who hold a qualification that is registered for practice in Australia, who have permanent resident status and are currently residing in Australia.
Level of Study: Postgraduate
Type: Scholarship
Value: Varies
Length of Study: 1 year, renewable for up to 2 further years
Frequency: Annual
Study Establishment: Institutions approved by the NHMRC such as teaching hospitals, universities and research institutes
Country of Study: Australia
No. of awards offered: Varies
Application Procedure: Available from the website at www.nhmrc.gov.au/funding/scholarships.htm
Closing Date: First Friday of August each year
Funding: Government
No. of awards given last year: 71
No. of applicants last year: 122

NHMRC/INSERM Exchange Fellowships

Subjects: Biomedical sciences.
Purpose: To enable Australian Fellows to work overseas on specific research projects in INSERM laboratories in France and vice versa.
Eligibility: Open to Australian citizens and permanent residents, who are not under bond to any foreign government, who hold a Doctorate in a medical, dental or related field of research or have submitted a thesis for such by December in the year of application, are actively engaged in such research in Australia and have no more than 2 years postdoctoral experience at the time of application.
Level of Study: Postdoctorate
Type: Fellowship
Value: Australian $59,000 and allowances per year
Length of Study: 4 years, the first 2 of which are to be spent in France and the final 2 in Australia
Frequency: Annual
Study Establishment: Institutions approved by the NHMRC, such as teaching hospitals, universities and research institutes, and INSERM laboratories in France
Country of Study: France or Australia
No. of awards offered: 1
Application Procedure: Applications forms available from the website.
Closing Date: First Friday of July each year
Funding: Government
No. of awards given last year: 1
No. of applicants last year: 5
Additional Information: This fellowship is awarded in association with l'Institut National de la Santé et de la Recherche Médicale (INSERM), France.

Peter Doherty Fellowships (Australian Biomedical)

Subjects: Biomedical sciences.
Purpose: To provide a vehicle for training in clinical and basic research in Australia, and to encourage persons of outstanding ability to make medical research a full-time career.
Eligibility: Open to Australian citizens or graduates from overseas with permanent Australian resident status who are not under bond to any foreign government. Candidates should hold a Doctorate in a medical, dental or related field of research or have submitted a thesis for such by December in the year of application, be actively engaged in such research in Australia or overseas and have no more than 2 years postdoctoral experience at the time of application.
Level of Study: Postdoctorate
Type: Fellowship
Value: Australian $59,000 and allowances per year
Length of Study: 4 years
Frequency: Annual
Study Establishment: Institutions approved by the NHMRC, such as teaching hospitals, universities and research institutes

Country of Study: Australia
No. of awards offered: Varies
Application Procedure: Application forms available from the website.
Closing Date: First Friday in July each year
Funding: Government
No. of awards given last year: 30
No. of applicants last year: 100

Public Health Fellowship (Australian)
Subjects: Public health.
Purpose: To provide full-time training in public health research in Australia.
Eligibility: Applicants should hold a Doctorate in a health-related field of research or have submitted a PhD by December in the year of application and have no more than 2 years postdoctoral experience. Open to Australian citizens or permanent residents.
Type: Fellowship
Value: Australian $59,000 and Australian $5,000
Length of Study: 4 years
Frequency: Annual
Study Establishment: Institutions approved by the NHMRC, such as teaching hospitals, universities and research institutes
Country of Study: Australia
No. of awards offered: Varies
Application Procedure: Application forms available from the website.
Closing Date: First Friday in July each year
Funding: Government
No. of awards given last year: 11
No. of applicants last year: 38

Sidney Sax Fellowship (Overseas Public Health)
Subjects: Public health.
Purpose: To provide full-time training in public health research overseas in Australia.
Eligibility: Applicants should hold a Doctorate in a health-related field of research or have submitted a PhD by December in the year of application and have no more than 2 years postdoctoral experience. Open to Australian citizens or permanent residents.
Type: Fellowship
Value: Australian $59,000 and allowances per year
Length of Study: 4 years
Frequency: Annual
Study Establishment: Institutions approved by the NHMRC, such as teaching hospitals, universities and research institutes
Country of Study: Any country
No. of awards offered: Varies
Application Procedure: Application forms available from the website.
Closing Date: First Friday in July each year
Funding: Government
No. of awards given last year: 3
No. of applicants last year: 9

Training Scholarship for Indigenous Health Research
Purpose: To encourage research with relevance to the health and well being of Aboriginal and Torres Strait Islander people.
Eligibility: Open to Australian citizens or Australian permanent residents enrolling in a diploma, certificate, an undergraduate degree or a postgraduate degree at a fully accredited institution, which will enable the applicant to pursue research relevant to Aboriginal and Torres Strait Islander health, healthcare, healthcare delivery or health research in the area of Aboriginal and Torres Strait Islander health.
Level of Study: Postdoctorate
Type: Scholarship
Length of Study: 1 year, renewable up to further 2 years
Frequency: Annual
Country of Study: Australia
Application Procedure: Available from the website at www.nhmrc.gov/funding/scholarships.htm
Closing Date: First Friday of August
Funding: Government
No. of awards given last year: 5
No. of applicants last year: 8

NATIONAL HEART FOUNDATION OF AUSTRALIA

411 King Street, West Melbourne, VIC, 3003, Australia
Tel: (61) 3 9321 1581
Fax: (61) 3 9326 3190
Email: research@heartfoundation.com.au
Website: www.heartfoundation.com.au
Contact: Research Manager

The National Heart Foundation of Australia is a non-government, non-profit health organization funded mostly by public donation. The Foundation's mission is to reduce suffering and death from heart, stroke and blood vessel disease in Australia. The Foundation funds biomedical, clinical and public health research, provides clinical leadership and develops health promotion strategies and initiatives.

National Heart Foundation of Australia Career Development Fellowship
Subjects: Cardiovascular disease and related disorders.
Purpose: To enable a senior Australian researcher of exceptional merit and proven record in the cardiovascular field to undertake independent research.
Eligibility: Open to Australian citizens and permanent residents only.
Level of Study: Research
Type: Fellowship
Value: Please contact the organization
Length of Study: 5 years, non-renewable
Frequency: Annual
Study Establishment: Universities, hospitals or research institutions
Country of Study: Australia
Application Procedure: Applicants must be nominated by the head of the host department or institution.
Funding: Private
Additional Information: Refer website for closing date for applications.

National Heart Foundation of Australia Overseas Research Fellowships
Subjects: Clinical, public health and biomedical research related to cardiovascular disease and related disorders.
Purpose: To allow Fellows to obtain skills in cardiovascular research.
Eligibility: Open to Australian citizens or permanent residents who are actively engaged in research in Australia on December 31st of the year prior to application.
Level of Study: Postdoctorate
Type: Fellowship
Value: Please contact the organization
Length of Study: 3 years
Frequency: Annual
Study Establishment: Approved institutions
Country of Study: Other
Application Procedure: Applicants must be nominated by the head of the host department or institution.
Funding: Private
Additional Information: Fellowships are awarded on the understanding that the Fellow will return to Australia to continue his or her career upon completion of the fellowship. Refer website for closing dates for applications.

National Heart Foundation of Australia Postdoctoral Research Fellowship
Subjects: Cardiovascular disease and related disorders.
Purpose: To award graduates who have demonstrated expertise and significant achievement in cardiovascular research.
Eligibility: Open to Australian citizens and permanent residents only.
Level of Study: Postdoctorate
Type: Fellowship
Value: Please contact the organization
Length of Study: 2 years
Frequency: Annual
Study Establishment: Universities, hospitals or research institutions
Country of Study: Australia

Application Procedure: Applicants must submit an application outlining a research proposal accompanied by the supervisor's reference and backing.
Funding: Private
Additional Information: Refer website for closing date for applications.

National Heart Foundation of Australia Postgraduate Biomedical Research Scholarship

Subjects: Cardiovascular disease and related disorders.
Purpose: To allow graduates to undertake a period of training in research under the full-time supervision and tuition of a responsible investigator.
Eligibility: Open to Australian citizens and permanent residents only.
Level of Study: Postgraduate
Type: Scholarship
Value: Please contact the organization
Length of Study: Up to 3 years
Frequency: Annual
Study Establishment: Universities, hospitals or research institutions
Country of Study: Australia
Application Procedure: Applicants must submit an application outlining a research proposal accompanied by the supervisor's reference and backing.
Funding: Private
Additional Information: Refer website for closing date for applications.

National Heart Foundation of Australia Postgraduate Clinical Research Scholarship

Subjects: Cardiovascular disease and related disorders.
Purpose: To enable medical graduates to undertake a period of training in research under the full-time supervision and tuition of a responsible investigator.
Eligibility: Open to Australian citizens and permanent residents only.
Level of Study: Postgraduate
Type: Scholarship
Value: Please contact the organization
Length of Study: 3 years
Frequency: Annual
Study Establishment: Universities, hospitals and research institutions
Country of Study: Australia
No. of awards offered: Varies
Application Procedure: Applicants must submit an application outlining a research proposal accompanied by the supervisor's reference and backing.
Funding: Private
Additional Information: Refer wesite for closing date for applications.

National Heart Foundation of Australia Postgraduate Public Health Research Scholarship

Subjects: Cardiovascular research and related disorders.
Purpose: To allow graduates to undertake a period of training in research under the full-time supervision and tuition of a responsible investigator.
Eligibility: Open to Australian citizens and permanent residents only.
Level of Study: Postgraduate
Type: Scholarship
Value: Please contact the organization
Length of Study: Up to 3 years
Frequency: Annual
Study Establishment: Universities, hospitals or research institutions
Country of Study: Australia
Application Procedure: Applicants must submit an application outlining a research proposal accompanied by the supervisor's reference and backing.
Funding: Private
Additional Information: Refer website for closing date for applications.

National Heart Foundation of Australia Research Grants-in-Aid

Subjects: Biomedical, clinical and public health research.
Purpose: To support research in the cardiovascular field.

Eligibility: Open to Australian citizens and permanent residents only.
Level of Study: Research
Type: Grant
Value: Please contact the organization
Length of Study: Up to 2 years
Frequency: Annual
Study Establishment: An approved institution
Country of Study: Australia
Application Procedure: Applicants must submit an application outlining research proposal. References are also required.
Closing Date: March 17, 2009
Funding: Private
Additional Information: Refer website for closing date for applications.

NATIONAL HEART FOUNDATION OF NEW ZEALAND

PO Box 17-160, Greenlane, Newmarket, Auckland, New Zealand
Tel: (64) 9 571 9191
Fax: (64) 9 571 9190
Email: info@nhf.org.nz
Website: www.heartfoundation.org.nz
Contact: Ms Helen Stewart, Research Grants Manager

The National Heart Foundation of New Zealand aims to promote good health and to reduce suffering and premature death from diseases of the heart and circulation. Grant advertisement for 2009 included. Please refer to website www.heartfoundation.org.nz for further information on research funding.

National Heart Foundation of New Zealand Fellowships

Subjects: Application's are particularly encouraged in areas that align with the National Heart Foundation's strategic priority objectives. For the list of objectives please visit the website.
Purpose: To promote the aims of the National Heart Foundation of New Zealand.
Eligibility: Normally open to New Zealand graduates only.
Level of Study: Postgraduate
Type: Fellowship/Scholarship
Value: Varies according to the determination of the Scientific Committee and within an annual budget
Frequency: Annual, 3 times per year
No. of awards offered: Varies
Application Procedure: Details available on the website www.heartfoundation.or.nz/research. The 'Guidelines for Research Applicants' is available as a PDF file.
Closing Date: June 1st
Funding: Private
No. of awards given last year: 9

National Heart Foundation of New Zealand Limited Budget Grants

Subjects: Applications are particularly encouraged in areas that align with National Heart Foundation's strategic priority objectives. For the list of objectives please visit the website.
Purpose: To further the aims of the National Heart Foundation of New Zealand.
Eligibility: Normally open to New Zealand graduates only.
Level of Study: Postgraduate
Type: Small project grant
Value: Varies, according to the determination of the Scientific Committee and within an annual budget
Frequency: 3 times per year
Country of Study: New Zealand
No. of awards offered: Varies
Application Procedure: Details are available on the website www.heartfoundation.org.nz
Closing Date: February 1st, June 1st or October 1st
Funding: Private
No. of awards given last year: 16
Additional Information: These grants cover small projects, e.g. less than New Zealand $15,000 and grants-in-aid.

National Heart Foundation of New Zealand Maori Cardiovascular Research Fellowship

Subjects: Cardiovascular health.
Purpose: To financially support graduates who propose to engage in research to improve Maori cardiovascular health.
Eligibility: Open to medical graduates or non-medical graduates enrolled for a higher degree. Preference will be given to those with a working knowledge of Te Reo Maori and who are committed to Maori health.
Level of Study: Doctorate, Postgraduate, Predoctorate
Type: Fellowship
Value: New Zealand $30,000
Length of Study: 2 years
Frequency: Every 2 years
Country of Study: New Zealand
No. of awards offered: 1
Application Procedure: Applications will be considered at the annual meeting of the Scientific Committee.
Closing Date: February 1st
Funding: Private
No. of awards given last year: 1

National Heart Foundation of New Zealand Project Grants

Subjects: Applications are particularly encouraged in areas that align with the National Heart Foundation's strategic priority objectives. For the list of objectives please visit the website.
Purpose: To provide short-term support for a single individual or a small group working on a clearly defined research project, which will promote the aims of the National Heart Foundation of New Zealand.
Eligibility: Normally open to New Zealand graduates only.
Level of Study: Postgraduate
Type: Grant
Value: Varies, according to the determination of the scientific committee and within an annual budget
Frequency: Annual
Country of Study: New Zealand
No. of awards offered: Varies
Application Procedure: Details are available on the website www.heartfoundation.org.nz/research. The 'Guidelines for Research Applicants' is available as a pdf file.
Closing Date: March 1st
Funding: Private
No. of awards given last year: 8
No. of applicants last year: 23

National Heart Foundation of New Zealand Senior Fellowship

Subjects: Cardiovascular disease.
Purpose: To support graduates from New Zealand who have trained as cardiologists or other scientists working in the field of cardiovascular research.
Eligibility: Applicants must possess an appropriate postgraduate degree or diploma. The maximum age for appointment will normally be 40 years.
Level of Study: Postgraduate
Type: Fellowship
Value: Individually determined in conjunction with the host institution according to the qualifications and seniority of the Fellow
Length of Study: Up to 3 years
Frequency: Every 3 years
Country of Study: New Zealand
No. of awards offered: 1
Application Procedure: Applicants should follow the format outlined in the revised 'A Guide to Applicants for Research and Other Grants' which is available from the website. Applications should be sent to Professor Norman Sharpe, Medical Director.
Closing Date: June 1st
Funding: Private
Additional Information: The fellowship must be taken up within 1 year of the award. Further research funding will require an application for project grant funds from the Foundation. Funding for conference expenses must be applied for separately.

National Heart Foundation of New Zealand Travel Grants

Subjects: Applications are particularly encouraged in areas that align with National Heart Foundation Strategic priority objectives.
Purpose: To enable medical or non-medical workers to travel in New Zealand or overseas for short-term study or to attend conferences.
Eligibility: Normally open to New Zealand graduates only.
Level of Study: Postgraduate
Type: Grant
Value: Varies, according to the determination of the scientific committee and within an annual budget
Frequency: 3 times per year
Country of Study: Any country
No. of awards offered: Varies
Application Procedure: Details are available on the website www.heartfoundation.org.nz/research. The 'Guidelines for Research Applicants' is available as a PDF file.
Closing Date: February 1st, June 1st or October 1st
Funding: Private
No. of awards given last year: 23

NATIONAL HISTORICAL PUBLICATIONS AND RECORDS COMMISSION (NHPRC)

National Archives and Records Administration, 700 Pennsylvania Avenue NW, Room 111, Washington, DC, 20408-0001, United States of America
Tel: (1) 202 501 5610
Fax: (1) 202 501 5601
Email: nancy.copp@nara.gov
Website: www.archives.gov
Contact: Nancy T. Copp, Management and Programme Analyst

The National Historical Publications and Records Commission (NHPRC) is the grantmaking affiliate of the National Archives and Records Administration (NARA). The Commission has defined its purpose to carry out its statutory mission to ensure understanding of the nation's past by promoting, nationwide, the identification, preservation and dissemination of essential historical documentation.

NHPRC Fellowship in Archival Administration

Subjects: Library and archive studies.
Purpose: To provide experience in management and administration for archivists.
Eligibility: Open to individuals who must have spent 2–5 years working as an archivist, and be United States of America citizens. While not required, it is desirable that applicants have the equivalent of two semesters of full-time graduate training in a programme containing an archival education component.
Level of Study: Professional development
Type: Fellowship
Value: The fellow's stipend is $40,000, with a benefit payment of $10,000
Length of Study: 9–12 months
Frequency: Annual
Country of Study: United States of America
No. of awards offered: 1
Application Procedure: Applicants must contact the Commission for guidelines and host institution information. This information is available before December of the preceding year.
Closing Date: Postmarked March 1st
Funding: Government

NHPRC Fellowship in Documentary Editing

Subjects: Documentary editing.
Purpose: To provide individuals with training in the field of historical documentary editing.
Eligibility: Open to candidates who hold PhD or have completed all requirements for the Doctorate except the dissertation. Candidates may be working on their dissertation and must be United States of America citizens.
Level of Study: Doctorate, Postdoctorate
Type: Fellowship
Value: The fellow's stipend is $40,000, with a benefit payment of $10,000
Length of Study: 11 months
Frequency: Annual

Country of Study: United States of America
No. of awards offered: 1
Application Procedure: Candidates must contact the Commission for guidelines and host institution information. This information is available before December of the preceding year.
Closing Date: Postmarked March 1st
Funding: Government
Additional Information: Further information is available from the website.

NATIONAL INSTITUTE FOR LABOR RELATIONS RESEARCH (NILRR)

5211 Port Royal Road, Suite 510 Springfield, VA, 22151, United States of America
Tel: (1) 703 3219606
Fax: (1) 703 3217342
Email: research@nilrr.org
Website: www.nilrr.org

The National Institute for Labor Relations Research's (NILRR) primary function is to act as a research facility for the general public, scholars and students. It provides the supplementary analysis and research necessary to expose the inequities of compulsory unionism.

The Applegate/Jackson/Parks Future Teacher Scholarship

Subjects: Journalism.
Purpose: To support students to pursue studies in journalism and related majors.
Eligibility: Open to graduate students majoring education or intending to become a teacher and attending an accredited institution of higher learning in the United States.
Level of Study: Doctorate, MBA
Type: Scholarship
Value: $1,000
Length of Study: 1 year
Frequency: Annual
No. of awards offered: 1
Application Procedure: Applicants must submit a complete formal application, a copy of the up-to-date transcript of grades and a type-written essay of 500 words demonstrating an interest in, and knowledge of, the right to work principle as it applies to educators.
Closing Date: December 31st
Funding: Private
No. of awards given last year: 1
No. of applicants last year: 123

For further information contact:

Website: www.nilrr.org/node/11

William B. Ruggles Right to Work Journalism Scholarship

Subjects: Journalism.
Purpose: To support students to pursue studies in journalism and related majors.
Eligibility: Open to graduate students attending an accredited institution of higher learning in USA and majoring in journalism or related majors.
Level of Study: Graduate, Postgraduate
Type: Scholarship
Value: US$2,000
Length of Study: 1 year
Frequency: Annual
Country of Study: United States of America
Application Procedure: Applicants must submit necessary application transcripts from accredited institution of higher learning in United States.
Closing Date: December 31st
Funding: Private
No. of awards given last year: 1
No. of applicants last year: 250

For further information contact:

Website: www.nilrr.org/ruggles1.htm

NATIONAL INSTITUTE OF GENERAL MEDICAL SCIENCES (NIGMS)

45 Center Drive, MSC 6200, Bethesda, MD, 20892-6200, United States of America
Tel: (1) 301 496 7301
Fax: (1) 301 402 0224
Email: info@nigms.nih.gov
Website: www.nigms.nih.gov
Contact: Ms Jilliene Mitchell, Information Development Specialist

The National Institute of General Medical Sciences (NIGMS) is one of the National Institutes of Health (NIH), the principal biomedical research agency of the Federal Government. NIGMS primarily supports basic biomedical research that lays the foundation for advances in disease diagnosis, treatment, and prevention.

MARC Faculty Predoctoral Fellowships

Subjects: Biomedical or behavioural sciences.
Purpose: Awards provide an opportunity for eligible faculty who lack the PhD degree (or equivalent) to obtain the research doctorate.
Eligibility: Open to full-time, permanent faculty members in a bio-medically related science or mathematics programme who have been at a minority or minority-serving institution for at least 3 years at the time of application. Candidates must be enrolled in, or have been accepted into, a PhD or combined MD-PhD training programme in the biomedical or behavioural sciences. Candidates must intend to return to the minority institution at the end of the training period.
Level of Study: Postgraduate, Predoctorate
Type: Fellowship
Value: An applicant may request a stipend equal to his or her annual salary, but not to exceed the stipend of a level 1 postdoctoral Fellow, currently valued at US$38,976. The applicant may also request tuition and fees as determined by the training institution as well as an allowance of US$2,750 per year for training-related costs
Frequency: Annual
Study Establishment: An institution in the United States of America
Country of Study: United States of America
No. of awards offered: Varies
Application Procedure: Applicants must write to the main address for details or telephone Dr Adolphus Toliver, at (1) 301 594 3900. Further details are also available from the website, www.nigms.nih.gov
Funding: Government

NIGMS Fellowship Awards for Minority Students

Subjects: Biomedical or behavioural sciences.
Purpose: These awards provide up to 5 years of support for research training leading to a PhD or equivalent research degree, a combined MD-PhD degree or another combined professional Doctorate-research PhD.
Eligibility: Open to highly qualified students who are members of minority groups that are underrepresented in the biomedical or behavioural sciences in the United States of America. These groups include African Americans, Hispanic Americans, Native Americans, including Alaska Natives and natives of the United States of America Pacific Islands.
Level of Study: Postgraduate, Predoctorate
Type: Fellowship
Value: An annual stipend of US$20,772, a tuition and fee allowance, and an annual institutional allowance of US$2,750, which may be used for travel to scientific meetings and for laboratory and other training expenses
Length of Study: Up to 5 years
Frequency: Annual
Study Establishment: An institution in the United States of America
Country of Study: United States of America
No. of awards offered: Varies
Application Procedure: Applicants must write to the main address for details or telephone Dr Adolphus Toliver, at (1) 301 594 3900. Further details are also available from the website, www.nigms.nih.gov
Funding: Government

NIGMS Fellowship Awards for Students With Disabilities

Subjects: Biomedical and behavioural sciences.

Purpose: These awards provide up to 5 years of support for research training leading to a PhD or equivalent research degree, combined MD-PhD degree or another combined professional doctorate/research PhD degree in the biomedical or behavioural science.

Eligibility: Open to principal investigators at domestic institutions holding an active NIGMS research grant, programme project grant, centre grant or co-operative agreement research programme with a reasonable period of research support remaining.

Level of Study: Postdoctorate, Predoctorate, Doctorate, Postgraduate, Graduate

Type: Fellowship

Value: Varies

Length of Study: 2 years or more

Frequency: Annual

Study Establishment: An institution in the United States of America

Country of Study: United States of America

No. of awards offered: Varies

Application Procedure: Applicants must write to the main address for details or telephone Dr Anthony René, at (1) 301 594 3833. Further details are also available from the website, www.nigms.nih.gov

Funding: Government

NIGMS Postdoctoral Awards

Subjects: Biomedical and behavioural sciences.

Purpose: NIGMS welcomes NRSA applications from eligible individuals who seek postdoctoral biomedical research training in areas related to the scientific programmes of the Institute.

Eligibility: Open to applicants who have received the doctoral degree (domestic or foreign) by the beginning date of the proposed award.

Level of Study: Postdoctorate

Value: Up to US$51,036 per year, based on the salary of the applicant at the time of the award

Frequency: Annual

Study Establishment: The institutional setting may be domestic or foreign, public or private

Country of Study: Any country

No. of awards offered: Varies

Application Procedure: Applicants must write to the main address for details or telephone Dr Alison Cole, at (1) 301 594 3349. Further details are also available from the website, www.nigms.nih.gov

Funding: Government

NIGMS Research Project Grants

Subjects: Biomedical and behavioural sciences.

Purpose: To support a discrete project related to the investigator's area of interest and competence.

Eligibility: Research Grants may be awarded to non-profit organizations and institutions, governments and their agencies, and occasionally to individuals who have access to adequate facilities and resources for conducting the research, as well as profit-making organizations. Foreign institutions and international organizations are also eligible to apply for these grants.

Level of Study: Postgraduate

Value: These grants may provide funds for reasonable costs of the research activity, as well as for salaries, equipment, supplies, travel and other related expenses

Frequency: Annual

Country of Study: United States of America

No. of awards offered: Varies

Application Procedure: Applicants must contact the Office of Extramural Outreach and Information Resources for details.

Funding: Government

For further information contact:

Office of Extramural Outreach and Information Resources, NIH, 6701 Rockledge Drive, MSC 7910, Room 6207, Bethesda, MD, 20892-7910, United States of America

Tel: (1) 301 435 0714

Email: grantsinfo@nih.gov

NIGMS Research Supplements for Underrepresented Minorities

Subjects: Biomedical and behavioural sciences.

Purpose: To help minority scientists and students develop their capabilities for independent research careers. Supplements are available to high school students, undergraduate students, post-baccalaureate, post-Master's degree and predoctoral students as well as minority individuals in postdoctoral training and minority staff and faculty.

Eligibility: Open to principal investigators at domestic institutions holding an active NIGMS research grant, programme project grant, centre grant or co-operative agreement research programme with a reasonable period of research support remaining.

Level of Study: Unrestricted

Type: Grant

Value: Varies

Length of Study: 2 years or more

Frequency: Annual

Study Establishment: An institution in the United States of America

Country of Study: United States of America

No. of awards offered: Varies

Application Procedure: Applicants must write to the main address for details or telephone Dr Anthony René, at (1) 301 594 3833. Further details are also available from the website, www.nigms.nih.gov

Funding: Government

NATIONAL INSTITUTE ON AGING

Building 31, Room 5C27, 31 Center Drive, MSC 2292, Bethesda, MD, 20892, United States of America
Tel: (1) 301 496 9322
Fax: (1) 301 402 2945
Email: mk46u@nih.gov
Website: www.nih.gov
Contact: Dr Miriam Kelty, Associate Director

The National Institute on Aging conducts and supports research and research training in all areas of biological ageing, the neuroscience and neuropsychology of ageing, geriatrics and the social and behavioural sciences of ageing.

NIH Research Grants

Subjects: The biology of ageing, the neuroscience and neuropsychology of ageing, geriatrics and clinical gerontology and the social and behavioural sciences of ageing.

Purpose: To support research and training in the biological, clinical, behavioural and social aspects of ageing mechanisms and processes.

Eligibility: Varies, depending on the mechanism, but generally open to United States of America citizens only.

Level of Study: Postdoctorate

Type: Grants, fellowships, career development awards and institutional training awards

Value: Varies

Length of Study: 1–5 years

Frequency: Annual, 3 cycles a year

Country of Study: The United States of America or others depending on mechanisms

No. of awards offered: Varies

Application Procedure: Applicants must download the application form, available on the website. NIH is transitioning to electronic transmission through grants.gov (www.nih.gov)

Closing Date: Deadlines are staggered. Please see website

Funding: Government

Contributor: The United States of America government

Additional Information: Some award mechanisms are limited to citizens and permanent residents of the United States of America. Others are open to applicants from any country. Further information is available on the website.

NATIONAL LEAGUE OF AMERICAN PEN WOMEN, INC. (NLAPW)

1300 17th Street NW, Washington, DC, 20036-1973, United States of America
Tel: (1) 202 785 1997
Fax: (1) 202 452 6868
Email: nlapw1@juno.com
Website: www.americanpenwomen.org
Contact: Ms Elaine Waidelich, National Scholarship Chairperson

The National League of American Pen Women (NLAPW) exists to promote women in the creative arts including art, writing and music.

Virginia Liebeler Biennial Grants for Mature Women (Art)

Subjects: Art.

Purpose: To advance creative purpose in art.

Eligibility: Open to women over 35 years of age who wish to pursue special work in their field of art, letters or music. Applicants must be citizens of the United States of America. Current and past recipients are not eligible for this award.

Level of Study: Unrestricted

Type: Grant

Value: US$1,000. The award may be used for college, framing, research or any creative purpose that furthers a career in the creative arts

Frequency: Every 2 years

Country of Study: United States of America

No. of awards offered: 1

Application Procedure: Applicants must; (a) send proof of age and United States of America citizenship (copy of birth certificate, passport ID page, voter's registration card and a driver's license or a state ID, if possible). Driver's license alone is not proof of citizenship; (b) enclose a 1 page cover letter describing how they intend to use the grant money, if awarded the grant, and any relevant information about themselves; (c) enclose a US$8 check made payable to NLAPW with submission; (d) enclose a stamped addressed envelope/mailer with sufficient postage for the return of the submission; (e) provide their name, address, telephone number and e-mail address on the cover page of submission; submit three 4X6 or larger colour prints (no slides): oil, watercolor, acrylic, mixed media, original works on paper etc. submit three 4X6 or larger photos of sculpture; and for photography, submit three 4X6 or larger prints in colour or black and white.

Closing Date: November 15th

Funding: Private

Contributor: NLAPW

No. of awards given last year: 6

No. of applicants last year: 150

Additional Information: Interested parties must send a stamped addressed envelope to receive current information.

For further information contact:

2315 Crown colony Dr, Arlington, TX, 76011, United States of America

Contact: Dr Bernice Reid

Virginia Liebeler Biennial Grants for Mature Women (Music)

Subjects: Music.

Purpose: To advance creative purpose in music.

Eligibility: Open to women over 35 years of age who wish to pursue special work in their field of art, letters or music. Applicants must be citizens of the United States of America. Current and past recipients are not eligible for this award.

Level of Study: Unrestricted

Type: Grant

Value: Minimum award of US$1,000

Frequency: Every 2 years

Country of Study: United States of America

No. of awards offered: 1

Application Procedure: Applicants must; (a) send proof of age and United States of America citizenship (copy of birth certificate, passport ID page, voter's registration card and a driver's license or a state ID, if possible). Driver's license alone is not proof of citizenship; (b) enclose a one-page cover letter describing how they intend to use the grant money, if awarded the grant, and any relevant information about themselves; (c) enclose a US$8 check made payable to NLAPW with the submission; (d) enclose a stamped addressed envelope/mailer with sufficient postage for the return of submission; and (e) provide their name, address, telephone number and e-mail address on the cover page of their submission. Applicants must also submit two compositions: 3-minute minimum performance time, 5-minute maximum performance time.

Closing Date: November 15th

Funding: Private

Contributor: NLAPW

No. of awards given last year: 6

No. of applicants last year: 100

Additional Information: Interested parties must send a stamped addressed envelope to receive current information.

For further information contact:

202 E Manford avenue Avenue Adq, Ohio, 45810, United States of America

Contact: Dr M.J.Sunny Zank

Virginia Liebeler Biennial Grants for Mature Women (Writing)

Subjects: Writing.

Purpose: To advance creative purpose in writing.

Eligibility: Open to women over 35 years of age who wish to pursue special work in their field of art, letters or music. Applicants must be citizens of the United States of America. Current and past recipients are not eligible for this award.

Level of Study: Unrestricted

Type: Grant

Value: US$1,000

Frequency: Every 2 years

Country of Study: United States of America

No. of awards offered: 1

Application Procedure: Applicants must (a) send proof of age and United States of America citizenship (copy of birth certificate, passport ID page, voter's registration card and a driver's license or a state ID, if possible). Driver's license alone is not proof of citizenship; (b) enclose a one-page cover letter describing how they intend to use the grant money, if awarded the grant, and any relevant information about themselves; (c) enclose a US$8 check made payable to NLAPW with their submission; (d) enclose a stamped addressed envelope/mailer with sufficient postage for the return of their submission; and (e) provide their name, address, telephone number and email address on the cover page of the submission. Applicants must submit either a published or unpublished manuscript in any or all of the following categories: article, drama, essay, first chapter of a novel, narrative outline of a complete novel, three poems, short-story or TV script. The entry is not to exceed 4,000 words.

Closing Date: November 15th

Funding: Private

Contributor: NLAPW

No. of awards given last year: 6

No. of applicants last year: 60

Additional Information: Interested parties must send a stamped addressed envelope to receive current information.

For further information contact:

37 Sonto Domingo Dt, Rancho Meroge, CA, 92270, United States of America

Contact: Dr Ann Lubell

NATIONAL LIBRARY OF AUSTRALIA

Canberra, ACT, 2600, Australia
Tel: (61) 2 6262 1258
Fax: (61) 2 6262 1516
Email: mayres@nla.gov.au
Contact: Dr Marie-Louise Ayres, Curator of Manuscripts

The National Library of Australia is responsible for developing and maintaining a comprehensive collection of Australian library materials and a strong collection of non-Australian publications, and for administering and co-ordinating a range of national bibliographical activities.

Harold White Fellowships

Subjects: There are few subject limitations but most fellowships fall within the categories of arts and humanities, fine and applied arts or social sciences.

Purpose: To promote the Library as a centre of scholarly activity and research, to encourage the scholarly and literary use of the collection and the production of publications based on them and to publicize the Library's collections.

Eligibility: Open to established scholars, writers and librarians from any country. Fellowships are not normally offered to candidates working for a higher degree.
Level of Study: Unrestricted
Type: Fellowship
Value: Australian $800 per week
Length of Study: 3–6 months
Frequency: Annual
Study Establishment: The National Library of Australia
Country of Study: Australia
No. of awards offered: 3–6
Application Procedure: Applicants must complete an application form available in the website www.nla.gov.au/grants/haroldwhite.
Closing Date: April 30th
Funding: Government
No. of awards given last year: 4
No. of applicants last year: 50
Additional Information: Normally, Fellows will be expected to give a public lecture and at least one seminar on the subject of their research during their tenure. At least three quarters of the fellowship time should be spent in Canberra.

THE NATIONAL MULTIPLE SCLEROSIS SOCIETY (NMSS)

733 3rd Avenue, New York, NY, 10017, United States of America
Tel: (1) 212 986 3240
Fax: (1) 212 986 7981
Email: patricia.olooney@nmss.org
Website: www.nationalmssociety.org
Contact: Grants Management Officer

The National Multiple Sclerosis Society (NMSS) is dedicated to ending the devastating effects of multiple sclerosis. Founded in 1946, NMSS supports more on multiple sclerosis (MS) research and provides professional education programmes and furthers MS advocacy efforts than any other MS organization in the world.

National Multiple Sclerosis Society Junior Faculty Awards

Subjects: Neurosciences related to multiple sclerosis.
Purpose: To enable highly qualified persons who have concluded their research training and have begun academic careers as independent investigators to undertake independent research.
Eligibility: Open to citizens of the United States of America holding a doctoral degree, and who have had sufficient research training at the pre- or postdoctoral levels to be capable of independent research. Individuals who have already carried out independent research for more than 5 years are not eligible.
Level of Study: Professional development
Value: Approx. US$75,000 per year
Length of Study: 5 years
Frequency: Annual
Study Establishment: An approved university, professional or research institute
Country of Study: United States of America
No. of awards offered: Varies
Application Procedure: Applicants must complete an application form.
Closing Date: August 15th
Funding: Private
No. of awards given last year: 1
No. of applicants last year: 4
Additional Information: The candidate will not be an employee of the Society but rather of the institution. It is expected that the institution will develop plans for continuing the candidate's appointment and for continued salary support beyond the 5-year period of the award. Fellows may not supplement their salary through private practice or consultation, nor accept another concurrent award. The grantee institution holds title to all equipment purchased with award funds.

National Multiple Sclerosis Society Pilot Research Grants

Subjects: Multiple sclerosis.
Purpose: To provide limited short-term support of novel high-risk research.

Eligibility: Open to suitably qualified investigators.
Level of Study: Research
Type: Research grant
Value: Up to US$40,000 in direct costs may be requested
Length of Study: 1 year
Frequency: Dependent on funds available
Country of Study: Any country
No. of awards offered: Varies
Application Procedure: Applicants must complete an application form.
Closing Date: Applications are accepted at any time
Funding: Private
No. of awards given last year: 58
No. of applicants last year: 121
Additional Information: Grants are awarded to an institution to support the research of the principal investigator. Progress reports are required.

National Multiple Sclerosis Society Postdoctoral Fellowships

Subjects: Multiple sclerosis.
Purpose: To provide postdoctoral training that will enhance the likelihood of performing meaningful and independent research relevant to multiple sclerosis.
Eligibility: Open to unusually promising recipients of MD or PhD degrees. Foreign nationals are welcome to apply for fellowships in the United States of America only. The Society will consider applications from established investigators who seek support to obtain specialized training in some field in which they are not expert, when such training will materially enhance their capacity to conduct more meaningful research. United States of America citizenship is not required for training in United States of America institutions but applicants who plan to train in other countries must be citizens of the United States of America.
Level of Study: Postdoctorate
Type: Fellowship
Value: Varies according to professional status, previous training, accomplishments in research and the pay scale of the institution in which the training is provided. Fellowships may be supplemented by other forms of support, with prior approval
Length of Study: 1–3 years
Frequency: Annual
Study Establishment: An institution of the candidate's choice
Country of Study: Any country
No. of awards offered: Varies
Application Procedure: Applicants must complete an application form.
Closing Date: August 15th
Funding: Private
No. of awards given last year: 24
No. of applicants last year: 65
Additional Information: Fellows are not considered employees of the Society but rather of the institution where the training is provided. The fellowship is to be administered in accordance with the prevailing policies of the sponsoring institution. It is the responsibility of the applicant to make all the necessary arrangements for their training with the mentor and institution of their choice.

National Multiple Sclerosis Society Research Grants

Subjects: Multiple sclerosis, the cause, prevention, alleviation and cure.
Purpose: To stimulate, co-ordinate and support fundamental or applied clinical or non-clinical research.
Eligibility: Open to suitably qualified investigators.
Level of Study: Professional development
Type: Research grant
Value: Funds may be used to pay the salaries of associated professional personnel, technical assistants and other non-professional personnel in proportion to the time spent directly on the project, in whole or in part. Salaries are made in accordance with the prevailing policies of the grantee institution. If requested, other expenses such as travel costs and fringe benefits may also be paid
Length of Study: 3 years
Country of Study: Any country
No. of awards offered: Varies

Application Procedure: Applicants must complete an application form.
Closing Date: February 1st for grants beginning on October 1st, August 1st for grants beginning on April 1st
Funding: Private
No. of awards given last year: 62
No. of applicants last year: 245
Additional Information: Grants are awarded to an institution to support the research of the principal investigator. Scientific equipment and supplies bought with grant funds become the property of the grantee institution. Progress reports are required and appropriate publication is expected.

NMSS Patient Management Care and Rehabilitation Grants

Subjects: Health and medical sciences, therapy/rehabilitation.
Purpose: To support investigators with an MD, PhD or equivalent degree to research patient management care and rehabilitation.
Eligibility: Open to citizens of the United States.
Level of Study: Doctorate, Postgraduate
Type: Grant
Value: US$2,00,000–3,00,000
Frequency: Annual
Country of Study: United States of America
No. of awards offered: 2–3
Closing Date: Early February and early August
No. of awards given last year: 5
No. of applicants last year: 21

NATIONAL ORCHESTRAL INSTITUTE

2110 Clarice Smith Performing Arts Center, University of Maryland, College Park, MD 20742-1620, United States of America
Tel: (1) 301 405 2317
Fax: (1) 301 314 9504
Email: noi@umd.edu
Website: www.noimusic.com

The National Orchestral Institute at the University of Maryland School of Music offers an intensive 4-week experience in orchestral musicianship and professional development for musicians on the threshold of their careers. Distinguished musicians and conductors work closely with participants to polish ensemble skills and orchestral excerpts.

National Orchestral Institute Scholarships

Subjects: Orchestral performance and chamber music.
Purpose: To provide an intensive 3-week orchestral training programme to enable musicians to rehearse and perform under internationally acclaimed conductors and study with principal musicians of the United States of America's foremost orchestras in preparation for careers as orchestral musicians.
Eligibility: Open to advanced musicians between 18 and 28 years of age, primarily students and postgraduates of United States of America universities, conservatories and colleges. Others, however, are welcome to apply, but must appear for an audition at the centre. String players, including harpists, who live more than 200 miles away from an audition centre, may audition by tape.
Level of Study: Unrestricted
Type: Scholarship
Value: Full tuition, room and boardscholarship worth over US$4,000
Length of Study: 4 weeks
Frequency: Annual
Study Establishment: The University of Maryland
Country of Study: United States of America
No. of awards offered: Approx. 100
Application Procedure: Applicants must submit an application, a fee of US$65, curriculum vitae and (optional) letter of recommendation.
Closing Date: Before the regional auditions
Funding: Government
Contributor: The University of Maryland
No. of awards given last year: 100
No. of applicants last year: 720
Additional Information: Personal auditions are required at one of the audition centres throughout the country.

THE NATIONAL ORGANIZATION FOR RARE DISORDERS (NORD)

PO Box 1968, 55 Kenosia Avenue, Danbury, CT, 06813-1968, United States of America
Tel: (1) 203 744 0100
Fax: (1) 203 798 2291
Email: lcataldo@rarediseases.org
Website: www.rarediseases.org
Contact: Ms Linda M Cataldo, Field Services Co-ordinator

The National Organization for Rare Disorders (NORD) is a federation of voluntary health organizations dedicated to helping people with rare (orphan) diseases and assisting the organizations that serve them. NORD is committed to the identification, treatment and cure of rare disorders through programmes of advocacy, education, research and service.

NORD/Rosoe Brady Lysosomal Storage Diseases Fellowships

Subjects: Genetics, new treatments and diagnostics, and/or epidemiology of lysosomal storage diseases in general, or a specific lysosomal storage disease.
Purpose: To assist physicians who desire to establish careers in lysosomal storage diseases and clinical medicine.
Eligibility: Open to all countries that adhere to the most recent guidelines for human subject protection as set forth by the NIH. Applicants should have earned an MD degree within the past 10 years.
Level of Study: Doctorate, Postdoctorate, Research
Type: Fellowship
Value: US$50,000–70,000 per year
Length of Study: 1 year, but renewable for a 2nd year
Frequency: Annual
Country of Study: Any country
No. of awards offered: 1
Application Procedure: Application forms and required attachments may be obtained directly from the website.
Closing Date: May 1st
Funding: Private
Contributor: Public donations
No. of awards given last year: 3
No. of applicants last year: 14

NATIONAL OSTEOPOROSIS FOUNDATION (NOF)

1232 22nd Street, NW, Washington, DC, 20037-1202, United States of America
Tel: (1) 202 223 2226
Fax: (1) 202 223 2237
Email: researchgrants@nof.org
Website: www.nof.org
Contact: Co-ordinator

The National Osteoporosis Foundation (NOF) is the United States of America's foremost voluntary, non-profit health organization dedicated to overcoming the widespread prevalence of osteoporosis. The Foundation provides up-to-date, medically sound information and programme materials on the prevention, diagnosis and treatment of osteoporosis through a network of individuals, healthcare professionals, organizations and the public.

National Osteoporosis Foundation Research Grants

Subjects: Epidemiology, pathogenesis and osteoporosis.
Purpose: To support clinical or translational research related to the epidemiology, pathogenesis, diagnosis and treatment of osteoporosis.
Eligibility: Applicants must have an MD, PhD or equivalent degree, United States of America citizenship or permanent resident status and be affiliated with non-profit institutions within the United States of America, its territories or the Commonwealth of Puerto Rico. Federal agencies and their employees are not eligible.
Level of Study: Research, Postdoctorate, Predoctorate, Young investigators
Type: Research grant
Value: US$57,000

Length of Study: 1 year
Frequency: Annual
Country of Study: United States of America
No. of awards offered: 3
Application Procedure: Applicants must visit the website for further information.
Closing Date: February 20th
Funding: Private
Contributor: Private donors
No. of awards given last year: 3
No. of applicants last year: 86
Additional Information: A primary focus of NOF is ensuring that adequate funding and researchers are available to support scientific research projects on osteoporosis prevention, diagnosis and treatment. Priority for funding are young investigators at the beginning or early stages of their faculty careers and within 4 years of completion of the postdoctoral training period.

NATIONAL PHYSICAL SCIENCE CONSORTIUM (NPSC)

USC-RAN 3716 South Hope Suite 348, Los Angeles, CA, 90007-4344, United States of America
Tel: (1) 213 743 2409/800 854 6772
Fax: (1) 213 743 2407
Email: jpowell@usc.edu
Website: www.npsc.org
Contact: Dr James L Powell, Executive Director

Established in 1987, the National Physical Science Consortium (NPSC) is headquartered in Los Angeles. It is a unique partnership between industry, government agencies and laboratories and higher education.

NPSC Fellowship in Physical Sciences

Subjects: Physical sciences.
Purpose: To increase the number of qualified citizens of the United States in the physical sciences and related engineering fields, emphasizing recruitment of a diverse applicant pool of women and historically underrepresented minorities.
Eligibility: Open to students who have at least 3.0 grade point average and are graduating seniors or graduate student (up to 2nd year) enrolled in a PhD programme.
Level of Study: Doctorate, Graduate
Type: Fellowship
Value: The charge to the employer for each student supported is US$21,000, of which $16,000 is the allowance to the student and $5,000 goes to NPSC to support its operations
Length of Study: 2–6 years
Frequency: Annual
Country of Study: United States of America
Application Procedure: Candidates must apply online.
Closing Date: November 5th
Additional Information: Members of underrepresented groups are encouraged to apply.

NATIONAL RADIO ASTRONOMY OBSERVATORY

520 Edgemont Road, Charlottesville, VA, 22903-2475, United States of America
Tel: (1) 434 296 0221
Fax: (1) 434 296 0278
Email: brodrigu@nrao.edu
Website: www.nrao.edu/administration/directors_office/jansky-postdocs.shtml
Contact: Jansky Fellowship

The National Radio Astronomy Observatory designs, builds and operates the world's most sophisticated and advanced radio telescopes (the VLA, VLBA, GBT and ALMA), providing scientists from around the world the means to study all aspects of astronomy from planets in our Solar System to the most distant galaxies.

Jansky Fellowship

Subjects: Astronomy radio astronomy instrumentation, computation and theory.
Purpose: To provide an opportunity for young scientists to establish themselves as independent researchers so that they may more effectively compete for permanent positions. The placement of fellows at institutions other than the NRAO will help foster closer scientific ties between the NRAO and the US astronomical community. Annual Jansky Fellows symposia are planned to ensure close contact among all Fellows and the NRAO.
Eligibility: Open to astronomers, physicists, electrical engineers and computer specialists. Preference will be given to recent PhD recipients.
Level of Study: Postdoctorate
Type: Fellowship
Value: US$58,000 per year with a research budget of US$10,000 per year for travel and computing requirements. In addition, page charge support, as well as vacation accrual, health insurance, and a moving allowance are provided, as well as up to US$3,000 per year to defray local institutional costs
Length of Study: 2 years, with a possibility of renewal for 1 further year
Frequency: Annual
Study Establishment: The Observatory's centres in Charlottesville, VA; Green Bank, WV; and Socorro, NM
Country of Study: Any country
No. of awards offered: Up to 3 appointments will be made annually for positions at any of the NRAO sites (Socorro, NM; Green Bank, WV; and Charlottesville, VA). Jansky Fellows are encouraged to spend time at universities working with collaborators during the course of their fellowship. In addition, up to 3 Jansky Fellowship appointments will be made annually for positions that may be located at a US university or research institute.
Application Procedure: Candidates normally commence in September or October. There is no application form. The initial letter should include a statement of the individual's research interests together with his or her own appraisal of his or her qualifications for carrying out research. Candidates should be single-sided with no staples. The application should have 3 letters of recommendation sent directly to the NRAO.
Closing Date: November 17th
Funding: Government
Contributor: The National Science Foundation
No. of awards given last year: 6
No. of applicants last year: 63
Additional Information: Research associates may formulate and carry out investigations either independently or in collaboration with others.

NATIONAL RESEARCH COUNCIL (NRC)

Fellowship Office, GR 346A, 500 5th Street, NW, Washington DC, 20001, United States of America
Tel: (1) 202 334 2872
Email: infofell@nas.edu
Website: www.nationalacademies.org

The National Research Council (NRC) is part of the National Academies, which also comprise the National Academy of Sciences, National Academy of Engineering and Institute of Medicine. They are private, non-profit institutions that provides science, technology and health policy advice under a congressional charter.

Ford Foundation Dissertation Fellowships for Minorities

Subjects: Literature/English/writing, history, foreign language, religion/theology, social sciences, political science, communications, physical sciences and mathematics and engineering-related technologies.
Purpose: To financially support underrepresented minorities in research-based fields of study.
Eligibility: Open to citizens of the United States of the following origin: Native-American, Alaska Native, Native Pacific Islander, African-American, Mexican-American or Puerto Rican. Applicants must also be full-time students.
Level of Study: Postgraduate, Research

Type: Fellowships
Value: US$21,500
Frequency: Annual
Country of Study: United States of America
No. of awards offered: 29
Application Procedure: Applicants must submit their application form, transcript, essay and reference letters.
Closing Date: November 12th

NATIONAL RESEARCH COUNCIL OF CANADA (NRC)

1200 Montreal Road, Building M-58, Ottawa, ON, K1A 0R6, Canada
Tel: (1) 613 993 9101
Fax: (1) 613 952 9907
Email: ra.coordinator@nrc-cnrc.gc.ca
Website: www.nrc-cnrc.gc.ca
Contact: Research Associates Co-ordinator

The National Research Council of Canada (NRC) is a dynamic, nationwide research and development organization committed to helping Canada realize its potential as an innovative and competitive nation.

NRC Research Associateships

Subjects: Biological sciences, biotechnology, chemistry, molecular sciences, chemical engineering and process technologies, electrical engineering, astrophysics, industrial materials research, construction, mechanical engineering, aeronautics, physics, photonics, microstructural sciences, plant biotechnology, biochemistry, microbiology or advanced structural ceramics, bioinformatics, fuel cells, genomics, nanotechnology, nutraceuticals, proteomics, ocean engineering, aerospace, measurement standards, communication and technologies.
Purpose: To give promising scientists and engineers an opportunity to work in a challenging research environment during the early stages of their research careers.
Eligibility: Open to nationals of any country, although preference will be given to Canadians and permanent residents of Canada. Applicants should have acquired a PhD in natural science or a Master's degree in an engineering field within the last 5 years or should expect to obtain their degree before taking up the associateship. Selections will be made on a competitive basis with a demonstrated ability to perform original research of high quality in the chosen field as the main criterion.
Level of Study: Postgraduate
Value: Canadian $49,489 plus $8,000 (terminable allowance) for a new PhD
Frequency: Annual
Study Establishment: Laboratories in the National Research Council of Canada
Country of Study: Any country
No. of awards offered: Approx. 50
Application Procedure: Applicants must fill out the online application form, available on the website www.careers-carrieres.nrc-cnrc.gc.ca
Closing Date: Applications are accepted at any time
Funding: Government
No. of awards given last year: 50
No. of applicants last year: 400
Additional Information: Salaries are revised annually. Further information is available from the website.

NATIONAL SCIENCE FOUNDATION (NSF)

Division of Earth Sciences, 4201 Wilson Boulevard Arlington, VA, 22230, United States of America
Tel: (1) 703 292 5111
Fax: (1) 703 292 9025
Email: info@nsf.gov
Website: www.nsf.gov
Contact: Division Director

The National Science Foundation (NSF) supports research in the areas of geology, geophysics, geochemistry, paleobiology and hydrology, including interdisciplinary or multidisciplinary proposals that may involve one or more of these disciplines.

NSF Doctoral Dissertation Improvement Grants

Subjects: Biological sciences.
Purpose: To provide partial support to Doctoral dissertation research and allow Doctoral candidates to conduct research in specialized facilities or field settings away from the home campus.
Eligibility: Open to students who have advanced to candidacy for a PhD degree to be eligible to submit a proposal. Also US institutions that are eligible for awards from the NSF may submit proposals.
Level of Study: Doctorate
Type: Grant
Value: US$3,000–12,000
Length of Study: 2 years
Frequency: Annual
Country of Study: United States of America
Closing Date: November 18th
Contributor: National Science Foundation

NATIONAL SEA GRANT COLLEGE

NOAA Sea Grant R-SG, NOAA RM 11718, 1355 EW Highway, Silver Springs, MD, 20910, United States of America
Tel: (1) 301 734 1077
Email: miguel.lugo@noaa.gov
Website: www.seagrant.noaa.gov
Contact: Dr Miguel A.Lugo, Program Officer

Sea Grant is a nationwide network administered through the National Oceanic and Atmospheric Administration (NOAA) of 30 university-based programmes that work with coastal communities. The organizations research and programmes promote better understanding, conservation and use of America's coastal resources. In short, Sea Grant is science serving America's coasts.

John A Knauss Marine Policy Fellowships

Subjects: Marine resource.
Purpose: To provide a unique educational experience to students who have an interest in ocean, coastal and Great Lakes resources and in the national policy decisions affecting those resources.
Eligibility: Open to all students regardless of citizenship. Applicants must be graduates or professionals in a marine or aquatic-related field at a United States accredited institution of higher education.
Level of Study: Postgraduate
Type: Fellowship
Value: US$43,500
Length of Study: 1 year
Frequency: Annual
Country of Study: United States of America
Application Procedure: Please visit www.seagrant.noaa.gov/knauss
Closing Date: February
Funding: Government

Sea Grant/NOAA Fisheries Fellowship

Subjects: Population dynamics and marine resource economics.
Purpose: To financially support and encourage qualified applicants to pursue careers in either population dynamics and stock assessment or in marine resource economics and also to increase available expertise related to these fields.
Eligibility: Applicants have to be PhD students in population dynamics or marine resource economics or related disciplines concentrating on the conservation and management of living marine resources.
Level of Study: Doctorate
Type: Fellowship
Value: US$38,500 per year
Length of Study: 2–3years
Frequency: Annual
Closing Date: January
Funding: Government

For further information contact:

Email: terry.smith@noaa.gov

THE NATIONAL SOCIETY OF HISPANIC MBAS (NSH MBA)

Scholarship America, One Scholarship Way, PO Box 297, Saint Peter, MN, 56082, United States of America
Tel: (1) 214 596 9338
Fax: (1) 214 596 9325
Email: jfarlinger@scholarshipamerica.org
Website: www.nshmba.org
Contact: Mr J Farlinger

The National Society of Hispanic MBAs, founded in 1988, is a non-profit organization. It exists to foster Hispanic leadership through management education and professional development.

NSHMBA
Subjects: Business administration.
Purpose: To provide financial assistance to outstanding Hispanics pursuing a Master's degree.
Eligibility: Open to citizens of the United States or legal permanent residents of Hispanic heritage with a grade point average of 3.0 on a 4.0 scale and are enrolled or plan to enrol in a Master's degree programme.
Level of Study: MBA
Type: Scholarship
Value: US$5,000–7,500
Frequency: Annual
Closing Date: April 30th
Additional Information: All queries should be directed to NSHMBA Scholarship Programme, Scholarship America – Julie Aretz, One Scholarship Way, PO Box 297, St Peter, MN 56082, United States of America, Tel: 507 931 1682.

NATIONAL TAIWAN UNIVERSITY

No 1, Section 4, Roosevelt Road, Taipei, 10617, Taiwan
Tel: (886) 2 2363 5251
Fax: (886) 2 2367 1909
Email: yiyunlee@cc.ee.ntu.edu.tw
Website: www.ee.ntu.edu.tw

The National Taiwan University (NTU) was founded by the Japanese in 1928. NTU is the most prestigious institution of higher education in Taiwan with the longest history and most diverse academic programmes, NTU has taken up the responsibility of promoting and advancing academic research and teaching in Taiwan.

Taiwan's Industrial Technology R&D Master Program for Foreign Students
Subjects: Engineering.
Purpose: To promote and advance academic research and teaching in Taiwan.
Eligibility: Open only to applicants who do not have overseas Chinese status and do not hold a Republic of China passport. Applicants must hold a Bachelor's degree or equivalent from a foreign university or independent institute and TOEFL is required for all applicants whose first language is not English.
Level of Study: Postgraduate
Type: Scholarship
Value: US$250 stipend per semester, tuition waived
Length of Study: 2 years
Frequency: Annual, Per semester
Country of Study: Taiwan
Application Procedure: Application forms are available online.
Closing Date: July 10th
Additional Information: Students are responsible for the remaining expenses, including transportation, books, dormitory and living expenses (Students with an awarded scholarship have to pay for their tuition).

For further information contact:

Website: www.ee.ntu.edu.tw/imaster/english/source

NATIONAL TRAPPERS ASSOCIATION (NTA)

NTA Headquarters, 2815 Washington Avenue, Bedford, IN, 47421-2247, United States of America
Tel: (1) 812 277 9670
Fax: (1) 812 277 9672
Email: ntaheadquarters@nationaltrappers.com
Website: www.nationaltrappers.com

The NTA, established in 1959, is an organization of dedicated individuals who have joined together to promote and protect the appropriate conservative use of our fur bearing species.

Charles L. Dobbins Memorial Scholarship
Subjects: Wildlife management.
Purpose: To encourage students majoring in a field of study pertaining to wildlife management or related topics.
Eligibility: Open to applicants who are members of a state or national trappers association.
Level of Study: Postgraduate
Type: Scholarship
Length of Study: US$250
Frequency: Annual
No. of awards offered: 12
Application Procedure: A completed application form must be submitted.
Closing Date: July 1st

For further information contact:

National Trappers Association, 4170 St Clair, Fallon, NV 89406
Contact: Jim Curran

NATIONAL UNION OF TEACHERS (NUT)

Strategy & Communications, Hamilton House, Mabledon Place, London, WC1H 9BD, England
Tel: (44) 20 7380 4704
Fax: (44) 20 7387 8458
Email: a.bush@nut.org.uk
Website: www.teachers.org.uk
Contact: Ms Angela Bush

NUT Page Scholarship
Subjects: A specific aspect of American education relevant to the recipient's own professional responsibilities.
Purpose: To promote the exchange of educational ideas between Britain and America.
Eligibility: Open to teaching members of the NUT aged 25–60 years, although 25–55 is preferred.
Level of Study: Professional development
Type: Scholarship
Value: Each up to UK £1,700 pro rata daily rate with complete hospitality in the United States of America provided by the English-Speaking Union of the United States of America
Length of Study: 2 weeks. The scholarship must be taken during the American academic year, which is September–May
Frequency: Annual
Country of Study: United States of America
No. of awards offered: 2
Application Procedure: Applicants must complete an application form. An outline and synopsis of the project must accompany the form along with a curriculum vitae and scholastic and personal testimonials.
Closing Date: December 22nd
Funding: Private
Contributor: NUT
No. of awards given last year: 2
No. of applicants last year: 100
Additional Information: The scholarship is limited to the individual teacher and neither the spouse nor partner can be included in the travel, accommodation or study arrangements. Recipients are required to report on their visit to teacher groups and educational meetings in the United States of America and on their return home.

NATIONAL UNIVERSITY OF IRELAND

Postgraduate Admissions Office, University Road, Galway, Ireland
Tel: (353) (0) 91 524411
Email: postgrad@nuigalway.ie

The national university of Ireland, founded in 1845 as Queen's College Galway, is now an institution with over 15,000 students in several facilities.

Lady Gregory Fellowship Scheme

Purpose: Humanities, languages and literatures, and social and behavioral sciences.
Eligibility: Open to students who are in their first year of PhD programme.
Level of Study: Doctorate
Type: Fellowship
Value: €20,000 per year
Length of Study: 3 years
Frequency: Annual
No. of awards offered: 3
Application Procedure: A completed application form and other required information must be sent. See website for further details.
Closing Date: March 3rd

For further information contact:

Office of Faculty of Arts Room 217A, First floor Arts Millenium Building NU1 Galway, university road, Galway, Ireland
Contact: Mr Mairead Ni Dhomhnaill

NATIONAL UNIVERSITY OF IRELAND GALWAY

Galway, Ireland
Tel: (353) 9 152 441
Fax: (353) 9 175 0436
Contact: MBA Admissions Officer

Charles Parsons Energy Research Award

Subjects: Microbial and biocatalytic fuel cell research.
Purpose: To focus on investigation and optimization of electron transfer reactions in biological fuel cells that can generate energy from diverse substrates. To focus the research on applications of pure- and mixed-culture microbial fuel cells, and biocatalytic enzyme-based fuel cells.
Eligibility: Open to engineering graduates.
Level of Study: Doctorate
Value: Up to €18,000 per year, plus payment of fees
Application Procedure: Applicants should include a curriculum vitae and the names of two academic referees.
Additional Information: The research will involve liaison with international collaborators, bench research and reporting. To this end, good inter-personal, written communication and networking skills are advantageous.

For further information contact:

Email: donal.leech@nuigalway.ie
Contact: Dr Dónal Leech

Masters Fellowship in Biomaterials

Subjects: Biomaterials.
Purpose: To encourage investigative work in developing blood-compatible biomaterials.
Eligibility: Open to candidates with Bachelor's Degree in polymer chemistry, polymer engineering, biomedical engineering or related sciences. Ideally, a First Class Honours track record is desirable.
Level of Study: Doctorate
Type: Fellowship
Value: Fees and a monthly stipend (IRCSET level)
Length of Study: 2 years
Frequency: Annual
Application Procedure: Applicants must send a curriculum vitae and the names of three referees with contact addresses.

Additional Information: This position is funded through Enterprise Ireland-Research Innovation Partnership Program.

For further information contact:

National Centre for Biomedical Engineering Science, National University of Ireland, Galway,
Tel: (353) 91 492758
Email: abhay.pandit@nuigalway.ie
Contact: Abahy Pandit, Professor in Biomedical Engineering

NATIONAL UNIVERSITY OF IRELAND, MAYNOOTH

Co. Kildare, Ireland
Tel: (353) 1 7086000
Fax: (353) 1 6289063
Email: fees.office@nuim.ie
Website: www.nuim.ie

Following two centuries of internationally renowned scholarly activity on the Maynooth campus, the National University of Ireland, Maynooth was established under the 1997 Universities Act as an autonomous member of the federal structure known as the National University of Ireland. With approximately 8,400 registered students, NUI, Maynooth has 26 academic departments which are organized into three Faculties: Arts, Celtic Studies and Philosophy; Science and Engineering; and Social Sciences. Building on a tradition of scholarship and excellence in all aspects of its teaching, learning, and research activities, within the liberal arts and sciences tradition NUI, Maynooth is committed to being a first-class research-led centre of learning and academic discovery.

John Hume Postgraduate Scholarships

Subjects: Arts, humanities, social sciences, sciences and engineering.
Purpose: To build on excellence in areas across the arts, humanities, social sciences, sciences and engineering.
Eligibility: Applicants must have a First or Upper Second-Class Honours Primary Degree (or equivalent) from Ireland, the EU or from any overseas university and intend to pursue a PhD degree at the University. Those who have commenced a research degree at NUI Maynooth prior to application will not be eligible.
Level of Study: Postgraduate, Research
Type: Scholarship
Value: €5000 per year plus payment of fees at EU level
Length of Study: Up to 3 years
Frequency: Annual
Study Establishment: NUI Maynooth
Country of Study: Ireland
No. of awards offered: 2
Application Procedure: Applicants must first make contact with a NUI Maynooth department or centre to discuss their suitability for a PhD programme. A list of departmental contacts is available on the website. Application for the scholarship can then be filed.
Closing Date: June 13th
No. of awards given last year: 30
Additional Information: Check website for further details.

For further information contact:

Office of Research and Graduate Studies, NUI Maynooth, Ireland
Tel: (353) 1 708 6018
Fax: (353) 1 7083359
Email: pgdean@nuim.ie
Website: http://graduatestudies.nuim.ie

NATIONAL UNIVERSITY OF SINGAPORE (NUS)

21 Lower Kent Ridge Road, Singapore, 119077, Singapore
Tel: (65) 6516 6666
Fax: (65) (0) 6775 9330
Email: gradenquiry@nus.edu.sg
Website: www.nus.edu.sg
Contact: Grants Management Officer

NUS aspires to be a dynamic connected knowledge community imbued with a no walls culture that promotes the free flow of talent and ideas. Individual members of our community enjoy access to diverse opportunities for intellectual and professional growth and in twin add value to NUS becoming a global knowledge enterprise.

Asian Development Bank-Japan Scholarship Program
Subjects: Public policy.
Purpose: To find further study in public policy implementation.
Eligibility: Open to residents of Asian Development Bank member countries currently enrolled at NUS. Upon completion of their study programmes, scholars are expected to contribute to the economic and social development of their home countries. Check website for further details.
Level of Study: Postgraduate
Type: Scholarship
Value: Singapore $250 per semester (one-time book allowance), tuition, health insurance, examination and other approved fees. Cost of travel from home country to Singapore on award of the scholarship and from Singapore to home country on graduation
Length of Study: 2 years for Master in public policy
Frequency: Annual
Study Establishment: Lee Kuan Yew School of Public Policy, National University of Singapore
Country of Study: Singapore
Application Procedure: Apply online.
Closing Date: Refer to website
Funding: Government
Contributor: Government
No. of awards given last year: 3
No. of applicants last year: 350

CapitaLand LKYSPP Scholarship
Subjects: Public administration.
Purpose: To find further study in public administration implementation.
Eligibility: Open to applicants of ASEAN countries (except Singapore), India, or the People's Republic of China.
Level of Study: Postgraduate
Type: Scholarship
Value: A monthly stipend, one-time book allowance, one-time settling-in allowance, shared housing, tuition, health insurance, examination and other approved fees. Cost of travel from home country to Singapore on award of the scholarship and from Singapore to home country on graduation
Length of Study: 1 year for Master in Public Administration
Frequency: Annual
Study Establishment: Lee Kuan Yew School of Public Policy, National University of Singapore
Country of Study: Singapore
No. of awards offered: 2
Application Procedure: Apply online.
Closing Date: Refer to website
Funding: Corporation
Contributor: CapitaLand

Hefner Scholarship
Subjects: Public administration.
Purpose: To find further study in public administration implementation.
Eligibility: Open to applicants of People's Republic of China or the United States of America.
Level of Study: Postgraduate
Type: Scholarship
Value: A monthly stipend, one-time book allowance, one-time settling-in allowance, shared housing, tuition, health insurance, examination and other approved fees. Cost of travel from home country to Singapore on award of the scholarship and from Singapore to home country on graduation
Length of Study: 1 year for Master in Public Administration
Frequency: Annual
Study Establishment: Lee Kuan Yew School of Public Policy, National University of Singapore

Country of Study: Singapore
No. of awards offered: 2
Application Procedure: Apply online.
Closing Date: Refer to website
Funding: Private
Contributor: Hefner

Law/Faculty Graduate Scholarship (FGS)
Subjects: Law.
Purpose: To reward an outstanding student of the faculty of Law.
Eligibility: Open to outstanding international applicants of any nationality (except Singapore citizens).
Level of Study: Postgraduate
Type: Scholarship
Value: A monthly stipend of Singapore $300, a one-off air travel allowance of S$700, health insurance and all approved NUS fees
Frequency: Annual
Study Establishment: National University of Singapore
Country of Study: Singapore

Lee Kong Chian Graduate Scholarships
Subjects: Any subject.
Purpose: To reward proven academic excellence, leadership and exceptional promise.
Eligibility: Open to any student enrolled as a candidate for a PhD programme at the university.
Level of Study: Postdoctorate
Type: Scholarship
Value: A monthly stipend of Singapore $3,000, all approved fees at NUS, an annual book allowance of Singapore $500, one-off air travel allowance of two return tickets of up to Singapore $4,000 (only for overseas students) and a one-off laptop allowance of Singapore $1,500
Frequency: Annual
Study Establishment: National University of Singapore
Country of Study: Singapore
No. of awards offered: 5
Closing Date: November 15th
Funding: Foundation
Contributor: Lee Foundation

Lee Kuan Yew School of Public Policy Graduate Scholarships (LKYSPPS)
Subjects: Public policy and public administration.
Purpose: To find further study in public policy and administration implementation.
Eligibility: Open to all nationalities (except Singapore).
Level of Study: Postgraduate
Type: Scholarship
Value: A monthly stipend, a one-time book allowance, a one-time settling-in allowance, shared housing, tuition, health insurance, examination and other approved fees, cost of travel from home country to Singapore on award of the scholarship and from Singapore to home country on graduation
Length of Study: 1 year (for public administration) and 2 years (for public policy)
Frequency: Annual
Study Establishment: Lee Kuan Yew School of Public Policy, National University of Singapore
Country of Study: Singapore
Application Procedure: Apply online.
Closing Date: Refer to website
Funding: Government
Contributor: Government

For further information contact:

Email: LKYSPPmpp@nus.edu.sg

Lien Foundation Scholarship for Social Service Leaders
Subjects: Public administration.
Purpose: To find further study in public administration implementation.
Eligibility: Open to Singapore citizens or permanent residents.
Level of Study: Postgraduate

Type: Scholarship
Value: A monthly allowance (for full-time candidates only), one-time allowance, tuition, health insurance, examination and other approved fees
Length of Study: 1 year for Master in Public Administration
Frequency: Annual
Study Establishment: Lee Kuan Yew School of Public Policy, National University of Singapore
Country of Study: Singapore
Application Procedure: Apply online.
Closing Date: Refer to website www.ncss.org.sg/lien
Funding: Private
Contributor: Hefner

National University of Singapore Research Scholarships

Subjects: Any subject.
Purpose: To reward outstanding graduates for research leading to a higher degree at the university.
Level of Study: Postgraduate
Type: Scholarship
Value: Monthly stipend of Singapore $1,500 and $2,300 (depending on nationality and type of programme), and a full tuition fee subsidy. No travel or other allowances are provided. PhD scholars who passed the qualifying exam will get an additional Singapore $500 per month
Length of Study: 2–4 years
Frequency: Annual
Study Establishment: National University of Singapore
Country of Study: Singapore
Additional Information: Research scholars may be asked to assist in departmental work for which they can earn up to Singapore $16,000 (gross) per annum at the current rate of remuneration. However, please note that the university does not guarantee employment to research scholars upon completion of their candidature.

NUS Graduate Scholarship for Asean Nationals

Subjects: Engineering, computing, science, law, dentistry, medicine, arts & social sciences, design and environmental studies.
Purpose: To enable a successful scholar to pursue full-time study.
Eligibility: Open to all Asean nationals, except Singaporeans.
Level of Study: Postgraduate
Type: Scholarship
Value: Payment of all NUS approved fees
Length of Study: 2–3 years
Frequency: Annual
Study Establishment: National University of Singapore
Country of Study: Singapore
No. of awards offered: 40
Application Procedure: Download application form from www.med.nus.edu.sg/registrar/sfau/gd-nusgsa.html/# degrees
Funding: Government

OCBC International Master in Public Policy Scholarship

Subjects: Public policy.
Purpose: To find further study in public policy implementation.
Eligibility: Open to applicants from China, Malaysia or Indonesia.
Level of Study: Postgraduate
Type: Scholarship
Value: A monthly stipend, one-time book allowance, one-time settling-in allowance, shared housing, tuition, health insurance, examination and other approved fees. Cost of travel from home country to Singapore on award of the scholarship and from Singapore to home country on graduation
Length of Study: 2 years for Master in Public Policy
Frequency: Annual
Study Establishment: Lee Kuan Yew School of Public Policy, National University of Singapore
Country of Study: Singapore
No. of awards offered: 3
Application Procedure: Apply online.
Closing Date: Refer to website
Funding: Corporation
Contributor: OCBC

Rodamas – LKYSPP Scholarship

Subjects: Public administration.
Purpose: To find further study in public administration implementation.

Eligibility: Open to Indonesian applicants.
Level of Study: Postgraduate
Type: Scholarship
Value: A monthly stipend, one-time book allowance, one-time settling-in allowance, shared housing, tuition, health insurance, examination and other approved fees. Cost of travel from home country to Singapore on award of the scholarship and from Singapore to home country on graduation
Length of Study: 1 year for Master in Public Administration
Frequency: Annual
Study Establishment: Lee Kuan Yew School of Public Policy, National University of Singapore
Country of Study: Singapore
No. of awards offered: 1
Application Procedure: Apply online.
Closing Date: Refer to website
Funding: Corporation
Contributor: PT Rodamas

Sequislife – LKYSPP Scholarship

Subjects: Public administration.
Purpose: To find further study in public administration implementation.
Eligibility: Open to applicants from Indonesia.
Level of Study: Postgraduate
Type: Scholarship
Value: A monthly stipend, one-time book allowance, one-time settling-in allowance, shared housing, tuition, health insurance, examination and other approved fees. Cost of travel from home country to Singapore on award of the scholarship and from Singapore to home country on graduation
Length of Study: 1 year for Master in Public Administration
Frequency: Annual
Study Establishment: Lee Kuan Yew School of Public Policy, National University of Singapore
Country of Study: Singapore
No. of awards offered: 1
Application Procedure: Apply online.
Closing Date: Refer to website
Funding: Corporation
Contributor: PT Sequislife

Singapore-MIT Alliance Graduate Fellowship

Subjects: Any subject.
Purpose: Singapore-MIT Alliance (SMA) is a collaboration between NUS and NTU in Singapore and MIT in the US to support dual degrees: either a master's degree from MIT and a master's degree from NUS/NTU; or a master's degree from MIT and a PhD from NUS/NTU; or a PhD degree from either NUS or NTU.
Level of Study: Graduate, Postgraduate
Type: Fellowship
Value: A monthly stipend of Singapore $1,500–2,500 in addition, full NUS or NTU and MIT tuition fee subsidy for the duration of the course, travel support to MIT and a living allowance of US$1,000 per month up to a mximum of between US$6,000 and 12,000, depending on the degree track
Length of Study: 18 months–5 years
Frequency: Annual
Study Establishment: National University of Singapore and Nanyang Technological University
Country of Study: Singapore
Application Procedure: Applicants must apply separately to both MIT and NUS/NTU for the dual degrees and only to NUS or NTU for direct Phd degree; applicants must also apply directly to SMA for an SMA Graduate Fellowship.
Closing Date: Between January and March
Funding: Government
Contributor: A*Star, Economic and Development Board (EDB), Ministry of Education (MOE), National University of Singapore (NUS) and Nanyang Technological University (NTU)
No. of applicants last year: 120

For further information contact:

Tel: 6516 4787
Fax: 6775 2920

Email: smart@nus.edu.sg
Website: www.sma.nus.edu.sg

Standard Chartered LKYSPP Scholarship
Subjects: Public administration and public policy.
Purpose: To find further study in public administration and public policy implementation.
Eligibility: Open to ASEAN countries (except Singapore), India, the People's Republic of China or the United Arab Emirates.
Level of Study: Postgraduate
Type: Scholarship
Value: A monthly stipend, one-time book allowance, one-time settling-in allowance, shared housing, tuition, health insurance, examination and other approved fees. Cost of travel from home country to Singapore on award of the scholarship and from Singapore to home country on graduation
Length of Study: 1 year for Master in Public Administration and, 2 years for Master in Public Policy
Frequency: Annual
Study Establishment: Lee Kuan Yew School of Public Policy, National University of Singapore
Country of Study: Singapore
No. of awards offered: 2
Application Procedure: Apply online.
Closing Date: Refer to website
Funding: Corporation
Contributor: Standard Chartered

Temasek Scholarship
Subjects: Public policy.
Purpose: To find further study in public policy implementation.
Eligibility: Open to nationals of permanent residents of member countries of ASEAN (except Singapore) and APEC (except Singapore).
Level of Study: Postgraduate
Type: Scholarship
Value: A monthly stipend, a one-time book allowance, a one-time settling-in allowance, shared housing, tuition, health insurance, examination and other approved fees. Cost of travel from home country to Singapore on award of the scholarship and from Singapore to home country on graduation
Length of Study: 2 years for Master in public policy
Frequency: Annual
Study Establishment: Lee Kuan Yew School of Public Policy, National University of Singapore
Country of Study: Singapore
Closing Date: Refer to website
Funding: Government
Contributor: Government

NATIONAL WILDLIFE FEDERATION (NWF)

11100 Wildlife Center Drive, Reston, VA, 20190, United States of America
Tel: (1) 800 822 9919
Email: campus@nwf.org
Website: www.nwf.org/campusecology
Contact: Director of Research

For more than a decade, National Wildlife Federation (NWF) has been helping to transform the nation's college and university campuses into living models of an ecologically sustainable society and training a new generation of environmental leaders. Campus Ecology supports and promotes positive and practical conservation projects on campus and beyond to protect wildlife by restoring habitat and slowing global warming.

Campus Ecology Fellowship Program
Subjects: Building design, composting, dining services, energy, landscaping, management systems, purchasing, transportation and waste reduction or water.
Purpose: To provide the opportunity to students to pursue their vision of an ecologically sustainable future, identify and implement innovative greening initiatives as relevant to their campus and community.

Eligibility: Open to former NWF interns following 1 year from their final work date.
Level of Study: Postgraduate
Type: Fellowships
Value: US$2,000 for direct project expenses or to cover cost of living
Frequency: Annual
Country of Study: United States of America
Closing Date: October 1st, November 14th and February 2nd
Contributor: National Wildlife Federation

NATURAL ENVIRONMENT RESEARCH COUNCIL (NERC)

Polaris House, North Star Avenue, Swindon, Wiltshire, SN2 1EU, England
Tel: (44) 17 9341 1500
Fax: (44) 17 9341 1501
Email: aval@nerc.ac.uk
Website: www.nerc.ac.uk/funding
Contact: Dr A E Allman, Process Manager

The Natural Environment Research Council (NERC) is one of the seven United Kingdom Research Councils that fund and manage research in the United Kingdom. NERC is the leading body in the United Kingdom for research, survey, monitoring and training in the environmental sciences. NERC supports research and training in universities and in its own centres, surveys and units.

NERC Advanced Research Fellowships
Subjects: Sciences of the natural environment
Purpose: To enable outstanding mid-career researchers develop into team leaders of international standing and devote themselves to personal research.
Eligibility: Open to candidates who hold a PhD and have had at least 2 years of research experience at the postdoctoral level at the time of application, although not necessarily in the United Kingdom. They must also have proven their ability as individual research workers.
Level of Study: Postdoctorate
Type: Fellowship
Value: Includes 80% of the full economic cost (FEC) of the proposal. NERC will provide funding for the fellow's salary costs in line with the agreed pay scales at the time of the award, with provision for future years
Length of Study: 5 years
Frequency: Annual
Study Establishment: Universities and other approved research institutes
Country of Study: United Kingdom
No. of awards offered: 5–10 per year
Application Procedure: Applicants must refer to the fellowship handbook and use the joint electronic submission application forms available via the NERC website.
Closing Date: October 30th
Funding: Government
No. of awards given last year: 6
No. of applicants last year: 38
Additional Information: All applications must carry the full support of the host institution, which will be expected to act as the Fellow's employer. As part of NERC's commitment to promote equal opportunities, all fellowships may be held by suitably qualified candidates on a full- or part-time basis, subject to the agreement of the host institution. The NERC is particularly keen to attract applications from scientists in the areas of applied mathematics, physics or strongly quantitative disciplines wishing to develop a career in environmental science.

NERC Masters Studentships
Subjects: Environmental sciences
Purpose: To allow postgraduate students to undertake courses, recognized by NERC, that lead to an MSc or MRes. These courses are designed to prepare students for employment in industry or the public sector, or to advance their study.
Eligibility: Open to British and EU citizens. EU citizens can only receive fees unless they have been resident in the UK for the preceding 3 years in which case they are eligible for a full award. Other

individuals with settled status in the UK may also be eligible. Candidates must hold an honours degree in an appropriate branch of science or technology. For research studentships (PhD/MPhil) this should be a first or upper second class honours degree. For an advanced course studentship (MSc) or research masters (MRes) it should be a first or second class honours degree.

Level of Study: Postgraduate, Predoctorate
Type: Studentship
Value: UK £8,280 maintenance grant per year for students outside London and UK £10,280 per year for students in London, payment of approved fees and assistance with travel and subsistence expenses under specified conditions, e.g. fieldwork
Length of Study: 1 year
Frequency: Annual
Study Establishment: Any approved Institute of Higher Education
Country of Study: United Kingdom
No. of awards offered: Approx. 290
Application Procedure: Individuals need to apply directly to the Master's courses, which have NERC funding. See website for further details.
Funding: Government
No. of awards given last year: 290
Additional Information: The list of departments with NERC PhD funding can be found at: www.nerc.ac.uk/funding/available/postgrad/awards/

NERC Postdoctoral Research Fellowships

Subjects: Sciences of the natural environment
Purpose: Early career development award to provide further postdoctoral experience and to support outstanding environmental scientists as they become independent investigators.
Eligibility: Candidates must hold a PhD or be able to demonstrate equivalent and relevant research experience. Applications will be accepted from PhD students but, if successful, awards may not start until NERC has received written confirmation of the outcome of the applicant's PhD viva. However, applicants are advised that some post-PhD experience can be an advantage when seeking a postdoctoral fellowship.
Level of Study: Postdoctorate, Postgraduate
Type: Fellowship
Value: Includes 80% of the full economic cost (FEC) of the proposal. NERC will provide funding for the fellow's salary costs in line with the agreed pay scales at the time of the award, with provision for future years
Length of Study: 3 years
Frequency: Annual
Study Establishment: Universities and other approved research institutes
Country of Study: United Kingdom
No. of awards offered: 20–25 per year
Application Procedure: Applicants must refer to the fellowship handbook and use the joint electronic submission (Je–S)application forms available via the NERC website.
Closing Date: October 30th (please check the website)
Funding: Government
No. of awards given last year: 23
No. of applicants last year: 104
Additional Information: All applications must carry the full support of the host institution, which will be expected to act as the Fellow's employer. As part of the NERC's commitment to promoting equal opportunities, all fellowships may be held by suitably qualified candidates on a full- or part-time basis, subject to the agreement of the host institution. The NERC is particularly keen to attract applications from scientists in the areas of mathematics, physics or other strongly quantitative disciplines wishing to develop a career in environmental science.

NERC Research (PhD) Studentships

Subjects: Environmental sciences.
Purpose: To enable students receive training in methods of research and to undertake research in particular scientific areas under the guidance of named supervisors and lead to the submission of a PhD thesis.
Eligibility: Open to British and EU citizens. EU citizens can only receive fees unless they have been resident in the UK for the preceding

3 years in which case they are eligible for a full award. Other individuals with settled status in the UK may also be eligible. Candidates must hold an honours degree in an appropriate branch of science or technology. For research studentships (PhD/MPhil) this should be a first or upper second class honours degree.

Level of Study: Postgraduate
Type: Studentship
Value: A maintenance grant of UK £12,940 per year for students outside London and UK £14,940 per year for students in London, the payment of approved fees and assistance with travel and subsistence expenses under specified conditions, e.g. fieldwork
Length of Study: Up to 3 1/2 years, part of which may be spent at an overseas institution
Frequency: Annual
Study Establishment: Any approved Institute of Higher Education
Country of Study: Other
No. of awards offered: Approx. 300
Application Procedure: Individuals need to apply directly to departments that have NERC funding. Check website for further details.
Funding: Government
No. of awards given last year: 350
Additional Information: The list of departments with NERC PhD funding can be found at: www.nerc.ac.uk/funding/available/postgrad/awards/

NATURAL HISTORY MUSEUM

Cromwell Road, London, SW7 5BD, England
Tel: (44) 20 7942 5530
Fax: (44) 20 7942 5841
Email: l.wylde@nhm.ac.uk
Website: www.nhm.ac.uk/science
Contact: L Wylde, Liaison Officer

The Natural History Museum's mission is to maintain and develop its collections and use them to promote the discovery, understanding, responsible use and enjoyment of the natural world.

Synthesys Visiting Fellowship

Subjects: Biological and Earth science
Purpose: To provide access for researchers so that they can undertake short visits to utilize the facilities of 20 major museums and botanic gardens within Europe, including the Natural History Museum and its associates, the Royal Botanical Gardens, Kew and the Royal Botanic Garden Edinburgh.
Eligibility: Open to applicants from the European Union member states, and associated and accession states.
Level of Study: Doctorate, Graduate, Postdoctorate, Predoctorate, Research, Unrestricted, Postgraduate
Value: International travel, accommodation, local travel and subsistence along with all access and facility costs
Length of Study: Up to 60 working days
Frequency: Annual, Twice a year
Study Establishment: The Natural History Museum, London
Country of Study: United Kingdom
No. of awards offered: 30 per call
Application Procedure: Applications must be completed. Website: www.synthesys.info
Closing Date: Please refer to the website
Funding: Government
Contributor: The European Union Programme
No. of awards given last year: 150
No. of applicants last year: 290
Additional Information: During the visit the user is assigned a host, according to their speciality. The role of the host is to familiarize the user with the department, collections and facilities and to give training where necessary. The visits are often collaborative, in which case the host will work directly with the user.

For further information contact:

Website: www.synthesys.info

NATURAL SCIENCES AND ENGINEERING RESEARCH COUNCIL OF CANADA (NSERC)

350 Albert Street, Ottawa, ON, K1A 1H5, Canada
Tel: (1) 613 995 5521
Fax: (1) 613 996 2589
Email: schol@nserc.ca
Website: www.nserc.ca
Contact: Corporate Account Executive

NSERC is Canada's instrument for promoting and supporting university research in the natural sciences and engineering, other than the health sciences. NSERC supports both basic university research through discovery grants and project research through partnerships among universities, governments and the private sector as well as the advanced training of highly qualified people.

Canada Postgraduate Scholarships (PGS)

Subjects: Natural sciences and engineering.
Eligibility: Open to a Canadian citizen or a permanent citizen of Canada, with a university degree in science or engineering, intending to pursue year full-time graduate study and research at the Master's or Doctorate level in one of the areas supported by NSERC with a first-class average in each of the last two completed years of study.
Level of Study: Postgraduate
Type: Fellowship
Value: Canadian $17,300 (Masters) per year for 1 year and Canadian $21,000 (Doctoral) per year for a maximum of 3 years
Length of Study: Up to 3 years
Frequency: Annual
Country of Study: Canada
No. of awards offered: 2
Application Procedure: Check website for further details.
Closing Date: November 15th
Contributor: Natural Sciences and Engineering Research Council of Canada (NSERC)

For further information contact:

National Sciences and Engineering Research Council of Canada (NSERC), Scholarships and Fellowships Division, 350 Albert Street (for courier mailings, add 10th Floor), Ontario, Ottawa, K1A 1H5, Canada
Fax: (1) 613 996 2589
Email: schol@nserc.ca
Website: www.nserc.gc.ca

Defence Research and Development Canada Postgraduate Scholarship Supplements

Subjects: Defence.
Purpose: To encourage and support graduates to carry out research of interest to DRDC; to increase contact between DRDC researchers and those at Canadian universities; and to foster graduate training potential candidates for possible employment at DRDC.
Eligibility: Open to candidates possessing a CGS, PGS or IPS award.
Level of Study: Postgraduate
Type: Scholarship
Value: $5,000 per year
Length of Study: 2 years
Frequency: Annual
Country of Study: Canada
No. of awards offered: 3
Application Procedure: Applicants must submit a copy Notification of Award document from NSERC, a copy of successful scholarship application (Form 200), and a statement of interest in R&D for defence/national security. Check website for further details.
Closing Date: June 1st
Contributor: Defence Research and Development Canada

For further information contact:

DRDC Postgraduate Scholarship Supplements Program, Department of National Defence, 305 Rideau Street, Ontario, Ottawa, K1A 0K2, Canada

Tel: (1) 613 992 0563
Fax: (1) 613 996-7063
Email: hr-rh@drdc-rddc.gc.ca

NSERC Postdoctoral Fellowships

Subjects: Engineering and natural sciences.
Purpose: To provide support to a core of the most promising researchers at a pivotal time in their careers. The fellowships are also intended to secure a supply of highly qualified Canadians with leading edge scientific and research skills for Canadian industry, government and universities.
Eligibility: Open to Canadian citizens or permanent residents residing in Canada, who have recently received, or will shortly receive a PhD from a Canadian university in one of the fields of research that NSERC supports.
Level of Study: Postdoctorate
Type: Fellowship
Value: Canadian $40,000 per year
Length of Study: 1 year, renewable for 1 additional year
Frequency: Annual
Study Establishment: A university or research institution of the Fellow's choice
Country of Study: Any country
No. of awards offered: 200–260
Application Procedure: Applicants must complete Form 200. Information is available on request.
Closing Date: October 15th
Funding: Government
No. of awards given last year: 254
No. of applicants last year: 1097
Additional Information: The information provided here is subject to change. Please visit the NSERC's website for up-to-date information.

NESTA

1 Plough Place, London, EC4A 1DE, United Kingdom
Tel: (44) (0) 20 7438 2500
Fax: (44) (0) 20 7438 2501
Email: nesta@nesta.org.uk
Website: www.nesta.org.uk

Nesta's Fellowship Programme gives creative and innovative individuals who have demonstrated exceptional talent and originality, the time, space, resources and support to develop their ideas, pursue their goals, experiment, and push at the boundaries of knowledge and practice.

NESTA Creative Pioneer Programme

Purpose: To encourage the growth of new generation of creative entrepreneurs.
Level of Study: Professional development
Type: Grant
Value: UK £35,000 start up finance and long-term mentoring
Length of Study: Continuous
Frequency: Annual
Study Establishment: NESTA Academy
Country of Study: United Kingdom
Application Procedure: Contact NESTA.
Closing Date: September 6th
Funding: Foundation
Contributor: NESTA Creative Investor

NESTA Crucible Fellowship

Purpose: To finance creative scientists and engineers-from astrophysicists to zoologists.
Level of Study: Professional development
Type: Fellowship
Value: Lab space, all travel fees and any other reasonable costs, such as child care
Length of Study: 1 year
Frequency: Annual
Study Establishment: NESTA Academy
Country of Study: United Kingdom
No. of awards offered: 30
Application Procedure: Contact NESTA.

Closing Date: November 30th
Contributor: NESTA Creative Investor

NESTA Dream Time Fellowship

Subjects: Technology, engineering, science, arts.
Purpose: To finance exceptional achievers wishing to take structured time away from their work to pursue ideas which will benefit both themselves and their sector.
Eligibility: Applicants must have at least 10 years of work experience in their field.
Level of Study: Professional development
Type: Fellowship
Value: UK £40,000
Length of Study: 1 year
Frequency: Annual
Study Establishment: NESTA Academy
Country of Study: United Kingdom
Application Procedure: Contact NESTA.
Closing Date: September
Funding: Foundation
Contributor: NESTA Creative Investor

NETHERLANDS ORGANIZATION FOR INTERNATIONAL CO-OPERATION IN HIGHER EDUCATION (NUFFIC)

Kortenaerkade 11, 2118 AX Den Haag, Po Box 29777, 2502-LT, The Hague, Netherlands
Tel: (31) 70 4260260
Fax: (31) 70 4260399
Email: nuffic@nuffic.nl
Website: www.nuffic.nl
Contact: Ms Rosalien van Santen, Information Officer

Since its founding in 1952, the Netherlands Organization for International Co-operation in Higher Education (NUFFIC) has been an independent, non-profit organization. Its mission is to foster international co-operation in higher education. Special attention is given to development co-operation.

NFP Netherlands Fellowships Programme for Development Co-operation

Subjects: All subjects offered by the Institutes for International Education in the Netherlands.
Purpose: To develop human potential through education and training mainly in the Netherlands with a view to diminishing qualitative and quantitative deficiencies in the availability of trained manpower in developing countries.
Eligibility: Open to candidates who have the education and work experience required for the course as well as an adequate command of the language in which it is conducted. This is usually English but sometimes French. The age limit is 40 for men and 45 for women. It is intended that candidates, upon completion of training, return to their home countries and resume their jobs. When several candidates with comparable qualifications apply, priority will be given to women. Candidates for a fellowship must be nominated by their employer and formal employment should be continued during the fellowship period.
Level of Study: Postgraduate
Type: Fellowship
Value: Normal living expenses, fees and health insurance. International travel expenses are provided only when the course lasts 3 months or longer
Length of Study: The duration of the course
Country of Study: The Netherlands
No. of awards offered: Varies
Application Procedure: Applicants must contact the Netherlands Embassy in their own country for information on nationality eligibility and on the application procedure. Information on the courses for which the fellowships are available can be obtained from the website.
Funding: Government
Additional Information: As a rule the candidate's government is required to state its formal support, except in the case of certain development-orientated non-government organizations. Further information is available from the website www.studyin.nl

NUFFIC-NFP Fellowships for Master's Degree Programmes

Subjects: Any subject on the list of eligible Master's degree programmes.
Purpose: To allow candidates to receive a postgraduate education and to earn either an MA, MSc or Professional Master's degree.
Eligibility: Applicant must be a national of one of 57 developing countries and have been admitted by a Dutch institution to one of the Master's degree programmes on the course list. Applicants who have received their education in any language other than English must provide International English Language Testing System scores (at least 5.5) or Test of English as a Foreign Language scores (at least 550).
Level of Study: Postgraduate
Type: Fellowship
Value: Tuition fees, cost of international travel, subsistence, books and health insurance
Length of Study: 9 months–2 years
Frequency: Annual
Study Establishment: A Dutch institution
Country of Study: The Netherlands
Application Procedure: Applicants may apply for an NFP fellowship through the Netherlands embassy or consulate in their own country. To do this, applicants must complete an NFP Master's degree programme application form and submit it together with all the required documents and information to the embassy or consulate well before the deadline. Forms can be obtained from the embassy or consulate or downloaded from the website, www.nuffic.nl/nfp
Additional Information: Applicants may not be employed by a large industrial, commercial and/or multinational firms.

For further information contact:

Contact the Netherlands embassy or consulate in home country

NUFFIC-NFP Fellowships for PhD Studies

Purpose: To allow candidates to pursue a PhD at one of 18 Dutch universities and institutes for international education.
Eligibility: Candidate must be a national of one of 57 developing countries and have been admitted to a Dutch institution as a PhD fellow. Priority will be given to female candidates and candidates from sub-Saharan Africa.
Level of Study: Doctorate
Type: Fellowship
Value: Up to €74,000
Length of Study: 4 years
Frequency: Annual
Study Establishment: Any one of 18 Dutch universities and institutes for international education. See list on website
Country of Study: The Netherlands
Application Procedure: After being accepted for admission to a Dutch institution, the candidate may submit a request for a PhD fellowship. Applicant must present a completed NFP PhD study application form to the Netherlands embassy or consulate in his/her own country. The application must be accompanied by the necessary documentation and by a research proposal that is supported by the supervisor(s). Form can be downloaded from website www.nuffic.nl/nfp
Closing Date: Before June 1st or October 1st
Additional Information: A large portion of the PhD research must take place in the candidate's home country.

For further information contact:

Contact the Netherlands embassy or consulate in home country

THE NETHERLANDS ORGANIZATION FOR SCIENTIFIC RESEARCH (NWO)

Lann van Nieuw Oost Indie 131, PO Box 93138, The Hague, NL-2509 AC, Netherlands
Tel: (31) (0) 70 344 06 40
Fax: (31) 70 385 0971
Email: nwo@nwo.nl
Website: www.nwo.nl
Contact: F.A.O. Grants Department

The Netherlands Organization for Scientific Research (NWO) is the central Dutch organization in the field of fundamental and strategic scientific research. NWO encompasses all fields of scholarship and consequently plays a key role in the development of science, technology and culture in the Netherlands. NWO is an independent organization that acts as the national research council in the Netherlands. NWO is the largest national sponsor of fundamental scientific research undertaken in the 13 Dutch universities and provides many types of funding for research driven by intellectual curiosity.

Dutch Russian Scientific Cooperation Programme
Subjects: Scientific research.
Purpose: To give a strong impulse to the scientific collaboration between the two countries.
Eligibility: Open to all talented Dutch researchers together with a Russian counterpart.
Level of Study: Postgraduate
Type: Fellowship
Value: €500,000
Length of Study: 5 years
No. of awards offered: 2
Closing Date: Sepetember 24th
Contributor: The Netherlands Organization for Scientific Research

Rubicon Programme
Subjects: Scientific research.
Purpose: To encourage talented researchers at Dutch Universities to dedicate themselves to a career in postdoctoral research.
Eligibility: Open to postgraduates who are currently engaged in Doctoral research.
Level of Study: Postdoctorate
Type: Grant
Value: €5.3 million a year
Length of Study: Up to 2 years
Application Procedure: A completed application form to be submitted via NOW's electronic submission system Iris.
Closing Date: April 1st, September 2nd and December 2nd.
Contributor: The Netherlands Ministry of Education, Culture and Science

For further information contact:

Tel: (0)70-3440 565
Email: rubicon@nwo.nl
Website: www.nwo.nl/rubicon
Contact: Coordinator Rubicon

WOTRO Integrated Programmes
Subjects: Development relevant research beyond MDG or thematic in the fields of poverty and hunger; global health and health systems; sustainable environment; global relationships.
Purpose: To support excellent demand-driven interdisciplinary research programmes to the benefit of development and societal issues in the South.
Eligibility: Applications must be submitted by a senior researcher affiliated at a Dutch academic institute together with a senior researcher from a developing country; the research team must include at least one (postdoc or PhD) researcher from a developing country; researchers must have appropriate degrees.
Level of Study: Postdoctorate, Doctorate
Type: Grant
Value: Salary costs, living allowances, communication and research costs to a maximum of €700,000
Length of Study: Up to 5 years (combining at least 2 doctorate and/or postdoctorate projects)
Frequency: Biannual
Application Procedure: Twice a year preliminary applications are selected. Selected applicants receive a grant for elaborating the application into a full proposal, in joint collaboration with scientific and non-scientific stakeholders.
Closing Date: February 17th
Contributor: WOTRO-Science for Global Development

THE NEUROBLASTOMA SOCIETY

Beverley House, Frilford, Abingdon, Oxfordshire, OX13 5NU, England
Tel: (44) 18 6539 1207
Email: info@nsoc.co.uk
Website: www.nsoc.co.uk
Contact: Antonya Cooper, Chairman

The Neuroblastoma Society was started in 1982 by a group of parents with children affected by neuroblastoma. The aim is to raise money to fund medical research towards better treatment and an eventual cure for this aggressive childhood tumour. The Society also aims to offer support to families affected by the disease.

Neuroblastoma Society Research Grants
Subjects: Paediatric oncology, specifically in neuroblastoma.
Purpose: To fund clinical research towards improvements in treatment and a cure for neuroblastoma.
Eligibility: There are no age or nationality restrictions but candidates must be based in the United Kingdom.
Value: Up to UK £35,000
Length of Study: 2–3 years
Frequency: Every 2 years
Study Establishment: A reputable research institution, usually a university or hospital
Country of Study: United Kingdom
No. of awards offered: Usually 3–4
Application Procedure: Applicants must apply to the Society for the terms of grant application. Application forms available on website.
Closing Date: Mid December
Funding: Private
Contributor: Members of the Society
No. of awards given last year: 6
No. of applicants last year: 12

THE NEW JERSEY STATE FEDERATION OF WOMEN'S CLUBS

Headquarter, 55 Labor Center Way, New Brunswick, NJ, 08901, United States of America
Tel: (1) 732 249 5474
Email: njsfwc@njsfwc.org
Website: www.njsfwc.org

The New Jersey State Federation of Women's Clubs is the largest volunteer women's service organization in the state and a member of the General Federation of Women's Clubs, which provides opportunities for education, leadership training and community service through participation in local clubs and enabling members to make a difference in the lives of others.

Margaret Yardley Fellowship
Subjects: All subjects.
Purpose: To help female students who are in financial need.
Eligibility: Open to female graduate or doctoral students, whose residence is in New Jersey, USA.
Level of Study: Doctorate, Postgraduate
Type: Fellowship
Value: US$1,000
Frequency: Annual
No. of awards offered: Varies
Application Procedure: Applicants must request applications prior to February 1st and requests must include a self-addressed, stamped envelope.
Closing Date: March 1st
Funding: Private
No. of awards given last year: 7
No. of applicants last year: 9

THE NEW JERSEY WATER ENVIRONMENT ASSOCIATION (NJWEA)

Department of Environmental Sciences, ENRSB, Cook College,
Rutgers University, 14 College Farm Road, New Brunswick, NJ,
08901 8551, United States of America
Tel: (1) 732 932 8078
Fax: (1) 732 932 8644
Email: strom@aesop.rutgers.edu
Website: www.njwea.org

The New Jersey Water Environment Association (NJWEA) is a non-profit educational organization dedicated to preserving and enhancing the water environment. NJWEA was founded in 1915 and is one of the oldest organization in the United States of America. With a membership of 2,800 engineers, operators, scientists, students and other professionals, the NJWEA is an environmental leader in New Jersey.

NJWEA Scholarship Award Program

Subjects: Environmental science and engineering.
Purpose: To further encourage highly capable individuals to continue studies in environmental science or engineering with a strong component in one or more areas of water pollution control and environmental protection or hazardous waste management.
Eligibility: Open to students who are enrolled in a full-time programme leading to a degree in environmental science, environmental engineering or a closely related field with an emphasis on appropriate technical aspects of environmental protection or water pollution control.
Level of Study: Postgraduate
Type: Scholarship and award
Value: US$1,500–2,500 each, and totaling $34,500 annually
Frequency: Annual
Country of Study: United States of America
No. of awards offered: 14
Application Procedure: Application forms can be downloaded from the website.
Closing Date: March 1st
Contributor: New Jersey Water Enviroment Association
Additional Information: The awards are based on academic performance, merit, scholastic ability and demonstrated interest in environmental science or engineering.

NEW SOUTH WALES ARCHITECTS REGISTRATION BOARD

Level 2, 156 Gloucester Street, Sydney, NSW, 2000, Australia
Tel: (61) 2 9241 4033
Fax: (61) 2 9241 6144
Email: mail@architects.nsw.gov.au
Website: www.architects.nsw.gov.au
Contact: Ms Mae Cruz, Deputy Registrar

Byera Hadley Travelling Scholarships

Subjects: Architecture.
Purpose: To allow candidates to undertake a course of study, research or other activity approved by the Board as contributing to the advancement of architecture.
Eligibility: Open to graduates or students of four accredited schools of architecture in New South Wales. Applicants must be Australian citizens.
Level of Study: Graduate, Postgraduate, Research
Type: Scholarship
Value: The total value of the combined awards is Australian $65,000, comprising two Registered Architect awards of Australian $30,000 and $11,000, one graduate award of Australian $8,000 and four student awards of Australian $4,000 each
Frequency: Annual
Country of Study: Any country
No. of awards offered: 7
Application Procedure: Applicants must write for details.
Closing Date: The deadline for all awards is July 30th
Funding: Private
Contributor: A bequest from the estate of the late Byera Hadley, an Australian architect

No. of awards given last year: 6
No. of applicants last year: 15
Additional Information: A report suitable for publication must be submitted within 12 months of the date of the award.

NSW Architects Registration Board Research Grant

Subjects: Any architectural topic approved by the board.
Purpose: To provide assistance to those wishing to undertake research on a topic approved by the Board to contribute to the advancement of architecture.
Eligibility: Open to candidates who are registered as architects in New South Wales.
Level of Study: Professional development
Value: Australian $20,000
Length of Study: 1 year
Frequency: Every 2 years
Country of Study: Australia
No. of awards offered: 1
Application Procedure: Applicants must write for details.
Funding: Government
No. of awards given last year: None
Additional Information: A report is to be submitted upon completion of tenure.

NEW SOUTH WALES MINISTRY OF THE ARTS

Level 9 St James Centre, 111 Elizabeth Street PO Box A226, NSW,
1235, Australia
Tel: (61) 2 92285533
Fax: (61) 2 92284722
Email: mail@arts.nsw.gov.au
Website: www.arts.nsw.gov.au

New South Wales Ministry of the Arts works closely with the State's 8 major cultural institutions, providing policy advice to Government on their operations.

Western Sydney Artists Fellowship

Subjects: Creative arts.
Purpose: To encourage artists and students in the field of creative arts.
Eligibility: Open to applicants who are residents of Western Sydney or whose practice is located primarily in Western Sydney.
Level of Study: Postgraduate
Type: Fellowship
Value: Australian $5,000–25,000
Length of Study: 1 year
Frequency: Annual
Study Establishment: New South Wales, Sydney Western Suburbs
Country of Study: Australia
Closing Date: September

NEW YORK FOUNDATION FOR THE ARTS (NYFA)

155 Avenue of the Americas, 6th Floor, New York, NY, 10013-1507,
United States of America
Tel: (1) 212 366 6900
Fax: (1) 212 366 1778
Email: deleget@nyfa.org
Website: www.nyfa.org

New York Foundation for the Arts (NYFA), founded in 1971, helps artists turn inspiration into art by giving more money and support to individual artists and arts organizations than any other comparable institution in the United States of America.

NYFA Artists' Fellowships

Subjects: Computer arts, crafts, cross-disciplinary/performative work, film, non-fiction literature, poetry,printmaking/drawing/artists' books and sculpture.
Purpose: To help the arts to flourish in New York State as well as nationally.

Eligibility: Open to residents of New York/any Indian national who is at least 18 years of age and not enrolled in any degree programme.
Level of Study: Professional development
Type: Fellowships
Value: US$7,000
Frequency: Annual
Application Procedure: Applicants must apply online.
Closing Date: October 3rd

NEW YORK STATE HISTORICAL ASSOCIATION

PO Box 800, 5798 State Highway 80, Cooperstown, NY 13326-0800, United States of America
Tel: (1) 607 547 1480
Fax: (1) 607 547 1405
Email: mason@nysha.org
Website: www.nysha.org
Contact: Ms Catherine Mason, Assistant Editor

The mission of the New York State Historical Association is to instil and cultivate, in a broad public audience, an informed appreciation of the diversity of the American past, especially as represented and exemplified by the history of New York State, in order to better understand the present.

Dixon Ryan Fox Manuscript Prize of the New York State Historical Association
Subjects: The history of New York state.
Purpose: To honour the best unpublished book-length monograph.
Eligibility: Open to nationals of any country. Biographies may be included. Fiction and poetry are not eligible entries.
Level of Study: Unrestricted
Type: Prize
Value: US$3,000 plus assistance in publishing
Length of Study: Dependent on the book length
Frequency: Annual
No. of awards offered: 1
Application Procedure: Applicants must submit two copies of the manuscript, typed and double-spaced with at least 1 inch margins.
Closing Date: January 20th
Funding: Private
No. of awards given last year: 0
No. of applicants last year: 6

NEW ZEALAND AGENCY FOR INTERNATIONAL DEVELOPMENT (NZAID)

195 Lambton Quay, Private Bag 18-901, Wellington, New Zealand
Tel: (64) 4 439 8200
Fax: (64) 4 439 8515
Email: enquiries@nzaid.govt.nz
Website: www.nzaid.govt.nz

NZAID is a government agency responsible for delivering New Zealand's Official Development Assistance (ODA) and for advising Ministers on development assistance policy and operations. Its main purpose is to give a distinctive profile and new focus to ODA programme. Its team of development specialists aim in reducing poverty. NZAID helps to eliminate poverty and fulfilling basic needs through development partnerships, particularly in the Pacific region, and also supports projects in Asia, Africa and Latin America.

Commonwealth Scholarships
Subjects: All subjects.
Purpose: To make a significant contribution to the development of candidate's home country for elimination of poverty and to address the human resource development needs of developing countries.
Eligibility: Open to candidates who have strong academic merit and preference will be given to candidates who nominate fields of study relevant to the development of their home country.
Level of Study: Postgraduate
Type: Scholarships

Value: Varies
Length of Study: For masters 2 years and doctorates 4 years
Frequency: Annual
Country of Study: New Zealand
No. of awards offered: 10
Application Procedure: For more details, see Commonwealth Scholarships and Fellowships Plan (CSFP) website.
Funding: Government
Contributor: New Zealand's International Aid and Development Agency (NZAID) and administered by the New Zealand Vice-Chancellors' Committee

New Zealand Development Scholarships (NZDS)
Subjects: All subjects.
Purpose: To enable the students to study in areas of developmental relevance and make a significant impact on return to their home countries.
Eligibility: Open to candidates who are citizens of an eligible developing country and not have New Zealand or Australian residence status or citizenship (excluding the Cook Islands), must normally be living in home country, have a B grade average (or higher) on most recently completed tertiary qualification, must not currently be studying, and not have been a recipient of any NZAID or other government scholarship within the last 12 months.
Level of Study: Postgraduate
Type: Scholarships
Value: Scholarships cover tuition fees, enrolment/orientation fees, return economy travel, medical insurance, and an allowance to meet course and basic living costs
Frequency: Annual
Country of Study: New Zealand
Application Procedure: Check the website for specific details.
Funding: Government
Contributor: The New Zealand Agency for International Development on behalf of the New Zealand Ministry of Foreign Affairs and Trade (MFAT)
Additional Information: NZDS has two categories, public and open. A candidate can only apply under one of the categories.

New Zealand Regional Development Scholarships
Subjects: All subjects.
Purpose: For Pacific Islanders to gain knowledge and skills in priority fields of study so that they can directly contribute to the sustainable development of key sectors in their home country.
Eligibility: Open to candidates who are citizens of a participating country (i.e. permanent residents are not eligible to apply), must be aged 17 or over before the scholarship start date, not hold another scholarship, or have held a New Zealand or Australian Government scholarship in the preceding 24 months at the time of application, satisfy the admission requirements of the education institution, and be able to take up the scholarship in the academic year for which it is offered.
Level of Study: Postgraduate
Type: Scholarships
Value: Tuition and enrolment fees, scholarship–related travel, an establishment allowance and a basic stipend
Length of Study: 2 years
Frequency: Every 2 years
Application Procedure: Applicants must apply directly to a nominating authority in their home country, nominating authority undertakes an initial screening of applications and sends shortlisted candidates to the NZRDS.
Funding: Government
Contributor: New Zealand Government's Official Development Assistance programme and is administered by NZAID. AusAID and NZAID jointly fund Regional Development Scholarships for the Cook Islands

Short-Term Training Awards (NZ)
Subjects: All subjects.
Purpose: To provide short-term vocational and/or skills courses or work attachments.
Eligibility: Open for the candidates of Pacific Islands, Latin America, and South East Asia. Eligibility varies according to the countries.
Type: Scholarships

Value: Payment of fees, return economy air fares, an establishment grant, a basic living allowance, and provision for health care
Length of Study: Up to 1 year
No. of awards offered: Varies
Application Procedure: Applicants must apply to the nominating authority in their home country responsible for selecting candidates for study or training abroad under development country programmes. Check website for further details.

THE NEW ZEALAND VICE CHANCELLORS COMMITTEE (NZVCC)

Level 11, 94 Dixon Street, PO Box 11915, Wellington, 6142, New Zealand
Tel: (64) 404 381 8500
Fax: (64) 404 381 8501
Email: kiri@nzvcc.ac.nz
Website: www.nzvcc.ac.nz
Contact: Kiri Manuera, Scholarships Manager

The New Zealand Vice Chancellors Committee (NZVCC) was established by the Universities Act 1961, which replaced the federal University of New Zealand with separate institutions. Today the Committee represents the interests of New Zealand's 8 universities. The NZVCC represents the interests of the New Zealand university system to government, its agencies and the public through a range of forums and communications from joint consultative groups to electronic and print publications.

The Association of University Staff Crozier Scholarship
Subjects: History, management, organization, economics, economic and social impact, sociology and pedagogy.
Purpose: To provide funds for individuals to undertake research towards an Honours, Master's or Doctoral degree and who are undertaking research or scholarly enquiry for a research project, theses or dissertation at a New Zealand or overseas university or research institution in the related fields.
Eligibility: Open to applicants who are citizens or permanent residents of New Zealand who have resided in New Zealand for at least 3 years.
Level of Study: Postgraduate
Type: Scholarship
Value: New Zealand $5,000
Frequency: Annual
Country of Study: New Zealand
Closing Date: October 1st
Contributor: New Zealand Vice Chancellors Committee Wellington

Cambridge Commonwealth Trust Prince of Wales Scholarship
Subjects: All subjects.
Purpose: To enable bright, young students of high academic ability to study at Cambridge University in Britain.
Eligibility: Open to citizens of New Zealand who wish to pursue a course of research leading to a PhD degree at Cambridge University. The candidate shoud have also applied for admission to Cambridge.
Level of Study: Doctorate, Research
Type: Scholarship
Value: The scholarship covers the University Composition Fee at the home rate along with a maintenance allowance
Length of Study: 3 years
Frequency: Annual
Study Establishment: Cambridge University
Country of Study: United Kingdom
Closing Date: October 1st

Claude McCarthy Fellowships
Subjects: All subjects.
Purpose: To enable graduates of a New Zealand university to undertake original work or research.
Eligibility: Open to any graduate of a New Zealand university.
Level of Study: Postgraduate, Doctorate
Type: Fellowship
Value: Varies, according to country of residence during tenure, and the project itself. Assistance for expenses incurred in travel,

employment of technical staff, special equipment, etc. may be provided
Length of Study: Usually no more than 1 year
Frequency: Annual
Country of Study: Any country
No. of awards offered: Varies, depending upon funds available, but usually 12–15
Application Procedure: Applicants must write for details.
Closing Date: August 1st
Funding: Private
Contributor: The Claude McCarthy Trust
Additional Information: Further information is available on request.

Dick and Mary Earle Scholarship in Technology
Subjects: Innovation and product development and bioprocess technology.
Purpose: To provide funds for individuals to undertake research towards a Masterate or Doctorate degree at a New Zealand university or research institution in related fields.
Eligibility: Open to candidates who are citizens or permanent residents of New Zealand, who have resided in New Zealand for at least 3 years and have completed the requirements for a BTech, BEng, BE degree or equivalent, with Honours at a New Zealand university.
Level of Study: Postgraduate
Type: Scholarships
Value: New Zealand $17,000 per year at Master's level and New Zealand $20,000 per year at PhD level
Frequency: Annual
Country of Study: New Zealand
No. of awards offered: 6
Closing Date: October 1st

Fish & Game New Zealand Research Scholarships
Subjects: Natural and physical sciences of fish and game, or the management of fish and game, social, cultural or political issues in the context of fish and game.
Purpose: To assist in the research of scientific, management, social, cultural and political issues related to New Zealand freshwater sportsfish and game birds.
Eligibility: Open to citizens or to permanent residents of New Zealand, who are studying full-time at Honour's, Master's, Doctoral or postdoctoral level at a New Zealand tertiary institution.
Level of Study: Research
Type: Research scholarship
Value: New Zealand $10,000
Frequency: Annual
Country of Study: New Zealand
No. of awards offered: 1
Closing Date: October 1st

Gordon Watson Scholarship
Subjects: International relationships and social and economic conditions.
Purpose: To enable the holder to study abroad questions of international relationships or social and economic conditions, at Masters or PhD level.
Eligibility: Candidates must be New Zealand citizens or permanent residents. Open to holders of an Honours degree, or a degree in theology from a university in New Zealand. Candidates must undertake to return to New Zealand after the scholarship period for not less than 2 years.
Level of Study: Postgraduate
Type: Scholarship
Value: New Zealand $12,000 per year
Length of Study: 3 years
Frequency: Annual
Study Establishment: Any approved university
No. of awards offered: 1
Application Procedure: Candidates must write for details.
Closing Date: March 1st
Funding: Private
Contributor: The Gordon Watson Trust
Additional Information: Further information is available on request.

L B Wood Travelling Scholarship

Subjects: All subjects.
Purpose: To allow graduates to undertake doctoral studies in the United Kingdom.
Eligibility: Open to all holders of postgraduate scholarships from any faculty of any university in New Zealand, provided that application is made within 3 years of the date of graduation.
Level of Study: Doctorate
Type: Scholarship
Value: New Zealand $3,000 per year, as a supplement to another postgraduate scholarship
Length of Study: Up to 3 years
Frequency: Annual
Study Establishment: A university or institution of university rank
Country of Study: United Kingdom
No. of awards offered: 1
Application Procedure: Applicants must write for details.
Closing Date: March 1st
Funding: Private
Contributor: The L B Wood Trust
Additional Information: Further information is available on request.

Shirtcliffe Fellowship

Subjects: Arts, science, law, commerce and agriculture.
Purpose: To assist students of outstanding ability and character who are graduates of a university in New Zealand, in the continuation of their doctoral studies in New Zealand or the Commonwealth.
Eligibility: Candidates for a doctoral scholarship awarded by a New Zealand university; andwhose degree is awarded in any faculty or school which, if that degree had been available in 1935, would in the opinion of the NZVCC be expected to have been awarded following a course of study in one or other of the faculties of arts, science, law, commerce or agriculture.
Level of Study: Doctorate
Type: Fellowship
Value: New Zealand $5,000 as a supplement to the postgraduate scholarship emolument
Length of Study: Up to 3 years
Frequency: Annual
Study Establishment: A suitable Institute of Higher Education
No. of awards offered: 1
Application Procedure: Candidates must write for details.
Closing Date: March 1st
Funding: Private
Additional Information: Further information is available on request.

William Georgetti Scholarships

Subjects: All subjects.
Purpose: To encourage postgraduate study and research in a field that is important to the social, cultural or economic development of New Zealand.
Eligibility: Candidates must be New Zealand citizens or permanent residents. Open to graduates who have been resident in New Zealand for 5 years immediately before application and who are preferably aged between 21 and 28 years.
Level of Study: Postgraduate
Type: Scholarship
Value: Up to New Zealand $10,000 for study in New Zealand and up to $20,000 per year for Masters study and $30,000 per year for doctoral study
Frequency: Annual
Study Establishment: Suitable universities
Country of Study: Any country
No. of awards offered: 12
Application Procedure: Applicants must write for details.
Closing Date: October 1st
Funding: Private
Contributor: The Georgetti Trust
Additional Information: Further information is available on request.

NEWBERRY LIBRARY

60 West Walton Street, Chicago, IL, 60610, United States of America
Tel: (1) 312 255 3666
Fax: (1) 312 255 3680
Email: research@newberry.org
Website: www.newberry.org
Contact: Ms Molly Schultz, Programme Assistant

The Newberry Library, open to the public without charge, is an independent research library and educational institution dedicated to the expansion and dissemination of knowledge in the humanities. With a broad range of books and manuscripts relating to the civilizations of Western Europe and the Americas, the Library's mission is to acquire and preserve research collections of such material, and to provide for and promote their effective use by a diverse community of users.

American Society for Eighteenth-Century Studies (ASECS) Fellowship

Subjects: Arts and humanities from 1660 to 1815.
Purpose: To support scholars wanting to use the Newberry's collections.
Eligibility: A fellowship holder must be an ABD graduate student or post-doctoral, holding the PhD. or equivalent degree at the time of the application.
Level of Study: Doctorate, Postdoctorate
Type: Fellowship
Value: $1,700 per month or $1,200 per month including housing in the Society's
Length of Study: 1 month
Frequency: Annual
Study Establishment: The Newberry Library
Country of Study: United States of America
No. of awards offered: 1
Application Procedure: Applicants must submit a completed application form, a description of the project and three letters of reference.
Closing Date: March 1st
Funding: Private
Contributor: ASECS
No. of awards given last year: 1
No. of applicants last year: 16

Arthur Weinberg Fellowship for Independent Scholars

Subjects: Humanities.
Purpose: To assist scholars working outside the academy who have demonstrated excellence through publishing and are working in a field appropriate to the Newberry's collections.
Eligibility: Open to all scholars but preference is given to those working on historical issues related to social justice or reform.
Level of Study: Unrestricted
Type: Fellowship
Value: US$1,600
Length of Study: 1 month
Frequency: Annual
Study Establishment: The Newberry Library
Country of Study: United States of America
No. of awards offered: Varies
Application Procedure: Applicants must write for details. Application forms can be downloaded from the website.
Closing Date: March 2nd
Funding: Private
No. of awards given last year: 1
No. of applicants last year: 1

Audrey Lumsden-Kouvel Fellowship

Subjects: Portuguese, Spanish, and Latin American studies are especially welcome, as are translation projects
Purpose: To enable scholars to use the Newberry's extensive holdings. The fellowship is intended to encourage scholars to pursue research at the Newberry during sabbaticals.
Eligibility: Open to postdoctoral scholars wishing to carry out extended research. Applicants must plan to be in continuous residence for at least 3 months. Preference will be given to projects focusing on romance cultures.
Level of Study: Postdoctorate
Type: Fellowship
Value: US$25,500

Length of Study: 6 months
Frequency: Annual
Study Establishment: The Newberry Library
Country of Study: United States of America
No. of awards offered: 1
Application Procedure: Applicants must write for details. Application forms can be downloaded from the website.
Closing Date: March 1st
Funding: Private
No. of awards given last year: 1
No. of applicants last year: 21

Committee on Institutional Co-operation Faculty Fellowship

Subjects: American Indian studies.
Purpose: To support research at the Newberry by CIC faculty.
Eligibility: Open to faculty members of a CIC institution.
Level of Study: Postdoctorate
Type: Fellowship
Value: US$40,000
Length of Study: A minimum of 9 months
Frequency: Annual
Study Establishment: The Newberry Library
Country of Study: United States of America
No. of awards offered: 1
Application Procedure: Applicants must contact the CIC programme at the D'Arcy McNickle Centre for American Indian history at mcnickle@newberry.org
Closing Date: January 6th
Funding: Government, private
Contributor: The Committee on Institutional Co-operation
No. of awards given last year: 1
Additional Information: In addition to carrying out this independent research, the CIC Faculty Fellow will lead a Spring seminar at the Library for graduate students at CIC institutions on a topic appropriate to the Newberry's collections and the expertise of the Fellow.

Frances C Allen Fellowships

Subjects: Humanities and social sciences.
Purpose: To encourage women of American Indian heritage in their studies through financial support.
Eligibility: Open to women of American Indian heritage who are pursuing an academic programme in any graduate or preprofessional field.
Level of Study: Postgraduate, Graduate
Type: Fellowship
Value: Varies according to need and may include travel expenses. Up to US$8,000 in approved expenses is available
Length of Study: 1 month–1 year
Frequency: Annual
Study Establishment: The Newberry Library
Country of Study: United States of America
No. of awards offered: Varies
Application Procedure: Applicants must write for details. Application forms can be downloaded from the website.
Closing Date: March 1st
Funding: Private
Contributor: The Frances C Allen Fund
No. of awards given last year: 4
No. of applicants last year: 5
Additional Information: Allen Fellows are expected to spend a significant part of their tenure in residence at the Newberry's D'Arcy McNickle Centre for American Indian History.

Frederick Burkhardt Residential Fellowships for Recently Tenured Scholars

Subjects: Humanities.
Purpose: To support long-term unusually ambitious projects in humanities and related social sciences.
Eligibility: Open to recently tenured humanists – scholars who will have begun their first tenured contracts by the aplication deadline but began their first tenured contracts no earlier than the fall semester or quarter. An applicant must be employed in a tenured position at a degree-granting academic institution in the US, remaining so for the duration of the fellowship.

Level of Study: Postdoctorate
Type: Fellowship
Value: $75,000
Length of Study: 1 academic year (normally 9 months)
Study Establishment: The Newberry Library
Country of Study: United States of America
No. of awards offered: 10
Application Procedure: Applicants must submit online application. It must include completed application form, proposal, bibliography, publications list, three reference letters and one institutional statement.
Closing Date: September 27th
Funding: Private
Contributor: The Andrew W. Mellon Foundation

For further information contact:

Website: http://ofa.acls.org

Herzog August Bibliothek Wolfenbüttel Fellowship

Subjects: Humanities.
Purpose: To enable a period of residence in Wolfenbüttel, Germany for study of the collections housed in the Herzog August Bibliothek.
Level of Study: Postdoctorate
Type: Fellowship
Value: €1,050 per month plus up to €1600 travel expenses
Length of Study: 2–12 months
Frequency: Annual
Study Establishment: The Herzog August Bibliothek in Wolfenbüttel
Country of Study: Germany
No. of awards offered: 1
Application Procedure: Applicants must write for details. Application forms may also be downloaded from the website.
Closing Date: January 31st
Funding: Private
No. of awards given last year: 1
No. of applicants last year: 2

For further information contact:

Herzog August Bibliothek, Postfach 13 64, D- 38299 Wolfenbüttel, United States of America
Tel: (1) 05331/808-208
Fax: (1) 05331/808-266
Contact: Dr Gillian Bepler Committee on Awards, The Newberry Library

Institute for the International Education of Students Faculty Fellowships

Subjects: Humanities.
Eligibility: Open to faculty members from any IES centre.
Level of Study: Postdoctorate
Value: $1,600 plus travel and lodging expenses
Length of Study: 2 month
Frequency: Annual
Study Establishment: The Newberry Library
Country of Study: United States of America
No. of awards offered: 2
Application Procedure: Applicants must submit an application, project description, curriculum vitae and letters of reference. Applicants should visit the wesite for further details and application forms.
Closing Date: March 1st
Funding: Private
Contributor: Institute for the International Education of Students
No. of awards given last year: 2
No. of applicants last year: 8

Lester J Cappon Fellowship in Documentary Editing

Subjects: Editing and archiving.
Purpose: To support historical editing projects based on Newberry materials.
Eligibility: Open to scholars who live outside the Chicago area.
Level of Study: Postdoctorate
Type: Fellowship
Value: Up to US$5,000
Length of Study: Varies

Frequency: Annual
Study Establishment: The Newberry Library
Country of Study: United States of America
No. of awards offered: 1
Application Procedure: Applicants must write for details. Application forms can be downloaded from the website.
Closing Date: March 1st
Funding: Private
Contributor: Lester J Cappon
No. of awards given last year: 2
No. of applicants last year: 3

Lloyd Lewis Fellowship in American History

Subjects: Any field of American history appropriate to the collections of the Newberry Library.
Purpose: To pursue projects in any area of American history appropriate to the Newberry's collections.
Eligibility: Open to established scholars, holding a PhD, who have demonstrated excellence in the field through publications. Foreign nationals may apply if they have resided in the United States of America for 3 or more years.
Level of Study: Postdoctorate
Type: Fellowship
Value: Up to US$50,400
Length of Study: 6–11 months
Frequency: Annual
Study Establishment: The Newberry Library
Country of Study: United States of America
No. of awards offered: Varies
Application Procedure: Candidates must write for details. Application forms can be downloaded from the website.
Closing Date: January 12th
Funding: Private
Contributor: The Lloyd Lewis Memorial Fund
No. of awards given last year: 1
No. of applicants last year: 25
Additional Information: Lewis Fellows participate in the Library's scholarly community through regular participation in seminars, colloquia and other events. Lewis Fellowships may be combined with sabbaticals or other stipendiary support. Candidates may ask to be considered for NEH and Mellon Fellowships at the time of their application.

Mellon Postdoctoral Research Fellowship

Subjects: Humanities.
Purpose: To support residential research and writing.
Eligibility: Open to postdoctoral scholars in any field of relevance to the Library's collection.
Level of Study: Postdoctorate
Type: Fellowship
Value: Up to US$50,400
Length of Study: 6–11 months
Frequency: Annual
Study Establishment: The Newberry Library
Country of Study: United States of America
No. of awards offered: Varies
Application Procedure: Applicants must write for details. Application forms can be downloaded from the website. Completed applications must include three letters of recommendation.
Closing Date: January 12th
Funding: Private
Contributor: The Mellon Foundation
No. of awards given last year: 3
No. of applicants last year: 94
Additional Information: Fellows will become part of Newberry's community of scholars, participating in biweekly fellows seminars, colloquial and other events.

Midwest Modern Language Association (MMLA) Fellowship

Subjects: Humanities.
Purpose: To support for work in residence at the Newberry.
Eligibility: Open to scholars with current MMLA membership at time of application and through the period of the fellowship.
Level of Study: Doctorate, Postdoctorate
Type: Fellowship

Value: $1,600
Length of Study: 1 month
Frequency: Annual
Study Establishment: The Newberry Library
Country of Study: United States of America
No. of awards offered: 1
Application Procedure: Candidates must submit an application, project description, curriculum vitae and letters of reference. Candidates should visit the website for further details and application forms.
Closing Date: March 1st
Funding: Private
Contributor: Midwest Modern Language Association
No. of applicants last year: 7

Monticello College Foundation Fellowship for Women

Subjects: Any field appropriate to the Library's collections.
Purpose: To offer young women the opportunity to undertake work in residence at the Library and to significantly enhance their careers through research and writing.
Eligibility: Open to women who hold a PhD and are in the early stages of their academic careers. This academic award is designed for a woman whose work gives clear promise of scholarly productivity and who would benefit significantly from 6 months of research, writing and participation in the intellectual life of the library. Other things being equal, preference is given to the applicant whose proposed study is concerned with the study of women.
Level of Study: Postdoctorate
Type: Fellowship
Value: US$25,500
Length of Study: 6 months
Frequency: Annual
Study Establishment: The Newberry Library
Country of Study: United States of America
No. of awards offered: 1
Application Procedure: Applicants must write for details. Application forms can be downloaded from the website.
Closing Date: January 10th
Funding: Private
Contributor: The Monticello College Foundation
No. of awards given last year: 1
No. of applicants last year: 27

National Endowment for the Humanities (NEH) Fellowships

Subjects: Any field appropriate to the Library's collections.
Purpose: To support projects in any field appropriate to the Library's collections
Eligibility: Open to citizens of the United States of America or foreign nationals who have been resident in the United States of America for 3 years, who are established scholars at the postdoctoral level or its equivalent. Preference is given to candidates who have not held major fellowships for 3 years preceding the proposed period of residency.
Level of Study: Postdoctorate
Type: Fellowships
Value: Up to US$50,400
Length of Study: 6–11 months
Frequency: Annual
Study Establishment: The Newberry Library
Country of Study: United States of America
No. of awards offered: Varies
Application Procedure: Candidates must write for an application form. Completed application forms must include all letters of reference. Application forms can be downloaded from the website.
Closing Date: January 10th
Funding: Government
Contributor: The NEH
No. of awards given last year: 3
No. of applicants last year: 79
Additional Information: Candidates may combine this award with sabbatical or other stipendiary support. Scholars conducting research in American history may also ask to be considered for the Lloyd Lewis Fellowship at the time of their application.

Newberry Library British Academy Fellowship for Study in Great Britain

Subjects: Humanities.

Purpose: To allow an individual to study in the United Kingdom in any field in which the Newberry's collections are strong.

Eligibility: Open to established scholars at the postdoctoral level or equivalent. Preference is given to readers and staff of the Newberry Library and to established Scholars who have previously used the Newberry Library.

Level of Study: Postdoctorate

Type: Fellowship

Value: A stipend of UK £1,350 per month while in the United Kingdom

Length of Study: Up to 3 months

Frequency: Annual

Country of Study: United Kingdom

No. of awards offered: Varies

Application Procedure: Applicants must write for details. Application forms can be downloaded from the website.

Closing Date: January 12th

Funding: Private

Contributor: The British Academy

No. of awards given last year: 1

No. of applicants last year: 3

Additional Information: The home institution is expected to continue to pay the Fellow's salary.

Newberry Library Ecole des Chartes Exchange Fellowship

Subjects: Renaissance studies.

Purpose: To enable a graduate student to study at the Ecole des Chartes in Paris.

Eligibility: Preference is given to graduate students at institutions in the Renaissance Centre Consortium.

Level of Study: Doctorate

Type: Fellowship

Value: Varies, but provides a monthly stipend and free tuition

Length of Study: 3 months

Frequency: Annual

Study Establishment: The Ecole des Chartes

Country of Study: France

No. of awards offered: Varies

Application Procedure: Applicants must write for details. Application forms can be downloaded from the website.

Closing Date: January 12th

Funding: Private

Contributor: The Ecole des Chartes

No. of awards given last year: 2

No. of applicants last year: 4

Additional Information: The Ecole des Chartes is the oldest institution in Europe specializing in the archival sciences, including palaeography, bibliography, textual editing and the history of the book.

Newberry Library Short-Term Fellowship in the History of Cartography

Subjects: The history of cartography.

Purpose: To financially support work in residence at the Newberry on projects related to the history of cartography.

Eligibility: Open to established scholars of any nationality, but limited to scholars who live outside the Chicago area.

Level of Study: Doctorate, Postdoctorate

Type: Fellowship

Value: US$1,600 per month

Length of Study: 1 week–2 months

Frequency: Annual

Study Establishment: The Newberry Library

Country of Study: United States of America

No. of awards offered: 1–2

Application Procedure: Applicants must submit an application, project description, curriculum vitae and letters of reference. Applicants must visit the website for further details and application forms.

Closing Date: March 2nd

Funding: Private

Contributor: Arthur Holzheimer

No. of awards given last year: 2

No. of applicants last year: 6

Newberry Library Short-Term Resident Fellowships for Individual Research

Subjects: Any field appropriate to the Library's collections.

Purpose: To provide access to Newberry's collections for those who live beyond commuting distance from Chicago.

Eligibility: Open to nationals of any country who hold a PhD degree or have completed all requirements for the degree except the dissertation. Awards are limited to scholars from outside the Chicago area.

Level of Study: Doctorate, Postdoctorate

Type: Fellowship

Value: US$1,600 per month

Length of Study: 1 week–2 months

Frequency: Annual

Study Establishment: The Newberry Library

Country of Study: United States of America

No. of awards offered: Varies

Application Procedure: Applicants must write for details. Application forms can be downloaded from the website.

Closing Date: March 2nd

Funding: Private

No. of awards given last year: 26

No. of applicants last year: 146

Northeast Modern Language Association (NEMLA) Fellowship

Subjects: Humanities.

Purpose: To support residential research at the library by members of NEMLA.

Eligibility: Open to scholars with current NEMLA membership at the time of application and through the period of the fellowship. Preference will be given to projects focusing on materials written in French, German, Italian or Spanish.

Level of Study: Doctorate, Postdoctorate

Value: $1,600

Length of Study: 1 month

Frequency: Annual

Study Establishment: The Newberry Library

Country of Study: United States of America

No. of awards offered: 1

Application Procedure: Applicants must submit an application, project description, curriculum vitae and letters of reference. Applicants should visit the website for further details and application forms.

Closing Date: March 2nd

Funding: Private

Contributor: Northeast Modern Language Association

No. of awards given last year: 1

No. of applicants last year: 2

South Central Modern Language Association Fellowship

Subjects: Humanities.

Purpose: To support residential research at the Library by members of the South Central Modern Language Association.

Eligibility: Open to scholars who live outside the Chicago area. Graduate students must have been SCMLA members for one year before applying. All other candidates must have been SCMLA members for two years before applying.

Level of Study: Doctorate

Type: Fellowship

Value: US$2,000

Length of Study: 1 month

Frequency: Annual

Study Establishment: The Newberry Library

Country of Study: United States of America

No. of awards offered: 1

Application Procedure: Candidates must write for details. Application forms can be downloaded from the website.

Closing Date: March 2nd

Funding: Private

Contributor: The South Central Modern Language Association

No. of awards given last year: 1

No. of applicants last year: 3

Susan Kelly Power and Helen Hornbeck Tanner Fellowship

Subjects: American Indian heritage.

Purpose: To support residential research.

Eligibility: Open to applicants with American Indian heritage.

Level of Study: Doctorate, Postdoctorate

Type: Fellowship
Value: US$1,600 per month
Length of Study: Up to 2 months
Frequency: Annual
Study Establishment: The Newberry Library
Country of Study: United States of America
No. of awards offered: 1
Application Procedure: Applicants must visit the website for application details and forms.
Closing Date: March 2nd
Funding: Private
No. of awards given last year: 1
No. of applicants last year: 2

Weiss/Brown Publication Subvention Award

Subjects: Humanities, particularly European civilization before 1700 in the areas of music, theatre, French or Italian literature or cultural studies.
Purpose: To subsidize the publication of a scholarly book and books.
Eligibility: Open to authors of books already accepted for publication.
Level of Study: Unrestricted
Type: Award
Value: Variable, up to US$15,000
Frequency: Annual
No. of awards offered: Varies
Application Procedure: Applicants must write for details. Application guidelines can be downloaded from the website. Applicants will be asked to provide detailed information regarding the publication and the subvention request.
Closing Date: January 12th
Funding: Private
Contributor: Roger Weiss and Howard Brown
No. of awards given last year: 1
No. of applicants last year: 4

NEWBY TRUST LIMITED

Hill Farm, Froxfield, Petersfield, Hampshire, GU32 1BQ, England
Tel: (44) 17 3082 7557
Email: info@newby-trust.org.uk
Website: www.newby-trust.org.uk
Contact: Miss W Gillam, Company Secretary

The Newby Trust Limited is a grant-giving charity working nationally, whose principal aims are to promote medical welfare, education and training and the relief of poverty.

Newby Trust Awards

Subjects: Grants are provided directly to universities or institutions in the United Kingdom to support education at the postgraduate or postdoctoral level.
Level of Study: Doctorate, Predoctorate, Postgraduate, Professional development
Type: Grant
Frequency: Annual
Study Establishment: United Kingdom universities or institutions
Country of Study: United Kingdom
No. of awards offered: Varies
Application Procedure: Individual applications are not accepted.
Funding: Private
Contributor: Funds from the Trust
No. of awards given last year: 135
No. of applicants last year: 600

NEWCASTLE UNIVERSITY

Manager, Student Financial Support, Newcastle University, 6 Kensington Terrace, Newcastle upon Tyne, NE1 7RU, United Kingdom
Tel: (44) 19 1222 5148
Fax: (44) 19 1222 5219
Email: international-scholarships@ncl.ac.uk
Website: www.ncl.ac.uk
Contact: Dr JWR Smith, Scholarships Officer

The Newcastle University, established in Newcastle in 1834, is one of the UK's leading universities and is known for its quality of teaching, outstanding research, and works with the regional and local communities, business and industry.

Alumni Tuition Fee Discount

Subjects: All subjects offered by the University, but some conditions apply
Purpose: To provide a discount for Newcastle University graduates.
Eligibility: Candidates for discounts must already have been offered a place to study at Newcastle University.
Level of Study: Graduate, Postgraduate, Doctorate, MBA, Research
Type: Other
Value: 10 per cent of the tuition fees
Length of Study: Duration of programme
Frequency: Annual
Study Establishment: Newcastle University
Country of Study: United Kingdom
Application Procedure: All eligible applicants who are offered a place to study at Newcastle University are considered for this discount. Applicants must check the website for details or contact the Student Financial Support Team.
Closing Date: September
Contributor: Newcastle University

International Family Discount (IFD)

Subjects: All subjects offered by the University.
Purpose: To provide a discount for international students.
Eligibility: Candidates for discounts must already have been offered a place to study at Newcastle University.
Level of Study: Graduate, Doctorate, MBA, Postgraduate, Research
Type: Other
Value: 10 per cent of the tuition fees
Length of Study: Duration of programme
Frequency: Annual
Study Establishment: Newcastle University
Country of Study: United Kingdom
Application Procedure: All eligible applicants who are offered a place to study at Newcastle University are invited to apply for one of these discounts. Applicants must check the website for details or contact the Student Financial Support Team.
Closing Date: September
Contributor: Newcastle University
No. of awards given last year: 25

Newcastle University International Postgraduate Scholarship (NUIPS)

Subjects: All subjects offered by the University.
Purpose: To provide a partial scholarship for international students.
Eligibility: Candidates for scholarships must already have been offered a place to study at Newcastle University.
Level of Study: Graduate, Postgraduate, MBA, Doctorate
Type: Partial scholarship
Value: UK £1,500 p.a
Length of Study: Duration of programme
Frequency: Annual
Study Establishment: Newcastle University
Country of Study: United Kingdom
No. of awards offered: Approx. 160
Application Procedure: All eligible applicants who are offered a place to study at Newcastle University are invited to apply for one of these scholarships. Applicants must check the website for details or contact the Student Financial Support Team.
Closing Date: May 22nd
Contributor: Newcastle University
No. of awards given last year: 60

NIJMEGEN CENTRE FOR MOLECULAR LIFE SCIENCES (NCMLS)

PO Box 9101, Nijmegen, 6500-HB, Netherlands
Tel: (31) 24 3610707
Fax: (31) 24 3610909
Email: info@ncmls.ru.nl
Website: www.ncmls.nl

Nijmegen Centre for Molecular Life Sciences (NCMLS) is a leading multidisciplinary research school within the domain of molecular mechanisms of disease and particularly in the fields of molecular medicine, cell biology and translational research.

NCMLS Tenure Track Research Fellowship

Subjects: Molecular life sciences.
Purpose: To establish an independent research group.
Eligibility: Open to candidates who have obtained their PhD and have recent international experience.
Level of Study: Research
Type: Fellowship
Value: Varies
Frequency: Annual
No. of awards offered: 1–2
Application Procedure: Applicants can download the expression of interest form from the website. Application can be sent to NCMLSFellow@ncmls.ru.nl
Closing Date: June 1st
Additional Information: All queries should be directed to Professor Dr Carl Figdor, Scientific Director.

NOAA COASTAL SERVICES CENTER

2234 South Hobson Avenue, Charleston, SC, 29405-2413,
United States of America
Tel: (1) 843 740 1200
Fax: (1) 843 740 1224
Email: csc.fellowships@noaa.gov
Website: www.csc.noaa.gov
Contact: Margaret Vanderwilt, Fellowship Programme Manager

The NOAA Coastal Services Center is an office within the National Oceanic and Atmospheric Administration that is devoted to serving the nation's state and local coastal resource management programmes.

NOAA Coastal Management Fellowship

Subjects: Natural resource management and environmental-related studies.
Purpose: To provide financial support to students with state coastal zone programmes to work on projects proposed by the state.
Eligibility: Open to students who will shortly complete a Master's, Doctoral or professional degree programme in natural resource management or environmental related studies at an accredited university in the United States.
Level of Study: Postgraduate
Type: Fellowships
Value: US$34,000
Length of Study: 2 years
Frequency: Annual
Country of Study: United States of America
No. of awards offered: 6
Application Procedure: Applicants must send in their transcript, interview references and curriculum vitae.
Closing Date: October 13th
Contributor: NOAA Coastal Services Center
Additional Information: Students from a broad range of environmental programmes are encouraged to apply.

NOAA Coral Management Assistantship

Subjects: Geography, natural resources, surveying, surveying technology, cartography and geographic information science.
Purpose: To provide assistantship to highly qualified recipients of Bachelor's and Master's degrees with hosts from coral management programmes within the United States Flag Pacific and Caribbean Islands.
Eligibility: Open to full-time students who are citizens of the United States.
Level of Study: Postgraduate
Type: Assistantship
Value: US$34,000
Length of Study: 2 years
Frequency: Annual
Country of Study: United States of America
No. of awards offered: 5
Contributor: NOAA Coastal Services Centre

NOAA Pacific Islands Assistantship Program

Subjects: Geography, natural resources, surveying, surveying technology, cartography and geographic information science.
Purpose: To support highly qualified recent recipients of Master's, Doctoral and professional degrees.
Eligibility: Open to full-time students who are citizens of the United States. Host for the applicants from each of the four Pacific Island coastal zone management (CZM) programmes: Hawaii, American Samoa, Guam and the Commonwealth of the Northern Mariana Islands is required.
Level of Study: Doctorate, Postgraduate
Type: Fellowships
Value: US$34,000–36,000
Length of Study: 2 years
Frequency: Annual
Country of Study: United States of America
No. of awards offered: 4
Application Procedure: Applicants must send in their interview and curriculum vitae details.

NORDIC AFRICA INSTITUTE (NAI)

PO Box 1703, Uppsala, SE75147, Sweden
Tel: (46) 18 562 200
Fax: (46) 18 562 290
Email: nai@nai.uu.se
Website: www.nai.uu.se
Contact: F.A.O. Grants Department

The Nordic Africa Institute (NAI) serves as a research, documentation and information centre on modern Africa for the Nordic countries. NAI also encourages research and studies on Africa in the Nordic countries and co-operation between Africa and Nordic researchers, as well as disseminating information about current African issues.

NAI Travel Scholarships for Research on Africa

Subjects: Anthropology, history, economics and human geography.
Purpose: To support research and preparation of research projects.
Eligibility: Open to researchers associated with Nordic universities, colleges and other research institutions. The applicants must have obtained a Bachelor's degree.
Level of Study: Research
Type: Travelling fellowship
Value: SEK 40,000
Frequency: Annual
Country of Study: Africa
No. of awards offered: 30–40
Application Procedure: Applicants must submit an application form, detailed plan of the project and copies of degree certificate and research permit.
Closing Date: January 15th
Additional Information: The format of the application form is available on the website.

NORTH ATLANTIC TREATY ORGANIZATION (NATO)

Public Diplomacy Division Office Nb 106 Boulevard Leopold III, 1110,
Brussels, Belgium
Tel: (32) 2 707 4111
Fax: (32) 2 707 5457
Email: natodoc@hq.nato.int
Website: www.nato.int
Contact: Academic Affairs Officer

The North Atlantic Treaty was signed in Washington on April 4, 1949, creating an alliance of 12 independent nations committed to each other's defence. Four more European nations later acceded to the Treaty between 1952 and 1982. On March 12, 1999, the Czech Republic, Hungary and Poland were welcomed into the Alliance, which now numbers 19 members.

Manfred Wörner Fellowship

Subjects: International relations.
Purpose: To honour the memory of the late Secretary General by focusing attention on his leadership in the transformation of the

alliance, including efforts at extending NATO's relations with CEE countries and promoting the principles and image of the Transatlantic partnership.
Eligibility: Open to applicants who are citizens of the EAPC countries with proven experience to carry out an important scholarly endeavour within the time limit of the Fellowship.
Level of Study: Professional development
Type: Fellowship
Value: 5,000 Euros including all travel costs
Frequency: Annual
Country of Study: Any country
Application Procedure: Application forms can be downloaded from the NATO website.
Closing Date: January 25th
Funding: Government

For further information contact:

Fax: 2 707 5457
Email: academics@hq.nato.int
Website: www.nato.int/acad/fellow/mwooe.htm

NORTH DAKOTA UNIVERSITY SYSTEM

600 East Boulevard, Bismarck, ND, 58505, United States of America
Tel: (1) 701 328 2960
Email: ndus.office@ndus.nodak.edu
Website: www.ndus.nodak.edu
Contact: Ms Rhonda Shaver, Co-ordinator

The North Dakota University System, governed by the State Board of Higher Education, comprises 11 public campuses.

North Dakota Indian Scholarship
Subjects: All subjects.
Purpose: To North Dakota's best and brightest high school graduates to encourage them to remain in North Dakota to obtain their post-secondary training.
Eligibility: Open to residents of North Dakota with a quarter degree of Indian blood who have been accepted for admission at an Institute of Higher Education or state vocational programme. Recipients must be enrolled full-time and have a grade point average above 2.0.
Level of Study: Doctorate, Postgraduate
Type: Scholarship
Value: US$500–2,000 per year
Frequency: Annual
Country of Study: United States of America
No. of awards offered: 45–50
Application Procedure: Applicants must complete an application form.
Closing Date: July 15th
Funding: Government
Contributor: The State
No. of awards given last year: 140

NORTH WEST CANCER RESEARCH FUND

22 Oxford Street, Liverpool, L7 7BL, England
Tel: (44) 15 1709 2919
Fax: (44) 15 1708 7997
Email: nwcrf@btclick.com
Website: www.cancerresearchnorthwest.co.uk
Contact: Mr A W Renison, General Secretary

North West Cancer Research Fund Research Project Grants
Subjects: All types of cancer, the mechanisms by which they arise and the way they exert their effects.
Purpose: To provide financial support for fundamental cancer research in northwest England and North and Mid-Wales.
Eligibility: Open to candidates undertaking cancer research studies at one of the universities named below in the Northwest. Grants are only available for travel costs associated with currently funded 3-year

cancer research projects. No grants are awarded for buildings or for the development of drugs.
Level of Study: Research
Type: Grant
Value: Approx. UK £35,000 per year
Length of Study: Usually 3 years
Frequency: Dependent on funds available
Study Establishment: The University of Liverpool, Lancaster University and the University of Wales, Bangor
Country of Study: North West England, North and Mid-Wales
Application Procedure: The NWCRF Scientific Committee meets twice a year. All applications are subject to peer review.
Closing Date: April 1st and October 1st
Funding: Individuals, private
Contributor: Voluntary donations
No. of awards given last year: 10
No. of applicants last year: 50

For further information contact:

NWCRF Scientific Committee Department of Medicine, Duncan Building, Daulby Street, Liverpool, L69 3BX, England
Email: ricketts@liverpool.ac.uk
Contact: The Secretary

NORWEGIAN INFORMATION SERVICE IN THE UNITED STATES

825 Third Avenue, 38th Floor, New York, NY 10022-7584, United States of America
Tel: (1) 212 421 7333
Fax: (1) 212 754 0583
Email: cg.newyork@mfa.no
Website: www.norway.org
Contact: Grants and Scholarships Department

American-Scandinavian Foundation Scholarships (ASF)
Subjects: All subjects.
Purpose: To encourage Scandinavians to undertake advanced study and research programmes in the United States.
Eligibility: Applicants must be Scandinavians over the age of 21, applicants from Denmark must be between 21 and 30 years. Applicants can be young professionals who have completed their formal education with related work experience in Scandinavia or Europe, or students who are currently enrolled in colleges and universities who need to undertake an internship. They should be fluent in English.
Level of Study: Postgraduate
Value: Grants are normally US$3,000, and fellowships can be up to US$18,000
Length of Study: 1 year
Frequency: Annual
Country of Study: United States of America
No. of awards offered: Varies
Application Procedure: Applicants must complete an application on ASF application forms, available on request from the Foundation.
Closing Date: November 8th
Funding: Foundation

John Dana Archbold Fellowship Program
Subjects: All subjects.
Purpose: To support educational exchange between the United States of America and Norway.
Eligibility: Open to citizens of the United States of America citizens aged 20–35, in good health and of good character. Qualified applicants must show evidence of a high level of competence in their chosen field, indicate a seriousness of purpose, and have a record of social adaptability. There is ordinarily no language requirement.
Level of Study: Postdoctorate, Postgraduate, Professional development, Research
Type: Fellowship
Value: Up to US$5,000. Individual grants vary, depending on the projected costs. Note that there will be no tuition at the University of Oslo. The maintenance stipend is sufficient to meet expenses for a single person. The travel allowance covers round trip airfare to Oslo
Length of Study: 1 year

Frequency: Annual
Study Establishment: The University of Oslo
No. of awards offered: 2
Application Procedure: Applicants must write to the Nansen Fund, Inc. for an application form.
Closing Date: February 1st
Funding: Private
Additional Information: The University of Oslo International Summer School offers orientation and Norwegian languages courses 6 weeks before the start of the regular academic year. For Americans, tuition is paid. Attendance is required. Americans visit Norway in even-numbered years and Norwegians visit the United States of America in odd-numbered years. For further information please contact the Nansen Fund, Inc.

For further information contact:

The Nansen Fund, Inc., 77 Saddlebrook Lane, Houston, TX, 77024, United States of America
Tel: (1) 713 680 8255

Memorial Fund of May 8th 1970

Subjects: All subjects.
Purpose: To promote cultural exchange between foreign countries and Norwegian residential experiential colleges by providing scholarships for residence, and to help prepare young people for everyday life in the community.
Eligibility: Open to candidates aged 18–22 years who do not have a permanent residence in Norway, and do not hold a Norwegian passport. Candidates must be planning to return to their home country after a year in Norway. Candidates must be aware of the kind of education the Memorial Fund bursaries cover, that being a year in a Norwegian residential colleges, not admission to education on a higher level, such as a university, or specialized training.
Level of Study: Norwegian Folk High School
Type: Scholarship
Value: The scholarship will cover board and lodging. In addition it is possible to apply for extra funds. Applicants from some countries may apply for required books and excursions arranged by the school. Also, extra support may be provided for short study trips and short courses before or after the school year. A fixed amount towards spending money may also be given. Normally the students must pay their own travelling expenses. The colleges do not charge tuition fees
Length of Study: 1 year
Frequency: Annual
Study Establishment: Norwegian residential experiential colleges
Country of Study: Norway
No. of awards offered: Approx. 25
Application Procedure: Applicants must request more information and application forms from the Memorial Fund of May 8th 1970 or to the nearest Norwegian Embassy. Applicants who require a scholarship to attend a Norwegian college should not apply to a them directly. In this case, the Board will place successful applicants at a college school based on their hobbies and interest. Residence permits must be applied for by each individual student when a scholarship has been granted.
Closing Date: November 1st
Funding: Government
No. of awards given last year: 25
No. of applicants last year: 700
Additional Information: A residential experiential college is a 1-year independent residential school, primarily for young adults, offering many non-traditional subjects of study. Each college has its own profile, but as a group, the Norwegian colleges teach classes covering almost all areas, including history, arts, crafts, music, sports, philosophy, theatre, photography etc.

For further information contact:

IKF, Grensen 9a N-0159 Oslo, Norway, Oslo, N-0159, Norway
Email: ikf@ikf.no

The Norway-America Association Awards

Subjects: All subjects.
Eligibility: Open to Norwegian who wish to study in the United States on the graduate level, must have completed their Bachelor's Degree before applying for these scholarships. The applicants must also be members of the Norway-America Association, and the membership fee is 200 NOK/year.

Level of Study: Postgraduate
Type: Award
Value: $2,000–20,000
Application Procedure: Check website for further details.
Closing Date: September 22nd
Additional Information: Norwegians who reside in Norway and plan to return to Norway after graduation are given preference in the selection process, and they cannot have studied for four or more years in the United States. Please contact the American-Scandinavian Foundation or the Norway-America Association directly in order to find the appropriate scholarship.

For further information contact:

The Norway–America Association, Rådhusgaten 23B, Oslo, 0158, Norway
Tel: (47) 47 23357160
Fax: (47) 47 23357175
Email: info@noram.no

The Norway-America Association Graduate & Research Stipend

Subjects: All subjects.
Purpose: To give the student substantial financial support for 1 year of studies in the United States.
Eligibility: Open to Norwegians and members of the Norway-America Association, and he/she must pay 250 NOK in administrative fees and are currently living in Norway, and intend to return to Norway after their graduation.
Level of Study: Graduate, Research
Value: $2,000–25,000
Application Procedure: Check website for further details.
Closing Date: September 22nd

For further information contact:

The Norway–America Association, Rådhusgaten 23B, Oslo, 0158, Norway
Tel: (47) 23357160
Fax: (47) 23357175
Email: info@noram.no
Website: www.noram.no/norsk/graduate_no.html

Norwegian Emigration Fund of 1975

Subjects: Emigration history and relations between the United States of America and Norway.
Purpose: To support for advanced or specialized study in Norway.
Eligibility: Open to citizens and residents of the United States of America. The fund may also give grants to institutions in the United States of America whose activities are primarily centred on the subjects mentioned.
Level of Study: Graduate, Postgraduate, Professional development
Type: Grant
Value: Norwegian Krone 5,000–20,000
Frequency: Annual
Country of Study: Norway
No. of awards offered: Varies
Application Procedure: Applicants must complete an application form and return it clearly marked Emigration Fund to Nordmanns-Forbundet. Applications as well as enclosures will not be returned.
Closing Date: February 1st
Funding: Government

Norwegian Marshall Fund

Subjects: Science and humanities.
Purpose: To provide financial support for Americans to come to Norway to conduct postgraduate study or research in areas of mutual importance to Norway and the United States of America, thereby increasing knowledge, understanding and strengthening the ties of friendship between the two countries.
Eligibility: Open to citizens of the United States of America, who have arranged with a Norwegian sponsor or research institution to pursue a research project or programme in Norway. Under special circumstances, the awards can be extended to Norwegians for study or research in the United States of America.
Level of Study: Research, Postgraduate
Type: Research grant

Value: The size of the individual grants depends on the research subject, purpose and the intended length of stay in Norway.
In previous years, the grants have varied from Norwegian Krone 10,000–30,000
Length of Study: Varies
Frequency: Annual
Study Establishment: Norwegian universities
Country of Study: Norway
No. of awards offered: 5–15
Application Procedure: Applicants must contact the Norway-America Association to receive an application. Application forms must be typewritten either in English or Norwegian and submitted in duplicate, including all supplementary materials. Each application must also be accompanied by a letter of support from the project sponsor or affiliated research institution in Norway. There is an application fee of Norwegian Krone 350.
Closing Date: March 23rd
Funding: Government

For further information contact:

The Norway-America Association, Rådhusgaten 23 B, Oslo, N-0158, Norway
Fax: (47) 2 335 7160
Email: info@noram.no
Website: www.noram.no

Norwegian Thanksgiving Fund Scholarship

Subjects: Fisheries, geology, glaciology, astronomy, social medicine and Norwegian culture.
Purpose: To provide eligible students to pursue theie studies.
Eligibility: Open to American graduate students.
Level of Study: Graduate
Type: Scholarship
Value: Up to US$3,000
Frequency: Annual
Country of Study: Norway
No. of awards offered: 1
Application Procedure: Candidates must contact the American Scandinavian Foundation.
Closing Date: November 1st
Funding: Individuals
Contributor: Former Norwegian students and friends

For further information contact:

The American Scandinavian Foundation, 58 Park Avenue, New York, NY, 10016, United States of America
Tel: (1) 212 879 9779
Fax: (1) 212 249 3444

The Professional Development Award

Subjects: All subjects.
Purpose: To help established professionals with a higher education who want to study within their own field of interest.
Eligibility: Open to Norwegian professionals who worked for at least 3 years after finishing his or her education as well as planning on doing special research or further study in their fields.
Level of Study: Postgraduate
Type: Award
Value: $5,000
Frequency: Annual
No. of awards offered: 2
Application Procedure: Check website for further details.
Additional Information: Candidates must be invited to apply for this award. There is also an administrative fee of 250 NOK, which must be deposited in bank account with number 7878.05.23025. Please contact the American-Scandinavian Foundation or the Norway-America Association directly in order to find the appropriate scholarship.

For further information contact:

The Norway–America Association, Cheryl Storø, Rådhusgaten 23B, Oslo, 0158, Norway
Tel: (47) 23357160
Fax: (47) 23357175
Email: info@noram.no

The Torskeklubben Stipend

Subjects: All subjects.
Purpose: To promote Norwegian-American relations through helping Norwegians come to the United States to study.
Eligibility: Open to Norwegians and must already be accepted at the Graduate School at the University of Minnesota before applying for the award.
Level of Study: Postgraduate
Value: Covers the tuition fees, but the applicant will also receive $7,500 from the club for 1 year at the school
Frequency: Annual
Application Procedure: Application forms are available upon request from the Norway-America Association and the Graduate School at the University of Minnesota or it can be downloaded from the website.
Closing Date: March 1st

For further information contact:

The Norway–America Association, Rådhusgaten 23B, Oslo, 0158, Norway
Tel: (47) 23357160
Fax: (47) 23357175
Email: info@noram.no
Website: www.grad.umn.edu/fellowships/norwegian_citizens

NORWICH JUBILEE ESPERANTO FOUNDATION

5 Craigenhill Road, Kilncadzow, Carluke, ML8 4QT, United Kingdom
Tel: (44) 15 5575 9166
Email: davidekelso@yahoo.co.uk
Website: www.esperanto-gb.org/nojef
Contact: Mr David Kelso, Secretary

A registered charitable trust established in 1967, the Norwich Jubilee Esperanto Foundation was founded for the advancement of education in the study and practice of Esperanto. It can pay travelling expenses to enable young persons who have shown efficiency in the study of Esperanto to visit approved United Kingdom venues or foreign countries. It also awards prizes and encourages research.

Norwich Jubilee Esperanto Foundation Grants-in-Aid

Subjects: Esperanto.
Purpose: To encourage thorough study of Esperanto by enabling young students to travel abroad or to approved United Kingdom venues and promote research into the teaching of Esperanto.
Eligibility: Open to citizens under 26 years of age of any country, who require financial assistance and who have a high standard of competence in Esperanto. An efficiency test may be required but there are no set academic or age requirements for research grants.
Level of Study: Unrestricted
Type: Travel grant
Value: Approx. UK £100–500, up to UK £1,500
Length of Study: From 1 week to several months
Frequency: Dependent on funds available
Study Establishment: Any venue approved by the Foundation
Country of Study: United Kingdom or Other
No. of awards offered: Varies
Application Procedure: Applicants must submit a letter of application in Esperanto. An application may be completed later.
Closing Date: Applications are accepted at any time provided an adequate margin is left for processing
Funding: Private
Contributor: Legacies from past supporters
No. of awards given last year: 10
No. of applicants last year: 30
Additional Information: Visitors to the United Kingdom will be expected to speak in Esperanto to schools or clubs.

NURSES EDUCATIONAL FUNDS, INC.

304 Park Avenue South, 11th Floor, New York, NY, 10010, United States of America
Tel: (1) 212 590 2443
Fax: (1) 212 590 2446
Email: info@n-e-f.org
Website: www.n-e-f.org

Nurses Educational Funds, Inc. is an independent, non-profit organization that grants scholarships to registered nurses for graduate study. It is governed by a board of trustees of nursing and business leaders, and is supported by contributions from corporations, foundations, nurses and individuals interested in the advancement of nursing.

Nurses' Educational Funds Fellowships and Scholarships

Subjects: Administration, supervision, education, clinical specialization and research. Any nursing-related field.
Purpose: To provide the opportunity to registered nurses who seek to qualify through advanced study in a degree programme.
Eligibility: Baccalaureate-prepared registered nurses residing in any one of the 50 states and the District of Columbia who are pursuing either a Master's or doctoral degree in nursing are eligible to apply for NEF scholarship monies.
Level of Study: Doctorate, Graduate
Type: Fellowship
Value: Please contact the organization
Frequency: Annual
Country of Study: United States of America
No. of awards offered: Varies
Application Procedure: Application available on the website.
Closing Date: March 1st
Funding: Individuals, corporation, private, trusts
No. of awards given last year: 24
No. of applicants last year: 130

OHIO ARTS COUNCIL

727 East Main Street, Columbus, OH, 43205-1796,
United States of America
Tel: (1) 614 466 2613
Email: webmaster@oac.state.oh.us
Website: www.oac.state.oh.us

The Ohio Arts Council is a state agency that funds and supports quality arts experiences to strengthen Ohio communities culturally, educationally and economically. It was created in 1965 to foster and encourage the development of the arts and assist the preservation of Ohio's cultural heritage.

Ohio Arts Council Individual Creativity Excellence Awards

Subjects: Interdisciplinary and performance art, criticism and music composition.
Purpose: To recognize and support the contributions of working artists to the cultural enrichment of the state.
Eligibility: Open to residents of Ohio who have lived in the state continuously for 1 year before the deadline and continue to remain an Ohio resident during the term of the award. Applicants cannot be students enrolled in any degree or certificate granting programme.
Level of Study: Postgraduate
Type: Fellowship
Value: US$5,000–10,000
Frequency: Annual
Country of Study: United States of America
Application Procedure: Applicants must submit application form B and supporting documents. Guidelines and application forms are available on the OAC website or upon request by writing to the address. All forms must be submitted to the OAC in printed format, rather than electronically.
Closing Date: September 1st
Funding: Government

OKLAHOMA SCHOOL OF ART

University of Oklahoma 520 Parrington Oval, Room 202 Norman, Oklahoma, 73019-0550, United States of America
Tel: (1) 405 325 2691
Fax: (1) 405 325 1668
Email: infoart.ou.edu
Website: http://art.ou.edu/

The School of Art is the largest, most comprehensive art school in Oklahoma, which provides excellent professional education and a focus for the study of visual arts. Additionally, the school is dedicated to promoting, pursuing and supporting creative activity and scholarly research in the visual arts.

Ben Barnett Scholarship

Subjects: Arts.
Eligibility: Any full-time Art majors admitted to either the MA or MFA degree program.
Level of Study: Postgraduate
Type: Scholarship
Value: $500–1,500
Frequency: Annual
Study Establishment: School of Art, University of Oklahoma
Country of Study: United States of America
No. of awards offered: 4–10
Application Procedure: See the website.
Closing Date: March 1st

Frances Weitzenhoffer Memorial Fellowship in Art History

Subjects: History of art.
Eligibility: Open to graduate students in art history.
Level of Study: Postgraduate
Type: Fellowship
Value: US$8,000
Frequency: Annual
Study Establishment: School of Arts, University of Oklahoma
Country of Study: United States of America
No. of awards offered: 1
Application Procedure: See the website.
Closing Date: March 1st

Glenis Horn Scholarship

Subjects: Sculpture.
Purpose: To support art students who are majoring in Sculpture.
Eligibility: Open to applicants majoring in Sculpture in the School of Art.
Level of Study: Professional development
Type: Scholarship
Value: US$500–2,500
Frequency: Annual
Study Establishment: School of Art, University of Oklahoma
Country of Study: United States of America
No. of awards offered: 1
Application Procedure: The School of Art Scholarship application may be downloaded from the website.
Closing Date: March 1st

Kim and Paul Moore Scholarship

Subjects: Arts.
Eligibility: Open to full-time Art majors admitted to the studio programme at the School of Arts.
Level of Study: Postgraduate
Type: Scholarship
Value: Varies
Frequency: Annual
Study Establishment: School of Art, University of Oklahoma
Country of Study: United States of America
No. of awards offered: Varies
Application Procedure: Contact the scholarship office.
Closing Date: March 1st

Selma Naifeh Scholarship Fund

Subjects: Painting.
Eligibility: Open to applicants who are residents of Oklahoma.
Level of Study: Postgraduate
Type: Scholarship
Value: US$500–2,500
Frequency: Annual
Study Establishment: School of Art, University of Oklahoma
Country of Study: United States of America
No. of awards offered: 1
Application Procedure: A completed application form must be sent to the scholarship office.
Closing Date: March 1st

OMOHUNDRO INSTITUTE OF EARLY AMERICAN HISTORY AND CULTURE

PO Box 8781, Williamsburg, VA, 23187-8781,
United States of America
Tel: (1) 757 221 1110
Fax: (1) 757 221 1047
Email: ieahc1@wm.edu
Website: http://oieahc.wm.edu
Contact: Ms Sally D Mason, Assistant to the Director

The Omohundro Institute of Early American History and Culture publishes books in its field of interest, the *William and Mary Quarterly* and a biannual newsletter, *Uncommon Sense*. It also sponsors conferences and colloquia and annually awards a 2-year NEH postdoctoral fellowship and a 1-year Andrew W Mellon postdoctoral research fellowship.

Andrew W Mellon Postdoctoral Research Fellowship at the Omohundro Institute

Subjects: The history and culture of North America's indigenous and immigrant peoples during the colonial, revolutionary and early national periods of the United States of America, and the related histories of Canada, the Caribbean, Latin America, the British Isles, Europe and Africa from 1500 to 1815.
Purpose: To revise the applicant's book manuscript into a first book that will make a distinguished contribution to scholarship, with publication by the Institute intended.
Eligibility: Applicants must not have previously published a book or have a book under contract, and must also have received their PhD at least 1 year prior to the application deadline.
Level of Study: Postdoctorate
Type: Fellowship
Value: US$45,000
Length of Study: 1 year, residential recommended but not mandatory
Frequency: Annual
Study Establishment: The Omohundro Institute of Early American History and Culture
Country of Study: United States of America
No. of awards offered: 1
Application Procedure: Applicants must complete an application form and submit this with a completed manuscript. Application forms are available on request and from the website.
Closing Date: November 1st
Funding: Private
Contributor: The Andrew W Mellon Foundation and the College of William and Mary
No. of awards given last year: 1
No. of applicants last year: 6

The National Endowment for Humanities (NEH) Institute Postdoctoral Fellowship

Subjects: The history and culture of North America's indigenous and immigrant peoples during the colonial, revolutionary and early national periods of the United States of America, and the related histories of Canada, the Caribbean, Latin America, the British Isles, Europe and Africa from 1500 to 1815.
Purpose: To revise a dissertation into a first book that will make a major contribution to the field of early American history and culture, for publication by the Institute.
Eligibility: Foreign nationals must have been in continuous residence in the United States for 3 years immediately preceding the date of their application for the Fellowship in order to be eligible for NEH funding
Level of Study: Postdoctorate
Type: Fellowship
Value: US$40,000 annually
Length of Study: 2 years
Frequency: Annual
Study Establishment: The Omohundro Institute of Early American History and Culture
Country of Study: United States of America
No. of awards offered: 1
Application Procedure: Applicants must complete an application form, available on written request or from the website.
Closing Date: November 1st

Funding: Government
Contributor: The NEH and the College of William and Mary
No. of awards given last year: 1
No. of applicants last year: 14

ONCOLOGY NURSING SOCIETY FOUNDATION (ONS)

125 Enterprise Drive, Pittsburgh, PA, 15275,
United States of America
Tel: (1) 412 859 6100
Fax: (1) 412 859 6162
Email: foundation@ons.org
Website: www.ons.org
Contact: Director of Research

The mission of the Oncology Nursing Society (ONS) is to promote excellence in oncology nursing and quality cancer care. ONS works to fulfil this mission by providing nurses and healthcare professionals with access to the highest quality educational programmes, cancer care resources, research opportunities and networks for peer support.

Aventis Research Fellowship

Subjects: Nursing, health and medical sciences.
Purpose: To financially support short-term postdoctorate oncology-specific research training.
Eligibility: Open to candidates who are registered nurses with interest in oncology and a completed Doctoral degree in nursing or a related discipline.
Level of Study: Postgraduate
Type: Fellowship
Value: Maximum $10,000 awarded to cover transportation, lodging, tuition, and other expenses. Up to $1,700 to attend ONS Congress in following year is also awarded
Frequency: Annual
Country of Study: United States of America
No. of awards offered: 1
Closing Date: June 1st
Funding: Foundation

ONS Breast Cancer Research Grant

Subjects: Oncology.
Purpose: To provide funding to support the ONS research agenda, which focuses on areas where gaps exist in the knowledge base for oncology nursing practice.
Eligibility: Open to the principal investigator who is actively involved in some aspect of cancer patient care, education or research.
Level of Study: Research
Type: Grant
Value: US$100,000 for 2 years for the research team
Length of Study: 2 years
Frequency: Annual
Country of Study: United States of America
Funding: Foundation
Contributor: ONS Foundation
Additional Information: Funding preference is given to projects that involve nurses in the design and conduct of the research activity.

ONS Foundation Research Awards

Subjects: Oncology nursing research, including research proposals related to AIDS, neuro-oncology, community health, cancer related genetics, nursing outcomes, oncology nursing education, symptom assessment and management, pain, palliative care, nausea and vomiting, neutropenia or biotherapy.
Purpose: To promote excellence in oncology nursing and quality cancer care.
Eligibility: Open to health professionals working in the field of oncology.
Level of Study: Unrestricted
Type: Research grant
Value: Generally US$3,000–10,000
Length of Study: 2 years

Frequency: Dependent on funds available
Country of Study: Any country
No. of awards offered: 28
Application Procedure: Applicants must complete an application form, available on request. They must also include a research proposal.
Closing Date: November 1st

For further information contact:

501 Holiday Drive, Pittsburgh, PA, 15220-2749, United States of America
Tel: (1) 412 921 7373
Fax: (1) 412 921 6565
Contact: Dr Gail A Mallory, Director of Research

ONS Genetech, Inc./Oncology Nursing Research Grant

Subjects: Nursing.
Purpose: To financially support the principal investigator actively involved in some aspect of care, education or research for patients with cancer.
Eligibility: Open to citizens of the United States only who are employees or relatives of employees in the designated career field.
Level of Study: Postgraduate
Type: Grant
Value: US$10,000
Frequency: Annual
Country of Study: United States of America
No. of awards offered: 1
Closing Date: October of each year
Funding: Foundation
Additional Information: Preference is given to projects that involve nurses in the design and conduct of the research activity and that promotes theoretically based oncology practice.

ONS Novartis Pharmaceuticals Post-Master's Certificate Scholarships

Subjects: Oncology nursing.
Purpose: To financially assist nurses in furthering their education.
Eligibility: Open to applicants who are enrolled in (or applying to) a postmaster's nurse practitioner certificate academic credit-bearing programme in an NLN or CCNE accredited school of nursing. The candidates must also have a previous Master's degree in nursing and a current license in and commitment to oncology nursing.
Level of Study: Postgraduate
Type: Scholarship
Value: US$3,000
Frequency: Annual
Country of Study: United States of America
Application Procedure: Applicants must submit their application form and transcripts along with the application fee.
Closing Date: February 1st

Ortho Biotech Products, L.P. Research Fellowship

Subjects: Nursing, health and medical sciences.
Purpose: To support short-term postdoctorate oncology-specific research training.
Eligibility: Open to applicants who are registered nurses with interest in oncology and have a completed Doctoral degree in nursing or a related discipline. Applicants must also demonstrate how study with a senior investigator helps career.
Level of Study: Postdoctorate
Type: Fellowship
Value: Maximum US$10,000 awarded to cover transportation, lodging, tuition and other expenses. Up to US$1,700 to attend ONS Congress in the following year is also awarded
Frequency: Annual
Country of Study: United States of America
No. of awards offered: 1
Closing Date: June 1st
Funding: Foundation
Contributor: ONS Foundation

THE ONTARIO COUNCIL ON GRADUATE STUDIES (OCGS)

180 Dundas Street West Suite 1100, Toronto, ON, M5G 1Z8, Canada
Tel: (1) 416 979 2165 ext 232
Fax: (1) 416 595 7392
Email: kpanesar@cou.on.ca
Website: http://ocgs.cou.on.ca

The Ontario Council on Graduate Studies (OCGS) is an affiliate of the Council of Ontario Universities (COU). OCGS strives to ensure quality research and education across Ontario. In order to achieve this, OCGS conducts quality reviews of research programmes that have been proposed for implementation in Ontario's universities. It also performs quality reviews of existing programmes on a 7 year cycle.

OCGS Women's Health Research Scholar Awards

Subjects: Women's health.
Purpose: To financially support research in and study of women's health at Ontario universities.
Eligibility: Open to students registered full-time in a Master's or Doctoral graduate programme at an Ontario university and sponsored and endorsed by a Dean of graduate studies at his or her university. For a postdoctoral award, applicant's must be engaged in full-time research at an Ontario university at the time of taking up the award.
Level of Study: Postgraduate, Doctorate, Postdoctorate
Type: Award
Value: Canadian $17,100 plus $1,000 research allowance for Master's award, $19,500 plus $2,000 research allowance for Doctoral awards and $39,000 plus $5,000 research allowance for postdoctoral awards
Length of Study: 2 year term for Master's and up to 3 years for Doctoral and postdoctoral programmes
Frequency: Annual
Country of Study: Canada
Application Procedure: Applicants must submit their application form, curriculum vitae, a statement of research to be undertaken during the period of graduate or postdoctoral study, transcripts and reference letters. Applications are available from the Deans office of Ontario universities or from the website.
Closing Date: January 31st
Funding: Foundation

ONTARIO FEDERATION OF ANGLERS & HUNTERS (OFAH)

4601 Guthrie Drive PO Box 2800, Peterborough, ON, K9J-8L5, Canada
Fax: (1) 705 748 9577
Email: ofah@ofah.org
Website: www.ofah.org
Tel: 705 748 OFAH 6324

The Ontario Federation of Anglers & Hunters (OFAH), Canada's leading conservation organization, is a non-profit, registered charity, which is dedicated to protecting woodland and wetland habitat, conserving precious fish and widlife stocks and promoting outdoor education.

OFAH Conservation Research Grants

Subjects: Conservation of natural resources.
Purpose: To financially support students who wish to pursue their research work in conservation research.
Level of Study: Research
Type: Research grant
Value: Canadian $2,000
Frequency: Annual
Country of Study: Canada
Application Procedure: Applicants must submit a completed application form, research proposal consisting of abstract, introduction, methods, research anticipated, literature cited and budget, curriculum vitae, transcripts and letter from supervising professor supporting the intended research project.
Closing Date: January 9th

ONTARIO PROBLEM GAMBLING RESEARCH CENTRE (OPGR)

150 Research Park Lane Suite 104, Guelph, ON, N1G-4T2, Canada
Tel: (1) 519 763 8049 ext 226
Fax: (1) 519 763 8521
Email: info@gamblingresearch.org
Website: www.gamblingresearch.org

In April 2000, Ontario Problem Gambling Research Centre (OPGR) was created as an arms length funding agency. The Ontario Government dedicates 2 per cent of the gross revenue from slot operations at the province's charity casinos and racetracks to a Problem Gambling Strategy.

OPGR Studentship Awards

Subjects: Problem gambling research.
Purpose: To develop the capacity in Ontario to conduct problem gambling research.
Eligibility: Open to candidates who are registered as full-time students in a Master's or Doctoral programme at a recognized Canadian university and anticipate completion of their programme within 3 years. Eligible applicants must be Canadian citizens or permanent residents of Canada at the time of application, must undertake problem gambling research as partial fulfilment of their Master's theses or Doctoral dissertation.
Level of Study: Doctorate, Postgraduate
Type: Studentship
Value: Masters program - $17,500 per year for up to 2 years Doctoral program - $20,000 per year for up to 3 years
Length of Study: 3 years for a Doctoral degree, 2 years for a Master's degree
Frequency: Annual
Country of Study: Canada
Application Procedure: Candidates must provide a completed application form, cover page, proposal, official transcripts, curriculum vitae, reference letter and confirmation letter from host university.
Closing Date: May 16th
Contributor: Ontario Problem Gambling Research Centre
Additional Information: This award can be pro-rated for up to 5 years provided that all requirements for the Doctoral programme will be completed by that date. Preference will be given to permanent Ontario residents studying at Ontario universities.

ONTARIO STUDENT ASSISTANCE PROGRAM (OSAP)

PO Box 4500, 189 Red River Road, 4th Floor, Thunder Bay, ON, P7B 6G9, Canada
Tel: (1) 807 343 7257
Website: http://osap.gov.on.ca

Minister of Education and the Minister of Training, Colleges and Universities are responsible for the administration of laws relating to education and skills training in Ontario.

Ontario Graduate Scholarship

Subjects: All subjects.
Purpose: To encourage excellence in graduate studies at the Master's and Doctoral levels.
Eligibility: Open to students who plan to be enrolled full-time in an approved graduate programme leading to a Master's or Doctoral degree. Candidates must be citizens or permanent residents of Canada.
Level of Study: Postgraduate, Doctorate
Type: Scholarships
Value: Canadian $5,000
Frequency: Annual
Study Establishment: Some selected universities
Country of Study: Canada
No. of awards offered: 2,000
Application Procedure: Applicants can send in paper or online application. For details see http://osap.gov.on.ca/eng/not_secure/ogsapply.htm.
Funding: Government
Contributor: Province of Ontario and the university

OPPENHEIM-JOHN DOWNES MEMORIAL TRUST

50 Broadway, London, Westminster, SW1H OBL, England
Tel: (44) (0) 20 7227 7000
Fax: (44) (0) 20 7222 3480
Website: www.oppenheimdownestrust.org/
Contact: Grants Management Officer

The Oppenheim-John Downes Memorial Trust makes annual awards in December to deserving artists of any kind unable to pursue their vocation by reason of poverty. Awards are restricted to persons over 30 years of age, who are natural born British subjects (S 34 of the Race Relations Act applies).

Oppenheim–John Downes Trust Grants

Subjects: Arts.
Purpose: To assist artists, musicians, writers, inventors, singers, actors and dancers of all descriptions who are unable to pursue their vocation by reason of their poverty.
Eligibility: Open to artists over 30 years of age, born in the British Isles of British parents and grandparents born after 1900. These qualifications are mandatory and applicants who do not qualify in all respects should not apply.
Level of Study: Unrestricted
Type: Grant
Value: UK £50–1,500 depending on requirement
Frequency: Annual
Country of Study: Any country
No. of awards offered: Approx. 30–40
Application Procedure: Applicants must write for details.
Closing Date: October 15th
Funding: Private
No. of awards given last year: 40
No. of applicants last year: 152

OREGON COLLEGE OF ART & CRAFT (OCAC)

8245 SW Barnes Road, Portland, OR, 97225, United States of America
Tel: (1) 503 297 5544
Email: sblack@ocac.edu
Website: www.ocac.edu
Contact: Sara Black, Extension Programme Director

Oregon College of Art & Craft (OCAC) is dedicated to excellence in teaching art through craft, contributing significantly to the continuity of contemporary craft as an artistic expression. The college traces its origins to 1907 when Julia Hoffman founded the Arts and Crafts Society to educate the public on the value of arts and crafts in daily life through art classes and exhibitions featuring the best examples of American crafts. Today OCAC is an accredited independent craft college offering studio classes in book arts, ceramics, drawing/painting, fibres, metals, photography and wood.

OCAC Junior Residency

Subjects: The college offers residencies that rotate through each of the studios: book arts, ceramics, drawing, fibres, metals, photography and wood.
Purpose: To encourage outstanding emerging artists to pursue a focused project in a stimulating art environment.
Eligibility: Open to citizens or permanent residents of the United States. Artists working in drawing/painting or fibres will be considered in the fall and those working in metals and photography for spring residency. The college defines emerging artists as postgraduates (post-MFA preferred) with less than 5 years experience as an exhibiting artist. Candidates from culturally diverse backgrounds are encouraged to apply.
Level of Study: Professional development
Type: Fellowship
Value: $1,200 fellowship, up to $500 reimbursement for travel to and from OCAC, up to $500 for materials and up to $100 for shipping the completed work
Length of Study: September–December or January–May

Frequency: Annual
Study Establishment: Oregon College of Arts and Craft
Country of Study: United States of America
No. of awards offered: 2 in fall and 2 in spring
Application Procedure: Applicants can download the application form from the website.
Closing Date: March 1st
Funding: Foundation
Contributor: The Collins Foundation
No. of awards given last year: 4
No. of applicants last year: 23
Additional Information: Housing on campus, $500 travel reimbursement, $500 materials reimbursement and a $1,200 fellowship stipend are provided to each junior resident. In addition, residents are invited to participate in a group show of resident work in the fall of the following year.

OREGON STUDENT ASSISTANCE COMMISSION (OSAC)

1500 Valley River Drive, Suite 100, Eugene, OR, 97401, United States of America
Tel: (1) 541 687 7400
Email: awardinfo@mercury.osac.state.or.us
Website: www.osac.state.or.us

Oregon Student Assistance Commission (OSAC) administers a variety of State of Oregon, Federal and privately funded student financial aid programmes for the benefit of Oregonians attending institutions of postgraduate education. This agency was formerly known as the Oregon State Scholarship Commission.

Lawrence R. Foster Memorial Scholarship

Subjects: Health and medical sciences.
Purpose: To offer one time award to students enrolled or planning to enrol in a public health degree programme.
Eligibility: Open to applicants working in the public health field or pursuing a graduate degree in public health. Applicants must be residents of Oregon.
Level of Study: Postgraduate
Type: Scholarships
Value: US$4,167
Frequency: Annual
Country of Study: United States of America
No. of awards offered: 0
Application Procedure: Applicants must submit an application form, transcript, financial need analysis, essay, 3 references and activity chart.
Closing Date: March 1st

For further information contact:

Tel: 800 452 8807
Contact: Director of Grant Programmes

ORENTREICH FOUNDATION FOR THE ADVANCEMENT OF SCIENCE, INC. (OFAS)

855 Route 301, Cold Spring, NY, 10516-9802, United States of America
Tel: (1) 845 265 4200
Fax: (1) 845 265 4210
Email: ofase@orentreich.org
Contact: N. F. Durr, Director for Scientific Affairs

The Orentreich Foundation for the Advancement of Science, Inc. (OFAS) is an operating private foundation that performs its own research and collaborates on projects of mutual interest.

OFAS Grants

Subjects: Areas of interest to the Foundation, including ageing, dermatology, endocrinology and serum markers for human diseases.
Purpose: To allow an individual to conduct collaborative biomedical research or research at the Foundation.

Eligibility: Open to applicants at or above the postgraduate level in science or medicine at an accredited research institution in the United States of America. There are, however, no citizenship restrictions.
Level of Study: Unrestricted
Type: Grant
Value: Varies, depending on the needs, nature and level of OFAS interest in the project
Frequency: Annual
Country of Study: United States of America
Application Procedure: Applicants must submit an outline of proposed joint or collaborative research, including, as a minimum, a brief overview of the current research in the field of interest, a statement of scientific objectives, a protocol summary, a curriculum vitae of the principal investigator, funding needed and total estimated project funding. Applications are reviewed quarterly. OFAS is usually the initiator of joint projects.
Closing Date: Applications may be submitted at any time
Funding: Foundation, private
Additional Information: Individuals who have a research question relating to a human disease or disease prevention factor for which there is adequate scientific basis for a serum marker to justify the use of the Serum Treasury, should submit a brief overview of a proposal. Researchers will be asked for additional information after the initial screening process. Proposals will be evaluated on an ongoing basis. In certain cases where the research applies directly to the primary interests of OFAS, limited grants to fund collaborative studies are available.

ORGANIZATION OF AMERICAN HISTORIANS (OAH)

PO Box 5457, Bloomington, IN, 47407-5457, United States of America
Tel: (1) 812 855 9852
Fax: (1) 812 855 0696/812 856 3340
Website: www.oah.org
Contact: Award and Prize Committee Coordinator

The Organization of American Historians (OAH) was founded in 1907 as the Mississippi Valley Historical Association and originally focused on the history of the Mississippi Valley. Now, national in scope and with approx. 11,000 members and subscribers, it is a large professional organization created and sustained for the investigation, study and teaching of American history.

Avery O Craven Award

Subjects: The coming of the Civil War, the Civil War years or the Era of Reconstruction, with the exception of works of purely military history.
Purpose: For the most original book on the coming of the Civil war, civil war years, or the era of reconstruction, with the exception of works of purely military history.
Type: Award
Value: US$500
Frequency: Annual
No. of awards offered: 1
Application Procedure: Applicants must visit the website www.oah.org/activities for complete application requirements. There is no standard application form and no application fee. Publishers are encouraged to enter one or more books in the competition.
Closing Date: October 1st
Contributor: OAH
No. of awards given last year: 1
No. of applicants last year: 41
Additional Information: The exception of works of purely military history recognizes and reflects the Quaker convictions of Avery Craven, President of the Organization of American Historians (1963–1964).

Binkley-Slephenson Award

Purpose: For the best scholarly article published in *The Journal of American History* during the preceding calendar year.
Value: US$500
Frequency: Annual
Application Procedure: Applicants must visit the website www.oah.org/activities for complete application requirements. There is no

standard application form and no application fee. Publishers are encouraged to enter one or more articles in the competition.
Closing Date: N/A
No. of awards given last year: 1
Additional Information: All articles published in the *The Journal of American History* during the preceding calendar year are considered.

David Thelen Award
Subjects: Past issues of continuity and change, as well as events or processes that began, developed or ended in what is now the United States of America.
Purpose: A biennial prize for the best article on American history published in a foreign language.
Eligibility: Comparative and international studies that fall within these guidelines are welcomed. This prize is not open to articles whose manuscripts were originally submitted for publication in English or by other people for whom English is their first language.
Type: Prize
Value: The winning article will be printed in *The Journal of American History* and its author awarded a US$500 subvention for refining the article's English translation
Frequency: Every 2 years
No. of awards offered: 1
Application Procedure: Applicants must visit the website www.oah.org/activities for complete application requirements. There is no standard application form and no application fee.
Closing Date: May 1st of odd-numbered years
Contributor: OAH
No. of awards given last year: 1
No. of applicants last year: 9

For further information contact:

Journal of American History (Committee Chair), 1215 East Atwater, Bloomington, IN, 47401, United States of America
Contact: Edward T. Linenthal, Editor

EBSCOhost America: History and Life Award
Subjects: American history.
Purpose: For scholarship in American history in the journal literature advancing new perspectives on accepted interpretations or previously unconsidered topics.
Eligibility: Open to entrants who have published an article in an American historical journal. Nominations and applications are welcome from both individuals and editors. Each entry must have been published within a specified time period, prior to the application deadline.
Type: Award
Value: US$750
Frequency: Every 2 years
No. of awards offered: 1
Application Procedure: Applicants should visit the website www.oah.org/activities for complete application requirements. There is no standard application form.
Closing Date: December 1st of even – numbered years
Contributor: EBSCOhost America: History & Life
No. of awards given last year: 1
No. of applicants last year: 53

Ellis W Hawley Prize
Subjects: Political economy, politics or institutions of the United States of America in its domestic or international affairs, from the Civil War to the present.
Purpose: For the best book-length historical study of the political economy politics, or institutions of the United States in its domestic or international affairs, from the civil war to the resent.
Eligibility: Eligible works shall include book-length historical studies, written in English and published during a given calendar year.
Type: Prize
Value: US$500
Frequency: Annual
No. of awards offered: 1
Application Procedure: Applicants should visit the website for complete application requirements. There is no standard application form and no application fee.
Closing Date: October 1st

No. of awards given last year: 2
No. of applicants last year: 63

Erik Barnouw Award
Subjects: American history.
Purpose: To recognize outstanding reporting or programming on network television, cable television or in a documentary film, concerned with American history, the study of American history, and/or the promotion of history.
Level of Study: Professional development
Type: Award
Value: US$1,000
Frequency: Annual
No. of awards offered: 1–2
Application Procedure: Applicants should visit the website for complete application requirements. There is no standard application form and no application fee. Companies are encouraged to enter one or more films in the competition.
Closing Date: December 1st
No. of awards given last year: 1
No. of applicants last year: 11

Frederick Jackson Turner Award
Subjects: American history.
Purpose: For an author's first book dealing with significant phase of American history.
Eligibility: The work must be the first book-length study of history published by the author. If the author has a PhD, he or she must have received it no more than 7 years prior to the submission of the manuscript for publication. The work must be published in the calendar year before the award is given.
Type: Award
Value: US$1,000
Frequency: Annual
No. of awards offered: 1
Application Procedure: Applicants should visit the website www.oah.org/activities for complete application requirements. There is no standard application form and no application fee.
Closing Date: October 1st
No. of awards given last year: 1
No. of applicants last year: 94

Huggins-Quarles Dissertation Award
Purpose: For graduate students of color at the dissertation research stage of their PhD programme.
Eligibility: Open to minority graduate students at the dissertation research stage of their PhD.
Level of Study: Postgraduate
Type: Award
Value: US $1,000 each if 2 wins. US$2,000 if 1 wins
Frequency: Annual
No. of awards offered: 1–2
Application Procedure: Applicants should visit the website www.oah.org/activities for complete application requirements. There is no standard application form and no application fee.
Closing Date: December 1st
No. of awards given last year: 2
No. of applicants last year: 10

James A Rawley Prize
Subjects: The history of race relations in the United States of America.
Purpose: To reward a book dealing with the history of race relations in the United States of America.
Type: Prize
Value: US$1,000
Frequency: Annual
No. of awards offered: 1
Application Procedure: Applicants should visit the website www.oah.org/activities for complete application requirements. There is no standard application form and no application fee. Publishers are encouraged to enter one or more books in the competition.
Closing Date: October 1st
No. of awards given last year: 1
No. of applicants last year: 68

Japanese Residencies Program

Subjects: American history and culture, native Americans, the West, social, economic and political history of the 20th century.

Purpose: To contribute to the expansion of personal scholarly networks between Japan and the United States of America.

Eligibility: Applicants must be current members of the OAH, have a PhD and be scholars of American history or culture. The committee invites applicants from previous competitions as well as new applicants to apply.

Level of Study: Professional development

Type: Residency

Value: Modest daily expenses, round-trip expenses to Japan and accommodation

Length of Study: 2 weeks

Frequency: Annual

Country of Study: Japan

Application Procedure: Applicants must visit the website www.oah.org/activities for complete application requirements. There is no standard application form and no application fees.

Closing Date: December 1st

Contributor: Japan–United States Friendship Commission

No. of awards given last year: 2

No. of applicants last year: 11

Additional Information: With generous support from the Japan–United States Friendship Commission, the OAH and the Japanese Association for American Studies send American scholars to Japanese Universities. During the residency, the selected scholars will give lectures and seminars in their speciality and provide individual consultation to Japanese scholars, graduate students and sometimes undergraduates studying American history and culture. Visitors will also participate in the collegial life of their host institutions.

John Higham Travel Grant Fund

Purpose: For graduate students to be used towards costs of attending the OAH/IEHS annual meeting.

Type: Travel grant

Value: US$500

Frequency: Annual

No. of awards offered: 3

Application Procedure: Applicants must visit the website www.oah.org/activities for complete application requirements. There is no standard application form and no application fee.

Closing Date: December 1st

No. of awards given last year: 3

No. of applicants last year: 4

Lawrence W. Levine Award

Subjects: American cultural history.

Purpose: To recognize scholarly and professional achievement in the field of American cultural history.

Eligibility: Open to applicants of any nationality.

Type: Award

Value: $2,000

Frequency: Annual

No. of awards offered: Varies

Application Procedure: Applicants must visit the website www.oah.org/activities for complete application requirements. There is no standard application form and no application fee.Publishers are encouraged to enter one or more books in the competition.

Closing Date: October 1st

No. of awards given last year: 1

No. of applicants last year: 49

Lerner-Scott Dissertation Prize

Subjects: United States of America women's history.

Purpose: For the best doctoral dissertation in US women's history.

Level of Study: Postdoctorate

Type: Prize

Value: US$1,000

Frequency: Annual

No. of awards offered: 1

Application Procedure: Applicants must visit the website www.oah.org/activities for complete application requirements. There is no standard application form and no application fee.

Closing Date: October 1st

No. of awards given last year: 1

No. of applicants last year: 15

Liberty Legacy Foundation Award

Subjects: American history and the civil rights movement.

Purpose: For the best book on any aspect of the struggle for civil rights in the United States, from the nation's founding to the present.

Eligibility: Open to writers and publishers writing a book on any historical aspect of the struggle for human civil rights in the United States of America. Each entry must be published within a specified time period prior to the application deadline.

Level of Study: Professional development

Type: Competition

Value: US$2,000

Frequency: Annual

Country of Study: United States of America

No. of awards offered: 1

Application Procedure: Applicants must visit the website www.oah.org/activities for complete application requirements. There is no standard application form and no application fees. Publishers are encouraged to enter one or more books in the competition.

Closing Date: October 1st

No. of awards given last year: 1

No. of applicants last year: Between 40 and 50

Additional Information: This award was inspired by the OAH President Darlene Clark Hine's call in her 2002 OAH presidential address for more research on the origins of the civil rights movement in the period before 1954.

Louis Pelzer Memorial Award

Subjects: Any period or topic in the history of the United States of America.

Purpose: For the best essay in American history by a graduate student.

Type: Award

Value: The winning essay will be published in *The Journal of American History*. The organization offers a prize of US$500

Frequency: Annual

Application Procedure: Applicants must visit the website www.oah.org/activities for complete application requirements. There is no standard application form and no application fee.

Closing Date: December 1st

No. of awards given last year: 1

No. of applicants last year: 18

Merle Curti Award

Subjects: American social and intellectual history.

Purpose: To recognize books in the fields of American social and intellectual history.

Type: Award

Value: US$2,000 if one wins; US$1,000 if two win

Frequency: Annual

No. of awards offered: 1

Application Procedure: Applicants must visit the website www.oah.org/activities for complete application requirements. There is no standard application form and no application fee. Publishers are encouraged to enter one or more books in the competition.

Closing Date: October 1st

Contributor: OAH

No. of awards given last year: 1

No. of applicants last year: 130

OAH Awards and Prizes

Subjects: American history.

Purpose: To recognize scholarly and professional achievement in the field of American history.

Eligibility: Open to applicants of any nationality.

Level of Study: Unrestricted

Type: Grant

Value: Varies, depending on award

Frequency: Other

No. of awards offered: Varies

Application Procedure: Applicants must visit the website www.oah.org/activities for complete application requirements. There is no standard application form and no application fee.

Closing Date: Deadlines vary
Contributor: OAH

OAH Darlene Clark Hine Award
Subjects: African-American women's and gender history.
Purpose: To honor the author and publisher of the best book on African-American women's and gender history.
Eligibility: Any author whose book on African-American women's and gender history is published between January 2008 and December 2009, and the publisher of the book.
Level of Study: Unrestricted
Type: Award
Value: US$2,000 for the author and a certificate of merit for the publisher
No. of awards offered: 1
Application Procedure: The author/publisher must send one copy of the book to each committee member of the organization before October 2009 in order to be considered for the award.
Closing Date: October 1st

Ray Allen Billington Prize
Subjects: American frontier history.
Purpose: To award the best book in American frontier history, defined broadly so as to include the pioneer periods of all geographical areas and comparisons between American frontiers and others.
Type: Award
Value: US$1,000
Frequency: Every 2 years
No. of awards offered: 1
Application Procedure: Applicants must visit the website www. oah.org/activities for complete application requirements. There is no standard application form and no application fees. Publishers are encouraged to enter one or more books in the competition.
Closing Date: October 1st of even – numbered years
Contributor: OAH
No. of awards given last year: 1
No. of applicants last year: 87

Richard W Leopold Prize
Subjects: Foreign policy, military affairs broadly construed, the historical activities of the federal government or a biography in one of the aforementioned areas.
Purpose: To improve contacts and interrelationships within the historical profession, where an increasing number of historically trained scholars hold distinguished positions in governmental agencies. It is awarded to the best book written by a historian connected with federal, state or municipal government.
Eligibility: The winner must have been employed in a government position for the last 5 years. If the author has accepted an academic position the book must have been published within 2 years from the time of the change.
Type: Prize
Value: US$1,500
Frequency: Every 2 years
No. of awards offered: 1
Application Procedure: Applicants must visit the website www. oah.org/activities for complete application requirements. There is no standard application form and no application fees. Publishers are encouraged to enter one or more books in the competition.
Closing Date: October 1st of odd – numbered years
No. of awards given last year: 1
No. of applicants last year: 23

Tachau Teacher of the year Award
Subjects: History.
Purpose: To recognize the contributions made by precollegiate and classroom teachers to improve history education.
Eligibility: Applicants must be precollegiate teachers engaged at least half time in history teaching, with exceptional ability in initiating projects that involve students in historical research. They should also demonstrate ability in working with museums, historical preservation societies or other public history associations, and in publishing or presenting scholarship that advances education or knowledge.
Level of Study: Professional development
Type: Award

Value: US$1,000, 1-year OAH membership and a 1-year subscription to the OAH Magazine of History. If the winner is an OAH member, the award will include a 1-year renewal of membership in the awardee's usual membership category. The winner's school will receive a certificate
Frequency: Annual
No. of awards offered: 1
Application Procedure: Applicants must visit the website www. oah.org/activities for complete application requirements. There is no standard application form and no application fees.
Closing Date: December 1st
No. of awards given last year: 1
No. of applicants last year: 9

Wiili Paul Adams Award
Subjects: American history, namely, the past and issues of continuity and change as well as events or processes that began, developed or ended in what is now the United States of America.
Purpose: For the best book on American history published in a foreign language.
Eligibility: This prize is not open to books whose manuscripts were originally submitted for publication in English or by people for whom English is their first language.
Type: Prize
Value: US$1,000
Frequency: Every 2 years
No. of awards offered: 1
Application Procedure: Applicants must visit the website www. oah.org/activities for complete application requirements. There is no standard application form and no application fees. Publisher are encouraged to enter one or more books in the competition.
Closing Date: May 1st in even years
Contributor: OAH
No. of awards given last year: 1
No. of applicants last year: 5

ORTHOPAEDIC RESEARCH AND EDUCATION FOUNDATION (OREF)

6300 N River Road, Suite 700, Rosemont, IL, 60018-4261, United States of America
Tel: (1) 847 698 9980
Fax: (1) 847 698 7806
Email: mcguire@oref.org
Website: www.oref.org
Contact: Mrs Jean McGuire, Vice President Grants

In 1955, leaders of the major professional organizations in the speciality, the American Orthopaedic Association, the American Academy of Orthopaedic Surgeons and the Orthopaedic Research Society, established the Orthopaedic Research and Education Foundation (OREF) as a means of supporting research and building the scientific base of clinical practice. Today, the Foundation raises over US$5 million per year and holds a unique place in medicine in the United States of America.

Clinical Research Training Fellowship
Subjects: Orthopaedics.
Purpose: To enable orthopaedic surgeons with research skills to manage health services and outcomes research.
Eligibility: Applicants must be orthopaedic surgeons in either Canada or the United States of America.
Level of Study: Postdoctorate
Type: Fellowship
Value: US$70,000 per year
Length of Study: 2 years
Frequency: Annual
Study Establishment: Participating institutions
Country of Study: United States of America
No. of awards offered: 1
Application Procedure: Applicants must make a formal application.
Closing Date: October 1st
Funding: Private
Contributor: Orthopaedic surgeons
No. of awards given last year: 1
No. of applicants last year: 4

517

OREF Career Development Award

Subjects: Orthopaedic surgery.
Purpose: To encourage a commitment to scientific research in orthopaedic surgery.
Eligibility: Applicants must be orthopaedic surgeons, and are not eligible if they are holders of the NIH ROI award.
Level of Study: Professional development
Type: Award
Value: Up to US$75,000 per year
Length of Study: 3 years
Frequency: Annual
Country of Study: United States of America or Canada
No. of awards offered: 2–3
Application Procedure: Applicants must make a formal application together with letters of recommendation.
Closing Date: August 1st
Funding: Private
Contributor: Orthopaedic surgeons
No. of awards given last year: 2
No. of applicants last year: 16

OREF Clinical Research Award

Subjects: Orthopaedics.
Purpose: To recognize outstanding clinical research related to musculoskeletal disease or injury.
Eligibility: Restricted to members of the American Academy of Orthopaedic Surgeons, the Orthopaedic Research Society (ORS), the Canadian Orthopaedic Association or the Canadian Orthopaedic Research Society. Alternatively, candidates may be sponsored by a member.
Level of Study: Professional development
Type: Award
Value: US$20,000
Length of Study: 1 year
Frequency: Annual
Country of Study: United States of America or Canada
No. of awards offered: 1
Application Procedure: Applicants must submit an original manuscript.
Closing Date: July 1st
Funding: Private
Contributor: Orthopaedic surgeons
No. of awards given last year: 1
No. of applicants last year: 9

OREF Prospective Clinical Research

Subjects: Orthopaedics.
Purpose: To provide funding for promising prospective clinical proposals.
Eligibility: Applicants must be orthopaedic surgeons.
Level of Study: Professional development
Type: Award
Value: Up to US$50,000 per year
Length of Study: 3 years
Frequency: Annual
Study Establishment: A medical centre
Country of Study: United States of America
No. of awards offered: 2
Application Procedure: Applicants must make a formal application.
Closing Date: August 1st
Funding: Private
Contributor: Orthopaedic surgeons
No. of awards given last year: 1
No. of applicants last year: 16

OREF Research Grants

Subjects: Sports medicine, surgery, rheumatology and treatment techniques.
Purpose: To encourage new investigators by providing seed money and start-up funding.
Eligibility: Open to orthopaedic surgeons who are principal investigators (PI) or co-PIs. PIs cannot have NIH ROI awards.
Level of Study: Postdoctorate
Type: Research grant
Value: Up to US$50,000

Length of Study: 2 years
Frequency: Annual
Study Establishment: A medical centre
Country of Study: United States of America
No. of awards offered: 9 to 12
Application Procedure: Applicants must make a formal application.
Closing Date: August 1st
Funding: Private
Contributor: Orthopaedic surgeons and corporations
No. of awards given last year: 7
No. of applicants last year: 58

OREF Resident Clinical Scientist Training Grants

Subjects: Orthopaedics.
Purpose: To encourage the development of research interests for residents and Fellows.
Eligibility: Applicants must be orthopaedic surgeon residents or Fellows in an approved residency programme in the United States of America.
Level of Study: Professional development
Type: Award
Value: US$15,000
Length of Study: 1 year
Frequency: Annual
Study Establishment: A medical centre
Country of Study: United States of America
No. of awards offered: 9–12
Application Procedure: Applicants must make a formal application.
Closing Date: August 1st
Funding: Private
Contributor: Orthopaedic surgeons
No. of awards given last year: 10
No. of applicants last year: 46

OUR WORLD-UNDERWATER SCHOLARSHIP SOCIETY

PO Box 4428, Chicago, IL 60680, United States of America
Tel: (1) 630 969 6690
Fax: (1) 630 969 6690
Email: vicepresident-EU@owuscholarship.org
Website: www.owuscholarship.org

The Our World Underwater Scholarship Society in an organization dedicated to promoting education in the underwater world.

Our World-Underwater Scholarship Society Scholarships

Subjects: Underwater-related disciplines.
Purpose: To provide hands-on intro to underwater and other aquatic-related endeavors.
Eligibility: Open to applicants who are certified scuba divers and above the age of 21 years. Refer to the website for further details.
Level of Study: Professional development
Type: Scholarship
Length of Study: 1 year
Frequency: Annual
No. of awards offered: 3
Application Procedure: Application form along with the required documents must be submitted before the deadline.
Closing Date: December 31st
Funding: Corporation
Contributor: Rolex Watch
No. of awards given last year: 3

PAINTING AND DECORATING CONTRACTORS OF AMERICA (PDCA)

1801 Park 270 Drive, Ste 220, St Louis, MD, 63146-3209, United States of America
Tel: (1) 800 332 7322
Fax: (1) 314 514 9417
Email: ihoren@pdca.org
Website: www.pdca.org

The PDCA was established in 1884 by a group of contractors to devise a means for assuring the public of the skill, honorable reputation, and probity of master painters.

A E Robert Friedman PDCA Scholarship

Subjects: All subjects.
Purpose: To provide scholastic and vocational aid.
Eligibility: Open to applicants who are under the age of 25 and are nominated by a PDCA member.
Level of Study: Postgraduate
Type: Scholarship
Value: Open to applicants who are under the age of 25 and are nominated by a PDCA member
Length of Study: US$1,500
Frequency: Annual
Application Procedure: See the website.
Closing Date: October 1st

PALOMA O'SHEA SANTANDER INTERNATIONAL PIANO COMPETITION

Calle Hernán Cortés 3, Santander, E-39003, Spain
Tel: (34) 94 231 1451
Fax: (34) 94 231 4816
Email: concurso@albeniz.com
Website: www.albeniz.com
Contact: A Kaufmann, Secretariat General

The Paloma O'Shea Santander International Piano Competition is one of the best rated competitions in the world. It provides an opportunity for exceptionally talented pianists to enhance their careers. The jury is composed of renowned musicians in order to ensure that grants are made in a fair and unbiased manner.

Paloma O'Shea Santander International Piano Competition

Subjects: Piano performance.
Purpose: To give support to young pianists of exceptional talent.
Eligibility: Open to pianists of any nationality under 29 years of age.
Level of Study: Unrestricted
Type: Competition
Value: approximately US$135,000
Length of Study: July 25th–August 7th
Frequency: Every 3 years
No. of awards offered: 7
Application Procedure: Applicants in the United States of America should contact Mrs Brookes McIntyre at the address below. Applicants from all other countries must contact the Secretariat General for details at the main address.
Closing Date: December 31st
Funding: Commercial, government, private
No. of awards given last year: 7
No. of applicants last year: 220
Additional Information: 20 pianists will participate in Santander in the First Phase with a performance of 50 minutes duration. Each one will be chosen from the pre-selection phase, which will be held in different cities of the world. 12 Participants will continue in the Second Phase and perform a recital of 40 minutes duration and a quintet for piano and strings. 6 pianists will go in the Semifinals and perform a concerto with chamber orchestra and a recital of 40 minutes duration. The final will consist of a concerto with symphony orchestra (3 finalists).

For further information contact:

PO Box 82743, Albuquerque, NM, 87198, United States of America
Tel: (1) 505 250 2341
Fax: (1) 505 265 8932
Contact: Mrs Brookes McIntyre

PAN AMERICAN HEALTH ORGANIZATION (PAHO) REGIONAL OFFICE OF THE WORLD HEALTH ORGANIZATION (WHO)

Regional Office for the Americas/Pan American Sanitary Bureau, 525 23rd Street NW, Washington, DC, 20037-2895, United States of America
Tel: (1) 202 974 3000
Fax: (1) 202 974 3663
Email: rgp@paho.org
Website: www.paho.org
Contact: Grants Administrator

The Pan American Health Organization (PAHO) is an international public health agency working to improve the health and living standards of the countries of the Americas. It serves as the specialized organization for health of the Inter-American System and as the regional office for the Americas of the World Health Organization.

PAHO Grants

Subjects: Public health studies.
Purpose: To contribute to the public health of the countries of the Americas (individual programme objectives vary). Programmes include graduate thesis grants, research training grants, regional research competitions (announced yearly) and special initiatives announced via the PAHO website.
Eligibility: Open to citizens and residents of Latin America and the Caribbean.
Level of Study: Graduate, Doctorate, Postgraduate, Research
Type: Research grant
Value: Please contact the organization
Study Establishment: Varies
Country of Study: Latin America or Caribbean countries only
No. of awards offered: Varies according to the programme
Application Procedure: Applicants must complete an application form. Guidelines and application forms are available from the website.
Closing Date: Varies according to the programme
Funding: Government
Contributor: Member states and their agencies

PARALYZED VETERANS OF AMERICA (PVA)

801,18th Street NW, Washington DC, 20006, United States of America
Tel: (1) 800 424 8200
Fax: (1) 202 416 7652
Email: info@pva.org
Website: www.pva.org

The Paralyzed Veterans of America (PVA), a congressionally chartered veterans service organization founded in 1946, has developed a unique expertise on a wide variety of issues involving the special needs of the members-veterans of the armed forces who have experienced spinal cord injury or dysfunction.

PVA Educational Scholarship Program

Subjects: Spinal cord injury or dysfunction.
Purpose: To provide financial support for PVA members so that they can achieve their goals in the academic arena.
Eligibility: Open to all PVA members and their families.
Level of Study: Postgraduate
Type: Scholarship
Value: US$1,000
Frequency: Annual
No. of awards offered: 10
Application Procedure: Details are available on the website.
Closing Date: June 1st

PARAPSYCHOLOGY FOUNDATION, INC.

PO Box 1562, New York, NY 10021-0043, United States of America
Tel: (1) 212 628 1550
Fax: (1) 212 628 1559
Email: info@parapsychology.org
Website: www.parapsychology.org
Contact: Vice President

Established in 1951, the Parapsychology Foundation acts as a clearinghouse for information about parapsychology. Essentially an administrative organization, it maintains one of the largest libraries to do with parapsychology, the Eileen J Garret Library, as well as supporting various programmes that include the library, a grant and scholarship programme, a conference and lecture programme, and a speaker's bureau and publishing programme.

D Scott Rogo Award for Parapsychological Literature

Subjects: Parapsychology.
Purpose: To provide support to authors working on a manuscript pertaining to the science of parapsychology.
Eligibility: Open to nationals of any country.
Level of Study: Unrestricted
Type: Award
Value: US$3,000
Length of Study: 1 year
Frequency: Annual
Country of Study: Any country
No. of awards offered: 1
Application Procedure: Applicants must submit a brief synopsis of the proposed contents of manuscript, a list of previous writings and a sample writing of assistance.
Closing Date: April 15th for notification on May 1st

Eileen J Garrett Scholarship

Subjects: Parapsychology.
Purpose: To assist students attending an accredited college or university in pursuing the academic study of the science of parapsychology.
Eligibility: Open to nationals of any country.
Level of Study: Unrestricted
Type: Scholarship
Value: US$3,000
Length of Study: 1 year
Frequency: Annual
Study Establishment: An accredited college or university
Country of Study: Any country
No. of awards offered: 1
Application Procedure: Applicants must submit samples of writings on the subject with an application form from the Foundation. Letters of reference are required from three individuals, familiar with the applicant's work and/or studies in parapsychology.
Closing Date: July 15th

For further information contact:

Email: office@parapsychology.org

Parapsychology Foundation Grant

Subjects: Parapsychology.
Purpose: To support original study, research and experiments in parapsychology.
Eligibility: Open to nationals of any country.
Level of Study: Unrestricted
Type: Grant
Value: Up to US$5,000
Length of Study: 1 year
Frequency: Annual
Country of Study: Any country
No. of awards offered: 10
Application Procedure: Applicants must contact the organization for details.
Closing Date: August 15th
Additional Information: Funding for the Foundation Grant is limited but applicants are still welcome to submit a proposal on the off chance that the programme will be reviewed.

PARKER B FRANCIS FELLOWSHIP PROGRAM

VA Puget Sound Health Care System, 1660S Columbian Way, 151L, Seattle, WA, 98108, United States of America
Tel: (1) 617 432 4099
Fax: (1) 617 277 2382
Email: brain@hsph.harvard.edu
Website: www.francisfellowships.org
Contact: Ms Deborah Snapp

A private foundation dedicated to creating current and future generations of well-rounded individuals who are creative, life-long learners, striving to achieve their fullest potential within their communities.

Parker B Francis Fellowship Program

Subjects: Pulmonary research.
Purpose: To support rising stars in the field of pulmonary research as they make the transition from postdoctoral trainees to independent researchers.
Eligibility: Ideally, open to applicants with between 2 and 7 years of postdoctoral research experience, published articles in leading journals and a clear trajectory in pulmonary research.
Level of Study: Postdoctorate
Type: Fellowship
Value: The total budget is limited to US$48,000 for the 1st year, US$50,000 for the 2nd and US$52,000 for the 3rd. These totals include a stipend plus fringe benefits and may include travel costs to a maximum of US$1,500. Direct research project costs and indirect costs are not covered
Length of Study: 3 years
Frequency: Annual
Country of Study: United States of America, Canada or Mexico
No. of awards offered: 15
Application Procedure: Applicants must submit a completed application form, biographical sketch and a brief statement of their career goals. They must also provide a letter from their mentor evaluating the applicant's qualifications and indicating their career goals in the field of pulmonary research, three letters of recommendation, a summary of the past training record of the primary mentor (including names of former trainees and their current positions, sources and level of support with grants pending and the extent of equipment and space for research training available to the primary mentor and trainee) and signatures of the primary mentor, department or division head and the fiscal officer responsible for administering the grant on the face page.
Closing Date: Mid-October
Funding: Private
Contributor: The Francis Family Foundation
No. of awards given last year: 15
No. of applicants last year: 69

THE PARKINSON'S DISEASE SOCIETY OF THE UNITED KINGDOM (PDS)

215 Vauxhall Bridge Road, London, SW1V 1EJ, England
Tel: (44) 20 7931 8080
Fax: (44) 20 7233 9908
Email: research@parkinsons.org.uk
Website: www.parkinsons.org.uk
Contact: Ms Catherine Fleming, Research Officer

The Parkinson's Disease Society of the United Kingdom (PDS) works with people who have Parkinson's disease, their families and health and social care professionals. The mission of the PDS is, through research, the conquest of Parkinson's disease and the alleviation of the suffering and distress it causes. The work of the PDS includes research into the cause, cure and prevention of the disease, improvements in treatments, and a helpline staffed by nurses offering advice on all aspects of Parkinson's disease including drug treatments, surgery, therapies, social and healthcare rights, benefits, driving, insurance and employment. The PDS also provides a wide range of publications, audio tapes and videos, a comprehensive education and training programme and a national network of field staff, branches and welfare visitors offering local information, support, advice and social activities.

PDS Career Development Awards

Subjects: Parkinson's disease.
Purpose: To support individuals who wish to specialise in Parkinson's disease research either by establishing their own research group or undertaking relevant research training. There are two types of awards, Senior Research Fellowships and Training Fellowships.
Eligibility: Applicants for Senior Research Fellowships should have significant experience at postdoctoral level and be looking to establish their own research group. For Training Fellowships, individuals should be qualified health and social care professionals who wish to undertake research training with the aim of achieving a higher research degree. All awards are tenable only at a United Kingdom university, NHS Trust, statutory social care instituition or other research instituition.
Level of Study: Research
Type: Award
Value: Covers applicant's salary and other research related costs
Length of Study: 5 years for Senior Research Fellowships and up to 3 years for Training Fellowships
Frequency: Annual
Study Establishment: United Kingdom University, NHS Trust, statutory Social Care organisation or other research institution
Country of Study: United Kingdom
No. of awards offered: Varies
Application Procedure: Application forms can be downloaded from the website.
Closing Date: December
Funding: Foundation

PDS Innovation Grants

Subjects: Parkinson's disease.
Purpose: Innovation grants are designed to support short, small-scale research projects and pilot studies that address novel ideas.
Eligibility: Applicants should hold employment contracts that extend beyond the period of the grant.
Level of Study: Research
Type: Grant
Value: Up to £15,000
Length of Study: Up to 12 months
Frequency: Twice per year
Study Establishment: United Kingdom University, NHS Trust, statutory social care organisation or other research institution
Country of Study: United Kingdom
No. of awards offered: Varies
Application Procedure: Application forms are available from the website or can be obtained by emailing to the PDS Reasearch Department.
Closing Date: March 6th, August 14th
Funding: Foundation

PDS Project Grant

Subjects: Medical sciences, neurology, neurosciences, biochemistry, toxicology, pathology, genetics, geriatrics and pharmacy.
Purpose: To support research into the causes, cure and prevention of Parkinson's disease, its care and effective treatments.
Eligibility: The Parkinson's Disease Society supports biomedical, health and social care and social policy research and wishes to encourage research related to improving the quality of life for people with Parkinson's. Applications are invited for project grants for up to 3 years. Grants are tenable only at a United Kingdom University or NHS Trust or statutory social care organization.
Level of Study: Postdoctorate, Professional development, Research
Type: Project grant
Value: To include at least one salary plus consumables and equipment
Length of Study: Up to 3 years
Frequency: Twice per year
Study Establishment: A recognized research institution, university or hospital in the United Kingdom
Country of Study: United Kingdom
No. of awards offered: Varies
Application Procedure: Applicants must complete an application form, which is available from the Society's website.
Closing Date: Please refer to the website (early April & early September)

Funding: Foundation, private
Contributor: Donations
No. of awards given last year: 13
Additional Information: For further details visit the Society's website.

PARTICLE PHYSICS AND ASTRONOMY RESEARCH COUNCIL (PPARC)

Polaris House, North Star Avenue, Swindon,
Wiltshire, SN2 1SZ, England
Tel: (44) 1793 442000
Fax: (44) 1793 442125
Email: steve.cann@pparc.ac.uk
Website: www.pparc.ac.uk
Contact: Mr Steve Cann, E & T Section

The PPARC is the UK's strategic science investment agency. By directing, coordinating and research, education and training in particle physics and astronomy, PPARC delivers world leading science, technologies and people for the UK.

PPARC Advanced Fellowships

Subjects: Particle physics, astronomy and solar system science.
Level of Study: Postdoctorate
Type: Fellowship
Value: £35,000 (approx. CAD$72,150)
Frequency: Annual
Country of Study: United Kingdom
No. of awards offered: 12
Application Procedure: Applications for a PPARC Fellowship must be submitted using the Je-S system.
Closing Date: October 15th
Additional Information: You may undertake up to a maximum of six hours teaching, including preparation each working week.

For further information contact:

Email: Clare.Heseltine@pparc.ac.uk
Contact: Clare Heseltine

PPARC CASE Studentship

Subjects: Science, engineering.
Purpose: To give promising students experience outside a purely academic environment.
Eligibility: Advice on eligibility should be sought from the Registrar's Office.
Level of Study: Postgraduate
Type: Studentship
Value: Tuition fees only
Length of Study: 3 months–3 years
Frequency: Annual
Country of Study: United Kingdom
Application Procedure: Contact the PPARC.
Closing Date: October 1st
Funding: Commercial

PPARC CASE-Plus Studentship

Subjects: Science and engineering.
Purpose: To help students become more effective in promoting technology transfer.
Eligibility: Advice on eligibility should be sought from the Registrar's Office.
Level of Study: Postgraduate
Type: Studentship
Value: Currently £370 per year in addition to the basic maintenance allowance
Length of Study: 3 years
Frequency: Annual
Country of Study: United Kingdom
Application Procedure: Contact the PPARC.
Closing Date: October 1st
Funding: Commercial

PPARC Daphne Jackson Fellowships

Subjects: Particle physics, particle astrophysics, solar system science and astronomy.
Purpose: To enable high-level engineers and scientists to return to their professions after a career break for family or other reasons.
Eligibility: Open to promising engineers and scientists who have taken a career break.
Level of Study: Postdoctorate, Research
Type: Fellowship
Value: Dependent on age and experience
Length of Study: 2 years
Frequency: Annual
Study Establishment: Any academic institution acceptable to the PPARC
Country of Study: United Kingdom
No. of awards offered: Varies
Application Procedure: Applicants must contact Jennifer Woolley, Trust Director, or Sue Smith, Fellowship Administrator, for application forms and further information.
Closing Date: Please write for details
Funding: Government
Additional Information: The Daphne Jackson Fellowship is also administered by the BBSRC and the EPSRC.

For further information contact:

The Daphne Jackson Trust, Department of Physics, University of Surrey, Guildford, Surrey, GU2 7XH, England
Tel: (44) 14 8368 9166

PPARC Gemini Studentship

Subjects: Astronomy.
Purpose: To enable promising South-American students to pursue a PhD in Great Britain.
Eligibility: Open to students from Argentina, Brazil or Chile only.
Level of Study: Doctorate
Type: Fellowship
Value: Agreed tuition costs and a maintenance allowance
Length of Study: 3 years
Frequency: Annual
Country of Study: United Kingdom
No. of awards offered: 3
Application Procedure: See website.
Closing Date: March 31st

PPARC Postdoctoral Fellowships

Subjects: Particle physics, astronomy and solar system science.
Level of Study: Postgraduate
Type: Fellowship
Value: All agreed salary, travel and subsistence, equipment, additional costs, and UK £1,500 stipend
Frequency: Annual
Country of Study: United Kingdom
No. of awards offered: 12
Application Procedure: Applications for a PPARC Fellowship must be submitted using the Je-S system.
Closing Date: October 12th
Additional Information: You may undertake up to a maximum of six hours teaching, including preparation each working week.

PPARC Postgraduate Studentships

Subjects: Particle physics, particle astrophysics, solar system science and astronomy.
Eligibility: Open to postgraduates from the United Kingdom and European Union countries.
Level of Study: Postgraduate
Type: Studentship
Length of Study: Up to 3 years
Frequency: Annual
Study Establishment: Any academic institution that is acceptable to the PPARC
Country of Study: United Kingdom
No. of awards offered: Approx. 185
Application Procedure: Applicants must refer to the PPARC website for application information.
Closing Date: July 31st

Funding: Government
Additional Information: Further information is available on request by emailing studentships@pparc.ac.uk

PPARC Spanish (IAC) Studentship

Subjects: Astronomy.
Purpose: To support students of the Instituto de Astrofiscia de Canarias (IAC), Tenerite, Spain pursuing a PhD in Great Britain.
Eligibility: Open to Spanish students of the Instituto de Astrofiscia de Canarias (IAC) only.
Level of Study: Doctorate
Type: Studentship
Value: Agreed tuition costs and a maintenance allowance
Length of Study: 3 years
Frequency: Annual
Country of Study: United Kingdom
No. of awards offered: 2
Application Procedure: See website.
Closing Date: March 31st

PASTEUR FOUNDATION

420 Lexington Avenue Suite 1654, New York, NY, 10170, United States of America
Tel: (1) 212 599 2050
Fax: (1) 212 599 2047
Email: PasteurUS@aol.com
Website: www.pasteurfoundation.org

Pasteur Foundation is located in New York city and works to introduce the research conducted at the Institut Pasteur to the American public, to develop exchanges between Pasteurian and United States scientists and to raise funds for Pasteurian research.

Pasteur Foundation Postdoctoral Fellowship Program

Subjects: Science.
Purpose: To provide financial assistance and develop international scientific exchanges.
Level of Study: Postdoctorate
Type: Fellowship
Value: US$70,000 per year
Length of Study: 3 years
Frequency: Annual
Application Procedure: Applicants must submit a passport-size photo, reprints of publications, letters of recommendation, letter of support and curriculum vitae.
Closing Date: September 11th

For further information contact:

Secrétariat de la Direction de l'Evaluation Scientifique Institut Pasteur 25 rue du Docteur Roux 75724 Paris Cedex 15, France
Contact: Dr Isabelle Saint Girons

PATERSON INSTITUTE FOR CANCER RESEARCH

Wilmslow Road, Withington, Manchester, M20 4BX, England
Tel: (44) 0161 446 3156
Fax: (44) 16 1446 3109
Email: gcowling@picr.man.ac.uk
Website: www.paterson.man.ac.uk
Contact: Dr Graham Cowling

The Paterson Institute for Cancer Research is a Cancer Research UK-funded centre for cancer research and now forms a part of the University of Manchester. It carries out cancer research in a large number of areas and has 18 research groups and around 250 scientists.

Paterson 4-Year Studentship

Subjects: Molecular and cellular basis of cancer and translational cancer research.
Purpose: To support study towards a PhD.
Eligibility: Open to candidates who have obtained a First or Second Class (Honours) Bachelor of Science Degree. International

First or 2.1 degree equivalent in biological science, medicine, or related subject.
Level of Study: Doctorate, Postgraduate
Type: Studentship
Value: UK £15,300 as stipend per year, university fees and bench fees
Length of Study: 4 years
Frequency: Annual, 3 times per year
Study Establishment: The University of Manchester
Country of Study: United Kingdom
No. of awards offered: Up to 10 per year
Application Procedure: www.paterson.man.ac.uk for details and download application form.
Closing Date: Refer the website
Funding: Private
Contributor: Cancer Research UK
No. of awards given last year: 8
No. of applicants last year: 320
Additional Information: All positions are advertised on the website. Self-funded students are accepted subject to qualifications and 3-year funding. Please use application form (website).

For further information contact:

Postgraduate Tutor, Paterson Institute
Email: gcowling@picr.man.ac.uk

THE PAUL & DAISY SOROS FELLOWSHIP PROGRAM

400 West 59th Street, New York, NY, 10019,
United States of America
Tel: (1) 212 547 6926
Fax: (1) 212 548 4623
Email: pdsoros_fellows@sorosny.org
Website: www.pdsoros.org

The Paul & Daisy Soros Fellowship for New Americans
Subjects: Any subject.
Purpose: To provide opportunities for continuing generations of able and accomplished New Americans to achieve leadership in their chosen fields.
Eligibility: Open to New Americans: resident aliens (Green Card Holders) naturalized US citizens and/or children of 2 naturalized parents.
Level of Study: Postdoctorate
Type: Fellowship
Value: US$20,000–30,000
Length of Study: 2 years
Study Establishment: Any accredited graduate University in the United States
Country of Study: United States of America
No. of awards offered: 30
Application Procedure: Apply online.
Closing Date: November 1st
Funding: Private
Contributor: Paul and Daisy Soros
No. of awards given last year: 30
No. of applicants last year: 84

THE PAUL FOUNDATION

Apeejay House, 15 Park Street, Kolkata, West Bengal,
700 016, India
Tel: (91) 033 22295455
Fax: (91) 033 22299596
Email: thepaulfoundation@apeejaygroup.com
Website: www.thepaulfoundation.org

The Paul Foundation has been conceived to promote the individuals quest for intellectual excellence. To pursue higher studies in India and abroad, the Foundation supports those Indians who have shown ability in their specific areas of interest, to give them an opportunity to develop their potential and be recognized as leaders.

The Paul Foundation Postgraduate Scholarship
Subjects: Humanities, social sciences, basic sciences, applied sciences, law, management, medicine, engineering, fine arts and the performing arts.
Purpose: To encourage outstanding scholars who have the ability to produce thoughtful and thought-provoking work and make a difference to society.
Eligibility: Open to applicants who are Indian citizens and have completed their graduation from a UGC-recognized Indian university.
Level of Study: Postgraduate, Doctorate
Type: Scholarship
Frequency: Annual
Country of Study: Any country
Application Procedure: A completed application form must be submitted.
Closing Date: February 28th
Funding: Foundation

THE PAULO CELLO COMPETITION

PO Box PL 1105, FIN-00101, Helsinki, Finland
Email: cello@paulo.fi
Website: www.cellocompetitionpaulo.org
Contact: Administrative Assistant

The Paulo Cello Competition organizes an international competition for cellists of all nations.

International Paulo Cello Competition
Subjects: Cello performance.
Eligibility: Open to cellists between 16 and 33 years of age.
Level of Study: Unrestricted
Type: Competition
Value: The 1st prize is €15,000, the 2nd prize is €12,000, the 3rd prize is €9,000 and the 4th, 5th and 6th prizes are €2,000
Frequency: Every 5 years
Country of Study: Finland
No. of awards offered: 6
Application Procedure: Applicants must write for a brochure, which contains details of the application and audition pieces.
Funding: Private
Contributor: The Paulo Foundation
No. of awards given last year: 6
No. of applicants last year: 77

PEMBROKE CENTER

172 Meeting Street Box I958, Brown University Providence, RI, 02912,
United States of America
Tel: (1) 401 863 2643/3466
Fax: (1) 401 863 1298
Email: Elizabeth_Weed@Brown.edu
Website: www.pembrokecenter.org
Contact: Elizabeth Weed, Director

The Pembroke Center was established in 1981 as a research centre on gender. Funded in its early years by the Ford Foundation, the National Endowment for the Humanities, and the Rockefeller Foundation, the Center now supports its programmes largely through its endowment, made possible by generous alumni and other donors.

Pembroke Center Post-Doctoral Fellowships
Subjects: All subjects.
Purpose: To encourage scholars to pursue research in any discipline.
Eligibility: Open to scholars from all disciplines. Recipients may not hold a tenured position.
Level of Study: Postdoctorate
Type: Fellowships
Value: US$50,000 plus supplement for health insurance
Length of Study: 9 months
Frequency: Annual
Study Establishment: Brown University
Country of Study: United States of America
No. of awards offered: 3

Application Procedure: For application forms contact Donna Good-now.
Closing Date: December 10th
No. of awards given last year: 3
Additional Information: The Center particularly encourages under-represented and minority scholars to apply.

For further information contact:

Email: Donna_Goodnow@brown.edu
Contact: Donna Goodnow

PEN AMERICAN CENTER

588 Broadway, Suite 303, New York, NY 10012, United States of America
Tel: (1) 212 334 1660
Fax: (1) 212 334 2181
Email: pen@pen.org, awards@pen.org
Website: www.pen.org

PEN American Center is a fellowship of writers dedicated to to ad-vance literature, depend free expression and foster international fel-lowship. The American Center is the largest of 141 international PEN centers worldwide.

The PEN Translation Fund Grants
Subjects: Translations of works of fiction, creative nonfiction, poetry and drama.
Purpose: The fund seeks to encourage translators to undertake projects they might not otherwise have had the means to attempt.
Eligibility: Works that have not previously appeared in English or have appeared only in an egregiously flawed translation are eligible.
Level of Study: Unrestricted
Type: Grant
Value: US$2,000–10,000
Frequency: Annual
Country of Study: Any country
Application Procedure: All applications must include the cover sheet with all the items filled in, a sample of the translation and a curriculum vitae of the translator. Seven hard copies of the translation with the completed applications must be submitted. Visit website: www.pen.org
Closing Date: January 14th
Funding: Private
No. of awards given last year: 1
Additional Information: Anthologies with multiple translators, works of literary criticism and scholarly or technical texts do not qualify. Project denied funding in previous years may not be resubmitted. Translators awarded grants by the fund are ineligible to reapply for 3 years after the year they receive a grant.

For further information contact:

Director of Literary Awards Translation Fund, PEN American Center
Email: nick@pen.org
Contact: Nick Burd

PEN Writer's Fund
Subjects: Professional writers in acute, emergency financial crisis.
Purpose: To assist professional published writers facing emergency situations.
Eligibility: Open to published professional writers and produced playwrights who have a traceable record of writing and publication.
Level of Study: Unrestricted
Type: Grant
Value: Up to US$2,000
Frequency: Dependent on funds available
Country of Study: United States of America & Canada
Application Procedure: Applicants must submit an application con-sisting of a two-page form, published writing samples, documentation of financial emergency, including bills, etc. and a professional curric-ulum vitae.
Funding: Private
No. of awards given last year: 40
Additional Information: A separate fund exists for writers and editors with AIDS who are in need of emergency assistance. The funds are

not for research purposes, to enable writers to complete unfinished projects, or to fund writing publications or organizations. Grants and loans are for unexpected emergencies only, for the support of working writers. PEN American Center also offers numerous annual awards to published writers to recognize distinguished writing, editing and translation.

PENINSULA SCHOOL OF MEDICINE AND DENTISTRY

Peninsula Medical School, The John Bull Building, Tamar Science Park, Research Way, Plymouth, PL6 8BU, England
Tel: (44) 01752 437000
Fax: (44) 01752 517842
Email: pmsenq@pms.ac.uk
Website: www.pms.ac.uk/pms/

Peninsula Medical School and Peninsula Dental School have come together in The Peninsula College of Medicine and Dentistry, a part-nership with the University of Exeter, University of Plymouth and the NHS in Devon and Cornwall. The Peninsula Medical School was es-tablished in 2000 and Peninsula Dental School was established in 2006. Postgraduate study, either at Masters level through taught programmes, or Doctorate level through research is available through the Peninsula College of Medicine & Dentistry Graduate School.

Peninsula College of Medicine and Dentistry PhD Studentships
Purpose: To attract PhD candidates of outstanding ability to join their exciting and rapidly expanding programme of internationally rated research.
Eligibility: Open to the suitably qualified graduates.
Level of Study: Doctorate
Type: Studentship
Value: £12,940
Frequency: Dependent on funds available
Study Establishment: Peninsula College of Medicine & Dentistry
Country of Study: England
Application Procedure: Check website for details.
Closing Date: See details of specific studentship
Contributor: Various sources

For further information contact:

Tel: 01752 437300
Email: pcmd-researchdegrees@pcmd.ac.uk

UNIVERSITY of PENNSYLVANIA

PENN HUMANITIES FORUM

University of Pennsylvania 3619 Locust Walk, Philadelphia, PA, 19104-6213, United States of America
Tel: (1) 215 898 8220
Fax: (1) 215 746 5946
Email: humanities@sas.upenn.edu
Website: www.humanities.sas.upenn.edu
Contact: Jennifer Conway, Associate Director

The Penn Humanities Forum promotes interdisciplinary collaboration across University of Pennsylvania departments and schools and be-tween the University and the Philadelphia region. Each year, a broad topic sets the theme for a research seminar for resident and visiting scholars, courses and public events involving Philadelphia's cultural institutions.

Mellon Postdoctoral Fellowships in the Humanities
Subjects: Humanities.
Purpose: To support research by untenured junior scholars.

Eligibility: Open to junior scholars who, at the time of application, have received a PhD (degree must be in hand no later than December of the year preceding the fellowship) but have not held it for more than 8 years nor been granted tenure. Applicants may not be tenured during the year of the fellowship. Research proposals must relate to the Forum's annual topic of study and are invited in all areas of humanistic studies, except educational curriculum-building and the performing arts. Other requirements include residency at the University of Pennsylvania and the teaching of one freshman seminar in each of the two semesters.
Level of Study: Postdoctorate
Type: Fellowship
Value: US$42,000 plus health insurance
Length of Study: 1 academic year, non-renewable
Frequency: Annual
Study Establishment: The University of Pennsylvania
Country of Study: United States of America
No. of awards offered: 5
Application Procedure: Applicants must complete an application form, which can be downloaded from the Forum's website.
Closing Date: October 15th
Funding: Foundation
No. of awards given last year: 5
No. of applicants last year: 200
Additional Information: Fellows may not normally hold other awards concurrently.

PERKINS SCHOOL OF THEOLOGY

Southern Methodist University, PO Box 750133 Dallas, TX, 75275-0133, United States of America
Tel: (1) 214 768 2293
Fax: (1) 214 768 2293
Email: theology@smu.edu
Website: www.smu.edu

Perkins School of Theology is one of the 13 seminaries of The United Methodist Church (and one of the only 5 university-related United Methodist theological schools), located in the heart of Dallas, Texas, with extension programmes in Houston/Galveston and San Antonio.

Diaconia Graduate Fellowships
Subjects: Theology.
Purpose: To supplement the financial resources of United Methodist students.
Eligibility: Open to consecrated diaconal ministers or ordained deacons and full-time Doctoral students.
Level of Study: Doctorate
Type: Fellowships
Value: US$10,000
Frequency: Annual
Application Procedure: Request for application forms can be sent to theology@smu.edu
Closing Date: February 1st
Contributor: Section of Deacons and Diaconal Ministries, General Board of Higher Education and Ministry, The United Methodist Church

For further information contact:

Diaconia Graduate Fellowships Section of Deacons and Diaconal Ministries PO Box 340007, Nashville, TN, 37203-0007
Tel: 615 340 7375
Email: www.sddm@gbhem.org

THE PERRY FOUNDATION

31 Rossendale, Chelmsford, Essex, CM1 2UA, England
Tel: (44) 12 4526 0805
Fax: (44) 12 4526 0805
Email: david.naylor@blueyonder.co.uk
Website: www.perryfoundation.co.uk
Contact: Mr D J Naylor, Secretary and Chief Executive

The Perry Foundation offers research awards and postgraduate scholarships in agriculture and related disciplines. Research awards are offered to universities and institutes in the United Kingdom and are normally for a 3-year period. Postgraduate scholarships are offered to holders of First or Second Class Degrees and are for a 3-year period leading to a PhD. Both research awards and postgraduate scholarships must be undertaken at a university, college or research establishment in the United Kingdom.

Perry Postgraduate Scholarships
Subjects: The production and utilization of crops for food and non-food uses, ecologically acceptable and sustainable farming systems, including, in particular, water and nutrient balances, integrated disease and pest control systems for both crops and livestock, socioeconomic studies in the occupation and use of land, the rural economy and infrastructure and developments in marketing. Projects must be of definable benefit to United Kingdom agriculture.
Purpose: To enable postgraduates undertake research and investigative work in agriculture and related fields and to build up a pool of highly competent researchers in the United Kingdom.
Eligibility: Applicants must hold a First or Upper Second Class (Honours) Degrees in appropriate subjects, and must have been offered a place at a university, college or other establishment in the United Kingdom that will lead to the award of a PhD.
Level of Study: Doctorate
Type: Postgraduate scholarships
Value: UK £12,940–14,940 p.a. maintenance stipend, UK £3,300 p.a. tuition fees, plus bench fees up to a maximum of UK £2,500 per academic year
Length of Study: 3–4 years
Frequency: Annual
Study Establishment: Universities, colleges, research establishments and institutes in the United Kingdom
Country of Study: United Kingdom
No. of awards offered: 3–4 per year
Application Procedure: Applicants must write to or email the Foundation Secretary for an application form. Full details will be provided to suitable applicants.
Closing Date: November 30th
Funding: Private
No. of awards given last year: 3
No. of applicants last year: 100+
Additional Information: Projects must be of definable benefit to United Kingdom agriculture.

Perry Research Awards
Subjects: The production and utilization of crops for food and non-food uses, ecologically acceptable and sustainable farming systems, including, in particular, water and nutrient balances, integrated disease and pest control systems for both crops and livestock, socioeconomic studies in the occupation and use of land, the rural economy and infrastructure and developments in marketing. Must be of definable benefit to United Kingdom agriculture.
Purpose: To support research projects at research establishments, universities and colleges in the United Kingdom and investigative work into agriculture and related fields.
Eligibility: Open to universities, colleges and research establishments in the United Kingdom
Level of Study: Research
Type: Research award
Value: Research awards are normally UK £15,000 per year maximum
Length of Study: Normally 3 years
Frequency: Annual
Study Establishment: Universities, colleges, institutes and research establishments
Country of Study: United Kingdom
No. of awards offered: 3–4, depending on the availability of funds
Application Procedure: Applicants must write to the Foundation Secretary for a brochure, which contains details of the application procedure and application forms. Applications submitted by individuals must be supported by their university, college, institute or other establishment.
Closing Date: November 30th for the postgraduate scholarships and October 31st for the research awards
Funding: Private
No. of awards given last year: 1
No. of applicants last year: 100+

Additional Information: The research awards must be of definable benefit to United Kingdom agriculture.

PFIZER INC.

Pfizer MAP Program, MedPoint Communications, 1603 Orrington Ave, Suite 1900, Evanston, IL, 60201, United States of America
Tel: (1) 800 382 7075
Fax: (1) 847 425 7028
Email: MAPInfo@medpt.com
Website: www.promisingminds.com
Contact: MAP Program Coordinator

As a reflection of our commitment to the advancement of healthcare, Pfizer Inc. is pleased to support medical innovation in a wide range of discipline through our Medical and Academic Partnership (MAP) grants and awards. Our Fellowships and Scholar Grants, which offer at career-building opportunities for academic researchers in basic, outcomes, and patient-oriented research, are key among these efforts. In addition, Pfizer Visiting Professorships continue to be a resource for in-depth, clinically focused exchange between medical scholars, host organizations and outside scholar-scientists. At Pfizer, we are proud to support the innovators and ideas that help make better treatments and cures possible.

ACCF/Pfizer Visiting Professorships in Cardiovascular Medicine

Subjects: Medicine.
Purpose: To provide opportunities for academic institutions to host a recognized expert for three days of educational exchange.
Eligibility: Open to U.S. medical schools and/or teaching hospitals.
Level of Study: Professional development
Type: Grant
Value: US$7,500
Length of Study: 3 days
Frequency: Annual
Country of Study: United States of America
No. of awards offered: 8
Application Procedure: See the website.
Closing Date: January 26th
Funding: Corporation
Contributor: The American College of Cardiology Foundation (ACCF) and Pfizer Inc

AUAER/Pfizer Visiting Professorships in Urology

Subjects: Medicine.
Purpose: To provide opportunities for academic institutions to host a recognized expert for 3 days of educational exchange.
Eligibility: Open to US medical schools and/or teaching hospitals.
Level of Study: Postgraduate, Professional development
Type: Grant
Value: US$7,500
Frequency: Annual
Country of Study: United States of America
No. of awards offered: Up to 10
Application Procedure: See the website.
Closing Date: January 26th
Funding: Corporation
Contributor: The American Urological Association Education and Research Inc

Pfizer Atorvastatin Research Awards Program

Subjects: Medicine.
Purpose: To support outstanding investigators at the early stages of their careers in academic research.
Eligibility: Open to US citizens who hold an MD or PhD.
Level of Study: Research
Type: Grant
Value: US$50,000
Length of Study: 2 years
Frequency: Annual
No. of awards offered: 20
Application Procedure: A proposal must be submitted. See the website for further information.
Closing Date: March 17th
Funding: Corporation

Pfizer Fellowship in Biological Psychiatry

Subjects: Biological psychiatry.
Purpose: To provide training opportunities for promoting young physicians who wish to pursue research in an academic environment.
Eligibility: Open to applicants who are the citizens of the United States.
Level of Study: Postdoctorate
Type: Grant
Value: US$65,000
Length of Study: 3 years
Frequency: Annual
Application Procedure: A complete form must be submitted.
Closing Date: December 9th

For further information contact:

UF college of medicine, 392-5398, United States of America
Contact: Dr Kristen Madsen, Director, Grants Programme Development

Pfizer Fellowships in Health Literary Clear Health Communication

Subjects: Medicine, health administration.
Purpose: To fund scientific research in health literary/clear health communication.
Eligibility: Open to US citizens who have undergone atleast 1 year of postdoctoral clinical training.
Level of Study: Doctorate, Professional development
Type: Fellowship
Value: US$130,000
Length of Study: 2 years
Frequency: Annual
No. of awards offered: 1
Application Procedure: See the website.
Closing Date: January 6th
Funding: Corporation

The Pfizer Fellowships in Rheumatology/Immunology

Subjects: Rheumatology and immunology.
Purpose: To provide training opportunities for promising young physicians who wish to pursue research in an academic environment.
Eligibility: Open to applicants who demonstrate a strong career interest in academic research in rheumatology and immunology.
Level of Study: Postdoctorate, Postgraduate
Type: Fellowship
Value: Upto eight awards of $7,500 each
Length of Study: 3 years
Frequency: Annual
Application Procedure: See the website.
Closing Date: February 5th
Funding: Commercial

For further information contact:

VF College of Medicine, 392-5398
Contact: Dr Kristen Madsen, Director, Grants Programme Development

Pfizer International HDL Research Awards Program

Subjects: Biology.
Purpose: To support outstanding investigators in the field of HDL biology.
Type: Grant
Value: US$110,000 per year
Length of Study: 2 years
Frequency: Annual
Application Procedure: See the website.
Closing Date: See the website
No. of awards given last year: 14

For further information contact:

International HDL Research Awards, 335 W. 16th Street., 4th Floor, New York, United States of America
Contact: Grants Co-ordinator

Pfizer Scholars Grants in Public Health
Subjects: Health administration.
Purpose: To support the career development of faculty.
Eligibility: Open to US citizens who demonstrate that at least 75 per cent their professional time will be devoted to research.
Level of Study: Postgraduate, Professional development
Type: Grant
Value: US$130,000
Length of Study: 2 years
Frequency: Annual
No. of awards offered: Up to 2
Application Procedure: See the website.
Closing Date: January 9th

Pfizer Visiting Professorship in Neurology
Subjects: Neurology.
Purpose: To bring new educational value to the institution.
Eligibility: Open to accredited US medical schools and/or affiliated teaching hospitals.
Level of Study: Postgraduate, Professional development
Type: Grant
Value: US$7,500 each
Length of Study: 3 days
Frequency: Annual
No. of awards offered: Up to 8
Application Procedure: See the website.
Closing Date: January 26th
Contributor: Pfizer Inc

Pfizer Visiting Professorships in Clear Health Literacy/ Clear Health Communication
Subjects: Health administration.
Purpose: To facilitate in-depth, educationally focused visits by prominent experts to US healthcare organizations.
Eligibility: Open to US medical schools and/or teaching hospitals.
Level of Study: Professional development
Type: Grant
Value: US$7,500 each
Length of Study: 3 days
Frequency: Annual
No. of awards offered: Up to 10
Application Procedure: See the website.
Closing Date: January 26th
Funding: Corporation

Pfizer Visiting Professorships in Diabetes
Subjects: Endocrinology.
Purpose: To bring new educational value to the institution.
Eligibility: Open to all accredited US medical schools (allopathic or osteopathic).
Level of Study: Postgraduate, Professional development
Type: Grant
Value: US$7,500 each
Length of Study: 3 days
Frequency: Annual
No. of awards offered: Up to 8
Application Procedure: See the website.
Closing Date: January 26th

Pfizer Visiting Professorships in Oncology
Subjects: Oncology.
Purpose: To advance oncology.
Eligibility: Open to accredited US. Medical schools, teaching hospitals and/or academic or community cancer centers.
Level of Study: Postgraduate, Professional development
Type: Grant
Value: US$7,500
Length of Study: 3 days
Frequency: Annual
No. of awards offered: Up to 8
Application Procedure: See the website.
Closing Date: January 26th
Funding: Corporation

Pfizer Visiting Professorships in Pulmonology
Subjects: Pulmonology.
Purpose: To bring new educational value to the institution.
Eligibility: Open to accredited US. Medical schools and/or affiliated teaching hospitals.
Level of Study: Postgraduate, Professional development
Type: Grant
Value: US$7,500 each
Length of Study: 3 days
Frequency: Annual
No. of awards offered: Up to 8
Application Procedure: See the website.
Closing Date: Febraury 5th

Pfizer Visiting Professorships Program
Subjects: Medicine.
Purpose: To create opportunities for selected institutions to invite a distinguished expert for three days of teaching.
Eligibility: Open to accredited medical schools and/or affiliated teaching hospitals.
Level of Study: Postgraduate
Type: Grant
Value: US$7,500 each
Frequency: Annual
No. of awards offered: Up to 10
Application Procedure: Applications available online.
Closing Date: January 26th

PHARMACEUTICAL RESEARCH AND MANUFACTURERS OF AMERICA FOUNDATION (PHRMAF)

950 F Street, N.W., Suite 300, Washington, DC, 20004, United States of America
Tel: (1) 202 572 7756
Fax: (1) 202 572 7799
Email: foundation@phrma.org
Website: www.phrmafoundation.org
Contact: Ms Eileen M McCarron, Executive Director

The Pharmaceutical Research and Manufacturers of America Foundation (PhRMAF) is a non-profit organization, established in 1965 to promote public health through scientific and medical research. It provides funding for research and for the education and training of scientists and physicians who have selected pharmacology, pharmaceutics, toxicology, informatics or health outcomes as a career choice.

PhRMAF Paul Calabresi Medical Student Research Fellowship
Subjects: Pharmacology, toxicology and clinical pharmacology.
Purpose: To support medical/dental students who have substantial interests in research and teaching careers in pharmacology/clinical pharmacology and who are willing to work full time in a specific research effort.
Eligibility: A candidate must be enrolled in a United States medical/dental school and have finished at least 1 year of the school curriculum. Priority consideration will be given to those candidates who project strong commitments to careers in the field of clinical pharmacology. Applicants must be citizens or permanent residents of the US.
Level of Study: Graduate, Postgraduate, Predoctorate
Type: Fellowship
Value: Maximum stipend of US $18,000
Length of Study: 3 months–2 years
Frequency: Annual
Study Establishment: An accredited school of medicine or dentistry
Country of Study: United States of America
Application Procedure: Requests for the Paul Calabresi Medical Student Research Fellowship are to be submitted online by the appropriate representative of the school or university.
Closing Date: August 1st
Funding: Private
No. of awards given last year: 3
Additional Information: Research projects involving animal subjects require a statement that the project will follow the guidelines set forth

by the NIH Guide for the Care and Use of Laboratory Animals and that the project will be performed, reviewed and approved by a faculty committee of the university. The recipient school is expected to submit an annual report on the disposition of the funds awarded by PhRMAF. A final report is due within 60 days after the conclusion of the grant. These reports must be signed by the recipient's sponsor. Any publications, speeches, presentations and other materials that stem directly from the research supported by this grant must acknowledge the support of PhRMAF. 3 reprints of each publication should be forwarded to PhRMAF for further information visit the Foundation's website.

PhRMAF Postdoctoral Fellowships in Health Outcomes Research

Subjects: Health outcomes research, patient-reported outcomes or pharmacoeconomics.
Purpose: To support well-trained graduates from PharmD, MD and PhD programmes who seek to further develop and refine their research skills through formal postdoctoral training.
Eligibility: Open to full-time students who are citizens or permanent residents of the United States of America. Applicants must have a firm commitment from a university in the United States of America before applying for a PhRMAF award. The department's chair will be expected to verify the applicant's doctoral candidacy.
Level of Study: Graduate, Postdoctorate, Postgraduate
Type: Fellowship
Value: US$40,000 stipend per year
Length of Study: 1–2 years
Frequency: Annual
Study Establishment: An accredited school of medicine, pharmacy, dentistry, public health or nursing
Country of Study: United States of America
No. of awards offered: Varies
Application Procedure: Applications must include a research plan written by the applicant, the mentor's research record and a description of how the mentored experience will enhance the applicant's career development in health outcomes research. Applications are to be submitted online by the appropriate representative of the school or university to the Executive Director at PhRMAF. Detailed application requirements are stated on the Foundation's website where applicants can download an application form and read the specific requirements for each award.
Closing Date: October 1st
Funding: Private

PhRMAF Postdoctoral Fellowships in Informatics

Subjects: Informatics.
Purpose: To support well-trained graduates from PhD programmes who seek to further develop and refine their informatics research skills through formal postdoctoral training.
Eligibility: Open to full-time students who are citizens or permanent residents of the United States of America. Applicants must have a firm commitment from a university in the United States of America before applying for a PhRMAF award. The department's chair will be expected to verify the applicant's doctoral candidacy.
Level of Study: Postdoctorate
Type: Fellowship
Value: US$40,000 per year
Length of Study: 1–2 years
Frequency: Annual
Country of Study: United States of America
No. of awards offered: Varies
Application Procedure: Applicants must submit an application including a research plan written by the applicant, the mentor's research record and a description of how the mentored experience will enhance the applicant's career development in informatics. Applications are to be submitted online by the appropriate representative of the school or university to the Executive Director of at PhRMAF. Detailed application requirements are stated on the Foundation's website where the applicant can download an application form and read the specific requirements for each award.
Closing Date: September 1st
Funding: Private
Additional Information: Research projects involving animal subjects require a statement that the project will follow the guidelines set forth

by the NIH Guide for the Care and Use of Laboratory Animals and that the project will be performed, reviewed and approved by a faculty committee of the university.

PhRMAF Postdoctoral Fellowships in Pharmaceutics

Subjects: Pharmaceutics.
Purpose: To encourage graduates to continue to develop and refine their pharmaceutics research skills through formal postdoctoral training.
Eligibility: Open to graduates from PhD programmes in pharmaceutics. Before an individual is eligible to apply for a PhRMAF award, the applicants must first have a firm commitment from a university in the United States of America. Applicants must be full-time students, and the department's chair is expected to verify the applicant's doctoral candidacy. All applicants must be citizens of the United States of America or permanent residents.
Level of Study: Postdoctorate, Postgraduate
Type: Fellowship
Value: US$40,000 stipend
Length of Study: 1–2 years
Frequency: Annual
Study Establishment: Schools of pharmacy in the United States of America
Country of Study: United States of America
No. of awards offered: Varies
Application Procedure: Applicants must visit the Foundation's website where detailed application requirements are stated and application forms can be downloaded. Applications must include a research plan written by the applicant, the mentor's research record and a description of how the mentored experience will enhance the applicant's career development in pharmaceutics. Applications are to be submitted online by the appropriate representative of the school or university to the Executive Director at PhRMAF.
Closing Date: April 1st
Funding: Private
Additional Information: Research projects involving animal subjects require a statement that the project will follow the guidelines set forth by the NIH Guide for the Care and Use of Laboratory Animals and that the project will be performed, reviewed and approved by a faculty committee of the university.

PhRMAF Postdoctoral Fellowships in Pharmacology/ Toxicology

Subjects: Pharmacology and toxicology.
Purpose: To facilitate career entry into pharmacology or toxicology at the level of postdoctoral training and to provide funding for recent graduates from PhD programmes who seek to develop research skills through formal postdoctoral training.
Eligibility: Open to applicants with a firm commitment from a university in the United States of America, prior to applying for a PhRMAF award. Applications must be submitted online by an accredited United States of America school and all applicants must be citizens of the United States of America or permanent residents.
Level of Study: Postdoctorate
Type: Fellowship
Value: US$40,000 stipend per year
Length of Study: 1–2 years
Frequency: Annual
Study Establishment: An accredited school of medicine, pharmacy, dentistry or veterinary medicine
Country of Study: United States of America
No. of awards offered: Varies
Application Procedure: Applicants must visit the Foundation's website where detailed application requirements are stated and application forms can be downloaded. Applications must be submitted online by the appropriate representative of the school or university to the Executive Director at PhRMAF. An application must include a research plan written by the applicant, a mentor's research record and a description of how the mentored experience will enhance the applicant's career development on pharmacology or toxicology.
Closing Date: September 1st
Funding: Private
Additional Information: Research projects involving animal subjects require a statement that the project will follow the guidelines set forth by the NIH Guide for the Care and Use of Laboratory Animals and that

the project will be performed, reviewed and approved by a faculty committee of the university.

PhRMAF Predoctoral Fellowships in Health Outcomes Research

Subjects: Health outcomes research, patient-reported outcomes and pharmacoeconomics.

Purpose: To support a student's PhD doctoral programme after coursework has been completed and the remaining training activity is the student's research project.

Eligibility: Open to applicants who have a firm commitment from a university in the United States of America. Applicants must be full-time students and the department's chair is expected to verify the applicant's doctoral candidacy. All applicants must be citizens of the United States of America or permanent residents.

Level of Study: Postgraduate

Type: Fellowship

Value: A stipend of US$20,000 per year, up to US$500 per year may be used for expenses associated with thesis preparation

Length of Study: 1–2 years

Frequency: Annual

Study Establishment: An accredited school of medicine, pharmacy, dentistry, public health or nursing

Country of Study: United States of America

No. of awards offered: Varies

Application Procedure: Applications are to be submitted online by the appropriate representative of the school or university to the Executive Director at PhRMAF. Detailed application requirements are stated on the Foundation's website where the applicant can download an application form and read the specific requirements for each award.

Closing Date: October 1st

Funding: Private

Additional Information: Research projects involving animal subjects require a statement that the project will follow the guidelines set forth by the NIH Guide for the Care and Use of Laboratory Animals and that the project will be performed, reviewed and approved by a faculty committee of the university.

PhRMAF Predoctoral Fellowships in Pharmaceutics

Subjects: Pharmaceutics.

Purpose: To support promising students during their thesis research.

Eligibility: Open to full-time students and citizens or permanent residents of the United States of America. Applicants must have a firm commitment from a university in the United States of America prior to applying for a PhRMAF award and the department's chair will be expected to verify the applicant's doctoral candidacy.

Level of Study: Postgraduate

Type: Fellowship

Value: A stipend of US$20,000 per year, which includes up to US$500 for expenses associated with thesis research

Length of Study: 1–2 years

Frequency: Annual

Study Establishment: A school of pharmacy

Country of Study: United States of America

No. of awards offered: Varies

Application Procedure: Applicants must visit the Foundation's website where detailed application requirements are stated and application forms can be downloaded. Applications must be submitted online by the appropriate representative of the school or university to the Executive Director of at PhRMAF.

Closing Date: October 1st

Funding: Private

Additional Information: Research projects involving animal subjects require a statement that the project will follow the guidelines set forth by the NIH Guide for the Care and Use of Laboratory Animals and that the project will be performed, reviewed and approved by a faculty committee of the university.

PhRMAF Predoctoral Fellowships in Pharmacology/Toxicology

Subjects: Pharmacology and toxicology.

Purpose: To support promising students during their thesis research.

Eligibility: Open to advanced students who have completed the bulk of their pre-thesis requirements and are starting their thesis research by the time the award is activated. Students just starting graduate

school should not apply. Before an individual is eligible to apply for a PhRMAF award, the applicant must have a firm commitment from a university in the United States of America. The applicant must be a citizen or permanent resident of the United States of America.

Level of Study: Predoctorate

Type: Fellowship

Value: A stipend of US$20,000 per year, which includes up to US$500 for expenses associated with thesis research

Length of Study: 1–2 years

Frequency: Annual

Study Establishment: An accredited school of medicine, pharmacy, dentistry or veterinary medicine

Country of Study: United States of America

No. of awards offered: Varies

Application Procedure: Applicants must visit the Foundation's website where detailed application requirements are stated and application forms can be downloaded. Applications must be submitted online by the appropriate representative of the school or university to the Executive Director at PhRMAF.

Closing Date: September 1st

Funding: Private

Additional Information: Research projects involving animal subjects require a statement that the project will follow the guidelines set forth by the NIH Guide for the Care and Use of Laboratory Animals and that the project will be performed, reviewed and approved by a faculty committee of the university.

PhRMAF Research Starter Grants in Health Outcomes Research

Subjects: Health outcomes research, patient-reported outcomes and pharmacoeconomics.

Purpose: To support individuals beginning independent research careers in academia.

Eligibility: Open to applicants sponsored by the school or university at which the research is to be conducted. Applicants must be appointed to an entry level tenure track or equivalent permanent position in a department or unit responsible for pharmaceutical activities as part of its core mission. All applicants must be citizens or permanent residents of the United States of America.

Level of Study: Graduate, Postgraduate

Type: Grant

Value: US$30,000 per year

Length of Study: 1–2 years

Frequency: Annual

Study Establishment: An accredited school of medicine, pharmacy, dentistry, public health or nursing

Country of Study: United States of America

No. of awards offered: Varies

Application Procedure: Applicants must visit the Foundations' website where detailed application requirements are stated and application forms can be downloaded. Applications must be submitted online by the appropriate representative of the school or university to the Executive Director of Development at PhRMAF. The description of an applicant's career goals and the departmental chair's description of institutional support for the applicant's salary are all important while evaluating an application.

Closing Date: October 1st

Funding: Private

Additional Information: Research projects involving animal subjects require a statement that the project will follow the guidelines set forth by the NIH Guide for the Care and Use of Laboratory Animals and that the project will be performed, reviewed and approved by a faculty committee of the university.

PhRMAF Research Starter Grants in Informatics

Subjects: Informatics.

Purpose: To offer support to new investigators beginning their independent research careers in academia at the faculty level.

Eligibility: Open to applicants sponsored by the school or university at which the research is to be conducted. Applicants must be appointed online to an entry level tenure track or equivalent permanent position in a department or unit responsible for informatics activities as part of its core mission. All applicants must be citizens or permanent residents of the United States of America.

Level of Study: Postdoctorate, Postgraduate, Graduate

Type: Grant
Value: US$30,000 per year
Length of Study: 1–2 years
Frequency: Annual
Country of Study: United States of America
No. of awards offered: Varies
Application Procedure: Applicants must visit the Foundation's website where detailed application requirements are stated and application forms can be downloaded. Applications must be submitted online by the appropriate representative of the school or university to the Executive Director at PhRMAF. The description of an applicant's career goals and the departmental chair's description of institutional support for the applicant's salary are all important while evaluating an application.
Closing Date: September 1st
Funding: Private
Additional Information: Research projects involving animal subjects require a statement that the project will follow the guidelines set forth by the NIH Guide for the Care and Use of Laboratory Animals and that the project will be performed, reviewed and approved by a faculty committee of the university.

PhRMAF Research Starter Grants in Pharmaceutics

Subjects: Pharmaceutics.
Purpose: To offer support to new investigators beginning their independent research careers in academia.
Eligibility: Open to applicants sponsored by the school or university at which the research is to be conducted. Applicants must be appointed to an entry level tenure track or equivalent permanent position in a department or unit responsible for pharmaceutical activities as part of its core mission. All applicants must be citizens or permanent residents of the United States of America.
Level of Study: Graduate, Postdoctorate, Postgraduate
Type: Grant
Value: US$30,000 per year for upto 2 years
Length of Study: 1–2 years
Frequency: Annual
Study Establishment: Schools of pharmacy
Country of Study: United States of America
No. of awards offered: Varies
Application Procedure: Applicants must visit the website where detailed application requirements are stated and application forms can be downloaded. Applications must be submitted online by the appropriate representative of the school or university to the Executive Director at PhRMAF. The description of an applicant's career goals and the departmental chair's description of institutional support for the applicant's salary are all important while evaluating an application.
Closing Date: October 1st
Funding: Private
Additional Information: Research projects involving animal subjects require a statement that the project will follow the guidelines set forth by the NIH Guide for the Care and Use of Laboratory Animals and that the project will be performed, reviewed and approved by a faculty committee of the university.

PhRMAF Research Starter Grants in Pharmacology/Toxicology

Subjects: Pharmacology and toxicology.
Purpose: To support individuals beginning independent research careers in academia.
Eligibility: Open to applicants sponsored by the school or university at which the research is to be conducted. Applicants must be appointed to an entry level tenure track or equivalent permanent position in a department or unit responsible for pharmacology or toxicology activities as part of its core mission. All applicants must be citizens or permanent residents of the United States of America.
Level of Study: Graduate, Postdoctorate, Postgraduate
Type: Grant
Value: US$30,000 per year for upto 2 years
Length of Study: 1–2 years
Frequency: Annual
Study Establishment: An accredited school of medicine, pharmacy, dentistry or veterinary medicine
Country of Study: United States of America

Application Procedure: Applicants must visit the website where detailed application requirements are stated and application forms can be downloaded. Applications must be submitted online by the appropriate representative of the school or university to the Executive Director of at PhRMAF. The description of an applicant's career goals and the departmental chair's description of institutional support for the applicant's salary are all important while evaluating an application.
Closing Date: September 1st
Funding: Private
Additional Information: Research projects involving animal subjects require a statement that the project will follow the guidelines set forth by the NIH Guide for the Care and Use of Laboratory Animals and that the project will be performed, reviewed and approved by a faculty committee of the university.

PhRMAF Sabbatical Fellowships in Health Outcomes Research

Subjects: Health outcomes research, patient-reported outcomes and pharmacoeconomics.
Purpose: To support faculty members at all levels with active research programmes and the opportunity to work at other institutions to learn new skills or develop new collaborations that will enhance their research and research training activities in health outcomes.
Eligibility: Open to citizens or permanent residents of the United States of America. Applicants are expected to have approval for a sabbatical leave from their home institution and to provide an endorsement from the mentor who will sponsor their visiting scientific activity. Matching funds must be provided through the university.
Level of Study: Professional development, Postdoctorate, Postgraduate
Type: Fellowship
Value: A stipend of up to US$40,000
Length of Study: 6 months–1 year
Frequency: Annual
Study Establishment: An accredited school of medicine, pharmacy, dentistry, public health or nursing
Country of Study: United States of America
No. of awards offered: Varies
Application Procedure: Applications are to be submitted online by the appropriate representative of the school or university to the Executive Director at PhRMAF. Detailed application requirements are stated on the Foundation's website where applicants can download an application form and read the specific requirements for each award.
Closing Date: October 1st
Funding: Private
Additional Information: Research projects involving animal subjects require a statement that the project will follow the guidelines set forth by the NIH Guide for the Care and Use of Laboratory Animals and that the project will be performed, reviewed and approved by a faculty committee of the university.

PhRMAF Sabbatical Fellowships in Informatics

Subjects: Informatics.
Purpose: To give faculty members at all levels with active research programmes an opportunity to work at other institutions and to develop new collaborations that will enhance their research and research training activities in informatics.
Eligibility: Applicants are expected to have approval for a sabbatical leave from their home institution and provide an endorsement from the mentor who will sponsor their visiting scientific activity. Matching funds must be provided through the university. All applicants must be citizens of the United States of America or permanent residents.
Level of Study: Postgraduate, Professional development, Postdoctorate
Type: Fellowship
Value: Up to US$40,000 stipend
Length of Study: 6 months–1 year
Frequency: Annual
Country of Study: United States of America
No. of awards offered: Varies
Application Procedure: Applications are to be submitted online by the appropriate representative of the school or university to the Executive Director of at PhRMAF. Detailed application requirements are stated on the Foundation's website where the applicant can download an application form and read the specific requirements for each award.

Closing Date: September 1st
Funding: Private
Additional Information: Research projects involving animal subjects require a statement that the project will follow the guidelines set forth by the NIH Guide for the Care and Use of Laboratory Animals and that the project will be performed, reviewed and approved by a faculty committee of the university.

PhRMAF Sabbatical Fellowships in Pharmaceutics

Subjects: Pharmaceutics.
Purpose: To enable pharmaceutics faculty members at all levels with active research programmes an opportunity to work at other institutions and to develop new collaborations that will enhance their research and research training activities in pharmaceutics.
Eligibility: Open to citizens of the United States of America or permanent residents. Applicants are expected to have approval for a sabbatical leave from their home institution and provide an endorsement from the mentor who will sponsor their sabbatical activity. Matching funds must be provided through the university.
Level of Study: Professional development, Postdoctorate, Postgraduate
Type: Fellowship
Value: A stipend of up to US$40,000
Length of Study: 6 months–1 year
Frequency: Annual
Study Establishment: An approved institute
Country of Study: United States of America
Application Procedure: Applicants must visit the Foundation's website where detailed application requirements are stated and application forms can be downloaded. Applications must be submitted online by the appropriate representative of the school or university to the Executive Director of at PhRMAF.
Closing Date: October 1st
Funding: Private
Additional Information: Research projects involving animal subjects require a statement that the project will follow the guidelines set forth by the NIH Guide for the Care and Use of Laboratory Animals and that the project will be performed, reviewed and approved by a faculty committee of the university.

PhRMAF Sabbatical Fellowships in Pharmacology/ Toxicology

Subjects: Pharmacology and toxicology.
Purpose: To give faculty members at all levels with active research programmes an opportunity to work at other institutions to learn new skills or develop new collaborations that will enhance their research and research training activities in pharmacology or toxicology.
Eligibility: Open to applicants with approval for sabbatical leave from their home institution and who can provide an endorsement from the mentor who will sponsor their visiting scientific activity. Matching funds must be provided through the university. All applicants must be citizens or permanent residents of the United States of America.
Level of Study: Professional development, Postgraduate, Postdoctorate
Type: Fellowship
Value: Up to US$40,000 stipend
Length of Study: 6 months–1 year
Frequency: Annual
Study Establishment: An accredited school of medicine, pharmacy, dentistry or veterinary medicine
Country of Study: United States of America
No. of awards offered: Varies
Application Procedure: Applicants must visit the Foundation's website where detailed application requirements are stated and application forms can be downloaded. Applications must be submitted online by the appropriate representative of the school or university to the Executive Director of at PhRMAF.
Closing Date: September 1st
Funding: Private
Additional Information: Research projects involving animal subjects require a statement that the project will follow the guidelines set forth by the NIH Guide for the Care and Use of Laboratory Animals and that the project will be performed, reviewed and approved by a faculty committee of the university.

THE PHI BETA KAPPA SOCIETY

1606 New Hampshire Avenue NW, Washington, DC, 20009,
United States of America
Tel: (1) 202 745 3235
Fax: (1) 202 986 1601
Email: awards@pbk.org
Website: www.pbk.org
Contact: Lucinda Morales, Co-ordinator of Society Events

The Phi Beta Kappa Society has pursued its mission of fostering and recognizing excellence in the liberal arts and sciences since 1776.

Mary Isabel Sibley Fellowship

Subjects: French language or literature in even-numbered years and Greek language, literature, history or archaeology in odd-numbered years.
Purpose: To recognize female scholars who have demonstrated their ability to carry out original research.
Eligibility: Open to unmarried women aged 25–35 who have demonstrated their ability to carry out original research. Candidates must hold a Doctorate or have fulfilled all the requirements for the Doctorate except the dissertation. There are no restrictions as to nationality and the award is not restricted to members of the Phi Beta Kappa Society.
Level of Study: Doctorate, Postdoctorate, Postgraduate
Type: Fellowship
Value: US$20,000
Length of Study: 1 year, non-renewable
Frequency: Annual
Country of Study: Any country
No. of awards offered: 1
Application Procedure: Applicants must complete an application form, available from the website, and submit this with transcripts and references.
Closing Date: January 15th
Funding: Private
No. of awards given last year: 1
No. of applicants last year: 50

The Walter J Jensen Fellowship for French Language, Literature and Culture

Subjects: French language, literature and culture.
Purpose: To help educators and researchers improve education in Standard French language, literature and culture and in the study of Standard French in the United States of America.
Eligibility: Candidates must be under 40 years of age and must be able to certify their career that will involve active use of the French language.
Level of Study: Postgraduate
Type: Fellowship
Value: US$10,000, with additional support available for airfare and, if applicable, support of dependant(s)
Length of Study: This 1-year-long fellowship includes 6 months of residence and study
Frequency: Annual
Country of Study: France
No. of awards offered: 1 per year
Application Procedure: Applicants must complete self-managed application form available in the website and submit it along with academic records, references, plans for study and proof of superior competence in French according to the standards established by the American Association for Teachers of French.
Closing Date: October 1st of each year
Funding: Private
Contributor: Dr Walter J Jensen
No. of awards given last year: 1
No. of applicants last year: 15
Additional Information: Preference may be given to, though the eligibility is not restricted to, members of Phi Beta Kappa and teachers at the high school level or above. Standard French is defined to exclude a focus on Creole, Quebecois and other dialects.

PHILHARMONIA ORCHESTRA

Martin Musical Scholarship Fund, 6th Floor,
The Tower Building, 11 York Road, London, SE1 7NX,
United Kingdom
Tel: (44) 020 7921 3900
Fax: (44) 020 7921 3950
Email: orchestra@philharmonia.co.uk
Website: www.philharmonia.co.uk
Contact: Mr Martyn Jones, Administrator

Emanual Hurwitz Award for Violinists of British Nationality

Subjects: Musical performance on violin only.
Purpose: To reward exceptional musical talent.
Eligibility: Open to British nationals only.
Level of Study: Postgraduate
Type: Award
Value: Varies
Frequency: Annual
Country of Study: Any country
No. of awards offered: Varies
Application Procedure: Applicants must write for details.
Closing Date: Please contact the organization

John E Mortimer Foundation Awards

Subjects: Musical performance on all instruments.
Purpose: To reward exceptional musical talent.
Eligibility: Applicants must write for details.
Level of Study: Postgraduate
Type: Award
Value: Prizes of varying value
Frequency: Annual
Country of Study: Any country
No. of awards offered: Varies
Application Procedure: Applicants must complete an application form and submit this with a stamped addressed envelope and a registration fee of UK £15.
Closing Date: December 1st

June Allison Award

Subjects: Musical performance on woodwind only.
Purpose: To assist exceptional musical talent with specialist and advanced study, and to help bridge the gap between study and fully professional status.
Eligibility: Applicants must write for details.
Level of Study: Postgraduate
Type: Award
Value: UK £500 plus recital
Frequency: Annual
Country of Study: Any country
Application Procedure: Applicants must complete an application form and submit this with a stamped addressed envelope and a non-returnable registration fee of UK £10.
Closing Date: December 1st

Martin Musical Scholarships

Subjects: Musical performance.
Purpose: To assist exceptional musical talent with specialist and advanced study and to help in bridging the gap between study and fully professional status.
Eligibility: Open to practising musicians as well as students who are instrumental performers, including pianists, preparing for a career on the concert platform either as a soloist or orchestral player, and are of no more than 25 years of age. Preference is given to United Kingdom citizens.
Level of Study: Postgraduate
Type: Scholarship
Value: Varies
Length of Study: 2 years, with a possibility of renewal
Frequency: Annual
No. of awards offered: Varies
Application Procedure: Applicants must complete an application form.
Closing Date: October 1st

Funding: Private
No. of awards given last year: 50
No. of applicants last year: 71
Additional Information: It is not the present policy of the Fund to support organists, singers, conductors, composers, academic students or piano accompanists.

Reginald Conway Memorial Award for String Performers

Subjects: Musical performance on strings only.
Purpose: To reward exceptional musical talent.
Eligibility: Applicants must write for details.
Level of Study: Postgraduate
Type: Award
Value: Varies
Frequency: Annual
Country of Study: Any country
Application Procedure: Applicants must write for details.
Closing Date: Please contact the organization

Sidney Perry Scholarship

Subjects: Musical performance.
Purpose: To support postgraduate study.
Eligibility: Open to nationals of any country.
Level of Study: Postgraduate
Type: Scholarship
Value: Varies
Length of Study: Up to 2 years
Frequency: Annual
Country of Study: Any country
No. of awards offered: Varies
Application Procedure: Applicants must complete an application form.
Closing Date: October 1st
No. of awards given last year: 3

PHILLIPS EXETER ACADEMY

20 Main Street, Exeter, NH, 03833-2460,
United States of America
Tel: (1) 603 777 3405
Fax: (1) 603 777 4393
Email: kcurwen@exeter.edu
Website: www.exeter.edu
Contact: Dr Kathleen Curwen, Dean of Faculty

Phillips Exeter Academy is a private secondary school with over 1,000 students.

George Bennett Fellowship

Subjects: Creative writing.
Purpose: To allow a person commencing a career as a writer the time and freedom from material considerations to complete a manuscript in progress.
Eligibility: Preference is given to writers who have not published a book with a major commercial publisher. Works must be in English.
Level of Study: Unrestricted
Type: Fellowship
Value: US$13,000 per year
Frequency: Annual
Study Establishment: Phillips Exeter Academy, Exeter, NH
Country of Study: United States of America
No. of awards offered: 1
Application Procedure: Applicants must send a manuscript, together with an application form, personal statement and US$10.
Closing Date: December 1st for the following academic year
Funding: Private
No. of awards given last year: 1
No. of applicants last year: 150
Additional Information: Duties include being in residence for 1 academic year while working on the manuscript and informal availability to student writers. For further information, please visit the Academy's website.

```
THE PHILLIPS
FOUNDATION
```

THE PHILLIPS FOUNDATION

1 Massachusetts Avenue, NW Suite 620, Washington DC, 20001,
United States of America
Tel: (1) 202 250 3887 ext 609
Email: jfarley@thephillipsfoundation.org
Website: www.thephillipsfoundation.org
Contact: John Farley

The Phillips Foundation is a non-profit organization founded in 1990 to
advance constitutional principles, a democratic society and a vibrant
free enterprise system.

The Phillips Foundation Journalism Fellowship Program
Subjects: Journalism (free market, history and law enforcement).
Purpose: To support working print journalist who share the same
mission as the Foundation.
Eligibility: Open to US citizens who are working journalists with less
than 10 years of professional experience in print journalism.
Level of Study: Professional development
Type: Fellowships
Value: US$75,000 + US$50,000 for full-time students, $25,000 for
part-time students
Length of Study: 1 year
Frequency: Annual
Country of Study: United States of America
Application Procedure: Applicants can download application forms
from the website www.thephillipsfoundation.org
Closing Date: March 1st
No. of awards given last year: 8

THE PIERRE ELLIOTT TRUDEAU FOUNDATION

1514 Doctor Penfield Avenue, Montreal, QC, H3G-1B9, Canada
Tel: (1) 514 938 0001
Fax: (1) 514 938 0046
Email: tfinfo@trudeaufoundation.ca
Website: www.trudeaufoundation.ca

The Pierre Elliott Trudeau Foundation seeks to promote outstanding
research in the social sciences and humanities and to foster a fruitful
dialogue between scholars and policymakers in government, business, voluntary sector, professions and the arts community.

Trudeau Foundation Doctoral Scholarships
Subjects: Social sciences and humanities.
Purpose: To support doctoral candidates pursuing research of com-
pelling present-day concern in areas touching upon 1 or more of the 4
themes of the Foundation: human rights and social justice, respon-
sible citizenship, Canada and the world, humans and their natural
environment.
Eligibility: Open to a Trudeau Scholar who is registered full-time in a
doctoral level programme approved by the Foundation.
Level of Study: Doctorate
Type: Scholarships
Value: Canadian $40,000
Length of Study: 4 years
Frequency: Annual
Country of Study: Canada
No. of awards offered: 15
Application Procedure: Applications to the Foundation must come
from the applicant's academic institution as a result of an internal
competition.
Closing Date: January 10th
Funding: Foundation
Contributor: Trudeau Foundation
Additional Information: An additional Canadian $20,000 per year
will be available to support research-related travel approved by the
Foundation, and to cover networking expenses associated with events

and joint projects undertaken within the framework of the Foundation's
programmes.

PLASTIC SURGERY EDUCATIONAL FOUNDATION (PSEF)

444 East Algonquin Road, Arlington Heights, IL, 60005, United States
of America
Tel: (1) 847 228 9900
Fax: (1) 847 228 9131
Email: cas@plasticsurgery.org
Website: www.plasticsurgery.org
Contact: Ms Mary Lewis

The mission of the Plastic Surgery Educational Foundation (PSEF) is
to develop and support domestic and international education as well
as research and public service activities of plastic surgeons.

Plastic Surgery Basic Research Grant
Subjects: Plastic surgery.
Purpose: To encourage young investigators to conduct clinical re-
search.
Eligibility: Open to plastic surgeons and holders of an MD or PhD
working in plastic surgery. Residents, Fellows and non-members of
the ASPRS or the PSEF require the sponsorship of a member or
candidate from the ASPRS or the PSEF or the American Society for
Aesthetic Plastic Surgery membership.
Level of Study: Postgraduate, Professional development
Value: Research seed money up to US$5,000
Length of Study: 1 year
Frequency: Annual
Country of Study: Any country
No. of awards offered: Approx. 20
Application Procedure: Applicants must complete an application
available on the website.
Closing Date: Mid-January
Funding: Private
Contributor: The Plastic Surgery Educational Foundation

Plastic Surgery Research Fellowship Award
Subjects: Cranofacial reconstructive, cleft lip and palate, paediatric
reconstruction.
Purpose: To encourage research and academic career development
in plastic and reconstructive surgery.
Eligibility: Open to surgical residents or Fellows, plastic surgery
residents planning to interrupt their training for a research experience
or recent residency graduates wishing to supplement their clinical
training with a research experience. Residents, Fellows and non-
members of the ASPS or the PSEF require the sponsorship of a
member or candidate for membership of the ASPS or the PSEF.
Level of Study: Professional development, Postgraduate
Type: Fellowship
Value: US$30,000
Length of Study: 1 year
Frequency: Annual
Country of Study: Any country
No. of awards offered: 2
Application Procedure: Applicants must complete an application
available on the website.
Closing Date: November 15th
Funding: Corporation, trusts
Contributor: Lyndon Peer and Fresh Start Surgical Gifts
No. of awards given last year: 3

PSEF Scientific Essay Contest
Subjects: Plastic surgery.
Eligibility: Open to persons involved in research in the field of plastic
surgery.
Level of Study: Postgraduate, Professional development
Type: Prize
Value: US$500–3,000
Length of Study: 1 year
Frequency: Annual
Country of Study: Any country
No. of awards offered: 8

Application Procedure: Applicants must submit manuscripts that contain the results of original clinical or basic science research in an area of importance to plastic and reconstructive surgery. Information on essay content and format are available on the website.
Closing Date: February 15th
Funding: Corporation, trusts
Contributor: Bernard G Sarnat MD, D Ralph Millard from the Plastic Surgery Society and the Plastic Surgery Educational Foundation, Integra Foundation
No. of awards given last year: 8
No. of applicants last year: 24
Additional Information: Check on Medicine Professionals, then check on Research.

PLAYMARKET

PO Box 9767, Te Aro, Wellington, New Zealand
Tel: (64) 4 382 8462
Fax: (64) 4 382 8461
Email: info@playmarket.org.nz
Website: www.playmarket.org.nz
Contact: Ms Dilys Grant, Director

Playmarket was founded in 1973 to assist New Zealand playwrights with a professional production of their scripts. For 25 years Playmarket has offered script assessment, development and agency services. Playmarket is at the heart of New Zealand theatre and its focus is on playwrights.

The Bruce Mason Playwriting Award
Subjects: Playwriting.
Purpose: To recognize achievement at the beginning of a career.
Eligibility: Open to all potential applicants.
Level of Study: Unrestricted
Type: Award
Value: New Zealand $7,000
Length of Study: 1 year
Frequency: Annual
Country of Study: New Zealand
No. of awards offered: 1
Application Procedure: Applicants can obtain full details of the competition directly from playmarket.
Closing Date: October
Funding: Commercial
Contributor: Independent Newspapers Limited
No. of awards given last year: 1
No. of applicants last year: 13
Additional Information: It is expected that the award will be used to write or complete a work for the theatre.

For further information contact:

Playmarket, Level 2, 16 Cambridge Terrace, Wellington, PO BOX 9767

THE POINT FOUNDATION

PO Box 11210, Chicago, IL, 60611, United States of America
Tel: (1) 775 782 5659
Fax: (1) 866 397 6468
Email: info@pointfoundation.org
Website: www.thepointfoundation.org

The Point Foundation provides financial support, mentoring and hope to meritorious students who are marginalized due to sexual orientation, gender expression or gender identity. The Foundation seeks the partnership of philanthropic individuals, corporations and foundations to supply financial support, professional guidance and a network of contacts for undergraduate, graduate and postgraduate students.

mtvU Point Scholarship
Subjects: All subjects.
Purpose: To support outstanding LGBT students (lesbian, gay, bisexual and transgender) who are underprivileged, especially those who have been abandoned by family and other support systems because of their sexual orientation or gender identity.

Eligibility: Open to applicants who attend an mtvU school. Both LGBT and non-LGBT students can apply provided they demonstrate leadership, scholastic achievement, participation in extracurricular activities and involvement in the LGBT community.
Level of Study: Postgraduate
Type: Scholarship
Value: US$10,000
Frequency: Annual
Country of Study: United States of America
Funding: Foundation

The Point Scholarship
Subjects: All subjects.
Purpose: To support outstanding LGBT students (lesbian, gay, bisexual and transgender) who are underprivileged, especially those who have been abandoned by family and other support systems because of their sexual orientation or gender identity.
Eligibility: Both LGBT and non-LGBT can apply provided they demonstrate leadership, scholastic achievement, participation in extracurricular activities and involvement in the LGBT community.
Level of Study: Postgraduate
Type: Scholarship
Value: US$2,000–12,000
Frequency: Annual
Country of Study: United States of America
No. of awards offered: Varies
Application Procedure: Applicants must complete an application online before the stated deadline at www.pointfoundation.org
Closing Date: February 9th
Funding: Foundation
No. of awards given last year: 27
No. of applicants last year: 1,344

POLLOCK-KRASNER FOUNDATION, INC.

863 Park Avenue, New York, NY, 10021, United States of America
Tel: (1) 212 517 5400
Fax: (1) 212 288 2836
Email: grants@pkf.org
Website: www.pkf.org
Contact: Programme Officer

The Pollock-Krasner Foundation's mission is to aid, internationally, those individuals who have worked as professional artists over a significant period of time.

Pollock-Krasner Foundation Grant
Subjects: Painting, sculpting, print-making, mixed media and installation art.
Purpose: To aid, internationally, individual artists of artistic merit with financial need.
Eligibility: Applicants may be painters, sculptors, print-makers, mixed media or installation artists. The Foundation has no age or geographic limits. Commercial artists, photographers, film-makers, craft-makers and students are not eligible.
Level of Study: Professional development
Type: Grant
Frequency: Annual
Application Procedure: Applicants must write, fax or email to the Foundation for an application and guidelines.
Closing Date: There is no deadline as grants are awarded throughout the year
Funding: Private
Additional Information: The Foundation does not fund academic study.

PONDICHERRY UNIVERSITY

R.V. Nagar Kalapet, Puducherry, Tamil Nadu, 605014, India
Website: www.pondiuni.org

The Pondicherry University, which was established in 1985 by the Government of India, is a teaching-cum-affiliating central University. The University is known for its advanced teaching leading to in-depth research, consultancy and extension activities.

Government of Pondicherry Fellowship

Subjects: Any subject.
Purpose: To provide financial assistance to students.
Eligibility: Open to students who are residents/natives of Pondicherry.
Level of Study: Doctorate
Type: Fellowship
Value: Rs 800/- per month and an annual contingency of Rs 3,000/- for 2 candidates pursuing research in Tamil/French leading to PhD
Frequency: Annual
Study Establishment: The Pondicherry University
Country of Study: India
No. of awards offered: 2
Application Procedure: A written application should be submitted for approval by the university authority.
Contributor: Government of Pondicherry

Pondicherry Junior Research Fellowship

Subjects: Any subject.
Purpose: To provide financial assistance to students.
Eligibility: The candidates must not be more than 28 years of age with a minimum of 55 per cent marks in a postgraduate degree or equivalent examination.
Level of Study: Doctorate, Postgraduate
Type: Fellowship
Value: Rs 8,000 per month for 2 years, enhanced to Rs 9,000 on completion of 2 years; also eligible for a contingent grant of Rs 20,000 per year
Length of Study: 2 years
Study Establishment: The Pondicherry University
Country of Study: India
Application Procedure: Application must submit written application.

Pondicherry Merit Scholarship

Subjects: Any subject.
Eligibility: Candidates must secure the highest percentage of marks in the postgraduate entrance examination.
Type: Scholarship
Value: Rs 500/- per month for semester 1 only
Length of Study: 2 years
Study Establishment: The Pondicherry University
Country of Study: India
Application Procedure: Applicants must submit a written application subject to the approval of the university.

Pondicherry Merit-Cum-Means Scholarship

Subjects: Any subject.
Purpose: To provide financial assistance to students.
Eligibility: Annual parental income of the student should not exceed Rs 30,000.
Level of Study: Postgraduate
Type: Scholarship
Value: Rs 500 per month for semester 1
Length of Study: 2 years
Frequency: Annual
Study Establishment: The Pondicherry University
Country of Study: India
No. of awards offered: 10 per cent of the students in each degree programme are eligible for this award
Application Procedure: Written application to be submitted for approval by the university.

THE POPULATION COUNCIL

Policy Research Division, One Dag Hammarskjold Plaza, New York, NY, 10017, United States of America
Tel: (1) 212 339 0500
Fax: (1) 212 755 6052
Email: pubinfo@popcouncil.org
Website: www.popcouncil.org
Contact: Fellowship Co-ordinator

The Population Council is an international non-profit, non-governmental institution that seeks to improve the well being and reproductive health of current and future generations around the world and to help achieve a humane, equitable and sustainable balance between people and resources. The Council conducts biomedical, social science and public health research and helps build research capacities in developing countries.

Fred H Bixby Fellowship Programme

Subjects: Population studies in combination with a social science discipline (demography, economics, sociology, anthropology, geography) public health or biomedical sciences.
Purpose: To expand training opportunities by allowing population specialists and biomedical researchers from developing countries to work with experienced mentors in the population Council's international network of offices. Fellowships are awarded to professionals in the early stages of their careers who have demonstrated commitment to remaining in their home countries or to returning home after working/studying abroad to build capacity in local institutions.
Eligibility: Candidates must have recently completed (within the last 5 years) or anticipate completing a Ph.D or equivalent degree in the social sciences, public health or biomedical sciences. Applicants must be legal citizens of a developing country who have a firm commitment to return home upon completion of their training programs.
Level of Study: Postdoctorate, Postgraduate, Professional development
Type: Fellowship
Value: A monthly stipend based on Fellowship location and years of experience and attendance at one professional meeting per year (including travel). An allowance for relocation and health insurance are also included
Length of Study: 1–2 years
Frequency: Annual
Study Establishment: One of the Population Council's international offices
No. of awards offered: Varies
Application Procedure: Applicants must submit an application form, research proposal and supporting documents in English. The application details and procedures can be found on the Bixby Fellowship website www.popcouncil.org/slr/bixby/bixby_home.html. Requests for information from the Fellowship Coordinator, which can be obtained by emailing to bixbyfellowship@popcouncil.org, should include a brief description of the candidate's academic and professional qualifications, a short statement about their research or study plans for the proposed Fellowship period and their curriculum vitae.
Closing Date: January 15th
Funding: Foundation
Contributor: Fred H Bixby Foundation
Additional Information: Selection will be based on the recommendation of the Fellowship Committee which consists of distinguished scholars in the field of population. Selection criteria will stress academic excellence, professional experience and prospective contribution to the population field. Prior to submitting a formal application to the Fellowship Office for consideration, Bixby applicants are required to seek sponsorship from at least one Population Council staff mentor, in consultation with the Fellowship coordinator.

Health and Population Innovation Fellowship Program

Subjects: Varies.
Purpose: To support mid-career individuals who have innovative ideas and the capacity to help shape public debate in the field of population, rights and reproductive health.
Level of Study: Professional development, Postdoctorate
Type: Fellowship
Length of Study: 1 year
Frequency: Annual
Study Establishment: The Population Council, New Delhi
Country of Study: India
No. of awards offered: 12
Application Procedure: Request application form.
Closing Date: September 15th
Funding: Foundation
Contributor: John D. and Catherine T. MacArthur Foundation
No. of awards given last year: 12

For further information contact:

Population Council, India Habitat Centre, Zone 5A, Ground Floor, Lodi Road, New Delhi, 110003

Tel: +91 11 24642901
Fax: 91 11 24642903
Email: fellowships@pcindia.org
Contact: Komal Saxena

Reproductive Biology and Immunology Postdoctoral Fellowship

Subjects: Physiology and biochemistry.
Eligibility: Foreign applicants must return to his/her own country upon completion of the fellowship.
Level of Study: Doctorate, Postdoctorate, Professional development
Type: Fellowship
Length of Study: 1–2 years
Frequency: Annual
Study Establishment: The Population Council's Centre for Biomedical Research
Country of Study: United States of America
No. of awards offered: Varies
Application Procedure: Contact the center for Biomedical Research.
Closing Date: No deadlines for submission
No. of awards given last year: 17

For further information contact:

Center for Biomedical Research, 1230 York Avenue, Box 773, New York, NY 10021

PRADER-WILLI SYNDROME ASSOCIATION UK

125a London Road, Derby, DE1 2QQ, England
Tel: (44) 13 3236 5676
Fax: (44) 13 3236 0401
Email: admin@pwsa-uk.demon.co.uk
Website: www.pwsa.uk.co.uk
Contact: Administrative Assistant

Prader-Willi Syndrome Association UK provides support and information to people with Prader- Willi Syndrome.

PWSA UK Research Grants

Subjects: Prader-Willi syndrome.
Purpose: To improve understanding and treatment of Prader-Willi Syndrome.
Level of Study: Unrestricted
Frequency: Dependent on funds available
Country of Study: United Kingdom
Application Procedure: Applicants must write or call the PWSA (UK) for information.
Funding: Private

PREHISTORIC SOCIETY

University College London, Institute of Archaeology, 31-34 Gordon Square, London, WC1H 0PY, England
Fax: (44) 20 7383 2572
Email: prehistoric@ucl.ac.uk
Website: www.ucl.ac.uk/prehistoric/
Contact: Ms Tessa Machling, Administrative Assistant

The Prehistoric Society is open to professionals and amateurs alike and has over 2,000 members worldwide. Its main activities are lectures, study tours and conferences and it publishes an annual journal (*PPS*) and a newsletter (*PAST*), which is published 3 times a year.

Prehistoric Society Conference Fund

Subjects: Archaeology, especially prehistoric.
Purpose: To finance attendance at international conferences.
Eligibility: Preference is given first to scholars from developing countries, whether they are members of the Society or not, then to members of the Society not qualified to apply for conference funds available to university staff. Other members of the Society are also eligible.
Level of Study: Postgraduate
Type: Travel grant

Value: UK £200–300
Length of Study: 1 year, renewals are considered
Frequency: Annual
Country of Study: Any country
No. of awards offered: 2
Application Procedure: Applicants must contact the Honorary Secretary for an application form.
Closing Date: January 31st
Funding: Private
Additional Information: Recipients are required to submit a short report on the conference to *PAST*, the Society's newsletter and their papers for the Society's proceedings if these are not to be included in a conference volume.

Prehistoric Society Research Fund Grant

Subjects: Prehistoric archaeology.
Purpose: To further research in prehistory by excavation or other means.
Eligibility: Open to all members of the Society. The Society may make specific conditions relating to individual applications.
Level of Study: Unrestricted
Type: Grant
Value: At the discretion of the Society
Length of Study: 1 year, renewals are considered
Frequency: Annual
Country of Study: Any country
No. of awards offered: Varies
Application Procedure: Applicants must complete an application form and include the names of two referees in their application.
Closing Date: January 31st
Funding: Private
Additional Information: Awards are made on the understanding that a detailed report will be made to the Society as to how the grant was spent.

Prehistoric Society Research Grant Conference Award

Subjects: Prehistoric archaeology.
Purpose: To fund initial projects and visits to conferences.
Eligibility: There are no eligibility restrictions.
Level of Study: Unrestricted
Value: Maximum of UK £500
Frequency: Annual
Application Procedure: Applicants must complete an application form.
Closing Date: January 1st
Funding: Private

THE PRESIDENT'S COMMISSION ON WHITE HOUSE FELLOWSHIPS

c/o O.P.M-Sheila Coates, 1900 E.Street, NW, Room B431, Washington, DC, 20415, United States of America
Tel: (1) (202) 395 4522
Fax: (1) 395-6179
Email: comments@whitehouse.gov
Website: www.whitehouse.gov/fellows
Contact: White House Fellowships

To maintain the healthy functioning of our system it is essential that we have a generous supply of leaders who have an understanding, gained first hand, of the challenges that our national government faces.

White House Fellowships

Subjects: Domestic and international policy studies.
Purpose: To offer exceptional young men and women first-handed experience working at the highest levels of the federal government.
Eligibility: Civilian employees of the Federal government are not eligible.
Level of Study: Postgraduate
Type: Fellowship
Value: A full-time, paid assistantship to the Vice President, Cabinet Securities, and other top-ranking government officials
Length of Study: 1 year
Frequency: Annual

Study Establishment: The White House
Country of Study: United States of America
Application Procedure: Application instructions are available on the website.
Closing Date: February 1st

PRESS GANEY ASSOCIATES INC.

404 Columbia Place, South Bend, IN, 46601, United States of America
Tel: (1) 800 232 8032
Fax: (1) 574 232 3485
Email: kleddy@pressganey.com
Website: www.pressganey.com
Contact: Ms Kelly Leddy, Research Specialist

The Press Ganey Associates, Inc. is the healthcare industry's top satisfaction measurement and improvement firm, serving more than 5,900 healthcare facilities and processing nearly 7,000,000 surveys annually. As one of the industry's market leaders, the company offers one of the world's largest comparative databases and unparalleled benchmarking opportunities.

Press Ganey Best Practices Research Program

Subjects: The subject of the grant is patient satisfaction in all aspects of the healthcare industry.
Purpose: To increase the systematic and rigorous study of patient satisfaction, through the funding of applied research that will identify best practices and that can be used throughout the healthcare industry.
Eligibility: There are no eligibility restrictions.
Level of Study: Research, Unrestricted
Value: US$10,000
Frequency: Annual
No. of awards offered: 5
Application Procedure: Applicants must visit the website or email Kelly Leddy at kleddy@pressganey.com for application procedures.
Closing Date: March 14th
Contributor: Press Ganey Associates
No. of awards given last year: 2
No. of applicants last year: 28

PRIMATE CONSERVATION INC.

1411 Shannock Road, Charlestown, RI, 02813-3726, United States of America
Tel: (1) 401 364 7140
Fax: (1) 401 364 6785
Email: nrowe@primate.org
Website: www.primate.org
Contact: The Grants Administrator

Primate Conservation Inc. gives small grants and matching funds for the conservation projects and studies of the least known and most endangered primates in their natural habitat.

Primate Conservation Inc. Grants

Subjects: Conservation and research projects on the least known and/or most endangered primates in habitat countries with wild populations.
Purpose: To protect and study the least known and/or most endangered primates in their natural habitats.
Eligibility: Applicants must be graduate students, qualified conservationists or primatologists.
Level of Study: Doctorate, Graduate, Postgraduate, Research
Type: Grant
Value: Average US$2,500 maximum US$5,000
Length of Study: 2 months–2 years
Frequency: Twice a year
No. of awards offered: Varies with each funding season
Application Procedure: Applicants must submit a grant proposal on forms that can be downloaded from the website, and submit four copies of the application to the institution's main address. Proposal must be typed, double spaced and in English. One copy of the proposal should be emailed to nrowe@primate.org

Closing Date: September 20th and Febuary 1st
Funding: Private
Contributor: Private donation
No. of awards given last year: 20
No. of applicants last year: 55

PRINCIPALITY OF LIECHTENSTEIN STATE EDUCATIONAL SUPPORT

PO Box 684, Principality of Liechtenstein, Vaduz, 9490, Switzerland
Tel: (41) 236 7681
Email: office@liechtenstein.li
Website: www.liechtenstein.li

The State provides educational assistance in the form of scholarships, loan, or contributions to expenses. Eligibility is determined on the basis of citizenship and the type of education.

Liechtenstein Scholarships and Loans

Subjects: All subjects.
Purpose: To awaken greater understanding of the Liechtenstein State by the domestic and foreign public.
Eligibility: Open to residents of Liechtenstein, expatriates or those whose mother, father, or spouse is a Liechtenstein citizen are eligible.
Level of Study: Postgraduate
Type: Scholarship
Frequency: Annual
Study Establishment: Liechtenstein Institute, Liechtenstein
Application Procedure: Applicants should first contact their chosen place of study.
Closing Date: No deadline
Funding: Government
Additional Information: All additional loans must be repaid within 6 years of completion of the course of study.

PROSTATE UK

10 Northfields Prospect, Putney Bridge Road, London, SW18 1PE, England
Tel: (44) 20 8877 5840
Fax: (44) 20 8877 2609
Email: info@prostateuk.org
Website: www.prostateuk.org
Contact: Chief Executive

Prostate UK is the working name of Prostate Research Campaign UK, a United Kingdom-registered charity (No. 1037063) that deals with all forms of prostate disease, benign and malignant (cancer). It seeks to limit the damage prostate diseases cause by funding medical research, raising awareness, training medical professionals and providing information. It provides free leaflets, videos, DVDs, a quarterly newsletter and a website.

Prostate UK Research Grants

Subjects: Research into prostate cancer, benign prostatic hyperplasia and prostatitis.
Purpose: To support research into both malignant and benign prostate diseases.
Eligibility: Available to English-speaking nationals of any country, of any mature age, resident in the United Kingdom and wishing to carry out research at a recognized United Kingdom hospital or institution into malignant or benign prostate disease. Bench space in a United Kingdom hospital/institution must be a prior condition for work to be carried out in the United Kingdom.
Level of Study: Professional development, Research
Value: 3 categories: UK £10,000, UK £25,000 and UK £50,000
Country of Study: United Kingdom
No. of awards offered: Dependent on funds available
Application Procedure: Advertisements appear once a year in *The British Medical Journal* and *The British Journal Of Urology International* inviting applicants to describe research projects they wish to undertake and to indicate the level of funding sought. The advertisements explains the application procedure.
Closing Date: Specified in relevant advertisements
Contributor: Charitable funds raised by Prostate UK

No. of awards given last year: Approx. 20
No. of applicants last year: Approx. 40

Prostate UK Training Grants

Subjects: Medical training relevant to the treatment of prostate cancer, benign prostatic hyperplasia and prostatitis.
Purpose: To support UK-based medical professionals for training relevant to the treatment of prostate diseases.
Eligibility: Available to English-speaking nationals of any country, of any mature age, resident in the United Kingdom and wishing to carry out training at a recognized United Kingdom or institution relevant to the treatment of malignant or benign prostate disease. A place at a United Kingdom hospital/institution is a prior condition.
Level of Study: Unrestricted
Type: Grant
Value: Up to £50,000
Country of Study: United Kingdom
No. of awards offered: Dependent on the funds available
Application Procedure: Advertisements appear once a year in *The British Medical Journal* and *The British Journal Of Urology International* inviting applicants to describe training they wish to undertake and to indicate the level of funding sought. These advertisements explain the application procedure.
Closing Date: December 15th
Contributor: Charitable funds raised by Prostate UK, the working name of Prostate Research Campaign UK
No. of awards given last year: Approx 8
No. of applicants last year: Approx 8

PULITZER CENTER ON CRISIS REPORTING

1779 Massachusetts Avenue, Suite 615, Washington, DC, 20036, United States of America
Tel: (1) 202 332 0900
Email: jsawyer@pulitzercenter.org
Website: www.pulitzercenter.org
Contact: Jon Sawyer, Director

The World Security Institute's Pulitzer Center on Crisis Reporting, established in 2006, intends to be a leader in sponsoring the independent reporting that media organizations are increasingly less willing to undertake on their own. It works towards raising the standard of coverage of global affairs, and to do so in a way that engages both the broad public and government policy makers.

Pulitzer Center on Crisis Reporting Travel Grants

Subjects: Journalism.
Purpose: To bring up issues that have gone unreported or underreported in the mainstream American media.
Eligibility: Open to all journalists, writers or filmmakers, staff journalists as well as freelancers of any nationality.
Level of Study: Professional development
Type: Travel grant
Value: US$3000 to 20,000
Frequency: Annual
Country of Study: United States of America
Application Procedure: Applicants must submit a proposed project, curriculum vitae, 3 recent writing samples and 3 references.
Additional Information: Applications should be submitted by email to info@pulitzercenter.org

PYMATUNING LABORATORY OF ECOLOGY (PLE)

University of Pittsburgh, 13142 Hartstown Road, Linesville, PA, 16424, United States of America
Tel: (1) 814 683 5813
Fax: (1) 814 683 2302
Email: pymlab@pitt.edu
Website: www.pitt.edu/~biology/pymatuning
Contact: Peter Quinby, Director

The Pymatuning Laboratory of Ecology (PLE) is a University of Pittsburgh field station dedicated to environmental education and ecological research. Situated on the shores of the Pymatuning Reservoir in North Western Pennsylvania, PLE's land includes woods, wet lands, successional fields and experimental agricultural lands. Researchers from nine institutions conduct projects ranging from community and ecosystem ecology to evolutionary genetics and behaviour.

Darbaker Botany Prize

Subjects: Botany.
Purpose: To award funds for the pursuit of excellent graduate and recent postdoctoral research in botany.
Eligibility: Applicants must be graduate students, recent PhDs or senior researchers initiating new research at PLE.
Level of Study: Doctorate, Postdoctorate, Postgraduate
Type: Research grant
Value: US$500–1,500
Length of Study: 1 year
Frequency: Annual
Study Establishment: PLE
Country of Study: United States of America
No. of awards offered: 1–3
Application Procedure: Applicants must request guidelines from the PLE or refer to the website.
Closing Date: February 1st
Funding: Private
No. of awards given last year: 1
No. of applicants last year: 2

QUEEN ELISABETH INTERNATIONAL MUSIC COMPETITION OF BELGIUM

20 rue aux Laines, B-1000 Brussels, Belgium
Tel: (32) 2 213 4050
Fax: (32) 2 514 3297
Email: info@qeimc.be
Website: www.qeimc.be
Contact: Secretariat

The Queen Elisabeth International Music Competition of Belgium is a non-profit association, located in Brussels, whose principal aim is to organize major international competitions for music virtuosos. In this way, the competition participates in the Belgian and international music world, and gives its support to young musicians.

Queen Elisabeth International Music Competition of Belgium

Subjects: Music: piano, voice, violin and composition.
Purpose: To provide career support for young pianists, singers, violinists and composers.
Eligibility: Open to musicians of any nationality who are at least 17 years of age and not older than 27 years for violin and piano, 30 years for singing and 40 years for composers. The competition is made up of a first round, a semi-final and a final round.
Level of Study: Unrestricted
Value: Prizes, awards and certificates along with cash prizes will be awarded
Frequency: Annual
Country of Study: Any country
No. of awards offered: 6
Application Procedure: Applicants must obtain an application form from the Secretariat of the Competition or via the website.
Closing Date: January 15th
Funding: Private
No. of applicants last year: Unrestricted
Additional Information: There are also master classes with jury members.

QUEEN MARGARET UNIVERSITY

Queen Margaret University Drive, Musselburgh, Edinburgh, EH21 6UU, United Kingdom
Tel: (44) 131 474 0000
Fax: (44) 131 474 0001
Website: www.qmuc.ac.uk
Contact: Professor Anthony Cohen, Principal

Queen Margaret University provides vocationally relevant education in business and enterprise; drama and creative industries; health, including international health; and social sciences, media and communication. Its internationally recognized research activity informs our teaching. With around 4,500 students, our small size allows us to offer students a highly supportive environment.

EMU International Student Postgraduate Scholarship
Subjects: All subjects.
Purpose: To assist and attract greater numbers of international students to postgraduate courses at Queen Margaret University.
Eligibility: Any self-funding, postgraduate international (non-European Union) student.
Level of Study: Graduate, MBA, Postgraduate
Value: UK £1,000
Frequency: Annual
Country of Study: United Kingdom
No. of awards offered: 10 per year
Application Procedure: Applicants must complete the application form and submit it to the International Office before the stated closing date, after accepting an offer of a place by the institution.
Closing Date: End of May each year
No. of awards given last year: 10
No. of applicants last year: 55

For further information contact:

Recruitment & International Liaison Office, Queen Margaret University, Queen Margaret University Drive, Musselburgh, EH21 6UU, Scotland

Postgraduate Student Allowance Scheme (PSAS) (Queen Margaret)
Subjects: Cultural management programmes, art therapy, audiology and international health scheme.
Purpose: International Health Scheme.
Eligibility: United Kingdom and European Union nationals living in Scotland on the relevant date (conditions apply).
Level of Study: Postgraduate
Value: UK £3,010 towards tuition fees and an income-assessed maintenance grant
Length of Study: 2 years, full-time
Frequency: Annual
Study Establishment: Queen Margaret University College
Country of Study: United Kingdom
No. of awards offered: 4
Application Procedure: Applicants must complete an application and send it to the SAAS, once nominated by the institution.
Funding: Government
Contributor: Students Awards Agency for Scotland (SAAS)
No. of awards given last year: 2
Additional Information: Students cannot apply directly to the SAAS. They must have accepted an offer of a place and be nominated by the institution.

For further information contact:

Tel: 44 (0)131 474 0000
Email: rilo@qmu.ac.uk

QUEEN MARY UNIVERSITY OF LONDON

Admissions and Research Student Office, London, E1 4NS, England
Tel: (44) 20 7882 5511
Fax: (44) 20 7882 5588
Email: admissions@qmul.ac.uk
Website: www.qmul.ac.uk
Contact: Mr Peter Smith, Admissions Assistant

Queen Mary is the fourth largest college in the University of London. Located on an attractive campus, it has more than 8,000 students studying in four faculties plus St Bartholomew's and the Royal London School of Medicine and Dentistry. Of these, more than 1,600 are pursuing postgraduate courses or undertaking research.

Queen Mary Research Studentships
Subjects: Arts, sciences, engineering, social sciences, law, medicine and dentistry.

Purpose: To provide the opportunity for full-time research leading towards an MPhil or PhD.
Eligibility: Open to suitably qualified candidates who hold at least an Upper second class (Honours) degree or equivalent at first degree level, but preferably a relevant Master's degree.
Level of Study: Research
Type: Studentship
Value: Maintenance at the current research council rate plus tuition fees
Length of Study: 3 years full-time subject to a satisfactory academic report
Frequency: Annual
Study Establishment: Queen Mary University of London
Country of Study: United Kingdom
No. of awards offered: 20+
Application Procedure: Applicants must contact the Admission and Recruitment Office for further application details.
Closing Date: Mid-Summer
Funding: Government
No. of awards given last year: 30
No. of applicants last year: 200+
Additional Information: These studentships are not available to existing Queen Mary research students.

THE QUEEN'S NURSING INSTITUTE

3 Albemarle Way, London, EC1V 4RQ, England
Tel: (44) 20 7549 1400
Fax: (44) 20 7490 1269
Email: mail@qni.org.uk
Website: www.qni.org.uk
Contact: Anne Pearson, Practice Development Manager

The Queen's Nursing Institute works to support and develop new and best nursing practice and innovation in primary care. Through this support we want to ensure that patients receive the highest standard of nursing in the community. Primary care has always been the highest priority and the Queen's Nursing Institute firmly believes in working in partnership with nurses to achieve its overall objectives.

Fund for Innovation
Subjects: Implementation of good practice, or a project or an idea, within the community.
Purpose: The QNI Fund for Innovation provides professional and financial support to community nurses wishing to undertake projects which improve services and/or develop practice in the care of patients at home and in the community.
Eligibility: Must be a qualified community nurse.
Level of Study: Postgraduate, Professional development, Research, Graduate
Type: Grant
Value: Upto UK £7,500
Length of Study: 1 year
Frequency: Annual
Study Establishment: The Queen's Nursing Institute
Country of Study: United Kingdom
No. of awards offered: Varies, usually 6–10
Application Procedure: Applicants must submit an application proposal and a curriculum vitae.
Closing Date: The closing dates vary. Please check the website for details
Funding: Private
Contributor: National Gardens Scheme
No. of awards given last year: 12

QUEENSLAND UNIVERSITY OF TECHNOLOGY (QUT)

Caboolture Campus, PO Box 1376, Caboolture, QLD, 4510, Australia
Tel: (61) 7 5433 7400
Fax: (61) 7 5433 7421
Email: caboolture@qut.edu.au
Website: www.rsc.qut.edu.au

QUT provides a career-oriented education which helps graduates find employment in their chosen career, in an environment which uses the latest technology to make learning stimulating and enjoyable. It provides information for students, staff and visitors about the resources of the University, its facilities and processes.

APAI Scholarships within Integrative Biology

Subjects: Plant science and biological sciences.
Eligibility: Open to citizens of Australia or permanent residents having Honours 1 Degree or equivalent.
Level of Study: Postgraduate
Type: Scholarship
Value: Australian $25,627
Length of Study: 3 years
Frequency: Annual
No. of awards offered: 2
Application Procedure: Check website for further details.
Closing Date: March 2nd

For further information contact:

School of Integrative Biology
Email: susanne.schmidt@uq.edu.au
Contact: Dr Susanne Schmidt, Senior Lecturer

ARC APAI – Alternative Engine Technologies

Subjects: Engineering and technology.
Eligibility: Open to citizens of Australia or New Zealand or permanent residents who have achieved Honours 1 or equivalent, or Honours 2a or equivalent.
Level of Study: Postdoctorate, Postgraduate
Type: Scholarship
Value: Australian $26,140
Length of Study: 3 years
Frequency: Annual
Country of Study: Australia
No. of awards offered: 1
Application Procedure: Check website for further details.
Closing Date: September 28th

For further information contact:

Queensland University of Technology, School of Engineering Systems, GPO Box 2434, Brisbane, QLD, 4001, Australia
Tel: (61) 7 3138 5174
Email: rong.situ@qut.edu.au
Website: www.rsc.qut.edu.au/future/scholarships/APAI.jsp
Contact: Dr Rong Situ

Institute of Health and Biomedical Innovation Awards

Subjects: Biomedical engineering, engineering and technology, medical and health sciences or physical sciences.
Purpose: To support living expenses.
Eligibility: Open for citizens of Australia or permanent residents who have achieved Honours 1 or equivalent, or Honours 2a or equivalent.
Level of Study: Doctorate, Postgraduate
Type: Award
Value: Australian $36,140
Length of Study: 2 years (Masters) or 3 years (PhD)
Frequency: Annual
Country of Study: Australia
No. of awards offered: 4
Application Procedure: Check website for further details.
Closing Date: October 12th

For further information contact:

Queensland University of Technology, IHBI, QUT, GPO Box 2434, Brisbane, QLD, 4001, Australia
Tel: (61) 7 3138 6056
Fax: (61) 7 3138 6039
Email: s.winn@qut.edu.au
Website: www.rsc.qut.edu.au/studentsstaff/scholarships/arw_domestic.jsp
Contact: Stella Winn, Research Services Manager

THE RADCLIFFE INSTITUTE FOR ADVANCED STUDY

34 Concord Avenue, Cambridge, MA, 02138, United States of America
Tel: (1) 617 495 8212
Fax: (1) 617 495 8136
Email: fellowships@radcliffe.edu
Website: www.radcliffe.edu
Contact: Administrator of Fellowships

The Radcliffe Institute for Advanced Study is a scholarly community where individuals pursue advanced work across a wide range of academic disciplines, professions and creative arts. Within this broad purpose, the Radcliffe Institute sustains a continuing commitment to the study of women, gender and society.

Radcliffe Institute for Advanced Study Fellowship Programme

Subjects: All subjects.
Purpose: To support women and men of exceptional promise and demonstrated accomplishment, who wish to pursue independent work.
Eligibility: Open to female and male scholars in any field who gained a doctorate or appropriate terminal degree at least 2 years prior to appointment, or creative writers and visual or performing artists with a record of significant accomplishment and equivalent professional experience. Special eligibility requirements apply to creative artists.
Level of Study: Postdoctorate, Research
Type: Fellowship
Value: Please consult the organization
Frequency: Annual
Study Establishment: Harvard University
Country of Study: United States of America
Application Procedure: Applicants must visit the website.
Closing Date: Please consult the organization
No. of awards given last year: 52

RADIO AND TELEVISION NEWS DIRECTORS FOUNDATION (RTNDF)

1600 K Street North West Suite 700, Washington, DC, 20006-2838, United States of America
Tel: (1) 202 659 6510
Fax: (1) 202 223 4007
Email: walts@rtndf.org
Website: www.rtndf.org
Contact: Mr Walt Swanston, Senior Project Director

The mission of the Radio and Television News Directors Foundation (RTNDF) is to promote excellence in electronic journalism through research, education and professional training in four principal programme areas: journalistic ethics and practices, the impact of technological change on electronic journalism, the role of electronic news in politics and public policy and cultural diversity in the electronic journalism profession.

RTNDF Fellowships

Subjects: Electronic journalism.
Eligibility: To support young journalists in radio or television with up to 10 years of experience.
Level of Study: Postgraduate, Professional development
Type: Fellowship
Value: Up to US$2,500
Frequency: Annual
Country of Study: United States of America
No. of awards offered: 4
Application Procedure: Applicants must download the application form from www.RTNDA.org
Closing Date: May 11th
Funding: Private
Additional Information: The awards include: the Michele Clark Fellowship for Minority News Professionals, the Jacque I Minotte Health Reporting Fellowship, the Vada and Barney Oldfield National Security Fellowship and NS Bienstock Fellowship for Minority Journalists.

RADIOLOGICAL SOCIETY OF NORTH AMERICA, INC. (RSNA)

820 Jorie Boulevard, Oak Brook, IL, 60523-2251, United States of America
Tel: (1) 630 571 7816
Fax: (1) 630 571 7837
Email: walter@rsna.org
Website: www.rsna.org
Contact: Mr Scott A Walter, Grant Review Process Manager

The Research and Education Foundation of the Radiological Society of North America (RSNA) provides grant support to medical students, residents, Fellows and full-time faculty members of departments of radiology, radiation oncology and nuclear medicine.

RSNA Education Seed Grant

Subjects: Radiologic sciences.
Purpose: To provide funding opportunities for individuals with an active interest in radiologic education.
Eligibility: Applicants must hold a faculty position in a department of radiology, radiation oncology, or nuclear medicine within a North American, educational institution and must have completed advanced training and be certified by the American Board of Radiology (or equivalent), or on track for certification. Applicants must not have received grant/contract amounts totaling $50,000 or more in a single calendar year as principal investigator.
Level of Study: Research
Type: Grant
Value: Up to $30,000, to support the preliminary or pilot phase of education projects, not to supplement major funding already secured. No salary support for the principal investigator will be provided
Frequency: Annual
Application Procedure: Application can be submitted online.
Closing Date: January 10th
Funding: Foundation

RSNA Educational Scholar Grant Program

Subjects: Radiology or related disciplines.
Purpose: To provide funding opportunities for individuals with an active interest in radiologic education.
Eligibility: Applications are accepted from individuals throughout the world. Candidate/co-principal investigator(s) must not be agents of any for-profit, commercial company in the radiologic sciences. Candidates may not submit more than one research or education grant application to the RSNA R&E Foundation per year. Recipients may not have concurrent RSNA grants.
Level of Study: Postgraduate, Predoctorate
Type: Grant
Value: Up to US$75,000 per year
Length of Study: 2 years
Frequency: Annual
No. of awards offered: 1
Application Procedure: Candidates must complete an application form, available from the website.
Closing Date: January 10th

RSNA International Radiology Program Educational Grant to 'Teach the Teachers' from Emerging Nations

Subjects: Radiology or related disciplines.
Purpose: To provide an opportunity for scientists and physicians in developed countries to use or develop educational materials specifically to educate the teachers in emerging countries who will return to their respective countries to improve clinical practice and education.
Eligibility: Open to individuals in the radiological sciences in developed countries throughout the world with the facilities and institutional support to establish the programme required to successfully compete for this grant.
Level of Study: Postgraduate
Type: Grant
Value: Up to US$100,000 per year. Each year's funding is based on successful progress towards the stated goals of the proposal. The Foundation does not pay institutional overhead costs or indirect costs
Length of Study: 3 years
Frequency: Annual

No. of awards offered: 1
Application Procedure: Applicants must complete an application form, available from the website.
Closing Date: June 1st

RSNA Medical Student Grant Program

Subjects: Radiology and related disciplines.
Purpose: To make radiology research opportunities available for medical students early in their training and encourage them to consider academic radiology as a career option.
Eligibility: Open to full-time medical students at an accredited North American medical school. Nominees must be citizens of a North American country or hold permanent resident status.
Type: Grant
Value: US$6,000
Length of Study: 1 year
Application Procedure: Applicants must be nominated by a current RSNA scholar grant recipient and work with the scholar on his or her designated research project.
Closing Date: There is no specific deadline. The scholar is notified of the option to nominate a medical student. The application must be prepared with the assistance of the nominating scholar

RSNA Research Fellow Program

Subjects: Medical sciences.
Purpose: To provide young investigators not yet professionally established in the radiological sciences an opportunity to gain further insight into scientific investigation and to develop competence in research techniques and methods.
Eligibility: Open to citizens or permanent residents of a North American country who have an MD, DO, DVM, DDS, DMD degree or equivalent as recognized by the American Medical Association. Individuals with a PhD or ScD, in addition to the appropriate medical degree, are not eligible for this award, although MD or PhDs who have their PhDs in areas other than medical research are eligible. Applicants should be near the end of their prescribed training and/or have completed the prerequisite training to sit for qualifying exams. Preference will be given to candidates who have a commitment from a North American educational institution for a faculty appointment after the fellowship is completed.
Level of Study: Doctorate, Postdoctorate, Postgraduate, Predoctorate
Type: Fellowship
Value: US$50,000 for 1 year as salary and/or non-personnel research expenses
Length of Study: 1 or 2 years
Frequency: Annual
No. of awards offered: 1
Application Procedure: Applicants must complete an application form, available from the website.
Closing Date: January 15th

RSNA Research Fellowship in Basic Radiologic Sciences

Subjects: Radiological sciences.
Purpose: To provide training and research opportunities for scientists who possess a PhD or equivalent degree to gain insight into scientific investigation and to develop competence in state-of-the-art research in basic radiological sciences.
Eligibility: Fellows must be within 5 years of completing their doctoral training in the radiological sciences and be eligible to join a department of diagnostic radiology, radiation oncology or nuclear medicine.
Level of Study: Postdoctorate
Type: Fellowship
Value: US$45,000 salary support for 1 year. Application for renewal for a 2nd year of salary support at US$50,000 will be considered based on progress towards the stated goals during the initial year. US$5,000 will be given to the institution each year to help cover direct expenses
Length of Study: Initially 1 year, further year by application
Frequency: Annual
Study Establishment: Any, which provides the necessary space, facilities and equipment
Country of Study: United States of America
No. of awards offered: Varies

Application Procedure: Applicants must download an application form from the website or contact the main organization address.
Closing Date: January 15th in same year. Award starts July 1st
Funding: Private
Additional Information: This programme is designed to promote and enhance the understanding and utilization of basic radiological sciences within departments of diagnostic radiology, radiation oncology and nuclear medicine. Research Fellows must be prepared to devote 100 per cent of their time to research under the guidance of a scientific advisor of their choice for the full-term of the fellowship.

RSNA Research Resident Program

Subjects: Radiology, radiation oncology and nuclear medicine.
Purpose: To provide opportunities for individuals to gain further insight into scientific investigation, and to develop competence in research and educational techniques and methods.
Eligibility: Open to citizens or permanent residents of a North American country. Applicants should be in residency training so that the award can occur during any year after the 1st year of training and should have an academic degree acceptable for a radiology residency.
Level of Study: Postgraduate
Type: Grant
Value: US$30,000 designed to replace a portion of the resident's salary
Length of Study: 1 year, non-renewable
Frequency: Annual
No. of awards offered: 1
Application Procedure: Applicants must complete an application form, available from the website.
Closing Date: January 15th

RSNA Research Scholar Grant Program

Subjects: Medical sciences.
Purpose: To support junior clinical faculty members and allow them to gain experience in research early in their academic careers.
Eligibility: Open to citizens or permanent residents of a North American country who have completed advanced training and are within 5 years of an initial faculty appointment at a North American educational institution. Applicants must also be board certified or eligible to sit for certifying exams and have not served or not currently be serving as principal investigator or co-principal investigator on grants or contracts totalling US$50,000 or more in a single calendar year.
Level of Study: Doctorate, Postdoctorate
Type: Award
Value: US$75,000 per year, payable to the institution, to be used exclusively as a stipend for the scholar
Length of Study: 2 years. In unusual circumstances, a 3rd year may be granted to provide bridge funding between the scholar award and additional funding obtained from other sources. A separate application is required to be considered for a 3rd year of funding
Frequency: Annual
No. of awards offered: 1
Application Procedure: Scholar applicants must be nominated by their host institution. If awarded, scholars will be required to take the Advanced Grant Writing Course offered through the RSNA Office of Research Development (ORD). Personal interviews will be conducted for selected finalists. Three letters of recommendation and a budget with details of the project and all sources of support are required.
Closing Date: January 15th

RSNA Research Seed Grant Program

Subjects: Diagnostic radiology, radiation oncology and nuclear medicine.
Purpose: To assist investigators in defining objectives and testing hypotheses before they apply for major grants from corporations, foundations or government agencies.
Eligibility: Applications are accepted from any country. Applicants must hold a full-time faculty position in an educational institution at the time the award commences and be in a department of diagnostic radiology, radiation oncology or nuclear medicine, having completed all advanced training. Applicants must not have served as a principal investigator co-principal investigator or co-investigator on grants totalling US$50,000 or more in a single calendar year. Any area of

radiology-related research is eligible including basic, clinical, developmental and healthcare planning, delivery and evaluation.
Type: Research grant
Value: US$30,000 or less, payable to the recipient's department in two equal instalments
Length of Study: 1 year
Application Procedure: Applicants must complete an application form, available from the website.
Closing Date: January 15th

The Rebecca Skelton Fund

REBECCA SKELTON FUND

Dance Department, University College Chichester, Chichester, West Sussex, PO19 6PE, England
Tel: (44) 01243 816470
Fax: (44) 01243 816080
Email: artsresearch@chi.ac.uk
Website: www.ucc.ac.uk

The fund provides financial assistance towards the cost of dance study. Rebecca Skelton who died in 2005 was an accomplished dance performer, choreographer and researcher whose work was an inspiration to many. This fund has been set up in her memory.

The Rebecca Skelton Scholarship

Subjects: Dance improvization; Skinner releasing technique, alignment therapy, Feldenkrais technique, Alexander technique and other body-mind practices that focus on an inner awareness and use of the proprioceptive communication system or inner sensory mode.
Purpose: To assist students to pursue a course of specific or advanced performance studies or an appropriate or dance research project.
Eligibility: Open to anyone pursuing dance studies at postgraduate level.
Level of Study: Postdoctorate, Doctorate, Postgraduate, Professional development, Research
Type: Scholarship
Value: UK £500
Frequency: Annual
Country of Study: United Kingdom
No. of awards offered: 1–4
Application Procedure: Application form on request.
Closing Date: January 12th
Funding: Foundation
Contributor: The Rebecca Skelton Fund
No. of awards given last year: 2
No. of applicants last year: 11

For further information contact:

Contact: Arts Research Administrator

REES JEFFREYS ROAD FUND

Merriewood, Horsell Park, Woking, Surrey, GU21 4LW, England
Tel: (44) 1483 750758
Fax: (44) 1483 750758
Email: briansmith@reesjeffreys.org
Website: www.reesjeffreys.org
Contact: Mr Brian Smith, Secretary

The Rees Jeffreys Road Fund makes grants for courses or research connected with roads and transportation. Within those subjects, it endows university teaching posts, pays bursaries for postgraduate students, sponsors research and contributes to research projects. It has a small budget for the provision of roadside rests and improving roadside environment.

Rees Jeffreys Road Fund Bursaries

Subjects: Transport scholarship and research that will lead to a better understanding of transport issues and offer the prospect of new thinking and ideas for dealing with contemporary transport issues.

Purpose: To facilitate postgraduate study or research into transport.

Eligibility: Open to candidates of any nationality who hold at least an Upper Second Class (Honours) Degree at a United Kingdom university.

Level of Study: Doctorate, Postgraduate

Type: Full bursaries for MSc students; transportation annual contributions to PhD research students

Value: Fees plus maintenance plus UK £1,000 for 1 year MSc courses; UK £3,000–6,000 per year for 1, 2 or 3-year Ph.D courses

Length of Study: 1–2 years

Frequency: Annual

Study Establishment: Universities and research institutions

Country of Study: United Kingdom

No. of awards offered: Approx. 5–7

Application Procedure: Applicants must be recommended by the intended institution of study.

Closing Date: July 1st for MSc courses

Funding: Private

No. of awards given last year: 6

No. of applicants last year: 21

Rees Jeffreys Road Fund Research Grants

Subjects: Transport.

Purpose: To facilitate research projects into roads and transportation.

Level of Study: Research

Value: UK £1,000–20,000, depending on the project

Frequency: Annual

Study Establishment: Universities and research institutions

Country of Study: United Kingdom

No. of awards offered: Approx. 10 per year

Application Procedure: Applicants must contact the secretary.

Closing Date: There is no fixed deadline. Applications will be considered by the Trustees at 1 of the 5 meetings each year

Funding: Private

No. of awards given last year: 12

No. of applicants last year: 30

REGENT'S BUSINESS SCHOOL LONDON (RBS LONDON)

Regent's College, London, Inner Circle, Regent's Park, NW1 4NS, United Kingdom
Tel: (44) 20 7487 7505
Fax: (44) 20 7487 7425
Email: rbsl@regents.ac.uk
Website: www.rbslondon.ac.uk

Regent's Business School London (RBS London) is one of the fastest growing business schools in the UK and follows an innovative postgraduate curriculum. Central to RBS London's ethos is a practitioner's focus. Industry level analysis and face to face interaction with managers in the international business community bring a practical dimension to your learning.

RBS London Academic Excellence Scholarships

Subjects: International business management.

Eligibility: These merit awards are awarded to students with strong academic achievements and potential.

Level of Study: Foundation programme, Graduate, Postgraduate

Type: Scholarship

Value: Up to 50 per cent of tuition fees is paid

Length of Study: 1 year

Frequency: Annual

Study Establishment: Regents Business School London

Country of Study: United Kingdom

No. of awards offered: 10

Application Procedure: Applicants must contact the school, or apply online and submit a 500 word statement for the attention of the scholarship committee stating why they should be considered for the award and what contribution they can make to the school.

Closing Date: There is no application deadline

Funding: International Office

Contributor: Individuals

No. of awards given last year: 7

No. of applicants last year: 30

Additional Information: Please contact the External Relations Office for further information.

RBS London Work-Study Scholarships

Subjects: International business management.

Purpose: To provide financial support to the students in need.

Eligibility: These merit awards are awarded to students with strong academic achievements and potential, who can combine study and work without interfering with their academic progress.

Level of Study: Foundation programme, Postgraduate, Professional development

Type: Scholarship

Value: Partial remission of tuition fees

Length of Study: 1 year

Frequency: Annual

Study Establishment: Regents Business School London

Country of Study: United Kingdom

No. of awards offered: 5 to 10 per year

Application Procedure: Apply online submit a 500-word statement for the attention of the scholarship committee.

Closing Date: There is no application deadline

Funding: International Office

No. of awards given last year: 5

No. of applicants last year: 10

Additional Information: Scholarship holders are required to work a specified number of hours per week (normally 10 hours, up to a maximum of 20 hours) during term time. Please contact the External Relations Office for further information.

For further information contact:

Regents Business School Candow (Admissions), External Relations, London, Regents College, Inner Circle, Regents Park, NW1 4NS, United Kingdom

THE REID TRUST FOR THE HIGHER EDUCATION OF WOMEN

53 Thornton Hill, Exeter, Devon, EX4 4NR, England
Contact: Mrs H M Harvey, Honorary Treasurer

The Reid Trust for the Higher Education of Women was founded in 1868 in connection with Bedford College for Women for the promotion and improvement of women's education. It is administered by a small committee of voluntary trustees.

Reid Trust For the Higher Education of Women

Subjects: All subjects.

Purpose: To promote the education of women.

Eligibility: Open to women educated in the United Kingdom who have appropriate academic qualifications and who wish to undertake further training or research in the United Kingdom.

Level of Study: Unrestricted

Type: Grant

Value: €250–1,000 each

Length of Study: Unrestricted

Frequency: Annual

Country of Study: United Kingdom

No. of awards offered: Usually 10–12

Application Procedure: Applicants must complete an application form, obtained by sending a stamped addressed envelope with a request.

Closing Date: May 31st

Funding: Private

No. of awards given last year: 12

No. of applicants last year: 60

REMEDI

Winterflood Securities Ltd, The Atrium Building, Cannon Bridge, 25 Dowgate Hill, London, EC4R 2GA, England
Tel: (44) 0207 384 2929
Fax: (44) 0207 731 8240
Email: rosie.wait@remedi.org.uk
Website: www.remedi.org.uk
Contact: Mrs R.J.Wait Director

REMEDI, founded in 1973, supports pioneering research into all aspects of disability and disease to improve the quality of life.

REMEDI Research Grants

Subjects: Diabetes, amputees, childhood eczema, osteoporosis, rehabilitation of the elderly, speech therapy, stroke, autism and head injury.

Purpose: To support pioneering research into all aspects of disability and disease. The Trustees are particularly interested in funding or part funding initial grants where applicants find it difficult to obtain funding through larger organizations.

Eligibility: Open to English-speaking applicants living and working in the United Kingdom.

Level of Study: Unrestricted

Type: Research grant

Value: Up to £150,000

Length of Study: 1–4 years

Frequency: Twice a year

Study Establishment: A hospital or university

Country of Study: United Kingdom

No. of awards offered: Varies

Application Procedure: Applicants must email the Director with a summary, including costs and start date on one side of A4-size paper. If the Chairman considers the research project to be of interest the Director will email an application form to be completed. Completed applications are sent to independent referees for peer review. The Trustees normally make awards twice a year in June and November.

Closing Date: Applications are accepted at any time

Funding: Private, trusts

Contributor: Trusts, companies and individuals

No. of awards given last year: 6

No. of applicants last year: 40

Additional Information: Grants will not be awarded for course fees, administration and university overheads. Trustees have decided to reduce the number of awards, but substantially increase the size of the grants.

For further information contact:

REMEDI, 14 Crondace road, London, SW6 4BB

REPORTERS COMMITTEE FOR FREEDOM OF THE PRESS

1101 Wilson Boulevard, Suite 1100, Arlington, VA 22209-2275, United States of America
Tel: (1) 703 807 2100
Fax: (1) 703 807 2109
Email: rcfp@rcfp.org
Website: www.rcfp.org
Contact: Ms Maria Gowen, Office Manager

The Reporters Committee for Freedom of the Press is a voluntary, unincorporated association of reporters and editors, dedicated to protecting the First Amendment interests of the news media. From its office in Arlington, Virginia, the Reporters Committee staff provide cost free legal defence and research services to journalists and their attorneys throughout the United States and also operate the FOI service centre to assist the news media with federal and state open records and open meetings issues.

Jack Nelson Legal Fellowship

Subjects: Media law.

Purpose: To financially support a recent law school graduate to pursue a postgraduate study.

Eligibility: To be eligible for the programme, candidates must have been granted a law degree no later than August. Significant experience in print or electronic news reporting and strong legal research and writing skills are required.

Level of Study: Postgraduate, Professional development

Type: Fellowship

Value: US$35,000 plus fully paid health benefits

Length of Study: 1 year

Frequency: Annual

Country of Study: United States of America

No. of awards offered: 1

Application Procedure: There is no application form. Applicants must submit a covering letter, curriculum vitae, contact details of three referees, news clips and a short legal writing sample to the attention of Lucy Daglish, Executive Director.

Closing Date: February 1st

Funding: Private

No. of awards given last year: 1

No. of applicants last year: 40

Additional Information: The Fellow will monitor significant developments in first amendment media law, assist with legal defense requirements from reporters, prepare legal memoranda, amicus briefs and other special projects. He or she will also write for The Reporter's Committee's publications, the quarterly magazine, *The News Media* and *The Law* and the bi-weekly newsletter, *News Media Update*.

Reporters Committee Legal Fellowship

Subjects: Media law.

Purpose: To financially support a recent law school graduate to pursue a postgraduate study.

Eligibility: Candidates must have received a law degree no later than August. Strong legal research and writing skills are required and a background in news reporting is very strongly preferred.

Level of Study: Postgraduate, Professional development

Type: Fellowship

Value: US$35,000 plus fully paid health benefits

Length of Study: 1 year, September–August

Frequency: Annual

Country of Study: United States of America

No. of awards offered: 1

Application Procedure: There is no application form, but the applicants should submit a covering letter, contact details of three referees, a short legal writing sample and new clips or one non-legal writing sample may be submitted in lieu of news clips. Email applications will not be accepted. Applications must be sent to Lucy Daglish, Executive Director.

Closing Date: February 1st

Funding: Private

No. of awards given last year: 1

No. of applicants last year: 40

Additional Information: Legal fellows monitor significant developments in first amendment media law, assist with legal defense requests from reporters, prepare legal memoranda, amicus briefs and other special projects. They write for the Committee's publications, the quarterly magazine, *The News Media* and *The Law* and the bi-weekly newsletter, *News Media Update*.

Robert R McCormick Tribune Foundation Legal Fellowship

Subjects: Media law.

Purpose: To financially support a law school graduate to pursue a postgraduate study.

Eligibility: Candidates must possess a law degree and be admitted to the Bar of any state. They must have a minimum of 2 or 3 years of postgraduate legal experience in a law firm, public interest group, government agency or judicial clerkship. Substantial experience in appellate brief writing is mandatory and strong legal research and writing skills is required. A background in news reporting is strongly preferred.

Level of Study: Postgraduate

Type: Fellowship

Value: US$46,000

Length of Study: 1 year

Frequency: Annual

Country of Study: United States of America

No. of awards offered: 1

Application Procedure: There is no application form. Applicants must submit a covering letter, curriculum vitae and contact details of three referees, a sample appellate brief and news clips or another short non-legal writing sample to Lucy Daglish, Executive Director.

Closing Date: March 2nd

Funding: Foundation, private

Contributor: Robert R McCormick Tribune Foundation

No. of awards given last year: 1

No. of applicants last year: 10

Additional Information: The Fellow will be expected to draft approx. six appellate amicus briefs in significant cases involving First Amendment media law issues during the fellowship. The legal Fellow will also monitor significant developments in media law, assist with responding to legal defence requests from reporters, prepare legal memoranda and other special projects. In addition, the legal Fellow will write for the Committee's publications, the quarterly magazine *The News Media* and *The Law* and the bi-weekly newsletter, *News Media Update*.

REPRESENTATION OF THE FLEMISH GOVERNMENT

Embassy of Belgium, 3330 Garfield Street NW, Washington, DC
20008, United States of America
Tel: (1) 202 625 5850
Fax: (1) 202 342 8346
Email: franm@wizard.net
Website: www.diplobel.us
Contact: Francoise Maertens, Representation Liaison Officer, the Government of Flanders

The Government of Flanders offers bursaries to permit students to continue their studies in Flanders.

Fellowship for American College Students

Subjects: Study or research at universities conservatories of music, art, music, humanities, social and political sciences, law, economics, sciences and medicine.
Purpose: To enable students to continue their education in Flanders, Belgium.
Eligibility: Citizens of the United States of America who are already studying for a first or doctoral degree. Candidates cannot be older than 35 years at the time of the application's deadline. Fellowship students cannot have other Belgian sources of income.
Level of Study: Doctorate, Graduate, Postdoctorate, Postgraduate, Predoctorate
Type: Fellowship
Value: A monthly stipend at a Flemish institution, reimbursement of tuition fees, health insurance and public liability insurance in accordance with Belgian law. There is no reimbursement of travel expenses
Length of Study: 10 months
Frequency: Annual
Study Establishment: Recognized institutes in Flanders
Country of Study: Belgium
No. of awards offered: 5
Application Procedure: Applicants must download an application form from the website or obtain one from the Cultural Officer at the Belgian Embassy in Washington DC.
Closing Date: January 31st
Funding: Government
Additional Information: The decision to grant a fellowship is made by the Ministry of the Flemish community after consultation with the prospective host institution.

RESEARCH CORPORATION (USA)

4703 E Camp Lowell Drive, Suite 201, Tucson, AZ, 85712,
United States of America
Tel: (1) 520 571 1111
Fax: (1) 520 571 1119
Email: awards@rescorp.org
Website: www.rescorp.org
Contact: Ms Dena McDuffie, Editor, Science Advancement Programme

The Research Corporation (USA) was one of the first United States of America foundations, and is the only one wholly devoted to the advancement of academic science. An endowed organization, it makes grants totalling US$5–7 million annually for independently proposed research in chemistry, physics and astronomy at United States of America and Canadian colleges and universities.

Cottrell College Science Awards

Subjects: Physics, chemistry and astronomy.

Purpose: To support significant research that contributes to the advancement of science.
Eligibility: Open to faculty members at public and private Institutes of Higher Education in the United States of America or Canada. The principal investigator must have an appointment in a department of astronomy, chemistry or physics and the department must offer at least baccalaureate, but not doctoral degrees. The institution must demonstrate its commitment by providing facilities and opportunities for faculty and student research.
Level of Study: Doctorate
Type: Research award
Value: Equipment and supplies, student Summer stipends of up to US$3,500 and a faculty Summer stipend of up to US$7,500
Length of Study: Up to 5 years, possibly renewable
Study Establishment: Public and private universities with non-PhD-granting departments of astronomy, chemistry or physics
Country of Study: United States of America or Canada
No. of awards offered: 100+
Application Procedure: Applicants must complete an application form and should visit the website for guidelines and application request forms.
Closing Date: November 15th or May 15th
Funding: Private
Contributor: Foundation endowment
No. of awards given last year: 93
No. of applicants last year: 262

Cottrell Scholars Awards

Subjects: Physics, chemistry and astronomy.
Purpose: To encourage excellence in both research and teaching.
Eligibility: Open to faculty in the 3rd year of a first tenure-track position.
Level of Study: Doctorate
Type: Award
Value: US$75,000, which may be flexibly applied in keeping with the applicants' approved programme
Frequency: Annual
Study Establishment: Universities with PhD-granting departments of physics, chemistry and astronomy
Country of Study: United States of America or Canada
No. of awards offered: Varies
Application Procedure: Applicants must complete an application form and should visit the website for guidelines and application request forms.
Closing Date: September 4th
Funding: Private
Contributor: Foundation endowment
No. of awards given last year: 12
No. of applicants last year: 122
Additional Information: Candidates must provide both a research and teaching plan for peer review.

RESOURCES FOR THE FUTURE (RFF)

1616 P Street NW, Washington, DC, 20036,
United States of America
Tel: (1) 202 328 5043
Fax: (1) 202 939 3460
Email: macauley@rff.org
Website: www.rff.org
Contact: Co-ordinator for Academic Programmes

Resources for the Future (RFF) is a non-profit and non-partisan think tank located in Washington, DC that conducts independent research rooted primarily in economics and other social sciences on environmental and natural resource issues.

Gilbert F White Postdoctoral Fellowship

Subjects: Social and policy sciences, environmental studies, energy and natural resources.
Purpose: To enable postdoctoral researchers to spend a year in residence conducting research in the social or policy sciences in areas related to the environment, energy or natural resources.

Eligibility: A strong economics background, or closely related discipline in the social or policy sciences, is required. Applicants must be postdoctorates.
Level of Study: Postdoctorate
Type: Fellowship
Value: Minimum award amount: $35000. Maximum award amount: $50000
Length of Study: 11 months
Frequency: Annual
Country of Study: United States of America
No. of awards offered: 2
Application Procedure: Applicants must submit a covering letter and curriculum vitae with a proposal relating to budget and three letters of recommendation. No application form is required. Application forms sent by fax or email will not be accepted.
Closing Date: February 27th
No. of awards given last year: 2

Joseph L Fisher Dissertation Award

Subjects: Economics, policy sciences, environment and natural resources.
Purpose: To support PhD students in their last year of dissertation research in economics or other policy sciences on issues related to the environment, energy or natural resources.
Eligibility: Open to all nationalities. Students must be in the final year of dissertation research or writing.
Level of Study: Doctorate
Type: Award
Value: US$12,000
Length of Study: 1 year
Frequency: Annual
Country of Study: Any country
No. of awards offered: Varies
Application Procedure: Applicants must submit a letter of application, a curriculum vitae, graduate transcripts, a one-page abstract of the dissertation, a technical summary of the dissertation, a letter from the department chair and two letters of recommendation. Applications sent by fax or email will not be accepted.
Closing Date: February 28th

RFF Fellowships in Environmental Regulatory Implementation

Subjects: Environmental studies and natural resources.
Purpose: To support research that documents the implementation and outcomes of environmental regulations.
Eligibility: Open to scholars from universities and research establishments who have a doctorate or equivalent degree or professional research experience.
Level of Study: Postdoctorate
Type: Fellowship
Value: Minimum award amount: $50000. Maximum award amount: $80000
Length of Study: 1–2 years
Frequency: Annual
Country of Study: United States of America
No. of awards offered: 2
Application Procedure: Applicants must submit a preproposal no longer than two pages, single spaced, with 11-point or larger font and 1-inch margins, containing full details of the proposed project. Applicants whose preproposals are selected for further review will then be invited to submit final proposals. These are limited to ten pages and are to follow a similar format. They must include all of the information contained in the preproposal but should offer further detailed description of the proposed research, anticipated contribution of the project and the importance of the results. Applicants must also include a curriculum vitae with the applicant's educational background, professional experience, a list of most relevant publications and honours and awards received. In addition, final proposals must include three letters of recommendation from fellow faculty members or colleagues. Applications sent by fax or email will not be accepted.
Closing Date: January 12th for preproposals and February 28th for final proposals
Funding: Private
No. of awards given last year: 3

RESUSCITATION COUNCIL (UK)

5th Floor, Tavistock House, North Tavistock Square, London, WC1H 9HR, England
Tel: (44) 20 7388 4678
Fax: (44) 20 7383 0773
Email: enquiries@resus.org.uk
Website: www.resus.org.uk
Contact: Dr David Gabbott, Chair, Research Subcommittee

The Resuscitation Council (UK) is the expert advisory body on the training and practice of resuscitation in the United Kingdom. It also actively pursues and promotes research in the field of resuscitation medicine.

Resuscitation Council Research Fellowships

Subjects: All aspects of the science, practice and teaching of resuscitation.
Purpose: To fund the wages of researchers based in the United Kingdom to conduct research into the science and practice of resuscitation medicine.
Eligibility: Open to research Fellows carrying out work in a suitable venue in the United Kingdom. Applicants must be full or associate members of the Resuscitation Council (UK).
Level of Study: Unrestricted
Type: Fellowship
Value: Basic salary level including National Insurance and Superannuation contributions. The salary would be at the appropriate point on the applicant's salary scale
Length of Study: Up to 2 years
Frequency: Dependent on funds available
Country of Study: United Kingdom
Application Procedure: Applicants should visit the website for application procedures.
Funding: Private
Contributor: The Resuscitation Council (UK)
No. of awards given last year: 4
No. of applicants last year: 5

Resuscitation Council Research Grants

Subjects: All aspects of the science, practice and teaching of resuscitation techniques.
Purpose: To provide grants up to a maximum of UK £10,000 for capital cost, data analysis and administrative support for research into the science and practice of resuscitation medicine.
Level of Study: Unrestricted
Type: Grant
Value: Up to UK £10,000
Frequency: Dependent on funds available
Country of Study: United Kingdom
Application Procedure: Applicants should visit the website: www.resus.org.uk for application details.
Closing Date: No closing dates. Applications are considered on a rolling basis
Funding: Private
Contributor: The Resuscitation Council, United Kingdom
No. of awards given last year: 4
No. of applicants last year: 7

RHODES COLLEGE

2000 North Parkway Memphis, Tennessee, 38112-1690, United States of America
Tel: (1) 901 843 3000
Email: Wottle@rhodes.edu
Website: www.rhodes.edu/

Rhodes, founded in 1848, seeks to graduate students with a lifelong passion for learning, a compassion for others, and the ability to translate academic study and personal concern into effective leadership and action in their communities and world.

Jacob K. Jarits Fellowships

Subjects: Humanities, arts and social sciences.
Purpose: Support for higher students in the areas of humanities, arts and social sciences.

Eligibility: Open to candidates who are US citizens, permanent residents of the US or citizens of any one of the freely associated states.
Type: Fellowship
Value: US$30,000 per year
Length of Study: Up to 4 years
Frequency: Annual
Study Establishment: Rhodes College
Country of Study: United States of America
No. of awards offered: 48
Application Procedure: Submit applications to the Rhodes Faculty post graduate scholarship committee 1 month prior to deadline.
Closing Date: October 1st, FAFSA by January 31st
Funding: Government
Contributor: The US Department of Education

For further information contact:

US Department of Education, DPE Teacher and student Development Programs Service Jacob K. Jarits Fellowships Program 1990 k street, N.W., 6th floor, Washington, DC 20006-8524
Tel: (202) 502-7542
Fax: (202) 502-7859
Website: www.ed.gov/programs/jacobjarits

Luce Scholars Program

Subjects: Any subject.
Purpose: To develop better cultural exchange between Asia and the US.
Eligibility: Open to US citizens with BA or equivalent degree, under 29 years of age with no significant exposure to Asia culture or study.
Level of Study: Postgraduate
Type: Scholarship
Length of Study: 1 year
Frequency: Annual
Country of Study: Asia
No. of awards offered: 15
Application Procedure: Requests for responsive or project grants should be submitted.
Closing Date: December 1st
Funding: Foundation
Contributor: Henry Luce Foundation

For further information contact:

The Henry Luce Foundation 111 West 50th street, New York, 10020
Tel: 212 489 7700
Website: www.hluce.org

Truman Scholarships

Subjects: Any subject.
Purpose: To support college juniors preparing for leadership in public service.
Eligibility: Candidates should be US citizens and full-time students pursuing a Bachelor's degree.
Value: US$26,000
Frequency: Annual
Study Establishment: Rhodes College
Country of Study: United States of America
No. of awards offered: 75–80 from 600 applications
Application Procedure: Download application from the website.
Closing Date: Early February
Funding: Foundation
Contributor: Truman Scholarship Foundation

For further information contact:

712 Jackson Place NW, Washington, DC 20006
Tel: (202) 395-4831
Fax: (202) 395-6995

Watson Fellowship

Purpose: To offer college graduates a year of independent study and travel outside the United States.
Eligibility: Candidates must be graduating seniors.
Type: Fellowship
Value: US$25,000
Frequency: Annual

No. of awards offered: Up to 50
Application Procedure: A fellowship form along with a project application proposal and details in not more than 5 pages should be submitted electronically.
Closing Date: Early November
Contributor: Thomas J. Watson Foundation

For further information contact:

Watson Fellowship Program, 293 South Main Street, Providence, RI 02903
Tel: 401 274 1952
Fax: 401 274 1954
Email: tjw@watsonfellowship.org
Contact: Thomas J

RHODES UNIVERSITY

PO Box 94, Grahamstown, 6139, South Africa
Tel: (27) 046 603 8936/8055
Fax: (27) 046 622 8822
Email: research-admin@ru.ac.za
Website: www.ru.ac.za/research
Contact: Dean of Research

Rhodes University is a small university campus in Grahamstown with one of the highest research outputs per capita in South Africa. The University offers excellent undergraduate and postgraduate education, and fosters personal development and leadership as well as team, social and communication skills amongst its diverse student body.

Allan Gray Senior Scholarship

Subjects: Commerce (accounting, economics, management and information systems).
Purpose: To encourage and enable previously disadvantaged South Africans to pursue their studies at Honours and Master's levels.
Eligibility: Open to previously disadvantaged South African students with the appropriate qualifications.
Level of Study: Postgraduate
Type: Scholarship
Value: South African Rand 35,000 for Honours and Rand 40,000 for Master's
Length of Study: 1 year, renewable upon reapplication for Master's
Frequency: Annual
Study Establishment: Rhodes University, Grahamstown
Country of Study: South Africa
No. of awards offered: 4
Application Procedure: Applicants must submit a curriculum vitae and a full academic record. Short-listed applicants will be required to complete an application form providing additional information and referee reports.
Closing Date: July 1st in the year preceding registration
Funding: Private
Contributor: Donor and investments
No. of awards given last year: 4
No. of applicants last year: Approx.35 per year
Additional Information: Postgraduate scholars must assist with teaching and/or research duties up to a maximum of 6 hours a week in their department of study, without additional remuneration. Awards are for full-time study in attendance at Rhodes University only.

Andrew Mellon Foundation Scholarship

Subjects: Humanities, commerce, education, law, pharmacy and science.
Purpose: To encourage and enable previously disadvantaged people to pursue their studies at the Honours, Master's or doctoral level at Rhodes University, as well as to enhance the recipients' ability to contribute to higher education in South Africa.
Eligibility: Open to previously disadvantaged individuals with the appropriate qualifications.
Level of Study: Postgraduate
Type: Scholarship
Value: South African Rand 35,000 for Honours, Rand 40,000 for Masters and Rand 60,000 for Doctoral
Length of Study: 1 year, renewable upon reapplication

Frequency: Annual
Study Establishment: Rhodes University, Grahamstown
Country of Study: South Africa
No. of awards offered: 25 at Honours level, 10 at Master's and Doctoral level
Application Procedure: Applicants must submit a curriculum vitae and a full academic record. Short-listed applicants will be required to complete an application form providing additional information and referee reports.
Closing Date: July 1st in the year preceding registration
Funding: Private
Contributor: Donor and investments
No. of awards given last year: 25 at Honours level, 10 at Master's or Doctoral level
No. of applicants last year: Approx. 250 per year
Additional Information: Scholars must assist with teaching and/or research duties up to a maximum of 6 hours a week in their department of study, without additional remuneration. Awards are for full-time study in attendance at Rhodes University only.

Henderson Postgraduate Scholarships

Subjects: Mathematical, physical, earth, life and pharmaceutical sciences, accountancy and information systems.
Purpose: To encourage and enable students to pursue their studies at the Master's and doctoral levels, and to enhance recipients' research abilities and produce internationally competitive graduates with an innovative, analytical, articulate and well-rounded desire to learn.
Eligibility: Open to South African citizens with appropriate qualifications.
Level of Study: Postgraduate
Type: Scholarship
Value: South African Rand 40,000 for Master's level and Rand 60,000 for Doctoral level
Length of Study: 1 year, renewable upon reapplication
Frequency: Annual
Study Establishment: Rhodes University, Grahamstown
Country of Study: South Africa
No. of awards offered: 4
Application Procedure: Applicants must submit a curriculum vitae and a full academic record. Short-listed applicants will be required to complete an application form, providing additional information and referee reports.
Closing Date: July 1st in the year preceding
Funding: Private
Contributor: Donor and investments
No. of awards given last year: 4
No. of applicants last year: Approx. 50
Additional Information: Scholars must assist with teaching and/or research duties up to a maximum of 6 hours a week in their department of study, without additional remuneration. Awards are for full-time study in attendance at Rhodes University only.

Hugh Kelly Fellowship

Subjects: All areas of science.
Purpose: To enable senior scientists to devote themselves to advanced work.
Eligibility: Open to suitable senior postdoctoral scientists with a very well-established research output record. Preference is given to candidates willing to accept appointments for at least 4 months. Applicants must be English speakers.
Level of Study: Postdoctorate, Research
Type: Fellowship
Value: Currently under review, but a package of approx. Rand 70,000. If the Fellow accepts an appointment for at least 4 months and is accompanied by a spouse, the spouse's air or rail fares will also be paid. University accommodation will be provided free of charge, but the provision of a telephone if available at the place of residence will be for the Fellow's personal account
Length of Study: Up to 1 year
Frequency: Every 2 years
Study Establishment: Rhodes University, Grahamstown
Country of Study: South Africa
No. of awards offered: 1
Application Procedure: Applicants must complete an application form, available from the Dean of Research or from the website.

Closing Date: July 31st of the year preceding the award
Funding: Private
Contributor: Donor and investments
No. of awards given last year: 1
No. of applicants last year: 6
Additional Information: The Fellow will be required to present a concise report on the work completed at the conclusion of the term of the fellowship.

Hugh Le May Fellowship

Subjects: All humanities.
Purpose: To enable senior scholars of standing in the humanities to devote themselves to advanced work.
Eligibility: Open to scholars from the humanities with a well-established research output record. Applicants must be English speaking.
Level of Study: Research
Type: Fellowship
Value: A return economy class air ticket from the Fellow's place of residence, furnished University accommodation and a small monthly cash stipend, free use of the University Library and sports facilities
Length of Study: 3–4 years, extended by mutual agreement and subject to the availability of funds
Study Establishment: Rhodes University, Grahamstown
Country of Study: South Africa
Application Procedure: Application forms to be completed, available from the Research Office or the website.
Closing Date: July 31st
Funding: Private
Contributor: Donor and investments
No. of awards given last year: 1
No. of applicants last year: 5
Additional Information: The Fellow will not be expected to undertake any teaching studies but will be required to present a report upon the work undertaken at the conclusion of the term of the Fellowship.

Patrick and Margaret Flanagan Scholarship

Subjects: All subjects.
Purpose: To enable South African women graduates to attend a university in the United Kingdom in order to obtain a higher postgraduate qualification.
Eligibility: Open to women graduates, preferably those who are English-speaking applicants of South African descent. Selection is based initially on academic merit, as well as broader qualities of intellect and character.
Level of Study: Postgraduate
Type: Scholarship
Value: South African Rand 180,000 per year
Length of Study: 2 years
Frequency: Annual
Study Establishment: Rhodes University, Grahamstown
Country of Study: United Kingdom
No. of awards offered: 1
Application Procedure: Applicants must submit a curriculum vitae and full academic record. Candidates shortlisted will be sent an application form or additional information and referee reports.
Closing Date: August 1st of the year prior to registration abroad
Funding: Private
Contributor: Donor and investments
No. of awards given last year: 1
No. of applicants last year: Approx. 50

Rhodes University Postdoctoral Fellowship and The Andrew Mellon Postdoctoral Fellowship

Subjects: All subjects (Rhodes University Postdoctoral Fellowship); humanities (Andrew Mellon Postdoctoral Fellowship).
Purpose: To enable scholars to devote themselves to advanced work, that will closely complement existing programmes in the host department.
Eligibility: Open to any postdoctoral scholars of standing, with research publications to their credit and of exceptional merit. Applicants must be English speakers.
Level of Study: Postdoctorate
Type: Fellowship
Value: South African Rand 100,000 per year with an additional allocation of Rand 10,000 for travel or research

Length of Study: 1 year, but may be extended by mutual agreement, subject to the availability of funds
Frequency: Annual
Study Establishment: Rhodes University, Grahamstown
Country of Study: South Africa
No. of awards offered: 2–3
Application Procedure: Applicants must be nominated. Nominations should be made through heads of departments and directors of research institutes at Rhodes University. Nominations must include a full curriculum vitae, research proposal and the name of three referees who may be consulted. Further information may be obtained from the Research Office or from the website.
Closing Date: July 31st of the year preceding the award
Funding: Private
Contributor: Donor and investments
No. of awards given last year: 4 for Rhodes University Postdoctoral Fellowship, 4 for Andrew Mellon Postdoctoral Fellowship
No. of applicants last year: 32
Additional Information: Fellows are not expected to undertake teaching duties.

Rhodes University Postgraduate Scholarship

Subjects: Humanities, commerce, education, law, pharmacy and science.
Purpose: To encourage and enable students to pursue their studies at the Master's and doctoral levels and enhance the recepients research abilities.
Eligibility: Open to students with the appropriate qualifications. Academic merit will override eligibility criteria.
Level of Study: Postgraduate
Type: Scholarship
Value: South African Rand 40,000 for Master's levels and Rand 60,000 for doctoral levels
Length of Study: 1 year, renewable upon reapplication
Frequency: Annual
Study Establishment: Rhodes University, Grahamstown
Country of Study: South Africa
No. of awards offered: 4
Application Procedure: Applicants must submit a curriculum vitae and a full academic record. Short-listed applicants will be required to complete an application form providing additional information and referee reports.
Closing Date: July 1st in the year preceding registration
Funding: Private
Contributor: Donor and investments
No. of awards given last year: 4
No. of applicants last year: Approx. 50
Additional Information: Scholars must assist with teaching and/or research duties up to a maximum of 6 hours per week in their department of study, without additional remuneration. Awards are for full-time study in attendance at Rhodes University only.

RICHARD III SOCIETY, AMERICAN BRANCH

2041 Christian Street, Philadelphia, PA, 19146, United States of America
Email: feedback@r3.org
Website: www.r3.org
Contact: Ms Laura Blanchard, Schallek Fellowships

The Richard III Society was founded in 1924 in England as The Fellowship of the White Boar and was renamed the Richard III Society in 1959. The American Branch was founded in 1961. Today, the Society has more than 4,000 members worldwide, and American Branch membership is more than 800.

William B Schallek Memorial Graduate Fellowship Award

Subjects: Medieval history.
Purpose: To support graduate study of 15th-century English history and culture.
Eligibility: Applicants must be citizens of the United States of America, have made an application for first citizenship papers or be permanent resident aliens enrolled at a recognized educational institution.

Level of Study: Doctorate
Type: Fellowship
Value: US$500–2,000 depending on the need and/or quality of applicant
Length of Study: 1 year, renewals will be considered
Frequency: Annual
Study Establishment: Recognized and accredited degree-granting institutions
Country of Study: Any country
No. of awards offered: 5
Application Procedure: Applicants must visit the website for guidelines, lists of past awards, their topics and application forms.
Closing Date: February 28th for the following academic year
No. of awards given last year: 3
No. of applicants last year: 7

RICS EDUCATION TRUST

12 Great George Street, London, SW1P 3AD, England
Tel: (44) 20 7334 3750
Fax: (44) 20 7334 3795
Email: aroberts@rics.org
Website: www.rics-educationtrust.org
Contact: Ms Amy Roberts

The Royal Institution of Chartered Surveyors (RICS) is the professional institution for the surveying profession.

RICS Education Trust Award

Subjects: The theory and practice of surveying in any of its disciplines including general practice, quantity surveying, building surveying, rural practice, planning and development, land surveying or minerals surveying.
Eligibility: Open to chartered surveyors and others carrying out research studies in relevant subjects.
Level of Study: Unrestricted
Type: Research grant
Value: Up to UK £5,000
Frequency: Twice a year
Country of Study: Any country
Application Procedure: Applicants must complete an application form, available to download online at www.rics-educationtrust.org
Closing Date: September 30th or February 28th
Funding: Commercial
Contributor: RICS
No. of awards given last year: 20
No. of applicants last year: 40

RMIT UNIVERSITY

Info Corner - Office for Prospective Students, GPO Box 2476V, Melbourne, VIC 3001, Australia
Tel: (61) 3 9925 2260
Fax: (61) 3 9925 3070
Email: study@rmit.edu.au
Website: www.rmit.edu.au

RMIT University is one of Australia's original and leading educational institutions producing some of Australia's most employable graduates. RMIT has an international reputation for excellence in work-relevant education professional and vocational education, high quality research, and engagement with the needs of industry and community.

Interior Design-Masters of Arts by Research

Subjects: Sculpture, film, theatre, journalism, visual arts, interior design and architecture.
Purpose: To offer a space within which candidates develop and contribute to the knowledge and possibilities of interior design.
Eligibility: Open to the candidates of any country who have a First Degree of RMIT with at least a credit average in the final undergraduate year or a deemed equivalent by RMIT to a First Degree of RMIT with at least a credit average in the final undergraduate year or evidence of experience.
Level of Study: Postgraduate

Length of Study: 2 years full-time (Masters) and 4 years part-time (PhD)
Application Procedure: Check website for further details.
Closing Date: October 31st
Funding: Government
Contributor: Commonwealth Government

For further information contact:

Tel: 03 9925 2819
Email: suzie.attiwill@rmit.edu.au
Contact: Ms Suzie Attiwill, Research Coordinator

ROB AND BESSIE WELDER WILDLIFE FOUNDATION

PO Drawer 1400, Sinton, TX, 78387, United States of America
Tel: (1) 361 364 2643
Fax: (1) 361 364 2650
Email: welderfoundation@welderwildlife.org
Website: www.welderwildlife.org
Contact: Dr Lynn Drawe, Director

The Rob and Bessie Welder Wildlife Foundation is a private non-profit foundation whose mission is to conduct research and education in wildlife management and closely related fields. The Welder Foundation operates a wildlife refuge on a commercial ranch in the midst of an active oil field.

Welder Wildlife Foundation Fellowship
Subjects: Wildlife ecology and management.
Purpose: To provide support to individual graduate student research.
Eligibility: Open to citizens of the United States of America or legal aliens registered at a United States of America university for a graduate degree. Priority is given to students who wish to work at the Welder Foundation Refuge or in the Coastal Bend Region of Texas.
Level of Study: Doctorate, Graduate
Type: Fellowship
Value: Up to US$18,000 per year, according to individual needs
Length of Study: The duration of a graduate degree programme
Frequency: Annual
Study Establishment: Any legitimate wildlife management or wildlife ecological department at any accredited university
Country of Study: United States of America
No. of awards offered: 10 at any given time, approx. 3 each year
Application Procedure: Applicants must write for details.
Closing Date: October 1st for fellowships to begin in January
Funding: Private
Contributor: Private endowment
No. of awards given last year: 2–3
No. of applicants last year: 15–20

ROBERT BOSCH FOUNDATION

CDS International, Inc., 440 Park Avenue South, 2nd Floor, New York, NY, 10016, United States of America
Tel: (1) (212) 497 3500
Fax: (1) 212 497 3535
Email: info@cdsintl.org
Website: www.cdsintl.org
Contact: Weingart Carolin, Programme assistant

The Robert Bosch Foundation is one of the largest German industry foundations. Many of the foundation's international exchange programmes are aimed at providing young people with opportunities to improve their knowledge of other countries and cultures and to build up networks among future leaders in Europe and the United States of America.

Robert Bosch Foundation Fellowships
Subjects: Business administration, economics, public affairs, public policy, political science, law, journalism and mass communication.
Purpose: To promote the advancement of American and German-European relations, and to broaden the participants' professional competence and cultural horizons.

Eligibility: Open to citizens of the United States of America between the ages of 23 and 34 years with a graduate or professional degree or equivalent work experience in the above subject areas. Candidates must provide evidence of outstanding professional or academic achievement and a strong knowledge of the German language. For those candidates who are outstanding in other areas but lack sufficient knowledge of German, the Foundation will provide language training prior to programme participation.
Level of Study: Professional development, Postgraduate
Type: Fellowship
Value: €1,800 per month stipend. Extra funding is available for family, language training and business travel
Length of Study: 9 months (September–May)
Frequency: Annual
Country of Study: Germany
No. of awards offered: 20
Application Procedure: Applicants must complete an application form and attend a personal interview. Please visit the website for more details.
Closing Date: October 15th
Funding: Private
Additional Information: Programme participants receive internships in German institutions such as the Federal Parliament, private corporation headquarters, mass media and other elements within the framework of government or commerce. Internships will be at a high level, closely related to senior officials. The programme will follow the following schedule: an intensive course on German language, political, economic and cultural affairs, work experience, a visit to Berlin and the former East Germany, a visit to the European Economic Community (EEC) and NATO headquarters in Brussels, a group visit to France for an overview of the political, economic and cultural perspective of another European country and a final programme evaluation in Stuttgart. All activities are conducted in German.

THE ROBERT WOOD JOHNSON FOUNDATION

Route 1 & College Road East, PO Box 2316, Princeton, NJ 08543-2316, United States of America
Tel: (1) 877 843 7953
Email: hss@rwjf.org
Website: www.rwjf.org

Established in 1972 in memory of Robert Wood Johnson, who founded Johnson & Johnson. The mission of the Robert Wood Johnson Foundationis to improve the health and healthcare of all Americans. Our goal is clear: to help Americans lead healthier lives and get the care they need

The Robert Wood Johnson Health & Society Scholars Program
Subjects: A broad range of factors affecting the nation's health.
Purpose: To build the nation's capacity for research, leadership and action.
Eligibility: For eligibility information, please visit our website, www.healthandsocietyscholars.org
Level of Study: Postdoctorate
Type: Scholarship
Value: Stipend of US$83,000 in the first year and US$86,000 in the second year
Length of Study: 2 years
Frequency: Annual
Study Establishment: One of six universities
Country of Study: United States of America
No. of awards offered: 18
Application Procedure: The application for the Robert Wood Johnson Health and Society Scholars program is done through an online application system available on our website www.healthandsociety-scholars.org
Closing Date: October 12th
Funding: Private
No. of awards given last year: 18

ROBERTO LONGHI FOUNDATION

Fondazione Roberto Longhi Via Benedetto Fortini 30, I-50125
Florence, Italy
Tel: (39) 55 658 0794
Fax: (39) 55 658 0794
Email: longhi@fondazionelonghi.it
Website: www.fondazionelonghi.it

The aim of the Roberto Longhi Foundation is to advance art historical studies. Applications are accepted annually from prospective Fellows who hold an advanced degree in art history. Fellows pursue individual and group research projects using the library and photo archive, participate in seminars and lectures by distinguished scholars at the Foundation and visit galleries, restorations and exhibitions.

Fondazione Roberto Longhi

Subjects: History of art.
Purpose: To aid those who want to seriously dedicate themselves to research in the history of art.
Eligibility: Open to citizens of Italy who possess a degree from an Italian university with a thesis in the history of art and to non-Italian citizens who have fulfilled the preliminary requirements for a doctoral degree in the history of art at an accredited university or an institution of equal standing. Students who have reached their 32nd birthday before the application deadline are not eligible.
Level of Study: Doctorate, Postgraduate
Type: Fellowship
Value: €600 per month
Length of Study: 9 months
Frequency: Annual
Study Establishment: The Foundation
Country of Study: Italy
No. of awards offered: Up to 10 or 12
Application Procedure: Applicants must submit an application containing their biographical data including place and date of birth, domicile, citizenship, transcript of undergraduate and graduate records, a copy of the degree thesis and of other original works, a curriculum vitae including knowledge of foreign languages both spoken and written, letters of reference from at least two persons of academic standing who are acquainted with the applicant's work, the subject of the research proposed and two passport size photographs.
Closing Date: May 15th
Funding: Private
Contributor: Private funds and capital endowment
No. of awards given last year: 10
No. of applicants last year: 30
Additional Information: Successful candidates must give an assurance that they will dedicate their full time to the research for which the fellowship is assigned. They may not enter into any connection with other institutions, they must live in Florence for the duration of the fellowship, excepting for travel required for their research. They may not exceed the periods of vacations fixed by the Institute and are required to attend seminars, lectures and other activities arranged by the Institute. The Fellows must, in addition, submit a written report at the end of their stay in Florence relating the findings of their individual research undertaken at the Longhi Foundation. Once approved by the scientific committee the Fellows research must be published only in the Foundations annual journal *Proporzioni*. Non-compliance with the above conditions will be considered sufficient grounds for the cancellation of a fellowship. Further information is available on request.

ROSL (ROYAL OVER-SEAS LEAGUE) ARTS

Over-Seas House, Park Place, St James's Street, London, SW1A 1LR, England
Tel: (44) 20 7408 0214 ext 219
Fax: (44) 20 7499 6738
Email: culture@rosl.org.uk
Website: www.rosl.org.uk
Contact: Ms Elaine Mitchener, Promotions Officer

The principal aim of the ROSL (Royal Over-Seas League) ARTS is to provide performance and exhibition opportunities for prize-winning artists and musicians early in their careers, bringing their work to the attention of the professional arts community, the media and the general public.

ROSL Annual Music Competition

Subjects: Musical performance, in four solo classes such as strings (including the harp and guitar), woodwind, brass and percussion, keyboard, singers and an ensemble class.
Purpose: To support and promote young Commonwealth musicians.
Eligibility: Open to citizens of the Commonwealth, including the United Kingdom and former Commonwealth countries, who are not more than 28 years of age for instrumentalists or 30 years of age for singers.
Level of Study: Professional development
Type: Competition
Value: Over UK £30,000 in prizes, including a UK £5,000 first prize
Frequency: Annual
Country of Study: Any country
No. of awards offered: Varies
Application Procedure: Applicants must see the website: www.roslarts.co.uk
Closing Date: January 14th
Funding: Commercial, individuals, private, trusts
No. of awards given last year: 19
No. of applicants last year: 500

ROTARY INTERNATIONAL

One Rotary Center 1560 Sherman Avenue, Evanston, IL, 60201-3698, United States of America
Tel: (1) 847 866 3000
Fax: (1) 847 328 8554
Email: scholarshipinquiries@rotaryintl.org
Website: www.rotary.org
Contact: Administrative Assistant

Rotary Internatyional is a worldwide organization of business and professional leaders that provides humanitarian service, encourages high ethical standards in all vocations and helps build goodwill and peace in the world. Approximately 1.2 million Rotarians belong to more than 32,000 clubs in more than 200 countries and geographical areas.

Rotary Ambassadorial Scholar Program

Subjects: All subjects.
Purpose: To develop a sense of purpose as ambassadors of goodwill and to further international understanding and world peace.
Eligibility: Open to applicants who are citizens of a country in which there are Rotary clubs. Initial application must be made through a Rotary club in the applicant's legal or permanent residence or place of full-time study or employment. Applicant must be proficient in the language of the proposed host country.
Level of Study: Postgraduate
Type: Scholarships
Value: Up to US$25,000. Covers round-trip transportation, 1 month of intensive language training, room and boarding and some educational supplies
Length of Study: 1 academic year of full-time graduate study
Frequency: Annual
Country of Study: Any country in which there is a Rotary Club
Application Procedure: Applications for the scholarship programme must be made through a Rotary Club. Every Club is eligible to submit Ambassadorial Scholar applications to the District.
Closing Date: October 1st
Additional Information: The scholarships are not appropriate for students seeking to continue studies already begun at a foreign institution.

Rotary Foundation Academic Year Ambassadorial Scholarships

Subjects: All subjects.
Purpose: To further international understanding and friendly relations among people of different countries.
Eligibility: Open to citizens of a country where there are Rotary clubs. The applicants should have completed more than 2 years of college-level coursework or equivalent professional experience before

commencing their scholarship studies. Applicants must be proficient in the language of the proposed host country.

Level of Study: Unrestricted

Type: Scholarship

Value: Round-trip transportation, tuition, room and board expenses, some educational supplies and 1 month of language training if necessary, totalling up to US$25,000 or its equivalent

Length of Study: 1 academic year

Frequency: Annual

Study Establishment: A study institution assigned by the Trustees of the Rotary Foundation

No. of awards offered: Varies

Application Procedure: Applicants should contact a local Rotary club for details.

Closing Date: Varies according to the local Rotary club, but between March 15th and July 15th. Applicants must apply over a year in advance

Funding: Private

Additional Information: Scholars will not be assigned to study in areas of a country where they have previously lived or studied for more than 6 months. During the study year, scholars are expected to be outstanding ambassadors of goodwill through appearances before Rotary clubs, schools, civic organizations and other forums. Upon completion of the scholarship, scholars are expected to share the experiences of understanding acquired during the study year with the people of their home countries. Candidates should contact local Rotary clubs for information on the availability of particular scholarships. Not all Rotary districts are able to offer scholarships. Further details are available from the website.

Rotary Foundation Cultural Ambassadorial Scholarships

Subjects: Cultural immersion and intensive language study.

Purpose: To further international understanding and friendly relations among people of different countries, and to make possible intensive language study and cultural immersion in another country.

Eligibility: Open to citizens of a country where there are Rotary clubs. The applicants should have completed more than 2 years of college-level coursework or equivalent professional experience before commencing their scholarship studies. Applicants must have completed more than 1 year of college level coursework or equivalent in the proposed language of study.

Level of Study: Unrestricted

Type: Scholarship

Value: Minimum award amount: $12000. Maximum award amount: $19000

Length of Study: 3 or 6 months

Frequency: Annual

Study Establishment: A language school assigned by the Trustees of the Rotary Foundation

Country of Study: Any country in which there is a Rotary Club

No. of awards offered: Varies

Application Procedure: Applicants should contact their local Rotary club for details. Applications are considered for candidates interested in studying Arabic, English, French, German, Hebrew, Italian, Japanese, Korean, Mandarin Chinese, Polish, Portuguese, Russian, Spanish, Swahili and Swedish.

Closing Date: Varies according to the local Rotary club, but between March 15th and July 15th. Applicants must apply over a year in advance

Funding: Private

Additional Information: During the study year, scholars are expected to be outstanding ambassadors of goodwill through appearances before Rotary clubs, schools, civic organizations and other forums. Candidates should contact local Rotary clubs for information on the availability of particular scholarships. Not all Rotary districts are able to offer scholarships. Further details are available from the website.

Rotary Foundation Multi-Year Ambassadorial Scholarships

Subjects: All subjects.

Purpose: To further international understanding and friendly relations among people of different countries and help defray the cost of pursuing a degree.

Eligibility: Open to citizens of a country where there are Rotary clubs. The applicants have completed more than 2 years of college-level coursework or equivalent professional experience before commencing their scholarship studies. Applicants must be proficient in the language of the proposed host country.

Level of Study: Graduate, Postgraduate, Unrestricted

Type: Scholarship

Value: The award provides a flat grant of US$12,000 or its equivalent per year to be applied towards the cost of a degree programme

Length of Study: 2 years

Frequency: Annual

Study Establishment: A foreign study institution approved by the trustees of the Rotary Foundation

Country of Study: Any country in which there is a Rotary Club

No. of awards offered: Varies

Application Procedure: Applicants should contact a local Rotary club for details.

Closing Date: Varies according to the local Rotary club, but between March 15th and July 15th. Applicants must apply over a year in advance

Funding: Private

Additional Information: Scholars will not be assigned to study in areas of a country where they have previously lived or studied for more than 6 months. During the study year, scholars are expected to be outstanding ambassadors of goodwill through appearances before Rotary clubs, schools, civic organizations and other forums. Upon completion of the scholarship, scholars are expected to share the experiences of understanding acquired during the study year with the people of their home countries. Candidates should contact local Rotary clubs for information on the availability of particular scholarships. Not all Rotary districts are able to offer scholarships. Further details are available from the website.

Rotary Grants for University Teachers

Subjects: All subjects of practical use to the host country.

Purpose: To build international understanding while strengthening higher education in low-income countries.

Eligibility: Open to candidates who have held a college or university appointment for 3 or more years and are proficient in the language of their prospective host country. Rotarians and relatives of rotarians are eligible.

Level of Study: Professional development

Type: Grant

Value: Up to US$12,500 for 3–5 months or up to US$22,500 for 6–10 months

Length of Study: 3–5 months or 6–10 months

Frequency: Annual, dependent on funds available

Study Establishment: A college/university located in a low-income country

Country of Study: Low-income countries only

No. of awards offered: Varies

Application Procedure: Applicants should contact a local Rotary club for details.

Closing Date: Varies according to the local Rotary club, but between March 15th and July 15th. Applicants must apply over a year in advance

Funding: Private

Additional Information: Grant recipients are expected to be outstanding ambassadors of goodwill to the people of their host and home countries through appearances to Rotary clubs. Not all Rotary districts are able to offer grants for university teachers. Further details are available from the website.

ROTARY YONEYAMA MEMORIAL FOUNDATION, INC.

3F Kokuryu Building, 2-6-15 Shiba Koen, Minato-ku, Tokyo, 105-0011, Japan
Tel: (81) 3 3434 8681
Fax: (81) 3 3578 8281
Website: www.rotary-yoneyama.org.jp/english
Contact: Administrative Assistant

The Rotary Yoneyama Memorial Foundation, Inc. has been growing in service and organization annually through the endorsement and co-operation of Japanese Rotaries. It awards scholarships to students not only from Asian countries but also from the rest of the world who are residents of Japan and studying or conducting research at Japanese Institutes of Higher Education.

Rotary Yoneyama Scholarship

Subjects: All subjects.

Purpose: The purpose of this programme is, by supporting motivated and excellent students from the world, to promote international and mutual understanding, develop international friendships and exchanges and make a contribution to create and maintain peace in the world.

Eligibility: Open to non-Japanese candidates under 45 years of age with a 'college student' visa for the purpose of studies and research.

Level of Study: Postgraduate, Doctorate, Graduate

Type: Scholarship

Value: ¥140,000 per month (graduate, postgraduate), ¥100,000 per month (undergraduate)

Length of Study: A maximum of 2 years

Frequency: Annual

Study Establishment: Colleges and universities

Country of Study: Japan

No. of awards offered: Varies

Application Procedure: Applicants should contact the Foundation for details or visit the website.

Closing Date: Please contact the organization

Funding: Private

Contributor: Rotarians in Japan

No. of awards given last year: 1,002 (sum total of all the scholarship programmes)

No. of applicants last year: 1,600

Additional Information: It is recommended that applicants contact the Foundation directly, since requirements for certain applicants can be conditional. Selection is extremely competitive, as the number of awards is limited.

THE ROYAL ACADEMY OF ENGINEERING

29 Great Peter Street, London, SW1P 3LW, England

Tel: (44) 20 7222 2688

Fax: (44) 20 7233 0054

Email: ian.bowbrick@raeng.org.uk

Website: www.raeng.org.uk

Contact: Ian Bowbrick, Scheme Manager

The Royal Academy of Engineering's objectives may be summarized as the pursuit, encouragement and maintenance of excellence in the whole field of engineering in order to promote the advancement of the science, art and the practice of engineering for the benefit of the public.

Exxon Mobil Teaching Fellowships

Subjects: Chemical, petroleum and mechanical engineering, geology.

Purpose: To encourage able young engineering and Earth science lecturers to remain in the education sector in their early years.

Eligibility: Open to well-qualified graduates, preferably with industrial experience and full-time lecturing posts at Institutes of Higher Education in the United Kingdom. Applicants should have been in their current posts for at least 1 year. The post must include the teaching of chemical, petroleum or mechanical engineering to undergraduates through courses that are accredited for registration with professional bodies for qualifications such as chartered engineer. For applicants whose career path has been graduation at the age of 22, followed by academic or industrial posts, the age limit is generally 32 years (at the closing date). Older candidates who have taken time out, e.g. for industrial experience, parenthood or voluntary service, will also be considered. Applicants should preferably be chartered engineers, or of equivalent professional status, or should be making progress towards this qualification.

Level of Study: Postdoctorate

Type: Fellowship

Value: UK £9,000

Length of Study: 4 years

Frequency: Annual

Study Establishment: The applicant's current university in the United Kingdom

Country of Study: United Kingdom

No. of awards offered: Up to 6

Application Procedure: Applicants must complete an application form.

Closing Date: October 1st

Funding: Commercial

Contributor: Exxon Mobile

Additional Information: A brochure is available on request. Enquiries about Exxon mobile university contacts should be sent to bowbricki@raeng.co.uk

Panasonic Trust Awards

Subjects: Engineering, particularly new engineering developments and new technologies.

Purpose: To encourage the technical updating and continuous professional development of qualified engineers through courses provided by United Kingdom Institutes of Higher Education at the Master's level.

Eligibility: Open to United Kingdom citizens who are qualified at the degree level in engineering or a related discipline. HND, HNC, OND, ONC or City and Guilds Full Technological Certificate qualifications are acceptable as a minimum. Applicants must be members, at any grade, of an engineering institution, working at the professional level in engineering in the United Kingdom and have several years of experience working at this level. Preference is given to those undertaking part-time modular Master's courses. The intended course of study must be relevant to the applicant's current or future career plans.

Level of Study: Professional development

Type: Award

Value: Usually 50 per cent of course fees up to a maximum of UK £1,000

Length of Study: The duration of the course

Frequency: Dependent on funds available

Country of Study: United Kingdom

No. of awards offered: Varies

Application Procedure: Applicants must write to the main address for application instructions, the application form and guidelines for employers and course co-ordinators.

Closing Date: Offered all year round

Funding: Private

Additional Information: Employers are expected to support an application in writing. The Trustees hope that the employer, once approached, might pay the full fees for the course. However, if this is not possible, a contribution from the employer is desirable. Applications must be supported by the course director or co-ordinator and confirm that the applicant is suitable for the course. Applications for grants of less than UK £1,000 should be submitted at least 4 weeks before the start of the course. Applications for larger grants should be submitted at least 6 weeks before the start of the course.

Royal Academy Engineering Professional Development

Subjects: Engineering.

Purpose: To ensure that the stills and knowledge of employees reflect the very latest in technological advances.

Eligibility: Open to UK citizens with a degree or HND/HNC in engineering or a closely allied subject. OND/ONC or City and Guilds Full Technological Certificate or NVQ level III qualifications are acceptable provided the individual has substantial industrial experience.

Level of Study: Professional development

Type: Grant

Value: Up to UK £15,000. In additions, prizes of UK £1,000 are being offered for each of the five most innovative applications

Length of Study: 1 year

Frequency: Annual

Country of Study: United Kingdom

Application Procedure: For further information please contact the scheme manager Ian Bowbrick at the Academy.

Closing Date: October 19th

For further information contact:

Email: Ian.bowbrick@raeng.org.uk

Royal Academy Executive Engineering Programme

Subjects: Engineering.

Purpose: To ensure that top engineering graduates continue to develop as professional engineers in order to provide UK industry with the high caliber technical and commercial managers required by world class enterprises.

Eligibility: Open to permanent members of United Kingdom Institutes of Higher Education with an approved engineering qualification.

Level of Study: Postgraduate

Type: Scholarship

Value: All training programme fees

Length of Study: 1 year

Frequency: Annual

Study Establishment: An industrial or commercial company

Country of Study: United Kingdom

Application Procedure: Visit the programme website.

Closing Date: Offered all year round

Funding: Foundation

Contributor: Gatsby Charitable Foundation

For further information contact:

Email: peter.revell@raeng.org.uk

Royal Academy of Engineering Industrial Secondment Scheme

Subjects: All fields of engineering.

Purpose: To provide financial support for the secondment of academic engineering staff to industrial companies within the United Kingdom.

Eligibility: Open to permanent members of United Kingdom Institutes of Higher Education with an approved engineering qualification, teaching some aspects of engineering. Preference may be given to junior staff without previous industrial experience or to more senior members whose industrial experience may have taken place some years earlier.

Level of Study: Unrestricted

Type: Grant

Value: Varies

Length of Study: Usually 3–6 months

Frequency: Dependent on funds available

Study Establishment: An industrial or commercial company

Country of Study: United Kingdom

No. of awards offered: Varies

Application Procedure: Applicants must submit a completed application form with a curriculum vitae, personal statement outlining the nature and objectives of the proposed secondment, letter of support from the applicant's head of department, statement from the applicant's employer detailing the financial aspects of the application, statement from the host company confirming the agreed work programme and defining the benefits of the secondment to the company and detailing any contribution costs that the company may wish to make. Application forms are available from the main address.

Funding: Government

No. of awards given last year: 18

No. of applicants last year: 26

Additional Information: The main objective is to obtain up-to-date industrial experience, to improve teaching capabilities and generally to foster academic industrial links. Contact Dr Imren Markesfor further information.

Royal Academy of Engineering International Travel Grants

Subjects: Engineering, materials technology and computing.

Purpose: To facilitate study visits overseas, generally for attendance at conferences, research institutions and/or industrial sites.

Eligibility: Open to postgraduate students, postdoctoral researchers, lecturers involved in research and chartered engineers in United Kingdom Institutes of Higher Education and in United Kingdom industry. Grants are not given to Fellows of The Royal Academy of Engineering, civil servants, employees of the British Museum or other government bodies. To be eligible for funding applicants must be United Kingdom or European Union nationals or United Kingdom permanent residents. There are no age restrictions.

Level of Study: Professional development, Doctorate, Postgraduate, Postdoctorate

Type: Travel grant

Value: 50 per cent of approved costs

Frequency: Dependent on funds available

No. of awards offered: Varies

Application Procedure: Applicants must submit a completed application form, nominating two referees of their choice, an abstract if an essay is being presented at a conference, publication list, photocopy of the personal details page from their passport, and a short paragraph of no more than 200 words, on a separate sheet of A4, justifying the relevance of the activity to their current work.

Closing Date: Applications are accepted at any time

Funding: Government

No. of awards given last year: Over 700

No. of applicants last year: Over 1,000

Additional Information: Applicants are urged to submit their forms at least 2 months prior to the departure date to enable APEX fares to be used.

Royal Academy of Engineering MacRobert Award

Subjects: The successful development of innovation in engineering or the other physical sciences.

Purpose: To recognize and reward outstanding contributions relating to innovation in engineering.

Eligibility: Open to individuals, independent teams and teams working for a firm, organization or laboratory. There should be no more than five members in a team.

Level of Study: Unrestricted

Type: Award

Value: UK £50,000 and a gold medal

Frequency: Annual

Country of Study: United Kingdom

No. of awards offered: 1

Application Procedure: Applicants must submit a 200–500 word summary of the engineering achievement, supported by 15 copies of relevant technical documentation. Further details and rules and conditions are available from the Royal Academy of Engineering.

Closing Date: January 30th

Funding: Private

No. of awards given last year: 1

Royal Academy Sir Angus Paton Bursary

Subjects: Engineering for development and water and environmental management.

Purpose: To study water and environmental management.

Eligibility: The bursary supports a suitably qualified engineer study a full-time Masters' degree course specifically related to water resources engineering or some other environmental technology.

Level of Study: Postgraduate

Type: Bursary

Value: UK £7,000

Length of Study: 1 year

Frequency: Annual

Country of Study: United Kingdom

No. of awards offered: 1

Application Procedure: For further information please contact the scheme manager Ian Bowbrick at the Academy.

Closing Date: Offered all year round

Funding: Private

Contributor: Sir Angus Paton

For further information contact:

Email: ian.bowbrick@raeng.org.uk

Royal Academy Visiting Professors Scheme

Subjects: Principles of engineering design, engineering design for sustainable development, integrated system design.

Purpose: To help universities to teach engineering design to undergraduates in a way that relates to real professional practice.

Level of Study: Doctorate, Postdoctorate, Research

Type: Fellowship

Length of Study: 1 year

Frequency: Annual

Country of Study: United Kingdom

No. of awards offered: 3

Application Procedure: Further information is available from the scheme manager Ian Bowbrick at the Academy.

Sainsbury Management Fellowships

Subjects: Engineering.
Purpose: To enable young chartered engineers of the highest career potential to undertake MBA courses at European business schools.
Eligibility: Open to United Kingdom citizens, who hold a First or Upper Second Class (Honours) Degree in engineering or a closely allied subject, have chartered engineer status or are making substantial progress towards it, have the potential and ambition to achieve senior management responsibility at an early age and be aged 26–34 years at the commencement of the proposed MBA course.
Level of Study: Postgraduate, Professional development, MBA
Type: Fellowship
Value: Course fees
Length of Study: 1 year
Frequency: Annual
Study Establishment: Awards are normally tenable at the following business schools: North America–Harvard, MIT, Stanford, Wharton, Columbia, Kellogg, University of Chicago; Europe–INSEAD (France), IMD (Switzerland), Erasmus (The Netherlands), IESE (Spain), SDA Bocconi (Italy)
Country of Study: Any country
No. of awards offered: 10
Application Procedure: Applicants must complete an application form, please contact the office for details.
Closing Date: Applications are accepted at any time
Funding: Private
Contributor: The Gatsby Charitable Foundation
No. of awards given last year: 10
No. of applicants last year: 46

Sainsbury Management Fellowships in the Life Sciences

Subjects: Life science.
Purpose: To support young scientists of high career potential to undertake activities related to their Personal Development Plans.
Eligibility: Open to UK citizens with a PhD in a bio-related subject, following a career compatible with the scheme's objectives in the UK. The applicants should be aged between 25 and 38 years.
Level of Study: Postgraduate
Type: Fellowship
Value: The award covers the cost of activities related to an individuals personal development plan, subject to approval
Frequency: Annual
Country of Study: Any country
Application Procedure: For further information please contact the scheme manager Ian Bowbrick at the Academy.
Closing Date: Offered all year round
Funding: Private
Contributor: Gatsby Charitable Foundation

For further information contact:

Email: ian.bowbrick@raeng.org.uk

ROYAL ACADEMY OF MUSIC

Marylebone Road, London, NW1 5HT, England
Tel: (44) 20 7873 7393
Fax: (44) 20 7873 7394
Email: go@ram.ac.uk
Website: www.ram.ac.uk
Contact: Examinations Officer

The Royal Academy of Music is a music college offering courses in music at postgraduate level. The Academy is part of the University of London.

Royal Academy of Music General Bursary Awards

Subjects: All relevant branches of music education and training.
Purpose: To help defray tuition fees and general living expenses for study at the Royal Academy of Music.
Eligibility: Open to any student offered a place at the Academy.
Level of Study: Postgraduate
Type: Scholarship/Bursary
Value: According to need and availability of funds
Length of Study: Normally for a complete academic year. Individual requirements may be imposed

Frequency: Annual
Study Establishment: The Royal Academy of Music
Country of Study: United Kingdom
No. of awards offered: Varies
Application Procedure: Applicants must complete an application form, which is sent automatically to all postgraduate students who are offered places.
Closing Date: January 31st for the following academic year
Funding: Trusts, commercial, individuals, private
No. of awards given last year: 115
No. of applicants last year: 219

ROYAL AERONAUTICAL SOCIETY

4 Hamilton Place, London, W1J 7BQ, England
Tel: (44) 20 7670 4300
Fax: (44) 20 7670 4309
Email: careers@raes.org.uk
Website: www.aerosociety.com
Contact: Careers Centre Manager

The Royal Aeronautical Society was founded in 1866 and is the only professional institution that covers all aspects of the aerospace industry including research, manufacture, operations and maintenance. Society membership unlocks a host of benefits for both the individual and organizations. Membership is open to anyone with an association or interest in aerospace.

Royal Aeronautical Society Centennial Scholarship Award

Subjects: Aeronautics and aerospace-related subjects such as aerospace engineering, safety, human factors, air transport management.
Purpose: To encourage the next generation of aerospace pioneers in the study of aeronautics and aerospace-related subjects and support of relevant projects to encourage young people into the field.
Eligibility: Open to students studying aerospace-related (e.g. aviation, aeronautical engineering, aeronautic-related) studies, and key organizations and research groups whose projects meet the aims and objectives of the fund.
Level of Study: Doctorate, Graduate, Postdoctorate, Postgraduate, Research, Relevant projects of national reach that meet the aims and objectives of the fund
Type: Scholarship
Value: As a guide, from UK £500 to 5,000
Length of Study: Most have already completed 1–2 years of relevant study
Frequency: Twice per year
Study Establishment: Not specified
Country of Study: Any country
No. of awards offered: Varies
Application Procedure: Applicants must complete an application form, available on request and provide all documentation specified in the form and accompanying guidelines.
Closing Date: March 31st - series 1, September 5th - series 2
Funding: Commercial, individuals
Contributor: A number of corporate, private and individual donors
No. of awards given last year: 32
No. of applicants last year: Approx. 55

ROYAL ANTHROPOLOGICAL INSTITUTE

50 Fitzroy Street, London, WTP 5BT, England
Tel: (44) 20 7387 0455
Fax: (44) 20 7383 4235
Email: admin@therai.org.uk
Website: www.therai.org.uk
Contact: Director of Grants

The Royal Anthropological Institute is a non-profit registered charity. It is entirely independent, with a Director and a small staff accountable to the Council, elected annually from the Fellowship. Council and Committee members and the editorial team of the Institute's principal journal, the *Journal of the Royal Anthropological Institute* (incorporating MAN), give their services without remuneration.

Emslie Horniman Anthropological Scholarship Fund

Subjects: Anthropology.
Purpose: To provide predoctoral grants for fieldwork in anthropology with a preference for research outside the United Kingdom.
Eligibility: Open to citizens of the United Kingdom, Commonwealth or Irish Republic who are university graduates or who can satisfy the trustees of their suitability for the study proposed. Preference is given to applicants whose proposals include fieldwork outside the United Kingdom. Graduates who already hold a doctorate in anthropology are not eligible. Open to individuals only, as no grants are given to expeditions or teams.
Level of Study: Postgraduate, Predoctorate
Type: Scholarship
Value: UK £1,000–9,500
Frequency: Annual
Country of Study: Any country
No. of awards offered: Approx. 10
Application Procedure: Applicants must request an application form.
Closing Date: March 31st
Funding: Private
No. of awards given last year: 6
No. of applicants last year: 41
Additional Information: No grants are available for library research, university fees or subsistence in the United Kingdom.

ROYAL COLLEGE OF MIDWIVES

15 Mansfield Street, London, W1G 9NH, England
Tel: (44) 20 7312 3535
Fax: (44) 20 7312 3536
Email: info@rcm.org.uk
Website: www.rcm.org.uk
Contact: S E MacDonald, Education and Research Manager

The Royal College of Midwives is the major professional organization for midwives in the United Kingdom, and aims to contribute to the art and science of midwifery knowledge and practice. The RCM awards and scholarships provide opportunities for the development of good practice ultimately improving the care provided to women, their babies and families.

Mary Seacole Nursing Development and Leadership Award

Subjects: Midwifery, nursing, health visiting, health service needs of ethnic minority communities.
Purpose: To provide an opportunity for the development of professional practice, service development and leadership potential of black and ethnic minority midwives, nurses and health visitors.
Eligibility: Applicants must be a nurse and, midwife or health visitor. Application should reflect the example set by Mary Seacole.
Level of Study: Professional development, Research, Doctorate, Graduate
Type: Leadership awards
Value: UK £12,500, Development award UK £6,000
Length of Study: 1 year
Frequency: Annual
Country of Study: United Kingdom
No. of awards offered: 4
Application Procedure: Applicants must send a stamped addressed envelope to the Royal College of Nursing (RCN) to obtain details and an application form.
Closing Date: June 15th
Funding: Government
Contributor: Department of Health
No. of awards given last year: 1
No. of applicants last year: 3

For further information contact:

Royal College of Nursing, 20 Cavendish Square, London, W1G 0RN, England
Contact: Award Officer, Mary Seacole Award,

RCM Midwifery Awards

Subjects: There are nine categories of awards which celebrate the range of work and achievement of midwives midwifery education, midwifery management or leadership, innovations in midwifery, Members' Champion award, promotion of normal birth, outstanding contribution to care of newborns, award for turning vision into reality, midwifery impact on child development, promoting effective midwifery in community settings and Student Vision award.
Purpose: To recognize and celebrate innovation in midwifery practice, education and research.
Eligibility: Applicants may be individuals or small groups but should meet the criteria of 1 of the 10 categories. Check the website for complete details: www.rcm.org.uk/college/annual-midwifery-awards/
Level of Study: Postgraduate, Professional development, Research
Value: Varies (up to UK £20,000 in total)
Frequency: Annual
Country of Study: Projects Based in United Kingdom – though some requiring travel may involve external activity
No. of awards offered: 10
Application Procedure: Applicants must apply in writing or email to the address given below. The application must be accompanied by a 500-word description of the project. Short-listed candidates will be asked to attend an interview.
Closing Date: November 1st
Funding: Commercial
Contributor: Several
No. of awards given last year: 10 awards in 10 categories
No. of applicants last year: 82

For further information contact:

Gothic House, 3 The Green, Richmond, Surrey, TW9 1PL, England
Email: mail@chamberdunn.co.uk
Contact: Chamberlain Dunn Associates

Ruth Davies Research Bursary

Subjects: Midwifery.
Purpose: To promote and develop midwifery research and practice.
Eligibility: Open to practicing midwives who are RCM members, who have basic knowledge, skills and understanding of the research process, have access to research support in their trust or Institutes of Higher Education and who have been in practice for 2 years or more.
Level of Study: Doctorate, Graduate, Postdoctorate, Postgraduate, Professional development, Research
Type: Bursary
Value: UK £5,000 per bursary
Length of Study: 1 year
Frequency: Annual
Country of Study: United Kingdom
No. of awards offered: 3
Application Procedure: Applicants must submit a succinct curriculum vitae covering the previous 5 years, a research proposal of no more than 2,500 words and letters of support from both employers and academics who are familiar with the applicant's work.
Closing Date: July 16th
Funding: Commercial
Contributor: Bounty
No. of awards given last year: 2
No. of applicants last year: 2 shortlisted

For further information contact:

Tel: 0207 312 3463
Email: marlyn.gennace@rcm.org.uk
Contact: Mrs Marlyn Gennace, Ruth Davies Research Bursary Administrator

ROYAL COLLEGE OF MUSIC

Prince Consort Road, London, SW7 2BS, United Kingdom
Tel: (44) 20 7591 4377
Fax: (44) 20 7591 4856
Email: dclark@rcm.ac.uk
Website: www.rcm.ac.uk
Contact: Mr Darren Clark, International and Awards Officer

The Royal College of Music, London, provides specialized musical education and professional training at the highest international level for performers and composers. This enables talented students to develop the musical skills, knowledge, understanding and resourcefulness that will equip them to contribute significantly to musical life in the United Kingdom and internationally.

Royal College of Music Scholarships

Subjects: Music performance, composition and conducting.
Purpose: To recognize merit in music performance, composition or conducting.
Eligibility: All those auditioning in person for a place at the Royal College of Music are considered for a scholarship at the time of their audition. Scholarships are awarded on the basis of merit and potential.
Level of Study: Postgraduate, Doctorate, Graduate
Type: Scholarship
Value: Up to UK £20,333 (full fees)
Length of Study: 1–4 years
Frequency: Annual
Study Establishment: Royal College of Music
Country of Study: United Kingdom
No. of awards offered: Approx. 200
Application Procedure: Applications are available on www.cukas.ac.uk/
Closing Date: October 1st
Funding: Private, trusts
No. of awards given last year: 120
No. of applicants last year: 1,600

ROYAL COLLEGE OF NURSING (RCN)

20 Cavendish Square, London, W1G 0RN, England
Tel: (44) 20 7409 3333
Email: scholarships@rcn.org.uk
Website: www.rcn.org.uk
Contact: Ms Moira Lambert, Awards Officer

The Royal College of Nursing of the United Kingdom (RCN) represents nurses and nursing, promotes excellence in practice and shapes health policies.

Barbers Company Clinical Nursing Scholarship

Subjects: All subjects related to nursing.
Purpose: To enable nurses making a career in clinical nursing to undertake further education, research or a clinical project.
Eligibility: The scholarship is offered for the fees or subsistence of a nurse, normally undertaking a taught Masters programme relevant to nursing or research in an academic department in the U.K., or at an approved academic department of nursing overseas.
Level of Study: Postgraduate, Doctorate, Predoctorate
Type: Scholarship
Value: UK £5,000 to be shared among the awardees
Frequency: Annual
Study Establishment: Universities
Country of Study: United Kingdom
No. of awards offered: Varies
Application Procedure: Applicants must send in their curriculum vitae plus a brief outline of about 500 words on the course/research or project and its intended application, to the address given below.
Closing Date: February 28th
Funding: Commercial
Contributor: Barber Surgeons (The Worshipful Company of Barbers)
No. of awards given last year: 3
No. of applicants last year: 35

For further information contact:

Royal College of Nursing Research Institute, School of Health and Social studies, University of Warwick, Coventry, CV4 7AL, England
Contact: PA to the Director

Ethicon Nurses Education Trust Fund

Subjects: Nursing, midwifery and health visiting.
Purpose: To further member's education and to enhance the standard of expertise in their chosen field of nursing.

Eligibility: Open to members of the RCN, Association for Perioperative Practice or Infection Prevention Society only.
Level of Study: Predoctorate, Doctorate, Graduate, Postdoctorate, Postgraduate, Professional development
Type: Grant
Value: Up to UK £1,000 each
Length of Study: Unrestricted
Frequency: Annual
Study Establishment: Unrestricted
Country of Study: Any country
No. of awards offered: Varies
Application Procedure: Applicants must contact Fitwise Drumcross Hall for an application form. Telephone no: 01506 811077.
Closing Date: March
Funding: Commercial
Contributor: Ethicon
No. of awards given last year: 15
No. of applicants last year: 45

For further information contact:

Fitwise Drumcross Hall, Bathgate, EH48 4JT, Scotland
Tel: (44) 01506 811077

Nuffield Trust/RCN/IHM Joint Travel Awards

Subjects: Nursing, midwifery and health visiting including public health, health policy and health education.
Purpose: To undertake a study overseas to pursue an area of innovation in health services. For nurses and healthcare managers to undertake joint study tours to improve patient experience.
Eligibility: Open to members of the RCN only.
Level of Study: Postgraduate, Professional development, Unrestricted, Research
Type: Fellowship
Value: Up to UK £5,000 each
Length of Study: Unrestricted
Frequency: Annual
Study Establishment: Unrestricted
Country of Study: Any country
No. of awards offered: Varies
Application Procedure: Applicants must send a stamped addressed envelope for application requirements. Enquiries are dealt with between February and April.
Closing Date: April
Funding: Private
Contributor: Nuffield Trust
No. of awards given last year: 2
No. of applicants last year: 3
Additional Information: Award scheme is under review in 2008.

For further information contact:

RCN/Nuffield Trust Awards, c/o Award Officer, Royal College of Nursing, 20 Cavendish Square, London, W1G 0RN, England

RCN Grants

Subjects: Nursing, midwifery and health visiting.
Purpose: To assist RCN members to enhance their professional skills, knowledge and competence. Pre-registration nursing students in RCN membership are also eligible.
Eligibility: Open to RCN members.
Level of Study: Predoctorate, Professional development, Research, Doctorate, Graduate, MBA, Postdoctorate, Postgraduate
Type: Grant
Value: Up to UK £500 each
Length of Study: Unrestricted
Frequency: Annual
Study Establishment: Unrestricted
Country of Study: Any country
No. of awards offered: Varies
Application Procedure: Applicants must request information by sending a stamped self-addressed envelope. Enquiries are dealt with between May and July.
Closing Date: August 1st
Funding: Trusts
Contributor: RCN Charitable Trust Funds

No. of awards given last year: 31
No. of applicants last year: 79

For further information contact:

RCN Grants (001-532), 20 Cavendish Square, London, W1G 0RN, England
Contact: Awards Officer

RCN Margaret Parkinson Scholarships

Subjects: Nursing and midwifery.
Purpose: To encourage graduates with a non-nursing degree to qualify as a nurse.
Eligibility: Open to graduates who have not yet started nurse training.
Level of Study: Postgraduate
Type: Scholarship
Value: Up to UK £1,000 each per annum
Length of Study: Unrestricted
Frequency: Annual
Study Establishment: Universities
Country of Study: United Kingdom
No. of awards offered: Varies
Application Procedure: Applicants must send a stamped self-addressed envelope to the Awards Officer. Enquiries will be dealt with between November and January.
Closing Date: February 1st
Funding: Private
Contributor: Margaret Parkinson Scholarship Fund
No. of awards given last year: 4
No. of applicants last year: 12

For further information contact:

RCN Margaret Parkinson Scholarships, 20 Cavendish square, London, W1G 0RN
Contact: Awards Officer

RCN Scholarships Fund

Subjects: Nursing, midwifery and health visiting including public health, health policy and health education.
Purpose: To provide funding for a project, study visit or course to facilitate professional development with an emphasis on education, leadership, management or dementia care.
Eligibility: Open to RCN members.
Level of Study: Doctorate, Research, Graduate, MBA, Postdoctorate, Postgraduate, Predoctorate, Professional development
Type: Scholarship
Value: Varies, up to UK £3,000 each
Length of Study: Unrestricted
Frequency: Annual
Study Establishment: Unrestricted
Country of Study: Any country
No. of awards offered: Varies
Application Procedure: Applicants must request information by sending a stamped addressed envelope. Enquiries are dealt with between February and April.
Closing Date: May 1st
Funding: Trusts
Contributor: RCN Charitable Trust Funds
No. of awards given last year: 7
No. of applicants last year: 29

For further information contact:

RCN Scholarships, c/o Awards Officer, Royal College of Nursing, 20 Cavendish Square, London, W1G 0RN, England

ROYAL COLLEGE OF OBSTETRICIANS AND GYNAECOLOGISTS (RCOG)

27 Sussex Place, Regent's Park, London, NW1 4RG, United Kingdom
Tel: (44) 20 7772 6285
Fax: (44) 20 7772 6359
Email: jhayman@rcog.org.uk
Website: www.rcog.org.uk
Contact: J. Hayman, Awards Administrator

The Royal College of Obstetricians and Gynaecologists (RCOG) is dedicated to the encouragement of the study, and the advancement of science and practice of obstetrics and gynaecology.

American Gynecological Club/Gynaecological Visiting Society Fellowship

Subjects: Obstetrics and gynaecology.
Purpose: To enable the recipient to visit, make contact with and gain knowledge from a specific centre offering new techniques or methods of clinical management within the speciality.
Eligibility: Open to specialist registrars in the United Kingdom, and to junior Fellows or those in residency programmes in the United States of America.
Level of Study: Professional development
Type: Fellowship
Value: UK £1,000
Frequency: Annual
Country of Study: United Kingdom or United States of America
No. of awards offered: 1
Application Procedure: Applicants must contact the Awards Secretary for details.
Closing Date: March 30th
No. of awards given last year: 1
No. of applicants last year: 3

Eden Travelling Fellowship

Subjects: Obstetrics and gynaecology.
Purpose: To enable the recipient to gain additional knowledge and experience in the pursuit of a specific research project in which he or she is currently engaged.
Eligibility: Open to medical graduates of not less than 2 years standing from any approved university in the United Kingdom or Commonwealth.
Level of Study: Postgraduate
Type: Fellowship
Value: Up to UK £5,000, according to the project undertaken
Frequency: Annual
Study Establishment: Another department of obstetrics and gynaecology or of closely related disciplines
Country of Study: Any country
No. of awards offered: 1
Application Procedure: Applicants must include information on qualifications, areas of interest and/or publications in a specified area, centres to be visited with confirmation of arrangements from the head of that centre, estimated costs and the names of two referees.
Closing Date: March 30th
No. of awards given last year: 1
No. of applicants last year: 5

Edgar Gentilli Prize

Subjects: Obstetrics and gynaecology.
Purpose: To recognize original work done on the cause, nature, recognition and treatment of any form of cancer of the female genital tract.
Eligibility: Unrestricted.
Type: Prize
Value: UK £750 plus book tokens up to a value of UK £250
Frequency: Annual
No. of awards offered: 1
Application Procedure: Applicants must submit results of their research in the form of an original manuscript, adequately referenced and written in a format comparable with that used for submission to a learned journal, or by means of reprint of a published article.
Closing Date: September 30th
No. of awards given last year: 1
No. of applicants last year: 5

Endometriosis Millennium Fund Award

Subjects: Endometriosis.
Purpose: To stimulate and encourage research, clinical or laboratory based, or to encourage clinicians to acquire extra clinical skills to manage patients.
Eligibility: Open to members of the College or members of the RCOG trainees register who are residents and working within the United Kingdom.

Level of Study: Postgraduate
Value: Up to UK £5,000
Frequency: Annual
Country of Study: United Kingdom
No. of awards offered: More than 1
Application Procedure: Applicants must submit an application in the requisite form, which can be downloaded from the website or can be obtained from the Awards Secretary at the RCOG. Application forms must be accompanied by two references from supervisors or senior colleagues and written confirmation of availability of laboratory space or access to surgical training in the host institution must be provided with the application. An undertaking that a structured typewritten report will be provided at the end of the grant period and that the source of grant will be acknowledged in any related publications must also be submitted.
Closing Date: March 30th
Contributor: The Endometriosis Millennium Fund
No. of awards given last year: 1
No. of applicants last year: 6
Additional Information: The award may only be used for the purpose approved by the Assessment Committee.

Ethicon Travel Awards

Subjects: Obstetrics and gynaecology.
Purpose: To promote international goodwill in the speciality.
Eligibility: Open to RCOG members who have passed both Part I and II of the membership exams. Members from the United Kingdom must be trainees and overseas members must not be in independent practice.
Level of Study: Postgraduate
Type: Travel grant
Value: Up to UK £1,000
Frequency: Twice per year
No. of awards offered: Up to 15
Application Procedure: Applicants must complete an application form, available from the Awards Secretary or from the website.
Closing Date: January 31st and July 31st
No. of awards given last year: 6
No. of applicants last year: 10
Additional Information: Travel must take place within 1 year of the award being made.

Green-Armytage and Spackman Travelling Scholarship

Subjects: Obstetrics and gynaecology.
Purpose: To allow applicants to visit centres where work similar to their own is being carried out.
Eligibility: Open to Fellows and members of the College. Applicants should have shown a special interest in some particular aspect of obstetrical or gynaecological practice.
Level of Study: Postgraduate
Type: Scholarship
Value: UK £4,000
Frequency: Annual
Country of Study: Any country
No. of awards offered: 1
Application Procedure: Applicants must include information on qualifications, areas of interest and/or publications in a specified area, centres to be visited with confirmation from the head of that centre, estimated costs and the names of two referees.
Closing Date: March 30th
No. of awards given last year: 1
No. of applicants last year: 2

Harold Malkin Prize

Subjects: Obstetrics and gynaecology.
Purpose: To reward those undertaking the best original work while holding a specialist registrar post in a hospital.
Eligibility: Open to RCOG members or membership candidates.
Level of Study: Professional development
Type: Prize
Value: 1st prize UK £250, 2nd prize UK £150
Frequency: Annual
No. of awards offered: 2
Application Procedure: Applicants must contact the Awards Secretary for details.

Closing Date: September 31st
No. of awards given last year: 2
No. of applicants last year: 4

Herbert Erik Reiss Memorial Case History Prize

Purpose: The prizes will be awarded to candidates who, in the opinion of the assessors, undertake the best presentation of a clinical case, including critical assessment and literature research, in a topic of obstetrics and gynaecology.
Eligibility: Open to medical students and junior doctors working in foundation years 1/2 in the UK and the Republic of Ireland.
Value: First prize is UK £400 and second prize is UK £200
Frequency: Annual
No. of awards offered: 2
Application Procedure: A maximum of 1,500 words with maximum of 10 references should be submitted. Please include a statement of contribution to the project and indicate the name and address of the supervisor. Only one submission per candidate is permitted.
Closing Date: September
No. of awards given last year: 2
No. of applicants last year: 25

John Lawson Prize

Purpose: The prize will be awarded to a candidate who, in the opinion of the assessors, undertakes the best article on a topic of obstetrics or gynaecology derived from work carried out in Africa between the tropics of Capricorn and Cancer.
Eligibility: Candidature is not restricted to fellows and members of the college.
Value: UK £150
Frequency: Annual
Application Procedure: The record of the work can be submitted by way of an original manuscript, adequately referenced and written in a format comparable to that used for submission to a learned journal, or by means of a reprint of a published article.
Closing Date: September
No. of awards given last year: 1
No. of applicants last year: 8
Additional Information: If joint authorship is involved then the candidate must identify his/her involvement in the publication.

Malcolm Black Travel Fellowship

Subjects: Obstetrics and gynaecology.
Purpose: To enable a College Member or Fellow of up to 5 years standing at the time of application, to travel either to the British Isles or from the British Isles abroad, for a period of time to extend postgraduate training courses or to visit centres of research or of particular expertise within the speciality of obstetrics and gynaecology.
Type: Travelling fellowship
Value: Travel and subsistence costs will be paid up to a maximum of UK £1,000
Frequency: Every 2 years
Closing Date: March
No. of awards given last year: 1
No. of applicants last year: 5

Overseas Fund

Subjects: Obstetrics and gynaecology.
Purpose: To allow individuals to travel to the United Kingdom for further training.
Eligibility: Open to RCOG members or the equivalent, working overseas.
Level of Study: Professional development
Type: Travel grant
Value: Up to UK £2,000
Frequency: Annual
No. of awards offered: Up to 8
Application Procedure: Applicants must see the website.
Closing Date: March 30th
No. of awards given last year: 1
No. of applicants last year: 3

Peter Huntingford Memorial Prize

Purpose: The prize is for presenting the best case history, clinical audit or a report of a research project in any aspect of fertility control in which the applicant is directly involved.
Eligibility: Open to doctors working in their foundation year or specialist training years 1 and/or 2 in the UK and the Republic of Ireland.
Value: First prize is UK £1,000 and second prize is UK £500
Frequency: Annual
No. of awards offered: 2
Application Procedure: A submission of no more than 1,500 words outlining the research with reference to publications (if any) is required. Please include a statement of the contribution to the project and indicate the name and address of the supervisor. Only one submission per candidate is permitted.
Closing Date: September
Contributor: British Pregnancy Advisory Service (BPAS)

RCOG Bernhard Baron Travelling Scholarships

Subjects: Obstetrics and gynaecology.
Purpose: To expand the recipient's knowledge in areas in which he or she already has some experience.
Eligibility: Open to Fellows and members of the College.
Level of Study: Postgraduate
Type: Scholarship
Value: Up to UK £6,000
Frequency: Annual
Country of Study: Any country
No. of awards offered: 2
Application Procedure: Applicants must contact the Awards Secretary for details.
Closing Date: March 30th
No. of awards given last year: 2
No. of applicants last year: 8

Richard Johanson Research Prize

Subjects: Obstetrics and gynaecology.
Purpose: To recognize the best research projects in any aspect of obstetrics and gynaecology.
Level of Study: Graduate
Value: First prize UK £250, second prize UK £100
Frequency: Annual
Country of Study: United Kingdom, Northern Ireland and Republic of Ireland
Application Procedure: Applicants should submit research outline no more than 1,500 words, with reference to publications (if any). The research must have been carried out during the applicant's undergraduate course and in a relevant department.
Closing Date: September
Funding: Private
No. of awards given last year: 2
No. of applicants last year: 34
Additional Information: Submissions may by sent by email or post (four copies of the typewritten submission on A4-size paper). Applicants must state clearly which award they are applying for and include their supervisor's name and address.

Tim Chard Case History Prize

Subjects: Obstetrics and gynaecology.
Purpose: To reward students showing the greatest understanding of a clinical problem in obstetrics and gynaecology.
Level of Study: Graduate
Value: First prize UK £500, second prize UK £250, third prize UK £100
Frequency: Annual
Study Establishment: An accredited medical school
Country of Study: United Kingdom, Northern Ireland and Republic of Ireland
Application Procedure: Applicants should submit one case history with discussion no longer than 1,500 words with 10 biographical references that includes the name and address of the applicant's supervisor. Submissions may be sent by email or post (four copies of the typewritten submission on A4-size paper). Applicants must state clearly which award they are applying for, and make separate applications for each. Applications that do not comply with the stipulations will not be accepted.

Closing Date: September
Funding: Private
Contributor: Bart's and the London School of Medicine
No. of awards given last year: 3
No. of applicants last year: 42

William Blair-Bell Memorial Lectureships in Obstetrics and Gynaecology

Subjects: Obstetrics and gynaecology.
Purpose: To allow an individual to give a lecture.
Eligibility: Open to Fellows or members of not more than 2 years standing.
Value: Honorarium of UK £500
Frequency: Annual
Application Procedure: Applicants must contact the Awards Secretary.
Closing Date: March 30th
No. of awards given last year: 1
No. of applicants last year: 5

Wyeth Historical Lecture

Subjects: Obstetrics and gynaecology with a strong historical content.
Purpose: To allow an individual to give a lecture on a current development in the field.
Eligibility: Open to RCOG Fellows and members.
Type: Other
Value: An honorarium of UK £400
Frequency: Annual
No. of awards offered: 1
Application Procedure: Applicants must contact the Awards Secretary for details.
Closing Date: March 30th
Funding: Private
Contributor: Wyeth Laboratories
No. of awards given last year: 1
No. of applicants last year: 3

THE ROYAL COLLEGE OF OPHTHALMOLOGISTS

17 Cornwall Terrace, London, NW1 4QW, England
Tel: (44) 20 7935 0702
Fax: (44) 20 7935 9838
Email: training@rcophth.ac.uk
Website: www.rcophth.ac.uk
Contact: Beth Barnes, Deputy

The college is responsible for promoting high standards of professional practice, setting curricula and conducting examinations and providing professional support and advice for ophthalmologists. The college runs an annual scientific congress and seminars for ophthalmologists and publishes a range of clinical guidelines.

The Dorey Bequest

Subjects: Ophthalmology.
Purpose: To provide personal travel expenses to members and Fellows of the Royal College of Ophthalmologists who are travelling abroad for research or training.
Eligibility: Members and Fellows of the Royal College of Ophthalmologists.
Level of Study: Postgraduate
Type: Travel award
Value: Generally UK £300–600 per award
Frequency: Annual
Country of Study: Any country
No. of awards offered: Varies
Application Procedure: An application form must be completed and copied five times and submitted with five copies of the candidate's curriculum vitae.
Closing Date: October 2nd
Funding: Private
No. of awards given last year: 2

Ethicon Foundation Fund Travel Award

Subjects: Ophthalmology.
Purpose: To prove financial assistance to members and Fellows of the Royal College of Ophthalmologists who are travelling abroad for research or training purposes.
Eligibility: Applicants must be members or Fellows of the Royal College of Ophthalmologists.
Level of Study: Postgraduate
Type: Travel award
Value: Generally UK £400–800 per award
Frequency: Annual
Country of Study: Any country
No. of awards offered: Varies
Application Procedure: An application form must be completed and copied five times and submitted with five copies of the candidates curriculum vitae.
Closing Date: November 6th
Funding: Commercial
Contributor: Ethicon Ltd
No. of awards given last year: 4

The Fight For Sight Award

Subjects: Ophthalmology.
Purpose: The award will be made in recognition of a significant piece of research (completed within 18 months prior to the closing date) in an area that falls within the remit of the charity. It is intended that the award will be used to further the education of the award winner by being sent on research-related activities including attendance at conferences and seminars on ophthalmology.
Eligibility: Applicants must be under 40 years of age.
Value: UK £5,000
Frequency: Annual
No. of awards offered: 1
Application Procedure: 5 copies each of the completed application form and the curriculum vitae, alongwith a supporting paper (published or otherwise) detailing a significant piece of research must be submitted.
Closing Date: February 13th
No. of awards given last year: 1

For further information contact:

Website: www.rcophth.ac.uk/education/travel awards
Contact: Miss Susannah Grant, The Education and Training Administrator

The Keeler Scholarship

Subjects: Ophthalmology.
Purpose: To enable the scholar to study, research or acquire special skills, knowledge or experience at a suitable location in the United Kingdom or elsewhere for a minimum period of 6 months.
Eligibility: Fellows, members and affiliate members of the college are eligible to apply for the scholarship. The trustees will give special consideration to candidates intending to make a career in ophthalmology in the United Kingdom.
Level of Study: Postgraduate
Type: Scholarship
Value: Up to UK £20,000
Frequency: Every 2 years
Country of Study: United Kingdom or elsewhere
No. of awards offered: 1
Application Procedure: 5 copies each of the application form duly completed and the candidate's curriculum vitae should be submitted.
Funding: Commercial
Contributor: Keeler Ltd
No. of awards given last year: 1

The Pfizer Ophthalmic Fellowship

Subjects: Ophthalmology.
Purpose: To enable the scholar to study, research or acquire special skills, knowledge or experience at a suitable location in the United Kingdom or elsewhere for a minimum period of 6 months.
Eligibility: Applicants must be Fellows, members or affiliates of the Royal College of Ophthalmologists, in good standing.
Level of Study: Postgraduate
Type: Fellowship

Value: Up to UK £35,000
Frequency: Annual
Country of Study: United Kingdom or elsewhere
No. of awards offered: 1
Application Procedure: 5 copies each of the application form duly completed and the candidate's curriculum vitae should be submitted.
Closing Date: October 23rd
Funding: Commercial
Contributor: Pfizer Ltd
No. of awards given last year: 1

Sir William Lister Award

Subjects: Ophthalmology.
Purpose: To provide personal travel expenses to citizens of the United Kingdom who are travelling abroad for research or training.
Eligibility: Applicants must be citizens of the United Kingdom and members or Fellows of the Royal College of Ophthalmologists.
Level of Study: Postgraduate
Type: Travel award
Value: Generally UK £400–600 per award
Frequency: Annual
Country of Study: Any country
No. of awards offered: Varies
Application Procedure: An application form must be completed and copied five times and submitted with five copies of the candidate's curriculum vitae.
Closing Date: October 2nd
Funding: Private
No. of awards given last year: 2

ROYAL COLLEGE OF ORGANISTS (RCO)

PO Box 56357, London, SE16 7XL, United Kingdom
Tel: (44) 5600 767208
Email: kim.gilbert@rco.org.uk
Website: www.rco.org.uk
Contact: Kim Gilbert, General Manager

The Royal College of Organists (RCO) is membership based. It promotes the art of organ playing as choral directing, and provides an organization with a library, events and examinations to further that object.

RCO Various Open Award Bequests

Purpose: To assist students who are training to become organists.
Eligibility: School and students in undergraduate and postgraduate education who are members of the college.
Level of Study: Postgraduate, Professional development, School and undergraduate
Type: Award
Value: Between UK £100 and UK £400 each
Frequency: Annual
Study Establishment: Various
No. of awards offered: Various
Application Procedure: Write for an application form.
Closing Date: April 18th
Funding: Private

For further information contact:

Email: admin@rco.org.uk
Contact: The Registrar

William Robertshaw Exhibition

Subjects: Organ playing.
Purpose: To offer financial support for organ student to use towards tuition fees and/or cost of sheet music.
Eligibility: Student organ who is member of RCO; membership is open to everyone on payment of subscription.
Level of Study: Postgraduate, Professional development, School and undergraduate
Value: UK £250 per annum
Frequency: Annual
No. of awards offered: Various
Application Procedure: Write for an application form.
Closing Date: April 18th
Funding: Private

ROYAL COLLEGE OF PAEDIATRICS AND CHILD HEALTH (RCPCH)

50 Hallam Street, London, W1W 6DE, England
Tel: (44) 20 7307 5600
Fax: (44) 020 7307 5601
Email: aaron.barham@rcpch.ac.uk
Website: www.rcpch.ac.uk
Contact: Mr Aaron Barham, Conference Organizer

The Royal College of Paediatrics and Child Health works to advance the art and science of paediatrics, to raise the standard of medical care provided to children, to educate and examine those concerned with health of children, and to advance the education of the public and, in particular, medical practitioners in child health.

Ashok Nathwani Visiting Fellowship
Subjects: Paediatrics.
Purpose: To enable young paediatricians from abroad to visit the United Kingdom.
Eligibility: Open to all Paediatricians.
Level of Study: Postdoctorate
Type: Fellowship
Value: A travel, accommodation and subsistence costs
Frequency: Annual
Country of Study: United Kingdom
Closing Date: August 24th

Douglas Hubble Travel Bursary
Subjects: Paediatrics and child health.
Purpose: To provide financial support for young pediatricians, or paediatric research workers, who contribute to the British paediatric practice.
Eligibility: Open to all young paediatricians or paediatric research workers below consultant status.
Level of Study: Postgraduate
Type: Award
Frequency: Every 2 years
Closing Date: August 24th
Funding: Foundation
Contributor: University of Birmingham and the Royal College of paediatrics and Child Health

For further information contact:

Royal College of Paediatrics and Child Health, 50 Hallam Street, London, W1W 6DE
Contact: Mrs Aaron Barham

Dr Michael Blacow Memorial Prize
Subjects: Paediatrics.
Purpose: To award the best plenary paper presented at the spring meeting.
Eligibility: Open to all trainee paediatricians.
Level of Study: Postgraduate
Type: Award
Value: UK £200
Frequency: Annual
Funding: Trusts, foundation
Contributor: The British Paediatric Association

Heinz Visiting and Travelling Fellowships
Subjects: Paediatrics.
Purpose: To enable paediatricians from any part of the Commonwealth to visit the United Kingdom and to attend the Spring meeting of the College, or to enable British paediatricians to spend time in a developing country.
Eligibility: Open to young paediatricians from any commonwealth country.
Level of Study: Professional development
Type: Fellowship
Value: Air fares and living expenses
Length of Study: Up to 12 weeks for Visiting Fellowships and up to 3 months for Travelling Fellowships
Frequency: Annual

Country of Study: United Kingdom for the visiting fellowship and up to three months for travelling fellowship
No. of awards offered: Varies
Application Procedure: Application form can be downloaded from the website.
Closing Date: August 24th
Funding: Corporation, private
Contributor: H J Heinz Company
No. of awards given last year: 3

RCPCH/Babes in Arms Fellowships
Subjects: Paediatrics.
Purpose: To support paediatricians researching into sudden infant death syndrome or associated problems.
Eligibility: Open to paediatricians in higher specialist praising.
Level of Study: Postdoctorate
Type: Fellowship
Value: UK £3,000
Frequency: Annual
Closing Date: August 24th

RCPCH/VSO Fellowship
Subjects: Paediatrics.
Purpose: To accredit 1 year placements in developing countries as part of higher specialist training in paediatrics.
Eligibility: Open to specialist registrars undertaking type 1 training.
Level of Study: Postgraduate
Type: Fellowship
Length of Study: 1 year
Frequency: Annual
Application Procedure: Contact VSO enquiries team for further information.

Young Investigator of the Year Medal
Subjects: Paediatrics.
Purpose: To award young medically qualified research worker for excellence in research.
Eligibility: Open to all young, medically qualified research workers.
Level of Study: Postgraduate
Type: Award
Value: UK £5,000 and medal plus UK £500 to the department in which they work for other expenses with their research
Frequency: Annual
No. of awards offered: 1
Application Procedure: All nominations are from the Head of Department. Direct applications are not accepted.
Funding: Foundation
Contributor: Sport Aiding Medical Research for Kids (SPARKS)

ROYAL COMMISSION FOR THE EXHIBITION OF 1851

Sherfield Building, Imperial College, London, SW7 2AZ, England
Tel: (44) 20 7594 8790
Fax: (44) 20 7594 8794
Email: royalcom1851@imperial.ac.uk
Website: www.royalcommission1851.org.uk
Contact: Mr Malcolm Shirley, Secretary

The Royal Commission for the Exhibition of 1851 is an educational trust supporting innovation and creativity in science, technology and occasionally the arts, almost always at postgraduate level. Apart from the competitive schemes listed, assistance is sometimes given to suitable charities or individuals.

Royal Commission Industrial Design Studentship
Subjects: Industrial design.
Purpose: To fund engineering and science graduates for a postgraduate industrial design course.
Eligibility: Open to United Kingdom nationals only with a first degree in engineering.
Level of Study: Postgraduate
Type: Studentship
Value: UK £10,000 per year plus materials and fees

Length of Study: 1–2 years
Frequency: Annual
Study Establishment: Universities
Country of Study: Any country
No. of awards offered: Approx. 7
Application Procedure: Applicants must complete an application form and submit this with the required enclosures. Forms available from the commission or its website.
Closing Date: April 24th
Funding: Private
Contributor: The profits from the Great Exhibition
No. of awards given last year: 7
No. of applicants last year: 18

Royal Commission Industrial Fellowships

Subjects: Industrial engineering and management.
Purpose: To allow able graduates working in industry to carry out research and development leading to a higher degree or other career milestone.
Eligibility: Open to United Kingdom nationals only with a degree in science or engineering who are working in or for a British company.
Level of Study: Doctorate, Postgraduate
Type: Fellowship
Value: 50 per cent of salary, up to a maximum of UK £21,000 per annum plus university fees London weighting and travel upto UK £3,500 per annum
Length of Study: 3 years
Frequency: Annual
Study Establishment: Any approved university/British company
Country of Study: United Kingdom
No. of awards offered: Approx. 8
Application Procedure: Applicants must complete an application form.
Closing Date: January 31st
Funding: Private
Contributor: The profits from the Great Exhibition
No. of awards given last year: 8
No. of applicants last year: 30

Royal Commission Research Fellowship

Subjects: Pure and applied sciences including mathematics and any branch of engineering.
Purpose: To give employed young scientists or engineers of exceptional promise the opportunity to conduct research.
Eligibility: Open to citizens of the United Kingdom, the British Commonwealth, or the Republics of Ireland or Pakistan.
Level of Study: Postdoctorate
Type: Fellowship
Value: UK £28,500 in year 1, UK £30,000 in years 2 and 3, plus a London (Overseas) Weighting of UK £2,500 per year
Length of Study: 3 years
Frequency: Annual
Study Establishment: Any approved university
Country of Study: Any country
No. of awards offered: Approx. 8
Application Procedure: Applicants must complete an application form online, available from the commission's website. Applications must be supported by professors of United Kingdom universities.
Closing Date: February 21st
Funding: Private
Contributor: The profits from the Great Exhibition
No. of awards given last year: 8
No. of applicants last year: 137

ROYAL GEOGRAPHICAL SOCIETY (WITH THE INSTITUTE OF BRITISH GEOGRAPHERS)

1 Kensington Gore, London, SW7 2AR, England
Tel: (44) 20 7591 3073
Fax: (44) 20 7591 3031
Email: grants@rgs.org
Website: www.rgs.org/grants
Contact: Grants Officer

The Royal Geographical Society (with the Institute of British Geographers) is the United Kingdom's learned society for geography and geographers and a professional body. It supports and promotes many aspects of geography including geographical research, education and teaching, field training and small expeditions, the public understanding and popularization of geography and the provision of geographical information.

30th International Geographical Congress Award

Subjects: Geography.
Purpose: To assist with the cost of attending an international geographical conference.
Eligibility: Applicants must be UK/EU nationals and must currently be employed by a UK Institute of Higher Education. Prefernce will be given to applicants within 6 years of completion of PhD. Attendance at AAG, CAG or the RGS-IBG Annual Conference is not eligible for support from this award.
Type: Award
Value: Up to £750
Frequency: Annual
No. of awards offered: 5
Application Procedure: Applicants must download the guidelines and application form from the website www.rgs.org/grants or contact the grants officer.
Closing Date: February 15

British Airways Travel Bursary

Subjects: Conservation related fieldwork outside the United Kingdom.
Purpose: To support conservation-related field research.
Eligibility: Open to applicants under 35 years who is an Established Researcher or at Postgraduate level Research and must be registered at a UK higher education instituition.
Level of Study: Research, Doctorate, Postgraduate, Early career research only
Type: Bursary
Value: Free return flight
Frequency: Annual
Country of Study: Outside the United Kingdom
No. of awards offered: 2
Application Procedure: Applicants must submit a typed proposal. Guidelines are available from the website www.rgs.org/grants
Funding: Corporation
Contributor: British Airways
No. of awards given last year: 2
No. of applicants last year: 11
Additional Information: Flights must be on existing BA routes. Some conditions apply.

EPSRC Geographical Research Grants

Subjects: Energy demand/use, climate change, sustainable urban environments.
Purpose: To support postdoctoral research in the Engineering and Physical Sciences Research Council's field of interest.
Eligibility: Open to individuals holding a PhD and affiliated with a UK institution. Preference is given to early career researchers (within 6 years of starting their PhD).
Level of Study: Doctorate, Postdoctorate, Research
Type: Grant
Value: Up to UK £3,000
Length of Study: Unspecified
Frequency: Annual
No. of awards offered: Varies
Application Procedure: Applicants must submit a completed application form. Applications and guidelines are available from the website www.rgs.org/grants
Closing Date: January 22nd
No. of awards given last year: 4
No. of applicants last year: 7

Geographical Club Award

Subjects: Geography.
Purpose: To support a postgraduate student (Masters or PhD) undertaking geographical fieldwork.
Eligibility: Applicants must be UK/EU nationals and must currently be registered for a Masters or PhD at a UK Institute of Higher Education.

563

Students who receive full funding from a Research Council or comparable levels of support from other sources with support for fieldwork/data collection are not eligible to apply.
Type: Award
Value: £1000
Frequency: Annual
No. of awards offered: 1
Application Procedure: Applicants must download the application guidelines from the website www.rgs.org/grants or contact the grants officer. There is no application form.
Closing Date: November 27th

Geographical Fieldwork Grants
Subjects: Geographical field work.
Purpose: To support UK-led research teams carrying out geographical field research and exploration overseas.
Eligibility: Open to multidisciplinary teams, rather than individuals, the majority of which must be British and over 19 years of age.
Level of Study: Postgraduate, Unrestricted, Undergraduate
Type: Grant
Value: UK £500–3,000
Length of Study: Must be over 6 weeks
Frequency: Twice a year
Country of Study: Outside the United Kingdom
No. of awards offered: Varies (upto approx 50)
Application Procedure: Applicants must complete an application form. These can be obtained from the Society's website or by writing to the Grants officer.
Closing Date: January 22nd or June 18th
No. of awards given last year: 40
No. of applicants last year: 60

Gilchrist Fieldwork Award
Subjects: Geography.
Purpose: To support original and challenging overseas fieldwork carried out by small teams of university academics and researchers.
Eligibility: The majority of team members must be British and hold established posts at University departments or equivalent research establishments. Team members may come from multiple establishments and teams must comprise up to 10 members.
Level of Study: Research
Type: Grant
Value: £15,000
Length of Study: At least 6 weeks
Frequency: Every 2 years
No. of awards offered: 1
Application Procedure: Applicants must submit a written proposal. Guidelines are available on the website.
No. of awards given last year: 1
No. of applicants last year: 16

Henrietta Hutton Research Grants
Subjects: Geographical field research.
Purpose: To support female geographers.
Eligibility: Open to female undergraduate/postgraduate geography students (under 25) who are registered at a UK higher education institution.
Level of Study: Postgraduate, Undergraduate
Type: Grant
Value: UK £500
Length of Study: Above 4 weeks
Frequency: Annual
No. of awards offered: 2
Application Procedure: Applicants must submit a written proposal. Guidelines are available from the website www.rgs.org/grants
Closing Date: January 22nd
No. of awards given last year: 2
No. of applicants last year: 21
Additional Information: Applicants who are members of other RGS-IBG supported teams may additionally apply for this award.

Hong Kong Research Grant
Subjects: Field research in The Greater China region, Taiwan, Macau, SAR and Hong Kong SAR, People's Republic of China.
Purpose: To support postgraduate research in greater China.

Eligibility: Open to candidates undertaking a PhD course.
Level of Study: Doctorate, Postgraduate
Type: Grant
Value: UK £2,500
Length of Study: Above 4 weeks
Frequency: Annual
Country of Study: Greater China
No. of awards offered: 1
Application Procedure: Applicants must submit a typed proposal. Guidelines are available from www.rgs.org/grants
Closing Date: November 26th
Contributor: Royal Geographical Society Hong Kong
No. of awards given last year: 1
No. of applicants last year: 8

Innovative Geography Teaching Grants
Subjects: Geography.
Purpose: To support new ideas in geography teaching at secondary level
Eligibility: Eligible to applicants teaching secondary aged pupils.
Level of Study: Secondary Teachers
Type: Grant
Value: Up to UK £800
Length of Study: Unspecified
Frequency: Annual
Country of Study: Worldwide
No. of awards offered: 5
Application Procedure: Applicants must submit a typed proposal. Guidelines are available at www.rgs.org/grants
Closing Date: October 15th
No. of awards given last year: 5
No. of applicants last year: 9
Additional Information: One award is usually reserved for NQTs or whose institution is an educational member of the society. All applicants must be teaching secondary school pupils.

Journey of a Lifetime Award
Subjects: Travel, geography.
Purpose: To support an inspiring journey and encourage new radio broadcast talent.
Eligibility: Unrestricted. Candidates must be able to attend interviews in person.
Level of Study: Unrestricted
Type: Travelling bursary
Value: UK £4,000
Length of Study: January–July
Frequency: Annual
Country of Study: Any country
No. of awards offered: 1
Application Procedure: Applicants must submit a written proposal.
Closing Date: September 24th
Funding: Private
No. of awards given last year: 1
No. of applicants last year: 150
Additional Information: The winner is trained by the BBC and records their journey for a BBC Radio 4 documentary.

Monica Cole Research Grant
Subjects: Physical geography.
Purpose: To support a female physical geographer undertaking original fieldwork overseas.
Eligibility: Open to female physical geographers only. Applicants must be registered at a United Kingdom university.
Level of Study: Postgraduate, Undergraduate
Type: Grant
Value: UK £1,000
Frequency: Annual
Country of Study: Outside the United Kingdom
No. of awards offered: 1
Application Procedure: Applicants must download guidelines from the website or contact the Grants officer. There is no application form.
Closing Date: January 22nd
Funding: Private
No. of awards given last year: 1
No. of applicants last year: 5

Neville Shulman Challenge Award

Subjects: The geographical sciences and exploration.
Purpose: To further the understanding and exploration of the planet, while promoting personal development through the intellectual or physical challenges involved.
Eligibility: Open to any United Kingdom national over the age of 25. PhD and MSc research students are not eligible.
Level of Study: Unrestricted
Type: Grant
Value: UK £10,000
Length of Study: Unrestricted
Frequency: Annual
Country of Study: Any country
No. of awards offered: 1
Application Procedure: Applicants must submit a proposal, following the guidelines, to the Grants officer by the closing date. There is no application form. Details are available from the website.
Closing Date: September 24th
Funding: Private
No. of awards given last year: 2
No. of applicants last year: 15
Additional Information: Project can be desk or field based and can be carried out in the UK or overseas. This award is not applicable to PhD and MSc research.

Peter Fleming Award

Subjects: Geographical research.
Purpose: For the advancement of geographical science.
Eligibility: Open to British individuals or teams. Applicants should either be working within a UK education institution or as an independent researcher within the UK.
Level of Study: Research
Type: Grant
Value: UK £9,000
Length of Study: Unspecified
Frequency: Annual
No. of awards offered: 1
Application Procedure: Applicants must submit a typed proposal.
Closing Date: November 26th
Funding: Private
No. of awards given last year: 1
No. of applicants last year: 8
Additional Information: Equipment costs should not be more than 10 per cent of total. Conference attendance will not be funded. Projects can be desk, lab or field based and can be carried out in the UK or overseas.

Ralph Brown Expedition Award

Subjects: Marine or aquatic environments.
Purpose: To support and encourage objectives that involve the study of rivers, inland or coastal wetlands or shallow marine environments.
Eligibility: Open to applicants over 25 from any country. The applicant must be a Fellow or Associate Fellow of the Society.
Level of Study: Research
Type: Grant
Value: UK £15,000
Frequency: Annual
Country of Study: Any country
No. of awards offered: 1
Application Procedure: Applicants must contact the Grants Co-ordinator or refer to the website for detailed guidelines.
Closing Date: November 26th
Funding: Private
No. of awards given last year: 1
No. of applicants last year: 10
Additional Information: The grant is awarded for the study of shallow marine environments, rivers, coral reefs and inland or coastal wetlands.

Ray Y. Gildea Jr. Award

Subjects: Geography education.
Purpose: To support innovation in teaching and learning in higher and secondary education directly beneficial to students of geography.

Eligibility: Applicants must currently be employed in the higher education sector or at the secondary school level either in UK or USA and actively teaching students.
Level of Study: Postgraduate, Teachers (secondary and higher)
Type: Grant
Value: UK £2,750
Frequency: Annual
No. of awards offered: 1
Application Procedure: There is no application form. Applicants are asked to submit a word-processed proposal to the Society's Grants Officer.
No. of awards given last year: 1
No. of applicants last year: 3

RGS-IBG Land Rover 'GO Beyond' Bursary

Subjects: Geography
Purpose: To promote a wider understanding and enjoyment of geography and to take the recipient beyond his or her normal limits and boundaries.
Eligibility: Must start and end in the UK. Teams of 2–6. Applicants must hold a clean UK driving licence and have 3 or more years of driving experience.
Level of Study: Unrestricted
Type: Grant
Value: £10,000 funding and the use of a Land Rover 110 Defender
Length of Study: Between March and October
Frequency: Annual
No. of awards offered: 1
Application Procedure: Guidelines available on website. No application form.
Closing Date: September 24th
No. of awards given last year: 1
No. of applicants last year: 100

RGS-IBG Postgraduate Research Awards

Subjects: Physical environment, conservation, sustainability, society, economy.
Purpose: For PhD students undertaking fieldwork/data collection. These awards are offered to individuals and aim to help students establish themselves in their particular field.
Eligibility: Currently registered for a PhD at a UK Higher Education Institution.
Level of Study: Doctorate, Postgraduate, PhD students
Type: Grant
Value: £2,000
Length of Study: Unspecified
Frequency: Annual
No. of awards offered: 6 (2 in each of the above subject area)
Application Procedure: Guidelines available on website. No application form.
Closing Date: November 26th
No. of awards given last year: 6
No. of applicants last year: 21

Slawson Awards

Subjects: Geographical fieldwork involving key development issues with high social value, including projects in geography-related disciplines such as anthropology and economics.
Purpose: To assist students intending to carry out geographical field research in developing countries to increase knowledge, awareness and understanding of the world in which we live.
Eligibility: Applicants must normally be United Kingdom citizens, currently be registered for a PhD at a United Kingdom Institute of Higher Education and be Fellows of the Society.
Level of Study: Doctorate, Postgraduate
Type: Grant
Value: Normally up to UK £3,000
Frequency: Annual
Country of Study: Outside the United Kingdom, preferably in developing countries
No. of awards offered: 1–2 awards.
Application Procedure: Applicants must submit a proposal, following the guidelines, to the Grants officer by the closing date. There is no application form and more details are available from the website.
Closing Date: February 5th

Funding: Private
No. of awards given last year: 2–3
No. of applicants last year: 13
Additional Information: Fieldwork must be outside UK and preferably in developing countries

Small Research Grants

Subjects: Geography.
Purpose: To provide grants for desk- or field-based research.
Eligibility: Applicants must be a fellow or member of the society. Preference to individual researchers within 10 years of the start of their PhD.
Level of Study: Postdoctorate, Research
Type: Grant
Value: Up to UK £3,000
Length of Study: Unspecified
Frequency: Annual
Country of Study: Unrestricted
No. of awards offered: Varies (4–10)
Application Procedure: An application form is available from the society's website or Grants officer.
Closing Date: January 22nd
No. of awards given last year: 10
No. of applicants last year: 30

Thesiger-Oman Research Fellowship

Subjects: Research in arid lands: physical environment and human environment.
Purpose: To support research in arid environments.
Eligibility: Applicants must be affiliated to a higher education instituition anywhere in the world and have held a PhD for at least 3 years.
Level of Study: Research, Postdoctorate
Type: Grant
Value: UK £8,000
Frequency: Annual
No. of awards offered: 2
Application Procedure: Guidelines can be downloaded from the website. No application form.
Closing Date: November 26th
No. of awards given last year: 2
No. of applicants last year: 5
Additional Information: One award is given to a project focused on the physical aspects of arid and semi-arid environments. Another award is given to a project focused on the human dimension of arid and semi-arid environments.

ROYAL HISTORICAL SOCIETY

University College London, Gower Street, London, WC1E 6BT, England
Tel: (44) 207 387 7532
Email: royalhistsoc@ucl.ac.uk
Website: www.royalhistoricalsociety.org
Contact: The Executive Secretary

The Royal Historical Society has limited funds to assist postgraduate students (and some others) with expenses incurred in the pursuit of advanced historical research. These funds are intended principally for postgraduate students registered for a research degree at United Kingdom Institutions of Higher Education, both full-time and part-time.

Royal Historical Society Postgraduate Research Support Grant

Subjects: History.
Purpose: To assist postgraduate students with expenses incurred in the pursuit of advanced historical research.
Eligibility: Applicants must be postgraduate students registered for a research degree at a United Kingdom Institution of Higher Education, either full-time or part-time, or individuals who have completed doctoral dissertations within the last 2 years and who are not in full-time employment.
Level of Study: Postgraduate
Type: Grant
Value: Approx. UK £250
Frequency: Annual

Study Establishment: United Kingdom Institutions of Higher Education
Country of Study: United Kingdom
Application Procedure: Applicants must download application form from website. Applications should include a well-costed budget, a proposal that indicates the scholarly value of the proposed project and letters of reference.
Additional Information: Preference will be given to members of the Royal Historical Society.

ROYAL HORTICULTURAL SOCIETY (RHS)

80 Vincent Square, London, SW1P 2PE, England
Tel: (44) 1483 212380
Fax: (44) 1483 212382
Email: bursaries@rhs.org.uk
Website: www.rhs.org.uk/learning/education/bursaries.htm
Contact: Secretary of RHS Bursaries Committee

The Royal Horticultural Society (RHS) is a membership charity holding a Royal Charter for horticulture. The Society promotes the science, art and practice of horticulture in all its branches through a wide range of educational, research and advisory activities. It also maintains some major gardens, shows and the internationally renowned Lindley Library.

Blaxall Valentine Trust Award

Subjects: Horticulture.
Purpose: To help finance worldwide plant collecting in natural habitats and study expeditions that will provide real benefits to horticulture.
Eligibility: Open to applicants worldwide, but preference is given to United Kingdom and Commonwealth citizens. Applicants should satisfy the Society that their health enables them to undertake the project proposed. Financial sponsorship will be available to both professional and amateur horticulturists and consideration for an award is not restricted to RHS members. Proposals may be made by individuals or group of individuals.
Level of Study: Unrestricted
Type: Bursary
Value: Funds are limited. High-cost projects are expected to receive supplementary finance from other sources, including personal contributions
Frequency: Annual
Country of Study: Any country
Application Procedure: Applicants must complete an application form available on request. Candidates may be called for interview.
Closing Date: December 15th, March 31st, June 30th or September 30th
Funding: Private
No. of awards given last year: 14

The Bullen Bursary

Subjects: Horticulture.
Purpose: To provide financial support for travel and/or accommodation to aid a project related to the study of herbs.
Eligibility: Open to UK nationals and to foreign nationals resident in the UK of any age, subject to the general conditions of application. Financial sponsorship is open to students and trainees in horticulture. Proposals may be made by individuals or groups.
Level of Study: Unrestricted
Type: Bursary
Value: Limited funds. High-cost projects are expected to receive supplementary finance from other sources, including personal contributions
Frequency: Annual
Country of Study: Any country
No. of awards offered: Unlimited
Application Procedure: Applicants must complete an application form, available on request. Alternatively, this can be downloaded from the RHS website: www.rhs.org.uk/Learning/Education/bursaries.htm
Closing Date: December 15th, March 31st, June 30th or September 30th
Funding: Private

Additional Information: Recipients must submit a factual report within 3 months of completion, along with an outline of achievements or difficulties, including any unusual problems encountered e.g. medical or political, and an account of expenses.

For further information contact:

RHS Garden Wisley, Woking, Surrey, GU23 6QB

Coke Trust Awards

Subjects: Horticulture.

Purpose: To broaden professional gardeners' and student gardeners' knowledge, skills and experience, and to finance horticultural projects that demonstrate a distinct educational or historic value, as submitted by institutions, charities or gardens.

Eligibility: Submissions are welcomed from applicants worldwide, but preference is given to United Kingdom and Commonwealth citizens. Applicants should preferably be within the age bracket of 20–35 years and satisfy the Society that their health enables them to undertake the project proposed. Financial sponsorship will be available to both professional and amateur horticulturists and consideration for an award is not restricted to RHS members.

Level of Study: Unrestricted

Type: Bursary

Value: Funds are limited. High-cost projects are expected to receive supplementary finance from other sources, including personal contributions

Frequency: Annual

Country of Study: United Kingdom

No. of awards offered: Unlimited

Application Procedure: Applicants must complete an application form, available on request.

Closing Date: December 15th, March 31st, June 30th or September 30th

Funding: Private

No. of awards given last year: 47

No. of applicants last year: 61

Additional Information: Recipients must submit a brief factual report within 3 months of completion, along with an outline of achievements or difficulties, including any unusual problems, e.g. medical or political, and an account of expenses.

For further information contact:

RHS Garden Wisley, Woking, Surrey, GU23 6QB

The Dawn Jolliffe Botanical Art Bursary

Subjects: Horticulture.

Purpose: To assist a botanical artist with the cost of exhibiting at one of the RHS shows or to travel in order to paint plants in their habitats.

Eligibility: Preference is given to botanical artists who are not yet established. Please note that submission of an application is dependent on notification from the RHS Picture Commitee that an applicant's botanical artwork is of a sufficient standard. For full details please contact the secretary of the picture commitee Tel No. 0207 821 3051.

Level of Study: Unrestricted

Type: Bursary

Value: Restricted to £1,000 annually, to be divided between two or more botanical artists

Frequency: Annual

Country of Study: United Kingdom or elsewhere

No. of awards offered: 1–2

Application Procedure: Applicants must complete an application form available on request.

Closing Date: June 30th

Funding: Private

No. of awards given last year: 3

No. of applicants last year: 5

Additional Information: The award was set up by the RHS on behalf of Mr Brian Jolliffe, who established the award in memory of his wife Dawn Jolliffe, a keen botanical artist.

For further information contact:

RHS Garden Wisley, Woking, Surrey, GU23 6QB

EA Bowles Memorial Bursary

Subjects: Horticulture.

Purpose: To aid a project regarding the horticultural work of EA Bowles, his garden at Myddelton House, Essex, or one of his particular horticultural interests, e.g., bulbs or alpines.

Eligibility: The award is open to students and trainees in horticulture and relevant related topics, e.g., garden history and design. There are no age restrictions.

Level of Study: Unrestricted

Type: Bursary

Value: UK £500

Frequency: Every 2 years

Country of Study: United Kingdom

No. of awards offered: Unlimited

Application Procedure: Applicants must complete an application form available on request.

Closing Date: December 15th, March 31st, June 30th or September 30th

Funding: Private

No. of awards given last year: None

Additional Information: The award was set up by the EA Bowles of Myddleton House Society in memory of EA Bowles VMH, one of the most eminent plantsmen of the first-half of the 20th century. Recipients must submit a brief factual report within 3 months of completion, along with an outline of achievements or difficulties, including any unusual problems e.g. medical or political and an account of expenses.

For further information contact:

RHS Garden Wisley, Woking, Surrey, GU23 6QB

Gurney Wilson Award

Subjects: Horticulture.

Purpose: To help finance horticulture-related projects and to further the interests of horticultural education as the RHS council deems fit.

Eligibility: Open to the candidates of any age who are UK nationals and foreign nationals residing in the UK, subject to the general conditions of application and who should be able to satisfy the Society that their health enables them to take a project proposed. Financial sponsorship is available to both professional and amateur horticulturists and consideration for an award is not restricted to RHS members. Proposals may be made by individuals or groups.

Level of Study: Unrestricted

Type: Bursary

Value: Limited funds. High-cost projects are expected to receive supplementary finance from other sources, including personal contributions

Frequency: Annual

Country of Study: Any country

No. of awards offered: Unlimited

Application Procedure: Applicants must complete an application form, available on request. Alternatively, this can be downloaded from the RHS website:www.rhs.org.uk/Learning/Education/bursaries.htm

Closing Date: December 15th, March 31st, June 30th or September 30th

Funding: Private

No. of awards given last year: 3

No. of applicants last year: N/A

Additional Information: Recipients must submit a factual report within 3 months of completion, along with an outline of achievements or difficulties, including any unusual problems encountered, e.g., medical or political, and an account of expenses.

For further information contact:

RHS Garden Wisley, Woking, Surrey, GU23 6QB

Jimmy Smart Memorial Bursary

Subjects: Horticulture.

Purpose: To provide financial support to a working (employed) gardener for travel and/or accommodation during visits overseas with the prime intention of seeing or studying plants and/or trees growing in their natural habitats. Applications to visit Australia or New Zealand are particularly encouraged, but other gardening-related travel may also be funded.

Eligibility: The award is open to experienced working gardeners in the British Isles, particularly those whose work includes responsibilities in relation to National Collections. There is no age restriction.
Level of Study: Unrestricted
Type: Bursary
Value: UK £1,000 maximum
Frequency: Annual
Country of Study: Any country
No. of awards offered: Unlimited
Application Procedure: Applicants must complete an application form available on request.
Closing Date: December 15th, March 31st, June 30th or September 30th
Funding: Private
No. of awards given last year: 1
No. of applicants last year: N/A
Additional Information: Recipients must submit a brief factual report within 3 months of completion, along with an outline of achievements or difficulties, including any unusual problems, e.g., medical or political, and an account of expenses. Applicants to visit Australia or New Zealand are particularly encouraged. Additional support may be offered to gardeners spending time in either of these countries.

For further information contact:

RHS Garden Wisley, Woking, Surrey, GU23 6QB

The Martin McLaren Horticultural Interchange Scholarship

Subjects: The program enables a British graduate to attend the first year of a Master's degree course at an American university at the Garden Club of America's 'Interchange Fellow'. The Martin McLaren Horticultural Interchange Scholarship provides a non-credit work experience/study program in Great Britain for an American exchange student, selected by the GCA Scholarship Committee.
Purpose: To provide a reciprocal exchange of British and American graduate students, aged 27 or under, in horticulture, landscape architecture, botany or environmental studies. The intent of the program is to foster cultural understanding, promote horticultural studies and exchange information in this field.
Eligibility: US and UK graduates specializing in horticulture, botany, landscape architecture or environmental studies.
Level of Study: Graduate
Type: Scholarship
Value: US$30,000 for the UK student whilst undergoing study in the USA. For the US student undergoing horticultural practical work placements in the UK for the 10 month scholarship period, the award currently pays a monthly allowance of £900. In addition to this, other contingency expenses will be covered if appropriate, e.g. attendance at a university to undertake an appropriate academic module deemed suitable for the student
Length of Study: 10 months
Frequency: Annual
Country of Study: United Kingdom or United States of America
No. of awards offered: 1
Application Procedure: Applicants must complete an application form, available on request. Applications can be downloaded from the RHS website www.rhs.org.Learning/Education/martinmclaren.htm
Closing Date: October 31st for UK applicants and November 15th for US applicants
Funding: Private

For further information contact:

Martin McLaren Scholarship Administrator, RHS Garden Wisley, Surrey, Wonking, GU23 6Q

Osaka Travel Award

Subjects: Horticultural-related study or work experience will be considered.
Purpose: To allow young people from the United Kingdom and Japan to study in each other's country and benefit from a cross-cultural exchange of ideas.
Eligibility: Open to British and Japanese citizens with a horticultural background. Applicants should preferably be within the age bracket of 20 and 35 years. Financial sponsorship will be available to both professional and amateur horticulturists and consideration for an award is

not restricted to RHS members. The awards are made to individuals, not to groups or expeditions.
Level of Study: Unrestricted
Type: Bursary
Value: Funds are limited. High-cost projects are expected to receive supplementary finance from other sources, including personal contributions
Frequency: Annual
No. of awards offered: 1–2
Application Procedure: Applicants must complete an application form, available on request.
Closing Date: December 15th, March 31st, June 30th or September 30th
Funding: Private
No. of awards given last year: 2
No. of applicants last year: N/A
Additional Information: Recipients must submit a brief factual report within 3 months of completion, along with an outline of achievements or difficulties and an account of expenses.

For further information contact:

RHS Garden Wisley, Woking, Surrey, GU23 6QB

Queen Elizabeth the Queen Mother Bursary

Subjects: Horticulture.
Purpose: To help finance related projects, e.g. study tours, horticulturally-related expeditions, minor research projects possibly working with an acknowledged expert on short-term research, taxonomic studies, specialized courses and programmes of study such as specific subject symposia. The award is reserved for proposals of particular excellence.
Eligibility: Submissions are welcomed from applicants worldwide but preference is given to United Kingdom and Commonwealth citizens. Applicants should preferably be within the age bracket of 20 and 35 years and satisfy the Society that their health enables them to undertake the project proposed. Financial sponsorship will be available to both professional and amateur horticulturists and consideration for an award is not restricted to RHS members. The awards are made to individuals, not to groups or expeditions.
Level of Study: Unrestricted
Type: Bursary
Value: Funds are limited. High-cost projects are expected to receive supplementary finance from other sources, including personal contributions
Frequency: Variable
Country of Study: Any country
No. of awards offered: 1–3
Application Procedure: Applicants must complete an application form, available on request. Candidates may be called for interview.
Closing Date: December 15th, March 31st, June 30th or September 30th
Funding: Private
No. of awards given last year: None
No. of applicants last year: N/A
Additional Information: Recipients must submit a brief factual report within 3 months of completion, along with an outline of achievements or difficulties, including any unusual problems, e.g. medical or political, and an account of expenses. Recipients must also be prepared to give a lecture on their project at the Society's headquarters at Vincent Square in London, within 18 months of completing the project.

For further information contact:

RHS Garden Wisley, Woking, Surrey, GU23 6QB

The RHS Environmental Bursary

Subjects: Awarded for an application of outstanding horticultural merit that concentrates on environmental issues such as water-wise gardening, research into drought-resistant plants, sustainability and other climate change issues that have a direct relevance to horticulture.
Purpose: Established in 2008 with the principal aim of encouraging an environmentally focused horticultural project.
Eligibility: Application is open to UK nationals and to foreign nationals resident in the UK, subject to the general conditions of application. There are no age restrictions. Applicants should be able to satisfy the Society that their health enables them to undertake the proposed

project. Financial scholarship is available to both professional and amateur horticulturists and consideration for an award is not restricted to RHS members. Proposals may be made by individual or groups.
Level of Study: Restricted to horticultural environmental issues
Type: Bursary
Value: Funds are limited. High-cost projects are expected to receive supplementary finance from other sources, including personal contributions
Frequency: Variable
Country of Study: Any country
No. of awards offered: Unlimited
Application Procedure: Applicants must complete an application form, available on request. Alternatively, this can be downloaded from the RHS website: www.rhs.org/uk/Learning/Education/bursaries.asp
Closing Date: December 15th, March 31st, June 30th or September 30th
Funding: Private
No. of awards given last year: None
No. of applicants last year: 1
Additional Information: Recipients must submit a factual report within 3 months of completion.

For further information contact:

RHS Garden Wisley, Woking, Surrey, GU23 6QB, United Kingdom

The Susan Pearson Memorial Traineeship Bursary

Subjects: The practical application of theoretical horticultural principles to present day practices and the highest standards of professional practice.
Purpose: To sponsor horticultural trainees undertaking up to one year of practical work experience in a recognized garden open to public.
Eligibility: Applicants must be British citizens. The Society particularly welcomes applications from individuals intending to pursue Continuing Professional Development (CPD) and/or complementary training provided by a local college/accredited learning centre.
Level of Study: Unrestricted
Type: Bursary
Country of Study: United Kingdom
No. of awards offered: Unlimited
Application Procedure: Applicants must complete an application form, available on request. Application can be downloaded from the website www.rhs.org.uk/Learning/Education/bursaries.asp
Closing Date: December 15th, March 31st, June 30th or September 30th
Funding: Private
No. of awards given last year: 0
No. of applicants last year: 0
Additional Information: Recipients must submit a factual report within 3 months of completion of the placement.

For further information contact:

RHS Garden Wisley, Surrey, Woking, GU23 6QB

The William Rayner Bursary

Subjects: Horticulture.
Purpose: To contribute significantly to horticultural career development.
Eligibility: Open to students and trainees in horticulture, along with working gardeners of any age who are UK nationals and foreign nationals residing in the UK, subject to the general conditions of application. Applicants should be able to satisfy the Society that their health enables them to take a project proposed.
Level of Study: Unrestricted
Type: Bursary
Value: Maximum £1,000 per year
Frequency: Annual
Country of Study: Any country
No. of awards offered: Unlimited
Application Procedure: Applicants must complete an application form, available on request. Alternatively, this can be downloaded from the RHS website:www.rhs.org.uk/Learning/Education/bursaries.htm
Closing Date: December 24th, March 31st, June 30th or September 30th
Funding: Private

No. of awards given last year: 1
No. of applicants last year: N/A
Additional Information: Recipients must submit a factual report within 3 months of completion, along with an outline of achievements or difficulties, including any unusual problems encountered e.g. medical or political, and an account of expenses.

For further information contact:

RHS Garden Wisley, Woking, Surrey, GU23 6QB

ROYAL IRISH ACADEMY

19 Dawson Street, Dublin 2, Ireland
Tel: (353) 1 676 2570
Fax: (353) 1 676 2346
Email: admin@ria.ie
Website: www.ria.ie
Contact: Ms Laura Mahoney, Assistant Executive Secretary

The Royal Irish Academy is the senior institution in Ireland for both the sciences and humanities. It publishes a number of journals and monographs. It is Ireland's national representative in a large number of international unions, and through its national committees runs conferences, lectures and workshops. It also manages a number of long-term research projects. The Academy participates in the Royal Society European Science Exchange Programmes in pure and applied science, in the British Academy European Exchange Programmes in the humanities, and in the Austrian, Hungarian, or Polish academy exchange schemes in science and the humanities. Small grants for work in all disciplines are available annually from the Academy's own funds.

Royal Irish Academy Gold Medals

Subjects: Physical and mathematical sciences, engineering science, life sciences, environment and geosciences, humanities, and social sciences in a rotation basis for a 4-year cycle.
Purpose: To an individual who has made a distinguished scholarly contribution to their subject.
Eligibility: Open to people who are resident in either Northern Ireland or the Republic of Ireland and have made an internationally recognised, substantial and distinguished contribution to their subject whilst working in Ireland.
Level of Study: Postdoctorate
Value: A gold medal
Frequency: Annual
Country of Study: Ireland
No. of awards offered: 2
Application Procedure: Applicant must be nominated independently by two scientists who are familiar with his/her work. At least one of whom must be a member of the Academy, and/or a member of one of the Academy committees, and/or the Head of an Irish Higher Education Institution.
Closing Date: May each year
Funding: Government
No. of awards given last year: 2
Additional Information: Two awards are awarded each year. Awards for humanities and social sciences are awarded biennially.

Royal Irish Academy Mobility Grants

Subjects: Humanities, social sciences and natural sciences.
Purpose: To provide small grants for short visits to any country supporting their primary research.
Level of Study: Postdoctorate, Professional development
Type: Fellowship
Value: Up to €2,500
Length of Study: Varies
Frequency: Annual
Country of Study: Other
Application Procedure: Applicants must complete an application form, available from the Academy.
Closing Date: Early October
Funding: Government

ROYAL PHILHARMONIC SOCIETY (RPS)

10 Stratford Place, London, W1C 1BA, England
Tel: (44) 20 7491 8110
Fax: (44) 20 7493 7463
Email: admin@royalphilharmonicsociety.org.uk
Website: www.royalphilharmonicsociety.org.uk
Contact: General Administrator

The Royal Philharmonic Society (RPS) offers support for young musicians and composers, sponsorship of new music events, debate and discussion about the future of music and has an active commissioning policy. It recognizes achievement through the prestigious annual RPS Music Awards and with the Society's Gold Medal. Full information is available on the RPS website.

RPS Composition Prize

Subjects: Musical composition.
Purpose: To encourage young composers.
Eligibility: Open to past and present registered students of any conservatoire or university within the United Kingdom, of any nationality, under the age of 29. Former winners are not eligible.
Level of Study: Graduate, Postgraduate
Type: Prize
Value: UK £3,000/£5000 commission plus a guaranteed performance of commissioned work
Frequency: Annual
No. of awards offered: 2
Application Procedure: Applicants must complete an application form. There is a UK £20 entry fee but this is free to RPS members.
Closing Date: March 31st annually
Funding: Private
No. of awards given last year: 2
No. of applicants last year: 70

THE ROYAL SCOTTISH ACADEMY (RSA)

The Mound, Edinburgh, EH2 2EL, Scotland
Tel: (44) (0) 131 225 6671
Fax: (44) (0) 131 220 6016
Email: info@royalscottishacademy.org
Website: www.royalscottishacademy.org
Contact: Secretary

Founded in 1826, the RSA, Scotland's foremost body of artists, has promoted the works of leading contemporary painters, sculptors, printmakers and architects. It also gives practical and financial help to young artists through scholarships as well as the annual Student's Exhibition.

The Alastair Salvesen Art Scholarship

Subjects: Painting in any medium.
Purpose: To encourage young painters who have made the transition from college to a working environment.
Eligibility: Open to painters who have been trained at one of four Scottish colleges of art in Aberdeen, Dundee, Edinburgh or Glasgow and are living and working in Scotland.
Level of Study: Postgraduate
Type: Scholarship
Value: Up to UK £10,000 depending on the plan submitted, and an exhibition that lasts approx. three weeks to take place in November or December in a gallery
Length of Study: 3–5 months
Frequency: Annual
Study Establishment: Any of the main art colleges
Country of Study: Scotland
No. of awards offered: 1
Application Procedure: Applicants must contact the RSA.
Closing Date: January 19th
Funding: Private
Contributor: The Alastair Salvesen Trust
No. of awards given last year: 1

The John Kinross Memorial Fund Student Scholarships/ RSA

Subjects: Painting, sculpture, architecture and printmaking.

Purpose: To allow young artists from the established training centres in Scotland to spend time in Italy.
Eligibility: Open to all final year and postgraduate students from the four main colleges of art in Scotland.
Level of Study: Postgraduate
Type: Scholarship
Value: UK £2,000
Length of Study: 3 months
Frequency: Annual
Country of Study: Italy
No. of awards offered: 13
Closing Date: Late April
Funding: Private
Contributor: The Kinross Scholarship Fund, which is administered by the RSA
No. of awards given last year: 15
No. of applicants last year: 80

Sir William Gillies Bequest-Hospitalfield Trust

Subjects: Painting, sculpture, architecture and printmaking.
Purpose: To provide young professional artists who are Scottish or have studied in Scotland, with a period for personal development and the exploration of new directions.
Eligibility: Open to all emerging professional artists.
Level of Study: Postgraduate
Type: Residency
Value: UK £1,666
Length of Study: 1 or 3 months
Frequency: Annual
Study Establishment: Hospitalfield House, Arbroath
Country of Study: Scotland
Application Procedure: Applicants must contact the RSA.
Closing Date: December
Funding: Private
Contributor: The Bequest Fund administered by the RSA

THE ROYAL SOCIETY OF CHEMISTRY

Burlington House Piccadilly, London, W1J 0BA, England
Tel: (44) (0) 20 7437 8656
Fax: (44) (0) 20 7437 8883
Email: langers@rsc.org
Website: www.rsc.org
Contact: Mr S S Langer

The Royal Society of Chemistry is the learned society for chemistry and the professional body for chemists in the United Kingdom with 46,000 members worldwide. The Society is a major publisher of chemical information, supports the teaching of chemistry at all levels, organizes hundreds of chemical meetings a year and is a leader in communicating science to the public. It is now the United Kingdom National Adhering Organization (NAO) to the International Union of Pure and Applied Chemistry (IUPAC).

Corday-Morgan Memorial Fund

Subjects: Chemistry.
Purpose: To allow members of any established chemical society or institute in the Commonwealth to visit chemical establishments in another Commonwealth country.
Eligibility: Open to citizens of, and those domiciled in, any Commonwealth country.
Level of Study: Professional development
Type: Grant
Value: Up to UK £500. The grants will complement, where appropriate, those for visits to developing countries available from the International Committee's fund, and funding would cover the additional travel costs involved, together with appropriate subsistence. Applicants should also see the Visits to Developing Countries awards
Frequency: Four times a year
Country of Study: Any country
No. of awards offered: Approx. 4
Application Procedure: Applicants must submit applications on the official form and will normally be considered within 1 month of receipt.
Closing Date: January 1st, April 1st, July 1st and October 1st
No. of awards given last year: 4

No. of applicants last year: 6
Additional Information: Applicants must be travelling to another country (not necessarily in the Commonwealth) and would normally stop en route to visit a third country that must be in the Commonwealth.

Hickinbottom/Briggs Fellowship
Subjects: Organic chemistry.
Purpose: To assist research.
Eligibility: Open to applicants domiciled in the United Kingdom or Republic of Ireland. Candidates must already hold a PhD or equivalent in chemistry and be not more than 36 years of age on October 31st.
Level of Study: Postdoctorate
Type: Fellowship
Value: Approx. UK £17,000/year
Length of Study: 3 years
Frequency: Dependent on funds available
Study Establishment: A British or Irish university or college
Country of Study: Other
No. of awards offered: 1
Application Procedure: Applicants must apply by application forms or be nominated.
Closing Date: June 1st
No. of awards given last year: 1

J W T Jones Travelling Fellowship
Subjects: Chemistry.
Purpose: To promote international co-operation, to enable chemists to carry out short-term studies in well established scientific centres abroad and to learn and use techniques not accessible to them in their own country.
Eligibility: Open to members of the Royal Society of Chemistry who hold at least a Master's or PhD degree in chemistry or a related subject and are already actively engaged in research. Candidates must produce evidence that the theoretical and practical knowledge or training to be acquired in the foreign laboratory will be beneficial to their scientific development and must also return to their country of origin upon termination of the fellowship.
Level of Study: Professional development
Type: Fellowship
Value: A lump sum of up to UK £5,000, designed to cover part or all of an economy class air or rail ticket and a subsistence allowance. It is expected that the institution of origin and/or the host institution will contribute to defray any remaining expenses incurred by the fellowship holder
Length of Study: Normally 1–3 months
Frequency: Four times a year
Country of Study: Any country
No. of awards offered: Approx. 6–8
Application Procedure: Applicants must apply for application forms, together with full details, from the International Affairs Officer.
Closing Date: January 1st, April 1st, July 1st or October 1st
No. of awards given last year: 7
No. of applicants last year: 12
Additional Information: Fellowships will not be awarded to attend scientific meetings. Applications will be considered by a Fellowship Committee and the holder will be required to submit a formal report on the work accomplished.

Royal Society of Chemistry Journals Grants for International Authors
Subjects: Chemistry.
Purpose: To allow international authors to visit other countries in order to collaborate in research, exchange research ideas and results, and to give or receive special expertise and training.
Eligibility: Open to anyone with a recent publication in any of the Society's journals. Those from the United Kingdom or Republic of Ireland are excluded.
Level of Study: Professional development
Type: Grant
Value: Up to £2500 cover travel and subsistence (but not research-related costs) and are available
Length of Study: Normally 1–3 months
Frequency: Four times a year
Country of Study: Any country

No. of awards offered: 100
Application Procedure: Candidates must apply for application forms, together with full details, from the International Affairs Officer.
Closing Date: January 1st, April 1st, July 1st or October 1st
No. of awards given last year: 83
No. of applicants last year: 107

Royal Society of Chemistry Research Fund
Subjects: Chemistry and chemical education.
Purpose: To provide financial support to those working in less affluent institutions.
Eligibility: Open to members of the Society.
Level of Study: Professional development
Type: Grant
Value: Up to UK £2,000 for the purchase of chemicals, equipment or for running expenses of research
Length of Study: 1 year
Frequency: Annual
Country of Study: Any country
No. of awards offered: 20–30
Closing Date: October 31st
No. of awards given last year: 30
No. of applicants last year: 50
Additional Information: Funds are limited, so preference will be given to those working in less well-endowed institutions. The Selection Committee is especially anxious to see inventive applications of a 'pump priming' nature. Members in developing countries should note particularly that additional funds have been made available by the Society's International Committee to provide grants for successful applicants from such countries. Preference will be given to those able to cite collaborative research projects with United Kingdom institutions.

Royal Society of Chemistry Visits to Developing Countries
Subjects: Chemistry.
Purpose: To promote international co-operation, specifically, to enable chemists to carry out short-term studies in well established scientific centres abroad and to learn and use techniques not accessible to them in their own country.
Eligibility: Open to members of the Society.
Level of Study: Professional development
Type: Grant
Value: Up to UK £500. The grants will complement, where appropriate, those for visits to Commonwealth countries, and funding would cover the additional travel costs involved, together with appropriate subsistence. Applicants should also see the Corday-Morgan Memorial Fund
Frequency: Four times a year
Country of Study: Any country
No. of awards offered: Approx. 4
Application Procedure: Applicants must submit applications on the official form and will normally be considered within 1 month of receipt.
Closing Date: January 1st, April 1st, July 1st and October 1st
No. of awards given last year: 2
No. of applicants last year: 2
Additional Information: Applicants must be travelling to another country and would normally stop en route to visit a third country. This must be a developing country.

THE ROYAL SOCIETY OF MEDICINE (RSM)

1 Wimpole Street, London, W1G 0AE, England
Tel: (44) (0) 20 7290 2900
Fax: (44) (0) 20 7290 2989
Email: jo.parkinson@rsm.ac.uk
Website: www.rsm.ac.uk
Contact: Section Manager Alademic Department

The Royal Society of Medicine (RSM) provides academic services and club facilities for its members as well as publishing a monthly journal and an annual bulletin, and providing over 400 educational conferences and meetings per year.

Adrian Tanner Prize

Subjects: Clinical case reports should be submitted to reflect the multidisciplinary nature of the care for surgical patients.
Purpose: To encourage surgical trainees submit the best clinical case reports.
Eligibility: Open to all surgeons in training.
Value: UK £250
Frequency: Annual
Study Establishment: Royal Society of Medicine - Surgery section
Country of Study: United Kingdom
No. of awards offered: 1
Application Procedure: Applicants should download an application form from www.rsm.ac.uk/awards
Closing Date: March 30th
No. of awards given last year: 1
No. of applicants last year: 50

For further information contact:

Email: surgery@rsm.ac.uk

Alan Emery Prize

Subjects: Genetics.
Purpose: To reward the best published research article in Medical Genetics in the past 2 years.
Eligibility: Open to candidates in an accredited training or research post in the UK.
Type: Prize
Value: £500 or £300 or 1 year membership of Royal Society of Medicine
Frequency: Annual
Application Procedure: Candidates must submit full copy of the article, curriculum vitae or covering letter explaining the significance of the publication.
Closing Date: March 31st
No. of awards given last year: 1
No. of applicants last year: 7

ASN Bursaries

Purpose: To enable ASN trainees to attend the ASN meeting.
Type: Bursary
Value: £750
Frequency: Annual
Country of Study: United Kingdom
No. of awards offered: 4
Application Procedure: Please visit website for further details.
Closing Date: July 24th
No. of awards given last year: 5
No. of applicants last year: 28

Cardiology Section Presidents Prize

Subjects: Cardiology.
Purpose: To reward original work for specialist registrar in cardiology.
Eligibility: Open to caridology trainees who have received all or part of their training at recognised centres of excellence in the UK. The subject of the presentation should represent original work.
Level of Study: Research
Type: Prize
Value: First prize - Commemoration medal and £1,000. Second prize - £500
Frequency: Annual
Study Establishment: Recognised centres of excellence in UK
Country of Study: United Kingdom
No. of awards offered: 2
Application Procedure: Candidates should submit an abstract of no more than 200 words.
Closing Date: May 1st
Contributor: Cardiology Section Funds
No. of awards given last year: 2
Additional Information: Presentation date: June 25th.

For further information contact:

Cardiology Section, Royal Society of Medicine, 1 Wimpole Street, London, WIG OAE

Catastrophes & Conflict Forum Medical Student Essay Prize

Eligibility: Open to candidates who are enrolled full-time at a UK medical school.
Level of Study: Postgraduate
Type: Prize
Value: £250
Frequency: Annual
Study Establishment: Royal Society of Medicine
Country of Study: United Kingdom
No. of awards offered: 1
Application Procedure: Candidates should submit an essay no longer than 1,500 words, emailed in Word format.
Closing Date: February 23rd
No. of awards given last year: 2
No. of applicants last year: 9

For further information contact:

Email: catastrophes@rsm.ac.uk

Clinical Forensic and Legal Medicine Section Case/Poster Presentation

Subjects: Clinical studies.
Purpose: To present a case or a poster in clinical studies.
Level of Study: Trainee and students
Value: £200 (case) and £100 (poster)
Frequency: Annual
No. of awards offered: Varies
Application Procedure: Please visit the website www.rsm.ac.uk/academ/awards/index for application form details.

Clinical Immunology & Allergy Section President's Prize

Subjects: Immunology or allergy.
Eligibility: Open to training grade doctors and young scientists (not above Specialist Registrar, Grade B Clinical Scientist or equivalent grade) with an immunological or allergy component of their clinical research.
Level of Study: Research, training graduate doctors and young scientists
Type: Prize
Value: £500
Frequency: Annual
No. of awards offered: 3
Application Procedure: Check website for further details.
Closing Date: March 20th
No. of awards given last year: 3
No. of applicants last year: 10

For further information contact:

Website: www.rsm.ac.uk/awards

Clinical Neurosciences Section Presidents Prize

Subjects: Neurology.
Purpose: To encourage clinical case presentation.
Eligibility: Trainees in neurosciences, including neurology, neurosurgery, neurophysiology, neuropathology or neuroradiology.
Level of Study: Trainee
Type: Prize
Length of Study: £300
Frequency: Every 2 years
No. of awards offered: Varies
Application Procedure: Submit a one A4 page (up to 500 words) summary of research carried out. Those considered to be the best will be asked to give a 15 minute presentation.

Clinocopath Meetings Best Presentations

Subjects: Clinicopathology.
Type: Prize
Value: £150
Frequency: Annual
Country of Study: United Kingdom
No. of awards offered: 1
Closing Date: August 10th

Contributor: Royal Society of Medicine
No. of awards given last year: 1
No. of applicants last year: 32

Gordon Holmes Prize

Subjects: Clinical neurosciences.
Purpose: To award a research prize in clinical neurosciences.
Level of Study: Neuro trainee
Type: Prize
Value: £300
Frequency: Every 2 years
No. of awards offered: Varies
Application Procedure: Please check the website www.rsm.ac.uk/awards/index

Innovation and Research in Palliative Care Prizes

Level of Study: Foundation programme, Postgraduate
Type: Prize
Value: First prize: £250, second prize: £100, third prize: £50
Frequency: Annual
No. of awards offered: 2
Contributor: Palliative Care Section

John Fry Prize

Subjects: Primary healthcare.
Purpose: To award best examples of practice-based research involving members of the primary health and social community, demonstrating and promoting effective team work.
Eligibility: Open to candidates currently working in primary healthcare in the UK excuding members of the RSM section of GP Council.
Level of Study: Unrestricted
Type: Prize
Value: £1,000 + 1 year membership
Frequency: Annual
Country of Study: United Kingdom
No. of awards offered: 1
Closing Date: February 28th
Funding: Private
Contributor: John Fry
No. of awards given last year: 1
No. of applicants last year: 4

For further information contact:

RSM, 1 Wimpole Street, London, W1G QAE
Contact: Nicole Leida

John of Arderne Medal

Subjects: Coloproctology.
Purpose: To award the presenter of the best paper presented at the short papers meeting of the section of coloproctology. Applicants have to submit an abstract for presentation at the meeting.
Eligibility: Open to applicants of any nationality.
Level of Study: Professional development
Type: Award
Value: Approx. UK £600
Frequency: Annual
Study Establishment: Varies
Country of Study: Any country
No. of awards offered: 1
Application Procedure: Further details are available from the RSM administrator.
Closing Date: September and November
Funding: Private
No. of awards given last year: 16
No. of applicants last year: 80

Karl Storz Travelling Scholarship

Subjects: Laryngology and rhinology.
Purpose: To assist with the cost of travel to overseas centres.
Eligibility: Open to senior registrars or consultants of not more than 2 years standing, who must be members of the section of laryngology and rhinology of the RSM.

Level of Study: Postdoctorate
Type: Scholarship
Value: UK £1,000
Frequency: Annual
Country of Study: Any country
No. of awards offered: 1
Application Procedure: Applicants must submit a paper to the RSM section of laryngology and rhinology. Further details are available from the RSM administrator.
Closing Date: December 7th
Funding: Commercial
Contributor: Karl Storz Endoscopy Limited
No. of awards given last year: 1
No. of applicants last year: 25
Additional Information: The recipient will be required to submit a brief report on the visit within 3 months of his or her return.

Malcolm Harrington Prize

Subjects: Occupational medicine.
Purpose: To award the work that is most likely to advance the study of occupational medicine in its broadest sense.
Eligibility: Open to occupational physician in training or within an year of achieving specialist accreditation.
Type: Prize
Value: £250
Frequency: Annual
Application Procedure: Candidates should submit an abstract of their own work (no longer than 200 words).
Closing Date: End of September
Funding: Private
Contributor: Professor Harrington
No. of awards given last year: 1
No. of applicants last year: 9

For further information contact:

Royal Society of Medicine, 1 Wimpole Street, London, W1G OAE, England

Norman Gamble Fund and Research Prize

Subjects: Otology.
Purpose: To support specific research projects.
Eligibility: Open to British nationals.
Level of Study: Unrestricted
Type: Prize
Value: UK £100 for the research prize and UK £1,500 for the grant-in-aid. Awards alternate every 2 years
Frequency: Annual
Country of Study: Any country
No. of awards offered: 1
Application Procedure: Further details are available from the RSM administrator.
Closing Date: December 9th
Funding: Private
No. of awards given last year: 1
No. of applicants last year: 4

Norman Tanner Prize

Subjects: Oncology.
Purpose: To encourage clinical registrars submit the best clinical paper.
Eligibility: Open to all trainee oncologists.
Value: UK £250
Frequency: Annual
Study Establishment: Royal Society of Medicine
Country of Study: United Kingdom
No. of awards offered: 1
Application Procedure: Applicants are requested to contact the Section Coordinator at oncology@rsm.ac.uk
Closing Date: April 27th
No. of awards given last year: 12
No. of applicants last year: 30

For further information contact:

Email: oncology@rsm.ac.uk

Ophthalmology Travelling Fellowship

Subjects: Ophthalmology.

Purpose: To enable British ophthalmologists to travel abroad with the intention of furthering the study or advancement of ophthalmology, or to enable foreign ophthalmologists to visit the United Kingdom for the same purpose.

Eligibility: Open to ophthalmologists in the British Isles of any nationality who have not attained an official consultant appointment, nor undertaken professional clinical work or equivalent responsibility for any substantial period before or during the execution of original work.

Level of Study: Professional development

Type: Fellowship

Value: UK £500–2,000

Frequency: Every 2 years

Study Establishment: Varies

Country of Study: Any country

No. of awards offered: Varies

Application Procedure: Applicants must apply to the academic administrator at RSM.

Closing Date: Entries are evaluated in December and May

No. of awards given last year: 4

No. of applicants last year: 6

Opthalmology Trainees Prize

Subjects: Ophthalmology.

Purpose: To encourage trainee ophthalmologists present research work and case reports to a knowledgeable and critical audience.

Eligibility: Open to all ophthalmologists in training.

Level of Study: Research, Postgraduate

Value: UK £150

Frequency: Annual

Study Establishment: Royal Society of Medicine

Country of Study: United Kingdom

No. of awards offered: 2 - one for best poster and one for best talk

Application Procedure: Applicants should download an application form from www.rsm.ac.uk/awards

Closing Date: March 30th

No. of awards given last year: 2

No. of applicants last year: 35

Orthopaedics Section President's Prize Papers

Eligibility: Open to all orthopaedic trainees.

Level of Study: Postgraduate

Type: Prize

Value: First prize: £500, second prize: £200, third prize: £100

Frequency: Annual

Study Establishment: Royal Society of Medicine

Country of Study: United Kingdom

No. of awards offered: 1

Application Procedure: Candidates should submit abstracts no longer than 200 words. The abstracts will be judged by a panel of experts, shortlisted and asked to be presented at a meeting.

Closing Date: May 5th

No. of awards given last year: 1

No. of applicants last year: 10

For further information contact:

Email: orthopaedics@rsm.ac.uk

RSM Mental Health Foundation Essay Prize

Subjects: Psychiatry.

Purpose: To award an essay.

Eligibility: Open to candidates practising medicine in the United Kingdom or the Republic of Ireland who are in training at any grade from senior house officer to senior registrar or equivalent. Applicants need not be members of RSM.

Type: Prize

Value: Varies, approx. UK £500–250 depending on available finance. It also includes a subscription to RSM if funds are available, 1st prize UK £750, 2nd prize UK £500

Frequency: Annual, SHO or SPR

Country of Study: United Kingdom

No. of awards offered: 2

Application Procedure: Essays should be submitted in triplicate to the RSM section of psychiatry.

Closing Date: Early January

Funding: Private

No. of applicants last year: 1

Additional Information: The subject is chosen by the Council. Essays should be approx. 5,000 words in length.

Sexual Health Trainee Prize

Eligibility: Trainees within 10 years of qualification.

Type: Prize

Value: £150

Length of Study: 10 years

Frequency: Annual

No. of awards offered: Varies

Application Procedure: Abstracts should be set out on A4 paper, double spaced and not more than 200 words in length. Only two abstracts are permitted per applicant and each applicant may only present one poster or one oral. Please visit the website www.rsm.ac.uk/academ/awards/index

Sylvia Lawler Prize

Subjects: Oncology.

Purpose: To encourage scientists and clinicians in training to present the best scientific paper and best clinical paper on oncology.

Eligibility: Open to all surgeons in training.

Level of Study: Postgraduate

Type: Grant

Value: UK £500

Frequency: Annual

Study Establishment: Royal Society of Medicine

Country of Study: United Kingdom

No. of awards offered: 2

Application Procedure: Applicants should download an application form from the website, www.rsm.ac.uk/awards and submit the same via email to surgery@rsm.ac.uk

Closing Date: November

No. of awards given last year: 1

No. of applicants last year: 50

For further information contact:

Email: surgery@rsm.ac.uk

Website: www.rsm.ac.uk/awards

Tim David Prize

Eligibility: Open to paediatric trainees.

Level of Study: Foundation programme, Postgraduate

Type: Prize

Value: First prize £150, one year's subscription to the RSM (worth up to £200) and membership of the Council of the Section of Paediatrics & Child Health for one year. There will also be a second prize of £100

Frequency: Annual

No. of awards offered: 2

Application Procedure: Candidates should submit abstracts.

Closing Date: December

Contributor: Paediatrics & Child Health Section, RSM

No. of awards given last year: 2

No. of applicants last year: 12

Trainees' Committee John Glyn Trainees' Prize

Eligibility: Open to trainees from any medical, dental, veterinary hospital or primary care speciality under the age of 40.

Level of Study: Foundation programme, Graduate, Postgraduate, Research

Type: Prize

Value: £400

Frequency: Annual

No. of awards offered: 1

Closing Date: April 27th

Contributor: Royal Society of Medicine

United Services Section Colt Foundation Research Prizes
Eligibility: Open to serving military officers in a training grade in general practice, a hospital or other speciality and are fellows of the RSM.
Level of Study: Postgraduate, serving military medical officers
Type: Prize
Value: First prize: £200, second prize: £100 (x5 each)
Frequency: Annual
Study Establishment: Royal Society of Medicine
Country of Study: United Kingdom
No. of awards offered: 1 (first prize), 5 (second prizes)
Application Procedure: Candidates should email the abstracts. The abstracts will be shortlisted by the panel and judged.
Closing Date: November 9th
Funding: Trusts
Contributor: Colt Foundation
No. of awards given last year: 1
No. of applicants last year: 15

For further information contact:

Email: united.services@rsm.ac.uk

Urology Section Clinicopathology Prize
Subjects: Urology.
Type: Prize
Value: £2,000
Frequency: Annual
No. of awards offered: 3
Closing Date: To be announced

For further information contact:

Website: www.rsm.ac.uk/awards

Urology Section Geoffrey Chisholm Prize
Subjects: Urology.
Purpose: To provide applicants the opportunity to be present at the prize meeting.
Eligibility: Open to members of the Urology section.
Level of Study: Trainee doctors
Type: Prize
Value: £2,000
No. of awards offered: 3
Closing Date: To be announced
No. of awards given last year: 3
No. of applicants last year: 30

For further information contact:

Website: www.rsm.ac.uk/awards

Urology Section Short Papers Prize
Subjects: Urology.
Type: Prize
Value: £2,000
Frequency: Annual
Closing Date: To be announced

For further information contact:

Website: www.rsm.ac.uk/awards

Urology Section Travelling Fellowship
Subjects: Urology.
Eligibility: Open to members of the Urology section.
Level of Study: Trainees
Type: Fellowship
Value: £1,000
Frequency: Annual
No. of awards offered: 1
Closing Date: To be announced

For further information contact:

Website: www.rsm.ac.uk

Venous Forum Spring Meeting Prizes
Eligibility: Open to non-consultants.

Level of Study: Postgraduate
Value: First prize: £250, second prize: £150
Frequency: Annual
Study Establishment: Royal Society of Medicine
Country of Study: United Kingdom
No. of awards offered: 1
Application Procedure: Candidates should email abstracts. Shortlisted candidates will be invited to present their papers.
Closing Date: February 13th
No. of awards given last year: 1
No. of applicants last year: 20

For further information contact:

Email: venous@rsm.ac.uk

Young Epidermologist Award
Subjects: Epidermology.
Purpose: To reward outstanding papers.
Eligibility: Open to candidates under 40 years of age.
Level of Study: Unrestricted
Type: Award
Value: £250
Frequency: Annual
Country of Study: United Kingdom
No. of awards offered: 1
Application Procedure: Please check website.
Closing Date: November 27th
No. of awards given last year: 1
No. of applicants last year: 9

ROYAL TOWN PLANNING INSTITUTE (RTPI)

41 Botolph Lane, London, EC3R 8DL,
England
Tel: (44) 20 7929 9473
Fax: (44) 20 7929 8199
Email: judy.woollett@rtpi.org.uk

The Royal Town Planning Institute (RTPI) was founded in 1914 and is a registered charity. Its aim is to advance the science and art of town planning in all its aspects, including local, regional and national planning for the benefit of the public. The Institute is primarily concerned with maintaining high standards of competence and conduct within the profession, promoting the role of planning within the country's social, economic and political structures, and presenting the profession's views on current planning issues.

George Pepler International Award
Subjects: Town and country planning or some particular aspect of planning theory and practice.
Purpose: To enable young people of any nationality to visit another country for a short period to study.
Eligibility: Open to persons under 30 years of age of any nationality.
Level of Study: Professional development, Research
Value: Up to UK £1,500
Length of Study: Short-term travel outside the United Kingdom for United Kingdom residents or for visits to the United Kingdom for applicants from abroad
Frequency: Every 2 years
Country of Study: Any country
No. of awards offered: 1
Application Procedure: Applicants must submit a statement showing the nature of the study visit proposed, together with an itinerary. Application forms are available on request from the RTPI.
Closing Date: March 31st
Funding: Private
Contributor: Trust fund
No. of awards given last year: 1
No. of applicants last year: 20
Additional Information: At the conclusion of the visit the recipient must submit a report.

RSM ERASMUS UNIVERSITY

MBA Programmes, Burgemeester Oudlaan 50,
3062 PA Rotterdam, PO Box 1738, Rotterdam,
3000 DR, Netherlands
Tel: (31) 10 408 2222
Fax: (31) 10 452 9509
Email: info@rsm.nl
Website: www.rsm.nl

As one of the world's top business schools, RSM is a centre of excellence and innovation for management education and research. Our goal is to empower individuals to succeed amid the complexities of modern international commerce and become the business leaders of tomorrow.

Handelsblatt/RSM Scholarship

Subjects: Business management.
Purpose: To assist nationals or residents of Germany to finance their MBA study.
Eligibility: Open to nationals and residents of Germany.
Level of Study: MBA
Type: Scholarship
Value: €36,000 (Full tuition fees)
Length of Study: 15 months
Frequency: Annual
Study Establishment: Erasmus University
Country of Study: Netherlands
No. of awards offered: 1
Application Procedure: Refer the website for further details.
Closing Date: July 15th
Funding: Commercial
Contributor: Handelsblatt Newpaper: Germany
No. of awards given last year: 1
No. of applicants last year: 6

NFP Netherlands Fellowship Programme

Subjects: Business management.
Purpose: To assist full-time MBA students financing MBA.
Eligibility: Open to residents of 57 countries as listed on the NUFFIC website with a preference for female candidates from sub-Saharan Africa.
Level of Study: MBA
Type: Fellowship
Value: €36,000 (full tuition), travel allowances and living expenses
Length of Study: 15 months
Frequency: Annual
Study Establishment: Erasmus University
Country of Study: Netherlands
No. of awards offered: 1
Application Procedure: Refer the website for further details.
Closing Date: March 1st
Funding: Government
Contributor: NUFFIC/Dutch Ministry of Foreign Affairs
No. of awards given last year: 1
No. of applicants last year: 6

RSM Alumni Scholarship

Subjects: Business management.
Purpose: To assist a financially needy MBA student in funding their study.
Level of Study: MBA
Type: Scholarship
Value: €10,000
Length of Study: 15 months
Frequency: Annual
Study Establishment: Erasmus University
Country of Study: Netherlands
No. of awards offered: 1
Application Procedure: Refer the website for further details.
Closing Date: July 15th
Funding: Private
Contributor: RSM Alumni Association
Additional Information: Students must be able to show clear financial need, that is, that they are not able to fully fund themselves.

RSM Erasmus University Dean's Fund Scholarship

Subjects: Business management.
Purpose: To assist full-time MBA students finance their study.
Level of Study: MBA
Type: Scholarship
Value: €5,000
Length of Study: 15 months
Frequency: Annual
Study Establishment: Erasmus University
Country of Study: Netherlands
No. of awards offered: 6
Application Procedure: Refer the website for further details.
Funding: Private
Contributor: RSM Erasmus University
No. of awards given last year: 5
No. of applicants last year: 45

RSM Erasmus University MBA Citizenship Scholarship

Subjects: Business Management.
Purpose: To assist full-time MBA students in financing their study.
Level of Study: MBA
Type: Scholarship
Value: €10,000
Length of Study: 15 months
Frequency: Annual
Study Establishment: Erasmus University
Country of Study: Netherlands
No. of awards offered: 3
Application Procedure: Refer the website for further details.
Funding: Private
Contributor: RSM Erasmus University
No. of awards given last year: 3
No. of applicants last year: 37
Additional Information: Applicants should be able to show a high level of international diversity in their background and experience.

RSM MBA Corporate Scholarship Programme

Subjects: Business management.
Purpose: To assist full-time MBA students to finance their study and to gain access to an internship and post-graduation employment with a company of their choice (within the programme).
Level of Study: MBA
Type: Scholarship
Value: €10,000 plus career coaching
Length of Study: 15 months
Frequency: Annual
Study Establishment: Erasmus University
Country of Study: Netherlands
No. of awards offered: Varies
Application Procedure: Refer the website for further details.
Closing Date: July 15th
Funding: Corporation
Contributor: Participating companies
No. of awards given last year: 9
No. of applicants last year: 55

RSM-Intermediair EMBA Scholarship

Subjects: Business management.
Purpose: To assist Dutch and Netherlands residential candidates and to finance their Executive MBA.
Eligibility: Applicants must be resident in the Netherlands.
Level of Study: MBA
Type: Scholarship
Value: €15,000
Length of Study: 2 years
Frequency: Annual
Study Establishment: Erasmus University
Country of Study: The Netherlands
No. of awards offered: 2
Application Procedure: See website.
Closing Date: December 1st
Funding: Commercial
Contributor: Intermediair
No. of awards given last year: 2
No. of applicants last year: 16

RSM-NTIO in Taiwan Scholarship

Subjects: Business management.
Purpose: To assist Taiwanese nationals in financing their MBA study in the Netherlands.
Eligibility: Open to candidates from Taiwan only.
Level of Study: MBA
Type: Scholarship
Value: €5,000 per award
Length of Study: 15 months
Frequency: Annual
Study Establishment: Erasmus University
Country of Study: The Netherlands
No. of awards offered: 2
Application Procedure: See website.
Closing Date: May 31st
Funding: Government
Contributor: Netherlands Education Support Office
No. of awards given last year: 2
No. of applicants last year: 8

RSM/Fundación BECA Scholarship

Subjects: Business management.
Purpose: To assist students from Mexico, Chile and Colombia finance their MBA study.
Eligibility: Open to residents of Mexico, Chile and Colombia.
Level of Study: MBA
Type: Scholarship
Value: €3,500 plus travel allowances
Length of Study: 15 months
Frequency: Annual
Study Establishment: Erasmus University
Country of Study: Netherlands
No. of awards offered: 3
Application Procedure: Refer the website for further details.
Closing Date: July 15th
Funding: Private
Contributor: Fundación BECA

RSM/NESO Mexico Scholarship

Subjects: Business management.
Purpose: To assist Mexican students finance their MBA.
Eligibility: Open to nationals of Mexico.
Level of Study: MBA
Type: Scholarship
Value: €10,000
Length of Study: 15 months
Frequency: Annual
Study Establishment: Erasmus University
Country of Study: Netherlands
No. of awards offered: 1
Application Procedure: Refer the website for further details.
Closing Date: May 31st
Funding: Government
Contributor: Netherlands Education Support Office

RSM/NESO Vietnam Scholarship

Subjects: Business management.
Purpose: To assist Vietnamese students finance their MBA study.
Eligibility: Open to nationals of Vietnam.
Level of Study: MBA
Type: Scholarship
Value: €18,000
Length of Study: 15 months
Frequency: Annual
Study Establishment: Erasmus University
Country of Study: Netherlands
No. of awards offered: 1
Application Procedure: Refer the website for further details.
Closing Date: May 31st
Funding: Government
Contributor: Netherlands Educational Support Office
No. of awards given last year: 1
No. of applicants last year: 4

RSPCA AUSTRALIA INC

PO Box 265, Deakin West, ACT 2600, Australia
Tel: (61) 02 6282 8300
Fax: (61) 02 6282 8311
Email: rspca@rspca.org.au
Website: www.rspca.org.au

The mission of RSPCA is to prevent cruelty to animals by actively promoting their care and protection and to be the leading authority in animal care and protection. The RSPCA shelters are one of the most visible parts of the Society's operations. RSPCA shelters receive more than 138,000 animals per year.

RSPCA Australia Alan White Scholarship for Animal Welfare Research

Subjects: General animal welfare issues.
Purpose: To encourage students to take an active interest in animal welfare issues, to support animal welfare research that might not otherwise attract funding, and to promote the objectives of the RSPCA within the research community.
Eligibility: Open to applicants who are enrolled in any accredited course at an Australian university. Applicants must also demonstrate a major commitment towards the involvement of animal welfare issues.
Level of Study: Postgraduate
Type: Scholarship
Value: Australian $7,000
Frequency: Annual
Country of Study: Australia
Application Procedure: Application forms can be downloaded from the website.
Closing Date: August 24th
Funding: Foundation
Contributor: RSPCA

For further information contact:

Contact: Chief Scientific Officer

RSPCA Australia Scholarship for Humane Animal Production Research

Subjects: Animal welfare issues in animal production.
Purpose: To encourage students to take an active interest in animal welfare issues, to support animal welfare research that might not otherwise attract funding, and to promote the objectives of the RSPCA within the research community.
Eligibility: Open to applicants who are enrolled in any accredited course at an Australian university. Applicants must also demonstrate a major commitment towards the involvement of animal welfare issues.
Type: Scholarship
Value: Australian $7,690
Frequency: Annual
Country of Study: Australia
Application Procedure: Application forms can be downloaded from the website.
Closing Date: August 28th
Funding: Foundation
Contributor: RSPCA

For further information contact:

Contact: Chief Scientific Officer

RURAL MATERNITY CARE RESEARCH

Suite 530-1501 West Broadway, Vancouver, BC, V6J-4Z6, Canada
Tel: (1) 604 742 1792
Fax: (1) 604 742 1798
Email: info@ruralmatresearch.com
Website: www.ruralmatresearch.net

Rural Maternity Care Research is a team of academic and community based researchers interested in rural maternity care. They believe their diversity of expertise, backgrounds and interests enhance their ability to comprehensively investigate the complexity of challenges and opportunities for rural maternity care in British Columbia.

Rural Maternity Care Doctoral Student Fellowship

Subjects: Maternity care.
Purpose: To enable a motivated Doctoral student researcher to join the interdisciplinary team investigating rural maternity care in British Columbia.
Eligibility: Open to citizens or permanent residents of Canada who are registered in a Doctoral programme in Canada.
Level of Study: Doctorate
Type: Fellowship
Value: Up to Canadian $45,000 (benefits included)
Length of Study: 18 months
Frequency: Annual
Country of Study: Canada
Application Procedure: Applicants must include the following documents in the application: cover letter, transcripts, curriculum vitae, contact information of 3 research referees and sample of the candidates writing preferably from an article published in a referred journal.
Closing Date: August 18th
Additional Information: The Fellow will be provided with office space in Vancouver, as well as access to and use of internet, printers and telephone and fax lines. Candidates from all academic disciplines are invited to apply. Candidates who may be completing coursework for their PhD programme, will be expected to contribute sufficient time to the RM-NET to develop a research focus area.

For further information contact:

Email: clin2@cw.bc.ca
Contact: Cynthia Lin Hsieh

Rural Maternity Care Research in Postdoctoral Fellowship

Subjects: Maternity care.
Purpose: To enable a motivated researcher to join their interdesciplinary team investigating rural maternity care in British Columbia.
Eligibility: Open to citizens or permanent residents of Canada, whose Doctoral requirements are completed in no more than 3 years before the application deadline unless the candidate has taken maternity leave after completion of the Doctorate.
Level of Study: Postdoctorate
Type: Fellowship
Value: Canadian $60,000 (benefits included)
Length of Study: 18 months
Frequency: Annual
Country of Study: Canada
Application Procedure: Applicants must include the following documents in the application: cover letter, transcripts, curriculum vitae, description of past research experiences, 2 letters of reference and contact information of 3 research referees.
Closing Date: August 18th
Additional Information: During the term period, the Fellow will be provided with office space in Vancouver and a portable PC, as well as access to and use of internet, printers and telephone and fax lines. Candidates from all academic disciplines are invited to apply.

RUSSELL SAGE FOUNDATION

112 East 64th Street, New York, NY, 10065, United States of America
Tel: (1) 212 750 6000
Fax: (1) 212 371 4761
Email: info@rsage.org
Website: www.russellsage.org
Contact: Vice President of Administration

The Russell Sage Foundation is the principal American foundation devoted exclusively to research in the social sciences. Located in New York City, the Foundation is a research centre, a funding source for studies by scholars at other academic and research institutions and an active member of the nation's social science community.

Russell Sage Foundation Visiting Scholar Appointments

Subjects: Social sciences.
Eligibility: Open to scholars in the social sciences. The Foundation particularly welcomes groups of visiting scholars who wish to collaborate on a specific project during their residence at the foundation. In order to develop these projects fully, support is sometimes provided for working groups prior to their arrival at the foundation. Awards are not made for the support of graduate degree work, nor for institutional support.
Level of Study: Doctorate, Postdoctorate
Type: Fellowship
Value: Varies
Length of Study: 1 academic year
Frequency: Annual
Study Establishment: The Foundation
Country of Study: Any country
No. of awards offered: Varies
Application Procedure: Applicants should consult the website or contact the organization for details.
Closing Date: October 15th prior to the year of residence
Funding: Foundation
No. of awards given last year: 21
No. of applicants last year: 110
Additional Information: Awardees are expected to offer the Foundation the right to publish any book-length manuscripts resulting from Foundation support.

RUTH ESTRIN GOLDBERG MEMORIAL FOR CANCER RESEARCH

885 Gloucester Road, Union, NJ, 07083, United States of America
Tel: (1) 908 688 1725
Email: goodfudgie@aol.com
Website: www.regm-cancer-research.us
Contact: Mrs Myrna Abramson, Past President

The Ruth Estrin Goldberg Memorial for Cancer Research is a foundation supporting cancer research.

Ruth Estrin Goldberg Memorial for Cancer Research

Subjects: Cancer research.
Purpose: To help fund cancer research in instituitions.
Eligibility: Open to candidates from the eastern United States of America, preferably New York, New Jersey, Pennsylvania, Connecticut, Massachusetts, Delaware or Maryland.
Level of Study: Unrestricted
Value: US$10,000–20,000
Length of Study: 1 year
Frequency: Annual
Country of Study: United States of America
No. of awards offered: 2
Application Procedure: Applicants must write for an application form and guidelines.
Closing Date: April 28th
Funding: Private
Contributor: Members and friends
No. of awards given last year: 2
No. of applicants last year: 10–15
Additional Information: The Ruth Estrin Goldberg Memorial for Cancer Research is a volunteer organization.

For further information contact:

653 Colonial Arms Road, Union, NJ, 07083, United States of America
Contact: Mrs Rhoda Goodman, Past President

RYERSON UNIVERSITY

350 Victoria Street, Toronto, ON, M5B-2K3, Canada
Tel: (1) 416 979 5000
Fax: (1) 416 979 5292
Email: awards@ryerson.ca
Website: www.ryerson.ca
Contact: Dr Judith Sandys, International Relations

Ryerson University was founded in 1948 as Ryerson Institute of Technology, established primarily as a training ground for the growing workforce of a booming post war economy. The Institute was a novel alternative to the traditional apprenticeship system of technical learning.

Ryerson Graduate Scholarship (RGS)

Subjects: All subjects.

Purpose: To attract and retain excellent graduate students and support them financially.

Eligibility: Open to Master's candidates with a minimum grade point average of at least 3.67. Renewal will require a minimum 1st year grade point average of 3.67, with no grade below 2.67. For a Doctoral candidate a minimum grade point average of at least 3.67 in their Master's programme is required.

Level of Study: Doctorate, Postgraduate

Type: Scholarship

Value: Canadian $7,000

Length of Study: 2–3 years

Study Establishment: Ryerson University

Country of Study: Canada

Funding: Private, individuals

Additional Information: Students who did not receive an entry scholarship, but who perform at the level required for scholarship renewal will be eligible to be considered for an RGS after their 1st year in a Ryerson graduate programme.

S S HUEBNER FOUNDATION FOR INSURANCE EDUCATION

3000 SH-DH, 3260 Locust Walk, Philadelphia, PA, 19104-6302, United States of America
Tel: (1) 215 898 9631
Fax: (1) 215 573 2218
Email: hcalvert@wharton.upenn.edu
Website: www.huebnergeneva.org
Contact: Associate Director

The S S Huebner Foundation is an educational foundation with the objective of promoting education and research in risk management and insurance. It provides PhD fellowships for the study of risk management and insurance economics at the Wharton School of the University of Pennsylvania, and publishes books and working papers.

S S Huebner Foundation for Insurance Education Predoctoral and Postdoctoral Fellowships

Subjects: Managerial science and applied economics, with a specialization in risk management and insurance economics.

Purpose: To increase the supply of college professors specializing in risk management and insurance economics.

Eligibility: Open to scholars who hold a Bachelor's degree from an accredited university or college and intend to pursue a teaching career in insurance.

Level of Study: Doctorate, Postdoctorate

Type: Fellowship

Value: Full tuition fees of the Wharton School of the University of Pennsylvania plus an annual living stipend of US$21,000

Length of Study: 4 years

Frequency: Annual

Study Establishment: The Wharton School of the University of Pennsylvania

Country of Study: United States of America

No. of awards offered: Varies

Application Procedure: Applicants must apply to the Wharton School doctoral programme for admission and to the Huebner Foundation for funding.

Closing Date: December 15th (Wharton admission), January 15th (Huebner funding)

Funding: Corporation, foundation, individuals

Contributor: Leading insurance companies in the United States and Canada

No. of awards given last year: 2

No. of applicants last year: 8

Additional Information: Candidates are required to certify that it is their intention to follow a teaching career in insurance and that they will major in insurance and risk management for a graduate degree. Applicants must take the admission test for graduate study in business. For information concerning these examinations, candidates should write directly to the Educational Testing Service (ETS). Applicants should apply separately and directly to the Wharton School Doctoral Programme Office for admission into the Insurance and Risk Management Doctoral Programme.

S.D.A.BOCCONI

Room 115 Via Bocconi, 8, Milan, 20136, Italy
Tel: (39) 02 5836 6875
Fax: (39) 02 5836 6890
Email: joanne.matthews@sdabocconi.it
Website: www.sdabocconi.it/en
Contact: Grants Enquiries

SDA School of Management enjoys recognition as a leading management school at an international level. Its mission is to educate men and women to be ready to act anywhere in the world, using their knowledge and imagination.

MPM Partial Tuition Fee Waivers

Subjects: Master of Public Management (MPM) is described as an MBA but focused on the international public sector. MPM is designed to prepare individuals for careers in Governmaental organizations, international institutions, NGOs and private businesses working with the public sector. The MPM programme provides a learning environment for participants from all 5 continents and is taught entirely in English.

Purpose: To provide partial tuition fee waivers for deserving candidates.

Eligibility: The MPM is open to candidates from different backgrounds and age groups. However, candidates with a background/interest in political science or international affairs will get the most from the MPM. Work experience is preferred but not essential.

Level of Study: Postgraduate

Type: Scholarship

Length of Study: 1 year

Frequency: Annual

Study Establishment: SDA Bocconi, Bocconi University, Milan

Country of Study: Italy

Application Procedure: Applicants must send a completed application form which is available online at www.sdabocconi.it/mpm along with a curriculum vitae, transcripts of the GMAT/GRE/TOEFL (or other) scores, 2 reference letters and 4 passport size photographs, in a sealed envelope, to the course Secretary.

Closing Date: July

Additional Information: MPM operates a rolling application process. Applications are assessed until the course is full. Candidates whose mother tongue is English or who have studied in institutions where the medium of instruction is English may request a waiver for the English language certificate such as TOEFL (or other).

For further information contact:

Room 115, SDA Bocconi, Via Bocconi, 8, Milan, 20136, Italy
Contact: Joanne Matthews, Secretary, MPM Master Division

SAINT ANDREW'S SOCIETY OF THE STATE OF NEW YORK SCHOLARSHIPS, THE CARNEGIE TRUST FOR THE UNIVERSITIES OF SCOTLAND

Andrew Carnegie House, Pittencrieff Street, DUNFERMLINE, Fife, KY12 8AW, Scotland
Tel: (44) 1383 724990
Fax: (44) 1383 749799
Email: jgray@carnegie-trust.org
Contact: Chairman, Scottish Selection Commitee

The Carnegie Trust for the Universities of Scotland administrates on behalf of the Saint Andrew's Society of the State of New York Scholarships to students of Scottish descent or birth for study at a university in the United States of America, within a radius of 250 miles from New York City or the Washington DC area.

Saint Andrew's Society of the State of New York Scholarship Fund

Subjects: All subjects.
Purpose: To support advanced study exchanges between the United States of America and Scotland.
Eligibility: Open to newly qualified graduates of a Scottish university or of Oxford or Cambridge. Candidates are required to have a Scottish background. The possession of an Honours degree is not essential. Personality and other qualities will influence the selection.
Level of Study: Postgraduate
Type: Scholarship
Value: US$20,000 to cover university tuition fees, room and board and transportation expenses
Length of Study: 1 academic year
Frequency: Annual
Study Establishment: A university within 250 miles of New York City or the Washington DC area
Country of Study: United States of America
No. of awards offered: 2
Application Procedure: Applicants must write for details. Each Scottish university will screen its own applicants and nominate one candidate to go forward to the final selection committee to be held in Edinburgh in early March. Oxford and Cambridge applicants should apply directly to the Society.
Closing Date: December
Funding: Private
No. of awards given last year: 2
No. of applicants last year: 7
Additional Information: Only in unusual circumstances will the Society consider other locations. Thereafter, the scholar is expected to spend a little time travelling in United States of America before returning to Scotland. Applications should be made via the principal of the university attended(ing) in the case of the Scottish universities.

SAMUEL H KRESS FOUNDATION

174 East 80th Street, New York, NY, 10021, United States of America
Tel: (1) 212 861 4993
Fax: (1) 212 628 3146
Email: wyman@kressfoundation.org
Website: www.kressfoundation.org

The Samuel H. Kress Foundation, since its creation in 1929, has devoted its resources almost exclusively to programmes related to European art. The Foundation devoted its resources to advancing the history, conservation, and enjoyment of the vast heritage of European art, architecture, and archaeology.

Samuel H Kress Foundation 2-Year Research Fellowships at Foreign Institutions

Subjects: Art history.
Purpose: To facilitate advanced dissertation research in association with a selected institute of art history in either Florence, Jerusalem, Leiden, London, Munich, Nicosia, Paris, Rome or Zurich.
Eligibility: Open to PhD candidates in the history of art for the completion of their dissertation research. Candidates must be citizens of the United States of America or matriculated at an institution in the United States of America.
Level of Study: Predoctorate
Type: Fellowship
Value: US$22,500 per year
Length of Study: 2 years
Frequency: Annual
Study Establishment: One of a number of art historical institutes in Florence, Jerusalem, Leiden, London, Munich, Nicosia, Paris, Rome or Zurich
No. of awards offered: 4
Application Procedure: Applicants must be nominated by their art history department. There is a limit of one applicant per department. The Foundation does not accept grant materials by fax.
Closing Date: November 30th
Funding: Private
No. of awards given last year: 4
No. of applicants last year: Approx. 25

Samuel H Kress Foundation Fellowships for Advanced Training in Fine Arts Conservation

Subjects: Specific areas of fine art conservation.
Purpose: To enable young American conservators to undertake post-MA advanced internships.
Eligibility: Open to those who have completed their academic training in conservation.
Level of Study: Postgraduate
Type: Fellowship
Value: US$30,000
Frequency: Annual
Study Establishment: Appropriate institutions
Country of Study: United States of America
No. of awards offered: 10
Application Procedure: Applicants must write for details. The Foundation does not accept grant materials by fax. Application procedures and contact information available at www.kressfoundation.org
Closing Date: Aprilst
Funding: Private
No. of applicants last year: Approx. 25–30
Additional Information: Emphasis is on hands-on training. These grants are not for the completion of degree programmes. Enquiries should be directed to Wyman Meers.

Samuel H Kress Foundation Travel Fellowships

Subjects: Art history.
Purpose: To facilitate travel for PhD candidates in the history of art to view materials essential for the completion of dissertation research.
Eligibility: Open to predoctoral candidates of universities at United States of America.
Level of Study: Doctorate
Type: Fellowship
Value: Varies between US$3,500–10,000
Frequency: Annual
Country of Study: Any country
No. of awards offered: 10–15
Application Procedure: Applicants must be nominated by their art history department. There is a limit of one applicant per department. The Foundation does not accept grant materials by fax. Procedures and forms available to download at www.kressfoundation.org
Closing Date: November 30th
Funding: Private
No. of awards given last year: 15
No. of applicants last year: Approx. 50

THE SAN FRANCISCO FOUNDATION (SFF)

225 Bush Street, Suite 500, San Francisco, CA, 94104, United States of America
Tel: (1) 415 733 8500
Fax: (1) 415 477 2783
Email: rec@sff.org
Website: www.sff.org

The San Francisco Foundation (SFF) is a leading agent of Bay Area philanthropy. They rank 7th in grant making and assets among the nation's community foundations. They cultivate a family of donors who share a commitment to the Bay Area. They give millions of dollars a year to build on community assets, respond to community needs and elevate public awareness.

Joseph Henry Jackson Literary Award

Subjects: Fiction (novel or short stories), nonfiction, prose and poetry.
Purpose: To support an author of an unpublished work in progress.
Eligibility: Open to residents of northern California or Nevada for 3 consecutive years who are between 20 and 35 years of age.
Level of Study: Postgraduate
Type: Award
Value: US$3,000
Frequency: Annual
Country of Study: United States of America
No. of awards offered: 1

Application Procedure: Applicants must submit manuscript of their unpublished work along with the application form, entry in a contest and stamped addressed envelope.

Closing Date: January 31st

Additional Information: In addition to the US$2,000 cash award, winners will be invited to participate in a public reading at Intersection for the Arts and the winning manuscripts will be permanently housed at UC Berkeley's Bancroft Library.

Phelan Award in Photography

Subjects: Photojournalism and photography.

Purpose: To recognize achievements in photography.

Eligibility: Open to people who have been born in California, but need not be a current resident.

Level of Study: Postgraduate

Type: Award

Value: US$3,750

Frequency: Every 2 years

Country of Study: United States of America

No. of awards offered: 2

Application Procedure: Applicants must submit application form, entry in a contest and stamped addressed envelope. They must also provide a copy of their birth certificate with their application.

Contributor: San Francisco Foundation

SAN FRANCISCO STATE UNIVERSITY (SFSU)

Students Services Building 110, 1600 Holloway Avenue, San Francisco, CA, 94132-4013, United States of America
Tel: (1) 415 338 2234/1111
Fax: (1) 415 338 0942
Email: mritter@sfsu.edu
Website: www.sfsu.edu

San Francisco State University (SFSU) is one of the nation's leading public urban universities. SFSU helps create and maintain an environment for learning that promotes respect for and appreciation of scholarship, freedom, human diversity and the cultural mosaic of the City of San Francisco. SFSU also provides a higher education for residents of the region and state, as well as the nation and world.

Robert Westwood Scholarship

Subjects: Arts, health, science and social services.

Purpose: To assist SFSU students who are living with HIV and plan to make a contribution in any field to communities affected by HIV.

Level of Study: Postgraduate

Type: Scholarship

Value: US$3,000

Frequency: Annual

Study Establishment: San Fransisco State University

Country of Study: United States of America

No. of awards offered: 1

Application Procedure: Applicants must submit a copy of the most recent SFSU academic transcript, along with a brief, typed essay discussing plans to incorporate academic work and degree at SFSU with service in the HIV community or in the area of HIV prevention.

Closing Date: October 28th

Additional Information: Applicants must submit a verification from the physician.

For further information contact:

Tel: 415 338 7339

Contact: Michael Ritter, Counseling and psychological services

SANSKRITI PRATISHTHAN

Head Office C-11 Qutab Institutional Area, New Delhi, 110-016, India
Tel: (91) 11 2696 3226/2652 7077
Fax: (91) 11 2685 3383
Email: fellowships@sanskritifoundation.org
Website: www.sanskritifoundation.org

Sanskriti Pratishthan is a non-profit organization that was established in 1978. Sanskriti Pratishthan perceives its role as that of a catalyst, in revitalizing cultural sensitivity in contemporary times.

Kalakriti Fellowship in Indian Classical Dance

Subjects: Indian classical dance.

Purpose: To encourage young artists to develop their potential and enhance their skills through intensive practice and/or incorporating different facets of their art.

Eligibility: Open to Indian nationals in the age group of 25–40. The candidates should have at least 10 years of initial training in Indian classical dance. The Fellows would be required to have given at least 2–3 solo performances to his/her credit in recognized forums.

Level of Study: Professional development

Type: Fellowships

Value: Indian Rupees 50,000

Length of Study: 10 months

Frequency: Annual

Application Procedure: Applicants must send their 2 page curriculum vitae and a writeup of approx. 500 words, explaining their project. Full postal and telephone contact details together with any email id should be submitted to facilitate contact. Few samples of previous work, project or performances should be submitted. The names and contact addresses/telephones of 2 referees should also be sent.

Funding: Foundation

Additional Information: The candidate should not be holding any other fellowship or working on any other project at the same time.

Mani Mann Fellowship in Indian Classical Vocal Music

Subjects: Indian classical music.

Purpose: To encourage promising young artists to advance in their field. This fellowship will enable the recipient to have the resources and time to dedicate to the art.

Eligibility: Open to Indian nationals in the age group of 25–40. Applicants must hold a degree/diploma from a recognized university or institution in the field and/or the candidates should have at least 10 years of initial training in Indian classical music.

Level of Study: Professional development

Type: Fellowship

Value: Indian Rupees 1,00,000

Length of Study: 3–12 months

Frequency: Annual

Country of Study: India

Application Procedure: Candidates should send their 2 page curriculum vitae and a writeup of approximately 500 words explaining their project. Full postal and telephone contact details together with any email id should be submitted to facilitate contact. Few samples of previous work, project or performances should be submitted. The names and contact addresses/telephones of 2 referees should also be sent.

Funding: Foundation

Prabha Dutt Fellowship in Journalism

Subjects: Journalism.

Purpose: To encourage young mid-career women journalists to develop their potential by pursuing meaningful projects without having to work under the pressures of short deadlines.

Eligibility: Open to women candidates who are Indian nationals and between 25 and 40 years of age. It is exclusively for print journalists.

Level of Study: Research

Type: Fellowships

Value: Indian Rupees 60,000

Length of Study: 10 months

Frequency: Annual

Country of Study: India

Application Procedure: Applicants must send a two page curriculum vitae and a write-up of about 250–300 words explaining their project. Full postal and telephone contact details together with any email Id should be submitted to facilitate contact, 5 samples of work published should be submitted. The names and contact addresses/telephones of 2 referees should also be sent.

Closing Date: August 31st

Funding: Foundation

Additional Information: The candidate should not be holding another fellowship or working on any other project at the same time.

SAVOY FOUNDATION

230 Foch Street, St Jean Sur Richelieu, QC, J3B 2B2, Canada
Tel: (1) 450 358 9779
Fax: (1) 450 346 1045
Email: epilepsy@savoy-foundation.ca
Website: www.savoy-foundation.ca
Contact: Secretary

The Savoy Foundation's main activity is to support and encourage research into epilepsy.

Savoy Foundation Postdoctoral and Clinical Research Fellowships

Subjects: Medical and behavioural science, as they relate to epilepsy.
Purpose: To support a full-time research project in the field of epilepsy.
Eligibility: Candidates must be scientists or medical specialists with a PhD or MD.
Level of Study: Postdoctorate, Postgraduate, Research
Type: Research grant
Value: Canadian $30,000
Length of Study: 1 year, in the first instance, but will be renewable once, exceptionally, on request
Frequency: Annual
Country of Study: Canada
No. of awards offered: Varies
Application Procedure: Applicants must contact the Foundation or visit the website for application forms and further information.
Closing Date: January 15th
Funding: Foundation, private
Contributor: The Savoy Foundation endowments
No. of awards given last year: 5
No. of applicants last year: 16

Savoy Foundation Research Grants

Subjects: Medical and behavioural science, as they relate to epilepsy.
Purpose: To support further research into epilepsy.
Eligibility: Only available to clinicians and established scientists.
Level of Study: Postdoctorate, Postgraduate, Research
Type: Research grant
Value: Up to Canadian $25,000
Frequency: Annual
Country of Study: Canada
No. of awards offered: Varies
Application Procedure: Applicants must contact the Foundation or visit the website for application forms and further information.
Closing Date: January 15th
Funding: Private, foundation
Contributor: The Savoy Foundation endowments
No. of awards given last year: 7
No. of applicants last year: 20
Additional Information: The grant is only available to Canadian citizens or for projects conducted in Canada.

Savoy Foundation Studentships

Subjects: Biomedicine, neurology and epileptology.
Purpose: To support training and research in a biomedical discipline, the health sciences or social sciences related to epilepsy.
Eligibility: Candidates must have a good university record, e.g. a BSc, MD or equivalent diploma and have ensured that a qualified researcher affiliated to a university or hospital will supervise his or her work. Concomitant registration in a graduate programme is encouraged. The awards are available to Canadian citizens or for projects conducted in Canada.
Level of Study: Doctorate, Postgraduate, Predoctorate
Type: Studentship
Value: The stipend will be Canadian $15,000 per year. An annual sum of Canadian $1,000 will be allocated to the laboratory or institution as additional support for the research project
Length of Study: 1–4 years
Frequency: Annual
Country of Study: Canada
No. of awards offered: Varies
Application Procedure: Applicants must contact the Foundation or visit the website for application forms and further information.

Closing Date: January 15th
Funding: Private, foundation
Contributor: The Savoy Foundation endowments
No. of awards given last year: 6
No. of applicants last year: 21

SCHOOL OF ORIENTAL AND AFRICAN STUDIES (SOAS)

University of London, Thornhaugh Street, Russell Square, London, WC1H 0XG, England
Tel: (44) 20 7074 5091
Fax: (44) 20 7074 5089
Email: as100@soas.ac.uk
Website: www.soas.ac.uk
Contact: Miss Alicia Sales, Scholarships Officer, Registry

The School of Oriental and African Studies (SOAS) regards its role as advancing the knowledge and understanding of the cultures and societies of Asia and Africa and of the School's academic disciplines through high-quality teaching and research.

A K S Postgraduate Korean Studies

Subjects: Korean studies, Korean literature, linguistics (Korean pathway only), Applied linguistics (Korean pathway only) or any other postgraduate degree related to Korean studies.
Purpose: Bursary towards tuition fees.
Level of Study: Postgraduate
Type: Bursary
Value: £4,090 towards tuition fees
Frequency: Annual
Study Establishment: SOAS
Country of Study: United Kingdom
Application Procedure: See website www.soas.ac.uk/scholarships for details.
Funding: Private
Contributor: Academy of Korean Studies

Ahmad Abu-Hakima Scholarship

Subjects: Any subject which includes the history of the modern Arab world.
Purpose: To offset tuition fees for a student taking a full-time master's programme which includes studying the history of the modern Arab world.
Eligibility: Those applicants having academic merit will be considered.
Type: Scholarship
Value: £1,250
Length of Study: 1 year
Study Establishment: SOAS
Country of Study: United Kingdom
Application Procedure: See website www.soas.ac.uk/scholarships for details.
Closing Date: March
Funding: Private

Bernard Buckman Scholarship

Subjects: Chinese studies with an emphasis on modern and contemporary China, although it is possible to study aspects of pre-modern China.
Purpose: To provide fee remission for a student taking a full-time MA course in Chinese studies.
Eligibility: Open to those candidates who qualify to pay for home or European Union tuition fees. Applicants must possess a good Honours Degree from a United Kingdom university or its equivalent.
Level of Study: Postgraduate
Type: Scholarship
Value: Home or European Union postgraduate fee
Length of Study: 1 year
Frequency: Annual
Study Establishment: SOAS
Country of Study: United Kingdom
No. of awards offered: 1

Application Procedure: Applicants must complete an application form, which can be obtained from the registry or downloaded from the website.
Closing Date: March
Funding: Private
No. of awards given last year: 1
No. of applicants last year: 7
Additional Information: Please see the website www.soas.ac.uk/scholarships or contact the organization for further information.

FELIX Scholarship

Subjects: Oriental and African studies in archeology, area studies, economics, ethnomusicology, history, law, languages, linguistics, phonetics, politics, religious study, social anthropology and development studies.
Purpose: For graduates of Indian universities commencing a master's course or researching for a doctoral degree.
Eligibility: A first class bachelor's degree from an Indian university or comparable Indian instituition. Applicants must be below 30 years of age.
Level of Study: Doctorate, Postgraduate
Type: Scholarship
Value: £10,980 per annum plus tuition fees
Length of Study: 1–3 years
Frequency: Annual
Study Establishment: SOAS
Country of Study: United Kingdom
No. of awards offered: 6
Application Procedure: See website www.soas.ac.uk/scholarships for details.
Closing Date: March
Funding: Private
No. of awards given last year: 6

HSBC SOAS Scholarships

Subjects: Sinology or Chinese literature.
Purpose: For UK or EU fee payers commencing a full-time master's course in Sinology or Chinese literature.
Eligibility: Applicants must possess or be about to complete a good honours degree, preferably first class, from a UK instituition or overseas equivalent. Applicants should not be above 25 years.
Level of Study: Postgraduate
Type: Scholarship
Value: £10,600 plus tuition fees at the home EU rate
Length of Study: 1 year
Frequency: Annual
Study Establishment: SOAS
Country of Study: United Kingdom
Application Procedure: see website www.soas.ac.uk/scholarships for details.
Closing Date: March
Contributor: HSBC

Ouseley Memorial Scholarship

Purpose: For a student taking a full-time reasearch degree, requiring the use of a Middle Eastern or Asian language.
Level of Study: Doctorate, Postgraduate
Type: Scholarship
Value: £6,000 for 1 year only
Study Establishment: SOAS
Country of Study: United Kingdom
No. of awards offered: 1
Application Procedure: See website www.soas.ac.uk/scholarships for details.
Closing Date: March
Funding: Private
No. of awards given last year: 1

SOAS Bursary

Subjects: Oriental and African studies in archaeology area studies, economics, ethnomusicology, history, law, languages, linguistics, phonetics, politics, religious studies, social anthropology and development studies.
Purpose: To provide financial assistance to study for a full-time taught Master's programme.

Eligibility: Applicants must possess a good Honours degree, preferably First Class, from a United Kingdom institution or overseas equivalent.
Level of Study: Postgraduate
Type: Bursary
Value: UK £8,300
Length of Study: 1 year, non-renewable
Frequency: Annual
Study Establishment: SOAS
Country of Study: United Kingdom
No. of awards offered: 8
Application Procedure: See website www.soas.ac.uk/scholarships for details.
Closing Date: March
Funding: Government
No. of awards given last year: 8
No. of applicants last year: 350

SOAS Open Scholarship

Subjects: Oriental and African studies in archeology, area studies, economics, ethnomusicology, history, law, languages, linguistics, phonetics, politics, religious studies, social anthropology and development studies.
Purpose: Partial remission of tuition fees.
Eligibility: Applicants must possess a good honours degree preferably first class from a UK institution or overseas equivalent.
Level of Study: Postgraduate
Type: Scholarship
Value: £4,000 for students liable to pay overseas fees; £2,000 for students are unable to pay UK or EU fees
Length of Study: 1 year
Frequency: Annual
Study Establishment: SOAS
Country of Study: United Kingdom
Application Procedure: See website www.soas.ac.uk/scholarship for details.
Closing Date: March
Funding: Government

SOAS Research Student Fellowships

Subjects: The languages and cultures of Africa, East Asia, Near and Middle East, South Asia and South- East Asia, focusing on anthropology and sociology, art and archaeology, development studies, economics, ethnomusicology, financial and management studies, history, law, linguistics, political studies and the study of religions.
Purpose: To support full-time research study at SOAS.
Eligibility: Applications are invited in respect of all subject areas offered by the School. Applicants must possess a good Master's degree from a United Kingdom university or its equivalent.
Level of Study: Doctorate
Type: Fellowship
Value: UK £10,600 plus remission of home or European Union fees
Length of Study: 3 years
Frequency: Annual
Study Establishment: SOAS
Country of Study: United Kingdom
No. of awards offered: 4
Application Procedure: Applicants must complete and submit an application form that can be downloaded from the website.
Closing Date: March
Funding: Government
No. of awards given last year: 4
No. of applicants last year: 120
Additional Information: See website www.soas.ac.uk/scholarships

Sochon Foundation Scholarship

Subjects: Korean studies, Korean literature, Korean study research.
Purpose: For a student undertaking a full-time postgraduate programme in Korean studies.
Level of Study: Doctorate, Postgraduate
Type: Scholarship
Length of Study: 1 year
Study Establishment: SOAS
Country of Study: United Kingdom

Application Procedure: See website www.soas.ac.uk/scholarships for details.
Closing Date: April
Funding: Foundation

William Ross Scholarship
Subjects: LLM.
Purpose: For a student of a developing country unable to pay overseas tuition fees.
Eligibility: Applicants from a developing country who must have a high level of academic achievements.
Level of Study: Postgraduate
Type: Scholarship
Value: Overseas tuition fees. Free accommodation at International Student House and food vouchers
Length of Study: 1 year
Frequency: Annual
Study Establishment: SOAS
Country of Study: United Kingdom
Application Procedure: See www.soas.ac.uk/scholarships for details.
Closing Date: March
Funding: Foundation

SCIENCE FOUNDATION IRELAND

Wilton Park House, Wilton Place, Dublin 2, Ireland
Fax: (353) 353 1 607 3201
Email: info@sfi.ie
Website: www.sfi.ie
Contact: William C Harris, Director

SFI Investigator Programme Grants
Subjects: Biotechnology and information and communications technology (ICT).
Purpose: To support fields of science and engineering that underpin biotechnology and ICT.
Eligibility: Applicants must be distinguished researchers in biotechnology and ICT.
Level of Study: Research
Type: Grant
Value: Up to €250,000 per year
Length of Study: Up to 4 years
Frequency: Annual
Application Procedure: Application forms and support notes can be downloaded from the website.
Funding: Foundation
Contributor: Science Foundation Ireland

SCOTTISH RITE CHARITABLE FOUNDATION OF CANADA (SRFC)

4 Queen Street South, Hamilton, ON, L8P-3R3, Canada
Tel: (1) 905 522 0033
Fax: (1) 905 522 3716
Email: info@srcf.ca
Website: www.srfc.ca
Contact: Manager Information Services

The Scottish Rite Charitable Foundation of Canada (SRFC) is a private charitable foundation, funded by donations and bequests from the 26,000 members of the ancient and accepted SRFC. The SRFC labours for the benefit of all Canadians, regardless of race or creed. Over the years millions of dollars have been disbursed to assist dedicated researchers in a search for the causes and cure of intellectual impairment.

SRFC Graduate Student Research Awards
Subjects: Health and medical sciences.
Purpose: To support students registered in a Doctoral research programme focused on the physical-biological or social aspects of intellectual impairment.

Eligibility: Open to candidates who are enrolled in a Doctoral programme at a Canadian university or research hospital. Applicants must be citizens or a permanent resident of Canada.
Level of Study: Doctorate
Type: Research award
Value: Up to Canadian $10,000
Length of Study: 2 years
Frequency: Annual
Country of Study: Canada
Application Procedure: Application package consists of the application form and application guide. Application form is available online.
Closing Date: April 30th
Funding: Foundation

SRFC Major Research Grant for Biomedical Research into Intellectual Impairment
Subjects: Health and medical sciences.
Purpose: To support biomedical research into intellectual impairment.
Eligibility: Open to researchers who have or are offered at least a 3 year academic appointment at a Canadian university or research hospital. Applicants must be Canadian citizens or permanent resident.
Level of Study: Research
Type: Research grant
Value: Canadian $35,000
Country of Study: Canada
No. of awards offered: 10
Application Procedure: Applicants must submit their application form and research proposal.
Closing Date: April 30th
Funding: Foundation
Additional Information: The focus of research should be on the causes and cure of the disease as opposed to the active treatment or palliative care.

SCOULOUDI FOUNDATION

The Institute of Historical Research, University of London, Senate House, London, WC1E 7HU, England
Tel: (44) 20 7862 8740
Fax: (44) 20 7862 8740
Email: james.lees@sas.ac.uk
Website: www.history.ac.uk
Contact: James Lees, Fellowships Officer

The IHR is an important resource and meeting place for scholars from all over the world. It contains an outstanding open access library, runs courses and major conferences, offers research fellowships and other awards and produces many significant research aids and tools.

Economic History Society Research Fellowships
Subjects: Economic and social history.
Purpose: To help candidates at an advanced stage of a PhD to complete their doctorates or to fund 1 year of postdoctoral study in history.
Eligibility: Open to postdoctoral candidates who have recently completed a doctoral degree in economic or social history or to graduates who are engaged in the completion of a doctoral degree in economic or social history and who have completed 2 years, but not more than 4 years of full-time or 8 years part-time research on their chosen topics. Fellowships are open to citizens of the United Kingdom or to candidates with a degree from a university in the United Kingdom.
Level of Study: Doctorate, Postdoctorate
Type: Fellowship
Value: In line with ESRC rates (approx. UK £12,000 per year)
Length of Study: 1 year
Frequency: Dependent on funds available
Study Establishment: An institute of historical research
Country of Study: England
No. of awards offered: 3
Application Procedure: Applicants must complete an application form, available from the Fellowship Officer in early January.
Closing Date: April 3rd
Funding: Foundation
Contributor: The Economic History Society
No. of awards given last year: 3

Scouloudi Foundation Historical Awards

Subjects: History or a related subject.

Purpose: To provide subsidies towards the cost of publishing a book or article in the field of history, incorporating an academic thesis or other scholarly work already accepted by a reputable publisher or learned journal or to pay for special expenses incurred in the completion of advanced historical work such as the cost of fares and subsistence during visits to libraries or record repositories.

Eligibility: Open to graduates of United Kingdom universities who possess a relevant Honours degree, or United Kingdom citizens with a similar qualification from a university outside the United Kingdom. These awards are not made for study or research towards a postgraduate qualification, e.g. work on thesis for higher degrees.

Type: Varies

Value: UK £100–1,000. Applicants should not ask for more than their minimum requirements for the year concerned

Frequency: Dependent on funds available, Publication

Study Establishment: None

Country of Study: Any country

No. of awards offered: Varies

Application Procedure: Applicants must complete an application form.

Closing Date: Early March

Funding: Private

Contributor: The Scouloudi Foundation

SEMICONDUCTOR RESEARCH CORPORATION (SRC)

PO Box 12053, Research Triangle Park, NC, 27709, United States of America
Tel: (1) 919 941 9400
Fax: (1) 919 941 9450
Email: students@src.org
Website: www.src.org
Contact: Fellowships Office

The Semiconductor Research Corporation (SRC) is a consortium of about 60 semiconductor manufacturers and equipment makers. The SRC manages a research portfolio in major research universities throughout the world. At any given time it supports about 700 advanced degree students on contract research, 45 graduate Fellows and 15 Master's scholars. The SRC supports a pragmatic approach to developing student programmes and provides industry interactions and other opportunities for its students.

SRC Master's Scholarship Program

Subjects: Electrical engineering, computer engineering, chemical engineering, mechanical engineering, materials science, physics and related areas.

Purpose: To attract underrepresented minorities and women to disciplines of interest to the semiconductor industry.

Eligibility: Open to students having United States of America citizenship or permanent resident status. Students are also required to be from underrepresented minorities, e.g. African American, Native American, Hispanic.

Level of Study: Postgraduate

Type: Scholarship

Value: Please contact the organization

Length of Study: 2 years or until completion of the Master's degree, whichever comes first

Frequency: Annual

Study Establishment: Universities having SRC-funded contracts. A list is available at the website

Country of Study: United States of America

No. of awards offered: Varies

Application Procedure: Applicants must complete an application form. Applications are distributed through SRC-funded faculty in November with a due date early in February. Applications are also distributed through other avenues outside the SRC community and applications are encouraged from non-SRC-funded colleges.

Closing Date: February 15th

Funding: Commercial

Contributor: The semiconductor industry

No. of awards given last year: 14

No. of applicants last year: 30

Additional Information: Recipients are required to be associated with an SRC-funded contract. Resources are available to assist qualified students in identifying suitable faculty within SRC-funded universities. SRC contracts support precompetitive research in areas of interest to the semiconductor industry.

SEOUL NATIONAL UNIVERSITY

San 56-1, Sillim-dong, Gwanak-gu, Seoul, 151-742, Korea
Tel: (82) 2 880 5488
Fax: (82) 2 871 6907
Email: snuadmit@snu.ac.kr
Website: www.snu.ac.kr
Contact: MBA Admissions Officer

Korea-Japan Cultural Association Scholarship

Subjects: Humanities and social-science.

Eligibility: Open to outstanding Japanese scholars receiving an education in Korea.

Level of Study: Postdoctorate, Postgraduate, Research

Type: Scholarship

Value: KRW 3,500,000

Length of Study: 1 academic year

Frequency: Annual

Study Establishment: Seoul National University

Country of Study: Korea

Application Procedure: Contact the Office of International Affairs.

Closing Date: March

Funding: Foundation

Contributor: Korea-Japan Cultural Association

For further information contact:

Tel: 2 880 8635
Fax: 2 880 8632
Email: yss@snu.ac.kr
Contact: Mr Sung Sub Yoon

Korean Government Scholarship

Subjects: Korean studies.

Purpose: To further international bilateral cultural agreement with Korea.

Eligibility: Applicants must be under 40 years of age as of September 1st.

Level of Study: Postgraduate, Research, Postdoctorate

Type: Scholarship

Value: All airfares, living expenses, tuition fees, research allowance, settling and repatriation allowance, language training expenses, dissertation publication costs and insurance

Frequency: Annual

Study Establishment: Seoul National University

Country of Study: Korea

Application Procedure: Contact the Korean Embassy in residing country or see website.

Closing Date: No deadline

Funding: Government

For further information contact:

Website: www.studyinkorea.go.kr

Overseas Korean Foundation Scholarship

Subjects: Korean studies.

Purpose: To support students with an outstanding academic record.

Eligibility: Preference is given to Korean students with majors related to Korean studies, in particular: language, literature, medicine, education or IT, which are beneficial to the development of Korea.

Level of Study: Postgraduate, Postdoctorate, Research

Type: Scholarship

Value: KRW 2,000,000

Length of Study: 1 year

Frequency: Annual

Application Procedure: Contact the Overseas Korean Foundation.

Closing Date: March–April

For further information contact:

Education Department, Overseas Korean Foundation, Seocho 2-dong, Seocho-gu, Seoul, (137-072)
Tel: 2 3463 5322 (ext. 405)
Fax: 2 3463 3999
Email: yhs6543@okf.or.kr
Contact: Coordinator

SHELBY CULLOM DAVIS CENTER FOR HISTORICAL STUDIES

129 Dickinson Hall, Princeton University, Princeton, NJ, 08544-1017, United States of America
Tel: (1) 609 258 4997
Fax: (1) 609 258 5326
Email: jhoule@Princeton.EDU
Website: www.princeton.edu
Contact: Ms Jennifer Houle, The Manager

The Davis center for historical studies was founded in 1968 to assure the continuance of excellence in scholarship and the teaching of history at Princeton University.

Shelby Cullom Davis Center Research Projects, Research Fellowships

Subjects: History.
Purpose: To support research.
Eligibility: Applicants must have completed a PhD.
Level of Study: Postdoctorate
Type: Fellowship
Length of Study: 1–2 semesters
Frequency: Annual
Study Establishment: Shelby Cullom Davis Center
Country of Study: United States of America
No. of awards offered: Varies
Application Procedure: Applications are available online.
Closing Date: December 1st
Funding: Private
No. of awards given last year: 7

SHORENSTEIN ASIA-PACIFIC RESEARCH CENTER (APARC)

Encina Hall, Room E301, 616 Serra Street, Stanford University, Stanford, CA, 94305-6055, United States of America
Tel: (1) 650 723 2408
Fax: (1) 650 723 6530
Email: sishi@stanford.edu
Website: www.aparc.stanford.edu

Shorenstein Asia-Pacific Research Center (APARC) is an important Stanford venue where faculty and students, visiting scholars and distinguished business and government leaders meet and exchange views on contemporary Asia and United States involvement in the region.

Shorenstein APARC Postdoctoral Research Fellowship in Korean Studies

Subjects: Contemporary political, economic and social change in the Asia-Pacific region.
Purpose: To financially support research and writing on Asia.
Eligibility: Open to candidates who have obtained a PhD.
Level of Study: Doctorate, Postdoctorate
Type: Fellowships
Value: Approx US$40,000
Length of Study: 1 year
Frequency: Annual
Country of Study: Asia
No. of awards offered: 3
Application Procedure: Applicants must submit a research proposal, a curriculum vitae and letters of recommendation.
Closing Date: Varies
Funding: Private

No. of awards given last year: 2
No. of applicants last year: 75 +

For further information contact:

Tel: 650 723 2408
Email: sishi@stanford.edu
Contact: sabrina Ishimatsu

SIDNEY SUSSEX COLLEGE

Cambridge, Cambridgeshire, CB2 3HU, England
Tel: (44) 12 2333 8810
Fax: (44) 12 2376 5744
Email: gradtutor@sid.cam.ac.uk
Website: www.sid.cam.ac.uk
Contact: Tutor for Graduate Students

Founded in 1596, Sidney Sussex College admits men and women as undergraduates and graduates. The college presently has 180 graduate students, including 100 working for the PhD degree. The college has excellent sporting, dramatic and musical facilities.

Evan Lewis Thomas Law Bursaries and Studentships

Subjects: Law.
Purpose: To support students carrying out research or taking advanced courses.
Eligibility: There are no eligibility restrictions. Candidates must have shown proficiency in Law and Jurisprudence, normally by obtaining a university degree in Law by August 2006, and they must be or become candidates for the PhD Degree, the Diploma in Legal Studies, the Diploma in International Law, the MPhil Degree (1 year course) in Criminology, or the LL.M Degree. Only candidates for the PhD Degree may apply for Evan Lewis Thomas Studentship offered by the College.
Level of Study: Doctorate, Postgraduate
Type: Studentships and bursaries
Length of Study: 1–3 years
Frequency: Annual
Study Establishment: The University of Cambridge
Country of Study: United Kingdom
No. of awards offered: 3–4
Application Procedure: Those wishing to apply for this award may either go to the link www.admin.cam.ac.uk/offices/gradstud/admissions/forms/Cambridge graduate.pdf and print pages 7–12 or make a copy of the corresponding on-line application pages. (this is the form you should have already completed for your application to the University) You must send this duplicate form directly to Sidney Sussex, fully completed, including the names of your references and your photograph. You must also send us a copy of your research proposal as submitted to the Faculty to which you have applied. Please do not send transcripts and indicate on the top of the front page of the application form as Even Lewis Thomas Studentship/Bursaries.
Closing Date: March 31st
Funding: Private
Contributor: Sidney Sussex College
Additional Information: For further information contact the Tutor for Graduate Students at gradtutor@sid.cam.ac.uk.

For further information contact:

Email: gradtutor@sid.cam.ac.uk

The Howard Research Studentship

Subjects: All subjects.
Purpose: To provide full support for research leading to a PhD degree.
Eligibility: Applicants must apply for a postgraduate place at the University of Cambridge. Preference is given to candidates under 26 years of age.
Level of Study: Doctorate
Type: Studentship
Length of Study: 3 years
Frequency: Annual
Study Establishment: The University of Cambridge
Country of Study: United Kingdom
No. of awards offered: 1

Application Procedure: Those wishing to apply for this award may either go to the link www.admin.cam.ac.uk/offices/gradstud/admissions/forms/Cambridge graduate.pdf and print pages 7–12 or make a copy of the corresponding online application pages (this is the form you should have already completed for your application to the University). You must send this duplicate form directly to Sidney Sussex, fully completed, including the names of your references and your photograph. You must also send us a copy of your research proposal as submitted to the Faculty to which you have applied. Please do not send transcripts and indicate on the top of the front page of the application form – The Sidney Sussex Studentship.

Closing Date: March 31st
Funding: Private
Contributor: Sidney Sussex College
Additional Information: For further information contact the Tutor for Graduate Students at gradtutor@sid.cam.ac.uk.

SIGMA THETA TAU INTERNATIONAL

550 West North Street, Indianapolis, IN, 46202, United States of America
Tel: (1) 888 434 7575
Fax: (1) 317 634 8188
Email: research@stti.iupui.edu
Website: www.nursingsociety.org
Contact: Tonna M.Thomas, Grants Administrative Coordinator

Sigma Theta Tau International exists to promote the development, dissemination and utilization of nursing knowledge. It is committed to improving the health of people worldwide through increasing the scientific base of nursing practice. In support of this mission, the society advances nursing leadership and scholarship, and furthers the utilization of nursing research in healthcare delivery as well as in public policy.

Doris Bloch Research Award
Subjects: Nursing.
Purpose: To encourage qualified nurses to contribute to the advancement of nursing through research. Multidisciplinary and international research is encouraged.
Eligibility: Applicants must be a registered nurse with a current licence, must have received a Master's degree, must have submitted an application package, must be ready to start the research project and must have signed a Sigma Theta Tau International research agreement. Allocation of funds is based on the quality of the proposed research, the future promise of the applicant and the applicant's research budget. Applications from novice researchers who have received no other national research funds are encouraged and will receive preference for funding, other aspects being equal. See website www.nursingsociety.org
Level of Study: Doctorate, Postdoctorate, Postgraduate, Predoctorate, Master's prepared
Type: Research grant
Value: Up to US$5,000
Frequency: Annual
Country of Study: Any country
No. of awards offered: 1
Application Procedure: All applications must be submitted via the online application system. See www.nursingsociety.org for information.
Closing Date: December 1st
Funding: Private
Contributor: Sigma Theta Tau International
No. of awards given last year: 1
Additional Information: Funding date is June 1st.

Rosemary Berkel Crisp Research Award
Subjects: Women's health, oncology and infant or child care.
Purpose: To support nursing research in the critical areas of women's health, oncology and pediatrics.
Eligibility: Open to registered nurses with a current licence who have a Master's or higher degree (those with baccalaureate degrees may be co-investigators), have submitted a complete research application package, are ready to initiate the research project and are Sigma Theta Tau International members. Some preference is given to applicants residing in Illinois, Missouri, Arkansas, Kentucky and Tennessee. See website www.nursingsociety.org. Some preference is given to applicants residing in Illinois, Missouri, Arkansas, Kentucky or Tennessee.
Level of Study: Postdoctorate, Doctorate, Postgraduate, Predoctorate, Master's prepared
Type: Research award
Value: US$5,000
Frequency: Annual
Country of Study: Any country
No. of awards offered: 1
Application Procedure: All applications must be submitted via the online application system. See www.nursingsociety.org for information.
Closing Date: December 1st
Funding: Private
Contributor: The Harry L Crisp II and Rosemary Berkel Crisp Foundation to Sigma Theta Tau International's Research Endowment
No. of awards given last year: 1
Additional Information: The allocation of funds is based on a research project in the area of women's health, oncology or paediatrics that is ready for implementation, the quality of the proposed research, future potential of the application, appropriateness of the research budget and feasibility of the time frame.

Sigma Theta Tau International Small Research Grants
Subjects: Nursing.
Purpose: To encourage nurses to contribute to the advancement of nursing through research.
Eligibility: Open to registered nurses with a current licence who have submitted a complete research application package, have a project ready for implementation, hold a Master's degree, are enrolled in a doctoral programme and have signed a Sigma Theta Tau International research agreement. See website www.nursingsociety.org
Level of Study: Doctorate, Postdoctorate, Postgraduate, Master's prepared
Type: Research grant
Value: Up to US$5,000
Frequency: Annual
Country of Study: Any country
No. of awards offered: 10–15
Application Procedure: All applications must be submitted via the online application system. See www.nursingsociety.org for information.
Closing Date: December 1st
Funding: Foundation, private
Additional Information: This grant has no specific focus; however, multidisciplinary, historical and international research is encouraged. The funding date is June 1st.

Sigma Theta Tau International/Alpha Eta Collaborative Research Grant
Subjects: Nursing.
Purpose: To provide a research grant, up to US $2,000, to Tau Lambda-at-Large chapter members for a new research project in Africa.
Eligibility: The applicant must be a member of the Tau Lambda-at-Large residing in Africa, must submit online a completed research application package and a signed research agreement, and should be ready to implement the research project when funding is received. The applicant should also submit a completed abstract to the Virginia Henderson International Nursing Research Library and credit grant research partners in all publications and presentations of the research, and a final report.
Level of Study: Doctorate, Postdoctorate, Postgraduate
Type: Research grant
Value: Up to US$2,000
Frequency: Annual
Country of Study: Africa
No. of awards offered: 1
Application Procedure: All applications must be submitted through the online submission system. See the website www.nursingsociety.org for information.
Closing Date: December 1st
Contributor: Alpha Eta chapter of Sigma Theta Tau International

Sigma Theta Tau International/American Association of Critical Care Nurses

Subjects: Critical care nursing practice.

Purpose: To encourage qualified nurses to contribute to the advancement of nursing through critical care nursing practice research.

Eligibility: Open to registered nurses with a current licence who have received a Master's degree and submitted a grant proposal relevant to critical care nursing practice. Research must be related to critical care nursing practice. See website www.nursingsociety.org

Level of Study: Doctorate, Postdoctorate, Postgraduate, Predoctorate, Master's prepared

Type: Research grant

Value: Up to US$10,000

Frequency: Annual

Country of Study: Any country

No. of awards offered: 1

Application Procedure: For application please contact the American Association of Critical Care Nurses, Department of Research.

Closing Date: October 1st

Funding: Foundation, private

Contributor: The American Association of Critical Care Nurses and Sigma Theta Tau International

Additional Information: January 1st is the funding date.

For further information contact:

American Association of Critical Care Nurses, Department of Research, 101 Columbia, Aliso Viejo, CA, 92656-1491, United States of America

Tel: (1) 949 362 2000

Fax: (1) 949 362 2020

Sigma Theta Tau International/American Association of Diabetes Educators Grant

Subjects: Diabetes education and care.

Purpose: To encourage qualified nurses to contribute to the enhancement of and availability of quality through diabetes education and care through nursing research.

Eligibility: The applicant must be a registered nurse but team members may be from other disciplines. The principal investigator must also have received a Master's degree, and have the ability to complete the project in 1 year from the funding date. Preference will be given to Sigma Theta Tau International members, other qualifications being equal. The grant must be dedicated to diabetes education and care research. See website www.nursingsociety.org

Level of Study: Doctorate, Postdoctorate, Postgraduate, Predoctorate, Master's prepared

Type: Research grant

Value: Up to US$6,000

Frequency: Annual

Country of Study: Any country

No. of awards offered: 1

Application Procedure: For application please contact American Association of Diabetes Educators (AADE).

Closing Date: October 1st

Funding: Foundation, private

Contributor: The American Association of Diabetes Educators and Sigma Theta Tau International

Additional Information: January 1st is the funding date.

For further information contact:

American Association of Diabetes Educators (AADE) Awards, 100 West Monroe Street, Suite 400, Chicago, IL, 60603, United States of America

Tel: (1) 312 424 2426

Fax: (1) 312 424 2427

Sigma Theta Tau International/American Nurses Foundation Grant

Subjects: Any clinical topic.

Purpose: To encourage the research career development of nurses through the support of research conducted by beginning nurse researchers, or experienced nurse researchers who are entering a new field of study.

Eligibility: Open to registered nurses with a current licence and a Master's degree who have submitted a complete research application package, are ready to start the research project and have signed a Sigma Theta Tau International Research agreement. Preference will be given to Sigma Theta Tau International members, other qualifications being equal. See website www.nursingsociety.org

Level of Study: Doctorate, Postdoctorate, Postgraduate, Predoctorate, Master's prepared

Type: Research grant

Value: Up to US$7,500

Frequency: Annual

Country of Study: Any country

No. of awards offered: 1

Application Procedure: Applicants must write for an information booklet and application form. Proposals should be sent to the Sigma Theta Tau International headquarters in even-numbered years (for which applicants should use the Sigma Theta Tau International application), and to the American Nurses Foundation in odd-numbered years (for which applicants should use the American Nurses Foundation application).

Closing Date: May 1st

Funding: Foundation, private

Contributor: The American Nurses Foundation (ANF) and Sigma Theta Tau International

Additional Information: Allocation of funds is based on the quality of the proposed research, the future promise of the applicant and the applicant's research budget. October is the funding month.

For further information contact:

8515 Georgia Avenue, Suite 400 West, Silver Spring, MD, United States of America

Tel: (1) 301 628 5227

Sigma Theta Tau International/Association of Nurses in AIDS Care Grant

Subjects: HIV prevention, symptom management, promotion of self-care and adherence.

Purpose: To encourage research career development of nurses through support of clinically oriented HIV/AIDS research and increase the number of HIV studies being done by nurses.

Eligibility: Open to candidates who have obtained a master's degree and/or are enrolled in a doctoral programme, must be a registered nurse with current license. For further information please see the website.

Level of Study: Research

Type: Grant

Value: $2,500

Length of Study: 1 year

Frequency: Annual

No. of awards offered: 1

Application Procedure: All applications must be submitted via the online submission system. See website www.nursingsociety.org for information.

Closing Date: April 3rd

Contributor: ANAC and Sigma Theta Tau International

Sigma Theta Tau International/Association of Perioperative Registered Nurses Foundation Grant

Subjects: Perioperative nursing practice.

Purpose: To encourage nurses to conduct research related to perioperative nursing practice and contribute to the development of perioperative nursing science.

Eligibility: Applicants must be a registered nurse with a current license in the perioperative setting, or a registered nurse who demonstrates interest in or significant contributions to nursing practice. The principal investigator must have, as a minimum, a Master's degree in nursing. Applicants must submit a completed Association of Perioperative Registered Nurses (AORN) research application. Membership of either organization is acceptable, but not required. See website www.nursingsociety.org

Level of Study: Doctorate, Postdoctorate, Postgraduate, Predoctorate, Master's prepared

Type: Research grant

Value: US$5,000. Allocation of funds is based on the quality of the research, the future promise of the applicant and the applicant's research budget
Frequency: Annual
Country of Study: Any country
No. of awards offered: 1
Application Procedure: Applicants must write to the AORN for an application form and general instructions.
Closing Date: April 1st
Funding: Foundation, private
Contributor: The Association of Perioperative Registered Nurses and Sigma Theta Tau International
Additional Information: July is the funding month.

For further information contact:

Association of Perioperative Registered Nurses (AORN), 2170 South Parker Road, Suite 300, Denver, CO, 80231-5711, United States of America
Tel: (1) 800 755 2676 ext. 277
Fax: (1) 303 750 2927
Email: sbeya@aorn.org
Website: www.aorn.org

Sigma Theta Tau International/Canadian Nurses Foundation Grant

Subjects: Nursing care.
Purpose: To support research on nursing care issues and build nursing research capacity.
Eligibility: Open to candidates who are registered nurses with current license and active members of Sigma Theta Tau International. Preference given to Canadian registered nurses with 4 current license. For further information please see the website.
Level of Study: Research
Type: Grant
Value: $4950
No. of awards offered: 1
Application Procedure: All applications must be submitted via the online submission system. See www.nursingsociety.org for further information.
Closing Date: December 1st
Contributor: Canadian Nurses Foundation and Sigma Theta Tau International

Sigma Theta Tau International/Emergency Nurses Association Foundation Grant

Subjects: Topics relating to the specialized practice of emergency nursing. All relevant subjects will be considered, although priority will be given to studies that relate to the Association's Research Initiatives, which include, but are not limited to, mechanisms to assure effective, efficient and quality emergency nursing care delivery systems, factors affecting healthcare cost, productivity and market forces to emergency services, ways to enhance health promotion and injury prevention, and mechanisms to assure quality and cost-effective educational programmes for emergency nursing.
Purpose: To encourage nursing research that will advance the specialized practice of emergency nursing.
Eligibility: Applicants must be a registered nurse, but team members may be from other disciplines. Applicants must have a Master's degree, submit a complete application with signed research agreement and be ready to or have already started the research project. See website www.nursingsociety.org
Level of Study: Doctorate, Postdoctorate, Postgraduate, Predoctorate, Master's prepared
Type: Research grant
Value: Up to US$6,000
Frequency: Annual
Country of Study: Any country
No. of awards offered: 1
Application Procedure: For application please contact Emergency Nurses Association (ENA) Foundation.
Closing Date: February 1st
Funding: Foundation, private
Contributor: The Emergency Nurses Association Foundation and Sigma Theta Tau International
Additional Information: July 1st is the funding date.

For further information contact:

Emergency Nurses Association (ENA) Foundation, 915 Lee Street, Des Plaines, IL, 60016-6569, United States of America
Tel: (1) 847 460 4100
Fax: (1) 847 460 4005

Sigma Theta Tau International/Hospice and Palliative Nurses Foundation Grant

Subjects: Hospice and palliative care nursing.
Purpose: To encourage qualified nurses to contribute to the advancement of nursing care through research.
Eligibility: Open to candidates who have obtained a Master's or Doctoral degree or are enrolled in a doctoral programme. The candidate must be a registered nurse with current license and must sign a research grant agreement. For further information please see the website.
Level of Study: Doctorate, Postdoctorate, Postgraduate, Predoctorate, Master's prepared
Type: Research grant
Value: Up to US$10,000
Frequency: Annual
No. of awards offered: 1
Application Procedure: All applications must be submitted via the online submission system. See www.nursingsociety.org for further information.
Closing Date: April 3rd
Funding: Foundation, private
Contributor: Sigma Theta Tau International and the Hospice and Palliative Nurses Foundation
Additional Information: The funding date is August 1st.

Sigma Theta Tau International/Joan K. Stout, RN, Research Grant

Subjects: Nursing.
Purpose: To advance ongoing evidence-based study by nurse researchers on the impact of the practice of simulation education in schools of nursing and clinical care settings.
Eligibility: The applicant should be a registered nurse with a current license, have a Master's degree or be enrolled in a doctoral program. The applicant should be ready to implement the rearch project when funding is received, complete the project within 1 year of funding, submit a completed abstract to the Virginia Henderson International Nursing Research Library and a final report to Sigma Theta Tau International.
Level of Study: Predoctorate, Postgraduate
Type: Research grant
Value: Up to $5,000
Frequency: Annual
Country of Study: Any country
No. of awards offered: 1
Application Procedure: A completed research application must be submitted through the online submission system. See www.nursingsociety.org for information.
Closing Date: July 1st
Funding: Foundation
Contributor: Sigma Theta Tau International Foundation

Sigma Theta Tau International/Midwest Nursing Research Society Research Grant

Subjects: Multi-disciplinary, historical and international research.
Purpose: To encourage qualified nurses to contribute to the advancement of nursing through research.
Eligibility: Open to candidates who have obtained a master's degree and/or are enrolled in a doctoral programme. The candidate must also be a registered nurse with current license and be a Midwest Nursing Research Society and a honor society member in good standing. For further information please see the website.
Level of Study: Doctorate, Postdoctorate, Postgraduate, Predoctorate, Master's prepared
Type: Research grant
Value: Up to US$2,500
Frequency: Annual
No. of awards offered: 1

Application Procedure: All applications must be submitted via the online submission system. See www.nursingsociety.org for information.
Closing Date: April 3rd
Funding: Foundation, private
Contributor: Sigma Theta Tau International and the Midwest Nursing Research Society
Additional Information: The funding date is August 1st.

Sigma Theta Tau International/National League for Nursing Grant (NLN)

Subjects: Nursing.
Purpose: To support research that advances the science of nursing education and learning through the use of technology in dissemination of knowledge.
Eligibility: The applicant must be a registered nurse with a current license, hold a master's or doctoral degree or be enrolled in a doctoral program. The applicant must complete a project within one year of funding and must sign a Research Grant Agreement. Preference will be given to Sigma Theta Tau International and National League for Nursing members.
Level of Study: Doctorate, Postdoctorate, Postgraduate, Predoctorate
Type: Grant
Value: Up to US$5,000
Country of Study: Any country
No. of awards offered: 1
Application Procedure: All applications must be submitted via the online submission system. See www.nursingsociety.org for information.
Closing Date: June 1st
Funding: Individuals
Additional Information: Funding date is 1st November.

Sigma Theta Tau International/Oncology Nursing Society Grant

Subjects: Clinical oncology.
Purpose: To simulate clinically related oncology nursing research.
Eligibility: Open to registered nurses who are actively involved in some aspect of cancer patient care, education or research and hold a Master's degree. Preference will be given to Sigma Theta Tau members, other qualifications being equal. See website www.nursingsociety.org
Level of Study: Doctorate, Postdoctorate, Postgraduate, Predoctorate, Master's prepared
Type: Research grant
Value: Up to US$10,000
Frequency: Annual
Country of Study: Any country
No. of awards offered: 1
Application Procedure: Applicants must send proposals for this grant to the Oncology Nursing Society.
Closing Date: November 1st
Funding: Foundation, private
Contributor: The Oncology Nursing Society and Sigma Theta Tau International
Additional Information: The funding date is March 15th.

For further information contact:

Oncology Nursing Society, 125 Enterprise Drive, RIDC Park West, Pittsburgh, PA, 15275-1214, United States of America
Tel: (1) 412 859 6100
Fax: (1) 877 369 5497
Website: www.ons.org

Sigma Theta Tau International/Rehabilitation Nursing Foundation Grant

Subjects: Rehabilitation nursing.
Purpose: To encourage research related to rehabilitation nursing.
Eligibility: The applicant must be a registered nurse in rehabilitation or a registered nurse who demonstrates interest in and significantly contributes to rehabilitation nursing. Proposals that address the clinical practice, educational or administrative dimensions of rehabilitation nursing are requested. Quantitative and qualitative research projects

will be accepted for review. The principal investigator must have a Master's degree in nursing and an ability to complete the project within 2 years of initial funding. See website www.nursingsociety.org
Level of Study: Doctorate, Postdoctorate, Postgraduate, Predoctorate, Master's prepared
Type: Research grant
Value: Up to US$4,000
Frequency: Annual
Country of Study: Any country
No. of awards offered: 1
Application Procedure: Applicants must write to the Rehabilitation Nursing Foundation for details.
Closing Date: February 1st
Funding: Foundation, private
Contributor: The Rehabilitation Nursing Foundation and Sigma Theta Tau International
Additional Information: The funding month is the following January.

For further information contact:

Rehabilitation Nursing Foundation, 4700 West Lake Avenue, Glenview, IL, 60025, United States of America
Tel: (1) 847 375 4710
Fax: (1) 847 375 4710
Email: info@rehabnurse.org

Sigma Theta Tau International/Southern Nursing Research Society Grant

Subjects: Nursing.
Purpose: To encourage qualified nurses to contribute to the advancement of nursing through research. Proposals for pilot and/or development research may be submitted for this grant.
Eligibility: The applicant must: be a registered nurse with a current license, hold at the minimum a Master's degree or its equivalent and/or be enrolled for a doctoral program, and be a member in good standing of both the STTI and SNRS. He or she must submit online a completed research application package and a signed research agreement, and should be ready to implement the research project when funding is received; however, the research may not be conducted as part of an academic degree. The applicant should also submit a completed abstract to STTI's Virginia Henderson International Nursing Research Library, an abstract for publication to SNRS, and credit grant research partners in all publications and presentations of the research, and a final report to STTI.
Level of Study: Postgraduate, Predoctorate
Type: Research grant
Value: Up to US $5,000
Frequency: Annual
Country of Study: Any country
No. of awards offered: 1
Application Procedure: All applications must be submitted via the online submisson system. See the website www.nursingsociety.org for information.
Closing Date: April 1st
Funding: Foundation
Contributor: Sigma Theta Tau International Foundation and Southern Nursing Research Society

Sigma Theta Tau International/The Council for the Advancement of Nursing Science

Subjects: Nursing.
Purpose: To encourage qualified nurses to improve the health of the world's people through research. Proposals for clinical, educational or historical research, including plans for disseminating the research findings, may be submitted for the grant.
Eligibility: Preference will be given to a Sigma Theta Tau International member who holds at the minimum a Master's degree or its equivalent. He or she must submit online a completed research application package and should be ready to implement the research project when funding is received. The applicant should also submit a completed abstract to STTI's Virginia Henderson International Nursing Research Library, a completed project abstract for presentation to the Sigma Theta Tau International or the Council for the Advancement of Nursing Science, and credit grant research partners in all publications and presentations of the research.
Level of Study: Postgraduate, Predoctorate

Type: Research grant
Value: Up to $5,000
Frequency: Annual
Country of Study: Any country
No. of awards offered: 1
Application Procedure: All applications must be submitted via the online submission system. See the website www.nursingsociety.org for information.
Closing Date: July 1st
Funding: Foundation
Contributor: Sigma Theta Tau International Foundation and The Council for the Advancement of Nursing Science
No. of awards given last year: 1

Sigma Theta Tau International/Virginia Henderson Clinical Research Grant

Subjects: Clinical research.
Purpose: To encourage the research career development of clinically based nurses through support of clinically orientated research.
Eligibility: Open to registered nurses actively involved in some aspect of healthcare delivery, education or research in a clinical setting, who are Theta Tau International members, hold a Master's degree in nursing or are enrolled in a doctoral programme. The allocation of funds is based on a research project ready for implementation, the quality of the proposed research, the future potential of the applicant, appropriateness of the research budget and feasibility of the time frame. See website www.nursingsociety.org
Level of Study: Doctorate, Postdoctorate, Postgraduate, Predoctorate, Master's prepared
Type: Research grant
Value: US$5,000
Frequency: Every 2 years
Country of Study: Any country
No. of awards offered: 1
Application Procedure: All applications must be submitted via the online submission system. See www.nursingsociety.org for information.
Closing Date: December 1st in odd-numbered years
Funding: Private
Contributor: The Virginia Henderson Clinical Research Endowment Fund
Additional Information: June is the funding month.

Sigma Theta Tau International/Western Institute of Nursing Research Grant

Subjects: Nursing.
Purpose: To encourage qualified nurses to contribute to the advancement of nursing through research.
Eligibility: Open to a registered nurse with a current license, who has a master's degree and/or is enrolled in a doctoral programme. The applicant must be a member of Western Institute of Nursing and Sigma Theta Tau International.
Level of Study: Doctorate, Postdoctorate, Postgraduate, Predoctorate, Master's prepared
Value: Up to US$2,500
Frequency: Annual
Country of Study: Any country
No. of awards offered: 1
Application Procedure: All applications must be submitted via the online submission system. See www.nursingsociety.org for information.
Closing Date: December 1st
Funding: Foundation
Contributor: Sigma Theta Tau International and the Western Institute of Nursing
Additional Information: The funding date is April 1st.

SILVERHILL INSTITUTE OF ENVIRONMENTAL RESEARCH AND CONSERVATION

Box 100, Schomberg, ON, L0G-1T0, Canada
Email: peter@silverhillinstitute.com
Website: www.silverhillinstitute.com
Contact: Dr Peter Homenuck, RPP

The Silverhill Institute of Environmental Research and Conservation was established as a charitable foundation in 2004. This foundation was established according to the Canada Corporations Act. It supports demonstration projects to develop, maintain and preserve wood lots. It also supports wetland protection and restoration as means for conservation and contributing to diversity and the protection of groundwater and surface water resources, and carries out research on environmental issues of the day.

Silverhill Institute of Environmental Research and Conservation Award

Subjects: Geography, environmental studies, ecology, biology, natural resources, planning, forestry and water resources.
Purpose: To financially support students for thesis/research projects that have an applied environmental or conservation focus and that have the potential to contribute in a direct way to society and/or provide specific community benefit.
Eligibility: Open only to graduate students for research (thesis or major paper) that is applied in nature and can be demonstrated to have community benefit or applicability.
Level of Study: Postgraduate, Research
Type: Grant
Value: Canadian $3,500 for the Summer season
Frequency: Annual
Study Establishment: University of Manitoba
Country of Study: Canada
No. of awards offered: Varies
Application Procedure: All applicants are to provide a 2 page summary of the proposed research along with the timeframe and workplan that will be undertaken. Application forms are available online.
Closing Date: February 28th
Additional Information: The grant will be paid out as follows: Canadian $2,500 upon selection and Canadian $1,000 upon receipt of a copy of the finished theses/product.

SIMON FRASER UNIVERSITY

8888 University Drive, Burnaby, BC, V5A 1S6, Canada
Tel: (1) 604 291 5310
Email: pchhina@sfu.ca
Website: www.business.sfu.ca
Contact: Ms Preet Virk, Manager, Donor Relations

Named after explorer Simon Fraser, SFU opened on September 9, 1965. Taking only 30 months to grow from the idea stage into an almost-completed campus with 2,500 students it was dubbed the "Instant University". The original campus has grown into three vibrant campuses in Burnaby, Vancouver and Surrey and SFU's reputation has grown into one of the innovative teaching, research, and community outreach.

The Canada Graduate Scholarship (CGS) Master's Program

Subjects: All subjects.
Eligibility: Open to those pursuing a first Graduate Degree.
Level of Study: Graduate
Type: Scholarship
Value: $17,500 per year
Length of Study: 1 year
Frequency: Annual
Application Procedure: Check website for further details.
Closing Date: November 5th

The Canada Graduate Scholarships Program (CGS)

Subjects: All subjects.
Eligibility: Open to candidates who are eligible to apply for the NSERC or SSHRC annual competition.
Value: $17,500
Length of Study: 1 year
Application Procedure: Check website for further details.
Contributor: NSERC and SSHRC
Additional Information: Applicants who apply for the NSERC or SSHRC annual competitions are also considered.

DCGS Doctoral Scholarships

Subjects: Humanities and social sciences.
Purpose: To provide doctoral support in the humanities and social sciences.
Eligibility: Open to Canadian citizens or permanent residents, who have completed a Master's Degree or at least 1 year of doctoral study and pursuing full time studies leading to a first PhD or its equivalent.
Level of Study: Postgraduate, Predoctorate
Type: Scholarship
Value: $35,000 per year
Length of Study: Up to 3 years
Frequency: Annual
Country of Study: Canada
Application Procedure: Candidates can avail information from the Office of the Dean of Graduate Studies, or check the website.
Closing Date: November 5th
Additional Information: The deadline for applications to the appropriate SFU department is approximately October 15th.

For further information contact:

Website: www.sshrc.ca

Methanex Graduate Scholarship in International Marketing

Subjects: International business and marketing.
Purpose: To recognize and reward an outstanding student pursuing an MBA at the Segal Graduate School of Business.
Eligibility: Open to a student with a demonstrated focus on international business and marketing.
Level of Study: Graduate
Type: Scholarship
Value: $5000
Frequency: Annual
Study Establishment: Segal Graduate School of Business
Country of Study: Canada
No. of awards offered: 1
Application Procedure: Check website for further information. Applications are accepted in January.

NSERC Industrial Post-Graduate Scholarships (IPS)

Subjects: Science and engineering.
Purpose: To encourage scholars to consider research careers in industry.
Eligibility: Open to highly qualified science and engineering graduates.
Level of Study: Graduate
Type: Scholarship
Value: $15,000 per year for up to 2 years plus company contribution of $6,000 minimum per year
Length of Study: Up to 2 years
Frequency: Annual
Country of Study: Canada
Application Procedure: Check website for further details.
Closing Date: May apply at any time

NSERC/MITACS Joint Industrial Postgraduate Scholarship (IPS)

Subjects: Mathematics.
Eligibility: Open to any graduate student in Simon Fraser University (SFU) using mathematics in their research.
Level of Study: Graduate
Type: Scholarship
Value: $22,000
Length of Study: Up to 3 years
Frequency: Annual
Study Establishment: Simon Fraser University (SFU)
Country of Study: Canada
Application Procedure: Check website address for further details.

Peter Legge Graduate Volunteer Leadership Award in Business

Subjects: Business administration.
Purpose: To provide financial support for graduate students pursuing or entering a degree at the Segal Graduate School of Business.

Eligibility: Open to graduate students pursuing a degree at the Segal Graduate School of Business.
Level of Study: Graduate
Type: Award
Value: $5,000
Frequency: Annual
Study Establishment: Segal Graduate School of Business
Country of Study: Bulgaria
Application Procedure: Check the website for further details.
Additional Information: Candidates must include the application for Private Graduate Scholarship along with the application, resume, cover letter, and letter of reference.

Phi Theta Kappa International Summit Scholarships

Subjects: All subjects.
Eligibility: Open to Phi Theta Kappa members with a minimum 3.75 Grade Point Average and have completed 30 credit hours.
Level of Study: Graduate
Type: Scholarship
Value: Canadian $3,500
No. of awards offered: Up to 3
Application Procedure: Candidates must apply through the website and also mail a package containing paper application form, original or photocopied, a one-page summary of achievements and activities, a copy of recent college transcript, and a copy of Phi Theta Kappa certificate of membership.
Closing Date: April 30th (for fall term), September 30th (for spring term), or January 31st (for summer term)
Additional Information: Students applying from outside Vancouver's Lower Mainland area may be eligible for a travel allowance of $500–1,000. Part-time students and students with a previous bachelor degree are not eligible.

For further information contact:

Entrance Scholarship Program, Student Recruitment, Student Services, MBC 3200, Burnaby, BC, V5A 1S6, Canada
Website: students.sfu.ca/ps

Scotiabank Graduate Scholarship for Women Entrepreneurs

Subjects: Business administration.
Purpose: To provide financial support for a female student enrolling for MBA.
Eligibility: Open to academically excellent female students enrolled full or part-time in an MBA program.
Level of Study: Graduate
Type: Scholarship
Value: $5,000
Frequency: Annual
Application Procedure: Check website for further details.
Additional Information: Candidates must submit a cover letter outlining entrepreneurial experience and a letter of reference from a business colleague or faculty member.

SSHRC Doctoral Fellowships

Subjects: All subjects.
Eligibility: Open to those who are currently in attendance at Simon Fraser University.
Level of Study: Postgraduate
Type: Fellowship
Value: $20,000 per year
Frequency: Annual
Application Procedure: Check website for further details.
Closing Date: Early October
Additional Information: Applications are ranked within subject areas by an SFU committee and recommended applications sent to SSHRC, which announces final results in April or May.

For further information contact:

Website: www.sshrc.ca

TCG International Graduate Scholarship in Business Administration

Subjects: Business administration.

Purpose: To support for a student in the MBA program.
Eligibility: Open to academically excellent (CGPA>3.5) graduates. Preference will be given to a BC resident.
Level of Study: Graduate
Type: Scholarship
Value: $8000
Frequency: Annual
No. of awards offered: 1
Application Procedure: Check website for further details. Applications are accepted in September.

Trudeau Foundation Doctoral Scholarship

Subjects: Social sciences and humanities.
Eligibility: Open to outstanding students who are in their first or second year of a PhD programme.
Level of Study: Doctorate, Postgraduate
Type: Scholarship
Value: $50,000
Length of Study: Up to 3 years
Frequency: Annual
No. of awards offered: 15
Application Procedure: Check website for further details.
Closing Date: December 1st
Additional Information: Research must be in one of the four themes of the foundation.

For further information contact:

Website: www.trudeaufoundation.ca

SIR HALLEY STEWART TRUST

22 Earith Road, Willingham, Cambridge, Cambridgeshire, CB24 5LS, England
Tel: (44) 19 5426 0707
Email: email@sirhalleystewart.org.uk
Website: www.sirhalleystewart.org.uk
Contact: Mrs Sue West, Administrator

The Sir Halley Stewart Trust has a Christian basis and is concerned with the development of body, mind and spirit, a just environment and international goodwill. The Trust aims to promote innovative research activities or developments. See www.sirhalley stewart.org.uk

Sir Halley Stewart Trust Grants

Subjects: Medical, social or religious research within certain priority areas.
Purpose: To assist pioneering research and development
Eligibility: Not open to general appeals, building, capital, running costs or personal education including educational and travel costs.
Level of Study: Doctorate, Postgraduate, Predoctorate, Research
Value: Salaries and relevant costs for innovative and imaginative young researchers in the region of UK £15,000–20,000
Length of Study: 2–3 years
Frequency: Dependent on funds available
Study Establishment: A United Kingdom charitable institution, e.g. a hospital, laboratory, university department or charitable organization
Country of Study: Mainly United Kingdom but some overseas, Africa (west/south) given priority
Application Procedure: Applicants must contact the Trust for further details. There is no application form. See website: www.sirhalleystewart.org.uk for the application process. Hard signed copies required by post. Preliminary enquiries available by email/phone call
Closing Date: Applications are accepted at any time
Funding: Private
No. of awards given last year: 47
No. of applicants last year: 537
Additional Information: Further information is available from the Trust's office by obtaining a copy of Notes for those Seeking Grants. The website contains the most up-to-date details.

SIR JOHN SOANE'S MUSEUM FOUNDATION

1040 First Avenue, No. 311, New York, NY, 10022, United States of America
Tel: (1) 212 223 2012
Fax: (1) 860 435 8019
Email: info@soanefoundation.com
Website: www.soanefoundation.com
Contact: Charles A Miller-III, Executive Director

The Sir John Soane's Museum Foundation assists the Museum in London to further Soane's commitment to educate and inspire the general and professional public in architecture and the fine and decorative arts. Programmes have attracted students, collectors, architects, decorators and arts enthusiasts since 1991 to its events, lectures, tours and dinners.

Sir John Soane's Museum Foundation Travelling Fellowship

Subjects: Art, architecture and the decorative arts.
Purpose: To enable scholars to pursue research projects related to the work of Sir John Soane's Museum and its collections.
Eligibility: Open to candidates enrolled in a graduate degree programme in a field appropriate to the Foundation's purpose.
Level of Study: Graduate, Postgraduate
Type: Fellowship
Value: US$5,000
Frequency: Annual
Study Establishment: The choice of the fellowship recipient
Country of Study: Usually the United States of America or the United Kingdom
No. of awards offered: 1
Application Procedure: Applicants must submit a formal proposal of not more than five pages describing the goal, scope and purpose of the research project, in addition to three letters of recommendation. An interview may be required.
Closing Date: March 1st
Funding: Foundation, private
Contributor: The Board of Directors and the Advisory Board
No. of awards given last year: 1
No. of applicants last year: 6
Additional Information: At the end of each research project the award recipient must submit a written documentation or a sketch book on the progress of the research as outlined in the original proposal with respect to goal, scope and allocation of funds, and give a lecture on the research, arranged by the Foundation. The scholar usually spends some time at Sir John Soane's Museum at 13 Lincoln's Inn Fields, London, studying architectural drawings, models and paintings.

SIR RICHARD STAPLEY EDUCATIONAL TRUST

North Street Farmhouse, Sheldwich, Near Faversham, Kent, ME13 0LN, England
Email: admin@stapleytrust.org
Website: www.stapleytrust.org
Contact: Mrs Christine Ford, Administrator

The Sir Richard Stapley Educational Trust awards grants to graduates studying for higher degrees without subject restriction. The Trust will support only one postgraduate degree at a university in the United Kingdom.

Sir Richard Stapley Educational Trust Grants

Subjects: Medical, dental and veterinary science and higher degrees in other subjects.
Purpose: To support postgraduate study.
Eligibility: Open to graduates holding a First Class (Honours) degree or an Upper Second Class (Honours) degree and who are more than 24 years of age on October 1st of the proposed academic year. Students in receipt of a substantial award from local authorities, the NHS Executive, Industry, Research Councils, the British Academy or other similar public bodies will not normally receive a grant from the Trust.

Courses not eligible include electives, diplomas, professional training and intercalated degrees. The Trust does not support students for full-time PhD studies beyond a 3rd year. Applicants must already be resident in the United Kingdom at the time of application.
Level of Study: Postgraduate
Type: Grant
Value: UK £300–1,000
Length of Study: Grants are awarded for 1 full academic year in the first instance
Frequency: Annual
Study Establishment: Any appropriate university
Country of Study: United Kingdom
No. of awards offered: Dependent on availability of funds
Application Procedure: Applicants making enquiries must include a large stamped addressed envelope. Application forms will be sent out and must be returned complete with one academic reference in sealed envelopes on or before March 31st. Applicants will be notified in June.
Closing Date: March 31st
Funding: Commercial, private
No. of awards given last year: 259
No. of applicants last year: 314
Additional Information: Grants are only paid upon receipt of official confirmation of participation in the course as well as confirmation that a financial shortfall still exists. All matters concerning application are communicated by email and letter only.

SIR ROBERT MENZIES MEMORIAL FOUNDATION

210 Clarendon Street, East Melbourne, VIC, Australia
Tel: (61) 394 195 699
Fax: (61) 394 177 049
Email: menzies@vicnet.net.au
Website: www.menziesfoundation.org.au
Contact: Ms S K Mackenzie, General Manager

The Sir Robert Menzies Memorial Foundation was formed as a memorial to Sir Robert Menzies in 1979. It is a non-profit and non-political organization with two principal activities. One is directed to the health and fitness of the Australian community and the other to the promotion of academic excellence.

The Robert Gordon Menzies Scholarship to Harvard
Subjects: All subjects.
Purpose: To encourage students who have gained admission to a Harvard graduate school.
Eligibility: Open to candidates who are Australian citizens who have graduated from an Australian university.
Level of Study: Postgraduate
Type: Scholarship
Value: US$50,000
Frequency: Annual
Study Establishment: Harvard University
Country of Study: United States of America
No. of awards offered: 1
Application Procedure: A completed application form with original academic transcripts must be submitted.
Closing Date: January 31st
Funding: Foundation
Contributor: The Harvard Club of Australia, the Menzies Foundation and the Australian National University
No. of awards given last year: 1
No. of applicants last year: 25

For further information contact:

Council and Boards Secretariat, 1.09 Chancelry Bld 10, The Australian National University, Canberra, ACT 0200, Australia
Contact: Scholarship Administrator and Selection Committee Secretary

Sir Robert Menzies Memorial Research Scholarships in the Allied Health Sciences
Subjects: Occupational therapy, speech pathology, physiotherapy, psychology, nursing, optometry and physical education.

Purpose: To allow an outstanding applicant to carry out doctoral research work that is likely to improve the health of Australians.
Eligibility: Open to Australian citizens of at least 5 years standing. Applicants will generally have completed the first year of their PhD project.
Level of Study: Doctorate, Postgraduate
Type: Scholarship
Value: Australian $25,000 free of income tax
Length of Study: 2 years
Frequency: Annual
Study Establishment: A tertiary institute with appropriate facilities
Country of Study: Australia
No. of awards offered: 2
Application Procedure: Applicants must complete and submit an application form, academic transcripts and other documents. Further information is available on request. Check the website for details.
Closing Date: June 30th
Funding: Private
Contributor: The Sir Robert Menzies Memorial Foundation
No. of awards given last year: 2
No. of applicants last year: 35

Sir Robert Menzies Memorial Scholarships in Law
Subjects: Law.
Purpose: To enable Australian citizens to pursue postgraduate studies in the United Kingdom, generally leading to a higher degree.
Eligibility: Open to Australian citizens of 5 years of standing with at least an Upper Second Class (Honours) Degree in law at the time of application.
Level of Study: Postgraduate
Type: Scholarship
Value: Tuition fees, return airfare, examination and other compulsory fees, an allowance of UK £8,600 p.a. and an additional allowance of UK £150 per month for spouse and UK £30 per month for each dependent child under 16
Length of Study: 1–2 years
Frequency: Annual
Study Establishment: Universities in UK
Country of Study: United Kingdom
No. of awards offered: 1–2
Application Procedure: Applicants must complete and submit an application form along with academic transcripts and other documents. Check website for details.
Closing Date: August 31st
Funding: Private
Contributor: The Sir Robert Menzies Memorial Trust in London, the Foreign and Commonwealth Office, the Australian Department of Education, Science and Training, and the Menzies Foundation in Australia
No. of awards given last year: 2
No. of applicants last year: 40

THE SKIDMORE, OWINGS AND MERRILL FOUNDATION

224 South Michigan Avenue, Suite 1000, Chicago, IL, 60604, United States of America
Tel: (1) 312 427 4202
Fax: (1) 312 360 4551
Email: somfoundation@som.com
Website: www.somfoundation.som.com
Contact: Ms Lisa Westerfield, Administrative Director

The mission of the Skidmore, Owings and Merrill Foundation is to identify and nuture emerging talent by sponsoring prestigious awards and traveling study grants to students of architecture, design, urban design and structural engineering. The SOM foundation identifies and supports individuals with the highest design aspirations, and enables them, through research and travel, to broaden their horizons and achieve excellence in their professional or academic careers. The foundation's goal is to instill in its fellows a heightened sense of reponsibility as future leaders in the design disciplines by offering them an opportunity to deepen their understanding of the complexities of the built environment.

SOM Prize and Travel Fellowship

Subjects: Architecture, design and urban design.
Purpose: To help young architects and designers to broaden their education and take an enlightened view of society's need to improve the built and natural environments.
Eligibility: Open to candidates of any citizenship who are graduating from a university in the United States of America. Fellowship winners must receive, prior to commencement of the fellowship, a Master's or Bachelor's degree in architecture. Students are eligible for nomination in the Spring of the academic year that they are due to graduate.
Level of Study: Graduate, Postgraduate
Type: Fellowship
Value: US$50,000 and US$20,000
Frequency: Annual
Study Establishment: Accredited schools, colleges or universities
Country of Study: United States of America
No. of awards offered: 1 grand prize and 1 travel fellowship
Application Procedure: Applicants must submit a portfolio with a proposed travel itinerary and a signed copyright release statement provided by the Foundation. Complete guidelines are available on request and on the website. Students must be nominated by the United States of America school of attendance.
Funding: Private
No. of awards given last year: 3
Additional Information: Information is sent to schools in January.

Structural Engineering Travelling Fellowship

Subjects: The role of aesthetics, innovation, efficiency and economy in the structural design of buildings, bridges and other structures.
Purpose: To foster an appreciation of the aesthetic potential inherent in the structural design of buildings, bridges and other major works of architecture and engineering.
Eligibility: Open to candidates of any citizenship who are graduating from a university in the United States of America with a Bachelor's, Master's or PhD degree in civil or architectural engineering and a specialization in structural engineering. Applicants must be nominated by the faculty and endorsed by the chair of the department from which they will receive the degree. Applicants must intend to enter the professional practice of structural engineering in the field of buildings or bridges.
Level of Study: Doctorate, Graduate, Postgraduate
Type: Fellowship
Value: US$10,000
Frequency: Annual
Study Establishment: Accredited schools
Country of Study: United States of America
No. of awards offered: 1
Application Procedure: Complete guidelines are available in the website.
Funding: Private
No. of awards given last year: 1
Additional Information: The fellowship hopes to encourage an awareness of the visual impact of structural engineering among engineering students and their schools. It also helps to strengthen the connection between aesthetics and efficiency, economy and innovation in structural design.

THE SMITH AND NEPHEW FOUNDATION

Heron House, 15 Adam Street, London, WC2N 6LA, England
Tel: (44) 20 7960 2276
Fax: (44) 20 7960 2298
Email: barbara.foster@smith-nephew.com
Website: www.snfoundation.org.uk
Contact: Ms Barbara Foster, Foundation Coordinator

To contribute to the development of a robust evidence base which will inform the identification of effective interventions for the management and prevention of skin breakdown and tissue integrity. To concentrate our effort on developing research capacity in this field.

Smith and Nephew Foundation Doctoral Nursing Research Studentship

Subjects: Nursing care of patients in the field of skin breakdown and tissue integrity.
Purpose: To influence and develop evidence-based nursing interventions in the field of skin breakdown and tissue integrity.
Eligibility: Applications are invited from outstanding nurse researchers who will contribute to the evidence base for the nursing care of patients with skin or tissue damage and vulnerability.
Level of Study: Doctorate
Type: Studentship
Value: Up to UK £90,000
Length of Study: Up to 3 years
Frequency: Annual
Country of Study: United Kingdom
No. of awards offered: 2 or 3
Application Procedure: Application forms must be completed. Shortlisted candidates are interviewed in London.
Closing Date: Advertised usually at the beginning of March with a closing date approximately 6 weeks later
Funding: Foundation
Contributor: The Smith and Nephew Foundation
No. of awards given last year: 3
No. of applicants last year: 6
Additional Information: Research which will contribute to the evidence base for the nursing care of patients with skin or tissue damage and vulnerability, particularly in the following areas: factors which influence the physiological response to tissue damage, the role of infection in delayed healing, factors which influence treatment decisions in skin/wound care and hidden cost of tissue damage. Applications which focus on research in other areas of skin, tissue damage or vulnerability will also be considered.

Smith and Nephew Foundation Postdoctoral Nursing Research Fellowship

Subjects: Nursing care of patients in the field of skin breakdown and tissue integrity.
Purpose: To influence and develop evidence-based nursing interventions in the field of skin breakdown and tissue integrity.
Eligibility: Applications are invited from potential Fellows and the proposed host research team or unit. The host research team must be a university school, faculty or department of nursing and have a proven track record of research and development in the nursing care of patients with skin damage or tissue damage or vulnerability.
Level of Study: Postdoctorate
Type: Fellowship
Value: Up to UK £120,000
Length of Study: Up to 3 years
Frequency: Annual
Country of Study: United Kingdom
No. of awards offered: 1
Application Procedure: Application forms must be completed. Shortlisted candidates are interviewed in London.
Closing Date: Advertised usually at the beginning of March with a closing date approximately 6 weeks later
Funding: Foundation
Contributor: The Smith and Nephew Foundation
No. of awards given last year: Nil
No. of applicants last year: Nil
Additional Information: Research which will contribute to the evidence base for the nursing care of patients with skin or tissue damage and vulnerability, particularly in the following areas: Factors which influence the physiological response to tissue damage, the role of infection in delayed healing, factors which influence treatment decisions in skin/wound care, hidden cost of tissue damage. Applications which focus on research in other areas of skin, or tissue damage or vulnerability will also be considered.

SMITHSONIAN ASTROPHYSICS OBSERVATORY (SAO)

60 Garden Street, Mail Stop 47, Cambridge, MA, 02138, United States of America
Email: predoc@cfa.harvard.edu
Website: www.cfa-www.harvard.edu
Contact: Christine A Crowley, Fellowship Programme Coordinator

SAO Predoctoral Fellowships

Subjects: Astronomy, astrophysics, atomic and molecular physics, planetary science, radio and geoastronomy, solar and stellar physics and theoretical astrophysics.
Purpose: To allow students from other institutions throughout the world to undertake their thesis research at the SAO.
Eligibility: Applicants must have completed their preliminary course work and examinations and be ready to begin dissertation research at the time of the award.
Level of Study: Predoctorate
Type: Fellowship
Value: A stipend of US$28,290. Some funds may also be available for relocation, travel and other expenses
Length of Study: 1 year, with a possibility of renewal for up to a total of 3 years
Frequency: Annual
Study Establishment: The Smithsonian Astrophysics Observatory
Country of Study: United States of America
No. of awards offered: Varies
Application Procedure: Applicants must directly contact Smithsonian scientists in their area of interest to discuss possible research topics. Applicants must complete an application form available from the website.
Closing Date: April 15th
No. of awards given last year: 11
No. of applicants last year: 12

SMITHSONIAN ENVIRONMENTAL RESEARCH CENTER (SERC)

PO Box 28, 647 Contees Wharf Road, Edgewater, MD, 21037-0028, United States of America
Tel: (1) 443 482 2217
Fax: (1) 443 482 2380
Email: gustafsond@si.edu
Website: www.serc.si.edu
Contact: Daniel E Gustafson, Jr

Smithsonian Environmental Research Center (SERC) is the world's leading research center for environmental studies of the coastal zone. For over 40 years, SERC has been involved in critical research, professional training for young scientists and environmental education.

SERC Postdoctoral Fellowships

Subjects: Soil and water science, forestry, fishery, Marine biology, botany, zoology, and chemistry.
Purpose: To financially support research at Smithsonian facilities or field stations.
Eligibility: Open to scholars who have held a PhD or equivalent for less than 7 years.
Level of Study: Postdoctorate
Type: Fellowship
Value: US$42,000 per year plus allowances
Length of Study: 3–12 months
Frequency: Annual
Application Procedure: Applicants can download the application from from the website. The completed application form, current curriculum vitae and a formal research proposal must be sent to the Smithsonian Office of Fellowships.
Closing Date: January 15th
Funding: Government
Additional Information: The Smithsonian Institution does not discriminate on grounds of race, creed, sex, age, marital status, condition of disability or national origin of any applicant.

For further information contact:

Office of Fellowships Smithsonian Institution PO Box 37012, 470 L'Enfant Plaza, SW, Washington DC, 20013 7012, United States of America

SERC Predoctoral Fellowships

Subjects: Soil and water science, forestry, fishery, Marine biology, botany, zoology, and chemistry.

Purpose: To facilitate the Smithsonian's scholarly interactions with students and scholars at universities, museums and other research institutions around the world.
Eligibility: Open to doctoral candidates who have completed preliminary course work and examinations and have been advanced to candidacy.
Level of Study: Predoctorate
Type: Fellowship
Value: US$27,000 per year plus allowances
Length of Study: 3–12 months
Frequency: Annual
Application Procedure: Applicants must download the form from the website and submit the completed form with their current curriculum vitae and a formal research proposal to Smithsonian Office of Fellowships.
Closing Date: January 15th
Funding: Government
Additional Information: The Smithsonian Institution does not discriminate on grounds of race, creed, sex, age, marital status, condition of disability or national origin of any applicant.

For further information contact:

Office of Research Training and Services Smithsonian Institution PO Box 37012 470 L'Enfant Plaza, SW, Washington DC, 20013 7012, United States of America

SERC Senior Fellowships

Subjects: Soil and water science, forestry, fishery, Marine biology, botany, zoology, and chemistry.
Purpose: To financially support research at Smithsonian facilities or field stations.
Eligibility: Open to candidates who have received the PhD or equivalent before January 15, 1992.
Level of Study: Research
Type: Fellowship
Value: US$40,000 per year plus allowances
Length of Study: 3–12 months
Frequency: Annual
Country of Study: United States of America
Application Procedure: Applicants can download the application form from the website. The completed application form, current curriculum vitae and a formal research proposal must be sent to the Smithsonian Institution Offfice of Fellowships.
Closing Date: January 15th
Additional Information: Senior fellowship applications may be submitted 2 years in advance.

For further information contact:

Office of Research Training and Services Smithsonian Institution PO Box 37012 470 L'Enfant Plaza, SW, Washington DC, 20013 7012, United States of America

SMITHSONIAN INSTITUTION-NATIONAL AIR AND SPACE MUSEUM

Office of Research Training and Services, Smithsonian Institution, 470 L'Enfant Plaza SW, Suite 7102, Washington, DC, 20024, United States of America
Tel: (1) 202 633 2648
Fax: (1) 202 786 2447
Email: NASM-Fellowships@si.edu
Website: www.si.edu/ofg/
Contact: Ms Collette Williams, Fellowships Programme Coordinator

A Verville Fellowship

Subjects: The history of aviation and space flights.
Purpose: To fund the analysis of major trends, developments and accomplishments in the history of aviation or space studies.
Eligibility: Open to all interested candidates who can demonstrate skills in research and writing. An advanced degree is not a requirement.
Level of Study: Postgraduate
Type: Fellowship

Value: A stipend of US$45,000 with limited additional funds available for travel and miscellaneous expenses
Length of Study: 9 months–1 year, normally beginning June 1st and October 1st
Country of Study: United States of America
No. of awards offered: 1
Application Procedure: Applicants must submit a summary description, research proposal, bibliography, estimated schedule, research budget, curriculum vitae and letters from three referees. Six copies of the complete application must be submitted. Further information and an application pack are available on request or downloadable from the website.
Closing Date: January 15th
Additional Information: Residence in the Washington, DC metropolitan area during the fellowship term is a requirement of this fellowship.

The Guggenheim Fellowships

Subjects: Historical research related to aviation and space.
Purpose: To promote research into, and writing about, the history of aviation and space flight.
Eligibility: Postdoctoral fellowships are open to applicants who have received a PhD degree or equivalent within 7 years of the beginning of the fellowship period. Predoctoral fellowships are open to applicants who have completed preliminary coursework and examinations and are engaged in dissertation research. All applicants must be able to speak and write fluently in English.
Level of Study: Postdoctorate, Predoctorate
Type: Fellowship
Value: Postdoctoral stipend US$30,000 for 1 year term and predoctoral stipend US$20,000 for 1year term, with limited additional funds available for travel and miscellaneous expenses
Length of Study: 3 months–1 year
Frequency: Annual
Study Establishment: A major portion of the research must be conducted at the Smithsonian Institution
Country of Study: United States of America
No. of awards offered: Varies
Application Procedure: Applicants must submit a summary description, research proposal, bibliography, estimated schedule, research budget, transcripts from all graduate institutions, English training with test scores and level of proficiency in reading, conversing and writing (if English is not the applicant's native language), a curriculum vitae and letters from 3 referees. 6 copies of the complete application must be submitted.
Closing Date: January 15th
Additional Information: Residence in the Washington, DC metropolitan area during the fellowship term is a requirement of the fellowship. Further information is available on the website.

Ramsay Fellowship in Naval Aviation History

Subjects: The history of aviation at sea and in naval service, particularly the United States of America Navy.
Eligibility: Open to all interested candidates who can demonstrate skills in research and writing. An advanced degree is not a requirement.
Level of Study: Postgraduate
Type: Fellowship
Value: A stipend of US$45,000 with additional limited funds available for travel and miscellaneous expenses
Length of Study: 9 months–1 year
Country of Study: United States of America
No. of awards offered: 1
Application Procedure: Applicants must submit a summary description, research proposal, bibliography, estimated schedule, research budget, curriculum vitae and letters from three referees. Six copies of the complete application must be submitted. Further information and an application pack are available on request or downloadable from the website.
Closing Date: January 15th
Additional Information: Residence in the Washington, DC metropolitan area during the fellowship term is a requirement of this fellowship. Further information is available on the website.

THE SNOWDON AWARD SCHEME

Unit 18, Oakhurst Business Park, Sothwater, Horsham, West Sussex, RH13 9RT, England
Tel: (44) 14 0373 2899
Fax: (44) 14 0373 3538
Email: info@snowdonawardscheme.org.uk
Website: www.snowdonawardscheme.org.uk
Contact: The Administrator

The Snowdon Award Scheme provides grants of up to UK £2,000 to physically disabled students for disability-related costs of further or higher education or training in the United Kingdom.

Snowdon Award Scheme Grants

Subjects: All subjects.
Purpose: To support physically impaired students for further or higher education or training in the United Kingdom.
Eligibility: Physically impaired students studying in the United Kingdom.
Level of Study: Postgraduate, Unrestricted
Type: Award
Value: UK £250–2,000 (UK £2,500 in exceptional circumstances)
Frequency: Annual
Study Establishment: All recognized further, higher education or training centres
Country of Study: United Kingdom
No. of awards offered: Up to 100 per year, depending on funds
Application Procedure: Applicants must submit an application form and at least four specialized references. The application form is available online from January to September.
Closing Date: May 31st
Funding: Commercial, individuals, private, trusts
Contributor: Trusts and commercial sponsors
No. of awards given last year: 86
No. of applicants last year: 126

SOCIAL SCIENCE RESEARCH COUNCIL (SSRC)

Fellowships Office, 810 7th Avenue, New York, NY, 10019, United States of America
Tel: (1) 212 377 2700
Fax: (1) 212 377 2727
Email: info@ssrc.org
Website: www.ssrc.org
Contact: Mr Director

Founded in 1923, the Social Science Research Council (SSRC) is an independent, non-governmental, non-profit international association devoted to the advancement of interdisciplinary research in the social sciences. The aim of the organization is to improve the quality of publicly available knowledge around the world.

The Dissertation Proposal Development Fellowship (DPDF)

Subjects: Humanities and social sciences.
Purpose: To help graduate students in the humanities and social sciences formulate doctoral dissertation proposals.
Eligibility: Open to graduate students in the early phase of their research.
Level of Study: Postgraduate, Research
Type: Fellowship
Value: Fellows up to US $5,000, research directors a stipend of US $10,000
Frequency: Annual
Application Procedure: Check website for further details.
Funding: Foundation
Contributor: Andrew W. Mellon Foundation

ESRC/SSRC Collaborative Visiting Fellowships

Subjects: Social sciences (including history).
Purpose: To encourage communication and cooperation between social scientists in Great Britain and the Americas.

Eligibility: Open to PhD scholars in the Americas, ESRC-supported centres, and holders of large grants awards or professorial fellowships in Britain.
Level of Study: Doctorate, Research
Type: Fellowship
Value: Up to US$9,500
Length of Study: 1–3 months
Frequency: Annual
No. of awards offered: Approximately 18
Application Procedure: Check website for further details.
Closing Date: April 16th
Additional Information: Please contact International Migration Program at the above address.

For further information contact:

Email: migration@ssrc.org
Website: www.esrc.ac.uk, and www.ssrc.org

SSRC Abe Fellowship Program

Subjects: Social sciences and related fields relevant to any one or combination of (i) traditional and non-traditional approaches to security and diplomacy; (ii) global and regional economic issues; (iii) the role of civil society.
Purpose: To encourage international multidisciplinary research on topics of pressing global concern and to foster the development of a new generation of researchers who are interested in policy-relevant topics of long-range importance and who are willing to become key members of a bilateral and global research network built around such topics.
Eligibility: Open to citizens of Japan and the US and to other nationals who can demonstrate serious and long-term affiliations in the research communities Japan or the US. Applicants must hold a PhD or have attained an equivalent level of professional experience as evaluated in their country of residence. Applications from researchers in non-academic professions are welcome.
Level of Study: Postdoctorate
Type: Fellowship
Value: Research and travel expenses as necessary for the completion of the research project in addition to limited salary replacement
Length of Study: Up to 1 year
Frequency: Annual
Study Establishment: An appropriate institution
Country of Study: United States of America
No. of awards offered: Approx. 14
Application Procedure: Applicants must submit an online application along with a writing sample, letter of reference and an optional language evaluation form.
Closing Date: September 1st
Funding: Foundation
Contributor: The Japan Foundation Center for Global Partnership
No. of awards given last year: 14
No. of applicants last year: 60–100
Additional Information: In addition to working on their research projects, Fellows will attend annual conferences and other events sponsored by the program, which will promote the development of an international network of scholars concerned with research on contemporary policy issues. Funds are provided by the Japan Foundation Center for Global Partnership. Further information is available by emailing abe@ssrc.org

For further information contact:

Website: http://soap.ssrc.org

SSRC Eurasia Program Postdoctoral Fellowships

Subjects: Social sciences and humanities with a specific focus on Eurasia.
Purpose: To support research and/or publication records and to further the recipients academic career.
Eligibility: Applicants for Postdoctoral Fellowships must have the PhD in hand at the time of application (ABDs will not be considered), and must have received the degree no more than 5 years prior to the application deadline. They must be citizens or permanent residents of the United States of America. Detailed information on eligibility criteria and conditions of awards will be in the application materials.
Level of Study: Doctorate, Postdoctorate

Type: Fellowship
Value: Up to $20,000
Length of Study: 18–24 months
Frequency: Annual
No. of awards offered: Varies
Application Procedure: Awards are made on the basis of evaluations and recommendations by the Title III Program Committee, an interdisciplinary committee and composed of scholars of the region. The committee rewards proposals with clarity of argument, purpose, theory, and method, written in a style accessible to readers outside the applicant's discipline. Applicants must submit a completed application, a narrative statement, a curriculum vitae and references. Full information is available online.
Closing Date: November 13th
Funding: Government
Contributor: US Department of State under the Program for Research and Training on Eastern Europe and the Independent States of the Former Soviet Union (Title VIII)
No. of awards given last year: Approx. 3
No. of applicants last year: Approx. 30
Additional Information: No funding is available for research on the Baltic States.

For further information contact:

Email: eurasia@ssrc.org
Website: http://programs.ssrc.org/eurasia/fellowships
Contact: SSRC, Eurasia Program

SSRC Eurasia Program Predissertation Training Fellowships

Subjects: The social sciences and humanities, with a specific focus on Eurasia.
Purpose: To provide graduate students with the opportunity to enhance their research skills in the field of Eurasian Studies.
Eligibility: Applicants for Predissertation Training Fellowships must be enrolled in a doctoral programme in the social sciences or humanities or equivalent degree, but not yet advanced to the PhD candidacy. ABD's are not eligible for these fellowships. They must be citizens or permanent residents of the United States of America. Detailed information on eligibility criteria and conditions of awards will be available in the application materials.
Level of Study: Doctorate, Graduate
Type: Fellowship
Value: Up to US$7,000
Length of Study: Up to 9 months
Frequency: Annual
Country of Study: United States of America
No. of awards offered: Varies
Application Procedure: Awards are made on the basis of evaluations and recommendations by the Title VIII Program Committee, an interdisciplinary committee composed of scholars of the region. The committee rewards proposals with clarity of argument, purpose, theory, and method, written a style accessible to readers outside the applicant's discipline. Applicants must submit a completed application, a narrative statement, transcripts, a course list and language evaluation form and references. Full information is available online.
Closing Date: November 13th
Funding: Government
Contributor: US Department of State under the Program for Research and Training on Eastern Europe and the Independent States of the Former Soviet Union (Title VIII)
No. of awards given last year: 2
No. of applicants last year: Approx. 20
Additional Information: No funding is available for research on the Baltic States.

For further information contact:

Email: eurasia@ssrc.org
Website: http://programs.ssrc.org/eurasia/fellowships
Contact: SSRC, Eurasia Program

SSRC Eurasia Title VIII Dissertation Write-Up Fellowships

Subjects: Social sciences and humanities, with a specific focus on Eurasia.

Purpose: To allow advanced graduate students to devote to the intellectual development of their projects and to write-up the results of their research.

Eligibility: Applicants for Dissertation Write-up Fellowships must have attained ABD status (must have completed all requirements for the PhD degree except for the dissertation) by the fellowship start date. They must be citizens or permanent residents of the United States of America. The Fellow's home institution is expected to make a cost-sharing contribution of no less than 10 per cent of the fellowship award. Detailed information on eligibility criteria and conditions of awards will be available in the application materials.

Level of Study: Doctorate, Graduate

Type: Fellowship

Value: Up to US$22,000

Length of Study: Up to 1 year

Frequency: Annual

No. of awards offered: Varies

Application Procedure: Awards are made on the basis of evaluations and recommendations by the Title VIII Program Committee, an interdisciplinary committee composed of scholars of the region. The committee rewards proposals with clarity of argument, purpose, theory and method, written in a style accessible to readers outside the applicant's discipline. Applicants must submit a completed application, a narrative statement, transcripts, a course list and language evaluation form, and references. Full information is available online.

Closing Date: November 13th

Funding: Government

Contributor: US Department of State under the Program for Research and Training on Eastern Europe and the Independent States of the Former Soviet Union (Title VIII)

No. of awards given last year: 6

No. of applicants last year: Approx. 40

Additional Information: No funding is available for research on the Baltic States.

For further information contact:

Email: eurasia@ssrc.org
Website: http://programs.ssrc.org/eurasia/fellowships
Contact: SSRC, Eurasia Program

SSRC International Dissertation Research Fellowship

Subjects: Non-US cultures and socities grounded in empirical and site-specific research (involving fieldwork, research in archival or manuscript collections, or quantitative data collection).

Purpose: To support distinguished graduate students in the humanities and social sciences conducting dissertation research outside the United States.

Eligibility: Open to full-time graduate students in the humanities and social sciences regardless of citizenship enrolled in doctoral programs in the United States. Applicants must complete all PhD requirements except on-site research by the time the fellowship begins.

Level of Study: Doctorate

Type: Fellowship

Value: Approx US$20,000

Length of Study: 9 months–1 year

Frequency: Annual

No. of awards offered: Approx. 75

Application Procedure: Applications are available on SSRC website.

Closing Date: November

Funding: Private

Contributor: The Andrew W Mellon Foundation

Additional Information: Applicants must contact the programme for further information by emailing idrf@ssrc.org

SSRC JSPS Postdoctoral Fellowship

Subjects: Social sciences and humanities.

Purpose: To provide qualified researchers with the opportunity to conduct research at leading universities and other research institutions in Japan.

Eligibility: Applicants must be US citizens or permanent residents at the time of application and submit proof of affiliation with an eligible host research institution in Japan as part of the application packet. Permanent residents must provide a copy of a permanent resident card. Citizens of other countries are eligible for the short-term fellowship (1–11 months) if they have completed a Master's or PhD

course at an institution of higher education in the US and, upon completing the course, have for at least three continuous years conducted high-level research at a university in the US. Applicants for long-term (12–24 months) fellowships must submit a copy of a PhD diploma dated no more than six years prior to applying. Check website for further details.

Level of Study: Doctorate, Postdoctorate

Type: Fellowship

Value: Round-trip airfare, insurance coverage for accidents and illness, a monthly stipend and settling-in allowance. Applicants will also be eligible for additional funds annually for research expenses for stays of 1–2 years and a domestic travel allowance for stays of 3–11 months

Length of Study: 16 days to 2 years

Frequency: Annual

Study Establishment: An approved institution

Country of Study: Japan

No. of awards offered: Up to 20

Application Procedure: Applications are available on http://fellowships.ssrc.org/japan/postdoc/

Closing Date: December

Funding: Government

Contributor: The Japan Society for the Promotion of Science

No. of awards given last year: 10–20

No. of applicants last year: 30–50

Additional Information: Fellows are selected by the Japan Society for the Promotion of Science based on nominations made by the SSRC Japan Advisory Board. Applicants will be notified of their nomination status by the following March. Successful applicants will be notified directly by JSPS in the summer.

SOCIAL SCIENCES AND HUMANITIES RESEARCH COUNCIL OF CANADA (SSHRC)

350 Albert Street, PO Box 1610, Ottawa, ON, K1P 6G4, Canada
Tel: (1) 613 992 8092
Fax: (1) 613 992 2803
Email: webgrant@sshrc.ca
Website: www.sshrc.ca

The Social Sciences and Humanities Research Council of Canada (SSHRC) is the federal agency responsible for promoting and supporting research and research training in the social sciences and humanities in Canada. SSHRC supports research on the economic, political, social and cultural dimensions of the human experience.

Aid to Research and Transfer Journals

Subjects: Social sciences and humanities.

Purpose: To assist in the effective dissemination of original research findings and in the transfer of knowledge to practitioners.

Eligibility: Open to candidates who are either Canadian citizens or permanent residents of Canada at the time of application and are established researchers in the social sciences or in the humanities. They must also be a member of the sponsoring institution or organization and not be under SSHRC sanction for financial or research misconduct. Check SSHRC website for further details.

Level of Study: Research

Type: Grant

Value: Check SSHRC website for further details

Frequency: Every 3 years

Country of Study: Canada

Application Procedure: Applicants must make the case for the funding requested. For full details on application visit the website.

Closing Date: June 30th

Funding: Government

Aid to Research Workshops and Conferences in Canada

Subjects: Arts and humanities and social sciences.

Purpose: To support workshops and conferences held in Canada that will facilitate essential knowledge transfer.

Eligibility: Applicants must be either Canadian citizens or permanent residents of Canada at the time of application, researchers or post-doctoral fellows, and members of the conference's or congress's organizing committee. Applicants for Conference grants must also be members in good standing of the international scholarly association in question, be affiliated with a Canadian university that agrees to administer the grant, and not be under SSHRC sanction for financial or research misconduct. For a conference to be eligible, it must take place after the date specified for SSHRC's announcement of competition results, have a defined theme in the Social sciences and Humanities, be held in Canada, not be receiving support for the same activity under another SSHRC program, not be an association's annual general meeting and charge registration. Check SSHRC website for further details.
Level of Study: Research
Type: Grant
Value: A maximum of Canadian $20,000–50,000 depending on number of participants
Country of Study: Canada
Application Procedure: Applicants must consult the organization or visit the website.
Closing Date: May 1st or November 1st
Funding: Government

Aid to Scholarly Publications

Subjects: Social sciences and humanities.
Purpose: To promote the sharing of research results by assisting the publication of individual works that make an important contribution to the advancement of knowledge.
Eligibility: Applicants must consult the Canadian Federation for the Humanities and Social Sciences website for eligibility requirements.
Level of Study: Postdoctorate, Research
Type: Grant
Frequency: Annual
Application Procedure: Applicants must refer to the website or email the Humanities and Social Sciences Federation of Canada.
Closing Date: Applications are accepted at any time
Funding: Government
Additional Information: The program is administered on behalf of SSHRC by the Humanities and Social Sciences Federation of Canada.

For further information contact:

The Humanities and Social Sciences Federation of Canada, 151 Slater Street, Ottawa, ON, K1P 5H3, Canada
Tel: (1) 613 238 6112 ext 350
Email: secaspp@fedcan.ca
Website: www.hssfc.ca

Aid to Small Universities

Subjects: Arts, humanities and social sciences.
Purpose: To enable the focused development of social sciences and humanities research capacity in small universities.
Eligibility: Open to institutions that have active degree-granting status for social sciences and humanities disciplines at the undergraduate level or beyond, and are institutional members of the Association of Universities and Colleges of Canada (AUCC), or institutional members of the AUCC and affiliated with an institution itself too large to be eligible for the ASU Program. Institutions applying must also have fewer than 250 full-time faculty in SSHRC fields and be independent of the federal government for the purpose of faculty employment status.
Level of Study: Research
Type: Grant
Value: Up to a maximum of Canadian $30,000
Length of Study: 3 years
Frequency: Every 3 years
Country of Study: Canada
Application Procedure: Applicants must contact the organization or visit the SSHRC website.
Closing Date: December
Funding: Government

Aileen D Ross Fellowship

Subjects: Sociology.

Purpose: To support an outstanding SSHRC Doctoral Award or Postdoctoral Fellowship holder who is conducting research in sociology, especially on poverty.
Eligibility: Open to Canadian citizens or permanent residents living in Canada at the time of application who are not under SSHRC sanction resulting from financial or research misconduct, or already in receipt of SSHRC, NSERC or CIHR funding to undertake or complete a previous doctoral or combined MA or PhD degree. At the time of taking up the award, applicants must have completed either a Master's degree or at least 1 year of doctoral study, and be pursuing either full-time studies leading to a PhD or equivalent, with a research specialization in sociology and with the intention of pursuing an academic career. Candidates wishing to study at a foreign university may only do so if at least one of their previous degrees was earned in Canada.
Level of Study: Doctorate, Postdoctorate
Type: Fellowship
Value: Canadian $10,000 plus the value of the fellowship
Length of Study: 1 year
Country of Study: Canada
No. of awards offered: 1
Application Procedure: Applicants must indicate their interest on their doctoral or postdoctoral application form.
Closing Date: Postdoctoral applications are due October 2nd. Doctoral application dates are set by the applicant's university
Funding: Government, trusts
Additional Information: Preference will be given to postdoctoral applicants.

Bora Laskin National Fellowship in Human Rights Research

Subjects: Human rights, as relevant to Canada.
Purpose: To support research, preferably of a multidisciplinary or interdisciplinary nature, and to develop Canadian expertise in the field of human rights, with an emphasis on themes and issues relevant to the Canadian human rights scene.
Eligibility: Open to Canadian citizens or permanent residents of Canada. Preference will be given to applicants with at least 5 years of proven research experience in their field, as this fellowship is not intended for scholars just beginning their research careers. The successful candidate must not be under SSHRC sanction for financial or research misconduct.
Level of Study: Research, Postdoctorate
Type: Fellowship
Value: Canadian $45,000 plus a research and travel allowance of Canadian $10,000
Length of Study: 1 year, non-renewable
Frequency: Annual
No. of awards offered: 1
Application Procedure: Applicants must complete an application form, available from the SSHRC website.
Closing Date: October 1st
Funding: Government

Canada Graduate Scholarship Program (CGS): Master's Scholarship

Subjects: Social sciences and humanities.
Purpose: To support graduate students working towards a Master's degree at a Canadian university.
Eligibility: Open to citizens or permanent residents of Canada who are applying for, or registered in a Master's programme in the social sciences or humanities at a Canadian university.
Level of Study: Graduate, Predoctorate
Type: Scholarship
Value: Canadian $17,500
Length of Study: 1 year
Frequency: Annual
Country of Study: Canada
No. of awards offered: Several hundred
Application Procedure: Applicants must visit the SSHRC website for further information.
Closing Date: Applicants must consult the programme description on the website to determine their applicant status, which in turn determines the application deadline
Funding: Government
No. of awards given last year: Hundreds
No. of applicants last year: Thousands

Canadian Initiative on Social Statistics: Data Training Schools

Subjects: Social sciences.

Purpose: To promote research and training in the application of Canadian social statistics.

Eligibility: Eligible applicants include research groups, departments and centres that are operating in a Canadian university. Eligible participants include students and researchers at a variety of levels.

Level of Study: Predoctorate, Research, Doctorate, Graduate, Postdoctorate

Type: Grant

Value: Up to Canadian $50,000 annually

Length of Study: 3 years

Frequency: Annual

Application Procedure: Applicants must visit the SSHRC website for application forms and instructions.

Community-University Research Alliances (CURA)

Subjects: Social sciences and humanities.

Purpose: To support research projects jointly developed and undertaken by post secondary institution-based researchers and community organizations.

Eligibility: Open to applicants who submit applications jointly by one or more postsecondary institutions and one or more organizations from the community. For further information check the SSHRC website.

Level of Study: Professional development, Postdoctorate, Research

Type: Grant

Value: Up to Canadian $200,000 annually over 5 years

Length of Study: Up to 5 years

Frequency: Annual

Country of Study: Canada

Application Procedure: Applicants must visit the SSHRC website for further information on the two-stage application process.

Closing Date: See programme description on website

Funding: Government

Image, Text, Sound and Technology: Summer Institute, Workshop and Conference Grants, and Research Grants

Subjects: Social sciences and humanities.

Purpose: To help scholars, especially in the humanities, apply innovative digital technologies to research on image, text and sound.

Eligibility: Applicants for the research grants must be researchers affiliated with Canadian postsecondary institutions. Canadian postsecondary institutions are eligible to apply for Summer Institute, Workshop and Conference grants.

Level of Study: Research

Type: Grant

Value: Up to Canadian $50,000

Length of Study: 1 year

Frequency: Annual

Country of Study: Canada

Application Procedure: Applicants must visit the SSHRC website for application information and forms.

Closing Date: See website

Funding: Government

International Opportunities Fund: Development and Project Grants

Subjects: Social sciences and humanities.

Purpose: To support developmental activities and projects.

Eligibility: Applicants must be researchers or research teams affiliated with Canadian postsecondary institutions.

Level of Study: Research

Type: Grant

Value: Development Grants: Up to Canadian $25,000. Project Grants: up to Canadian $75,000

Length of Study: 1 year

Frequency: 4 times per annum

Application Procedure: Applicants must visit the SSHRC website for application forms and instructions.

Closing Date: Please see website

Jules and Gabrielle Léger Fellowship

Subjects: The Crown and Governor General in a parliamentary democracy.

Purpose: To promote better understanding of the diverse contributions of the crown and its representatives to all aspects of Canadian life.

Eligibility: Open to Canadian citizens or permanent residents of Canada. Applicants must be affiliated with a post secondary institution not be under SSHRC sanction for financial or research misconduct. Preference will be given to applicants with at least five years of proven research experience in their field.

Level of Study: Postdoctorate, Research

Type: Fellowship

Value: Canadian $40,000, plus Canadian $10,000 for research and travel costs

Length of Study: 1 year, non-renewable

Frequency: Every 2 years

Study Establishment: A recognized Canadian post secondary institution

Country of Study: Any country

No. of awards offered: 1

Application Procedure: Applicants must visit the SSHRC website for full application details.

Closing Date: October 1st

Funding: Government

Knowledge Impact in Society

Subjects: Social sciences and humanities.

Purpose: To support university-based knowledge mobilization initiatives that will enable non-university stockholders to benefit from existing social sciences and humanities research.

Eligibility: The programme offers institutional grants, which are available only to universities eligible for SSHRC Institutional Grants. Applicants must check SSHRC website for full details.

Level of Study: Research

Type: Grant

Value: Up to Canadian $100,000 per annum

Length of Study: Up to 3 years

Frequency: Annual

Application Procedure: Applicants must visit the website for application forms and instructions.

Closing Date: Visit website

Funding: Government

Major Collaborative Research Initiatives (MCRI)

Subjects: Arts, humanities and social sciences.

Purpose: To strengthen Canadian research capacity in the humanities and social sciences by promoting high-quality, broadly based innovative, collaborative research and unique student training opportunities in a collaborative interdisciplinary, inter-postsecondary institution research environment.

Eligibility: Open to leading scholars with a solid track record and past experience in collaborative research, student training and grant management. Please check the program description on the SSHRC website.

Level of Study: Research

Type: Grant

Value: Up to Canadian $2.5 million over 7 years, with a minimum budget of Canadian $100,000 per year. A Canadian $20,000 development fund will also be offered to assist the research team's planning and preparation for its formal application

Length of Study: 7 years

Frequency: Annual

Application Procedure: Applications must be submitted by the Project Director on behalf of the research team. There is a two-stage application process, the first being a letter of intent, followed by a formal application.

Closing Date: January 31st for the first stage and September 1st for the second

Funding: Government

Northern Research Development Program

Subjects: Social sciences and humanities.

Purpose: To support research in and about the Canadian North, with emphasis on involving local stakeholders.

Eligibility: Open to individual researchers or groups of researchers affiliated with Canadian postsecondary institutions or from other organizations whose proposed activites include significant involvement of researchers affiliated with Canadian postsecondary institutions. For further details check the SSHRC website.
Level of Study: Research
Type: Grant
Value: Up to Canadian $40,000
Length of Study: Up to 2 years
Frequency: Annual
Country of Study: Canada
Application Procedure: Applicants must visit the SSHRC website for application information, forms and instructions.
Closing Date: See programme description on website
Funding: Government

Queen's Fellowships

Subjects: Canadian studies.
Purpose: To assist an outstanding candidate who intends to enter a doctoral program in the relevant field.
Eligibility: Open to Canadian citizens and permanent residents who, by the time of taking up the fellowship, will have completed 1 year of graduate study or all the requirements for the master's degree beyond the bachelor's (honours) degree or its equivalent, and will be registered in a program of studies leading to a PhD or its equivalent. This award is offered to one or two outstanding and successful doctoral fellowship candidates.
Level of Study: Doctorate
Type: Fellowship
Value: Tuition fees and travel to the main place of tenure and travel for research purposes
Length of Study: 1 year, non-renewable
Frequency: Annual
Study Establishment: A recognized university
Country of Study: Canada
No. of awards offered: 1–2
Application Procedure: Applicants cannot apply for this award, but are automatically eligible if they intend to study Canadian studies at a Canadian university. The Queen's Fellowship is not a program, but a special award given to a doctoral fellow.
Funding: Government

Sport Participation Research Initiative: Research Grants

Subjects: Social sciences and humanities.
Purpose: To support policy-relevant research about participation in sport in Canada.
Eligibility: Open to individuals and research teams must be affiliated with Canadian postsecondary institutions who are working in one or more of the target areas of interest. For further information check the SSHRC website.
Level of Study: Research
Type: Grant
Value: Up to Canadian $100,000 per year
Length of Study: Up to 3 years
Frequency: Annual
Country of Study: Canada
Application Procedure: Applicants must visit the SSHRC website for application forms and instructions.
Funding: Government

SSHRC Doctoral Awards

Subjects: Social sciences and humanities.
Purpose: To develop research skills and to assist in the training of highly qualified academic personnel by supporting students who demonstrate a high standard of scholarly achievement.
Eligibility: Open to Canadian citizens or permanent residents living in Canada at the time of application, who are not under SSHRC sanction resulting from financial or research misconduct, or already in receipt of SSHRC, NSERC or CIHR funding to undertake or complete a previous doctoral or combined MA/PhD degree. At the time of taking up the award applicants must have completed either a Master's degree or at least 1 year of doctoral study, and be pursuing either full-time studies leading to a PhD or equivalent. Candidates wishing to study at a foreign university may only do so if at least one of their previous degrees was earned in Canada.

Level of Study: Doctorate
Type: Fellowship/Scholarship
Value: SSHRC doctoral fellowships: Canadian $20,000 per year, up to and including the 4th year of doctoral study (tenable in Canada and abroad); CGS doctoral scholarship: Canadian $35,000 per year for 3 years (tenable only at Canadian universities)
Length of Study: 1–4 years
Frequency: Annual
Study Establishment: Any recognized universities
Country of Study: SSHRC doctoral fellowships: tenable in Canada or abroad; CGS doctoral scholarships: tenable in Canada only
No. of awards offered: Varies
Application Procedure: Applicants must complete an application form along with a detailed description. Forms are available from the SSHRC website.
Closing Date: For applicants registered at a Canadian university, the university sets the deadline; for all others, November 15th
Funding: Government

SSHRC Institutional Grants

Subjects: Social sciences and humanities.
Purpose: To help universities develop and maintain a solid base of research and research-related activities.
Eligibility: Open to Canadian postsecondary institutions only.
Level of Study: Postgraduate
Type: Research grant
Value: Minimum Canadian $5,000 per annum
Length of Study: 3 years
Frequency: Annual
Country of Study: Canada
No. of awards offered: Varies
Application Procedure: Applicants must complete an application form available from the SSHRC website.
Closing Date: See the website
Funding: Government

SSHRC Postdoctoral Fellowships

Subjects: Social sciences and humanities.
Purpose: To support the most promising new scholars and to assist them in establishing a research base at an important time in their research career.
Eligibility: Open to candidates who are Canadian citizens or permanent residents living in Canada at the time of application. They must also be able to demonstrate skill in research, not be under SSHRC sanction resulting from financial or research misconduct and have earned their doctorate from a recognized university no more than 3 years prior to the competition deadline or have completed their degree within 6 years prior to the competition deadline, but have had their career interrupted or delayed for the purpose of child-rearing. Candidates must also have finalized arrangements for affiliation with a recognized university or research institution and have applied not more than twice before for a SSHRC postdoctoral fellowship. At the time of taking up the award, applicants must have completed all requirements for the doctoral degree, must intend to engage in full-time postdoctoral research for the period of the award and not hold or have held a tenure or tenure-track position.
Level of Study: Postdoctorate
Type: Fellowship
Value: Up to Canadian $38,000 per year, plus a research allowance of up to Canadian $5,000
Length of Study: A minimum of 1 year and a maximum of 2 years
Frequency: Annual
Study Establishment: For applicants who earned their doctorate at a Canadian University, there is no restriction on the location of the tenure
Country of Study: Any country, under certain conditions
No. of awards offered: Approx. 100
Application Procedure: Applicants must complete an application form available in the SSHRC website.
Closing Date: October 1st
Funding: Government
No. of awards given last year: 140
No. of applicants last year: 558
Additional Information: Applicants wishing to hold their award at a foreign university may do so only if their PhD was earned at a Canadian university.

SSHRC Research Development Initiatives

Subjects: Humanities, the social and cognitive sciences and the educational sciences.
Purpose: To support research that explores new conceptual and methodological perspectives and directions. The program supports research that both assesses and elicits the changing directions of research and the evolution of relevant disciplines.
Eligibility: Candidates should visit the SSHRC website for eligibility requirements.
Level of Study: Research
Value: A maximum of Canadian $40,000
Length of Study: Up to 2 years
Frequency: 3 times a year
Application Procedure: Applicants must visit the SSHRC website for further details as there are two parts to the application process, a form and a project description.
Closing Date: See website
Funding: Government

SSHRC Standard Research Grants

Subjects: Social sciences and humanities.
Purpose: To support and develop excellence in research, with the research projects proposed by the researchers themselves.
Eligibility: Open to scholars who are Canadian citizens or permanent residents of Canada and who are affiliated with a Canadian university or recognized postsecondary institution. Applicants must have met all requirements for the PhD by April of the year in which the grant is awarded.
Level of Study: Research
Type: Research grant
Value: Up to a maximum of Canadian $100,000 per year, but not totalling more than Canadian $250,000 over a 3-year period. A minimum budget of Canadian $7,000 in at least one of the years is required unless the applicant is at an institution not receiving a SSHRC institutional Grant
Length of Study: Grants in support of research programs will ordinarily be expected to cover 3-year periods
Frequency: Annual
Study Establishment: An approved institution
Country of Study: Any country
No. of awards offered: Varies
Application Procedure: Applicants must visit the SSHRC website for full application details.
Closing Date: October 15th
Funding: Government
No. of applicants last year: Approx. 1,800

SSHRC Strategic Research Grants

Subjects: Social sciences and humanities.
Purpose: To support targeted research and research-related activities in areas of national importance. SSHRC offers many separate programs to support strategic research. See the website for current offerings.
Eligibility: Applicants should visit the website for requirements.
Level of Study: Research
Type: Grant
Frequency: Annual
Country of Study: Canada
Application Procedure: Applicants must visit the website for full application details.
Closing Date: Varies according to program
Funding: Trusts, foundation, government

Thérèse F Casgrain Fellowship

Subjects: Women and social change in Canada.
Purpose: To carry out research in the field of social justice, particularly in the defence of individual rights and the promotion of the economic and social interests of Canadian women.
Eligibility: Open to Canadian citizens or permanent residents. At the time of taking up the fellowship, the successful candidate must have obtained a doctorate or an equivalent advanced professional degree, as well as have proven research experience and not be under SSHRC sanction for financial or research misconduct.
Level of Study: Postdoctorate
Type: Fellowship

Value: Canadian $40,000, paid in three instalments, of which up to Canadian $10,000 may be used for travel and research expenses
Length of Study: 1 year, non-renewable
Frequency: Every 2 years
Country of Study: Canada
No. of awards offered: 1
Application Procedure: Applicants must complete an application form, available from the website. Application forms and instructions are available on the SSHRC website.
Closing Date: October 1st
Funding: Private
Contributor: The Thérèse F Casgrain Foundation
No. of awards given last year: 1
No. of applicants last year: 21
Additional Information: The fellowship was created by the Thérèse F Casgrain Foundation and is administered by the Social Sciences and Humanities Research Council. Affiliation with a university or an appropriate research institute or similar organization is desirable, but is not a condition of the award. Recipients must submit a final report to the Foundation outlining conclusions of the research, accompanied by a complete financial statement for all expenses.

SOCIAL WORKERS EDUCATIONAL TRUST

British Association of Social Workers, 16 Kent Street, Birmingham, West Midlands, B5 6RD, England
Tel: (44) 12 1622 3911
Fax: (44) 12 1622 4860
Email: swet@basw.co.uk
Website: www.socialworkerseducationaltrust.org
Contact: Ms Gill Aslett, Honorary Secretary

The Social Workers Educational Trust offers grants and scholarships to experienced social workers for postqualifying training or research, with the overall aim of improving social work practice in the United Kingdom.

Anne Cummins Scholarship

Subjects: Health-related social work.
Purpose: To support study or research on health-related social work practice.
Eligibility: Open to qualified social workers who have completed 2 years of work practice postqualification, resident in the United Kingdom.
Level of Study: Professional development, Postgraduate
Type: Scholarship
Value: UK £1,000–1,500
Frequency: Annual
Country of Study: United Kingdom
No. of awards offered: 1
Application Procedure: Applicants must complete an application form. Details and forms are available on written request from the Trust. Applicants should state whether their application is for a grant or scholarship. Applications can be downloaded from the website www.socialworkerseducationaltrust.org
Funding: Private
No. of awards given last year: 1

SOCIETY FOR PROMOTION OF ROMAN STUDIES

Senate House, Malet Street, London, WC1E 7HU, England
Tel: (44) 20 7862 8727
Fax: (44) 20 7862 8728
Email: office@romansociety.org
Website: www.romansociety.org
Contact: Dr Helen M Cockle, Secretary of Society

The Society for the Promotion of Roman Studies aims to promote the study of history, architecture, archaeology, language, literature and the art of Italy and the Roman Empire, including Roman Britain, from the earliest times to about 700 AD.

Hugh Last and Donald Atkinson Funds Committee Grants

Subjects: The history, archaeology, language, literature and art of Italy and the Roman Empire including Roman Britain.

Purpose: To assist in the undertaking, completion or publication of work that relates to any of the general scholarly purposes of the Roman Society.

Eligibility: Open to applicants of graduate, postgraduate or post-doctoral status or the equivalent, usually of United Kingdom nationality.

Level of Study: Graduate, Postdoctorate, Postgraduate, Research

Type: Grant

Value: Varies, but usually UK £200–1,500

Frequency: Annual

No. of awards offered: 20

Application Procedure: Applicants must ensure that two references are sent directly to the Society. Completion of an application form is not essential.

Closing Date: January 15th

Funding: Private

No. of awards given last year: 20

No. of applicants last year: 31

Additional Information: Grants for the organization of conferences or colloquia and symposia will only be considered in exceptional circumstances.

SOCIETY FOR TECHNICAL COMMUNICATION

901 North Stuart Street, Suite 904, Arlington, VA 22203, United States of America
Tel: (1) 4522-4114 extn 208
Fax: (1) (703) 522 2075
Email: maurice@stc.org
Website: www.stc.org
Contact: Maurice Martin

The Society for Technical Communication is an individual membership organization dedicated to advancing the arts and sciences of technical communication.

STC International Scholarship Program

Subjects: Technical writing.

Purpose: To assist students who are pursuing programmes in some area of technical communication.

Eligibility: Open to full-time students studying communication of information about technical subjects.

Level of Study: Postgraduate

Type: Scholarship

Value: US$1,500

Frequency: Annual

Study Establishment: Society for Technical Communication

Application Procedure: A completed application form must be sent. See the website for complete details.

Closing Date: February 15th

For further information contact:

Scholarships 901 North Stuart Street, Suite 904, Arlington, VA 22203-1822

SOCIETY FOR THE ARTS IN RELIGIOUS AND THEOLOGICAL STUDIES (SARTS)

United Theological Seminary of the Twin Cities, 3000 5th Street NW, New Brighton, MN, 55112, United States of America
Tel: (1) 651 962 5337
Fax: (1) 651 962 5310
Email: wyates@unitedseminary-mn.org
Website: www.artsmag.org
Contact: Wilson Yates

The Society for the Arts in Religious and Theological Studies (SARTS) was organized to provide a forum for scholars and artists interested in the intersections between theology, religion and the arts to share thoughts, challenge ideas, strategize approaches in the classroom and to advance the discipline in theological and religious studies.

Luce Fellowships

Subjects: Intersection of theology and art.

Purpose: To enhance and expand the conversation on theology and art.

Eligibility: Open to candidates teaching theology as a faculty member at an accredited postsecondary educational institution or graduate students

Level of Study: Graduate, Research

Type: Fellowships

Value: US$6,000 (for teachers) $3,500 (for graduate students)

Length of Study: 1 year

Frequency: Annual

No. of awards offered: 2

Application Procedure: Applicants must submit an information sheet, curriculum vitae, a project abstract, a formal proposal, a budget and 2 letters of recommendation.

Closing Date: June 15th

For further information contact:

University of St Thomas, Mail JRC 153 2115 Summit Avenue, St Paul, MN, 55105, United States of America
Email: kjvrudny@stthomas.edu
Contact: Kimberly Vrudny

THE SOCIETY FOR THE PROMOTION OF HELLENIC STUDIES

Senate House, Malet Street, London, WC1E 7HU, England
Tel: (44) 20 7862 8730
Fax: (44) 20 7862 8731
Email: officehellenicsociety@org.uk
Website: www-hellenicsociety.org.uk
Contact: Secretary

The Society for the Promotion of Hellenic Studies, generally known as the Hellenic Society, was founded in 1879 to advance the study of Greek language, literature, history, art and archaeology in the ancient, Byzantine and modern periods.

The Dover Fund

Subjects: Greek language and papyri.

Purpose: To further the study of the history of the Greek language in any period from the Bronze Age to the 15th century AD, and to further the edition and exegesis of Greek texts from any period within those same limits.

Eligibility: Open to currently registered research students and lecturers, teaching Fellows, research Fellows, postdoctoral Fellows and research assistants who are within the first 5 years of their appointment.

Level of Study: Doctorate, Postdoctorate, Postgraduate

Type: Grant

Value: Grants will be made for such purposes as books, photography, including microfilm and photocopying, and towards the costs of visits to libraries, museums and sites. The sums awarded will vary according to the needs of the applicant, but most grants will be in the range of UK £50–250. Larger grants may be made from time to time at the discretion of the awards committee

Frequency: Annual

Study Establishment: The Society for the Promotion of Hellenic Studies

Country of Study: United Kingdom

No. of awards offered: Varies

Application Procedure: Applicants must complete an application form, available from the Society. Applications should be marked for the attention of the Dover Fund and sent to the main address.

Closing Date: February 14th of the year in which the award is sought

Funding: Private

Contributor: Membership subscriptions

No. of awards given last year: 3

No. of applicants last year: 8

THE SOCIETY FOR THE PSYCHOLOGICAL STUDY OF SOCIAL ISSUES (SPSSI)

SPSSI Central Office, 208 I Street NE, Washington, DC, 20002-4340, United States of America
Tel: (1) 202 675 6956
Fax: (1) 202 675 6902
Email: awards@spssi.org
Website: www.spssi.org
Contact: Susan Dudley, Administrative Director

The Society for the Psychological Study of Social Issues (SPSSI) is an interdisciplinary, international organization of over 3,000 social scientists who share an interest in research on the psychological aspects of important social issues. The Society's goals are to increase the understanding of social issues through research and its dissemination and to support policy efforts consistent with such research.

Clara Mayo Grants

Subjects: Aspects of sexism, racism and prejudice.
Purpose: To support masters' thesis or pre-dissertation research on aspects of sexism, racism, or prejudice.
Eligibility: Individuals who are SPSSI members and who have matriculated in graduate programs in psychology, applied social science, and related disciplines. A student who is applying for a Grants-In-Aid may not apply for the Clara Mayo award in the same award year. Applicants may submit only one Mayo application per calendar year. Proposals that include a college or university agreement to match the amount requested will be favored, but proposals without matching funds will also be considered.
Level of Study: Graduate, Postgraduate
Type: Research grant
Value: Up to US$1,000
Frequency: Biannual
Country of Study: Any country
No. of awards offered: Up to 4
Application Procedure: The Application should include: 1. A cover sheet stating title of thesis proposal, name of investigator, address, phone, and if possible, fax and e-mail; 2. An abstract of no more than 100 words summarizing the proposed research; 3. Project purposes, theoretical rationale, research methodology, and analytic procedures to be employed; 4. Relevance of research to SPSSI goals and funding criteria; 5. Status of human subjects review process (which must be satisfactorily completed before grant funds can be forwarded); 6. Clear statement of type of degree program applicant is enrolled in (e.g., terminal master's program); 7. Faculty advisor's recommendation, including certification that the proposal is for a master's thesis or for pre-dissertation research; 8. Specific amount requested, including a budget; 9. If available, an institutional letter of agreement to match the funds requested. Recommended length for points (1) through (4) of the application is 5–7 double-spaced, 12-point font, typed pages.
Closing Date: May 8th or October 9th
Funding: Private
No. of awards given last year: 5
No. of applicants last year: 10
Additional Information: Incomplete applications will be returned. Late applications may be held until the next deadline.

Louise Kidder Early Career Award

Subjects: Social and community psychology.
Purpose: To recognize social issues researchers who have made substantial contributions to the field early in their careers.
Eligibility: Nominees should be social issues investigators who have made substantial contributions to social issues research within 5 years of receiving a graduate degree and who have demonstrated the potential to continue such contributions. Nominees need not be current SPSSI members.
Level of Study: Postdoctorate, Professional development
Type: Award
Value: US$500 plus plaque
Frequency: Annual
Country of Study: Any country
No. of awards offered: 1
Application Procedure: The online application form should be completed and sent as an email attachment. For further details visit the website.

Closing Date: June 30th
Funding: Private
No. of awards given last year: 1
No. of applicants last year: 10
Additional Information: Late applications will be retained for the next year. The winner will be announced by August 15th.

Otto Klineberg Intercultural and International Relations Award

Subjects: Intercultural and international relations.
Purpose: To recognize the best paper or article of the year on intercultural or international relations.
Eligibility: Entries can be either unpublished manuscripts, in press papers or books, or papers or books published no more than 18 months prior to the submission deadline. Entries cannot be returned. The competition is open to non-members, as well as members of SPSSI, and graduate students are especially urged to submit papers. The originality of the contribution, whether theoretical or empirical, will be given special weight.
Level of Study: Doctorate, Graduate, Postdoctorate, Postgraduate
Type: Prize
Value: US$1,000
Frequency: Annual
Country of Study: Any country
No. of awards offered: 1
Application Procedure: The online application form should be completed and sent as an email attachment. For further details visit the website.
Closing Date: February 15th
Funding: Private
No. of awards given last year: 1
No. of applicants last year: 8
Additional Information: Late applications will be retained for the next year.

SPSSI Applied Social Issues Internship Program

Subjects: The application of social principles to social issues in cooperation with a community or government organization, public interest group or other not-for-profit entity that will benefit directly from the project.
Purpose: To encourage research that is conducted in cooperation with a community or government organization, public interest group or other not-for-profit entity that will benefit directly from the project.
Eligibility: Open to college seniors, graduate students and 1st year postdoctorates in psychology, applied social science and related disciplines. Applicants must be SPSSI members.
Level of Study: Graduate, Postdoctorate, Postgraduate
Type: Grant
Value: US$300–2,500 to cover research costs, community organizing, Summer stipends, etc
Frequency: Annual
Country of Study: Any country
No. of awards offered: Varies
Application Procedure: The Application should include: a) A 3–6 page proposal including the proposed budget and a cover sheet with your name, address, phone number, e-mail address and title of your proposal. If an intervention is planned, the proposal should carefully describe the theoretical rationale for the intervention, specifically how the effectiveness of the program will be assessed and the plan to disseminate the findings to relevant parties and policy makers. b) A short resume. c) A letter from a faculty sponsor/supervisor of the project, a statement concerning protection for participants if relevant and any funds that the sponsoring organization will use to support the intern's research. d) A letter from an organizational sponsor (waived if the applicant is proposing to organize a group) that endorses the intern's research activities, describes how the organization will potentially benefit from the work, and outlines any funds the organization will use to support the intern's research.
Closing Date: April 10th
Funding: Private
No. of awards given last year: 1
No. of applicants last year: 5
Additional Information: Late applications will be retained for the next year. Cost sharing by sponsoring department or organization is desirable.

SPSSI Grants-in-Aid Program

Subjects: Scientific research in social problem areas related to the basic interests and goals of SPSSI and particularly those that are not likely to receive support from traditional sources.
Purpose: To support scientific research in social problem areas related to the basic interests and goals of SPSSI
Eligibility: Applicant must be a member of SPSSI. Applicants may submit only one application per deadline. If applied to the Clara Mayo Grant in the same award year he/she is not eligible for GIA. Individuals may submit a joint application.
Level of Study: Doctorate, Graduate, Postdoctorate, Postgraduate
Type: Grant
Value: Up to US$2,000 for postdoctoral work and up to US$1,000 for graduate student research that must be matched by the student's university
Frequency: Biannual
Country of Study: Any country
No. of awards offered: Varies
Application Procedure: The Application should include: 1. A cover sheet with your name, address, phone number, e-mail address and title of the proposal. 2. An abstract of 100 words or less summarizing the proposed research. 3. Project purposes, theoretical rationale, and research methodology and analytical procedures to be employed. 4. Relevance of research to SPSSI goals and Grants-in-Aid criteria. 5. Status of human subjects review process (which must be satisfactorily completed before grant funds can be forwarded). 6. Resume of investigator (a faculty sponsor's recommendation must be provided if the investigator is a graduate student; support is seldom awarded to students who have not yet reached the dissertation stage). 7. Specific amount requested, including a budget. For co-authored submissions, please indicate only one name and institution to which a check should be jointly issued if selected for funding.
Closing Date: May 14th and October 15th
Funding: Private
Contributor: The Sophie and Shirley Cohen Memorial Fund and membership contributions
No. of awards given last year: Approx. 10
No. of applicants last year: Approx.18
Additional Information: Late applications may be held until the next deadline. Proposals for highly timely and event-oriented research may be submitted at any time during the year to be reviewed within one month of receipt on an ad hoc basis. If yours is a time-sensitive application, please indicate that on the outside of the envelope.

SPSSI Social Issues Dissertation Award

Subjects: Social issues in psychology or in a social science with psychological subject matter.
Purpose: To encourage excellence in socially relevant research.
Eligibility: Open to doctoral dissertations in psychology (or in a social science with psychology subject matter) accepted between March 1st of the year preceding that of application and March 1st of the year of application. In the award year (July 1 to June 30) an individual or group may only submit one paper to one SPSSI paper award (amongst Allport, Klineberg and Dissertation awards).
Level of Study: Postgraduate
Type: Prize
Value: First prize of US$750 and a second prize of US$500
Frequency: Annual
Country of Study: Any country
No. of awards offered: 2
Application Procedure: A 500-word summary of the dissertation. The summary should include title, rationale, methods, and results of dissertation, as well as its implications for social problems. Please also include a cover sheet that states the title of your dissertation, your name, postal and e-mail addresses, phone number, and university granting the degree.
Closing Date: May 1st
Funding: Private
No. of awards given last year: 2
No. of applicants last year: 15
Additional Information: Applicants will be notified of their status by July. Finalist will be asked to provide certification by the dissertation advisor of the acceptance date of the dissertation and four copies of dissertation. Final decision will be announced by September 1st.

THE SOCIETY FOR THE SCIENTIFIC STUDY OF SEXUALITY (SSSS)

PO Box 416, Allentown, PA 18105-0416, United States of America
Tel: (1) 610 530 2483
Fax: (1) 610 530 2485
Email: thesociety@sexscience.org
Website: www.sexscience.org
Contact: Mr David L Fleming, Executive Director

The Society for the Scientific Study of Sexuality (SSSS) is an international organization dedicated to the advancement of knowledge about sexuality. The Society brings together an interdisciplinary group of professionals who believe in the importance of both production of quality research and the clinical, educational and social applications of research related to all aspects of sexuality.

FSSS Grants-in-Aid Program

Subjects: Human sexuality.
Level of Study: Unrestricted
Type: Grant
Value: US$1,000
Length of Study: 1 year
Frequency: Annual
No. of awards offered: Varies
Application Procedure: Contact the society.
Closing Date: No deadline for applications
Funding: Foundation
Contributor: The foundation for the scientific Study of sexuality
Additional Information: Preference will be given to research areas unlikely to receive support from other sources.

SSSS Student Research Grants

Subjects: Human sexuality.
Eligibility: Applicants must be a member of the SSSS.
Level of Study: Doctorate, Postgraduate
Type: Scholarship
Value: US$1,000
Length of Study: 1 year
Frequency: Annual
No. of awards offered: 2
Application Procedure: Contact the society or check website for details.
Closing Date: February 1st and September 1st
Funding: Foundation
Contributor: The Foundation for the Scientific study of sexuality

SOCIETY FOR THE STUDY OF FRENCH HISTORY

Department of Modern History, University of St Andrews, St Katharine's Lodge, The Scores, Saint Andrews, Fife, KY16 9AL, Scotland
Tel: (44) 1334 462 886
Fax: (44) 1334 462 927
Email: st29@st-andrews.ac.uk
Website: www.frenchhistorysociety.ac.uk
Contact: Dr Stephen Tyre, Secretary

The Society for the Study of French History was established to encourage research into French history. It offers a forum where scholars, teachers and students can meet and exchange ideas. It also offers bursaries for research and conferences to postgraduates in Britian and Ireland undertaking research into French history.

Society for the Study of French History Bursaries

Subjects: Any aspect of French history.
Purpose: To enable postgraduates undertake research in French history. To enable postgraduates attend conferences concerning French history.
Eligibility: Open to postgraduate students registered at a United Kingdom or Republic of Ireland university. Students at any level at postgraduate study may apply, provided that their dissertation is on some aspect of French history.
Level of Study: Postgraduate
Type: Bursary
Value: Up to UK £500

Length of Study: Dependent on the project for which the award is given
Frequency: Annual
Country of Study: France
No. of awards offered: Up to 20
Application Procedure: Applicants must give details of the research being pursued and the use to which the money would be put, along with the names of two referees. Applicants are responsible for writing to their referees. Successful applicants will be required to submit, in the first instance, a brief outline of their research proposal and then, after the research trip, a synopsis of their findings, both for publication on the Society's website. Application forms can be downloaded from the Society's website: www.frenchhistorysociety.ac.uk/bursaries.htm
Closing Date: March 16th
Funding: Private
Contributor: The Society for the Study of French History
No. of awards given last year: 13
No. of applicants last year: 14

THE SOCIETY FOR THEATRE RESEARCH

PO Box 53971, London, SW15 64L, England
Email: e.cottis@btinternet.com
Website: www.str.org.uk
Contact: Chairman, Research Awards Sub-Committee

The Society for Theatre Research was founded in 1948 for all those interested in the history and techniques of British theatre. It publishes annually one or more books, newsletters and three issues of the journal *Theatre Notebook*, holds lecture meetings and other events, and gives an annual book prize as well as grants for theatre research.

Society for Theatre Research Awards
Subjects: The history and practice of the British theatre, including music hall, opera, dance and other associated performing arts.
Purpose: To aid research into the history and practice of British theatre.
Eligibility: Applicants should normally be 18 years of age or over, but there is no other restriction on their status, nationality or the location of the research.
Level of Study: Unrestricted
Value: From a total of approx. UK £5,000. Major awards are normally UK £1,000–1,500 and other awards are normally UK £200–500
Frequency: Annual
Country of Study: Any country
No. of awards offered: 2 major awards and a number of lesser awards
Application Procedure: Applicants must write to the Chairman of the Research Awards Sub-Committee after October 1st of the preceding year for an application form and guidance notes. All applications and enquiries must be made by post to the Society's accommodation address.
Closing Date: February 1st
Funding: Private
Contributor: Members' subscriptions, donations and bequests
No. of awards given last year: 9
No. of applicants last year: 25
Additional Information: While applicants will need to show evidence of the value of the research and a scholarly approach, they are by no means restricted to professional academics. Many awards, including major ones, have previously been made to theatre practitioners and amateur researchers who are encouraged to apply. The Society also welcomes proposals which in their execution extend the methods and techniques of historiography. In coming to its decisions, the Society will consider the progress already made by the applicants and the possible availability of other grants.

SOCIETY OF ACTUARIES

475 North Martingale Road, Suite 600, Schaumburg, IL, 60173-2226, United States of America
Tel: (1) 847 706 3500
Fax: (1) 847 706 3599
Email: eschulty@soa.org
Website: www.soa.org
Contact: Erika Schulty, Business Manager

The Committee on Knowledge Extension research of the Society of Actuaries and the AERF committee of the Actuarial Foundation carry out research and education projects in actuarial science and studies specific projects that could be advanced under this mechanism.

The AERF/CKER Individual Grants Competition
Subjects: Actuarial science.
Purpose: To produce publications that will advance actuarial science, especially with regard to practical applications.
Eligibility: Proposals are invited from members of the eight sponsoring actuarial organizations (AAA, ASPA, CIA, CAS, CONAC, CCA, SoA and TAF), from faculty members of universities or colleges who have teaching and research responsibilities in actuarial or related fields and by others who are qualified by knowledge and experience to contribute to their goals.
Level of Study: Unrestricted
Type: Grant
Value: Varies, approx. US$10,000–15,000
Length of Study: Projects should generally be of less than 1 year in duration
Frequency: Annual
Country of Study: Any country
No. of awards offered: Varies
Application Procedure: Applicants must submit a letter of intent and an application form.
Funding: Private
Contributor: The Society of Actuaries, The Actuarial Foundation and the Casualty Actuarial Society and individuals
No. of awards given last year: 7
No. of applicants last year: 27
Additional Information: The project may be either theoretical or empirical in nature. A key criteria is that the project should have the potential to contribute significantly to the advancement of knowledge in actuarial science. The Actuarial Foundation and the SOA give preference to projects relating to current policy issues or having direct applications and those that further the basic or continuing education of actuaries. Proposals for innovative developments in actuarial education are also considered by The Actuarial Foundation and the SOA. More information is available from the website.

SOCIETY OF APOTHECARIES OF LONDON

Black Friars Lane, London, EC4V 6EJ, England
Tel: (44) 20 7236 1189
Fax: (44) 20 7329 3177
Email: clerk@apothecaries.org
Website: www.apothecaries.org
Contact: Wallington Smith, Clerk

Gillson Scholarship in Pathology
Subjects: Pathology.
Purpose: To encourage original research in any branch of pathology.
Eligibility: Open to candidates under 35 years of age who are either licenciates or freemen of the Society, or who will obtain the licence or the freedom within 6 months of election to the scholarship.
Level of Study: Postgraduate
Type: Scholarship
Value: UK £1,800 in total. Payments are made twice annually for the duration of the scholarship
Length of Study: 3 years, renewable for a second term of 3 years
Frequency: Every 3 years
Country of Study: Any country
No. of awards offered: 1
Application Procedure: Applicants must submit two testimonials and present evidence of their attainments and capabilities as shown by any papers already published, and a detailed record of any pathological work already done. Candidates should also state where the research will be undertaken.
Closing Date: December 1st
Funding: Private
Additional Information: Preference is given to the candidate who is engaged in the teaching of medical science or in its research. Scholars are required to submit an interim report at the end of the first 6 months

of tenure, and a complete report 1 month prior to the end of the 3rd year. Any published results should also be submitted to the Society.

SOCIETY OF ARCHITECTURAL HISTORIANS (SAH)

1365 North Astor Street, Chicago, Illionis, 60610-2144,
United States of America
Tel: (1) 312 573 1365
Fax: (1) 312 573 1141
Email: ksturm@sah.org
Website: www.sah.org/

SAH is an international not-for-profit membership organization that promotes the study and preservation of the built environment worldwide. The Society serves scholars, professionals in allied fields and the interested general public.

Annual Meeting Fellowship - Beverly Willis Architectural Foundation Travel Fellowship
Subjects: Gender issues in the history of architecture, landscape architecture and associated fields.
Purpose: To advance the status of women in architecture.
Eligibility: Applicants must be members of the SAH.
Level of Study: Doctorate
Type: Fellowship
Value: US$1,500 travel stipend
Frequency: Annual
Country of Study: United States of America
No. of awards offered: 1
Application Procedure: Apply online.
Closing Date: November 1st

For further information contact:

Contact: Kathy Sturm, Manager, Meetings and Tours

Edilia and Francois-Auguste de Montequin Fellowship
Subjects: Spanish, Portugese and Ibero-American architecture.
Eligibility: Applicants must be members of the SAH.
Level of Study: Doctorate, Postdoctorate
Type: Fellowship
Value: US$2,000–6,000 stipend
Length of Study: 1 year
Frequency: Annual
No. of awards offered: 2
Application Procedure: Apply online.
Closing Date: October 15th
Funding: Foundation
Contributor: The Auguste de Montequin Foundation

Edilia and François-Auguste de Montequin Fellowship in Iberian and Latin American Architecture
Subjects: Spanish, Portuguese or Ibero American architecture, including colonial architecture produced by the Spaniards in the Philippines and what is today the United States of America.
Purpose: To fund travel for research into Spanish, Portuguese and Ibero American architecture.
Eligibility: Open to SAH members who are junior Scholars, including graduate students.
Level of Study: Doctorate, Postdoctorate, Postgraduate
Type: Fellowship
Value: US$2,000 for junior scholars awarded each year and US$6,000 for senior scholars offered every 2 years
Frequency: Annual for junior scholars and every 2 years for senior scholars
Country of Study: Any country
No. of awards offered: 2
Application Procedure: Applicants must complete an application form, available on request by writing to SAH for guidelines or visiting the SAH website.
Closing Date: October 20th
Funding: Private
No. of awards given last year: 1
No. of applicants last year: 5

Keepers Preservation Education Fund Fellowship
Subjects: Historic preservation.
Purpose: To enable a graduate student to attend the annual meeting of the Society, held each April.
Eligibility: Open to members of any nationality who are currently engaged in the study of historic preservation.
Level of Study: Doctorate, Postdoctorate, Postgraduate
Type: Fellowship
Value: grants can range from several hundred dollars to larger sums, awarded at the discretion of the board of trustees
Frequency: Annual
Country of Study: Any country
No. of awards offered: 1
Application Procedure: Applicants must write to SAH for application guidelines or download an application from the Society's website.
Closing Date: November 15th
Funding: Private
No. of awards given last year: 1
No. of applicants last year: 7

Rosann Berry Fellowship
Subjects: Architectural history or an allied field, e.g. city planning, landscape architecture, decorative arts or historic preservation.
Purpose: To enable a student engaged in advanced graduate study to attend the annual meeting of the Society.
Eligibility: Open to persons of any nationality who have been members of SAH for at least 1 year prior to the meeting, and who are currently engaged in advanced graduate study, normally beyond the Master's level, that involves some aspect of the history of architecture or of one of the fields closely allied to it.
Level of Study: Postdoctorate, Postgraduate
Type: Fellowship
Value: US$1000 travel stipend and complimentary meeting registration
Frequency: Annual
Country of Study: Any country
No. of awards offered: 1
Application Procedure: Applicants must complete an application form, available on request by writing to SAH for guidelines or visiting the SAH website.
Closing Date: November 15th
Funding: Private
No. of awards given last year: 1
No. of applicants last year: 15

SAH Fellowships for Senior Scholars
Subjects: European artistic traditions before 1,800.
Eligibility: Applicants must be members of the SAH.
Level of Study: Doctorate, Postdoctorate
Type: Fellowship
Value: US$1,000 travel stipend
Frequency: Annual
Country of Study: United States of America
No. of awards offered: 10
Application Procedure: Apply online.

SAH Study Tour Fellowship
Subjects: South Indian architecture of historical significance.
Eligibility: Applicants must be members of the SAH.
Level of Study: Doctorate
Type: Fellowship
Length of Study: 30–40 days
Frequency: Annual
Country of Study: India
No. of awards offered: Varies
Application Procedure: Contact the Society.
Closing Date: December 28th

Sally Kress Tompkins Fellowship
Subjects: Architectural history and historic preservation.
Purpose: To enable an architectural history student to work as an intern on an Historic American Buildings Survey project, during the summer.
Eligibility: Open to architectural history and historic preservation students.
Level of Study: Postdoctorate, Doctorate, Postgraduate
Type: Fellowship

Value: US$10,000
Length of Study: 12 weeks
Frequency: Annual
Country of Study: United States of America
No. of awards offered: 1
Application Procedure: Applicants must submit an application including a sample of work, a letter of recommendation from a faculty member, and a United States Government Standard Form 171, available from HABS or most United States government personnel offices. Applications should be sent to the Sally Kress Tompkins Fellowship. Applicants not selected for the Tomkins Fellowship will be considered for other HABS Summer employment opportunities. For more information, please contact Catherine C Laudie, HABS/HAER Co-ordinator.
Closing Date: November through January
Funding: Government
No. of awards given last year: 1
No. of applicants last year: 7

For further information contact:

The Sally Kress Tompkins Fellowship, c/o HABS/HAER, National Park Service, 1849C Street NW, Washington, DC, 2270-20240, United States of America

Samuel H. Kress Foundation Fellowships for Speakers
Subjects: Nationally significant buildings and sites.
Eligibility: Applicants must be members of the SAH.
Level of Study: Doctorate, Postdoctorate
Type: Fellowship
Value: US$ 9,800 stipend
Length of Study: 12 weeks
Frequency: Annual
Study Establishment: HABS Washington Office
Country of Study: United States of America
Application Procedure: Apply online.
Closing Date: February 1st
Funding: Foundation
Contributor: The Historic American Building Survey (HABS)

Scott Opler Fellowships for New Scholars
Subjects: Architectural history.
Eligibility: Applicants must be members of the SAH.
Level of Study: Postgraduate, Postdoctorate
Type: Fellowship
Value: A full 1 year membership to the Society of Architectural Historians
Length of Study: 1 year
Frequency: Annual
Country of Study: United States of America
No. of awards offered: 1
Closing Date: November 15th

For further information contact:

Contact: Kathy Sturm, Manager, Meetings and Tours

Spiro Kostof Annual Meeting Fellowship
Subjects: Architectural history.
Purpose: To enable an advanced graduate student in architectural history to attend the annual meeting of the Society of Architectural Historians.
Eligibility: Open to Doctoral candidates only who have been members of the SAH for at least 1 year.
Level of Study: Doctorate, Predoctorate
Type: Fellowship
Value: US$500 travel stipend and complimentary meeting registration
Frequency: Annual
No. of awards offered: 1
Application Procedure: Applicants must write for an application form, available after June 1st by mail or by visiting the website.
Closing Date: November 15th
Funding: Commercial, private
Contributor: The Society of Architectural Historians
No. of awards given last year: 1
No. of applicants last year: 15

THE SOCIETY OF AUTHORS

84 Drayton Gardens, London, SW10 9SB, England
Tel: (44) 020 7373 6642
Fax: (44) 020 7373 5768
Email: info@societyofauthors.net
Website: www.societyofauthors.org
Contact: The Administration Office

The Society of Authors is a non-profit making organization, founded in 1884, to protect the rights and further the interests of authors, mainly by giving bursaries, advice and help to members. It administers prizes and grants for authors.

The Authors' Foundation Grant
Subjects: Authorship.
Purpose: To provide grants to writers to assist them while writing books.
Eligibility: To apply the author must meet either of these conditions: the author has been commissioned by a commercial British publishers to write a work of fiction, poetry or non-fiction and needs funding. The author is without contractual commitment by a publisher but has least one book published already.
Level of Study: Professional development
Type: Grant
Value: UK £1,000–4,000
Length of Study: 1 year
Frequency: Every six months
Country of Study: United Kingdom
Application Procedure: Please check the website for more details.
Closing Date: April 30th and September 30th
Funding: Foundation
Contributor: The Authors' Foundation
No. of awards given last year: 50
No. of applicants last year: 250
Additional Information: Editors, translators and screenwriters are not eligible.

Elizabeth Longford Grants
Subjects: Historical biography.
Eligibility: Please check The Author's Foundation for specific eligibility details for this grant.
Level of Study: Professional development
Type: Grant
Value: UK £2,500
Frequency: Every six months
Country of Study: United Kingdom
Application Procedure: Please check the website for more details.
Closing Date: April 30th and September 30th
Funding: Private
Contributor: Flora Fraser and Peter Soros
No. of awards given last year: 2

Great Britain Sasakawa Foundation Grants
Subjects: Authorship relating to Japanese culture or society.
Eligibility: Preference will be given to authors whose work helps to interpret modern Japan to the English-speaking world.
Level of Study: Professional development
Type: Grant
Value: UK £2,500
Length of Study: 1 year
Frequency: Annual
Country of Study: United Kingdom
Application Procedure: Contact Paula Johnson at the Authors' Foundation or check the website for more details.
Closing Date: April 30th and September 30th
Funding: Foundation
Contributor: Sasakawa Foundation

The K. Blundell Trust Grant
Subjects: Authorship.
Purpose: To support British authors who need funding for important research, travel or other expenditure.
Eligibility: Applicants must be British by birth, resident in the UK, under the age of 40 and their work must contribute to the 'greater understanding of existing social and economic organization'. They must have had one book published.

Level of Study: Professional development
Type: Grant
Value: UK £1,000–4,000
Length of Study: 1 year
Frequency: Every six months
Country of Study: United Kingdom
Application Procedure: See the website for guidelines; submissions by fax or email are not acceptable.
Closing Date: April 30th and September 30th
Funding: Trusts
Contributor: K. Blundell Trust
No. of awards given last year: 8
No. of applicants last year: 25
Additional Information: No author may apply twice to the Trust within one 12 month period; grants will not be awarded to cover publication costs.

Michael Meyer Award

Subjects: Authorship.
Eligibility: Please check The Author's Foundation for specific eligibility details for this grant.
Level of Study: Professional development
Type: Grant
Frequency: Annual
Country of Study: United Kingdom
No. of awards offered: 1or 2
Application Procedure: Please check the website for more details.
Closing Date: April 30th and September 30th
Funding: Trusts
Contributor: The late Michael Meyer
No. of awards given last year: 2

SOCIETY OF CHILDREN'S BOOK WRITERS AND ILLUSTRATORS (SCBWI)

8271 Beverly Boulevard, Los Angeles, CA 90048, United States of America
Tel: (1) 323 782 1010
Fax: (1) 323 782 1892
Email: scbwi@scbwi.org
Website: www.scbwi.org
Contact: Mr Stephen Mooser, President

The Society of Children's Book Writers and Illustrators (SCBWI) is an organization of 22,000 writers, illustrators, editors, agents and publishers of children's books, television, film and multimedia.

Barbara Karlin Grant

Subjects: Children's picture books.
Purpose: To assist picture book writers in the completion of a specific project.
Eligibility: Open to both full and associate members of the Society who have never had a picture book published. The grant is not available for a project for which there is already a contract.
Level of Study: Unrestricted
Type: Grant
Value: The full grant is US$1,500 and the runner-up grant is US$500
Frequency: Annual
Country of Study: Any country
No. of awards offered: 1
Application Procedure: Applicants must write for details.
Closing Date: May 15th
Funding: Private
No. of awards given last year: 2
No. of applicants last year: 75

Don Freeman Memorial Grant-in-Aid

Subjects: Children's picture books.
Purpose: To enable picture-book artists to further their understanding, training and work in the picture-book genre.
Eligibility: Open to both full and associate members of the Society who, as artists, seriously intend to make picture books their chief contribution to the field of children's literature.
Level of Study: Unrestricted
Type: Grant

Value: The full grant is US$1,500 and the runner-up grant is US$500
Frequency: Annual
Country of Study: Any country
No. of awards offered: 2
Application Procedure: Applicants must submit an application to the Society. Receipt of the application will be acknowledged.
Closing Date: Application requests should be submitted by June 15th and completed applications should be submitted by February 10th
Funding: Private
No. of awards given last year: 2
No. of applicants last year: 48

SCBWI General Work-in-Progress Grant

Subjects: Children's literature.
Purpose: To assist children's book writers in the completion of a specific project.
Eligibility: Open to both full and associate members of the Society. The grant is not available for a project for which there is already a contract. Recipients of previous grants are not eligible to apply for any further SCBWI grants.
Level of Study: Unrestricted
Type: Grant
Value: The full grant is US$1,500 and the runner-up grant is US$500
Frequency: Annual
Country of Study: Any country
No. of awards offered: 1 full grant and 1 runner-up grant
Application Procedure: Applicants must write for details.
Closing Date: May 1st
Funding: Private
No. of awards given last year: 2
No. of applicants last year: 123

SCBWI Grant for a Contemporary Novel for Young People

Subjects: Children's literature.
Purpose: To assist children's book writers in the completion of a specific project.
Eligibility: Open to both full and associate members of the Society. The grant is not available for a project for which there is already a contract. Recipients of previous grants are not eligible to apply for any further SCBWI Grants.
Level of Study: Unrestricted
Type: Grant
Value: The full grant is US$1,500 and the runner-up grant is US$500
Frequency: Annual
Country of Study: Any country
No. of awards offered: 1 full grant and 1 runner-up grant
Application Procedure: Applicants must write for details.
Closing Date: May 1st
Funding: Private
No. of awards given last year: 2
No. of applicants last year: 110

SCBWI Grant for Unpublished Authors

Subjects: Children's literature.
Purpose: To assist children's book writers in the completion of a specific project.
Eligibility: Open to both full and associate members of the Society who have never had a book published. The grant is not available for a project for which there is already a contract. Recipients of previous grants are not eligible to apply for any further SCBWI Grants.
Level of Study: Unrestricted
Type: Grant
Value: The full grant is US$1,500 and the runner-up grant is US$500
Frequency: Annual
Country of Study: Any country
No. of awards offered: 1 full grant and 1 runner-up grant
Closing Date: May 1st
Funding: Private
No. of awards given last year: 2
No. of applicants last year: 45

SCBWI Nonfiction Research Grant

Subjects: Children's literature.
Purpose: To assist children's book writers in the completion of a specific project.

Eligibility: Open to both full and associate members of the Society. The grant is not available for a project for which there is already a contract. Recipients of previous grants are not eligible to apply for any further SCBWI Grants.
Level of Study: Unrestricted
Type: Grant
Value: The full grant is US$1,500 and the runner-up grant is US$500
Frequency: Annual
Country of Study: Any country
No. of awards offered: 1 full grant and 1 runner-up grant
Application Procedure: Applicants must write for details.
Closing Date: May 1st
Funding: Private
No. of awards given last year: 1
No. of applicants last year: 75

SOCIETY OF ENVIRONMENTAL TOXICOLOGY AND CHEMISTRY (SETAC)

1010 North 12th Avenue, Pensacola, FL, 32501-3367,
United States of America
Tel: (1) 850 469 1500
Fax: (1) 850 469 9778
Email: setac@setaceu.org
Website: www.setac.org

The Society of Environmental Toxicology and Chemistry (SETAC) is a non-profit, worldwide professional society comprised of individuals and institutions who support the development of principles and practices for protection, enhancement and management of sustainable environmental quality and ecosystem integrity.

Procter & Gamble Fellowship for Doctoral Research in Environmental Science

Subjects: Environmental sciences.
Purpose: To promote the advancement and application of scientific research, education in the environmental sciences and the use of science in environmental policy and decision making.
Eligibility: Open to Doctoral students whose research area and academic standing are consistent with the research topics.
Level of Study: Doctorate
Type: Fellowships
Value: US$15,000
Length of Study: 1 year
Frequency: Annual
Application Procedure: Applicants must submit electronically a description of the dissertation research, a curriculum vitae and a letter of support from the dissertation director.
Closing Date: September 1st
Additional Information: The award is paid to the recipient's institution, so it is necessary that an authorized representative approve the application on behalf of the institution and certify that none of the award will be spent on overhead.

For further information contact:

Europe Avenue de la Toison d'Or 67 B-1060, Brussels, FL, 32501-3367, Belgium
Tel: (32) 850 469 1500
Fax: (32) 850 469 9978
Contact: Bart Bosveld, Executive Director

SOCIETY OF EXPLORATION GEOPHYSICISTS FOUNDATION (SEG)

SEG Foundation PO 702740, Tulsa, OK, 74170-2740, United States of America
Tel: (1) 918 497 5500
Fax: (1) 918 497 5560
Email: scholarships@seg.org
Website: www.seg.org
Contact: SEG Scholarship Committee

The Society of Exploration Geophysicists Foundation (SEG) began a programme of encouraging the establishment of scholarship funds by companies and individuals in the field of geophysics in 1956. In 1963, the Foundation's activities were expanded to include grants-in-aid.

SEG Scholarships

Subjects: Applied geophysics and related fields.
Purpose: To encourage careers in applied geophysics and related fields.
Eligibility: Open to citizens of any non-sanctioned country who are entering undergraduate or graduate level and have above average grades and an aptitude for physics, mathematics, and geology.
Level of Study: Unrestricted
Type: Scholarship
Value: US$500–14,000 per academic year. Average awards are approx. US$1,500
Length of Study: 1 academic year, may be eligible for renewal
Frequency: Annual
Country of Study: Any country
No. of awards offered: Varies
Application Procedure: Applicants must submit a completed application form accompanied by 3 years of transcripts and 2 letters of recommendation from faculty members who are familiar with the applicant's academic work.
Closing Date: February 1st of the year in which the award is made
Funding: Corporation, individuals, private, trusts, commercial
No. of awards given last year: 150
No. of applicants last year: 500
Additional Information: More than US$200,000 was granted in scholarships during the 2006–2007 academic year.

SOCIETY OF ORTHOPAEDIC MEDICINE

PO Box 204, Woolton, L25 7WA, England
Tel: (44) 0845 680 1608
Fax: (44) 0845 680 1618
Email: admin@somed.org
Website: www.somed.org

The Society of Orthopaedic Medicine is a non-profit making organization offering grants for work within musculoskeletal medicine.

SOM Research Grant

Subjects: Musculoskeletal and orthopaedic medicine.
Purpose: To assist those undertaking programmes of study that will increase knowledge in the field of orthopaedic medicine and enhance their professional development.
Eligibility: Applications are considered from those who may be undertaking a research degree leading to an MPhil, a research degree leading to a PhD/DProf, a pilot study or a presentation at a conference. Grants are also available for equipment. Must be member of society of Orthopaedic medicine.
Level of Study: Postdoctorate, Predoctorate, Professional development, Graduate
Value: Up to UK £5,000. UK £2,000 of this allocation will be available in the form of smaller grants of up to UK £500
Frequency: Annual
Country of Study: United Kingdom
No. of awards offered: Varies according to funds
Application Procedure: Applicants must complete an application form available from the organization.
Closing Date: Applications are accepted all year round
Funding: Commercial
No. of awards given last year: 5
No. of applicants last year: 8

SOCIETY OF WOMEN ENGINEERS (SWE)

230 East Ohio Street, Suite 400, Chicago, IL, 60611,
United States of America
Tel: (1) 312 596 5223
Fax: (1) 312 596 5252
Email: hq@swe.org
Website: www.swe.org
Contact: Ms Betty Shanahan, Executive Director

The Society of Women Engineers (SWE) was founded in 1950, and is a non-profit educational service organization. SWE is the driving force that establishes engineering as a highly desirable career aspiration for women. SWE empowers women to succeed and advance in those aspirations and be recognized for their life-changing contributions and achievements as engineers and leaders.

B K Krenzer Memorial Re-Entry Scholarship

Subjects: Engineering.

Purpose: To assist women in obtaining the credentials necessary to re-enter the job market as engineers.

Eligibility: Open to women who have been out of the job market as well as out of school for a minimum of 2 years. Recipients may be entering any year of an engineering programme, as full-time or part-time students. Preference is given to graduate engineers desiring to return to the workforce following a period of temporary retirement.

Level of Study: Graduate, Postgraduate, Undergraduate

Type: Scholarship

Value: US$2,000

Frequency: Annual

Study Establishment: An ABET or CSB accredited programme

Country of Study: United States of America

No. of awards offered: 1

Application Procedure: Application forms are available from the website.

Closing Date: May 15th

Funding: Private

No. of awards given last year: 1

Lydia I Pickup Memorial Scholarship

Subjects: Engineering and computer science.

Purpose: To advance the applicant's career in engineering or computer science.

Eligibility: Open only to women majoring in engineering or computer science at a college or university with an ABET accredited programme.

Level of Study: Doctorate, Graduate, Undergraduate

Type: Scholarship

Value: US$4,000

Frequency: Annual

Country of Study: United States of America

No. of awards offered: 1

Application Procedure: Application forms are available from the website.

Closing Date: Continuous

Funding: Private

No. of awards given last year: 1

Olive Lynn Salembier Scholarship

Subjects: Engineering and computer science.

Purpose: To aid women who have been out of the engineering market and out of school to obtain the credentials necessary to re-enter the job market as an engineer.

Eligibility: Open to women who have not practised engineering or been enrolled in an engineering or other university or college programme in the past 2 years. Applicants must be citizens of the United States of America. Recipients may be entering any graduate year, including doctoral programmes, as full-time or part-time students.

Level of Study: Graduate, Doctorate, Undergraduate

Type: Scholarship

Value: US$2,000

Frequency: Annual

Country of Study: United States of America

No. of awards offered: 1

Application Procedure: Application forms are available from the website.

Closing Date: May 15th

Funding: Private

No. of awards given last year: 1

SWE Caterpillar Scholarship

Subjects: Any engineering subject.

Purpose: To support women in engineering careers.

Eligibility: Applicants must be women engineering students and members of SWE in SWE regions C,D,H or I.

Level of Study: Graduate, Doctorate

Type: Scholarship

Value: US$2,400

Frequency: Annual

Country of Study: United States of America

No. of awards offered: 3

Application Procedure: Application forms are available from the website.

Closing Date: February 1st

Funding: Corporation

Contributor: Caterpillar Inc

No. of awards given last year: 3

SWE Electronics for Imaging Scholarship

Subjects: Engineering.

Purpose: To encourage women engineers to attain graduate engineering degrees.

Eligibility: Open only to women engineering students.

Level of Study: Doctorate, Graduate, Undergraduate

Type: Scholarship

Value: US$4,000

Frequency: Annual

Country of Study: United States of America

No. of awards offered: 4

Application Procedure: Application forms are available from the website.

Closing Date: February 1st

Funding: Corporation

Contributor: Electronics for Imaging

No. of awards given last year: 4

SWE General Motors Foundation Graduate Scholarship

Subjects: Mechanical engineering, electrical engineering, chemical engineering, industrial engineering, materials science and engineering or manufacturing engineering.

Purpose: To encourage women engineers to attain high levels of education and professional achievement.

Eligibility: Applicants must have a career interest in the automotive industry or manufacturing, and have demonstrated leadership potential.

Level of Study: Doctorate, Graduate, Postgraduate

Type: Scholarship

Value: US$3,000, plus a travel grant of US$500 for each recipient to attend the SWE National Conference

Frequency: Annual

Study Establishment: See the website for list of schools

Country of Study: United States of America

No. of awards offered: 3

Application Procedure: Application forms are available from the website.

Closing Date: February 1st

Funding: Corporation, foundation

Contributor: General Motors Foundation

No. of awards given last year: 1

SWE Microsoft Corporation Scholarships

Subjects: Computer science and computer engineering.

Purpose: To encourage women engineers to attain a high level of education and professional achievement.

Eligibility: Open only to women majoring in engineering or computer science in a college or university with an ABET-accredited programme. Applicants must be citizens of the United States of America.

Level of Study: Graduate, Undergraduate

Type: Scholarship

Value: US$2,500

Frequency: Annual

Study Establishment: A college or university

Country of Study: United States of America

No. of awards offered: 2

Application Procedure: Application forms are available from the website.

Closing Date: March 1st

Funding: Corporation

Contributor: The Microsoft Corporation

No. of awards given last year: 2

Additional Information: Further information is available on the website.

SWE Past Presidents Scholarships

Subjects: Engineering.

Eligibility: Open only to women majoring in engineering or computer science in a college or university with an ABET accredited programme. United States of America citizenship is required.
Level of Study: Doctorate, Graduate, Postgraduate
Type: Scholarship
Value: US$1,200
Frequency: Annual
Country of Study: United States of America
No. of awards offered: 2
Application Procedure: Application forms are available from the website.
Closing Date: February 1st
Funding: Private
No. of awards given last year: 2

SWE/Bentley Graduate Merit Scholarship
Subjects: MBA.
Purpose: To pursue a full-time MBA at Bentley's McCallum Graduate School of Business.
Eligibility: African American, Latina, Asian or Native American women are especially eligible to apply.
Level of Study: MBA
Type: Scholarship
Value: US$12,615–63,075
Frequency: Annual
Study Establishment: The Bentley McCallum Graduate School of Business
Country of Study: United States of America
No. of awards offered: 1
Application Procedure: Application forms are available from the website.
Closing Date: March 1st
Funding: Private
Contributor: Bentley College
No. of awards given last year: 1

SOCRATES SCULPTURE PARK

Broadway at Vernon Boulevard, PO Box 6259 Long Island City, NY, 11106, United States of America
Tel: (1) 718 956 1819
Fax: (1) 718 626 1533
Email: info@socratessculpturepark.org
Website: www.socratessculpturepark.org

Socrates Sculpture Park was an abandoned riverside landfill and illegal dumpsite until 1986 when a coalition of artists and community members, under the leadership of artist Mark di Suvero, transformed it into an open studio and exhibition space for artists and a neighbourhood park for local residents. Today it is an internationally renowned outdoor museum and artist residency programme that also serves as a vital New York City park offering a wide variety of public services.

Socrates Sculpture Park Emerging Artist Fellowship Program
Subjects: Sculpture.
Purpose: To provide artists with opportunities to create and exhibit large-scale work in a unique environment that encourages strong interaction between artists, artworks and the public.
Eligibility: Open to artists who are not yet well established, are New York State residents and are in need of financial assistance.
Level of Study: Professional development
Type: Fellowship
Value: US$4,000
Length of Study: 2–6 months
Frequency: Annual
Country of Study: United States of America
Application Procedure: Applicants can download the application form from the website. The completed application form along with a curriculum vitae, references, slide script and proposal must be submitted.
Closing Date: January 30th
Additional Information: Grants and fellowships are not available to artists who are enrolled in a school, college or university programme.

SOIL AND WATER CONSERVATION SOCIETY (SWCS)

945 SW Ankeny Road, Ankeny, Iowa 50023-9723, United States of America
Tel: (1) 515 289 2331
Fax: (1) 515 289 1227
Email: sueann.lynes@swcs.org
Website: www.swcs.org

The Soil and Water Conservation Society (SWCS) fosters the science and the art of soil, water and related natural resource management to achieve sustainability. The SWCS promotes and practices an ethic recognizing the interdependence of people and the environment.

The Kenneth E. Grant Scholarship
Subjects: Soil science, water science and related natural resource management.
Purpose: To actively promote multi-disciplinary research.
Level of Study: Postgraduate
Type: Scholarship
Value: US$1,300
Length of Study: 1 year
Frequency: Annual
No. of awards offered: 1
Application Procedure: Apply online.
Closing Date: February 13th

SONS OF THE REPUBLIC OF TEXAS

1717 8th Street, Bay City, TX, 77414, United States of America
Tel: (1) 979 245 6644
Fax: (1) 979 244 3819
Email: srttexas@srttexas.org
Website: www.srttexas.org
Contact: Administrative Assistant

Sons of the Republic of Texas seeks to perpetuate the memory and spirit of the men and women who settled Texas and won its independence through great personal sacrifice and dedication to the cause of freedom.

Presidio La Bahia Award
Subjects: History.
Purpose: To promote the suitable preservation of relics, appropriate dissemination of data and research into Texas heritage, with particular emphasis on the Spanish colonial period.
Eligibility: Open to all persons interested in the Spanish colonial influence on Texas culture.
Level of Study: Unrestricted
Type: Award
Value: The 1st prize is a minimum of US$1,200, and the 2nd and 3rd prizes are the divided balance from the total amount available of US$2,000 at the discretion of the judges
Frequency: Annual
Study Establishment: Any suitable institution
Country of Study: Any country
No. of awards offered: 3
Application Procedure: Applicants must submit four copies of published writings to the office. Galley proofs are not acceptable.
Closing Date: Entries are accepted from June 1st to September 30th
Funding: Private
No. of awards given last year: 1
Additional Information: Research writings have, in the past, proved to be the most successful type of entry. However, consideration will be given to other literary forms, art, architecture and archaeological discovery. For projects other than writing, contestants should furnish a description of the proposed entry, so that the Chairman may issue specific instructions.

Summerfield G Roberts Award
Subjects: History.
Purpose: To encourage literary effort and research about historical events and personalities during the days of the Republic of Texas 1836–1846, and to stimulate interest in the period.

Eligibility: Open to all writers.
Level of Study: Unrestricted
Type: Award
Value: US$2,500
Frequency: Annual
Study Establishment: Any suitable institution
Country of Study: Any country
No. of awards offered: 1
Application Procedure: Manuscripts must be written or published during the calendar year for which the award is given. There is no word limit. No entry may be submitted more than one time. The manuscripts must be mailed (5 copies, for the use of the judges) to the General Office of the Sons of the Republic of Texas.
Closing Date: January 15th
Funding: Private
No. of awards given last year: 1
Additional Information: The award was made possible through the generosity of Mr and Mrs Summerfield G Roberts.

THE SOROPTIMIST FOUNDATION OF CANADA

13311 Yonge Street, Suite 104, Richmond Hill, ON, L4E 3L6, Canada
Tel: (1) 905-773-9927
Email: corinne@cmrlaw.ca
Website: www.soroptimistfoundation.ca
Contact: Corinne Rivers,

The Soroptimist Foundation was established in 1963 by incorporation under the laws of Canada, for charitable, scientific, literary and educational purposes.

Soroptimist Foundation of Canada Grants for Women
Subjects: All subjects.
Purpose: To financially assist women who wish to complete their studies for careers that will improve the quality of the lives of women and girls.
Eligibility: Open only to women candidates who are citizens of Canada.enrolled in an accredited Canadian university and will work in Canada for a minimum of 2 years after completion of the degree course
Level of Study: Postgraduate
Type: Grant
Value: Canadian $7,500
Frequency: Annual
Country of Study: Canada
No. of awards offered: 4
Application Procedure: Applicants must send completed application forms and all required additional documents before the closing date.Please see the website www.soroptimistfoundation.ca for further details.
Closing Date: January 31st
Funding: Foundation
No. of awards given last year: 4
No. of applicants last year: 110

For further information contact:

For Eastern Canada: 35 Dakin Crescent, Cambridge, ON, N1S-3X1, Canada
Email: rsanders@sentex.net
Contact: Alison Sanders, Grants Manager For Western Canada: 3107 Highland Boulevard, North Vancouver, BC, V7R 0X5
Contact: Jean Violette

SOROS FOUNDATION

400 West 59th Street, New York, NY, 10019, United States of America
Tel: (1) 212 547 6926
Fax: (1) 212 548 4623
Email: pdsoros_fellows@sorosny.org
Website: www.pdsoros.org
Contact: Mr Peter Byrne

The Soros Foundation was founded by Hungarian immigrants and American philanthropists in December 1997 with a charitable trust of 50 million dollars. Their reasons for doing so were several. They wished to give back to the country that had afforded them and their children such great opportunities and felt a fellowship programme was an appropriate vehicle.

Paul and Daisy Soros Fellowships for New Americans
Subjects: Engineering, medicine, law, social work, humanities, social sciences, sciences, fine arts and performing arts.
Purpose: To provide opportunities for continuing generations of able and accomplished New Americans to achieve leadership in their chosen fields.
Eligibility: Open to resident aliens, who have been naturalized as citizens of United States or whose parents are both naturalized citizens. Applicants must either have a Bachelor's degree or be in their final year of undergraduate study and must not be older than 30 years of age as of November 1st.
Level of Study: Doctorate, Graduate, Postgraduate
Type: Fellowships
Value: US$20,000 (paid in two installments) and a tuition grant of one-half the tuition cost of the United States graduate programme attended by the Fellow (up to US$16,000 per academic year)
Length of Study: 2 years
Frequency: Annual
Study Establishment: Any accredited graduate programme
Country of Study: United States of America
No. of awards offered: 30
Application Procedure: Applicants must submit a completed online application form, 2 essays on specified topics, 1–2 page curriculum vitae, 3 recommendation letters, transcripts and provide a photocopy of the test scores of Graduate Management Admission Test, MCAT, Graduate Record Examination and LSAT.
Closing Date: December
Additional Information: Individuals are expected to retain loyalty and a sense of commitment to their country of origin as well as to the United States, but is intended to support individuals who will continue to regard the United States as their principal residence and focus of national identity.

THE SOUTH AFRICAN INSTITUTE OF INTERNATIONAL AFFAIRS (SAIIA)

Jan Smuts House, PO Box 31596, Johannesburg, Braamfontein, 2017, South Africa
Tel: (27) 11 339 2021
Fax: (27) 11 339 2154
Email: info@saiia.org.za
Website: www.saiia.org.za
Contact: Mr Jonathan Stead, Director of Operations

The South African Institute of International Affairs (SAIIA) is an independent, non-governmental foreign policy think tank, whose purpose is to encourage wider and more informed interest in international affairs and public education and to focus on policy-relevant research.

SAIIA Bradlow Fellowship
Subjects: Social and behavioural sciences.
Purpose: To provide travel costs and a stipend to enable a senior scholar to reside at the Institute in order to research a subject of importance to South Africa's international relations.
Eligibility: Open to senior scholars.
Level of Study: Research
Type: Fellowship
Value: The stipend covers living expenses and a return economy-class airfare from the candidate's place of residence
Length of Study: 4–6 months
Frequency: Annual
Study Establishment: SAIIA
Country of Study: South Africa
No. of awards offered: 1
Application Procedure: Applicants must send a curriculum vitae including a short research proposal of not more than 1,000 words to the Director of Studies.
Funding: Private
Contributor: The Bradlow Foundation
No. of awards given last year: 1

SAIIA Konrad Adenauer Foundation Research Internship

Subjects: Politics, international relations, journalism and economics.
Purpose: To enable research interns to enroll at the University of Witwatersrand for a Master's degree by coursework while simultaneously working at SAIIA.
Eligibility: Open to South African citizens under 30 years of age.
Level of Study: Postgraduate
Type: Internship
Length of Study: 10 months
Frequency: Annual
Study Establishment: SAIIA and the University of Witwatersrand
Country of Study: South Africa
No. of awards offered: 3
Application Procedure: Applicants must send a curriculum vitae, names and contact details of three referees, letter of motivation, outline of research interests in the field of international relations, three written references, June results and academic transcripts of previous degree and one example of written work not exceeding 3,000 words on a topic of choice.
Closing Date: October 8th
Funding: Foundation
Contributor: Konrad Adenauer Foundation
No. of awards given last year: 2
No. of applicants last year: 32

For further information contact:

Email: grobbelaarn@saiia.wits.ac.za

SOUTH AFRICAN MEDICAL RESEARCH COUNCIL (SAMRC)

Research Grants Administration, PO Box 19070, Tygerberg, 7505, South Africa
Tel: (27) 21 938 0227
Fax: (27) 21 938 0368
Email: info@mrc.ac.za
Website: www.mrc.ac.za
Contact: Mrs Marina Jenkins, Research Grants Administration

The South African Medical Research Council's (SAMRC) brief is to undertake excellent research, which can be implemented to improve the health of all South Africans. Research priorities are regularly established through broad consultation. The SAMRC's mission is to improve the health, status and quality of life of the nation through excellence in scientific research.

SAMRC Local Postdoctoral Scholarships

Subjects: Health sciences.
Purpose: To create opportunities for recent postdoctoral scientists who are otherwise lost to the system and country.
Eligibility: Open to candidates who have completed a Doctorate research in any field in the health sciences.
Level of Study: Postdoctorate
Type: Scholarships
Value: Varies
Length of Study: 3 years
Frequency: Annual
Country of Study: South Africa
Application Procedure: Applicants must submit a research plan, institutional and ethics approval for the project, proof of source of funding for the research project and 3 referees reports.
Closing Date: September 30th

SAMRC Post MBChB and BChD Grants

Subjects: Health sciences.
Purpose: To provide an opportunity for full-time research training for medical doctors as part of their development towards a Master's degree.
Eligibility: Open to recent MBChB or BChD graduates who are registered with the health professions council and have completed their internship and community service and registered for a Master's degree in a specialist field or a research area.
Level of Study: Postgraduate
Type: Grant

Value: South African Rand 80,000 per year
Length of Study: 4 years
Frequency: Annual
Country of Study: South Africa
Application Procedure: Applicants must submit their applications to the MRC through the institution's postgraduate bursary office.
Closing Date: June 30th

SOUTHDOWN TRUST

Holmbush, 64 High Street, Findon, West Sussex, BN14 0SY, England
Contact: Mr John G Wyatt

The Southdown Trust is a small charity that gives limited help to individuals for educational purposes.

Southdown Trust Awards

Subjects: All subjects except law, drama and music, dance, journalism, sociology, women's studies, business studies, arts, sports, IT, counselling, peace studies. Only educational costs are supported. Grants are not made for equipment such as computers.
Purpose: To encourage personal initiative, education and concern for others.
Eligibility: Open mainly to United Kingdom citizens but other nationalities are considered.
Value: Varies, usually UK £25–500
Frequency: Dependent on funds available
Country of Study: United Kingdom
No. of awards offered: Varies
Application Procedure: All applicants must apply directly. No applications are accepted through agencies. There are no application forms. Applicants must write giving full details and include a stamped addressed envelope. All letters must be signed.
Closing Date: May 1st, November 1st
Funding: Private
No. of awards given last year: 106
No. of applicants last year: 1500
Additional Information: Not eligible for PhDs.

SOUTHEAST ASIA URBAN ENVIRONMENTAL MANAGEMENT APPLICATIONS (SEA-UEMA)

School of Environment, Resources and Development, Asian Institute of Technology PO Box 4, Klong Luang, Pathumthani, 12120, Thailand
Tel: (66) 02 5245777
Fax: (66) 02 5162126/5248338
Email: uemapplications@ait.ac.th
Website: www.sea-uema.ait.ac.th

The Canadian International Development Agency and the Asian Institute of Technology have entered into a contribution agreement on urban environmental management. This is in the form of Southeast Asia Urban Environmental Management Applications (SEA-UEMA) Project, which aims to improve the urban environmental management policies and good practices in the region.

SEA-UEMA Post-doctoral Research Fellowships

Subjects: Urban environmental management practices and policies.
Purpose: To contribute to the improvements of urban environmental conditions in Southeast Asia.
Eligibility: Open to candidates from the Canadian ODA eligible Southeast Asian countries who hold a Doctoral degree.
Level of Study: Postdoctorate
Type: Fellowships
Value: Baht 50,000 per month plus Baht 1,50,000 as research fund and other benefits
Length of Study: 1 year
Frequency: Annual
Application Procedure: Applicants must submit an application form along with curriculum vitae, reprints of publications and a research proposal.
Closing Date: July 15th

Additional Information: For further inquiries please contact Mr Vikas Nitivattaranon, Assistant Professor. Email:bimal@ait.ac.th; Tel: 02 5246399.

SOUTHERN AFRICAN MUSIC RIGHTS ORGANIZATION (SAMRO) ENDOWMENT FOR THE NATIONAL ARTS

PO Box 31609, Braamfontein, 2017, South Africa
Tel: (27) 11 489 5000
Fax: (27) 11 403 1934
Email: customerservices@samro.org.za
Website: www.samro.org.za
Contact: J C Otto, Liaison & Research Officer

Southern African Music Rights Organization (SAMRO) is Southern Africa's society of composers and lyricists, administering the performing, transmission and broadcasting rights in the musical works of its members and the members of its affiliated societies. Through the SAMRO Endowment for the National Arts (SENA), it encourages the developement of the arts by combining funding with support and advisory services to individuals and organisations to enable them to further their music education, composer careers and more.

SAMRO Intermediate Bursaries for Composition Study In Southern Africa

Subjects: Music.
Purpose: To support music composition study as a major subject in either the western art, choral or jazz popular music genres.
Eligibility: Open to citizens of South Africa, Botswana, Lesotho and Swaziland who have met the requirements for proceeding to the 3rd, 4th or honours year of a senior undergraduate degree or equivalent diploma course. Applicants must have been born after February 15th, 1974. For those entering any year of a Master's or doctoral degree, the age limit is 32. Older students are considered in special circumstances.
Level of Study: Postgraduate
Type: Bursary
Value: Rand 9,000 for 3rd, 4th and honours year students and Rand 6,000 for Master's or doctoral degrees
Length of Study: 1 year
Frequency: Annual
Study Establishment: A university, institute of technology or other recognized statutory institute of tertiary education approved by the trustees
Country of Study: South Africa, Botswana, Lesotho, or Swaziland
No. of awards offered: 10
Application Procedure: Applicants must complete an application form.
Closing Date: February 15th
Funding: Private
Contributor: SAMRO
No. of awards given last year: 4
No. of applicants last year: 5
Additional Information: Applicants must produce an official letter of acceptance for entering any year of a Master's or doctoral degree.

SAMRO Overseas Scholarship

Subjects: Music.
Purpose: To encourage music study at the postgraduate level in the western art/choral or jazz popular music genres.
Eligibility: Open to postgraduate students who are citizens of South Africa, Botswana, Lesotho or Swaziland. The age limit is 34 years.
Level of Study: Postgraduate
Type: Scholarship
Value: Rand 160,000 plus travel expenses of up to Rand 10,000
Length of Study: 2 years
Frequency: Annual
Study Establishment: An institute or educational entity approved by the SAMRO Endowment for the National Arts (SENA)
Country of Study: United Kingdom, Europe or North America
No. of awards offered: 2
Application Procedure: Applicants must complete an application form.

Closing Date: April 30th
Funding: Private
Contributor: SAMRO
No. of awards given last year: 2
No. of applicants last year: 13

SAMRO Postgraduate Bursaries for Indigenous African Music Study

Subjects: Music.
Purpose: To encourage the study of indigenous African music at the postgraduate level in either the traditional, western art/choral or jazz popular music genres.
Eligibility: Open to postgraduate students who are citizens of South Africa, Botswana, Lesotho or Swaziland. The age limit is 40 years.
Level of Study: Postgraduate
Type: Bursary
Value: Rand 5,500
Length of Study: 5 years
Frequency: Annual
Study Establishment: A university or other recognized statutory institute of tertiary education approved by the trustees and situated in SAMRO's current territory of operation
Country of Study: South Africa, Botswana, Lesotho, or Swaziland
No. of awards offered: 6
Application Procedure: Applicants must complete an application form.
Closing Date: February 15th
Funding: Private
Contributor: SAMRO
No. of awards given last year: 4
No. of applicants last year: 5
Additional Information: Applicants must produce an official letter of acceptance from a recognized tertiary institute of learning. They must have acceptance into the 1st year or any subsequent year of a postgraduate degree in indigenous African music at such an institute.

THE SPENCER FOUNDATION

625 North Michigan Avenue Suite 1600, Chicago, IL, 60611, United States of America
Tel: (1) 312 274 6526
Fax: (1) 312 337 0282
Email: abrinkman@spencer.org
Website: www.spencer.org
Contact: Annie Brinkman, Program Administrator

The Spencer Foundation was established in 1962 by Lyle M. Spencer. The Foundation is committed to supporting high quality investigation of education through its research programmes and to strengthening and renewing the educational research community through its fellowship and training programmes and related activities.

Spencer Foundation Dissertation Fellowship Program

Subjects: Education.
Purpose: To encourage a new generation of scholars from a wide range of disciplines and professional fields to undertake research relevant to the improvement of education.
Eligibility: Open to candidates for the Doctoral degree at a graduate school within the United States of America.
Level of Study: Doctorate
Type: Fellowship
Value: US$25,000
Frequency: Annual
Country of Study: United States of America
Application Procedure: Applicants must apply online. In addition to the completed application form they must submit a list of publications/presentations, a dissertation abstract, a narrative discussion of the dissertation, a work plan, 2 letters of recommendation and a graduate transcript.
Closing Date: November 2nd

For further information contact:

Email: fellows@spencer.org

ST VINCENT'S INSTITUTE (SVI)

41 Victoria Parade, Fitzroy, VIC 3065, Australia
Tel: (61) 03 9288 2480
Fax: (61) 03 9416 2676
Email: pgscholarships2009@svi.edu.au
Website: www.svi.edu.au
Contact: Dr Robyn Starr, Postgraduate Student Coordinator

St Vincent's Institute (SVI) conducts programs of basic and clinical research into diseases that have a high impact on the community and is focused on exploring both disease causes and prevention, with a commitment to discovering practical and far-reaching solutions to diseases that impact on the everyday life of people around the world.

SVI Foundation Postgraduate Student Award

Subjects: Medical research.
Purpose: To provide valuable financial support for outstanding students commencing their PhD training at SVI.
Eligibility: Open to First Class (Honours) students commencing full time study towards a PhD at St Vincent's Institute. Students need to successfully apply for a full PhD stipend (APA, Dora Lush etc.) to be eligible for this award. This is intended to be a top up award for those students receiving full PhD scholarships.
Level of Study: Doctorate, Graduate
Type: Award
Value: $5,000 per year
Length of Study: 3 years
Frequency: Annual
Study Establishment: St Vincent's Institute
Country of Study: Australia
No. of awards offered: Up to 2
Application Procedure: Check website for further details.
Closing Date: October 31st
Funding: Foundation
No. of awards given last year: 2
No. of applicants last year: 7
Additional Information: Scholarships will be awarded on the basis of the applicant's academic excellence and research potential. An interview with the selection panel may be required.

THE STANLEY MEDICAL RESEARCH INSTITUTE

8401 Connecticut Avenue, Suite 200, Chevy Chase, MD, 20815, United States of America
Tel: (1) 301 571 0760
Fax: (1) 301 571 0769
Email: marter@stanleyresearch.org
Website: www.stanleyresearch.org
Contact: Ms Rhoda Marte

SMRI is a nonprofit organization that supports research designed to find better treatments for schizophrenia and bipolar disorder. Approximately 75 per cent of its annual expenditures are devoted to the direct clinical testing of new treatments. 25 per cent is earmarked for research on the causes of these illness.

Stanley Medical Research Institute Postdoctoral Research Fellowship Program

Subjects: Psychiatry and mental health-causes and treatment of schizophrenia and bipolar disorder.
Purpose: To attract top-quality scientists to specific areas of research in severe mental illness.
Eligibility: Open to researchers worldwide. Applicants must be a doctorate or equivalent professional and must not be more than 2 years past receipt of their doctoral degree.
Level of Study: Postdoctorate, Research
Type: Research fellowship
Value: Up to US$150,000 spread over 2 years including indirect costs of up to 15 per cent as part of the total grant budget
Length of Study: 2 years
Frequency: Annual
Country of Study: Any country
No. of awards offered: 1

Application Procedure: Interested applicants must apply online at the website. Detailed instructions for application are available in a printable format (PDF).
Closing Date: January 15th
Funding: Foundation, individuals
Additional Information: Top priority will be given to applications that address the following questions: (a) Synthesis or screening of compounds to be tested against molecular targets identified for servere mental illness (schizophrenia, bipolar disorder, servere depression). (b) Pharmacokinetic and toxicological characterization of potential drugs for servere mental illness. (c) Ethnopharmacology, i.e., discovery or characterization of potentially useful psychoactive compounds from non-Western medical traditions.

Stanley Medical Research Institute Research Grants Program

Subjects: Psychiatry and mental health: causes and treatment of schizophrenia and bipolar disorder.
Purpose: To support researchers at all levels of development in fields related to the cause and treatment of schizophrenia and bipolar disorder, as well as from other areas of medicine and biology who wish to initiate new projects in this field.
Eligibility: Open to researchers worldwide. Applicants must be a doctorate or equivalent professional.
Level of Study: Research
Type: Research grant
Value: US$5,000 per year; indirect costs may be paid up to 15 per cent as part of the total grant budget
Length of Study: 2 years
Frequency: Annual
Country of Study: Any country
Application Procedure: Interested applicants must apply online at the SMRI website. Detailed instructions for application are available in a printable formate(PDF).
Closing Date: March 1st
Funding: Individuals, private, foundation

Stanley Medical Research Institute Treatment Trial Grants Program

Subjects: Psychology and mental health: treatments for schizophrenia and bipolar disorder.
Purpose: To support researchers and facilitate the direct testing of new treatments for schizophrenia and bipolar disorder. This programme supports projects involving human subjects and testing a therapeutic intervention (medication; device; putative medication including plant substances and nutritional; psychotherapy).
Eligibility: Open to researchers worldwide. Applicants must be a Doctorate or equivalent professional.
Level of Study: Research
Type: Research grant
Value: US$900,000
Length of Study: 3 years
Frequency: Annual
Country of Study: Any country
Application Procedure: Interested applicants must apply online at the SMRI website. Detailed instructions for application are available in printable format (PDF).
Closing Date: March 1st and October 1st
Funding: Foundation, individuals
Additional Information: Please check the master list of Stanley Medical Research Institute awarded trials on the website prior to completing the application. If we are supporting trials with the compound you propose, we are unlikely to support an additional trial until results are available.

STANLEY SMITH (UK) HORTICULTURAL TRUST

Cory Lodge, PO Box 365, Cambridge, Cambridgeshire, CB2 1HR, England
Tel: (44) 12 2333 6299
Fax: (44) 12 2333 6278
Email: jc240@cam.ac.uk
Contact: Mr James Cullen, Director

The Stanley Smith (UK) Horticultural Trust supports projects that contribute to the development of the art and science of horticulture, i.e. garden conservation and restoration, education and training, publications and travel.

Stanley Smith (UK) Horticultural Trust Awards

Subjects: Horticulture. The Trust supports individual projects in all aspects (including training) of amenity horticulture and some aspects of commercial horticulture.
Eligibility: Open to institutions and individuals. All projects are judged entirely on merit and there are no eligibility requirements, but grants are not awarded for students to take academic or diploma courses of any kind.
Level of Study: Unrestricted
Type: Varies
Value: Varies
Length of Study: Dependent on the nature of the project
Frequency: Twice a year
Country of Study: Any country
No. of awards offered: Varies
Application Procedure: Applicants must apply to the Trust. Trustees allocate awards in Spring and Autumn.
Closing Date: February 15th and August 15th
Funding: Private
Contributor: Donations
No. of awards given last year: 30
No. of applicants last year: 150

STATE LIBRARY OF NEW SOUTH WALES

Macquarie Street, Sydney, NSW 2000, Australia
Tel: (61) 02 9273 1414
Fax: (61) 02 9273 1255
Email: library@sl.nsw.gov.au
Website: www.sl.nsw.gov.au
Contact: Mitchell Librarian

The State Library of New South Wales is the premier reference and research library in New South Wales. The Library consists of the State Reference Library and the Mitchell Library, which contains the renowned Australian research collections pertaining to the history of Australia and the Southwest Pacific region.

Blake Dawson Waldron Prize for Business Literature

Subjects: Australian corporate and commercial literature, histories, accounts and analyses of corporate affairs as well as biographies of business men and women.
Purpose: To encourage the highest standards of commentary in the fields of business and finance.
Eligibility: The author must be a living Australian citizen or hold permanent resident status. The work must have primary reference to business or financial affairs, business or financial institutions or people directly associated with business and financial affairs, be written in the English language, published in book form and consist of a minimum of 50,000 words.
Level of Study: Professional development
Type: Prize
Length of Study: Australian $30,000
Frequency: Annual
Study Establishment: State Library of New South Wales
Country of Study: Australia
Application Procedure: All nominations must be made on the appropriate form, be submitted with five copies of the nominated work and be accompanied by an entry fee of Australian $66 per title to be eligible for consideration. A separate form must be completed for each nomination. See State Library of NSW website www.sl.nsw.gov.au/awards/
Closing Date: September 17th
Funding: Private

For further information contact:

Education and Client Liaison Branch, State Library of New South Wales, Australia
Email: smartin@sl.nsw.gov.au
Contact: Stephen Martin, Senior Project Officer

C H Currey Memorial Fellowship

Subjects: Australian history.
Purpose: To promote the writing of Australian history from original sources of information, preferably making use of the collection of the State Library of New South Wales.
Eligibility: Applicants may be residents or non-residents of Australia. Preference will normally be given to applications that support research on a topic or project that is not being pursued as part of a higher degree programme.
Level of Study: Professional development
Type: Fellowship
Value: Australian $20,000
Length of Study: 1 year
Frequency: Annual
Study Establishment: The State Library of New South Wales
Country of Study: Australia
Application Procedure: Applications should be made on forms available from the State Library or the website www.sl.nsw.gov.au/awards/
Closing Date: September 15th

Jean Arnot Memorial Fellowship

Subjects: Librarianship.
Purpose: To reward an outstanding original paper of no more than 5,000 words on any aspect of librarianship by a female librarian or a female student of librarianship.
Eligibility: The author must be a professional librarian or a student at an Australian school of librarianship. The submitted paper must be an outstanding original paper on any aspect of librarianship.
Level of Study: Professional development
Type: Fellowship
Value: Australian $1,000
Length of Study: 1 year
Frequency: Annual
Study Establishment: State Library of New South Wales
Country of Study: Australia
No. of awards offered: 1
Application Procedure: Applicants must complete an application form, available on request. See State Library of NSW website www.sl.nsw.gov.au/awards/
Closing Date: March 30th
Funding: Private
Contributor: National Council of Women of New South Wales Incorporated and the Australian Federation of Business and Professional Women's Association Inc

For further information contact:

Collection Management Services and Mitchell Librarian, State Library of New South Wales, Australia
Email: eellis@sl.nsw.gov.au
Contact: Elizabeth Ellis, Assistant State Librarian

Kathleen Mitchell Award

Subjects: Writing, literature.
Purpose: To reward a novel by an Australian author.
Eligibility: Applicants must be an Australian author under 30 years of age.
Value: Australian $7,500
Frequency: Every 2 years
Study Establishment: The State Library of New South Wales
Country of Study: Australia
Application Procedure: Applicants must complete an application form, available on request.
Funding: Private

Miles Franklin Literary Award

Subjects: Australian literature.
Purpose: To promote excellence in Australian literature.
Eligibility: Novel must be of the highest literary merit and must present Australian life in any of its phases. Novels submitted must have been published in the year of entry of the award.
Level of Study: Professional development
Type: Award
Value: Australian $42,000
Frequency: Annual

Application Procedure: Application forms can be downloaded from the website www.trustco.com.au/awards/miles_franklin.htm, see also State library of NSW website www.sl.nsw.gov.au/awards/
Closing Date: December 10th
Funding: Individuals

For further information contact:

Cauz Group, Australia
Tel: (61) 02 9332 1559
Fax: (61) 02 9332 1298
Email: trustawards@cauzgroup.com.au
Contact: Petrea Salter

Milt Luger Fellowships

Subjects: Australian life, history and culture using the resources of the state library.
Purpose: For projects which investigate and document aspects of Australian life, history and culture.
Eligibility: Persons aged between 18 and 25 years.
Type: Fellowship
Value: US$5,000 and US$3,000
Study Establishment: The state library of NSW
Country of Study: Australia
No. of awards offered: 2 Awards
Application Procedure: Applicants must complete an application form, available on request. See State Library of NSW website www.sl.nsw.gov.au/awards/
Closing Date: July 31st
Funding: Private

For further information contact:

Mitchell Library Office, State Library of New South Wales, Macquarie Street, Sydney, Australia
Tel: (61) 02 9273 1467
Fax: (61) 02 9273 1245
Email: awards@sl.nsw.gov.au
Website: www.sl.nsw.gov.au/awards/
Contact: Margaret Bjork

Nancy Keesing Fellowship

Subjects: Australian life and culture.
Purpose: To promote the State Library of New South Wales as a centre of research into Australian life and culture and to provide a readily accessible record of the fellowship project.
Eligibility: Applicants may be either residents or non-residents of Australia. Preference will normally be given to applications that support research on a topic or project that is not being pursued as part of higher degree programme.
Level of Study: Professional development
Type: Fellowship
Value: Australian $10,000
Length of Study: 1 year
Frequency: Annual
Study Establishment: State Library of New South Wales
Country of Study: Australia
Application Procedure: Applications must be made on forms available from the State Library or the website www.sl.nsw.gov.au/awards/
Closing Date: September 15th
Funding: Private

National Biography Award

Subjects: Writing.
Purpose: To encourage the highest standards of writing in the fields of biography and autobiography and to promote public interest in biography and autobiography.
Eligibility: The author must be a living Australian citizen or hold permanent resident status. The work must be classified as either biography or autobiography, be written in the English language, published in book form and consist of a minimum of 50,000 words.
Level of Study: Professional development
Type: Award
Value: Australian $20,000
Frequency: Annual
Study Establishment: The State Library of New South Wales
Country of Study: Australia

Application Procedure: All nominations must be made on the appropriate form and be accompanied by an entry fee of Australian $55 to be eligible for consideration. Five copies of the nominated work must be submitted. A separate form must be completed for each nomination. See state library of NSW website www.sl.nsw.gov.au/awards/
Closing Date: October 26th
Funding: Individuals, private
Contributor: Geoffrey Cains

Nita B Kibble Literary Awards: Dobbie Literary Award

Subjects: Writing.
Purpose: To reward a first published work by a woman author of fiction or nonfiction classifiable as 'Life Writing'.
Eligibility: Open to a first published work of fiction or nonfiction classifiable as 'Life Writing' by a woman author.
Value: Australian $2,500
Frequency: Annual
Study Establishment: The State Library of New South Wales
Country of Study: Australia
Application Procedure: Applicants must complete an application form, available on request.
Funding: Private

Nita B Kibble Literary Awards: Kibble Literary Awards

Subjects: Writing.
Purpose: To reward women writers of a published book of fiction or nonfiction classifiable as 'Life Writing'.
Eligibility: Open to women writers of a published book of fiction or nonfiction classifiable as 'Life Writing'.
Value: Australian $20,000
Frequency: Annual
Study Establishment: The State Library of New South Wales
Country of Study: Australia
Application Procedure: Applicants must complete an application form, available on request.
Closing Date: December
Funding: Private

State Librarian's Metcalfe Fellowship at UNSW

Subjects: Librarianship.
Purpose: To fund the study of Librarianship.
Type: Fellowship
Value: US$2,500
Frequency: Periodic
Study Establishment: The State Library of New South Wales
Country of Study: Australia
Application Procedure: Applicants must complete an application form, available on request. See State Library of NSW website: www.sl.nsw.gov.au/awards/
Funding: Private

Visiting Scholars-in-Residence (Council of Australian State Libraries Honorary Fellowship; Library Council of New South Wales Honorary Fellowship)

Subjects: All subjects relevant to the Library's collections. (Awarded to two second top shortlisted candidates for the C.H. Currey Memorial Fellowship and the Nancy Keesing Memorial Fellowship).
Purpose: To assist visiting scholars-in-residence to undertake research on specific subjects with a strong emphasis on the library's collections.
Eligibility: Applicants may be residents or non-residents of Australia.
Level of Study: Professional development
Type: Research fellowship
Value: N/A
Length of Study: 1 year
Frequency: Annual
Study Establishment: State Library of New South Wales
Country of Study: Australia
No. of awards offered: 2
Application Procedure: Applicants must complete an application form, available on request. See state library of NSW website www.sl.nsw.gov.au/awards/
Funding: Trusts

STATISTICAL SOCIETY OF CANADA

577 King Edward Avenue, Ottawa, Ontario, K1N 6N5, Canada
Tel: (1) 613 562 5320
Fax: (1) 613 565 6774
Email: info@ssc.ca
Website: www.ssc.ca
Contact: Sudhir Paul, Chair, Pierre Robillard Award

The Statistical Society of Canada provides a forum for discussion and interaction among individuals involved in all aspects of the statistical sciences. It publishes a newsletter, Liaison as well as a scientific journal, *The Canadian Journal of Statistics*. The Society also organises annual scientific meetings and short courses on professional development.

Pierre Robillard Award

Subjects: Statistics.
Purpose: To recognize the best PhD thesis defended at a Canadian university and written in a field covered by the Canadian Journal of Statistics.
Eligibility: Open to all postgraduates who have made a potential impact on the statistical sciences.
Level of Study: Doctorate
Type: Award
Value: A certificate, a monetary prize of Canadian $1,000 and 1 years membership of the Society
Frequency: Annual
Country of Study: Canada
No. of awards offered: 1
Application Procedure: Applicants must submit four copies of the thesis together with a covering letter from the thesis supervisor.
Closing Date: February 15th
No. of awards given last year: 1
No. of applicants last year: 8
Additional Information: The committee may decide that none of the submitted theses merits the award.

For further information contact:

University of Windsor, Department of Mathematics and Statistics, 1-109 Lambton Tower, Windsor, ON, N9B 3P4, Canada
Contact: Dr Sudhir Paul

STELLENBOSCH UNIVERSITY

Private Bay XI, Matieland, 7602, South Africa
Tel: (27) (0) 808 9111
Fax: (27) (0) 21 808 3822
Email: usbritz@sun.ac.za
Website: www.samro.org.za

The raison Dé of the chemistry of Stellenbosch is to create and sustain, in commitment to the academic ideal of excellent scholarly and scientific practice, an environment within which knowledge can be discovered, shared and applied for the benefit of the community.

Harry Crossley Doctoral Fellowship

Subjects: Any subject, with the exception of theology and political science.
Purpose: To reward academically above-average students.
Eligibility: Open to full-time students registered at Stellenbosch University in any postgraduate degree programme except theology and political science.
Level of Study: Doctorate
Type: Fellowship
Value: South African Rand 80,000
Length of Study: 2 years
Frequency: Annual
Study Establishment: Stellenbosch University
Country of Study: South Africa
Application Procedure: Request application.
Closing Date: September 30th
Funding: Foundation
Contributor: Harry Crossley Foundation
No. of awards given last year: 50
No. of applicants last year: 350

For further information contact:

The Office for Postgraduate Bursaries Division for Research Development Administration Building Block A, Room A 2069
Tel: 021 808 4208/2957
Fax: 021 808 2739
Email: beursnavrae_nagraads@sun.ac.za

Harry Crossley Master's Bursary

Subjects: Any subject, with the exception of theology and political science.
Purpose: To reward academically above-average studens.
Eligibility: To full-time students registered at Stellenbosch University in any postgraduate degree programme except theology and political science.
Level of Study: Postgraduate
Type: Bursary
Value: South African Rand 60,000
Length of Study: 2 years
Frequency: Annual
Study Establishment: Stellenbosch University
Country of Study: South Africa
Application Procedure: Request application form.
Closing Date: September 30th
Funding: Foundation
Contributor: Harry Crossley Foundation
No. of awards given last year: 50
No. of applicants last year: 350

For further information contact:

The Office for Postgraduate Busaries Division for Research Development Administrator Building Block A, Room A 2069
Tel: 021 808 4208/2957
Fax: 021 808 2739
Email: beursnavrae_nagraads@sun.ac.za

Stellenbosch Merit Bursary Award

Subjects: Any subject.
Purpose: To reward academically above-average students.
Eligibility: Available to full-time students registered at Stellenbosch University in any postgraduate degree programme.
Level of Study: Postgraduate
Type: Bursary
Value: South African Rand 4,100–34,700
Length of Study: Up to 3 years
Frequency: Annual
Study Establishment: Stellenbosch University
Country of Study: South Africa
Application Procedure: Students must submit an application and a certified copy of a complete, official academic record.
Closing Date: December 9th
Contributor: Stellenbosch University
No. of awards given last year: 340
No. of applicants last year: Approx. 700

For further information contact:

Office for postgraduate bursaries
Tel: (021) 808-4208
Fax: 021 808 2739
Email: beursnavrae_nagraads@sun.ac.za

Stellenbosch Rector's Grants for Successing Against the Odds

Subjects: Any subject.
Purpose: To award students who have achieved exceptional success despite difficult circumstances.
Eligibility: Open to candidates who satisfy the admission requirements of the University and who can provide proof of exceptional achievement despite handicaps and/or specific physical, educational or social challenges.
Level of Study: Postgraduate
Type: Grant
Value: South African Rand 50,000
Length of Study: Up to 3 years
Frequency: Annual

Study Establishment: Stellenbosch University
Country of Study: South Africa
No. of awards offered: 3
Application Procedure: Students must submit a complete application form accompanied by a curriculum vitae and 2 references.
Closing Date: September 30th
Funding: Foundation
Contributor: Andrew Mellon Foundation
No. of awards given last year: 3
No. of applicants last year: 100

For further information contact:

Office for Postgraduate Bursaries
Tel: 021 8084208
Fax: 021 808 2739
Email: beursnavrae_nagraads@sun.ac.za

STOUT RESEARCH CENTRE, VICTORIA UNIVERSITY OF WELLINGTON

PO Box 600, Wellington, New Zealand
Tel: (64) 4 465 5305
Fax: (64) 4 463 5439
Email: lydia.wevers@vuw.ac.nz
Website: www.vuw.ac.nz/stout-centre
Contact: Dr Lydia Wevers, Director

The Stout Research Center was established in 1984 to encourage scholarly inquiry into New Zealand society, history and culture, and to provide a focus for the collegial atmosphere and exchange of ideas that enrich the quality of research.

J D Stout Fellowship

Subjects: New Zealand society, history and culture.
Purpose: To encourage research.
Eligibility: Open to distinguished scholars from New Zealand and abroad.
Level of Study: Postdoctorate
Type: Fellowship
Value: New Zealand $52,348–76,160
Length of Study: 1 year
Frequency: Annual
Study Establishment: The Stout Research Centre
Country of Study: New Zealand
No. of awards offered: 1
Application Procedure: Applicants must write for details.
Closing Date: August 1st of the year preceding the fellowship
Funding: Trusts
Contributor: Stout Trust

STROKE ASSOCIATION

Stroke House, 240 City Road, London, EC1V 2PR, England
Tel: (44) 20 7566 0300
Fax: (44) 020 7490 2686
Email: research@stroke.org.uk
Website: www.stroke.org.uk
Contact: Ms M. Bendix, Research Officer

The Stroke Association funds research into rehabilitation, treatment and better methods of rehabilitation, and helps stroke patients and their families directly through community services. It campaigns, educates and informs to increase knowledge of stroke at all levels of society and it acts as a voice for everyone affected by stroke.

Stroke Association Clinical Fellowships

Subjects: The prevention, treatment and rehabilitation of strokes.
Purpose: To equip a trainee for a career in the field.
Eligibility: Awarded to a department in the United Kingdom that can provide an educational programme and the expert supervision required to enable a specialist registrar to gain the appropriate clinical experience required for a career in stroke.
Level of Study: Professional development
Type: Fellowship
Value: UK £40,000

Length of Study: 1 year
Frequency: Annual
Study Establishment: Suitable universities and medical schools
Country of Study: United Kingdom
No. of awards offered: 2
Application Procedure: Applicants must respond to advertisements in the *British Medical Journal* in October of each year. Application forms are available from the website.
Closing Date: Usually March
Funding: Private
No. of awards given last year: 2
Additional Information: Fellowships are assessed by peer review. Awards are made in March.

Stroke Association Research Project Grants

Subjects: Stroke research encompassing epidemiology, prevention, acute treatment, assessment and rehabilitation, psychology of stroke and stroke in ethnic minorities.
Purpose: To advance research into stroke.
Eligibility: Open to medically qualified and other clinically active researchers in the United Kingdom in the relevant fields. Applications are judged by peer review on their merit without limitations of age. Applicants can be from any country but must be based in the United Kingdom.
Level of Study: Research, Postdoctorate
Type: Project grant
Value: Salaries for researchers and support staff, some equipment costs, consumables and essential travel. No other overheads, advertising etc. are covered. The maximum award is normally UK £60,000 per year
Length of Study: 1–3 years
Frequency: Twice a year
Study Establishment: A suitable university or hospital in the United Kingdom
Country of Study: United Kingdom
No. of awards offered: Approx. 30 ongoing at any point in time
Application Procedure: Application forms are available from the website.
Closing Date: As advertised, usually February and July
Funding: Private
Contributor: Donations
No. of awards given last year: 11
No. of applicants last year: 80

Stroke Association Therapy Research Bursaries

Subjects: Stroke research.
Purpose: To provide a research training programme and appropriate supervision to equip a trainee for a career in stroke research.
Eligibility: Open to nurses and therapists, but consideration will be given to other health professionals. They will be awarded to departments that can demonstrate a track record and current participation in stroke research.
Level of Study: Postgraduate, Professional development
Type: Bursary
Value: UK £30,000 per year
Length of Study: Up to 3 years
Frequency: Annual
Study Establishment: Suitable universities and hospitals
Country of Study: United Kingdom
No. of awards offered: 2
Application Procedure: Applicants must respond to advertisements in *Therapy Weekly* in October of each year. Application forms are available from the website.
Closing Date: Usually January
Funding: Private
No. of awards given last year: 2

THE STUDENT AWARDS AGENCY FOR SCOTLAND

Gyleview House, 3 Redheughs Rigg, Edinburgh, EH12 9HH, Scotland
Tel: (44) 845 111 1711
Fax: (44) 13 1244 5887
Email: saas.geu@scotland.gsi.gov.uk
Website: www.saas.gov.uk
Contact: Mr Victor Abela

The brief of the Student Awards Agency for Scotland is to administer the Students' Allowances Scheme, the Postgraduate Students' Allowances Scheme and the Nursing and Midwifery Student Bursary Scheme.

SAAS-Arts and Humanities Postgraduate Scholarships

Subjects: Arts and humanities.
Eligibility: Open to students enrolled in a postgraduate programme in the Arts and Humanities Graduate School.
Level of Study: Postgraduate
Type: Scholarship
Value: UK £9,000
Length of Study: 1 year
Frequency: Annual
Study Establishment: Arts and Humanities Graduate School
Country of Study: United Kingdom
Application Procedure: Application form can be downloaded from the website.
Closing Date: March 31st

SWANSEA UNIVERSITY

Singleton Park, Swansea, Wales, SA2 8PP, United Kingdom
Tel: (44) 0 1792 205678
Fax: (44) 0 1792 295157
Email: sro@swansea.ac.uk
Website: www.swan.ac.uk

Swansea University has nearly 12,000 students and offers over 500 undergraduate and 150 postgraduate courses in a wide range of subject areas, from American Studies to Zoology. A full range of social, cultural, and sporting amenities complements the campus lifestyle and contributes to the strong sense of community. Recent surveys and league tables have consistently placed Swansea among the top 20 Universities in the UK for teaching quality and student satisfaction.

Civil and Computational Research Centre–PhD Studentships

Subjects: Computational mechanics.
Purpose: To strengthen research excellence and to broaden its application to other areas of engineering.
Eligibility: Open to Masters or Bachelor students with a First Class Honours or a good 2.1 degree in a suitable engineering, mathematical or scientific discipline, and who are in the field of computational mechanics and related to any of the established research themes of the Civil and Computational Research Centre. UK residents are eligible for a full studentship and EU residents are eligible only for home/EU tuition fees.
Level of Study: Doctorate, Graduate
Type: Studentship
Value: Full studentship of £12,500 stipend per year plus tuition fees (Up to £14,000 for a first class student)
Length of Study: 3 years
Frequency: Annual
Study Establishment: Swansea University
Country of Study: United Kingdom
No. of awards offered: 2
Application Procedure: Check the website for further details.
Closing Date: Please contact us for details
Additional Information: Students are advised to apply as soon as possible.

For further information contact:

Email: O.Hassan@swansea.ac.uk
Contact: Professor Oubay Hassan

International Scholarships

Subjects: Available in all academic schools.
Eligibility: Awards are available to postgraduate applicants from outside the EU. Other eligibility criteria may apply. Please contact us for details.
Level of Study: Postgraduate
Value: Variable
Length of Study: Masters - 1 year; PhD - 3 years

Frequency: Annual
Study Establishment: Swansea University
Country of Study: United Kingdom
Application Procedure: Please contact your academic school of interest.

For further information contact:

Email: international@swansea.ac.uk

The James Callaghan Scholarships

Subjects: Applications can be made to any academic school.
Eligibility: Research students from Commonwealth member countries are eligible to apply. Awards are available for full-time or part-time MPhil or PhD studies.
Level of Study: Doctorate, Predoctorate
Type: Scholarship
Value: Contribution towards tuition fees
Length of Study: MPhil - 1 year; PhD - 3 years
Frequency: Annual
Study Establishment: Swansea University
Country of Study: United Kingdom
Application Procedure: Please contact us for an application form.

For further information contact:

Postgraduates Admissions Office, Swansea University, Wales
Email: postgraduate.admissions@swansea.ac.uk

PhD Fees-only Bursaries

Subjects: Normally available in all subject areas. Please check our website www.swansea.org.uk/postgraduate for details.
Eligibility: Open to good Master's graduates from the UK/EU who will be commencing PhD studies at Swansea University for the first time in September.
Type: Scholarship
Value: Covers UK/EU tuition fees
Length of Study: 3 years
Frequency: Annual
Study Establishment: Swansea University
Country of Study: United Kingdom
No. of awards offered: Approx. 10
Application Procedure: Please contact us for an application form.
No. of awards given last year: 10

For further information contact:

Postgraduate Admissions Office, Swansea University, Wales
Email: postgraduate.admissions@swansea.ac.uk

PhD Studentships

Subjects: Normally available in all subject areas. Please check our website www.swansea.ac.uk/postgraduate for details.
Eligibility: Open to good Masters graduates from the UK/EU who will be commencing PhD studies at Swansea University for the first time in September.
Level of Study: Doctorate
Type: Scholarship
Value: Tuition fees plus maintenance grant of approx. £12,940 per annum
Length of Study: 3 years
Frequency: Annual
Study Establishment: Swansea University
Country of Study: United Kingdom
No. of awards offered: Approx. 10
Application Procedure: Please contact us for an application form.
No. of awards given last year: 10

For further information contact:

Postgraduate Admissions Office, Swansea University, Wales
Email: postgraduate.admissions@swansea.ac.uk

Taught Masters Bursaries

Subjects: Available in all academic schools.
Eligibility: Open to good honours graduates from the UK/EU who will be commencing Masters studies for the first time in September.
Level of Study: Postdoctorate

Type: Scholarship
Value: £1500 towards tuition fees
Length of Study: I year full time or 2 years part time
Frequency: Annual
Study Establishment: Swansea University
Country of Study: United Kingdom
No. of awards offered: 160
Application Procedure: Please contact us for an application form.
No. of awards given last year: 160

For further information contact:

Postgraduate Admissions Office, Swansea University, Wales
Email: postgraduate.admissions@swansea.ac.uk

SWEDISH INFORMATION SERVICE

One Dag Hammarskjold Plaza, 885 Second Avenue, 45th Floor,
New York, NY 10017, United States of America
Tel: (1) 1 212 583 2550
Fax: (1) 212 755 2732
Email: generalkonsulat.new-york@foreign.ministry.se
Website: www.swedennewyork.com
Contact: Consulate General of Sweden

The Section for culture and Public Affairs of the Consulate General of Sweden in New York works to promote awareness in the United States of America of Swedish cultural achievement and advancement in scientific research and development, and contributes to the formation of public opinion and policy in an international context.

Bicentennial Swedish-American Exchange Fund

Subjects: Politics, public administration, working life, human environment, mass media, business and industry, education or culture.
Purpose: To provide an opportunity for those in a position to influence public opinion and contribute to the development of their society to make an intensive research trip to Sweden.
Eligibility: Applicants should be citizens or permanent residents of the United States of America. People who have made recurrent visits to or resided in Sweden will only be considered in exceptional circumstances. The grant may not be used to finance participation in conferences or regular ongoing vocational or academic courses. If co-applicants on the same project are selected, the grant will be divided between them. The grant may be used in conjunction with scholarships from other sources.
Level of Study: Research
Type: Travel grant
Value: Krona 30,000 or the equivalent in United States of America dollars to partially cover transportation and living expenses
Length of Study: 2–4 weeks intensive research
Frequency: Annual
Country of Study: Sweden
No. of awards offered: 2
Application Procedure: Application forms are available from the website or can be requested directly from the Swedish Information Service, during the month of November. As a signature is required, application forms should be printed out and signed before sending in the post. Two letters of recommendation are also required. Email applications are not accepted. Application forms to be filled in by hand may be requested by post along with a stamped addressed envelope.
Closing Date: November 30th
Funding: Government
Contributor: The Swedish Institute in Stockholm, Sweden
No. of awards given last year: 5
No. of applicants last year: 40
Additional Information: The project must be completed within 1 year of receipt of the grant. A report must be submitted to the Swedish Information Service 6 months after the research trip is completed. Award recipients are announced during the month of May.

The SASS Swedish Travel Grants

Subjects: Politics, public administration, working life, human environment, mass media, business and industry, education and culture.
Level of Study: Postgraduate
Type: Grant
Value: US$1,000

Frequency: Annual
Country of Study: Sweden
No. of awards offered: Varies
Application Procedure: Contact the Institute.
Closing Date: April 15th
Funding: Government
Contributor: The Swedish Institute in Stockholm

SWEDISH INSTITUTE (SI)

Skeppsbron 2 Box 7434, Stockholm, 103-91, Sweden
Tel: (46) 8 453 78 00
Fax: (46) 8 20 72 48
Email: si@si.se
Website: www.si.se

Swedish Institute SI is entrusted with the task to inform the world about Sweden and to organise exchanges with other countries in the spheres of culture, education, research and public life in general.

Anna Lindh Swedish-Turkish Scholarships

Subjects: Human rights law.
Purpose: To advance the field of European studies.
Eligibility: Open to Turkish students only.
Level of Study: Postgraduate
Type: Scholarship
Value: All tuition fees, plus travel allowance
Frequency: Annual
Country of Study: Sweden
Application Procedure: Apply online.
Closing Date: September
Funding: Government
Contributor: Consulate General of Swedish in Istanbul

SWINBURNE UNIVERSITY OF TECHNOLOGY

PO Box 218, Hawthorn, VIC, 3122, Australia
Tel: (61) 613 9214 8000
Fax: (61) 3 9818 3648
Email: webmaster@swin.edu.au
Website: www.swinburne.edu.au/index.php
Contact: MBA Admissions Officer

It provides career-orientated education and as a university with a commitment to research. The University maintains a strong technology base and important links with industry, complemented by a number of innovative specialist research centres which attract a great deal of international interest. A feature of many Swinburne undergraduate courses is the applied vocational emphasis and direct industry application through Industry Based Learning (IBL) programs. Swinburne was a pioneer of IBL program which places students directly in industry for vocational employment as an integral part of the course structure. Swinburne is committed to the transfer of lifelong learning skills. It is heavily involved in international initiatives and plays a significant part in the internationalization of Australia's tertiary education system.

Endeavour International Postgraduate Research Scholarship (EIPRS)

Subjects: All subjects.
Purpose: To maintain and develop international research linkages and specifically aims to attract top quality international postgraduate students to areas of research strength in the Australian higher education sector and support Australia's research effort.
Eligibility: Open to a citizen of a country other than Australia and New Zealand. Please check the website for further details.
Level of Study: Doctorate, Research
Type: Research scholarship
Value: To cover tuition costs and the cost of overseas student health cover. No living allowance is provided
Length of Study: 3 years (Research Doctorate) and 2 years (Research Masters)
Application Procedure: Check website for further details.
Closing Date: August 31st

For further information contact:

Building 60Wm, Level 7, 60 William Street, Hawthorn campus
Tel: 9214 5547 or 9214 8744
Email: ehill@swin.edu.au, jamathews@swin.edu.au
Website: www.swinburne.edu.au/research/schols.htm

International Postgraduate Research Scholarship (IPRS)

Subjects: All subjects.
Eligibility: Open to citizens of all overseas countries except New Zealand who have completed at least 4 years (or equivalent) of tertiary education studies at a high level of achievement. Plus students must demonstrate English Language proficiency: IELTS.
Level of Study: Doctorate, Postgraduate
Type: Research scholarship
Value: Covers the tuition fees only
Application Procedure: Complete an application for admission to research higher degree candidature and scholarship and mail/courier or you can scan your application forms in and email them.
Closing Date: Last Friday of October
Contributor: Australian Department of Education, Science and Training (DEST)

For further information contact:

Website: www.international.swinburne.edu.au/apply/research.html

Swinburne University Centenary Postgraduate Research Award (SUCPRA)

Subjects: All subjects.
Purpose: To assist with general living costs.
Eligibility: Open to domestic or an international student undertaking a higher degree by research. Please check the website for further details.
Level of Study: Doctorate, Research
Type: Research award
Value: Varies
Length of Study: 3 years (Research Doctorate) and 2 years (Research Masters)
Application Procedure: Please check website for further details.

For further information contact:

Building 60Wm, Level 7, 60 William Street, Hawthorn campus
Tel: 9214 5547 or 9214 8744
Email: ehill@swin.edu.au, jamathews@swin.edu.au
Website: www.swinburne.edu.au/research/schols.htm

The Swinburne University Chancellor's Centenary Research Scholarship (CCRS)

Subjects: All subjects.
Purpose: To award students of exceptional research potential to undertake a higher degree by research (HDR).
Eligibility: Open to a local or an international student undertaking a higher degree by research (HDR) with Bachelor Degree with First Class Honours. For further details, please check the website.
Level of Study: Doctorate
Type: Research scholarship
Value: $25,000 (normally tax-free)
Length of Study: 3 years
Frequency: Annual
Application Procedure: Check website for further details.

For further information contact:

Building 60Wm, Level 7, 60 William Street, Hawthorn campus
Tel: 9214 5547 or 9214 8744
Email: ehill@swin.edu.au, jamathews@swin.edu.au
Website: www.swinburne.edu.au/research/schols.htm

Vice Chancellor's Centenary Research Scholarship (VCCRS)

Subjects: All subject.
Purpose: To assist with general living costs.
Eligibility: Open to domestic or an international student who have completed a Bachelor Degree with First Class Honours and are of

exceptional research potential undertaking a higher degree by research (HDR). For further details, please check the website.
Level of Study: Research
Type: Research scholarship
Value: Varies
Length of Study: 3 years (Research Doctorate) and 2 years (Research Masters)
Application Procedure: Check website for further details.

For further information contact:

Building 60Wm, Level 7, 60 William Street, Hawthorn campus
Tel: 9214 5547 or 9214 8744
Email: ehill@swin.edu.au, jamathews@swin.edu.au
Website: www.swinburne.edu.au/research/schols.htm

SWISS FEDERAL INSTITUTE OF TECHNOLOGY ZÜRICH

International Instituitional Affairs, Rämistrasse 101, Zurich, CH-8092, Switzerland
Tel: (41) 44 632 2141
Fax: (41) 44 632 1264
Email: international@sl.ethz.ch
Website: www.master.ethz.ch
Contact: Anders Hagstrom

The Swiss Federal Institute of Technology Zurich is a science and technology university with an outstanding research record. Excellent research conditions, state-of-the-art infrastructure and an attractive urban environment add up to the ideal setting for creative personalities.

ETH Zurich Excellence Scholarship and Opportunity Award

Subjects: Architecture, engineering, (civil, mechanical, electrical, production, rural and surveying), computer science, materials science, chemistry, physics, mathematics, biology, environmental sciences, earth sciences, pharmacy, agriculture and forestry, international relations, political science.
Eligibility: Open to graduates in one of the discipline represented at ETH Zurich with very good academic record.
Level of Study: Postgraduate
Type: Scholarship
Value: Swiss Francs 1,750 per month plus tuition fees
Length of Study: 15 months–2years
Frequency: Annual
Study Establishment: ETH Zurich
Country of Study: Switzerland
No. of awards offered: 20
Application Procedure: Applications must be made to the appropriate address. See www.master.ethz.ch for further information.
Closing Date: March 15th and September 30th
Funding: Foundation, government
Contributor: ETH Zurich Foundation
No. of awards given last year: 23
No. of applicants last year: 290

SYNGENTA FOUNDATION

WRO-1002.11.52, Postfach CH-4002, Basel, Switzerland
Tel: (41) 61 323 5634
Fax: (41) 61 323 7200
Website: www.syngentafoundation.com
Contact: Grants Enquiries

Syngenta Foundation awards

Subjects: All subjects.
Eligibility: Open to candidates from African nations.
Type: Award
Value: Varies
Country of Study: Developing countries
No. of awards offered: Variable year to year
Application Procedure: Open

Additional Information: The Syngenta Foundation does not have a formal award mechanism. It awards people within the projects in developing countries on an ad hoc basis.

For further information contact:

Syngenta Foundation, Schwarzwalpallee 215, Bases, Switzerland, 4002

SYRACUSE UNIVERSITY

303 Bowne Hall, Syracuse, NY 13244, United States of America
Tel: (1) 315 443 4492
Fax: (1) 315 443 3423
Email: grad@syr.edu
Website: www.gradsch.syr.edu

Syracuse University is a non-profit, private student research university. Its mission is to promote learning through teaching, research, scholarship, creative accomplishment and service.

African American Studies Graduate Fellowships

Subjects: Any subject.
Purpose: To support new continuing graduate students across disciplines whose work supports that of the African American/Pan African studies program and who will make a intellectual contribution to the life of the Department of African American studies.
Eligibility: Open to African American fellows enrolled in at least one three-credit graduate course each semester in the African American Studies program for the duration of their award.
Level of Study: Postgraduate, Doctorate
Type: Fellowship
Value: US$12,050 for Master's and US$20,150 for doctoral students plus a full-time tuition scholarship (Up to 30 credits for the academic year)
Frequency: Annual
No. of awards offered: 6
Application Procedure: Applicants must send their application along with a letter of intent and should indicate interest in this award.
Closing Date: January 10th

Hursky Fellowship

Subjects: Ukrainian language and literature, linguistics and culture.
Purpose: To a full-time graduate student of Ukranian background enrolled for the study of Ukranian language and literature, Ukrainian linguistics and, culture.
Eligibility: Open to graduate students with a Ukrainian background enrolled in Maxwell School of Citizenship and Public Affairs or the College of Arts and Sciences, or any SU graduate whose area of study is the Ukraine or included Ukrainian topics.
Type: Fellowship
Value: A stipend of US$10,000 plus a tuition scholarship for 24 credits for the academic year
Frequency: Annual

McNair Scholars Program

Purpose: To increase the number of low-income, first-generation and underrepresented minority college students who pursue and complete the doctoral degree.
Eligibility: Open to the candidates who were McNair Scholars at their undergraduate instituions.
Level of Study: Doctorate, Postgraduate
Type: Fellowship
Value: US$12,050 for Master's students and US$20,150 for doctoral students plus a full-tuition scholarship (up to 30 credits for the academic year)
Frequency: Annual
No. of awards offered: 6

STEM Doctoral Fellowship

Subjects: Science, technology, engineering and maths disciplines.
Purpose: To support doctoral students in the field of science, technology, engineering and maths from underrepresented group of US or its permanent residents.
Eligibility: Open to members of an underrepresented group who are US citizens or permanent residents.

Level of Study: Doctorate
Value: US$20,150 plus tuition scholarship
Frequency: Annual
No. of awards offered: 5

Syracuse University Graduate Fellowship

Subjects: All subjects.
Purpose: To provide a full support package during a student's term of study.
Eligibility: Open to nationals of any country.
Level of Study: Unrestricted
Type: Fellowship
Value: US$12,050 stipend for Master, US$20,150 stipend for PhD plus tuition scholarship
Length of Study: 1–6 years
Frequency: Annual
Study Establishment: Syracuse University
Country of Study: United States of America
No. of awards offered: Varies by school/college
Application Procedure: Applicants must apply through admission application.
Closing Date: January 10th
Funding: Private
Contributor: The Syracuse University Graduate School
No. of awards given last year: Varies
No. of applicants last year: 250

THE TAN KAH KEE FOUNDATION

Secretariat 5 Toh Tuck Link, 596224, Singapore
Tel: (65) 6463 8464
Fax: (65) 6462 1192
Email: tkkf@wspc.com.sg
Website: www.tkk.wspc.com.sg

The mission of The Tan Kah Kee Foundation is to carry on the charity works and to foster the Tan Kah Kee spirit in entrepreneurship and dedication to education. Over the years, the Foundation has been actively engaged in the promotion of education and culture. Today, its influence has been extended beyond the Chinese Community in Singapore and has begun to reach out to the region.

Tan Kah Kee Postgraduate Scholarship

Subjects: All subjects.
Purpose: To provide financial assistance to students pursuing their postgraduate studies.
Eligibility: Open to citizens and permanent residents of Singapore who are pursuing full-time Master's degree or PhD in any discipline, regardless of race or religion. Candidates are appraised on their academic achievements, outstanding personal character and bilingual capabilities.
Level of Study: Doctorate, Postgraduate
Type: Scholarship
Value: Singaporean $10,000 for overseas students, Singaporean $7,000 for local universities
Frequency: Annual
Application Procedure: Applicants can download the application form from the website.
Funding: Foundation
Contributor: Tan Kah Kee Foundation
Additional Information: Application is open in May every year. Shortlisted applicants will be informed to attend an interview in the month of June or July.

TANTE MARIE'S COOKING SCHOOL

271 Francisco Street, San Francisco, CA 94133, United States of America
Tel: (1) 415 788 6699
Fax: (1) 415 788 8924
Email: peggy@tantemarie.com
Website: www.tantemarie.com

Tante Marie's Cooking School, located in San Francisco was founded as a full-time school in 1979. It is one of the first schools of fine cooking offering all-day, year-round classes for people who are serious about cooking well. Graduates from Tante Marie's have interesting and varied careers. In addition to offering professional courses for people wanting to begin a career in culinary or pastry, Tante Marie's welcomes interested avocational students in the Evening Series, Weekend Workshops, One-Day Workshops and Cooking Vacations. There are also cooking parties on weekend evenings where groups of up to 30 people cook together. The emphasis at Tante Marie's is in building confidence in the kitchen.

Tante Marie's Cooking School Scholarship

Subjects: Cooking.
Purpose: To make the candidates learn cooking professionally.
Eligibility: Open to candidates who are 24 years of age or older and exhibit a high degree of motivation.
Level of Study: Unrestricted
Type: Scholarship
Value: US$5,000
Length of Study: 6 months
Frequency: Annual
Country of Study: United States of America
Application Procedure: Check website for further details.
Funding: Private

TEAGASC (IRISH AGRICULTURE AND FOOD DEVELOPMENT AUTHORITY)

Oak Park, Carlow, Ireland
Tel: (353) 59 917 0200
Fax: (353) 59 918 2097
Email: Debbie.murphy@teagasc.ie
Website: www.teagasc.ie
Contact: Debbie Murphy

Teagasc (Irish Agriculture and Food Development Authority) is the parastatal body responsible for agricultural and food research, farm advisory services and farmer education in the Republic of Ireland. Its research programme includes foods, dairy cows, beef cattle, pigs, sheep, crops, horticulture, environment, rural economics and sociology at eight research centres.

Teagasc Walsh Fellowships

Subjects: Any subject relevant to food and agriculture in Ireland, e.g. animal sciences, plant sciences, physical or earth sciences, environment, economics and rural development.
Purpose: To support MSc and PhD projects on topics relevant to the overall Teagasc research programme on agriculture and food.
Eligibility: Applicants must be college faculty members who, in co-operation with Teagasc researchers, submit proposals relevant to the Teagasc programme on agriculture and food in Ireland. If successful, they then select postgraduate students for MSc or PhD programmes as Walsh Fellows. Applications are not accepted from individual students or for taught non-research postgraduate courses.
Level of Study: Research, Doctorate, Postgraduate
Type: Fellowship
Value: €21,000 per year to cover a postgraduate stipend and all fees. A limited provision for materials and travel is also available
Length of Study: Up to 2 years for an MSc, maximum of 3 years for a PhD
Frequency: Annual
Study Establishment: Any third-level college, in association with a Teagasc Research Centre
Country of Study: Ireland
No. of awards offered: Approx. 40
Application Procedure: Applicants must apply for an information brochure, which includes an application form, available on request. Students who wish to apply for a pre-awarded fellowship should check the Teagasc website (www.teagasc.ie) that contains a complete list of fellowships awarded with supervisor contact details.
Closing Date: Mid-December for university faculty applicants. Students begin fellowships in the autumn of the following year
Funding: Government
Contributor: Teagasc's own resources, via the Irish Government and the European Union agri-food industry
No. of awards given last year: 40

No. of applicants last year: 120
Additional Information: The full list of awarded fellowships are posted on the Teagasc website (www.teagasc.ie) mid-April annually.

THE TECHNISCHE UNIVERSITEIT DELFT (TUD)

Post bus 5, 2600 AA Delft, Netherlands
Tel: (31) 15 2785404
Fax: (31) 15 2781855
Email: voorlichting@tudelft.nl
Website: www.tudelft.nl/msc

Founded in 1842, the Delft University of Technology is the oldest, largest, and most comprehensive technical university in the Netherlands. It is an establishment of both national importance and significant international standing. Renowned for its high standard of education and research, TU Delft collaborates with other educational establishments and research institutes, both within and outside of the Netherlands. TU Delft aims at being an 'interactive partner' to social issues, committed to answering its multifaceted demands and initiating changes to benefit people in the future.

The Shell Centenary Scholarship Fund, Netherlands

Subjects: All master programmes under the TSCSF scholarship scheme.
Purpose: To give students the opportunity to study at the TUD and gain skills that will make a long-term contribution to the further development of their countries.
Eligibility: Open to candidates who are nationals of and resident in any country other than the ones listed in 'Additional Information' and aged 35 or under, intending to study a subject that will be of significant value in aiding the sustainable development of their home country, fluent in spoken and written English, and neither a current nor former employee of the Royal Dutch/Shell Group of companies.
Level of Study: Postgraduate
Type: Scholarship
Value: Full-cost scholarship including tuition fees, international travel, living allowances and health insurance
Length of Study: 2 years
Frequency: Annual
Country of Study: Netherlands
No. of awards offered: 6
Application Procedure: Applicants must have been admitted to a MSc programme of TU Delft, the International Office will subsequently send you the application form by email, the International Office will check your application on the basis of the Royal Dutch/Shell criteria.
Closing Date: February 1st (for applying MSc), March 28th (for scholarship)
Contributor: TUD with support from The Shell Centenary Scholarship Fund (TSCSF)
Additional Information: Countries not eligible: Australia, Austria, Belgium, Canada, Cyprus, Czech Republic, Denmark, Estonia, Finland, France, Germany, Greece, Hungary, Iceland, Ireland, Italy, Japan, Latvia, Lithuania, Luxembourg, Malta, The Netherlands, New Zealand, Norway, Poland, Portugal, Slovenia, Slovakia, Spain, Sweden, Switzerland, United Kingdom and United States.

For further information contact:

International Office, Julianalaan 134, 2628 BL Delft, Netherlands
Tel: (31) 15 278 5690
Email: msc2@tudelft.nl
Website: www.tudelft.nl/msc

TEL AVIV UNIVERSITY (TAU)

PO Box 39040, Tel Aviv, 69978, Israel
Tel: (972) 0 3 640 8111
Email: tauinfo@post.tau.ac.il
Website: www.tau.ac.il

Tel Aviv University (TAU) was founded in 1956 and is located in Israel's cultural, financial and industrial heartland, TAU is the largest university in Israel and the biggest Jewish university in the world. TAU offers an extensive range of programmes in the arts and sciences.

TAU Scholarships

Subjects: History and contemporary music.
Purpose: To encourage innovative and interdisciplinary research that cuts across traditional boundaries and paradigms.
Eligibility: Open to candidates who have registered for their Doctoral or postdoctoral degree.
Level of Study: Doctorate, Postdoctorate
Type: Scholarships
Value: US$15,000
Frequency: Annual
No. of awards offered: 20
Application Procedure: Applicants can download the application form from the website. The completed application form along with a curriculum vitae and one 2 page description of research project with a list of publications is to be sent.
Closing Date: March 15th and December 15th
Additional Information: Applications if sent by email, must be directed to ddprize@post.tau.ac.il

For further information contact:

The Lowy School for Overseas Students, Center Building, Tel-Aviv University, Ramat Aviv, Tel Aviv, 69978, Israel
Contact: Ms Smadar Fisher, Director, Dan David Prize

TENOVUS SCOTLAND

Small Research Grants, 234 St Vincent Street, Glasgow, G2 5RJ, Scotland
Tel: (44) 14 1221 6268
Fax: (44) 12 9231 1433
Email: gen.sec@talk21.com
Website: www.tenovus-scotland.org.uk
Contact: E R Read, General Secretary

Tenovus Scotland supports innovative and pilot medical research projects carried out by young researchers who may not have a track record, across the full spectrum of Medicine and Dentistry.

Tenovus Scotland Small Research Grants

Subjects: Medicine, dentistry, medical sciences and allied areas.
Purpose: To foster high-quality research within the healthcare professions in Scotland.
Eligibility: Medical professionals of Scotland. (1) No restrictions on age although preference is for young researchers seeking to establish a track record. (2) Grants conditional on the work being carried out in a Scottish University/Teaching at an NHS Trust Hospital. (3) No restriction on nationality provided they meet the above criteria.
Level of Study: Research
Type: Grant
Value: Normally up to UK £10,000 or part thereof
Country of Study: Scotland
Application Procedure: Application forms must be filled, applications from investigators lacking support in the early stages of a new project are encouraged. Applications may be invited for salary support or for research studentships.
Closing Date: February 15th and September15th
Funding: Trusts, individuals
No. of awards given last year: 54
No. of applicants last year: 81

THE MINISTRY OF FISHERIES

ASB Bank House, 101-103 The Terrace, Wellington, PO Box 1020, New Zealand
Tel: (64) 470 2600
Fax: (64) 819 4601
Email: mfishfeedback@fish.govt.nz
Website: www.fish.govt.nz/en-nz/default.htm

Ministry of Fisheries PG Scholarships in Quantitative Fisheries Science

Subjects: Fisheries science.
Purpose: To allow graduate students to develop expertise in quantitative fisheries science and encourage postgraduate students to

contribute to priority research areas identified by the New Zealand government
Eligibility: Open to applicants with majors or minors in mathematics, statistics, biology, economics or computer science.
Level of Study: Postgraduate
Type: Scholarship
Value: $30,000 per year for PhD and up to $25,000 per year for Masters
Length of Study: 3 years (PhD) and up to 2 years (Masters)
Frequency: Annual
No. of awards offered: Varies
Application Procedure: Applicants should contact Rebecca Lawton for details.
Closing Date: November 30th
Contributor: In collaboration with NIWA
Additional Information: Research is most likely to be carried out a a NIWA facility. Preference will be given to New Zealand citizens.

For further information contact:

The Ministry of Fisheries
Tel: 04 819 4251
Email: rebecca.lawton@fish.govt.nz
Contact: Rebecca Lawton

THE NATIONAL BUREAU OF ASIAN RESEARCH (NBR)

1215 Fourth Avenue, Suite 1600, Seattle, WA 98161-1011, United States of America
Tel: (1) 206 632 7370
Fax: (1) 206 632 7487
Email: nbr@nbr.org
Website: www.nbr.org

NBR is a nonprofit, nonpartisan research institution dedicated to informing and strengthening policy. NBR conducts advanced research on politics and security, economics and trade, and health and societal issues, with emphasis on those of interest to the United States.

The Next Generation: Leadership in Asian Affairs Fellowship

Subjects: China's energy insecurity, military modernization in Asia, early health policy, central Asia's changing geopolitics, globalization or Chinese economic development, trends in Islamic education in South Asia, China–Southeast Asia relations.
Purpose: To further the professional development of Asian specialists in the year just after the completion of their Master's degree.
Eligibility: Open to citizens or permanent residents of the United States who have obtained a Master's degree.
Level of Study: Research
Type: Fellowships
Value: US$32,500 salary per year as well as travel and research-related expenses
Length of Study: 1 year
Frequency: Annual
Country of Study: United States of America
No. of awards offered: 4
Application Procedure: Candidates must submit an online cover letter, curriculum vitae, 750 word essay stating the purpose of applying and 3 written references.
Closing Date: January 16th
Funding: Corporation, foundation, government
No. of awards given last year: 3

For further information contact:

Email: nextgen@nbr.org

THE ROYAL SOCIETY OF EDINBURGH

22-26 George Street, Edinburgh, Scotland, EH2 2PQ, United Kingdom
Tel: (44) 131-240-5000
Fax: (44) 0131-240-5024
Email: afraser@royalsoced.org.uk
Website: www.royalsoced.org.uk
Contact: Anne Fraser, Research Awards Manager

The Royal Society of Edinburgh awards research fellowships and scholarships to candidates based in Scotland.

Auber Bequest

Subjects: All subjects.

Purpose: To provide assistance for the furtherance of academic research.

Eligibility: Open to naturalized British citizens or individuals wishing to acquire British nationality who are over 60 years of age, resident in Scotland or England and are bona fide scholars engaged in academic, but not industrial, research. Applicants should not have been British nationals at birth, nor held dual British nationality, and must have since acquired British nationality.

Level of Study: Unrestricted

Value: Varies, not normally exceeding UK £3,000

Length of Study: Up to 2 years

Frequency: Every 2 years

Country of Study: Other

No. of awards offered: Varies

Application Procedure: Applicants must complete an application form, available from the Research Awards Manager or from the RSE website www.royalsoced.org.uk

Closing Date: January 23rd

Funding: Private

Contributor: The Auber Bequest

BP/RSE Research Fellowships

Subjects: Mechanical engineering, chemical engineering, control engineering, solid state sciences, information technology, non-biological chemistry and geological sciences.

Purpose: To support independent research in specific fields.

Eligibility: Open to persons of all nationalities who have a PhD or equivalent qualification. Applicants should have 2–6 years postdoctoral research experience and must show they have a capacity for innovative research and a substantial volume of published work relevant to their proposed field of study.

Level of Study: Postdoctorate, Research

Type: Fellowship

Value: Salaries within the scale points 23–37 for research and analogous staff in Institutes of Higher Education with annual increments and superannuation benefits. Financial support towards expenses involved in carrying out the research is available, up to UK £6,000 for travel and subsistence each year

Length of Study: Up to 3 years

Frequency: Annual

Study Establishment: Any Institute of Higher Education in Scotland approved for the purpose by the Council of the Society

Country of Study: Scotland

No. of awards offered: 1

Application Procedure: Applicants must complete an application form, available from the Research Awards coordinator or the RSE website. Candidates must negotiate directly with the relevant head of department of the proposed host institution.

Closing Date: January 30th

Funding: Trusts

Contributor: British Petroleum (BP) – BP Trust

No. of awards given last year: 1

No. of applicants last year: 24

Additional Information: Fellows will be expected to devote their full time to research and will not be allowed to hold other paid appointments without the express permission of the Council of the RSE.

CRF (Caledonian Research Foundation)/RSE European Visiting Research Fellowships

Subjects: Archaeology, art and architecture, economics and economic history, geography, history, jurisprudence, linguistics, literature and philology, philosophy and religious studies and social sciences.

Purpose: To create a two-way flow of visiting scholars in arts and letters and social sciences between Scotland and continental Europe.

Eligibility: Open to members of the academic staff of a Scottish Institute of Higher Education or equivalent continental European institution. Applicants from continental Europe must be nominated by members of staff from a Scottish Institute of Higher Education.

Level of Study: Professional development

Type: Fellowship

Value: Up to UK £6,000 for visits of 6 months, which is reduced pro-rata for shorter visits, to cover actual costs of travel, subsistence and relevant study costs

Length of Study: 2–6 months

Frequency: Annual

Study Establishment: A Scottish Institute of Higher Education or a recognized Institute of Higher Education in a continental European country

Country of Study: Other

No. of awards offered: 8

Application Procedure: Applicants must complete an application form, available from the Research Awards Co-ordinator or the RSE website.

Closing Date: Early November

Funding: Private

Contributor: The Caledonian Research Foundation

No. of awards given last year: 8

No. of applicants last year: 22

Additional Information: Successful applicants will be required to submit a report within 2 months of the end of the visit.

John Moyes Lessells Travel Scholarships

Subjects: All forms of engineering.

Purpose: To enable well-qualified engineering graduates of Scottish Institutes of Higher Education to study some aspect of their profession overseas.

Eligibility: Applicants must be graduates with an Honours or higher degree in engineering from a Scottish Institute of Higher Education or who are currently pursuing a postgraduate degree in engineering at a Scottish university.

Level of Study: Postdoctorate, Professional development, Graduate, Postgraduate, Predoctorate

Type: Scholarship

Value: Normally up to UK £15,000 per year. Additional research or travel expenditure may be sanctioned

Length of Study: Initially for 1 year but shorter periods or extension for a second year may be considered. Acceptance of a scholarship implies a willingness to spend at least 2 years in the UK following the period of tenure

Frequency: Annual

Country of Study: Other

No. of awards offered: Varies

Application Procedure: Applicants must complete an application form, available from the Research Awards Manager or the RSE website.

Closing Date: March 27th

Funding: Private

No. of awards given last year: 5

No. of applicants last year: 10

Scottish Government Personal Research Fellowships

Subjects: All subjects.

Purpose: To encourage independent research in any discipline.

Eligibility: Open to persons of all nationalities who have a PhD or equivalent qualification. Applicants must have between 2–6 years of postdoctoral experience. They must also show that they have a capacity for innovative research and have a substantial volume of published work relevant to their proposed field of study.

Level of Study: Postdoctorate, Research

Type: Fellowship

Value: Annual stipends are within the scale points 23–37 for research and analogous staff in Institutes of Higher Education with annual increments and superannuation benefits. Expenses of up to UK £6,000 each year for travel and attendance at meetings or incidentals may be reimbursed. No support payments are available to the institution but Fellows may seek support for their research from other sources

Length of Study: Up to 5 years full-time research

Frequency: Annual

Study Establishment: Any Institute of Higher Education, research institution or industrial laboratory approved for the purpose by the Council of the Society

Country of Study: Scotland

No. of awards offered: 6

Application Procedure: Applicants must complete an application form, available from the Research Awards Co-ordinator or the RSE website. Applicants should negotiate directly with the proposed host institution.

Closing Date: Late March
Funding: Government
Contributor: The Scottish Government
No. of awards given last year: 6
No. of applicants last year: 42
Additional Information: Fellows may not hold other paid appointments without the express permission of the Council, but teaching or seminar work appropriate to their special knowledge may be acceptable.

Scottish Government/RSE Support Research Fellowships

Subjects: All subjects. The fellowships are awarded in fields likely to enhance the transfer of ideas and technology from the research community into wealth creation and improvement of the quality of life and encourage better uses of resources in Scotland.
Purpose: To enable or support Fellows to take study leave, either in their own institutions or elsewhere, while remaining in continuous employment with their present employer.
Eligibility: Candidates must be existing members of staff who have held a permanent appointment for not less than 5 years in any Institution of Higher Education in Scotland. Applicants should be employed on the lecturer grade or equivalent.
Level of Study: Professional development, Research
Type: Fellowship
Value: The actual cost of replacement staff will be reimbursed according to the Lecturer A scale (maximum Point 37) with the placement determined by the employer. Superannuation costs and employer's National Insurance contributions will also be reimbursed
Length of Study: Up to 1 year of full-time research
Frequency: Annual
Study Establishment: Any Institute of Higher Education, research institution or industrial laboratory approved for the purpose by the Council of the Society
Country of Study: Scotland
No. of awards offered: 3
Application Procedure: Applicants must complete an application form, available from the Research Awards office or the RSE website. Applicants must negotiate directly with the proposed host institution.
Closing Date: Late March
Funding: Government
Contributor: The Scottish Government
No. of awards given last year: 3
No. of applicants last year: 8
Additional Information: Further information is available on request or on the website.

THIRD WORLD ACADEMY OF SCIENCES (TWAS)

The Abdus Salam International Centre for Theoretical Physics, Strada Costiera 11, I-34014 Trieste, Italy
Tel: (39) 40 224 0327
Fax: (39) 40 224 0559
Email: info@twas.org
Website: www.twas.org
Contact: Professor Mohamed H A Hassan, Executive Director

The Third Word Academy of Sciences (TWAS) is an autonomous international organization that promotes and supports excellence in scientific research and helps build research capacity in the South.

CAS-TWAS Fellowship for Postdoctoral Research in China

Subjects: All areas of the natural sciences.
Purpose: To enable scholars who wish to pursue postdoctoral research to undertake research in laboratories or institutes of the Chinese Academy of Sciences.
Eligibility: Candidates must have a PhD and be nationals of a developing country other than China. They must also be regularly employed at a research or teaching institution in their home country. The maximum age limit is 40 years.
Level of Study: Postdoctorate
Type: Fellowship

Value: Covers food, accommodation and international travel, no provision for family members
Length of Study: Up to 1 year
Frequency: Annual
Study Establishment: CAS
Country of Study: China
No. of awards offered: Up to 15
Application Procedure: Applicants must send one copy of the application form to TWAS and three copies to CAS. Application forms can be obtained from the TWAS website.
Closing Date: August 31st
Funding: Government
Contributor: Chinese Academy of Sciences (CAS) and TWAS
Additional Information: CAS has 5 academic divisions, 11 local branches, 84 research institutes and 3 universities or colleges, distributed throughout the country.

For further information contact:

Division of International Organization Programmes, Chinese Academy of Sciences, 52 Sanlihe Road, Beijing, 100864, China
Contact: Mr Wang Zhenyu, Deputy Director

CAS-TWAS Fellowship for Postgraduate Research in China

Subjects: All areas of the natural sciences.
Purpose: To carry out research towards the final year of a PhD programme in China.
Eligibility: Candidates must have a Master's degree in natural sciences, be nationals of a developing country other than China and be registered for a PhD in their home country. The maximum age limit is 35 years.
Level of Study: Postgraduate
Type: Fellowship
Value: Covers food, accommodation and international travel. There is no provision for family members
Length of Study: 1 year
Frequency: Annual
Study Establishment: CAS
Country of Study: China
No. of awards offered: Up to 20
Application Procedure: Applicants must send one copy of the application form to TWAS and three copies to CAS. Application forms can be obtained from the TWAS website.
Closing Date: August 31st
Funding: Government
Contributor: Chinese Academy of Sciences (CAS) and TWAS
No. of awards given last year: New
Additional Information: CAS has 5 academic divisions, 11 local branches, 84 research institutes and 3 universities or colleges distributed throughout the country.

For further information contact:

Division of International Organization Programmes, Chinese Academy of Sciences, 52 Sanlihe Road, Beijing, 100864, China
Contact: Mr Wang Zhengu, Deputy Director

CAS-TWAS Fellowship for Visiting Scholars in China

Subjects: All areas of the natural sciences.
Purpose: To pursue advanced research in the natural sciences.
Eligibility: Applicants must have a PhD, a regular research assignment and at least 5 years postdoctoral research experience. Chinese nationals are not eligible. The maximum age limit is 55 years.
Level of Study: Research
Type: Fellowship
Length of Study: 1–3 months
Frequency: Annual
Study Establishment: CAS
Country of Study: China
No. of awards offered: Up to 15
Application Procedure: Applicants must send one copy of the application to TWAS and 3 copies to CAS. Application forms can be obtained from the TWAS website.
Closing Date: August 31st
Funding: Government
Contributor: Chinese Academy of Sciences (CAS) and TWAS

Additional Information: CAS has 5 academic divisions, 11 local branches, 84 research institutes and 3 universities or colleges distributed throughout the country.

For further information contact:

Division of International Organization Programmes, Chinese Academy of Sciences, 52 Sanlihe Road, Beijing, 100864, China
Contact: Mr Wang Zhenyu, Deputy Director

CNPq-TWAS Doctoral Fellowships in Brazil

Subjects: All areas of the natural sciences.
Purpose: To enable scholars from developing countries (other than Brazil) to undertake research in Brazil.
Eligibility: Applicants must hold a Master's degree or equivalent, and be proficient in either English, French, Portuguese or Spanish. Open to nationals of a developing country other than Brazil. The maximum age limit is 30 years.
Level of Study: Postgraduate
Type: Fellowship
Value: Covers food, accommodation and international travel, no provision for family members
Length of Study: Up to 4 years
Frequency: Annual
Country of Study: Brazil
No. of awards offered: Up to 40
Application Procedure: Applicants must complete an application form, available on request or from the website www.twas.org
Closing Date: August 31st
Funding: Government
Contributor: Brazilian ministry of science and technology, the Conselho Nacional de Desenvolvimento Cientifico e Tecnologico (CNPq) and TWAS
No. of awards given last year: New award

CNPq-TWAS Fellowships for Postdoctoral Research in Brazil

Subjects: All areas of the natural sciences.
Purpose: To enable scholars to pursue postdoctoral research in Brazil.
Eligibility: Applicants must have a PhD in the natural sciences, be proficient in English, French, Portuguese or Spanish and must be regularly employed at a research or teaching institution in their home country. Open to nationals of developing countries other than Brazil. The maximum age limit is 40 years.
Level of Study: Postdoctorate
Type: Fellowship
Value: Covers food, accommodation and international travel, no provision for family members
Length of Study: 6 months–1 year
Frequency: Annual
Country of Study: Brazil
No. of awards offered: Up to 10
Application Procedure: Applicants must complete an application form, available on request or from the website www.twas.org
Closing Date: August 31st
Funding: Government
Contributor: Brazilian Ministry of Science and Technology, the Conselho Nacional de Desenvolvimento Cientifico e Tecnologico (CNPq) and TWAS

CSIR (Council of Scientific and Industrial Research)/ TWAS Fellowship for Postgraduate Research

Subjects: Newly emerging areas of science and technology.
Purpose: To enable scholars from developing countries (other than India) who wish to pursue postgraduate research to undertake research in laboratories or institutes of the CSIR.
Eligibility: Candidates must have a Master's or equivalent degree in science or engineering and should be a regular employee in a developing country (other than India) and be holding a research assignment.
Level of Study: Postgraduate
Type: Fellowship
Value: A monthly stipend of Rs 8,000 per month, extendable to Rs 9,000 in the final year, plus a contingency grant of Rs 20,000

Length of Study: 2–3 years
Frequency: Annual
Study Establishment: CSIR research laboratories or institutes
Country of Study: India
No. of awards offered: Varies
Application Procedure: One copy of the application should be sent to TWAS and three copies to CSIR. Application forms are available on request or from the website www.twas.org or www.ictp.trieste.it/~twas/hg/csir_postgrad_form.html
Closing Date: June 30th
Funding: Government
Contributor: CSIR (India), the Italian Ministry of Foreign Affairs and the Directorate General for Development Co-operation
No. of awards given last year: 8
Additional Information: CSIR is the premier scientific organization of India, and has a network of research laboratories covering wide areas of scientific and industrial research. Further information is available on the CSIR website www.csir.res.in

For further information contact:

International S&T Affairs Directorate, Council for Scientific and Industrial Research (CSIR), Anusandhan Bhavan, 2 Rafi Marg, New Delhi, 110001, India
Fax: (91) 11 2371 0618
Email: rprasad@csir.res.in
Contact: Dr B K Ramprasad, Senior Deputy Advisor

CSIR (The Council of Scientific and Industrial Research)/ TWAS Fellowship for Postdoctoral Research

Subjects: Newly emerging areas of science and technology.
Purpose: To enable scholars from developing countries (other than India) who wish to pursue postdoctoral research to undertake research in laboratories or institutes of the CSIR.
Eligibility: The minimum qualification requirement is a PhD degree in science or technology. Applicants must be regular employees in a developing country (but not India) and should hold a research assignment.
Level of Study: Postdoctorate
Type: Fellowship
Value: A monthly stipend of Rs 11,500 for a maximum of 1 year, plus a contingency grant of Rs 20,000 per year
Length of Study: Up to 1 year
Frequency: Annual
Study Establishment: CSIR research laboratories or institutes
Country of Study: India
No. of awards offered: Varies
Application Procedure: Applicants must complete an application form, available on request or from the website.
Closing Date: June 30th
Funding: Government
Contributor: CSIR (India), the Italian Ministry of Foreign Affairs and the Directorate General for Development Co-operation
No. of awards given last year: 4
Additional Information: CSIR is the premier civil scientific organization of India, which has a network of research laboratories covering wide areas of industrial research. Further information is available on the CSIR website www.csir.res.in

For further information contact:

Senior Deputy Advisor, CSIR (The Council of Scientific and Industrial Research), Anusandhan Bhavan, 2 Rafi Marg, New Delhi, 110001, India
Tel: (91) 11 331 6751
Fax: (91) 11 371 0618
Email: rprasad@csirhq.ren.nic.in
Contact: Dr B K Ramprasad

DBT-TWAS Biotechnology Fellowship for Postdoctoral Studies in India

Subjects: All areas of biotechnology.
Purpose: To support postdoctoral research in biotechnology in India.
Eligibility: Applicants must have a Master's degree in science or engineering or an equivalent degree and must be a national of a developing country. Indian nationals are not eligible. The maximum age

limit is 40 years. Fellowships for PhD will be awarded only to candidates who are already registered for PhD in a university in their home country or willing to register in India

Level of Study: Postgraduate

Type: Fellowship

Value: Rs 11,500, plus a house rent allowance, medical coverage and an Rs 20,000 contingency grant paid to the host institution

Length of Study: 1 year

Frequency: Annual

Study Establishment: More than 80 listed universities and research institutions

Country of Study: India

No. of awards offered: Up to 10

Application Procedure: Applicants must complete an application form, available on request or from the website www.twas.org

Closing Date: August 31st

Funding: Government

Contributor: Indian Department of Biotechnology (DBT) and TWAS

DBT-TWAS Biotechnology Fellowships for Postgraduate Studies in India

Subjects: All areas of biotechnology.

Purpose: To carry out research leading to a PhD in biotechnology.

Eligibility: Applicants must have a Master's degree in science, engineering or equivalent, must be a national of a developing country (except India) and must be registered for a PhD or be willing to register in India. The maximum age limit is 30 years.

Level of Study: Postdoctorate

Type: Fellowship

Value: Rs 8,000 during the first 2 years, rising to Rs 9,000 in the 3rd year. An Rs 20,000 contingency grant is provided to the host institution. Medical coverage and subsidized housing is also provided

Length of Study: Up to 3 years

Frequency: Annual

Study Establishment: More than 80 listed universities and research institutions

Country of Study: India

No. of awards offered: Up to 40

Application Procedure: Applicants must complete an application form, available on request or from the website.

Closing Date: August 31st

Funding: Government

Contributor: Indian Department of Biotechnology (DBT) and TWAS

ICSU-TWAS-UNESCO-UNU/IAS Visiting Scientist Programme

Subjects: All areas of science other than mathematics or physics.

Purpose: To provide institutions and research grants in the South, especially in least developed countries (LDCs), with the opportunity to establish long-term links with world leaders in science and help build scientific capacity in their country.

Eligibility: Candidate must be an internationally renowned expert.

Level of Study: Research, Professional development

Type: Consultancy

Value: Travel plus a US$500 honorarium. Local costs will be covered by the host institution

Length of Study: Minimum of 1 month

Frequency: Annual

Study Establishment: Teaching and research institutions

Country of Study: Any developing country, preference will be given to LDCs

Application Procedure: Applicants must complete an application form, available on request or from the website.

Closing Date: October 1st

Funding: International Office, government

Contributor: International Council for Science (ICSU), United Nations Educational, Scientific and Cultural Organization (UNESCO), United Nations University/Institute for Advanced Studies (UNU/IAS) and TWAS

No. of awards given last year: 16 visits

Additional Information: A similar programme for mathematics and physics is run by the Abdus Salam International Centre for Theoretical Physics (ICTP). See the website www.ictp.trieste.it/www-users/oea/vs for more information.

The Trieste Science Prize

Subjects: Biological sciences, chemical sciences, agricultural sciences, Earth, space, ocean and atmospheric sciences, engineering sciences, mathematics, medical sciences, physics and astronomy.

Purpose: To honour outstanding scientists living and working in developing countries.

Eligibility: Candidates must be nationals of developing countries living and working in the South. Individuals who have won the Nobel Prize, Tokyo/Kyoto Prize, Gafoord Prize or Abel Prize are not eligible.

Level of Study: Research

Type: Prize

Value: US$50,000 each

Frequency: Annual

Country of Study: Any developing country

No. of awards offered: 2

Application Procedure: Nomination forms must be downloaded from the website www.twas.org and accompanied by a 5–6 page biographical sketch outlining the nominee's major scientific achievements, pre-prints of up to 20 publications and a complete list of publications.

Closing Date: January 31st

Funding: Commercial, private

Contributor: Illycaffè, Trieste

TWAS Fellowships for Research and Advanced Training

Subjects: All fields of basic sciences.

Purpose: To enhance the research of young promising scientists, specifically those at the beginning of their research career, and to help them to foster links for future collaboration.

Eligibility: Open to nationals of developing countries with permanent positions in universities or research institutes in developing countries holding a PhD or equivalent. Candidates must not be older than 40 years and preference will be given to candidates from less developed countries.

Level of Study: Postdoctorate

Type: Fellowship

Value: Travel support and monthly subsistence of up to US$300. Living expenses are usually obtained from local sources

Length of Study: 3 months–1 year

Frequency: Annual

Country of Study: Developing countries

No. of awards offered: Varies

Application Procedure: Applicants must complete an application form, available on request or from the website.

Closing Date: October 1st

Funding: Government

Contributor: The Italian Ministry of Foreign Affairs and the Directorate General for Development Co-operation

Additional Information: Further information is available on the website.

TWAS Grants for Scientific Meetings in Developing Countries

Subjects: Agricultural, biological, chemical, engineering or geological and medical sciences.

Purpose: To encourage international scientific meetings in Third World countries.

Eligibility: Open to organizers of international scientific meetings in developing countries. Special consideration is given to those meetings that are likely to benefit the scientific community in the Third World and to promote regional and international co-operation in developing science and its applications to the problems of the Third World.

Level of Study: Postgraduate, Professional development

Type: Travel grant

Value: Up to US$3,000 for travel expenses of principal speakers from abroad and/or participants from the region

Frequency: Annual

Country of Study: Developing countries

No. of awards offered: Varies

Application Procedure: Applicants must complete an application form, available on request or from the website.

Closing Date: June 1st for meetings held between January and June of the following year, and December 1st for meetings held between July and December of the following year

Funding: Government

Contributor: The Italian Ministry of Foreign Affairs and the Directo-rate General for Development Co-operation
No. of awards given last year: 30
Additional Information: Grants are not offered for meetings in Physics and Mathematics.

TWAS Prizes

Subjects: Medical sciences, biology, chemistry, mathematics and physics, agricultural sciences, engineering sciences and earth sciences.
Purpose: To recognize and support outstanding achievements made by scientists from developing countries. Prizes are awarded to those scientists whose research work has significantly contributed to the advancement of science.
Eligibility: Open to nationals of developing countries who are, as a rule, working and living in these countries. Consideration is given to proven achievements judged particularly by their national and inter-national impact. Members of TWAS are not eligible for such awards.
Level of Study: Postgraduate, Professional development, Doctorate, Postdoctorate
Type: Prize
Value: US$10,000 plus a plaque on which major contributions of the award winner are mentioned
Frequency: Annual
Country of Study: Developing countries
No. of awards offered: 8
Application Procedure: Applicants must be designated on the nomination form. The nomination must be accompanied by a one- to two-page biographical sketch of the nominee including their major scientific accomplishments, a list of twelve of the candidate's most significant publications as well as a complete list of publications and a curriculum vitae. Nominations for the awards are invited from all members of the TWAS as well as from academies, national research councils, universities and scientific institutions in developing countries and advanced countries. A nomination form is available on request or can be downloaded from the website www.twas.org
Closing Date: March 31st. Nominations received after the deadline will be considered in the next year
Funding: Government
Contributor: The Italian Ministry of Foreign Affairs and the Directo-rate General for Development Co-operation
No. of awards given last year: 8
Additional Information: The awards are usually presented on a special occasion, normally coinciding with the general meeting of the Academy and/or a general conference organized by the Academy. Recipients of awards are expected to give lectures about the work for which the awards have been made. Further information is available on the website.

TWAS Prizes to Young Scientists in Developing Countries

Subjects: Biology, chemistry, mathematics or physics, rotated an-nually.
Purpose: To enable science academies and research councils in developing countries to award prizes to scientists in their countries.
Eligibility: Open to academies and research councils in developing countries. The age limit for prize winners is 40 years.
Level of Study: Postgraduate
Type: Prize
Value: Usually US$2,000
Frequency: Annual
Country of Study: Developing countries
No. of awards offered: More than 30
Application Procedure: Applicants must write for details to info@twas.org or see the website.
Funding: Government
Contributor: The Italian Ministry of Foreign Affairs and the Directo-rate General for Development Co-operation
No. of awards given last year: 23

TWAS Research Grants

Subjects: Biology, chemistry, mathematics and physics.
Purpose: To reinforce and promote scientific research in basic sci-ences in the Third World, to strengthen the endogenous capacity in science and to reduce the exodus of scientific talents from the South.

Eligibility: Applicants must be nationals of developing countries with an advanced academic degree, some research experience and must hold positions at universities or research institutions in developing countries.
Level of Study: Postdoctorate, Doctorate, Professional development, Postgraduate
Value: Up to US$10,000. Grants are to be used to purchase scientific equipment, consumable laboratory supplies and scientific literature (textbooks and proceedings only)
Length of Study: 1 year
Frequency: Annual
Country of Study: Developing countries
No. of awards offered: Varies
Application Procedure: Applicants must complete an application form available on request or from the website. Applications must be submitted in English.
Closing Date: July 1st or December 1st
Funding: Government
Contributor: The Italian Ministry of Foreign Affairs, the Directorate General for Development Co-operation and the Swedish Agency for Research Co-operation with Developing Countries
No. of awards given last year: 90
Additional Information: Further information is available on the re-quest.

TWAS Spare Parts for Scientific Equipment

Subjects: Biology, chemistry and physics.
Purpose: The programme has been established in response to the current difficulty faced by several laboratories in the Third World to obtain badly needed spares and replacement parts for scientific equipment that is required for their experimental research.
Eligibility: Applicants must be research group leaders at universities or research institutes in developing countries.
Level of Study: Professional development
Type: Grant
Value: Up to US$1,000 including insurance and freight charges
Country of Study: Developing countries
No. of awards offered: Varies
Application Procedure: Applicants must first contact the suppliers and obtain a proforma invoice, valid for 3–6 months, including cost, insurance and freight charges for the items they require. Applicants must submit a completed application form with the proforma invoice from the supplier. Application forms are available on request or from the website.
Closing Date: Applications are accepted at any time
Funding: Government
Contributor: The Italian Ministry of Foreign Affairs and the Directo-rate General for Development Co-operation
No. of awards given last year: 30
Additional Information: Applications by email will not be accepted.

TWAS UNESCO Associateship Scheme

Subjects: Biology, chemistry, physics, mathematics, engineering, agricultural sciences, medical sciences and earth sciences.
Purpose: To alleviate the problem of isolated talented scientists in developing countries, and strengthen the research programmes of centres of excellence in the South.
Eligibility: Open to associates among the most eminent and prom-ising researchers in developing countries. Special consideration is given to scientists from isolated institutions in developing countries.
Level of Study: Postdoctorate, Professional development
Value: Travel costs plus US$300 per month for incidental local ex-penses. The host centre provides local hospitality and research fa-cilities
Length of Study: 3 years, plus the entitlement to visit the Centre twice for a period of 2–3 months each time. There is a possibility of renewal for a further 3 years depending on funds available
Frequency: Annual
Study Establishment: There are over 116 centres
Country of Study: Developing countries
No. of awards offered: Varies
Application Procedure: Applicants must complete an application form, available on request or from the website.

Closing Date: December 1st
Funding: Government
Contributor: UNESCO, the Italian Ministry for Foreign Affairs and the Directorate General for Development Co-operation

TWAS-S N Bose National Centre for Basic Sciences Postgraduate Fellowships in Physical Sciences

Subjects: Physical sciences.
Purpose: To carry out research leading to a PhD in the physical sciences.
Eligibility: Applicant must have a Master's degree in physics, mathematics or physical chemistry, must be a national of a developing country (other than India) and be employed at a research institution. The maximum age limit is 30 years.
Level of Study: Postgraduate
Type: Fellowship
Value: Rs 8,000 during the first 2 years, rising to Rs 9,000 in the 3rd year. A Rs 20,000 containing grant is provided to the host institution. Travel and subsidized accommodation are covered
Length of Study: Up to 5 years
Frequency: Annual
Study Establishment: S N Bose National Centre for Basic Sciences
Country of Study: India
No. of awards offered: Up to 5
Application Procedure: Applicants must complete an application form, available on request or from the website.
Closing Date: August 31st
Funding: Government
Contributor: S N Bose National Centre for Basic Sciences, Kolkata, India and TWAS
Additional Information: For further information see the website www.bose.res.in

THE THOMSON FOUNDATION

37 Park Place, Cardiff, CF10 3BB, Wales
Tel: (44) 29 2035 3060
Fax: (44) 29 2035 3061
Email: enquiries@thomfound.co.uk
Website: www.thomsonfoundation.co.uk
Contact: Mr Gareth Price

The Thomson Foundation provides practical, intensive training both in the United Kingdom and abroad, along with a wide range of consultancies to journalists, managers, technicians and production staff in television, radio and the press.

Thomson Foundation Scholarship

Subjects: Journalism, radio or television broadcasting, internet publishing and photojournalism.
Purpose: To enable recipients to attend Thomson Foundation training courses in Britain.
Eligibility: Open to professional journalists and broadcasters with at least 3 years of full-time experience.
Level of Study: Professional development
Type: Scholarship
Value: Varies
Length of Study: Varies, usually a 12-week Summer course or a shorter 4-week course
Study Establishment: The Thomson Foundation
Country of Study: United Kingdom
No. of awards offered: Varies
Application Procedure: Applicants must complete an application form, available from the Foundation, for the courses they wish to apply for.
Closing Date: April 15th
Funding: Private, government
Contributor: The British Foreign Office Chevening Scholarship Scheme
No. of awards given last year: 6
No. of applicants last year: 20
Additional Information: Annual 3-month courses in television, radio and press journalism run from June to September.

THURGOOD MARSHALL COLLEGE FUND (TMCF)

80 Maiden Lane, Suite 2204, New York, NY, 10038, United States of America
Tel: (1) 212 573 8888
Fax: (1) 212 573 8497
Email: emhall@tmcfund.org
Website: www.thurgoodmarshallfund.org

The Thurgood Marshall College Fund (TMCF) was established in 1987 to carry on Justice Marshall's legacy of equal access to higher education by supporting exceptional merit scholars attending America's public historically Black colleges and universities. More than 5000 Thurgood Marshall Scholars have graduated and are making valuable contributions to science, technology, government, human service, business, education and various communities.

Philip Morris USA Thurgood Marshall Scholarship

Subjects: Biology, business, chemistry, computer science, economics, engineering, finance and physics.
Purpose: To aid students who demonstrated financial need and the potential for success.
Eligibility: Open to citizens of the United States and current full-time students of Florida A&M, North Carolina A&T, Winston-Salem State, Howard University, Virginia State or Norfolk State Universities.
Level of Study: Postgraduate
Type: Scholarships
Value: Up to US$5,000
Length of Study: 1 year
Frequency: Annual
Country of Study: United States of America
No. of awards offered: 17
Application Procedure: A completed application form should be submitted to the TMSF College Coordinator.
Funding: Foundation

For further information contact:

90 William Street, Suite 1203, New York, NY, 10038, United States of America
Contact: Philip Morris

TMCF Scholarships

Subjects: Creative and performing arts.
Purpose: To financially support outstanding students.
Eligibility: Open to candidates who are academically exceptional in the creative and performing arts requiring financial help.
Type: Scholarship
Value: US$2,200 per semester and payment of tuition fees, accommodation and books
Frequency: Annual
Application Procedure: Completed applications must be submitted along with the required attachments. Visit: www.aiplef.org/donors/
Funding: Foundation

For further information contact:

AIPLEF Scholarship, 80 Maiden Lane, Suite 2204, New York, NY 10038
Email: jessica.barnes@tmcfund.org

TOKYU FOUNDATION FOR INBOUND STUDENTS

1-21-6 Dogenzaka, Shibuya Ku, Tokyo, 150-0043, Japan
Tel: (81) 3 3461 0844
Fax: (81) 3 5458 1696
Email: info@tokyu-f.jp
Website: www.tokyu-f.jp
Contact: Mr Takashi Izumi, Managing Director & Secretary General

The Tokyu Foundation for Inbound Students grant scholarships to postgraduate students studying in Japan from Asia-pacific areas.

Tokyu Scholarship

Subjects: All subjects.
Purpose: To promote international exchange by fostering the development of international goodwill between Japan and her neighbours in Asia and the Pacific and contributing to international co-operation and cultural exchange in the broadest possible sense.
Eligibility: Open to applicants from Asian countries who will be able to explain about their research plan in Japanese.
Level of Study: Postgraduate
Type: Scholarship
Value: ¥160,000 per month per student
Length of Study: Up to 2 years
Frequency: Annual
Country of Study: Japan
No. of awards offered: 20–25
Application Procedure: Download application form from the website.
Closing Date: November 10th
Funding: Commercial
Contributor: Tokyu Corporation
No. of awards given last year: 21
No. of applicants last year: 869
Additional Information: Applicants must travel to Japan at their own cost and be admitted to enter university postgraduate school.

TOLEDO COMMUNITY FOUNDATION

608 Madison Avenue, Suite 1540, Toledo, OH, 43604-1151, United States of America
Tel: (1) 419 241 5049
Fax: (1) 419 242 5549
Email: toledocf@toledocf.org
Website: www.toledocf.org

The Toledo Community Foundation, Inc. is a public, charitable foundation that exists to improve the quality of life in the Toledo region.

Charles Z. Moore Memorial Scholarship Fund

Subjects: Music.
Purpose: To encourage students pursuing a course of study in music with an emphasis on Jazz studies.
Eligibility: Open to residents of northwest Ohio or Southeast Michigan who demonstrate the talent, interest and ability needed to pursue the study of Jazz.
Level of Study: Professional development
Type: Scholarship
Frequency: Annual
Country of Study: United States of America
Application Procedure: A completed scholarship application form and support materials must be sent.
Closing Date: March 30th

Edith Franklin Pottery Scholarship

Subjects: Ceramic arts.
Purpose: To assist promising and accomplished potters in obtaining additional education or training in the ceramic arts.
Eligibility: Open to all applicants who are current residents of northwest Ohio Lenawee or Monroe Countries in Michigan with individual motivation, ability and potential.
Level of Study: Professional development
Type: Scholarship
Length of Study: US$7,000
Frequency: Annual
Study Establishment: Any recognized college, university or nonprofit organization
Country of Study: United States of America
Application Procedure: A completed scholarship application form must be sent.
Closing Date: February 28th

Harold W. Wott-IEEE Toledo Section Scholarship Fund

Subjects: Engineering.
Purpose: To support students studying in the engineering field.
Eligibility: Open to applicants attending institutions or universities in northwestern Ohio and southeastern Michigan.
Level of Study: Postgraduate

Type: Scholarship
Value: US$1,000
Frequency: Annual
Country of Study: United States of America
No. of awards offered: Varies
Application Procedure: A completed application form and required attachments and transcripts must be sent.
Closing Date: March 2nd

TOMSK POLYTECHNIC UNIVERSITY

Institute for International Education, 30 Lenin Prospect, Tomsk, 634050, Russia
Tel: (7) 3822 563304
Fax: (7) 3822 563299
Email: iie@tpu.ru
Website: www.iie.tpu.ru

Tomsk Polytechnic University was founded in 1896 and is the oldest technical educational institution in the Asian part of Russia. Since that time, the university scholars and graduates have greatly contributed to the Russian science, education, culture and industry development.

Tomsk Polytechnic University International Scholarship

Subjects: All subjects available at the university.
Purpose: To financially support outstanding students.
Eligibility: Open to candidates with an average of 80 per cent marks at graduation, who are not older than 40 years of age.
Level of Study: Doctorate, Postgraduate
Type: Scholarships
Value: Varies
Length of Study: From 1 to 3 years
Frequency: Annual
Study Establishment: Tomsk Polytechnic University
Country of Study: Russia
No. of awards offered: 5
Application Procedure: Applicants can download the application form from the website. The completed application form and educational certificates must be submitted.
Closing Date: August 15th
Funding: Corporation, government
Contributor: Ministry of Russian Federation
No. of awards given last year: 3
No. of applicants last year: 50
Additional Information: Applications are to be submitted by fax at 3822 563304 or by email to iie@tpu.ru

TOURETTE SYNDROME ASSOCIATION, INC. (TSA)

42-40 Bell Boulevard, Suite 205, Bayside, NY, 11361-2874, United States of America
Tel: (1) 718 224 2999
Fax: (1) 718 279 9596
Email: ts@tsa-usa.org
Website: www.tsa-usa.org
Contact: Ms Sue Levi-Pearl, Vice President, Medical & Scientific Programmes

The Tourette Syndrome Association, Inc. (TSA), founded in 1972, is the only national voluntary non-profit membership organization dedicated to identifying the cause, finding the cure and controlling the effects of Tourette Syndrome. Members include individuals with the disorder, their relatives and other interested, concerned people. The Association develops and disseminates educational material to individuals, professionals and agencies in the fields of healthcare, education and government, co-ordinates support services to help people and their families cope with the problems that occur with Tourette Syndrome and funds research that will ultimately find the cause of and cure for it and, at the same time, lead to improved medications and treatments.

TSA Research Grant and Fellowship Program

Subjects: Clinical and basic science relevant to Tourette Syndrome.

Purpose: To foster basic and clinical research related to the causes or treatment of Tourette Syndrome.

Eligibility: Open to candidates who have an MD, PhD or equivalent qualifications. Previous experience in the field of movement disorders is desirable, but not essential. Fellowships are intended for young postdoctoral investigators in the early stages of their careers.

Level of Study: Postdoctorate, Research

Type: Research grant

Value: Varies, depending upon the category and applicants's experience within that category, and is usually US$5,000–75,000. Postdoctoral grants (fellowships) are up to US$40,000

Length of Study: 1 year

Frequency: Annual

Study Establishment: Any institution with adequate facilities

Country of Study: Any country

No. of awards offered: Varies

Application Procedure: Applicants must submit a letter of intent briefly describing the scientific basis of the proposed project. For further information and deadlines please see the website www.tsa-usa.org/research/html

Closing Date: October of each year

Funding: Private

No. of awards given last year: 21

No. of applicants last year: 82

Additional Information: The Association provides up to 10 per cent of overhead or indirect costs within the total amount budgeted.

TOXICOLOGY EDUCATION FOUNDATION (TEF)

PO Box 31021, Raleigh, NC, 27622-1021, United States of America
Tel: (1) 919 676 4666
Fax: (1) 919 841 5042
Email: tefhq@toxedfoundation.org
Website: www.toxedfoundation.org

The mission of TFE is to encourage, support and promote charitable and educational activities that increase the public understanding of toxicology.

Alleghery-ENCRC Student Research Award

Subjects: Toxicology.

Purpose: To support a student's thesis, dissertation and summer research project in toxicology and to encourage them to formulate and conduct meaningful research.

Eligibility: Open to students who are members in good standing of AE-SOT. The student's advisor must also be a member in good standing and submit a letter concerning availability.

Level of Study: Graduate

Type: Award

Value: Up to $1,000

Frequency: Annual

Country of Study: United States of America

No. of awards offered: 1

Application Procedure: Applicants must send four copies of completed application form alongwith a project description and budget.

Closing Date: May 30th

For further information contact:

CDC/NIOSH MS 2015, 1095 Willowdale Road, Morgatown, WV, 26505, United States of America
Email: LBattelli@cdc.gov
Contact: Lori Battelli

Colgate-Palmolive Grants for Alternative Research

Subjects: Reproductive and developmental toxicology, neurotoxicology, systemic toxicology, sensitization and acute toxicity.

Purpose: To identify and support efforts that promote, develop, refine or validate scientifically acceptable animal alternative methods to facilitate the safety assessment of new chemicals and formulations.

Level of Study: Research

Type: Research grant

Value: US$10,000–40,000

Frequency: Annual

Country of Study: United States of America

Application Procedure: Application is available online. A research plan, budget, curriculum vitae and a letter from the institution must be sent.

Closing Date: August 9th

Funding: Private

Contributor: Colgate-Palmolive

No. of awards given last year: 5

Colgate-Palmolive Postdoctoral Fellowship Award in In Vitro Toxicology

Subjects: Toxicology.

Purpose: To advance the development of alternatives to animal testing in toxicological research.

Eligibility: Open to postdoctoral trainees employed by academic institutions. The applicants or postdoctoral advisors must be members or pending members of SOT.

Level of Study: Postdoctorate

Type: Fellowship

Value: Includes a stipend and research-related costs of up to US$38,500 per year

Length of Study: 1 year

Frequency: Every 2 years, alternate year

Country of Study: United States of America

Application Procedure: Applicants must submit their curriculum vitae, transcripts, research proposal, budget and recommendation letters. Applicants must also supply a description of the research to be performed.

Closing Date: October 9th

Contributor: Colgate-Palmolive

Additional Information: Preference is for applicants in their first year of study beyond the PhD, MD or DVM degree. Funding for second year is contingent upon satisfactory research progress.

For further information contact:

Website: www.toxicology.org/ai/af/awards.aspx

Food Safety SS Burdock Group Travel Award

Subjects: Food safety toxicology.

Purpose: To cover travel expenses for a student to attend the Annual Meeting.

Eligibility: Open to full-time graduate students with research interests in toxicology. Students in their early graduate training, who have not attended any SOT Annual Meeting are encouraged to apply.

Level of Study: Graduate

Value: Up to $500

Frequency: Annual

Country of Study: United States of America

No. of awards offered: 1

Application Procedure: Applicants must send a letter of request indicating that he/she is enrolled in good standing in a doctoral training programme. The applicant must also state how the research and training relate to food safety.

Closing Date: January 20th

For further information contact:

Genevieve Body

Regulation and Safety SS Travel Award

Subjects: Toxicology.

Purpose: To help defray the costs of travel to the SOT meeting.

Eligibility: Open to students submitting a poster or making a presentation at the SOT meeting.

Type: Travel award

Value: US$1,000 plus a plaque

Frequency: Annual

Country of Study: United States of America

No. of awards offered: 4–5

Application Procedure: Applicants must fill an application form and an abstract of work preserved.

For further information contact:

Email: jtmacgror@earthlink.net
Contact: James TMacGregor

Robert L. Dixon International Travel Award

Subjects: Reproductive toxicology.
Purpose: To give financially assist students studying in the area of reproductive toxicology.
Eligibility: Open to applicants enrolled full-time in a PhD programme studying reproductive toxicology and are student members of SOT.
Level of Study: Doctorate, Graduate
Type: Award
Value: Includes a stipend of US$2,000 for travel costs to enable students to attend the International Congress of Toxicology meeting
Frequency: Every 3 years
Country of Study: United States of America and abroad
Application Procedure: Applicants must submit a completed application form, reference letter, graduate transcripts and lists of complete citations of the original work.
Closing Date: December 31st
Contributor: Toxicology Education Foundation

For further information contact:

Email: tefhq@toxedfoundation.org

THE TOYOTA FOUNDATION

37F, Shinjuku-Mitsui Building, 2-1-1, Nishi-Shinjuku, Shinjuku-Ku, Tokyo, Japan
Tel: (81) 3 3344 1701
Fax: (81) 3 3342 6911
Email: admin@toyotafound.or.jp
Website: www.toyotafound.or.jp

The Toyota Foundation was established in 1974 as a multi-purpose grant-making foundation. It provides financial assistance to carry out projects in Japan and other countries, mainly in the developing world, that address timely issues in a variety of fields.

The Toyota Foundation Research Programme

Subjects: All subjects.
Purpose: To support research.
Eligibility: Open to candidates of all nationalities studying a doctoral programme.
Type: Scholarship
Value: Varies
Length of Study: 1–2 years
Frequency: Annual
Application Procedure: See the website.
Funding: Foundation
Contributor: The Toyota Foundation

TRANSPORTATION ASSOCIATION OF CANADA FOUNDATION

2323 St Laurent Boulevard, Ottawa, ON, K1G 4J8, Canada
Tel: (1) 613 736 1350, ext. 235
Fax: (1) 613 736 1395
Email: secretariat@tac-atc.ca
Website: www.tac-atc.ca
Contact: Ms Susan Killam, Secretary-Treasurer

The Transportation Association of Canada Foundation has a mandate to support the educational and research needs of the Canadian transportation industry.

TAC Foundation – 3M Canada Company Scholarship

Subjects: Transportation-related disciplines.
Eligibility: Open only to the Canadian candidates or landed immigrants who are admissible to a postgraduate studies program or already registered as full-time graduate students having a minimum grade point average of B.
Level of Study: Postgraduate
Type: Scholarship
Value: $5,000
Length of Study: 4 years
Application Procedure: Check the website for further details.
Contributor: 3M Canada Company

TAC Foundation – Albert M. Stevens Scholarship

Subjects: Transportation-related disciplines.
Purpose: To contribute to maintain high quality transportation expertise in Canada.
Eligibility: Open only to the Canadian candidates or landed immigrants who are admissible to a postgraduate studies programme or already registered as full-time graduate students having a minimum grade point average of B.
Level of Study: Postgraduate
Type: Scholarship
Value: $5,000
Length of Study: 4 years
Application Procedure: Applicants must send application form (including a two page resume) to the TAC Foundation.
Closing Date: March 1st
Funding: Individuals
Contributor: Albert M. Stevens

TAC Foundation – BA Group Scholarship

Subjects: Transportation planning or transportation engineering.
Purpose: To encourage students to acquire the full range of technical skills required contributing to the development of superior transportation solutions.
Eligibility: Open only to the Canadian candidates or landed immigrants who are admissible to a postgraduate studies program or already registered as full-time graduate students having a minimum grade point average of B.
Level of Study: Postgraduate
Type: Scholarship
Value: $5,000
Length of Study: 4 years
Application Procedure: Applicants must send application form (including a two page resume) to the TAC Foundation.
Closing Date: March 1st
Contributor: BA Group Transportation Consultants

TAC Foundation – Cement Association of Canada Scholarship

Subjects: Transportation-related disciplines.
Purpose: To recognize the importance of education in the transportation field.
Eligibility: Open only to the Canadian candidates or landed immigrants who are admissible to a postgraduate studies program or already registered as full-time graduate students having a minimum grade point average of B.
Level of Study: Postgraduate
Type: Scholarship
Value: $5,000
Length of Study: 4 years
Application Procedure: Applicants must send application form (including a two page resume) to the TAC Foundation.
Closing Date: March 1st
Contributor: Cement Association of Canada

TAC Foundation – Delcan Corporation Scholarship

Subjects: Transportation-related disciplines.
Eligibility: Open only to the Canadian candidates or landed immigrants who are admissible to a postgraduate studies program or already registered as full-time graduate students having a minimum grade point average of B.
Level of Study: Postgraduate
Type: Scholarship
Value: $5,000
Length of Study: 4 years
Application Procedure: Applicants must send application form (including a two page resume) to the TAC Foundation.
Closing Date: March 1st
Contributor: Delcan Corporation

TAC Foundation – EBA Engineering Consultants Ltd Scholarship

Subjects: Transportation engineering.
Eligibility: Open only to the Canadian candidates or landed immigrants who are admissible to a postgraduate studies program or al-

ready registered as full-time graduate students having a minimum grade point average of B.
Level of Study: Postgraduate
Type: Scholarship
Value: $5,000
Length of Study: 4 years
Application Procedure: Applicants must send application form (including a two page resume) to the TAC Foundation.
Closing Date: March 1st
Contributor: EBA Engineering Consultants Limited
Additional Information: Preference is given in the areas of design, construction, maintenance and operation of roadway transportation systems in rural and urban environments.

TAC Foundation – IBI Group scholarship

Subjects: Transportation-related disciplines.
Purpose: To attract and prepare transportation planners, providers, funders, and users for a career in the transportation industry.
Eligibility: Open only to the Canadian candidates or landed immigrants who are admissible to a postgraduate studies program or already registered as full-time graduate students having a minimum grade point average of B.
Level of Study: Postgraduate
Type: Scholarship
Value: $5,000
Length of Study: 4 years
Application Procedure: Applicants must send application form (including a two page resume) to the TAC Foundation.
Closing Date: March 1st
Contributor: IBI Group

TAC Foundation – iTRANS Consulting Scholarship

Subjects: Transportation-related disciplines.
Purpose: To foster education, innovation, and research in transportation planning and transportation engineering.
Eligibility: Open only to the Canadian candidates or landed immigrants who are admissible to a postgraduate studies program or already registered as full-time graduate students having a minimum grade point average of B.
Level of Study: Postgraduate
Type: Scholarship
Value: $10,000
Length of Study: 4 years
Application Procedure: Applicants must send application form (including a two page resume) to the TAC Foundation.
Closing Date: March 1st
Contributor: iTRANS Consulting

TAC Foundation – Municipalities Scholarship

Subjects: Transportation-related disciplines.
Purpose: To attract and prepare transportation planners, providers, funders, and users for a career in the transportation industry.
Eligibility: Open only to the Canadian candidates or landed immigrants who are admissible to a postgraduate studies program or already registered as full-time graduate students having a minimum grade point average of B.
Level of Study: Postgraduate
Type: Scholarship
Value: $3,000
Length of Study: 4 years
Application Procedure: Applicants must send application form (including a two page resume) to the TAC Foundation.
Closing Date: March 1st
Contributor: Municipalities

TAC Foundation – ND LEA Scholarship

Subjects: Transportation-related disciplines.
Purpose: To develop Canadian-educated engineers and planners in transportation and related planning and environmental disciplines.
Eligibility: Open only to the Canadian candidates or landed immigrants who are admissible to a postgraduate studies program or already registered as full-time graduate students having a minimum grade point average of B.
Level of Study: Postgraduate
Type: Scholarship

Value: $5,000
Length of Study: 4 years
Application Procedure: Applicants must send application form (including a two page resume) to the TAC Foundation.
Closing Date: March 1st
Contributor: ND LEA

TAC Foundation – Provinces and Territories Scholarship

Subjects: Transportation-related disciplines.
Purpose: To attract and prepare transportation planners, providers, funders, and users for a career in the transportation industry.
Eligibility: Open only to the Canadian candidates or landed immigrants who are admissible to a postgraduate studies program or already registered as full-time graduate students having a minimum grade point average of B.
Level of Study: Postgraduate
Type: Scholarship
Value: $5,000
Length of Study: 4 years
Application Procedure: Applicants must send application form (including a two page resume) to the TAC Foundation.
Closing Date: March 1st
Contributor: Provinces and territories

TAC Foundation – Stantec Consulting Scholarship

Subjects: Transportation engineering.
Purpose: To encourage students to continue their postgraduate studies in the field of transportation engineering and to contribute to the cost-effective mobility upon which our society is based.
Eligibility: Open only to the Canadian candidates or landed immigrants who are admissible to a postgraduate studies program or already registered as full-time graduate students having a minimum grade point average of B.
Level of Study: Postgraduate
Type: Scholarship
Value: $5,000
Length of Study: 4 years
Application Procedure: Applicants must send application form (including a two page resume) to the TAC Foundation.
Closing Date: March 1st
Contributor: Stantec Consulting Limited

TAC Foundation – Waterloo Alumni Scholarship

Subjects: Transportation-related disciplines.
Purpose: To continue the tradition of providing financial assistance to postgraduate students in the broad area of transportation.
Eligibility: Open only to the Canadian candidates or landed immigrants who are admissible to a postgraduate studies program or already registered as full-time graduate students having a minimum grade point average of B.
Level of Study: Postgraduate
Type: Scholarship
Value: $7,500
Length of Study: 4 years
Application Procedure: Applicants must send application form (including a two page resume) to the TAC Foundation.
Closing Date: March 1st
Contributor: University of Waterloo Alumni who are past recipients of Transportation Association of Canada scholarships
Additional Information: Preference will be given to qualified candidates pursuing their work in the pavement field.

TAC Foundation Scholarships

Subjects: Road and transportation-related disciplines.
Eligibility: Open to Canadian citizens and landed immigrants who hold university degrees and who are acceptable to the university at which they plan to carry out their studies in the transportation field. See website for full details.
Level of Study: Graduate, Postgraduate
Type: Scholarship

Value: Canadian $3,000–5,000, with one Canadian $10,000 scholarship
Length of Study: 1 year
Frequency: Annual
Study Establishment: Universities
Country of Study: Other
No. of awards offered: 15
Application Procedure: Online applications only.
Closing Date: The first working day in March. Applicants should check the website for the exact date, which varies each year
Funding: Commercial, government, private
No. of awards given last year: 31
Additional Information: Scholarships currently offered are from the DELCAN Corporation, Stantec Consulting Limited, provincial and territorial governments of Canada, ND LEA, EBA Engineering Consultants Limited, Dillon Consulting Limited, 3M Company, BA Group, IBI Group, Armtec, UMA Engineering, iTRANS Consulting, Cement Association of Canada, Waterloo Alumni, Albert Stewens, Mccormick Rawkin.

TREE RESEARCH & EDUCATION ENDOWMENT FUND

Tree Fund, 711 E. Roosevelt Rd., Wheaton, IL, 60187, United States of America
Tel: (1) (630) 221 8127
Fax: (1) (630) 690 0702
Email: treefund@treefund.org
Website: www.treefund.org
Contact: Ms Cindy Stachowski

To identify and fund projects and programmes that advance knowledge in the field of arboriculture and urban forestry that benefit people, trees and the environment.

Hyland R Johns Grant Program

Subjects: Arboricultural, urban and community forestry.
Purpose: To provide funding for research.
Eligibility: Open to qualified researchers of any nationality.
Level of Study: Postgraduate
Type: Research grant
Value: US$7,500–25,000
Length of Study: 2–3 years
Frequency: Annual
Country of Study: Any country
Application Procedure: Applicants must complete an application form.
Closing Date: May 31st
Funding: Private
Contributor: ISA members
No. of awards given last year: 7
No. of applicants last year: 39

John Z Duling Grant Program

Subjects: Arboricultural, urban and community forestry.
Purpose: To provide money to support projects.
Eligibility: Open to qualified researchers of any nationality.
Level of Study: Postgraduate
Type: Research grant
Value: A maximum of US$7,500. Funds cannot be used for expenses associated with attendance at colleges and universities, e.g. tuition, books or laboratory fees
Length of Study: 1–3 years
Frequency: Annual
Country of Study: Any country
No. of awards offered: 5–10
Application Procedure: Applicants must complete a 2 page application form, available from the ISA Research Trust.
Closing Date: November 1st
Funding: Private
Contributor: International Society of Arboriculture (ISA), National Arborist Association
No. of awards given last year: 10
No. of applicants last year: Approx. 60

TRIANGLE COMMUNITY FOUNDATION

324 Blackwell Street, Suite 1220, Durham, NC, 27701, United States of America
Tel: (1) 919 474 8370
Fax: (1) 919 941 9208
Email: info@trianglecf.org
Website: www.trianglecf.org

Triangle Community Foundation connects philanthropic resources with community needs, creates opportunity for enlightened change and encourages philanthropy as a way of life.

Shaver-Hitchings Scholarship

Purpose: To provide financial aid and honour individuals with a commitment to helping others in the area of drug and alcohol addiction.
Eligibility: Applicants must reside in Chatham, Durham, Orange or Wake countries, and be enrolled or planning to enroll in graduate school, a physician assistant programme of study or continue a programme in which the applicant is already enrolled. The student need not be pursuing a degree in addictive disorders, but must show demonstrated commitment to working with others in that field during or before graduate studies, preferably as a volunteer.
Level of Study: Graduate
Type: Scholarship
Value: US$1,500
Frequency: Annual
Country of Study: United States of America
Application Procedure: Application forms are available online.
Closing Date: March 15th
Funding: Foundation
Contributor: Triangle Community Foundation
No. of awards given last year: 1
No. of applicants last year: 6
Additional Information: The scholarship is available to any graduate student, physician's assistant or medical student in the Triangle area who has worked (preferably as a volunteer) to help others with alcoholism, drug abuse and addictive disorder treatment or with preventive education on the subject of addiction.

TROPICAL AGRICULTURAL RESEARCH AND HIGHER EDUCATION CENTER (CATIE)

Turrialba, 7170, Costa Rica
Tel: (506) 556 1016
Fax: (506) 558 2044
Email: posgrado@catie.ac.cr
Website: www.catie.ac.cr
Contact: Dean of the Graduate School

The Tropical Agricultural Research and Higher Education Center (CATIE) is an international, non-profit, regional, scientific and educational institution. Its main purpose is research and education in agricultural sciences, natural resources and related subjects in the American tropics, with emphasis on Central America and the Caribbean.

Scholarship opportunities linked to CATIE's Postgraduate Program including CATIE scholarship forming part of the Scholarship-Loan Program

Subjects: Ecological agriculture, biotechnology and genetic resources, management and conservation of tropical forestry and biodiversity, tropical woodlands, tropical agroforestry, tropical crop protection and improvement, integrated watershed management and protected areas and environmental socioeconomics and rural enterprise development.
Purpose: To develop specialized intellectual capital in clean technology, tropical agriculture, natural resources management and human resources in the American tropics.
Eligibility: Priority is given to citizens of Belize, Guatemala, El Salvador, Honduras, Nicaragua, Panama, Costa Rica, Mexico, Venezuela, Colombia, the Dominican Republic, Bolivia and Paraguay.
Level of Study: Doctorate, Postgraduate

Type: Scholarship
Value: Tuition and fees
Length of Study: 2 years for a Master's degree and 3–4 years for a PhD
Frequency: Annual
Country of Study: Costa Rica
No. of awards offered: CATIE offers approximately 30 scholarships per year. Scholarships from other sources vary in origin and number. Information is available on the CATIE website.
Application Procedure: Applicants must undertake an admission process that constitutes 75 per cent for curricular evaluation and 25 per cent for a domiciliary examination. Please refer to the CATIE website for full instructions.
Closing Date: Applications are accepted at any time, but the evaluation deadline for Scholarship-Loan Program is late October. Other sources of financing have specific requirements available on CATIE website. These change considerably over time
Funding: Foundation, government, international office, private
Contributor: ASDI, OAS, CATIE, DAAD, Russell Train (WWF), CONACYT (Mexico), Ford Foundation, FUNDAYACUCHO (Venezuela), Gobierno de Noruega, Kellogg Foundation, Fundación Pablo Garcia (México). Joint/Japan World Bank. USAID provided the original donation for the endowment financing the Scholarship-Loan Program
No. of awards given last year: 34 in the Scholarship-Loan Program. Over 25 students received funding from alternative sources.
No. of applicants last year: 350

UCLA CENTER FOR 17TH AND 18TH CENTURY STUDIES AND THE WILLIAM ANDREWS CLARK MEMORIAL LIBRARY

310 Royce Hall, UCLA, Los Angeles, CA, 90095-1404, United States of America
Tel: (1) 310 206 8552
Fax: (1) 310 206 8577
Email: c1718cs@humnet.ucla.edu
Website: www.humnet.ucla.edu/humnet/c1718cs
Contact: Fellowship Co-ordinator

The UCLA Center for 17th and 18th-century Studies provides a forum for the discussion of central issues in the field of early modern studies, facilitates research and publication, supports scholarship and encourages the creation of interdisciplinary, cross-cultural programmes that advance the understanding of this important period. The William Andrews Clark Memorial Library, administered by the Center, is known for its collections of rare books and manuscripts concerning 17th and 18th-century Britain and Europe, Oscar Wilde and the 1890s, the history of printing, and certain aspects of the American West.

Ahmanson and Getty Postdoctoral Fellowships

Subjects: Arts and humanities, religious studies and social sciences.
Purpose: To encourage participation by junior scholars in the Center's year-long interdisciplinary core programmes.
Eligibility: Open to postdoctoral scholars who have received their PhD in the last 6 years and whose research pertains to the theme as announced by the Library.
Level of Study: Postdoctorate
Type: Fellowship
Value: US$37,500
Length of Study: 3 consecutive academic quarters
Frequency: Annual
Study Establishment: UCLA and the William Andrews Clark Memorial Library
Country of Study: United States of America
No. of awards offered: Up to 4
Application Procedure: Applicants must submit an application form, a curriculum vitae, a proposal statement, a bibliography and three letters of reference.
Closing Date: February 1st
Funding: Private
Contributor: The Ahmanson Foundation of Los Angeles and the Getty Trust
No. of awards given last year: 4
No. of applicants last year: 30

Additional Information: The award is theme-based and is announced each year. The series intends to be interdisciplinary, with emphasis on both literary and historical perspectives. Participating Fellows will be expected to make a substantive contribution to programme seminars.

ASECS (American Society for 18th-Century Studies)/ Clark Library Fellowships

Subjects: The Restoration and the 18th century.
Eligibility: Open to members of ASECS who are postdoctoral scholars and hold a PhD or equivalent at the time of application. The award is also open to advanced doctoral candidates who are members of ASECS.
Level of Study: Postdoctorate
Type: Fellowship
Value: US$2,500
Length of Study: 1 month
Frequency: Annual
Study Establishment: UCLA and the William Andrews Clark Memorial Library
Country of Study: United States of America
No. of awards offered: Varies
Application Procedure: Applicants must submit an application form, a curriculum vitae, a proposal statement, a bibliography and three letters of reference.
Closing Date: February 1st
Funding: Government
Contributor: ASECS and the Clark Library Endowment
No. of awards given last year: 1
No. of applicants last year: 40

Clark Library Short-Term Resident Fellowships

Subjects: Research relevant to the Library's holdings.
Eligibility: Open to PhD scholars or equivalent who are involved in advanced research.
Level of Study: Postdoctorate
Type: Fellowship
Value: US$2,500 per month
Length of Study: 1–3 months
Frequency: Annual
Study Establishment: UCLA and the William Andrews Clark Memorial Library
Country of Study: United States of America
No. of awards offered: Varies
Application Procedure: Applicants must submit an application form, a curriculum vitae, a proposal statement, a bibliography and three letters of reference.
Closing Date: February 1st
Funding: Government, private
Contributor: The Ahmanson Foundation and the Clark Library Endowment
No. of awards given last year: 16
No. of applicants last year: 60

Clark Predoctoral Fellowships

Subjects: Seventeenth- and eighteenth-century studies or one of the other areas represented in the Clark's collections.
Purpose: To support dissertation research.
Eligibility: Open to advanced doctoral students at the University of California whose dissertation concerns an area appropriate to the collections of the Clark Library.
Level of Study: Predoctorate
Type: Fellowship
Value: US$7,500
Length of Study: 3 months
Frequency: Annual
Study Establishment: UCLA and the William Andrews Clark Memorial Library
Country of Study: United States of America
No. of awards offered: Varies
Application Procedure: Applicants must submit an application form, a curriculum vitae, a proposal statement, a bibliography and three letters of reference.
Closing Date: February 1st
Funding: Private

Contributor: The Ahmanson Foundation
No. of awards given last year: 3
No. of applicants last year: 9

Clark-Huntington Joint Bibliographical Fellowship

Subjects: Early modern literature and history and other areas where the sponsoring libraries have common strengths.
Purpose: To support bibliographical research.
Level of Study: Professional development, Postdoctorate
Type: Fellowship
Value: US$5,000
Length of Study: 2 months
Frequency: Annual
Study Establishment: The Clark Library and the Huntington Library
Country of Study: United States of America
No. of awards offered: 1
Application Procedure: Applicants must submit an application form, a curriculum vitae, a proposal statement, a bibliography and three letters of reference.
Closing Date: February 1st
Funding: Private
No. of awards given last year: 1
No. of applicants last year: 15

For further information contact:

William Andrews Clark Memorial Library, 2520 Cimarron Street, Los Angeles, CA, 90018-2098, United States of America
Contact: Fellowship Co-ordinator

Kanner Fellowship In British Studies

Subjects: British history and culture.
Eligibility: Open to both postdoctoral and predoctoral scholars.
Level of Study: Postdoctorate, Predoctorate
Type: Fellowship
Value: US$7,500
Length of Study: 3 months
Frequency: Annual
Application Procedure: Applicants must submit an application form, a curriculum vitae, proposal statement, a bibliography and three letters of reference.
Closing Date: February 1st
Funding: Private
Contributor: Penny Kanner
No. of awards given last year: 1
No. of applicants last year: 12

THE UKRAINIAN FRATERNAL ASSOCIATION (UFA)

371 N 9th Avenue, Scranton, PA 18504-2005,
United States of America
Tel: (1) 570 342 0937
Fax: (1) 570 347 5649
Email: fratrag@aol.com

Since 1939 the Association has always been, and continues to be, an ardent supporter of our youth. They represent the future of our society and our communities. From them we will draw our future leaders.

Eugene R. & Elinor R. Kotur Scholarship

Subjects: Any subject.
Eligibility: Applicant must be of Ukranian ancestry a member of the Association and enrolled at an approved university or college.
Level of Study: Postgraduate
Type: Scholarship
Value: US$250,000
Length of Study: 1–3 years
Frequency: Annual
Country of Study: United States of America
Application Procedure: Contact the association.
Closing Date: May 31st
Funding: Trusts
Contributor: Eugene & Elinor Kotur
No. of awards given last year: 6

UNITED CHURCH OF CHRIST (UCC)

700 Prospect Avenue East, Cleveland, OH, 44115-1100,
United States of America
Tel: (1) 216 736 3849
Website: www.ucc.org
Contact: William R Johnson, Ministry Team

The United Church of Christ (UCC) was founded in 1957 as the union of several different Christian traditions. The UCC is one of the most diverse Christian churches in the United States of America.

William R Johnson Scholarship

Subjects: Theology.
Purpose: To affirm the long-standing conviction of the UCC that sexual orientation should not be a barrier to ordination.
Eligibility: Open to candidates enrolled in an American Theological School accredited seminary and have proof of both local membership in a UCC. Must be open about their sexual orientation.
Level of Study: Postgraduate
Type: Scholarship
Value: US$2,500
Frequency: Annual

UNITED NATIONS DEVELOPMENT PROGRAMME (UNDP)

304 East 45th Street FF-10th Floor, New York, NY, 10017,
United States of America
Email: ohr.recruitment.hq@undp.org
Website: www.undp.org

The UNDP launched the Local Initiative Facility for Urban Environment (LIFE) as a global pilot programme at the Earth summit in Rio de Janeiro in 1992. The programme uses environmental deprivation as the entry point for achieving sustainable human development.

UNDP's Local Initiative Facility for Urban Environment (LIFE) Global Programme

Subjects: Urban environmental development.
Purpose: To promote local-local dialogue and partnership between NGOs, CBOs, Local Governments and the private sector for improving conditions of the urban poor.
Eligibility: Application for need-based participatory, community-based projects in Urban poor communities.
Level of Study: Professional development
Type: Grant
Value: Up to US$50,000
Frequency: Annual
Funding: Government
Contributor: Life

UNITED STATES CENTER FOR ADVANCED HOLOCAUST STUDIES

United States Holocaust Memorial Museum,
100 Raoul Wallenberg Place South West, Washington,
DC, 20024-2126, United States of America
Tel: (1) 202 314 7829
Fax: (1) 202 479 9726
Email: visiting_scholars@ushmm.org
Website: www.ushmm.org
Contact: Ms Traci Rucker, Visiting Scholar Programs

The United States Holocaust Memorial Museum is the United States of America's national institution for the documentation, study and interpretation of Holocaust history, and serves as the country's memorial to the millions of people murdered during the Holocaust. The Center for Advanced Holocaust Studies fosters research in Holocaust and genocide studies.

United States Holocaust Memorial Museum Center for Advanced Holocaust Studies Visiting Scholar Programs

Subjects: History, political science, literature, philosophy, sociology, religion and other disciplines, as they relate to the study of the Holocaust.

Purpose: To support research and writing in the fields of Holocaust and genocide studies.

Eligibility: Fellowships are awarded to candidates working on their dissertations (ABD), postdoctoral researchers and senior scholars. Applicants must be affiliated with an academic and/or research institution when applying for a fellowship. Immediate postdocs and faculty between appointments will also be considered.

Level of Study: Doctorate, Postdoctorate

Type: Fellowship

Value: All awards include a monthly stipend, direct travel to and from Washington, DC and visa assistance, if necessary. The Museum provides office space, postage, and access to a computer, telephone, facsimile machine and photocopier

Length of Study: 3–9 months

Frequency: Annual

Country of Study: United States of America

No. of awards offered: Varies

Application Procedure: Applicants must consult the Museum's website or contact Traci Rucker, Programme Assistant, for application forms and information.

Closing Date: November. Please consult the website for updated information about deadlines

Funding: Private

No. of awards given last year: 25

For further information contact:

Visiting Scholar Programs, Center for Advanced Holocaust Studies, United States Holocaust Memorial Museum, 100 Raoul Wallenberg Place SW, Washington, DC 20024-2126

UNITED STATES EDUCATIONAL FOUNDATION IN INDIA (USEFI)

Fulbright House 12 Hailey Road, New Delhi, 110001, India
Tel: (91) 91 11 2332 8944/48
Fax: (91) 2332 9718
Email: info@fulbright-india.org
Website: www.fulbright-india.org
Contact: Programme Officer

The activities of the United States Educational Foundation in India (USEFI) may be broadly categorized as the administration of the Fulbright Exchange Fellowships for Indian and United States scholars and professionals, and the provision of educational advising services to help Indian students wishing to pursue higher education in the United States. USEFI also works for the promotion of dialogue among fulbrighters and their communities as an outgrowth of educational exchange.

Fulbright Doctoral and Professional Research Fellowships

Subjects: The United States Special education, conflict resolution, museum studies, arts/culture management and heritage conservation.

Eligibility: Open to Indian citizens resident in India at the time of application who have not been to the United States of America in the previous 3 years. Applicants must have a high level of academic and professional achievement, proficiency in English and be in good health. Applicants must be registered for a PhD at an Indian institution at least 1 year prior to application. The fellowship is also open to professionals with postgraduate degrees who are working in areas where study of IPR or special education would be helpful to their institutions.

Level of Study: Predoctorate, Professional development

Type: Fellowship

Value: Maintenance in the United States of America, affiliation fees, health insurance and round trip economy class airfare

Length of Study: Up to 9 months

Frequency: Annual

Country of Study: United States of America

No. of awards offered: 6–7

Application Procedure: Application material can be downloaded from the website.

Closing Date: July 16th

Funding: Foundation

Contributor: USEFI

No. of awards given last year: 6

No. of applicants last year: 71

Fulbright Master's Fellowship for Leadership Development

Subjects: Public administration, economics, communication studies and environment.

Purpose: The programme is specially targeted at highly motivated individuals who demonstrate leadership qualities.

Eligibility: Open to Indian citizens resident in India at the time of application who have not been to the United States of America in the preceding 3 years. Applicants must have completed an equivalent of a US Bachelor's degree from a recognized Indian university with at least 55 per cent marks. Applicants should either possess a 4 year Bachelors degree or a completed master's degree, if the Bachelor's degree is of less than 4 years duration.

Level of Study: Postgraduate

Type: Fellowship

Value: Maintenance in the United States of America, affiliation fees, health insurance and round trip economy air fare, limited allowance for books

Length of Study: Up to 6 months

Frequency: Annual

Country of Study: United States of America

No. of awards offered: 4–6

Application Procedure: Applicants must complete an application form. Requests for application materials must state the applicant's academic and professional qualifications, date of birth, current position and grant category and be accompanied by a 7 by 10 inch stamped addressed envelope. Requests for application materials must be sent to the USEFI offices in the applicant's region or alternatively can be downloaded from the website.

Closing Date: July 15th

Funding: Government

Contributor: USEFI

No. of applicants last year: 45

Additional Information: Further information is available on request from USEFI.

Fulbright Senior Research Fellowships

Subjects: The United States of America education, society and development, and management.

Purpose: To provide scholars with the opportunity to undertake research on contemporary issues and concerns.

Eligibility: Open to Indian citizens resident in India at the time of application who have not been to the United States of America in the preceding 3 years. Applicants must have a high level of academic and professional achievement, proficiency in English and be in good health. Applicants must be employed as full-time faculty members in an Indian college, university or research institution, or as a full-time professional at an Indian non-profit organization, hold a PhD degree or have equivalent published work and be under 50 years of age.

Level of Study: Postdoctorate

Type: Grant

Value: Round trip travel, monthly stipend, university affiliation fees, health insurance and a modest settling in allowance, dependent allowance and round trip travel for one dependent

Length of Study: Up to 8 months

Frequency: Annual

Study Establishment: A university or research institution

Country of Study: United States of America

No. of awards offered: 4–5

Application Procedure: Application information can be downloaded from the website.

Closing Date: July 15th

Funding: Foundation

Contributor: USEFI

No. of awards given last year: 4

No. of applicants last year: 162

Additional Information: Applicants must demonstrate the relevance of the proposed research to India and/or the United States, its applicability in India, its benefit to the applicant's institution and the need to carry it out in the United States.

Fulbright Teacher Exchange Program

Subjects: Designed for Indian secondary school teachers (9th to 12th grades) of English, mathematics, and science to participate in direct exchanges of positions with US teachers for semester.

Purpose: To provide Indian teachers the opportunity to work within a US school system and experience US society and culture similarly US teachers will work in an Indian school set up and share their expertise.

Eligibility: Open to Indian citizens resident in India at the time of application who have not been to the United States of America in the preceding 3 years. Applicants must have a high level of academic and professional achievement, proficiency in English and be in good health. Applicants must have a Master's degree in English, mathematics or science subjects with a teacher training degree and be a full-time teacher (9th to 12th grades) in a recognized secondary school for at least 5 years.

Level of Study: Professional development, Postgraduate, Secondary school

Type: Fellowship

Value: Round trip travel, moderate monthly stipend, health insurance

Length of Study: One semester

Frequency: Annual

Country of Study: United States of America

No. of awards offered: 7

Application Procedure: Applicants must complete an application form. Requests for application materials must state the applicant's academic and professional qualifications, date of birth, current position and grant category and be accompanied by a 7 by 10 inch stamped addressed envelope. Requests for application materials must be sent to the USEFI offices in the applicant's region. Alternatively, applicants can download information from the USEFI website.

Closing Date: July 16th

Funding: Government

Contributor: USEFI

No. of applicants last year: 109

Additional Information: Further information is available on request from USEFI.

Fulbright Visiting Lecturer Fellowships

Subjects: Humanities and social sciences.

Purpose: To allow scholars to share their expertise on contemporary issues significant to India and the United States of America.

Eligibility: Open to Indian citizens resident in India at the time of application who have not been to the United States of America in the preceding 3 years. Applicants must have a high level of academic and professional achievement, proficiency in English and be in good health. Applicants must be permanent full-time faculty members at an Indian college, university or research institute, hold a PhD degree or have equivalent published work, have at least 10 years of college or university level teaching experience and be no more than 50 years of age.

Level of Study: Postdoctorate

Type: Grant

Value: Round trip travel, monthly stipend, university fees, health insurance and a modest settling in allowance

Length of Study: 4 months

Frequency: Annual

Country of Study: United States of America

No. of awards offered: 2–3

Application Procedure: Applicants must complete an application form. Requests for application materials must state the applicant's academic and professional qualifications, date of birth, current position and grant category and be accompanied by a 7 by 10 inch stamped addressed envelope. Requests for application materials must be sent to the USEFI offices in the applicant's region or can be downloaded from the USEFI website.

Closing Date: July 16th

Funding: Foundation

Contributor: USEFI

No. of awards given last year: 8

No. of applicants last year: 44

International Fulbright Science and Technology Award

Subjects: Aeronautics and astronomics, aeronautical engineering, astronomy, planetary sciences, biology, chemistry, computer sciences, engineering-electrical, chemical, civil, mechanical, ocean and petroleum, environmental science, geology, earth and atmospheric sciences, information sciences engineering, materials science engineering, mathematics, neuroscience, brain and cognitive sciences, oceanography and physics.

Purpose: To enable deserving students to study in accredited institutions in the United States.

Eligibility: Open to applicants who have high level of academic or professional achievements and have completed equivalent of a United States Bachelor's degree from a recognized Indian university with at least 60 per cent marks. Applicants must possess a 4 year Bachelor's degree or a completed Master's degree. The candidates must also possess a valid Indian Passport.

Level of Study: Doctorate

Type: Scholarships

Value: A monthly stipend for up to 3 years, health insurance, round-trip air travel, J-1 visa for up to 5 years, books and equipment, research and professional conference allowances and tuition fees

Length of Study: 3 years

Frequency: Annual

Country of Study: United States of America

No. of awards offered: 25

Application Procedure: A completed application form must be sent before the deadline.

Closing Date: July 31st

Funding: Government

Contributor: The Bureau of Educational and Cultural Affairs of the United States Department

USEFI Fulbright-CII Fellowships for Leadership in Management

Subjects: Leadership in management.

Purpose: To enable business managers to attend a management programme in the United States of America.

Eligibility: Open to Indian business managers. Age limit, preferably not above 40, Nationality: Indian, Designed for: Mid-level Managers in Indian Industries.

Level of Study: Professional development

Type: Fellowship

Length of Study: 10 weeks

Frequency: Annual

Study Establishment: Carnegie Mellon University

Country of Study: United States of America

No. of awards offered: 5–6

Application Procedure: Applicants must complete an application form, available from the CII.

Closing Date: January 31st

Funding: Corporation, foundation

Contributor: USEFI and employers of selected Managers

No. of awards given last year: 8

No. of applicants last year: 49

Additional Information: For further information contact the Confederation of Indian Industry (CII).

For further information contact:

Confederation of Indian Industry, Mantosh Sondhi Centre, 23, Institutional Area, Lodi Road, New Delhi, 110 003, India
Tel: (91) 24629994-7 Ext. 367
Fax: (91) 24601298, 24626149
Email: ls.rajeshwari@ciionline.org
Contact: Ms S Rajeshwari, Executive Officer

USEFI Hubert H Humphrey Fellowships

Subjects: Agricultural development/agricultural economics; communications/journalism, drug abuse education, treatment and prevention, economic development educational planning and administration, finance and banking HIV/AIDS policy and prevention, human resource management, law and human rights, natural resources and environmental management, nonproliferation studies, public health policy and management, public policy analysis and public administration, technology policy and management, prevention of trafficking in persons and policy development and management for anti-trafficking efforts, teacher training and curriculum development, and urban regional planning.

Purpose: To bring accomplished mid-level professionals from developing countries to the United States for 10 months of non-degree graduate study and related professional experiences.

Eligibility: Open to Indian citizens resident in India at the time of application who have not been to the United States of America in the previous 3 years. Applicants must have a high level of academic and professional achievement, proficiency in English and be in good health. Preferably applicants will have a first class master's or a professional degree of at least 4 year's duration. Applicants must have at least 5 years of substantial professional experience in the respective field and not be more than 40 years of age. Applicants applying for the fellowships in drug abuse must hold a PhD or equivalent degree in the health, behavioural or social sciences or an MD.

Level of Study: Professional development

Type: Fellowship

Value: Tuition and fees, a monthly maintenance allowance, modest allowance for books and supplies, round trip international travel to the host institution and domestic travel to Washington, DC and/or Minnesota workshops

Length of Study: 10 months

Frequency: Annual

Country of Study: United States of America

No. of awards offered: Varies

Application Procedure: Applicants must complete an application form. Requests for application materials must state the applicant's academic and professional qualifications, date of birth, current position and grant category and be accompanied by a 7 by 10 inch stamped addressed envelope. Requests for application materials must be sent to the USEFI offices in the applicant's region. Alternatively, applications can be downloaded from the USEFI website.

Closing Date: June 30th

Funding: Government

Contributor: Bureau of Educational and Cultural Affairs, US Department of State, Washington, DC

No. of awards given last year: 9

No. of applicants last year: 57

UNITED STATES INSTITUTE OF PEACE (USIP)

1200 17th Street North West, Suite 200, Washington, DC, 20036-3011, United States of America
Tel: (1) 202 429 3842
Fax: (1) 202 429 6063
Email: grant_program@usip.org
Website: www.usip.org
Contact: Ms Cornelia Haggart, Senior Programme Assistant

The United States Institute of Peace (USIP) is mandated by the Congress to promote education and training, research and public information programmes on means to promote international peace and resolve international conflicts without violence. The Institute meets this mandate through an array of programmes, including grants, fellowships, conferences and workshops, library services, publications and other educational activities.

Jennings Randolph Program for International Peace Dissertation Fellowship

Subjects: A broad range of disciplines and interdisciplinary fields.

Purpose: To support dissertations that explore the sources and nature of international conflict, and strategies to prevent or end conflict and to sustain peace.

Eligibility: Open to applicants of all nationalities who are enrolled in an accredited college or university in the United States of America. Applicants must have completed all requirements for the degree except the dissertation by the commencement of the award.

Level of Study: Doctorate

Type: Fellowship

Value: US$20,000, which may be used to support dissertation writing or field research

Length of Study: 1 year

Frequency: Annual

Study Establishment: The student's home university or site of fieldwork

Country of Study: United States of America

No. of awards offered: 10

Application Procedure: Applicants must complete a web-based application form, available on the Institute's website.

Closing Date: January 5th

Funding: Government

No. of awards given last year: 10

Additional Information: The programme does not support work involving partisan political and policy advocacy or policy making for any government or private organization.

For further information contact:

Tel: 202 429 3853
Email: jrprogram@usip.org
Contact: Miss Shira Lowinger, Program Coordinator

Jennings Randolph Program for International Peace Senior Fellowships

Subjects: Preventive diplomacy, ethnic and regional conflicts, peacekeeping and peace operations, peace settlements, postconflict reconstruction and reconciliation, democratization and the rule of law, cross-cultural negotiations, United States of America policy in the 21st century and related subjects.

Purpose: To use the recipient's existing knowledge and skills towards a fruitful endeavour in the international peace and conflict management field, and to help bring the perspectives of this field into the Fellow's own career.

Eligibility: Open to outstanding practitioners and scholars from a broad range of backgrounds. The competition is open to citizens of any country who have specific interest and experience in international peace and conflict management. Candidates would typically be senior academics, but applicants who hold at least a Bachelor's degree from a recognized university will also be considered.

Type: Fellowship

Value: A stipend, an office with computer and voicemail and a part-time research assistant

Length of Study: Up to 10 months

Frequency: Annual

Study Establishment: USIP

Country of Study: United States of America

No. of awards offered: 8–10

Application Procedure: Applicants must complete a web-based application form, available on request from the Institute or from the website.

Closing Date: September 15th

Funding: Government

No. of awards given last year: 8

No. of applicants last year: 89

For further information contact:

Tel: 202 429 3886
Email: jrprogram@usip.org
Contact: Miss Shira Lowinger, Program Coordinator

USIP Annual Grant Competition

Subjects: Topic areas of interest to the Institute include, but are not restricted to, international conflict resolution, diplomacy, negotiation theory, functionalism and track-two diplomacy, methods of third party dispute settlement, international law, international organizations and collective security, deterrence and balance of power, arms control, psychological theories about international conflict, the role of non-violence and non-violent sanctions, moral and ethical thought about conflict and conflict resolution and theories about relationships among political institutions, human rights and conflict.

Purpose: To provide financial support for research, education and training, and the dissemination of information on international peace and conflict resolution.

Eligibility: The Institute may provide grant support to non-profit organizations and individuals from both the United States of America and other countries. These include institutions of post-secondary, community and secondary education, public and private education, training and research institutions and libraries. Although the Institute can provide grant support to individuals, it prefers that an institutional affiliation be established. The Institute will not accept applications that list members of the Institute's Board of Directors or staff as participants, consultants or project personnel. In addition, any application that lists the Institute as a collaborator in the project will not be accepted.

Level of Study: Postdoctorate, Research, Education, Training

Type: Grant

Value: Most awards fall in the range of US$25,000–45,000, although somewhat larger grants are also awarded. The amount of any grant is based on the proposed budget and on negotiations with successful applicants

Length of Study: 1–2 years

Frequency: Annual

No. of awards offered: Approx. 35

Application Procedure: Applicants must complete an application form, available on request from the Institute or from the website.

Closing Date: October 1st

Funding: Government

No. of awards given last year: 39

No. of applicants last year: 239

USIP Priority Grant-making Competition

Subjects: Check website for specific details.

Purpose: To provide financial support for research, education and training, and the dissemination of information on international peace and conflict resolution.

Eligibility: Open to non-profit organizations and individuals from both the United States of America and other countries. These include institutions of post-secondary, community and secondary education, public and private education, training or research institutions and libraries. Although the Institute can provide grant support to individuals, it prefers that an institutional affiliation be established. The Institute will not accept applications that list as participants, consultants or project personnel members of the Institute's Board of Directors or staff. In addition, any application that lists the Institute as a collaborator in the project will not be accepted.

Level of Study: Postdoctorate, Research, Education, training

Type: Grant

Value: Most awards fall in the range of US$45,000–100,000. The amount of any grant is based on the proposed budget and on negotiations with successful applicants

Length of Study: 1–2 years

Frequency: Rolling deadline

No. of awards offered: Approx. 35

Application Procedure: Applicants must complete an application form, available on request from the Institute or from the website.

Funding: Government

No. of awards given last year: 29

No. of applicants last year: 100

Additional Information: For further informaiton see the website.

UNIVERSITIES FEDERATION FOR ANIMAL WELFARE (UFAW)

The Old School, Brewhouse Hill, Wheathampstead, Hertfordshire, AL4 8AN, England

Tel: (44) 15 8283 1818

Fax: (44) 15 8283 1414

Email: scioff@ufaw.org.uk

Website: www.ufaw.org.uk

Contact: Scientific Officer

The Universities Federation for Animal Welfare (UFAW) is an independent, scientific and educational animal welfare charity concerned with improving knowledge and understanding of animals' needs in order to promote high standards of welfare for farm, companion, laboratory and captive wild animals and those with which we interact in the wild.

UFAW 3Rs Liaison Group Research Studentship

Subjects: The UFAW 3Rs Liaison Group is a coalition of pharmaceutical companies, contract research organizations, laboratory animal breeders and animal welfare organizations, formed by UFAW in 1998.

Purpose: To fund research that is likely to lead to practical solutions that advance the welfare of laboratory animals.

Eligibility: Open to nationals of any country studying in the United Kingdom.

Level of Study: Doctorate

Value: A maximum of UK £25,000 per annum for up to 3 years

Length of Study: 3 years

Frequency: Dependent on funds available

Country of Study: United Kingdom

Application Procedure: Application for this award is by a two-stage process. Initially, supervisors are required to submit a brief Concept Note, available from the UFAW website or by emailing the UFAW Scientific Officer at scioff@ufaw.org.uk. Following assessment of these concept notes, selected applicants are invited to submit more detailed proposals prepared jointly by the supervisor and the PhD candidate.

Funding: Private

Additional Information: Please visit the UFAW website (www.afaw. org.uk) to check whether this award is currently open.

UFAW Animal Welfare Research Training Scholarships

Subjects: UFAW would particularly like to encourage applications in the following fields:development of methodologies aimed at elucidation of the neurological basis of sentience in animals; developments in approaches to alleviating welfare problems in farmed, companion and/ or laboratory animals through breeding; developments in detection and alleviation of pain;developments of methods of welfare/quality of life assessment. However, UFAW does not wish to exclude potentially valuable projects in other aspects of animal welfare science and applications for work in other areas will also be considered.

Purpose: To encourage high-quality science likely to lead to substantial advances in animal welfare and to enable promising graduates to start a career in animal welfare science.

Eligibility: Open to nationals of any country studying in the United Kingdom.

Level of Study: Doctorate

Type: Scholarship

Value: Science graduates: UK £16,283 rising to £19,230 for the 3rd year (London weighting £18,211 rising to £21,507 for the 3rd year), and veterinary graduates: UK £17,097 rising to £20,192for the 3rd year (London weighting £19,121 rising to £22,583 for the 3rd year). In addition, research costs up to UK £10,000 research costs per annum and approved tuition fees up to £3,235 will be met.(Applications for tuition fees in excess of this amount may be considered.)

Length of Study: 3 years

Frequency: Dependent on funds available

Country of Study: United Kingdom

Application Procedure: Application for this award is by a two-stage process. Initially, supervisors are required to submit a brief Concept Note available from the UFAW website www.ufaw.org.uk or by emailing the UFAW Scientific Officer at scioff@ufaw,org.uk. Following assessment of these concept notes selected applicants will then be invited to submit more detailed proposals prepared jointly by the supervisor and PhD candidate.

Funding: Private

Additional Information: Please visit the UFAW website www.ufaw. org.uk to check whether award is currently open.

UFAW Companion Animal Welfare Award

Subjects: The UFAW Companion Animal Welfare Award scheme is an annual, international competition open to all individuals and organizations working in the field of companion animal welfare science and technology. Interested applicants are invited to apply to UFAW detailing how their innovation is likely to, or already has, led to welfare improvements in companion animals. UFAW would particularly like to encourage applications relating to the following fields: Genetic welfare problems; detection and alleviation of pain; diagnoses and treatment of painful disease. However, UFAW does not wish to exclude potentially valuable projects dealing with other aspects of companion animal welfare and applications in other relevant fields will also be welcomed.

Purpose: To recognize significant innovations or advances for the welfare of companion animals.

Eligibility: Applications are invited from individuals or organizations in the field of companion animal welfare science and technology. Applicants may be based in the UK or internationally.

Level of Study: Unrestricted
Value: UK £1,000
Frequency: Annual
Country of Study: Any country
Application Procedure: Applicants must complete a Companion Animal Welfare Award application form available for download from the UFAW website or by emailing the UFAW Scientific Officer at scioff@ufaw.org.uk. Applicants should present an evidence-based, scientifically-informed case and the relevance to animal welfare should be made clear. Key points to be considered include the number of companion animals likely to benefit, and the severity and duration of the welfare problem addressed.
Closing Date: November 21st
Funding: Private

UFAW Research and Project Awards

Subjects: Full or part funding for self-contained projects or initial funding for studies that may lead to further investigation or welfare benefits. Awards can be used to supplement current work, to extend previous projects that promote animal welfare or to support non-research projects that promote animal welfare, such as preparation and publication of books and teaching materials.
Purpose: To encourage fundamental and high-quality research that is likely to lead to substantial improvements in animal welfare.
Eligibility: Open to nationals of any country.
Level of Study: Unrestricted
Type: Grant
Value: UK £3,500+ (rarely in excess of UK £10,000)
Length of Study: For the duration of the approved works
Frequency: Dependent on funds available
Country of Study: Any country
No. of awards offered: Varies
Application Procedure: Applicants must submit an application form available for download from the UFAW website www.ufaw.org.uk or by emailing the UFAW Scientific Officer at scioff@ufaw.org.uk
Closing Date: Considered at approx. 3-month intervals
Funding: Private
Additional Information: Annual progress reports are required within 1 month of the anniversary of the start date and a final report must be submitted within 3 months of the completion date.

UFAW SAWI Fund

Subjects: UFAW SAWI is keen to identify and support projects through which high quality science can lead to major animal welfare benefits in Israel. Funds are available via a number of routes including UFAW SAWI Small Project and Travel Awards, UFAW SAWI Research and Project Awards, UFAW SAWI Vacation Scholarship Awards, and a postgraduate scholarship for an Israeli student to undertake study in animal welfare science in the UK.
Purpose: To promote animal welfare in Israel.
Eligibility: Please visit the UFAW website for further information on individual SAWI grants.
Length of Study: Varies
Frequency: Dependent on funds available
Application Procedure: Application forms may be downloaded from the UFAW website (www.ufaw.org.uk) or by contacting the UFAW scientific officer at scioff@ufaw.org.uk
Funding: Private

UFAW Small Project and Travel Awards

Subjects: Through its Small Project and Travel Awards (up to £3,500) UFAW supports a variety of activities for the benefit of animal welfare. Applications may be made for: the purchase of equipment; organization of educational meetings, lectures and courses; publication, translation or transmission of information on animal welfare; and for other small projects in support of UFAW's objectives. Particularly welcomed are applications for pilot studies where there is a likelihood of successful completion leading to further, more substantial work. Please note, all applications are judged on their merits for animal welfare and (in the case of research applications) their scientific quality.
Purpose: To support research projects and other activities for the benefit of animal welfare.

Eligibility: Open to nationals of any country.
Level of Study: Unrestricted
Type: Grant
Value: Up to UK £3,500
Length of Study: For the duration of the approved works
Frequency: Dependent on funds available
Country of Study: Any country
Application Procedure: Applicants must complete a Small Project and Travel Award application form available for download from the UFAW website www.ufaw.org.uk or by emailing the UFAW Scientific Officer at scioff@ufaw.org.uk
Closing Date: Considered at approx. 3-month intervals
Funding: Private
Additional Information: A report is required on completion of the project.

UFAW Vacation Scholarships

Subjects: Research that is likely to provide new insight into the subjective mental experiences of animals relevant to their welfare and at understanding their needs and preferences, and also applied research aimed at developing practical solutions to animal welfare problems.
Purpose: To encourage students to develop their interests in animal welfare and their abilities for animal welfare research.
Eligibility: Applications are welcome from individuals studying at universities or colleges in the United Kingdom or an overseas institution at which there is a UFAW University Links representative. Students will be usually undertaking courses in the agricultural, biological, medical, veterinary or zoological sciences. Applicants need a nominated supervisor to oversee the project.
Level of Study: Graduate
Type: Scholarship
Value: UK £140 subsistence and UK £30 departmental expenses for each week of study
Length of Study: Maximum of 8 weeks
Frequency: Annual
No. of awards offered: Up to 15
Application Procedure: Applicants must complete a Vacation Scholarship application form available for download from the UFAW website www.ufaw.org.uk or by emailing the UFAW Scientific Officer at scioff@ufaw.org.uk
Closing Date: February 28th
Funding: Private
No. of awards given last year: 12
No. of applicants last year: 28
Additional Information: Successful applicants must submit a written report to UFAW by November of the year in which the project was undertaken.

UFAW Wild Animal Welfare Award

Subjects: The UFAW Wild Animal Welfare Award scheme is a annual, international competition open to all individual or organizations working in the field of wild animal welfare. UFAW would particularly like to encourage applications regarding advances in alleviating or preventing anthropogenic harm to the welfare of free-living wild animals including work to improve the humaneness of rodent 'pest' control, work toward the control of wildlife disease, of anthropogenic origin (infectitious or non-infectitious), improved methods of capture, handling or marking for field studies. However, UFAW does not wish to exclude projects dealing with other aspects of wild animal welfare and applications in other relevant fields will also be welcomed.
Purpose: To recognize significant innovations or advances for the welfare of wild animals.
Eligibility: Applications are invited from individuals or organizations working in relevant areas including research, management, conservation, control and reintroduction of wild animals. Applicants may be based in the UK or internationally.
Value: UK £1,000
Frequency: Annual
Application Procedure: Applicants must complete a Wild Animal Welfare Award application form, available for download from the UFAW website (www.ufaw.org.uk) or by emailing the UFAW Scientific Officer at scioff@ufaw.org.uk
Closing Date: December 7th

UNIVERSITY COLLEGE DUBLIN (UCD)

Belfield, Dublin 4, Ireland
Tel: (353) 1 716 2921
Fax: (353) 1 269 7262
Email: ucdresearch@ucd.ie
Website: www.ucd.ie
Contact: Simon Doloson

University College Dublin (UCD) was founded in the mid 19th century and is a dynamic, modern university. It is committed to becoming one of the top 30 research universities in the European Union, where cutting edge research and scholarship will create a stimulating intellectual environment, the ideal surroundings for learning and discovery.

SRG Postdoctoral Fellowships

Subjects: Semantics, verification and software engineering.
Purpose: To develop into a world-class research group in systems and software technology.
Eligibility: Open to candidates who have obtained a PhD in computer science or mathematics.
Level of Study: Postdoctorate
Type: Fellowships
Value: €35,866–39,337
Length of Study: 18 months–3 years
Frequency: Annual
Study Establishment: University College Dublin (UCD)
Country of Study: Ireland
No. of awards offered: 2
Additional Information: For general information or applications, mail to aquigley@ucd.ie

For further information contact:

Website: http://srg.cs.ucd.ie

UNIVERSITY COLLEGE FOR THE CREATIVE ARTS

New Dover Road, Canterbury, Kent,
CT1 3AN, United Kingdom
Tel: (44) 44 0 1227 817302
Fax: (44) 44 0 1227 817500
Email: admissions@ucreative.ac.uk
Website: www.ucreative.ac.uk

The University College for the Creative Arts at Canterbury, Epsom, Farnham, Maidstone and Rochester provides inspiring courses in art, design, architecture, media and communication. With around 6,500 students enrolled on more than 80 different courses, the College is one of the United Kingdom's leading providers of specialist art and design education. The College's key strength lies in the breadth of specialist, academic disciplines that it offers. Providing students with a ladder of opportunity, the College enables talented individuals to progress from further education through to undergraduate and postgraduate study and on to employment or creative practice.

MA (Taught) Postgraduate Scholarships

Subjects: Creative arts.
Eligibility: Full or part-time home/EU or overseas postgraduate students.
Level of Study: Postgraduate
Type: Scholarship
Value: UK £1,200 (full-time) or UK £600 (part-time)
Frequency: Annual
Study Establishment: University College for the Creative Arts
Country of Study: United Kingdom
No. of awards offered: 100
Application Procedure: Check website for further details.
Closing Date: September
Funding: Government
Additional Information: Send the application forms to the college registar at the relevant college.

UNIVERSITY COLLEGE LONDON

Gower Street, London, WC1E 6BT, United Kingdom
Tel: (44) 20 7679 2005/4167
Fax: (44) 20 7691 3112
Email: postmaster@ucl.ac.uk
Website: www.ucl.ac.uk

Just 175 years ago, the benefits of a university education in England were restricted to men who were members of the Church of England; University College London (UCL) was founded to challenge that discrimination. UCL was the first university to be established in England after Oxford and Cambridge, providing a progressive alternative to those institutions social exclusivity, religious restrictions and academic constraints. UCL is the largest of over 50 colleges and institutes that make up the federal University of London.

A C Gimson Scholarships in Phonetics and Linguistics

Subjects: Phonetics and linguistics.
Purpose: To financially support MPhil/PhD research.
Eligibility: United Kingdom, European Union and overseas students are eligible to apply.
Level of Study: Doctorate, Postgraduate, Research
Type: Scholarship
Value: UK £1,000
Frequency: Annual
Study Establishment: University College London
Country of Study: United Kingdom
No. of awards offered: 2
Application Procedure: Applicants should write indicating their intention to compete for the bursaries to the department.
Closing Date: June 1st

For further information contact:

Department of Phonetics and Linguistics
Tel: 44 0 20 7679 3262
Email: s.anyadi@ling.ucl.ac.uk
Contact: Ms Stefanie Anyadi

A J Ayer-Sumitomo Corporation Scholarship in Philosophy

Subjects: Philosophy.
Purpose: To financially support MPhil/PhD research.
Eligibility: United Kingdom, European Union and overseas students are eligible to apply.
Level of Study: Doctorate, Postgraduate, Research
Type: Scholarship
Value: Up to UK £800
Frequency: Annual
Study Establishment: University College London
Country of Study: United Kingdom
Application Procedure: No separate application is required. All who are admitted to research programmes in philosophy will automatically be considered for the scholarship. Any queries should be directed to the department.
Additional Information: Decisions regarding this award will be made in September.

For further information contact:

Department of Philosophy
Tel: 44 0 20 7679 7115
Email: philosophy@ucl.ac.uk
Contact: Mr Richard Edwards

Abbey "1 UCL" Excellence/Endeavour Award

Purpose: To foster the notion of UCL as a community, and to highlight, celebrate and reward outstanding academic achievement or endeavour by current students in a non-academic field.
Eligibility: Applicants should refer to the website for full details on eligibility.
Level of Study: Postgraduate
Type: Scholarship
Value: £1,000
Frequency: Annual
No. of awards offered: 10

Application Procedure: Applicants should refer to the website for further information on application procedures, forms and deadlines.

Abbey Master's Scholarship
Purpose: To assist the most academically able students from leading universities in each of the Santander network countries to pursue a Master's programme at UCL.
Eligibility: Applicants should refer to the website for full details on eligibility.
Level of Study: Postgraduate
Type: Scholarship
Value: UK £2,000 or 5,000, depending on other funding held by the scholar
Frequency: Annual
No. of awards offered: Up to 10
Application Procedure: Applicants should refer to the website for further information on application procedures, forms and deadlines.

Alfred Bader Prize in Organic Chemistry
Subjects: Organic chemistry.
Purpose: To financially support MPhil/PhD research.
Level of Study: Doctorate, Postgraduate, Research
Type: Scholarship
Value: UK £1,000
Frequency: Annual
Study Establishment: University College London
Country of Study: United Kingdom
No. of awards offered: 1
Application Procedure: Applicants must contact the department.
Closing Date: Check the website for closing date
Additional Information: The award will be announced in October.

For further information contact:

Department of Chemistry
Tel: (44) 20 7679 4650
Fax: (44) 20 7679 7463
Email: m.l.jabore@ucl.ac.uk
Contact: Ms Mary Lau Jabore

Amelia Zollner IPPR/UCL Internship Award
Purpose: The Amelia Zollner IPPR/UCL Internship Award was founded in 2007 in memory of UCL student Ameial Zollner. IPPR and UCI co-fund an annual, approximately 3-month London-based IPPR internship reserved for a recent UCL graduate as a stepping stone to working in policy or politics. The internship will normally run from October through December, but can take place at any time of the year.
Eligibility: 1. Applicants must be final year UCL students, about to graduate (Bachelors, Masters or Research degree) in any area, interested in and passionate about policy and politics, current affairs and social justice, and the work of IPPR, as well as enthusiastic about political research. 2. Applicants can come from any country, but must be able to work in the UK (UK/EU nationals or holders of valid work permit). 3. Applicants should have some research skills, and need to be committed to the aims of IPPR of wanting to build a fair, more democratic and environmentally sustainable world.
Level of Study: Postgraduate, Research, Graduate
Type: Internship
Value: UK £5,000 or the equivalent of the current IPPR salary for the duration of the internship
Length of Study: 3 months
Frequency: Annual
Country of Study: United Kingdom
Application Procedure: Applications should be made direct to IPPR and submitted preferably by email to intern@ippr.org
Closing Date: May 11th
No. of applicants last year: 48

For further information contact:

Internships IPPR, 30-32 Southampton Street, London, WC2 7RA, United Kingdom
Tel: (44) 020 7470 6133
Email: k.holdway@ippr.org
Website: www.ippr.org.uk

Archibald Richardson Scholarship for Mathematics
Subjects: Pure mathematics.
Purpose: To financially support students to pursue MPhil/PhD research.
Eligibility: United Kingdom, European Union and overseas applicants are eligible to apply. A candidate must be a student of U.C.L. and must have obtained first class honours in pure mathematics at the Bachelor Degree examination to engage him/her to do research work in this subject.
Level of Study: Doctorate, Postgraduate, Research
Type: Scholarship
Value: UK £3,000
Frequency: Annual
Study Establishment: University College London
Country of Study: United Kingdom
No. of awards offered: 1
Application Procedure: Applicants must contact the department. Applicants must give particulars of their academic record and of the work they intend to pursue in the event of the scholarship being awarded to them.
Closing Date: May 15th

For further information contact:

Department of Mathematics, United Kingdom
Tel: (44) 44 (0) 20 7679 2839
Fax: (44) 44 (0) 20 7383 5519
Email: h.higgins@ucl.ac.uk
Contact: Ms Helen Higgins

Arts and Humanities Faculty Postgraduate Research Studentship
Subjects: The award is given for academic excellence. Applicants should be intending to pursue a course of stuyd leading to a PhD degreee in the faculty of Arts and Humanities
Purpose: To provide financial asssitance to students admitted for MPhil/PhD degree studies in the Faculty of Arts and Humanities at UCL.
Eligibility: Applicants should contact the Faculty of Arts and Humanities for full details on eligibility.
Level of Study: Doctorate, Postgraduate, Research
Type: Scholarship
Value: For 1 year, each £5,000 (for 3); for 2 years, £6,500 for 2 overseas scholarships, subject to revision at the end of year 1
Frequency: Dependent on funds available
No. of awards offered: Up to 5
Application Procedure: Applicants should refer to the website for further information.
Closing Date: March 16th
Contributor: Faculty of Arts and Humanities
No. of awards given last year: 5
No. of applicants last year: Approx. 10

For further information contact:

Website: www.ucl.ac.uk/ah/pages.studentships

Bentham Scholarships
Subjects: Law.
Purpose: To financially support prospective LLM students.
Eligibility: Applicants must be overseas students from outside the European Union. An applicant must have accepted an offer (either conditional or unconditional) to read for the LLM at UCL to be eligible.
Level of Study: Postgraduate
Type: Scholarship
Value: UK £2,000
Frequency: Annual
Study Establishment: University College London
Country of Study: United Kingdom
No. of awards offered: 10
Application Procedure: Application forms are available from the department at the address given below.
Closing Date: May 31st
No. of awards given last year: 3
Additional Information: The scholarships will be based on academic merit. The faculty will only consider these applicants who have firmly accepted their offer of admission to the LLM by May 31st.

For further information contact:

Faculty of Laws, University College London, Bentham House, Endsleigh Gardens, London, WC1H 0EG, United Kingdom
Tel: (44) 20 7679 1441
Fax: (44) 20 7209 3470
Email: graduatelaw@ucl.ac.uk
Contact: The Graduate Officer

Bioprocessing Graduate Scholarship

Subjects: Biochemical engineering.
Purpose: To financially support study leading to an MPhil/PhD.
Eligibility: Open to students resident outside the United Kingdom and pursuing the MSc or MPhil or PhD research in the department of biomedical engineering.
Level of Study: Doctorate, Postgraduate
Type: Scholarship
Value: Up to a maximum of UK £11,000 per year. This sum can be set against tuition fees and/or be received as maintenance allowance payable in quarterly installments
Length of Study: Maximum of 4 calendar years
Frequency: Annual
Study Establishment: University College London
Country of Study: United Kingdom
Application Procedure: Applicants must contact the department at the address given below or the British Council Office in Colombo.
Closing Date: May 15th
Funding: Trusts
No. of applicants last year: 8

For further information contact:

Department of Biochemical Engineering, University College London, Torrington Place, London, United Kingdom
Tel: (44) 20 7679 3796
Email: nigelth@ucl.ac.uk
Contact: Professor Nigel Titchener-Hooker

Brain Research Trust Prize and Medical Research Council Studentships

Subjects: Neurology or Clinical Neurosciences
Purpose: To financially support MPhil/PhD research students.
Eligibility: Open to United Kingdom, European Union and overseas students. Overseas fee-paying students should be aware that only home tuition fee (EU rates) is included in the award.
Level of Study: Doctorate, Postgraduate, Research
Type: Studentship
Value: Stipend, tuition fees at UK/EU rate, consumables + travel budget
Length of Study: 3 or 4 years
Frequency: Annual
Study Establishment: UCL Institute of Neurology
Country of Study: United Kingdom
No. of awards offered: 5+
Application Procedure: Applicants should contact the UCL Institute of Neurology.
Funding: Government, trusts
Contributor: The Brian Research Trust and Medical Research Council
No. of awards given last year: 4
No. of applicants last year: 90

For further information contact:

Email: education.unit@ion.ucl.ac.uk
Website: www.ion.ucl.ac.uk

British Chevening/UCL Israel Alumni/Chaim Herzog Award

Subjects: All subjects. Preference given to public policy, economics and history.
Purpose: To financially support postgraduate study.
Eligibility: Applicants must be Master's students of Israeli nationality residing in Israel. Please refer to the website for further details.
Level of Study: Postgraduate
Type: Scholarship
Value: Tuition fees, return airfare and living expenses

Frequency: Annual
Study Establishment: University College London
Country of Study: United Kingdom
Application Procedure: Applicants should refer to the website for details.
Closing Date: Refer to website

For further information contact:

Tel: 44 0 20 7679 2005/4167
Website: www.ucl.ac.uk/scholarships

Chief Justice Scholarships for Students from India

Subjects: Law.
Purpose: To financially support prospective LLM students.
Eligibility: Applicants must be overseas students from India. An applicant must have accepted an offer (either conditional or unconditional) to read for the LLM at UCL to be eligible.
Level of Study: Postgraduate
Type: Scholarship
Value: UK £2,000
Frequency: Annual
Study Establishment: University College London
Country of Study: United Kingdom
No. of awards offered: 10
Application Procedure: Application forms are available from the department.
Closing Date: May 31st
No. of awards given last year: 1
Additional Information: The scholarships will be based on academic merit. The faculty will only consider these applicants who have firmly accepted their offer of admission to the LLM by May 31st.

For further information contact:

Faculty of Laws
Tel: 44 0 20 7679 1441
Fax: 44 0 20 7209 3470
Email: graduatelaw@ucl.ac.uk
Contact: The Graduate Officer

Civil and Environmental Engineering Graduate Scholarship

Subjects: Civil and environmental engineering.
Purpose: To financially support MPhil/PhD study.
Eligibility: Applicants should hold or except to obtain a First Class (Honours) Degree or equivalent. Applicants should have been offered a place at UCL and should firmly have accepted that offer or be intending to do so. They can be from any country outside the European Union.
Level of Study: Doctorate, Postgraduate
Type: Scholarship
Value: UK £5,000 per year
Length of Study: 3 years
Frequency: Annual
Study Establishment: University College London
Country of Study: United Kingdom
No. of awards offered: 1
Application Procedure: Applicants should write indicating their intention to compete for the scholarship to the department.
Closing Date: July 31st
Additional Information: If the applicant has not already applied to UCL, please complete a graduate application form and enclose it with the scholarship application.

For further information contact:

Lecturer in Environmental Engineering, Department of Civil and Environmental Engineering
Tel: (44) 20 7679 7994
Fax: (44) 20 7380 0986
Email: m.khraisheh@ucl.ac.uk
Contact: Dr Majeda Khraisheh

Clinical Psychology Awards

Subjects: Clinical psychology.
Purpose: To financially support doctorate study.

Eligibility: United Kingdom and European Union students are eligible to apply.
Level of Study: Doctorate
Type: Scholarship
Value: Salary, tuition fees and travelling expenses
Frequency: Annual
Study Establishment: University College London
Country of Study: United Kingdom
No. of awards offered: 42
Application Procedure: Applicants should contact the department via Clearing House, Leeds.
Closing Date: December 1st
Funding: Government
No. of awards given last year: 42
Additional Information: Clinical Psychology Awards are salaried positions with the Camden & Islington Community Mental Health Trust.

For further information contact:

The Clearing House for Postgraduate Courses in Clinical Psychology, Fairbairn House, 7175 Clarendon Road, Leeds, LSZ 9PL
Tel: (44) 20 7436 4276
Website: www.leeds.ac.uk/chpccp

CSC/UCL/FCO Chevening Scholarship

Subjects: Public policy.
Purpose: To financially support students pursuing a 1-year taught MSc degree programme.
Eligibility: Applicants should be citizens and residents of the People's Republic of China. Students pursuing a 1-year taught MSc degree programme in public policy are eligible to apply.
Level of Study: Postgraduate
Type: Scholarship
Value: Tuition fees, a monthly stipend for living expenses and other agreed allowances
Length of Study: 1 year
Frequency: Annual
Study Establishment: University College London
Country of Study: United Kingdom
No. of awards offered: 9
Application Procedure: Applicants should contact the China Scholarship Council at the address given below.
Additional Information: Applicants are expected to return to China at the end of their period of study. The scholarships are awarded on the basis of academic merit.

For further information contact:

China Scholarship Council, 160 Fuxingmennei Street, Beijing, 100031, PR, China
Tel: (86) 10 6641 3119

David Pearce Research Scholarship

Subjects: Economics.
Purpose: To provide financial assistance to students admitted for MPhil/PhD degree studies in the faculty of Arts and Humanities at UCL.
Eligibility: Applicants should contact the Department of Economics for full details on eligibility.
Level of Study: Postgraduate, Research
Type: Scholarship
Value: Fees and £13,000 plus maintenance
Frequency: Annual
No. of awards offered: Up to 3
Application Procedure: Applicants should contact the Department for further information.
Closing Date: April 1st

For further information contact:

Website: www.econ.ucl.ac.uk

Dawes Hicks Postgraduate Scholarships in Philosophy

Subjects: Philosophy.
Purpose: To financially support postgraduate research.

Eligibility: United Kingdom, European Union and overseas students are eligible to apply.
Level of Study: Postgraduate, Research
Type: Scholarship
Value: Up to UK £5,000
Frequency: Annual
Study Establishment: University College London
Country of Study: United Kingdom
Application Procedure: No separate application is required. All who are admitted to research programmes in philosophy will automatically be considered for the scholarship. Any queries should be directed to the department.
Additional Information: Decisions regarding this award will be made in September.

For further information contact:

Department of Philosophy
Tel: 44 0 20 7679 7115
Email: philosophy@ucl.ac.uk
Contact: Mr Richard Edwards

The Denys Holland Scholarship

Purpose: The Denys Holland Scholarship aims to support undergraduate students from any country, who would be unable to study at UCL without financial help, and who can demonstrate their intention to make full use of the activities offered by UCL and the Student Union.
Eligibility: 1. Applicants should be holding an offer of admission to UCL for full-time undergraduate study in any department. 2. Applicants should be in financial hardship, and be able to demonstrate that without the scholarship they would be unable to study at UCL.
3. Applicants should be preferably aged 25 or below at the time of commencing their studies. 4. Applicants should be able to demonstrate that they have broad interests and intend to be actively involved in and contribute to the life of the College.
Level of Study: Undergraduate
Type: Scholarship
Value: UK £9,300 per annum, subject to an annual inflationary increase
Length of Study: 13 years
Frequency: Annual
Study Establishment: University College London
Country of Study: United Kingdom
Application Procedure: Applicants will be required to detail their current outside interests and indicate areas of non-academic activity which they would hope to pursue while a student. They will also have to provide information on their financial circumstances and other sources of income being sought. Applicants must apply for admission to UCL through UCAS (www.ucas.ac.uk) and submit the completed UCL Denys Holland Scholarship Application Form by the deadline.
Closing Date: August 1st
Funding: Private

For further information contact:

UCL Scholarships, The Registry, University College London, Gower Street, London, WC1E 6BT, United Kingdom

Department of Communities and Local Government (formally Office of the Deputy Prime Minister)

Subjects: Spatial planning and international planning.
Purpose: To financially support full-time study.
Eligibility: Open to candidates who take up full time study only with residence restrictions, already holding or offer for the MSC spatial planning or MSC international planning, 2:1 or equivalent (except in exceptional circumstances).
Level of Study: Postgraduate
Type: Bursary
Value: Tuition fees at UK/EU rate plus (For UK/EU nationals only) along with a quarterly stipend of £1,500
Length of Study: 1 year
Frequency: Annual
Study Establishment: University College London
Country of Study: United Kingdom
Application Procedure: Applications are available from www.esrc.ac.uk (ESRC) and should be sent to the department. Potentially eligible candidates will be contacted by the department.

Closing Date: Second Friday in June
Funding: Government
Contributor: Department of Communities and Local Government
No. of awards given last year: 7
No. of applicants last year: 16

For further information contact:

Barlett School of Planning, Wates House, 22, Gordon Street, London, WC1H 0QB,
Tel: 44 0 20 7679 7501
Email: j.hillmore@ucl.ac.uk
Contact: Judith Hillmore

Department of Geography Teaching/Computing Assistantships

Subjects: Geography.
Purpose: To financially support teaching and computer assistants.
Eligibility: Applicants should be United Kingdom or European Union students. Overseas students who can apply the balance of fees to the higher rate, including those receiving an Overseas Research Students award for this purpose.
Level of Study: Doctorate, Postgraduate
Type: Assistantship
Value: Stipend based on that paid by the United Kingdom Research Councils and fees at the Home/European Union rate
Frequency: Every 3 years
Study Establishment: University College London
Country of Study: United Kingdom
No. of awards offered: Up to 4 teaching/computer assistantships
Application Procedure: Applicants must contact the Department of Geography.
Closing Date: July 7th

For further information contact:

Tel: 44 0 20 7679 0500
Website: www.geog.ucl.ac.uk/admission

Dorothy Hodgkin Postgraduate Award

Purpose: To enable top-quality science, engineering, medicine, social science and technology students from India, China, Hong Kong, Brazil, South Africa, Russia and the developing world (as defined by the OECD) to study for PhDs in highly rated UK research environments.
Eligibility: Applicants should refer to the website for full details on eligibility.
Level of Study: Postgraduate, Research
Type: Scholarship
Value: Full overseas tuition fees plus annual maintenance up to £14,600 per annum
Frequency: Annual
No. of awards offered: Varies
Application Procedure: Applicants should refer to the website for further information on application procedures, forms and deadlines.

Edwin Power Scholarship

Subjects: Applied Mathematics.
Purpose: To support a graduate student to the Department of Mathematics for Master's study or PhD research in Applied Mathematics.
Level of Study: Postgraduate, Research
Type: Scholarship
Value: UK £400, subject to annual renewal based on satisfactory progress
Length of Study: 3 years
Frequency: Annual
Study Establishment: University College London
Country of Study: United Kingdom
Application Procedure: Candidates wishing to apply for the Scholarship must send written notice of their intention to apply for the Scholarship to the Head of the Department of Mathematics at UCL.
Closing Date: August 15th

For further information contact:

University College London, Gower Street, London, WC1E 6BT
Tel: 44 (0) 20 7679 2839

Fax: 44 (0) 20 7383 2839
Contact: Ms Helen Higgins

Eleanor Grove Scholarships for Women Students

Subjects: German language and literature.
Purpose: To promote and encourage study and proficiency in German.
Eligibility: Candidate must be a woman student of the college. The scholarship will be awarded to assist a student who is reading for a higher degree, or, in special cases, to enable a BA student to study German abroad.
Type: Scholarship
Value: £950
Frequency: Annual
Study Establishment: University college or elsewhere approved by the Faculty of Arts and Humanities
Country of Study: United Kingdom
No. of awards offered: 2
Application Procedure: Candidate must send written notice of her intention to compete for a scholarship to the graduate tutor. Candidate must give particulars of the research work which she intends to pursue in the event of the scholarship being awarded to her, and of the place or places where she intends to pursue it.
Closing Date: May 25th
No. of awards given last year: 2
No. of applicants last year: 2

For further information contact:

Email: german@ucl.ac.uk
Contact: Dr Stephanie Bird

Fielden Research Scholarship

Subjects: German language and literature.
Purpose: To financially support MPhil/PhD study.
Eligibility: Applicants must have applied for a place for graduate study at UCL.
Level of Study: Doctorate, Graduate, Postgraduate
Type: Scholarship
Value: UK £500
Frequency: Annual
Study Establishment: University College London
Country of Study: United Kingdom
Application Procedure: Applicants must contact the department. If the applicants have not applied to UCL they must complete a graduate application form and enclose it with the scholarship application.
Closing Date: May 25th
No. of awards given last year: 1
No. of applicants last year: 1

For further information contact:

Department of German
Contact: Dr Stephanie Bird

Follett Scholarship

Subjects: Philosophy.
Purpose: To financially support MPhil/PhD research.
Eligibility: United Kingdom, European Union and overseas students are eligible to apply.
Level of Study: Postgraduate, Research, Doctorate
Type: Scholarship
Value: Up to UK £13,000
Frequency: Annual
Study Establishment: University College London
Country of Study: United Kingdom
Application Procedure: No separate application is required. Applicants who are admitted to research programmes in philosophy will automatically be considered for the scholarship. Any queries should be directed to the department.
Additional Information: Decisions regarding this award will be made in September.

For further information contact:

Department of Philosophy
Tel: (44) 20 7679 7115

Fax: (44) 20 7679 3336
Email: philosophy@ucl.ac.uk
Contact: Mr Richard Edwards

Franz Sondheimer Bursary Fund

Subjects: Chemistry.
Purpose: To financially support MPhil/PhD research.
Eligibility: Preference is given to overseas applicants.
Level of Study: Doctorate, Postgraduate, Research
Type: Scholarship
Value: Approx. UK £2,000
Study Establishment: University College London
Country of Study: United Kingdom
No. of awards offered: 1
Application Procedure: Applicants must contact the department.
Closing Date: May 1st
No. of awards given last year: 1
No. of applicants last year: 2

For further information contact:

Department of Chemistry
Tel: (44) 20 7679 4650
Fax: (44) 20 7679 7463
Email: m.l.jabore@ucl.ac.uk
Contact: Ms Mary Lou Jabore

Frederick Bonnart-Braunthal Scholarship

Subjects: Tackling the causes and consequences of intolerance (religious, racial and cultural prejudices).
Purpose: To financially support students who plan to explore the nature of religious, racial and cultural prejudices, and to find ways of combating them.
Eligibility: Open to prospective MPhil/PhD candidates with a First Class (Honours) Degree or equivalent are eligible to apply.
Level of Study: Doctorate, Research
Type: Scholarship
Value: UK £12,000 per year
Length of Study: Duration of course
Frequency: Annual
Study Establishment: University College London
Country of Study: United Kingdom
No. of awards offered: Up to 2
Application Procedure: Please check the website for further details about application procedures and deadlines.
Closing Date: March 1st
No. of awards given last year: 1

For further information contact:

Entrance Scholarships Office, Registrar's Division
Tel: (44) 20 7679 2005/4167
Website: www.ucl.ac.uk/scholarships

Gaitskell MSc Scholarship

Subjects: Economics.
Purpose: To financially support full-time Master's study in the department of Economics.
Eligibility: Open to candidates who have applied for a place for graduate study at UCL and are not already receiving full financial support from other sources for fees and living costs.
Level of Study: Postgraduate
Type: Scholarship
Value: UK£5,000
Frequency: Annual
Study Establishment: University College London
Country of Study: United Kingdom
No. of awards offered: Up to 4
Application Procedure: Candidates should send an acadmic curriculum vitae and a letter of no more than 500 words describing their areas of interest in the discipline.
Closing Date: May 15th

For further information contact:

Department of Economics
Tel: (44) 20 7679 5861

Fax: (44) 20 7616 2775
Email: d.fauvrelle@ucl.ac.uk
Contact: Ms Daniella Fauvrelle

Gay Clifford Fees Award for Outstanding Women Students

Subjects: Arts and humanities, social and historical sciences.
Purpose: To financially support postgraduate study.
Eligibility: Open to prospective female Master's degree students in the faculties of Arts and Humanities and Social and Historical Sciences with a First Class (Honours) undergraduate Degree or equivalent.
Level of Study: Postgraduate
Type: Scholarship
Value: UK £2,500 (Deducted from tuition fees)
Frequency: Annual
Study Establishment: University College London
Country of Study: United Kingdom
No. of awards offered: 4
Application Procedure: Applicants should refer to the website for further information about the application procedures and deadlines.
Closing Date: March 1st
No. of awards given last year: 3
Additional Information: Awarded in memory of Gay Clifford (1943–1998), academic and poet.

For further information contact:

Entrance Scholarships Office, Registrar's Division
Tel: (44) 20 7679 2005/4167
Website: www.ucl.ac.uk/scholarships

The George Melhuish Postgraduate Scholarship

Subjects: Philosophy.
Purpose: To financially support postgraduate research.
Eligibility: Open to United Kingdom, European Union and overseas applicants.
Level of Study: Postgraduate, Research
Type: Scholarship
Value: Up to UK £3,700
Frequency: Annual
Study Establishment: University College London
Country of Study: United Kingdom
Application Procedure: No separate application is required. Applicants who are admitted to research programmes in philosophy will automatically be considered for the scholarship. Any queries should be directed to the department.
Additional Information: Decision regarding this award will be made in September.

For further information contact:

Department of Philosophy
Tel: 44 0 20 7679 7115
Email: philosophy@ucl.ac.uk
Contact: Mr Richard Edwards

Graduate UCL Research Scholarship

Subjects: Any subject
Purpose: To attract high-quality students to undertake research at UCL.
Eligibility: Open to prospective MPhil/PhD candidates with a United Kingdom First Class (Honours) Degree or equivalent and first year MPhil/PhD candidates who have registered on or after the scholarship deadline. Applicants must be admitted to or currently registered at UCL for full-time or part-time MPhil/PhD or engineering research, and should hold or expect to achieve at least a UK 2:1 honours undergraduate degree or equivalent qualification.
Level of Study: Doctorate, Research
Type: Scholarship
Value: UK/EU fees plus annual maintenance allowance of £14,600
Length of Study: 3 years
Frequency: Annual
Study Establishment: University College London
Country of Study: United Kingdom
No. of awards offered: 15

Application Procedure: Applicants should refer to the website for further information about the application procedures and deadlines.
Closing Date: Refer to website
No. of awards given last year: 15
Additional Information: Overseas fee-payers are strongly advised to apply for an Overseas Research Student (ORS) award, which can be held together with a Graduate School Research Scholarship.

For further information contact:

Entrance Scholarships Office, Registrar's Division
Tel: (44) 20 7579 2005/4167
Website: www.ucl.ac.uk/scholarships

Ian Karten Charitable Trust Scholarship (Hebrew and Jewish Studies)

Subjects: Hebrew and Jewish studies.
Purpose: To financially support postgraduate study.
Eligibility: Applicants must have applied for a place for graduate study at UCL. Available to prospective students of the MA language, culture and history: Hebrew and Jewish Studies, Holocaust studies and Modern Israeli Studies.
Level of Study: Graduate
Type: Scholarship
Value: UK £1,000 each
Frequency: Annual
Study Establishment: University College London
Country of Study: United Kingdom
No. of awards offered: 4
Application Procedure: Applicants should contact the department. If the applicants have not applied to UCL they must complete a graduate application form and enclose it with the scholarship application.
Closing Date: June 1st
Funding: Trusts
No. of awards given last year: 4
No. of applicants last year: 5

For further information contact:

Department of Hebrew and Jewish Studies
Tel: (44) 20 7679 3028
Fax: (44) 20 7209 1026
Email: n.f.lochery@ucl.ac.uk
Contact: Dr Neil Lochery

J J Sylvester Scholarship

Subjects: Mathematics.
Purpose: To financially support MPhil/PhD research.
Eligibility: United Kingdom, European Union and overseas students are eligible to apply.
Level of Study: Postgraduate, Doctorate, Research
Type: Scholarship
Value: UK £500 per year
Frequency: Annual
Study Establishment: University College London
Country of Study: United Kingdom
No. of awards offered: 1
Application Procedure: Applicants must contact the department.

For further information contact:

Department of Mathematics, United Kingdom
Tel: (44) 44 (0) 20 7679 2839
Fax: (44) 44 (0) 20 7383 5519
Email: h.higgins@ucl.ac.uk
Contact: Ms Helen Higgins

Jacobsen Scholarship in Philosophy

Subjects: Philosophy.
Purpose: To financially support MPhil/PhD research.
Eligibility: Open to United Kingdom, European Union and overseas students.
Level of Study: Doctorate, Postgraduate, Research
Type: Scholarship
Value: Up to UK £9,500
Frequency: Annual
Study Establishment: University College London

Country of Study: United Kingdom
Application Procedure: No separate application is required. Applicants who are admitted to research programmes in philosophy will automatically be considered for the scholarship. Any queries should be directed to the department.
Additional Information: Decisions regarding this award will be made in September.

For further information contact:

Department of Philosophy
Tel: 44 0 20 7679 7115
Email: philosophy@ucl.ac.uk
Contact: Mr Richard Edwards

The James Lanner Memorial Scholarship

Subjects: Economics, environmental resource economics.
Purpose: To financially support students to pursue MPhil/PhD in Economics.
Eligibility: Candidates should have applied for a place for graduate study at UCL. Open to prospective students of the MSc in Economics, MSc in environmental resource economics or MPhil/PhD in Economics.
Level of Study: Postgraduate
Type: Scholarship
Value: UK £5,000
Frequency: Annual
Study Establishment: University College London
Country of Study: United Kingdom
Application Procedure: Candidates should send an academic curriculum vitae and a letter of no more than 500 words describing their areas in interest in the discipline.
Closing Date: May 15th
Additional Information: Preference is given to candidates who intend to specialize in international economics or an issues of economic policy in Europe.

For further information contact:

Department of Economics
Tel: (44) 20 7679 5861
Fax: (44) 20 7616 2775
Email: d.fauvrelle@ucl.ac.uk
Contact: Ms Daniella Fauvrelle

Jevons Memorial Scholarship in Economic Science

Subjects: Economics.
Purpose: To financially support MPhil/PhD study.
Eligibility: Candidates must have graduated or be a candidate for graduation in the term in which the award is made. Previous tenure of the scholarship does not debar candidate from competing on a second occasion. Normally the scholar elected must pursue a course of study and research for a higher degree at UCL.
Level of Study: Doctorate, Postgraduate
Type: Scholarship
Value: UK £55
Frequency: Annual
Study Establishment: University College London
Country of Study: United Kingdom
Application Procedure: Applicants should send particulars of the research work they intend to pursue plus an academic curriculum vitae to the department. If the applicant has not applied to UCL, they must complete a graduate application form and enclose it with the scholarship application.
Closing Date: May 15th

For further information contact:

Department of Economics
Tel: (44) 20 7679 5861
Fax: (44) 20 7916 2775
Email: d.fauvrelle@ucl.ac.uk
Contact: Ms Daniella Fauvrelle

John Carr Scholarship for Students from Africa and the Caribbean

Subjects: Law.

Purpose: To financially support prospective LLM students.
Eligibility: Applicants must be overseas students from Africa and the Caribbean. An applicant must have accepted an offer (either conditional or unconditional) to read for the LLM at UCL to be eligible.
Level of Study: Postgraduate
Type: Scholarship
Value: UK £2,000
Frequency: Annual
Study Establishment: University College London
Country of Study: United Kingdom
No. of awards offered: 10
Application Procedure: Application forms are available from the department.
Closing Date: May 31st
Additional Information: The scholarships will be based on academic merit. The faculty will only consider those applicants who have firmly accepted their offer of admission to the LLM by May 31st.

For further information contact:

Faculty of Laws
Tel: 44 0 20 7679 1441
Fax: 44 0 20 7209 3470
Email: graduatelaw@ucl.ac.uk
Contact: The Graduate Officer

John Lyon UCL Master's Scholarship

Purpose: To enable UCL undergraduates from certain boroughs of London to pursue a one-year taught Master's programme at UCL.
Eligibility: Applicants should refer to the website for full details on eligibility.
Level of Study: Postgraduate
Type: Scholarship
Value: £14,500 for fees and maintenance
Length of Study: 1 year
Frequency: Annual
No. of awards offered: Up to 2
Application Procedure: Applicants should refer to the website for further information on application procedures, forms and deadlines.

John Stuart Mill Scholarship in Philosophy of Mind and Logic

Subjects: Philosophy.
Purpose: To financially support MPhil/PhD research.
Eligibility: Open to United Kingdom, European Union and overseas applicants.
Level of Study: Research, Doctorate, Postgraduate
Type: Scholarship
Value: Up to UK £1,400
Frequency: Annual
Study Establishment: University College London
Country of Study: United Kingdom
Application Procedure: No separate application is required. All who are admitted to research programmes in philosophy will automatically be considered for the scholarship. Any queries should be directed to the department.
Additional Information: Decision regarding this award will be made in September.

For further information contact:

Department of Philosophy
Tel: 44 0 20 7679 7115
Email: philosophy@ucl.ac.uk
Contact: Mr Richard Edwards

Joseph Hume Scholarship

Subjects: Law.
Purpose: To financially support LLM students or MPhil/PhD research.
Eligibility: Open to LLM students and students with a Master's degree. Normally the scholar elected must pursue a course of study and research for the LLM, or MPhil degree in the faculty of law at UCL.
Level of Study: Doctorate, Postgraduate, Research
Type: Scholarship
Value: UK £1,600
Frequency: Annual

Study Establishment: University College London
Country of Study: United Kingdom
No. of awards offered: 1
Application Procedure: Application forms are available from the department. Candidates must give particulars of their academic record and of the research work they intend to pursue.
Closing Date: August 1st
No. of awards given last year: 2

For further information contact:

Faculty of Laws
Tel: 0 20 7679 1441
Fax: 0 20 7209 3470
Email: graduatelaw@ucl.ac.uk
Contact: The Graduate Officer

Karim Rida Said Foundation/UCL Joint Scholarship

Subjects: All subjects.
Purpose: To financially support taught Master's study students.
Eligibility: Applicants must be Master's students from Iraq, Jordan, Lebanon, Palestine or Syria.
Level of Study: Doctorate, Postgraduate, Research
Type: Scholarship
Value: Full or partial support for tuition fees and maintenance, depending on financial need and availability of other grants to applicants
Frequency: Annual
Study Establishment: University College London
Country of Study: United Kingdom
No. of awards offered: Approx. 510
Application Procedure: Applicants should refer to the website for further information.
Closing Date: January 31st; May 1st for United Kingdom resident applicants
No. of awards given last year: 6

For further information contact:

Tel: 0 20 7679 2005/4167
Website: www.ucl.ac.uk/scholarships

Keeling Scholarship

Subjects: Philosophy.
Purpose: To financially support MPhil/PhD research.
Eligibility: United Kingdom, European Union and overseas students are eligible to apply.
Level of Study: Postgraduate, Research, Doctorate
Type: Scholarship
Value: United Kingdom/European Union tuition fees plus a bursary
Frequency: Annual
Study Establishment: University College London
Country of Study: United Kingdom
Application Procedure: No separate application is required. Applicants who are admitted to research programmes in philosophy will automatically be considered for the scholarship. Any queries should be directed to the department.
Additional Information: Decisions regarding this award will be made in September.

For further information contact:

Department of Philosophy
Tel: 44 0 20 7679 7115
Email: philosophy@ucl.ac.uk
Contact: Mr Richard Edwards

KWOK Foundation Scholarship

Subjects: Archaeology.
Purpose: To support Chinese students admitted to UCL to undertake research at the Institute of Archaeology.
Eligibility: Applicants should contact the Institute of Archaeology for full details on eligibility.
Level of Study: Postgraduate, Research
Type: Scholarship
Value: Fees and maintenance
Frequency: Annual
Study Establishment: University College London

Country of Study: United Kingdom
No. of awards offered: Up to 3
Application Procedure: Applicants should contact the Institute of Archaeology for further information.

For further information contact:

Website: www.ucl.ac.uk/archaeology/china-archaeology

Liver Group PhD Studentship

Subjects: Hepatology.
Purpose: To financially support students to pursue MPhil/PhD research.
Eligibility: Open to United Kingdom and European Union applicants.
Level of Study: Doctorate, Research, Postgraduate
Type: Scholarship
Value: United Kingdom/European Union tuition fees plus a maintenance allowance (1st year approx. UK £14,500)
Length of Study: 3 years
Frequency: Dependent on funds available
Study Establishment: Royal Free and University College Medical School, UCL-Hampstead campus
Country of Study: United Kingdom
No. of awards offered: 1
Application Procedure: Applicants should contact the department.
Closing Date: May 1st
Funding: Foundation
Contributor: The Liver Group Charity
No. of awards given last year: 1

For further information contact:

Centre for Hepatology, Department of Medicine (Royal Free Campus), Royal Free and University College Medicine School, Rowland Hill Street, Hampstead, London, NW3 2PF, United Kingdom
Tel: (44) 20 7433 2854
Fax: (44) 20 7433 2852
Email: c.selden@medsch.ucl.ac.uk
Contact: Dr Clare Selden

The Lloyd's Register Scholarship for Marine Engineering and Naval Architecture

Subjects: Marine engineering and naval architecture.
Purpose: To financially support postgraduate study in Marine Engineering and Naval Architecture.
Eligibility: Any country students are eligible to apply. All students must apply in writing. Consideration will be given to those with low financial means.
Level of Study: Postgraduate
Type: Scholarship
Value: UK £10,000
Frequency: Annual
Study Establishment: University College London
Country of Study: United Kingdom
No. of awards offered: 1
Application Procedure: Applicants should write indicating their interest in being considered for this scholarship to the department through e-mail to charlotte@meng.ucl.ac.uk
Closing Date: June 1st
Funding: Commercial
Contributor: Lloyd's Register
No. of awards given last year: 1
No. of applicants last year: 10
Additional Information: Only one award is currently available.

For further information contact:

Department of Mechanical Engineering
Tel: (44) 20 7679 3907
Fax: (44) 20 7388 0180
Email: info@meng.ucl.ac.uk
Contact: The Graduate Tutor

Margaret Richardson Scholarship

Subjects: German.
Purpose: To financially support MPhil/PhD study.

Eligibility: Open to applicants should have applied for a place for graduate study at UCL and have upper-second class degree or equivalent in German or a related field of study to enable them to do research work in this subject. Previous tenure of the scholarship does not debar a candidate from competing on a second occasion.
Level of Study: Graduate, Doctorate, Postgraduate
Type: Scholarship
Value: UK £2,800
Frequency: Annual
Study Establishment: University College London
Country of Study: United Kingdom
Application Procedure: Applicants should contact the department. If the applicant has not applied to UCL, they must complete a graduate application form and enclose it with the scholarship application. The application must give particulars of the research work which they intend to pursue in the event of the scholarship being awarded to them.
Closing Date: May 2th

For further information contact:

Department of German
Tel: (44) 20 7679 3104
Fax: (44) 20 7813 0168
Email: stephanie.bird@ucl.ac.uk
Contact: Dr Stephanie Bird

Master of the Rolls Scholarship For Commonwealth Students

Subjects: Law.
Purpose: To financially support prospective LLM students.
Eligibility: Applicants must be overseas students from the Commonwealth countries. An applicant must have accepted an offer (either conditional or unconditional) to read for the LLM at UCL.
Level of Study: Postgraduate
Type: Scholarship
Value: UK £2,000
Frequency: Annual
Study Establishment: University College London
Country of Study: United Kingdom
No. of awards offered: 10
Application Procedure: Application forms are available from the department.
Closing Date: May 31st
No. of awards given last year: 1
Additional Information: The scholarships will be based on academic merit. The faculty will only consider these applicants who have firmly accepted their offer of admission to the LLM by May 31st.

For further information contact:

Faculty of Laws
Tel: 44 0 20 7679 1441
Fax: 44 0 20 7209 3470
Email: graduatelaw@ucl.ac.uk
Contact: The Graduate Officer

Master's Degree Awards in Archaeology

Subjects: Archaeology.
Purpose: To financially support MA and MSc programmes in the Institute of Archaeology.
Eligibility: Open to students on MA and MSc programmes in UCL's institute of archaeology.
Level of Study: Postgraduate
Type: Scholarship
Value: Approx. UK £1,000
Frequency: Annual
Study Establishment: University College London
Country of Study: United Kingdom
Application Procedure: Applicants must contact the department.
Closing Date: Mid-March, check the department website for details

For further information contact:

Institute of Archaeology
Tel: (44) 20 7679 7495
Fax: (44) 20 7383 2572

Email: ethan.cochrane@ucl.ac.uk
Contact: Dr Ethan Cochrane

Mayer de Rothschild Scholarship in Pure Mathematics
Subjects: Pure Mathematics.
Eligibility: Open to students of the college who have attended for not less than 5 terms a course of study in pure mathematics.
Value: £275 per year
Application Procedure: Applicants must send a written notice of their intention to compete for a scholarship to the registrar of the college. For further information please visit the website.
Closing Date: May 15th

Monica Hulse Scholarship
Subjects: Mathematics.
Eligibility: Open to graduate students in the department of mathematics in the first year of their Master's course or PhD. The applicant should not be in receipt of any other special funding.
Type: Scholarship
Value: £1,000
Frequency: Annual
Application Procedure: Applicants must send written notice of their intention prior to the start of the academic year alongwith an academic curriculum vitae.
Closing Date: May

For further information contact:

The Graduate Tutor
Contact: Department of Mathematics

NHS Bursaries
Subjects: Speech and Language Sciences.
Purpose: To financially support postgraduate study.
Eligibility: Open to United Kingdom and European Union applicants only who have applied for a place for graduate study at UCL.
Level of Study: Postgraduate
Type: Bursary
Value: United Kingdom/European Union tuition fees. United Kingdom residents will also normally be eligible for a means tested bursary
Frequency: Annual
Study Establishment: University College London
Country of Study: United Kingdom
Application Procedure: There is no separate bursary application form. Application procedure is an automatic process once an offer of a place has been made.
Additional Information: When an offer of a place has been made, the NHS Student Grants unit will contact the applicant directly.

For further information contact:

Tel: 0 20 7679 4202
Email: n.wilkins@ucl.ac.uk
Contact: Natalie Wilkins

OSI/UCL-SSEES/FCO Chevening Scholarship
Subjects: Slavonic and East European Studies.
Purpose: To financially support postgraduate research.
Eligibility: Applicants must be registered in one of the following programmes: MA in political economy of Russia and Eastern Europe, MA in politics, security and integration, and MA in Central and South East European Studies.
Level of Study: Postgraduate
Type: Scholarship
Value: Full tuition fees, monthly stipend and other agreed allowances including return economy airfare
Frequency: Annual
Study Establishment: University College London
Country of Study: United Kingdom
No. of awards offered: 5
Application Procedure: For information on applications procedure please visit the website.
Closing Date: February 1st
No. of awards given last year: 5

Overseas Research Students (ORS) Award
Purpose: To attract high-quality international students to the UK to undertake research.
Eligibility: Applicants should refer to the website for full details on eligibility.
Level of Study: Postgraduate, Research
Type: Scholarship
Value: Overseas fees minus UK/EU fees; UCL covers UK/EU fees where no further fee funding is held
Frequency: Annual
No. of awards offered: Varies
Application Procedure: Applicants should refer to the website for further information on application procedures, forms and deadlines.

Perren Studentship
Subjects: Astronomy.
Purpose: To financially support graduate study and research.
Eligibility: United Kingdom, European Union and overseas applicants are eligible to apply.
Level of Study: Postgraduate, Research
Type: Studentship
Value: Full home/EU fees + stipend
Length of Study: 3 years
Frequency: Every 2 years
Study Establishment: University College London
Country of Study: United Kingdom
No. of awards offered: 1
Application Procedure: Applicants should provide particulars of their academic record and of the work that they intend to pursue to the department.
Closing Date: February 16th
Funding: Trusts
Contributor: Perren Fund
No. of awards given last year: 1
No. of applicants last year: 47

For further information contact:

Department of Physics and Astronomy
Tel: (44) 20 7679 3943
Contact: Mrs Christine Johnston

Physics and Astronomy Departmental Studentship Grant
Subjects: Physics or Astronomy related study.
Purpose: To support physics and astronomy related study.
Eligibility: UK, EU and Overseas applicants with co-funding.
Level of Study: Research
Type: Studentship
Value: Full home/Eu fees + stipend
Length of Study: 3 years
Frequency: Every 3 years
Study Establishment: University College London
Country of Study: United Kingdom
No. of awards offered: 1
Closing Date: February 16th
Funding: Government
Contributor: University College London
No. of awards given last year: 0
No. of applicants last year: N/A

For further information contact:

Department of Physics and Astronomy
Tel: 020 7679 3943
Contact: Mrs Christine Johnston

The Professor Denys Holland and Cowan Cheung Scholarship
Purpose: To provide financial need for studies at UCL.
Eligibility: 1. Applicants must be holders of Hong Kong Permanent Identity Cards or Chinese citizens who have received full-time education in Hong Kong and/or China for no less than 5 of the 8 years immediately prior to the start of study at UCL. 2. Applicants must hold an offer of admission to full-time undergraduate study at UCL in any area except Medicine which they have firmly accepted or intend to do so. 3. Applicants must be self-financing and liable to pay tuition fees at

the rate for overseas students. 4. Applicants should be in financial need and unable to fund their planned studies at UCL without financial help.

Level of Study: Undergraduate
Value: UK£10,000 toward tuition fees for a maximum of four years
Frequency: Annual
Study Establishment: United College London
Country of Study: United Kingdom
Application Procedure: Completed UG HK application form should be submitted along with required documentation as detailed in the form to UCL Scholarships.
Closing Date: April 1st
Additional Information: Interviews will be held in Hong Kong and applicants invited for interview will be required to present themselves for interview in Hong Kong at applicants' own expense.

For further information contact:

UCL Scholarships, The Registry, University College London, Gower Street, London, WC1E 6BT, United Kingdom
Tel: (44) 44 (0)20 7679 2724

R B Hounsfield Scholarship in Traffic Engineering
Subjects: Traffic engineering.
Purpose: To financially support MPhil/PhD research in Traffic Engineering in the Department of Civil and Environmental Engineering.
Eligibility: Candidates should hold or expect to obtain a First Class (Honours) Degree or equivalent and should have been offered a place at UCL and have firmly accepted that offer or be intending to do so.
Level of Study: Postgraduate, Research, Doctorate
Type: Scholarship
Value: Not less than UK £120
Frequency: Dependent on funds available
Study Establishment: University College London
Country of Study: United Kingdom
Application Procedure: No application is necessary. Enquiries should be directed to the department.
Closing Date: May 15th
Additional Information: If the applicant has not already applied to UCL, please complete a graduate application form and enclose it with the scholarship application.

For further information contact:

Centre for Transport Studies
Tel: (44) 20 7679 1554
Fax: (44) 20 7679 1567
Email: civengenquiries@ucl.ac.uk
Contact: Professor R L Mackett

Research Degree Scholarships in Anthropology
Subjects: Anthropology.
Purpose: To financially support research in the field of anthropology.
Level of Study: Doctorate, Postgraduate, Research
Type: Scholarship
Value: United Kingdom/European Union tuition fees
Frequency: Annual
Study Establishment: University College London
Country of Study: United Kingdom
No. of awards offered: Up to 4
Application Procedure: Applicants must contact the department.
Closing Date: April 30th
No. of awards given last year: 4
No. of applicants last year: 12

For further information contact:

Department of Anthropology
Tel: (44) 20 7679 8622
Fax: (44) 20 7679 8632
Email: d.goforth@ucl.ac.uk
Website: www.ucl.ac.uk/anthropology
Contact: Ms Diana Goforth

Ricardo Scholarship
Subjects: Economics.
Purpose: To financially support study and research.

Eligibility: Applicants should have applied for a place for graduate study at UCL.
Level of Study: Doctorate, Postgraduate, Research
Type: Scholarship
Value: UK £950
Frequency: Annual
Study Establishment: University College London
Country of Study: United Kingdom
Application Procedure: Applicants should send particulars of the research work they intend to pursue plus an academic curriculum vitae.
Closing Date: May 15th

For further information contact:

Department of Economics, London,
Tel: (44) 20 7679 5861
Fax: (44) 20 7616 2775
Email: d.fauvrelle@ucl.ac.uk
Contact: Ms Fauvrelle Daniella

Richard Chattaway Scholarship
Subjects: History of modern warfare from 1870.
Purpose: To financially support MPhil/PhD study.
Eligibility: Open to applicants who have applied for a graduate study at UCL. The scholar selected must pursue research for a higher degree at UCL. Receipt of the scholarship must be acknowledged in any publication or research paper which has benefitted from it.
Level of Study: Doctorate, Postgraduate
Type: Scholarship
Value: UK £2,000
Frequency: Annual
Study Establishment: University College London
Country of Study: United Kingdom
Application Procedure: Applicants must contact the department. If the applicants have not already applied to UCL they must complete a graduate application form and enclose it with the scholarship application. Applicants must include particulars of the research work they intend to pursue in the event of the scholarship being awarded to them.
Closing Date: May 15th
Funding: Individuals
Contributor: Private donation in honour of Richard Chattaway
No. of awards given last year: 1

For further information contact:

Department of History
Tel: (44) 20 7679 3897
Fax: (44) 20 7413 8394
Email: n.miller@ucl.ac.uk
Contact: Professor Nicola Miller, Head of the Department

Shell Centenary and Shell Chevening Scholarships
Purpose: To support educational advancement and co-operation worldwide by providing opportunities to study in the UK to students and young professionals from overseas who can demonstrate the potential to become leaders and decision-makers in their own countries.
Eligibility: Applicants should refer to the website for full details on eligibility.
Level of Study: Postgraduate
Type: Scholarship
Value: Tuition fees, maintenance, accomodation and return airfare
Frequency: Annual
No. of awards offered: 8
Application Procedure: Applicants should refer to the website for further information on application procedures, forms and deadlines.

Simon LI/UCL China Law Scholarship
Subjects: Law
Purpose: To financially support chinese students admitted to UCL to pursue PhD studies.
Eligibility: Open to citizens of the People's Republic of China other than Hong Kong who are graduates of Tsinghua University. Candidates joining UCL's LLM programme are also eligible.
Type: Scholarship

Value: Tuition fees, return travel and living expenses
Frequency: Annual
Study Establishment: University College London
Country of Study: United Kingdom
No. of awards offered: 1 (full-time)
Application Procedure: Candidates should first contact the Law Faculty of Beijing University. Short-listed candidates must submit no later than May 15th, a UCL graduate application form together with a written notice of their intention to compete for the scholarship. Candidates should also submit an essay of about 1,200–1,500 words on the subject 'How I shall contribute to the development of the legal system in China' and demonstrate in the essay their desire to do so.
Closing Date: February 11th
Contributor: Simon Li and his family, UCL and the China Scholarship Council
Additional Information: The initial short-listing of candidates will be managed by the China Scholarship Council (CSC) working with the Law Faculty of Beijing University. It is a condition that the award holders will return to China upon completion of their study at UCL. For further information contact the Entrance Scholarships Office.

Sir Frederick Pollock Scholarship for Students from North America
Subjects: LLM.
Purpose: To financially support prospective LLM students.
Eligibility: Applicants must be overseas students from North America. An applicant must have accepted an offer (either conditional or unconditional) to read for the LLM at UCL to be eligible.
Level of Study: Postgraduate
Type: Scholarship
Value: £2,000
Frequency: Annual
Country of Study: United Kingdom
No. of awards offered: 10
Application Procedure: Application forms are available from the department.
Closing Date: May 31st
Additional Information: The scholarships will be based on academic merit. The faculty will only consider those applicants who have firmly accepted their offer of admission to the LLM by May 31st.

For further information contact:

Faculty of Laws
Tel: 44 0 20 7679 1441
Fax: 44 0 20 7209 3470
Email: graduatelaw@ucl.ac.uk
Contact: The Graduate Officer

Sir George Jessel Studentship in Mathematics
Subjects: Mathematics.
Purpose: To financially support MPhil/PhD research.
Eligibility: Applicants must be graduates of University College London. Normally, the student elected must pursue a course of study and research for a higher degree at U.C.L.
Level of Study: Doctorate, Postgraduate, Research
Type: Studentship
Value: UK £1,800
Frequency: Annual
Study Establishment: University College London
Country of Study: United Kingdom
No. of awards offered: 1
Application Procedure: Applicants must contact the department.

For further information contact:

Department of Mathematics
Tel: (44) 20 7679 2839
Fax: (44) 20 7383 5519
Email: h.higgins@ucl.ac.uk
Contact: Ms Helen Higgins

Sir James Lighthill Scholarship
Subjects: Applied mathematics.
Purpose: To financially support MPhil/PhD research.

Eligibility: United Kingdom, European Union and overseas students are eligible to apply.
Level of Study: Postgraduate, Doctorate, Research
Type: Scholarship
Value: Up to £500 per year
Frequency: Annual
Study Establishment: University College London
Country of Study: United Kingdom
Application Procedure: Applicants must contact the department.

For further information contact:

Department of Mathematics
Tel: 20 7679 2839
Email: h.higgins@ucl.ac.uk
Contact: Ms Helen Higgins

Sir John Salmond Scholarship for Students from Australia and New Zealand
Subjects: Law.
Purpose: To financially support prospective LLM students.
Eligibility: Applicants must be overseas students from Australia and New Zealand. An applicant must have accepted an offer (either conditional or unconditional) to read for the LLM at UCL to be eligible.
Level of Study: Postgraduate
Type: Scholarship
Value: UK £2,000
Frequency: Annual
Study Establishment: University College London
Country of Study: United Kingdom
No. of awards offered: 10
Application Procedure: Application forms are available from the department.
Closing Date: May 31st
Additional Information: The scholarships will be based on academic merit. The faculty will only consider these applicants who have firmly accepted their offer of admission to the LLM by May 31st.

For further information contact:

Faculty of Laws
Tel: 44 0 20 7679 1441
Fax: 44 0 20 7209 3470
Email: graduatelaw@ucl.ac.uk
Contact: The Graduate Officer

Sully Scholarship
Subjects: Psychology.
Purpose: To financially support MPhil/PhD research.
Eligibility: Open to United Kingdom, European Union and overseas applicants and awarded to the best existing MPhil student after one year with the best performance (written and oral) at the December upgrade. There is no restriction on age, nationality, residency, etc.
Level of Study: Doctorate, Postgraduate, Research
Type: Scholarship
Value: UK £2,200
Frequency: Annual
Study Establishment: University College London
Country of Study: United Kingdom
No. of awards offered: 1
Application Procedure: There is no separate application and the award is given to an outstanding student who is registered in the department's PhD programme and is in the second year of study.
No. of awards given last year: 1

For further information contact:

Department of Psychology
Tel: 44 0 20 7679 5332
Fax: 44 0 20 7430 4276
Email: psychology-pg-enquiries@ucl.ac.uk
Contact: Head of the Department

Teaching Assistantships (Economics)
Subjects: Economics.
Purpose: To financially support MPhil/PhD students.

Eligibility: MPhil/PhD students who have successfully completed their 1st year in the department.
Level of Study: Doctorate
Type: Assistantship
Value: UK £11,000
Frequency: Annual
Study Establishment: University College London
Country of Study: United Kingdom

Ted Hollis Scholarship

Subjects: Wetland hydrology and conservation.
Purpose: To financially support a student pursuing research leading to a PhD.
Eligibility: Open to United Kingdom, European Union and overseas students who have applied for a place for graduate study at UCL. The scholar elected must pursue research leading to a PhD in geography at UCL.
Level of Study: Doctorate
Type: Scholarship
Value: Full time home fees plus maintenance grant equivalent to NERC (London rate)
Frequency: Every 3 years
Study Establishment: University College London
Country of Study: United Kingdom
No. of awards offered: 1
Application Procedure: Applicants must contact the department at the address given below. If the applicants have not applied to UCL they must complete a graduate application form and enclose it with the scholarship application. Candidates should send particulars of the research work they intend to pursue in the event of the scholarship being awarded to them.
Closing Date: May 15th

For further information contact:

Graduate Admissions, Department of Geography, University College London, Gower Street, London, WC1E 6BT, United Kingdom
Tel: (44) 20 7679 5500

Thomas Witherden Batt Scholarship

Subjects: Life sciences and mathematical and physical sciences.
Purpose: To financially support students to pursue MPhil/PhD research.
Eligibility: Open to United Kingdom nationals only.
Level of Study: Doctorate, Postgraduate, Research
Type: Scholarship
Frequency: Annual
Study Establishment: University College London
Country of Study: United Kingdom
Application Procedure: Applicants should contact the department.

For further information contact:

Faculty of Mathematical and Physical Sciences
Tel: (44) 20 7679 3359

UCL Celebration 60 Scholarship

Purpose: To celebrate 60 year's presence of the British Council in Hong Kong by giving Hong Kong students the chance to experience UK education.
Eligibility: 1. Applicants should be permanent residents of the Hong Kong Special Administrative Region of PR China. 2. Applicants should not be working or studying in the UK at the time of application. 3. Applicants should have applied for admission to a one-year taught Master's degree programme in any department at UCL. 4. Applicants should have received an offer of admission to UCL by March 1st.
Level of Study: Postgraduate
Type: Scholarship
Value: Covers full tuition fees for the scholar selected
Length of Study: 1 year
Study Establishment: United College London
Country of Study: United Kingdom
No. of awards offered: 1
Application Procedure: Information and online admissions application is available from the prospective student pages of the UCL website www.ucl.ac.uk

Closing Date: February 28th
Contributor: United College London

For further information contact:

British Council, Hong Kong
Website: www.britishcouncil.org/hongkong

UCL Global Excellence Scholarship

Purpose: To reward academic excellence among new UCL students.
Eligibility: Applicants should refer to the website for full details on eligibility.
Level of Study: Postgraduate
Type: Scholarship
Value: £5,000
Frequency: Annual
No. of awards offered: 16
Application Procedure: Applicants should refer to the website for further information on application procedures, forms and deadlines.

UCL Graduate Research Scholarships for Cross-Disciplinary Training

Subjects: All subjects.
Purpose: To support students in acquiring research skills and knowledge from a different discipline that can be applied in their normal area of research.
Eligibility: Applicants must be admitted to or currently registered at UCL for full-time MPhil/PhD or Engineering research and in receipt of three years funding for their normal MPhil/PhD or Engineering programme.
Level of Study: Doctorate, Postgraduate
Type: Scholarship
Value: Tuition fees at the UK/EU rate plus maintanance allowance of £14,600
Length of Study: 1 year
Frequency: Annual
Study Establishment: University College London
Country of Study: United Kingdom
No. of awards offered: Up to 4
Application Procedure: Applicants should refer to the website for further details about the application procedures and deadlines.
Closing Date: Refer to the website
No. of awards given last year: 4

For further information contact:

Entrance Scholarships Office, Registrar's Division
Tel: (44) 20 7679 2005/4167
Website: www.ucl.ac.uk/scholarships

The UCL Hong Kong Alumni Scholarship

Purpose: To provide financial need for studies at UCL.
Eligibility: 1. Applicants must be holders of Hong Kong Permanent Identity Cards or Chinese citizens who have received full-time education in Hong Kong and/or China for no less than 5 of the 8 years immediately prior to the start of the study at UCL. 2. Applicants must hold an offer of admission to full-time undergraduate study at UCL – in any area except Medicine – which they have firmly accepted or intend to do so. 3. Applicants must be self-financing and liable to pay tuition fees at the rate for overseas students. 4. Applicants should be in financial need and unable to fund their planned studies at UCL without financial help.
Type: Scholarship
Value: UK £10,000 toward tuition fees for a maximum of 4 years
Length of Study: 4 years
Study Establishment: United College London
Country of Study: United Kingdom
No. of awards offered: 1
Application Procedure: Completed UG HK application form should be submitted along with the required documentationas detailed in the form to UCL Scholarships.
Closing Date: April 1st
Additional Information: Interviews will be held in Hong Kong and applicants invited for the interview will be required to present themselves for interview in Hong Kong at applicants' own expense.

For further information contact:

UCL Scholarships, The Registry, University College London, Gower Street, London, WC1E 6BT, United Kingdom
Fax: (44) 44 (0) 20 7679 2724

UCL Marshall Scholarships

Purpose: To strengthen the enduring relationship between the British and American people, their governments and their institutions.
Eligibility: 1. Applicants must fulfil the eligibility criteria required for a Marshall Scholarship and have been selected for a Marshall Scholarship. 2. Applicants must have been selected by the MACC Committees to study at UCL. 3. Applicants must have followed the usual admission procedures at UCL and be holding an offer of admission to pursue graduate studies in any subject available at UCL.
Level of Study: Graduate
Type: Scholarship
Length of Study: 2 years
Frequency: Annual
Study Establishment: University College London
Country of Study: United Kingdom
No. of awards offered: 1
Application Procedure: Application is available at the website www.marshallscholarship.org/

UCL Simon Li Graduate Scholarship Fund

Purpose: To support Chinese students admitted to UCL to undertake research, and who are supported by the China Research Council (CSC).
Eligibility: Applicants should refer to the website for full details on eligibility.
Level of Study: Postgraduate, Research
Type: Scholarship
Value: Fees and/or maintenance
Frequency: Annual
No. of awards offered: Variable
Application Procedure: Applicants should refer to the website for further information on application procedures, forms and deadlines.

UCL UPC Progression Scholarships

Purpose: To encourage University Preparatory Certificate for Science and Engineering (UPCSE) and University Preparatory Certificate for Humanities and Social Sciences (UPCH) students to continue to undergraduate study at UCL and recruit new students into UCL's UPCSE and UPCH programmes.
Eligibility: Candidates will be enrolled on UCL's UPCSE or UPCH programme and admitted for undergraduate studies at UCL.
Level of Study: Undergraduate
Type: Scholarship
Value: UK £5,000 per annum for the duration of the undergraduate programme. Scholarships will be applied to fees with any remainder paid as a maintenance allowance
Study Establishment: University College London
Country of Study: United Kingdom
No. of awards offered: 2
Application Procedure: All UCL UPCSE/UPCH students holding an offer of admission for undergraduate studies at UCL will be considered.

UCL Vinson Chu Graduate Scholarship Fund

Purpose: To support Chinese students admitted to UCL to undertake research, and who are supported by the China Research Council (CSC).
Eligibility: Applicants should refer to the website for full details on eligibility.
Level of Study: Postgraduate, Research
Type: Scholarship
Value: Fees and/or maintenance
Frequency: Annual
No. of awards offered: Varies
Application Procedure: Applicants should refer to the website for further information on application, procedures, forms and deadlines.

UCL Wellcome Trust Vacation Scholarships

Purpose: To provide promising undergraduates 'hands-on' research experience during the summer vacation and to encourage them to consider a career in research.
Eligibility: Applicants must be undergraduate students registered at a university within the UK or Ireland (including UCL) who are currently enrolled in the middle year(s) of their undergraduate degree in a basic science, veterinary science or dentistry; or are currently enrolled between the end of their second year and the end of their penultimate year of a medical degree; and have secured a vacation research project placement at UCL in an area of biomedicine.
Level of Study: Undergraduate
Type: Scholarship
Value: Each award consists of a weekly stipend of a maximum of for a maximum of 8 weeks over the summer vacations. The weekly stipend rate is for scholarships for placements at UCL is UK £190 (2008 rate)
Study Establishment: University College London
Country of Study: United Kingdom
Application Procedure: Completed application forms must be submitted both electronically as an email attachment and as a hard copy with original signatures.

UCL-UWC Undergraduate International Outreach Bursaries

Purpose: To enable graduates of a UWC, who are financially unable to study in the UK, to pursue full-time undergraduate studies at UCL.
Eligibility: 1. Applicants must be a final-year IB diploma student attending a United World College, or in case of candidates coming from Waterford KaMhlaba UWC, have completed their studies in the preceding calendar year. 2. Applicants must have before or by January applied for admission through UCAS to a full-time undergraduate degree programme of study at UCL. 3. Applicants must be liable to pay tuition fees at the rate applicable to Overseas students, as assessed by UCL. 4. Applicants must lack the financial means necessary to pursue undergraduate degree studies at UCL.
Level of Study: Graduate
Type: Bursary
Value: Each bursary will consist of full tuition fees and a maintenance allowance for the duration of the student's programme of study, as well as international economy air travel to/from the UK at the beginning and end of the bursary-holder's degree programme. The maintenance of allowance will normally rise each year in line with inflation but at the absolute discretion of UCL
Frequency: Annual
Study Establishment: University College London
Country of Study: United Kingdom
No. of awards offered: 2
Application Procedure: For information about undergraduate admission to UCL, please see www.ucl.ac.uk/prospective-students/undergraduate-study/application-and-entry.ucas/
Closing Date: March 15th
No. of applicants last year: 3

The Vinson Chu Charitable Foundation Scholarship

Purpose: To provide financial need for studies at UCL.
Eligibility: 1. Applicants must be holders of Hong Kong Permanent Identity Cards or Chinese citizens who have received full-time education in Hong Kong and/or China for no less than 5 of the 8 years immediately prior to the start of study at UCL. 2. Applicants must hold an offer of admission to full-time undergraduate study at UCL in any area except medicine which they have firmly accepted or intend to do so. 3. Applicants must be self-financing and liable to pay tuition fees at the rate for overseas students. 4. Applicants should be in financial need and unable to fund their planned studies at UCL without financial help.
Level of Study: Undergraduate
Type: Scholarship
Value: UK £10,000 toward tuition fees for a maximum of 4 years
Study Establishment: United College London
Country of Study: United Kingdom
No. of awards offered: 1

Application Procedure: Completed UG HK application form must be submitted along with the required documentation as detailed in the form to UCL Scholarships.

Additional Information: Interviews will be held in Hong Kong and applicants invited for interview will be required to present themselves for interview in Hong Kong at applicants' own expense.

For further information contact:

UCL Scholarships, The Registry, University College London, Gower Street, London, WC1E 6BT, United Kingdom
Tel: (44) 44 (0)20 7679 2724

Vinson Chu/UCL China Law

Subjects: Law.
Purpose: To financially support graduate students.
Eligibility: Open to citizens of the People's Republic of China, other than Hong Kong who are graduates of Beijing University. Applicants joining UCL's LLM programme are also eligible.
Level of Study: Postgraduate
Type: Scholarship
Value: Tuition fees, return travel and living expenses
Frequency: Annual
Study Establishment: University College London
Country of Study: United Kingdom
No. of awards offered: 1 (full-time)
Application Procedure: Candidates should first contact the Law Faculty at Beijing University. Short-listed candidates must submit no later than May 15th a UCL graduate application form together with a written notice of their intention to compete for the scholarship. Applicants should also submit an essay of about 1,200–1,500 words on the subject 'How I shall contribute to the development of the legal system in China' and demonstrate in the essay their desire to do so.
Closing Date: May 15th
Contributor: Vinson Chu family, UCL and the China Scholarship Council
Additional Information: The initial short-listing of candidates will be managed by the China Scholarship Council (CSC) working with the Law Faculty of Beijing University. It is a condition that the award holders will return to China upon completion of their study at UCL.

For further information contact:

Entrance Scholarships Office

W M Gorman Graduate Research Scholarship

Subjects: Economics.
Purpose: To financially support students entering the first year of the MPhil/PhD degree in department of Economics.
Eligibility: Open to candidates who have applied for a place for graduate study at UCL.
Level of Study: Doctorate, Postgraduate
Type: Scholarship
Value: UK £9,000
Frequency: Annual
Study Establishment: University College London
Country of Study: United Kingdom
No. of awards offered: Up to 8
Application Procedure: Candidates should send an academic curriculum vitae and a letter of no more than 500 words describing the particulars of the research work they intend to pursue.
Closing Date: May 15th
Additional Information: The scholarship will be awarded to students who are not already receiving full financial support from other sources for fees and living costs, and will be, awarded on the basis of academic merit.

For further information contact:

Department of Economics
Tel: 20 7679 5861
Fax: 20 7916 2775
Email: d.fauvrelle@ucl.ac.uk
Contact: Ms Daniella Fauvrelle

UNIVERSITY INSTITUTE OF EUROPEAN STUDIES

Via Maria Vittoria 26, I-10123 Turin, Italy
Tel: (39) 011 839 4660
Fax: (39) 011 839 4664
Email: info@iuse.it
Website: www.iuse.it
Contact: Ms Maria Grazia Goiettina, Course Secretariat

The University Institute of European Studies promotes international relations and European integration by organizing academic activities. The Institute has a comprehensive library in international law and economics. Since 1952 the Institute has been a European Documentation Centre (EDC), thus receiving all official publications of European institutions.

International Trade Law Postgraduate Scholarships

Subjects: International trade law focusing on the origin and evolution of international trade, instruments and rules of the main economic international organizations, sources of law in international trade, legal aspects of international contracts in international trade, conflict of laws, modes of payment taxation, arbitration and dispute resolution.
Purpose: To allow students to attend the postgraduate course on international trade law, jointly organized by the University Institute of European Studies and the International Trading Centre of the ILO.
Eligibility: Open to Italian and foreign graduates in law, business and economics. Candidates from Turin are not eligible.
Level of Study: Postgraduate
Type: Scholarship
Value: Part of the accommodation expenses or registration fees
Length of Study: 3 months
Frequency: Annual
Study Establishment: The ILO Turin Centre
Country of Study: Italy
No. of awards offered: Varies
Application Procedure: Candidates should fill in the application form, obtainable from the Secretariat or the website (http://tradelaw.iuse.it/). Copies of the applicant's degrees, including a transcript of academic records and a certificate of English knowledge, should be attached.
Closing Date: Mid-January
Funding: Private
No. of awards given last year: 8
No. of applicants last year: 250
Additional Information: The course aims to provide candidates with a common approach to the main legal issues in international trade law and contract drafting. Lecturers are prominent Italian and international experts, university professors or practitioners and senior officials of international institutions. The course, usually held in Spring, is in English. The number of participants is limited and full-time participation is required throughout the programme.

Law & Business in Europe Fellowships

Subjects: The programme has been designed in the field of European economic law, business and competition, such as: European Governance (European institutions and policies, economic freedoms, external policies); Competition (antitrust, multilateral relations, state aids, public procurement, public utilities, intellectual properties); Enterprises (European company law, EU small and medium size enterprises (SMEs) policies, financial transparency, customer protection, tax law and modes of payment, e-commerce, information society); European Financial Support (structural funds, European programmes and regional policy, EU projects). Participants will be also exposed to EU gateway and databases and EU recruitment procedures.
Purpose: To allow students to attend the Law & Business in Europe: Post Graduate Course in Economic Law and Competition in European Union, jointly organised by the University Institute of European Studies and the Centre for Studies Federalism.
Eligibility: Open to Italian and foreign graduates in law, business, economics, political science or with equivalent qualifications and undergraduates in the final year of attendance (provided they are on schedule with their exams).
Level of Study: Postgraduate
Type: Fellowship
Value: Part of accommodation expenses and/or registration fees

Length of Study: 11 weeks
Frequency: Annual
Study Establishment: Collegio Carlo Alberto, Moncalieri (Turin)
Country of Study: Italy
No. of awards offered: Varies
Application Procedure: Candidates should fill in the application form, which may be obtained from the L.B.E. course secretariat or downloadable from the website http://lbeurope.iuse.it. Copies of the official degree certificates with the official lists of academic results, a complete curriculam vitae (including postal and e-mail adresses) and where the applicant's mother tongue is not English a certification of proficience in English must be enclosed within the application form.
Closing Date: Mid-June
Funding: Foundation
Contributor: Compagnia di San Paolo, Turin (Italy)
No. of awards given last year: 8
No. of applicants last year: 100
Additional Information: This course, aims at providing young graduates with specific and practical competencies on EU regulations and markets, including competition and regional policies. Lecturers are prominent Italian and international experts, University professors, senior officials from regional and international institutions (mainly from EU), business managers, law consultants and practitioners. The course is taught in English. Full-time attendance is required throughout the programme.

THE UNIVERSITY OF ADELAIDE

National Wine Centre of Australia, Corner of Botanic and Hackney Road, Adelaide, SA, 5005, Australia
Tel: (61) 61 8 8303 3355
Fax: (61) 61 8 8303 7444
Email: student.centre@adelaide.edu.au
Website: www.adelaide.edu.au
Contact: Adelaide Graduate Centre

University of Adelaide was established in 1874 and has been amongst Australia's leading universities. Its contribution to the wealth and wellbeing of South Australia and Australia as a whole in all fields of endeavour has been enormous. The university is committed to producing graduates recognised worldwide for their creativity, knowledge and skills, as well as their culture and tolerance.

Adelaide Postgraduate Coursework Scholarships
Subjects: All subjects.
Eligibility: Open only to the citizens of Australia or permanent residents who have achieved Honours 1 or equivalent.
Level of Study: Postgraduate
Type: Scholarship
Value: Australian $20,427 per year
Length of Study: 2 years
Frequency: Annual
Study Establishment: University of Adelaide
Country of Study: Australia
No. of awards offered: 2
Application Procedure: Applicants must apply directly to the scholarship provider. Check website for further details.
Closing Date: October 31st

For further information contact:

Adelaide Graduate Centre, Adelaide University, Adelaide, South Australia, 5005, Australia
Tel: (61) 08 8303 3044
Fax: (61) 08 8223 3394
Email: adrienne.gorringe@adelaide.edu.au
Website: www.adelaide.edu.au/GSSO

Adelaide Scholarships International
Subjects: All subjects.
Purpose: To attract high quality overseas postgraduate students to areas of research strength in the University of Adelaide to support its research effort.
Eligibility: Open only to the citizens of Australia or permanent residents who have achieved Honours 1 or equivalent.
Level of Study: Postgraduate

Type: Scholarships
Value: Australian $20, 427 per year
Length of Study: 2 years (Masters) or 3 years (PhD)
Frequency: Annual
Study Establishment: University of Adelaide
Country of Study: Australia
No. of awards offered: 10
Application Procedure: Candidates must apply directly to the university. Check the website for further details.
Closing Date: August 31st
Contributor: Adelaide University

For further information contact:

Email: student.centre@adelaide.edu.au
Website: www.international.adelaide.edu.au/

Ferry Scholarship – UniSA
Subjects: Chemistry and physics.
Purpose: To promote study and research into the scientific fields of physics and chemistry.
Eligibility: Open only to the citizens of Australia below the age of 25 who have achieved Honours 1 or equivalent.
Level of Study: Postgraduate
Type: Scholarship
Value: Australian $25,118 per year
Length of Study: 2 years (Masters) or 3 years (PhD)
Frequency: Annual
Study Establishment: Flinders University, The University of Adelaide, University of South Australia
Country of Study: Australia
No. of awards offered: 1
Application Procedure: Applicants must apply directly to the university. Check the website for further details.
Closing Date: October 31st
Funding: Individuals
Contributor: Late Cedric Arnold Seth Ferry

For further information contact:

University of South Australia, Australian Admissions and Scholarships
Tel: 8302 3967
Email: jenni.critcher@unisa.edu.au
Contact: Jenni Critcher

The G O Lawrence Scholarship
Subjects: Operative dentistry, crown and bridgework, endodontics, related dental materials, implantology and those parts of paedodontics which involved the above treatments.
Purpose: To enable students to undertake postgraduate study or research in the fields of operative dentistry, crown and bridgework, endodontics, related dental materials, implantology and those parts of paedodontics which involved the above treatments.
Eligibility: Open to candidates who are postgraduate and undertake study or research in fields of operative dentistry, crown and bridgework, endodontics, related dental materials, implantology and those parts of paedodontics which involved the above treatments. However, the relevance of the applicant's research topic is considered when deeming eligibility.
Level of Study: Postgraduate
Type: Scholarship
Value: $20,427
Application Procedure: Check website for further details.
Closing Date: October 31st

Grape and Wine Research and Development Corporation Honours Scholarships
Subjects: Viticulture.
Purpose: To help attract an increasing number of postgraduate students to the fields of wine and viticultural research.
Eligibility: Scholarships will be awarded on the basis of academic excellence, the quality of an applicant's curriculum vitae and the likelihood of the candidate's future involvement in the wine industry.
Level of Study: Postgraduate

Type: Scholarships
Value: Australian $6,000
Frequency: Annual
Country of Study: Australia
No. of awards offered: 7
Application Procedure: Application forms can be downloaded from the website.
Closing Date: December
Contributor: Australian Wine Industry and the Australian Government

For further information contact:

Website: www.gwrdc.com.au/applicationForms.asp

The Herbert Gill-Williams Scholarship

Subjects: Dentistry.
Purpose: To support a full-time candidate of outstanding merit to undertake further research studies in dentistry at Adelaide University.
Eligibility: Open to the full-time candidates who have Honours Degree of Bachelor of Science in dentistry and have been accepted into a programme of study leading to a research degree in the Dental School. Check website for further details.
Level of Study: Postgraduate
Type: Scholarship
Value: $20,427
Length of Study: 1 year
Application Procedure: Check website for further details.
Closing Date: October 31st

The Oliver Rutherford-Turner Scholarship

Subjects: Dentistry.
Purpose: Assist students to undertake a higher degree in a field of dentistry.
Eligibility: Open only to the permanent residents of Australia and New Zealand with a 4 year undergraduate degree or equivalent, (First Class Honours degree or equivalent for Australians) with minimum English language proficiency. Check website for further details.
Level of Study: Postgraduate
Type: Scholarship
Value: Australian $20,427
Application Procedure: Check website for further details.
Closing Date: October 31st
Funding: Private
Contributor: Bequest from the late Oliver Rutherford Turner

Scholarships in Plant Cell Physiology

Subjects: Plant cell physiology.
Purpose: To improve the nutritional qualities of crop plants allowing the fortification of animal and human diets without adversely affecting crop plant.
Eligibility: Open only to the citizens of Australia who have achieved Honours 1 or equivalent, or Honours 2a or equivalent.
Level of Study: Postgraduate
Type: Scholarship
Value: Australian $27,500 per year
Length of Study: 3 years
Frequency: Annual
Study Establishment: The University of Adelaide
Country of Study: Australia
No. of awards offered: 1
Application Procedure: Applicants must apply directly to the university. Check website for further details.
Closing Date: August 31st
Contributor: Adelaide University

For further information contact:

Plant Research Centre, University of Adelaide, PMB 1, Glen Osmond, South Australia, 5064, Australia
Tel: (61) 08 8303 8145
Email: matthew.gillam@adelaide.edu.au
Website: www.adelaide.edu.au/GSSO
Contact: Dr Matthew Gillam

UNIVERSITY OF ALBERTA

Killam Centre for Advanced Studies, 2-29 Triffo Mall Edmonton, Alberta, T6G 2E1, Canada
Tel: (1) 780 492 3499
Fax: (1) 780 492 0692
Email: grad.services@ualberta.ca
Website: www.gradstudies.ualberta.ca

Opened in 1908, the University of Alberta has a long tradition of scholarly achievements and commitment to excellence in teaching, research and service to the community. It is one of Canada's five largest research-intensive universities, with an annual research income from external sources of more than Canadian $300 million. It participates in 18 of 21 of the Federal Networks of Centres of Excellence, which link industries, universities and governments in applied research and development.

Grant Notley Memorial Postdoctoral Fellowship

Subjects: The politics, history, economy or society of Western Canada and related fields.
Purpose: To encourage scholars of superior research ability who graduated within the last 3 years.
Eligibility: Open to citizens of any country, must have completed a doctoral degree or will do so in the immediate future, must have obtained doctorate degree from a university other than University of Alberta, must not currently hold a postdoc or be employed at the University of Alberta, must not hold or have held any other fellowships, must not hold faculty position, fellowship holders should be likely to contribute to the advancement of learning. Fellowships are only tenable at the University of Alberta. Applicants must visit the website for additional information.
Level of Study: Postdoctorate
Type: Fellowship
Value: Canadian $44,000 per year and a non-renewable research grant of Canadian $4,000
Length of Study: 2 years
Frequency: Annual
Study Establishment: The University of Alberta
Country of Study: Canada
No. of awards offered: 1
Application Procedure: Applicants must visit the website for application information.
Closing Date: December 16th
Funding: Private
No. of awards given last year: 1
No. of applicants last year: 9

Izaak Walton Killam Memorial Scholarships

Subjects: All subjects.
Eligibility: Open to candidates of any nationality who are registered in, or are admissible to, a doctoral programme at the University. Scholars must have completed at least 1 year of graduate work prior to beginning the scholarship. Applicants must be nominated by the department in which they plan to pursue their doctoral studies.
Level of Study: Doctorate
Type: Scholarship
Value: Canadian $27,000 per year plus a non-renewable research grant of Canadian $2,000, tuition and fees
Length of Study: 2 years from May 1st or September 1st, subject to review after the 1st year
Frequency: Annual
Study Establishment: The University of Alberta
Country of Study: Canada
No. of awards offered: Approx. 20
Application Procedure: Applicants must visit the website for application information.
Closing Date: March 2nd for the submission of nominations from departments. Please check with the department for their internal deadline
Funding: Private
No. of awards given last year: 13
No. of applicants last year: 115

Queen Elizabeth II Scholarships-Doctoral

Subjects: All subjects.

Eligibility: Open to Canadian citizens or permanent residents at the date of application who have completed at least 1 year of graduate study and who are registered in a full-time doctoral programme at the University of Alberta. Applicants must be nominated by the department in which they plan to pursue their studies. Students registered as qualifying graduates or probationary students are not eligible.
Level of Study: Doctorate
Type: Fellowship
Value: Canadian $15,000 for commencement in May and Canadian $7,500 for commencement in September
Length of Study: 8 months from September 1st or January 1st (4 months)
Frequency: Annual
Study Establishment: The University of Alberta
Country of Study: Canada
No. of awards offered: Approx. 234
Application Procedure: Visit the website for application information.
Closing Date: Departments may submit nominations from departments. Please check with the department for their internal deadline
Funding: Government
No. of awards given last year: 217
No. of applicants last year: 732
Additional Information: Recipients must carry out a full-time research programme during the Summer months.

Queen Elizabeth II Scholarships-Master's

Subjects: All subjects.
Eligibility: Open to Canadian citizens or permanent residents who are entering or continuing, at the date of application, in a full-time Master's programme at the University of Alberta. Applicants must be nominated by the department in which they plan to pursue their studies. Students registered as qualifying graduates or probationary students are not eligible.
Level of Study: Graduate
Type: Scholarship
Value: Canadian $9,300 for commencement in May, Canadian $6,200 for commencement in September
Length of Study: 8 months from September 1st or January 1st (4 months)
Frequency: Annual
Study Establishment: The University of Alberta
Country of Study: Canada
No. of awards offered: Approx. 242
Application Procedure: Applicants must visit the website for application information.
Closing Date: February 1st for the submission of nominations from departments. Please check with the department for their internal deadline
Funding: Government
No. of awards given last year: 242
No. of applicants last year: 744
Additional Information: Recipients must carry out a full-time research programmes during the summer months.

Walter H Johns Graduate Fellowship

Subjects: All subjects.
Eligibility: Open to students registered full-time in a Graduate Degree programme who are receiving an eligible scholarship of less than $30,000 from NSERC, SSHRC, or CIHR.
Level of Study: Postgraduate
Type: Fellowship
Value: Canadian $4,435
Application Procedure: Check website for further details.
Closing Date: January 5th and September 5th

For further information contact:

Faculty of Graduate Studies and Research, Killam Centre for Advanced Studies, 2-29 Triffo Hall
Website: www.gradstudies.ualberta.ca

THE UNIVERSITY OF AUCKLAND

Private Bag 92019, Auckland Mail Centre, Auckland, 1142, New Zealand
Tel: (64) 64 9 373 7999
Email: rfatialofa.patolo@auckland.ac.nz
Website: www.auckland.ac.nz

The University of Auckland is New Zealand's pre-eminent research-led University. Established in 1883, it has grown into an international centre of learning and academic excellence and now is the largest university in New Zealand. Its mission is to be an internationally recognised, research-led university, known for the excellence in teaching, research, and service to its local, national and international communities. It aims to be a vibrant and intellectually challenging place of learning and nurturing a community of scholars who share a passion for discovery, the advance of knowledge and human progress.

Anne Bellam Scholarship

Subjects: Music.
Purpose: To assist students to further their musical education overseas.
Eligibility: The candidate must be under 30 years of age and a citizen of New Zealand, must have compeleted or will complete in the year of application any degree or diploma in performance or any postgraduate music degree at the University of Auckland.
Level of Study: Postgraduate
Type: Scholarship
Value: Up to $30,000 for study overseas and up to $10,000 for study at the University of Auckland
Length of Study: 1 year
Frequency: Annual
Study Establishment: University of Auckland
Country of Study: New Zealand
Application Procedure: The candidate must supply, one week in advance of examination, an outline of his proposed study plans and itinerary.
Closing Date: September 30th
Funding: Government

For further information contact:

Faculty of Creative Arts and Industries: School of Music, Auckland, New Zealand
Email: scholarships@auckland.ac.nz
Website: www.auckland.ac.nz/scholarships

Arthington Davy Scholarship

Subjects: Any subject.
Purpose: To study and research in areas which will significantly contribute to the development of Tonga.
Eligibility: The candidate must be a Tongan citizen, born to Tongan parents and possess a first University degree.
Level of Study: Research
Type: Scholarship
Value: The Arthington Davy Scholarship may cover the cost of part of the cost of a postgraduate study or research programme
Study Establishment: Trinity College
Country of Study: United Kingdom
Application Procedure: The candidate must submit a complete curriculum vitae and academic record, proof of Tongan origin, details of the intended postgraduate study preferably with a letter of conditional acceptance from the University concerned, full details of tuition fees and living expenses and of finances available from the student's own resources or elsewhere and the names of two academic referees.
Closing Date: November 30th (for course commencing in March or April), May 31st (for course commencing in September or October)
Funding: Commercial, foundation, individuals, private

For further information contact:

Trinity College, Cambridge, CB2 1TQ, United Kingdom
Email: hf202@hermes.cam.ac.uk
Contact: Tutor for Advanced Studies

Asian Development Bank Japan Scholarship

Subjects: Envrionmental science, development studies, international business and engineering.

Eligibility: The candidate must possess a minimum English language requirement for entry into postgraduate study at the University of Auckland. IELTS with an overall score of 6.5 and no band less than 6.0 or a TOEFL paper-based 575 with a TWE of 4.5 or computer-based 233 with a TWE of 4.5.
Level of Study: Postgraduate
Type: Scholarship
Value: Tuition fee at the University of Auckland, Airfare from his or her home country to Auckland, New Zealand, Basic cost of living in Auckland, Health and medical insurance in New Zealand, and Airfare from Auckland, New Zealand, to the scholar's home country at the conclusion of his or her course of study.
Study Establishment: University of Auckland
Country of Study: New Zealand
Application Procedure: Applications can be filled online.
Closing Date: June 1st
Funding: Government, private
Contributor: Asian Development Bank and Government of Japan

For further information contact:

The University of Auckland, Auckland International, Private Bag 92018, Auckland, New Zealand
Email: information@adbj.org
Website: www.adb.org

International College of Auckland PhD Scholarship in Plant Sciences

Subjects: Plant Science.
Purpose: To assist eminent Chinese scholars from nominated areas of China to study plant sciences at the University of Auckland and to promote links between China and New Zealand in the field of plant sciences.
Eligibility: The candidate must possess a PhD in the field of plant science and who has paid the fees, or arranged to pay the fees, for full–time enrolment in the School of Biological Sciences.
Level of Study: Postdoctorate
Type: Scholarship
Value: $20,000 per year. The scholarship's emolument will be paid as a tuition/compulsory fees credit and the balance as a fortnightly stipend
Length of Study: 3 years
Frequency: Annual
Study Establishment: University of Auckland
Country of Study: New Zealand
No. of awards offered: 1
Application Procedure: The candidate must submit the completed application form along with the curriculum vitae and atleast two academic reference letters.
Closing Date: October 1st
Funding: Government
Contributor: The International College of Auckland

For further information contact:

Scholarships Office, Room 012, Clock tower, Ground floor, 22 Princes Street, Auckland Central, Auckland, New Zealand
Email: scholarships@auckland.ac.nz

NZ Development Scholarship – Public Category

Subjects: Any subject.
Eligibility: The candidate must be a possess a degree in any discipline.
Level of Study: Postgraduate
Type: Scholarship
Value: Covers tuition fee, airfare, cost of living, health and medical insurance, education of dependant children
Study Establishment: University of Auckland
Country of Study: New Zealand
Application Procedure: The candidate must submit his application form through his home nominating authority. The New Zealand Ministry of Foreign Affairs and Trade seeks placements and decides which institution, polytechnic or university the candidate may study at in New Zealand.
Funding: Government
Contributor: Ministry of Foreign Affairs and Trade, Government of New Zealand

For further information contact:

Website: http://mft.gov.nz

NZ International Doctoral Research (NZIDRS) Scholarship

Subjects: Any subject.
Purpose: To provide financial support for postgraduate students from designated countries seeking doctoral degrees by research in New Zealand universities.
Eligibility: The candidate must hold an 'A' average or equivalent in their studies, meet the requirements for entry into a research-based doctoral degree programme at a New Zealand university.
Level of Study: Doctorate, Research
Type: Research scholarship
Value: The scholarship funding covers tuition fees, a monthly living allowance ($1,708.33 per month), a travel allowance (up to $2,000), a health insurance allowance ($600), an establishment allowance ($500), and a book and thesis allowance ($800)
Length of Study: 3 years
Study Establishment: University of Auckland
Country of Study: New Zealand
Application Procedure: The candidate must complete the application form in English and attach supporting documents as stipulated in the application form.
Closing Date: July 15th
Funding: Government
Contributor: Government of New Zealand

For further information contact:

The Education New Zealand Trust, PO Box 10-500, Wellington, New Zealand
Tel: (64) 64 4 4720788
Fax: (64) 64 4 4712828
Email: scholarships@educationnz.org.nz
Website: www.nzeducated.com/scholarships/documents/NZIDRSApplicationform.doc
Contact: Scholarships Manager

NZAID Development Scholarship (NZDS) – Open Category

Subjects: Any subject.
Eligibility: The candidate must possess minimum English language requirements for entry into the University of Auckland postgraduate study. IELTS (International English Language Testing System Certificate) with an overall score of 6.5 and no band less than 6.0 or a TOEFL (Test of English as a Foreign Language) paper based 575 with a TWE of 4.5 or computer based 233.
Level of Study: Postgraduate
Type: Scholarship
Value: Tuition, enrollment/orientation fees, return economy fare travel, medical insurance and provision for students to meet course and basic living costs
Study Establishment: University of Auckland
Country of Study: New Zealand
Application Procedure: Application form can be downloaded from the website.
Closing Date: June 1st
Funding: Government
Contributor: New Zealand Agency for International Development and the Ministry of Foreign Affairs

For further information contact:

Auckland International Student Information Centre, Auckland, New Zealand
Tel: (64) 64 9 3737599 extn 87556
Fax: (64) 64 9 373 7405
Email: rfatialofa.patolo@auckland.ac.nz

Property Institute of New Zealand Postgraduate Scholarship

Subjects: Real property.
Purpose: To promote postgraduate study in the field of real property.
Eligibility: The candidate must possess a Master's degree or full-time PhD candidate and has the paid the fees, or arranged to pay the fees,

for study in the Department of Property at Lincoln University, Massey University or The University of Auckland.
Level of Study: Doctorate
Type: Scholarship
Value: $1,500
Length of Study: 1 year
Frequency: Annual
Study Establishment: University of Auckland
Country of Study: New Zealand
No. of awards offered: 2
Closing Date: May 1st and March 31st
Funding: Government
Contributor: Property Institute of New Zealand

For further information contact:

The Scholarships Office, The University of Auckland, Private Bag 92019, Auckland, New Zealand
Tel: (64) (09) 373 7599 ext: 87494
Fax: (64) (09) 308 2309
Email: scholarships@auckland.ac.nz

Reardon Postgraduate Scholarship in Music

Subjects: Music.
Purpose: To honour and in memory of Daniel Patrick Reardon and Kathleen Mary Reardon.
Eligibility: The candidate must possess a degree or diploma with a specialisation in Performance in the year of the award.
Level of Study: Postgraduate
Type: Scholarship
Value: $4,500
Length of Study: 1 year
Frequency: Annual
Study Establishment: University of Auckland
Country of Study: New Zealand
No. of awards offered: 1
Closing Date: September 30th
Funding: Government
Contributor: Reardon Memorial Music Trust

For further information contact:

Faculty of Creative Arts and Industries: School of Music, University of Auckland, Auckland, New Zealand
Email: scholarships@auckland.ac.nz
Website: www.auckland.ac.nz/scholarships

University of Auckland Commonwealth Scholarship

Subjects: Any subject.
Purpose: The scholarships are available to students to be enrolled at the University of Auckland for the Degree of Doctor of Philosophy; another approved Doctorate or a Master's degree.
Eligibility: The candidate must be a citizen of Commonwealth of Nations, including Australian, British and Canadian citizens. The candidate must be tenable for a maximum of 36 months for a PhD candidate or 21 months for a Master's candidate.
Level of Study: Doctorate, Postgraduate
Type: Scholarship
Value: New Zealand $15,000 per year plus fees and other allowances
Study Establishment: University of Auckland
Country of Study: New Zealand
Application Procedure: The candidate must send the application for UA Commonwealth Scholarships must be made through the appropriate organization in the scholar's home country on the Commonwealth Scholarship application form.
Closing Date: Varies
Funding: Government

For further information contact:

Scholarships Office, Student Administration, The University of Auckland, Private Bag 92019, Auckland Mail Centre, Auckland, New Zealand
Tel: (64) 64 9 373 7599 ext 87494
Fax: (64) 64 9 308 2309
Email: scholarships @auckland.ac.nz

The University of Auckland Doctoral Scholarship

Subjects: Any subject.
Purpose: To assist and encourage students to pursue doctoral studies at The University of Auckland
Eligibility: The candidate must be a citizen or a permanent resident of New Zealand.
Level of Study: Doctorate
Type: Scholarship
Value: Up to $25,000 plus compulsory fees
Length of Study: 3 years
Frequency: Annual
Study Establishment: University of Auckland
Country of Study: New Zealand
No. of awards offered: Varies
Application Procedure: The candidate must fill the application form and send it to the Scholarships office. The selection will be made on the basis of merit.
Closing Date: November 1st
Funding: Government

For further information contact:

Scholarships Office, University of Auckland, Auckland, New Zealand
Email: scholarships@auckland.ac.nz
Website: www.auckland.ac.nz/scholarships

University of Auckland Fulbright Scholarship

Subjects: Any subject.
Purpose: To encourage and facilitate study for approved postgraduate degrees at the University of Auckland by candidates already selected to hold Fulbright Awards.
Eligibility: The candidate must be a citizen of the United States of America and intending to take up Fulbright Awards to study in New Zealand and should enrol for a full-time at the University of Auckland for an approved Master's or Doctoral degree.
Level of Study: Doctorate, Postgraduate
Type: Scholarship
Value: $15,000 per year plus research/tuition fees
Frequency: Annual
Study Establishment: University of Auckland
Country of Study: New Zealand
No. of awards offered: 3
Application Procedure: The candidate must send the completed application form to the Scholarships office.
Closing Date: No closing date
Funding: Government

For further information contact:

Scholarships Office, Student Administration, The University of Auckland, Private Bag 92019, Auckland Mail Centre, Auckland, 1142, New Zealand
Tel: (64) 64 9 373 7599 ext 87494
Fax: (64) 64 9 308 2309
Email: internationalscholarships@auckland.ac.nz

The University of Auckland International Doctoral Fees Bursary

Subjects: Any subject.
Purpose: To assist international students from all countries who wish to pursue doctoral studies.
Eligibility: Permanent citizens and residents of Australia and New Zealand are not eligible for the scholarship.
Level of Study: Doctorate
Type: Bursary
Value: New Zealand $ 25,000
Frequency: Annual
Study Establishment: University of Auckland
Country of Study: New Zealand
No. of awards offered: Up to 10
Application Procedure: The application form can be obtained from the Scholarships Office, University of Auckland.
Closing Date: August 1st
Funding: Government

For further information contact:

Scholarhips Office, University of Auckland, Private Bag 92019, Auckland Mail Centre, Auckland, 1142, New Zealand
Email: c.tuu@auckland.ac.nz
Website: www.auckland.ac.nz/uoa/for/currentstudents/money/

University of Auckland International Doctoral Scholarship

Subjects: Any subject.
Purpose: To assist international students from all countries who wish to pursue doctoral studies.
Eligibility: The scholarship is available to international students from all countries who wish to pursue Doctoral studies on a full-time basis. Permanent citizens and residents of Australia and New Zealand are not eligible for the scholarship.
Level of Study: Doctorate
Type: Scholarship
Value: New Zealand $25,000, in the form of a fortnightly stipend
Frequency: Annual
Study Establishment: University of Auckland
Country of Study: New Zealand
No. of awards offered: 4
Application Procedure: The application form can be obtained from the Scholarships Office, University of Auckland.
Closing Date: August 1st
Funding: Government

For further information contact:

Scholarships Office, University of Auckland, Private Bag 92019, Auckland Mail Centre, Auckland, 1142, New Zealand
Email: c.tuu@auckland.ac.nz
Website: www.auckland.ac.nz/uoa/for/currentstudents/money/

University of Auckland Maori and Pacific Graduate Scholarships (Doctoral Study)

Subjects: Any subject.
Purpose: To assist Maori and Pacific students enrolled full-time at The University of Auckland for the Degree of Doctor of Philosophy or the research component of another approved Doctorate.
Eligibility: The candidate must be a Maori or Pacific student who are citizens or permanent residents of New Zealand.
Level of Study: Doctorate
Type: Scholarships
Value: Up to $25,000 plus compulsory fees
Length of Study: Up to 3 years
Frequency: Annual
Study Establishment: University of Auckland
Country of Study: New Zealand
No. of awards offered: Varies
Application Procedure: The candidate must fill up the application form and send it to the Scholarships office. Selection will be made on the basis of merit.
Closing Date: November 1st
Funding: Government

For further information contact:

Scholarships Office, University of Auckland, Auckland, New Zealand
Email: scholarships@auckland.ac.nz
Website: www.auckland.ac.nz/scholarships

University of Auckland Maori and Pacific Graduate Scholarships (Masters/Honours/PGDIP)

Subjects: Any subject.
Purpose: To assist and encourage Maori and Pacific students to pursue Masters, Honours and PGDip courses at The University of Auckland.
Eligibility: The candidate must be a Maori or Pacific student who are citizens or permanent residents of New Zealand.
Level of Study: Graduate, Postgraduate
Type: Scholarship
Value: Up to $10,000 plus compulsory fees
Length of Study: 1 year
Frequency: Annual
Study Establishment: University of Auckland

Country of Study: New Zealand
No. of awards offered: Varies
Application Procedure: The candidate must fill up the application form and send it to the Scholarships office. The Selection Committee will assess the application form.
Closing Date: November 1st
Funding: Government

For further information contact:

Scholarships Office, University of Auckland, Auckland, New Zealand
Email: scholarships@auckland.ac.nz
Website: www.auckland.ac.nz/scholarships

University of Auckland Masters/Honours/PGDIP Scholarships

Subjects: Any subject.
Eligibility: The candidate must be a citizen or a permanent resident of New Zealand. In case of a Master's degree, the candidate must be tenable until the date for completion of the requirements for the degree as specified in the General Regulations – Masters degrees.
Level of Study: Graduate, Postgraduate
Type: Scholarship
Value: Up to $10,000 per year plus compulsory fees
Length of Study: 1 year
Frequency: Annual
Study Establishment: University of Auckland
Country of Study: New Zealand
No. of awards offered: Varies
Application Procedure: The candidate must fill the application form and send it to the Scholarships office. Selection will be made on the basis of merit.
Closing Date: November 1st
Funding: Government

For further information contact:

Scholarships Office, University of Auckland, Auckland, New Zealand
Email: scholarships@auckland.ac.nz
Website: www.auckland.ac.nz/scholarships

University of Auckland Senior Health Research Scholarships

Subjects: Health.
Purpose: To attract health professionals to return to the University to study full-time for a PhD in a health-related field.
Eligibility: The candidate must be a citizen or a permanent resident of New Zealand and who have worked for 3 years as a health professional.
Level of Study: Doctorate
Value: $40,000 plus compulsory fees
Length of Study: 3 years
Frequency: Annual
Study Establishment: University of Auckland
Country of Study: New Zealand
No. of awards offered: 3
Application Procedure: The candidate must submit an application form and send it to the Scholarships office. Selection shall be made on the basis of merit.
Closing Date: November 1st
Funding: Government

For further information contact:

Scholarships Office, University of Auckland, Auckland, New Zealand
Email: scholarships@auckland.ac.nz
Website: www.auckland.ac.nz/scholarships

UNIVERSITY OF BALLARAT

Vice-Chancellor's Office, University Drive, Mt Helen, VIC, 3350, Australia
Tel: (61) 3 5327 9000
Fax: (61) 3 5327 9704
Email: international@ballarat.edu.au
Website: www.ballarat.edu.au

The University of Ballarat is Australia's only regional, multi-sector University acknowledged for its excellence in education, training, and research, committed to providing high quality services to students, the community, and the industry. It provides educational and training programs from apprenticeships, certificates and diplomas to post-graduate qualifications, masters, and doctorates by research. International students at the University come from over 25 different countries to participate in a diverse range of TAFE and higher education programmes. The University is proud of its track record in business innovation and entrepreneurship, research, consulting, and educational programs, and promoting new technology in products and services through scientific and industrial research.

Australian Postgraduate Award Research Scholarship

Subjects: Behavioural and cognitive sciences, business and management, education, engineering and technology, human movement and sports science, information, computing and communication sciences, mathematical sciences, nursing, science, social sciences, humanities and arts.
Purpose: To support students and professional doctorates undertaking research.
Eligibility: Open to candidates who have a First Class (Honours) Degree or equivalent.
Level of Study: Postdoctorate, Research
Type: Scholarship
Value: Australian $20,007 per year
Frequency: Annual
Study Establishment: The University of Ballarat
Country of Study: Australia
No. of awards offered: 6
Application Procedure: Check website for further details.
Closing Date: October 31st
Funding: Government
Additional Information: It is required that the study starts no earlier than February 1st.

For further information contact:

PO Box 663, Ballarat, Victoria, 3350, Australia
Tel: (61) 03 5327 9508
Fax: (61) 03 5327 9602
Email: s.murphy@ballarat.edu.au
Website: www.ballarat.edu.au/ard/ubresearch/graduate_studies/index.shtml
Contact: Sarah Murphy, Administrative Assistant

International Postgraduate Research Scholarship

Subjects: All subjects.
Purpose: To provide overseas student health care cover and a stipend.
Eligibility: Open to citizens of all countries except Australia and New Zealand, to candidates with First Class (Honours) Degree or equivalent.
Level of Study: Research
Type: Scholarship
Value: Australian $19,231 per year
Length of Study: 2 years (Masters) and 3 years (PhD)
Frequency: Annual
Study Establishment: The University of Ballarat
Country of Study: Australia
No. of awards offered: 1
Application Procedure: Check website for further details. Application are open from January 1st.
Closing Date: October 31st
Funding: Government
Additional Information: The study should start no earlier than February 1st.

For further information contact:

PO Box 663, Ballarat, Victoria, 3350, Australia
Tel: (61) 03 5327 9508
Fax: (61) 03 5327 9602
Email: s.murphy@ballarat.edu.au
Website: www.ballarat.edu.au/ard/ubresearch/graduate_studies/index.shtml
Contact: Sarah Murphy, Administrative Assistant

Special Overseas Student Scholarship (SOSS)

Subjects: All subjects.
Eligibility: Open to citizens of all countries except Australia, who have achieved First Class (Honours) or equivalent.
Level of Study: Research
Type: Scholarship
Value: Australian $19,231 per year
Length of Study: 3 years
Frequency: Annual
Study Establishment: The University of Ballarat
Country of Study: Australia
No. of awards offered: 1
Application Procedure: Check website for further details. Applications are open from January 1st.
Closing Date: October 31st
Additional Information: The study should start no earlier than January 1st.

For further information contact:

PO Box 663, Ballarat, Victoria, 3350
Tel: 03 5327 9508
Fax: 03 5327 9602
Email: s.murphy@ballarat.edu.au
Website: www.ballarat.edu.au/ard/research/graduate_studies/index.shtml
Contact: Sarah Murphy, Administrative Assistant

University of Ballarat Part Postgraduate Research Scholarship

Subjects: Behavioural and cognitive sciences, business and management, education, engineering and technology, human movement and sports science, information, computing and communication sciences, mathematical sciences, nursing, science, or social sciences, humanities and arts.
Eligibility: Open to citizens of Australia or permanent residents who have achieved First Class (Honours) or equivalent.
Level of Study: Postgraduate, Research
Type: Scholarship
Value: Australian $20,007 per year
Length of Study: 3 years (PhD and Professional Doctorate) and 1.5 years (Masters)
Frequency: Biannual
Study Establishment: University of Ballarat
Country of Study: Australia
No. of awards offered: 5
Application Procedure: Check website for further details. Applications are open from January 3rd.
Closing Date: October 31st
Additional Information: The study should start no earlier than February 1st.

For further information contact:

PO Box 663, Ballarat, Victoria, 3350, Australia
Tel: (61) 03 5327 9508
Fax: (61) 03 5327 9602
Email: s.murphy@ballarat.edu.au
Website: www.ballarat.edu.au/ard/research/graduate_studies/index.shtml
Contact: Sarah Murphy, Administrative Assistant

University of Ballarat Postgraduate Research Scholarship

Subjects: Behavioural and cognitive sciences, business and management, education, engineering and technology, human movement and sports science, information, computing and communication sciences, mathematical sciences, nursing, science, social sciences, humanities and arts.
Purpose: To assist students in postgraduate research.
Eligibility: Open to those who have achieved First Class (Honours) or equivalent. Awards are restricted to Australian citizens or those with residence status and current University of Ballarat IPRS Awardees.
Level of Study: Research, Postgraduate
Type: Scholarship
Value: Australian $19,231 per year

Frequency: Annual
Study Establishment: University of Ballarat
Country of Study: Australia
No. of awards offered: 5
Application Procedure: Check website for further details. Applications are from January 3rd.
Closing Date: October 31st
Additional Information: This scholarship is paid fortnightly. The study should start no earlier than February 1st.

For further information contact:

PO Box 663, Ballarat, Victoria, 3350, Australia
Tel: (61) 03 5327 9508
Fax: (61) 03 5327 9602
Email: s.murphy@ballarat.edu.au
Website: www.ballarat.edu.au/ard/research/graduate_studies/index.shtml
Contact: Sarah Murphy, Administrative Assistant

University of Ballarat Publication Award (UBPA)

Subjects: All subjects.
Purpose: To lift the publications profile of the University by providing financial support to postgraduate students following submission of their theses.
Eligibility: Open to postgraduate candidates who have recently submitted theses.
Level of Study: Postgraduate
Type: Award
Value: Up to $3,000
Length of Study: 2 months
Frequency: Annual
No. of awards offered: Up to 6
Application Procedure: Check website for further details.

UNIVERSITY OF BERGEN

Post Box 7800, N-5020 Bergen, Norway
Tel: (47) 55 580000
Fax: (47) 55 58 96 43
Email: post@fa.uib.no
Website: www.uib.no

The university of Bergen is a young, modern university, which is Norway's International university. The academic profile of the university has two major focuses marine research and co-operation with developing countries.

The Holberg International Memorial Prize/The Holberg Prize

Subjects: Arts and humanities, social science, law and theology.
Purpose: To honor scholars who have made outstanding, internationally recognized contributions to research interdisciplinary work.
Eligibility: Open to outstanding researchers from the relevant academic fields.
Level of Study: Postgraduate
Type: Award
Value: Norwegian Kroner 4.5 million (Approx. US $750,000)
Frequency: Annual
Application Procedure: See the website: www.holbergprisen.no/HP_prisen/en_hp_utlysning.html for details.
Closing Date: January 20th
Funding: Foundation

UNIVERSITY OF BIRMINGHAM

Division of Student Life, Edgbaston, Birmingham, West Midlands, B15 2TT, England
Tel: (44) 121 414 3142
Fax: (44) 0121 414 6637
Email: j.e.bryan@bham.ac.uk
Website: www.as.bham.ac.uk/funding
Contact: Joanne Bryan, Student Funding Manager

The University of Birmingham is a leading research institution, offering a wide range of programmes, high teaching and research standards, and excellent facilities for academic work.

A E Hills Scholarship

Subjects: Any subjects.
Purpose: To support students who have registered for full-time higher studies.
Eligibility: Open to all students who wish to pursue higher degrees.
Level of Study: Postgraduate
Type: Scholarship
Value: Tuition fees at home rate and maintenance
Length of Study: 1 year
Frequency: Annual
Study Establishment: The University of Birmingham
Country of Study: United Kingdom
No. of awards offered: 1
Application Procedure: Schools are asked to nominate their top 2 candidates. Awards are made on academic performance.
Closing Date: Mid-June
Funding: Private
No. of awards given last year: 1
No. of applicants last year: 23

Adrian Brown Scholarship

Subjects: Chemical engineering and biosciences related to brewing sciences and technology.
Eligibility: Open to all students reading a research degree.
Type: Scholarship
Value: Tuition fees and maintenance at research council rates
Length of Study: Tenable for period of study subject to satisfactory progress
Frequency: Dependent on funds available
Study Establishment: The University of Birmingham
Country of Study: United Kingdom
No. of awards offered: 1
Application Procedure: Contact the student funding office at the university for details. Recommendation from the Head of school is required.
Funding: Private

AHRC Studentships

Subjects: Arts and humanities.
Purpose: To support research among the postgraduate community.
Eligibility: UK/EU students.
Level of Study: Postgraduate
Type: Studentship
Value: Majority are fees and maintenance
Length of Study: Normally 3–4 years
Frequency: Annual
Study Establishment: University of Birmingham
Country of Study: United Kingdom
No. of awards offered: Varies
Application Procedure: Applicants must contact schools/departments concerned.
Closing Date: Expected Spring 2009
Additional Information: Due to changes in the AHRC award system current grant availability and applications process for 2009/2010 are not yet known.

BBSRC Studentships

Subjects: Biological sciences.
Purpose: To support research among the postgraduate community.
Eligibility: UK/EU students.
Level of Study: Postgraduate
Type: Studentship
Value: Majority are fees and maintenance
Length of Study: Normally 3–4 years
Frequency: Annual
Study Establishment: University of Birmingham
Country of Study: United Kingdom
No. of awards offered: Varies

Application Procedure: Applicants must contact schools/departments concerned.
No. of awards given last year: 53

Dinshaw Bursary
Subjects: Theology.
Purpose: To support students reading for a research degree.
Eligibility: These bursaries are awarded on the basis of academic merit and financial need. They are mainly aimed at existing students.
Level of Study: Postgraduate
Type: Bursary
Value: £1,000
Length of Study: 1 year
Frequency: Annual
Study Establishment: University of Birmingham
Country of Study: United Kingdom
No. of awards offered: 1
Application Procedure: Details can be obtained from the Student Funding Office or the Department of Theology.
Closing Date: December
Funding: Private

Dudley Docker Research Scholarship
Subjects: Engineering or science discipline
Eligibility: Open to exisiting students at the University of Birmingham who have graduated in a pure or applied science and continuing to undertake research.
Type: Scholarship
Value: UK£1000 towards tuition fees
Frequency: Annual
Study Establishment: The University of Birmingham
Country of Study: United Kingdom
No. of awards offered: 2
Application Procedure: Students are nominated from school only. Applicant must be a current student at the university.
Funding: Private
No. of awards given last year: 2
No. of applicants last year: 3

Edna Pearson Scholarship
Subjects: History.
Purpose: To support students reading for a research degree.
Eligibility: Candidates must also apply to AHRB or equivalent.
Level of Study: Postgraduate
Type: Scholarship
Value: Tuition fees at home rates only/maintenance variable
Length of Study: 1 year
Frequency: Dependent on funds available
Study Establishment: University of Birmingham
Country of Study: United Kingdom
No. of awards offered: 1
Application Procedure: Check website for further details.
Funding: Private
Additional Information: Students need to be nominated by the School of Historical Studies.

EPSRC Studentships
Subjects: Engineering sciences.
Purpose: To support research among the postgraduate community.
Eligibility: UK/EU students.
Level of Study: Postgraduate
Type: Studentship
Value: Majority are fees and maintenance
Length of Study: Varies – normally 3–4 years
Frequency: Annual
Study Establishment: University of Birmingham
Country of Study: United Kingdom
No. of awards offered: Varies normally 34 years
Application Procedure: Applicants must contact schools/departments concerned.
No. of awards given last year: 113

ESRC Studentships
Subjects: Research and taught programmes is ESRC approved areas of study.

Eligibility: Open to home students only.
Type: Scholarship
Frequency: Annual
Study Establishment: The University of Birmingham
Country of Study: United Kingdom
Application Procedure: Application forms from school should be submitted.
Closing Date: April 30th
No. of awards given last year: 72

Francis Corder Clayton Scholarship
Subjects: Arts.
Eligibility: Open only to existing students of the university.
Level of Study: Postgraduate
Type: Scholarship
Value: Tuition fees at home rate
Length of Study: 1 year
Frequency: Annual
Study Establishment: The University of Birmingham
Country of Study: United Kingdom
No. of awards offered: 1
Application Procedure: Schools are asked to nominate their top 2 candidates. Awards are made on academic performance.
Closing Date: Mid-June
Funding: Private
No. of awards given last year: 1
No. of applicants last year: 6

Guest, Keen and Nettlefolds Scholarship
Subjects: Engineering.
Purpose: To support students reading for a research degree.
Eligibility: This scholarship is open to engineering graduates who wish to undertake postgraduate work in the University of Birmingham. Applicants must be current students at the university.
Level of Study: Postgraduate
Type: Scholarship
Value: Dependent on funds
Length of Study: 1 year
Frequency: Dependent on funds available
Study Establishment: The University of Birmingham
Country of Study: United Kingdom
No. of awards offered: 1
Application Procedure: Students need to be nominated by the school of engineering. Details can be obtained from the student funding office.
Funding: Private

Haywood Scholarship
Subjects: History of art.
Purpose: To support students reading for a research degree.
Eligibility: Candidates must also apply to AHRB or equivalent.
Level of Study: Postgraduate
Type: Scholarship
Value: Tuition fees at home rates only/maintenance variable
Length of Study: 1 year
Frequency: Dependent on funds available
Study Establishment: University of Birmingham
Country of Study: United Kingdom
No. of awards offered: 1
Application Procedure: Check website for further details.
Funding: Private
Additional Information: Students need to be nominated by the School of Historical Studies.

Joseph Chamberlain Scholarship
Subjects: Business, engineering, public policy and social sciences.
Purpose: Entrance scholarship for students wishing to pursue a higher degree at the University of Birmingham.
Eligibility: Open to students whose parents or guardians have been bona fide residents of the former west midlands country for 4 years prior to the start of the course or who have fulfilled the residency criteria themselves.
Level of Study: Postgraduate
Value: Tuition fees (at home rate) and maintenance at research council rates

Length of Study: 1 year
Frequency: Annual
Study Establishment: The University of Birmingham
Country of Study: United Kingdom
No. of awards offered: 1
Application Procedure: Contact the student funding office at the university. Student must be nominated by their school.
Closing Date: Mid-June
Funding: Private
No. of awards given last year: 1
No. of applicants last year: 4

Kirkcaldy Scholarship

Subjects: Business, public policy and social sciences.
Purpose: To support exisiting students who wish to pursue higher studies.
Eligibility: Open to all students registered for full-time higher degrees, that have been declared ineligible for public funds.
Level of Study: Postgraduate
Type: Scholarship
Value: Tution fees at home rate and maintenance
Length of Study: 1 year
Frequency: Annual
Study Establishment: The University of Birmingham
Country of Study: United Kingdom
No. of awards offered: 1
Application Procedure: Schools are asked to nominate their top 2 candidates. Awards are made on academic performance.
Closing Date: Mid-June
Funding: Private
No. of awards given last year: 1
No. of applicants last year: 6

Leventis Studentships

Subjects: Modern Greek studies.
Purpose: To support students reading for a research degree.
Eligibility: Candidates must also apply to AHRB or equivalent.
Level of Study: Postgraduate
Type: Studentship
Value: Tuition fees Home/EU
Length of Study: 1 year
Frequency: Dependent on funds available
Study Establishment: University of Birmingham
Country of Study: United Kingdom
No. of awards offered: 3
Application Procedure: Application forms can be obtained from postgraduate office within the School of Historical Studies.
Closing Date: June 4th
Funding: Private

MRC Studentships

Subjects: Medical sciences.
Purpose: To support research among the postgraduate community.
Eligibility: UK/EU students, though there are various criteria.
Level of Study: Postgraduate
Type: Studentship
Value: Majority are fees and maintenance
Length of Study: Varies – normally 3–4 years
Frequency: Annual
Study Establishment: University of Birmingham
Country of Study: United Kingdom
No. of awards offered: Varies normally 34 years
Application Procedure: Applicants must contact schools/departments concerned.
No. of awards given last year: 42

NERC Studentships

Subjects: Goegraphical and earth sciences.
Purpose: To support research among the postgraduate community.
Eligibility: UK/EU students, though there are various criteria.
Level of Study: Postgraduate
Type: Studentship
Value: Majority are fees and maintenance
Length of Study: Varies – normally 3–4 years
Frequency: Annual

Study Establishment: University of Birmingham
Country of Study: United Kingdom
No. of awards offered: Varies 34 years
Application Procedure: Applicants must contact schools/departments concerned.
No. of awards given last year: 25

Neville Chamberlain Scholarship

Subjects: Humanities subjects. Preference will be given to studies focusing on modern political, social and economic history, especially concerning Great Britain and its 19th-century sphere of influence.
Purpose: To provide financial assistance to students wishing to study for a higher degree.
Eligibility: Open to non United Kingdom students with a good Honours Degree who have been offered and have accepted admission to study for a higher degree in a humanities subject. Proficiency in English is essential.
Level of Study: Postgraduate
Type: Scholarship
Value: Tuition fees at home rate
Length of Study: 1 year, renewable as funding allows
Frequency: Dependent on funds available
Study Establishment: The University of Birmingham
Country of Study: United Kingdom
No. of awards offered: 1
Application Procedure: Schools are asked to nominate their top 2 candidates. Awards are made on academic performance.
Closing Date: Mid-June
Funding: Private
Contributor: The family of Neville Chamberlain
No. of awards given last year: 1
No. of applicants last year: 4

Paul Ramsay MSc Computer Science Bursary

Subjects: Computer Science.
Purpose: To support outstanding students with priority given to those from a low income background.
Eligibility: The bursary will be awarded to home/EU Masters students in need of financial assistance.
Level of Study: Postgraduate
Type: Bursary
Value: Tuition fees at home rate
Length of Study: 1 year
Frequency: Annual
Study Establishment: University of Birmingham
Country of Study: United Kingdom
No. of awards offered: 2
Application Procedure: Application forms can be obtained from the School of Computer Science or downloaded from the website.
Funding: Private
Contributor: Paul and Yuanbi Ramsay

Paul Ramsay PhD Computer Science Studentship

Subjects: Computer Science.
Purpose: To support outstanding students with priority given to those from a low income background.
Eligibility: The bursary will be awarded to home/EU PhD students in need of financial assistance.
Level of Study: Postgraduate
Type: Studentship
Value: Tuition fees at home rate plus maintenance
Length of Study: 1 year
Frequency: Annual
Study Establishment: University of Birmingham
Country of Study: United Kingdom
No. of awards offered: 1
Application Procedure: Check website for further details.
Funding: Private
Contributor: Paul and Yuanbi Ramsay
Additional Information: Students need to be nominated by the School of Computer Science.

Richard Fenwick Scholarship

Subjects: Any subject except medicine, dentistry and health sciences.

Purpose: To encourage students who wish to pursue higher studies.
Eligibility: Open to all students who desire to obtain higher degrees.
Level of Study: Postgraduate
Type: Scholarship
Value: Tuition fees at home rate plus maintenance
Length of Study: 1 year
Frequency: Annual
Study Establishment: The University of Birmingham
Country of Study: United Kingdom
Application Procedure: Applications are sent out to schools, success is based on academic performance, school will select their top two candidates to put forward for the award.
Closing Date: Mid-June
Funding: Private
No. of awards given last year: 1
No. of applicants last year: 21

STFC Studentships

Subjects: Physical sciences.
Purpose: To support research among the postgraduate community.
Eligibility: UK/EU students, though there are various criteria.
Level of Study: Postgraduate
Type: Studentship
Value: Majority are fees and maintenance
Length of Study: Normally 3–4 years
Frequency: Annual
Study Establishment: University of Birmingham
Country of Study: United Kingdom
No. of awards offered: Varies
Application Procedure: Applicants must contact Schools/Departments concerned.
Closing Date: April 1st
No. of awards given last year: 27

TI Group Scholarship

Subjects: Studying on a programme within the School of Engineering and intend to pursue a scientific or technological career in the manufacturing industry.
Purpose: To support students wishing to pursue a career in manufacturing.
Eligibility: Priority will be given to students who supply evidence of financial need.
Level of Study: Postgraduate
Type: Scholarship
Value: £5,000
Length of Study: 1 year (renewable)
Frequency: Annual
Study Establishment: University of Birmingham
Country of Study: United Kingdom
No. of awards offered: 5
Application Procedure: Details can be obtained from the Student Funding Office or the School of Engineering.
Closing Date: December
Funding: Private

University of Birmingham Alumni Scholarship

Subjects: Any subject.
Purpose: To support attending the University of Birmingham.
Eligibility: Candidates must either be an alumnus of the university, or the son or daughter of an alumnus. Preference will be given to students reading a research degree.
Level of Study: Postgraduate
Type: Scholarship
Value: Tuition fees at home rate
Length of Study: Up to 3 years
Frequency: Dependent on funds available
Study Establishment: The University of Birmingham
Country of Study: United Kingdom
No. of awards offered: 3
Application Procedure: This is a school nomination scholarship. The school will nominate 2 candidates based on academic performance.
Closing Date: Mid-June
Funding: Private
No. of awards given last year: 1
No. of applicants last year: 14

UNIVERSITY OF BREMEN

Building SFG, area 3260, Enrique Schmidt road 7, Bremen, 28359, Germany
Tel: (49) 49 421 218 60334
Fax: (49) 49 421 218 4770
Email: arici@uni-bremen.de
Website: www.uni-bremen.de

University of Bremen was set up as a Science complex in the early 1970s but could gain importance only after 1980s when the mathematics professor Jurgen Timm was elected in 1982. The result is increasingly higher levels in the research rankings, national recognition, a number of endowment professorships, the profiling of interdisciplinary scientific focuses nine DFG sponsored collaborative research centres and, sensationally, the Research Center of Ocean Margins embedded in the earth sciences with the emphasis on Global Change in the Marine Realm; one of only three – initially – national research centers of the DFG (German Research Foundation). From 1996 until 2001 the University of Bremen (along with six other universities in Germany) has been participating in a pilot scheme for structural reform of university administration, funded by the Volkswagen Foundation.

Studentships in the Life Sciences Graduate Program

Subjects: Life sciences.
Purpose: To attract the very best students worldwide to our American-type BSc and MSc degree programs.
Eligibility: Applicants should have outstanding undergraduate records in the biological, chemical, or physical sciences and show great promise of successful careers in research.
Level of Study: Graduate
Value: Waiver of the study fees at IUB, and a monthly allowance to cover food, housing, and personal expenses, and are guaranteed for two years
No. of awards offered: 10
Application Procedure: Check website for details.
Closing Date: February 1st and May 1st
Funding: Private
Additional Information: Students who do well in the MSc stage can, after 18 months, directly transfer to their PhD thesis work without MSc thesis and examination. This is dependent on an offer of financial suppport from a faculty member.

University of Bremen PhD studentship

Subjects: Social Sciences.
Eligibility: Open for the candidates who have obtained post graduation in MA or equivalent and have a good command on English.
Level of Study: Postgraduate
Value: €1000 per month
Length of Study: 3 years
No. of awards offered: 9
Application Procedure: Applications can be downloaded from the website.
Closing Date: March 1st
Funding: Private
Contributor: Volkswagen Foundation
Additional Information: Funding is also available for empirical research and travel. As the University of Bremen intends to increase the proportion of female employees in science, women are particularly encouraged to apply. In case of equal personal aptitudes and qualification disabled persons will be given priority.

For further information contact:

University of Bremen, Postfach 330440, Bremen, 28334, Germany
Website: www.gsss.uni-bremen.de
Contact: Dr Steffen Mau

UNIVERSITY OF BRISTOL

Student Funding Office, Senate House (Ground Floor), Tyndall Avenue, Bristol, BS8 1TH, England
Tel: (44) 11 7331 7972
Fax: (44) 11 7331 7873
Email: student-funding@bris.ac.uk
Website: www.bristol.ac.uk
Contact: Ms Jane Fitzwalier, Student Funding Manager

The University of Bristol is committed to providing high-quality teaching and research in all its designated fields.

International Postgraduate Scholarships – Taught Master's programmes

Subjects: All subjects.
Eligibility: Open to candidates holding an offer for a taught post-graduate programme at the University of Bristol.
Level of Study: Postgraduate
Type: Scholarship (MSc)
Value: £2,000
Study Establishment: University of Bristol
Country of Study: United Kingdom
No. of awards offered: 10
Application Procedure: Check website for further details.
Closing Date: June 30th

For further information contact:

International Recruitment Office, University of Bristol Union, Queens Road, Clifton, Bristol, Clifton, BS8 1LN, United Kingdom
Email: iro@bristol.ac.uk
Website: www.bristol.ac.uk/international/recruit/scholarships/scholarships
Contact: International Scholarship Administrator

University of Bristol Postgraduate Scholarships

Subjects: Any research topic that is covered in the work of the department within the University.
Purpose: To recruit high-quality research students.
Eligibility: Open to new PhD research students with at least an Upper Second Class (Honours) Degree or equivalent. Home/European Union Overseas students must be registered as full-time. Overseas students are only awarded a scholarship if they are successful in obtaining an Overseas Research Student (ORS) award. All scholars must be registered and in attendance for a research degree at the University.
Level of Study: Doctorate
Type: Scholarship
Value: At least UK £8,000 towards living costs plus home tuition fees
Length of Study: 3 years
Frequency: Annual
Study Establishment: University of Bristol
Country of Study: United Kingdom
No. of awards offered: 19 Home/European Union plus a commitment to fund all successful ORS award holders
Application Procedure: Applicants should contact the department where they intend to carry out their research in the first instance, and should look at the Student Funding Office website for up-to-date information on the application process either – www.bristol.ac.uk/student funding/overseas_pg/ors.html for overseas students or www.bristol.ac.uk/student funding/home_pg/schols.html for UK and EU students.
Closing Date: May 1st for Home/European Union (although some faculties may vary); February 16th for overseas applicants
Funding: Private
Contributor: University of Bristol
No. of awards given last year: Approx. 50 in total
No. of applicants last year: 200 (overseas only)

UNIVERSITY OF BRITISH COLUMBIA (UBC)

2329 West Mall, Vancouver, B.C., V6T 1Z2, Canada
Tel: (1) 604 822 4556
Fax: (1) 604 822 5802
Email: graduate.awards@ubc.ca
Website: www.grad.ubc.ca
Contact: Ms Jiffin Arboleda, Awards Administrator

The University of British Columbia (UBC) is one of North America's major research universities. The Faculty of Graduate Studies has 6,500 students and is a national leader in interdisciplinary study and research, with 98 departments, 18 interdisciplinary research units, 9 interdisciplinary graduate programmes, 2 graduate residential colleges and 1 scholarly journal.

Izaak Walton Killam Postdoctoral Fellowships

Subjects: All subjects.
Purpose: To support all areas of academic research.
Eligibility: Open to candidates who show superior ability in research and have obtained, within 2 academic years of the anticipated commencement date of the fellowship, a doctorate at a university other than UBC. Graduates of UBC are not normally eligible.
Level of Study: Postdoctorate
Type: Fellowship
Value: Canadian $46,000 per year and Canadian $6,000 travel allowance for duration of the award
Length of Study: 2 years, subject to satisfactory progress at the end of the 1st year
Frequency: Annual
Study Establishment: UBC
Country of Study: Canada
No. of awards offered: 6–12 per year
Application Procedure: Applicants must submit an application form, academic transcripts and three reference letters to the appropriate department. For information and application forms, please visit the website.
Closing Date: November 15th
Funding: Private
Contributor: Izaak Walton Killam Memorial Fund
No. of awards given last year: 4
No. of applicants last year: 200
Additional Information: Candidates are responsible for contacting the appropriate department at the University to ensure that their proposed research project is acceptable and may be undertaken under the supervision of a member of the department.

THE UNIVERSITY OF CALGARY

Faculty of Graduate Studies, Earth Sciences Building, Room 720, 2500 University Drive North West, Calgary, AB, T2N 1N4, Canada
Tel: (1) 403 220 5690
Fax: (1) 403 289 7635
Email: gsaward@ucalgary.ca
Website: www.grad.ucalgary.ca
Contact: Ms Connie Baines, Graduate Scholarship Officer

The University of Calgary is a place of education and scholarly inquiry. Its mission is to seek truth and disseminate knowledge and it aims to pursue this mission with integrity for the benefit of the people of Alberta, Canada and other parts of the world.

Alberta Law Foundation Graduate Scholarship

Subjects: Natural resources, energy and environmental law.
Eligibility: Open to full-time graduates who are registered in or admissible to a programme of studies leading to a Master's degree in the Faculty of Law at the University of Calgary.
Level of Study: Postgraduate
Type: Scholarship
Value: Canadian $14,000 each
Length of Study: 1 year, non-renewable
Frequency: Annual
Study Establishment: The University of Calgary
Country of Study: Canada
No. of awards offered: 10
Application Procedure: Applicants must complete an application form, available from the Director of the graduate programme at the Faculty of Law.
Closing Date: December 15th
Additional Information: In cases where no suitable application is received no awards will be made.

Honourable N D McDermid Graduate Scholarship in Law

Subjects: Law.
Eligibility: Open to graduate students enrolled on a full-time basis in the LLM programme in the Faculty of Law at the University of Calgary.
Level of Study: Postgraduate
Type: Scholarship

Value: Canadian $12,000
Length of Study: 1 year
Frequency: Annual
Study Establishment: The University of Calgary
Country of Study: Canada
No. of awards offered: 2
Application Procedure: Applicants must complete an application form, available from the Dean's office.
Closing Date: December 15th
Additional Information: The scholarship is not renewable. In cases where no suitable applications are received the award will not be made.

Izaak Walton Killam Memorial Scholarships

Subjects: All subjects.
Eligibility: Open to qualified graduates of any university who are admissible to a doctoral programme at the University of Calgary. Applicants must have completed at least 1 year of graduate study prior to taking up the award.
Level of Study: Doctorate, Postgraduate
Type: Scholarship
Value: Canadian $25,000. If approved, award holders may also receive up to Canadian $3,000 over the full-term of appointment for special equipment and/or travel in direct connection with the PhD research
Length of Study: 1 year, renewable for a further year upon presentation of evidence of satisfactory progress. Further renewal is available in open competition
Frequency: Annual
Study Establishment: The University of Calgary
Country of Study: Canada
No. of awards offered: 4–5
Application Procedure: Applicants must complete an online application form, available from the University Of Calgary Faculty of Graduate Studies website at: www.grad.ucalgary.ca/funding/htm/scholarship_app_guidelines.htm
Closing Date: February 1st
No. of awards given last year: 4–5

Peter C Craigie Memorial Scholarship

Subjects: Humanities.
Eligibility: Open to full-time registrants from any country who are registered in and have completed one term of study in a programme of studies leading to an MA degree in a department of the Faculty of Humanities. The recipient must have an outstanding scholastic record and will have been or be involved in activities contributing to the general welfare of the university committee.
Level of Study: Postgraduate
Type: Scholarship
Value: Canadian $4,000
Length of Study: 1 year
Frequency: Every 2 years
Study Establishment: The University of Calgary
Country of Study: Canada
No. of awards offered: 1
Application Procedure: Applicants must apply to the Faculty of Humanities in the first instance. Recommendations from the Faculty will be submitted for consideration and approval by the University Graduate Scholarship Committee.
Closing Date: May 1st
Contributor: Peter C. Craigie Memorial Scholarship Fund

Queen Elizabeth II Graduate Scholarships

Subjects: All subjects.
Eligibility: Candidates must be registered in, or admissible to, a programme leading to a Master's or doctoral degree. The award is restricted to Canadian citizens and landed immigrants.
Level of Study: Doctorate, Postgraduate
Type: Fellowship/Scholarship
Value: The Master's level scholarship consists of Canadian $9,300 per year and the doctoral level scholarship of Canadian $10,500 per year
Length of Study: 1 year, renewable in open competition
Frequency: Annual
Study Establishment: The University of Calgary

Country of Study: Canada
No. of awards offered: 60–70
Application Procedure: Applicants must complete an application form, available from the directors of graduate studies of the departments concerned.
Closing Date: February 1st
Additional Information: Students whose awards begin in May are expected to carry out a full-time research programme during the Summer months.

Sheriff Willoughby King Memorial Scholarship

Subjects: Prevention of family violence and the treatment of the victims of family violence.
Eligibility: Open to candidates registered in the Faculty of Graduate Studies at the University of Calgary who are pursuing a Master of Social Work degree. Candidates must be Canadian citizens.
Level of Study: Postgraduate
Type: Scholarship
Value: Canadian $5,000
Length of Study: 1 year
Frequency: Annual
Study Establishment: The University of Calgary
Country of Study: Canada
No. of awards offered: 1 to a candidate studying in the area of treatment and 1 to a candidate studying in the area of prevention
Application Procedure: Applicants must apply to the Faculty of Social Work. Recommendations from the Faculty will be considered by the University Graduate Scholarship Committee at its annual meeting. Awards are made on the basis of academic excellence.
Closing Date: February 1st
No. of awards given last year: 1 to a candidate studying in the area of treatment and 1 to a candidate studying in the area of prevention

University of Calgary Faculty of Law Graduate Scholarship

Subjects: Natural resources, energy and environmental law.
Eligibility: Open to full-time graduate students who are registered in or admissible to a programme of studies leading to a Master's degree in the Faculty of Law.
Level of Study: Postgraduate
Type: Scholarship
Value: Up to Canadian $10,500
Length of Study: 1 year, non-renewable
Frequency: Annual
Study Establishment: The University of Calgary
Country of Study: Canada
No. of awards offered: 1
Application Procedure: Applicants must complete an application form, available from the graduate programme director at the Faculty of Law. Awards will be recommended by a committee of the Faculty of Law based upon academic excellence.
Closing Date: December 15th
Additional Information: In cases where no suitable applications are received no awards will be made.

William H Davies Medical Research Scholarship

Subjects: Medicine.
Eligibility: Open to qualified graduates of any recognized university who will be registered in the Faculty of Graduate Studies at the University of Calgary. Successful candidates must conduct their research programme within the Faculty of Medicine.
Level of Study: Postgraduate
Type: Scholarship
Value: Canadian $3,000–11,000 depending on qualifications, experience and graduate programme
Length of Study: 4 months–1 year, renewable in open competition
Study Establishment: The University of Calgary
Country of Study: Canada
No. of awards offered: More than 1
Application Procedure: Applicants must apply to the Assistant Dean of Medical Science in the first instance. The Graduate Scholarship Committee will make the final decision based on departmental recommendations. Awards are made on the basis of academic excellence.
Closing Date: May 1st

673

UNIVERSITY OF CALIFORNIA, BERKELEY

Graduate Services, Graduate Fellowships Office, 318 Sproul Hall #5900, Berkeley, CA 94720 5900, United States of America
Tel: (1) 510 642 0672
Fax: (1) 510 643 1524
Email: gradfell@berkeley.edu
Website: www.grad.berkeley.edu

Founded in the wake of the gold rush by the leaders of the newly established 31st state, the university of California's flagship campus at Berkeley has become one of the preeminent universities in the world. Its early guiding lights, charged with providing education (both "practical" and "classical") for the state's people, gradually established a distinguished faculty (with 20 Nobel laureates to date), a stellar research library, and more than 350 academic programs.

Albert Newman Fellowship for Visually Impaired Students
Subjects: All subjects.
Purpose: To encourage substantially visually impaired graduate students who demonstrate scholastic achievement.
Eligibility: Applicant must be substantially visually impaired.
Level of Study: Graduate
Type: Fellowship
Frequency: Annual
Application Procedure: Applicants must submit completed application and supporting documents.
Closing Date: April 18th

Chancellor's Dissertation-Year Fellowship
Subjects: Humanities and social sciences.
Purpose: To support outstanding students in the humanities and social sciences.
Eligibility: Applicants must be advanced to candidacy at the time of the award and expect to finish their dissertations during the fellowship year.
Level of Study: Doctorate
Type: Fellowship
Value: US$18,000, with an additional US$2,000 if the dissertation is completed before the deadline, plus fees/tuition.
Length of Study: 1 year
Frequency: Annual
Study Establishment: University of California–Berkeley
Country of Study: United States of America
No. of awards offered: 13
Application Procedure: The applicant must submit a letter from the department or group chair supporting the nomination, a letter from the dissertation adviser describing the importance of the dissertation project, the Report on Progress in Candidacy in the Doctoral Programme form signed by the dissertation adviser, a copy of the Chancellor's Dissertation Year Fellowship application, a detailed outline of the dissertation, a 1 page summary of the dissertation in nontechnical language, a copy of the latest chapter completed or other substantive work as evidence of progress on dissertation and an unofficial copy of the University of California–Berkeley graduate transcript showing date of advancement to candidacy.
Closing Date: March 2nd

Conference Travel Grants
Subjects: All subjects.
Purpose: To allow students to attend professional conferences.
Eligibility: Applicant must be registered graduate students in good academic standing. They must be in the final stages of their graduate work and planning to present a paper on their dissertation research at the conference they are attending.
Type: Grant
Value: Maximum US$500
Study Establishment: University of California–Berkeley
Country of Study: United States of America
No. of awards offered: 1
Application Procedure: Applicants must submit an application form and one letter of support from their graduate advisor attesting to the

academic merit of the trip. Applications can be obtained from the website.
Closing Date: 3 weeks before the date of travel

Dr and Mrs James C Y Soong Fellowship
Subjects: All subjects.
Purpose: To financially support graduate students from Taiwan.
Eligibility: Applicants must have graduated from a fully accredited, 4-year college or university in Taiwan, with a grade point average of 3.7 (A-) or higher, must be a citizen of the Republic of China and have lived in Taiwan consecutively for at least 10 years and must have demonstrated financial need in pursuit of advanced degrees.
Level of Study: Graduate
Type: Fellowship
Value: The fellowship may be renewed one time
Length of Study: 1 year
Frequency: Annual
Study Establishment: University of California–Berkeley
Country of Study: United States of America
Application Procedure: Applicant must submit a completed application form, available from the website, a one-page typewritten statement of purpose, a copy of the University of California–Berkeley transcript, the international student financial information form and a letter of support from the department chair.
Closing Date: April 10th

Elizabeth Roboz Einstein Fellowship
Subjects: Neurosciences.
Purpose: To fund doctoral candidates in the neurosciences relating to human development.
Eligibility: Applicants must have demonstrated distinguished scholarship as well as the ability to conduct research at an advanced level.
Level of Study: Doctorate
Type: Fellowship
Value: US$4,000
Length of Study: 1 semester
Frequency: Annual
Study Establishment: University of California–Berkeley
Country of Study: United States of America
No. of awards offered: 2
Application Procedure: Applicants must submit a completed application form, two letters of recommendation in sealed envelopes, a copy of the latest University of California–Berkeley transcript and a one-page description of the research project.
Closing Date: November 14th

Foreign Language and Area Studies (FLAS) Fellowships
Subjects: Foreign languages, humanities, social sciences, area and international studies and professional fields.
Purpose: To ensure continued national competence in modern foreign languages and area and international studies.
Eligibility: Candidates must be graduate students and citizens, nationals or permanent residents of the United States of America.
Level of Study: Graduate
Type: Award
Value: US$15,000 and fees
Frequency: Annual
Study Establishment: University of California–Berkeley
Country of Study: United States of America
Application Procedure: Incoming students should apply using the Graduate Application for Admission and Fellowships, which should be submitted directly to their departments by the departmental deadlines.
Closing Date: January 26th

Mentored Research Award
Subjects: All subjects.
Purpose: To provide academically promising graduate students an opportunity to conduct doctoral research, acquire sophisticated research skills and strengthen their working relationships with faculty advisers.
Eligibility: The applicant must be a citizen or permanent resident of the United States of America who demonstrates high academic potential and promise and whose background and life experiences enhance the diversity within the department or discipline. Generally for 3rd and 4th year students.

Level of Study: Doctorate
Type: Fellowship
Value: US$14,000 plus registration fees
Length of Study: 1 year
Frequency: Annual
Study Establishment: University of California–Berkeley
Country of Study: United States of America
No. of awards offered: 15
Application Procedure: Each nominating department must submit a letter from the department or group chair supporting the nomination and confirming eligibility; a letter from the proposed mentor describing plans for mentoring the student and past mentoring experience; a letter from the student describing his or her academic progress to date, the nature of the research project in which she or he will be involved, its importance to the student's academic career, and how this award would help the student to achieve his or her goals; a copy of the Mentored Research Award application; and unofficial copies of all graduate transcripts.
Closing Date: March 2nd

Paul J Alexander Memorial Fellowship
Subjects: Ancient history.
Purpose: To encourage the study of Byzantine, ancient and medieval history.
Eligibility: Advanced University of California, Berkeley graduate students studying in the general area of ancient history are invited to apply.
Level of Study: Graduate
Type: Fellowship
Value: Approx. US$4,000
Application Procedure: Applicants must submit an application form, available from the website. The application must also include a letter of endorsement from the applicant's sponsor, a copy of the latest University of California–Berkeley transcript and a one-page description of the dissertation research.
Closing Date: November 12th
Additional Information: A student can receive this award only once during his/her academic career.

University of California Dissertation-Year Fellowship
Subjects: All subjects.
Purpose: To support the writing of a doctoral dissertation.
Eligibility: Applicants must be citizens or permanent residents of the United States of America who demonstrate high academic potential and promise and whose backgrounds and life experiences enhance the level of diversity within the department or discipline. Applicants must be advanced to candidacy for the PhD at the time of nomination.
Level of Study: Doctorate
Type: Fellowship
Value: US$18,000 plus a travel allowance and registration fees as well as an additional US$2,000 if the dissertation is submitted before the deadline
Length of Study: 1 year
Frequency: Annual
Study Establishment: University of California–Berkeley
Country of Study: United States of America
No. of awards offered: 12
Application Procedure: Each nominating department must submit a letter from the department or group chair supporting the nomination, a letter from the dissertation adviser describing the importance of the dissertation project, an outline of dissertation progress signed by the dissertation adviser, a copy of the UC Dissertation-Year Fellowship application, a detailed outline of the dissertation, a 1-page summary of the dissertation in non-technical language, a copy of the latest chapter completed or other substantive work as evidence of progress on the dissertation and unofficial copies of all graduate transcripts.
Closing Date: March 2nd

UNIVERSITY OF CALIFORNIA, LOS ANGELES (UCLA)

Department of Sociology, 2201 Hershey, Los Angeles, CA, 90095-1551, United States of America
Tel: (1) 310 825 3232
Email: grusky@ucla.edu
Website: www.ucla.edu
Contact: Mr Oscar Grusky

UCLA is a leader in many fields, pursuing its mission through excellence in education, research and service. Its faculty, students, and staff work together to advance knowledge in the sciences, humanities and professional fields, address contemporary issues and improve the quality of life.

Charles F Scott Fellowship
Eligibility: Applicants should be graduate students with baccalaureates from UCLA, consideration may be given to students with baccalaureates from other UC campuses.
Type: Fellowship
Value: Up to $15,000 each as fees
No. of awards offered: Varies
Application Procedure: Applicants must provide evidence that they are enrolled in a course of study that prepares them for leadership in national, state or local governmental administration.

Dr Ursula Mandel Scholarship
Subjects: Scientific fields related, allied or of value to the medical field.
Eligibility: Applicants must have a doctorate as their degree objective. MD and DDS students are not eligible.
Value: Up to $15,000 each as fees
No. of awards offered: Varies

Eugene V Cota-Robles Fellowship
Subjects: College or university teaching and research.
Purpose: To provide access to higher education for students who might otherwise find it difficult or impossible to successfully pursue graduate study.
Eligibility: Candidates must be either US citizens or permanent residents and should demonstrate high potential and promise. Individuals from cultural, racial, linguistic, geographic and socioeconomic backgrounds that are currently underrepresented in graduate education are especially encouraged to participate in the programme. Candidates must be nominated by their department/school. Students pursuing MD or DDS degrees are not eligible for this programme.
Level of Study: Postdoctorate
Type: Fellowship
Value: Stipend of $20,000 plus registration fees and nonresident tuition (for the first year only) if necessary. During the second, third and fourth years it provides support in the form of a Graduate Research Mentorship Award on activation of the award by the student and the department
Length of Study: 4 years
No. of awards offered: Varies
Application Procedure: Candidates must complete both the Fellowship Application for Entering Graduate Student and the Diversity Fellowships–Supplemental Application and submitted along with Admission Application's Statement of Purpose essay on contributions to the University's diversity mission.
Contributor: University of California Office of the President and the UCLA Graduate Division

Gordon Hein Memorial Scholarship
Subjects: Any subject.
Purpose: To support blind graduate students.
Eligibility: Awards are made on the basis of the student's financial need during the fellowship year and academic record.
Level of Study: Graduate
Type: Scholarship
Value: $5,000 each
Frequency: Dependent on funds available
No. of awards offered: Varies
Application Procedure: Applicants must submit verification of their blindness (e.g. letter from a physician or from the Office for students with Disabilities) and a completed Free Application for Federal Student Aid (FAFSA) or UCLA Financial Statement with the application.

Graduate Opportunity Fellowship Program (GOFP)
Purpose: To provide access to higher education for students who might otherwise find it difficult or impossible to successfully pursue graduate study.
Eligibility: Applicants must be either US citizens or permanent residents and should demonstrate high potential and promise. Individuals

from cultural, racial, linguistic, geographic and socioeconomic backgrounds that are currently underrepresented in graduate education are especially encouraged to participate in the programme. Students pursuing doctoral degrees (e.g. MD, PhD, DDS, etc.) are not eligible for this programme.
Level of Study: Postgraduate
Type: Fellowship
Value: $12,500 stipend plus registration fees (and non-resident tuition if necessary)
Length of Study: 1 year
No. of awards offered: Varies
Application Procedure: Applicants must complete both the Fellowship Application for Entering Graduate Student and the Diversity Fellowships-Supplemental Application and submitted along with Admission Application's Statement of Purpose essay on contributions to the University's diversity mission.

Karekin Der Avedisian Memorial Endowment Fund
Subjects: American studies.
Level of Study: Graduate
Value: Approx. $1,000
No. of awards offered: 1
Application Procedure: Applicants may show financial need (via a Free Application for Federal Students Aid (FAFSA) or a UCLA Financial Statement submitted at time of application) or outstanding academic ability.

Kasper and Siroon Hovannisian Fellowship
Subjects: Armenian studies with preference given to American history.
Type: Fellowship
Value: Up to $10,000 as fees
No. of awards offered: 1
Application Procedure: Applicants should provide a statement of their projected plan of study along with the application.

Malcolm R Stacey Memorial Scholarship
Subjects: Engineering.
Eligibility: Candidates should be Jewish graduate student in any area of engineering.
Level of Study: Graduate
Type: Scholarship
Value: Up to $5,000. Amount of award is based on financial need during the fellowship year, as determined by the Financial Aid Office
No. of awards offered: Varies
Application Procedure: Candidates should submit a completed FAFSA or UCLA Financial Statement with the application.
Contributor: University of California Office of the President

Mangasar M Mangasarian Scholarship
Eligibility: Applicants must be of Armenian descent and provide evidence that at least one parent is Armenian. Awards are made on the basis of candidates' academic records.
Level of Study: Graduate
Type: Scholarship
Value: Up to $10,000 each as fees
Frequency: Dependent on funds available
No. of awards offered: Varies

Non resident Tuition Fellowships/Registration Fee Grants
Eligibility: Applicants must be enrolled in a full-time programme of study and may not be recipients of awards from federal, state or private foundations that provide tuition coverage. Non resident tuition fellowships are not available for students financially sponsored by foreign governments.
Type: Fellowship or Grant
Value: To cover either the non resident tuition or the registration fees and living expenses
No. of awards offered: Varies
Closing Date: December 15th
Additional Information: Contact the department for further details.

Paulson Scholarship Fund
Eligibility: Applicants must be nationals of Sweden.

Level of Study: Graduate
Type: Scholarship
Value: Up to $6,000
No. of awards offered: Varies

Rose and Sam Gilbert Fellowship
Eligibility: Applicants should be graduate students who attended UCLA as undergraduates for at least 2 years and participated on men's or women's athletic teams (intramural teams are not eligible).
Value: Up to $10,000 each
No. of awards offered: Approx. 2

Steven J Sackler Scholarship
Eligibility: Offered to graduate or undergraduate student who had or is experiencing cancer and who can demonstrate financial need for the fellowship year.
Level of Study: Graduate
Type: Scholarship
Value: Up to $5,000
No. of awards offered: 1
Application Procedure: Applicants must provide a letter from a physician verifying the condition and submit a completed Free Application for Federal Student Aid (FAFSA) or a UCLA Financial Statement. Final selection will be made by the Sackler family.

UCLA Competitive Edge
Subjects: Science, technology, engineering, mathematics.
Purpose: To provide awardees with research and professional development experiences to enhance their success in UCLA Doctoral in the fields of science, technology, engineering and mathematics (STEM) programmes.
Eligibility: Applicants must be admitted or entering Doctoral students in the fields of STEM with strong interest in pursuing a faculty or research position. Applicants must also be US citizens or permanent residents and, in accordance with the NSF, have backgrounds underrepresented in STEM doctoral programmes.
Level of Study: Doctorate
Type: Award
Value: Provides faculty-guided research and mentoring, as well as academic and professional workshops
Length of Study: 6 weeks
Contributor: National Science Foundation (NSF) Alliance for Graduate Education and the Professoriate (AGEP)

Werner R Scott Fund
Eligibility: Applicants should be Caucasian graduate students who are residents of Hawaii.
Type: Funding support
Value: Up to $8,000 as fees
No. of awards offered: Varies

Will Rogers Memorial Fellowship
Purpose: To support graduate students with physical disabilities in any field of study.
Eligibility: Applicants should be graduate students with physical disabilities in any field of study.
Level of Study: Graduate
Type: Fellowship
Value: Up to $10,000 each as fees
No. of awards offered: Varies
Application Procedure: Applicants must submit verification of their physical disability (e.g. letter from a physician or from the Office for Students with Disabilities) with the application.

UNIVERSITY OF CAMBRIDGE

University Registry, The Old Schools, Cambridge, Cambridgeshire, CB2 1TN, England
Tel: (44) 12 2333 2317
Fax: (44) 12 2333 2332
Email: dmh14@cam.ac.uk
Website: www.admin.cam.ac.uk
Contact: D M Holburn, Acting Senior Tutor

The University of Cambridge is a loose confederation of faculties, colleges and other bodies. The colleges are mainly concerned with the teaching of their undergraduate students through tutorials and supervisions and the academic support of both graduate and undergraduate students, while the University employs professors, readers, lecturers and other teaching and administrative staff who provide the formal teaching in lectures, seminars and practical classes. The University also administers the University Library.

Allen, Meek and Reed Scholarship (Bursary)

Eligibility: Applicants must be registered as MPhil in the academic year. Applications are restricted to full-time students. Scholars must already possess a degree from the University of Cambridge (including the Certificate of Advanced Study in Mathematics) or be about to graduate during the competition period.
Type: Bursary
Value: Maximum £5,000
Length of Study: 1 year
Application Procedure: Should apply through the department.
Closing Date: July 1st
Contributor: the Allen, Meek and Read (AMR) Fund

Dorothy Hodgkin Postgraduate Award

Eligibility: Applicants must be registered for an PhD programme. Candidate offered admission to an MPhil programme are not eligible. Continuing students may be registered for an MPhil. Limited to candidates from specific countries. Candidates must have applied for an ORS award.
Type: Award
Value: Approx. £12,300 p.a. (university composition plus college fees and maintenance stipend)
Length of Study: 3 years
Frequency: Annual
No. of awards offered: Approx. 7
Application Procedure: Successful candidates are selected from the ORS ranked list. There is no seperate application form for this competition.
Closing Date: December 15th
Contributor: the UK Research Councils and industrial partners

For further information contact:

Email: kfw20@admin.cam.ac.uk

Le Bas Scholarsips (Bursary)

Subjects: Literature.
Purpose: To offer a limited number of bursaries to the best students in the study of literature and who intend to continue to a PhD.
Eligibility: Candidates must have registered for MPhil. Applications are restricted to full-time students, undertaking study in the field of literature.
Type: Bursary
Value: Maximum £5,000
Length of Study: 1 year
Application Procedure: Candidates must apply through the department. Check website for further details.
Closing Date: June 1st

UNIVERSITY OF CAMBRIDGE, JUDGE BUSINESS SCHOOL

Trumpington Street, Cambridge, Cambridgeshire, CB2 1AG, England
Tel: (44) 12 2333 9700
Fax: (44) 12 2333 9701
Email: enquiries@jims.cam.ac.uk
Website: www.jims.cam.ac.uk
Contact: Mrs Natacha Wilson

The Judge Business School is the University of Cambridge's business school. Founded in 1990, it offers a portfolio of management programmes, including the Cambridge MBA. Accredited by AMBA and EQUIS, the business school now hosts one of the largest concentrations of interdisciplinary business and management research activity in Europe.

Director's Scholarships

Subjects: MBA.
Purpose: To help outstanding candidates with the cost of the Cambridge MBA.
Eligibility: The scholarships are merit based; Recipients usually have an exceptional academic background, strong GMAT score, and have enjoyed considerable success in their careers to date.
Level of Study: MBA
Type: Scholarship
Value: UK £5,000
Length of Study: 1 year
Frequency: Annual
Study Establishment: Judge Business School, University of Cambridge
Country of Study: United Kingdom
No. of awards offered: Approx. 10
Application Procedure: All applicants who are offered a place on the MBA programme are automatically considered.
Closing Date: June 6th
Funding: Private
Contributor: Judge Business School
No. of awards given last year: 10
No. of applicants last year: 150 (all admitted students are considered)
Additional Information: As the number of scholarships is limited, candidates who apply early in the admissions round are more likely to receive this award.

N Boustany MBA Scholarship

Subjects: MBA.
Purpose: To enable a Lebanese national to attend the Cambridge MBA on a full scholarship.
Eligibility: Open to candidates of all nations although priority given to Lebanese nationals, who have obtained a good Honours Degree from a recognized university and have at least 3 years of full-time, real-world experience. Candidates will need to demonstrate a high intellectual potential, practical common sense and the ability to put ideas into action. They also need to be highly motivated with a strong desire to learn. Applicants will be asked to take the Test of English as a Foreign Language (TOEFL) where applicable and the Graduate Management Admission Test (GMAT).
Level of Study: MBA
Type: Scholarship
Value: US$30,000 including full tuition and travelling expenses
Length of Study: 2 years
Frequency: Every 2 years
Study Establishment: Judge Business School, University of Cambridge
Country of Study: United Kingdom
No. of awards offered: 1
Application Procedure: Applicants must email their curriculum vitae to admissions@boustany-foundation.org. Applicants must also be applying for the Cambridge MBA programme.
Closing Date: May 15th
Funding: Foundation
Contributor: The Nabil Boustany Foundation
No. of awards given last year: 1
No. of applicants last year: 4
Additional Information: The scholarship recipient is normally required to spend a summer internship, carrying no salary, within a Lebanese organization. Applicants must be accepted into the Cambridge MBA programme.

For further information contact:

1 avenue des Citronniers, Monte Carlo, 98000, Monaco
Fax: (377) 77 93 15 05 56
Email: info@boustany-foundation.org
Website: www.jbs.cam.ac.uk
Contact: Mr M Tamar

Sainsbury Bursaries

Subjects: MBA.
Purpose: To support students engaged in charitable, voluntary or public sector work in areas such as housing, health and education,

local economic development and social services, as it is difficult for such candidates to secure sponsorship from their employers.
Eligibility: Preference will be given to applicants from the United Kingdom but exceptional candidates working for international aid agencies based outside the United Kingdom will be given consideration. It is expected that applicants will contribute to the sectors in the United Kingdom after completion of the MBA. Candidates must have completed 3 years of work within the charitable, voluntary or public sector prior to submitting their application. The applicants for the 2-year integrated course must have a placement set up within an organization in the charitable, voluntary or public sector. Candidates must also show evidence of a career plan showing how they would use the skills and knowledge gained during the MBA course to develop their career within the charitable, voluntary or public sector.
Level of Study: MBA
Type: Bursary
Value: Ranges from UK £14,000–28,000 at the discretion of The Sainsbury Bursary Scheme Committee
Length of Study: 1 year
Frequency: Annual
Study Establishment: Judge Business School, University of Cambridge
Country of Study: United Kingdom
No. of awards offered: 5
Application Procedure: Applicants must complete and submit an application form for the MBA along with a covering letter, indicating that they would also like to apply for a Sainsbury Bursary, to the Judge Business School.
Closing Date: June 5th
Funding: Private
Contributor: The Monument Trust
No. of awards given last year: 3
No. of applicants last year: 3
Additional Information: The Monument Trust is one of the Sainsbury Family Charitable Trusts.

St Catharine's College Benavitch Scholarships

Subjects: MBA.
Purpose: To encourage exceptional candidates to pursue the Cambridge MBA.
Eligibility: Candidates should apply for admission to the Cambridge MBA in the normal way, but must also send a covering letter with their application form explaining in not more than 300 words the contribution they expect to make to business and society in the future.
Level of Study: MBA
Type: Scholarship
Value: UK £10,000
Length of Study: 1 year
Frequency: Annual
Study Establishment: Judge Business School, University of Cambridge
Country of Study: United Kingdom
No. of awards offered: 5
Application Procedure: First class degree, GPA above 3.7 (out of 4) or equivalent from a recognised university Minimum GMAT score of 700 3 years' full-time post-graduation work experience.
Closing Date: March 15th
Funding: Private
Contributor: The late Maurice Benavitch and his late wife Natalie
Additional Information: Recipients of Benavitch Scholarships will become members of St Catharine's College, Cambridge and be given the option to live in single, college-owned accommodation (some married accommodation may be offered, subject to availability).

UNIVERSITY OF CANTERBURY

College of Arts, University of Canterbury, Private Bag 4800, Christchurch, New Zealand
Tel: (64) 3 364 2426 (ext: 6426)
Fax: (64) 3 364 2683
Email: michelle.payton@canterbury.ac.nz
Website: www.canterbury.ac.nz
Contact: Ms Michelle Payton, Human Resource Administrator

The University of Canterbury offers a variety of subjects in a few flexible degree structures, namely, first and postgraduate degrees in arts, commerce, education, engineering, fine arts, forestry, law, music and science. At Canterbury, research and teaching are closely related, and while this feature shapes all courses, it is very marked at the postgraduate level.

University of Canterbury Alumni Association Scholarships

Eligibility: Awarded annually to the top students from nominated faculties.
Level of Study: Postgraduate
Type: Scholarship
Value: $5,000
Length of Study: 1 year
Frequency: Annual
No. of awards offered: 2
Application Procedure: No application necessary.
Closing Date: November 1st

University of Canterbury and Creative New Zealand Ursula Bethell Residency in Creative Writing

Subjects: Creative writing, fiction, poetry, scriptwriting and literary nonfiction.
Purpose: To foster New Zealand writing by providing a full-time opportunity for a writer to work in an academic environment.
Eligibility: Open to authors of proven merit who are normally resident in New Zealand and to New Zealand nationals temporarily resident overseas.
Level of Study: Unrestricted
Type: Fellowship
Value: Emolument at the rate of New Zealand $52,600
Length of Study: Up to 1 year
Frequency: Dependent on funds available
Study Establishment: University of Canterbury
Country of Study: New Zealand
No. of awards offered: 1
Application Procedure: Applicants must submit details of published writing and work in progress, and include a proposal of work to be undertaken during the appointment.
Funding: Government
No. of awards given last year: 30
Additional Information: The appointment will be made on the basis of published or performed writing of high quality. Conditions of appointment should be obtained from the Human Resources Department before applying, available in August from: hr@arts.canterbury.ac.nz

University of Canterbury Doctoral Scholarship – Students with Disabilities

Purpose: To provide an incentive for students with high academic achievement who have a significant disability.
Level of Study: Doctorate
Type: Scholarship
Value: $20,000 per year plus tuition fees (NZ domestic rate)
Length of Study: Up to 4 years
Application Procedure: Applicants must contact the scholarship office.
Closing Date: October 15th
Additional Information: The scholarship may not be held with a University of Canterbury Doctoral Scholarship. The general conditions for the scholarship are as for the University of Canterbury Doctoral Scholarship regulations.

University of Canterbury Doctoral Scholarships

Purpose: To support full-time or part-time study towards a PhD degree at the University of Canterbury.
Eligibility: Open to international students who meet the academic requirements for enrolment in a PhD.
Level of Study: Doctorate
Type: Scholarship
Value: $20,000 plus tuition fees at NZ domestic rate
Length of Study: 3 years
Frequency: Annual

Application Procedure: Applicants must contact the scholarship office.
Closing Date: May 15th and October 15th,

University of Canterbury International Doctoral Scholarship

Purpose: To provide support for international students with high academic achievement.
Eligibility: Applicants must be international students (New Zealand citizens and permanent residents are not eligible to apply). They must meet the academic requirements for enrolling in a PhD undertaking or planning to undertake full-time study.
Level of Study: Doctorate
Type: Scholarship
Value: $25,000 per year for thesis tuition fees at NZ domestic rate and economy return airfare
Length of Study: Up to 3 years
No. of awards offered: 5
Application Procedure: The applicants must contact the scholarship office.
Closing Date: October 15th

University of Canterbury Masters Scholarship – Students with Disabilities

Purpose: To provide an incentive for students who have a significant disability with high academic achievement.
Eligibility: Open to candidates with disabilities.
Level of Study: Doctorate, Postdoctorate
Type: Scholarship
Value: $12,000 per year plus tuition fees (NZ domestic rate)
Length of Study: Up to 2 years
Application Procedure: Applicants must contact the scholarship office.
Closing Date: October 15th
Additional Information: The scholarship may not be held with a University of Canterbury Masters Scholarship. The general conditions for the scholarship are as for the University of Canterbury Masters Scholarship regulations.

University of Canterbury Masters Scholarships

Purpose: To support a full-time or part-time study towards the research year of a Masters degree at the University of Canterbury.
Level of Study: Postgraduate
Type: Scholarship
Value: $12,000 plus tuition fees (NZ domestic rate)
Length of Study: 1 year
Frequency: Annual
No. of awards offered: 40
Application Procedure: Applicants must contact the scholarship office.
Closing Date: May 15th and October 15th

Wood Technology Research Centre – Postgraduate Scholarships

Subjects: Chemical engineering.
Purpose: To develop a computer model to simulate energy flow and energy efficiency in wood and wood product processing industry.
Level of Study: Postgraduate
Type: Scholarship
Value: $24,000 per year for PhD and $18,000 per year for ME
Length of Study: 3 years for PhD and 1 year and 6 months for ME
Additional Information: Case studies will be conducted for manufacturing of Laminated Veneer Lumber (LVL) and Medium Density Fibreboard (MDF). The project will be conduced in collaboration with the University of Otago and a wood processing company.

For further information contact:

Wood Technology Centre, Department of Chemical and Process Engineering, University of Canterbury, Christchurch, New Zealand
Tel: (64) 64 3 364 2538
Fax: (64) 64 3 364 2063
Email: shusheng.pang@canterbury.ac.nz
Contact: Dr Shusheng Pang, Associate Professor and Director

UNIVERSITY OF CENTRAL LANCASHIRE (UCLAN)

University of Central Lancashire, Preston,
PR1 2HE, United Kingdom
Tel: (44) 44 0 1772 201201
Email: uadmissions@uclan.ac.uk
Website: www.uclan.ac.uk

UCLan is the sixth largest university in the UK ranked in the leading third of the UK's modern universities with around 30,000 students studying at Preston and is the leading modern university in the North West of England. During the last 10 years the University has spent over £77 million in providing a modern, state-of-the-art learning environment, including campus-wide free Internet access via an extensive computer network, and a new library open seven days a week.

Sports and Arts Related Scholarships

Purpose: To support artistic and sporting talent of the future in China.
Eligibility: Open to Chinese students applying to relevant UCLan undergraduate or postgraduate programme. Applicants must not be in receipt of a full fee scholarship from any other source.
Level of Study: Graduate
Type: Scholarship
Value: £2,000
No. of awards offered: 10
Application Procedure: Check website for further details.
Closing Date: August 24th
Additional Information: Scholarships will be awarded for prior academic and personal achievement in the chosen area of study based on information supplied in the scholarship application form. Students will also get the opportunity to discuss their academic background as well as apply for these scholarships on the same day therefore students are advised to bring their transcript, English language score and references with them.

For further information contact:

Email: cbmagee@uclan.ac.uk

THE UNIVERSITY OF CINCINNATI

Department of Electrical and Computer Engineering and Computer Science, 2600 Clifton Avenue, Cincinnati, OH, 45221-0030, United States of America
Tel: (1) 513 556 4756
Fax: (1) 513 556 6245
Email: dpa@ececs.uc.edu
Website: www.uc.edu
Contact: Dr Dharma P Agrawal, Admissions Committee

The University of Cincinnati offers students a balance of educational excellence and real world experience. Since its founding in 1819, University of Cincinnati has been the source of many discoveries creating positive change for society.

Ohio Board of Regents (OBR) Distinguished Doctoral Research Fellowship

Subjects: Computer science.
Purpose: To provide opportunity to highly qualified researchers.
Level of Study: Doctorate
Type: Fellowship
Value: US$24,000 per year plus tuition
Length of Study: 2 years
Frequency: Annual
Study Establishment: University of Cincinnati
Country of Study: United States of America
Closing Date: March 15th
Contributor: Ohio Board of Regents (OBR)
Additional Information: All queries should be directed to dpa@ececs.uc.edu

UNIVERSITY OF DELAWARE

Department of History, Newark, DE, 19716, United States of America
Tel: (1) 302 831 8226
Fax: (1) 302 831 1538
Email: pato@udel.edu
Website: www.udel.edu
Contact: Ms Patricia H Orendorf, Administrative Assistant

The Department of History offers MA and PhD programmes in American and European history and more limited graduate study Ancient, African, Asian, Latin American, and Middle Eastern history. In conjunction with these, it offers special programmes in the history of industrialization, material culture studies, American Civilization, and museum studies.

E Lyman Stewart Fellowship

Subjects: History.
Purpose: To provide a programme of graduate study leading to an MA or PhD degree for students who plan careers as museum professionals, historical agency administrators or seek careers in college teaching and public history.
Eligibility: Open to nationals of any country.
Level of Study: Graduate, Predoctorate, Doctorate
Type: Fellowship
Value: US$15,200 plus tuition
Study Establishment: University of Delaware
Country of Study: United States of America
No. of awards offered: 6–8
Application Procedure: Applicants must submit an application form, transcripts, Graduate Record Examination (GRE) scores, Test of English as a Foreign Language (TOEFL) scores where applicable, plus three letters of recommendation and a writing sample.
Closing Date: January 15th
Funding: Private
No. of awards given last year: 7
No. of applicants last year: 21
Additional Information: This is a residential programme.

Fellowships in the University of Delaware Hagley Program

Subjects: The history of industrialization (broadly defined to include business, economics, labour and social history) and the history of science and technology.
Purpose: To provide a programme of graduate study leading to an MA or PhD degree for students who seek careers in college teaching and public history.
Eligibility: Open to graduates of any nationality seeking degrees in American or European history or the history of science and technology.
Level of Study: Predoctorate, Doctorate, Graduate
Type: Fellowship
Value: US$14,000 for Master's and doctoral candidates. All tuition fees for university courses are paid
Length of Study: 1 year, renewable once for those seeking a terminal MA and up to three times for those seeking the doctorate
Frequency: Annual
Study Establishment: University of Delaware
Country of Study: United States of America
No. of awards offered: Approx. 2–3
Application Procedure: Fellows are selected upon Graduate Record Examination scores, recommendations, undergraduate grade index, work experience and personal interviews.
Closing Date: January 15th
Funding: Private
No. of awards given last year: 3
No. of applicants last year: 16
Additional Information: This is a residential programme.

UNIVERSITY OF DUBLIN, TRINITY COLLEGE

Graduate Studies Office, Arts Building, Trinity College, Dublin 2, Ireland
Tel: (353) 1 896 1166
Email: gradinfo@tcd.ie
Website: www.tcd.ie/graduate_studies
Contact: Bernadette Curtis

The University of Dublin, Trinity College was founded in 1592 and is the oldest university in Ireland. Trinity College is the sole constituent college of the University. Trinity is now ranked in the top 20 European universities (13th) and 53rd in the world by international employers.

Claude and Vincenette Pichois Research Award

Subjects: French literature.
Purpose: To support research in 19th and/or 20th century french literature.
Eligibility: Open to all candidates.
Level of Study: Research
Type: Scholarship
Value: €16,000 per annum
Length of Study: 3 years
Frequency: Every 3 years
Country of Study: Ireland
Application Procedure: Applications should be mailed to Graduate Studies Office, Trinity College.
Contributor: Claude and Vincenette Pichois Memorial Fund

Cluff Memorial Studentship

Subjects: History.
Purpose: To support postgraduate study in history.
Eligibility: Open to all candidates in history.
Level of Study: Research
Type: Studentship
Value: €2,285 per annum
Length of Study: 1–3 years
Frequency: Dependent on funds available
Country of Study: Ireland
Application Procedure: Applications should be mailed to the Professor of Modern history, Trinity College Dublin.
Funding: Individuals
Contributor: Mr W.V.Cluff

E.C. Smith Scholarship in Pathology

Subjects: Pathology.
Purpose: To support research in pathology.
Eligibility: Open to all candidates.
Level of Study: Research
Type: Scholarship
Value: €9,523 per annum
Length of Study: 2 years
Frequency: Every 3 years
Country of Study: Ireland
Application Procedure: Applications should be mailed to the Graduate Studies Office, Trinity College.

Elrington Scholarship

Subjects: Theology.
Purpose: To support theological research.
Eligibility: Open to all candidates in theology and/or divinity and/or related academic disciplines.
Level of Study: Research
Type: Scholarship
Value: €3,174
Length of Study: 2 years
Frequency: Every 2 years
Country of Study: Ireland
Application Procedure: Applications should be mailed to the Professor of Theology, University of Dublin, Trinity College.

Frances E. Moran Research Studentship

Subjects: Law.
Purpose: To support research in Irish law.
Eligibility: Open to all candidates.
Level of Study: Research
Type: Studentship
Value: €1,841–2,222 plus full fees cover
Length of Study: 1 year
Frequency: Annual
Country of Study: Ireland
Application Procedure: Applications should be mailed to the Regius, Professor of Laws, Trinity College.

Henry Flood Research Scholarship

Subjects: Irish.
Purpose: To support research in the area of Irish folk and language studies.
Eligibility: Open to all candidates.
Level of Study: Research
Type: Scholarship
Value: €8,000 plus EU fee cover per annum
Length of Study: 1–2 years
Frequency: Annual
Country of Study: Ireland
Application Procedure: Applications should be mailed to the Professor of Irish, University of Dublin, Trinity College.

Home Hewson Scholarship

Subjects: Music, theatre, literature and visual arts.
Purpose: To support studies in music, literature, theatre and visual arts.
Eligibility: Open to all candidates.
Level of Study: Research
Type: Scholarship
Value: €2,539 (approx) per annum
Length of Study: 1–3 years
Frequency: Dependent on funds available
Country of Study: Ireland
Application Procedure: Applications should be mailed to the Professor of Music, University of Dublin, Trinity College.

Postgraduate Research Studentships

Purpose: To support theological research.
Eligibility: Open to new entrants to the full-time research register.
Level of Study: Research
Type: Scholarship
Value: €8,000 plus full fees cover per annum
Length of Study: 3 years
Frequency: Annual
Country of Study: Ireland
Application Procedure: Completed application form must be submitted to the organization.

Postgraduate Travelling Scholarship in Medicine and Surgery

Subjects: Medicine and Surgery.
Purpose: To encourage younger graduates to undertake further work in specialised aspects of medicine and surgery, including the acquisition of modern techniques and the carrying out of research.
Eligibility: Open to all candidates.
Level of Study: Research
Type: Scholarship
Value: €22,220 (plus the Sheppard Memorial Prize value €5,078)
Length of Study: 1 year
Frequency: Annual
Country of Study: Ireland
Application Procedure: Applications should be mailed to the Graduate Studies Office, Trinity College.
Contributor: John Banks Fund, E. Hallaran Bennett Fund, Bicentenary Fund and Dr H. Hutchinson Stewart Fund

Postgraduate Ussher Fellowships

Purpose: To support research students.
Eligibility: Open to new entrants to the full time research register.
Level of Study: Research
Type: Fellowship
Value: €16,000 plus full cover of fees per annum
Length of Study: 3 years
Frequency: Annual
Country of Study: Ireland
Application Procedure: Completed application must be submitted to Trinity College Dublin.

Professor D.A. Webb Scholarship

Subjects: Botany.
Purpose: To support research in botany.
Eligibility: Open to all candidates.

Level of Study: Research
Type: Scholarship
Value: €6,348
Length of Study: 1 year
Frequency: Dependent on funds available
Country of Study: Ireland
Application Procedure: Applications should be mailed to the Curator of the Herbarium, Trinity College.

Raq O'sMeara Research Fund

Subjects: Medicine.
Purpose: To support research in the field of cancer and allied disorders.
Eligibility: Open to all candidates.
Level of Study: Research
Type: Scholarship
Value: €10,158
Frequency: Every 2 years
Country of Study: Ireland
Application Procedure: Applications should be mailed to the Dean of the Health Sciences faculty.
Contributor: Marie Curie Memorial Foundation

RB McDowell Ussher Fellowship

Subjects: Modern history.
Purpose: To support research in modern history.
Eligibility: Open to students registered for a higher degree by research leading to a PhD in modern history.
Level of Study: Research
Type: Fellowship
Value: €16,680 plus full fees cover per annum
Length of Study: 3 years
Frequency: Every 3 years
Country of Study: Ireland
Application Procedure: Completed application must be submitted to Trinity College Dublin.
Contributor: London Trust for Trinity College Dublin

White Postgraduate Fellowship

Subjects: Irish art history.
Purpose: To support research in Irish Art History.
Eligibility: Open to all candidates.
Level of Study: Research
Type: Fellowship
Value: €15,000 (plus full fee cover) per annum
Length of Study: 3 years
Frequency: Annual
Country of Study: Ireland
Application Procedure: Applications should be mailed to Irish Art Research Centre, Trinity College.

UNIVERSITY OF EAST ANGLIA (UEA)

Faculty of Arts and Humanities, School of Literature and Creative Writing, Norwich, Norfolk, NR4 7TJ, England
Tel: (44) 16 0359 2810
Fax: (44) 16 0350 7728
Email: v.striker@uea.ac.uk
Website: www.uea.ac.uk
Contact: Fellowship Administrator

The University of East Anglia (UEA) is organized into 23 schools of study encompassing arts and humanities, health, sciences and social sciences. These are supported by central service and administration departments.

Charles Pick Fellowship

Subjects: Fictional and nonfictional literature.
Purpose: To assist and support the work of a new and as yet unpublished writer of fiction or nonfictional prose and to give promising writers time to devote to the development of their talent.
Eligibility: Open to applicants of all ages and nationalities who are writers of fiction or nonfictional prose in English. Applicants must not yet have had a book published, but all applicants must provide a

reference from either an editor, agent or accredited teacher of creative writing to be sent directly to the Charles Pick Fellowship.
Level of Study: Professional development
Type: Fellowship
Value: UK £10,000 plus free accommodation provided on the university campus
Length of Study: 6 months, starting September 1st
Frequency: Annual
Study Establishment: University of East Anglia
Country of Study: United Kingdom
No. of awards offered: 1
Application Procedure: Applicants must submit a completed application form together with a typescript of an original unpublished piece of fiction or nonfiction. This should not be more than 2,500 words, written in English. Emailed and faxed applications and any application form sent without a reference will not be accepted. Late references will also not be accepted. There will be no interviews but candidates will be judged on the quality and promise of their writing, the project they describe and their reference. They will also be expected to provide reasonable proof of writing progress on occasion during their residency. Application documents are available at www.uea.ac.uk/LIT
Closing Date: January 31st
Funding: Private
No. of awards given last year: 1
No. of applicants last year: 160
Additional Information: The Charles Pick Fellowship is dedicated to the memory of the distinguished publisher and literary agent, Charles Pick, whose career began in 1933 and continued until shortly before his death in January 2000. He encouraged young writers at the start of their careers with introductions to other writers as well as practical and financial help. The new fellowship seeks to continue this spirit of encouragement by giving support to the work of a new and as yet, unpublished writer of fictional or nonfictional prose. Please note that for the purposes of this fellowship, nonfictional prose includes, for example, biography, memoir and travel writing but not critical or historical monographs based on academic research.

David T K Wong Fellowship

Subjects: Writing.
Purpose: To support promising writers in producing a work of fiction set in the Far East.
Eligibility: Open to all writers whose projects deal with some aspect of life in the Far East.
Level of Study: Professional development
Type: Fellowship
Value: UK £26,000
Length of Study: 1 academic year
Frequency: Annual
Study Establishment: UEA
Country of Study: United Kingdom
No. of awards offered: 1
Application Procedure: Applicants must obtain further information and application forms by writing to the School of Literature and Creative Writing at UEA, Norwich NR4 7TJ or visiting the website www.uea.ac.uk/LIT
Closing Date: January 31st
Funding: Private
Contributor: David T K Wong
No. of awards given last year: 1
No. of applicants last year: 50
Additional Information: The Far East is defined as Brunei, Cambodia, Hong Kong, Indonesia, Japan, Korea, Laos, Macau, Malaysia, Mongolia, Myanmar, Peoples' Republic of China, Philippines, Singapore, Taiwan, Thailand and Vietnam.

THE UNIVERSITY OF EDINBURGH

Old College, South Bridge, Edinburgh, EH8 9YL, Scotland
Tel: (44) 13 1651 4067
Fax: (44) 13 1650 8223
Email: registry@ed.ac.uk
Website: www.scholarships.ed.ac.uk
Contact: Robert Lawrie The Scholarships and Student Finance Office

The University of Edinburgh is an international centre of excellence in research and teaching, with outstanding resources and facilities for postgraduate students across the whole range of academic disciplines. More than 160 taught postgraduate programmes are available, with around 130 academic units offering subjects for degrees by research.

American Friends of the University of Edinburgh Scholarship

Subjects: All subjects.
Purpose: To foster good relations with students from the United States of America and to enhance graduate study opportunities for deserving students.
Eligibility: Applicants must hold a United States of America passport.
Level of Study: Postgraduate
Type: Scholarship
Value: One scholarship at US$5,000 and two at US$2,000
Frequency: Annual
Study Establishment: The University of Edinburgh
Country of Study: Scotland
No. of awards offered: 2
Application Procedure: Applicants must complete an application form, available from the Scholarship and Student Finance Office, and enclose a copy of their degree transcript as well as two academic references in sealed envelopes.
Closing Date: April 1st
Contributor: The University of Edinburgh USA Development Trust, Inc
No. of awards given last year: 3

Birzeit Chevening Scholarship

Subjects: Any subject offered by the University.
Purpose: To assist graduates of Berzeit University who apply for a one-year taught Master's degree in any subject offered by the University of Edinburgh.
Eligibility: Graduates of Berzeit University with outstanding academic ability, an excellent command of written and spoken English and substantially relevant work experience can apply. They should have a commitment to contribute significantly to the development of Palestinian society.
Level of Study: Graduate
Type: Scholarship
Value: The scholarship will cover tuition fees, a monthly stipend and return flights
Length of Study: 1 year
Study Establishment: The University of Edinburgh
Country of Study: Scotland
Application Procedure: Please contact the British Council for further details.

College of Medicine and Veterinary Medicine PhD Studentship

Subjects: Eight PhD studentships for prospective PhD candidates who are required to select their research project from 30 available projects.
Eligibility: Applicants should hold, or expect to obtain a first or upper second class (Honours) degree or equivalent qualification in a relevant subject.
Level of Study: Doctorate
Type: Scholarship
Value: An annual stipend of UK £12,940 per academic year, payment of tuition fees at the United Kingdom/European Union rate, payment of bench fees and an annual conference allowance
Study Establishment: The University of Edinburgh
Country of Study: Scotland
No. of awards offered: 8
Application Procedure: Applicants are asked to select from the 30 projects on offer, and to submit a completed application form. Applications not using the application form may not be accepted. Applicants are also required to arrange for two confidential referee reports to be submitted by the closing date.
Closing Date: February 1st
Additional Information: For further information please check the website www.mvm.ed.ac.uk/gradschool/apply/funding.htm

For further information contact:

College of Medicine and Veterinary Medicine, University of Edinburgh, Queens Medical Research Institute, 47 Little France Crescent, Edinburgh, EH16 4TJ
Contact: Dorothy Watson

The Craig Mathieson China Master's Scholarship
Subjects: All subjects.
Purpose: To support full-time study leading to a Master's degree in any discipline.
Eligibility: Open to Chinese citizens who are normally resident in China and who are entering a full-time Master's programme at the University of Edinburgh.
Level of Study: Postgraduate
Type: Scholarship
Value: UK £5,000
Length of Study: 1 year
Frequency: Annual
Study Establishment: The University of Edinburgh
Country of Study: Scotland
No. of awards offered: 1
Application Procedure: Applicants must complete an application form available from the Scholarships and Student Finance Office, and enclose a copy of their degree transcript as well as two academic references in sealed envelopes.
Closing Date: April 1st
No. of awards given last year: 1

The Denwyn Dobby Scholarship
Subjects: Philosophy, psychology and language sciences.
Purpose: To support full-time research in the Koestler Parapsychology Unit in the School of Philosophy, Psychology and Language Sciences.
Eligibility: Open to students who are entering a full-time research degree within the Koestler Parapsychology Unit in the School of Philosophy, Psychology and Language Sciences. For details, please visit the website www.scholarships.ed.ac.uk/postgraduate/colleges/koestler.htm
Level of Study: Postgraduate, Research
Type: Scholarship
Value: United Kingdom tuition fees plus an appropriate living allowance as determined by the Koestler Chair
Length of Study: Tenable for 1 year in the first instance. Renewable for 2 further years pending satisfactory progress
Frequency: Annual
Study Establishment: The University of Edinburgh
Country of Study: Scotland
No. of awards offered: 1
Application Procedure: Candidates should send a written notice of their intention to compete for the scholarships to the Koestler Professor of parapsychology. Along with their application, candidates should submit a statement of not more than 1,500 words explaining their research project and how the award will assist them to carry out their research in parapsychology.
Closing Date: April 14th
No. of awards given last year: 1

For further information contact:

School of Philosophy, Psychology and Language Sciences, 7 George Square, Edinburgh, EH8 9SZ, Scotland

Malaysia Chevening Scholarship
Subjects: International law, economics, international and European politics, sustainable energy systems, environment and development, environmental protection and management, environmental sustainability, e-science, high performance computing and informatics.
Purpose: To enable a Malaysian student to undertake a one-year taught Master's degree at the University of Edinburgh.
Eligibility: Please contact the British Council.
Level of Study: Graduate
Type: Scholarship
Length of Study: 1 year
Study Establishment: The University of Edinburgh

Country of Study: Scotland
Application Procedure: Please contact the British Council.

Russia Chevening Scholarship
Subjects: Comparative public policy, ecological economics, economics/economic finance - Scottish graduate programme, environment and development, environmental protection and management, environmental sustainability, European law, European Union politics and law, forest geosciences, geosciences (by research), global environmental change (by research), global health management/health administration, innovation, technology and law, international and European politics, law, international law, law and society, nationalism studies, policy studies, public health policy (global health), public health policy (public-private partnerships), public health research, science and technology studies, sustainable energy systems.
Purpose: To enable a Russian student to undertake a one-year taught Master's degree at the University of Edinburgh.
Eligibility: Open to Russian students.
Type: Scholarship
Value: The scholarship will cover tuition fees, a monthly stipend and return flights
Length of Study: 1 year
Study Establishment: The University of Edinburgh
Country of Study: Scotland
Application Procedure: Details of the Russia Scholarship Scheme can be obtained from the British Council.
Closing Date: October 10th

Shell Centenary Scholarships and Shell Centenary Chevening Scholarships at Edinburgh
Subjects: Applied sciences and technology, including environmental sciences.
Eligibility: Students from countries that are not present or applicant members of the Organization for Economic Co-operation and Development (OECD). Candidates should be resident in one of the non-OECD countries and be intending to return to the country concerned at the end of the period of study. They should normally already hold a degree equivalent to a United Kingdom First Class (Honours) Degree or be expecting to obtain such a degree before the start of their proposed course.
Level of Study: Postgraduate
Type: Scholarship
Value: The scholarships covers tuition fees, accommodation, maintenance costs and a return airfare for the scholarship holder
Length of Study: 1 year
Frequency: Annual
Study Establishment: University of Edinburgh
Country of Study: Scotland
No. of awards offered: 6
Application Procedure: Applicants must apply separately for admission to the University of Edinburgh making a clear statement that they wish to be considered for a Shell Scholarship.
Closing Date: March 1st
No. of awards given last year: 6

The University of Edinburgh China and Hong Kong Scholarship
Subjects: To support full-time study leading to a Master's degree in any discipline.
Purpose: To support full-time study leading to a Master's degree in any discipline.
Eligibility: Open to Chinese citizens who are normally resident in China or the Hong Kong SAR and who are entering a full-time Master's programme at the University of Edinburgh.
Level of Study: Postgraduate
Type: Scholarship
Value: 1 year - Full tuition fees
Length of Study: 1 year
Frequency: Annual
Study Establishment: The University of Edinburgh
Country of Study: Scotland
No. of awards offered: 1
Application Procedure: Applicants must complete an application form available from the Scholarships and Student Finance, and

enclose a copy of their degree transcript as well as two academic references in sealed envelopes.
Closing Date: April 1st
No. of awards given last year: 1

University of Edinburgh College of Humanities and Social Science Research Studentships and Scholarships
Subjects: All subjects.
Eligibility: Students should hold, or expect to obtain, a First Class or Upper Second Class (Honours) Degree from the United Kingdom or the overseas equivalent. Candidates who have progressed to obtain a Master's degree with distinction will also be considered.
Level of Study: Doctorate, MPhil, MLitt
Type: Studentship and scholarship
Value: United Kingdom tuition fees and a maintenance allowance broadly equivalent to those of the United Kingdom Research Councils and the British Academy. Research costs may also be paid. Studentship value Tuition fees of UK/Eu rate, annual stipend and research expenses. Scholarship value Tuition fees (UK/EU rate) and research expenses.
Frequency: Annual
Study Establishment: The University of Edinburgh
Country of Study: Scotland
Application Procedure: Candidates must be recommended for a studentship by the head of the school in which they wish to study. Candidates who wish to be nominated should contact the relevant school office.
Closing Date: February 26th
Additional Information: For further information please see the website www.hss.ed.ac.uk/postgraduate

For further information contact:

College of Humanities and Social Sciences, Postgraduate office, 1st floor, David Hume Towers, George square, Edinburgh, EH8 9JY

The University of Edinburgh International Master's Scholarships
Subjects: All subjects.
Purpose: To support full-time study leading to a Master's degree in any discipline.
Eligibility: Open to one year Master's students from certain eligible countries as detailed at: www.scholarships.ed.ac.uk/postgraduate/internat/other.htm
Level of Study: Postgraduate
Type: Scholarship
Value: UK £3,000
Length of Study: 1 year
Frequency: Annual
Study Establishment: The University of Edinburgh
Country of Study: Scotland
No. of awards offered: At least 20
Application Procedure: Applicants must complete an application form available from the Scholarships and Student Finance Office, and enclose a copy of their degree transcript as well as two academic references in sealed envelopes.
Closing Date: April 1st
Contributor: University of Edinburgh
No. of awards given last year: 42

The University of Edinburgh ORS Linked Scholarship
Subjects: All subjects.
Eligibility: Open to overseas postgraduate research students in any discipline who are in receipt of an Overseas Research Student (OR-SAS) Award.
Level of Study: Postgraduate
Type: Scholarship
Value: United Kingdom/European Union tuition fees
Length of Study: A maximum of 3 years
Frequency: Annual
Study Establishment: The University of Edinburgh
No. of awards offered: 8
Application Procedure: As all ORSAS applicants are automatically considered, no separate application is required for these scholarships.
No. of awards given last year: 8

The University of Edinburgh UK/EU Master's Scholarships
Subjects: Any subject offered by the University.
Purpose: To assist UK/EU students who have been accepted by the University to study on a one year full-time Master's programme in any subject area by covering a part of their tuition fees.
Eligibility: The scholarships will be awarded to UK/EU citizens who have been accepted for admission on a full-time basis for a postgraduate Master's programme in any subject offered by the University. Candidates must have or expect to obtain a UK first class or upper second class Honours degree or the overseas equivalent before applying for admission.
Level of Study: Graduate
Type: Scholarship
Value: Up to £4850
Length of Study: 1 year
Study Establishment: University of Edinburgh
Country of Study: Scotland
No. of awards offered: 12
Application Procedure: Applicants can download an application form or request one from The Scholarships and Students Finance Office of the University. A completed application form along with a copy of the degree transcript and two academic references should be sent.
Closing Date: May 1st

For further information contact:

Tel: 13 1651 4070
Fax: 13 1651 4066
Email: scholarships@ed.ac.uk

Wellcome Trust 4-Year PhD Programme Studentships
Subjects: The cellular and molecular basis of disease.
Eligibility: Students should be from a life sciences background and should hold, or expect to obtain, at least an Upper Second Class (Honours) Degree.
Level of Study: Doctorate
Type: Studentship
Value: Tax-free stipend (UK £14,200–16,400), tuition fees and research costs
Frequency: Annual
Study Establishment: The University of Edinburgh
Country of Study: Scotland
No. of awards offered: 5
Application Procedure: Students wishing to apply should supply a covering letter, a curriculum vitae, a one page statement supporting their application and stating the reasons for wishing to follow this programme of research training. Applicants should also have three reference reports sent directly to the graduate school.
Closing Date: January 5th
No. of awards given last year: 5

For further information contact:

The University of Edinburgh, Swann Building, King's Buildings, Mayfield Road, Edinburgh, EH9 3JR
Contact: Programme Secretary, Life Sciences Graduate Programme

UNIVERSITY OF ESSEX

Graduate Admissions Office, University of Essex, Wivenhoe Park, Colchester, C04 3SQ, England
Tel: (44) 12 0687 2719
Fax: (44) 12 0687 2808
Email: pgadmit@essex.ac.uk
Website: www.essex.ac.uk
Contact: Marketing Officer (Postgraduate)

The University of Essex is one of the United Kingdom's leading academic institutions, rated tenth nationally in the most recent Research Assessment Exercise. It offers degrees and research opportunities across 19 academic departments (including government and sociology, which both have 6-star research ratings) and numerous research centres of world renown. As a result the teaching that we provide is informed by leading world-class researchers.

Access to Learning Fund
Subjects: All subjects.
Purpose: To support home students with study.
Eligibility: Applicants must be home students.
Level of Study: Unrestricted
Type: Grant
Value: According to individual needs
Frequency: Annual
Study Establishment: University of Essex
Country of Study: United Kingdom
Application Procedure: Applicants must contact Student Support.
Funding: Government
Contributor: ALF

AHRC Doctoral Award for PhD in History
Subjects: History from 1500 AD to present day.
Purpose: Support research students.
Eligibility: Applicants must be postgraduate students. Research must be humanities based.
Level of Study: Postgraduate
Type: Scholarship
Value: British full-time: fees and maintenance of around UK £12,600 part-time: fees and around UK £250 per annum EU: dependent on residency status
Frequency: Annual
Study Establishment: University of Essex
Country of Study: United Kingdom
Application Procedure: Applicants must contact the department concerned.
Contributor: AHRC

AHRC Research Preparations Masters Scheme for History
Subjects: History from 1500 AD to present day.
Purpose: Support MA Student (full-time home or EU).
Eligibility: Applicants must be postgraduate students. Study must be humanities based. Must have first or high 2.1.
Level of Study: Postgraduate
Type: Scholarship
Value: British-fees and around UK £8,800 maintenance EU-dependent an residency status
Length of Study: One year
Frequency: Annual
Study Establishment: University of Essex
Country of Study: United Kingdom
Application Procedure: Applicants must contact the department concerned.
Contributor: AHRB

Art History Bursary
Subjects: Art history and theory.
Purpose: To support postgraduate study.
Eligibility: Applicants must be postgraduates.
Level of Study: Postgraduate
Type: Bursary
Value: Approx UK £1,200
Frequency: Dependent on funds available
Study Establishment: University of Essex
Country of Study: United Kingdom
No. of awards offered: 1
Application Procedure: Applicants must contact the department concerned.
Funding: Foundation, private

BBSRC Studentship
Subjects: Biological sciences.
Purpose: To support postgraduate biological science students.
Eligibility: Open to applicants who are biological science postgraduates, but mathematics or computing graduates may be eligible depending on the project.
Level of Study: Postgraduate
Type: Studentship
Value: £12,940
Length of Study: 3 years
Frequency: Annual

Study Establishment: University of Essex
Country of Study: United Kingdom
No. of awards offered: None for October 2009
Application Procedure: Applicants must contact the department concerned.
Funding: Government
Contributor: BBSRC
No. of awards given last year: 1
No. of applicants last year: 20

British Marshall Scholarships
Subjects: All research degrees.
Purpose: Support American students doing a research degree.
Eligibility: Applicants must be postgraduate students. American students applying for full-time degree.
Level of Study: Postgraduate, Research
Type: Scholarship
Value: Tuition fees, living expenses, annual book grant, thesis grant, research and daily travel grant, fares to and from the US
Frequency: Annual
Study Establishment: University of Essex
Country of Study: United Kingdom
Application Procedure: Applicants must contact the department concerned. See www.marshallscholarship.org
Closing Date: Mid-October of year before tenure
Funding: Foundation

For further information contact:

Email: macc@acu.ac.uk
Website: www.marshallscholarships.org

Canon Collins Trust
Subjects: All postgraduate subjects.
Purpose: To support postgraduate study.
Eligibility: Commonwealth students.
Level of Study: Postgraduate
Value: Maintenance and tuition fees for taught study; partial funding for PhD study
Frequency: Annual
Study Establishment: University of Essex
Country of Study: United Kingdom
Closing Date: March
Funding: Government
Contributor: Partnership with British Foreign and Commonwealth Office

For further information contact:

Website: www.canoncollins.org.uk

Department of Biological Sciences Studentships
Subjects: Biological sciences.
Purpose: To support postgraduate biological science students.
Eligibility: Open to applicants who are biological science postgraduates, mathematics or computing graduates are also eligible depending on the project.
Level of Study: Postgraduate
Type: Studentship
Value: £10,500
Length of Study: 3 years (+6 months)
Frequency: Annual
Study Establishment: University of Essex
Country of Study: United Kingdom
No. of awards offered: 2 or 3
Application Procedure: Applicants must contact the department concerned.
Contributor: University of Essex
No. of awards given last year: 2
No. of applicants last year: 15

Department of Economics 1+3 and +3 Quota Awards and Competition Awards
Subjects: Economics.
Purpose: To support postgraduate study.

Eligibility: Applicants must be postgraduates. Applicants must be from UK and EU.
Level of Study: Postgraduate
Type: Studentship
Value: Fees and maintenance for home students. Fees only for European Union students
Frequency: Annual
Study Establishment: University of Essex
Country of Study: United Kingdom
No. of awards offered: Not yet known
Application Procedure: Applicants must contact the department concerned.
Closing Date: Mid-March
Contributor: ESRC
No. of awards given last year: 3 Quota
No. of applicants last year: 15

Department of Language and Linguistics AHRC Scholarships

Subjects: Linguistics, syntax, phonology or English language and linguistics; theoretical historical and descriptive linguistics.
Purpose: To support postgraduate and PhD study in linguistics.
Eligibility: Open to students in linguistics who propose to take MA or PhD and have high prior academic achievement.
Level of Study: Doctorate, Postgraduate
Type: Scholarship
Value: Covers fees and maintenance for UK students and only fees for EU students
Length of Study: 1 or 3 years
Frequency: Annual
Study Establishment: University of Essex
Country of Study: United Kingdom
Application Procedure: For applications contact angelina@essex.ac.uk
Closing Date: March
Contributor: AHRC
No. of awards given last year: 1
No. of applicants last year: 1
Additional Information: Applicants not selected for AHRC are automatically considered for University of Essex scholarships.

Department of Language and Linguistics ESRC + 3 Studentships

Subjects: Social linguistics, psycho linguistics, computational linguistics, language acquisition, applied linguistics, english language teaching.
Purpose: To support postgraduate and PhD study in linguistics.
Eligibility: Open to postgraduate students in linguistics who are embarking on PhD and already have suitable training and high academic achievement.
Level of Study: Doctorate, Postgraduate
Type: Scholarship
Value: Fees and maintenance for students from United Kingdom; only fees for students from European Union
Length of Study: 3 years
Frequency: Annual
Study Establishment: University of Essex
Country of Study: United Kingdom
Application Procedure: For applications contact angelina@essex.ac.uk
Closing Date: March
Contributor: ESRC
Additional Information: Unsuccessful candidates are considered for University of Essex scholarships.

Department of Language and Linguistics ESRC 1+3 Studentships

Subjects: Socio linguistics, psycho linguistics, computational linguistics, language acquisition, applied linguistics, english language teaching.
Purpose: To support postgraduate and Phd study in linguistics.
Eligibility: Open to postgraduate students in linguistics proposing to take an MA for training, followed by PhD, and who have high academic achievement.
Level of Study: Doctorate, Postgraduate

Type: Scholarship
Value: Fees and maintenance for students from United Kingdom; only fees for students from European Union
Length of Study: 4 years
Frequency: Annual
Study Establishment: University of Essex
Country of Study: United Kingdom
Application Procedure: For applications contact angelina@essex.ac.uk
Closing Date: March
Contributor: ESRC
Additional Information: Unsuccessful candidates are considered for University of Essex scholarships.

Department of Language and Linguistics ORSAS Award

Subjects: All areas of linguistics, applied linguistics, sociolinguistics, psycholinguistics, english language teaching.
Purpose: Support PhD study in Linguistics.
Eligibility: Students from all countries outside UK and EU with high academic background wishing to take PhD (3 years) or already in the first year of the PhD.
Level of Study: Doctorate
Type: Scholarship
Value: Difference between home student fee and overseas student fee
Length of Study: 2 or 3 years
Frequency: Annual
Study Establishment: University of Essex
Country of Study: United Kingdom
Application Procedure: Contact angelina@essex.ac.uk
Closing Date: January
Contributor: ORSAS
No. of applicants last year: 6
Additional Information: Unsuccessful ORSAS applicants are automatically considered for University of Essex scholarships. Successful applicants automatically get a University of Essex scholarship to pay the balance of fees not covered by ORSAS.

Department of Psychology Scholarships

Subjects: Psychology.
Purpose: To support PhD research.
Eligibility: Home or European Union students with a First Class or a High Second Class (Honours) Degree in psychology or related discipline are eligible to apply.
Level of Study: Doctorate
Type: Student bursary
Value: UK £9,000 maintenance per year plus fees
Length of Study: 3 years
Frequency: Dependent on funds available
Study Establishment: University of Essex
Country of Study: United Kingdom
No. of awards offered: 2
Application Procedure: Applicants must first apply for a PhD and then appear for an interview on offer of admission.
Closing Date: May 27th
Contributor: University of Essex and the Department of Psychology
No. of awards given last year: Two

Don Pike Award

Subjects: Philosophy of social science.
Purpose: Support students over the age of 21 working in one field of philosophy of social sciences at postgraduate or undergraduate level.
Eligibility: Applicants must be students working on philosophy of social science.
Level of Study: Unrestricted
Type: Scholarship
Value: UK £250 towards purchase of books and expenses in preparing a thesis or dissertation
Frequency: Annual
Study Establishment: University of Essex
Country of Study: United Kingdom
Application Procedure: Applicants must contact the department concerned.
Funding: Trusts

EPSRC Department of Psychology Studentship

Subjects: Psychology.
Purpose: To support PhD research.
Eligibility: Home or European Union students with a First Class or High Second Class (Honours) Degree in psychology or a related discipline are eligible to apply.
Level of Study: Doctorate
Type: Student bursary
Value: Usually maintenance equivalent to ESCR rate plus fees for home students. Fees only for European Union students
Length of Study: 3 years
Frequency: Dependent on funds available
Study Establishment: University of Essex
Country of Study: United Kingdom
No. of awards offered: Dependent on funds available
Application Procedure: Applicants must first apply for admission to a PhD programme.
Closing Date: July
Contributor: EPSRC

EPSRC School of Computer Science and Electronic Engineering Research Studentship

Subjects: Electronic systems engineering, computer science, applied physics
Purpose: To support postgraduate study.
Eligibility: Applicants must be graduates holding a good UK honours degree or overseas equivalent and preferably a Masters degree.
Level of Study: Doctorate, Postgraduate, Research
Type: Scholarship
Value: Fees and maintenance for UK and EU students resident in the UK for 3 years prior to commencing the course. Fees only for other students
Frequency: Annual
Study Establishment: University of Essex
Country of Study: United Kingdom
Application Procedure: Applicants must submit a formal application for PhD by research and state on the form that they wish to be considered for an EPSRC studentship.
Contributor: EPSRC
No. of awards given last year: 6

For further information contact:

School of Computer Science and Engineering, University of Essex, Wivenhoe Park, Colchester, CO4 3SQ
Contact: Postgraduate Research Administrator

ESRC +3 (PhD research) History Studentship

Subjects: History from 1500 AD to present day.
Purpose: Support full or part-time home/EU student undertake PhD.
Eligibility: Open to postgraduate students undertaking social science based research and successfully completed an ESRC recognised degree.
Level of Study: Postgraduate
Type: Scholarship
Value: British full-time: tuition fees and maintenance of around UK £12,300, British part-time: tuition fees only, EU: level of support depends on residential status
Frequency: Annual
Study Establishment: University Essex
Country of Study: United Kingdom
Application Procedure: Applicants must contact the department concerned.
Contributor: ESRC

ESRC 1+3 Department of Psychology Studentship

Subjects: Psychology.
Purpose: To support PhD research.
Eligibility: Home or European Union students with a First Class or High Second Class (Honours) Degree in psychology or a related discipline are eligible to apply.
Level of Study: Postgraduate, 1-year Master's in research methods followed by a 3 year doctorate
Type: Student bursary
Value: Up to UK £12,000 maintenance plus fees for home students; fees only for European Union students

Length of Study: 4 years
Frequency: Annual
Study Establishment: University of Essex
Country of Study: United Kingdom
Application Procedure: Applicants must first apply for admission to a PhD programme. Their application is then submitted by the department to the ESRC national competition.
Closing Date: April
Contributor: ESRC
No. of awards given last year: 1

ESRC 1+3 History Studentship

Subjects: History from 1500 AD to the present day.
Purpose: To support student in pursuing an MA and PhD in history.
Eligibility: Open to British and EU full or part-time students proposing to undertake social science based research and having been accepted on the MA researching history in Britain.
Level of Study: Postgraduate
Type: Studentship
Value: British students-tuition fees and maintenance of up to UK £12,300 for full-time study, fees only for part time EU-level of support depends on residential status
Length of Study: 4 years
Frequency: Annual
Study Establishment: University of Essex
Country of Study: United Kingdom
Application Procedure: Applicants must contact the department concerned.
Contributor: University of Essex ESRC

ESRC+3 Department of Psychology Studentship

Subjects: Psychology.
Purpose: To support PhD research.
Eligibility: Home or European Union students with a First Class or High Second Class (Honours) Degree in psychology or a related discipline are eligible to apply. Applicants must hold an ESRC-approved MSc in psychological research methods.
Level of Study: Doctorate
Type: Student bursary
Value: Up to UK £12,000 maintenance plus fees for home students fees only for European Union students
Length of Study: 3 years
Frequency: Annual
Study Establishment: University of Essex
Country of Study: United Kingdom
No. of awards offered: National competition
Application Procedure: Applicants must first apply for admission to a PhD programme. Their application will then be submitted by the department to the ESRC national competition.
Closing Date: April
Contributor: ESRC
No. of awards given last year: 1

Essex Rotary University Travel Grants

Subjects: All subjects.
Purpose: To support students to spend time studying abroad.
Eligibility: Applicants must be a students at the University of Essex.
Level of Study: Unrestricted
Type: Grant
Frequency: Annual
Study Establishment: University of Essex
Country of Study: United Kingdom
No. of awards offered: 2
Application Procedure: Applicants must send a statement (not exceeding 500 words) indicating what they would do with a rotary travel grant.
Closing Date: Monday of the 2nd week of the Summer term
Funding: Trusts
Contributor: Rotary clubs in Essex
No. of awards given last year: 2
Additional Information: Successful applicants may be invited to give not more than 3 to Rotary Clubs is Essex on their return. See website www.ac.uk/academic/docs/cal/stship.shtm

Giulia Mereu Scholarships

Subjects: LLM International Human Rights Law.
Purpose: Support a student on the University of Essex LLM in International Human Rights Law.
Eligibility: Applicants must be postgraduate students on the LLM in International Human Rights Law at Essex and must hold a firm offer from the school.
Type: Scholarship
Value: Equivalent to home/EU fees
Length of Study: One year
Frequency: Annual
Study Establishment: University of Essex
Country of Study: United Kingdom
No. of awards offered: One
Application Procedure: Applicants must contact the department concerned.
Closing Date: June 12th
Funding: Trusts
Contributor: Family and friends of Giulia Mereu
No. of awards given last year: 1

MA in Literature, Film, and Theatre Studies Scholarship

Subjects: Department of literature, film and theatre studies.
Purpose: To support MA study.
Eligibility: Open to postgraduate students who already have an offer of a place to study MA in the department.
Level of Study: Postgraduate
Type: Scholarship
Value: To cover Home/EU fees
Length of Study: 1 year
Frequency: Annual
Study Establishment: University of Essex
Country of Study: United Kingdom
No. of awards offered: 2
Application Procedure: Applicants must contact the department concerned.
Contributor: University of Essex
No. of awards given last year: 2

National Federation of Business and Professional Women's Clubs Travel Grants

Subjects: All subjects.
Purpose: To enable full-time female postgraduates to travel for research/studies.
Eligibility: Female full-time postgraduates at the University of Essex.
Level of Study: Postgraduate
Type: Grant
Value: Approx. UK £175
Frequency: Annual
Study Establishment: University of Essex
Country of Study: United Kingdom
No. of awards offered: 1
Application Procedure: See the University website.
Contributor: National Federation of Business and Professional Women's clubs
No. of awards given last year: 1

NERC Studentships

Subjects: Biological sciences.
Purpose: To support postgraduate biological science students.
Eligibility: Applicants must be biological science postgraduates.
Level of Study: Postgraduate
Type: Studentship
Value: £12,940
Length of Study: 3 years (+6 months)
Frequency: Annual
Study Establishment: University of Essex
Country of Study: United Kingdom
No. of awards offered: Usually 3
Application Procedure: Please contact the department concerned.
Funding: Government
Contributor: NERC
No. of awards given last year: 2
No. of applicants last year: 22

ORSAS Awards

Subjects: All subjects.
Purpose: To support international students wanting to undertake postgraduate PhD study.
Eligibility: Overseas Postgraduates.
Level of Study: Postgraduate
Type: Scholarship
Value: Difference between home and overseas tuition fees
Frequency: Annual
Study Establishment: University of Essex
Country of Study: United Kingdom
Application Procedure: Applicants must see the University website and contact the department in which they wish to study.
Closing Date: Application packs are available from departments after November
Funding: Government
Contributor: ORSAS

Oscar Arias Scholarship

Subjects: All subjects.
Purpose: To enable students of Costa Rican nationality to pursue a full-time Master's or doctoral study at Essex.
Eligibility: Costa Rican nationals.
Level of Study: Postgraduate
Type: Scholarship
Length of Study: 1 year, renewable for not more than 2 further years
Frequency: Annual
Study Establishment: University of Essex
Country of Study: United Kingdom
No. of awards offered: 1
Application Procedure: Applicants must be recommended by the British Ambassador in San Jose, who receives nominations from the University.
Funding: International Office, government
Contributor: Foreign office and British Council

PhD in Literature, Film and Theatre Studies Studentship

Subjects: Literature, film, and theatre studies.
Purpose: To support PhD study.
Eligibility: Applicants must be new prospective PhD students with the offer of a place in the institution.
Level of Study: Postgraduate
Type: Scholarship
Value: UK £4,000 for up to 3 years study
Frequency: Annual
Study Establishment: University of Essex
Country of Study: United Kingdom
No. of awards offered: 2
Application Procedure: Applicants must contact the department concerned.
Contributor: University of Essex
No. of awards given last year: 2

Philosophy Graduate Awards

Subjects: Philosophy.
Purpose: To support postgraduate students studying in the Department of Philosophy.
Eligibility: Applicants must be applying to study in the Department of Philosophy at postgraduate level.
Level of Study: Doctorate, Postgraduate
Type: Studentship
Value: Up to £3,000 for home/EU. Up to £6,000 for overseas
Length of Study: 3 years for research (subject to satisfactory progression); 1 year for 1–year study
Frequency: Annual
Study Establishment: University of Essex
Country of Study: United Kingdom
No. of awards offered: 3
Application Procedure: Applicants must complete an application form, available from the department's website.
Closing Date: July 1st
Contributor: University of Essex
No. of awards given last year: 3

Postgraduate Research Studentship

Subjects: Mathematical sciences.
Purpose: To support postgraduate research and taught MSc schemes.
Eligibility: Applicants must be postgraduates.
Level of Study: Postgraduate
Type: Scholarship
Value: Up to UK £2,000
Study Establishment: University of Essex
Country of Study: United Kingdom
Application Procedure: Applicants must contact the department concerned.
Closing Date: Spring
Contributor: University of Essex

Poulter Studentship

Subjects: Science and archaeology.
Purpose: To enable full-time University of Essex graduates to study archaeology or natural science at graduate level.
Eligibility: Applicants must be University of Essex graduates.
Level of Study: Postgraduate
Type: Studentship
Value: Related to amount given by research councils
Length of Study: 1 year in the first instance, renewable for not more than 2 years
Frequency: Dependent on funds available
Study Establishment: University of Essex
Country of Study: United Kingdom
No. of awards offered: Not yet allocated
Application Procedure: Applicants must visit the website.
Closing Date: Spring
Funding: Trusts
Contributor: Bequest from the late H W Poulter

School of Computer Science and Electronic Engineering University Scholarship

Subjects: Computer science, electronic engineering, applied physics
Purpose: Support postgraduate study.
Eligibility: Applicants must be postgraduate students. Students must be home or EU or overseas students who have secured an ORS award or partial funding or are able to partially self-fund.
Level of Study: Postgraduate, Doctorate, Research
Type: Scholarship
Value: Depends on funds available
Frequency: Annual
Study Establishment: University of Essex
Country of Study: United Kingdom
No. of awards offered: 2
Application Procedure: Applicants must submit a formal application for PhD by research and state on the form that they wish to be considered for a scholarship.
Closing Date: Mid Jan for overseas students who want to considered for ORS and university scholarship. July 1st for home/EU applicants
Contributor: University of Essex
No. of awards given last year: 3

For further information contact:

School of Computer Science and Electronic Engineering, University of Essex, Wivenhoe Park, Colchester, CO4 3SQ
Contact: Postgraduate Research Administrator

School of Law AHRC Scholarships

Subjects: Law.
Purpose: Support studies that are arts and humanities based.
Eligibility: Applicants must be postgraduate students whose studies have an arts/humanities basis.
Level of Study: Postgraduate, Research
Type: Scholarship
Value: Fees and maintenance
Frequency: Annual
Study Establishment: University of Essex
Country of Study: United Kingdom
Application Procedure: Applicants must contact the department concerned.
Contributor: AHRC

Sir Eric Berthoud Travel Grant

Subjects: All subjects.
Purpose: To support full-time students wishing to travel as part of their studies/research.
Eligibility: Applicants must be students at the University of Essex.
Level of Study: Unrestricted
Type: Grant
Frequency: Annual
Study Establishment: University of Essex
Country of Study: United Kingdom
Application Procedure: Applicants must visit the website for details.
Funding: Trusts
Contributor: Bequest from Sir Eric Berthoud

Sociology PhD Studentships

Subjects: Sociology.
Purpose: To support PhD students studying within the Department of Sociology.
Eligibility: All.
Level of Study: Postgraduate
Type: Scholarship
Value: Up to UK £1,000
Frequency: Annual
Study Establishment: University of Essex
Country of Study: United Kingdom
Application Procedure: Applicants must contact the department for more information.
Closing Date: Applications considered by research committee which meets three times a year: Deadline for applications is week 5, 19 and 33
Contributor: University of Essex

Travel Grants

Subjects: All subjects.
Purpose: To support students who need additional financial assistance.
Eligibility: Graduate students.
Level of Study: Postgraduate
Type: Grant
Frequency: Annual
Study Establishment: University of Essex
Country of Study: United Kingdom
No. of awards offered: 1–2
Application Procedure: Applicants can obtain application forms from Registry.
Closing Date: Monday of the 2nd week of the Summer term
Contributor: University of Essex
No. of awards given last year: 1–2

University of Essex MA Scholarships

Subjects: History from 1500 AD to the present.
Purpose: To support postgraduates within the Department of History.
Eligibility: Applicants must be postgraduate history students.
Level of Study: Postgraduate
Type: Studentship
Value: UK £1,500–3,000
Length of Study: One year
Frequency: Annual
Study Establishment: University of Essex
Country of Study: United Kingdom
Application Procedure: Applicants must contact the department concerned.
Closing Date: Spring
Contributor: University of Essex
No. of awards given last year: 4
Additional Information: Please note that this university award can not be held concurrently with either research council funding or other external awards.

University of Essex PhD Scholarship

Subjects: History from 1500 AD to the present.
Purpose: To support a PhD student within the Department of History.
Eligibility: Applicants must be PhD students.
Level of Study: Postgraduate
Type: Studentship

Value: Up to UK £8,000
Frequency: Annual
Study Establishment: University of Essex
Country of Study: United Kingdom
Application Procedure: Applicants must contact the department concerned.
Closing Date: Spring
Contributor: University of Essex
No. of awards given last year: 3

University of Essex Scholarships

Subjects: Economics.
Purpose: To support MSc study.
Eligibility: Applicants must be MSc students in the department.
Level of Study: Postgraduate
Type: Studentship
Value: Up to full funding
Length of Study: 1 year
Frequency: Annual
Study Establishment: University of Essex
Country of Study: United Kingdom
No. of awards offered: Variable
Application Procedure: Applicants must apply for an MSc scheme and then apply separately for funds.
Closing Date: April 30th
Contributor: University of Essex

University of Essex Scholarships

Subjects: Law.
Purpose: To support research students.
Eligibility: Applicants must be postgraduate research students with an offer for MPhil or PhD in the school of law.
Level of Study: Research
Type: Scholarship
Value: Fees and same maintenance
Length of Study: Up to 3 years
Frequency: Annual
Study Establishment: University of Essex
Country of Study: United Kingdom
Application Procedure: Applicants must contact the department concerned.
Contributor: University of Essex

University of Essex Scholarships

Subjects: Economics.
Purpose: To support postgraduate study.
Eligibility: Talented postgraduate students from any country.
Level of Study: Postgraduate
Type: Scholarship
Value: Variable
Frequency: Annual
Study Establishment: University of Essex
Country of Study: United Kingdom
No. of awards offered: Varies
Application Procedure: Applicants can obtain an application form from the Department of Economics.
Closing Date: May
No. of awards given last year: 4
No. of applicants last year: 19

University of Essex Scholarships Given by Department of Language and Linguistics

Subjects: All areas of linguistics, applied linguistics, sociolinguistics, psycholinguistics and English language teaching
Purpose: Support postgraduate study in linguistics.
Eligibility: Open to postgraduate students in linguistics from all countries.
Level of Study: Postgraduate
Type: Scholarship
Value: Part fees and maintanence fees
Frequency: Annual
Study Establishment: University of Essex
Country of Study: United Kingdom
No. of awards offered: Depends on funds available.

Application Procedure: Students who apply for ESRC, AHRC or ORSAS funding and fail to obtain it are automatically considered for Essex scholarships when the result of those competitions are known. For applications contact angelina@essex.ac.uk
Closing Date: August
Contributor: University of Essex

UNIVERSITY OF EXETER

Postgraduate Administration Office, Northcote House, The Queen's Drive, Exeter, Devon, EX4 4QJ, England
Tel: (44) 13 9226 3097
Fax: (44) 13 9226 3108
Email: gradfunding@exeter.ac.uk
Website: www.exeter.ac.uk/gradschool
Contact: Mrs Katrina Jones, Administrative Officer

The University of Exeter combines a reputation of national and international excellence in research with a record of established excellence in teaching. Providing a superb environment in which to live and work, the University of Exeter is representative of the best in university education in the United Kingdom.

Andrew Stratton Scholarship

Subjects: Engineering and science.
Purpose: To help to support postgraduate study
Eligibility: Studying for taught Masters in Engineering or science – International only
Level of Study: Postgraduate
Type: Scholarship
Value: Upto UK £1,000
Length of Study: 1 year
Frequency: Dependent on funds available
Study Establishment: The University of Exeter
Country of Study: United Kingdom
No. of awards offered: 1
Application Procedure: Applicants must contact Postgraduate Administration office for further details.
Closing Date: April 30th
No. of awards given last year: 2
No. of applicants last year: 10
Additional Information: Further information is available on request.

Anning Morgan Bursary

Subjects: All subjects.
Purpose: To financially support postgraduate study.
Eligibility: Open to students residing in Duchy of Cornwall prior to entry or during their postgraduate studies.
Level of Study: Postgraduate
Type: Bursary
Value: Upto £750
Length of Study: Maximum 2 years
Frequency: Dependent on funds available
Study Establishment: University of Exeter
Country of Study: United Kingdom
No. of awards offered: 1
Application Procedure: Application forms available from postgraduate administration office.
Closing Date: June 30th
No. of awards given last year: 1
No. of applicants last year: 14
Additional Information: Further information available on request.

British Council Awards and Scholarships for International Students

Subjects: All subjects offered by the University.
Purpose: To allow international students to pursue postgraduate study.
Eligibility: Open to candidates for research degrees who have obtained at least an Upper Second Class (Honours) Degree or its equivalent.
Level of Study: Postgraduate
Type: Scholarship
Value: Varies
Length of Study: Varies

Frequency: Annual
Study Establishment: The University of Exeter
Country of Study: United Kingdom
No. of awards offered: Varies
Application Procedure: Applicants must obtain details from the British Council representative in the applicant's own country.
Closing Date: Please contact the organization
Funding: Government
Additional Information: Further information is available on request.

For further information contact:

Contact British Council

Commonwealth Scholarship Plan
Subjects: All subjects.
Purpose: To allow students to pursue postgraduate study.
Eligibility: Open to students from Commonwealth countries who do not already hold scholarships from their own country.
Level of Study: Postgraduate
Type: Scholarship
Value: Varies, but includes payment of tuition fees
Frequency: Annual
Study Establishment: The University of Exeter
Country of Study: United Kingdom
No. of awards offered: Varies
Application Procedure: Applicants must apply well in advance in their country of permanent residence through the Commonwealth Scholarship Agency.
Closing Date: Please contact the organization
Funding: Government
Additional Information: Further information is available on request.

Cornwall Heritage Trust Bursary
Subjects: All subjects centering on Cornwall's heritage.
Purpose: To support the tuition fees of the applicants.
Eligibility: Open to one or more postgraduate students producing dissertations/theses centred on any aspect of cornwall's heritage.
Level of Study: Postgraduate
Type: Bursary
Value: Upto UK £1,000
Length of Study: 1 year
Frequency: Dependent on funds available
Study Establishment: The University of Exeter
Country of Study: United Kingdom
No. of awards offered: 1 or more
Application Procedure: Applicants should contact Postgraduate administration office.
Closing Date: June 30th
Funding: Trusts
No. of awards given last year: 3
No. of applicants last year: 4
Additional Information: Further information is available on request.

Exeter Research Scholarships
Subjects: All subjects.
Purpose: To fund MPhil and PhD study.
Eligibility: International students studying MPhil or PhD.
Level of Study: Postgraduate, Research
Type: Scholarship
Value: Full international fees
Length of Study: 3 years
Frequency: Annual
Study Establishment: University of Exeter
Country of Study: United Kingdom
No. of awards offered: Varies
Application Procedure: Applicants should apply through ORSAS scheme. Application forms available from graduate school website. Application forms to be sent from school through which student will be studying.
Closing Date: February 8th
No. of awards given last year: 12
No. of applicants last year: 77

Full-Fee Master's Scholarships
Subjects: Selected taught Masters in the arts, business, education, humanities and social sciences and science.
Purpose: Full fee waiver offered to students who best demonstrate the potential to progress to doctoral study.
Eligibility: Applicants who demonstrate exceptional academic ability such as a first class honours or direct equivalent, and the potential to progress to doctoral study based on a submitted research proposal and personal statement will be considered.
Level of Study: Graduate, Postgraduate
Type: Scholarship
Value: Full fee waiver of the taught Master's programme irrespective of fee status
Length of Study: 1 year
Frequency: Annual
Study Establishment: The University of Exeter
Country of Study: United Kingdom
No. of awards offered: 18
Application Procedure: Application forms can be downloaded from the website www.exeter.ac.uk/scholarships/postgraduate/fullmasters
Closing Date: March 31st
Funding: Corporation
No. of awards given last year: 15
No. of applicants last year: 185
Additional Information: Applications will only be considered from students who have received an offer of a place on a taught Master's programme at the University.

For further information contact:

Scholarship Administrator, Admissions Office, Laver Building, North Park Road, Exeter EX4 4QE, United Kingdom
Email: admissions-scholarships@exeter.ac.uk

Jonathan Young Scholarship
Subjects: Subjects covered by School of Business and Economics and School of Humanities and Social sciences.
Purpose: To finance travel in support of furtherance of studies of research.
Eligibility: Postgraduate or Undergraduate studying in School of Business and Economics or School of Humanities and Social sciences.
Level of Study: Postgraduate, Undergraduate
Type: Scholarship
Value: Upto £1,000
Length of Study: 1 year
Frequency: Dependent on funds available
Study Establishment: University of Exeter
Country of Study: United Kingdom
No. of awards offered: 1 or more
Application Procedure: Application forms available from postgraduate administration office.
Closing Date: November 14th
Funding: Private
No. of awards given last year: 3
No. of applicants last year: 10

Tom Davis Scholarship
Subjects: Any subject.
Purpose: Payment of part-time fees for Taught Masters Programme
Eligibility: Students ordinarily resident in Devon with preference given to those ordinarily resident in Exeter studying Master's degree.
Level of Study: Postgraduate
Type: Scholarship
Value: Part-time fees
Length of Study: 2 years maximum
Frequency: Dependent on funds available
Study Establishment: University of Exeter
Country of Study: United Kingdom
No. of awards offered: 1
Application Procedure: Application forms available from postgraduate administration office.
Closing Date: April 30th

University of Exeter Chapel Choir Choral and Organ Scholarship

Purpose: Annual scholarships offered to choral and organ practitioners to aid in recitals on behalf of the chapel choir.
Eligibility: Based on audition. The Director of Chapel Music will invite for competitive audition on the basis of applications demonstrating a high level of competence and experience plus details of two referees familiar with the applicant's ability.
Level of Study: Doctorate, Graduate, MBA, Postgraduate, Research
Type: Scholarship
Value: Up to a maximum of £1000. £400 per annum for choral scholars, £700 per annum for senior organ scholars, £300 per annum for junior organ scholars
Length of Study: 1 year initially but may be renewed for the duration of study, where appropriate
Frequency: Annual
Study Establishment: The University of Exeter
Country of Study: United Kingdom
No. of awards offered: 10 - choral and 2 - organ
Application Procedure: Applicants can contact the Director for more information and request an application form.
Closing Date: February 13th
Funding: Corporation, trusts
No. of awards given last year: 5
No. of applicants last year: 43
Additional Information: From the 10 choral scholarships available, 4 are offered to sopranos, 2 each for other voice parts of atto (male and female), tenor and bass. The award for senior organ scholarship status will require recipients to direct the choir when required.

For further information contact:

University of Exeter, Amory Building, Rennes Drive, Exeter EX4 4RJ, United Kingdom
Email: ajmusson@exeter.ac.uk
Contact: Professor Anthony Musson, Director of Chapel Music

University of Exeter Departmental Research Scholarships

Subjects: All subjects.
Purpose: To fund MPhil and PhD study.
Eligibility: Open to all international applicants for PhD and MPhil/PhD programmes.
Level of Study: Postgraduate, Research, Doctorate
Type: Scholarship
Value: Full fees
Length of Study: 3 years
Frequency: Annual
Study Establishment: The University of Exeter
Country of Study: United Kingdom
No. of awards offered: Varies
Application Procedure: Applicants should make enquiries to the school in which they wish to study.
Contributor: University of Exeter

University of Exeter Graduate Research Assistantships

Subjects: All subjects.
Purpose: To assist students by offering them a top-quality scheme that offers excellent career development opportunities.
Eligibility: Open to MPhil and PhD students.
Level of Study: Doctorate, Postgraduate, Research
Type: Other
Value: Fees and maintenance at research council rates
Length of Study: 4 years
Frequency: Annual
Study Establishment: The University of Exeter
Country of Study: United Kingdom
No. of awards offered: Varies
Application Procedure: Applicants must visit the website of the school in which they wish to study.
Additional Information: Further details of this scheme are available from the website. Graduate research assistants are required to undertake 2 days of research a week for a research team in addition to their own research.

University of Exeter Graduate Teaching Assistantships (GTA)

Subjects: All subjects.
Purpose: To assist students by offering them a top-quality scheme that offers excellent career development opportunities.
Eligibility: Open to MPhil and PhD students.
Level of Study: Doctorate, Postgraduate, Research
Type: Other
Value: Fees and maintenance at research council rates
Length of Study: Up to 4 years
Frequency: Annual
Study Establishment: The University of Exeter
Country of Study: United Kingdom
No. of awards offered: Varies
Application Procedure: Applicants must visit the website of the school in which they wish to study.
Closing Date: Please contact the organization
Additional Information: Further details of this scheme are available from the Graduate School website. GTAs are given full training with SEDA accreditation and are expected to teach for up to 150 hours per year.

University of Exeter Sports Scholarships

Subjects: Sports.
Purpose: To assist students of outstanding sporting ability who show evidence of achievement or potential at international or national level.
Eligibility: Performers from any sport considered, but emphasis is placed on cricket, golf, hockey, rugby, sailing and tennis. Both male and female athletes in these sports.
Level of Study: Graduate, Postgraduate
Type: Scholarship
Value: Up to maximum of £1,000 (For all sporting expenses/discounted accommodation costs)
Length of Study: 1 year initially, but may be renewed for an additional 2 years
Frequency: Annual
Study Establishment: The University of Exeter
Country of Study: United Kingdom
No. of awards offered: Varies
Application Procedure: Applicants must contact Nick Beasant.
Closing Date: January 31st

For further information contact:

University of Exeter, Sports Park Stocker Road, Exeter, EX4 4QN, England
Tel: n.e.beasant@ex.ac.uk
Contact: Nick Beasant, Sports Performance Manager

UNIVERSITY OF GLAMORGAN

Pontypridd, Wales, CF37 1DL, Wales
Tel: (44) (0) 1443 654 450
Fax: (44) (0) 1443 654 050
Email: enquiries@glam.ac.uk
Website: www.glam.ac.uk
Contact: Enquiries and Admissions Unit

The University of Glamorgan is a dynamic institution with an exceptional record for academic excellence, teaching and research. Glamorgan offers first class teaching, excellent facilities and outstanding academic support.

Crawshays Rugby Scholarship

Subjects: All subjects.
Purpose: To support talented young rugby players through higher education at the University.
Eligibility: Open to applicants who are rugby players studying at the University of Glamorgan.
Level of Study: Postgraduate
Type: Scholarship
Value: UK £1,000
Frequency: Annual
Study Establishment: University of Glamorgan
Country of Study: United Kingdom
Application Procedure: For further details contact the university.

Closing Date: September 1st
Contributor: Crawshay's Welsh RFC

For further information contact:

Sardis Road, Pontypridd RFC
Contact: Clive Jones, Director of Rugby

The University of Glamorgan Sports Scholarships

Subjects: Sports.
Purpose: To support potential elite athletes and sports people who are competing at national and international level in their chosen field.
Eligibility: Open to students studying on the Treforest or Glyntaff Campus.
Level of Study: Professional development
Type: Scholarship
Value: UK £500, a one-off kit grant of £150 in the first year, an annual grant of £150 to use in the University's excellent sports centre
Frequency: Annual
Country of Study: United Kingdom
Application Procedure: Contact the university for further details.
Closing Date: December 1st

UNIVERSITY OF GLASGOW

6 University Gardens, Glasgow, G12 8QQ, Scotland
Tel: (44) 0141 330 6828
Email: e.queune@admin.gla.ac.uk
Website: www.gla.ac.uk
Contact: Emily Queune, Faculty of Arts Office

The University of Glasgow is a major research led university operating in an international context, which aims to provide education through the development of learning in a research environment, to undertake fundamental, strategic and applied research and to sustain and add value to Scottish culture, to the natural environment and to the national economy.

Adam Smith Research Foundation PhD Scholarships

Subjects: Public policy, governance and social justice, work, ethics and technology, people places and change, macroeconomics, business and finance, legal and political thought.
Purpose: To promote and sustain research within the UK, European and international arenas.
Eligibility: Open to candidates in any of the faculty's constituent departments: accounting and finance; central and East European studies; centre for drugs misuse research; economic and social history; economics; School of Law; management; politics, sociology, anthropology and applied social sciences; urban studies.
Level of Study: Doctorate
Type: Scholarship
Value: UK/EU rate of £3,168 or the overseas rate of £8,800
Length of Study: 3 years
Frequency: Annual
No. of awards offered: 4
Application Procedure: Candidates should apply for entry to PhD in a department in the faculty in the usual way www.gla.ac.uk/lbss/graduateschool/applications.html
Closing Date: May 1st
Funding: Foundation
Contributor: Adam Smith Research Foundation

Alexander and Dixon Scholarship (Bryce Bequest)

Subjects: English literature.
Eligibility: Open to the citizens of United Kingdom or a European Union national.
Level of Study: Doctorate
Type: Scholarship
Value: £3,500 fees only
Length of Study: 3 years
No. of awards offered: 2
Application Procedure: The application should consist of a 500-word case for support and a brief covering letter, including the proposed title of the thesis, the name(s) of the proposed supervisor(s), and give the applicant's e-mail and other contact details.
Closing Date: June 21st

For further information contact:

Department Office, Department of English Literature, University of Glasgow, Glasgow, G12 8QQ, United Kingdom
Email: a.macmillan@englit.arts.gla.ac.uk
Website: www.arts.gla.ac.uk/SESLL/EngLit/grad.htm
Contact: Anna Macmillan

Alexander and Margaret Johnstone Postgraduate Research Scholarships

Subjects: Arts.
Eligibility: Open to students intending a research degree in the faculty of arts in a department rated 5 or 5* in the research assessment exercise.
Level of Study: Doctorate
Type: Research scholarship
Value: Tuition fees at the Home/EU student rate, plus stipend of between £6,000 and £7,000
Application Procedure: Check website for further details.
Funding: Government

For further information contact:

Faculty of Arts Office, University of Glasgow, 6 University Gardens, Glasgow, G12 8QQ, United Kingdom
Tel: (44) 0141 330 6828
Email: e.queune@admin.gla.ac.uk
Contact: Emily Queune

Bellahouston Bequest Fund

Subjects: Arts and science.
Eligibility: Open to postgraduate students undertaking a Masters Degree course in the faculty of Arts.
Level of Study: Postgraduate
Type: Scholarship
Value: £1000
Length of Study: 1 year (arts and engineering) and 2 years (science)
Frequency: Annual
No. of awards offered: 2
Application Procedure: The candidate must contact the clerk of the faculty of arts. Check website for further information.
Closing Date: July 31st
Additional Information: Preference will be given to the Glaswegians.

For further information contact:

University of Glasgow, Glasgow, G12 8QQ, United Kingdom
Tel: (44) 44 0141 330 2000
Email: ugs@archives.gla.ac.uk
Contact: Clerk of the Faculty of Arts

British Federation of Women Graduates (BFWG)

Subjects: All subjects.
Purpose: To encourage applicants to become members of the Federation to help promote better links between female graduates throughout the world.
Eligibility: Open to female graduate with academic excellence. Research students of all nationalities who will be studying in the United Kingdom are eligible for the scholarship.
Level of Study: Graduate, Research
Type: Scholarship and award
Value: Range upwards from £1,000 with the average award being around £3,000
Country of Study: United Kingdom
Application Procedure: Check website for further details.
Closing Date: April 2nd
Funding: Private
Additional Information: Male graduates and female undergraduates are not eligible.

For further information contact:

4 Mandeville Courtyard, 142 Battersea Park Road, London, SW11 4NB, United Kingdom
Email: info@bfwg.org.uk
Website: www.bfwg.org.uk

The Catherine Mackichan Trust

Subjects: Scottish history.
Eligibility: Open to applications from academic centres worldwide, schools, colleges and individuals or groups.
Level of Study: Research
Type: Award
Value: £350
Length of Study: 1 year
Frequency: Annual
No. of awards offered: 4
Application Procedure: Check website for further details.
Funding: Trusts
Contributor: The Catherine Mackichan Trust

For further information contact:

Catherine Mackichan Trust, School of Scottish Studies, 2729 George Square, Edinburgh, EH8, United Kingdom
Contact: I Fraser, Vice Chairman

Dorothy Hodgkin Postgraduate Awards

Subjects: Engineering and physical sciences, physics and astronomy and biological sciences.
Purpose: To support the highest calibre doctoral students from developing countries to undertake their PhD in the UK.
Eligibility: This award is only open to student nationals from India, China, Hong Kong, Brazil, South Africa, Russia and the developing world, as defined by the OECD.
Level of Study: Research
Value: £90,000
Length of Study: 3 years
Frequency: Annual
Study Establishment: Glasgow University
Country of Study: Scotland
No. of awards offered: 1–3
Application Procedure: Please check the website for details.
Funding: Commercial, government
Contributor: UK Research Councils and Industrial Partners

Eglington Fellowship for Postgraduate Study

Subjects: Arts.
Eligibility: Open to candidates possessing a graduate degree.
Level of Study: Graduate
Type: Fellowship
Value: £500 per year
Length of Study: 3 years
Application Procedure: Check website for further details.
Closing Date: August 1st

For further information contact:

Faculty Office, 2nd floor, 6 University Gardens, Glasgow, United Kingdom
Website: www.gsah.arts.gla.ac.uk/html/eglington.html
Contact: Clerk of the Arts Faculty

Faculty of Medicine Studentships

Subjects: Medicine.
Eligibility: Open to candidates having an upper second or first class degree in a relevant subject. Overseas applicants will be required to obtain an ORS in addition to a scholarship or studentship awarded by the faculty or the division/section.
Level of Study: Postgraduate, Doctorate, Research
Type: Scholarship
Study Establishment: University of Glasgow
Country of Study: United Kingdom
Application Procedure: Check website for details regarding postgraduate research and postgraduate taught programmes.
Closing Date: December 14th
Additional Information: Applicants should enclose a referee's report, degree transcripts, proof of English language proficiency, a curriculum vitae and an approval of title in principle.

For further information contact:

Wolfson Medical School Building, University Avenue, University of Glasgow, Glasgow, G12 8QQ, United Kingdom

Website: www.gla.ac.uk/faculties/medicine/gradschool/applications.html
Contact: Faculty of Medicine Graduate School

Faculty Studentships

Subjects: Adult education, higher education including teacher education and teachers work, innovation in curriculum policy and practice, critical and cultural perspectives on education.
Purpose: To provide funding for PhD students.
Eligibility: As per university eligibility for a PhD.
Level of Study: Doctorate
Type: Scholarship
Value: Home fees plus stipend of £12,400
Length of Study: 3 years
Frequency: Annual
Country of Study: Scotland
No. of awards offered: 1
Application Procedure: Normal university procedures. Please check the website for applications.
Closing Date: February
Contributor: Faculty of Education
No. of awards given last year: 1
No. of applicants last year: 10
Additional Information: Applications are invited based on the faculty research strengths.

Glasgow Educational & Marshall Trust Award

Subjects: All subjects.
Eligibility: Open to the candidates who are above 18 years of age and a resident of Glasgow within one of the following post code areas: G1–5, G11/12, G14/15, G20, G22/23, G31, G34, G40–42, G45, 51.
Type: Grant
Value: £50–1,000
Length of Study: 1 year
Study Establishment: Glasgow Educational and Marshall Trust
Country of Study: United Kingdom
Application Procedure: Check website for further details.
Closing Date: April 30th

For further information contact:

Glasgow Educational and Marshall Trust, 21 Beaton Road, Glasgow, G41 4NW, United Kingdom
Tel: (44) 0141 423 2169
Contact: Secretary and Treasurers

Henry Dryerre Scholarship in Medical and Veterinary Physiology

Subjects: Medical and Veterinary Physiology.
Eligibility: Open to candidates holding a degree of a Scottish University with first class honours or, if in their final year, to be expected to achieve first class honours.
Level of Study: Postgraduate
Type: Scholarship
Value: Varies
Frequency: Every 3 years
Application Procedure: The candidate must submit the application form through a member of staff on the appropriate Henry Dryerre Nomination Form.

For further information contact:

The Carnegie Trust for the Universities of Scotland, Cameron House, Abbey Park Place, Dunfermline, KY12 7P
Website: www.carnegie-trust.org/our_schemes.htm
Contact: Assistant Secretary

James Watt Research Scholarships

Subjects: Engineering, support for PhD studies in engineering at the University of Glasgow.
Level of Study: Postgraduate
Type: Scholarship
Value: Stipend at the level recommended by the Research Council plus a contribution towards tuition fees
Country of Study: United Kingdom

Application Procedure: Please see the website www.gla.ac.uk/faculties/engineering/gradschool

John & James Houston Crawford Scholarship

Subjects: Veterinary medicine.
Purpose: To assist the advanced study or research into the bovine and equine animals.
Eligibility: Open to university graduates or qualified veterinary surgeons.
Level of Study: Postgraduate
Type: Scholarship
Length of Study: 1–2 years
Frequency: Every 2 years
Study Establishment: Institution approved by the faculty of veterinary medicine
Country of Study: United Kingdom
Application Procedure: Applications to be submitted to the clerk of the Faculty of Veterinary Medicine.
Closing Date: June 1st
Additional Information: Preference is given to graduates in veterinary medicine of the University of Glasgow.

For further information contact:

Faculty of Veterinary Medicine, University of Glasgow Veterinary School, Bearsden, Glasgow, G61 1QH, Scotland

John Crawford Scholarship

Subjects: Veterinary medicine.
Purpose: To assist the advanced study or research into equine animals, with particular reference to blood stock breeding and its improvement.
Eligibility: Open to university graduates of veterinary medicine and qualified veterinary surgeons.
Level of Study: Postgraduate
Type: Scholarship
Value: Please consult the organization
Frequency: Every 2 years
Study Establishment: The University of Glasgow
Country of Study: United Kingdom
Application Procedure: Applicants must write for details.
Additional Information: Preference is given to graduates in veterinary medicine of the University of Glasgow.

For further information contact:

Faculty of Veterinary Medicine, University of Glasgow Veterinary School, Bearsden, Glasgow, G61 1QH, Scotland

Lord Kelvin/Adam Smith Postgraduate Scholarships

Subjects: All subjects.
Purpose: To enable the University to recruit outstanding postgraduate research students to a range of innovative, boundary-crossing research developments.
Eligibility: Open to postgraduate students.
Level of Study: Postgraduate
Type: Scholarship
Value: £12,600
Length of Study: 4 years
Frequency: Annual
No. of awards offered: 10
Application Procedure: Check website for further details.
Funding: Trusts

For further information contact:

United Kingdom
Email: lauren-currie@enterprise.gla.ac.uk
Contact: Lauren Currie, Postgraduate Research Secretary,

Mac Robertson Travel Scholarship

Subjects: All subjects.
Purpose: To provide funding which will enrich and further the award-holder's academic experience and research achievements.
Eligibility: Open to postgraduate research students.
Level of Study: Postgraduate, Research
Type: Scholarship

Value: £2,000–3,000
Length of Study: 1 year
Frequency: Annual
Study Establishment: Glasgow University
Application Procedure: Check website for further details.
Closing Date: April 22nd

For further information contact:

Postgraduate Research Office, 10 The Square, Glasgow, G12 8QQ, United Kingdom
Tel: (44) 0141 330 1989
Website: www.gla.ac.uk/scholarships/travelscholarships
Contact: Lauren Currie

Overseas Research Student Awards Scheme (ORS)

Subjects: All subjects.
Purpose: To support overseas research students of outstanding merit and research potential.
Eligibility: To students who are classed as international student for fee purposes.
Level of Study: Research
Value: The difference between home/EU fee element and international fees
Frequency: Annual
Study Establishment: Glasgow University
Country of Study: Scotland
No. of awards offered: 20
Application Procedure: Please check the website http://glas.ac.uk for applications and further details. Applications should be completed and returned to the relevant faculty office.
Closing Date: January 31st
Funding: Government

R. Harper Brown Memorial Scholarship

Subjects: All subjects.
Purpose: To honour the late R. Harper Brown and to assist in defraying the cost of an American (US) college student's study at a university in Scotland.
Eligibility: Open to the candidates who are graduating seniors in high school with an acceptance and intention to attend university in Scotland or a student in an accredited American (US) college or university looking for a study-abroad experience.
Level of Study: Graduate
Type: Scholarship
Application Procedure: Check website for further details.
Closing Date: Between January 1st and March 31st
Funding: Private
Contributor: The Illinois Saint Andrew Society

For further information contact:

Tel: 847 967 2725
Email: dforlow@yahoo.com
Contact: David Forlow

Ross Scholarship

Subjects: History.
Purpose: To encourage the extraction of Scottish material from archives outside Scotland relating to all aspects of the history of Scotland, the Scottish people and Scottish influence abroad.
Eligibility: Open to candidates possessing a degree in MLitt.
Level of Study: Research
Type: Scholarship
Value: £1,000
Length of Study: 1 year
Frequency: Annual
No. of awards offered: 1
Application Procedure: The candidate must submit a letter outlining a dissertation research proposal including the planned topic and archival research plans.
Closing Date: July 1st
Contributor: Trustees of the Ross Fund

For further information contact:

9 University Gardens, University of Glasgow, Glasgow, G12 8HQ, United Kingdom
Email: c.leriguer@arts.gla.ac.uk
Contact: Christelle LeRiguer

Royal Historical Society: Postgraduate Research Support Grants

Subjects: History.
Purpose: To assist postgraduate students in the pursuit of advanced historical research.
Eligibility: The candidate must be a postgraduate student registered for a research degree at United Kingdom Institute of Higher Education.
Level of Study: Postgraduate, Research
Type: Grant
Application Procedure: Check website for further details.
Closing Date: January 14th, February 18th, May 6th, June 18th, September 9th and November 12th
Contributor: Royal Historical Society

For further information contact:

Website: www.rhs.ac.uk/postgrad.htm#grant

Saint Andrew's Society of the State of New York Scholarship Fund

Subjects: All subjects.
Eligibility: Open to candidates who are either graduates of a Scottish university or of Oxford or Cambridge and have completed their first degree course.
Level of Study: Graduate
Type: Scholarship
Value: Not less than US $20,000 each
Frequency: Annual
Country of Study: United States of America
No. of awards offered: 2
Application Procedure: The candidate must arrange for references from two academic referees to be submitted in the appropriate referee forms.
Closing Date: December 3rd
Funding: Trusts
Contributor: Saint Andrew's Society of the State of New York

For further information contact:

Senate Office, Gilbert Scott Building, University of Glasgow, University Avenue, Glasgow, G12 8QQ, United Kingdom
Email: c.omand@admin.gla.ac.uk
Contact: Catherine Omand

Stevenson Exchange Scholarships

Subjects: All subjects.
Purpose: To promote friendly relations between the students of Scotland, Germany, France and Spain.
Eligibility: Open to current or recent students of French, German or Spanish universities who intend to study at any university in Scotland.
Level of Study: Postdoctorate
Type: Scholarship
Value: Varies
Application Procedure: Check website for further details.

For further information contact:

1 The Square, University of Glasgow, Glasgow, G12 8QQ, United Kingdom
Tel: (44) 0141 330 4241
Fax: (44) 0141 330 4045
Email: l.buchan@admin.gla.ac.uk
Contact: Linda Buchan, Exchange Co-ordinator

The Sue Green Bursary

Subjects: Archaeology.
Purpose: To support a postgraduate student in the Department of Archaeology at the University of Glasgow.
Eligibility: Open to postgraduate students.
Level of Study: Postgraduate, Research

Type: Bursary
Value: £500
Application Procedure: The candidate must send an application in the form of a short research proposal (c. 500 words) and an accompanying brief curriculum vitae. Check website for further details.
Closing Date: August 31st
Funding: Private
Contributor: The Sue Green Bursary

For further information contact:

Department of Archaeology, University of Glasgow, Glasgow, G12 8QQ, United Kingdom
Contact: Head of the Department

Synergy Scholarship

Purpose: To enhance existing synergy collaborations or assist in creating new areas of synergy collaborations between Glasgow and Strathclyde universities.
Eligibility: The project must be jointly supervised in one university and a second supervisor in the other university.
Level of Study: Research
Value: £12,923 for maintenance
Length of Study: 3 years
Frequency: Annual
Study Establishment: University of Scotland
Country of Study: Scotland
No. of awards offered: 1–2
Application Procedure: Application forms are available in the website. Forms should be completed and returned to the relevant faculty office.
Closing Date: January 31st
Additional Information: The project must be jointly supervised in one university and a second supervisor in the other university. Please check the wesite for more details.

University of Glasgow Postgraduate Research Scholarships

Subjects: All subjects.
Purpose: To assist with research towards a PhD degree.
Eligibility: Open to candidates of any nationality who are proficient in English and who have obtained a first or an upper second class (Honours) Degree or equivalent.
Level of Study: Postgraduate
Type: Scholarship
Value: Please consult the organization
Length of Study: 3 year's maximum award
Frequency: Annual
Study Establishment: The University of Glasgow
Country of Study: Scotland
Application Procedure: Applicants must refer to the University's application for graduate studies form that covers application for admission and scholarship. Please refer to the notes for applicants issued with the application form for address details.
Closing Date: Please refer to institution website
Funding: Private
Contributor: Endowments
Additional Information: Scholars from outside the European Union will be expected to make up the difference between the home fee and the overseas fee.

For further information contact:

Postgraduate Research Office, Research & Enterprise, 10 The Square, University of Glasgow, Glasgow, G12 8QQ
Tel: 0141 330 1989
Fax: 0141 330 5856

William and Margaret Kesson Award for Postgraduate Study

Subjects: Arts.
Purpose: To enable a student to undertake study leading to a postgraduate degree in the faculty of arts.
Eligibility: Open to candidates of Scottish or English nationality possessing a graduate degree.
Level of Study: Graduate

Type: Scholarship
Length of Study: 3 years
Application Procedure: Check website for further details.
Closing Date: May 1st

For further information contact:

Faculty of Arts, United Kingdom
Contact: Clerk of the Faculty

William Barclay Memorial Scholarship

Subjects: Biblical studies, theology and church history or any subject falling within the faculty of the divinity.
Purpose: To provide an opportunity for a scholar to pursue full-time study or to undertake research.
Eligibility: Open to any suitably qualified graduate of theology from a university outside the United Kingdom.
Level of Study: Postgraduate
Type: Scholarship
Value: £3500
Frequency: Annual
Study Establishment: The Faculty of Divinity at the University of Glasgow
Country of Study: Scotland
Application Procedure: Applicants must request postgraduate study application material. The PG form is used for the Barclay application.
Funding: Private

For further information contact:

Faculty of Divinity, Glasgow, G12 8QQ, Scotland
Tel: (44) 141 330 6525
Fax: (44) 141 330 4943

Wingate Scholarships

Subjects: All subjects.
Purpose: To support creative or original work of intellectual, scientific, artistic, social or enviromental value.
Eligibility: Open for mature candidates and those from non-traditional academic backgrounds without any upper age limit.
Level of Study: Unrestricted
Type: Scholarship
Value: The average total award is about £6,500 and the maximum in any one year is £10,000.
Length of Study: 1 year
Frequency: Annual
Application Procedure: Check website for further details.

For further information contact:

Queen Anne Business Center, 28 Broadway, London, SW1H 9JX, United Kingdom
Website: www.wingate.org.uk/scholarships/overview.php

UNIVERSITY OF GUELPH

50 Stone Road East, Suite 158, Guelph, ON, N1G-2W1, Canada
Tel: (1) 519 824 4120
Fax: (1) 519 767 1693
Email: sinclair@registrar.uoguelph.ca
Website: www.uoguelph.ca
Contact: Associate Registrar

The University of Guelph is renowned in Canada and around the world as a research-intensive and learner-centred institution and for its commitment to open learning, internationalism and collaboration. Their vision is to be Canada's leader in creating, transmitting and applying knowledge to improve the social, cultural and economic quality of life of people in Canada and around the world.

The Brock Doctoral Scholarship

Subjects: All subjects.
Purpose: To financially support Doctoral students to attain a high level of academic achievement and to make significant teaching and research contributions.
Eligibility: Open to students with sustained outstanding academic performance, evidence of strong teaching and research skills,

demonstrated outstanding communication skills and excellent potential for research and teaching as assessed by the College Dean.
Level of Study: Doctorate
Type: Scholarship
Value: Canadian $10,000 per semester
Length of Study: 6 years
Frequency: Annual
Study Establishment: University of Guelph
Country of Study: Canada
Application Procedure: Students entering a Doctoral programme should apply to their College Dean by February 1st with a curriculum vitae, which must then be forwarded to Graduate Program Services by February 15th, with the Dean's written assessment of the candidate's research and teaching potential attached.
Closing Date: February 15th
Additional Information: The Brock Doctoral Scholarship is one of the most prestigious Doctoral awards available at the University. It is hoped that award holders will be mentors for future Brock Doctoral Scholarship winners.

Dairy Farmer's of Ontario Doctoral Research Assistantships

Subjects: Animal and herd health, management systems for dairy cattle, nutrition, economic aspects of milk production and marketing or the processing, quality and use of dairy products.
Purpose: To provide research assistantship to outstanding students entering a Doctoral programme.
Eligibility: Open to Doctoral applicants, with at least a First Class (A) average in the most recently completed 2 years of academic study.
Level of Study: Doctorate, Research
Type: Assistantship
Value: Canadian $20,000
Length of Study: 3 years
Frequency: Annual
Study Establishment: University of Guelph
Country of Study: Canada
Application Procedure: The assistantship application letter from the student should include a 1 page research proposal and name the proposed graduate faculty adviser at the University of Guelph. The assistantship application letter and graduate application file will be circulated to, and selection made by, an intercollege committee that includes the Dean of Graduate Studies.
Closing Date: October

THE UNIVERSITY OF HONG KONG

Pok Fu Lam Road, Hong Kong, China
Tel: (86) 2859 2111
Fax: (86) 2858 2549
Email: gradsch.@hkucc.hku.hk
Website: www.hku.hk

The University of Hong Kong, as a pre-eminent international university in Asia, seeks to sustain and enhance its excellence as an institution of higher learning through outstanding teaching and world-class research, so as to produce well-rounded graduates with the abilities to provide leadership within the societies they serve.

Hui Pun Hing Scholarship for Postgraduate Research Overseas

Subjects: Sciences including medicine.
Purpose: To provide scholarship to a student who intends to pursue postgraduate research studies in the field of science, including medicine and who is expected to make a significant contribution to the development of the chosen specialization on his/her return from study abroad.
Eligibility: Open to students who have obtained a Bachelor's degree or a Master's degree or both at the University of Hong Kong including medicine and to those who intend to pursue postgraduate research studies in the field of Science.
Level of Study: Postgraduate, Research
Value: Up to a maximum of HK $100,000
Length of Study: 3 years at most
Frequency: Annual
Study Establishment: The University of Hong Kong

Country of Study: China
No. of awards offered: 1
Application Procedure: Open application
Funding: Trusts
Contributor: Hui Pun Hing Endowment Fund
No. of awards given last year: 1
No. of applicants last year: 1

Peter Vine Postgraduate Law Scholarship

Subjects: Law
Purpose: To provide scholarships, (1) outstanding LLB graduates of the Faculty of Law of University of Hong Kong to undertake one year of full-time study overseas for the degree of Master of Laws or its equivalent and (2) for outstanding Law graduates from universities in Mainland China undertaking one year full-time study at the University of Hong Kong in the Postgraduate Diploma in Common Law/Master of Common Law programme.
Eligibility: Open to LLB graduates of the University of Hong Kong and Law graduates from universities in Mainland China
Level of Study: Graduate, Postgraduate
Type: Scholarship
Value: HK $60,000 each for category (1), a total of not more than HK $144,000 for category (2)
Length of Study: 1 year
Frequency: Annual
Study Establishment: The University of Hong Kong
Country of Study: China
No. of awards offered: 5
Application Procedure: Open application but nomination from the Faculty of Law is required
Funding: Foundation
Contributor: The Peter Vine Charitable Foundation
No. of awards given last year: 2
No. of applicants last year: 2

THE UNIVERSITY OF KENT

School of Drama, Film and Visual Art, Canterbury, Kent, CT2 7NZ,
United Kingdom
Tel: (44) (0) 1227 764 000
Fax: (44) 12 2782 7077
Email: web-team@kent.ac.uk
Website: www.kent.ac.uk
Contact: The Registry

The University of Kent is a UK higher education institution funded by the Higher Education Funding Council for England (HEFCE). The university provides education of excellent quality characterized by flexibility and inter disciplinarily and informed by research and scholarship, meeting the lifelong needs of diversity students.

Computing Laboratory Scholarship

Subjects: Theoretical computer science, systems, architecture, applied and interdisciplinary informatics cognitive systems, pervasive computing, information systems security, computing education.
Purpose: To support postgraduate studies towards a PhD.
Eligibility: Candidates are expected to hold an Upper Second Class (Honours) Degree.
Level of Study: Doctorate, Postgraduate
Type: Scholarship
Value: £1,000
Length of Study: 3 years
Frequency: Annual
Study Establishment: The University of Kent
Country of Study: United Kingdom
No. of awards offered: 5
Application Procedure: Applicants must enclose a covering letter and indicate their area of interest. See website www.cs.kent.ac.uk/research/pg/funding/bursary_app.html
Closing Date: June 15th
Funding: Government
No. of awards given last year: 4
No. of applicants last year: Approx. 150
Additional Information: Please contact the Computing Laboratory at computer-science@kent.ac.uk

EPSRC Doctoral Training Awards for Computer Science

Subjects: Applied and interdisciplinary informatics, cognitive systems, computing education, information systems security, pervasive computing, systems, architecture and theoretical computer science.
Purpose: To support postgraduate studies towards a PhD.
Eligibility: Primarily open to United Kingdom nationals although European Union citizens may qualify in special circumstances.
Level of Study: Doctorate, Postgraduate
Type: Award
Value: Covers tuition fees at the home/EU rate plus a maintenance grant. The maintenance grant varys in amount, but may be up to a maximum which is equivalent to the Research Councils
Length of Study: 3 years
Frequency: Annual
Study Establishment: The University of Kent
Country of Study: United Kingdom
No. of awards offered: 5
Application Procedure: Candidates must complete the application form available at www.cs.kent.ac.uk/research/pg/funding/bursary_app.html
Closing Date: April 9th
Funding: Government
Contributor: EPSRC
No. of awards given last year: 4
No. of applicants last year: Approx 150
Additional Information: Please contact the computing laboratory at computer-science@kent.ac.uk

EPSRC Grant for School of Physical Sciences

Subjects: Physical sciences, study in materials science and applied optics.
Purpose: To support research.
Eligibility: Open to candidates who hold or expect to obtain a First Class (Honours) Degree. They should also be citizens of one of the European Union countries.
Level of Study: Doctorate, Postgraduate
Type: Grant
Value: Tuition fees plus the maintenance bursary at the same rate as provided by the EPSRC
Length of Study: 3 years
Frequency: Annual
Study Establishment: The University of Kent
Country of Study: United Kingdom
No. of awards offered: 3
Application Procedure: Applicants must complete an application form.
Closing Date: There is no fixed closing date
Funding: Government
Contributor: EPSRC
No. of awards given last year: 3
No. of applicants last year: 15
Additional Information: Holders of the studentships are required to undertake a small amount of teaching assistance.

Ian Gregor Scholarship

Subjects: American literature, postcolonial literature, Anglo-Irish literature, Shakespeare and renaissance studies, Dickens and Victorian studies, modern poetry, theory and cultural ethnography.
Purpose: To support a candidate registered for taught or research MA programmes in English.
Eligibility: Candidates are expected to hold at least an Upper Second Class (Honours) Degree or equivalent. Candidates should also have applied for an external scholarship, such as AHRB.
Level of Study: Graduate, Postgraduate
Type: Scholarship
Value: Home fees plus UK £500. An equivalent contribution towards fees will be made for overseas students
Length of Study: 1 year
Frequency: Annual
Study Establishment: The University of Kent
Country of Study: United Kingdom
No. of awards offered: 1
Application Procedure: Candidates must complete the postgraduate application form, indicating in the appropriate section that they are interested in being considered for departmental scholarships.

A covering letter supporting the scholarship application should be attached.
Closing Date: May 30th
Funding: Trusts
No. of awards given last year: 1

Kent Law School Studentships and Bursaries
Subjects: Banking law, carriage of goods, company law, comparative law, computers and the law, criminal law and penology, critical legal studies, environmental law, emergency powers, European comparative and human rights law, family law, gender, sexuality and law, immigration law, intellectual property law, international law and human rights, international economic and trade law, labor law, law and multiculturalism, legal services, legal theory, modern legal history, multinationals and the law, and private law.
Purpose: To provide funding for 1 year in the first instance, extended to a maximum of 3 years (for registered students only) based on satisfactory progress (including upgrading to a PhD). The retention of the posts will be subject to a review of progress and performance in both research and teaching after the 1st year.
Eligibility: Candidates should hold an Upper Second Class (Honours) Degree or a good postgraduate taught degree in law.
Level of Study: Doctorate, Postgraduate, Research
Type: Studentship
Value: (£12,940 in 2008/09) and tuition fees paid at the home/EU rate (£3,500 in 2008/09)
Length of Study: 1–3 years
Frequency: Annual
Study Establishment: The University of Kent
Country of Study: United Kingdom
No. of awards offered: 3
Application Procedure: Applicants must submit to the University's recruitment and admissions office a research proposal, curriculum vitae and covering letter with an application for their chosen research degree. They should also ensure that the recruitment and admissions office receives two referees' reports by the closing date for applications. Applications are available at http://records.kent.ac.uk/external/admissions/pg-application.php
Closing Date: February 13th
Funding: Private
Contributor: Kent Law School
No. of awards given last year: 2
No. of applicants last year: 20–30
Additional Information: Holders of the studentships will be expected to teach for a maximum of 4 hours per week in term time on an undergraduate law module, at the direction of the head of department. For further information contact the Kent Law school at kls-pgoffice@kent.ac.uk

Maurice Crosland History of Science Studentship
Subjects: Grant is designed to support postgraduate research in the history of science and technology (excluding history of medicine). The emphasis is on the history of science and technology in cultural contexts (e.g. religion).
Purpose: To fund research to PhD level.
Eligibility: Open to qualified applicants of any nationality.
Level of Study: Doctorate, Postgraduate, Research
Type: Studentship
Value: Home fees plus a maintenance bursary
Length of Study: 3 years
Frequency: Dependent on funds available
Study Establishment: The University of Kent
Country of Study: United Kingdom
No. of awards offered: 1
Application Procedure: Applicants must apply to Professor Crosbie Smith. Candidates should submit a detailed curriculum vitae together with a 500-word description of their preferred research topic. They may wish to discuss this informally with Professor Crosbie Smith first.
Closing Date: June 1st
Funding: Private
No. of awards given last year: 2
No. of applicants last year: 5

For further information contact:

Centre for History of Science, Technology & Medicine, Rutherford College, University of Kent at Canterbury, Canterbury, Kent, CT2 7NX, England

Tel: (44) 12 2776 4000
Fax: (44) 12 2782 7258
Contact: Professor Crosbie Smith

University of Kent Department of Biosciences
Subjects: Cancer research, cell and developmental biology, infectious diseases and protein science.
Purpose: To support research.
Eligibility: Primarily open to United Kingdom nationals although European Union citizens may qualify in special circumstances. Candidates should hold an Upper Second Class (Honours) Degree.
Level of Study: Doctorate, Postgraduate, Research
Value: Home tuition fees and a maintenance bursary at the same rate as that provided by the Research Councils
Length of Study: 3 years
Frequency: Annual
Study Establishment: The University of Kent
Country of Study: United Kingdom
No. of awards offered: 7
Application Procedure: Applicants should contact the Department of Biosciences for further information via email to bio-admin@kent.ac.uk
Closing Date: July 31st
Funding: Government
Contributor: BBSRC
No. of awards given last year: 7

University of Kent Department of Economics Bursaries
Subjects: Labour economics, money and development, international finance and trade, migration, defence and energy economics, macro economics, ganne theory and econometrics.
Purpose: To support research.
Eligibility: Candidates must have at least a taught Master's degree in economics.
Level of Study: Doctorate, Postgraduate, Research
Type: Bursary
Value: Up to the equivalent of home fees and/or a maintenance grant of UK £6,000
Length of Study: 3 years
Frequency: Dependent on funds available
Study Establishment: The University of Kent
Country of Study: United Kingdom
No. of awards offered: 2
Application Procedure: Applicants must enclose a separate letter proposing their wish to apply for the bursary along with their university PhD application form. A link to the online application form can be found on the department's website www.ukc.ac.uk/economics/students/postgrad/MPhil/PhD.html
Closing Date: May
Funding: Government
No. of awards given last year: 2
Additional Information: Candidates should note that 4–6 hours of teaching per week and acceptable progress in the programme of study will be expected of the student. The bursary will be subject to review each year.

University of Kent Department of Electronics Studentships
Subjects: Electronics, including image processing and vision, embedded systems, broadband and wireless communications and electronic instrumentation.
Purpose: To enable well-qualified students to undertake research programmes within the department.
Eligibility: Candidates are expected to hold an Upper Second Class (Honours) Degree or equivalent in an appropriate subject, and be nationals of one of the European Union countries.
Level of Study: Doctorate, Postgraduate, Research
Type: Studentship
Value: Research Council studentships are at a fixed rate determined annually by EPSRC. Departmental bursaries depend on individual circumstances
Length of Study: 3 years
Frequency: Annual
Study Establishment: The University of Kent
Country of Study: United Kingdom
No. of awards offered: Varies

Application Procedure: Applicants should contact the Department of Electronics.
Closing Date: June
Funding: Government
Contributor: EPSRC
No. of awards given last year: 5
No. of applicants last year: 10

For further information contact:

Department of Electronics, University of Kent, Canterbury, Kent, CT2 7NT, England
Email: ee-admissions-pg@kent.ac.uk
Contact: Professor J Z Wang

University of Kent Department of Politics and International Relations Bursary

Subjects: European studies, international relations and international political economy, intergovernmental co-operation in the European Union, political theory and law, politics and conflict analysis.
Purpose: To support research.
Eligibility: Open to candidates accepted for research study.
Level of Study: Doctorate, Postgraduate
Type: Bursary
Value: Home fees
Length of Study: 3 years
Frequency: Annual
Study Establishment: The University of Kent
Country of Study: United Kingdom
No. of awards offered: 5
Application Procedure: Applicants must apply by letter to the head of the department after being accepted for research study.
Closing Date: Applications may be submitted at any time. Deadline for following academic year is the end of March
No. of awards given last year: 5
No. of applicants last year: 7
Additional Information: A maximum of 6 hours of teaching per week will be required.

University of Kent Department of Psychology Studentship

Subjects: Social psychology, cognitive psychology, neuropsychology, health psychology, developmental psychology, forensic psychology.
Purpose: To support research studies.
Eligibility: Candidates should hold or expect to obtain at least an Upper Second Class (Honours) Degree.
Level of Study: Postgraduate, Research
Type: Studentship
Value: Tuition fees at the UK rate plus a maintenance bursary (at the same rate as provided by the ESRC)
Length of Study: 3 years
Frequency: Annual
Study Establishment: The University of Kent
Country of Study: United Kingdom
No. of awards offered: 1
Application Procedure: Applicants must complete an application form.
Closing Date: End of July or mid-August
Funding: Private
Contributor: The University of Kent
No. of awards given last year: 2
No. of applicants last year: 30–40
Additional Information: A maximum of 6 hours of teaching per week will be required.

University of Kent English Scholarship

Subjects: American literature, postcolonial literature, Anglo-Irish literature, Shakespeare and renaissance studies, Dickens and Victorian Studies, modern poetry, theory and cultural ethnography, eighteenth century and creative writing.
Purpose: To support research.
Eligibility: Candidates are expected to hold at least an Upper Second Class (Honours) Degree or equivalent.
Level of Study: Doctorate, Postgraduate, Research
Type: Research grant

Value: Home tuition fees for up to 3 years for up to 3 years full-time study. A stipend of £3,500 (subject to change) for the first year of study. Teaching is offered to bursary students in their second and third years
Length of Study: 3 years
Frequency: Annual
Study Establishment: The University of Kent
Country of Study: United Kingdom
No. of awards offered: Several
Application Procedure: Candidates must complete the postgraduate application form, indicating in the appropriate section that they are interested in being considered for departmental scholarships.
Closing Date: May 30th
Funding: Private
No. of awards given last year: 2

University of Kent Institute of Mathematics, Statistics and Actuarial Science (IMSAS)

Subjects: Mathematics or statistics.
Purpose: To support studies at the IMSAS.
Eligibility: Candidates for scholarships should hold a First Class (Honours) Degree in mathematics or a related subject.
Level of Study: Doctorate
Type: Studentship
Value: Tuition fees plus the maintenance bursary at the same rate as provided by the EPSRC
Length of Study: 3 years
Frequency: Dependent on funds available
Study Establishment: The University of Kent
Country of Study: United Kingdom
No. of awards offered: 3
Application Procedure: Candidates should complete an application form for postgraduate study and indicate that they wish to be considered for this award.
Closing Date: May 31st
Funding: Private
No. of awards given last year: 5
No. of applicants last year: 36
Additional Information: Holders of the studentships are required to undertake a small amount of teaching assistance. For more information, please email imspg-admiss@ukc.ac.uk or see the website www.kent.ac.uk/IMS

University of Kent Postgraduate Funding Awards

Subjects: Social policy, sociology, criminology, environmental, women's studies or urban studies.
Purpose: To support research.
Eligibility: Candidates should hold a First Class or an Upper Second Class (Honours) Degree.
Level of Study: Doctorate, Postgraduate, Predoctorate, (not available to MA/MSc students)
Type: Award
Value: Up to 4 awards at UK £9,000 for full-time students, up to 10 awards at UK £4,000 for full-time students or UK £2,000 for a part-time student
Length of Study: 3 years
Frequency: Annual
Study Establishment: The University of Kent, School of Social Policy, Sociology and Social Research
Country of Study: United Kingdom
No. of awards offered: Up to 14
Application Procedure: Applicants must contact The Admissions Secretary, School of Social Policy, Canterbury, Kent, Sociology or Social Research, CT2 7NF, or email: socio-office@kent.ac.uk
Closing Date: June
Funding: Government
No. of awards given last year: 8
Additional Information: A maximum of 2 hours of teaching per week will be required.

University of Kent School of Drama, Film and Visual Arts Scholarships

Subjects: Drama, including performance-making process and theory, theatre history and practice as research film studies, including varied aspects of film aesthetics, film theory and film history as well as research by practice. History and philosophy of art, including contemporary aesthetics and the history of art thoery, the photograph, and the historical interplay of image, theory and institutions from the renaissance to the present.

Purpose: To support research.

Eligibility: Candidates are expected to hold an Upper Second Class (Honours) Degree and be a citizen of one of the European Union countries.

Level of Study: Postgraduate, Research

Type: Bursary - fees only

Value: To cover home fees only

Length of Study: The bursary is 1 year

Frequency: Annual, One initial bursary for one year only. Opportunity to reapply on a competitive basis

Study Establishment: The University of Kent

Country of Study: United Kingdom

No. of awards offered: 7

Application Procedure: Applicants must indicate their interest on the postgraduate application form.

Closing Date: July 31st

No. of awards given last year: 8

No. of applicants last year: 19

Additional Information: Some teaching or research assistant work may be required.

For further information contact:

Email: k.j.goddard@kent.ac.uk

University of Kent School of European Culture and Languages Scholarships

Subjects: European and Latin American literary, linguistic and cultural studies (French, German, Hispanic studies, Italian and comparative literary studies), philosophy (with special expertise in moral and political philosophy, aesthetics, philosophy of mind, philosophical logic and paradoxes, Bayesian epistemology and artificial intelligence), religious studies (modern theology, Christian ethics, mysticism and religious experience, religion and film, psychology of religion and cultural study of cosmology and divination) and the literature, history and archaeology of classical World (including Britain and Gaul).

Purpose: To support research.

Eligibility: Candidates are expected to hold a First Class (Honours) Degree or a minimum Upper Second Class (Honours) Degree and be a citizen of one of the European Union countries.

Level of Study: Postgraduate, Research

Type: Scholarships

Value: Offers three full fee bursaries for full-time and part-time research degrees. These bursaries classed as UK/EU for the purpose of fees, cover the payment of tuition fees (currently £3,350 per annum full time and £1,710 for part time). Funding in the second and third years is subject to satisfactory progress

Length of Study: 3 years

Frequency: Annual

Study Establishment: The University of Kent

Country of Study: United Kingdom

No. of awards offered: Varies (up to 4)

Application Procedure: Application is via School of European Culture and Language website at www.kent.ac.uk/secl/researchcentres/graduate/funding.html

Closing Date: May 1st

Funding: Government

No. of awards given last year: 3

No. of applicants last year: 7

Additional Information: Some part-time teaching may be required.

University of Kent School of European Culture and Languages Studentships

Subjects: European and Latin American literary, linguistic and cultural studies (French, German, Hispanic studies, Italian and comparative literary studies), philosophy (with special expertise in moral and political philosophy, aesthetics, philosophy of mind, philosophical logic and paradoxes, Bayesian epistemology and artificial intelligence), religious studies (modern theology, Christian ethics, mysticism and religious experience, religion and film, psychology of religion and cultural study of cosmology and divination) and the literature, history and archaeology of classical World (including Britain and Gaul).

Purpose: To support research.

Eligibility: Candidates are expected to hold a First Class (Honours) Degree or a minimum Upper Second Class (Honours) Degree and be a citizen of one of the European Union countries.

Level of Study: Postgraduate, Research

Type: Studentship

Value: Offers three full fee bursaries for full-time and part-time research degrees. These bursaries classed as UK or EU for the purpose of fees, cover the payment of tuition fees (currently £3,350 per annum full time and £1,710 for part time). Funding in the second and third years is subject to satisfactory progress

Length of Study: 3 years

Frequency: Annual

Study Establishment: The University of Kent

Country of Study: United Kingdom

No. of awards offered: Varies (up to 4)

Application Procedure: Application is via School of European Culture and Language website at www.kent.ac.uk/secl/researchcentres/graduate/funding.html

Closing Date: June 27th

Funding: Government

No. of awards given last year: 5

No. of applicants last year: 13

University of Kent School of Physical Sciences

Subjects: Physical sciences, study in materials science, applied optics or astronomy and space science.

Eligibility: Candidates should hold an Upper Second Class (Honours) Degree or equivalent EU degree and be a citizen of one of the European Union countries or equivalent EU degree.

Level of Study: Postgraduate, Doctorate

Type: Studentship

Value: Home/EU fees plus maintenance at Research Council Rate

Length of Study: 3 years

Country of Study: United Kingdom

No. of awards offered: 4

Application Procedure: Applicants must contact Dr Chris Solomon, School of Physical Sciences or by email c.j.solomon@kent.ac.uk

Closing Date: June

Funding: Commercial, government

Contributor: The University of Kent

No. of awards given last year: 4

No. of applicants last year: 30

University of Kent Sociology Studentship

Subjects: Sociology, social policy, criminology, environmental social science, social work and urban studies.

Purpose: To support research.

Eligibility: Candidates should hold a First Class or Upper Second Class (Honours) Degree.

Level of Study: Postgraduate, (Not available to MA/MSc students)

Type: Studentship

Value: Up to 2 awards at UK £9,250 for full-time students, up to 2 awards at UK £3,250 for full-time students or UK £2,000 for a part-time student, up to 2 awards at UK £12,600 plus £3,270 fees, 2 ESRC 1 + 3 awards

Length of Study: 3 years

Frequency: Annual

Study Establishment: The University of Kent

Country of Study: United Kingdom

No. of awards offered: Up to 9

Application Procedure: Candidates must contact: The Graduate Admissions Secretary, School of Social Research, Kent, CTZ 7NP England or email: socio-office@kent.ac.uk

Closing Date: March 20th

Funding: Government

No. of awards given last year: 9

UNIVERSITY OF KWAZULU-NATAL

Howard College, King George V Avenue, Glenwood, Durban, 4041, South Africa

Tel: (27) 27 (0) 31 260 2212

Fax: (27) (0) 31 260 2384

Email: harrian@nu.ac.za

Website: www.ukzn.ac.za

The Ernest Oppenheimer Memorial Trust Overseas Study Grant

Subjects: Any subject.
Purpose: To finance the costs of overseas study where the specialization cannot be pursued locally.
Level of Study: Postgraduate
Type: Grant
Value: Varies
Length of Study: 1–3 years
Frequency: Annual
Study Establishment: Any approved overseas university
Country of Study: Any country other than South Africa
No. of awards offered: Varies
Application Procedure: Applicants should submit a detailed motivation for support to the manager of the trust accompanied by: a current curriculum vitae, intended place of study and a full disclosure of personal financial position.
Funding: Trusts
Contributor: The Ernest Oppenheimer Memorial Trust
Additional Information: Third party applications are not accepted.

For further information contact:

The Ernest Openheiner Memorial Trust, PO Box 61593, Marshalltown, 2017
Tel: 011 497 8120
Fax: 011 834 286
Contact: Mr PM Hollesen, The Manager

THE UNIVERSITY OF LEEDS

Postgraduate Scholarships Research Student Administrator, Leeds, West Yorkshire, LS2 9JT, England
Tel: (44) 11 3343 4007
Fax: (44) 113 343 3774
Email: s.woodruff@adm.leeds.ac.uk
Website: http://scholarships.leeds.ac.uk
Contact: Ms J Y Findlay, Senior Assistant Registrar

The University of Leeds aims to promote excellence and to achieve and sustain international standing in higher education teaching, learning and research, and to serve a wide range of student constituencies, social and professional communities and industrial, commercial and government agencies, locally, nationally and internationally.

Akroyd, Brotherton and Brown Scholarship

Subjects: Biological sciences, engineering, environment, mathematics and physical sciences, medicine and health.
Purpose: To provide postgraduate scholarships for UK and EU research students of high calibre.
Eligibility: Candidates must be from the UK or an EU country (or eligible to pay fees at the UK rate) and be commencing PhD study for the first time. Candidates must hold at least a UK upper second class honours degree or equivalent.
Level of Study: Doctorate
Type: Scholarship
Value: Fees at the UK rate plus a maintenance allowance
Length of Study: Up to 3 years, subject to satisfactory progress
Frequency: Annual
Study Establishment: University of Leeds
Country of Study: United Kingdom
No. of awards offered: 1
Application Procedure: An application form must be completed and returned to the Postgraduate Scholarships Office by the relevant date.
Closing Date: June 1st
Funding: Private
No. of awards given last year: 1
No. of applicants last year: 46

Canon Collins Trust-FCO Chevening-University of Leeds Scholarships

Subjects: Majority of subjects.
Purpose: To provide awards to students of high academic calibre, who demonstrate both academic excellence and the potential to

become leaders, decision makers and opinion formers in their own countries.
Eligibility: Open to candidates from Angola, Botswana, Lesotho, Malawi Mozambique, Namibia, South Africa, Swaziland, Zambia or Zimbabwe. Applicants must already hold a degree of equivalent standard to a UK upper second class honours degree. An adequate standard of english is required.
Level of Study: Postgraduate
Type: Scholarship
Value: Academic fees, living expenses, other allowances, economy return airfares
Length of Study: 1 year
Frequency: Annual
Study Establishment: The University of Leeds
Country of Study: United Kingdom
No. of awards offered: Up to 10
Application Procedure: Applicants must complete an application form available on request from the Canon Collins Trust.
Closing Date: February 28th
Funding: Government, private
No. of awards given last year: 10
No. of applicants last year: Not known

For further information contact:

Canon Collins Trust, 2 The Ivories, 6 Northampton Street, London, N1 2HY, England
Email: info@canoncollins.org.uk

Collection of Small Endowed Awards

Subjects: Art, business education, social sciences, law, performance, visual arts, communications.
Purpose: To provide postgraduate scholarships for UK and EU Master's students of high calibre.
Eligibility: Candidates from the UK or other countries wishing to undertake study for a Master's degree. Candidates must hold at least a UK upper second class honours degree or equivalent.
Level of Study: Postgraduate
Type: Scholarship
Value: Fees at the UK/EU rate plus a maintenance allowance
Length of Study: 1 year
Frequency: Annual
Study Establishment: University of Leeds
Country of Study: United Kingdom
No. of awards offered: 1
Application Procedure: An application form must be completed and returned to the Postgraduate Scholarships Office by the relevant date.
Closing Date: June 12th
Funding: Private

Commonwealth Shared Scholarship Scheme

Subjects: Subjects related to the economic, social and technological development of the student's home country.
Purpose: To provide scholarships to students of high academic calibre from developing Commonwealth countries.
Eligibility: Applicants must already have obtained a United Kingdom Upper Second Class (Honours) Degree or equivalent. An adequate standard of English is also required and candidates must be nationals of, or permanently resident in, a developing Commonwealth country.
Level of Study: Postgraduate
Type: Scholarship
Value: Academic fees, living expenses, other allowances, economy return airfares
Length of Study: 1 year
Frequency: Annual
Study Establishment: The University of Leeds
Country of Study: United Kingdom
No. of awards offered: Up to 7
Application Procedure: Applicants must complete an application form.
Closing Date: April 1st
Funding: Government, private
No. of awards given last year: 5
No. of applicants last year: 208

Emma and Leslie Reid Scholarship

Subjects: Diseases of the heart or brain.
Purpose: To provide postgraduate scholarships for UK and EU research students of high calibre.
Eligibility: Candidates must be from the UK or an EU country (or eligible to pay fees at the UK rate) and be commencing PhD study for the first time. Candidates must hold at least a UK upper second class honours degree or equivalent.
Level of Study: Doctorate
Type: Scholarship
Value: Fees at the UK rate plus a maintenance allowance
Length of Study: Up to 3 years, subject to satisfactory progress
Frequency: Annual
Study Establishment: University of Leeds
Country of Study: United Kingdom
No. of awards offered: 1
Application Procedure: An application form must be completed and returned to the Postgraduate Scholarships office by the relevant date.
Closing Date: June 1st
Funding: Private
No. of awards given last year: 3
No. of applicants last year: 5

Frank Stell Scholarship

Subjects: Biology, agricultural science, social and political science.
Purpose: To provide postgraduate scholarships for UK research students of high calibre.
Eligibility: Candidates must be commencing PhD study for the first time and hold at least a UK upper second class honours degree or equivalent. Candidates should be resident, or have parents resident within the former administrative area of the County Council of the West Riding of Yorkshire.
Level of Study: Doctorate
Type: Scholarship
Value: Fees at the UK rate plus a maintenance allowance
Length of Study: Up to 3 years, subject to satisfactory progress
Frequency: Annual
Study Establishment: University of Leeds
Country of Study: United Kingdom
No. of awards offered: 2
Application Procedure: An application form must be completed and returned to the Scholarships Office by the relevant date.
Closing Date: June 2nd
Funding: Private

Full Fee Scholarship

Subjects: Any subject.
Purpose: To provide postgraduate scholarships for UK and EU mastership students of high calibre.
Eligibility: Candidates from the UK or other EU countries wishing to undertake study for a master's degree.
Level of Study: Postgraduate
Type: Scholarship
Value: Fees at the UK rate
Length of Study: 12 months
Frequency: Annual
Study Establishment: University of Leeds
Country of Study: United Kingdom
No. of awards offered: Up to 10
Application Procedure: An Application form must be completed and returned to the Postgraduate Scholarships Office by the relevant date.
Closing Date: June 12th
Contributor: University of Leeds
No. of awards given last year: 15
No. of applicants last year: 352
Additional Information: Awards available for full and part-time.

Henry Ellison Scholarship

Subjects: Chemistry or physics.
Purpose: To provide postgraduate scholarships for UK and EU research students of high calibre.
Eligibility: Candidates must be from the UK or an EU country (or eligible to pay fees at the UK rate) and be commencing PhD study for the first time. Candidates must hold at least a UK upper second class honours degree or equivalent and be a University of Leeds graduate.

Level of Study: Doctorate
Type: Scholarship
Value: Fees at the UK rate plus a maintenance allowance
Length of Study: Up to 3 years, subject to satisfactory progress
Frequency: Annual
Study Establishment: University of Leeds
Country of Study: United Kingdom
No. of awards offered: 2
Application Procedure: An application form must be completed and returned to the Postgraduate Scholarships Office by the relevant date.
Closing Date: June 1st
Funding: Private
No. of awards given last year: 2
No. of applicants last year: 3
Additional Information: One award is available within the School of Chemistry and one award is available in the School of Physics and Astronomy for 2009.

John Henry Garner Scholarship

Subjects: Research on matters relating to chemical and biological surveys of rivers and streams and the pollution, prevention and purification of sewage and trade effluents in the area previously known as the West Riding of Yorkshire.
Purpose: To provide postgraduate scholarships for UK and EU research students of high calibre.
Eligibility: Candidates must be from the UK or an EU country (or eligible to pay fees at the UK rate) and be commencing PhD study for the first time. Candidates must hold at least a UK upper second class honours degree or equivalent.
Level of Study: Doctorate
Type: Scholarship
Value: Fees at the UK rate plus a maintenance allowance
Length of Study: Up to 3 years, subject to satisfactory progress
Frequency: Annual
Study Establishment: University of Leeds
Country of Study: United Kingdom
No. of awards offered: 1
Application Procedure: An application form must be completed and returned to the Scholarships Office by the relevant date.
Closing Date: June 2nd
Funding: Private

Joseph Wright Scholarship

Subjects: English, German.
Purpose: To provide postgraduate scholarships for UK and EU research students of high calibre.
Eligibility: Candidates must be from the UK or an EU country (or be eligible to pay fees at the UK rate) and be commencing PhD study for the first time. Candidates must hold at least a UK upper second class honours degree or equivalent.
Level of Study: Doctorate
Type: Scholarship
Value: Fees at the UK rate plus a maintenance allowance
Length of Study: Up to 3 years, subject to satisfactory progress
Frequency: Annual
Study Establishment: University of Leeds
Country of Study: United Kingdom
No. of awards offered: 1
Application Procedure: An application form must be completed and returned to the Postgraduate Scholarships Office by the relevant date.
Closing Date: June 1st
Funding: Private

Kulika Charitable Trust-FCO Chevening-University of Leeds Scholarships

Subjects: Engineering, environment, finance (Not MBA), communications studies, development studies, education.
Purpose: To provide postgraduate scholarships to students of high academic calibre, who demonstrate both academic excellence and the potential to become leaders, decision makers and opinion formers in their own countries.
Eligibility: Open to Ugandan nationals living in Uganda. Applicants must hold at least an upper second class degree from a Ugandan instituition, or a degree of equivalent standard to a UK upper second

class honours degree, and should normally have 3 years relevant experience. Applicants should usually be under 36 years of age.
Level of Study: Postgraduate
Type: Scholarship
Value: Academic fees, living expenses, other allowances, economy return airfares
Length of Study: 1 year
Frequency: Annual
Study Establishment: The University of Leeds
Country of Study: United Kingdom
No. of awards offered: Up to 3
Application Procedure: Applicants must apply via an application form after acceptance into a taught course. Application forms for the scholarship are available from Kulika Uganda.
Closing Date: January 30th
Funding: Government, private
No. of applicants last year: Not known

For further information contact:

Kulika Uganda, Kampala, PO Box 11330, Uganda

Lowson Scholarship
Subjects: Chemistry.
Purpose: To provide postgraduate scholarships for UK and EU research students of high calibre.
Eligibility: Candidates must be from the UK or an EU country (or be eligible to pay fees at the UK rate) and be commencing PhD study for the first time. Candidates must hold at least a UK upper second class honours degree or equivalent.
Level of Study: Doctorate
Type: Scholarship
Value: Fees at the UK rate plus a maintenance allowance
Length of Study: Up to 3 years, subject to satisfactory progress
Frequency: Annual
Study Establishment: University of Leeds
Country of Study: United Kingdom
No. of awards offered: 1
Application Procedure: An application form must be completed and returned to the Postgraduate Scholarships Office by the relevant date.
Funding: Private

Mary and Alice Smith Memorial Scholarship
Subjects: Research into the prevention or cure of cancer or heart disease.
Purpose: To provide postgraduate scholarships for UK research students of high calibre.
Eligibility: Candidates must be British and be commencing PhD study for the first time. Candidates must hold at least a UK upper second class honours degree or equivalent.
Level of Study: Doctorate
Type: Scholarship
Value: Fees at the UK rate plus a maintenance allowance
Length of Study: Up to 3 years, subject to satisfactory progress
Frequency: Annual
Study Establishment: University of Leeds
Country of Study: United Kingdom
No. of awards offered: 1
Application Procedure: An application form must be completed and returned to the Postgraduate Scholarships Office by the relevant date.
Closing Date: June 1st
Funding: Private
No. of awards given last year: 1
No. of applicants last year: 4

Overseas Research Students Awards Scheme
Subjects: All subjects.
Purpose: To provide postgraduate scholarships for international research students of high calibre.
Eligibility: Open to international research students of outstanding merit and research potential. Applicants must have obtained at least a United Kingdom Upper Second Class (Honours) Degree or equivalent. An adequate knowledge of English is required.
Level of Study: Postgraduate, Doctorate
Type: Scholarship
Value: Partial academic fees

Length of Study: Up to 3 years, subject to satisfactory academic performance
Frequency: Annual
Study Establishment: The University of Leeds
Country of Study: United Kingdom
Application Procedure: Applicants must complete an application form.
Closing Date: January 31st
Funding: Government
No. of awards given last year: 27
No. of applicants last year: 482

Shell Centenary/Shell Centenary Chevening Scholarships
Subjects: Engineering geology, exploration geophysics, structural geology with geophysics, geochemistry, hydrogeology, environmental geochemistry, environmental engineering and project management, international construction management and engineering, engineering project management, sustainable waste management, combustion and energy, computational fluid dynamics, automotive engineering, mechanical engineering, fire and explosion engineering, modern digital and radio frequency wireless communications, advanced textiles and performance clothing, catchments dynamics and management, geographical information systems, infrastructure asset engineering and management, transport planning, transport planning and engineering, transport planning and the environment, energy and environment, advanced chemical engineering, structural engineering.
Purpose: To provide postgraduate scholarships to students of high academic calibre, who demonstrate both academic excellence and the potential to become leaders, decision makers and opinion formers in their own countries.
Eligibility: Open to candidates who have obtained, or are about to obtain, a United Kingdom First Class (Honours) Degree or equivalent. An excellent knowledge of English is required. Candidates must be under 35 years of age. Candidates should be nationals of and resident in any country other than Australia, Austria, Belgium, Canada, Denmark, Finland, France, Germany, Greece, Iceland, Ireland, Italy, Japan, Luxembourg, The Netherlands, New Zealand, Norway, Portugal, Spain, Sweden, Switzerland, United Kingdom and United States of America.
Level of Study: Postgraduate
Type: Scholarship
Value: Academic fees, living expenses, other allowances, economy return airfares
Length of Study: 1 year
Frequency: Annual
Study Establishment: The University of Leeds
Country of Study: United Kingdom
No. of awards offered: 6
Application Procedure: Applicants must apply by application form.
Closing Date: March 1st
Funding: Commercial, government, private
No. of awards given last year: 5
No. of applicants last year: 224

Stanley Burton Research Scholarship
Subjects: Music or fine art.
Purpose: To provide postgraduate scholarships for UK research students of high calibre.
Eligibility: Candidates must be British and be commencing PhD study for the first time. Candidates must hold at least a UK upper second class honours degree or equivalent.
Level of Study: Doctorate
Type: Scholarship
Value: Fees at the UK rate plus a maintenance allowance
Length of Study: Up to 3 years, subject to satisfactory progress
Frequency: Annual
Study Establishment: University of Leeds
Country of Study: United Kingdom
No. of awards offered: 1
Application Procedure: An application form must be completed and returned to the Postgraduate Scholarships Office by the relevant date.
Closing Date: June 1st
Funding: Private
No. of awards given last year: 1
No. of applicants last year: 3

Additional Information: One award is available within the School of Fine Art, History of Art and Cultural Studies in 2009.

University of Leeds – FCO Chevening Award for Vietnamese Students

Subjects: Economics, international relations, law/criminal justice studies, political science, international security, business studies, development studies, finance and banking, public administration, environmental studies/engineering, journalism, human rights/democracy.
Purpose: To provide postgraduate scholarships to Vietnamese students of high calibre, who demonstrate both academic excellence and the potential to become leaders, decision makers and opinion formers in their own country.
Eligibility: Open to candidates from Vietnam who have obtained at least a UK upper second class honours degree or equivalent and has an adequate standard of English.
Level of Study: Postgraduate
Type: Scholarship
Value: Academic fees, maintenance allowance, return airfare, other allowances
Length of Study: 12 months
Frequency: Annual
Study Establishment: University of Leeds
Country of Study: United Kingdom
No. of awards offered: 1
Application Procedure: Applications should be made through the British Council in Vietnam.
Closing Date: November 23rd
Funding: Government

University of Leeds Fully Funded International Research Scholarships (FIRS)

Subjects: All subjects.
Purpose: To provide postgraduate scholarships for international research students of high calibre.
Eligibility: Candidates must be eligible to pay fees at the international rate and be commencing PhD study for the first time. Candidates must hold at least a UK upper second class honours degree or equivalent.
Level of Study: Doctorate
Type: Scholarship
Value: Fees at the international rate plus a maintenance allowance
Length of Study: Up to 3 years, subject to satisfactory progress
Frequency: Annual
Study Establishment: University of Leeds
Country of Study: United Kingdom
No. of awards offered: 12
Application Procedure: An application form must be completed and returned to the Postgraduate Scholarships Office by the relevant date.
Closing Date: January 31st
Contributor: University

University of Leeds International Research Scholarships

Subjects: All subjects.
Purpose: To provide postgraduate scholarships for international research students of high calibre.
Eligibility: Applicants must have applied for an ORSAS award and be commencing PhD research degree study for the 1st time. Applicants must be eligible to pay fees at the international fee rate and hold a degree equivalent to a United Kingdom first class honours degree.
Level of Study: Doctorate, Postgraduate
Type: Scholarship
Value: Full maintenance scholarships of UK £12,900 or partial maintenance scholarship of UK £2,500
Length of Study: Up to 3 years
Frequency: Annual
Study Establishment: The University of Leeds
Country of Study: United Kingdom
No. of awards offered: Up to 5 full awards and upto 3 partial awards
Application Procedure: Applicants must complete an application for the ORSAS awards.
Closing Date: January 31st
Funding: Private
No. of awards given last year: 5 Full, 3 Partial
No. of applicants last year: 411

University Research Scholarships

Subjects: All subjects.
Purpose: To provide postgraduate scholarships for UK and EU research students of high calibre.
Eligibility: Candidates must be from the UK or an EU country (or eligible to pay fees at the UK rate) and be commencing PhD study for the first time. Candidates must hold at least a UK upper second class honours degree or equivalent.
Level of Study: Doctorate
Type: Scholarship
Value: Fees at the UK rate plus a maintenance allowance
Length of Study: Up to 3 years, subject to satisfactory progress
Frequency: Annual
Study Establishment: University of Leeds
Country of Study: United Kingdom
No. of awards offered: 18
Application Procedure: An application form must be completed and returned to the Postgraduate Scholarships Office by the relevant date.
Closing Date: Variable according to Faculty. Please check the website for details. http://scholarships.leeds.ac.uk
No. of awards given last year: 18
No. of applicants last year: 249

W B Crump Scholarship

Subjects: Areas relating to the economic, social and industrial history, archaeology, geography, botany of the north of England generally, in Yorkshire and the Pennines in particular.
Purpose: To provide postgraduate scholarships for UK and EU research students of high calibre.
Eligibility: Candidates must be from the UK or an EU country (or be eligible to pay fees at the UK rate) and be commencing PhD study for the first time. Candidates must hold at least a UK upper second class honours degree or equivalent.
Level of Study: Doctorate
Type: Scholarship
Value: Fees at the UK rate plus a maintenance allowance
Length of Study: Up to 3 years, subject to satisfactory progress
Frequency: Annual
Study Establishment: University of Leeds
Country of Study: United Kingdom
No. of awards offered: 1
Application Procedure: An application form must be completed and returned to the Postgraduate Scholarships Office by the relevant date.
Closing Date: June 1st
Funding: Private

White Rose Studentships

Subjects: Project based, subjects to be confirmed.
Purpose: To provide postgraduate scholarships for UK and EU research students of high calibre.
Eligibility: Candidates must be from the UK or an EU country (or eligible to pay fees at the UK rate) and be commencing PhD study for the first time. Candidates must hold at least a UK upper second class honours degree or equivalent.
Level of Study: Doctorate
Type: Scholarship
Value: Fees at the UK rate plus a maintenance allowance
Length of Study: Up to 3 years, subject to satisfactory progress
Frequency: Annual
Study Establishment: University of Leeds
Country of Study: United Kingdom
No. of awards offered: 4
Application Procedure: An application form must be completed and returned to the Postgraduate Scholarships Office by the relevant date.
Closing Date: April 17th
Funding: Private
No. of awards given last year: 4
No. of applicants last year: 28
Additional Information: The University of Leeds is offering four White Rose Research Studentships, in collaboration with the Universities of Sheffield and York, for students from the United Kingdom and from European Union Countries commencing full-time PhD study in October.

UNIVERSITY OF LONDON INSTITUTE IN PARIS

9-11 rue de Constantine, F-75340 Paris
Cedex 07, France
Tel: (33) 1 44 11 73 76
Fax: (33) 145 503 155
Email: c.miller@ulip.lon.ac.uk
Website: www.ulip.lon.ac.uk
Contact: The Dean

The University of London Institute in Paris is a United Kingdom Institute of Higher Education devoted to the study of French language, literature and culture.

Quinn, Nathan and Edmond Scholarships

Subjects: An area in which the institute can provide supervision in the field of humanities relating to France.
Purpose: To assist postgraduate research in France.
Eligibility: Open to graduates who possess sufficient knowledge of French to pursue their proposed studies.
Level of Study: Doctorate, Postdoctorate, Postgraduate
Type: Scholarship
Value: Depending on the funds available and the needs of the candidates, scholarships are of the order of UK £500 per month
Length of Study: Upto 1 year
Frequency: Dependent on funds available
Study Establishment: University of London Institute in Paris
Country of Study: France
No. of awards offered: Dependent on availability of funds
Application Procedure: Application forms can be downloaded from the website.
Closing Date: May 31st
Funding: Private
Contributor: Trust funds
No. of awards given last year: 2
No. of applicants last year: 2
Additional Information: Scholarships cannot be held concurrently with other major awards. These scholarships are intended for research and not for those following taught courses.

THE UNIVERSITY OF MANCHESTER

Oxford Road, Manchester, M13 9PL, United Kingdom
Tel: (44) 161 306 6000
Email: m.barnes@manchester.ac.uk
Website: www.manchester.ac.uk
Contact: Louise Barnes

The University of Manchester is Britain's largest single site university with a proud history of achievement and an ambitious agenda for the future. The University has an exceptional record of generating and sharing new ideas, and the quality, breadth and volume of its research activity is unparalleled in Britain.

IDPM Taught Postgraduate Scholarship Scheme

Subjects: Development studies.
Eligibility: Open to citizens of any country (excluding Andorra, Australia, Austria, Belgium, Bermuda, Canada, Cyprus, Denmark, Faroe Islands, Finland, France, Germany, Greece, Hong Kong, Iceland, Ireland, Israel, Italy, Japan, Liechtenstein, Luxembourg, Macau, Monaco, Netherlands, New Zealand, Norway, Portugal, San Marino, Singapore, Slovenia, South Korea, Spain, Sweden, Switzerland, Taiwan, United Kingdom, United States, Vatican City) who are holding a first degree, have not previously studied for 1 year or more in the UK or any other developed country, and have received an offer to study from IDPM.
Level of Study: Postgraduate
Type: Scholarship
Value: UK £2,000
Frequency: Annual
No. of awards offered: 3
Application Procedure: Check website for further details.
Closing Date: June 30th

For further information contact:

University of Manchester, Harold Hankins Building, Room 5.31, Precinct Centre, Oxford Road, Manchester, M13 9PL, United Kingdom
Email: paul.arrowsmith@manchester.ac.uk
Website: www.sed.manchester.ac.uk/
Contact: Paul Arrowsmith, School of Environment & Development, Admissions Office

Manchester-China Scholarship Council Joint Postgraduate Scholarship Programme

Subjects: Telecommunication and information technology, life science and public health, material science and new material, energy sources and environment, engineering science and applied social sciences and WTO-related areas.
Purpose: To provide scholarships to the nationals of PR China who wish to pursue their PhD at the University of Manchester.
Eligibility: Open to students who are citizens and permanent residents of PR China and who hold a Master's degree from one of the 38 Chinese universities under 985 Programme.
Level of Study: Doctorate, Postgraduate
Type: Scholarships
Value: UK £4,800
Length of Study: 3 years
Frequency: Annual
Study Establishment: University of Manchester
Country of Study: United Kingdom
No. of awards offered: 10
Application Procedure: Applicants must complete the standard postgraduate application form and return it together with: Academic transcripts, English language qualification, 2 reference letters and a research proposal.
Closing Date: April 20th

UNIVERSITY OF MANITOBA

Department of English, 623 Fletcher Argue Building, Winnipeg, MB, R3T 5V5, Canada
Tel: (1) 204 474 7365
Fax: (1) 204 474-7669
Email: english@umanitoba.ca
Website: www.umanitoba.ca
Contact: Dr Mark Libin

The University of Manitoba is the province's largest, most comprehensive and only research intensive post secondary educational institution. It was founded in 1877. In a typical year, the university has an enrolment of 24,542 undergraduate students and 3,021 graduate students. The University offers 82 degrees, 51 at the undergraduate level. Most academic units offer Graduate studies programmes leading to Master's or Doctoral degrees.

University of Manitoba Graduate Fellowship

Subjects: English literature.
Purpose: To provide fellowships to students who wish to pursue higher studies in english literature.
Eligibility: Open to students who have maintained high grades and made satisfactory progress in full-time graduate programme.
Level of Study: Doctorate, Postgraduate
Type: Fellowships
Value: Canadian $16,000 for PhD, Canadian $12,000 for MA
Length of Study: 2–4 years
Frequency: Annual
Study Establishment: University of Manitoba
Country of Study: Canada
No. of awards offered: 2
Application Procedure: Application for these fellowships will be invited in September each year. Application forms are available on the Faculty of Graduate Studies website at www.umanitoba.ca/faculties/graduate_studies/funding/index.html
Closing Date: January 5th

University of Manitoba Teaching Assistantships

Subjects: English literature.

Purpose: To financially support students enrolled in full-time PhD programme.
Eligibility: Open to full-time students registered in a PhD programme who may apply for positions as lecturers or seminar leaders in the first year literature courses.
Level of Study: Doctorate
Type: Assistantship
Value: Varies
Length of Study: 3–4 years
Frequency: Dependent on funds available
Study Establishment: University of Manitoba
Country of Study: Canada
Application Procedure: To view current postings and obtain an application form students can log on to www.umanitoba.ca/admin/human_resources/employment
Funding: Trusts

UNIVERSITY OF MELBOURNE

Scholarships Office, Melbourne, VIC 3010, Australia
Tel: (61) (3) 8344 4000
Fax: (61) (3) 8344 5104
Email: pg-schools@unimelb.edu.au
Website: www.services.unimelb.edu.au

The University of Melbourne has a long and distinguished tradition of excellence in teaching and research. It is the leading research institution in Australia and enjoys a reputation for the high quality of its research programmes, consistently winning the largest share of national competitive research funding.

A.O. Capell Scholarship

Subjects: All subjects.
Eligibility: Open to APA and MRS candidates having completed tertiary studies that are equivalent to a 4 years Australian degree with a minimum result of First Class Honours and currently enrolled in, a research higher degree.
Level of Study: Postgraduate
Type: Scholarship
Value: $25,000 per year and other benefits as per the APA
Length of Study: 1 year
Frequency: Every 3 years
Study Establishment: University of Melbourne
Country of Study: Australia
No. of awards offered: 3
Application Procedure: Check website for further details.
Closing Date: October 31st
Funding: Private
Contributor: A.O. Capell Scholarship Fund, Stella Mary Langford Scholarship Fund, and the Henry & Louisa Williams Bequest

Baillieu Research Scholarship

Subjects: Medicine, law, commerce, economics and architecture.
Eligibility: Open to lineal descendants of Australian soldiers and sailors killed, blinded or permanently incapacitated while engaged in war service, with priority being given to World War I service.
Level of Study: Postgraduate
Type: Scholarship
Value: $19,040 per year and other benefits as per the MRS
Frequency: Annual
Application Procedure: Applicants should lodge to the Melbourne Scholarships office the SCHOLS online application indicating that they wish to be considered for the Baillieu Research Scholarship and documents to verify that they are a lineal descendent of an Australian solider or sailor killed, blinded or permanently incapacitated while engaged in war service.
Closing Date: October 31st
Funding: Private
Contributor: Baillieu Research Scholarship Fund

Dairy Postgraduate Scholarships and Awards

Subjects: Dairy farming and dairy manufacturing.
Purpose: To enable students for research contributing to the technical areas relevant to dairy farming and dairy manufacturing operations.

Eligibility: Open to citizens or permanent residents of Australia.
Level of Study: Postgraduate
Type: Scholarship
Value: Australian $25,000 stipend plus Australian $3,000 per year
Frequency: Annual
Country of Study: Australia
Application Procedure: To apply for this scholarship one must apply direct to the faculty.
Closing Date: October 20th

For further information contact:

Dairy Australia Limited, Australia
Tel: (61) 03 9694 3810
Fax: (61) 03 9694 3701
Email: research@dairyaustralia.com.au
Website: www.dairyaustralia.com.au

Ernst and Grace Matthaei Research Scholarship

Subjects: Optics.
Eligibility: Open to an APA or MRS applicant undertaking studies in the field of optics.
Level of Study: Postgraduate
Type: Scholarship
Value: $22,000 per year and other benefits as per the APA
Frequency: Annual
Country of Study: Australia
Application Procedure: Applicants must indicate on SCHOLS, the online application service, their interest in being considered for the scholarship.
Closing Date: October 31st
Contributor: Ernst and Grace Matthaei Bequest

Fay Marles Scholarships

Subjects: Human rights.
Purpose: To provide financial support to students of indigenous Australian descent, with disabilities and whose academic career has been adversely affected.
Eligibility: Open to applicants who are citizens of Australia or New Zealand or Australian permanent residents. Applicants must provide evidence to show they meet at least 1 of the following criteria: student of indigenous Australian descent, student whose academic career has been adversely affected or student with a disability.
Level of Study: Postgraduate
Type: Scholarships
Value: Up to Australian $8,660 per year
Frequency: Annual
Study Establishment: University of Melbourne
Country of Study: Australia
No. of awards offered: 10
Additional Information: For further information please visit www.services.unimelb.edu.au/scholarship

Fred Knight Research Scholarship

Subjects: All subjects.
Eligibility: Open to APA and MRS candidates having completed tertiary studies that are equivalent to a 4 years Australian degree with a minimum result of First Class Honours and currently enrolled in a research higher degree.
Level of Study: Postgraduate
Type: Scholarship
Value: $6,800 for 1 year in addition to an APA or MRS
Frequency: Annual
Country of Study: Australia
Application Procedure: Check website for further details.
Closing Date: October 31st
Funding: Private
Contributor: Fred Knight Research Scholarship Fund

Grimwade Scholarship

Subjects: All subjects.
Eligibility: Open to highest-ranked PhD applicant from interstate or New Zealand on the recommendation of the Miegunyah Fund Committee.
Level of Study: Doctorate
Type: Scholarship

Value: $25,000 per year, and a $2,500 relocation grant is provided in the first year
Frequency: Annual
No. of awards offered: 1
Application Procedure: Check website for further details.
Funding: Private
Contributor: Russell and Mab Grimwade Miegunyah Fund

The Helen Macpherson Smith Scholarships

Subjects: Science, humanities and social sciences.
Eligibility: Open to outstanding women who are entering postgraduate study.
Level of Study: Postgraduate
Type: Scholarship
Value: $4,000 approx. payment in addition to an APA or MRS
Frequency: Annual
Country of Study: Australia
No. of awards offered: 2
Application Procedure: Check website for further details.
Funding: Trusts
Contributor: Helen Macpherson Smith Trust

Henry James Williams Scholarship

Subjects: All subjects.
Eligibility: Open to APA and MRS candidates having completed tertiary studies that are quivalent to a 4 year Australian degree with a minimum result of First Class Honours and currently enrolled in a research higher degree.
Level of Study: Postgraduate
Type: Scholarship
Value: $25,000 per year and other benefits as per the APA
Length of Study: 3 years
Frequency: Annual
No. of awards offered: 3
Application Procedure: Check website for further details.
Closing Date: October 31st
Funding: Private
Contributor: A.O. Capell Scholarship Fund, the Stella Mary Langford Scholarship Fundand Henry & Louisa Williams Bequest

Human Rights Scholarship

Subjects: Human rights.
Purpose: To support international and local students who will be undertaking postgraduate studies in the human rights field and who are able to demonstrate their commitment to the peaceful advancement of respect for human rights.
Eligibility: Open to applicants who are able to demonstrate their commitment to the peaceful advancement of respect for human rights extends beyond their academic studies, a high H2A (i.e. 78–79 per cent and above) minimum grade average and must be planning to commence or be currently enrolled in a postgraduate diploma, Masters by coursework, Doctorate by coursework or research higher degree in the human rights field at the University of Melbourne.
Level of Study: Postgraduate
Type: Scholarship
Value: Living allowance of $22,000 per year, relocation grant of $2,500, relocation allowance and thesis allowance of up to $420 for Masters and $840 for PhD and other Doctorate by research candidates
Frequency: Annual
Country of Study: Australia
No. of awards offered: 2
Application Procedure: Local applicants must submit to three complete sets (one original or certified and two copies) of the documents listed on the document checklist. International applicants must submit three sets (one original and two copies) of the International HRS Application Form.
Closing Date: October 31st

Melbourne International Fee Remission Scholarships

Subjects: All subjects offered by the University.
Purpose: To enable graduates to undertake a research higher degree in any discipline.

Eligibility: Please see www.services.unimelb.edu/scholarships/pgrad for full details.
Level of Study: Postgraduate, Research
Type: Scholarship
Value: Full tuition fees
Length of Study: Up to 2 years at the Master's level and up to 3 years at the PhD and research doctorate level. A 6-month extension is possible at the research doctorate level
Frequency: Annual
Study Establishment: The University of Melbourne
Country of Study: Australia
No. of awards offered: 150. Available only to international students
Application Procedure: International applicants who have not already commenced the course for which they seek scholarship will automatically be considered for scholarship if they receive an unconditional offer of a place in a research higher degree course. Information about applying for courses is available at www.services.unimelb.edu.au/admissions/apply/. A separate application form is not required.
Closing Date: August 31st
Funding: Government
Contributor: Scholarship fund
No. of awards given last year: 60
No. of applicants last year: 500

Melbourne Research Scholarships

Subjects: All subjects offered by the University.
Purpose: To enable graduates to undertake a research higher degree in any discipline.
Eligibility: Please see www.services.unimelb.edu.au/scholarships/pgrad for full details.
Level of Study: Doctorate, Postgraduate, Research
Type: Scholarship
Value: Australian $19,040 per year, payable fortnightly
Length of Study: Up to 2 years at the Master's level and up to 3 years at the PhD and research doctorate level. A 6-month extension is possible at the research doctorate level
Frequency: Annual
Study Establishment: The University of Melbourne
Country of Study: Australia
No. of awards offered: 220, of which approx. 95 may be awarded to international students
Application Procedure: International applicants who have not already commenced the course for which they seek scholarship will automatically be considered for scholarship if they receive an unconditional offer of a place in a research higher degree course. Information about applying for courses is available at www.services.unimelb.edu.au/admissions/apply/. A separate application form is not required.
Closing Date: October 31st for Australian citizens and residents in the main selection round, and September 15th for international students. A small number of scholarships may be available throughout the year subject to availability
Funding: Government
Contributor: Scholarship fund
No. of awards given last year: 210
No. of applicants last year: 1,000

PhD Scholarship: Research in Health Law and Policy

Subjects: Health law and policy.
Purpose: To research into policy issues at the intersection of the legal and health care systems in Australia.
Eligibility: Open to applicants holding an Honours Degree in law. Prior training in statistics or quantitative methods will be highly valued.
Level of Study: Doctorate
Type: Scholarship
Value: Australian $25,600 per year
Length of Study: 3 years
Frequency: Annual
Study Establishment: Melbourne Law School or School of Population Health
Country of Study: Australia
Application Procedure: Check website for further details.
Contributor: ARC

For further information contact:

Centre for Health Programs, Policy and Economics, School of Population Health
Tel: 8344 0710
Contact: Joy Yeadon

PhDs in Bio nanotechnology

Subjects: Bio nanotechnology.
Eligibility: Open to those who have achieved Honours 2a or equivalent.
Level of Study: Postgraduate, Research
Type: Scholarship
Value: Australian $19,616 per year
Length of Study: 2 years (Masters) and 3 years (PhD)
Frequency: Annual
Study Establishment: University of Melbourne
Country of Study: Australia
No. of awards offered: 3
Application Procedure: Applicants must apply directly to the scholarship provider. Check website for further details.
Closing Date: July 21st
Contributor: University of Melbourne

For further information contact:

Chemical and Biomolecular Engineering, Australia
Email: fcaruso@unimelb.edu.au
Website: www.cnst.unimelb.edu.au
Contact: Professor Frank Caruso, Federation Fellow

Pratt Foundation Scholarship

Subjects: All subjects.
Eligibility: Open to high-ranking Victorian applicant with a higher research degree.
Level of Study: Postgraduate
Type: Scholarship
Value: $25,000 per year and other benefits as per the APA
Frequency: Annual
Country of Study: Australia
No. of awards offered: 1
Application Procedure: Check website for further details.
Funding: Foundation
Contributor: Pratt Foundation

Rae and Edith Bennett Travelling Scholarship

Subjects: All subjects.
Purpose: To enable students and graduates of the University of Melbourne to undertake postgraduate study or research in the United Kingdom.
Eligibility: Open to students and graduates of the University of Melbourne who can demonstrate outstanding academic merit and promise.
Level of Study: Postgraduate
Type: Scholarship
Value: $60,000 per year
Frequency: Annual
Country of Study: Australia
No. of awards offered: 2
Application Procedure: Applicants must provide official transcript/s of all tertiary study, a curriculum vitae, an outline of the proposed study or research, evidence of acceptance into a postgraduate course, or research program at a tertiary institution in the United Kingdom, a completed Estimated Budget form and two academic references and one personal reference.
Closing Date: June 30th
Funding: Private
Contributor: Rae and Edith Bennett Travelling Scholarship Fund

Sir Arthur Sims Travelling Scholarship

Subjects: All subjects.
Purpose: To enable graduates of Australian universities to undertake postgraduate study or research in United Kingdom.
Eligibility: Open to graduates of Australian universities who can demonstrate outstanding academic merit and promise. Applicants

must be born in Australia or have parents who have been Australian residents for 7 years or more.
Level of Study: Postgraduate, Research
Type: Scholarship
Value: $20,000 per year
Length of Study: 1–3
Country of Study: United Kingdom
Application Procedure: Check website for further details.
Closing Date: June 30th
Funding: Private
Contributor: Sir Arthur Sims Traveling Scholarship Fund

For further information contact:

Website: www.jason.edu

Sir John and Lady Higgins Research Scholarship

Subjects: Industrial chemistry and biochemistry.
Purpose: For the development of the pastoral and agricultural industries.
Eligibility: Open to students undertaking a research higher degree in the fields of industrial chemistry and biochemistry.
Level of Study: Research
Type: Scholarship
Value: $22,000 per year and other benefits as per the APA
Frequency: Every 2 years
Country of Study: Australia
No. of awards offered: 1
Application Procedure: Applicants must indicate on SCHOLS, the online application service, their interest for this scholarship and explain how their research in industrial chemistry and biochemistry relates directly to the study and development of the pastoral and agricultural industries. Check website for more details.
Closing Date: October 31st

Sir Thomas Naghten Fitzgerald Scholarship

Subjects: Medical and health sciences.
Eligibility: Open to candidates studied or currently studying at The University of Melbourne.
Level of Study: Postgraduate
Type: Scholarship
Value: $8,000 (maximum)
Frequency: Annual
Study Establishment: University of Melbourne
Country of Study: Australia
No. of awards offered: 1
Application Procedure: Check website for further details.
Closing Date: October 31st
Funding: Government

For further information contact:

The University of Melbourne, Parkville, Victoria, 3010, Australia
Email: jyv@unimelb.edu.au
Website: www.mdhs.unimelb.edu.au
Contact: Joan Vosen, Medicine Faculty

Stella Mary Langford Scholarship

Subjects: All subjects.
Eligibility: Open to highly ranked applicants for an APA or MRS.
Level of Study: Unrestricted
Type: Scholarship
Value: $25,000 per year and other benefits as per the APA
Length of Study: 3 years
Frequency: Annual
Country of Study: Australia
No. of awards offered: 3
Application Procedure: Check website for further details.
Funding: Private
Contributor: A.O. Capell Scholarship Fund, Henry & Louisa Williams Bequest, and Stella Mary Langford Scholarship Fund

Viola Edith Reid Bequest Scholarship

Subjects: Medicine.
Eligibility: Open for study in Australia. There are no restrictions on citizenship.

Level of Study: Postgraduate, Research
Type: Scholarship
Value: $22,000 maximum per award
Frequency: Annual
Study Establishment: University of Melbourne
Country of Study: Australia
No. of awards offered: 1
Application Procedure: Check website for further details.
Closing Date: October 31st
Funding: Government

For further information contact:

The University of Melbourne, Parkville, Victoria, 3010, Australia
Tel: (61) 61 8344 4019
Fax: (61) 9347 7854
Email: jyv@unimelb.edu.au
Website: www.mdhs.unimelb.edu.au
Contact: Joan Vosen, Medicine Faculty

UNIVERSITY OF MICHIGAN

42 Maynard Street, Ann Arbor, MI, 48109-1399, United States of America
Tel: (1) 734 647 1844
Fax: (1) 734 764 7084
Email: drath@umich.edu
Website: www.umich.edu
Contact: Joe Serwach

University of Michigan is Internationally renowned for research and education. The University offers a wide variety of degree programmes for undergraduate and graduate students.

Knight-Wallace Fellowship

Subjects: Journalism.
Purpose: To provide financial aid, broaden perspectives, nurture intellectual growth and inspire personal transformation.
Eligibility: Open to full-time journalists with 5 years experience and whose work appears regularly as an employee or freelance in the United States.
Level of Study: Professional development
Type: Stipendiary
Value: US$55,000
Length of Study: 8 months
Frequency: Annual
Country of Study: United States of America
No. of awards offered: 12
Application Procedure: Applicants can download the application form from the website. The completed application form along with a study plan, autobiographical statement and work samples must be submitted.
Closing Date: February 1st
Additional Information: There are no academic prerequisites.

For further information contact:

Knight-Wallace Fellows Wallace House 620 Oxford Road University of Michigan, Ann Arbor, MI, 48104-2635, United States of America
Website: www.kwfellows.org
Contact: Charles R Eisendrath, Director

UNIVERSITY OF MONTANA (UM)

Financial Aid Office, 2nd Floor, Emma B. Lommasson Center, Griz Central, 32 Campus Drive, Missoula, MT 59812, United States of America
Tel: (1) 406 243 0211
Email: dss@umontana.edu
Website: www.umt.edu

University of Montana is a magnet not only for top-notch teachers and researchers, but also for students from across the country and around the globe. Students receive a high-quality, well-rounded education and training for professional careers in the University's three colleges – arts and sciences, forestry and conservation, and technology – and six schools – journalism, law, business, education, pharmacy and the

fine arts. A city within a city – with its own eateries, stores, medical facilities, banking and postal services, and zip code – UM has an increasingly diverse population and rich culture. The University has nurtured a tradition of cultural and scientific exploration.

Erasmus Scholarships

Subjects: English, environmental studies, history, law, philosophy, political science, foreign languages, interdisciplinary studies.
Eligibility: Open to the full-time UM students of all nationalities including freshmen, transfer students and graduate students.
Level of Study: Graduate
Type: Scholarships
Value: $500–4,000
Length of Study: 1 year (renewable)
Frequency: Annual
No. of awards offered: 35
Closing Date: February 1st

UNIVERSITY OF NEBRASKA AT OMAHA (UNO)

College of Business Adminstration, University of Nebraska at Omaha, Omaha, 6001 Dodge Street, NE, 68182-0048, United States of America
Tel: (1) 402 554 2341
Fax: (1) 402 554 4036
Email: cba@unomaha.edu/mba
Website: www.mba.unomaha.edu
Contact: MBA Admissions Officer

The University of Nebraska at Omaha's (UNO) College of Business Administration offers a dynamic, challenging Master's programme designed to help students acquire the knowledge, perspective and skills necessary for success in the marketplace of today and tomorrow. The goal of the programme is to develop leaders who have the ability to incorporate change, use information technology to resolve problems and make sound business decisions. The curriculum focuses on results with an emphasis on how to excel in a rapidly changing world.

UNO Graduate Assistantships

Subjects: MBA, MACC, MA/ECM and MS/ECM.
Eligibility: Open to qualified students who are enrolled in a graduate degree programme.
Level of Study: Graduate, MBA
Value: A waiver of tuition costs up to 12 hours of graduate credit per semester
Frequency: Every 2 years
Study Establishment: UNO
Country of Study: United States of America
No. of awards offered: 1–3 each semester
Application Procedure: Applicants must make enquiries in their department about the availability of assistantships, the procedures for applying, and the details of when the application and supporting credentials should be on file in the department or school for consideration. Applicants must complete application for graduate assistantships and submit a curriculum vitae and supporting materials.
Closing Date: June 1st
No. of awards given last year: 1–3
No. of applicants last year: 40

UNIVERSITY OF NEVADA, LAS VEGAS (UNLV)

Graduate College, 4505 Maryland Parkway, Box 451010, Las Vegas, NV, 89154-6031, United States of America
Tel: (1) 702 895 3621
Fax: (1) 702 895 5944
Email: scrhelp@unlv.nevada.edu
Website: www.unlv.edu
Contact: Administrative Officer

UNLV Alumni Association Graduate Scholarships

Subjects: All subjects.

Purpose: To reward outstanding graduate students.
Eligibility: Applicants must have completed at least 12 credits of graduate study at UNLV, have a minimum undergraduate and graduate grade point average of 3.5 and enrol for six or more graduate credits in each semester of the scholarship year.
Level of Study: Graduate, MBA
Type: Scholarship
Value: US$1,000
Length of Study: 1 year
Frequency: Annual
Study Establishment: UNLV
Country of Study: United States of America
No. of awards offered: 3
Application Procedure: Applicants must telephone (1) 702 895 3320 or write for application forms or further information.
Closing Date: March 1st

UNLV Graduate Assistantships

Subjects: All subjects.
Purpose: To offer financial assistance and support to students admitted to any graduate degree programme.
Eligibility: Open to students who have already been admitted to any graduate degree programme.
Level of Study: Graduate, MBA
Value: A 9 month stipend of US$10,000 for Master's level assistantships plus tuition and fee waivers
Length of Study: 1 year
Frequency: Annual
Study Establishment: UNLV
Country of Study: United States of America
No. of awards offered: Varies
Application Procedure: Applicants must send applications and all supporting materials to the Dean of the Graduate College.
Closing Date: March 1st or November 1st for the Spring assistantship. Applications may be accepted after this date in the event of an unexpected opening for the Autumn semester. On some rare occasions an assistantship is available for the Spring semester
Additional Information: Graduate assistants must carry a minimum of 6 semester hours of credit and are expected to spend 20 hours per week on departmental duties such as instruction or research.

UNLV James F Adams/GSA Scholarship

Subjects: All subjects.
Purpose: To recognize the academic achievements of graduate students.
Eligibility: Applicants must have completed at least 12 credits of graduate study at UNLV, have a minimum undergraduate and graduate grade point average of 3.5 and enrol for six or more graduate credits in each semester of the scholarship year.
Level of Study: Graduate, MBA
Type: Scholarship
Value: US$1,000
Length of Study: Varies
Frequency: Annual
Study Establishment: UNLV
Country of Study: United States of America
No. of awards offered: 6
Application Procedure: Applicants must telephone (1) 702 895 3320, or write for application forms or further information.
Closing Date: March 1st

UNIVERSITY OF NEW BRUNSWICK (UNB)

PO Box 4400 Station A, Fredericton, NB, E3B 5A3, Canada
Tel: (1) 506 453 4666
Fax: (1) 506 453 4599
Email: chantelo@unbsj.ca
Website: www.unb.ca
Contact: Robert Chanteloup

The University of New Brunswick (UNB) was founded in 1785. It is the oldest, public English language comprehensive university in Canada. The University offers over 60 graduate diploma and degree programmes in the faculties of arts, science, engineering, forestry and environmental management, computer science, kinesiology, nursing, business administration and education.

Dr William S. Lewis Doctoral Fellowships

Subjects: Science and humanities.
Purpose: To support incoming University of New Brunswick Doctoral students who have the potential to be regional, national and international leaders in research and the dissemination of knowledge.
Eligibility: Open to Doctorate students with academic excellence and depending on the candidate's contribution to the field.
Level of Study: Doctorate
Type: Fellowship
Value: Canadian $25,000
Length of Study: Up to 4 years
Frequency: Annual
Country of Study: Canada
Closing Date: February 1st
Funding: Individuals

UNIVERSITY OF NEW ENGLAND (UNE)

Research Grants Office, Armidale, NSW 2351, Australia
Tel: (61) 2 6773 3333
Fax: (61) 2 6773 3100
Email: phonebook@une.edu.au
Website: www.une.edu.au

UNE is internationally recognized as one of the best teaching and research universities. Yearly, the university offers students more than $2.5 million in scholarships, prizes, and bursaries and more than $18 million for staff and students involved in research. It provides distance education for the students. Its scholars and scientists have established international reputations through their contributions in areas such as rural science, agricultural economics, educational administration, linguistics and archaeology.

A S Nivison Memorial Scholarship

Subjects: Pasture improvement, animal husbandry, farm management, wool research or promotion, water conservation and environmental protection.
Eligibility: Applicants must be a citizen or a permanent resident of Australia undertaking PhD or Research Masters.
Level of Study: Doctorate
Type: Scholarship
Value: $5,000
Length of Study: 1 year
Frequency: Annual
Country of Study: Australia
Application Procedure: Check website for further details.
Closing Date: April 30th
Funding: Private
Contributor: Nivision family

For further information contact:

Australia
Tel: (61) 61 2 6773 3745
Email: pgscholarships@une.edu.au
Contact: Belinda Keogh

CRC Spatial Information PhD Scholarship

Subjects: Agriculture.
Purpose: To produce long-lasting outcomes relating to understanding how complex decision-making processes can be improved using spatial and other data.
Eligibility: Applicants must hold a Class 1 or 2A Honours (or equivalent) Degree in a suitable discipline, and be a citizen or permanent resident of Australia. A valid driver's licence is also a necessary requirement.
Level of Study: Doctorate
Type: Scholarship
Value: $28,000 per year, tax-free
Frequency: Annual
Study Establishment: University of New England
Country of Study: Australia

Application Procedure: Applicants should send a letter outlining suitability for the position, accompanied by a brief curriculum vitae (including contact details of two referees) and a copy of academic transcripts.
Funding: Government

For further information contact:

Centre for Sustainable Farming Systems
Tel: 02 6773 2436
Email: jim.scott@une.edu.au
Contact: Professor Jim Scott

CRDC Postgraduate Scholarship

Subjects: Cotton research.
Purpose: To enhance the environmental, economic and social performance of the Australian cotton industry.
Eligibility: Applicants must be Australian citizens, studying at an Australian university and interested in working in the Australian cotton industry to pursue postgraduate studies relating to the cotton industry or its related community activities.
Level of Study: Postgraduate
Type: Scholarship
Value: $32,000 per year
Length of Study: 3 years
Frequency: Annual
Study Establishment: University of New England
Country of Study: Australia, New Zealand or South Africa
Application Procedure: Check website for further details.
Closing Date: September 1st
Funding: Government
Contributor: Cotton Research and Development Corporation (CRDC)
Additional Information: Projects may relate to any field of cotton-related research.

For further information contact:

Cotton Research and Development Corporation, 2 Lloyd Street, Narrabri, New South Wales, Australia
Tel: (61) 02 6792 4088
Fax: (61) 02 6792 4400
Email: research@crdc.com.au
Website: www.crdc.com.au

PhD Scholarship in Animal Breeding

Subjects: Animal breeding.
Purpose: To investigate aspects of sow feed intake and its impact on reproductive performance and longevity.
Eligibility: Applicants should be well versed in statistics and/or animal breeding units at a tertiary level and computing and data analysis skills is highly desirable.
Level of Study: Doctorate
Type: Scholarship
Value: Australian $28,000 per year
Length of Study: 3 years
Frequency: Annual
Study Establishment: University of New England
Country of Study: Australia
Application Procedure: Check website une.edu.au/imp/courses/sciences/postgrad.php
Closing Date: June 30th
Contributor: Australian Pork CRC

For further information contact:

Tel: 02 6773 3788
Email: kbunter2@une.edu.au
Contact: Dr Kim Bunter

PhD Scholarship: Molecular Factors in Plant–microbe Associations

Subjects: Molecular biology.
Purpose: To study the molecular aspect of the interaction between the fungal pathogen and the plant.
Eligibility: Applicants must hold a Class 1 or 2A Honours (or equivalent) Degree in a suitable discipline, and be an citizen or permanent resident of Australia.

Level of Study: Doctorate
Type: Scholarship
Value: $26,000 per year, tax-free
Length of Study: 3 years
Frequency: Annual
Study Establishment: University of New England
Country of Study: Australia
Application Procedure: Applicants should send a letter outlining their suitability for the position, accompanied by a brief curriculum vitae (including contact details of two referees) and a copy of their academic transcripts.
Funding: Government

For further information contact:

Molecular and Cellular Biology, School of Science and Technology
Tel: 02 6773 2708
Fax: 02 6773 3267
Email: lperegge@une.edu.au
Contact: Dr Lily Pereg-Grek

PhD Scholarship: Weed Ecology

Subjects: Ecology.
Purpose: To manage the species through a series of field and controlled environment experiments on emergence, growth, reproduction and spread of environment experiments on emergence, growth, reproduction and spread of fleabane species.
Eligibility: Applicants must hold a Class 1 or 2A Honours (or equivalent) Degree in a suitable discipline, and be an citizen or permanent resident of Australia.
Level of Study: Doctorate
Type: Scholarship
Value: $26,000 per year, tax-free
Length of Study: 3 years
Study Establishment: University of New England
Country of Study: Australia
Application Procedure: Applicants should send a letter outlining their suitability for the position accompanied by a brief curriculum vitae (including contact details of two referees) and a copy of their academic transcripts.
Closing Date: April 27th
Funding: Government

For further information contact:

School of Rural Science and Agriculture, University of Armidale, New South Wales, 2351, Australia
Tel: (61) 02 6773 3238
Email: bsindel@une.edu.au
Contact: Brian Sindel, Associate Professor

UNE Mary Dolan Memorial Travelling Scholarship

Subjects: Archaeology.
Purpose: To encourage students to travel to undertake work at an archaeological site as members of a team.
Eligibility: Applicants must currently be enrolled at the University of New England and must have completed at least 2 years of study at either undergraduate or postgraduate level, in disciplines of study ranging from the ancient world through the medieval world and on into the modern historical world.
Level of Study: Postgraduate
Type: Scholarship
Value: Up to $3,000
Frequency: Annual
Study Establishment: University of New England
Country of Study: Australia
Application Procedure: Check website, www.prod.une.edu.au/research-services/forms/refereesreport.pdf
Closing Date: October 19th
Funding: Government

University of New England Postgraduate Equity Scholarship

Subjects: Any subject.
Eligibility: Applicants must be citizens of Australia or New Zealand and be a Aboriginal or Torres Strait Islander, non-English speaking

background person, student with a disability or woman from non-traditional area.
Level of Study: Postgraduate
Type: Scholarship
Value: Australian $19,231 per year
Length of Study: 2 years (Masters) or 3 years (PhD)
Frequency: Annual
Study Establishment: University of New England
Country of Study: Australia, New Zealand or South Africa
No. of awards offered: 2
Application Procedure: Check website for further details.
Funding: Government

For further information contact:

University of New England, Armidale, NSW 2351, Australia
Email: aharris@une.edu.au
Website: www.une.edu.au/reseach-services/grants/
Contact: Thea Harris, Scholarships Administrative Assistant

University of New England Research Scholarship
Subjects: Any subject.
Eligibility: Applicants must have achieved Honours 1 or equivalent, or Masters or equivalent.
Type: Scholarship
Value: Australian $19,616
Length of Study: 3 years (PhD) and 2 years (Masters)
Frequency: Annual
Study Establishment: University of New England
Country of Study: Australia
No. of awards offered: Varies
Application Procedure: Check the website, www.une.edu.au/research-services/grants/ for further details.
Closing Date: October 31st
Funding: Government

For further information contact:

University of New England, Armidale, NSW 2351, Australia
Tel: (61) 6773 3571
Fax: (61) 6773 3543
Email: aharris@une.edu.au
Website: www.une.edu.au/research-services/grants/
Contact: Thea Harris, Scholarships Administrative Assistant

UNIVERSITY OF NEW HAMPSHIRE

The Family Research Laboratory, Department of Sociology, Horton Social Science Center, Durham, NH, 03824, United States of America
Tel: (1) 603 862 2594
Fax: (1) 603 862 1122
Email: murray.straus@unh.edu
Website: www.unh.edu
Contact: Mr Murray Straus, Co-Director

The Family Research Laboratory at the University of New Hampshire conducts research studies of interest to state and national policy makers and citizens. Studies include a national survey of families and youth, and the 30-nation international dating violence study. Staff and faculty members associated with the laboratory give lectures and workshops to professionals and provide information to the public about family violence and related family issues. The Family Violence Research Programme, which is part of the laboratory, is the first and only research programme concerned with all aspects of family violence and related phenomena. The laboratory maintains a library of about 2,500 books and sponsors national conferences.

University of New Hampshire Postdoctoral Fellowships For Research on Family Violence
Subjects: Family violence including physical, sexual and psychological maltreatment of children, partners in marital, cohabiting and dating relationships and maltreatment of the elderly by members of their family.
Purpose: To provide training and experience in research into all aspects of family violence.
Eligibility: Open to citizens or permanent residents of the United States of America.

Level of Study: Postdoctorate
Type: Fellowship
Length of Study: 1 or 2 years
Frequency: Annual
Study Establishment: The Family Research Laboratory at the University of New Hampshire
Country of Study: United States of America
No. of awards offered: 4
Application Procedure: Applicants must send a brief letter, publications and arrange for three letters of recommendation. Applications are available from the website www.unh.edu/fri
Funding: Government
Contributor: The National Institute of Mental Health
No. of awards given last year: 4
No. of applicants last year: 35

UNIVERSITY OF NEW MEXICO (UNM)

Department of Computer Science, Mail Stop MS Col 1130, University of NM, Albuquerque, NM, 87131, United States of America
Tel: (1) 505 277 0111
Fax: (1) 505 277 6927
Email: csinfo@cs.unm.edu
Website: www.unm.edu
Contact: The Postgraduate Admissions Office

University of New Mexico (UNM), a Hispanic-Serving Institution, represents a wide cross-section of cultures and backgrounds. It was founded in1889. UNM boasts outstanding faculty members and includes a Nobel Laureate, MacArthur Fellows and several members of the national academies.

New Mexico Information Technology Fellowships
Subjects: Computer science.
Purpose: To financially support students and strengthen New Mexico's technology base.
Eligibility: Open to candidates who have obtained an undergraduate degree with a grade point average of 3.5.
Level of Study: Doctorate, Postgraduate
Type: Fellowships
Value: US$25,000 per year
Length of Study: 2–4 years
Frequency: Annual
Country of Study: United States of America
Closing Date: February 15th

THE UNIVERSITY OF NEW SOUTH WALES (UNSW)

Scholarships and Financial Support, Sydney, NSW, 2052, Australia
Tel: (61) 02 9385 1000
Fax: (61) 02 938 500706
Email: scholarships@unsw.edu.au
Website: www.unsw.edu.au

University of New South Wales (UNSW) is one of Australia's leading research and teaching universities. UNSW takes great pride in the broad range and high quality of teaching programmes. UNSW's teaching gains strength, vitality and currency both from their research activities and from their international nature.

APAI Scholarship in Metallurgy/Materials
Subjects: Metallurgy, materials engineering.
Purpose: To undertake blast furnace research in collaboration with industry.
Eligibility: Open to Australian citizens or permanent residents with a good Honours or equivalent degree.
Level of Study: Doctorate, Postgraduate
Type: Scholarship
Value: Stipend of Australian $24,851 per year and up to Australian $6,000 per year supplement to outstanding candidates
Length of Study: 3–3.5 years
Frequency: Annual
Study Establishment: School of Materials Science and Engineering
Application Procedure: Check website for further details.

For further information contact:

Website: www.materials.unsw.edu.au/

College of Fine Arts Research Scholarship
Subjects: Fine arts.
Purpose: To provide financial assistance to students pursuing a PhD.
Eligibility: Open to full-time PhD students from any country
Level of Study: Doctorate
Type: Scholarship
Value: Australian $18,000 per year
Length of Study: 2 years
Frequency: Annual
Study Establishment: University of New South Wales
Country of Study: Australia
Application Procedure: Application forms are available at the COFA Student Centre on the UNSW Scholarships website.
Closing Date: September 30th
Additional Information: To assist in the selection process, UNSW may also request applicants to provide, orally or in writing, further information. Applicants can also submit the application to Melanie Cheung at the COFA Student Centre.

For further information contact:

Email: l.mitchell@unsw.edu.au
Contact: Leah Mitchell

PhD Scholarship in Materials Science and Engineering
Subjects: Materials science and engineering.
Purpose: To support research on metal dusting.
Eligibility: Open to citizens of Australia or permanent residents holding high Honours Degree in science.
Level of Study: Postgraduate, Research
Type: Scholarship
Value: Australian $30,000 per year
Length of Study: 3 years
Frequency: Annual
Study Establishment: University of New South Wales
Country of Study: Australia
No. of awards offered: 1
Application Procedure: Check website for further details.
Closing Date: Not specified

For further information contact:

UNSW, Kensington, NSW, 2052, Australia
Tel: (61) 93854322
Fax: (61) 93855956
Email: d.young@unsw.edu.au
Website: www.materials.unsw.edu.au
Contact: David Young, (Professor) Science/Materials

PhD Scholarships in Environmental Microbial Genomics
Subjects: Environmental microbiology, microbial genomics.
Purpose: To attract the nations strongest candidates capable of pursuing PhD studies in the genomics of environmental microorganisms.
Eligibility: Open to candidates having Honours Degree in BSc or MSc in bioinformatics and/or microbiology, with some experience in microbial genomics, environmental microbiology and ecology or molecular microbiology.
Level of Study: Doctorate, Postgraduate
Type: Scholarship
Value: Australian $30,000
No. of awards offered: 3
Application Procedure: Check website for further details.

For further information contact:

Email: r.cavicchioli@unsw.edu.au
Contact: Rick Cavicchioli

The Senior Artists from Asia College of Fine Arts Research Scholarship
Subjects: Fine arts.

Purpose: To provide financial assistance to full-time Master's (by research) students.
Eligibility: Open only to full-time Master's (by research) students who are citizens of an Asian country and normally resident in Asia.
Level of Study: Postgraduate
Type: Scholarship
Value: Payment of programme fees
Frequency: Annual
Study Establishment: University of New South Wales
Country of Study: Australia
Application Procedure: Application forms are available at the COFA Student Centre or on the UNSW Scholarships website.
Closing Date: October 31st

Vida Rees Scholarship in Pediatrics
Subjects: Medicine.
Purpose: To support Australian students to undertake research in paediatrics.
Eligibility: Open to applicants who are undertaking an Honours project or postgraduate research in paediatrics and selection will be based on academic merit, demonstrated ability and leadership qualities, potential to contribute to the wider life of the university and consideration of financial need.
Level of Study: Postgraduate
Type: Bursary
Value: Australian $1,000
Length of Study: 1 year
Frequency: Annual
Study Establishment: University of New South Wales
Country of Study: Australia
Closing Date: October 31st

Viktoria Marinov Scholarship of Art
Subjects: Creative arts.
Purpose: To financially assist female artists who are proposing to undertake the Master of Art or Master of Fine Arts course.
Eligibility: Open to female artists under the age of 35 years who are proposing to undertake the Master of Art or Master of Fine Arts course.
Level of Study: Postgraduate
Type: Bursary
Value: Australian $5,000
Length of Study: 1 year
Frequency: Annual
Study Establishment: New South Wales, Sydney City Central and Eastern Suburbs
Country of Study: Australia
Closing Date: January 31st

For further information contact:

Email: j.elliot@unsw.edu.au
Contact: Joanna Elliot

THE UNIVERSITY OF NEWCASTLE

Research Division University of Newcastle, Callaghan, NSW 2308, Australia
Tel: (61) 02 4921 65387
Fax: (61) 02 4921 6908
Email: research@newcastle.edu.au
Website: www.newcastle.edu.au/research/rhd/
Contact: Jackie Walkom, Office of Graduate Studies

The University of Newcastle is one of Australia's top ten research universities. The University has over 1,200 research degree candidates enrolled in five faculties, incorporating a wide range of disciplines including architecture, building, humanities, social sciences, education, economics, management, engineering, computer science, law, medicine, nursing, health sciences, music, drama and creative arts, physcial and natural sciences, mathematics and information technology. Scholarships are available to support research degree candidates in most disciplines. About 90 new scholarships are awarded each year.

Australian Government Postgraduate Awards

Subjects: All subjects.
Purpose: To support students undertaking full-time higher research degree programmes.
Eligibility: Open to Australian and New Zealand citizens who are permanent residents. Applicants must have completed 4 years of full-time undergraduate study and gained a First Class (Honours) Degree or equivalent award.
Level of Study: Doctorate, Postgraduate, Research
Type: Scholarship
Value: A living allowance of approx. Australian $20,000 per year which is tax-exempt and index-linked. Allowances for relocation and thesis production may also be provided
Length of Study: 2 years full-time study for research Master's candidates or 3 years full-time for PhD candidates
Frequency: Annual
Study Establishment: Any university
Country of Study: Australia
No. of awards offered: Approx. 40
Application Procedure: Applicants must complete an application form from the Office of Graduate Studies or from the website.
Closing Date: October 31st
Funding: Government

Chemical Engineering Scholarship

Subjects: Chemical Engineering.
Purpose: To develop models capable of simulating temporal and spatial characteristics of rainfall fields over large river basins using novel approaches to hierarchical modelling, storm clustering, advection and calibration. The models will provide continuous simulation support for the design and assessment of water-related infrastructure.
Eligibility: Open only to the postgraduates who are the citizens of Australia or the permanent residents of Australia.
Level of Study: Postgraduate
Type: Scholarship
Value: Australian $25,118 (per year)
Length of Study: 2 years (Masters) and 3 years (PhD)
Frequency: Annual
Country of Study: Australia
No. of awards offered: 4
Application Procedure: Application form and the Research Higher Degree prospectus from can be downloaded from the website.
Closing Date: July 1st

For further information contact:

University of Newcastle, Australia
Tel: (61) 02 4921 6038
Email: George.Kuczera@newcastle.edu.au
Website: www.newcastle.edu.au/research/rhd/prospective.html
Contact: Professor George Kuczera

Commercialisation Training Scheme (CTS)

Subjects: All subjects.
Eligibility: Open to the citizens of Australia and New Zealand or its permanent residents who are enrolled in a research higher degree and will also be enrolled in a commercialization training programme or have a research higher degree thesis under examination with only 6 months full-time or part-time equivalent study remaining in the commercialization training programme.
Level of Study: Research
Type: Scholarship
Value: $5,281
Length of Study: 28 weeks
Application Procedure: Check website for further details.

Endeavour International Postgraduate Research Scholarship

Subjects: All subjects.
Eligibility: Open to the residents of any country except Australia and New Zealand who have achieved Honours 1 or equivalent and meet the minimum English Language proficiency level.
Level of Study: Postgraduate, Research
Type: Scholarship
Value: Australian $19,616 per year
Length of Study: 2 years (Masters) and 3 years (PhD)

Frequency: Annual
Country of Study: Australia
No. of awards offered: 8
Application Procedure: Apply directly to the university. Applications can be downloaded from the website. For further details please visit www.jason.edu.au/
Closing Date: September 30th

For further information contact:

Website: www.newcastle.edu.au/research/rhd/scholarships.html

The Gowrie Scholarship Trust Fund Research Scholarships

Subjects: All subjects.
Eligibility: Open to the members and children of the members of the Forces including, grandchildren or other lineal descendants of such members and to the residents of Australia and Australian soldiers who are the graduates of Australian universities or to others who have completed a course of tertiary education at other recognized institutions in Australia.
Level of Study: Research
Type: Research scholarship
Value: $4,000 per year
Length of Study: 2 years
Frequency: Annual
No. of awards offered: 1–2
Application Procedure: Check website for further details.
Closing Date: October 31st
Funding: Trusts
Contributor: The Gowrie Trust Fund

For further information contact:

The Gowrie Scholarship Trust Fund, 3/32 Beaconsfield Rd, Mosman, NSW, 2088, Australia
Tel: (61) 02 99603458
Contact: The Secretary

Newcastle University Civil Engineering and Geosciences Scholarship

Subjects: Engineering Geology, Environmental Biogeochemistry and Sustainable Management of the Water Environment.
Eligibility: Open to preferably UK students, EU countries candidates can also apply.
Level of Study: Postgraduate
Type: Scholarship
Value: Varies
No. of awards offered: Varies
Application Procedure: Check website for further details.
Contributor: NERC or EPSRC sources

For further information contact:

Website: www.ceg.ncl.ac.uk/postgrad/pgt/fundingpg

Palliative Care in Cancer Scholarship

Subjects: Health Research and Psycho-oncology.
Purpose: To undertake a PhD in behavioural cancer research.
Eligibility: Open to the candidates who have achieved Honours 1 or equivalent.
Level of Study: Postgraduate
Type: Scholarship
Value: Australian $19,616 per year
Length of Study: 3 years
Frequency: Annual
Country of Study: Australia
No. of awards offered: 1
Application Procedure: Apply direct to faculty. Check website for more details.
Closing Date: December 31st

For further information contact:

Website: www.newcastle.edu.au

PhD Scholarship in Coal Utilization in Thermal and Coking Applications

Subjects: Chemical engineering, mechanical engineering, and chemistry.
Purpose: To undertake research on particular coal properties which determine its utilization potential.
Eligibility: Open to the engineering and the science graduates who have an Honours Degree in chemical or mechanical engineering or chemistry.
Level of Study: Doctorate
Type: Scholarship
Value: Australian $20,000 per year
Application Procedure: Check website for further details.

For further information contact:

University of Newcastle
Tel: 61 2 49 21 6179
Email: Terry.Wall@newcastle.edu.au
Contact: Professor Terry Wall

Postgraduate Research Scholarship in Physics

Subjects: Physics.
Eligibility: Open to the residents of Australia and New Zealand or the permanent residents of Australia who have an Honours 1 or 2A or a Masters Degree.
Level of Study: Postgraduate, Research
Type: Scholarship
Value: $19,616 per year
Length of Study: 3 years
Frequency: Annual
Application Procedure: Check website for more details.
Closing Date: July 1st
Contributor: ARC Discovery-projects

For further information contact:

School of Mathematical and Physical Sciences, Callaghan, NSW 2308, Australia
Tel: (61) 61 2 4921 6653
Fax: (61) 61 2 4921 6907
Email: vicki.keast@newcastle.edu.au
Website: www.newcastle.edu.au
Contact: Dr Vicki Keast

Scholarship in Cancer Prevention

Subjects: Cancer prevention.
Eligibility: Open to the candidates who have achieved Honours 1 or equivalent.
Level of Study: Postgraduate, Research
Type: Scholarship
Value: Australian $19,616 per year
Length of Study: 3 years
Frequency: Annual
Country of Study: Australia
No. of awards offered: 1
Application Procedure: Apply direct to faculty. Check website for further details.
Closing Date: December 31st

For further information contact:

Website: www.newcastle.edu.au

Space-Time Model-Rainfall Fields Scholarship

Subjects: Environmental engineering.
Purpose: Development and implementation of computer models for hydrologic applications.
Eligibility: Open to the candidates who have achieved Honours 1 or equivalent.
Level of Study: Postgraduate, Research
Type: Scholarship
Value: Australian $25,000 per year
Length of Study: 3 years
Frequency: Annual
Country of Study: Australia
No. of awards offered: 1

Application Procedure: Apply directly to the scholarship provider. Check website for further details.
Closing Date: October 31st

For further information contact:

Website: www.newcastle.edu.au

University of Newcastle International Postrgraduate Research Scholarship

Subjects: All subjects.
Eligibility: Open to the candidates from any country except Australia and New Zealand who have achieved Honours 1 or equivalent.
Level of Study: Postgraduate
Type: Scholarship
Value: Australian $20,000 per year
Length of Study: 2 years (Masters) or 3 years (PhD)
Frequency: Annual
Country of Study: Australia
No. of awards offered: 25
Application Procedure: Check website for further details.
Closing Date: August 31st

For further information contact:

Website: www.Jason.edu.au

University of Newcastle Postgraduate Research Scholarship Central

Subjects: All subjects.
Eligibility: Open to the residents of Australia and New Zealand or permanent residents who have achieved Honours 1 or equivalent and have completed at least 4 years of undergraduate study.
Level of Study: Postgraduate, Research
Type: Scholarship
Value: Australian $19,616 per year
Length of Study: 2 years (Masters) and 3 years (PhD)
Frequency: Annual
Country of Study: Australia
No. of awards offered: 30
Application Procedure: Check website for further details.
Closing Date: October 31st

For further information contact:

Research Higher Degrees, The Chancellery Eastern Wing, University Drive, Callaghan, NSW 2308, Australia
Tel: (61) 02 4921 6537
Fax: (61) 02 4921 6908
Email: research@newcastle.edu.au
Website: www.newcastle.edu.au

UNIVERSITY OF NOTRE DAME: COLLEGE OF ARTS AND LETTERS

Office of the Dean, 100 O'Shaughnessy Hall, Notre Dame, IN, 46556, United States of America
Tel: (1) 574 631 7085
Fax: (1) 574 631 7743
Email: aldean@nd.edu
Website: http://al.nd.edu

University of Notre Dame: College of Arts and Letters offers one of the finest liberal arts educations in the nation. Its Division of the Humanities was recently ranked 12th among private universities, while the social sciences continue their ascent in the national rankings. College of Arts and Letters is the largest and oldest of the University's 4 colleges.

The Erskine A. Peters Dissertation Year Fellowship at Notre Dame

Subjects: Arts, humanities, social sciences and theological disciplines.
Purpose: To provide an opportunity for African American scholars at the beginning of their academic careers to experience life at a major Catholic research university.

Eligibility: Open to African-American Doctoral candidates who have completed all degree requirements with the exception of the dissertation.
Level of Study: Postgraduate, Research
Type: Fellowship
Value: US$25,000 stipend and US$2,000 research budget
Length of Study: 10 months
Frequency: Annual
Country of Study: United States of America
Application Procedure: Applicants may apply online.
Closing Date: December 1st
No. of awards given last year: 3

For further information contact:

Department of Africana Studies
Tel: 574 631 5628
Fax: 574 631 3587
Email: astudies@nd.edu
Website: http://africana.nd.edu

THE UNIVERSITY OF NOTTINGHAM

Graduate School, University Park, Nottingham, Nottinghamshire, NG7 2RD, England
Tel: (44) 11 5951 4608
Fax: (44) 11 584 67799
Email: graduate-school@nottingham.ac.uk
Website: www.nottingham.ac.uk/gradschool
Contact: Ms Claire Palmer, PG Funding and Services Manager

The University of Nottingham is a community of students and staff dedicated to bringing out the best in all of its members. It aims to provide the finest possible environment for teaching, learning and research and has a well-known record of success.

University of Nottingham Doctoral Training Awards
Subjects: All subjects offered by the University.
Purpose: To promote research.
Eligibility: Open to graduates of all nationalities.
Level of Study: Postgraduate, Predoctorate
Type: PhD scholarship
Value: Minimum of UK £12,900 maintenance per year where appropriate, plus payment of fees at the home or European Union rate
Length of Study: 3 years leading to PhD submission given adequate academic progress
Frequency: Annual
Study Establishment: The University of Nottingham
Country of Study: United Kingdom
No. of awards offered: More than 75
Application Procedure: Applicants must contact the individual schools for information. Applicants must apply to the school where they intend to study.
Closing Date: Please contact the individual schools for information
Contributor: University of Nottingham
No. of awards given last year: Over 75
Additional Information: The scholarships are awarded internally to the schools and/or institutes. It is then up to those schools receiving awards to advertise the scholarship and set an application deadline.

University of Nottingham Weston Scholarships
Subjects: All subjects from a prescribed list.
Purpose: To provide promising students with full-time home or European Union fees.
Eligibility: There are no eligibility restrictions.
Level of Study: Postgraduate
Type: Studentship
Value: Home or European Union fees only
Length of Study: Usually 1 year full-time
Frequency: Annual
Study Establishment: The University of Nottingham
Country of Study: United Kingdom
No. of awards offered: 4
Application Procedure: Applicants must submit applications to the individual schools and contact them for details. Applicants must apply to the school where they intend to study.

Closing Date: Please contact the individual schools for information
Funding: Trusts
No. of awards given last year: 4
Additional Information: The scholarships are awarded internally to four schools and/or institutes on a competitive basis. It is then up to those schools receiving awards to advertise the scholarship and set an application deadline.

UNIVERSITY OF OTAGO

Scholarships Office, PO Box 56, Dunedin, New Zealand
Tel: (64) 3 479 1100 ext 5291
Fax: (64) 3 479 5650
Email: pgschols@otago.ac.nz
Website: www.otago.ac.nz
Contact: Mr Eddy Vande Pol, Manager, PhD Scholarship

The University of Otago has over 17,000 students, most of whom are based at the Dunedin campus, which is the oldest campus in New Zealand. The University has four divisions: the Division of Commerce (School of Business), the Division of Health Sciences, the Division of Humanities and the Division of Science. The University has a School of Medicine in Christchurch and Wellington, and a campus in Auckland.

Neuropsychology Scholarships
Subjects: Neuropsychology.
Purpose: To investigate how visual information is used by humans in the learning of new skills.
Eligibility: Open to applicants with an undergraduate qualification and a background or interest in cognitive science or neuropsychology. The project would suit a self-motivated person who is able to work well with participants and patients and other members on the study team. A working knowledge of the software package MATLAB and experience in programming with its language, is highly desirable.
Level of Study: Postgraduate
Type: Scholarship
Value: New Zealand $12,000 per year for 2 years maximum, plus a maximum of New Zealand $4,000 per year towards tuition fees
Application Procedure: Applicants must enquire in the first instance to the director of the Cognitive Science programme.
Contributor: Marsden Fund of the Royal Society of New Zealand

For further information contact:

Tel: 64 3 4795269
Fax: 64 3 4798335
Email: lfranz@psy.otago.ac.nz
Contact: Dr Elizabeth Franz

University of Otago International Scholarships
Subjects: All subjects.
Purpose: To assist with funding for study.
Eligibility: Open to all international applicants intending to study at the University of Otago who would normally be charged international fees.
Level of Study: Postgraduate, Research
Type: Scholarship
Value: Master's scholarships New Zealand $13,000
Length of Study: 1 year for their Master's study
Frequency: Annual
Study Establishment: The University of Otago
Country of Study: New Zealand
No. of awards offered: 4
Application Procedure: Applicants must complete the application for international study at the University of Otago, available from the website.
Closing Date: November 1st
No. of awards given last year: 4 Master's

University of Otago Master's Awards
Subjects: All subjects.
Purpose: To fund research towards a Master's degree.
Eligibility: Open to permanent residents or citizens of New Zealand or Australia, and to citizens of France and Germany with a minimum

qualification of a First Class (Honours) Degree who are entering the thesis year of a Master's degree.
Level of Study: Postgraduate, Research
Type: Scholarship
Value: New Zealand $13,000 per year plus fees
Length of Study: 1 year
Frequency: Annual
Study Establishment: The University of Otago
Country of Study: New Zealand
No. of awards offered: 68
Application Procedure: Applicants must complete an application form, available from the website.
Closing Date: November 1st
No. of applicants last year: 207

University of Otago PhD Scholarships

Subjects: All subjects.
Purpose: To fund research towards a PhD degree.
Eligibility: Open to applicants of any country but must be primarily resident in New Zealand during study.
Level of Study: Doctorate, Research
Type: Scholarship
Value: New Zealand $20,000, plus fees
Length of Study: 3 years
Frequency: Annual
Study Establishment: The University of Otago
Country of Study: New Zealand
No. of awards offered: 162
Application Procedure: Applicants must complete an application form, available from the website.
Closing Date: November 1st
No. of applicants last year: 378

University of Otago Prestigious PhD Scholarships

Subjects: All subjects.
Purpose: To fund research towards a PhD degree.
Eligibility: Open to applicants of any country but must be primarily resident in New Zealand during study.
Level of Study: Doctorate, Research
Type: Scholarship
Value: New Zealand $25,000, plus fees
Length of Study: 3 years
Frequency: Annual
Study Establishment: The University of Otago
Country of Study: New Zealand
No. of awards offered: 10
Application Procedure: Applicants must complete an application form, available from the website.
Closing Date: November 1st
No. of applicants last year: 378

UNIVERSITY OF OXFORD

University Offices, Wellington Square, Oxford, Oxfordshire, OX1 2JD, England
Tel: (44) 18 6527 0000
Fax: (44) 18 6527 0708
Email: admissions@stcatz.ox.ac.uk
Website: www.ox.ac.uk
Contact: Ms Clare Woodcock, Information Officer

African Studies: ORISHA

Subjects: African studies.
Purpose: To assist graduate students with fees and travel expenses.
Eligibility: Open to African studies applicants who have completed MSc.
Level of Study: Postgraduate
Value: £10,000 plus travel expenses
Length of Study: 1 year
Closing Date: January 23rd

For further information contact:

Website: www.africanstudies.ox.ac.uk/prospective_students/scholarships/orisha

African Studies: Southern African Students Fund (SASF)

Subjects: African studies.
Purpose: To assist graduate students with fees, maintenance and travel expenses.
Eligibility: Open to African studies applicants who have completed MSc.
Level of Study: Postgraduate
Type: Funding support
Value: University fees, college fees, maintenance award of around £9,000 and travel expenses
Length of Study: 1 year
Closing Date: January 23rd

For further information contact:

Website: www.africanstudies.ox.ac.uk/prospective_students/scholarships/southern_african_students_fund

AHRC Block Grant Partnership Studentships

Subjects: Various Arts and Humanities degrees.
Eligibility: Open to UK nationals or those able to demonstrate relevant connection with the UK.
Level of Study: Postgraduate, Research
Type: Studentship
Value: University fee, college fee and maintenance (varied value). Fees-only awards for non UK, EU students
Length of Study: 1–3 years
Application Procedure: Applicants must visit the university website for application procedure.
Closing Date: January
Additional Information: Applicants must visit the university website for further details.

For further information contact:

Website: www.humanities.ox.ac.uk/graduate_study/ahrc

Balliol College Dervorguilla Scholarship

Subjects: Arts and social sciences.
Purpose: To help scholars who have gained admission for a higher degree in Balliol college.
Eligibility: Students starting a new course who are liable for University fees at the Overseas rate. Preference wil be given to students studying at Oxford for the first time.
Level of Study: Postdoctorate, Postgraduate, Research
Type: Scholarship
Value: £4,000–£6,000 per annum
Length of Study: Up to 3 years
Frequency: Annual
Study Establishment: Balliol College, University of Oxford
Country of Study: United Kingdom
No. of awards offered: Up to 2
Application Procedure: Applicants must write for details.
Closing Date: 23 January
Contributor: Balliol College, University of Oxford, and the Clarendon Fund Award
Additional Information: Preference wil be given to students studying at Oxford for the first time. Can be held in conjunction with the University Clarendon Awards (see central awards table)

For further information contact:

Tutor for Graduate Admissions, Balliol College, University of Oxford, Oxford, OX1 3BJ, England
Website: www.balliol.ox.ac.uk/applying/graduates/

Balliol College Gregory Kulkes Scholarships in Law

Subjects: Law.
Purpose: To assist new students pursue studies in law at Balliol colllege.
Eligibility: Open to all students starting a new course at Balliol.
Level of Study: Postgraduate, Research
Type: Scholarship
Value: £2,000–£4,000 per annum
Length of Study: Up to 3 years
Frequency: Annual
Study Establishment: Balliol College, University of Oxford

Country of Study: United Kingdom
No. of awards offered: Up to 2
Application Procedure: Applicants must contact the tutor for graduate admissions at Balliol College.
Closing Date: 23 January
Funding: Private
Contributor: Balliol College and the Clarendon Fund Award
Additional Information: Can be held in conjunction with the University Clarendon Awards.

For further information contact:

Tutor for Graduate Admissions, Balliol College, University of Oxford, Oxford, OX1 3BJ, England
Website: www.balliol.ox.ac.uk/applying/graduates/

Balliol College: Domus Award
Subjects: All subjects.
Purpose: To assist fresh graduates with their university and college fees.
Eligibility: All students starting a new course.
Level of Study: Postgraduate, Research
Type: Award
Value: £2,000–£4,000 per year
Length of Study: Up to 3 years
Application Procedure: There is no closing date for this award.
Closing Date: August 31st

For further information contact:

Website: www.balliol.ox.ac.uk/applying/graduates/

Balliol College: Foley-Béjar Scholarships
Subjects: All subjects.
Purpose: To appoint three Scholars who have who have gained an offer of admission to read for a higher degree at Balliol College.
Eligibility: Open to students starting a new course at Balliol. Eligibility criteria are (a) 5 or more years' residence in Mexico, Spain, Ireland or Northern Ireland and (b) birth in this country, or birth of one parent in this country.
Level of Study: Postgraduate, Research
Type: Scholarship
Value: £7,000 per year
Length of Study: Up to 3 years
Application Procedure: Open to students starting a new course at Balliol. Eligibility criteria are (a) 5 or more years' residence in Mexico, Spain, Ireland or Northern Ireland, and (b) birth in this country, or birth of one parent in this country. 2 - 3 awards available.
Closing Date: January 23rd

For further information contact:

Website: www.balliol.ox.ac.uk/applying/graduates/

Balliol College: JT Hamilton Scholarship in Physics
Subjects: Physics.
Purpose: To appoint a Scholar who has gained an offer of admission to read for a higher degree in physics at Balliol College.
Eligibility: Open to all students starting a new course at Balliol.
Level of Study: Postgraduate, Research
Type: Scholarship
Value: Approx. £13,000 per year
Length of Study: Up to 3 years
Application Procedure: Can be held in conjunction with the University Clarendon Awards.
Closing Date: January 23rd

For further information contact:

Website: www.balliol.ox.ac.uk/applying/graduates/

Balliol College: Marvin Bower Scholarship
Subjects: Management and business studies (except MBA), economics, international relations and mathematics.
Purpose: To assist new students pursue studies in law at Balliol College.
Eligibility: Open to all students starting a new course at Balliol.
Level of Study: Postgraduate, Research

Type: Scholarship
Value: At least £5,000 per annum
Length of Study: Up to 3 years
Frequency: Dependent on funds available
Study Establishment: Balliol College, University of Oxford
Country of Study: United Kingdom
No. of awards offered: 1
Application Procedure: Applicants must write for details.
Closing Date: 23 January
Contributor: Balliol College and the Clarendon Fund Award
Additional Information: Can be held in conjunction with the University Clarendon Awards.

For further information contact:

Tutor for Graduate Admissions, Balliol College, University of Oxford, Oxford, OX1 3BJ, England
Website: www.balliol.ox.ac.uk/applying/graduates/

Biochemistry: BBSRC Doctoral Training Awards
Subjects: Molecular biochemistry and chemical biology.
Purpose: To train a new generation of researchers at the Chemistry–Biochemistry interface.
Eligibility: Open to candidates who fulfil residence and academic eligibility for UK Research Council Funding, normally UK nationals who have resided in the UK since 1/9/2006.
Level of Study: Research
Type: Award
Value: University fees, college fees and £13,200 for maintenance
Length of Study: 4 years
Closing Date: January 7th

For further information contact:

Website: www.bioch.ox.ac.uk/studentships

Biochemistry: BBSRC Doctoral Training Awards in Collaboration With Industry (CASE)
Subjects: Molecular biochemistry and chemical biology.
Purpose: To receive high quality research training in collaboration with an industrial partner.
Eligibility: Open to candidates who must fulfil residence and academic eligibility for UK Research Council Funding, normally UK nationals who have resided in the UK since 1/9/2006.
Level of Study: Research
Value: University fees, college fees and £15,700 for maintenance
Length of Study: 3 or 4 years
Closing Date: January 7th

For further information contact:

Website: www.bioch.ox.ac.uk/studentships

Biochemistry: BBSRC Fees-only Doctoral Training Awards
Subjects: Molecular biochemistry and chemical biology.
Purpose: To train a new generation of researchers at the Chemistry–Biochemistry interface.
Eligibility: Open to candidates who must fulfil residence and academic eligibility for UK Research Council Funding for non-UK EU candidates, normally EU nationals who have resided in the EU since 1/9/2006.
Level of Study: Research
Value: University fees and college fees
Length of Study: 4 years
Closing Date: January 7th

For further information contact:

Website: www.bioch.ox.ac.uk/studentships

Biochemistry: EPSRC Doctoral Training Award
Subjects: Biophysics and biochemistry.
Purpose: To assist graduate students with fees and maintenance.
Eligibility: Open to candidates who must fulfil residence and academic eligibility for UK Research Council Funding, normally UK nationals who have resided in the UK since 1/9/2006.

Level of Study: Research
Type: Award
Value: University fees, college fees and £13,200 for maintenance
Length of Study: 4 years
Closing Date: January 7th

For further information contact:

Website: www.bioch.ox.ac.uk/studentships

Brasenose College: Brasenose/Clarendon Linked Awards

Subjects: All subjects.
Purpose: To enable academically outstanding students to take up their places at Oxford.
Eligibility: Open to overseas students newly on course in 2009/2010.
Level of Study: Postgraduate, Research
Type: Award
Value: The joint studentships will provide full funding of fees and maintenance
Length of Study: Up to 3 years
No. of awards offered: 2–4
Closing Date: January 23rd
Additional Information: See Student Funding Services website for details on Clarendon Awards: www.admin.ox.ac.uk/studentfunding/scholarship_profiles/clarendon.shtml.

For further information contact:

Website: www.bnc.ox.ac.uk/340/graduate-admissions-37/scholarships-191.html

Brasenose College: Brasenose/Department Linked awards

Subjects: Humanities/social sciences.
Purpose: To enable academically outstanding students to take up their places at Oxford.
Eligibility: All new students liable for home/EU rate fees.
Level of Study: Postgraduate, Research
Type: Award
Value: The joint studentships will provide full funding of fees and a full maintenance stipend at AHRC levels
Length of Study: Up to 4 years
No. of awards offered: 2–4
Additional Information: Closing date is as advertised on departmental websites.

For further information contact:

Website: www.bnc.ox.ac.uk/340/graduate-admissions-37/scholarships-191.html

Business School (Saïd): Dean's Latin America and Africa Scholarship

Subjects: MBA.
Purpose: To support an exceptional MBA student from Latin America or Africa.
Eligibility: Open to permanent residents of Latin America and Africa.
Level of Study: MBA, Postgraduate
Type: Scholarship
Value: £10,000
Length of Study: 1 year

For further information contact:

Website: www.sbs.ox.ac.uk/MBA/Fees/Scholarships.htm

Business School (Saïd): Entrepreneurial British Women Scholarship

Subjects: MBA.
Purpose: To support a talented and entrepreneurial British woman to undertake an MBA at the Sad Business School.
Eligibility: Open to female candidates who are citizens or permanent residents of the UK.
Level of Study: Postgraduate, MBA
Type: Scholarship
Value: £25,000
Length of Study: 1 year

For further information contact:

Website: www.sbs.ox.ac.uk/MBA/Fees/Scholarships.htm

Business School (Saïd): Man Group Plc Scholarship

Subjects: MBA and MFE.
Purpose: To assist graduate students with fees and a living allowance.
Eligibility: Candidates must have a strong academic or professional background in finance and a desire to enter into or continue in this field upon completion of their studies.
Level of Study: MBA, Postgraduate
Type: Scholarship
Value: Full scholarship
Length of Study: 1 year
Closing Date: June 1st
Additional Information: Candidates must have a strong academic or professional background in finance and a desire to enter into or continue in this field upon completion of their studies.

For further information contact:

Website: www.sbs.ox.ac.uk/MBA/Fees/Scholarships.htm

Business School (Saïd): OBA Australia Boston Consulting Group Scholarship

Subjects: MBA and MFE.
Purpose: To undertake a postgraduate business degree at the Sad Business School.
Eligibility: Open to nationals or permanent residents of Australia and New Zealand.
Level of Study: MBA, Postgraduate
Type: Scholarship
Value: AUD$40,000
Length of Study: 1 year

For further information contact:

Website: www.sbs.ox.ac.uk/MBA/Fees/Scholarships.htm

Business School (Saïd): Registrar's University of Oxford Scholarship

Subjects: EMBA.
Purpose: To assist graduate students with fees and a living allowance.
Eligibility: Open to all.
Level of Study: MBA, Postgraduate
Type: Scholarship
Value: Programme cost
Length of Study: 2 years
Closing Date: July 1st
Additional Information: Contact Diana.Hulin@admin.ox.ac.uk for further details.

Business School (Saïd): Skoll Scholarship

Subjects: MBA.
Purpose: To give social entrepreneurs the knowledge, skills and networks they need to turn ideas into reality; and deepen their conviction for doing so.
Eligibility: Open to candidates who can demonstrate evidence of the personal qualities strongly correlated with social entrepreneurship.
Level of Study: MBA, Postgraduate
Type: Scholarship
Value: Cover porgramme fees and an allowance for living expenses
Length of Study: 1 year

For further information contact:

Website: www.sbs.ox.ac.uk/MBA/Fees/Scholarships.htm

Cardiovascular Medicine: British Heart Foundation (BHF)

Subjects: Cardiovascular medicine.
Purpose: To assist graduate students with fees and maintenance.
Eligibility: Open to candidates who must comply with BHF residency requirements.
Level of Study: Research
Type: Residency

Value: University fees, college fees and £16,853 for maintenance
Length of Study: 4 years

For further information contact:

Website: www.cardiov.ox.ac.uk/Students/BHF-4-year-Graduate-Programme

Cardiovascular Medicine: Medical Research Council (MRC) Studentship

Subjects: Cardiovascular medicine.
Purpose: To assist graduate students with fees and maintenance.
Eligibility: Open to candidates who must comply with MRC residency requirements.
Level of Study: Research
Type: Studentship
Value: University fees, college fees and at least £12,940 for maintenance
Length of Study: 3 years
Additional Information: Please contact barbara.casadei@cardiov.ox.ac.uk for more details.

Chemistry: BBSRC Studentships

Subjects: Chemical biology.
Purpose: To assist graduate students with fees and a living allowance.
Eligibility: Open to candidates are home/EU applicants and have completed DPhil.
Level of Study: Doctorate, Research
Type: Studentship
Value: University and college fees paid. UK residents also receive a maintenance allowance of at least £12,900 per year
Length of Study: 4 years, 1st year rotation of supervisors
Closing Date: January 23rd
Additional Information: Joint program with Biochemistry, applicants can apply to Chemical Biology or Biochemistry.

For further information contact:

Website: www.bioch.ox.ac.uk/aspsite/index.asp?pageid=390

Chemistry: Cancer Research UK Studentships

Subjects: Organic chemistry.
Purpose: To provide a comprehensive training in medicinal chemistry as applied to the design, synthesis and biological evaluation of small molecule anticancer agents.
Eligibility: Open to all.
Level of Study: Research
Type: Studentship
Value: Fees at home rate and maintenance allowance
Length of Study: 4 years
Closing Date: December 1st
Additional Information: Administered by Pharmacology.

For further information contact:

Website: www.pharm.ox.ac.uk/jobvacancies/MedChem

Chemistry: EPSRC Doctoral Training Grant Studentships

Subjects: Organic chemistry, inorganic chemistry, physical and theoretical chemistry.
Purpose: To assist graduate students with fees and maintenance.
Eligibility: Open to home/EU applicants who have completed DPhil.
Level of Study: Research
Type: Studentship
Value: University and college fees paid. UK residents also receive a maintenance allowance of at least £12,900 per year
Length of Study: 3 years. A further extension of up to 1 year may be possible
Closing Date: January 23rd

For further information contact:

Website: www.chem.ox.ac.uk/graduatestudies/

Chemistry: EPSRC/BBSRC Individual Studentships

Subjects: Organic chemistry, chemical biology, inorganic chemistry, physical and theoretical chemistry.

Purpose: To assist graduate students with fees and maintenance.
Eligibility: Open to home/EU applicants who have completed DPhil only.
Level of Study: Research
Type: Studentship
Value: University and college fees paid. UK residents also receive a maintenance allowance of at least £12,900 per year
Length of Study: 3 years
Additional Information: Supervisors may get funding for specific projects, which will be advertised seperately to other funding.

For further information contact:

Website: www.chem.ox.ac.uk/graduatestudies/

Chemistry: Newton Abraham Scholarship in Chemical Sciences

Subjects: Organic chemistry, chemical biology, inorganic chemistry, physical and theoretical chemistry.
Purpose: To assist graduate students with fees and maintenance.
Eligibility: Open to candidates who have completed DPhil.
Level of Study: Research
Type: Scholarship
Value: University and college fees at the home student rate, plus a minimum of £12,900 per year maintenance allowance
Length of Study: 3 years. Under special circumstances, the award may be extended for an extra 6 months
Closing Date: January 23rd

For further information contact:

Website: www.chem.ox.ac.uk/graduatestudies/

Chemistry: Research Project Studentships and EPSRC Industrial CASE Studentships

Subjects: Organic chemistry, inorganic chemistry, physical and theoretical chemistry.
Purpose: To assist graduate students with fees and maintenance.
Eligibility: Please check website for details.
Level of Study: Research
Value: University and college fees paid, plus a minimum of £12,900 per year maintenance allowance
Length of Study: 3 or 3 years, depending on the sponsor

For further information contact:

Website: www.chem.ox.ac.uk/graduatestudies/

China Centre Postgraduate Scholarship

Subjects: Humanities and social sciences.
Purpose: To assist graduate students with fees and a living allowance.
Eligibility: Check website for details.
Level of Study: Research
Type: Scholarship
Value: £14,000 per year (tuition/college fees, some living expenses)
Length of Study: 3 years
Frequency: Every 2 years
Closing Date: March 13th

For further information contact:

Website: www.chinacentre.ox.ac.uk/news/items/china_centre_postgraduate_scholarship

Chinese Ministry of Education-University of Oxford Scholarships

Subjects: All subjects.
Purpose: To provide Chinese students who demonstrate both academic excellence and leadership potential the opportunity to study for a DPhil at the University of Oxford.
Eligibility: Open to candidates from mainland China. Candidates must have graduated or intend to graduate by October 2009 from one of the 211 Project universities and must be able to demonstrate both academic excellence and leadership potential.
Level of Study: Research
Type: Scholarships

Value: University and college fees; grant for living costs; return air travel to/from UK
Length of Study: Up to 4 years coterminous with fee liability
Closing Date: January 23rd

For further information contact:

Website: www.admin.ox.ac.uk/studentfunding/scholarship_profiles/cmeoxford.shtml

Christ Church: Alberto del Vicario Scholarship

Subjects: Engineering.
Purpose: To provide a scholarship for EU graduate students in Engineering at Christ Church.
Eligibility: Open to EU nationals only.
Level of Study: Postgraduate, Research
Type: Scholarship
Value: Maximum £3,750
Length of Study: Up to 3 years
Closing Date: May 1st

For further information contact:

Website: www.chch.ox.ac.uk

Christ Church: American Friends Scholarship

Subjects: All subjects.
Purpose: The American Friends Scholarship has been established by American alumni of Christ Church to permit qualified Americans to further their education at Christ Church in any academic field or area of interest.
Eligibility: American nationals only.
Level of Study: Postgraduate, Research
Type: Scholarship
Value: Maximum £4,000
Length of Study: 1 year
Frequency: Annual
Study Establishment: Christ Church, University of Oxford
Country of Study: United Kingdom
No. of awards offered: Varies
Application Procedure: Applicants must apply for the scholarship when applying for admission.
Closing Date: 01 May
Funding: Private

For further information contact:

The Tutor for Graduates' Secretary, Christ Church, Oxford, Oxfordshire, OX1 1DP, England
Website: www.chch.ox.ac.uk

Christ Church: Myers Scholarship

Subjects: All subjects.
Purpose: Established by Christ Church alumnus Allan Myers to enable Australian graduate students to pursue postgraduate studies at Christ Church.
Eligibility: Australian nationals only.Must be a graduate student. Preference given to students studying Law.
Level of Study: Postgraduate, Research
Type: Scholarship
Value: Maximum £6,000
Length of Study: 1 year
Frequency: Annual
Study Establishment: Christ Church, University of Oxford
Country of Study: United Kingdom
No. of awards offered: 1
Application Procedure: Applications may be made by students on admission to Christ Church, University of Oxford.
Closing Date: 1 May
Funding: Private

For further information contact:

Tutor for Graduates' Secretary, Christ Church, Oxford, Oxfordshire, OX1 1DP, England
Website: www.chch.ox.ac.uk

Clarendon Fund Linked Awards

Subjects: All subjects.
Purpose: To enable academically outstanding students to take up their places at Oxford.
Eligibility: Open to overseas candidates (Clarendon Award holders).
Level of Study: Research, Postgraduate
Type: Award
Value: £4,000
Length of Study: 1 year, possible renewal
Closing Date: January 23rd

For further information contact:

Website: www.admin.ox.ac.uk/studentfunding/scholarship_profiles/clarendon.shtml

Clarendon Fund Scholarships

Subjects: All subjects.
Purpose: To enable academically outstanding students to take up their places at Oxford.
Eligibility: Open to candidates who are liable to pay fees at overseas rate.
Level of Study: Postgraduate, Research
Type: Scholarships
Value: Most awards are full (tuition/college fees and grant for living expenses at UK Research Council rate); some are fees only (tuition/college fees)
Length of Study: Period of fee liability. A few awards may be made for two courses, i.e., MSc+DPhil or MPhil+Dphil
No. of awards offered: 120
Closing Date: January 23rd

For further information contact:

Website: www.admin.ox.ac.uk/studentfunding/scholarship_profiles/Clarendon.shtml

Clarendon Scholarships in Chemistry

Subjects: Organic chemistry, chemical biology, inorganic chemistry, physical and theoretical chemistry.
Purpose: To assist graduate students with fees and maintenance.
Eligibility: Open to overseas students only.
Level of Study: Research
Type: Scholarship
Value: University and college fees paid, plus a minimum of £12,900 maintenance allowance per year
Length of Study: 3 years
Closing Date: January 23rd
Additional Information: Candidates are advised to apply by application deadline 1, but if possible applications will also be considered by application deadline 2; please see website.

For further information contact:

Website: www.chem.ox.ac.uk/graduatestudies/

Clarendon Scholarships in Computer Science

Subjects: Computer science.
Purpose: To assist graduate students with fees and maintenance.
Eligibility: Open to overseas students only.
Level of Study: Research
Type: Scholarship
Value: University and college fees paid, plus a minimum of £12,900-maintenance allowance per year. Some fees only awards may be made
Length of Study: 3 years
Closing Date: January 23rd
No. of awards given last year: 2–3

For further information contact:

Website: www.comlab.ox.ac.uk/news/opportunities.html

Clarendon Scholarships in Engineering Science

Subjects: Engineering science.
Purpose: To assist graduate students with fees and maintenance.
Eligibility: Open to overseas students only.
Level of Study: Research
Type: Scholarships

Value: University and college fees paid, plus a minimum of £12,900 maintenance allowance per year
Length of Study: 3 years
Closing Date: November 21st
Additional Information: Candidates are advised to apply by application deadline 1, but if possible applications will also be considered by application deadline 2; please see website.

For further information contact:

Website: www.eng.ox.ac.uk/postgrad/studentships.html

Clarendon Scholarships in Materials

Subjects: Materials science.
Purpose: To assist graduate students with fees and maintenance.
Eligibility: Open to candidates who have completed DPhil programme and are overseas students.
Level of Study: Research
Value: University and college fees, plus a minimum of £12,900 maintenance allowance
Length of Study: Normally 3 years
Closing Date: November 21st
No. of awards given last year: 1 or 2
Additional Information: Typically we award 1 or 2 Clarendon Scholarships each year, but this number depends on the funding announcements made by the sponsors. Candidates are advised to apply by application deadline 1.

For further information contact:

Website: www.materials.ox.ac.uk/admissions/postgraduate/newprojects.html

Clarendon Scholarships in Physics

Subjects: Physics.
Purpose: To assist graduate students with fees and maintenance.
Eligibility: Varies.
Level of Study: Research
Type: Scholarships
Value: University and college fees, plus a minimum of £12,900 per year maintenance allowance
Length of Study: Normally 3 years
Closing Date: January 23rd
Additional Information: Typically we get 4–6 Clarendon Scholarships each year, but the number depends on the funding announcements made by the sponsors.

For further information contact:

Website: www.physics.ox.ac.uk/admissions/postgrad.htm

Clinical Neurology: MRC Studentship

Subjects: Clinical neurology.
Purpose: To assist graduate students with fees and maintenance.
Eligibility: Open to home/EU applicants only.
Level of Study: Research
Type: Studentship
Value: University fees and college fees; maintenace for UK students
Length of Study: 3 years
No. of awards offered: 1
Closing Date: January 9th

For further information contact:

Website: www.clneuro.ox.ac.uk/graduate-studies

Commonwealth Scholarship and Fellowship Plan

Subjects: All subjects.
Purpose: To assist graduate students with fees and living allowance.
Eligibility: Open to new and continuing students. Commonwealth citizens and British-protected persons who are permanently resident in a Commonwealth country (not UK).
Level of Study: Postgraduate, Research
Type: Scholarship
Value: University and college fees, travel to UK, full grant for living costs, occasionally other allowances
Length of Study: Full course duration
Closing Date: December 31st

Additional Information: Preference is given to DPhil students.

For further information contact:

Website: www.cscuk.org.uk

Computing Laboratory: Departmental Funding

Subjects: Computer science.
Purpose: To assist graduate students with fees and maintenance.
Eligibility: Varies.
Level of Study: Research
Type: Funding support
Value: University and college fees paid, plus a minimum of £12,900 maintenance allowance per year
Length of Study: 3 years
Closing Date: January 23rd
Additional Information: A limited amount of departmental funding is available each year and will be mainly used to support students who have some form of funding but not sufficient to allow them to take up their place.

For further information contact:

Website: www.comlab.ox.ac.uk/news/opportunities.html

Computing Laboratory: EPSRC Doctoral Training Grant Studentships

Subjects: Computer science.
Purpose: To assist graduate students with fees and maintenance.
Eligibility: Open to home/EU candidates with DPhil only.
Level of Study: Doctorate, Research
Type: Studentship
Value: University and college fees paid. UK residents also receive a maintenance allowance of at least £12,900 per year
Length of Study: 3.5 years. A further extension of up to 6 months may be possible
Closing Date: January 23rd
Additional Information: Between 3 and 5 studentships are available each year, dependent on the annual funding announcement by EPSRC.

For further information contact:

Website: www.comlab.ox.ac.uk/news/opportunities.html

Corpus Christi College: Corpus Development Studentship

Subjects: Economics for development, global governance and diplomacy, forced migration.
Purpose: To support students pursuing their degree through Queen Elizabeth House.
Eligibility: Open to candidates from the developing world studying for a degree run through Queen Elizabeth House.
Level of Study: Postgraduate, Research
Type: Studentship
Value: University fee, college fee and £8,000 living expenses
Length of Study: 1 year

For further information contact:

Website: www.ccc.ox.ac.uk/

Criminology: ESRC 1+3/ +3 Nomination (Quota) Studentship

Subjects: Criminology and criminal justice.
Purpose: To assist graduate students with fees and maintenance.
Eligibility: Open to UK/EU residents; the 1+3 award is open to applicants for the MSc Criminology and Criminal Justice (Research Methods); applicants for the +3 award should have completed PhD in Criminology applications.
Level of Study: Postgraduate, Research
Type: Studentship
Value: University fees and college fees. UK residents are eligible for maintenance allowance (2008–2009 level: £12,940)

Length of Study: Up to 4 years (depending on point of entry to studies)

For further information contact:

Website: www.crim.ox.ac.uk/graduate/funding.htm; www.esrc.ac.uk

Doctoral Training Centre-MPLS: Clarendon Awards – Systems Biology Doctoral Training Centre

Subjects: Life science, mathematics and physics.
Purpose: To assist graduate students with fees and maintenance.
Eligibility: Open to overseas candidates only.
Level of Study: Research
Type: Award
Value: College and university fees plus maintenance allowance of £12,900
Length of Study: 4 years
Closing Date: November 21st
Additional Information: Candidates are advised to apply by application deadline 1, but if possible applications will also be considered by application deadline 2; please see website.

For further information contact:

Website: www.dtc.ox.ac.uk

Dorothy Hodgkin Postgraduate Awards

Subjects: Social sciences, MPLS and medical sciences.
Purpose: To study for doctoral degrees in highly rated UK research environments.
Eligibility: Open to candidates from Hong Kong, Russia and the developing world.
Level of Study: Postgraduate, Research
Type: Award
Value: University and college fees; full grant for living costs. May occasionally include small allowances
Length of Study: Full course duration
No. of awards offered: Varies
Closing Date: July 25th
Additional Information: Candidates must have equivalent of a UK first class honours degree from a prestigious academic institution. Awards are tenable only in departments RAE-rated 5 or 5* and these vary by year – check with the department to see if they have bid for any awards.

For further information contact:

Website: www.admin.ox.ac.uk/studentfunding/scholarship_profiles/ DHPA.shtml

Dulverton and Michael Wills Scholarships

Subjects: All subjects.
Purpose: To assist graduate students with fees and maintenance.
Eligibility: Open to candidates from Albania, Armenia, Azerbaijan, Belarus, Bosnia, Bulgaria, Croatia, Georgia, Hungary, Latvia, Lithuania, the Former Yugoslav Republic of Macedonia, Moldova, Montenegro, Poland, Romania, Serbia, Slovakia and Ukraine.
Level of Study: Postgraduate, Research
Type: Scholarships
Value: Full awards to cover university and college fees plus grant for living costs. Partial awards depending on candidate's financial circumstances
Length of Study: Full course duration
Closing Date: January 23rd

For further information contact:

Website: www.admin.ox.ac.uk/io/funding/Dulverton.shtml

Earth Sciences: Boise Studentship in Earth Sciences

Subjects: Earth sciences.
Purpose: To assist graduate students with fees and maintenance.
Eligibility: Open to candidates with 2.1 degree or higher.
Level of Study: Research
Type: Studentship
Value: University and college fees paid and a maintenance allowance of £12,500 per year

Length of Study: Normally 3 years, which can be extended in some cases
Additional Information: The Department will have one studentship available for 2009 entry. Candidates are advised to apply directly to the Department as advertised on the website, deadline to be confirmed.

For further information contact:

Website: www.earth.ox.ac.uk/research/postgradeg.htm

Earth Sciences: Clarendon Scholarship in Earth Sciences

Subjects: Earth sciences.
Purpose: To assist graduate students with fees and maintenance.
Eligibility: Open to overseas candidates with a first class degree.
Level of Study: Research
Type: Scholarship
Value: University and college fees, also maintenance allowance of £12,500 per year
Length of Study: Normally 3 years, which can be extended in some cases
Additional Information: The Department expects to have at least one Clarendon Scholarship for 2009 entry. Candidates are advised to apply directly to the Department as advertised on the website, deadline to be confirmed.

For further information contact:

Website: www.earth.ox.ac.uk/research/postgradeg.htm

Earth Sciences: STFC Studentships in Earth Sciences

Subjects: Earth sciences.
Purpose: To assist graduate students with fees and maintenance.
Eligibility: Open to home or EU candidates usually 2.1 degree or higher.
Level of Study: Research
Type: Studentship
Value: University and college fees paid. Home students also receive a maintenance allowance of £12,500 per year
Length of Study: Between 3 and 4 years depending on the project
Additional Information: The Department occasionally has one or more STFC studentships, to be confirmed. An EU national who has studied for an undergraduate degree at a UK university during the 3 years leading up to the application may be classed as a UK resident.

For further information contact:

Website: www.earth.ox.ac.uk/research/postgradeg.htm

Economics - ESRC Quota Award

Subjects: Economics.
Purpose: To assist graduate students with fees and maintenance.
Eligibility: Open to home/EU candidates with a Mphil and DPhil Economics.
Level of Study: Doctorate, Research
Type: Award
Value: Maintenance and fees (depending on residency)
Length of Study: Up to 4 years (depending on point of entry to studies)
Closing Date: November 21st

For further information contact:

Website: www.economics.ox.ac.uk/index.php/graduate

Education: ESRC

Subjects: Education.
Purpose: To assist graduate students with fees and maintenance.
Eligibility: Open to home/EU candidates.
Level of Study: Doctorate, Research
Type: Award
Value: University fees, college fees and maintenance allowance
Length of Study: 4 years
Closing Date: Januray 23rd

For further information contact:

Website: www.education.ox.ac.uk/courses/DPhil/ssublinkna/ index.php

Education: Talbot Scholarship
Subjects: Education.
Purpose: To assist graduate students with fees.
Eligibility: Open to female candidates.
Level of Study: Doctorate, Research
Type: Scholarship
Value: University fees and college fees
No. of awards offered: 3 years
Closing Date: January 23rd

For further information contact:

Website: www.education.ox.ac.uk/courses/DPhil/ssublinkna/index.php

Engineering Doctorate (Eng.D.) Studentships
Subjects: Engineering science.
Purpose: To assist graduate students with fees and maintenance.
Eligibility: Open to home/EU candidates.
Level of Study: Research
Type: Studentship
Value: University and College fees paid, plus a minimum of £12,900 maintenance allowance per year and a contribution from the sponsoring company
Length of Study: 4 years
Additional Information: The Engineering Doctorate (Eng.D) is a four-year research degree undertaken in collaboration with an industrial company. These studentships will be advertised on the Department of Engineering Science website. Closing date is as advertised by the department.

For further information contact:

Website: www.eng.ox.ac.uk/postgrad/studentships.html

Engineering Science: EPSRC Doctoral Training Grant Studentships
Subjects: Engineering science.
Purpose: To assist graduate students with fees and maintenance.
Eligibility: Open to home/EU candidates with a DPhil.
Level of Study: Research
Type: Studentship
Value: University and college fees paid. UK residents also receive a maintenance allowance of at least £12,900 per year
Length of Study: 3 years. A further extension of up to 1 year may be possible
Closing Date: March 13th
Additional Information: Between 5 and 8 studentships are available each year, dependent on the annual funding announcement by EPSRC.

For further information contact:

Website: www.eng.ox.ac.uk/postgrad/studentships.html

Engineering Science: Medtronic Scholarships
Subjects: Biomedical engineering.
Purpose: To assist graduate students with fees.
Eligibility: Open to home/EU female and/or minority candidates only.
Level of Study: Research
Type: Scholarships
Value: $25,000 or its GBP equivalent
Length of Study: 1 year
Closing Date: March 13th

For further information contact:

Website: www.eng.ox.ac.uk/postgrad/studentships.html

Engineering Science: Sloane-Robinson Scholarships
Subjects: Biomedical engineering.
Purpose: To assist graduate students with fees.
Eligibility: Open to candidates from developing countries including Eastern Europe.
Level of Study: Research
Type: Scholarships
Value: $10,000 or its GBP equivalent
Length of Study: 1 year
Closing Date: March 13th

For further information contact:

Website: www.eng.ox.ac.uk/postgrad/studentships.html

Engineering Science: VenCap Scholarship
Subjects: Biomedical engineering and commercial entrepreneurship.
Purpose: To assist graduate students with fees and maintenance.
Eligibility: Open to home/EU and overseas applicants with a DPhil.
Level of Study: Research
Type: Scholarship
Value: University fees, college fees and a maintenance maintenance allowance of at least £12,900 per year for 3 years
Length of Study: 3 years of DPhil study and 1 year of paid work experience
Additional Information: This scholarship will enable a graduate student to undertake 3 fully-funded years of DPhil study and 1 year of paid work experience with a top venture capital firm operating in the MedTech sector. Deadlines are as advertised on the Department of Engineering.

For further information contact:

Website: www.eng.ox.ac.uk/postgrad/studentships.html

English Faculty: E.K.Chambers Studentship
Subjects: English literature.
Purpose: To assist graduate students with fees and maintenance.
Eligibility: Open to a candidate with good classical attainments (Classics 'A' Levels) who has graduated from a subject other than single honours English.
Level of Study: Postgraduate
Type: Studentship
Value: University fee and maintenance grant of around £8,800

For further information contact:

Website: www.english.ox.ac.uk

English Faculty: Faculty Studentships
Subjects: English literature and language.
Purpose: To assist graduate students with fees and maintenance.
Eligibility: Open to all candidates.
Level of Study: Postgraduate
Type: Studentship
Value: University fee and maintenance grant of around £8,803
Length of Study: Depending on course length
Additional Information: All students applying for English graduate courses will automatically be considered.

For further information contact:

Website: www.english.ox.ac.uk

English Faculty: Violet Vaughan Morgan Studentship
Subjects: English literature and language.
Purpose: To assist graduate students with fees and maintenance.
Eligibility: Open to candidates from UK or Commonwealth nationals.
Level of Study: Postgraduate
Type: Studentship
Value: University fee and maintenance grant of around £8,801
Length of Study: Depending on course length (usually for 1 year M.St course)
Additional Information: All students applying for English graduate courses will automatically be considered.

For further information contact:

Website: www.english.ox.ac.uk

EPSRC Doctoral Training Grant Studentships in Condensed Matter Physics, Atomic & Laser Physics etc
Subjects: Condensed matter physics, atomic and laser physics, and theoretical physics.
Purpose: To assist graduate students with fees and maintenance.

Eligibility: Open to UK/EU candidates with a DPhil only; EU students are eligible for fees only unless a first degree was taken in the UK in the period immediately prior to the award, in which case a maintenance stipend may be included.
Level of Study: Research
Type: Studentship
Value: University and college fees, plus a minimum of £12,940 per year maintenance allowance
Closing Date: January 23rd
Additional Information: Typically we award about 10 DTA studentships each year, but this number depends on the annual funding announcement made by the sponsors.

EPSRC DTA Studentships in Materials

Subjects: Materials science.
Purpose: To assist graduate students with fees and maintenance.
Eligibility: Open to candidates with a DPhil programme only.
Level of Study: Research
Type: Studentship
Value: University & college fees, plus a maintenance allowance of £12,900 which the sponsors may increase by £2,000
Length of Study: $3\frac{1}{2}$ years
Closing Date: November 21st
Additional Information: EU students are eligible for fees only unless first degree was taken in the UK in the period immediately prior to the award, in which case they may be eligible for maintenance allowance. Typically 10 of these studentships are awarded each year.

For further information contact:

Website: www.materials.ox.ac.uk/admissions/postgraduate/newprojects.html

EPSRC Life Sciences Interface Doctoral Training Centre Studentships

Subjects: Mathematics and physical science.
Purpose: To assist graduate students with fees and maintenance.
Eligibility: Open to home/EU candidates only who have achieved a minimum of 2:1 or equivalent in their undergraduate degree.
Level of Study: Research
Type: Studentship
Value: University and college fees paid. UK residents also receive a maintenance allowance of at least £12,900 per year
Length of Study: 4 years
Additional Information: EU students are eligible for fees only unless first degree was taken in the UK in the period immediately prior to the award, in which case they may be eligible for maintenance allowance. Up to 15 awards available annually. Please refer to website for closing dates.

For further information contact:

Website: www.dtc.ox.ac.uk

EPSRC Project Studentships in Condensed Matter Physics, Atomic & Laser Physics and Theoretical Physics

Subjects: Condensed matter physics and atomic and laser physics.
Purpose: To assist graduate students with fees and maintenance.
Eligibility: Open only to UK/EU/overseas candidates with a DPhil; EU students are eligible for fees only unless a first degree was taken in the UK in the period immediately prior to the award, in which case a maintenance allowance may be included.
Level of Study: Research
Type: Studentship
Value: University and college fees, plus a minimum of £12,940 per year maintenance allowance
Length of Study: Normally between 3–4 years depending on the project
Closing Date: January 23rd
Additional Information: These are for specific EPSRC funded projects; the number varies from year to year but is typically between 10–15 each year.

For further information contact:

Website: www.physics.ox.ac.uk/admissions/postgrad.htm

EPSRC Studentships in Earth Sciences

Subjects: Earth sciences.
Purpose: To assist graduate students with fees and maintenance.
Eligibility: Open to home or EU candidates with a usually 2.1 degree or higher.
Level of Study: Research
Type: Studentship
Value: University and college fees paid. Home students also receive a maintenance allowance of £12,500 per year
Length of Study: Normally 3 years, which can be extended in some cases
Additional Information: The Department occasionally has one or more EPSRC studentships, to be confirmed. An EU national who has studied for an undergraduate degree at a UK university during the 3 years leading up to the application may be classed as a UK resident.

For further information contact:

Website: www.earth.ox.ac.uk/research/postgradeg.htm

EPSRC Systems Biology Doctoral Training Centre Studentships

Subjects: Life science, mathematics and physical science.
Purpose: To assist graduate students with fees and maintenance.
Eligibility: Open only to home/EU candidates who have achieved a minimum of 2:1 or equivalent in their undergraduate degree.
Type: Studentship
Value: University and college fees paid. UK residents also receive a maintenance allowance of at least £12,900 per year
Length of Study: 4 years
Additional Information: EU students are eligible for fees only unless first degree was taken in the UK in the period immediately prior to the award, in which case they may be eligible for maintenance allowance. Up to 15 awards available annually. Closing date to be confirmed – please check website for details.

For further information contact:

Website: www.dtc.ox.ac.uk

Exeter College: SKP Scholarship

Subjects: Any subject which would lead to the economic development of India, all subjects in the medical sciences and maths, physical and life sciences divisions, and also all subjects in the humanities division, excluding film aesthetics and medieval studies.
Purpose: To study the factors leading to the economic development of India.
Eligibility: Open to candidates who have been awarded a University Clarendon Award and is an Indian citizen and is resident in India, has taken his or her undergraduate degree at an Indian institution of Higher Education and intends to return to India after graduation.
Level of Study: Postgraduate, Research
Type: Scholarship
Value: Full living allowance (in line with British Council)
Length of Study: Up to 3 years
Closing Date: January 23rd

For further information contact:

Website: www.exeter.ox.ac.uk/news/studentships

Experimental Psychology ESRC 1+3 Award

Subjects: Experimental psychology.
Purpose: To assist graduate students with fees and maintenance.
Eligibility: Open to home/EU candidates only. Candidates will need to have gained a 2:1 or above in a Psychology degree.
Level of Study: Doctorate, Postgraduate
Type: Award
Value: University fees and college fees; maintenance for UK students
Length of Study: 4 years
Closing Date: March 13th

For further information contact:

Website: www.psy.ox.ac.uk/graduate/funding

Experimental Psychology MRC DTA Award

Subjects: Experimental psychology.

Purpose: To assist graduate students with fees and maintenance.
Eligibility: Open to home/EU candidates only. Candidates will need to have gained a 2:1 or above in a Psychology degree and/or successfully completed a Masters.
Level of Study: Research
Type: Award
Value: University fees and college fees; maintenance for UK students
Length of Study: 3 years
Closing Date: March 13th
Additional Information: Home/EU applicants only. Candidates will need to have gained a 2:1 or above in a Psychology Degree and/or successfully completed a masters.

For further information contact:

Website: www.psy.ox.ac.uk/graduate/funding

Experimental Psychology Open ESRC + 3 Award

Subjects: Experimental psychology.
Purpose: To assist graduate students with fees and maintenance.
Eligibility: Open to home/EU candidates only. Ideally candidates should have successfully completed/or about to complete the MSc in Psychological Research Course.
Level of Study: Doctorate, Research
Type: Award
Value: University fees and college fees; maintenance for UK students
Length of Study: 3 years
Closing Date: March 13th
Additional Information: This is an "Open" Award and competition is competitive with other candidates from other universities.

For further information contact:

Website: www.psy.ox.ac.uk/graduate/funding

Felix Scholarships

Subjects: All subjects.
Purpose: To enable first class Indian students to pursue graduate studies at the University of Oxford, University of Reading and the School of Oriental and African Studies, University of London (SOAS).
Eligibility: Open to Indian graduates with a first-class Bachelor's degree from a University or comparable institution in India; must be under 30 years of age.
Level of Study: Postgraduate, Research
Type: Scholarships
Value: University and college fees; full grant for living costs; return air travel to/from UK
Length of Study: Up to 3 years
No. of awards offered: 7
Closing Date: January 23rd
Additional Information: Check website for subject specifications.

For further information contact:

Website: www.admin.ox.ac.uk/studentfunding/scholarship_profiles/Felix.shtml

Fountain Court Chambers Graduate Law Scholarship

Subjects: Legal studies.
Purpose: To assist graduate students with fees.
Eligibility: Open to home/EU and non-EU candidates.
Level of Study: Doctorate, Postgraduate, Research
Type: Scholarship
Value: £10,000
Length of Study: 1 year
Closing Date: June 20th

For further information contact:

Website: http://denning.law.ox.ac.uk/postgraduate/scholarships.shtml

Freshfields Bruckhaus Deringer Scholarships (Law)

Subjects: Legal studies.
Purpose: To assist graduate students with fees and a living allowance.
Eligibility: Varies.
Level of Study: Doctorate, Postgraduate, Research

Type: Scholarships
Value: To be confirmed
Length of Study: 1 year
Closing Date: June 20th

For further information contact:

Website: http://denning.law.ox.ac.uk/postgraduate/scholarships.shtml

Fulbright Scholarships

Subjects: All subjects.
Purpose: To assist graduate students with fees.
Eligibility: Open to new graduate students with US citizenship.
Level of Study: Postgraduate, Research
Type: Scholarships
Value: Full funding for one year
Length of Study: 1 year
Closing Date: October 20th
Additional Information: If you are currently enrolled in an undergraduate or graduate program at a U.S. college or university, you must apply through the Fulbright Program Adviser (FPA) on your campus.

For further information contact:

Website: www.iie.org

Geography: ESRC 1 + 3 Quota

Subjects: Nature, society and environmental policy, and geography.
Purpose: To assist graduate students with fees and maintenance.
Eligibility: Open to candidates from UK only. Students take MSc Nature, society and environmental policy in first year and then move onto DPhil.
Level of Study: Doctorate, Postgraduate, Research
Type: Studentship
Value: All fees and a maintenance grant
Length of Study: 4 years
Closing Date: February 1st

For further information contact:

Website: www.ouce.ox.ac.uk/graduate/

Geography: Hitachi Chemical Europe Scholarship with Linacre College

Subjects: Environmental change and management.
Purpose: To assist graduate students with fees and maintenance.
Eligibility: Preference will be given to a student from China, Central or South America but students with limited resources from other countries are not excluded.
Level of Study: Research
Type: Scholarship
Value: College fee plus contribution of £1,000 towards maintenance costs
Length of Study: 1 year
Closing Date: March 13th

For further information contact:

Website: www.eci.ox.ac.uk/teaching/msc/scholarships.php

Geography: Louwes Scholarship

Subjects: Water science, policy and management.
Purpose: To assist graduate students with fees, maintenance and travel expenses.
Eligibility: Open to all nationalities but applications from developing countries are particularly welcome and all applicants must have a demonstrable interest in water issues and developing countries.
Level of Study: Postgraduate
Type: Scholarship
Value: All fees and maintenance grant of £10,000 and contribution towards travel from the scholar's country of residence
Length of Study: 1 year
Closing Date: May 1st

For further information contact:

Website: www.ouce.ox.ac.uk/graduate/

Geography: NERC DPhil Quota
Subjects: Geography.
Purpose: To assist graduate students with fees and maintenance.
Eligibility: Open to UK candidates only.
Level of Study: Doctorate, Research
Value: All fees and a maintenance grant
Length of Study: 3 years
Additional Information: Closing date to be confirmed - please contact the department for more information.

For further information contact:

Website: www.ouce.ox.ac.uk/graduate/

Geography: NERC Quota
Subjects: Biodiversity, conservation and management.
Purpose: To assist graduate students with fees and maintenance.
Eligibility: Open to UK candidates only.
Level of Study: Postgraduate
Type: Studentship
Value: All fees and a maintenance grant
Length of Study: 1 year
Closing Date: February 1st

For further information contact:

Website: www.ouce.ox.ac.uk/graduate/

Geography: Water Conservators Scholarship
Subjects: Water science, policy and management.
Purpose: To assist graduate students with fees.
Eligibility: Open to all nationalities but applicants must have a demonstrable interest in and passion for water issues.
Level of Study: Postgraduate
Type: Scholarship
Value: £4,000
Length of Study: 1 year
Closing Date: May 1st
Additional Information: Open to all nationalities but applicants must have a demonstrable interest in and passion for water issues.

For further information contact:

Website: www.ouce.ox.ac.uk/graduate/

Graduate Scholarship in Medieval and Modern Languages with Keble College
Subjects: Medieval and modern languages.
Purpose: To assist graduate students with fees, maintenance and accomodation.
Eligibility: All eligible doctoral applicants submitting applications before the third gathered field will automatically be considered, irrespective of choice of college, provided that they have applied for other funded awards (if eligible).
Level of Study: Research
Type: Scholarship
Value: University fee at UK/EU rate; maintenance grant of £5,000. Additional benefits include some dining rights and guaranteed accommodation in 1st year
Length of Study: Up to 3 years
Closing Date: January 18th

For further information contact:

Website: www.mod-langs.ox.ac.uk/prizes/#keble

Graduate Scholarship in Medieval and Modern Languages with Merton College
Subjects: Medieval and modern languages.
Purpose: To assist graduate students with fees and a living allowance.
Eligibility: All eligible doctoral applicants submitting applications before the third gathered field will automatically be considered, irrespective of choice of college, provided that they have applied for other funded awards (if eligible).
Level of Study: Research
Type: Scholarship

Value: University fee at UK/EU rate; allowance of £5,000 to assist with college fees and/or maintenance
Length of Study: Up to 3 years
Closing Date: January 18th

For further information contact:

Website: www.mod-langs.ox.ac.uk/prizes/#merton

Graduate Scholarship in Medieval and Modern Languages with Somerville College
Subjects: Medieval and modern languages.
Purpose: To assist graduate students with fees, maintenance and accomodation.
Eligibility: All eligible doctoral applicants submitting applications before the third gathered field will automatically be considered, irrespective of choice of college, provided that they have applied for other funded awards (if eligible).
Level of Study: Research
Type: Scholarship
Value: University fee at UK/EU rate; maintenance grant of £6,000. Additional benefits include some dining rights and guaranteed accommodation in 1st year
Length of Study: Up to 3 years
Closing Date: January 18th

For further information contact:

Website: www.mod-langs.ox.ac.uk/prizes/#somerville

Green Templeton College: Leyland Scholarships
Subjects: Management studies.
Purpose: To study any management studies programme.
Eligibility: Open to candidate pursuing a research degree, or pursuing a taught Masters degree or a candidate of other EU nationality pursuing any postgraduate degree or to an overseas candidate pursuing any postgraduate degree.
Level of Study: MBA, Postgraduate, Research
Type: Scholarship
Value: £4,000
Length of Study: 1 year
Closing Date: April 3rd

For further information contact:

Website: www.gtc.ox.ac.uk/admissions/scholarships-and-awards/for-dphil-students.html

Green Templeton College: Templeton Scholarships
Subjects: Management studies.
Purpose: To undertake management studies.
Eligibility: Open to candidates who have applied for and been awarded a Clarendon scholarship, and is only tenable at Green Templeton College.
Level of Study: MBA, Postgraduate, Research
Type: Scholarship
Value: £4,000
Length of Study: 1 year
Closing Date: April 3rd

For further information contact:

Website: www.gtc.ox.ac.uk/admissions/scholarships-and-awards/for-dphil-students.html

Harris Manchester College: Second BA Scholarships
Subjects: Law, theology, english, human sciences, economics and management.
Purpose: To assist graduate students with fees.
Eligibility: Open to candidates in new second BA in law, theology, english, human sciences, economics and management. Awards will be made on academic merit. The scholarships are primarily for those who already have, or will have, a good first degree.
Type: Scholarship
Value: £9,000 for two years or £6,000 for three years
Length of Study: 2 or 3 years
Closing Date: October 15th

For further information contact:

Website: www.hmc.ox.ac.uk/prizesandscholarships.html

Hill Foundation Scholarships
Subjects: All subjects.
Purpose: To enable Russians of very high academic ability to undertake a period of study at Oxford University before returning to develop their careers in the Russian Federation.
Eligibility: Open to nationals of the Russian Federation or first generation Israelis of Russian descent. Candidates should normally not be more than 25 years of age.
Level of Study: Postgraduate, Research
Value: University and college fees; full grant for living costs
Length of Study: Full course duration
No. of awards offered: Varies
Closing Date: January 23rd
Additional Information: Maximum age normally 35. If Israeli, the candidate must be first generation Israeli of Russian descent.

For further information contact:

Website: www.admin.ox.ac.uk/studentfunding/scholarship_profiles/Hill.shtml

International Development: Corpus Christi Graduate Studentship in Development
Subjects: Economics for development, forced migration, and global governance and diplomacy.
Purpose: To assist graduate students with fees and maintenance.
Eligibility: Open to candidates having a citizenship in (and normal residence in) a developing country as defined by the United Nations, with a preference for candidates from Sub-Saharan Africa.
Level of Study: Postgraduate
Type: Studentship
Value: University fee, college fee and £8,000 maintenance allowance
Length of Study: 1 year

For further information contact:

Website: www.qeh.ox.ac.uk

International Development: Department of Economics Scholarship
Subjects: Economics for development.
Purpose: To assist graduate students with fees.
Eligibility: Open to all.
Level of Study: Postgraduate
Type: Scholarship
Value: £20,000
Length of Study: 1 year
Closing Date: January 23rd

For further information contact:

Website: www.qeh.ox.ac.uk; www.econ.ox.ac.uk

International Development: MSc in Forced Migration Scholarships
Subjects: Forced migration.
Purpose: To explore forced migration through a thesis, a group research essay, and a range of required courses.
Eligibility: Open to all.
Level of Study: Postgraduate
Type: Scholarships
Value: Amount to be confirmed
Length of Study: 1 year
Closing Date: January 23rd

For further information contact:

Website: www.rsc.ox.ac.uk

International Development: QEH Scholarship
Subjects: Development studies.
Purpose: To assist graduate students with fees and maintenance.

Eligibility: Open to candidates having a citizenship of (and normal residence in) a developing country as defined by the United Nations, with a preference for candidates from Sub-Saharan Africa.
Level of Study: Research
Type: Scholarship
Value: University fees and college fees. A maintenance allowance may also be made
Length of Study: Up to 3 years
Closing Date: January 23rd

For further information contact:

Website: www.qeh.ox.ac.uk

International Development: QEH Scholarships
Subjects: Economics for development, forced migration and global governance and diplomacy.
Purpose: To assist graduate students with fees and maintenance.
Eligibility: Open to candidates having a citizenship of (and normal residence in) a developing country as defined by the United Nations, with a preference for candidates from Sub-Saharan Africa.
Level of Study: Postgraduate
Type: Scholarships
Value: University fees, college fees and £8,000 maintenance allowance
Length of Study: 1 year

For further information contact:

Website: www.qeh.ox.ac.uk; www.rsc.ox.ac.uk

International Development: QEH Scholarships
Subjects: Development studies.
Purpose: To assist graduate students with fees and maintenance.
Eligibility: Open to candidates having citizenship of (and normal residence in) a developing country as defined by the United Nations, with a preference for candidates from Sub-Saharan Africa.
Level of Study: Research
Type: Scholarships
Value: University fees, college fees and £8,000 maintenance allowance
Length of Study: 2 years
Closing Date: January 23rd

For further information contact:

Website: www.qeh.ox.ac.uk

Internet Institute: PGP Scholarship
Subjects: DPhil Information, Communication and the Social Sciences & MSc Social Science of the Internet.
Eligibility: Open to all Doctoral students on the basis of academic merit.
Level of Study: Doctorate, Postgraduate, Research
Value: £10,000
Length of Study: 1 year
Frequency: Annual
Closing Date: Please contact the department for more information
Contributor: Internet Institute

For further information contact:

Website: www.oii.ox.ac.uk/teaching/dphil/apply.cfm

Jesus College Alun Hughes Scholarship
Subjects: DPhil in languages and cultures of Polynesisa or Micronesia, including the relationship and interaction of such cultures and languages with those of Melanesia.
Purpose: To study the languages and cultures of Polynesia or Micronesia, including the relationship and interaction of such cultures and languages with those of Melanesia.
Eligibility: Open to all applicants.
Level of Study: Doctorate, Postgraduate, Research
Type: Scholarship
Value: University and College fees. Full maintainance allowance and a research allowance of around £1500 per year
Length of Study: Up to 4 years

Application Procedure: The closing date is usually in January pre-ceeding entry. Please contact the college for further information.
Closing Date: January 1st

For further information contact:

Website: www.jesus.ox.ac.uk/admissions/graduateadmissions.php#section9

Jesus College Sir Richard Southwood Scholarship

Subjects: Ecology, particularly with an entomological focus.
Purpose: To study ecology, particularly with an entomological focus.
Eligibility: Open to graduate students.
Level of Study: Doctorate, MBA, Postgraduate, Research
Type: Scholarship
Value: Stipend at the rate paid by the UK's Natural Environment Research Council (currently £12,600 per year); university fees and college fees (at the overseas or Home/EU rate as applicable); and a research and conference allowance of up to £1,500 per year
Length of Study: 3 years (including probationary research year)
No. of awards offered: 2
Closing Date: January 23rd

For further information contact:

Website: www.jesus.ox.ac.uk/notices/southwoodscholarship.php

Karim Rida Said Scholarships

Subjects: All subjects.
Purpose: To support students from the Middle East to study for a Masters degree at Oxford.
Eligibility: Open to new graduate students from Iraq, Jordan, Lebanon, Palestine and Syria taking one-year Master's degrees. Candidates must be under 40 years old.
Level of Study: Postgraduate
Type: Scholarships
Value: University and college fees; full grant for living costs; return air fare to/from UK. Some partial grants are also available
Length of Study: 1 year
Closing Date: January 23rd

For further information contact:

Website: www.admin.ox.ac.uk/studentfunding/scholarship_profiles/KRSF.shtml

Keble College/Gwynne Jones Award

Subjects: All subjects.
Purpose: To enable students from Sierra Leonne or those Yoruba-speaking countries to pursue a postgraduate research degree.
Eligibility: Open to candiates from Sierra Leone or those Yoruba-speaking inhabitants of Nigeria.
Level of Study: Postgraduate, Research
Type: Award
Value: £11,500
Length of Study: Up to 3 years
Closing Date: March 1st

For further information contact:

Website: www.keble.ox.ac.uk/admissions/graduate/graduate-scholarships-1

Keble College: Keble De Breyne

Subjects: All subjects.
Purpose: To assist research students with fees.
Eligibility: Open to candidates with any research degree.
Level of Study: Postgraduate, Research
Type: Award
Value: £5,000
Length of Study: Up to 3 years
No. of awards offered: 2
Closing Date: March 1st

For further information contact:

Website: www.keble.ox.ac.uk/admissions/graduate/graduate-scholarships-1

Keble College: Keble Sloane-Robinson/Clarendon Awards

Subjects: All subjects.
Purpose: To assist research students with fees.
Level of Study: Research
Type: Award
Value: £5,000
Length of Study: Up to 3 years
No. of awards offered: 5
Closing Date: January 23rd

For further information contact:

Website: www.keble.ox.ac.uk/admissions/graduate/graduate-scholarships-1

Lady Margaret Hall: The LMH Studentship for Canadian Studies

Subjects: All subjects.
Eligibility: Open to candidates who are UK nationals or Canadians permanently resident in the UK.
Level of Study: Research
Value: £2,000 and a right to college accommodation (to be charged to the award holder at the prevailing rates) and limited SCR dining rights
Length of Study: Renewable annually until the end of the course, or of fee liability, whichever is first
Closing Date: January 2nd

For further information contact:

Website: www.lmh.ox.ac.uk

Latin American Centre: Banco Santander, Oxford University

Subjects: Latin American studies, public policy in Latin America and Latin American studies.
Purpose: To assist graduate students with fees.
Eligibility: Open to candidates studying for a 1 or 2 year degree in Latin American Studies who have the intention of continuing their studies at doctoral level and be residents of one of the following countries: Argentina, Brazil, Chile, Colombia, Mexico, Portugal, Puerto Rico.
Level of Study: Postgraduate, Research
Type: Award
Value: £10,000
Length of Study: One year. Not renewable
Closing Date: November 21st

Latin American Centre: Ronaldo Falconer, LAC Scholarship, St Antony's College

Subjects: Latin American studies, public policy in Latin America and Latin American studies.
Purpose: To assist graduate students with fees.
Eligibility: Open to candidates studying for a 1 or 2 year degree in Latin American Studies and be residents of Costa Rica of any nationality.
Level of Study: Postgraduate, Research
Type: Scholarship
Value: £4,500
Length of Study: Up to 2 years
Closing Date: March 13th

For further information contact:

Website: www.lac.ox.ac.uk/prospective_students/lorem_ipsum_dolor_sit_amet3/funding

Law, Faculty of: Commercial Bar

Subjects: Law.
Purpose: To assist graduate students with fees.
Eligibility: Open to all gradutes.
Level of Study: Research
Value: £7,500
Length of Study: 1 year
Closing Date: June 20th

For further information contact:

Website: http://denning.law.ox.ac.uk/postgraduate/scholarships.shtml

Law, Faculty of: Graduate Assistance Fund
Subjects: Legal studies and law.
Purpose: To assist graduate students with fees.
Eligibility: Open to all.
Level of Study: Postgraduate, Research
Type: Funding support
Value: Up to £7,500
Length of Study: 1 year
Closing Date: June 20th

For further information contact:

Website: http://denning.law.ox.ac.uk/postgraduate/scholarships.shtml

Law, Faculty of: Linklaters Scholarship
Subjects: Law.
Purpose: To assist graduate students with fees.
Eligibility: Open to all.
Level of Study: Postgraduate
Type: Scholarship
Value: £15,000
Length of Study: 1 year
Closing Date: June 20th

For further information contact:

Website: http://denning.law.ox.ac.uk/postgraduate/scholarships.shtml

Law, Faculty of: Peter Birks Memorial Scholarship
Subjects: Legal studies and law.
Purpose: To assist graduate students with fees.
Eligibility: Open to all.
Level of Study: Postgraduate, Research
Type: Scholarship
Value: £5,000
Length of Study: 1 year
Closing Date: June 20th

For further information contact:

Website: http://denning.law.ox.ac.uk/postgraduate/scholarships.shtml

Law, Faculty of: Winter Williams Studentships
Subjects: Legal studies and law.
Purpose: To assist graduate students with fees.
Eligibility: Open to all.
Level of Study: Postgraduate, Research
Type: Studentship
Value: £7,500
Length of Study: 1 year
Frequency: Annual
Closing Date: June 20th

For further information contact:

Website: http://denning.law.ox.ac.uk/postgraduate/scholarships.shtml

Life and Environmental Sciences: Clarendon Awards - Life Sciences Interface Doctoral Training Centre
Subjects: Mathematics and physical science.
Purpose: To assist graduate students with fees and maintenance.
Eligibility: Open to overseas candidates only.
Level of Study: Research
Type: Award
Value: College and university fees plus maintenance allowance of £12,900
Length of Study: 4 years
Closing Date: November 21st

Additional Information: Candidates are advised to apply by application deadline 1, but if possible applications will also be considered by application deadline 2; please see website.

For further information contact:

Website: www.dtc.ox.ac.uk

Linacre College Canadian National Scholarship
Subjects: All subjects.
Purpose: To enable suitably qualified Canadian nationality students intending to read for a post graduate degree
Eligibility: Canadian nationals only.
Level of Study: Graduate, Postgraduate, Research
Type: Scholarship
Value: £5,000
Length of Study: 1 year
Frequency: May not be available every year
Study Establishment: Linacre College, University of Oxford
Country of Study: United Kingdom
Application Procedure: Applicants must write for details or visit the website www.linacre.ox.ac.uk
Closing Date: 31 March
Contributor: Canadian National

For further information contact:

The College Secretary, Linacre College, Oxford, Oxfordshire, OX1 3JA, England
Website: www.linacre.ox.ac.uk/scholarships

Linacre College Coca-Cola Water Sustainability Scholarships
Subjects: MSc courses in Environmental change and management; water science policy and management; nature, society and environmental policy; biodiversity, conservation and management.
Purpose: To enable graduate students to work in the Oxford University Centre for the environment.
Eligibility: All.
Level of Study: Postgraduate
Type: Scholarship
Value: University and college fees plus £3,183 maintenance
Length of Study: 1 year
Frequency: Dependent on funds available
Study Establishment: Linacre College, University of Oxford
Country of Study: United Kingdom
No. of awards offered: 2
Application Procedure: Application form available from the college secretary Linacre College, Oxford OX1 3JA or from the website: www.linacre.ox.ac.uk
Closing Date: Please see the website
Contributor: The Coca-Cola Foundation

For further information contact:

Linacre college, Oxford, OX1 3JA
Website: www.linacre.ox.ac.uk/Linacre/about-linacre/current-members/scholarships
Contact: The College Secretary

Linacre College Euopean Blaschko Visiting Research Scholarship
Subjects: Pharmacology,Anatomical neuropharmacology.
Purpose: To enable European students to carry out research for 1 year in the department of pharmacology or the MRC anatomical neuropharmacology unit.
Eligibility: EU nationals only.
Level of Study: Postgraduate, Research
Type: Scholarship
Value: College and university visiting student fees; stipend cost of travel from scholar's home country
Length of Study: 2 years
Frequency: Annual
Study Establishment: Linacre College, University of Oxford
Country of Study: United Kingdom
Closing Date: 01 April
Funding: Private

Additional Information: Please contact: Professor A D Smith, Department of Pharmacology, Oxford OX1 3QT info@pharm.ox.ac.uk

For further information contact:

Head of the Department of Pharmacology, Mansfield Road, Oxford, Oxfordshire, OX1 3QT, England
Website: www.linacre.ox.ac.uk/Linacre/about-linacre/current-members/scholarships

Linacre College Mary Blaschko Graduate Scholarship

Subjects: Arts & Humanities research degrees.
Purpose: To enable students pursue a research degree in the arts and humanities
Eligibility: Open to all.
Level of Study: Research
Type: Scholarship
Value: College fees
Length of Study: Up to 2 years
Frequency: Annual, May not be available every year
Study Establishment: Linacre College, University of Oxford
Country of Study: United Kingdom
No. of awards offered: 3
Application Procedure: Applicants must write for details. Forms are also available from www.linacre.ox.ac.uk
Closing Date: 31 January
Funding: Private

For further information contact:

Tutor for Admissions, Linacre College, St Cross Road, Oxford, Oxfordshire, OX1 3JA, England
Website: www.linacre.ox.ac.uk/scholarships

Linacre College Norman and Ivy Lloyd Scholarship

Subjects: MSc Environmental change and management.
Purpose: To enable a student from developing Commonwealth countries to undertake an MSc course in Environmental change and management.
Eligibility: Must be from a developing Commonwealth country.
Level of Study: Postgraduate
Type: Scholarship
Value: University fees college fees and maintenance allowance
Length of Study: 1 year
Frequency: Annual
Study Establishment: Linacre College, University of Oxford
Country of Study: United Kingdom
No. of awards offered: Varies
Application Procedure: Applicants must write for details.No separate application required. This scholarship will be linked to a Commonwealth Shared Scholarship or University Clarendon award. Please see the College's website for details.
Closing Date: Please write for details
Funding: Private

For further information contact:

Environmental Change Institute, 5 Mansfield Road, Oxford, Oxfordshire, OX1 3TB, England
Website: www.linacre.ox.ac.uk/scholarships
Contact: Dr J Boardman

Linacre College: A.J Hosier Studentship

Subjects: Husbandry; Agricultural Economics or Statistics; Applied Agricultural Science.
Purpose: To fund graduate study.
Eligibility: UK citizens who are Honours graduates of a UK University.
Level of Study: Postgraduate, Research
Type: Studentship
Value: Up to £4,000
Length of Study: 1 year
Study Establishment: Linacre College, University of Oxford
Country of Study: United Kingdom
No. of awards offered: Varies
Application Procedure: Applicants must contact the College Secretary for further details.

Closing Date: 30 May
Additional Information: UK citizens who are Honours graduates of a UK University

For further information contact:

Linacre College, Oxford, Oxfordshire, OX1 3JA, England
Website: www.linacre.ox.ac.uk/scholarships
Contact: College Secretary

Linacre College: Applied Materials DPhil Scholarship

Subjects: Research degree in either materials or environment science.
Purpose: To assist graduate students with fees.
Eligibility: Open to all.
Level of Study: Research
Type: Scholarship
Value: £6,500
Length of Study: Up to 3 years

For further information contact:

Website: www.linacre.ox.ac.uk/scholarships

Linacre College: Applied Materials MSc Scholarship

Subjects: Environmental change and management.
Purpose: To assist graduate students with fees and a living allowance.
Eligibility: Open to all.
Level of Study: Postgraduate
Type: Scholarship
Length of Study: 1 year

For further information contact:

School of Geography, Oxford, OUCE, OX1 3QY
Email: enquiries@ouce.ox.ac.uk
Contact: Director of Graduate Studies

Linacre College: EPA Cephalosporin Scholarship

Subjects: Biological, medical and chemical sciences.
Purpose: To assist graduate students with fees.
Eligibility: Open to all graduate students.
Level of Study: Postgraduate, Research
Type: Scholarship
Value: College fees
Length of Study: Up to 2 years depending on fee liability
No. of awards offered: 1

For further information contact:

Sir William Dunn School of Pathology, Oxford, OX1 3RE
Email: administration@path.ox.ac.uk
Website: www.linacre.ox.ac.uk/Linacre/about-linacre/current-members/scholarships
Contact: Director of Graduate Studies

Linacre College: Hitachi Chemical Europe Scholarship

Subjects: Environmental change and management.
Purpose: To assist graduate students with fees and a living allowance.
Eligibility: Open to all.
Level of Study: Postgraduate
Type: Scholarship
Value: College fees + £1,000
Length of Study: 1 year
Closing Date: March 14th
Additional Information: Preference given to applicant from China or Central/South America.

For further information contact:

School of Geography, OUCE, Oxford,
Email: enquiries@ouce.ox.ac.uk
Website: www.linacre.ox.ac.uk/Linacre/about-linacre/current-members/scholarships
Contact: Director of Graduate Studies

Linacre College: Linacre Rausing Scholarship

Subjects: English research.
Purpose: To assist EU nationals only pursue a degree in English research.
Eligibility: EU nationals only.
Level of Study: Postgraduate
Type: Scholarship
Value: £4,000
Length of Study: Up to 3 years
Frequency: Annual, Varies, not available every year
Study Establishment: Linacre College, University of Oxford
Country of Study: United Kingdom
No. of awards offered: 2
Application Procedure: No separate application required. Please contact: Director of Graduate Studies, English Faculty, Oxford OX1 3UQ english.office@ell.ox.ac.uk.

For further information contact:

Website: www.linacre.ox.ac.uk

Linares-Rivas

Subjects: All subjects.
Purpose: To assist graduate students with fees and living allowance.
Eligibility: Open to new graduate students from Spain. Candidates should normally either be studying or recently graduated from a Spanish university.
Level of Study: Postgraduate, Research
Type: Scholarship
Value: University and college fees; grant towards living costs
Length of Study: 1 year
No. of awards offered: 1
Closing Date: January 23rd

For further information contact:

Website: www.admin.ox.ac.uk/studentfunding/scholarship_profiles/LinaresRiv.shtml

Lincoln College Keith Murray Senior Scholarship

Subjects: All subjects.
Purpose: To permit students from outside the UK to undertake postgraduate study at Oxford University.
Eligibility: All non-EU nationals.
Level of Study: Doctorate, Postgraduate, Research
Type: Scholarship
Value: All university and college fees plus a substantial contribution towards living expenses
Length of Study: 2 years, with possibility of renewal for a third year
Frequency: Every 2 years
Study Establishment: Lincoln College, University of Oxford
Country of Study: United Kingdom
No. of awards offered: 1
Application Procedure: Applicants must write for details.
Closing Date: 12 January
Funding: Private
Additional Information: Applicants must make a simultaneous application to ORS (see central awards table). Candidates will be chosen on basis of academic merit and potential for active contribution to college life.

For further information contact:

The Rector's Office, Lincoln College, Oxford, Oxfordshire, OX1 3DR, England
Website: www.lincoln.ox.ac.uk/content/view/678/85/

Lincoln College Sloane Robinson Foundation Graduate Awards

Subjects: All subjects.
Purpose: To fund those intending to pursue research programmes at Oxford.
Eligibility: Open to all.
Level of Study: Doctorate, Graduate, MBA
Value: £5,000
Length of Study: One year, with the possibility of renewal on applying
Frequency: Annual

Study Establishment: Lincoln College, University of Oxford
Country of Study: United Kingdom
No. of awards offered: 4
Application Procedure: Information will be made available when the college makes a conditional offer to candidates. Please see website www.lincoln.ox.ac.uk for further details
Closing Date: August 1st
Funding: Foundation
Additional Information: Successful candidates must show evidence of both academic merit and financial need.

For further information contact:

Oxford, OX1 3DR
Website: www.lincoln.ox.ac.uk/content/view/678/85/
Contact: Admissions Office, Lincoln College

Lincoln College: Polonsky Foundation Grants

Subjects: All subjects.
Purpose: To financially assist meritorious student.
Eligibility: All non-EU nationals.
Level of Study: Postgraduate
Type: Grant
Value: £4,700
Length of Study: One year, with the possibility of re-application for renewal
Frequency: Annual
No. of awards offered: 3
Closing Date: 01 August

For further information contact:

Website: www.lincoln.ox.ac.uk/content/view/678/85/

Magdalen College: Hichens MBA/MFE Awards

Subjects: Management.
Purpose: To assist graduate students with accomodation.
Eligibility: Open to all.
Level of Study: MBA, Postgraduate
Type: Award
Value: Free accommodation in college for the year
Length of Study: 1 year
Frequency: Annual
No. of awards offered: 3

For further information contact:

Website: www.magd.ox.ac.uk/admissions_graduate/scholarships.shtml

Magellan Prize with St Catherines College

Subjects: Language, literature, culture or history of the Portuguese-speaking world.
Purpose: To study the language, literature, culture or history of the Portuguese-speaking world.
Eligibility: Open to graduates of literature.
Level of Study: Postgraduate, Research
Type: Prize
Value: £3,000 plus a non-stipendiary graduate scholarship at St Catherines College
Length of Study: 1 year
Closing Date: March 14th
Additional Information: The award holder will be expected to move to St Catherines College if they are not already placed there.

For further information contact:

Website: www.mod-langs.ox.ac.uk/prizes/index.php#Magellan

Mansfield College: Elfan Rees Scholarship

Subjects: Theology.
Purpose: To commencing studies towards a higher degree in the field of theology.
Level of Study: Postdoctorate, Postgraduate
Type: Scholarship
Value: £3,000
Length of Study: 2 years
Frequency: Once in every 4 years

Closing Date: March 13th

For further information contact:

Website: www.mansfield.ox.ac.uk/prospective/studying/graduate-studies/scholarships-and-awards.html

Mathematical Institute: Clarendon Scholarships

Subjects: Mathematics.
Purpose: To assist graduate students with fees and a living allowance.
Eligibility: Open to overseas candidates only.
Level of Study: Research
Type: Scholarships
Value: University and college fees paid, plus a minimum of £12,900 living expenses per year
Length of Study: 3 years
Closing Date: November 21st
Additional Information: Around 3 awards usually made. Candidates are advised to apply by application deadline 1, but if possible applications will also be considered by application deadline 2; please see website.

For further information contact:

Website: www.maths.ox.ac.uk/prospective-students/graduate/procedures/non-epsrc

Mathematical Institute: EPSRC Doctoral Training Grant Studentships

Subjects: Mathematics.
Purpose: To assist graduate students with fees and maintenance.
Eligibility: Open to home/EU candidates with DPhil.
Level of Study: Research
Type: Studentship
Value: University and college fees paid. UK residents also receive a maintenance allowance of at least £12,900 per year
Length of Study: 3.5 years
No. of awards offered: 12
Additional Information: An EU national who has studied for an undergraduate degree at a UK university during the 3 years leading up to the application may be classed as a UK resident. Closing date as advertised on departmental website.

For further information contact:

Website: www.maths.ox.ac.uk/prospective-students/graduate/procedures/epsrc

Mathematical Institute: Research Project Studentships and EPSRC CASE Studentships

Subjects: Mathematics.
Purpose: To assist graduate students with fees and maintenance.
Eligibility: Varies.
Level of Study: Research
Type: Studentship
Value: Usually university and college fees paid, plus a minimum of £12,900 per year maintenance allowance
Length of Study: 3.5 years
Additional Information: These awards are individually advertised on the departmental website. Closing date in line with departmental deadlines.

For further information contact:

Website: www.maths.ox.ac.uk

Merdeka Scholarships

Subjects: Economics, finance, investment, law and actuarial science.
Purpose: To support those wishing to undertake postgraduate study at the University of Oxford.
Eligibility: Open to candidates who must be Malaysian citizens.
Level of Study: Postgraduate, Research
Type: Scholarships
Value: Tuition and college fees; grant for living expenses at UK Research Council rate
Length of Study: One year, renewable annually

Closing Date: January 12th

For further information contact:

Website: www.oxcis.ac.uk/merdeka

Merton College Greendale Scholarship

Subjects: All subjects.
Purpose: To enable a Swiss national or a resident who is a graduate of a Swiss university to study at Oxford.
Eligibility: Only open to Swiss nationals or residents.
Level of Study: Postgraduate, Research
Type: Scholarship
Value: University and college fees and grant for living costs
Length of Study: Up to 3 years
Frequency: Annual
Study Establishment: Merton College, University of Oxford
Country of Study: United Kingdom
No. of awards offered: 1
Application Procedure: Further particulars and application forms are available from the Merton College website www.merton.ox.ac.uk/vacancies/index.htm or from the Secretary for Graduates.
Closing Date: August 31st
Funding: Private

For further information contact:

Merton College, Oxford, Oxfordshire, OX1 4JD, England
Email: julie.gerhardi@merton.ox.ac.uk
Website: www.merton.ox.ac.uk/graduateadmissions/application.shtml#gs
Contact: College Admissions Officer

Merton College Merton Domus B Scholarships

Subjects: All for which the College normally considers.
Purpose: To enable UK/EU students pursue studies at Merton College.
Eligibility: Home/EU applicants.
Level of Study: Research, Graduate, Postgraduate
Type: Scholarship
Value: All fees plus maintenance award
Length of Study: Up to 4 years
Frequency: Annual
Study Establishment: Merton College, University of Oxford
Country of Study: United Kingdom
No. of awards offered: 2
Application Procedure: Further particulars and application forms are available from the Merton College website www.merton.ox.ac.uk/vacancies/index.htm or from the Secretary for Graduates.
Closing Date: August 28

For further information contact:

Merton College, Oxford, Oxfordshire, OX1 4JD, England
Email: julie.gerhardig@merton.ox.ac.uk
Website: www.merton.ox.ac.uk/vacancies/index.shtml
Contact: Admissions Office

Merton College: Four Merton Domus A Joint Scholarships with the University's Clarendon Fund

Subjects: All subjects.
Purpose: To assist graduate students with fees.
Eligibility: Open to all.
Level of Study: Postgraduate
Type: Scholarship
Value: Maintenance award from the college (around £13,290 for 2009–2010)
Frequency: Annual
Closing Date: January 23rd

Museveni Scholarship

Subjects: Economics.
Purpose: To support Africans wishing to pursue economic research at the Oxford University for the degree of DPhil.
Eligibility: Open to African students.
Level of Study: Research
Type: Scholarship

Value: £10,000
Length of Study: Up to 3 years
Additional Information: The proposed DPhil topic must be relevant to African economies.

For further information contact:

Website: www.csae.ox.ac.uk/scholarships/Museveni/Mscholar.html

NERC Studentships in Earth Sciences
Subjects: Earth sciences.
Purpose: To assist graduate students with fees and maintenance.
Eligibility: Open to home or EU candidates usually with a 2.1 degree or higher.
Level of Study: Research
Type: Studentship
Value: University and college fees paid. Home students also receive a maintenance allowance of £12,500 per year
Length of Study: Normally 3 years, which can be extended in some cases
Additional Information: The Department will have a number of NERC studentships, to be confirmed. An EU national who has studied for an undergraduate degree at a UK university during the 3 years leading up to the application may be classed as a UK resident.

For further information contact:

Website: www.earth.ox.ac.uk/research/postgradeg.htm

New College: 1379 Society Awards
Subjects: All subjects.
Purpose: To assist graduate students with fees.
Eligibility: Open to all candidates, but preference for students studying for a research degree.
Level of Study: Postgraduate, Research
Type: Award
Value: Up to £10,000
Length of Study: Duration of fee liability
No. of awards offered: 1

For further information contact:

Website: www.new.ox.ac.uk/Prospective_Students/Graduate_Entry/Awards.php

New College: Brandon Fradd Scholarship
Subjects: All subjects.
Purpose: To assist graduate students with fees.
Eligibility: Open to all.
Level of Study: Postgraduate, Research
Type: Scholarship
Value: £5,000 per year
Length of Study: Up to 3 years

New College: Clarendon Scholarship
Purpose: To assist graduate students with fees and a living allowance.
Eligibility: Open to overseas candidates.
Type: Scholarship
Value: £5,000 a year towards a graduate student's maintenance costs
Closing Date: January 23rd

For further information contact:

Website: www.new.ox.ac.uk/Prospective_Students/Graduate_Entry/Awards.php

New College: Peter Smart Scholarship
Subjects: All subjects.
Purpose: To assist graduate students with fees.
Eligibility: Open to all, but preference for students studying for a research degree.
Level of Study: Postgraduate, Research
Type: Scholarship
Value: £5,000 per year

New College: Ralph Oppenheimer Scholarship

Subjects: English.
Purpose: To assist graduate students with fees.
Eligibility: Open to all.
Level of Study: Postgraduate, Research
Type: Scholarship
Value: £5,000 per year
Length of Study: Duration of fee liability

New College: Reynolds Scholarship
Subjects: History or modern languages.
Purpose: To assist graduate students with fees and a living allowance.
Eligibility: Open to all.
Level of Study: Postgraduate
Type: Scholarship
Value: Home/EU fees plus equivalent of an AHRC studentship
Length of Study: 1 year

For further information contact:

Website: www.new.ox.ac.uk/Prospective_Students/Graduate_Entry/Awards.php

New College: Stewart Millman Scholarship
Subjects: Management research.
Purpose: To assist students with research funds/travel grants for a degree in MSc or DPhil in Management Research.
Eligibility: Open to all.
Level of Study: Doctorate, Postgraduate, Research
Type: Scholarship
Value: £15,000 per year
Length of Study: Duration of fee liability
Additional Information: Closing date to be confirmed - please contact the college for more information.

New College: Wykeham Scholarship
Subjects: History and biochemistry/plant sciences.
Purpose: To assist students with research funds and travel.
Eligibility: Open to home/EU students.
Level of Study: Postgraduate, Research
Value: College fee plus £6,500 per year (College fee plus half a standard research council maintenance award; other half to be matched by the relevant faculty)
Length of Study: Duration of fee liability
No. of awards offered: 2
Application Procedure: Applicants can download an application form from the website www.new.ox.ac.uk/Prospective_Students/Graduate_Entry/Awards.php and also send a letter explaining their suitability.
Additional Information: Closing date to be confirmed - please contact the college for more information.

For further information contact:

Website: www.new.ox.ac.uk/Prospective_Students/Graduate_Entry/Awards.php

Noon Foundation/OSI/Chevening/Oxford Scholarships
Subjects: All subjects.
Purpose: To support scholars from Pakistan to study at leading universities in the United Kingdom.
Eligibility: Open to new graduate students from Pakistan (normally those who have not already studied for a degree outside Pakistan).
Level of Study: Postgraduate, Research
Type: Scholarships
Value: Full or partial awards to cover university and college fees and a full grant for living costs
Length of Study: Up to 3 years
Closing Date: January 23rd

For further information contact:

Website: www.admin.ox.ac.uk/studentfunding/scholarship_profiles/Noon.shtml

Nuffield College: JK Swire Memorial Scholarship
Subjects: Social sciences.
Purpose: To assist students in payment of university fees for their studies.

Eligibility: Open to nationals of Hong Kong and China.
Level of Study: Postgraduate, Research
Type: Scholarship
Value: University and college fees and maintenance allowance
Length of Study: Up to 4 years
No. of awards offered: Varies
Application Procedure: There is no separate application procedure. Students who have been admitted will automatically be considered for the scholarship grant.
Additional Information: Closing date to be confirmed - please contact the college for more information.

For further information contact:

Website: www.nuffield.ox.ac.uk/general/prospectus/funding.aspx

Nuffield College: Nuffield Sociology Studentships

Subjects: Sociology.
Purpose: To assist doctoral students with their university and their college fees.
Eligibility: Open to doctoral students.
Level of Study: Doctorate, Research
Type: Studentship
Value: University fees (at home/EU rate), college fees and maintenance allowance up to £9,000
Length of Study: Up to 3 years
Frequency: Annual
No. of awards offered: Up to 2
Application Procedure: There is separate application procedure. For details please see the website www.nuffield.ox.ac.uk/general/prospectus/funding.aspx.
Additional Information: Not available to Oxford students transferring from a Masters course.

For further information contact:

Website: www.nuffield.ox.ac.uk/general/prospectus/funding.aspx

Nuffield College: Nuffield Studentships

Subjects: Social sciences.
Purpose: To assist students in the payment of fees and provide support for maintenance.
Eligibility: Open to all.
Level of Study: Postgraduate, Research
Type: Studentship
Value: Up to £15,500 (home/EU students) Up to £22,000 (overseas students)
Length of Study: Up to 4 years
No. of awards offered: varies
Application Procedure: There is no separate application procedure. For further details please see the website www.nuffield.ox.ac.uk/general/prospectus/funding.aspx.

For further information contact:

Website: www.nuffield.ox.ac.uk/general/prospectus/funding.aspx

Oriel College: Sir Walter Raleigh Scholarship

Subjects: Environmental change and management.
Purpose: To assist a student studying at the Environmental Change Institute for an MSc degree in Environmental Change and Management.
Eligibility: Open to first-year students only.
Level of Study: Postgraduate
Type: Scholarship
Value: £4,000
Length of Study: 1 year
Frequency: Annual
No. of awards offered: 1
Application Procedure: Applicants can download an application form from the website www.ox.ac.uk/admissions/index.html or obtain one from the Academic Office or the Environmental Change Institute.
Closing Date: March 31st
Additional Information: The successful applicant will be expected to transfer their application to Oriel College if they have already been accepted by another College. Please contact: Academic Assistant (Admissions) (admissions@oriel.ox.ac.uk).

ORISHA (Oxford Research in the Scholarship and Humanities of Africa) Studentship

Subjects: African studies, social and cultural anthropology, archaeology, development studies, history, human geography, literature, politics, international relations and religious studies.
Purpose: To assist graduate students with fees.
Eligibility: Open to new and existing students; also DPhil students who have completed fee liability but have run out of support to cover other costs. Successful candidate (if not already a member of an Oxford College) may be offered a place at St Antony's or St Cross.
Level of Study: Postgraduate, Research
Type: Studentship
Value: University fees at home rate plus grant for living costs. Exceptionally, supplement to cover (partially or fully) the difference between home and overseas fees
Length of Study: Up to 2 years, possible extension for third or fourth year
Closing Date: March 13th

For further information contact:

Website: www.africanstudies.ox.ac.uk/prospective_students/scholarships/orisha

Orthopaedic Surgery: Overseas Bursary

Subjects: Orthopaedic surgery.
Purpose: To assist graduate students with fees.
Eligibility: Open to medical graduates.
Level of Study: Research
Type: Bursary
Value: This award funds the difference between home/EU and overseas rate university fees
Length of Study: 2 or 3 years
Additional Information: Awarded to outstanding overseas students who wish to undertake Research by MSc or Dphil. Closing date to be confirmed - please contact the department for more information.

OSI/FCO Chevening Scholarships

Subjects: Humanities, social sciences and environmental sciences.
Purpose: To assist graduate students with fees and living allowance.
Eligibility: Open to new graduate students from Albania, Armenia, Belarus, Bosnia, Croatia, Georgia, Kazakhstan, Kyrgyzstan, Macedonia, Moldova, Russia, Serbia, Ukraine, Uzbekistan.
Level of Study: Postgraduate
Type: Scholarships
Value: University and college fees, travel to/from Oxford and grant for living costs
Length of Study: 1 year
No. of awards offered: Up to 15
Closing Date: Januray 23rd
Additional Information: One-year Master's degrees or research as a visiting student only.

For further information contact:

Website: www.admin.ox.ac.uk/studentfunding/scholarship_profiles/OSIFCOChev.shtml

Overseas Research Scheme (ORS) Awards

Subjects: All subjects.
Purpose: To help outstanding overseas research students to take up places to study at British universities.
Eligibility: Open to graduate students liable to pay university fees at overseas rate. Open to new research students or those going into their second year. Eligible degrees are: DPhil, MPhil with a thesis, MLitt and some MSt courses.
Level of Study: Postgraduate, Research
Type: Award
Value: Difference between UK/EU and overseas university fee
Length of Study: Up to 3 years
Closing Date: January 23rd
Additional Information: Please note that HEFCE recently announced that it would be phasing out ORS funding from 2009/2010: www.hefce.ac.uk/pubs/circlets/2008/cl18_08/. It is therefore highly unlikely that many new awards will be available.

For further information contact:

Website: www.admin.ox.ac.uk/studentfunding/scholarship_profiles/ ORS.shtml

Oxford Australia Fund Scholarships (James Fairfax and College-Linked Awards)
Subjects: All subjects.
Purpose: To assist graduate students with fees and living allowance.
Eligibility: Open to new students from Australia. Candidates should normally be under the age of 30 on January 1st in the year in which the scholarship is to be taken up. Candidates must have a Bachelor's degree with first or upper second class honours or equivalent from a recognised university.
Level of Study: Postgraduate, Research
Type: Scholarships
Value: Varies by scheme but a minimum of AUD$12,000 per year towards living expenses
Length of Study: Up to 3 years
Closing Date: January 23rd

For further information contact:

Website: www.admin.ox.ac.uk/studentfunding/scholarship_profiles/ OxfordAus.shtml

Oxford Centre for Islamic Studies (OCIS) Scholarship
Subjects: Islamic studies.
Purpose: To assist graduate students with fees and living allowance.
Eligibility: Open to UK students from Muslim communities and students from developing countries in Asia and Africa (exact countries to be confirmed).
Level of Study: Postgraduate, Research
Type: Scholarship
Value: University and college fees; full grant for living costs
Length of Study: Period of fee liability
Closing Date: January 23rd

For further information contact:

Website: www.admin.ox.ac.uk/studentfunding/scholarship_profiles/ index.shtml

Oxford Internet Institute Scholarship
Subjects: Information, communication and social sciences.
Purpose: To assist graduate students with fees.
Eligibility: Open to all.
Level of Study: Postgraduate, Research
Type: Scholarship
Value: £11,206
Length of Study: 1 year

For further information contact:

Website: www.oii.ox.ac.uk/teaching/dphil/apply.cfm

Oxford Kobe Scholarships
Subjects: All subjects.
Purpose: To enable Japanese graduate students to study at Oxford.
Eligibility: Open to new graduate students with Japanese citizenship.
Level of Study: Postgraduate, Research
Type: Scholarships
Value: University and college fees, full grant for living costs and return air travel to/from UK
Length of Study: Up to 3 years
Closing Date: January 23rd

For further information contact:

Website: www.admin.ox.ac.uk/studentfunding/scholarship_profiles/ OxfordKobe.shtml

Oxford Marshall Scholarships
Subjects: All subjects.
Purpose: To assist graduate students with fees and living allowance.
Eligibility: Open to new graduate students with US citizenship.
Level of Study: Postgraduate, Research
Type: Scholarships

Value: University and college fees, grant for living costs, travel and some additional expenses
Length of Study: 2 years, possibly 3
Closing Date: October 1st

For further information contact:

Website: www.marshallscholarship.org

Pathology (William Dunn School): Departmental Studentships
Subjects: Pathology.
Purpose: To assist graduate students with fees and travel costs.
Eligibility: Open to all candidates.
Level of Study: Research
Type: Studentship
Value: Fees at home/EU rate, research and travel costs (£1,300 per year), and stipend (£15,000 per year)
Length of Study: 4 years
Closing Date: January 9th

For further information contact:

Website: www.path.ox.ac.uk

Pembroke College: Gordon Aldrick Scholarship
Subjects: Chinese cultural studies.
Purpose: To assist scholars in Chinese cultural studies.
Eligibility: Open to candidates beginning a two or three-year research degree at Oxford.
Level of Study: Research
Type: Scholarship
Value: £3,000 per year
Length of Study: Tenable for up to three years whilst the recipient is liable to pay University and College fees. Automatically renewed each year if satisfactory academic progess is made
Frequency: Annual
No. of awards offered: 1
Application Procedure: Intending candidates should apply in Section L of the Oxford University graduate application form or notify the Admissions & Access Officer at Pembroke.
Closing Date: May 1st

For further information contact:

Website: www.pmb.ox.ac.uk/Students/Graduate_Students/ Scholarships_Awards/Graduate_Scholarships.php

Pembroke College: Pembroke Graduate Scholarships
Subjects: Any, but preferred subjects are history, theology, politics or biochemistry.
Purpose: To assist UK, EU or overseas Master's degree applicants progressing to a research degree.
Eligibility: Open to candidates beginning a two or three-year research degree at Oxford.
Level of Study: Research
Type: Scholarships
Value: £4,500 per year
Length of Study: Tenable for up to 3 years whilst the recipient is liable to pay university and college fees. Automatically renewed each year if satisfactory academic progess being made
No. of awards offered: 3
Application Procedure: Intending candidates should apply in Section L of the Oxford University graduate application form or notify the Admissions & Access Officer at Pembroke.
Closing Date: May 1st

For further information contact:

Website: www.pmb.ox.ac.uk/Students/Graduate_Students/ Scholarships_Awards/Graduate_Scholarships.php

Pembroke College: Stanley Ho Scholarship
Subjects: Chinese studies.
Purpose: To assist applicants who are eligible to pay university and college fees and who have been accepted to read a research degree in Oxford University in Pembroke college.

Eligibility: Open to candidates beginning a two or three-year research degree at Oxford.
Level of Study: Research
Type: Scholarship
Value: £9,000 per year
Length of Study: Tenable for up to 3 years whilst the recipient is liable to pay university and college fees. Automatically renewed each year if satisfactory academic progess being made
No. of awards offered: 1
Application Procedure: Intending candidates should apply in Section L of the Oxford University graduate application form or notify the Admissions & Access Officer at Pembroke.
Closing Date: May 1st

For further information contact:

Website: www.pmb.ox.ac.uk/Students/Graduate_Students/Scholarships_Awards/Graduate_Scholarships.php

Pembroke College: TEPCO Scholarship

Subjects: Japanese studies.
Purpose: To assist applicants in Japanese studies as an extension to their postdoctoral awards.
Eligibility: Open to candidates beginning a two or three-year research degree at Oxford.
Level of Study: Research
Type: Scholarship
Value: £3,000 per year
Length of Study: Tenable for up to 3 years whilst the recipient is liable to pay university and college fees. Automatically renewed each year if satisfactory academic progess being made
No. of awards offered: 1
Application Procedure: Intending candidates should apply in Section L of the Oxford University graduate application form or notify the Admissions & Access Officer at Pembroke.
Closing Date: May 1st

For further information contact:

Website: www.pmb.ox.ac.uk/Students/Graduate_Students/Scholarships_Awards/Graduate_Scholarships.php

Pembroke Venezuela Scholarship

Subjects: Medical or biological sciences.
Purpose: To assist graduates of Venezuelan nationality undertaking postgraduate study at Oxford University, with preference for graduates studying medical or biological sciences.
Level of Study: Research
Type: Scholarship
Value: £12,000 per year
Length of Study: Up to 3 years
No. of awards offered: 1
Application Procedure: Intending candidates should apply in Section L of the Oxford University graduate application form or notify the Admissions & Access Officer at Pembroke.
Closing Date: May 1st

For further information contact:

Website: www.pmb.ox.ac.uk/Students/Graduate_Students/Scholarships_Awards/Graduate_Scholarships.php

Pharmacology: BBSRC DPhil Studentship

Subjects: Pharmacology.
Purpose: To embark on a career in the pharmaceutical industry as well as in academic research.
Eligibility: Open to all home/EU candidates.
Level of Study: Research
Type: Studentship
Value: Home students: Full university and college fees, maintenance allowance, support with travel to conferences. EU students: full fees only
Length of Study: 3 years
Closing Date: April 30th

For further information contact:

Website: www.pharm.ox.ac.uk/jobvacancies/studentship

Pharmacology: BBSRC MSc Studentship

Subjects: Pharmacology.
Purpose: To embark on a career in the pharmaceutical industry as well as in academic research.
Eligibility: Open to all home/EU candidates.
Level of Study: Postgraduate
Type: Studentship
Value: Home students: Full university and college fees, maintenance allowance, support with travel to conferences. EU students: full fees only
Length of Study: 1 year
Closing Date: April 30th

For further information contact:

Website: www.pharm.ox.ac.uk/jobvacancies/bbsrcstudentship

Pharmacology: CRUK Scholarship in Medicinal Chemistry

Subjects: Medicinal chemistry.
Purpose: To assist graduate students with fees and maintenance.
Eligibility: Open to all home/EU candidates for the MSc Medicinal chemistry.
Level of Study: Postgraduate
Type: Scholarship
Value: Home students: Full university and college fees, maintenance allowance, support with travel to conferences. EU students: full fees only
Length of Study: 4 years (1 year MSc and 3 years DPhil)
Closing Date: April 30th
Additional Information: This scholarship supports students taking the MSC and then subsequent DPhil in the Medicinal chemistry course.

For further information contact:

Website: www.pharm.ox.ac.uk/jobvacancies/MedChem

Pharmacology: Departmental Scholarship

Subjects: Pharmacology.
Purpose: To assist graduate students with fees and maintenance.
Eligibility: Open to all candidates.
Level of Study: Research
Type: Scholarship
Value: Home students: Full university and college fees, maintenance allowance. EU students: full fees only
Length of Study: 3 years
Closing Date: April 30th

For further information contact:

Website: www.pharm.ox.ac.uk/jobvacancies/studentship

Physics: Joint Department-College Scholarships

Subjects: Physics.
Purpose: To assist graduate students with fees and maintenance.
Eligibility: Open to UK/EU candidates with a DPhil.
Level of Study: Research
Type: Scholarships
Value: University and college fees, plus a minimum of £12,940 per year maintenance allowance
Length of Study: Normally 3 years, which can be extended in some cases
Additional Information: Typically only one or two across the whole physics department. Closing date to be confirmed - please contact the department for more information.

For further information contact:

Website: www.physics.ox.ac.uk/admissions/postgrad.htm

Physics: NERC Studentships in Atmospheric Physics

Subjects: Atmospheric, oceanic and planetary physics.
Purpose: To assist graduate students with fees and maintenance.
Eligibility: Open to UK/EU candidates with a DPhil only;
EU students are eligible for fees only unless a first degree was taken in the UK in the period immediately prior to the

award, in which case a maintenance allowance may be included.
Level of Study: Research
Type: Studentship
Value: University and college fees, plus a minimum of £12,940 per year maintenance allowance
Length of Study: Normally 3 years with a possible further extension of up to 1 year
Closing Date: January 23rd
Additional Information: Typically we award 3 or 4 studentships each year, but this number depends on the annual funding announcement made by the sponsors.

For further information contact:

Website: www.physics.ox.ac.uk/admissions/postgrad.htm

Pirie-Reid Scholarship

Subjects: All subjects.
Purpose: To benefit Scottish students coming to Oxford.
Eligibility: Open to candidates domiciled or educated in Scotland. Preference is given to candidates who have not studied at Oxford before.
Level of Study: Postgraduate, Research
Type: Scholarship
Value: University and college fees, full grant for living costs. Partial grants are also available
Length of Study: Period of fee liability
Closing Date: January 23rd

For further information contact:

Website: www.admin.ox.ac.uk/studentfunding/scholarship_profiles/piriereid.shtml

Plant Sciences: BBSRC DTA Studentships in Plant Sciences

Subjects: Biochemistry and cell biology, comparative developmental genetics, and evolution, ecology and systematics.
Purpose: To assist graduate students with fees and maintenance.
Eligibility: Open to home/EU candidates only. EU students are eligible for fees only.
Level of Study: Research
Type: Studentship
Value: University and college fees, plus a minimum of £12,900 maintenance allowance per year
Length of Study: 3 or 4 years depending on research area
Closing Date: January 23rd
Additional Information: An EU national who has studied for an undergraduate degree at a UK university during the 3 years leading up to the application will be classed as a UK resident.

For further information contact:

Website: http://dps.plants.ox.ac.uk/plants/students/postgraduates/default.aspx

Plant Sciences: Christopher Welch Scholarship

Subjects: Biological sciences.
Purpose: To assist graduate students with fees and maintenance.
Eligibility: Open to all.
Level of Study: Research
Type: Scholarship
Value: University and college fees (at the rate for "Home" students), plus £13,500 maintenance allowance per year
Length of Study: 2 years, but may be extended for a third year. Under special circumstances, the award may be extended for an extra 6 months
Closing Date: January 23rd

For further information contact:

Website: http://dps.plants.ox.ac.uk/plants/students/postgraduates/default.aspx

Plant Sciences: Clarendon Scholarship

Subjects: Biochemistry and cell biology, comparative developmental genetics, and evolution, ecology and systematics.

Purpose: To assist graduate students with fees and maintenance.
Eligibility: Open to overseas candidates only.
Level of Study: Research
Type: Scholarship
Value: University and college fees, plus a minimum of £12,900 maintenance allowance per year
Length of Study: 3 years
Closing Date: November 21st
Additional Information: Candidates are advised to apply by application deadline 1, but if possible applications will also be considered by application deadline 2.

For further information contact:

Website: http://dps.plants.ox.ac.uk/plants/students/postgraduates/default.aspx

Plant Sciences: Newton Abraham Scholarship

Subjects: Biological sciences.
Purpose: To assist graduate students with fees and maintenance.
Eligibility: Open to all.
Level of Study: Research
Type: Scholarship
Value: University and college fees at the home student rate, plus £12,900 per year maintenance allowance
Length of Study: 3 years. Under special circumstances, the award may be extended for an extra 6 months
Closing Date: March 13th

For further information contact:

Website: http://dps.plants.ox.ac.uk/plants/students/postgraduates/default.aspx

Politics and International Relations: ESRC Open Competition Nomination

Subjects: Politics and international relations.
Purpose: To assist graduate students with fees and maintenance.
Eligibility: Open to DPhil candidates only.
Level of Study: Research
Type: Studentship
Value: College fees, around £3,300 towards university fee. Home students will receive maintenance allowance
Length of Study: 3 years for applicants who apply for the DPhil directly. 4 years for applicants who approach the doctorate via an MPhil or an MSc degree
Closing Date: May 1st

For further information contact:

Website: www.politics.ox.ac.uk/prospective/grad/funding.asp#esrc_and_ahrc

Politics and International Relations: ESRC Quota Award Studentships

Subjects: Politics and international relations.
Purpose: To assist graduate students with fees and maintenance.
Eligibility: Open to DPhil candidates only.
Level of Study: Research
Type: Studentship
Value: College fees, around £3,300 towards university fee. Home students will receive maintenance allowance
Length of Study: 3 years for applicants who apply for the DPhil directly. 4 years for applicants who approach the doctorate via an MPhil or an MSc degree
Closing Date: May 1st

For further information contact:

Website: www.politics.ox.ac.uk/prospective/grad/funding.asp#esrc_and_ahrc

Primary Health Care: MRC Studentships

Subjects: Primary health care.
Purpose: To assist graduate students with fees and maintenance.
Eligibility: Open to all home/EU candidates.
Level of Study: Research

Type: Studentship
Value: University fees, college fees and maintenance allowance
Length of Study: 3 years
Closing Date: March 13th
Additional Information: Contact christelle.kervella@dphpc.ox.ac.uk or gabriela.romo@dphpc.ox.ac.uk for more details.

Project Studentships in Materials (Various Sponsors) and EPSRC Industrial CASE Studentships

Subjects: Materials science.
Purpose: To assist graduate students with fees and maintenance.
Eligibility: Varies.
Level of Study: Research
Type: Studentship
Value: University and college fees, plus a maintenance allowance of £12,900 which the sponsors may increase by £2,000
Length of Study: Normally $3\frac{1}{2}$ years
Closing Date: November 21st
Additional Information: Typically about 10 studentships of these types are awarded each year, but this number depends on the funding announcements made by the sponsors (industry, research councils, EC, Govt).

For further information contact:

Website: www.materials.ox.ac.uk/admissions/postgraduate/newprojects.html

Public Health: Johnson & Johnson

Subjects: Global health science.
Purpose: To assist graduate students with fees and maintenance.
Eligibility: Open to candidates from Eastern Europe/Russia, Latin America, Africa, Asia.
Level of Study: Postgraduate
Type: Scholarships
Value: University fees, college fees and maintenance allowance
Length of Study: 1 year
Closing Date: March 13th

For further information contact:

Website: www.publichealth.ox.ac.uk/gradstu/globalhealth/funding

Public Health: Li Ka Shing

Subjects: Global health science.
Purpose: To assist graduate students with fees and maintenance.
Eligibility: Open to candidates from China.
Level of Study: Postgraduate
Type: Scholarship
Value: University fees, college fees and maintenance allowance
Length of Study: 1 year
Closing Date: March 13th
Additional Information: For further infomration please contact ghs@dphpc.ox.ac.uk

Public Health: MRC Studentships

Subjects: Public health.
Purpose: To assist graduate students with fees and maintenance.
Eligibility: Open to home/EU applicants.
Level of Study: Research
Type: Studentship
Value: University fees, college fees and maintenance allowance
Length of Study: 3 years
Closing Date: March 13th
Additional Information: Contact christelle.kervella@dphpc.ox.ac.uk for further details.

Public Health: MRC Studentships

Subjects: Global health science.
Purpose: To assist graduate students with fees and maintenance.
Eligibility: Open to home/EU applicants.
Level of Study: Postgraduate
Type: Studentship
Value: University fees and maintenance. Please note that applicants will have to cover college fees
Length of Study: 1 year

Closing Date: January 9th

For further information contact:

Website: www.publichealth.ox.ac.uk/gradstu/globalhealth/funding

Queen's College Cyril and Phillis Long Studenthsip

Subjects: Varies.
Purpose: To enable students pursue subjects as advertised by the International Office.
Eligibility: Overseas students.
Level of Study: Postgraduate
Type: Studentship
Value: Equivalent of Research Council maintenance grant
Length of Study: 2–3 years depending on course length. Automatically renewed if satisfactory academic progress is made
Frequency: Annual
Study Establishment: The Queen's College, University of Oxford
Country of Study: United Kingdom
No. of awards offered: 1
Application Procedure: Award associated with a Clarendon Fund Award. Applications will be considered as part of the Clarendon Award process.
Closing Date: January 23rd
Funding: Private

For further information contact:

International Office, University Offices, Wellington Square, Oxford, OX1 2JD, England
Website: www.admin.ox.ac.uk/studentfunding/scholarship_profiles/clarendon.shtml

Raffy Manoukian Scholarships

Subjects: Ancient history, biochemistry, classics, economics, English language and literature, history, international relations, law, mathematical and physical sciences, medical sciences, medieval and modern languages and politics.
Purpose: To promote Armenians who would otherwise be unable to study at Oxford.
Eligibility: Open to new graduate students who are Armenian nationals or those with parent(s) of Armenian nationality; must be aged under 25 on October 1st 2009.
Level of Study: Postgraduate, Research
Type: Scholarships
Value: University and college fees; full grant for living costs
Length of Study: Full course duration
Closing Date: January 23rd

For further information contact:

Website: www.admin.ox.ac.uk/studentfunding/scholarship_profiles/RaffyMan.shtml

Reach Oxford (Formerly Oxford Student Scholarships)

Subjects: All except Medicine.
Purpose: To students from developing countries who, for political or financial reasons, or because equivalent educational facilities do not exist, cannot study for a degree in their own countries.
Eligibility: New undergraduate students from low income countries: Afghanistan, Albania, Algeria, Angola, Antigua and Barbuda, Armenia, Argentina, Azerbaijan, Bangladesh, Barbados, Belarus, Belize, Benin, Bhutan, Bolivia, Bosnia and Herzegovina, Botswana, Brazil, Burk.
Type: Scholarships
Value: University and college fees; full grant for living costs. May also include return airfare to/from UK
Length of Study: Full course duration
No. of awards offered: 3
Closing Date: 20 February
Additional Information: The scholarship is only open to students who have a conditional or unconditional place to study at Oxford in 2009/10. Awards are not tenable to read medicine.

For further information contact:

Website: www.admin.ox.ac.uk/studentfunding/scholarship_profiles/ReachOx.shtml

Regent's Park College: Henman Scholarship
Subjects: Theology.
Purpose: To assist graduate students with fees.
Eligibility: Open to overseas students.
Level of Study: Postgraduate, Research
Type: Scholarship
Value: Up to £3,600 towards fees
Length of Study: Sum is awarded over 2 years
Closing Date: May 20th

Regent's Park College: Studentships of the Centre for Christianity and Culture
Subjects: Theology.
Purpose: To assist graduate students with fees.
Eligibility: Open to all.
Level of Study: Postgraduate, Research
Type: Studentship
Value: College fees
Length of Study: Awarded for 1 year but may be extended up to 3 years
Closing Date: May 20th

Research Project Studentships in Engineering Science (Various Sponsors) and EPSRC Industrial CASE
Subjects: Engineering science.
Purpose: To assist graduate students with fees and maintenance.
Eligibility: Varies.
Level of Study: Research
Type: Studentship
Value: University and college fees paid, plus a minimum of £12,900 per year maintenance allowance
Length of Study: Up to 3 years, depending on the sponsor
Additional Information: These studentships become available at various points throughout the year and are advertised on the Department of Engineering Science website.

For further information contact:

Website: www.eng.ox.ac.uk/postgrad/studentships.html

Rhodes Scholarships
Subjects: All except MBA.
Purpose: To assist graduate students with fees and living allowance.
Eligibility: Open to candidates from Australia, Bermuda, Commonwealth, Caribbean, Canada, Germany, India, Jamaica, Kenya, New Zealand, Pakistan, Southern Africa, USA, Zambia and Zimbabwe. Candidates must be aged between 19 and 25.
Level of Study: Postgraduate, Research
Type: Scholarships
Value: University and college fees; full grant for living costs
Length of Study: 1, 2 or 3 years
Additional Information: Check website for more details.

For further information contact:

Website: www.rhodeshouse.ox.ac.uk/infoscholar.htm

Russian and East European Studies CEELBAS Studentship
Subjects: Russian and East European studies.
Purpose: To assist graduate students with fees and maintenance.
Eligibility: Open to all.
Level of Study: Research
Type: Studentship
Value: University fees and college fees. UK students (and EU students with at least 3 years residency in the UK) also receive a maintenance allowance
Length of Study: 2 years
Closing Date: March 13th

For further information contact:

Website: www.ceelbas.ac.uk www.rees.ox.ac.uk

Said Business School Scholarship
Subjects: Management research.
Purpose: To assist graduate students with fees.
Eligibility: Open to all.
Level of Study: Postgraduate
Type: Scholarship
Value: 50% of the university fees
Length of Study: 1 year
Closing Date: June 1st

For further information contact:

Website: www.sbs.ox.ac.uk

Santander Abbey Scholarships
Subjects: All except BCL, MJur, MBA, EMBA, MFE and PGCE.
Purpose: To assist graduate students with fees and living allowance.
Eligibility: Open to candidates from Argentina, Brazil, Chile, Colombia, Mexico, Portugal, Puerto Rico, Spain, Uruguay and Venezuela. Candidates must be intending to continue studies at doctoral level.
Level of Study: Postgraduate
Type: Scholarships
Value: £10,000 for living expenses
Length of Study: One year, non-renewable
No. of awards offered: 8
Closing Date: January 23rd

For further information contact:

Website: www.admin.ox.ac.uk/studentfunding/scholarship_profiles/santander.shtml

Sasakawa Fund Scholarships
Subjects: Japanese studies.
Purpose: To be applied to the advancement within Oxford University of knowledge and understanding of Japan.
Eligibility: Open to Japanese students or students who will require a period of study in Japan to fulfil their programme of study at Oxford.
Level of Study: Postgraduate, Research
Type: Scholarships
Value: Up to £5,000 per year
Length of Study: 1 year, renewable for maximum of 3 years
No. of awards offered: Up to 2
Closing Date: January 23rd

For further information contact:

Website: www.admin.ox.ac.uk/studentfunding/scholarship_profiles/Sasakawa.shtml

Scatcherd European Scholarships
Subjects: All subjects.
Purpose: To assist graduate students with fees and living allowance.
Eligibility: Open to nationals of any European country except UK and Turkey (includes Russian Federation and other countries west of the Urals).
Level of Study: Postgraduate, Research
Type: Scholarships
Value: University and college fees; full grant for living costs
Length of Study: Full course duration
No. of awards offered: Varies
Closing Date: January 23rd

For further information contact:

Website: www.admin.ox.ac.uk/studentfunding/scholarship_profiles/Scatcherd.shtml

Shell Centenary Scholarships and Shell Centenary Chevening Scholarships
Subjects: African studies, applied statistics, applied and computational mathematics, biodiversity, conservation and management, law, computer science, criminology and criminal justice, drylands science and management and economics.

Purpose: To assist graduate students with fees, living allowance and travel costs.
Eligibility: Open to nationals of any country except Australia, Austria, Belgium, Canada, Denmark, Finland, France, Germany, Greece, Iceland, Ireland, Italy, Japan, Luxembourg, Netherlands, New Zealand, Norway, Portugal, Spain, Sweden, Switzerland, UK and USA. Candidates should normally be aged between 25 and 35.
Level of Study: Postgraduate
Type: Scholarships
Value: University and college fees, full grant for living costs, arrival allowance and return air travel to/from UK
Length of Study: 1 year
Closing Date: January 23rd

For further information contact:

Website: www.admin.ox.ac.uk/studentfunding/scholarship_profiles/Shell.shtml

Social Policy and Social Work: The Barnett Scholarship Fund

Subjects: Social policy or social intervention.
Purpose: To assist graduate students with fees.
Eligibility: Open to all.
Level of Study: Research
Value: £3,000
Length of Study: 1 year
Closing Date: July 24th

For further information contact:

Website: www.spsw.ox.ac.uk/students/prospective/admissions/the-barnett-scholarship-fund.html

Sociology: Departmental Bursaries

Subjects: Sociology.
Purpose: To assist graduate students with fees.
Eligibility: Open to all.
Level of Study: Postgraduate, Research
Type: Bursary
Value: Home/EU fees equivalent
Length of Study: 1 year
Closing Date: April 1st

For further information contact:

Website: www.sociology.ox.ac.uk/apply/funding.asp

Sociology: ESRC Quota Studentships

Subjects: Sociology.
Purpose: To support postgraduate training in the social sciences.
Eligibility: Open to all.
Level of Study: Postgraduate, Research
Type: Studentship
Value: University fees, college fees and maintenance allowance
Length of Study: Up to 4 years (depending on point of entry to studies)
Closing Date: April 1st

For further information contact:

Website: www.esrc.ac.uk/ESRCInfoCentre/opportunities/postgraduate/

Sociology: ESRC Studentship Competition

Subjects: Sociology.
Purpose: To support postgraduate training in the social sciences.
Eligibility: Open to all.
Level of Study: Postgraduate, Research
Type: Studentship
Value: University fees, college fees and maintenance allowance
Length of Study: Up to 4 years (depending on point of entry to studies)
Closing Date: March 1st

For further information contact:

Website: www.esrc.ac.uk/ESRCInfoCentre/opportunities/postgraduate/

Sociology: Nuffield Full Funded Studentships

Subjects: Sociology.
Purpose: To assist graduate students with fees and maintenance.
Eligibility: Open to all.
Level of Study: Doctorate, Research
Type: Studentship
Value: Home/EU fees maintenance allowance
Length of Study: 3 years
Closing Date: May 1st
Additional Information: Candidates must apply to Nuffield College.

For further information contact:

Website: www.nuffield.ox.ac.uk/general/prospectus/funding.aspx

Somerville Graduate Scholarship in Biochemistry, in Association with Department of Biochemistry

Subjects: Biochemistry.
Purpose: To assist graduate students with their fees and a living allowance.
Eligibility: Open to candidates applying for a DPhil.
Level of Study: Research
Type: Scholarship
Value: Departmental Studentship: university fees; living allowance at the level of a national research council studentship; training grant. Somerville Scholarship: college fee waived; some SCR dining rights; right to college room at usual rate, for first year
Length of Study: Departmental studentship: 4 years, subject to satisfactory progress being made. College scholarship: 2 years in first instance, with possible renewal considered on request
No. of awards offered: Varies
Application Procedure: Applicants can download a form from the website www.some.ox.ac.uk.

For further information contact:

Website: www.some.ox.ac.uk

Somerville Graduate Scholarship in Chemistry, in Association with Department of Chemistry

Subjects: Chemistry.
Purpose: To assist graduate students in chemistry with fees and a living allowance.
Eligibility: Open to candidates applying for a DPhil.
Level of Study: Doctorate, Research
Type: Scholarship
Value: Departmental Studentship: university fees and a living allowance per year at the level of a national research council studentship. Somerville Scholarship: college fee waived; some SCR dining rights; right to college room at usual rate, for first year
Length of Study: Departmental Studentship: 3 years, subject to satisfactory progress being made. College Scholarship: 2 years in first instance, with possible renewal considered on request
Application Procedure: Applicants can download a form from the website www.some.ox.ac.uk.
Additional Information: Department automatically considers DPhil applications for studentship/scholarship. This scholarship is available for those starting a course during the academic year 2008/2009, and it is hoped that it will be offered for those starting during 2009/2010.

For further information contact:

Website: www.some.ox.ac.uk

Somerville Graduate Scholarship in Classics, in Partnership with Faculty of Classics

Subjects: Classical languages and literatures and ancient history.
Purpose: To assist graduate students in classics with fees and a living allowance.
Eligibility: Open to candidates applying for a DPhil.
Level of Study: Doctorate, Research
Type: Scholarship
Value: Faculty Studentship: £9,000 per year. Somerville Scholarship: college fee waived; £5,000 per year; some SCR dining rights; right to college room at usual rate, for first year
Length of Study: 3 years, subject to satisfactory progress being made

Application Procedure: Applicants can download a form from the website www.some.ox.ac.uk.

For further information contact:

Website: www.some.ox.ac.uk

Somerville Graduate Scholarship in Modern Languages, in Association with Faculty of Medieval & Modern Languages

Subjects: Medieval and modern languages.
Purpose: To assist graduate students in modern languages with fees and a living allowance.
Eligibility: Open to candidates applying for a DPhil.
Level of Study: Doctorate, Research
Type: Scholarship
Value: Faculty contribution: university fees. Somerville contribution: college fee waived; £6,000 per year; some SCR dining rights; right to college room at usual rate, for first year
Length of Study: 3 years, subject to satisfactory progress being made
Application Procedure: Applicants can download a form from the website www.some.ox.ac.uk.

For further information contact:

Website: www.some.ox.ac.uk

Somerville Graduate Scholarship in Philosophy, in Association with Faculty of Philosophy

Subjects: Philosophy.
Purpose: To assist graduate students in philosophy with fees and a living allowance.
Eligibility: Open to candidates applying for a BPhil or DPhil.
Level of Study: Doctorate, Research
Type: Scholarship
Value: Faculty contribution: university fees; maintenance grant at the level of AHRC studentship (unless AHRC funding obtained). Somerville contribution: college fee waived (if AHRC funding application unsuccessful); £1,000 per year; some SCR dining rights; right to college room at usual rate, for first year
Length of Study: 1 year in first instance. Renewable for two further years subject to satisfactory progress (and successful transfer from BPhil to DPhil, if applicable)
Application Procedure: Applicants can download a form from the website www.some.ox.ac.uk.

For further information contact:

Website: www.some.ox.ac.uk

Somerville Graduate Scholarship in Politics/International Relations, in Association with Department of Politics and International Relations

Subjects: Politics or international relations.
Purpose: To assist graduate students in politics/international relations with fees and a living allowance.
Eligibility: Open to candidates applying for a DPhil in politics or international relations.
Level of Study: Doctorate, Research
Type: Scholarship
Value: Department contribution: university fees; maintenance grant of £6,000 per year. Somerville contribution: college fee waived; maintenance grant of £6,000 per year; some SCR dining rights; right to college room at usual rate, for first year
Length of Study: Up to 3 years, subject to satisfactory progress
Application Procedure: Applicants can download a form from the website www.some.ox.ac.uk.
Additional Information: Department automatically considers DPhil applications for scholarship. This scholarship is available for those starting a course during the academic year 2008/2009, and it is hoped that it will be offered for those starting during 2009/2010.

For further information contact:

Website: www.some.ox.ac.uk

Somerville Graduate Scholarship in Zoology, in Association with Department of Zoology

Subjects: Zoology.

Purpose: To assist graduate students in zoology with fees and a living allowance.
Eligibility: Open to candidates applying for a DPhil.
Level of Study: Doctorate, Research
Type: Scholarship
Value: Departmental Studentship: university fees; living allowance per year at the level of a national research council studentship. Somerville Scholarship: college fee waived; some SCR dining rights; right to college room at usual rate, for first year
Length of Study: Departmental Studentship: 3 years, subject to satisfactory progress being made. College Scholarship: 2 years in first instance, with possible renewal considered on request
Additional Information: Department automatically considers DPhil applications for scholarship. This scholarship is available for those starting a course during the academic year 2008/2009, and it is hoped that it will be offered for those starting during 2009/2010.

For further information contact:

Website: www.some.ox.ac.uk

St Anne's College: Irene Jamieson & St Anne's Scholarship

Subjects: Humanities or social sciences.
Purpose: To assist fresh graduates with their university and college fees.
Eligibility: Open to UK and EU graduates. All degrees except BA and one-year degrees. Application form included with offer of college membership.
Level of Study: Research
Type: Scholarship
Value: College fees
Length of Study: 1 year, renewable for second
Application Procedure: Applicants can apply online. Please see the website www.st.anne.ox.ac.uk.
Closing Date: May 31st

For further information contact:

Website: www.st-annes.ox.ac.uk/study/graduate/resschol.html

St Anne's College: Iris Murdoch Scholarship

Subjects: All subjects.
Purpose: To assist fresh graduates with their university and college fees.
Eligibility: Open to UK and EU graduates. All degrees except BA and one-year degrees. Application form included with offer of college membership.
Level of Study: Research
Type: Scholarship
Value: College fees
Length of Study: 1 year, renewable for second
Application Procedure: Applicants can apply online. Please see the website www.st.anne.ox.ac.uk.
Closing Date: May 31st

For further information contact:

Website: www.st-annes.ox.ac.uk/study/graduate/resschol.html

St Anne's College: Olwyn Rhys Scholarship

Subjects: Medieval romance language and literature.
Purpose: To assist fresh graduates with their university and college fees.
Eligibility: Open to all graduate students. Application form included with offer of college membership.
Level of Study: Postgraduate, Research
Value: College fees
Length of Study: 1 year, renewable for second
Application Procedure: Applicants can apply online. Please see the website www.st.anne.ox.ac.uk.
Closing Date: May 31st
Additional Information: Your degree must include the study of medieval romance language and literature.

For further information contact:

Website: www.st-annes.ox.ac.uk/study/graduate/resschol.html

St Anne's College: Una Goodwin Scholarship

Subjects: MPLS or medical sciences.

Purpose: To assist fresh graduates with their university and college fees.

Eligibility: Open to UK and EU graduates. All degrees except BA and one-year degrees. Application form included with offer of college membership.

Level of Study: Research

Type: Scholarship

Value: College fees

Length of Study: 1 year, renewable for second

Application Procedure: Applicants can apply online. Please see the website www.st.anne.ox.ac.uk

Closing Date: May 31st

For further information contact:

Website: www.st-annes.ox.ac.uk/study/graduate/resschol.html

St Antony's College Southern African Students Fund Scholarship

Subjects: MSc in African studies.

Purpose: To assist students who have studied in one of the universities in South Africa, Botswana, Lesotho, Swaziland, Namibia, Zimbabwe, Mozambique, Zambia, and Malawi and are residents of that country pursue a post graduate course in African studies.

Eligibility: Open to students who have been to university in, and are resident in, any one of the following countries: South Africa, Botswana, Lesotho, Swaziland, Namibia, Zimbabwe, Mozambique, Zambia, and Malawi.

Level of Study: Graduate, Postgraduate

Type: Scholarship

Value: University and college fees, and a maintenance allowance

Length of Study: One year

Application Procedure: Refer www.sant.ox.ac.uk/study/afschol.shtml for further details.

For further information contact:

Email: african.studies@sant.ox.ac.uk

Website: www.sant.ox.ac.uk/study/scholarships.html

St Antony's College The Ronaldo Falconer Scholarship

Subjects: Any subject in which the college specialises.

Purpose: To assist graduate students who have already undertaken higher studies in Costa Rica and who wish to study for a higher degree in any of the subjects in which the college specialises.

Eligibility: Open to graduate students who have already undertaken higher education in Costa Rica. For closing date information, please contact Latin American Centre: enquiries@lac.ox.ac.uk

Level of Study: Graduate, Postgraduate, Research

Type: Scholarship

Value: University and college fees, maintenance and some travel costs

Length of Study: Up to 3 years

Frequency: Annual

Study Establishment: St Antony's College, University of Oxford

Country of Study: United Kingdom

Application Procedure: Applicants must write for details. Please contact Latin American Centre: enquiries@lac.ox.ac.uk for further information.

Closing Date: Please write for details

Funding: Private

For further information contact:

Latin American Centre, St Antony's College, Oxford, OX2 6UF, England

Email: enquiries@lac.ox.ac.uk

Website: www.sant.ox.ac.uk/study/scholarships.html

Contact: The Director

St Antony's College The Sir John Swire Scholarship

Subjects: Any subject in which the college specialises

Purpose: To assist graduates from North-east and South-east Asia who wish to study for a higher degree in any of the subjects in which the college specialise

Eligibility: Open to graduate students from North-east and South-east Asia.

Level of Study: Research, Graduate, Postgraduate, New scholarship offers when current scholars completes

Type: Scholarship

Value: University and college fees, maintenance and some travel costs

Length of Study: Up to 3 years

Study Establishment: St Antony's College, University of Oxford

Country of Study: United Kingdom

No. of awards offered: 1

Application Procedure: Applicants must write for details or check the website www.sant.ox.ac.uk

Closing Date: March 31st

Funding: Commercial

For further information contact:

St Antony's College, Oxford, Oxfordshire, OX2 6JF, England

Website: www.sant.ox.ac.uk/study/scholarships.html

Contact: College Secretary

St Antony's College: Swire Centenary/Cathay Pacific (Japan)

Subjects: All subjects.

Purpose: To assist fresh graduates with their university and college fees.

Eligibility: Open to permanent residents of Japan.

Level of Study: Postgraduate, Research

Value: University and college fees, grant for living expenses, and some travel costs

Length of Study: 2 years, possible extension for further 2 years

Application Procedure: Applicants can see the website www.sant.ox.ac.uk/study/scholarships.shtml.

For further information contact:

Website: www.sant.ox.ac.uk/study/scholarships.shtml

Contact: College Secretary, St Antony's

St Antony's College: Swire/Cathay Pacific (Hong Kong)

Subjects: All subjects.

Purpose: To assist fresh graduates with their university and college fees.

Eligibility: Open to permanent residents of Hong Kong.

Level of Study: Postgraduate, Research

Value: University and college fees, grant for living expenses, and some travel costs

Length of Study: 2 years, possible extension for further 2 years

For further information contact:

Website: www.sant.ox.ac.uk/study/scholarships.shtml

Contact: College Secretary, St Antony's

St Catherine's College College Scholarship (Sciences)

Subjects: Sciences (mathematical, physical and life sciences, medical sciences)

Purpose: To assist students who are, or will be reading for an Oxford University DPhil, MLitt, or MSc by research degree.

Eligibility: Open to new graduate students commencing graduate study at Oxford and to current graduate students who will have completed no more than 2 years of research degree study at Oxford and restricted to Indian nationals.

Level of Study: Graduate, Research

Type: Scholarship

Value: £2,000 per year

Length of Study: Up to 3 years while the recepient is liable for university and college fees

Frequency: Annual

Study Establishment: St Catherine's College, University of Oxford

Country of Study: United Kingdom

No. of awards offered: Up to 3

Application Procedure: See www.stcatz.ox.ac.uk for details.
Closing Date: March

For further information contact:

St Catherine's College, Oxford, Oxfordshire, OX1 3UJ, England
Fax: (44) 186 527 1768
Email: academic.registrar@stcatz.ox.ac.uk
Website: www.stcatz.ox.ac.uk/admissions_pages/scholarships.htm
Contact: Academic Registrar

St Catherine's College Graduate Scholarship in the Arts

Subjects: Humanities and social sciences.
Purpose: To assist graduates who are, or will be reading for an Oxford University DPhil, MLitt, or MSc by research degree.
Eligibility: Open to new graduate students commencing graduate study at Oxford and to current graduate students who will have completed no more than 2 years of research degree study at Oxford and restricted to Indian nationals.
Level of Study: Graduate, Research
Type: Scholarship
Value: £2,000 per year
Length of Study: Up to 3 years while the recepient is liable for university and college fees
Frequency: Annual
Study Establishment: St Catherine's College, University of Oxford
Country of Study: United Kingdom
No. of awards offered: Up to 3
Application Procedure: See www.stcatz.ox.ac.uk for details
Closing Date: March

For further information contact:

St Catherine's College, Oxford, Oxfordshire, OX1 3UJ, England
Fax: (44) 186 527 1768
Email: academic.registrar@stcatz.ox.ac.uk
Website: www.stcatz.ox.ac.uk/admissions_pages/scholarships.htm
Contact: Academic Registrar

St Catherine's College Great Eastern Scholarship

Subjects: All subjects.
Purpose: To assist students who are, or will be reading for an Oxford University DPhil, MLitt, or MSc by research degree.
Eligibility: Open to new graduate students commencing graduate study at Oxford and to current graduate students who will have completed no more than 2 years of research degree study at Oxford and restricted to Indian nationals.
Level of Study: Graduate, Research
Type: Scholarship
Value: UK £2,000 per year
Length of Study: Up to 3 years while the student is liable for university and college fees
Frequency: Dependent on funds available
Study Establishment: St Catherine's College, University of Oxford
Country of Study: United Kingdom
No. of awards offered: 1
Application Procedure: See the website www.stcatz.ox.ac.uk for details.
Closing Date: March

For further information contact:

St Catherine's College, Oxford, Oxfordshire, OX1 3UJ, England
Email: academic.registrar@stcatz.ox.ac.uk
Website: www.stcatz.ox.ac.uk/admissions_pages/scholarships.htm
Contact: Academic Registrar

St Catherine's College Overseas Scholarship

Subjects: All subjects.
Purpose: To assist students who are, or will be reading for an Oxford University DPhil, MLitt, or MSc by research degree.
Eligibility: Open to new graduate students commencing graduate study at Oxford and to current graduate students who will have completed no more than 2 years of research degree study at Oxford and restricted to Indian nationals.
Level of Study: Graduate, Postgraduate, Research
Type: Scholarship

Value: £2,000 per year + limited High Table dining rights
Length of Study: Up to 3 years while student is liable for fees
Frequency: Annual
Study Establishment: St Catherine's College, University of Oxford
Country of Study: United Kingdom
No. of awards offered: Up to 3
Application Procedure: See www.stcatz.ox.ac.uk for details.
Closing Date: 13 March

For further information contact:

St Catherine's College, Oxford, Oxfordshire, OX1 3UJ, England
Fax: (44) 186 527 1732
Email: academic.registrar@stcatz.ox.ac.uk
Website: www.stcatz.ox.ac.uk/admissions_pages/scholarships.htm
Contact: Academic Registrar

St Catherine's College: Leathersellers' Company Graduate Scholarship

Subjects: Biochemistry, chemistry, computing, earth sciences, engineering science, materials, mathematics, physics, plant sciences, statistics or zoology
Purpose: To assist students who are, or will be reading for an Oxford University DPhil, MLitt, or MSc by research degree.
Eligibility: Open to new graduate students commencing graduate study at Oxford and to current graduate students who will have completed no more than 2 years of research degree study at Oxford and restricted to Indian nationals.
Level of Study: Graduate, Research
Type: Scholarship
Value: UK £3,000 per year
Length of Study: Up to 3 years while the recepient is liable for university and college fees
Frequency: Annual
Study Establishment: St Catherine's College, University of Oxford
Country of Study: United Kingdom
No. of awards offered: Up to 3
Application Procedure: See www.stcatz.ox.ac.uk for details.
Closing Date: March

For further information contact:

St Catherine's College, Manor Road, Oxford, Oxfordshire, OX1 3UJ, England
Fax: (44) 186 527 1768
Email: academic.registrar@stcatz.ox.ac.uk
Website: www.stcatz.ox.ac.uk/admissions_pages/scholarships.htm
Contact: Academic Registrar

St Catherine's College: Magellan Prize

Subjects: Language, literature, culture, or history of the Portuguese-speaking world.
Purpose: To assist fresh graduates with their university and college fees.
Eligibility: Open to all graduate students.
Level of Study: Postgraduate, Research
Type: Prize
Value: £3,000 per year + limited high table dining rights
Length of Study: 1 year
Application Procedure: For application details, visit the website www.sant.ox.ac.uk/study/scholarships.shtml.

For further information contact:

Website: www.stcatz.ox.ac.uk/admissions_pages/scholarships.htm

St Cross College Graduate Studentship in Sociology

Subjects: Sociology.
Purpose: To assist graduate students with fees and maintenance.
Eligibility: Open to all.
Level of Study: Research
Type: Scholarship
Value: University fees, college fees and maintenance allowance of £6,000
Length of Study: 3 years
Closing Date: March 1st
Additional Information: Candidates must apply to St Cross College.

For further information contact:

Website: www.stx.ox.ac.uk/admissions/funding/graduate_
studentship_in_sociol

St Cross College: Graduate Studentship in Archaeology
Subjects: Archaeology.
Purpose: To assist graduate students with fees.
Eligibility: Open to all.
Level of Study: Doctorate, Research
Type: Studentship
Value: £4,000 per year
Length of Study: Up to 3 years of study
Closing Date: January 23rd

For further information contact:

Website: www.stx.ox.ac.uk/admissions/funding/graduate_
studentship_in_archae

St Cross College: The Robin & Nadine Wells Scholarship
Subjects: All subjects.
Purpose: To provide financial assistance to an academically merito-
rious graduate student who has been accepted into both an accredited
one year's Masters programme at the University of Oxford and St
Cross College.
Eligibility: Open to candidates who have been unsuccessful in a UK
or University of Oxford (e.g. Clarendon, Beit) funding competition.
Level of Study: Research, Postgraduate
Type: Scholarship
Value: £5,000 per year
Length of Study: One year - not renewable

For further information contact:

Website: www.stx.ox.ac.uk/admissions/funding/the_robin_nadine_
wells_scholar

St Edmund Hall: William R. Miller Postgraduate Award
Subjects: All subjects.
Purpose: To assist graduate students with fees and accomodation.
Eligibility: Open to all graduate students.
Level of Study: Postgraduate, Research
Type: Award
Value: A rent-free college room (to the value of £4,800 per year) is
offered
Length of Study: 1 year, renewal for one further year upon reappli-
cation
Frequency: Annual
No. of awards offered: 3
Closing Date: May 1st

For further information contact:

Website: www.seh.ox.ac.uk

St Hugh's College Wei Lun Foundation Graduate Scholarship
Subjects: All subjects.
Purpose: To assist graduate students with fees and a living allow-
ance.
Eligibility: Open to candidates from the People's Republic of China
only.
Level of Study: Postgraduate, Research
Type: Scholarship
Value: Can be used to cover fees and/or maintenance. Up to a total
value of £10,000
Length of Study: 2 years
Closing Date: August 20th

For further information contact:

Website: www.st-hughs.ox.ac.uk/Graduate_Courses/Graduate_
Studentships/index.php

St John's College: College Scholarships
Subjects: All subjects.
Purpose: To assist graduate students with fees and a living allow-
ance.
Eligibility: Four new graduate scholarships are available at St John's
College.The awards are intended to assist students, of proven out-
standing academic excellence, who are starting a research degree.
Level of Study: Research
Type: Scholarship
Value: All fees (at home/EU rate only) plus a maintenance allowance
Length of Study: Up to 4 years, subject to satisfactory progress
No. of awards offered: 4

For further information contact:

Website: www.sjc.ox.ac.uk

St John's College: Kendrew Scholarship
Subjects: All subjects.
Purpose: To assist students, of proven outstanding academic ex-
cellence, who are starting a research degree.
Eligibility: Open to candidates from all application deadlines, who
secure a place at St John's College. There is no separate application
form for the Kendrew Scholarships, decisions will be based on the
information as provided in the university application.
Level of Study: Postgraduate, Research
Type: Scholarship
Value: All fees plus a maintenance allowance
Length of Study: Up to 3 years, subject to satisfactory progress
Closing Date: March 13th
Additional Information: Open to applicants from all application
deadlines, who secure a place at St John's College. There is no
separate application form for the Kendrew Scholarships, decisions
will be based on the information as provided in your University
Application.

For further information contact:

Website: www.sjc.ox.ac.uk

Statistics: Clarendon Scholarship in Statistics
Subjects: Statistics.
Purpose: To assist graduate students with fees and maintenance.
Eligibility: Open to overseas applicants only.
Level of Study: Research
Type: Scholarship
Value: University and college fees paid, plus a minimum of £12,900
maintenance allowance per year
Length of Study: 3 years
Closing Date: November 21st
Additional Information: At least one Clarendon Scholarship is
awarded for entry in October 2009. Candidates are advised to apply
by application deadline 1, but if possible applications will also be
considered by application deadline 2; please see website.

For further information contact:

Website: www.stats.ox.ac.uk/prospective_students/research_
degrees/DPhil_funding

Statistics: EPSRC Studentships
Subjects: Statistics.
Purpose: To assist graduate students with fees and maintenance.
Eligibility: Open to UK and EU citizens only. The candidates must be
accepted for a DPhil in Statistics starting October 2009.
Level of Study: Research
Type: Studentship
Value: University and college fees, plus a minimum of £12,900
maintenance allowance per year
Length of Study: Maximum 3.5 years
Additional Information: Applicants who have not been ordinarily
resident in the UK for the past 3 years may be eligible for fees-only
awards. Up to 3 studentships are available each year, dependent on
the annual funding announcement by EPSRC.

For further information contact:

Website: www.stats.ox.ac.uk/prospective_students/research_
degrees/DPhil_funding

Statistics: Teaching Assistant Bursaries

Subjects: Statistics.
Purpose: To assist graduate students with fees and maintenance.
Eligibility: Open to all.
Level of Study: Research
Type: Bursary
Value: University and college fees, plus a minimum of £12,900 maintenance allowance per year
Length of Study: Maximum 3 years
Additional Information: Must demonstrate satisfactory performance as a teaching assistant as a condition of renewal. Deadlines are advertised at www.stats.ox.ac.uk/prospective_students/research_degrees/DPhil_funding

For further information contact:

Website: www.stats.ox.ac.uk/prospective_students/research_degrees/DPhil_funding

STFC Studentships in Particle Physics, Astrophysics, Theoretical Physics

Subjects: Particle physics (experiment and theory), astrophysics (experiment and thoery) and atmospheric physics.
Purpose: To assist graduate students with fees and maintenance.
Eligibility: Open UK/EU students with a DPhil only; EU students are eligible for fees only unless a first degree was taken in the UK in the period immediately prior to the award, in which case a maintenance maintenance allowance may be included.
Level of Study: Research
Type: Studentship
Value: University and college fees, plus a minimum of £12,940 per year maintenance allowance
Length of Study: Normally 3 years with a possible further extension of up to 1 year
Closing Date: January 23rd
Additional Information: Typically, we award about 19 STFC studentships a year: 9 to Particle Physics (experiment), 3 Particle Physics (theory) and 7 to Astrophysics (experiment and theory). The exact number depends on the funding announcement made by the sponsors.

For further information contact:

Website: www.physics.ox.ac.uk/admissions/postgrad.htm

Trinity College Cecil Lubbock Memorial Scholarship

Subjects: Humanities and social sciences
Purpose: To promote research in philosophy.
Eligibility: Home students of research degrees. Please note interest on application form, having checked college website to see whether the award is available for 2008 entry.
Level of Study: Doctorate, Research
Type: Scholarship
Value: £10,000 (all fees and some maintenance)
Length of Study: 1–4 years (period of fee liability)
Frequency: Dependent on funds available
Study Establishment: Trinity college, University of Oxford
Country of Study: United Kingdom
No. of awards offered: 1
Application Procedure: Candidates who wish to be considered for the scholarship should apply on the university application form. Please see www.trinity.ox.ac.uk for details.

For further information contact:

Website: www.trinity.ox.ac.uk/admissions/funding/
Contact: Academic Administrator

Trinity College MB Grabowski Fund Postgraduate Scholarship in Polish Studies

Subjects: Modern history or Modern languages for carrying out research in Polish studies.
Purpose: To promote graduate studies in Polish.
Eligibility: Open to all
Level of Study: Doctorate, Postgraduate, Research
Type: Scholarship
Value: £6000 pa

Length of Study: Variable
Frequency: Dependent on funds available
Study Establishment: Trinity college, University of Oxford
Country of Study: United Kingdom
No. of awards offered: 1
Application Procedure: Candidates who wish to be considered for the scholarship should apply on the university application form. Please see www.admin.ox.ac.uk/postgraduate for further details.
Closing Date: May 1st
Additional Information: .

For further information contact:

Website: www.trinity.ox.ac.uk/admissions/

Trinity College Said MBA and EMBA Scholarships

Subjects: MBA/EMBA
Purpose: To promote graduate education in business administration.
Eligibility: Open to all
Level of Study: MBA, Postgraduate, Research
Type: Scholarship
Value: College fees
Length of Study: 1 year
Frequency: Annual
Study Establishment: Trinity College, University of Oxford
Country of Study: United Kingdom
No. of awards offered: 2 (MBA), 1 (EMBA)
Application Procedure: Candidates who wish to be considered should apply on the university application form. Please see www.admin.ox.ac.uk/postgraduate for details.
Closing Date: May 1st
Additional Information: 2 for MBA, 1 for EMBA. Please note interest on application form.

For further information contact:

Website: www.trinity.ox.ac.uk/admissions/

Trinity College: Birkett Scholarships in Environmental Studies

Subjects: MSc in Environmental change and management
Purpose: To promote graduate education in the environment.
Eligibility: Open to all
Level of Study: Research
Type: Scholarship
Value: £3,500
Length of Study: 1 year
Frequency: Annual
Study Establishment: Trinity College, University of Oxford
Country of Study: United Kingdom
No. of awards offered: 2
Application Procedure: Candidates who wish to be considered for the scholarship should apply on the university application form. Please see www.admin.ox.ac.uk/postgraduate for details.
Closing Date: March 1st

For further information contact:

Website: www.trinity.ox.ac.uk/admissions/

Trinity College: Michael and Judith Beloff Scholarship

Subjects: Civil law.
Purpose: To assist graduate students with fees.
Eligibility: Open to postgraduate students intending to study for a BCL Degree, with preference to someone intending to practise at the Bar of England and Wales.
Level of Study: Postgraduate
Type: Scholarship
Value: £6,500 per year
Length of Study: 1 year
Closing Date: January 1st

For further information contact:

Website: www.trinity.ox.ac.uk/admissions/

University College: Bartlett Scholarship

Subjects: All subjects.

Purpose: To assist graduate students with fees.
Eligibility: Open to candidates intending to study for a DPhil (preference for North American applicants).
Level of Study: Research
Type: Scholarships
Value: Up to £3,500
Length of Study: Up to 3 years

For further information contact:

Website: www.univ.ox.ac.uk/postgraduate/financial_1/scholarships_and_studentships/

University College: CEPL
Subjects: Law.
Purpose: To assist graduate students with fees.
Eligibility: Awarded annually to candidates embarking on a one-year research degree, or entering the final year of a DPhil.
Level of Study: Research
Type: Studentship
Value: £6,000 for 1 year
Length of Study: 1 year only

For further information contact:

Website: http://denning.law.ox.ac.uk/postgraduate/scholarships.shtml

University College: Chellgren
Subjects: All subjects, but with a preference for Economics.
Purpose: To assist graduate students with fees.
Eligibility: Open to all candidates.
Level of Study: Postgraduate, Research
Value: £4,000 per year
Length of Study: Up to three years
Additional Information: Closing date to be confirmed - please contact the college for more information.

For further information contact:

Website: www.univ.ox.ac.uk/postgraduate/financial_1/scholarships_and_studentships/

University College: Clarendon Linked Award
Subjects: All subjects (MPLS).
Purpose: To assist graduate students with fees.
Eligibility: Open to candidates who are overseas graduates.
Level of Study: Postgraduate, Research
Value: £7,000 per year (including college fees)
Length of Study: Up to 3 years
Closing Date: January 23rd
Additional Information: In association with the Clarendon Fund awards.

For further information contact:

Website: www.admin.ox.ac.uk/studentfunding/scholarship_profiles/clarendon.shtml

University College: Clarendon Linked Award
Subjects: Social Sciences.
Purpose: To assist graduate students with fees.
Eligibility: Open to candidates who are overseas graduates.
Level of Study: Postgraduate, Research
Value: £7,000 per year (including college fees)
Length of Study: Up to 3 years
Closing Date: January 23rd
Additional Information: In association with the Clarendon Fund awards.

For further information contact:

Website: www.admin.ox.ac.uk/studentfunding/scholarship_profiles/clarendon.shtml

University College: Loughman
Subjects: All subjects.
Purpose: To assist graduate students with fees.

Eligibility: Open to all.
Level of Study: Postgraduate, Research
Value: £4,000 per year
Length of Study: Up to 3 years

For further information contact:

Website: www.univ.ox.ac.uk/postgraduate/financial_1/scholarships_and_studentships/

University College: Old Members' Trust Graduate Scholarship
Subjects: All subjects.
Purpose: To assist graduate students with fees.
Eligibility: Open to candidates intending to read for a DPhil.
Level of Study: Research
Type: Scholarship
Value: £5,000 per year
Length of Study: Up to 3 years

For further information contact:

Website: www.univ.ox.ac.uk/postgraduate/financial_1/scholarships_and_studentships/

University College: Senior Scholarship
Subjects: All subjects.
Purpose: To assist graduate students with fees.
Eligibility: Open to candidates intending to read for a DPhil.
Level of Study: Research
Type: Scholarship
Value: £7,000 per year
Length of Study: Up to 3 years

For further information contact:

Website: www.univ.ox.ac.uk/postgraduate/financial_1/scholarships_and_studentships/

University College: Swire Scholarship (Taiwan)
Subjects: Non-clinical Science subjects.
Purpose: To assist graduate students with fees, maintenance allowance and travel costs.
Eligibility: Open to candidates who are citizens of Taiwan reading for a DPhil.
Level of Study: Research
Type: Scholarship
Value: Fees, maintenance and some travel costs
Length of Study: Up to 3 years

For further information contact:

Website: www.univ.ox.ac.uk/postgraduate/financial_1/scholarships_and_studentships/

University of Oxford Croucher Scholarship
Subjects: Natural sciences, technology or medicine.
Purpose: To provide students who are able to demonstrate academic excellence with the opportunity to pursue postgraduate research study at the University of Oxford.
Eligibility: Open to permanent Hong Kong residents who have a first class honours or equivalent in first degree or a substantive postgraduate degree at Master's level or above.
Level of Study: Research
Type: Scholarship
Value: Tuition and college fees; grant for living expenses at UK Research Council rate
Length of Study: Period of fee liability
No. of awards offered: 4
Closing Date: November 21st

For further information contact:

Website: www.admin.ox.ac.uk/studentfunding/scholarship_profiles/croucher.shtml

Wadham College Brookman Organ Scholarship
Subjects: All subjects.

Purpose: To assist an organisation scholar who has been given admission to read for a higher degree in the university.
Eligibility: Open to all.
Level of Study: Research, Postgraduate
Type: Scholarship
Value: Approximate value of college fee, plus benefits
Length of Study: 1 year, possible renewal
Frequency: At close of existing scholars course of studies
Study Establishment: Wadham College, University of Oxford
Country of Study: United Kingdom
No. of awards offered: 1
Application Procedure: Applicants must apply to The Registrar, Wadham College. See www.wadham.ox.ac.uk for details.
Funding: Trusts
Contributor: Endowed by late E. W. M. Brookman, an old member of the college, in memory of his son, John M Brookman (1926–1980)
Additional Information: Entails certain chapel and choir duties. For more information, please contact admissions@wadh.ox.ac.uk. Closing date to be confirmed - please contact the college for more information.

For further information contact:

Wadham College, Oxford, Oxfordshire, OX1 3PN, England
Website: www.wadham.ox.ac.uk
Contact: The Registrar

Wadham College: Graduate Computing Assistant

Subjects: All subjects.
Purpose: To assist graduate students with fees and accomodation.
Eligibility: Open to all.
Level of Study: Postgraduate, Research
Value: Approximate value of college fee, as stipend, plus free accommodation
Length of Study: 1 year, possible renewal
Additional Information: For further details, please contact admissions@wadh.ox.ac.uk.

Weidenfeld Scholarships

Subjects: All subjects.
Purpose: To cultivate the leaders of tomorrow primarily from Eastern Europe, Central Asia, Russia, the Middle East and North Africa by providing outstanding university graduates and young professionals with the opportunity to pursue graduate studies at the University of Oxford.
Eligibility: Open to new graduate students from Afghanistan, Albania, Algeria, Armenia, Azerbaijan, Bahrain, Belarus, Bosnia and Herzegovina, Bulgaria, Croatia, Czech Republic, Egypt, Estonia, FYR Macedonia, Georgia, Hungary, Iran, Iraq, Israel, Jordan, Kazakhstan, Kuwait, Kyrgyzstan, Latvia, Lebanon, Libya, Lithuania, Mongolia, Montenegro, Morocco, Oman, Palestinian Authority, Poland, Qatar, Moldova, Romania, Russian Federation, Saudi Arabia, Serbia, Slovakia, Slovenia, Sudan, Syrian Arab Republic, Tajikistan, Tunisia, Turkey, Turkmenistan, Ukraine, United Arab Emirates, United States, Uzbekistan, Western Sahara and Yemen.
Level of Study: Postgraduate, Research
Type: Scholarships
Value: Tuition and college fees; grant for living expenses at UK Research Council rate
Length of Study: Full course duration
No. of awards offered: Up to 40–50
Closing Date: January 23rd

For further information contact:

Website: www.admin.ox.ac.uk/studentfunding/scholarship_profiles/Weidenfeld.shtml

Worcester College: Clarendon Fund Linked Award

Subjects: Humanities.
Purpose: To assist graduate students with fees.
Eligibility: Open to candidates who are overseas students.
Level of Study: Postgraduate, Research
Type: Award
Value: College fees
Length of Study: 1 year

For further information contact:

Website: www.admin.ox.ac.uk/studentfunding/scholarship_profiles/clarendon.shtml

Worcester College: Laycock Graduate Studentship in Egyptology

Subjects: Egyptology.
Purpose: To assist graduate students with fees.
Eligibility: Open to candidates who are holders of Oxford undergraduate or advanced degrees by examination.
Level of Study: Postgraduate, Research
Type: Studentship
Value: £6,000 per year
Length of Study: Up to 3 years
Additional Information: Further information and closing date available by e-mailing graduate.enquiries@worc.ox.ac.uk

Zaharoff Graduate Scholarship

Subjects: French.
Purpose: To assist graduate students with fees and maintenance.
Eligibility: All eligible doctoral applicants studying French submitting applications before the third gathered field will automatically be considered, irrespective of choice of college, provided that they have applied for other funded awards (if eligible).
Level of Study: Research, Doctorate
Type: Scholarship
Value: University fees at UK/EU rate; maintenance grant at the value of a full AHRC award
Length of Study: Up to 3 years
Closing Date: January 18th

For further information contact:

Website: www.mod-langs.ox.ac.uk/prizes/index.php#Zahschol

Zoology: Christopher Welch Scholarship in Biological Sciences

Subjects: Zoology.
Purpose: To assist graduate students with fees and maintenance.
Eligibility: Open to candidates with DPhil programme only.
Level of Study: Research
Type: Scholarship
Value: University and college fees at the home student rate, plus a minimum of £13,600 per year maintenance allowance (2007/2008 figure)
Length of Study: 2 years, but may be extended for a third year. Under special circumstances, the award may be extended for an extra 6 months
Closing Date: January 23rd
Additional Information: Generally these will be advertised with a closing date to coincide with application deadline 2, but if possible applications will also be considered subsequent to this; please see website.

For further information contact:

Website: www.zoo.ox.ac.uk/students/postgrad/prospective_students.htm

Zoology: Newton Abraham Scholarship in Biological Sciences

Subjects: Zoology is one of a number of departments that compete for this scholarship each year.
Purpose: To assist graduate students with fees and maintenance.
Eligibility: Open to candidates with DPhil programme only.
Level of Study: Research
Type: Scholarship
Value: University and college fees at the home student rate, plus a minimum of £12,900 per year maintenance allowance
Length of Study: 3 years. Under special circumstances, the award may be extended for an extra 6 months
Closing Date: January 23rd
Additional Information: Generally these will be advertised with a closing date to coincide with Application Deadline 2, but if possible

applications will also be considered subsequent to this; please see website.

For further information contact:

Website: www.zoo.ox.ac.uk/students/postgrad/prospective_students.htm

UNIVERSITY OF PUNE

Institute of Bioinformatics & Biotechnology (IBB), Ganeshkhind, Maharashtra, Pune, 411007, India
Tel: (91) 020-5656061
Fax: (91) 91-20-25690087
Email: directoribb@unipune, chopade@unipune.ernet.in
Website: www.unipune.ernet.in
Contact: Director

The University stands for humanism and tolerance, for reason for adventure of ideas and for the search of truth. It stands for the forward march of the human race towards even higher objectives. If the universities discharge their duties adequately then it is well with the nation and the people – Jawaharlal Nehru.

Department of Biotechnology (DBT) - Junior Research Fellowship

Subjects: Biotechnology and applied biology.
Purpose: To support candidates pursuing research in areas of biotechnology and applied biology.
Eligibility: Open to candidates from the centres supported by the DBT, New Delhi.
Level of Study: Research
Type: Fellowship
Value: Rs 8,000 per month; Rs 9,000 for SRF; and a research contingency of Rs 30,000 per year
Length of Study: 5 years
Frequency: Annual
Study Establishment: University of Pune
Country of Study: India
Application Procedure: A written application along with application fee of Rs 500 in the form of a DD in favour of – Registrar, University of Pune.
Contributor: Government of India

For further information contact:

Department of Biotechnology University of Pune, Pune, 411 007, India
Contact: Professor J. K. Pal, Co-ordinator, DBJ-JRF Programme

THE UNIVERSITY OF QUEENSLAND

Research and Postgraduate Studies, Cumbrae-Stewart Building, Brisbane, QLD, 4072, Australia
Tel: (61) 7 3365 2033/4838
Fax: (61) 7 3365 4455/6941
Email: scholarships@research.uq.edu.au
Website: www.uq.edu.au

The University of Queensland has an outstanding profile in the Australian and international research community. It maintains a world-class, comprehensive programme of research and research training, underpinned by state-of-the-art infrastructure and a commitment to rewarding excellence. As one of Australia's premier universities, UQ attracts researchers and students of outstanding calibre.

The Accenture Scholarship in ITEE

Subjects: Information technology and electrical engineering.
Purpose: To financially assist students to study in the field of information technology and electrical engineering.
Eligibility: Applicants must be enrolled in an Honours programme in the Bachelor of Information Technology, Bachelor of Science or Bachelor of Engineering.
Level of Study: Postgraduate
Type: Scholarship
Value: Australian $1,500
Length of Study: 1 year
Frequency: Annual

Study Establishment: University of Queensland
Country of Study: Australia
Closing Date: May
Funding: Foundation, government

Alumni Association – Elizabeth Usher Memorial Travelling Scholarship

Subjects: Any subject.
Purpose: To assist a research higher degree student to travel overseas to present a research paper or poster at an international conference.
Eligibility: Open to candidates who have graduated from the University of Queensland not more than 5 years ago. The applicants must be enrolled (full-time or part-time) for a PhD and must be in their second or full-time equivalent yera of study for the PhD.
Level of Study: Postgraduate
Type: Scholarship
Value: $2,500
Frequency: Annual
Country of Study: Australia
No. of awards offered: 1
Application Procedure: Applicants must send a completed application form.
Closing Date: June 20th
Funding: Individuals
Contributor: Bequest from the estate of the late Elizabeth Catherine Usher AO
No. of awards given last year: 1
No. of applicants last year: 14
Additional Information: Consideration will be given to applicant's work during the entire postgraduate career, their aptitude for original research and the extent to which participation in this conference will benefit Australia.

For further information contact:

Research Scholarships, Research and Research Training Division, The University of Queensland, Queensland 4072, Brisbane, Australia

APAI Scholarships within Integrative Biology

Subjects: Integrative biology.
Purpose: To characterize the newly generated polyploid trees using molecular, physiological and/or field investigations.
Level of Study: Doctorate, Postgraduate
Type: Scholarship
Value: $25,118 per year (non–taxable)
Length of Study: 3 years
Frequency: Annual
No. of awards offered: 2
Application Procedure: Candidates must contact Dr Susanne Schmidt (susanne.schmidt@uq.edu.au), Dr Peer Schenk (p.schenk@uq.edu.au) or Professor Christa Critchley (c.critchley@uq.edu.au) for more information.

Australian Postgraduate Awards

Subjects: Any subject.
Purpose: To provide a living allowance for research higher degree candidates to undertake a PhD or MPhil.
Eligibility: Open to candidates who hold or expect to hold a Bachelor's degree with Honours Class I or equivalent results. They must be an Australian citizen, permanent Australian resident or a citizen of New Zealand.
Level of Study: Postgraduate
Type: Scholarship
Value: $19,616
Length of Study: 3 years
Frequency: Annual
Country of Study: Australia
No. of awards offered: 140
Application Procedure: Applicants must send in completed application forms.
Closing Date: Mid-October
Funding: Government
Contributor: Australian Government
No. of awards given last year: 186
No. of applicants last year: 430

For further information contact:

Research Scholarships, Research and Research Training Division, The University of Queensland QLD 4072, Brisbane, Australia

The Baillieu Research Scholarship
Subjects: Medicine, law, commerce, economics, architecture, planning.
Purpose: To assist a research higher degree student.
Eligibility: Open to candidates enrolled or eligible to enrol in a research higher degree, not more than 35 years of age and preference shall be given to graduates of not more than 5 years standing.
Level of Study: Postgraduate
Type: Scholarship
Value: $5,000
Length of Study: 1 year
Frequency: Annual
Country of Study: Australia
No. of awards offered: 1
Application Procedure: Applicants must send a completed application form.
Closing Date: August 4th
Contributor: Established in 1954 by a gift of $9,677.42 under the provisions of the Repatriation Fund (Baillieu Gift) Act of 1937
No. of awards given last year: 1
No. of applicants last year: 8
Additional Information: Preference shall be given to a lineal descendant of an Australian soldier or sailor who served in World War I and suffered death, blindness of total capacity. Note that if you do not meet this preference criterion you are still eligible to apply.

For further information contact:

Research Scholarships, Office of Research and Postgraduate Studies, The University of Queensland QLD 4072, Brisbane, Australia

The Constantine Aspromourgos Memorial Scholarship for Greek Studies
Subjects: Greek studies.
Purpose: To assist a research higher degree student studying at least 1 area of Greek studies.
Eligibility: Open to candidates who have obtained their Bachelors or Masters degrees and are undertaking a postgraduate programme involving studies which pertain to at least one area of Greek studies.
Level of Study: Postgraduate
Type: Scholarship
Value: $3,950
Length of Study: 1 year
Frequency: Annual
Country of Study: Australia
No. of awards offered: 1
Application Procedure: Applicants must send a completed application form.
Closing Date: March 27th
Funding: Individuals
Additional Information: The Scholarship is also open to candidates who are undertaking the programme as a student of another university acceptable to the committee, or this university, provided that some part of the programme involves studies at another university.

For further information contact:

Faculty of Arts, Forgan Smith Building, The University of Queensland QLD 4072
Contact: Executive Dean

Dr Rosamond Siemon Postgraduate Renal Research Scholarship
Subjects: Medical sciences.
Purpose: To support a research higher degree candidate to undertake multidisciplinary, collaborative research into renal disease, repair and regeneration.
Eligibility: Open to candidates who are enrolled or intend to enrol in a research higher degree at the University of Queensland and who demonstrate a high level of academic acheivement and ability.
Level of Study: Postgraduate
Type: Scholarship

Value: The value of the scholarship is $30,000 per year consisting of a stipend of $20,000 and a direct research cost allowance of $10,000
Length of Study: 3 years
Frequency: Annual
Country of Study: Australia
No. of awards offered: 1
Application Procedure: Applicants must send a proposed research project description, certified copies of academic transcripts, academic Curriculum vitae, including publications and 3 letters of recommendation.
Closing Date: November 20th
Funding: Individuals
Contributor: Dr Rosamond Siemon
Additional Information: Research Scholarships Refree Report Form can be used. This can be accessed from www.uq.edu.au/grad-school/scholarship-forms

For further information contact:

Research Scholarships, Office of Research and Postgraduate Studies, The University of Queensland QLD 4072, Brisbane, Australia
Contact: Professor Melissa Little

E.M.A and M.C Henker Postgraduate Medical Research Scholarship
Subjects: Medical Sciences.
Purpose: To assist a research higher degree student to undertake medical research.
Eligibility: Open to MBBS graduates of not more than 8 years standing seeking to undertake medical research. Preference shall be given to applicants who: enrol full-time PhD or MPhil degree; demonstrate that they are involved or have arranged involvement in an existing research project; and demonstrate an intention to transfer to an NHMRC Medical Postgraduate Research Scholarship at the termination of this scholarship.
Level of Study: Postgraduate
Type: Scholarship
Value: $28,600
Length of Study: Scholarship will be held for 1 year, but extension for a further year may be granted if progress has been excellent and there are good reasons for failure to find alternative funding
Frequency: Dependent on funds available
Country of Study: Australia
No. of awards offered: 1
Application Procedure: Application form must be completed.
Closing Date: July
Funding: Individuals
Contributor: Miss Edith M.A. Henker and Miss Minnie C. Henker
No. of awards given last year: 1
No. of applicants last year: 1
Additional Information: Scholarship shall consist of: a stipend commensurate with the stipend associated with an NH&MRC Medical Postgraduate Research Scholarship; and a school maintenance grant to support the scholar's research of an amount determined by the Head, School of Medicine for each year.

The E.S Cornwall Memorial Scholarship
Subjects: Engineering.
Purpose: The object of the scholarship is to enable UQ Engineering graduates to obtain special experience abroad in aspects of the electricity supply industry so that the industry in Australia may benefit by the knowledge and experience thus gained by them.
Eligibility: Preference will be given to applicants who have between 3 and 5 years industry experience.
Level of Study: Postgraduate
Type: Scholarship
Value: $2,400
Length of Study: Period between 9 and 18 months, in accordance with a programme approved by the Advisory Commitee
Frequency: Dependent on funds available
Country of Study: Australia
No. of awards offered: 1
Application Procedure: Application form must be completed.
Closing Date: May 31st
Contributor: University of Queensland

Edwin Tooth Scholarship

Subjects: Medicine, public health.
Purpose: To assist a research higher degree student to undertake full-time study towards a PhD.
Eligibility: Applicants must be eligible to enrol in a PhD. Research must be conducted within the biological and chemical sciences faculty or within the schools for medicine or population health.
Level of Study: Postgraduate
Type: Scholarship
Value: Up to $28,600
Length of Study: 2 years initially with the possibility of a further year
Frequency: Dependent on funds available
Country of Study: Australia
No. of awards offered: 1
Application Procedure: Application form must be completed.
Closing Date: July 5th
Funding: Individuals
Contributor: Bequest in the will of Sir Edwin Tooth
No. of awards given last year: 1
No. of applicants last year: 8

Endeavour International Postgraduate Research Scholarship (IPRS)

Subjects: Any subject.
Purpose: This scholarship covers tuition fees and health cover for International students undertaking a PhD or MPhil.
Eligibility: The IPRS programmes enables outstanding international students to undertake an MPhil or PhD in areas of research strength at Australian universities to gain experience with leading Australian researchers.
Level of Study: Postgraduate
Type: Scholarship
Value: Tuition fees and health cover (including health cover for spouse and dependents)
Length of Study: For an initial period of 3 years for PhD and 2 years for MPhil study
Frequency: Annual
Country of Study: Australia
No. of awards offered: 30
Application Procedure: To apply just complete the International Student Application for Research Studies – MPhil or PhD from the university website paying attention to the section on scholarships.
Closing Date: August 31st
Funding: Government
Contributor: Australian Government Department of Education, Science and Training (DEST)
No. of awards given last year: 30
No. of applicants last year: 435
Additional Information: For more information please visit the Commonwealth Department of Education, Science and Training website. All enquiries from prospective international students regarding this award should be directed to the UQ International Education Directorate.

For further information contact:

International Admissions Section, The University of Queensland, Level 2, JD Story Building, Brisbane, Queensland, 4072, Australia
Contact: The Manager

Graduate School Research Travel Grant (GSRTG)

Subjects: Any subject.
Purpose: To fund students to travel to access resources in Australia or overseas that have enabled them to speed up progress on and enhance the quality of their thesis.
Eligibility: Applicants must be enrolled for a PhD or MPhil degree, must be confirmed PhD or MPhil candidates by the closing date – no exceptions, who have previously held a GSRTG are not eligible, grants will not be made retrospectively. Applicants are ineligible if they are already undertaking the research travel at the time of application closing date and if the need for this research travel was identified in the initial research proposal.
Level of Study: Postgraduate
Type: Grant
Value: Australia/New Zealand: up to $2,000; Indonesia/Papua New Guinea/Pacific Islands/Southeast Asia: up to $3,000; Other overseas destinations: up to $5,000
Frequency: Bi-annual
Country of Study: Australia
No. of awards offered: Up to 80
Application Procedure: Application form must be completed.
Closing Date: March and August
Contributor: University of Queensland
No. of awards given last year: Round 1: 42, Round 2: 37
No. of applicants last year: Round 1: 56, Round 2: 43
Additional Information: These grants do not fund essential research travel signalled in the initial research proposal since that should be met from other grants or school funds; GSRTGs are not intended for consultation and Conference travel will not be funded. Preference will be given to travel that was unforeseen at the time of confirmation of candidature. Travel to workshops where new specialist techniques are taught may be funded in special cases; these require a strong and well supported argument, clearly indicating how this training will benefit the timely submission of the thesis. Successful applicants must be enrolled full-time for the duration of their travel and travel must commence within 6 months of the grant being offered. Students enrolled in a PhD by Cotutelle, in International Collaborative Mode or in a similar international collaborative arrangement must satisfy the same eligibility criteria as all other GSRTG applicants.

Herdsman Fellowship in Medical Science

Subjects: Medicine, related health sciences.
Purpose: The fellowship is open to graduates in medicine or related health sciences enrolled full-time for a PhD on a topic related to the medical problems of the aged.
Eligibility: Applicants must be graduates in medicine or related health sciences, enrol full-time for a PhD, and be undertaking a research topic related to the medical problems of the aged.
Level of Study: Postgraduate
Type: Fellowship
Value: $19,616
Length of Study: Fellowship shall initially be for 1 year but may be extended by the commitee for further terms of 1 year up to a total of 3 years
Frequency: As tenure falls vacant
Country of Study: Australia
No. of awards offered: 1
Application Procedure: Applications must consist of: covering letter addressing the Herdsman Fellowship Rules, in particular point 2, academic Curriculum vitae, 2 referee reports. No strict format is required; however the Research Scholarships generic Referee Report may be used.
Closing Date: August 31st
Contributor: Maintained by the income from a bequest of $260,000 from Mrs Rose Herdsman
No. of awards given last year: 1
No. of applicants last year: 1

For further information contact:

Faculty of Health Sciences, University of Queensland, Brisbane, 4072, Australia
Email: s.tett@pharmacy.uq.edu.au
Contact: Professor Susan Tett, Deputy Executive Dean and Director of Research

PhD Scholarship in Immunology and Immunogenetics

Subjects: Immunology.
Purpose: To provide the foundations for the development of treatments based on the genetic findings.
Eligibility: Open to a dynamic, intelligent and diligent PhD candidate (Australian or international) with either a clinical or a relevant basic science background to take forward the project.
Level of Study: Doctorate
Type: Scholarship
Value: Australian $25,000 per year
Length of Study: 3 years
Frequency: Annual
Study Establishment: The University of Queensland
Country of Study: Australia
No. of awards offered: 1
Application Procedure: Candidates must contact Prof. Brown for more information.

Closing Date: August 20th
Additional Information: International applicants must cover tuition fees ($27,000 per year).

For further information contact:

Diamantina Institute for Cancer, Immunology & Metabolic Medicine, Level 4 Research Wing, Princess Alexandra Hospital, Ipswich Road
Tel: 07 3240 2870
Email: matt.brown@uq.edu.au
Contact: Professor Matt Brown

Queensland Cancer Fund PhD Scholarships
Subjects: Any involving cancer research.
Purpose: For any field related to cancer research.
Eligibility: Candidates must be ordinarily resident in Queensland, be an Australian citizen or hold a visa or passport allowing them to work or study in Queensland.
Level of Study: Postgraduate
Type: Scholarship
Value: $22,100 (stipend amount to be indexed annually to CPI – no extension allowed)
Length of Study: 3 years
Frequency: Annual
Country of Study: Australia
No. of awards offered: 3
Application Procedure: Application forms and further information is available from the Queensland Cancer website: www.qldcancer.com.au/research/qcf_grantd/PhDScholarships.htm
Funding: Corporation
Contributor: Queensland Cancer fund
No. of awards given last year: 2
No. of applicants last year: 2

R.N. Hammon Scholarship
Subjects: Science, engineering, medicine, dentistry, architecture, agriculture and veterinary science, and other fields of study.
Purpose: To assist Australian Aboriginal and/or Torres Strait Island students for further studies.
Eligibility: Open to Australian Aboriginal and/or Torres Strait Island students who have successfully completed at least one year of an undergraduate or postgraduate program and are enrolling on a full-time basis for a subsequent year of that program, or for a further program.
Level of Study: Postgraduate
Type: Scholarship
Value: Australian $2,000 per year
Frequency: Annual
Study Establishment: The University of Queensland, Queensland University of Technology, University of Southern Queensland, Central Queensland University, or Queensland Colleges of TAFE
Country of Study: Australia
Application Procedure: Candidates can download the application form and referee report form from the website.
Additional Information: The Selection Committee shall take into account the academic merit or technical excellence, any other scholarship, bursary, award or benefit, whether governmental or otherwise, to which the applicant is entitled; and social and economic need.

For further information contact:

Tel: 07 33651984
Email: ugscholarships@uq.edu.au

Sister Janet Mylonas Memorial Scholarship
Subjects: Any involving cancer research.
Purpose: To assist a student undertaking a research higher degree involving cancer research.
Eligibility: Open to students who are commencing a programme at the University which either directly involves cancer research or will prepare the students to undertake cancer research in the future, and satisfy the Selection Committee that they are most likely to engage in cancer research during the tenure of the scholarship or in the future.
Level of Study: Postgraduate
Type: Scholarship
Value: Up to $28,600 plus direct research cost allowance
Length of Study: 3 years

Frequency: Annual
Country of Study: Australia
No. of awards offered: 1
Application Procedure: Applicants must submit an application form.
Closing Date: July 5th
Contributor: Income bequeathed to the university by late Stelios Demetrion Mylonas
No. of awards given last year: 1
No. of applicants last year: 4

Sustainable Tourism CRC – Climate Change PhD
Subjects: Commerce, management, tourism and services.
Purpose: To develop a tourism consumer decision-making model that focuses on climate change as a driver of consumer choice and apply it to Australian tourism market.
Eligibility: Open to candidates who have achieved First Class (Honours) Degree or equivalent.
Level of Study: Postgraduate, Research
Type: Scholarship
Value: Australian $19,930 per year
Length of Study: 3 years
Frequency: Annual
Study Establishment: The University of Queensland
Country of Study: Australia
No. of awards offered: 1
Application Procedure: Candidates must contact Jane Malady for application forms.
Contributor: Sustainable Tourism CRC and University of Queensland
Additional Information: For further information on topic and research proposal contact Prof Ballantyne at r.ballantyne@uq.edu.au.

For further information contact:

STCRC Education Program, Sustainable Tourism CRC
Tel: 61 7 5552 9063
Email: Jane@crctourism.com.au
Website: www.crctourism.com.au
Contact: Jane Malady

University of Queensland International Living Allowance Scholarships (UQILAS)
Subjects: Any subject.
Purpose: It provides a living allowance to international students who have been awarded an Endeavour International Postgraduate Research Scholarship (IPRS).
Eligibility: The IPRS programme enables outstanding international students to undertake an MPhil or PhD in areas of research strength at Australian universities to gain experience with leading Australian researchers.
Level of Study: Postgraduate
Type: Scholarship
Value: $19,616 p.a
Length of Study: 3 years for PhD and 2 years for MPhil
Frequency: Annual
Country of Study: Australia
No. of awards offered: 50
Application Procedure: IPRS application should be completed on the International Student Application for Research Studies – MPhil or PhD.
Closing Date: August 31st
Contributor: University of Queensland
No. of awards given last year: 42
No. of applicants last year: 435

For further information contact:

International Admissions Section, The University of Queensland, Level 2, JD Story Building, Brisbane, Queensland, 4072
Contact: The Manager

The UQ AHURI PhD Scholarship
Subjects: Any subject.
Purpose: The scholarship holder is required to undertake research on a topic related to the research and policy areas included in the AHURI research agenda.

Eligibility: Applicants must be an Australian citizen, permanent resident or New Zealand citizen at the application closing date; may be any age; must meet the University's English proficiency requirements; must enrol for a full-time research higher degree (part-time awards are available in exceptional circumstances); must hold or expect to hold a Bachelor's degree with Honours Class I, or a qualification deemed equivalent. This qualification must be in a relevant field; must have completed at least 4 years of full-time equivalent tertiary education.
Level of Study: Postgraduate
Type: Scholarship
Value: $19,616
Length of Study: 3 years
Frequency: Annual
Country of Study: Australia
No. of awards offered: 1
Application Procedure: Application form.
Closing Date: July
Contributor: University of Queensland
Additional Information: The student awarded the UQ AHURI PhD scholarship may also be recommended for an AHURI 'top-up' scholarship of $7,000 p.a. to supplement the AHURI PhD scholarship.

UQ International Research Award (UQIRA)

Subjects: Any subject.
Purpose: The UQIRA is funded by the University of Queensland and covers tuition fees and health cover for international students for an initial period of 3 years for PhD and 2 years for MPhil study. They are awarded during the annual Endeavour IPRS round.
Eligibility: As for the Endeavour International Postgraduate Research Scholarship (IPRS). Please see UQ website.
Level of Study: Postgraduate
Type: Award
Value: Tuition fees and health cover (including health cover for spouse and dependents)
Length of Study: 3 years for PhD and 2 years for MPhil
Frequency: Annual
Country of Study: Australia
No. of awards offered: Approx. 20
Application Procedure: These scholarships are awarded during the Endeavour International Postgraduate Research Scholarship (IPRS) round. As with the IPRS, applications should be completed on the International Student Application for Research Studies – MPhil or PhD. All applicants considered for the IPRS will be automatically considered for a UQ International Research Award.
Closing Date: September 19th
Contributor: University of Queensland
No. of awards given last year: 19
No. of applicants last year: 21

For further information contact:

International Admissions Section, University of Queensland, Level 2, JD Story Building, Brisbane, Queensland, 4072, Australia
Contact: The Manager

UQ Joint Research Scholarships (UQJRS)

Subjects: Any subject.
Purpose: It enables schools, centres or institute (through their Head of School/Postgraduate Coordinator) to nominate high quality commencing or enrolled research higher degree candidates. The UQ Graduate School shares the cost for these scholarships with schools, centres or institutes.
Eligibility: Nominees will be selected on the following criteria: academic merit; research potential or demonstrated research performance, including publications, seminar/conference papers and timely confirmation (if applicable); match with the university, faculty or school research strength.
Level of Study: Postgraduate
Type: Scholarship
Value: $19,616
Length of Study: 3 years for PhD and 2 years for MPhil
Frequency: Bi-annual
Country of Study: Australia
No. of awards offered: Approx. 40
Application Procedure: Students do not submit an application form for these scholarships, but must register an expression of interest with

their school. Heads of School/Postgraduate Coordinators must justify and provide supporting evidence for each nomination and provide ratings for research potential or demonstrated research performance. Schools may require nominees to provide academic references.
Closing Date: February
Contributor: University of Queensland
No. of awards given last year: 40
No. of applicants last year: 96

UQ Mid Year Scholarships (UQMYS)

Subjects: Any subject.
Purpose: A limited number of Mid Year Scholarships are available to students completing a Bachelor's degree with Honours Class I or equivalent qualification in semester 1 and who intend on commencing a research higher degree immediately in semester 2.
Eligibility: Applicants must be a Australian citizen, Australian permanent resident or New Zealand citizen as at the application closing date, must have completed a Bachelor's degree with Honours Class I, or a qualification deemed equivalent, in semester 1. This qualification must be in a relevant field. Applicants must enrol for a full-time research higher degree by August 25th and may be of any age.
Level of Study: Postgraduate
Type: Scholarship
Value: $19,616
Length of Study: 3 years
Frequency: Annual
Country of Study: Australia
No. of awards offered: Approx. 20
Application Procedure: Application form.
Closing Date: June
Contributor: University of Queensland
No. of awards given last year: 23
No. of applicants last year: 34

UQ Research Scholarship (UQRS)

Subjects: Any subject.
Purpose: It enables recently confirmed students who have demonstrated the strength of their research potential during their first year of candidature to work on their research higher degree full-time with scholarship support.
Eligibility: Check website for detailed eligibility criteria.
Level of Study: Postgraduate
Type: Scholarship
Value: $19,616 p.a
Length of Study: Up to 3 years
Frequency: Bi-annual
Country of Study: Australia
No. of awards offered: Approx. 20
Application Procedure: Students do not submit an application form, but must register an expression of interest with their school. Heads of School/Postgraduate Coordinators will complete a UQCS Nomination form to provide evidence in support of each nomination.
Closing Date: May and September
Contributor: University of Queensland
No. of awards given last year: Round 1: 40, Round 2: 25
No. of applicants last year: Round 1: 44, Round 2: 31

UQ Research Scholarships (UQRS)

Subjects: Any subject.
Purpose: To provide a living allowance for research higher degree candidates (PhD or MPhil).
Eligibility: Applicants may be of any age, must hold or expect to hold a Bachelor's degree with Honours Class I or equivalent results by December 31st and must be an Australian citizen, Australian permanent resident or New Zealand citizen as at the application closing date.
Level of Study: Postgraduate
Type: Scholarship
Value: $19,616
Length of Study: 3 years
Frequency: Annual
Country of Study: Australia
No. of awards offered: 35
Application Procedure: Application form.
Contributor: University of Queensland

No. of awards given last year: 38
No. of applicants last year: 433
Additional Information: The University of Queensland offers successful applicants who relocate more than 250 km to take up an APA or UQPRS a $1,100 Establishment Allowance. This is in addition to the Travel/Removal Allowance.

UQ Return to Research Scholarships (UQRTRS)
Subjects: Any subject.
Purpose: To assist women re-entering an academic or research career which has been interrupted, delayed or otherwise disrupted by family or other commitments.
Eligibility: Applicants may be of any age and must: have been interrupted, delayed or otherwise disrupted from an academic or research career by family or other commitments for at least 5 years; be an Australian citizen, Australian permanent resident or New Zealand citizen as at the application closing date; meet the university's English proficiency requirements; enrol for a full-time research higher degree before March 26th (part-time awards are available, check guidelines); hold a Bachelor's degree with Honours Class I or IIA or a qualification deemed equivalent. The qualification must be in a relevant field; have completed at least 4 years of full-time equivalent tertiary education.
Level of Study: Postgraduate
Type: Scholarship
Value: $19,616
Length of Study: 3 years
Frequency: Annual
Country of Study: Australia
No. of awards offered: 2
Application Procedure: Application form.
Closing Date: October
Contributor: University of Queensland
No. of awards given last year: 2
No. of applicants last year: 22

Venerable Archdeacon E L Hayes Postgraduate Scholarship
Subjects: Australian studies, literature and history.
Purpose: To provide support for research in the fields of Australian literature and/or historical sources.
Eligibility: Open to full-time internal students of the University of Queensland who are enrolled in a course leading to a Master's or Doctorate of Philosophy.
Level of Study: Postgraduate
Type: Scholarship
Value: Australian $ 19,231
Length of Study: 3 years
Frequency: Annual
Study Establishment: Brisbane Metropolitan and Ipswich West Moreton, Queensland
Country of Study: Australia

THE UNIVERSITY OF READING

Whiteknights, PO Box 217, Reading, Berkshire, RG6 6AH, England
Tel: (44) 11 8987 5123
Fax: (44) 11 8931 4404
Email: studenthelp@reading.ac.uk
Website: www.rdg.ac.uk
Contact: Student Financial Support Office

The University of Reading offers postgraduate taught and research degree courses in all the traditional subject areas except medical sciences. Vocational courses are also offered. Research work in many areas is of international renown.

University of Reading Arts and Humanities Studentship
Subjects: Research areas within those covered by the Faculty of Arts and Humanities.
Purpose: To enable students to obtain a doctoral degree.
Level of Study: Doctorate, Postgraduate
Type: Studentship
Value: Composition fee at the home standard rate plus a maintenance award related to that paid by the relevant United Kingdom Research Council

Length of Study: 3 years
Frequency: Annual
Study Establishment: The University of Reading
Country of Study: United Kingdom
No. of awards offered: Varies
Application Procedure: Applicants must complete an application form, available from the Faculty Office via email, faspg@reading.ac.uk. Eligible applicants are expected to apply for, and accept if offered, a scholarship from the relevant United Kingdom Research Council or an ORS award.
Closing Date: End of January of the year of entry
Funding: Private

University of Reading Felix Scholarship
Subjects: All subjects.
Eligibility: Open to international postgraduate taught and research students who have Indian citizenship, under 30 years of age holding at least a first class honours degree and who have not studied outside India.
Level of Study: Postgraduate
Type: Scholarship
Value: All tuition fees and generous allowances for clothes, books, and a return flight home
Length of Study: 1–3 years
Frequency: Annual
Study Establishment: University of Reading
Country of Study: United Kingdom
No. of awards offered: 1
Application Procedure: Contact The Student Financial Support Office at the Carrington Building.
Closing Date: January 31st
Funding: Trusts
Contributor: The Felix Trust
No. of awards given last year: 6
No. of applicants last year: 120

For further information contact:

Tel: (0) 118 378 4245

University of Reading General Overseas Scholarships
Subjects: All subjects, subject to the availability of appropriate supervision at the University.
Purpose: To enable students to obtain a doctoral degree.
Eligibility: Open to applicants who hold a first degree qualification and pay international fees.
Level of Study: Doctorate, Postgraduate
Type: Studentship
Value: Full tuition fees and maintenance at a rate related to that offered by the relevant United Kingdom Funding Council
Length of Study: Up to 3 years
Frequency: Annual
Study Establishment: The University of Reading
Country of Study: United Kingdom
No. of awards offered: 5
Application Procedure: Applicants must fulfil the eligibility criteria and express an interest in the scholarships to be considered. They are also requested to contact The Student Financial Support Office at the Carrington Building.
Closing Date: Please contact the University for ascertaining this information
Funding: Private
Contributor: University of Reading
No. of awards given last year: 3
No. of applicants last year: 135

University of Reading Graduate School for the Social Sciences Studentships
Subjects: Social sciences.
Purpose: To enable students to obtain a doctoral degree.
Level of Study: Postgraduate, Doctorate
Type: Scholarship
Value: Composition fee at the home standard rate plus a maintenance award related to the rate paid by the relevant Research Council; also some smaller awards
Length of Study: Up to 3 years

Frequency: Annual
Study Establishment: The University of Reading
Country of Study: United Kingdom
No. of awards offered: Up to 10
Application Procedure: Applicants must complete an application form available from the Faculty Office via email, faspg@reading.ac.uk
Closing Date: End of January of the year of entry
Funding: Private
Contributor: The University of Reading
No. of awards given last year: 4

University of Reading MSc Intelligent Buildings Scholarship

Subjects: Construction management and engineering.
Eligibility: In order to be considered for this Scholarship you must hold the offer of a place on the MSc Intellegent Buildings course.
Level of Study: Postgraduate
Type: Scholarship
Value: UK £3,000
Length of Study: 1 year
Frequency: Annual
Study Establishment: University of Reading
Country of Study: United Kingdom
No. of awards offered: 1
Application Procedure: Contact Gulay Ozkan, Programme Coordinator at the School of Construction Management and Engineering.
Closing Date: August 30th
Contributor: The Happold Trust

For further information contact:

Tel: (0) 118 378 6254
Email: g.ozkan@rdg.ac.uk

University of Reading Postgraduate Studentship

Subjects: All subjects, subject to the availability of appropriate supervision at the University.
Purpose: To enable students to obtain a doctoral degree.
Eligibility: Open to candidates holding a first degree qualification.
Level of Study: Doctorate, Postgraduate
Type: Studentship
Value: The composition fee at the home standard rate plus a maintenance award related to the relevant Research Council rate
Length of Study: Up to 3 years
Frequency: Annual
Study Establishment: The University of Reading
Country of Study: United Kingdom and Australia
No. of awards offered: 4
Application Procedure: Applicants must be nominated to the Financial Support Office. Full details are available on the Funding search page of The University of Reading website (www.reading.ac.uk).
Closing Date: February of the year of entry
Funding: Private
Contributor: The University of Reading
No. of awards given last year: 4
No. of applicants last year: 90
Additional Information: Applications are assessed on the quality of their research proposal and shortlisted applicants will be asked to attend an interview.

UNIVERSITY OF REGINA

Scholarship and Award Office, Faculty of Graduate Studies, North Residence N.110.23737 Wascana Parkway, Regina, SK, S4S-0A2, Canada
Tel: (1) 306 585 4161
Fax: (1) 306 585 4893
Email: grad.studies@uregina.ca
Website: www.uregina.ca/gradstudies
Contact: Ms Ann Bishop, Faculty of Research Studies

Founded as Regina College in 1911, the University of Regina became an affiliated junior college of the University of Saskatchewan in 1925 and acquired degree granting status in 1959. The University achieved academic autonomy in 1974. The Faculty of Graduate Studies and

Research offers a wide range of programmes such as social justice, culture and heritage, energy and the environment, health and informatics.

China-Canada Scholars Exchange Program

Subjects: All subjects.
Purpose: To support Canadian scholars and students who wish to study or do research in subject areas related to China in the Chinese universities that are open to Chinese Government Scholarship recipients.
Eligibility: Open to applicants who are faculty members at Canadian Universities or students who have a Bachelor's degree or are enrolled in a graduate programme.
Level of Study: Graduate, Postgraduate, Research
Type: Scholarship
Value: The scholarship covers the cost of basic living allowance, payment of tuition fees, on-campus accommodation, medical insurance and teaching and research materials
Length of Study: 4–12 months
Frequency: Annual
Application Procedure: Applicants must submit 5 copies of each of the following: a completed application form, a detailed study or research proposal indicating objectives, duration of the proposed stay, methodologies, 2 letters of reference, academic transcripts and a certificate of degree letter verifying the graduation time by the dean.
Closing Date: February 1st
Contributor: China Scholarship Council
Additional Information: Preference will be given to those candidates whose research is related to the study of China.

For further information contact:

Education Office the Chinese Embassy in Canada 80 Cobourg Street, Ottawa, ON, K1N-8H1, Canada
Tel: (1) 613 789 6312
Fax: (1) 613 789 0262
Website: www.chinaembassycanada.org

UNIVERSITY OF SHEFFIELD

Western Bank, Sheffield, S10 2TN, United Kingdom
Tel: (44) 114 222 2000
Fax: (44) 114 2223739
Email: grad.school@sheffield.ac.uk
Website: www.shef.ac.uk

The University's history dates back to 1828, when the Sheffield School of Medicine was founded, and the University Charter was granted in 1905. With 25,000 students, from 116 countries, and almost 6000 staff, it is one of the leading universities of United Kingdom.

Dorothy Hodgkin Postgraduate Awards

Subjects: All subjects.
Purpose: To enable top-quality applicants to undertake doctoral research at the University.
Eligibility: Open to prospective international students only.
Level of Study: Postgraduate, Research
Type: Studentship
Value: Up to a maximum of £75,000 per award to cover tuition fees and living expenses
Frequency: Annual
Study Establishment: University of Sheffield
No. of awards offered: 2
Application Procedure: Candidates can check the website for further details.

University of Sheffield Postgraduate International Scholarships

Subjects: Arts and sciences.
Purpose: To provide opportunities to Russian students of high academic standing.
Eligibility: Open to candidates who are Russian by birth or permanently domiciled in Russia and must hold an offer of a study place for entry.
Level of Study: Postgraduate
Type: Scholarships

Value: UK £ 2,000
Length of Study: 1 year
Frequency: Annual
Country of Study: Russia
Application Procedure: Candidates will be sent a postgraduate International Scholarships application form automatically if they are eligible.
Additional Information: Applicants cannot apply for the scholarship before being offered a study place at Sheffield.

White Rose Studentships

Subjects: Plant biology.
Purpose: Collaborative research networks within the three White Rose Universities.
Eligibility: Open to United Kingdom, European Union, and international applicants who will register with the University for a PhD degree.
Level of Study: Postgraduate, Research
Type: Studentship
Value: United Kingdom, European Union tuition fee bursary + stipend (approx £12,900)
Length of Study: 3 years
Frequency: Annual
Study Establishment: One of the three White Rose Universities
No. of awards offered: 1
Application Procedure: Candidates can check the website for further details.
Additional Information: International applicants are only eligible if they can show sufficient funds to cover the difference between the United Kingdom and international students tuition fee.

For further information contact:

Email: s.beecroft@shef.ac.uk
Contact: Simon Beecroft

UNIVERSITY OF SOUTH AUSTRALIA

GPO Box 2471, Adelaide, SA, 5001, Australia
Tel: (61) 8 8302 6611/3615
Fax: (61) 8 8302 2466/3997
Email: research.international@unisa.edu.au
Website: www.unisa.edu.au

The University of South Australia is an innovative and successful institution with a distinctive profile. It is committed to educating professionals, creating and applying knowledge and serving the community.

Aboriginal Advancement League Study Grants

Subjects: All subjects.
Purpose: To help Australian Indigenous and Torres Strait Islander students of the University of South Australia and Flinders University who are enrolled in a postgraduate or Medical Degree.
Eligibility: Open to Australian Indigenous and Torres Strait Islander (permanent residents of South Australia) and students of the University of South Australia and Flinders University, who have enrolled in a postgraduate or Medical Degree.
Level of Study: Postgraduate
Type: Study grant
Value: $5000(Full-Time)
Frequency: Annual
Study Establishment: University of South Australia and Flinders University
Country of Study: Australia
Application Procedure: Check website for further details.
Closing Date: March 31st
Additional Information: Part-time grants are also awarded on a pro rata basis. For further information please check www.unisa.edu.au/scholarship/Ab_Advancement_League_appform

The AFUW–SA Inc Trust Fund Bursary

Subjects: All subjects.
Purpose: To assist women undertaking postgraduate studies.
Eligibility: Open to women undertaking postgraduate degrees by coursework at Australian universities.
Level of Study: Postgraduate
Type: Bursary

Value: $4,000
Frequency: Annual
Study Establishment: Australian universities
Country of Study: Australia
Application Procedure: Candidates must apply on forms available from the AFUW website from October to February.
Closing Date: March 1st
Funding: Trusts
Contributor: The Australian Federation of University Women – South Australia Inc (AFUW–SA Inc) Trust Fund
Additional Information: All bursaries are envisaged primarily as short-term aids and must be used within 1 year of the date of award.

For further information contact:

GPO Box 634, Adelaide, 5001, Australia
Website: www.afuwsa-bursaries.com.au

The Diamond Jubilee Bursary

Subjects: All subjects.
Purpose: To assist men and women undertaking postgraduate studies.
Eligibility: Open to men and women undertaking a postgraduate degree by coursework at a South Australian university.
Level of Study: Postgraduate
Type: Bursary
Value: $4,000
Frequency: Annual
Study Establishment: Australian universities
Country of Study: Australia
Application Procedure: Candidates must apply on forms available from the AFUW website from October to February.
Closing Date: March 1st
Contributor: The Australian Federation of University Women – South Australia Inc (AFUW–SA Inc) Trust Fund
Additional Information: All bursaries are envisaged primarily as short-term aids and must be used within 1 year of the date of award.

For further information contact:

GPO Box 634, Adelaide, 5001, Australia
Website: www.afuwsa-bursaries.com.au

Division of Business Student Mobility Scholarships

Subjects: Business programme.
Purpose: To assist business students undertaking an international exchange (via the UniSA International Student Exchange Program) at a partner university.
Eligibility: Open to both undergraduate and postgraduate coursework students enrolled in a Division of Business program and are participating in exchange for the first time.
Level of Study: Postgraduate
Type: Scholarship
Value: $5000 for Institutional Partner Scholarships, $2500 for Student Mobility Scholarships.$5,000 for institutional partner scholarships, $2,500 for postgraduate mobility scholarships, $2,500 for undergraduate mobility scholarships
Frequency: Annual
Application Procedure: For extended criteria and application details, please contact: Ms Sarah Oolyer-Braham.

For further information contact:

Student Mobility and Academic Administration, Business Division Office
Tel: 08 8302 0880
Email: sarah.collyer-braham@unisa.edu.au
Contact: Ms Sarah Collyer-Braham, Administrative Officer

Donald Dyer Scholarship – Public Relations & Communication Management

Subjects: Public relations, communication management.
Purpose: To encourage research of an original nature leading to the advancement of knowledge in public relations and communication.
Eligibility: Open to candidates who have achieved First Class (Honours) or equivalent. Candidates from discipline areas such as public relations, communication, marketing or advertising are encouraged to apply.

Level of Study: Postgraduate, Research
Type: Scholarship
Value: Australian $22,200 per annum(tax-free) Plus one return travel airfare between the candidate's home location and Adelaide, and organised by the University
Frequency: Annual
Study Establishment: University of South Australia
Country of Study: Australia
No. of awards offered: 1
Application Procedure: Check website for further details.
Closing Date: October 29th
Contributor: Bequest from the estate of the Late Sylvia Dyer

For further information contact:

School of Communication
Tel: 08 8302 4493
Fax: 08 8302 4745
Email: david.brittan@unisa.edu.au
Website: www.unisa.edu.au/cppc/DyerScholarship.asp
Contact: David Brittan, (Postgraduate Research) Education Administrator

Ferry Scholarship

Subjects: Physics and chemistry.
Purpose: Promoting study and research in physics and chemistry.
Eligibility: Open to Australian citizens under the age of 25 years on January 1st of the year of the award, who have completed at least 4 years of tertiary education studies, have a First Class (Honours) (or equivalent undergraduate degree), and have enrolled as full–time students for a Master's Degree or Doctorate by research in chemistry or physics.
Level of Study: Postgraduate
Type: Scholarship
Value: A stipend which provides an exemption from tuition fees, allowances, and leave provisions
Length of Study: Up to 3 years (Doctorate) and 2 years (Masters Degree)
Frequency: Annual
Application Procedure: Applications can be filled online.
Closing Date: October 31st
Contributor: Bequest from the late Cedric Arnold Seth Ferry

For further information contact:

Australian Admissions and Scholarships, University of South Australia
Tel: 8302 3967
Email: jenni.critcher@unisa.edu.au
Website: www.unisa.edu.au/resdegrees/howtoapply/default.asp
Contact: Jenni Critcher

International Postgraduate Research Scholarships (IPRS)

Subjects: All subjects.
Purpose: To attract international postgraduate students to study for a higher degree by research in Australia and support Australia's research effort.
Eligibility: Available to international research candidates generally with first-class honours degree or equivalent.
Level of Study: Postgraduate, Doctorate
Type: Research scholarship
Value: Australian $19,231 per year
Frequency: Annual
Study Establishment: The University of South Australia
Country of Study: Any country
Application Procedure: Applicants must submit an application form, which can be obtained from the website.
Closing Date: End of August
Funding: Government
Contributor: Department of Education, Science and Training (DEST)
No. of awards given last year: 6
No. of applicants last year: 160

The Jean Gilmore, Thenie Baddams and Daphne Elliot Bursaries

Subjects: All subjects.
Purpose: To assist women undertaking postgraduate studies.

Eligibility: Open to women enrolled for research towards a PhD or Masters at Australian universities.
Level of Study: Postgraduate
Type: Bursary
Value: $6,000
Frequency: Annual
Study Establishment: Australian universities
Country of Study: Australia
Application Procedure: Candidates must apply on forms available from the AFUW website from October to February.
Closing Date: March 1st
Funding: Trusts
Contributor: The Australian Federation of University Women – South Australia Inc (AFUW–SA Inc) Trust Fund
Additional Information: All bursaries are envisaged primarily as short-term aids and must be used within 1 year of the date of award.

For further information contact:

GPO Box 634, Adelaide, 5001, Australia
Website: www.afuwsa-bursaries.com.au

Lewis O'Brien Scholarship

Subjects: Education, arts, and social sciences.
Purpose: To assist and encourage Aboriginal and Torres Strait Islander people in postgraduate study in a field of particular relevance and potential benefit to the Indigenous Australian community.
Eligibility: Open to Aboriginal and Torres Strait Islander people eligible to undertake a postgraduate program in the division of education, arts and social sciences.
Level of Study: Postgraduate
Type: Scholarship
Value: Maximum $10,000 per year
Frequency: Annual
Country of Study: Australia
Application Procedure: Candidates must contact Ms Jillian Mille for further information.
Closing Date: February 24th
Contributor: Division of Education, Arts and Social Sciences

For further information contact:

Tel: 08 8302 9151
Fax: 08 8302 7034
Email: jillian.miller@unisa.edu.au
Contact: Jillian Miller, Coordinator Indigenous Support Services

Margaret George Award

Subjects: Archival research, history.
Purpose: To encourage and facilitate use of National Archives collection by promoting archival research in Australia and encouraging scholarly use of its holdings.
Eligibility: Open to postgraduate degree holders, historians, academics, independent researchers, or journalists with a talent for research.
Level of Study: Postgraduate
Type: Award
Value: Up to $10,000
Frequency: Annual
Country of Study: Australia
Application Procedure: Check website for further details.
Closing Date: June 30th
Additional Information: Successful applicants may undertake their award at any time from the date of the announcement of the award until June 30th the following year.

For further information contact:

National Archives of Australia in Canberra, Australia
Tel: (61) 02 6212 3986
Fax: (61) 02 6212 3699
Email: derina.mclaughlin@naa.gov.au
Website: www.naa.gov.au/about_us/margaret_george.html
Contact: Derina McLaughlin

The Padnendadlu Postgraduate Bursary

Subjects: All subjects.
Purpose: To assist women undertaking postgraduate studies.

Eligibility: Open to Indigenous Australian women undertaking postgraduate degrees at South Australian universities.
Level of Study: Postgraduate
Type: Bursary
Value: $5,000 (research) and $4,000 (coursework)
Frequency: Annual
Study Establishment: South Australian universities
Country of Study: Australia
Application Procedure: Candidates must apply on forms available from the AFUW website from October to February.
Closing Date: March 1st
Contributor: The Australian Federation of University Women – South Australia Inc (AFUW–SA Inc) Trust Fund
Additional Information: All bursaries are envisaged primarily as short–term aids and must be used within 1 year of the date of award.

For further information contact:

GPO Box 634, Adelaide, 5001, Australia
Website: www.afuwsa-bursaries.com.au

Trevor Prescott Memorial Scholarship

Subjects: All subjects.
Purpose: To help youth in the South Australian community to advance their careers through further postgraduate studies.
Eligibility: Open to students between 20 and 30 years of age who desire to do further postgraduate studies or equivalent.
Level of Study: Unrestricted
Type: Scholarship
Value: Up to $20,000 and may be divided between more than 1 recipient
Frequency: Annual
Application Procedure: Check website for further details.
Closing Date: June 30th
Funding: Foundation
Contributor: The Masonic Foundation Inc
Additional Information: Preference is not given to a Freemason or to a member of the family for the scholarship.

For further information contact:

The Masonic Foundation Inc, Australia
Tel: (61) 08 8443 9909
Fax: (61) 08 8443 9928
Email: masfound@senet.com.au
Website: www.freemasonrysaust.org.au/foundation.html

UNIVERSITY OF SOUTHAMPTON

Corporate and Marketing Services Highfield, Southampton, Hampshire, SO17 1BJ, England
Tel: (44) 23 8059 4730
Fax: (44) 23 8059 5789
Email: admissns@soton.ac.uk
Website: www.soton.ac.uk
Contact: Student Marketing Office

The University of Southampton was granted its Royal Charter in 1952. Today, the University is one of the United Kingdom's top ten research universities, offering a wide range of postgraduate taught and research courses in engineering, science, mathematics, law, arts, social sciences, medicine and health and life sciences.

University of Southampton Engineering Doctorate

Subjects: Engineering, physical sciences, mathematics.
Purpose: To provide financial assistance to graduate students with their studies and research.
Eligibility: Open to candidates who hold a good Honours degree and are eligible for admission to the academic school in which they intend to study.
Level of Study: Doctorate
Type: Studentship
Value: Enhanced stipend plus tuition fees and travel costs
Length of Study: 4 years
Frequency: Annual
Study Establishment: The University of Southampton
Country of Study: United Kingdom

No. of awards offered: 10
Application Procedure: Applicants should make initial enquiries to the academic school in which they intend to study.
Closing Date: Varies
Funding: Commercial, government

University of Southampton Postgraduate Studentships

Subjects: All subjects.
Purpose: To provide financial assistance to graduate students with their studies and research.
Eligibility: Open to candidates who hold a good Honours Degree and are eligible for admission to the academic school in which they intend to study.
Level of Study: Doctorate, MBA, Postgraduate, Research
Type: Studentship
Value: Varies; (awards may cover tuition fees and/or maintenance)
Length of Study: The duration of the course of study and research
Frequency: Annual
Study Establishment: The University of Southampton
Country of Study: United Kingdom
No. of awards offered: Varies
Application Procedure: Applicants should make initial enquiries to the academic school in which study is to be undertaken.
Closing Date: Varies
Funding: Commercial, government
Additional Information: Applicants should contact each academic school for further details.

World Universities Network (WUN) International Research Mobility Scheme

Subjects: A wide range of subject areas reflecting the research interest of the WUN network.
Purpose: To support research visits to WUN partner universities in the United States of America, China and Europe.
Eligibility: Open to candidates currently registered for an MPhil or PhD degree in one of the University of Southampton's schools.
Level of Study: Doctorate, Postdoctorate, Postgraduate, Research
Type: Scholarship (travel and subsistence grant)
Value: Varies, usually up to around UK £5,000
Length of Study: The duration of the research visit, which is normally between 1 and 6 months
Frequency: Annual, annual budget but awards made twice a year in November and March
Study Establishment: Partner Universities
Country of Study: United States of America, China, Norway, Netherlands
No. of awards offered: Varies
Application Procedure: Applicants must make initial enquiries to the head of the academic school in which they are registered for their research degree. Information can also be obtained from the WUN coordinator via Email at elisa@soton.ac.uk
Closing Date: November 30th, March 15th
Contributor: The University of Southampton
No. of awards given last year: 8
No. of applicants last year: 10
Additional Information: For subject details see the website at www.wun.ac.uk

UNIVERSITY OF STRATHCLYDE

16 Richmond Street, Glasgow, G1 1XQ, Scotland
Tel: (44) 14 1552 4400
Email: s.kirk@mis.strath.ac.uk
Website: www.strath.ac.uk
Contact: Mr Jim Wilson, Senior International Adviser

British Gas (BG) Group/Strathclyde/Chevening Scholarships

Subjects: Engineering, applied science, business administration.
Purpose: The scholarships are intended for candidates who will benefit from a year's study in the United Kingdom before beginning or resuming key positions in their countries.
Eligibility: Applicants must be a First Class (Honours) Degree and minimum 1-year work experience. Applicants should not have undertaken full-time study in the last 2 years.

Level of Study: Postgraduate
Type: Scholarship
Value: Tuition fees, living costs and air fare
Length of Study: 1 year
Frequency: Annual
Study Establishment: University of Strathclyde
Country of Study: United Kingdom
Application Procedure: Application forms are available from local BG managers, British embassies in the countries mentioned or can be downloaded from the website.
Closing Date: Februaury 28th
Funding: Corporation, government
Contributor: BG group, University of Strathclyde, Foreign and Commonwealth Office
No. of awards given last year: 8
Additional Information: Nationals of Argentina, Bolivia, Brazil, Cambodia, Egypt, India, Israel, Libya, Kazakhstan, Palestine, Phillippines, Singapore, Thailand, Trinidad, Tobago and Tunisia are eligible.

Department for International Development (DFID) Shared Scholarships Scheme

Subjects: All subjects.
Purpose: To assist students from developing Commonwealth countries to come to the United Kingdom for a 1-year taught Master's degree.
Eligibility: Candidates must be of outstanding academic calibre. They should not be employed by a government or a parastatal organization and should be below 35 years of age. Candidates must be nationals of developing commonwealth countries.
Level of Study: Postgraduate
Type: Scholarship
Value: Tuition fees, living costs and air fare
Length of Study: 1 year
Frequency: Annual
Study Establishment: University of Strathclyde
Country of Study: United Kingdom
Application Procedure: Application forms and more information are available from the website.
Closing Date: Mid-April
Funding: Government
No. of awards given last year: 4
No. of applicants last year: 200

International Scholarships

Subjects: All subjects.
Purpose: To assist applicants and students who are seeking sources of financial assistance to pursue full-time postgraduate study at the University of Strathclyde.
Eligibility: Applicants should be new students of outstanding academic calibre who are about to begin a 1-year full-time taught Master's course in September.
Level of Study: Postgraduate
Type: Scholarship
Value: Up to UK £4,000 (maximum)
Length of Study: 1 year
Frequency: Annual
Study Establishment: University of Strathclyde
Country of Study: United Kingdom
Application Procedure: Application forms can be downloaded from the website.
Closing Date: May 25th
Funding: International Office
Contributor: International Office, Strathclyde University
Additional Information: For more information, applicants can visit the website. Eligibility is restricted to nationals of Argentina, Bolivia, Brazil, Canada, China, Egypt, India, Indonesia, Kazakhstan, Korea, Malaysia, Mexico, Norway, Oman, Russia, Singapore, Taiwan, Thailand, Trinidad, Tunisia and USA.

John Mather Scholarship

Subjects: Postgraduate instructional courses in business administration and management, economics, hospitality management and tourism.
Purpose: To encourage potential rising stars in the business world, selected on the basis of academic merit.

Eligibility: Open to students from the vicinity of the former Strathclyde Region area enrolled in postgraduate instructional courses.
Level of Study: Postgraduate
Type: Scholarship
Value: UK £5,000
Length of Study: 1 year
Frequency: Annual
Study Establishment: Strathclyde Business School
Country of Study: United Kingdom
No. of awards offered: 5
Application Procedure: Applicants must be nominated by their Head of Department on forms available from the Faculty Officer.
Closing Date: July 23rd
Funding: Trusts
Contributor: John Mather Charitable Trust
No. of awards given last year: 4
No. of applicants last year: 10

For further information contact:

Email: e.leiper@mis.strath.ac.uk

Mac Robertson Travelling Scholarship

Subjects: All subjects.
Purpose: To provide funding that will enrich and further the award holder's academic experience and research achievements.
Eligibility: Applicants should be postgraduate research students currently registered at Strathclyde or Glasgow Universities.
Level of Study: Research
Type: Scholarship
Value: UK £2,000–3,000
Length of Study: Varies
Frequency: Annual
Study Establishment: University of Strathclyde
Country of Study: United Kingdom
Application Procedure: Application forms can be downloaded from the website www.strath.ac.uk
Funding: Individuals
Contributor: Mac Robertson
No. of awards given last year: 11
No. of applicants last year: 20
Additional Information: The aim of the scheme is to provide funding which will enrich and further the award holder's experience and research achievements.

For further information contact:

Email: cathy.bonner@mis.strath.ac.uk

Overseas Research Students Awards Scheme (ORSAS)

Subjects: All subjects.
Purpose: To assist overseas applicants and students who are seeking sources of financial assistance to pursue full-time postgraduate research study at the University of Strathclyde.
Eligibility: Candidates must have a First Class (Honours) Degree or equivalent. Candidates entering the 3rd year of a PhD are not eligible. Candidates from European Union countries are not eligible.
Level of Study: Research
Type: Scholarship
Value: The balance between the overseas and United Kingdom/European Union rate for tuition fees
Length of Study: Up to 3 years
Frequency: Annual
Study Establishment: University of Strathclyde
Country of Study: United Kingdom
Application Procedure: Application forms can be downloaded from the website.
Closing Date: February 28th
Funding: Government
Contributor: HE Funding Councils
No. of awards given last year: 7
No. of applicants last year: 100

For further information contact:

Room 738, Livingstone Tower, 76 Richmond Street, Glasgow, G1 1XH
Contact: Graduate Office

Pakistan 50th Anniversary Fund

Subjects: Engineering, computing and business management.
Purpose: To provide an opportunity for well-qualified but needy Pakistan nationals to pursue 1-year MSc study in the United Kingdom.
Eligibility: Applicants should be Pakistan nationals with a First Class (Honours) Degree from a recognized Pakistan university.
Level of Study: Postgraduate
Type: Scholarship
Value: Tuition fees, living costs, return travel and other expenses
Length of Study: 1 year
Frequency: Annual
Study Establishment: University of Strathclyde
Country of Study: United Kingdom
Application Procedure: Application forms will be available from British Council offices in Pakistan, or can be downloaded from the website, normally in February.
Closing Date: May 1st
Funding: Foundation
Contributor: Scottish Pakistani Association
No. of awards given last year: 2

University of Strathclyde and Glasgow Synergy Scholarships

Subjects: All subjects, but the project must be jointly supervised between Glasgow and Strathclyde universities.
Purpose: To assist applicants and students who are seeking sources of financial assistance to pursue full-time postgraduate research study at the University of Strathclyde.
Eligibility: Applicants should be PhD candidates of outstanding academic merit.
Level of Study: Doctorate
Type: Scholarship
Value: UK £12,600 per year
Length of Study: Up to 3 years
Frequency: Annual
Study Establishment: University of Strathclyde
Country of Study: United Kingdom
Application Procedure: Applicants seeking nomination for the awards should contact the department they wish to join. Existing research students should contact their head of department or supervisor.
Closing Date: Check the website
Funding: International Office
Contributor: University
Additional Information: For more information, visit the website www.strath.gla.ac.uk/synergy

For further information contact:

Email: synergy@gla.ac.uk

University of Strathclyde Scholarships

Subjects: All subjects.
Purpose: To assist applicants and students who are seeking sources of financial assistance to pursue full-time research study at the University of Stratclyde.
Eligibility: Applicants should be research students of outstanding academic merit.
Level of Study: Doctorate, Research
Type: Scholarship
Value: These awards pay a competitive maintenance allowance in many cases at basic research council rate. In the absence of other funding, university will also consider meeting tuition fee costs
Length of Study: Up to 3 years
Frequency: Annual
Study Establishment: University of Strathclyde
Country of Study: United Kingdom
Application Procedure: Applicants seeking nomination for the awards should contact the department they wish to join. Existing research students should contact their head of department or supervisor.
Closing Date: There is no central deadline. Each faculty sets its own deadline dates
Funding: International Office
Contributor: University
No. of awards given last year: 25
Additional Information: For more information, visit the website www.strath.ac.uk.

UNIVERSITY OF SUSSEX

Postgraduate Office, Sussex House, Falmer, Brighton, East Sussex, BN1 9RH, England
Tel: (44) 12 7360 6755
Fax: (44) 12 7367 8335
Email: pg.admissions@sussex.ac.uk
Website: www.sussex.ac.uk
Contact: Mr Terry O'Donnell

The University of Sussex is one of the United Kingdom's foremost research institutions. The University boasts a distinguished faculty that includes 17 Fellows of the Royal Society and four Fellows of the British Academy. The University has around 15,000 students, 25 per cent of whom are postgraduates.

Chancellor's International Scholarships

Subjects: Scholarships are available in all subjects at all schools (except the Institute of Development Studies and Brighton and Sussex medical school).
Purpose: To provide scholarships to new overseas fee-paying students at the postgraduate taught degree level.
Eligibility: Candidates must have applied for and accepted a place to start a postgraduate degree (e.g. MA, MSc, LLM, postgraduate studies and graduate diploma) at the University of Sussex.
Level of Study: Graduate, Postgraduate
Type: Scholarship
Value: UK £2,500
Length of Study: Duration of the degree programme
Frequency: Annual
Study Establishment: University of Sussex
Country of Study: United Kingdom
No. of awards offered: 40
Application Procedure: Completed application forms should be returned by email, post or fax.
Closing Date: May 1st
Funding: Private
Additional Information: Scholarships are awarded on the basis of academic merit and potential.

For further information contact:

International and Study Abroad Office, Mantell Building, University of Sussex, Falmer, Brighton, BN1 9RF, United Kingdom
Fax: (44) 12 7367 8640
Email: cisscholarships@sussex.ac.uk

Economic and Social Development Scholarship

Subjects: Anthropolgy, gender studies, development studies, industrial relations, economics, human rights, education and migration studies.
Purpose: Intended for students intending to contribute to the development of their home countries.
Eligibility: Nationals from Brazil, India, Pakistan or Sri Lanka who have not previously studied in the UK are eligible. The applicants are liable to pay the overseas fees.
Level of Study: Postgraduate
Type: Scholarship
Value: Fee waiver of UK £5,000
Length of Study: 1 year Master's
Frequency: Annual
Study Establishment: University of Sussex
Country of Study: United Kingdom
Application Procedure: Application forms can be downloaded from the website www.sussex.ac.uk and sent to the university after filling in the same.
Closing Date: March 31st
No. of awards given last year: 2

Geoff Lockwood Scholarship

Subjects: All subjects.
Purpose: To encourage high-calibre graduate applications for MSc programmes.
Eligibility: The scholarship is only available to a fully self-financing UK MSc candidate who holds an offer of a place for admission.
Level of Study: Postgraduate
Type: Scholarship

Value: UK £1,000 per annum for tuition fees
Length of Study: 1 year
Frequency: Annual
Study Establishment: University of Sussex
Country of Study: United Kingdom
No. of awards offered: 1
Application Procedure: Applicants should first apply for an MSc place in the school of SPRU for admission. Eligible candidates are automatically considered. Applicants are strongly encouraged to provide a supporting statement.
Closing Date: July 24th
Contributor: George Lockwood
Additional Information: Applications received the closing date will be considered for an MSc place but not for the Geoff Lockwood scholarship.

Helen McMurray Scholarship

Subjects: MA in opera and music theatre.
Purpose: To provide financial support to a student from the UK or EU taking an MA course in opera and music theatre.
Eligibility: Applicants should be UK/EU nationals who have been accepted unconditionally for the MA course in Opera and Music Theatre.
Level of Study: Postgraduate
Type: Scholarship
Value: UK £8,975
Length of Study: 1 year
Study Establishment: University of Sussex
Country of Study: United Kingdom
No. of awards offered: 1
Application Procedure: Applications should be submitted with one reference supporting the case for financial need and should reach the university before the closing date.
Closing Date: May 29th
Funding: Private
Contributor: Helen McMurray
No. of applicants last year: 1

International Security Scholarship

Subjects: International security.
Purpose: Fee waiver for international students doing a Master's degree in international security at the university.
Level of Study: Postgraduate
Type: Scholarship
Value: UK £3,500
Length of Study: 1 year
Frequency: Annual
Application Procedure: Application forms can be downloaded from the website www.sussex.ac.uk and sent to the university after filling in the same.
Closing Date: May 1st
Additional Information: Applicants may not simultaneously hold a Chancellor's International Scholarship.

Mangement and Finance Scholarships

Subjects: Corporate and financial risk management, international accounting, finance and strategy, international management, management and entrepreneurship, management and finance, managing knowledge and intellectual property, science and technology policy, technology and innovation management.
Purpose: Offered in conjunction with the launch of a new Master's degree in the areas of management and finance at Sussex in 2009. Scholarships will be awarded to students who possess the highest academic ability and potential (not made out on the basis of potential need).
Eligibility: Applicants can apply for any one of the above-mentioned courses and should be classified as paying "home tuition fees" for the courses which commence in October.
Type: Scholarship
Value: UK£1,000 bursary for home students; UK£3,500 fee waiver for international students
Frequency: Annual
Study Establishment: University of Sussex
Country of Study: United Kingdom
Application Procedure: Applications duly filled in should be sent to the Scholarships and Bursaries Office.

Closing Date: April 1st (for UK/EU applicants); May 1st (for international students)
Additional Information: For further information please contact Janet French at J.french@sussex.ac.uk

Sussex International Research Scholarships

Subjects: Postgraduate research study (full-time).
Purpose: To enable students undertaking full-time postgraduate research study to pay the difference between the international student and the UK/EU tuition fees.
Eligibility: Applicants must have been accepted (conditionally or unconditionally) as a full-time postgraduate research student and be able to pay the overseas (nonUK/EU) rate of fees. Those who already have a PhD/DPhil or equivalent degree are not eligible.
Level of Study: Doctorate, Postdoctorate, Postgraduate
Value: The difference between the international student and the UK/EU tuition fees
Length of Study: 3 years
Frequency: 1 year initially which can be renewed subject to satisfactory progress up to a maximum of 3 terms or 3 academic years
Study Establishment: Sussex University
Country of Study: United Kingdom
Application Procedure: SIRS application forms duly filled in should be sent to the Scholarships andBursarise office at Sussex University.
Closing Date: March 20th

SYLFF Fellowship

Subjects: Development studies, international relations, anthropology.
Purpose: Educating graduate students with high potential for future leadership in international affairs.
Eligibility: UK citizens or citizens of East European states listed on the website.
Level of Study: Postgraduate
Type: Fellowship
Value: Fee remission
Length of Study: 1 year
Frequency: Annual
Study Establishment: Sussex University
Country of Study: United Kingdom
No. of awards offered: 2
Closing Date: March 31st
Funding: Foundation
Contributor: Tokyo Foundation
No. of awards given last year: 2

USA Friends Scholarship

Subjects: Open to all subjects excludin IDS programmes.
Purpose: Rewarding academic merit.
Eligibility: Applicants must be US citizens.
Type: Scholarship
Value: US $5,000
Length of Study: 1 year
Frequency: Annual
Study Establishment: Sussex University
Country of Study: United Kingdom
No. of awards offered: Approx.4
Application Procedure: Application forms can be downloaded from the website www.sussex.ac.uk and sent to the university after filling in the same.
Closing Date: May 1st
Funding: Individuals
No. of awards given last year: 4

THE UNIVERSITY OF SYDNEY

Research Office, Jane Foss Russell Building, G02, Sydney, NSW, 2006, Australia
Tel: (61) 2 8627 8112
Fax: (61) 2 8627 8145
Email: research.training@usyd.edu.au
Website: www.usyd.edu.au/to/training
Contact: Mrs Carmen NG, Research Scholarships

The role of the University of Sydney is to create, preserve, transmit, extend and apply knowledge through teaching, research, creative works and other forms of scholarship. In carrying out its role, the University affirms its commitment to the values and goals of institutional autonomy, recognizes the importance of ideas and intellectual freedom to pursue critical and open enquiry, as well as social responsibility, tolerance, honesty and respect, as the hallmarks of relationships throughout the University community. It also understands the needs and expectations of those whom it serves and constantly improves the quality and delivery of its services.

Alexander Hugh Thurland Scholarship

Subjects: Agriculture.
Eligibility: Open to the graduates from other universities with relevant degree.
Level of Study: Research, Doctorate, Postgraduate
Type: Scholarship
Value: Australian $20,427 per year
Length of Study: 2 years for Masters by research candidates and 3 years with a possible 6-month extension for research doctoral candidates
Frequency: Dependent on funds available
Study Establishment: The University of Sydney
Country of Study: Australia
Application Procedure: Check website www. agri.usud. edu.au/ for further details.
Funding: Trusts

For further information contact:

Faculty of Agriculture, Food and Natural Resources, JRA McMillan Building, AO5, The University of Sydney, NSW, 2006, Australia
Tel: (61) (61) 2 9351 6926
Fax: (61) (61) 2 9351 2945
Email: agriculture.pg@usud.edu.au

Australian Postgraduate Award (APA)

Subjects: All subjects.
Purpose: To enable candidates with exceptional research potential to undertake a higher degree by research.
Eligibility: Open to Australian citizens and permanent residents, and citizens of New Zealand.
Level of Study: Postgraduate, Doctorate, Research
Type: Scholarship
Value: Australian $20,427 per year
Length of Study: 2 years for Research Master's by research candidates, and 3 years with a possible 6-month extension for Research Doctorate candidates
Frequency: Annual
Study Establishment: The University of Sydney
Country of Study: Australia
No. of awards offered: 163
Application Procedure: Applicants must complete a form, available from the Research Office between late August and October. Forms can also be downloaded from the website or emailed on request.
Closing Date: October 31st
Funding: Government
Contributor: Australian Government
No. of awards given last year: 163

Endeavour International Postgraduate Research Scholarships (EIPRS) and University of Sydney International Postgraduate Awards (IPA)

Subjects: All subjects.
Purpose: To support candidates with exceptional research potential.
Eligibility: Open to suitably qualified graduates eligible to commence a higher degree by research. Australia and New Zealand citizens and Australian permanent residents are not eligible to apply.
Level of Study: Doctorate, Postgraduate, Research
Type: Scholarship
Value: Tuition fees for IPRS, and for IPA Australian $20,427 per year
Length of Study: 2 years for the Master's by research candidates, and 3 years with a possible 6-month extension for PhD candidates
Frequency: Annual
Study Establishment: The University of Sydney
Country of Study: Australia
No. of awards offered: 34

Application Procedure: Applicants must complete an application form for admission available from the International Office.
Closing Date: July 31st for Semester 1, December 31st for Semester 2
Funding: Government
Contributor: Australian Government and University of Sydney
No. of awards given last year: 34

For further information contact:

International Office, Jane Foss Russell Building G02, Sydney, NSW, 2006, Australia
Tel: (61) 2 8627 8353
Fax: (61) 2 8627 8388
Email: infoschol@io.usyd.edu.au
Contact: Scholarships

University of Sydney – China Scholarship Council Research Schemes

Subjects: Areas of study that meets Chinese and Australian national research priorities.
Eligibility: Open to the citizens of the People's Republic of China, who are currently not working or studying in Australia and will normally be from leading Chinese research universities, including 985 Program Universities.
Level of Study: Doctorate, MBA, Postgraduate
Type: Studentship
Value: Living allowance, tuition scholarship, airfare
Length of Study: Up to 3 years
Study Establishment: University of Sydney
Country of Study: Australia
No. of awards offered: Up to 11
Application Procedure: Check website for further details.
Closing Date: December 19th
Funding: Government
Contributor: Chinese government and the University of Sydney
Additional Information: Preference will be given to applicants working in areas of study that meet Chinese and Australian National research priorities.

For further information contact:

Website: www.usyd.edu.au/fstudent/international/postgrad/coetscsc.shtml

University of Sydney - China Scholarship Council Early Career Research Scholars Scheme

Subjects: All subjects.
Eligibility: Open to the applicants from leading Chinese research universities who hold a doctorate and be citizens of the People's Republic of China and not be currently working or studying in Australia.
Level of Study: Postdoctorate, Research
Type: Fellowship
Value: Living expenses, international airfare, office accommodation
Length of Study: 1 year
Frequency: Dependent on funds available
Country of Study: Australia
No. of awards offered: 2
Application Procedure: Check website for further details.
Funding: Government
Contributor: University of Sydney
Additional Information: Preference will be given to applicants working in areas of study that meet Chinese and Australian.

For further information contact:

Old Teachers College A22, The University of Sydney, NSW, 2006, Australia
Website: www.usyd.edu.au/fstudent/international/postgrad/costs/
Contact: International Development Manager

University of Sydney International Scholarship (USydIS)

Subjects: All subjects.
Purpose: To attract top quality international postgraduate students to undertake research projects to enhance the University's research activities.

Eligibility: Open to eligible international postgraduate students eligible to commencea higher degree by research.
Level of Study: Doctorate, Research, Postgraduate
Type: Scholarship
Value: Tuition fees and living allowance of Australian $20,427 per year
Length of Study: 2 years for masters by research candidates, and 3 years with a possible 6-month extension for research doctorate extension
Frequency: Annual
Study Establishment: University of Sydney
Country of Study: Australia
Application Procedure: Applicants must complete an application for admission form available from the International Office.
Closing Date: July 31st for Semester 1, December 31st for Semester 2
Contributor: University of Sydney

For further information contact:

International Office, Jane Foss Russell Building GO2, Sydney, NSW, 2006, Australia
Tel: (61) (61) 2 8627 8353
Fax: (61) (61) 2 8627 8388

University of Sydney Postgraduate Award (UPA)
Subjects: All subjects.
Purpose: To enable candidates with exceptional research potential to undertake a higher degree by research.
Eligibility: Open to Australian citizens and permanent residents and New Zealand citizens.
Level of Study: Doctorate, Postgraduate, Research
Type: Scholarship
Value: Australian $20,427 per year
Length of Study: 2 years for the Research Master's by research candidates, and 3 years with a possible 6-month extension for Research Doctorate candidates
Frequency: Annual
Study Establishment: University of Sydney
Country of Study: Australia
No. of awards offered: 125
Application Procedure: Applicants must complete a form, available from the Research Office between late August and October. Forms can also be downloaded from the website or emailed on request.
Closing Date: October 31st
Funding: Government
Contributor: University of Sydney

UNIVERSITY OF TASMANIA

Private Bag 45, Hobart, TAS 7001, Australia
Tel: (61) 3 6226 2766
Fax: (61) 3 6226 7497
Email: scholarships@research.utas.edu.au
Website: www.research.utas.edu.au/gr
Contact: Graduate Research Unit

The University of Tasmania was officially founded on January 1st 1890, by an Act of the Colony's Parliament and was only the fourth university to be established in 19th century Australia. The university represents areas of significant research strengths and substantial teaching endeavours.

Victoria League for Commonwealth Friendship Medical Research Trust
Subjects: Research into dementia, heart complaints or cancer.
Purpose: To provide support and guidance to deserving candidates for medical research and related fields.
Eligibility: Open to students who have completed at least 4 years of tertiary education studies and have achieved at least an upper Second Class Honours Degree or equivalent and who are citizens or permanent residents of Australia.
Level of Study: Postgraduate
Type: Fellowship
Value: Australian $ 20,007
Length of Study: 3 years

Frequency: Every 3 years
Study Establishment: University of Tasmania
Country of Study: Australia
Closing Date: October 31st
Funding: Trusts
No. of awards given last year: 1

UNIVERSITY OF ULSTER

Research Office, Cromore Road, Coleraine, Co. Londonderry, BT52 1SA, Northern Ireland
Tel: (44) (28) 7032 4729
Fax: (44) (28) 7032 4905
Email: hj.campbell@ulster.ac.uk
Website: www.ulster.ac.uk
Contact: Mrs H Campbell, Administrative Assistant

The University of Ulster is a dynamic and innovative institution, which is very proud of its excellent track record in the education and training of researchers. Our doctoral graduates can demonstrate outstanding achievements in advancing knowledge and making breakthroughs of relevance to the economic, social and cultural development of society.

Vice Chancellor's Research Scholarships (VCRS)
Subjects: All subjects.
Purpose: To assist candidates of a high academic standard to complete research degrees (PhD).
Eligibility: Applicants must have or expect to obtain the minimum of an upper second class Honours degree in a specific research area (as advertised). Applications are invited from UK, European Union and overseas students. Only candidates who are new applicants to PhD will be eligible.
Level of Study: Doctorate, Postgraduate
Type: Scholarship
Value: Fees and maintenance grant
Length of Study: Up to 3 years
Frequency: Annual
Study Establishment: University of Ulster
Country of Study: United Kingdom
No. of awards offered: Varies
Application Procedure: Applicants must complete an application form.
Closing Date: Check the website
Funding: Private
No. of awards given last year: 30
No. of applicants last year: 700
Additional Information: VCRS awards are not available for applicants for any other research degree or for any candidate who has previously registered for a PhD, or anyone who has already obtained a PhD. Further information is available on the website www.ulster.ac.uk/research study

UNIVERSITY OF UTAH

Admissions Office, 201 S 1460 E Rm. 250 S, Salt Lake City, UT, 84112-9057, United States of America
Tel: (1) 801 581 7281
Fax: (1) 801 585 7864
Email: admissions@sa.utah.edu
Website: www.utah.edu/home/index.uofu

The mission of University College is to assist new, transfer and transitioning students, through academic advising, to develop and implement individual plans for achieving educational and life goals.

Liberal Education Scholarships
Subjects: All subjects.
Purpose: To support students chosen an approved program abroad to complete their studies in their field.
Eligibility: Open to candidates of all nationalities and ages who are in need of liberal education credit and have matriculated status, 3.0 cumulative GPA, completed 36 hours of residence at the University of Utah prior to departure, full-time status (at least 2 out of 3 quarters during the year prior to departure) 6 weeks study program, priority will

be given to students who will be sophomores or juniors during their study abroad program.
Type: Scholarship
Value: $1,000–1,500
Frequency: Biannual
No. of awards offered: 12 (every 6 months)
Application Procedure: Completed applications should be sent to the center's address.
Closing Date: November (for program beginning in winter and spring), March (for summer and fall)

For further information contact:

159 University Union, Salt Lake City, Utah, 841 12, United States of America

THE UNIVERSITY OF WAIKATO

Gate 1 Knighton Road Private Bag 3105, Hamilton, New Zealand
Tel: (64) 7 856 2889
Fax: (64) 7 838 4300
Email: info@waikato.ac.nz
Website: www.waikato.ac.nz/home.shtml

The University of Waikato through high quality teaching and research aims to deliver a world class education and research portfolio and a full dynamic university experience which is distinctive in character and pursue strong international linkages to advance knowledge.

Acorn Foundation Eva Trowbridge Scholarship
Subjects: All subjects.
Purpose: To support the people of Tauranga and the Western Bay of Plenty community.
Eligibility: Adult students (25 years and over) studying at the University of Waikato's Tauranga campus and residing in the areas administered by Tauranga City Council or Western Bay of Plenty District Council are eligible for the award.
Type: Scholarship
Value: $3,000 per year
Length of Study: 1 year
Frequency: Annual
Country of Study: New Zealand
Closing Date: August 31st
Contributor: Acorn Foundation
Additional Information: The Scholarship will be paid in one lump sum to the successful applicant.

For further information contact:

The Scholarships Office, ITS Building, The University of Waikato, Private Bag 3105, Hamilton, 3240, New Zealand
Tel: (64) 07 838 4964 or 07 858 5195
Email: scholarships@waikato.ac.nz

Alan Turing Prize
Subjects: Computer science and mathematics.
Purpose: To encourage students to develop strong joint interests in computer science and mathematics.
Eligibility: Open to students who have strong interest in computer science and mathematics.
Level of Study: Research
Length of Study: 3 years
Frequency: Annual
Application Procedure: Check website for further details.
Contributor: Council of the University of Waikato

Alumni Master's Scholarship
Subjects: All subjects.
Purpose: To support a student who has graduated with a degree of the University of Waikato and is enrolled for a Masters Degree at this university in the year of tenure.
Eligibility: Open to New Zealand citizens or permanent residents who have qualified for a first degree from the University of Waikato and be enrolled full-time for a Masters degree at the University of Waikato in the year of tenure. The candidate must be in their final year of study for the degree.
Level of Study: Postgraduate

Value: $5,500 plus actual tuition fees up to a maximum of $4,000
Length of Study: 1 year
Application Procedure: Check website for further details.
Closing Date: October 31st
Additional Information: The Scholarship will be awarded to a student who demonstrates academic merit; who is active in university affairs and who contributes to the activities of the School or Faculty in which they are enrolled; who demonstrates willingness to maintain an active relationship with the Alumni programme; who demonstrates willingness to attend Alumni functions and promotional activities; who is considered to be a good ambassador for the University of Waikato and the Alumni Association.

For further information contact:

The Scholarships Office, ITS Building, The University of Waikato, Private Bag 3105, Hamilton, 3105, New Zealand
Tel: (64) 07 838 4964 or 07 858 5195
Email: scholarships@waikato.ac.nz

Chamber of Commerce Tauranga Business Scholarship
Subjects: Management Studies.
Purpose: For the benefit of members of the Tauranga Chamber of Commerce to assist the recipient to undertake study at postgraduate level.
Eligibility: Open to citizens or permanent residents of New Zealand having a tertiary or relevant professional qualification; must have a minimum of 5 years' relevant work experience; must own or be employed by a business or organization which is a member of the Tauranga, Chamber of Commerce; must have the support of his/her employer and currently not enrolled in a Postgraduate Diploma in Management Studies with the Waikato, Management School, University of Waikato. Check website for further details.
Level of Study: Postgraduate
Type: Scholarship
Value: The value of the scholarship is usually equivalent to 1 year's fees (a total of four papers)
Length of Study: Above 2 years
Frequency: Annual
Application Procedure: Check website for further details.
Closing Date: September 30th

For further information contact:

The Scholarships Office, ITS Building, The University of Waikato, Private Bag 3105, Hamilton, New Zealand
Tel: (64) 07 838 4964 or 07 858 5195
Email: scholarships@waikato.ac.nz

Evelyn Stokes Memorial Doctoral Scholarship
Subjects: Geography, Tourism and Environmental Planning.
Eligibility: Open to candidates enrolled or intending to enroll in an approved full-time programme of study at the University of Waikato in the years of tenure of the scholarship. Applicants who have undertaken study outside the University of Waikato must supply a full verified copy of their academic transcript(s) from their previous institution(s).
Level of Study: Doctorate
Type: Scholarship
Value: $5,000
Length of Study: 3 years
Frequency: Annual
Application Procedure: Check website for further details.
Closing Date: October 31st in the year prior to that in which the award will be taken up
Additional Information: The Scholarship will end on the completion of doctoral study, or after 3 years, whichever is the earlier date, provided that the candidate is enrolled during this time in an appropriate programme of studies. Completion takes place when the postgraduate studies committee has accepted the report of the examiners and recommends the awarding of the degree.

For further information contact:

The Scholarships Office, ITS Building, The University of Waikato, Private Bag 3105, Hamilton, New Zealand
Tel: (64) 07 838 4964 or 07 858 5195
Email: scholarships@waikato.ac.nz

Faculty of Arts and Social Sciences Honours Awards

Subjects: Arts, humanities and social sciences.
Purpose: To support students enrolling in a master's degree based on academic merit.
Eligibility: Open to applicants who are New Zealand citizens or permanent residents with high academic caliber and enrolling in a master's degree in the faculty of arts and social sciences.
Level of Study: Postgraduate
Type: Award
Value: NZ $1,000
Frequency: Annual
Study Establishment: University of Waikato
Country of Study: New Zealand
No. of awards offered: 40
Application Procedure: For further details please check website www.waikato.ac.nz/research/scholarships
Closing Date: March 7th and July 18th
Contributor: School of Science and Engineering

Faculty of Arts and Social Sciences Masters Thesis Awards

Subjects: Humanities, arts and social sciences.
Purpose: To assist students enrolling in a Master's degree in the faculty of Arts and Social sciences.
Eligibility: Open to all Master's enrolling in the faculty of arts and social sciences.
Level of Study: Postgraduate
Type: Award
Value: Up to Canadian $2,000
Length of Study: 1 year
Frequency: Annual
Study Establishment: University of Waikato
Country of Study: New Zealand
No. of awards offered: 20
Application Procedure: Application forms and information available on www.waikato.ac.nz/research/scholarships
Closing Date: March 7th and July 18th
Contributor: The International Council for Canadian studies (ICCS)

Hilary Jolly Memorial Scholarship

Subjects: Fresh water ecology
Purpose: To encourage research in the field of fresh water ecology at the University of Waikato at Master's or Doctoral level.
Eligibility: Open to New Zealand citizens or permanent residents who are enrolled for a Master's degree at the university in the area of fresh water ecology.
Level of Study: Doctorate, Postgraduate
Type: Scholarship
Value: Master's–$6,000 plus tuition fees. Doctoral–$15,000 plus tuition fees
Length of Study: 2 years for Master's and 3 years for doctorate
Frequency: Dependent on funds available
Study Establishment: University of Waikato
Country of Study: New Zealand
No. of awards offered: 1
Application Procedure: A completed application form must be submitted to the scholarship office at the university. Application forms are available on www.waikato.ac.nz/research/scholarships
Closing Date: October 31st

Lee Foundation Grants

Subjects: All subjects.
Eligibility: Open to citizens and residents of Singapore or Malaysia, must have completed at least 1 year of study or are studying at the University of Waikato in Hamilton.
Type: Grant
Value: $500
Application Procedure: Check website for further details.
Closing Date: April 30th
Additional Information: Grants are awarded on the basis of above average academic performance.

For further information contact:

The Scholarships Office, The University of Waikato, Private Bag 3105, Hamilton, New Zealand
Email: scholarships@waikato.ac.nz

The Michael Baldwin Memorial Scholarship

Subjects: All subjects.
Purpose: To commemorate Michael's commitment to teaching and to assist people in their educational endeavours.
Eligibility: Open to students who are citizens of Papua New Guinea. Preference will be given to applicants who can demonstrate a need for financial support in order to undertake tertiary study. Candidates must be current or intending students, who will be enrolled in an approved full–time programme of study at The University of Waikato in the year of tenure of the scholarship.
Value: $5,000 per year, the recipient of a scholarship may re-apply in a subsequent year
Length of Study: 1 year
Frequency: Annual
No. of awards offered: 1
Application Procedure: Applications should include a personal statement indicating how the scholarship will benefit the candidate's particular circumstances and aspirations and must give certified details of the candidate's academic history, accompanied by copies of two recent testimonials.
Closing Date: October 31st in the year prior to that in which the award will be taken up

MTKS Education Fund International Scholarships

Subjects: All subjects.
Purpose: To enhance the applicant's academic and professional development.
Eligibility: Applicants must be Assistant Lecturers or Lecturers at Waikato Management School on a fixed-term contract of at least 9 months or on the permanent staff.
Type: Scholarship
Value: New Zealand $5,000
Frequency: Annual
No. of awards offered: 2
Application Procedure: Applicants should submit an application form and Chairperson's certificate supporting the application, an application letter and curriculum vitae.
Closing Date: April 1st

For further information contact:

Scholarships Office, University of Waikato, Private Bag 3105 ITS Building, Gate 1, Knighton Road, Hamilton, New Zealand

New Zealand Federation of University Women Emmy Noether Prize in Mathematics

Subjects: Mathematics.
Eligibility: Open for the outstanding woman student studying first year mathematics in that year at the University.
Type: Prize
Value: $1,500
Frequency: Annual
Application Procedure: Check website for further details.
Contributor: Federation of University Women to the University of Waikato
Additional Information: All women students enrolled in first year mathematics courses in any 1 year will be considered without application as candidates for the award of the prize in that year.

New Zealand Tourism Research Scholarships

Subjects: Tourism.
Purpose: To increase research targeted to the needs of the tourism industry.
Eligibility: Open to New Zealand citizens or permanent residents who are undertaking a tourism-related research thesis.
Type: Scholarship
Value: $15,000
Length of Study: 1 year
Frequency: Annual
No. of awards offered: 7
Application Procedure: For further information and application forms, visit www.tourism.govt.nz
Closing Date: April 30th and October 31st
Funding: Government
Contributor: The Ministry of Tourism

Price Water House Coopers Masters Scholarship

Subjects: Business management.
Purpose: To assist students undertaking Master level research in a business relevant topic in the areas of accounting finance or economics.
Eligibility: Open to New Zealand citizens or permanent residents undertaking Master level research in a business relevant topic in the areas of accounting finance or economics.
Type: Scholarship
Value: US$20,000
Length of Study: 1 year
Frequency: Annual
Study Establishment: Waikato Management School
Country of Study: New Zealand
No. of awards offered: 1
Application Procedure: Further information and application forms are available from the website.
Closing Date: November 15th
Contributor: The Gallagher Group

For further information contact:

Website: www.waikato.ac.nz/research/scholarships

Priority One Management Scholarship

Subjects: Management studies.
Eligibility: Open to citizens or permanent residents of New Zealand who have a tertiary or relevant professional qualification with a minimum of 5 years relevant work experience, own or be employed by a business or organization which is a member of Priority One, have the support of his/her employer, must not already be enrolled in a Postgraduate Diploma in Management Studies with the Waikato, Management School, University of Waikato, not have been a previous recipient of any Waikato Management School, University of Waikato.
Level of Study: Postgraduate
Type: Scholarship
Value: Equivalent to 1 year's fees
Length of Study: 2 years
Frequency: Annual
Application Procedure: Check website for further details.
Closing Date: September 30th in the year preceding the postgraduate diploma study

For further information contact:

The Scholarships Office, ITS Building, The University of Waikato, Private Bag 3105, Hamilton, New Zealand
Tel: (64) 07 838 4964 or 07 858 5195
Email: scholarships@waikato.ac.nz

Science Admission Fees Scholarships

Subjects: Science and engineering
Purpose: To provide financial assistance to science students.
Eligibility: Open to New Zealand citizens or permanent residents enrolling in science faculty.
Level of Study: Postgraduate
Type: Scholarship
Value: NZ $4,000
Frequency: Annual
Study Establishment: University of Waikato
Country of Study: New Zealand
No. of awards offered: 10
Application Procedure: Further information can be found on www.waikato.ac.nz/research/scholarships
Closing Date: December 30th

Science and Engineering Masters Fees Award

Subjects: Science and engineering.
Purpose: To support students pursuing Master's degree in school of science and engineering.
Eligibility: Open to New Zealand citizens or permanent residents enrolling for science master's study.
Level of Study: Postgraduate
Type: Scholarship
Value: $2,000 credited to fees
Frequency: Annual
Study Establishment: University of Waikato

Country of Study: New Zealand
No. of awards offered: 15
Application Procedure: Further information and application forms are available on www.waikato.ac.nz/research/scholarships
Closing Date: February 17th

Sir Edmund Hillary Scholarship Programme

Subjects: Any subject.
Purpose: To support students to achieve a high academic standard and excellence in sports or creative and performing arts.
Eligibility: Open to New Zealand citizens or permanent residents who can demonstrate academic achievement and excellence in either a sporting code or a performing or creative arts.
Level of Study: Graduate, Postgraduate
Type: Scholarship
Value: Tuition fees and associated charges
Length of Study: 1 year, renewable for period of degree, up to maximum 4 years
Frequency: Annual
Study Establishment: University of Waikato
Country of Study: New Zealand
No. of awards offered: Varies
Application Procedure: Further information available on the website www.waikato.ac.nz/research/scholarships
Closing Date: October 31st
No. of awards given last year: 40

Ted Zorn Waikato Alumni Award For Management Communication

Subjects: Management studies.
Purpose: To provide an opportunity for peer recognition of graduates of the department who have, since their graduation, distinguished themselves in a field of management communication.
Eligibility: Open to candidates holding a responsible position in an organization or in a project, sustainability and/or workplace wellbeing; must know the use of creativity and initiative in performing the responsibilities of the position. Check website for further details.
Level of Study: Postgraduate
Type: Award
Value: $1,000
Frequency: Annual
Application Procedure: Check website for further details.
Closing Date: November 30th

For further information contact:

Department of Management Communication, The University of Waikato, Private Bag 3105, Hamilton, New Zealand
Email: jbeaton@waikato.ac.nz
Contact: Jean Beaton

The University of Waikato Doctoral Scholarships

Subjects: All subjects.
Purpose: To support candidates applying for doctoral studies.
Eligibility: Open to New Zealand citizens or permanent residents enrolling in a doctoral degree.
Level of Study: Doctorate
Type: Scholarship
Value: $22,000 plus tuition fees per annum
Length of Study: 3 years
Frequency: Annual, Twice a year
Study Establishment: University of Waikato
Country of Study: New Zealand
Application Procedure: Contact the scholarships office at the university. Applications are available on www.waikato.ac.nz/research/scholarships
Closing Date: October 31th and April 30th

University of Waikato Masters Research Scholarships

Subjects: All subjects.
Purpose: To encourage research at the University, principally by assisting with course-related costs.
Eligibility: Open to citizens and permanent residents of New Zealand who have qualified for a first degree and be enrolled full-time for a first

Masters or Master of Philosophy degree at the University of Waikato in the year of tenure.

Level of Study: Postgraduate
Type: Research grant
Value: $12,000, of which $3,500 is to be applied to tuition fees for the Master's Degree. The remaining $8,500 will be paid out in two installments of $4,250
Length of Study: 1 year
Frequency: Annual
No. of awards offered: Up to 60 awards
Application Procedure: Check website for further details.
Closing Date: October 31st and April 30th annually
Additional Information: Should a student also hold another fees scholarship, the University of Waikato Masters Research Scholarship will pay the balance of any fees (up to $3,500).

For further information contact:

The Scholarships Office, ITS Building, The University of Waikato, Private Bag 3105, Hamilton, New Zealand
Tel: (64) 07 858 5136 or 07 858 5195
Email: scholarships@waikato.ac.nz

WMS International Exchange Scholarships

Eligibility: Applicants must have completed at least 1 year of study at the Waikato Management School and be eligible to apply for exchange programmes, must have been accepted into a University of Waikato exchange programme, should apply to institutions listed as recommended institutions, should be New Zealand citizens or permanent residents of New Zealand and should be full-time students at the Waikato Management School.
Level of Study: Postgraduate
Type: Scholarship
Value: $2,500 for students participating in exchange programmes in Europe; $2,000 for students participating in exchange programmes in USA, Canada and Mexico; and $1,500 for students participating in exchange programmes in Asia
Frequency: Annual, Twice a year
No. of awards offered: 10
Application Procedure: Applicants should submit an International Exchange Scholarship Application Form, an application letter and curriculum vitae.
Closing Date: August 15th for A Semester exchanges and March 15th for B Semester exchanges

For further information contact:

Scholarships Office, University of Waikato, ITS Building, Private Bag 3105, Gate 1, Knighton Road, Hamilton, New Zealand

UNIVERSITY OF WALES, LAMPETER

Lampeter, Ceredigion, SA48 7ED, Wales
Tel: (44) 15 7042 2351
Fax: (44) 15 7042 3423
Email: t.rodervick@lamp.ac.uk
Website: www.lamp.ac.uk
Contact: Ms Gwawr Davies, Registry Administrator

At Lampeter, research is greatly prized by our academic staff and we can offer a wide range of supervision in the humanities and social sciences. There is simply no other long-established university with our pedigree that operates on such an intimate scale.

Delahaye Memorial Benefaction

Subjects: Theology.
Purpose: To financially support a graduate of UWL who is accepted to read Honours Theology at Cambridge.
Eligibility: Graduates.
Level of Study: Graduate
Value: UK £100
Frequency: Annual
Study Establishment: Magdalene College, University of Cambridge
Country of Study: United Kingdom
No. of awards offered: 1
Application Procedure: Applications for postgraduate awards should be made to the Postgraduate Office, which writes, during the

Michaelmas term, to all registered postgraduate students reminding them of the awards and enclosing the official application forms.
Closing Date: March 7th
No. of awards given last year: None
No. of applicants last year: None

Helen McCormack Turner Memorial Scholarship

Subjects: All subjects.
Purpose: The applicant must be a postgraduate student who graduated recently from the University of Wales, Lampeter.
Eligibility: The recipient must be less than 25 years of age on August 1st and must be registered to support graduates pursuing research for the degrees of MPhil or PhD.
Type: Scholarship
Value: UK £250
Frequency: Annual
No. of awards offered: 1
Application Procedure: Applications for postgraduate awards should be made to the Postgraduate Office, which writes, during the Michaelmas term, to all registered postgraduate students reminding them of the awards and enclosing the official application forms.
Closing Date: March 7th
No. of awards given last year: 1
No. of applicants last year: 1

Herbert Hughes Scholarship

Subjects: Theology.
Purpose: To support postgraduate or undergraduate students of any discipline who intend to serve in the Ministry of the Church in Wales.
Eligibility: Postgraduate or undergraduate. (Preference may be given to candidates from the parish of Silian, Ceredigion).
Type: Scholarship
Value: UK £250
No. of awards offered: 1
Application Procedure: Applications for postgraduate awards should be made to the Postgraduate Office, which writes, during the Michaelmas term, to all registered postgraduate students reminding them of the awards and enclosing the official application forms.
Closing Date: March 7th
No. of awards given last year: 1
No. of applicants last year: 1

Mary Radcliffe Scholarship

Subjects: Theology.
Purpose: To support graduates of UWL to study theology.
Eligibility: Applicants must be graduates of UWL.
Level of Study: Graduate
Type: Scholarship
Value: UK £175
Frequency: Annual
No. of awards offered: 1
Application Procedure: Applications for postgraduate awards should be made to the Postgraduate Office, which writes, during the Michaelmas term, to all registered postgraduate students reminding them of the awards and enclosing the official application forms.
Closing Date: March 7th
No. of awards given last year: 1
No. of applicants last year: 1

RHYS Curzon-Jones Scholarship

Subjects: Theology.
Purpose: To support a postgraduate student of any discipline who is a candidate for Holy Orders in the Church in Wales.
Type: Scholarship
Value: UK £50
Frequency: Annual
No. of awards offered: 1
Application Procedure: Applications for postgraduate awards should be made to the Postgraduate Office, which writes, during the Michaelmas term, to all registered postgraduate students reminding them of the awards and enclosing the official application forms.
Closing Date: March 7th
No. of awards given last year: None
No. of applicants last year: None

Ridley Lewis Bursary

Subjects: All subjects.
Purpose: To support a postgraduate student funding his/her studies in whole or in part from his/her own resources.
Eligibility: Applicants must be postgraduate students.
Type: Bursary
Value: UK £75
Frequency: Annual
No. of awards offered: 1
Application Procedure: Applications for postgraduate awards should be made to the Postgraduate Office, which writes, during the Michaelmas term, to all registered postgraduate students reminding them of the awards and enclosing the official application forms.
Closing Date: March 7th
No. of awards given last year: 1
No. of applicants last year: 29

W D Llewelyn Memorial Benefaction

Subjects: All subjects.
Purpose: To support graduates of UWL for further degrees or research at Lampeter or at other universities.
Eligibility: Applicants must be graduates of UWL.
Value: Six awards of UK £100 each
Length of Study: 1 year
Frequency: Annual
No. of awards offered: 6
Application Procedure: Applications for postgraduate awards should be made to the Postgraduate Office, which writes, during the Michaelmas term, to all registered postgraduate students reminding them of the awards and enclosing the official application forms.
Closing Date: March 7th
No. of awards given last year: 6
No. of applicants last year: 16

UNIVERSITY OF WALES, NEWPORT

Caerleon Campus, PO Box 179, Newport, NP18 3YG, Wales
Tel: (44) (01633) 432432
Fax: (44) (01633) 432432
Email: uic@newport.ac.uk
Website: www3.newport.ac.uk/

The University of Wales, Newport, has been involved in higher education for more than 80 years, and its roots go back even further to the first Mechanics Institute in the town, which opened in 1841.

Pilcher Senior Research Fellowship

Subjects: Welsh and Celtic studies.
Purpose: To support a student in advanced research in the fields of Welsh and Celtic studies.
Level of Study: Postdoctorate
Type: Fellowship
Frequency: As needed
Study Establishment: University of Wales
Country of Study: Wales
Application Procedure: Applicants must check with the website or the University.
Funding: Private
Contributor: The late Sophia Margaretta Pilcher

The Stott Fellowship

Subjects: Welsh and Celtic studies.
Purpose: To support a student in advanced research in the fields of Welsh and Celtic studies.
Level of Study: Postgraduate
Type: Fellowship
Frequency: As needed
Study Establishment: University of Wales
Country of Study: Wales
Application Procedure: Applicants must check with the website or the University.
Funding: Private
Contributor: Miss Muriel Stott of Colwyn Bay

UNIVERSITY OF WARWICK

Coventry, CV4 7AL, England
Tel: (44) 24 7652 3523
Fax: (44) 24 7646 1606
Email: studentfunding@warwick.ac.uk
Website: www.warwick.ac.uk

The University of Warwick offers an exciting range of doctoral, research-based and taught Master's programmes in the humanities, sciences, social sciences and medicine. In the 2001 Research Assessment Exercise, Warwick was ranked 5th in the United Kingdom for research quality. Postgraduate students make up around 35 per cent of Warwick's 18,000 students. The University is located in the heart of England, adjacent to the city of Coventry and on the border with Warwickshire.

Bangladesh Postgraduate Award (Warwick Manufacturing Group)

Subjects: WMG (Warwick Manufacturing Group) taught masters courses.
Purpose: To support Master's Bangladeshi students at WMG.
Eligibility: Applicants must be nationals of Bangladesh, classed as international fee-payer, not currently registered for a taught masters course at the University of Warwick and should have received an offer of a place from WMG at Warwick.
Level of Study: Postgraduate
Type: Scholarship
Value: UK £5,000
Length of Study: 1 year
Frequency: Dependent on funds available
Study Establishment: University of Warwick
Country of Study: United Kingdom
No. of awards offered: 1
Application Procedure: Applicants must complete an online application form.
Closing Date: May 9th
Contributor: University of Warwick
Additional Information: Non-renewable, deducted from tuition fees, for taught masters only.

For further information contact:

Website: www.warwick.ac.uk/go/scholarships

China Postgraduate Award

Subjects: Any subject.
Purpose: To support Master's students from China at Warwick.
Eligibility: Applicants must be nationals of the Peoples Republic of China, classed as international fee-payer, not currently registered for a taught masters course at the University of Warwick and should have received an offer of a place at Warwick.
Level of Study: Postgraduate
Type: Scholarship
Value: UK £4,000
Length of Study: 1 year
Frequency: Dependent on funds available
Study Establishment: University of Warwick
Country of Study: United Kingdom
No. of awards offered: 1
Application Procedure: Applicants must complete an online application form.
Closing Date: May 9th
Funding: International Office
Contributor: University of Warwick

Additional Information: Non-renewable, deducted from tuition fees, for taught masters only.

For further information contact:

Website: www.warwick.ac.uk/go/scholarships

COLOMBIA Postgraduate Awards (Warwick Manufacturing Group/Colfuturo)

Subjects: WMG (Warwick Manufacturing Group) taught masters courses.

Purpose: To support Master's Columbian students at WMG.
Eligibility: Applicants should be nationals of Columbia, not currently registered on a postgraduate course at the University, and should have received an offer of a place from WMG. Only students who have been awarded a COLFUTURO scholarship-loan are eligible.
Level of Study: Postgraduate
Type: Scholarship
Value: full tuition fees
Length of Study: 1 year
Frequency: Dependent on funds available
Study Establishment: University of Warwick UK
Country of Study: United Kingdom
No. of awards offered: 5
Application Procedure: Applicants must apply via COLFUTURO.
Contributor: WMG/COLFUTURO
Additional Information: Non-renewable, for taught masters only.

For further information contact:

Email: yosoyfuturo@colfuturo.com.co

COLOMBIA Postgraduate Awards (Warwick Manufacturing Group/ICETEX)

Subjects: WMG (Warwick Manufacturing Group) taught masters courses.
Purpose: To support Master's Columbian students at WMG.
Eligibility: Applicants should be nationals of Colombia and classed as international fee-payer. Applicants can be registered on Undergraduate courses at the University of Warwick, but should have received a place at Warwick. Only students who have been awarded a Icetex scholarship-loan are eligible.
Level of Study: Postgraduate
Type: Scholarship
Value: Full tuition fees
Length of Study: 1 year
Frequency: Dependent on funds available
Study Establishment: University of Warwick
Country of Study: United Kingdom
No. of awards offered: 5
Application Procedure: Applicants must apply via Icetex website www.icetex.gov.co
Contributor: WMG/ICETEX
Additional Information: Non-renewable, for taught masters only.

For further information contact:

Website: www.icetex.gov.co/

COLOMBIA Postgraduate Awards (Warwick/Colfuturo)

Subjects: Any except MBA or WMG courses.
Purpose: To support Colubmian students on postgradaute courses at Warwick.
Eligibility: Applicants should be nationals of Columbia and classed as an international fee-payer. Applicants can be registered on an Undergraduate course at the University of Warwick, but should have received a place on a Postgraduate Taught Master's course at Warwick. Only students who have been awarded a COLFUTURO scholarship-loan are eligible.
Level of Study: Postgraduate
Type: Scholarship
Value: tuition fees
Length of Study: 1 year
Frequency: Dependent on funds available
Study Establishment: University of Warwick

Country of Study: United Kingdom
No. of awards offered: Variable
Application Procedure: Application should be submitted via COLFUTURO.
Funding: International Office
Contributor: COLFUTURO
Additional Information: Non-renewable, for taught masters only.

For further information contact:

Email: yosoyfuturo@colfuturo.com.co

INDIA Postgraduate Awards

Subjects: Any subject.
Purpose: To support students from India at Warwick
Eligibility: Applicants must be nationals of India, classed as international fee-payer and should have received an offer of a place at Warwick for 2008 entry. Applicants can be registered on Undergraduate courses or Taught Master's courses at the University of Warwick.
Level of Study: Postgraduate
Type: Scholarship
Value: £5,000
Length of Study: 1–3 years
Frequency: Dependent on funds available
Study Establishment: University of Warwick
Country of Study: United Kingdom
No. of awards offered: 4
Application Procedure: Applicants must complete an online application form.
Closing Date: May 11th
Funding: International Office
Contributor: University of Warwick
Additional Information: Non-renewable, deducted from tuition fees, for taught masters and research.

For further information contact:

Website: www.warwick.ac.uk/go/scholarships

INDIA Postgraduate Awards (LLM)

Subjects: Law.
Purpose: To support students from India on LLM programme at Warwick.
Eligibility: Applicants should be nationals of India and classed as international fee-payer. Applicants can be registered on Undergraduate courses at the University of Warwick, but should have received a place for taught master courses at Warwick Law School.
Level of Study: Postgraduate
Type: Scholarship
Value: UK £3,000
Length of Study: 1 year
Frequency: Dependent on funds available
Study Establishment: University of Warwick
Country of Study: United Kingdom
No. of awards offered: 3
Application Procedure: Applicants must complete an online application form.
Closing Date: May 11th
Contributor: Warwick Law School
No. of awards given last year: 3
Additional Information: Non-renewable, deducted from tuition fees, for taught masters only.

For further information contact:

Website: www.warwick.ac.uk/go/scholarships

INDIA Postgraduate Awards (Warwick Manufacturing Group)

Subjects: WMG (Warwick Manufacturing Group) taught masters courses.
Purpose: To support Master's Indian students at WMG.
Eligibility: Applicants must be nationals of India, classed as international fee-payer, not currently registered for a taught masters course at the University of Warwick and should have received an offer of a place from WMG at Warwick.
Level of Study: Postgraduate
Type: Scholarship
Value: Two awards of £5,000 each, one award of £3,000, and ten awards of £2,000
Length of Study: 1 year
Frequency: Dependent on funds available
Study Establishment: University of Warwick
Country of Study: United Kingdom
Application Procedure: Applicants must complete an online application form.
Closing Date: May 11th
Contributor: University of Warwick
No. of awards given last year: 2

Additional Information: Non-renewable, deducted from tuition fees, for taught masters only.

For further information contact:

Website: www.warwick.ac.uk/go/scholarships

Japan Postgraduate Award

Subjects: Any subject.
Purpose: To support Master's students from Japan at Warwick.
Eligibility: Applicants must be nationals of Japan, classed as international fee-payer, not currently registered for a taught masters course at the University of Warwick and should have received an offer of a place at Warwick.
Level of Study: Postgraduate
Type: Scholarship
Value: UK £5,000 each
Length of Study: 1 year
Frequency: Dependent on funds available
Study Establishment: University of Warwick
Country of Study: United Kingdom
No. of awards offered: 2
Application Procedure: Applicants must complete an online application form.
Closing Date: May 11th
Funding: International Office
Contributor: University of Warwick
No. of awards given last year: 2
Additional Information: Non-renewable, deducted from tuition fees, for taught masters only.

For further information contact:

Website: www.warwick.ac.uk/go/scholarships

KARIM RIDA SAID FOUNDATION Postgraduate Award (KRSF/Warwick)

Subjects: Any subject.
Purpose: To support students from the Middle Eastern region on Postgraduate courses at Warwick.
Eligibility: Applicants should be Jordanian, Iraqi, Lebanese, Palestinian or Syrian nationals and be resident in the Middle East. Applicants should meet all other eligibility criteria as set by KRSF and awards will only be offered to applicants who already hold an offer of a place at Warwick.
Level of Study: Postgraduate
Type: Scholarship
Length of Study: 1 year
Study Establishment: University of Warwick
Country of Study: United Kingdom
No. of awards offered: 1
Application Procedure: Applications are submitted via KRSF website www.krsf.org/whatwedo/masters
Funding: International Office
Contributor: KRSF
No. of awards given last year: 2
Additional Information: Non-renewable, for taught masters only.

For further information contact:

International Office, University of Warwick, Coventry, CV4 8UW, United Kingdom
Tel: (44) 24 7652 2469
Email: J.C.Inegbedion@warwick.ac.uk
Contact: Jon Inegbedion

Korea Postgradaute Award

Subjects: Any subject.
Purpose: To support Master's students from Korea at Warwick.
Eligibility: Applicants must be nationals of Korea, classed as international fee-payer, not currently registered for a taught masters course at the University of Warwick and should have received an offer of a place at Warwick.
Level of Study: Postgraduate
Type: Scholarship
Value: UK £5,000
Length of Study: 1 year
Frequency: Dependent on funds available

Study Establishment: University of Warwick
Country of Study: United Kingdom
No. of awards offered: 1
Application Procedure: Applicants must complete an online application form.
Closing Date: May 11th
Funding: International Office
Contributor: University of Warwick
No. of awards given last year: 1
Additional Information: Non-renewable, deducted from tuition fees, for taught masters only.

For further information contact:

Website: www.warwick.ac.uk/go/scholarships

Lord Rootes Memorial Fund

Subjects: Economic, environmental, social and technological problems.
Purpose: To support a student's or society's project.
Eligibility: Applicants must be either full-time or part-time postgraduate or undergraduate students belonging to a student society at the University of Warwick
Level of Study: Unrestricted
Type: Grant
Value: From UK £100–£3,000 for individuals or groups. £5,000 for a project of outstanding merit
Length of Study: At least 2 years
Frequency: Annual
Study Establishment: University of Warwick
Country of Study: United Kingdom
No. of awards offered: Variable
Application Procedure: Applicants must submit an application form plus a detailed project proposal of up to six A4 pages including financial plan. Short-listed applicants are interviewed.
Closing Date: January 8th
Funding: Private
Contributor: Lord Rootes Memorial Fund
No. of awards given last year: 13
No. of applicants last year: 38

MEXICO Postgraduate Award (Chevening/Brockmann/Warwick)

Subjects: Any subject (except MBA)
Purpose: To support Mexican students on a Postgraduate course at Warwick.
Eligibility: Applicants should be nationals of Mexico, not currently registered at the University of Warwick and should have received an offer of a place at Warwick.
Level of Study: Postgraduate
Type: Scholarship
Value: Full tuition fees plus maintanence
Length of Study: 1 year
Study Establishment: University of Warwick
Country of Study: United Kingdom
No. of awards offered: 1
Application Procedure: Applicants must complete an application.
Closing Date: May 9
Funding: Government
Contributor: The Foreign and Commonwealth Office and the Brockmann Foundation
No. of awards given last year: 1
Additional Information: Non-renewable

For further information contact:

The British Council, Lope de Vega, 316, Col Chapultepec Morales, Delègacion Miguel Hidalgo, CP 11570, DF, Mexico
Tel: (52) 44 24 7657 2686
Email: ana_delcarmen@hotmail.com
Contact: Ana Galllegos, Adviser for Latin America - International Office

MEXICO Postgraduate Awards (Warwick Manufacturing Group)

Subjects: WMG (Warwick Manufacturing Group) taught masters courses.

Purpose: To support Master's Mexican students at WMG.
Eligibility: Applicants must be nationals of Mexico, classed as international fee-payer, not currently registered for a taught masters course at the University of Warwick and should have received an offer of a place from WMG at Warwick.
Level of Study: Postgraduate
Type: Scholarship
Value: UK £5,000
Length of Study: 1 year
Frequency: Dependent on funds available
Study Establishment: University of Warwick
Country of Study: United Kingdom
No. of awards offered: 2
Application Procedure: Applicants must complete an online application form.
Closing Date: May 11th
Contributor: University of Warwick
No. of awards given last year: 2
Additional Information: Non-renewable, deducted from tuition fees, for taught masters only.

For further information contact:

Website: www.warwick.ac.uk/go/scholarships

MIDDLE EAST AND NORTH AFRICA Postgraduate Award (Warwick Manufacturing Group)

Subjects: WMG (Warwick Manufacturing Group) taught masters courses.
Purpose: To support Master's students from the Middle East and northern Africa region at WMG.
Eligibility: Applicants must be nationals of one of the country within the region of Middle East and Northern Africa, classed as international fee-payer, not currently registered for a taught masters course at the University of Warwick and should have received an offer of a place from WMG at Warwick.
Level of Study: Postgraduate
Type: Scholarship
Value: UK £5,000
Length of Study: 1 year
Frequency: Dependent on funds available
Study Establishment: University of Warwick
Country of Study: United Kingdom
No. of awards offered: 1
Application Procedure: Applicants must complete an online application form.
Closing Date: May 11th
Contributor: University of Warwick
No. of awards given last year: 1
Additional Information: Non-renewable, deducted from tuition fees, for taught masters only.

For further information contact:

Website: www.warwick.ac.uk/go/scholarships

MIDEPLAN Chile Postgraduate Award (Warwick Manufacturing Group)

Subjects: WMG (Warwick Manufacturing Group) taught masters courses.
Purpose: To support Master's students from Chile at WMG.
Eligibility: Applicants should be nationals of Chile and can be registered on an Undergraduate courses at the University of Warwick, but should have received a place at Warwick. Only students who have been awarded a Mideplan scholarship-loan are eligible.
Level of Study: Postgraduate
Type: Scholarship
Value: £1000
Length of Study: 1 year
Frequency: Dependent on funds available
Study Establishment: University of Warwick
Country of Study: United Kingdom
No. of awards offered: 5
Application Procedure: Applicants must apply via MIDEPLAN.

Contributor: WMG/MIDEPLAN
Additional Information: Non-renewable, deducted from tuition fees, for taught masters only.

For further information contact:

Website: www.mideplan.cl/final/index.php

NORTH AMERICA Postgraduate Awards

Subjects: Any subject.
Purpose: To support Master's students from North America at Warwick.
Eligibility: Applicants must be nationals of the USA or Canada, classed as international fee-payer, not currently registered for a taught masters course at the University of Warwick and should have received an offer of a place at Warwick.
Level of Study: Postgraduate
Type: Scholarship
Value: UK £4,000
Length of Study: 1 year
Frequency: Dependent on funds available
Study Establishment: University of Warwick
Country of Study: United Kingdom
No. of awards offered: 4
Application Procedure: Applicants must complete an online application form.
Closing Date: May 11th
Funding: International Office
Contributor: University of Warwick
No. of awards given last year: 4
Additional Information: Non-renewable, deducted from tuition fees, for taught masters only.

For further information contact:

Website: www.warwick.ac.uk/go/scholarships

PAKISTAN Postgraduate Awards

Subjects: Any subject.
Purpose: To support students from Pakistan at Warwick.
Eligibility: Applicants must be nationals of Pakistan, classed as international fee-payer and should have received an offer of a place at Warwick. Applicants can be registered on Undergraduate courses or Taught Master's courses at the University of Warwick, but are not eligible for this scholarship if applying for a second Taught Master's course at the University of Warwick.
Level of Study: Postgraduate
Type: Scholarship
Value: UK £5,000
Length of Study: 1–3 years
Frequency: Dependent on funds available
Study Establishment: University of Warwick
Country of Study: United Kingdom
No. of awards offered: 2
Application Procedure: Applicants must complete an online application form.
Closing Date: May 11th
Funding: International Office
Contributor: University of Warwick
No. of awards given last year: 2
Additional Information: Non-renewable, deducted from tuition fees, for taught masters and research.

For further information contact:

Website: www.warwick.ac.uk/go/scholarships

PAKISTAN Postgraduate Awards (Warwick Manufacturing Group)

Subjects: WMG (Warwick Manufacturing Group) taught masters courses.
Purpose: To support Master's Pakistani students at WMG.
Eligibility: Applicants should be nationals of Pakistan, not currently registered on a postgraduate course at the University, and should have received an offer of a place from WMG.
Level of Study: Postgraduate
Type: Scholarship

Value: Full tuition fees
Length of Study: 1 year
Frequency: Dependent on funds available
Study Establishment: University of Warwick
Country of Study: United Kingdom
No. of awards offered: 2
Application Procedure: Applicants must be accepted by the HEC for the award before applying for the WMG contribution. Applicants must apply to HEC Pakistan.
Contributor: HEC Pakistan
Additional Information: Non-renewable, for taught masters only.

Politics and International Studies Postgraduate Award

Subjects: Politics and International Studies.
Purpose: To support Master's students at the Department of Politics and International Studies at Warwick.
Eligibility: Applicants should be nationals of one of the following countries Africa, America, South Asia, South East Asia. Should have received an offer of a place to study one of the taught master courses offered by the Department of Politics and International Studies at Warwick.
Level of Study: Postgraduate
Type: Scholarship
Value: UK £3,500
Length of Study: 1 year
Frequency: Dependent on funds available
Study Establishment: University of Warwick
Country of Study: United Kingdom
No. of awards offered: 8
Application Procedure: Applicants must complete an online application form.
Closing Date: May 11th
Contributor: University of Warwick
No. of awards given last year: 8
Additional Information: Non-renewable, deducted from tuition fees, for taught masters only.

For further information contact:

Website: www.warwick.ac.uk/go/scholarships

Russia/CIS/Turkey Law Postgradaute Award

Subjects: Law.
Purpose: To support students from Russia, CIS and Turkey on LLM programme at Warwick.
Eligibility: Applicants should be nationals of Russia, Armenia, Azerbaijan, Belarus, Georgia, Kazakhstan, Kyrgyzstan, Moldova, Tajikistan, Turkey, Turkmenista, Ukraine, or Uzbekistan and classed as international fee-payer. Applicants can be registered on Undergraduate courses at the University of Warwick, but should have received a place for taught master courses at Warwick Law School.
Level of Study: Postgraduate
Type: Scholarship
Value: UK £2,000
Length of Study: 1 year
Frequency: Dependent on funds available
Study Establishment: University of Warwick
Country of Study: United Kingdom
No. of awards offered: 2
Application Procedure: Applicants must complete an online application form.
Closing Date: May 11th
Contributor: Warwick Law School
No. of awards given last year: 2
Additional Information: Non-renewable, deducted from tuition fees, for taught masters only.

For further information contact:

Website: www.warwick.ac.uk/go/scholarships

School of Law - Brazil Postgraduate Award

Subjects: Law.
Purpose: To support students from Brazil on LLM programme at Warwick.
Eligibility: Open to prospective full–time postgraduate students in any postgraduate degree within the Law School. Applicants can be registered on Undergraduate courses at the University of Warwick, but should have received a place for taught master courses at Warwick Law School.
Level of Study: Postgraduate
Type: Scholarship
Value: 50% towards tuition fees
Length of Study: 1 year
Frequency: Dependent on funds available
Study Establishment: University of Warwick
Country of Study: United Kingdom
No. of awards offered: 2
Application Procedure: Applicants must complete an online application form.
Closing Date: May 9th
Contributor: Warwick Law School
Additional Information: Non-renewable, deducted from tuition fees, for taught masters only.

For further information contact:

The British Council, Ed. Centro Empresarial Varig, SCN Quadra 04, Bloco B, Torre Oeste Conjunto 202, Brasilia, DF 70710-926, Brazil
Email: paula.nascimento@britishcouncil.org.br
Website: www.warwick.ac.uk/go/scholarships

SOUTH ASIA Postgraduate Awards (LLM)

Subjects: Law.
Purpose: To support students from South Asia and South East Asia on LLM programme at Warwick.
Eligibility: Applicants should be nationals of South Asia or South East Asia and classed as international fee-payer. Applicants can be registered on Undergraduate courses at the University of Warwick, but should have received a place for taught master courses at Warwick Law School.
Level of Study: Postgraduate
Type: Scholarship
Value: UK £2,000
Length of Study: 1 year
Frequency: Dependent on funds available
Study Establishment: University of Warwick
Country of Study: United Kingdom
No. of awards offered: 3
Application Procedure: Applicants must complete an online application form.
Closing Date: May 11th
Contributor: Warwick Law School
No. of awards given last year: 3
Additional Information: Non-renewable, deducted from tuition fees, for taught masters only.

For further information contact:

Website: www.warwick.ac.uk/go/scholarships

SOUTH EAST ASIA Postgraduate Awards (LLM)

Subjects: Any subject.
Purpose: To support Master's students from South East Asian region at Warwick.
Eligibility: Applicants must be nationals of one of the country within the region of South East Asia, classed as international fee-payer, not currently registered for a taught masters course at the University of Warwick and should have received an offer of a place at Warwick.
Level of Study: Postgraduate
Type: Scholarship
Value: £4,000
Length of Study: 1 year
Frequency: Dependent on funds available
Study Establishment: University of Warwick
Country of Study: United Kingdom
No. of awards offered: 3
Application Procedure: Applicants must complete an online application form.
Closing Date: May 11th
Funding: International Office
Contributor: University of Warwick
Additional Information: Non-renewable, deducted from tuition fees, for taught masters only.

For further information contact:

Website: www.warwick.ac.uk/go/scholarships

Sub-Saharan Africa Postgraduate Award
Subjects: Any subject.
Purpose: To support Master's students from Sub-Saharan Africa region at Warwick.
Eligibility: Applicants must be nationals of one of the country within the region of Sub-Saharan Africa, classed as international fee-payer, not currently registered for a taught masters course at the University of Warwick and should have received an offer of a place at Warwick.
Level of Study: Postgraduate
Type: Scholarship
Value: UK £9,000
Length of Study: 1 year
Frequency: Dependent on funds available
Study Establishment: University of Warwick
Country of Study: United Kingdom
No. of awards offered: 1
Application Procedure: Applicants must complete an online application form.
Closing Date: May 11th
Funding: International Office
Contributor: University of Warwick
No. of awards given last year: 1
Additional Information: Non-renewable, deducted from tuition fees, for taught masters only.

For further information contact:

Website: www.warwick.ac.uk/go/scholarships

SUB-SAHARAN AFRICA Postgraduate Awards (Warwick Manufacturing Group)
Subjects: WMG (Warwick Manufacturing Group) taught masters courses.
Purpose: To support Master's African students at WMG.
Eligibility: Applicants must be nationals of one of the country within the region of Sub-Saharan Africa, classed as international fee-payer, not currently registered for a taught masters course at the University of Warwick and should have received an offer of a place from WMG at Warwick.
Level of Study: Postgraduate
Type: Scholarship
Value: UK £5,000
Length of Study: 1 year
Frequency: Dependent on funds available
Study Establishment: University of Warwick
Country of Study: United Kingdom
No. of awards offered: 2
Application Procedure: Applicants must complete an online application form.
Closing Date: May 11th
Contributor: University of Warwick
No. of awards given last year: 2
Additional Information: Non-renewable, deducted from tuition fees, for taught masters only.

For further information contact:

Website: www.warwick.ac.uk/go/scholarships

Taiwan Postgraduate Award
Subjects: Any subject.
Purpose: To support Master's students from Taiwan at Warwick.
Eligibility: Applicants should be nationals of Taiwan, not currently registered on a postgraduate course at the University of Warwick and should have received an offer of a place at Warwick.
Level of Study: Postgraduate
Type: Scholarship
Value: UK £5,000
Length of Study: 1 year
Frequency: Dependent on funds available
Study Establishment: University of Warwick
Country of Study: United Kingdom
No. of awards offered: 2

Application Procedure: Applicants must complete an online application form.
Closing Date: May 11th
Funding: International Office
Contributor: University of Warwick
No. of awards given last year: 2
Additional Information: Non-renewable, deducted from tuition fees, for taught masters only.

For further information contact:

Website: www.warwick.ac.uk/go/scholarships

TAIWAN Postgraduate Awards (Warwick Manufacturing Group)
Subjects: WMG (Warwick Manufacturing Group) taught masters courses.
Purpose: To support Master's Taiwanese students at WMG.
Eligibility: Applicants must be nationals of Taiwan, classed as international fee-payer, not currently registered for a taught masters course at the University of Warwick and should have received an offer of a place from WMG at Warwick.
Level of Study: Postgraduate
Type: Scholarship
Value: UK £5,000
Length of Study: 1 year
Frequency: Dependent on funds available
Study Establishment: University of Warwick
Country of Study: United Kingdom
No. of awards offered: 2
Application Procedure: Applicants must complete an online application form.
Closing Date: May 11th
Contributor: University of Warwick
No. of awards given last year: 2
Additional Information: Non-renewable, deducted from tuition fees, for taught masters only.

For further information contact:

Website: www.warwick.ac.uk/go/scholarships

THAILAND Postgraduate Awards
Subjects: Any subject.
Purpose: To support Master's Thai students at WMG.
Eligibility: Applicants must be nationals of Thailand, classed as international fee-payer, not currently registered for a taught masters course at the University of Warwick and should have received an offer of a place from WMG at Warwick.
Level of Study: Postgraduate
Type: Scholarship
Value: UK £2,500
Length of Study: 1 year
Frequency: Dependent on funds available
Study Establishment: University of Warwick
Country of Study: United Kingdom
No. of awards offered: 4
Application Procedure: Applicants must complete an online application form.
Closing Date: May 11th
Contributor: University of Warwick
Additional Information: Non-renewable, deducted from tuition fees, for taught masters only.

For further information contact:

Website: www.warwick.ac.uk/go/scholarships

TURKEY Postgraduate Awards (Warwick Manufacturing Group)
Subjects: WMG (Warwick Manufacturing Group) taught masters courses.
Purpose: To support Master's Turkish students at WMG.
Eligibility: Applicants should be nationals of Turkey, not currently registered on a postgraduate course at the University of Warwick and should have received an offer of a place from WMG.
Level of Study: Postgraduate

Type: Scholarship
Value: UK £3,000
Length of Study: 1 year
Frequency: Dependent on funds available
Study Establishment: University of Warwick
Country of Study: United Kingdom
No. of awards offered: 15
Application Procedure: All applicants who have received an offer of a place from WMG will automatically be considered for the scholarship, no additional application is required.
Contributor: University of Warwick
No. of awards given last year: 15
Additional Information: Non-renewable, deducted from tuition fees, for taught masters only.

For further information contact:

Website: www.warwick.ac.uk/go/scholarships

University of Warwick Music Scholarships

Subjects: Music.
Purpose: To support students with outstanding musical ability.
Eligibility: Applicants should be undergraduate or postgraduate students, should have applied for admission to the University for a full-time scheme and have satisfied the entry requirements.
Level of Study: Postgraduate
Type: Scholarship
Value: UK £450 per year (with an additional subsidy on music tuition fees)
Length of Study: Up to 3 years
Study Establishment: University of Warwick
Country of Study: United Kingdom
No. of awards offered: 10
Application Procedure: Application forms are available online or from the Music Centre Secretary.
Closing Date: February 10th in proposed calendar year of entry
Funding: Private
No. of awards given last year: 4
No. of applicants last year: 40

VIETNAM Postgraduate Award

Subjects: Any subject.
Purpose: To fund a Vietnamese student on a postgraduate course at Warwick.
Eligibility: Applicants should be nationals of Vietnam, not currently registered on a postgraduate course at the University of Warwick and should have received an offer of a place at Warwick.
Level of Study: Postgraduate
Type: Scholarship
Value: £3,000
Length of Study: 1 year
Frequency: reviewed every year
Study Establishment: University of Warwick
Country of Study: United Kingdom
No. of awards offered: 1
Application Procedure: Applications must be submitted via British Council Vietnam.
Closing Date: May 11th
Funding: International Office
Contributor: British Council
No. of awards given last year: 1
Additional Information: Non-renewable.

For further information contact:

Website: www.britishcouncil.org/vietnam-education-chevening-scholarships.htm

Warwick French Department Bursaries

Subjects: French culture and thought, French studies.
Purpose: To support students registered for an MA in French studies.
Eligibility: Open to candidates who apply for admission to the MA programme through the normal application procedures via Warwick Graduate School. Candidates may be asked to attend an interview and/or to submit a sample of written work, a brief description of circumstances and/or motivations to departmental bursary, to the

Department's Director of Graduate Studies at the time of application to the MA.
Level of Study: Postgraduate
Type: Scholarship
Value: UK/EU fee remission
Length of Study: 1 year full-time/2 years part-time
Frequency: Dependent on funds available
Study Establishment: University of Warwick
Country of Study: United Kingdom
No. of awards offered: 3
Application Procedure: There is no separate application form. Applicants must apply through normal application procedures via Warwick Graduate School available on www2.warwick.ac.uk/study/postgraduate/.
Closing Date: February 14th
Contributor: University of Warwick
No. of awards given last year: 4
No. of applicants last year: 4

For further information contact:

Website: www2.warwick.ac.uk/study/postgraduate/

UNIVERSITY OF WATERLOO

Graduate Studies Office, Needles Hall, Room 2072, Waterloo, ON, N2L 3G1, Canada
Tel: (1) 519 888 4567, ext. 35411, 36745
Fax: (1) (1) 519 888 8009
Email: hmussar@uwaterloo.ca
Website: www.uwaterloo.ca
Contact: Heidi Mussar, Manager, Graduate Studies Financial Aid Programs

The University of Waterloo has long been recognized as the most innovative university in Canada. The University is committed to advancing learning and knowledge through teaching, research, and scholarship in our faculties, colleges, and schools. Our six faculties include applied health sciences, arts, engineering, environmental studies, mathematics, and science.

Industrial Postgraduate Scholarship 1 (NSERC IPS)

Subjects: Science and engineering.
Purpose: To encourage scholars to consider research careers in industry where they will be able to contribute to strengthening Canadian innovation.
Eligibility: Open to citizen or permanent resident of Canada, with a degree in science or engineering from a university whose standing is acceptable to NSERC, have certification from the Dean of Graduate Studies that the applicant has a first-class academic standing (a grade of 'A'); and be pursuing full- or part-time graduate studies in the natural sciences or engineering at an eligible Canadian university.
Level of Study: Postgraduate
Type: Scholarship
Value: $21,000 per year
Length of Study: 2 years
Application Procedure: The applicants should contact the Senior Manager, Graduate Studies Financial Aid Programs.
Funding: Government
Contributor: NSERC

UNIVERSITY OF WESTERN AUSTRALIA

35 Stirling Highway, Crawley, WA, 6009, Australia
Tel: (61) 8 9380 2490, 8 6488 6000
Fax: (61) 8 9380 1919, 8 6488 1380
Email: international@uwa.edu.au
Website: www.uwa.edu.au

Since its establishment in 1911, the University of Western Australia has helped to shape the careers of more than 75,000 graduates. Their success reflects the UWA's balanced coverage of disciplines in the arts, sciences and professions.

Postgraduate Top Up Scholarships in Offshore Engineering and Naval Architecture

Subjects: Offshore engineering and naval architecture.
Purpose: To provide students with quality professional training, education, research and development within the petroleum industry.
Eligibility: Open to International self-funding students or candidates who qualify for an Australian postgraduate award or university postgraduate award.
Level of Study: Postgraduate
Type: Scholarships
Value: Tax free top up scholarships in the range of Australian $ 5,000–20,000
Frequency: Annual
Study Establishment: University of Western Australia
Country of Study: Australia
No. of awards offered: 5
Closing Date: October 31st for Australian and New Zealand applications, August 31st for International applications

The Science & Innovation Studentship Award

Subjects: Science.
Purpose: To promote innovation in areas of key technologies.
Eligibility: Open to citizens of Australia or permanent residents who have completed 2 years, or more, full-time study in a science degree at a recognized Western Australian University.
Level of Study: Postgraduate
Type: Studentship
Value: Australian $7,000 per year
Frequency: Annual
Study Establishment: Curtin University of Technology, Edith Cowan University, Murdoch University, The University of Notre Dame, The University of Western Australia
No. of awards offered: 20
Application Procedure: Check website for further details.
Closing Date: September 14

For further information contact:

100 Plain Street, EAST PERTH, WA, 6004, Australia
Tel: (61) 08 9222 3333
Fax: (61) 08 9222 3862
Email: krystle.mccormick@doir.wa.gov.au
Website: www.doir.wa.gov.au/studentship
Contact: Krystle McCormick, Studentship Co-ordinator, The Office of Science, Technology and Innovation

Sir Charles and Lady Court Music Fund

Subjects: Music.
Purpose: To assist music graduates to obtain more advanced musical experience outside Western Australia.
Eligibility: Open to graduates holding the degree of Bachelor of music or Bachelor of music education, (pass or honours) or Bachelor of arts with a major in music (pass or honours) of the University of Western Australia.
Level of Study: Postgraduate
Type: Award
Application Procedure: Check website for further details.
Funding: Trusts

Society of Petroleum Engineers Western Australia Scholarships

Subjects: Petroleum engineering.
Purpose: To encourage students to specialize in the fields of study that may lead to a professional career in petroleum engineering.
Eligibility: Open to citizens or permanent residents of Australia who are enrolled in full-time study in oil and gas engineering at the University of Western Australia.
Level of Study: Postgraduate
Type: Scholarships
Value: Australian $ 2,500
Length of Study: 1 year
Frequency: Annual
Study Establishment: University of Western Australia
Country of Study: Australia
No. of awards offered: 5

Closing Date: February
Contributor: Western Australian Section of the Society of Petroleum Engineers (SPE-WA)
Additional Information: The award of scholarships will be based on the written applications only.

For further information contact:

Dept of Petroleum Engineering ARRC 26 Dick Perry Avenue, Kensington, Western Australia, 6151, Australia
Contact: Geoffrey Weir, SPE WA Scholarship Chairman

Tunley Postgraduate Music Scholarship

Subjects: Music.
Purpose: To encourage and support an outstanding graduate in music to undertake a full-time PhD course at the University.
Eligibility: Open to citizens or permanent residents of Australia enrolling full-time in the PhD course, and intending to undertake a research project approved by the head of the school of music.
Level of Study: Postgraduate
Type: Scholarship
Value: Equivalent to the stipend of the University Postgraduate Award
Length of Study: 3 years
Study Establishment: School of Music at The University of Western Australia
Country of Study: Australia
No. of awards offered: 1
Application Procedure: Applications, using the application form available from the Scholarships Office, must be submitted to the Scholarships Office. Check website for further details.

Water and Health Scholarships

Subjects: Medical microbiology, earth sciences, or public health and health services.
Purpose: To position graduates favourably with respect to future employment opportunities through research projects in the area of public health impacts of recycled water use.
Eligibility: Open to Australian candidates with a broad range of backgrounds.
Level of Study: Postgraduate
Type: Scholarship
Value: $30,000 per year
Length of Study: 3 years
Frequency: Annual
Study Establishment: The University of Western Australia
Country of Study: Australia
No. of awards offered: Varies
Application Procedure: Check website for further details.
Closing Date: July 6th
Additional Information: Applications are open from June 13th.

For further information contact:

School of Population Health (M431), 35 Stirling Highway, Crawley, WA, 6009, Australia
Tel: (61) 61 8 6488 7804
Email: Angus.Cook@uwa.edu.au
Website: www.publichealth.uwa.edu.au/welcome/research/ehr/ehr-home
Contact: Dr Angus Cook, Research Fellow, The University of Western Australia

Western Australian CSIRO–University Postgraduate Scholarships

Subjects: Geology, geophysics, or metallurgy.
Purpose: To enhance research into minerals and energy exploration, extraction and processing.
Eligibility: Open to citizens of Australia enrolling for postgraduate research.
Level of Study: Postgraduate
Type: Scholarship
Value: Australian $25,000 per year
Length of Study: 3 years
Country of Study: Australia
No. of awards offered: Varies
Application Procedure: Check website for further details.

For further information contact:

Tel: 08 6488 3027
Email: campbell.thomson@uwa.edu.au
Website: www.scholarships.uwa.edu.au/home/postgrad/multi/wacups
Contact: Dr Campbell Thomson, Director Research Services

THE UNIVERSITY OF WESTERN ONTARIO

1151 Richmond Street, Ontario, N6A 3K7, Canada
Tel: (1) 519-661-2111
Website: www.registrar.uwo.ca/FinancialServices/index.cfm
Contact: Grants Department

The University of Western Ontario is a modern, well-equipped university offering programmes in all major academic disciplines. With its enrollment of over 25,000 students, the University of Western Ontario is the 5th largest Canadian university and the second largest university in Ontario.

University of Western Ontario Senior Visiting Fellowship

Subjects: Research interests span a wide range of theory and experiment from mathematical physics through chemistry, physics, macro and micro-electronics to many aspects of the biosciences and medicine.
Purpose: To bring established senior scientists to the Centre for Interdisciplinary Studies in Chemical Physics to work on problems that are interdisciplinary in nature and of interest to Centre members.
Eligibility: Open to senior scientific researchers of established standing. There are no nationality restrictions.
Level of Study: Postdoctorate
Type: Fellowship
Value: Varies
Length of Study: 3 months–1 year
Frequency: Annual
Study Establishment: The Centre
Country of Study: Canada
No. of awards offered: Varies
Application Procedure: Applicants must complete an application form, available on the website.
Closing Date: October of the year preceding tenure
Funding: Government

UNIVERSITY OF WESTMINSTER

35 Marylebone Road, London, NW1 5LS, England
Tel: (44) 0 20 7915 5511
Fax: (44) 0 20 7911 5858
Email: studentfinance@wmin.ac.uk, scholarships@wmin.ac.uk
Website: www.wmin.ac.uk

The University of Westminster is giving generous financial support to many of its students so that they can get on with their studies rather than worrying about finances.

Alumni Scholarships

Subjects: All subjects.
Eligibility: Open to graduates progressing to a full-time Masters Degree at the University of West Minster.
Level of Study: Postgraduate
Type: Scholarship
Value: £2,000 tuition fee waivers
Application Procedure: Check website for further details.
Funding: Government

David Faddy Scholarships

Subjects: Photojournalism.
Eligibility: Open to full-time students holding an offer for the full-time MA photojournalism or MA photographic studies.
Level of Study: Postgraduate
Type: Scholarship

Value: £2,500 tuition fee waivers
Application Procedure: Check website for further details.
Funding: Private
Contributor: Richard Jenkins and Maureen Amar

Diplomatic Academy Scholarships

Subjects: Diplomatic studies.
Eligibility: Open to students pursuing full-time MA diplomatic studies based in London or at the Paris Centre.
Level of Study: Postgraduate
Type: Scholarship
Value: Full tuition fee waivers
No. of awards offered: 2
Application Procedure: Check website for further details.

EU Acceding and Candidate Countries Scholarship

Subjects: All subjects.
Eligibility: Open to students from Bulgaria, Croatia, Romania and Turkey holding an offer for any full-time Masters Degree.
Level of Study: Postgraduate
Type: Scholarship
Value: Full tuition fee waiver
Application Procedure: Check website for further details.
Contributor: International Students House

Fiona McDiarmid/Sky Bursary

Subjects: Journalism.
Eligibility: Open to students accepted onto the postgraduate diploma in journalism (broadcasting), with excellent potential as a broadcast journalist.
Level of Study: Postgraduate
Type: Bursary
Value: £2,000 tuition fee waiver
Application Procedure: Check website for further details.
Additional Information: Applicants must submit a 300 word essay explaining how they will benefit from the course.

MA English Literature Scholarships

Subjects: English literature.
Eligibility: Open to citizens of North America and EU member states holding an offer for the full-time MA English literature.
Level of Study: Postgraduate
Type: Scholarship
Value: 50 per cent tuition fee waivers
No. of awards offered: 2
Application Procedure: Check website for further details.
Funding: Government

MA European Studies

Subjects: European studies.
Eligibility: Open to students holding an offer for the full-time MA European studies.
Level of Study: Postgraduate
Type: Award
Value: Full tuition fee waiver
Application Procedure: Check website for further details.

MA Fashion Design and Enterprise Scholarship

Subjects: Fashion design.
Eligibility: Open to students of United Kingdom holding an offer for the full-time MA fashion design and enterprise.
Level of Study: Postgraduate
Type: Scholarship
Value: £5,000 covering fees and living expenses
Application Procedure: Check website for further details.
Funding: Government

MA Music Business Management Scholarship

Subjects: Music business management.
Eligibility: Open to students of United Kingdom holding an offer for the full-time or part-time MA music business management.

Level of Study: Postgraduate
Type: Scholarship
Value: Full tuition fee waiver and £5,000 towards living expenses
Frequency: Annual
Study Establishment: University of West Minister
Country of Study: United Kingdom
Application Procedure: Check website for further details.
Closing Date: July 2nd
Funding: Private
Contributor: V2 Music

MA Public Communication and Public Relations Scholarships

Subjects: Public relations.
Eligibility: Open to students holding an offer for the full-time or part-time course.
Level of Study: Postgraduate
Type: Scholarship
Value: Full tuition fee waiver for full-time student and part-time student
No. of awards offered: 2
Application Procedure: Check website for further details.
Funding: Government

MA Urban Design

Subjects: Urban design.
Eligibility: Open to students holding an offer for the full-time MA urban design.
Level of Study: Postgraduate
Type: Scholarship
Value: £3,000 towards living expenses and 50 per cent tuition fee waiver
Application Procedure: Check website for further details.
Funding: Private
Contributor: Barton Willmore architectural practice

MBA Scholarships

Subjects: Business administration.
Eligibility: Open to students holding an offer for the full-time MBA degree.
Level of Study: Postgraduate
Type: Scholarship
Value: 50 per cent tuition fee waivers
Application Procedure: Check website for further details.
Closing Date: August 1st
Funding: Government

Media, Arts and Design Scholarship

Subjects: Media, arts and design.
Eligibility: Open to students holding an offer for any full-time Masters in the school of media, arts and design.
Level of study: Postgraduate
Type: Scholarship
Value: Full tuition fee waiver, accommodation, living expenses and flights to and from London
Application Procedure: Check website for further details.

Part Fee Waiver Scholarships

Subjects: All subjects.
Eligibility: Open to students from UK/EU countries holding an offer for a full-time Masters Degree.
Level of Study: Postgraduate
Type: Scholarship
Value: £2,000 tuition fee waivers
Application Procedure: Check website for further details.
Funding: Government

Quintin Hogg PhD Scholarships

Subjects: All subjects.
Purpose: To pursue research at the University and improve their English prior to the studies.

Eligibility: Open to students planning to pursue their PhD at the University.
Level of Study: Doctorate
Value: Full tuition fee waivers, accommodation, living expenses, flights to and from London
Application Procedure: Check website for further details.
Funding: Trusts

Regent Campus Scholarship (Poland)

Subjects: Social Sciences, humanities and languages.
Eligibility: Open to students from Poland holding an offer for a full-time Masters Degree within the School of Law or the School of Social Sciences, Humanities and Languages (SSHL).
Level of Study: Postgraduate
Type: Scholarship
Value: Full tuition fee waiver, accommodation, living expenses and flights to and from London
Application Procedure: Check website for further details.

Westminster Business School (WBS) Scholarships

Subjects: All subjects excluding MBA.
Eligibility: Open to students holding an offer for any full-time Masters Degree, excluding MBA, within Westminster Business School.
Level of Study: Postgraduate
Type: Scholarship
Value: Full tuition fee waivers
No. of awards offered: 6
Application Procedure: Check website for further details.

UNIVERSITY OF WOLLONGONG (UOW)

Academic Registrar's Division Building 36, Wollongong, NSW 2522, Australia
Tel: (61) 2 4221 3555
Fax: (61) 2 4221 4322
Email: scholarships@uow.edu.au
Website: www.uow.edu.au
Contact: Mr Tim McDonald, Postgraduate Research Scholarships Officer

The UOW is a university of international standing with an enviable record of achievement in teaching and research, which aims to nurture quality graduates who are experts in their fields and who can work anywhere in the world.

Eurobodalla Shire Council Residential Scholarships

Purpose: To support the students in their first year of studies at UOW.
Eligibility: Applicants must intend to enroll at University of Wollongong, Wollongong Campus.
Level of Study: Postgraduate
Type: Scholarship
Value: Australian $1,500
Length of Study: 1 year
Frequency: Annual
Study Establishment: University of Wollongong, Wollongong campus
No. of awards offered: 3
Application Procedure: Applicants must apply with copies of recent academic records and a brief resume.
Closing Date: February 26th
Contributor: Eurobodalla Shire Council
No. of awards given last year: 3

Marketing Research Innovation Centre PhD Scholarship

Subjects: Commerce, management, tourism and services.
Purpose: To conduct research in the area of qualitative and quantitative methods, market segmentation, brand image studies and advertising experiments.
Eligibility: Open to applicants who have an excellent tertiary track record, experience with conducting academic research.
Level of Study: Postgraduate, Research
Type: Scholarship

Value: Australian $20,000 per year
Length of Study: 3 years
Frequency: Annual
Country of Study: Australia
No. of awards offered: 1
Application Procedure: Candidates can check the website for further details.

For further information contact:

Marketing Research Innovation Centre, School of Management and Marketing, University of Wollongong, Wollongong, NSW 2522, Australia
Fax: (61) 02 4221 3862
Email: sarad@uow.edu.au
Website: www.uow.edu.au/commerce/mark/mric.html
Contact: Professor Sara Dolnicar, Professor

UOW Academic Excellence Regional Scholarship

Purpose: To recognize academic excellence.
Eligibility: Candidates must be from Iilwarra, Southern Sydney, South Western Sydney, Southern Highlands and/or the South Coast of New South Wales.
Level of Study: Postgraduate
Type: Scholarship
Value: Australian $3,000
Length of Study: 1 years
Frequency: Annual
Study Establishment: University of Wollongong
Country of Study: Australia
No. of awards offered: 100
Application Procedure: Apply online.
Closing Date: October

UOW Engineering Scholarships

Subjects: Engineering, materials, mechanical, mechatronics, mining, physics, medical radiation physics, photonics.
Purpose: To award students for academic excellence.
Eligibility: Open to students with strong academic records. Student must not hold any other scholarship or cadetship.
Level of Study: Postgraduate
Type: Scholarship
Value: Australian $3,000
Length of Study: 1 year
Frequency: Annual
Study Establishment: University of Wollongong
Country of Study: Australia
No. of awards offered: 30 (15 of the scholarships will be reserved for women)
Application Procedure: Apply online.
Closing Date: October
Contributor: Bluescope steel Industrial markets and Bluescope steel research laboratories port kembla

UOW Iron & Steel Society Scholarships

Subjects: Materials Engineering.
Purpose: To support students enrolled in a Bachelor of Engineering degree in Materials Engineering.
Eligibility: Candidate must join the Iron & Steel Society before completion of the degree.
Level of Study: Postgraduate
Type: Scholarship
Value: Australian $10,000 p.a
Length of Study: 4 years
Frequency: Annual
Study Establishment: University of Wollongong
Country of Study: Australia
No. of awards offered: 2
Application Procedure: Apply online.
Closing Date: October
Funding: Commercial
Contributor: BlueScope Steel Ltd
Additional Information: There is an opportunity for vacation employment at BlueScope Steel Ltd. Please contact Debby Porter at the scholarships office.

UOW Loftus Education Centre Teaching Innovation

Subjects: Mathematics, science.
Purpose: To support students with a proven interest in mathematics and/or science.
Eligibility: Applicants must be commencing study as a first-year, full-time undergraduate student in the Bachelor of Science Education or the Bachelor of Mathematics Education at the UOW Loftus Education center.
Level of Study: Postgraduate
Type: Scholarship
Value: Australian $6,000
Length of Study: 4 years
Frequency: Annual
Study Establishment: University of Wollongong
Country of Study: Australia
No. of awards offered: 5
Application Procedure: Apply online.
Closing Date: October
Contributor: Loftus education centre

UOW Work-Integrated Learning Scholarship

Purpose: To reward outstanding academic achievements.
Eligibility: Open to students with outstanding academic achievements.
Level of Study: Postgraduate
Type: Scholarship
Value: Australian $3,000–9,300
Frequency: Annual
Study Establishment: University of Wollongong
Country of Study: Australia
No. of awards offered: Varies
Application Procedure: Apply online.
Closing Date: October
Additional Information: Scholarship holders are required to undertake a period, usually 6–10 weeks of professional work experience each year with an appropriate sponsor organization.

For further information contact:

Uniadvice University of Wollongong, NSW 2522, Australia
Tel: (61) 1300 367 869
Fax: (61) 612 4221 3233
Email: uniadvice@uow.edu.au

US DEPARTMENT OF EDUCATION

Fulbright-Hays Programme, 1990 K Street NW, 6th Floor,
Washington DC, 20006-8521,
United States of America
Tel: (1) 202 502 7632
Fax: (1) 202 502 7860
Email: karla.verbryckblock@ed.gov
Website: www.ed.gov

The US Department of Education is the agency of the federal government that establishes policy, administers and co-ordinates most federal assistance to education. The Department's mission is to serve American students and to ensure that all have equal access to education and to promote excellence in various schools.

Fulbright Hays Doctoral Dissertation Research Abroad Program

Subjects: All subjects.
Purpose: To assist PhD students in carrying out dissertation research in other countries.
Eligibility: Open to US citizens or nationals who are Doctoral candidates enrolled in a PhD programme in the United States.
Level of Study: Doctorate
Type: Scholarship
Value: Varies
Length of Study: six to twelve months
Frequency: Annual
Country of Study: United States of America

Application Procedure: Applicants must submit a completed application form and proof of enrollment in a Doctoral programme.
Closing Date: Late October or early November

For further information contact:

Website: www.ed.gov/offices/OPE/HEP/iegps

THE US-UK FULBRIGHT COMMISSION

Fulbright House, 62 Doughty Street, London, WC1N 2JZ, England
Tel: (44) 20 7404 6880
Fax: (44) 20 7404 6834
Email: programmes@fulbright.co.uk
Website: www.fulbright.co.uk
Contact: Ms Michael Scott-Kline, Director

The US-UK Fulbright Commission has a programme of awards offered annually to citizens of the United Kingdom and United States of America.

Fulbright British Friends of HBS MBA Awards
Subjects: MBA.
Purpose: To enable British candidates to participate in Harvard Business School MBA programmes.
Eligibility: Open to citizens of the United Kingdom. Applicants must hold the minimum of an Upper Second Class (Honours) Degree and be able to demonstrate leadership qualities.
Level of Study: MBA, Postgraduate
Type: Scholarship
Value: Tuition fees for the 1st academic year, limited sickness and accident coverage and visa sponsorship and processing
Length of Study: 9 months
Frequency: Annual
Study Establishment: Harvard Business School
Country of Study: United States of America
No. of awards offered: 24
Application Procedure: Applicants must complete an application form.
Closing Date: Early April
Funding: Government, individuals
Contributor: The British Friends of Harvard Business School
No. of awards given last year: 3
No. of applicants last year: 20

For further information contact:

Website: www.fulbright.co.uk

Fulbright Distinguished Scholar Awards
Subjects: All subjects.
Purpose: To enable scholars to carry out lecturing and research in the United Kingdom.
Eligibility: PhD requried.
Level of Study: Postdoctorate, Professional development, Research, Lecture
Value: UK £2,500 per month
Length of Study: 3 months–10 months
Frequency: Annual
Study Establishment: An approved Institute of Higher Education
Country of Study: United Kingdom
No. of awards offered: 24
Application Procedure: Applicants must submit a formal application.
Closing Date: August 1st
Funding: Government
No. of awards given last year: 5

For further information contact:

Council for International Exchange of Scholars (CIES), 3007 Tilden Street North West, Suite 5M, Washington DC, 20008-3009, United States of America
Tel: (1) 202 686 6245
Website: www.cies.org

Fulbright Distinguished Scholar Awards
Subjects: All subjects.
Purpose: To allow outstanding academics or professionals who are established or potential leaders in their field to undertake a period of professional development in the United States of America.

Eligibility: Open to citizens of the United Kingdom with an affiliation to one academic institution in the United States of America. Proof of this affiliation and details of its nature are necessary. Medical doctors intending to work with patients in any capacity while in the United States of America are not eligible. Awards are not available for peripatetic visits or attendance at conferences only.
Level of Study: Research, Postdoctorate, Professional development
Type: Fellowship
Value: An award of UK £2,500 per month (not to exceed £25,000), visa paperwork fees and visa paid by the Commission, and health and accident insurance
Length of Study: A minimum stay of 3 months
Frequency: Annual
Country of Study: United States of America
No. of awards offered: 2
Application Procedure: Applicants must draw up a detailed project outline and provide evidence that a United States of America institution will agree to act as host and supervisor. Lecturers and researchers must have an invitation from the host institution. Completed applications should reach the Commission by the deadline and may not be emailed.
Closing Date: May 31st
Funding: Government
No. of awards given last year: 2
No. of applicants last year: 50

For further information contact:

Website: www.fulbright.co.uk

Fulbright Graduate Student Awards
Subjects: All subjects.
Purpose: To enable students to pursue postgraduate study or research in the United Kingdom.
Eligibility: Open to citizens of the United States of America, normally resident in the United States of America. Applicants must have a minimum grade point average of 3.5 and be able to demonstrate evidence of leadership qualities. Applicants should be adventurous and be able to demonstrate that they will maximize academic, social and cultural opportunities available in the United Kingdom. A full description of the selection criteria is available from the website.
Level of Study: Doctorate, Postgraduate, Research
Value: Up to UK£20,000 and health insurance
Length of Study: 9 months (1 academic year)
Frequency: Annual
Study Establishment: Any approved Institute of Higher Education
Country of Study: United Kingdom
No. of awards offered: 814
Application Procedure: Applicants must submit a formal application.
Closing Date: October
Funding: Government
Contributor: The United States and United Kingdom governments
No. of awards given last year: 12
No. of applicants last year: approx. 450
Additional Information: A telephone interview is required of shortlisted candidates.

For further information contact:

Institute of International Education, 809 United Nations Plaza, New York, NY, 10017, United States of America
Tel: (1) 212 984 5466
Fax: (1) 212 984 5465
Website: www.iie.org
Contact: Student Program Division

Fulbright Police Research Fellowships
Subjects: Policing.
Purpose: To enable serving police officers to spend 3–6 months in the United States of America researching an aspect of policing.
Eligibility: Open to United Kingdom police officers and staff (all ranks).
Level of Study: Professional development
Type: Fellowship
Value: UK £10,000
Length of Study: 3 months minimum
Frequency: Annual

Study Establishment: An approved United States of America Institute of Higher Education or police force
Country of Study: United States of America
No. of awards offered: 2
Application Procedure: Applicants must complete a formal application.
Closing Date: May 31st
Funding: Government
No. of awards given last year: 2
No. of applicants last year: 6
Additional Information: Short-listed candidates will usually be interviewed in June.

For further information contact:

Website: www.fulbright.co.uk

Fulbright Postgraduate Student Awards
Subjects: All subjects (journalism, film and MBA awards are offered in other categories.
Purpose: To enable students to pursue postgraduate study or research in the United States of America.
Eligibility: Candidates should hold a minimum of an Upper Second Class (Honours) Degree (or equivalent) and demonstrate outstanding leadership qualities.
Level of Study: Doctorate, Postgraduate
Value: Up to US$40,000, health insurance, visa processing
Length of Study: A minimum of 9 months
Frequency: Annual
Study Establishment: An approved Institute of Higher Education
Country of Study: United States of America
No. of awards offered: 10–16
Application Procedure: Applicants must submit a formal application. Applications can be obtained www.fulbright.co.uk website.
Closing Date: May 31st
Funding: Government
No. of awards given last year: 10
No. of applicants last year: 300
Additional Information: Short-listed candidates will be interviewed in mid-February.

Fulbright-AstraZeneca Research Scholarship
Subjects: Cell biology, molecular biology, bioinformatics, biochemistry and chemistry.
Purpose: To enable a postdoctoral scientist to carry out research at a top centre in the United States of America.
Eligibility: Open to United Kingdom scientists.
Level of Study: Postdoctorate
Type: Scholarship
Value: UK £20,000 plus round-trip travel, limited sickness and accident coverage and visa sponsorship and processing
Length of Study: A minimum of 10 months
Frequency: Annual
Study Establishment: An approved establishment in the USA
Country of Study: United States of America
No. of awards offered: 1
Application Procedure: Applicants must complete an application form.
Closing Date: May 31st
Funding: Government, private
Contributor: AstraZeneca Plc
No. of awards given last year: 1
No. of applicants last year: 20
Additional Information: Short-listed candidates will usually be interviewed in Summer 2009.

For further information contact:

Website: www.fulbright.co.uk

The Fulbright-Bristol University Award
Purpose: To enable a US ciitizen to pursue postgraduate study in the United Kingdom at the University of Bristol.
Eligibility: Applicant must be a US citizen (resident anywhere but the UK), and a graduating seniro, hold a B.S./B.A. degree, Master's or doctoral degree candidate, young professional or artist.
Level of Study: Postgraduate

Value: Up to UK£20,000, limited sickness and accident benefit coverage and participation in a number of Fulbright Scholar events including the Fulbright Forum in January are also included
Frequency: Annual
Study Establishment: University of Bristol
Country of Study: United Kingdom
No. of awards offered: 1
Application Procedure: A two-page statement of proposed study or research and one-page personal statement along with the online application form.
Closing Date: October 20th
Additional Information: For more information, please visit www.bristol.ac.uk/prospectus/postgraduate and http://us.fulbrightonline.org/program_country.html?id = 112

For further information contact:

University of Bristol, Senate House, Tyndall Avenue, Bristol, BS8 1TH, United Kingdom
Tel: (44) 44 (0) 117 928 9000
Website: www.bristol.ac.uk

The Fulbright-Coventry Award in Automotive Design
Subjects: Automotive Design.
Purpose: To enable a US citizen to pursue a Master's degree in Automotive Design.
Eligibility: Applicant should be a US citizen (resident anywhere but the UK), and a graduating senior, holding a B.S./B.A. degree, master's or doctoral degree candidate, young professional or artist.
Level of Study: Doctorate, Graduate, Postgraduate
Type: Award
Value: Up to UK£20,000, limited sickness and accident benefit coverage, as well as participation in a number of Fulbright Scholar events including the Fulbright Forum in January
Frequency: Annual
Study Establishment: Coventry University
Country of Study: United Kingdom
No. of awards offered: 1
Application Procedure: Please visit the website http://us.fulbrightonline.org/applynow.html for applications.
Closing Date: October

For further information contact:

Website: www.coventry.ac.uk/courses/postgraduate-full-time-a-z/a/381

The Fulbright-Edinburgh University Award
Subjects: All subjects.
Purpose: To enable a US citizen to pursue postgraduate study in the United Kingdom at the University of Bristol.
Eligibility: Applicant must be a US citizen (resident anywhere but the UK), and a graduating senior, holding a B.S./B.A. degree, master's or doctoral degree candidate, young professional or artist.
Level of Study: Doctorate, Graduate, Postgraduate
Type: Award/Grant
Value: Up to UK£20,000, limited sickness and accident benefit coverage, as well as participation in a number of Fulbright Scholar events including the Fulbright Forum in January are also included
Frequency: Annual
Study Establishment: University of Edinburgh
Country of Study: United Kingdom
No. of awards offered: 1
Application Procedure: Please visit the website http://us.fulbrightonline.org/applynow.html
Closing Date: October
Additional Information: For more information, visit www.ed.ac.uk/studying/postgraduate and http://us.fulbrightonline.org/program_country.html?id = 112

For further information contact:

United Kingdom
Tel: (44) +44 (0) 131 651 4221
Email: Robert.Lawrie@ed.ac.uk
Contact: Ms Lawrie Robert, Head of Scholarships & Student Finance

The Fulbright-Glasgow University Award

Subjects: All subjects.

Purpose: To enable a US citizen to pursue postgraduate study in the United Kingdom at Glasgow University.

Eligibility: Applicant should be a US citizen (resident anywhere but the UK), and a graduating senior, hold a B.S./B.A. degree, master's or doctoral degree candidate, young professional or artist.

Level of Study: Postgraduate

Type: Award

Value: UK£20,000. From the £20,000 tuition fees will be deducted and the remainder will be paid in installments directly to the grantee. the first of which is typically given upon arrival in the UK

Frequency: Annual

Study Establishment: Glasgow University

Country of Study: United Kingdom

No. of awards offered: 1

Application Procedure: Please visit http://us.fulbrightonline.org/applynow.html for application details.

Closing Date: October

Additional Information: For more information, visit www.gla.ac.uk/postgraduate/ and http://us.fulbrightonline.org/program_country.html?id=112

Fulbright-Glasgow Urban Lab Distinguished Chair Award

Purpose: To contribute to the development of curriculum and research agenda of the Glasgow Urban Lab and to undertake a series of public lectures in Glasgow and other major Scottish cities.

Eligibility: Applicant should possess Ph.D. or equivalent professional/terminal degree (including a master's depending on the field) as appropriate at the time of the application.

Level of Study: Postdoctorate

Type: Award

Value: UK£25,000 plus accommodation. Limited sickness and accident benefit coverage as well as participation in a number of Fulbright Scholar events including the Fulbright Forum in January are also included

Study Establishment: Glasgow School of Art, Mackintosh School of Architecture

Country of Study: Scotland

No. of awards offered: 1

Application Procedure: Please visit www.cies.org/Chairs/Apply.htm for application details.

Closing Date: August

Fulbright-King's College London Distinguished Scholar Award

Subjects: All subjects.

Purpose: To support research at King's College, London.

Eligibility: Applicant must be a PhD or equivalent professional/terminal degree (including a master's depending on the field) as appropriate at the time of application.

Level of Study: Postdoctorate

Type: Award

Value: UK£10,000. Limited sickness and accident benefit coverage as well as participation in a number of Fulbright Scholar events including the Fulbright Forum in January are also included

Frequency: Annual

Study Establishment: King's College London

Country of Study: United Kingdom

No. of awards offered: 1

Application Procedure: Please visit www.cies.org/us_scholars/us_awards for application details.

Closing Date: Early August

Additional Information: For more information, visit www.cies.org/us_scholars/us_awards/index.html and www.kcl.ac.uk/

The Fulbright-Leeds University Award

Subjects: All subjects.

Purpose: To enable a US citizen to pursue postgraduate study in the United Kingdom at the University of Leeds.

Eligibility: Applicant must be a US citizen (resident anywhere but the UK), and a graduating senior, hold a B.S./B.A. degree, master's or doctoral degree candidate, young professional or artist.

Level of Study: Postgraduate

Type: Award

Value: Up to Uk£20,000, limited sickness and accident benefit coverage, as well as participation in a number of Fulbright Scholar events including the Fulbright Forum in January are also included

Frequency: Annual

Study Establishment: University of Leeds

Country of Study: United Kingdom

No. of awards offered: 1

Application Procedure: Please visit the website http://us.fulbright-online.org/applynow.html

Closing Date: October

Additional Information: For more information, please visit www.leeds.ac.uk and http://us.fulbrightonline.org/program_country.html?id=112.

Fulbright-Leeds University Distinguished Chair Award

Subjects: All subjects.

Purpose: To contribute to the intellectual life of Leeds University through seminars, public lectures and curriculum development in any discipline.

Eligibility: Applicant must be a PhD or equivalent professional/terminal degree (including a master's depending on the field) as appropriate at the time of application.

Level of Study: Postdoctorate

Type: Award

Value: UK£25,000 plus accommodation. Limited sickness and accident benefit coverage as well as participation in a number of Fulbright Scholar events including the Fulbright Forum in January are also included

Study Establishment: Leeds University

Country of Study: United Kingdom

No. of awards offered: 1

Application Procedure: Please visit the website www.cies.org/Chairs/Apply.htm

Closing Date: August

Additional Information: For more information, please visit www.cies.org/Chairs, www.cies.org/Chairs/2009/area2.htm and www.leeds.ac.uk

The Fulbright-Liverpool University Award

Subjects: All subjects.

Purpose: To enable a US citizen to pursue postgraduate study in the United Kingdom at the University of Liverpool.

Eligibility: Applicant must be a US citizen (resident anywhere but the UK), and a graduating senior, holding a B.S./B.A. degree, master's or doctoral degree candidate, young professional or artist.

Level of Study: Doctorate, Graduate, Postgraduate

Type: Award

Value: Up to UK£20,000, limited sickness and accident benefit coverage as well as participation in a number of Fulbright Scholar events including the Fulbright Forum in January

Frequency: Annual

Study Establishment: University of Liverpool

Country of Study: United Kingdom

No. of awards offered: 1

Application Procedure: Please visit the website http://us.fulbright-online.org/applynow.html

Closing Date: October

Additional Information: For more information, visit www.liverpool.ac.uk and http://us.fulbrightonline.org/program_country.html?id=112.

Fulbright-LSE Government Studies Award

Purpose: To enable a US citizen to pursue postgraduate study in the United Kingdom at the London School of Economics and Political Science (LSE).

Eligibility: Applicant must be a US citizen (resident anywhere but the UK), and a graduating senior, holding a B.S./B.A. degree, master's or doctoral degree candidate, young professional or artist.

Level of Study: Doctorate, Graduate, Postgraduate

Type: Award

Value: Up to UK£20,000, limited sickness and accident benefit coverage, as well as participation in a number of Fulbright Scholar events including the Fulbright Forum in January

Frequency: Annual

Study Establishment: London School of Economics and Political Science (LSE)

Country of Study: United Kingdom
No. of awards offered: 1
Application Procedure: Please visit the website http://us.fulbright-online.org/applynow.html for application details.
Closing Date: October
Additional Information: For more information, visit www.ise.ac.uk/collections/government/, http://us.fulbrightonline.org/program_country.html?id = 112 and www.fulbright.co.uk/awards/us/postgrad/traditional.html#LSE

Fulbright-Multiple Sclerosis Society Research Award
Subjects: All subjects.
Purpose: To enable a UK citizen to pursue research in clinical or biomedical aspects of MS or the social or economic conditions of sufferers, at any accredited US institution, for a minimum of 12 months.
Eligibility: Applicant must be a UK citizen (resident anywhere but the US), holding a doctoral degree or equivalent professional training or experience at the time of application.
Level of Study: Postdoctorate
Type: Award
Value: Approximately UK£75,000, plus limted sickness and accident benefit coverage, visa sponsorship and processing and participation in a number of Fulbright Scholar events
Frequency: Annual
Country of Study: United States of America
No. of awards offered: 1
Application Procedure: Formal applications are made online via the USUK Fulbright Commission: www.fulbright.co.uk
Closing Date: May 31st
Additional Information: For more information, visit www.fulbright.co.uk and www.cies.org/vs_scholars/vs_awards/

Fulbright-Queen's University Belfast Anglophone Irish Writing Distinguished Scholar Award
Subjects: Language and Literature (Non-US).
Purpose: To support the research and teaching/lecturing of Anglophone Irish Literature from the 18th century through to contemporary writing at Queen's University Belfast.
Eligibility: Applicant must be a PhD or equivalent professional/terminal degree (including a master's depending on the field) as appropriate at the time of application.
Level of Study: Postdoctorate
Type: Award
Value: UK£15,000. Dedicated housing will be offered. Limited sickness and accident benefit coverage as well as participation in a number of Fulbright Scholar events including the Fulbright Forum in January are also included
Study Establishment: Queen's University Belfast
Country of Study: United Kingdom
Application Procedure: Please visit the website www.cies.org/us_scholars/us_awards/Eligibility.htm for application details.
Closing Date: August
Additional Information: For more information, visit www.cies.org/us_scholars/us_awards/index.html, www.qub.ac.uk/schools/SchoolofEnglish/ and www.qub.ac.uk/schools/SeamusHeaneyCentreforPoetry/

Fulbright-Queen's University Belfast Anglophone Irish Writing Distinguished Scholar Award
Subjects: Creative Writing.
Purpose: To enable teaching/lecturing, writing and public readings of their own work at Queen's University Belfast.
Eligibility: Applicant must be a PhD or equivalent professional/terminal degree (including a master's depending on the field) as appropriate at the time of application.
Level of Study: Postdoctorate
Type: Award
Value: UK£15,000. Dedicated housing will be offered. Limited sickness and accident benefit coverag as well as participation in a number of Fulbright Scholar events including the Fulbright Forum in January are also included
No. of awards offered: 1
Application Procedure: Please visit the website www.cies.org/us_scholars/us_awards/

Closing Date: August
Additional Information: For more information, visit www.cies.org/us_scholars/us_awards/index.html, www.qub.ac.uk/schools/SchoolofEnglish/ and www.qub.ac.uk/schools/SeamusHeaneyCentrefor
Poetry/

Fulbright-Robertson Visiting Professorship in British History
Subjects: British history or Western civilization (any specialisation).
Purpose: To enable a British scholar to spend 10 months lecturing in British history at Westminster College, Fulton, Missouri.
Eligibility: Open to scholars of British history, with 1–2 years of experience of teaching undergraduates.
Level of Study: Professional development
Value: Up to US$50,000 plus round-trip travel for the grantee and up to four accompanying dependants
Length of Study: 10 months
Frequency: Annual
Study Establishment: Westminster College, Fulton, Missouri
Country of Study: United States of America
No. of awards offered: 1
Application Procedure: Applicants must submit a formal application with two references.
Closing Date: May 31st
Funding: Private
Contributor: Westminster College, Fulton, Missouri
No. of awards given last year: 1
No. of applicants last year: 5

The Fulbright-Sussex University Award
Subjects: All subjects.
Purpose: To enable a US citizen to pursue postgraduate study in the United Kingdom at the University of Sussex.
Eligibility: Applicant must be a US citizen (resident anywhere but th UK), and a graduating senior, holding a B.S./B.A. degree, master's or doctoral degree candidate, young professional or artist.
Level of Study: Doctorate, Graduate, Postgraduate
Type: Award
Value: Up to UK£20,000. Limited sickness and accident benefit coverage, and participation in a number of Fulbright Scholar events including the Fulbright Forum in January are included as well
Frequency: Annual
Study Establishment: University of Sussex
Country of Study: United Kingdom
No. of awards offered: 1
Application Procedure: Please visit the website http://us.fulbrightonline.org/applynow.html for application details.
Closing Date: October
Additional Information: For more information, visit www.sussex.ac.uk/pgstudy and http://us.fulbrightonline.org/program_country.html?id = 112.

The Fulbright-University College Falmouth Media Award
Subjects: Media.
Purpose: To enable a US citizen to pursue a postgraduate degree in media studies at University College, Falmouth.
Eligibility: Applicant must be a US citizen (resident anywhere but the UK), and a graduating senior, holding a B.S./B.A. degree, master's or doctoral degree candidate, young professional or artist.
Level of Study: Postgraduate, Doctorate, Graduate
Type: Award
Value: UK£15,000. An additional allowance of up to £1,000 is available to support engagement with (travel) UK publishing and/or media companies. Limited sickness and accident benefit coverage as well as participation in a number of Fulbright Scholar events including the Fulbright Forum in January are also included
Frequency: Annual
Study Establishment: University College Falmouth
Country of Study: United Kingdom
No. of awards offered: 1
Application Procedure: Please visit the website http://us.fulbrightonline.org/applynow.html for application details.
Closing Date: October

Additional Information: For more information, visit www.fal-mouth.ac.uk/201/courses-7/postgraduate-courses-43.html and http://us.fulbrightonline.org/program_country.html?id = 112

The Fulbright-University College London Award

Subjects: All subjects.
Purpose: To enable a US citizen to pursue postgraduate study in the United Kingdom at the University College London.
Eligibility: Applicant must be a US citizen (resident anywhere but the UK), and a graduating senior, holding a B.S./B.A. degree, master's or doctoral degree candidate, young professional or artist.
Level of Study: Doctorate, Graduate, Postgraduate
Type: Award
Value: UK£20,000. From the £20,000 tuition fees will be deducted and the remainder will be paid in installments directly to the grantee, the first of which is typically given upon arrival in the UK
Frequency: Annual
Study Establishment: University College London
Country of Study: United Kingdom
No. of awards offered: 1
Application Procedure: Please visit the website http://us.fulbright-online.org/applynow.html
Closing Date: October
Additional Information: For more information, visit www.grad.ucl.ac.uk and http://us.fulbrightonline.org/program_country.html?id = 112

Fulbright-University of the Arts London Distinguished Chair Award

Subjects: Art, communications, history, philosophy.
Purpose: To pursue research, lecture, teach and/or contribute to the curriculum at TrAIN, a department of the University of the Arts London.
Eligibility: Applicant must be a PhD or equivalent professional/terminal degree (including a master's depending on the field) as appropriate at the time of application.
Level of Study: Postdoctorate
Type: Award
Value: UK£25,000 plus accommodation. Limited sickness and accident benefit coverage as well as participation in a number of Fulbright Scholar events including the Fulbright Forum in January are also included
Study Establishment: University of Arts London
Country of Study: United Kingdom
No. of awards offered: 1
Application Procedure: Please visit the website www.cies.org/Chairs/Apply.htm for application details.
Closing Date: August

The Fulbright-Warwick University Award

Subjects: All subjects.
Purpose: To enable a US citizen to pursue a postgraduate study in the United Kingdom in any field at the University of Warwick.
Eligibility: Applicant must be a US citizen (resident anywhere but the UK), and a graduating senior, holding a B.S./B.A. degree, master's or doctoral degree candidate, young professional or artist.
Level of Study: Graduate, Doctorate, Postgraduate
Type: Award
Value: Up to UK£20,000, limited sickness and accident benefit coverage, as well as participation in a number of Fulbright Scholar events including the Fulbright Forum in January
Frequency: Annual
Study Establishment: University of Warwick
Country of Study: United Kingdom
No. of awards offered: 1
Closing Date: October
Additional Information: For more information, visit www.warwick.ac.uk/study/postgraduate and http://us.fulbrightonline.org/program_country.html?id = 112

UK Fulbright Alistair Cooke Award in Journalism

Subjects: Journalism.
Purpose: To finance an aspiring journalist.
Eligibility: US nationals.
Level of Study: Postgraduate
Type: Scholarship

Value: Up to UK £20,000
Length of Study: 9 months
Frequency: Annual
Country of Study: United Kingdom
No. of awards offered: 1
Application Procedure: See website www.iie.org
Closing Date: Late October
Funding: Government
No. of awards given last year: 1

US Fulbright Alistair Cooke Award in Journalism

Subjects: Journalism.
Purpose: To finance an aspiring journalist.
Eligibility: UK nationals and EU nationals residents in the UK.
Level of Study: Postgraduate
Type: Scholarship
Value: Up to US$40,000, health insurance, visa sponsorship and processing
Length of Study: 9 months
Frequency: Annual
Country of Study: United States of America
No. of awards offered: 1
Application Procedure: For applications, please visit the website www.fulbright.co.uk
Closing Date: May 31st
Funding: Government
No. of awards given last year: 1

For further information contact:

Fulbright House, 62 Doughty Street, London, WCIN ZJ7

US-UK Fulbright Commission, Criminal Justice and Police Research Fellowships

Subjects: Policing.
Purpose: To enable active domestic police officers and staff to extend their professional expertise and experience in conducting research into any aspect of policing, in the UK.
Eligibility: Applicants should ideally hold a Bachelor's degree in criminal justice, police studies or a related discipline within the social sciences.
Level of Study: Professional development
Value: UK £10,000
Length of Study: Between 3 and 6 months
Frequency: Annual
Study Establishment: Institutes of Higher Education or a police force
Country of Study: United Kingdom
No. of awards offered: 2
Application Procedure: Applicants must complete an application form available from the Council for the International Exchange of Scholars (CIES) www.cies.org
Closing Date: August 1st
Funding: Government
No. of awards given last year: 2
No. of applicants last year: 3

For further information contact:

3007 Tilden Street, Suite 5M, Washington DC, 2008-3009, United States of America

VALPARAISO UNIVERSITY

Lilly Fellows Program, Linwood House 1401 Linwood Avenue, Valparaiso, IN, 46383 6493, United States of America
Tel: (1) 219 464 5317
Fax: (1) 219 464 5496
Email: University.Relations@valpo.edu
Website: www.lillyfellows.org

Valparaiso University was founded in 1859 by Methodists, with approximately 4,000 students from most states and more than 40 countries. The university, which is nearly 150 years old offers more than 70 fields of study.

Lilly Postdoctoral Teaching Fellowship Program

Subjects: Arts and humanities.
Purpose: To strengthen the quality of church-related institutions of higher learning for the 21st century.
Eligibility: Open to new scholar-teachers who have obtained a PhD and are interested in the relationship between Christianity and the academic vocation and are seriously considering a career at a church-related college or university.
Level of Study: Postgraduate, Teaching
Type: Fellowships
Value: US$45,000 per year
Length of Study: 2 years
Frequency: Annual
Country of Study: United States of America
No. of awards offered: 3
Application Procedure: Applicants must submit a curriculum vitae, a graduate transcript, 2 letters of recommendation and an essay or personal statement.
Closing Date: December 16th
Additional Information: All queries should be directed to lillyfellows.program@valpo.edu. For further information contact The Selection Committee Lilly Fellows Program at the above address.

VATICAN FILM LIBRARY

Mellon Fellowship Program, Pius XII Memorial Library, Saint Louis University, 3650 Lindell Boulevard, St Louis, MO, 63108 3302, United States of America
Tel: (1) 314 977 3090
Fax: (1) 314 977 3108
Email: vfl@slu.edu
Website: www.slu.edu/libraries/vfl

The Vatican Film Library at Saint Louis University in St Louis, Missouri, is a microfilm repository for the Vatican Library manuscripts housed in Rome and a research centre for medieval and Renaissance manuscripts studies in general. The research collections contain a wide range of primary source manuscript materials on microfilm, microfiche and in digital reproduction, in addition to slides and printed facsimile editions ranging in date from the 5th to the 19th centuries, and a large number of incunabula and early-printed books also on microfilm and microfiche. At the core of these collections are the microfilmed copies of approximately three-quarters of the Vatican Library's Greek, Latin and Western European vernacular manuscripts, as well as Hebrew, Ethiopic and Arabic manuscripts.

Vatican Film Library Mellon Fellowship

Subjects: Classical languages and literature, palaeography, scriptural and patristic studies, history, philosophy and sciences in the Middle ages and the Renaissance and early Romance literature. There are also opportunities for supported research in the history of music, manuscript illumination, mathematics and technology, theology, liturgy, Roman and canon law or political theory.
Purpose: To assist scholars wishing to conduct research in the manuscript collections in the Vatican Film Library at Saint Louis University.
Eligibility: Open to candidates who are at the postdoctoral level, or graduate students formally admitted to PhD candidacy and working on their dissertation.
Level of Study: Graduate, Doctorate, Postgraduate, Predoctorate, Research, Postdoctorate
Type: Fellowship
Value: Travel expenses and per diem expenses (currently US$73)
Length of Study: 2–8 weeks
Study Establishment: The Vatican Film Library
Country of Study: United States of America
Application Procedure: Applicants must write, in the first instance, to describe the topic of the planned research and to indicate the exact dates during which support is desired. A formal application should then be submitted, which should include a cover letter stating the title and proposed dates of research, a detailed statement of the project proposal of not more than two or three pages in length, a list of the manuscripts or other archival materials to be consulted, a selective bibliography of primary and secondary sources relating to the research topic and a curriculum vitae. Applications submitted by PhD

candidates should also include a letter of recommendation from their advisor with reference to the applicant's palaeographical and language.
Closing Date: March 1st for research in June to August, June 1st for research in September to December and October 1st for research in January to May

VERNE CATT MCDOWELL CORPORATION

PO Box 1336, Albany, OR, 97321-0440, United States of America
Tel: (1) 541 926 6829
Contact: Ms Emily Killin, Business Manager

The Verne Catt McDowell Scholarship educates pastoral ministers of the Christian Church (Disciples of Christ) by providing supplementary financial grants to graduate theology students.

Verne Catt McDowell Corporation Scholarship

Subjects: Religion, theology and church administration.
Purpose: To provide supplemental financial grants to men and women for graduate theological education for ministry in the Christian Church (Disciples of Christ) denomination.
Eligibility: All scholarship candidates must be ministers ordained or studying to meet the requirements to be ordained as a minister in the Christian Church (Disciples of Christ). Candidates must be members of the Christian Church (Disciples of Christ) denomination. Preference is given to Oregon graduates and citizens of the United States of America.
Level of Study: Postgraduate
Type: Scholarship
Value: Average: $3000
Length of Study: 1–3 years
Frequency: Annual
Study Establishment: A graduate institution of theological education, accredited by the general assembly of the Christian Church (Disciples of Christ)
Country of Study: United States of America
No. of awards offered: 5
Application Procedure: Applicants must complete an application form and provide details of qualifications, transcripts, 3 references and state where they obtained information about the scholarship. An interview may be requested.
Closing Date: May 1st
Funding: Private
Contributor: I A McDowell
No. of awards given last year: 6
No. of applicants last year: 12

VERNON WILLEY TRUST-GUARDIAN TRUST COMPANY

PO Box 9, Christchurch, 8001, New Zealand
Tel: (64) 3 379 0645
Fax: (64) 3 366 7616
Email: gary_anderson@nzgt.co.nz
Website: www.nzgt.co.nz
Contact: Mr G Anderson

Vernon Willey Trust Awards

Subjects: The sheep and wool industry of New Zealand.
Purpose: To assist with research and education into the production, processing and marketing of wool and the general development of the industry for the national benefit of New Zealand.
Eligibility: Open to New Zealand citizens, permanent New Zealand residents or overseas researchers working in New Zealand.
Level of Study: Doctorate, Postdoctorate
Type: Fellowship
Value: Varies, usually between New Zealand $30,000–35,000
Length of Study: Up to 3 years
Frequency: Dependent on funds available
Country of Study: New Zealand
No. of awards offered: 1

Application Procedure: Applicants must complete an application form.
Closing Date: March 15th
Funding: Private
No. of awards given last year: 4
No. of applicants last year: 6
Additional Information: Applicants for financial grants must satisfy the Committee that their activities are of general or public benefit. The results of the research or studies are expected to be covered by material suitable for publication in recognized scientific or technical journals.

VICTORIA UNIVERSITY

PO Box 14428, Melbourne, VIC 8001,
Australia
Tel: (61) 9919 4659
Fax: (61) 9689 4069
Email: lesley.birch@vu.edu.au
Website: www.vu.edu.au
Contact: Ms Lesley Birch

Victoria University is one of Australia's leading universities, where challenging conventional thinking is not only encouraged but also expected. It has 11 campuses and sites, 46,000 enrolled students, 7,900 international students from over 30 countries, 700 courses in higher education and TAFE.

Victoria University Research Scholarships

Subjects: All subjects.
Purpose: To support students undertaking Master's research and research Doctorates.
Eligibility: Open to citizens or permanent residents of Australia who have achieved Honours 1 or equivalent having studied at or currently studying at Victoria University of Technology.
Level of Study: Postgraduate
Type: Scholarship
Value: Australian $18,000
Length of Study: 1 year
Frequency: Annual
Study Establishment: Victoria University
Country of Study: Australia
Closing Date: March 31st, July 31st, October 31st

For further information contact:

Tel: 03 9688 4659
Fax: 03 9688 4559
Email: Lesley.Birch@vu.edu.au
Contact: Ms Lesley Birch, Postgraduate Scholarships Officer

VICTORIA UNIVERSITY OF WELLINGTON

Office of Research and Postgraduate Study, 10 Kelburn Parade, PO Box 600, Wellington, New Zealand
Tel: (64) 4 463 5113, 4 472 1000
Fax: (64) 4 496 5454, 4 499 4601
Email: scholarships-office@vuw.ac.nz
Website: www.vuw.ac.nz
Contact: Scholarship Office

Victoria University of Wellington is a thriving community of over 20,000 students of all nationalities. Victoria has a reputation for academic excellence and the calibre of its research. Scholarships are available in all disciplines.

Vice-Chancellor's Strategic Doctoral Research Scholarships

Subjects: All subjects.
Eligibility: Applicants are expected to have the equivalent of a New Zealand First Class Honours Degree and skills and research experience appropriate for the topic.
Level of Study: Doctorate, Research
Type: Scholarship

Value: $20,000 per year
Frequency: Annual
Study Establishment: Victoria University
Country of Study: New Zealand
Application Procedure: Application forms must be forwarded to the scholarships manager. Topics are advertised at www.ac.nz/scholarships from March 1 each year.
Closing Date: May 15th
Contributor: Victoria University
No. of awards given last year: 10
No. of applicants last year: 35

For further information contact:

Scholarships Office, Office of Research and Postgraduate Study, Victoria University of Wellington, PO Box 600, Wellington, New Zealand
Tel: (64) 4 463 5113 or 0 4 463 7493
Email: Scholarships-Office@vuw.ac.nz
Contact: Scholarships Manager

Victoria University of Wellington PhD Scholarships

Subjects: All subjects.
Purpose: To provide financial assistance to Doctoral students.
Eligibility: Open to students who are about to commence their Doctoral studies. The selection is based on academic merit.
Level of Study: Doctorate, Postgraduate
Type: Scholarship
Value: New Zealand $20,000 plus tuition fees
Length of Study: 3 years
Frequency: Three times each year
Study Establishment: Victoria University
Country of Study: New Zealand
Application Procedure: Application forms available from www.victoria.ac.nz/scholarships
Closing Date: February, June and Novermber
Contributor: Victoria University
No. of awards given last year: 80
No. of applicants last year: 300

For further information contact:

Email: scholarships-office@vuw.ac.nz

VICTORIAN INSTITUTE OF FORENSIC MEDICINE (VIFM)

57-83 Kavanagh Street, Southbank 3006, VIC, Australia
Tel: (61) 9684 4444
Fax: (61) 9682 7353
Email: assist@vifm.org
Website: www.vifm.org

The VIFM is a body corporate with perpetual succession that was established by the Coroners Act 1985. VIFM aims to provide timely, high quality and high value forensic medicine and related services, including teaching and research, for Victoria.

VIFM Scholarship in Forensic Medicine

Subjects: Forensic medicine.
Purpose: To support students who are likely to make a significant contribution to the field of forensic medicine.
Eligibility: Open to all medical graduates from developing countries.
Level of Study: Postgraduate
Type: Scholarship
Value: Cost of tuition fees and accommodation
Length of Study: 2 years
Frequency: Dependent on funds available
Country of Study: Any country
Application Procedure: Mid-December. See the website.
Funding: International Office
Contributor: Victorian Institute of Forensic Medicine
No. of awards given last year: 1

VILLA I TATTI: THE HARVARD UNIVERSITY CENTER FOR ITALIAN RENAISSANCE STUDIES

Via di Vincigliata 26, 50135 Florence, Italy
Tel: (39) 055 603 251
Fax: (39) 055 603 383
Email: info@itatti.it
Website: www.itatti.it

Villa I Tatti is devoted to advanced study of the Italian Renaissance in all its aspects, the history of art, political, economic and social history, the history of science, philosophy and religion and the history of literature and music.

Craig Hugh Smyth Visiting Fellowship

Subjects: Italian Renaissance.
Purpose: To establish an intellectual community where fruitful interchange of ideas can take place.
Eligibility: Open to librarians, full-time editors and university and museum administrators.
Level of Study: Postgraduate, Research
Type: Fellowships
Value: US$5,000 per month
Length of Study: 2–3 months
Frequency: Annual
No. of awards offered: 3
Application Procedure: Applicants can apply online or send hard copy of their application.
Closing Date: April 15th

For further information contact:

Fellowship Application Office

Villa I Tatti Fellowships

Subjects: Italian Renaissance.
Purpose: To establish an intellectual community in which a fruitful interchange of ideas can take place.
Eligibility: Open to candidates who have completed all the requirements of the PhD, the DPhil, the dottorato di ricerca or an equivalent Doctorate at the time of application, including submission and examination of the theses.
Level of Study: Postdoctorate
Type: Fellowships
Value: US$50,000–55,000
Length of Study: 1 year
Frequency: Annual
No. of awards offered: 15
Application Procedure: Applicants can submit online or mail a hard copy to both Cambridge and Florence addresses.
Closing Date: October 15th
Additional Information: If submitting a hard copy application, the application and supporting materials must be sent to the Cambridge address too: Fellowship Application Office, Villa I Tatti, Harvard University, 124 Mount Auburn Street, Cambridge, MA 02138-5795, United States of America (Tel: 617 496 8724).

THE VINAVER TRUST

45 Albert Street, Western Hill, Durham, DH1 4RJ, England
Tel: (44) 19 1386 8898
Email: G.N.Bromiley@durham.ac.uk
Contact: Dr G.N. Bromiley, Secretary-Treasurer

The Eugène Vinaver Memorial Trust exists to promote research into Arthurian studies, as defined by the International Arthurian Society. It offers subventions to publishers to facilitate the publication of scholarly works; it also offers grants to postgraduate students pursuing research in the Arthurian field.

Barron Bequest

Subjects: Any field of Arthurian studies.
Purpose: To support postgraduate research in Arthurian studies.

Eligibility: Open to graduates of any university of the United Kingdom or the Republic of Ireland.
Level of Study: Postgraduate Research
Type: Grant
Value: Up to UK £1,250 towards academic fees
Length of Study: 1 year. Candidates may apply for further years on a basis of parity with those applying for the first time
Frequency: Annual
Country of Study: United Kingdom, Republic of Ireland
No. of awards offered: Varies
Application Procedure: For application details applicants must contact Dr W. H. Jackson at the address given below.
Closing Date: April 30th
Funding: Private
Contributor: The Eugène Vinaver Memorial Trust
No. of awards given last year: 2
No. of applicants last year: 4

For further information contact:

School of Modern Languages, University of St Andrews, Buchanan Building, Union Street, St Andrews, Fife, KY16 9PH
Email: whj@st-andrews.ac.uk
Contact: Dr W.H Jackson, Administrator of the Research Support Fund

VISUAL COMMUNICATIONS (VC)

120 Judge John Aiso Street, Los Angeles, CA, 90012-3805, United States of America
Tel: (1) 213 680 4462
Fax: (1) 213 687 4848
Email: kennedy@vconline.org
Website: www.vconline.org
Contact: Kennedy Kabasares

Visual Communications (VC) is the premier Asian Pacific media arts center in the United States of America with a history of more than 30 years. It promotes intercultural understanding through the production, presentation and preservation of honest and sensitive stories about Asian Pacific people.

Armed with a Camera Fellowship

Subjects: Photography.
Purpose: To cultivate a new generation of Asian Pacific American media artists committed to preserving the legacy and vision of VC.
Eligibility: Open to candidates of Asian Pacific descent, who are 30 years of age or below, and are residents of California and have had previous work experience in the VC Film fest, Chili visions, any other VC exhibition and/or any film festival.
Level of Study: Professional development
Type: Fellowships
Value: US$500
Length of Study: 4 months
Frequency: Annual
No. of awards offered: 10
Closing Date: December 2nd

VOLKSWAGEN FOUNDATION

Kastanienalle 35, Hannover, 30519, Germany
Tel: (49) (0) 511 8381 0
Fax: (49) 511 838 1344
Email: info@volkswagen-stiftung.de
Website: www.volkswagen-stiftung.de

For detailed information, please visit the homepage: www.volkswagen-stiftung.de/index

Volkswagen Foundation Between Europe and the Orient Programme Grants

Subjects: Humanities, social science, natural science (including theoretical medicine) and engineering science.
Purpose: To provide funding aimed at stimulating the research interest of German scholars in the region as well as promoting cooperation projects, and to secure the active participation of scholars

and scientists of all disciplines working in the region of Central Asia and the Caucasus.

Eligibility: Open to highly qualified young scientists from those states in Central Asia and the Caucasus that became independent following the collapse of the Soviet Union, especially Armenia, Azerbaijan, Georgia, Kazakhstan, Uzbekistan, Tadzhikistan, Turkmenistan and Kyrgystan. The funding initiative also includes Afghanistan and some parts of the Russian Federation in the lower Volga (Tatarstan, Bashkortostan) and the northern Caucasus regions.

Level of Study: Research

Type: Grant

Value: Varies with the project. The Foundation expects the German partner to administer the allocated funds. For further details on funding, see the Foundation's website

Length of Study: 2–3 years for research projects, 2–3 years for individual scholarships and 6–12 months for research visits, co-operation or training visits

Study Establishment: German universities or research institutes

Country of Study: Germany

Application Procedure: Applicants need not be submitted on a special form. In the case of joint projects involving scholars and academic institutions in the region (also applications for funding visits to Germany), the German partner needs to submit the application on behalf of all participants. For further details see the Foundation's website.

Closing Date: There are no firm application deadlines

Additional Information: Special consideration will be given to research projects that investigate the political, socio-economic, cultural or natural characteristics of these regions with a view to gain a better understanding of the complex interplay between these factors.

VON KARMAN INSTITUTE FOR FLUID DYNAMICS (VKI)

Chausse de Waterloo 72, B-1640 Rhode-Saint-Genese, Belgium
Tel: (32) 2 359 9611
Fax: (32) 2 359 9600
Email: secretariat@vki.ac.be
Website: www.vki.ac.be

The Von Karman Institute for Fluid Dynamics (VKI) is an international postgraduate training and research centre specializing in the fluid dynamic aspects of aircraft, spacecraft, turbomachines, wind flows and industrial processes.

VKI Fellowship

Subjects: Fluid dynamics.

Purpose: To support the living costs of recipients who attend the VKI postgraduate diploma course.

Eligibility: Open to citizens of NATO countries, with the exception of Canada, Denmark, Greece, the Netherlands and the United Kingdom, who have the equivalent of a 5 year engineering degree. Applicants must have a working knowledge of English.

Level of Study: Postgraduate

Type: Fellowship

Value: Varies

Length of Study: 9 months

Frequency: Annual

Study Establishment: The VKI

Country of Study: Belgium

No. of awards offered: Varies

Application Procedure: Applicants must submit two application forms, one endorsed by the RTO National Delegate (NATO Research and Technology Organization). Copies of college transcripts and 3 references are required.

Closing Date: Applications received before March 1st will be given priority

Funding: Government

No. of awards given last year: 21

No. of applicants last year: 52

Additional Information: Please contact the organization or visit the website for further details.

W EUGENE SMITH MEMORIAL FUND, INC.

c/o International Center of Photography, 1133, Avenue of the Americas, New York, NY, 10036, United States of America
Tel: (1) 212 857 0038
Website: www.smithfund.org
Contact: Ms Helen Marcus, President

The W Eugene Smith Memorial Fund, established in 1979, is a memorial fund to honour W. Eugene Smith 's compassionate dedication exhibited during his 45 year career as a photographic essayist.

W Eugene Smith Grant in Humanistic Photography

Subjects: Photojournalism.

Purpose: To support a photographer working on a project in the humanistic tradition of W Eugene Smith, in order to continue to pursue the work.

Eligibility: Open to outstanding photographers of any nationality.

Level of Study: Professional development

Type: Grant

Value: One grant of US$30,000 with a possible second grant of US$5,000

Frequency: Annual

Country of Study: Any country

No. of awards offered: 2

Application Procedure: Applicants must send a stamped addressed envelope for application information. Application form must be completed, also obtained from website www.smithfund.org

Closing Date: July 15th

Funding: Commercial

No. of awards given last year: 2

No. of applicants last year: 171

For further information contact:

W Eugene Smith Fund, c/o ICP, 1133 Ave of Americas, NYC 10036

W. F. ALBRIGHT INSTITUTE OF ARCHAEOLOGICAL RESEARCH (AIAR)

26 Salah ed-Din Street, PO Box 19096, Jerusalem, 91190, Israel
Tel: (972) 2 628 8956
Fax: (972) 2 626 4424
Email: manager@albright.org.il
Website: www.aiar.org

The W. F. Albright Institute of Archaeological Research (AIAR) was founded in 1900 as the American School of Oriental Research in Jerusalem, AIAR provides a base for a broad range of American led scholarly research projects in ancient eastern studies, from the prehistoric to the early Islamic periods. Located in a historic building in Jerusalem, the Albright offers fellowships for Doctoral and postdoctoral studies and maintains residential and research facilities for its Fellows, including an extensive library.

Samuel H. Kress Fellowship

Subjects: Achitecture, art history, archaeology and classical studies.

Purpose: To promote the participation of students and scholars in archaeological research from all over the world.

Eligibility: Open to students studying at the institutions in the United States.

Level of Study: Doctorate

Type: Fellowship

Value: US$18,500

Length of Study: 10 months

Frequency: Annual

Closing Date: October 15th

Additional Information: All queries should be directed to Dr Joan R Branham, Chair Albright Fellowship Committee, Department of Art and Art History, Providence College, Providence, RI-02918, United States of America Tel: 401 865 1789; Fax: 401 865 1036; Email: jbranham@providence.edu

WALT DISNEY STUDIOS

Writing Fellowship Programme, 500 South Buena Vista Street, Burbank, CA, 91521-4016, United States of America

Tel: (1) 818 560 6894
Email: abc.fellowships@cbc.com
Website: abctalentdevelopment.com

The Walt Disney Company is one of the largest media and entertainment corporations in the world. Founded on October 16, 1923, by brothers Walt and Roy Disney as a small animation studio, today it is one of the largest Hollywood studios and also owns 9 theme parks and several television networks, including the American Broadcasting Company (ABC).

The Walt Disney Studios and ABC Entertainment Writing Fellowship Program

Subjects: Feature film and television.
Purpose: To seek out and employ culturally and ethnically diverse new writers.
Eligibility: Open to all writers.
Level of Study: Professional development
Type: Fellowships
Value: US$50,000
Length of Study: 1 year
Frequency: Annual
No. of awards offered: 15
Application Procedure: Applicants can download the application form from the website.
Closing Date: June 23rd
Additional Information: Members with Writers Guild of America (WGA) credits are also eligible for this programme and can apply via Employment Access Department at 323 782 4648.

THE WARBURG INSTITUTE

University of London, Woburn Square, London, WC1H 0AB, England

Tel: (44) 20 7862 8949
Fax: (44) 20 7862 8955
Email: warburg@sas.ac.uk
Website: www.warburg.sas.ac.uk
Contact: E A Witchell, Administrative Assistant

The Warburg Institute is concerned with the interdisciplinary study of continuities between the ancient Mediterranean civilizations and the cultural and intellectual history of postclassical Europe before 1800 AD. Its collections are arranged to encourage research into the processes by which different fields of thought and art interact.

Albin Salton Fellowship

Subjects: Cultural and intellectual history that led to the formation of a new worldview, understood in the broadest cultural, political and socioeconomic terms as Europe developed contacts with the world in the late medieval, renaissance and early modern periods and that world came into contact with Europe.
Purpose: To enable a young scholar spend 2 months at the Warburg Institute, pursuing research.
Eligibility: Fellowships are generally for young scholars in the early stages of their career; Candidates may be pre- or postdoctorates, but must have completed at least 1 year of research on their doctoral dissertation by the time they apply. Postdoctoral candidates, must normally have been awarded their doctorate within the preceding five academic years. If it was awarded before, then they should explain the reasons for any interruption in their academic career in a covering letter.
Level of Study: Doctorate, Postdoctorate
Type: Research fellowship
Value: Applicants domiciled abroad: UK £2,100; Domiciled applicants: UK £1,600
Length of Study: 2 months
Frequency: Annual
Study Establishment: The Warburg Institute, London
Country of Study: United Kingdom
No. of awards offered: 1
Application Procedure: Applications should be made by letter to the Director, enclosing a curriculum vitae, an outline of proposed

research, particulars of grants received, if any, for the same project. The names and addresses of 2 or 3 academic referees who have agreed to support the application should also be submitted.
Closing Date: December 1st
Funding: Private
No. of awards given last year: 1
Additional Information: Applications may be sent by post or fax, but not by email.

Brian Hewson Crawford Fellowship

Subjects: The classical tradition.
Purpose: To support research into any aspect of the classical tradition.
Eligibility: Fellowships are generally intended for scholars in the early stages of their career. Candidates may be pre or postdoctoral, but must have completed at least 1 year of research on their doctoral dissertation by the time they submit their application. Postdoctoral candidates must normally have been awarded their doctorate within the preceding 5 years. If their doctorate was awarded before this they should explain the reasons for any interruption in their academic career in a covering letter.
Level of Study: Doctorate, Postdoctorate
Type: Fellowship
Value: For those based in the United Kingdom it varies: for those based overseas UK £2,000
Length of Study: 2 months
Frequency: Annual
Study Establishment: The Warburg Institute, London
Country of Study: United Kingdom
No. of awards offered: 1
Application Procedure: Applications should be made by letter to the Director enclosing a full curriculum vitae comprising name, date of birth, address (including email address) and present occupation, school and university education, degrees, teaching and research experience, list of publications, an outline of proposed research (of not more than two pages), particulars of grants received, if any, on the same subject and the names and addresses of 2 or 3 persons who have agreed to write, without further invitation, in support of the application.
Closing Date: December 1st
Funding: Private
No. of awards given last year: 1
Additional Information: Those employed as professor, lecturer or equivalent in a university or learned institution may normally hold an award only if they are taking unpaid leave for the whole of the period. The fellowship may not be held concurrently with another fellowship or award. Applications may be sent by post or fax, but not by e-mail.

Frances A Yates Fellowships

Subjects: Any aspect of cultural and intellectual history with emphasis on the medieval and renaissance periods. Preference will be given to those areas of knowledge to which Dame Frances made a contribution.
Purpose: To promote research in any aspect of cultural and intellectual history.
Eligibility: Fellowships are generally intended for young scholars in the early stages of their career. Candidates may be pre- or postdoctorates, but must have completed at least 1 year's research on their doctoral dissertation before they apply. Postdoctoral candidates, must normally have been awarded their doctorate within the preceding five academic years. If their doctorate was awarded earlier, they should explain the reason for any interruption in their academic career in a covering letter.
Level of Study: Doctorate, Postdoctorate
Type: Fellowship
Value: For those based in UK £2,650–3,500; for those based overseas: UK £2,100, £3,050 and £4,000
Length of Study: The long-term fellowship is 1–3 years, not normally renewable, and short-term fellowships are 2–4 months, non-renewable
Frequency: Annual
Study Establishment: The Warburg Institute, London
Country of Study: United Kingdom
No. of awards offered: Several short-term awards

Application Procedure: Applications should be made by letter to the Director, (enclosing) a curriculum vitae, outline of proposed research and particulars of grants received, if any, for the same subject. The names and addresses of three persons who have agreed to write, without further invitation, in support of the application should also be submitted.
Closing Date: December 1st of preceeding year
Funding: Private
No. of awards given last year: 5 short-term
Additional Information: Applications must not be sent by email. The long-term fellowship is not offered every year.

Grete Sondheimer Fellowship

Subjects: Any aspect of cultural and intellectual history with the emphasis on the medieval and renaissance period.
Purpose: To promote research in any aspect of cultural and intellectual history.
Eligibility: The fellowships are generally intended for scholars in the early stages of their careers. Candidates must have completed at least 1 year research on their doctoral dissertation by the time they submit their application for a fellowship and, if postdoctoral, must normally have been awarded their doctorate within the preceeding 5 years after 1st October 2001. If their doctorate was awarded before this date, they should explain the reasons for any interruptions in their academic career in a covering letter.
Level of Study: Doctorate, Postdoctorate
Type: Fellowship
Value: For those based in UK £1,600 to £2,650; for those based overseas £2,100 to £3,050
Length of Study: 2 or 3 months
Frequency: Annual
Study Establishment: The Warburg Institute, London
Country of Study: United Kingdom
No. of awards offered: 1
Application Procedure: Applications should be made by letter to the Director enclosing a curriculum vitae along with an outline of proposed research project and details of grants received, if any, for the same project. The names and addresses of 2 or 3 academic referees, who will write in support of the application should also be submitted.
Closing Date: December 1st of the preceeding year
Funding: Private
No. of awards given last year: 1
Additional Information: Application may not be sent by email, but should be sent by post or fax.

Henri Frankfort Fellowship

Subjects: The intellectual and cultural history of the ancient Near East, with reference to society, art, architecture, religion, philosophy and science; the relations between the cultures of Mesopotamia, Egypt and the Aegean, and their influence on later civilizations.
Purpose: To promote research into the history of the ancient near east.
Eligibility: Fellowships are generally intended for young scholars in the early stages of their career. Candidates may be pre- or postdoctorates, but must have completed at least 1 year of research on their doctoral dissertation before they apply. Postdoctoral candidates must normally have been awarded their doctorate within the preceding five academic years. If their doctorate was awarded before this, candidates should explain the reason for any interruption in their academic career in a covering letter.
Level of Study: Doctorate, Postdoctorate
Type: Fellowship
Value: For those based in UK: UK £1,600 and 2,650; for those based overseas: UK £2,100 and 3,050
Length of Study: 2–3 months
Frequency: Annual
Study Establishment: The Warburg Institute, London
Country of Study: United Kingdom
No. of awards offered: 1
Application Procedure: Applications should be made by letter to the Director (enclosing a curriculum vitae, outline of proposed research and particulars of grants received, if any, for the same subject). The names and addresses of two or three persons who have agreed to write, without further invitation, in support of the application should also be submitted.
Closing Date: December 1st of the preceeding year

Funding: Private
No. of awards given last year: 1
Additional Information: This fellowship not intended to support archaeological excavation. Application must not be sent by email.

Warburg Mellon Research Fellowship

Subjects: Humanities in the pre-1800 period.
Purpose: To fund Eastern European scholars in the humanities.
Eligibility: Fellows should have obtained a doctorate or equivalent experience. Fellowships are intended for postdoctoral scholars in the earlier stages of their career. Preference will be given to those who have not previously held an award under the Mellon Fellowship programme at any of the participating institutions. Candidates who have held 2 Mellon Fellowships or 1 within the last 3 years are not eligible to apply.
Level of Study: Postdoctorate
Type: Fellowship
Value: Sterling equivalent of US$11,500 each
Length of Study: 3 months; 2 of the 3 months must fall within the Institute's terms
Frequency: Annual
Study Establishment: The Warburg Institute. The applicant may teach elsewhere with the permission of the Director
Country of Study: United Kingdom
No. of awards offered: Three 3-month fellowships
Application Procedure: Applications should be made by letter to the Director. A curriculum vitae giving full details, an outline of proposed research, particulars of grants received earlier, two or three references and samples of published or written work should be submitted if possible.
Closing Date: April 3rd
Funding: Private
Contributor: Andrew W. Mellon Foundation
No. of awards given last year: 3
Additional Information: Applications may be sent by post or fax but not by email. Fellowships are open to Bulgarian, Czech, Estonian, Hungarian, Latvian, Lithuanian, Polish, Romanian and Slovakian scholars. Candidates should not be permanently resident outside the countries concerned.

WARWICK BUSINESS SCHOOL

University of Warwick, Coventry, CV4 7AL, England
Tel: (44) 24 7652 4306
Fax: (44) 24 7652 3719
Email: enquiries@wbs.ac.uk
Website: www.wbs.ac.uk
Contact: Ms Diana Holton, Assistant Communications Manager

Warwick Business School is an international school with 330 staff and 4,500 students from 130 countries worldwide, and is accredited with management associations in North America, Europe and the United Kingdom. Its high-calibre research feeds into top-quality teaching on undergraduate, specialist Master's, doctoral, MBA and MPA degrees.

ESRC Awards (For Doctoral Study)

Subjects: Finance, industrial, employment relations, knowledge management and networks.
Purpose: To allow the candidates to pursue the WBS Doctoral Programme.
Eligibility: Open to students applying for entry into the full-time WBS Doctoral Programme subject to the research being relevant.
Level of Study: Doctorate
Value: Refer to the Warwick Business School website for further details
Length of Study: 3 years (full-time)
Frequency: Annual
Study Establishment: Warwick Business School
Country of Study: United Kingdom
Application Procedure: Procedures vary according to the scholarship relevant to the area of interest.
Funding: Government

ESRC PhD in Finance

Subjects: Finance.
Purpose: To allow candidates to pursue the WBS Doctoral Programme.

Eligibility: Open to students applying for entry into the full-time Warwick Business School PhD in Finance programme.
Level of Study: Doctorate
Frequency: Annual
Study Establishment: Warwick Business School
Country of Study: United Kingdom
No. of awards offered: ESRC Quota awards
Application Procedure: Procedures vary accoding to the scholarship relevant to the area of interest.
Funding: Government

Warwick Busines School Scholarships (For Masters Study)

Subjects: Finance and economics, business management, economics, management science, marketing and operational research, financial maths, marketing and strategy, international European employment relations, information systems and management, management science and operational research, business analytics and consulting, management and organizational analysis, industrial relations and managing human relations.
Purpose: To allow candidates to pursue full-time and part-time specialist Masters courses.
Eligibility: Open to students applying for full-time and part-time masters courses. Please refer to the website for eligibility criteria.
Level of Study: Postgraduate
Type: Scholarship
Value: UK £2,000–8075. Refer website for further details
Length of Study: 1 year (full-time), 2 years (part-time)
Frequency: Annual
Study Establishment: Warwick Business School
Country of Study: United Kingdom
No. of awards offered: 23
Application Procedure: All applicants to the courses will automatically be considered for the scholarships.
Additional Information: See website for details.

Warwick Busines School Scholarships (For MPA Study)

Subjects: MPA (Master in Public Administration).
Purpose: To allow candidates to pursue the Warwick MPA course.
Eligibility: Applicants need to meet the academic director at the time they apply to the course. Statement must be within 1,000 words explaining how applicant will contribute to the MPA and how they expect to benefit from the course. In addition, if appropriate, information regarding to financial position may be outlined.
Level of Study: Postgraduate, Professional development
Type: Scholarship
Value: Covers 50 per cent of the tuition fees
Length of Study: 1 year (full-time), 3 years (part-time)
Frequency: Dependent on funds available
Study Establishment: Warwick Busines School
Country of Study: United Kingdom
No. of awards offered: Up to 2 awards of 50% of fees
Application Procedure: All applicants to the programme will be automatically considered for the scholarship.
Closing Date: Mid-July to for entry in October, mid-October for entry in January
No. of awards given last year: 2
No. of applicants last year: 4

Warwick Business School PhD in Finance Scholarships (for Doctoral Study)

Subjects: Finance.
Purpose: To allow candidates to pursue the WBS Doctoral Programme.
Eligibility: Open to students applying for entry into the full-time Warwick Business School PhD in Finance programme.
Level of Study: Doctorate
Value: Refer the Warwick Business School website for further details
Length of Study: 3 years (full time)
Frequency: Dependent on funds available
Study Establishment: Warwick Business School
Country of Study: United Kingdom
Application Procedure: Procedures vary according to the scholarship relevant to the area of interest.

Warwick Business School Scholarships (For Doctoral Study)

Subjects: Finance, industrial, employment relations, knowledge mangement and networks.
Purpose: To allow candidates to pursue the WBS Doctoral Programme.
Eligibility: Open to students applying for entry into the full-time Warwick Doctoral Programme, subject to research area being relevant.
Level of Study: Doctorate
Type: Bursary and scholarship
Value: Refer the Warwick Business School website for further details
Length of Study: 3 years (full-time)
Frequency: Dependent on funds available
Study Establishment: Warwick Business School
Country of Study: United Kingdom
Application Procedure: Procedures vary according to the scholarship relevant to the area of interest.

Warwick Business School Scholarships (For full-time MBA Study)

Subjects: MBA by full-time study
Purpose: To allow candidates to pursue the Warwick MBA course.
Eligibility: Open to students applying for full-time.
Level of Study: MBA, Professional development
Type: Scholarship
Value: The scholarships provide up to 50 per cent of the tuition fees, up to a maximum of UK £12,000 for full-time MBA applicants
Length of Study: 1 year
Frequency: Annual
Study Establishment: Warwick Business School
Country of Study: United Kingdom
No. of awards offered: 20
Application Procedure: All applicants to the programme will automatically be considered for the scholarship.
Closing Date: Full-time July 31st

Warwick Business School Scholarships (For MBA Study via Distance Learning)

Subjects: MBA by distance learning
Purpose: To allow candidates to pursue the distance-learning MBA course.
Eligibility: All international candidates for distance learning applying for the programme are eligible.
Level of Study: MBA
Type: Scholarship
Value: Up to UK £2,500
Length of Study: 3 years
Study Establishment: Warwick Business School
Country of Study: United Kingdom
No. of awards offered: 12
Application Procedure: All applicants to the Distance Learning MBA will automatically be considered.
Closing Date: Please see the website

WASHINGTON UNIVERSITY

Graduate School of Arts and Sciences, Box 1187, 1 Brookings Drive, St Louis, MO, 63130, United States of America
Tel: (1) 314 935 6818
Fax: (1) 314 935 4887
Email: graduateschool@artsci.wustl.edu
Website: www.artsci.wustl.edu
Contact: Ms Nancy P Pope, Associate Dean

Washington University has a diverse offering of events, disciplines, people, and resources that create unlimited possibilities for discovery and growth. Arts & sciences signals a curriculum and place, a core of teaching, learning, and discovery at Washington University.

Mr and Mrs Spencer T Olin Fellowships for Women

Subjects: All subjects.
Purpose: To encourage women of exceptional promise to prepare for professional careers.

Eligibility: Open to female graduates of a baccalaureate institution in the United States of America who plan to prepare for a career in higher education or the professions. Applicants must meet the admission requirements of their graduate or professional school at Washington University. Preference will be given to those who wish to study for the highest earned degree in their chosen field, do not already hold an advanced degree, and are not currently enrolled in a graduate or professional degree programme.
Level of Study: Doctorate, Graduate
Type: Fellowship
Value: Full tuition and in some cases a living expense stipend
Length of Study: 1 year, renewable for up to 4 years, or until the completion of the degree programme, whichever comes first
Frequency: Annual
Study Establishment: Washington University
Country of Study: United States of America
No. of awards offered: Approx. 10
Application Procedure: Applicants must complete an application form. Finalists must be interviewed on campus at the expense of the University.
Closing Date: February 1st
Funding: Private
Contributor: The Monticello College Foundation
No. of awards given last year: 10
No. of applicants last year: 375
Additional Information: Candidates must also make concurrent application to the department or school of Washington University in which they plan to study.

Washington University Chancellor's Graduate Fellowship Program

Subjects: Arts and sciences, business, engineering and social work.
Purpose: To encourage students who are interested in becoming college or university professors, and who bring diversity to the campus environment.
Eligibility: Open to doctoral candidates. Applicants must meet the admission requirements of their graduate or professional school at Washington University, and provide evidence that they will contribute to diversity on our campus.
Level of Study: Doctorate, Graduate
Type: Fellowship
Value: Doctoral candidates will receive full tuition plus US$24,500 stipend and allowances
Length of Study: 5 years, subject to satisfactory academic progress
Frequency: Annual
Study Establishment: Washington University
Country of Study: United States of America
No. of awards offered: 5–6
Application Procedure: Applicants must complete an application form. Finalists will be interviewed on the campus at the expense of the University. Applications should be addressed to Assistant Dean, Sheri Notaro.
Closing Date: January 25th
No. of awards given last year: 9
No. of applicants last year: 105
Additional Information: The fellowship includes other Washington University programmes providing final disciplinary training for prospective college professors.

WEIMAR CLASSIC FOUNDATION

Burgplatz 4, 99423 Weimar, Germany
Tel: (49) 03643 545 0
Fax: (49) 03643 545 454
Email: info@klassiksiftung.de
Website: www.klassik-stiftung.de/
Contact: Grants Department

Weimar Classic Foundation Research Scholarships

Subjects: Academic, literary and artistic projects on the cultural history of Europe from the 18th to the 20th century.
Eligibility: Applicants are required to hold a doctorate or show a proof of comparable academic, literary or artistic achievement.
Level of Study: Research
Type: Scholarship

Value: €1,000 per month
Length of Study: 1–6 months (extension possible)
Country of Study: Germany
Application Procedure: Applications need not be submitted on a special form.
Closing Date: There are no firm application deadlines. The selection committee meets in June and December
Additional Information: The Foundation particularly supports: academic, literary and artistic projects funded from budgetary funds; research projects on the Goethe era primarily by foreign academics and funded by the Fritz Thyssen Foundation; and work by young academics on the historical critical edition of Arnim's works, funded by the Globus Holding.

WEIZMANN INSTITUTE OF SCIENCE

Feinberg Graduate School, PO Box 26, IL-76100 Rehovot, Israel
Tel: (972) 8 934 4553
Fax: (972) 8 934 4114
Email: adi.shimron@weizmann.ac.il
Website: www.weizmann.ac.il/feinberg
Contact: The Grants Management Officer

The Weizmann Institute of Science is one of the top-ranking multidisciplinary research institutions in the world. Noted for its wide-ranging exploration of the sciences and technology, the Institute houses 2,400 scientists, technicians and research students devoted to a better understanding of nature and our place within it.

Weizmann Institute of Science MSc Fellowships

Subjects: Life sciences, including brain research, cell biology, molecular genetics, biochemistry, biophysics, immunology, biological regulation, plant sciences and bioinformatics; chemistry, including physical, theoretical, organic, biological, environmental sciences and energy research and material sciences; physics, including theoretical, experimental, applied, semiconductor and biological; and mathematics, including pure and applied, computer science and science teaching.
Purpose: To enable study at the Feinberg Graduate School of the Weizmann Institute of Science.
Eligibility: Open to holders of a BSc degree from an accredited Institute of Higher Education in Israel or of an equivalent degree from a recognized overseas university.
Level of Study: Postgraduate
Type: Fellowship
Value: Living expenses
Length of Study: 2 years
Frequency: Annual
Study Establishment: The Institute
Country of Study: Israel
Application Procedure: Applicants must write for details.
Closing Date: May 31st
Funding: Private
No. of awards given last year: 270
No. of applicants last year: 700

Weizmann Institute of Science PhD Fellowships

Subjects: Life sciences, including brain research, cell biology, molecular genetics, biochemistry, biophysics, immunology, biological regulation, plant sciences and bioinformatics, chemistry, including physical, theoretical, organic, biological, environmental sciences and energy research and material sciences; physics, including theoretical, experimental, applied, semiconductor and biological, and mathematics, including pure and applied, computer science or science teaching.
Purpose: To enable study at the Feinberg Graduate School of the Weizmann Institute of Science.
Eligibility: Open to holders of an MSc or MD degree.
Level of Study: Doctorate
Type: Fellowship
Value: Living expenses
Length of Study: 4.5 years
Frequency: Annual
Study Establishment: The Institute

Country of Study: Israel
Application Procedure: Applicants must write for details.
Funding: Private
No. of awards given last year: 700
Additional Information: A special programme is offered to students wishing to take a direct BSc to PhD route.

Weizmann Institute of Science Postdoctoral Fellowships Program

Subjects: Life sciences, including brain research, cell biology, molecular genetics, biochemistry, biophysics, immunology, biological regulation, plant sciences and bioinformatics; chemistry, including physical, theoretical, organic, biological, environmental sciences and energy research and material sciences; physics, including theoretical, experimental, applied, semiconductor and biological; and mathematics, including pure and applied, computer science or science teaching.
Purpose: To enable study at the Feinberg Graduate School of the Weizmann Institute of Science.
Eligibility: Open to holders of a PhD degree.
Level of Study: Postdoctorate
Type: Fellowship
Value: Living expenses
Length of Study: 1–3 years
Frequency: Annual
Study Establishment: The Institute
Country of Study: Israel
Application Procedure: Applicants must write for details.
Closing Date: January 1st and May 15th
Funding: Private

THE WELDER WILDLIFE FOUNDATION

PO Box 1400, Sinton, TX, 78387, United States of America
Tel: (1) 361 364 2643
Fax: (1) 361 364 2650
Email: welderfoundation@welderwildlife.org
Website: www.welderwildlife.org

The Welder Wildlife Foundation is a private, non-profit foundation established in 1954. The Foundation has gained international recognition through its research programme. The primary purpose of the Foundation is to conduct research and education in the field of wildlife management and conservation and other closely related fields. As a private foundation their purpose and operation remain unhindered by outside political or institutional pressures.

Rob and Bessie Welder Wildlife Foundation's Graduate Research Scholarship Program

Subjects: Animal behaviour, biology, botany, conservation education, ecology, mammalogy, ornithology, parasitology, range science, veterinary pathology and wildlife sciences.
Purpose: To conduct research and education in the field of wildlife management and conservation and other closely related fields.
Eligibility: Open to applicants whose research interests relate to wildlife management and conservation or a closely related area. Students must have a minimum Graduate Record Examination score of 1,100 and a B average in the last 2 years of undergraduate or graduate work.
Level of Study: Doctorate, Master of Science
Type: Scholarship
Value: US$1,400 per month for full-time Master's candidates and US$1,600 per month for PhD candidates, which includes living costs, tuition fees and books
Frequency: Annual
Country of Study: United States of America
Application Procedure: Applications and abbreviated proposals may be submitted in letter form and must be signed by a qualified member of the faculty at the parent university.
Closing Date: October 1st
Funding: Foundation, private
No. of awards given last year: 11
No. of applicants last year: 20

WELLBEING OF WOMEN

27 Sussex Place, London, NW1 4SP, England
Tel: (44) 20 7772 6458
Fax: (44) 20 7724 7725
Email: ahayson.wellbeingofwomen@rcog.org.uk
Website: www.wellbeingofwomen.org.uk
Contact: Mrs Ann Hayson, Research Grants Manager

Wellbeing of Women is the only UK charity funding vital research into all aspects of reproductive health in three key areas; gynaecological cancers, pregnancy and birth, and quality of life problems.

Wellbeing of Women Entry-Level Scholarship

Subjects: All subjects of relevance to obstetrics, gynaecology.
Purpose: To provide Pump-Priming funds to enable trainees to be exposed to a research environment to obtain pilot data for bids for definitive funding.
Eligibility: Work must be undertaken in the UK. Applications must be from individuals who have not previously been involved in substantial research projects.
Level of Study: Graduate
Type: Scholarship
Value: A maximum of UK £20,000
Length of Study: 1–3 years
Frequency: Annual
Study Establishment: A hospital or university
Country of Study: United Kingdom
No. of awards offered: Varies depending on the amount of disposable income
Application Procedure: Applicants must write for details or access the website.
Closing Date: March
Funding: Commercial, individuals, private, trusts
No. of awards given last year: 2
No. of applicants last year: 13

Wellbeing of Women Project Grants

Subjects: All subjects of relevance to obstetrics and gynaecology.
Purpose: To fund research projects.
Eligibility: Open to specialists in any obstetrics/gynaecology interrelated field.
Level of Study: Research, Professional development
Type: Grant
Value: A maximum of UK £150,000 over 3 years
Length of Study: 1–3 years
Frequency: Annual
Study Establishment: A hospital or university
Country of Study: United Kingdom
No. of awards offered: Varies depending on the amount of disposable income
Application Procedure: Applicants must write for details or access the website.
Closing Date: September
Funding: Commercial, individuals, private, trusts
No. of awards given last year: 5
No. of applicants last year: 55

Wellbeing of Women/RCOG Research Training Fellowship

Subjects: All subjects of relevance to obstetrics and gynaecology.
Purpose: To fund training in basic science or clinical research techniques and methodology for a medical graduate embarking upon a career in obstetrics and gynaecology.
Eligibility: Research training fellowships are to be undertaken in the UK.
Level of Study: Postdoctorate, Postgraduate, Research
Type: Fellowship
Value: The upper limit for this award is UK £150,000
Length of Study: 1–3 years
Frequency: Annual
Study Establishment: A hospital or university
Country of Study: United Kingdom
No. of awards offered: Varies depending on the amount of disposable income

Application Procedure: Applicants must write for details or access the website.
Closing Date: March
Funding: Individuals, private, trusts
No. of awards given last year: 2
No. of applicants last year: 14

WELLCHILD INTERNATIONAL

16 Royal Crescent, Cheltenham, Gloucester, GL50 3OA, England
Tel: (44) 12 4253 0007
Fax: (44) 12 4253 0008
Email: info@wellchild.org.uk
Website: www.wellchild.org.uk
Contact: The Administrator

WellChild is committed to getting sick children better, whatever their illness, through care, support and research.

WellChild Pump-Priming Grants
Subjects: Diseases in children.
Purpose: To enable a student to run a pilot study.
Level of Study: Doctorate, Postdoctorate, Postgraduate
Type: Grant
Value: Up to UK £30,000
Frequency: Annual
Study Establishment: Accredited institute in the United Kingdom
Country of Study: United Kingdom
Application Procedure: Applicants must download application and guidelines from the website.
Closing Date: September 26th
Funding: Private
Additional Information: Assessment by peer review and the Scientific Medical Advisory Committee.

WellChild Research Fellowships
Subjects: Diseases in children.
Purpose: To support clinicians working towards the development of their own research projects.
Level of Study: Postdoctorate, Doctorate, Postgraduate
Type: Fellowship
Value: Appropriate salary costs
Length of Study: Up to 3 years
Frequency: Annual
Study Establishment: Accredited institute in the United Kingdom
Country of Study: United Kingdom
Application Procedure: Applicants must download application and guidelines from the website.
Closing Date: September 26th
Funding: Private
Additional Information: Assessment by peer review and the Scientific Medical Advisory Committee.

WELLCOME TRUST

215 Euston Road, London, NW1 2BE, England
Tel: (44) 20 7611 8888
Fax: (44) 20 7611 8545
Email: contact@wellcome.ac.uk
Website: www.wellcome.ac.uk

The Wellcome Trust's mission is to foster and promote research with the aim of improving human and animal health. The Trust funds most areas of biomedical research and funds research in the history of medicine, biomedical ethics and public engagement of science.

Wellcome Trust Grants
Subjects: Biomedical sciences, from the basic sciences related to medicine to the clinical aspects of medicine and veterinary medicine. The Trust also operates a portfolio of schemes to support research in the history of medicine, biomedical ethics and the public engagement of science.
Purpose: To foster and promote research with the aim of improving human and animal health. The Trust aims to: (a) Support research to increase understanding of health and disease, and its societal context;

(b) support the development and use of knowledge to create health benefit; (c) engage with society to foster an informed climate within which biomedical research can flourish; (d) foster a research community and individual researchers who can contribute to the advancement and use of knowledge; (e) promote the best conditions for research and the use of knowledge.
Eligibility: Eligible institutions in the UK and Republic of Ireland are normally universities, medical schools, or NHS Trusts. Institutions outside the UK and Republic of Ireland must confirm their status with the Wellcome Trust for research grants. Principal applicants are established researchers who are applying from an eligible institution and are able to sign up to the Trust's grant conditions, and normally hold an academic or research post (or equivalent) and have at least 5 yeas' postdoctoral or equivalent research experience. Check website for further details.
Level of Study: Doctorate, Postdoctorate, Postgraduate, Professional development, Research
Type: Research grant or fellowship
Value: Varies
Length of Study: Varies
Frequency: Applications are considered throughout the year
No. of awards offered: Varies
Application Procedure: Applications can be submitted via online application system.
Closing Date: Please visit the website for scheme deadlines
Contributor: Endowment
No. of awards given last year: 951
No. of applicants last year: 2736
Additional Information: The Wellcome Trust is one of the most richly endowed of all charitable institutions that fund general medical research in the United Kingdom. The Governors review their policy annually in response to proposals from their advisory committees and professional staff.

WENNER-GREN FOUNDATION FOR ANTHROPOLOGICAL RESEARCH

470 Park Avenue South, 8th Floor, New York, NY, 10016, United States of America
Tel: (1) 212 683 5000
Fax: (1) 212 683 9151
Email: inquiries@wennergren.org
Website: www.wennergren.org
Contact: The Fellowships Office

The Wenner-Gren Foundation for Anthropological Research supports research, conferences, training, archiving and collaboration in all branches of anthropology, including cultural and social anthropology, ethnology, biological and physical anthropology, archaeology and anthropological linguistics, and in closely related disciplines concerned with human origins, development and variation.

Hunt Postdoctoral Fellowships
Subjects: Anthropology.
Purpose: To aid the writeup of research results.
Eligibility: Open to scholars within 10 years of the receipt of their PhD.
Level of Study: Postdoctorate
Type: Fellowship
Value: Up to US$40,000
Frequency: Twice a year
Application Procedure: Applications can be downloaded from the website and must be submitted online.
Closing Date: November 1st and May 1st
No. of awards given last year: 9
No. of applicants last year: 89
Additional Information: Qualified scholars are eligible without regard to nationality or institutional affiliation.

Wenner-Gren Foundation Dissertation Fieldwork Grants
Subjects: Anthropology.
Purpose: To aid doctoral dissertation or thesis research.
Level of Study: Doctorate
Type: Grant
Value: Up to US$25,000

Frequency: Twice a year
Application Procedure: Applicants must complete a formal application on an up-to-date form that should be downloaded from the website and should be submitted online.
Closing Date: May 1st and November 1st
No. of awards given last year: 109
No. of applicants last year: 662

Wenner-Gren Foundation Post-PhD Grants
Subjects: Anthropology.
Purpose: To support a researcher in postdoctoral fieldwork.
Level of Study: Postdoctorate
Type: Grant
Value: Up to US$25,000
Frequency: Twice a year
Application Procedure: Applicants must download an up-to-date form from the website.
Closing Date: November 1st and May 1st
No. of awards given last year: 42
No. of applicants last year: 220

WESLEYAN UNIVERSITY

Center for the Humanities, Middletown, CT, 06459-0069, United States of America
Tel: (1) 860 685 3044
Fax: (1) 860 685 2171
Email: bkeating@wesleyan.edu
Website: www.wesleyan.edu
Contact: Ms Brenda Keating, Administrative Assistant

Wesleyan University offers instruction in 41 departments and programmes and 50 major fields of study and awards the Bachelor of Arts and graduate degrees. Master's degrees are awarded in 11 fields of study and doctoral degrees in 6. Students may choose from about 960 courses each year and may be asked to devise, with the faculty, some 1,500 individual tutorials and lessons.

Andrew W Mellon Postdoctoral Fellowship
Subjects: Humanities and humanistic social sciences.
Purpose: To provide scholars with free time to further their own work in a cross-disciplinary setting, and to associate them with a distinguished faculty.
Eligibility: Open to persons who have received their PhD within the last 4 years. Scholars who have received their PhD degree after June 2004 in any field of inquiry in the humanities or humanistic social sciences, broadly conceived, are invited to apply.
Level of Study: Postdoctorate
Type: Fellowship
Value: US$40,000
Frequency: Annual
Country of Study: Any country
No. of awards offered: 1
Application Procedure: Applicants must request a brochure detailing the application process. There is no formal application form. Applicants should refer to the Center for the Humanities website for instructions on how to apply.
Closing Date: November 1st
Funding: Private
No. of awards given last year: 2
No. of applicants last year: 285
Additional Information: The Fellow must reside in Middletown during the tenure of the fellowship, give one public lecture and teach one course for 20 students.

WILFRID LAURIER UNIVERSITY

75 University Avenue West, Waterloo, ON, N2L 3C5, Canada
Tel: (1) 519 884 1970
Fax: (1) 519 884 8826
Email: ahecht@wlu.ca
Website: www.wlu.ca
Contact: Mr Al Hecht, International Relations

Wilfrid Laurier University is well known for offering an extremely high quality academic experience as well as for cultivating a closely-knit undergraduate and graduate student population. Wilfrid Laurier University is committed to continuing to provide the educational experiences and environment that foster such development and nurture what can best be described as the Laurier spirit

Hans Viessmann International Scholarship
Subjects: All subjects.
Purpose: To assist students wanting to study in Germany.
Level of Study: Postgraduate
Type: Scholarship
Value: Canadian $1,050
Length of Study: 1 year
Frequency: Annual
Country of Study: Germany
Application Procedure: Contact University.
Closing Date: June

President Marsden Scholarship
Subjects: All subjects.
Purpose: To reward a strong student who best exemplifies the mission of Laurier.
Level of Study: Postgraduate
Type: Scholarship
Value: Canadian $3,900
Length of Study: 1 year
Frequency: Annual
Study Establishment: Laurier University
Country of Study: Canada
No. of awards offered: 1
Application Procedure: Apply online.
Closing Date: September 29th

Ross and Doris Dixon Special Needs Awards
Subjects: All subjects.
Purpose: To create a positive environment for students with special needs.
Eligibility: No restrictions.
Level of Study: Postgraduate
Type: Scholarship
Value: Varies
Length of Study: 1 year
Frequency: Annual
Study Establishment: Laurier University
Country of Study: Canada
No. of awards offered: 20
Application Procedure: Apply online.
Closing Date: September 29th
Funding: Trusts
Contributor: Ross and Doris Dixon

Viessmann/Marburg Travel Scholarship
Subjects: All subjects.
Purpose: To assist students wanting to study in Germany.
Level of Study: Postgraduate
Type: Scholarship
Value: €767
Length of Study: 1 year
Frequency: Annual
Study Establishment: An approved place of study in Marburg
Country of Study: Germany
Application Procedure: Contact University.
Closing Date: June

Wilfrid Laurier University Postdoctoral Fellowship
Subjects: All subjects.
Purpose: To provide full-time research opportunities for recent graduates who wish to pursue independent and collaborative research under the supervision of Laurier faculty.
Eligibility: Applicants must be within 5 years of the completion of all PhD requirements.
Level of Study: Postdoctorate
Type: Fellowship
Length of Study: 1–2 years

Study Establishment: Wilfrid Laurier University
Country of Study: Canada
Application Procedure: Self-funded applicants must submit a copy of their SSHRC or NSERC PDF application, curriculum vitae and a detailed research plan for each year. Applicants who wish to teach will be interviewed by the chair.

William and Marion Marr Graduate Award
Subjects: All subjects.
Purpose: To aid graduate students with special needs.
Level of Study: Postgraduate
Type: Scholarship
Value: Canadian $1,000
Length of Study: 1 year
Frequency: Annual
Study Establishment: Laurier University
Country of Study: Canada
Application Procedure: Apply online.
Closing Date: September 29th
Funding: Private
Contributor: Dr and Mrs Marr

WLU Graduate Incentive Scholarships
Subjects: All subjects.
Purpose: To reward graduate students who are successful in major external scholarship competitions.
Level of Study: Postgraduate
Type: Scholarship
Value: Varies
Frequency: Annual
Study Establishment: Laurier University
Country of Study: Canada
No. of awards offered: Varies
Application Procedure: Contact University.
Closing Date: No deadline

WLU Graduate Scholarships
Subjects: All subjects.
Level of Study: Postgraduate
Type: Scholarship
Value: Canadian $1,000
Length of Study: 1 year
Frequency: Annual
Study Establishment: Laurier university
Country of Study: Canada
Application Procedure: Apply online.
Closing Date: August 25th
Additional Information: A scholarship is awarded on academic merit, not financial need.

WLU President's Scholarship
Subjects: All subjects.
Purpose: To reward significant contribution to the community as a volunteer or to the discipline as a scholar.
Level of Study: Postgraduate
Type: Scholarship
Value: Canadian $1,985
Length of Study: 1 year
Frequency: Annual
Study Establishment: Laurier University
Country of Study: Canada
Application Procedure: Apply online.
Closing Date: October 24th
Funding: Trusts
Contributor: Dr Neale H Taylor

WLU Student International Travel Scholarship
Subjects: All subjects.
Purpose: To assist Laurier students with travel costs associated with an academic exchange programme.
Level of Study: Postgraduate
Type: Scholarship
Value: Varies
Length of Study: 1 year
Frequency: Annual

Study Establishment: An approved University or Institute
Application Procedure: Contact University.
Closing Date: June

WILLIAM HONYMAN GILLESPIE SCHOLARSHIP TRUST

Tods Murray LLP, Edinburgh Quay, 133 Fountain Bridge, Edinburgh, EH3 9AG, Scotland
Tel: (44) 131 656 2000
Fax: (44) 131 656 2020
Email: maildesk@todsmurray.com
Contact: Trustees

William Honyman Gillespie Scholarships
Subjects: Theology.
Purpose: To allow the recipient to engage in a full-time approved scheme of theological studies or research.
Eligibility: Open to graduates of a theological college of one of the Scottish universities.
Level of Study: Postgraduate
Type: Scholarship
Value: UK £1,000 per year
Length of Study: 2 years
Frequency: Annual
Study Establishment: An approved university or similar institution
Country of Study: Any country
No. of awards offered: Varies, usually 1 to 2
Application Procedure: Applicants must submit applications through the principal of the theological college of which the applicant is a graduate. Application guidelines are available from the Trust or the candidate's university department.
Closing Date: May 15th
Funding: Private
No. of awards given last year: 2
No. of applicants last year: 2

WILLIAM J. CUNLIFFE SCIENTIFIC AWARDS

Department of Dermatology, Venereology, Allergology and Immunology, Dessau Medical center, Auenweg 38, Dessau, 06847, Germany
Tel: (49) 340 501 4000
Fax: (49) 340 501 4025
Email: info@cunliffe-awards.org
Website: www.cunliffe-awards.org
Contact: Professor Dr Christos C. Zouboulis, Chairman of the Executive Committee

The William J Cunliffe Scientific Awards aim to recognize and encourage innovative and outstanding research in the areas of endocrine dermatology and skin pharmacology, conferring great benefit upon understanding the function of the pilosebaceous unit as well as the pathophysiology and treatment of its disease.

William J Cunliffe Scientific Awards
Subjects: The significance of skin, and especially of the pilosebaceous unit, as hormone target and endocrine organ, the development of new molecules to target skin diseases and the understanding of the molecular action of therapeutic compounds.
Purpose: The William J Cunliffe Scientific Awards aim to recognize and encourage innovative and outstanding research in the areas of endocrine dermatology and skin pharmacology.
Eligibility: Open to persons for any nationality. Living individuals or public or private institutions of any nation, are eligible for nomination.
Level of Study: Professional development
Type: Lectureship/Prize
Value: €12,500 (prize), €15,000 (lectureship)
Length of Study: Nominees will be considered for the year of their nomination
Frequency: Annual
No. of awards offered: 1 per year (major)

Application Procedure: Applicants must complete an application form. Guidelines can be found on the website www.cunliffe-awards. org. Applicants should be nominated.
Closing Date: May 31st
Funding: Corporation
Contributor: Galderma
No. of awards given last year: 2
No. of applicants last year: 8

WILSON ORNITHOLOGICAL SOCIETY

Fort Collins Science Centre, 2150 Centre Avenue, Building C, Fort Collins, CO, 80526-8118, United States of America
Tel: (1) 970 226 9466
Email: rbpayne@umich.edu
Website: www.ummz.lsa.umich.edu/birds/wos.html
Contact: The Administrative Assistant

Founded in 1888 and named after Alexander Wilson, the father of American ornithology, the Wilson Ornithological Society publishes a scientific journal, the *Wilson Journal of Ornithology*, holds annual meetings, provides research awards and maintains an outstanding research library.

George A Hall/Harold F Mayfield Award
Subjects: Any aspect of ornithology.
Purpose: To encourage and stimulate research projects on birds, by amateurs and students.
Eligibility: Open to independent researchers without access to funds and facilities available at colleges, universities or governmental agencies. The award is restricted to non-professionals.
Level of Study: Unrestricted
Type: Award
Value: US$1,000
Frequency: Annual
Country of Study: Any country
No. of awards offered: 1
Application Procedure: An application form must be completed and submitted with three letters of recommendation and a research proposal. Forms are available from the website.
Closing Date: February 1st
Funding: Private

Louis Agassiz Fuertes Award
Subjects: Any aspect of ornithology.
Eligibility: Open to all ornithologists, although graduate students and young professionals are preferred. Any avian researcher is eligible.
Level of Study: Unrestricted
Type: Award
Value: US$2,500
Frequency: Annual
No. of awards offered: 1
Application Procedure: Application forms are available from the website.
Closing Date: February 1st
No. of awards given last year: 37

THE WINGATE SCHOLARSHIPS

Queen Anne Business Centre, 28 Broadway, London, SW1H 9JX, England
Email: clark@wingate.org.uk
Website: www.wingatescholarships.org.uk
Contact: Ms Faith Clark, Administrator

Wingate Scholarships are awarded to exceptional individuals who need financial support to undertake creative or original work of intellectual, scientific, artistic, social or environmental value of great potential or proven excellence, and to outstanding musicians for advanced training.

Wingate Scholarships
Subjects: All subjects except fine arts, performing arts (except music), business courses or courses leading to professional qualifications and electives.

Purpose: To fund creative or original work of intellectual, scientific, artistic, social or environmental value and advanced music study.
Eligibility: Open to United Kingdom, Commonwealth, former Commonwealth, Irish, Israeli or other European Union country citizens provided that they are and have been resident in the United Kingdom for at least 3 years. Applicants must be over 24 years of age. No upper age limit is prescribed. No academic qualifications are necessary.
Level of Study: Doctorate, Postdoctorate, Research
Type: Scholarship
Value: Costs of a project, which may last for up to 3 years. This is an average of UK £6,500 to a maximum of UK £10,000 in any 1 year
Length of Study: 1–3 years
Frequency: Annual, Independent research
Study Establishment: Any approved institute
Country of Study: Any country
No. of awards offered: Approx. 40–50
Application Procedure: Applicants must complete application forms, available from the administrator (send an A4 S.A.E) or the website. Applicants must be able to satisfy the Scholarship Committee that they need financial support to undertake the work projected, and show why the proposed work (if it takes the form of academic research) is unlikely to attract the Research Council, British Academy or any other major agency funding.
Closing Date: February 1st
Funding: Private
Contributor: HHW Foundation
No. of awards given last year: 52
No. of applicants last year: 500
Additional Information: The scholarships are not awarded for professional qualifications, taught courses or electives, or in the following subject areas: performing arts, fine art, business studies. Musicians are eligible for advanced training, but apart from that, all applicants must have projects that are personal to them and involve either creative or original work.

WINSTON CHURCHILL FOUNDATION OF THE USA

600 Madison Avenue, 16th Floor, New York, NY 10022-1615, United States of America
Tel: (1) 212 752 3200
Fax: (1) 212 246 8330
Email: info@winstonchurchillfoundation.org
Website: www.winstonchurchillfoundation.org/Index.html
Contact: Mr Peter C. Patrikis, Executive Director

The Winston Churchill Foundation of the United States was established in 1959 as an expression of American admiration for one of the great leaders of the free world. The foundation was established to encourage and enable outstanding American students to attend graduate school at Churchill College, Cambridge University.

Winston Churchill Foundation Scholarship
Subjects: Engineering, mathematics, computer science and natural and physical sciences.
Purpose: To encourage the development of American scientific and technological talent and foster Anglo-American ties.
Eligibility: Open to citizens of the United States of America only. Applicants must be enrolled in one of 102 institutions participating in the programme, may not have enrolled a PhD and must be no older than 26 years at the time of taking up the scholarships.
Level of Study: Postgraduate
Type: Scholarship
Value: Approx. US$45,000–50,000
Length of Study: 1 year
Frequency: Annual
Study Establishment: Churchill College, the University of Cambridge
Country of Study: United Kingdom
No. of awards offered: 13
Application Procedure: Applicants must apply through their sponsoring institution.
Closing Date: November 12th
Funding: Foundation
No. of awards given last year: 12
No. of applicants last year: 100

WINSTON CHURCHILL MEMORIAL TRUST (AUS)

GPO Box 1536, Canberra City, ACT, 2601, Australia
Tel: (61) 26 2478 333
Fax: (61) 26 2498 944
Email: churchilltrust@bigpond.com
Website: www.churchilltrust.com.au
Contact: Ms Louise Stenhouse, Senior Executive Officer, Finance and Administration

The principal objective of the Winston Churchill Memorial Trust (Aus) is to perpetuate and honour the memory of Sir Winston Churchill by awarding memorial Fellowships known as Churchill Fellowships.

Churchill Fellowships

Subjects: All subjects.
Purpose: To enable Australian citizens over the age of 18 to undertake an overseas research project of a kind that is not available in Australia.
Eligibility: All Australian citizens over the age of 18 years are eligible to apply. Merit of the proposal and benefit to the Australian community at either a local, State or National level are the primary tests. Applications to further tertiary qualifications will not be eligible.
Level of Study: Unrestricted
Type: Fellowship
Value: Approx. Australian $25,000, return economy airfare to the country or countries to be visited and a living allowance plus fees if approved
Length of Study: 4–8 weeks, depending upon the project
Frequency: Annual
Study Establishment: 1965
Country of Study: Any country
No. of awards offered: Over 100 per year
Application Procedure: Applicants must complete and submit an application form supported by 2 references. For an application form, contact the National Office or visit the website.
Closing Date: Last day of February
Funding: Private
No. of awards given last year: 120
No. of applicants last year: 976
Additional Information: Applicants need to apply in their state or territory of residence. Deatils are contained in the application package. Further information is available from the National Office on 1800 777 231 (Australia) or on the web at www.churchill trust.com.au

WINSTON CHURCHILL MEMORIAL TRUST (UK)

15 Queen's Gate Terrace, London, SW7 5PR, England
Tel: (44) 20 7584 9315
Fax: (44) 20 7581 0410
Email: office@wcmt.org.uk
Website: www.wcmt.org.uk
Contact: Ms S Matthews, Trust Office Manager

Each year the trust awards fellowships to 100 British citizens to carry out Travelling Fellowships overseas for the benefit of country, community and international goodwill. Different categories of fellowships are awarded each year, e.g. conservation of the environment, agriculture and horticulture, science and technology, adventure, exploration and leaders of expeditions.

Winston Churchill Memorial Trust (UK) Travelling Fellowships

Subjects: Approx. 10 categories that vary annually and are representative of culture, social and public service, technology, commerce and industry, agriculture and nature, recreation and adventure.
Purpose: To enable British citizens from all walks of life and all ages to travel abroad in pursuit of a worthwhile purpose and so to contribute more to their trade or profession, their community and their country.
Eligibility: Open to British citizens resident in the UK whose purposes must be covered by one of the categories chosen for the year.

Level of Study: Unrestricted
Type: Fellowship
Value: The average award is UK £5,500. This covers all travel and living expenses by individual assessment. The fellowship scheme does not cover attending courses, academic studies, student grants or gap year projects
Length of Study: 4–8 weeks
Frequency: Annual
Country of Study: Any country
No. of awards offered: Approx. 100
Application Procedure: Applicants must complete an application form.
Closing Date: Mid-October
Funding: Private
Contributor: The public
No. of awards given last year: 100
No. of applicants last year: 941
Additional Information: Award winners are announced at the beginning of February, and Fellows may travel after April 1st.

WINTERTHUR

Winterthur Museum and Country Estate, Winterthur, DE, 19735, United States of America
Tel: (1) 800 448 3883
Email: webmaster@winterthur.org
Website: www.winterthur.org

Winterthur, an American country estate, is the former home of Henry Francis du Pont (1880–1969), an avid antiques collector and horticulturist. Winterthur is an ideal centre for the interdisciplinary study of America's artistic, cultural, social, and intellectual past, Winterthur offers academic programmes for college credit as well as fellowship opportunities. Researchers can find a wealth of resources awaiting them in the Winterthur Library.

Winterthur National Endowment for the Humanities Fellowships

Subjects: American history.
Purpose: To encourage critical inquiry that will further the understanding of American history and visual and material culture.
Eligibility: Open to scholars pursuing advanced research who are citizens of the United States or residents for 3 years.
Level of Study: Research
Type: Fellowships
Value: US$40,000
Length of Study: 4–12 months
Frequency: Annual
Country of Study: United States of America
Application Procedure: Applicants can download the application form from the website.
Closing Date: January 15th
Additional Information: For further information contact Kay Collins at the above address.

For further information contact:

Office of Academic Programmes Winterthur Museum, Wilmington, DE, 19735, United States of America
Contact: Kay Collins

THE WOLF AVIATION FUND

2060 State Highway 595, Gavilan Community, New Mexico, Lindrith, 87029, United States of America
Tel: (1) 215 977 2099, 505 774 0029
Email: mail@wolf-aviation.org
Website: www.wolf-aviation.org
Contact: The Grants Administrator

The Wolf Aviation Fund was established in the wills of Alfred L. and Constance C. Wolf. The Wolf Foundation hopes to help people and projects that benefit general aviation by identifying talented, worthy individuals - often working in collaboration with others - and worthwhile projects and providing them support.

Wolf Aviation Fund Grants Program

Subjects: Aviation.
Purpose: To promote and support the advancement of personal air transportation by seeking and funding the most promising individuals and worthy projects which advance the field of general aviation.
Level of Study: Postgraduate
Value: Varies
Frequency: Annual
No. of awards offered: Varies
Application Procedure: For more details please visit the website.
Closing Date: November 15th
Additional Information: In preparing proposals the foundation strongly encourages applicants to browse the Resources section and learn how to find out what kinds of grants might be available from any source and to learn in general how to properly prepare grant requests.

WOLF BLASS WINES INTERNATIONAL

97 Sturt Highway, Nuriootpa, Adelaide, SA, Australia
Tel: (61) 08 8568 7311
Email: cellardoor@wolfblass.com.au
Website: www.wolfblass.com.au/brands/wolfblass/index.asp

Wolf Blass Wines International is public listed company and one of the Australia's top sellers of red and white wine. It is one of the best Australian wine-producing company. As they have for almost 30 years, Wolf Blass wines continue to delight wine lovers all over the world.

Wolf Blass Australian Winemaking Independent Study Scholarship

Subjects: Winemaking.
Purpose: To support independent study related to winemaking in Australia.
Eligibility: Open to culinary professional to conduct research and writing related to Australian winemaking and culinary traditions.
Type: Scholarship
Value: Australian $5,000
Country of Study: Australia
No. of awards offered: 1
Application Procedure: All applicants are required to include a project proposal, an itemized budget detailing the use of this award and a tentative travel schedule with dates and locations. Check website for further details.
Additional Information: Applicant is additionally required to provide a current resume to qualify for this scholarship.

For further information contact:

304W, Liberty Street, Suite 201, Kentucky, Louisville, 40202, United States of America
Tel: (1) 800 928 4227 Ext 264
Fax: (1) 502 589 3602
Email: tgribbins@hqtrs.com
Website: www.theculinarytrust.org

WOLF FOUNDATION

39 Hamaapilim Street, PO Box 398, IL-46103 Herzlia Bet, Israel
Tel: (972) 9 955 7120
Fax: (972) 9 954 1253
Email: wolffund@netvision.net.il
Website: www.wolffund.org.il
Contact: Mr Yaron Gruder, Director General

The Wolf Foundation was established in 1976 by Dr Ricardo Wolf (1887–1981), inventor, diplomat and philanthropist, and his wife Francisca Subirana-Wolf (1900–1981), in order to promote science and art for the benefit of mankind.

Wolf Foundation Prizes

Subjects: In science the fields are agriculture, chemistry, mathematics, medicine and physics, and in the arts the fields are architecture, music, painting and sculpture.
Purpose: To recognize the achievements of outstanding scientists and artists in the interest of mankind and friendly relations among people.
Eligibility: There are no eligibility restrictions.

Level of Study: Postgraduate
Type: Prize
Value: The prize in each field consists of a diploma and US$100,000
Frequency: Annual
Country of Study: Any country
No. of awards offered: 4 prizes in sciences and 1 in the arts
Application Procedure: Applicants must request an application form.
Closing Date: August 31st
Funding: Private
Contributor: The founder, Richard Wolf
No. of awards given last year: 5 fields, to 10 recipients

THE WOLFSON FOUNDATION

8 Queen Anne Street, London, W1G 9LD, England
Tel: (44) 20 7323 5730
Fax: (44) 20 7323 3241
Website: www.wolfson.org.uk
Contact: The Executive Secretary

The aim of the Wolfson Foundation is the advancement of the arts and humanities, science, health and education. Grants are given to back excellence and talent, and provide support for promising projects that may be under funded, particularly for renovation and equipment. The emphasis is on science and technology, research, education, health and the arts.

Wolfson Foundation Grants

Subjects: Medicine and healthcare, including the prevention of disease, and the care and treatment of the sick, disadvantaged and disabled, research, science, technology and education, particularly where benefits may accrue to the development of industry or commerce in the United Kingdom and the arts and humanities, including libraries, museums, galleries, theatres, academies or historic buildings.
Eligibility: Open to registered charities and to exempt charities such as universities. Eligible applications from registered charities for contributions to appeals will normally be considered only when at least 50 per cent of that appeal has already been raised. Grants to universities for research and scholarship are normally made under the umbrella of designated competitive programmes in which vice chancellors and principals are invited to participate from time to time. Applications from university researchers are not considered outside these programmes. Grants are not made to private individuals.
Level of Study: Postgraduate, Research
Type: Grant
Value: The Trustees make several types of grants, which are not necessarily independent of each other. Capital Project Grants may contribute towards the cost of erecting a new building or extension, or of renovating and refurbishing existing buildings. Equipment Grants supply equipment for specific purposes and/or furnishing and fittings. Recurrent costs are not normally provided
Frequency: Twice a year
Country of Study: United Kingdom or Israel or The Commonwealth countries
No. of awards offered: Varies
Application Procedure: Applicants must submit in writing a brief outline of the project with one copy of the organization's most recent audited accounts before embarking on a detailed proposal.
Closing Date: March 1st or September 1st
Funding: Private
No. of awards given last year: 382
No. of applicants last year: 1,200

THE WOLFSONIAN-FLORIDA INTERNATIONAL UNIVERSITY

1001 Washington Avenue, Miami Beach, FL, 33139, United States of America
Tel: (1) 305 531 1001
Fax: (1) 305 531 2133
Email: research@thewolf.fiu.edu
Website: www.wolfsonian.fiu.edu
Contact: Mr Jonathan Mogul, Fellowship Co-ordinator

The Wolfsonian-Florida International University is a museum and research centre that promotes the examination of modern material culture. Through exhibitions, publications, scholarships, educational programmes and public presentations, the Wolfsonian strives to enhance the understanding of objects as agents and reflections of social, cultural, political and technological change. The collection includes works on paper, furniture, paintings, sculpture, glass, textiles, ceramics, books and many other kinds of objects.

Wolfsonian-FIU Fellowship

Subjects: Modern material and visual culture.
Purpose: To conduct research on the Wolfsonian's collection of objects and library materials from the period 1885 to 1945, including decorative arts, works on paper, books and ephemera.
Eligibility: The programme is open to holder of Master's or doctoral degrees, PhD candidates, and to other who have a record of significant professional achievement in relevant fields.
Level of Study: Doctorate, Postdoctorate, Professional development
Type: Fellowship
Value: Approx. US$425 per week plus travel and accommodation
Length of Study: Approx. 3–5 weeks
Frequency: Annual
Study Establishment: The Wolfsonian-Florida International University
Country of Study: United States of America
No. of awards offered: Varies, approx. 5
Application Procedure: Applicants must complete an application form and submit this with three letters of recommendation.
Contact the Fellowship Co-ordinator for details and application materials. Applicants may also download programme information and an application form from the website www.wolfsonian.fiu.edu/education/research/
Closing Date: December 31st
No. of awards given last year: 5
No. of applicants last year: 26

WOMEN BAND DIRECTORS INTERNATIONAL (WBDI)

7424 Whistlestop Drive, Austin, TX, 78749, United States of America
Tel: (1) 512 496 3591
Fax: (1) 512 841 3811
Email: dgorzycki@austin.rr.com
Website: www.womenbanddirectors.org
Contact: Diane Gorzycki, Scholarships Chair

Women Band Directors International (WBDI) is an organization in which every woman band director is represented at the international level, regardless of the length of her experience or the level at which she works. It is the only international organization for women band directors.

WBDI Scholarship Awards

Subjects: Music education.
Purpose: To support young college women presently preparing to be band directors.
Eligibility: Any female student enrolled in college and majoring in music education with the purpose of becoming a band director.
Level of Study: Unrestricted
Type: Scholarship
Value: US$1,500
Frequency: Annual
Country of Study: United States of America
No. of awards offered: 5
Application Procedure: Download the application from our website-essay, 2 letters of recommendations transcript, statement of philosophy, completed application.
Closing Date: December 1st
Funding: Private
No. of awards given last year: 4
No. of applicants last year: 50 per year

WOMEN OF THE EVANGELICAL LUTHERAN CHURCH IN AMERICA (ELCA)

8765 W. Higgins Road, Chicago, IL 60631-4101, United States of America
Tel: (1) 800 638 3522, ext. 2730
Fax: (1) 773 380 2419
Email: women.elca@elca.org
Website: www.womenoftheelca.org/

The mission of ELCA is to mobilize women to act boldly on their faiths. As an organization with an anti-racist identity, it offers opportunities for growth by cross-cultural ministry and leadership development.

Amelia Kemp Scholarship

Subjects: All subjects.
Purpose: To provide assistance to women studying for a career other than the ordained ministry.
Eligibility: Open to female citizens of the United States who are members of the ELCA.
Level of Study: Professional development
Type: Scholarship
Value: US$1,000
Length of Study: 1 year
Frequency: Annual
Country of Study: United States of America
Application Procedure: A completed application form must be submitted.
Closing Date: February 15th
Contributor: Lutheran Church in America

Arne Administrative Leadership Scholarship

Subjects: Church administration.
Purpose: To provide assistance to ELCA women interested in reaching the top of their field as an administrator.
Eligibility: Open to women citizens of the United States who are members of the ELCA.
Level of Study: Professional development
Type: Scholarship
Value: Upto US$2,000
Frequency: Annual
Application Procedure: See the website.
Closing Date: February 15th

Belmer/Flora Prince Scholarship

Subjects: Theology.
Purpose: To assist ELCA women as they prepare for ELCA service abroad.
Eligibility: Open to women citizens of the United States who are members of the ELCA.
Level of Study: Professional development
Type: Scholarship
Value: US$1,500
Frequency: Annual
Country of Study: United States of America
Application Procedure: Application forms are available on the website.
Closing Date: February 15th
Contributor: Lutheran Church in America

Chilstrom Scholarship for Ordained Ministry

Subjects: Theology.
Purpose: To provide assistance to ELCA women during their final year at an ELCA seminary.
Eligibility: Open to women candidates of the United States who are members of the ELCA.
Level of Study: Professional development
Type: Scholarship
Value: US$700–2,000
Frequency: Annual
Application Procedure: Application form available on the website.
Closing Date: February 15th

WOMEN'S INTERNATIONAL LEAGUE FOR PEACE AND FREEDOM (WILPF)

PO Box 28, CH-1211 Geneva 20, Switzerland
Tel: (41) 22 919 7080
Fax: (41) 22 919 7081
Email: inforequest@wilpf.ch
Website: www.wilpf.ch
Contact: The Internships Programme

Founded in 1915 to protest against the war then raging in Europe, the Women's International League for Peace and Freedom (WILPF) aims to bring together women of different political and philosophical conviction, united in their determination to study, make known and help abolish the political, social, economic and psychological causes of war and to work for a constructive peace.

WILPF Internship in Disarmament
Subjects: Disarmament, in the context of the United Nations (UN) and international organizations.
Purpose: To focus on the work of the UN and non-governmental organizations (NGOs) in promoting and strengthening their efforts for disarmament and the peaceful settlement of conflict.
Eligibility: The internships are reserved for women in recognition of the fact that women remain largely excluded from positions concerned with questions of foreign policy and international relations, although their presence in these crucial areas is much needed. Priority is given to women between 20 and 30 years of age and preference is given to WILPF members. Fluency in oral and written English is essential, and Spanish and French speaking skills are an advantage for the work of the interns.
Level of Study: Graduate, Postgraduate, Professional development
Type: Internship
Value: Round-trip travel from home to Geneva and a small stipend that covers basic living expenses in an expensive city. Accommodation is also provided
Length of Study: From mid-January to mid-December
Frequency: Annual
Study Establishment: WILPF, Geneva
Country of Study: Switzerland
No. of awards offered: 1
Application Procedure: All applications must be submitted as a hard copy in English and should state clearly the internship for which the application is submitted. Applications must include a curriculum vitae, a covering letter giving reasons for wanting to follow the programme, a 1,000 to 1,500 word essay about a disarmament issue stating why this is of interest and two recommendations from non-family members. Emails and incomplete applications will not be considered. Please check the website www.wilpf.ch for further details.
Closing Date: July 30th
Funding: Private
Additional Information: The intern follows the sessions of the UN conference or Disarmament and meeting of UN agencies, as well as participating in non-governmental organization meetings and WILPF activities.

WILPF Internship in Human Rights
Subjects: Human rights in the context of the United Nations (UN) and international organizations.
Purpose: To provide leadership training for young women. To focus on the annual session of the UN Human Rights Council (HRC), its working groups, the Committee on Economic Social and Cultural Rights and meetings of UN Agencies.
Eligibility: The internships are reserved for women in recognition of the fact that women remain largely excluded from positions concerned with questions of foreign policy and international relations, although their presence in these crucial areas is much needed. Priority is given to women between 20 and 30 years of age, and preference is given to WILPF members. Fluency in oral and written English is essential and Spanish and French speaking skills are an advantage for the work of the interns.
Level of Study: Graduate, Postgraduate, Professional development
Type: Internship
Value: Round-trip travel from home to Geneva and a small stipend that covers basic living expenses in an expensive city. Accommodation is also provided

Length of Study: Early March–Early May
Frequency: Annual
Study Establishment: WILPF, Geneva
Country of Study: Switzerland
No. of awards offered: 1
Application Procedure: All applications must be submitted as a hard copy in English and should state clearly the internship for which the application is submitted. Applications must include a curriculum vitae, a covering letter giving reasons for wanting to follow the programme, a 1,000 to 1,500 word essay about a human rights issue stating why this is of interest and 2 recommendations from non-family members. Emails and incomplete applications will not be considered. Please check website for further details.
Closing Date: July 30th of the previous year
Funding: Private
No. of awards given last year: 1
No. of applicants last year: 75
Additional Information: The intern follows the sessions of the UN on Human Rights Council, its working group, the Committee on Economic Social and Cultural Rights and meetings of UN Agencies, as well as participating in non-governmental organization meetings and WILPF activities.

WOMEN'S RESEARCH AND EDUCATION INSTITUTE (WREI)

1828 L Street, NW, #801, Washington, DC, WA, 20036-5104, United States of America
Tel: (1) 202 332 2275
Email: WREI@WREI.org
Website: www.wrei.org
Contact: Fellowship Programme

Founded in 1977, Women's Research and Education Institute (WREI) is an independent, non-profit, non-partisan organization governed by a board of directors that includes leading Americans from many fields who are committed to equality for women. Its mission is to inform and help shape the public policy debate on issues affecting women and their roles in the family, workplace and public arena.

WREI Congressional Fellowships on Women and Public Policy
Subjects: Public policy.
Purpose: To encourage more effective participation by women in the formulation of public policy. To train feminist leaders in legislative procedure at the national level.
Eligibility: Open to students who are currently in, or have recently completed a graduate or professional degree programme at an accredited institution in the United States.
Level of Study: Graduate, Postgraduate
Type: Fellowship
Value: Stipends for tuition and living expenses
Frequency: Annual
Country of Study: United States of America
Application Procedure: Application forms can be downloaded from the website www.wrei.org every year in January. Please note that applications sent by fax are not accepted.
Closing Date: Mid-May. Please check the website www.wrei.org
Funding: Corporation, foundation, individuals
No. of awards given last year: 6
No. of applicants last year: 35–40
Additional Information: Fellows are selected on the basis of academic competence as well as their demonstrated interest in the public policy process. They are expected to be articulate and adaptable and to have strong writing skills.

WOMEN'S STUDIO WORKSHOP (WSW)

PO Box 489, Rosendale, NY, 12472, United States of America
Tel: (1) 845 658 9133
Fax: (1) 845 658 9031
Email: info@wsworkshop.org
Website: www.wsworkshop.org
Contact: Ms Ann Kalmbach, Executive Director

The Women's Studio Workshop (WSW) is an artist-run workshop with facilities for printmaking, papermaking, photography, book arts and ceramics. WSW supports the creation of new work through studio residency and annual book arts grant programmes and an ongoing subsidized fellowship programme. WSW offers studio-based educational programming in the above disciplines through its annual Summer Arts Institute.

Studio Residency Grant

Subjects: Books, printmaking papermaking, photography and clay.
Purpose: To provide artists with time and resources to create a new body of work or to edition a new bookwork.
Eligibility: Open to all national and international applicants. Emerging artists are encouraged to apply.
Level of Study: Unrestricted
Type: Grant
Value: A stipend of up to US$2,000 plus materials of up to US$700 and housing
Length of Study: 6 weeks
Frequency: Annual
Study Establishment: WSW
Country of Study: United States of America
No. of awards offered: 2
Application Procedure: Applicants must submit an application form, a one-page project description on a separate sheet of paper, a curriculum vitae, ten slides of recent work, a slide script including title, medium, size and date and a stamped addressed envelope, for return of materials. Forms are available from the website.
Closing Date: April 1st
Funding: Foundation, government
No. of awards given last year: 2
No. of applicants last year: 80

WSW Artists Fellowships

Subjects: Intaglio, water-based silkscreen, photography, papermaking or ceramics, letterpress, book arts, ceramics.
Purpose: To provide a time for artists to explore new ideas in a dynamic and co-operative community of women artists in a rural environment.
Eligibility: Open to women artists only.
Level of Study: Unrestricted
Type: Fellowship
Value: The award includes on-site housing and unlimited access to the studios. Cost to artists will be US$200 per week, including their own material
Length of Study: Each fellowship is 2–4 weeks long. Fellowship opportunities are from September to June
Frequency: Annual
Study Establishment: WSW
Country of Study: United States of America
No. of awards offered: 10–20
Application Procedure: Applicants must complete an application form, available on request or online at the website.
Closing Date: March 15th or November 1st
Funding: Government, private
Contributor: Private foundations
No. of awards given last year: 25
No. of applicants last year: 100

WSW Artists' Book Residencies

Subjects: Artists books.
Purpose: To enable artists to produce a limited edition book work at the Women's Studio Workshop.
Level of Study: Unrestricted
Type: Residency grant
Value: A stipend of up to US$2,000, plus materials of up to US$700 and housing
Length of Study: 6 weeks
Frequency: Annual
Study Establishment: WSW
Country of Study: United States of America
No. of awards offered: Varies, usually 3–5
Application Procedure: Applicants must submit an application including a one-page description of the proposed project, the medium or media used to print the book, the number of pages, page size, edition number, a structural dummy, materials budget, a curriculum vitae,

10 slides and a stamped addressed envelope for return of materials. Applications are reviewed by past grant recipients and a WSW staff artist. Applicants should write for an application form or download one from the website.
Closing Date: November 15th
Funding: Government, private
Contributor: Private foundations
No. of awards given last year: 2
No. of applicants last year: 150

WSW Hands-On-Art Visiting Artist Project

Subjects: Artist's books.
Purpose: To assist an emerging artist in the creation of a new artist's book, while also working with school children in WSW's studio-based Art-In-Education programme.
Eligibility: Open to all artists. Emerging artists are encouraged to apply.
Level of Study: Unrestricted
Type: Grant
Value: A stipend of up to US$3,200, plus materials of up to US$1000 and housing
Length of Study: 8 weeks
Frequency: Annual
Study Establishment: WSW
Country of Study: United States of America
No. of awards offered: 2
Application Procedure: Applicants must apply through a two-part application. Artists apply to WSW, WSW juries and then applies to other funding sources. Artists must submit a one-page description of their intended artist book project, including details of the medium to be used for printing the book, number of pages, page size, edition size (100 preferred), a structural dummy, materials budget, a curriculum vitae, a one-page description of relevant work experience with young people, ten slides of recent work and a stamped addressed envelope.
Closing Date: March 15 or November 15
Funding: Foundation, government
No. of awards given last year: 2
No. of applicants last year: 30

WSW Internships

Subjects: Book arts, papermaking, printmaking, ceramics and photography.
Purpose: To provide opportunities for young artists to continue development of their work in a supportive environment, while learning studio skills and responsibilities.
Eligibility: Open to emerging and established female artists.
Level of Study: Unrestricted
Type: Internship
Value: US$300 per month plus housing
Length of Study: 2–12 months
Frequency: Annual
Study Establishment: WSW
Country of Study: United States of America
No. of awards offered: 5
Application Procedure: Applicants must submit a curriculum vitae, 10–20 slides with slide list, 3 current letters of reference, a letter of interest that addresses the question of why an internship at WSW would be important and a stamped addressed envelope.
Closing Date: February 15 for studio,summer, Arts, Administration internships. November 15 for ceramics internships
Funding: Government, private
Contributor: Private foundations
No. of awards given last year: 6
No. of applicants last year: 150

THE WOODROW WILSON NATIONAL FELLOWSHIP FOUNDATION

PO Box 5281, Princeton, NJ, 08543-5281, United States of America
Tel: (1) 609 452 7007
Fax: (1) 609 452 0066
Email: jlp@woodrow.org
Website: www.woodrow.org
Contact: Ms Judith L Pinch

The Woodrow Wilson National Fellowship Foundation, an independent, non-profit organization, attempts to maximize human potential through education. The Foundation seeks to sponsor excellence in education and thus develop a new generation of leaders.

Andrew W Mellon Fellowships in Humanistic Studies

Subjects: Humanistic studies.

Purpose: To allow exceptionally promising students to prepare for careers of teaching and scholarship in humanistic studies by providing top-level, competitive, portable awards, and to contribute to the continuity of teaching and research of the highest order in America's colleges and universities.

Eligibility: Open to college seniors or recent graduates who are citizens of the United States of America or permanent residents entering into a programme leading to a PhD in the humanities. Applicants must not be enrolled in a graduate or professional study or hold an MA degree.

Level of Study: Doctorate

Type: Fellowship

Value: US$17,500 plus tuition and mandated fees

Length of Study: 1 year

Frequency: Annual

Country of Study: United States of America or Canada

No. of awards offered: 85

Application Procedure: Applicants must provide their full name, current address and telephone number, their address in March, details of their undergraduate institution, major and year of graduation, the intended discipline in graduate school, details of their mailing address and United States of America mail or email. These must be provided by mail, phone, fax or email.

Closing Date: Early December

Funding: Foundation, private

Contributor: The Andrew W Mellon Foundation

No. of awards given last year: 85

Charlotte W Newcombe Doctoral Dissertation Fellowships

Subjects: Topics of religious or ethical values in all fields.

Purpose: To encourage new and significant research.

Eligibility: Open to students enrolled in doctoral programmes in the humanities and social sciences at a university in the United States of America. Students must have completed all predissertation requirements by November 1st.

Level of Study: Doctorate

Type: Fellowship

Value: US$19,000

Length of Study: 1 year, full-time

Frequency: Annual

Study Establishment: Any appropriate graduate school

Country of Study: United States of America

No. of awards offered: Approx. 30

Application Procedure: Applicants must write for details.

Closing Date: November 14th

Funding: Private

No. of awards given last year: 35

No. of applicants last year: 450

The Millicent C. McIntosh Fellowship

Subjects: Humanities.

Purpose: These fellowships are specifically intended for recently tenured faculty who would benefit from additional time and resources.

Level of Study: Postgraduate

Type: Fellowship

Value: A US$15,000 stipend

Length of Study: 1 year

Frequency: Annual

No. of awards offered: 6

Application Procedure: Contact the Foundation.

Closing Date: March 31st

Funding: Private

Contributor: Gladys Krieble Delmas Foundation

For further information contact:

Tel: 609 452 7007 ext. 301
Email: mcintoshfellowship@woodrow.org

Woodrow Wilson Dissertation Fellowship in Women's Studies

Subjects: Women's studies, the history, education and psychology of women and women's health.

Purpose: To assist those writing dissertations.

Eligibility: Open to doctoral candidates at American universities who have completed all the requirements for the degree course, except the dissertation.

Level of Study: Doctorate

Type: Grant

Value: US$3,000

Length of Study: 1 year

Frequency: Annual

Country of Study: United States of America

No. of awards offered: 20

Application Procedure: Applicants must write for details.

Closing Date: October 11th

Funding: Private

No. of awards given last year: 25

No. of applicants last year: 250

Woodrow Wilson Teaching Fellowship

Subjects: Arts and sciences education.

Level of Study: Professional development

Type: Fellowship

Length of Study: 1 year

Frequency: Annual

No. of awards offered: 1

Closing Date: Please visit website

Funding: Private

For further information contact:

Tel: 609 452 7007 ext. 305
Email: caddeau@woodrow.org

Woodrow Wilson Visiting Fellows

Subjects: All subjects.

Purpose: To encourage the flow of ideas between the academic and non-academic sectors of society.

Level of Study: Postgraduate

Type: Fellowships

Value: US$5,000

Length of Study: 1 year

Frequency: Annual

Application Procedure: Contact the Foundation.

Funding: Private

Contributor: Lilly Endowment

For further information contact:

Visiting Fellows Program
Tel: 609 452 7007 ext. 181
Email: sanford@woodrow.org
Contact: Beverly Sanford, Director

WOODS HOLE OCEANOGRAPHIC INSTITUTION (WHOI)

Woods Hole Oceanographic Institution Bell House, MS #39 221 Oyster Pond Road, Woods Hole, MA, 02543-1531, United States of America
Tel: (1) 508 289 2219
Fax: (1) 508 457 2188
Email: information@whoi.edu
Website: www.whoi.edu/education
Contact: Janet Fields, Coordinator

The Woods Hole Oceanographic Institution is a private, independent, non-profit corporation dedicated to research and higher education at the frontiers of ocean science. Its primary mission is to develop and effectively communicate a fundamental understanding of the processes and characteristics governing how the oceans function and how they interact with the Earth as a whole.

CICOR Postdoctoral Scholar Fellowship in Coastal Oceanography, Climate or Marine Ecosystems

Subjects: Coastal ocean and near shore processes, the ocean's participation in climate and climate variability and marine ecosystem processes analysis.

Purpose: To build ties between WHOI investigators and colleagues at NOAA laboratories and to develop co-operative NOAA funded research at academic institutions in the Northeastern United States of America. The fellowship also aims to further the education and training of recent recipients of doctoral degrees in the marine sciences.

Eligibility: Applicants must have received their doctoral degree within the past 4 years, completed if full in biology, physics, microbiology, molecular biology, chemistry, geology, geophysics, oceanography, meteorology, engineering or mathematics. Candidates should have a command of the English language. Candidates holding a WHOI appointment at the post-PhD level the 12 months prior to the scholar application deadline are not eligible.

Level of Study: Postdoctorate

Type: Fellowship

Value: US$54,000 per year, eligible for health insurance and limited support for travel expenses, equipment, supplies and special services

Length of Study: 18 months

Frequency: Annual

Study Establishment: Woods Hole Oceanographic Institution

Country of Study: United States of America

Closing Date: January 15th

Funding: Government

Additional Information: Award holders work in the laboratory under the general supervision of an appropriate member of the staff, but are expected to work independently on research problems of their own choice.

For further information contact:

Clark laboratory, MS #31, Woods Hole Oceanographic Institution, 266 Woods Hole Road, Woods Hole, Massachusetts, 02543-1541, United States of America
Contact: Academic Programs Office

NOSAMS Postdoctoral Fellowships in Marine Radiocarbon Studies and in Accelerator Mass Spectrometry

Subjects: Radiocarbon research.

Purpose: To attract outstanding individuals interested in either or both, studies of radiocarbon in oceanic systems and developments in accelerator mass spectrometry and related techniques. Typical projects include diverse studies of the biogeochemical cycling of carbon, the detection and tracing of pollutants in natural systems and paleoceanographic and paleoclimatic investigations of all kinds.

Eligibility: Applicants must have received their doctoral degree before taking up their appointment at Woods Hole. They should have related research interests. Applications from physicists, chemists and biologists as well as from oceanographers are specifically invited.

Level of Study: Postdoctorate

Type: Fellowship

Value: $54,000 per year, eligible for health insurance and limited support for travel expenses, equipment, supplies and special services

Length of Study: 18 months

Frequency: Annual

Study Establishment: Woods Hole Oceanographic Institution

Country of Study: United States of America

Closing Date: December1st

For further information contact:

Clark Laboratory, MS #31, Woods Hole Oceanographic Institution, 266 Woods Hole Road, Woods Hole, Massachusetts, 02543-1541, United States of America
Contact: Academic Programs Office

WHOI Geophysical Fluid Dynamics (GFD) Fellowships

Subjects: Classical fluid dynamics, physical oceanography, engineering, geophysics, meteorology, astrophysics, planetary atmospheres, geological fluid dynamics, hydromagnetics, physics and applied mathematics.

Purpose: To bring together graduate students and researchers from a variety of fields who share a common interest in the non linear dynamics of rotating, stratified fields.

Eligibility: There are no eligibility restrictions.

Level of Study: Graduate

Type: Fellowships

Value: A stipend of US$4,900 and travel allowance

Length of Study: 10 weeks

Frequency: Annual

Study Establishment: Woods Hole Oceanographic Institution

Country of Study: United States of America

No. of awards offered: Up to 10

Application Procedure: Application forms may be obtained from the GFD section of the education website or by writing directly to the Fellowship Committee.

Closing Date: February 15th

Funding: Government

Contributor: The United States office of Naval Research and the United States National Science Foundation

WHOI Marine Policy Fellowship Program

Subjects: Economic, legal and policy issues that arise from use of the world's oceans.

Purpose: To provide support and experience to research fellows interested in marine policy issues, to provide opportunities for interdisciplinary application of social sciences and natural sciences to marine policy problems, and to conduct research and convey information necessary for the development of effective local, national and international ocean policy.

Eligibility: Applicants must have completed a doctoral level degree or possess equivalent professional qualifications through career experience. The center also welcomes experienced professionals who can arrange a leave or sabbatical.

Level of Study: Postdoctorate

Type: Fellowship

Value: $54,000 and eligibility for health insurance and research and travel funds

Length of Study: 1 year

Frequency: Annual

Study Establishment: Woods Hole Oceanographic Institution

Country of Study: United States of America

No. of awards offered: Varies

Application Procedure: A completed application form, a statement of proposed research, a current curriculum vitae including educational background and work experience, transcripts of college and university records and at least 3 personal references.

Closing Date: January 15th

For further information contact:

Clarks laboratory, MS #31, Woods Hole Oceanographic Institution, Woods Hole, Massachusetts, 02543-1541, United States of America
Contact: Academic Programs Office

WHOI Postdoctoral Scholarship Program

Subjects: Applied ocean physics and engineering, biology, marine chemistry and geochemistry, geology and geophysics, physical oceanography.

Purpose: To further education and training of the applicant with primary emphasis placed on the individual's research promise.

Eligibility: Open to applicants who have received their doctoral degree within the past 2–3 years, completed in full. Candidate should have a command of the English language. Candidates holding a WHOI appointment at the post-PhD level during the 12 months prior to the Scholar application deadline are not eligible.

Level of Study: Postdoctorate

Type: Scholarship

Value: A stipend of US$54,000 per year, eligible for health insurance and limited support for travel expenses, equipment, supplies and special services

Length of Study: 18 months

Study Establishment: Woods Hole Oceanographic Institution

Country of Study: United States of America

No. of awards offered: 5–6 departmental awards, 4 institute awards

Closing Date: January 15th

For further information contact:

Clark Laboratory, MS #31, Woods Hole Oceanographic Institution, Woods Hole, Massachusetts, 02543-1541, United States of America
Contact: Academic Programs Office

WORCESTER POLYTECHNIC INSTITUTE (WPI)

100 Institute Road, Worcester, MA, 01609-2280, United States of America
Tel: (1) 508 831 5000/5671
Fax: (1) 508 831 5776
Email: gaann@cs.wpi.edu
Website: www.wpi.edu
Contact: Dr Matthew Ward, GAANN Director

Worcester Polytechnic Institute (WPI) was founded in Worcester, MA, in 1865 and was one of the nation's earliest technological universities. From the very beginning, it has taken a unique approach to science and technology education. There are over 20 WPI's project centres throughout North America and Central America, Africa, Australia, Asia and Europe.

Graduate Assistance in Areas of National Need (GAANN) Award

Subjects: Computer science.
Purpose: To make important contributions to the computer science research community.
Eligibility: Open to citizens or permanent residents of the United States pursuing a PhD in computer science.
Level of Study: Doctorate
Type: Fellowships
Value: US$30,000 per year
Length of Study: 3 years
Frequency: Annual
Country of Study: United States of America
No. of awards offered: 5
Application Procedure: Applicants must send a letter of intent, curriculum vitae and a description of any coursework or research completed.

WORLD BANK INSTITUTE

1818 H Street, Washington, NW, DC 20433, United States of America
Tel: (1) 202 473 1000
Fax: (1) 202 477 6391
Email: pic@worldbank.org
Website: www.worldbank.org
Contact: Communications Officer

One of the largest sources of funding and knowledge for transition and development councils; The World Bank uses its financial resources, staff and extensive experience to help developing countries reduce poverty, increase economic growth and improve their quality of life.

World Bank Grants Facility for Indigenous Peoples

Subjects: Indigenous culture, intellectual property and human rights.
Purpose: To support sustainable and culturally appropriate development projector planed and implemented by and for Indigenous People.
Eligibility: Applicants must belong to an Indigenous Peoples' community or organization.
Level of Study: Professional development, Research
Value: 20 per cent of total project cost ranging between US$10,000 and US$30,000
Frequency: Annual
Application Procedure: A complete application, not more than 10 pages, should be submitted.
Closing Date: November 15th
Contributor: The World Bank

For further information contact:

World Bank Grants Facility for Indigenous Peoples, Social Development Department, Mailstop MC 5-52b, World Bank, 1818 H Street, Washington, NW, DC 20433, United States of America

Fax: (1) 1 202 522 1669
Email: indigenouspeoples@worldbank.org

World Bank Small Grant Program

Subjects: Civil engagement.
Purpose: To strengthen the voice and influence of poor and marginalized groups.
Eligibility: Visit the website, requester and proposals should not be sent to the World Bank Office in Washington, DC.
Level of Study: Postgraduate
Type: Grant
Value: US$3,000–7,000 with a maximum of US$15,000
Frequency: Annual
Application Procedure: Guidelines and application forms available from the participating World Bank country office.
Closing Date: The small grants program makes decisions only once a year by June; applicant organizations should apply at least four to six months in advance of the date of the grant activity
Contributor: The World Bank

WORLD METEOROLOGICAL ORGANIZATION (WMO)

Education & Training Department, 7 bis Avenue de la Paix, Case postale No 2300 CH-1211 Geneva, Switzerland
Tel: (41) 22 730 81 11
Fax: (41) 22 730 81 81
Email: wmo@wmo.int
Website: www.wmo.ch
Contact: Director

The World Meteorological Organization (WMO) is an inter-governmental organization with a membership of 185 member states and territories. It originated from the International Meteorological Organization, which was founded in 1873. Set up in 1950, WMO became the specialized agency of the United Nations for meteorology, weather and climate, operational hydrology and related sciences.

WMO Education and Training Fellowships

Subjects: Atmospheric science, meteorology, operational hydrology and related sciences.
Purpose: To educate and train meteorological personnel on individually tailored or group-study training programmes.
Eligibility: Open to nationals from WMO member countries. Potential candidates should meet the requirements for academic qualifications, relevant experience, language proficiency, age limits and other specific requirements, as stipulated by the host training institutions concerned.
Level of Study: Professional development
Type: Fellowship
Value: According to United Nations rates
Length of Study: Varies
Frequency: Dependent on funds available
Study Establishment: Dependent on the required training or education
Country of Study: The applicants home country
No. of awards offered: Approx. 300
Application Procedure: Applicants must be designated officially through the permanent representative with WMO, which will normally be the Director of the National Meteorological Service in the requesting country concerned.
Funding: Government
Contributor: United Nation Development Programme (UNDP), Trust Funds and the Voluntary Co-operation Programme (VCP) and the Regular Budget (RB) of WMO
No. of awards given last year: 310
No. of applicants last year: 590

WORLD WILDLIFE FUND (WWF)

US Headquarters 1250, NW 24th Street PO Box 97180, Washington, 20090-7180, United States of America
Tel: (1) 202 293 4800
Email: membership@wwfus.org
Website: www.worldwildlife.org

World Wildlife Fund (WWF) is known to everyone by its panda logo, WWF leads international efforts to protect endangered species and their habitats. Now in its 5th decade, WWF works in more than 100 countries around the globe to conserve the diversity of life on earth.

WWF Fuller Fellowships

Subjects: Natural and social sciences.
Purpose: To help scientists to address research questions that will powerfully inform and improve the practice of biodiversity conservation.
Eligibility: Open to candidates who have obtained a Doctoral degree.
Level of Study: Postdoctorate
Type: Fellowships
Value: US$50,000 per year plus additional benefits
Length of Study: 2 years
Frequency: Annual
No. of awards offered: 2
Application Procedure: Applicants can apply online.
Closing Date: November 15th
Additional Information: The fellowship is not applicable to employees of WWF-US or immediate family members of WWF-US employees.

WWF Prince Bernhard Scholarship for Nature Conservation

Subjects: Any field that is directly relevant to the delivery and promotion of conservation.
Purpose: To provide financial support to individuals who wish to pursue professional training or formal studies that will help them to contribute more effectively to conservation efforts in their country.
Eligibility: Open to candidates from developing countries, central and eastern Europe and the Middle East.
Level of Study: Postgraduate
Type: Scholarship
Value: Swiss Franc 10,000
Frequency: Annual
Closing Date: January 12th
Contributor: World Wide Fund for Natures international programme based in Gland, Switzerland

THE WORSHIPFUL COMPANY OF FOUNDERS

The Old Estate Office, Fifty One Firle, Lewes, East Sussex, BN8 6LQ, England
Tel: (44) 01273 858700
Fax: (44) 01273 858900
Email: FoundersCompany@aol.com
Website: www.foundersco.org.uk
Contact: A.J. Gillett

Malcolm Ray Travelling Scholarship

Subjects: Materials engineering.
Purpose: To help candidates advance both personal skills and professional knowledge.
Eligibility: Open to applicants studying materials engineering and who are under the age of 28, and can put forward an imaginative and testing project outside the UK.
Level of Study: Postgraduate, Professional development
Type: Scholarship
Value: UK £3,000
Frequency: Every 2 years
No. of awards offered: 1
Closing Date: April 20th
Funding: Trusts
Contributor: Malcolm Ray Travelling Scholarship
No. of awards given last year: 2

THE WORSHIPFUL COMPANY OF MUSICIANS

6th Floor, 2 London Wall Buildings, London, EC2M 5PP, England
Tel: (44) 20 7496 8980
Fax: (44) 20 7588 3633
Email: clerk@wcom.org.uk
Website: www.wcom.org.uk
Contact: Ms Margaret Alford, Clerk

The Worshipful Company of Musicians supports young musicians particularly in the wilderness years between graduating and setting out on their musical careers.

Allcard Grants

Subjects: Music.
Purpose: To support the advanced training of performers at home or abroad for string, voice or piano accompanists, and wind instruments in exceptional circumstances.
Eligibility: Open to individuals wishing to undertake a relevant training or research programme. The grants are not available for courses leading either to a first degree at a university or to a diploma at a college of music, and only in exceptional circumstances will assistance towards the cost of a 4th or 5th year at a college of music be considered. Grants are not available towards the purchase of instruments. Applicants must have studied at a British institution for at least 3 years.
Level of Study: Postgraduate
Type: Grant
Value: Up to UK £3,000
Frequency: Annual
Country of Study: Any country
No. of awards offered: A limited number
Application Procedure: Applicants must be nominated by principals or heads of music departments at the Royal Academy of Music, the Royal College of Music, the Guildhall School of Music, the Royal Northern College of Music, the Royal Scottish Academy of Music, the Welsh College of Music, the Birmingham Conservatoire, the Trinity College of Music, City University, Huddersfield University, Goldsmiths or other university departments.
Closing Date: Applications are to be made after January 1st and before April 30th
No. of awards given last year: 4
No. of applicants last year: 30

Carnwath Scholarship

Subjects: Music.
Purpose: To support young pianists.
Eligibility: Open to any person permanently resident in the United Kingdom and 21–25 years of age. The scholarship is intended only for the advanced student who has successfully completed a solo performance course at a college of music.
Level of Study: Postgraduate
Type: Scholarship
Value: UK £4,150 per year
Length of Study: Up to 2 years
Frequency: Every 2 years
Country of Study: United Kingdom
No. of awards offered: 1
Application Procedure: Applicants must be nominated by principals of the Royal Academy of Music, the Guildhall School of Music, the Royal Northern College of Music, the Royal Scottish Academy of Music, Trinity College of Music, London College of Music, the Welsh College of Music, the Birmingham School of Music or the Royal College of Music. No application should be made directly to the Worshipful Company of Musicians.
Closing Date: June 1st in the year of the award

John Clementi Collard Fellowship

Subjects: Music.
Eligibility: Open to professional musicians of standing and experience who show excellence in one or more of the higher branches of musical activity, such as composition, research and performance including conducting.
Level of Study: Postgraduate
Type: Fellowship
Value: UK £5,000 per year
Length of Study: 1 year
Frequency: Dependent on funds available, approx. every 3 years
Country of Study: United Kingdom
No. of awards offered: 1
Application Procedure: Applicants must be nominated by professors of music at Oxford, Cambridge or London Universities, directors of the Royal College of Music, principals of the Royal Academy of Music, the Guildhall School of Music or the Royal Northern College of Music. No

application should be made directly to the Worshipful Company of Musicians.

Maisie Lewis Young Artists Fund

Subjects: Musical performance.
Purpose: To assist young artists of outstanding ability who wish to acquire experience on the professional soloist concert platform.
Eligibility: Open to instrumentalists including organists up to 28 years of age and to singers of up to 32 years of age.
Level of Study: Postgraduate
Value: Reimbursement of recitalists' expenses
Frequency: Annual
Country of Study: United Kingdom
No. of awards offered: 4–6 half recitals per year
Application Procedure: Applicants must complete an application form, available from January 1st.
No. of awards given last year: 4
No. of applicants last year: 80
Additional Information: Auditions are held in March.

THE XEROX FOUNDATION

6th Floor/PO Box 4505, 45 Glover Avenue, Norwalk, CT 06856-4505, United States of America
Tel: (1) 800 275 9376
Email: xtmsp@rballiance.com
Website: www.xerox.com
Contact: Dr Joseph M. Cahalan

Xerox Foundation is a US$15.7 billion technology and services enterprise that helps businesses deploy Smarter Document Management strategies and find better ways to work. Its intent is to constantly lead with innovative technologies, products and services that customers can depend upon to improve business results.

Xerox Technical Minority Scholarship

Subjects: Chemistry, engineering, optics, software, information management systems and physics and material science.
Purpose: To provide funding to minority students enrolled in one of the technical sciences or engineering disciplines.
Eligibility: Open to citizens of the United States or visa-holding permanent residents of African American, Asian, Pacific Island, Native American, Native Alaskan or Hispanic descent. Applicants must have grade point average of 3.0 or better.
Level of Study: Postgraduate
Type: Scholarship
Value: US$1,000–10,000 (depending on tuition balance, academic excellence and classification)
Frequency: Annual
Country of Study: United States of America
Application Procedure: Applicants must submit the completed application form along with a curriculum vitae.
Closing Date: September 15th

For further information contact:

Xerox Technical Minority Scholarship Programme office

YIVO INSTITUTE FOR JEWISH RESEARCH

15 West 16th Street, New York, NY, 10011-6301, United States of America
Tel: (1) 212 294 6139
Fax: (1) 212 292 1892
Email: pglasser@yivo.cjh.org
Website: www.yivoinstitute.org
Contact: Dr Paul Glasser, Associate Dean, Senior Research Associate

YIVO Institute for Jewish Research was founded in 1925, in Vilna, Poland as the Yiddish Scientific Institute, the YIVO Institute for Jewish Research is dedicated to the history and culture of Ashkenazi Jewry and to its influence in the Americas.

Abraham and Rachela Melezin Fellowship

Subjects: Jewish educational networks in Lithuania.
Purpose: To support doctoral and postdoctoral research on Jewish educational networks in Lithuania, with emphasis on pre-war Vilna and the Vilna region.
Level of Study: Doctorate, Postdoctorate
Type: Fellowship
Value: US$1,500
Length of Study: 1–3 months
Frequency: Annual
Study Establishment: YIVO Library and Archives
Country of Study: United States of America
Application Procedure: Applicants must send a covering letter, curriculum vitae, research proposal and 2 letters of support through regular mail, fax or email.
Closing Date: December 31st
Additional Information: A written summary of one's research is required; a public lecture is optional.

For further information contact:

Email: pglasser@yivo.cjh.org
Contact: Dr Paul Glasser

Abram and Fannie Gottlieb Immerman and Abraham Nathan and Bertha Daskal Weinstein Memorial Fellowship

Subjects: Jews of Courland and Latvia.
Purpose: To support travel for PhD dissertation research in archives and libraries of the Baltic states with preference given to research on the Jews of Courland and Latvia.
Eligibility: For those engaged in PhD dissertation research in archives and libraries of the Baltic states with preference given to research on the Jews of Courland and Latvia.
Level of Study: Doctorate
Type: Fellowship
Value: US$2,000
Frequency: Every 2 years
Application Procedure: Applicants must send a covering letter, curriculum vitae, research proposal and 2 letters of support through regular mail, fax or email.
Closing Date: December 31st

For further information contact:

Email: pglasser@yivo.cjh.org
Contact: Dr Paul Glasser

Aleksander and Alicja Hertz Memorial Fellowship

Subjects: Polish-Jewish history.
Purpose: To encourage research on Jewish-Polish relations and Jewish contributions to Polish literature and culture.
Level of Study: Postdoctorate, Doctorate
Type: Fellowship
Value: US$1,500
Length of Study: 1–3 months
Frequency: Annual
Country of Study: United States of America
Application Procedure: Applicants must send their curriculum vitae, research proposal and 2 letters of support through regular mail, fax or email.
Closing Date: December 31st

For further information contact:

Email: pglasser@yivo.cjh.org
Contact: Dr Paul Glasser, Chair Fellowship Committee

Dina Abramowicz Emerging Scholar Fellowship

Subjects: Eastern European Jewish studies.
Purpose: To support a significant scholarly publication that may encompass the revision of a doctoral dissertation.
Level of Study: Postdoctorate
Type: Fellowship
Value: US$3,000
Length of Study: 2–3 months
Frequency: Annual

Application Procedure: Applicants must send their curriculum vitae, a research proposal and 2 letters of support through regular mail, fax or email.
Closing Date: December 31st

For further information contact:

Email: pglasser@yivo.cjh.org
Contact: Dr Paul Glasser, Chair, Fellowship Committee

Dora and Mayer Tendler Fellowship

Subjects: Jewish studies.
Purpose: To support graduate research in Jewish studies with preference given to research in YIVO collections.
Eligibility: Graduate applicants must carry out original research in the field of Jewish studies and give a written summary of the research carried out.
Level of Study: Doctorate
Type: Fellowship
Value: US$3,000
Frequency: Annual
Study Establishment: YIVO collections
Country of Study: United States of America
Application Procedure: Applicants must send a covering letter, curriculum vitae, research proposal and 2 letters of support through regular mail, fax or email.
Closing Date: December 31st
Additional Information: A public lecture at the end of the tenure of the Fellowship is optional.

For further information contact:

Email: pglasser@yivo.cjh.org
Contact: Dr Paul Glasser, Chairman - Fellowship Committee

Joseph Kremen Memorial Fellowship

Subjects: Eastern European Jewish music.
Purpose: To financially assist researchers at the YIVO Archives and Library.
Level of Study: Postgraduate, Research
Type: Fellowship
Value: US$1,000
Frequency: Annual
Application Procedure: Applicants must send their curriculum vitae, research proposal and 2 letters of support by regular mail, fax or email.
Closing Date: December 31st

For further information contact:

Email: pglasser@yivo.cjh.org
Contact: Dr Paul Glasser, Chair Fellowship Committee

Maria Salit-Gitelson Tell Memorial Fellowship

Subjects: Lithuanian Jewish history.
Purpose: To support original doctoral or postdoctoral research in the field of Lithuanian Jewish history, the city of Vilnus in particular, at the YIVO Library and Archives.
Eligibility: Applicants must carry out original doctoral or postdoctoral research in the field of Lithuanian Jewish history and give a public lecture at the end of the tenure of the Fellowship.
Level of Study: Doctorate, Postdoctorate
Type: Fellowship
Value: US $1,500
Length of Study: 1–3 months
Frequency: Annual
Study Establishment: YIVO Library and Archives
Country of Study: United States of America
Application Procedure: Applicants must send a covering letter, curriculum vitae, research proposal and 2 letters of support through regular mail, fax or email.
Closing Date: December 31st

For further information contact:

Email: pglasser@yivo.cjh.org
Contact: Dr Paul Glasser, Chairman - Fellowship Committee

Natalie and Mendel Racolin Memorial Fellowship

Subjects: East European Jewish history.

Purpose: To support original doctoral or postdoctoral research in the field of East European Jewish history at the YIVO Library and Archives.
Eligibility: Applicants must carry out original doctoral or postdoctoral research in the field of East European Jewish history and give a public lecture at the end of the tenure of the Fellowship.
Level of Study: Doctorate, Postdoctorate
Type: Fellowship
Value: US$1,500
Length of Study: 1–3 months
Frequency: Annual
Study Establishment: YIVO Library and Archives
Country of Study: United States of America
Application Procedure: Applicants must send a covering letter, curriculum vitae, research proposal and 2 letters of support through regular mail, fax or email.
Closing Date: December 31st

For further information contact:

Email: pglasser@yivo.cjh.org
Contact: Dr Paul Glasser, Chairman - Fellowship Committee

Professor Bernard Choseed Memorial Fellowship

Subjects: East European Jewish studies.
Purpose: To financially support doctoral and postdoctoral students who conduct research.
Level of Study: Doctorate, Postdoctorate
Type: Fellowship
Value: US$7,500
Length of Study: 1–3 months
Frequency: Annual
Country of Study: United States of America
Application Procedure: Applicants must submit a curriculum vitae, a research proposal and 2 letters of support through regular mail, fax or email.
Closing Date: Decemeber 31st

For further information contact:

Email: pglasser@yivo.cjh.org
Contact: Dr Paul Glasser, Chair, Fellowship Committee

Rose and Isidore Drench Memorial Fellowship

Subjects: American Jewish history with a focus on Jewish labour movement.
Purpose: To encourage research in American Jewish history.
Level of Study: Doctorate, Postdoctorate
Type: Fellowship
Value: US$2,500
Length of Study: 1–3 months
Frequency: Annual
Application Procedure: Applicants must submit their curriculum vitae, a research proposal and 2 letters of support through regular mail, fax or email.
Closing Date: December 31st

For further information contact:

Email: pglasser@yivo.cjh.org
Contact: Dr Paul Glasser, Chair Fellowship Committee

Samuel and Flora Weis Research Fellowship

Subjects: Polish Jewry or Polish-Jewish relations during the Holocaust period.
Purpose: To support research on the destruction of Polish Jewry or on Polish-Jewish relations during the Holocaust period.
Eligibility: Applicants must carry out original research on the destruction of Polish Jewry or on Polish-Jewish relations during the Holocaust period and give a written summary of the research carried out. The research should result in a scholarly publication.
Level of Study: Doctorate
Type: Fellowship
Value: US$2,500
Frequency: Annual

Application Procedure: Applicants must send a covering letter, curriculum vitae, research proposal and 2 letters of support through regular mail, fax or email.
Closing Date: December 31st
Additional Information: A public lecture at the end of the tenure of the Fellowship is optional.

For further information contact:

Email: pglasse@yivo.cjh.org
Contact: Dr Paul Glasser, Chairman - Fellowship Committee

Vivian Lefsky Hort Memorial Fellowship
Subjects: Yiddish literature.
Purpose: To support original doctoral or postdoctoral research in the field of Yiddish literature.
Eligibility: Applicants must carry out original doctoral or postdoctoral research in Yiddish literature and give a public lecture at the end of the tenure of the Fellowship.
Level of Study: Doctorate, Postdoctorate
Type: Fellowship
Value: US $2,000
Length of Study: 1–3 months
Frequency: Annual
Study Establishment: YIVO Library and Archives
Country of Study: United States of America
Application Procedure: Applicants must send a covering letter, curriculum vitae, research proposal and 2 letters of support through regular mail, fax or email.
Closing Date: December 31st

For further information contact:

Email: pglasser@yivo.cjh.org
Contact: Dr Paul Glasser

Vladimir and Pearl Heifetz Memorial Fellowship in Eastern European Jewish Music
Subjects: Eastern European Jewish Music.
Purpose: To assist undergraduate, graduate and postgraduate researchers defray expenses connected with research in YIVO's music collection at the YIVO Archives and Library.
Eligibility: Undergraduate, graduate and postgraduate researchers who will carry on research in YIVO's music collection at the YIVO Archives and Library.
Level of Study: Graduate, Postgraduate
Type: Fellowship
Value: US$1,500
Frequency: Annual
Study Establishment: YIVO's music collection
Country of Study: United States of America
Application Procedure: Applicants must send a covering letter, curriculum vitae, research proposal and 2 letters of support through regular mail, fax or email.
Closing Date: December 31st
Funding: Foundation
Additional Information: A written summary of one's research is required; a public lecture is optional.

For further information contact:

Email: pglasser@yivo.cjh.org
Contact: Dr Paul Glasser, Chaiman-Fellowship Committee

Workmen's Circle/Dr Emanuel Patt Visiting Professorship
Subjects: Eastern European Jewish Studies.
Purpose: To support postdoctoral research at the YIVO Library and Archives.
Level of Study: Postdoctorate
Type: Fellowship
Value: US$5,000
Length of Study: 3 months
Frequency: Annual
Study Establishment: YIVO Library and Archives
Country of Study: United States of America
Application Procedure: Applicants must send a covering letter, curriculum vitae, research proposal and 2 letters of support through regular mail, fax or email.

Closing Date: December 31st
Additional Information: The visiting faculty member should give a public lecture at the end of the award's tenure.

For further information contact:

Email: pglasser@yivo.cjh.org
Contact: Dr Paul Glasser

YONSEI UNIVERSITY

134 Sinchon-dong, Seodaemun-gu, Seoul, 120-749, Korea
Tel: (82) 2 212 33291-4
Fax: (82) 2 392 3321
Email: gsis@yonsei.ac.kr
Website: www.yonsci.ac.kr/yu/eng/contact.html
Contact: Seung Hyun Kim, Admissions Officer

Yonsei University offers Master's and PhD programmes in English.

Hwa Am Scholarship
Subjects: All subjects.
Purpose: To financially assist students.
Eligibility: Students with promise in the field of international co-operation are eligible to apply.
Level of Study: Postgraduate
Type: Scholarship
Value: Approx. US$2000, up to US$4000
Length of Study: 1 semester
Frequency: Each semester
Study Establishment: GSIS
Country of Study: Korea
No. of awards offered: 2–3
Application Procedure: Applicants are selected by the GSIS.
Closing Date: The end of May for Autumn entry and the end of November for Spring entry
Funding: Private
Contributor: Korean Air
No. of applicants last year: 2

International Students Award
Subjects: All subjects.
Purpose: To financially assist students.
Eligibility: Open to incoming students from respective continents with good academic records and in need of financial support.
Type: Award
Value: US$770–3,077
Length of Study: 1 semester
Frequency: Each semester
Study Establishment: GSIS
Country of Study: Korea
No. of awards offered: 2–3 from each continent
Application Procedure: Applicants must complete an application form which can be found on the Yonsei GSIS homepage at gsis.yonsei.ac.kr/html/content.asp?code=004002002.
Closing Date: The end of May for Autumn entry
Funding: Private
No. of awards given last year: 3

Korea Foundation Fellowship
Subjects: Korean studies.
Purpose: To financially assist foreign students specializing in Korean studies.
Eligibility: Korean nationals are not eligible to apply.
Level of Study: Doctorate, Postgraduate
Type: Fellowship
Value: US$2,000 per semester
Length of Study: 1 year
Frequency: Annual, Applications reviewed each spring
Study Establishment: GSIS
Country of Study: Korea
No. of awards offered: 3–5
Application Procedure: Applicants must complete an application form which can be found on the Korea Foundation homepage at www.kf.or.kr

Closing Date: The end of May for Autumn entry and the end of November for Spring entry
Funding: Private
Contributor: Korean Foundation

Korea-Japan Cultural Association Scholarship
Subjects: All subjects.
Purpose: To financially assist students.
Eligibility: Open to Japanese students with good academic records.
Level of Study: Doctorate, Postgraduate
Type: Scholarship
Value: US$1,347
Length of Study: 1 semester
Frequency: Each semester
Study Establishment: GSIS
Country of Study: Korea
No. of awards offered: 1–2
Application Procedure: Applicants are selected by KJCAS.
Closing Date: The end of May for Autumn entry and the end of November for Spring entry
Funding: Private
No. of awards given last year: 1

POSCO Asia Fellowship at Yonsei GSIS
Subjects: Any subject.
Purpose: To encourage students who pursue a Master's degree at the Graduate School of International Studies (GSIS) at Yonsei University.
Eligibility: A Bachelor's degree or an equivalent degree.
Level of Study: Postgraduate
Type: Fellowship
Value: Tuition fee of US $9,600 with monthly stipend of US $950
Length of Study: 2 years
Study Establishment: Yonsei University GSIS
Country of Study: Korea
Application Procedure: Please refer to GSIS website http://gsis.yonsei.ac.kr
Closing Date: May 15th

Underwood Fellowship
Subjects: All subjects.
Purpose: To financially assist students with a high grade point average and a commitment to good citizenship.
Eligibility: Korean nationals and continuing international students with a high GPA and commitment to good citizenship are eligible to apply.
Level of Study: Postgraduate
Type: Fellowship
Value: Approx. US$1,670
Length of Study: 1 semester
Frequency: Each semester
Study Establishment: GSIS
Country of Study: Korea
No. of awards offered: 3–4
Application Procedure: Applicants must complete an application form.
Closing Date: The end of May for Autumn entry and the end of November for Spring entry
Funding: Private
Contributor: CBOL Corporation

Yonsei University Incoming Students Award
Subjects: All subjects.
Purpose: To financially assist students.
Eligibility: Incoming students who show outstanding academic potential.
Level of Study: Doctorate, Postgraduate
Value: Up to full tuition scholarship (only for first semester)
Length of Study: 1 semester
Frequency: Every semester
Study Establishment: GSIS
Country of Study: Korea
No. of awards offered: Up to 10
Application Procedure: Applicants are selected by the GSIS.
Closing Date: The end of May for Autumn entry
Funding: Private
No. of awards given last year: 12

YORKSHIRE SCULPTURE PARK

Bretton Hall, West Bretton, Wakefield, Yorkshire, WF4 4LG, England
Tel: (44) 19 2483 0579
Fax: (44) 19 2480 0044
Email: info@ysp.co.uk
Website: www.ysp.co.uk
Contact: Mr Peter Murray, Administrator

Yorkshire Sculpture Park is one of Europe's leading open-air art organizations, showing modern and contemporary work by leading United Kingdom and international artists.

Feiweles Trust Bursary
Subjects: Dance, music, art, sculpture.
Purpose: To support an artist at the beginning of his or her career, after training.
Level of Study: Postgraduate
Type: Bursary
Value: UK £10,000
Length of Study: 3 months
Frequency: Annual
Study Establishment: Workshops within the community
Country of Study: United Kingdom
Application Procedure: Applicants must send a letter, explaining exactly how the bursary would benefit the development of their career and a full curriculum vitae.
Closing Date: February 20th
Funding: Private
Contributor: Feiweles Trust
Additional Information: It is expected that the appointed artists will use this bursary experience to develop their own artistic practice. A different art form is supported each year.

YORKVILLE UNIVERSITY

1149 Smythe Street, Fredericton, NB, E3B-3H4, Canada
Tel: (1) 506 454 1220
Fax: (1) 506 454 1221
Email: info@yorkvilleu.ca
Website: www.yorkvilleu.ca

Yorkville University, established in 2003 in Fredericton, New Brunswick, is private and non-denominational, specializing in practice-oriented graduate level academic programmes.

Jacob Markovitz Memorial Scholarship
Subjects: Counselling psychology.
Purpose: To support graduate students in the helping professions at a number of academic institutions.
Eligibility: Open to all students with Canadian citizenship or with landed immigrant status in Canada who are registered in a programme at the Yorkville University. Only first time applicants are eligible to apply.
Level of Study: Postgraduate
Type: Scholarship
Value: 50 per cent of first year tuition
Frequency: Annual
Study Establishment: Yorkville University
Country of Study: Canada
No. of awards offered: 2–4
Closing Date: November 24th
Funding: Trusts
Contributor: Jacob Markovitz Memorial Scholarship Fund
Additional Information: If granted a scholarship one must maintain a 3.0 average in each trimester for the duration of the scholarship grant.

YOSHIDA SCHOLARSHIP FOUNDATION

3-22-1 Kamezawa, Sumida-ku, Tokyo, 130-8521, Japan
Fax: (81) 81 3 5610 8104
Email: webmaster@ysf.or.jp
Website: www.ysf.or.jp/en/indexe.html

The Yoshida Scholarship Foundation was founded through the advocacy of the late Mr. Tadao Yoshida. It aims to contribute to society by financially assisting and providing students of excellent nature with equal opportunities of education.

Yoshida Scholarship

Subjects: Natural science or engineering except medical, dental, and veterinary.
Eligibility: Open to candidates under 30 years for Master degree and under 35 years for Doctor's degree course.
Level of Study: Doctorate, Postgraduate
Type: Scholarship
Value: Stipend (¥150,000), matriculation fee and tuition fee (¥2,500,000), housing allowance–large city (¥40,000), other city (¥20,000)–family allowance (¥20,000) and travel expenses
Length of Study: Master degree – 2 years and doctor degree – 3 years
Frequency: Annual
Country of Study: Japan
No. of awards offered: 7
Application Procedure: Applicants are required to be admitted by one of the following universities and receive recommendation: University of Tokyo, Tokyo Institute of Technology, Keio University, Waseda University, Kyoto University, Doshisha University and Kwansei Gakuin University.
Contributor: Yoshida Scholarship Foundation
No. of applicants last year: 7
Additional Information: 1 student each year will be recommended by the 7 universities.

ZAMI INC

PO Box 2502, Decatur, GA, 30031, United States of America
Tel: (1) 404 370 0920
Email: audrelordescholarship@zami.org
Website: www.zami.org

ZAMI Inc. is a non-profit collective for gay and lesbians of African descent residing in the Atlanta Metropolitan area. ZAMI's primary mission is to empower and affirm the lives of lesbians of African descent through scholarships, leadership development, support discussion groups, social activities, drum performances, outreach and education. The organization also provides a forum and affirming space for the voices of lesbian writers of colour.

Audre Lorde Scholarship Fund

Subjects: All subject.
Purpose: To recognize lesbian and gay men of colour who are making significant contributions to their communities.
Eligibility: Open to lesbian or gay men of colour who are graduates from the United States. Lesbians and gay men who are 40 years of age are also strongly encouraged to apply.
Level of Study: Graduate, Postgraduate
Type: Scholarships

Value: US$1,000
Frequency: Annual
Country of Study: United States of America
No. of awards offered: 13
Application Procedure: Application forms can be downloaded from the website.
Closing Date: May 1st

ZONTA INTERNATIONAL FOUNDATION

557 West Randolph Street, Chicago, IL, 60661 2202, United States of America
Tel: (1) 312 930 5848
Fax: (1) 312 930 0951
Email: aubides@zonta.org
Website: www.zonta.org
Tel: 190200 UT
Contact: Ms Ana L Ubides, Programme Co-ordinator

The Foundation is a worldwide service organization of executives in business and the professions working together to advance the status of women. The Amelia Earhart Fellowship was established in 1938 in honour of Amelia Earhart, famed pilot and member of Zonta International.

Zonta Amelia Earhart Fellowships

Subjects: Aerospace-related sciences and aerospace-related engineering.
Purpose: The Fellowships are granted to women pursuing PhD/Doctoral degrees in aerospace related sciences and engineering.
Eligibility: Open to women of any nationality who demonstrate a superior academic record in the field of aerospace-related sciences and engineering.
Level of Study: Doctorate
Type: Fellowship
Value: US$10,000
Frequency: Annual
Study Establishment: Any University
No. of awards offered: Approx. 35
Application Procedure: The Zonta International Amelia Earhart Fellowship committee reviews and recommends recipients to the Zonta International Board of Directors. All applicants will be notified of their status by the end of April.
Closing Date: November 15th
Funding: Foundation
No. of awards given last year: 35
No. of applicants last year: 97
Additional Information: Recipients are not permitted to defer the Fellowship although Zonta will consider a new application the following year.

SUBJECT AND ELIGIBILITY GUIDE TO AWARDS

AGRICULTURE, FORESTRY AND FISHERY

General
Agronomy
Animal husbandry and animal production
  Sericulture
Horticulture and viticulture
Crop husbandry and crop production
Agriculture and farm management
Agricultural economics
Food science and production
  Meat and poultry
  Dairy
  Fish
  Oenology
  Brewing
  Harvest technology
Soil and water science
  Water management
  Soil conservation
Veterinary medicine
Tropical/Sub-tropical agriculture
Forestry
  Forest soils
  Forest biology
  Forest pathology
  Forest products
  Forest economics
  Forest management
Fishery
  Aquaculture

ARCHITECTURE AND TOWN PLANNING

General
Structural architecture
Architectural restoration
Environmental design
Landscape architecture
Town and community planning
Regional planning

ARTS AND HUMANITIES

General
Interpretation and translation
Writing (authorship)
Native language and literature
Modern languages and literatures
  English
  French
  Spanish
  Germanic languages
  German
  Swedish
  Danish
  Norwegian
  Italian
  Portuguese
  Romance languages
  Modern Greek
  Dutch
  Baltic languages
  Celtic languages
  Finnish
  Russian
  Slavonic languages (others)
  Hungarian
  Fino Ugrian languages
  European languages (others)
  Altaic languages
  Arabic
  Hebrew

Chinese
Korean
Japanese
Indian languages
Iranic languages
African Languages
Amerindian languages
Austronesian and oceanic languages
Classical languages and literatures
  Latin
  Classical Greek
  Sanskrit
Linguistics and philology
  Applied linguistics
  Psycholinguistics
  Grammar
  Semantics and terminology
  Phonetics
  Logopedics
Comparative literature
History
  Prehistory
  Ancient civilisations
  Medieval history
  Modern history
  Contemporary history
Archaeology
Philosophy
  Philosophical schools
  Metaphysics
  Logic
  Ethics

BUSINESS ADMINISTRATION AND MANAGEMENT

General
Business studies
International business
Secretarial studies
Business machine operation
Business computing
Management systems and techniques
Accountancy
Real estate
Marketing and sales management
Insurance management
Finance, banking and investment
Personnel management
Labour/industrial relations
Public administration
Institutional administration
MBA

EDUCATION AND TEACHER TRAINING

General
Nonvocational subjects education
  Education in native language
  Foreign languages education
  Mathematics education
  Science education
  Humanities and social science education
  Physical education
  Literacy education
Vocational subjects education
  Agricultural education
  Art education
  Commerce/business education
  Computer education

Technology education
Health education
Home economics education
Industrial arts education
Music education
Pre-school education
Primary education
Secondary education
Adult education
Special education
  Education of the gifted
  Education of the handicapped
  Education of specific learning disabilities
  Education of foreigners
  Education of natives
  Education of the socially disadvantaged
  Bilingual/bicultural education
Teacher trainers education
Higher education teacher training
Educational science
  International and comparative education
  Philosophy of education
  Curriculum
  Teaching and learning
  Educational research
  Educational technology
  Educational and student counselling
  Educational administration
  Educational testing and evaluation
  Distance education

ENGINEERING

General
Surveying and mapping science
Engineering drawing/design
Chemical engineering
Civil, construction and transportation engineering
Environmental and Sanitary Engineering
Safety engineering
Electrical/electronic and telecommunications engineering
Computer engineering
Industrial and management engineering
Metallurgical engineering
Production engineering
Materials engineering
Mining and minerals engineering
Petroleum engineering
Energy engineering
Nuclear engineering
Mechanical/electromechanical engineering
Hydraulic/pneumatic engineering
Sound engineering
Automotive engineering
Measurement/precision engineering
Control engineering (robotics)
Aeronautical and aerospace engineering
Marine engineering and naval architecture
Agricultural engineering

Forestry engineering
Bioengineering and biomedical engineering

FINE AND APPLIED ARTS

General
History and Philosophy of Art
  Aesthetics
Art management
Drawing and painting
Sculpture
Handicrafts
Music
  Musicology
  Music theory and composition
  Conducting
  Singing
  Musical instruments (performance)
  Religious music
  Jazz and popular music
  Opera
Drama
Dancing
Photography
Cinema and television
Design
  Interior design
  Furniture design
  Fashion design
  Textile design
  Graphic design
  Industrial design
  Display and stage design

HOME ECONOMICS

General
Household management
Clothing and sewing
Nutrition
Child care/child development
House arts and environment

LAW

General
History of law
Comparative law
International law
Human rights
Labour law
Maritime law
Law of the air
Notary studies
Civil law
Commercial law
Public law
  Constitutional law
  Administrative law
  Fiscal law
Criminal law
Canon law
Islamic law
European community law

MASS COMMUNICATION AND INFORMATION SCIENCE

General
Journalism
Radio/television broadcasting
Public relations and publicity

Mass communication
Media studies
Communications skills
Library science
Museum studies and
  conservation
Museum management
Restoration of works of art
Documentation techniques and
  archiving

MATHEMATICS AND COMPUTER SCIENCE

General
Statistics
Actuarial science
Applied mathematics
Computer science
Artificial intelligence
Systems analysis

MEDICAL SCIENCES

General
Public health and hygiene
  Social/preventive medicine
  Dietetics
  Sports medicine
Health administration
Medicine and surgery
  Anaesthesiology
  Cardiology
  Dermatology
  Endocrinology
  Epidemiology
  Gastroenterology
  Geriatrics
  Gynaecology and obstetrics
  Haematology
  Hepathology
  Nephrology
  Neurology
  Oncology
  Ophthalmology
  Otorhinolaryngology
  Parasitology
  Pathology
  Paediatrics
  Plastic surgery
  Pneumology
  Psychiatry and mental health
  Rheumatology
  Urology
  Virology
  Tropical medicine
  Venereology
Rehabilitation medicine and
  therapy
Nursing
Medical auxiliaries
Midwifery
Radiology
Treatment techniques
Medical technology
Dentistry and stomatology
  Oral pathology
  Orthodontics
  Periodontics
  Community dentistry
Dental technology
  Prosthetic dentistry
Pharmacy
Biomedicine
Optometry

Podiatry
Forensic medicine and dentistry
Acupuncture
Homeopathy
Chiropractic
Osteopathy
Traditional eastern medicine

NATURAL SCIENCES

General
Biological and life sciences
  Anatomy
  Biochemistry
  Biology
  Histology
  Biophysics and molecular biology
  Biotechnology
  Botany
  Plant pathology
  Embryology and reproduction
    biology
  Genetics
  Immunology
  Marine biology
  Limnology
  Microbiology
  Neurosciences
  Parasitology
  Pharmacology
  Physiology
  Toxicology
  Zoology
Chemistry
  Analytical chemistry
  Inorganic chemistry
  Organic chemistry
  Physical chemistry
Earth and geological sciences
  Geochemistry
  Geography (Scientific)
  Geology
  Mineralogy and crystallography
  Petrology
  Geophysics and seismology
  Palaeontology
Physics
  Atomic and molecular physics
  Nuclear physics
  Optics
  Solid state physics
  Thermal physics
Astronomy and astrophysics
Atmosphere science/
  meteorology
  Arctic studies
  Arid land studies
Oceanography

RECREATION, WELFARE, PROTECTIVE SERVICES

General
Police and law enforcement
Criminology
Fire protection/control
Military science
Civil security
Peace and disarmament
Social welfare and social work
  Public and community services
Vocational counselling
Environmental studies
  Ecology
  Natural resources
  Environmental management
  Wildlife and pest management

Physical education and sports
  Sports management
  Sociology of sports
Leisure studies
Parks and recreation

RELIGION AND THEOLOGY

General
Religious studies
  Christian
  Jewish
  Islam
  Asian religious studies
  Agnosticism and Atheism
  Ancient religions
Religious education
Holy writings
Religious practice
Church administration (pastoral
  work)
Theological studies
Comparative religion
Sociology of religion
History of religion
Esoteric practices

SERVICE TRADES

General
Hotel and restaurant
Hotel management
Cooking and catering
Retailing
Tourism

SOCIAL AND BEHAVIOURAL SCIENCES

General
  Economics
  Economic history
  Economic and finance policy
  Taxation
  Econometrics
  Industrial and production
    economics
Political science and
  government
  Comparative politics
International relations
Sociology
  History of societies
  Comparative sociology
  Social policy
  Social institutions
  Social communication problems
  Futurology
Demography
Anthropology
  Ethnology
  Folklore
Women's studies
Urban Studies
Rural studies
Cognitive sciences
Psychology
  Experimental psychology
  Social and community psychology
  Clinical psychology
  Personality psychology
  Industrial/organisational psychology

Psychometrics
Educational psychology
Geography (social and
  economic)
Development studies
Area and cultural studies
  North African
  Subsahara African
  African studies
  African American
  Native American
  Hispanic American
  American
  Canadian
  Asian
  South Asian
  East Asian
  Southeast Asian
  European (EC)
  Eastern European
  Western European
  Nordic
  Caribbean
  Latin American
  Pacific area
  Aboriginal
  Middle Eastern
  Islamic
  Jewish
Preservation of cultural
  heritage
Ancient civilisations
  (Egyptology, Assyriology)

TRADE, CRAFT AND INDUSTRIAL TECHNIQUES

General
Food processing techniques
Building trades
Electrical/electronic
  equipment and maintenance
  techniques
Metal trades techniques
Mechanical equipment and
  maintenance techniques
Wood technology
Heating, air conditioning and
  refrigeration technology
Leather techniques
Textile techniques
Paper and packaging
  technology
Graphic arts techniques
  Printing
  Publishing and book trade
Laboratory techniques
Optical technology

TRANSPORT AND COMMUNICATIONS

General
Air transport
Marine transport and nautical
  science
Railway transport
Road transport
Transport management
Transport economics
Postal services
Telecommunications services

ANY SUBJECT

ANY SUBJECT

Any Country

A E Hills Scholarship 668
A E Robert Friedman PDCA Scholarship 519
AAH Visiting Scholar Programmes 132
Adelphi University Athletic Grants 7
Adelphi University Dean's Award 7
Adelphi University Presidential Scholarship 7
Adelphi University Provost Scholarship 7
Adelphi University Trustee Scholarship 8
AFFDU Grants 163
AFUW Australian Capital Territory Bursary 164
AFUW Georgina Sweet Fellowship 164
AFUW Western Australian Bursaries 164
AFUW William and Elizabeth Fisher Scholarship 134
Alexander Graham Bell Scholarship Awards 14
Alumni Tuition Fee Discount 505
Anglo-Jewish Association Bursary 101
Anning Morgan Bursary 690
ANU Doctoral Fellowships 137
ANU Graduate School Scholarships 137
ANU PhD Scholarships 137
Arthington Davy Scholarship 663
ASFDU/SVA International Fellowship 164
AUC Arabic Language Fellowships 96
BFWG Funds for Women Graduates–Charitable Foundation Grants
and Emergency Grants 290
BFWG Scholarships 166
British Council Awards and Scholarships for International Students
690
British Federation Crosby Hall Fellowship 381
British Federation of Women Graduates (BFWG) 693
Burkey Family Memorial Scholarship 446
Caledonian Scholarship 181
Carnegie Grants 219
Carnegie Scholarships 219
Celgene/Hsanz Educational Grants 329
China-Canada Scholars Exchange Program 756
Commonwealth Scholarships 242
The Conservation Guest Scholar Program 316
Cornwall Heritage Trust Bursary 691
David Myers Research Scholarship 413
David Phillips Fellowships 151
Descendants of the Signers of the Declaration of Independence
Scholarships 265
DFG Mercator Programme Guest Professorships 266
DFG Priority Programme Funds 266
DFG Research Training Grant 266
Diamond Jubilee Bursary 134
Doreen McCarthy, Barbara Crase, Cathy Candler and Brenda Nettle
Bursaries 134
Dorothy Hodgkin Postgraduate Awards 694
Dorothy Leet Grants 382
Elise Richter Program 142
Endeavour International Postgraduate Research Scholarship (IPRS)
752
EURYI–Award 142
Falconer Madan Award 150
Friedrich Wilhelm Bessel Research Award 16
Fulbright Hays Doctoral Dissertation Research Abroad Program 779
GET Grants 318
Gowrie Research Scholarship 258
Graduate UCL Research Scholarship 651
Griffith University Postgraduate Research Scholarships 326
Gypsy Lore Society Young Scholar's Prize in Romani Studies 328
Hayek Fund for Scholars 363
Heather Latz Bursary 135
Heinrich Böll Foundation Doctoral Scholarships 337
Heinrich Böll Foundation Scholarships for Postgraduate Studies 337
Heinz Maier–Leibnitz Prize 267
Herbert Hughes Scholarship 768

Hott Fellowship Awards 329
The Howard Research Studentship 586
Humboldt Research Award 17
Humboldt Research Fellowships for Postdoctoral Researchers 18
Hwa Am Scholarship 809
IBM PhD Fellowship Program 350
Ida Smedley MacLean Fellowship 382
IFUWA Amy Rustomjee International Scholarship 166
International Postgraduate Research Scholarship 667
International Students Award 809
Izaak Walton Killam Memorial Scholarships 662
Izaak Walton Killam Memorial Scholarships 662
Izaak Walton Killam Postdoctoral Fellowships 672
Jack Kent Cooke Scholarship 396
James Cook University Postgraduate Research Scholarship 397
Japanese Grant Aid for Human Resource Development Scholarship
391
JAUW International Fellowship 167
Jean Gilmore, Thenie Baddams and Daphne Elliott Bursary 135
Jennings Randolph Program for International Peace Dissertation
Fellowship 643
John W O'Brien Graduate Fellowship 244
Josephine De Kármán Fellowships 406
JSPS Postdoctoral Fellowships for Foreign Researchers 399
L B Wood Travelling Scholarship 501
Lee Kong Chian Graduate Scholarships 491
Leverhulme Trust Emeritus Fellowships 420
Leverhulme Trust Research Fellowships 420
Leverhulme Trust Study Abroad Studentships 420
Library Research Grants 316
Lise Meitner Program 142
Lord Rootes Memorial Fund 771
Mac Robertson Travelling Scholarship 760
Margaret Yardley Fellowship 497
Marquette University Graduate Assistantship 434
Marquette University Women's Club Fellowship
Max Planck Research Award 18
Melbourne International Fee Remission Scholarships 708
Melbourne Research Scholarships 708
Memorial Fund of May 8th 1970 508
Michigan Society of Fellows Postdoctoral Fellowships 448
Missouri State University Graduate Assistantships 451
Monash Graduate Scholarship 455
Moscow University Touro Corporate Scholarships 458
Moscow University Touro Universal Scholarships 458
Mr and Mrs Spencer T Olin Fellowships for Women 791
mtvU Point Scholarship 534
National University of Singapore Research Scholarships 492
Netherlands Fellowship Programme 271
New Zealand Development Scholarships (NZDS) 499
New Zealand Postgraduate Study Abroad Award (NZPSAA) 275
Newby Trust Awards 505
NKA Ellen Gleditsch Scholarship 167
NZ Development Scholarship – Public Category 664
NZ International Doctoral Research (NZIDRS) Scholarship 664
NZAID Development Scholarship (NZDS) – Open Category 664
Onassis Foreigners' Fellowship Programme Educational Scholarships
Category C 15
Onassis Foreigners' Fellowships Programme Research Grants
Category AII 15
Overseas Field Trip Grant 295
Peel Studentship Trust Award 415
Pembroke Center Post-Doctoral Fellowships 523
Phi Theta Kappa International Summit Scholarships 592
The Point Scholarship 534
Professorial Fellowships 152
Quintin Hogg PhD Scholarships 778
Radcliffe Institute for Advanced Study Fellowship Programme 540
Research Development Fellowships 152
RHYS Curzon-Jones Scholarship 768
Ridley Lewis Bursary 769
Rotary Ambassadorial Scholar Program 551
Rotary Foundation Academic Year Ambassadorial Scholarships 551
Rotary Foundation Multi-Year Ambassadorial Scholarships 552
Rotary Grants for University Teachers 552
Rotary Yoneyama Scholarship 553

African Nations

Australia

Canada

Caribbean Countries

East European Countries

European Union

Middle East

New Zealand

West European Countries

AGRICULTURE, FORESTRY AND FISHERY

GENERAL

Any Country

African Nations

Australia

Alexander Hugh Thurland Scholarship 763
CRC Spatial Information PhD Scholarship 711
Fulbright Postdoctoral Fellowships 140
Fulbright Postgraduate Awards 140
GRDC Grains Industry Research Scholarships 323
GRDC In-Service Training 324
GRDC Industry Development Awards 324
GRDC Senior Fellowships 324
MINTRAC Postgraduate Scholarship 451
R.N. Hammon Scholarship 753
Victoria Fellowships 264
Wingate Scholarships 697

Canada

Canadian Window on International Development 380
IDRC Doctoral Research Awards 380
NSERC Postdoctoral Fellowships 495
Olin Fellowship 125
Wingate Scholarships 697

Caribbean Countries

Canadian Window on International Development 380
CAS-TWAS Fellowship for Postdoctoral Research in China 629
CAS-TWAS Fellowship for Postgraduate Research in China 629
CAS-TWAS Fellowship for Visiting Scholars in China 629
CNPq-TWAS Doctoral Fellowships in Brazil 630
CNPq-TWAS Fellowships for Postdoctoral Research in Brazil 630
CSIR (Council of Scientific and Industrial Research)/TWAS Fellowship for Postgraduate Research 630
CSIR (The Council of Scientific and Industrial Research)/TWAS Fellowship for Postdoctoral Research 630
IDRC Doctoral Research Awards 380
IFS Research Grants 382
TWAS Fellowships for Research and Advanced Training 631
TWAS Grants for Scientific Meetings in Developing Countries 631
TWAS Prizes 632
TWAS Prizes to Young Scientists in Developing Countries 632
TWAS Research Grants 632
TWAS Spare Parts for Scientific Equipment 632
TWAS UNESCO Associateship Scheme 632

East European Countries

IDRC Doctoral Research Awards 380

European Union

Sir William Roberts Scholarship 146
Wingate Scholarships 697

Middle East

ABCCF Student Grant 102
CAS-TWAS Fellowship for Postdoctoral Research in China 629
CAS-TWAS Fellowship for Postgraduate Research in China 629
CAS-TWAS Fellowship for Visiting Scholars in China 629
CNPq-TWAS Doctoral Fellowships in Brazil 630
CNPq-TWAS Fellowships for Postdoctoral Research in Brazil 630
CSIR (Council of Scientific and Industrial Research)/TWAS Fellowship for Postgraduate Research 630
CSIR (The Council of Scientific and Industrial Research)/TWAS Fellowship for Postdoctoral Research 630
IDRC Doctoral Research Awards 380
IFS Research Grants 382
NUFFIC-NFP Fellowships for Master's Degree Programmes 496
The Trieste Science Prize 631
TWAS Fellowships for Research and Advanced Training 631
TWAS Grants for Scientific Meetings in Developing Countries 631
TWAS Prizes 632
TWAS Prizes to Young Scientists in Developing Countries 632
TWAS Research Grants 632
TWAS Spare Parts for Scientific Equipment 632
TWAS UNESCO Associateship Scheme 632

New Zealand

Alexander Hugh Thurland Scholarship 763
C. Alma Baker Postgraduate Scholarship 436
Vernon Willey Trust Awards 785
Wingate Scholarships 697

South Africa

Canadian Window on International Development 380
CAS-TWAS Fellowship for Postdoctoral Research in China 629
CAS-TWAS Fellowship for Postgraduate Research in China 629
CAS-TWAS Fellowship for Visiting Scholars in China 629
CNPq-TWAS Doctoral Fellowships in Brazil 630
CNPq-TWAS Fellowships for Postdoctoral Research in Brazil 630
CSIR (Council of Scientific and Industrial Research)/TWAS Fellowship for Postgraduate Research 630
CSIR (The Council of Scientific and Industrial Research)/TWAS Fellowship for Postdoctoral Research 630
IDRC Doctoral Research Awards 380
IFS Research Grants 382
NUFFIC-NFP Fellowships for Master's Degree Programmes 496
The Trieste Science Prize 631
TWAS Fellowships for Research and Advanced Training 631
TWAS Grants for Scientific Meetings in Developing Countries 631
TWAS Prizes 632
TWAS Prizes to Young Scientists in Developing Countries 632
TWAS Research Grants 632
TWAS Spare Parts for Scientific Equipment 632
TWAS UNESCO Associateship Scheme 632
Wingate Scholarships 697

United Kingdom

Aberystwyth Postgraduate Research Studentships 4
Hilda Martindale Exhibitions 341
Linacre College: A.J Hosier Studentship 732
Mr and Mrs David Edward Memorial Award 145
Neville Shulman Challenge Award 565
Sir William Roberts Scholarship 146
Wingate Scholarships 697

United States of America

Budweiser Conservation Scholarship 475
Congress Bundestag Youth Exchange for Young Professionals 221
DEED (Demonstration of Energy-Efficient Developments) Student Research Grant/Internship 80
Foundation for Science and Disability Student Grant Fund 302
Fulbright Distinguished Chairs Program 248
Norwegian Thanksgiving Fund Scholarship 509
Olin Fellowship 125

West European Countries

Mr and Mrs David Edward Memorial Award 145
Sir William Roberts Scholarship 146

AGRONOMY

Any Country

ETH Zurich Excellence Scholarship and Opportunity Award 624
Perry Postgraduate Scholarships 525
Teagasc Walsh Fellowships 626
University of Otago International Scholarships 717

African Nations

Canadian Window on International Development 380
IDRC Doctoral Research Awards 380

Australia

Wingate Scholarships 697

Canada

Canadian Window on International Development 380
CIC Montreal Medal 232
IDRC Doctoral Research Awards 380
Wingate Scholarships 697

Caribbean Countries

Canadian Window on International Development 380
IDRC Doctoral Research Awards 380

East European Countries

IDRC Doctoral Research Awards 380

European Union

Sir William Roberts Scholarship 146
Wingate Scholarships 697

Middle East

IDRC Doctoral Research Awards 380

New Zealand

Wingate Scholarships 697

South Africa

Canadian Window on International Development 380
IDRC Doctoral Research Awards 380
Wingate Scholarships 697

United Kingdom

Mr and Mrs David Edward Memorial Award 145
Perry Research Awards 525
Sir William Roberts Scholarship 146
Wingate Scholarships 697

West European Countries

Mr and Mrs David Edward Memorial Award 145
Sir William Roberts Scholarship 146

ANIMAL HUSBANDRY AND ANIMAL PRODUCTION

Any Country

ETH Zurich Excellence Scholarship and Opportunity Award 624
Perry Postgraduate Scholarships 525
PhD Scholarship in Animal Breeding 712
RSPCA Australia Alan White Scholarship for Animal Welfare Research 577
RSPCA Australia Scholarship for Humane Animal Production Research 577
Scholarship opportunities linked to CATIE's Postgraduate Program including CATIE scholarship forming part of the Scholarship-Loan Program 638
Teagasc Walsh Fellowships 626
Thesiger-Oman Research Fellowship 566
TSA Research Grant and Fellowship Program 634
UFAW Animal Welfare Research Training Scholarships 644
UFAW Research and Project Awards 645
UFAW Small Project and Travel Awards 645
UFAW Vacation Scholarships 645
University of Bristol Postgraduate Scholarships 672

African Nations

Canadian Window on International Development 380
IDRC Doctoral Research Awards 380

Australia

A S Nivison Memorial Scholarship 711
MINTRAC Postgraduate Scholarship 451
Wingate Scholarships 697

Canada

Canadian Window on International Development 380
Dairy Farmer's of Ontario Doctoral Research Assistantships 697
IDRC Doctoral Research Awards 380
Wingate Scholarships 697

Caribbean Countries

Canadian Window on International Development 380
IDRC Doctoral Research Awards 380

East European Countries

IDRC Doctoral Research Awards 380

European Union

Sir William Roberts Scholarship 146
Wingate Scholarships 697

Middle East

IDRC Doctoral Research Awards 380

New Zealand

Vernon Willey Trust Awards 785
Wingate Scholarships 697

South Africa

Canadian Window on International Development 380
IDRC Doctoral Research Awards 380
Wingate Scholarships 697

United Kingdom

Aberystwyth Postgraduate Research Studentships 4
Linacre College: A.J Hosier Studentship 732
Perry Research Awards 525
Sir William Roberts Scholarship 146
Wingate Scholarships 697

West European Countries

Sir William Roberts Scholarship 146

SERICULTURE

Any Country

Perry Postgraduate Scholarships 525

African Nations

IDRC Doctoral Research Awards 380

Australia

Wingate Scholarships 697

Canada

IDRC Doctoral Research Awards 380
Wingate Scholarships 697

Caribbean Countries

IDRC Doctoral Research Awards 380

East European Countries

IDRC Doctoral Research Awards 380

European Union

Wingate Scholarships 697

Middle East

IDRC Doctoral Research Awards 380

New Zealand

Wingate Scholarships 697

South Africa

IDRC Doctoral Research Awards 380
Wingate Scholarships 697

United Kingdom

Perry Research Awards 525
Wingate Scholarships 697

HORTICULTURE AND VITICULTURE

Any Country

Anne S. Chatham Fellowship in Medicinal Botany 451
Blaxall Valentine Trust Award 566
The Bullen Bursary 566
The Dawn Jolliffe Botanical Art Bursary 567
Grape and Wine Research and Development Corporation Honours
    Scholarships 661
Gurney Wilson Award 567
Herb Society of America Research Grant 338
HSA Grant for Educators 338
Perry Postgraduate Scholarships 525
Queen Elizabeth the Queen Mother Bursary 568
Stanley Smith (UK) Horticultural Trust Awards 618
Teagasc Walsh Fellowships 626
The William Rayner Bursary 569

African Nations

Canadian Window on International Development 380
IDRC Doctoral Research Awards 380

Australia

Wingate Scholarships 697

Canada

Canadian Window on International Development 380
Horticultural Research Institute Grants 346
IDRC Doctoral Research Awards 380
Wingate Scholarships 697

Caribbean Countries

Canadian Window on International Development 380
IDRC Doctoral Research Awards 380

East European Countries

IDRC Doctoral Research Awards 380

European Union

Sir William Roberts Scholarship 146
Wingate Scholarships 697

Middle East

IDRC Doctoral Research Awards 380

New Zealand

Wingate Scholarships 697

South Africa

Canadian Window on International Development 380
IDRC Doctoral Research Awards 380
Wingate Scholarships 697

United Kingdom

Coke Trust Awards 567
The Dawn Jolliffe Botanical Art Bursary 567
Jerusalem Botanical Gardens Scholarship 305
Jimmy Smart Memorial Bursary 567
The Martin McLaren Horticultural Interchange Scholarship 568
Martin McLaren Horticultural Scholarship 367
Osaka Travel Award 568
Perry Research Awards 525
Sir William Roberts Scholarship 146
The Susan Pearson Memorial Traineeship Bursary 569
Wingate Scholarships 697

United States of America

Budweiser Conservation Scholarship 475
Horticultural Research Institute Grants 346
The Martin McLaren Horticultural Interchange Scholarship 568

West European Countries

Sir William Roberts Scholarship 146

CROP HUSBANDRY AND CROP PRODUCTION

Any Country

Anne S. Chatham Fellowship in Medicinal Botany 451
Perry Postgraduate Scholarships 525
Teagasc Walsh Fellowships 626
University of Bristol Postgraduate Scholarships 672

African Nations

The Bentley Cropping Systems Fellowship 380
Canadian Window on International Development 380
IDRC Doctoral Research Awards 380
IFS Research Grants 382

Australia

Wingate Scholarships 697

Canada

The Bentley Cropping Systems Fellowship 380
Canadian Window on International Development 380
IDRC Doctoral Research Awards 380
Wingate Scholarships 697

Caribbean Countries

The Bentley Cropping Systems Fellowship 380
Canadian Window on International Development 380
IDRC Doctoral Research Awards 380
IFS Research Grants 382

East European Countries

The Bentley Cropping Systems Fellowship 380
IDRC Doctoral Research Awards 380

European Union

Sir William Roberts Scholarship 146
Wingate Scholarships 697

Middle East

The Bentley Cropping Systems Fellowship 380
IDRC Doctoral Research Awards 380
IFS Research Grants 382

New Zealand

Wingate Scholarships 697

South Africa

The Bentley Cropping Systems Fellowship 380
Canadian Window on International Development 380
IDRC Doctoral Research Awards 380
IFS Research Grants 382
Wingate Scholarships 697

United Kingdom

Aberystwyth Postgraduate Research Studentships 4
Linacre College: A.J Hosier Studentship 732
Martin McLaren Horticultural Scholarship 367
Mr and Mrs David Edward Memorial Award 145
Perry Research Awards 525
Sir William Roberts Scholarship 146
Wingate Scholarships 697

West European Countries

Mr and Mrs David Edward Memorial Award 145
Sir William Roberts Scholarship 146

AGRICULTURE AND FARM MANAGEMENT

Any Country

AFFDU Monique Fouet Grant 163
CRCWQT Young Water Scientist of the Year Scholarship 245
Perry Postgraduate Scholarships 525

RICS Education Trust Award 549
Teagasc Walsh Fellowships 626
University of Bristol Postgraduate Scholarships 672

African Nations

The Bentley Cropping Systems Fellowship 380
Canadian Window on International Development 380
IDRC Doctoral Research Awards 380

Australia

A S Nivison Memorial Scholarship 711
Wingate Scholarships 697

Canada

The Bentley Cropping Systems Fellowship 380
Canadian Window on International Development 380
IDRC Doctoral Research Awards 380
Wingate Scholarships 697

Caribbean Countries

The Bentley Cropping Systems Fellowship 380
Canadian Window on International Development 380
IDRC Doctoral Research Awards 380

East European Countries

The Bentley Cropping Systems Fellowship 380
IDRC Doctoral Research Awards 380

European Union

Sir William Roberts Scholarship 146
Wingate Scholarships 697

Middle East

The Bentley Cropping Systems Fellowship 380
IDRC Doctoral Research Awards 380

New Zealand

Wingate Scholarships 697

South Africa

The Bentley Cropping Systems Fellowship 380
Canadian Window on International Development 380
IDRC Doctoral Research Awards 380
Wingate Scholarships 697

United Kingdom

Aberystwyth Postgraduate Research Studentships 4
Harry Steele-Bodger Memorial Travelling Scholarship 178
Perry Research Awards 525
Sir William Roberts Scholarship 146
Wingate Scholarships 697

United States of America

Appraisal Institute Education Trust Scholarship 102
DEED (Demonstration of Energy-Efficient Developments) Student
    Research Grant/Internship 80

West European Countries

Sir William Roberts Scholarship 146

AGRICULTURAL ECONOMICS

Any Country

Gilbert F White Postdoctoral Fellowship 545
Joseph L Fisher Dissertation Award 546
Perry Postgraduate Scholarships 525
RICS Education Trust Award 549
Scholarship opportunities linked to CATIE's Postgraduate Program
    including CATIE scholarship forming part of the Scholarship-Loan
    Program 638
Teagasc Walsh Fellowships 626
University of Bristol Postgraduate Scholarships 672

African Nations

The Bentley Cropping Systems Fellowship 380
Canadian Window on International Development 380
IDRC Doctoral Research Awards 380

Australia

Wingate Scholarships 697

Canada

The Bentley Cropping Systems Fellowship 380
Canadian Window on International Development 380
Community Forestry: Trees and People-John G Bene Fellowship
    380
Horticultural Research Institute Grants 346
IDRC Doctoral Research Awards 380
Wingate Scholarships 697

Caribbean Countries

The Bentley Cropping Systems Fellowship 380
Canadian Window on International Development 380
IDRC Doctoral Research Awards 380

East European Countries

The Bentley Cropping Systems Fellowship 380
IDRC Doctoral Research Awards 380

European Union

Department of Agriculture and Rural Development (DARD) for
    Northern Ireland 253
Sir William Roberts Scholarship 146
Wingate Scholarships 697

Middle East

The Bentley Cropping Systems Fellowship 380
IDRC Doctoral Research Awards 380

New Zealand

Wingate Scholarships 697

South Africa

The Bentley Cropping Systems Fellowship 380
Canadian Window on International Development 380
IDRC Doctoral Research Awards 380
Wingate Scholarships 697

United Kingdom

Aberystwyth Postgraduate Research Studentships 4
Department of Agriculture and Rural Development (DARD) for
    Northern Ireland 253
Linacre College: A.J Hosier Studentship 732
Perry Research Awards 525
Sir William Roberts Scholarship 146
Wingate Scholarships 697

United States of America

Appraisal Institute Education Trust Scholarship 102
DEED (Demonstration of Energy-Efficient Developments) Student
    Research Grant/Internship 80
Fulbright Senior Specialists Program 249
Horticultural Research Institute Grants 346

West European Countries

Sir William Roberts Scholarship 146

FOOD SCIENCE AND PRODUCTION

Any Country

ETH Zurich Excellence Scholarship and Opportunity Award 624
IFT Graduate Fellowships 366
Marcel Loncin Research Prize 366
Perry Postgraduate Scholarships 525

Teagasc Walsh Fellowships 626
University of Bristol Postgraduate Scholarships 672

African Nations

IDRC Doctoral Research Awards 380
IFS Research Grants 382
International Postgraduate Research Scholarships (IPRS) 413

Australia

MINTRAC Postgraduate Scholarship 451
Wingate Scholarships 697

Canada

IDRC Doctoral Research Awards 380
International Postgraduate Research Scholarships (IPRS) 413
Wingate Scholarships 697

Caribbean Countries

IDRC Doctoral Research Awards 380
IFS Research Grants 382
International Postgraduate Research Scholarships (IPRS) 413

East European Countries

FEMS Fellowship 290
IDRC Doctoral Research Awards 380
International Postgraduate Research Scholarships (IPRS) 413

European Union

Sir William Roberts Scholarship 146
Wingate Scholarships 697

Middle East

IDRC Doctoral Research Awards 380
IFS Research Grants 382
International Postgraduate Research Scholarships (IPRS) 413

New Zealand

Wingate Scholarships 697

South Africa

IDRC Doctoral Research Awards 380
IFS Research Grants 382
International Postgraduate Research Scholarships (IPRS) 413
Wingate Scholarships 697

United Kingdom

FEMS Fellowship 290
International Postgraduate Research Scholarships (IPRS) 413
Perry Research Awards 525
Sir William Roberts Scholarship 146
Wingate Scholarships 697

United States of America

International Postgraduate Research Scholarships (IPRS) 413

West European Countries

FEMS Fellowship 290
International Postgraduate Research Scholarships (IPRS) 413
Sir William Roberts Scholarship 146

MEAT AND POULTRY

Any Country

Perry Postgraduate Scholarships 525
Teagasc Walsh Fellowships 626

Australia

MINTRAC Postgraduate Scholarship 451
Wingate Scholarships 697

Canada

Wingate Scholarships 697

European Union

Wingate Scholarships 697

New Zealand

Vernon Willey Trust Awards 785
Wingate Scholarships 697

South Africa

Wingate Scholarships 697

United Kingdom

Perry Research Awards 525
Wingate Scholarships 697

DAIRY

Any Country

Iager Dairy Scholarship 472
Perry Postgraduate Scholarships 525
Teagasc Walsh Fellowships 626

Australia

Wingate Scholarships 697

Canada

Dairy Farmer's of Ontario Doctoral Research Assistantships 697
Wingate Scholarships 697

European Union

Wingate Scholarships 697

New Zealand

Wingate Scholarships 697

South Africa

Wingate Scholarships 697

United Kingdom

Perry Research Awards 525
Wingate Scholarships 697

FISH

Any Country

Postgraduate Research Studentship 689

Australia

Wingate Scholarships 697

Canada

Olin Fellowship 125
Wingate Scholarships 697

European Union

Wingate Scholarships 697

New Zealand

Wingate Scholarships 697

South Africa

Wingate Scholarships 697

United Kingdom

Wingate Scholarships 697

United States of America
Olin Fellowship 125

OENOLOGY

Australia
Wingate Scholarships 697

Canada
Wingate Scholarships 697

European Union
Wingate Scholarships 697

New Zealand
Wingate Scholarships 697

South Africa
Wingate Scholarships 697

United Kingdom
Wingate Scholarships 697

BREWING

Australia
Wingate Scholarships 697

Canada
Wingate Scholarships 697

European Union
Wingate Scholarships 697

New Zealand
Wingate Scholarships 697

South Africa
Wingate Scholarships 697

United Kingdom
Wingate Scholarships 697

HARVEST TECHNOLOGY

Any Country
Perry Postgraduate Scholarships 525

Australia
Wingate Scholarships 697

Canada
Wingate Scholarships 697

European Union
Wingate Scholarships 697

New Zealand
Wingate Scholarships 697

South Africa
Wingate Scholarships 697

United Kingdom
Perry Research Awards 525
Wingate Scholarships 697

SOIL AND WATER SCIENCE

Any Country
Andrew Mellon Foundation Scholarship 547
Earthwatch Field Research Grants 272
Edmund Niles Huyck Preserve, Inc. Graduate and Postgraduate
    Grants 274
ETH Zurich Excellence Scholarship and Opportunity Award 624
Gilbert F White Postdoctoral Fellowship 545
Horton (Hydrology) Research Grant 56
Joseph L Fisher Dissertation Award 546
Lindbergh Grants 228
National Geographic Conservation Trust Grant 244
NERC Advanced Research Fellowships 493
NERC Postdoctoral Research Fellowships 494
Perry Postgraduate Scholarships 525
Rhodes University Postgraduate Scholarship 549
Scholarship opportunities linked to CATIE's Postgraduate Program
    including CATIE scholarship forming part of the Scholarship-Loan
    Program 638
SERC Postdoctoral Fellowships 596
SERC Predoctoral Fellowships 596
SERC Senior Fellowships 596
St Catherine's College Graduate Scholarship in the Arts
Teagasc Walsh Fellowships 626
Thesiger-Oman Research Fellowship 566
Utilities and Service Industries Training (USIT) 254
Victoria University of Wellington PhD Scholarships 786

African Nations
Austrian Academy of Sciences, MSc Course in Limnology and
    Wetland Ecosystems 141
Canadian Window on International Development 380
IDRC Doctoral Research Awards 380
International Postgraduate Research Scholarships (IPRS) 413
Master Studies in Physical Land Resources Scholarship 379
School of Applied Sciences Overseas Scholarships 254

Australia
School of Applied Sciences Overseas Scholarships 254
Wingate Scholarships 697

Canada
Canadian Window on International Development 380
CWRA Dillon Consulting Scholarship/Ken Thomson Scholarship 216
IDRC Doctoral Research Awards 380
International Postgraduate Research Scholarships (IPRS) 413
School of Applied Sciences Overseas Scholarships 254
Wingate Scholarships 697

Caribbean Countries
Canadian Window on International Development 380
IDRC Doctoral Research Awards 380
International Postgraduate Research Scholarships (IPRS) 413
Master Studies in Physical Land Resources Scholarship 379
School of Applied Sciences Overseas Scholarships 254

East European Countries
IDRC Doctoral Research Awards 380
International Postgraduate Research Scholarships (IPRS) 413
School of Applied Sciences Overseas Scholarships 254

European Union
Department of Agriculture and Rural Development (DARD) for
    Northern Ireland 253
NERC Masters Studentships 493
NERC Research (PhD) Studentships 494
Sir William Roberts Scholarship 146
Wingate Scholarships 697

Middle East
IDRC Doctoral Research Awards 380
International Postgraduate Research Scholarships (IPRS) 413

Master Studies in Physical Land Resources Scholarship 379
School of Applied Sciences Overseas Scholarships 254

New Zealand

School of Applied Sciences Overseas Scholarships 254
Wingate Scholarships 697

South Africa

Canadian Window on International Development 380
Henderson Postgraduate Scholarships 548
IDRC Doctoral Research Awards 380
International Postgraduate Research Scholarships (IPRS) 413
Master Studies in Physical Land Resources Scholarship 379
School of Applied Sciences Overseas Scholarships 254
Wingate Scholarships 697

United Kingdom

Aberystwyth Postgraduate Research Studentships 4
Department of Agriculture and Rural Development (DARD) for
    Northern Ireland 253
Douglas Bomford Trust 253
International Postgraduate Research Scholarships (IPRS) 413
The Lorch MSc Student Bursary 253
Mr and Mrs David Edward Memorial Award 145
Natural Environment Research Council (NERC) Masters Studentships
    253
NERC Masters Studentships 493
NERC Research (PhD) Studentships 494
Panasonic Trust Fellowships 253
Perry Research Awards 525
Sir William Roberts Scholarship 146
Wingate Scholarships 697

United States of America

Budweiser Conservation Scholarship 475
DEED (Demonstration of Energy-Efficient Developments) Student
    Research Grant/Internship 80
Earthwatch Fellowships 272
International Postgraduate Research Scholarships (IPRS) 413
The Kenneth E. Grant Scholarship 613
School of Applied Sciences Overseas Scholarships 254

West European Countries

International Postgraduate Research Scholarships (IPRS) 413
Mr and Mrs David Edward Memorial Award 145
Sir William Roberts Scholarship 146

WATER MANAGEMENT

Any Country

Geography: Water Conservators Scholarship 728
IWMI PhD Scholarship 392
Jennings Randolph Program for International Peace Dissertation
    Fellowship 643
Linacre College Coca-Cola Water Sustainability Scholarships 731
NERC Advanced Research Fellowships 493
NERC Postdoctoral Research Fellowships 494
Perry Postgraduate Scholarships 525
Ralph Brown Expedition Award 565
Scholarship opportunities linked to CATIE's Postgraduate Program
    including CATIE scholarship forming part of the Scholarship-Loan
    Program 638
Thesiger-Oman Research Fellowship 566
Utilities and Service Industries Training (USIT) 254
Victoria University of Wellington PhD Scholarships 786

African Nations

Canadian Window on International Development 380
IDRC Doctoral Research Awards 380
International Postgraduate Research Scholarships (IPRS) 413
School of Applied Sciences Overseas Scholarships 254

Australia

MINTRAC Postgraduate Scholarship 451
School of Applied Sciences Overseas Scholarships 254
Wingate Scholarships 697

Canada

Canadian Window on International Development 380
CWRA Dillon Consulting Scholarship/Ken Thomson Scholarship
    216
Horticultural Research Institute Grants 346
IDRC Doctoral Research Awards 380
International Postgraduate Research Scholarships (IPRS) 413
Olin Fellowship 125
School of Applied Sciences Overseas Scholarships 254
Wingate Scholarships 697

Caribbean Countries

Canadian Window on International Development 380
IDRC Doctoral Research Awards 380
International Postgraduate Research Scholarships (IPRS) 413
School of Applied Sciences Overseas Scholarships 254

East European Countries

IDRC Doctoral Research Awards 380
International Postgraduate Research Scholarships (IPRS) 413
School of Applied Sciences Overseas Scholarships 254

European Union

Department of Agriculture and Rural Development (DARD) for
    Northern Ireland 253
NERC Masters Studentships 493
NERC Research (PhD) Studentships 494
Wingate Scholarships 697

Middle East

IDRC Doctoral Research Awards 380
International Postgraduate Research Scholarships (IPRS) 413
School of Applied Sciences Overseas Scholarships 254

New Zealand

School of Applied Sciences Overseas Scholarships 254
Wingate Scholarships 697

South Africa

Canadian Window on International Development 380
IDRC Doctoral Research Awards 380
International Postgraduate Research Scholarships (IPRS) 413
School of Applied Sciences Overseas Scholarships 254
Wingate Scholarships 697

United Kingdom

Department of Agriculture and Rural Development (DARD) for
    Northern Ireland 253
Douglas Bomford Trust 253
International Postgraduate Research Scholarships (IPRS) 413
Mr and Mrs David Edward Memorial Award 145
Natural Environment Research Council (NERC) Masters Studentships
    253
NERC Masters Studentships 493
NERC Research (PhD) Studentships 494
Panasonic Trust Fellowships 253
Perry Research Awards 525
Wingate Scholarships 697

United States of America

ACWA Scholarship 120
Clair A. Hill Scholarship 120
DEED (Demonstration of Energy-Efficient Developments) Student
    Research Grant/Internship 80
Earthwatch Fellowships 272
Horticultural Research Institute Grants 346
International Postgraduate Research Scholarships (IPRS) 413
The Kenneth E. Grant Scholarship 613

Olin Fellowship 125
School of Applied Sciences Overseas Scholarships 254

West European Countries

International Postgraduate Research Scholarships (IPRS) 413
Mr and Mrs David Edward Memorial Award 145

SOIL CONSERVATION

Any Country

NERC Advanced Research Fellowships 493
NERC Postdoctoral Research Fellowships 494
Perry Postgraduate Scholarships 525
Scholarship opportunities linked to CATIE's Postgraduate Program
    including CATIE scholarship forming part of the Scholarship-Loan
    Program 638
Trinity College: Birkett Scholarships in Environmental Studies 747
Victoria University of Wellington PhD Scholarships 786

African Nations

The Bentley Cropping Systems Fellowship 380
Canadian Window on International Development 380
IDRC Doctoral Research Awards 380
International Postgraduate Research Scholarships (IPRS) 413
Master Studies in Physical Land Resources Scholarship 379

Australia

Wingate Scholarships 697

Canada

The Bentley Cropping Systems Fellowship 380
Canadian Window on International Development 380
IDRC Doctoral Research Awards 380
International Postgraduate Research Scholarships (IPRS) 413
Wingate Scholarships 697

Caribbean Countries

The Bentley Cropping Systems Fellowship 380
Canadian Window on International Development 380
IDRC Doctoral Research Awards 380
International Postgraduate Research Scholarships (IPRS) 413
Master Studies in Physical Land Resources Scholarship 379

East European Countries

The Bentley Cropping Systems Fellowship 380
IDRC Doctoral Research Awards 380
International Postgraduate Research Scholarships (IPRS) 413
Synthesys Visiting Fellowship 494
WWF Prince Bernhard Scholarship for Nature Conservation 806

European Union

Department of Agriculture and Rural Development (DARD) for
    Northern Ireland 253
NERC Masters Studentships 493
NERC Research (PhD) Studentships 494
Synthesys Visiting Fellowship 494
Wingate Scholarships 697

Middle East

The Bentley Cropping Systems Fellowship 380
IDRC Doctoral Research Awards 380
International Postgraduate Research Scholarships (IPRS) 413
Master Studies in Physical Land Resources Scholarship 379
WWF Prince Bernhard Scholarship for Nature Conservation 806

New Zealand

Wingate Scholarships 697

South Africa

The Bentley Cropping Systems Fellowship 380
Canadian Window on International Development 380

IDRC Doctoral Research Awards 380
International Postgraduate Research Scholarships (IPRS) 413
Master Studies in Physical Land Resources Scholarship 379
Wingate Scholarships 697

United Kingdom

Aberystwyth Postgraduate Research Studentships 4
Department of Agriculture and Rural Development (DARD) for
    Northern Ireland 253
International Postgraduate Research Scholarships (IPRS) 413
Mr and Mrs David Edward Memorial Award 145
NERC Masters Studentships 493
NERC Research (PhD) Studentships 494
Perry Research Awards 525
Synthesys Visiting Fellowship 494
Wingate Scholarships 697

United States of America

DEED (Demonstration of Energy-Efficient Developments) Student
    Research Grant/Internship 80
Earthwatch Fellowships 272
International Postgraduate Research Scholarships (IPRS) 413
The Kenneth E. Grant Scholarship 613

West European Countries

International Postgraduate Research Scholarships (IPRS) 413
Mr and Mrs David Edward Memorial Award 145
Synthesys Visiting Fellowship 494

VETERINARY MEDICINE

Any Country

The Airey Neave Trust Scholarship 12
Horserace Betting Levy Board Senior Equine Clinical Scholarships
    345
Horserace Betting Levy Board Veterinary Research Training Scho-
    larship 345
John & James Houston Crawford Scholarship 695
John Crawford Scholarship 695
Perry Postgraduate Scholarships 525
Sir Richard Stapley Educational Trust Grants 593
UFAW Animal Welfare Research Training Scholarships 644
UFAW Research and Project Awards 645
UFAW Small Project and Travel Awards 645
UFAW Vacation Scholarships 645
University of Bristol Postgraduate Scholarships 672
Wellcome Trust Grants 794

Australia

R.N. Hammon Scholarship 753
Wingate Scholarships 697

Canada

Dodge Foundation Frontiers for Veterinary Medicine Fellowships
    312
Wingate Scholarships 697

East European Countries

FEMS Fellowship 290

European Union

Henry Dryerre Scholarship in Medical and Veterinary Physiology 694
Sir William Roberts Scholarship 146
Wingate Scholarships 697

New Zealand

Wingate Scholarships 697

South Africa

Wingate Scholarships 697

United Kingdom

FEMS Fellowship 290
Harry Steele-Bodger Memorial Travelling Scholarship 178
Perry Research Awards 525
Sir William Roberts Scholarship 146
Wingate Scholarships 697

United States of America

Dodge Foundation Frontiers for Veterinary Medicine Fellowships
312

West European Countries

FEMS Fellowship 290
Henry Dryerre Scholarship 182
Sir William Roberts Scholarship 146

TROPICAL/SUB-TROPICAL AGRICULTURE

Any Country

Earthwatch Field Research Grants 272
Lindbergh Grants 228
National Geographic Conservation Trust Grant 244
Scholarship opportunities linked to CATIE's Postgraduate Program
including CATIE scholarship forming part of the Scholarship-Loan
Program 638

African Nations

The Bentley Cropping Systems Fellowship 380
Canadian Window on International Development 380
IDRC Doctoral Research Awards 380
IFS Research Grants 382
Master Studies in Physical Land Resources Scholarship 379

Australia

Wingate Scholarships 697

Canada

The Bentley Cropping Systems Fellowship 380
Canadian Window on International Development 380
IDRC Doctoral Research Awards 380
Wingate Scholarships 697

Caribbean Countries

The Bentley Cropping Systems Fellowship 380
Canadian Window on International Development 380
IDRC Doctoral Research Awards 380
IFS Research Grants 382
Master Studies in Physical Land Resources Scholarship 379

East European Countries

The Bentley Cropping Systems Fellowship 380
IDRC Doctoral Research Awards 380

European Union

Sir William Roberts Scholarship 146
Wingate Scholarships 697

Middle East

The Bentley Cropping Systems Fellowship 380
IDRC Doctoral Research Awards 380
IFS Research Grants 382
Master Studies in Physical Land Resources Scholarship 379

New Zealand

Wingate Scholarships 697

South Africa

The Bentley Cropping Systems Fellowship 380
Canadian Window on International Development 380
IDRC Doctoral Research Awards 380
IFS Research Grants 382

Master Studies in Physical Land Resources Scholarship 379
Wingate Scholarships 697

United Kingdom

Mr and Mrs David Edward Memorial Award 145
Sir William Roberts Scholarship 146
Wingate Scholarships 697

United States of America

Earthwatch Fellowships 272

West European Countries

Mr and Mrs David Edward Memorial Award 145
Sir William Roberts Scholarship 146

FORESTRY

Any Country

Anne S. Chatham Fellowship in Medicinal Botany 451
Earthwatch Field Research Grants 272
Edmund Niles Huyck Preserve, Inc. Graduate and Postgraduate
Grants 274
ETH Zurich Excellence Scholarship and Opportunity Award 624
Gilbert F White Postdoctoral Fellowship 545
Hyland R Johns Grant Program 638
International Tropical Timber Organization (ITTO) Fellowship
Programme 389
John Z Duling Grant Program 638
Joseph L Fisher Dissertation Award 546
Lindbergh Grants 228
National Geographic Conservation Trust Grant 244
Scholarship opportunities linked to CATIE's Postgraduate Program
including CATIE scholarship forming part of the Scholarship-Loan
Program 638
SERC Postdoctoral Fellowships 596
SERC Predoctoral Fellowships 596
SERC Senior Fellowships 596
Silverhill Institute of Environmental Research and Conservation Award
591
Teagasc Walsh Fellowships 626

African Nations

The Bentley Cropping Systems Fellowship 380
IDRC Doctoral Research Awards 380
IFS Research Grants 382

Australia

Wingate Scholarships 697

Canada

The Bentley Cropping Systems Fellowship 380
Community Forestry: Trees and People-John G Bene Fellowship 380
IDRC Doctoral Research Awards 380
Wingate Scholarships 697

Caribbean Countries

The Bentley Cropping Systems Fellowship 380
IDRC Doctoral Research Awards 380
IFS Research Grants 382

East European Countries

The Bentley Cropping Systems Fellowship 380
IDRC Doctoral Research Awards 380

European Union

Wingate Scholarships 697

Middle East

The Bentley Cropping Systems Fellowship 380
IDRC Doctoral Research Awards 380
IFS Research Grants 382

New Zealand

Wingate Scholarships 697

South Africa

The Bentley Cropping Systems Fellowship 380
IDRC Doctoral Research Awards 380
IFS Research Grants 382
Wingate Scholarships 697

United Kingdom

Mr and Mrs David Edward Memorial Award 145
Perry Research Awards 525
Wingate Scholarships 697

United States of America

Budweiser Conservation Scholarship 475
Earthwatch Fellowships 272

West European Countries

Mr and Mrs David Edward Memorial Award 145

FOREST SOILS

Any Country

Edmund Niles Huyck Preserve, Inc. Graduate and Postgraduate
   Grants 274
International Tropical Timber Organization (ITTO) Fellowship
   Programme 389

Australia

Wingate Scholarships 697

Canada

Wingate Scholarships 697

East European Countries

Synthesys Visiting Fellowship 494

European Union

Synthesys Visiting Fellowship 494
Wingate Scholarships 697

New Zealand

Wingate Scholarships 697

South Africa

Wingate Scholarships 697

United Kingdom

Mr and Mrs David Edward Memorial Award 145
Synthesys Visiting Fellowship 494
Wingate Scholarships 697

United States of America

Earthwatch Fellowships 272

West European Countries

Mr and Mrs David Edward Memorial Award 145
Synthesys Visiting Fellowship 494

FOREST BIOLOGY

Any Country

Anne S. Chatham Fellowship in Medicinal Botany 451
Edmund Niles Huyck Preserve, Inc. Graduate and Postgraduate
   Grants 274
Future Conservationist Awards 244

International Tropical Timber Organization (ITTO) Fellowship
   Programme 389
Silverhill Institute of Environmental Research and Conservation Award
   591

African Nations

The Bentley Cropping Systems Fellowship 380

Australia

Wingate Scholarships 697

Canada

The Bentley Cropping Systems Fellowship 380
Wingate Scholarships 697

Caribbean Countries

The Bentley Cropping Systems Fellowship 380

East European Countries

The Bentley Cropping Systems Fellowship 380
Synthesys Visiting Fellowship 494

European Union

Synthesys Visiting Fellowship 494
Wingate Scholarships 697

Middle East

The Bentley Cropping Systems Fellowship 380

New Zealand

Wingate Scholarships 697

South Africa

The Bentley Cropping Systems Fellowship 380
Wingate Scholarships 697

United Kingdom

Mr and Mrs David Edward Memorial Award 145
Synthesys Visiting Fellowship 494
Wingate Scholarships 697

United States of America

Earthwatch Fellowships 272

West European Countries

Mr and Mrs David Edward Memorial Award 145
Synthesys Visiting Fellowship 494

FOREST PATHOLOGY

Any Country

Anne S. Chatham Fellowship in Medicinal Botany 451
Edmund Niles Huyck Preserve, Inc. Graduate and Postgraduate
   Grants 274
International Tropical Timber Organization (ITTO) Fellowship
   Programme 389

Australia

Wingate Scholarships 697

Canada

Wingate Scholarships 697

European Union

Wingate Scholarships 697

New Zealand

Wingate Scholarships 697

South Africa

Wingate Scholarships 697

United Kingdom

Mr and Mrs David Edward Memorial Award 145
Wingate Scholarships 697

United States of America

Earthwatch Fellowships 272

West European Countries

Mr and Mrs David Edward Memorial Award 145

FOREST PRODUCTS

Any Country

Anne S. Chatham Fellowship in Medicinal Botany 451
International Tropical Timber Organization (ITTO) Fellowship Programme 389

Australia

Wingate Scholarships 697

Canada

Wingate Scholarships 697

European Union

Wingate Scholarships 697

New Zealand

Wingate Scholarships 697

South Africa

Wingate Scholarships 697

United Kingdom

Mr and Mrs David Edward Memorial Award 145
Wingate Scholarships 697

United States of America

Earthwatch Fellowships 272

West European Countries

Mr and Mrs David Edward Memorial Award 145

FOREST ECONOMICS

Any Country

International Tropical Timber Organization (ITTO) Fellowship Programme 389
Scholarship opportunities linked to CATIE's Postgraduate Program
including CATIE scholarship forming part of the Scholarship-Loan
Program 638

Australia

Wingate Scholarships 697

Canada

Wingate Scholarships 697

European Union

Wingate Scholarships 697

New Zealand

Wingate Scholarships 697

South Africa

Wingate Scholarships 697

United Kingdom

Mr and Mrs David Edward Memorial Award 145
Wingate Scholarships 697

West European Countries

Mr and Mrs David Edward Memorial Award 145

FOREST MANAGEMENT

Any Country

Anne S. Chatham Fellowship in Medicinal Botany 451
Edmund Niles Huyck Preserve, Inc. Graduate and Postgraduate
Grants 274
International Tropical Timber Organization (ITTO) Fellowship
Programme 389
Scholarship opportunities linked to CATIE's Postgraduate Program
including CATIE scholarship forming part of the Scholarship-Loan
Program 638
Trinity College: Birkett Scholarships in Environmental Studies 747

Australia

Wingate Scholarships 697

Canada

Community Forestry: Trees and People-John G Bene Fellowship 380
Wingate Scholarships 697

European Union

Wingate Scholarships 697

New Zealand

Wingate Scholarships 697

South Africa

Wingate Scholarships 697

United Kingdom

Mr and Mrs David Edward Memorial Award 145
Wingate Scholarships 697

United States of America

Earthwatch Fellowships 272

West European Countries

Mr and Mrs David Edward Memorial Award 145

FISHERY

Any Country

Andrew Mellon Foundation Scholarship 547
CICOR Postdoctoral Scholar Fellowship in Coastal Oceanography,
Climate or Marine Ecosystems 804
Earthwatch Field Research Grants 272
NRC Research Associateships 488
Postgraduate Research Studentship 689
Ralph Brown Expedition Award 565
Rhodes University Postgraduate Scholarship 549
SERC Postdoctoral Fellowships 596
SERC Predoctoral Fellowships 596
SERC Senior Fellowships 596
UFAW Animal Welfare Research Training Scholarships 644
UFAW Research and Project Awards 645
UFAW Small Project and Travel Awards 645
UFAW Vacation Scholarships 645
Victoria University of Wellington PhD Scholarships 786

African Nations

Austrian Academy of Sciences, MSc Course in Limnology and
Wetland Ecosystems 141

IDRC Doctoral Research Awards 380
IFS Research Grants 382

Australia

Wingate Scholarships 697

Canada

IDRC Doctoral Research Awards 380
Olin Fellowship 125
Wingate Scholarships 697

Caribbean Countries

IDRC Doctoral Research Awards 380
IFS Research Grants 382

East European Countries

IDRC Doctoral Research Awards 380

European Union

Wingate Scholarships 697

Middle East

IDRC Doctoral Research Awards 380
IFS Research Grants 382

New Zealand

Fish & Game New Zealand Research Scholarships 500
Wingate Scholarships 697

South Africa

IDRC Doctoral Research Awards 380
IFS Research Grants 382
Wingate Scholarships 697

United Kingdom

Mr and Mrs David Edward Memorial Award 145
Wingate Scholarships 697

United States of America

Budweiser Conservation Scholarship 475
Olin Fellowship 125
Sea Grant/NOAA Fisheries Fellowship 488

West European Countries

Mr and Mrs David Edward Memorial Award 145

AQUACULTURE

Any Country

Victoria University of Wellington PhD Scholarships 786

Australia

Wingate Scholarships 697

Canada

Wingate Scholarships 697

East European Countries

Synthesys Visiting Fellowship 494

European Union

Synthesys Visiting Fellowship 494
Wingate Scholarships 697

New Zealand

Wingate Scholarships 697

South Africa

Henderson Postgraduate Scholarships 548
Wingate Scholarships 697

United Kingdom

Mr and Mrs David Edward Memorial Award 145
Synthesys Visiting Fellowship 494
Wingate Scholarships 697

West European Countries

Mr and Mrs David Edward Memorial Award 145
Synthesys Visiting Fellowship 494

ARCHITECTURE AND TOWN PLANNING

GENERAL

Any Country

Akademie Schloss Solitude Fellowships 12
The Alastair Salvesen Art Scholarship 570
ARI PhD Research Scholarship 114
ASCSA Advanced Fellowships 82
ASCSA Fellowships 82
CRF (Caledonian Research Foundation)/RSE European Visiting
    Research Fellowships 628
Edilia and François-Auguste de Montequin Fellowship in Iberian and
    Latin American Architecture 608
ETH Zurich Excellence Scholarship and Opportunity Award 624
Frederick Douglass Institute Postdoctoral Fellowship 304
Grace and Clark Fyfe Architecture Masters Scholarships 320
Grace and Clark Fyfe Architecture PhD Scholarship 320
Henrietta Hutton Research Grants 564
Honda Prize 343
Hong Kong Research Grant 564
International Postgraduate Research Scholarship 667
John Keppie Scholarship 321
The John Kinross Memorial Fund Student Scholarships/RSA 570
La Trobe University Postgraduate Scholarship 414
Lindbergh Grants 228
Matsumae International Foundation Research Fellowship 436
Ohio Arts Council Individual Creativity Excellence Awards 510
Rosann Berry Fellowship 608
Samuel H. Kress Fellowship 788
Sir William Gillies Bequest-Hospitalfield Trust 570
Small Research Grants 566
SOM Prize and Travel Fellowship 595
Spiro Kostof Annual Meeting Fellowship 609
TIACA Walter H. Johnson, Jr. Scholarship Award 375
University of Reading MSc Intelligent Buildings Scholarship 756
Wolf Foundation Prizes 799
Wolfsonian-FIU Fellowship 800

African Nations

ABCCF Student Grant 102
ECOPOLIS Graduate Research and Design Awards 380
George Pepler International Award 575
International Postgraduate Research Scholarships (IPRS) 413
Neville Chamberlain Scholarship 670
NUFFIC-NFP Fellowships for Master's Degree Programmes 496

Australia

Baillieu Research Scholarship 707
Byera Hadley Travelling Scholarships 498
Fulbright Postdoctoral Fellowships 140
Fulbright Postgraduate Awards 140
George Pepler International Award 575
Marten Bequest Travelling Scholarships 220
Neville Chamberlain Scholarship 670
NSW Architects Registration Board Research Grant 498
R.N. Hammon Scholarship 753
Wingate Scholarships 697

Canada

ECOPOLIS Graduate Research and Design Awards 380
George Pepler International Award 575

International Postgraduate Research Scholarships (IPRS) 413
J B C Watkins Award 199
Neville Chamberlain Scholarship 670
Wingate Scholarships 697

Caribbean Countries

ECOPOLIS Graduate Research and Design Awards 380
George Pepler International Award 575
International Postgraduate Research Scholarships (IPRS) 413
Neville Chamberlain Scholarship 670

East European Countries

ECOPOLIS Graduate Research and Design Awards 380
George Pepler International Award 575
International Postgraduate Research Scholarships (IPRS) 413
Neville Chamberlain Scholarship 670

European Union

AHRC Doctoral Awards Scheme 109
CBRL Travel Grant 248
Department of Communities and Local Government (formally Office of
  the Deputy Prime Minister) 649
Neville Chamberlain Scholarship 670
Research Preparation Master's Scheme
Wingate Scholarships 697

Middle East

ABCCF Student Grant 102
AUC Nadia Niazi Mostafa Fellowship in Islamic Art and Architecture
  97
ECOPOLIS Graduate Research and Design Awards 380
George Pepler International Award 575
International Postgraduate Research Scholarships (IPRS) 413
Neville Chamberlain Scholarship 670
NUFFIC-NFP Fellowships for Master's Degree Programmes 496

New Zealand

George Pepler International Award 575
Neville Chamberlain Scholarship 670
Wingate Scholarships 697

South Africa

ECOPOLIS Graduate Research and Design Awards 380
George Pepler International Award 575
International Postgraduate Research Scholarships (IPRS) 413
Neville Chamberlain Scholarship 670
NUFFIC-NFP Fellowships for Master's Degree Programmes 496
Wingate Scholarships 697

United Kingdom

AHRC Doctoral Awards Scheme 109
CBRL Research Award 248
CBRL Travel Grant 248
Department of Communities and Local Government (formally Office of
  the Deputy Prime Minister) 649
Frank Knox Fellowships at Harvard University 302
George Pepler International Award 575
Giles Worsley Travel Fellowship 174
Hilda Martindale Exhibitions 341
International Postgraduate Research Scholarships (IPRS) 413
Kennedy Scholarships 409
Leverhulme Scholarships for Architecture 321
Research Preparation Master's Scheme
Rome Scholarship in Architecture 175
Sargant Fellowship 176
Wingate Scholarships 697

United States of America

American Academy in Rome Fellowships in Design Art 24
Annual Meeting Fellowship - Beverly Willis Architectural Foundation
  Travel Fellowship 608
ASOR W.F. Albright Institute of Archaeological Research/National
  Endowment of the Humanities Fellowships 84

Congress Bundestag Youth Exchange for Young Professionals 221
Fulbright Distinguished Chairs Program 248
Fulbright Senior Specialists Program 249
George Pepler International Award 575
Howard Brown Rickard Scholarship 474
International Postgraduate Research Scholarships (IPRS) 413
Kennedy Research Grants 405
Kress Fellowship in the Art and Archaeology of Jordan 35
Neville Chamberlain Scholarship 670
North Dakota Indian Scholarship 507
Rotch Travelling Scholarship 155
SAH Fellowships for Senior Scholars 608
Samuel H. Kress Fellowship 788
Scott Opler Fellowships for New Scholars 609

West European Countries

George Pepler International Award 575
International Postgraduate Research Scholarships (IPRS)
  413
Janson Johan Helmich Scholarships and Travel Grants 398
Neville Chamberlain Scholarship 670

STRUCTURAL ARCHITECTURE

Any Country

ETH Zurich Excellence Scholarship and Opportunity Award 624
MacDowell Colony Residencies 429
Structural Engineering Travelling Fellowship 595

African Nations

ECOPOLIS Graduate Research and Design Awards 380
International Postgraduate Research Scholarships (IPRS) 413

Australia

Wingate Scholarships 697

Canada

ECOPOLIS Graduate Research and Design Awards 380
International Postgraduate Research Scholarships (IPRS) 413
Wingate Scholarships 697

Caribbean Countries

ECOPOLIS Graduate Research and Design Awards 380
International Postgraduate Research Scholarships (IPRS) 413

East European Countries

ECOPOLIS Graduate Research and Design Awards 380
International Postgraduate Research Scholarships (IPRS) 413

European Union

Wingate Scholarships 697

Middle East

ECOPOLIS Graduate Research and Design Awards 380
International Postgraduate Research Scholarships (IPRS) 413

New Zealand

Wingate Scholarships 697

South Africa

ECOPOLIS Graduate Research and Design Awards 380
International Postgraduate Research Scholarships (IPRS) 413
Wingate Scholarships 697

United Kingdom

International Postgraduate Research Scholarships (IPRS) 413
Wingate Scholarships 697

United States of America

International Postgraduate Research Scholarships (IPRS) 413

West European Countries

International Postgraduate Research Scholarships (IPRS) 413

ARCHITECTURAL RESTORATION

Any Country

ASCSA Advanced Fellowships 82
Earthwatch Field Research Grants 272
Edilia and François-Auguste de Montequin Fellowship in Iberian and
    Latin American Architecture 608
Keepers Preservation Education Fund Fellowship 608
NEH Fellowships 83
Rosann Berry Fellowship 608
Sir John Soane's Museum Foundation Travelling Fellowship 593
Spiro Kostof Annual Meeting Fellowship 609

African Nations

ECOPOLIS Graduate Research and Design Awards 380

Australia

Wingate Scholarships 697

Canada

ECOPOLIS Graduate Research and Design Awards 380
Wingate Scholarships 697

Caribbean Countries

ECOPOLIS Graduate Research and Design Awards 380

East European Countries

ECOPOLIS Graduate Research and Design Awards 380

European Union

Wingate Scholarships 697

Middle East

ECOPOLIS Graduate Research and Design Awards 380

New Zealand

Wingate Scholarships 697

South Africa

ECOPOLIS Graduate Research and Design Awards 380
Wingate Scholarships 697

United Kingdom

Wingate Scholarships 697

United States of America

ACC Fellowship Grants Program 115
American Academy in Rome Fellowships in Design Art 24
Sally Kress Tompkins Fellowship 608

ENVIRONMENTAL DESIGN

Any Country

ETH Zurich Excellence Scholarship and Opportunity Award 624
Ohio Arts Council Individual Creativity Excellence Awards 510
Stanley Smith (UK) Horticultural Trust Awards 618

African Nations

ECOPOLIS Graduate Research and Design Awards 380
IDRC Evaluation Research Awards 381
International Postgraduate Research Scholarships (IPRS) 413

Australia

Wingate Scholarships 697

Canada

ECOPOLIS Graduate Research and Design Awards 380

Horticultural Research Institute Grants 346
IDRC Evaluation Research Awards 381
International Postgraduate Research Scholarships (IPRS)
    413
Jim Bourque Scholarship 103
Wingate Scholarships 697

Caribbean Countries

ECOPOLIS Graduate Research and Design Awards 380
IDRC Evaluation Research Awards 381
International Postgraduate Research Scholarships (IPRS) 413

East European Countries

ECOPOLIS Graduate Research and Design Awards 380
IDRC Evaluation Research Awards 381
International Postgraduate Research Scholarships (IPRS) 413

European Union

AHRC Doctoral Awards Scheme 109
Professional Preparation Master's Scheme
Research Preparation Master's Scheme
Wingate Scholarships 697

Middle East

ECOPOLIS Graduate Research and Design Awards 380
IDRC Evaluation Research Awards 381
International Postgraduate Research Scholarships (IPRS)
    413

New Zealand

Wingate Scholarships 697

South Africa

ECOPOLIS Graduate Research and Design Awards 380
IDRC Evaluation Research Awards 381
International Postgraduate Research Scholarships (IPRS) 413
Wingate Scholarships 697

United Kingdom

AHRC Doctoral Awards Scheme 109
International Postgraduate Research Scholarships (IPRS) 413
Professional Preparation Master's Scheme
Research Preparation Master's Scheme
Wingate Scholarships 697

United States of America

Horticultural Research Institute Grants 346
International Postgraduate Research Scholarships (IPRS) 413

West European Countries

International Postgraduate Research Scholarships (IPRS) 413

LANDSCAPE ARCHITECTURE

Any Country

Dumbarton Oaks Fellowships and Junior Fellowships 271
MacDowell Colony Residencies 429
Ohio Arts Council Individual Creativity Excellence Awards 510
Stanley Smith (UK) Horticultural Trust Awards 618

African Nations

International Postgraduate Research Scholarships (IPRS) 413

Australia

Wingate Scholarships 697

Canada

Horticultural Research Institute Grants 346
International Postgraduate Research Scholarships (IPRS) 413
Rome Scholarship in Landscape Architecture 176
Wingate Scholarships 697

Caribbean Countries

International Postgraduate Research Scholarships (IPRS) 413

East European Countries

International Postgraduate Research Scholarships (IPRS) 413

European Union

AHRC Doctoral Awards Scheme 109
Professional Preparation Master's Scheme
Research Preparation Master's Scheme
Wingate Scholarships 697

Middle East

International Postgraduate Research Scholarships (IPRS) 413

New Zealand

Wingate Scholarships 697

South Africa

International Postgraduate Research Scholarships (IPRS) 413
Wingate Scholarships 697

United Kingdom

AHRC Doctoral Awards Scheme 109
International Postgraduate Research Scholarships (IPRS) 413
Martin McLaren Horticultural Scholarship 367
Professional Preparation Master's Scheme
Research Preparation Master's Scheme
Rome Scholarship in Landscape Architecture 176
Wingate Scholarships 697

United States of America

American Academy in Rome Fellowships in Design Art 24
Horticultural Research Institute Grants 346
International Postgraduate Research Scholarships (IPRS) 413

West European Countries

International Postgraduate Research Scholarships (IPRS) 413

TOWN AND COMMUNITY PLANNING

Any Country

ETH Zurich Excellence Scholarship and Opportunity Award 624
RICS Education Trust Award 549

African Nations

ECOPOLIS Graduate Research and Design Awards 380
George Pepler International Award 575
IDRC Evaluation Research Awards 381
International Postgraduate Research Scholarships (IPRS) 413

Australia

George Pepler International Award 575
Wingate Scholarships 697

Canada

ECOPOLIS Graduate Research and Design Awards 380
George Pepler International Award 575
IDRC Evaluation Research Awards 381
International Postgraduate Research Scholarships (IPRS) 413
Public Safety and Emergency Preparedness Canada Research
   Fellowship in Honour of Stuart Nesbitt White 123
TAC Foundation Scholarships 637
Wingate Scholarships 697

Caribbean Countries

ECOPOLIS Graduate Research and Design Awards 380
George Pepler International Award 575
IDRC Evaluation Research Awards 381
International Postgraduate Research Scholarships (IPRS) 413

East European Countries

ECOPOLIS Graduate Research and Design Awards 380
George Pepler International Award 575
IDRC Evaluation Research Awards 381
International Postgraduate Research Scholarships (IPRS)
   413

European Union

Department of Communities and Local Government (formally Office of
   the Deputy Prime Minister) 649
Wingate Scholarships 697

Middle East

ECOPOLIS Graduate Research and Design Awards 380
George Pepler International Award 575
IDRC Evaluation Research Awards 381
International Postgraduate Research Scholarships (IPRS) 413

New Zealand

George Pepler International Award 575
Wingate Scholarships 697

South Africa

ECOPOLIS Graduate Research and Design Awards 380
George Pepler International Award 575
IDRC Evaluation Research Awards 381
International Postgraduate Research Scholarships (IPRS) 413
Wingate Scholarships 697

United Kingdom

Department of Communities and Local Government (formally Office of
   the Deputy Prime Minister) 649
George Pepler International Award 575
International Postgraduate Research Scholarships (IPRS) 413
Wingate Scholarships 697

United States of America

American Academy in Rome Fellowships in Design Art 24
DEED (Demonstration of Energy-Efficient Developments) Student
   Research Grant/Internship 80
George Pepler International Award 575
International Postgraduate Research Scholarships (IPRS) 413

West European Countries

George Pepler International Award 575
International Postgraduate Research Scholarships (IPRS) 413

REGIONAL PLANNING

Any Country

ETH Zurich Excellence Scholarship and Opportunity Award
   624

African Nations

George Pepler International Award 575
IDRC Evaluation Research Awards 381
International Postgraduate Research Scholarships (IPRS) 413

Australia

George Pepler International Award 575
Wingate Scholarships 697

Canada

George Pepler International Award 575
IDRC Evaluation Research Awards 381
International Postgraduate Research Scholarships (IPRS) 413
Public Safety and Emergency Preparedness Canada Research
   Fellowship in Honour of Stuart Nesbitt White 123
TAC Foundation Scholarships 637
Wingate Scholarships 697

Caribbean Countries

George Pepler International Award 575
IDRC Evaluation Research Awards 381
International Postgraduate Research Scholarships (IPRS) 413

East European Countries

George Pepler International Award 575
IDRC Evaluation Research Awards 381
International Postgraduate Research Scholarships (IPRS) 413

European Union

Department of Communities and Local Government (formally Office of
    the Deputy Prime Minister) 649
Wingate Scholarships 697

Middle East

George Pepler International Award 575
IDRC Evaluation Research Awards 381
International Postgraduate Research Scholarships (IPRS) 413

New Zealand

George Pepler International Award 575
Wingate Scholarships 697

South Africa

George Pepler International Award 575
IDRC Evaluation Research Awards 381
International Postgraduate Research Scholarships (IPRS) 413
Wingate Scholarships 697

United Kingdom

Department of Communities and Local Government (formally Office of
    the Deputy Prime Minister) 649
George Pepler International Award 575
International Postgraduate Research Scholarships (IPRS) 413
Wingate Scholarships 697

United States of America

George Pepler International Award 575
International Postgraduate Research Scholarships (IPRS) 413

West European Countries

George Pepler International Award 575
International Postgraduate Research Scholarships (IPRS) 413

ARTS AND HUMANITIES

GENERAL

Any Country

AAS Reese Fellowship 27
AAS-North East Modern Language Association Fellowship 27
ACLS/Chiang Ching-kuo Foundation (CCK) New Perspectives on
    Chinese Culture and Society 48
AFUW Western Australian Bursaries 164
AISLS Dissertation Planning Grant 60
Akademie Schloss Solitude Fellowships 12
American Historical Print Collectors Society Fellowship 27
American Society for Eighteenth-Century Studies (ASECS) Fellow-
    ship 501
Andrew W Mellon Postdoctoral Fellowship 795
Andrew W. Mellon Foundation/ACLS Early Career Fellowships
    Program Dissertation Completion Fellowships 48
Andrew W. Mellon/ACLS Recent Doctoral Recipients Fellowships 48
ARI (Senior) Visiting Fellowships 114
ARI PhD Research Scholarship 114
ARI Postdoctoral Fellowships 115
ARIT Fellowship Program 80
Arthur Weinberg Fellowship for Independent Scholars 501
ASCSA Advanced Fellowships 82

ASCSA Fellowships 82
ASECS (American Society for 18th-Century Studies)/Clark Library
    Fellowships 639
AUC Assistantships 96
AUC Graduate Merit Fellowships 97
AUC Ryoichi Sasakawa Young Leaders Graduate Scholarship 97
AUC University Fellowships 98
Audrey Lumsden-Kouvel Fellowship 501
Australian Postgraduate Award Research Scholarship
Austro-American Association of Boston Stipend 143
Balliol College Dervorguilla Scholarship 718
Banff Centre Financial Assistance 144
Barry Bloomfield Bursary 150
BIAA Post-Doctoral Research Fellowship 168
BIAA Research Scholarship 168
BIAA Study Grants 168
BIAA Travel Grants 168
Bibliographical Society Small Grants 150
British Academy Overseas Conference Grants 158
British Academy Research Development Awards (BARDAs) 158
British Academy Small Research Grants 158
British Academy Worldwide Congress Grant 159
British Conference Grants 159
CAGS UMI Dissertation Awards 199
Camargo Fellowships 182
CARTI Junior Fellowships 225
Charlotte W Newcombe Doctoral Dissertation Fellowships 803
Chiang Ching Kuo Foundation Doctoral Fellowships 232
CINS Graduate Scholarship 208
Clark-Huntington Joint Bibliographical Fellowship 640
Concordia University Graduate Fellowships 243
David J Azrieli Graduate Fellowship 243
Delahaye Memorial Benefaction 768
The Dissertation Proposal Development Fellowship (DPDF) 597
Donald Dyer Scholarship – Public Relations & Communication
    Management 757
Drawn to Art Fellowship 27
Earthwatch Field Research Grants 272
The Erskine A. Peters Dissertation Year Fellowship at Notre Dame
    716
Frances A Yates Fellowships 789
Frances C Allen Fellowships 502
Franklin Research Grant Program 73
Frederick Burkhardt Residential Fellowships for Recently Tenured
    Scholars 502
The Fredson Bowers Award 150
Gay Clifford Fees Award for Outstanding Women Students 651
The Getty Foundation Curatorial Research Fellowships 316
The Getty Foundation Postdoctoral Fellowships 316
Graduate Dissertation Research Fellowship 448
Graduate Summer Travel Grants 449
Harold White Fellowships 484
Helen McCormack Turner Memorial Scholarship 768
Helen Wallis Fellowship 170
Henrietta Hutton Research Grants 564
Henry Moore Institute Research Fellowship 338
Herbert Hughes Scholarship 768
Herzog August Bibliothek Wolfenbüttel Fellowship 502
The Holberg International Memorial Prize/The Holberg Prize 668
Hong Kong Research Grant 564
HRC Visiting Fellowships 347
IAUW International Scholarship 166
IHS Humane Studies Fellowships 363
Institute for Advanced Studies in the Humanities Visiting Research
    Fellowships 362
Institute for Advanced Study Postdoctoral Residential Fellowships 363
Institute of Irish Studies Research Fellowships 367
International Visiting Scholarship 156
Irish Research Funds 394
J Franklin Jameson Fellowship 58
Jacob Hirsch Fellowship 83
Jacob's Pillow Intern Program
John Hume Postgraduate Scholarships 490
Journey of a Lifetime Award 564
JSPS Award for Eminent Scientists 398
JSPS Invitation Fellowship Programme for Research in Japan 399

Kanner Fellowship In British Studies 640
Kennan Institute Short-Term Grants 408
Lewis Walpole Library Fellowship 421
Library Resident Research Fellowships 74
Lilly Postdoctoral Teaching Fellowship Program 785
Linacre College Mary Blaschko Graduate Scholarship 732
Lincoln College Sloane Robinson Foundation Graduate Awards 733
Lindbergh Grants 228
Lloyd Lewis Fellowship in American History 503
M Alison Frantz Fellowship in Post-Classical Studies at the Gennadius Library 83
Mary Isabel Sibley Fellowship 531
Mary Radcliffe Scholarship 768
Mellon Postdoctoral Fellowships in the Humanities 524
Mellon Postdoctoral Research Fellowship 503
Minda de Gunzberg Graduate Dissertation Writing Fellowship 449
Monash International Postgraduate Research Scholarship (MIPRS) 455
Monash University Silver Jubilee Postgraduate Scholarship 455
Monticello College Foundation Fellowship for Women 503
NEH Fellowships 83
Newberry Library British Academy Fellowship for Study in Great Britain 503
Newberry Library Ecole des Chartes Exchange Fellowship 504
Newberry Library Short-Term Resident Fellowships for Individual Research 504
Nila Banton Smith Research Dissemination Support Grant 387
Paul D. Fleck Fellowships in the Arts 144
Paul Mellon Centre Rome Fellowship 175
Peter C Craigie Memorial Scholarship 673
Postdoctoral Fellowship in Academic Libraries for Humanists 251
Queen Mary Research Studentships 539
Research Grants for Getty Scholars and Visiting Scholars 317
Residential Grants at the Getty Center and Getty Villa 317
Rhodes University Postdoctoral Fellowship and The Andrew Mellon Postdoctoral Fellowship 548
Rhodes University Postgraduate Scholarship 549
RHYS Curzon-Jones Scholarship 768
Ridley Lewis Bursary 769
Robert Westwood Scholarship 581
Royal Irish Academy Mobility Grants 569
Sabbatical Fellowship for the Humanities and Social Sciences 74
SCBWI Grant for Unpublished Authors 610
Senior Fellowships 353
Sir Allan Sewell Visiting Fellowship 326
Sir Richard Stapley Educational Trust Grants 593
SOAS Open Scholarship 583
Society for the Humanities Postdoctoral Fellowships 246
South Central Modern Language Association Fellowship 504
St Catherine's College Graduate Scholarship in the Arts
Stanley G French Graduate Fellowship 244
Trudeau Foundation Doctoral Scholarships 533
United States Holocaust Memorial Museum Center for Advanced Holocaust Studies Visiting Scholar Programs 641
University of Ballarat Postgraduate Research Scholarship
University of Kent School of Drama, Film and Visual Arts Scholarships 700
University of Otago International Scholarships 717
University of Otago PhD Scholarships 718
University of Otago Prestigious PhD Scholarships 718
University of Reading Arts and Humanities Studentship 755
University of Southampton Postgraduate Studentships 759
USA – Getty Foundation Research Grants for Predoctoral and Postdoctoral Fellowships 317
Vera Moore International Postgraduate Research Scholarships 455
Victoria University of Wellington PhD Scholarships 786
Viktoria Marinov Scholarship of Art 714
Villa Predoctoral and Postdoctoral Fellowships 317
W D Llewelyn Memorial Benefaction 769
Weiss/Brown Publication Subvention Award 505
Wolfsonian-FIU Fellowship 800
Woodrow Wilson Dissertation Fellowship in Women s Studies
World Universities Network (WUN) International Research Mobility Scheme 759

African Nations

AUC African Graduate Fellowship 96
International Postgraduate Research Scholarships (IPRS) 413
International Postgraduate Research Scholarships (IPRS) 413
NUFFIC-NFP Fellowships for Master's Degree Programmes 496
ORSAS Awards 688

Australia

AAH Humanities Travelling Fellowships 132
Asialink Residency Program 111
Australian Postgraduate Awards 413
Dunlop Asia Fellowships 115
Fulbright Postdoctoral Fellowships 140
International Postgraduate Research Scholarships (IPRS) 413
Japanese Government (Monbukagakusho) Scholarships Research Category 400
Lewis O'Brien Scholarship
Literative Key Organisations Triennial 128
Literature Program 129
Literature Skills and Arts Development 129
Marten Bequest Travelling Scholarships 220
ORSAS Awards 688
Robert Helpmann Scholarship 112
University of Ballarat Part Postgraduate Research Scholarship 667
University of Otago Master's Awards 717
Western Sydney Artists Fellowship 498
Wingate Scholarships 697
Women and Arts Fellowship 113

Canada

Aid to Research and Transfer Journals 599
Aid to Research Workshops and Conferences in Canada
Aid to Scholarly Publications 600
Aid to Small Universities 600
Canada Graduate Scholarship Program (CGS): Master's Scholarship 600
Canadian Initiative on Social Statistics: Data Training Schools 601
CAPI Student Fellowship for Thesis Research 226
Community-University Research Alliances (CURA) 601
DCGS Doctoral Scholarships 592
Dr William S. Lewis Doctoral Fellowships 711
Frank Knox Memorial Fellowships 123
Guggenheim Fellowships to Assist Research and Artistic Creation (USA and Canada) 406
Image, Text, Sound and Technology: Summer Institute, Workshop and Conference Grants, and Research Grants 601
International Postgraduate Research Scholarships (IPRS) 413
International Postgraduate Research Scholarships (IPRS) 413
J W McConnell Memorial Fellowships 243
JCCA Graduate Education Scholarship 400
JSPS Summer Programme 399
Knowledge Impact in Society 601
Konrad Adenauer Research Award for Canadian Scholars in the Humanities and Social Sciences 18
KRESS/ARIT Pre-Doctoral Fellowship in the History of Art and Archaeology 81
Major Collaborative Research Initiatives (MCRI) 601
Mary McNeill Scholarship in Irish Studies 368
Mellon Postdoctoral Fellowships 246
Ministry Fellowship 308
North American Doctoral Fellowship 308
Northern Research Development Program 601
ORSAS Awards 688
Sport Participation Research Initiative: Research Grants 602
SSHRC Doctoral Awards 602
SSHRC Institutional Grants 602
SSHRC Postdoctoral Fellowships 602
SSHRC Research Development Initiatives 603
SSHRC Standard Research Grants 603
SSHRC Strategic Research Grants 603
Vatican Film Library Mellon Fellowship 785
Wingate Scholarships 697

Caribbean Countries

East European Countries

European Union

Middle East

New Zealand

South Africa

United Kingdom

United States of America

SSRC JSPS Postdoctoral Fellowship 599
Vatican Film Library Mellon Fellowship 785
Virginia Liebeler Biennial Grants for Mature Women (Writing) 484
Washington University Chancellor's Graduate Fellowship Program 792

West European Countries

David Baumgardt Memorial Fellowship 417
Freie Universität Berlin John-F.-Kennedy-Institut für Nordamerikastudien Research Grants 304
Fritz Halbers Fellowship 417
German Historical Institute Doctoral and Postdoctoral Fellowships 313
International Postgraduate Research Scholarships (IPRS) 413
International Postgraduate Research Scholarships (IPRS) 413
JSPS Summer Programme 399
Lady Gregory Fellowship Scheme 490
Mr and Mrs David Edward Memorial Award 145
University of Kent School of Drama, Film and Visual Arts Scholarships 700
University of Otago Master's Awards 717

INTERPRETATION AND TRANSLATION

Any Country

Aldo and Jeanne Scaglione Prize for a Translation of a Literary Work 452
Aldo and Jeanne Scaglione Prize for Translation of a Scholarly Study of Literature 453
Banff Centre Financial Assistance 144
BIAA Post-Doctoral Research Fellowship 168
BIAA Research Scholarship 168
BIAA Study Grants 168
Camargo Fellowships 182
Fenia and Yaakov Leviant Memorial Prize in Yiddish Studies 453
Henry Moore Institute Research Fellowship 338
Jacob's Pillow Intern Program
Lois Roth Award for a Translation of Literary Work 454
MacDowell Colony Residencies 429
Paul D. Fleck Fellowships in the Arts 144
The PEN Translation Fund Grants 524
SOAS Open Scholarship 583

European Union

AHRC Doctoral Awards Scheme 109
CBRL Travel Grant 248
MA in Literature, Film, and Theatre Studies Scholarship 688
PhD in Literature, Film and Theatre Studies Studentship 688
Professional Preparation Master's Scheme
Research Preparation Master's Scheme

United Kingdom

AHRC Doctoral Awards Scheme 109
CBRL Research Award 248
CBRL Travel Grant 248
Professional Preparation Master's Scheme
Research Preparation Master's Scheme
University of Kent School of European Culture and Languages Scholarships 701
University of Kent School of European Culture and Languages Studentships 701

United States of America

ACC Fellowship Grants Program 115
ITBE Graduate Scholarship 352

West European Countries

University of Kent School of European Culture and Languages Scholarships 701
University of Kent School of European Culture and Languages Studentships 701

WRITING (AUTHORSHIP)

Any Country

AAS Reese Fellowship 27
Alfred Bradley Bursary Award 146
Antiquarian Booksellers Award 150
Banff Centre Financial Assistance 144
Barbara Karlin Grant 610
BIAA Study Grants 168
Camargo Fellowships 182
Charles Pick Fellowship 681
David T K Wong Fellowship 682
Fine Arts Work Center in Provincetown Fellowships 291
George Bennett Fellowship 532
Glenn E and Barbara Hodsdon Ullyot Scholarship 230
Hambidge Residency Program Scholarships 331
Henry Moore Institute Research Fellowship 338
IHS Film & Fiction Scholarships 363
Liberty Legacy Foundation Award 516
MacDowell Colony Residencies 429
Miles Franklin Literary Award 221
MLA Prize for a Distinguished Scholarly Edition 454
MLA Prize for a First Book 454
MLA Prize for Independent Scholars 454
National Association of Composers Young Composers Competition 467
Paul D. Fleck Fellowships in the Arts 144
PEN Writer's Fund
SCBWI General Work-in-Progress Grant 610
SCBWI Grant for a Contemporary Novel for Young People 610
SCBWI Grant for Unpublished Authors 610
SCBWI Nonfiction Research Grant 610
Watson Davis and Helen Miles Davis Prize 343
William Flanagan Memorial Creative Persons Center 277

African Nations

International Postgraduate Research Scholarships (IPRS) 413
ORSAS Awards 688

Australia

Blake Dawson Waldron Prize for Business Literature 618
Literature New Work 128
Literature Presentation and Promotion 129
Marten Bequest Travelling Scholarships 220
National Biography Award 619
ORSAS Awards 688
OZCO Literature Fellowships 130
OZCO Literature Grants Initiative: Write in Your Face 130
Wingate Scholarships 697

Canada

Canada Council Grants for Professional Artists 198
Canada Council Travel Grants 198
International Postgraduate Research Scholarships (IPRS) 413
ORSAS Awards 688
Wingate Scholarships 697

Caribbean Countries

International Postgraduate Research Scholarships (IPRS) 413
ORSAS Awards 688

East European Countries

ArtsLink Independent Projects 221
ArtsLink Residencies 222
International Postgraduate Research Scholarships (IPRS) 413
ORSAS Awards 688

European Union

AHRC Doctoral Awards Scheme 109
CBRL Travel Grant 248
MA in Literature, Film, and Theatre Studies Scholarship 688
PhD in Literature, Film and Theatre Studies Studentship 688
Professional Preparation Master's Scheme

Research Preparation Master's Scheme
Wingate Scholarships 697

Middle East

International Postgraduate Research Scholarships (IPRS) 413
ORSAS Awards 688

New Zealand

The Bruce Mason Playwriting Award 534
ORSAS Awards 688
University of Canterbury and Creative New Zealand Ursula Bethell
 Residency in Creative Writing 678
Wingate Scholarships 697

South Africa

International Postgraduate Research Scholarships (IPRS) 413
ORSAS Awards 688
Wingate Scholarships 697

United Kingdom

Aberystwyth Postgraduate Research Studentships 4
AHRC Doctoral Awards Scheme 109
The Airey Neave Research Fellowships 11
The Authors' Foundation Grant
CBRL Research Award 248
CBRL Travel Grant 248
Elizabeth Longford Grants 609
ESU Chautauqua Institution Scholarships 280
Great Britain Sasakawa Foundation Grants 609
International Postgraduate Research Scholarships (IPRS) 413
The K. Blundell Trust Grant 609
Michael Meyer Award 610
Oppenheim–John Downes Trust Grants 513
Professional Preparation Master's Scheme
Research Preparation Master's Scheme
Wingate Scholarships 697

United States of America

ASOR W.F. Albright Institute of Archaeological Research/National
 Endowment of the Humanities Fellowships 84
British Marshall Scholarships 685
Ernest Hemingway Research Grants 405
Fulbright Senior Specialists Program 249
Hurston-Wright Legacy Award 349
International Postgraduate Research Scholarships (IPRS) 413
Joseph Henry Jackson Literary Award 580
Kennedy Research Grants 405
McKnight Artists Fellowship for Screenwriters 467
Nelson Algren Awards 233
ORSAS Awards 688
PEN Writer's Fund
Virginia Liebeler Biennial Grants for Mature Women (Art) 484
Virginia Liebeler Biennial Grants for Mature Women (Music) 484
Virginia Liebeler Biennial Grants for Mature Women (Writing) 484

West European Countries

International Postgraduate Research Scholarships (IPRS) 413

NATIVE LANGUAGE AND LITERATURE

Any Country

BIAA Post-Doctoral Research Fellowship 168
BIAA Research Scholarship 168
BIAA Study Grants 168
Committee on Institutional Co-operation Faculty Fellowship 502
Earthwatch Field Research Grants 272
Frederick Douglass Institute Postdoctoral Fellowship 304
Frederick Douglass Institute Predoctoral Dissertation Fellowship 304
Gypsy Lore Society Young Scholar's Prize in Romani Studies 328
Institute of Irish Studies Research Fellowships 367
The Metchie J E Budka Award of the Kosciuszko Foundation 412

Onassis Foreigners' Fellowships Programme Research Grants
 Category AI 15
SOAS Open Scholarship 583
Susan Kelly Power and Helen Hornbeck Tanner Fellowship 504

African Nations

International Postgraduate Research Scholarships (IPRS) 413

Australia

Asialink Residency Program 111
NSW Premier's Literary Awards
NSW Premier's Translation Prize
Wingate Scholarships 697

Canada

International Postgraduate Research Scholarships (IPRS) 413
Mary McNeill Scholarship in Irish Studies 368
Ministry of Education, Science and Culture (Iceland) Scholarships in
 Icelandic Studies 449
Wingate Scholarships 697

Caribbean Countries

International Postgraduate Research Scholarships (IPRS) 413

East European Countries

International Postgraduate Research Scholarships (IPRS) 413
Ministry of Education, Science and Culture (Iceland) Scholarships in
 Icelandic Studies 449

European Union

AHRC Doctoral Awards Scheme 109
CBRL Travel Grant 248
Professional Preparation Master's Scheme
Research Preparation Master's Scheme
Wingate Scholarships 697

Middle East

International Postgraduate Research Scholarships (IPRS)
 413

New Zealand

Wingate Scholarships 697

South Africa

International Postgraduate Research Scholarships (IPRS) 413
Wingate Scholarships 697

United Kingdom

AHRC Doctoral Awards Scheme 109
BACS Travel Awards 160
CBRL Research Award 248
CBRL Travel Grant 248
International Postgraduate Research Scholarships (IPRS) 413
Ministry of Education, Science and Culture (Iceland) Scholarships in
 Icelandic Studies 449
Pilcher Senior Research Fellowship 769
Professional Preparation Master's Scheme
Research Preparation Master's Scheme
The Stott Fellowship 769
University of Kent School of European Culture and Languages
 Scholarships 701
University of Kent School of European Culture and Languages
 Studentships 701
Wingate Scholarships 697

United States of America

Ford Foundation Dissertation Fellowships for Minorities 487
International Postgraduate Research Scholarships (IPRS) 413
Mary McNeill Scholarship in Irish Studies 368
Ministry of Education, Science and Culture (Iceland) Scholarships in
 Icelandic Studies 449

West European Countries

MODERN LANGUAGES AND LITERATURES

Any Country

African Nations

Australia

Canada

Caribbean Countries

East European Countries

European Union

Middle East

New Zealand

South Africa

International Postgraduate Research Scholarships (IPRS) 413
ORSAS Awards 688
Wingate Scholarships 697

United Kingdom

Aberystwyth Postgraduate Research Studentships 4
AHRC Doctoral Awards Scheme 109
BAAS Short Term Awards 159
CBRL Research Award 248
CBRL Travel Grant 248
ESU Chautauqua Institution Scholarships 280
International Postgraduate Research Scholarships (IPRS) 413
John Speak Trust Scholarships 156
Professional Preparation Master's Scheme
Research Preparation Master's Scheme
University of Kent School of European Culture and Languages
    Scholarships 701
University of Kent School of European Culture and Languages
    Studentships 701
Wingate Scholarships 697

United States of America

AAS-National Endowment for the Humanities Visiting Fellowships 27
ACLS Frederick Burkhardt Fellowship 27
ARCE Fellowships 80
British Marshall Scholarships 685
CIA Graduate Studies Program Scholarship 225
Edouard Morot-Sir Fellowship in Literature 361
Foreign Language and Area Studies (FLAS) Fellowships 674
Fulbright Distinguished Chairs Program 248
Fulbright Senior Specialists Program 249
Gilbert Chinard Fellowships 361
International Postgraduate Research Scholarships (IPRS) 413
IREX Individual Advanced Research Opportunities 388
ITBE Graduate Scholarship 352
Kennedy Research Grants 405
Mary McNeill Scholarship in Irish Studies 368
Michael and Marie Marucci Scholarship 475
ORSAS Awards 688
SSRC JSPS Postdoctoral Fellowship 599
Summer Language Study Grants in Turkey for Graduate Studies 369
Virginia Liebeler Biennial Grants for Mature Women (Writing) 484
The Walter J Jensen Fellowship for French Language, Literature and
    Culture 531

West European Countries

International Postgraduate Research Scholarships (IPRS) 413
Lady Gregory Fellowship Scheme 490
University of Kent School of European Culture and Languages
    Scholarships 701
University of Kent School of European Culture and Languages
    Studentships 701

ENGLISH

Any Country

Acadia Graduate Awards 5
Ahmanson and Getty Postdoctoral Fellowships 639
Aldo and Jeanne Scaglione Prize for Studies in Germanic Languages
    and Literatures 453
Aldo and Jeanne Scaglione Prize for Studies in Slavic Languages and
    Literatures 453
ASECS (American Society for 18th-Century Studies)/Clark Library
    Fellowships 639
AUC Writing Center Graduate Fellowships 98
Barbara Thom Postdoctoral Fellowship 347
Barron Bequest 787
CC-CS Scholarship Program 223
Clark Library Short-Term Resident Fellowships 639
Clark Predoctoral Fellowships 639
Clark-Huntington Joint Bibliographical Fellowship 640
David T K Wong Fellowship 682

Delahaye Memorial Benefaction 768
ETS Summer Internship Program for Graduate Students 276
Helen McCormack Turner Memorial Scholarship 768
Herbert Hughes Scholarship 768
Ian Gregor Scholarship 698
Kanner Fellowship In British Studies 640
La Trobe University Postgraduate Scholarship 414
Lewis Walpole Library Fellowship 421
Library Company of Philadelphia and Historical Society of Pennsyl-
    vania Research Fellowships in American History and Culture 422
Linacre College: Linacre Rausing Scholarship 733
Mary Radcliffe Scholarship 768
Mellon Fellowships 348
Mina P Shaughnessy Prize 454
Queen Mary Research Studentships 539
Rhodes University Postdoctoral Fellowship and The Andrew Mellon
    Postdoctoral Fellowship 548
RHYS Curzon-Jones Scholarship 768
Ridley Lewis Bursary 769
Thank-Offering to Britain Fellowships 159
Theodora Bosanquet Bursary 291
United States Holocaust Memorial Museum Center for Advanced
    Holocaust Studies Visiting Scholar Programs 641
University of Bristol Postgraduate Scholarships 672
University of Kent English Scholarship 700
University of Manitoba Graduate Fellowship 706
University of Manitoba Teaching Assistantships 706
University of Otago International Scholarships 717
University of Otago PhD Scholarships 718
University of Otago Prestigious PhD Scholarships 718
University of Southampton Postgraduate Studentships 759
W D Llewelyn Memorial Benefaction 769
William Sanders Scarborough Prize 454
World Universities Network (WUN) International Research Mobility
    Scheme 759

African Nations

International Postgraduate Research Scholarships (IPRS) 413

Australia

University of Otago Master's Awards 717
Wingate Scholarships 697

Canada

International Postgraduate Research Scholarships (IPRS) 413
Wingate Scholarships 697

Caribbean Countries

International Postgraduate Research Scholarships (IPRS) 413

East European Countries

International Postgraduate Research Scholarships (IPRS) 413

European Union

AHRC Doctoral Awards Scheme 109
Alexander and Dixon Scholarship (Bryce Bequest) 693
CBRL Travel Grant 248
Joseph Wright Scholarship 703
PhD Studentships 107
Professional Preparation Master's Scheme
Research Preparation Master's Scheme
Wingate Scholarships 697

Middle East

International Postgraduate Research Scholarships (IPRS) 413

New Zealand

University of Otago Master's Awards 717
Wingate Scholarships 697

South Africa

International Postgraduate Research Scholarships (IPRS) 413
Wingate Scholarships 697

United Kingdom

Aberystwyth Postgraduate Research Studentships 4
AHRC Doctoral Awards Scheme 109
Alexander and Dixon Scholarship (Bryce Bequest) 693
BAAS Short Term Awards 159
CBRL Travel Grant 248
English Faculty: Violet Vaughan Morgan Studentship 725
International Postgraduate Research Scholarships (IPRS) 413
Joseph Wright Scholarship 703
Mr and Mrs David Edward Memorial Award 145
PhD Studentships 107
Professional Preparation Master's Scheme
Research Preparation Master's Scheme
Wingate Scholarships 697

United States of America

ASOR W.F. Albright Institute of Archaeological Research/National
  Endowment of the Humanities Fellowships 84
The Berg Family Endowed Scholarship 456
British Marshall Scholarships 685
Ernest Hemingway Research Grants 405
ETS Summer Internship Program for Graduate Students 276
Fulbright Distinguished Chairs Program 248
Fulbright Senior Specialists Program 249
Fulbright Teacher Exchange 307
International Postgraduate Research Scholarships (IPRS) 413
MA English Literature Scholarships 777
National Endowment for the Humanities Fellowships 348

West European Countries

International Postgraduate Research Scholarships (IPRS) 413
Mr and Mrs David Edward Memorial Award 145
PhD Studentships 107
University of Otago Master's Awards 717

FRENCH

Any Country

Ahmanson and Getty Postdoctoral Fellowships 639
Aldo and Jeanne Scaglione Prize for French and Francophone
  Literary Studies 452
ASECS (American Society for 18th-Century Studies)/Clark Library
  Fellowships 639
Barron Bequest 787
Camargo Fellowships 182
Clark Library Short-Term Resident Fellowships 639
Clark Predoctoral Fellowships 639
Clark-Huntington Joint Bibliographical Fellowship 640
Claude and Vincenette Pichois Research Award 680
La Trobe University Postgraduate Scholarship 414
Lewis Walpole Library Fellowship 421
Mary Isabel Sibley Fellowship 531
Queen Mary Research Studentships 539
Quinn, Nathan and Edmond Scholarships 706
Society for the Study of French History Bursaries 606
United States Holocaust Memorial Museum Center for Advanced
  Holocaust Studies Visiting Scholar Programs 641
University of Bristol Postgraduate Scholarships 672
University of Otago International Scholarships 717
University of Otago PhD Scholarships 718
University of Otago Prestigious PhD Scholarships 718
University of Southampton Postgraduate Studentships 759
Warwick French Department Bursaries 775
World Universities Network (WUN) International Research Mobility
  Scheme 759

African Nations

International Postgraduate Research Scholarships (IPRS) 413

Australia

French Government Postgraduate Scholarships 279
University of Otago Master's Awards 717
Wingate Scholarships 697

Canada

Edouard Morot-Sir Fellowship in Literature 361
Gilbert Chinard Fellowships 361
Harmon Chadbourn Rorison Fellowship 361
International Postgraduate Research Scholarships (IPRS) 413
Wingate Scholarships 697

Caribbean Countries

International Postgraduate Research Scholarships (IPRS) 413

East European Countries

International Postgraduate Research Scholarships (IPRS) 413

European Union

AHRC Doctoral Awards Scheme 109
Professional Preparation Master's Scheme
Research Preparation Master's Scheme
Wingate Scholarships 697

Middle East

International Postgraduate Research Scholarships (IPRS) 413

New Zealand

University of Otago Master's Awards 717
Wingate Scholarships 697

South Africa

International Postgraduate Research Scholarships (IPRS) 413
Wingate Scholarships 697

United Kingdom

Aberystwyth Postgraduate Research Studentships 4
AHRC Doctoral Awards Scheme 109
International Postgraduate Research Scholarships (IPRS)
  413
Mr and Mrs David Edward Memorial Award 145
Professional Preparation Master's Scheme
Research Preparation Master's Scheme
University of Kent School of European Culture and Languages
  Scholarships 701
University of Kent School of European Culture and Languages
  Studentships 701
Wingate Scholarships 697

United States of America

British Marshall Scholarships 685
Edouard Morot-Sir Fellowship in Literature 361
Fulbright Teacher Exchange 307
Gilbert Chinard Fellowships 361
Harmon Chadbourn Rorison Fellowship 361
International Postgraduate Research Scholarships (IPRS) 413
The Walter J Jensen Fellowship for French Language, Literature and
  Culture 531

West European Countries

International Postgraduate Research Scholarships (IPRS) 413
Mr and Mrs David Edward Memorial Award 145
University of Kent School of European Culture and Languages
  Scholarships 701
University of Kent School of European Culture and Languages
  Studentships 701
University of Otago Master's Awards 717

SPANISH

Any Country

Ahmanson and Getty Postdoctoral Fellowships 639
ASECS (American Society for 18th-Century Studies)/Clark Library
  Fellowships 639
Barron Bequest 787
CC-CS Scholarship Program 223

Clark Library Short-Term Resident Fellowships 639
Clark Predoctoral Fellowships 639
Clark-Huntington Joint Bibliographical Fellowship 640
Exeter College Queen Sofia Research Fellowship 288
Katherine Singer Kovacs Prize 453
Queen Mary Research Studentships 539
United States Holocaust Memorial Museum Center for Advanced
    Holocaust Studies Visiting Scholar Programs 641
University of Bristol Postgraduate Scholarships 672
University of Southampton Postgraduate Studentships 759
World Universities Network (WUN) International Research Mobility
    Scheme 759

Australia

Wingate Scholarships 697

Canada

Wingate Scholarships 697

European Union

AHRC Doctoral Awards Scheme 109
PhD Studentships 107
Professional Preparation Master's Scheme
Research Preparation Master's Scheme
Wingate Scholarships 697

New Zealand

Wingate Scholarships 697

South Africa

Wingate Scholarships 697

United Kingdom

Aberystwyth Postgraduate Research Studentships 4
AHRC Doctoral Awards Scheme 109
Mr and Mrs David Edward Memorial Award 145
PhD Studentships 107
Professional Preparation Master's Scheme
Research Preparation Master's Scheme
University of Kent School of European Culture and Languages
    Scholarships 701
University of Kent School of European Culture and Languages
    Studentships 701
Wingate Scholarships 697

United States of America

British Marshall Scholarships 685
Fulbright Teacher Exchange 307

West European Countries

Mr and Mrs David Edward Memorial Award 145
PhD Studentships 107
University of Kent School of European Culture and Languages
    Scholarships 701
University of Kent School of European Culture and Languages
    Studentships 701

GERMANIC LANGUAGES

Any Country

Ahmanson and Getty Postdoctoral Fellowships 639
Aldo and Jeanne Scaglione Prize for Studies in Germanic Languages
    and Literatures 453
Austro-American Association of Boston Stipend 143
Barron Bequest 787
Clark Library Short-Term Resident Fellowships 639
Clark Predoctoral Fellowships 639
Clark-Huntington Joint Bibliographical Fellowship 640
Queen Mary Research Studentships 539
United States Holocaust Memorial Museum Center for Advanced
    Holocaust Studies Visiting Scholar Programs 641

Australia

Wingate Scholarships 697

Canada

Wingate Scholarships 697

European Union

AHRC Doctoral Awards Scheme 109
Professional Preparation Master's Scheme
Research Preparation Master's Scheme
Wingate Scholarships 697

New Zealand

Wingate Scholarships 697

South Africa

Wingate Scholarships 697

United Kingdom

AHRC Doctoral Awards Scheme 109
Professional Preparation Master's Scheme
Research Preparation Master's Scheme
Wingate Scholarships 697

United States of America

Congress Bundestag Youth Exchange for Young Professionals 221

GERMAN

Any Country

Ahmanson and Getty Postdoctoral Fellowships 639
Aldo and Jeanne Scaglione Prize for Studies in Germanic Languages
    and Literatures 453
ASECS (American Society for 18th-Century Studies)/Clark Library
    Fellowships 639
Austro-American Association of Boston Stipend 143
Barron Bequest 787
Clark Library Short-Term Resident Fellowships 639
Clark Predoctoral Fellowships 639
Clark-Huntington Joint Bibliographical Fellowship 640
Fielden Research Scholarship 650
Queen Mary Research Studentships 539
United States Holocaust Memorial Museum Center for Advanced
    Holocaust Studies Visiting Scholar Programs 641
University of Bristol Postgraduate Scholarships 672
University of Otago International Scholarships 717
University of Otago PhD Scholarships 718
University of Otago Prestigious PhD Scholarships 718
University of Southampton Postgraduate Studentships 759
World Universities Network (WUN) International Research Mobility
    Scheme 759

Australia

University of Otago Master's Awards 717
Wingate Scholarships 697

Canada

Wingate Scholarships 697

European Union

AHRC Doctoral Awards Scheme 109
Joseph Wright Scholarship 703
Professional Preparation Master's Scheme
Research Preparation Master's Scheme
Wingate Scholarships 697

New Zealand

University of Otago Master's Awards 717
Wingate Scholarships 697

South Africa

Wingate Scholarships 697

United Kingdom

Aberystwyth Postgraduate Research Studentships 4
AHRC Doctoral Awards Scheme 109
Joseph Wright Scholarship 703
Mr and Mrs David Edward Memorial Award 145
Professional Preparation Master's Scheme
Research Preparation Master's Scheme
University of Kent School of European Culture and Languages
    Scholarships 701
University of Kent School of European Culture and Languages
    Studentships 701
Wingate Scholarships 697

United States of America

British Marshall Scholarships 685
Congress Bundestag Youth Exchange for Young Professionals 221
Fulbright Teacher Exchange 307

West European Countries

Eugen and Ilse Seibold Award 266
Mr and Mrs David Edward Memorial Award 145
University of Kent School of European Culture and Languages
    Scholarships 701
University of Kent School of European Culture and Languages
    Studentships 701
University of Otago Master's Awards 717

SWEDISH

Any Country

Aldo and Jeanne Scaglione Prize for Studies in Germanic Languages
    and Literatures 453
Barron Bequest 787
United States Holocaust Memorial Museum Center for Advanced
    Holocaust Studies Visiting Scholar Programs 641

Australia

Wingate Scholarships 697

Canada

Wingate Scholarships 697

European Union

AHRC Doctoral Awards Scheme 109
Professional Preparation Master's Scheme
Research Preparation Master's Scheme
Wingate Scholarships 697

New Zealand

Wingate Scholarships 697

South Africa

Wingate Scholarships 697

United Kingdom

AHRC Doctoral Awards Scheme 109
Professional Preparation Master's Scheme
Research Preparation Master's Scheme
Wingate Scholarships 697

DANISH

Any Country

Aldo and Jeanne Scaglione Prize for Studies in Germanic Languages
    and Literatures 453
Barron Bequest 787
United States Holocaust Memorial Museum Center for Advanced
    Holocaust Studies Visiting Scholar Programs 641

Australia

Wingate Scholarships 697

Canada

Wingate Scholarships 697

European Union

AHRC Doctoral Awards Scheme 109
Professional Preparation Master's Scheme
Research Preparation Master's Scheme
Wingate Scholarships 697

New Zealand

Wingate Scholarships 697

South Africa

Wingate Scholarships 697

United Kingdom

AHRC Doctoral Awards Scheme 109
Professional Preparation Master's Scheme
Research Preparation Master's Scheme
Wingate Scholarships 697

NORWEGIAN

Any Country

Aldo and Jeanne Scaglione Prize for Studies in Germanic Languages
    and Literatures 453
Barron Bequest 787
United States Holocaust Memorial Museum Center for Advanced
    Holocaust Studies Visiting Scholar Programs 641

Australia

Wingate Scholarships 697

Canada

Wingate Scholarships 697

European Union

AHRC Doctoral Awards Scheme 109
Professional Preparation Master's Scheme
Research Preparation Master's Scheme
Wingate Scholarships 697

New Zealand

Wingate Scholarships 697

South Africa

Wingate Scholarships 697

United Kingdom

AHRC Doctoral Awards Scheme 109
Professional Preparation Master's Scheme
Research Preparation Master's Scheme
Wingate Scholarships 697

United States of America

Fulbright Teacher Exchange 307
Norwegian Emigration Fund of 1975 508

ITALIAN

Any Country

Ahmanson and Getty Postdoctoral Fellowships 639
Aldo and Jeanne Scaglione Prize for Italian Studies 452
ASECS (American Society for 18th-Century Studies)/Clark Library
    Fellowships 639
Barron Bequest 787
Clark Library Short-Term Resident Fellowships 639
Clark Predoctoral Fellowships 639
Clark-Huntington Joint Bibliographical Fellowship 640

Howard R Marraro Prize 453
United States Holocaust Memorial Museum Center for Advanced
    Holocaust Studies Visiting Scholar Programs 641
University of Bristol Postgraduate Scholarships 672

Australia

Wingate Scholarships 697

Canada

Wingate Scholarships 697

European Union

AHRC Doctoral Awards Scheme 109
Professional Preparation Master's Scheme
Research Preparation Master's Scheme
Wingate Scholarships 697

New Zealand

Wingate Scholarships 697

South Africa

Wingate Scholarships 697

United Kingdom

Aberystwyth Postgraduate Research Studentships 4
AHRC Doctoral Awards Scheme 109
Balsdon Fellowship 174
Professional Preparation Master's Scheme
Research Preparation Master's Scheme
Rome Awards 175
Rome Fellowship 175
Rome Scholarships in Ancient, Medieval and Later Italian Studies
    176
University of Kent School of European Culture and Languages
    Scholarships 701
University of Kent School of European Culture and Languages
    Studentships 701
Wingate Scholarships 697

United States of America

British Marshall Scholarships 685
Gladys Krieble Delmas Foundation Grants 319

West European Countries

University of Kent School of European Culture and Languages
    Scholarships 701
University of Kent School of European Culture and Languages
    Studentships 701

PORTUGUESE

Any Country

Barron Bequest 787
CC-CS Scholarship Program 223
Katherine Singer Kovacs Prize 453
United States Holocaust Memorial Museum Center for Advanced
    Holocaust Studies Visiting Scholar Programs 641
University of Bristol Postgraduate Scholarships 672
University of Southampton Postgraduate Studentships 759
World Universities Network (WUN) International Research Mobility
    Scheme 759

Australia

Wingate Scholarships 697

Canada

Wingate Scholarships 697

European Union

AHRC Doctoral Awards Scheme 109
Professional Preparation Master's Scheme

Research Preparation Master's Scheme
Wingate Scholarships 697

New Zealand

Wingate Scholarships 697

South Africa

Wingate Scholarships 697

United Kingdom

AHRC Doctoral Awards Scheme 109
Professional Preparation Master's Scheme
Research Preparation Master's Scheme
Wingate Scholarships 697

United States of America

British Marshall Scholarships 685

ROMANCE LANGUAGES

Any Country

Ahmanson and Getty Postdoctoral Fellowships 639
ASECS (American Society for 18th-Century Studies)/Clark Library
    Fellowships 639
Camargo Fellowships 182
Clark Library Short-Term Resident Fellowships 639
Clark Predoctoral Fellowships 639
Clark-Huntington Joint Bibliographical Fellowship 640
United States Holocaust Memorial Museum Center for Advanced
    Holocaust Studies Visiting Scholar Programs 641
University of Bristol Postgraduate Scholarships 672

Australia

Wingate Scholarships 697

Canada

Gilbert Chinard Fellowships 361
Harmon Chadbourn Rorison Fellowship 361
Wingate Scholarships 697

European Union

AHRC Doctoral Awards Scheme 109
Professional Preparation Master's Scheme
Research Preparation Master's Scheme
Wingate Scholarships 697

New Zealand

Wingate Scholarships 697

South Africa

Wingate Scholarships 697

United Kingdom

AHRC Doctoral Awards Scheme 109
Professional Preparation Master's Scheme
Research Preparation Master's Scheme
University of Kent School of European Culture and Languages
    Scholarships 701
University of Kent School of European Culture and Languages
    Studentships 701
Wingate Scholarships 697

United States of America

Gilbert Chinard Fellowships 361
Harmon Chadbourn Rorison Fellowship 361

West European Countries

University of Kent School of European Culture and Languages
    Scholarships 701
University of Kent School of European Culture and Languages
    Studentships 701

MODERN GREEK

Any Country

M Alison Frantz Fellowship in Post-Classical Studies at the Gennadius Library 83
Mary Isabel Sibley Fellowship 531
NEH Fellowships 83
United States Holocaust Memorial Museum Center for Advanced Holocaust Studies Visiting Scholar Programs 641

African Nations

Scholarships for Greek Language Studies in Greece 325

Australia

The Constantine Aspromourgos Memorial Scholarship for Greek Studies 751
Wingate Scholarships 697

Canada

Wingate Scholarships 697

East European Countries

Scholarships for Greek Language Studies in Greece 325

European Union

AHRC Doctoral Awards Scheme 109
Professional Preparation Master's Scheme
Research Preparation Master's Scheme
Wingate Scholarships 697

Middle East

Scholarships for Greek Language Studies in Greece 325

New Zealand

Wingate Scholarships 697

South Africa

Wingate Scholarships 697

United Kingdom

AHRC Doctoral Awards Scheme 109
Hector and Elizabeth Catling Bursary 173
Professional Preparation Master's Scheme
Research Preparation Master's Scheme
Wingate Scholarships 697

DUTCH

Any Country

Aldo and Jeanne Scaglione Prize for Studies in Germanic Languages and Literatures 453
Barron Bequest 787
United States Holocaust Memorial Museum Center for Advanced Holocaust Studies Visiting Scholar Programs 641

Australia

Wingate Scholarships 697

Canada

Wingate Scholarships 697

European Union

AHRC Doctoral Awards Scheme 109
Professional Preparation Master's Scheme
Research Preparation Master's Scheme
Wingate Scholarships 697

New Zealand

Wingate Scholarships 697

South Africa

Wingate Scholarships 697

United Kingdom

AHRC Doctoral Awards Scheme 109
Professional Preparation Master's Scheme
Research Preparation Master's Scheme
Wingate Scholarships 697

BALTIC LANGUAGES

Any Country

M Alison Frantz Fellowship in Post-Classical Studies at the Gennadius Library 83
United States Holocaust Memorial Museum Center for Advanced Holocaust Studies Visiting Scholar Programs 641

Australia

Wingate Scholarships 697

Canada

Wingate Scholarships 697

European Union

AHRC Doctoral Awards Scheme 109
Professional Preparation Master's Scheme
Research Preparation Master's Scheme
Wingate Scholarships 697

New Zealand

Wingate Scholarships 697

South Africa

Wingate Scholarships 697

United Kingdom

AHRC Doctoral Awards Scheme 109
Professional Preparation Master's Scheme
Research Preparation Master's Scheme
Wingate Scholarships 697

United States of America

IREX Individual Advanced Research Opportunities 388

CELTIC LANGUAGES

Any Country

Barron Bequest 787
Cornwall Heritage Trust Bursary 691
Delahaye Memorial Benefaction 768
Dublin Institute for Advanced Studies Scholarship in Celtic Studies 270
Helen McCormack Turner Memorial Scholarship 768
Henry Flood Research Scholarship 681
Herbert Hughes Scholarship 768
Mary Radcliffe Scholarship 768
RHYS Curzon-Jones Scholarship 768
Ridley Lewis Bursary 769
W D Llewelyn Memorial Benefaction 769

Australia

Wingate Scholarships 697

Canada

Wingate Scholarships 697

European Union

AHRC Doctoral Awards Scheme 109
Professional Preparation Master's Scheme

Research Preparation Master's Scheme
Wingate Scholarships 697

New Zealand

Wingate Scholarships 697

South Africa

Wingate Scholarships 697

United Kingdom

Aberystwyth Postgraduate Research Studentships 4
AHRC Doctoral Awards Scheme 109
Mr and Mrs David Edward Memorial Award 145
Professional Preparation Master's Scheme
Research Preparation Master's Scheme
Wingate Scholarships 697

West European Countries

Mr and Mrs David Edward Memorial Award 145

FINNISH

Any Country

United States Holocaust Memorial Museum Center for Advanced
  Holocaust Studies Visiting Scholar Programs 641

Australia

Wingate Scholarships 697

Canada

Wingate Scholarships 697

European Union

AHRC Doctoral Awards Scheme 109
Professional Preparation Master's Scheme
Research Preparation Master's Scheme
Wingate Scholarships 697

New Zealand

Wingate Scholarships 697

South Africa

Wingate Scholarships 697

United Kingdom

AHRC Doctoral Awards Scheme 109
Professional Preparation Master's Scheme
Research Preparation Master's Scheme
Wingate Scholarships 697

United States of America

Fulbright Teacher Exchange 307

RUSSIAN

Any Country

Aldo and Jeanne Scaglione Prize for Studies in Slavic Languages and
  Literatures 453
Barron Bequest 787
Kennan Institute Short-Term Grants 408
Queen Mary Research Studentships 539
United States Holocaust Memorial Museum Center for Advanced
  Holocaust Studies Visiting Scholar Programs 641
University of Bristol Postgraduate Scholarships 672

Australia

Wingate Scholarships 697

Canada

Wingate Scholarships 697

European Union

AHRC Doctoral Awards Scheme 109
Professional Preparation Master's Scheme
Research Preparation Master's Scheme
Wingate Scholarships 697

New Zealand

Wingate Scholarships 697

South Africa

Wingate Scholarships 697

United Kingdom

AHRC Doctoral Awards Scheme 109
Professional Preparation Master's Scheme
Research Preparation Master's Scheme
Wingate Scholarships 697

United States of America

IREX Individual Advanced Research Opportunities 388
Kennan Institute Research Scholarship 408

SLAVONIC LANGUAGES (OTHERS)

Any Country

Aldo and Jeanne Scaglione Prize for Studies in Slavic Languages and
  Literatures 453
CIUS Research Grants 209
Helen Darcovich Memorial Doctoral Fellowship 209
Kennan Institute Short-Term Grants 408
Marusia and Michael Dorosh Master's Fellowship 209
The Metchie J E Budka Award of the Kosciuszko Foundation
  412
Neporany Doctoral Fellowship 210
Trinity College MB Grabowski Fund Postgraduate Scholarship in
  Polish Studies 747
United States Holocaust Memorial Museum Center for Advanced
  Holocaust Studies Visiting Scholar Programs 641

Australia

Wingate Scholarships 697

Canada

Wingate Scholarships 697

European Union

AHRC Doctoral Awards Scheme 109
Professional Preparation Master's Scheme
Research Preparation Master's Scheme
Wingate Scholarships 697

New Zealand

Wingate Scholarships 697

South Africa

Wingate Scholarships 697

United Kingdom

AHRC Doctoral Awards Scheme 109
Professional Preparation Master's Scheme
Research Preparation Master's Scheme
Wingate Scholarships 697

United States of America

IREX Individual Advanced Research Opportunities
  388
Kennan Institute Research Scholarship 408
The Kosciuszko Foundation Year Abroad Program
  411

HUNGARIAN

Any Country

United States Holocaust Memorial Museum Center for Advanced
    Holocaust Studies Visiting Scholar Programs 641

Australia

Wingate Scholarships 697

Canada

Wingate Scholarships 697

European Union

AHRC Doctoral Awards Scheme 109
Professional Preparation Master's Scheme
Research Preparation Master's Scheme
Wingate Scholarships 697

New Zealand

Wingate Scholarships 697

South Africa

Wingate Scholarships 697

United Kingdom

AHRC Doctoral Awards Scheme 109
Professional Preparation Master's Scheme
Research Preparation Master's Scheme
Wingate Scholarships 697

United States of America

Fulbright Teacher Exchange 307
IREX Individual Advanced Research Opportunities 388

FINO UGRIAN LANGUAGES

Any Country

United States Holocaust Memorial Museum Center for Advanced
    Holocaust Studies Visiting Scholar Programs 641

Australia

Wingate Scholarships 697

Canada

Wingate Scholarships 697

European Union

AHRC Doctoral Awards Scheme 109
Professional Preparation Master's Scheme
Research Preparation Master's Scheme
Wingate Scholarships 697

New Zealand

Wingate Scholarships 697

South Africa

Wingate Scholarships 697

United Kingdom

AHRC Doctoral Awards Scheme 109
Professional Preparation Master's Scheme
Research Preparation Master's Scheme
Wingate Scholarships 697

EUROPEAN LANGUAGES (OTHERS)

Any Country

United States Holocaust Memorial Museum Center for Advanced
    Holocaust Studies Visiting Scholar Programs 641

Australia

Wingate Scholarships 697

Canada

Wingate Scholarships 697

European Union

AHRC Doctoral Awards Scheme 109
Professional Preparation Master's Scheme
Research Preparation Master's Scheme
Wingate Scholarships 697

New Zealand

Wingate Scholarships 697

South Africa

Wingate Scholarships 697

United Kingdom

Aberystwyth Postgraduate Research Studentships 4
AHRC Doctoral Awards Scheme 109
Professional Preparation Master's Scheme
Research Preparation Master's Scheme
Wingate Scholarships 697

United States of America

Summer Language Study Grants in Turkey for Graduate Studies 369

ALTAIC LANGUAGES

Australia

Wingate Scholarships 697

Canada

Wingate Scholarships 697

European Union

AHRC Doctoral Awards Scheme 109
Professional Preparation Master's Scheme
Research Preparation Master's Scheme
Wingate Scholarships 697

New Zealand

Wingate Scholarships 697

South Africa

Wingate Scholarships 697

United Kingdom

AHRC Doctoral Awards Scheme 109
Professional Preparation Master's Scheme
Research Preparation Master's Scheme
Wingate Scholarships 697

United States of America

Summer Language Study Grants in Turkey for Graduate Studies 369

ARABIC

Any Country

AUC International Graduate Fellowships in Arabic Studies, Middle
    East Studies and Sociology/Anthropology 97
AUC Teaching Arabic as a Foreign Language Fellowships 98
British Academy Ancient Persia Fund 158
SOAS Bursary 583
SOAS Research Student Fellowships 583

Australia

Wingate Scholarships 697

Canada

Wingate Scholarships 697

European Union

AHRC Doctoral Awards Scheme 109
CBRL Travel Grant 248
Professional Preparation Master's Scheme
Research Preparation Master's Scheme
Wingate Scholarships 697

New Zealand

Wingate Scholarships 697

South Africa

Wingate Scholarships 697

United Kingdom

AHRC Doctoral Awards Scheme 109
CBRL Research Award 248
CBRL Travel Grant 248
Professional Preparation Master's Scheme
Research Preparation Master's Scheme
Wingate Scholarships 697

United States of America

ARCE Fellowships 80
Fulbright Teacher Exchange 307

HEBREW

Any Country

Barron Bequest 787
IAUW International Scholarship 166
Jacob Hirsch Fellowship 83
SOAS Bursary 583
SOAS Research Student Fellowships 583
United States Holocaust Memorial Museum Center for Advanced
   Holocaust Studies Visiting Scholar Programs 641

Australia

Wingate Scholarships 697

Canada

JCCA Graduate Education Scholarship 400
Wingate Scholarships 697

European Union

AHRC Doctoral Awards Scheme 109
CBRL Travel Grant 248
Professional Preparation Master's Scheme
Research Preparation Master's Scheme
Wingate Scholarships 697

New Zealand

Wingate Scholarships 697

South Africa

Wingate Scholarships 697

United Kingdom

AHRC Doctoral Awards Scheme 109
CBRL Research Award 248
CBRL Travel Grant 248
Professional Preparation Master's Scheme
Research Preparation Master's Scheme
Wingate Scholarships 697

United States of America

JCCA Graduate Education Scholarship 400

CHINESE

Any Country

An Wang Postdoctoral Fellowship 289
SOAS Bursary 583
SOAS Research Student Fellowships 583
United States Holocaust Memorial Museum Center for Advanced
   Holocaust Studies Visiting Scholar Programs 641

Australia

Wingate Scholarships 697

Canada

Wingate Scholarships 697

European Union

AHRC Doctoral Awards Scheme 109
Bernard Buckman Scholarship 582
Professional Preparation Master's Scheme
Research Preparation Master's Scheme
Wingate Scholarships 697

New Zealand

Wingate Scholarships 697

South Africa

Wingate Scholarships 697

United Kingdom

AHRC Doctoral Awards Scheme 109
Bernard Buckman Scholarship 582
Professional Preparation Master's Scheme
Research Preparation Master's Scheme
Wingate Scholarships 697

United States of America

Blakemore Freeman Fellowships for Advanced Asian Language Study
   154
Blakemore Refresher Grants: Short-Term Grants for Advanced Asian
   Language Study 154

West European Countries

Bernard Buckman Scholarship 582

KOREAN

Any Country

A K S Postgraduate Korean Studies 582
SOAS Bursary 583
SOAS Research Student Fellowships 583
SOCHOW Foundation Scholarship 583

Australia

Wingate Scholarships 697

Canada

Wingate Scholarships 697

European Union

AHRC Doctoral Awards Scheme 109
Professional Preparation Master's Scheme
Research Preparation Master's Scheme
Wingate Scholarships 697

New Zealand

Wingate Scholarships 697

South Africa

Wingate Scholarships 697

United Kingdom

AHRC Doctoral Awards Scheme 109
Professional Preparation Master's Scheme
Research Preparation Master's Scheme
Wingate Scholarships 697

United States of America

Blakemore Freeman Fellowships for Advanced Asian Language Study 154
Blakemore Refresher Grants: Short-Term Grants for Advanced Asian Language Study 154

JAPANESE

Any Country

Harvard Postdoctoral Fellowships in Japanese Studies 277
SOAS Bursary 583
SOAS Research Student Fellowships 583
United States Holocaust Memorial Museum Center for Advanced Holocaust Studies Visiting Scholar Programs 641
Western Australian Government Japanese Studies Scholarship 263

Australia

Wingate Scholarships 697

Canada

Wingate Scholarships 697

European Union

AHRC Doctoral Awards Scheme 109
Professional Preparation Master's Scheme
Research Preparation Master's Scheme
Wingate Scholarships 697

New Zealand

Wingate Scholarships 697

South Africa

Wingate Scholarships 697

United Kingdom

AHRC Doctoral Awards Scheme 109
Professional Preparation Master's Scheme
Research Preparation Master's Scheme
Wingate Scholarships 697

United States of America

Blakemore Freeman Fellowships for Advanced Asian Language Study 154
Blakemore Refresher Grants: Short-Term Grants for Advanced Asian Language Study 154

West European Countries

Eugen and Ilse Seibold Award 266

INDIAN LANGUAGES

Any Country

IFUWA Sarojini Naidu Memorial Scholarship 167
SOAS Bursary 583
SOAS Research Student Fellowships 583

Australia

Wingate Scholarships 697

Canada

Wingate Scholarships 697

European Union

AHRC Doctoral Awards Scheme 109
Professional Preparation Master's Scheme
Research Preparation Master's Scheme
Wingate Scholarships 697

New Zealand

Wingate Scholarships 697

South Africa

Wingate Scholarships 697

United Kingdom

AHRC Doctoral Awards Scheme 109
Professional Preparation Master's Scheme
Research Preparation Master's Scheme
Wingate Scholarships 697

IRANIC LANGUAGES

Any Country

British Academy Ancient Persia Fund 158
SOAS Bursary 583
SOAS Research Student Fellowships 583

African Nations

British School of Archaeology in Iraq Grants 169

Australia

British School of Archaeology in Iraq Grants 169
Wingate Scholarships 697

Canada

British School of Archaeology in Iraq Grants 169
Wingate Scholarships 697

European Union

AHRC Doctoral Awards Scheme 109
Professional Preparation Master's Scheme
Research Preparation Master's Scheme
Wingate Scholarships 697

New Zealand

British School of Archaeology in Iraq Grants 169
Wingate Scholarships 697

South Africa

British School of Archaeology in Iraq Grants 169
Wingate Scholarships 697

United Kingdom

AHRC Doctoral Awards Scheme 109
British School of Archaeology in Iraq Grants 169
Professional Preparation Master's Scheme
Research Preparation Master's Scheme
Wingate Scholarships 697

AFRICAN LANGUAGES

Any Country

Frederick Douglass Institute Postdoctoral Fellowship 304
Frederick Douglass Institute Predoctoral Dissertation Fellowship 304
Rhodes University Postdoctoral Fellowship and The Andrew Mellon Postdoctoral Fellowship 548
SOAS Bursary 583
SOAS Research Student Fellowships 583

Australia

Wingate Scholarships 697

Canada

Wingate Scholarships 697

European Union

AHRC Doctoral Awards Scheme 109
Professional Preparation Master's Scheme
Research Preparation Master's Scheme
Wingate Scholarships 697

New Zealand

Wingate Scholarships 697

South Africa

Wingate Scholarships 697

United Kingdom

AHRC Doctoral Awards Scheme 109
British Institute in Eastern Africa Minor Grants 169
Professional Preparation Master's Scheme
Research Preparation Master's Scheme
Wingate Scholarships 697

AMERINDIAN LANGUAGES

Any Country

Frederick Douglass Institute Postdoctoral Fellowship 304
Frederick Douglass Institute Predoctoral Dissertation Fellowship
   304

Australia

Wingate Scholarships 697

Canada

Wingate Scholarships 697

European Union

AHRC Doctoral Awards Scheme 109
Professional Preparation Master's Scheme
Research Preparation Master's Scheme
Wingate Scholarships 697

New Zealand

Wingate Scholarships 697

South Africa

Wingate Scholarships 697

United Kingdom

AHRC Doctoral Awards Scheme 109
BACS Travel Awards 160
Professional Preparation Master's Scheme
Research Preparation Master's Scheme
Wingate Scholarships 697

AUSTRONESIAN AND OCEANIC LANGUAGES

Any Country

Frederick Douglass Institute Postdoctoral Fellowship 304
Frederick Douglass Institute Predoctoral Dissertation Fellowship 304

Australia

Wingate Scholarships 697

Canada

Wingate Scholarships 697

European Union

AHRC Doctoral Awards Scheme 109
Professional Preparation Master's Scheme

Research Preparation Master's Scheme
Wingate Scholarships 697

New Zealand

Wingate Scholarships 697

South Africa

Wingate Scholarships 697

United Kingdom

AHRC Doctoral Awards Scheme 109
Professional Preparation Master's Scheme
Research Preparation Master's Scheme
Wingate Scholarships 697

CLASSICAL LANGUAGES AND LITERATURES

Any Country

Aldo and Jeanne Scaglione Prize for a Translation of a Literary Work
   452
Aldo and Jeanne Scaglione Prize for Comparative Literary Studies
   452
ASCSA Advanced Fellowships 82
ASCSA Fellowships 82
BIAA Post-Doctoral Research Fellowship 168
BIAA Research Scholarship 168
BIAA Study Grants 168
British Academy Overseas Conference Grants 158
British Academy Postdoctoral Fellowships 158
British Academy Research Development Awards (BARDAs)
   158
British Academy Small Research Grants 158
British Academy Worldwide Congress Grant 159
British Conference Grants 159
Center for Hellenic Studies Junior Fellowships 223
Charlotte W Newcombe Doctoral Dissertation Fellowships 803
CRF (Caledonian Research Foundation)/RSE European Visiting
   Research Fellowships 628
Dumbarton Oaks Fellowships and Junior Fellowships 271
Findel Scholarships and Schneider Scholarships 340
Frances A Yates Fellowships 789
Graduate Dissertation Research Fellowship 448
Graduate Summer Travel Grants 449
Grete Sondheimer Fellowship 790
Hugh Le May Fellowship 548
Jacob Hirsch Fellowship 83
James Russell Lowell Prize 453
Lois Roth Award for a Translation of Literary Work 454
M Alison Frantz Fellowship in Post-Classical Studies at the Gennadius
   Library 83
Mary Isabel Sibley Fellowship 531
Minda de Gunzberg Graduate Dissertation Writing Fellowship 449
MLA Prize for a Distinguished Scholarly Edition 454
MLA Prize for a First Book 454
MLA Prize for Independent Scholars 454
Onassis Foreigners' Fellowship Programme Educational Scholarships
   Category B 15
St Catherine's College Graduate Scholarship in the Arts
University of Bristol Postgraduate Scholarships 672
University of Otago International Scholarships 717
University of Otago PhD Scholarships 718
University of Otago Prestigious PhD Scholarships 718

African Nations

Harry Crossley Doctoral Fellowship 620
ORSAS Awards 688

Australia

AAH Humanities Travelling Fellowships 132
ORSAS Awards 688
University of Otago Master's Awards 717
Wingate Scholarships 697

Canada

ORSAS Awards 688
Vatican Film Library Mellon Fellowship 785
Wingate Scholarships 697

Caribbean Countries

ORSAS Awards 688

East European Countries

Brian Hewson Crawford Fellowship 789
Freie Universität Berlin John-F.-Kennedy-Institut für Nordamerikastu-
    dien Research Grants 304
ORSAS Awards 688
Warburg Mellon Research Fellowship 790

European Union

AHRC Doctoral Awards Scheme 109
CBRL Travel Grant 248
Freie Universität Berlin John-F.-Kennedy-Institut für Nordamerikastu-
    dien Research Grants 304
MA in Literature, Film, and Theatre Studies Scholarship 688
Professional Preparation Master's Scheme
Research Preparation Master's Scheme
School of Law AHRC Scholarships 689
Warburg Mellon Research Fellowship 790
Wingate Scholarships 697

Middle East

ORSAS Awards 688

New Zealand

ORSAS Awards 688
University of Otago Master's Awards 717
Wingate Scholarships 697

South Africa

Harry Crossley Doctoral Fellowship 620
ORSAS Awards 688
Wingate Scholarships 697

United Kingdom

AHRC Doctoral Awards Scheme 109
CBRL Research Award 248
CBRL Travel Grant 248
Frances A Yates Fellowships 789
Grete Sondheimer Fellowship 790
Professional Preparation Master's Scheme
Research Preparation Master's Scheme
School of Law AHRC Scholarships 689
University of Kent School of European Culture and Languages
    Scholarships 701
University of Kent School of European Culture and Languages
    Studentships 701
Wingate Scholarships 697

United States of America

British Marshall Scholarships 685
Fulbright Distinguished Chairs Program 248
ORSAS Awards 688
SSRC JSPS Postdoctoral Fellowship 599
Vatican Film Library Mellon Fellowship 785

West European Countries

Brian Hewson Crawford Fellowship 789
Freie Universität Berlin John-F.-Kennedy-Institut für Nordamerikastu-
    dien Research Grants 304
University of Kent School of European Culture and Languages
    Scholarships 701
University of Kent School of European Culture and Languages
    Studentships 701
University of Otago Master's Awards 717

LATIN

Any Country

Grete Sondheimer Fellowship 790
Hugh Last and Donald Atkinson Funds Committee Grants 604

Australia

Wingate Scholarships 697

Canada

Wingate Scholarships 697

East European Countries

Warburg Mellon Research Fellowship 790

European Union

AHRC Doctoral Awards Scheme 109
Professional Preparation Master's Scheme
Research Preparation Master's Scheme
Warburg Mellon Research Fellowship 790
Wingate Scholarships 697

New Zealand

Wingate Scholarships 697

South Africa

Wingate Scholarships 697

United Kingdom

Access to Learning Fund 685
AHRC Doctoral Awards Scheme 109
Balsdon Fellowship 174
Grete Sondheimer Fellowship 790
Hugh Last Fellowship 175
Professional Preparation Master's Scheme
Research Preparation Master's Scheme
Rome Awards 175
Rome Fellowship 175
Rome Scholarships in Ancient, Medieval and Later Italian Studies
    176
University of Kent School of European Culture and Languages
    Scholarships 701
University of Kent School of European Culture and Languages
    Studentships 701
Wingate Scholarships 697

United States of America

Fulbright Teacher Exchange 307

West European Countries

University of Kent School of European Culture and Languages
    Scholarships 701
University of Kent School of European Culture and Languages
    Studentships 701

CLASSICAL GREEK

Any Country

ASCSA Advanced Fellowships 82
ASCSA Fellowships 82
Center for Hellenic Studies Junior Fellowships 223
Delahaye Memorial Benefaction 768
Grete Sondheimer Fellowship 790
Helen McCormack Turner Memorial Scholarship 768
Herbert Hughes Scholarship 768
Mary Isabel Sibley Fellowship 531
Mary Radcliffe Scholarship 768
NEH Fellowships 83
Onassis Foreigners' Fellowship Programme Educational Scholarships
    Category B 15
RHYS Curzon-Jones Scholarship 768

Ridley Lewis Bursary 769
W D Llewelyn Memorial Benefaction 769

Australia

The Constantine Aspromourgos Memorial Scholarship for Greek
    Studies 751
Wingate Scholarships 697

Canada

Wingate Scholarships 697

European Union

AHRC Doctoral Awards Scheme 109
Professional Preparation Master's Scheme
Research Preparation Master's Scheme
Wingate Scholarships 697

New Zealand

Wingate Scholarships 697

South Africa

Wingate Scholarships 697

United Kingdom

AHRC Doctoral Awards Scheme 109
The Dover Fund 604
Grete Sondheimer Fellowship 790
Hector and Elizabeth Catling Bursary 173
Professional Preparation Master's Scheme
Research Preparation Master's Scheme
University of Kent School of European Culture and Languages
    Scholarships 701
University of Kent School of European Culture and Languages
    Studentships 701
Wingate Scholarships 697

United States of America

Fulbright Teacher Exchange 307

West European Countries

University of Kent School of European Culture and Languages
    Scholarships 701
University of Kent School of European Culture and Languages
    Studentships 701

SANSKRIT

Any Country

SOAS Bursary 583
SOAS Open Scholarship 583
SOAS Research Student Fellowships 583

Australia

Wingate Scholarships 697

Canada

Wingate Scholarships 697

European Union

AHRC Doctoral Awards Scheme 109
Professional Preparation Master's Scheme
Research Preparation Master's Scheme
Wingate Scholarships 697

New Zealand

Wingate Scholarships 697

South Africa

Wingate Scholarships 697

United Kingdom

AHRC Doctoral Awards Scheme 109
Professional Preparation Master's Scheme
Research Preparation Master's Scheme
Wingate Scholarships 697

LINGUISTICS AND PHILOLOGY

Any Country

Aldo and Jeanne Scaglione Prize for French and Francophone
    Literary Studies 452
Aldo and Jeanne Scaglione Prize for Studies in Germanic Languages
    and Literatures 453
Aldo and Jeanne Scaglione Prize for Studies in Slavic Languages and
    Literatures 453
ASCSA Advanced Fellowships 82
ASCSA Fellowships 82
BIAA Post-Doctoral Research Fellowship 168
BIAA Research Scholarship 168
BIAA Study Grants 168
British Academy Overseas Conference Grants 158
British Academy Postdoctoral Fellowships 158
British Academy Small Research Grants 158
British Conference Grants 159
Camargo Fellowships 182
CRF (Caledonian Research Foundation)/RSE European Visiting
    Research Fellowships 628
ETS Postdoctoral Fellowships 276
Fondation Fyssen Postdoctoral Study Grants 297
Graduate Dissertation Research Fellowship 448
Graduate Summer Travel Grants 449
Gypsy Lore Society Young Scholar's Prize in Romani Studies 328
Jacob Hirsch Fellowship 83
James Russell Lowell Prize 453
Kenneth W Mildenberger Prize 453
La Trobe University Postgraduate Scholarship 414
M Alison Frantz Fellowship in Post-Classical Studies at the Gennadius
    Library 83
Marusia and Michael Dorosh Master's Fellowship 209
Mina P Shaughnessy Prize 454
Minda de Gunzberg Graduate Dissertation Writing Fellowship 449
MLA Prize for a Distinguished Bibliography 454
MLA Prize for a First Book 454
MLA Prize for Independent Scholars 454
NEH Fellowships 83
Neporany Doctoral Fellowship 210
Onassis Foreigners' Fellowships Programme Research Grants
    Category AI 15
Phillips Fund Grants for Native American Research 74
Queen Mary Research Studentships 539
SOAS Bursary 583
SOAS Open Scholarship 583
SOAS Research Student Fellowships 583
St Catherine's College Graduate Scholarship in the Arts
United States Holocaust Memorial Museum Center for Advanced
    Holocaust Studies Visiting Scholar Programs 641
University of Otago International Scholarships 717
University of Otago PhD Scholarships 718
University of Otago Prestigious PhD Scholarships 718
University of Southampton Postgraduate Studentships 759
World Universities Network (WUN) International Research Mobility
    Scheme 759

African Nations

British School of Archaeology in Iraq Grants 169
Department of Language and Linguistics ORSAS Award 686
ORSAS Awards 688

Australia

AAH Humanities Travelling Fellowships 132
Australian Postgraduate Awards 413
British School of Archaeology in Iraq Grants 169
Department of Language and Linguistics ORSAS Award 686

ORSAS Awards 688
University of Otago Master's Awards 717
Wingate Scholarships 697

Canada

British School of Archaeology in Iraq Grants 169
Department of Language and Linguistics ORSAS Award 686
Gilbert Chinard Fellowships 361
Harmon Chadbourn Rorison Fellowship 361
ORSAS Awards 688
Wingate Scholarships 697

Caribbean Countries

Department of Language and Linguistics ORSAS Award 686
ORSAS Awards 688

East European Countries

ORSAS Awards 688

European Union

AHRC Doctoral Awards Scheme 109
CBRL Travel Grant 248
Department of Language and Linguistics AHRC Scholarships 686
Department of Language and Linguistics ESRC + 3 Studentships
Department of Language and Linguistics ESRC 1 + 3 Studentships
ESRC 1 + 3 Awards and + 3 Awards
Professional Preparation Master's Scheme
Research Preparation Master's Scheme
Wingate Scholarships 697

Middle East

Department of Language and Linguistics ORSAS Award 686
ORSAS Awards 688

New Zealand

Australian Postgraduate Awards 413
British School of Archaeology in Iraq Grants 169
Department of Language and Linguistics ORSAS Award 686
ORSAS Awards 688
University of Otago Master's Awards 717
Wingate Scholarships 697

South Africa

British School of Archaeology in Iraq Grants 169
Department of Language and Linguistics ORSAS Award 686
ORSAS Awards 688
Wingate Scholarships 697

United Kingdom

Access to Learning Fund 685
AHRC Doctoral Awards Scheme 109
British School of Archaeology in Iraq Grants 169
CBRL Research Award 248
CBRL Travel Grant 248
Department of Language and Linguistics AHRC Scholarships 686
Department of Language and Linguistics ESRC + 3 Studentships
Department of Language and Linguistics ESRC 1 + 3 Studentships
ESRC 1 + 3 Awards and + 3 Awards
Mr and Mrs David Edward Memorial Award 145
NHS Bursaries 655
Professional Preparation Master's Scheme
Research Preparation Master's Scheme
Wingate Scholarships 697

United States of America

British Marshall Scholarships 685
Department of Language and Linguistics ORSAS Award 686
ETS Postdoctoral Fellowships 276
Fulbright Distinguished Chairs Program 248
Fulbright Senior Specialists Program 249
Gilbert Chinard Fellowships 361
Harmon Chadbourn Rorison Fellowship 361
IREX Individual Advanced Research Opportunities 388

ITBE Graduate Scholarship 352
ORSAS Awards 688
SSRC JSPS Postdoctoral Fellowship 599

West European Countries

ESRC 1 + 3 Awards and + 3 Awards
Mr and Mrs David Edward Memorial Award 145
University of Otago Master's Awards 717

APPLIED LINGUISTICS

Any Country

A C Gimson Scholarships in Phonetics and Linguistics 646
Camargo Fellowships 182
Kenneth W Mildenberger Prize 453
Mina P Shaughnessy Prize 454
Quinn, Nathan and Edmond Scholarships 706

African Nations

Department of Language and Linguistics ORSAS Award 686
International Postgraduate Research Scholarships (IPRS) 413

Australia

Australian Postgraduate Awards 413
Department of Language and Linguistics ORSAS Award 686
Wingate Scholarships 697

Canada

Department of Language and Linguistics ORSAS Award 686
International Postgraduate Research Scholarships (IPRS) 413
Wingate Scholarships 697

Caribbean Countries

Department of Language and Linguistics ORSAS Award 686
International Postgraduate Research Scholarships (IPRS) 413

East European Countries

International Postgraduate Research Scholarships (IPRS) 413

European Union

AHRC Doctoral Awards Scheme 109
Department of Language and Linguistics ESRC 1 + 3 Studentships
Professional Preparation Master's Scheme
Research Preparation Master's Scheme
Wingate Scholarships 697

Middle East

Department of Language and Linguistics ORSAS Award 686
International Postgraduate Research Scholarships (IPRS) 413

New Zealand

Australian Postgraduate Awards 413
Department of Language and Linguistics ORSAS Award 686
Wingate Scholarships 697

South Africa

Department of Language and Linguistics ORSAS Award 686
International Postgraduate Research Scholarships (IPRS) 413
Wingate Scholarships 697

United Kingdom

Access to Learning Fund 685
AHRC Doctoral Awards Scheme 109
Department of Language and Linguistics ESRC 1 + 3 Studentships
International Postgraduate Research Scholarships (IPRS) 413
Mr and Mrs David Edward Memorial Award 145
Professional Preparation Master's Scheme
Research Preparation Master's Scheme
University of Kent School of European Culture and Languages
    Scholarships 701
Wingate Scholarships 697

United States of America

British Marshall Scholarships 685
Department of Language and Linguistics ORSAS Award 686
Fulbright Distinguished Chairs Program 248
Fulbright Senior Specialists Program 249
International Postgraduate Research Scholarships (IPRS) 413

West European Countries

International Postgraduate Research Scholarships (IPRS)
   413
Mr and Mrs David Edward Memorial Award 145
University of Kent School of European Culture and Languages
   Scholarships 701

PSYCHOLINGUISTICS

Any Country

A C Gimson Scholarships in Phonetics and Linguistics 646
Association for Women in Science Educational Foundation Predoc-
   toral Awards 118
Fondation Fyssen Postdoctoral Study Grants 297
Kenneth W Mildenberger Prize 453
Mina P Shaughnessy Prize 454

African Nations

Department of Language and Linguistics ORSAS Award 686

Australia

Australian Postgraduate Awards 413
Department of Language and Linguistics ORSAS Award 686
Wingate Scholarships 697

Canada

Department of Language and Linguistics ORSAS Award 686
Wingate Scholarships 697

Caribbean Countries

Department of Language and Linguistics ORSAS Award 686

European Union

Department of Language and Linguistics ESRC 1 + 3 Studentships
Professional Preparation Master's Scheme
Wingate Scholarships 697

Middle East

Department of Language and Linguistics ORSAS Award 686

New Zealand

Australian Postgraduate Awards 413
Department of Language and Linguistics ORSAS Award 686
Wingate Scholarships 697

South Africa

Department of Language and Linguistics ORSAS Award 686
Wingate Scholarships 697

United Kingdom

Access to Learning Fund 685
Department of Language and Linguistics ESRC 1 + 3 Studentships
Mr and Mrs David Edward Memorial Award 145
Professional Preparation Master's Scheme
Wingate Scholarships 697

United States of America

British Marshall Scholarships 685
Department of Language and Linguistics ORSAS Award 686

West European Countries

Mr and Mrs David Edward Memorial Award 145

GRAMMAR

Any Country

A C Gimson Scholarships in Phonetics and Linguistics 646
AUC Writing Center Graduate Fellowships 98
Camargo Fellowships 182
Findel Scholarships and Schneider Scholarships 340
Kenneth W Mildenberger Prize 453
Mina P Shaughnessy Prize 454

African Nations

Department of Language and Linguistics ORSAS Award 686

Australia

Australian Postgraduate Awards 413
Department of Language and Linguistics ORSAS Award 686
Wingate Scholarships 697

Canada

Department of Language and Linguistics ORSAS Award 686
Wingate Scholarships 697

Caribbean Countries

Department of Language and Linguistics ORSAS Award 686

European Union

AHRC Doctoral Awards Scheme 109
Professional Preparation Master's Scheme
Research Preparation Master's Scheme
Wingate Scholarships 697

Middle East

Department of Language and Linguistics ORSAS Award 686

New Zealand

Australian Postgraduate Awards 413
Department of Language and Linguistics ORSAS Award 686
Wingate Scholarships 697

South Africa

Department of Language and Linguistics ORSAS Award 686
Wingate Scholarships 697

United Kingdom

Access to Learning Fund 685
AHRC Doctoral Awards Scheme 109
Mr and Mrs David Edward Memorial Award 145
Professional Preparation Master's Scheme
Research Preparation Master's Scheme
Wingate Scholarships 697

United States of America

British Marshall Scholarships 685
Department of Language and Linguistics ORSAS Award 686
Fulbright Distinguished Chairs Program 248
Fulbright Senior Specialists Program 249

West European Countries

Mr and Mrs David Edward Memorial Award 145

SEMANTICS AND TERMINOLOGY

Any Country

A C Gimson Scholarships in Phonetics and Linguistics 646
Camargo Fellowships 182
SRG Postdoctoral Fellowships 646

Australia

Australian Postgraduate Awards 413
Wingate Scholarships 697

Canada

Wingate Scholarships 697

European Union

AHRC Doctoral Awards Scheme 109
Professional Preparation Master's Scheme
Research Preparation Master's Scheme
Wingate Scholarships 697

New Zealand

Australian Postgraduate Awards 413
Wingate Scholarships 697

South Africa

Wingate Scholarships 697

United Kingdom

Access to Learning Fund 685
AHRC Doctoral Awards Scheme 109
Mr and Mrs David Edward Memorial Award 145
Professional Preparation Master's Scheme
Research Preparation Master's Scheme
Wingate Scholarships 697

United States of America

British Marshall Scholarships 685
Fulbright Distinguished Chairs Program 248
Fulbright Senior Specialists Program 249

West European Countries

Mr and Mrs David Edward Memorial Award 145

PHONETICS

Any Country

A C Gimson Scholarships in Phonetics and Linguistics 646
Camargo Fellowships 182

Australia

Australian Postgraduate Awards 413
Wingate Scholarships 697

Canada

Wingate Scholarships 697

European Union

AHRC Doctoral Awards Scheme 109
Professional Preparation Master's Scheme
Research Preparation Master's Scheme
Wingate Scholarships 697

New Zealand

Australian Postgraduate Awards 413
Wingate Scholarships 697

South Africa

Wingate Scholarships 697

United Kingdom

Access to Learning Fund 685
AHRC Doctoral Awards Scheme 109
Mr and Mrs David Edward Memorial Award 145
Professional Preparation Master's Scheme
Research Preparation Master's Scheme
Wingate Scholarships 697

United States of America

British Marshall Scholarships 685

West European Countries

Mr and Mrs David Edward Memorial Award 145

LOGOPEDICS

Australia

Wingate Scholarships 697

Canada

Wingate Scholarships 697

European Union

AHRC Doctoral Awards Scheme 109
Professional Preparation Master's Scheme
Research Preparation Master's Scheme
Wingate Scholarships 697

New Zealand

Wingate Scholarships 697

South Africa

Wingate Scholarships 697

United Kingdom

Access to Learning Fund 685
AHRC Doctoral Awards Scheme 109
Mr and Mrs David Edward Memorial Award 145
Professional Preparation Master's Scheme
Research Preparation Master's Scheme
Wingate Scholarships 697

United States of America

British Marshall Scholarships 685

West European Countries

Mr and Mrs David Edward Memorial Award 145

COMPARATIVE LITERATURE

Any Country

Ahmanson and Getty Postdoctoral Fellowships 639
Aldo and Jeanne Scaglione Prize for Comparative Literary Studies 452
Aldo and Jeanne Scaglione Prize for French and Francophone Literary Studies 452
Aldo and Jeanne Scaglione Prize for Italian Studies 452
Aldo and Jeanne Scaglione Prize for Studies in Germanic Languages and Literatures 453
Aldo and Jeanne Scaglione Prize for Studies in Slavic Languages and Literatures 453
ASCSA Advanced Fellowships 82
ASCSA Fellowships 82
ASECS (American Society for 18th-Century Studies)/Clark Library Fellowships 639
BIAA Post-Doctoral Research Fellowship 168
BIAA Research Scholarship 168
BIAA Study Grants 168
British Academy Overseas Conference Grants 158
British Academy Postdoctoral Fellowships 158
British Academy Research Development Awards (BARDAs) 158
British Academy Small Research Grants 158
British Academy Worldwide Congress Grant 159
British Conference Grants 159
Camargo Fellowships 182
CC-CS Scholarship Program 223
Charlotte W Newcombe Doctoral Dissertation Fellowships 803
ChLA Beiter Graduate Student Research Grant 233
ChLA Faculty Research Grant 233
Clark Library Short-Term Resident Fellowships 639
Clark Predoctoral Fellowships 639
Clark-Huntington Joint Bibliographical Fellowship 640
CRF (Caledonian Research Foundation)/RSE European Visiting Research Fellowships 628
Fenia and Yaakov Leviant Memorial Prize in Yiddish Studies 453
Graduate Dissertation Research Fellowship 448

HISTORY

Any Country

African Nations

British Institute in Eastern Africa Graduate Attachments 169
British School of Archaeology in Iraq Grants 169
IDRC Evaluation Research Awards 381
ORISHA (Oxford Research in the Scholarship and Humanities of
Africa) Studentship 736
ORSAS Awards 688

Australia

AAH Humanities Travelling Fellowships 132
Australian Postgraduate Awards 413
British School of Archaeology in Iraq Grants 169
NSW Premier's History Awards
ORSAS Awards 688
University of Otago Master's Awards 717
Wingate Scholarships 697

Canada

British School of Archaeology in Iraq Grants 169
CFUW Margaret Dale Philp Award 207
Edouard Morot-Sir Fellowship in Literature 361
Gilbert Chinard Fellowships 361
Harmon Chadbourn Rorison Fellowship 361
IDRC Evaluation Research Awards 381
Mary McNeill Scholarship in Irish Studies 368
ORSAS Awards 688
Vatican Film Library Mellon Fellowship 785
Wingate Scholarships 697

Caribbean Countries

ESRC/SSRC Collaborative Visiting Fellowships 597
IDRC Evaluation Research Awards 381
ORSAS Awards 688

East European Countries

Brian Hewson Crawford Fellowship 789
Freie Universität Berlin John-F.-Kennedy-Institut für Nordamerikastu-
dien Research Grants 304
IDRC Evaluation Research Awards 381
ORSAS Awards 688
Warburg Mellon Research Fellowship 790
Young Scholars Forum 314

European Union

AHRC Doctoral Award for PhD in History 685
AHRC Doctoral Awards Scheme 109
AHRC Research Preparations Masters Scheme for History
685
CBRL Travel Grant 248
ESRC +3 (PhD research) History Studentship
ESRC 1+3 History Studentship
Freie Universität Berlin John-F.-Kennedy-Institut für Nordamerikastu-
dien Research Grants 304
Professional Preparation Master's Scheme
Research Preparation Master's Scheme
Warburg Mellon Research Fellowship 790
Wingate Scholarships 697

Middle East

IDRC Evaluation Research Awards 381
ORSAS Awards 688

New Zealand

The Association of University Staff Crozier Scholarship 500
Australian Postgraduate Awards 413
British School of Archaeology in Iraq Grants 169
ORSAS Awards 688
University of Otago Master's Awards 717
Wingate Scholarships 697

South Africa

British School of Archaeology in Iraq Grants 169
IDRC Evaluation Research Awards 381

ORSAS Awards 688
Wingate Scholarships 697

United Kingdom

Aberystwyth Postgraduate Research Studentships 4
Access to Learning Fund 685
AHRC Doctoral Award for PhD in History 685
AHRC Doctoral Awards Scheme 109
AHRC Research Preparations Masters Scheme for History 685
BAAS Short Term Awards 159
BACS Travel Awards 160
British Institute in Eastern Africa Graduate Attachments 169
British Institute in Eastern Africa Minor Grants 169
British School of Archaeology in Iraq Grants 169
CBRL Research Award 248
CBRL Travel Grant 248
ESRC +3 (PhD research) History Studentship
ESRC 1+3 History Studentship
ESRC/SSRC Collaborative Visiting Fellowships 597
Frances A Yates Fellowships 789
Fulbright-Robertson Visiting Professorship in British History 783
Grete Sondheimer Fellowship 790
Mr and Mrs David Edward Memorial Award 145
Prix du Québec Award 160
Professional Preparation Master's Scheme
Research Preparation Master's Scheme
Ross Scholarship 695
Wingate Scholarships 697
Young Scholars Forum 314

United States of America

AAS-National Endowment for the Humanities Visiting Fellowships 27
Annual Meeting Fellowship - Beverly Willis Architectural Foundation
Travel Fellowship 608
ARCE Fellowships 80
Arthur M. Schlesinger, Jr. Fellowship 405
ASOR W.F. Albright Institute of Archaeological Research/National
Endowment of the Humanities Fellowships 84
The Berg Family Endowed Scholarship 456
British Marshall Scholarships 685
Earthwatch Fellowships 272
Edilia and Francois-Auguste de Montequin Fellowship 608
Edouard Morot-Sir Fellowship in Literature 361
Ford Foundation Dissertation Fellowships for Minorities 487
Fulbright Distinguished Chairs Program 248
Fulbright Senior Specialists Program 249
German Historical Institute Doctoral and Postdoctoral Fellowships 313
German Historical Institute Summer Seminar in Germany 313
German Historical Institute Transatlantic Doctoral Seminar in German
History 313
Gilbert Chinard Fellowships 361
Gladys Krieble Delmas Foundation Grants 319
Harmon Chadbourn Rorison Fellowship 361
IREX Individual Advanced Research Opportunities 388
IREX Short-Term Travel Grants 389
James Madison Fellowship Program 398
Kennan Institute Research Scholarship 408
Kennedy Research Grants 405
Louis Pelzer Memorial Award 516
Marine Corps History College Internships 433
Mary McNeill Scholarship in Irish Studies 368
Michael and Marie Marucci Scholarship 475
The National Endowment for Humanities (NEH) Institute Postdoctoral
Fellowship 511
NHPRC Fellowship in Documentary Editing 481
Norwegian Emigration Fund of 1975 508
ORSAS Awards 688
SAH Fellowships for Senior Scholars 608
SAH Study Tour Fellowship 608
Samuel H. Kress Fellowship 788
Samuel H. Kress Foundation Fellowships for Speakers 609
Scott Opler Fellowships for New Scholars 609
SSRC Abe Fellowship Program 598
SSRC JSPS Postdoctoral Fellowship 599
Vatican Film Library Mellon Fellowship 785

Winterthur National Endowment for the Humanities Fellowships 798
Young Scholars Forum 314

West European Countries

Brian Hewson Crawford Fellowship 789
Freie Universität Berlin John-F.-Kennedy-Institut für Nordamerikastudien Research Grants 304
German Historical Institute Doctoral and Postdoctoral Fellowships 313
German Historical Institute Transatlantic Doctoral Seminar in German History 313
Mr and Mrs David Edward Memorial Award 145
University of Otago Master's Awards 717
Young Scholars Forum 314

PREHISTORY

Any Country

Albert J Beveridge Grant 58
ASCSA Advanced Fellowships 82
ASCSA Fellowships 82
Bernadotte E Schmitt Grants 58
Earthwatch Field Research Grants 272
Henry Moore Institute Research Fellowship 338
Institute for Advanced Study Postdoctoral Residential Fellowships 363
J Franklin Jameson Fellowship 58
Jacob Hirsch Fellowship 83
Littleton-Griswold Research Grant 59
Mary Isabel Sibley Fellowship 531
NEH Fellowships 83
Prehistoric Society Conference Fund 536
Prehistoric Society Research Fund Grant 536
Prehistoric Society Research Grant Conference Award 536

African Nations

British School of Archaeology in Iraq Grants 169

Australia

Australian Postgraduate Awards 413
British School of Archaeology in Iraq Grants 169
Wingate Scholarships 697

Canada

British School of Archaeology in Iraq Grants 169
Wingate Scholarships 697

European Union

AHRC Doctoral Awards Scheme 109
CBRL Travel Grant 248
Professional Preparation Master's Scheme
Research Preparation Master's Scheme
Wingate Scholarships 697

New Zealand

Australian Postgraduate Awards 413
British School of Archaeology in Iraq Grants 169
Wingate Scholarships 697

South Africa

British School of Archaeology in Iraq Grants 169
Wingate Scholarships 697

United Kingdom

AHRC Doctoral Awards Scheme 109
Balsdon Fellowship 174
British Institute in Eastern Africa Minor Grants 169
British School of Archaeology in Iraq Grants 169
CBRL Research Award 248
CBRL Travel Grant 248
Hector and Elizabeth Catling Bursary 173
Professional Preparation Master's Scheme
Research Preparation Master's Scheme
Rome Awards 175

Rome Fellowship 175
Rome Scholarships in Ancient, Medieval and Later Italian Studies 176
University of Kent School of European Culture and Languages Scholarships 701
University of Kent School of European Culture and Languages Studentships 701
Wingate Scholarships 697

West European Countries

University of Kent School of European Culture and Languages Scholarships 701
University of Kent School of European Culture and Languages Studentships 701

ANCIENT CIVILISATIONS

Any Country

Albert J Beveridge Grant 58
ASCSA Advanced Fellowships 82
ASCSA Fellowships 82
Bernadotte E Schmitt Grants 58
Center for Hellenic Studies Junior Fellowships 223
Delahaye Memorial Benefaction 768
Dumbarton Oaks Fellowships and Junior Fellowships 271
Earthwatch Field Research Grants 272
Frances M Schwartz Fellowship 71
Grete Sondheimer Fellowship 790
Helen McCormack Turner Memorial Scholarship 768
Henri Frankfort Fellowship 790
Henry Moore Institute Research Fellowship 338
Herbert Hughes Scholarship 768
Hugh Last and Donald Atkinson Funds Committee Grants 604
Hugh Le May Fellowship 548
Institute for Advanced Study Postdoctoral Residential Fellowships 363
J Franklin Jameson Fellowship 58
Jacob Hirsch Fellowship 83
Littleton-Griswold Research Grant 59
Mary Isabel Sibley Fellowship 531
Mary Radcliffe Scholarship 768
NEH Fellowships 83
RHYS Curzon-Jones Scholarship 768
Ridley Lewis Bursary 769
W D Llewelyn Memorial Benefaction 769

African Nations

British School of Archaeology in Iraq Grants 169

Australia

British School of Archaeology in Iraq Grants 169
Wingate Scholarships 697

Canada

British School of Archaeology in Iraq Grants 169
Wingate Scholarships 697

East European Countries

British Academy Stein-Arnold Exploration Fund 158

European Union

AHRC Doctoral Awards Scheme 109
CBRL Travel Grant 248
Professional Preparation Master's Scheme
Research Preparation Master's Scheme
Wingate Scholarships 697

New Zealand

British School of Archaeology in Iraq Grants 169
Wingate Scholarships 697

South Africa

British School of Archaeology in Iraq Grants 169
Wingate Scholarships 697

United Kingdom

AHRC Doctoral Awards Scheme 109
Balsdon Fellowship 174
British Academy Stein-Arnold Exploration Fund 158
British Institute in Eastern Africa Minor Grants 169
British School of Archaeology in Iraq Grants 169
CBRL Research Award 248
CBRL Travel Grant 248
The Dover Fund 604
Grete Sondheimer Fellowship 790
Hector and Elizabeth Catling Bursary 173
Hugh Last Fellowship 175
Professional Preparation Master's Scheme
Research Preparation Master's Scheme
Rome Awards 175
Rome Fellowship 175
Rome Scholarships in Ancient, Medieval and Later Italian Studies 176
University of Kent School of European Culture and Languages Scholarships 701
University of Kent School of European Culture and Languages Studentships 701
Wingate Scholarships 697

United States of America

ARCE Fellowships 80
Earthwatch Fellowships 272

West European Countries

University of Kent School of European Culture and Languages Scholarships 701
University of Kent School of European Culture and Languages Studentships 701

MEDIEVAL HISTORY

Any Country

Albert J Beveridge Grant 58
ASCSA Fellowships 82
Barbara Thom Postdoctoral Fellowship 347
Barron Bequest 787
Bernadotte E Schmitt Grants 58
Camargo Fellowships 182
Clark-Huntington Joint Bibliographical Fellowship 640
Delahaye Memorial Benefaction 768
Dumbarton Oaks Fellowships and Junior Fellowships 271
Economic History Society Research Fellowships 584
Grete Sondheimer Fellowship 790
Helen McCormack Turner Memorial Scholarship 768
Henry Moore Institute Research Fellowship 338
Herbert Hughes Scholarship 768
Hugh Le May Fellowship 548
Institute for Advanced Study Postdoctoral Residential Fellowships 363
Institute of Irish Studies Research Fellowships 367
Isobel Thornley Research Fellowship 367
J Franklin Jameson Fellowship 58
Jacob Hirsch Fellowship 83
Littleton-Griswold Research Grant 59
M Alison Frantz Fellowship in Post-Classical Studies at the Gennadius Library 83
Mary Isabel Sibley Fellowship 531
Mary Radcliffe Scholarship 768
Mellon Fellowships 348
NEH Fellowships 83
Neil Ker Memorial Fund 159
Queen Mary Research Studentships 539
RHYS Curzon-Jones Scholarship 768
Ridley Lewis Bursary 769
Roy G. Neville Fellowship 231
Royal History Society Fellowship 367
Scouloudi Fellowships 367
W D Llewelyn Memorial Benefaction 769

Australia

Wingate Scholarships 697

Canada

Mary McNeill Scholarship in Irish Studies 368
Medieval History Seminar 314
Wingate Scholarships 697

East European Countries

Medieval History Seminar 314
Young Scholars Forum 314

European Union

AHRC Doctoral Awards Scheme 109
CBRL Travel Grant 248
Professional Preparation Master's Scheme
Research Preparation Master's Scheme
Wingate Scholarships 697

New Zealand

Wingate Scholarships 697

South Africa

Wingate Scholarships 697

United Kingdom

Aberystwyth Postgraduate Research Studentships 4
AHRC Doctoral Awards Scheme 109
Balsdon Fellowship 174
British Institute in Eastern Africa Minor Grants 169
CBRL Research Award 248
CBRL Travel Grant 248
Grete Sondheimer Fellowship 790
Hector and Elizabeth Catling Bursary 173
Medieval History Seminar 314
Mr and Mrs David Edward Memorial Award 145
Professional Preparation Master's Scheme
Research Preparation Master's Scheme
Rome Awards 175
Rome Fellowship 175
Rome Scholarships in Ancient, Medieval and Later Italian Studies 176
University of Kent School of European Culture and Languages Scholarships 701
University of Kent School of European Culture and Languages Studentships 701
Wingate Scholarships 697
Young Scholars Forum 314

United States of America

ARCE Fellowships 80
Earthwatch Fellowships 272
Mary McNeill Scholarship in Irish Studies 368
Medieval History Seminar 314
National Endowment for the Humanities Fellowships 348
William B Schallek Memorial Graduate Fellowship Award 549
Young Scholars Forum 314

West European Countries

Medieval History Seminar 314
Mr and Mrs David Edward Memorial Award 145
University of Kent School of European Culture and Languages Scholarships 701
University of Kent School of European Culture and Languages Studentships 701
Young Scholars Forum 314

MODERN HISTORY

Any Country

AAS Joyce Tracy Fellowship 26
Adelle and Erwin Tomash Fellowship in the History of Information Processing 228

CONTEMPORARY HISTORY

CBRL Travel Grant 248
ESRC +3 (PhD research) History Studentship
ESRC 1+3 History Studentship
EUI Postgraduate Scholarships 287
Fulbright-Robertson Visiting Professorship in British History 783
Hector and Elizabeth Catling Bursary 173
Research Preparation Master's Scheme
Rome Awards 175
Rome Fellowship 175
Rome Scholarships in Ancient, Medieval and Later Italian Studies 176
Wingate Scholarships 697
Young Scholars Forum 314

United States of America

British Marshall Scholarships 685
Fritz Stern Dissertation Prize 313
Fulbright Senior Specialists Program 249
German Historical Institute Doctoral and Postdoctoral Fellowships 313
Japanese Residencies Program 516
Mary McNeill Scholarship in Irish Studies 368
National Endowment for the Humanities Fellowships 348
ORSAS Awards 688
Thyssen-Heideking Fellowship 314
Young Scholars Forum 314

West European Countries

Elisabeth Barker Fund 159
EUI Postgraduate Scholarships 287
German Historical Institute Doctoral and Postdoctoral Fellowships 313
Kade-Heideking Fellowship 313
Young Scholars Forum 314

ARCHAEOLOGY

Any Country

ASCSA Advanced Fellowships 82
ASCSA Fellowships 82
ASCSA Research Fellowship in Environmental Studies 82
ASCSA Research Fellowship in Faunal Studies 82
ASCSA Research Fellowship in Geoarchaeology 82
Association for Women in Science Educational Foundation Predoc-
    toral Awards 118
BIAA Post-Doctoral Research Fellowship 168
BIAA Research Scholarship 168
BIAA Study Grants 168
British Academy Overseas Conference Grants 158
British Academy Postdoctoral Fellowships 158
British Academy Small Research Grants 158
British Academy Worldwide Congress Grant 159
British Conference Grants 159
Center for Hellenic Studies Junior Fellowships 223
CIUS Research Grants 209
Claude C. Albritton, Jr. Scholarships 310
CRF (Caledonian Research Foundation)/RSE European Visiting
    Research Fellowships 628
Delahaye Memorial Benefaction 768
Earthwatch Field Research Grants 272
Findel Scholarships and Schneider Scholarships 340
Fondation Fyssen Postdoctoral Study Grants 297
Frances M Schwartz Fellowship 71
Graduate Dissertation Research Fellowship 448
Helen McCormack Turner Memorial Scholarship 768
Henry Moore Institute Research Fellowship 338
Herbert Hughes Scholarship 768
Hugh Last and Donald Atkinson Funds Committee Grants 604
Institute of Irish Studies Research Fellowships 367
J Lawrence Angel Fellowship in Human Skeletal Studies
Jacob Hirsch Fellowship 83
La Trobe University Postgraduate Scholarship 414
Marusia and Michael Dorosh Master's Fellowship 209
Mary Isabel Sibley Fellowship 531
Mary Radcliffe Scholarship 768
Master's Degree Awards in Archaeology
NEH Fellowships 83

Neporany Doctoral Fellowship 210
NERC Advanced Research Fellowships 493
NERC Postdoctoral Research Fellowships 494
Onassis Foreigners' Fellowships Programme Research Grants
    Category AI 15
Poulter Studentship 689
Prehistoric Society Conference Fund 536
Prehistoric Society Research Fund Grant 536
Prehistoric Society Research Grant Conference Award 536
RHYS Curzon-Jones Scholarship 768
Ridley Lewis Bursary 769
Samuel H. Kress Fellowship 788
SOAS Bursary 583
SOAS Open Scholarship 583
SOAS Research Student Fellowships 583
St Catherine's College Graduate Scholarship in the Arts
University of Bristol Postgraduate Scholarships 672
University of Southampton Postgraduate Studentships 759
W D Llewelyn Memorial Benefaction 769
World Universities Network (WUN) International Research Mobility
    Scheme 759

African Nations

British Institute in Eastern Africa Graduate Attachments 169
British School of Archaeology in Iraq Grants 169
ORISHA (Oxford Research in the Scholarship and Humanities of
    Africa) Studentship 736

Australia

AAH Humanities Travelling Fellowships 132
Australian Postgraduate Awards 413
British School of Archaeology in Iraq Grants 169
UNE Mary Dolan Memorial Travelling Scholarship 712
Wingate Scholarships 697

Canada

British School of Archaeology in Iraq Grants 169
KRESS/ARIT Pre-Doctoral Fellowship in the History of Art and
    Archaeology 81
Mary McNeill Scholarship in Irish Studies 368
Wingate Scholarships 697

European Union

AHRC Doctoral Awards Scheme 109
CBRL Travel Grant 248
NERC Masters Studentships 493
NERC Research (PhD) Studentships 494
Professional Preparation Master's Scheme
Research Preparation Master's Scheme
W B Crump Scholarship 705
Wingate Scholarships 697

New Zealand

Australian Postgraduate Awards 413
British School of Archaeology in Iraq Grants 169
Wingate Scholarships 697

South Africa

British School of Archaeology in Iraq Grants 169
Wingate Scholarships 697

United Kingdom

AHRC Doctoral Awards Scheme 109
Balsdon Fellowship 174
British Institute in Eastern Africa Graduate Attachments 169
British Institute in Eastern Africa Minor Grants 169
British School of Archaeology in Iraq Grants 169
CBRL Research Award 248
CBRL Travel Grant 248
The Dover Fund 604
Hector and Elizabeth Catling Bursary 173
Mr and Mrs David Edward Memorial Award 145
NERC Masters Studentships 493

NERC Research (PhD) Studentships 494
Professional Preparation Master's Scheme
Research Preparation Master's Scheme
Rome Awards 175
Rome Fellowship 175
Rome Scholarships in Ancient, Medieval and Later Italian Studies 176
Tim Potter Memorial Award 177
University of Kent School of European Culture and Languages Scholarships 701
University of Kent School of European Culture and Languages Studentships 701
W B Crump Scholarship 705
Wingate Scholarships 697

United States of America

ACC Fellowship Grants Program 115
ACC Humanities Fellowship Program 115
ARCE Fellowships 80
Earthwatch Fellowships 272
Fulbright Distinguished Chairs Program 248
Fulbright Senior Specialists Program 249
IREX Individual Advanced Research Opportunities 388
Kennan Institute Research Scholarship 408
Kress Fellowship in the Art and Archaeology of Jordan 35
KRESS/ARIT Pre-Doctoral Fellowship in the History of Art and Archaeology 81
Mary McNeill Scholarship in Irish Studies 368
Samuel H. Kress Fellowship 788
SSRC JSPS Postdoctoral Fellowship 599

West European Countries

Mr and Mrs David Edward Memorial Award 145
University of Kent School of European Culture and Languages Scholarships 701
University of Kent School of European Culture and Languages Studentships 701

PHILOSOPHY

Any Country

A J Ayer-Sumitomo Corporation Scholarship in Philosophy 646
Ahmanson and Getty Postdoctoral Fellowships 639
ASCSA Advanced Fellowships 82
ASCSA Fellowships 82
ASECS (American Society for 18th-Century Studies)/Clark Library Fellowships 639
BIAA Post-Doctoral Research Fellowship 168
BIAA Research Scholarship 168
BIAA Study Grants 168
British Academy Overseas Conference Grants 158
British Academy Postdoctoral Fellowships 158
British Academy Research Development Awards (BARDAs) 158
British Academy Small Research Grants 158
British Academy Worldwide Congress Grant 159
British Conference Grants 159
Camargo Fellowships 182
Center for Hellenic Studies Junior Fellowships 223
Charlotte W Newcombe Doctoral Dissertation Fellowships 803
Clark Library Short-Term Resident Fellowships 639
Clark Predoctoral Fellowships 639
CRF (Caledonian Research Foundation)/RSE European Visiting Research Fellowships 628
Dawes Hicks Postgraduate Scholarships in Philosophy 649
Delahaye Memorial Benefaction 768
Exeter College Senior Scholarship in Theology 289
Findel Scholarships and Schneider Scholarships 340
Follett Scholarship 650
Frances A Yates Fellowships 789
The George Melhuish Postgraduate Scholarship 651
Graduate Dissertation Research Fellowship 448
Graduate Summer Travel Grants 449
Grete Sondheimer Fellowship 790
Helen McCormack Turner Memorial Scholarship 768

Henry Moore Institute Research Fellowship 338
Herbert Hughes Scholarship 768
Hugh Le May Fellowship 548
IHS Humane Studies Fellowships 363
IHS Summer Graduate Research Fellowship 363
Institute for Advanced Study Postdoctoral Residential Fellowships 363
Jacob Hirsch Fellowship 83
Jacobsen Scholarship in Philosophy 652
John Stuart Mill Scholarship in Philosophy of Mind and Logic 653
Jonathan Young Scholarship 691
Kanner Fellowship In British Studies 640
Keeling Scholarship 653
Kennan Institute Short-Term Grants 408
M Alison Frantz Fellowship in Post-Classical Studies at the Gennadius Library 83
Mary Radcliffe Scholarship 768
Minda de Gunzberg Graduate Dissertation Writing Fellowship 449
NEH Fellowships 83
Onassis Foreigners' Fellowships Programme Research Grants Category AI 15
Philosophy Graduate Awards 688
Queen Mary Research Studentships 539
Rhodes University Postdoctoral Fellowship and The Andrew Mellon Postdoctoral Fellowship 548
RHYS Curzon-Jones Scholarship 768
Ridley Lewis Bursary 769
St Catherine's College Graduate Scholarship in the Arts
United States Holocaust Memorial Museum Center for Advanced Holocaust Studies Visiting Scholar Programs 641
University of Bristol Postgraduate Scholarships 672
University of Otago International Scholarships 717
University of Otago PhD Scholarships 718
University of Otago Prestigious PhD Scholarships 718
University of Southampton Postgraduate Studentships 759
W D Llewelyn Memorial Benefaction 769
World Universities Network (WUN) International Research Mobility Scheme 759

African Nations

ORSAS Awards 688

Australia

AAH Humanities Travelling Fellowships 132
Australian Postgraduate Awards 413
ORSAS Awards 688
University of Otago Master's Awards 717
Wingate Scholarships 697

Canada

ORSAS Awards 688
Vatican Film Library Mellon Fellowship 785
Wingate Scholarships 697

Caribbean Countries

ORSAS Awards 688

East European Countries

ORSAS Awards 688
Warburg Mellon Research Fellowship 790

European Union

AHRC Doctoral Awards Scheme 109
CBRL Travel Grant 248
Jacobsen Scholarship in Philosophy 652
Professional Preparation Master's Scheme
Research Preparation Master's Scheme
Warburg Mellon Research Fellowship 790
Wingate Scholarships 697

Middle East

ORSAS Awards 688

New Zealand

Australian Postgraduate Awards 413
ORSAS Awards 688
University of Otago Master's Awards 717
Wingate Scholarships 697

South Africa

ORSAS Awards 688
Wingate Scholarships 697

United Kingdom

Access to Learning Fund 685
AHRC Doctoral Awards Scheme 109
Balsdon Fellowship 174
CBRL Research Award 248
CBRL Travel Grant 248
ESU Chautauqua Institution Scholarships 280
Frances A Yates Fellowships 789
Grete Sondheimer Fellowship 790
Jacobsen Scholarship in Philosophy 652
Professional Preparation Master's Scheme
Research Preparation Master's Scheme
Rome Awards 175
Rome Fellowship 175
Rome Scholarships in Ancient, Medieval and Later Italian Studies 176
Trinity College Cecil Lubbock Memorial Scholarship 747
University of Kent School of European Culture and Languages
   Scholarships 701
University of Kent School of European Culture and Languages
   Studentships 701
Wingate Scholarships 697

United States of America

The Berg Family Endowed Scholarship 456
British Marshall Scholarships 685
Fulbright Distinguished Chairs Program 248
Fulbright Senior Specialists Program 249
Kennan Institute Research Scholarship 408
ORSAS Awards 688
SSRC JSPS Postdoctoral Fellowship 599
Vatican Film Library Mellon Fellowship 785

West European Countries

University of Kent School of European Culture and Languages
   Scholarships 701
University of Kent School of European Culture and Languages
   Studentships 701
University of Otago Master's Awards 717

PHILOSOPHICAL SCHOOLS

Any Country

Ahmanson and Getty Postdoctoral Fellowships 639
ASCSA Advanced Fellowships 82
ASECS (American Society for 18th-Century Studies)/Clark Library
   Fellowships 639
Camargo Fellowships 182
Clark Library Short-Term Resident Fellowships 639
Clark Predoctoral Fellowships 639
Clark-Huntington Joint Bibliographical Fellowship 640
Henry Moore Institute Research Fellowship 338
Kanner Fellowship In British Studies 640
NEH Fellowships 83
United States Holocaust Memorial Museum Center for Advanced
   Holocaust Studies Visiting Scholar Programs 641

Australia

Wingate Scholarships 697

Canada

Wingate Scholarships 697

European Union

AHRC Doctoral Awards Scheme 109
Professional Preparation Master's Scheme
Research Preparation Master's Scheme
Wingate Scholarships 697

New Zealand

Wingate Scholarships 697

South Africa

Wingate Scholarships 697

United Kingdom

AHRC Doctoral Awards Scheme 109
Hector and Elizabeth Catling Bursary 173
Professional Preparation Master's Scheme
Research Preparation Master's Scheme
University of Kent School of European Culture and Languages
   Scholarships 701
University of Kent School of European Culture and Languages
   Studentships 701
Wingate Scholarships 697

United States of America

British Marshall Scholarships 685

West European Countries

University of Kent School of European Culture and Languages
   Scholarships 701
University of Kent School of European Culture and Languages
   Studentships 701

METAPHYSICS

Any Country

ASCSA Advanced Fellowships 82
Camargo Fellowships 182
Kanner Fellowship In British Studies 640
NEH Fellowships 83

Australia

Wingate Scholarships 697

Canada

Wingate Scholarships 697

European Union

AHRC Doctoral Awards Scheme 109
Professional Preparation Master's Scheme
Research Preparation Master's Scheme
Wingate Scholarships 697

New Zealand

Wingate Scholarships 697

South Africa

Wingate Scholarships 697

United Kingdom

AHRC Doctoral Awards Scheme 109
Professional Preparation Master's Scheme
Research Preparation Master's Scheme
University of Kent School of European Culture and Languages
   Scholarships 701
University of Kent School of European Culture and Languages
   Studentships 701
Wingate Scholarships 697

United States of America

British Marshall Scholarships 685

West European Countries

University of Kent School of European Culture and Languages
Scholarships 701
University of Kent School of European Culture and Languages
Studentships 701

LOGIC

Any Country

ASCSA Advanced Fellowships 82
Camargo Fellowships 182
John Stuart Mill Scholarship in Philosophy of Mind and Logic 653
Kanner Fellowship In British Studies 640
NEH Fellowships 83

Australia

Wingate Scholarships 697

Canada

Wingate Scholarships 697

European Union

AHRC Doctoral Awards Scheme 109
Professional Preparation Master's Scheme
Research Preparation Master's Scheme
Wingate Scholarships 697

New Zealand

Wingate Scholarships 697

South Africa

Wingate Scholarships 697

United Kingdom

AHRC Doctoral Awards Scheme 109
Professional Preparation Master's Scheme
Research Preparation Master's Scheme
University of Kent School of European Culture and Languages
Scholarships 701
University of Kent School of European Culture and Languages
Studentships 701
Wingate Scholarships 697

United States of America

British Marshall Scholarships 685

West European Countries

University of Kent School of European Culture and Languages
Scholarships 701
University of Kent School of European Culture and Languages
Studentships 701

ETHICS

Any Country

ASCSA Advanced Fellowships 82
Camargo Fellowships 182
Charlotte W Newcombe Doctoral Dissertation Fellowships 803
CIHR Fellowships Program 210
Delahaye Memorial Benefaction 768
Helen McCormack Turner Memorial Scholarship 768
Herbert Hughes Scholarship 768
Kanner Fellowship In British Studies 640
Mary Radcliffe Scholarship 768
NEH Fellowships 83
RHYS Curzon-Jones Scholarship 768
Ridley Lewis Bursary 769
United States Holocaust Memorial Museum Center for Advanced
Holocaust Studies Visiting Scholar Programs 641
W D Llewelyn Memorial Benefaction 769

Australia

Wingate Scholarships 697

Canada

Wingate Scholarships 697

European Union

AHRC Doctoral Awards Scheme 109
Professional Preparation Master's Scheme
Research Preparation Master's Scheme
Wingate Scholarships 697

New Zealand

Wingate Scholarships 697

South Africa

Wingate Scholarships 697

United Kingdom

AHRC Doctoral Awards Scheme 109
ESU Chautauqua Institution Scholarships 280
Professional Preparation Master's Scheme
Research Preparation Master's Scheme
University of Kent School of European Culture and Languages
Scholarships 701
University of Kent School of European Culture and Languages
Studentships 701
Wingate Scholarships 697

United States of America

British Marshall Scholarships 685

West European Countries

University of Kent School of European Culture and Languages
Scholarships 701
University of Kent School of European Culture and Languages
Studentships 701

BUSINESS ADMINISTRATION AND MANAGEMENT

GENERAL

Any Country

Andrew Mellon Foundation Scholarship 547
ARI PhD Research Scholarship 114
Ashridge Management College-Full-Time MBA and Executive MBA
Scholarships 114
AUC Assistantships 96
AUC Graduate Merit Fellowships 97
AUC University Fellowships 98
Australian Postgraduate Award Research Scholarship
Bray Leadership Scholarship 446
Concordia University Graduate Fellowships 243
Curtin Business School Doctoral Scholarship 258
David J Azrieli Graduate Fellowship 243
Delahaye Memorial Benefaction 768
Donald Dyer Scholarship – Public Relations & Communication
Management 757
Ernst Meyer Prize 376
Field Psych Trust Grant 291
Geneva Association 376
Helen McCormack Turner Memorial Scholarship 768
Henry Belin du Pont Dissertation Fellowship in Business, Technology
and Society 329
Herbert Hughes Scholarship 768
International Association for the Study of Insurance Economics
Research Grants 376
International Postgraduate Research Scholarship 667
ISM Doctoral Dissertation Grant In Supply Management 363

ISM Senior Research Fellowship Program 364
Jonathan Young Scholarship 691
Lincoln College Sloane Robinson Foundation Graduate Awards 733
Mary Radcliffe Scholarship 768
Monash International Postgraduate Research Scholarship (MIPRS) 455
Monash University Silver Jubilee Postgraduate Scholarship 455
Queen Mary Research Studentships 539
RBS London Academic Excellence Scholarships 543
RBS London Work-Study Scholarships 543
Rhodes University Postdoctoral Fellowship and The Andrew Mellon
   Postdoctoral Fellowship 548
Rhodes University Postgraduate Scholarship 549
RHYS Curzon-Jones Scholarship 768
Ridley Lewis Bursary 769
Shirtcliffe Fellowship 501
Sir Allan Sewell Visiting Fellowship 326
Stanley G French Graduate Fellowship 244
Ted Zorn Waikato Alumni Award For Management Communication 767
TIACA Walter H. Johnson, Jr. Scholarship Award 375
Tomsk Polytechnic University International Scholarship 634
University of Ballarat Postgraduate Research Scholarship
University of Southampton Postgraduate Studentships 759
Vera Moore International Postgraduate Research Scholarships 455
W D Llewelyn Memorial Benefaction 769
World Universities Network (WUN) International Research Mobility
   Scheme 759

African Nations

ABCCF Student Grant 102
AUC African Graduate Fellowship 96
ECOPOLIS Graduate Research and Design Awards 380
International Postgraduate Research Scholarships (IPRS) 413
International Postgraduate Research Scholarships (IPRS) 413
NUFFIC-NFP Fellowships for Master's Degree Programmes 496
Shell Centenary Chevening Scholarships for Postgraduate Study 196

Australia

ADB-Japan Scholarship Program 116
DOI Women in Freight, Logistics and Marine Management Scholar-
   ship 264
Fulbright Postdoctoral Fellowships 140
Fulbright Postgraduate Awards 140
International Postgraduate Research Scholarships (IPRS) 413
University of Ballarat Part Postgraduate Research Scholarship 667
Wingate Scholarships 697

Canada

Bank of Montréal Pauline Varnier Fellowship 243
Canada Graduate Scholarship Program (CGS): Master's Scholarship
   600
Community-University Research Alliances (CURA) 601
ECOPOLIS Graduate Research and Design Awards 380
International Postgraduate Research Scholarships (IPRS) 413
International Postgraduate Research Scholarships (IPRS) 413
J W McConnell Memorial Fellowships 243
JCCA Graduate Education Scholarship 400
Major Collaborative Research Initiatives (MCRI) 601
Public Safety and Emergency Preparedness Canada Research
   Fellowship in Honour of Stuart Nesbitt White 123
SSHRC Doctoral Awards 602
SSHRC Postdoctoral Fellowships 602
SSHRC Research Development Initiatives 603
Wingate Scholarships 697

Caribbean Countries

ADB-Japan Scholarship Program 116
ECOPOLIS Graduate Research and Design Awards 380
International Postgraduate Research Scholarships (IPRS) 413
International Postgraduate Research Scholarships (IPRS) 413

East European Countries

ECOPOLIS Graduate Research and Design Awards 380
International Postgraduate Research Scholarships (IPRS) 413
International Postgraduate Research Scholarships (IPRS) 413

European Union

ESRC 1 + 3 Awards and + 3 Awards
International Postgraduate Research Scholarships (IPRS) 413
University of Southampton Engineering Doctorate 759
Wingate Scholarships 697

Middle East

ABCCF Student Grant 102
ECOPOLIS Graduate Research and Design Awards 380
International Postgraduate Research Scholarships (IPRS) 413
International Postgraduate Research Scholarships (IPRS) 413
NUFFIC-NFP Fellowships for Master's Degree Programmes 496

New Zealand

The Association of University Staff Crozier Scholarship 500
Chamber of Commerce Tauranga Business Scholarship 765
Priority One Management Scholarship 767
Wingate Scholarships 697
WMS International Exchange Scholarships 768

South Africa

Allan Gray Senior Scholarship 547
ECOPOLIS Graduate Research and Design Awards 380
International Postgraduate Research Scholarships (IPRS) 413
International Postgraduate Research Scholarships (IPRS) 413
NUFFIC-NFP Fellowships for Master's Degree Programmes 496
Wingate Scholarships 697

United Kingdom

Aberystwyth Postgraduate Research Studentships 4
ESRC 1 + 3 Awards and + 3 Awards
Fulbright British Friends of HBS MBA Awards 780
Hilda Martindale Exhibitions 341
International Postgraduate Research Scholarships (IPRS) 413
International Postgraduate Research Scholarships (IPRS) 413
John Mather Scholarship 760
Mr and Mrs David Edward Memorial Award 145
University of Southampton Engineering Doctorate 759
Wingate Scholarships 697

United States of America

AIGC Accenture American Indian Scholarship Fund 59
Bicentennial Swedish-American Exchange Fund 623
Billings Broadcasters MSU-Billings Media Scholarship 456
British Marshall Scholarships 685
Congress Bundestag Youth Exchange for Young Professionals 221
Fulbright Distinguished Chairs Program 248
Fulbright Senior Specialists Program 249
International Postgraduate Research Scholarships (IPRS) 413
International Postgraduate Research Scholarships (IPRS) 413
IREX Individual Advanced Research Opportunities 388
IREX Short-Term Travel Grants 389
Jacki Tuckfield Memorial Graduate Business Scholarship Fund 396
JCCA Graduate Education Scholarship 400
Kennan Institute Research Scholarship 408
North Dakota Indian Scholarship 507
NSHMBA 489
Robert Bosch Foundation Fellowships 550
Washington University Chancellor's Graduate Fellowship Program 792

West European Countries

ESRC 1 + 3 Awards and + 3 Awards
International Postgraduate Research Scholarships (IPRS) 413
International Postgraduate Research Scholarships (IPRS) 413
Janson Johan Helmich Scholarships and Travel Grants 398
Mr and Mrs David Edward Memorial Award 145

BUSINESS STUDIES

Any Country

The Airey Neave Trust Scholarship 12
The Cámara de Comercio Scholarship 351

ETS Summer Internship Program for Graduate Students 276
IESE AECI/Becas MAE 351
IESE Alumini Association Scholarships 351
IESE Donovan Data Systems Anniversary 351
IESE Private Foundation Scholarships 352
IESE Trust Scholarships 352
ISM Doctoral Dissertation Grant In Supply Management 363
ISM Senior Research Fellowship Program 364
Kennan Institute Short-Term Grants 408
La Trobe University Postgraduate Scholarship 414
Marshall Memorial Fellowship 315

European Union

ESRC 1 + 3 Awards and + 3 Awards
Ficosa International Scholarship 351
Fundación Ramón Areces Scholarship 351

South Africa

Allan Gray Senior Scholarship 547

United Kingdom

Aberystwyth Postgraduate Research Studentships 4
ESRC 1 + 3 Awards and + 3 Awards
MA Music Business Management Scholarship 777
Mr and Mrs David Edward Memorial Award 145

United States of America

British Marshall Scholarships 685
Congress Bundestag Youth Exchange for Young Professionals 221
ETS Summer Internship Program for Graduate Students 276
Fulbright Senior Specialists Program 249
Jacki Tuckfield Memorial Graduate Business Scholarship Fund 396
Philip Morris USA Thurgood Marshall Scholarship 633

West European Countries

ESRC 1 + 3 Awards and + 3 Awards
Mr and Mrs David Edward Memorial Award 145

INTERNATIONAL BUSINESS

Any Country

Frederick Douglass Institute Postdoctoral Fellowship 304
Frederick Douglass Institute Predoctoral Dissertation Fellowship 304
ISM Doctoral Dissertation Grant In Supply Management 363
ISM Senior Research Fellowship Program 364
Jennings Randolph Program for International Peace Dissertation
  Fellowship 643
Kennan Institute Short-Term Grants 408
Law & Business in Europe Fellowships 660
Rhodes University Postdoctoral Fellowship and The Andrew Mellon
  Postdoctoral Fellowship 548
Scholarship opportunities linked to CATIE's Postgraduate Program
  including CATIE scholarship forming part of the Scholarship-Loan
  Program 638
Shorenstein APARC Postdoctoral Research Fellowship in Korean
  Studies 586
Tomsk Polytechnic University International Scholarship 634
UNO Graduate Assistantships 710

Australia

Wingate Scholarships 697

Canada

Wingate Scholarships 697

European Union

ESRC 1 + 3 Awards and + 3 Awards
Transatlantic Fellows Program 315
Wingate Scholarships 697

New Zealand

Wingate Scholarships 697

South Africa

Wingate Scholarships 697

United Kingdom

Aberystwyth Postgraduate Research Studentships 4
ESRC 1 + 3 Awards and + 3 Awards
John Mather Scholarship 760
John Speak Trust Scholarships 156
Wingate Scholarships 697

United States of America

British Marshall Scholarships 685
Congress Bundestag Youth Exchange for Young Professionals 221
Fulbright Distinguished Chairs Program 248
Fulbright Senior Specialists Program 249
Kennan Institute Research Scholarship 408
Transatlantic Fellows Program 315

West European Countries

ESRC 1 + 3 Awards and + 3 Awards

BUSINESS COMPUTING

Any Country

Jacob's Pillow Intern Program
Rhodes University Postdoctoral Fellowship and The Andrew Mellon
  Postdoctoral Fellowship 548
University of Southampton Postgraduate Studentships 759
World Universities Network (WUN) International Research Mobility
  Scheme 759

United Kingdom

John Mather Scholarship 760

United States of America

British Marshall Scholarships 685
Congress Bundestag Youth Exchange for Young Professionals 221

MANAGEMENT SYSTEMS AND TECHNIQUES

Any Country

ISM Doctoral Dissertation Grant In Supply Management 363
ISM Senior Research Fellowship Program 364
Queen Mary Research Studentships 539
Rhodes University Postdoctoral Fellowship and The Andrew Mellon
  Postdoctoral Fellowship 548
Warwick Busines School Scholarships (For Masters Study) 791

African Nations

Shell Centenary Scholarships and Shell Centenary Chevening
  Scholarships at Edinburgh 683

Canada

Sloan Industry Studies Fellowships 19
Warwick Busines School Scholarships (For Masters Study) 791

Caribbean Countries

Shell Centenary Scholarships and Shell Centenary Chevening
  Scholarships at Edinburgh 683

East European Countries

Shell Centenary Scholarships and Shell Centenary Chevening
  Scholarships at Edinburgh 683
Warwick Busines School Scholarships (For Masters Study) 791

Middle East

Shell Centenary Scholarships and Shell Centenary Chevening
    Scholarships at Edinburgh 683

New Zealand

The Association of University Staff Crozier Scholarship 500

South Africa

Shell Centenary Scholarships and Shell Centenary Chevening
    Scholarships at Edinburgh 683

United Kingdom

Aberystwyth Postgraduate Research Studentships 4
John Mather Scholarship 760

United States of America

Campus Ecology Fellowship Program 493
Congress Bundestag Youth Exchange for Young Professionals 221
Jacki Tuckfield Memorial Graduate Business Scholarship Fund 396
Sloan Industry Studies Fellowships 19
Warwick Busines School Scholarships (For Masters Study) 791

West European Countries

Shell Centenary Scholarships and Shell Centenary Chevening
    Scholarships at Edinburgh 683
Warwick Busines School Scholarships (For Masters Study) 791

ACCOUNTANCY

Any Country

Jacob's Pillow Intern Program
La Trobe University Postgraduate Scholarship 414
Rhodes University Postdoctoral Fellowship and The Andrew Mellon
    Postdoctoral Fellowship 548
UNO Graduate Assistantships 710
World Universities Network (WUN) International Research Mobility
    Scheme 759

European Union

ESRC 1 + 3 Awards and + 3 Awards

South Africa

Allan Gray Senior Scholarship 547
Henderson Postgraduate Scholarships 548

United Kingdom

Aberystwyth Postgraduate Research Studentships 4
ESRC 1 + 3 Awards and + 3 Awards
John Mather Scholarship 760
Mr and Mrs David Edward Memorial Award 145

United States of America

British Marshall Scholarships 685
Congress Bundestag Youth Exchange for Young Professionals 221
Fellowships for Minority Doctoral Students 61
Jacki Tuckfield Memorial Graduate Business Scholarship Fund 396
Kenneth W. Heikes Family Endowed Scholarship 457

West European Countries

ESRC 1 + 3 Awards and + 3 Awards
Mr and Mrs David Edward Memorial Award 145

REAL ESTATE

Any Country

RICS Education Trust Award 549

United States of America

Appraisal Institute Education Trust Scholarship 102
Minorities and Women Educational Scholarship Program 102

MARKETING AND SALES MANAGEMENT

Any Country

Jacob's Pillow Intern Program
Warwick Busines School Scholarships (For Masters Study) 791

Canada

Horticultural Research Institute Grants 346
Warwick Busines School Scholarships (For Masters Study) 791

East European Countries

Warwick Busines School Scholarships (For Masters Study) 791

European Union

ESRC 1 + 3 Awards and + 3 Awards

United Kingdom

Aberystwyth Postgraduate Research Studentships 4
ESRC 1 + 3 Awards and + 3 Awards
John Mather Scholarship 760

United States of America

Billings Broadcasters MSU-Billings Media Scholarship 456
British Marshall Scholarships 685
Congress Bundestag Youth Exchange for Young Professionals 221
Fulbright Distinguished Chairs Program 248
Fulbright Senior Specialists Program 249
Horticultural Research Institute Grants 346
Jacki Tuckfield Memorial Graduate Business Scholarship Fund 396
Warwick Busines School Scholarships (For Masters Study) 791

West European Countries

ESRC 1 + 3 Awards and + 3 Awards
Warwick Busines School Scholarships (For Masters Study) 791

INSURANCE MANAGEMENT

Any Country

Ernst Meyer Prize 376
Geneva Association 376
International Association for the Study of Insurance Economics
    Research Grants 376
S S Huebner Foundation for Insurance Education Predoctoral and
    Postdoctoral Fellowships 579

Canada

S S Huebner Foundation for Insurance Education Predoctoral and
    Postdoctoral Fellowships 579

United Kingdom

Mr and Mrs David Edward Memorial Award 145

United States of America

Jacki Tuckfield Memorial Graduate Business Scholarship Fund
    396

West European Countries

Mr and Mrs David Edward Memorial Award 145

FINANCE, BANKING AND INVESTMENT

Any Country

CCAF Junior Research Fellowship 239
German Chancellor Fellowships for Prospective Leaders 17
Gold and Silver Scholarships 145
ICMA Centre Doctoral Scholarship 350
S S Huebner Foundation for Insurance Education Predoctoral and
    Postdoctoral Fellowships 579
University of Southampton Postgraduate Studentships 759

Warwick Busines School Scholarships (For Masters Study) 791
World Universities Network (WUN) International Research Mobility
Scheme 759

African Nations

Kulika Charitable Trust-FCO Chevening-University of Leeds Scholarships 703

Australia

ADB Fully Funded Internships 116

Canada

Daniel B. Goldberg Scholarship 323
Minorities in Government Finance Scholarship 323
S S Huebner Foundation for Insurance Education Predoctoral and
Postdoctoral Fellowships 579
Warwick Busines School Scholarships (For Masters Study) 791

Caribbean Countries

ADB Fully Funded Internships 116

East European Countries

German Chancellor Fellowships for Prospective Leaders 17
Warwick Busines School Scholarships (For Masters Study) 791

European Union

ESRC 1 + 3 Awards and + 3 Awards

United Kingdom

Aberystwyth Postgraduate Research Studentships 4
ESRC 1 + 3 Awards and + 3 Awards
John Mather Scholarship 760
Mr and Mrs David Edward Memorial Award 145

United States of America

Appraisal Institute Education Trust Scholarship 102
British Marshall Scholarships 685
Daniel B. Goldberg Scholarship 323
Fulbright Senior Specialists Program 249
German Chancellor Fellowships for Prospective Leaders 17
Jacki Tuckfield Memorial Graduate Business Scholarship Fund 396
Minorities and Women Educational Scholarship Program 102
Minorities in Government Finance Scholarship 323
Warwick Busines School Scholarships (For Masters Study) 791

West European Countries

ESRC 1 + 3 Awards and + 3 Awards
Mr and Mrs David Edward Memorial Award 145
Warwick Busines School Scholarships (For Masters Study) 791

PERSONNEL MANAGEMENT

Any Country

University of Southampton Postgraduate Studentships 759
World Universities Network (WUN) International Research Mobility
Scheme 759

Canada

Horticultural Research Institute Grants 346

European Union

ESRC 1 + 3 Awards and + 3 Awards

United Kingdom

ESRC 1 + 3 Awards and + 3 Awards
John Mather Scholarship 760

United States of America

Fulbright Senior Specialists Program 249
Horticultural Research Institute Grants 346
Jacki Tuckfield Memorial Graduate Business Scholarship Fund 396

West European Countries

ESRC 1 + 3 Awards and + 3 Awards

LABOUR/INDUSTRIAL RELATIONS

Any Country

Mackenzie King Travelling Scholarship 429
Warwick Busines School Scholarships (For Masters Study)
791

Canada

Warwick Busines School Scholarships (For Masters Study) 791

East European Countries

Warwick Busines School Scholarships (For Masters Study) 791

United Kingdom

Mr and Mrs David Edward Memorial Award 145

United States of America

Fulbright Distinguished Chairs Program 248
Fulbright Senior Specialists Program 249
Warwick Busines School Scholarships (For Masters Study) 791

West European Countries

Mr and Mrs David Edward Memorial Award 145
Warwick Busines School Scholarships (For Masters Study) 791

PUBLIC ADMINISTRATION

Any Country

Fulbright Institutional Linkages Program 306
German Chancellor Fellowships for Prospective Leaders 17
Kirkcaldy Scholarship 670
Metropolitan Museum of Art Summer Internships for Graduate
Students 447
Warwick Busines School Scholarships (For MPA Study) 791

African Nations

Cannon Collins Scholarship 425

Australia

Wingate Scholarships 697

Canada

Frank Knox Memorial Fellowships 123
Public Safety and Emergency Preparedness Canada Research
Fellowship in Honour of Stuart Nesbitt White 123
Wingate Scholarships 697

East European Countries

German Chancellor Fellowships for Prospective Leaders 17

European Union

Wingate Scholarships 697

New Zealand

Wingate Scholarships 697

South Africa

Cannon Collins Scholarship 425
Wingate Scholarships 697

United Kingdom

Frank Knox Fellowships at Harvard University 302
Kennedy Scholarships 409
Warwick Busines School Scholarships (For MPA Study) 791
Wingate Scholarships 697

United States of America

American Academy in Berlin Prize Fellowships 24
Congress Bundestag Youth Exchange for Young Professionals 221
Fulbright Distinguished Chairs Program 248
German Chancellor Fellowships for Prospective Leaders 17
IREX Individual Advanced Research Opportunities 388
Mike M. Masaoka Congressional Fellowship 400

INSTITUTIONAL ADMINISTRATION

Any Country

Jacob's Pillow Intern Program

Australia

Wingate Scholarships 697

Canada

Wingate Scholarships 697

European Union

Wingate Scholarships 697

New Zealand

Wingate Scholarships 697

South Africa

Wingate Scholarships 697

United Kingdom

Wingate Scholarships 697

MBA

Any Country

Ashridge Management College-Full-Time MBA and Executive MBA
Scholarships 114
The Cámara de Comercio Scholarship 351
Clemson Graduate Assistantships 238
Director's Scholarships 677
ESADE MBA Scholarships 284
Gold and Silver Scholarships 145
Handelsblatt/RSM Scholarship 576
IESE Alumini Association Scholarships 351
IESE Private Foundation Scholarships 352
The IMD MBA Future Leaders Scholarships 384
INSEAD Asia Enterprise Fund Scholarship 358
INSEAD Elmar Schulte Diversity Scholarship 359
INSEAD L'Oréal Scholarship 360
INSEAD Sasakawa (SYLLF) Scholarships 360
Lancaster MBA Director's Leadership Scholarships 415
Lancaster MBA Open Scholarships 415
Missouri State University Carr Foundation Scholarship 451
Missouri State University Graduate Assistantships 451
Missouri State University Robert and Charlotte Bitter Graduate
Scholarship 451
Nestlé Scholarship for Women 385
NTU Alumni Scholarship 463
NTU MBA Scholarship 464
RSM Alumni Scholarship 576
RSM Erasmus University Dean's Fund Scholarship
RSM Erasmus University MBA Citizenship Scholarship 576
RSM MBA Corporate Scholarship Programme 576
RSM-Intermediair EMBA Scholarship 576
St Catharine's College Benavitch Scholarships 678
SWE/Bentley Graduate Merit Scholarship 613
Trinity College Said MBA and EMBA Scholarships 747
University of Southampton Postgraduate Studentships 759
UNLV Alumni Association Graduate Scholarships 710
UNLV Graduate Assistantships 711
UNLV James F Adams/GSA Scholarship 711
UNO Graduate Assistantships 710

Warwick Business School Scholarships (For Doctoral Study) 791
Warwick Business School Scholarships (For full-time MBA Study) 791
World Universities Network (WUN) International Research Mobility
Scheme 759

African Nations

INSEAD Alumni Fund (IAF) Diversity Scholarship(s) 358
INSEAD Eli Lilly and Company Innovation Scholarship 359
Shell and IMD MBA Alumni Scholarships 385
Warwick Business School Scholarships (For MBA Study via Distance
Learning) 791

Australia

NTU APEC Scholarship 463
Shell and IMD MBA Alumni Scholarships 385
Warwick Business School Scholarships (For MBA Study via Distance
Learning) 791

Canada

Bank of Montréal Pauline Varnier Fellowship 243
Frank Knox Memorial Fellowships 123
INSEAD Canadian Foundation Scholarship 359
INSEAD Eli Lilly and Company Innovation Scholarship 359
JCCA Graduate Education Scholarship 400
NTU APEC Scholarship 463
Shell and IMD MBA Alumni Scholarships 385
Warwick Business School Scholarships (For full-time MBA Study) 791
Warwick Business School Scholarships (For MBA Study via Distance
Learning) 791

Caribbean Countries

INSEAD Alumni Fund (IAF) Diversity Scholarship(s) 358

East European Countries

INSEAD Alumni Fund (IAF) Diversity Scholarship(s) 358
INSEAD Eli Lilly and Company Innovation Scholarship 359
INSEAD Sisley-Marc d'Ornano Scholarship 360
N Boustany MBA Scholarship 677
Shell and IMD MBA Alumni Scholarships 385
Warwick Business School Scholarships (For full-time MBA Study) 791
Warwick Business School Scholarships (For MBA Study via Distance
Learning) 791

European Union

Ficosa International Scholarship 351
Fundación Ramón Areces Scholarship 351
Shell and IMD MBA Alumni Scholarships 385
Warwick Business School Scholarships (For MBA Study via Distance
Learning) 791

Middle East

INSEAD Alumni Fund (IAF) Diversity Scholarship(s) 358
INSEAD Eli Lilly and Company Innovation Scholarship 359
Shell and IMD MBA Alumni Scholarships 385
Warwick Business School Scholarships (For MBA Study via Distance
Learning) 791

New Zealand

NTU APEC Scholarship 463
Shell and IMD MBA Alumni Scholarships 385
Warwick Business School Scholarships (For MBA Study via Distance
Learning) 791

South Africa

INSEAD Alumni Fund (IAF) Diversity Scholarship(s) 358
Shell and IMD MBA Alumni Scholarships 385
Warwick Business School Scholarships (For MBA Study via Distance
Learning) 791

United Kingdom

Aberystwyth Postgraduate Research Studentships 4
Frank Knox Fellowships at Harvard University 302
Fulbright British Friends of HBS MBA Awards 780

INSEAD Henry Grunfeld Foundation Scholarship 359
INSEAD Lord Kitchener National Memorial Scholarship 360
INSEAD Louis Franck Scholarship 360
John Mather Scholarship 760
Postgraduate Student Allowance Scheme (PSAS) (Queen Margaret) 539
Sainsbury Bursaries 677
Sainsbury Management Fellowships 555
Shell and IMD MBA Alumni Scholarships 385
Warwick Business School Scholarships (For MBA Study via Distance Learning) 791

United States of America

ASOL Orchestra Management Fellowship Program 95
INSEAD Judith Connelly Delouvrier Scholarship 359
Jacki Tuckfield Memorial Graduate Business Scholarship Fund 396
JCCA Graduate Education Scholarship 400
NTU APEC Scholarship 463
Shell and IMD MBA Alumni Scholarships 385
Warwick Business School Scholarships (For full-time MBA Study) 791
Warwick Business School Scholarships (For MBA Study via Distance Learning) 791

West European Countries

INSEAD Belgian Alumni and Council Scholarship Fund 358
INSEAD Børsen/Danish Council Scholarship 358
INSEAD Elof Hansson Scholarship Fund 359
INSEAD Giovanni Agnelli Scholarship 359
Shell and IMD MBA Alumni Scholarships 385
Warwick Business School Scholarships (For full-time MBA Study) 791
Warwick Business School Scholarships (For MBA Study via Distance Learning) 791

EDUCATION AND TEACHER TRAINING

GENERAL

Any Country

Acadia Graduate Awards 5
Andrew Mellon Foundation Scholarship 547
The Applegate/Jackson/Parks Future Teacher Scholarship 482
AUC Teaching Arabic as a Foreign Language Fellowships 98
AUC Teaching English as a Foreign Language Fellowships 98
Australian Postgraduate Award Research Scholarship
Blance E Woolls Scholarship for School Library Media Service 149
Concordia University Graduate Fellowships 243
David J Azrieli Graduate Fellowship 243
Doctoral Dissertation Scholarship 149
ETS Postdoctoral Fellowships 276
Faculty Studentships 694
Field Psych Trust Grant 291
Helen Darcovich Memorial Doctoral Fellowship 209
HSA Grant for Educators 338
Jacob's Pillow Intern Program
John Hume Postgraduate Scholarships 490
Kennan Institute Short-Term Grants 408
La Trobe University Postgraduate Scholarship 414
Lindbergh Grants 228
Monash International Postgraduate Research Scholarship (MIPRS) 455
Monash University Silver Jubilee Postgraduate Scholarship 455
Neporany Doctoral Fellowship 210
NUT Page Scholarship 489
Rhodes University Postdoctoral Fellowship and The Andrew Mellon Postdoctoral Fellowship 548
Rhodes University Postgraduate Scholarship 549
Royal Irish Academy Mobility Grants 569
Sarah Rebecca Reed Award 149
Sir Allan Sewell Visiting Fellowship 326
Snowdon Award Scheme Grants 597
Southdown Trust Awards 615
Spencer Foundation Dissertation Fellowship Program 616

Stanley G French Graduate Fellowship 244
United States Holocaust Memorial Museum Center for Advanced Holocaust Studies Visiting Scholar Programs 641
University of Ballarat Postgraduate Research Scholarship
University of Otago International Scholarships 717
University of Otago PhD Scholarships 718
University of Otago Prestigious PhD Scholarships 718
USIP Annual Grant Competition 643
USIP Priority Grant-making Competition 644
Vera Moore International Postgraduate Research Scholarships 455

African Nations

ABCCF Student Grant 102
International Postgraduate Research Scholarships (IPRS) 413
International Postgraduate Research Scholarships (IPRS) 413
NUFFIC-NFP Fellowships for Master's Degree Programmes 496

Australia

Australian Postgraduate Awards 413
Council of Catholic School Parents (NSW) Indigenous Postgraduate Scholarship (IES) 133
Fulbright Postdoctoral Fellowships 140
Fulbright Postgraduate Awards 140
Fulbright Professional Award for Vocational Education and Training 141
International Postgraduate Research Scholarships (IPRS) 413
Lewis O'Brien Scholarship
University of Ballarat Part Postgraduate Research Scholarship 667
University of Otago Master's Awards 717
Wingate Scholarships 697

Canada

Canada Graduate Scholarship Program (CGS): Master's Scholarship 600
Community-University Research Alliances (CURA) 601
International Postgraduate Research Scholarships (IPRS) 413
International Postgraduate Research Scholarships (IPRS) 413
J W McConnell Memorial Fellowships 243
JCCA Graduate Education Scholarship 400
Jim Bourque Scholarship 103
Major Collaborative Research Initiatives (MCRI) 601
SSHRC Doctoral Awards 602
SSHRC Research Development Initiatives 603
SSHRC Standard Research Grants 603
Wingate Scholarships 697

Caribbean Countries

International Postgraduate Research Scholarships (IPRS) 413
International Postgraduate Research Scholarships (IPRS) 413

East European Countries

International Postgraduate Research Scholarships (IPRS) 413
International Postgraduate Research Scholarships (IPRS) 413

European Union

All Saints Educational Trust Personal Scholarships 20
International Postgraduate Research Scholarships (IPRS) 413
Wingate Scholarships 697

Middle East

ABCCF Student Grant 102
International Postgraduate Research Scholarships (IPRS) 413
International Postgraduate Research Scholarships (IPRS) 413
NUFFIC-NFP Fellowships for Master's Degree Programmes 496

New Zealand

Australian Postgraduate Awards 413
University of Otago Master's Awards 717
Wingate Scholarships 697

South Africa

International Postgraduate Research Scholarships (IPRS) 413
International Postgraduate Research Scholarships (IPRS) 413

NUFFIC-NFP Fellowships for Master's Degree Programmes 496
Wingate Scholarships 697
Wolfson Foundation Grants 799

United Kingdom

Aberystwyth Postgraduate Research Studentships 4
All Saints Educational Trust Corporate Awards 20
All Saints Educational Trust Personal Scholarships 20
Frank Knox Fellowships at Harvard University 302
Fulbright-Robertson Visiting Professorship in British History 783
Goldsmiths' Company Science for Society Courses
International Postgraduate Research Scholarships (IPRS) 413
International Postgraduate Research Scholarships (IPRS) 413
Wingate Scholarships 697
Winston Churchill Memorial Trust (UK) Travelling Fellowships 798
Wolfson Foundation Grants 799

United States of America

AIGC Accenture American Indian Scholarship Fund 59
ASME Graduate Teaching Fellowship Program 93
Bicentennial Swedish-American Exchange Fund 623
ETS Postdoctoral Fellowships 276
Fulbright Senior Specialists Program 249
Fulbright Teacher Exchange 307
International Postgraduate Research Scholarships (IPRS) 413
International Postgraduate Research Scholarships (IPRS) 413
IREX Individual Advanced Research Opportunities 388
IREX Short-Term Travel Grants 389
JCCA Graduate Education Scholarship 400
Kennan Institute Research Scholarship 408
NEA Foundation Learning and Leadership Grants 473
NEA Foundation Student Achievement Grants 473
North Dakota Indian Scholarship 507
Nurses' Educational Funds Fellowships and Scholarships 510
Sally S Jacobsen Scholarship 475

West European Countries

International Postgraduate Research Scholarships (IPRS) 413
International Postgraduate Research Scholarships (IPRS) 413
University of Otago Master's Awards 717

NONVOCATIONAL SUBJECTS EDUCATION

Any Country

Camargo Fellowships 182
Snowdon Award Scheme Grants 597

United Kingdom

Fund for Innovation 539

United States of America

The Walter J Jensen Fellowship for French Language, Literature and Culture 531

EDUCATION IN NATIVE LANGUAGE

Any Country

AUC Writing Center Graduate Fellowships 98
ETS Summer Internship Program for Graduate Students 276

Canada

Horticultural Research Institute Grants 346

United Kingdom

Aberystwyth Postgraduate Research Studentships 4
Mr and Mrs David Edward Memorial Award 145

United States of America

ETS Summer Internship Program for Graduate Students 276
Fulbright Teacher Exchange 307
Horticultural Research Institute Grants 346

West European Countries

Mr and Mrs David Edward Memorial Award 145

FOREIGN LANGUAGES EDUCATION

Any Country

AUC Arabic Language Fellowships 96
Camargo Fellowships 182
ETS Postdoctoral Fellowships 276
ETS Summer Internship Program for Graduate Students 276
Norwich Jubilee Esperanto Foundation Grants-in-Aid 509

Canada

Edouard Morot-Sir Fellowship in Literature 361
Gilbert Chinard Fellowships 361
Harmon Chadbourn Rorison Fellowship 361

United Kingdom

Aberystwyth Postgraduate Research Studentships 4
Prix du Québec Award 160

United States of America

Edouard Morot-Sir Fellowship in Literature 361
ETS Postdoctoral Fellowships 276
ETS Summer Internship Program for Graduate Students 276
ETS Sylvia Taylor Johnson Minority Fellowship in Educational Measurement 276
Fulbright Teacher Exchange 307
Gilbert Chinard Fellowships 361
Harmon Chadbourn Rorison Fellowship 361
The Walter J Jensen Fellowship for French Language, Literature and Culture 531

MATHEMATICS EDUCATION

Any Country

ETS Postdoctoral Fellowships 276
ETS Summer Internship Program for Graduate Students 276
Research/Visiting Scientist Fellowships 8

United Kingdom

Goldsmiths' Company Science for Society Courses
Mr and Mrs David Edward Memorial Award 145

United States of America

ETS Postdoctoral Fellowships 276
ETS Summer Internship Program for Graduate Students 276
ETS Sylvia Taylor Johnson Minority Fellowship in Educational Measurement 276

West European Countries

Mr and Mrs David Edward Memorial Award 145

SCIENCE EDUCATION

Any Country

Carski Foundation Distinguished Undergraduate Teaching Award 86
Crohn's and Colitis Foundation Career Development Award 255
Crohn's and Colitis Foundation Research Fellowship Awards 255
ETS Postdoctoral Fellowships 276
ETS Summer Internship Program for Graduate Students 276
Glenn E and Barbara Hodsdon Ullyot Scholarship 230
Gordon Cain Fellowship 230
Hastings Center International Visiting Scholars Program 332
IAU Travel Grant 377
Joseph H. Hazen Education Prize 342
Société de Chimie Industrielle (American Section) Fellowship 231
UFAW Animal Welfare Research Training Scholarships 644

UFAW Research and Project Awards 645
UFAW Small Project and Travel Awards 645
UFAW Vacation Scholarships 645

African Nations

Hastings Center International Visiting Scholars Program 332

Australia

APAI Water Resources Management Scholarship 326
Hastings Center International Visiting Scholars Program 332
Hsanz Travel Grant 329

Canada

CIC Award for Chemical Education 231

Caribbean Countries

Hastings Center International Visiting Scholars Program 332

East European Countries

Hastings Center International Visiting Scholars Program 332

Middle East

Hastings Center International Visiting Scholars Program 332

New Zealand

APAI Water Resources Management Scholarship 326
Hastings Center International Visiting Scholars Program 332
Hsanz Travel Grant 329

South Africa

Hastings Center International Visiting Scholars Program 332

United Kingdom

Aberystwyth Postgraduate Research Studentships 4
Goldsmiths' Company Science for Society Courses
Hastings Center International Visiting Scholars Program 332

United States of America

Earthwatch Fellowships 272
ETS Postdoctoral Fellowships 276
ETS Summer Internship Program for Graduate Students 276
NIH Research Grants 483
Woodrow Wilson Teaching Fellowship 803

West European Countries

Hastings Center International Visiting Scholars Program 332

HUMANITIES AND SOCIAL SCIENCE EDUCATION

Any Country

ACLS/Chiang Ching-kuo Foundation (CCK) New Perspectives on Chinese Culture and Society 48
Andrew W. Mellon/ACLS Recent Doctoral Recipients Fellowships 48
Bernadotte E Schmitt Grants 58
BIAA Post-Doctoral Research Fellowship 168
BIAA Research Scholarship 168
BIAA Study Grants 168
CAGS UMI Dissertation Awards 199
Doctoral Fellowships 352
ETS Postdoctoral Fellowships 276
ETS Summer Internship Program for Graduate Students 276
Hastings Center International Visiting Scholars Program 332
HFG Foundation Dissertation Fellowships 332
Innovative Geography Teaching Grants 564
J Franklin Jameson Fellowship 58
Jacob Hirsch Fellowship 83
John Hume Postgraduate Scholarships 490
Joseph H. Hazen Education Prize 342
National Fellowships 353
Research Grants for Getty Scholars and Visiting Scholars 317
Senior Fellowships 353

Shorenstein APARC Postdoctoral Research Fellowship in Korean Studies 586
Trudeau Foundation Doctoral Scholarships 533
USA – Getty Foundation Research Grants for Predoctoral and Postdoctoral Fellowships 317
Villa Predoctoral and Postdoctoral Fellowships 317

African Nations

Canadian Window on International Development 380
Hastings Center International Visiting Scholars Program 332
IDRC Doctoral Research Awards 380
International Postgraduate Research Scholarships (IPRS) 413

Australia

Hastings Center International Visiting Scholars Program 332

Canada

Canadian Window on International Development 380
CIES Fellowship Program 273
Dr William S. Lewis Doctoral Fellowships 711
IDRC Doctoral Research Awards 380
International Postgraduate Research Scholarships (IPRS) 413

Caribbean Countries

Canadian Window on International Development 380
Hastings Center International Visiting Scholars Program 332
IDRC Doctoral Research Awards 380
International Postgraduate Research Scholarships (IPRS) 413

East European Countries

Hastings Center International Visiting Scholars Program 332
IDRC Doctoral Research Awards 380
International Postgraduate Research Scholarships (IPRS) 413

European Union

All Saints Educational Trust Personal Scholarships 20

Middle East

German Israeli Foundation Young Scientist's Programme
Hastings Center International Visiting Scholars Program 332
IDRC Doctoral Research Awards 380
International Postgraduate Research Scholarships (IPRS) 413
Research Grant (GIF) 314

New Zealand

Hastings Center International Visiting Scholars Program 332

South Africa

Canadian Window on International Development 380
Hastings Center International Visiting Scholars Program 332
IDRC Doctoral Research Awards 380
International Postgraduate Research Scholarships (IPRS) 413

United Kingdom

All Saints Educational Trust Corporate Awards 20
All Saints Educational Trust Personal Scholarships 20
BIAA/SPBS Fieldwork Award 168
Fulbright-Robertson Visiting Professorship in British History 783
Hastings Center International Visiting Scholars Program 332
International Postgraduate Research Scholarships (IPRS) 413
Mr and Mrs David Edward Memorial Award 145
Ray Y. Gildea Jr. Award 565

United States of America

ACOR-CAORC Fellowship 34
ACOR-CAORC Postgraduate Fellowships 34
ASOR Mesopotamian Fellowship 83
ASOR W.F. Albright Institute of Archaeological Research/National Endowment of the Humanities Fellowships 84
Bicentennial Swedish-American Exchange Fund Travel Grants 245
Earthwatch Fellowships 272
Ernest Hemingway Research Grants 405

ETS Postdoctoral Fellowships 276
ETS Summer Internship Program for Graduate Students 276
International Postgraduate Research Scholarships (IPRS) 413
James Madison Fellowship Program 398
Kennedy Research Grants 405
ONR Summer Faculty Research 84
Ray Y. Gildea Jr. Award 565
Woodrow Wilson Teaching Fellowship 803

West European Countries

German Israeli Foundation Young Scientist's Programme
Hastings Center International Visiting Scholars Program 332
International Postgraduate Research Scholarships (IPRS) 413
Mr and Mrs David Edward Memorial Award 145
Research Grant (GIF) 314

PHYSICAL EDUCATION

Any Country

Adelphi University Athletic Grants 7
ETS Postdoctoral Fellowships 276

African Nations

International Postgraduate Research Scholarships (IPRS) 413

Australia

Our World-Underwater Scholarship Society Scholarships 518

Canada

International Postgraduate Research Scholarships (IPRS) 413
JCCA Graduate Education Scholarship 400

Caribbean Countries

International Postgraduate Research Scholarships (IPRS) 413

East European Countries

International Postgraduate Research Scholarships (IPRS) 413

European Union

Our World-Underwater Scholarship Society Scholarships 518

Middle East

International Postgraduate Research Scholarships (IPRS) 413

New Zealand

Our World-Underwater Scholarship Society Scholarships 518

South Africa

International Postgraduate Research Scholarships (IPRS) 413

United Kingdom

International Postgraduate Research Scholarships (IPRS) 413
Mr and Mrs David Edward Memorial Award 145

United States of America

Adelphi University Athletic Grants 7
ETS Postdoctoral Fellowships 276
International Postgraduate Research Scholarships (IPRS) 413
JCCA Graduate Education Scholarship 400
Our World-Underwater Scholarship Society Scholarships 518

West European Countries

International Postgraduate Research Scholarships (IPRS) 413
Mr and Mrs David Edward Memorial Award 145

LITERACY EDUCATION

Any Country

Albert J Harris Award 386
AUC Writing Center Graduate Fellowships 98

Dina Feitelson Research Award 386
Elva Knight Research Grant 387
ETS Postdoctoral Fellowships 276
ETS Summer Internship Program for Graduate Students 276
Helen M Robinson Award 387
International Reading Association Outstanding Dissertation of the
    Year Award 387
International Reading Association Teacher as Researcher Grant 387
Jeanne S Chall Research Fellowship 387
Nila Banton Smith Research Dissemination Support Grant 387
Steven A Stahl Research Grant 388

African Nations

International Postgraduate Research Scholarships (IPRS) 413
Reading/Literacy Research Fellowship 387

Australia

Reading/Literacy Research Fellowship 387

Canada

International Postgraduate Research Scholarships (IPRS) 413

Caribbean Countries

International Postgraduate Research Scholarships (IPRS) 413
Reading/Literacy Research Fellowship 387

East European Countries

International Postgraduate Research Scholarships (IPRS) 413
Reading/Literacy Research Fellowship 387

Middle East

International Postgraduate Research Scholarships (IPRS) 413
Reading/Literacy Research Fellowship 387

New Zealand

Reading/Literacy Research Fellowship 387

South Africa

International Postgraduate Research Scholarships (IPRS) 413
Reading/Literacy Research Fellowship 387

United Kingdom

International Postgraduate Research Scholarships (IPRS) 413
Reading/Literacy Research Fellowship 387

United States of America

ETS Postdoctoral Fellowships 276
ETS Summer Internship Program for Graduate Students 276
International Postgraduate Research Scholarships (IPRS) 413

West European Countries

International Postgraduate Research Scholarships (IPRS) 413
Reading/Literacy Research Fellowship 387

VOCATIONAL SUBJECTS EDUCATION

Any Country

American Cancer Society UICC International Fellowships for Begin-
    ning Investigators (ACSBI) 389
Faculty Studentships 694
Snowdon Award Scheme Grants 597

Australia

Fulbright Professional Award for Vocational Education and Training 141

United Kingdom

Hilda Martindale Exhibitions 341

United States of America

NFID Advanced Vaccinology Course Travel Grant 476

AGRICULTURAL EDUCATION

Any Country

UFAW Animal Welfare Research Training Scholarships 644
UFAW Research and Project Awards 645
UFAW Small Project and Travel Awards 645
UFAW Vacation Scholarships 645

Australia

MINTRAC Postgraduate Scholarship 451

Canada

Horticultural Research Institute Grants 346

United States of America

Horticultural Research Institute Grants 346

ART EDUCATION

Any Country

Henry Moore Institute Research Fellowship 338
International Paulo Cello Competition 523
Jacob's Pillow Intern Program
Metropolitan Museum of Art Roswell L Gilpatric Internship 447
Metropolitan Museum of Art Summer Internships for College Students 447
Metropolitan Museum of Art Summer Internships for Graduate Students 447
MICA Fellowship 435

African Nations

International Postgraduate Research Scholarships (IPRS) 413

Canada

International Postgraduate Research Scholarships (IPRS) 413

Caribbean Countries

International Postgraduate Research Scholarships (IPRS) 413

East European Countries

International Postgraduate Research Scholarships (IPRS) 413

Middle East

International Postgraduate Research Scholarships (IPRS) 413

South Africa

International Postgraduate Research Scholarships (IPRS) 413

United Kingdom

The Costume Society Student Bursary 247
The Costume Society Yarwood Award 247
International Postgraduate Research Scholarships (IPRS) 413

United States of America

ACC Humanities Fellowship Program 115
Dodge Foundation Visual Arts Initiative 312
International Postgraduate Research Scholarships (IPRS) 413
Virginia Liebeler Biennial Grants for Mature Women (Art) 484

West European Countries

International Postgraduate Research Scholarships (IPRS) 413

COMMERCE/BUSINESS EDUCATION

Australia

Baillieu Research Scholarship 707

COMPUTER EDUCATION

Any Country

ETS Summer Internship Program for Graduate Students 276

African Nations

International Postgraduate Research Scholarships (IPRS) 413

Canada

International Postgraduate Research Scholarships (IPRS) 413

Caribbean Countries

International Postgraduate Research Scholarships (IPRS) 413

East European Countries

International Postgraduate Research Scholarships (IPRS) 413

Middle East

International Postgraduate Research Scholarships (IPRS) 413

South Africa

International Postgraduate Research Scholarships (IPRS) 413

United Kingdom

International Postgraduate Research Scholarships (IPRS) 413

United States of America

ETS Summer Internship Program for Graduate Students 276
International Postgraduate Research Scholarships (IPRS) 413

West European Countries

International Postgraduate Research Scholarships (IPRS) 413

TECHNOLOGY EDUCATION

Any Country

Blance E Woolls Scholarship for School Library Media Service 149
Doctoral Dissertation Scholarship 149
ETS Postdoctoral Fellowships 276
Exxon Mobil Teaching Fellowships 553
Sarah Rebecca Reed Award 149

United States of America

DEED (Demonstration of Energy-Efficient Developments) Student Research Grant/Internship 80
Earthwatch Fellowships 272
ETS Postdoctoral Fellowships 276

HEALTH EDUCATION

Any Country

AFSP Distinguished Investigator Awards 55
AFSP Pilot Grants 55
AFSP Postdoctoral Research Fellowships 55
AFSP Standard Research Grants 55
AFSP Young Investigator Award 56
Allen Foundation Grants 20
American Cancer Society UICC International Fellowships for Beginning Investigators (ACSBI) 389
ASBAH Research Grant 118
Breast Cancer Campaign Project Grants 157
Breast Cancer Campaign Small Pilot Grants 157
FSSS Grants-in-Aid Program 606
Hastings Center International Visiting Scholars Program 332
UICC International Cancer Research Technology Transfer Fellowships (ICRETT) 390

African Nations

Hastings Center International Visiting Scholars Program 332

Australia

Hastings Center International Visiting Scholars Program 332

Canada

JCCA Graduate Education Scholarship 400

Caribbean Countries

Hastings Center International Visiting Scholars Program 332

East European Countries

FEMS Fellowship 290
Hastings Center International Visiting Scholars Program 332

Middle East

Hastings Center International Visiting Scholars Program 332

New Zealand

Hastings Center International Visiting Scholars Program 332

South Africa

Hastings Center International Visiting Scholars Program 332

United Kingdom

FEMS Fellowship 290
Fund for Innovation 539
Hastings Center International Visiting Scholars Program 332
Resuscitation Council Research Fellowships 546
Resuscitation Council Research Grants 546

United States of America

JCCA Graduate Education Scholarship 400
NFID Advanced Vaccinology Course Travel Grant 476
Nurses' Educational Funds Fellowships and Scholarships 510
Pfizer Fellowships in Health Literary Clear Health Communication 526
Pfizer Visiting Professorships in Clear Health Literacy/Clear Health
    Communication 527
PhRMAF Postdoctoral Fellowships in Health Outcomes Research 528
PhRMAF Predoctoral Fellowships in Health Outcomes Research 529
PhRMAF Research Starter Grants in Health Outcomes Research 529
PhRMAF Sabbatical Fellowships in Health Outcomes Research 530

West European Countries

FEMS Fellowship 290
Hastings Center International Visiting Scholars Program 332

HOME ECONOMICS EDUCATION

European Union

All Saints Educational Trust Personal Scholarships 20

United Kingdom

All Saints Educational Trust Personal Scholarships 20

MUSIC EDUCATION

Any Country

Davis and Lyons Bursaries in Music 237
Royal Academy of Music General Bursary Awards 555
WBDI Scholarship Awards 800

Australia

Australian Music Foundation Award 136

European Union

Hezekiah Wardwell Fellowships 17

United States of America

ACC Humanities Fellowship Program 115

PRE-SCHOOL EDUCATION

Any Country

ETS Postdoctoral Fellowships 276
ETS Summer Internship Program for Graduate Students 276
Faculty Studentships 694

African Nations

International Postgraduate Research Scholarships (IPRS) 413

Canada

International Postgraduate Research Scholarships (IPRS) 413
JCCA Graduate Education Scholarship 400

Caribbean Countries

International Postgraduate Research Scholarships (IPRS) 413

East European Countries

International Postgraduate Research Scholarships (IPRS) 413

Middle East

International Postgraduate Research Scholarships (IPRS) 413

South Africa

International Postgraduate Research Scholarships (IPRS) 413

United Kingdom

International Postgraduate Research Scholarships (IPRS) 413

United States of America

ETS Postdoctoral Fellowships 276
ETS Summer Internship Program for Graduate Students 276
ETS Sylvia Taylor Johnson Minority Fellowship in Educational
    Measurement 276
International Postgraduate Research Scholarships (IPRS) 413
JCCA Graduate Education Scholarship 400

West European Countries

International Postgraduate Research Scholarships (IPRS) 413

PRIMARY EDUCATION

Any Country

ETS Postdoctoral Fellowships 276
ETS Summer Internship Program for Graduate Students 276
Faculty Studentships 694
University of Southampton Postgraduate Studentships 759
World Universities Network (WUN) International Research Mobility
    Scheme 759

African Nations

International Postgraduate Research Scholarships (IPRS) 413

Canada

International Postgraduate Research Scholarships (IPRS) 413

Caribbean Countries

International Postgraduate Research Scholarships (IPRS) 413

East European Countries

International Postgraduate Research Scholarships (IPRS) 413

European Union

All Saints Educational Trust Personal Scholarships 20

Middle East

International Postgraduate Research Scholarships (IPRS) 413

South Africa

International Postgraduate Research Scholarships (IPRS) 413

United Kingdom

Aberystwyth Postgraduate Research Studentships 4
All Saints Educational Trust Personal Scholarships 20
International Postgraduate Research Scholarships (IPRS) 413
Mr and Mrs David Edward Memorial Award 145

United States of America

ETS Postdoctoral Fellowships 276
ETS Summer Internship Program for Graduate Students 276
ETS Sylvia Taylor Johnson Minority Fellowship in Educational
    Measurement 276
International Postgraduate Research Scholarships (IPRS) 413

West European Countries

International Postgraduate Research Scholarships (IPRS) 413
Mr and Mrs David Edward Memorial Award 145

SECONDARY EDUCATION

Any Country

ETS Postdoctoral Fellowships 276
ETS Summer Internship Program for Graduate Students 276
Faculty Studentships 694
Innovative Geography Teaching Grants 564
University of Southampton Postgraduate Studentships 759
World Universities Network (WUN) International Research Mobility
    Scheme 759

African Nations

International Postgraduate Research Scholarships (IPRS) 413

Canada

International Postgraduate Research Scholarships (IPRS) 413

Caribbean Countries

International Postgraduate Research Scholarships (IPRS) 413

East European Countries

FEMS Fellowship 290
International Postgraduate Research Scholarships (IPRS) 413

European Union

All Saints Educational Trust Personal Scholarships 20

Middle East

International Postgraduate Research Scholarships (IPRS) 413

South Africa

International Postgraduate Research Scholarships (IPRS) 413

United Kingdom

Aberystwyth Postgraduate Research Studentships 4
All Saints Educational Trust Personal Scholarships 20
FEMS Fellowship 290
International Postgraduate Research Scholarships (IPRS) 413
Mr and Mrs David Edward Memorial Award 145
Ray Y. Gildea Jr. Award 565

United States of America

ETS Postdoctoral Fellowships 276
ETS Summer Internship Program for Graduate Students 276
ETS Sylvia Taylor Johnson Minority Fellowship in Educational
    Measurement 276
International Postgraduate Research Scholarships (IPRS) 413

Ray Y. Gildea Jr. Award 565
The Walter J Jensen Fellowship for French Language, Literature and
    Culture 531

West European Countries

FEMS Fellowship 290
International Postgraduate Research Scholarships (IPRS) 413
Mr and Mrs David Edward Memorial Award 145

ADULT EDUCATION

Any Country

ETS Postdoctoral Fellowships 276
ETS Summer Internship Program for Graduate Students 276
Faculty Studentships 694
Snowdon Award Scheme Grants 597
University of Southampton Postgraduate Studentships 759
World Universities Network (WUN) International Research Mobility
    Scheme 759

African Nations

International Postgraduate Research Scholarships (IPRS) 413

Canada

International Postgraduate Research Scholarships (IPRS) 413

Caribbean Countries

International Postgraduate Research Scholarships (IPRS) 413

East European Countries

International Postgraduate Research Scholarships (IPRS) 413

Middle East

International Postgraduate Research Scholarships (IPRS) 413

South Africa

International Postgraduate Research Scholarships (IPRS) 413

United Kingdom

International Postgraduate Research Scholarships (IPRS) 413
Ray Y. Gildea Jr. Award 565

United States of America

ETS Postdoctoral Fellowships 276
ETS Summer Internship Program for Graduate Students 276
ETS Sylvia Taylor Johnson Minority Fellowship in Educational
    Measurement 276
International Postgraduate Research Scholarships (IPRS) 413
Ray Y. Gildea Jr. Award 565

West European Countries

International Postgraduate Research Scholarships (IPRS) 413

SPECIAL EDUCATION

Any Country

ETS Postdoctoral Fellowships 276
ETS Summer Internship Program for Graduate Students 276
Faculty Studentships 694
Snowdon Award Scheme Grants 597

Canada

JCCA Graduate Education Scholarship 400

United States of America

ACRES Scholarship 49
ETS Postdoctoral Fellowships 276
ETS Summer Internship Program for Graduate Students 276

ETS Sylvia Taylor Johnson Minority Fellowship in Educational
    Measurement 276
JCCA Graduate Education Scholarship 400

EDUCATION OF THE GIFTED

United States of America

ETS Sylvia Taylor Johnson Minority Fellowship in Educational
    Measurement 276

EDUCATION OF THE HANDICAPPED

Any Country

ASBAH Research Grant 118
ETS Postdoctoral Fellowships 276
ETS Summer Internship Program for Graduate Students 276
Snowdon Award Scheme Grants 597

United States of America

ACRES Scholarship 49
ETS Postdoctoral Fellowships 276
ETS Summer Internship Program for Graduate Students 276
ETS Sylvia Taylor Johnson Minority Fellowship in Educational
    Measurement 276
Nurses' Educational Funds Fellowships and Scholarships 510
Sally S Jacobsen Scholarship 475

EDUCATION OF SPECIFIC LEARNING DIS-ABILITIES

Any Country

ASBAH Research Grant 118
ETS Summer Internship Program for Graduate Students 276
University of Southampton Postgraduate Studentships 759
World Universities Network (WUN) International Research Mobility
    Scheme 759

United Kingdom

Mr and Mrs David Edward Memorial Award 145

United States of America

ACRES Scholarship 49
ETS Summer Internship Program for Graduate Students 276
Nurses' Educational Funds Fellowships and Scholarships 510

West European Countries

Mr and Mrs David Edward Memorial Award 145

EDUCATION OF FOREIGNERS

Any Country

AUC Arabic Language Fellowships 96

United Kingdom

Mr and Mrs David Edward Memorial Award 145

United States of America

Fulbright Teacher Exchange 307
Japanese Residencies Program 516

West European Countries

Mr and Mrs David Edward Memorial Award 145

EDUCATION OF NATIVES

African Nations

International Postgraduate Research Scholarships (IPRS) 413

Canada

International Postgraduate Research Scholarships (IPRS) 413

Caribbean Countries

International Postgraduate Research Scholarships (IPRS) 413

East European Countries

International Postgraduate Research Scholarships (IPRS) 413

Middle East

International Postgraduate Research Scholarships (IPRS) 413

South Africa

International Postgraduate Research Scholarships (IPRS) 413

United Kingdom

International Postgraduate Research Scholarships (IPRS) 413

United States of America

Fulbright Teacher Exchange 307
International Postgraduate Research Scholarships (IPRS) 413

West European Countries

International Postgraduate Research Scholarships (IPRS) 413

EDUCATION OF THE SOCIALLY DISADVANTAGED

Any Country

ETS Summer Internship Program for Graduate Students 276
Frederick Douglass Institute Postdoctoral Fellowship 304

United States of America

ACRES Scholarship 49
ETS Summer Internship Program for Graduate Students 276

BILINGUAL/BICULTURAL EDUCATION

Any Country

Neporany Doctoral Fellowship 210

United Kingdom

Aberystwyth Postgraduate Research Studentships 4
Mr and Mrs David Edward Memorial Award 145

United States of America

Fulbright Teacher Exchange 307

West European Countries

Mr and Mrs David Edward Memorial Award 145

TEACHER TRAINERS EDUCATION

Any Country

ETS Postdoctoral Fellowships 276
ETS Summer Internship Program for Graduate Students 276
Faculty Studentships 694
Weizmann Institute of Science MSc Fellowships 792
Weizmann Institute of Science PhD Fellowships 792

African Nations

International Postgraduate Research Scholarships (IPRS) 413

Australia

Japanese Government (Monbukagakusho) Scholarships In-Service
    Training for Teachers Category 400

Canada

International Postgraduate Research Scholarships (IPRS) 413

Caribbean Countries

International Postgraduate Research Scholarships (IPRS) 413

East European Countries

International Postgraduate Research Scholarships (IPRS) 413

European Union

All Saints Educational Trust Personal Scholarships 20

Middle East

International Postgraduate Research Scholarships (IPRS) 413

South Africa

International Postgraduate Research Scholarships (IPRS) 413

United Kingdom

Aberystwyth Postgraduate Research Studentships 4
All Saints Educational Trust Corporate Awards 20
All Saints Educational Trust Personal Scholarships 20
International Postgraduate Research Scholarships (IPRS) 413
Mr and Mrs David Edward Memorial Award 145
Ray Y. Gildea Jr. Award 565

United States of America

ETS Postdoctoral Fellowships 276
ETS Summer Internship Program for Graduate Students 276
International Postgraduate Research Scholarships (IPRS) 413
Ray Y. Gildea Jr. Award 565

West European Countries

International Postgraduate Research Scholarships (IPRS) 413
Mr and Mrs David Edward Memorial Award 145

HIGHER EDUCATION TEACHER TRAINING

Any Country

ETS Postdoctoral Fellowships 276
ETS Summer Internship Program for Graduate Students 276
University of Bristol Postgraduate Scholarships 672

United Kingdom

Mr and Mrs David Edward Memorial Award 145
Ray Y. Gildea Jr. Award 565

United States of America

ETS Postdoctoral Fellowships 276
ETS Summer Internship Program for Graduate Students 276
Ray Y. Gildea Jr. Award 565
The Walter J Jensen Fellowship for French Language, Literature and
    Culture 531

West European Countries

Mr and Mrs David Edward Memorial Award 145

EDUCATIONAL SCIENCE

Any Country

Camargo Fellowships 182
ETS Postdoctoral Fellowships 276
Faculty Studentships 694
IAU Travel Grant 377
Lindbergh Grants 228
SERC Postdoctoral Fellowships 596
SERC Predoctoral Fellowships 596
SERC Senior Fellowships 596
University of Bristol Postgraduate Scholarships 672

University of Southampton Postgraduate Studentships 759
Weizmann Institute of Science MSc Fellowships 792
Weizmann Institute of Science PhD Fellowships 792
World Universities Network (WUN) International Research Mobility
    Scheme 759

European Union

All Saints Educational Trust Personal Scholarships 20
Collection of Small Endowed Awards 702
ESRC 1 + 3 Awards and + 3 Awards

United Kingdom

All Saints Educational Trust Corporate Awards 20
All Saints Educational Trust Personal Scholarships 20
Collection of Small Endowed Awards 702
ESRC 1 + 3 Awards and + 3 Awards

United States of America

ETS Postdoctoral Fellowships 276
Kennedy Research Grants 405
SSRC Abe Fellowship Program 598
SSRC JSPS Postdoctoral Fellowship 599

West European Countries

ESRC 1 + 3 Awards and + 3 Awards

INTERNATIONAL AND COMPARATIVE EDUCATION

Any Country

Camargo Fellowships 182
Frederick Douglass Institute Predoctoral Dissertation Fellowship
    304

African Nations

Nicholas Hans Comparative Education Scholarship 365

Australia

Nicholas Hans Comparative Education Scholarship 365
Wingate Scholarships 697

Canada

Nicholas Hans Comparative Education Scholarship 365
Wingate Scholarships 697

Caribbean Countries

Nicholas Hans Comparative Education Scholarship 365

East European Countries

Nicholas Hans Comparative Education Scholarship 365

European Union

Transatlantic Fellows Program 315
Wingate Scholarships 697

Middle East

Nicholas Hans Comparative Education Scholarship 365

New Zealand

Nicholas Hans Comparative Education Scholarship 365
Wingate Scholarships 697

South Africa

Nicholas Hans Comparative Education Scholarship 365
Wingate Scholarships 697

United Kingdom

Prix du Québec Award 160
Wingate Scholarships 697

United States of America

Fulbright Teacher Exchange 307
Nicholas Hans Comparative Education Scholarship 365
Transatlantic Fellows Program 315

West European Countries

Nicholas Hans Comparative Education Scholarship 365

PHILOSOPHY OF EDUCATION

Any Country

Camargo Fellowships 182
Faculty Studentships 694
Frederick Douglass Institute Postdoctoral Fellowship 304

African Nations

International Postgraduate Research Scholarships (IPRS) 413

Australia

Wingate Scholarships 697

Canada

International Postgraduate Research Scholarships (IPRS) 413
Wingate Scholarships 697

Caribbean Countries

International Postgraduate Research Scholarships (IPRS) 413

East European Countries

International Postgraduate Research Scholarships (IPRS) 413

European Union

Wingate Scholarships 697

Middle East

International Postgraduate Research Scholarships (IPRS) 413

New Zealand

Wingate Scholarships 697

South Africa

International Postgraduate Research Scholarships (IPRS) 413
Wingate Scholarships 697

United Kingdom

International Postgraduate Research Scholarships (IPRS) 413
Wingate Scholarships 697

United States of America

International Postgraduate Research Scholarships (IPRS) 413

West European Countries

International Postgraduate Research Scholarships (IPRS) 413

CURRICULUM

Any Country

Faculty Studentships 694
Jacob's Pillow Intern Program
Lindbergh Grants 228

African Nations

International Postgraduate Research Scholarships (IPRS) 413

Canada

International Postgraduate Research Scholarships (IPRS) 413

Caribbean Countries

International Postgraduate Research Scholarships (IPRS) 413

East European Countries

International Postgraduate Research Scholarships (IPRS) 413

Middle East

International Postgraduate Research Scholarships (IPRS) 413

South Africa

International Postgraduate Research Scholarships (IPRS) 413

United Kingdom

International Postgraduate Research Scholarships (IPRS) 413
Mr and Mrs David Edward Memorial Award 145
Ray Y. Gildea Jr. Award 565

United States of America

International Postgraduate Research Scholarships (IPRS) 413
Ray Y. Gildea Jr. Award 565

West European Countries

International Postgraduate Research Scholarships (IPRS) 413
Mr and Mrs David Edward Memorial Award 145

TEACHING AND LEARNING

Any Country

AUC Writing Center Graduate Fellowships 98
Dina Feitelson Research Award 386
ETS Postdoctoral Fellowships 276
ETS Summer Internship Program for Graduate Students 276
Faculty Studentships 694
International Reading Association Teacher as Researcher Grant 387
Jeanne S Chall Research Fellowship 387
Lindbergh Grants 228

African Nations

International Postgraduate Research Scholarships (IPRS) 413

Canada

International Postgraduate Research Scholarships (IPRS) 413

Caribbean Countries

International Postgraduate Research Scholarships (IPRS) 413

East European Countries

International Postgraduate Research Scholarships (IPRS) 413

European Union

All Saints Educational Trust Personal Scholarships 20
ESRC 1 + 3 Awards and + 3 Awards

Middle East

International Postgraduate Research Scholarships (IPRS) 413

South Africa

International Postgraduate Research Scholarships (IPRS) 413

United Kingdom

All Saints Educational Trust Corporate Awards 20
All Saints Educational Trust Personal Scholarships 20
ESRC 1 + 3 Awards and + 3 Awards
International Postgraduate Research Scholarships (IPRS) 413
Mr and Mrs David Edward Memorial Award 145
Ray Y. Gildea Jr. Award 565

United States of America

ETS Postdoctoral Fellowships 276
ETS Summer Internship Program for Graduate Students 276
ETS Sylvia Taylor Johnson Minority Fellowship in Educational
    Measurement 276
International Postgraduate Research Scholarships (IPRS) 413

Nurses' Educational Funds Fellowships and Scholarships 510
Ray Y. Gildea Jr. Award 565

West European Countries

ESRC 1+3 Awards and +3 Awards
International Postgraduate Research Scholarships (IPRS) 413
Mr and Mrs David Edward Memorial Award 145

EDUCATIONAL RESEARCH

Any Country

Albert J Harris Award 386
ChLA Beiter Graduate Student Research Grant 233
ChLA Faculty Research Grant 233
Dina Feitelson Research Award 386
Elva Knight Research Grant 387
ETS Postdoctoral Fellowships 276
ETS Summer Internship Program for Graduate Students 276
Faculty Studentships 694
Helen M Robinson Award 387
IAU Travel Grant 377
International Reading Association Teacher as Researcher Grant 387
Jeanne S Chall Research Fellowship 387
Lindbergh Grants 228

African Nations

International Postgraduate Research Scholarships (IPRS) 413
Reading/Literacy Research Fellowship 387

Australia

Reading/Literacy Research Fellowship 387
Wingate Scholarships 697

Canada

International Postgraduate Research Scholarships (IPRS) 413
Wingate Scholarships 697

Caribbean Countries

International Postgraduate Research Scholarships (IPRS) 413
Reading/Literacy Research Fellowship 387

East European Countries

International Postgraduate Research Scholarships (IPRS) 413
Reading/Literacy Research Fellowship 387

European Union

Wingate Scholarships 697

Middle East

International Postgraduate Research Scholarships (IPRS) 413
Reading/Literacy Research Fellowship 387

New Zealand

Reading/Literacy Research Fellowship 387
Wingate Scholarships 697

South Africa

International Postgraduate Research Scholarships (IPRS) 413
Reading/Literacy Research Fellowship 387
Wingate Scholarships 697

United Kingdom

Aberystwyth Postgraduate Research Studentships 4
All Saints Educational Trust Corporate Awards 20
International Postgraduate Research Scholarships (IPRS) 413
Mr and Mrs David Edward Memorial Award 145
Reading/Literacy Research Fellowship 387
Wingate Scholarships 697

United States of America

Earthwatch Fellowships 272
ETS Postdoctoral Fellowships 276

ETS Summer Internship Program for Graduate Students 276
ETS Sylvia Taylor Johnson Minority Fellowship in Educational
    Measurement 276
International Postgraduate Research Scholarships (IPRS) 413
Nurses' Educational Funds Fellowships and Scholarships 510

West European Countries

International Postgraduate Research Scholarships (IPRS) 413
Mr and Mrs David Edward Memorial Award 145
Reading/Literacy Research Fellowship 387

EDUCATIONAL TECHNOLOGY

Any Country

ETS Postdoctoral Fellowships 276
ETS Summer Internship Program for Graduate Students 276
Faculty Studentships 694
Lindbergh Grants 228

African Nations

International Postgraduate Research Scholarships (IPRS) 413

Canada

International Postgraduate Research Scholarships (IPRS) 413

Caribbean Countries

International Postgraduate Research Scholarships (IPRS) 413

East European Countries

International Postgraduate Research Scholarships (IPRS) 413

Middle East

International Postgraduate Research Scholarships (IPRS) 413

South Africa

International Postgraduate Research Scholarships (IPRS) 413

United Kingdom

International Postgraduate Research Scholarships (IPRS) 413

United States of America

Earthwatch Fellowships 272
ETS Postdoctoral Fellowships 276
ETS Summer Internship Program for Graduate Students 276
International Postgraduate Research Scholarships (IPRS) 413
Nurses' Educational Funds Fellowships and Scholarships 510

West European Countries

International Postgraduate Research Scholarships (IPRS) 413

EDUCATIONAL AND STUDENT COUNSELLING

Any Country

ETS Summer Internship Program for Graduate Students 276

African Nations

International Postgraduate Research Scholarships (IPRS) 413

Canada

International Postgraduate Research Scholarships (IPRS) 413

Caribbean Countries

International Postgraduate Research Scholarships (IPRS) 413

East European Countries

International Postgraduate Research Scholarships (IPRS) 413

Middle East

International Postgraduate Research Scholarships (IPRS) 413

South Africa

International Postgraduate Research Scholarships (IPRS) 413

United Kingdom

International Postgraduate Research Scholarships (IPRS) 413

United States of America

ETS Summer Internship Program for Graduate Students 276
International Postgraduate Research Scholarships (IPRS) 413

West European Countries

International Postgraduate Research Scholarships (IPRS) 413

EDUCATIONAL ADMINISTRATION

Any Country

ETS Summer Internship Program for Graduate Students 276
Fulbright Institutional Linkages Program 306
Jacob's Pillow Intern Program

African Nations

International Postgraduate Research Scholarships (IPRS) 413

Canada

International Postgraduate Research Scholarships (IPRS) 413

Caribbean Countries

International Postgraduate Research Scholarships (IPRS) 413

East European Countries

International Postgraduate Research Scholarships (IPRS) 413

European Union

All Saints Educational Trust Personal Scholarships 20

Middle East

International Postgraduate Research Scholarships (IPRS) 413

South Africa

International Postgraduate Research Scholarships (IPRS) 413

United Kingdom

All Saints Educational Trust Corporate Awards 20
All Saints Educational Trust Personal Scholarships 20
International Postgraduate Research Scholarships (IPRS) 413

United States of America

ETS Summer Internship Program for Graduate Students 276
ETS Sylvia Taylor Johnson Minority Fellowship in Educational
    Measurement 276
Fulbright Teacher and Administrator Exchange Awards – Elementary
    & High School Administrator 306
International Postgraduate Research Scholarships (IPRS) 413
Nurses' Educational Funds Fellowships and Scholarships 510

West European Countries

International Postgraduate Research Scholarships (IPRS) 413

EDUCATIONAL TESTING AND EVALUATION

Any Country

ASBAH Research Grant 118
ETS Postdoctoral Fellowships 276
ETS Summer Internship Program for Graduate Students 276

African Nations

International Postgraduate Research Scholarships (IPRS) 413

Australia

Wingate Scholarships 697

Canada

International Postgraduate Research Scholarships (IPRS) 413
Wingate Scholarships 697

Caribbean Countries

International Postgraduate Research Scholarships (IPRS) 413

East European Countries

International Postgraduate Research Scholarships (IPRS) 413

European Union

Wingate Scholarships 697

Middle East

International Postgraduate Research Scholarships (IPRS) 413

New Zealand

Wingate Scholarships 697

South Africa

International Postgraduate Research Scholarships (IPRS) 413
Wingate Scholarships 697

United Kingdom

International Postgraduate Research Scholarships (IPRS) 413
Wingate Scholarships 697

United States of America

ETS Postdoctoral Fellowships 276
ETS Summer Internship Program for Graduate Students 276
ETS Sylvia Taylor Johnson Minority Fellowship in Educational
    Measurement 276
International Postgraduate Research Scholarships (IPRS) 413

West European Countries

International Postgraduate Research Scholarships (IPRS) 413

DISTANCE EDUCATION

Any Country

Faculty Studentships 694

ENGINEERING

GENERAL

Any Country

The Airey Neave Trust Scholarship 12
Association for Women in Science Educational Foundation Predoc-
    toral Awards 118
AUC Assistantships 96
AUC Laboratory Instruction Graduate Fellowships in Engineering and
    Computer Science 97
AUC University Fellowships 98
Australian Postgraduate Award Research Scholarship 667
B K Krenzer Memorial Re-Entry Scholarship 612
The Bernard Butler Trust Fund 395
Berthold Leibinger Innovation Prize 148
BITS HP Labs India PhD Fellowship 152
BRI PhD Scholarships 156
CAGS UMI Dissertation Awards 199
Concordia University Graduate Fellowships 243

DAGSI Research Fellowships 261
David J Azrieli Graduate Fellowship 243
DOI Women in Science, Engineering, Technology and Construction
    Scholarship 264
Donald Julius Groen Prizes 372
Doshisha University Harris Science School Foundation Grant 270
ETH Zurich Excellence Scholarship and Opportunity Award 624
Exxon Mobil Teaching Fellowships 553
French–Australian Cotutelle 258
Guest, Keen and Nettlefolds Scholarship 669
Honda Prize 343
Horton (Hydrology) Research Grant 56
John Hume Postgraduate Scholarships 490
John Moyes Lessells Travel Scholarships 628
Lincoln College Sloane Robinson Foundation Graduate Awards 733
Lydia I Pickup Memorial Scholarship 612
Matsumae International Foundation Research Fellowship 436
Mintek Bursaries 450
Monash International Postgraduate Research Scholarship (MIPRS)
    455
Monash University Silver Jubilee Postgraduate Scholarship 455
NJWEA Scholarship Award Program 498
NRC Research Associateships 488
Queen Mary Research Studentships 539
Rice-Cullimore Scholarship 93
Royal Academy of Engineering Industrial Secondment Scheme 554
Royal Academy of Engineering MacRobert Award 554
Royal Irish Academy Mobility Grants 569
Scottish Government Personal Research Fellowships 628
Scottish Government/RSE Support Research Fellowships 629
Sir Allan Sewell Visiting Fellowship 326
Sir James McNeill Foundation Postgraduate Scholarship 455
St Catherine's College: Leathersellers' Company Graduate Scholar-
    ship
Stanley G French Graduate Fellowship 244
SWE Electronics for Imaging Scholarship 612
Taiwan's Industrial Technology R&D Master Program for Foreign
    Students 489
TIACA Walter H. Johnson, Jr. Scholarship Award 375
University of Ballarat Postgraduate Research Scholarship
University of Bristol Postgraduate Scholarships 672
Utilities and Service Industries Training (USIT) 254
Vera Moore International Postgraduate Research Scholarships 455
World Universities Network (WUN) International Research Mobility
    Scheme 759

African Nations

ABCCF Student Grant 102
Andrew Stratton Scholarship 690
ANSTI/DAAD Postgraduate Fellowships 9
AUC African Graduate Fellowship 96
The Bernard Butler Trust Fund 395
CAS-TWAS Fellowship for Postdoctoral Research in China 629
CAS-TWAS Fellowship for Postgraduate Research in China 629
CAS-TWAS Fellowship for Visiting Scholars in China 629
CNPq-TWAS Doctoral Fellowships in Brazil 630
CNPq-TWAS Fellowships for Postdoctoral Research in Brazil 630
CSIR (Council of Scientific and Industrial Research)/TWAS Fellowship
    for Postgraduate Research 630
CSIR (The Council of Scientific and Industrial Research)/TWAS
    Fellowship for Postdoctoral Research 630
International Postgraduate Research Scholarships (IPRS) 413
International Postgraduate Research Scholarships (IPRS) 413
Lindemann Trust Fellowships 280
School of Applied Sciences Overseas Scholarships 254
The Trieste Science Prize 631
TWAS Fellowships for Research and Advanced Training 631
TWAS Grants for Scientific Meetings in Developing Countries 631
TWAS Prizes 632
TWAS Spare Parts for Scientific Equipment 632

Australia

ADB-Japan Scholarship Program 116
Andrew Stratton Scholarship 690
APAI Water Resources Management Scholarship 326

ARC APAI – Alternative Engine Technologies 540
Australian Postgraduate Awards 413
The Bernard Butler Trust Fund 395
DOI Women in Freight, Logistics and Marine Management
    Scholarship 264
French Government Postgraduate Scholarships 279
Fulbright Postdoctoral Fellowships 140
Fulbright Postgraduate Awards 140
Institute of Health and Biomedical Innovation Awards 540
International Postgraduate Research Scholarships (IPRS) 413
Lindemann Trust Fellowships 280
MINTRAC Postgraduate Scholarship 451
R.N. Hammon Scholarship 753
School of Applied Sciences Overseas Scholarships 254
University of Ballarat Part Postgraduate Research Scholarship 667
Victoria Fellowships 264
Wingate Scholarships 697

Canada

Andrew Stratton Scholarship 690
The Bernard Butler Trust Fund 395
Canada Postgraduate Scholarships (PGS) 495
Engineers Canada's National Scholarship Program
Industrial Postgraduate Scholarship 1 (NSERC IPS) 775
International Postgraduate Research Scholarships (IPRS) 413
International Postgraduate Research Scholarships (IPRS) 413
J W McConnell Memorial Fellowships 243
Kenneth Sutherland Memorial Cambridge Scholarship 192
Lindemann Trust Fellowships 280
NSERC Postdoctoral Fellowships 495
School of Applied Sciences Overseas Scholarships 254
Sloan Industry Studies Fellowships 19
William and Margaret Brown Cambridge Scholarship for PhD Study 198
Wingate Scholarships 697

Caribbean Countries

ADB-Japan Scholarship Program 116
Andrew Stratton Scholarship 690
The Bernard Butler Trust Fund 395
CAS-TWAS Fellowship for Postdoctoral Research in China 629
CAS-TWAS Fellowship for Postgraduate Research in China 629
CAS-TWAS Fellowship for Visiting Scholars in China 629
CNPq-TWAS Doctoral Fellowships in Brazil 630
CNPq-TWAS Fellowships for Postdoctoral Research in Brazil 630
CSIR (Council of Scientific and Industrial Research)/TWAS Fellowship
    for Postgraduate Research 630
CSIR (The Council of Scientific and Industrial Research)/TWAS
    Fellowship for Postdoctoral Research 630
International Postgraduate Research Scholarships (IPRS) 413
International Postgraduate Research Scholarships (IPRS) 413
School of Applied Sciences Overseas Scholarships 254
TWAS Fellowships for Research and Advanced Training 631
TWAS Grants for Scientific Meetings in Developing Countries 631
TWAS Prizes 632
TWAS Spare Parts for Scientific Equipment 632

East European Countries

The Bernard Butler Trust Fund 395
CERN Technical Student Programme 227
International Postgraduate Research Scholarships (IPRS) 413
International Postgraduate Research Scholarships (IPRS) 413
School of Applied Sciences Overseas Scholarships 254
Volkswagen Foundation Between Europe and the Orient Programme
    Grants 787

European Union

The Bernard Butler Trust Fund 395
International Postgraduate Research Scholarships (IPRS) 413
University of Southampton Engineering Doctorate 759
Wingate Scholarships 697

Middle East

ABCCF Student Grant 102
Andrew Stratton Scholarship 690

The Bernard Butler Trust Fund 395
CAS-TWAS Fellowship for Postdoctoral Research in China 629
CAS-TWAS Fellowship for Postgraduate Research in China 629
CAS-TWAS Fellowship for Visiting Scholars in China 629
CNPq-TWAS Doctoral Fellowships in Brazil 630
CNPq-TWAS Fellowships for Postdoctoral Research in Brazil 630
CSIR (Council of Scientific and Industrial Research)/TWAS Fellowship
    for Postgraduate Research 630
CSIR (The Council of Scientific and Industrial Research)/TWAS
    Fellowship for Postdoctoral Research 630
IDB Merit Scholarship for High Technology 395
IDB Scholarship Programme in Science and Technology 395
International Postgraduate Research Scholarships (IPRS) 413
International Postgraduate Research Scholarships (IPRS) 413
School of Applied Sciences Overseas Scholarships 254
The Trieste Science Prize 631
TWAS Fellowships for Research and Advanced Training 631
TWAS Grants for Scientific Meetings in Developing Countries 631
TWAS Prizes 632
TWAS Spare Parts for Scientific Equipment 632

New Zealand

Andrew Stratton Scholarship 690
APAI Water Resources Management Scholarship 326
ARC APAI – Alternative Engine Technologies 540
Australian Postgraduate Awards 413
The Bernard Butler Trust Fund 395
Lindemann Trust Fellowships 280
School of Applied Sciences Overseas Scholarships 254
Wingate Scholarships 697

South Africa

Andrew Stratton Scholarship 690
The Bernard Butler Trust Fund 395
CAS-TWAS Fellowship for Postdoctoral Research in China 629
CAS-TWAS Fellowship for Postgraduate Research in China 629
CAS-TWAS Fellowship for Visiting Scholars in China 629
CNPq-TWAS Doctoral Fellowships in Brazil 630
CNPq-TWAS Fellowships for Postdoctoral Research in Brazil 630
CSIR (Council of Scientific and Industrial Research)/TWAS Fellowship
    for Postgraduate Research 630
CSIR (The Council of Scientific and Industrial Research)/TWAS
    Fellowship for Postdoctoral Research 630
International Postgraduate Research Scholarships (IPRS) 413
International Postgraduate Research Scholarships (IPRS) 413
Lindemann Trust Fellowships 280
School of Applied Sciences Overseas Scholarships 254
The Trieste Science Prize 631
TWAS Fellowships for Research and Advanced Training 631
TWAS Grants for Scientific Meetings in Developing Countries 631
TWAS Prizes 632
TWAS Spare Parts for Scientific Equipment 632
Wingate Scholarships 697
Wolfson Foundation Grants 799

United Kingdom

The Bernard Butler Trust Fund 395
CERN Technical Student Programme 227
Frank Knox Fellowships at Harvard University 302
Grundy Educational Trust 327
Hilda Martindale Exhibitions 341
International Postgraduate Research Scholarships (IPRS) 413
International Postgraduate Research Scholarships (IPRS) 413
James Watt Research Scholarships 694
Kennedy Scholarships 409
Lindemann Trust Fellowships 280
Panasonic Trust Awards 553
Panasonic Trust Fellowships 253
Royal Academy Engineering Professional Development 553
Royal Academy Executive Engineering Programme 553
Royal Academy of Engineering International Travel Grants 554
Royal Academy Sir Angus Paton Bursary 554
Royal Academy Visiting Professors Scheme 554
Royal Commission Industrial Fellowships 563
Royal Commission Research Fellowship 563

Sainsbury Management Fellowships 555
University of Southampton Engineering Doctorate 759
Wingate Scholarships 697
Wolfson Foundation Grants 799

United States of America

Air Force Summer Faculty Fellowship Program 84
Andrew Stratton Scholarship 690
The Bernard Butler Trust Fund 395
Congress Bundestag Youth Exchange for Young Professionals 221
DEED (Demonstration of Energy-Efficient Developments) Student
    Research Grant/Internship 80
Early American Industries Association Research Grants Program 272
Elisabeth M and Winchell M Parsons Scholarship 93
Ford Foundation Dissertation Fellowships for Minorities 487
Foundation for Science and Disability Student Grant Fund 302
Fulbright Senior Specialists Program 249
The Graduate Fellowship Award 340
Howard Brown Rickard Scholarship 474
International Postgraduate Research Scholarships (IPRS) 413
International Postgraduate Research Scholarships (IPRS) 413
Jefferson Science Fellows at the U.S. Department of State 466
Krell Institute Computational Science Graduate Fellowship Program
    412
Marie Tharp Visiting Fellowships 239
Marjorie Roy Rothermel Scholarship 93
National Academics Christine Mirzayan Science and Technology
    Policy Graduate Fellowship Program 466
NDSEG Fellowship Program 84
North Dakota Indian Scholarship 507
Olive Lynn Salembier Scholarship 612
ONR Summer Faculty Research 84
Pasteur Foundation Postdoctoral Fellowship Program 522
Renate W Chasman Scholarship 180
School of Applied Sciences Overseas Scholarships 254
Sloan Industry Studies Fellowships 19
SMART Scholarship for Service Program 85
SWE Past Presidents Scholarships 612
Washington University Chancellor's Graduate Fellowship Program
    792
Winston Churchill Foundation Scholarship 797
Xerox Technical Minority Scholarship 807

West European Countries

The Bernard Butler Trust Fund 395
CERN Technical Student Programme 227
International Postgraduate Research Scholarships (IPRS) 413
International Postgraduate Research Scholarships (IPRS) 413
Janson Johan Helmich Scholarships and Travel Grants 398
Royal Academy of Engineering International Travel Grants 554

SURVEYING AND MAPPING SCIENCE

Any Country

AAGS Graduate Fellowship Award 46
AAGS Joseph F. Dracup Scholarship Award 46
Berntsen International Scholarship in Surveying Technology 46
ETH Zurich Excellence Scholarship and Opportunity Award 624
John Moyes Lessells Travel Scholarships 628
RICS Education Trust Award 549
The Schonstedt Scholarships in Surveying 46
Small Research Grants 566

African Nations

Canadian Window on International Development 380
Civil and Environmental Engineering Graduate Scholarship 648
International Postgraduate Research Scholarships (IPRS) 413

Australia

Civil and Environmental Engineering Graduate Scholarship 648
Fulbright Postgraduate Student Award for Science and Engineering
    140
Wingate Scholarships 697

Canada

Canadian Window on International Development 380
International Postgraduate Research Scholarships (IPRS) 413
Wingate Scholarships 697

Caribbean Countries

Canadian Window on International Development 380
Civil and Environmental Engineering Graduate Scholarship 648
International Postgraduate Research Scholarships (IPRS) 413

East European Countries

Civil and Environmental Engineering Graduate Scholarship 648
International Postgraduate Research Scholarships (IPRS) 413

European Union

Wingate Scholarships 697

Middle East

Civil and Environmental Engineering Graduate Scholarship 648
International Postgraduate Research Scholarships (IPRS) 413

New Zealand

Civil and Environmental Engineering Graduate Scholarship 648
Wingate Scholarships 697

South Africa

Canadian Window on International Development 380
Civil and Environmental Engineering Graduate Scholarship 648
International Postgraduate Research Scholarships (IPRS) 413
Wingate Scholarships 697

United Kingdom

International Postgraduate Research Scholarships (IPRS) 413
Wingate Scholarships 697

United States of America

The Cady McDonnell Memorial Scholarship 46
Civil and Environmental Engineering Graduate Scholarship 648
DEED (Demonstration of Energy-Efficient Developments) Student
    Research Grant/Internship 80
International Postgraduate Research Scholarships (IPRS) 413
NOAA Coral Management Assistantship 506
NOAA Pacific Islands Assistantship Program 506
Tri State Surveying and Photogrammetry Kris M. Kunze Memorial
    Scholarship 46

West European Countries

Civil and Environmental Engineering Graduate Scholarship 648
International Postgraduate Research Scholarships (IPRS) 413

ENGINEERING DRAWING/DESIGN

Any Country

John Moyes Lessells Travel Scholarships 628

African Nations

International Postgraduate Research Scholarships (IPRS) 413

Australia

Fulbright Postgraduate Student Award for Science and Engineering
    140
Wingate Scholarships 697

Canada

International Postgraduate Research Scholarships (IPRS) 413
TAC Foundation Scholarships 637
Wingate Scholarships 697

Caribbean Countries

International Postgraduate Research Scholarships (IPRS) 413

East European Countries

International Postgraduate Research Scholarships (IPRS) 413

European Union

Wingate Scholarships 697

Middle East

International Postgraduate Research Scholarships (IPRS) 413

New Zealand

Wingate Scholarships 697

South Africa

International Postgraduate Research Scholarships (IPRS) 413
Wingate Scholarships 697

United Kingdom

International Postgraduate Research Scholarships (IPRS) 413
Wingate Scholarships 697

United States of America

DEED (Demonstration of Energy-Efficient Developments) Student
    Research Grant/Internship 80
International Postgraduate Research Scholarships (IPRS) 413
Winston Churchill Foundation Scholarship 797

West European Countries

International Postgraduate Research Scholarships (IPRS) 413

CHEMICAL ENGINEERING

Any Country

ACS PRF Type SE Grants 37
Adrian Brown Scholarship 668
BP/RSE Research Fellowships 628
CIC Fellowships 214
ETH Zurich Excellence Scholarship and Opportunity Award 624
Exxon Mobil Teaching Fellowships 553
HFSPO Cross-Disciplinary Fellowships 383
IFT Graduate Fellowships 366
John Moyes Lessells Travel Scholarships 628
Marcel Loncin Research Prize 366
Postgraduate Research Studentship 689
Tomsk Polytechnic University International Scholarship 634
University of Bristol Postgraduate Scholarships 672
University of Western Ontario Senior Visiting Fellowship 777
Utilities and Service Industries Training (USIT) 254
Welch Foundation Scholarship 391
Wood Technology Research Centre – Postgraduate Scholarships 679

African Nations

Bioprocessing Graduate Scholarship 648
International Postgraduate Research Scholarships (IPRS) 413
Shell Centenary/Shell Centenary Chevening Scholarships 704

Australia

Bioprocessing Graduate Scholarship 648
Chemical Engineering Scholarship 715
Fulbright Postgraduate Student Award for Science and Engineering
    140
Wingate Scholarships 697

Canada

Bioprocessing Graduate Scholarship 648
CIC Award for Chemical Education 231
CIC Catalysis Award 231
CIC Macromolecular Science and Engineering Lecture Award 231
CIC Medal 232
CIC Montreal Medal 232
CNC/IUPAC Travel Awards 214
CSCT Norman and Marion Bright Memorial Award 232

International Postgraduate Research Scholarships (IPRS) 413
Wingate Scholarships 697

Caribbean Countries

Bioprocessing Graduate Scholarship 648
International Postgraduate Research Scholarships (IPRS) 413
Shell Centenary/Shell Centenary Chevening Scholarships 704

East European Countries

Bioprocessing Graduate Scholarship 648
International Postgraduate Research Scholarships (IPRS) 413
VKI Fellowship 788

European Union

Bioprocessing Graduate Scholarship 648
Wingate Scholarships 697

Middle East

Bioprocessing Graduate Scholarship 648
International Postgraduate Research Scholarships (IPRS) 413
Shell Centenary/Shell Centenary Chevening Scholarships 704

New Zealand

Bioprocessing Graduate Scholarship 648
Wingate Scholarships 697

South Africa

Bioprocessing Graduate Scholarship 648
International Postgraduate Research Scholarships (IPRS) 413
Shell Centenary/Shell Centenary Chevening Scholarships 704
Wingate Scholarships 697

United Kingdom

International Postgraduate Research Scholarships (IPRS) 413
Wingate Scholarships 697

United States of America

Air Force Summer Faculty Fellowship Program 84
Bioprocessing Graduate Scholarship 648
Congress Bundestag Youth Exchange for Young Professionals 221
DEED (Demonstration of Energy-Efficient Developments) Student
  Research Grant/Internship 80
Earle B. Barnes Award for Leadership in Chemical Research
  Management 38
International Postgraduate Research Scholarships (IPRS) 413
Krell Institute Computational Science Graduate Fellowship Program
  412
NPSC Fellowship in Physical Sciences 487
ONR Summer Faculty Research 84
SRC Master's Scholarship Program 585
SWE Caterpillar Scholarship 612
SWE General Motors Foundation Graduate Scholarship 612
VKI Fellowship 788
Winston Churchill Foundation Scholarship 797

West European Countries

Bioprocessing Graduate Scholarship 648
International Postgraduate Research Scholarships (IPRS) 413
VKI Fellowship 788

CIVIL, CONSTRUCTION AND TRANSPORTATION ENGINEERING

Any Country

The Bernard Butler Trust Fund 395
De Paepe-Willems Award 386
EREF Scholarships in Waste Management Research and Education
  281
ETH Zurich Excellence Scholarship and Opportunity Award 624
John Moyes Lessells Travel Scholarships 628
Johnson's Wax Research Fellowship

NRC Research Associateships 488
QUEST Institution of Civil Engineers Continuing Education Award 370
QUEST Institution of Civil Engineers Overseas Travel Awards 370
Rees Jeffreys Road Fund Bursaries 542
RICS Education Trust Award 549
Structural Engineering Travelling Fellowship 595
University of Bristol Postgraduate Scholarships 672
University of Southampton Postgraduate Studentships 759
World Universities Network (WUN) International Research Mobility
  Scheme 759

African Nations

The Bernard Butler Trust Fund 395
Civil and Environmental Engineering Graduate Scholarship 648
International Postgraduate Research Scholarships (IPRS) 413
Shell Centenary/Shell Centenary Chevening Scholarships 704

Australia

The Bernard Butler Trust Fund 395
Civil and Environmental Engineering Graduate Scholarship 648
Fulbright Postgraduate Student Award for Science and Engineering
  140
Wingate Scholarships 697

Canada

The Bernard Butler Trust Fund 395
CWRA Dillon Consulting Scholarship/Ken Thomson Scholarship 216
International Postgraduate Research Scholarships (IPRS) 413
TAC Foundation – 3M Canada Company Scholarship 636
TAC Foundation – Albert M. Stevens Scholarship 636
TAC Foundation – BA Group Scholarship 636
TAC Foundation – Cement Association of Canada Scholarship 636
TAC Foundation – Delcan Corporation Scholarship 636
TAC Foundation – EBA Engineering Consultants Ltd Scholarship 636
TAC Foundation – IBI Group scholarship 637
TAC Foundation – iTRANS Consulting Scholarship 637
TAC Foundation – Municipalities Scholarship 637
TAC Foundation – ND LEA Scholarship 637
TAC Foundation – Provinces and Territories Scholarship
TAC Foundation – Stantec Consulting Scholarship 637
TAC Foundation – Waterloo Alumni Scholarship 637
TAC Foundation Scholarships 637
Wingate Scholarships 697

Caribbean Countries

The Bernard Butler Trust Fund 395
Civil and Environmental Engineering Graduate Scholarship 648
International Postgraduate Research Scholarships (IPRS) 413
Shell Centenary/Shell Centenary Chevening Scholarships 704

East European Countries

The Bernard Butler Trust Fund 395
CERN Technical Student Programme 227
Civil and Environmental Engineering Graduate Scholarship 648
International Postgraduate Research Scholarships (IPRS) 413

European Union

The Bernard Butler Trust Fund 395
Civil and Computational Research Centre–PhD Studentships 622
New Castle University Civil Engineering and Geosciences Scholarship
  715
University of Southampton Engineering Doctorate 759
Wingate Scholarships 697

Middle East

The Bernard Butler Trust Fund 395
Civil and Environmental Engineering Graduate Scholarship 648
International Postgraduate Research Scholarships (IPRS) 413
Shell Centenary/Shell Centenary Chevening Scholarships 704

New Zealand

The Bernard Butler Trust Fund 395
Civil and Environmental Engineering Graduate Scholarship 648
Wingate Scholarships 697

South Africa

The Bernard Butler Trust Fund 395
Civil and Environmental Engineering Graduate Scholarship 648
International Postgraduate Research Scholarships (IPRS) 413
Shell Centenary/Shell Centenary Chevening Scholarships 704
Wingate Scholarships 697

United Kingdom

The Bernard Butler Trust Fund 395
CERN Technical Student Programme 227
Civil and Computational Research Centre–PhD Studentships 622
International Postgraduate Research Scholarships (IPRS) 413
New Castle University Civil Engineering and Geosciences Scholarship 715
University of Southampton Engineering Doctorate 759
Wingate Scholarships 697

United States of America

AGC The Saul Horowitz, Jr. Memorial Graduate Award 117
Air Force Summer Faculty Fellowship Program 84
The Bernard Butler Trust Fund 395
Civil and Environmental Engineering Graduate Scholarship 648
DEED (Demonstration of Energy-Efficient Developments) Student Research Grant/Internship 80
International Postgraduate Research Scholarships (IPRS) 413
Krell Institute Computational Science Graduate Fellowship Program 412
TAC Foundation – Stantec Consulting Scholarship 637
Winston Churchill Foundation Scholarship 797

West European Countries

The Bernard Butler Trust Fund 395
CERN Technical Student Programme 227
Civil and Environmental Engineering Graduate Scholarship 648
International Postgraduate Research Scholarships (IPRS) 413

ENVIRONMENTAL AND SANITARY ENGINEERING

Any Country

The Bernard Butler Trust Fund 395
EREF Scholarships in Waste Management Research and Education 281
John Moyes Lessells Travel Scholarships 628
Lindbergh Grants 228
QUEST Institution of Civil Engineers Overseas Travel Awards 370
Small Research Grants 566
Space-Time Model-Rainfall Fields Scholarship 716
Tomsk Polytechnic University International Scholarship 634
Utilities and Service Industries Training (USIT) 254
World Universities Network (WUN) International Research Mobility Scheme 759

African Nations

The Bernard Butler Trust Fund 395
Canadian Window on International Development 380
Civil and Environmental Engineering Graduate Scholarship 648
International Postgraduate Research Scholarships (IPRS) 413
School of Applied Sciences Overseas Scholarships 254
Shell Centenary/Shell Centenary Chevening Scholarships 704

Australia

The Bernard Butler Trust Fund 395
Civil and Environmental Engineering Graduate Scholarship 648
Fulbright Postgraduate Student Award for Science and Engineering 140
School of Applied Sciences Overseas Scholarships 254
Wingate Scholarships 697

Canada

The Bernard Butler Trust Fund 395
Canadian Window on International Development 380

CWRA Dillon Consulting Scholarship/Ken Thomson Scholarship 216
Horticultural Research Institute Grants 346
International Postgraduate Research Scholarships (IPRS) 413
School of Applied Sciences Overseas Scholarships 254
TAC Foundation Scholarships 637
Wingate Scholarships 697

Caribbean Countries

The Bernard Butler Trust Fund 395
Canadian Window on International Development 380
Civil and Environmental Engineering Graduate Scholarship 648
International Postgraduate Research Scholarships (IPRS) 413
School of Applied Sciences Overseas Scholarships 254
Shell Centenary/Shell Centenary Chevening Scholarships 704

East European Countries

The Bernard Butler Trust Fund 395
CERN Technical Student Programme 227
Civil and Environmental Engineering Graduate Scholarship 648
International Postgraduate Research Scholarships (IPRS) 413
School of Applied Sciences Overseas Scholarships 254
VKI Fellowship 788

European Union

The Bernard Butler Trust Fund 395
Department of Agriculture and Rural Development (DARD) for Northern Ireland 253
Wingate Scholarships 697

Middle East

The Bernard Butler Trust Fund 395
Civil and Environmental Engineering Graduate Scholarship 648
International Postgraduate Research Scholarships (IPRS) 413
School of Applied Sciences Overseas Scholarships 254
Shell Centenary/Shell Centenary Chevening Scholarships 704

New Zealand

The Bernard Butler Trust Fund 395
Civil and Environmental Engineering Graduate Scholarship 648
School of Applied Sciences Overseas Scholarships 254
Wingate Scholarships 697

South Africa

The Bernard Butler Trust Fund 395
Canadian Window on International Development 380
Civil and Environmental Engineering Graduate Scholarship 648
International Postgraduate Research Scholarships (IPRS) 413
School of Applied Sciences Overseas Scholarships 254
Shell Centenary/Shell Centenary Chevening Scholarships 704
Wingate Scholarships 697

United Kingdom

The Bernard Butler Trust Fund 395
CERN Technical Student Programme 227
Department of Agriculture and Rural Development (DARD) for Northern Ireland 253
Douglas Bomford Trust 253
International Postgraduate Research Scholarships (IPRS) 413
Wingate Scholarships 697

United States of America

The Bernard Butler Trust Fund 395
Civil and Environmental Engineering Graduate Scholarship 648
DEED (Demonstration of Energy-Efficient Developments) Student Research Grant/Internship 80
Horticultural Research Institute Grants 346
International Postgraduate Research Scholarships (IPRS) 413
Krell Institute Computational Science Graduate Fellowship Program 412
School of Applied Sciences Overseas Scholarships 254
VKI Fellowship 788
Winston Churchill Foundation Scholarship 797

West European Countries

The Bernard Butler Trust Fund 395
CERN Technical Student Programme 227
Civil and Environmental Engineering Graduate Scholarship 648
International Postgraduate Research Scholarships (IPRS) 413
VKI Fellowship 788

SAFETY ENGINEERING

Any Country

John Moyes Lessells Travel Scholarships 628
University of Southampton Postgraduate Studentships 759

African Nations

International Postgraduate Research Scholarships (IPRS) 413

Australia

Fulbright Postgraduate Student Award for Science and Engineering 140
Wingate Scholarships 697

Canada

International Postgraduate Research Scholarships (IPRS) 413
Public Safety and Emergency Preparedness Canada Research Fellowship in Honour of Stuart Nesbitt White 123
TAC Foundation Scholarships 637
Wingate Scholarships 697

Caribbean Countries

International Postgraduate Research Scholarships (IPRS) 413

East European Countries

CERN Technical Student Programme 227
International Postgraduate Research Scholarships (IPRS) 413

European Union

University of Southampton Engineering Doctorate 759
Wingate Scholarships 697

Middle East

International Postgraduate Research Scholarships (IPRS) 413

New Zealand

Wingate Scholarships 697

South Africa

International Postgraduate Research Scholarships (IPRS) 413
Wingate Scholarships 697

United Kingdom

Aberystwyth Postgraduate Research Studentships 4
CERN Technical Student Programme 227
International Postgraduate Research Scholarships (IPRS) 413
University of Southampton Engineering Doctorate 759
Wingate Scholarships 697

United States of America

DEED (Demonstration of Energy-Efficient Developments) Student Research Grant/Internship 80
International Postgraduate Research Scholarships (IPRS) 413
Winston Churchill Foundation Scholarship 797

West European Countries

CERN Technical Student Programme 227
International Postgraduate Research Scholarships (IPRS) 413

ELECTRICAL/ELECTRONIC AND TELECOMMUNICATIONS ENGINEERING

Any Country

The Accenture Scholarship in ITEE 750
Bursaries 144
D H Thomas Travel Bursary 370
Essex Rotary University Travel Grants 687
ETH Zurich Excellence Scholarship and Opportunity Award 624
HFSPO Cross-Disciplinary Fellowships 383
HFSPO Short-Term Fellowships 384
Hudswell Bequest Travelling Fellowships 370
Hudswell International Research Scholarships 370
IEEE Fellowship in Electrical History 351
IET Master's Degree Scholarship 371
IET Postgraduate Scholarships 371
IET Younger Members Conference Bursary 371
J R Beard Travelling Fund 371
John Moyes Lessells Travel Scholarships 628
Johnson's Wax Research Fellowship
Leonard Research Grant 371
Leslie H Paddle Scholarship 371
Milwaukee Foundation's Frank Rogers Bacon Research Assistantship
National Federation of Business and Professional Women's Clubs Travel Grants
NRC Research Associateships 488
Princess Royal Scholarship 372
Queen Mary Research Studentships 539
Robinson Research Scholarship 372
Singapore-MIT Alliance Graduate Fellowship 492
Sir Eric Berthoud Travel Grant 689
Taiwan's Industrial Technology R&D Master Program for Foreign Students 489
University of Bristol Postgraduate Scholarships 672
University of Southampton Postgraduate Studentships 759
University of Western Ontario Senior Visiting Fellowship 777
Victoria University of Wellington PhD Scholarships 786
World Universities Network (WUN) International Research Mobility Scheme 759

African Nations

International Postgraduate Research Scholarships (IPRS) 413
ORSAS Awards 688
Shell Centenary/Shell Centenary Chevening Scholarships 704

Australia

Fulbright Postgraduate Student Award for Science and Engineering 140
ORSAS Awards 688
Wingate Scholarships 697

Canada

Canadian Commonwealth Scholarship and Fellowship Plan 201
International Postgraduate Research Scholarships (IPRS) 413
ORSAS Awards 688
Wingate Scholarships 697

Caribbean Countries

International Postgraduate Research Scholarships (IPRS) 413
ORSAS Awards 688
Shell Centenary/Shell Centenary Chevening Scholarships 704

East European Countries

CERN Technical Student Programme 227
International Postgraduate Research Scholarships (IPRS) 413
ORSAS Awards 688

European Union

EPSRC School of Computer Science and Electronic Engineering Research Studentship 687
University of Kent Department of Electronics Studentships 699
University of Southampton Engineering Doctorate 759
Wingate Scholarships 697

893

Middle East

International Postgraduate Research Scholarships (IPRS) 413
ORSAS Awards 688
Shell Centenary/Shell Centenary Chevening Scholarships 704

New Zealand

ORSAS Awards 688
Wingate Scholarships 697

South Africa

International Postgraduate Research Scholarships (IPRS) 413
ORSAS Awards 688
Shell Centenary/Shell Centenary Chevening Scholarships 704
Wingate Scholarships 697

United Kingdom

Access to Learning Fund 685
CERN Technical Student Programme 227
EPSRC School of Computer Science and Electronic Engineering
    Research Studentship 687
International Postgraduate Research Scholarships (IPRS) 413
Lord Lloyd of Kilgerran Memorial Prize 371
Mr and Mrs David Edward Memorial Award 145
University of Kent Department of Electronics Studentships 699
University of Southampton Engineering Doctorate 759
Wingate Scholarships 697

United States of America

Air Force Summer Faculty Fellowship Program 84
British Marshall Scholarships 685
Congress Bundestag Youth Exchange for Young Professionals 221
DEED (Demonstration of Energy-Efficient Developments) Student
    Research Grant/Internship 80
International Postgraduate Research Scholarships (IPRS) 413
Krell Institute Computational Science Graduate Fellowship Program
    412
NPSC Fellowship in Physical Sciences 487
ONR Summer Faculty Research 84
ORSAS Awards 688
SRC Master's Scholarship Program 585
SWE Caterpillar Scholarship 612
SWE General Motors Foundation Graduate Scholarship 612
Winston Churchill Foundation Scholarship 797

West European Countries

CERN Technical Student Programme 227
International Postgraduate Research Scholarships (IPRS) 413
Mr and Mrs David Edward Memorial Award 145
University of Kent Department of Electronics Studentships 699

COMPUTER ENGINEERING

Any Country

Bursaries 144
CDI Internship 223
ESRF Postdoctoral Fellowships 287
ETH Zurich Excellence Scholarship and Opportunity Award 624
HFSPO Cross-Disciplinary Fellowships 383
HFSPO Short-Term Fellowships 384
Hudswell Bequest Travelling Fellowships 370
Hudswell International Research Scholarships 370
IEEE Fellowship in Electrical History 351
IET Master's Degree Scholarship 371
IET Postgraduate Scholarships 371
IET Younger Members Conference Bursary 371
J R Beard Travelling Fund 371
John Moyes Lessells Travel Scholarships 628
La Trobe University Postgraduate Scholarship 414
Queen Mary Research Studentships 539
SRG Postdoctoral Fellowships 646
SWE Microsoft Corporation Scholarships 612
Tomsk Polytechnic University International Scholarship 634

University of Bristol Postgraduate Scholarships 672
University of Southampton Postgraduate Studentships 759
University of Western Ontario Senior Visiting Fellowship 777
Victoria University of Wellington PhD Scholarships 786

African Nations

International Postgraduate Research Scholarships (IPRS) 413
School of Applied Sciences Overseas Scholarships 254

Australia

Fulbright Postgraduate Student Award for Science and Engineering
    140
School of Applied Sciences Overseas Scholarships 254
Wingate Scholarships 697

Canada

International Postgraduate Research Scholarships (IPRS) 413
School of Applied Sciences Overseas Scholarships 254
Wingate Scholarships 697

Caribbean Countries

International Postgraduate Research Scholarships (IPRS) 413
School of Applied Sciences Overseas Scholarships 254

East European Countries

CERN Technical Student Programme 227
ESRF Thesis Studentships 287
International Postgraduate Research Scholarships (IPRS) 413
School of Applied Sciences Overseas Scholarships 254

European Union

Civil and Computational Research Centre–PhD Studentships 622
EPSRC School of Computer Science and Electronic Engineering
    Research Studentship 687
Microsoft Research European PhD Scholarship Programme 448
University of Kent Department of Electronics Studentships 699
University of Southampton Engineering Doctorate 759
Wingate Scholarships 697

Middle East

International Postgraduate Research Scholarships (IPRS) 413
School of Applied Sciences Overseas Scholarships 254

New Zealand

School of Applied Sciences Overseas Scholarships 254
Wingate Scholarships 697

South Africa

International Postgraduate Research Scholarships (IPRS) 413
School of Applied Sciences Overseas Scholarships 254
Wingate Scholarships 697

United Kingdom

Aberystwyth Postgraduate Research Studentships 4
CERN Technical Student Programme 227
Civil and Computational Research Centre–PhD Studentships 622
EPSRC School of Computer Science and Electronic Engineering
    Research Studentship 687
ESRF Thesis Studentships 287
International Postgraduate Research Scholarships (IPRS) 413
Mr and Mrs David Edward Memorial Award 145
Royal Academy of Engineering International Travel Grants 554
University of Kent Department of Electronics Studentships 699
University of Southampton Engineering Doctorate 759
Wingate Scholarships 697

United States of America

Air Force Summer Faculty Fellowship Program 84
British Marshall Scholarships 685
Congress Bundestag Youth Exchange for Young Professionals 221
DEED (Demonstration of Energy-Efficient Developments) Student
    Research Grant/Internship 80

International Postgraduate Research Scholarships (IPRS) 413
ONR Summer Faculty Research 84
School of Applied Sciences Overseas Scholarships 254
SRC Master's Scholarship Program 585
SWE General Motors Foundation Graduate Scholarship 612
Winston Churchill Foundation Scholarship 797

West European Countries

CERN Technical Student Programme 227
ESRF Thesis Studentships 287
International Postgraduate Research Scholarships (IPRS) 413
Microsoft Research European PhD Scholarship Programme 448
Mr and Mrs David Edward Memorial Award 145
Royal Academy of Engineering International Travel Grants 554
University of Kent Department of Electronics Studentships 699

INDUSTRIAL AND MANAGEMENT ENGINEERING

Any Country

ETH Zurich Excellence Scholarship and Opportunity Award 624
John Moyes Lessells Travel Scholarships 628
Johnson's Wax Research Fellowship
University of Bristol Postgraduate Scholarships 672

African Nations

International Postgraduate Research Scholarships (IPRS) 413
School of Applied Sciences Overseas Scholarships 254
Shell Centenary/Shell Centenary Chevening Scholarships 704

Australia

Fulbright Postgraduate Student Award for Science and Engineering 140
School of Applied Sciences Overseas Scholarships 254
Wingate Scholarships 697

Canada

International Postgraduate Research Scholarships (IPRS) 413
School of Applied Sciences Overseas Scholarships 254
Wingate Scholarships 697

Caribbean Countries

International Postgraduate Research Scholarships (IPRS) 413
School of Applied Sciences Overseas Scholarships 254
Shell Centenary/Shell Centenary Chevening Scholarships 704

East European Countries

International Postgraduate Research Scholarships (IPRS) 413
School of Applied Sciences Overseas Scholarships 254

European Union

Wingate Scholarships 697

Middle East

International Postgraduate Research Scholarships (IPRS) 413
School of Applied Sciences Overseas Scholarships 254
Shell Centenary/Shell Centenary Chevening Scholarships 704

New Zealand

School of Applied Sciences Overseas Scholarships 254
Wingate Scholarships 697

South Africa

International Postgraduate Research Scholarships (IPRS) 413
School of Applied Sciences Overseas Scholarships 254
Shell Centenary/Shell Centenary Chevening Scholarships 704
Wingate Scholarships 697

United Kingdom

International Postgraduate Research Scholarships (IPRS) 413
Royal Commission Industrial Fellowships 563
Wingate Scholarships 697

United States of America

Air Force Summer Faculty Fellowship Program 84
Congress Bundestag Youth Exchange for Young Professionals 221
DEED (Demonstration of Energy-Efficient Developments) Student Research Grant/Internship 80
International Postgraduate Research Scholarships (IPRS) 413
ONR Summer Faculty Research 84
School of Applied Sciences Overseas Scholarships 254
SWE Caterpillar Scholarship 612
SWE General Motors Foundation Graduate Scholarship 612
Winston Churchill Foundation Scholarship 797

West European Countries

International Postgraduate Research Scholarships (IPRS) 413

METALLURGICAL ENGINEERING

Any Country

John Moyes Lessells Travel Scholarships 628
Malcolm Ray Travelling Scholarship 806
Stanley Elmore Fellowship Fund 368
Welch Foundation Scholarship 391

African Nations

International Postgraduate Research Scholarships (IPRS) 413
School of Applied Sciences Overseas Scholarships 254

Australia

APAI Scholarship in Metallurgy/Materials 713
Fulbright Postgraduate Student Award for Science and Engineering 140
PhD Scholarship in Materials Science and Engineering 714
School of Applied Sciences Overseas Scholarships 254
Western Australian CSIRO–University Postgraduate Scholarships 776
Wingate Scholarships 697

Canada

International Postgraduate Research Scholarships (IPRS) 413
School of Applied Sciences Overseas Scholarships 254
Wingate Scholarships 697

Caribbean Countries

International Postgraduate Research Scholarships (IPRS) 413
School of Applied Sciences Overseas Scholarships 254

East European Countries

International Postgraduate Research Scholarships (IPRS) 413
School of Applied Sciences Overseas Scholarships 254

European Union

Wingate Scholarships 697

Middle East

International Postgraduate Research Scholarships (IPRS) 413
School of Applied Sciences Overseas Scholarships 254

New Zealand

School of Applied Sciences Overseas Scholarships 254
Wingate Scholarships 697

South Africa

International Postgraduate Research Scholarships (IPRS) 413
School of Applied Sciences Overseas Scholarships 254
Wingate Scholarships 697

United Kingdom

International Postgraduate Research Scholarships (IPRS) 413
Wingate Scholarships 697

United States of America

Air Force Summer Faculty Fellowship Program 84
DEED (Demonstration of Energy-Efficient Developments) Student
    Research Grant/Internship 80
International Postgraduate Research Scholarships (IPRS) 413
School of Applied Sciences Overseas Scholarships 254
Winston Churchill Foundation Scholarship 797

West European Countries

International Postgraduate Research Scholarships (IPRS) 413

PRODUCTION ENGINEERING

Any Country

ETH Zurich Excellence Scholarship and Opportunity Award 624
John Moyes Lessells Travel Scholarships 628
Postgraduate Research Studentship 689
Singapore-MIT Alliance Graduate Fellowship 492

African Nations

International Postgraduate Research Scholarships (IPRS) 413
School of Applied Sciences Overseas Scholarships 254

Australia

Fulbright Postgraduate Student Award for Science and Engineering
    140
School of Applied Sciences Overseas Scholarships 254
Wingate Scholarships 697

Canada

International Postgraduate Research Scholarships (IPRS) 413
School of Applied Sciences Overseas Scholarships 254
Wingate Scholarships 697

Caribbean Countries

International Postgraduate Research Scholarships (IPRS) 413
School of Applied Sciences Overseas Scholarships 254

East European Countries

International Postgraduate Research Scholarships (IPRS) 413
School of Applied Sciences Overseas Scholarships 254

European Union

Wingate Scholarships 697

Middle East

International Postgraduate Research Scholarships (IPRS) 413
School of Applied Sciences Overseas Scholarships 254

New Zealand

Dick and Mary Earle Scholarship in Technology 500
School of Applied Sciences Overseas Scholarships 254
Wingate Scholarships 697

South Africa

International Postgraduate Research Scholarships (IPRS) 413
School of Applied Sciences Overseas Scholarships 254
Wingate Scholarships 697

United Kingdom

International Postgraduate Research Scholarships (IPRS) 413
Panasonic Trust Fellowships 253
Wingate Scholarships 697

United States of America

DEED (Demonstration of Energy-Efficient Developments) Student
    Research Grant/Internship 80
International Postgraduate Research Scholarships (IPRS) 413
School of Applied Sciences Overseas Scholarships 254
Winston Churchill Foundation Scholarship 797

West European Countries

International Postgraduate Research Scholarships (IPRS) 413

MATERIALS ENGINEERING

Any Country

ESRF Postdoctoral Fellowships 287
ETH Zurich Excellence Scholarship and Opportunity Award 624
HFSPO Cross-Disciplinary Fellowships 383
HFSPO Short-Term Fellowships 384
John Moyes Lessells Travel Scholarships 628
Johnson's Wax Research Fellowship
Malcolm Ray Travelling Scholarship 806
Queen Mary Research Studentships 539
Singapore-MIT Alliance Graduate Fellowship 492
University of Southampton Postgraduate Studentships 759
University of Western Ontario Senior Visiting Fellowship 777
Welch Foundation Scholarship 391
World Universities Network (WUN) International Research Mobility
    Scheme 759

African Nations

International Postgraduate Research Scholarships (IPRS) 413
School of Applied Sciences Overseas Scholarships 254

Australia

APAI Scholarship in Metallurgy/Materials 713
Fulbright Postgraduate Student Award for Science and Engineering
    140
PhD Scholarship in Materials Science and Engineering 714
School of Applied Sciences Overseas Scholarships 254
UOW Iron & Steel Society Scholarships 779
Wingate Scholarships 697

Canada

International Postgraduate Research Scholarships (IPRS) 413
School of Applied Sciences Overseas Scholarships 254
TAC Foundation Scholarships 637
Wingate Scholarships 697

Caribbean Countries

International Postgraduate Research Scholarships (IPRS) 413
School of Applied Sciences Overseas Scholarships 254

East European Countries

CERN Technical Student Programme 227
International Postgraduate Research Scholarships (IPRS) 413
School of Applied Sciences Overseas Scholarships 254

European Union

IPTME (Materials) Scholarships 427
University of Southampton Engineering Doctorate 759
Wingate Scholarships 697

Middle East

International Postgraduate Research Scholarships (IPRS) 413
School of Applied Sciences Overseas Scholarships 254

New Zealand

School of Applied Sciences Overseas Scholarships 254
Wingate Scholarships 697

South Africa

International Postgraduate Research Scholarships (IPRS) 413
School of Applied Sciences Overseas Scholarships 254
Wingate Scholarships 697

United Kingdom

Aberystwyth Postgraduate Research Studentships 4
CERN Technical Student Programme 227
International Postgraduate Research Scholarships (IPRS) 413

Royal Academy of Engineering International Travel Grants 554
Society for Underwater Technology (SUT) 254
University of Southampton Engineering Doctorate 759
Wingate Scholarships 697

United States of America

Air Force Summer Faculty Fellowship Program 84
DEED (Demonstration of Energy-Efficient Developments) Student Research Grant/Internship 80
International Postgraduate Research Scholarships (IPRS) 413
Krell Institute Computational Science Graduate Fellowship Program 412
ONR Summer Faculty Research 84
School of Applied Sciences Overseas Scholarships 254
SRC Master's Scholarship Program 585
SWE Caterpillar Scholarship 612
SWE General Motors Foundation Graduate Scholarship 612
Winston Churchill Foundation Scholarship 797

West European Countries

CERN Technical Student Programme 227
International Postgraduate Research Scholarships (IPRS) 413
Royal Academy of Engineering International Travel Grants 554

MINING AND MINERALS ENGINEERING

Any Country

Bosworth Smith Trust Fund 368
G Vernon Hobson Bequest 368
John Moyes Lessells Travel Scholarships 628
NERC Advanced Research Fellowships 493
NERC Postdoctoral Research Fellowships 494
The Tom Seaman Travelling Scholarship 368

African Nations

International Postgraduate Research Scholarships (IPRS) 413

Australia

Edgar Pam Fellowship 368
Fulbright Postgraduate Student Award for Science and Engineering 140
Wingate Scholarships 697

Canada

Edgar Pam Fellowship 368
International Postgraduate Research Scholarships (IPRS) 413
Wingate Scholarships 697

Caribbean Countries

International Postgraduate Research Scholarships (IPRS) 413

East European Countries

International Postgraduate Research Scholarships (IPRS) 413
Synthesys Visiting Fellowship 494

European Union

NERC Masters Studentships 493
NERC Research (PhD) Studentships 494
Synthesys Visiting Fellowship 494
Wingate Scholarships 697

Middle East

International Postgraduate Research Scholarships (IPRS) 413

New Zealand

Edgar Pam Fellowship 368
Wingate Scholarships 697

South Africa

Edgar Pam Fellowship 368
International Postgraduate Research Scholarships (IPRS) 413
Wingate Scholarships 697

United Kingdom

Edgar Pam Fellowship 368
International Postgraduate Research Scholarships (IPRS) 413
Mining Club Award 368
NERC Masters Studentships 493
NERC Research (PhD) Studentships 494
Synthesys Visiting Fellowship 494
Wingate Scholarships 697

United States of America

DEED (Demonstration of Energy-Efficient Developments) Student Research Grant/Internship 80
International Postgraduate Research Scholarships (IPRS) 413
Winston Churchill Foundation Scholarship 797

West European Countries

International Postgraduate Research Scholarships (IPRS) 413
Synthesys Visiting Fellowship 494

PETROLEUM ENGINEERING

Any Country

ACS PRF Type SE Grants 37
Exxon Mobil Teaching Fellowships 553
John Moyes Lessells Travel Scholarships 628
NERC Advanced Research Fellowships 493
NERC Postdoctoral Research Fellowships 494
Postgraduate Top Up Scholarships in Offshore Engineering and Naval Architecture 776

Australia

Fulbright Postgraduate Student Award for Science and Engineering 140
Society of Petroleum Engineers Western Australia Scholarships 776
Wingate Scholarships 697

Canada

Wingate Scholarships 697

European Union

NERC Masters Studentships 493
NERC Research (PhD) Studentships 494
Wingate Scholarships 697

New Zealand

Wingate Scholarships 697

South Africa

Wingate Scholarships 697

United Kingdom

NERC Masters Studentships 493
NERC Research (PhD) Studentships 494
Wingate Scholarships 697

United States of America

Air Force Summer Faculty Fellowship Program 84
DEED (Demonstration of Energy-Efficient Developments) Student Research Grant/Internship 80
Winston Churchill Foundation Scholarship 797

ENERGY ENGINEERING

Any Country

ASHRAE Grants-in-Aid for Graduate Students 91
Earthwatch Field Research Grants 272
Energy Fellowships 423
ETH Zurich Excellence Scholarship and Opportunity Award 624
Hudswell International Research Scholarships 370
IET Master's Degree Scholarship 371

IET Younger Members Conference Bursary 371
J R Beard Travelling Fund 371
John Moyes Lessells Travel Scholarships 628
Lindbergh Grants 228
NERC Advanced Research Fellowships 493
NERC Postdoctoral Research Fellowships 494
Tomsk Polytechnic University International Scholarship 634

African Nations

School of Applied Sciences Overseas Scholarships 254
Shell Centenary/Shell Centenary Chevening Scholarships 704

Australia

Fulbright Postgraduate Student Award for Science and Engineering
140
School of Applied Sciences Overseas Scholarships 254
Wingate Scholarships 697

Canada

School of Applied Sciences Overseas Scholarships 254
Wingate Scholarships 697

Caribbean Countries

School of Applied Sciences Overseas Scholarships 254
Shell Centenary/Shell Centenary Chevening Scholarships 704

East European Countries

School of Applied Sciences Overseas Scholarships 254
VKI Fellowship 788

European Union

NERC Masters Studentships 493
NERC Research (PhD) Studentships 494
Wingate Scholarships 697

Middle East

School of Applied Sciences Overseas Scholarships 254
Shell Centenary/Shell Centenary Chevening Scholarships 704

New Zealand

School of Applied Sciences Overseas Scholarships 254
Wingate Scholarships 697

South Africa

School of Applied Sciences Overseas Scholarships 254
Shell Centenary/Shell Centenary Chevening Scholarships 704
Wingate Scholarships 697

United Kingdom

NERC Masters Studentships 493
NERC Research (PhD) Studentships 494
Society for Underwater Technology (SUT) 254
Wingate Scholarships 697

United States of America

Air Force Summer Faculty Fellowship Program 84
DEED (Demonstration of Energy-Efficient Developments) Student
    Research Grant/Internship 80
ONR Summer Faculty Research 84
School of Applied Sciences Overseas Scholarships 254
VKI Fellowship 788
Winston Churchill Foundation Scholarship 797

West European Countries

VKI Fellowship 788

NUCLEAR ENGINEERING

Any Country

Alan F Henry/Paul A Greebler Scholarship 69
ETH Zurich Excellence Scholarship and Opportunity Award 624

John and Muriel Landis Scholarship Awards 70
John Moyes Lessells Travel Scholarships 628

Australia

Fulbright Postgraduate Student Award for Science and Engineering 140
Wingate Scholarships 697

Canada

Wingate Scholarships 697

East European Countries

CERN Technical Student Programme 227

European Union

Wingate Scholarships 697

New Zealand

Wingate Scholarships 697

South Africa

Wingate Scholarships 697

United Kingdom

CERN Technical Student Programme 227
Wingate Scholarships 697

United States of America

Air Force Summer Faculty Fellowship Program 84
DEED (Demonstration of Energy-Efficient Developments) Student
    Research Grant/Internship 80
Everitt P Blizard Scholarship 70
James F Schumar Scholarship 70
Krell Institute Computational Science Graduate Fellowship Program
    412
ONR Summer Faculty Research 84
Robert A Dannels Memorial Scholarship 70
Verne R Dapp Memorial Scholarship 71
Walter Meyer Scholarship 71
Winston Churchill Foundation Scholarship 797

West European Countries

CERN Technical Student Programme 227

MECHANICAL/ELECTROMECHANICAL ENGINEERING

Any Country

ASHRAE Grants-in-Aid for Graduate Students 91
BP/RSE Research Fellowships 628
ESRF Postdoctoral Fellowships 287
ETH Zurich Excellence Scholarship and Opportunity Award 624
Exxon Mobil Teaching Fellowships 553
HFSPO Short-Term Fellowships 384
Hudswell International Research Scholarships 370
James Clayton Awards 372
James Clayton Overseas Conference Travel for Senior Engineers 372
James Clayton Postgraduate Hardship Award 372
James Watt International Medal 373
John Moyes Lessells Travel Scholarships 628
Queen Mary Research Studentships 539
Singapore-MIT Alliance Graduate Fellowship 492
Tomsk Polytechnic University International Scholarship 634
University of Bristol Postgraduate Scholarships 672
University of Southampton Postgraduate Studentships 759
World Universities Network (WUN) International Research Mobility
    Scheme 759

African Nations

International Postgraduate Research Scholarships (IPRS) 413
School of Applied Sciences Overseas Scholarships 254
Shell Centenary/Shell Centenary Chevening Scholarships 704

Australia

Fulbright Postgraduate Student Award for Science and Engineering 140
School of Applied Sciences Overseas Scholarships 254
Wingate Scholarships 697

Canada

Horticultural Research Institute Grants 346
International Postgraduate Research Scholarships (IPRS) 413
School of Applied Sciences Overseas Scholarships 254
TAC Foundation Scholarships 637
Wingate Scholarships 697

Caribbean Countries

International Postgraduate Research Scholarships (IPRS) 413
School of Applied Sciences Overseas Scholarships 254
Shell Centenary/Shell Centenary Chevening Scholarships 704

East European Countries

CERN Technical Student Programme 227
International Postgraduate Research Scholarships (IPRS) 413
School of Applied Sciences Overseas Scholarships 254
VKI Fellowship 788

European Union

University of Southampton Engineering Doctorate 759
Wingate Scholarships 697

Middle East

International Postgraduate Research Scholarships (IPRS) 413
School of Applied Sciences Overseas Scholarships 254
Shell Centenary/Shell Centenary Chevening Scholarships 704

New Zealand

School of Applied Sciences Overseas Scholarships 254
Wingate Scholarships 697

South Africa

International Postgraduate Research Scholarships (IPRS) 413
School of Applied Sciences Overseas Scholarships 254
Shell Centenary/Shell Centenary Chevening Scholarships 704
Wingate Scholarships 697

United Kingdom

CERN Technical Student Programme 227
International Postgraduate Research Scholarships (IPRS) 413
University of Southampton Engineering Doctorate 759
Wingate Scholarships 697

United States of America

Air Force Summer Faculty Fellowship Program 84
ASME Graduate Teaching Fellowship Program 93
Congress Bundestag Youth Exchange for Young Professionals 221
DEED (Demonstration of Energy-Efficient Developments) Student Research Grant/Internship 80
Elisabeth M and Winchell M Parsons Scholarship 93
Horticultural Research Institute Grants 346
International Postgraduate Research Scholarships (IPRS) 413
Krell Institute Computational Science Graduate Fellowship Program 412
Marjorie Roy Rothermel Scholarship 93
NPSC Fellowship in Physical Sciences 487
School of Applied Sciences Overseas Scholarships 254
SRC Master's Scholarship Program 585
SWE Caterpillar Scholarship 612
SWE General Motors Foundation Graduate Scholarship 612
VKI Fellowship 788
Winston Churchill Foundation Scholarship 797

West European Countries

CERN Technical Student Programme 227
International Postgraduate Research Scholarships (IPRS) 413
VKI Fellowship 788

HYDRAULIC/PNEUMATIC ENGINEERING

Any Country

Horton (Hydrology) Research Grant 56
John Moyes Lessells Travel Scholarships 628

African Nations

International Postgraduate Research Scholarships (IPRS) 413

Australia

Fulbright Postgraduate Student Award for Science and Engineering 140
Wingate Scholarships 697

Canada

CWRA Dillon Consulting Scholarship/Ken Thomson Scholarship 216
Horticultural Research Institute Grants 346
International Postgraduate Research Scholarships (IPRS) 413
Wingate Scholarships 697

Caribbean Countries

International Postgraduate Research Scholarships (IPRS) 413

East European Countries

International Postgraduate Research Scholarships (IPRS) 413

European Union

Wingate Scholarships 697

Middle East

International Postgraduate Research Scholarships (IPRS) 413

New Zealand

Wingate Scholarships 697

South Africa

International Postgraduate Research Scholarships (IPRS) 413
Wingate Scholarships 697

United Kingdom

International Postgraduate Research Scholarships (IPRS) 413
Wingate Scholarships 697

United States of America

DEED (Demonstration of Energy-Efficient Developments) Student Research Grant/Internship 80
Horticultural Research Institute Grants 346
International Postgraduate Research Scholarships (IPRS) 413
Winston Churchill Foundation Scholarship 797

West European Countries

International Postgraduate Research Scholarships (IPRS) 413

SOUND ENGINEERING

Any Country

ASA Frederick V. Hunt Postdoctoral Research Fellowship 5
IET Younger Members Conference Bursary 371
John Moyes Lessells Travel Scholarships 628
University of Southampton Postgraduate Studentships 759
World Universities Network (WUN) International Research Mobility Scheme 759

Australia

Fulbright Postgraduate Student Award for Science and Engineering 140
Wingate Scholarships 697

Canada

Wingate Scholarships 697

East European Countries

VKI Fellowship 788

European Union

University of Southampton Engineering Doctorate 759
Wingate Scholarships 697

New Zealand

Wingate Scholarships 697

South Africa

Wingate Scholarships 697

United Kingdom

University of Southampton Engineering Doctorate 759
Wingate Scholarships 697

United States of America

ASA Frederick V. Hunt Postdoctoral Research Fellowship 5
VKI Fellowship 788
Winston Churchill Foundation Scholarship 797

West European Countries

VKI Fellowship 788

AUTOMOTIVE ENGINEERING

Any Country

Hudswell Bequest Travelling Fellowships 370
IET Younger Members Conference Bursary 371
John Moyes Lessells Travel Scholarships 628
University of Bristol Postgraduate Scholarships 672
University of Southampton Postgraduate Studentships 759
World Universities Network (WUN) International Research Mobility
    Scheme 759

African Nations

International Postgraduate Research Scholarships (IPRS) 413
School of Applied Sciences Overseas Scholarships 254
Shell Centenary/Shell Centenary Chevening Scholarships 704

Australia

Fulbright Postgraduate Student Award for Science and Engineering
    140
School of Applied Sciences Overseas Scholarships 254
Wingate Scholarships 697

Canada

International Postgraduate Research Scholarships (IPRS) 413
School of Applied Sciences Overseas Scholarships 254
Wingate Scholarships 697

Caribbean Countries

International Postgraduate Research Scholarships (IPRS) 413
School of Applied Sciences Overseas Scholarships 254
Shell Centenary/Shell Centenary Chevening Scholarships 704

East European Countries

International Postgraduate Research Scholarships (IPRS) 413
School of Applied Sciences Overseas Scholarships 254

European Union

University of Southampton Engineering Doctorate 759
Wingate Scholarships 697

Middle East

International Postgraduate Research Scholarships (IPRS) 413
School of Applied Sciences Overseas Scholarships 254
Shell Centenary/Shell Centenary Chevening Scholarships 704

New Zealand

School of Applied Sciences Overseas Scholarships 254
Wingate Scholarships 697

South Africa

International Postgraduate Research Scholarships (IPRS)
    413
School of Applied Sciences Overseas Scholarships 254
Shell Centenary/Shell Centenary Chevening Scholarships 704
Wingate Scholarships 697

United Kingdom

Aberystwyth Postgraduate Research Studentships 4
Grand Prix Mechanics Charitable Trust Fund 253
International Postgraduate Research Scholarships (IPRS) 413
University of Southampton Engineering Doctorate 759
Wingate Scholarships 697

United States of America

International Postgraduate Research Scholarships (IPRS) 413
School of Applied Sciences Overseas Scholarships 254
Winston Churchill Foundation Scholarship 797

West European Countries

International Postgraduate Research Scholarships (IPRS) 413

MEASUREMENT/PRECISION ENGINEERING

Any Country

ESRF Postdoctoral Fellowships 287
IET Younger Members Conference Bursary 371
John Moyes Lessells Travel Scholarships 628

African Nations

International Postgraduate Research Scholarships (IPRS) 413

Australia

Fulbright Postgraduate Student Award for Science and Engineering
    140
Wingate Scholarships 697

Canada

International Postgraduate Research Scholarships (IPRS) 413
Wingate Scholarships 697

Caribbean Countries

International Postgraduate Research Scholarships (IPRS) 413

East European Countries

ESRF Thesis Studentships 287
International Postgraduate Research Scholarships (IPRS) 413

European Union

Wingate Scholarships 697

Middle East

International Postgraduate Research Scholarships (IPRS) 413

New Zealand

Wingate Scholarships 697

South Africa

International Postgraduate Research Scholarships (IPRS) 413
Wingate Scholarships 697

United Kingdom

ESRF Thesis Studentships 287
International Postgraduate Research Scholarships (IPRS) 413
Wingate Scholarships 697

United States of America

Air Force Summer Faculty Fellowship Program 84
International Postgraduate Research Scholarships (IPRS) 413
Winston Churchill Foundation Scholarship 797

West European Countries

ESRF Thesis Studentships 287
International Postgraduate Research Scholarships (IPRS) 413

CONTROL ENGINEERING (ROBOTICS)

Any Country

ASPRS Ta Liang Memorial Award 89
BP/RSE Research Fellowships 628
ETH Zurich Excellence Scholarship and Opportunity Award
  624
HFSPO Cross-Disciplinary Fellowships 383
Hudswell Bequest Travelling Fellowships 370
Hudswell International Research Scholarships 370
IET Master's Degree Scholarship 371
IET Postgraduate Scholarships 371
IET Younger Members Conference Bursary 371
John Moyes Lessells Travel Scholarships 628
Postgraduate Research Studentship 689

African Nations

International Postgraduate Research Scholarships (IPRS) 413
School of Applied Sciences Overseas Scholarships 254

Australia

Fulbright Postgraduate Student Award for Science and Engineering
  140
School of Applied Sciences Overseas Scholarships 254
Wingate Scholarships 697

Canada

ASPRS Robert N. Colwell Memorial Fellowship 89
Horticultural Research Institute Grants 346
International Postgraduate Research Scholarships (IPRS) 413
School of Applied Sciences Overseas Scholarships 254
Wingate Scholarships 697

Caribbean Countries

International Postgraduate Research Scholarships (IPRS) 413
School of Applied Sciences Overseas Scholarships 254

East European Countries

International Postgraduate Research Scholarships (IPRS) 413
School of Applied Sciences Overseas Scholarships 254

European Union

Wingate Scholarships 697

Middle East

International Postgraduate Research Scholarships (IPRS) 413
School of Applied Sciences Overseas Scholarships 254

New Zealand

School of Applied Sciences Overseas Scholarships 254
Wingate Scholarships 697

South Africa

International Postgraduate Research Scholarships (IPRS) 413
School of Applied Sciences Overseas Scholarships 254
Wingate Scholarships 697

United Kingdom

Aberystwyth Postgraduate Research Studentships 4
International Postgraduate Research Scholarships (IPRS) 413
Wingate Scholarships 697

United States of America

Air Force Summer Faculty Fellowship Program 84
ASPRS Robert N. Colwell Memorial Fellowship 89
Horticultural Research Institute Grants 346
International Postgraduate Research Scholarships (IPRS) 413
School of Applied Sciences Overseas Scholarships 254
Winston Churchill Foundation Scholarship 797

West European Countries

International Postgraduate Research Scholarships (IPRS) 413

AERONAUTICAL AND AEROSPACE ENGINEERING

Any Country

A Verville Fellowship 596
F.L. Scarf Award 56
The Guggenheim Fellowships 597
Hudswell Bequest Travelling Fellowships 370
Hudswell International Research Scholarships 370
IET Postgraduate Scholarships 371
IET Younger Members Conference Bursary 371
John Moyes Lessells Travel Scholarships 628
Lindbergh Grants 228
NRC Research Associateships 488
Queen Mary Research Studentships 539
Ramsay Fellowship in Naval Aviation History 597
University of Bristol Postgraduate Scholarships 672
University of Southampton Postgraduate Studentships 759
World Universities Network (WUN) International Research Mobility
  Scheme 759
Zonta Amelia Earhart Fellowships 811

African Nations

International Postgraduate Research Scholarships (IPRS) 413

Australia

Fulbright Postgraduate Student Award for Science and Engineering 140
Wingate Scholarships 697

Canada

Canadian Space Agency Supplements Postgraduate Scholarships 214
International Postgraduate Research Scholarships (IPRS) 413
Wingate Scholarships 697

Caribbean Countries

International Postgraduate Research Scholarships (IPRS) 413

East European Countries

International Postgraduate Research Scholarships (IPRS) 413
VKI Fellowship 788

European Union

University of Southampton Engineering Doctorate 759
Wingate Scholarships 697

Middle East

International Postgraduate Research Scholarships (IPRS) 413

New Zealand

Wingate Scholarships 697

South Africa

International Postgraduate Research Scholarships (IPRS) 413
Wingate Scholarships 697

United Kingdom

International Postgraduate Research Scholarships (IPRS) 413
University of Southampton Engineering Doctorate 759
Wingate Scholarships 697

United States of America

Air Force Summer Faculty Fellowship Program 84
International Postgraduate Research Scholarships (IPRS) 413
Krell Institute Computational Science Graduate Fellowship Program 412
ONR Summer Faculty Research 84
VKI Fellowship 788
Winston Churchill Foundation Scholarship 797

West European Countries

International Postgraduate Research Scholarships (IPRS) 413
VKI Fellowship 788

MARINE ENGINEERING AND NAVAL ARCHITECTURE

Any Country

CICOR Postdoctoral Scholar Fellowship in Coastal Oceanography, Climate or Marine Ecosystems 804
De Paepe-Willems Award 386
John A Knauss Marine Policy Fellowships 488
John Moyes Lessells Travel Scholarships 628
The Lloyd's Register Scholarship for Marine Engineering and Naval Architecture
Postgraduate Top Up Scholarships in Offshore Engineering and Naval Architecture 776
University of Southampton Postgraduate Studentships 759
World Universities Network (WUN) International Research Mobility Scheme 759

African Nations

School of Applied Sciences Overseas Scholarships 254

Australia

Fulbright Postgraduate Student Award for Science and Engineering 140
School of Applied Sciences Overseas Scholarships 254
Wingate Scholarships 697

Canada

School of Applied Sciences Overseas Scholarships 254
Wingate Scholarships 697

Caribbean Countries

School of Applied Sciences Overseas Scholarships 254

East European Countries

School of Applied Sciences Overseas Scholarships 254

European Union

University of Southampton Engineering Doctorate 759
Wingate Scholarships 697

Middle East

School of Applied Sciences Overseas Scholarships 254

New Zealand

School of Applied Sciences Overseas Scholarships 254
Wingate Scholarships 697

South Africa

School of Applied Sciences Overseas Scholarships 254
Wingate Scholarships 697

United Kingdom

Society for Underwater Technology (SUT) 254
University of Southampton Engineering Doctorate 759
Wingate Scholarships 697

United States of America

Air Force Summer Faculty Fellowship Program 84
School of Applied Sciences Overseas Scholarships 254
Sea Grant/NOAA Fisheries Fellowship 488

AGRICULTURAL ENGINEERING

Any Country

Hong Kong Research Grant 564
John Moyes Lessells Travel Scholarships 628
Lindbergh Grants 228
QUEST Institution of Civil Engineers Overseas Travel Awards 370
Teagasc Walsh Fellowships 626

African Nations

Canadian Window on International Development 380
IDRC Doctoral Research Awards 380
International Postgraduate Research Scholarships (IPRS) 413
School of Applied Sciences Overseas Scholarships 254

Australia

Fulbright Postgraduate Student Award for Science and Engineering 140
School of Applied Sciences Overseas Scholarships 254
Wingate Scholarships 697

Canada

Canadian Window on International Development 380
CWRA Dillon Consulting Scholarship/Ken Thomson Scholarship 216
IDRC Doctoral Research Awards 380
International Postgraduate Research Scholarships (IPRS) 413
School of Applied Sciences Overseas Scholarships 254
Wingate Scholarships 697

Caribbean Countries

Canadian Window on International Development 380
IDRC Doctoral Research Awards 380
International Postgraduate Research Scholarships (IPRS) 413
School of Applied Sciences Overseas Scholarships 254

East European Countries

IDRC Doctoral Research Awards 380
International Postgraduate Research Scholarships (IPRS) 413
School of Applied Sciences Overseas Scholarships 254

European Union

Wingate Scholarships 697

Middle East

IDRC Doctoral Research Awards 380
International Postgraduate Research Scholarships (IPRS) 413
School of Applied Sciences Overseas Scholarships 254

New Zealand

School of Applied Sciences Overseas Scholarships 254
Wingate Scholarships 697

South Africa

Canadian Window on International Development 380
IDRC Doctoral Research Awards 380
International Postgraduate Research Scholarships (IPRS) 413
School of Applied Sciences Overseas Scholarships 254
Wingate Scholarships 697

United Kingdom

International Postgraduate Research Scholarships (IPRS) 413
Wingate Scholarships 697

United States of America

Air Force Summer Faculty Fellowship Program 84
DEED (Demonstration of Energy-Efficient Developments) Student Research Grant/Internship 80
International Postgraduate Research Scholarships (IPRS) 413
School of Applied Sciences Overseas Scholarships 254
SWE Caterpillar Scholarship 612

West European Countries

International Postgraduate Research Scholarships (IPRS) 413

FORESTRY ENGINEERING

Any Country

Henrietta Hutton Research Grants 564
Hong Kong Research Grant 564
John Moyes Lessells Travel Scholarships 628
Lindbergh Grants 228
Small Research Grants 566

African Nations

Canadian Window on International Development 380
IDRC Doctoral Research Awards 380

Australia

Fulbright Postgraduate Student Award for Science and Engineering 140
Wingate Scholarships 697

Canada

Canadian Window on International Development 380
IDRC Doctoral Research Awards 380
Wingate Scholarships 697

Caribbean Countries

Canadian Window on International Development 380
IDRC Doctoral Research Awards 380

East European Countries

IDRC Doctoral Research Awards 380

European Union

Wingate Scholarships 697

Middle East

IDRC Doctoral Research Awards 380

New Zealand

Wingate Scholarships 697

South Africa

Canadian Window on International Development 380
IDRC Doctoral Research Awards 380
Wingate Scholarships 697

United Kingdom

Wingate Scholarships 697

United States of America

Air Force Summer Faculty Fellowship Program 84

BIOENGINEERING AND BIOMEDICAL ENGINEERING

Any Country

Action Medical Research Project Grants 6
Action Medical Research Training Fellowship 7
Alberta Heritage Full-Time Studentship 13
Charles Parsons Energy Research Award 490

ESRF Postdoctoral Fellowships 287
ETH Zurich Excellence Scholarship and Opportunity Award 624
Fellowships for Biomedical Engineering Research 148
Hastings Center International Visiting Scholars Program 332
HFSPO Cross-Disciplinary Fellowships 383
HFSPO Short-Term Fellowships 384
Hudswell Bequest Travelling Fellowships 370
Hudswell International Research Scholarships 370
IEEE Fellowship in Electrical History 351
IET Postgraduate Scholarships 371
IET Younger Members Conference Bursary 371
J R Beard Travelling Fund 371
John Moyes Lessells Travel Scholarships 628
Lindbergh Grants 228
Queen Mary Research Studentships 539
Singapore-MIT Alliance Graduate Fellowship 492
Welch Foundation Scholarship 391

African Nations

Hastings Center International Visiting Scholars Program 332
International Postgraduate Research Scholarships (IPRS) 413
School of Applied Sciences Overseas Scholarships 254

Australia

Australian Clinical Research Postdoctoral Fellowship 477
Biomedical (Dora Lush) and Public Health Postgraduate Scholarships 477
C J Martin Fellowships (Overseas Biomedical) 477
Career Development Awards 477
Fulbright Postgraduate Student Award for Science and Engineering 140
Hastings Center International Visiting Scholars Program 332
Howard Florey Centenary Fellowship 478
Industry Fellowships 478
Institute of Health and Biomedical Innovation Awards 540
NHMRC Medical and Dental and Public Health Postgraduate Research Scholarships 478
NHMRC/INSERM Exchange Fellowships 478
Peter Doherty Fellowships (Australian Biomedical) 478
School of Applied Sciences Overseas Scholarships 254
Training Scholarship for Indigenous Health Research 479
Wingate Scholarships 697

Canada

International Postgraduate Research Scholarships (IPRS) 413
School of Applied Sciences Overseas Scholarships 254
Wingate Scholarships 697

Caribbean Countries

Hastings Center International Visiting Scholars Program 332
International Postgraduate Research Scholarships (IPRS) 413
School of Applied Sciences Overseas Scholarships 254

East European Countries

Engineering Science: Sloane-Robinson Scholarships 725
ESRF Thesis Studentships 287
FEMS Fellowship 290
Hastings Center International Visiting Scholars Program 332
International Postgraduate Research Scholarships (IPRS) 413
School of Applied Sciences Overseas Scholarships 254
VKI Fellowship 788

European Union

Wingate Scholarships 697

Middle East

Hastings Center International Visiting Scholars Program 332
International Postgraduate Research Scholarships (IPRS) 413
School of Applied Sciences Overseas Scholarships 254

New Zealand

Hastings Center International Visiting Scholars Program 332
School of Applied Sciences Overseas Scholarships 254

FINE AND APPLIED ARTS

GENERAL

African Nations

Australia

Canada

International Postgraduate Research Scholarships (IPRS) 413
International Postgraduate Research Scholarships (IPRS) 413
J W McConnell Memorial Fellowships 243
Wingate Scholarships 697

Caribbean Countries

Guggenheim Fellowships to Assist Research and Artistic Creation
(Latin America and the Caribbean) 405
International Postgraduate Research Scholarships (IPRS) 413
International Postgraduate Research Scholarships (IPRS) 413

East European Countries

Andrew W Mellon Foundation East-Central European Fellowships in
the Humanities 362
ArtsLink Residencies 222
International Postgraduate Research Scholarships (IPRS) 413
International Postgraduate Research Scholarships (IPRS) 413

European Union

AHRC Doctoral Awards Scheme 109
CBRL Travel Grant 248
International Postgraduate Research Scholarships (IPRS) 413
Professional Preparation Master's Scheme
Research Preparation Master's Scheme
School of Art and Design Scholarships 428
Wingate Scholarships 697

Middle East

AUC Nadia Niazi Mostafa Fellowship in Islamic Art and Architecture
97
International Postgraduate Research Scholarships (IPRS) 413
International Postgraduate Research Scholarships (IPRS) 413

New Zealand

Wingate Scholarships 697

South Africa

International Postgraduate Research Scholarships (IPRS) 413
International Postgraduate Research Scholarships (IPRS) 413
Wingate Scholarships 697
Wolfson Foundation Grants 799

United Kingdom

Aberystwyth Postgraduate Research Studentships 4
AHRC Doctoral Awards Scheme 109
BIAA Travel Grants 168
CBRL Research Award 248
CBRL Travel Grant 248
ESU Chautauqua Institution Scholarships 280
Glasgow and West of Scotland Postgraduate Scholarships 320
Hilda Martindale Exhibitions 341
International Postgraduate Research Scholarships (IPRS) 413
International Postgraduate Research Scholarships (IPRS) 413
Oppenheim–John Downes Trust Grants 513
Portia Geach Memorial Award 221
Professional Preparation Master's Scheme
Research Preparation Master's Scheme
Rome Scholarships in the Fine Arts 176
Sargant Fellowship in Critical and Curatorial Studies 176
University of Kent School of Drama, Film and Visual Arts Scholarships
700
Wingate Scholarships 697
Wolfson Foundation Grants 799

United States of America

ACC Fellowship Grants Program 115
American Academy in Berlin Prize Fellowships 24
Artist Trust/WSAC Fellowships 109
ArtsLink Projects 222
BNS Arts Administrator Renewal Fellowship 153
Congress Bundestag Youth Exchange for Young Professionals 221
Eric Robert Anderson Memorial Scholarship 456
Fellowship for American College Students 545

Fulbright Distinguished Chairs Program 248
Fulbright Senior Specialists Program 249
Grants for Artist Projects (GAP) Program 109
Guggenheim Fellowships to Assist Research and Artistic Creation
(USA and Canada) 406
Harriet Hale Woolley Scholarships 297
International Postgraduate Research Scholarships (IPRS) 413
International Postgraduate Research Scholarships (IPRS) 413
Kress Fellowship in the Art and Archaeology of Jordan 35
Louise Wallace Hackney Fellowship 72
The Nadine Blacklock Nature Photography for Women 153
National Endowment for the Humanities Fellowships 348
Nellie Mae Rowe Fellowship 331
North Dakota Indian Scholarship 507
OCAC Junior Residency 513
Rabun Gap-Nacoochee School Teaching Fellowship 331
Twining Humber Award for Lifetime Artistic Achievement 109
Virginia Liebeler Biennial Grants for Mature Women (Art) 484
Virginia Liebeler Biennial Grants for Mature Women (Music) 484
Virginia Liebeler Biennial Grants for Mature Women (Writing) 484

West European Countries

International Postgraduate Research Scholarships (IPRS) 413
International Postgraduate Research Scholarships (IPRS) 413
University of Kent School of Drama, Film and Visual Arts Scholarships
700

HISTORY AND PHILOSOPHY OF ART

Any Country

Ahmanson and Getty Postdoctoral Fellowships 639
Albert J Beveridge Grant 58
American Historical Print Collectors Society Fellowship 27
ASCSA Advanced Fellowships 82
ASCSA Fellowships 82
ASECS (American Society for 18th-Century Studies)/Clark Library
Fellowships 639
Barbara Thom Postdoctoral Fellowship 347
Bernadotte E Schmitt Grants 58
BIAA Post-Doctoral Research Fellowship 168
BIAA Research Scholarship 168
BIAA Study Grants 168
BIAA Travel Grants 168
British Academy Overseas Conference Grants 158
British Academy Postdoctoral Fellowships 158
British Academy Research Development Awards (BARDAs) 158
British Academy Small Research Grants 158
British Academy Worldwide Congress Grant 159
British Conference Grants 159
Camargo Fellowships 182
Clark Library Short-Term Resident Fellowships 639
Clark Predoctoral Fellowships 639
Clark-Huntington Joint Bibliographical Fellowship 640
Drawn to Art Fellowship 27
Edilia and François-Auguste de Montequin Fellowship in Iberian and
Latin American Architecture 608
Essex Rotary University Travel Grants 687
Fondazione Roberto Longhi 551
Frances A Yates Fellowships 789
Frances Weitzenhoffer Memorial Fellowship in Art History 510
Frederick Douglass Institute Postdoctoral Fellowship 304
Frederick Douglass Institute Predoctoral Dissertation Fellowship 304
The Getty Foundation Collaborative Research Grants 316
The Getty Foundation Curatorial Research Fellowships 316
The Getty Foundation Postdoctoral Fellowships 316
Graduate Dissertation Research Fellowship 448
Graduate Summer Travel Grants 449
Grete Sondheimer Fellowship 790
Helen Wallis Fellowship 170
Henry Moore Institute Research Fellowship 338
Hugh Last and Donald Atkinson Funds Committee Grants 604
Huntington Short-Term Fellowships 348
Institute for Advanced Study Postdoctoral Residential Fellowships 363
Jacob Hirsch Fellowship 83

Jay and Deborah Last Fellowship in American History Visual Culture 28
Kanner Fellowship In British Studies 640
Keepers Preservation Education Fund Fellowship 608
Kennan Institute Short-Term Grants 408
Lewis Walpole Library Fellowship 421
Library Company of Philadelphia and Historical Society of Pennsylvania Research Fellowships in American History and Culture 422
Lifchez/Stronach Curatorial Internship 447
Littleton-Griswold Research Grant 59
M Alison Frantz Fellowship in Post-Classical Studies at the Gennadius Library 83
Mellon Fellowships 348
Metropolitan Museum of Art Summer Internships for College Students 447
Metropolitan Museum of Art Summer Internships for Graduate Students 447
Minda de Gunzberg Graduate Dissertation Writing Fellowship 449
National Federation of Business and Professional Women's Clubs Travel Grants
NEH Fellowships 83
Paul Mellon Centre Rome Fellowship 175
Residential Grants at the Getty Center and Getty Villa 317
Rhodes University Postdoctoral Fellowship and The Andrew Mellon Postdoctoral Fellowship 548
Rosann Berry Fellowship 608
Samuel H Kress Foundation 2-Year Research Fellowships at Foreign Institutions 580
Samuel H Kress Foundation Fellowships for Advanced Training in Fine Arts Conservation 580
Samuel H Kress Foundation Travel Fellowships 580
Shorenstein APARC Postdoctoral Research Fellowship in Korean Studies 586
Sir Eric Berthoud Travel Grant 689
Society for the Study of French History Bursaries 606
Spiro Kostof Annual Meeting Fellowship 609
St Catherine's College Graduate Scholarship in the Arts
United States Holocaust Memorial Museum Center for Advanced Holocaust Studies Visiting Scholar Programs 641
University of Bristol Postgraduate Scholarships 672
University of Kent School of Drama, Film and Visual Arts Scholarships 700
University of Southampton Postgraduate Studentships 759
Victoria University of Wellington PhD Scholarships 786
White Postgraduate Fellowship 681
Wolfsonian-FIU Fellowship 800
World Universities Network (WUN) International Research Mobility Scheme 759

African Nations

International Postgraduate Research Scholarships (IPRS) 413
ORSAS Awards 688

Australia

AAH Humanities Travelling Fellowships 132
ORSAS Awards 688
Wingate Scholarships 697

Canada

Gilbert Chinard Fellowships 361
Harmon Chadbourn Rorison Fellowship 361
International Postgraduate Research Scholarships (IPRS) 413
KRESS/ARIT Pre-Doctoral Fellowship in the History of Art and Archaeology 81
ORSAS Awards 688
Vatican Film Library Mellon Fellowship 785
Wingate Scholarships 697

Caribbean Countries

International Postgraduate Research Scholarships (IPRS) 413
ORSAS Awards 688

East European Countries

International Postgraduate Research Scholarships (IPRS) 413
Mellon Postdoctoral Fellowships In Turkey For East European Scholars 81
ORSAS Awards 688
Warburg Mellon Research Fellowship 790

European Union

AHRC Doctoral Awards Scheme 109
Professional Preparation Master's Scheme
Research Preparation Master's Scheme
Warburg Mellon Research Fellowship 790
Wingate Scholarships 697

Middle East

International Postgraduate Research Scholarships (IPRS) 413
ORSAS Awards 688

New Zealand

ORSAS Awards 688
Wingate Scholarships 697

South Africa

International Postgraduate Research Scholarships (IPRS) 413
ORSAS Awards 688
Wingate Scholarships 697

United Kingdom

Aberystwyth Postgraduate Research Studentships 4
Access to Learning Fund 685
AHRC Doctoral Awards Scheme 109
Balsdon Fellowship 174
BIAA Travel Grants 168
The Costume Society Museum Placement Award 246
The Costume Society Student Bursary 247
Frances A Yates Fellowships 789
Frank Knox Fellowships at Harvard University 302
Giles Worsley Travel Fellowship 174
Grete Sondheimer Fellowship 790
Hector and Elizabeth Catling Bursary 173
International Postgraduate Research Scholarships (IPRS) 413
Kennedy Scholarships 409
The Pilgrim Trust Grants 476
Professional Preparation Master's Scheme
Research Preparation Master's Scheme
Rome Awards 175
Rome Fellowship 175
Rome Scholarships in Ancient, Medieval and Later Italian Studies 176
Sargant Fellowship in Critical and Curatorial Studies 176
University of Kent School of Drama, Film and Visual Arts Scholarships 700
Wingate Scholarships 697

United States of America

ACC Fellowship Grants Program 115
ARCE Fellowships 80
British Marshall Scholarships 685
Fulbright Distinguished Chairs Program 248
Fulbright Senior Specialists Program 249
Gilbert Chinard Fellowships 361
Gladys Krieble Delmas Foundation Grants 319
Harmon Chadbourn Rorison Fellowship 361
International Postgraduate Research Scholarships (IPRS) 413
IREX Individual Advanced Research Opportunities 388
Kennan Institute Research Scholarship 408
KRESS/ARIT Pre-Doctoral Fellowship in the History of Art and Archaeology 81
National Endowment for the Humanities Fellowships 348
ORSAS Awards 688
Sally Kress Tompkins Fellowship 608
SSRC JSPS Postdoctoral Fellowship 599
Vatican Film Library Mellon Fellowship 785

West European Countries

International Postgraduate Research Scholarships (IPRS) 413
University of Kent School of Drama, Film and Visual Arts Scholarships 700

AESTHETICS

Any Country

ASCSA Fellowships 82
BIAA Post-Doctoral Research Fellowship 168
BIAA Research Scholarship 168
BIAA Study Grants 168
British Academy Overseas Conference Grants 158
British Academy Worldwide Congress Grant 159
British Conference Grants 159
Camargo Fellowships 182
Henry Moore Institute Research Fellowship 338
Kanner Fellowship In British Studies 640
United States Holocaust Memorial Museum Center for Advanced Holocaust Studies Visiting Scholar Programs 641

African Nations

International Postgraduate Research Scholarships (IPRS) 413

Australia

Wingate Scholarships 697

Canada

International Postgraduate Research Scholarships (IPRS) 413
Wingate Scholarships 697

Caribbean Countries

International Postgraduate Research Scholarships (IPRS) 413

East European Countries

International Postgraduate Research Scholarships (IPRS) 413

European Union

AHRC Doctoral Awards Scheme 109
Professional Preparation Master's Scheme
Research Preparation Master's Scheme
Wingate Scholarships 697

Middle East

International Postgraduate Research Scholarships (IPRS) 413

New Zealand

Wingate Scholarships 697

South Africa

International Postgraduate Research Scholarships (IPRS) 413
Wingate Scholarships 697

United Kingdom

AHRC Doctoral Awards Scheme 109
International Postgraduate Research Scholarships (IPRS) 413
Professional Preparation Master's Scheme
Research Preparation Master's Scheme
University of Kent School of European Culture and Languages Scholarships 701
University of Kent School of European Culture and Languages Studentships 701
Wingate Scholarships 697

United States of America

ACC Fellowship Grants Program 115
British Marshall Scholarships 685
International Postgraduate Research Scholarships (IPRS) 413
SSRC JSPS Postdoctoral Fellowship 599

West European Countries

International Postgraduate Research Scholarships (IPRS) 413
University of Kent School of European Culture and Languages Scholarships 701
University of Kent School of European Culture and Languages Studentships 701

ART MANAGEMENT

Any Country

BIAA Travel Grants 168
The Getty Foundation Curatorial Research Fellowships 316
Jacob's Pillow Intern Program
Metropolitan Museum of Art Summer Internships for College Students 447
Metropolitan Museum of Art Summer Internships for Graduate Students 447
WSW Internships 802

African Nations

International Postgraduate Research Scholarships (IPRS) 413

Australia

Wingate Scholarships 697

Canada

International Postgraduate Research Scholarships (IPRS) 413
Wingate Scholarships 697

Caribbean Countries

International Postgraduate Research Scholarships (IPRS) 413

East European Countries

ArtsLink Independent Projects 221
ArtsLink Residencies 222
International Postgraduate Research Scholarships (IPRS) 413

European Union

AHRC Doctoral Awards Scheme 109
Professional Preparation Master's Scheme
Research Preparation Master's Scheme
Wingate Scholarships 697

Middle East

International Postgraduate Research Scholarships (IPRS) 413

New Zealand

Wingate Scholarships 697

South Africa

International Postgraduate Research Scholarships (IPRS) 413
Wingate Scholarships 697

United Kingdom

AHRC Doctoral Awards Scheme 109
BIAA Travel Grants 168
International Postgraduate Research Scholarships (IPRS) 413
Professional Preparation Master's Scheme
Research Preparation Master's Scheme
Sargant Fellowship in Critical and Curatorial Studies 176
Wingate Scholarships 697

United States of America

ACC Fellowship Grants Program 115
Congress Bundestag Youth Exchange for Young Professionals 221
International Postgraduate Research Scholarships (IPRS) 413

West European Countries

International Postgraduate Research Scholarships (IPRS) 413

DRAWING AND PAINTING

Any Country

Abbey Harris Mural Fund 3
Akademie Schloss Solitude Fellowships 12
The Alastair Salvesen Art Scholarship 570
ASCSA Advanced Fellowships 82
Austro-American Association of Boston Stipend 143
Banff Centre Financial Assistance 144
Camargo Fellowships 182
The Dawn Jolliffe Botanical Art Bursary 567
Don Freeman Memorial Grant-in-Aid 610
Fine Arts Work Center in Provincetown Fellowships 291
Frederick Douglass Institute Postdoctoral Fellowship 304
Frederick Douglass Institute Predoctoral Dissertation Fellowship 304
Gottlieb Foundation Emergency Assistance Grants 8
Gottlieb Foundation Individual Support Grants 8
Hambidge Residency Program Scholarships 331
Haystack Scholarship 333
Jacob Hirsch Fellowship 83
The John Kinross Memorial Fund Student Scholarships/RSA 570
MacDowell Colony Residencies 429
Mackendrick Scholarship 321
MICA Fellowship 435
Ohio Arts Council Individual Creativity Excellence Awards 510
Paul D. Fleck Fellowships in the Arts 144
Pollock-Krasner Foundation Grant 534
Rhodes University Postdoctoral Fellowship and The Andrew Mellon Postdoctoral Fellowship 548
Sir William Gillies Bequest-Hospitalfield Trust 570
St Catherine's College Graduate Scholarship in the Arts
University of Southampton Postgraduate Studentships 759
William and Mary Armour Fellowships 322
Wolf Foundation Prizes 799
World Universities Network (WUN) International Research Mobility Scheme 759

African Nations

International Postgraduate Research Scholarships (IPRS) 413

Australia

AAH Humanities Travelling Fellowships 132
Fulbright Postgraduate Student Award for the Visual and Performing Arts 140
Marten Bequest Travelling Scholarships 220
Portia Geach Memorial Award 221

Canada

Canada Council Grants for Professional Artists 198
Canada Council Travel Grants 198
CFUW Elizabeth Massey Award 207
International Postgraduate Research Scholarships (IPRS) 413
Vatican Film Library Mellon Fellowship 785

Caribbean Countries

International Postgraduate Research Scholarships (IPRS) 413

East European Countries

ArtsLink Independent Projects 221
ArtsLink Residencies 222
International Postgraduate Research Scholarships (IPRS) 413

European Union

AHRC Doctoral Awards Scheme 109
Professional Preparation Master's Scheme
Research Preparation Master's Scheme

Middle East

AICF Sharett Scholarship Program 24
International Postgraduate Research Scholarships (IPRS) 413

South Africa

International Postgraduate Research Scholarships (IPRS) 413

United Kingdom

Abbey Awards 3
Abbey Fellowships in Painting 173
Abbey Scholarship in Painting 174
Aberystwyth Postgraduate Research Studentships 4
AHRC Doctoral Awards Scheme 109
Arts Council England Helen Chadwick Fellowship 174
Arts Council of Northern Ireland Fellowship 174
The Dawn Jolliffe Botanical Art Bursary 567
Derek Hill Foundation Scholarship 174
ESU Chautauqua Institution Scholarships 280
Friends of Israel Educational Foundation Young Artist Award 305
Hector and Elizabeth Catling Bursary 173
International Postgraduate Research Scholarships (IPRS) 413
Portia Geach Memorial Award 221
Professional Preparation Master's Scheme
Research Preparation Master's Scheme
Rome Scholarships in the Fine Arts 176
Sainsbury Scholarship in Painting and Sculpture 176
Sargant Fellowship 176

United States of America

Abbey Awards 3
Abbey Fellowships in Painting 173
Abbey Scholarship in Painting 174
ACC Fellowship Grants Program 115
Fulbright Senior Specialists Program 249
Harriet Hale Woolley Scholarships 297
International Postgraduate Research Scholarships (IPRS) 413
John F and Anna Lee Stacey Scholarships 404
Selma Naifeh Scholarship Fund 510
Twining Humber Award for Lifetime Artistic Achievement 109
Vatican Film Library Mellon Fellowship 785
Virginia Liebeler Biennial Grants for Mature Women (Art) 484
Virginia Liebeler Biennial Grants for Mature Women (Music) 484
Virginia Liebeler Biennial Grants for Mature Women (Writing) 484

West European Countries

International Postgraduate Research Scholarships (IPRS) 413

SCULPTURE

Any Country

The Alastair Salvesen Art Scholarship 570
ASCSA Advanced Fellowships 82
ASCSA Fellowships 82
Banff Centre Financial Assistance 144
Camargo Fellowships 182
Fine Arts Work Center in Provincetown Fellowships 291
Frederick Douglass Institute Predoctoral Dissertation Fellowship 304
Glenis Horn Scholarship 510
Gottlieb Foundation Emergency Assistance Grants 8
Gottlieb Foundation Individual Support Grants 8
Hambidge Residency Program Scholarships 331
Haystack Scholarship 333
Henry Moore Institute Research Fellowship 338
Hugh Last and Donald Atkinson Funds Committee Grants 604
Jacob Hirsch Fellowship 83
John Keppie Scholarship 321
The John Kinross Memorial Fund Student Scholarships/RSA 570
MacDowell Colony Residencies 429
MICA Fellowship 435
NEH Fellowships 83
Ohio Arts Council Individual Creativity Excellence Awards 510
Paul D. Fleck Fellowships in the Arts 144
Pollock-Krasner Foundation Grant 534
Rhodes University Postdoctoral Fellowship and The Andrew Mellon Postdoctoral Fellowship 548
Sir William Gillies Bequest-Hospitalfield Trust 570
St Catherine's College Graduate Scholarship in the Arts
Studio Residency Grant 802
University of Southampton Postgraduate Studentships 759

Wolf Foundation Prizes 799
World Universities Network (WUN) International Research Mobility Scheme 759

African Nations

International Postgraduate Research Scholarships (IPRS) 413

Australia

AAH Humanities Travelling Fellowships 132
Fulbright Postgraduate Student Award for the Visual and Performing Arts 140
Marten Bequest Travelling Scholarships 220

Canada

Canada Council Grants for Professional Artists 198
Canada Council Travel Grants 198
CFUW Elizabeth Massey Award 207
International Postgraduate Research Scholarships (IPRS) 413

Caribbean Countries

International Postgraduate Research Scholarships (IPRS) 413

East European Countries

ArtsLink Independent Projects 221
ArtsLink Residencies 222
International Postgraduate Research Scholarships (IPRS) 413

European Union

AHRC Doctoral Awards Scheme 109
Professional Preparation Master's Scheme
Research Preparation Master's Scheme

Middle East

AICF Sharett Scholarship Program 24
International Postgraduate Research Scholarships (IPRS) 413

South Africa

International Postgraduate Research Scholarships (IPRS) 413

United Kingdom

AHRC Doctoral Awards Scheme 109
Arts Council England Helen Chadwick Fellowship 174
Arts Council of Northern Ireland Fellowship 174
ESU Chautauqua Institution Scholarships 280
Hector and Elizabeth Catling Bursary 173
International Postgraduate Research Scholarships (IPRS) 413
Professional Preparation Master's Scheme
Research Preparation Master's Scheme
Rome Scholarships in the Fine Arts 176
Sainsbury Scholarship in Painting and Sculpture 176
Sargant Fellowship 176

United States of America

ACC Fellowship Grants Program 115
Edith Franklin Pottery Scholarship 634
Fulbright Senior Specialists Program 249
Harriet Hale Woolley Scholarships 297
International Postgraduate Research Scholarships (IPRS) 413
Socrates Sculpture Park Emerging Artist Fellowship Program 613
Twining Humber Award for Lifetime Artistic Achievement 109
Virginia Liebeler Biennial Grants for Mature Women (Art) 484
Virginia Liebeler Biennial Grants for Mature Women (Music) 484
Virginia Liebeler Biennial Grants for Mature Women (Writing) 484

West European Countries

International Postgraduate Research Scholarships (IPRS) 413

HANDICRAFTS

Any Country

Hambidge Residency Program Scholarships 331
Haystack Scholarship 333

HSA Grant for Educators 338
Ohio Arts Council Individual Creativity Excellence Awards 510

African Nations

International Postgraduate Research Scholarships (IPRS) 413

Australia

AAH Humanities Travelling Fellowships 132
Fulbright Postgraduate Student Award for the Visual and Performing Arts 140
Wingate Scholarships 697

Canada

International Postgraduate Research Scholarships (IPRS) 413
Wingate Scholarships 697

Caribbean Countries

International Postgraduate Research Scholarships (IPRS) 413

East European Countries

International Postgraduate Research Scholarships (IPRS) 413

European Union

AHRC Doctoral Awards Scheme 109
Professional Preparation Master's Scheme
Research Preparation Master's Scheme
Wingate Scholarships 697

Middle East

International Postgraduate Research Scholarships (IPRS) 413

New Zealand

Wingate Scholarships 697

South Africa

International Postgraduate Research Scholarships (IPRS) 413
Wingate Scholarships 697

United Kingdom

AHRC Doctoral Awards Scheme 109
The Costume Society Student Bursary 247
The Costume Society Yarwood Award 247
International Postgraduate Research Scholarships (IPRS) 413
Professional Preparation Master's Scheme
Research Preparation Master's Scheme
Wingate Scholarships 697

United States of America

ACC Fellowship Grants Program 115
International Postgraduate Research Scholarships (IPRS) 413
Twining Humber Award for Lifetime Artistic Achievement 109
Virginia Liebeler Biennial Grants for Mature Women (Art) 484

West European Countries

International Postgraduate Research Scholarships (IPRS) 413
Janson Johan Helmich Scholarships and Travel Grants 398

MUSIC

Any Country

Ahmanson and Getty Postdoctoral Fellowships 639
Akademie Schloss Solitude Fellowships 12
Allcard Grants 806
Alvin H Johnson AMS 50 Dissertation One Year Fellowships 68
AMS Subventions for Publications 68
AMSA World Piano Competition 68
ARD International Music Competition Munich 104
Arthur Rubinstein International Piano Master Competition 108
ASCSA Advanced Fellowships 82
Austro-American Association of Boston Stipend 143
Banff Centre Financial Assistance 144

African Nations

Australia

Canada

Caribbean Countries

European Union

Middle East

New Zealand

South Africa

United Kingdom

United States of America

ASCAP Foundation Morton Gould Young Composer Awards
ASOL Orchestra Management Fellowship Program 95
Charles Z. Moore Memorial Scholarship Fund 634
Fromm Foundation Commission 305
Fulbright Senior Specialists Program 249
Gilbert Chinard Fellowships 361
Harmon Chadbourn Rorison Fellowship 361
Harriet Hale Woolley Scholarships 297
Howard Mayer Brown Fellowship 69
MetLife Creative Connections 443
Music Alive 443
Otto Kinkeldey Award 69
TMCF Scholarships 633
Vatican Film Library Mellon Fellowship 785
Virginia Liebeler Biennial Grants for Mature Women (Art) 484
Virginia Liebeler Biennial Grants for Mature Women (Music) 484
Virginia Liebeler Biennial Grants for Mature Women (Writing) 484

West European Countries

Donatella Flick Conducting Competition 269
Maisie Lewis Young Artists Fund 807
Mr and Mrs David Edward Memorial Award 145
University of Otago Master's Awards 717

MUSICOLOGY

Any Country

Ahmanson and Getty Postdoctoral Fellowships 639
Alvin H Johnson AMS 50 Dissertation One Year Fellowships 68
AMS Subventions for Publications 68
ASECS (American Society for 18th-Century Studies)/Clark Library
   Fellowships 639
British Academy Overseas Conference Grants 158
British Academy Small Research Grants 158
British Academy Worldwide Congress Grant 159
British Conference Grants 159
Camargo Fellowships 182
Clark Library Short-Term Resident Fellowships 639
Clark Predoctoral Fellowships 639
Clark-Huntington Joint Bibliographical Fellowship 640
Earthwatch Field Research Grants 272
Findel Scholarships and Schneider Scholarships 340
Kanner Fellowship In British Studies 640
Kurt Weill Foundation for Music Grants Program 412
Noah Greenberg Award 69
Paul A Pisk Prize 69
Royal College of Music Scholarships 557
Society for the Study of French History Bursaries 606
United States Holocaust Memorial Museum Center for Advanced
   Holocaust Studies Visiting Scholar Programs 641

Australia

Wingate Scholarships 697

Canada

Alfred Einstein Award 68
Howard Mayer Brown Fellowship 69
Otto Kinkeldey Award 69
Wingate Scholarships 697

East European Countries

Mellon Postdoctoral Fellowships In Turkey For East European
   Scholars 81

European Union

AHRC Doctoral Awards Scheme 109
Professional Preparation Master's Scheme
Research Preparation Master's Scheme
Wingate Scholarships 697

New Zealand

Wingate Scholarships 697

South Africa

SAMRO Postgraduate Bursaries for Indigenous African Music Study
   616
Wingate Scholarships 697

United Kingdom

AHRC Doctoral Awards Scheme 109
Frank Knox Fellowships at Harvard University 302
Kennedy Scholarships 409
Mr and Mrs David Edward Memorial Award 145
Professional Preparation Master's Scheme
Research Preparation Master's Scheme
Wingate Scholarships 697

United States of America

ACC Fellowship Grants Program 115
Alfred Einstein Award 68
American Academy in Berlin Prize Fellowships 24
ARCE Fellowships 80
Fulbright Distinguished Chairs Program 248
Fulbright Senior Specialists Program 249
Gladys Krieble Delmas Foundation Grants 319
Howard Mayer Brown Fellowship 69
IREX Individual Advanced Research Opportunities 388
Otto Kinkeldey Award 69
Virginia Liebeler Biennial Grants for Mature Women (Music) 484

West European Countries

Mr and Mrs David Edward Memorial Award 145

MUSIC THEORY AND COMPOSITION

Any Country

Camargo Fellowships 182
Cleveland Institute of Music Scholarships and Accompanying
   Fellowships 238
Hambidge Residency Program Scholarships 331
MacDowell Colony Residencies 429
National Association of Composers Young Composers Competition
   467
Ohio Arts Council Individual Creativity Excellence Awards 510
Queen Elisabeth International Music Competition of Belgium 538
Royal College of Music Scholarships 557
RPS Composition Prize 570
Susan and Graeme Mc Donald Music Scholarships 144
United States Holocaust Memorial Museum Center for Advanced
   Holocaust Studies Visiting Scholar Programs 641
Wolf Foundation Prizes 799

Australia

Countess of Munster Musical Trust Awards 252
Wingate Scholarships 697

Canada

Countess of Munster Musical Trust Awards 252
Robert Fleming Prize 199
Wingate Scholarships 697

European Union

AHRC Doctoral Awards Scheme 109
Professional Preparation Master's Scheme
Research Preparation Master's Scheme
Wingate Scholarships 697

Middle East

AICF Sharett Scholarship Program 24

New Zealand

Countess of Munster Musical Trust Awards 252
Wingate Scholarships 697

South Africa

Countess of Munster Musical Trust Awards 252
SAMRO Intermediate Bursaries for Composition Study In Southern
Africa 616
SAMRO Overseas Scholarship 616
Wingate Scholarships 697

United Kingdom

AHRC Doctoral Awards Scheme 109
Countess of Munster Musical Trust Awards 252
Frank Knox Fellowships at Harvard University 302
Kennedy Scholarships 409
Mr and Mrs David Edward Memorial Award 145
Professional Preparation Master's Scheme
Research Preparation Master's Scheme
Wingate Scholarships 697

United States of America

ACC Fellowship Grants Program 115
American Academy in Berlin Prize Fellowships 24
American Music Center Composer Assistance Program 68
ASCAP Foundation Morton Gould Young Composer Awards
Commissioning Music/USA 442
Fromm Foundation Commission 305
Virginia Liebeler Biennial Grants for Mature Women (Art) 484
Virginia Liebeler Biennial Grants for Mature Women (Music) 484
Virginia Liebeler Biennial Grants for Mature Women (Writing) 484

West European Countries

Mr and Mrs David Edward Memorial Award 145

CONDUCTING

Any Country

Cleveland Institute of Music Scholarships and Accompanying
Fellowships 238
Royal College of Music Scholarships 557
WBDI Scholarship Awards 800
Wolf Foundation Prizes 799

Australia

Wingate Scholarships 697

Canada

Wingate Scholarships 697

European Union

AHRC Doctoral Awards Scheme 109
Professional Preparation Master's Scheme
Research Preparation Master's Scheme
Wingate Scholarships 697

Middle East

AICF Sharett Scholarship Program 24

New Zealand

Wingate Scholarships 697

South Africa

Wingate Scholarships 697

United Kingdom

AHRC Doctoral Awards Scheme 109
Mr and Mrs David Edward Memorial Award 145
Professional Preparation Master's Scheme
Research Preparation Master's Scheme
Wingate Scholarships 697

United States of America

ACC Fellowship Grants Program 115
Virginia Liebeler Biennial Grants for Mature Women (Music) 484

West European Countries

Donatella Flick Conducting Competition 269
Mr and Mrs David Edward Memorial Award 145

SINGING

Any Country

ARD International Music Competition Munich 104
Associated Board of the Royal Schools of Music Scholarships
117
Banff Centre Financial Assistance 144
Cleveland Institute of Music Scholarships and Accompanying
Fellowships 238
Feiweles Trust Bursary 810
Hambidge Residency Program Scholarships 331
International Robert Schumann Competition 392
Loren L Zachary National Vocal Competition for Young Opera Singers
426
Marcella Sembrich Memorial Voice Scholarship Competition 411
Maria Callas International Music Competition 125
MBF Music Education Awards 461
Miriam Licette Scholarships 462
Paul D. Fleck Fellowships in the Arts 144
Prize Winner of the ARD International Music Competition Munich
104
Queen Elisabeth International Music Competition of Belgium 538
Richard Tauber Prize for Singers 101
Royal College of Music Scholarships 557
Susan and Graeme Mc Donald Music Scholarships 144

African Nations

ROSL Annual Music Competition 551

Australia

Australian Music Foundation Award 136
Countess of Munster Musical Trust Awards 252
Marten Bequest Travelling Scholarships 220
ROSL Annual Music Competition 551
Sir Robert William Askin Operatic Travelling Scholarship
Wingate Scholarships 697

Canada

Countess of Munster Musical Trust Awards 252
ROSL Annual Music Competition 551
Ruth Watson Henderson Choral Competition 235
Wingate Scholarships 697

Caribbean Countries

ROSL Annual Music Competition 551

European Union

AHRC Doctoral Awards Scheme 109
Philip and Dorothy Green Award for Young Concert Artists in
Association with Making Music 430
Professional Preparation Master's Scheme
Research Preparation Master's Scheme
Wingate Scholarships 697

Middle East

AICF Sharett Scholarship Program 24

New Zealand

Countess of Munster Musical Trust Awards 252
ROSL Annual Music Competition 551
Wingate Scholarships 697

South Africa

Countess of Munster Musical Trust Awards 252
ROSL Annual Music Competition 551
SAMRO Overseas Scholarship 616
Wingate Scholarships 697

United Kingdom

AHRC Doctoral Awards Scheme 109
Countess of Munster Musical Trust Awards 252
Philip and Dorothy Green Award for Young Concert Artists in
    Association with Making Music 430
Professional Preparation Master's Scheme
Research Preparation Master's Scheme
ROSL Annual Music Competition 551
Wingate Scholarships 697

United States of America

ACC Fellowship Grants Program 115
Virginia Liebeler Biennial Grants for Mature Women (Music) 484

MUSICAL INSTRUMENTS (PERFORMANCE)

Any Country

AMSA World Piano Competition 68
ARD International Music Competition Munich 104
Arthur Rubinstein International Piano Master Competition 108
Associated Board of the Royal Schools of Music Scholarships 117
Banff Centre Financial Assistance 144
Budapest International Music Competition 180
Chopin Piano Competition 410
Clara Haskil Competition 237
Cleveland Institute of Music Scholarships and Accompanying
    Fellowships 238
Eric Thompson Charitable Trust for Organists 283
Foundation Busoni International Piano Competition 289
Guilhermina Suggia Gift 461
Hambidge Residency Program Scholarships 331
Hattori Foundation Awards 333
Henry Rudolf Meisels Bursary Awards 416
International Beethoven Piano Competition Vienna 377
International Frederic Chopin Piano Competition 303
International Géza Anda Piano Competition 317
International Harp Contest in Israel 383
International Paulo Cello Competition 523
International Robert Schumann Competition 392
International Violin Competition–Premio Paganini 392
John E Mortimer Foundation Awards 532
June Allison Award 532
Leeds International Pianoforte Competition Award 416
London International String Quartet Competition 426
Manoug Parikian Award 461
Maria Callas International Music Competition 125
Martin Musical Scholarships 532
MBF Music Education Awards 461
National Orchestral Institute Scholarships 486
Noah Greenberg Award 69
Paloma O'Shea Santander International Piano Competition 519
Paul D. Fleck Fellowships in the Arts 144
Peter Whittingham Award 462
Prize Winner of the ARD International Music Competition Munich 104
Queen Elisabeth International Music Competition of Belgium 538
RCO Various Open Award Bequests 561
Reginald Conway Memorial Award for String Performers
Royal College of Music Scholarships 557
Sidney Perry Scholarship 532
Susan and Graeme Mc Donald Music Scholarships 144
William Robertshaw Exhibition 561
Wolf Foundation Prizes 799

African Nations

ROSL Annual Music Competition 551

Australia

Australian Music Foundation Award 136
Countess of Munster Musical Trust Awards 252
Marten Bequest Travelling Scholarships 220
ROSL Annual Music Competition 551
Wingate Scholarships 697

Canada

Countess of Munster Musical Trust Awards 252
ROSL Annual Music Competition 551
Wingate Scholarships 697

Caribbean Countries

ROSL Annual Music Competition 551

East European Countries

ArtsLink Independent Projects 221
ArtsLink Residencies 222

European Union

AHRC Doctoral Awards Scheme 109
Philip and Dorothy Green Award for Young Concert Artists in
    Association with Making Music 430
Professional Preparation Master's Scheme
Research Preparation Master's Scheme
Wingate Scholarships 697

Middle East

AICF Sharett Scholarship Program 24

New Zealand

Countess of Munster Musical Trust Awards 252
ROSL Annual Music Competition 551
Wingate Scholarships 697

South Africa

Countess of Munster Musical Trust Awards 252
ROSL Annual Music Competition 551
SAMRO Overseas Scholarship 616
Wingate Scholarships 697

United Kingdom

AHRC Doctoral Awards Scheme 109
Countess of Munster Musical Trust Awards 252
Emanual Hurwitz Award for Violinists of British Nationality 532
Mr and Mrs David Edward Memorial Award 145
Philip and Dorothy Green Award for Young Concert Artists in
    Association with Making Music 430
Professional Preparation Master's Scheme
Research Preparation Master's Scheme
ROSL Annual Music Competition 551
Wingate Scholarships 697

United States of America

ACC Fellowship Grants Program 115
ASOL Orchestra Management Fellowship Program 95
J P Morgan Chase Regrant Program for Small Ensembles 442
MetLife Creative Connections 443
Music Alive 443

West European Countries

Maisie Lewis Young Artists Fund 807
Mr and Mrs David Edward Memorial Award 145

RELIGIOUS MUSIC

Any Country

Jacob Hirsch Fellowship 83
Kanner Fellowship In British Studies 640
Royal College of Music Scholarships 557
United States Holocaust Memorial Museum Center for Advanced
    Holocaust Studies Visiting Scholar Programs 641

Australia

Wingate Scholarships 697

Canada

Wingate Scholarships 697

European Union

AHRC Doctoral Awards Scheme 109
Professional Preparation Master's Scheme
Research Preparation Master's Scheme
Wingate Scholarships 697

New Zealand

Wingate Scholarships 697

South Africa

Wingate Scholarships 697

United Kingdom

AHRC Doctoral Awards Scheme 109
Professional Preparation Master's Scheme
Research Preparation Master's Scheme
Wingate Scholarships 697

United States of America

ACC Fellowship Grants Program 115
IREX Individual Advanced Research Opportunities 388
Virginia Liebeler Biennial Grants for Mature Women (Music) 484

JAZZ AND POPULAR MUSIC

Any Country

Banff Centre Financial Assistance 144
Frederick Douglass Institute Postdoctoral Fellowship 304
Frederick Douglass Institute Predoctoral Dissertation Fellowship 304
Kurt Weill Foundation for Music Grants Program 412
MBF Music Education Awards 461
Paul D. Fleck Fellowships in the Arts 144
Peter Whittingham Award 462
Susan and Graeme Mc Donald Music Scholarships 144

Australia

Wingate Scholarships 697

Canada

Wingate Scholarships 697

European Union

AHRC Doctoral Awards Scheme 109
Professional Preparation Master's Scheme
Research Preparation Master's Scheme
Wingate Scholarships 697

Middle East

AICF Sharett Scholarship Program 24

New Zealand

Wingate Scholarships 697

South Africa

SAMRO Intermediate Bursaries for Composition Study In Southern
  Africa 616
SAMRO Overseas Scholarship 616
Wingate Scholarships 697

United Kingdom

AHRC Doctoral Awards Scheme 109
Professional Preparation Master's Scheme
Research Preparation Master's Scheme
Wingate Scholarships 697

United States of America

ACC Fellowship Grants Program 115
Charles Z. Moore Memorial Scholarship Fund 634
Virginia Liebeler Biennial Grants for Mature Women (Music) 484

OPERA

Any Country

Banff Centre Financial Assistance 144
Camargo Fellowships 182
Cleveland Institute of Music Scholarships and Accompanying
  Fellowships 238
Kurt Weill Foundation for Music Grants Program 412
Loren L Zachary National Vocal Competition for Young Opera Singers
  426
Maria Callas International Music Competition 125
MBF Music Education Awards 461
Paul D. Fleck Fellowships in the Arts 144
Queen Elisabeth International Music Competition of Belgium 538
Royal College of Music Scholarships 557
Society for the Study of French History Bursaries 606

Australia

Countess of Munster Musical Trust Awards 252
Marten Bequest Travelling Scholarships 220
Sir Robert William Askin Operatic Travelling Scholarship
Wingate Scholarships 697

Canada

Countess of Munster Musical Trust Awards 252
Wingate Scholarships 697

European Union

AHRC Doctoral Awards Scheme 109
Professional Preparation Master's Scheme
Research Preparation Master's Scheme
Wingate Scholarships 697

Middle East

AICF Sharett Scholarship Program 24

New Zealand

Countess of Munster Musical Trust Awards 252
Wingate Scholarships 697

South Africa

Countess of Munster Musical Trust Awards 252
Wingate Scholarships 697

United Kingdom

AHRC Doctoral Awards Scheme 109
Countess of Munster Musical Trust Awards 252
Professional Preparation Master's Scheme
Research Preparation Master's Scheme
Wingate Scholarships 697

United States of America

ACC Fellowship Grants Program 115
Virginia Liebeler Biennial Grants for Mature Women (Music) 484

DRAMA

Any Country

AIIS Senior Performing and Creative Arts Fellowships 61
Akademie Schloss Solitude Fellowships 12
Alfred Bradley Bursary Award 146
ASCSA Advanced Fellowships 82
ASCSA Fellowships 82
Austro-American Association of Boston Stipend 143
Banff Centre Financial Assistance 144
British Academy Overseas Conference Grants 158
British Academy Research Development Awards (BARDAs) 158
British Academy Small Research Grants 158
British Academy Worldwide Congress Grant 159
British Conference Grants 159
Fine Arts Work Center in Provincetown Fellowships 291

Home Hewson Scholarship 681
Jacob Hirsch Fellowship 83
Kanner Fellowship In British Studies 640
La Trobe University Postgraduate Scholarship 414
MacDowell Colony Residencies 429
NEH Fellowships 83
Ohio Arts Council Individual Creativity Excellence Awards 510
Onassis Foreigners' Fellowships Programme Research Grants
  Category AI 15
Paul D. Fleck Fellowships in the Arts 144
Queen Mary Research Studentships 539
Quinn, Nathan and Edmond Scholarships 706
Rhodes University Postdoctoral Fellowship and The Andrew Mellon
  Postdoctoral Fellowship 548
Society for Theatre Research Awards 607
University of Bristol Postgraduate Scholarships 672
University of Kent School of Drama, Film and Visual Arts Scholarships
  700
Victoria University of Wellington PhD Scholarships 786

Australia

AAH Humanities Travelling Fellowships 132
Fulbright Postgraduate Student Award for the Visual and Performing
  Arts 140
Marten Bequest Travelling Scholarships 220
Theatre Initiative Dramaturgy Fellowship 131
Theatre Initiative-Playing the World 131

Canada

Canada Council Grants for Professional Artists 198
J B C Watkins Award 199

East European Countries

ArtsLink Independent Projects 221
ArtsLink Residencies 222

European Union

AHRC Doctoral Awards Scheme 109
MA in Literature, Film, and Theatre Studies Scholarship 688
PhD in Literature, Film and Theatre Studies Studentship 688
Professional Preparation Master's Scheme
Research Preparation Master's Scheme

Middle East

AICF Sharett Scholarship Program 24

United Kingdom

Aberystwyth Postgraduate Research Studentships 4
AHRC Doctoral Awards Scheme 109
The Costume Society Student Bursary 247
The Costume Society Yarwood Award 247
Professional Preparation Master's Scheme
Research Preparation Master's Scheme
University of Kent School of Drama, Film and Visual Arts Scholarships
  700

United States of America

ACC Fellowship Grants Program 115
British Marshall Scholarships 685
Fulbright Senior Specialists Program 249
TMCF Scholarships 633
Virginia Liebeler Biennial Grants for Mature Women (Music) 484

West European Countries

University of Kent School of Drama, Film and Visual Arts Scholarships
  700

DANCING

Any Country

Akademie Schloss Solitude Fellowships 12
ASCSA Advanced Fellowships 82

ASCSA Fellowships 82
Banff Centre Financial Assistance 144
British Academy Overseas Conference Grants 158
British Academy Research Development Awards (BARDAs)
  158
British Academy Small Research Grants 158
British Academy Worldwide Congress Grant 159
British Conference Grants 159
Earthwatch Field Research Grants 272
Feiweles Trust Bursary 810
Hambidge Residency Program Scholarships 331
Jacob Hirsch Fellowship 83
Jacob's Pillow Intern Program
NEH Fellowships 83
Onassis Foreigners' Fellowships Programme Research Grants
  Category AI 15
Paul D. Fleck Fellowships in the Arts 144
Queen Mary Research Studentships 539
The Rebecca Skelton Scholarship 542
Rhodes University Postdoctoral Fellowship and The Andrew Mellon
  Postdoctoral Fellowship 548
University of Kent School of Drama, Film and Visual Arts Scholarships
  700

Australia

AAH Humanities Travelling Fellowships 132
Dance Artform Development 127
Dance Cite International des Arts Residency 127
Dance New Work Creative Development 127
Dance New Work Production 127
Dance Presentation and Promotion 128
Dance Program 128
Dance Skill and Arts Development–Skills Development for Young
  Emerging Artists 128
Fulbright Postgraduate Student Award for the Visual and Performing
  Arts 140
Lady Mollie Isabelle Askin Ballet Travelling Scholarship 220
Marten Bequest Travelling Scholarships 220
OZCO Dance Fellowship 130
OZCO Dance Grant Initiative: Take Your Partner 130

Canada

Canada Council Grants for Professional Artists 198

East European Countries

ArtsLink Independent Projects 221
ArtsLink Residencies 222

European Union

AHRC Doctoral Awards Scheme 109
Professional Preparation Master's Scheme
Research Preparation Master's Scheme

Middle East

AICF Sharett Scholarship Program 24

United Kingdom

AHRC Doctoral Awards Scheme 109
Professional Preparation Master's Scheme
Research Preparation Master's Scheme
University of Kent School of Drama, Film and Visual Arts Scholarships
  700

United States of America

ACC Fellowship Grants Program 115
Fulbright Senior Specialists Program 249
TMCF Scholarships 633

West European Countries

University of Kent School of Drama, Film and Visual Arts Scholarships
  700

PHOTOGRAPHY

Any Country

Akademie Schloss Solitude Fellowships 12
AMIA Kodak Fellowship in Film Preservation 121
Banff Centre Financial Assistance 144
British Academy Overseas Conference Grants 158
British Academy Research Development Awards (BARDAs) 158
British Academy Small Research Grants 158
British Academy Worldwide Congress Grant 159
British Conference Grants 159
Camargo Fellowships 182
CCP Ansel Adams Research Fellowship 223
Hambidge Residency Program Scholarships 331
Jacob's Pillow Intern Program
Library Company of Philadelphia and Historical Society of Pennsyl-
vania Research Fellowships in American History and Culture 422
Light Work Artist-in-Residence Program 423
MacDowell Colony Residencies 429
MICA Fellowship 435
Ohio Arts Council Individual Creativity Excellence Awards 510
Onassis Foreigners' Fellowships Programme Research Grants
Category AI 15
Paul D. Fleck Fellowships in the Arts 144
Rhodes University Postdoctoral Fellowship and The Andrew Mellon
Postdoctoral Fellowship 548
University of Kent School of Drama, Film and Visual Arts Scholarships
700
W Eugene Smith Grant in Humanistic Photography 788
WSW Artists Fellowships 802
WSW Artists' Book Residencies 802
WSW Hands-On-Art Visiting Artist Project 802
WSW Internships 802

Australia

Fulbright Postgraduate Student Award for the Visual and Performing
Arts 140

Canada

Canada Council Grants for Professional Artists 198

East European Countries

ArtsLink Residencies 222

European Union

AHRC Doctoral Awards Scheme 109
Professional Preparation Master's Scheme
Research Preparation Master's Scheme

Middle East

AICF Sharett Scholarship Program 24

United Kingdom

AHRC Doctoral Awards Scheme 109
Arts Council England Helen Chadwick Fellowship 174
Professional Preparation Master's Scheme
Research Preparation Master's Scheme
Rome Scholarships in the Fine Arts 176
Sargant Fellowship 176
University of Kent School of Drama, Film and Visual Arts Scholarships
700

United States of America

ACC Fellowship Grants Program 115
ACC Humanities Fellowship Program 115
Fulbright Senior Specialists Program 249
Individual Photographer's Fellowship 3
The Nadine Blacklock Nature Photography for Women 153
Phelan Award in Photography 581
Twining Humber Award for Lifetime Artistic Achievement 109
Virginia Liebeler Biennial Grants for Mature Women (Art) 484
Virginia Liebeler Biennial Grants for Mature Women (Music) 484
Virginia Liebeler Biennial Grants for Mature Women (Writing) 484

West European Countries

Janson Johan Helmich Scholarships and Travel Grants 398
University of Kent School of Drama, Film and Visual Arts Scholarships
700

CINEMA AND TELEVISION

Any Country

Akademie Schloss Solitude Fellowships 12
AMIA Kodak Fellowship in Film Preservation 121
Austro-American Association of Boston Stipend 143
Banff Centre Financial Assistance 144
British Academy Overseas Conference Grants 158
British Academy Research Development Awards (BARDAs) 158
British Academy Small Research Grants 158
British Academy Worldwide Congress Grant 159
British Conference Grants 159
CDI Internship 223
Home Hewson Scholarship 681
MacDowell Colony Residencies 429
Ohio Arts Council Individual Creativity Excellence Awards 510
Onassis Foreigners' Fellowships Programme Research Grants
Category AI 15
Paul D. Fleck Fellowships in the Arts 144
Queen Mary Research Studentships 539
Quinn, Nathan and Edmond Scholarships 706
Rhodes University Postdoctoral Fellowship and The Andrew Mellon
Postdoctoral Fellowship 548
University of Bristol Postgraduate Scholarships 672
University of Kent School of Drama, Film and Visual Arts Scholarships
700
The Walt Disney Studios and ABC Entertainment Writing Fellowship
Program 789

Australia

AAH Humanities Travelling Fellowships 132
Fulbright Postgraduate Student Award for the Visual and Performing
Arts 140

Canada

Canada Council Grants for Professional Artists 198
CanWest Global System Broadcasters of the Future Awards 235

European Union

AHRC Doctoral Awards Scheme 109
Professional Preparation Master's Scheme
Research Preparation Master's Scheme

Middle East

AICF Sharett Scholarship Program 24

United Kingdom

Aberystwyth Postgraduate Research Studentships 4
AHRC Doctoral Awards Scheme 109
Professional Preparation Master's Scheme
Research Preparation Master's Scheme
University of Kent School of Drama, Film and Visual Arts Scholarships
700
University of Kent School of European Culture and Languages
Scholarships 701
University of Kent School of European Culture and Languages
Studentships 701

United States of America

ACC Fellowship Grants Program 115
ACC Humanities Fellowship Program 115
AMIA Scholarship Program 121
Fulbright Distinguished Chairs Program 248
Fulbright Senior Specialists Program 249
IREX Individual Advanced Research Opportunities 388
McKnight Artist Fellowship for Filmmakers 467
SSRC JSPS Postdoctoral Fellowship 599

Virginia Liebeler Biennial Grants for Mature Women (Music) 484
Virginia Liebeler Biennial Grants for Mature Women (Writing) 484

West European Countries

Janson Johan Helmich Scholarships and Travel Grants 398
University of Kent School of Drama, Film and Visual Arts Scholarships 700
University of Kent School of European Culture and Languages Scholarships 701
University of Kent School of European Culture and Languages Studentships 701

DESIGN

Any Country

Akademie Schloss Solitude Fellowships 12
Austin Merrills Scholarship 319
British Academy Overseas Conference Grants 158
British Academy Research Development Awards (BARDAs) 158
British Academy Worldwide Congress Grant 159
DOG Digital Scholarship 320
Editorial, Design, and Video Internships in Educational Media 447
Hambidge Residency Program Scholarships 331
Haystack Scholarship 333
MICA Fellowship 435
MICA International Fellowship Award 436
Ohio Arts Council Individual Creativity Excellence Awards 510
University of Southampton Postgraduate Studentships 759
Victoria University of Wellington PhD Scholarships 786
Wolfsonian-FIU Fellowship 800
World Universities Network (WUN) International Research Mobility Scheme 759

African Nations

International Postgraduate Research Scholarships (IPRS) 413

Australia

Fulbright Postgraduate Student Award for the Visual and Performing Arts 140

Canada

Frank Knox Memorial Fellowships 123
International Postgraduate Research Scholarships (IPRS) 413

Caribbean Countries

International Postgraduate Research Scholarships (IPRS) 413

East European Countries

ArtsLink Independent Projects 221
Designs for Life 126
International Postgraduate Research Scholarships (IPRS) 413

European Union

AHRC Doctoral Awards Scheme 109
Design and Technology Scholarships 427
Designs for Life 126
Professional Preparation Master's Scheme
Research Preparation Master's Scheme
School of Art and Design Scholarships 428

Middle East

AICF Sharett Scholarship Program 24
International Postgraduate Research Scholarships (IPRS) 413

South Africa

International Postgraduate Research Scholarships (IPRS) 413

United Kingdom

AHRC Doctoral Awards Scheme 109
Bellahouston Bequest Scholarship 319

The Costume Society Student Bursary 247
The Costume Society Yarwood Award 247
Designs for Life 126
International Postgraduate Research Scholarships (IPRS) 413
Professional Preparation Master's Scheme
Research Preparation Master's Scheme

United States of America

Congress Bundestag Youth Exchange for Young Professionals 221
Fulbright Senior Specialists Program 249
The George and Viola Hoffman Fund 119
International Postgraduate Research Scholarships (IPRS) 413
Virginia Liebeler Biennial Grants for Mature Women (Art) 484
Virginia Liebeler Biennial Grants for Mature Women (Music) 484
Virginia Liebeler Biennial Grants for Mature Women (Writing) 484

West European Countries

Designs for Life 126
International Postgraduate Research Scholarships (IPRS) 413
Janson Johan Helmich Scholarships and Travel Grants 398

INTERIOR DESIGN

Any Country

ASID/Joel Polsky-Fixtures Furniture Academic Achievement Award 92
ASID/Joel Polsky-Fixtures Furniture Prize 92
ASID/Mabelle Wilhelmina Boldt Memorial Scholarship 92
Ohio Arts Council Individual Creativity Excellence Awards 510
Wolfsonian-FIU Fellowship 800

African Nations

International Postgraduate Research Scholarships (IPRS) 413

Canada

International Postgraduate Research Scholarships (IPRS) 413

Caribbean Countries

International Postgraduate Research Scholarships (IPRS) 413

East European Countries

International Postgraduate Research Scholarships (IPRS) 413

European Union

AHRC Doctoral Awards Scheme 109
Professional Preparation Master's Scheme
Research Preparation Master's Scheme

Middle East

International Postgraduate Research Scholarships (IPRS) 413

South Africa

International Postgraduate Research Scholarships (IPRS) 413

United Kingdom

AHRC Doctoral Awards Scheme 109
International Postgraduate Research Scholarships (IPRS) 413
Professional Preparation Master's Scheme
Research Preparation Master's Scheme

United States of America

American Academy in Rome Fellowships in Design Art 24
International Postgraduate Research Scholarships (IPRS) 413
Virginia Liebeler Biennial Grants for Mature Women (Art) 484

West European Countries

International Postgraduate Research Scholarships (IPRS) 413

FURNITURE DESIGN

Any Country

Haystack Scholarship 333
Ohio Arts Council Individual Creativity Excellence Awards
  510
Wolfsonian-FIU Fellowship 800

African Nations

International Postgraduate Research Scholarships (IPRS) 413

Canada

International Postgraduate Research Scholarships (IPRS) 413

Caribbean Countries

International Postgraduate Research Scholarships (IPRS) 413

East European Countries

Designs for Life 126
International Postgraduate Research Scholarships (IPRS)
  413

European Union

AHRC Doctoral Awards Scheme 109
Designs for Life 126
Professional Preparation Master's Scheme
Research Preparation Master's Scheme

Middle East

International Postgraduate Research Scholarships (IPRS)
  413

South Africa

International Postgraduate Research Scholarships (IPRS) 413

United Kingdom

AHRC Doctoral Awards Scheme 109
Designs for Life 126
International Postgraduate Research Scholarships (IPRS)
  413
Professional Preparation Master's Scheme
Research Preparation Master's Scheme

United States of America

International Postgraduate Research Scholarships (IPRS) 413

West European Countries

Designs for Life 126
International Postgraduate Research Scholarships (IPRS) 413

FASHION DESIGN

Any Country

CSA Adele Filene Travel Award 247
CSA Stella Blum Research Grant 247
CSA Travel Research Grant 248
Ohio Arts Council Individual Creativity Excellence Awards 510
Wolfsonian-FIU Fellowship 800

African Nations

International Postgraduate Research Scholarships (IPRS) 413

Canada

International Postgraduate Research Scholarships (IPRS) 413

Caribbean Countries

International Postgraduate Research Scholarships (IPRS) 413

East European Countries

International Postgraduate Research Scholarships (IPRS) 413

European Union

AHRC Doctoral Awards Scheme 109
Professional Preparation Master's Scheme
Research Preparation Master's Scheme

Middle East

AICF Sharett Scholarship Program 24
International Postgraduate Research Scholarships (IPRS) 413

South Africa

International Postgraduate Research Scholarships (IPRS) 413

United Kingdom

AHRC Doctoral Awards Scheme 109
The Costume Society Museum Placement Award 246
The Costume Society Patterns of Fashion Award 246
The Costume Society Student Bursary 247
The Costume Society Yarwood Award 247
International Postgraduate Research Scholarships (IPRS) 413
MA Fashion Design and Enterprise Scholarship 777
Professional Preparation Master's Scheme
Research Preparation Master's Scheme

United States of America

International Postgraduate Research Scholarships (IPRS) 413

West European Countries

International Postgraduate Research Scholarships (IPRS) 413

TEXTILE DESIGN

Any Country

CSA Adele Filene Travel Award 247
CSA Stella Blum Research Grant 247
CSA Travel Research Grant 248
Hambidge Residency Program Scholarships 331
Haystack Scholarship 333
HWSDA Scholarship Program 331
Ohio Arts Council Individual Creativity Excellence Awards 510
Wolfsonian-FIU Fellowship 800

African Nations

International Postgraduate Research Scholarships (IPRS) 413
Shell Centenary/Shell Centenary Chevening Scholarships 704

Canada

International Postgraduate Research Scholarships (IPRS) 413

Caribbean Countries

International Postgraduate Research Scholarships (IPRS) 413
Shell Centenary/Shell Centenary Chevening Scholarships 704

East European Countries

Designs for Life 126
International Postgraduate Research Scholarships (IPRS) 413

European Union

AHRC Doctoral Awards Scheme 109
Designs for Life 126
Professional Preparation Master's Scheme
Research Preparation Master's Scheme

Middle East

AICF Sharett Scholarship Program 24
International Postgraduate Research Scholarships (IPRS) 413
Shell Centenary/Shell Centenary Chevening Scholarships 704

South Africa

International Postgraduate Research Scholarships (IPRS) 413
Shell Centenary/Shell Centenary Chevening Scholarships 704

United Kingdom

AHRC Doctoral Awards Scheme 109
The Costume Society Patterns of Fashion Award 246
The Costume Society Student Bursary 247
The Costume Society Yarwood Award 247
Designs for Life 126
International Postgraduate Research Scholarships (IPRS) 413
Professional Preparation Master's Scheme
Research Preparation Master's Scheme

United States of America

International Postgraduate Research Scholarships (IPRS) 413

West European Countries

Designs for Life 126
International Postgraduate Research Scholarships (IPRS) 413

GRAPHIC DESIGN

Any Country

Hambidge Residency Program Scholarships 331
Haystack Scholarship 333
Jacob's Pillow Intern Program
MICA Fellowship 435
MICA International Fellowship Award 436
Ohio Arts Council Individual Creativity Excellence Awards 510
Wolfsonian-FIU Fellowship 800

African Nations

International Postgraduate Research Scholarships (IPRS) 413

Canada

International Postgraduate Research Scholarships (IPRS) 413

Caribbean Countries

International Postgraduate Research Scholarships (IPRS) 413

East European Countries

Designs for Life 126
International Postgraduate Research Scholarships (IPRS) 413

European Union

AHRC Doctoral Awards Scheme 109
Designs for Life 126
Professional Preparation Master's Scheme
Research Preparation Master's Scheme

Middle East

AICF Sharett Scholarship Program 24
International Postgraduate Research Scholarships (IPRS) 413

South Africa

International Postgraduate Research Scholarships (IPRS) 413

United Kingdom

AHRC Doctoral Awards Scheme 109
Designs for Life 126
International Postgraduate Research Scholarships (IPRS) 413
Professional Preparation Master's Scheme
Research Preparation Master's Scheme

United States of America

American Academy in Rome Fellowships in Design Art 24
International Postgraduate Research Scholarships (IPRS) 413
Virginia Liebeler Biennial Grants for Mature Women (Art) 484
Virginia Liebeler Biennial Grants for Mature Women (Writing) 484

West European Countries

Designs for Life 126
International Postgraduate Research Scholarships (IPRS) 413

INDUSTRIAL DESIGN

Any Country

Breast Cancer Campaign Project Grants 157
Ohio Arts Council Individual Creativity Excellence Awards 510
Wolfsonian-FIU Fellowship 800

African Nations

International Postgraduate Research Scholarships (IPRS) 413

Canada

International Postgraduate Research Scholarships (IPRS) 413

Caribbean Countries

International Postgraduate Research Scholarships (IPRS) 413

East European Countries

Designs for Life 126
International Postgraduate Research Scholarships (IPRS) 413

European Union

AHRC Doctoral Awards Scheme 109
Designs for Life 126
IPTME (Materials) Scholarships 427
Professional Preparation Master's Scheme
Research Preparation Master's Scheme

Middle East

AICF Sharett Scholarship Program 24
International Postgraduate Research Scholarships (IPRS) 413

South Africa

International Postgraduate Research Scholarships (IPRS) 413

United Kingdom

AHRC Doctoral Awards Scheme 109
Designs for Life 126
Industrial Design Studentship 427
International Postgraduate Research Scholarships (IPRS) 413
Professional Preparation Master's Scheme
Research Preparation Master's Scheme
Royal Commission Industrial Design Studentship 562

United States of America

American Academy in Rome Fellowships in Design Art 24
International Postgraduate Research Scholarships (IPRS) 413

West European Countries

Designs for Life 126
International Postgraduate Research Scholarships (IPRS) 413

DISPLAY AND STAGE DESIGN

Any Country

Banff Centre Financial Assistance 144
Ohio Arts Council Individual Creativity Excellence Awards 510
Paul D. Fleck Fellowships in the Arts 144

African Nations

International Postgraduate Research Scholarships (IPRS) 413

Canada

International Postgraduate Research Scholarships (IPRS) 413

Caribbean Countries

International Postgraduate Research Scholarships (IPRS) 413

East European Countries

International Postgraduate Research Scholarships (IPRS) 413

European Union

AHRC Doctoral Awards Scheme 109
Professional Preparation Master's Scheme
Research Preparation Master's Scheme

Middle East

AICF Sharett Scholarship Program 24
International Postgraduate Research Scholarships (IPRS) 413

South Africa

International Postgraduate Research Scholarships (IPRS) 413

United Kingdom

AHRC Doctoral Awards Scheme 109
The Costume Society Patterns of Fashion Award 246
The Costume Society Student Bursary 247
International Postgraduate Research Scholarships (IPRS) 413
Professional Preparation Master's Scheme
Research Preparation Master's Scheme

United States of America

International Postgraduate Research Scholarships (IPRS) 413

West European Countries

International Postgraduate Research Scholarships (IPRS) 413

HOME ECONOMICS

GENERAL

Any Country

Frederick Douglass Institute Postdoctoral Fellowship 304
Frederick Douglass Institute Predoctoral Dissertation Fellowship 304

Australia

Fulbright Postgraduate Awards 140

European Union

All Saints Educational Trust Personal Scholarships 20

United Kingdom

All Saints Educational Trust Corporate Awards 20
All Saints Educational Trust Personal Scholarships 20

United States of America

North Dakota Indian Scholarship 507

CLOTHING AND SEWING

Any Country

CSA Adele Filene Travel Award 247
CSA Stella Blum Research Grant 247
CSA Travel Research Grant 248

NUTRITION

Any Country

Allen Foundation Grants 20
Earthwatch Field Research Grants 272
University of Otago International Scholarships 717
University of Otago PhD Scholarships 718
University of Otago Prestigious PhD Scholarships 718

African Nations

International Postgraduate Research Scholarships (IPRS) 413

Australia

University of Otago Master's Awards 717

Canada

International Postgraduate Research Scholarships (IPRS) 413

Caribbean Countries

International Postgraduate Research Scholarships (IPRS) 413

East European Countries

International Postgraduate Research Scholarships (IPRS) 413

European Union

Akroyd, Brotherton and Brown Scholarship 702

Middle East

International Postgraduate Research Scholarships (IPRS) 413

New Zealand

University of Otago Master's Awards 717

South Africa

International Postgraduate Research Scholarships (IPRS) 413

United Kingdom

Akroyd, Brotherton and Brown Scholarship 702
International Postgraduate Research Scholarships (IPRS) 413

United States of America

International Postgraduate Research Scholarships (IPRS) 413
Nurses' Educational Funds Fellowships and Scholarships 510

West European Countries

International Postgraduate Research Scholarships (IPRS) 413
University of Otago Master's Awards 717

CHILD CARE/CHILD DEVELOPMENT

Any Country

Earthwatch Field Research Grants 272
Tim Brighouse Scholarship 153

LAW

GENERAL

Any Country

AALL and West-George A Strait Minority Scholarship Endowment 30
AALL James F Connolly LexisNexis Academic and Library Solutions
   Scholarship 31
The Airey Neave Trust Scholarship 12
Alberta Law Foundation Graduate Scholarship 672
Andrew Mellon Foundation Scholarship 547
ARI PhD Research Scholarship 114
Australian Postgraduate Award Research Scholarship
British Academy Overseas Conference Grants 158
British Academy Postdoctoral Fellowships 158
British Academy Research Development Awards (BARDAs) 158
British Academy Small Research Grants 158
British Academy Worldwide Congress Grant 159
British Conference Grants 159
CIUS Research Grants 209
Evan Lewis Thomas Law Bursaries and Studentships 586
Field Psych Trust Grant 291
Giulia Mereu Scholarships 688

H Thomas Austern Memorial Writing Competition–Food and Drug Law Institute(FDLI) 298
Helen Darcovich Memorial Doctoral Fellowship 209
The Holberg International Memorial Prize/The Holberg Prize 668
Honourable N D McDermid Graduate Scholarship in Law 672
IALS Visiting Fellowship in Law Librarianship 364
IALS Visiting Fellowship in Legislative Studies 365
IALS Visiting Fellowships 365
IHS Humane Studies Fellowships 363
IHS Summer Graduate Research Fellowship 363
Institute for Advanced Studies in the Humanities Visiting Research Fellowships 362
Kennan Institute Short-Term Grants 408
Kent Law School Studentships and Bursaries 699
La Trobe University Postgraduate Scholarship 414
Lincoln College Sloane Robinson Foundation Graduate Awards 733
Mackenzie King Open Scholarship 429
Mackenzie King Travelling Scholarship 429
Maxwell Boulton QC Fellowship 437
Monash International Postgraduate Research Scholarship (MIPRS) 455
Monash University Silver Jubilee Postgraduate Scholarship 455
Neporany Doctoral Fellowship 210
Queen Mary Research Studentships 539
Rhodes University Postdoctoral Fellowship and The Andrew Mellon Postdoctoral Fellowship 548
Rhodes University Postgraduate Scholarship 549
Royal Irish Academy Mobility Grants 569
Shirtcliffe Fellowship 501
Sir Allan Sewell Visiting Fellowship 326
SOAS Bursary 583
SOAS Research Student Fellowships 583
Thank-Offering to Britain Fellowships 159
TIACA Walter H. Johnson, Jr. Scholarship Award 375
United States Holocaust Memorial Museum Center for Advanced Holocaust Studies Visiting Scholar Programs 641
University of Bristol Postgraduate Scholarships 672
University of Calgary Faculty of Law Graduate Scholarship 673
University of Essex Scholarships 690
University of Otago International Scholarships 717
University of Otago PhD Scholarships 718
University of Otago Prestigious PhD Scholarships 718
Vera Moore International Postgraduate Research Scholarships 455
World Universities Network (WUN) International Research Mobility Scheme 759

African Nations

Balliol College Gregory Kulkes Scholarships in Law 718
IDRC Doctoral Research Awards 380
International Postgraduate Research Scholarships (IPRS) 413
NUFFIC-NFP Fellowships for Master's Degree Programmes 496

Australia

Australian Postgraduate Awards 413
Baillieu Research Scholarship 707
Balliol College Gregory Kulkes Scholarships in Law 718
Fulbright Postdoctoral Fellowships 140
Fulbright Postgraduate Awards 140
International Postgraduate Research Scholarships (IPRS) 413
The Lionel Murphy Australian Postgraduate Scholarships 424
The Lionel Murphy Overseas Postgraduate Scholarships 424
Sir Robert Menzies Memorial Scholarships in Law 594
University of Otago Master's Awards 717
Wingate Scholarships 697

Canada

Balliol College Gregory Kulkes Scholarships in Law 718
CAPSLE Fellowship 200
CIALS Cambridge Scholarships 188
IDRC Doctoral Research Awards 380
International Postgraduate Research Scholarships (IPRS) 413
The Right Honorable Paul Martin Sr. Scholarship 208
Vatican Film Library Mellon Fellowship 785
Viscount Bennett Fellowship 200
Wingate Scholarships 697

Caribbean Countries

Balliol College Gregory Kulkes Scholarships in Law 718
IDRC Doctoral Research Awards 380
International Postgraduate Research Scholarships (IPRS) 413

East European Countries

Andrew W Mellon Foundation East-Central European Fellowships in the Humanities 362
Balliol College Gregory Kulkes Scholarships in Law 718
IDRC Doctoral Research Awards 380
International Postgraduate Research Scholarships (IPRS) 413

European Union

AHRC Doctoral Awards Scheme 109
CBRL Travel Grant 248
ESRC 1+3 Awards and +3 Awards
International Postgraduate Research Scholarships (IPRS) 413
PhD Studentships 107
Professional Preparation Master's Scheme
Research Preparation Master's Scheme
Wingate Scholarships 697

Middle East

Balliol College Gregory Kulkes Scholarships in Law 718
IDRC Doctoral Research Awards 380
International Postgraduate Research Scholarships (IPRS) 413
NUFFIC-NFP Fellowships for Master's Degree Programmes 496

New Zealand

Australian Postgraduate Awards 413
Balliol College Gregory Kulkes Scholarships in Law 718
University of Otago Master's Awards 717
Wingate Scholarships 697

South Africa

Allan Gray Senior Scholarship 547
Balliol College Gregory Kulkes Scholarships in Law 718
IDRC Doctoral Research Awards 380
International Postgraduate Research Scholarships (IPRS) 413
NUFFIC-NFP Fellowships for Master's Degree Programmes 496
Wingate Scholarships 697

United Kingdom

Aberystwyth Postgraduate Research Studentships 4
AHRC Doctoral Awards Scheme 109
Balsdon Fellowship 174
CBRL Research Award 248
CBRL Travel Grant 248
ESRC 1+3 Awards and +3 Awards
Frank Knox Fellowships at Harvard University 302
Hilda Martindale Exhibitions 341
International Postgraduate Research Scholarships (IPRS) 413
Kennedy Scholarships 409
PhD Studentships 107
Professional Preparation Master's Scheme
Research Preparation Master's Scheme
Rome Awards 175
Rome Fellowship 175
Rome Scholarships in Ancient, Medieval and Later Italian Studies 176
Wingate Scholarships 697

United States of America

ACLS/New York Public Library Fellowship 48
American Academy in Berlin Prize Fellowships 24
ARCE Fellowships 80
Balliol College Gregory Kulkes Scholarships in Law 718
British Marshall Scholarships 685
Congress Bundestag Youth Exchange for Young Professionals 221
Fellowship for American College Students 545
Fulbright Distinguished Chairs Program 248
Fulbright Senior Specialists Program 249
Howard Brown Rickard Scholarship 474
International Postgraduate Research Scholarships (IPRS) 413

IREX Individual Advanced Research Opportunities 388
IREX Short-Term Travel Grants 389
National Academics Christine Mirzayan Science and Technology
   Policy Graduate Fellowship Program 466
Robert Bosch Foundation Fellowships 550
Vatican Film Library Mellon Fellowship 785

West European Countries

Balliol College Gregory Kulkes Scholarships in Law 718
ESRC 1 + 3 Awards and + 3 Awards
International Postgraduate Research Scholarships (IPRS) 413
Janson Johan Helmich Scholarships and Travel Grants 398
PhD Studentships 107
University of Otago Master's Awards 717

HISTORY OF LAW

Any Country

Ahmanson and Getty Postdoctoral Fellowships 639
ASCSA Advanced Fellowships 82
ASCSA Fellowships 82
ASECS (American Society for 18th-Century Studies)/Clark Library
   Fellowships 639
British Academy Postdoctoral Fellowships 158
Clark Library Short-Term Resident Fellowships 639
Clark Predoctoral Fellowships 639
Clark-Huntington Joint Bibliographical Fellowship 640
CRF (Caledonian Research Foundation)/RSE European Visiting
   Research Fellowships 628
Findel Scholarships and Schneider Scholarships 340
Hugh Last and Donald Atkinson Funds Committee Grants 604
J Franklin Jameson Fellowship 58
Jacob Hirsch Fellowship 83
Kanner Fellowship In British Studies 640
Littleton-Griswold Research Grant 59
M Alison Frantz Fellowship in Post-Classical Studies at the Gennadius
   Library 83
NEH Fellowships 83
Society for the Study of French History Bursaries 606
United States Holocaust Memorial Museum Center for Advanced
   Holocaust Studies Visiting Scholar Programs 641
University of Essex Scholarships 690

Australia

Wingate Scholarships 697

Canada

Viscount Bennett Fellowship 200
Wingate Scholarships 697

European Union

AHRC Doctoral Awards Scheme 109
Professional Preparation Master's Scheme
Research Preparation Master's Scheme
Wingate Scholarships 697

New Zealand

Wingate Scholarships 697

South Africa

Wingate Scholarships 697

United Kingdom

AHRC Doctoral Awards Scheme 109
Hector and Elizabeth Catling Bursary 173
Professional Preparation Master's Scheme
Research Preparation Master's Scheme
Wingate Scholarships 697

United States of America

ACLS/New York Public Library Fellowship 48
British Marshall Scholarships 685

Fulbright Senior Specialists Program 249
Kennan Institute Research Scholarship 408

COMPARATIVE LAW

Any Country

Fernand Braudel Senior Fellowships 287
Hastings Center International Visiting Scholars Program 332
Jean Monnet Fellowships 288
Max Weber Fellowships 288
United States Holocaust Memorial Museum Center for Advanced
   Holocaust Studies Visiting Scholar Programs 641
University of Bristol Postgraduate Scholarships 672
University of Essex Scholarships 690

African Nations

Hastings Center International Visiting Scholars Program 332

Australia

Hastings Center International Visiting Scholars Program 332
Wingate Scholarships 697

Canada

Jules and Gabrielle Léger Fellowship 601
Viscount Bennett Fellowship 200
Wingate Scholarships 697

Caribbean Countries

Hastings Center International Visiting Scholars Program 332

East European Countries

EUI Postgraduate Scholarships 287
Hastings Center International Visiting Scholars Program 332

European Union

AHRC Doctoral Awards Scheme 109
EUI Postgraduate Scholarships 287
PhD Studentships 107
Professional Preparation Master's Scheme
Research Preparation Master's Scheme
Wingate Scholarships 697

Middle East

EUI Postgraduate Scholarships 287
Hastings Center International Visiting Scholars Program 332

New Zealand

Hastings Center International Visiting Scholars Program 332
Wingate Scholarships 697

South Africa

Hastings Center International Visiting Scholars Program 332
Wingate Scholarships 697

United Kingdom

AHRC Doctoral Awards Scheme 109
BACS Travel Awards 160
EUI Postgraduate Scholarships 287
Hastings Center International Visiting Scholars Program 332
PhD Studentships 107
Prix du Québec Award 160
Professional Preparation Master's Scheme
Research Preparation Master's Scheme
Wingate Scholarships 697

United States of America

ACLS/New York Public Library Fellowship 48
British Marshall Scholarships 685
Fulbright Distinguished Chairs Program 248
Fulbright Senior Specialists Program 249
Kennan Institute Research Scholarship 408

West European Countries

EUI Postgraduate Scholarships 287
Hastings Center International Visiting Scholars Program 332
PhD Studentships 107

INTERNATIONAL LAW

Any Country

Fernand Braudel Senior Fellowships 287
Gilbert Murray Trust Junior Awards 318
Giulia Mereu Scholarships 688
Graduate Institute of International Studies (HEI-Geneva) Scholarships 323
Hague Academy of International Law/Scholarships for Sessions of Courses 330
Hastings Center International Visiting Scholars Program 332
IAUW International Scholarship 166
International Trade Law Postgraduate Scholarships 660
Jean Monnet Fellowships 288
Jennings Randolph Program for International Peace Dissertation Fellowship 643
Jennings Randolph Program for International Peace Senior Fellowships 643
Max Weber Fellowships 288
Paul H. Nitze School of Advanced International Studies (SAIS) Financial Aid and Fellowships 155
United States Holocaust Memorial Museum Center for Advanced Holocaust Studies Visiting Scholar Programs 641
University of Bristol Postgraduate Scholarships 672
University of Essex Scholarships 690
University of Southampton Postgraduate Studentships 759
USIP Annual Grant Competition 643
USIP Priority Grant-making Competition 644
World Universities Network (WUN) International Research Mobility Scheme 759

African Nations

Canadian Window on International Development 380
Hague Academy of International Law/Doctoral Scholarships 330
Hastings Center International Visiting Scholars Program 332
IDRC Doctoral Research Awards 380

Australia

Hastings Center International Visiting Scholars Program 332
The Lionel Murphy Australian Postgraduate Scholarships 424
Wingate Scholarships 697

Canada

Canadian Window on International Development 380
IDRC Doctoral Research Awards 380
Viscount Bennett Fellowship 200
Wingate Scholarships 697

Caribbean Countries

Canadian Window on International Development 380
Hastings Center International Visiting Scholars Program 332
IDRC Doctoral Research Awards 380

East European Countries

EUI Postgraduate Scholarships 287
Hastings Center International Visiting Scholars Program 332
IDRC Doctoral Research Awards 380

European Union

AHRC Doctoral Awards Scheme 109
CBRL Travel Grant 248
EUI Postgraduate Scholarships 287
PhD Studentships 107
Professional Preparation Master's Scheme
Research Preparation Master's Scheme
Wingate Scholarships 697

Middle East

EUI Postgraduate Scholarships 287
Hastings Center International Visiting Scholars Program 332
IDRC Doctoral Research Awards 380

New Zealand

Hastings Center International Visiting Scholars Program 332
Wingate Scholarships 697

South Africa

Canadian Window on International Development 380
Hastings Center International Visiting Scholars Program 332
IDRC Doctoral Research Awards 380
Wingate Scholarships 697

United Kingdom

Aberystwyth Postgraduate Research Studentships 4
AHRC Doctoral Awards Scheme 109
The Airey Neave Research Fellowships 11
CBRL Research Award 248
CBRL Travel Grant 248
EUI Postgraduate Scholarships 287
Hastings Center International Visiting Scholars Program 332
PhD Studentships 107
Professional Preparation Master's Scheme
Research Preparation Master's Scheme
Wingate Scholarships 697

United States of America

ACLS/New York Public Library Fellowship 48
British Marshall Scholarships 685
Fulbright Senior Specialists Program 249
Kennan Institute Research Scholarship 408

West European Countries

EUI Postgraduate Scholarships 287
Hastings Center International Visiting Scholars Program 332
PhD Studentships 107

HUMAN RIGHTS

Any Country

ALA Eli M Oboler Memorial Award 63
Fernand Braudel Senior Fellowships 287
Giulia Mereu Scholarships 688
Hastings Center International Visiting Scholars Program 332
HFG Research Program 332
HRC Visiting Fellowships 347
Human Rights Scholarship 708
Jean Monnet Fellowships 288
Jennings Randolph Program for International Peace Dissertation Fellowship 643
Jennings Randolph Program for International Peace Senior Fellowships 643
Max Weber Fellowships 288
Paul H. Nitze School of Advanced International Studies (SAIS) Financial Aid and Fellowships 155
United States Holocaust Memorial Museum Center for Advanced Holocaust Studies Visiting Scholar Programs 641
University of Bristol Postgraduate Scholarships 672
University of Essex Scholarships 690
USIP Annual Grant Competition 643
USIP Priority Grant-making Competition 644
WILPF Internship in Disarmament 801
WILPF Internship in Human Rights 801
World Bank Grants Facility for Indigenous Peoples 805

African Nations

Canadian Window on International Development 380
Hastings Center International Visiting Scholars Program 332
IDRC Doctoral Research Awards 380
World Bank Grants Facility for Indigenous Peoples 805

European Union

AHRC Doctoral Awards Scheme 109
Professional Preparation Master's Scheme
Research Preparation Master's Scheme
Wingate Scholarships 697

New Zealand

Wingate Scholarships 697

South Africa

Wingate Scholarships 697

United Kingdom

AHRC Doctoral Awards Scheme 109
Professional Preparation Master's Scheme
Research Preparation Master's Scheme
Wingate Scholarships 697

United States of America

British Marshall Scholarships 685

LAW OF THE AIR

Any Country

United States Holocaust Memorial Museum Center for
   Advanced Holocaust Studies Visiting Scholar Programs
   641
University of Essex Scholarships 690

Australia

Wingate Scholarships 697

Canada

Viscount Bennett Fellowship 200
Wingate Scholarships 697

European Union

AHRC Doctoral Awards Scheme 109
Professional Preparation Master's Scheme
Research Preparation Master's Scheme
Wingate Scholarships 697

New Zealand

Wingate Scholarships 697

South Africa

Wingate Scholarships 697

United Kingdom

AHRC Doctoral Awards Scheme 109
Professional Preparation Master's Scheme
Research Preparation Master's Scheme
Wingate Scholarships 697

United States of America

British Marshall Scholarships 685

NOTARY STUDIES

Any Country

University of Essex Scholarships 690

Canada

Viscount Bennett Fellowship 200

United States of America

British Marshall Scholarships 685

CIVIL LAW

Any Country

H Thomas Austern Memorial Writing Competition–Food and Drug Law
   Institute(FDLI) 298
Trinity College: Michael and Judith Beloff Scholarship 747
United States Holocaust Memorial Museum Center for Advanced
   Holocaust Studies Visiting Scholar Programs 641
University of Bristol Postgraduate Scholarships 672
University of Essex Scholarships 690
University of Southampton Postgraduate Studentships 759
World Universities Network (WUN) International Research Mobility
   Scheme 759

African Nations

International Postgraduate Research Scholarships (IPRS) 413

Australia

The Lionel Murphy Australian Postgraduate Scholarships 424
The Lionel Murphy Overseas Postgraduate Scholarships 424
Wingate Scholarships 697

Canada

International Postgraduate Research Scholarships (IPRS) 413
Viscount Bennett Fellowship 200
Wingate Scholarships 697

Caribbean Countries

International Postgraduate Research Scholarships (IPRS) 413

East European Countries

International Postgraduate Research Scholarships (IPRS) 413

European Union

AHRC Doctoral Awards Scheme 109
Professional Preparation Master's Scheme
Research Preparation Master's Scheme
Wingate Scholarships 697

Middle East

International Postgraduate Research Scholarships (IPRS) 413

New Zealand

Wingate Scholarships 697

South Africa

International Postgraduate Research Scholarships (IPRS) 413
Wingate Scholarships 697

United Kingdom

AHRC Doctoral Awards Scheme 109
International Postgraduate Research Scholarships (IPRS) 413
Professional Preparation Master's Scheme
Research Preparation Master's Scheme
Wingate Scholarships 697

United States of America

British Marshall Scholarships 685
Fulbright Senior Specialists Program 249
International Postgraduate Research Scholarships (IPRS) 413

West European Countries

International Postgraduate Research Scholarships (IPRS) 413

COMMERCIAL LAW

Any Country

H Thomas Austern Memorial Writing Competition–Food and Drug Law
   Institute(FDLI) 298
International Trade Law Postgraduate Scholarships 660

Queen Mary Research Studentships 539
University of Bristol Postgraduate Scholarships 672
University of Essex Scholarships 690
University of Southampton Postgraduate Studentships 759
World Universities Network (WUN) International Research Mobility
    Scheme 759

African Nations

International Postgraduate Research Scholarships (IPRS) 413

Canada

International Postgraduate Research Scholarships (IPRS) 413
Viscount Bennett Fellowship 200

Caribbean Countries

International Postgraduate Research Scholarships (IPRS) 413

East European Countries

International Postgraduate Research Scholarships (IPRS) 413

European Union

AHRC Doctoral Awards Scheme 109
PhD Studentships 107
Professional Preparation Master's Scheme
Research Preparation Master's Scheme

Middle East

International Postgraduate Research Scholarships (IPRS) 413

South Africa

International Postgraduate Research Scholarships (IPRS) 413

United Kingdom

Aberystwyth Postgraduate Research Studentships 4
AHRC Doctoral Awards Scheme 109
International Postgraduate Research Scholarships (IPRS) 413
PhD Studentships 107
Professional Preparation Master's Scheme
Research Preparation Master's Scheme

United States of America

British Marshall Scholarships 685
International Postgraduate Research Scholarships (IPRS) 413

West European Countries

International Postgraduate Research Scholarships (IPRS) 413
PhD Studentships 107

PUBLIC LAW

Any Country

Fernand Braudel Senior Fellowships 287
Jack Nelson Legal Fellowship 544
Jean Monnet Fellowships 288
Max Weber Fellowships 288
Reporters Committee Legal Fellowship 544
Robert R McCormick Tribune Foundation Legal Fellowship 544
United States Holocaust Memorial Museum Center for Advanced
    Holocaust Studies Visiting Scholar Programs 641
University of Bristol Postgraduate Scholarships 672
University of Essex Scholarships 690
University of Southampton Postgraduate Studentships 759
World Universities Network (WUN) International Research Mobility
    Scheme 759
WREI Congressional Fellowships on Women and Public Policy 801

African Nations

Canadian Window on International Development 380
IDRC Doctoral Research Awards 380
International Postgraduate Research Scholarships (IPRS) 413

Australia

The Lionel Murphy Australian Postgraduate Scholarships 424
The Lionel Murphy Overseas Postgraduate Scholarships 424

Canada

Canadian Window on International Development 380
IDRC Doctoral Research Awards 380
International Postgraduate Research Scholarships (IPRS) 413
Jules and Gabrielle Léger Fellowship 601
Viscount Bennett Fellowship 200

Caribbean Countries

Canadian Window on International Development 380
IDRC Doctoral Research Awards 380
International Postgraduate Research Scholarships (IPRS) 413

East European Countries

EUI Postgraduate Scholarships 287
IDRC Doctoral Research Awards 380
International Postgraduate Research Scholarships (IPRS) 413

European Union

AHRC Doctoral Awards Scheme 109
EUI Postgraduate Scholarships 287
PhD Studentships 107
Professional Preparation Master's Scheme
Research Preparation Master's Scheme

Middle East

EUI Postgraduate Scholarships 287
IDRC Doctoral Research Awards 380
International Postgraduate Research Scholarships (IPRS) 413

South Africa

Canadian Window on International Development 380
IDRC Doctoral Research Awards 380
International Postgraduate Research Scholarships (IPRS) 413

United Kingdom

AHRC Doctoral Awards Scheme 109
EUI Postgraduate Scholarships 287
International Postgraduate Research Scholarships (IPRS) 413
PhD Studentships 107
Professional Preparation Master's Scheme
Research Preparation Master's Scheme

United States of America

British Marshall Scholarships 685
Fulbright Senior Specialists Program 249
International Postgraduate Research Scholarships (IPRS) 413
WREI Congressional Fellowships on Women and Public Policy
    801

West European Countries

EUI Postgraduate Scholarships 287
International Postgraduate Research Scholarships (IPRS) 413
PhD Studentships 107

CONSTITUTIONAL LAW

Any Country

ALA John Philip Immroth Award for Intellectual Freedom 64
H Thomas Austern Memorial Writing Competition–Food and Drug Law
    Institute(FDLI) 298
Jack Nelson Legal Fellowship 544
Reporters Committee Legal Fellowship 544
Robert R McCormick Tribune Foundation Legal Fellowship 544
United States Holocaust Memorial Museum Center for Advanced
    Holocaust Studies Visiting Scholar Programs 641
University of Essex Scholarships 690

European Union

AHRC Doctoral Awards Scheme 109
PhD Studentships 107
Professional Preparation Master's Scheme
Research Preparation Master's Scheme

United Kingdom

AHRC Doctoral Awards Scheme 109
BACS Travel Awards 160
PhD Studentships 107
Professional Preparation Master's Scheme
Research Preparation Master's Scheme

United States of America

British Marshall Scholarships 685
Fulbright Senior Specialists Program 249

West European Countries

PhD Studentships 107

ADMINISTRATIVE LAW

Any Country

H Thomas Austern Memorial Writing Competition–Food and Drug Law Institute(FDLI) 298
United States Holocaust Memorial Museum Center for Advanced Holocaust Studies Visiting Scholar Programs 641
University of Essex Scholarships 690

European Union

AHRC Doctoral Awards Scheme 109
PhD Studentships 107
Professional Preparation Master's Scheme
Research Preparation Master's Scheme

United Kingdom

AHRC Doctoral Awards Scheme 109
PhD Studentships 107
Professional Preparation Master's Scheme
Research Preparation Master's Scheme

United States of America

British Marshall Scholarships 685

West European Countries

PhD Studentships 107

FISCAL LAW

Any Country

University of Essex Scholarships 690

European Union

AHRC Doctoral Awards Scheme 109
PhD Studentships 107
Professional Preparation Master's Scheme
Research Preparation Master's Scheme

United Kingdom

AHRC Doctoral Awards Scheme 109
PhD Studentships 107
Professional Preparation Master's Scheme
Research Preparation Master's Scheme

United States of America

British Marshall Scholarships 685

West European Countries

PhD Studentships 107

CRIMINAL LAW

Any Country

United States Holocaust Memorial Museum Center for Advanced Holocaust Studies Visiting Scholar Programs 641
University of Bristol Postgraduate Scholarships 672
University of Essex Scholarships 690
University of Southampton Postgraduate Studentships 759
World Universities Network (WUN) International Research Mobility Scheme 759

Australia

CRC Grants 254

Canada

Viscount Bennett Fellowship 200

European Union

AHRC Doctoral Awards Scheme 109
PhD Studentships 107
Professional Preparation Master's Scheme
Research Preparation Master's Scheme

United Kingdom

AHRC Doctoral Awards Scheme 109
PhD Studentships 107
Professional Preparation Master's Scheme
Research Preparation Master's Scheme

United States of America

British Marshall Scholarships 685
Fulbright Senior Specialists Program 249
US-UK Fulbright Commission, Criminal Justice and Police Research Fellowships 784

West European Countries

PhD Studentships 107

CANON LAW

Any Country

University of Essex Scholarships 690

European Union

AHRC Doctoral Awards Scheme 109
Professional Preparation Master's Scheme
Research Preparation Master's Scheme

United Kingdom

AHRC Doctoral Awards Scheme 109
Professional Preparation Master's Scheme
Research Preparation Master's Scheme

United States of America

British Marshall Scholarships 685

ISLAMIC LAW

Any Country

USIP Priority Grant-making Competition 644

European Union

AHRC Doctoral Awards Scheme 109
CBRL Travel Grant 248
Professional Preparation Master's Scheme
Research Preparation Master's Scheme

United Kingdom

AHRC Doctoral Awards Scheme 109
CBRL Research Award 248

CBRL Travel Grant 248
Professional Preparation Master's Scheme
Research Preparation Master's Scheme

United States of America

ARCE Fellowships 80

EUROPEAN COMMUNITY LAW

Any Country

Fernand Braudel Senior Fellowships 287
Jean Monnet Fellowships 288
Law & Business in Europe Fellowships 660
Max Weber Fellowships 288
Paul H. Nitze School of Advanced International Studies (SAIS)
 Financial Aid and Fellowships 155
United States Holocaust Memorial Museum Center for Advanced
 Holocaust Studies Visiting Scholar Programs 641
University of Essex Scholarships 690
University of Southampton Postgraduate Studentships 759
World Universities Network (WUN) International Research Mobility
 Scheme 759

East European Countries

EUI Postgraduate Scholarships 287

European Union

AHRC Doctoral Awards Scheme 109
EUI Postgraduate Scholarships 287
PhD Studentships 107
Research Preparation Master's Scheme

Middle East

EUI Postgraduate Scholarships 287

United Kingdom

Aberystwyth Postgraduate Research Studentships 4
AHRC Doctoral Awards Scheme 109
EUI Postgraduate Scholarships 287
PhD Studentships 107
Research Preparation Master's Scheme

United States of America

British Marshall Scholarships 685

West European Countries

EUI Postgraduate Scholarships 287
PhD Studentships 107

MASS COMMUNICATION AND INFORMATION SCIENCE

GENERAL

Any Country

Adelle and Erwin Tomash Fellowship in the History of Information
 Processing 228
Andrew Mellon Foundation Scholarship 547
AUC Graduate Merit Fellowships 97
AUC University Fellowships 98
BITS HP Labs India PhD Fellowship 152
Concordia University Graduate Fellowships 243
David J Azrieli Graduate Fellowship 243
ETS Summer Internship Program for Graduate Students 276
Field Psych Trust Grant 291
IHS Humane Studies Fellowships 363
John A Knauss Marine Policy Fellowships 488
Journey of a Lifetime Award 564
Monash International Postgraduate Research Scholarship (MIPRS) 455

NTU Asian Communication Resource Centre (ACRC) Fellowship
 Award 464
Rhodes University Postdoctoral Fellowship and The Andrew Mellon
 Postdoctoral Fellowship 548
Rhodes University Postgraduate Scholarship 549
Scottish Government Personal Research Fellowships 628
Scottish Government/RSE Support Research Fellowships 629
Shorenstein APARC Postdoctoral Research Fellowship in Korean
 Studies 586
Sir Allan Sewell Visiting Fellowship 326
Stanley G French Graduate Fellowship 244
United States Holocaust Memorial Museum Center for Advanced
 Holocaust Studies Visiting Scholar Programs 641
University of Otago International Scholarships 717
University of Otago PhD Scholarships 718
University of Otago Prestigious PhD Scholarships 718
Vera Moore International Postgraduate Research Scholarships 455
Victoria University of Wellington PhD Scholarships 786

African Nations

ABCCF Student Grant 102
AUC African Graduate Fellowship 96
International Postgraduate Research Scholarships (IPRS) 413
NUFFIC-NFP Fellowships for Master's Degree Programmes 496

Australia

Fulbright Postdoctoral Fellowships 140
Fulbright Postgraduate Awards 140
Google Australia Anita Borg Memorial Scholarship 322
University of Otago Master's Awards 717
Wingate Scholarships 697

Canada

Community-University Research Alliances (CURA) 601
International Postgraduate Research Scholarships (IPRS) 413
J W McConnell Memorial Fellowships 243
Major Collaborative Research Initiatives (MCRI) 601
SSHRC Doctoral Awards 602
SSHRC Standard Research Grants 603
Wingate Scholarships 697

Caribbean Countries

International Postgraduate Research Scholarships (IPRS) 413

East European Countries

International Postgraduate Research Scholarships (IPRS) 413

European Union

AHRC Doctoral Awards Scheme 109
Professional Preparation Master's Scheme
Research Preparation Master's Scheme
Wingate Scholarships 697

Middle East

ABCCF Student Grant 102
International Postgraduate Research Scholarships (IPRS) 413
NUFFIC-NFP Fellowships for Master's Degree Programmes 496

New Zealand

University of Otago Master's Awards 717
Wingate Scholarships 697

South Africa

International Postgraduate Research Scholarships (IPRS) 413
NUFFIC-NFP Fellowships for Master's Degree Programmes 496
Wingate Scholarships 697
Wolfson Foundation Grants 799

United Kingdom

Aberystwyth Postgraduate Research Studentships 4
AHRC Doctoral Awards Scheme 109
Hilda Martindale Exhibitions 341
International Postgraduate Research Scholarships (IPRS) 413

JOURNALISM

RADIO/TELEVISION BROADCASTING

IHS Film & Fiction Scholarships 363
The McGee Journalism Fellowship in Southern Africa 378
Rhodes University Postdoctoral Fellowship and The Andrew Mellon
   Postdoctoral Fellowship 548
RTNDF Fellowships 540

African Nations

International Postgraduate Research Scholarships (IPRS) 413
Thomson Foundation Scholarship 633

Canada

BBM Scholarship 200
International Postgraduate Research Scholarships (IPRS) 413

Caribbean Countries

International Postgraduate Research Scholarships (IPRS) 413
Thomson Foundation Scholarship 633

East European Countries

International Postgraduate Research Scholarships (IPRS) 413
Thomson Foundation Scholarship 633

European Union

AHRC Doctoral Awards Scheme 109
Professional Preparation Master's Scheme
Research Preparation Master's Scheme

Middle East

International Postgraduate Research Scholarships (IPRS) 413
Thomson Foundation Scholarship 633

South Africa

International Postgraduate Research Scholarships (IPRS) 413
Thomson Foundation Scholarship 633

United Kingdom

Aberystwyth Postgraduate Research Studentships 4
AHRC Doctoral Awards Scheme 109
International Postgraduate Research Scholarships (IPRS) 413
Professional Preparation Master's Scheme
Research Preparation Master's Scheme

United States of America

Fulbright Senior Specialists Program 249
International Postgraduate Research Scholarships (IPRS) 413
Knight International Press Fellowship 378
Virginia Liebeler Biennial Grants for Mature Women (Writing) 484

West European Countries

International Postgraduate Research Scholarships (IPRS) 413

PUBLIC RELATIONS AND PUBLICITY

Any Country

Donald Dyer Scholarship – Public Relations & Communication
   Management 757
Jacob's Pillow Intern Program
Kennan Institute Short-Term Grants 408
Metropolitan Museum of Art Roswell L Gilpatric Internship 447
Metropolitan Museum of Art Summer Internships for College Students
   447
Metropolitan Museum of Art Summer Internships for Graduate
   Students 447
Onassis Foreigners' Fellowships Programme Research Grants
   Category AI 15
United States Holocaust Memorial Museum Center for Advanced
   Holocaust Studies Visiting Scholar Programs 641

African Nations

International Postgraduate Research Scholarships (IPRS) 413

Canada

International Postgraduate Research Scholarships (IPRS) 413

Caribbean Countries

International Postgraduate Research Scholarships (IPRS) 413

East European Countries

International Postgraduate Research Scholarships (IPRS) 413

Middle East

International Postgraduate Research Scholarships (IPRS) 413

South Africa

International Postgraduate Research Scholarships (IPRS) 413

United Kingdom

International Postgraduate Research Scholarships (IPRS) 413
MA Public Communication and Public Relations Scholarships 778

United States of America

Billings Broadcasters MSU-Billings Media Scholarship 456
Fulbright Senior Specialists Program 249
International Postgraduate Research Scholarships (IPRS) 413
Kennan Institute Research Scholarship 408
Knight International Press Fellowship 378
Virginia Liebeler Biennial Grants for Mature Women (Writing) 484

West European Countries

International Postgraduate Research Scholarships (IPRS) 413

MASS COMMUNICATION

Any Country

German Chancellor Fellowships for Prospective Leaders 17
The McGee Journalism Fellowship in Southern Africa 378
United States Holocaust Memorial Museum Center for Advanced
   Holocaust Studies Visiting Scholar Programs 641

African Nations

Canadian Window on International Development 380
International Postgraduate Research Scholarships (IPRS) 413

Australia

AAH Humanities Travelling Fellowships 132

Canada

BBM Scholarship 200
Canadian Window on International Development 380
International Postgraduate Research Scholarships (IPRS) 413
Jim Bourque Scholarship 103

Caribbean Countries

Canadian Window on International Development 380
International Postgraduate Research Scholarships (IPRS) 413

East European Countries

German Chancellor Fellowships for Prospective Leaders 17
International Postgraduate Research Scholarships (IPRS) 413

Middle East

International Postgraduate Research Scholarships (IPRS) 413

South Africa

Canadian Window on International Development 380
International Postgraduate Research Scholarships (IPRS) 413

United Kingdom

Aberystwyth Postgraduate Research Studentships 4
International Postgraduate Research Scholarships (IPRS) 413

United States of America

Billings Broadcasters MSU-Billings Media Scholarship 456
DEED (Demonstration of Energy-Efficient Developments) Student
   Research Grant/Internship 80
Fulbright Distinguished Chairs Program 248
Fulbright Senior Specialists Program 249
German Chancellor Fellowships for Prospective Leaders 17
International Postgraduate Research Scholarships (IPRS) 413
IREX Short-Term Travel Grants 389
Knight International Press Fellowship 378
Robert Bosch Foundation Fellowships 550
Virginia Liebeler Biennial Grants for Mature Women (Writing) 484

West European Countries

International Postgraduate Research Scholarships (IPRS) 413

MEDIA STUDIES

Any Country

AAS Joyce Tracy Fellowship 26
Marshall Memorial Fellowship 315
The McGee Journalism Fellowship in Southern Africa 378
Rhodes University Postdoctoral Fellowship and The Andrew Mellon
   Postdoctoral Fellowship 548
United States Holocaust Memorial Museum Center for Advanced
   Holocaust Studies Visiting Scholar Programs 641
Victoria University of Wellington PhD Scholarships 786

African Nations

International Postgraduate Research Scholarships (IPRS) 413

Australia

AAH Humanities Travelling Fellowships 132
Australian Postgraduate Awards 413

Canada

International Postgraduate Research Scholarships (IPRS) 413

Caribbean Countries

International Postgraduate Research Scholarships (IPRS) 413

East European Countries

International Postgraduate Research Scholarships (IPRS) 413

European Union

AHRC Doctoral Awards Scheme 109
ESRC 1 + 3 Awards and + 3 Awards
Research Preparation Master's Scheme

Middle East

International Postgraduate Research Scholarships (IPRS) 413

New Zealand

Australian Postgraduate Awards 413

South Africa

International Postgraduate Research Scholarships (IPRS) 413

United Kingdom

Aberystwyth Postgraduate Research Studentships 4
AHRC Doctoral Awards Scheme 109
ESRC 1 + 3 Awards and + 3 Awards
International Postgraduate Research Scholarships (IPRS) 413
Research Preparation Master's Scheme

United States of America

Fulbright Distinguished Chairs Program 248
Fulbright Senior Specialists Program 249
International Postgraduate Research Scholarships (IPRS) 413
SSRC JSPS Postdoctoral Fellowship 599
Virginia Liebeler Biennial Grants for Mature Women (Writing) 484

West European Countries

ESRC 1 + 3 Awards and + 3 Awards
International Postgraduate Research Scholarships (IPRS) 413

COMMUNICATIONS SKILLS

Any Country

Donald Dyer Scholarship – Public Relations & Communication
   Management 757
Fulbright Institutional Linkages Program 306
IHS Humane Studies Fellowships 363
STC International Scholarship Program 604

African Nations

International Postgraduate Research Scholarships (IPRS) 413

Australia

Community Cultural Development Category A 127
Community Cultural Development Category B 127
Community Cultural Development Category C 127
Community Cultural Development Presentation and Promotion 127

Canada

BBM Scholarship 200
International Postgraduate Research Scholarships (IPRS) 413

Caribbean Countries

International Postgraduate Research Scholarships (IPRS) 413

East European Countries

International Postgraduate Research Scholarships (IPRS) 413

European Union

ESRC 1 + 3 Awards and + 3 Awards

Middle East

International Postgraduate Research Scholarships (IPRS) 413

South Africa

International Postgraduate Research Scholarships (IPRS) 413

United Kingdom

ESRC 1 + 3 Awards and + 3 Awards
International Postgraduate Research Scholarships (IPRS) 413

United States of America

British Marshall Scholarships 685
Fulbright Senior Specialists Program 249
International Postgraduate Research Scholarships (IPRS) 413
Virginia Liebeler Biennial Grants for Mature Women (Writing) 484

West European Countries

ESRC 1 + 3 Awards and + 3 Awards
International Postgraduate Research Scholarships (IPRS) 413

LIBRARY SCIENCE

Any Country

AALL and West-George A Strait Minority Scholarship Endowment 30
AALL James F Connolly LexisNexis Academic and Library Solutions
   Scholarship 31
AALL LexisNexis/John R Johnson Memorial Scholarship Endowment
   31
ALA 3M/NMRT Professional Development Grant 62
ALA AASL Frances Henne Award 62
ALA AASL Highsmith Research Grant 62
ALA AASL Information Technology Pathfinder Award 62
ALA Beta Phi Mu Award 62
ALA Bogle-Pratt International Library Travel Fund 62

African Nations

Australia

Canada

Caribbean Countries

East European Countries

European Union

Middle East

New Zealand

South Africa

United Kingdom

United States of America

West European Countries

MUSEUM STUDIES AND CONSERVATION

Any Country

ASCSA Advanced Fellowships 82
ASCSA Fellowships 82
CIUS Research Grants 209
CSA Adele Filene Travel Award 247
CSA Stella Blum Research Grant 247
CSA Travel Research Grant 248
Doctoral Dissertation Scholarship 149
J Franklin Jameson Fellowship 58
Jacob Hirsch Fellowship 83
M Alison Frantz Fellowship in Post-Classical Studies at the Gennadius Library 83
Metropolitan Museum of Art Roswell L Gilpatric Internship 447
Metropolitan Museum of Art Summer Internships for College Students 447
Metropolitan Museum of Art Summer Internships for Graduate Students 447
NEH Fellowships 83
United States Holocaust Memorial Museum Center for Advanced Holocaust Studies Visiting Scholar Programs 641
University of Southampton Postgraduate Studentships 759
Victoria University of Wellington PhD Scholarships 786
World Universities Network (WUN) International Research Mobility Scheme 759

African Nations

International Postgraduate Research Scholarships (IPRS) 413

Australia

Wingate Scholarships 697

Canada

International Postgraduate Research Scholarships (IPRS) 413
Wingate Scholarships 697

Caribbean Countries

International Postgraduate Research Scholarships (IPRS) 413

East European Countries

International Postgraduate Research Scholarships (IPRS) 413
Synthesys Visiting Fellowship 494

European Union

AHRC Doctoral Awards Scheme 109
CBRL Travel Grant 248
Professional Preparation Master's Scheme
Research Preparation Master's Scheme
Synthesys Visiting Fellowship 494
Wingate Scholarships 697

Middle East

International Postgraduate Research Scholarships (IPRS) 413

New Zealand

Wingate Scholarships 697

South Africa

International Postgraduate Research Scholarships (IPRS) 413
Wingate Scholarships 697

United Kingdom

AHRC Doctoral Awards Scheme 109
CBRL Research Award 248
CBRL Travel Grant 248
International Postgraduate Research Scholarships (IPRS) 413
Professional Preparation Master's Scheme
Research Preparation Master's Scheme
Synthesys Visiting Fellowship 494
Tim Potter Memorial Award 177
Wingate Scholarships 697

United States of America

ACC Humanities Fellowship Program 115
British Marshall Scholarships 685
Fulbright Senior Specialists Program 249
International Postgraduate Research Scholarships (IPRS) 413
SSRC JSPS Postdoctoral Fellowship 599

West European Countries

International Postgraduate Research Scholarships (IPRS) 413
Synthesys Visiting Fellowship 494

MUSEUM MANAGEMENT

Any Country

ASCSA Advanced Fellowships 82
ASCSA Fellowships 82
J Franklin Jameson Fellowship 58
Metropolitan Museum of Art Roswell L Gilpatric Internship 447
Metropolitan Museum of Art Summer Internships for College Students 447
Metropolitan Museum of Art Summer Internships for Graduate Students 447
The Tiffany & Co. Foundation Curatorial Internship in American Decorative Arts 447

African Nations

International Postgraduate Research Scholarships (IPRS) 413

Australia

Wingate Scholarships 697

Canada

International Postgraduate Research Scholarships (IPRS) 413
Wingate Scholarships 697

Caribbean Countries

International Postgraduate Research Scholarships (IPRS) 413

East European Countries

International Postgraduate Research Scholarships (IPRS) 413
Synthesys Visiting Fellowship 494

European Union

AHRC Doctoral Awards Scheme 109
CBRL Travel Grant 248
Professional Preparation Master's Scheme
Research Preparation Master's Scheme
Synthesys Visiting Fellowship 494
Wingate Scholarships 697

Middle East

International Postgraduate Research Scholarships (IPRS) 413

New Zealand

Wingate Scholarships 697

South Africa

International Postgraduate Research Scholarships (IPRS) 413
Wingate Scholarships 697

United Kingdom

AHRC Doctoral Awards Scheme 109
CBRL Research Award 248
CBRL Travel Grant 248
The Costume Society Museum Placement Award 246
International Postgraduate Research Scholarships (IPRS) 413
Professional Preparation Master's Scheme
Research Preparation Master's Scheme
Synthesys Visiting Fellowship 494
Wingate Scholarships 697

United States of America

AMIA Scholarship Program 121
British Marshall Scholarships 685
Fulbright Senior Specialists Program 249
International Postgraduate Research Scholarships (IPRS) 413
NHPRC Fellowship in Archival Administration 481

West European Countries

International Postgraduate Research Scholarships (IPRS) 413
Synthesys Visiting Fellowship 494

RESTORATION OF WORKS OF ART

Any Country

AMIA Kodak Fellowship in Film Preservation 121
ASCSA Advanced Fellowships 82
ASCSA Fellowships 82
Henry Moore Institute Research Fellowship 338
Jacob Hirsch Fellowship 83
M Alison Frantz Fellowship in Post-Classical Studies at the Gennadius Library 83
Metropolitan Museum of Art Roswell L Gilpatric Internship 447
Metropolitan Museum of Art Summer Internships for College Students 447
Metropolitan Museum of Art Summer Internships for Graduate Students 447
NEH Fellowships 83

African Nations

International Postgraduate Research Scholarships (IPRS) 413

Australia

Wingate Scholarships 697

Canada

International Postgraduate Research Scholarships (IPRS) 413
Wingate Scholarships 697

Caribbean Countries

International Postgraduate Research Scholarships (IPRS) 413

East European Countries

International Postgraduate Research Scholarships (IPRS) 413

European Union

AHRC Doctoral Awards Scheme 109
CBRL Travel Grant 248
Professional Preparation Master's Scheme
Research Preparation Master's Scheme
Wingate Scholarships 697

Middle East

International Postgraduate Research Scholarships (IPRS) 413

New Zealand

Wingate Scholarships 697

South Africa

International Postgraduate Research Scholarships (IPRS) 413
Wingate Scholarships 697

United Kingdom

AHRC Doctoral Awards Scheme 109
CBRL Research Award 248
CBRL Travel Grant 248
International Postgraduate Research Scholarships (IPRS) 413
Professional Preparation Master's Scheme
Research Preparation Master's Scheme
Wingate Scholarships 697

United States of America

AMIA Scholarship Program 121
Fulbright Senior Specialists Program 249
International Postgraduate Research Scholarships (IPRS) 413
Virginia Liebeler Biennial Grants for Mature Women (Writing) 484

West European Countries

International Postgraduate Research Scholarships (IPRS) 413

DOCUMENTATION TECHNIQUES AND ARCHIVING

Any Country

Albert J Beveridge Grant 58
AMIA Kodak Fellowship in Film Preservation 121
ASCSA Advanced Fellowships 82
ASCSA Fellowships 82
Bernadotte E Schmitt Grants 58
Doctoral Dissertation Scholarship 149
Eugene Garfield Doctoral Dissertation Fellowship 149
J Franklin Jameson Fellowship 58
Jacob's Pillow Intern Program
Lester J Cappon Fellowship in Documentary Editing 502
Littleton-Griswold Research Grant 59
Metropolitan Museum of Art Roswell L Gilpatric Internship 447
Metropolitan Museum of Art Summer Internships for College Students 447
Metropolitan Museum of Art Summer Internships for Graduate Students 447
NEH Fellowships 83
Victoria University of Wellington PhD Scholarships 786

African Nations

International Postgraduate Research Scholarships (IPRS) 413

Australia

Wingate Scholarships 697

Canada

International Postgraduate Research Scholarships (IPRS) 413
Wingate Scholarships 697

Caribbean Countries

International Postgraduate Research Scholarships (IPRS) 413

East European Countries

International Postgraduate Research Scholarships (IPRS) 413

European Union

AHRC Doctoral Awards Scheme 109
CBRL Travel Grant 248
Professional Preparation Master's Scheme
Research Preparation Master's Scheme
Wingate Scholarships 697

Middle East

International Postgraduate Research Scholarships (IPRS) 413

New Zealand

Wingate Scholarships 697

South Africa

International Postgraduate Research Scholarships (IPRS) 413
Wingate Scholarships 697

United Kingdom

Aberystwyth Postgraduate Research Studentships 4
AHRC Doctoral Awards Scheme 109
CBRL Research Award 248
CBRL Travel Grant 248

International Postgraduate Research Scholarships (IPRS) 413
Professional Preparation Master's Scheme
Research Preparation Master's Scheme
Wingate Scholarships 697

United States of America

Fulbright Senior Specialists Program 249
International Postgraduate Research Scholarships (IPRS) 413
NHPRC Fellowship in Archival Administration 481
NHPRC Fellowship in Documentary Editing 481

West European Countries

International Postgraduate Research Scholarships (IPRS) 413

MATHEMATICS AND COMPUTER SCIENCE

GENERAL

Any Country

Abdus Salam ICTP Fellowships 4
AFUW Western Australian Bursaries 164
Alain Bensoussan Fellowship Programme 286
Alan Turing Prize 765
Andrew Mellon Foundation Scholarship 547
Association for Women in Science Educational Foundation
    Predoctoral Awards 118
AUC Assistantships 96
AUC University Fellowships 98
Australian Postgraduate Award Research Scholarship
BRI PhD Scholarships 156
CICOR Postdoctoral Scholar Fellowship in Coastal Oceanography,
    Climate or Marine Ecosystems 804
Concordia University Graduate Fellowships 243
CSCMP George A Gecowets Graduate Scholarship Program 250
David J Azrieli Graduate Fellowship 243
ETH Zurich Excellence Scholarship and Opportunity Award 624
HFSPO Cross-Disciplinary Fellowships 383
HFSPO Short-Term Fellowships 384
Honda Prize 343
Hugh Kelly Fellowship 548
Institute Development Fellowships 152
International Postgraduate Research Scholarship 667
John Hume Postgraduate Scholarships 490
La Trobe University Postgraduate Scholarship 414
Lincoln College Sloane Robinson Foundation Graduate Awards 733
Matsumae International Foundation Research Fellowship 436
Monash International Postgraduate Research Scholarship (MIPRS)
    455
Postgraduate Research Studentship 689
Queen Mary Research Studentships 539
Rhodes University Postdoctoral Fellowship and The Andrew Mellon
    Postdoctoral Fellowship 548
Rhodes University Postgraduate Scholarship 549
Royal Irish Academy Mobility Grants 569
Scottish Government Personal Research Fellowships 628
Scottish Government/RSE Support Research Fellowships 629
SEG Scholarships 611
Shorenstein APARC Postdoctoral Research Fellowship in Korean
    Studies 586
Sir Allan Sewell Visiting Fellowship 326
Sir George Jessel Studentship in Mathematics 657
SRG Postdoctoral Fellowships 646
St Catherine's College: Leathersellers' Company Graduate
    Scholarship
Stanley G French Graduate Fellowship 244
University of Ballarat Postgraduate Research Scholarship
University of Bristol Postgraduate Scholarships 672
University of Otago International Scholarships 717
University of Otago PhD Scholarships 718
University of Otago Prestigious PhD Scholarships 718
Vera Moore International Postgraduate Research Scholarships 455

Victoria University of Wellington PhD Scholarships 786
Weizmann Institute of Science MSc Fellowships 792
Weizmann Institute of Science PhD Fellowships 792
Weizmann Institute of Science Postdoctoral Fellowships Program 793
WHOI Geophysical Fluid Dynamics (GFD) Fellowships 804
Wolf Foundation Prizes 799

African Nations

ABCCF Student Grant 102
ANSTI/DAAD Postgraduate Fellowships 9
CAS-TWAS Fellowship for Postdoctoral Research in China 629
CAS-TWAS Fellowship for Postgraduate Research in China 629
CAS-TWAS Fellowship for Visiting Scholars in China 629
CNPq-TWAS Doctoral Fellowships in Brazil 630
CNPq-TWAS Fellowships for Postdoctoral Research in Brazil 630
CSIR (Council of Scientific and Industrial Research)/TWAS Fellowship
    for Postgraduate Research 630
CSIR (The Council of Scientific and Industrial Research)/TWAS
    Fellowship for Postdoctoral Research 630
International Postgraduate Research Scholarships (IPRS) 413
International Postgraduate Research Scholarships (IPRS) 413
Lindemann Trust Fellowships 280
NUFFIC-NFP Fellowships for Master's Degree Programmes 496
PTDF Cambridge Scholarships 195
The Trieste Science Prize 631
TWAS Fellowships for Research and Advanced Training 631
TWAS Grants for Scientific Meetings in Developing Countries 631
TWAS Prizes 632
TWAS Prizes to Young Scientists in Developing Countries 632
TWAS Research Grants 632
TWAS Spare Parts for Scientific Equipment 632
TWAS UNESCO Associateship Scheme 632

Australia

Faculty of Science and Engineering Research Awards (FSERA) 292
Fulbright Postdoctoral Fellowships 140
Fulbright Postgraduate Awards 140
International Postgraduate Research Scholarships (IPRS) 413
Lindemann Trust Fellowships 280
NBCF Postdoctoral Fellowship 469
University of Otago Master's Awards 717
Victoria Fellowships 264
Wingate Scholarships 697

Canada

International Postgraduate Research Scholarships (IPRS) 413
International Postgraduate Research Scholarships (IPRS) 413
J W McConnell Memorial Fellowships 243
Killam Research Fellowships 199
Lindemann Trust Fellowships 280
NSERC Postdoctoral Fellowships 495
Vatican Film Library Mellon Fellowship 785
Wingate Scholarships 697

Caribbean Countries

CAS-TWAS Fellowship for Postdoctoral Research in China 629
CAS-TWAS Fellowship for Postgraduate Research in China 629
CAS-TWAS Fellowship for Visiting Scholars in China 629
CNPq-TWAS Doctoral Fellowships in Brazil 630
CNPq-TWAS Fellowships for Postdoctoral Research in Brazil 630
CSIR (Council of Scientific and Industrial Research)/TWAS Fellowship
    for Postgraduate Research 630
CSIR (The Council of Scientific and Industrial Research)/TWAS
    Fellowship for Postdoctoral Research 630
International Postgraduate Research Scholarships (IPRS) 413
International Postgraduate Research Scholarships (IPRS) 413
TWAS Fellowships for Research and Advanced Training 631
TWAS Grants for Scientific Meetings in Developing Countries 631
TWAS Prizes 632
TWAS Prizes to Young Scientists in Developing Countries 632
TWAS Research Grants 632
TWAS Spare Parts for Scientific Equipment 632
TWAS UNESCO Associateship Scheme 632

East European Countries

CERN Technical Student Programme 227
International Postgraduate Research Scholarships (IPRS) 413
International Postgraduate Research Scholarships (IPRS) 413

European Union

International Postgraduate Research Scholarships (IPRS) 413
University of Kent Institute of Mathematics, Statistics and Actuarial Science (IMSAS) 700
University of Southampton Engineering Doctorate 759
Wingate Scholarships 697

Middle East

ABCCF Student Grant 102
CAS-TWAS Fellowship for Postdoctoral Research in China 629
CAS-TWAS Fellowship for Postgraduate Research in China 629
CAS-TWAS Fellowship for Visiting Scholars in China 629
CNPq-TWAS Doctoral Fellowships in Brazil 630
CNPq-TWAS Fellowships for Postdoctoral Research in Brazil 630
CSIR (Council of Scientific and Industrial Research)/TWAS Fellowship for Postgraduate Research 630
CSIR (The Council of Scientific and Industrial Research)/TWAS Fellowship for Postdoctoral Research 630
IDB Merit Scholarship for High Technology 395
IDB Scholarship Programme in Science and Technology 395
International Postgraduate Research Scholarships (IPRS) 413
International Postgraduate Research Scholarships (IPRS) 413
KFAS Kuwait Prize 413
NUFFIC-NFP Fellowships for Master's Degree Programmes 496
The Trieste Science Prize 631
TWAS Fellowships for Research and Advanced Training 631
TWAS Grants for Scientific Meetings in Developing Countries 631
TWAS Prizes 632
TWAS Prizes to Young Scientists in Developing Countries 632
TWAS Research Grants 632
TWAS Spare Parts for Scientific Equipment 632
TWAS UNESCO Associateship Scheme 632

New Zealand

Faculty of Science and Engineering Research Awards (FSERA) 292
Lindemann Trust Fellowships 280
University of Otago Master's Awards 717
Wingate Scholarships 697

South Africa

CAS-TWAS Fellowship for Postdoctoral Research in China 629
CAS-TWAS Fellowship for Postgraduate Research in China 629
CAS-TWAS Fellowship for Visiting Scholars in China 629
CNPq-TWAS Doctoral Fellowships in Brazil 630
CNPq-TWAS Fellowships for Postdoctoral Research in Brazil 630
CSIR (Council of Scientific and Industrial Research)/TWAS Fellowship for Postgraduate Research 630
CSIR (The Council of Scientific and Industrial Research)/TWAS Fellowship for Postdoctoral Research 630
Henderson Postgraduate Scholarships 548
International Postgraduate Research Scholarships (IPRS) 413
International Postgraduate Research Scholarships (IPRS) 413
Lindemann Trust Fellowships 280
NUFFIC-NFP Fellowships for Master's Degree Programmes 496
The Trieste Science Prize 631
TWAS Fellowships for Research and Advanced Training 631
TWAS Grants for Scientific Meetings in Developing Countries 631
TWAS Prizes 632
TWAS Prizes to Young Scientists in Developing Countries 632
TWAS Research Grants 632
TWAS Spare Parts for Scientific Equipment 632
TWAS UNESCO Associateship Scheme 632
Wingate Scholarships 697
Wolfson Foundation Grants 799

United Kingdom

Aberystwyth Postgraduate Research Studentships 4
CERN Technical Student Programme 227
Frank Knox Fellowships at Harvard University 302

Grundy Educational Trust 327
International Postgraduate Research Scholarships (IPRS) 413
International Postgraduate Research Scholarships (IPRS) 413
Kennedy Scholarships 409
Leverhulme Scholarships for Architecture 321
Lindemann Trust Fellowships 280
Mr and Mrs David Edward Memorial Award 145
Royal Commission Research Fellowship 563
University of Kent Institute of Mathematics, Statistics and Actuarial Science (IMSAS) 700
University of Southampton Engineering Doctorate 759
Wingate Scholarships 697
Wolfson Foundation Grants 799

United States of America

Air Force Summer Faculty Fellowship Program 84
British Marshall Scholarships 685
Congress Bundestag Youth Exchange for Young Professionals 221
DEED (Demonstration of Energy-Efficient Developments) Student Research Grant/Internship 80
Fellowships for Minority Doctoral Students 61
Ford Foundation Dissertation Fellowships for Minorities 487
Foundation for Science and Disability Student Grant Fund 302
Fulbright Senior Specialists Program 249
International Postgraduate Research Scholarships (IPRS) 413
International Postgraduate Research Scholarships (IPRS) 413
Krell Institute Computational Science Graduate Fellowship Program 412
Naval Research Laboratory Post Doctoral Fellowship Program 84
NDSEG Fellowship Program 84
North Dakota Indian Scholarship 507
ONR Summer Faculty Research 84
Pasteur Foundation Postdoctoral Fellowship Program 522
PhRMAF Postdoctoral Fellowships in Informatics 528
PhRMAF Research Starter Grants in Informatics 529
PhRMAF Sabbatical Fellowships in Informatics 530
Renate W Chasman Scholarship 180
SMART Scholarship for Service Program 85
Vatican Film Library Mellon Fellowship 785
Winston Churchill Foundation Scholarship 797

West European Countries

CERN Technical Student Programme 227
International Postgraduate Research Scholarships (IPRS) 413
International Postgraduate Research Scholarships (IPRS) 413
Janson Johan Helmich Scholarships and Travel Grants 398
Mr and Mrs David Edward Memorial Award 145
University of Otago Master's Awards 717

STATISTICS

Any Country

Acadia Graduate Awards 5
ASQ Ellis R. Ott Scholarship for Applied Statistics and Quality Management 90
Australian Postgraduate Award Research Scholarship
ETH Zurich Excellence Scholarship and Opportunity Award 624
ETS Postdoctoral Fellowships 276
Hugh Kelly Fellowship 548
International Postgraduate Research Scholarship 667
NCAR Graduate Visitor Programme 471
NCAR Postdoctoral Appointments in the Advanced Study Program 471
Pierre Robillard Award 620
Postgraduate Research Studentship 689
Queen Mary Research Studentships 539
Rhodes University Postdoctoral Fellowship and The Andrew Mellon Postdoctoral Fellowship 548
Sir James McNeill Foundation Postgraduate Scholarship 455
University of Ballarat Postgraduate Research Scholarship
University of Bristol Postgraduate Scholarships 672
Victoria University of Wellington PhD Scholarships 786

African Nations

IDRC Evaluation Research Awards 381
International Postgraduate Research Scholarships (IPRS) 413

Australia

Australian Clinical Research Postdoctoral Fellowship 477
Wingate Scholarships 697

Canada

Gertrude M. Cox Scholarship 95
IDRC Evaluation Research Awards 381
International Postgraduate Research Scholarships (IPRS) 413
Wingate Scholarships 697

Caribbean Countries

IDRC Evaluation Research Awards 381
International Postgraduate Research Scholarships (IPRS) 413

East European Countries

IDRC Evaluation Research Awards 381
International Postgraduate Research Scholarships (IPRS) 413

European Union

ESRC 1+3 Awards and +3 Awards
Statistics: EPSRC Studentships 746
University of Kent Institute of Mathematics, Statistics and Actuarial Science (IMSAS) 700
Wingate Scholarships 697

Middle East

IDRC Evaluation Research Awards 381
International Postgraduate Research Scholarships (IPRS) 413

New Zealand

Wingate Scholarships 697

South Africa

Allan Gray Senior Scholarship 547
IDRC Evaluation Research Awards 381
International Postgraduate Research Scholarships (IPRS) 413
Wingate Scholarships 697

United Kingdom

ESRC 1+3 Awards and +3 Awards
International Postgraduate Research Scholarships (IPRS) 413
James Watt Research Scholarships 694
Mr and Mrs David Edward Memorial Award 145
Statistics: EPSRC Studentships 746
University of Kent Institute of Mathematics, Statistics and Actuarial Science (IMSAS) 700
Wingate Scholarships 697

United States of America

Air Force Summer Faculty Fellowship Program 84
British Marshall Scholarships 685
ETS Postdoctoral Fellowships 276
ETS Sylvia Taylor Johnson Minority Fellowship in Educational Measurement 276
Fulbright Senior Specialists Program 249
Gertrude M. Cox Scholarship 95
International Postgraduate Research Scholarships (IPRS) 413
NCAR Faculty Fellowship Programme 471
Winston Churchill Foundation Scholarship 797

West European Countries

ESRC 1+3 Awards and +3 Awards
International Postgraduate Research Scholarships (IPRS) 413
Mr and Mrs David Edward Memorial Award 145

ACTUARIAL SCIENCE

Any Country

The AERF/CKER Individual Grants Competition 607
ETH Zurich Excellence Scholarship and Opportunity Award 624
ETS Postdoctoral Fellowships 276
Postgraduate Research Studentship 689
Sir James McNeill Foundation Postgraduate Scholarship 455
University of Ballarat Postgraduate Research Scholarship

African Nations

International Postgraduate Research Scholarships (IPRS) 413

Australia

NBCF Doctoral Scholarship 469

Canada

International Postgraduate Research Scholarships (IPRS) 413

Caribbean Countries

International Postgraduate Research Scholarships (IPRS) 413

East European Countries

International Postgraduate Research Scholarships (IPRS) 413

Middle East

International Postgraduate Research Scholarships (IPRS) 413

South Africa

International Postgraduate Research Scholarships (IPRS) 413

United Kingdom

International Postgraduate Research Scholarships (IPRS) 413
Mr and Mrs David Edward Memorial Award 145

United States of America

British Marshall Scholarships 685
ETS Postdoctoral Fellowships 276
Fulbright Senior Specialists Program 249
International Postgraduate Research Scholarships (IPRS) 413
Winston Churchill Foundation Scholarship 797

West European Countries

International Postgraduate Research Scholarships (IPRS) 413
Mr and Mrs David Edward Memorial Award 145

APPLIED MATHEMATICS

Any Country

CICOR Postdoctoral Scholar Fellowship in Coastal Oceanography, Climate or Marine Ecosystems 804
ETH Zurich Excellence Scholarship and Opportunity Award 624
ETS Postdoctoral Fellowships 276
Hugh Kelly Fellowship 548
Institut Mittag-Leffler Grants 361
Institute for Advanced Study Postdoctoral Residential Fellowships 363
International Postgraduate Research Scholarship 667
La Trobe University Postgraduate Scholarship 414
NCAR Graduate Visitor Programme 471
NCAR Postdoctoral Appointments in the Advanced Study Program 471
NERC Postdoctoral Research Fellowships 494
Postgraduate Research Studentship 689
Queen Mary Research Studentships 539
Rhodes University Postdoctoral Fellowship and The Andrew Mellon Postdoctoral Fellowship 548
Sir James Lighthill Scholarship 657
Sir James McNeill Foundation Postgraduate Scholarship 455
University of Ballarat Postgraduate Research Scholarship
University of Bristol Postgraduate Scholarships 672
University of Western Ontario Senior Visiting Fellowship 777

Victoria University of Wellington PhD Scholarships 786
Weizmann Institute of Science MSc Fellowships 792
Weizmann Institute of Science PhD Fellowships 792
Weizmann Institute of Science Postdoctoral Fellowships Program 793

African Nations

International Postgraduate Research Scholarships (IPRS) 413

Australia

NBCF Doctoral Scholarship 469
NBCF Postdoctoral Fellowship 469
Wingate Scholarships 697

Canada

International Postgraduate Research Scholarships (IPRS) 413
Wingate Scholarships 697

Caribbean Countries

International Postgraduate Research Scholarships (IPRS) 413

East European Countries

International Postgraduate Research Scholarships (IPRS) 413

European Union

University of Kent Institute of Mathematics, Statistics and Actuarial
Science (IMSAS) 700
Wingate Scholarships 697

Middle East

International Postgraduate Research Scholarships (IPRS) 413

New Zealand

Wingate Scholarships 697

South Africa

International Postgraduate Research Scholarships (IPRS) 413
Wingate Scholarships 697

United Kingdom

Aberystwyth Postgraduate Research Studentships 4
International Postgraduate Research Scholarships (IPRS) 413
University of Kent Institute of Mathematics, Statistics and Actuarial
Science (IMSAS) 700
Wingate Scholarships 697

United States of America

Air Force Summer Faculty Fellowship Program 84
British Marshall Scholarships 685
ETS Postdoctoral Fellowships 276
Fulbright Senior Specialists Program 249
The Graduate Fellowship Award 340
International Postgraduate Research Scholarships (IPRS) 413
Krell Institute Computational Science Graduate Fellowship Program
412
NCAR Faculty Fellowship Programme 471
NPSC Fellowship in Physical Sciences 487
Winston Churchill Foundation Scholarship 797

West European Countries

International Postgraduate Research Scholarships (IPRS) 413

COMPUTER SCIENCE

Any Country

Acadia Graduate Awards 5
Adelle and Erwin Tomash Fellowship in the History of Information
Processing 228
AUC Graduate Merit Fellowships 97
AUC Laboratory Instruction Graduate Fellowships in Engineering and
Computer Science 97
Australian Postgraduate Award Research Scholarship

BP/RSE Research Fellowships 628
Bursaries 144
CERN Summer Student Programme 227
Computing Laboratory Scholarship 698
DAGSI Research Fellowships 261
ESRF Postdoctoral Fellowships 287
ETH Zurich Excellence Scholarship and Opportunity Award 624
ETS Postdoctoral Fellowships 276
ETS Summer Internship Program for Graduate Students 276
HFSPO Long-Term Fellowships 383
Hugh Kelly Fellowship 548
Institute for Advanced Study Postdoctoral Residential Fellowships 363
International Postgraduate Research Scholarship 667
La Trobe University Postgraduate Scholarship 414
Lydia I Pickup Memorial Scholarship 612
Microsoft Fellowship 448
Microsoft Research India PhD Fellowships 448
NCAR Graduate Visitor Programme 471
NCAR Postdoctoral Appointments in the Advanced Study Program 471
New Mexico Information Technology Fellowships 713
NFB Computer Science Scholarship 475
Ohio Board of Regents (OBR) Distinguished Doctoral Research
Fellowship 679
Postgraduate Research Studentship 689
Queen Mary Research Studentships 539
Rhodes University Postdoctoral Fellowship and The Andrew Mellon
Postdoctoral Fellowship 548
School of Computer Science and Electronic Engineering University
Scholarship 689
SWE Microsoft Corporation Scholarships 612
Tomsk Polytechnic University International Scholarship 634
University of Ballarat Postgraduate Research Scholarship
University of Bristol Postgraduate Scholarships 672
Victoria University of Wellington PhD Scholarships 786
Weizmann Institute of Science MSc Fellowships 792
Weizmann Institute of Science PhD Fellowships 792
Weizmann Institute of Science Postdoctoral Fellowships Program 793

African Nations

IDRC Evaluation Research Awards 381
International Postgraduate Research Scholarships (IPRS) 413
Shell Centenary Scholarships and Shell Centenary Chevening
Scholarships at Edinburgh 683

Australia

Google Australia Anita Borg Memorial Scholarship 322
NBCF Doctoral Scholarship 469
NBCF Postdoctoral Fellowship 469
Wingate Scholarships 697

Canada

IDRC Evaluation Research Awards 381
International Postgraduate Research Scholarships (IPRS) 413
Public Safety and Emergency Preparedness Canada Research
Fellowship in Honour of Stuart Nesbitt White 123
Wingate Scholarships 697

Caribbean Countries

IDRC Evaluation Research Awards 381
International Postgraduate Research Scholarships (IPRS) 413
Shell Centenary Scholarships and Shell Centenary Chevening
Scholarships at Edinburgh 683

East European Countries

CERN Technical Student Programme 227
IDRC Evaluation Research Awards 381
International Postgraduate Research Scholarships (IPRS) 413
Shell Centenary Scholarships and Shell Centenary Chevening
Scholarships at Edinburgh 683

European Union

Computing Laboratory: EPSRC Doctoral Training Grant Studentships
723
EPSRC Doctoral Training Awards for Computer Science 698

Microsoft Research European PhD Scholarship Programme 448
University of Southampton Engineering Doctorate 759
Wingate Scholarships 697

Middle East

IDRC Evaluation Research Awards 381
International Postgraduate Research Scholarships (IPRS) 413
Shell Centenary Scholarships and Shell Centenary Chevening
　　Scholarships at Edinburgh 683

New Zealand

Wingate Scholarships 697

South Africa

IDRC Evaluation Research Awards 381
International Postgraduate Research Scholarships (IPRS) 413
Shell Centenary Scholarships and Shell Centenary Chevening
　　Scholarships at Edinburgh 683
Wingate Scholarships 697

United Kingdom

Aberystwyth Postgraduate Research Studentships 4
CERN Technical Student Programme 227
Computing Laboratory: EPSRC Doctoral Training Grant Studentships
　　723
EPSRC Doctoral Training Awards for Computer Science 698
International Postgraduate Research Scholarships (IPRS) 413
Ohio Board of Regents (OBR) Distinguished Doctoral Research
　　Fellowship 679
University of Southampton Engineering Doctorate 759
Wingate Scholarships 697

United States of America

Air Force Summer Faculty Fellowship Program 84
British Marshall Scholarships 685
DEED (Demonstration of Energy-Efficient Developments) Student
　　Research Grant/Internship 80
ETS Postdoctoral Fellowships 276
ETS Summer Internship Program for Graduate Students 276
Foundation for Science and Disability Student Grant Fund 302
Fulbright Distinguished Chairs Program 248
Fulbright Senior Specialists Program 249
Graduate Assistance in Areas of National Need (GAANN) Award 805
The Graduate Fellowship Award 340
International Postgraduate Research Scholarships (IPRS) 413
Krell Institute Computational Science Graduate Fellowship Program
　　412
National Federation of the Blind Computer Science Scholarship 475
NCAR Faculty Fellowship Programme 471
NPSC Fellowship in Physical Sciences 487
Ohio Board of Regents (OBR) Distinguished Doctoral Research
　　Fellowship 679
Olive Lynn Salembier Scholarship 612
Philip Morris USA Thurgood Marshall Scholarship 633
PhRMAF Postdoctoral Fellowships in Informatics 528
PhRMAF Research Starter Grants in Informatics 529
PhRMAF Sabbatical Fellowships in Informatics 530
Winston Churchill Foundation Scholarship 797

West European Countries

CERN Technical Student Programme 227
EPSRC Doctoral Training Awards for Computer Science 698
International Postgraduate Research Scholarships (IPRS) 413
Microsoft Research European PhD Scholarship Programme 448
Shell Centenary Scholarships and Shell Centenary Chevening
　　Scholarships at Edinburgh 683

ARTIFICIAL INTELLIGENCE

Any Country

Australian Postgraduate Award Research Scholarship
BP/RSE Research Fellowships 628

Bursaries 144
ETS Postdoctoral Fellowships 276
International Postgraduate Research Scholarship 667
La Trobe University Postgraduate Scholarship 414
Queen Mary Research Studentships 539
School of Computer Science and Electronic Engineering University
　　Scholarship 689
University of Ballarat Postgraduate Research Scholarship
University of Bristol Postgraduate Scholarships 672
Victoria University of Wellington PhD Scholarships 786

African Nations

International Postgraduate Research Scholarships (IPRS) 413
Shell Centenary Scholarships and Shell Centenary Chevening
　　Scholarships at Edinburgh 683

Australia

NBCF Doctoral Scholarship 469
NBCF Postdoctoral Fellowship 469
Wingate Scholarships 697

Canada

International Postgraduate Research Scholarships (IPRS) 413
Wingate Scholarships 697

Caribbean Countries

International Postgraduate Research Scholarships (IPRS) 413
Shell Centenary Scholarships and Shell Centenary Chevening
　　Scholarships at Edinburgh 683

East European Countries

International Postgraduate Research Scholarships (IPRS) 413
Shell Centenary Scholarships and Shell Centenary Chevening
　　Scholarships at Edinburgh 683

European Union

Wingate Scholarships 697

Middle East

International Postgraduate Research Scholarships (IPRS) 413
Shell Centenary Scholarships and Shell Centenary Chevening
　　Scholarships at Edinburgh 683

New Zealand

Wingate Scholarships 697

South Africa

International Postgraduate Research Scholarships (IPRS)
　　413
Shell Centenary Scholarships and Shell Centenary Chevening
　　Scholarships at Edinburgh 683
Wingate Scholarships 697

United Kingdom

Aberystwyth Postgraduate Research Studentships 4
International Postgraduate Research Scholarships (IPRS) 413
Wingate Scholarships 697

United States of America

Air Force Summer Faculty Fellowship Program 84
British Marshall Scholarships 685
ETS Postdoctoral Fellowships 276
International Postgraduate Research Scholarships (IPRS)
　　413
Winston Churchill Foundation Scholarship 797

West European Countries

International Postgraduate Research Scholarships (IPRS)
　　413
Shell Centenary Scholarships and Shell Centenary Chevening
　　Scholarships at Edinburgh 683

SYSTEMS ANALYSIS

Any Country

Australian Postgraduate Award Research Scholarship
Bursaries 144
HFSPO Long-Term Fellowships 383
International Postgraduate Research Scholarship 667
La Trobe University Postgraduate Scholarship 414
University of Ballarat Postgraduate Research Scholarship
University of Bristol Postgraduate Scholarships 672
Victoria University of Wellington PhD Scholarships 786

African Nations

International Postgraduate Research Scholarships (IPRS) 413
Shell Centenary Scholarships and Shell Centenary Chevening
    Scholarships at Edinburgh 683

Australia

NBCF Doctoral Scholarship 469
NBCF Postdoctoral Fellowship 469

Canada

International Postgraduate Research Scholarships (IPRS) 413

Caribbean Countries

International Postgraduate Research Scholarships (IPRS) 413
Shell Centenary Scholarships and Shell Centenary Chevening
    Scholarships at Edinburgh 683

East European Countries

CERN Technical Student Programme 227
International Postgraduate Research Scholarships (IPRS) 413
Shell Centenary Scholarships and Shell Centenary Chevening
    Scholarships at Edinburgh 683

Middle East

International Postgraduate Research Scholarships (IPRS) 413
Shell Centenary Scholarships and Shell Centenary Chevening
    Scholarships at Edinburgh 683

South Africa

International Postgraduate Research Scholarships (IPRS) 413
Shell Centenary Scholarships and Shell Centenary Chevening
    Scholarships at Edinburgh 683

United Kingdom

Aberystwyth Postgraduate Research Studentships 4
CERN Technical Student Programme 227
International Postgraduate Research Scholarships (IPRS) 413

United States of America

Air Force Summer Faculty Fellowship Program 84
British Marshall Scholarships 685
International Postgraduate Research Scholarships (IPRS) 413
PhRMAF Postdoctoral Fellowships in Informatics 528
PhRMAF Research Starter Grants in Informatics 529
PhRMAF Sabbatical Fellowships in Informatics 530
Winston Churchill Foundation Scholarship 797

West European Countries

CERN Technical Student Programme 227
International Postgraduate Research Scholarships (IPRS) 413
Shell Centenary Scholarships and Shell Centenary Chevening
    Scholarships at Edinburgh 683

MEDICAL SCIENCES

GENERAL

Any Country

AACR Career Development Awards in Cancer Research 28
AACR Gertrude B. Elion Cancer Research Award 28

AACR Research Fellowships 29
AACR Scholar-in-Training Awards 29
Action Medical Research Project Grants 6
Action Medical Research Training Fellowship 7
Alberta Heritage Clinical Fellowships 12
Alberta Heritage Full-Time Fellowships 13
Alberta Heritage Full-Time Studentship 13
Alberta Heritage Part-Time Fellowships 13
Alberta Heritage Part-Time Studentship 13
Alzheimer's Society Research Grants
American Cancer Society UICC International Fellowships for
    Beginning Investigators (ACSBI) 389
American Herpes Foundation Stephen L Sacks Investigator Award 58
ANRF Research Grants 104
Ataxia Research Grant 468
BackCare Research Grants 144
Barbers Company Clinical Nursing Scholarship 557
Behavioral Sciences Postdoctoral Fellowships 282
Beit Memorial Fellowships for Medical Research 147
Berthold Leibinger Innovation Prize 148
BIAL Award 149
Brain Research Trust Prize and Medical Research Council
    Studentships 648
Breast Cancer Campaign PhD Studentships 157
Breast Cancer Campaign Project Grants 157
Breast Cancer Campaign Scientific Fellowships 157
Breast Cancer Campaign Small Pilot Grants 157
BRI PhD Scholarships 156
British Skin Foundation Small Grants 177
Broad Medical Research Program for Inflammatory Bowel Disease
    Grants 178
CAGS UMI Dissertation Awards 199
Cancer Research Society, Inc. (Canada) Postdoctoral Fellowships
    218
CCFF Scholarships 202
CCFF Small Conference Grants 203
CCFF Visiting Scientist Awards 204
CIHR Fellowships Program 210
Colt Foundation PhD Fellowship 239
Concordia University Graduate Fellowships 243
CRF (Caledonian Research Foundation)/RSE Personal Research
    Fellowships 182
Diabetes UK Equipment Grant 268
Diabetes UK Project Grants 269
Direct Research on Ataxia-Telangiectasia 3
Dr Hadwen Trust Research Assistant or Technician 270
Dr Hadwen Trust Research Fellowship 270
Dr Vincent Cristofalo Memorial Fund, Cecille Gould Memorial Fund
    Award in Cancer Research, Richard Shepherd Fellowship 54
Exeter College Monsanto Senior Research Fellowship 288
Exeter College Staines Medical Research Fellowship 289
Faculty of Medicine Studentships 694
Field Psych Trust Grant 291
Foulkes Foundation Fellowship 298
Hastings Center International Visiting Scholars Program 332
Health Services Research Training Fellowships and Palliative Care
    Fellowships 334
Honda Prize 343
HRB Project Grants-General 334
HRB Summer Student Grants 334
HRB Translational Research Programmes 335
Humane Research Trust Grant 347
IAUW International Scholarship 166
ICS Young Investigator Award (Research Grants) 374
ICSU-TWAS-UNESCO-UNU/IAS Visiting Scientist Programme 631
IFER Graduate Fellowship Program 382
JDRF Career Development Award 406
JDRF Innovative Grant 407
JDRF Postdoctoral Fellowships 407
Karl Storz Travelling Scholarship 573
Kay Kendall Leukaemia Fund Research Fellowship 408
Lincoln College Sloane Robinson Foundation Graduate Awards 733
Lindbergh Grants 228
Matsumae International Foundation Research Fellowship 436
Melville Trust for Care and Cure of Cancer Research Fellowships 443
Melville Trust for Care and Cure of Cancer Research Grants 443

African Nations

Australia

Canada

Caribbean Countries

CSIR (Council of Scientific and Industrial Research)/TWAS Fellowship for Postgraduate Research 630
CSIR (The Council of Scientific and Industrial Research)/TWAS Fellowship for Postdoctoral Research 630
Hastings Center International Visiting Scholars Program 332
International Postgraduate Research Scholarships (IPRS) 413
International Postgraduate Research Scholarships (IPRS) 413
ORSAS Awards 688
TWAS Fellowships for Research and Advanced Training 631
TWAS Grants for Scientific Meetings in Developing Countries 631
TWAS Prizes 632
TWAS Prizes to Young Scientists in Developing Countries 632
TWAS Research Grants 632
TWAS Spare Parts for Scientific Equipment 632
TWAS UNESCO Associateship Scheme 632

East European Countries

Hastings Center International Visiting Scholars Program 332
International Postgraduate Research Scholarships (IPRS) 413
International Postgraduate Research Scholarships (IPRS) 413
ORSAS Awards 688

European Union

Henry Dryerre Scholarship in Medical and Veterinary Physiology 694
International Postgraduate Research Scholarships (IPRS) 413
Wingate Scholarships 697

Middle East

CAS-TWAS Fellowship for Postdoctoral Research in China 629
CAS-TWAS Fellowship for Postgraduate Research in China 629
CAS-TWAS Fellowship for Visiting Scholars in China 629
CNPq-TWAS Doctoral Fellowships in Brazil 630
CNPq-TWAS Fellowships for Postdoctoral Research in Brazil 630
CSIR (Council of Scientific and Industrial Research)/TWAS Fellowship for Postgraduate Research 630
CSIR (The Council of Scientific and Industrial Research)/TWAS Fellowship for Postdoctoral Research 630
Hastings Center International Visiting Scholars Program 332
IDB Scholarship Programme in Science and Technology 395
International Postgraduate Research Scholarships (IPRS) 413
International Postgraduate Research Scholarships (IPRS) 413
NUFFIC-NFP Fellowships for Master's Degree Programmes 496
ORSAS Awards 688
The Trieste Science Prize 631
TWAS Fellowships for Research and Advanced Training 631
TWAS Grants for Scientific Meetings in Developing Countries 631
TWAS Prizes 632
TWAS Prizes to Young Scientists in Developing Countries 632
TWAS Research Grants 632
TWAS Spare Parts for Scientific Equipment 632
TWAS UNESCO Associateship Scheme 632

New Zealand

Harkness Fellowships in Healthcare Policy 240
Hastings Center International Visiting Scholars Program 332
Hsanz Travel Grant 329
ORSAS Awards 688
Training Scholarship for Indigenous Health Research 479
University of Otago Master's Awards 717
Wingate Scholarships 697

South Africa

CAS-TWAS Fellowship for Postdoctoral Research in China 629
CAS-TWAS Fellowship for Postgraduate Research in China 629
CAS-TWAS Fellowship for Visiting Scholars in China 629
CNPq-TWAS Doctoral Fellowships in Brazil 630
CNPq-TWAS Fellowships for Postdoctoral Research in Brazil 630
CSIR (Council of Scientific and Industrial Research)/TWAS Fellowship for Postgraduate Research 630
CSIR (The Council of Scientific and Industrial Research)/TWAS Fellowship for Postdoctoral Research 630
Hastings Center International Visiting Scholars Program 332
International Postgraduate Research Scholarships (IPRS) 413
International Postgraduate Research Scholarships (IPRS) 413

NUFFIC-NFP Fellowships for Master's Degree Programmes 496
ORSAS Awards 688
The Trieste Science Prize 631
TWAS Fellowships for Research and Advanced Training 631
TWAS Grants for Scientific Meetings in Developing Countries 631
TWAS Prizes 632
TWAS Prizes to Young Scientists in Developing Countries 632
TWAS Research Grants 632
TWAS Spare Parts for Scientific Equipment 632
TWAS UNESCO Associateship Scheme 632
Wingate Scholarships 697
Wolfson Foundation Grants 799

United Kingdom

American Gynecological Club/Gynaecological Visiting Society Fellowship 558
British Lung Foundation Project Grants 170
Frank Knox Fellowships at Harvard University 302
Fund for Innovation 539
Gilchrist Fieldwork Award 318
Goldsmiths' Company Science for Society Courses
Grundy Educational Trust 327
Harkness Fellowships in Healthcare Policy 240
Hastings Center International Visiting Scholars Program 332
Hilda Martindale Exhibitions 341
International Postgraduate Research Scholarships (IPRS) 413
International Postgraduate Research Scholarships (IPRS) 413
James and Grace Anderson Trust Research Grant 397
Joan Dawkins Research Grant 171
Kennedy Scholarships 409
Moynihan Travelling Fellowship 122
MRC Industrial Collaborative Studentships 439
MRC Master's Studentships
MRC Research Studentships 440
Postgraduate Student Allowance Scheme (PSAS) (Queen Margaret) 539
Resuscitation Council Research Fellowships 546
Resuscitation Council Research Grants 546
Royal Commission Research Fellowship 563
Wellbeing of Women/RCOG Research Training Fellowship 793
Wingate Scholarships 697
Wolfson Foundation Grants 799

United States of America

The A. Jean Ayres Award 72
ADA Career Development Awards 51
Alcohol Beverage Medical Research Foundation Research Project Grant 14
American Gynecological Club/Gynaecological Visiting Society Fellowship 558
AOTF Certificate of Appreciation 72
Aventis Research Fellowship 511
Diversity Program in Neuroscience Postdoctoral Fellowship 76
Dr Marie E Zakrzewski Medical Scholarship 411
Fellowship for American College Students 545
Florence P Kendall Doctoral Scholarships 301
Foundation for Science and Disability Student Grant Fund 302
Fulbright Senior Specialists Program 249
Howard Brown Rickard Scholarship 474
International Postgraduate Research Scholarships (IPRS) 413
International Postgraduate Research Scholarships (IPRS) 413
John E Fogarty International Research Scientist Development Award 404
Lawrence R. Foster Memorial Scholarship 514
March of Dimes Research Grants 431
National Academics Christine Mirzayan Science and Technology Policy Graduate Fellowship Program 466
National Headache Foundation Research Grant 476
National Osteoporosis Foundation Research Grants 486
New Investigator Fellowships Training Initiative (NIFTI) 301
NMSS Patient Management Care and Rehabilitation Grants 486
North Dakota Indian Scholarship 507
Nurses' Educational Funds Fellowships and Scholarships 510
ORSAS Awards 688
Ortho Biotech Products, L.P. Research Fellowship 512

Parker B Francis Fellowship Program 520
Pasteur Foundation Postdoctoral Fellowship Program 522
Pfizer Atorvastatin Research Awards Program 526
Pfizer Fellowships in Health Literary Clear Health Communication 526
The Pfizer Fellowships in Rheumatology/Immunology 526
Pfizer International HDL Research Awards Program 526
Pfizer Visiting Professorships Program 527
PhRMAF Postdoctoral Fellowships in Health Outcomes Research 528
PhRMAF Predoctoral Fellowships in Health Outcomes Research 529
PhRMAF Research Starter Grants in Health Outcomes Research 529
PhRMAF Sabbatical Fellowships in Health Outcomes Research 530
Promotion of Doctoral Studies (PODS) 302
Research Grants (FPT) 302
The Robert Wood Johnson Health & Society Scholars Program 550
RSNA Research Fellow Program 541
RSNA Research Scholar Grant Program 542
Scholarships for Émigrés from the FSU in the Health Professions 401
SNM Pilot Research Grants in Nuclear Medicine/Molecular Imaging 275
Vatican Film Library Mellon Fellowship 785

West European Countries

Hastings Center International Visiting Scholars Program 332
Henry Dryerre Scholarship 182
International Postgraduate Research Scholarships (IPRS) 413
International Postgraduate Research Scholarships (IPRS) 413
MRC Industrial Collaborative Studentships 439
MRC Master's Studentships
MRC Research Studentships 440
University of Otago Master's Awards 717

PUBLIC HEALTH AND HYGIENE

Any Country

AACR Scholar-in-Training Awards 29
AFSP Distinguished Investigator Awards 55
AFSP Pilot Grants 55
AFSP Postdoctoral Research Fellowships 55
AFSP Standard Research Grants 55
AFSP Young Investigator Award 56
Alzheimer's Society Research Grants
American Cancer Society UICC International Fellowships for Beginning Investigators (ACSBI) 389
Barbers Company Clinical Nursing Scholarship 557
CCFF Special Travel Allowances 203
CIHR Fellowships Program 210
Colt Foundation PhD Fellowship 239
Greenwall Fellowship 406
Health Services Research Training Fellowships and Palliative Care Fellowships 334
HFG Research Program 332
Hong Kong Research Grant 564
HRB Project Grants-General 334
HRB Translational Research Programmes 335
Meningitis Research Foundation Project Grant 445
The Pedro Zamora Public Policy Fellowship 11
Postgraduate Research Bursaries (Epilepsy Action) 282
Robert Westwood Scholarship 581
Sir Allan Sewell Visiting Fellowship 326
University of Bristol Postgraduate Scholarships 672

African Nations

ABCCF Student Grant 102
Canadian Window on International Development 380
ECOPOLIS Graduate Research and Design Awards 380
IARC Postdoctoral Fellowships for Training in Cancer Research 374
IDRC Doctoral Research Awards 380
International Postgraduate Research Scholarships (IPRS) 413
Shell Centenary Scholarships and Shell Centenary Chevening Scholarships at Edinburgh 683

Australia

Asthma Research Postgraduate Scholarships 124
Asthma Research Project Grants 124
Australian Clinical Research Postdoctoral Fellowship 477
Australian Health Inequities Program Research Scholarship 292
Biomedical (Dora Lush) and Public Health Postgraduate Scholarships 477
The Cancer Council NSW Research Project Grants 217
Career Development Awards 477
Howard Florey Centenary Fellowship 478
NBCF Doctoral Scholarship 469
NBCF Postdoctoral Fellowship 469
Neil Hamilton Fairley Fellowships (Overseas Clinical) 478
NHMRC Medical and Dental and Public Health Postgraduate Research Scholarships 478
NHMRC Public Health Postgraduate Scholarships 294
Public Health Fellowship (Australian) 479
Sidney Sax Fellowship (Overseas Public Health) 479
Training Scholarship for Indigenous Health Research 479
Wingate Scholarships 697

Canada

Alcohol Beverage Medical Research Foundation Research Project Grant 14
Canadian Window on International Development 380
CBS Postdoctoral Fellowship (PDF) 201
CIHR Canadian Graduate Scholarships Doctoral Awards 210
CIHR Doctoral Research Awards 210
ECOPOLIS Graduate Research and Design Awards 380
Frank Knox Memorial Fellowships 123
Idea Grants 215
IDRC Doctoral Research Awards 380
International Postgraduate Research Scholarships (IPRS) 413
PAHO Grants 519
Policy Research Grants 215
Research Planning Grants 216
Researcher Travel Grant 216
Wingate Scholarships 697
Workshop and Learning Opportunity Grants 216

Caribbean Countries

Canadian Window on International Development 380
ECOPOLIS Graduate Research and Design Awards 380
IARC Postdoctoral Fellowships for Training in Cancer Research 374
IDRC Doctoral Research Awards 380
International Postgraduate Research Scholarships (IPRS) 413
PAHO Grants 519
Shell Centenary Scholarships and Shell Centenary Chevening Scholarships at Edinburgh 683

East European Countries

ECOPOLIS Graduate Research and Design Awards 380
IARC Postdoctoral Fellowships for Training in Cancer Research 374
IDRC Doctoral Research Awards 380
International Postgraduate Research Scholarships (IPRS) 413
Shell Centenary Scholarships and Shell Centenary Chevening Scholarships at Edinburgh 683

European Union

Public Health: MRC Studentships 740
Wingate Scholarships 697

Middle East

ABCCF Student Grant 102
ECOPOLIS Graduate Research and Design Awards 380
IARC Postdoctoral Fellowships for Training in Cancer Research 374
IDRC Doctoral Research Awards 380
International Postgraduate Research Scholarships (IPRS) 413
Shell Centenary Scholarships and Shell Centenary Chevening Scholarships at Edinburgh 683

New Zealand

Australian Health Inequities Program Research Scholarship 292
Training Scholarship for Indigenous Health Research 479
University of Auckland Senior Health Research Scholarships 666
Wingate Scholarships 697

South Africa

Canadian Window on International Development 380
ECOPOLIS Graduate Research and Design Awards 380
IARC Postdoctoral Fellowships for Training in Cancer Research 374
IDRC Doctoral Research Awards 380
International Postgraduate Research Scholarships (IPRS) 413
SAMRC Local Postdoctoral Scholarships 615
Shell Centenary Scholarships and Shell Centenary Chevening
    Scholarships at Edinburgh 683
Wingate Scholarships 697

United Kingdom

Fund for Innovation 539
International Postgraduate Research Scholarships (IPRS) 413
Nuffield Trust/RCN/IHM Joint Travel Awards 557
Public Health: MRC Studentships 740
Wingate Scholarships 697

United States of America

Alcohol Beverage Medical Research Foundation Research Project
    Grant 14
The Commonwealth Fund/Harvard University Fellowship in Minority
    Health Policy 239
Fulbright Senior Specialists Program 249
International Postgraduate Research Scholarships (IPRS) 413
IREX Individual Advanced Research Opportunities 388
Lung Health (LH) Research Dissertation Grants 66
NBRC/AMP Gareth B Gish, MS RRT Memorial Postgraduate
    Recognition Award 29
NIH Research Grants 483
Nurses' Educational Funds Fellowships and Scholarships 510
Packer Fellowships 240
PAHO Grants 519
Parker B Francis Respiratory Research Grant 29
Pfizer Scholars Grants in Public Health 527
PhRMAF Postdoctoral Fellowships in Health Outcomes Research 528
PhRMAF Predoctoral Fellowships in Health Outcomes Research 529
PhRMAF Research Starter Grants in Health Outcomes Research 529
PhRMAF Sabbatical Fellowships in Health Outcomes Research 530
William F Miller, MD Postgraduate Education Recognition Award 29

West European Countries

International Postgraduate Research Scholarships (IPRS) 413
Shell Centenary Scholarships and Shell Centenary Chevening
    Scholarships at Edinburgh 683

SOCIAL/PREVENTIVE MEDICINE

Any Country

AACR Career Development Awards in Cancer Research 28
AACR Research Fellowships 29
AFSP Distinguished Investigator Awards 55
AFSP Pilot Grants 55
AFSP Postdoctoral Research Fellowships 55
AFSP Standard Research Grants 55
AFSP Young Investigator Award 56
Alzheimer's Society Research Grants
American Cancer Society UICC International Fellowships for Begin-
    ning Investigators (ACSBI) 389
ASBAH Research Grant 118
BackCare Research Grants 144
Barbers Company Clinical Nursing Scholarship 557
Breast Cancer Campaign PhD Studentships 157
Breast Cancer Campaign Project Grants 157
Breast Cancer Campaign Scientific Fellowships 157
Breast Cancer Campaign Small Pilot Grants 157
CCFF Fellowships 202
CCFF Special Travel Allowances 203
CCFF Studentships 203
CRF Research Grant 236
Distinguished Research Award 103
Earthwatch Field Research Grants 272
Fight for Sight Awards 291

FSSS Grants-in-Aid Program 606
Hastings Center International Visiting Scholars Program 332
HDA Research Project Grants 348
Heart Research UK Novel and Emerging Technologies Grant 336
The IASO New Investigator Award 376
Meningitis Research Foundation Project Grant 445
PDS Project Grant 521
Queen Mary Research Studentships 539
Savoy Foundation Postdoctoral and Clinical Research Fellowships
    582
Savoy Foundation Research Grants 582
Savoy Foundation Studentships 582
Sir Halley Stewart Trust Grants 593
University of Bristol Postgraduate Scholarships 672
Wellbeing of Women Project Grants 793

African Nations

Canadian Window on International Development 380
Hastings Center International Visiting Scholars Program 332
IARC Postdoctoral Fellowships for Training in Cancer Research 374
IDRC Doctoral Research Awards 380
International Postgraduate Research Scholarships (IPRS) 413
UICC Trish Greene International Cancer Nursing Training Fellowships
    390

Australia

Asthma Research Postgraduate Scholarships 124
Asthma Research Project Grants 124
Hastings Center International Visiting Scholars Program 332
National Heart Foundation of Australia Overseas Research
    Fellowships 479
NBCF Doctoral Scholarship 469
NBCF Postdoctoral Fellowship 469

Canada

Canadian Window on International Development 380
CCFF Senior Scientist Research Training Award 203
IDRC Doctoral Research Awards 380
International Postgraduate Research Scholarships (IPRS) 413

Caribbean Countries

Canadian Window on International Development 380
Hastings Center International Visiting Scholars Program 332
IARC Postdoctoral Fellowships for Training in Cancer Research 374
IDRC Doctoral Research Awards 380
International Postgraduate Research Scholarships (IPRS) 413
UICC Trish Greene International Cancer Nursing Training Fellowships
    390

East European Countries

Hastings Center International Visiting Scholars Program 332
IARC Postdoctoral Fellowships for Training in Cancer Research 374
IDRC Doctoral Research Awards 380
International Postgraduate Research Scholarships (IPRS) 413
UICC Trish Greene International Cancer Nursing Training Fellowships
    390

Middle East

Hastings Center International Visiting Scholars Program 332
IARC Postdoctoral Fellowships for Training in Cancer Research 374
IDRC Doctoral Research Awards 380
International Postgraduate Research Scholarships (IPRS) 413
UICC Trish Greene International Cancer Nursing Training Fellowships
    390

New Zealand

Hastings Center International Visiting Scholars Program 332
National Heart Foundation of New Zealand Fellowships 480
National Heart Foundation of New Zealand Limited Budget Grants 480
National Heart Foundation of New Zealand Maori Cardiovascular
    Research Fellowship 481
National Heart Foundation of New Zealand Project Grants 481
National Heart Foundation of New Zealand Travel Grants 481

South Africa

Canadian Window on International Development 380
Hastings Center International Visiting Scholars Program 332
IARC Postdoctoral Fellowships for Training in Cancer Research 374
IDRC Doctoral Research Awards 380
International Postgraduate Research Scholarships (IPRS) 413
UICC Trish Greene International Cancer Nursing Training Fellowships 390

United Kingdom

Hastings Center International Visiting Scholars Program 332
International Postgraduate Research Scholarships (IPRS) 413
Postgraduate Student Allowance Scheme (PSAS) (Queen Margaret) 539
Samuel Strutt Research Grant 171
Sue McCarthy Travelling Scholarship 328
T P Gunton Research Grant 171

United States of America

Damon Runyon Fellowship Award 260
Florence P Kendall Doctoral Scholarships 301
Fulbright Senior Specialists Program 249
International Postgraduate Research Scholarships (IPRS) 413
New Investigator Fellowships Training Initiative (NIFTI) 301
Nurses' Educational Funds Fellowships and Scholarships 510
Promotion of Doctoral Studies (PODS) 302
Research Grants (FPT) 302
Shaver-Hitchings Scholarship 638

West European Countries

Hastings Center International Visiting Scholars Program 332
International Postgraduate Research Scholarships (IPRS) 413

DIETETICS

Any Country

Barbers Company Clinical Nursing Scholarship 557
Breast Cancer Campaign Project Grants 157
Breast Cancer Campaign Scientific Grants 157
Breast Cancer Campaign Small Pilot Grants 157
Heart Research UK Novel and Emerging Technologies Grant 336

Australia

NBCF Doctoral Scholarship 469
NBCF Postdoctoral Fellowship 469

New Zealand

National Heart Foundation of New Zealand Fellowships 480
National Heart Foundation of New Zealand Limited Budget Grants 480
National Heart Foundation of New Zealand Maori Cardiovascular Research Fellowship 481
National Heart Foundation of New Zealand Project Grants 481
National Heart Foundation of New Zealand Travel Grants 481

United Kingdom

PWSA UK Research Grants 536
Sue McCarthy Travelling Scholarship 328

United States of America

Nurses' Educational Funds Fellowships and Scholarships 510

SPORTS MEDICINE

Any Country

Barbers Company Clinical Nursing Scholarship 557
Colt Foundation PhD Fellowship 239
OREF Career Development Award 518
OREF Prospective Clinical Research 518
OREF Research Grants 518
OREF Resident Research Award 518

SOM Research Grant 611
University of Bristol Postgraduate Scholarships 672

African Nations

International Postgraduate Research Scholarships (IPRS) 413

Australia

NBCF Doctoral Scholarship 469
NBCF Postdoctoral Fellowship 469

Canada

Clinical Research Training Fellowship 517
Idea Grants 215
International Postgraduate Research Scholarships (IPRS) 413
OREF Clinical Research Award 518
Research Planning Grants 216
Researcher Travel Grant 216

Caribbean Countries

International Postgraduate Research Scholarships (IPRS) 413

East European Countries

International Postgraduate Research Scholarships (IPRS) 413

Middle East

International Postgraduate Research Scholarships (IPRS) 413

South Africa

International Postgraduate Research Scholarships (IPRS) 413

United Kingdom

Duke of Edinburgh Prize for Sports Medicine 369
International Postgraduate Research Scholarships (IPRS) 413
Sir Robert Atkins Award 369

United States of America

British Marshall Scholarships 685
Clinical Research Training Fellowship 517
Florence P Kendall Doctoral Scholarships 301
International Postgraduate Research Scholarships (IPRS) 413
New Investigator Fellowships Training Initiative (NIFTI) 301
Nurses' Educational Funds Fellowships and Scholarships 510
OREF Clinical Research Award 518
Promotion of Doctoral Studies (PODS) 302
Ralph S. Paffenbarger-Blair Fund for Epidemiological Research on Physical Activity. 45
Research Grants (FPT) 302

West European Countries

International Postgraduate Research Scholarships (IPRS) 413

HEALTH ADMINISTRATION

Any Country

AAOHN Professional Development Scholarship 32
AFSP Distinguished Investigator Awards 55
AFSP Pilot Grants 55
AFSP Postdoctoral Research Fellowships 55
AFSP Standard Research Grants 55
AFSP Young Investigator Award 56
Barbers Company Clinical Nursing Scholarship 557
CIHR Fellowships Program 210
Hastings Center International Visiting Scholars Program 332
Health Services Research Training Fellowships and Palliative Care Fellowships 334
HRB Project Grants-General 334
IRSST Graduate Studies Scholarships 360
La Trobe University Postgraduate Scholarship 414
OCGS Women's Health Research Scholar Awards
The Pedro Zamora Public Policy Fellowship 11
Press Ganey Best Practices Research Program 537

Savoy Foundation Postdoctoral and Clinical Research Fellowships 582
Savoy Foundation Research Grants 582
Savoy Foundation Studentships 582
Sir Allan Sewell Visiting Fellowship 326
University of Bristol Postgraduate Scholarships 672

African Nations

ABCCF Student Grant 102
Hastings Center International Visiting Scholars Program 332
International Postgraduate Research Scholarships (IPRS) 413

Australia

The Cancer Council NSW Research Project Grants 217
Harkness Fellowships in Healthcare Policy 240
Hastings Center International Visiting Scholars Program 332
NBCF Doctoral Scholarship 469
NBCF Postdoctoral Fellowship 469
Wingate Scholarships 697

Canada

CIHR Canadian Graduate Scholarships Doctoral Awards 210
CIHR Doctoral Research Awards 210
Idea Grants 215
International Postgraduate Research Scholarships (IPRS) 413
Métis Centre Fellowship Program 446
PAHO Grants 519
Public Safety and Emergency Preparedness Canada Research Fellowship in Honour of Stuart Nesbitt White 123
Research Planning Grants 216
Researcher Travel Grant 216
Wingate Scholarships 697

Caribbean Countries

Hastings Center International Visiting Scholars Program 332
International Postgraduate Research Scholarships (IPRS) 413
PAHO Grants 519

East European Countries

Hastings Center International Visiting Scholars Program 332
International Postgraduate Research Scholarships (IPRS) 413

European Union

Wingate Scholarships 697

Middle East

ABCCF Student Grant 102
Hastings Center International Visiting Scholars Program 332
International Postgraduate Research Scholarships (IPRS) 413

New Zealand

Harkness Fellowships in Healthcare Policy 240
Hastings Center International Visiting Scholars Program 332
Wingate Scholarships 697

South Africa

Hastings Center International Visiting Scholars Program 332
International Postgraduate Research Scholarships (IPRS) 413
Wingate Scholarships 697

United Kingdom

Harkness Fellowships in Healthcare Policy 240
Hastings Center International Visiting Scholars Program 332
International Postgraduate Research Scholarships (IPRS) 413
Nuffield Trust/RCN/IHM Joint Travel Awards 557
Wingate Scholarships 697

United States of America

British Marshall Scholarships 685
Congress Bundestag Youth Exchange for Young Professionals 221
International Postgraduate Research Scholarships (IPRS) 413
Lung Health (LH) Research Dissertation Grants 66

NMSS Patient Management Care and Rehabilitation Grants 486
Nurses' Educational Funds Fellowships and Scholarships 510
Packer Fellowships 240
PAHO Grants 519
Pfizer Fellowships in Health Literary Clear Health Communication 526
Pfizer Scholars Grants in Public Health 527
Pfizer Visiting Professorships in Clear Health Literacy/Clear Health Communication 527
PhRMAF Postdoctoral Fellowships in Health Outcomes Research 528
PhRMAF Sabbatical Fellowships in Health Outcomes Research 530
SSRC Abe Fellowship Program 598

West European Countries

Hastings Center International Visiting Scholars Program 332
International Postgraduate Research Scholarships (IPRS) 413

MEDICINE AND SURGERY

Any Country

AACR Scholar-in-Training Awards 29
Action Medical Research Project Grants 6
Action Medical Research Training Fellowship 7
The Airey Neave Trust Scholarship 12
The Anne S. Chatham Fellowship 309
BackCare Research Grants 144
Barbers Company Clinical Nursing Scholarship 557
Brain Research Trust Prize and Medical Research Council Student-ships 648
Breast Cancer Campaign PhD Studentships 157
Breast Cancer Campaign Project Grants 157
Breast Cancer Campaign Scientific Fellowships 157
Breast Cancer Campaign Small Pilot Grants 157
Broad Medical Research Program for Inflammatory Bowel Disease Grants 178
Career Development Program 419
CCFF Scholarships 202
CCFF Visiting Scientist Awards 204
CIHR Fellowships Program 210
Clinical Scholar Research Award 375
Collaborative Career Development Fellowship in Stem Cell Research 439
Cooley's Anemia Foundation Research Fellowship 245
Daland Fellowships in Clinical Investigation 73
Dr Hadwen Trust Research Assistant or Technician 270
Dr Hadwen Trust Research Fellowship 270
ESSO Training Fellowships 286
FRAXA Grants and Fellowships 303
Frontiers in Anesthesia Research Award 375
Heart Research UK Novel and Emerging Technologies Grant 336
HRB Translational Research Programmes 335
Hypertension Trust Studentship 349
ISH Postdoctoral Award 301
Islamic Organization for Medical Sciences Prize 413
John of Arderne Medal 573
Leslie Bernstein Grant 25
Lister Institute Research Prizes 424
Malcolm Harrington Prize 573
Meningitis Research Foundation Project Grant 445
NORD/Rosoe Brady Lysosomal Storage Diseases Fellowships 486
OREF Career Development Award 518
OREF Prospective Clinical Research 518
OREF Research Grants 518
OREF Resident Research Award 518
PDS Project Grant 521
Postgraduate Research Bursaries (Epilepsy Action) 282
Queen Mary Research Studentships 539
RESTRACOMP Research Fellowship 346
Savoy Foundation Postdoctoral and Clinical Research Fellowships 582
Savoy Foundation Research Grants 582
Savoy Foundation Studentships 582
Sigma Theta Tau International/Association of Perioperative Registered Nurses Foundation Grant 588
Sir Richard Stapley Educational Trust Grants 593

Sir Thomas Naghten Fitzgerald Scholarship 709
Teaching Recognition Award 375
Translational Research Program 143
University of Bristol Postgraduate Scholarships 672
University of Southampton Postgraduate Studentships 759
Viola Edith Reid Bequest Scholarship 709
Wellbeing of Women Project Grants 793
Wellcome Trust Grants 794
William J Cunliffe Scientific Awards 796
World Universities Network (WUN) International Research Mobility Scheme 759

African Nations

TWAS Grants for Scientific Meetings in Developing Countries 631
TWAS Prizes 632
TWAS Research Grants 632
TWAS UNESCO Associateship Scheme 632

Australia

Asthma Research Postgraduate Scholarships 124
Asthma Research Project Grants 124
Australian Clinical Research Postdoctoral Fellowship 477
The Baillieu Research Scholarship 751
Baillieu Research Scholarship 707
Biomedical (Dora Lush) and Public Health Postgraduate Scholarships 477
C J Martin Fellowships (Overseas Biomedical) 477
The Cancer Council NSW Research Project Grants 217
Career Development Awards 477
Foundation for High Blood Pressure Research Postdoctoral Fellowship 300
Howard Florey Centenary Fellowship 478
Industry Fellowships 478
NBCF Doctoral Scholarship 469
NBCF Postdoctoral Fellowship 469
Neil Hamilton Fairley Fellowships (Overseas Clinical) 478
NHMRC Medical and Dental and Public Health Postgraduate Research Scholarships 478
NHMRC/INSERM Exchange Fellowships 478
Peter Doherty Fellowships (Australian Biomedical) 478
Public Health Fellowship (Australian) 479
Sidney Sax Fellowship (Overseas Public Health) 479
Training Scholarship for Indigenous Health Research 479

Canada

Canadian Commonwealth Scholarship and Fellowship Plan 201
CCFF Research Grants 202
CIHR Canadian Graduate Scholarships Doctoral Awards 210
CIHR Doctoral Research Awards 210
Clinical Research Training Fellowship 517
CTS Research Fellowship Program 215
Leslie Bernstein Investigator Development Grant 25
Leslie Bernstein Resident Research Grants 26
OREF Clinical Research Award 518
Research Planning Grants 216

Caribbean Countries

TWAS Grants for Scientific Meetings in Developing Countries 631
TWAS Prizes 632
TWAS Research Grants 632
TWAS UNESCO Associateship Scheme 632

East European Countries

ECTS Career Establishment Award 284
ECTS Exchange Scholarship Grants 284

European Union

ECTS Career Establishment Award 284
ECTS Exchange Scholarship Grants 284
Hypertension Trust Fellowship 349
Hypertension Trust Studentship 349

Middle East

TWAS Grants for Scientific Meetings in Developing Countries 631
TWAS Prizes 632
TWAS Research Grants 632
TWAS UNESCO Associateship Scheme 632

New Zealand

Training Scholarship for Indigenous Health Research 479

South Africa

TWAS Grants for Scientific Meetings in Developing Countries 631
TWAS Prizes 632
TWAS Research Grants 632
TWAS UNESCO Associateship Scheme 632

United Kingdom

Adrian Tanner Prize 572
British Lung Foundation Project Grants 170
Clinical Research Fellowships 106
ECTS Career Establishment Award 284
ECTS Exchange Scholarship Grants 284
Hypertension Trust Fellowship 349
Hypertension Trust Studentship 349
Moynihan Travelling Fellowship 122
Orthopaedic Clinical Research Fellowship 107
Sue McCarthy Travelling Scholarship 328
Wellbeing of Women Entry-Level Scholarship 793
Wellbeing of Women/RCOG Research Training Fellowship 793

United States of America

AFAR Research Grants 52
CAMS Scholarship 234
Clinical Research Training Fellowship 517
The Glenn/AFAR Breakthroughs in Gerontology Awards 53
The Julie Martin Mid-Career Award in Aging Research 53
Leslie Bernstein Investigator Development Grant 25
Leslie Bernstein Resident Research Grants 26
Medical Student Training in Aging Research (MSTAR) Program 53
Nurses' Educational Funds Fellowships and Scholarships 510
OREF Clinical Research Award 518
Paul Beeson Career Development Award in Aging Research 53
Sigvaris Travelling Fellowship 99

West European Countries

ECTS Career Establishment Award 284
ECTS Exchange Scholarship Grants 284

ANAESTHESIOLOGY

Any Country

Action Medical Research Project Grants 6
BackCare Research Grants 144
Barbers Company Clinical Nursing Scholarship 557
Clinical Scholar Research Award 375
Frontiers in Anesthesia Research Award 375
Queen Mary Research Studentships 539
Teaching Recognition Award 375
University of Bristol Postgraduate Scholarships 672

Australia

NBCF Doctoral Scholarship 469
NBCF Postdoctoral Fellowship 469

United Kingdom

Resuscitation Council Research Fellowships 546
Resuscitation Council Research Grants 546

United States of America

AFAR Research Grants 52
FAER Mentored Research Training Grant (MRTG) 299
FAER Research Education Grant 299

FAER Research Fellowship Grant 299
The Glenn/AFAR Breakthroughs in Gerontology Awards 53
NIGMS Postdoctoral Awards 483
NIGMS Research Supplements for Underrepresented Minorities 483
Nurses' Educational Funds Fellowships and Scholarships 510
Paul Beeson Career Development Award in Aging Research 53

CARDIOLOGY

Any Country

AHAF National Heart Foundation 58
Barbers Company Clinical Nursing Scholarship 557
Cooley's Anemia Foundation Research Fellowship 245
Heart Research UK Novel and Emerging Technologies Grant 336
Hypertension Trust Studentship 349
Lister Institute Research Prizes 424
National Heart Foundation of New Zealand Senior Fellowship 481
Queen Mary Research Studentships 539
University of Bristol Postgraduate Scholarships 672

Australia

National Heart Foundation of Australia Career Development
    Fellowship 479
National Heart Foundation of Australia Overseas Research
    Fellowships 479
National Heart Foundation of Australia Postdoctoral Research
    Fellowship 479
National Heart Foundation of Australia Postgraduate Biomedical
    Research Scholarship 480
National Heart Foundation of Australia Postgraduate Clinical Re-
    search Scholarship 480
National Heart Foundation of Australia Postgraduate Public Health
    Research Scholarship 480
National Heart Foundation of Australia Research Grants-in-Aid

Canada

AHA Fellowships 58
Alcohol Beverage Medical Research Foundation Research Project
    Grant 14

European Union

Hypertension Trust Fellowship 349
Hypertension Trust Studentship 349

New Zealand

National Heart Foundation of New Zealand Fellowships 480
National Heart Foundation of New Zealand Limited Budget Grants 480
National Heart Foundation of New Zealand Maori Cardiovascular
    Research Fellowship 481
National Heart Foundation of New Zealand Project Grants 481
National Heart Foundation of New Zealand Travel Grants 481

United Kingdom

Helen Lawson Research Grant 170
Hypertension Trust Fellowship 349
Hypertension Trust Studentship 349
Josephine Lansdell Research Grant 171
Resuscitation Council Research Fellowships 546
Resuscitation Council Research Grants 546
Sue McCarthy Travelling Scholarship 328

United States of America

ACCF/Pfizer Visiting Professorships in Cardiovascular Medicine 526
AFAR Research Grants 52
AHA Fellowships 58
Alcohol Beverage Medical Research Foundation Research Project
    Grant 14
The Glenn/AFAR Breakthroughs in Gerontology Awards 53
Heart and Stroke Foundation of Canada Visiting Scientist Program 336
Nurses' Educational Funds Fellowships and Scholarships 510
Paul Beeson Career Development Award in Aging Research 53
Pfizer Atorvastatin Research Awards Program 526

DERMATOLOGY

Any Country

Action Medical Research Project Grants 6
Barbers Company Clinical Nursing Scholarship 557
British Skin Foundation Small Grants 177
CERIES Research Award 227
DEBRA UK Research Grant Scheme
Lister Institute Research Prizes 424
Medical Elective Funding and Annual Essay Competition 418
OFAS Grants 514
Queen Mary Research Studentships 539
University of Bristol Postgraduate Scholarships 672
William J Cunliffe Scientific Awards 796

Australia

The Cancer Council NSW Research Project Grants 217

United States of America

AFAR Research Grants 52
The Glenn/AFAR Breakthroughs in Gerontology Awards 53
Nurses' Educational Funds Fellowships and Scholarships 510
Paul Beeson Career Development Award in Aging Research 53

ENDOCRINOLOGY

Any Country

Action Medical Research Project Grants 6
Barbers Company Clinical Nursing Scholarship 557
Cooley's Anemia Foundation Research Fellowship 245
Diabetes UK Equipment Grant 268
Diabetes UK Project Grants 269
Diabetes UK Small Grant Scheme 269
HRB Translational Research Programmes 335
Lister Institute Research Prizes 424
NARSAD Distinguished Investigator Awards 465
NARSAD Independent Investigator Awards 465
NARSAD Young Investigator Awards 465
OFAS Grants 514
Queen Mary Research Studentships 539
University of Bristol Postgraduate Scholarships 672
Wellbeing of Women Project Grants 793
William J Cunliffe Scientific Awards 796

Australia

The Cancer Council NSW Research Project Grants 217

Canada

Alcohol Beverage Medical Research Foundation Research Project
    Grant 14

East European Countries

ECTS Career Establishment Award 284
ECTS Exchange Scholarship Grants 284

European Union

ECTS Career Establishment Award 284
ECTS Exchange Scholarship Grants 284

United Kingdom

DRWF Open Funding 268
DRWF Research Fellowship 268
ECTS Career Establishment Award 284
ECTS Exchange Scholarship Grants 284
PWSA UK Research Grants 536
Wellbeing of Women Entry-Level Scholarship 793
Wellbeing of Women/RCOG Research Training Fellowship 793

United States of America

ADA Career Development Awards 51
ADA Clinical Research Grants 51

ADA Junior Faculty Awards 51
ADA Mentor-Based Postdoctoral Fellowship Program 52
ADA Research Awards 52
AFAR Research Grants 52
Alcohol Beverage Medical Research Foundation Research Project Grant 14
Clinical Scholars Program 52
The Glenn/AFAR Breakthroughs in Gerontology Awards 53
NIH Research Grants 483
Nurses' Educational Funds Fellowships and Scholarships 510
Paul Beeson Career Development Award in Aging Research 53
Pfizer Visiting Professorships in Diabetes 527

West European Countries

ECTS Career Establishment Award 284
ECTS Exchange Scholarship Grants 284

EPIDEMIOLOGY

Any Country

Action Medical Research Project Grants 6
AFSP Distinguished Investigator Awards 55
AFSP Pilot Grants 55
AFSP Postdoctoral Research Fellowships 55
AFSP Standard Research Grants 55
AFSP Young Investigator Award 56
AHAF Alzheimer's Disease Research Grant 57
AHAF National Heart Foundation 58
Alzheimer's Society Research Grants
Ataxia UK PhD Studentship 124
Ataxia UK Research Fellowship in Friedreich's ataxia
Ataxia UK Research Grant 124
Ataxia UK Travel Award 124
BackCare Research Grants 144
Barbers Company Clinical Nursing Scholarship 557
Breast Cancer Campaign Project Grants 157
Career Development Program 419
CBS Graduate Fellowship Program 200
CGD Research Trust Grants 236
Health Services Research Training Fellowships and Palliative Care Fellowships 334
HRB Project Grants-General 334
HRB Translational Research Programmes 335
ICR Studentships 365
Lister Institute Research Prizes 424
Meningitis Research Foundation Project Grant 445
NARSAD Distinguished Investigator Awards 465
NARSAD Independent Investigator Awards 465
NARSAD Young Investigator Awards 465
OFAS Grants 514
Queen Mary Research Studentships 539
Savoy Foundation Postdoctoral and Clinical Research Fellowships 582
Savoy Foundation Studentships 582
Translational Research Program 143
TSA Research Grant and Fellowship Program 634
University of Bristol Postgraduate Scholarships 672

African Nations

Canadian Window on International Development 380
IARC Postdoctoral Fellowships for Training in Cancer Research 374
IDRC Doctoral Research Awards 380
IDRC Internship Awards 381

Australia

The Cancer Council NSW Research Project Grants 217
CDRF Project Grants 236
CDRF Research Fellowship 236
NBCF Doctoral Scholarship 469
NBCF Postdoctoral Fellowship 469

Canada

Alcohol Beverage Medical Research Foundation Research Project Grant 14
Canadian Window on International Development 380
CBS Postdoctoral Fellowship (PDF) 201
CTS Research Fellowship Program 215
Heritage Health Research Career Renewal Awards 14
IDRC Doctoral Research Awards 380
IDRC Internship Awards 381
Rural Maternity Care Doctoral Student Fellowship 578

Caribbean Countries

Canadian Window on International Development 380
IARC Postdoctoral Fellowships for Training in Cancer Research 374
IDRC Doctoral Research Awards 380
IDRC Internship Awards 381

East European Countries

CDRF Project Grants 236
CDRF Research Fellowship 236
FEMS Fellowship 290
IARC Postdoctoral Fellowships for Training in Cancer Research 374
IDRC Doctoral Research Awards 380

Middle East

IARC Postdoctoral Fellowships for Training in Cancer Research 374
IDRC Doctoral Research Awards 380
IDRC Internship Awards 381

New Zealand

National Heart Foundation of New Zealand Fellowships 480
National Heart Foundation of New Zealand Limited Budget Grants 480
National Heart Foundation of New Zealand Maori Cardiovascular Research Fellowship 481
National Heart Foundation of New Zealand Project Grants 481
National Heart Foundation of New Zealand Travel Grants 481

South Africa

Canadian Window on International Development 380
IARC Postdoctoral Fellowships for Training in Cancer Research 374
IDRC Doctoral Research Awards 380
IDRC Internship Awards 381

United Kingdom

British Lung Foundation Project Grants 170
CDRF Project Grants 236
CDRF Research Fellowship 236
FEMS Fellowship 290

United States of America

AFAR Research Grants 52
Alcohol Beverage Medical Research Foundation Research Project Grant 14
CDRF Project Grants 236
CDRF Research Fellowship 236
The Glenn/AFAR Breakthroughs in Gerontology Awards 53
Lung Health (LH) Research Dissertation Grants 66
NFID Advanced Vaccinology Course Travel Grant 476
Nurses' Educational Funds Fellowships and Scholarships 510
Paul Beeson Career Development Award in Aging Research 53
Pfizer International HDL Research Awards Program 526
PhRMAF Postdoctoral Fellowships in Health Outcomes Research 528
PhRMAF Predoctoral Fellowships in Health Outcomes Research 529
PhRMAF Research Starter Grants in Health Outcomes Research 529
PhRMAF Sabbatical Fellowships in Health Outcomes Research 530

West European Countries

CDRF Project Grants 236
CDRF Research Fellowship 236
FEMS Fellowship 290

GASTROENTEROLOGY

Any Country

Action Medical Research Project Grants 6
AGA June and Donald O Castell, MD, Esophageal Clinical Research Award 299
AGA R Robert and Sally D Funderburg Research Scholar Award in Gastric Biology Related to Cancer 300
AGA Research Scholar Awards 300
AGA Student Research Fellowship Awards 300
Barbers Company Clinical Nursing Scholarship 557
Broad Medical Research Program for Inflammatory Bowel Disease Grants 178
CGD Research Trust Grants 236
Crohn's and Colitis Foundation Career Development Award 255
Crohn's and Colitis Foundation Research Fellowship Awards 255
Crohn's and Colitis Foundation Senior Research Award 255
Crohn's and Colitis Foundation Student Research Fellowship Awards 255
HRB Translational Research Programmes 335
Lister Institute Research Prizes 424
Pilot Research Awards 300
Queen Mary Research Studentships 539
Sir Halley Stewart Trust Grants 593
University of Bristol Postgraduate Scholarships 672

Australia

The Cancer Council NSW Research Project Grants 217

Canada

Alcohol Beverage Medical Research Foundation Research Project Grant 14

United Kingdom

CORE Fellowships and Grants 245

United States of America

AFAR Research Grants 52
AGA Fellowship to Faculty Transition Awards 299
Alcohol Beverage Medical Research Foundation Research Project Grant 14
The Glenn/AFAR Breakthroughs in Gerontology Awards 53
Nurses' Educational Funds Fellowships and Scholarships 510
Paul Beeson Career Development Award in Aging Research 53

GERIATRICS

Any Country

ADDF Grants Program 22
AFSP Distinguished Investigator Awards 55
AFSP Pilot Grants 55
AFSP Postdoctoral Research Fellowships 55
AFSP Standard Research Grants 55
AFSP Young Investigator Award 56
Alzheimer's Research Trust, Clinical Research Fellowship
Alzheimer's Research Trust, Emergency Support Grant
Alzheimer's Research Trust, Major Project or Programme
Alzheimer's Research Trust, Network Co-operation Grant
Alzheimer's Research Trust, Pilot Project Grant
Alzheimer's Research Trust, Research Fellowships
Alzheimer's Society Research Grants
Barbers Company Clinical Nursing Scholarship 557
Dr Vincent Cristofalo Memorial Fund, Cecille Gould Memorial Fund Award in Cancer Research, Richard Shepherd Fellowship 54
HRB Translational Research Programmes 335
Lister Institute Research Prizes 424
NARSAD Distinguished Investigator Awards 465
NARSAD Independent Investigator Awards 465
NARSAD Young Investigator Awards 465
PDS Project Grant 521
Sir Halley Stewart Trust Grants 593
Stroke Association Research Project Grants 621
University of Bristol Postgraduate Scholarships 672

Canada

Alcohol Beverage Medical Research Foundation Research Project Grant 14

United Kingdom

REMEDI Research Grants 544

United States of America

ACR/REF Association of Subspecialty Professors Junior Career Development Award in Geriatric Medicine Award 43
AFAR Research Grants 52
Alcohol Beverage Medical Research Foundation Research Project Grant 14
The Glenn/AFAR Breakthroughs in Gerontology Awards 53
NIH Research Grants 483
Nurses' Educational Funds Fellowships and Scholarships 510
Paul Beeson Career Development Award in Aging Research 53

GYNAECOLOGY AND OBSTETRICS

Any Country

Action Medical Research Project Grants 6
BackCare Research Grants 144
Barbers Company Clinical Nursing Scholarship 557
Eden Travelling Fellowship 558
Edgar Gentilli Prize 558
Ethicon Travel Awards 559
FSSS Grants-in-Aid Program 606
Green-Armytage and Spackman Travelling Scholarship 559
Harold Malkin Prize 559
HRB Translational Research Programmes 335
Lister Institute Research Prizes 424
Meningitis Research Foundation Project Grant 445
MRC Royal College of Obstetricians and Gynaecologists (RCOG) Training Fellowship 440
Overseas Fund 559
Queen Mary Research Studentships 539
RCOG Bernhard Baron Travelling Scholarships 560
University of Bristol Postgraduate Scholarships 672
Wellbeing of Women Project Grants 793

Australia

The Cancer Council NSW Research Project Grants 217

Canada

ACOG Bayer Health Care Pharmaceticals Research Award in Long Term Contraception 40
ACOG/Bayer Health Care Pharmaceuticals Research Award in Contraceptive Counseling 40
ACOG/Kenneth Gottesfeld-Charles Hohler Memorial Foundation Research Award in Ultrasound 41
ACOG/Ortho Women's Health and Urology Academic Training Fellowships in Obstetrics and Gynecology
Warren H Pearse/Wyeth Pharmaceuticals Women's Health Policy Research Award 42

United Kingdom

American Gynecological Club/Gynaecological Visiting Society Fellowship 558
Endometriosis Millennium Fund Award 558
REMEDI Research Grants 544
Richard Johanson Research Prize 560
Tim Chard Case History Prize 560
Wellbeing of Women Entry-Level Scholarship 793
Wellbeing of Women/RCOG Research Training Fellowship 793
William Blair-Bell Memorial Lectureships in Obstetrics and Gynaecology 560
Wyeth Historical Lecture 560

United States of America

ACOG Bayer Health Care Pharmaceticals Research Award in Long
  Term Contraception 40
ACOG/Bayer Health Care Pharmaceuticals Research Award in
  Contraceptive Counseling 40
ACOG/Kenneth Gottesfeld-Charles Hohler Memorial Foundation
  Research Award in Ultrasound 41
ACOG/Ortho Women's Health and Urology Academic Training
  Fellowships in Obstetrics and Gynecology
AFAR Research Grants 52
American Gynecological Club/Gynaecological Visiting Society
  Fellowship 558
The Glenn/AFAR Breakthroughs in Gerontology Awards 53
Nurses' Educational Funds Fellowships and Scholarships 510
Paul Beeson Career Development Award in Aging Research 53
Warren H Pearse/Wyeth Pharmaceuticals Women's Health Policy
  Research Award 42

HAEMATOLOGY

Any Country

Action Medical Research Project Grants 6
Barbers Company Clinical Nursing Scholarship 557
Career Development Program 419
CBS Graduate Fellowship Program 200
Cooley's Anemia Foundation Research Fellowship 245
Elimination of Leukaemia Fund Travelling and Training Fellowships
  278
Friends of José Carreras International Leukemia Foundation E D
  Thomas Postdoctoral Fellowship 305
Gordon Piller Studentships 419
HRB Translational Research Programmes 335
ICR Studentships 365
Kay Kendall Leukaemia Fund Research Fellowship 408
Lady Tata Memorial Trust Scholarships 414
Leukaemia Research Clinical Research Training Fellowships 419
Leukaemia Research Grant Programme 419
Lister Institute Research Prizes 424
Meningitis Research Foundation Project Grant 445
Queen Mary Research Studentships 539
Translational Research Program 143
University of Bristol Postgraduate Scholarships 672

Australia

Baikie Award 329
The Cancer Council NSW Research Project Grants 217
Leukaemia Foundation PhD Scholarships 418
Leukaemia Foundation Postdoctoral Fellowship 418
New Investigator Scholarships 329

Canada

Alcohol Beverage Medical Research Foundation Research Project
  Grant 14
American Society of Hematology Minority Medical Student Award
  Program 91
CBS Postdoctoral Fellowship (PDF) 201
LLSC Awards 419

New Zealand

Baikie Award 329
New Investigator Scholarships 329

United Kingdom

Annual Scientific Meeting Scholarships for Haematology Professionals 177
REMEDI Research Grants 544

United States of America

AFAR Research Grants 52
Alcohol Beverage Medical Research Foundation Research Project
  Grant 14

American Society of Hematology Minority Medical Student Award
  Program 91
The Glenn/AFAR Breakthroughs in Gerontology Awards 53
Nurses' Educational Funds Fellowships and Scholarships 510
Paul Beeson Career Development Award in Aging Research 53

HEPATHOLOGY

Any Country

AGA June and Donald O Castell, MD, Esophageal Clinical Research
  Award 299
AGA R Robert and Sally D Funderburg Research Scholar Award in
  Gastric Biology Related to Cancer 300
AGA Research Scholar Awards 300
AGA Student Research Fellowship Awards 300
Barbers Company Clinical Nursing Scholarship 557
Cooley's Anemia Foundation Research Fellowship 245
HRB Translational Research Programmes 335
Lister Institute Research Prizes 424
Pilot Research Awards 300

Canada

Alcohol Beverage Medical Research Foundation Research Project
  Grant 14
Canadian Liver Foundation Graduate Studentships 212
Canadian Liver Foundation Operating Grant 212

East European Countries

Liver Group PhD Studentship 654

European Union

Liver Group PhD Studentship 654

United Kingdom

CORE Fellowships and Grants 245
Liver Group PhD Studentship 654

United States of America

AFAR Research Grants 52
AGA Fellowship to Faculty Transition Awards 299
Alcohol Beverage Medical Research Foundation Research Project
  Grant 14
The Glenn/AFAR Breakthroughs in Gerontology Awards 53
Nurses' Educational Funds Fellowships and Scholarships 510
Paul Beeson Career Development Award in Aging Research 53

NEPHROLOGY

Any Country

Barbers Company Clinical Nursing Scholarship 557
HRB Translational Research Programmes 335
Lister Institute Research Prizes 424
LSA Medical Research Grant 428

Australia

Australian Kidney Foundation Medical Research Grants and
  Scholarships 409
Australian Kidney Foundation Seeding and Equipment Grants 409

Canada

ASN-ASP Junior Development Grant in Geriatric Nephrology 94

New Zealand

ASN-ASP Junior Development Grant in Geriatric Nephrology 94

United Kingdom

Kidney Research UK Non-clinical Senior Fellowships 409
Kidney Research UK Research Project and Innovation Grants 410
Kidney Research UK Training Fellowships/Career Development
  Fellowships 410

PhD Studentships 107
Samuel Strutt Research Grant 171

United States of America

AFAR Research Grants 52
ASN-ASP Junior Development Grant in Geriatric Nephrology 94
The Glenn/AFAR Breakthroughs in Gerontology Awards 53
Nurses' Educational Funds Fellowships and Scholarships 510
Paul Beeson Career Development Award in Aging Research 53

NEUROLOGY

Any Country

Action Medical Research Project Grants 6
ADDF Grants Program 22
AFSP Distinguished Investigator Awards 55
AFSP Pilot Grants 55
AFSP Postdoctoral Research Fellowships 55
AFSP Standard Research Grants 55
AFSP Young Investigator Award 56
AHAF Alzheimer's Disease Research Grant 57
AHAF National Heart Foundation 58
Alzheimer's Research Trust, Clinical Research Fellowship
Alzheimer's Research Trust, Emergency Support Grant
Alzheimer's Research Trust, Equipment Grant
Alzheimer's Research Trust, Major Project or Programme
Alzheimer's Research Trust, Network Co-operation Grant
Alzheimer's Research Trust, PhD Scholarship
Alzheimer's Research Trust, Pilot Project Grant
Alzheimer's Research Trust, Research Fellowships
Alzheimer's Society Research Grants
American Tinnitus Association Scientific Research Grants 96
ASBAH Research Grant 118
Ataxia UK PhD Studentship 124
Ataxia UK Research Fellowship in Friedreich's ataxia
Ataxia UK Research Grant 124
Ataxia UK Travel Award 124
BackCare Research Grants 144
Barbers Company Clinical Nursing Scholarship 557
Batten Disease Support and Research Association Research Grant
    Awards 146
The Betty Cuthbert Postgraduate Scholarship 459
The Cart Fund, Inc. 53
CRF Research Grant 236
Direct Research on Ataxia-Telangiectasia 3
Epilepsy Research UK Fellowship 283
Epilepsy Research UK Research Grant 283
FRAXA Grants and Fellowships 303
HDA Research Project Grants 348
HDA Studentship 348
Herbert H Jasper Fellowship 327
HFG Research Program 332
HRB Translational Research Programmes 335
Jeanne Timmins Costello Fellowships 457
Lister Institute Research Prizes 424
LSA Medical Research Grant 428
MDA Grant Programs 460
Meningitis Research Foundation Project Grant 445
MND Research Project Grants 458
NARSAD Distinguished Investigator Awards 465
NARSAD Independent Investigator Awards 465
NARSAD Young Investigator Awards 465
National Multiple Sclerosis Society Pilot Research Grants 485
National Multiple Sclerosis Society Postdoctoral Fellowships 485
National Multiple Sclerosis Society Research Grants 485
PDS Project Grant 521
Post-Doctoral Research Fellowship 462
Postgraduate Research Bursaries (Epilepsy Action) 282
Preston Robb Fellowship 457
Queen Mary Research Studentships 539
Savoy Foundation Postdoctoral and Clinical Research Fellowships
    582
Savoy Foundation Research Grants 582
Savoy Foundation Studentships 582

Stroke Association Research Project Grants 621
Student Research Fellowship 462
TSA Research Grant and Fellowship Program 634
University of Bristol Postgraduate Scholarships 672
William P. Van Wagenen Fellowship 32

African Nations

William P. Van Wagenen Fellowship 32

Australia

William P. Van Wagenen Fellowship 32

Canada

Alcohol Beverage Medical Research Foundation Research Project
    Grant 14
Herbert H Jasper Fellowship 327
William P. Van Wagenen Fellowship 32

Caribbean Countries

William P. Van Wagenen Fellowship 32

East European Countries

Linacre College Euopean Blaschko Visiting Research Scholarship 731
William P. Van Wagenen Fellowship 32

European Union

Clinical Neurology: MRC Studentship 723

Middle East

William P. Van Wagenen Fellowship 32

New Zealand

William P. Van Wagenen Fellowship 32

South Africa

William P. Van Wagenen Fellowship 32

United Kingdom

Clinical Neurology: MRC Studentship 723
Doris Hillier Research Grant 170
Guillain-Barré Syndrome Support Group Research Fellowship 328
MND PhD Studentship Award 458
REMEDI Research Grants 544
Vera Down Research Grant 171
William P. Van Wagenen Fellowship 32

United States of America

AFAR Research Grants 52
Alcohol Beverage Medical Research Foundation Research Project
    Grant 14
Diversity Program in Neuroscience Postdoctoral Fellowship 76
The Glenn/AFAR Breakthroughs in Gerontology Awards 53
National Multiple Sclerosis Society Junior Faculty Awards 485
NIH Research Grants 483
NREF Research Fellowship 31
NREF Young Clinician Investigator Award 31
Nurses' Educational Funds Fellowships and Scholarships 510
Paul Beeson Career Development Award in Aging Research 53
Pfizer Visiting Professorship in Neurology 527
PVA Educational Scholarship Program 519

West European Countries

Linacre College Euopean Blaschko Visiting Research Scholarship 731

ONCOLOGY

Any Country

AACR Career Development Awards in Cancer Research 28
AACR Gertrude B. Elion Cancer Research Award 28
AACR Research Fellowships 29
AACR Scholar-in-Training Awards 29

Action Cancer Pilot Grants 6
Action Cancer Project Grant 6
Action Cancer Research Studentship 6
American Cancer Society UICC International Fellowships for
   Beginning Investigators (ACSBI) 389
Barbers Company Clinical Nursing Scholarship 557
Breast Cancer Campaign PhD Studentships 157
Breast Cancer Campaign Project Grants 157
Breast Cancer Campaign Scientific Fellowships 157
Breast Cancer Campaign Small Pilot Grants 157
Cancer Research Society, Inc. (Canada) Operating Grants 218
Career Development Program 419
CCS Feasibility Grants 469
Dr Vincent Cristofalo Memorial Fund, Cecille Gould Memorial Fund
   Award in Cancer Research, Richard Shepherd Fellowship 54
Elimination of Leukaemia Fund Travelling and Training Fellowships
   278
ESSO Training Fellowships 286
Friends of José Carreras International Leukemia Foundation E D
   Thomas Postdoctoral Fellowship 305
Gordon Piller Studentships 419
HRB Translational Research Programmes 335
ICR Studentships 365
Leukaemia Research Clinical Research Training Fellowships 419
Leukaemia Research Grant Programme 419
Lister Institute Research Prizes 424
Melville Trust for Care and Cure of Cancer Research Fellowships 443
Melville Trust for Care and Cure of Cancer Research Grants 443
NCIC Clinical Research Fellowship 470
NCIC Equipment Grants for New Investigators 470
NCIC Post-PhD Research Fellowships 470
NCIC Research Grants for New Investigators 470
NCIC Research Grants to Individuals 470
NCIC Research Studentships 471
NCIC Travel Awards for Senior Level PhD Students 471
Neuroblastoma Society Research Grants 497
OFAS Grants 514
ONS Breast Cancer Research Grant 511
ONS Foundation Research Awards 511
ONS Novartis Pharmaceuticals Post-Master's Certificate Scholarships
   512
Paterson 4-Year Studentship 522
Prostate UK Research Grants 537
Queen Mary Research Studentships 539
Strategic Research Program on Genomics and Proteomics of
   Metastasic Cancer 218
Sylvia Lawler Prize 574
Translational Research Program 143
UICC International Cancer Research Technology Transfer Fellow-
   ships (ICRETT) 390
UICC Yamagiwa-Yoshida Memorial International Cancer Study
   Grants 390
University of Bristol Postgraduate Scholarships 672
Wellbeing of Women Project Grants 793

African Nations

IARC Postdoctoral Fellowships for Training in Cancer Research
   374
UICC International Cancer Technology Transfer Training Workshops
   390
UICC Trish Greene International Cancer Nursing Training Fellowships
   390

Australia

The Cancer Council NSW Research Project Grants 217
Leukaemia Foundation PhD Scholarships 418
Leukaemia Foundation Postdoctoral Fellowship 418
NBCF Doctoral Scholarship 469
NBCF Postdoctoral Fellowship 469
Pilot Study Grants 469
Queensland Cancer Fund PhD Scholarships 753
Research Project Grants 217
Sister Janet Mylonas Memorial Scholarship 753
UICC Asia-Pacific Cancer Society Training Grants 390

Canada

Alcohol Beverage Medical Research Foundation Research Project
   Grant 14
Idea Grants 215
Knowledge Synthesis Grant 215
LLSC Awards 419
Research Planning Grants 216
Researcher Travel Grant 216
Student Research Grant 216

Caribbean Countries

IARC Postdoctoral Fellowships for Training in Cancer Research 374
UICC International Cancer Technology Transfer Training Workshops
   390
UICC Trish Greene International Cancer Nursing Training Fellowships
   390

East European Countries

ECTS Career Establishment Award 284
ECTS Exchange Scholarship Grants 284
IARC Postdoctoral Fellowships for Training in Cancer Research 374
UICC International Cancer Technology Transfer Training Workshops
   390
UICC Trish Greene International Cancer Nursing Training Fellowships
   390

European Union

ECTS Career Establishment Award 284
ECTS Exchange Scholarship Grants 284

Middle East

IARC Postdoctoral Fellowships for Training in Cancer Research 374
UICC International Cancer Technology Transfer Training Workshops
   390
UICC Trish Greene International Cancer Nursing Training Fellowships
   390

New Zealand

UICC Asia-Pacific Cancer Society Training Grants 390

South Africa

IARC Postdoctoral Fellowships for Training in Cancer Research 374
UICC International Cancer Technology Transfer Training Workshops
   390
UICC Trish Greene International Cancer Nursing Training Fellowships
   390

United Kingdom

British Lung Foundation Project Grants 170
ECTS Career Establishment Award 284
ECTS Exchange Scholarship Grants 284
Paterson 4-Year Studentship 522
Prostate UK Research Grants 537
Samuel Strutt Research Grant 171
Sylvia Lawler Prize 574
T P Gunton Research Grant 171
Wellbeing of Women Entry-Level Scholarship 793
Wellbeing of Women/RCOG Research Training Fellowship 793

United States of America

AFAR Research Grants 52
AHNS Pilot Research Grant 57
AHNS Surgeon Scientist Career Development Award (with AAOHNS)
   57
AHNS Young Investigator Award (with AAOHNS) 57
AHNS-ACS Career Development Award 57
Alcohol Beverage Medical Research Foundation Research Project
   Grant 14
Aventis Research Fellowship 511
BTS Research Grant 156
Damon Runyon Clinical Investigator Award 260
Damon Runyon Fellowship Award 260
Damon Runyon Scholar Award 260

The Glenn/AFAR Breakthroughs in Gerontology Awards 53
LRF New Investigator Research Grant 420
Nurses' Educational Funds Fellowships and Scholarships 510
Ortho Biotech Products, L.P. Research Fellowship 512
Paul Beeson Career Development Award in Aging Research 53
Pfizer Atorvastatin Research Awards Program 526
Pfizer Visiting Professorships in Oncology 527
Ruth Estrin Goldberg Memorial for Cancer Research 578

West European Countries

ECTS Career Establishment Award 284
ECTS Exchange Scholarship Grants 284

OPHTHALMOLOGY

Any Country

Action Medical Research Project Grants 6
AHAF Macular Degeneration Research 57
AHAF National Glaucoma Research 57
Barbers Company Clinical Nursing Scholarship 557
CNIB Winston Gordon Award 212
The Dorey Bequest 560
The E. (Ben) & Mary Hochhausen Access Technology Research
   Award 213
Ethicon Foundation Fund Travel Award 561
Fight for Sight Awards 291
HRB Translational Research Programmes 335
The Keeler Scholarship 561
Lister Institute Research Prizes 424
LSA Medical Research Grant 428
MRC Royal College of Surgeons of Edinburgh Clinical Research
   Training Fellowship 440
Ophthalmology Travelling Fellowship 574
Ross Purse Doctoral Fellowship 213
University of Bristol Postgraduate Scholarships 672

Australia

NHMRC Centre of Clinical Eye Research: PhD Scholarships 294

Canada

Alcohol Beverage Medical Research Foundation Research Project
   Grant 14
CNIB Baker Fellowship Fund 212
Tuck MacPhee Award 213

New Zealand

NHMRC Centre of Clinical Eye Research: PhD Scholarships 294

United Kingdom

Guide Dogs Ophthalmic Research Grant 327
The Pfizer Ophthalmic Fellowship 561
Sir William Lister Award 561

United States of America

AFAR Research Grants 52
Alcohol Beverage Medical Research Foundation Research Project
   Grant 14
The Glenn/AFAR Breakthroughs in Gerontology Awards 53
Nurses' Educational Funds Fellowships and Scholarships 510
Paul Beeson Career Development Award in Aging Research 53

OTORHINOLARYNGOLOGY

Any Country

Action Medical Research Project Grants 6
American Tinnitus Association Scientific Research Grants 96
Barbers Company Clinical Nursing Scholarship 557
HRB Translational Research Programmes 335
Karl Storz Travelling Scholarship 573
Lister Institute Research Prizes 424

Canada

American Otological Society Research Grants 72
American Otological Society Research Training Fellowships 73

United Kingdom

Norman Gamble Fund and Research Prize 573

United States of America

AFAR Research Grants 52
American Otological Society Research Grants 72
American Otological Society Research Training Fellowships 73
The Glenn/AFAR Breakthroughs in Gerontology Awards 53
Nurses' Educational Funds Fellowships and Scholarships 510
Paul Beeson Career Development Award in Aging Research
   53

PARASITOLOGY

Any Country

Barbers Company Clinical Nursing Scholarship 557
HRB Translational Research Programmes 335
Lister Institute Research Prizes 424
Rob and Bessie Welder Wildlife Foundation's Graduate Research
   Scholarship Program 793
Sir Halley Stewart Trust Grants 593

African Nations

Canadian Window on International Development 380
IDRC Doctoral Research Awards 380
International Postgraduate Research Scholarships (IPRS) 413

Canada

Canadian Window on International Development 380
IDRC Doctoral Research Awards 380
International Postgraduate Research Scholarships (IPRS) 413

Caribbean Countries

Canadian Window on International Development 380
IDRC Doctoral Research Awards 380
International Postgraduate Research Scholarships (IPRS) 413

East European Countries

FEMS Fellowship 290
IDRC Doctoral Research Awards 380
International Postgraduate Research Scholarships (IPRS) 413
Synthesys Visiting Fellowship 494

European Union

Synthesys Visiting Fellowship 494

Middle East

IDRC Doctoral Research Awards 380
International Postgraduate Research Scholarships (IPRS) 413

South Africa

Canadian Window on International Development 380
IDRC Doctoral Research Awards 380
International Postgraduate Research Scholarships (IPRS) 413

United Kingdom

FEMS Fellowship 290
International Postgraduate Research Scholarships (IPRS) 413
Synthesys Visiting Fellowship 494

United States of America

International Postgraduate Research Scholarships (IPRS)
   413
Nurses' Educational Funds Fellowships and Scholarships
   510
Paul Beeson Career Development Award in Aging Research
   53

West European Countries

FEMS Fellowship 290
International Postgraduate Research Scholarships (IPRS) 413
Synthesys Visiting Fellowship 494

PATHOLOGY

Any Country

AHAF National Heart Foundation 58
Barbers Company Clinical Nursing Scholarship 557
Breast Cancer Campaign PhD Studentships 157
Breast Cancer Campaign Project Grants 157
Breast Cancer Campaign Scientific Fellowships 157
Breast Cancer Campaign Small Pilot Grants 157
Broad Medical Research Program for Inflammatory Bowel Disease
  Grants 178
Career Development Program 419
CCFF Fellowships 202
CCFF Special Travel Allowances 203
CCFF Studentships 203
E.C. Smith Scholarship in Pathology 680
Gillson Scholarship in Pathology 607
HRB Translational Research Programmes 335
Lister Institute Research Prizes 424
Meningitis Research Foundation Project Grant 445
NARSAD Distinguished Investigator Awards 465
NARSAD Independent Investigator Awards 465
NARSAD Young Investigator Awards 465
PDS Project Grant 521
Queen Mary Research Studentships 539
Student Research Fund 120
TSA Research Grant and Fellowship Program 634
University of Bristol Postgraduate Scholarships 672

African Nations

International Postgraduate Research Scholarships (IPRS) 413

Australia

The Cancer Council NSW Research Project Grants 217
NBCF Doctoral Scholarship 469
NBCF Postdoctoral Fellowship 469

Canada

Alcohol Beverage Medical Research Foundation Research Project
  Grant 14
CBS Postdoctoral Fellowship (PDF) 201
CTS Research Fellowship Program 215
International Postgraduate Research Scholarships (IPRS) 413

Caribbean Countries

International Postgraduate Research Scholarships (IPRS) 413

East European Countries

International Postgraduate Research Scholarships (IPRS) 413

Middle East

International Postgraduate Research Scholarships (IPRS) 413

South Africa

International Postgraduate Research Scholarships (IPRS) 413

United Kingdom

British Lung Foundation Project Grants 170
International Postgraduate Research Scholarships (IPRS) 413

United States of America

AFAR Research Grants 52
Alcohol Beverage Medical Research Foundation Research Project
  Grant 14
The Glenn/AFAR Breakthroughs in Gerontology Awards 53
International Postgraduate Research Scholarships (IPRS) 413

Nurses' Educational Funds Fellowships and Scholarships 510
Paul Beeson Career Development Award in Aging Research 53

West European Countries

International Postgraduate Research Scholarships (IPRS) 413

PAEDIATRICS

Any Country

Action Medical Research Project Grants 6
ASBAH Research Grant 118
Ashok Nathwani Visiting Fellowship 562
BackCare Research Grants 144
Barbers Company Clinical Nursing Scholarship 557
CGD Research Trust Grants 236
FRAXA Grants and Fellowships 303
HRB Translational Research Programmes 335
ICR Studentships 365
LSA Medical Research Grant 428
Meningitis Research Foundation Project Grant 445
Neuroblastoma Society Research Grants 497
Postgraduate Research Bursaries (Epilepsy Action) 282
Queen Mary Research Studentships 539
RCPCH/Babes in Arms Fellowships 562
RCPCH/VSO Fellowship 562
RESTRACOMP Research Fellowship 346
Savoy Foundation Postdoctoral and Clinical Research Fellowships
  582
Savoy Foundation Research Grants 582
Savoy Foundation Studentships 582
Sir Halley Stewart Trust Grants 593
Translational Research Program 143
University of Bristol Postgraduate Scholarships 672

Australia

The Cancer Council NSW Research Project Grants 217

Canada

CTS Research Fellowship Program 215

East European Countries

ECTS Career Establishment Award 284
ECTS Exchange Scholarship Grants 284

European Union

ECTS Career Establishment Award 284
ECTS Exchange Scholarship Grants 284

United Kingdom

Barbara Ansell Fellowships in Paediatric Rheumatology 105
BDF Newlife-Full and Small Grants Schemes 153
British Lung Foundation Project Grants 170
ECTS Career Establishment Award 284
ECTS Exchange Scholarship Grants 284
PWSA UK Research Grants 536
REMEDI Research Grants 544
Resuscitation Council Research Fellowships 546
Resuscitation Council Research Grants 546
WellChild Pump-Priming Grants 794
WellChild Research Fellowships 794

United States of America

Florence P Kendall Doctoral Scholarships 301
New Investigator Fellowships Training Initiative (NIFTI) 301
Nurses' Educational Funds Fellowships and Scholarships 510
Paul Beeson Career Development Award in Aging Research 53
Promotion of Doctoral Studies (PODS) 302
Research Grants (FPT) 302

West European Countries

ECTS Career Establishment Award 284
ECTS Exchange Scholarship Grants 284

PLASTIC SURGERY

Any Country

BAPRAS Student Bursaries 160
BAPRAS Travelling Bursary 161
Barbers Company Clinical Nursing Scholarship 557
HRB Translational Research Programmes 335
Leslie Bernstein Grant 25
Meningitis Research Foundation Project Grant 445
Paton/Masser Memorial Fund 161
Plastic Surgery Basic Research Grant 533
Plastic Surgery Research Fellowship Award 533
PSEF Scientific Essay Contest 533

Canada

Leslie Bernstein Investigator Development Grant 25
Leslie Bernstein Resident Research Grants 26

United States of America

Leslie Bernstein Investigator Development Grant 25
Leslie Bernstein Resident Research Grants 26
Nurses' Educational Funds Fellowships and Scholarships 510
Paul Beeson Career Development Award in Aging Research 53

PNEUMOLOGY

Any Country

Action Medical Research Project Grants 6
Barbers Company Clinical Nursing Scholarship 557
Fungal Research Trust Travel Grants 308
HRB Translational Research Programmes 335

Canada

Alcohol Beverage Medical Research Foundation Research Project Grant 14
CTS Research Fellowship Program 215
Parker B Francis Fellowship Program 520

United Kingdom

British Lung Foundation Project Grants 170
H C Roscoe Research Grant 170
The James Trust Research Grant 171

United States of America

Alcohol Beverage Medical Research Foundation Research Project Grant 14
Lung Health (LH) Research Dissertation Grants 66
Nurses' Educational Funds Fellowships and Scholarships 510
Parker B Francis Fellowship Program 520
Paul Beeson Career Development Award in Aging Research 53

PSYCHIATRY AND MENTAL HEALTH

Any Country

ADDF Grants Program 22
AFSP Distinguished Investigator Awards 55
AFSP Pilot Grants 55
AFSP Postdoctoral Research Fellowships 55
AFSP Standard Research Grants 55
AFSP Young Investigator Award 56
Alzheimer's Research Trust, Clinical Research Fellowship
Alzheimer's Research Trust, Emergency Support Grant
Alzheimer's Research Trust, Equipment Grant
Alzheimer's Research Trust, Major Project or Programme
Alzheimer's Research Trust, Network Co-operation Grant
Alzheimer's Research Trust, PhD Scholarship
Alzheimer's Research Trust, Pilot Project Grant
Alzheimer's Research Trust, Research Fellowships
Alzheimer's Society Research Grants
BackCare Research Grants 144
Barbers Company Clinical Nursing Scholarship 557

Distinguished Research Award 103
FRAXA Grants and Fellowships 303
FSSS Grants-in-Aid Program 606
HDA Research Project Grants 348
HDA Studentship 348
HRB Translational Research Programmes 335
LSA Medical Research Grant 428
Meningitis Research Foundation Project Grant 445
NARSAD Distinguished Investigator Awards 465
NARSAD Independent Investigator Awards 465
NARSAD Young Investigator Awards 465
PDS Project Grant 521
Postgraduate Research Bursaries (Epilepsy Action) 282
Queen Mary Research Studentships 539
Savoy Foundation Postdoctoral and Clinical Research Fellowships 582
Savoy Foundation Research Grants 582
Savoy Foundation Studentships 582
Stanley Medical Research Institute Postdoctoral Research Fellowship Program 617
Stanley Medical Research Institute Treatment Trial Grants Program 617
TSA Research Grant and Fellowship Program 634
University of Bristol Postgraduate Scholarships 672

African Nations

International Postgraduate Research Scholarships (IPRS) 413

Australia

The Cancer Council NSW Research Project Grants 217

Canada

Alcohol Beverage Medical Research Foundation Research Project Grant 14
Heritage Health Research Career Renewal Awards 14
International Postgraduate Research Scholarships (IPRS) 413
Research Planning Grants 216

Caribbean Countries

International Postgraduate Research Scholarships (IPRS) 413

East European Countries

International Postgraduate Research Scholarships (IPRS) 413

Middle East

International Postgraduate Research Scholarships (IPRS) 413

South Africa

International Postgraduate Research Scholarships (IPRS) 413

United Kingdom

International Postgraduate Research Scholarships (IPRS) 413
Margaret Temple Research Grant 171
PWSA UK Research Grants 536
REMEDI Research Grants 544
RSM Mental Health Foundation Essay Prize 574

United States of America

AACAP Educational Outreach Program for Child and Adolescent Psychiatry Residents (former Travel Grant Program) 25
AFAR Research Grants 52
Air Force Summer Faculty Fellowship Program 84
Alcohol Beverage Medical Research Foundation Research Project Grant 14
British Marshall Scholarships 685
International Postgraduate Research Scholarships (IPRS) 413
Jeanne Spurlock Minority Medical Student Clinical Fellowship in Child and Adolescent Psychiatry 25
Jeanne Spurlock Research Fellowship in Drug Abuse and Addiction for Minority Medical Students 25
Nurses' Educational Funds Fellowships and Scholarships 510
Paul Beeson Career Development Award in Aging Research 53

West European Countries

International Postgraduate Research Scholarships (IPRS) 413

RHEUMATOLOGY

Any Country

Action Medical Research Project Grants 6
ANRF Research Grants 104
Arthritis Society Research Fellowships 108
BackCare Research Grants 144
Barbers Company Clinical Nursing Scholarship 557
Dr Vincent Cristofalo Memorial Fund, Cecille Gould Memorial Fund
    Award in Cancer Research, Richard Shepherd Fellowship 54
HRB Translational Research Programmes 335
Lister Institute Research Prizes 424
Metro A Ogryzlo International Fellowship 108
OREF Career Development Award 518
OREF Prospective Clinical Research 518
OREF Research Grants 518
OREF Resident Research Award 518
Queen Mary Research Studentships 539
University of Bristol Postgraduate Scholarships 672

African Nations

Metro A Ogryzlo International Fellowship 108

Australia

CDRF Project Grants 236
CDRF Research Fellowship 236
Metro A Ogryzlo International Fellowship 108

Canada

Alcohol Beverage Medical Research Foundation Research Project
    Grant 14
Arthritis Society Research Fellowships 108
Clinical Research Training Fellowship 517
Geoff Carr Lupus Fellowship 108
OREF Clinical Research Award 518

Caribbean Countries

Metro A Ogryzlo International Fellowship 108

East European Countries

ACR/REF Physician Scientist Development Award 44
CDRF Project Grants 236
CDRF Research Fellowship 236
ECTS Career Establishment Award 284
ECTS Exchange Scholarship Grants 284
Metro A Ogryzlo International Fellowship 108

European Union

ECTS Career Establishment Award 284
ECTS Exchange Scholarship Grants 284

Middle East

Metro A Ogryzlo International Fellowship 108

New Zealand

Metro A Ogryzlo International Fellowship 108

South Africa

Metro A Ogryzlo International Fellowship 108

United Kingdom

Allied Health Professionals Educational Training Bursaries 105
Allied Health Professionals Training Fellowships 105
Barbara Ansell Fellowships in Paediatric Rheumatology 105
Career Development Fellowships 106
CDRF Project Grants 236
CDRF Research Fellowship 236
Clinical Research Fellowships 106

Doris Hillier Research Grant 170
ECTS Career Establishment Award 284
ECTS Exchange Scholarship Grants 284
Educational Research Fellowships 106
Equipment Grants 106
Orthopaedic Clinical Research Fellowship 107
PhD Studentships 107
Programme Grants 107
Project Grants 107
REMEDI Research Grants 544
Travelling Fellowships 107

United States of America

ACF/REF/Paula De Merieux Rheumatology Fellowship Award 42
ACR REF Lawren H. Daltroy Fellowship in Patient-Clinician
    Communication 42
ACR REF/Amgen/Wyeth Rheumatology Fellowship Training Award 43
ACR REF/Ephraim P. Engleman Endowed Resident Research
    Preceptorship 43
ACR/REF Amgen Pediatric Rheumatology Research Award 43
ACR/REF Association of Subspecialty Professors Junior Career
    Development Award in Geriatric Medicine Award 43
ACR/REF Clinical Investigator Fellowship Award 43
ACR/REF Clinician Scholars Educator Award 44
ACR/REF Health Professional New Investigator Award 44
AFAR Research Grants 52
Alcohol Beverage Medical Research Foundation Research Project
    Grant 14
CDRF Project Grants 236
CDRF Research Fellowship 236
Clinical Research Training Fellowship 517
The Glenn/AFAR Breakthroughs in Gerontology Awards 53
Nurses' Educational Funds Fellowships and Scholarships 510
OREF Clinical Research Award 518
Paul Beeson Career Development Award in Aging Research 53

West European Countries

CDRF Project Grants 236
CDRF Research Fellowship 236
ECTS Career Establishment Award 284
ECTS Exchange Scholarship Grants 284
Metro A Ogryzlo International Fellowship 108

UROLOGY

Any Country

Action Medical Research Project Grants 6
ASBAH Research Grant 118
Barbers Company Clinical Nursing Scholarship 557
CRF Research Grant 236
HRB Translational Research Programmes 335
ICR Studentships 365
Lister Institute Research Prizes 424
Prostate UK Research Grants 537
Queen Mary Research Studentships 539
Wellbeing of Women Project Grants 793

Australia

Australian Kidney Foundation Medical Research Grants and
    Scholarships 409
Australian Kidney Foundation Seeding and Equipment Grants 409
The Cancer Council NSW Research Project Grants 217

United Kingdom

Prostate UK Research Grants 537
Wellbeing of Women/RCOG Research Training Fellowship 793

United States of America

AFAR Research Grants 52
AUAER/Pfizer Visiting Professorships in Urology 526
The Glenn/AFAR Breakthroughs in Gerontology Awards 53
Nurses' Educational Funds Fellowships and Scholarships 510
Paul Beeson Career Development Award in Aging Research 53

VIROLOGY

Any Country

Action Medical Research Project Grants 6
Barbers Company Clinical Nursing Scholarship 557
Career Development Program 419
CBS Graduate Fellowship Program 200
Dr Vincent Cristofalo Memorial Fund, Cecille Gould Memorial Fund
  Award in Cancer Research, Richard Shepherd Fellowship 54
HRB Translational Research Programmes 335
Lister Institute Research Prizes 424
NARSAD Distinguished Investigator Awards 465
NARSAD Independent Investigator Awards 465
NARSAD Young Investigator Awards 465
Queen Mary Research Studentships 539
Translational Research Program 143

African Nations

IARC Postdoctoral Fellowships for Training in Cancer Research
  374

Canada

CBS Postdoctoral Fellowship (PDF) 201

Caribbean Countries

IARC Postdoctoral Fellowships for Training in Cancer Research 374

East European Countries

FEMS Fellowship 290
IARC Postdoctoral Fellowships for Training in Cancer Research 374

Middle East

IARC Postdoctoral Fellowships for Training in Cancer Research
  374

South Africa

IARC Postdoctoral Fellowships for Training in Cancer Research 374

United Kingdom

British Lung Foundation Project Grants 170
FEMS Fellowship 290
H C Roscoe Research Grant 170

United States of America

Nurses' Educational Funds Fellowships and Scholarships 510
Paul Beeson Career Development Award in Aging Research 53

West European Countries

FEMS Fellowship 290

TROPICAL MEDICINE

Any Country

Barbers Company Clinical Nursing Scholarship 557
Earthwatch Field Research Grants 272
Fungal Research Trust Travel Grants 308
HRB Translational Research Programmes 335
Lister Institute Research Prizes 424
Meningitis Research Foundation Project Grant 445
Sir Halley Stewart Trust Grants 593

African Nations

Canadian Window on International Development 380
IDRC Doctoral Research Awards 380
IDRC Internship Awards 381

Canada

Canadian Window on International Development 380
IDRC Doctoral Research Awards 380
IDRC Internship Awards 381

Caribbean Countries

Canadian Window on International Development 380
IDRC Doctoral Research Awards 380
IDRC Internship Awards 381

East European Countries

IDRC Doctoral Research Awards 380

Middle East

IDRC Doctoral Research Awards 380
IDRC Internship Awards 381

South Africa

Canadian Window on International Development 380
IDRC Doctoral Research Awards 380
IDRC Internship Awards 381

United States of America

Nurses' Educational Funds Fellowships and Scholarships 510
Paul Beeson Career Development Award in Aging Research 53

VENEREOLOGY

Any Country

Barbers Company Clinical Nursing Scholarship 557
HRB Translational Research Programmes 335
Lister Institute Research Prizes 424

United States of America

Nurses' Educational Funds Fellowships and Scholarships 510
Paul Beeson Career Development Award in Aging Research 53

REHABILITATION MEDICINE AND THERAPY

Any Country

Action Medical Research Project Grants 6
Action Medical Research Training Fellowship 7
Alberta Heritage Full-Time Studentship 13
Alzheimer's Society Research Grants
Ataxia UK PhD Studentship 124
Ataxia UK Research Fellowship in Friedreich's ataxia
Ataxia UK Research Grant 124
Ataxia UK Travel Award 124
BackCare Research Grants 144
Barbers Company Clinical Nursing Scholarship 557
CCFF Fellowships 202
CCFF Special Travel Allowances 203
Clinical Research Training Fellowship in Nursing and Midwifery 333
CRF Research Grant 236
DEBRA UK Research Grant Scheme
HDA Research Project Grants 348
Heart Research UK Novel and Emerging Technologies Grant 336
HRB Project Grants-General 334
HRB Translational Research Programmes 335
Meningitis Research Foundation Project Grant 445
MND Research Project Grants 458
PDS Project Grant 521
Postgraduate Research Bursaries (Epilepsy Action) 282
Savoy Foundation Postdoctoral and Clinical Research Fellowships
  582
Savoy Foundation Research Grants 582
Savoy Foundation Studentships 582
Sigma Theta Tau International/Rehabilitation Nursing Foundation
  Grant 590
SOM Research Grant 611
University of Southampton Postgraduate Studentships 759
World Universities Network (WUN) International Research Mobility
  Scheme 759

African Nations

International Postgraduate Research Scholarships (IPRS) 413

Australia

Australian Clinical Research Postdoctoral Fellowship 477
Biomedical (Dora Lush) and Public Health Postgraduate Scholarships 477
C J Martin Fellowships (Overseas Biomedical) 477
The Cancer Council NSW Research Project Grants 217
Career Development Awards 477
Howard Florey Centenary Fellowship 478
Industry Fellowships 478
NBCF Doctoral Scholarship 469
NBCF Postdoctoral Fellowship 469
Neil Hamilton Fairley Fellowships (Overseas Clinical) 478
NHMRC Medical and Dental and Public Health Postgraduate Research Scholarships 478
NHMRC/INSERM Exchange Fellowships 478
Peter Doherty Fellowships (Australian Biomedical) 478
Public Health Fellowship (Australian) 479
Repatriation General Hospital Department of Rehabilitation and Aged Care: Health Professionals Research Scholarship 296
Sidney Sax Fellowship (Overseas Public Health) 479
Sir Robert Menzies Memorial Research Scholarships in the Allied Health Sciences 594
Training Scholarship for Indigenous Health Research 479

Canada

Alberta Heritage Health Research Studentship 13
CCFF Senior Scientist Research Training Award 203
CIHR Doctoral Research Awards 210
CTS Research Fellowship Program 215
International Postgraduate Research Scholarships (IPRS) 413

Caribbean Countries

International Postgraduate Research Scholarships (IPRS) 413

East European Countries

ECTS Career Establishment Award 284
ECTS Exchange Scholarship Grants 284
International Postgraduate Research Scholarships (IPRS) 413

European Union

ECTS Career Establishment Award 284
ECTS Exchange Scholarship Grants 284

Middle East

International Postgraduate Research Scholarships (IPRS) 413

New Zealand

National Heart Foundation of New Zealand Fellowships 480
National Heart Foundation of New Zealand Limited Budget Grants 480
National Heart Foundation of New Zealand Maori Cardiovascular Research Fellowship 481
National Heart Foundation of New Zealand Project Grants 481
National Heart Foundation of New Zealand Travel Grants 481
Repatriation General Hospital Department of Rehabilitation and Aged Care: Health Professionals Research Scholarship 296
Training Scholarship for Indigenous Health Research 479

South Africa

International Postgraduate Research Scholarships (IPRS) 413

United Kingdom

British Lung Foundation Project Grants 170
Doris Hillier Research Grant 170
ECTS Career Establishment Award 284
ECTS Exchange Scholarship Grants 284
Guillain-Barré Syndrome Support Group Research Fellowship 328
Hilda Martindale Exhibitions 341
International Postgraduate Research Scholarships (IPRS) 413
MND PhD Studentship Award 458
Owen Shaw Award 237
Postgraduate Student Allowance Scheme (PSAS) (Queen Margaret) 539
REMEDI Research Grants 544

United States of America

Damon Runyon Fellowship Award 260
Damon Runyon Scholar Award 260
Florence P Kendall Doctoral Scholarships 301
International Postgraduate Research Scholarships (IPRS) 413
New Investigator Fellowships Training Initiative (NIFTI) 301
NIH Research Grants 483
NMSS Patient Management Care and Rehabilitation Grants 486
Nurses' Educational Funds Fellowships and Scholarships 510
Promotion of Doctoral Studies (PODS) 302
Research Grants (FPT) 302

West European Countries

ECTS Career Establishment Award 284
ECTS Exchange Scholarship Grants 284
International Postgraduate Research Scholarships (IPRS) 413

NURSING

Any Country

AFSP Distinguished Investigator Awards 55
AFSP Pilot Grants 55
AFSP Postdoctoral Research Fellowships 55
AFSP Standard Research Grants 55
AFSP Young Investigator Award 56
Alberta Heritage Full-Time Studentship 13
Alzheimer's Society Research Grants
Australian Postgraduate Award Research Scholarship
Barbers Company Clinical Nursing Scholarship 557
Breast Cancer Campaign PhD Studentships 157
Breast Cancer Campaign Project Grants 157
Breast Cancer Campaign Scientific Fellowships 157
Breast Cancer Campaign Small Pilot Grants 157
CCFF Special Travel Allowances 203
CCFF Studentships 203
Clinical Research Training Fellowship in Nursing and Midwifery 333
Doris Bloch Research Award 587
Essex Rotary University Travel Grants 687
FSSS Grants-in-Aid Program 606
Hastings Center International Visiting Scholars Program 332
HRB Project Grants-General 334
HRB Translational Research Programmes 335
La Trobe University Postgraduate Scholarship 414
March of Dimes Graduate Nursing Scholarship 431
MND Research Project Grants 458
Myasthenia Gravis Nursing Research Fellowship 462
ONS Foundation Research Awards 511
ONS Novartis Pharmaceuticals Post-Master's Certificate Scholarships 512
PDS Project Grant 521
Postgraduate Research Bursaries (Epilepsy Action) 282
RCN Grants 557
RCN Scholarships Fund 558
Rosemary Berkel Crisp Research Award 587
Sigma Theta Tau International Small Research Grants 587
Sigma Theta Tau International/American Association of Critical Care Nurses 588
Sigma Theta Tau International/American Association of Diabetes Educators Grant 588
Sigma Theta Tau International/American Nurses Foundation Grant 588
Sigma Theta Tau International/Association of Perioperative Registered Nurses Foundation Grant 588
Sigma Theta Tau International/Emergency Nurses Association Foundation Grant 589
Sigma Theta Tau International/Hospice and Palliative Nurses Foundation Grant 589
Sigma Theta Tau International/Midwest Nursing Research Society Research Grant 589
Sigma Theta Tau International/National League for Nursing Grant (NLN) 590
Sigma Theta Tau International/Oncology Nursing Society Grant 590
Sigma Theta Tau International/Virginia Henderson Clinical Research Grant 591

Sir Allan Sewell Visiting Fellowship 326
Sir Eric Berthoud Travel Grant 689
University of Ballarat Postgraduate Research Scholarship

African Nations

ABCCF Student Grant 102
Hastings Center International Visiting Scholars Program 332
International Postgraduate Research Scholarships (IPRS) 413
ORSAS Awards 688

Australia

Australian Clinical Research Postdoctoral Fellowship 477
Biomedical (Dora Lush) and Public Health Postgraduate Scholarships 477
Career Development Awards 477
Hastings Center International Visiting Scholars Program 332
Hazel Hawke Research Grant in Dementia Care 22
Howard Florey Centenary Fellowship 478
NBCF Doctoral Scholarship 469
NBCF Postdoctoral Fellowship 469
Neil Hamilton Fairley Fellowships (Overseas Clinical) 478
NHMRC Medical and Dental and Public Health Postgraduate Research Scholarships 478
ORSAS Awards 688
Public Health Fellowship (Australian) 479
Sidney Sax Fellowship (Overseas Public Health) 479
Sir Robert Menzies Memorial Research Scholarships in the Allied Health Sciences 594
Training Scholarship for Indigenous Health Research 479
University of Ballarat Part Postgraduate Research Scholarship 667

Canada

Alberta Heritage Health Research Studentship 13
CIHR Doctoral Research Awards 210
CNF Scholarships and Fellowships 213
CTS Research Fellowship Program 215
International Postgraduate Research Scholarships (IPRS) 413
ORSAS Awards 688
Research Planning Grants 216
Rural Maternity Care Doctoral Student Fellowship 578
Rural Maternity Care Research in Postdoctoral Fellowship 578
Sigma Theta Tau International/Canadian Nurses Foundation Grant 589

Caribbean Countries

Hastings Center International Visiting Scholars Program 332
International Postgraduate Research Scholarships (IPRS) 413
ORSAS Awards 688

East European Countries

Hastings Center International Visiting Scholars Program 332
International Postgraduate Research Scholarships (IPRS) 413
ORSAS Awards 688

Middle East

ABCCF Student Grant 102
Hastings Center International Visiting Scholars Program 332
International Postgraduate Research Scholarships (IPRS) 413
ORSAS Awards 688

New Zealand

Hastings Center International Visiting Scholars Program 332
ORSAS Awards 688
Training Scholarship for Indigenous Health Research 479

South Africa

DENOSA Bursaries, Scholarships and Grants 262
Hastings Center International Visiting Scholars Program 332
International Postgraduate Research Scholarships (IPRS) 413
ORSAS Awards 688

United Kingdom

Access to Learning Fund 685
British Lung Foundation Project Grants 170

Ethicon Nurses Education Trust Fund 557
Fund for Innovation 539
Hastings Center International Visiting Scholars Program 332
International Postgraduate Research Scholarships (IPRS) 413
MND PhD Studentship Award 458
Mr and Mrs David Edward Memorial Award 145
Nuffield Trust/RCN/IHM Joint Travel Awards 557
RCN Margaret Parkinson Scholarships 558
Resuscitation Council Research Fellowships 546
Resuscitation Council Research Grants 546
Smith and Nephew Foundation Doctoral Nursing Research Studentship 595
Smith and Nephew Foundation Postdoctoral Nursing Research Fellowship 595

United States of America

Aventis Research Fellowship 511
British Marshall Scholarships 685
International Postgraduate Research Scholarships (IPRS) 413
Lung Health (LH) Research Dissertation Grants 66
Nurses' Educational Funds Fellowships and Scholarships 510
ONS Genetech, Inc./Oncology Nursing Research Grant 512
ORSAS Awards 688
Ortho Biotech Products, L.P. Research Fellowship 512
PhRMAF Postdoctoral Fellowships in Health Outcomes Research 528
PhRMAF Predoctoral Fellowships in Health Outcomes Research 529
PhRMAF Research Starter Grants in Health Outcomes Research 529
PhRMAF Sabbatical Fellowships in Health Outcomes Research 530
Scholarships for Émigrés from the FSU in the Health Professions 401

West European Countries

Hastings Center International Visiting Scholars Program 332
International Postgraduate Research Scholarships (IPRS) 413
Mr and Mrs David Edward Memorial Award 145

MEDICAL AUXILIARIES

Any Country

Barbers Company Clinical Nursing Scholarship 557
HRB Project Grants-General 334
HRB Translational Research Programmes 335

African Nations

International Postgraduate Research Scholarships (IPRS) 413

Australia

Australian Clinical Research Postdoctoral Fellowship 477
Biomedical (Dora Lush) and Public Health Postgraduate Scholarships 477
C J Martin Fellowships (Overseas Biomedical) 477
Career Development Awards 477
Howard Florey Centenary Fellowship 478
NBCF Doctoral Scholarship 469
NBCF Postdoctoral Fellowship 469
Neil Hamilton Fairley Fellowships (Overseas Clinical) 478
NHMRC Medical and Dental and Public Health Postgraduate Research Scholarships 478
NHMRC/INSERM Exchange Fellowships 478
Public Health Fellowship (Australian) 479
Sidney Sax Fellowship (Overseas Public Health) 479
Training Scholarship for Indigenous Health Research 479

Canada

International Postgraduate Research Scholarships (IPRS) 413

Caribbean Countries

International Postgraduate Research Scholarships (IPRS) 413

East European Countries

International Postgraduate Research Scholarships (IPRS) 413

Middle East

International Postgraduate Research Scholarships (IPRS) 413

New Zealand

Training Scholarship for Indigenous Health Research 479

South Africa

International Postgraduate Research Scholarships (IPRS) 413

United Kingdom

International Postgraduate Research Scholarships (IPRS) 413

United States of America

International Postgraduate Research Scholarships (IPRS) 413
Nurses' Educational Funds Fellowships and Scholarships 510

West European Countries

International Postgraduate Research Scholarships (IPRS) 413

MIDWIFERY

Any Country

ANRF Research Grants 104
Barbers Company Clinical Nursing Scholarship 557
CIHR Fellowships Program 210
Clinical Research Training Fellowship in Nursing and Midwifery 333
HRB Project Grants-General 334
HRB Translational Research Programmes 335
RCN Grants 557
RCN Scholarships Fund 558
Wellbeing of Women Project Grants 793

African Nations

International Postgraduate Research Scholarships (IPRS) 413

Australia

Australian Clinical Research Postdoctoral Fellowship 477
Biomedical (Dora Lush) and Public Health Postgraduate Scholarships 477
Career Development Awards 477
Howard Florey Centenary Fellowship 478
NBCF Doctoral Scholarship 469
NBCF Postdoctoral Fellowship 469
Neil Hamilton Fairley Fellowships (Overseas Clinical) 478
NHMRC Medical and Dental and Public Health Postgraduate Research Scholarships 478
Public Health Fellowship (Australian) 479
Sidney Sax Fellowship (Overseas Public Health) 479
Training Scholarship for Indigenous Health Research 479

Canada

International Postgraduate Research Scholarships (IPRS) 413
Rural Maternity Care Doctoral Student Fellowship 578
Rural Maternity Care Research in Postdoctoral Fellowship 578

Caribbean Countries

International Postgraduate Research Scholarships (IPRS) 413

East European Countries

International Postgraduate Research Scholarships (IPRS) 413

Middle East

International Postgraduate Research Scholarships (IPRS) 413

New Zealand

Training Scholarship for Indigenous Health Research 479

South Africa

International Postgraduate Research Scholarships (IPRS) 413

United Kingdom

Ethicon Nurses Education Trust Fund 557
International Postgraduate Research Scholarships (IPRS) 413
Mary Seacole Nursing Development and Leadership Award 556
Mr and Mrs David Edward Memorial Award 145
Nuffield Trust/RCN/IHM Joint Travel Awards 557
RCM Midwifery Awards 556
RCN Margaret Parkinson Scholarships 558
Richard Johanson Research Prize 560
Ruth Davies Research Bursary 556
Smith and Nephew Foundation Doctoral Nursing Research Studentship 595
Smith and Nephew Foundation Postdoctoral Nursing Research Fellowship 595
Tim Chard Case History Prize 560
Wellbeing of Women Entry-Level Scholarship 793
Wellbeing of Women/RCOG Research Training Fellowship 793

United States of America

International Postgraduate Research Scholarships (IPRS) 413
Nurses' Educational Funds Fellowships and Scholarships 510

West European Countries

International Postgraduate Research Scholarships (IPRS) 413
Mr and Mrs David Edward Memorial Award 145

RADIOLOGY

Any Country

AACR Scholar-in-Training Awards 29
Alice Ettinger Distinguished Achievement Award 30
BackCare Research Grants 144
Barbers Company Clinical Nursing Scholarship 557
Breast Cancer Campaign PhD Studentships 157
Breast Cancer Campaign Project Grants 157
Breast Cancer Campaign Scientific Fellowships 157
Breast Cancer Campaign Small Pilot Grants 157
Career Development Program 419
CIHR Fellowships Program 210
Eleanor Montague Distinguished Resident Award in Radiation Oncology 30
HRB Project Grants-General 334
HRB Translational Research Programmes 335
Lucy Frank Squire Distinguished Resident Award in Diagnostic Radiology 30
Marie Sklodowska-Curie Award 30
RSNA International Radiology Program Educational Grant to 'Teach the Teachers' from Emerging Nations 541
RSNA Research Seed Grant Program 542
Translational Research Program 143

African Nations

International Postgraduate Research Scholarships (IPRS) 413

Australia

Australian Clinical Research Postdoctoral Fellowship 477
Biomedical (Dora Lush) and Public Health Postgraduate Scholarships 477
C J Martin Fellowships (Overseas Biomedical) 477
The Cancer Council NSW Research Project Grants 217
Career Development Awards 477
Howard Florey Centenary Fellowship 478
Industry Fellowships 478
NBCF Doctoral Scholarship 469
NBCF Postdoctoral Fellowship 469
Neil Hamilton Fairley Fellowships (Overseas Clinical) 478
NHMRC Medical and Dental and Public Health Postgraduate Research Scholarships 478
NHMRC/INSERM Exchange Fellowships 478
Peter Doherty Fellowships (Australian Biomedical) 478
Training Scholarship for Indigenous Health Research 479

Canada

International Postgraduate Research Scholarships (IPRS) 413

Caribbean Countries

International Postgraduate Research Scholarships (IPRS) 413

East European Countries

International Postgraduate Research Scholarships (IPRS) 413

Middle East

International Postgraduate Research Scholarships (IPRS) 413

New Zealand

Training Scholarship for Indigenous Health Research 479

South Africa

International Postgraduate Research Scholarships (IPRS) 413

United Kingdom

International Postgraduate Research Scholarships (IPRS) 413
Mr and Mrs David Edward Memorial Award 145

United States of America

Cassen Post-Doctoral Fellowships 275
Damon Runyon Fellowship Award 260
International Postgraduate Research Scholarships (IPRS) 413
Nurses' Educational Funds Fellowships and Scholarships 510
RSNA Educational Scholar Grant Program 541
RSNA Medical Student Grant Program 541
RSNA Research Fellowship in Basic Radiologic Sciences 541
RSNA Research Resident Program 542

West European Countries

International Postgraduate Research Scholarships (IPRS) 413
Mr and Mrs David Edward Memorial Award 145

TREATMENT TECHNIQUES

Any Country

ADDF Grants Program 22
AFSP Distinguished Investigator Awards 55
AFSP Pilot Grants 55
AFSP Postdoctoral Research Fellowships 55
AFSP Standard Research Grants 55
AFSP Young Investigator Award 56
Alzheimer's Society Research Grants
American Tinnitus Association Scientific Research Grants 96
BackCare Research Grants 144
Barbers Company Clinical Nursing Scholarship 557
Breast Cancer Campaign PhD Studentships 157
Breast Cancer Campaign Project Grants 157
Breast Cancer Campaign Scientific Fellowships 157
Breast Cancer Campaign Small Pilot Grants 157
Broad Medical Research Program for Inflammatory Bowel Disease
   Grants 178
BRPS Research Grants 172
Career Development Program 419
CCFF Fellowships 202
CCFF Special Travel Allowances 203
CCFF Studentships 203
Colgate-Palmolive Grants for Alternative Research 635
Cooley's Anemia Foundation Research Fellowship 245
CRF Research Grant 236
DEBRA UK Research Grant Scheme
FRAXA Grants and Fellowships 303
HDA Studentship 348
Heart Research UK Novel and Emerging Technologies Grant 336
HRB Project Grants-General 334
HRB Translational Research Programmes 335
Meningitis Research Foundation Project Grant 445
NORD/Rosoe Brady Lysosomal Storage Diseases Fellowships 486

OREF Career Development Award 518
OREF Prospective Clinical Research 518
OREF Research Grants 518
OREF Resident Research Award 518
PDS Project Grant 521
Postgraduate Research Bursaries (Epilepsy Action) 282
SOM Research Grant 611
Stroke Association Research Project Grants 621
Translational Research Program 143

African Nations

International Postgraduate Research Scholarships (IPRS) 413

Australia

Australian Clinical Research Postdoctoral Fellowship 477
Biomedical (Dora Lush) and Public Health Postgraduate Scholarships
   477
C J Martin Fellowships (Overseas Biomedical) 477
The Cancer Council NSW Research Project Grants 217
Career Development Awards 477
Howard Florey Centenary Fellowship 478
Industry Fellowships 478
NBCF Doctoral Scholarship 469
NBCF Postdoctoral Fellowship 469
Neil Hamilton Fairley Fellowships (Overseas Clinical) 478
NHMRC Medical and Dental and Public Health Postgraduate
   Research Scholarships 478
NHMRC/INSERM Exchange Fellowships 478
Public Health Fellowship (Australian) 479
Queensland Cancer Fund PhD Scholarships 753
Sidney Sax Fellowship (Overseas Public Health) 479
Sir Robert Menzies Memorial Research Scholarships in the Allied
   Health Sciences 594
Training Scholarship for Indigenous Health Research 479

Canada

CIHR Doctoral Research Awards 210
Clinical Research Training Fellowship 517
International Postgraduate Research Scholarships (IPRS) 413
OREF Clinical Research Award 518

Caribbean Countries

International Postgraduate Research Scholarships (IPRS) 413

East European Countries

International Postgraduate Research Scholarships (IPRS) 413

Middle East

International Postgraduate Research Scholarships (IPRS) 413

New Zealand

Training Scholarship for Indigenous Health Research 479

South Africa

International Postgraduate Research Scholarships (IPRS) 413

United Kingdom

British Lung Foundation Project Grants 170
International Postgraduate Research Scholarships (IPRS) 413
Owen Shaw Award 237
REMEDI Research Grants 544
Resuscitation Council Research Fellowships 546
Resuscitation Council Research Grants 546

United States of America

The BSN-Jobst Inc. Research Award 99
Clinical Research Training Fellowship 517
Damon Runyon Scholar Award 260
International Postgraduate Research Scholarships (IPRS) 413
National Headache Foundation Research Grant 476
Nurses' Educational Funds Fellowships and Scholarships 510
OREF Clinical Research Award 518

West European Countries

International Postgraduate Research Scholarships (IPRS) 413

MEDICAL TECHNOLOGY

Any Country

Action Medical Research Project Grants 6
Action Medical Research Training Fellowship 7
Alzheimer's Society Research Grants
Barbers Company Clinical Nursing Scholarship 557
Breast Cancer Campaign PhD Studentships 157
Breast Cancer Campaign Project Grants 157
Breast Cancer Campaign Scientific Fellowships 157
Breast Cancer Campaign Small Pilot Grants 157
BRPS Research Grants 172
Career Development Program 419
CCFF Fellowships 202
CCFF Special Travel Allowances 203
CCFF Studentships 203
Cooley's Anemia Foundation Research Fellowship 245
Dr Hadwen Trust Research Assistant or Technician 270
Dr Hadwen Trust Research Fellowship 270
ESRF Postdoctoral Fellowships 287
Hastings Center International Visiting Scholars Program 332
HDA Studentship 348
Heart Research UK Novel and Emerging Technologies Grant 336
HRB Project Grants-General 334
HRB Translational Research Programmes 335
Meningitis Research Foundation Project Grant 445
MND Research Project Grants 458
PDS Project Grant 521
Queen Mary Research Studentships 539
Savoy Foundation Postdoctoral and Clinical Research Fellowships 582
Savoy Foundation Studentships 582
Translational Research Program 143

African Nations

Hastings Center International Visiting Scholars Program 332

Australia

Australian Clinical Research Postdoctoral Fellowship 477
Biomedical (Dora Lush) and Public Health Postgraduate Scholarships 477
C J Martin Fellowships (Overseas Biomedical) 477
Career Development Awards 477
Hastings Center International Visiting Scholars Program 332
Howard Florey Centenary Fellowship 478
Industry Fellowships 478
NBCF Doctoral Scholarship 469
NBCF Postdoctoral Fellowship 469
Neil Hamilton Fairley Fellowships (Overseas Clinical) 478
NHMRC Medical and Dental and Public Health Postgraduate Research Scholarships 478
NHMRC/INSERM Exchange Fellowships 478
Peter Doherty Fellowships (Australian Biomedical) 478
Training Scholarship for Indigenous Health Research 479

Canada

CCFF Senior Scientist Research Training Award 203
CIHR Doctoral Research Awards 210

Caribbean Countries

Hastings Center International Visiting Scholars Program 332

East European Countries

ESRF Thesis Studentships 287
Hastings Center International Visiting Scholars Program 332

Middle East

Hastings Center International Visiting Scholars Program 332

New Zealand

Hastings Center International Visiting Scholars Program 332
Training Scholarship for Indigenous Health Research 479

South Africa

Hastings Center International Visiting Scholars Program 332

United Kingdom

BDF Newlife-Full and Small Grants Schemes 153
British Lung Foundation Project Grants 170
ESRF Thesis Studentships 287
Hastings Center International Visiting Scholars Program 332
MND PhD Studentship Award 458
Resuscitation Council Research Fellowships 546
Resuscitation Council Research Grants 546

United States of America

Nurses' Educational Funds Fellowships and Scholarships 510

West European Countries

ESRF Thesis Studentships 287
Hastings Center International Visiting Scholars Program 332

DENTISTRY AND STOMATOLOGY

Any Country

Barbers Company Clinical Nursing Scholarship 557
HRB Project Grants-General 334
HRB Translational Research Programmes 335
National Association of Dental Assistants Annual Scholarship Award 468
Queen Mary Research Studentships 539
Sir Richard Stapley Educational Trust Grants 593
University of Bristol Postgraduate Scholarships 672
Wellcome Trust Grants 794
Winifred E Preedy Postgraduate Bursary 135

Australia

Australian Clinical Research Postdoctoral Fellowship 477
Career Development Awards 477
Howard Florey Centenary Fellowship 478
Industry Fellowships 478
Neil Hamilton Fairley Fellowships (Overseas Clinical) 478
NHMRC Medical and Dental and Public Health Postgraduate Research Scholarships 478
NHMRC/INSERM Exchange Fellowships 478
Peter Doherty Fellowships (Australian Biomedical) 478
R.N. Hammon Scholarship 753
Training Scholarship for Indigenous Health Research 479

Canada

DCF Biennial Research Award 263
DCF Fellowships for Teacher/Researcher Training 263
Frank Knox Memorial Fellowships 123

New Zealand

Training Scholarship for Indigenous Health Research 479

United States of America

CAMS Scholarship 234
Scholarships for Émigrés from the FSU in the Health Professions 401

ORAL PATHOLOGY

Any Country

Barbers Company Clinical Nursing Scholarship 557
National Association of Dental Assistants Annual Scholarship Award 468
Queen Mary Research Studentships 539

ORTHODONTICS

Any Country

Barbers Company Clinical Nursing Scholarship 557
National Association of Dental Assistants Annual Scholarship Award 468
Queen Mary Research Studentships 539
University of Bristol Postgraduate Scholarships 672

PERIODONTICS

Any Country

Barbers Company Clinical Nursing Scholarship 557
National Association of Dental Assistants Annual Scholarship Award 468
Queen Mary Research Studentships 539
University of Bristol Postgraduate Scholarships 672

COMMUNITY DENTISTRY

Any Country

Barbers Company Clinical Nursing Scholarship 557
National Association of Dental Assistants Annual Scholarship Award 468
Queen Mary Research Studentships 539

DENTAL TECHNOLOGY

Any Country

Barbers Company Clinical Nursing Scholarship 557
HRB Translational Research Programmes 335
National Association of Dental Assistants Annual Scholarship Award 468
Queen Mary Research Studentships 539

Australia

Career Development Awards 477
Howard Florey Centenary Fellowship 478
Industry Fellowships 478
Neil Hamilton Fairley Fellowships (Overseas Clinical) 478
NHMRC Medical and Dental and Public Health Postgraduate Research Scholarships 478
NHMRC Medical and Dental Postgraduate Research Scholarships 294
NHMRC/INSERM Exchange Fellowships 478
Peter Doherty Fellowships (Australian Biomedical) 478
Training Scholarship for Indigenous Health Research 479

Canada

CIHR Doctoral Research Awards 210
DCF Biennial Research Award 263
DCF Fellowships for Teacher/Researcher Training 263

New Zealand

Training Scholarship for Indigenous Health Research 479

United States of America

ADA Foundation Allied Dental Health Scholarship 51

PROSTHETIC DENTISTRY

Any Country

Barbers Company Clinical Nursing Scholarship 557
National Association of Dental Assistants Annual Scholarship Award 468
Queen Mary Research Studentships 539
University of Bristol Postgraduate Scholarships 672

Australia

Victoria Fellowships 264

PHARMACY

Any Country

AACR Scholar-in-Training Awards 29
ADDF Grants Program 22
AFSP Distinguished Investigator Awards 55
AFSP Pilot Grants 55
AFSP Postdoctoral Research Fellowships 55
AFSP Standard Research Grants 55
AFSP Young Investigator Award 56
Alzheimer's Research Trust, Clinical Research Fellowship
Alzheimer's Research Trust, Emergency Support Grant
Alzheimer's Research Trust, Equipment Grant
Alzheimer's Research Trust, Major Project or Programme
Alzheimer's Research Trust, Network Co-operation Grant
Alzheimer's Research Trust, PhD Scholarship
Alzheimer's Research Trust, Pilot Project Grant
Alzheimer's Research Trust, Research Fellowships
Alzheimer's Society Research Grants
Andrew Mellon Foundation Scholarship 547
Barbers Company Clinical Nursing Scholarship 557
Breast Cancer Campaign PhD Studentships 157
Breast Cancer Campaign Project Grants 157
Breast Cancer Campaign Scientific Fellowships 157
Breast Cancer Campaign Small Pilot Grants 157
Career Development Program 419
HRB Project Grants-General 334
HRB Translational Research Programmes 335
Hugh Kelly Fellowship 548
NARSAD Distinguished Investigator Awards 465
NARSAD Independent Investigator Awards 465
NARSAD Young Investigator Awards 465
PDS Project Grant 521
Postgraduate Research Bursaries (Epilepsy Action) 282
Queen Mary Research Studentships 539
Rhodes University Postdoctoral Fellowship and The Andrew Mellon Postdoctoral Fellowship 548
Rhodes University Postgraduate Scholarship 549
Savoy Foundation Postdoctoral and Clinical Research Fellowships 582
Savoy Foundation Studentships 582
Translational Research Program 143

African Nations

International Postgraduate Research Scholarships (IPRS) 413

Australia

Asthma Research Postgraduate Scholarships 124
Asthma Research Project Grants 124
Australian Clinical Research Postdoctoral Fellowship 477
Biomedical (Dora Lush) and Public Health Postgraduate Scholarships 477
Career Development Awards 477
Howard Florey Centenary Fellowship 478
Industry Fellowships 478
Peter Doherty Fellowships (Australian Biomedical) 478
Training Scholarship for Indigenous Health Research 479

Canada

CTS Research Fellowship Program 215
International Postgraduate Research Scholarships (IPRS) 413

Caribbean Countries

International Postgraduate Research Scholarships (IPRS) 413

East European Countries

International Postgraduate Research Scholarships (IPRS) 413

Middle East

International Postgraduate Research Scholarships (IPRS) 413

New Zealand

Training Scholarship for Indigenous Health Research 479

South Africa

International Postgraduate Research Scholarships (IPRS) 413

United Kingdom

International Postgraduate Research Scholarships (IPRS) 413

United States of America

International Postgraduate Research Scholarships (IPRS) 413
PhRMAF Postdoctoral Fellowships in Health Outcomes Research 528
PhRMAF Postdoctoral Fellowships in Pharmaceutics 528
PhRMAF Postdoctoral Fellowships in Pharmacology/Toxicology 528
PhRMAF Predoctoral Fellowships in Health Outcomes Research 529
PhRMAF Predoctoral Fellowships in Pharmaceutics 529
PhRMAF Research Starter Grants in Health Outcomes Research 529
PhRMAF Research Starter Grants in Pharmaceutics 530
PhRMAF Sabbatical Fellowships in Health Outcomes Research 530
PhRMAF Sabbatical Fellowships in Pharmaceutics 531
Scholarships for Émigrés from the FSU in the Health Professions 401

West European Countries

International Postgraduate Research Scholarships (IPRS) 413

BIOMEDICINE

Any Country

AACR Scholar-in-Training Awards 29
ADDF Grants Program 22
AFSP Distinguished Investigator Awards 55
AFSP Pilot Grants 55
AFSP Postdoctoral Research Fellowships 55
AFSP Standard Research Grants 55
AFSP Young Investigator Award 56
AHAF Alzheimer's Disease Research Grant 57
AHAF Macular Degeneration Research 57
AHAF National Glaucoma Research 57
AHAF National Heart Foundation 58
AIDS International Training and Research Programme (AITRP) 403
Alzheimer's Research Trust, Clinical Research Fellowship
Alzheimer's Research Trust, Emergency Support Grant
Alzheimer's Research Trust, Equipment Grant
Alzheimer's Research Trust, Major Project or Programme
Alzheimer's Research Trust, Network Co-operation Grant
Alzheimer's Research Trust, PhD Scholarship
Alzheimer's Research Trust, Pilot Project Grant
Alzheimer's Research Trust, Research Fellowships
Alzheimer's Society Research Grants
Association for Women in Science Educational Foundation Predoctoral Awards 118
Barbers Company Clinical Nursing Scholarship 557
Batten Disease Support and Research Association Research Grant Awards 146
Career Development Program 419
Coltman Scholarship 261
Department of Biological Sciences Studentships 685
Diabetes UK Project Grants 269
Diabetes UK Small Grant Scheme 269
Dr Hadwen Trust Research Assistant or Technician 270
Dr Hadwen Trust Research Fellowship 270
Dr Vincent Cristofalo Memorial Fund, Cecille Gould Memorial Fund Award in Cancer Research, Richard Shepherd Fellowship 54
FRAXA Grants and Fellowships 303
Hastings Center International Visiting Scholars Program 332
Heart Research UK Novel and Emerging Technologies Grant 336
HRB Clinical Research Training Fellowships 334
HRB Project Grants-General 334
HRB Translational Research Programmes 335
ICR Studentships 365
MND Research Project Grants 458
MRC Career Development Award 439
MRC Clinical Research Training Fellowships 439
MRC Clinician Scientist Fellowship 439
MRC Royal College of Surgeons of England Training Fellowship 441
MRC Senior Clinical Fellowship 441

MRC Senior Non-Clinical Fellowship 441
MRC Special Training Fellowships in Bioinformatics, Neuroinformatics and Computational Biology 441
MRC Special Training Fellowships in Health Services and Health of the Public Research 441
MRC/Academy of Medical Sciences Tenure Track Clinician Scientist Fellowship 442
Muscular Dystrophy Research Grants 461
NARSAD Distinguished Investigator Awards 465
NARSAD Independent Investigator Awards 465
NARSAD Young Investigator Awards 465
OFAS Grants 514
PhD Scholarships (B.I.F.) 154
Queen Mary Research Studentships 539
RESTRACOMP Research Fellowship 346
Savoy Foundation Postdoctoral and Clinical Research Fellowships 582
Savoy Foundation Studentships 582
Translational Research Program 143
Wellcome Trust Grants 794

African Nations

Fogarty International Research Collaboration Award (FIRCA) 404
Hastings Center International Visiting Scholars Program 332
International Postgraduate Research Scholarships (IPRS) 413

Australia

Australian Clinical Research Postdoctoral Fellowship 477
Biomedical (Dora Lush) and Public Health Postgraduate Scholarships 477
C J Martin Fellowships (Overseas Biomedical) 477
Career Development Awards 477
Hastings Center International Visiting Scholars Program 332
Howard Florey Centenary Fellowship 478
Industry Fellowships 478
NBCF Doctoral Scholarship 469
NBCF Postdoctoral Fellowship 469
NHMRC Medical and Dental and Public Health Postgraduate Research Scholarships 478
NHMRC/INSERM Exchange Fellowships 478
Peter Doherty Fellowships (Australian Biomedical) 478
Training Scholarship for Indigenous Health Research 479

Canada

Alcohol Beverage Medical Research Foundation Research Project Grant 14
CTS Research Fellowship Program 215
International Postgraduate Research Scholarships (IPRS) 413
Research Planning Grants 216

Caribbean Countries

Hastings Center International Visiting Scholars Program 332
International Postgraduate Research Scholarships (IPRS) 413

East European Countries

FEMS Fellowship 290
Fogarty International Research Collaboration Award (FIRCA) 404
Hastings Center International Visiting Scholars Program 332
International Postgraduate Research Scholarships (IPRS) 413

European Union

EPSRC Grant for School of Physical Sciences 698

Middle East

Fogarty International Research Collaboration Award (FIRCA) 404
Hastings Center International Visiting Scholars Program 332
International Postgraduate Research Scholarships (IPRS) 413

New Zealand

Hastings Center International Visiting Scholars Program 332
Training Scholarship for Indigenous Health Research 479

South Africa

Hastings Center International Visiting Scholars Program 332
International Postgraduate Research Scholarships (IPRS) 413

United Kingdom

BBSRC Studentship 685
British Lung Foundation Project Grants 170
EPSRC Grant for School of Physical Sciences 698
FEMS Fellowship 290
Hastings Center International Visiting Scholars Program 332
International Postgraduate Research Scholarships (IPRS) 413
MND PhD Studentship Award 458
MRC Industrial Collaborative Studentships 439
MRC Research Studentships 440
NERC Studentships 145
Sue McCarthy Travelling Scholarship 328
University of Kent School of Physical Sciences 701

United States of America

AFAR Research Grants 52
Alcohol Beverage Medical Research Foundation Research Project
    Grant 14
Fogarty International Research Collaboration Award (FIRCA)
    404
International Postgraduate Research Scholarships (IPRS) 413
MARC Faculty Predoctoral Fellowships 482
NIGMS Fellowship Awards for Minority Students 482
NIGMS Fellowship Awards for Students With Disabilities 483
NIGMS Postdoctoral Awards 483
NIGMS Research Project Grants 483
NIGMS Research Supplements for Underrepresented Minorities
    483

West European Countries

EPSRC Grant for School of Physical Sciences 698
FEMS Fellowship 290
Fogarty International Research Collaboration Award (FIRCA) 404
Hastings Center International Visiting Scholars Program 332
International Postgraduate Research Scholarships (IPRS) 413
MRC Industrial Collaborative Studentships 439
MRC Research Studentships 440
University of Kent School of Physical Sciences 701

OPTOMETRY

Any Country

Barbers Company Clinical Nursing Scholarship 557
CNIB Winston Gordon Award 212
College of Optometrists Postgraduate Scholarships 238
The E. (Ben) & Mary Hochhausen Access Technology Research
    Award 213
Fight for Sight Awards 291
HRB Project Grants-General 334
Ross Purse Doctoral Fellowship 213
University of Bristol Postgraduate Scholarships 672

Australia

Australian Clinical Research Postdoctoral Fellowship 477
Biomedical (Dora Lush) and Public Health Postgraduate Scholarships
    477
Career Development Awards 477
Howard Florey Centenary Fellowship 478
Industry Fellowships 478
Neil Hamilton Fairley Fellowships (Overseas Clinical) 478
NHMRC Medical and Dental and Public Health Postgraduate
    Research Scholarships 478
Sir Robert Menzies Memorial Research Scholarships in the Allied
    Health Sciences 594
Training Scholarship for Indigenous Health Research 479

Canada

Tuck MacPhee Award 213

New Zealand

Training Scholarship for Indigenous Health Research 479

PODIATRY

Any Country

BackCare Research Grants 144
Barbers Company Clinical Nursing Scholarship 557
CIHR Fellowships Program 210
HRB Project Grants-General 334

African Nations

International Postgraduate Research Scholarships (IPRS) 413

Australia

Australian Clinical Research Postdoctoral Fellowship 477
Biomedical (Dora Lush) and Public Health Postgraduate Scholarships
    477
Howard Florey Centenary Fellowship 478
Neil Hamilton Fairley Fellowships (Overseas Clinical) 478

Canada

International Postgraduate Research Scholarships (IPRS) 413

Caribbean Countries

International Postgraduate Research Scholarships (IPRS) 413

East European Countries

International Postgraduate Research Scholarships (IPRS) 413

Middle East

International Postgraduate Research Scholarships (IPRS) 413

South Africa

International Postgraduate Research Scholarships (IPRS) 413

United Kingdom

International Postgraduate Research Scholarships (IPRS) 413

United States of America

International Postgraduate Research Scholarships (IPRS) 413

West European Countries

International Postgraduate Research Scholarships (IPRS) 413

FORENSIC MEDICINE AND DENTISTRY

Any Country

Barbers Company Clinical Nursing Scholarship 557
HRB Project Grants-General 334

African Nations

International Postgraduate Research Scholarships (IPRS) 413

Australia

Biomedical (Dora Lush) and Public Health Postgraduate Scholarships
    477
Career Development Awards 477
Howard Florey Centenary Fellowship 478
Peter Doherty Fellowships (Australian Biomedical) 478

Canada

International Postgraduate Research Scholarships (IPRS) 413

Caribbean Countries

International Postgraduate Research Scholarships (IPRS) 413
VIFM Scholarship in Forensic Medicine 786

East European Countries

International Postgraduate Research Scholarships (IPRS) 413

Middle East

International Postgraduate Research Scholarships (IPRS) 413
VIFM Scholarship in Forensic Medicine 786

South Africa

International Postgraduate Research Scholarships (IPRS) 413
VIFM Scholarship in Forensic Medicine 786

United Kingdom

International Postgraduate Research Scholarships (IPRS) 413

United States of America

International Postgraduate Research Scholarships (IPRS) 413

West European Countries

International Postgraduate Research Scholarships (IPRS) 413

ACUPUNCTURE

Any Country

BackCare Research Grants 144
Barbers Company Clinical Nursing Scholarship 557
Breast Cancer Campaign PhD Studentships 157
Breast Cancer Campaign Project Grants 157
Breast Cancer Campaign Scientific Fellowships 157
Breast Cancer Campaign Small Pilot Grants 157
HRB Project Grants-General 334
PDS Project Grant 521
Postgraduate Research Bursaries (Epilepsy Action) 282

Australia

Biomedical (Dora Lush) and Public Health Postgraduate Scholarships
477

HOMEOPATHY

Any Country

Barbers Company Clinical Nursing Scholarship 557
Breast Cancer Campaign PhD Studentships 157
Breast Cancer Campaign Project Grants 157
Breast Cancer Campaign Scientific Fellowships 157
Breast Cancer Campaign Small Pilot Grants 157
HRB Project Grants-General 334
PDS Project Grant 521
Postgraduate Research Bursaries (Epilepsy Action) 282

Australia

Biomedical (Dora Lush) and Public Health Postgraduate Scholarships
477

CHIROPRACTIC

Any Country

BackCare Research Grants 144
Barbers Company Clinical Nursing Scholarship 557
CRF Research Grant 236
HRB Project Grants-General 334

African Nations

International Postgraduate Research Scholarships (IPRS) 413

Australia

Australian Clinical Research Postdoctoral Fellowship 477
Biomedical (Dora Lush) and Public Health Postgraduate Scholarships
477

Canada

International Postgraduate Research Scholarships (IPRS) 413

Caribbean Countries

International Postgraduate Research Scholarships (IPRS) 413

East European Countries

International Postgraduate Research Scholarships (IPRS) 413

Middle East

International Postgraduate Research Scholarships (IPRS) 413

South Africa

International Postgraduate Research Scholarships (IPRS) 413

United Kingdom

International Postgraduate Research Scholarships (IPRS) 413

United States of America

International Postgraduate Research Scholarships (IPRS) 413

West European Countries

International Postgraduate Research Scholarships (IPRS) 413

OSTEOPATHY

Any Country

BackCare Research Grants 144
Barbers Company Clinical Nursing Scholarship 557
HRB Project Grants-General 334

Australia

Australian Clinical Research Postdoctoral Fellowship 477
Biomedical (Dora Lush) and Public Health Postgraduate Scholarships
477

Canada

Alcohol Beverage Medical Research Foundation Research Project
Grant 14

United States of America

Alcohol Beverage Medical Research Foundation Research Project
Grant 14

TRADITIONAL EASTERN MEDICINE

Any Country

Alzheimer's Society Research Grants
Barbers Company Clinical Nursing Scholarship 557
HRB Project Grants-General 334
Postgraduate Research Bursaries (Epilepsy Action) 282

Australia

NBCF Doctoral Scholarship 469
NBCF Postdoctoral Fellowship 469

NATURAL SCIENCES

GENERAL

Any Country

AACR Scholar-in-Training Awards 29
ACS Ahmed Zewail Award in Ultrafast Science and Technology 36
AHRC Studentships 227
The Airey Neave Trust Scholarship 12
AMNH Annette Kade Graduate Student Fellowship Program

African Nations

Australia

Canada

Andrew Stratton Scholarship 690
Canada Postgraduate Scholarships (PGS) 495
CCFF Research Grants 202
CIC Montreal Medal 232
Frank Knox Memorial Fellowships 123
GSA Research Grants 310
Guggenheim Fellowships to Assist Research and Artistic Creation
    (USA and Canada) 406
Industrial Postgraduate Scholarship 1 (NSERC IPS) 775
International Postgraduate Research Scholarships (IPRS) 413
International Postgraduate Research Scholarships (IPRS) 413
J W McConnell Memorial Fellowships 243
JSPS Summer Programme 399
NSERC Postdoctoral Fellowships 495
Parker B Francis Fellowship Program 520
Vatican Film Library Mellon Fellowship 785
William and Margaret Brown Cambridge Scholarship for PhD Study
    198
Wingate Scholarships 697

Caribbean Countries

Andrew Stratton Scholarship 690
CAS-TWAS Fellowship for Postdoctoral Research in China 629
CAS-TWAS Fellowship for Postgraduate Research in China 629
CAS-TWAS Fellowship for Visiting Scholars in China 629
CNPq-TWAS Doctoral Fellowships in Brazil 630
CNPq-TWAS Fellowships for Postdoctoral Research in Brazil 630
CSIR (Council of Scientific and Industrial Research)/TWAS Fellowship
    for Postgraduate Research 630
CSIR (The Council of Scientific and Industrial Research)/TWAS
    Fellowship for Postdoctoral Research 630
Guggenheim Fellowships to Assist Research and Artistic Creation
    (Latin America and the Caribbean) 405
International Postgraduate Research Scholarships (IPRS) 413
International Postgraduate Research Scholarships (IPRS) 413
Master Studies in Physical Land Resources Scholarship 379
TWAS Fellowships for Research and Advanced Training 631
TWAS Grants for Scientific Meetings in Developing Countries 631
TWAS Prizes 632
TWAS Prizes to Young Scientists in Developing Countries 632
TWAS Research Grants 632
TWAS Spare Parts for Scientific Equipment 632
TWAS UNESCO Associateship Scheme 632

East European Countries

International Postgraduate Research Scholarships (IPRS) 413
International Postgraduate Research Scholarships (IPRS) 413
Synthesys Visiting Fellowship 494
University of Sheffield Postgraduate International Scholarships 756
Volkswagen Foundation Between Europe and the Orient Programme
    Grants 787

European Union

International Postgraduate Research Scholarships (IPRS) 413
NERC Masters Studentships 493
NERC Research (PhD) Studentships 494
Synthesys Visiting Fellowship 494
Wingate Scholarships 697

Middle East

ABCCF Student Grant 102
Andrew Stratton Scholarship 690
CAS-TWAS Fellowship for Postdoctoral Research in China 629
CAS-TWAS Fellowship for Postgraduate Research in China 629
CAS-TWAS Fellowship for Visiting Scholars in China 629
CNPq-TWAS Doctoral Fellowships in Brazil 630
CNPq-TWAS Fellowships for Postdoctoral Research in Brazil 630
CSIR (Council of Scientific and Industrial Research)/TWAS Fellowship
    for Postgraduate Research 630
CSIR (The Council of Scientific and Industrial Research)/TWAS
    Fellowship for Postdoctoral Research 630
International Postgraduate Research Scholarships (IPRS) 413
International Postgraduate Research Scholarships (IPRS) 413

KFAS Kuwait Prize 413
Master Studies in Physical Land Resources Scholarship 379
NUFFIC-NFP Fellowships for Master's Degree Programmes 496
The Trieste Science Prize 631
TWAS Fellowships for Research and Advanced Training 631
TWAS Grants for Scientific Meetings in Developing Countries 631
TWAS Prizes 632
TWAS Prizes to Young Scientists in Developing Countries 632
TWAS Research Grants 632
TWAS Spare Parts for Scientific Equipment 632
TWAS UNESCO Associateship Scheme 632

New Zealand

Andrew Stratton Scholarship 690
Australian Postgraduate Awards 413
Fish & Game New Zealand Research Scholarships 500
PhD Scholarships 137
University of Otago Master's Awards 717
Wingate Scholarships 697

South Africa

Andrew Stratton Scholarship 690
CAS-TWAS Fellowship for Postdoctoral Research in China 629
CAS-TWAS Fellowship for Postgraduate Research in China 629
CAS-TWAS Fellowship for Visiting Scholars in China 629
CNPq-TWAS Doctoral Fellowships in Brazil 630
CNPq-TWAS Fellowships for Postdoctoral Research in Brazil 630
CSIR (Council of Scientific and Industrial Research)/TWAS Fellowship
    for Postgraduate Research 630
CSIR (The Council of Scientific and Industrial Research)/TWAS
    Fellowship for Postdoctoral Research 630
International Postgraduate Research Scholarships (IPRS) 413
International Postgraduate Research Scholarships (IPRS) 413
Master Studies in Physical Land Resources Scholarship 379
NUFFIC-NFP Fellowships for Master's Degree Programmes 496
SAMRC Post MBChB and BChD Grants 615
The Trieste Science Prize 631
TWAS Fellowships for Research and Advanced Training 631
TWAS Grants for Scientific Meetings in Developing Countries 631
TWAS Prizes 632
TWAS Prizes to Young Scientists in Developing Countries 632
TWAS Research Grants 632
TWAS Spare Parts for Scientific Equipment 632
TWAS UNESCO Associateship Scheme 632
Wingate Scholarships 697
Wolfson Foundation Grants 799

United Kingdom

Aberystwyth Postgraduate Research Studentships 4
Bellahouston Bequest Fund 693
Frank Knox Fellowships at Harvard University 302
Geographical Fieldwork Grants 564
Gilchrist Fieldwork Award 318
Goldsmiths' Company Science for Society Courses
Grundy Educational Trust 327
International Postgraduate Research Scholarships (IPRS) 413
International Postgraduate Research Scholarships (IPRS) 413
JSPS Summer Programme 399
Kennedy Scholarships 409
Llewellyn and Mary Williams Scholarship 145
Mr and Mrs David Edward Memorial Award 145
NERC Masters Studentships 493
NERC Research (PhD) Studentships 494
Neville Shulman Challenge Award 565
Perry Research Awards 525
Royal Commission Research Fellowship 563
Synthesys Visiting Fellowship 494
Wingate Scholarships 697
Wolfson Foundation Grants 799

United States of America

ACOR-CAORC Postgraduate Fellowships 34
Air Force Summer Faculty Fellowship Program 84
Andrew Stratton Scholarship 690

Budweiser Conservation Scholarship 475
CAORC Multi-Country Research Fellowship Program For Advanced Multi-Country Research 249
Congress Bundestag Youth Exchange for Young Professionals 221
Earthwatch Fellowships 272
ETS Postdoctoral Fellowships 276
Fellowship for American College Students 545
Foundation for Science and Disability Student Grant Fund 302
Fulbright Senior Specialists Program 249
The Glenn/AFAR Breakthroughs in Gerontology Awards 53
GSA Research Grants 310
Guggenheim Fellowships to Assist Research and Artistic Creation (USA and Canada) 406
Howard Brown Rickard Scholarship 474
International Postgraduate Research Scholarships (IPRS) 413
International Postgraduate Research Scholarships (IPRS) 413
Jefferson Science Fellows at the U.S. Department of State 466
JSPS Summer Programme 399
Naval Research Laboratory Post Doctoral Fellowship Program 84
NDSEG Fellowship Program 84
North Dakota Indian Scholarship 507
Norwegian Marshall Fund 508
ONR Summer Faculty Research 84
Parker B Francis Fellowship Program 520
Pasteur Foundation Postdoctoral Fellowship Program 522
Renate W Chasman Scholarship 180
SMART Scholarship for Service Program 85
Vatican Film Library Mellon Fellowship 785
Washington University Chancellor's Graduate Fellowship Program 792
Winston Churchill Foundation Scholarship 797

West European Countries

BAEF Alumni Award 147
International Postgraduate Research Scholarships (IPRS) 413
International Postgraduate Research Scholarships (IPRS) 413
JSPS Summer Programme 399
Llewellyn and Mary Williams Scholarship 145
Mr and Mrs David Edward Memorial Award 145
Synthesys Visiting Fellowship 494
University of Otago Master's Awards 717

BIOLOGICAL AND LIFE SCIENCES

Any Country

AAC Research Grants 26
AACR Scholar-in-Training Awards 29
Alberta Heritage Full-Time Fellowships 13
Alberta Heritage Full-Time Studentship 13
Alzheimer's Society Research Grants
Anne S. Chatham Fellowship in Medicinal Botany 451
Association for Women in Science Educational Foundation Predoctoral Awards 118
BFWG Johnstone and Florence Stoney Studentship 165
Breast Cancer Campaign PhD Studentships 157
Breast Cancer Campaign Project Grants 157
Breast Cancer Campaign Scientific Fellowships 157
Breast Cancer Campaign Small Pilot Grants 157
Broad Medical Research Program for Inflammatory Bowel Disease Grants 178
Career Development Program 419
CBS Graduate Fellowship Program 200
Collaborative Career Development Fellowship in Stem Cell Research 439
Colt Foundation PhD Fellowship 239
Department of Biological Sciences Studentships 685
Direct Research on Ataxia-Telangiectasia 3
EMBO Long-Term Fellowships in Molecular Biology 285
EMBO Short-Term Fellowships in Molecular Biology 285
Ernst Mayr Travel Grant 461
ESRF Postdoctoral Fellowships 287
Essex Rotary University Travel Grants 687
ETH Zurich Excellence Scholarship and Opportunity Award 624
Foulkes Foundation Fellowship 298

Future Conservationist Awards 244
Graduate Research Travel Scholarship 281
Hastings Center International Visiting Scholars Program 332
Heart Research UK Novel and Emerging Technologies Grant 336
HFG Research Program 332
HFSPO Long-Term Fellowships 383
HFSPO Program Grant 383
HFSPO Short-Term Fellowships 384
HFSPO Young Investigator Grant 384
Horton (Hydrology) Research Grant 56
HRB Project Grants-General 334
HRB Translational Research Programmes 335
Hugh Kelly Fellowship 548
Hypertension Trust Studentship 349
ICSU-TWAS-UNESCO-UNU/IAS Visiting Scientist Programme 631
International Postgraduate Research Scholarship 667
J Lawrence Angel Fellowship in Human Skeletal Studies
Lindbergh Grants 228
Lister Institute Research Prizes 424
LSRF 3-Year Postdoctoral Fellowships 423
Mount Desert Island New Investigator Award 459
MRC Career Development Award 439
MRC Clinical Research Training Fellowships 439
MRC Clinician Scientist Fellowship 439
MRC Royal College of Surgeons of Edinburgh Clinical Research Training Fellowship 440
MRC Royal College of Surgeons of England Training Fellowship 441
MRC Senior Non-Clinical Fellowship 441
MRC Special Training Fellowships in Health Services and Health of the Public Research 441
MRC/Academy of Medical Sciences Tenure Track Clinician Scientist Fellowship 442
Muscular Dystrophy Research Grants 461
NARSAD Distinguished Investigator Awards 465
NARSAD Independent Investigator Awards 465
NARSAD Young Investigator Awards 465
National Geographic Conservation Trust Grant 244
NCMLS Tenure Track Research Fellowship 506
NERC Advanced Research Fellowships 493
NERC Postdoctoral Research Fellowships 494
NRC Research Associateships 488
NSF Doctoral Dissertation Improvement Grants 488
Perry Postgraduate Scholarships 525
Postgraduate Research Studentship 689
Queen Mary Research Studentships 539
Rhodes University Postdoctoral Fellowship and The Andrew Mellon Postdoctoral Fellowship 548
RSPCA Australia Alan White Scholarship for Animal Welfare Research 577
RSPCA Australia Scholarship for Humane Animal Production Research 577
Savoy Foundation Studentships 582
Singapore-MIT Alliance Graduate Fellowship 492
Sir Eric Berthoud Travel Grant 689
St Catherine's College College Scholarship (Sciences)
Studentships in the Life Sciences Graduate Program 671
SVI Foundation Postgraduate Student Award 617
Teagasc Walsh Fellowships 626
Tibor T Polgar Fellowship 347
Translational Research Program 143
UFAW Animal Welfare Research Training Scholarships 644
UFAW Research and Project Awards 645
UFAW Small Project and Travel Awards 645
UFAW Vacation Scholarships 645
University of Bristol Postgraduate Scholarships 672
University of Otago International Scholarships 717
University of Otago PhD Scholarships 718
University of Otago Prestigious PhD Scholarships 718
University of Southampton Postgraduate Studentships 759
Victoria University of Wellington PhD Scholarships 786
Weizmann Institute of Science MSc Fellowships 792
Weizmann Institute of Science PhD Fellowships 792
Weizmann Institute of Science Postdoctoral Fellowships Program 793
Wellcome Trust Grants 794
William J Cunliffe Scientific Awards 796

NIH Research Grants 483
ORSAS Awards 688
Paul Beeson Career Development Award in Aging Research 53
Pfizer International HDL Research Awards Program 526
Sea Grant/NOAA Fisheries Fellowship 488
Washington University Chancellor's Graduate Fellowship Program 792
Winston Churchill Foundation Scholarship 797

West European Countries

ESRF Thesis Studentships 287
FEMS Fellowship 290
Hastings Center International Visiting Scholars Program 332
Llewellyn and Mary Williams Scholarship 145
Mr and Mrs David Edward Memorial Award 145
Shell Centenary Scholarships and Shell Centenary Chevening
    Scholarships at Edinburgh 683
University of Otago Master's Awards 717

ANATOMY

Any Country

Alzheimer's Society Research Grants
CBS Graduate Fellowship Program 200
EMBO Short-Term Fellowships in Molecular Biology 285
HRB Project Grants-General 334
HRB Summer Student Grants 334
Hugh Kelly Fellowship 548
JILA Postdoctoral Research Associateship and Visiting Fellowships 401
Mount Desert Island New Investigator Award 459
NARSAD Distinguished Investigator Awards 465
NARSAD Independent Investigator Awards 465
NARSAD Young Investigator Awards 465
Queen Mary Research Studentships 539
TSA Research Grant and Fellowship Program 634
UFAW Animal Welfare Research Training Scholarships 644
UFAW Research and Project Awards 645
UFAW Small Project and Travel Awards 645
UFAW Vacation Scholarships 645
University of Bristol Postgraduate Scholarships 672
University of Otago International Scholarships 717
University of Otago PhD Scholarships 718
University of Otago Prestigious PhD Scholarships 718
Victoria University of Wellington PhD Scholarships 786

Australia

University of Otago Master's Awards 717

Canada

Research Planning Grants 216

New Zealand

University of Otago Master's Awards 717

United Kingdom

Aberystwyth Postgraduate Research Studentships 4
Mr and Mrs David Edward Memorial Award 145

United States of America

Paul Beeson Career Development Award in Aging Research 53
Washington University Chancellor's Graduate Fellowship Program 792

West European Countries

Mr and Mrs David Edward Memorial Award 145
University of Otago Master's Awards 717

BIOCHEMISTRY

Any Country

AFSP Distinguished Investigator Awards 55
AFSP Pilot Grants 55
AFSP Postdoctoral Research Fellowships 55

AFSP Standard Research Grants 55
AFSP Young Investigator Award 56
Agnes Fay Morgan Research Award 392
AHAF Alzheimer's Disease Research Grant 57
AHAF Macular Degeneration Research 57
AHAF National Heart Foundation 58
Alzheimer's Research Trust, Clinical Research Fellowship
Alzheimer's Research Trust, Emergency Support Grant
Alzheimer's Research Trust, Equipment Grant
Alzheimer's Research Trust, Major Project or Programme
Alzheimer's Research Trust, Network Co-operation Grant
Alzheimer's Research Trust, PhD Scholarship
Alzheimer's Research Trust, Pilot Project Grant
Alzheimer's Research Trust, Research Fellowships
Alzheimer's Society Research Grants
The Biochemical Society General Travel Fund 151
Breast Cancer Campaign PhD Studentships 157
Breast Cancer Campaign Project Grants 157
Breast Cancer Campaign Scientific Fellowships 157
Breast Cancer Campaign Small Pilot Grants 157
Career Development Program 419
CBS Graduate Fellowship Program 200
CGD Research Trust Grants 236
Department of Biological Sciences Studentships 685
Direct Research on Ataxia-Telangiectasia 3
Dr Vincent Cristofalo Memorial Fund, Cecille Gould Memorial Fund
    Award in Cancer Research, Richard Shepherd Fellowship 54
Earthwatch Field Research Grants 272
EMBO Long-Term Fellowships in Molecular Biology 285
EMBO Short-Term Fellowships in Molecular Biology 285
EMBO Young Investigator 286
ESRF Postdoctoral Fellowships 287
ETH Zurich Excellence Scholarship and Opportunity Award 624
Exeter College Monsanto Senior Research Fellowship 288
Foulkes Foundation Fellowship 298
Gladys Anderson Emerson Scholarship 393
Heart Research UK Novel and Emerging Technologies Grant 336
HRB Postdoctoral Research Fellowships 334
HRB Project Grants-General 334
HRB Summer Student Grants 334
HRB Translational Research Programmes 335
Hugh Kelly Fellowship 548
ICR Studentships 365
Iota Sigma Pi Centennial Award 393
John J. Wasmuth Postdoctoral Fellowships 339
The Krebs Memorial Scholarship 151
La Trobe University Postgraduate Scholarship 414
Lister Institute Research Prizes 424
LSRF 3-Year Postdoctoral Fellowships 423
Meningitis Research Foundation Project Grant 445
MND Research Project Grants 458
Muscular Dystrophy Research Grants 461
NARSAD Distinguished Investigator Awards 465
NARSAD Independent Investigator Awards 465
NARSAD Young Investigator Awards 465
NCAR Graduate Visitor Programme 471
NCAR Postdoctoral Appointments in the Advanced Study Program
    471
NRC Research Associateships 488
PDS Project Grant 521
Queen Mary Research Studentships 539
Reproductive Biology and Immunology Postdoctoral Fellowship 536
Rhodes University Postdoctoral Fellowship and The Andrew Mellon
    Postdoctoral Fellowship 548
Savoy Foundation Postdoctoral and Clinical Research Fellowships
    582
Savoy Foundation Studentships 582
St Catherine's College: Leathersellers' Company Graduate Scholar-
    ship
Teagasc Walsh Fellowships 626
Translational Research Program 143
University of Bristol Postgraduate Scholarships 672
University of Otago International Scholarships 717
University of Otago PhD Scholarships 718
University of Otago Prestigious PhD Scholarships 718
Victoria University of Wellington PhD Scholarships 786

Weizmann Institute of Science MSc Fellowships 792
Weizmann Institute of Science PhD Fellowships 792
Weizmann Institute of Science Postdoctoral Fellowships Program 793
Wellcome Trust Grants 794
William J Cunliffe Scientific Awards 796
Wood-Whelan Research Fellowships 391

African Nations

IDRC Doctoral Research Awards 380
ORSAS Awards 688
TWAS Grants for Scientific Meetings in Developing Countries 631

Australia

ORSAS Awards 688
University of Otago Master's Awards 717

Canada

Alcohol Beverage Medical Research Foundation Research Project
    Grant 14
CBS Postdoctoral Fellowship (PDF) 201
CIC Award for Chemical Education 231
CIC Montreal Medal 232
IDRC Doctoral Research Awards 380
L'ORÉAL Canada For Women in Science Fellowships, With Support
    of the Canadian Commission for UNESCO 123
ORSAS Awards 688

Caribbean Countries

IDRC Doctoral Research Awards 380
ORSAS Awards 688
TWAS Grants for Scientific Meetings in Developing Countries 631

East European Countries

ESRF Thesis Studentships 287
FEMS Fellowship 290
IDRC Doctoral Research Awards 380
Liver Group PhD Studentship 654
ORSAS Awards 688

European Union

Liver Group PhD Studentship 654
Plant Sciences: BBSRC DTA Studentships in Plant Sciences 739

Middle East

IDRC Doctoral Research Awards 380
ORSAS Awards 688
TWAS Grants for Scientific Meetings in Developing Countries 631

New Zealand

ORSAS Awards 688
University of Otago Master's Awards 717

South Africa

Henderson Postgraduate Scholarships 548
IDRC Doctoral Research Awards 380
ORSAS Awards 688
TWAS Grants for Scientific Meetings in Developing Countries 631

United Kingdom

Aberystwyth Postgraduate Research Studentships 4
Access to Learning Fund 685
BBSRC Studentship 685
Biochemistry: BBSRC Doctoral Training Awards 719
Biochemistry: BBSRC Doctoral Training Awards in Collaboration With
    Industry (CASE) 719
Biochemistry: EPSRC Doctoral Training Award 719
British Lung Foundation Project Grants 170
ESRF Thesis Studentships 287
FEMS Fellowship 290
Fulbright-AstraZeneca Research Scholarship 781
Liver Group PhD Studentship 654
Llewellyn and Mary Williams Scholarship 145
MND PhD Studentship Award 458

Mr and Mrs David Edward Memorial Award 145
Plant Sciences: BBSRC DTA Studentships in Plant Sciences 739
Sue McCarthy Travelling Scholarship 328
University of Kent Department of Biosciences 699

United States of America

AFAR Research Grants 52
Alcohol Beverage Medical Research Foundation Research Project
    Grant 14
British Marshall Scholarships 685
The Glenn/AFAR Breakthroughs in Gerontology Awards 53
Krell Institute Computational Science Graduate Fellowship Program
    412
MARC Faculty Predoctoral Fellowships 482
NCAR Faculty Fellowship Programme 471
NIGMS Fellowship Awards for Minority Students 482
NIGMS Fellowship Awards for Students With Disabilities 483
NIGMS Postdoctoral Awards 483
NIGMS Research Project Grants 483
NIGMS Research Supplements for Underrepresented Minorities 483
ONR Summer Faculty Research 84
ORSAS Awards 688
Paul Beeson Career Development Award in Aging Research 53
Washington University Chancellor's Graduate Fellowship Program
    792

West European Countries

ESRF Thesis Studentships 287
FEMS Fellowship 290
Llewellyn and Mary Williams Scholarship 145
Mr and Mrs David Edward Memorial Award 145
University of Kent Department of Biosciences 699
University of Otago Master's Awards 717

BIOLOGY

Any Country

Acadia Graduate Awards 5
AFSP Distinguished Investigator Awards 55
AFSP Pilot Grants 55
AFSP Postdoctoral Research Fellowships 55
AFSP Standard Research Grants 55
AFSP Young Investigator Award 56
AHAF National Glaucoma Research 57
AHAF National Heart Foundation 58
Anne S. Chatham Fellowship in Medicinal Botany 451
Breast Cancer Campaign PhD Studentships 157
Breast Cancer Campaign Project Grants 157
Breast Cancer Campaign Scientific Fellowships 157
Breast Cancer Campaign Small Pilot Grants 157
Broad Medical Research Program for Inflammatory Bowel Disease
    Grants 178
Career Development Program 419
CERIES Research Award 227
The CFUW/A Vibert Douglas International Fellowship 382
CGD Research Trust Grants 236
Department of Biological Sciences Studentships 685
Direct Research on Ataxia-Telangiectasia 3
Earthwatch Field Research Grants 272
Edmund Niles Huyck Preserve, Inc. Graduate and Postgraduate
    Grants 274
EMBO Long-Term Fellowships in Molecular Biology 285
EMBO Short-Term Fellowships in Molecular Biology 285
EMBO Young Investigator 286
Ernst Mayr Travel Grant 461
ESRF Postdoctoral Fellowships 287
ETH Zurich Excellence Scholarship and Opportunity Award 624
Exeter College Monsanto Senior Research Fellowship 288
Foulkes Foundation Fellowship 298
Horton (Hydrology) Research Grant 56
Hugh Kelly Fellowship 548
Institute for Advanced Study Postdoctoral Residential Fellowships 363
Jennifer Robinson Memorial Scholarship 103
Johnson's Wax Research Fellowship

African Nations

Australia

Canada

Caribbean Countries

East European Countries

European Union

Middle East

New Zealand

South Africa

United Kingdom

United States of America

School of Applied Sciences Overseas Scholarships 254
Washington University Chancellor's Graduate Fellowship Program
792

West European Countries

ESRF Thesis Studentships 287
Eugen and Ilse Seibold Award 266
Llewellyn and Mary Williams Scholarship 145
Microsoft Research European PhD Scholarship Programme 448
Mr and Mrs David Edward Memorial Award 145
Synthesys Visiting Fellowship 494
University of Otago Master's Awards 717

HISTOLOGY

Any Country

Alzheimer's Society Research Grants
Breast Cancer Campaign PhD Studentships 157
Breast Cancer Campaign Project Grants 157
Breast Cancer Campaign Scientific Fellowships 157
Breast Cancer Campaign Small Pilot Grants 157
EMBO Short-Term Fellowships in Molecular Biology 285
HRB Postdoctoral Research Fellowships 334
HRB Project Grants-General 334
HRB Summer Student Grants 334
HRB Translational Research Programmes 335
Hugh Kelly Fellowship 548
Lister Institute Research Prizes 424
Meningitis Research Foundation Project Grant 445
Muscular Dystrophy Research Grants 461
Savoy Foundation Postdoctoral and Clinical Research Fellowships
582
Savoy Foundation Studentships 582
TSA Research Grant and Fellowship Program 634
University of Otago International Scholarships 717
University of Otago PhD Scholarships 718
University of Otago Prestigious PhD Scholarships 718
Victoria University of Wellington PhD Scholarships 786

Australia

University of Otago Master's Awards 717

New Zealand

University of Otago Master's Awards 717

United Kingdom

Llewellyn and Mary Williams Scholarship 145
Mr and Mrs David Edward Memorial Award 145

United States of America

Paul Beeson Career Development Award in Aging Research 53

West European Countries

Llewellyn and Mary Williams Scholarship 145
Mr and Mrs David Edward Memorial Award 145
University of Otago Master's Awards 717

BIOPHYSICS AND MOLECULAR BIOLOGY

Any Country

Abdus Salam ICTP Fellowships 4
AHAF Alzheimer's Disease Research Grant 57
AHAF Macular Degeneration Research 57
AHAF National Glaucoma Research 57
AHAF National Heart Foundation 58
Alzheimer's Society Research Grants
Breast Cancer Campaign PhD Studentships 157
Breast Cancer Campaign Project Grants 157
Breast Cancer Campaign Scientific Fellowships 157
Breast Cancer Campaign Small Pilot Grants 157

Broad Medical Research Program for Inflammatory Bowel Disease
Grants 178
Career Development Program 419
CBS Graduate Fellowship Program 200
CGD Research Trust Grants 236
Department of Biological Sciences Studentships 685
Direct Research on Ataxia-Telangiectasia 3
Dr Vincent Cristofalo Memorial Fund, Cecille Gould Memorial Fund
Award in Cancer Research, Richard Shepherd Fellowship 54
EMBO Long-Term Fellowships in Molecular Biology 285
EMBO Short-Term Fellowships in Molecular Biology 285
EMBO Young Investigator 286
ESRF Postdoctoral Fellowships 287
ETH Zurich Excellence Scholarship and Opportunity Award 624
Exeter College Monsanto Senior Research Fellowship 288
Fanconi Anemia Research Award 290
Foulkes Foundation Fellowship 298
FRAXA Grants and Fellowships 303
HRB Postdoctoral Research Fellowships 334
HRB Project Grants-General 334
HRB Summer Student Grants 334
Hugh Kelly Fellowship 548
ICR Studentships 365
Lister Institute Research Prizes 424
The LMB Cambridge Scholarships for PhD Study 192
LSA Medical Research Grant 428
LSRF 3-Year Postdoctoral Fellowships 423
Meningitis Research Foundation Project Grant 445
MND Research Project Grants 458
Mount Desert Island New Investigator Award 459
Muscular Dystrophy Research Grants 461
NARSAD Distinguished Investigator Awards 465
NARSAD Independent Investigator Awards 465
NARSAD Young Investigator Awards 465
NCMLS Tenure Track Research Fellowship 506
NRC Research Associateships 488
PDS Project Grant 521
Perry Postgraduate Scholarships 525
Postgraduate Research Studentship 689
Queen Mary Research Studentships 539
Rhodes University Postdoctoral Fellowship and The Andrew Mellon
Postdoctoral Fellowship 548
Savoy Foundation Postdoctoral and Clinical Research Fellowships 582
Savoy Foundation Studentships 582
St Catherine's College: Leathersellers' Company Graduate
Scholarship
Translational Research Program 143
TSA Research Grant and Fellowship Program 634
University of Bristol Postgraduate Scholarships 672
University of Otago International Scholarships 717
University of Otago PhD Scholarships 718
University of Otago Prestigious PhD Scholarships 718
Victoria University of Wellington PhD Scholarships 786
Weizmann Institute of Science MSc Fellowships 792
Weizmann Institute of Science PhD Fellowships 792
Weizmann Institute of Science Postdoctoral Fellowships Program 793
Wellcome Trust Grants 794
Wood-Whelan Research Fellowships 391

African Nations

IARC Postdoctoral Fellowships for Training in Cancer Research 374
IDRC Doctoral Research Awards 380
ORSAS Awards 688

Australia

The Cancer Council NSW Research Project Grants 217
ORSAS Awards 688
PhD Scholarship: Molecular Factors in Plant–microbe Associations
712
University of Otago Master's Awards 717

Canada

Alcohol Beverage Medical Research Foundation Research Project
Grant 14
IDRC Doctoral Research Awards 380

L'ORÉAL Canada For Women in Science Fellowships, With Support
of the Canadian Commission for UNESCO 123
ORSAS Awards 688

Caribbean Countries

IARC Postdoctoral Fellowships for Training in Cancer Research 374
IDRC Doctoral Research Awards 380
ORSAS Awards 688

East European Countries

ECTS Career Establishment Award 284
ECTS Exchange Scholarship Grants 284
ESRF Thesis Studentships 287
FEMS Fellowship 290
IARC Postdoctoral Fellowships for Training in Cancer Research 374
IDRC Doctoral Research Awards 380
ORSAS Awards 688

European Union

ECTS Career Establishment Award 284
ECTS Exchange Scholarship Grants 284

Middle East

IARC Postdoctoral Fellowships for Training in Cancer Research 374
IDRC Doctoral Research Awards 380
ORSAS Awards 688

New Zealand

ORSAS Awards 688
University of Otago Master's Awards 717

South Africa

IARC Postdoctoral Fellowships for Training in Cancer Research 374
IDRC Doctoral Research Awards 380
ORSAS Awards 688

United Kingdom

Aberystwyth Postgraduate Research Studentships 4
Access to Learning Fund 685
BBSRC Studentship 685
Biochemistry: EPSRC Doctoral Training Award 719
British Lung Foundation Project Grants 170
ECTS Career Establishment Award 284
ECTS Exchange Scholarship Grants 284
ESRF Thesis Studentships 287
FEMS Fellowship 290
MND PhD Studentship Award 458
Mr and Mrs David Edward Memorial Award 145
NERC Studentships 145

United States of America

Alcohol Beverage Medical Research Foundation Research Project
Grant 14
British Marshall Scholarships 685
The Graduate Fellowship Award 340
Krell Institute Computational Science Graduate Fellowship Program
412
MARC Faculty Predoctoral Fellowships 482
NIGMS Fellowship Awards for Minority Students 482
NIGMS Fellowship Awards for Students With Disabilities 483
NIGMS Postdoctoral Awards 483
NIGMS Research Project Grants 483
NIGMS Research Supplements for Underrepresented Minorities 483
ORSAS Awards 688
Paul Beeson Career Development Award in Aging Research 53
Washington University Chancellor's Graduate Fellowship Program
792

West European Countries

ECTS Career Establishment Award 284
ECTS Exchange Scholarship Grants 284
ESRF Thesis Studentships 287
FEMS Fellowship 290

Mr and Mrs David Edward Memorial Award 145
University of Otago Master's Awards 717

BIOTECHNOLOGY

Any Country

ADDF Grants Program 22
Alzheimer's Society Research Grants
Breast Cancer Campaign PhD Studentships 157
Breast Cancer Campaign Project Grants 157
Breast Cancer Campaign Scientific Fellowships 157
Breast Cancer Campaign Small Pilot Grants 157
Career Development Program 419
Department of Biological Sciences Studentships 685
EMBO Long-Term Fellowships in Molecular Biology 285
EMBO Short-Term Fellowships in Molecular Biology 285
EMBO Young Investigator 286
ETH Zurich Excellence Scholarship and Opportunity Award 624
Foulkes Foundation Fellowship 298
FRAXA Grants and Fellowships 303
Fungal Research Trust Travel Grants 308
Hastings Center International Visiting Scholars Program 332
Heart Research UK Novel and Emerging Technologies Grant 336
HRB Postdoctoral Research Fellowships 334
HRB Project Grants-General 334
HRB Summer Student Grants 334
Hugh Kelly Fellowship 548
IAS-STS Fellowship Programme 362
Meningitis Research Foundation Project Grant 445
Muscular Dystrophy Research Grants 461
NARSAD Distinguished Investigator Awards 465
NARSAD Independent Investigator Awards 465
NARSAD Young Investigator Awards 465
NRC Research Associateships 488
Perry Postgraduate Scholarships 525
Postgraduate Research Studentship 689
Promega Biotechnology Research Award 87
Queen Mary Research Studentships 539
Rhodes University Postdoctoral Fellowship and The Andrew Mellon
Postdoctoral Fellowship 548
Savoy Foundation Postdoctoral and Clinical Research Fellowships 582
Savoy Foundation Studentships 582
Scholarship opportunities linked to CATIE's Postgraduate Program
including CATIE scholarship forming part of the Scholarship-Loan
Program 638
Teagasc Walsh Fellowships 626
Tomsk Polytechnic University International Scholarship 634
UFAW Animal Welfare Research Training Scholarships 644
UFAW Research and Project Awards 645
UFAW Small Project and Travel Awards 645
UFAW Vacation Scholarships 645
University of Otago International Scholarships 717
University of Otago PhD Scholarships 718
University of Otago Prestigious PhD Scholarships 718
Victoria University of Wellington PhD Scholarships 786
William J Cunliffe Scientific Awards 796

African Nations

Bioprocessing Graduate Scholarship 648
DBT-TWAS Biotechnology Fellowship for Postdoctoral Studies in
India 630
DBT-TWAS Biotechnology Fellowships for Postgraduate Studies in
India 631
Hastings Center International Visiting Scholars Program 332
IDRC Doctoral Research Awards 380
International Postgraduate Research Scholarships (IPRS) 413
ORSAS Awards 688
TWAS Grants for Scientific Meetings in Developing Countries 631

Australia

Bioprocessing Graduate Scholarship 648
Hastings Center International Visiting Scholars Program 332
ORSAS Awards 688
University of Otago Master's Awards 717

Canada

Bioprocessing Graduate Scholarship 648
Canadian Commonwealth Scholarship and Fellowship Plan 201
IDRC Doctoral Research Awards 380
International Postgraduate Research Scholarships (IPRS) 413
L'ORÉAL Canada For Women in Science Fellowships, With Support
of the Canadian Commission for UNESCO 123
ORSAS Awards 688

Caribbean Countries

Bioprocessing Graduate Scholarship 648
DBT-TWAS Biotechnology Fellowship for Postdoctoral Studies in
India 630
DBT-TWAS Biotechnology Fellowships for Postgraduate Studies in
India 631
Hastings Center International Visiting Scholars Program 332
IDRC Doctoral Research Awards 380
International Postgraduate Research Scholarships (IPRS) 413
ORSAS Awards 688
TWAS Grants for Scientific Meetings in Developing Countries 631

East European Countries

Bioprocessing Graduate Scholarship 648
FEMS Fellowship 290
Hastings Center International Visiting Scholars Program 332
IDRC Doctoral Research Awards 380
International Postgraduate Research Scholarships (IPRS) 413
Liver Group PhD Studentship 654
ORSAS Awards 688

European Union

Bioprocessing Graduate Scholarship 648
Liver Group PhD Studentship 654

Middle East

Bioprocessing Graduate Scholarship 648
DBT-TWAS Biotechnology Fellowship for Postdoctoral Studies in
India 630
DBT-TWAS Biotechnology Fellowships for Postgraduate Studies in
India 631
Hastings Center International Visiting Scholars Program 332
IDRC Doctoral Research Awards 380
International Postgraduate Research Scholarships (IPRS) 413
ORSAS Awards 688
TWAS Grants for Scientific Meetings in Developing Countries 631

New Zealand

Bioprocessing Graduate Scholarship 648
Hastings Center International Visiting Scholars Program 332
ORSAS Awards 688
University of Otago Master's Awards 717

South Africa

Bioprocessing Graduate Scholarship 648
DBT-TWAS Biotechnology Fellowship for Postdoctoral Studies in
India 630
DBT-TWAS Biotechnology Fellowships for Postgraduate Studies in
India 631
Hastings Center International Visiting Scholars Program 332
Henderson Postgraduate Scholarships 548
IDRC Doctoral Research Awards 380
International Postgraduate Research Scholarships (IPRS) 413
ORSAS Awards 688
TWAS Grants for Scientific Meetings in Developing Countries 631

United Kingdom

Aberystwyth Postgraduate Research Studentships 4
Access to Learning Fund 685
BBSRC Studentship 685
British Lung Foundation Project Grants 170
FEMS Fellowship 290
Hastings Center International Visiting Scholars Program 332
International Postgraduate Research Scholarships (IPRS) 413
Liver Group PhD Studentship 654
Martin McLaren Horticultural Scholarship 367
Mr and Mrs David Edward Memorial Award 145
NERC Studentships 145
Perry Research Awards 525
University of Kent Department of Biosciences 699

United States of America

Air Force Summer Faculty Fellowship Program 84
Bioprocessing Graduate Scholarship 648
British Marshall Scholarships 685
The Graduate Fellowship Award 340
International Postgraduate Research Scholarships (IPRS)
413
Krell Institute Computational Science Graduate Fellowship Program
412
MARC Faculty Predoctoral Fellowships 482
NIGMS Fellowship Awards for Minority Students 482
NIGMS Fellowship Awards for Students With Disabilities 483
NIGMS Postdoctoral Awards 483
NIGMS Research Project Grants 483
NIGMS Research Supplements for Underrepresented Minorities
483
ONR Summer Faculty Research 84
ORSAS Awards 688

West European Countries

Bioprocessing Graduate Scholarship 648
FEMS Fellowship 290
Hastings Center International Visiting Scholars Program 332
International Postgraduate Research Scholarships (IPRS)
413
Mr and Mrs David Edward Memorial Award 145
University of Kent Department of Biosciences 699
University of Otago Master's Awards 717

BOTANY

Any Country

The Anne S. Chatham Fellowship 309
Anne S. Chatham Fellowship in Medicinal Botany 451
ASCSA Research Fellowship in Environmental Studies 82
Darbaker Botany Prize 538
Earthwatch Field Research Grants 272
Edmund Niles Huyck Preserve, Inc. Graduate and Postgraduate
Grants 274
EMBO Long-Term Fellowships in Molecular Biology 285
EMBO Short-Term Fellowships in Molecular Biology 285
EMBO Young Investigator 286
ETH Zurich Excellence Scholarship and Opportunity Award
624
Grants for Orchid Research 72
Hugh Kelly Fellowship 548
Jessup and McHenry Awards 4
La Trobe University Postgraduate Scholarship 414
National Geographic Conservation Trust Grant 244
NERC Advanced Research Fellowships 493
NERC Postdoctoral Research Fellowships 494
Perry Postgraduate Scholarships 525
Queen Mary Research Studentships 539
Rhodes University Postdoctoral Fellowship and The Andrew Mellon
Postdoctoral Fellowship 548
Rob and Bessie Welder Wildlife Foundation's Graduate Research
Scholarship Program 793
SERC Postdoctoral Fellowships 596
SERC Predoctoral Fellowships 596
SERC Senior Fellowships 596
St Catherine's College: Leathersellers' Company Graduate
Scholarship
Stanley Smith (UK) Horticultural Trust Awards 618
Teagasc Walsh Fellowships 626
University of Bristol Postgraduate Scholarships 672
University of Otago International Scholarships 717
University of Otago PhD Scholarships 718

University of Otago Prestigious PhD Scholarships 718
Victoria University of Wellington PhD Scholarships 786

African Nations

Canadian Window on International Development 380
IDRC Doctoral Research Awards 380

Australia

Scholarships in Plant Cell Physiology 662
University of Otago Master's Awards 717
Wingate Scholarships 697

Canada

Canadian Window on International Development 380
IDRC Doctoral Research Awards 380
L'ORÉAL Canada For Women in Science Fellowships, With Support
  of the Canadian Commission for UNESCO 123
Wingate Scholarships 697

Caribbean Countries

Canadian Window on International Development 380
IDRC Doctoral Research Awards 380

East European Countries

IDRC Doctoral Research Awards 380
Synthesys Visiting Fellowship 494

European Union

NERC Masters Studentships 493
NERC Research (PhD) Studentships 494
Synthesys Visiting Fellowship 494
W B Crump Scholarship 705
Wingate Scholarships 697

Middle East

IDRC Doctoral Research Awards 380

New Zealand

University of Otago Master's Awards 717
Wingate Scholarships 697

South Africa

Canadian Window on International Development 380
Henderson Postgraduate Scholarships 548
IDRC Doctoral Research Awards 380
Wingate Scholarships 697

United Kingdom

Aberystwyth Postgraduate Research Studentships 4
Jerusalem Botanical Gardens Scholarship 305
Llewellyn and Mary Williams Scholarship 145
Martin McLaren Horticultural Scholarship 367
Mr and Mrs David Edward Memorial Award 145
NERC Masters Studentships 493
NERC Research (PhD) Studentships 494
Perry Research Awards 525
Synthesys Visiting Fellowship 494
W B Crump Scholarship 705
Wingate Scholarships 697

United States of America

Budweiser Conservation Scholarship 475
Earthwatch Fellowships 272
Fulbright Senior Specialists Program 249
Washington University Chancellor's Graduate Fellowship Program
  792

West European Countries

Llewellyn and Mary Williams Scholarship 145
Mr and Mrs David Edward Memorial Award 145
Synthesys Visiting Fellowship 494
University of Otago Master's Awards 717

PLANT PATHOLOGY

Any Country

ASCSA Research Fellowship in Environmental Studies 82
Department of Biological Sciences Studentships 685
Earthwatch Field Research Grants 272
EMBO Long-Term Fellowships in Molecular Biology 285
EMBO Short-Term Fellowships in Molecular Biology 285
EMBO Young Investigator 286
ETH Zurich Excellence Scholarship and Opportunity Award 624
Hugh Kelly Fellowship 548
LSRF 3-Year Postdoctoral Fellowships 423
National Geographic Conservation Trust Grant 244
NERC Advanced Research Fellowships 493
NERC Postdoctoral Research Fellowships 494
Perry Postgraduate Scholarships 525
Queen Mary Research Studentships 539
Scholarship opportunities linked to CATIE's Postgraduate Program
  including CATIE scholarship forming part of the Scholarship-Loan
  Program 638
St Catherine's College: Leathersellers' Company Graduate
  Scholarship
Teagasc Walsh Fellowships 626
University of Otago International Scholarships 717
University of Otago PhD Scholarships 718
University of Otago Prestigious PhD Scholarships 718
Victoria University of Wellington PhD Scholarships 786
Weizmann Institute of Science MSc Fellowships 792
Weizmann Institute of Science PhD Fellowships 792
Weizmann Institute of Science Postdoctoral Fellowships Program
  793
White Rose Studentships 705

African Nations

Canadian Window on International Development 380
IDRC Doctoral Research Awards 380
ORSAS Awards 688

Australia

APAI Scholarships within Integrative Biology 540
ORSAS Awards 688
University of Otago Master's Awards 717
Wingate Scholarships 697

Canada

Canadian Window on International Development 380
IDRC Doctoral Research Awards 380
ORSAS Awards 688
Wingate Scholarships 697

Caribbean Countries

Canadian Window on International Development 380
IDRC Doctoral Research Awards 380
ORSAS Awards 688

East European Countries

IDRC Doctoral Research Awards 380
ORSAS Awards 688

European Union

NERC Masters Studentships 493
NERC Research (PhD) Studentships 494
White Rose Studentships 705
Wingate Scholarships 697

Middle East

IDRC Doctoral Research Awards 380
ORSAS Awards 688

New Zealand

ORSAS Awards 688
University of Otago Master's Awards 717
Wingate Scholarships 697

South Africa

Canadian Window on International Development 380
IDRC Doctoral Research Awards 380
ORSAS Awards 688
Wingate Scholarships 697

United Kingdom

Aberystwyth Postgraduate Research Studentships 4
Access to Learning Fund 685
BBSRC Studentship 685
Llewellyn and Mary Williams Scholarship 145
Martin McLaren Horticultural Scholarship 367
Mr and Mrs David Edward Memorial Award 145
NERC Masters Studentships 493
NERC Research (PhD) Studentships 494
NERC Studentships 145
Perry Research Awards 525
University of Kent Department of Biosciences 699
White Rose Studentships 705
Wingate Scholarships 697

United States of America

Earthwatch Fellowships 272
ORSAS Awards 688

West European Countries

Llewellyn and Mary Williams Scholarship 145
Mr and Mrs David Edward Memorial Award 145
University of Kent Department of Biosciences 699
University of Otago Master's Awards 717

EMBRYOLOGY AND REPRODUCTION BIOLOGY

Any Country

BackCare Research Grants 144
EMBO Long-Term Fellowships in Molecular Biology 285
EMBO Short-Term Fellowships in Molecular Biology 285
EMBO Young Investigator 286
Foulkes Foundation Fellowship 298
FSSS Grants-in-Aid Program 606
Hastings Center International Visiting Scholars Program 332
HRB Postdoctoral Research Fellowships 334
HRB Project Grants-General 334
HRB Summer Student Grants 334
HRB Translational Research Programmes 335
Hugh Kelly Fellowship 548
Lister Institute Research Prizes 424
LSRF 3-Year Postdoctoral Fellowships 423
Mount Desert Island New Investigator Award 459
Perry Postgraduate Scholarships 525
Queen Mary Research Studentships 539
Rhodes University Postdoctoral Fellowship and The Andrew Mellon Postdoctoral Fellowship 548
UFAW Animal Welfare Research Training Scholarships 644
UFAW Research and Project Awards 645
UFAW Small Project and Travel Awards 645
UFAW Vacation Scholarships 645
University of Otago International Scholarships 717
University of Otago PhD Scholarships 718
University of Otago Prestigious PhD Scholarships 718
Weizmann Institute of Science MSc Fellowships 792
Weizmann Institute of Science PhD Fellowships 792
Weizmann Institute of Science Postdoctoral Fellowships Program 793
Wellbeing of Women Project Grants 793
Wellcome Trust Grants 794

African Nations

Hastings Center International Visiting Scholars Program 332

Australia

Hastings Center International Visiting Scholars Program 332
Neil Hamilton Fairley Fellowships (Overseas Clinical) 478
University of Otago Master's Awards 717

Caribbean Countries

Hastings Center International Visiting Scholars Program 332

East European Countries

Hastings Center International Visiting Scholars Program 332

Middle East

Hastings Center International Visiting Scholars Program 332

New Zealand

Hastings Center International Visiting Scholars Program 332
University of Otago Master's Awards 717

South Africa

Hastings Center International Visiting Scholars Program 332

United Kingdom

Aberystwyth Postgraduate Research Studentships 4
Hastings Center International Visiting Scholars Program 332
Llewellyn and Mary Williams Scholarship 145
Mr and Mrs David Edward Memorial Award 145
Perry Research Awards 525
Wellbeing of Women Entry-Level Scholarship 793
Wellbeing of Women/RCOG Research Training Fellowship 793

United States of America

Fulbright Senior Specialists Program 249

West European Countries

Hastings Center International Visiting Scholars Program 332
Llewellyn and Mary Williams Scholarship 145
Mr and Mrs David Edward Memorial Award 145
University of Otago Master's Awards 717

GENETICS

Any Country

ADDF Grants Program 22
AFSP Distinguished Investigator Awards 55
AFSP Pilot Grants 55
AFSP Postdoctoral Research Fellowships 55
AFSP Standard Research Grants 55
AFSP Young Investigator Award 56
AHAF Alzheimer's Disease Research Grant 57
AHAF Macular Degeneration Research 57
Alzheimer's Research Trust, Clinical Research Fellowship
Alzheimer's Research Trust, Emergency Support Grant
Alzheimer's Research Trust, Equipment Grant
Alzheimer's Research Trust, Major Project or Programme
Alzheimer's Research Trust, Network Co-operation Grant
Alzheimer's Research Trust, PhD Scholarship
Alzheimer's Research Trust, Pilot Project Grant
Alzheimer's Research Trust, Research Fellowships
Alzheimer's Society Research Grants
ANRF Research Grants 104
ASBAH Research Grant 118
Ataxia UK PhD Studentship 124
Ataxia UK Research Fellowship in Friedreich's ataxia
Ataxia UK Research Grant 124
Ataxia UK Travel Award 124
Breast Cancer Campaign PhD Studentships 157
Breast Cancer Campaign Project Grants 157
Breast Cancer Campaign Scientific Fellowships 157
Breast Cancer Campaign Small Pilot Grants 157
Broad Medical Research Program for Inflammatory Bowel Disease Grants 178

African Nations

Australia

Canada

Caribbean Countries

East European Countries

European Union

Middle East

New Zealand

South Africa

United Kingdom

United States of America

The Glenn/AFAR Breakthroughs in Gerontology Awards 53
International Postgraduate Research Scholarships (IPRS) 413
MARC Faculty Predoctoral Fellowships 482
NIGMS Fellowship Awards for Minority Students 482
NIGMS Fellowship Awards for Students With Disabilities 483
NIGMS Postdoctoral Awards 483
NIGMS Research Project Grants 483
NIGMS Research Supplements for Underrepresented Minorities 483
NIH Research Grants 483
Paul Beeson Career Development Award in Aging Research 53
Pfizer International HDL Research Awards Program 526
PhRMAF Postdoctoral Fellowships in Informatics 528
PhRMAF Research Starter Grants in Informatics 529
PhRMAF Sabbatical Fellowships in Informatics 530
Washington University Chancellor's Graduate Fellowship Program 792

West European Countries

ECTS Career Establishment Award 284
ECTS Exchange Scholarship Grants 284
FEMS Fellowship 290
Hastings Center International Visiting Scholars Program 332
International Postgraduate Research Scholarships (IPRS) 413
Llewellyn and Mary Williams Scholarship 145
Mr and Mrs David Edward Memorial Award 145
Shell Centenary Scholarships and Shell Centenary Chevening Scholarships at Edinburgh 683
University of Otago Master's Awards 717

IMMUNOLOGY

Any Country

AACR Scholar-in-Training Awards 29
Abbott Laboratories Award in Clinical and Diagnostic Immunology 85
AHAF Macular Degeneration Research 57
Alzheimer's Society Research Grants
ANRF Research Grants 104
Broad Medical Research Program for Inflammatory Bowel Disease Grants 178
Career Development Program 419
CBS Graduate Fellowship Program 200
CGD Research Trust Grants 236
CRF Research Grant 236
Department of Biological Sciences Studentships 685
Dr Vincent Cristofalo Memorial Fund, Cecille Gould Memorial Fund Award in Cancer Research, Richard Shepherd Fellowship 54
EMBO Long-Term Fellowships in Molecular Biology 285
EMBO Short-Term Fellowships in Molecular Biology 285
EMBO Young Investigator 286
ETH Zurich Excellence Scholarship and Opportunity Award 624
Foulkes Foundation Fellowship 298
Fungal Research Trust Travel Grants 308
Gordon Piller Studentships 419
HRB Postdoctoral Research Fellowships 334
HRB Project Grants-General 334
HRB Summer Student Grants 334
HRB Translational Research Programmes 335
Leukaemia Research Clinical Research Training Fellowships 419
Leukaemia Research Grant Programme 419
Lister Institute Research Prizes 424
LSRF 3-Year Postdoctoral Fellowships 423
Meningitis Research Foundation Project Grant 445
Mount Desert Island New Investigator Award 459
Muscular Dystrophy Research Grants 461
NARSAD Distinguished Investigator Awards 465
NARSAD Independent Investigator Awards 465
NARSAD Young Investigator Awards 465
National Multiple Sclerosis Society Research Grants 485
NRC Research Associateships 488
Queen Mary Research Studentships 539
Rhodes University Postdoctoral Fellowship and The Andrew Mellon Postdoctoral Fellowship 548
Savoy Foundation Postdoctoral and Clinical Research Fellowships 582

Savoy Foundation Studentships 582
Teagasc Walsh Fellowships 626
Translational Research Program 143
TSA Research Grant and Fellowship Program 634
University of Otago International Scholarships 717
University of Otago PhD Scholarships 718
University of Otago Prestigious PhD Scholarships 718
Victoria University of Wellington PhD Scholarships 786
Weizmann Institute of Science MSc Fellowships 792
Weizmann Institute of Science PhD Fellowships 792
Weizmann Institute of Science Postdoctoral Fellowships Program 793
Wellbeing of Women Project Grants 793
Wellcome Trust Grants 794
William J Cunliffe Scientific Awards 796

African Nations

ORSAS Awards 688

Australia

The Cancer Council NSW Research Project Grants 217
Neil Hamilton Fairley Fellowships (Overseas Clinical) 478
ORSAS Awards 688
University of Otago Master's Awards 717

Canada

CBS Postdoctoral Fellowship (PDF) 201
Eli Lilly and Company Research Award 86
L'ORÉAL Canada For Women in Science Fellowships, With Support of the Canadian Commission for UNESCO 123
ORSAS Awards 688

Caribbean Countries

ORSAS Awards 688

East European Countries

FEMS Fellowship 290
ORSAS Awards 688

Middle East

ORSAS Awards 688

New Zealand

ORSAS Awards 688
University of Otago Master's Awards 717

South Africa

ORSAS Awards 688

United Kingdom

Aberystwyth Postgraduate Research Studentships 4
Access to Learning Fund 685
BBSRC Studentship 685
Clinical Immunology & Allergy Section President's Prize 572
FEMS Fellowship 290
Llewellyn and Mary Williams Scholarship 145
Mr and Mrs David Edward Memorial Award 145
NERC Studentships 145
Wellbeing of Women/RCOG Research Training Fellowship 793

United States of America

AFAR Research Grants 52
Air Force Summer Faculty Fellowship Program 84
British Marshall Scholarships 685
Eli Lilly and Company Research Award 86
The Glenn/AFAR Breakthroughs in Gerontology Awards 53
MARC Faculty Predoctoral Fellowships 482
NFID Advanced Vaccinology Course Travel Grant 476
NIGMS Fellowship Awards for Students With Disabilities 483
NIGMS Postdoctoral Awards 483
NIGMS Research Project Grants 483
NIGMS Research Supplements for Underrepresented Minorities 483
NIH Research Grants 483
ORSAS Awards 688

Paul Beeson Career Development Award in Aging Research 53
Pfizer Atorvastatin Research Awards Program 526
Washington University Chancellor's Graduate Fellowship Program 792

West European Countries

FEMS Fellowship 290
Llewellyn and Mary Williams Scholarship 145
Mr and Mrs David Edward Memorial Award 145
University of Otago Master's Awards 717

MARINE BIOLOGY

Any Country

CICOR Postdoctoral Scholar Fellowship in Coastal Oceanography,
   Climate or Marine Ecosystems 804
Department of Biological Sciences Studentships 685
Earthwatch Field Research Grants 272
EMBO Long-Term Fellowships in Molecular Biology 285
EMBO Short-Term Fellowships in Molecular Biology 285
EMBO Young Investigator 286
ETH Zurich Excellence Scholarship and Opportunity Award 624
Hugh Kelly Fellowship 548
John A Knauss Marine Policy Fellowships 488
Mount Desert Island New Investigator Award 459
NERC Advanced Research Fellowships 493
NERC Postdoctoral Research Fellowships 494
NRC Research Associateships 488
Postgraduate Research Studentship 689
Queen Mary Research Studentships 539
Rhodes University Postdoctoral Fellowship and The Andrew Mellon
   Postdoctoral Fellowship 548
SERC Postdoctoral Fellowships 596
SERC Predoctoral Fellowships 596
SERC Senior Fellowships 596
Tibor T Polgar Fellowship 347
UFAW Research and Project Awards 645
University of Otago International Scholarships 717
University of Otago PhD Scholarships 718
University of Otago Prestigious PhD Scholarships 718
Victoria University of Wellington PhD Scholarships 786

African Nations

Canadian Window on International Development 380
IDRC Doctoral Research Awards 380
ORSAS Awards 688

Australia

Noel and Kate Monkman Postgraduate Award 397
ORSAS Awards 688
University of Otago Master's Awards 717
Wingate Scholarships 697

Canada

Canadian Window on International Development 380
IDRC Doctoral Research Awards 380
ORSAS Awards 688
Wingate Scholarships 697

Caribbean Countries

Canadian Window on International Development 380
IDRC Doctoral Research Awards 380
ORSAS Awards 688

East European Countries

FEMS Fellowship 290
IDRC Doctoral Research Awards 380
ORSAS Awards 688
Synthesys Visiting Fellowship 494

European Union

NERC Masters Studentships 493
NERC Research (PhD) Studentships 494

Synthesys Visiting Fellowship 494
Wingate Scholarships 697

Middle East

IDRC Doctoral Research Awards 380
ORSAS Awards 688

New Zealand

ORSAS Awards 688
University of Otago Master's Awards 717
Wingate Scholarships 697

South Africa

Canadian Window on International Development 380
Henderson Postgraduate Scholarships 548
IDRC Doctoral Research Awards 380
ORSAS Awards 688
Wingate Scholarships 697

United Kingdom

Aberystwyth Postgraduate Research Studentships 4
Access to Learning Fund 685
BBSRC Studentship 685
FEMS Fellowship 290
Llewellyn and Mary Williams Scholarship 145
Mr and Mrs David Edward Memorial Award 145
NERC Masters Studentships 493
NERC Research (PhD) Studentships 494
NERC Studentships 145
Society for Underwater Technology (SUT) 254
Synthesys Visiting Fellowship 494
Wingate Scholarships 697

United States of America

British Marshall Scholarships 685
Budweiser Conservation Scholarship 475
Earthwatch Fellowships 272
ORSAS Awards 688
Sea Grant/NOAA Fisheries Fellowship 488

West European Countries

FEMS Fellowship 290
Llewellyn and Mary Williams Scholarship 145
Mr and Mrs David Edward Memorial Award 145
Synthesys Visiting Fellowship 494
University of Otago Master's Awards 717

LIMNOLOGY

Any Country

Earthwatch Field Research Grants 272
Edmund Niles Huyck Preserve, Inc. Graduate and Postgraduate
   Grants 274
EMBO Short-Term Fellowships in Molecular Biology 285
ETH Zurich Excellence Scholarship and Opportunity Award 624
Hugh Kelly Fellowship 548
NERC Advanced Research Fellowships 493
NERC Postdoctoral Research Fellowships 494
Rhodes University Postdoctoral Fellowship and The Andrew Mellon
   Postdoctoral Fellowship 548
University of Otago International Scholarships 717
University of Otago PhD Scholarships 718
University of Otago Prestigious PhD Scholarships 718
Victoria University of Wellington PhD Scholarships 786

African Nations

Austrian Academy of Sciences, MSc Course in Limnology and
   Wetland Ecosystems 141

Australia

University of Otago Master's Awards 717

East European Countries

FEMS Fellowship 290

European Union

NERC Masters Studentships 493
NERC Research (PhD) Studentships 494

New Zealand

University of Otago Master's Awards 717

United Kingdom

FEMS Fellowship 290
Llewellyn and Mary Williams Scholarship 145
Mr and Mrs David Edward Memorial Award 145
NERC Masters Studentships 493
NERC Research (PhD) Studentships 494

United States of America

Earthwatch Fellowships 272

West European Countries

FEMS Fellowship 290
Llewellyn and Mary Williams Scholarship 145
Mr and Mrs David Edward Memorial Award 145
University of Otago Master's Awards 717

MICROBIOLOGY

Any Country

Abbott-ASM Lifetime Achievement Award 85
ASBAH Research Grant 118
ASM Graduate Microbiology Teaching Award 85
BD Award for Research in Clinical Microbiology 85
bioMérieux Sonnenwirth Award for Leadership in Clinical Microbiology 86
Broad Medical Research Program for Inflammatory Bowel Disease Grants 178
Career Development Program 419
Carski Foundation Distinguished Undergraduate Teaching Award 86
CBS Graduate Fellowship Program 200
Department of Biological Sciences Studentships 685
Dr Vincent Cristofalo Memorial Fund, Cecille Gould Memorial Fund Award in Cancer Research, Richard Shepherd Fellowship 54
Edmund Niles Huyck Preserve, Inc. Graduate and Postgraduate Grants 274
EMBO Long-Term Fellowships in Molecular Biology 285
EMBO Short-Term Fellowships in Molecular Biology 285
EMBO Young Investigator 286
ESRF Postdoctoral Fellowships 287
ETH Zurich Excellence Scholarship and Opportunity Award 624
Foulkes Foundation Fellowship 298
Fungal Research Trust Travel Grants 308
Gen-Probe Joseph Award 86
HRB Postdoctoral Research Fellowships 334
HRB Project Grants-General 334
HRB Summer Student Grants 334
HRB Translational Research Programmes 335
Hugh Kelly Fellowship 548
ICAAC Young Investigator Award 86
La Trobe University Postgraduate Scholarship 414
Lister Institute Research Prizes 424
LSRF 3-Year Postdoctoral Fellowships 423
Meningitis Research Foundation Project Grant 445
Merck Irving S. Sigal Memorial Award 87
NARSAD Distinguished Investigator Awards 465
NARSAD Independent Investigator Awards 465
NARSAD Young Investigator Awards 465
NERC Advanced Research Fellowships 493
NERC Postdoctoral Research Fellowships 494
NRC Research Associateships 488
Procter & Gamble Award in Applied and Environmental Microbiology 87

Queen Mary Research Studentships 539
Raymond W. Sarber Award 87
Rhodes University Postdoctoral Fellowship and The Andrew Mellon Postdoctoral Fellowship 548
Roche Diagnostics Alice C. Evans Award 87
Royal Irish Academy Gold Medals 569
sanofi-aventis US Award 87
Scherago-Rubin Award 88
Siemens Healthcare Diagnostics Young Investigator Award 88
Teagasc Walsh Fellowships 626
Translational Research Program 143
University of Bristol Postgraduate Scholarships 672
University of Otago International Scholarships 717
University of Otago PhD Scholarships 718
University of Otago Prestigious PhD Scholarships 718
USFCC/J. Roger Porter Award 88
Weizmann Institute of Science MSc Fellowships 792
Weizmann Institute of Science PhD Fellowships 792
Weizmann Institute of Science Postdoctoral Fellowships Program 793
Wellcome Trust Grants 794
William A Hinton Research Training Award 88

African Nations

IARC Postdoctoral Fellowships for Training in Cancer Research 374
International Postgraduate Research Scholarships (IPRS) 413

Australia

The Cancer Council NSW Research Project Grants 217
Neil Hamilton Fairley Fellowships (Overseas Clinical) 478
University of Otago Master's Awards 717
Wingate Scholarships 697

Canada

CBS Postdoctoral Fellowship (PDF) 201
Eli Lilly and Company Research Award 86
International Postgraduate Research Scholarships (IPRS) 413
L'ORÉAL Canada For Women in Science Fellowships, With Support of the Canadian Commission for UNESCO 123
Research Planning Grants 216
Wingate Scholarships 697

Caribbean Countries

IARC Postdoctoral Fellowships for Training in Cancer Research 374
International Postgraduate Research Scholarships (IPRS) 413

East European Countries

ESRF Thesis Studentships 287
FEMS Fellowship 290
IARC Postdoctoral Fellowships for Training in Cancer Research 374
International Postgraduate Research Scholarships (IPRS) 413
Synthesys Visiting Fellowship 494

European Union

NERC Masters Studentships 493
NERC Research (PhD) Studentships 494
Synthesys Visiting Fellowship 494
Wingate Scholarships 697

Middle East

IARC Postdoctoral Fellowships for Training in Cancer Research 374
International Postgraduate Research Scholarships (IPRS) 413

New Zealand

University of Otago Master's Awards 717
Wingate Scholarships 697

South Africa

Henderson Postgraduate Scholarships 548
IARC Postdoctoral Fellowships for Training in Cancer Research 374
International Postgraduate Research Scholarships (IPRS) 413
Wingate Scholarships 697

United Kingdom

Aberystwyth Postgraduate Research Studentships 4
Access to Learning Fund 685
BBSRC Studentship 685
ESRF Thesis Studentships 287
FEMS Fellowship 290
International Postgraduate Research Scholarships (IPRS) 413
Llewellyn and Mary Williams Scholarship 145
Mr and Mrs David Edward Memorial Award 145
NERC Masters Studentships 493
NERC Research (PhD) Studentships 494
NERC Studentships 145
Synthesys Visiting Fellowship 494
University of Kent Department of Biosciences 699
Wingate Scholarships 697

United States of America

AFAR Research Grants 52
British Marshall Scholarships 685
Eli Lilly and Company Research Award 86
The Glenn/AFAR Breakthroughs in Gerontology Awards 53
International Postgraduate Research Scholarships (IPRS) 413
MARC Faculty Predoctoral Fellowships 482
NIGMS Fellowship Awards for Minority Students 482
NIGMS Fellowship Awards for Students With Disabilities 483
NIGMS Postdoctoral Awards 483
NIGMS Research Project Grants 483
NIGMS Research Supplements for Underrepresented Minorities 483
Paul Beeson Career Development Award in Aging Research 53
Washington University Chancellor's Graduate Fellowship Program 792

West European Countries

ESRF Thesis Studentships 287
FEMS Fellowship 290
International Postgraduate Research Scholarships (IPRS) 413
Llewellyn and Mary Williams Scholarship 145
Mr and Mrs David Edward Memorial Award 145
Synthesys Visiting Fellowship 494
University of Kent Department of Biosciences 699
University of Otago Master's Awards 717

NEUROSCIENCES

Any Country

ADDF Grants Program 22
AFSP Distinguished Investigator Awards 55
AFSP Pilot Grants 55
AFSP Postdoctoral Research Fellowships 55
AFSP Standard Research Grants 55
AFSP Young Investigator Award 56
AHAF Alzheimer's Disease Research Grant 57
AHAF National Glaucoma Research 57
Alzheimer's Research Trust, Clinical Research Fellowship
Alzheimer's Research Trust, Emergency Support Grant
Alzheimer's Research Trust, Equipment Grant
Alzheimer's Research Trust, Major Project or Programme
Alzheimer's Research Trust, Network Co-operation Grant
Alzheimer's Research Trust, PhD Scholarship
Alzheimer's Research Trust, Pilot Project Grant
Alzheimer's Research Trust, Research Fellowships
Alzheimer's Society Research Grants
ASBAH Research Grant 118
Ataxia UK PhD Studentship 124
Ataxia UK Research Fellowship in Friedreich's ataxia
Ataxia UK Research Grant 124
Ataxia UK Travel Award 124
CRF Research Grant 236
Direct Research on Ataxia-Telangiectasia 3
Dr Vincent Cristofalo Memorial Fund, Cecille Gould Memorial Fund Award in Cancer Research, Richard Shepherd Fellowship 54
EMBO Long-Term Fellowships in Molecular Biology 285
EMBO Short-Term Fellowships in Molecular Biology 285

EMBO Young Investigator 286
Epilepsy Research UK Fellowship 283
Epilepsy Research UK Research Grant 283
ETH Zurich Excellence Scholarship and Opportunity Award 624
Fondation Fyssen Postdoctoral Study Grants 297
Foulkes Foundation Fellowship 298
FRAXA Grants and Fellowships 303
Herbert H Jasper Fellowship 327
HRB Postdoctoral Research Fellowships 334
HRB Project Grants-General 334
HRB Summer Student Grants 334
HRB Translational Research Programmes 335
Hugh Kelly Fellowship 548
John J. Wasmuth Postdoctoral Fellowships 339
Lister Institute Research Prizes 424
LSA Medical Research Grant 428
LSRF 3-Year Postdoctoral Fellowships 423
MDA Grant Programs 460
Meningitis Research Foundation Project Grant 445
MND Research Project Grants 458
Muscular Dystrophy Research Grants 461
NARSAD Distinguished Investigator Awards 465
NARSAD Independent Investigator Awards 465
NARSAD Young Investigator Awards 465
National Multiple Sclerosis Society Research Grants 485
NRC Research Associateships 488
PDS Project Grant 521
Queen Mary Research Studentships 539
Rhodes University Postdoctoral Fellowship and The Andrew Mellon Postdoctoral Fellowship 548
Savoy Foundation Postdoctoral and Clinical Research Fellowships 582
Savoy Foundation Research Grants 582
Savoy Foundation Studentships 582
Teagasc Walsh Fellowships 626
TSA Research Grant and Fellowship Program 634
UFAW Animal Welfare Research Training Scholarships 644
UFAW Research and Project Awards 645
UFAW Small Project and Travel Awards 645
UFAW Vacation Scholarships 645
University of Otago International Scholarships 717
University of Otago PhD Scholarships 718
University of Otago Prestigious PhD Scholarships 718
Victoria University of Wellington PhD Scholarships 786
Weizmann Institute of Science MSc Fellowships 792
Weizmann Institute of Science PhD Fellowships 792
Weizmann Institute of Science Postdoctoral Fellowships Program 793
Wellcome Trust Grants 794
William P. Van Wagenen Fellowship 32

African Nations

IARC Postdoctoral Fellowships for Training in Cancer Research 374
William P. Van Wagenen Fellowship 32

Australia

Neil Hamilton Fairley Fellowships (Overseas Clinical) 478
University of Otago Master's Awards 717
William P. Van Wagenen Fellowship 32

Canada

Alcohol Beverage Medical Research Foundation Research Project Grant 14
Herbert H Jasper Fellowship 327
L'ORÉAL Canada For Women in Science Fellowships, With Support of the Canadian Commission for UNESCO 123
William P. Van Wagenen Fellowship 32

Caribbean Countries

IARC Postdoctoral Fellowships for Training in Cancer Research 374
William P. Van Wagenen Fellowship 32

East European Countries

ECTS Career Establishment Award 284
ECTS Exchange Scholarship Grants 284

IARC Postdoctoral Fellowships for Training in Cancer Research 374
William P. Van Wagenen Fellowship 32

European Union

ECTS Career Establishment Award 284
ECTS Exchange Scholarship Grants 284

Middle East

IARC Postdoctoral Fellowships for Training in Cancer Research 374
William P. Van Wagenen Fellowship 32

New Zealand

University of Otago Master's Awards 717
William P. Van Wagenen Fellowship 32

South Africa

Henderson Postgraduate Scholarships 548
IARC Postdoctoral Fellowships for Training in Cancer Research 374
William P. Van Wagenen Fellowship 32

United Kingdom

ECTS Career Establishment Award 284
ECTS Exchange Scholarship Grants 284
MND PhD Studentship Award 458
Mr and Mrs David Edward Memorial Award 145
William P. Van Wagenen Fellowship 32

United States of America

AFAR Research Grants 52
Alcohol Beverage Medical Research Foundation Research Project
    Grant 14
Diversity Program in Neuroscience Doctoral Fellowship 75
Florence P Kendall Doctoral Scholarships 301
The Glenn/AFAR Breakthroughs in Gerontology Awards 53
Krell Institute Computational Science Graduate Fellowship Program
    412
NIH Research Grants 483
NREF Research Fellowship 31
NREF Young Clinician Investigator Award 31
Paul Beeson Career Development Award in Aging Research 53
Pfizer Atorvastatin Research Awards Program 526
Promotion of Doctoral Studies (PODS) 302
Washington University Chancellor's Graduate Fellowship Program
    792

West European Countries

ECTS Career Establishment Award 284
ECTS Exchange Scholarship Grants 284
Mr and Mrs David Edward Memorial Award 145
University of Otago Master's Awards 717

PARASITOLOGY

Any Country

Broad Medical Research Program for Inflammatory Bowel Disease
    Grants 178
Edmund Niles Huyck Preserve, Inc. Graduate and Postgraduate
    Grants 274
EMBO Long-Term Fellowships in Molecular Biology 285
EMBO Short-Term Fellowships in Molecular Biology 285
EMBO Young Investigator 286
HRB Postdoctoral Research Fellowships 334
HRB Project Grants-General 334
HRB Summer Student Grants 334
HRB Translational Research Programmes 335
Lister Institute Research Prizes 424
NERC Advanced Research Fellowships 493
NERC Postdoctoral Research Fellowships 494
UFAW Animal Welfare Research Training Scholarships 644
University of Otago International Scholarships 717
University of Otago PhD Scholarships 718
University of Otago Prestigious PhD Scholarships 718

Victoria University of Wellington PhD Scholarships 786
Wellcome Trust Grants 794

African Nations

Canadian Window on International Development 380
IDRC Doctoral Research Awards 380

Australia

Neil Hamilton Fairley Fellowships (Overseas Clinical) 478
University of Otago Master's Awards 717

Canada

Canadian Window on International Development 380
CBS Postdoctoral Fellowship (PDF) 201
IDRC Doctoral Research Awards 380
L'ORÉAL Canada For Women in Science Fellowships, With Support
    of the Canadian Commission for UNESCO 123

Caribbean Countries

Canadian Window on International Development 380
IDRC Doctoral Research Awards 380

East European Countries

FEMS Fellowship 290
IDRC Doctoral Research Awards 380
Synthesys Visiting Fellowship 494

European Union

NERC Masters Studentships 493
NERC Research (PhD) Studentships 494
Synthesys Visiting Fellowship 494

Middle East

IDRC Doctoral Research Awards 380

New Zealand

University of Otago Master's Awards 717

South Africa

Canadian Window on International Development 380
IDRC Doctoral Research Awards 380

United Kingdom

Aberystwyth Postgraduate Research Studentships 4
FEMS Fellowship 290
Llewellyn and Mary Williams Scholarship 145
Mr and Mrs David Edward Memorial Award 145
NERC Masters Studentships 493
NERC Research (PhD) Studentships 494
Synthesys Visiting Fellowship 494

United States of America

Earthwatch Fellowships 272

West European Countries

FEMS Fellowship 290
Llewellyn and Mary Williams Scholarship 145
Mr and Mrs David Edward Memorial Award 145
Synthesys Visiting Fellowship 494
University of Otago Master's Awards 717

PHARMACOLOGY

Any Country

AACR Scholar-in-Training Awards 29
AAPS/AFPE Gateway to Research Scholarships 54
ADDF Grants Program 22
AFSP Distinguished Investigator Awards 55
AFSP Pilot Grants 55
AFSP Postdoctoral Research Fellowships 55
AFSP Standard Research Grants 55
AFSP Young Investigator Award 56

PHYSIOLOGY

Any Country

AHAF National Heart Foundation 58
Alzheimer's Society Research Grants
Broad Medical Research Program for Inflammatory Bowel Disease Grants 178
CBS Graduate Fellowship Program 200
Colt Foundation PhD Fellowship 239
EMBO Long-Term Fellowships in Molecular Biology 285
EMBO Short-Term Fellowships in Molecular Biology 285
EMBO Young Investigator 286
FSSS Grants-in-Aid Program 606
Heart Research UK Novel and Emerging Technologies Grant 336
HRB Postdoctoral Research Fellowships 334
HRB Project Grants-General 334
HRB Summer Student Grants 334
HRB Translational Research Programmes 335
Hugh Kelly Fellowship 548
Lister Institute Research Prizes 424
LSRF 3-Year Postdoctoral Fellowships 423
Meningitis Research Foundation Project Grant 445
MND Research Project Grants 458
Mount Desert Island New Investigator Award 459
Muscular Dystrophy Research Grants 461
NARSAD Distinguished Investigator Awards 465
NARSAD Independent Investigator Awards 465
NARSAD Young Investigator Awards 465
NERC Advanced Research Fellowships 493
NERC Postdoctoral Research Fellowships 494
Postgraduate Scholarship Program–Physiology (Quality Control) 139
Postgraduate Scholarship–Physiology (Biochemistry/Haematology) 139
Reproductive Biology and Immunology Postdoctoral Fellowship 536
Rhodes University Postdoctoral Fellowship and The Andrew Mellon Postdoctoral Fellowship 548
Savoy Foundation Postdoctoral and Clinical Research Fellowships 582
Savoy Foundation Studentships 582
Sports Physiology Postgraduate Scholarship–Fatigue and Recovery 140
SSSS Student Research Grants 606
UFAW Animal Welfare Research Training Scholarships 644
UFAW Research and Project Awards 645
UFAW Small Project and Travel Awards 645
UFAW Vacation Scholarships 645
University of Bristol Postgraduate Scholarships 672
University of Otago International Scholarships 717
University of Otago PhD Scholarships 718
University of Otago Prestigious PhD Scholarships 718
Victoria University of Wellington PhD Scholarships 786
Weizmann Institute of Science MSc Fellowships 792
Weizmann Institute of Science PhD Fellowships 792
Weizmann Institute of Science Postdoctoral Fellowships Program 793
Wellcome Trust Grants 794
William J Cunliffe Scientific Awards 796

Australia

Investigation of the Human Intestinal Nervous System 293
Neil Hamilton Fairley Fellowships (Overseas Clinical) 478
University of Otago Master's Awards 717

Canada

Alcohol Beverage Medical Research Foundation Research Project Grant 14
L'ORÉAL Canada For Women in Science Fellowships, With Support of the Canadian Commission for UNESCO 123

European Union

NERC Masters Studentships 493
NERC Research (PhD) Studentships 494

New Zealand

University of Otago Master's Awards 717

South Africa

Henderson Postgraduate Scholarships 548

United Kingdom

Aberystwyth Postgraduate Research Studentships 4
Llewellyn and Mary Williams Scholarship 145
MND PhD Studentship Award 458
Mr and Mrs David Edward Memorial Award 145
NERC Masters Studentships 493
NERC Research (PhD) Studentships 494

United States of America

AFAR Research Grants 52
Alcohol Beverage Medical Research Foundation Research Project Grant 14
APS Conference Student Award 74
APS Mass Media Science and Engineering Fellowship 74
APS Minority Travel Fellowship Awards 75
Caroline tum Suden/Frances Hellebrandt Professional Opportunity Awards 75
The Glenn/AFAR Breakthroughs in Gerontology Awards 53
MARC Faculty Predoctoral Fellowships 482
NIGMS Fellowship Awards for Minority Students 482
NIGMS Fellowship Awards for Students With Disabilities 483
NIGMS Postdoctoral Awards 483
NIGMS Research Project Grants 483
NIGMS Research Supplements for Underrepresented Minorities 483
NIH Research Grants 483
Porter Physiology Fellowships for Minorities 75
Procter and Gamble Professional Opportunity Awards 75

West European Countries

Llewellyn and Mary Williams Scholarship 145
Mr and Mrs David Edward Memorial Award 145
University of Otago Master's Awards 717

TOXICOLOGY

Any Country

Alleghery-ENCRC Student Research Award 635
Alzheimer's Society Research Grants
CAAT Research Grants 406
Colgate-Palmolive Grants for Alternative Research 635
Colgate-Palmolive Postdoctoral Fellowship Award in In Vitro Toxicology 635
Colt Foundation PhD Fellowship 239
Dr Vincent Cristofalo Memorial Fund, Cecille Gould Memorial Fund Award in Cancer Research, Richard Shepherd Fellowship 54
EMBO Short-Term Fellowships in Molecular Biology 285
HRB Postdoctoral Research Fellowships 334
HRB Project Grants-General 334
HRB Summer Student Grants 334
HRB Translational Research Programmes 335
Hugh Kelly Fellowship 548
Lister Institute Research Prizes 424
Mount Desert Island New Investigator Award 459
Muscular Dystrophy Research Grants 461
NERC Advanced Research Fellowships 493
NERC Postdoctoral Research Fellowships 494
PDS Project Grant 521
Regulation and Safety SS Travel Award 635
Rhodes University Postdoctoral Fellowship and The Andrew Mellon Postdoctoral Fellowship 548
Robert L. Dixon International Travel Award 636
UFAW Animal Welfare Research Training Scholarships 644
UFAW Research and Project Awards 645
UFAW Small Project and Travel Awards 645
UFAW Vacation Scholarships 645
University of Otago International Scholarships 717
University of Otago PhD Scholarships 718
University of Otago Prestigious PhD Scholarships 718
Victoria University of Wellington PhD Scholarships 786
Wellcome Trust Grants 794

African Nations

IARC Postdoctoral Fellowships for Training in Cancer Research 374

Australia

Neil Hamilton Fairley Fellowships (Overseas Clinical) 478
University of Otago Master's Awards 717

Caribbean Countries

IARC Postdoctoral Fellowships for Training in Cancer Research 374

East European Countries

IARC Postdoctoral Fellowships for Training in Cancer Research 374
Synthesys Visiting Fellowship 494

European Union

NERC Masters Studentships 493
NERC Research (PhD) Studentships 494
Synthesys Visiting Fellowship 494

Middle East

IARC Postdoctoral Fellowships for Training in Cancer Research 374

New Zealand

University of Otago Master's Awards 717

South Africa

IARC Postdoctoral Fellowships for Training in Cancer Research 374

United Kingdom

Aberystwyth Postgraduate Research Studentships 4
Llewellyn and Mary Williams Scholarship 145
Mr and Mrs David Edward Memorial Award 145
NERC Masters Studentships 493
NERC Research (PhD) Studentships 494
Synthesys Visiting Fellowship 494

United States of America

AFAR Research Grants 52
AFPE Predoctoral Fellowships 55
The Glenn/AFAR Breakthroughs in Gerontology Awards 53
MARC Faculty Predoctoral Fellowships 482
NIGMS Fellowship Awards for Students With Disabilities 483
NIGMS Postdoctoral Awards 483
NIGMS Research Project Grants 483
NIGMS Research Supplements for Underrepresented Minorities 483
PhRMAF Postdoctoral Fellowships in Pharmacology/Toxicology 528
PhRMAF Predoctoral Fellowships in Pharmacology/Toxicology 529
PhRMAF Research Starter Grants in Pharmacology/Toxicology 530
PhRMAF Sabbatical Fellowships in Health Outcomes Research 530
PhRMAF Sabbatical Fellowships in Informatics 530
PhRMAF Sabbatical Fellowships in Pharmacology/Toxicology 531

West European Countries

Llewellyn and Mary Williams Scholarship 145
Mr and Mrs David Edward Memorial Award 145
Synthesys Visiting Fellowship 494
University of Otago Master's Awards 717

ZOOLOGY

Any Country

AMNH Annette Kade Graduate Student Fellowship Program
AMNH Research Fellowships 67
Böhlke Memorial Endowment Fund 4
Career Development Program 419
Earthwatch Field Research Grants 272
Edmund Niles Huyck Preserve, Inc. Graduate and Postgraduate Grants 274
EMBO Short-Term Fellowships in Molecular Biology 285
Ernst Mayr Travel Grant 461
ETH Zurich Excellence Scholarship and Opportunity Award 624

George A Hall/Harold F Mayfield Award 797
Hugh Kelly Fellowship 548
Jessup and McHenry Awards 4
La Trobe University Postgraduate Scholarship 414
Louis Agassiz Fuertes Award 797
Mount Desert Island New Investigator Award 459
NERC Advanced Research Fellowships 493
NERC Postdoctoral Research Fellowships 494
Primate Conservation Inc. Grants 537
Queen Mary Research Studentships 539
Rhodes University Postdoctoral Fellowship and The Andrew Mellon Postdoctoral Fellowship 548
Rob and Bessie Welder Wildlife Foundation's Graduate Research Scholarship Program 793
SERC Postdoctoral Fellowships 596
SERC Predoctoral Fellowships 596
SERC Senior Fellowships 596
Tibor T Polgar Fellowship 347
Translational Research Program 143
UFAW Animal Welfare Research Training Scholarships 644
UFAW Research and Project Awards 645
UFAW Small Project and Travel Awards 645
UFAW Vacation Scholarships 645
University of Bristol Postgraduate Scholarships 672
University of Otago International Scholarships 717
University of Otago PhD Scholarships 718
University of Otago Prestigious PhD Scholarships 718
Victoria University of Wellington PhD Scholarships 786

African Nations

Primate Conservation Inc. Grants 537

Australia

University of Otago Master's Awards 717
Wingate Scholarships 697

Canada

Wingate Scholarships 697

East European Countries

Synthesys Visiting Fellowship 494

European Union

NERC Masters Studentships 493
NERC Research (PhD) Studentships 494
Synthesys Visiting Fellowship 494
Wingate Scholarships 697

New Zealand

University of Otago Master's Awards 717
Wingate Scholarships 697

South Africa

Henderson Postgraduate Scholarships 548
Wingate Scholarships 697

United Kingdom

Aberystwyth Postgraduate Research Studentships 4
Llewellyn and Mary Williams Scholarship 145
Mr and Mrs David Edward Memorial Award 145
NERC Masters Studentships 493
NERC Research (PhD) Studentships 494
Synthesys Visiting Fellowship 494
Wingate Scholarships 697

United States of America

Budweiser Conservation Scholarship 475
Earthwatch Fellowships 272
PhRMAF Sabbatical Fellowships in Informatics 530

West European Countries

Llewellyn and Mary Williams Scholarship 145
Mr and Mrs David Edward Memorial Award 145

CIC Montreal Medal 232
CNC/IUPAC Travel Awards 214
Corday-Morgan Memorial Fund 570
Cottrell College Science Awards 545
Cottrell Scholars Awards 545
CSCT Norman and Marion Bright Memorial Award 232
Ichikizaki Fund for Young Chemists 214
International Postgraduate Research Scholarships (IPRS) 413
L'ORÉAL Canada For Women in Science Fellowships, With Support
    of the Canadian Commission for UNESCO 123
Lindemann Trust Fellowships 280
ORSAS Awards 688
School of Applied Sciences Overseas Scholarships 254
Wingate Scholarships 697

Caribbean Countries

International Postgraduate Research Scholarships (IPRS) 413
ORSAS Awards 688
School of Applied Sciences Overseas Scholarships 254
TWAS Fellowships for Research and Advanced Training 631
TWAS Grants for Scientific Meetings in Developing Countries 631
TWAS Prizes 632
TWAS Prizes to Young Scientists in Developing Countries 632
TWAS Research Grants 632
TWAS Spare Parts for Scientific Equipment 632
TWAS UNESCO Associateship Scheme 632
TWAS-S N Bose National Centre for Basic Sciences Postgraduate
    Fellowships in Physical Sciences 633

East European Countries

ESRF Thesis Studentships 287
International Postgraduate Research Scholarships (IPRS) 413
ORSAS Awards 688
School of Applied Sciences Overseas Scholarships 254

European Union

EPSRC Grant for School of Physical Sciences 698
ESPRC Studentships 427
Henry Ellison Scholarship 703
Microsoft Research European PhD Scholarship Programme 448
Wingate Scholarships 697

Middle East

ABCCF Student Grant 102
International Postgraduate Research Scholarships (IPRS) 413
ORSAS Awards 688
School of Applied Sciences Overseas Scholarships 254
The Trieste Science Prize 631
TWAS Fellowships for Research and Advanced Training 631
TWAS Grants for Scientific Meetings in Developing Countries 631
TWAS Prizes 632
TWAS Prizes to Young Scientists in Developing Countries 632
TWAS Research Grants 632
TWAS Spare Parts for Scientific Equipment 632
TWAS UNESCO Associateship Scheme 632
TWAS-S N Bose National Centre for Basic Sciences Postgraduate
    Fellowships in Physical Sciences 633

New Zealand

Corday-Morgan Memorial Fund 570
Lindemann Trust Fellowships 280
ORSAS Awards 688
School of Applied Sciences Overseas Scholarships 254
University of Otago Master's Awards 717
Wingate Scholarships 697

South Africa

Corday-Morgan Memorial Fund 570
Henderson Postgraduate Scholarships 548
International Postgraduate Research Scholarships (IPRS) 413
Lindemann Trust Fellowships 280
ORSAS Awards 688
School of Applied Sciences Overseas Scholarships 254
The Trieste Science Prize 631

TWAS Fellowships for Research and Advanced Training 631
TWAS Grants for Scientific Meetings in Developing Countries 631
TWAS Prizes 632
TWAS Prizes to Young Scientists in Developing Countries 632
TWAS Research Grants 632
TWAS Spare Parts for Scientific Equipment 632
TWAS UNESCO Associateship Scheme 632
TWAS-S N Bose National Centre for Basic Sciences Postgraduate
    Fellowships in Physical Sciences 633
Wingate Scholarships 697

United Kingdom

Access to Learning Fund 685
BBSRC Studentship 685
Corday-Morgan Memorial Fund 570
Eli Lilly Scholarship 427
EPSRC Grant for School of Physical Sciences 698
ESRF Thesis Studentships 287
Fulbright-AstraZeneca Research Scholarship 781
Henry Ellison Scholarship 703
International Postgraduate Research Scholarships (IPRS) 413
Lindemann Trust Fellowships 280
Mr and Mrs David Edward Memorial Award 145
NERC Studentships 145
Royal Commission Research Fellowship 563
Wingate Scholarships 697

United States of America

ACS Award in Colloid and Surface Chemistry 37
ACS PRF Supplements for Underrepresented Minority Research
    (SUMR) 37
ACS Stanley C. Israel Regional Award 38
AFAR Research Grants 52
Air Force Summer Faculty Fellowship Program 84
Cottrell College Science Awards 545
Cottrell Scholars Awards 545
Earle B. Barnes Award for Leadership in Chemical Research
    Management 38
Fulbright Senior Specialists Program 249
The Glenn/AFAR Breakthroughs in Gerontology Awards 53
The Graduate Fellowship Award 340
International Postgraduate Research Scholarships (IPRS) 413
Irving Langmuir Award in Chemical Physics 39
Krell Institute Computational Science Graduate Fellowship Program
    412
MARC Faculty Predoctoral Fellowships 482
McDonnell Center Astronaut Fellowships in the Space Sciences
    437
National Energy Technology (NETL) Methane Hydrates Fellowship
    Programs (MHFP) 467
NCAR Faculty Fellowship Programme 471
NIGMS Fellowship Awards for Minority Students 482
NIGMS Fellowship Awards for Students With Disabilities 483
NIGMS Postdoctoral Awards 483
NIGMS Research Project Grants 483
NIGMS Research Supplements for Underrepresented Minorities
    483
ONR Summer Faculty Research 84
ORSAS Awards 688
Philip Morris USA Thurgood Marshall Scholarship 633
School of Applied Sciences Overseas Scholarships 254
Washington University Chancellor's Graduate Fellowship Program
    792
Winston Churchill Foundation Scholarship 797
Xerox Technical Minority Scholarship 807

West European Countries

EPSRC Grant for School of Physical Sciences 698
ESRF Thesis Studentships 287
International Postgraduate Research Scholarships (IPRS) 413
Janson Johan Helmich Scholarships and Travel Grants 398
Microsoft Research European PhD Scholarship Programme 448
Mr and Mrs David Edward Memorial Award 145
University of Otago Master's Awards 717

ANALYTICAL CHEMISTRY

Any Country

Alzheimer's Society Research Grants
BP/RSE Research Fellowships 628
ETH Zurich Excellence Scholarship and Opportunity Award 624
Hugh Kelly Fellowship 548
JILA Postdoctoral Research Associateship and Visiting Fellowships 401
NRC Research Associateships 488
Queen Mary Research Studentships 539
Rhodes University Postdoctoral Fellowship and The Andrew Mellon Postdoctoral Fellowship 548
Teagasc Walsh Fellowships 626
Tomsk Polytechnic University International Scholarship 634
University of Bristol Postgraduate Scholarships 672
Victoria University of Wellington PhD Scholarships 786

African Nations

International Postgraduate Research Scholarships (IPRS) 413

Australia

Fulbright Postgraduate Student Award for Science and Engineering 140

Canada

CSCT Norman and Marion Bright Memorial Award 232
International Postgraduate Research Scholarships (IPRS) 413

Caribbean Countries

International Postgraduate Research Scholarships (IPRS) 413

East European Countries

International Postgraduate Research Scholarships (IPRS) 413

Middle East

International Postgraduate Research Scholarships (IPRS) 413

South Africa

International Postgraduate Research Scholarships (IPRS) 413

United Kingdom

Hector and Elizabeth Catling Bursary 173
International Postgraduate Research Scholarships (IPRS) 413
Mr and Mrs David Edward Memorial Award 145

United States of America

Air Force Summer Faculty Fellowship Program 84
International Postgraduate Research Scholarships (IPRS) 413
ONR Summer Faculty Research 84
Washington University Chancellor's Graduate Fellowship Program 792

West European Countries

International Postgraduate Research Scholarships (IPRS) 413
Mr and Mrs David Edward Memorial Award 145

INORGANIC CHEMISTRY

Any Country

Alzheimer's Society Research Grants
BP/RSE Research Fellowships 628
ETH Zurich Excellence Scholarship and Opportunity Award 624
F. Albert Cotton Award in Synthetic Inorganic Chemistry 39
Hugh Kelly Fellowship 548
JILA Postdoctoral Research Associateship and Visiting Fellowships 401
NRC Research Associateships 488
Queen Mary Research Studentships 539
Rhodes University Postdoctoral Fellowship and The Andrew Mellon Postdoctoral Fellowship 548

University of Bristol Postgraduate Scholarships 672
Victoria University of Wellington PhD Scholarships 786
Weizmann Institute of Science MSc Fellowships 792
Weizmann Institute of Science PhD Fellowships 792
Weizmann Institute of Science Postdoctoral Fellowships Program 793

African Nations

International Postgraduate Research Scholarships (IPRS) 413

Australia

Fulbright Postgraduate Student Award for Science and Engineering 140

Canada

International Postgraduate Research Scholarships (IPRS) 413

Caribbean Countries

International Postgraduate Research Scholarships (IPRS) 413

East European Countries

International Postgraduate Research Scholarships (IPRS) 413

European Union

Chemistry: EPSRC Doctoral Training Grant Studentships 721
EPSRC Grant for School of Physical Sciences 698

Middle East

International Postgraduate Research Scholarships (IPRS) 413

South Africa

International Postgraduate Research Scholarships (IPRS) 413

United Kingdom

Chemistry: EPSRC Doctoral Training Grant Studentships 721
EPSRC Grant for School of Physical Sciences 698
Hector and Elizabeth Catling Bursary 173
International Postgraduate Research Scholarships (IPRS) 413
Mr and Mrs David Edward Memorial Award 145
University of Kent School of Physical Sciences 701

United States of America

Air Force Summer Faculty Fellowship Program 84
International Postgraduate Research Scholarships (IPRS) 413
ONR Summer Faculty Research 84
Washington University Chancellor's Graduate Fellowship Program 792

West European Countries

EPSRC Grant for School of Physical Sciences 698
International Postgraduate Research Scholarships (IPRS) 413
Mr and Mrs David Edward Memorial Award 145
University of Kent School of Physical Sciences 701

ORGANIC CHEMISTRY

Any Country

ACS Award for Creative Work in Synthetic Organic Chemistry 36
ACS Roger Adams Award in Organic Chemistry 37
Alzheimer's Society Research Grants
Arthur C. Cope Scholar Awards 38
BP/RSE Research Fellowships 628
Ernest Guenther Award in the Chemistry of Natural Products 38
ETH Zurich Excellence Scholarship and Opportunity Award 624
Hugh Kelly Fellowship 548
JILA Postdoctoral Research Associateship and Visiting Fellowships 401
NRC Research Associateships 488
Queen Mary Research Studentships 539
Rhodes University Postdoctoral Fellowship and The Andrew Mellon Postdoctoral Fellowship 548
Tomsk Polytechnic University International Scholarship 634

University of Bristol Postgraduate Scholarships 672
Victoria University of Wellington PhD Scholarships 786
Weizmann Institute of Science MSc Fellowships 792
Weizmann Institute of Science PhD Fellowships 792
Weizmann Institute of Science Postdoctoral Fellowships Program 793

African Nations

International Postgraduate Research Scholarships (IPRS) 413

Australia

Fulbright Postgraduate Student Award for Science and Engineering 140

Canada

Boehringer Ingelheim Award for Organic or Bioorganic Chemistry 214
Ichikizaki Fund for Young Chemists 214
International Postgraduate Research Scholarships (IPRS) 413

Caribbean Countries

International Postgraduate Research Scholarships (IPRS) 413

East European Countries

International Postgraduate Research Scholarships (IPRS) 413

European Union

Chemistry: EPSRC Doctoral Training Grant Studentships 721
EPSRC Grant for School of Physical Sciences 698

Middle East

International Postgraduate Research Scholarships (IPRS) 413

South Africa

International Postgraduate Research Scholarships (IPRS) 413

United Kingdom

Chemistry: EPSRC Doctoral Training Grant Studentships 721
EPSRC Grant for School of Physical Sciences 698
Hickinbottom/Briggs Fellowship 571
International Postgraduate Research Scholarships (IPRS) 413
Mr and Mrs David Edward Memorial Award 145
University of Kent School of Physical Sciences 701

United States of America

Air Force Summer Faculty Fellowship Program 84
International Postgraduate Research Scholarships (IPRS) 413
Krell Institute Computational Science Graduate Fellowship Program 412
ONR Summer Faculty Research 84
Washington University Chancellor's Graduate Fellowship Program 792

West European Countries

EPSRC Grant for School of Physical Sciences 698
International Postgraduate Research Scholarships (IPRS) 413
Mr and Mrs David Edward Memorial Award 145
University of Kent School of Physical Sciences 701

PHYSICAL CHEMISTRY

Any Country

Alzheimer's Society Research Grants
BP/RSE Research Fellowships 628
CBS Graduate Fellowship Program 200
ETH Zurich Excellence Scholarship and Opportunity Award 624
Hugh Kelly Fellowship 548
JILA Postdoctoral Research Associateship and Visiting Fellowships 401
NRC Research Associateships 488
Peter Debye Award in Physical Chemistry 39
Queen Mary Research Studentships 539
Rhodes University Postdoctoral Fellowship and The Andrew Mellon Postdoctoral Fellowship 548

Tomsk Polytechnic University International Scholarship 634
University of Bristol Postgraduate Scholarships 672
Victoria University of Wellington PhD Scholarships 786
Weizmann Institute of Science MSc Fellowships 792
Weizmann Institute of Science PhD Fellowships 792
Weizmann Institute of Science Postdoctoral Fellowships Program 793
Welch Foundation Scholarship 391

African Nations

International Postgraduate Research Scholarships (IPRS) 413
TWAS-S N Bose National Centre for Basic Sciences Postgraduate Fellowships in Physical Sciences 633

Australia

Fulbright Postgraduate Student Award for Science and Engineering 140

Canada

CBS Postdoctoral Fellowship (PDF) 201
International Postgraduate Research Scholarships (IPRS) 413

Caribbean Countries

International Postgraduate Research Scholarships (IPRS) 413
TWAS-S N Bose National Centre for Basic Sciences Postgraduate Fellowships in Physical Sciences 633

East European Countries

International Postgraduate Research Scholarships (IPRS) 413

European Union

Chemistry: EPSRC Doctoral Training Grant Studentships 721
EPSRC Grant for School of Physical Sciences 698

Middle East

International Postgraduate Research Scholarships (IPRS) 413
TWAS-S N Bose National Centre for Basic Sciences Postgraduate Fellowships in Physical Sciences 633

South Africa

International Postgraduate Research Scholarships (IPRS) 413
TWAS-S N Bose National Centre for Basic Sciences Postgraduate Fellowships in Physical Sciences 633

United Kingdom

Chemistry: EPSRC Doctoral Training Grant Studentships 721
EPSRC Grant for School of Physical Sciences 698
International Postgraduate Research Scholarships (IPRS) 413
Mr and Mrs David Edward Memorial Award 145
University of Kent School of Physical Sciences 701

United States of America

Air Force Summer Faculty Fellowship Program 84
International Postgraduate Research Scholarships (IPRS) 413
Krell Institute Computational Science Graduate Fellowship Program 412
ONR Summer Faculty Research 84
PhRMAF Research Starter Grants in Pharmaceutics 530
Washington University Chancellor's Graduate Fellowship Program 792

West European Countries

EPSRC Grant for School of Physical Sciences 698
International Postgraduate Research Scholarships (IPRS) 413
Mr and Mrs David Edward Memorial Award 145
University of Kent School of Physical Sciences 701

EARTH AND GEOLOGICAL SCIENCES

Any Country

AAC Research Grants 26
ACS PRF Type SE Grants 37

American Association of Petroleum Geologists Foundation Grants-in-Aid 32
AMNH Research Fellowships 67
ASCSA Research Fellowship in Environmental Studies 82
ASCSA Research Fellowship in Geoarchaeology 82
Association for Women in Science Educational Foundation Predoctoral Awards 118
BFWG Eila Campbell Scholarship 164
BFWG Johnstone and Florence Stoney Studentship 165
BIAA Post-Doctoral Research Fellowship 168
CICOR Postdoctoral Scholar Fellowship in Coastal Oceanography, Climate or Marine Ecosystems 804
Earthwatch Field Research Grants 272
ESRF Postdoctoral Fellowships 287
ETH Zurich Excellence Scholarship and Opportunity Award 624
Horton (Hydrology) Research Grant 56
Hudson River Graduate Fellowships 346
Hugh Kelly Fellowship 548
ICSU-TWAS-UNESCO-UNU/IAS Visiting Scientist Programme 631
Lindbergh Grants 228
McDonnell Graduate Fellowship in the Space Sciences 437
National Geographic Conservation Trust Grant 244
NCAR Graduate Visitor Programme 471
NCAR Postdoctoral Appointments in the Advanced Study Program 471
NERC Advanced Research Fellowships 493
NERC Postdoctoral Research Fellowships 494
Queen Mary Research Studentships 539
Rhodes University Postdoctoral Fellowship and The Andrew Mellon Postdoctoral Fellowship 548
Robert K. Fahnestock Memorial Award 311
SEG Scholarships 611
St Catherine's College College Scholarship (Sciences)
St Catherine's College: Leathersellers' Company Graduate Scholarship
Teagasc Walsh Fellowships 626
University of Bristol Postgraduate Scholarships 672
University of Otago International Scholarships 717
University of Otago PhD Scholarships 718
University of Otago Prestigious PhD Scholarships 718
University of Southampton Postgraduate Studentships 759
University of Western Ontario Senior Visiting Fellowship 777
Victoria University of Wellington PhD Scholarships 786
Weizmann Institute of Science MSc Fellowships 792
Weizmann Institute of Science PhD Fellowships 792
Weizmann Institute of Science Postdoctoral Fellowships Program 793
WHOI Geophysical Fluid Dynamics (GFD) Fellowships 804
Wolf Foundation Prizes 799
World Universities Network (WUN) International Research Mobility Scheme 759

African Nations

ABCCF Student Grant 102
International Postgraduate Research Scholarships (IPRS) 413
Master Studies in Physical Land Resources Scholarship 379
PTDF Cambridge Scholarships 195
School of Applied Sciences Overseas Scholarships 254
The Trieste Science Prize 631
TWAS Fellowships for Research and Advanced Training 631
TWAS Grants for Scientific Meetings in Developing Countries 631
TWAS Prizes 632
TWAS Prizes to Young Scientists in Developing Countries 632
TWAS Research Grants 632
TWAS Spare Parts for Scientific Equipment 632
TWAS UNESCO Associateship Scheme 632

Australia

Fulbright Postgraduate Student Award for Science and Engineering 140
School of Applied Sciences Overseas Scholarships 254
Wingate Scholarships 697

Canada

ASPRS Robert N. Colwell Memorial Fellowship 89
Geomatics Canada Scholarship Program 208

GSA Research Grants 310
International Postgraduate Research Scholarships (IPRS) 413
Public Safety and Emergency Preparedness Canada Research Fellowship in Honour of Stuart Nesbitt White 123
School of Applied Sciences Overseas Scholarships 254
Wingate Scholarships 697

Caribbean Countries

International Postgraduate Research Scholarships (IPRS) 413
Master Studies in Physical Land Resources Scholarship 379
School of Applied Sciences Overseas Scholarships 254
TWAS Fellowships for Research and Advanced Training 631
TWAS Grants for Scientific Meetings in Developing Countries 631
TWAS Prizes 632
TWAS Prizes to Young Scientists in Developing Countries 632
TWAS Research Grants 632
TWAS Spare Parts for Scientific Equipment 632
TWAS UNESCO Associateship Scheme 632

East European Countries

ESRF Thesis Studentships 287
International Postgraduate Research Scholarships (IPRS) 413
School of Applied Sciences Overseas Scholarships 254
Synthesys Visiting Fellowship 494

European Union

CBRL Travel Grant 248
EPSRC Studentships in Earth Sciences 726
NERC Masters Studentships 493
NERC Research (PhD) Studentships 494
NERC Studentships in Earth Sciences 735
Synthesys Visiting Fellowship 494
Wingate Scholarships 697

Middle East

ABCCF Student Grant 102
International Postgraduate Research Scholarships (IPRS) 413
Master Studies in Physical Land Resources Scholarship 379
School of Applied Sciences Overseas Scholarships 254
The Trieste Science Prize 631
TWAS Fellowships for Research and Advanced Training 631
TWAS Grants for Scientific Meetings in Developing Countries 631
TWAS Prizes 632
TWAS Prizes to Young Scientists in Developing Countries 632
TWAS Research Grants 632
TWAS Spare Parts for Scientific Equipment 632
TWAS UNESCO Associateship Scheme 632

New Zealand

School of Applied Sciences Overseas Scholarships 254
Wingate Scholarships 697

South Africa

Henderson Postgraduate Scholarships 548
International Postgraduate Research Scholarships (IPRS) 413
Master Studies in Physical Land Resources Scholarship 379
School of Applied Sciences Overseas Scholarships 254
The Trieste Science Prize 631
TWAS Fellowships for Research and Advanced Training 631
TWAS Grants for Scientific Meetings in Developing Countries 631
TWAS Prizes 632
TWAS Prizes to Young Scientists in Developing Countries 632
TWAS Research Grants 632
TWAS Spare Parts for Scientific Equipment 632
TWAS UNESCO Associateship Scheme 632
Wingate Scholarships 697

United Kingdom

Aberystwyth Postgraduate Research Studentships 4
CBRL Research Award 248
CBRL Travel Grant 248
EPSRC Studentships in Earth Sciences 726
ESRF Thesis Studentships 287

Geographical Fieldwork Grants 564
International Postgraduate Research Scholarships (IPRS) 413
Mr and Mrs David Edward Memorial Award 145
NERC Masters Studentships 493
NERC Research (PhD) Studentships 494
NERC Studentships in Earth Sciences 735
Royal Commission Research Fellowship 563
Synthesys Visiting Fellowship 494
Wingate Scholarships 697

United States of America

Air Force Summer Faculty Fellowship Program 84
ASPRS Robert N. Colwell Memorial Fellowship 89
Earthwatch Fellowships 272
Fulbright Senior Specialists Program 249
The Graduate Fellowship Award 340
GSA Research Grants 310
International Postgraduate Research Scholarships (IPRS) 413
Krell Institute Computational Science Graduate Fellowship Program 412
Marie Tharp Visiting Fellowships 239
McDonnell Center Astronaut Fellowships in the Space Sciences 437
NCAR Faculty Fellowship Programme 471
ONR Summer Faculty Research 84
School of Applied Sciences Overseas Scholarships 254
Washington University Chancellor's Graduate Fellowship Program 792
Winston Churchill Foundation Scholarship 797

West European Countries

Albert Maucher Prize 265
ESRF Thesis Studentships 287
International Postgraduate Research Scholarships (IPRS) 413
Janson Johan Helmich Scholarships and Travel Grants 398
Mr and Mrs David Edward Memorial Award 145
Synthesys Visiting Fellowship 494

GEOCHEMISTRY

Any Country

ACS PRF Type SE Grants 37
American Association of Petroleum Geologists Foundation
    Grants-in-Aid 32
Anne U White Fund 119
BP/RSE Research Fellowships 628
Earthwatch Field Research Grants 272
Establishing the Source of Gas in Australia's Offshore Petroleum
    Basins–Scholarship 258
ETH Zurich Excellence Scholarship and Opportunity Award 624
Hugh Kelly Fellowship 548
NERC Advanced Research Fellowships 493
NERC Postdoctoral Research Fellowships 494
Tomsk Polytechnic University International Scholarship 634
University of Bristol Postgraduate Scholarships 672
Victoria University of Wellington PhD Scholarships 786
Weizmann Institute of Science MSc Fellowships 792
Weizmann Institute of Science PhD Fellowships 792
Weizmann Institute of Science Postdoctoral Fellowships Program 793

African Nations

International Postgraduate Research Scholarships (IPRS) 413
Shell Centenary/Shell Centenary Chevening Scholarships 704

Australia

Fulbright Postgraduate Student Award for Science and Engineering
    140

Canada

GSA Research Grants 310
International Postgraduate Research Scholarships (IPRS) 413

Caribbean Countries

International Postgraduate Research Scholarships (IPRS) 413
Shell Centenary/Shell Centenary Chevening Scholarships 704

East European Countries

International Postgraduate Research Scholarships (IPRS) 413
Synthesys Visiting Fellowship 494

European Union

NERC Masters Studentships 493
NERC Research (PhD) Studentships 494
Synthesys Visiting Fellowship 494

Middle East

International Postgraduate Research Scholarships (IPRS) 413
Shell Centenary/Shell Centenary Chevening Scholarsips 704

South Africa

International Postgraduate Research Scholarships (IPRS) 413
Shell Centenary/Shell Centenary Chevening Scholarships 704

United Kingdom

Aberystwyth Postgraduate Research Studentships 4
Hector and Elizabeth Catling Bursary 173
International Postgraduate Research Scholarships (IPRS) 413
Mr and Mrs David Edward Memorial Award 145
NERC Masters Studentships 493
NERC Research (PhD) Studentships 494
Synthesys Visiting Fellowship 494

United States of America

Air Force Summer Faculty Fellowship Program 84
The Graduate Fellowship Award 340
GSA Research Grants 310
International Postgraduate Research Scholarships (IPRS) 413
Krell Institute Computational Science Graduate Fellowship Program
    412
ONR Summer Faculty Research 84
Washington University Chancellor's Graduate Fellowship Program
    792

West European Countries

International Postgraduate Research Scholarships (IPRS) 413
Mr and Mrs David Edward Memorial Award 145
Synthesys Visiting Fellowship 494

GEOGRAPHY (SCIENTIFIC)

Any Country

AAG Dissertation Research Grants 118
AAG General Research Fund 119
Earthwatch Field Research Grants 272
ETH Zurich Excellence Scholarship and Opportunity Award 624
Hugh Kelly Fellowship 548
Innovative Geography Teaching Grants 564
J. Warren Nystrom Award 119
Journey of a Lifetime Award 564
Monica Cole Research Grant 564
NERC Advanced Research Fellowships 493
NERC Postdoctoral Research Fellowships 494
Queen Mary Research Studentships 539
RGS-IBG Land Rover 'GO Beyond' Bursary 565
Silverhill Institute of Environmental Research and Conservation Award
    591
Small Research Grants 566
St Catherine's College Graduate Scholarship in the Arts
Thesiger-Oman Research Fellowship 566
University of Bristol Postgraduate Scholarships 672
Victoria University of Wellington PhD Scholarships 786
Weizmann Institute of Science Postdoctoral Fellowships Program 793

African Nations

Canadian Window on International Development 380
IDRC Doctoral Research Awards 380
International Postgraduate Research Scholarships (IPRS) 413
Master Studies in Physical Land Resources Scholarship 379

School of Applied Sciences Overseas Scholarships 254
Shell Centenary/Shell Centenary Chevening Scholarships 704

Australia

Australian Health Inequities Program Research Scholarship 292
Fulbright Postgraduate Student Award for Science and Engineering 140
School of Applied Sciences Overseas Scholarships 254

Canada

Canadian Window on International Development 380
GSA Research Grants 310
IDRC Doctoral Research Awards 380
International Postgraduate Research Scholarships (IPRS) 413
School of Applied Sciences Overseas Scholarships 254

Caribbean Countries

Canadian Window on International Development 380
IDRC Doctoral Research Awards 380
International Postgraduate Research Scholarships (IPRS) 413
Master Studies in Physical Land Resources Scholarship 379
School of Applied Sciences Overseas Scholarships 254
Shell Centenary/Shell Centenary Chevening Scholarships 704

East European Countries

Freie Universität Berlin John-F.-Kennedy-Institut für Nordamerikastudien Research Grants 304
IDRC Doctoral Research Awards 380
International Postgraduate Research Scholarships (IPRS) 413
School of Applied Sciences Overseas Scholarships 254
Synthesys Visiting Fellowship 494

European Union

Freie Universität Berlin John-F.-Kennedy-Institut für Nordamerikastudien Research Grants 304
NERC Masters Studentships 493
NERC Research (PhD) Studentships 494
RGS-IBG Postgraduate Research Awards 565
Synthesys Visiting Fellowship 494

Middle East

IDRC Doctoral Research Awards 380
International Postgraduate Research Scholarships (IPRS) 413
Master Studies in Physical Land Resources Scholarship 379
School of Applied Sciences Overseas Scholarships 254
Shell Centenary/Shell Centenary Chevening Scholarships 704

New Zealand

Australian Health Inequities Program Research Scholarship 292
School of Applied Sciences Overseas Scholarships 254

South Africa

Canadian Window on International Development 380
IDRC Doctoral Research Awards 380
International Postgraduate Research Scholarships (IPRS) 413
Master Studies in Physical Land Resources Scholarship 379
School of Applied Sciences Overseas Scholarships 254
Shell Centenary/Shell Centenary Chevening Scholarships 704

United Kingdom

Aberystwyth Postgraduate Research Studentships 4
Geographical Fieldwork Grants 564
Geography: ESRC 1 + 3 Quota
Geography: NERC DPhil Quota 728
Geography: NERC Quota 728
International Postgraduate Research Scholarships (IPRS) 413
NERC Masters Studentships 493
NERC Research (PhD) Studentships 494
Neville Shulman Challenge Award 565
Peter Fleming Award 565
Ray Y. Gildea Jr. Award 565
RGS-IBG Postgraduate Research Awards 565
Synthesys Visiting Fellowship 494

United States of America

Air Force Summer Faculty Fellowship Program 84
ASOR W.F. Albright Institute of Archaeological Research/National Endowment of the Humanities Fellowships 84
Budweiser Conservation Scholarship 475
CIA Graduate Studies Program Scholarship 225
GSA Research Grants 310
International Postgraduate Research Scholarships (IPRS) 413
Krell Institute Computational Science Graduate Fellowship Program 412
Michael and Marie Marucci Scholarship 475
NOAA Coral Management Assistantship 506
NOAA Pacific Islands Assistantship Program 506
Ray Y. Gildea Jr. Award 565
S.E. Dwornik Student Paper Awards 311
School of Applied Sciences Overseas Scholarships 254

West European Countries

Freie Universität Berlin John-F.-Kennedy-Institut für Nordamerikastudien Research Grants 304
International Postgraduate Research Scholarships (IPRS) 413
Synthesys Visiting Fellowship 494

GEOLOGY

Any Country

Acadia Graduate Awards 5
ACS PRF Type SE Grants 37
Alexander Sisson Award 309
American Association of Petroleum Geologists Foundation Grants-in-Aid 32
ASCSA Research Fellowship in Geoarchaeology 82
BP/RSE Research Fellowships 628
Bruce L. "Biff" Reed Award 309
Earthwatch Field Research Grants 272
Establishing the Source of Gas in Australia's Offshore Petroleum Basins–Scholarship 258
ETH Zurich Excellence Scholarship and Opportunity Award 624
G Vernon Hobson Bequest 368
Gladys W Cole Memorial Research Award 310
Hugh Kelly Fellowship 548
John Montagne Fund 310
NERC Advanced Research Fellowships 493
NERC Postdoctoral Research Fellowships 494
Queen Mary Research Studentships 539
Rhodes University Postdoctoral Fellowship and The Andrew Mellon Postdoctoral Fellowship 548
Sediment and Asphaltite Transport by Canyon Upwelling – Top Up Scholarship 259
SEG Scholarships 611
Tomsk Polytechnic University International Scholarship 634
University of Bristol Postgraduate Scholarships 672
Victoria University of Wellington PhD Scholarships 786
Weizmann Institute of Science Postdoctoral Fellowships Program 793

African Nations

Canadian Window on International Development 380
IDRC Doctoral Research Awards 380
International Postgraduate Research Scholarships (IPRS) 413
Lindemann Trust Fellowships 280
Master Studies in Physical Land Resources Scholarship 379
Shell Centenary/Shell Centenary Chevening Scholarships 704

Australia

Edgar Pam Fellowship 368
Fulbright Postgraduate Student Award for Science and Engineering 140
Lindemann Trust Fellowships 280
Western Australian CSIRO–University Postgraduate Scholarships 776

Canada

Canadian Window on International Development 380
Edgar Pam Fellowship 368

GSA Research Grants 310
IDRC Doctoral Research Awards 380
International Postgraduate Research Scholarships (IPRS) 413
Lindemann Trust Fellowships 280

Caribbean Countries

Canadian Window on International Development 380
IDRC Doctoral Research Awards 380
International Postgraduate Research Scholarships (IPRS) 413
Master Studies in Physical Land Resources Scholarship 379
Shell Centenary/Shell Centenary Chevening Scholarships 704

East European Countries

IDRC Doctoral Research Awards 380
International Postgraduate Research Scholarships (IPRS) 413
Synthesys Visiting Fellowship 494

European Union

NERC Masters Studentships 493
NERC Research (PhD) Studentships 494
Synthesys Visiting Fellowship 494

Middle East

IDRC Doctoral Research Awards 380
International Postgraduate Research Scholarships (IPRS) 413
Master Studies in Physical Land Resources Scholarship 379
Shell Centenary/Shell Centenary Chevening Scholarships 704

New Zealand

Edgar Pam Fellowship 368
Lindemann Trust Fellowships 280

South Africa

Canadian Window on International Development 380
Edgar Pam Fellowship 368
IDRC Doctoral Research Awards 380
International Postgraduate Research Scholarships (IPRS) 413
Lindemann Trust Fellowships 280
Master Studies in Physical Land Resources Scholarship 379
Shell Centenary/Shell Centenary Chevening Scholarships 704

United Kingdom

Aberystwyth Postgraduate Research Studentships 4
Edgar Pam Fellowship 368
Hector and Elizabeth Catling Bursary 173
International Postgraduate Research Scholarships (IPRS) 413
Lindemann Trust Fellowships 280
Mr and Mrs David Edward Memorial Award 145
NERC Masters Studentships 493
NERC Research (PhD) Studentships 494
Synthesys Visiting Fellowship 494

United States of America

Air Force Summer Faculty Fellowship Program 84
The Graduate Fellowship Award 340
GSA Research Grants 310
International Postgraduate Research Scholarships (IPRS) 413
Norwegian Thanksgiving Fund Scholarship 509
Washington University Chancellor's Graduate Fellowship Program
  792

West European Countries

International Postgraduate Research Scholarships (IPRS) 413
Mr and Mrs David Edward Memorial Award 145
Synthesys Visiting Fellowship 494

MINERALOGY AND CRYSTALLOGRAPHY

Any Country

BP/RSE Research Fellowships 628
ESRF Postdoctoral Fellowships 287

ETH Zurich Excellence Scholarship and Opportunity Award 624
Lipman Research Award 311
The Mineral and Rock Physics Outstanding Student Award
NERC Advanced Research Fellowships 493
NERC Postdoctoral Research Fellowships 494
Queen Mary Research Studentships 539
Rhodes University Postdoctoral Fellowship and The Andrew Mellon
  Postdoctoral Fellowship 548
University of Bristol Postgraduate Scholarships 672
Victoria University of Wellington PhD Scholarships 786
Weizmann Institute of Science MSc Fellowships 792
Weizmann Institute of Science PhD Fellowships 792
Weizmann Institute of Science Postdoctoral Fellowships Program 793

African Nations

International Postgraduate Research Scholarships (IPRS) 413

Australia

Fulbright Postgraduate Student Award for Science and Engineering
  140

Canada

GSA Research Grants 310
International Postgraduate Research Scholarships (IPRS) 413

Caribbean Countries

International Postgraduate Research Scholarships (IPRS) 413

East European Countries

ESRF Thesis Studentships 287
International Postgraduate Research Scholarships (IPRS) 413
Synthesys Visiting Fellowship 494

European Union

NERC Masters Studentships 493
NERC Research (PhD) Studentships 494
Synthesys Visiting Fellowship 494

Middle East

International Postgraduate Research Scholarships (IPRS) 413

South Africa

International Postgraduate Research Scholarships (IPRS) 413

United Kingdom

ESRF Thesis Studentships 287
Hector and Elizabeth Catling Bursary 173
International Postgraduate Research Scholarships (IPRS) 413
NERC Masters Studentships 493
NERC Research (PhD) Studentships 494
Synthesys Visiting Fellowship 494

United States of America

Air Force Summer Faculty Fellowship Program 84
The Graduate Fellowship Award 340
GSA Research Grants 310
International Postgraduate Research Scholarships (IPRS) 413

West European Countries

ESRF Thesis Studentships 287
International Postgraduate Research Scholarships (IPRS) 413
Synthesys Visiting Fellowship 494

PETROLOGY

Any Country

American Association of Petroleum Geologists Foundation
  Grants-in-Aid 32
BP/RSE Research Fellowships 628
ETH Zurich Excellence Scholarship and Opportunity Award 624
Lipman Research Award 311

NERC Advanced Research Fellowships 493
NERC Postdoctoral Research Fellowships 494
Rhodes University Postdoctoral Fellowship and The Andrew Mellon
    Postdoctoral Fellowship 548
Tomsk Polytechnic University International Scholarship 634
Victoria University of Wellington PhD Scholarships 786

Australia

Fulbright Postgraduate Student Award for Science and Engineering
    140

Canada

GSA Research Grants 310

East European Countries

Synthesys Visiting Fellowship 494

European Union

NERC Masters Studentships 493
NERC Research (PhD) Studentships 494
Synthesys Visiting Fellowship 494

United Kingdom

Hector and Elizabeth Catling Bursary 173
NERC Masters Studentships 493
NERC Research (PhD) Studentships 494
Synthesys Visiting Fellowship 494

United States of America

Air Force Summer Faculty Fellowship Program 84
GSA Research Grants 310

West European Countries

Synthesys Visiting Fellowship 494

GEOPHYSICS AND SEISMOLOGY

Any Country

Abdus Salam ICTP Fellowships 4
ACS PRF Type SE Grants 37
American Association of Petroleum Geologists Foundation Grants-in-
    Aid 32
BP/RSE Research Fellowships 628
Dublin Institute for Advanced Studies Scholarship in Astronomy,
    Astrophysics and Geophysics 270
Earthwatch Field Research Grants 272
ETH Zurich Excellence Scholarship and Opportunity Award 624
Hugh Kelly Fellowship 548
JILA Postdoctoral Research Associateship and Visiting Fellowships 401
NERC Advanced Research Fellowships 493
NERC Postdoctoral Research Fellowships 494
Rhodes University Postdoctoral Fellowship and The Andrew Mellon
    Postdoctoral Fellowship 548
SEG Scholarships 611
University of Bristol Postgraduate Scholarships 672
Victoria University of Wellington PhD Scholarships 786
Weizmann Institute of Science MSc Fellowships 792
Weizmann Institute of Science PhD Fellowships 792
Weizmann Institute of Science Postdoctoral Fellowships Program 793
WHOI Postdoctoral Scholarship Program 804

African Nations

International Postgraduate Research Scholarships (IPRS) 413
Lindemann Trust Fellowships 280
Shell Centenary/Shell Centenary Chevening Scholarships 704

Australia

Fulbright Postgraduate Student Award for Science and Engineering
    140
Lindemann Trust Fellowships 280
Western Australian CSIRO–University Postgraduate Scholarships 776

Canada

GSA Research Grants 310
International Postgraduate Research Scholarships (IPRS) 413
Lindemann Trust Fellowships 280

Caribbean Countries

International Postgraduate Research Scholarships (IPRS) 413
Shell Centenary/Shell Centenary Chevening Scholarships 704

East European Countries

International Postgraduate Research Scholarships (IPRS) 413
Synthesys Visiting Fellowship 494

European Union

NERC Masters Studentships 493
NERC Research (PhD) Studentships 494
Synthesys Visiting Fellowship 494

Middle East

International Postgraduate Research Scholarships (IPRS) 413
Shell Centenary/Shell Centenary Chevening Scholarships 704

New Zealand

Lindemann Trust Fellowships 280

South Africa

International Postgraduate Research Scholarships (IPRS) 413
Lindemann Trust Fellowships 280
Shell Centenary/Shell Centenary Chevening Scholarships 704

United Kingdom

Hector and Elizabeth Catling Bursary 173
International Postgraduate Research Scholarships (IPRS) 413
Lindemann Trust Fellowships 280
NERC Masters Studentships 493
NERC Research (PhD) Studentships 494
Synthesys Visiting Fellowship 494

United States of America

Air Force Summer Faculty Fellowship Program 84
The Graduate Fellowship Award 340
GSA Research Grants 310
International Postgraduate Research Scholarships (IPRS) 413
Krell Institute Computational Science Graduate Fellowship Program
    412
Washington University Chancellor's Graduate Fellowship Program
    792

West European Countries

International Postgraduate Research Scholarships (IPRS) 413
Synthesys Visiting Fellowship 494

PALAEONTOLOGY

Any Country

ACS PRF Type SE Grants 37
American Association of Petroleum Geologists Foundation Grants-in-
    Aid 32
AMNH Annette Kade Graduate Student Fellowship Program
ASCSA Research Fellowship in Environmental Studies 82
ASCSA Research Fellowship in Faunal Studies 82
ASCSA Research Fellowship in Geoarchaeology 82
BP/RSE Research Fellowships 628
Charles A. & June R.P. Ross Research Fund 309
Earthwatch Field Research Grants 272
ESRF Postdoctoral Fellowships 287
ETH Zurich Excellence Scholarship and Opportunity Award 624
Fondation Fyssen Postdoctoral Study Grants 297
Hugh Kelly Fellowship 548
Jessup and McHenry Awards 4
NERC Advanced Research Fellowships 493

NERC Postdoctoral Research Fellowships 494
University of Bristol Postgraduate Scholarships 672
Victoria University of Wellington PhD Scholarships 786
W Storrs Cole Memorial Research Award 311

Australia

Fulbright Postgraduate Student Award for Science and Engineering 140

Canada

GSA Research Grants 310

East European Countries

ESRF Thesis Studentships 287
Synthesys Visiting Fellowship 494

European Union

NERC Masters Studentships 493
NERC Research (PhD) Studentships 494
Synthesys Visiting Fellowship 494

United Kingdom

ESRF Thesis Studentships 287
Hector and Elizabeth Catling Bursary 173
NERC Masters Studentships 493
NERC Research (PhD) Studentships 494
Synthesys Visiting Fellowship 494

United States of America

Air Force Summer Faculty Fellowship Program 84
Earthwatch Fellowships 272
GSA Research Grants 310

West European Countries

ESRF Thesis Studentships 287
Synthesys Visiting Fellowship 494

PHYSICS

Any Country

Abdus Salam ICTP Fellowships 4
Association for Women in Science Educational Foundation Predoctoral Awards 118
Breast Cancer Campaign PhD Studentships 157
Breast Cancer Campaign Project Grants 157
Breast Cancer Campaign Scientific Fellowships 157
Breast Cancer Campaign Small Pilot Grants 157
CICOR Postdoctoral Scholar Fellowship in Coastal Oceanography, Climate or Marine Ecosystems 804
Dublin Institute for Advanced Studies Scholarship in Theoretical Physics 271
ESRF Postdoctoral Fellowships 287
Essex Rotary University Travel Grants 687
ETH Zurich Excellence Scholarship and Opportunity Award 624
HFSPO Cross-Disciplinary Fellowships 383
HFSPO Short-Term Fellowships 384
Horton (Hydrology) Research Grant 56
Hugh Kelly Fellowship 548
ICR Studentships 365
La Trobe University Postgraduate Scholarship 414
Lindbergh Grants 228
Marie Curie Fellowships for Early Stage Training at CERN
McDonnell Graduate Fellowship in the Space Sciences 437
NCAR Graduate Visitor Programme 471
NCAR Postdoctoral Appointments in the Advanced Study Program 471
NRC Research Associateships 488
Queen Mary Research Studentships 539
Rhodes University Postdoctoral Fellowship and The Andrew Mellon Postdoctoral Fellowship 548
SEG Scholarships 611
Sir Eric Berthoud Travel Grant 689

St Catherine's College College Scholarship (Sciences)
St Catherine's College: Leathersellers' Company Graduate Scholarship
University of Bristol Postgraduate Scholarships 672
University of Otago International Scholarships 717
University of Otago PhD Scholarships 718
University of Otago Prestigious PhD Scholarships 718
University of Southampton Postgraduate Studentships 759
University of Western Ontario Senior Visiting Fellowship 777
Victoria University of Wellington PhD Scholarships 786
Weizmann Institute of Science MSc Fellowships 792
Weizmann Institute of Science PhD Fellowships 792
Weizmann Institute of Science Postdoctoral Fellowships Program 793
WHOI Geophysical Fluid Dynamics (GFD) Fellowships 804
Wolf Foundation Prizes 799
World Universities Network (WUN) International Research Mobility Scheme 759

African Nations

ABCCF Student Grant 102
International Postgraduate Research Scholarships (IPRS) 413
Lindemann Trust Fellowships 280
ORSAS Awards 688
PTDF Cambridge Scholarships 195
The Trieste Science Prize 631
TWAS Fellowships for Research and Advanced Training 631
TWAS Grants for Scientific Meetings in Developing Countries 631
TWAS Prizes 632
TWAS Prizes to Young Scientists in Developing Countries 632
TWAS Research Grants 632
TWAS Spare Parts for Scientific Equipment 632
TWAS UNESCO Associateship Scheme 632
TWAS-S N Bose National Centre for Basic Sciences Postgraduate Fellowships in Physical Sciences 633

Australia

Ferry Scholarship 758
Fulbright Postgraduate Student Award for Science and Engineering 140
Lindemann Trust Fellowships 280
ORSAS Awards 688
Postgraduate Research Scholarship in Physics 716
Wingate Scholarships 697

Canada

Cottrell College Science Awards 545
Cottrell Scholars Awards 545
International Postgraduate Research Scholarships (IPRS) 413
L'ORÉAL Canada For Women in Science Fellowships, With Support of the Canadian Commission for UNESCO 123
Lindemann Trust Fellowships 280
ORSAS Awards 688
Wingate Scholarships 697

Caribbean Countries

International Postgraduate Research Scholarships (IPRS) 413
ORSAS Awards 688
TWAS Fellowships for Research and Advanced Training 631
TWAS Grants for Scientific Meetings in Developing Countries 631
TWAS Prizes 632
TWAS Prizes to Young Scientists in Developing Countries 632
TWAS Research Grants 632
TWAS Spare Parts for Scientific Equipment 632
TWAS UNESCO Associateship Scheme 632
TWAS-S N Bose National Centre for Basic Sciences Postgraduate Fellowships in Physical Sciences 633

East European Countries

CERN Technical Student Programme 227
ESRF Thesis Studentships 287
International Postgraduate Research Scholarships (IPRS) 413
ORSAS Awards 688
PPARC Postgraduate Studentships 522

European Union

EPSRC Doctoral Training Grant Studentships in Condensed Matter Physics, Atomic & Laser Physics etc 725
EPSRC Grant for School of Physical Sciences 698
EPSRC Project Studentships in Condensed Matter Physics, Atomic & Laser Physics and Theoretical Physics 726
Henry Ellison Scholarship 703
Microsoft Research European PhD Scholarship Programme 448
Physics: Joint Department-College Scholarships 738
Physics: NERC Studentships in Atmospheric Physics 738
Wingate Scholarships 697

Middle East

ABCCF Student Grant 102
International Postgraduate Research Scholarships (IPRS) 413
ORSAS Awards 688
The Trieste Science Prize 631
TWAS Fellowships for Research and Advanced Training 631
TWAS Grants for Scientific Meetings in Developing Countries 631
TWAS Prizes 632
TWAS Prizes to Young Scientists in Developing Countries 632
TWAS Research Grants 632
TWAS Spare Parts for Scientific Equipment 632
TWAS UNESCO Associateship Scheme 632
TWAS-S N Bose National Centre for Basic Sciences Postgraduate Fellowships in Physical Sciences 633

New Zealand

Lindemann Trust Fellowships 280
ORSAS Awards 688
Postgraduate Research Scholarship in Physics 716
Wingate Scholarships 697

South Africa

Henderson Postgraduate Scholarships 548
International Postgraduate Research Scholarships (IPRS) 413
Lindemann Trust Fellowships 280
ORSAS Awards 688
The Trieste Science Prize 631
TWAS Fellowships for Research and Advanced Training 631
TWAS Grants for Scientific Meetings in Developing Countries 631
TWAS Prizes 632
TWAS Prizes to Young Scientists in Developing Countries 632
TWAS Research Grants 632
TWAS Spare Parts for Scientific Equipment 632
TWAS UNESCO Associateship Scheme 632
TWAS-S N Bose National Centre for Basic Sciences Postgraduate Fellowships in Physical Sciences 633
Wingate Scholarships 697

United Kingdom

Aberystwyth Postgraduate Research Studentships 4
Access to Learning Fund 685
CERN Technical Student Programme 227
EPSRC Doctoral Training Grant Studentships in Condensed Matter Physics, Atomic & Laser Physics etc 725
EPSRC Grant for School of Physical Sciences 698
EPSRC Project Studentships in Condensed Matter Physics, Atomic & Laser Physics and Theoretical Physics 726
ESRF Thesis Studentships 287
Goldsmiths' Company Science for Society Courses
Henry Ellison Scholarship 703
International Postgraduate Research Scholarships (IPRS) 413
Lindemann Trust Fellowships 280
Physics: Joint Department-College Scholarships 738
Physics: NERC Studentships in Atmospheric Physics 738
PPARC Daphne Jackson Fellowships 522
PPARC Postgraduate Studentships 522
Royal Commission Research Fellowship 563
Thomas Witherden Batt Scholarship 658
Wingate Scholarships 697

United States of America

Air Force Summer Faculty Fellowship Program 84
British Marshall Scholarships 685
Cottrell College Science Awards 545
Cottrell Scholars Awards 545
Ford Foundation Dissertation Fellowships for Minorities 487
Fulbright Senior Specialists Program 249
The Graduate Fellowship Award 340
International Postgraduate Research Scholarships (IPRS) 413
Irving Langmuir Award in Chemical Physics 39
Krell Institute Computational Science Graduate Fellowship Program 412
McDonnell Center Astronaut Fellowships in the Space Sciences 437
NCAR Faculty Fellowship Programme 471
NPSC Fellowship in Physical Sciences 487
ONR Summer Faculty Research 84
ORSAS Awards 688
Philip Morris USA Thurgood Marshall Scholarship 633
Washington University Chancellor's Graduate Fellowship Program 792
Winston Churchill Foundation Scholarship 797
Xerox Technical Minority Scholarship 807

West European Countries

CERN Technical Student Programme 227
EPSRC Grant for School of Physical Sciences 698
ESRF Thesis Studentships 287
International Postgraduate Research Scholarships (IPRS) 413
Janson Johan Helmich Scholarships and Travel Grants 398
Microsoft Research European PhD Scholarship Programme 448
PPARC Postgraduate Studentships 522

ATOMIC AND MOLECULAR PHYSICS

Any Country

ESRF Postdoctoral Fellowships 287
ETH Zurich Excellence Scholarship and Opportunity Award 624
IFT Graduate Fellowships 366
Institute for Advanced Study Postdoctoral Residential Fellowships 363
JILA Postdoctoral Research Associateship and Visiting Fellowships 401
Marcel Loncin Research Prize 366
NRC Research Associateships 488
SAO Predoctoral Fellowships 596
Victoria University of Wellington PhD Scholarships 786
Weizmann Institute of Science MSc Fellowships 792
Weizmann Institute of Science PhD Fellowships 792
Weizmann Institute of Science Postdoctoral Fellowships Program 793
Welch Foundation Scholarship 391

African Nations

TWAS-S N Bose National Centre for Basic Sciences Postgraduate Fellowships in Physical Sciences 633

Caribbean Countries

TWAS-S N Bose National Centre for Basic Sciences Postgraduate Fellowships in Physical Sciences 633

East European Countries

ESRF Thesis Studentships 287

European Union

EPSRC Doctoral Training Grant Studentships in Condensed Matter Physics, Atomic & Laser Physics etc 725
EPSRC Project Studentships in Condensed Matter Physics, Atomic & Laser Physics and Theoretical Physics 726

Middle East

TWAS-S N Bose National Centre for Basic Sciences Postgraduate Fellowships in Physical Sciences 633

South Africa

TWAS-S N Bose National Centre for Basic Sciences Postgraduate
Fellowships in Physical Sciences 633

United Kingdom

EPSRC Doctoral Training Grant Studentships in Condensed Matter
Physics, Atomic & Laser Physics etc 725
EPSRC Project Studentships in Condensed Matter Physics, Atomic &
Laser Physics and Theoretical Physics 726
ESRF Thesis Studentships 287
PPARC Advanced Fellowships 521
PPARC Postdoctoral Fellowships 522

United States of America

Air Force Summer Faculty Fellowship Program 84
DEED (Demonstration of Energy-Efficient Developments) Student
Research Grant/Internship 80
Krell Institute Computational Science Graduate Fellowship Program
412

West European Countries

ESRF Thesis Studentships 287

NUCLEAR PHYSICS

Any Country

Alan F Henry/Paul A Greebler Scholarship 69
ETH Zurich Excellence Scholarship and Opportunity Award 624
John and Muriel Landis Scholarship Awards 70
Victoria University of Wellington PhD Scholarships 786
Weizmann Institute of Science MSc Fellowships 792
Weizmann Institute of Science PhD Fellowships 792
Weizmann Institute of Science Postdoctoral Fellowships Program 793

East European Countries

CERN Technical Student Programme 227

United Kingdom

CERN Technical Student Programme 227

United States of America

Air Force Summer Faculty Fellowship Program 84
DEED (Demonstration of Energy-Efficient Developments) Student
Research Grant/Internship 80
Everitt P Blizard Scholarship 70
Krell Institute Computational Science Graduate Fellowship Program
412
Walter Meyer Scholarship 71

West European Countries

CERN Technical Student Programme 227

OPTICS

Any Country

Abdus Salam ICTP Fellowships 4
BP/RSE Research Fellowships 628
Ernst and Grace Matthaei Research Scholarship 707
ESRF Postdoctoral Fellowships 287
ETH Zurich Excellence Scholarship and Opportunity Award 624
JILA Postdoctoral Research Associateship and Visiting Fellowships 401
Tomsk Polytechnic University International Scholarship 634
Victoria University of Wellington PhD Scholarships 786
Weizmann Institute of Science MSc Fellowships 792
Weizmann Institute of Science PhD Fellowships 792
Weizmann Institute of Science Postdoctoral Fellowships Program 793

East European Countries

CERN Technical Student Programme 227
ESRF Thesis Studentships 287

European Union

EPSRC Grant for School of Physical Sciences 698

United Kingdom

CERN Technical Student Programme 227
EPSRC Grant for School of Physical Sciences 698
ESRF Thesis Studentships 287
University of Kent School of Physical Sciences 701

United States of America

Air Force Summer Faculty Fellowship Program 84
Krell Institute Computational Science Graduate Fellowship
Program 412
Xerox Technical Minority Scholarship 807

West European Countries

CERN Technical Student Programme 227
EPSRC Grant for School of Physical Sciences 698
ESRF Thesis Studentships 287
University of Kent School of Physical Sciences 701

SOLID STATE PHYSICS

Any Country

Abdus Salam ICTP Fellowships 4
BP/RSE Research Fellowships 628
ESRF Postdoctoral Fellowships 287
ETH Zurich Excellence Scholarship and Opportunity Award 624
JILA Postdoctoral Research Associateship and Visiting Fellowships
401
Tomsk Polytechnic University International Scholarship 634
Victoria University of Wellington PhD Scholarships 786
Weizmann Institute of Science MSc Fellowships 792
Weizmann Institute of Science PhD Fellowships 792
Weizmann Institute of Science Postdoctoral Fellowships Program 793
Welch Foundation Scholarship 391

African Nations

TWAS-S N Bose National Centre for Basic Sciences Postgraduate
Fellowships in Physical Sciences 633

Caribbean Countries

TWAS-S N Bose National Centre for Basic Sciences Postgraduate
Fellowships in Physical Sciences 633

East European Countries

CERN Technical Student Programme 227
ESRF Thesis Studentships 287

European Union

EPSRC Grant for School of Physical Sciences 698

Middle East

TWAS-S N Bose National Centre for Basic Sciences Postgraduate
Fellowships in Physical Sciences 633

South Africa

TWAS-S N Bose National Centre for Basic Sciences Postgraduate
Fellowships in Physical Sciences 633

United Kingdom

Aberystwyth Postgraduate Research Studentships 4
CERN Technical Student Programme 227
EPSRC Grant for School of Physical Sciences 698
ESRF Thesis Studentships 287
University of Kent School of Physical Sciences 701

United States of America

Air Force Summer Faculty Fellowship Program 84
Krell Institute Computational Science Graduate Fellowship Program
412

West European Countries

CERN Technical Student Programme 227
EPSRC Grant for School of Physical Sciences 698
ESRF Thesis Studentships 287
University of Kent School of Physical Sciences 701

THERMAL PHYSICS

Any Country

ETH Zurich Excellence Scholarship and Opportunity Award 624
JILA Postdoctoral Research Associateship and Visiting Fellowships 401
Tomsk Polytechnic University International Scholarship 634
Victoria University of Wellington PhD Scholarships 786
Weizmann Institute of Science MSc Fellowships 792
Weizmann Institute of Science PhD Fellowships 792
Weizmann Institute of Science Postdoctoral Fellowships Program 793

African Nations

International Postgraduate Research Scholarships (IPRS) 413

Canada

International Postgraduate Research Scholarships (IPRS) 413

Caribbean Countries

International Postgraduate Research Scholarships (IPRS) 413

East European Countries

International Postgraduate Research Scholarships (IPRS) 413

Middle East

International Postgraduate Research Scholarships (IPRS) 413

South Africa

International Postgraduate Research Scholarships (IPRS) 413

United Kingdom

International Postgraduate Research Scholarships (IPRS) 413

United States of America

Air Force Summer Faculty Fellowship Program 84
DEED (Demonstration of Energy-Efficient Developments) Student Research Grant/Internship 80
International Postgraduate Research Scholarships (IPRS) 413
Krell Institute Computational Science Graduate Fellowship Program 412

West European Countries

International Postgraduate Research Scholarships (IPRS) 413

ASTRONOMY AND ASTROPHYSICS

Any Country

Abdus Salam ICTP Fellowships 4
Association for Women in Science Educational Foundation Predoctoral Awards 118
Dublin Institute for Advanced Studies Scholarship in Astronomy, Astrophysics and Geophysics 270
ETH Zurich Excellence Scholarship and Opportunity Award 624
Hugh Kelly Fellowship 548
IAU Travel Grant 377
Institute for Advanced Study Postdoctoral Residential Fellowships 363
Jansky Fellowship 487
JILA Postdoctoral Research Associateship and Visiting Fellowships 401
McDonnell Graduate Fellowship in the Space Sciences 437
NCAR Postdoctoral Appointments in the Advanced Study Program 471
NRC Research Associateships 488
Perren Studentship 655

Queen Mary Research Studentships 539
Rhodes University Postdoctoral Fellowship and The Andrew Mellon Postdoctoral Fellowship 548
SAO Predoctoral Fellowships 596
St Catherine's College College Scholarship (Sciences)
St Catherine's College: Leathersellers' Company Graduate Scholarship
University of Bristol Postgraduate Scholarships 672
University of Southampton Postgraduate Studentships 759
Victoria University of Wellington PhD Scholarships 786
Weizmann Institute of Science MSc Fellowships 792
Weizmann Institute of Science PhD Fellowships 792
WHOI Geophysical Fluid Dynamics (GFD) Fellowships 804
Wolf Foundation Prizes 799
World Universities Network (WUN) International Research Mobility Scheme 759

African Nations

Lindemann Trust Fellowships 280
PTDF Cambridge Scholarships 195
The Trieste Science Prize 631
TWAS Fellowships for Research and Advanced Training 631
TWAS Grants for Scientific Meetings in Developing Countries 631
TWAS Prizes 632
TWAS Research Grants 632
TWAS Spare Parts for Scientific Equipment 632
TWAS UNESCO Associateship Scheme 632

Australia

Lindemann Trust Fellowships 280
Wingate Scholarships 697

Canada

Cottrell College Science Awards 545
Cottrell Scholars Awards 545
Lindemann Trust Fellowships 280
Wingate Scholarships 697

Caribbean Countries

TWAS Fellowships for Research and Advanced Training 631
TWAS Grants for Scientific Meetings in Developing Countries 631
TWAS Prizes 632
TWAS Research Grants 632
TWAS Spare Parts for Scientific Equipment 632
TWAS UNESCO Associateship Scheme 632

East European Countries

PPARC Postgraduate Studentships 522

European Union

EPSRC Grant for School of Physical Sciences 698
PPARC Spanish (IAC) Studentship 522
STFC Studentships in Particle Physics, Astrophysics, Theoretical Physics 747
Wingate Scholarships 697

Middle East

The Trieste Science Prize 631
TWAS Fellowships for Research and Advanced Training 631
TWAS Grants for Scientific Meetings in Developing Countries 631
TWAS Prizes 632
TWAS Research Grants 632
TWAS Spare Parts for Scientific Equipment 632
TWAS UNESCO Associateship Scheme 632

New Zealand

Lindemann Trust Fellowships 280
Wingate Scholarships 697

South Africa

Henderson Postgraduate Scholarships 548
Lindemann Trust Fellowships 280
The Trieste Science Prize 631

TWAS Fellowships for Research and Advanced Training 631
TWAS Grants for Scientific Meetings in Developing Countries 631
TWAS Prizes 632
TWAS Research Grants 632
TWAS Spare Parts for Scientific Equipment 632
TWAS UNESCO Associateship Scheme 632
Wingate Scholarships 697

United Kingdom

Aberystwyth Postgraduate Research Studentships 4
EPSRC Grant for School of Physical Sciences 698
Goldsmiths' Company Science for Society Courses
Lindemann Trust Fellowships 280
PPARC Advanced Fellowships 521
PPARC Daphne Jackson Fellowships 522
PPARC Postdoctoral Fellowships 522
PPARC Postgraduate Studentships 522
Royal Commission Research Fellowship 563
STFC Studentships in Particle Physics, Astrophysics, Theoretical
    Physics 747
University of Kent School of Physical Sciences 701
Wingate Scholarships 697

United States of America

Air Force Summer Faculty Fellowship Program 84
Cottrell College Science Awards 545
Cottrell Scholars Awards 545
Fulbright Senior Specialists Program 249
The Graduate Fellowship Award 340
Krell Institute Computational Science Graduate Fellowship Program
    412
McDonnell Center Astronaut Fellowships in the Space Sciences 437
Norwegian Thanksgiving Fund Scholarship 509
ONR Summer Faculty Research 84
Winston Churchill Foundation Scholarship 797

West European Countries

EPSRC Grant for School of Physical Sciences 698
ESO Fellowship 286
PPARC Postgraduate Studentships 522
University of Kent School of Physical Sciences 701

ATMOSPHERE SCIENCE/METEOROLOGY

Any Country

AAC Research Grants 26
Abdus Salam ICTP Fellowships 4
AMS Graduate Fellowship in the History of Science 67
Association for Women in Science Educational Foundation Predoc-
    toral Awards 118
BFWG Johnstone and Florence Stoney Studentship 165
CICOR Postdoctoral Scholar Fellowship in Coastal Oceanography,
    Climate or Marine Ecosystems 804
Earthwatch Field Research Grants 272
ETH Zurich Excellence Scholarship and Opportunity Award 624
ICSU-TWAS-UNESCO-UNU/IAS Visiting Scientist Programme 631
McDonnell Graduate Fellowship in the Space Sciences 437
National Geographic Conservation Trust Grant 244
NCAR Graduate Visitor Programme 471
NCAR Postdoctoral Appointments in the Advanced Study Program 471
NERC Advanced Research Fellowships 493
NERC Postdoctoral Research Fellowships 494
Queen Mary Research Studentships 539
Victoria University of Wellington PhD Scholarships 786
Weizmann Institute of Science MSc Fellowships 792
Weizmann Institute of Science PhD Fellowships 792
WHOI Geophysical Fluid Dynamics (GFD) Fellowships 804
WMO Education and Training Fellowships 805
Wolf Foundation Prizes 799

African Nations

The Trieste Science Prize 631
TWAS Fellowships for Research and Advanced Training 631

TWAS Grants for Scientific Meetings in Developing Countries 631
TWAS Prizes 632
TWAS Research Grants 632
TWAS Spare Parts for Scientific Equipment 632
TWAS UNESCO Associateship Scheme 632

Australia

Wingate Scholarships 697

Canada

Wingate Scholarships 697

Caribbean Countries

TWAS Fellowships for Research and Advanced Training 631
TWAS Grants for Scientific Meetings in Developing Countries 631
TWAS Prizes 632
TWAS Research Grants 632
TWAS Spare Parts for Scientific Equipment 632
TWAS UNESCO Associateship Scheme 632

European Union

NERC Masters Studentships 493
NERC Research (PhD) Studentships 494
Wingate Scholarships 697

Middle East

The Trieste Science Prize 631
TWAS Fellowships for Research and Advanced Training 631
TWAS Grants for Scientific Meetings in Developing Countries 631
TWAS Prizes 632
TWAS Research Grants 632
TWAS Spare Parts for Scientific Equipment 632
TWAS UNESCO Associateship Scheme 632

New Zealand

Wingate Scholarships 697

South Africa

Henderson Postgraduate Scholarships 548
The Trieste Science Prize 631
TWAS Fellowships for Research and Advanced Training 631
TWAS Grants for Scientific Meetings in Developing Countries 631
TWAS Prizes 632
TWAS Research Grants 632
TWAS Spare Parts for Scientific Equipment 632
TWAS UNESCO Associateship Scheme 632
Wingate Scholarships 697

United Kingdom

NERC Masters Studentships 493
NERC Research (PhD) Studentships 494
Wingate Scholarships 697

United States of America

Air Force Summer Faculty Fellowship Program 84
The Graduate Fellowship Award 340
NCAR Faculty Fellowship Programme 471
Winston Churchill Foundation Scholarship 797

West European Countries

Janson Johan Helmich Scholarships and Travel Grants 398

ARCTIC STUDIES

Any Country

AAC Research Grants 26
Earthwatch Field Research Grants 272
NERC Advanced Research Fellowships 493
NERC Postdoctoral Research Fellowships 494
Victoria University of Wellington PhD Scholarships 786

European Union

NERC Masters Studentships 493
NERC Research (PhD) Studentships 494

United Kingdom

NERC Masters Studentships 493
NERC Research (PhD) Studentships 494

United States of America

Air Force Summer Faculty Fellowship Program 84
Norwegian Thanksgiving Fund Scholarship 509

ARID LAND STUDIES

Any Country

Earthwatch Field Research Grants 272
NERC Advanced Research Fellowships 493
NERC Postdoctoral Research Fellowships 494
Victoria University of Wellington PhD Scholarships 786

European Union

NERC Masters Studentships 493
NERC Research (PhD) Studentships 494

United Kingdom

NERC Masters Studentships 493
NERC Research (PhD) Studentships 494

United States of America

Air Force Summer Faculty Fellowship Program 84

OCEANOGRAPHY

Any Country

AMS Graduate Fellowship in the History of Science 67
Association for Women in Science Educational Foundation Predoctoral Awards 118
CICOR Postdoctoral Scholar Fellowship in Coastal Oceanography, Climate or Marine Ecosystems 804
Earthwatch Field Research Grants 272
Horton (Hydrology) Research Grant 56
Hugh Kelly Fellowship 548
ICSU-TWAS-UNESCO-UNU/IAS Visiting Scientist Programme 631
National Geographic Conservation Trust Grant 244
NCAR Graduate Visitor Programme 471
NCAR Postdoctoral Appointments in the Advanced Study Program 471
NERC Advanced Research Fellowships 493
NERC Postdoctoral Research Fellowships 494
Queen Mary Research Studentships 539
Ralph Brown Expedition Award 565
Rhodes University Postdoctoral Fellowship and The Andrew Mellon Postdoctoral Fellowship 548
University of Southampton Postgraduate Studentships 759
Victoria University of Wellington PhD Scholarships 786
Weizmann Institute of Science MSc Fellowships 792
Weizmann Institute of Science PhD Fellowships 792
WHOI Geophysical Fluid Dynamics (GFD) Fellowships 804
WHOI Marine Policy Fellowship Program 804
WHOI Postdoctoral Scholarship Program 804
Wolf Foundation Prizes 799

African Nations

The Trieste Science Prize 631
TWAS Fellowships for Research and Advanced Training 631
TWAS Grants for Scientific Meetings in Developing Countries 631
TWAS Research Grants 632
TWAS Spare Parts for Scientific Equipment 632

Australia

Wingate Scholarships 697

Canada

GSA Research Grants 310
Wingate Scholarships 697

Caribbean Countries

TWAS Fellowships for Research and Advanced Training 631
TWAS Grants for Scientific Meetings in Developing Countries 631
TWAS Research Grants 632
TWAS Spare Parts for Scientific Equipment 632

European Union

NERC Masters Studentships 493
NERC Research (PhD) Studentships 494
Wingate Scholarships 697

Middle East

The Trieste Science Prize 631
TWAS Fellowships for Research and Advanced Training 631
TWAS Grants for Scientific Meetings in Developing Countries 631
TWAS Research Grants 632
TWAS Spare Parts for Scientific Equipment 632

New Zealand

Wingate Scholarships 697

South Africa

The Trieste Science Prize 631
TWAS Fellowships for Research and Advanced Training 631
TWAS Grants for Scientific Meetings in Developing Countries 631
TWAS Research Grants 632
TWAS Spare Parts for Scientific Equipment 632
Wingate Scholarships 697

United Kingdom

NERC Masters Studentships 493
NERC Research (PhD) Studentships 494
Wingate Scholarships 697

United States of America

Air Force Summer Faculty Fellowship Program 84
Budweiser Conservation Scholarship 475
DEED (Demonstration of Energy-Efficient Developments) Student Research Grant/Internship 80
Earthwatch Fellowships 272
The Graduate Fellowship Award 340
GSA Research Grants 310
NCAR Faculty Fellowship Programme 471
Winston Churchill Foundation Scholarship 797

RECREATION, WELFARE, PROTECTIVE SERVICES

GENERAL

Any Country

Australian Postgraduate Award Research Scholarship
Field Psych Trust Grant 291
Griffith University Postgraduate Research Scholarships 326
International Postgraduate Research Scholarship 667
Jennings Randolph Program for International Peace Senior Fellowships 643
La Trobe University Postgraduate Scholarship 414
Lee Kuan Yew School of Public Policy Graduate Scholarships (LKYSPPS) 491
Monash International Postgraduate Research Scholarship (MIPRS) 455
Monash University Silver Jubilee Postgraduate Scholarship 455
Sir Allan Sewell Visiting Fellowship 326

Thesiger-Oman Research Fellowship 566
Vera Moore International Postgraduate Research Scholarships 455

African Nations

International Postgraduate Research Scholarships (IPRS) 413
International Postgraduate Research Scholarships (IPRS) 413

Australia

Fulbright Postdoctoral Fellowships 140
Fulbright Postgraduate Awards 140
International Postgraduate Research Scholarships (IPRS) 413
Wingate Scholarships 697

Canada

International Postgraduate Research Scholarships (IPRS) 413
International Postgraduate Research Scholarships (IPRS) 413
Toyota Earth Day Scholarship Program 235
Wingate Scholarships 697

Caribbean Countries

International Postgraduate Research Scholarships (IPRS) 413
International Postgraduate Research Scholarships (IPRS) 413

East European Countries

International Postgraduate Research Scholarships (IPRS) 413
International Postgraduate Research Scholarships (IPRS) 413

European Union

International Postgraduate Research Scholarships (IPRS) 413
Wingate Scholarships 697

Middle East

International Postgraduate Research Scholarships (IPRS) 413
International Postgraduate Research Scholarships (IPRS) 413

New Zealand

Wingate Scholarships 697

South Africa

International Postgraduate Research Scholarships (IPRS) 413
International Postgraduate Research Scholarships (IPRS) 413
Wingate Scholarships 697

United Kingdom

Hilda Martindale Exhibitions 341
International Postgraduate Research Scholarships (IPRS) 413
International Postgraduate Research Scholarships (IPRS) 413
Wingate Scholarships 697

United States of America

AIGC Accenture American Indian Scholarship Fund 59
International Postgraduate Research Scholarships (IPRS) 413
International Postgraduate Research Scholarships (IPRS) 413
North Dakota Indian Scholarship 507

West European Countries

International Postgraduate Research Scholarships (IPRS) 413
International Postgraduate Research Scholarships (IPRS) 413

POLICE AND LAW ENFORCEMENT

United Kingdom

Fulbright Police Research Fellowships 780

United States of America

Fulbright Senior Specialists Program 249
US-UK Fulbright Commission, Criminal Justice and Police Research
Fellowships 784

CRIMINOLOGY

Any Country

Essex Rotary University Travel Grants 687
HFG Research Program 332
Sir Eric Berthoud Travel Grant 689
St Catherine's College Graduate Scholarship in the Arts
United States Holocaust Memorial Museum Center for
Advanced Holocaust Studies Visiting Scholar Programs
641

African Nations

ORSAS Awards 688

Australia

CRC Grants 254
ORSAS Awards 688
Wingate Scholarships 697

Canada

ORSAS Awards 688
SSHRC Doctoral Awards 602
SSHRC Standard Research Grants 603
Wingate Scholarships 697

Caribbean Countries

ORSAS Awards 688

East European Countries

ORSAS Awards 688

European Union

Criminology: ESRC 1 + 3/ + 3 Nomination (Quota) Studentship
ESRC 1 + 3 Awards and + 3 Awards
Wingate Scholarships 697

Middle East

ORSAS Awards 688

New Zealand

ORSAS Awards 688
Wingate Scholarships 697

South Africa

ORSAS Awards 688
Wingate Scholarships 697

United Kingdom

Aberystwyth Postgraduate Research Studentships 4
Criminology: ESRC 1 + 3/ + 3 Nomination (Quota) Studentship
ESRC 1 + 3 Awards and + 3 Awards
Mr and Mrs David Edward Memorial Award 145
Wingate Scholarships 697

United States of America

British Marshall Scholarships 685
IREX Short-Term Travel Grants 389
Kennedy Research Grants 405
ORSAS Awards 688

West European Countries

ESRC 1 + 3 Awards and + 3 Awards
Mr and Mrs David Edward Memorial Award 145

FIRE PROTECTION/CONTROL

United Kingdom

Aberystwyth Postgraduate Research Studentships 4

MILITARY SCIENCE

Any Country

CDI Internship 223
HFG Research Program 332
United States Holocaust Memorial Museum Center for Advanced
Holocaust Studies Visiting Scholar Programs 641

Canada

Department of National Defence Security and Defence Forum
Internship Program 122
Department of National Defence Security and Defence Forum MA
Scholarship Program 122
Department of National Defense Security and Defence Forum PhD
Scholarship Program Including the Dr Ronald Baker Doctoral
Scholarship 122
Department of National Defense Security and Defense Forum
Postdoctoral Fellowship including the R B Byers Postdoctoral
Fellowship 123

United Kingdom

Aberystwyth Postgraduate Research Studentships 4

United States of America

IREX Short-Term Travel Grants 389

CIVIL SECURITY

Any Country

CDI Internship 223
USIP Annual Grant Competition 643
USIP Priority Grant-making Competition 644

African Nations

Canadian Window on International Development 380
IDRC Doctoral Research Awards 380

Canada

Canadian Window on International Development 380
Department of National Defence Security and Defence Forum
Internship Program 122
Department of National Defence Security and Defence Forum MA
Scholarship Program 122
Department of National Defense Security and Defence Forum PhD
Scholarship Program Including the Dr Ronald Baker Doctoral
Scholarship 122
Department of National Defense Security and Defense Forum
Postdoctoral Fellowship including the R B Byers Postdoctoral
Fellowship 123
IDRC Doctoral Research Awards 380
Public Safety and Emergency Preparedness Canada Research
Fellowship in Honour of Stuart Nesbitt White 123
SSHRC Standard Research Grants 603
The Yitzhak Rabin Fellowship Fund for the Advancement of Peace
and Tolerance 318

Caribbean Countries

Canadian Window on International Development 380
IDRC Doctoral Research Awards 380

East European Countries

IDRC Doctoral Research Awards 380

Middle East

IDRC Doctoral Research Awards 380

South Africa

Canadian Window on International Development 380
IDRC Doctoral Research Awards 380

United Kingdom

Aberystwyth Postgraduate Research Studentships 4

United States of America

IREX Short-Term Travel Grants 389
Kennan Institute Research Scholarship 408
Robert Bosch Foundation Fellowships 550
SSRC Abe Fellowship Program 598

PEACE AND DISARMAMENT

Any Country

CDI Internship 223
HFG Research Program 332
The Sally Davis Scholarship 445
United States Holocaust Memorial Museum Center for Advanced
Holocaust Studies Visiting Scholar Programs 641
University of Southampton Postgraduate Studentships 759
USIP Annual Grant Competition 643
USIP Priority Grant-making Competition 644
WILPF Internship in Disarmament 801

African Nations

Canadian Window on International Development 380
IDRC Doctoral Research Awards 380

Australia

The Lionel Murphy Australian Postgraduate Scholarships 424
The Lionel Murphy Overseas Postgraduate Scholarships 424

Canada

Canadian Window on International Development 380
IDRC Doctoral Research Awards 380
SSHRC Doctoral Awards 602
SSHRC Standard Research Grants 603

Caribbean Countries

Canadian Window on International Development 380
IDRC Doctoral Research Awards 380

East European Countries

IDRC Doctoral Research Awards 380

Middle East

IDRC Doctoral Research Awards 380

South Africa

Canadian Window on International Development 380
IDRC Doctoral Research Awards 380

United Kingdom

Aberystwyth Postgraduate Research Studentships 4

United States of America

British Marshall Scholarships 685
Fulbright Senior Specialists Program 249
Herbert Scoville Jr Peace Fellowship 339
IREX Short-Term Travel Grants 389
Kennan Institute Research Scholarship 408
SSRC Abe Fellowship Program 598

SOCIAL WELFARE AND SOCIAL WORK

Any Country

BackCare Research Grants 144
Memorial Foundation for Jewish Culture International Scholarship
Programme for Community Service 444
Robert Westwood Scholarship 581
S. Leonard Syme Training Fellowships in Work & Health 364
St Catherine's College Graduate Scholarship in the Arts
United States Holocaust Memorial Museum Center for Advanced
Holocaust Studies Visiting Scholar Programs 641
University of Bristol Postgraduate Scholarships 672

University of Southampton Postgraduate Studentships 759
Victoria University of Wellington PhD Scholarships 786
World Universities Network (WUN) International Research Mobility
Scheme 759

African Nations

International Postgraduate Research Scholarships (IPRS) 413

Australia

Dunlop Asia Fellowships 115
Wingate Scholarships 697

Canada

Canadian Millenium Excellence Awards 235
International Postgraduate Research Scholarships (IPRS) 413
JCCA Graduate Education Scholarship 400
Sheriff Willoughby King Memorial Scholarship 673
SSHRC Doctoral Awards 602
SSHRC Standard Research Grants 603
Terry Fox Humanitarian Award 235
Wingate Scholarships 697

Caribbean Countries

International Postgraduate Research Scholarships (IPRS) 413

East European Countries

International Postgraduate Research Scholarships (IPRS) 413

European Union

ESRC 1+3 Awards and +3 Awards
Wingate Scholarships 697

Middle East

International Postgraduate Research Scholarships (IPRS) 413

New Zealand

Wingate Scholarships 697

South Africa

International Postgraduate Research Scholarships (IPRS) 413
Wingate Scholarships 697

United Kingdom

Aberystwyth Postgraduate Research Studentships 4
ESRC 1+3 Awards and +3 Awards
International Postgraduate Research Scholarships (IPRS) 413
Mr and Mrs David Edward Memorial Award 145
Wingate Scholarships 697

United States of America

AIGC Accenture American Indian Scholarship Fund 59
Congress Bundestag Youth Exchange for Young Professionals 221
CSWE Doctoral Fellowships in Social Work for Ethnic Minority
Students Preparing for Leadership Roles in Mental Health and/or
Substance Abuse 252
CSWE Doctoral Fellowships in Social Work for Ethnic Minority
Students Specializing in Mental Health 252
Fulbright Senior Specialists Program 249
International Postgraduate Research Scholarships (IPRS) 413
IREX Short-Term Travel Grants 389
JCCA Graduate Education Scholarship 400
Robert Bosch Foundation Fellowships 550
SSRC Abe Fellowship Program 598
Washington University Chancellor's Graduate Fellowship Program
792

West European Countries

ESRC 1+3 Awards and +3 Awards
International Postgraduate Research Scholarships (IPRS) 413
Mr and Mrs David Edward Memorial Award 145

PUBLIC AND COMMUNITY SERVICES

Any Country

ASBAH Research Grant 118
Memorial Foundation for Jewish Culture International Scholarship
Programme for Community Service 444
Victoria University of Wellington PhD Scholarships 786

African Nations

International Postgraduate Research Scholarships (IPRS) 413

Australia

Advanced Community Care Scholarship 292

Canada

International Postgraduate Research Scholarships (IPRS) 413
JCCA Graduate Education Scholarship 400
SSHRC Doctoral Awards 602

Caribbean Countries

International Postgraduate Research Scholarships (IPRS) 413

East European Countries

International Postgraduate Research Scholarships (IPRS) 413

Middle East

International Postgraduate Research Scholarships (IPRS) 413

South Africa

International Postgraduate Research Scholarships (IPRS) 413

United Kingdom

International Postgraduate Research Scholarships (IPRS) 413

United States of America

AIGC Accenture American Indian Scholarship Fund 59
American Academy in Berlin Prize Fellowships 24
Congress Bundestag Youth Exchange for Young Professionals 221
International Postgraduate Research Scholarships (IPRS) 413
JCCA Graduate Education Scholarship 400
Mike M. Masaoka Congressional Fellowship 400

West European Countries

International Postgraduate Research Scholarships (IPRS) 413

ENVIRONMENTAL STUDIES

Any Country

ACS Award for Creative Advances in Environmental Science and
Technology 36
Alberta Law Foundation Graduate Scholarship 672
American Association of Petroleum Geologists Foundation
Grants-in-Aid 32
ASCSA Research Fellowship in Environmental Studies 82
BIAA Post-Doctoral Research Fellowship 168
BIAA Research Scholarship 168
BIAA Study Grants 168
BIAA Travel Grants 168
British Airways Travel Bursary 563
The CFUW/A Vibert Douglas International Fellowship 382
CRCWQT Young Water Scientist of the Year Scholarship 245
Earthwatch Field Research Grants 272
Edmund Niles Huyck Preserve, Inc. Graduate and Postgraduate
Grants 274
EREF Scholarships in Waste Management Research and Education
281
George A Hall/Harold F Mayfield Award 797
German Chancellor Fellowships for Prospective Leaders 17

Gilbert F White Postdoctoral Fellowship 545
Grants for Young Scholars with Research Projects Abroad 322
Hastings Center International Visiting Scholars Program 332
Honda Prize 343
Hudson River Graduate Fellowships 346
IIASA Postdoctoral Program 384
Joseph L Fisher Dissertation Award 546
Journey of a Lifetime Award 564
Lindbergh Grants 228
Louis Agassiz Fuertes Award 797
Monica Cole Research Grant 564
NCAR Graduate Visitor Programme 471
NCAR Postdoctoral Appointments in the Advanced Study Program 471
NERC Advanced Research Fellowships 493
NERC Postdoctoral Research Fellowships 494
NJWEA Scholarship Award Program 498
Procter & Gamble Fellowship for Doctoral Research in Environmental Science 611
Ralph Brown Expedition Award 565
RFF Fellowships in Environmental Regulatory Implementation 546
RGS-IBG Land Rover 'GO Beyond' Bursary 565
Rhodes University Postdoctoral Fellowship and The Andrew Mellon Postdoctoral Fellowship 548
Robin Rousseau Memorial Mountain Achievement Scholarship 235
The Sally Davis Scholarship 445
Scholarship opportunities linked to CATIE's Postgraduate Program including CATIE scholarship forming part of the Scholarship-Loan Program 638
Sir Eric Berthoud Travel Grant 689
Small Research Grants 566
St Catherine's College Graduate Scholarship in the Arts
Teagasc Walsh Fellowships 626
Tibor T Polgar Fellowship 347
Trinity College: Birkett Scholarships in Environmental Studies 747
University of Bristol Postgraduate Scholarships 672
University of Southampton Postgraduate Studentships 759
Ursula M. Händel Animal Welfare Prize 267
Utilities and Service Industries Training (USIT) 254
Victoria University of Wellington PhD Scholarships 786
World Universities Network (WUN) International Research Mobility Scheme 759

African Nations

Canadian Window on International Development 380
Hastings Center International Visiting Scholars Program 332
IDRC Doctoral Research Awards 380
IDRC Internship Awards 381
International Postgraduate Research Scholarships (IPRS) 413
Kulika Charitable Trust-FCO Chevening-University of Leeds Scholarships 703
NUFFIC-NFP Fellowships for Master's Degree Programmes 496
ORSAS Awards 688
School of Applied Sciences Overseas Scholarships 254
Shell Centenary Scholarships and Shell Centenary Chevening Scholarships at Edinburgh 683

Australia

APAI Water Resources Management Scholarship 326
Fulbright Postgraduate Student Award for Science and Engineering 140
Hastings Center International Visiting Scholars Program 332
The Lionel Murphy Australian Postgraduate Scholarships 424
The Lionel Murphy Overseas Postgraduate Scholarships 424
ORSAS Awards 688
School of Applied Sciences Overseas Scholarships 254
Victoria Fellowships 264
Wingate Scholarships 697

Canada

Canadian Commonwealth Scholarship and Fellowship Plan 201
Canadian Window on International Development 380
Community Forestry: Trees and People-John G Bene Fellowship 380
Horticultural Research Institute Grants 346
IDRC Doctoral Research Awards 380

IDRC Internship Awards 381
International Postgraduate Research Scholarships (IPRS) 413
ORSAS Awards 688
School of Applied Sciences Overseas Scholarships 254
Wingate Scholarships 697

Caribbean Countries

Canadian Window on International Development 380
Hastings Center International Visiting Scholars Program 332
IDRC Doctoral Research Awards 380
IDRC Internship Awards 381
International Postgraduate Research Scholarships (IPRS) 413
ORSAS Awards 688
School of Applied Sciences Overseas Scholarships 254
Shell Centenary Scholarships and Shell Centenary Chevening Scholarships at Edinburgh 683

East European Countries

German Chancellor Fellowships for Prospective Leaders 17
Hastings Center International Visiting Scholars Program 332
IDRC Doctoral Research Awards 380
Intel Public Affairs Russia Grant 373
International Postgraduate Research Scholarships (IPRS) 413
ORSAS Awards 688
School of Applied Sciences Overseas Scholarships 254
Shell Centenary Cambridge Scholarships (Countries Outside of the Commonwealth) 196
Shell Centenary Scholarships and Shell Centenary Chevening Scholarships at Edinburgh 683
Synthesys Visiting Fellowship 494

European Union

Akroyd, Brotherton and Brown Scholarship 702
Department of Agriculture and Rural Development (DARD) for Northern Ireland 253
John Henry Garner Scholarship 703
NERC Masters Studentships 493
NERC Research (PhD) Studentships 494
Synthesys Visiting Fellowship 494
Wingate Scholarships 697

Middle East

Hastings Center International Visiting Scholars Program 332
IDRC Doctoral Research Awards 380
IDRC Internship Awards 381
International Postgraduate Research Scholarships (IPRS) 413
NUFFIC-NFP Fellowships for Master's Degree Programmes 496
ORSAS Awards 688
School of Applied Sciences Overseas Scholarships 254
Shell Centenary Cambridge Scholarships (Countries Outside of the Commonwealth) 196
Shell Centenary Scholarships and Shell Centenary Chevening Scholarships at Edinburgh 683

New Zealand

APAI Water Resources Management Scholarship 326
Hastings Center International Visiting Scholars Program 332
ORSAS Awards 688
School of Applied Sciences Overseas Scholarships 254
Wingate Scholarships 697

South Africa

Canadian Window on International Development 380
Hastings Center International Visiting Scholars Program 332
IDRC Doctoral Research Awards 380
IDRC Internship Awards 381
International Postgraduate Research Scholarships (IPRS) 413
NUFFIC-NFP Fellowships for Master's Degree Programmes 496
ORSAS Awards 688
School of Applied Sciences Overseas Scholarships 254
Shell Centenary Scholarships and Shell Centenary Chevening Scholarships at Edinburgh 683
Wingate Scholarships 697

United Kingdom

Aberystwyth Postgraduate Research Studentships 4
Access to Learning Fund 685
Akroyd, Brotherton and Brown Scholarship 702
BIAA Travel Grants 168
Department of Agriculture and Rural Development (DARD) for
  Northern Ireland 253
Douglas Bomford Trust 253
Geographical Fieldwork Grants 564
Hastings Center International Visiting Scholars Program 332
International Postgraduate Research Scholarships (IPRS) 413
John Henry Garner Scholarship 703
Leverhulme Scholarships for Architecture 321
Mr and Mrs David Edward Memorial Award 145
NERC Masters Studentships 493
NERC Research (PhD) Studentships 494
Neville Shulman Challenge Award 565
Peter Fleming Award 565
Synthesys Visiting Fellowship 494
Wingate Scholarships 697

United States of America

British Marshall Scholarships 685
Congress Bundestag Youth Exchange for Young Professionals 221
Earthwatch Fellowships 272
Environmental Leadership Fellowships 281
FFGC Scholarship in Environmental Issues 297
Fulbright Senior Specialists Program 249
German Chancellor Fellowships for Prospective Leaders 17
Horticultural Research Institute Grants 346
International Postgraduate Research Scholarships (IPRS) 413
IREX Short-Term Travel Grants 389
Marie Tharp Visiting Fellowships 239
NCAR Faculty Fellowship Programme 471
NOAA Coastal Management Fellowship 506
ORSAS Awards 688
School of Applied Sciences Overseas Scholarships 254
SSRC Abe Fellowship Program 598
Welder Wildlife Foundation Fellowship 550

West European Countries

Hastings Center International Visiting Scholars Program 332
International Postgraduate Research Scholarships (IPRS) 413
Janson Johan Helmich Scholarships and Travel Grants 398
Mr and Mrs David Edward Memorial Award 145
Shell Centenary Scholarships and Shell Centenary Chevening
  Scholarships at Edinburgh 683
Synthesys Visiting Fellowship 494

ECOLOGY

Any Country

AAC Research Grants 26
BES Early Career Project Grants 161
BES Overseas Bursary 162
BES Small Ecological Project (SEPG) Grants 162
BES Specialist Course Grants 162
BIAA Post-Doctoral Research Fellowship 168
BIAA Research Scholarship 168
BIAA Study Grants 168
BIAA Travel Grants 168
The CFUW/A Vibert Douglas International Fellowship 382
Darbaker Botany Prize 538
Earthwatch Field Research Grants 272
Edmund Niles Huyck Preserve, Inc. Graduate and Postgraduate
  Grants 274
George A Hall/Harold F Mayfield Award 797
Honda Prize 343
Hudson River Graduate Fellowships 346
Louis Agassiz Fuertes Award 797
NERC Advanced Research Fellowships 493
NERC Postdoctoral Research Fellowships 494
Postgraduate Research Studentship 689

Primate Conservation Inc. Grants 537
Rhodes University Postdoctoral Fellowship and The Andrew Mellon
  Postdoctoral Fellowship 548
Rob and Bessie Welder Wildlife Foundation's Graduate Research
  Scholarship Program 793
Scholarship opportunities linked to CATIE's Postgraduate Program
  including CATIE scholarship forming part of the Scholarship-Loan
  Program 638
Silverhill Institute of Environmental Research and Conservation Award
  591
Student Support for Attendance at BES and Specialist Group 162
Tibor T Polgar Fellowship 347
Tomsk Polytechnic University International Scholarship 634
University of Southampton Postgraduate Studentships 759
Victoria University of Wellington PhD Scholarships 786

African Nations

Canadian Window on International Development 380
IDRC Doctoral Research Awards 380
IDRC Internship Awards 381
International Postgraduate Research Scholarships (IPRS) 413
Primate Conservation Inc. Grants 537

Australia

Fulbright Postgraduate Student Award for Science and Engineering
  140
PhD Scholarship: Weed Ecology 712
Victoria Fellowships 264
Wingate Scholarships 697

Canada

Canadian Window on International Development 380
IDRC Doctoral Research Awards 380
IDRC Internship Awards 381
International Postgraduate Research Scholarships (IPRS) 413
Wingate Scholarships 697

Caribbean Countries

Canadian Window on International Development 380
IDRC Doctoral Research Awards 380
IDRC Internship Awards 381
International Postgraduate Research Scholarships (IPRS) 413
Travel Grants for Ecologists from Developing Countries to Attend BES
  Meetings 162

East European Countries

IDRC Doctoral Research Awards 380
International Postgraduate Research Scholarships (IPRS) 413
Synthesys Visiting Fellowship 494

European Union

Department of Agriculture and Rural Development (DARD) for
  Northern Ireland 253
NERC Masters Studentships 493
NERC Research (PhD) Studentships 494
Plant Sciences: BBSRC DTA Studentships in Plant Sciences 739
Synthesys Visiting Fellowship 494
Wingate Scholarships 697

Middle East

IDRC Doctoral Research Awards 380
IDRC Internship Awards 381
International Postgraduate Research Scholarships (IPRS) 413
Travel Grants for Ecologists from Developing Countries to Attend BES
  Meetings 162

New Zealand

Wingate Scholarships 697

South Africa

Canadian Window on International Development 380
IDRC Doctoral Research Awards 380
IDRC Internship Awards 381

International Postgraduate Research Scholarships (IPRS) 413
Travel Grants for Ecologists from Developing Countries to Attend BES
  Meetings 162
Wingate Scholarships 697

United Kingdom

Aberystwyth Postgraduate Research Studentships 4
BIAA Travel Grants 168
Department of Agriculture and Rural Development (DARD) for
  Northern Ireland 253
International Postgraduate Research Scholarships (IPRS) 413
Mr and Mrs David Edward Memorial Award 145
NERC Masters Studentships 493
NERC Research (PhD) Studentships 494
Plant Sciences: BBSRC DTA Studentships in Plant Sciences 739
Synthesys Visiting Fellowship 494
Wingate Scholarships 697

United States of America

British Marshall Scholarships 685
Congress Bundestag Youth Exchange for Young Professionals 221
Earthwatch Fellowships 272
FFGC Scholarship in Ecology 297
Fulbright Senior Specialists Program 249
International Postgraduate Research Scholarships (IPRS) 413
Welder Wildlife Foundation Fellowship 550

West European Countries

International Postgraduate Research Scholarships (IPRS) 413
Mr and Mrs David Edward Memorial Award 145
Synthesys Visiting Fellowship 494

NATURAL RESOURCES

Any Country

Alberta Law Foundation Graduate Scholarship 672
American Association of Petroleum Geologists Foundation Grants-in-
  Aid 32
BIAA Post-Doctoral Research Fellowship 168
BIAA Research Scholarship 168
BIAA Study Grants 168
BIAA Travel Grants 168
Canadian Embassy Faculty Enrichment Program 205
CRCWQT Young Water Scientist of the Year Scholarship 245
Earthwatch Field Research Grants 272
Edmund Niles Huyck Preserve, Inc. Graduate and Postgraduate
  Grants 274
Hudson River Graduate Fellowships 346
NERC Advanced Research Fellowships 493
NERC Postdoctoral Research Fellowships 494
Postgraduate Research Studentship 689
Rhodes University Postdoctoral Fellowship and The Andrew Mellon
  Postdoctoral Fellowship 548
Scholarship opportunities linked to CATIE's Postgraduate Program
  including CATIE scholarship forming part of the Scholarship-Loan
  Program 638
Silverhill Institute of Environmental Research and Conservation Award
  591
Tibor T Polgar Fellowship 347
University of Calgary Faculty of Law Graduate Scholarship 673
Victoria University of Wellington PhD Scholarships 786

African Nations

Canadian Window on International Development 380
IDRC Doctoral Research Awards 380
IDRC Internship Awards 381
International Postgraduate Research Scholarships (IPRS) 413
School of Applied Sciences Overseas Scholarships 254

Australia

Fulbright Postgraduate Student Award for Science and Engineering
  140
School of Applied Sciences Overseas Scholarships 254

Victoria Fellowships 264
Wingate Scholarships 697

Canada

Canadian Window on International Development 380
CWRA Dillon Consulting Scholarship/Ken Thomson Scholarship 216
IDRC Doctoral Research Awards 380
IDRC Internship Awards 381
International Postgraduate Research Scholarships (IPRS) 413
School of Applied Sciences Overseas Scholarships 254
Wingate Scholarships 697

Caribbean Countries

Canadian Window on International Development 380
IDRC Doctoral Research Awards 380
IDRC Internship Awards 381
International Postgraduate Research Scholarships (IPRS) 413
School of Applied Sciences Overseas Scholarships 254

East European Countries

IDRC Doctoral Research Awards 380
International Postgraduate Research Scholarships (IPRS) 413
School of Applied Sciences Overseas Scholarships 254
Synthesys Visiting Fellowship 494

European Union

Department of Agriculture and Rural Development (DARD) for
  Northern Ireland 253
NERC Masters Studentships 493
NERC Research (PhD) Studentships 494
Synthesys Visiting Fellowship 494
Wingate Scholarships 697

Middle East

IDRC Doctoral Research Awards 380
IDRC Internship Awards 381
International Postgraduate Research Scholarships (IPRS)
  413
School of Applied Sciences Overseas Scholarships 254

New Zealand

School of Applied Sciences Overseas Scholarships 254
Wingate Scholarships 697

South Africa

Canadian Window on International Development 380
IDRC Doctoral Research Awards 380
IDRC Internship Awards 381
International Postgraduate Research Scholarships (IPRS) 413
School of Applied Sciences Overseas Scholarships 254
Wingate Scholarships 697

United Kingdom

BIAA Travel Grants 168
Department of Agriculture and Rural Development (DARD) for
  Northern Ireland 253
Douglas Bomford Trust 253
International Postgraduate Research Scholarships (IPRS) 413
Mr and Mrs David Edward Memorial Award 145
NERC Masters Studentships 493
NERC Research (PhD) Studentships 494
Synthesys Visiting Fellowship 494
Wingate Scholarships 697

United States of America

Campus Ecology Fellowship Program 493
Congress Bundestag Youth Exchange for Young Professionals
  221
Earthwatch Fellowships 272
Fulbright Senior Specialists Program 249
International Postgraduate Research Scholarships (IPRS) 413
NOAA Coastal Management Fellowship 506
NOAA Coral Management Assistantship 506

NOAA Pacific Islands Assistantship Program 506
School of Applied Sciences Overseas Scholarships 254
Welder Wildlife Foundation Fellowship 550

West European Countries

International Postgraduate Research Scholarships (IPRS) 413
Mr and Mrs David Edward Memorial Award 145
Synthesys Visiting Fellowship 494

ENVIRONMENTAL MANAGEMENT

Any Country

BIAA Post-Doctoral Research Fellowship 168
BIAA Research Scholarship 168
BIAA Study Grants 168
BIAA Travel Grants 168
Earthwatch Field Research Grants 272
EREF Scholarships in Waste Management Research and Education 281
Hudson River Graduate Fellowships 346
Linacre College Coca-Cola Water Sustainability Scholarships 731
NERC Advanced Research Fellowships 493
NERC Postdoctoral Research Fellowships 494
NJWEA Scholarship Award Program 498
Postgraduate Research Studentship 689
Rhodes University Postdoctoral Fellowship and The Andrew Mellon Postdoctoral Fellowship 548
Scholarship opportunities linked to CATIE's Postgraduate Program including CATIE scholarship forming part of the Scholarship-Loan Program 638
Stanley Smith (UK) Horticultural Trust Awards 618
Tibor T Polgar Fellowship 347
Tomsk Polytechnic University International Scholarship 634
UFAW Animal Welfare Research Training Scholarships 644
UFAW Research and Project Awards 645
UFAW Small Project and Travel Awards 645
UFAW Vacation Scholarships 645
University of Calgary Faculty of Law Graduate Scholarship 673
Victoria University of Wellington PhD Scholarships 786

African Nations

Canadian Window on International Development 380
IDRC Doctoral Research Awards 380
IDRC Internship Awards 381
International Postgraduate Research Scholarships (IPRS) 413
School of Applied Sciences Overseas Scholarships 254

Australia

Dunlop Asia Fellowships 115
Fulbright Postgraduate Student Award for Science and Engineering 140
School of Applied Sciences Overseas Scholarships 254
Victoria Fellowships 264
Wingate Scholarships 697

Canada

Canadian Window on International Development 380
CWRA Dillon Consulting Scholarship/Ken Thomson Scholarship 216
Horticultural Research Institute Grants 346
IDRC Doctoral Research Awards 380
IDRC Internship Awards 381
International Postgraduate Research Scholarships (IPRS) 413
School of Applied Sciences Overseas Scholarships 254
Wingate Scholarships 697

Caribbean Countries

Canadian Window on International Development 380
IDRC Doctoral Research Awards 380
IDRC Internship Awards 381
International Postgraduate Research Scholarships (IPRS) 413
School of Applied Sciences Overseas Scholarships 254

East European Countries

IDRC Doctoral Research Awards 380
International Postgraduate Research Scholarships (IPRS) 413
School of Applied Sciences Overseas Scholarships 254
Synthesys Visiting Fellowship 494

European Union

Department of Agriculture and Rural Development (DARD) for Northern Ireland 253
NERC Masters Studentships 493
NERC Research (PhD) Studentships 494
Synthesys Visiting Fellowship 494
Wingate Scholarships 697

Middle East

Geography: Hitachi Chemical Europe Scholarship with Linacre College 727
IDRC Doctoral Research Awards 380
IDRC Internship Awards 381
International Postgraduate Research Scholarships (IPRS) 413
School of Applied Sciences Overseas Scholarships 254

New Zealand

School of Applied Sciences Overseas Scholarships 254
Wingate Scholarships 697

South Africa

Canadian Window on International Development 380
IDRC Doctoral Research Awards 380
IDRC Internship Awards 381
International Postgraduate Research Scholarships (IPRS) 413
School of Applied Sciences Overseas Scholarships 254
Wingate Scholarships 697

United Kingdom

Aberystwyth Postgraduate Research Studentships 4
BIAA Travel Grants 168
Department of Agriculture and Rural Development (DARD) for Northern Ireland.253
Douglas Bomford Trust 253
International Postgraduate Research Scholarships (IPRS) 413
Mr and Mrs David Edward Memorial Award 145
NERC Masters Studentships 493
NERC Research (PhD) Studentships 494
Synthesys Visiting Fellowship 494
Wingate Scholarships 697

United States of America

Congress Bundestag Youth Exchange for Young Professionals 221
Earthwatch Fellowships 272
Fulbright Senior Specialists Program 249
Horticultural Research Institute Grants 346
International Postgraduate Research Scholarships (IPRS) 413
School of Applied Sciences Overseas Scholarships 254
Welder Wildlife Foundation Fellowship 550

West European Countries

International Postgraduate Research Scholarships (IPRS) 413
Mr and Mrs David Edward Memorial Award 145
Synthesys Visiting Fellowship 494

WILDLIFE AND PEST MANAGEMENT

Any Country

BIAA Post-Doctoral Research Fellowship 168
BIAA Research Scholarship 168
BIAA Study Grants 168
BIAA Travel Grants 168
Charles L. Dobbins Memorial Scholarship 489
Earthwatch Field Research Grants 272
Hudson River Graduate Fellowships 346
John H. Borden Scholarship 281

NERC Advanced Research Fellowships 493
NERC Postdoctoral Research Fellowships 494
Rhodes University Postdoctoral Fellowship and The Andrew Mellon
  Postdoctoral Fellowship 548
Rob and Bessie Welder Wildlife Foundation's Graduate Research
  Scholarship Program 793
RSPCA Australia Alan White Scholarship for Animal Welfare
  Research 577
Scholarship opportunities linked to CATIE's Postgraduate Program
  including CATIE scholarship forming part of the Scholarship-Loan
  Program 638
Tibor T Polgar Fellowship 347
UFAW Animal Welfare Research Training Scholarships 644
UFAW Research and Project Awards 645
UFAW Small Project and Travel Awards 645
UFAW Vacation Scholarships 645
Victoria University of Wellington PhD Scholarships 786

African Nations

Canadian Window on International Development 380
IDRC Doctoral Research Awards 380
IDRC Internship Awards 381
International Postgraduate Research Scholarships (IPRS) 413

Australia

Victoria Fellowships 264
Wingate Scholarships 697

Canada

Canadian Window on International Development 380
IDRC Doctoral Research Awards 380
IDRC Internship Awards 381
International Postgraduate Research Scholarships (IPRS) 413
Wingate Scholarships 697

Caribbean Countries

Canadian Window on International Development 380
IDRC Doctoral Research Awards 380
IDRC Internship Awards 381
International Postgraduate Research Scholarships (IPRS) 413

East European Countries

IDRC Doctoral Research Awards 380
International Postgraduate Research Scholarships (IPRS) 413

European Union

NERC Masters Studentships 493
NERC Research (PhD) Studentships 494
Wingate Scholarships 697

Middle East

IDRC Doctoral Research Awards 380
IDRC Internship Awards 381
International Postgraduate Research Scholarships (IPRS) 413

New Zealand

Wingate Scholarships 697

South Africa

Canadian Window on International Development 380
IDRC Doctoral Research Awards 380
IDRC Internship Awards 381
International Postgraduate Research Scholarships (IPRS) 413
Wingate Scholarships 697

United Kingdom

BIAA Travel Grants 168
International Postgraduate Research Scholarships (IPRS) 413
Mr and Mrs David Edward Memorial Award 145
NERC Masters Studentships 493
NERC Research (PhD) Studentships 494
Wingate Scholarships 697

United States of America

Congress Bundestag Youth Exchange for Young Professionals 221
Earthwatch Fellowships 272
Fulbright Senior Specialists Program 249
International Postgraduate Research Scholarships (IPRS) 413
Welder Wildlife Foundation Fellowship 550

West European Countries

International Postgraduate Research Scholarships (IPRS) 413
Mr and Mrs David Edward Memorial Award 145

PHYSICAL EDUCATION AND SPORTS

Any Country

Acadia Graduate Awards 5
Australian Postgraduate Award Research Scholarship
Biomechanics Postgraduate Scholarship (General Sports) 138
Department of Biological Sciences Studentships 685
Essex Rotary University Travel Grants 687
Explorers Club Exploration Fund 289
Indigenous Sporting Excellence Scholarships 138
The Katrina Mihaere Scholarship 425
MSc Bursaries 145
National Coaching Scholarship Program 139
Performance Analysis Scholarship 139
Postgraduate Scholarship–Biomechanics (Swimming) 139
Rhodes University Postdoctoral Fellowship and The Andrew Mellon
  Postdoctoral Fellowship 548
Sir Eric Berthoud Travel Grant 689
Sport Leadership Grants for Women Program 140
University of Ballarat Postgraduate Research Scholarship
University of Bristol Postgraduate Scholarships 672
University of Exeter Sports Scholarships 692
University of Otago International Scholarships 717
University of Otago PhD Scholarships 718
University of Otago Prestigious PhD Scholarships 718

African Nations

International Postgraduate Research Scholarships (IPRS) 413
ORSAS Awards 688

Australia

ORSAS Awards 688
Physiotherapy Postgraduate Scholarship 139
University of Ballarat Part Postgraduate Research Scholarship 667

Canada

International Postgraduate Research Scholarships (IPRS) 413
JCCA Graduate Education Scholarship 400
ORSAS Awards 688

Caribbean Countries

International Postgraduate Research Scholarships (IPRS) 413
ORSAS Awards 688

East European Countries

International Postgraduate Research Scholarships (IPRS) 413
ORSAS Awards 688

European Union

Loughborough Sports Scholarships 428
Mountaineering Council of Scotland Climbing and Mountaineering
  Bursary 459

Middle East

International Postgraduate Research Scholarships (IPRS) 413
ORSAS Awards 688

New Zealand

Fish & Game New Zealand Research Scholarships 500
ORSAS Awards 688
Sir Edmund Hillary Scholarship Programme 767

South Africa

International Postgraduate Research Scholarships (IPRS) 413
ORSAS Awards 688

United Kingdom

Aberystwyth Postgraduate Research Studentships 4
Access to Learning Fund 685
Alpine Ski Club Kenneth Smith Scholarship 172
BBSRC Studentship 685
BMC Grant 172
International Postgraduate Research Scholarships (IPRS) 413
Mr and Mrs David Edward Memorial Award 145
NERC Studentships 145

United States of America

AAC Mountaineering Fellowship Fund Grants 26
British Marshall Scholarships 685
International Postgraduate Research Scholarships (IPRS) 413
JCCA Graduate Education Scholarship 400
ORSAS Awards 688

West European Countries

International Postgraduate Research Scholarships (IPRS) 413
Mr and Mrs David Edward Memorial Award 145

SPORTS MANAGEMENT

Any Country

Harness Track of America Scholarship 331
University of Bristol Postgraduate Scholarships 672

African Nations

International Postgraduate Research Scholarships (IPRS) 413
School of Applied Sciences Overseas Scholarships 254

Australia

Dunlop Asia Fellowships 115
Our World-Underwater Scholarship Society Scholarships 518
School of Applied Sciences Overseas Scholarships 254

Canada

International Postgraduate Research Scholarships (IPRS) 413
JCCA Graduate Education Scholarship 400
School of Applied Sciences Overseas Scholarships 254

Caribbean Countries

International Postgraduate Research Scholarships (IPRS) 413
School of Applied Sciences Overseas Scholarships 254

East European Countries

International Postgraduate Research Scholarships (IPRS) 413
School of Applied Sciences Overseas Scholarships 254

European Union

Our World-Underwater Scholarship Society Scholarships 518
The University of Glamorgan Sports Scholarships 693

Middle East

International Postgraduate Research Scholarships (IPRS) 413
School of Applied Sciences Overseas Scholarships 254

New Zealand

Fish & Game New Zealand Research Scholarships 500
Our World-Underwater Scholarship Society Scholarships 518
School of Applied Sciences Overseas Scholarships 254

South Africa

International Postgraduate Research Scholarships (IPRS) 413
School of Applied Sciences Overseas Scholarships 254

United Kingdom

Aberystwyth Postgraduate Research Studentships 4
International Postgraduate Research Scholarships (IPRS) 413
Mr and Mrs David Edward Memorial Award 145
The University of Glamorgan Sports Scholarships 693

United States of America

British Marshall Scholarships 685
Congress Bundestag Youth Exchange for Young Professionals 221
International Postgraduate Research Scholarships (IPRS) 413
JCCA Graduate Education Scholarship 400
Our World-Underwater Scholarship Society Scholarships 518
School of Applied Sciences Overseas Scholarships 254

West European Countries

International Postgraduate Research Scholarships (IPRS) 413
Mr and Mrs David Edward Memorial Award 145

SOCIOLOGY OF SPORTS

African Nations

International Postgraduate Research Scholarships (IPRS) 413

Australia

Our World-Underwater Scholarship Society Scholarships 518

Canada

International Postgraduate Research Scholarships (IPRS) 413
JCCA Graduate Education Scholarship 400

Caribbean Countries

International Postgraduate Research Scholarships (IPRS) 413

East European Countries

International Postgraduate Research Scholarships (IPRS) 413

European Union

ESRC 1+3 Awards and +3 Awards
Our World-Underwater Scholarship Society Scholarships 518

Middle East

International Postgraduate Research Scholarships (IPRS) 413

New Zealand

Our World-Underwater Scholarship Society Scholarships 518

South Africa

International Postgraduate Research Scholarships (IPRS) 413

United Kingdom

Aberystwyth Postgraduate Research Studentships 4
ESRC 1+3 Awards and +3 Awards
International Postgraduate Research Scholarships (IPRS) 413
Mr and Mrs David Edward Memorial Award 145

United States of America

British Marshall Scholarships 685
International Postgraduate Research Scholarships (IPRS) 413
JCCA Graduate Education Scholarship 400
Our World-Underwater Scholarship Society Scholarships 518

West European Countries

ESRC 1+3 Awards and +3 Awards
International Postgraduate Research Scholarships (IPRS) 413
Mr and Mrs David Edward Memorial Award 145

Australia

AAH Humanities Travelling Fellowships 132
Fulbright Postgraduate Awards 140
Hastings Center International Visiting Scholars Program 332
Wingate Scholarships 697

Canada

J W McConnell Memorial Fellowships 243
Killam Research Fellowships 199
Ministry Fellowship 308
North American Doctoral Fellowship 308
SSHRC Doctoral Awards 602
SSHRC Standard Research Grants 603
Vatican Film Library Mellon Fellowship 785
Wingate Scholarships 697

Caribbean Countries

Hastings Center International Visiting Scholars Program 332

East European Countries

Andrew W Mellon Foundation East-Central European Fellowships in
the Humanities 362
Hastings Center International Visiting Scholars Program 332
Mellon Postdoctoral Fellowships In Turkey For East European
Scholars 81

European Union

AHRC Doctoral Awards Scheme 109
All Saints Educational Trust Personal Scholarships 20
CBRL Travel Grant 248
Professional Preparation Master's Scheme
Research Preparation Master's Scheme
Wingate Scholarships 697

Middle East

Hastings Center International Visiting Scholars Program 332

New Zealand

Hastings Center International Visiting Scholars Program 332
Wingate Scholarships 697

South Africa

Hastings Center International Visiting Scholars Program 332
Wingate Scholarships 697

United Kingdom

AHRC Doctoral Awards Scheme 109
All Saints Educational Trust Corporate Awards 20
All Saints Educational Trust Personal Scholarships 20
Balsdon Fellowship 174
BIAA Travel Grants 168
CBRL Research Award 248
CBRL Travel Grant 248
Frank Knox Fellowships at Harvard University 302
Hastings Center International Visiting Scholars Program 332
Kennedy Scholarships 409
Mr and Mrs David Edward Memorial Award 145
Professional Preparation Master's Scheme
Research Preparation Master's Scheme
Rome Awards 175
Rome Fellowship 175
Rome Scholarships in Ancient, Medieval and Later Italian Studies 176
Wingate Scholarships 697

United States of America

Dissertation Fellowship for African Americans 308
Doctoral Fellowship for African-Americans 308
Ford Foundation Dissertation Fellowships for Minorities 487
Fulbright Senior Specialists Program 249
Kennan Institute Research Scholarship 408
Ministry Fellowship 308
NEH ARIT-National Endowment for the Humanities Fellowships for
Research in Turkey 81

North American Doctoral Fellowship 308
SSRC JSPS Postdoctoral Fellowship 599
Vatican Film Library Mellon Fellowship 785

West European Countries

Hastings Center International Visiting Scholars Program 332
Mr and Mrs David Edward Memorial Award 145

RELIGIOUS STUDIES

Any Country

Ahmanson and Getty Postdoctoral Fellowships 639
ASECS (American Society for 18th-Century Studies)/Clark Library
Fellowships 639
BIAA Post-Doctoral Research Fellowship 168
BIAA Research Scholarship 168
BIAA Study Grants 168
BIAA/SPHS Fieldwork Award 168
British Academy Overseas Conference Grants 158
British Academy Postdoctoral Fellowships 158
British Academy Research Development Awards (BARDAs) 158
British Academy Small Research Grants 158
Clark Library Short-Term Resident Fellowships 639
Clark Predoctoral Fellowships 639
Clark-Huntington Joint Bibliographical Fellowship 640
CRF (Caledonian Research Foundation)/RSE European Visiting
Research Fellowships 628
Delahaye Memorial Benefaction 768
Faculty Studentships 694
Findel Scholarships and Schneider Scholarships 340
Frederick Douglass Institute Postdoctoral Fellowship 304
Frederick Douglass Institute Predoctoral Dissertation Fellowship 304
Helen McCormack Turner Memorial Scholarship 768
Herbert Hughes Scholarship 768
Institute of European History Fellowships 366
M Alison Frantz Fellowship in Post-Classical Studies at the Gennadius
Library 83
Mary Radcliffe Scholarship 768
NEH Fellowships 83
RHYS Curzon-Jones Scholarship 768
Ridley Lewis Bursary 769
SOAS Open Scholarship 583
SOAS Research Student Fellowships 583
USIP Annual Grant Competition 643
USIP Priority Grant-making Competition 644
Victoria University of Wellington PhD Scholarships 786
W D Llewelyn Memorial Benefaction 769

African Nations

IDRC Evaluation Research Awards 381
ORISHA (Oxford Research in the Scholarship and Humanities of
Africa) Studentship 736

Australia

AAH Humanities Travelling Fellowships 132
Wingate Scholarships 697

Canada

Bishop Thomas Hoyt Jr Fellowship 238
IDRC Evaluation Research Awards 381
Ministry Fellowship 308
North American Doctoral Fellowship 308
Wingate Scholarships 697

Caribbean Countries

IDRC Evaluation Research Awards 381

East European Countries

IDRC Evaluation Research Awards 381

European Union

AHRC Doctoral Awards Scheme 109
All Saints Educational Trust Personal Scholarships 20

CBRL Travel Grant 248
Professional Preparation Master's Scheme
Research Preparation Master's Scheme
Wingate Scholarships 697

Middle East

IDRC Evaluation Research Awards 381

New Zealand

Wingate Scholarships 697

South Africa

IDRC Evaluation Research Awards 381
Wingate Scholarships 697

United Kingdom

AHRC Doctoral Awards Scheme 109
All Saints Educational Trust Personal Scholarships 20
Balsdon Fellowship 174
BIAA/SPBS Fieldwork Award 168
CBRL Research Award 248
CBRL Travel Grant 248
Mr and Mrs David Edward Memorial Award 145
Professional Preparation Master's Scheme
Research Preparation Master's Scheme
Rome Awards 175
Rome Fellowship 175
Rome Scholarships in Ancient, Medieval and Later Italian Studies 176
University of Kent School of European Culture and Languages Scholarships 701
University of Kent School of European Culture and Languages Studentships 701
Wingate Scholarships 697

United States of America

ARCE Fellowships 80
Bishop Thomas Hoyt Jr Fellowship 238
Dissertation Fellowship for African Americans 308
Doctoral Fellowship for African-Americans 308
Fulbright Senior Specialists Program 249
Ministry Fellowship 308
North American Doctoral Fellowship 308
SSRC JSPS Postdoctoral Fellowship 599

West European Countries

Mr and Mrs David Edward Memorial Award 145
University of Kent School of European Culture and Languages Scholarships 701
University of Kent School of European Culture and Languages Studentships 701

CHRISTIAN

Any Country

Ahmanson and Getty Postdoctoral Fellowships 639
ASCSA Advanced Fellowships 82
ASECS (American Society for 18th-Century Studies)/Clark Library Fellowships 639
BIAA Post-Doctoral Research Fellowship 168
BIAA Research Scholarship 168
BIAA Study Grants 168
Clark Library Short-Term Resident Fellowships 639
Clark Predoctoral Fellowships 639
Clark-Huntington Joint Bibliographical Fellowship 640
Louisville Institute Dissertation Fellowship Program 428
M Alison Frantz Fellowship in Post-Classical Studies at the Gennadius Library 83
NEH Fellowships 83
United States Holocaust Memorial Museum Center for Advanced Holocaust Studies Visiting Scholar Programs 641

Australia

Wingate Scholarships 697

Canada

Wingate Scholarships 697

European Union

AHRC Doctoral Awards Scheme 109
All Saints Educational Trust Personal Scholarships 20
PhD Studentships 107
Professional Preparation Master's Scheme
Research Preparation Master's Scheme
Wingate Scholarships 697

New Zealand

Wingate Scholarships 697

South Africa

Wingate Scholarships 697

United Kingdom

AHRC Doctoral Awards Scheme 109
All Saints Educational Trust Personal Scholarships 20
Mr and Mrs David Edward Memorial Award 145
PhD Studentships 107
Professional Preparation Master's Scheme
Research Preparation Master's Scheme
University of Kent School of European Culture and Languages Scholarships 701
University of Kent School of European Culture and Languages Studentships 701
Wingate Scholarships 697

United States of America

Verne Catt McDowell Corporation Scholarship 785

West European Countries

Mr and Mrs David Edward Memorial Award 145
PhD Studentships 107
University of Kent School of European Culture and Languages Scholarships 701
University of Kent School of European Culture and Languages Studentships 701

JEWISH

Any Country

Ahmanson and Getty Postdoctoral Fellowships 639
ASCSA Advanced Fellowships 82
ASECS (American Society for 18th-Century Studies)/Clark Library Fellowships 639
Bernard and Audre Rapoport Fellowships 431
BIAA Post-Doctoral Research Fellowship 168
BIAA Research Scholarship 168
BIAA Study Grants 168
Clark Library Short-Term Resident Fellowships 639
Clark Predoctoral Fellowships 639
Clark-Huntington Joint Bibliographical Fellowship 640
Delahaye Memorial Benefaction 768
Ethel Marcus Memorial Fellowship 431
Helen McCormack Turner Memorial Scholarship 768
Herbert Hughes Scholarship 768
IAUW International Scholarship 166
Jacob Hirsch Fellowship 83
The Joseph and Eva R Dave Fellowship 432
Loewenstein-Wiener Fellowship Awards 432
M Alison Frantz Fellowship in Post-Classical Studies at the Gennadius Library 83
Marguerite R Jacobs Memorial Award 432
Mary Radcliffe Scholarship 768
Memorial Foundation for Jewish Culture International Doctoral Scholarships 443

Memorial Foundation for Jewish Culture International Fellowships in Jewish Studies 444

Memorial Foundation for Jewish Culture International Scholarship Programme for Community Service 444

Memorial Foundation for Jewish Culture Scholarships for Post-Rabbinical Students 444

The Natalie Feld Memorial Fellowship 432

NEH Fellowships 83

The Rabbi Harold D Hahn Memorial Fellowship 432

The Rabbi Joachin Prinz Memorial Fellowship 432

Rabbi Levi A Olan Memorial Fellowship 433

Rabbi Theodore S Levy Tribute Fellowship 433

RHYS Curzon-Jones Scholarship 768

Ridley Lewis Bursary 769

SOAS Bursary 583

SOAS Open Scholarship 583

Starkoff Fellowship 433

United States Holocaust Memorial Museum Center for Advanced Holocaust Studies Visiting Scholar Programs 641

W D Llewelyn Memorial Benefaction 769

Australia

Wingate Scholarships 697

Canada

JCCA Graduate Education Scholarship 400

Wingate Scholarships 697

European Union

AHRC Doctoral Awards Scheme 109

PhD Studentships 107

Professional Preparation Master's Scheme

Research Preparation Master's Scheme

Wingate Scholarships 697

New Zealand

Wingate Scholarships 697

South Africa

Wingate Scholarships 697

United Kingdom

AHRC Doctoral Awards Scheme 109

Mr and Mrs David Edward Memorial Award 145

PhD Studentships 107

Professional Preparation Master's Scheme

Research Preparation Master's Scheme

Wingate Scholarships 697

United States of America

JCCA Graduate Education Scholarship 400

Maurice and Marilyn Cohen Fund for Doctoral Dissertation Fellowships in Jewish Studies 301

West European Countries

Mr and Mrs David Edward Memorial Award 145

PhD Studentships 107

ISLAM

Any Country

Ahmanson and Getty Postdoctoral Fellowships 639

ASCSA Advanced Fellowships 82

BIAA Post-Doctoral Research Fellowship 168

BIAA Research Scholarship 168

BIAA Study Grants 168

Delahaye Memorial Benefaction 768

Helen McCormack Turner Memorial Scholarship 768

Herbert Hughes Scholarship 768

M Alison Frantz Fellowship in Post-Classical Studies at the Gennadius Library 83

Mary Radcliffe Scholarship 768

NEH Fellowships 83

RHYS Curzon-Jones Scholarship 768

Ridley Lewis Bursary 769

SOAS Bursary 583

SOAS Open Scholarship 583

W D Llewelyn Memorial Benefaction 769

Australia

Wingate Scholarships 697

Canada

Wingate Scholarships 697

European Union

AHRC Doctoral Awards Scheme 109

PhD Studentships 107

Professional Preparation Master's Scheme

Research Preparation Master's Scheme

Wingate Scholarships 697

New Zealand

Wingate Scholarships 697

South Africa

Wingate Scholarships 697

United Kingdom

AHRC Doctoral Awards Scheme 109

PhD Studentships 107

Professional Preparation Master's Scheme

Research Preparation Master's Scheme

Wingate Scholarships 697

United States of America

ARCE Fellowships 80

West European Countries

PhD Studentships 107

ASIAN RELIGIOUS STUDIES

Any Country

Ahmanson and Getty Postdoctoral Fellowships 639

BIAA Post-Doctoral Research Fellowship 168

BIAA Research Scholarship 168

BIAA Study Grants 168

SOAS Bursary 583

SOAS Open Scholarship 583

Australia

Wingate Scholarships 697

Canada

Wingate Scholarships 697

European Union

AHRC Doctoral Awards Scheme 109

Professional Preparation Master's Scheme

Research Preparation Master's Scheme

Wingate Scholarships 697

New Zealand

Wingate Scholarships 697

South Africa

Wingate Scholarships 697

United Kingdom

AHRC Doctoral Awards Scheme 109

Professional Preparation Master's Scheme

Research Preparation Master's Scheme

University of Kent School of European Culture and Languages
  Scholarships 701
University of Kent School of European Culture and Languages
  Studentships 701
Wingate Scholarships 697

United States of America

SSRC JSPS Postdoctoral Fellowship 599

West European Countries

University of Kent School of European Culture and Languages
  Scholarships 701
University of Kent School of European Culture and Languages
  Studentships 701

AGNOSTICISM AND ATHEISM

Any Country

BIAA Post-Doctoral Research Fellowship 168
BIAA Research Scholarship 168
BIAA Study Grants 168

Australia

Wingate Scholarships 697

Canada

Wingate Scholarships 697

European Union

AHRC Doctoral Awards Scheme 109
Professional Preparation Master's Scheme
Research Preparation Master's Scheme
Wingate Scholarships 697

New Zealand

Wingate Scholarships 697

South Africa

Wingate Scholarships 697

United Kingdom

AHRC Doctoral Awards Scheme 109
Professional Preparation Master's Scheme
Research Preparation Master's Scheme
Wingate Scholarships 697

ANCIENT RELIGIONS

Any Country

ASCSA Advanced Fellowships 82
ASCSA Fellowships 82
BIAA Post-Doctoral Research Fellowship 168
BIAA Research Scholarship 168
BIAA Study Grants 168
Hugh Last and Donald Atkinson Funds Committee Grants 604
Jacob Hirsch Fellowship 83
M Alison Frantz Fellowship in Post-Classical Studies at the Gennadius
  Library 83
Mary Isabel Sibley Fellowship 531
NEH Fellowships 83
SOAS Bursary 583

Australia

Wingate Scholarships 697

Canada

Wingate Scholarships 697

European Union

AHRC Doctoral Awards Scheme 109
Professional Preparation Master's Scheme

Research Preparation Master's Scheme
Wingate Scholarships 697

New Zealand

Wingate Scholarships 697

South Africa

Wingate Scholarships 697

United Kingdom

AHRC Doctoral Awards Scheme 109
Hector and Elizabeth Catling Bursary 173
Professional Preparation Master's Scheme
Research Preparation Master's Scheme
Wingate Scholarships 697

United States of America

ARCE Fellowships 80

RELIGIOUS EDUCATION

Any Country

BIAA Post-Doctoral Research Fellowship 168
BIAA Research Scholarship 168
BIAA Study Grants 168
Dempster Fellowship 309
Faculty Studentships 694

African Nations

International Postgraduate Research Scholarships (IPRS) 413

Canada

International Postgraduate Research Scholarships (IPRS) 413
Ministry Fellowship 308
North American Doctoral Fellowship 308

Caribbean Countries

International Postgraduate Research Scholarships (IPRS) 413

East European Countries

International Postgraduate Research Scholarships (IPRS) 413

European Union

All Saints Educational Trust Personal Scholarships 20
CBRL Travel Grant 248

Middle East

International Postgraduate Research Scholarships (IPRS) 413

South Africa

International Postgraduate Research Scholarships (IPRS) 413

United Kingdom

All Saints Educational Trust Personal Scholarships 20
CBRL Research Award 248
CBRL Travel Grant 248
International Postgraduate Research Scholarships (IPRS) 413
Mr and Mrs David Edward Memorial Award 145
University of Kent School of European Culture and Languages
  Scholarships 701
University of Kent School of European Culture and Languages
  Studentships 701

United States of America

Dissertation Fellowship for African Americans 308
Doctoral Fellowship for African-Americans 308
International Postgraduate Research Scholarships (IPRS) 413
Ministry Fellowship 308
North American Doctoral Fellowship 308

West European Countries

International Postgraduate Research Scholarships (IPRS) 413
Mr and Mrs David Edward Memorial Award 145
University of Kent School of European Culture and Languages
    Scholarships 701
University of Kent School of European Culture and Languages
    Studentships 701

HOLY WRITINGS

Any Country

BIAA Post-Doctoral Research Fellowship 168
BIAA Research Scholarship 168
BIAA Study Grants 168
SOAS Bursary 583
SOAS Research Student Fellowships 583

Australia

AAH Humanities Travelling Fellowships 132
Wingate Scholarships 697

Canada

Wingate Scholarships 697

European Union

AHRC Doctoral Awards Scheme 109
CBRL Travel Grant 248
Professional Preparation Master's Scheme
Research Preparation Master's Scheme
Wingate Scholarships 697

New Zealand

Wingate Scholarships 697

South Africa

Wingate Scholarships 697

United Kingdom

AHRC Doctoral Awards Scheme 109
CBRL Research Award 248
CBRL Travel Grant 248
Professional Preparation Master's Scheme
Research Preparation Master's Scheme
Wingate Scholarships 697

United States of America

ARCE Fellowships 80

RELIGIOUS PRACTICE

Any Country

SOAS Bursary 583
SOAS Research Student Fellowships 583

Canada

Ministry Fellowship 308

European Union

AHRC Doctoral Awards Scheme 109
CBRL Travel Grant 248
Professional Preparation Master's Scheme
Research Preparation Master's Scheme

United Kingdom

AHRC Doctoral Awards Scheme 109
CBRL Research Award 248
CBRL Travel Grant 248
Mr and Mrs David Edward Memorial Award 145
Professional Preparation Master's Scheme

Research Preparation Master's Scheme
University of Kent School of European Culture and Languages
    Scholarships 701
University of Kent School of European Culture and Languages
    Studentships 701

United States of America

Ministry Fellowship 308

West European Countries

Mr and Mrs David Edward Memorial Award 145
University of Kent School of European Culture and Languages
    Scholarships 701
University of Kent School of European Culture and Languages
    Studentships 701

CHURCH ADMINISTRATION (PASTORAL WORK)

Canada

Ministry Fellowship 308

European Union

AHRC Doctoral Awards Scheme 109
CBRL Travel Grant 248
Professional Preparation Master's Scheme
Research Preparation Master's Scheme

United Kingdom

AHRC Doctoral Awards Scheme 109
CBRL Research Award 248
CBRL Travel Grant 248
Hilda Martindale Exhibitions 341
Mr and Mrs David Edward Memorial Award 145
Professional Preparation Master's Scheme
Research Preparation Master's Scheme

United States of America

Arne Administrative Leadership Scholarship 800
Ministry Fellowship 308
Verne Catt McDowell Corporation Scholarship 785

West European Countries

Mr and Mrs David Edward Memorial Award 145

THEOLOGICAL STUDIES

Any Country

BIAA Research Scholarship 168
BIAA Study Grants 168
British Academy Overseas Conference Grants 158
British Academy Small Research Grants 158
Delahaye Memorial Benefaction 768
Essex Rotary University Travel Grants 687
Faculty Studentships 694
Findel Scholarships and Schneider Scholarships 340
Helen McCormack Turner Memorial Scholarship 768
Herbert Hughes Scholarship 768
Institute of European History Fellowships 366
M Alison Frantz Fellowship in Post-Classical Studies at the Gennadius
    Library 83
Mary Radcliffe Scholarship 768
RHYS Curzon-Jones Scholarship 768
Ridley Lewis Bursary 769
University of Bristol Postgraduate Scholarships 672
W D Llewelyn Memorial Benefaction 769
William Honyman Gillespie Scholarships 796

African Nations

ORSAS Awards 688

Australia

AAH Humanities Travelling Fellowships 132
ORSAS Awards 688
Wingate Scholarships 697

Canada

Ministry Fellowship 308
North American Doctoral Fellowship 308
ORSAS Awards 688
Wingate Scholarships 697

Caribbean Countries

ORSAS Awards 688

East European Countries

ORSAS Awards 688

European Union

AHRC Doctoral Awards Scheme 109
CBRL Travel Grant 248
Professional Preparation Master's Scheme
Research Preparation Master's Scheme
Wingate Scholarships 697

Middle East

ORSAS Awards 688

New Zealand

ORSAS Awards 688
Wingate Scholarships 697

South Africa

ORSAS Awards 688
Wingate Scholarships 697

United Kingdom

Access to Learning Fund 685
AHRC Doctoral Awards Scheme 109
CBRL Research Award 248
CBRL Travel Grant 248
Hector and Elizabeth Catling Bursary 173
Hilda Martindale Exhibitions 341
Mr and Mrs David Edward Memorial Award 145
Professional Preparation Master's Scheme
Research Preparation Master's Scheme
University of Kent School of European Culture and
  Languages Scholarships 701
University of Kent School of European Culture and Languages
  Studentships 701
Wingate Scholarships 697

United States of America

ASOR W.F. Albright Institute of Archaeological Research/
  National Endowment of the Humanities Fellowships
  84
Chilstrom Scholarship for Ordained Ministry 800
Dissertation Fellowship for African Americans
  308
Doctoral Fellowship for African-Americans 308
ELCA Educational Grant Program 288
Ministry Fellowship 308
North American Doctoral Fellowship 308
ORSAS Awards 688

West European Countries

Mr and Mrs David Edward Memorial Award 145
University of Kent School of European Culture and Languages
  Scholarships 701
University of Kent School of European Culture and Languages
  Studentships 701

COMPARATIVE RELIGION

Any Country

Ahmanson and Getty Postdoctoral Fellowships 639
ASECS (American Society for 18th-Century Studies)/Clark Library
  Fellowships 639
BIAA Post-Doctoral Research Fellowship 168
BIAA Research Scholarship 168
BIAA Study Grants 168
British Academy Overseas Conference Grants 158
British Academy Small Research Grants 158
Camargo Fellowships 182
Clark Library Short-Term Resident Fellowships 639
Clark Predoctoral Fellowships 639
Clark-Huntington Joint Bibliographical Fellowship
  640
Delahaye Memorial Benefaction 768
Faculty Studentships 694
Findel Scholarships and Schneider Scholarships
  340
Helen McCormack Turner Memorial Scholarship
  768
Herbert Hughes Scholarship 768
Institute of European History Fellowships 366
M Alison Frantz Fellowship in Post-Classical Studies at the Gennadius
  Library 83
Mary Isabel Sibley Fellowship 531
Mary Radcliffe Scholarship 768
RHYS Curzon-Jones Scholarship 768
Ridley Lewis Bursary 769
SOAS Bursary 583
SOAS Research Student Fellowships 583
University of Bristol Postgraduate Scholarships 672
Victoria University of Wellington PhD Scholarships
  786
W D Llewelyn Memorial Benefaction 769

Australia

AAH Humanities Travelling Fellowships 132
Wingate Scholarships 697

Canada

Wingate Scholarships 697

European Union

AHRC Doctoral Awards Scheme 109
CBRL Travel Grant 248
Professional Preparation Master's Scheme
Research Preparation Master's Scheme
Wingate Scholarships 697

New Zealand

Wingate Scholarships 697

South Africa

Wingate Scholarships 697

United Kingdom

AHRC Doctoral Awards Scheme 109
CBRL Research Award 248
CBRL Travel Grant 248
Mr and Mrs David Edward Memorial Award 145
Professional Preparation Master's Scheme
Research Preparation Master's Scheme
Wingate Scholarships 697

United States of America

SSRC JSPS Postdoctoral Fellowship 599

West European Countries

Mr and Mrs David Edward Memorial Award 145

SOCIOLOGY OF RELIGION

Any Country

Ahmanson and Getty Postdoctoral Fellowships 639
ASECS (American Society for 18th-Century Studies)/Clark Library
    Fellowships 639
BIAA Post-Doctoral Research Fellowship 168
BIAA Research Scholarship 168
BIAA Study Grants 168
British Academy Overseas Conference Grants 158
British Academy Small Research Grants 158
Camargo Fellowships 182
Clark Library Short-Term Resident Fellowships 639
Clark Predoctoral Fellowships 639
Clark-Huntington Joint Bibliographical Fellowship 640
Delahaye Memorial Benefaction 768
Findel Scholarships and Schneider Scholarships 340
Helen McCormack Turner Memorial Scholarship 768
Herbert Hughes Scholarship 768
M Alison Frantz Fellowship in Post-Classical Studies at the Gennadius
    Library 83
Mary Radcliffe Scholarship 768
NEH Fellowships 83
RHYS Curzon-Jones Scholarship 768
Ridley Lewis Bursary 769
SOAS Bursary 583
SOAS Research Student Fellowships 583
University of Bristol Postgraduate Scholarships 672
Victoria University of Wellington PhD Scholarships 786
W D Llewelyn Memorial Benefaction 769

African Nations

IDRC Evaluation Research Awards 381

Australia

AAH Humanities Travelling Fellowships 132
Wingate Scholarships 697

Canada

IDRC Evaluation Research Awards 381
Wingate Scholarships 697

Caribbean Countries

IDRC Evaluation Research Awards 381

East European Countries

IDRC Evaluation Research Awards 381

European Union

AHRC Doctoral Awards Scheme 109
CBRL Travel Grant 248
Wingate Scholarships 697

Middle East

IDRC Evaluation Research Awards 381

New Zealand

Wingate Scholarships 697

South Africa

IDRC Evaluation Research Awards 381
Wingate Scholarships 697

United Kingdom

AHRC Doctoral Awards Scheme 109
CBRL Research Award 248
CBRL Travel Grant 248
Mr and Mrs David Edward Memorial Award 145
University of Kent School of European Culture and Languages
    Scholarships 701
University of Kent School of European Culture and Languages
    Studentships 701
Wingate Scholarships 697

United States of America

British Marshall Scholarships 685
Fulbright Senior Specialists Program 249
SSRC JSPS Postdoctoral Fellowship 599

West European Countries

Mr and Mrs David Edward Memorial Award 145
University of Kent School of European Culture and Languages
    Scholarships 701
University of Kent School of European Culture and Languages
    Studentships 701

HISTORY OF RELIGION

Any Country

Ahmanson and Getty Postdoctoral Fellowships 639
Albert J Beveridge Grant 58
ASCSA Fellowships 82
ASECS (American Society for 18th-Century Studies)/Clark Library
    Fellowships 639
Bernadotte E Schmitt Grants 58
BIAA Post-Doctoral Research Fellowship 168
BIAA Research Scholarship 168
BIAA Study Grants 168
British Academy Overseas Conference Grants 158
British Academy Research Development Awards (BARDAs) 158
British Academy Small Research Grants 158
Camargo Fellowships 182
Clark Library Short-Term Resident Fellowships 639
Clark-Huntington Joint Bibliographical Fellowship 640
Delahaye Memorial Benefaction 768
Earthwatch Field Research Grants 272
Findel Scholarships and Schneider Scholarships 340
Helen McCormack Turner Memorial Scholarship 768
Herbert Hughes Scholarship 768
Institute of European History Fellowships 366
M Alison Frantz Fellowship in Post-Classical Studies at the Gennadius
    Library 83
Mary Radcliffe Scholarship 768
NEH Fellowships 83
Queen Mary Research Studentships 539
RHYS Curzon-Jones Scholarship 768
Ridley Lewis Bursary 769
SOAS Bursary 583
SOAS Research Student Fellowships 583
University of Bristol Postgraduate Scholarships 672
Victoria University of Wellington PhD Scholarships 786
W D Llewelyn Memorial Benefaction 769

Australia

AAH Humanities Travelling Fellowships 132
Wingate Scholarships 697

Canada

Wingate Scholarships 697

European Union

AHRC Doctoral Awards Scheme 109
CBRL Travel Grant 248
Professional Preparation Master's Scheme
Research Preparation Master's Scheme
Wingate Scholarships 697

New Zealand

Wingate Scholarships 697

South Africa

Wingate Scholarships 697

United Kingdom

AHRC Doctoral Awards Scheme 109
CBRL Research Award 248

CBRL Travel Grant 248
Mr and Mrs David Edward Memorial Award 145
Professional Preparation Master's Scheme
Research Preparation Master's Scheme
Wingate Scholarships 697

United States of America

British Marshall Scholarships 685
Fritz Stern Dissertation Prize 313
SSRC JSPS Postdoctoral Fellowship 599
Thyssen-Heideking Fellowship 314

West European Countries

Kade-Heideking Fellowship 313
Mr and Mrs David Edward Memorial Award 145

ESOTERIC PRACTICES

Any Country

BIAA Research Scholarship 168
CRF (Caledonian Research Foundation)/RSE European Visiting
    Research Fellowships 628

European Union

CBRL Travel Grant 248

United Kingdom

CBRL Research Award 248
CBRL Travel Grant 248
University of Kent School of European Culture and Languages
    Scholarships 701
University of Kent School of European Culture and Languages
    Studentships 701

United States of America

SSRC JSPS Postdoctoral Fellowship 599

West European Countries

University of Kent School of European Culture and Languages
    Scholarships 701
University of Kent School of European Culture and Languages
    Studentships 701

SERVICE TRADES

GENERAL

Any Country

Field Psych Trust Grant 291

African Nations

International Postgraduate Research Scholarships (IPRS) 413
NUFFIC-NFP Fellowships for Master's Degree Programmes 496

Australia

Fulbright Postdoctoral Fellowships 140

Canada

International Postgraduate Research Scholarships (IPRS) 413

Caribbean Countries

International Postgraduate Research Scholarships (IPRS) 413

East European Countries

International Postgraduate Research Scholarships (IPRS) 413

Middle East

International Postgraduate Research Scholarships (IPRS) 413
NUFFIC-NFP Fellowships for Master's Degree Programmes 496

South Africa

International Postgraduate Research Scholarships (IPRS) 413
NUFFIC-NFP Fellowships for Master's Degree Programmes 496

United Kingdom

Hilda Martindale Exhibitions 341
International Postgraduate Research Scholarships (IPRS) 413
Postgraduate Student Allowance Scheme (PSAS) (Queen Margaret)
    539

United States of America

Congress Bundestag Youth Exchange for Young Professionals 221
International Postgraduate Research Scholarships (IPRS) 413

West European Countries

International Postgraduate Research Scholarships (IPRS) 413
Janson Johan Helmich Scholarships and Travel Grants 398

HOTEL AND RESTAURANT

Any Country

The Julia Child Endowment Fund Scholarship 257

African Nations

International Postgraduate Research Scholarships (IPRS) 413

Australia

BMHS Hospitality and Tourism Management Scholarship 154
Le Cordon Bleu Master of Arts in Gastronomy Scholarship 415
Le Cordon Bleu Master of Business Administration Scholarship. 416

Canada

International Postgraduate Research Scholarships (IPRS) 413

Caribbean Countries

International Postgraduate Research Scholarships (IPRS) 413

East European Countries

International Postgraduate Research Scholarships (IPRS) 413

Middle East

International Postgraduate Research Scholarships (IPRS) 413

South Africa

International Postgraduate Research Scholarships (IPRS) 413

United Kingdom

International Postgraduate Research Scholarships (IPRS) 413

United States of America

Congress Bundestag Youth Exchange for Young Professionals 221
International Postgraduate Research Scholarships (IPRS) 413

West European Countries

International Postgraduate Research Scholarships (IPRS) 413

HOTEL MANAGEMENT

Any Country

The Julia Child Endowment Fund Scholarship 257
Savoy Educational Trust Scholarships 425

African Nations

International Postgraduate Research Scholarships (IPRS) 413

Australia

BMHS Hospitality and Tourism Management Scholarship 154
Le Cordon Bleu Master of Arts in Gastronomy Scholarship 415
Le Cordon Bleu Master of Business Administration Scholarship. 416

Canada

International Postgraduate Research Scholarships (IPRS) 413

Caribbean Countries

International Postgraduate Research Scholarships (IPRS) 413

East European Countries

International Postgraduate Research Scholarships (IPRS) 413

Middle East

International Postgraduate Research Scholarships (IPRS) 413

South Africa

International Postgraduate Research Scholarships (IPRS) 413

United Kingdom

International Postgraduate Research Scholarships (IPRS) 413
John Mather Scholarship 760

United States of America

Congress Bundestag Youth Exchange for Young Professionals 221
International Postgraduate Research Scholarships (IPRS) 413

West European Countries

International Postgraduate Research Scholarships (IPRS) 413

COOKING AND CATERING

Any Country

James Beard Scholarship 397
James Beard Scholarship II 397
The Julia Child Endowment Fund Scholarship 257
Tante Marie's Cooking School Scholarship

Australia

Le Cordon Bleu Master of Arts in Gastronomy Scholarship 415
Le Cordon Bleu Master of Business Administration Scholarship. 416

United States of America

Charlie Trotter s Culinary Education Foundation Culinary Study Scholarship
Congress Bundestag Youth Exchange for Young Professionals 221
IDDBA Graduate Scholarships 379

RETAILING

African Nations

International Postgraduate Research Scholarships (IPRS) 413

Canada

International Postgraduate Research Scholarships (IPRS) 413

Caribbean Countries

International Postgraduate Research Scholarships (IPRS) 413

East European Countries

International Postgraduate Research Scholarships (IPRS) 413

Middle East

International Postgraduate Research Scholarships (IPRS) 413

South Africa

International Postgraduate Research Scholarships (IPRS) 413

United Kingdom

International Postgraduate Research Scholarships (IPRS) 413

United States of America

Congress Bundestag Youth Exchange for Young Professionals 221
International Postgraduate Research Scholarships (IPRS) 413

West European Countries

International Postgraduate Research Scholarships (IPRS) 413

TOURISM

Any Country

Healy Scholarship 94
Jacob's Pillow Intern Program
Savoy Educational Trust Scholarships 425
Tomsk Polytechnic University International Scholarship 634
Victoria University of Wellington PhD Scholarships 786

African Nations

IDRC Evaluation Research Awards 381
International Postgraduate Research Scholarships (IPRS) 413
NUFFIC-NFP Fellowships for Master's Degree Programmes 496

Australia

BMHS Hospitality and Tourism Management Scholarship 154

Canada

IDRC Evaluation Research Awards 381
International Postgraduate Research Scholarships (IPRS) 413

Caribbean Countries

IDRC Evaluation Research Awards 381
International Postgraduate Research Scholarships (IPRS) 413

East European Countries

IDRC Evaluation Research Awards 381
International Postgraduate Research Scholarships (IPRS) 413

Middle East

IDRC Evaluation Research Awards 381
International Postgraduate Research Scholarships (IPRS) 413
NUFFIC-NFP Fellowships for Master's Degree Programmes 496

South Africa

IDRC Evaluation Research Awards 381
International Postgraduate Research Scholarships (IPRS) 413
NUFFIC-NFP Fellowships for Master's Degree Programmes 496

United Kingdom

International Postgraduate Research Scholarships (IPRS) 413
John Mather Scholarship 760

United States of America

Congress Bundestag Youth Exchange for Young Professionals 221
International Postgraduate Research Scholarships (IPRS) 413
Southern California Chapter/Pleasant Hawaiian 95

West European Countries

International Postgraduate Research Scholarships (IPRS) 413

SOCIAL AND BEHAVIOURAL SCIENCES

GENERAL

Any Country

ACLS/Chiang Ching-kuo Foundation (CCK) New Perspectives on Chinese Culture and Society 48
The Airey Neave Trust Scholarship 12
AISLS Dissertation Planning Grant 60
Alberta Heritage Clinical Fellowships 12

African Nations

Ernest Hemingway Research Grants 405
ETS Summer Internship Program for Graduate Students 276
Fellowship for American College Students 545
Ford Foundation Dissertation Fellowships for Minorities 487
Foundation for Science and Disability Student Grant Fund 302
German Historical Institute Doctoral and Postdoctoral Fellowships 313
Guggenheim Fellowships to Assist Research and Artistic Creation (USA and Canada) 406
International Postgraduate Research Scholarships (IPRS) 413
International Postgraduate Research Scholarships (IPRS) 413
IREX Individual Advanced Research Opportunities 388
IREX Policy-Connect Collaborative Research Grants Program 388
IREX Short-Term Travel Grants 389
Kennan Institute Research Scholarship 408
Kennedy Research Grants 405
Marie Tharp Visiting Fellowships 239
North Dakota Indian Scholarship 507
Norwegian Thanksgiving Fund Scholarship 509
ONR Summer Faculty Research 84
ORSAS Awards 688
Sloan Industry Studies Fellowships 19
SSRC Abe Fellowship Program 598
SSRC Eurasia Program Postdoctoral Fellowships 598
SSRC Eurasia Title VIII Dissertation Write-Up Fellowships 598
SSRC JSPS Postdoctoral Fellowship 599

West European Countries

ESRC 1+3 Awards and +3 Awards
German Historical Institute Doctoral and Postdoctoral Fellowships 313
International Postgraduate Research Scholarships (IPRS) 413
International Postgraduate Research Scholarships (IPRS) 413
Lady Gregory Fellowship Scheme 490
Mr and Mrs David Edward Memorial Award 145
University of Kent School of Physical Sciences 701

ECONOMICS

Any Country

AIER Summer Fellowship 59
Alzheimer's Society Research Grants
Association for Women in Science Educational Foundation Predoctoral Awards 118
Balliol College: Marvin Bower Scholarship 719
BIAA Study Grants 168
Canadian Embassy Faculty Enrichment Program 205
CCAF Junior Research Fellowship 239
CRF (Caledonian Research Foundation)/RSE European Visiting Research Fellowships 628
Curtin Business School Doctoral Scholarship 258
Eli Ginzberg Award 344
Ernst Meyer Prize 376
Fernand Braudel Senior Fellowships 287
Gaitskell MSc Scholarship 651
Geneva Association 376
German Chancellor Fellowships for Prospective Leaders 17
Graduate Dissertation Research Fellowship 448
Graduate Institute of International Studies (HEI-Geneva) Scholarships 323
Graduate Summer Travel Grants 449
Hagley Museum and Library Grants-in-Aid of Research 329
Harry S Truman Library Institute Dissertation Year Fellowships 332
Houblon-Norman Fellowships/George Fellowships 346
IIASA Postdoctoral Program 384
Institute for Advanced Study Postdoctoral Residential Fellowships 363
International Association for the Study of Insurance Economics Research Grants 376
The James Lanner Memorial Scholarship 652
Jean Monnet Fellowships 288
Max Weber Fellowships 288
Minda de Gunzberg Graduate Dissertation Writing Fellowship 449
NAI Travel Scholarships for Research on Africa 506
Paul H. Nitze School of Advanced International Studies (SAIS) Financial Aid and Fellowships 155
Queen Mary Research Studentships 539

Rhodes University Postdoctoral Fellowship and The Andrew Mellon Postdoctoral Fellowship 548
Ricardo Scholarship 656
Russell Sage Foundation Visiting Scholar Appointments 578
S S Huebner Foundation for Insurance Education Predoctoral and Postdoctoral Fellowships 579
SAIIA Bradlow Fellowship 614
Shorenstein APARC Postdoctoral Research Fellowship in Korean Studies 586
SOAS Open Scholarship 583
Teaching Assistantships (Economics) 657
Teagasc Walsh Fellowships 626
Thank-Offering to Britain Fellowships 159
Tomsk Polytechnic University International Scholarship 634
University of Bristol Postgraduate Scholarships 672
University of Essex Scholarships 690
University of Kent Department of Economics Bursaries 699
University of Otago International Scholarships 717
University of Otago PhD Scholarships 718
University of Otago Prestigious PhD Scholarships 718
University of Southampton Postgraduate Studentships 759
Victoria University of Wellington PhD Scholarships 786
W M Gorman Graduate Research Scholarship 660
World Universities Network (WUN) International Research Mobility Scheme 759

African Nations

Canadian Window on International Development 380
IDRC Doctoral Research Awards 380
IDRC Internship Awards 381
International Postgraduate Research Scholarships (IPRS) 413
Museveni Scholarship 734
ORSAS Awards 688
Shell Centenary Chevening Scholarships for Postgraduate Study 196

Australia

ADB-Japan Scholarship Program 116
APA(I) – Innovation, Competition and Economic Performance 257
Australian Health Inequities Program Research Scholarship 292
Baillieu Research Scholarship 707
The Baillieu Research Scholarship 751
ORSAS Awards 688
Wingate Scholarships 697

Canada

Alcohol Beverage Medical Research Foundation Research Project Grant 14
Canadian Commonwealth Scholarship and Fellowship Plan 201
Canadian Home Economics Association (CHEA) Fellowship 206
Canadian Window on International Development 380
CIES Fellowship Program 273
Gilbert Chinard Fellowships 361
Harmon Chadbourn Rorison Fellowship 361
IDRC Doctoral Research Awards 380
IDRC Internship Awards 381
International Postgraduate Research Scholarships (IPRS) 413
ORSAS Awards 688
Public Safety and Emergency Preparedness Canada Research Fellowship in Honour of Stuart Nesbitt White 123
S S Huebner Foundation for Insurance Education Predoctoral and Postdoctoral Fellowships 579
Wingate Scholarships 697

Caribbean Countries

ADB-Japan Scholarship Program 116
Canadian Window on International Development 380
IDRC Doctoral Research Awards 380
IDRC Internship Awards 381
International Postgraduate Research Scholarships (IPRS) 413
ORSAS Awards 688

East European Countries

EUI Postgraduate Scholarships 287
German Chancellor Fellowships for Prospective Leaders 17

IDRC Doctoral Research Awards 380
International Postgraduate Research Scholarships (IPRS) 413
ORSAS Awards 688
Shell Centenary Cambridge Scholarships (Countries Outside of the
Commonwealth) 196

European Union

CBRL Travel Grant 248
Department of Economics 1 + 3 and + 3 Quota Awards and
Competition Awards
Economics - ESRC Quota Award 724
ESRC 1 + 3 Awards and + 3 Awards
EUI Postgraduate Scholarships 287
Wingate Scholarships 697

Middle East

EUI Postgraduate Scholarships 287
IDRC Doctoral Research Awards 380
IDRC Internship Awards 381
International Postgraduate Research Scholarships (IPRS) 413
ORSAS Awards 688
Shell Centenary Cambridge Scholarships (Countries Outside of the
Commonwealth) 196

New Zealand

APA(I) – Innovation, Competition and Economic Performance 257
Australian Health Inequities Program Research Scholarship 292
ORSAS Awards 688
Wingate Scholarships 697

South Africa

Canadian Window on International Development 380
IDRC Doctoral Research Awards 380
IDRC Internship Awards 381
International Postgraduate Research Scholarships (IPRS) 413
ORSAS Awards 688
SAIIA Konrad Adenauer Foundation Research Internship 615
Wingate Scholarships 697

United Kingdom

Aberystwyth Postgraduate Research Studentships 4
Access to Learning Fund 685
Balsdon Fellowship 174
CBRL Research Award 248
CBRL Travel Grant 248
Department of Economics 1 + 3 and + 3 Quota Awards and
Competition Awards
Economics - ESRC Quota Award 724
ESRC 1 + 3 Awards and + 3 Awards
EUI Postgraduate Scholarships 287
International Postgraduate Research Scholarships (IPRS) 413
John Mather Scholarship 760
Mr and Mrs David Edward Memorial Award 145
Rome Awards 175
Rome Fellowship 175
Rome Scholarships in Ancient, Medieval and Later Italian Studies 176
Wingate Scholarships 697

United States of America

Alcohol Beverage Medical Research Foundation Research Project
Grant 14
ARCE Fellowships 80
British Marshall Scholarships 685
CIA Graduate Studies Program Scholarship 225
Fellowship for American College Students 545
Fulbright Distinguished Chairs Program 248
Fulbright Senior Specialists Program 249
German Chancellor Fellowships for Prospective Leaders 17
Gilbert Chinard Fellowships 361
Harmon Chadbourn Rorison Fellowship 361
International Postgraduate Research Scholarships (IPRS) 413
IREX Individual Advanced Research Opportunities 388
IREX Short-Term Travel Grants 389
Kennedy Research Grants 405

NIH Research Grants 483
ORSAS Awards 688
Robert Bosch Foundation Fellowships 550
Sea Grant/NOAA Fisheries Fellowship 488
SSRC Abe Fellowship Program 598
SSRC JSPS Postdoctoral Fellowship 599
Washington University Chancellor's Graduate Fellowship Program
792

West European Countries

ESRC 1 + 3 Awards and + 3 Awards
EUI Postgraduate Scholarships 287
International Postgraduate Research Scholarships (IPRS) 413
Mr and Mrs David Edward Memorial Award 145

ECONOMIC HISTORY

Any Country

AIER Summer Fellowship 59
BIAA Study Grants 168
Camargo Fellowships 182
CRF (Caledonian Research Foundation)/RSE European Visiting
Research Fellowships 628
Findel Scholarships and Schneider Scholarships 340
Frederick Douglass Institute Postdoctoral Fellowship 304
Frederick Douglass Institute Predoctoral Dissertation Fellowship 304
Gordon Cain Fellowship 230
Graduate Dissertation Research Fellowship 448
Graduate Summer Travel Grants 449
Harry S Truman Library Institute Dissertation Year Fellowships 332
Herbert Hoover Presidential Library Association Travel Grants 338
IHS Summer Graduate Research Fellowship 363
Institute for Advanced Study Postdoctoral Residential Fellowships 363
Institute of European History Fellowships 366
Library Company of Philadelphia and Historical Society of
Pennsylvania Research Fellowships in American History and
Culture 422
Library Company of Philadelphia Dissertation Fellowships 422
Minda de Gunzberg Graduate Dissertation Writing Fellowship 449
Paul H. Nitze School of Advanced International Studies (SAIS)
Financial Aid and Fellowships 155
Queen Mary Research Studentships 539
Rhodes University Postdoctoral Fellowship and The Andrew Mellon
Postdoctoral Fellowship 548
Roosevelt Institute Research Grant 303
Russell Sage Foundation Visiting Scholar Appointments 578
SOAS Open Scholarship 583
University of Bristol Postgraduate Scholarships 672
University of Essex Scholarships 690
Victoria University of Wellington PhD Scholarships 786

African Nations

International Postgraduate Research Scholarships (IPRS) 413
ORSAS Awards 688

Australia

ORSAS Awards 688
Wingate Scholarships 697

Canada

International Postgraduate Research Scholarships (IPRS) 413
ORSAS Awards 688
Wingate Scholarships 697

Caribbean Countries

International Postgraduate Research Scholarships (IPRS) 413
ORSAS Awards 688

East European Countries

International Postgraduate Research Scholarships (IPRS) 413
ORSAS Awards 688

European Union

CBRL Travel Grant 248
Department of Economics 1 + 3 and + 3 Quota Awards and
    Competition Awards
ESRC 1 + 3 Awards and + 3 Awards
W B Crump Scholarship 705
Wingate Scholarships 697

Middle East

International Postgraduate Research Scholarships (IPRS) 413
ORSAS Awards 688

New Zealand

ORSAS Awards 688
Wingate Scholarships 697

South Africa

International Postgraduate Research Scholarships (IPRS) 413
ORSAS Awards 688
Wingate Scholarships 697

United Kingdom

Aberystwyth Postgraduate Research Studentships 4
Access to Learning Fund 685
BACS Travel Awards 160
Balsdon Fellowship 174
CBRL Research Award 248
CBRL Travel Grant 248
Department of Economics 1 + 3 and + 3 Quota Awards and
    Competition Awards
ESRC 1 + 3 Awards and + 3 Awards
International Postgraduate Research Scholarships (IPRS) 413
Mr and Mrs David Edward Memorial Award 145
Prix du Québec Award 160
Rome Awards 175
Rome Fellowship 175
Rome Scholarships in Ancient, Medieval and Later Italian Studies 176
W B Crump Scholarship 705
Wingate Scholarships 697

United States of America

ARCE Fellowships 80
British Marshall Scholarships 685
Fritz Stern Dissertation Prize 313
Fulbright Distinguished Chairs Program 248
Fulbright Senior Specialists Program 249
International Postgraduate Research Scholarships (IPRS) 413
ORSAS Awards 688
SSRC Abe Fellowship Program 598
SSRC JSPS Postdoctoral Fellowship 599
Thyssen-Heideking Fellowship 314

West European Countries

ESRC 1 + 3 Awards and + 3 Awards
International Postgraduate Research Scholarships (IPRS) 413
Kade-Heideking Fellowship 313
Mr and Mrs David Edward Memorial Award 145

ECONOMIC AND FINANCE POLICY

Any Country

BIAA Study Grants 168
Fernand Braudel Senior Fellowships 287
Harry S Truman Library Institute Dissertation Year Fellowships 332
Jean Monnet Fellowships 288
Max Weber Fellowships 288
Paul H. Nitze School of Advanced International Studies (SAIS)
    Financial Aid and Fellowships 155
Queen Mary Research Studentships 539
S S Huebner Foundation for Insurance Education Predoctoral and
    Postdoctoral Fellowships 579
University of Bristol Postgraduate Scholarships 672

University of Essex Scholarships 690
Victoria University of Wellington PhD Scholarships 786

African Nations

International Postgraduate Research Scholarships (IPRS) 413
ORSAS Awards 688

Australia

ORSAS Awards 688
Wingate Scholarships 697

Canada

International Postgraduate Research Scholarships (IPRS) 413
ORSAS Awards 688
S S Huebner Foundation for Insurance Education Predoctoral and
    Postdoctoral Fellowships 579
Wingate Scholarships 697

Caribbean Countries

International Postgraduate Research Scholarships (IPRS) 413
ORSAS Awards 688

East European Countries

EUI Postgraduate Scholarships 287
International Postgraduate Research Scholarships (IPRS) 413
ORSAS Awards 688

European Union

CBRL Travel Grant 248
Department of Economics 1 + 3 and + 3 Quota Awards and
    Competition Awards
ESRC 1 + 3 Awards and + 3 Awards
EUI Postgraduate Scholarships 287
Wingate Scholarships 697

Middle East

EUI Postgraduate Scholarships 287
International Postgraduate Research Scholarships (IPRS) 413
ORSAS Awards 688

New Zealand

ORSAS Awards 688
Wingate Scholarships 697

South Africa

International Postgraduate Research Scholarships (IPRS) 413
ORSAS Awards 688
Wingate Scholarships 697

United Kingdom

Aberystwyth Postgraduate Research Studentships 4
Access to Learning Fund 685
BACS Travel Awards 160
CBRL Research Award 248
CBRL Travel Grant 248
Department of Economics 1 + 3 and + 3 Quota Awards and
    Competition Awards
ESRC 1 + 3 Awards and + 3 Awards
EUI Postgraduate Scholarships 287
International Postgraduate Research Scholarships (IPRS) 413
John Mather Scholarship 760
Mr and Mrs David Edward Memorial Award 145
Wingate Scholarships 697

United States of America

British Marshall Scholarships 685
Fulbright Distinguished Chairs Program 248
Fulbright Senior Specialists Program 249
International Postgraduate Research Scholarships (IPRS) 413
IREX Short-Term Travel Grants 389
ORSAS Awards 688
SSRC Abe Fellowship Program 598
SSRC JSPS Postdoctoral Fellowship 599

West European Countries

ESRC 1 + 3 Awards and + 3 Awards
EUI Postgraduate Scholarships 287
International Postgraduate Research Scholarships (IPRS) 413
Mr and Mrs David Edward Memorial Award 145

TAXATION

Any Country

AIER Summer Fellowship 59
Rhodes University Postdoctoral Fellowship and The Andrew Mellon
   Postdoctoral Fellowship 548
University of Bristol Postgraduate Scholarships 672
University of Essex Scholarships 690
Victoria University of Wellington PhD Scholarships 786

African Nations

International Postgraduate Research Scholarships (IPRS) 413
ORSAS Awards 688

Australia

ORSAS Awards 688
Wingate Scholarships 697

Canada

Alcohol Beverage Medical Research Foundation Research Project
   Grant 14
International Postgraduate Research Scholarships (IPRS) 413
ORSAS Awards 688
Wingate Scholarships 697

Caribbean Countries

International Postgraduate Research Scholarships (IPRS) 413
ORSAS Awards 688

East European Countries

International Postgraduate Research Scholarships (IPRS) 413
ORSAS Awards 688

European Union

Department of Economics 1 + 3 and + 3 Quota Awards and
   Competition Awards
Wingate Scholarships 697

Middle East

International Postgraduate Research Scholarships (IPRS) 413
ORSAS Awards 688

New Zealand

ORSAS Awards 688
Wingate Scholarships 697

South Africa

International Postgraduate Research Scholarships (IPRS) 413
ORSAS Awards 688
Wingate Scholarships 697

United Kingdom

Aberystwyth Postgraduate Research Studentships 4
Access to Learning Fund 685
Department of Economics 1 + 3 and + 3 Quota Awards and
   Competition Awards
International Postgraduate Research Scholarships (IPRS) 413
Wingate Scholarships 697

United States of America

Alcohol Beverage Medical Research Foundation Research Project
   Grant 14
British Marshall Scholarships 685
International Postgraduate Research Scholarships (IPRS) 413
ORSAS Awards 688

SSRC Abe Fellowship Program 598
SSRC JSPS Postdoctoral Fellowship 599

West European Countries

International Postgraduate Research Scholarships (IPRS) 413

ECONOMETRICS

Any Country

Alzheimer's Society Research Grants
Fernand Braudel Senior Fellowships 287
Institute for Advanced Study Postdoctoral Residential Fellowships 363
Jean Monnet Fellowships 288
Paul H. Nitze School of Advanced International Studies (SAIS)
   Financial Aid and Fellowships 155
Queen Mary Research Studentships 539
S S Huebner Foundation for Insurance Education Predoctoral and
   Postdoctoral Fellowships 579
University of Bristol Postgraduate Scholarships 672
University of Essex Scholarships 690
University of Southampton Postgraduate Studentships 759
Victoria University of Wellington PhD Scholarships 786
World Universities Network (WUN) International Research Mobility
   Scheme 759

African Nations

International Postgraduate Research Scholarships (IPRS) 413
ORSAS Awards 688

Australia

ORSAS Awards 688
Wingate Scholarships 697

Canada

Alcohol Beverage Medical Research Foundation Research Project
   Grant 14
International Postgraduate Research Scholarships (IPRS) 413
ORSAS Awards 688
S S Huebner Foundation for Insurance Education Predoctoral and
   Postdoctoral Fellowships 579
Wingate Scholarships 697

Caribbean Countries

International Postgraduate Research Scholarships (IPRS) 413
ORSAS Awards 688

East European Countries

EUI Postgraduate Scholarships 287
International Postgraduate Research Scholarships (IPRS) 413
ORSAS Awards 688

European Union

Department of Economics 1 + 3 and + 3 Quota Awards and
   Competition Awards
ESRC 1 + 3 Awards and + 3 Awards
EUI Postgraduate Scholarships 287
Wingate Scholarships 697

Middle East

EUI Postgraduate Scholarships 287
International Postgraduate Research Scholarships (IPRS) 413
ORSAS Awards 688

New Zealand

ORSAS Awards 688
Wingate Scholarships 697

South Africa

International Postgraduate Research Scholarships (IPRS) 413
ORSAS Awards 688
Wingate Scholarships 697

SOCIAL AND BEHAVIOURAL SCIENCES

United Kingdom

Access to Learning Fund 685
Department of Economics 1 + 3 and + 3 Quota Awards and
 Competition Awards
ESRC 1 + 3 Awards and + 3 Awards
EUI Postgraduate Scholarships 287
International Postgraduate Research Scholarships (IPRS) 413
Mr and Mrs David Edward Memorial Award 145
Wingate Scholarships 697

United States of America

Alcohol Beverage Medical Research Foundation Research Project
 Grant 14
British Marshall Scholarships 685
International Postgraduate Research Scholarships (IPRS) 413
ORSAS Awards 688
Sea Grant/NOAA Fisheries Fellowship 488
SSRC Abe Fellowship Program 598
SSRC JSPS Postdoctoral Fellowship 599

West European Countries

ESRC 1 + 3 Awards and + 3 Awards
EUI Postgraduate Scholarships 287
International Postgraduate Research Scholarships (IPRS) 413
Mr and Mrs David Edward Memorial Award 145

INDUSTRIAL AND PRODUCTION ECONOMICS

Any Country

BIAA Study Grants 168
Houblon-Norman Fellowships/George Fellowships 346
S S Huebner Foundation for Insurance Education Predoctoral and
 Postdoctoral Fellowships 579
University of Essex Scholarships 690
Victoria University of Wellington PhD Scholarships 786

African Nations

International Postgraduate Research Scholarships (IPRS) 413
ORSAS Awards 688

Australia

ORSAS Awards 688
Wingate Scholarships 697

Canada

International Postgraduate Research Scholarships (IPRS) 413
ORSAS Awards 688
S S Huebner Foundation for Insurance Education Predoctoral and
 Postdoctoral Fellowships 579
Wingate Scholarships 697

Caribbean Countries

International Postgraduate Research Scholarships (IPRS) 413
ORSAS Awards 688

East European Countries

International Postgraduate Research Scholarships (IPRS) 413
ORSAS Awards 688

European Union

Department of Economics 1 + 3 and + 3 Quota Awards and
 Competition Awards
ESRC 1 + 3 Awards and + 3 Awards
Wingate Scholarships 697

Middle East

International Postgraduate Research Scholarships (IPRS) 413
ORSAS Awards 688

New Zealand

ORSAS Awards 688
Wingate Scholarships 697

South Africa

International Postgraduate Research Scholarships (IPRS) 413
ORSAS Awards 688
Wingate Scholarships 697

United Kingdom

Aberystwyth Postgraduate Research Studentships 4
Access to Learning Fund 685
Department of Economics 1 + 3 and + 3 Quota Awards and
 Competition Awards
ESRC 1 + 3 Awards and + 3 Awards
International Postgraduate Research Scholarships (IPRS) 413
Mr and Mrs David Edward Memorial Award 145
Wingate Scholarships 697

United States of America

British Marshall Scholarships 685
International Postgraduate Research Scholarships (IPRS) 413
ORSAS Awards 688
SSRC Abe Fellowship Program 598
SSRC JSPS Postdoctoral Fellowship 599

West European Countries

ESRC 1 + 3 Awards and + 3 Awards
International Postgraduate Research Scholarships (IPRS) 413
Mr and Mrs David Edward Memorial Award 145

POLITICAL SCIENCE AND GOVERNMENT

Any Country

Acadia Graduate Awards 5
AFFDU Monique Fouet Grant 163
Ahmanson and Getty Postdoctoral Fellowships 639
ASECS (American Society for 18th-Century Studies)/Clark Library
 Fellowships 639
Association for Women in Science Educational Foundation Predoc-
 toral Awards 118
Balliol College: Marvin Bower Scholarship 719
BIAA Post-Doctoral Research Fellowship 168
BIAA Research Scholarship 168
BIAA Study Grants 168
BIAA Travel Grants 168
BIAA/SPHS Fieldwork Award 168
British Academy Overseas Conference Grants 158
British Academy Postdoctoral Fellowships 158
British Academy Small Research Grants 158
British Academy Worldwide Congress Grant 159
British Conference Grants 159
Camargo Fellowships 182
CDI Internship 223
Clark Predoctoral Fellowships 639
Clark-Huntington Joint Bibliographical Fellowship 640
Essex Rotary University Travel Grants 687
ETH Zurich Excellence Scholarship and Opportunity Award 624
Frederick Douglass Institute Postdoctoral Fellowship 304
Frederick Douglass Institute Predoctoral Dissertation Fellowship 304
German Chancellor Fellowships for Prospective Leaders 17
Gilbert F White Postdoctoral Fellowship 545
Graduate Dissertation Research Fellowship 448
Graduate Institute of International Studies (HEI-Geneva) Scholarships
 323
Graduate Summer Travel Grants 449
Grant Notley Memorial Postdoctoral Fellowship 662
Harry S Truman Library Institute Dissertation Year Fellowships 332
Herbert Hoover Presidential Library Association Travel Grants 338
HFG Research Program 332
IHS Summer Graduate Research Fellowship 363
Institute for Advanced Study Postdoctoral Residential Fellowships 363
Institute of Irish Studies Research Fellowships 367
Jennings Randolph Program for International Peace Dissertation
 Fellowship 643
Joseph L Fisher Dissertation Award 546
Kennan Institute Short-Term Grants 408

Lee Kuan Yew School of Public Policy Graduate Scholarships (LKYSPPS) 491
M Alison Frantz Fellowship in Post-Classical Studies at the Gennadius Library 83
Marshall Memorial Fellowship 315
Marusia and Michael Dorosh Master's Fellowship 209
Minda de Gunzberg Graduate Dissertation Writing Fellowship 449
Onassis Foreigners' Fellowships Programme Research Grants Category AI 15
Paul H. Nitze School of Advanced International Studies (SAIS) Financial Aid and Fellowships 155
Queen Mary Research Studentships 539
Rhodes University Postdoctoral Fellowship and The Andrew Mellon Postdoctoral Fellowship 548
Roosevelt Institute Research Grant 303
Russell Sage Foundation Visiting Scholar Appointments 578
Shorenstein APARC Postdoctoral Research Fellowship in Korean Studies 586
Sir Eric Berthoud Travel Grant 689
SOAS Bursary 583
SOAS Research Student Fellowships 583
St Catherine's College Graduate Scholarship in the Arts
Thank-Offering to Britain Fellowships 159
United States Holocaust Memorial Museum Center for Advanced Holocaust Studies Visiting Scholar Programs 641
University of Bristol Postgraduate Scholarships 672
University of Kent Department of Politics and International Relations Bursary 700
University of Southampton Postgraduate Studentships 759
Victoria University of Wellington PhD Scholarships 786
Wallace Scholarships 278
World Security Institute Internship 223
World Universities Network (WUN) International Research Mobility Scheme 759

African Nations

Canadian Window on International Development 380
IDRC Doctoral Research Awards 380
IDRC Internship Awards 381
International Postgraduate Research Scholarships (IPRS) 413
ORSAS Awards 688

Australia

ORSAS Awards 688
Wingate Scholarships 697

Canada

Canadian Window on International Development 380
Gilbert Chinard Fellowships 361
Harmon Chadbourn Rorison Fellowship 361
IDRC Doctoral Research Awards 380
IDRC Internship Awards 381
International Postgraduate Research Scholarships (IPRS) 413
Jules and Gabrielle Léger Fellowship 601
Mary McNeill Scholarship in Irish Studies 368
ORSAS Awards 688
Sloan Industry Studies Fellowships 19
William and Margaret Brown Cambridge Scholarship for PhD Study 198
Wingate Scholarships 697

Caribbean Countries

Canadian Window on International Development 380
IDRC Doctoral Research Awards 380
IDRC Internship Awards 381
International Postgraduate Research Scholarships (IPRS) 413
ORSAS Awards 688

East European Countries

German Chancellor Fellowships for Prospective Leaders 17
IDRC Doctoral Research Awards 380
International Postgraduate Research Scholarships (IPRS) 413
ORSAS Awards 688

European Union

CBRL Travel Grant 248
ESRC 1 + 3 Awards and + 3 Awards
Politics Scholarships 428
Wingate Scholarships 697

Middle East

IDRC Doctoral Research Awards 380
IDRC Internship Awards 381
International Postgraduate Research Scholarships (IPRS) 413
ORSAS Awards 688

New Zealand

ORSAS Awards 688
Wingate Scholarships 697

South Africa

Canadian Window on International Development 380
IDRC Doctoral Research Awards 380
IDRC Internship Awards 381
International Postgraduate Research Scholarships (IPRS) 413
ORSAS Awards 688
SAIIA Konrad Adenauer Foundation Research Internship 615
Wingate Scholarships 697

United Kingdom

Aberystwyth Postgraduate Research Studentships 4
Access to Learning Fund 685
BACS Travel Awards 160
Balsdon Fellowship 174
BIAA Travel Grants 168
CBRL Research Award 248
CBRL Travel Grant 248
ESRC 1 + 3 Awards and + 3 Awards
International Postgraduate Research Scholarships (IPRS) 413
Ray Y. Gildea Jr. Award 565
Rome Awards 175
Rome Fellowship 175
Rome Scholarships in Ancient, Medieval and Later Italian Studies 176
Wingate Scholarships 697

United States of America

ARCE Fellowships 80
Arthur M. Schlesinger, Jr. Fellowship 405
Bicentennial Swedish-American Exchange Fund 623
British Marshall Scholarships 685
Budweiser Conservation Scholarship 475
California Senate Fellows 222
Dirksen Congressional Research Grants Program 269
EAI Fellows Program on Peace, Governance and Development in East Asia 273
Fellowship for American College Students 545
Fulbright Distinguished Chairs Program 248
Fulbright Senior Specialists Program 249
German Chancellor Fellowships for Prospective Leaders 17
Gilbert Chinard Fellowships 361
Harmon Chadbourn Rorison Fellowship 361
International Postgraduate Research Scholarships (IPRS) 413
IREX Individual Advanced Research Opportunities 388
IREX Short-Term Travel Grants 389
James Madison Fellowship Program 398
Jesse M. Unruh Assembly Fellowship Program 222
Kennan Institute Research Scholarship 408
Kennedy Research Grants 405
Marjorie Kovler Fellowship 405
Mary McNeill Scholarship in Irish Studies 368
Michael and Marie Marucci Scholarship 475
ORSAS Awards 688
Ray Y. Gildea Jr. Award 565
Robert Bosch Foundation Fellowships 550
Sloan Industry Studies Fellowships 19
SSRC Abe Fellowship Program 598
SSRC JSPS Postdoctoral Fellowship 599
Washington University Chancellor's Graduate Fellowship Program 792

White House Fellowships 536
World Security Institute Internship 223

West European Countries

ESRC 1 + 3 Awards and + 3 Awards
International Postgraduate Research Scholarships (IPRS) 413

COMPARATIVE POLITICS

Any Country

Balliol College: Marvin Bower Scholarship 719
BIAA Study Grants 168
Camargo Fellowships 182
ETH Zurich Excellence Scholarship and Opportunity Award 624
Fernand Braudel Senior Fellowships 287
Institute of Irish Studies Research Fellowships 367
Jean Monnet Fellowships 288
Max Weber Fellowships 288
Paul H. Nitze School of Advanced International Studies (SAIS)
    Financial Aid and Fellowships 155
Queen Mary Research Studentships 539
SOAS Open Scholarship 583
United States Holocaust Memorial Museum Center for Advanced
    Holocaust Studies Visiting Scholar Programs 641
University of Bristol Postgraduate Scholarships 672
Victoria University of Wellington PhD Scholarships 786

African Nations

International Postgraduate Research Scholarships (IPRS) 413
ORSAS Awards 688

Australia

ORSAS Awards 688
Wingate Scholarships 697

Canada

International Postgraduate Research Scholarships (IPRS) 413
Jules and Gabrielle Léger Fellowship 601
Mary McNeill Scholarship in Irish Studies 368
ORSAS Awards 688
Wingate Scholarships 697

Caribbean Countries

International Postgraduate Research Scholarships (IPRS) 413
ORSAS Awards 688

East European Countries

EUI Postgraduate Scholarships 287
Freie Universität Berlin John-F.-Kennedy-Institut für
    Nordamerikastudien Research Grants 304
International Postgraduate Research Scholarships (IPRS) 413
ORSAS Awards 688
Young Scholars Forum 314

European Union

CBRL Travel Grant 248
ESRC 1 + 3 Awards and + 3 Awards
EUI Postgraduate Scholarships 287
Freie Universität Berlin John-F.-Kennedy-Institut für
    Nordamerikastudien Research Grants 304
Wingate Scholarships 697

Middle East

EUI Postgraduate Scholarships 287
International Postgraduate Research Scholarships (IPRS) 413
ORSAS Awards 688

New Zealand

ORSAS Awards 688
Wingate Scholarships 697

South Africa

International Postgraduate Research Scholarships (IPRS) 413
ORSAS Awards 688
Wingate Scholarships 697

United Kingdom

Aberystwyth Postgraduate Research Studentships 4
Access to Learning Fund 685
CBRL Research Award 248
CBRL Travel Grant 248
ESRC 1 + 3 Awards and + 3 Awards
EUI Postgraduate Scholarships 287
International Postgraduate Research Scholarships (IPRS) 413
Wingate Scholarships 697
Young Scholars Forum 314

United States of America

ARCE Fellowships 80
British Marshall Scholarships 685
Fritz Stern Dissertation Prize 313
Fulbright Senior Specialists Program 249
International Postgraduate Research Scholarships (IPRS) 413
IREX Individual Advanced Research Opportunities 388
IREX Short-Term Travel Grants 389
Mary McNeill Scholarship in Irish Studies 368
ORSAS Awards 688
SSRC Abe Fellowship Program 598
SSRC JSPS Postdoctoral Fellowship 599
Thyssen-Heideking Fellowship 314
Young Scholars Forum 314

West European Countries

ESRC 1 + 3 Awards and + 3 Awards
EUI Postgraduate Scholarships 287
Freie Universität Berlin John-F.-Kennedy-Institut für
    Nordamerikastudien Research Grants 304
International Postgraduate Research Scholarships (IPRS) 413
Kade-Heideking Fellowship 313
Young Scholars Forum 314

INTERNATIONAL RELATIONS

Any Country

Balliol College: Marvin Bower Scholarship 719
BIAA Post-Doctoral Research Fellowship 168
BIAA Research Scholarship 168
BIAA Study Grants 168
BIAA Travel Grants 168
British Academy Overseas Conference Grants 158
British Academy Postdoctoral Fellowships 158
British Academy Small Research Grants 158
British Academy Worldwide Congress Grant 159
British Conference Grants 159
CDI Internship 223
Edward R Murrow Fellowship for Foreign Correspondents 251
Essex Rotary University Travel Grants 687
ETH Zurich Excellence Scholarship and Opportunity Award 624
Fernand Braudel Senior Fellowships 287
Frederick Douglass Institute Postdoctoral Fellowship 304
Frederick Douglass Institute Predoctoral Dissertation Fellowship 304
Gilbert Murray Trust Junior Awards 318
Graduate Dissertation Research Fellowship 448
Graduate Summer Travel Grants 449
HFG Research Program 332
Institute of Current World Affairs Fellowships 365
Jean Monnet Fellowships 288
Jennings Randolph Program for International Peace Dissertation
    Fellowship 643
Joseph L Fisher Dissertation Award 546
Kennan Institute Short-Term Grants 408
M Alison Frantz Fellowship in Post-Classical Studies at the Gennadius
    Library 83
Mackenzie King Travelling Scholarship 429

Marusia and Michael Dorosh Master's Fellowship 209
Max Weber Fellowships 288
Minda de Gunzberg Graduate Dissertation Writing Fellowship 449
Otto Klineberg Intercultural and International Relations Award 605
Paul H. Nitze School of Advanced International Studies (SAIS)
  Financial Aid and Fellowships 155
Rhodes University Postdoctoral Fellowship and The Andrew Mellon
  Postdoctoral Fellowship 548
SAIIA Bradlow Fellowship 614
Sir Eric Berthoud Travel Grant 689
SOAS Bursary 583
SOAS Research Student Fellowships 583
St Catherine's College Graduate Scholarship in the Arts
Theodore Lentz Fellowship in Peace and Conflict Resolution
  Research 417
Theodore Lentz Postdoctoral or Sabbatical Fellowship in Peace and
  Conflict Resolution Research 224
United States Holocaust Memorial Museum Center for Advanced
  Holocaust Studies Visiting Scholar Programs 641
University of Bristol Postgraduate Scholarships 672
University of Kent Department of Politics and International Relations
  Bursary 700
University of Southampton Postgraduate Studentships 759
Victoria University of Wellington PhD Scholarships 786
WILPF Internship in Disarmament 801
WILPF Internship in Human Rights 801
World Security Institute Internship 223
World Universities Network (WUN) International Research Mobility
  Scheme 759

African Nations

IDRC Internship Awards 381
International Postgraduate Research Scholarships (IPRS) 413
ORISHA (Oxford Research in the Scholarship and Humanities of
  Africa) Studentship 736
ORSAS Awards 688

Australia

ORSAS Awards 688
Wingate Scholarships 697

Canada

Gilbert Chinard Fellowships 361
Harmon Chadbourn Rorison Fellowship 361
IDRC Internship Awards 381
International Postgraduate Research Scholarships (IPRS) 413
Manfred Wörner Fellowship 506
ORSAS Awards 688
Wingate Scholarships 697

Caribbean Countries

IDRC Internship Awards 381
International Postgraduate Research Scholarships (IPRS) 413
ORSAS Awards 688

East European Countries

EUI Postgraduate Scholarships 287
International Postgraduate Research Scholarships (IPRS) 413
Manfred Wörner Fellowship 506
ORSAS Awards 688

European Union

CBRL Travel Grant 248
ESRC 1 + 3 Awards and + 3 Awards
EUI Postgraduate Scholarships 287
Politics Scholarships 428
Transatlantic Community Foundation Fellowship 315
Transatlantic Fellows Program 315
Wingate Scholarships 697

Middle East

EUI Postgraduate Scholarships 287
IDRC Internship Awards 381

International Postgraduate Research Scholarships (IPRS) 413
ORSAS Awards 688

New Zealand

Gordon Watson Scholarship 500
ORSAS Awards 688
Wingate Scholarships 697

South Africa

IDRC Internship Awards 381
International Postgraduate Research Scholarships (IPRS) 413
ORSAS Awards 688
SAIIA Konrad Adenauer Foundation Research Internship 615
Wingate Scholarships 697

United Kingdom

Aberystwyth Postgraduate Research Studentships 4
Access to Learning Fund 685
Balsdon Fellowship 174
BIAA Travel Grants 168
CBRL Research Award 248
CBRL Travel Grant 248
ESRC 1 + 3 Awards and + 3 Awards
ESU Chautauqua Institution Scholarships 280
EUI Postgraduate Scholarships 287
International Postgraduate Research Scholarships (IPRS) 413
Manfred Wörner Fellowship 506
Rome Awards 175
Rome Fellowship 175
Rome Scholarships in Ancient, Medieval and Later Italian Studies
  176
Wingate Scholarships 697

United States of America

ARCE Fellowships 80
British Marshall Scholarships 685
CFR International Affairs Fellowship Program in Japan 250
CFR International Affairs Fellowships 251
CIA Graduate Studies Program Scholarship 225
EAI Fellows Program on Peace, Governance and Development in
  East Asia 273
Edward R Murrow Fellowship for Foreign Correspondents 251
Fritz Stern Dissertation Prize 313
Fulbright Distinguished Chairs Program 248
Fulbright Senior Specialists Program 249
Gilbert Chinard Fellowships 361
Harmon Chadbourn Rorison Fellowship 361
International Postgraduate Research Scholarships (IPRS)
  413
IREX Individual Advanced Research Opportunities 388
IREX Short-Term Travel Grants 389
Kennan Institute Research Scholarship 408
Manfred Wörner Fellowship 506
Manfred Wörner Seminar 315
Michael and Marie Marucci Scholarship 475
The Next Generation: Leadership in Asian Affairs Fellowship
  627
Norwegian Emigration Fund of 1975 508
ORSAS Awards 688
Pasteur Foundation Postdoctoral Fellowship Program 522
Program Enhancement Grant 206
SSRC Abe Fellowship Program 598
SSRC JSPS Postdoctoral Fellowship 599
Thyssen-Heideking Fellowship 314
Transatlantic Community Foundation Fellowship 315
Transatlantic Fellows Program 315
World Security Institute Internship 223

West European Countries

ESRC 1 + 3 Awards and + 3 Awards
EUI Postgraduate Scholarships 287
International Postgraduate Research Scholarships (IPRS) 413
Kade-Heideking Fellowship 313
Manfred Wörner Fellowship 506

SOCIOLOGY

Any Country

Acadia Graduate Awards 5
AFSP Young Investigator Award 56
Ahmanson and Getty Postdoctoral Fellowships 639
Alzheimer's Society Research Grants
Anne Cummins Scholarship 603
ASCSA Fellowships 82
Association for Women in Science Educational Foundation
    Predoctoral Awards 118
AUC International Graduate Fellowships in Arabic Studies, Middle
    East Studies and Sociology/Anthropology 97
Behavioral Sciences Postdoctoral Fellowships 282
BIAA Post-Doctoral Research Fellowship 168
BIAA Research Scholarship 168
BIAA Study Grants 168
BIAA Travel Grants 168
BIAA/SPHS Fieldwork Award 168
British Academy Overseas Conference Grants 158
British Academy Postdoctoral Fellowships 158
British Academy Small Research Grants 158
British Academy Worldwide Congress Grant 159
British Conference Grants 159
BSA Support Fund 177
Camargo Fellowships 182
Charlotte W Newcombe Doctoral Dissertation Fellowships 803
Clark-Huntington Joint Bibliographical Fellowship 640
CSA Stella Blum Research Grant 247
CSA Travel Research Grant 248
Don Pike Award 686
Eli Ginzberg Award 344
Essex Rotary University Travel Grants 687
Fernand Braudel Senior Fellowships 287
FSSS Grants-in-Aid Program 606
Graduate Dissertation Research Fellowship 448
Graduate Summer Travel Grants 449
Gypsy Lore Society Young Scholar's Prize in Romani Studies 328
Harold D. Lasswell Award 344
Harold White Fellowships 484
HFG Research Program 332
HRB Postdoctoral Research Fellowships 334
Institute for Advanced Study Postdoctoral Residential Fellowships 363
Jean Monnet Fellowships 288
Jennings Randolph Program for International Peace Dissertation
    Fellowship 643
John L Stanley Award 344
Jonathan Young Scholarship 691
Joshua Feigenbaum Award 344
Kennan Institute Short-Term Grants 408
Lee Kuan Yew School of Public Policy Graduate Scholarships
    (LKYSPPS) 491
M Alison Frantz Fellowship in Post-Classical Studies at the Gennadius
    Library 83
Marine Corps History Research Grants 434
Martinus Nijhoff Award 345
Marusia and Michael Dorosh Master's Fellowship 209
Max Weber Fellowships 288
Minda de Gunzberg Graduate Dissertation Writing Fellowship 449
Onassis Foreigners' Fellowships Programme Research Grants
    Category AI 15
Postgraduate Research Bursaries (Epilepsy Action) 282
Rhodes University Postdoctoral Fellowship and The Andrew Mellon
    Postdoctoral Fellowship 548
Robert K Merton Award 345
Russell Sage Foundation Visiting Scholar Appointments 578
Shorenstein APARC Postdoctoral Research Fellowship in Korean
    Studies 586
Sir Eric Berthoud Travel Grant 689
Sir Halley Stewart Trust Grants 593
Slawson Awards 565
SOAS Bursary 583
SOAS Open Scholarship 583
SOAS Research Student Fellowships 583
St Catherine's College Graduate Scholarship in the Arts

Teagasc Walsh Fellowships 626
United States Holocaust Memorial Museum Center for Advanced
    Holocaust Studies Visiting Scholar Programs 641
University of Bristol Postgraduate Scholarships 672
University of Southampton Postgraduate Studentships 759
Victoria University of Wellington PhD Scholarships 786
World Universities Network (WUN) International Research Mobility
    Scheme 759

African Nations

Canadian Window on International Development 380
IDRC Doctoral Research Awards 380
IDRC Internship Awards 381
International Postgraduate Research Scholarships (IPRS) 413
ORSAS Awards 688

Australia

ORSAS Awards 688
Wingate Scholarships 697

Canada

Bishop Thomas Hoyt Jr Fellowship 238
Canadian Commonwealth Scholarship and Fellowship Plan 201
Canadian Window on International Development 380
CIES Fellowship Program 273
Gilbert Chinard Fellowships 361
Harmon Chadbourn Rorison Fellowship 361
Idea Grants 215
IDRC Doctoral Research Awards 380
IDRC Internship Awards 381
International Postgraduate Research Scholarships (IPRS) 413
ORSAS Awards 688
Research Planning Grants 216
Rural Maternity Care Doctoral Student Fellowship 578
Sloan Industry Studies Fellowships 19
Wingate Scholarships 697

Caribbean Countries

Canadian Window on International Development 380
IDRC Doctoral Research Awards 380
IDRC Internship Awards 381
International Postgraduate Research Scholarships (IPRS) 413
ORSAS Awards 688

East European Countries

EUI Postgraduate Scholarships 287
IDRC Doctoral Research Awards 380
International Postgraduate Research Scholarships (IPRS) 413
ORSAS Awards 688

European Union

CBRL Travel Grant 248
ESRC 1 + 3 Awards and + 3 Awards
EUI Postgraduate Scholarships 287
Wingate Scholarships 697

Middle East

EUI Postgraduate Scholarships 287
IDRC Doctoral Research Awards 380
IDRC Internship Awards 381
International Postgraduate Research Scholarships (IPRS) 413
ORSAS Awards 688

New Zealand

The Association of University Staff Crozier Scholarship 500
ORSAS Awards 688
Wingate Scholarships 697

South Africa

Canadian Window on International Development 380
IDRC Doctoral Research Awards 380
IDRC Internship Awards 381
International Postgraduate Research Scholarships (IPRS) 413

ORSAS Awards 688
Wingate Scholarships 697

United Kingdom

Access to Learning Fund 685
Balsdon Fellowship 174
BIAA Travel Grants 168
BSA Support Fund 177
CBRL Research Award 248
CBRL Travel Grant 248
ESRC 1+3 Awards and +3 Awards
EUI Postgraduate Scholarships 287
Hector and Elizabeth Catling Bursary 173
International Postgraduate Research Scholarships (IPRS) 413
Mr and Mrs David Edward Memorial Award 145
Rome Awards 175
Rome Fellowship 175
Rome Scholarships in Ancient, Medieval and Later Italian Studies 176
Slawson Awards 565
University of Kent Sociology Studentship 701
Wingate Scholarships 697

United States of America

ASA Minority Fellowship Program 95
Bishop Thomas Hoyt Jr Fellowship 238
British Marshall Scholarships 685
EAI Fellows Program on Peace, Governance and Development in East Asia 273
Fulbright Distinguished Chairs Program 248
Fulbright Senior Specialists Program 249
Gilbert Chinard Fellowships 361
Harmon Chadbourn Rorison Fellowship 361
International Postgraduate Research Scholarships (IPRS) 413
IREX Individual Advanced Research Opportunities 388
IREX Short-Term Travel Grants 389
Kennan Institute Research Scholarship 408
ORSAS Awards 688
Sloan Industry Studies Fellowships 19
SSRC Abe Fellowship Program 598
SSRC JSPS Postdoctoral Fellowship 599
University of New Hampshire Postdoctoral Fellowships For Research on Family Violence 713

West European Countries

ESRC 1+3 Awards and +3 Awards
EUI Postgraduate Scholarships 287
International Postgraduate Research Scholarships (IPRS) 413
Mr and Mrs David Edward Memorial Award 145
University of Kent Sociology Studentship 701

HISTORY OF SOCIETIES

Any Country

Ahmanson and Getty Postdoctoral Fellowships 639
Albert J Beveridge Grant 58
ASCSA Advanced Fellowships 82
Bernadotte E Schmitt Grants 58
Bernard and Audre Rapoport Fellowships 431
Camargo Fellowships 182
CIUS Research Grants 209
Clark-Huntington Joint Bibliographical Fellowship 640
CSA Adele Filene Travel Award 247
Earthwatch Field Research Grants 272
Ethel Marcus Memorial Fellowship 431
Findel Scholarships and Schneider Scholarships 340
Frederick Douglass Institute Postdoctoral Fellowship 304
Frederick Douglass Institute Predoctoral Dissertation Fellowship 304
The Joseph and Eva R Dave Fellowship 432
Liberty Legacy Foundation Award 516
Library Company of Philadelphia and Historical Society of Pennsylvania Research Fellowships in American History and Culture 422
Littleton-Griswold Research Grant 59

Loewenstein-Wiener Fellowship Awards 432
M Alison Frantz Fellowship in Post-Classical Studies at the Gennadius Library 83
Marguerite R Jacobs Memorial Award 432
The Natalie Feld Memorial Fellowship 432
NEH Fellowships 83
Queen Mary Research Studentships 539
The Rabbi Harold D Hahn Memorial Fellowship 432
The Rabbi Joachin Prinz Memorial Fellowship 432
Rabbi Levi A Olan Memorial Fellowship 433
Rabbi Theodore S Levy Tribute Fellowship 433
Rhodes University Postdoctoral Fellowship and The Andrew Mellon Postdoctoral Fellowship 548
Society for the Study of French History Bursaries 606
Starkoff Fellowship 433
Victoria University of Wellington PhD Scholarships 786

African Nations

ORSAS Awards 688

Australia

ORSAS Awards 688
Wingate Scholarships 697

Canada

ORSAS Awards 688
Wingate Scholarships 697

Caribbean Countries

ORSAS Awards 688

East European Countries

ORSAS Awards 688
Young Scholars Forum 314

European Union

ESRC 1+3 Awards and +3 Awards
Wingate Scholarships 697

Middle East

ORSAS Awards 688

New Zealand

ORSAS Awards 688
Wingate Scholarships 697

South Africa

ORSAS Awards 688
Wingate Scholarships 697

United Kingdom

Access to Learning Fund 685
British Institute in Eastern Africa Minor Grants 169
ESRC 1+3 Awards and +3 Awards
Mr and Mrs David Edward Memorial Award 145
Wingate Scholarships 697
Young Scholars Forum 314

United States of America

ARCE Fellowships 80
ASOR Mesopotamian Fellowship 83
British Marshall Scholarships 685
Earthwatch Fellowships 272
Fritz Stern Dissertation Prize 313
Fulbright Senior Specialists Program 249
Japanese Residencies Program 516
Kennedy Research Grants 405
ORSAS Awards 688
SSRC Abe Fellowship Program 598
SSRC JSPS Postdoctoral Fellowship 599
Thyssen-Heideking Fellowship 314
Young Scholars Forum 314

West European Countries

ESRC 1 + 3 Awards and + 3 Awards
Kade-Heideking Fellowship 313
Mr and Mrs David Edward Memorial Award 145
Young Scholars Forum 314

COMPARATIVE SOCIOLOGY

Any Country

Camargo Fellowships 182
Earthwatch Field Research Grants 272
M Alison Frantz Fellowship in Post-Classical Studies at the Gennadius
    Library 83
Rhodes University Postdoctoral Fellowship and The Andrew Mellon
    Postdoctoral Fellowship 548
University of Bristol Postgraduate Scholarships 672
Victoria University of Wellington PhD Scholarships 786

African Nations

ORSAS Awards 688

Australia

ORSAS Awards 688
Wingate Scholarships 697

Canada

Alcohol Beverage Medical Research Foundation Research Project
    Grant 14
ORSAS Awards 688
Wingate Scholarships 697

Caribbean Countries

ORSAS Awards 688

East European Countries

ORSAS Awards 688
Young Scholars Forum 314

European Union

ESRC 1 + 3 Awards and + 3 Awards
Wingate Scholarships 697

Middle East

ORSAS Awards 688

New Zealand

ORSAS Awards 688
Wingate Scholarships 697

South Africa

ORSAS Awards 688
Wingate Scholarships 697

United Kingdom

Access to Learning Fund 685
ESRC 1 + 3 Awards and + 3 Awards
Mr and Mrs David Edward Memorial Award 145
Wingate Scholarships 697
Young Scholars Forum 314

United States of America

Alcohol Beverage Medical Research Foundation Research Project
    Grant 14
ARCE Fellowships 80
British Marshall Scholarships 685
Fritz Stern Dissertation Prize 313
Fulbright Senior Specialists Program 249
ORSAS Awards 688
SSRC Abe Fellowship Program 598
SSRC JSPS Postdoctoral Fellowship 599
Thyssen-Heideking Fellowship 314
Young Scholars Forum 314

West European Countries

ESRC 1 + 3 Awards and + 3 Awards
Kade-Heideking Fellowship 313
Mr and Mrs David Edward Memorial Award 145
Young Scholars Forum 314

SOCIAL POLICY

Any Country

AFSP Distinguished Investigator Awards 55
AFSP Pilot Grants 55
AFSP Postdoctoral Research Fellowships 55
AFSP Standard Research Grants 55
AFSP Young Investigator Award 56
Fernand Braudel Senior Fellowships 287
Frederick Douglass Institute Postdoctoral Fellowship 304
Frederick Douglass Institute Predoctoral Dissertation Fellowship
    304
Harold D. Lasswell Award 344
Hastings Center International Visiting Scholars Program 332
HRB Summer Student Grants 334
Jean Monnet Fellowships 288
John L Stanley Award 344
Joshua Feigenbaum Award 344
M Alison Frantz Fellowship in Post-Classical Studies at the Gennadius
    Library 83
Martinus Nijhoff Award 345
Max Weber Fellowships 288
Paul H. Nitze School of Advanced International Studies (SAIS)
    Financial Aid and Fellowships 155
PDS Project Grant 521
Rhodes University Postdoctoral Fellowship and The Andrew Mellon
    Postdoctoral Fellowship 548
Robert K Merton Award 345
Sir Halley Stewart Trust Grants 593
University of Bristol Postgraduate Scholarships 672
University of Kent Postgraduate Funding Awards 700
Victoria University of Wellington PhD Scholarships 786
WILPF Internship in Disarmament 801
WILPF Internship in Human Rights 801

African Nations

Hastings Center International Visiting Scholars Program
    332
IDRC Doctoral Research Awards 380
IDRC Internship Awards 381
International Postgraduate Research Scholarships (IPRS) 413
ORSAS Awards 688

Australia

CRC Grants 254
Hastings Center International Visiting Scholars Program 332
ORSAS Awards 688
Wingate Scholarships 697

Canada

Alcohol Beverage Medical Research Foundation Research Project
    Grant 14
Idea Grants 215
IDRC Doctoral Research Awards 380
IDRC Internship Awards 381
International Postgraduate Research Scholarships (IPRS) 413
ORSAS Awards 688
Research Planning Grants 216
Wingate Scholarships 697

Caribbean Countries

Hastings Center International Visiting Scholars Program 332
IDRC Doctoral Research Awards 380
IDRC Internship Awards 381
International Postgraduate Research Scholarships (IPRS) 413
ORSAS Awards 688

East European Countries

EUI Postgraduate Scholarships 287
Hastings Center International Visiting Scholars Program 332
IDRC Doctoral Research Awards 380
International Postgraduate Research Scholarships (IPRS) 413
ORSAS Awards 688

European Union

ESRC 1+3 Awards and +3 Awards
EUI Postgraduate Scholarships 287
Wingate Scholarships 697

Middle East

EUI Postgraduate Scholarships 287
Hastings Center International Visiting Scholars Program 332
IDRC Doctoral Research Awards 380
IDRC Internship Awards 381
International Postgraduate Research Scholarships (IPRS) 413
ORSAS Awards 688

New Zealand

Hastings Center International Visiting Scholars Program 332
ORSAS Awards 688
Wingate Scholarships 697

South Africa

Hastings Center International Visiting Scholars Program 332
IDRC Doctoral Research Awards 380
IDRC Internship Awards 381
International Postgraduate Research Scholarships (IPRS) 413
ORSAS Awards 688
Wingate Scholarships 697

United Kingdom

Access to Learning Fund 685
BACS Travel Awards 160
ESRC 1+3 Awards and +3 Awards
EUI Postgraduate Scholarships 287
Hastings Center International Visiting Scholars Program 332
International Postgraduate Research Scholarships (IPRS) 413
Mr and Mrs David Edward Memorial Award 145
Prix du Québec Award 160
University of Kent School of Physical Sciences 701
Wingate Scholarships 697

United States of America

Alcohol Beverage Medical Research Foundation Research Project
   Grant 14
ARCE Fellowships 80
British Marshall Scholarships 685
Fulbright Senior Specialists Program 249
International Postgraduate Research Scholarships (IPRS) 413
NIH Research Grants 483
ORSAS Awards 688
Special Initiatives Research Fellowship 50
SSRC Abe Fellowship Program 598
SSRC JSPS Postdoctoral Fellowship 599

West European Countries

ESRC 1+3 Awards and +3 Awards
EUI Postgraduate Scholarships 287
Hastings Center International Visiting Scholars Program 332
International Postgraduate Research Scholarships (IPRS) 413
Mr and Mrs David Edward Memorial Award 145
University of Kent School of Physical Sciences 701

SOCIAL INSTITUTIONS

Any Country

HRB Summer Student Grants 334
M Alison Frantz Fellowship in Post-Classical Studies at the Gennadius
   Library 83

Rhodes University Postdoctoral Fellowship and The Andrew Mellon
   Postdoctoral Fellowship 548
University of Bristol Postgraduate Scholarships 672
Victoria University of Wellington PhD Scholarships 786

African Nations

IDRC Internship Awards 381
International Postgraduate Research Scholarships (IPRS) 413
ORSAS Awards 688

Australia

ORSAS Awards 688
Wingate Scholarships 697

Canada

Alcohol Beverage Medical Research Foundation Research Project
   Grant 14
IDRC Internship Awards 381
International Postgraduate Research Scholarships (IPRS) 413
ORSAS Awards 688
Wingate Scholarships 697

Caribbean Countries

IDRC Internship Awards 381
International Postgraduate Research Scholarships (IPRS) 413
ORSAS Awards 688

East European Countries

International Postgraduate Research Scholarships (IPRS) 413
ORSAS Awards 688

European Union

ESRC 1+3 Awards and +3 Awards
Wingate Scholarships 697

Middle East

IDRC Internship Awards 381
International Postgraduate Research Scholarships (IPRS) 413
ORSAS Awards 688

New Zealand

ORSAS Awards 688
Wingate Scholarships 697

South Africa

IDRC Internship Awards 381
International Postgraduate Research Scholarships (IPRS) 413
ORSAS Awards 688
Wingate Scholarships 697

United Kingdom

Access to Learning Fund 685
ESRC 1+3 Awards and +3 Awards
International Postgraduate Research Scholarships (IPRS) 413
Mr and Mrs David Edward Memorial Award 145
Wingate Scholarships 697

United States of America

Alcohol Beverage Medical Research Foundation Research Project
   Grant 14
ARCE Fellowships 80
British Marshall Scholarships 685
Fulbright Senior Specialists Program 249
International Postgraduate Research Scholarships (IPRS) 413
NIH Research Grants 483
ORSAS Awards 688
SSRC Abe Fellowship Program 598
SSRC JSPS Postdoctoral Fellowship 599

West European Countries

ESRC 1+3 Awards and +3 Awards
International Postgraduate Research Scholarships (IPRS) 413
Mr and Mrs David Edward Memorial Award 145

SOCIAL COMMUNICATION PROBLEMS

Any Country

BackCare Research Grants 144
Harold D. Lasswell Award 344
HRB Summer Student Grants 334
John L Stanley Award 344
Joshua Feigenbaum Award 344
Martinus Nijhoff Award 345
NCAR Postdoctoral Appointments in the Advanced Study Program 471
Rhodes University Postdoctoral Fellowship and The Andrew Mellon Postdoctoral Fellowship 548
Robert K Merton Award 345
University of Bristol Postgraduate Scholarships 672
Victoria University of Wellington PhD Scholarships 786

African Nations

International Postgraduate Research Scholarships (IPRS) 413
ORSAS Awards 688

Australia

ORSAS Awards 688
Wingate Scholarships 697

Canada

Alcohol Beverage Medical Research Foundation Research Project Grant 14
International Postgraduate Research Scholarships (IPRS) 413
ORSAS Awards 688
Wingate Scholarships 697

Caribbean Countries

International Postgraduate Research Scholarships (IPRS) 413
ORSAS Awards 688

East European Countries

International Postgraduate Research Scholarships (IPRS) 413
ORSAS Awards 688

European Union

ESRC 1 + 3 Awards and + 3 Awards
Wingate Scholarships 697

Middle East

International Postgraduate Research Scholarships (IPRS) 413
ORSAS Awards 688

New Zealand

ORSAS Awards 688
Wingate Scholarships 697

South Africa

International Postgraduate Research Scholarships (IPRS) 413
ORSAS Awards 688
Wingate Scholarships 697

United Kingdom

Access to Learning Fund 685
ESRC 1 + 3 Awards and + 3 Awards
International Postgraduate Research Scholarships (IPRS) 413
Mr and Mrs David Edward Memorial Award 145
Wingate Scholarships 697

United States of America

Alcohol Beverage Medical Research Foundation Research Project Grant 14
British Marshall Scholarships 685
Fulbright Senior Specialists Program 249
International Postgraduate Research Scholarships (IPRS) 413
NIH Research Grants 483
ORSAS Awards 688

SSRC Abe Fellowship Program 598
SSRC JSPS Postdoctoral Fellowship 599

West European Countries

ESRC 1 + 3 Awards and + 3 Awards
International Postgraduate Research Scholarships (IPRS) 413
Mr and Mrs David Edward Memorial Award 145

FUTUROLOGY

Any Country

Harold D. Lasswell Award 344
John L Stanley Award 344
Joshua Feigenbaum Award 344
Martinus Nijhoff Award 345
Robert K Merton Award 345

African Nations

ORSAS Awards 688

Australia

ORSAS Awards 688
Wingate Scholarships 697

Canada

ORSAS Awards 688
Wingate Scholarships 697

Caribbean Countries

ORSAS Awards 688

East European Countries

ORSAS Awards 688

European Union

ESRC 1 + 3 Awards and + 3 Awards
Wingate Scholarships 697

Middle East

ORSAS Awards 688

New Zealand

ORSAS Awards 688
Wingate Scholarships 697

South Africa

ORSAS Awards 688
Wingate Scholarships 697

United Kingdom

BACS Travel Awards 160
ESRC 1 + 3 Awards and + 3 Awards
Wingate Scholarships 697

United States of America

ARCE Fellowships 80
British Marshall Scholarships 685
ORSAS Awards 688
SSRC Abe Fellowship Program 598
SSRC JSPS Postdoctoral Fellowship 599

West European Countries

ESRC 1 + 3 Awards and + 3 Awards

DEMOGRAPHY

Any Country

Alzheimer's Society Research Grants
Association for Women in Science Educational Foundation Predoctoral Awards 118

Australia

Canada

European Union

New Zealand

South Africa

United Kingdom

United States of America

West European Countries

ANTHROPOLOGY

Any Country

African Nations

British Institute in Eastern Africa Graduate Attachments 169
Canadian Window on International Development 380
IDRC Doctoral Research Awards 380
IDRC Internship Awards 381
ORISHA (Oxford Research in the Scholarship and Humanities of
Africa) Studentship 736
Primate Conservation Inc. Grants 537

Australia

Wingate Scholarships 697

Canada

Alcohol Beverage Medical Research Foundation Research Project
Grant 14
Canadian Window on International Development 380
IDRC Doctoral Research Awards 380
IDRC Internship Awards 381
Mary McNeill Scholarship in Irish Studies 368
Wingate Scholarships 697
The Yitzhak Rabin Fellowship Fund for the Advancement of Peace
and Tolerance 318

Caribbean Countries

Canadian Window on International Development 380
IDRC Doctoral Research Awards 380
IDRC Internship Awards 381

East European Countries

IDRC Doctoral Research Awards 380
Research Degree Scholarships in Anthropology 656

European Union

CBRL Travel Grant 248
ESRC 1 + 3 Awards and + 3 Awards
Wingate Scholarships 697

Middle East

IDRC Doctoral Research Awards 380
IDRC Internship Awards 381

New Zealand

Wingate Scholarships 697

South Africa

Canadian Window on International Development 380
IDRC Doctoral Research Awards 380
IDRC Internship Awards 381
Wingate Scholarships 697

United Kingdom

Balsdon Fellowship 174
BIAA Travel Grants 168
British Institute in Eastern Africa Graduate Attachments 169
CBRL Research Award 248
CBRL Travel Grant 248
Emslie Horniman Anthropological Scholarship Fund 556
ESRC 1 + 3 Awards and + 3 Awards
Hector and Elizabeth Catling Bursary 173
Prix du Québec Award 160
Research Degree Scholarships in Anthropology 656
Rome Awards 175
Rome Fellowship 175
Rome Scholarships in Ancient, Medieval and Later Italian Studies 176
Slawson Awards 565
Wingate Scholarships 697

United States of America

ACC Fellowship Grants Program 115
Alcohol Beverage Medical Research Foundation Research Project
Grant 14
ARCE Fellowships 80

ASOR W.F. Albright Institute of Archaeological Research/National
Endowment of the Humanities Fellowships 84
Earthwatch Fellowships 272
Fulbright Senior Specialists Program 249
IREX Individual Advanced Research Opportunities 388
IREX Short-Term Travel Grants 389
Kennan Institute Research Scholarship 408
Mary McNeill Scholarship in Irish Studies 368
NIH Research Grants 483
SSRC Abe Fellowship Program 598
SSRC JSPS Postdoctoral Fellowship 599
Washington University Chancellor's Graduate Fellowship Program 792

West European Countries

ESRC 1 + 3 Awards and + 3 Awards
Research Degree Scholarships in Anthropology 656

ETHNOLOGY

Any Country

ASCSA Fellowships 82
Earthwatch Field Research Grants 272
Fondation Fyssen Postdoctoral Study Grants 297
Institute of Irish Studies Research Fellowships 367
M Alison Frantz Fellowship in Post-Classical Studies at the Gennadius
Library 83
NEH Fellowships 83
SOAS Open Scholarship 583
Victoria University of Wellington PhD Scholarships 786

Australia

Wingate Scholarships 697

Canada

Mary McNeill Scholarship in Irish Studies 368
Wingate Scholarships 697

European Union

CBRL Travel Grant 248
ESRC 1 + 3 Awards and + 3 Awards
Wingate Scholarships 697

New Zealand

Wingate Scholarships 697

South Africa

Wingate Scholarships 697

United Kingdom

CBRL Research Award 248
CBRL Travel Grant 248
ESRC 1 + 3 Awards and + 3 Awards
Wingate Scholarships 697

United States of America

ACC Fellowship Grants Program 115
ARCE Fellowships 80
Bicentennial Swedish-American Exchange Fund Travel Grants 245
Earthwatch Fellowships 272
Mary McNeill Scholarship in Irish Studies 368
SSRC JSPS Postdoctoral Fellowship 599

West European Countries

ESRC 1 + 3 Awards and + 3 Awards

FOLKLORE

Any Country

ASCSA Fellowships 82
Earthwatch Field Research Grants 272

Institute of Irish Studies Research Fellowships 367
M Alison Frantz Fellowship in Post-Classical Studies at the Gennadius
    Library 83
NEH Fellowships 83
Victoria University of Wellington PhD Scholarships 786

Australia

Wingate Scholarships 697

Canada

Mary McNeill Scholarship in Irish Studies 368
Wingate Scholarships 697

European Union

CBRL Travel Grant 248
ESRC 1 + 3 Awards and + 3 Awards
Wingate Scholarships 697

New Zealand

Wingate Scholarships 697

South Africa

Wingate Scholarships 697

United Kingdom

CBRL Research Award 248
CBRL Travel Grant 248
ESRC 1 + 3 Awards and + 3 Awards
Wingate Scholarships 697

United States of America

ACC Fellowship Grants Program 115
ARCE Fellowships 80
Earthwatch Fellowships 272
Mary McNeill Scholarship in Irish Studies 368
SSRC JSPS Postdoctoral Fellowship 599

West European Countries

ESRC 1 + 3 Awards and + 3 Awards

WOMEN'S STUDIES

Any Country

AAUW Rose Sidgwick Memorial Fellowship 163
AAUW/IFUW International Fellowships 163
Ahmanson and Getty Postdoctoral Fellowships 639
ASCSA Advanced Fellowships 82
ASCSA Fellowships 82
ASECS (American Society for 18th-Century Studies)/Clark Library
    Fellowships 639
BIAA Post-Doctoral Research Fellowship 168
BIAA Research Scholarship 168
BIAA Study Grants 168
BIAA Travel Grants 168
British Academy Overseas Conference Grants 158
British Academy Postdoctoral Fellowships 158
British Academy Small Research Grants 158
British Academy Worldwide Congress Grant 159
British Conference Grants 159
Camargo Fellowships 182
Clark Library Short-Term Resident Fellowships 639
Clark Predoctoral Fellowships 639
Clark-Huntington Joint Bibliographical Fellowship 640
Essex Rotary University Travel Grants 687
Frederick Douglass Institute Postdoctoral Fellowship 304
Frederick Douglass Institute Predoctoral Dissertation Fellowship 304
FSSS Grants-in-Aid Program 606
Graduate Dissertation Research Fellowship 448
Graduate Summer Travel Grants 449
Hastings Center International Visiting Scholars Program 332
HFG Research Program 332
IFUW International Fellowships 166

Institute for Advanced Study Postdoctoral Residential Fellowships 363
Jennings Randolph Program for International Peace Dissertation
    Fellowship 643
Kennan Institute Short-Term Grants 408
La Trobe University Postgraduate Scholarship 414
Lee Kuan Yew School of Public Policy Graduate Scholarships
    (LKYSPPS) 491
Library Company of Philadelphia and Historical Society of Pennsyl-
    vania Research Fellowships in American History and Culture 422
M Alison Frantz Fellowship in Post-Classical Studies at the Gennadius
    Library 83
Margaret W. Rossiter History of Women in Science Prize 342
Marusia and Michael Dorosh Master's Fellowship 209
Minda de Gunzberg Graduate Dissertation Writing Fellowship 449
NEH Fellowships 83
Russell Sage Foundation Visiting Scholar Appointments 578
Sir Eric Berthoud Travel Grant 689
Slawson Awards 565
Society for the Study of French History Bursaries 606
St Catherine's College Graduate Scholarship in the Arts
United States Holocaust Memorial Museum Center for Advanced
    Holocaust Studies Visiting Scholar Programs 641
University of Bristol Postgraduate Scholarships 672
University of Glasgow Postgraduate Research Scholarships 696
University of Otago International Scholarships 717
University of Otago PhD Scholarships 718
University of Otago Prestigious PhD Scholarships 718
Victoria University of Wellington PhD Scholarships 786
Wolfsonian-FIU Fellowship 800
Woodrow Wilson Dissertation Fellowship in Women s Studies

African Nations

Canadian Window on International Development 380
Hastings Center International Visiting Scholars Program 332
IDRC Doctoral Research Awards 380
IDRC Internship Awards 381
International Postgraduate Research Scholarships (IPRS) 413
ORSAS Awards 688

Australia

Hastings Center International Visiting Scholars Program 332
NBCF Doctoral Scholarship 469
NBCF Postdoctoral Fellowship 469
ORSAS Awards 688
Wingate Scholarships 697

Canada

Alcohol Beverage Medical Research Foundation Research Project
    Grant 14
Canadian Window on International Development 380
Gilbert Chinard Fellowships 361
Harmon Chadbourn Rorison Fellowship 361
Idea Grants 215
IDRC Doctoral Research Awards 380
IDRC Internship Awards 381
International Postgraduate Research Scholarships (IPRS) 413
ORSAS Awards 688
Research Planning Grants 216
Thérèse F Casgrain Fellowship 603
Wingate Scholarships 697

Caribbean Countries

Canadian Window on International Development 380
Hastings Center International Visiting Scholars Program 332
IDRC Doctoral Research Awards 380
IDRC Internship Awards 381
International Postgraduate Research Scholarships (IPRS) 413
ORSAS Awards 688

East European Countries

Hastings Center International Visiting Scholars Program 332
IDRC Doctoral Research Awards 380
International Postgraduate Research Scholarships (IPRS) 413
ORSAS Awards 688

European Union

CBRL Travel Grant 248
ESRC 1+3 Awards and +3 Awards
Wingate Scholarships 697

Middle East

Hastings Center International Visiting Scholars Program 332
IDRC Doctoral Research Awards 380
IDRC Internship Awards 381
International Postgraduate Research Scholarships (IPRS) 413
ORSAS Awards 688

New Zealand

Hastings Center International Visiting Scholars Program 332
ORSAS Awards 688
Wingate Scholarships 697

South Africa

Canadian Window on International Development 380
Hastings Center International Visiting Scholars Program 332
IDRC Doctoral Research Awards 380
IDRC Internship Awards 381
International Postgraduate Research Scholarships (IPRS) 413
ORSAS Awards 688
Wingate Scholarships 697

United Kingdom

Access to Learning Fund 685
Balsdon Fellowship 174
BIAA Travel Grants 168
CBRL Research Award 248
CBRL Travel Grant 248
ESRC 1+3 Awards and +3 Awards
Hastings Center International Visiting Scholars Program 332
Hector and Elizabeth Catling Bursary 173
International Postgraduate Research Scholarships (IPRS) 413
Mr and Mrs David Edward Memorial Award 145
Rome Awards 175
Rome Fellowship 175
Rome Scholarships in Ancient, Medieval and Later Italian Studies 176
Slawson Awards 565
University of Kent School of European Culture and Languages
   Scholarships 701
University of Kent School of European Culture and Languages
   Studentships 701
Wingate Scholarships 697

United States of America

AAUW Eleanor Roosevelt Fund Award 33
Alcohol Beverage Medical Research Foundation Research Project
   Grant 14
Annual Meeting Fellowship - Beverly Willis Architectural Foundation
   Travel Fellowship 608
ARCE Fellowships 80
British Marshall Scholarships 685
Fulbright Distinguished Chairs Program 248
Fulbright Senior Specialists Program 249
Gilbert Chinard Fellowships 361
Harmon Chadbourn Rorison Fellowship 361
International Postgraduate Research Scholarships (IPRS) 413
IREX Individual Advanced Research Opportunities 388
IREX Short-Term Travel Grants 389
Kennan Institute Research Scholarship 408
ORSAS Awards 688
Samuel H. Kress Foundation Fellowships for Speakers 609
SSRC JSPS Postdoctoral Fellowship 599
University of New Hampshire Postdoctoral Fellowships For Research
   on Family Violence 713

West European Countries

ESRC 1+3 Awards and +3 Awards
Hastings Center International Visiting Scholars Program 332
International Postgraduate Research Scholarships (IPRS) 413

Mr and Mrs David Edward Memorial Award 145
University of Kent School of European Culture and Languages
   Scholarships 701
University of Kent School of European Culture and Languages
   Studentships 701

URBAN STUDIES

Any Country

ASCSA Fellowships 82
BIAA Post-Doctoral Research Fellowship 168
BIAA Research Scholarship 168
BIAA Study Grants 168
BIAA Travel Grants 168
British Academy Overseas Conference Grants 158
British Academy Postdoctoral Fellowships 158
British Academy Small Research Grants 158
British Academy Worldwide Congress Grant 159
British Conference Grants 159
Eli Ginzberg Award 344
Frederick Douglass Institute Postdoctoral Fellowship 304
Frederick Douglass Institute Predoctoral Dissertation Fellowship 304
Gypsy Lore Society Young Scholar's Prize in Romani Studies 328
Harold D. Lasswell Award 344
HFG Research Program 332
Jennings Randolph Program for International Peace Dissertation
   Fellowship 643
John L Stanley Award 344
Joseph L Fisher Dissertation Award 546
Joshua Feigenbaum Award 344
Kennan Institute Short-Term Grants 408
Lee Kuan Yew School of Public Policy Graduate Scholarships
   (LKYSPPS) 491
M Alison Frantz Fellowship in Post-Classical Studies at the Gennadius
   Library 83
Martinus Nijhoff Award 345
Queen Mary Research Studentships 539
Robert K Merton Award 345
Russell Sage Foundation Visiting Scholar Appointments 578
Slawson Awards 565
University of Bristol Postgraduate Scholarships 672
University of Glasgow Postgraduate Research Scholarships 696
University of Kent Postgraduate Funding Awards 700
Victoria University of Wellington PhD Scholarships 786
Wolfsonian-FIU Fellowship 800

African Nations

Canadian Window on International Development 380
IDRC Doctoral Research Awards 380
IDRC Internship Awards 381
International Postgraduate Research Scholarships (IPRS) 413

Australia

Wingate Scholarships 697

Canada

Alcohol Beverage Medical Research Foundation Research Project
   Grant 14
Canadian Window on International Development 380
IDRC Doctoral Research Awards 380
IDRC Internship Awards 381
International Postgraduate Research Scholarships (IPRS) 413
Wingate Scholarships 697

Caribbean Countries

Canadian Window on International Development 380
IDRC Doctoral Research Awards 380
IDRC Internship Awards 381
International Postgraduate Research Scholarships (IPRS) 413

East European Countries

IDRC Doctoral Research Awards 380
International Postgraduate Research Scholarships (IPRS) 413

European Union

ESRC 1+3 Awards and +3 Awards
Wingate Scholarships 697

Middle East

IDRC Doctoral Research Awards 380
IDRC Internship Awards 381
International Postgraduate Research Scholarships (IPRS) 413

New Zealand

Wingate Scholarships 697

South Africa

Canadian Window on International Development 380
IDRC Doctoral Research Awards 380
IDRC Internship Awards 381
International Postgraduate Research Scholarships (IPRS) 413
Wingate Scholarships 697

United Kingdom

Balsdon Fellowship 174
BIAA Travel Grants 168
ESRC 1+3 Awards and +3 Awards
International Postgraduate Research Scholarships (IPRS) 413
Rome Awards 175
Rome Fellowship 175
Rome Scholarships in Ancient, Medieval and Later Italian Studies
    176
Slawson Awards 565
University of Kent Sociology Studentship 701
Wingate Scholarships 697

United States of America

Alcohol Beverage Medical Research Foundation Research Project
    Grant 14
American Academy in Rome Fellowships in Design Art 24
ARCE Fellowships 80
Fulbright Senior Specialists Program 249
International Postgraduate Research Scholarships (IPRS)
    413
IREX Individual Advanced Research Opportunities 388
Kennan Institute Research Scholarship 408
SAH Study Tour Fellowship 608
Samuel H. Kress Foundation Fellowships for Speakers 609
SSRC Abe Fellowship Program 598
SSRC JSPS Postdoctoral Fellowship 599

West European Countries

ESRC 1+3 Awards and +3 Awards
International Postgraduate Research Scholarships (IPRS) 413
University of Kent Sociology Studentship 701

RURAL STUDIES

Any Country

ASCSA Fellowships 82
BIAA Post-Doctoral Research Fellowship 168
BIAA Research Scholarship 168
BIAA Study Grants 168
BIAA Travel Grants 168
British Academy Overseas Conference Grants 158
British Academy Postdoctoral Fellowships 158
British Academy Small Research Grants 158
British Academy Worldwide Congress Grant 159
British Conference Grants 159
Earthwatch Field Research Grants 272
Jennings Randolph Program for International Peace Dissertation
    Fellowship 643
Joseph L Fisher Dissertation Award 546
Kennan Institute Short-Term Grants 408
M Alison Frantz Fellowship in Post-Classical Studies at the Gennadius
    Library 83

Rhodes University Postdoctoral Fellowship and The Andrew Mellon
    Postdoctoral Fellowship 548
Scholarship opportunities linked to CATIE's Postgraduate Program
    including CATIE scholarship forming part of the Scholarship-Loan
    Program 638
Slawson Awards 565
Teagasc Walsh Fellowships 626
University of Glasgow Postgraduate Research Scholarships 696
Victoria University of Wellington PhD Scholarships 786

African Nations

Canadian Window on International Development 380
IDRC Doctoral Research Awards 380
IDRC Internship Awards 381
International Postgraduate Research Scholarships (IPRS) 413

Australia

Wingate Scholarships 697

Canada

Alcohol Beverage Medical Research Foundation Research Project
    Grant 14
Canadian Window on International Development 380
IDRC Doctoral Research Awards 380
IDRC Internship Awards 381
International Postgraduate Research Scholarships (IPRS) 413
Wingate Scholarships 697

Caribbean Countries

Canadian Window on International Development 380
IDRC Doctoral Research Awards 380
IDRC Internship Awards 381
International Postgraduate Research Scholarships (IPRS) 413

East European Countries

IDRC Doctoral Research Awards 380
International Postgraduate Research Scholarships (IPRS) 413

European Union

ESRC 1+3 Awards and +3 Awards
Wingate Scholarships 697

Middle East

IDRC Doctoral Research Awards 380
IDRC Internship Awards 381
International Postgraduate Research Scholarships (IPRS) 413

New Zealand

Wingate Scholarships 697

South Africa

Canadian Window on International Development 380
IDRC Doctoral Research Awards 380
IDRC Internship Awards 381
International Postgraduate Research Scholarships (IPRS) 413
Wingate Scholarships 697

United Kingdom

Aberystwyth Postgraduate Research Studentships 4
BIAA Travel Grants 168
ESRC 1+3 Awards and +3 Awards
International Postgraduate Research Scholarships (IPRS) 413
Slawson Awards 565
Wingate Scholarships 697

United States of America

Alcohol Beverage Medical Research Foundation Research Project
    Grant 14
ARCE Fellowships 80
International Postgraduate Research Scholarships (IPRS) 413
IREX Individual Advanced Research Opportunities 388
Kennan Institute Research Scholarship 408

SAH Study Tour Fellowship 608
SSRC Abe Fellowship Program 598
SSRC JSPS Postdoctoral Fellowship 599

West European Countries

ESRC 1 + 3 Awards and + 3 Awards
International Postgraduate Research Scholarships (IPRS)
413

COGNITIVE SCIENCES

Any Country

Alzheimer's Society Research Grants
Association for Women in Science Educational Foundation
Predoctoral Awards 118
BackCare Research Grants 144
BIAA Post-Doctoral Research Fellowship 168
BIAA Research Scholarship 168
BIAA Study Grants 168
BIAA Travel Grants 168
British Academy Overseas Conference Grants 158
British Academy Postdoctoral Fellowships 158
British Academy Small Research Grants 158
British Academy Worldwide Congress Grant 159
British Conference Grants 159
ETS Summer Internship Program for Graduate Students
276
Gilbert F White Postdoctoral Fellowship 545
HRB Postdoctoral Research Fellowships 334
Jennings Randolph Program for International Peace Dissertation
Fellowship 643
Joseph L Fisher Dissertation Award 546
MRC Career Development Award 439
MRC Clinical Research Training Fellowships 439
MRC Clinician Scientist Fellowship 439
MRC Royal College of Surgeons of Edinburgh Clinical Research
Training Fellowship 440
MRC Royal College of Surgeons of England Training Fellowship
441
MRC Senior Non-Clinical Fellowship 441
MRC Special Training Fellowships in Health Services and Health of
the Public Research 441
MRC/Academy of Medical Sciences Tenure Track Clinician Scientist
Fellowship 442
PDS Project Grant 521
UFAW Research and Project Awards 645
UFAW Small Project and Travel Awards 645
UFAW Vacation Scholarships 645
University of Glasgow Postgraduate Research Scholarships 696
Victoria University of Wellington PhD Scholarships 786
Wellcome Trust Grants 794

African Nations

International Postgraduate Research Scholarships (IPRS) 413
Shell Centenary Scholarships and Shell Centenary Chevening
Scholarships at Edinburgh 683

Australia

Career Development Awards 477
Wingate Scholarships 697

Canada

Alcohol Beverage Medical Research Foundation Research Project
Grant 14
International Postgraduate Research Scholarships (IPRS)
413
Wingate Scholarships 697

Caribbean Countries

International Postgraduate Research Scholarships (IPRS) 413
Shell Centenary Scholarships and Shell Centenary Chevening
Scholarships at Edinburgh 683

East European Countries

International Postgraduate Research Scholarships (IPRS) 413
Shell Centenary Scholarships and Shell Centenary Chevening
Scholarships at Edinburgh 683

European Union

ESRC 1 + 3 Awards and + 3 Awards
Wingate Scholarships 697

Middle East

International Postgraduate Research Scholarships (IPRS) 413
Shell Centenary Scholarships and Shell Centenary Chevening
Scholarships at Edinburgh 683

New Zealand

Wingate Scholarships 697

South Africa

International Postgraduate Research Scholarships (IPRS) 413
Shell Centenary Scholarships and Shell Centenary Chevening
Scholarships at Edinburgh 683
Wingate Scholarships 697

United Kingdom

BIAA Travel Grants 168
ESRC 1 + 3 Awards and + 3 Awards
International Postgraduate Research Scholarships (IPRS) 413
Mr and Mrs David Edward Memorial Award 145
Wingate Scholarships 697

United States of America

Alcohol Beverage Medical Research Foundation Research Project
Grant 14
British Marshall Scholarships 685
ETS Summer Internship Program for Graduate Students 276
Fulbright Senior Specialists Program 249
International Postgraduate Research Scholarships (IPRS) 413
Kennan Institute Research Scholarship 408
NDSEG Fellowship Program 84
NIH Research Grants 483
SMART Scholarship for Service Program 85
SSRC JSPS Postdoctoral Fellowship 599

West European Countries

ESRC 1 + 3 Awards and + 3 Awards
International Postgraduate Research Scholarships (IPRS) 413
Mr and Mrs David Edward Memorial Award 145
Shell Centenary Scholarships and Shell Centenary Chevening
Scholarships at Edinburgh 683

PSYCHOLOGY

Any Country

Acadia Graduate Awards 5
AFSP Distinguished Investigator Awards 55
AFSP Pilot Grants 55
AFSP Postdoctoral Research Fellowships 55
AFSP Standard Research Grants 55
AFSP Young Investigator Award 56
Albert Ellis Institute Clinical Fellowship 12
Alberta Heritage Clinical Fellowships 12
Alberta Heritage Full-Time Fellowships 13
Alberta Heritage Full-Time Studentship 13
Alberta Heritage Part-Time Fellowships 13
Alberta Heritage Part-Time Studentship 13
Alzheimer's Society Research Grants
Association for Women in Science Educational Foundation
Predoctoral Awards 118
BackCare Research Grants 144
Behavioral Sciences Postdoctoral Fellowships 282
Benton Meier Neuropsychology Scholarships 77
BIAA Post-Doctoral Research Fellowship 168

African Nations

Australia

Canada

Caribbean Countries

East European Countries

European Union

Middle East

New Zealand

South Africa

United Kingdom

Counseling Psychology Fund 77
ESRC 1 + 3 Awards and + 3 Awards
ESRC + 3 Department of Psychology Studentship
International Postgraduate Research Scholarships (IPRS) 413
James Watt Research Scholarships 694
Mr and Mrs David Edward Memorial Award 145
Wingate Scholarships 697

United States of America

Alcohol Beverage Medical Research Foundation Research Project Grant 14
Andrew Stratton Scholarship 690
British Marshall Scholarships 685
ETS Postdoctoral Fellowships 276
ETS Summer Internship Program for Graduate Students 276
Fulbright Distinguished Chairs Program 248
Fulbright Senior Specialists Program 249
International Postgraduate Research Scholarships (IPRS) 413
IREX Individual Advanced Research Opportunities 388
IREX Short-Term Travel Grants 389
Kennan Institute Research Scholarship 408
Lung Health (LH) Research Dissertation Grants 66
NIH Research Grants 483
ORSAS Awards 688
SSRC JSPS Postdoctoral Fellowship 599
University of New Hampshire Postdoctoral Fellowships For Research on Family Violence 713
Washington University Chancellor's Graduate Fellowship Program 792

West European Countries

ESRC 1 + 3 Awards and + 3 Awards
International Postgraduate Research Scholarships (IPRS) 413
Mr and Mrs David Edward Memorial Award 145

EXPERIMENTAL PSYCHOLOGY

Any Country

Alzheimer's Society Research Grants
D Scott Rogo Award for Parapsychological Literature 520
Eileen J Garrett Scholarship 520
NARSAD Distinguished Investigator Awards 465
NARSAD Independent Investigator Awards 465
NARSAD Young Investigator Awards 465
Parapsychology Foundation Grant 520
TSA Research Grant and Fellowship Program 634
UFAW Research and Project Awards 645
UFAW Small Project and Travel Awards 645
UFAW Vacation Scholarships 645
University of Bristol Postgraduate Scholarships 672
Victoria University of Wellington PhD Scholarships 786

African Nations

International Postgraduate Research Scholarships (IPRS) 413
ORSAS Awards 688

Australia

Career Development Awards 477
Howard Florey Centenary Fellowship 478
Neil Hamilton Fairley Fellowships (Overseas Clinical) 478
NHMRC Medical and Dental and Public Health Postgraduate Research Scholarships 478
ORSAS Awards 688
Training Scholarship for Indigenous Health Research 479
Victoria Fellowships 264
Wingate Scholarships 697

Canada

International Postgraduate Research Scholarships (IPRS) 413
ORSAS Awards 688
Wingate Scholarships 697

Caribbean Countries

International Postgraduate Research Scholarships (IPRS) 413
ORSAS Awards 688

East European Countries

International Postgraduate Research Scholarships (IPRS) 413
ORSAS Awards 688

European Union

ESRC 1 + 3 Awards and + 3 Awards
Wingate Scholarships 697

Middle East

International Postgraduate Research Scholarships (IPRS) 413
ORSAS Awards 688

New Zealand

ORSAS Awards 688
Training Scholarship for Indigenous Health Research 479
Wingate Scholarships 697

South Africa

International Postgraduate Research Scholarships (IPRS) 413
ORSAS Awards 688
Wingate Scholarships 697

United Kingdom

ESRC 1 + 3 Awards and + 3 Awards
International Postgraduate Research Scholarships (IPRS) 413
Mr and Mrs David Edward Memorial Award 145
Wingate Scholarships 697

United States of America

British Marshall Scholarships 685
International Postgraduate Research Scholarships (IPRS) 413
NIH Research Grants 483
ORSAS Awards 688
Washington University Chancellor's Graduate Fellowship Program 792

West European Countries

ESRC 1 + 3 Awards and + 3 Awards
International Postgraduate Research Scholarships (IPRS) 413
Mr and Mrs David Edward Memorial Award 145

SOCIAL AND COMMUNITY PSYCHOLOGY

Any Country

Alzheimer's Society Research Grants
BackCare Research Grants 144
Breast Cancer Campaign Project Grants 157
D Scott Rogo Award for Parapsychological Literature 520
Eileen J Garrett Scholarship 520
Frederick Douglass Institute Postdoctoral Fellowship 304
Frederick Douglass Institute Predoctoral Dissertation Fellowship 304
Harold D. Lasswell Award 344
HFG Research Program 332
John L Stanley Award 344
Joshua Feigenbaum Award 344
Louise Kidder Early Career Award 606
Martinus Nijhoff Award 345
Parapsychology Foundation Grant 520
PDS Project Grant 521
Postgraduate Research Bursaries (Epilepsy Action) 282
Rhodes University Postdoctoral Fellowship and The Andrew Mellon Postdoctoral Fellowship 548
Shelby Cullom Davis Center Research Projects, Research Fellowships 586
SPSSI Applied Social Issues Internship Program 605
SPSSI Grants-in-Aid Program 605
SPSSI Social Issues Dissertation Award 606

Teagasc Walsh Fellowships 626
Victoria University of Wellington PhD Scholarships 786

African Nations

International Postgraduate Research Scholarships (IPRS) 413
ORSAS Awards 688

Australia

Australian Clinical Research Postdoctoral Fellowship 477
Biomedical (Dora Lush) and Public Health Postgraduate Scholarships 477
The Cancer Council NSW Research Project Grants 217
Career Development Awards 477
CRC Grants 254
Hazel Hawke Research Grant in Dementia Care 22
Howard Florey Centenary Fellowship 478
Neil Hamilton Fairley Fellowships (Overseas Clinical) 478
NHMRC Medical and Dental and Public Health Postgraduate
    Research Scholarships 478
ORSAS Awards 688
Public Health Fellowship (Australian) 479
Sidney Sax Fellowship (Overseas Public Health) 479
Training Scholarship for Indigenous Health Research 479
Wingate Scholarships 697

Canada

Idea Grants 215
International Postgraduate Research Scholarships (IPRS) 413
ORSAS Awards 688
Research Planning Grants 216
Wingate Scholarships 697

Caribbean Countries

International Postgraduate Research Scholarships (IPRS) 413
ORSAS Awards 688

East European Countries

International Postgraduate Research Scholarships (IPRS) 413
ORSAS Awards 688

European Union

ESRC 1+3 Awards and +3 Awards
Wingate Scholarships 697

Middle East

International Postgraduate Research Scholarships (IPRS) 413
ORSAS Awards 688

New Zealand

ORSAS Awards 688
Training Scholarship for Indigenous Health Research 479
Wingate Scholarships 697

South Africa

International Postgraduate Research Scholarships (IPRS) 413
ORSAS Awards 688
Wingate Scholarships 697

United Kingdom

ESRC 1+3 Awards and +3 Awards
International Postgraduate Research Scholarships (IPRS) 413
Mr and Mrs David Edward Memorial Award 145
Wingate Scholarships 697

United States of America

British Marshall Scholarships 685
International Postgraduate Research Scholarships (IPRS) 413
NIH Research Grants 483
ORSAS Awards 688
Washington University Chancellor's Graduate Fellowship Program 792

West European Countries

ESRC 1+3 Awards and +3 Awards
International Postgraduate Research Scholarships (IPRS) 413
Mr and Mrs David Edward Memorial Award 145

CLINICAL PSYCHOLOGY

Any Country

The Airey Neave Trust Scholarship 12
Albert Ellis Institute Clinical Fellowship 12
Alzheimer's Society Research Grants
BackCare Research Grants 144
HRB Project Grants-General 334
NARSAD Distinguished Investigator Awards 465
NARSAD Independent Investigator Awards 465
NARSAD Young Investigator Awards 465
PDS Project Grant 521
Postgraduate Research Bursaries (Epilepsy Action) 282
Rhodes University Postdoctoral Fellowship and The Andrew Mellon
    Postdoctoral Fellowship 548
Sully Scholarship 657
TSA Research Grant and Fellowship Program 634
Victoria University of Wellington PhD Scholarships 786

African Nations

International Postgraduate Research Scholarships (IPRS) 413
ORSAS Awards 688

Australia

Australian Clinical Research Postdoctoral Fellowship 477
Biomedical (Dora Lush) and Public Health Postgraduate Scholarships 477
The Cancer Council NSW Research Project Grants 217
Career Development Awards 477
Howard Florey Centenary Fellowship 478
NBCF Doctoral Scholarship 469
NBCF Postdoctoral Scholarship 469
Neil Hamilton Fairley Fellowships (Overseas Clinical) 478
NHMRC Medical and Dental and Public Health Postgraduate
    Research Scholarships 478
ORSAS Awards 688
Public Health Fellowship (Australian) 479
Sidney Sax Fellowship (Overseas Public Health) 479
Training Scholarship for Indigenous Health Research 479
Victoria Fellowships 264

Canada

International Postgraduate Research Scholarships (IPRS) 413
ORSAS Awards 688

Caribbean Countries

International Postgraduate Research Scholarships (IPRS) 413
ORSAS Awards 688

East European Countries

International Postgraduate Research Scholarships (IPRS) 413
ORSAS Awards 688

European Union

Clinical Psychology Awards 648

Middle East

International Postgraduate Research Scholarships (IPRS) 413
ORSAS Awards 688

New Zealand

ORSAS Awards 688
Training Scholarship for Indigenous Health Research 479

South Africa

International Postgraduate Research Scholarships (IPRS) 413
ORSAS Awards 688

United Kingdom

Clinical Psychology Awards 648
International Postgraduate Research Scholarships (IPRS) 413
Mr and Mrs David Edward Memorial Award 145
PWSA UK Research Grants 536

United States of America

British Marshall Scholarships 685
International Postgraduate Research Scholarships (IPRS) 413
MFP Mental Health and Substance Abuse Services Doctoral Fellowship 76
NIH Research Grants 483
ORSAS Awards 688
University of New Hampshire Postdoctoral Fellowships For Research on Family Violence 713
Washington University Chancellor's Graduate Fellowship Program 792

West European Countries

International Postgraduate Research Scholarships (IPRS) 413
Mr and Mrs David Edward Memorial Award 145

PERSONALITY PSYCHOLOGY

Any Country

Alzheimer's Society Research Grants
BackCare Research Grants 144
Victoria University of Wellington PhD Scholarships 786

African Nations

International Postgraduate Research Scholarships (IPRS) 413

Canada

International Postgraduate Research Scholarships (IPRS) 413

Caribbean Countries

International Postgraduate Research Scholarships (IPRS) 413

East European Countries

International Postgraduate Research Scholarships (IPRS) 413

European Union

ESRC 1 + 3 Awards and + 3 Awards

Middle East

International Postgraduate Research Scholarships (IPRS) 413

South Africa

International Postgraduate Research Scholarships (IPRS) 413

United Kingdom

ESRC 1 + 3 Awards and + 3 Awards
International Postgraduate Research Scholarships (IPRS) 413
Mr and Mrs David Edward Memorial Award 145
PWSA UK Research Grants 536

United States of America

British Marshall Scholarships 685
International Postgraduate Research Scholarships (IPRS) 413
NIH Research Grants 483

West European Countries

ESRC 1 + 3 Awards and + 3 Awards
International Postgraduate Research Scholarships (IPRS) 413
Mr and Mrs David Edward Memorial Award 145

INDUSTRIAL/ORGANISATIONAL PSYCHOLOGY

Any Country

BackCare Research Grants 144
Institute for Advanced Study Postdoctoral Residential Fellowships 363
Rhodes University Postdoctoral Fellowship and The Andrew Mellon Postdoctoral Fellowship 548
Victoria University of Wellington PhD Scholarships 786

African Nations

International Postgraduate Research Scholarships (IPRS) 413
ORSAS Awards 688

Australia

ORSAS Awards 688

Canada

International Postgraduate Research Scholarships (IPRS) 413
ORSAS Awards 688

Caribbean Countries

International Postgraduate Research Scholarships (IPRS) 413
ORSAS Awards 688

East European Countries

International Postgraduate Research Scholarships (IPRS) 413
ORSAS Awards 688

European Union

ESRC 1 + 3 Awards and + 3 Awards

Middle East

International Postgraduate Research Scholarships (IPRS) 413
ORSAS Awards 688

New Zealand

ORSAS Awards 688

South Africa

International Postgraduate Research Scholarships (IPRS) 413
ORSAS Awards 688

United Kingdom

ESRC 1 + 3 Awards and + 3 Awards
International Postgraduate Research Scholarships (IPRS) 413
Mr and Mrs David Edward Memorial Award 145

United States of America

British Marshall Scholarships 685
International Postgraduate Research Scholarships (IPRS) 413
ORSAS Awards 688

West European Countries

ESRC 1 + 3 Awards and + 3 Awards
International Postgraduate Research Scholarships (IPRS) 413
Mr and Mrs David Edward Memorial Award 145

PSYCHOMETRICS

Any Country

Alzheimer's Society Research Grants
ETS Summer Internship Program for Graduate Students 276
NARSAD Distinguished Investigator Awards 465
NARSAD Independent Investigator Awards 465
NARSAD Young Investigator Awards 465
Victoria University of Wellington PhD Scholarships 786

African Nations

ORSAS Awards 688

Australia

ORSAS Awards 688

Canada

ORSAS Awards 688

Caribbean Countries

ORSAS Awards 688

East European Countries

ORSAS Awards 688

Middle East

ORSAS Awards 688

New Zealand

ORSAS Awards 688

South Africa

ORSAS Awards 688

United Kingdom

Mr and Mrs David Edward Memorial Award 145

United States of America

British Marshall Scholarships 685
ETS Summer Internship Program for Graduate Students 276
NIH Research Grants 483
ORSAS Awards 688
University of New Hampshire Postdoctoral Fellowships For Research
    on Family Violence 713

West European Countries

Mr and Mrs David Edward Memorial Award 145

EDUCATIONAL PSYCHOLOGY

Any Country

BackCare Research Grants 144
John L Stanley Award 344
Joshua Feigenbaum Award 344
Martinus Nijhoff Award 345
Rhodes University Postdoctoral Fellowship and The Andrew Mellon
    Postdoctoral Fellowship 548
University of Bristol Postgraduate Scholarships 672
Victoria University of Wellington PhD Scholarships 786

African Nations

ORSAS Awards 688

Australia

ORSAS Awards 688
Wingate Scholarships 697

Canada

ORSAS Awards 688
Wingate Scholarships 697

Caribbean Countries

ORSAS Awards 688

East European Countries

ORSAS Awards 688

European Union

ESRC 1+3 Awards and +3 Awards
Wingate Scholarships 697

Middle East

ORSAS Awards 688

New Zealand

ORSAS Awards 688
Wingate Scholarships 697

South Africa

ORSAS Awards 688
Wingate Scholarships 697

United Kingdom

ESRC 1+3 Awards and +3 Awards
Mr and Mrs David Edward Memorial Award 145
PWSA UK Research Grants 536
Wingate Scholarships 697

United States of America

British Marshall Scholarships 685
ORSAS Awards 688

West European Countries

ESRC 1+3 Awards and +3 Awards
Mr and Mrs David Edward Memorial Award 145

GEOGRAPHY (SOCIAL AND ECONOMIC)

Any Country

AAG General Research Fund 119
Ahmanson and Getty Postdoctoral Fellowships 639
ASCSA Fellowships 82
Association for Women in Science Educational Foundation
    Predoctoral Awards 118
BIAA Post-Doctoral Research Fellowship 168
BIAA Research Scholarship 168
BIAA Study Grants 168
BIAA Travel Grants 168
BIAA/SPHS Fieldwork Award 168
British Academy Overseas Conference Grants 158
British Academy Postdoctoral Fellowships 158
British Academy Small Research Grants 158
British Academy Worldwide Congress Grant 159
British Airways Travel Bursary 563
British Conference Grants 159
CRF (Caledonian Research Foundation)/RSE European Visiting
    Research Fellowships 628
Earthwatch Field Research Grants 272
Gypsy Lore Society Young Scholar's Prize in Romani Studies 328
Harold D. Lasswell Award 344
Innovative Geography Teaching Grants 564
J. Warren Nystrom Award 119
John L Stanley Award 344
Joseph L Fisher Dissertation Award 546
Joshua Feigenbaum Award 344
Journey of a Lifetime Award 564
Kennan Institute Short-Term Grants 408
M Alison Frantz Fellowship in Post-Classical Studies at the Gennadius
    Library 83
Martinus Nijhoff Award 345
Monica Cole Research Grant 564
NCAR Graduate Visitor Programme 471
NCAR Postdoctoral Appointments in the Advanced Study Program
    471
Queen Mary Research Studentships 539
RGS-IBG Land Rover 'GO Beyond' Bursary 565
Rhodes University Postdoctoral Fellowship and The Andrew Mellon
    Postdoctoral Fellowship 548
Robert K Merton Award 345
Slawson Awards 565
Small Research Grants 566
St Catherine's College Graduate Scholarship in the Arts
Teagasc Walsh Fellowships 626
Thesiger-Oman Research Fellowship 566
University of Bristol Postgraduate Scholarships 672
University of Otago International Scholarships 717
University of Otago PhD Scholarships 718

University of Otago Prestigious PhD Scholarships 718
University of Southampton Postgraduate Studentships 759
Victoria University of Wellington PhD Scholarships 786
World Universities Network (WUN) International Research Mobility
  Scheme 759

African Nations

IDRC Doctoral Research Awards 380
IDRC Internship Awards 381
International Postgraduate Research Scholarships (IPRS) 413

Australia

Wingate Scholarships 697

Canada

Canadian Commonwealth Scholarship and Fellowship Plan 201
IDRC Doctoral Research Awards 380
IDRC Internship Awards 381
International Postgraduate Research Scholarships (IPRS) 413
Wingate Scholarships 697

Caribbean Countries

IDRC Doctoral Research Awards 380
IDRC Internship Awards 381
International Postgraduate Research Scholarships (IPRS) 413

East European Countries

Freie Universität Berlin John-F.-Kennedy-Institut für
  Nordamerikastudien Research Grants 304
IDRC Doctoral Research Awards 380
International Postgraduate Research Scholarships (IPRS) 413

European Union

Akroyd, Brotherton and Brown Scholarship 702
CBRL Travel Grant 248
Department of Geography Teaching/Computing Assistantships 650
EPSRC Geographical Research Grants 563
ESRC 1+3 Awards and +3 Awards
Freie Universität Berlin John-F.-Kennedy-Institut für
  Nordamerikastudien Research Grants 304
John Henry Garner Scholarship 703
RGS-IBG Postgraduate Research Awards 565
W B Crump Scholarship 705
Wingate Scholarships 697

Middle East

IDRC Doctoral Research Awards 380
IDRC Internship Awards 381
International Postgraduate Research Scholarships (IPRS) 413

New Zealand

Wingate Scholarships 697

South Africa

IDRC Doctoral Research Awards 380
IDRC Internship Awards 381
International Postgraduate Research Scholarships (IPRS) 413
Wingate Scholarships 697

United Kingdom

Aberystwyth Postgraduate Research Studentships 4
Akroyd, Brotherton and Brown Scholarship 702
Balsdon Fellowship 174
BIAA Travel Grants 168
CBRL Research Award 248
CBRL Travel Grant 248
Department of Geography Teaching/Computing Assistantships 650
EPSRC Geographical Research Grants 563
ESRC 1+3 Awards and +3 Awards
Geographical Fieldwork Grants 564
Grundy Educational Trust 327
International Postgraduate Research Scholarships (IPRS) 413
John Henry Garner Scholarship 703

Neville Shulman Challenge Award 565
Peter Fleming Award 565
Ray Y. Gildea Jr. Award 565
RGS-IBG Postgraduate Research Awards 565
Rome Awards 175
Rome Fellowship 175
Rome Scholarships in Ancient, Medieval and Later Italian Studies
  176
Slawson Awards 565
W B Crump Scholarship 705
Wingate Scholarships 697

United States of America

Budweiser Conservation Scholarship 475
Fulbright Distinguished Chairs Program 248
Fulbright Senior Specialists Program 249
IGU Travel Grant 119
International Postgraduate Research Scholarships (IPRS) 413
IREX Individual Advanced Research Opportunities 388
IREX Short-Term Travel Grants 389
Kennan Institute Research Scholarship 408
NCAR Faculty Fellowship Programme 471
Ray Y. Gildea Jr. Award 565
SSRC Abe Fellowship Program 598
SSRC JSPS Postdoctoral Fellowship 599
Visiting Geographical Scientist Program 119

West European Countries

ESRC 1+3 Awards and +3 Awards
Freie Universität Berlin John-F.-Kennedy-Institut für
  Nordamerikastudien Research Grants 304
International Postgraduate Research Scholarships (IPRS) 413

DEVELOPMENT STUDIES

Any Country

BIAA Post-Doctoral Research Fellowship 168
BIAA Research Scholarship 168
BIAA Study Grants 168
BIAA Travel Grants 168
British Academy Postdoctoral Fellowships 158
Earthwatch Field Research Grants 272
Gilbert F White Postdoctoral Fellowship 545
Gilbert Murray Trust Junior Awards 318
Harold D. Lasswell Award 344
Hastings Center International Visiting Scholars Program 332
IDPM Taught Postgraduate Scholarship Scheme 706
Institute for Advanced Study Postdoctoral Residential Fellowships
  363
John L Stanley Award 344
Joseph L Fisher Dissertation Award 546
Joshua Feigenbaum Award 344
Kennan Institute Short-Term Grants 408
M Alison Frantz Fellowship in Post-Classical Studies at the Gennadius
  Library 83
Martinus Nijhoff Award 345
Paul H. Nitze School of Advanced International Studies (SAIS)
  Financial Aid and Fellowships 155
Rhodes University Postdoctoral Fellowship and The Andrew Mellon
  Postdoctoral Fellowship 548
Robert K Merton Award 345
Slawson Awards 565
Small Research Grants 566
SOAS Bursary 583
SOAS Research Student Fellowships 583
St Catherine's College Graduate Scholarship in the Arts
Teagasc Walsh Fellowships 626
University of Bristol Postgraduate Scholarships 672
Victoria University of Wellington PhD Scholarships 786
WILPF Internship in Human Rights 801
World Bank Cambridge Scholarships for Postgraduate Study
  198
World Bank Grants Facility for Indigenous Peoples 805

African Nations

Canadian Window on International Development 380
Hastings Center International Visiting Scholars Program 332
IDRC Doctoral Research Awards 380
IDRC Evaluation Research Awards 381
IDRC Internship Awards 381
International Postgraduate Research Scholarships (IPRS) 413
Kulika Charitable Trust-FCO Chevening-University of Leeds
  Scholarships 703
World Bank Grants Facility for Indigenous Peoples 805

Australia

Hastings Center International Visiting Scholars Program 332
Wingate Scholarships 697

Canada

Alcohol Beverage Medical Research Foundation Research Project
  Grant 14
Canadian Window on International Development 380
Community Forestry: Trees and People-John G Bene Fellowship 380
IDRC Doctoral Research Awards 380
IDRC Evaluation Research Awards 381
IDRC Internship Awards 381
International Postgraduate Research Scholarships (IPRS) 413
Organization of American States (OAS) Fellowships Programs 201
Wingate Scholarships 697

Caribbean Countries

Canadian Window on International Development 380
Hastings Center International Visiting Scholars Program 332
IDRC Doctoral Research Awards 380
IDRC Evaluation Research Awards 381
IDRC Internship Awards 381
International Postgraduate Research Scholarships (IPRS) 413

East European Countries

Hastings Center International Visiting Scholars Program 332
IDRC Doctoral Research Awards 380
IDRC Evaluation Research Awards 381
International Postgraduate Research Scholarships (IPRS) 413

European Union

CBRL Travel Grant 248
ESRC 1 + 3 Awards and + 3 Awards
Wingate Scholarships 697

Middle East

Hastings Center International Visiting Scholars Program 332
IDRC Doctoral Research Awards 380
IDRC Evaluation Research Awards 381
IDRC Internship Awards 381
International Postgraduate Research Scholarships (IPRS) 413

New Zealand

Hastings Center International Visiting Scholars Program 332
Wingate Scholarships 697

South Africa

Canadian Window on International Development 380
Hastings Center International Visiting Scholars Program 332
IDRC Doctoral Research Awards 380
IDRC Evaluation Research Awards 381
IDRC Internship Awards 381
International Postgraduate Research Scholarships (IPRS) 413
SAIIA Konrad Adenauer Foundation Research Internship 615
Wingate Scholarships 697

United Kingdom

BIAA Travel Grants 168
CBRL Research Award 248
CBRL Travel Grant 248
ESRC 1 + 3 Awards and + 3 Awards
Geographical Fieldwork Grants 564

Goldsmiths' Company Science for Society Courses
Hastings Center International Visiting Scholars Program 332
International Postgraduate Research Scholarships (IPRS) 413
Slawson Awards 565
Wingate Scholarships 697

United States of America

Alcohol Beverage Medical Research Foundation Research Project
  Grant 14
Budweiser Conservation Scholarship 475
International Postgraduate Research Scholarships (IPRS) 413
IREX Individual Advanced Research Opportunities 388
IREX Short-Term Travel Grants 389
Kennan Institute Research Scholarship 408
SSRC Abe Fellowship Program 598
SSRC JSPS Postdoctoral Fellowship 599

West European Countries

ESRC 1 + 3 Awards and + 3 Awards
Hastings Center International Visiting Scholars Program 332
International Postgraduate Research Scholarships (IPRS) 413

AREA AND CULTURAL STUDIES

Any Country

AAS Joyce Tracy Fellowship 26
Ahmad Abu-Hakima Scholarship 582
AISF Scholarship 125
Albert J Beveridge Grant 58
Albin Salton Fellowship 789
An Wang Postdoctoral Fellowship 289
Andrew W Mellon Postdoctoral Fellowship 795
ASCSA Fellowships 82
ASCSA Research Fellowship in Environmental Studies 82
ASCSA Research Fellowship in Faunal Studies 82
ASCSA Research Fellowship in Geoarchaeology 82
Australian Bicentennial (Australia) Scholarships and Fellowships 410
Austro-American Association of Boston Stipend 143
Bernadotte E Schmitt Grants 58
Bernard and Audre Rapoport Fellowships 431
BIAA Post-Doctoral Research Fellowship 168
BIAA Research Scholarship 168
BIAA Study Grants 168
BIAA Travel Grants 168
BIAA/SPHS Fieldwork Award 168
British Academy Overseas Conference Grants 158
British Academy Postdoctoral Fellowships 158
British Academy Sino-British Fellowship Trust 158
British Academy Small Research Grants 158
British Academy Worldwide Congress Grant 159
British Conference Grants 159
C H Currey Memorial Fellowship 618
Camargo Fellowships 182
CDI Internship 223
CSA Adele Filene Travel Award 247
CSA Stella Blum Research Grant 247
CSA Travel Research Grant 248
Dina Abramowicz Emerging Scholar Fellowship 807
Earthwatch Field Research Grants 272
Ethel Marcus Memorial Fellowship 431
Frederick Douglass Institute Postdoctoral Fellowship 304
Frederick Douglass Institute Predoctoral Dissertation Fellowship 304
Graduate Dissertation Research Fellowship 448
Graduate Summer Travel Grants 449
Gypsy Lore Society Young Scholar's Prize in Romani Studies 328
Harold D. Lasswell Award 344
Harvard Postdoctoral Fellowships in Japanese Studies 277
HFG Research Program 332
IFUWA Sarojini Naidu Memorial Scholarship 167
Institute for Advanced Study Postdoctoral Residential Fellowships 363
Irish Research Funds 394
The Isi Leibler Prize 261
John L Stanley Award 344
The Joseph and Eva R Dave Fellowship 432

Caribbean Countries

Canadian Window on International Development 380

European Union

AHRC Doctoral Awards Scheme 109
Professional Preparation Master's Scheme
Research Preparation Master's Scheme

South Africa

Canadian Window on International Development 380

United Kingdom

AHRC Doctoral Awards Scheme 109
Professional Preparation Master's Scheme
Research Preparation Master's Scheme

United States of America

ARCE Fellowships 80

SUBSAHARA AFRICAN

Any Country

Bernadotte E Schmitt Grants 58
Frederick Douglass Institute Postdoctoral Fellowship 304
Frederick Douglass Institute Predoctoral Dissertation Fellowship 304
SAIIA Bradlow Fellowship 614

African Nations

Canadian Window on International Development 380

Canada

Canadian Window on International Development 380

Caribbean Countries

Canadian Window on International Development 380

European Union

AHRC Doctoral Awards Scheme 109
Professional Preparation Master's Scheme
Research Preparation Master's Scheme

South Africa

Canadian Window on International Development 380

United Kingdom

AHRC Doctoral Awards Scheme 109
Professional Preparation Master's Scheme
Research Preparation Master's Scheme

AFRICAN STUDIES

Any Country

Bernadotte E Schmitt Grants 58
Frederick Douglass Institute Postdoctoral Fellowship 304
Frederick Douglass Institute Predoctoral Dissertation Fellowship 304
Huggins-Quarles Dissertation Award 515
Paul H. Nitze School of Advanced International Studies (SAIS) Financial Aid and Fellowships 155
Rhodes University Postdoctoral Fellowship and The Andrew Mellon Postdoctoral Fellowship 548
SAIIA Bradlow Fellowship 614

African Nations

British Institute in Eastern Africa Graduate Attachments 169
Canadian Window on International Development 380

Canada

Canadian Window on International Development 380

Caribbean Countries

Canadian Window on International Development 380

European Union

AHRC Doctoral Awards Scheme 109
Professional Preparation Master's Scheme
Research Preparation Master's Scheme

South Africa

Canadian Window on International Development 380

United Kingdom

AHRC Doctoral Awards Scheme 109
British Institute in Eastern Africa Graduate Attachments 169
British Institute in Eastern Africa Minor Grants 169
Professional Preparation Master's Scheme
Research Preparation Master's Scheme

AFRICAN AMERICAN

Any Country

Albert J Beveridge Grant 58
Frederick Douglass Institute Postdoctoral Fellowship 304
Frederick Douglass Institute Predoctoral Dissertation Fellowship 304
Huggins-Quarles Dissertation Award 515
Library Company of Philadelphia and Historical Society of Pennsylvania Research Fellowships in American History and Culture 422
Wolfsonian-FIU Fellowship 800

European Union

AHRC Doctoral Awards Scheme 109
Professional Preparation Master's Scheme
Research Preparation Master's Scheme

United Kingdom

AHRC Doctoral Awards Scheme 109
Professional Preparation Master's Scheme
Research Preparation Master's Scheme

United States of America

Fulbright Distinguished Chairs Program 248
Fulbright Senior Specialists Program 249

NATIVE AMERICAN

Any Country

Albert J Beveridge Grant 58
Frederick Douglass Institute Postdoctoral Fellowship 304
Frederick Douglass Institute Predoctoral Dissertation Fellowship 304
Library Company of Philadelphia and Historical Society of Pennsylvania Research Fellowships in American History and Culture 422

European Union

AHRC Doctoral Awards Scheme 109
Professional Preparation Master's Scheme
Research Preparation Master's Scheme

United Kingdom

AHRC Doctoral Awards Scheme 109
Professional Preparation Master's Scheme
Research Preparation Master's Scheme

United States of America

Fulbright Senior Specialists Program 249

HISPANIC AMERICAN

Any Country

Albert J Beveridge Grant 58
Frederick Douglass Institute Postdoctoral Fellowship 304
Frederick Douglass Institute Predoctoral Dissertation Fellowship 304
Library Company of Philadelphia and Historical Society of Pennsylvania Research Fellowships in American History and Culture 422

European Union

AHRC Doctoral Awards Scheme 109
Professional Preparation Master's Scheme
Research Preparation Master's Scheme

United Kingdom

AHRC Doctoral Awards Scheme 109
Professional Preparation Master's Scheme
Research Preparation Master's Scheme
University of Kent School of European Culture and Languages Scholarships 701
University of Kent School of European Culture and Languages Studentships 701

United States of America

Fulbright Senior Specialists Program 249

West European Countries

University of Kent School of European Culture and Languages Scholarships 701
University of Kent School of European Culture and Languages Studentships 701

AMERICAN

Any Country

AAS American Society for 18th Century Studies Fellowships 26
AAS Joyce Tracy Fellowship 26
AAS Kate B and Hall J Peterson Fellowships 27
Albert J Beveridge Grant 58
Donald Groves Fund 71
Library Company of Philadelphia and Historical Society of Pennsylvania Research Fellowships in American History and Culture 422
Library Company of Philadelphia Dissertation Fellowships 422
United States Holocaust Memorial Museum Center for Advanced Holocaust Studies Visiting Scholar Programs 641
Wolfsonian-FIU Fellowship 800

European Union

AHRC Doctoral Awards Scheme 109
Professional Preparation Master's Scheme
Research Preparation Master's Scheme

United Kingdom

AHRC Doctoral Awards Scheme 109
BAAS Short Term Awards 159
Professional Preparation Master's Scheme
Research Preparation Master's Scheme

United States of America

AAS-National Endowment for the Humanities Visiting Fellowships 27
Fulbright Distinguished Chairs Program 248
Fulbright Senior Specialists Program 249

CANADIAN

Any Country

Albert J Beveridge Grant 58
Canadian Embassy Faculty Enrichment Program 205
Grant Notley Memorial Postdoctoral Fellowship 662

Canada

Department of National Defence Security and Defence Forum Internship Program 122
Department of National Defence Security and Defence Forum MA Scholarship Program 122
Department of National Defense Security and Defence Forum PhD Scholarship Program Including the Dr Ronald Baker Doctoral Scholarship 122
Department of National Defense Security and Defense Forum Postdoctoral Fellowship including the R B Byers Postdoctoral Fellowship 123
Jules and Gabrielle Léger Fellowship 601
Lorraine Allison Scholarship 103
Queen's Fellowships 602

European Union

AHRC Doctoral Awards Scheme 109
Professional Preparation Master's Scheme
Research Preparation Master's Scheme

United Kingdom

AHRC Doctoral Awards Scheme 109
BACS Travel Awards 160
Prix du Québec Award 160
Professional Preparation Master's Scheme
Research Preparation Master's Scheme

ASIAN

Any Country

AISF Scholarship 125
An Wang Postdoctoral Fellowship 289
Bernadotte E Schmitt Grants 58
Harvard Postdoctoral Fellowships in Japanese Studies 277
Hong Kong Research Grant 564
IFUWA Sarojini Naidu Memorial Scholarship 167
SAIIA Bradlow Fellowship 614
Western Australian Government Japanese Studies Scholarship 263

European Union

AHRC Doctoral Awards Scheme 109
Professional Preparation Master's Scheme
Research Preparation Master's Scheme

United Kingdom

AHRC Doctoral Awards Scheme 109
Professional Preparation Master's Scheme
Research Preparation Master's Scheme

United States of America

SSRC JSPS Postdoctoral Fellowship 599

SOUTH ASIAN

Any Country

AIIS Junior Research Fellowships 61
AIIS Senior Research Fellowships 61
AIIS Senior Scholarly/Professional Development Fellowships 61
Bernadotte E Schmitt Grants 58
Hong Kong Research Grant 564

African Nations

Canadian Window on International Development 380
International Postgraduate Research Scholarships (IPRS) 413

Canada

Canadian Window on International Development 380
International Postgraduate Research Scholarships (IPRS) 413

Caribbean Countries

Canadian Window on International Development 380
International Postgraduate Research Scholarships (IPRS) 413

East European Countries

International Postgraduate Research Scholarships (IPRS) 413

European Union

AHRC Doctoral Awards Scheme 109
Professional Preparation Master's Scheme
Research Preparation Master's Scheme

Middle East

International Postgraduate Research Scholarships (IPRS) 413

South Africa

Canadian Window on International Development 380
International Postgraduate Research Scholarships (IPRS) 413

United Kingdom

AHRC Doctoral Awards Scheme 109
International Postgraduate Research Scholarships (IPRS) 413
Professional Preparation Master's Scheme
Research Preparation Master's Scheme

United States of America

International Postgraduate Research Scholarships (IPRS) 413

West European Countries

International Postgraduate Research Scholarships (IPRS) 413

EAST ASIAN

Any Country

Bernadotte E Schmitt Grants 58
SAIIA Bradlow Fellowship 614

African Nations

Canadian Window on International Development 380
International Postgraduate Research Scholarships (IPRS) 413

Canada

Canadian Window on International Development 380
International Postgraduate Research Scholarships (IPRS) 413

Caribbean Countries

Canadian Window on International Development 380
International Postgraduate Research Scholarships (IPRS) 413

East European Countries

International Postgraduate Research Scholarships (IPRS) 413

European Union

AHRC Doctoral Awards Scheme 109
Bernard Buckman Scholarship 582
Professional Preparation Master's Scheme
Research Preparation Master's Scheme

Middle East

International Postgraduate Research Scholarships (IPRS) 413

South Africa

Canadian Window on International Development 380
International Postgraduate Research Scholarships (IPRS) 413

United Kingdom

AHRC Doctoral Awards Scheme 109
Bernard Buckman Scholarship 582
International Postgraduate Research Scholarships (IPRS) 413

Professional Preparation Master's Scheme
Research Preparation Master's Scheme

United States of America

ACC Fellowship Grants Program 115
International Postgraduate Research Scholarships (IPRS) 413
SSRC JSPS Postdoctoral Fellowship 599

West European Countries

Bernard Buckman Scholarship 582
International Postgraduate Research Scholarships (IPRS) 413

SOUTHEAST ASIAN

Any Country

Bernadotte E Schmitt Grants 58
Harold White Fellowships 484
SAIIA Bradlow Fellowship 614

African Nations

Canadian Window on International Development 380
International Postgraduate Research Scholarships (IPRS) 413

Canada

Canadian Window on International Development 380
International Postgraduate Research Scholarships (IPRS) 413

Caribbean Countries

Canadian Window on International Development 380
International Postgraduate Research Scholarships (IPRS) 413

East European Countries

International Postgraduate Research Scholarships (IPRS) 413

European Union

AHRC Doctoral Awards Scheme 109
Professional Preparation Master's Scheme
Research Preparation Master's Scheme

Middle East

International Postgraduate Research Scholarships (IPRS) 413

South Africa

Canadian Window on International Development 380
International Postgraduate Research Scholarships (IPRS) 413

United Kingdom

AHRC Doctoral Awards Scheme 109
International Postgraduate Research Scholarships (IPRS) 413
Professional Preparation Master's Scheme
Research Preparation Master's Scheme

United States of America

ACC Fellowship Grants Program 115
International Postgraduate Research Scholarships (IPRS) 413

West European Countries

International Postgraduate Research Scholarships (IPRS) 413

EUROPEAN (EC)

Any Country

Austro-American Association of Boston Stipend 143
Bernadotte E Schmitt Grants 58
Camargo Fellowships 182
Irish Research Funds 394
NEH Fellowships 83
Paul H. Nitze School of Advanced International Studies (SAIS)
    Financial Aid and Fellowships 155

European Union

AHRC Doctoral Awards Scheme 109
Professional Preparation Master's Scheme
Research Preparation Master's Scheme

United Kingdom

AHRC Doctoral Awards Scheme 109
Ministry of Education, Science and Culture (Iceland) Scholarships in
    Icelandic Studies 449
Professional Preparation Master's Scheme
Research Preparation Master's Scheme

United States of America

Ministry of Education, Science and Culture (Iceland) Scholarships in
    Icelandic Studies 449
Norwegian Thanksgiving Fund Scholarship 509

West European Countries

Ministry of Education, Science and Culture (Iceland) Scholarships in
    Icelandic Studies 449

CARIBBEAN

Any Country

Albert J Beveridge Grant 58
Frederick Douglass Institute Postdoctoral Fellowship 304
Frederick Douglass Institute Predoctoral Dissertation Fellowship 304
Huggins-Quarles Dissertation Award 515
Milt Luger Fellowships 619

African Nations

Canadian Window on International Development 380

Canada

Canadian Window on International Development 380

Caribbean Countries

Canadian Window on International Development 380

European Union

AHRC Doctoral Awards Scheme 109
Professional Preparation Master's Scheme
Research Preparation Master's Scheme

South Africa

Canadian Window on International Development 380

United Kingdom

AHRC Doctoral Awards Scheme 109
Professional Preparation Master's Scheme
Research Preparation Master's Scheme

LATIN AMERICAN

Any Country

Albert J Beveridge Grant 58
Australian Bicentennial (Australia) Scholarships and Fellowships 410
British Academy 44th International Congress of Americanists Fund 157
Frederick Douglass Institute Postdoctoral Fellowship 304
Frederick Douglass Institute Predoctoral Dissertation Fellowship 304
Paul H. Nitze School of Advanced International Studies (SAIS)
    Financial Aid and Fellowships 155
SAIIA Bradlow Fellowship 614

African Nations

Canadian Window on International Development 380

Canada

Canadian Window on International Development 380

Caribbean Countries

Canadian Window on International Development 380

European Union

AHRC Doctoral Awards Scheme 109
Professional Preparation Master's Scheme

South Africa

Canadian Window on International Development 380

United Kingdom

AHRC Doctoral Awards Scheme 109
Professional Preparation Master's Scheme
University of Kent School of European Culture and Languages
    Scholarships 701
University of Kent School of European Culture and Languages
    Studentships 701

West European Countries

University of Kent School of European Culture and Languages
    Scholarships 701
University of Kent School of European Culture and Languages
    Studentships 701

PACIFIC AREA

Any Country

C H Currey Memorial Fellowship 618

European Union

AHRC Doctoral Awards Scheme 109
Professional Preparation Master's Scheme
Research Preparation Master's Scheme

United Kingdom

AHRC Doctoral Awards Scheme 109
Professional Preparation Master's Scheme
Research Preparation Master's Scheme

United States of America

CFR International Affairs Fellowship Program in Japan 250

ABORIGINAL

Any Country

Frederick Douglass Institute Postdoctoral Fellowship 304
Frederick Douglass Institute Predoctoral Dissertation Fellowship 304
Harold White Fellowships 484

African Nations

International Postgraduate Research Scholarships (IPRS) 413

Australia

AIATSIS Conference Support Grants 136
AIATSIS Research Grants Program 136

Canada

International Postgraduate Research Scholarships (IPRS) 413

Caribbean Countries

International Postgraduate Research Scholarships (IPRS) 413

East European Countries

International Postgraduate Research Scholarships (IPRS) 413

European Union

AHRC Doctoral Awards Scheme 109
Professional Preparation Master's Scheme
Research Preparation Master's Scheme

Middle East

International Postgraduate Research Scholarships (IPRS) 413

New Zealand

AIATSIS Conference Support Grants 136

South Africa

International Postgraduate Research Scholarships (IPRS) 413

United Kingdom

AHRC Doctoral Awards Scheme 109
International Postgraduate Research Scholarships (IPRS) 413
Professional Preparation Master's Scheme
Research Preparation Master's Scheme

United States of America

International Postgraduate Research Scholarships (IPRS) 413

West European Countries

International Postgraduate Research Scholarships (IPRS) 413

MIDDLE EASTERN

Any Country

Ahmad Abu-Hakima Scholarship 582
ASCSA Advanced Fellowships 82
AUC International Graduate Fellowships in Arabic Studies, Middle
    East Studies and Sociology/Anthropology 97
Bernadotte E Schmitt Grants 58
Jacob Hirsch Fellowship 83
M Alison Frantz Fellowship in Post-Classical Studies at the Gennadius
    Library 83
NEH Fellowships 83
Paul H. Nitze School of Advanced International Studies (SAIS)
    Financial Aid and Fellowships 155
SAIIA Bradlow Fellowship 614
United States Holocaust Memorial Museum Center for Advanced
    Holocaust Studies Visiting Scholar Programs 641

African Nations

British School of Archaeology in Iraq Grants 169
Canadian Window on International Development 380

Australia

British School of Archaeology in Iraq Grants 169

Canada

British School of Archaeology in Iraq Grants 169
Canadian Window on International Development 380

Caribbean Countries

Canadian Window on International Development 380

European Union

AHRC Doctoral Awards Scheme 109
CBRL Travel Grant 248
Professional Preparation Master's Scheme
Research Preparation Master's Scheme

New Zealand

British School of Archaeology in Iraq Grants 169

South Africa

British School of Archaeology in Iraq Grants 169
Canadian Window on International Development 380

United Kingdom

AHRC Doctoral Awards Scheme 109
British School of Archaeology in Iraq Grants 169
CBRL Research Award 248

CBRL Travel Grant 248
Professional Preparation Master's Scheme
Research Preparation Master's Scheme

United States of America

ARCE Fellowships 80
ASOR Mesopotamian Fellowship 83
ASOR W.F. Albright Institute of Archaeological Research/National
    Endowment of the Humanities Fellowships 84

ISLAMIC

Any Country

ASCSA Advanced Fellowships 82
Bernadotte E Schmitt Grants 58
Jacob Hirsch Fellowship 83
M Alison Frantz Fellowship in Post-Classical Studies at the Gennadius
    Library 83
NEH Fellowships 83
Paul H. Nitze School of Advanced International Studies (SAIS)
    Financial Aid and Fellowships 155

African Nations

Oxford Centre for Islamic Studies (OCIS) Scholarship 737

European Union

AHRC Doctoral Awards Scheme 109
CBRL Travel Grant 248
Professional Preparation Master's Scheme
Research Preparation Master's Scheme

United Kingdom

AHRC Doctoral Awards Scheme 109
CBRL Research Award 248
CBRL Travel Grant 248
Oxford Centre for Islamic Studies (OCIS) Scholarship 737
Professional Preparation Master's Scheme
Research Preparation Master's Scheme

United States of America

ARCE Fellowships 80
IREX Individual Advanced Research Opportunities 388

JEWISH

Any Country

ASCSA Advanced Fellowships 82
Bernadotte E Schmitt Grants 58
Bernard and Audre Rapoport Fellowships 431
Dina Abramowicz Emerging Scholar Fellowship 807
Ethel Marcus Memorial Fellowship 431
IAUW International Scholarship 166
The Joseph and Eva R Dave Fellowship 432
Loewenstein-Wiener Fellowship Awards 432
M Alison Frantz Fellowship in Post-Classical Studies at the Gennadius
    Library 83
Marguerite R Jacobs Memorial Award 432
The Natalie Feld Memorial Fellowship 432
NEH Fellowships 83
Professor Bernard Choseed Memorial Fellowship 808
The Rabbi Harold D Hahn Memorial Fellowship 432
The Rabbi Joachin Prinz Memorial Fellowship 432
Rabbi Levi A Olan Memorial Fellowship 433
Rabbi Theodore S Levy Tribute Fellowship 433
Starkoff Fellowship 433
Touro National Heritage Trust Fellowship 403
United States Holocaust Memorial Museum Center for Advanced
    Holocaust Studies Visiting Scholar Programs 641

Canada

JCCA Graduate Education Scholarship 400

European Union

AHRC Doctoral Awards Scheme 109
CBRL Travel Grant 248
Professional Preparation Master's Scheme
Research Preparation Master's Scheme

United Kingdom

AHRC Doctoral Awards Scheme 109
CBRL Research Award 248
CBRL Travel Grant 248
Professional Preparation Master's Scheme
Research Preparation Master's Scheme

United States of America

JCCA Graduate Education Scholarship 400
LBI/DAAD Fellowship for Research at the Leo Baeck Institute, New York 417
LBI/DAAD Fellowships for Research in the Federal Republic of Germany 418
Maurice and Marilyn Cohen Fund for Doctoral Dissertation Fellowships in Jewish Studies 301

PRESERVATION OF CULTURAL HERITAGE

Any Country

Albert J Beveridge Grant 58
ASCSA Advanced Fellowships 82
ASCSA Fellowships 82
Bernadotte E Schmitt Grants 58
Bernard and Audre Rapoport Fellowships 431
BIAA Post-Doctoral Research Fellowship 168
BIAA Research Scholarship 168
BIAA Study Grants 168
BIAA Travel Grants 168
BIAA/SPHS Fieldwork Award 168
British Academy Postdoctoral Fellowships 158
CSA Adele Filene Travel Award 247
CSA Stella Blum Research Grant 247
CSA Travel Research Grant 248
Ethel Marcus Memorial Fellowship 431
Irish Research Funds 394
Jacob Hirsch Fellowship 83
Jennings Randolph Program for International Peace Dissertation Fellowship 643
The Joseph and Eva R Dave Fellowship 432
Loewenstein-Wiener Fellowship Awards 432
M Alison Frantz Fellowship in Post-Classical Studies at the Gennadius Library 83
Marguerite R Jacobs Memorial Award 432
Milt Luger Fellowships 619
The Natalie Feld Memorial Fellowship 432
NEH Fellowships 83
The Rabbi Harold D Hahn Memorial Fellowship 432
The Rabbi Joachin Prinz Memorial Fellowship 432
Rabbi Levi A Olan Memorial Fellowship 433
Rabbi Theodore S Levy Tribute Fellowship 433
Starkoff Fellowship 433
United States Holocaust Memorial Museum Center for Advanced Holocaust Studies Visiting Scholar Programs 641
Victoria University of Wellington PhD Scholarships 786

African Nations

International Postgraduate Research Scholarships (IPRS) 413

Australia

Wingate Scholarships 697

Canada

International Postgraduate Research Scholarships (IPRS) 413
Wingate Scholarships 697

Caribbean Countries

International Postgraduate Research Scholarships (IPRS) 413

East European Countries

International Postgraduate Research Scholarships (IPRS) 413
Synthesys Visiting Fellowship 494

European Union

CBRL Travel Grant 248
Synthesys Visiting Fellowship 494
Wingate Scholarships 697

Middle East

International Postgraduate Research Scholarships (IPRS) 413

New Zealand

Wingate Scholarships 697

South Africa

International Postgraduate Research Scholarships (IPRS) 413
Wingate Scholarships 697

United Kingdom

Balsdon Fellowship 174
BIAA Travel Grants 168
BIAA/SPBS Fieldwork Award 168
CBRL Research Award 248
CBRL Travel Grant 248
International Postgraduate Research Scholarships (IPRS) 413
Synthesys Visiting Fellowship 494
Wingate Scholarships 697

United States of America

ACC Fellowship Grants Program 115
David Baumgardt Memorial Fellowship 417
Earthwatch Fellowships 272
Fritz Halbers Fellowship 417
Fulbright Senior Specialists Program 249
International Postgraduate Research Scholarships (IPRS) 413
SSRC Abe Fellowship Program 598

West European Countries

David Baumgardt Memorial Fellowship 417
Fritz Halbers Fellowship 417
International Postgraduate Research Scholarships (IPRS) 413
Synthesys Visiting Fellowship 494

ANCIENT CIVILISATIONS (EGYPTOLOGY, ASSYRIOLOGY)

Any Country

ASCSA Advanced Fellowships 82
ASCSA Fellowships 82
ASCSA Research Fellowship in Environmental Studies 82
ASCSA Research Fellowship in Faunal Studies 82
ASCSA Research Fellowship in Geoarchaeology 82
BIAA Post-Doctoral Research Fellowship 168
BIAA Research Scholarship 168
BIAA Study Grants 168
BIAA Travel Grants 168
BIAA/SPHS Fieldwork Award 168
British Academy Postdoctoral Fellowships 158
Frances M Schwartz Fellowship 71
Grants for ANS Summer Seminar in Numismatics 71
J Lawrence Angel Fellowship in Human Skeletal Studies
Jacob Hirsch Fellowship 83
NEH Fellowships 83
SOAS Research Student Fellowships 583

African Nations

British School of Archaeology in Iraq Grants 169

Australia

AAH Humanities Travelling Fellowships 132
British School of Archaeology in Iraq Grants 169
Wingate Scholarships 697

Canada

British School of Archaeology in Iraq Grants 169
Wingate Scholarships 697

European Union

AHRC Doctoral Awards Scheme 109
CBRL Travel Grant 248
Professional Preparation Master's Scheme
Research Preparation Master's Scheme
Wingate Scholarships 697

New Zealand

British School of Archaeology in Iraq Grants 169
Wingate Scholarships 697

South Africa

British School of Archaeology in Iraq Grants 169
Wingate Scholarships 697

United Kingdom

AHRC Doctoral Awards Scheme 109
BIAA Travel Grants 168
BIAA/SPBS Fieldwork Award 168
British School of Archaeology in Iraq Grants 169
CBRL Research Award 248
CBRL Travel Grant 248
Professional Preparation Master's Scheme
Research Preparation Master's Scheme
Wingate Scholarships 697

TRADE, CRAFT AND INDUSTRIAL TECHNIQUES

GENERAL

Any Country

Concordia University Graduate Fellowships 243
David J Azrieli Graduate Fellowship 243
Frederick Douglass Institute Postdoctoral Fellowship 304
Frederick Douglass Institute Predoctoral Dissertation Fellowship 304
Henry Moore Institute Research Fellowship 338
Honda Prize 343
Matsumae International Foundation Research Fellowship 436
Stanley G French Graduate Fellowship 244

Australia

Fulbright Postgraduate Awards 140

Canada

J W McConnell Memorial Fellowships 243

United Kingdom

Hilda Martindale Exhibitions 341
Oppenheim–John Downes Trust Grants 513

United States of America

Congress Bundestag Youth Exchange for Young Professionals 221
DEED (Demonstration of Energy-Efficient Developments) Student
  Research Grant/Internship 80
Early American Industries Association Research Grants Program 272
North Dakota Indian Scholarship 507

West European Countries

Janson Johan Helmich Scholarships and Travel Grants 398

FOOD PROCESSING TECHNIQUES

Any Country

Baking Industry Scholarship 60
Teagasc Walsh Fellowships 626

United States of America

Congress Bundestag Youth Exchange for Young Professionals 221

BUILDING TRADES

United States of America

Congress Bundestag Youth Exchange for Young Professionals 221
Early American Industries Association Research Grants Program 272

ELECTRICAL/ELECTRONIC EQUIPMENT AND MAINTENANCE TECHNIQUES

United States of America

Congress Bundestag Youth Exchange for Young Professionals 221
DEED (Demonstration of Energy-Efficient Developments) Student
  Research Grant/Internship 80

METAL TRADES TECHNIQUES

United States of America

Congress Bundestag Youth Exchange for Young Professionals 221
DEED (Demonstration of Energy-Efficient Developments) Student
  Research Grant/Internship 80
Early American Industries Association Research Grants Program 272

MECHANICAL EQUIPMENT AND MAINTENANCE TECHNIQUES

United States of America

Congress Bundestag Youth Exchange for Young Professionals 221
DEED (Demonstration of Energy-Efficient Developments) Student
  Research Grant/Internship 80
Early American Industries Association Research Grants Program 272

WOOD TECHNOLOGY

United States of America

Congress Bundestag Youth Exchange for Young Professionals 221
DEED (Demonstration of Energy-Efficient Developments) Student
  Research Grant/Internship 80
Early American Industries Association Research Grants Program 272

HEATING, AIR CONDITIONING AND REFRIGERATION TECHNOLOGY

Any Country

ASHRAE Grants-in-Aid for Graduate Students 91

United States of America

Congress Bundestag Youth Exchange for Young Professionals 221
DEED (Demonstration of Energy-Efficient Developments) Student
  Research Grant/Internship 80

LEATHER TECHNIQUES

African Nations

CSIR (Council of Scientific and Industrial Research)/TWAS Fellowship
  for Postgraduate Research 630
CSIR (The Council of Scientific and Industrial Research)/TWAS
  Fellowship for Postdoctoral Research 630

Caribbean Countries

CSIR (Council of Scientific and Industrial Research)/TWAS Fellowship for Postgraduate Research 630
CSIR (The Council of Scientific and Industrial Research)/TWAS Fellowship for Postdoctoral Research 630

Middle East

CSIR (Council of Scientific and Industrial Research)/TWAS Fellowship for Postgraduate Research 630
CSIR (The Council of Scientific and Industrial Research)/TWAS Fellowship for Postdoctoral Research 630

South Africa

CSIR (Council of Scientific and Industrial Research)/TWAS Fellowship for Postgraduate Research 630
CSIR (The Council of Scientific and Industrial Research)/TWAS Fellowship for Postdoctoral Research 630

United States of America

Congress Bundestag Youth Exchange for Young Professionals 221
Early American Industries Association Research Grants Program 272

TEXTILE TECHNIQUES

Any Country

CSA Adele Filene Travel Award 247
CSA Stella Blum Research Grant 247
CSA Travel Research Grant 248
Earthwatch Field Research Grants 272
Haystack Scholarship 333
Weavers Postgraduate Textiles Scholarships 321

United States of America

Congress Bundestag Youth Exchange for Young Professionals 221
Early American Industries Association Research Grants Program 272

PAPER AND PACKAGING TECHNOLOGY

Any Country

WSW Internships 802

United States of America

Congress Bundestag Youth Exchange for Young Professionals 221
Early American Industries Association Research Grants Program 272

GRAPHIC ARTS TECHNIQUES

Any Country

Henry Moore Institute Research Fellowship 338
WSW Hands-On-Art Visiting Artist Project 802
WSW Internships 802

United States of America

Billings Broadcasters MSU-Billings Media Scholarship 456
Early American Industries Association Research Grants Program 272
Virginia Liebeler Biennial Grants for Mature Women (Art) 484

PRINTING

Any Country

Henry Moore Institute Research Fellowship 338
Library Company of Philadelphia and Historical Society of Pennsylvania Research Fellowships in American History and Culture 422
WSW Artists Fellowships 802
WSW Artists' Book Residencies 802
WSW Hands-On-Art Visiting Artist Project 802
WSW Internships 802

East European Countries

FEMS Fellowship 290

United Kingdom

FEMS Fellowship 290

United States of America

Early American Industries Association Research Grants Program 272
Virginia Liebeler Biennial Grants for Mature Women (Art) 484
Virginia Liebeler Biennial Grants for Mature Women (Writing) 484

West European Countries

FEMS Fellowship 290

PUBLISHING AND BOOK TRADE

Any Country

Henry Moore Institute Research Fellowship 338
Library Company of Philadelphia and Historical Society of Pennsylvania Research Fellowships in American History and Culture 422
WSW Artists Fellowships 802
WSW Artists' Book Residencies 802
WSW Hands-On-Art Visiting Artist Project 802
WSW Internships 802

East European Countries

FEMS Fellowship 290

United Kingdom

FEMS Fellowship 290

United States of America

Early American Industries Association Research Grants Program 272
Virginia Liebeler Biennial Grants for Mature Women (Writing) 484

West European Countries

FEMS Fellowship 290

LABORATORY TECHNIQUES

United States of America

Congress Bundestag Youth Exchange for Young Professionals 221

OPTICAL TECHNOLOGY

Any Country

Berthold Leibinger Innovation Prize 148

United States of America

Congress Bundestag Youth Exchange for Young Professionals 221

TRANSPORT AND COMMUNICATIONS

GENERAL

Any Country

Australian Postgraduate Award Research Scholarship
Concordia University Graduate Fellowships 243
CSCMP Distinguished Service Award 250
CSCMP Doctoral Dissertation Award 250
David J Azrieli Graduate Fellowship 243
Henrietta Hutton Research Grants 564
Honda Prize 343
Journey of a Lifetime Award 564

Lee Kuan Yew School of Public Policy Graduate Scholarships
(LKYSPPS) 491
Matsumae International Foundation Research Fellowship 436
Rees Jeffreys Road Fund Bursaries 542
Rees Jeffreys Road Fund Research Grants 543
Small Research Grants 566
Stanley G French Graduate Fellowship 244
University of Southampton Postgraduate Studentships 759
World Universities Network (WUN) International Research Mobility
Scheme 759

African Nations

ABCCF Student Grant 102
International Postgraduate Research Scholarships (IPRS) 413
NUFFIC-NFP Fellowships for Master's Degree Programmes 496
Shell Centenary/Shell Centenary Chevening Scholarships 704

Australia

DOI Women in Freight, Logistics and Marine Management
Scholarship 264
Fulbright Postdoctoral Fellowships 140
Fulbright Postgraduate Awards 140
Wingate Scholarships 697

Canada

International Postgraduate Research Scholarships (IPRS) 413
J W McConnell Memorial Fellowships 243
NSERC Postdoctoral Fellowships 495
TAC Foundation Scholarships 637
Wingate Scholarships 697

Caribbean Countries

International Postgraduate Research Scholarships (IPRS) 413
Shell Centenary/Shell Centenary Chevening Scholarships 704

East European Countries

International Postgraduate Research Scholarships (IPRS) 413

European Union

ESRC 1 + 3 Awards and + 3 Awards
Wingate Scholarships 697

Middle East

ABCCF Student Grant 102
International Postgraduate Research Scholarships (IPRS) 413
NUFFIC-NFP Fellowships for Master's Degree Programmes 496
Shell Centenary/Shell Centenary Chevening Scholarships 704

New Zealand

Wingate Scholarships 697

South Africa

International Postgraduate Research Scholarships (IPRS) 413
NUFFIC-NFP Fellowships for Master's Degree Programmes 496
Shell Centenary/Shell Centenary Chevening Scholarships 704
Wingate Scholarships 697

United Kingdom

ESRC 1 + 3 Awards and + 3 Awards
Hilda Martindale Exhibitions 341
International Postgraduate Research Scholarships (IPRS) 413
Kennedy Scholarships 409
Wingate Scholarships 697

United States of America

Congress Bundestag Youth Exchange for Young Professionals 221
International Postgraduate Research Scholarships (IPRS) 413
North Dakota Indian Scholarship 507

West European Countries

ESRC 1 + 3 Awards and + 3 Awards
International Postgraduate Research Scholarships (IPRS) 413
Janson Johan Helmich Scholarships and Travel Grants 398

AIR TRANSPORT

African Nations

International Postgraduate Research Scholarships (IPRS) 413

Australia

DOI Women in Freight, Logistics and Marine Management
Scholarship 264

Canada

International Postgraduate Research Scholarships (IPRS) 413

Caribbean Countries

International Postgraduate Research Scholarships (IPRS) 413

East European Countries

International Postgraduate Research Scholarships (IPRS) 413

Middle East

International Postgraduate Research Scholarships (IPRS) 413

South Africa

International Postgraduate Research Scholarships (IPRS) 413

United Kingdom

International Postgraduate Research Scholarships (IPRS) 413

United States of America

Congress Bundestag Youth Exchange for Young Professionals
221
International Postgraduate Research Scholarships (IPRS) 413

West European Countries

International Postgraduate Research Scholarships (IPRS) 413

MARINE TRANSPORT AND NAUTICAL SCIENCE

Any Country

De Paepe-Willems Award 386
Ralph Brown Expedition Award 565

Australia

DOI Women in Freight, Logistics and Marine Management
Scholarship 264

United States of America

Congress Bundestag Youth Exchange for Young Professionals
221

RAILWAY TRANSPORT

African Nations

International Postgraduate Research Scholarships (IPRS) 413

Australia

DOI Women in Freight, Logistics and Marine Management
Scholarship 264

Canada

International Postgraduate Research Scholarships (IPRS) 413

Caribbean Countries

International Postgraduate Research Scholarships (IPRS) 413

East European Countries

International Postgraduate Research Scholarships (IPRS) 413

Middle East
International Postgraduate Research Scholarships (IPRS) 413

South Africa
International Postgraduate Research Scholarships (IPRS) 413

United Kingdom
International Postgraduate Research Scholarships (IPRS) 413

United States of America
Congress Bundestag Youth Exchange for Young Professionals 221
International Postgraduate Research Scholarships (IPRS) 413

West European Countries
International Postgraduate Research Scholarships (IPRS) 413

ROAD TRANSPORT

Any Country
Rees Jeffreys Road Fund Bursaries 542
Rees Jeffreys Road Fund Research Grants 543

African Nations
International Postgraduate Research Scholarships (IPRS) 413

Australia
DOI Women in Freight, Logistics and Marine Management Scholarship 264

Canada
International Postgraduate Research Scholarships (IPRS) 413
TAC Foundation Scholarships 637

Caribbean Countries
International Postgraduate Research Scholarships (IPRS) 413

East European Countries
International Postgraduate Research Scholarships (IPRS) 413

Middle East
International Postgraduate Research Scholarships (IPRS) 413

South Africa
International Postgraduate Research Scholarships (IPRS) 413

United Kingdom
International Postgraduate Research Scholarships (IPRS) 413

United States of America
Congress Bundestag Youth Exchange for Young Professionals 221
International Postgraduate Research Scholarships (IPRS) 413

West European Countries
International Postgraduate Research Scholarships (IPRS) 413

TRANSPORT MANAGEMENT

African Nations
International Postgraduate Research Scholarships (IPRS) 413
Shell Centenary/Shell Centenary Chevening Scholarships 704

Australia
DOI Women in Freight, Logistics and Marine Management Scholarship 264
Wingate Scholarships 697

Canada
International Postgraduate Research Scholarships (IPRS) 413
TAC Foundation Scholarships 637
Wingate Scholarships 697

Caribbean Countries
International Postgraduate Research Scholarships (IPRS) 413
Shell Centenary/Shell Centenary Chevening Scholarships 704

East European Countries
International Postgraduate Research Scholarships (IPRS) 413

European Union
ESRC 1+3 Awards and +3 Awards
Wingate Scholarships 697

Middle East
International Postgraduate Research Scholarships (IPRS) 413
Shell Centenary/Shell Centenary Chevening Scholarships 704

New Zealand
Wingate Scholarships 697

South Africa
International Postgraduate Research Scholarships (IPRS) 413
Shell Centenary/Shell Centenary Chevening Scholarships 704
Wingate Scholarships 697

United Kingdom
ESRC 1+3 Awards and +3 Awards
International Postgraduate Research Scholarships (IPRS) 413
Wingate Scholarships 697

United States of America
Congress Bundestag Youth Exchange for Young Professionals 221
DEED (Demonstration of Energy-Efficient Developments) Student Research Grant/Internship 80
International Postgraduate Research Scholarships (IPRS) 413

West European Countries
ESRC 1+3 Awards and +3 Awards
International Postgraduate Research Scholarships (IPRS) 413

TRANSPORT ECONOMICS

Any Country
Rees Jeffreys Road Fund Bursaries 542
Rees Jeffreys Road Fund Research Grants 543

African Nations
International Postgraduate Research Scholarships (IPRS) 413

Australia
DOI Women in Freight, Logistics and Marine Management Scholarship 264

Canada
International Postgraduate Research Scholarships (IPRS) 413
TAC Foundation Scholarships 637

Caribbean Countries
International Postgraduate Research Scholarships (IPRS) 413

East European Countries
International Postgraduate Research Scholarships (IPRS) 413

European Union
ESRC 1+3 Awards and +3 Awards

Middle East

International Postgraduate Research Scholarships (IPRS) 413

South Africa

International Postgraduate Research Scholarships (IPRS) 413

United Kingdom

ESRC 1+3 Awards and +3 Awards
International Postgraduate Research Scholarships (IPRS) 413

United States of America

Congress Bundestag Youth Exchange for Young Professionals
221
DEED (Demonstration of Energy-Efficient Developments) Student
Research Grant/Internship 80
International Postgraduate Research Scholarships (IPRS) 413

West European Countries

ESRC 1+3 Awards and +3 Awards
International Postgraduate Research Scholarships (IPRS) 413

POSTAL SERVICES

United States of America

Congress Bundestag Youth Exchange for Young Professionals
221

TELECOMMUNICATIONS SERVICES

Any Country

Essex Rotary University Travel Grants 687
Sir Eric Berthoud Travel Grant 689

African Nations

International Postgraduate Research Scholarships (IPRS) 413
ORSAS Awards 688

Australia

ORSAS Awards 688

Canada

International Postgraduate Research Scholarships (IPRS) 413
ORSAS Awards 688

Caribbean Countries

International Postgraduate Research Scholarships (IPRS) 413
ORSAS Awards 688

East European Countries

International Postgraduate Research Scholarships (IPRS) 413
ORSAS Awards 688

Middle East

International Postgraduate Research Scholarships (IPRS) 413
ORSAS Awards 688

New Zealand

ORSAS Awards 688

South Africa

International Postgraduate Research Scholarships (IPRS) 413
ORSAS Awards 688

United Kingdom

Access to Learning Fund 685
International Postgraduate Research Scholarships (IPRS) 413

United States of America

Congress Bundestag Youth Exchange for Young Professionals
221
International Postgraduate Research Scholarships (IPRS) 413
ORSAS Awards 688

West European Countries

International Postgraduate Research Scholarships (IPRS) 413

INDEX OF AWARDS

INDEX OF DISCONTINUED AWARDS

Acadia University
Acadia University Research Fund

Alexander von Humboldt Foundation
Linked Postdoctoral Awards for Scientists and Engineers

Alzheimer's Association Australia
AAR Janssen Cilag Dementia Research Grant
AAR Rosemary Foundation Travel Project Grant-Dementia Research
AAR/CRC Joint Postgraduate Research Scholarship in Social
    Research and Dementia
Hunter Postgraduate Scholarship
Rosemary Foundation Loader Research Scholarship

American Association for the Advancement of Science (AAAS)
Canon National Parks Science Scholars Program

American College of Obstetricians and Gynecologists (ACOG)
ACOG/3M Pharmaceuticals Research Award in Human
    Papillomavirus

American Congress on Surveying and Mapping (ACSM)
NSPS Forum for Equal Opportunity/Mary Feindt Scholarship

American Federation for Aging Research (AFAR)
Ellison Medical Foundation/AFAR Senior Postdoctoral Research
    Program
The Fannie E. Rippel Foundation/AFAR New Investigator Awards on
    Gender Differences in Aging

American Indian Graduate Center (AIGC)
AIGC-EPA Tribal Lands Environmental Science Scholarship

American Society for Engineering Education (ASEE)
ASEE Helen T Carr Fellowship Program

Arthritis Australia
ARA–AFA Heald Fellowship
Arthritis Australia Grants–Scholarships
Helen Moran Memorial Grant
Kilimanjaro–Ascent for Arthritis Research Grant
Ray and Pam Robinson Award for Rheumatology Research

Arthritis Research Campaign
Educational Project Grants The

Arthritis Society
Arthritis Society Industry Program The

Arts Council of Wales
The Arts Council of Wales Fiction Factory Grant
Community Dance Wales Grants
Cultural Enterprise Service Grant
Forget About it Film & TV Grant
Organic Films/Fertile Ground Ltd. Grant
Wales One World Film Festival Grant
Welsh Independent Dance Grant

Association of British Science Writers
ABSW Student Bursaries funded by the Wellcome Trust

Austrian Academy of Sciences
Austrian Academy of Sciences, Short Course–Tropical Limnology
Institute for Limnology Postgraduate Training Fellowships

Bangor University
University Studentships

British Journal of Surgery
British Journal of Surgery Research Bursaries

British Medical Association (BMA)
Albert McMaster Research Grant
Charlotte Eyck Research Grant
Helen Tomkinson Research Grant
Insole Research Grant
John William Clark Research Grant

British School at Rome (BSR)
SAIA Rome Scholarship in Architecture
Wingate Rome Scholarship in the Fine Arts

Budapest International Music Competition
International Carl Flesch Violin Competition

Canadian Blood Services (CBS)
CBS Research Fellowship In Haemostasis (RFH)

Canadian Bureau for International Education (CBIE)
Canada-Latin America-Caribbean Awards
DFAIT Doctoral Student Research Program The

Chemical Institute of Canada
CIC Environmental Improvement Award

Cranfield University
Engineering and Physical Science Research Council (EPSRC)
    Awards – Collaborative Training Award (CTA) and Masters Training
    Packages (MTP)
Silsoe Awards
Waste and Resource Management RAEng Awards
Williams F1-Cranfield Motorsport Bursaries

Dr Hadwen Trust for Humane Research
Dr Hadwen Trust for Humane Research Grants

Dr M Aylwin Cotton Foundation
Cotton Research Fellowships

Embassy of France in Australia
Ministry of Foreign Affairs (France) International Teaching
    Fellowships

Epilepsy Research UK
Epilepsy Research Foundation Equipment Grant

European Calcified Tissue Society
ECTS Eastern European Young Investigator Grants

European Commission
Marie Curie Development Host Fellowships

European Molecular Biology Organization (EMBO)
EMBO Award for Communication in the Life Sciences
EMBO Science Writing Prize

Heart Research UK
Heart Research UK Basic Science Medical Research Grant
Heart Research UK Clinical Medical Research Grant The

Horowitz Foundation for Social Policy
Horowitz Foundation for Social Policy Grant The

Huntington
W M Keck Foundation Fellowship for Young Scholars

International Development Research Centre (IDRC)
The Acacia ICT R&D Grants Programme
Ecosystem Approaches to Human Health Graduate Awards

**International Federation of Library Associations and Institutions
    (IFLA)**
Hans-Peter Geh Grant for Conference Participation

International Foundation for Science (IFS)
IFS Carolina MacGillavry Fellowship

John Carter Brown Library at Brown University
NEH Research Fellowship

Kidney Research UK
NKRF Special Project Grants

La Trobe University
La Trobe University Postdoctoral Research Fellowship

Lancaster University
Lancaster University International Bursaries The

Life Course Center
National Research Service Award for Mental Health and Adjustment in
    the Life Course The

Musicians Benevolent Fund (MBF)
Ian Fleming Charitable Trust Music Education Awards
MBF Awards for Accompanists and Repetiteurs
MBF Charles Leggett Awards
Myra Hess Trust
Sybil Tutton Awards

Nanyang Technological University (NTU)
NTU SCCCF Business Scholarship

National Center for Atmospheric Research (NCAR)
NCAR IAI/NCAR Postdoctoral Fellowship The

National Education Association (NEA) Foundation for the Improvement of Education
NEA Foundation Fine Arts Grant Program

National Strength and Conditioning Association (NSCA)
GNC Nutritional Research Grant
NSCA Graduate Research Grant
NSCA Minority Scholarship
NSCA Power Systems Professional Scholarship
NSCA Women's Scholarship
SSG Christopher Falkel Scholarship
Velocity Sports Performance Challenge Scholarship
Young Investigator Grant

National University of Singapore (NUS)
National University of Singapore Fellowships
Sanwa Bank Foundation Research Fellowship The

Netherlands Organization for Scientific Research (NWO)
WOTRO DC Fellowships

New South Wales Architects Registration Board
Client Service Excellence Award The

Norah Howell Charitable Trust
The Norah Howell Music Awards

Organization of American Historians (OAH)
White House Historical Association Fellowships

Philharmonia Orchestra
Trevor Snoad Memorial Trust The

Population Council
Population Council Fellowships in Population and Social Sciences

Radio and Television News Directors Foundation (RTNDF)
Capitol Hill News Internships

Roche Research Foundation
Roche Research Foundation

Royal Aeronautical Society
Handley Page Award

Royal College of Midwives
Hospital Savings Association (HSA) Charitable Trust Scholarships

Royal College of Music
Royal College of Music Junior Fellowship in Performance History
Royal College of Music Junior Scholarship

Royal Horticultural Society (RHS)
RHS Financial Awards

Royal Irish Academy
Eoin O'Mahony Bursary
Royal Irish Academy Award in Biochemistry
Royal Irish Academy Award in Nutritional Sciences
Royal Irish Academy Award in Pharmacology and Toxicology
Royal Irish Academy Science Writing Competition The

Royal Literary Fund RLF
RLF Fellowships

RSM Erasmus University
RSM-Antoinette Scholarship
RSM-ING Bank Loan Programme
RSM-NESO in Beijing Scholarship

Sigma Theta Tau International
Sigma Theta Tau International/The Long-Term Care Point-of-Care Diagnostics Research Grant

Social Science Research Council (SSRC)
Berlin Program for Advanced German and European Studies
SSRC Africa Program Advanced Research Grants
SSRC Africa Program Dissertation Fellowships
SSRC Africa Program Predissertation Fellowships
SSRC Japan Studies Dissertation Workshop
SSRC Program on the Corporation as a Social Institution Fellowships
SSRC Sexuality Research Fellowship Program
SSRC South Asia Regional Fellowship Program: Fellowships for the Study of Migration
SSRC South Asia Regional Fellowship Program: Fellowships for the Study of Sexuality
SSRC Summer Institute on International Migration

Social Sciences and Humanities Research Council of Canada (SSHRC)
Boreas: Histories from the North-Environments, Movements, Narratives
Canadian Forest Service Graduate Supplements
Geomatics for Informed Decisions (GEOIDE) Networks of Centers of Excellence Graduate Supplement Program
Virtual Scholar in Residence Program

South African Council for English Education (SACEE)
Norah Taylor Bursary
SACEE EX-PCE Bursary

Swiss Federal Institute of Technology Zürich
Swiss Federal Institute of Technology Scholarships

United Daughters of the Confederacy
Mrs Simon Baruch University Award

University College London
AHW Beck Memorial Scholarship
Child Health Research Appeal Trust Studentship
CSC/UCL Graduate Scholarship
OSI UCL Chevening Scholarship

University of Birmingham
Carlyle & Porter Scholarships
Charles Grant Robertson Scholarship
Geoffrey Shepherd Scholarship
Golden Jubilee Scholarships
Kenward Memorial Fellowship The

University of Edinburgh
Sir Gordon and Lady Ivy Wu Scholarship
The University of Edinburgh Canadian Master's Scholarships
The University of Edinburgh Indian Master's Scholarships
The University of Edinburgh Japanese Master's Scholarship
The University of Edinburgh Thai Master's Scholarship

University of Essex
MRC Studentship

University of Exeter
Anthony Parsons Memorial Scholarship
University of Exeter Overseas Research Students Award Scheme The

University of Leeds
BEIT Trust-FCO Chevening-University of Leeds Scholarships
Boothman, Reynolds and Smithells Scholarship
BP-FCO Chevening-University of Leeds Scholarships
Tetley and Lupton Scholarships for International Students for Research Study

University of London Institute in Paris
Hamilton Studentship

University of Otago
University of Otago Dr Sulaiman Daud 125th Jubilee International Postgraduate Scholarship The

University of Reading
University of Reading Access to Learning Fund
University of Reading Career Development Loan
University of Reading Dorothy Hodgkin Postgraduate Award
University of Reading Music Scholarship
University of Reading Research Endowment Trust Fund (RETF) The

University of Sydney
PhD Scholarship Healthcare Services for Older People
PhD Scholarship to Advance Aquaculture in Australasia

University of Victoria
The Alexander, Holburn, Beaudin & Lang Scholarship
The Baker & McKenzie Prize in Asia-Pacific Comparative Law
The Blakes Scholars Scholarship Award
The David Roberts Prize in Legal Writing
The Diana M. Priestly Memorial Scholarship Award
The Guild, Yule & Company Advocacy Award
The Howard Petch Scholarship in Law
Victoria Bar Association Founders Committee Award

University of Warwick
Argentina Chevening Scholarship
University of Warwick Postgraduate Award (Caribbean)

University of Warwick Postgraduate Award (Latin America)
University of Warwick Postgraduate Award (Nigeria)
University of Warwick Psychology Department Studentship (Master's)
University of Warwick Psychology Department Studentship (PhD)

Victoria University of Wellington
Curtis-Gordon Research Scholarships in Chemistry The

Warburg Institute
Sophia Fellowship

Women's Studio Workshop (WSW)
Geraldine R Dodge Residency Grant

Yonsei University
Kwanjeong Scholarship for Chinese Young Leaders
Scholarship for Academic Excellence

INDEX OF AWARDING ORGANISATIONS

International Harp Contest in Israel, 383
International Human Frontier Science Program Organization
    (HFSPO), 383
International Institute for Applied Systems Analysis (IIASA), 384
International Institute for Management Development (IMD), 384
International Navigation Association (PIANC), 386
International Peace Scholarship Fund, 386
International Reading Association, 386
International Research and Exchange Board (IREX), 388
International Tropical Timber Organization (ITTO), 389
International Union Against Cancer (UICC), 389
International Union for Vacuum Science and Technology (IUVSTA),
    391
International Union of Biochemistry and Molecular Biology (IUBMB),
    391
International University of Japan, 391
International Violin Competition–Premio Paganini, 392
International Water Management Institute (IWMI), 392
Internationaler Robert-Schumann-Wettbewerb Zwickau, 392
Iota Sigma Pi, 392
Ireland Alliance, 393
Irish Research Council for the Humanities and Social Sciences
    (IRCHSS), 394
Irish-American Cultural Institute (IACI), 394
Islamic Development Bank (IDB), 395
IWHM Bernard Butler Trust Fund, 395
J N Tata Endowment, 395
J.H. Stewart Reid Memorial Fellowship Trust, 395
Jack Kent Cooke Foundation, 396
Jacki Tuckfield Memorial Graduate Business Scholarship Fund
    (JTMGBSF), 396
Jacob's Pillow Dance, 396
James and Grace Anderson Trust, 397
James Beard Foundation, 397
James Cook University, 397
James Madison Memorial Fellowship Foundation, 398
James Pantyfedwen Foundation, 398
Janson Johan Helmich Og Marcia Jansons Legat, 398
Japan Society for the Promotion of Science (JSPS), 398
Japanese American Citizens League (JACL), 399
Japanese Government, 400
Jewish Community Centers Association (JCCA), 400
Jewish Foundation for Education of Women, 401
JILA (formerly Joint Institute for Laboratory Astrophysics), 401
John Carter Brown Library at Brown University, 401
John E Fogarty International Center (FIC) for Advanced Study in the
    Health Sciences, 403
John F and Anna Lee Stacey Scholarship Fund, 404
John F. Kennedy Library Foundation, 405
John Simon Guggenheim Memorial Foundation, 405
Johns Hopkins University, 406
Josephine De Kármán Fellowship Trust, 406
Juvenile Diabetes Foundation International/The Diabetes Research
    Foundation, 406
Kaiser Family Foundation (KFF), 407
Katholieke Universiteit Leuven, 407
Kay Kendall Leukaemia Fund, 408
Kennan Institute , 408
Kennedy Memorial Trust, 408
Kidney Health Australia, 409
Kidney Research UK, 409
King's College London, 410
Kosciuszko Foundation, 410
Krell Institute, 412
Kurt Weill Foundation for Music, 412
Kuwait Foundation for the Advancement of Science (KFAS), 413
La Trobe University, 413
Lady Tata Memorial Trust, 414
Lahore University of Management Sciences (LUMS), 414
Lancaster University, 414
Lancaster University Management School, 415
Le Cordon Bleu Australia, 415
Le Cordon Bleu Ottawa, 416
League of United Latin American Citizens (LULAC), 416
Leeds International Pianoforte Competition, 416
Lentz Peace Research Association (LPRA), 417
Leo Baeck Institute (LBI), 417
LEPRA, 418
Leukaemia Foundation, 418
Leukaemia Research Fund, 419

Leukemia & Lymphoma Society of Canada (LLSC), 419
Leukemia and Lymphoma Society, 419
Leukemia Research Foundation (LRF), 420
Leverhulme Trust, 420
Lewis & Clark College, 421
Lewis Walpole Library, 421
Library and Information Technology Association (LITA), 421
Library Company of Philadelphia, 422
Life Sciences Research Foundation (LSRF), 422
Light Work, 423
Link Foundation, 423
Lionel Murphy Foundation, 423
Lister Institute of Preventive Medicine, 424
London Goodenough Association of Canada, 424
London Mathematical Society, 424
London Metropolitan University, 425
London School of Economics (LSE), 426
London String Quartet Foundation, 426
Loren L Zachary Society for the Performing Arts, 426
Los Alamos National Laboratory (LANL), 427
Loughborough University, 427
Louisville Institute, 428
Lowe Syndrome Association (LSA), 428
Luiss University of Rome (LUR), 429
MacDowell Colony, 429
Mackenzie King Scholarship Selection Committee, 429
Macquarie University, 430
Making Music, The National Federation of Music Societies (NFMS),
    430
Manitoba Library Association (MLA), 430
March of Dimes Birth Defects Foundation, 431
Marcus Center of The American Jewish Archives, 431
Marine Corps Historical Center, 433
Marines' Memorial Association, 434
Marquette University, 434
Marshall Aid Commemoration Commission, 435
Maryland Institute College of Art (MICA), 435
Massey University, 436
Matsumae International Foundation, 436
McDonnell Center for the Space Sciences, 437
McGill University, 437
Medical Library Association (MLA), 437
Medical Research Council (MRC), 439
Medical Research Scotland, 442
Meet The Composer, Inc., 442
Melville Trust for Care and Cure of Cancer, 443
Memorial Foundation for Jewish Culture, 443
Memorial University of Newfoundland (MUN), 444
Meningitis Research Foundation, 445
Mesa State College, 446
Métis Centre at NAHO, 446
Metropolitan Museum of Art, 446
Michigan Society of Fellows, 447
Microsoft Research, 448
Minda de Gunzburg Center for European Studies (CES) at Harvard
    University, 448
Minerva Foundation, 449
Ministry of Education, Science and Culture (Iceland), 449
Ministry of Environment & Forests (MoEF) Government of India, 450
Mintek, 450
MINTRAC National Meat Industry Training Advisory Council Limited,
    450
Missouri Botanical Garden, 451
Missouri State University, 451
Mizutani Foundation for Glycoscience, 452
Modern Language Association of America (MLA), 452
Monash University, 455
Montana State University-Billings, 456
Montreal Neurological Institute, 457
Morris K Udall Foundation, 458
Moscow University Touro, 458
Motor Neurone Disease Association, 458
Mount Desert Island Biological Laboratory, 459
Mountaineering Council of Scotland (MCofS), 459
Multiple Sclerosis Research Australia (MSRA), 459
Multiple Sclerosis Society of Canada (MSSC), 459
Muscular Dystrophy Association (MDA), 460
Muscular Dystrophy Campaign of Great Britain and Northern Ireland,
    460
Museum of Comparative Zoology, 461